THE ULTIMATE PRACTICAL GUIDE TO
SCRAPBOOKING

THE ULTIMATE PRACTICAL GUIDE TO
SCRAPBOOKING

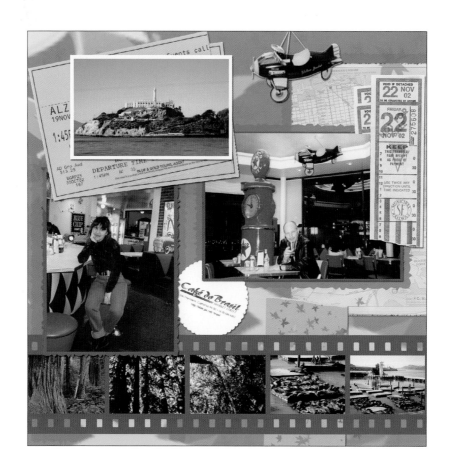

CREATING FABULOUS LASTING
MEMORY JOURNALS TO CHERISH

contributing editor: Alison Lindsay

HERMES
HOUSE

This edition is published by Hermes House,
an imprint of Anness Publishing Ltd, Blaby Road, Wigston,
Leicestershire LE18 4SE; info@anness.com

www.hermeshouse.com; www.annesspublishing.com

If you like the images in this book and would like to investigate using
them for publishing, promotions or advertising, please visit our
website www.practicalpictures.com for more information.

Publisher: Joanna Lorenz
Editorial Director: Helen Sudell
Editors: Ann Kay and Simona Hill
Designer: Terry Jeavons
Photographers: Mark Wood and Paul Bricknell
Editorial Reader: Emily Adenipekun
Production Manager: Steve Lang

ETHICAL TRADING POLICY
At Anness Publishing we believe that business should be conducted
in an ethical and ecologically sustainable way, with respect for the
environment and a proper regard to the replacement of the natural
resources we employ.
As a publisher, we use a lot of wood pulp to make high-quality paper
for printing, and that wood commonly comes from spruce trees. We
are therefore currently growing more than 750,000 trees in three
Scottish forest plantations: Berrymoss (130 hectares/320 acres),
West Touxhill (125 hectares/305 acres) and Deveron Forest
(75 hectares/185 acres). The forests we manage contain more than
3.5 times the number of trees employed each year in making paper
for the books we manufacture.
Because of this ongoing ecological investment programme, you, as
our customer, can have the pleasure and reassurance of knowing that
a tree is being cultivated on your behalf to naturally replace the
materials used to make the book you are holding.
Our forestry programme is run in accordance with the UK
Woodland Assurance Scheme (UKWAS) and will be certified by the
internationally recognized Forest Stewardship Council (FSC). The FSC
is a non-government organization dedicated to promoting
responsible management of the world's forests. Certification ensures
forests are managed in an environmentally sustainable and socially
responsible way. For further information about this scheme, go to
www.annesspublishing.com/trees

PUBLISHER'S NOTE
Although the advice and information in this book are believed to be
accurate and true at the time of going to press, neither the authors
nor the publisher can accept any legal responsibility or liability for any
errors or omissions that may have been made nor for any
inaccuracies nor for any loss, harm or injury that comes about from
following instructions or advice in this book.

CONTENTS

INTRODUCTION

In the early days of photography, having a picture taken was a notable event. It generally involved a visit to a professional photographer's studio, and the resulting prints – though they might be small and hard to see in tones of sepia or grey – were treasured and displayed in silver frames or ornate albums. Now we live in an age where photography is all around us. It is easier than ever before to take beautiful, detailed, interesting photographs whenever we want, and yet many good prints languish in boxes or drawers. The burgeoning craft of scrapbooking is all about displaying them as they deserve to be seen. But scrapbooks are more than just photograph albums: on their pages you can present your favourite pictures in beautiful, creative settings, accompanied by all the details you need to keep your memories of special times alive and fresh, to enjoy now and to pass down to future generations.

This comprehensive guide includes everything you need to get you started, whatever your artistic ability, with practical tips and inspiring suggestions for pages of originality and style. The opening

▼ *Christmas is a good subject for scrapbooks and there is always plenty of decorative material to hand.*

▲ *Old black-and-white photographs show how times change when compared to today's colour prints.*

section details the different kinds of materials and equipment you can choose from to make your pages and sets out easy techniques for mounting and editing photographs, creating backgrounds and making decorations. It also explores a range of styles and shows how to achieve each look. In the second part of the book, 120 step-by-step projects put the basic techniques into practice, with inspirational results. They are grouped around popular themes such as Children, Weddings, Travel and Family History, to help you decide how to organize your own collections.

Before you begin work on your first page, you need to decide on the size of the album you will use, as this will dictate the size of the layout. Most of the projects in this book are based on 30cm/12in square pages, on which there is plenty of space to mount a good selection of pictures and embellish them creatively. Scrapbooking suppliers offer a huge range of paper, card and other materials in this popular size. Alternatively, you could go for the slightly smaller 21 x 28cm/8½ x 11in. This has the advantage that you can print material on A4 paper to fit it, but it can be more difficult to arrange all the items you want on a single page or double-page spread. Smaller size albums are also available, such as 20cm/8in square, and can be useful if you want to create mini-albums as gifts. Of course, you can also make your own albums and covers in any size you wish, and there are some great ideas in this book for displaying your designs in one-off albums and other unusual ways.

Albums use a number of different binding systems: with three-ring bindings it is easy to move pages around, but they hold a limited number of pages, and the rings make it difficult to display double-page layouts effectively. This is not a problem with post-bound or strap-bound albums, which can expand to take more pages as your collection grows. Whatever you choose, always look for albums and papers that are of "archival" quality, made with acid-free and lignin-free materials, so that your precious prints don't deteriorate once they are mounted.

Like many other aspects of life, the digital revolution plays a vital part in many areas of scrapbooking. Digital cameras and image-editing software have opened up all kinds of photographic possibilities. With no need to buy film, you can take as

▼ *Children are a perennially popular subject for scrapbooks, and children will love looking at their own photographs.*

▲ *Photographs of a family trip to the seaside take on a nostalgic appearance when embellished with 1950s memorabilia.*

many experimental pictures as you like and play around with novel formats, colour and special effects. An internet connection gives you access to online craft suppliers, sources of templates and fonts, and special interest groups with whom you can discuss your projects and display your favourites in virtual galleries. There is now a growing trend towards virtual scrapbooking, in which stickers, borders and charms are replaced by digital versions entirely assembled and displayed on screen.

However, it's certainly not necessary to have a computer in order to enjoy scrapbooking to the full. This craft's great attraction derives from the fact that it is a wonderfully back-to-basics pastime. Good layouts combine artistic flair with genuine hands-on skills with paper, card, fabrics and natural materials. Like the quilting and knitting bees of previous generations, communal scrapbooking events (known as "crops") are strengthening social networks everywhere. As you trim, glue and assemble the elements of your pages, you can rediscover all the enthusiasm and satisfaction you felt when compiling a scrapbook as a child, in the knowledge that you are safeguarding and enhancing your treasured family memorabilia for your own children and for future generations.

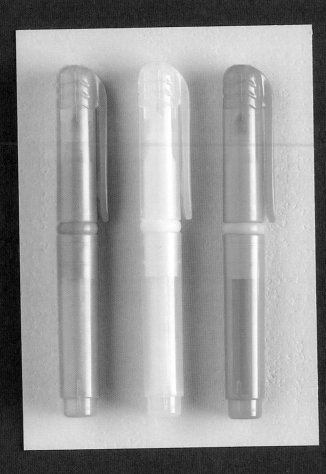

Getting started

Creating album pages is about encapsulating life's precious moments in a way that feels right for you. As you gain experience you'll have plenty of ideas for presentation and develop your own personal style. There are lots of ways to make exciting scrapbooks, and there are tips to guide you through your ideas to help you make the best of irreplaceable prints and memorabilia.

Craft stores are bursting with seductive pieces of kit and decorative materials, and it's very easy to get carried away buying stickers, die stamps and fancy cutters that appeal to your sense of colour and style before you have any clear idea of what you'll do with them. This section offers a guide to the materials and equipment available, to help you match the possibilities to the items you want to display. Step-by-step instructions will take you through all the different photographic and craft techniques you need to make beautiful, meaningful pages.

EQUIPMENT AND MATERIALS

It's easy to get carried away by the vast range of fancy punches, stamps and stickers available for scrapbooking. Start with the basics – album pages, scissors and adhesive – and add to your collection gradually as you develop your themes.

Cutting tools

Whatever the style of your albums, impeccably accurate cutting is essential for good-looking results. Bad trimming can ruin your precious pictures, so invest in good scissors and knives.

Metal ruler and craft knife

These give total control over where and how you cut. The knife blade should always be retracted or covered when not in use. If safety is a concern, a guillotine or trimmer may be a better option.

Straight trimmer or guillotine

Use this to trim paper or photographs with straight edges. All trimmers have a grid printed or embossed on to the cutting surface, to help you measure accurately. Some have interchangeable blades that cut patterned lines as well as straight ones.

Speciality cutters

There are all kinds of cutters available that make it easy to cut photographs and mats into decorative shapes. Placing a template over a photograph allows you to see what size to cut. Templates and cutters are only suitable for use together.

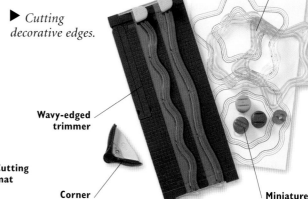

▶ *Cutting decorative edges.*

Template sheets

Shaped plastic templates

Wavy-edged trimmer

Corner cutter

Miniature knives

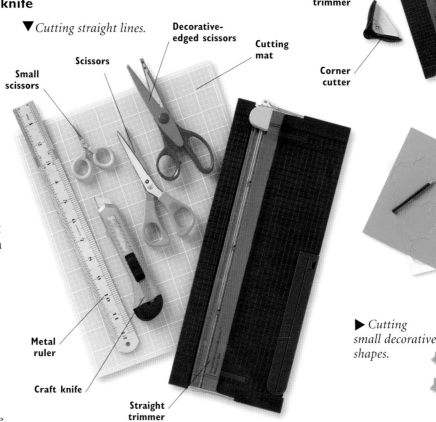

▼ *Cutting straight lines.*

Small scissors

Scissors

Decorative-edged scissors

Cutting mat

Metal ruler

Craft knife

Straight trimmer

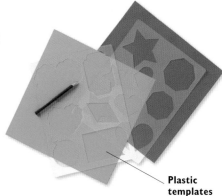

Plastic templates

▶ *Cutting small decorative shapes.*

Punches

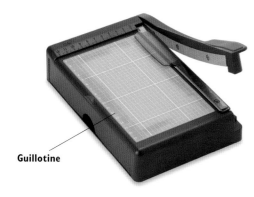

Guillotine

Templates

A wide range of lightweight templates provide different cropping options, and are easy to store. Use a pencil with the template to trace a shape on to a photograph or paper, then cut along the drawn line with scissors.

Punches

Simple small shapes look striking when punched in coloured card. Larger shapes can also be used to cut out the important part of a photograph. Shaped punches are available in hundreds of designs, and can be combined for added impact: for example, several hearts can be assembled together to create the petals of a flower.

Scissors

It is useful to have two pairs of scissors: a large pair for cutting straight lines and a small pair for trimming around decorative shapes and templates. Blades with pointed tips make it easier to cut out intricate shapes.

Decorative-edged scissors

Used sparingly, these add a fancy touch to mats and trims, although it is advisable not to use them on photographs. They work best when cutting a straight edge or a gentle curve.

Adhesives

Many different kinds of adhesive will work well on paper and card (card stock). Make sure any you use are labelled acid-free so that your photographs will not deteriorate when in contact with them.

Glue sticks

These are a cheap and easy way to stick light items such as punched shapes, but some glue sticks are not strong enough to hold photographs in position permanently. Although the glue takes some time to dry, it does not need to be left flat while drying.

Spray adhesive

Both permanent and repositionable adhesives are available in spray form – the latter allows for something that is stuck down to be peeled off and then reapplied. Spray outside or in a well-ventilated room, so that the fumes can disperse. To prevent the spray going everywhere, it is a good idea to place items in a large box, and direct the spray into that. No drying time is required.

Foam pads

These can be used to raise an element on a layout, making it appear three-dimensional. For greater height, you can stick two or more pads together before mounting your item. Use scissors to trim the pads if they are too large, but clean the scissor blades afterwards.

Glue dots and glue lines

These are available in different sizes and thicknesses, and with permanent or repositionable adhesive. The glue is tacky and will hold most items securely. No drying time is required.

Double-sided tape

Whether as a single sheet, pre-cut into squares, or on a continuous roll, this is a clean, easy way to glue most items. Long strips can be used to created borders, by applying a piece of tape, removing the backing, then pouring beads or glitter over the exposed tape. Use the same technique with small shapes punched from a sheet. No drying time is required.

Tape applicators

These dispensers allow for the convenient application of a square or line of adhesive, making it easy to glue the edge of unusual or angled shapes.

Refills are available for most designs, making them economical too. No drying time is required.

PVA (white) glue

This will hold most items in place, including awkward or three-dimensional items such as shells or charms. The work must be left flat while the glue dries. To cover an album or box, brush glue diluted with water over a sheet of paper and wrap it around the sides.

Photo corners

If you prefer to avoid gluing your photographs permanently, mount them with photo corners. Because the adhesive is on the corner and not the photograph, the picture can be removed later if necessary. Clear photo corners are the most useful, but coloured ones are also available. Gold, silver or black look good on heritage or wedding layouts. No drying time is required.

Masking tape

This is useful for temporarily attaching stencils to a layout, or for lifting stickers from their backing sheet.

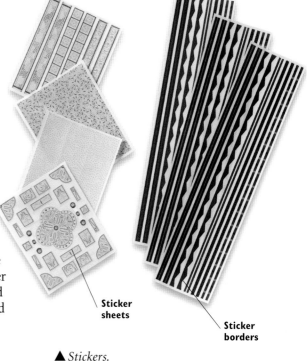

Sticker sheets

Sticker borders

▲ *Stickers.*

Glue for vellum

Specially made "invisible" glue dots are needed when working with vellum, to avoid the adhesive showing through the sheet. Alternatively, it can be attached using spray adhesive.

Stickers

As well as being a decorative element, stickers can be positioned to attach vellum, photographs or journaling blocks to a layout. Choose large scale stickers if you want to stick a heavy item down.

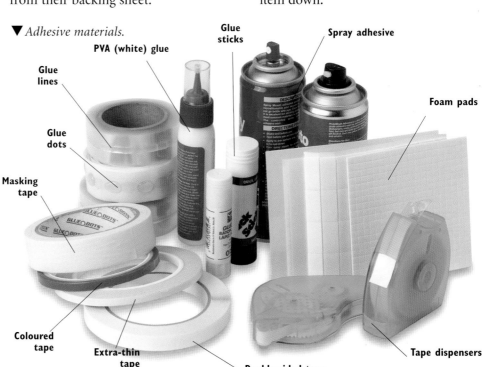

▼ *Adhesive materials.*

Glue lines

PVA (white) glue

Glue sticks

Spray adhesive

Glue dots

Masking tape

Foam pads

Coloured tape

Extra-thin tape

Double-sided tape

Tape dispensers

Paper and card

Good paper makes a world of difference to your designs, so always buy the best quality you can afford, and make sure it is acid-free to keep your photographs in perfect condition.

Page kits

Sometimes helpful for beginners, page kits combine paper with matching stickers or other embellishments and offer an easy way to create co-ordinated layouts quickly. They are designed to suit a range of themes and cover many different subjects.

Self-coloured card (stock)

This is the basis for many scrapbook pages, and its firmness provides an ideal surface to support photographs and embellishments. Card may be smooth or textured to resemble natural surfaces such as linen. It is available from art and craft suppliers, as single sheets or in multi-packs. Save scraps for paper piecing and matting photos.

Patterned paper

There are thousands of patterned papers available to match almost any theme, event or mood. Papers may be purchased individually, in books or multi-packs; the latter offer better value, but not all the sheets may be to your taste. A folder of patterned paper scraps is useful since many layouts can be attractively embellished using small scraps of paper.

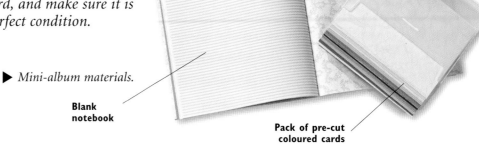

▶ *Mini-album materials.*

Blank notebook

Pack of pre-cut coloured cards

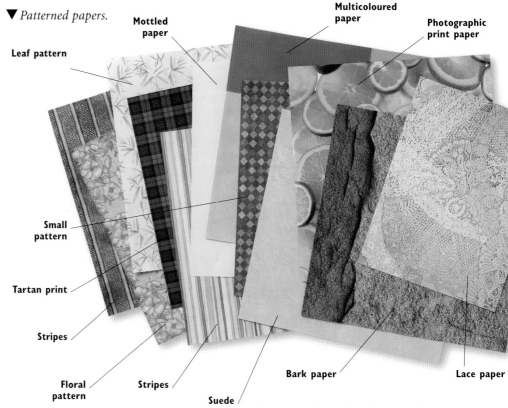

▼ *Patterned papers.*

Mottled paper

Multicoloured paper

Photographic print paper

Leaf pattern

Small pattern

Tartan print

Stripes

Floral pattern

Stripes

Suede paper

Bark paper

Lace paper

▼ *Self-coloured card.*

Glitter card

Textured and embossed paper

These tactile papers give a design texture and depth without adding bulk. Some papers resemble leather or fabric, while others have stitching or metallic embossing to add richness.

Mulberry paper

The fibres used to create this paper are light but very strong. Do not use scissors to cut the paper; instead, "draw" a damp paintbrush across the paper, then tear apart, leaving soft, feathery edges.

Photographic print paper

Some patterned papers offer photographic or naturalistic representations of everyday objects. These can overwhelm a layout if they compete with your own photographs, so restrict them to accents.

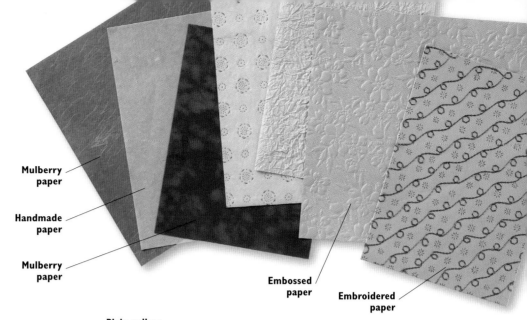

▶ *Textured and embossed papers.*

Mulberry paper

Handmade paper

Mulberry paper

Embossed paper

Embroidered paper

Suede paper
This mimics the texture and appearance of real suede, and so is perfect for representing that material.

Glitter and pearlescent paper
The soft sheen of pearlescent paper is ideal for baby or wedding layouts, while brighter glitter sheets can be used as colourful accents for party pages.

Cut and mini-album packs
Pre-cut small paper packs are available for matting or mini-albums.

Lace papers
These delicate papers mimic the soft colours and patterns of lace without adding weight to the pages, and are perfect for wedding or heritage layouts.

Vellum
Being translucent, vellum gives a soft look to paper or photographs placed underneath it. Patterned vellum can be layered over plain or patterned paper to create a romantic look, and mini-envelopes made from vellum half-conceal the souvenirs they hold. If a photograph you want to use is a little out of focus, you can disguise this by slipping it behind vellum.

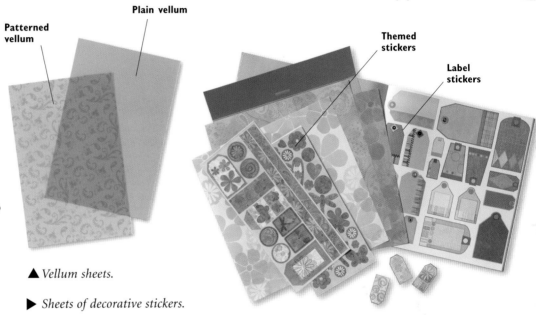

Patterned vellum

Plain vellum

Themed stickers

Label stickers

▲ *Vellum sheets.*

▶ *Sheets of decorative stickers.*

ALBUM BINDINGS

Your album can be of any size, but you will probably find that a 30cm/12in square format offers the best scope for creating satisfying layouts. Loose-leaf albums give the most flexibility, and there are basically three methods of binding pages into them.

Ring binder albums
These are the cheapest way to display layouts, which can be slipped into clear plastic page protectors. Extra page protectors can be added to expand the album. As the ring binding lies between the two pages and distracts the eye, ring binders are best used to present single-page layouts.

Post-bound albums
These albums conceal the posts binding the page protectors together, so a double layout can be viewed without distracting elements. They are available in a wide range of sizes and designs. Extra page protectors may be inserted by unscrewing the posts and adding extenders.

Strap-hinge albums
Plastic hinges slide through loops on the spines of these album pages to create an infinitely extendable album. Each page is an integral part of this kind of album, so background paper needs to be glued on top (known as "wallpapering") to change the layout base.

Notebooks
Any kind of notebook may be used as a scrapbook, especially if a smaller gift album is being created. Decorate plain notebooks by painting or covering with paper, and add embellishments for a unique look. Don't forget to leave room for a title page before the first layout.

Embellishments

This is where the fun really starts, but it's important to keep the focus of attention on your own photographs and memorabilia: make sure the decorative elements enhance the theme of your page rather than dominate it.

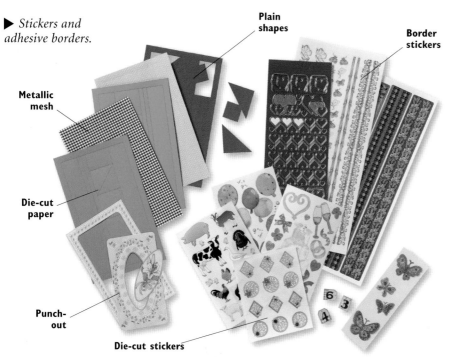

▶ *Stickers and adhesive borders.*

Plain shapes

Border stickers

Metallic mesh

Die-cut paper

Punch-out

Die-cut stickers

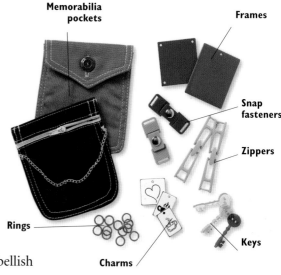

Multi-shape template

Adhesive mesh strip

Slide mounts

▶ *Photo mounts and templates.*

Memorabilia pockets

Frames

Snap fasteners

Zippers

Rings

Charms

Keys

▲ *Fabric pockets and attachments add interest to a layout.*

Stickers

A staple of scrapbooking, stickers are available in every conceivable colour, size and design, and make it easy to embellish a page quickly. Popular characters are represented on stickers, as well as traditional themes such as Christmas and weddings. If you want to make a sticker more substantial, apply it to white card and cut round it, then mount the shape on a foam pad.

Fabric stickers

These are printed on fabric to add textural interest to a layout. For a homespun look, fray some of the threads at the edges of the sticker.

3D stickers

These are built up from two or more layers of card, ready to be added to a page. Popular themes include babies and travel, and many are also suitable for making greetings cards.

Punch-outs

Shapes die-cut from sheets of card are known as punch-outs, as they need to be pressed out of the backing sheet. They are usually simple shapes, and may be coloured. Printed shapes, or those carrying titles, embellish a layout quickly, and can create a consistent style throughout an album.

Stamping

Use stamps to create a theme on background paper. Stamped images can be coloured, cut out and used like stickers to lend an accent colour or design to a layout. Choose inks in colours that complement the layout, or scribble a felt-tip pen over a stamp, spray lightly with water, then press down. Alphabet stamps are useful for titles.

▼ *Collect postcards, currency and timetables as travel mementoes.*

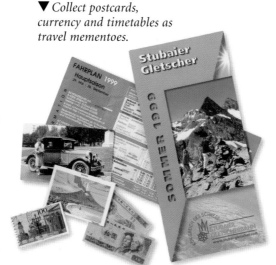

Paint

Acrylic paint can be used to create any design on backing paper, and the huge range of colours available means you can match any shade in a photograph. Ready-mixed paint in tubes is easy to apply and very fine lines can be drawn using the nib.

Templates

All kinds of templates are available to help you customize layouts. They are an economical option since it's easy to create many different looks with just one template.

Fibres

Lengths of fibre add softness and texture to layouts, and provide contrast with the flatness and hard edges of card and paper. Luxurious knitting wool or ribbons can also be used. Mixed packs can be bought already colour co-ordinated. Try wrapping fibres round the bottom of a photograph, or threading a handful through a tag.

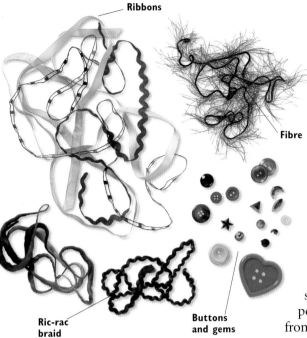

Ribbons

Fibre

Ric-rac braid

Buttons and gems

▲ *Fibres, braids and buttons can be used as borders for pictures or to hold items in place.*

Buttons and gems

Stitch or stick these to a layout as embellishments, or to anchor journaling blocks. You could use a gem to dot the "i" in a title, or scatter several in the corner of a photograph. Delicate pearl buttons are especially suited to baby themes or heritage layouts.

Memorabilia

Real or replica memorabilia adds significance to a layout. When you go travelling, for example, save ephemera such as tickets, timetables and restaurant bills to combine with your photographs. Failing the real thing, you can buy a replica pack. Foreign stamps, used or unused, and paper currency are other authentic additions.

Memorabilia pockets

Tuck small items of memorabilia in pockets to keep them safe but accessible. Pockets that have clear fronts allow you to see what's inside without taking it out.

Attachments

There are lots of specialist attachments available now, which can be kept as they are or further embellished by sanding, painting or stitching. Tuck a special souvenir in a pre-made pocket, or hang a key or zipper pull from a length of ribbon.

Metal

Embellishments sold for scrapbooks have been specially coated to prevent damage to layouts. Use brads or eyelets to fix vellum or tags in place. Thread ribbon or fibres through charms, or place a tiny key next to a heart. Photo turns are attached with brads and can hold hidden journaling closed but accessible. For quick attachment of ribbons, use coloured staples.

Adhesive mesh

This is available in strips or sheets and quickly adds texture to a layout. Dab ink or chalk over the surface then peel off, to give a shadowed texture pattern on paper.

Slide mounts

Cover these in paper or paint, then use as tiny picture frames or to highlight part of a photograph.

Paper charms

Embossed printed and foiled charms can be cut out and added to layouts.

▼ *Paper charms.*

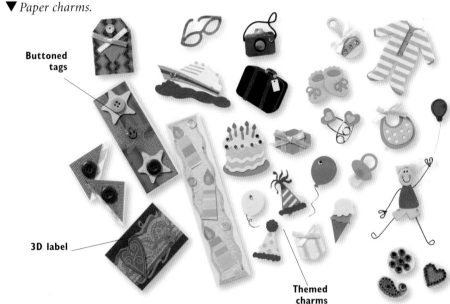

Buttoned tags

3D label

Themed charms

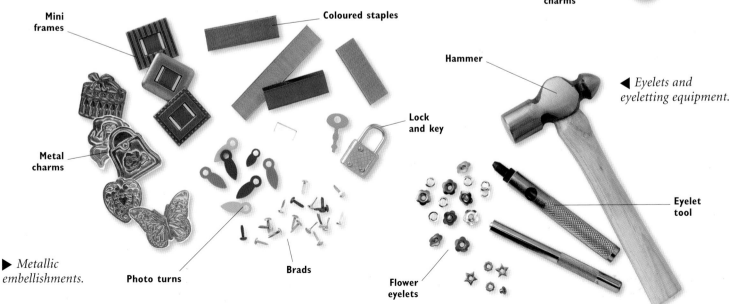

Mini frames

Coloured staples

Hammer

◀ *Eyelets and eyeletting equipment.*

Metal charms

Lock and key

Eyelet tool

◀ *Metallic embellishments.*

Photo turns

Brads

Flower eyelets

Lettering

The words you add to your layouts add an all-important dimension. Use the title to establish the theme of the page, bringing out the character of the layout in your treatment of the main word or perhaps an illuminated initial.

Letter templates

Use these in reverse to trace individual letters on to the back of your chosen paper, then flip over, to avoid having to erase pencil lines. Or use right side up to trace a title directly on to a layout, then colour with pencils or pens.

Letter stickers

The quickest and easiest way to add titles to your pages is with adhesive stickers. Align the bases of the letters along a ruler or use a special plastic guide for curved lines of lettering. Mix colours and styles for a fun approach. Letter squares can be used in both positive and negative forms, making them versatile and economical. Tweezers or a crocodile clip are useful in helping to place letter stickers accurately.

Cut-out letters

These are available in sheets or as part of themed paper collections, and make good decorative initials. Cut them out individually and glue down, or mount on foam pads for added dimension. A large number of styles are available to suit any scrapbook theme.

Buttons

Some manufacturers offer sets of letters in a range of different formats, such as small buttons. You could glue or stitch them on to a layout, or thread a name on thin ribbon and drape it over a photograph. Use a single button for the initial letter of a word to highlight it.

▼ *Lettering stickers and tools.*

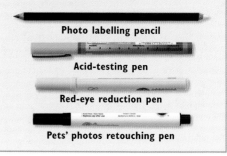

Photo labelling pencil

Acid-testing pen

Red-eye reduction pen

Pets' photos retouching pen

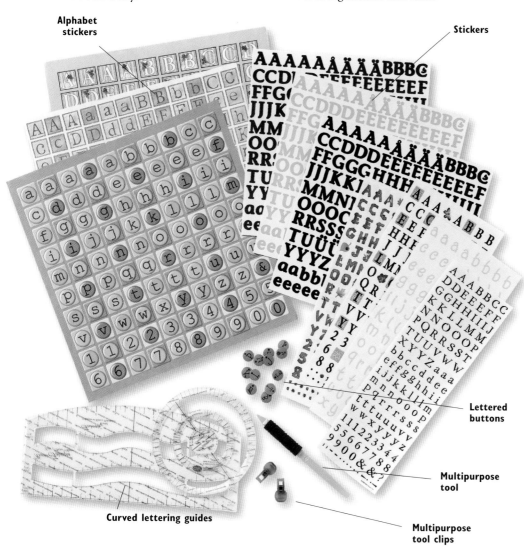

Alphabet stickers

Stickers

Lettered buttons

Multipurpose tool

Curved lettering guides

Multipurpose tool clips

▲ *Use lettering templates to trace individual letters for titles, then fill in with ink or pens or cut out and glue in place on the page.*

Tools for journaling

While titles and captions can identify the people in the pictures, journaling goes further, explaining the background to an event and capturing its mood. Writing by hand adds a personal touch.

▶ *Fibre-tipped pens are easy to use and available in a wide range of colours and widths.*

Plain lettering

Wedding template

Decorative lettering

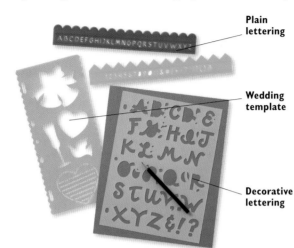

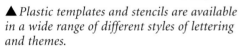

▲ *Plastic templates and stencils are available in a wide range of different styles of lettering and themes.*

◀ *Printed journaling blocks can be filled in by hand and then glued on to the album page.*

Templates
Scrapbooking templates in decorative shapes can be used to help you fit and align journaling. Trace one of the shapes on to the page and draw in guidelines with a soft pencil. Rub out the lines when the text is complete. Alternatively, draw round the shape and cut it out of contrasting paper. Add the journaling, erase the guidelines, then glue the paper shape on the layout.

Writing guide
Rest this on the paper and rest your pen lightly on the top of the wire loops as you write. The flexible loops will bend out of the way for the tails of letters descending below the level of the line.

Pens
Fibre-tip pens give good, even coverage. Use the tip for fine writing, and the side to create striking titles.

Fine-tipped pens
Use these when a lot of information has to be written in a small space, as their fine point allows for very neat writing. Fine tips can also be used to decorate titles drawn with thicker pens.

Gel pens
Manufactured in a wide range of colours, gel pens are a scrapbooker's staple. Metallic shades look good on dark paper.

Paint pens
These draw a wide, opaque line of colour, perfect for large titles or for outlining photographs instead of matting.

Computer fonts
A computer will give you access to an almost limitless range of fonts and sizes available for titles and journaling. Titles can be printed out and mounted on a layout, but for a more striking effect, print a title in reverse and cut it out, then flip it over and add to the page. Printing in reverse means any lines will not be seen on the finished layout.

Printed journaling boxes
Sets of journaling boxes offer pre-made titles and sayings to add to a layout, along with some blanks for you to record personal information. These are often produced to coordinate with paper sets, making it easy to complete a layout.

▶ *Fibre-tipped and gel pens are suitable for titles and journaling.*

Flexible nylon loops

▲ *A writing guide keeps your handwriting horizontal when journaling without obstructing the movement of the pen.*

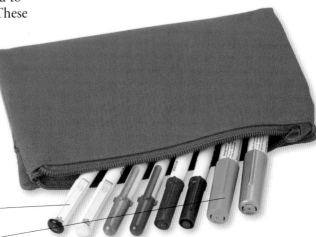

Fine-tipped pens

Round-tipped pens

CREATIVE IMAGE-MAKING

Whether you're sorting through boxes of old family pictures or taking new ones with your album in mind, these ideas will help you develop your visual sense and explore imaginative ways of using photographs to create some really arresting images.

Taking good photographs

The craft of scrapbooking sprang from a desire to present photographs of family and friends in a creative and meaningful way, and good photographs are the heart of every album page. So here are some tips to help you take more effective pictures for really stunning layouts. Modern cameras, equipped with high-quality lenses, built-in automatic exposure meters and sophisticated auto-focusing systems, can do nearly all the work for you. Unless you choose to manage your camera's settings manually for creative effects, you really can just point and shoot terrific pictures. However, technical quality is meaningless if your pictures are badly composed, coarsely lit or just lifeless.

Whether you're using a state-of-the-art SLR or a disposable camera, you need to train your eye to make the most of light, colour and form, and learn how to see your subject as the camera sees it to achieve the effective results you want.

Even if you are a good photographer, you are bound to have some pictures that don't come out right, with too much background or foreground, subjects disappearing off the edge of the photo or, if you've used flash, people with red eyes. All is not lost: there are ways of improving many pictures that will enable you to display them.

Photographing people

Whether they're formally posed or candid shots, photographs of people should aim to convey their true character. Most people feel ill-at-ease or put on some kind of show when you first point a lens at them, so it's best to take lots of pictures. Children, especially, will soon forget about the camera's presence if they're busy playing, leaving you to get your best photographs.

For candid shots, a telephoto or zoom lens means your subjects need not be aware of the camera at all. It will also throw the foreground and background out of focus, adding emphasis to the subject, which is just what you want.

Lighting

The traditional instruction to "shoot with the sun behind you" when taking pictures outdoors tends to produce the flattest effect. If your subject is a person looking at the camera, this position will leave them squinting uncomfortably. It can be much more effective to move them into the shade of a tree or a building, where the indirect light will be much more flattering and the contrasts less extreme, making it possible to capture every detail.

If you are taking pictures in direct light, it's best to move yourself or your subject so that the light is coming from one side. This is easiest to achieve when the sun is low in the sky – early in the morning or in the late afternoon (which photographers call the "magic hour"). Indoors, a similar atmospheric sidelight can be provided by daylight coming through a window, which is wonderful for portraits.

Composing pictures

As you look through the viewfinder, or at the LCD screen of a digital camera, it's easy to concentrate too hard on the main subject of your picture, but it's important to see how the whole picture works within the frame. Before you focus and shoot, move the camera around to find the best angle. If necessary, change your position entirely to get a better angle, or to bring in some foreground interest.

Think about the background too: try to find an angle that gives a background that's attractive but not distracting, and look out for ugly details like power lines. If anyone appears to have a tree growing out of their head, move slightly to one side to avoid the problem.

▼ *Here the photographer has successfully used the rule of thirds to make a visually interesting image, but has tilted the camera so that the horizon is not level.*

even remedy pictures that are crooked by cropping a little: draw a new frame parallel with the horizon in the photograph and trim all the edges to produce a straight image.

Red eyes

If people are looking straight at the camera when you take pictures using flash, the light reflects on their retinas, causing their eyes to shine red. Professional photographers use lights set at a distance from the camera to avoid this problem, and some compact cameras that rely on inbuilt flash have a "red-eye reduction" setting, which can help. Another solution is to take pictures when your subjects are not looking directly into the lens.

If you do want to use photographs in which people looking directly at the camera have red eyes, you can improve your prints using a red-eye pen, available from photograhic suppliers. This is a dark green marker pen that successfully counteracts the red, leaving the eyes looking dark. Simply colour in all the red eyes visible on the photograph, taking care not to mark the rest of the faces. The ink is permanent so the colour will not smudge, and your pictures will look much better.

◀▲ Red eyes appear when a subject is looking directly at the camera when the flash goes off. The problem is easy to rectify with a red-eye pen. Use it like a felt-tipped pen to mask out the unwanted red tones.

If you're photographing people, move in as close as you can to fill the frame. Alternatively, use a zoom lens – this also has the advantage of flattening the perspective, which has a flattering effect. With children, crouch or kneel to get yourself down to their level.

Try turning the camera on its side. A vertical, or "portrait", format is often better for pictures of people, but that's not always the case. If you're taking the photograph in an interesting setting,

▼If you forget to check what's going on in the background of a picture while focusing on smiling faces, you can end up with an object appearing to grow out of someone's head.

including more of the the surroundings in a "landscape" format may convey more information about your subject. For example, you might portray a keen gardener in the context of the garden that they have created.

The most interesting pictures rarely have the main subject right in the centre. Photographers tend to follow the "rule of thirds", which involves visualizing a grid dividing the picture vertically and horizontally into three. Placing your subject on one of the four points where the imaginary lines intersect gives a harmonious composition.

Cropping prints

If you have a photograph where the main focus is too far off to one side, or the subject is set against a busy, distracting background, it is easy to crop the picture to eliminate the unnecessary parts and balance up the composition.

Rather than cutting off the unwanted part of the picture by eye and ending up with a lopsided picture, cut out two L-shaped pieces of black card (card stock). You can use these to form a rectangular frame of any size so that you can judge the part of the picture you want to use. Adjust the L-shapes backwards and forwards until you find the crop that looks best, then mark the print with a pencil. Cut along the marked lines using a craft knife and metal ruler and working on a cutting mat. Cropping pictures will give you a variety of different-sized prints, which can often add interest to album pages. You can

▲ Everyone has the odd print like this in their collection: most of the sky can simply be cropped away to focus on the main subject.

▶ Many badly framed pictures can be redeemed by judicious cropping, but try out your ideas with an adjustable frame, easily made from two pieces of black card, before you start cutting up a print.

Tinting photographs

Black-and-white photographs, particularly those that have not faded with age, can sometimes look stark in a photograph album. One way to enliven them and give them more interest is to tint them with coloured inks.

1 Select the photographs to be hand-tinted. Pour some water mixed with the ink thinner solution into a shallow tray. Using a pair of tweezers, add one photograph at a time to the solution.

2 Place the wet photo on a board and wipe the excess water from it using a cloth. The photo should be damp rather than wet, or the ink will run where the water is rather than where you want it to go.

3 Pour a little thinner solution into a palette and add a drop of ink. Apply the colour gently using a fine paintbrush and wait for it to be dispersed by the damp print before adding more. Test the colours to see how different they appear once dry.

4 Add touches of colour to the hair, eyes and lips. Darken the colour as necessary to suit the person in the photograph. Finally, add a few touches of colour to the clothing. Leave the photograph to dry thoroughly before mounting it.

COLOURING MEDIA

Oil-based inks specially formulated for colouring photographs are available in a range of colours and are sold with a thinner solution that can be used to prepare the surface of the print and to dilute the colour. Special marker pens are also available, and can be easier to use for small areas of colour, though the use of a brush can give a more authentic period look. You could also experiment with other media, such as coloured pencils.

The degree to which the colour "takes" will depend on the type of paper used to make the print: if possible select matt prints for colouring as the surface has more grip and will hold the ink more successfully than gloss.

Traditionally, when all photography was in black and white, the most common use for hand-colouring was to add flesh tones to portraits, and doing this will give your prints a period feel. When painting faces, however, take care not to overdo the inking, or your pictures will end up looking like caricatures. If you add too much colour to start with it cannot easily be removed. Use very dilute inks and test all the colours first on a copy of the photograph to ensure that you are happy with the effect and so that you do not risk ruining the original print.

VIRTUAL HAND-TINTING

If you have image-editing software, such as Adobe Photoshop, on your computer, you can apply all kinds of colour effects before making prints. In the example shown here the colourful background was felt to be too dominant and has been selectively converted to black and white so that the album pages stand out more strongly. If you wish to "age" existing black-and-white prints digitally you can scan the images into the computer and add effects such as sepia toning, vignetting or hand-tinting, then print new copies.

Making a photographic mosaic

Try this simple technique to give added interest to an image with bold shapes and colours, or to create an overall pattern from a more detailed picture. Simply cut the print up into a series of small squares and then reassemble it on a coloured background, leaving narrow spaces between the shapes. Mosaic works best on more abstract subjects, or shots of the natural world like these two flower pictures. If you are working with pictures of people, don't make any cuts through the faces as this will alter their proportions.

  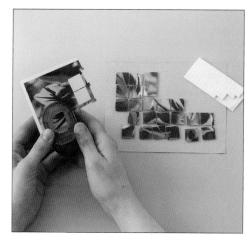

1 Working on a cutting mat, use a clear ruler and a sharp knife to cut the picture into strips of equal width, 2.5–3cm/1–1¼in wide. Cut each strip into squares, keeping them in the correct order as you work to avoid ending up with a jigsaw. A 10 × 15cm/4 × 6in print can be divided into 24 squares each measuring 2.5cm/1in; larger prints can be cut into more squares, or larger squares, as desired.

2 Decide how much space you want around the completed mosaic and how wide to make the distance between the squares. Lightly rule a border on to your chosen backing paper. Starting at the bottom left corner, stick down the first row of squares, making sure that the gaps between them are regular. Continue working upwards until you reach the end of the last row.

3 For a less structured approach, try using a punch to cut out the squares. This method leaves larger, irregular spaces between the picture elements and the finished look resembles a traditional mosaic made from tesserae. Adhesive foam pads add an extra dimension to the finished image. Make sure you are going to punch out a complete square by opening the little flap underneath the cutter and inserting the photograph face down in the punch.

NOW TRY THIS

These two mosaics show complementary variations on the technique. A photograph of russet, gold and green branches takes on an abstract feel when divided into squares, while a picture of rich autumnal foliage provides the perfect frame for a study of a noble tree.

Making a photographic patchwork

Traditional patchwork blocks have a strong geometry, which provides a ready-made framework for floral photographs. Designs such as the hexagonal "Grandmother's Flower Garden" are ideal for showing off your favourite garden pictures, and flowers such as primulas, pansies and apple blossom are reminiscent of the pretty prints on old-fashioned dressmaking fabrics. Look for formal carpet bedding, fields of colourful crops or wild flowers, and take both wide-angle and close-up photographs of them to use in creating your own interpretations of these patterns.

NOW TRY THIS

This bright chequerboard is made up of alternate squares: one a close-up of a poppy flower, the other a wider shot of the field in which it grew. Both pictures were given a pop art look by digitally increasing the contrast and brightness of the original images. The squares butt up to each other so that no background shows through.

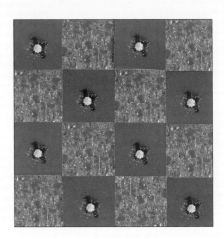

1 Use a patchwork template to cut out a series of hexagons from your prints – you will need to make several copies of each photograph. The centre of each motif is cut from a single close-up and the six hexagons that surround it are made from pictures of massed flowers in a bed.

2 Take time to arrange the shapes before sticking them down, making sure that you have enough of each type. Starting at the bottom left corner, glue six patterned hexagons around a plain coloured one. Leaving a 6mm/¼in space all around, make more interlocking motifs to fill the page. Trim the edges flush with the background.

Weaving photographic images

This technique requires planning, but the results are well worth it and often produce unexpected effects. Experiment by combining a black-and-white and a coloured copy of the same photograph to create extra depth, as shown with the picture of a Japanese news stand, or by weaving an abstract photograph of texture with a landscape. Weaving works best on landscape or abstract images: as with photographic mosaics, avoid using close-up portraits.

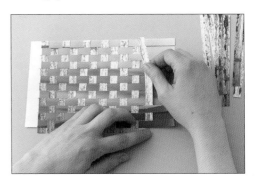

1 For a square weave, cut the black-and-white version of the picture into horizontal strips 2cm/³⁄4in wide, stopping just short of one end so that they remain joined together. Use a sharp knife and a transparent ruler, and work carefully on a cutting mat. Cut the coloured picture into separate vertical strips of the same width.

2 Weave the first strip from the left of the coloured picture under and over the black-and-white strips. Take the second strip and weave it under the alternate strips: repeat this to the end, making sure that they are all at right angles and that the space between them is minimal. Secure the ends of the strips with double-sided tape and display the finished piece in a window mount.

3 To create a basket weave, in which the horizontal strips form rectangles and the vertical ones squares, leave a 3mm/⅛in gap between the short strips. Two very different pictures – one of a stunning coastal sunset and the other of a rusting iron shed – are combined in this weave. They work well together because they have very similar colour schemes.

Making panoramas and compositions

Panoramic cameras are fun to use but you don't actually need one to make your own panorama. If you take two or more photographs from the same viewpoint, turning the camera slightly each time, you can then trim and stick the photographs together to make a long, narrow view. You can also use variations on this technique to create extended panoramas from just a single image or use your imagination to combine different images, with surprising results.

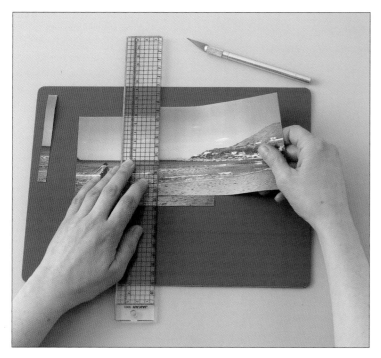

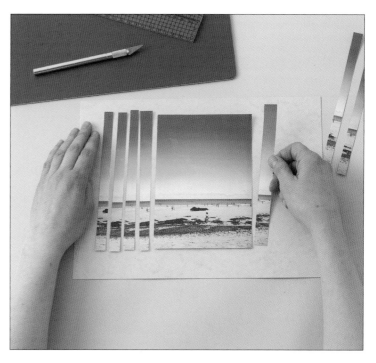

▲ If you are making a joined panorama remember that photographs tend be slightly darker towards the edges (a natural consequence of producing a rectangular image with a round lens) so it's best not to butt untrimmed vertical edges together. Instead, overlap the pictures to see how much of the image they share, then trim half this width from one picture. Put them together with the trimmed photo on top, align a ruler with the trimmed edge, slide away the top picture and trim the bottom one.

▲ Turn a single portrait-format view into an extended landscape, or composite panorama, by combining two identical prints. Cut strips of varying width from each side of one photograph and mount them either side of your main image. If you leave narrow spaces between them, it is less obvious that they simply repeat the image rather than extending it.

▲ An interesting variation on the composite panorama is to use two very different but related pictures to encapsulate memories of an event or place. Here a photograph of a Greek flag is interspersed with a geometric abstract view of buildings clinging to the steep hillside of the Cycladic island of Syros. Staggering the strips adds to the geometric nature of the images.

▲ A quick way to join two similar pictures is to find an obvious vertical line or strong outline along the edge of one of them and cut along it. You can then overlay this edge across the other picture. Although the two pictures used here were not taken from the same spot, they share the same colours and tonal range, so give the effect of two people appearing in the same photograph.

▲ *A great way to produce a multifaceted image of an event or scene is as a photo-composite, in the style of artist David Hockney. To do this, take lots of pictures from different angles and combine them in a collage. This view of the lake and Palm House at the Royal Botanic Gardens in Kew, London, includes several photographs of the same pair of swans, creating the illusion of a larger flock.*

Transferring photographs on to fabric

Several types of special paper are available for transferring photographs on to fabric. Your pictures will not be damaged by the process but it must be undertaken at a photocopy bureau. Copy several photographs together on to one sheet. Make sure you have enough transfers to allow for experimentation and mistakes. Some photographs do not work well on transfer paper, such as those with dark backgrounds or lots of contrast, so be prepared for some trial and error.

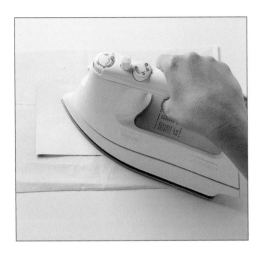

1 Stick the photographs lightly on to a piece of plain paper. Take this to a colour copy bureau together with the transfer paper, which needs to be fed one sheet at a time through the paper tray. (Have the photographs copied using a normal colour process to check the colour before they are copied on to the transfer paper.) Trim around a transfer and place it face down on a plain natural fabric with a close weave, such as calico, which will withstand heat and pressure. Referring to the manufacturer's instructions, press with a hot iron. If a lot of pressure is required, it may be advisable to work on a sturdy table protected with several layers of blanket.

2 Carefully peel off the transfer backing in an even movement to reveal the transferred image. Allow the fabric to cool before using it. Refer to the transfer paper manufacturer's instructions for washing and aftercare. A more expensive, but generally foolproof method of photo transfer is to have the process done professionally at a copy bureau that prints T-shirts with your own images.

NOW TRY THIS

This endearing photograph of a much-loved pet required special treatment. The image was transferred on to a piece of natural linen and the vintage-style fabric that forms the frame was carefully selected to echo the paisley quilt the kitten is sitting on. A narrow lace edging and pearl buttons complete the frame.

NOW TRY THIS

This sophisticated cloth book would make a wonderful keepsake for a young child. Take close-up photographs of familiar scenes around the child's house and garden and transfer them on to a coarsely woven fabric such as linen or calico to give them a canvas-like texture. Trim each one to 12.5cm/5in square and tack (baste) it to a 16.5 x 18cm/6¹/₂ x 7in felt rectangle, allowing a 2cm/³/₄in border around three sides and a wider border at the spine. Attach with a decorative machine stitch, then assemble the pages and stitch along the spine. You could also embellish the pages with embroidered messages, printed text or other appliquéd decoration.

Making a kaleidoscope

The multi-faceted image inside a kaleidoscope is created by reflecting an image between two angled mirrors to produce a repeating, symmetrical pattern. With patience it is possible to make your own photographic version: the effect is stunning, complex, and can be slightly surreal, as with this reinterpretation of a Venetian canal scene. You will need eight prints of the same picture, four of them reversed.

I Draw a square on acetate or tracing paper and divide it diagonally to make a triangular template. Cut it out and use to make two sets of four triangles from the photographs. Clear acetate will enable you to position the template accurately so that the images are identical, with one set a mirror image of the other.

2 Mark a square sheet of paper into eight equal sections: these will be your guidelines for assembling the pattern. Matching the sides of the images exactly, glue the segments in place, making sure that each one lies next to its mirror image.

3 You can then trim the finished pattern as you wish: into a square, a four-point star or, as here, a circle. Mark the circumference with a pair of compasses and cut around the pencil line.

4 If you choose an image that is already symmetrical you can make a kaleidoscope from four, six or eight prints without having to reverse them. Here, the iconic image of the Eiffel Tower is surrounded by pictures of a period shop front to create a unique souvenir of Paris.

NOW TRY THIS

Here, eight diamonds form the design known in patchwork as the LeMoyne Star, giving the original flower image an abstract quality.

Framing and mounting photographs

There are many possible ways to frame your favourite photographs and cards. All the ideas shown here are quick and easy to do and look very effective, both in album pages and as fresh ways of displaying photographs in frames. Try them on your own layouts, or use them as inspiration for your original ideas.

CUTTING PAPER FRAMES

Single or multiple borders in paper or thin card (stock), known as mats, are a simple way to present a picture, but must be accurately cut for successful results. Choose colours that match or contrast effectively with the dominant colours in the photographs, and make sure that each successive border balances the photograph and is evenly positioned around the picture.

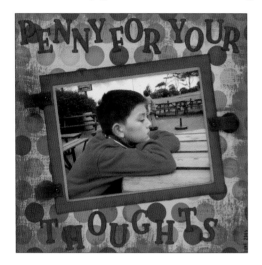

▲ On this album page attention is focused on a single image by mounting it in a double mat in two colours. The opening in the top layer is cut a little larger to expose a narrow contrasting inner border.

▲ In this charming treatment the paper border is arranged some way away from the edge of the photograph, so that the background acts as an inner frame. A spray of die-cut daisies completes the effect.

▲ Multiple paper frames in a simple colour scheme are a great way to give unity to a diverse collection of photographs and other memorabilia. Extra layers can be added to disguise differences of size.

▼ For this stacked technique the subject is cut out first and used as the template for the border shapes, each drawn 6mm/¼in larger than the layer above. The careful choice of graduated tones, complementing the bird's plumage, gives a subtle three-dimensional effect.

▲ Here the background colour matches the vehicle, and contrast is provided by the square black frames, each of which has a window a little larger than the cut-out photograph, leaving a striking band of colour around each picture.

USING TEMPLATES

Plastic templates are available in a host of different shapes and sizes, from simple geometric forms to outlines of cats and Christmas trees. You can also draw and cut your own from many sources. Basic shapes such as ovals are useful guides for trimming photographs accurately, and are easy to use.

1 Position a template over the part of the photograph you want to use and draw around the outline with a pencil.

2 Use a small, sharp pair of scissors to cut carefully around the pencil line.

▲ *Use a set of templates in graduated sizes to cut a series of mats or frames to fit around your picture.*

1 Cut out a narrow frame from a photograph with a lot of background to draw attention to the focal point.

2 Turn the cut-out section by 45 degrees and replace it between the central area and the border to complete the frame.

▲ *Alternatively, cut away the outer sections of the picture in regular shapes, then offset them slightly and glue to a backing sheet.*

▲ *For a rainbow effect, use a template to cut a succession of circles, then offset them.*

▲ *Make a frame to suit your subject, like this porthole for an underwater theme.*

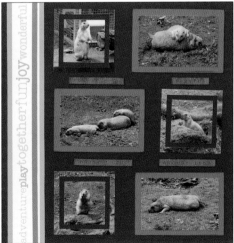

▲ *Different framing methods are unified here by consistent use of colour and shape.*

TEARING PAPER FRAMES

Torn paper shapes can add softness and a change of texture to your layouts, but it's a good idea to use the effect sparingly, as it can easily become too dominant. Combine it with neat, straight edges for contrast, or make a mosaic of lots of small-scale torn edges using different colours for a subtle collage.

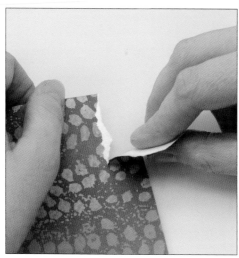

1 Tearing paper or card (stock) that is coloured the same shade all through gives a soft textured edge. The feathery lines are good for recreating textures such as teddy bear fur, or for layering to create backgrounds resembling water, clouds or grass. Tearing with the grain of the paper gives a straighter edge than tearing against the grain, so practise to see the effects you can achieve. To make it easier to tear a shape, try drawing with a dampened paintbrush along the line you want to tear.

2 Patterned paper is usually printed and has a white core. Tearing the paper will reveal this. Tearing towards yourself with the pattern uppermost produces a white edge, which highlights the tear. If you don't want to make a feature of this, tear the paper from the other side so that the rough white edge is concealed under the printed top layer. This is a good choice when you want to create a softer line, perhaps when overlapping torn edges to create a change of colour.

▲ *A sheet of torn mulberry paper in a toning colour makes a lovely textural border for a picture. Tearing this paper pulls out the fibres to make a softly fringed edge. The paper should be dampened where you want it to part. For a straight tear, fold it and wet the folded edge then gently pull it apart. For the more random tearing used here, dampen the paper by drawing curves and shapes with a wet paintbrush or cotton bud (swab).*

DECORATING PAPER FRAMES

You can use pre-printed stickers, but it is easy to make your own frames to suit a particular theme. Trace motifs from books or magazines on to plain paper and adjust the scale on a photocopier if necessary to make a template. Draw around or trace the design on to coloured paper and cut out as many shapes as you need, then glue them on to your album page.

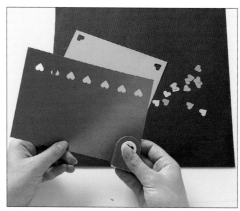

▲ *Specially shaped edging scissors are available in many different designs, and you can use these to create smart decorative effects on coloured paper frames.*

▲ *You can decorate the corners of frames with a punched motif, or punch rows of decorative holes all round the edge. Keep the shapes to decorate the rest of the album page.*

▲ *Use a template to cut decorative shapes from appropriately coloured paper to highlight the theme of an album page, and let them overlap the picture frames.*

▲ *Create an informal look by making a frame from printed stickers. Mount the photograph on a plain background then mass the stickers in groups around it, overlapping the edges and each other.*

▲ *A pricked design makes a pretty, lacy edging for a simple paper frame. Draw the design lightly in pencil then prick evenly along the lines with a bodkin, resting the frame on a soft surface such as a cork tile.*

▲ *Use a stamp of a frame and bright ink to make a frame on plain coloured paper. Cut out a wavy edge for a funky look.*

NOW TRY THIS

Instead of framing pictures, try mounting them over blocks of bright colour to create a collage effect, then frame them with groups of flowers in co-ordinating shades. These could be stickers or your own photographs, carefully cut out.

1 Select individual flowerheads to match the colours in your pictures and cut them out, carefully eliminating any background.

2 Arrange the coloured paper shapes for the background and glue in place, then position the photographs.

3 Arrange the flower cut-outs to create a scattered effect over the background areas, co-ordinating the colours and allowing the petals to overlap the edges of the photographs.

BACKGROUND TREATMENTS

Rather than have plain backgrounds to the pages in your album, decorate them with stamps, stencils, stickers and paint effects in colours and themes that are sympathetic to your photographs. Choose subdued, muted shades for subtle compositions, or be more adventurous and experiment with unusual combinations of colour and pattern.

Choosing colours

The background should flatter the photographs rather than overpower them and its style needs to be in keeping with the subject matter. But you need not restrict your choice to a single colour or design: try making up collages of interesting textures and patterns. Include greetings cards, wrapping paper, children's artwork, and even fabric swatches.

1 Allow the photographs to dictate your choice of background colours, rather than choosing a paper and hoping the pictures will match it. Hold your images against a wide variety of colours and patterns before making your choice. Here the photograph is overpowered by the colour of the background paper.

▲ *Once you have decided on the images you want to mount, think about colours and motifs that underline their theme. These gold papers suit a wedding layout and the heart is a traditional symbol. Play around with combinations of papers until you find a good balance between images and background.*

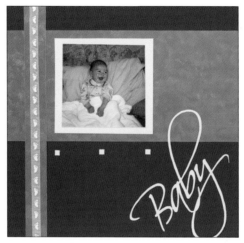

▲ *Blue is the traditional colour scheme for a baby boy, but the dark blue background overlaid with simple bands of lighter tones, with only tiny dashes of baby blue, give this simple treatment a modern look.*

2 Orange and green are opposite each other on the colour wheel, so they complement each other well and the cooler colour tends to recede, making the picture of the pumpkins stand out as the focal point. Against this background you could use accents of orange and other warm, toning colours such as peach and gold to accompany the image.

▲ *Do not shy away from patterned backgrounds; these scraps of delicately patterned wallpaper work beautifully with each other and the warm tones of the cat.*

▲ *If you place the same images on a different background, with colours that clash with the photographs, you can instantly see that it is an unsuitable combination.*

Using patterns

Patterned backgrounds help to give layouts a distinctive style, but need to be carefully chosen to avoid dominating the images and other elements that you may choose to add to the page. Make sure the colours and contrasts in the photographs are strong enough to stand out from the background.

MONOCHROME SCHEMES

An easy way to begin experimenting with pattern is to restrict your use of colour.

1 Gather together a selection of papers, patterned and plain, in a single colour. Experiment by overlapping them or placing them next to each other until you find an arrangement you like. Choose one as the background, and cut a few rectangles or strips from the other papers.

2 For this layout, cut a rectangle of plain blue paper 18 × 25cm/7 × 10in and a strip 5 × 30cm/2 × 12in from another pattern. Stick the rectangle to the left-hand side of the page, 2.5cm/1in in from the top, bottom and left side. Arrange the patterned strip horizontally across the page so it overlaps the lower part of the rectangle. Mat the photographs and add them to the layout.

▲ *Using the same design in a different colour scheme and with different subjects changes the look entirely. Here, the monochromatic green layout includes touches of pale yellow in the flower and buttons to pick up the yellow details in the photographs.*

COMBINING PATTERNED PAPERS

Many ranges of patterned paper are specially designed to be used in combination, making it easy to create interesting backgrounds.

1 This design mimics a wall with wallpaper and a dado rail, the perfect place to display a few photos. Choose a 30cm/12in square sheet of paper for the background and cut a strip of another paper 10cm/4in wide.

2 Glue the strip to the bottom of the page and cover the join with a length of toning ribbon. Arrange two large photographs on the upper part of the page. With a button and an extra length of ribbon, suspend a smaller photo from the ribbon "rail".

▲ *These two papers harmonize perfectly because although the patterns contrast in shape and scale they are printed in the same range of colours. When mixing patterns, go for colours in the same tonal family and try teaming stripes with floral designs, or look for the same motifs in different sizes.*

USING STRIPES AS BORDERS

If you are combining striped and patterned paper, the stripes can be cut up to form a border around the page and frames for the photographs.

1 Choose a paper with wide stripes, and cut four identical strips 4 x 30cm/1 1/2 x 12in. Mount one on each side of the page, matching the stripes. Glue another along the bottom and mitre the corners by cutting diagonally through both layers.

2 Add the last strip at the top of the page, making sure the strips correspond as before, and mitre the two top corners. Mat your selection of photographs in toning shades and mount on the page.

▲ *Four black-and-white photographs of disparate subjects are neatly unified with this simple treatment, which does not distract attention from the pictures.*

USING BOLD PATTERNS

Some patterned papers are bold and dramatic but won't overwhelm photographs if they are paired with strong images or colours. Close-ups of faces or objects work best.

1 Choose a patterned paper that includes as many of the colours in your choice of photographs as possible. Here the bright pinks and oranges pick up the colours of the flowers and the vivid stripes convey the exuberance of spring blossom.

2 Pick shades from the patterned paper to mat the photos: this will help them stand out from the background. Add embellishments that match the colour and theme of the layout.

▶ *The pretty ribbons on this page are chosen to match the striped paper, while the little flower buttons echo the springtime theme.*

Collage techniques

Building up a multilayered background using different papers allows you to introduce a satisfying variety of texture and colour.

USING MULBERRY PAPER

Mulberry paper is available plain or printed, and some sheets incorporate pieces of flowers or leaves, making perfect backgrounds for pictures with a pastoral or garden theme. Its soft feathered edges are very attractive.

1 Choose a selection of papers that match the tones of the photograph. Strips of paper will be used to extend the bands of colour in the sky. To tear them, dip a paintbrush in water then trace a line on the paper. Pull the paper apart while it is wet.

2 Build up the scene with torn strips of mulberry paper; a different shade is created when two colours of the paper overlap. Mat the photograph in black, so that its straight edges form a striking contrast with the soft outlines of the mulberry paper, and mount it on the background.

▲ *This lovely photograph of a sunset has an almost abstract quality, and the collage background made with torn strips of mulberry paper extends the scene very effectively. The dark foreground, reduced to a silhouette in the fading light, is matched by a sheet of black paper covering the lower part of the page.*

MAKING A PAPER COLLAGE

Subtle colour effects can be achieved by building up small pieces of torn paper in a range of toning colours. Begin by tearing a good quantity of the colours you need before applying any glue.

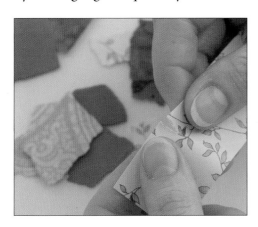

1 Tear the paper into small pieces of a fairly even size, aiming to make rounded shapes. Tear away the straight edges of the paper so that they are roughly torn on all sides.

2 Glue the pieces to the background in a group, overlapping them and mixing the colours at random. If you want to create the effect of falling leaves, you could add a scattering of isolated pieces.

3 Add details to the collage if you wish by stamping motifs or drawing them in with a fibre-tipped pen in a toning colour.

▶ *Here a photograph is enhanced by a colour-co-ordinated collage in subdued colours that has been aged with stamping.*

USING COLLAGED PAPER

Some patterned papers have a collage-effect design, with elements scattered across the paper. If you cut around parts of these, you can slide photographs underneath to look as if they are part of the overall design.

1 Mark with a pencil where a corner or edge of the photograph intersects with an element in the pattern. Use a craft knife to trim along the edge of the pattern.

2 Make more slits across the page to accommodate the photographs you wish to include. Mat the photos and slide them under the flaps.

▲ *Single elements, such as the suitcase on this travel-themed layout, can be trimmed from another sheet of patterned paper and added as embellishments.*

COLOUR BLOCKING

This is an easy technique to master, especially for beginners and when using a monochromatic colour scheme. Photographs and other elements can sit neatly within one block or overlap across several. This design for a 30cm/12in album page is based on a grid of 8 x 8 squares.

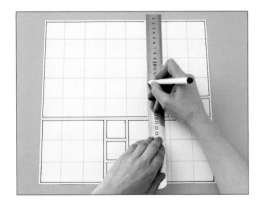

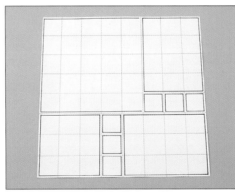

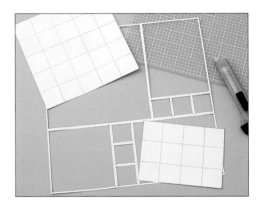

1 Using a grid of 4cm/1½in squares, design the blocks for your layout.

2 Rule 6mm/¼in margins between the blocks and all round the edge of the sheet.

3 Use a craft knife and ruler to cut each template piece out of the grid.

4 Draw round each template on the back of patterned paper and cut out. Use a different paper for each section.

5 Glue the cut-out papers on to a background sheet of 30cm/12in card (stock), following the original layout.

6 Add photographs, embellishments and journaling as desired.

NOW TRY THIS

Traditional patchwork patterns include lots of designs that can be adapted to scrapbooking. This one is called "Shoo Fly" and is a simple combination of squares and triangles in a balanced design to which photographs can be added.

1 Choose one 30cm/12in square paper for the background. From a different paper, cut three 10cm/4in squares. Cut two of these in half diagonally.

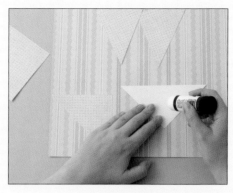

2 Position the background square centrally on the page, and arrange one triangle diagonally across each corner. Glue in place.

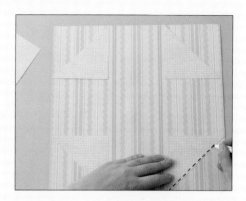

3 Add lines of "stitching" around the patches with a black pen to mimic running stitch and blanket stitch. Glue the remaining square in the centre.

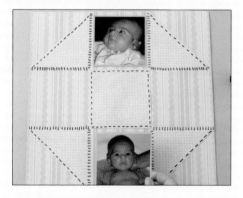

4 Arrange the photographs and embellishments between the patches.

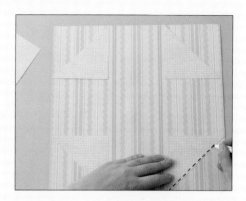

◀ *The patchwork theme is enhanced with drawn-in stitching and lettering designed to resemble appliqué.*

MAKING A SILHOUETTE

This makes an interesting treatment for a photograph of someone in profile. Cut the profile out of black or coloured card (card stock) to form an accompaniment to the photo. You can use the photograph as your guide for the silhouette, or you could draw your own version.

1 Using a computer or photocopier, enlarge the photograph to the desired size for the silhouette and glue to a sheet of dark card.

2 Cut carefully around the outline of the person in the print using a pair of sharp-pointed scissors.

3 Reverse the silhouette and add it to the layout, positioning it to balance the original photograph.

Adding paint, chalk and ink

Instead of using printed paper, you can create your own unique patterns to form tailor-made backgrounds for your collections. If you don't feel confident about your painting and drawing skills, just choose from the host of ready-made stencils and stamps available, and work with colour-washed backgrounds.

PAINTING BACKGROUNDS

For interesting textural effects, make patterns in wet paint. You can try a variety of objects such as the blunt end of a paintbrush, a cocktail stick (toothpick) or a wooden skewer, drawing simple curls, spirals and stars. Or cut a comb from stiff cardboard and draw it through the paint.

1 Mix some acrylic paint with wallpaper paste to make a thick paste. With a wide brush, paint the surface of a sheet of heavy cartridge (construction) paper using even strokes in one direction. Use a comb to make patterns in the wet paint.

2 Draw the comb in two directions for a woven pattern, or use random strokes for bark-like effects. Allow the paper to dry completely. If it buckles, press the back with a cool iron, then leave it between heavy books to keep it flat.

ANTIQUING

Paper with an aged look can be useful for heritage layouts, either as a background, as part of a collage, or for titles and journaling.

1 To achieve an antique effect, brush a strong solution of tea over the surface of white paper. Allow to dry, then press with a cool iron if necessary to flatten. The paper can then be torn or cut up to use in a collage. You could also try singeing the edges to add to the effect.

RUBBER STAMPING

There are literally hundreds of rubber stamps available on the market nowadays, so you will always be able to find something to complement your album page designs. You could use small motifs for surface decoration, or large scale designs that form an all-over background pattern.

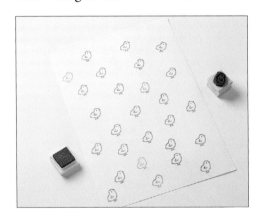

1 Use a single motif to stamp an all-over design on to plain paper to create a patterned background. Press the stamp in the ink pad, then press it on the paper, taking care not to smudge. Repeat as desired. Apply the images in a random pattern, or rule faint pencil guidelines.

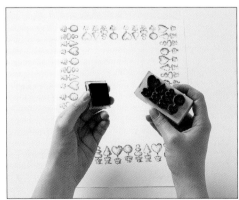

2 The elongated shape of this topiary stamp makes it ideal for a border design. If you want a symmetrical design, measure the stamp and work out how many repeats will fit the page. Ensure the stamp aligns with the edge, and that each new print lines up with the designs already stamped.

3 Rubber-stamped designs can be enhanced very simply by colouring the motifs lightly with coloured pencils. You could also try using various kinds of paint to achieve different effects.

USING CHALKS

Sets of acid-free chalks are available in various ranges of different shades and can be used to create very soft colour effects on very light or very dark papers. To extend the tones of a photograph across a full layout, use chalks to recreate the scene, or use them to tint embossed paper.

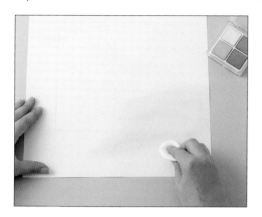

1 Measure the photograph, subtract 1cm/⅜in from each side, and trace the dimensions on to a 30cm/12in square sheet of white card (stock). With a pad of cotton wool (ball), pick up some coloured chalk and rub it across the page.

2 Continue to build up the chalk scene, matching the shades used in the photograph and using a clean pad for each new colour. For details such as the path and fence posts, use a cotton bud (swab) or the applicator supplied with the chalk to draw finer lines.

3 Leave the page overnight, to allow the chalks to settle into the paper. Finally, add the photograph in the marked area.

COMBINING CHALKS AND STAMPING

Used together, rubber stamps and chalks enable you to combine fine pictorial detail with soft colouring. You can either use the chalks to fill in the stamped motifs or rub them over the paper to create a mist of colour over the whole page before applying the stamped image.

1 Choose rubber stamp motifs to match the theme of the page and stamp them at random over the background sheet using a range of coloured inks. Using a cotton wool pad (ball) rub chalks in toning colours across the page to create a soft wash of background colour. Leave the page for a few hours to allow the chalk to settle into the paper, then add the matted photographs and embellishments.

▶ *The smaller photograph of a leafy country track inspired the choice of leaf stamps in soft autumn shades for this background. The chalks harmonize well with the horse's colouring, and a length of real ribbon provides the finishing touch.*

STENCILLING

Charming backgrounds can be created using stencils, which work well with paints, oil sticks or chalks. Stencils are easy to cut from manila card or clear acetate, and you can work from templates or draw your own. Hundreds of ready-cut designs are also available in craft stores.

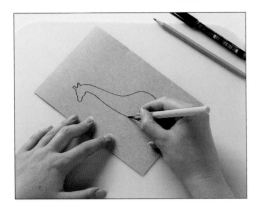

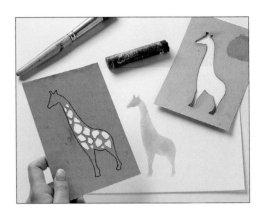

1 Trace the design and transfer it to stencil card. Working on a cutting mat and using a craft knife cut out each shape, taking care not to cut through any "bridges" holding elements of the design in place.

2 Using an oil stick or appropriate paint, and a large stencil brush, dab paint on to the chosen area using the stencil. Lift the stencil carefully to avoid smudging the edges and leave to dry.

3 Add details with a second stencil. Leave to dry.

▼ *Stencilled animals and a Noah's ark make a lovely setting for a young child's picture.*

EMBELLISHING THE PAGES

Adding the final decorative touches is often the most enjoyable part of assembling your album pages. The elements you use should enhance the photographs and complement the background.

Papercraft

Keep a collection of offcuts of interesting papers for these delicate decorations, which use precise folding and cutting to create pretty three-dimensional ornaments, from decorative tags and envelopes to classic origami flowers.

▲ *The photographs here have been enhanced with rolled paper frames.*

PAPER ROLLING

Rolled paper edgings and frames work particularly well when you use paper that is printed differently on each side, as the rolling exposes the contrasting pattern or colour.

1 To create a rolled heart, draw the shape on the back of the paper and cut a series of slashes from the centre to the edge.

2 Roll a dampened cotton bud (swab) along the cut edges to soften the fibres. Turn the paper over and roll each section towards the edge of the shape.

3 Glue a photograph or embellishment in the centre of the heart motif.

MAKING A LACÉ DESIGN

Pronounced "lassay", this technique works best when cut from two-sided card (stock). It can be cut using a metal template (you can buy lots of different designs) or you can devise your own using a pair of compasses or a protractor. Small patterned cuts are made in the card and the cut piece is bent over to form a bicoloured design.

1 Transfer the template to the wrong side of the card using a pencil (the lines will be erased later).

2 Using a sharp craft knife, cut neatly along the lines from end to middle. Erase the pencil marks and turn the card over.

3 Lift one petal and fold it backwards. Once all the petals are folded, tuck each one under the edge of the previous point.

PAPER APPLIQUÉ

Appliqué literally means "applied". Usually appliqué is a technique used with fabric in the art of patchwork. Here it is used with paper. Cut-out shapes in paper or card (stock) of different colours or patterns can be stacked together to create three-dimensional motifs. Here the appliqué effect is emphasized by lines of decorative "stitches" drawn around the card patches. Attaching the motif by means of sticky foam pads raises it a little above the surface, so that the butterfly seems to hover over the flowers.

1 Trace the outlines of the butterfly and the applied panels for the wings and copy them on to a sheet of card to make templates. Cut out all the pieces.

2 Select sheets of card in four different colours. Draw round the templates for the basic shape and the body in one colour, and divide the smaller coloured details between the remaining sheets, keeping the design symmetrical.

3 Cut out all the pieces of the butterfly.

4 Using a fine-tipped black pen, draw lines of small "stitches" around the edge of each coloured shape. Glue the shapes to the butterfly's wings. Create a pair of antennae from a length of fine silver wire, curling the ends tightly, and glue to the head. Attach the body to the wings using foam pads to give a three-dimensional effect, and use more foam pads to anchor the butterfly to the background.

▶ *This cut-out butterfly, floating a little above the surface of the album page, softens what would otherwise be a very rigid layout of squares, and is perfectly in keeping with the floral theme. The colours of the panels on its wings are repeated in the picture mats.*

QUILLING

Thin strips of finely rolled paper are arranged into pictorial images suitable for scrapbooking. This traditional craft requires a special tool and narrow strips of plain coloured paper, which you can buy specially cut. It is possible to cut them yourself but they must be precisely the same width all along their length. Once you've mastered your first roll (it's very easy) you can make this pretty flower.

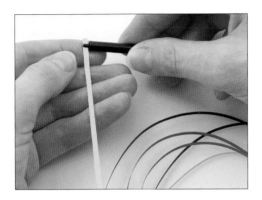

1 Make the leaves first. Slide one end of a green strip into the notch on the quilling tool.

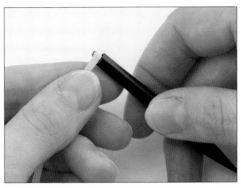

2 Roll the paper tightly and evenly on to the tool.

3 Gently ease the rolled paper off the tool and allow it to uncoil to the desired size. Glue the end and hold until dry.

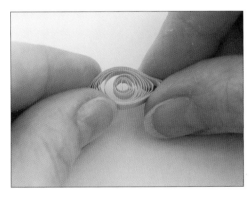

4 Pinch the edges of the circle on opposite sides, using your thumbs and forefingers.

5 Make four red coils for the petals. Make two pinches close to each other, and press the rest of the circle down towards them.

6 Roll a tight black coil for the centre. Cut a stem from green paper and assemble the pieces to complete the poppy.

DECORATING TAGS

Tags are quick-to-make scrapbook embellishments and use only small quantities of materials. You can use a die-cutting machine or templates, or make the shape by just snipping the corners off a rectangle.

1 Snip two corners off a rectangle of card. Punch a hole for the string and shape the other two corners with a corner cutter.

2 Embellish the tag as desired. In this case ribbons and ribbon roses were used and the tag was tied with coloured fibres.

▲ *Use simple tags to hold pictures or text, or just as decoration. They can be glued to a page or hung by ribbon ties.*

MAKING POCKETS

As vellum is translucent, you can use this simple pocket for photos, or just slip some journaling or souvenirs such as tickets inside.

1 Cut out a pocket template and draw around it on vellum.

2 Fold in the side and bottom flaps. Glue the flaps and attach to the layout.

▼ *Vellum allows you to see what's inside the pocket without taking it out.*

MAKING MINI-ENVELOPES

A tiny envelope adds excitement to a page, and could be used to hold small treasures such as a handful of confetti in a wedding album, a scrap of lace or even a lock of hair. Or you could inscribe a secret message on a little card and tuck it inside.

1 Draw around an envelope template and cut out.

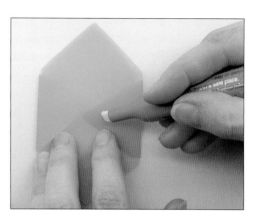

2 Fold in three of the corners and glue the overlapping edges. Fold down the top.

▶ *For a page celebrating the arrival of a baby girl, you could decorate some little envelopes with pretty labels and tiny pink bows.*

PLASTIC POCKETS

Cut a pocket from the lower edge of a stationery folder. Staple the sides together and insert a memento. Staple the top closed or leave it open so that the contents can be taken out.

Cut two squares from a plastic folder and pierce holes around the edges. Attach a memento or decorations to one piece using double-sided tape. Lace the sides together with cord and knot the ends.

MAKING POP-UP PAGES

Proper pop-ups like these party balloons work only on pages that aren't in page protectors, since it's the action of the pages opening out that makes the pop-up rise. You can, however, arrange lifting flaps on single pages inside page protectors, either by cutting a slit for them or by sticking them to the outside with another, cut-down, page protector to cover them. These pages are good for children's themes.

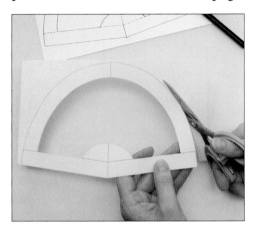

1 Transfer the pop-up template at the back of the book to white card (stock) and cut it out. Score along the dotted lines. Fold the bottom struts up and the arch back.

▼*A pop-up is a dramatic ornament for a strap or post-bound album.*

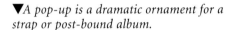

2 Apply adhesive to the bottom of the two struts, then glue the whole pop-up in place across two pages of the album. Following the templates, cut out the four balloons and two presents from plain card in a range of bright colours.

3 Wrap a ribbon round each present and tie ribbons round the ends of the balloons. Stick the parcels on the base of the pop-up, and balloons on the arch, making sure they will not jam the pop-up when it closes. Stick the tails of the balloons behind the parcels. Add photographs to the layout.

MAKING AN ORIGAMI SHIRT

This traditional craft of paper folding can be successfully exploited for scrapbooking designs. This clever little design really does look just like a tiny shirt, and makes a lovely embellishment for pictures of children playing at dressing up, or perhaps dressed for a special occasion. All the creases need to be sharp and accurate.

1 Cut a piece of patterned paper 10 × 20cm/4 × 8in. Fold in half lengthwise, then unfold. Fold down 1.5cm/½in from the narrow top edge. Fold over again.

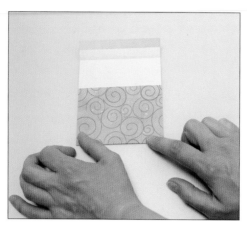

2 Unfold the two folds at the top, and fold up 7cm/2¾in from the bottom edge.

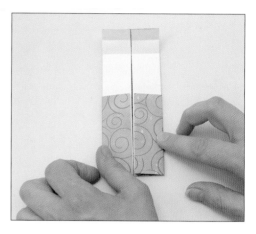

3 Fold the two long edges in to meet in the centre.

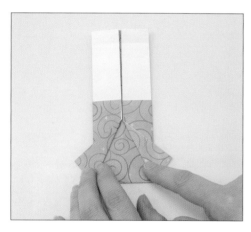

4 Fold out the bottom corners (these will form the sleeves).

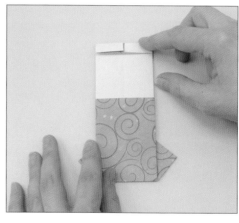

5 Turn over and fold the top edge down once, along the pre-existing crease.

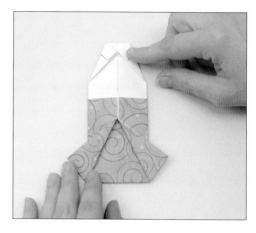

6 Turn over again and fold the top corners into the centre to form the collar.

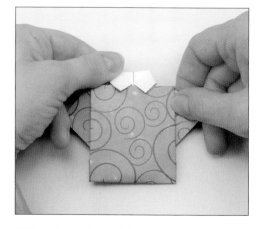

7 Fold in half horizontally, so that the original lower edge just touches the outer corners of the collar.

8 Tuck the points of the collar over the folded edge to complete the shirt. Add a bead necklace or a ribbon tie.

▲ *For this page the shirt is neatly trimmed with a necklace threaded with a child's initial, and is accompanied by a little skirt made by concertina pleating a strip of paper in a toning colour. Photo mats using the two papers tie the whole scheme together.*

TEA BAG FOLDING

This technique gets its unusual name because its inventor made her first fold using a colourful tea bag envelope. It's also known as miniature kaleidoscopic origami, and you can buy or download sheets printed with small patterned squares. The easiest design is a rosette, which can be used as a decorative element or as the "O" in a word like "snow" or "love".

1 Cut out eight patterned tea bag squares from a printed sheet.

2 Fold the first square diagonally, with the patterned side inside.

3 Unfold and turn the paper over so the back of the square is facing you.

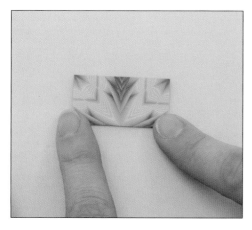

4 Fold the square in half horizontally, taking the bottom edge up to the top edge.

5 Unfold it, then fold it in half vertically, taking the right edge to the left edge with the patterned side inside. Unfold.

6 With the patterned side facing you, push the valley folds in and bring the two uncreased quarters of the square together.

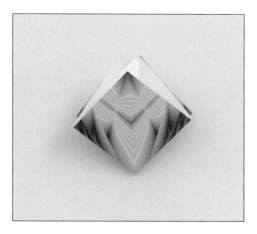

7 Fold all the remaining squares in the same way, then take one in your fingers, with the peak down and the open folds to the top.

8 Open the fold on one side, and spread some glue on it. Slide the next square, peak down, in between these two sticky sides, and press to make the glue stick.

9 Go round the circle, adding each square in the same way until the rosette is complete, then glue the last section over the first.

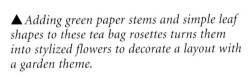

▲ *Adding green paper stems and simple leaf shapes to these tea bag rosettes turns them into stylized flowers to decorate a layout with a garden theme.*

10 Glue a cluster of beads or sequins in the centre to complete the decoration.

IRIS FOLDING

This technique creates intricate spiralling designs using folded strips of paper arranged like the panels of a camera iris. It is an ingenious method of creating curved forms using only straight components, and looks very effective when mounted inside an aperture. Experiment with combinations of plain and patterned paper or contrasting colours.

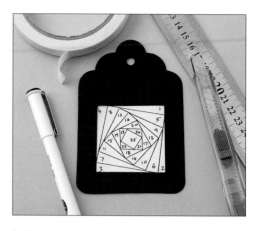

1 Choose four different shades of paper and cut into strips 2cm/¾in wide.

2 Fold each strip in half lengthwise and glue the two sides together, right sides out.

3 Cut a 5cm/2in aperture in black card (stock) and use low-tack masking tape to fix the template temporarily within the aperture. The pattern will be built up backwards, so place the black card face down on the table, with the template below.

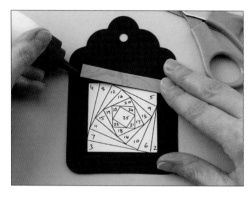

4 Cut a piece 6cm/2¼in long from a length of brown paper. Line it up to cover the triangle labelled 1, with the folded edge towards the centre. Glue the edges of the strip to stick it down (be careful not to get any adhesive on the template below).

5 Take a 6cm/2¼in length of pink paper, and glue it in position to cover the section marked 2 on the template.

6 Take a 6cm/2¼in length of blue paper, and glue it in position to cover the section marked 3 on the template.

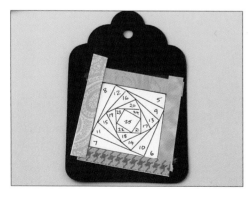

7 Take a 6cm/2¼in length of green paper, and glue it in position to cover the section marked 4 on the template.

8 Continue round the spiral, adding paper strips as follows: brown (5), pink (6), blue (7), green (8), brown (9), pink (10), blue (11), green (12), brown (13), pink (14), blue (15), green (16), brown (17), pink (18), blue (19), green (20), brown (21), pink (22) blue (23), green (24).

9 The strips spiral into the centre, leaving a square hole (section 25 on the template).

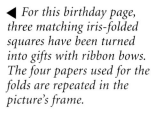

▲ *This six-petalled flower design accentuates the spiralling shapes created in iris folding. This time just three different papers have been used, and a paper stem and leaves have been added to complete the picture.*

◀ *For this birthday page, three matching iris-folded squares have been turned into gifts with ribbon bows. The four papers used for the folds are repeated in the picture's frame.*

10 Cover the central hole by gluing on a square of brown paper.

11 Turn the card over and remove the template to reveal the completed design.

12 Turn the square into a house with a brown triangle for the roof and a folded paper chimney.

Adding metal and wire

Eyelets, wire decorations and metal tags add lustre and a change of texture to your layouts. Make sure hard materials of this kind are well protected and positioned so that they will not damage your precious photographs.

EMBOSSING METAL

Foil of around 38 gauge is suitable for embossing, working on the back to create a raised pattern, or on the front to indent a pattern.

1 To make a tag, draw round a card tag on a sheet of foil using an embossing tool or dry ballpoint pen and a ruler.

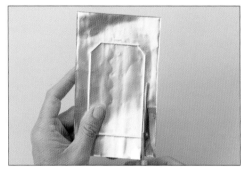

2 Cut out the tag with old scissors, trimming 2mm/¹⁄₈in outside the embossed line. Punch a hole in the top of the tag.

▲ *A simple outline of evenly spaced dots makes a pretty decoration for small metal picture frames.*

3 Place the tag face down on thick cardboard and emboss a row of dots inside the marked line. Add other motifs as desired and glue on a photograph or message.

◀ *For extra charm add some small motifs such as stylized flower shapes or these simple stars.*

USING WIRE

Fine wire in silver, gold and other colours can be twisted into delicate coils and curls and used in conjunction with paper decorations, fabric or ribbon flowers, sequins or clay ornaments.

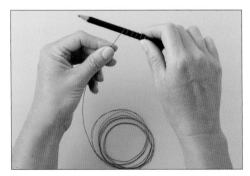

1 To make a coil, wrap some coloured wire around a pencil, then slide it off and trim.

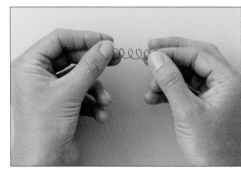

2 Flatten the coils with your fingers and glue the wire in place on the layout.

▲ *A wire coil makes an offbeat stem for a punched flower decoration in shiny plastic.*

INSERTING BRADS

Brads or paper fasteners are a decorative way to attach pictures.

1 To attach a picture to a tag, cut a small slit in each corner of the picture, and corresponding slits in the tag.

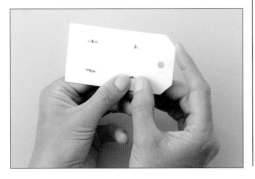

2 Push in the brads and open out the pins on the back, pressing them flat. Cover with small pieces of sticky tape if desired.

▲ *Brads can be used to hold layers of papers and embellishments together or they can be used for purely decorative purposes.*

▼ *This picture is held in place on its mount with eyelets in each corner, through which a length of fibre fringe has been threaded.*

INSERTING EYELETS

Eyelets can be used to hold several layers of paper or card together; in addition they provide holes through which ribbon or string can be laced.

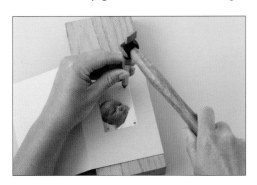

1 Glue the picture to the card, then place it on a block of wood. To make holes for the eyelets, place an eyelet punch in one corner of the picture and tap it sharply with a tack hammer. Repeat at each corner. Insert an eyelet into the first hole, through both picture and card.

2 Turn the card over. Place the pointed end of the eyelet setter into the collar of the eyelet, and tap it sharply with a tack hammer. This will split and flatten the collar. Repeat for the remaining eyelets.

►*Outsize coloured metal eyelets threaded with string make an eye-catching trimming for a plain frame.*

Adding texture and ornament

Relief effects add subtle interest to a page. Embossed motifs can underline a theme and draw attention to the tactile quality of lovely paper, while glitter and sequins add a change of texture as well as sparkle. Use tiny beads or model your own motifs for three-dimensional embellishments.

BLIND (DRY) EMBOSSING

If you are using good paper with an interesting texture, embossed motifs make the most of its quality and lend an extra dimension to a layout.

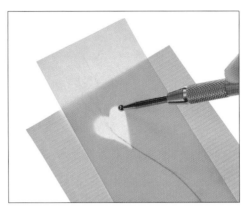

1 Draw your chosen motif on a piece of card (stock). Using a craft knife and working on a cutting mat, cut out the motif to make a stencil for embossing.

2 Place the stencil on a lightbox, if you have one, and lay a sheet of watercolour paper on top. Use an embossing tool to press into the paper, through the stencil. This is now the back of your paper. Reposition the paper to repeat the embossed motif as many times as required.

▲ *It's possible to use real objects as templates for embossed designs. On very smooth paper you could try a finely detailed object such as a coin, while on heavily textured paper greater relief is needed. Here, a flat scallop shell has been used to embossed rough handmade paper with a bold design.*

SHRINKING PLASTIC

1 Using felt-tipped pens, draw a design on the rough side of a piece of shrink plastic. If the plastic does not have a rough side, sand it lightly first with fine glass paper. The image should be no larger than 12.5 x 10cm/5 x 4in. Bear in mind that it will become seven times smaller and the colours will intensify.

2 Cut out the image, leaving a narrow border all round. Bake the plastic in an oven for a few minutes following the manufacturer's instructions. It will twist and turn then become flat. Remove the image, which will be pliable, and place a weight such as a book on top for a few moments to keep it flat while it cools and sets.

◄ *Embossed on thick, soft watercolour paper this simple heart motif gains complexity when repeated and overlapped in a soft curve, creating an engaging interplay of light and shade.*

GLITTER AND SEQUINS

If you want to add a little sparkle to a photograph, glitter paint is easy to control, allowing you to highlight fine details of the image. This product is particularly effective on black-and-white photographs.

1 Apply glitter paint to selected areas of a picture via the nozzle of the container or using a fine paintbrush.

2 Attach some small cabouchon jewellery stones to the glitter paint, using a pair of tweezers to position them accurately.

3 Gently drop sequins and sequin dust on the glitter paint. Shake off the excess.

RAISED (WET) EMBOSSING

In wet embossing, a design is stamped on the paper then coated with embossing powder, which is fused with the stamped design using heat to produce a raised motif. Embossing powders and inks are available in many colours as well as metallic and pearlized finishes.

1 Press the stamp into the ink pad and stamp an image on to the paper where required. While the ink is still wet, sprinkle embossing powder over the image. Make sure it is completely covered, then pour the excess powder back into the pot.

2 Use a dry paintbrush to gently brush away any excess embossing powder from the paper.

3 Switch on a heat gun. Holding it about 10cm/4in from the surface of the paper, gently blow heat over the embossing powder until it melts and flows together to make a raised image.

LOOSE GLITTER

Glitter needs to be attached to the paper using glue, usually painted on with a brush, so broad effects are easier to achieve than fine detail.

1 Using an old paintbrush, draw the design in PVA (white) glue. Sprinkle on the glitter.

2 Shake off the excess glitter on to a sheet of scrap paper then pour it back into the container.

BEADS

Small glass beads can be strung on thread using a beading needle or threaded on to fine wire: 0.4mm is a suitable thickness to use.

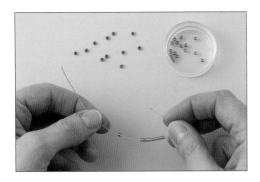

◀ Mount a photograph on card using spray adhesive. Resting on a cutting mat, use an awl to pierce holes at each end where you wish to add wires. Thread coloured wire up through one hole, bending back the end on the underside to keep the wire in place. Thread on a few beads. Insert the wire through the next hole. Bend back the wire to hold it in place on the underside, and snip off the excess with wirecutters. Repeat to attach wires between all the holes.

▲ In this celebratory layout, coils of fine wire frame the pictures in the central panel.

BEADED FLOWER

Glass rocaille beads are available in a range of exciting colours and add sparkle and colour to layouts. When threaded on wire they can be manipulated easily to make motifs.

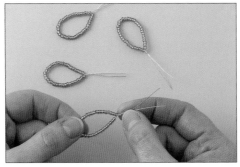

I Bend back 3cm/1¼in of one end of a 12.5cm/5in length of fine wire to stop the beads slipping off. Thread on rocaille beads to a point 3cm/1¼in from the other end.

2 Twist the wire ends together under the beads to make a loop. Repeat to make four petals. Pierce the centre of a piece of card and poke the wire ends through the hole.

3 Stick the wire ends to the underside of the card with sticky tape. Splay the petals open on the front of the card and sew on a button to form the centre of the flower.

TASSELS

Little tassels made of silky thread are a charming trimming for elements such as small books containing journaling. They are quick and easy to make using embroidery thread (floss).

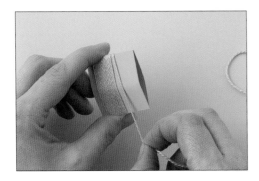

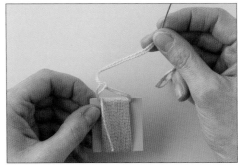

I To make a tassel 4cm/1½in long, cut out a rectangle of card (card stock) measuring 8 × 4cm/3¼ × 1½in and fold it in half, parallel with the short edges. (Cut a larger rectangle of card to make a bigger tassel.) Bind thread around the card many times.

2 Fold a 40cm/16in length of thread in half and thread the ends through the eye of a large needle. Slip the needle behind the strands close to the fold then insert the needle through the loop of thread and pull tightly.

3 Slip the point of a scissor blade between the card layers and cut through the strands. Thread the needle with single thread and bind it tightly around the top of the tassel. Insert the needle into the tassel to lose the end of the thread. Trim the ends level.

Using modelling clay

*Polymer and air-drying clays are ideal for moulding small three-dimensional motifs. Their fine texture enables
you to create very detailed objects. Polymer clay needs to be baked in a domestic oven; air-drying clay hardens over
about 24 hours. Glue motifs in place using strong epoxy glue.*

CUTTING CLAY

For flat motifs, roll the clay out on a
smooth cutting mat using a rolling pin.
Rolling guides, such as two pieces of
plywood placed on each side of the clay,
guarantee an even thickness.

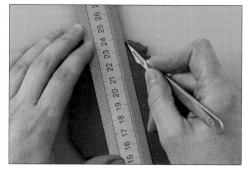

I Cut the clay with a craft knife. Cut
straight edges against a metal ruler.

2 Use cookie cutters to stamp motifs then
pull away the excess clay.

MAKING POLYMER CLAY MOTIFS

Complex motifs are easier to make if you first break the shapes down into a series of
geometric forms, such as cylinders, cones, spheres and rectangles. These basic shapes
can be pressed together and refined using modelling tools.

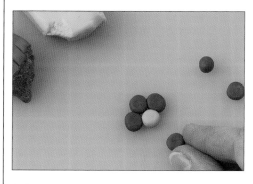

I To make a flower, roll a ball of polymer
clay for the centre and six matching balls
for the petals. Flatten all the balls and press
the petals around the centre.

2 Shape the petals by impressing them
close to the flower centre using the pointed
handle of an artist's brush.

3 Roll a ball for a bear's head. and three
smaller balls for the muzzle and ears. Flatten
all the balls and press together. Impress the
ears with the handle of an artist's brush.

4 Press on a tiny ball of black clay for
the nose. Stamp the eyes with the glass
head of a dressmaker's pin and use the
point to indent a line down the muzzle.

STAMPING CLAY

For repeated motifs, flat shapes of polymer or air-drying clay can be stamped with any object with an interesting profile. Novelty
buttons, for example, make good stamps. If the button has a shank, you can hold this to stamp the button into the clay. Bonsai
wire (from specialist nurseries) is ideal for making wire stamping tools for curls and spirals as it is thick but very pliable.

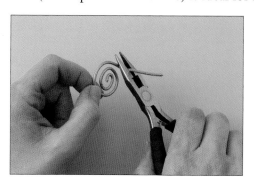

◀**I** To make a wire stamping tool,
shape the wire using jewellery pliers.
Bend the free end up at 90 degrees to
form a handle.

▶ **2** Hold the handle and stamp the motif
on to polymer or air-drying clay.

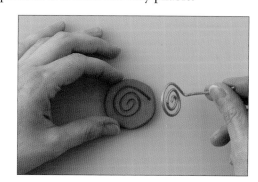

SEWING AND FABRICS

You can use fabrics and fibres of all kinds to add texture and variety to your album pages, and all can be enhanced with decorative stitching and embroidery, by hand or machine. Bold stitches also look good on paper and card (stock). If you are machine sewing on paper use a new needle.

STRAIGHT STITCH

Use plain machine stitching to join fabrics to paper or card (stock).

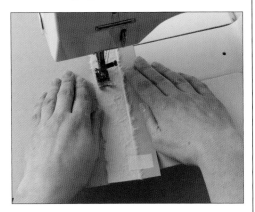

▲ For decorative effect or to apply a contrast coloured border, tear or cut a strip of paper or fabric. Tape it to the background with masking tape at the top and bottom. Stitch the strip with a straight stitch either in a straight line or meander in a wavy line. Remove the masking tape. Pull the thread ends to the wrong side and knot them. Cut off the excess thread.

ZIG-ZAG

In a contrasting colour, zig-zag stitch makes a decorative border.

▲ Stick a photograph in place with paper glue. Stitch along the edges of the photo with a zig-zag stitch, pivoting the stitching at the corners. Pull the thread ends to the wrong side and knot them. Cut off the excess thread.

SATIN STITCH

Decorative lines of satin stitch can be worked on paper, card or fabric.

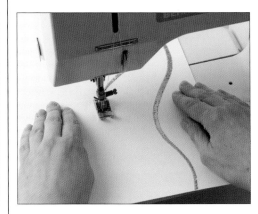

▲ To work a line of satin stitch on card (card stock) or fabric, gradually increase and decrease the width of the zig-zag stitch as you stitch. These lines are sewn with a shaded thread in random wavy lines. If you prefer, draw guidelines lightly with a pencil first. Pull the thread ends to the wrong side and knot them. Cut off the excess thread.

SATIN STITCH MOTIF

For a simple fabric motif, work the outline in satin stitch, using either matching or contrasting thread, then cut it out and attach with glue.

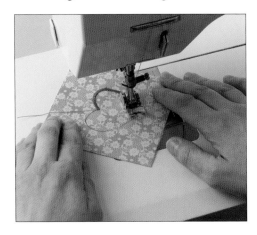

I Draw the outline of the motif on fabric. Stitch along the line with a close zig-zag stitch, pivoting the stitching at any corners, until you return to the starting point. Pull the ends of the threads to the wrong side and knot them. Cut off the excess thread.

2 Use a pair of sharp embroidery scissors to cut away the fabric close to the stitching.

RUNNING STITCH

To keep your stitches perfectly even and avoid tearing paper or card (card stock), it's best to make the holes first using an awl.

1 Stick the photograph in place with paper glue. Resting on a cutting mat, pierce a row of holes along two opposite edges of the picture, using an awl or paper piercer.

2 Knot the end of a length of fine cord. Thread the cord in and out of the holes. Knot the cord on the last hole and cut off the excess. Repeat on the opposite edge.

CROSS STITCH

Use thick embroidery thread (floss) to make large-scale cross stitches.

1 Stick the photograph in position with spray adhesive and "sew" along the top and bottom edges with a row of large cross stitches using embroidery thread. To make it easier to sew, pierce a hole at each end of the cross with an awl, resting on a cutting mat. Knot the thread ends on the underside to start and finish.

GUIDE HOLES FOR HAND SEWING

Instead of piercing holes individually, try using your sewing machine, set to a long stitch length: the holes will be perfectly even and straight.

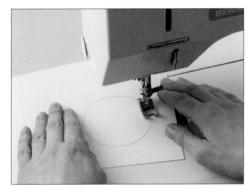

1 To create a frame or line of evenly spaced holes to sew through, first draw your design lightly with a pencil. Stitch with a straight stitch but no thread. Rub away the pencil marks with an eraser.

2 Sew in and out of the holes with thread. Knot the thread ends on the underside to start and finish. A photo or charm can be stuck within the frame.

▲ *A felt cover with a border of bold blanket stitching is a pretty treatment for a mini-album containing baby pictures.*

Working with fabric

A box of fabric scraps can be a real treasure trove when you are designing layouts. Materials such as net won't fray and looks lovely when gathered. Sheer organza is especially useful for subtle effects.

APPLIQUÉ

Bonding web is a fusible webbing used to apply fabric to fabric. It is simply ironed on, prevents fraying and is ideal for appliqué work.

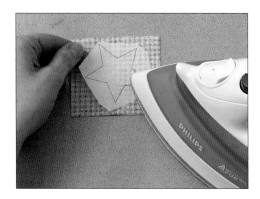

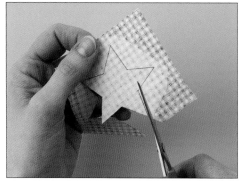

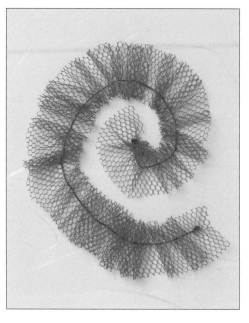

1 Draw your motif, in reverse if not symmetrical, on the paper backing of the bonding web. Roughly cut out the shape and iron it on to the wrong side of the fabric.

2 Cut out the design. Peel off the backing paper and position the motif right side up on the background. Press with a hot iron to fuse it in place. Oversew the edges by hand or with a machine satin stitch if you wish.

▲ *To make a pretty net spiral decoration, cut a 50 x 1.5cm/20 x ⅝in strip of net. Run a gathering thread along one long edge. Pull up the gathers until the strip is 15cm/6in long. Curl the strip and glue it in a spiral shape to your background using all-purpose household glue.*

ORGANZA LAYERS

This sheer fabric is available in many colours, some shot with silver or gold for exciting effects.

1 Cut a motif such as this tree from fabric or paper and stick it to the background card (card stock) with spray adhesive.

2 Tear strips of organza fabric. Use spray adhesive to stick the strips across the card overlapping or singly in bands. Trim the organza level with the edges of the card. Glue on sequins to complete the picture.

▶ *Sheer fabrics such as organza can be layered to create depth and interesting tonal effects. Here the raw edges also suggest grass.*

TIE-DYEING

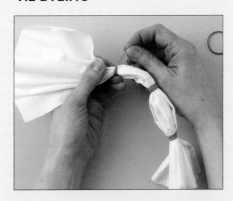

1 Wash and dry a piece of 100 per cent cotton fabric. Roughly gather the fabric in tight accordion folds and bind tightly with elastic bands where you want paler stripes in the design.

2 Dampen the fabric. Wearing protective gloves, plunge the fabric bundle into a bowl of cold water dye made up according to the manufacturer's instructions.

3 After the required soaking time, wash the fabric, rinse until the water runs clear, remove the bands and smooth it out to reveal the effect. Leave to dry then press with a hot iron.

NET SKIRT

A scrap of gathered net can be turned into a beautiful ballgown in no time.

▼ Cut a 14 × 6cm/5½ × 2½in rectangle of net. Gather one short edge tightly. Press a piece of iron-on interfacing to the wrong side of some matching fabric and cut out a bodice shape about 2.5cm/1in across. Glue the bodice and skirt to the background and attach a stick-on jewel at the waist.

RIBBON WEAVING

It's worth experimenting with ribbons of different widths to see what effects you can create. Once you're happy with the design, iron-on interfacing keeps it in place.

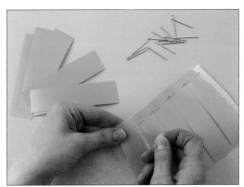

1 Cut a piece of iron-on interfacing to the finished size of your panel adding a 1cm/⅜in margin at each edge. Matching the depth of the interfacing, cut enough lengths for the "warp" ribbons to fit along one edge. Lay them on the adhesive side of the interfacing and pin them in place along the top edge.

▶ **3** Press the ribbons with a hot iron to fuse them to the interfacing, removing the pins as you work. Press the raw edges under.

2 Cut enough lengths of contrasting "weft" ribbons to fit along one side edge. Weave the first ribbon in and out of the warp ribbons, passing it over one and under the next until you reach the opposite edge. Repeat to form a chequered pattern and pin all the ends in place.

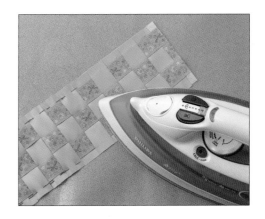

◀ *A tiny evening dress, easily made from scraps of fabric, would make a romantic detail for a party or prom layout.*

LETTERING SKILLS

While pictures are the focal points of scrapbook layouts, titles, captions and written details are crucial to creating lasting souvenirs that keep your memories intact. Word-processing software and the thousands of available fonts enable you to establish a host of different moods and characters for your pages, but writing by hand stamps them with a unique personality – yours. Perfect calligraphy isn't essential, but practising a few of the techniques that go towards mastering this traditional skill can be helpful in improving the grace and legibility of your own handwriting.

BASIC PENMANSHIP

A broad nib, pen or brush is the essential tool for calligraphy. When you hold the pen in your hand the flat tip forms an angle to the horizontal writing line (called the pen angle). It takes some adjustment to use this sort of tool after using pointed pens and pencils, so practising basic strokes is helpful.

Writing position

To produce beautiful work you need a relaxed posture, so spend some time adjusting your position so that you are comfortable. You may like to work on a drawing board resting on a table top, or secured to the edge of a table so that the paper is on gentle slope. If you prefer, you can rest the board on your lap, or flat on a table, resting your weight on your non-writing arm so that you have free movement with your pen.

Remember to place some extra sheets beneath the paper you are working on to act as padding: this will help the flexibility of the nib and stop it scratching the paper and spattering ink. Attach the writing sheets securely to the board with masking tape.

Light should fall evenly on your working area; although good daylight is best, you can also use an adjustable lamp to light the page.

Terminology

Calligraphy uses special terms to describe the consituent parts of letters and words and the way they are written. The style or "hand" in which the writing is created is composed of "letterforms". These are divided into capital, or "upper-case" letters and smaller "lower-case" letters. Most text is written in the latter because they are easier to read than solid blocks of capitals.

The "x-height" is the height of the full letter in capitals or the main body of

◄ *Calligraphy pens are available with different size nibs. This type of pen can be used with different colours and consistencies of ink.*

small letters, excluding "ascenders" and "descenders", which extend above or below the line of the text.

Calligraphers use pencil guidelines to ensure that their strokes are correctly placed on the page, and the two most important are those drawn to mark the top and bottom of the x-height.

Forming strokes

When you write with a normal pen, it can easily be moved round the page. When you are using a calligraphy pen this is not possible because the nib resists against the paper and may cause an ink blot or mark. For this reason, letters are made from several separate strokes, lifting the pen between them. For example, the letter "o" is made using two strokes, with one pen lift, while a small "d" is made in three strokes and other letters may require four. Practise slowly to start with.

Three strokes

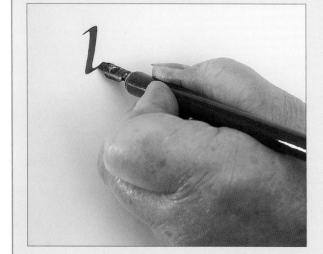

WRITING WITH THE LEFT HAND

If you are left-handed you should sit to the right of the paper and tuck the left elbow into the waist, twisting the wrist so as to hold the pen at the required angle. Special left-oblique nibs are available to minimize the amount that the wrist needs to be bent, but if you can manage with straight-edged nibs the left-hander will have a greater choice of nibs available to them.

Four strokes

PRACTICE STROKES

To begin with it is helpful to practise just keeping the whole nib edge against the paper.

Practise simple curves and angles before you form any letters. Zig-zag patterns will show you the thinnest and thickest marks the nib is capable of.

PEN ANGLES

Holding the pen at the same angle to the writing line for every letter is an essential discipline to create letters that work well together. Practise first on spare paper. A line of differently angled letters will look odd.

Resist the temptation to move the wrist as you would in standard writing. As you complete each letter, check that you are keeping the same pen angle: it is easy to change without noticing. Zig-zag patterns, made at the correct angle for the alphabet you are using, can be a useful warming up exercise before writing.

LAYING OUT TEXT

Having decided what you are going to write, you need to plan where each word will fall and work out how much space it will take up, so that the page looks balanced and harmonious. Think about the relative importance of titles – and hence which will be larger or smaller.

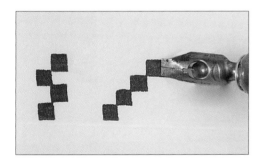

1 Determine the x-height of an alphabet using a "ladder" of nib widths. Holding the nib at 90 degrees to the baseline, make a clear mark, then move the pen up and repeat for the required number of widths.

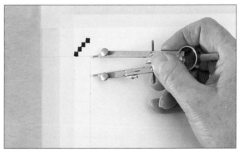

2 Measure the height of the ladder and use this measurement to mark the x-height down both sides of the paper, then join the marks up with a ruler and pencil. If you have a T-square you can mark one side only.

3 When ruling guidelines for lower-case letters, leave the equivalent of two x-heights between each line of text to allow for ascenders and descenders. For capitals, you can leave one x-height or even less.

4 When you are going to write mostly in lower case with the occasional capital, rule as for lower case and gauge the height of the capital letters by eye.

5 Once you start writing, it is important to be aware of letter spacing and awkward combinations, such as the "r" and "a" above: move them closer to create a natural space.

6 Adjusting letter spacing helps to make the text more legible by evening out the frequency of downstrokes: leave more space between adjacent uprights, as above.

Foundational hand

To grasp the principles of calligraphy it is best to start by learning an alphabet. The Foundational, or Round, hand was devised by the British calligrapher Edward Johnston (1872–1944), who is credited with reviving the art of penmanship and lettering in the modern age.

▶ *The numerals and letters of the alphabet are written in a specific order. Follow the numbers on the digits and letters opposite to achieve the best effect.*

The Foundational hand is simply crafted, based on the circle made by two overlapping strokes of the pen, and is written with a constant pen angle of 30 degrees and few pen lifts. It is the constant angle that produces the characteristic thick and thin strokes of the letterforms. Johnston based his design for the lower-case letters on the Ramsey Psalter, a late tenth-century English manuscript now in the British Library. The capitals, however, are based on carved letterforms used in ancient Rome, and their elegant proportions relate to the geometry of a circle within a square.

The basic rules

Foundational hand is a formal, upright script, in which each letter is made up of two or more strokes. The letters should be evenly spaced for easy reading. An important characteristic of this hand is that the top curves of "c" and "r" are slightly flattened to help the eye travel along the line of writing.

The x-height is four nib-widths. Turn the pen sideways to make four adjacent squares with the nib, then rule your guidelines that distance apart. The ascenders and descenders should be less than three-quarters of the x-height (two or three nib-widths). The capital letters should be just two nib-widths above the x-height and do not look right if they are any higher. Hold the nib at a constant angle of 30 degrees for all letters except for diagonals, where the first stroke is made with a pen angle of 45 degrees.

Practice exercises

Almost all the letterforms of this hand relate to the circle and arches, so practise by drawing controlled crescent moon shapes, beginning and ending on a thin point. These semicircles can then be attached to upright stems to create rounded letterforms, or they can be extended into a downstroke to form arches. Begin high up and inside the stem to create a strong, rounded arch. Rounded serifs are used on entry and exit strokes to embellish the letters.

GROUPS

Round or circular

cbpdqoe

Note where the thin parts of the letters are. The first stroke of these letters should be a clean semicircular sweep, producing a shape like a crescent moon. Start at the top and move the pen downwards. The left and right edges of the pen form the circles.

Arched

lmnrhau

The arch joins the stem high up. Beginning with the pen in the stem, draw outwards in a wide curve, following the "o" form. Start the letters with a strong, curved serif and end with a smaller curved serif. Keep the pen angle at 30 degrees throughout.

Diagonal

wxyzkv

For the first stroke, hold the pen at the steeper angle of 45 degrees. This will prevent the stroke from being too thick. Take care not to make any curve on this stroke. Revert to a pen angle of 30 degrees for the second stroke.

Ungrouped

fgsijt

Keep the pen angle at 30 degrees for these letters. Follow the smooth shape of the "o" when drawing curves. Crossbars should sit just below the top line, and should protrude to nearly the width of the curve.

STROKES

(1st = red, 2nd= blue, 3rd = green)

The letter "o" is made by two overlapping semicircular strokes, which produce the characteristic oval shape inside the letter. The back of the "e" does not quite follow the "o", but is flattened so it appears balanced. The top joins just above halfway.

For "a" draw an arch continuing into a straight stroke. The bowl begins halfway down the stem. The "u" follows the same line as an "n" but upside down, producing a strong arch with no thin hairlines. Add the stem last.

Start the ascender for "k" three nib-widths above the x-height. The second stroke is a continuous movement forming a right-angle. The pen angle is steepened for the first stroke of "v" and the second begins with a small serif. The two should sit upright.

The base of the first stroke of the "j" curves inwards to cup the preceeding letter "i". The second begins with a small serif and joins the base. The dot above the j is formed last. Start the "t" above the top line. The crossbar forms the second stroke, just below the top line.

1 2 3 4 5 6 7 8 9 0

A B C D E F G
H I J K L M N
O P Q R S T U
V W X Y Z & Æ

a b c d e f g
h i j k l m n
o p q r s t u
v w x y z &

? æ ě ü é ß .,:;

DIGITAL SCRAPBOOKING

There is a whole range of software available for digital scrapping. Some of the programs that came free with your computer, printer or digital camera, such as simple layout software, or image-viewing and editing programs, are essential scrapbooking tools. Specific digital scrapbooking software is also available and is easy to use to import photographs and design elements to your pages. For those wishing to work at an advanced level, professional image-editing software enables you to create a vast range of effects on photographs and layouts.

SCRAPBOOKING SOFTWARE

If you enjoy scrapbooking and also like working on a computer, you will enjoy all the possibilities of creativity offered by designing your scrapbook pages on screen. Being able to undo, redo, or make several different versions of your ideas and see them side by side without wasting any paper, is a joy. Your computer and printer, with various software packages, give you all the basics you need to design and print great pages. If you also have a scanner, digital camera and access to the internet you will have even more creative options. There are many scrapbooking websites, which offer a variety of e-papers, borders and embellishments at high resolution, allowing you to make good-quality prints. They sell templates and even ready-made pages – so all you need to do is position your photos.

Each site has its own style: some elements look very high-tech and computer generated, whereas others have a more traditional feel. If you need inspiration you can browse through the galleries on the sites, which are full of exciting ideas. There are many software tutorials to help you out, too.

▼ *Scrapbooking websites such as scrapgirls.com offer themed collections of background designs, overlays, embellishments, and everything you need to compile your digital pages.*

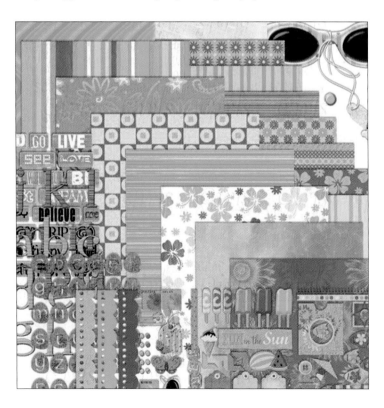

CREATING DIGITAL PAGES

Even the most basic software can be used to create backgrounds and make different shapes and frames to contain photographs and journaling. You can either use these in traditional scrapbook layouts by printing all the elements individually to arrange together on paper, or print the finished page. You can buy a whole range of papers to print on, and experiment with coloured and textured papers, and even fabric.

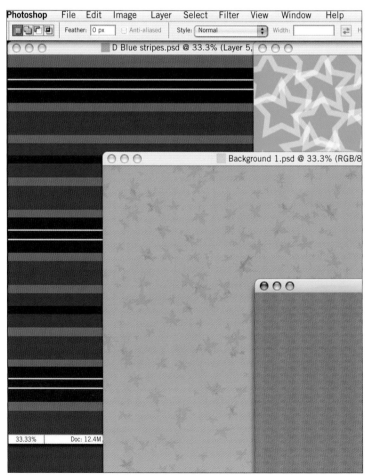

I To begin your page using image-editing software such as Photoshop, set the design area to 30 x 30cm/12 x 12in (it can later be reduced to 20 x 20cm/8 x 8in if you want to print on to A4 paper). For good printing quality use 300dpi (dots per inch) when creating and importing images, and experiment with different filters and effects. The stripes on the left were achieved by colouring rectangles then repeating down the page.

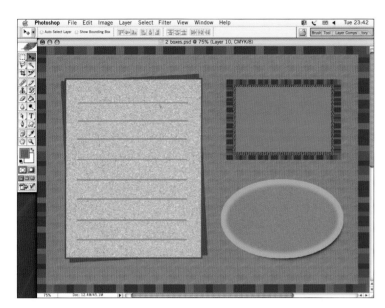

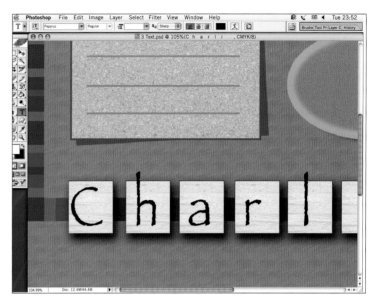

2 Squares, circles, stars and more can be created to make boxes, borders and embellishments, then coloured and treated with different filters and effects. Here the striped background has been used to create a stripy border. In the journaling panel on the left, a textured surface and rules imitate notepaper. The shape was duplicated then twisted a little and re-coloured to give a shadow effect. Another shadow under the oval shape gives it a three-dimensional feel. You can resize and reshape the elements as much as you like, until you are happy with the basic layout.

3 The beauty of creating journal boxes on screen is that you can type your story straight into the box, and then edit it and resize the type or the box until everything fits beautifully and you have exactly the look you want to achieve. Your computer will come with a basic range of fonts installed, and many more are available if you want to create a particular look. They can be enlarged, emboldened, italicized and capitalized and all will look different. Special effects for titles and other text include drop shadows, 3-D effects and outline lettering, and you can of course type in any colour to fit the mood of the layout. Alternatively, you can print the empty boxes and write the text by hand for a traditional look, or print your text on clear film and superimpose it on a printed background.

DRAWING A SOLID OBJECT

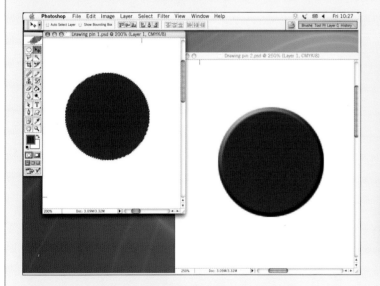

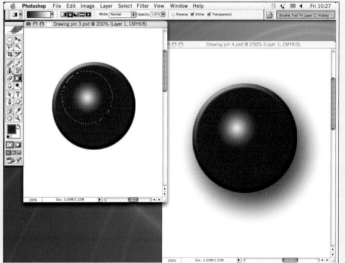

1 Try using imaging software to create the illusion of solid objects such as this drawing pin (thumb tack). Create a circle and colour it, using the eyedropper tool to pick a colour from one of your photos. Create a bevel edge using the Bevel and Emboss layer style. Here a smooth inner bevel has been added with a shading angle of 120 degrees. Play with the settings until you are happy with the effect.

2 To add a little shine to the surface of the pin, create a smaller circle on the surface. Choose Radial Gradient in the gradient tool menu and scale to make the area of shine as big or small as you want it. Here it has been set at 56 degrees. Finally add a shadow to relate the pin to the background, at the same angles of 120 degrees. You can now scale the image down to a realistic size and use it to "pin" your photograph to the page.

Scanning and using digital images

A scanner is definitely useful if you have an archive of traditional photographs you want to scrapbook digitally. All your old family photos can be scanned too, so all your relatives can have their own copies. As well as photographic prints, both colour and black and white, most scanners can also be used to copy transparencies and negatives. And of course your traditional paper scrapbook pages can be scanned, to be stored or refined digitally, or emailed to your friends.

Making a scan

1 Fit as many photos on to the scanner bed as possible, as they can be cropped individually once they are scanned. Work at 300dpi or, for small photos that you may want to use at, say, three times the original size, at 900dpi. Save and name the scan.

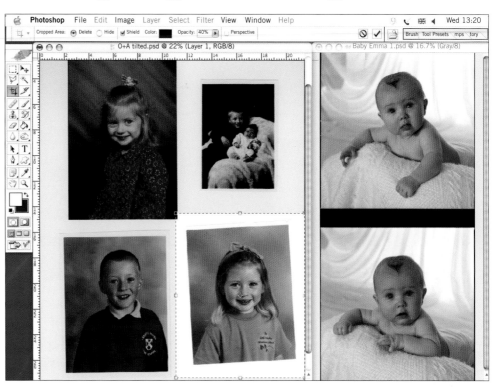

2 Crop out the picture you want to use, and save and rename it as a separate file. If the picture is a bit wonky, which often happens when scanning prints, or even upside down, it can be turned around easily in increments of 90 degrees or less, until it is straight. Check the alignments using the guides on the screen.

DIGITAL PHOTO FILES

If you have a digital camera, all your photographs can be downloaded straight to your computer using the software supplied with the camera. The pictures are then ready to use on digital scrapbook pages, or can be printed to use traditionally. Store each set of digital photos in a folder and label as you would ordinary prints.

You can store your photographs, and other scrapbooking material, on your computer, but they will take up a lot of memory. You should certainly delete any bad pictures so they do not take up valuable space, and it is best to copy all your pictures on to CDs or DVDs, so that you have back-up copies.

Use your camera for backgrounds such as beach, grass and sky, as well as other elements such as signs, tickets, labels and buttons. With these and elements from other sources you can build up a library of digital papers, embellishments and typography to use whenever you want.

NOW TRY THIS

1 Scan your photograph. Add a white border to imitate a print, by increasing the canvas size, before you bring it on to the album page. Duplicate the image box, twist by a few degrees, re-colour and put behind the photograph to give the semi-shadow effect.

2 Create stripes for the background, matching colours from the photo using the eyedropper tool.

3 Take a patch of colour from the photo background to use for the decorative boxes to the right of the photograph. Reshape one of these boxes to add the cross bands at the bottom and right of the page.

4 Create individual text boxes with shadows and add type to create the title.

5 You can make the drawing pins (thumb tacks) digitally as here, or print the page and then add buttons and other three-dimensional embellishments to the printed version. For best results use a good quality printing paper, and allow plenty of time for the inks to dry.

▲ *The denim dungarees Jack is wearing in the colour photograph provided the inspiration for this layout. The background is a picture of the garment itself, digitally augmented with stripes and lettering, and the photograph has been vignetted in a shape that fits neatly on to the pocket.*

▲ *A single scanned photograph of this pampered pet on his favourite cushion has been used three times at different scales, and the tartan rug in the picture also forms the background design. Don't forget that you can use a scanner to create digital images of fabrics and printed papers as well as photographs. The frames, name tag and stitching are all digital embellishments.*

USING A SCANNER FOR SPECIAL EFFECTS

As well as creating digital images from your photographic prints and negatives, you can use a scanner like a camera to create pictures of a whole host of other items that you might want to use on your scrapbook page. Different patterns and textures for backgrounds, traditional embellishments such as buttons, bows, lace, ribbon or photo corners can all be scanned to be used on your pages. All those tickets and other ephemera from your travels can be scanned in to go with the photos. In fact, if you can pick it up, then you can usually scan it! The flatter the item, the better the scan.

▲ *Woven fabric, denim from a pair of jeans, a piece of knitwear, flower petals and a child's painting have been scanned here. Fabric needs to be pulled taut across the scanner bed to avoid creases, unless of course you are after a creased effect. As with photographs, you can crop around the area that you want to use after making the scan. The scans can be used as they are, or layers, colours and other effects can be added to tone them down, creating more abstract patterns.*

1 Create a border around the knitwear background by duplicating the background, cutting out a row of stitching, copying this to the other side, then copying and rotating to make the other two sides of the square. Use the same method to make the edging around the photograph.

2 A felt flower with contrasting stitching is used here to embellish the frame. Having scanned the motif, use the lasso tool to cut it out and drag it on to your page. It can be resized as necessary and dropped into position. It can also be copied and used again and again in different sizes. Add a little shadow behind the motifs to enhance the realistic effect.

▲ *The final touch to this pretty layout is a row of simple felt shapes embroidered with the letters of the child's name. The pink knitted frame is a good match for this photograph, but you could of course change the colour if you wanted to use this texture in a different context.*

IMPROVING YOUR PHOTOS

Once you have your photos in digital format, there are a number of easy ways to enhance the quality of both black and white and colour photographs. Even the most basic picture-editing software packages will allow you to improve the colour or composition, or restore damaged prints. Always make a copy of the original scan to work on, so that you can refer back to it or start again if you don't like the new effect.

Cropping out distracting objects

If you find you have an awkward or distracting object in the background, or foreground, like this overhanging roof, it can often easily be cropped out using the crop or selection tool. Experiment with cropping even further to focus more on the subjects.

Improving colour

Here the picture on the left is too light and the contrast and colour have been improved using the automatic settings. To refine the result further you could alter the contrast and brightness controls manually, and add the colours individually in the colour balance panel.

Improving the sky

A featureless or dull sky is easily improved. First select the sky area using the wand or lasso tool. Select a suitable sky colour to go with the foreground, then select linear gradient in the gradient tool. Draw a vertical line with the mouse to add the gradient colour – the longer the line the more colour there will be in the background. Experiment with the gradient until you are happy with it.

Retouching

If you don't want to crop into the background of a picture, you may be able to remove a distracting object by retouching. Use the clone tool initially, to delete the object and match the area with the rest of the background. Then use the healing brush to soften any harsh edges. This method can be used to eliminate red eye, too.

Making a focal point

You can blur the background if it is too distracting and you want to focus attention on the subject. Use the lasso tool to draw around the subject and make a clipping path. Invert the path to make the background the working area. Now choose Radial Blur in the filter menu. Decide how much blur to apply and position the blur centre: in this case it has been moved down below the centre of the image so that the effect circulates around the subjects.

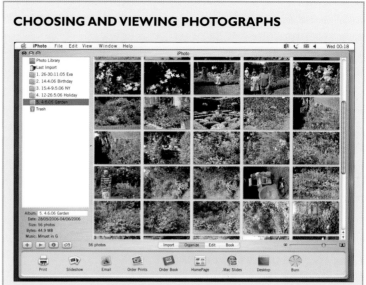

CHOOSING AND VIEWING PHOTOGRAPHS

Photo-viewing software is often supplied with your camera, printer or computer. It allows photographs to be imported from a digital camera and then viewed as large or small as needed. Viewing a group of photographs together as thumbnails makes it easier to make the best selection for a scrapbook page. You can arrange your picture library in folders or albums and add titles. Some software allows you to do a little picture editing too. You can rotate photos to view them the right way round, crop to improve framing and even create a slideshow. You can also import your finished digital pages to be viewed as a slideshow.

IMPROVING BLACK-AND-WHITE PHOTOGRAPHS

As with colour photographs, black-and-white pictures can easily be improved with the addition of special effects.

Brightening dark pictures

If a photograph is too dark, as on the left, make it brighter using the brightness control and lessen the contrast to lighten it. Use the curves and levels controls to refine the image. The sharpness can be improved too, which can be helpful with some older photos.

Repairing creases and tears

When old photos have been stored for a long time, they may be creased or damaged. They may also be stained and spotted with damp or mould. The clone tool and the healing brush are both easy to use to retouch any damaged areas, and tears, spots and even small holes can be repaired very effectively.

Creating tints and duotones

Copy the image (converting to greyscale if it is colour) then choose Duotone from the image menu. This allows you to create the photo in two, three or even four colours of your choice. Be careful – some colours, such as green, can make a photo look strange. Warm sepia works well with old photos. The duotones above show the effects created using orange (100y, 100m), yellow (100y) and finally magenta (100m).

Eliminating creased corners

Old photos often have creased or bent corners. If the damage is too bad to retouch in the digital version, you could try this effect. Draw an oval shape around the subject, then invert the selection so the background is selected and delete it. The edge of the photo is softened, or vignetted, by feathering, in this case by 30 pixels, before hitting delete. This gives a soft, period feel to the picture.

NOW TRY THIS

1 Scan a sheet of brown paper for the background. Add brush marks around the edges to create the effect of antique paper.

2 Add a white border to the photo, by increasing the canvas size before you bring it on to the page. Position it on the page, resizing to fit. Add a rectangular text box below and add the title.

3 Make a tag, or download a tag from a scrapbooking website. Position it at an angle in the corner of the page. Select a rectangular section of the tag. Copy this and enlarge it down the left side of the page. Tone down the colour by adding a semi-opaque layer over it.

4 Scan in photo corners, paper reinforcements and ribbon. Position the paper reinforcements, then add the ribbon as if threaded through them. Resize and crop to fit. Duplicate the ribbon and position it over the tag. Twist it around until it looks right and crop the length a bit. Add the photo corners. Finally, add a little shadow to all the elements to give a three-dimensional effect.

CREATING A TORN PAPER EFFECT

Torn paper is a good effect to master for use in your digital scrapbook pages. A real piece of paper can be torn and scanned, but it may not be quite the right shape. You can learn to alter the shape and size of a real paper scan or you can create a mock effect. Once you know how to create the effect with your software, this method can be used on any shape you need.

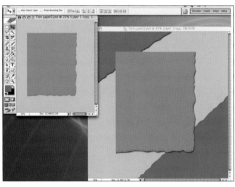

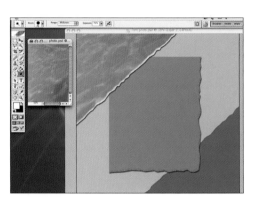

1 Create and colour a rectangle. Make a jagged line around two sides with the lasso tool. Join up the shape and hit delete.

2 Add noise in the filters menu and adjust the levels, making the torn area lighter or darker to suit your needs. This gives a jagged torn edge effect on two sides of the rectangular sheet.

3 This effect can be added to the edge of a photograph. Apply the torn paper method as described in steps 1 and 2, then use the dodge tool along the jagged edge so that it appears white like a tear in a real print.

CREATING A CALENDAR

Once you are into digital scrapbooking it is very easy to create your own calendar, adding seasonal effects. Scrapbooking websites offer many different calendar templates. Some can be created on the website and then downloaded to print (you will need broadband for this). Others are just like digital scrapbook templates and can be downloaded and designed as usual.

1 For this October page, create an autumn background from leaf-patterned paper with an opaque layer over it to soften the colour. Add numbered boxes, duplicating the required amount. Add the days of the week above each column.

2 Import the photos, resizing and moving them around until you are happy with the composition. Using the eyedropper to pick out a dark colour from one of the photos, add a border and shadows to both pictures.

3 Add a contrasting band at the top by creating a rectangular box and using the eyedropper to colour it. Add noise to create texture and place it behind the top of the upper photo. Duplicate the band and position one at the bottom of the page. Duplicate again and position the middle band across the foot of the lower photo.

4 Position the word "October" along the middle band, and add a shadow so that it stands out. Finally, using the leafy brush, spatter a few leaves in the bottom corner.

UPLOADING PAGES

Having made your digital page, you can save it to disc for posterity, and print as many copies as you like. The brilliant thing about digital pages is that you can also email them to friends, and even upload them on to one of the many websites that allow you to show them. If your pages are saved at 300dpi you should first reduce the resolution to 72dpi. This generally makes your page small enough to be emailed and uploaded on to the web. Follow the instructions given on the website for uploading your material for display.

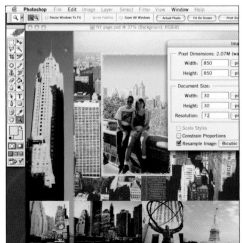

CREATING A PHOTOGRAPHIC BACKGROUND

Photographic backgrounds can be very effective provided they don't distract too much attention from the main subject. There are many ways to avoid this, such as keeping the background to a solid colour, reducing the opacity of the background image, throwing it out of focus or applying a filter.

1 Duplicate the background layer twice. On the top layer create a box around the area to be full strength, invert and crop out the background. You can check the crop by just viewing that layer. If you want to soften the edges, feather the crop.

2 Click on the layer below. Reduce the opacity, or strength, of the background in the layers menu until you get the effect you want: in this case the background has an opacity of 60 per cent.

3 To enhance the subject further, enlarge the full-strength area. Here this was subtly done by keeping the edge of the grass in line with the background. A soft shadow was added to lift it off the page.

CREATING A PANORAMA AND MONTAGE

Various programs are available to stitch panoramas together, but you can do this yourself. It works best if the pictures are taken from the same standpoint.

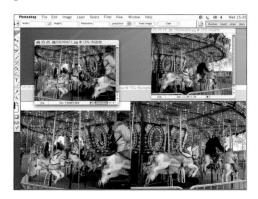

1 If you have an assortment of photos, choose the ones that match up best. Bring them on to the same page, resize as necessary and nudge along to find the best match. Enlarge the canvas to accommodate the photos.

2 To add people to the scene, cut them out using the lasso tool, and move across to the panorama. They can be flipped, rotated and resized to fit. Use this method to add as many images as you need.

3 After adding all the images and adjusting them to fit into the scene, look at the edge of the final photo. If it is uneven it can be cropped, and the page area altered so that it fits a page or across a spread.

▲ *The photograph of New York used as the background was given a painted effect using Fresco in the filter menu. In the main photo, Ink Outlines was used for the distant view, and Glass Distort noise effect has been added around the edge to soften it. A variety of city scenes have been added around the edges of the page to enhance the mood.*

Styles to suit

For inspiration for the style of your scrapbook pages you need generally look no further than the photographs you want to display and your knowledge of their subjects. So while a collection of old family photographs, for instance, might seem to warrant a "traditional" treatment, your partying forebears enjoying their cocktails might look happier in chic Art Deco black and silver frames to echo their sharp suits and stylish dresses.

   The fun is in relating your backgrounds and decorations to the contents of the pictures, and it's important that the photographs always have a starring role: the thousands of patterns and ornaments available from scrapbooking stores should never be allowed to overwhelm the personal elements of your displays.

Keeping it traditional

The photograph albums and scrapbooks of earlier generations have a wonderfully evocative look. It can be fun to adopt their look, either with squared up presentations of photographs, or with a twist, by adding in memorabilia that has been digitally scanned or enhanced. Keep the presentation quite formal, with the pictures squarely mounted in narrow borders or in old-fashioned photo corners, and add handwritten captions.

▼ *This page crowded with lots of tickets and other bits and pieces evokes the eventful days of a memorable trip to San Francisco. It has been digitally created, and makes use of the standard elements of a traditional scrapbook.*

▶ *Athough created digitally, this layout looks back to an earlier era with its metal corners and hand-tinted black and white pictures.*

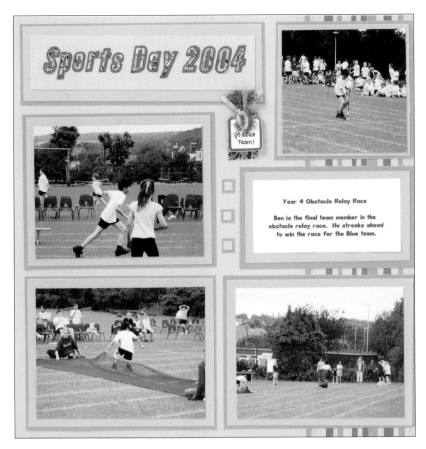

▲ The camouflage theme is taken from the uniforms in the picture and the titling and black border give a period feel.

▲ Here the pictures telling the story of the children's race almost fill the page, apart from a small panel describing what happened, and are squarely arranged with little embellishment.

▶ The dog's formal pose in this photograph has inspired an equally formal presentation in a double frame with bound corners.

▼ This record of a day at the zoo uses matching frames for all the pictures. The string detail is based on old album bindings.

▲ An old map has been used as the background to this Caribbean beach scene and neatly imitates the look of the sand where the boat sits in readiness to head out to sea.

Bold graphics

Crisp geometric shapes and repeating patterns can make really effective settings for strong images, or if you are using digital images, you could make a feature of the graphics within the photograph by repeating and blurring edges.

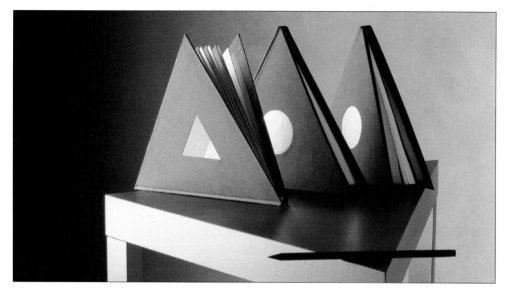

▲ *To create a smart, unified look for a multivolume set of family albums, go for matching or co-ordinated bindings in formal designs. Choose colours that suit your home décor so you'll want to have them on show.*

▲ *Albums need not be square: these striking triangular volumes have an Oriental feel and demand a modern, minimalist treatment on the pages inside.*

▶ *Papers printed in strong graphic designs like these make wonderful album covers. If you want to mix them up, look for designs of equal strength and scale, or use the same motifs in different sizes or colours.*

▼ *Die-cut patterns create a strong graphic effect when they are set against a background in a contrasting colour, as in this pretty ribbon-tied folder.*

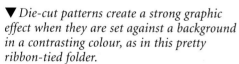

▲ Although the carousel is a very traditional subject, the modern technique of digital splicing has resulted in an image that forces you to take a second look.

◀ Image-editing software has been used to add some eye-catching stripes to this digitally created scrapbook page.

▼ Royalty-free images from old black and white engravings can be photocopied and added to paper collages to make lovely album covers, cards and gift tags.

Fabric and stitch

If you are skilled with a needle, there are lots of creative ways to introduce textiles and stitching into your scrapbooking, from embroidered album covers to painted or printed silk panels or braided embellishments.

▼ *A small embroidery can become a front cover feature of a special album cover. This motif would be appropriate for a gardener.*

▶ *This small-scale book cover has been made by appliquéing small squares to a background fabric and satin stitching the raw edges.*

▲ *Thick woven cotton or linen makes a lovely album cover, trimmed with embroidered titling and decorative blanket stitch and closed with two buttoned bands.*

◀ *For a contemporary decoration for the front of an album cover stitch small strips of evenly-spaced brightly coloured silk fabrics in a column to one side.*

▶ *Use transfer paper to copy a favourite photo on to fine fabric such as silk to form the centrepiece of an appliquéd panel.*

Heritage

Most families have collections of photographs and ephemera handed down from previous generations, and it can be very rewarding to identify and mount them in albums to preserve them for the future. Good heritage layouts can be powerful evocations of the period when the pictures were taken.

▼ *Copies of letters to home and other contemporary memorabilia make moving additions to wartime pages.*

▲ *Try to get older relatives to help you identify the subjects of photographs in your old family albums.*

◄ *Treasured souvenirs of long-ago trips deserve to be properly displayed and preserved for the future.*

▼ *A decorative collage in period style can make the most of simple but precious family snaps.*

▲ When you're assembling a family group like this, the photographs themselves may all be simple portraits, but with personal knowledge of the subjects of the pictures you can choose appropriate backgrounds that help to show what the people were really like.

▼ For old photographs that are to be out on display, use old materials in muted colours to frame them. Here an antique cream piece of card (stock) immediately frames the photograph, and the outer frame is made from coloured corrugated cardboard, which picks up the darkest tones in the photograph.

▲ If you've inherited old family albums they're likely to be crammed with small black and white or sepia prints. It can be effective to reflect some of that style in your new album, but it's often possible to improve the images greatly by scanning and enhancing faded prints and reprinting them on a larger scale.

Natural inspiration

Don't forget your scrapbook when you're out and about: as well as bringing home photographs, gather natural objects such as shells, leaves and flowers that will help you build up a complete picture of the places you visited.

▲ *This display box is a lovely way to bring together a photograph of a happy day on the beach with the collection of seashells you made while you were there.*

◀ *Instead of portraying a particular place, water has been chosen as the theme for this layout, bringing together diverse natural scenes. However, all the photographs used were taken in similar weather conditions, so the colours give the page a very unified feel.*

▼ *Handmade paper makes the perfect cover for an album on a natural theme. This sheet incorporates delicate scattered flower petals, and pressed flowers have been used to decorate the title panel. A simple undyed raffia tie holds it all together.*

▲ *This cover, decorated with a collage of leaves and flowers and bound with string, would be perfect for an album recording a garden tour.*

▲ The complex frame-within-a-frame used in this layout, combined with the unusual view in the photograph, creates the effect of a window opening in the page, through which you can see the view of the tree beyond. The embellishment of leafy twigs is clearly related to the picture.

▲ As well as taking photographs of views and landscapes when you're on holiday, you can use your camera to record interesting abstract images and close-ups for fantastic borders and backgrounds in future scrapbooks.

◀ Pretty pressed flowers form the focal point on this handmade album cover. The cover is made from textured paper, which has a handmade quality to it. The flowers can be collected fresh in spring and summer and pressed at home.

▼ Trinket boxes are a delightful way to store small treasures that are unsuitable for your album pages because of their shape. Beautify plain boxes with patterned papers and embellishments such as pressed flowers and leaves.

Simple colour schemes

A monochrome treatment is an obvious choice for a collection of black-and-white photographs, but it can also be extremely effective with pictures in which the colour range is fairly limited. Don't limit your ideas to black and white but explore other single colours that match or contrast well with your images.

▼ *A delicately decorated photograph box makes an elegant minimal presentation for a silver wedding souvenir.*

◀ *Although these striking seascapes are in colour the effect is almost monochromatic, and the simple black and white layout suits them perfectly.*

▼ *A crowded layout including photographs of all the members of a family is full of interest, and keeping it all in black and white gives a simple, graphic look.*

▲ *This all-white frame is intricately designed and texturally interesting, but doesn't distract attention from the photograph inside.*

▼ *Paper printed with a toile de Jouy design goes well with a strong collection of black-and-white photographs, though the plain black background is needed to keep all the images clear and well defined. The effect is softened with a purple border and ribbons.*

◀ *A fragile collection of old sepia prints can be overpowered by stark black-and-white or any strong colours, and looks best with gentle, faded tones.*

▲ *A photographic background, such as this drift of rose petals created for a wedding album, can have its opacity level reduced and be printed in just one or two colours, so that it does not compete visually with the photographs on the pages.*

◀ *In many older photograph albums the pages are of matt black paper, and this can still make a very effective and dramatic setting for both black and white and colour prints.*

▲ *A white wedding album luxuriously bound in white leather or vellum demands perfectly matted prints and a restrained approach to page layouts.*

Bold colours

When you are mounting photographs of happy children playing with brightly coloured toys or running about on a sunny beach, your backgrounds can be as bold and bright as possible to create an explosion of colour. You can either pick up one of the strong colours in the pictures and use a matching or contrasting tone for the whole setting, or go for a multicoloured effect, using all the colours of the rainbow for a really eye-catching layout.

▲ *The yellow background forming a frame around each of the cut-outs of this car has the effect of making them glow.*

◀ *Children's drawings and paintings, especially their self-portraits, make great additions to your layouts. Cut round both artwork and photographs to create amusing collages, and get them to help you with planning the pages.*

▼ *Here the layout is bold and bright but uses a limited colour palette and achieves a patterned quality by repeating two pictures all round the border. It also promises an irresistible surprise under the central flap.*

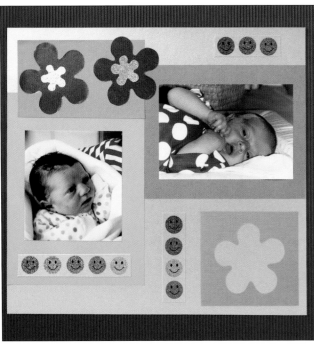

▲ *The two pictures on this layout are very different in character but the colour and black and white have been successfully linked by the shifting tones and consistent shapes of the frames and embellishments.*

▶ *Simple lacing through punched holes creates an eye-catching border for this name tag.*

▼ *This pretty garden of flower babies against a background the colour of a summer sky makes a sweet cover for a family album.*

▲ *This lovely page exhibits the finished results of the bold creative session that is in full swing in the photograph.*

◀ *The simplest shapes cut out of handmade or bark paper and cleverly combined make beautiful original tags and cards.*

▼ *Using a different bright colour for each page of a basic ring-bound album turns into it a really striking display that needs no further ornamentation.*

▲ *This digital scrapbook page takes the colour and movement of the sea as its theme, using a section of the photograph itself as part of the background.*

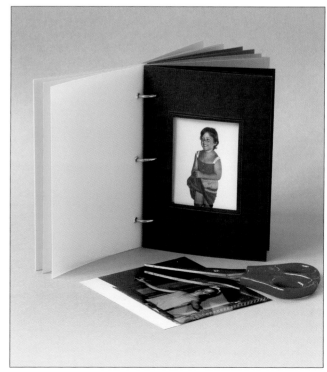

Pale and pastel

Delicately coloured photographs can easily be overwhelmed by a layout that includes strong or dark colours. Softer, paler tones mix and match well with each other and can be used to create a very feminine look, or to give a period setting for a collection of old and perhaps faded prints.

▼ *This pretty floral pattern looks right for the date of the photograph and its colours set off the sepia print perfectly. Toning stripes provide a crisp finishing touch.*

▶ *For a lovely, light-hearted wedding album cover, paste a scattering of tissue paper confetti shapes in mixed pastel colours over a sheet of soft handmade paper.*

Florence

Age 17.

1940

◀ *Pale blue for a boy is enriched by the framing bands of deep blue and the toning pale shades of olive and brown in the background, which carefully echo the soft colours in the photograph.*

◀ *The ice blues of this layout emphasize the coldness of the snow in the photograph. Although the picture was taken in sunny weather there is no colour to warm it up.*

▲ *An enchanting little dog gets her own flowery setting in delicate colours that are just right for her light fur and small size. The daisy chain is threaded with a light touch across the bottom of the page. The simple colour scheme works well.*

▲ *Wearing a pale pink dress, this baby girl is given a traditionally coloured setting on a digitally created page. Touches of warmer pinks add interest to the treatment.*

▶ *The large spots on the girl's clothing were the starting point for this simple design, in which the colours are kept muted and pale so that the picture is the strongest element.*

Shabby chic

Mix-and-match patterns and textures with a confident hand for an eclectic, layered look with a timeless feel. This kind of treatment goes wonderfully with old family photographs and ornate memorabilia, evoking the richness of family history and the way in which possessions are gradually acquired and collected together in a home to make a harmonious whole.

▲ *Handmade papers in soft colours, which can often be found with flower petals or leaves incorporated in their surface, mix beautifully with pressed flowers, ribbons and other scraps to make albums and folders.*

◄ *Scrapbooking websites offer a host of different patterned papers, which can be used for onscreen layouts or downloaded and printed. Ornate historical patterns set off the elaborate dresses of past generations.*

▼ *There are plenty of gift wrap papers or poster-size prints available that can be cut to size and reused as attractive and decorative covers for an album. Choose a print that is appropriate for the contents.*

▲ *Colour-printed die-cut scraps were collected in the 19th century to fill scrapbooks and make decorative collages on items such as trays and screens. Reproductions are now available to add instant Victorian charm to cards and tags.*

▼ *Richly patterned and gilded paper is ideal for embellishments such as envelopes and pouches to hold small treasures. Fasten their flaps with paper or silk flowers to complete the ornate effect.*

▲ *In the 19th century, the sending of greetings cards became extremely popular and many elaborate designs were produced, featuring flowers and hearts, intricate paper lace and ribbons. Their complexity and delicate charm provides inspiration for newly crafted displays in period style.*

▲ *A collage made up of old-fashioned items of ephemera immediately sets the tone for shabby chic. You could use this kind of background as a means of displaying old black-and-white photographs.*

▲ *The exuberant colours of mass-produced Victorian prints and scraps reflect the enthusiasm with which chromolithography, the first system of mass-market colour printing, was greeted when it appeared in the 1830s.*

◄ *Evoke the period of early photography with an abundance of intricate detail in scraps of lace and frills, printed patterns and rich textures. Delicate pressed flowers enhance the faded beauty of old textiles and photographs.*

Journaling

The text you add to your pages adds crucial meaning to the images, filling in all the details you know about when and where the pictures were taken and what was happening at the time, as well as identifying the people featured in them. There are many creative ways to add journaling so that it is not only informative but also becomes an intrinsic and attractive part of the design.

▲ *If you have original letters to accompany your photographs, they can be copied and used as part of your display, or tucked safely into envelopes attached to the pages.*

Victory in Europe
V.E. Day Celebrations

This photo is of my Mum, Nan and Aunty Bar. The huge teapot was probably borrowed from the Street warden who would have used it in the Air Raid Shelter to make Tea during the raids.
My Mum was Fifteen years old when the war ended and had been Bombed out of her house twice. There were Ammunition Factories in Ashton so were a major target for enemy Bomber Planes during the war.

My Grandad, pictured here with his friends was still in Europe on V.E. day, his job as a Despatch rider meant he was one of the first people inside the Concentration Camps when the war ended, and witnessed firsthand the horrors that Hitler had inflicted on the Jewish people .

Street party held at Foxcote road, Ashton, Bristol

▲ *Old-fashioned wax seals and stamps can be purchased at craft stores. They can add the finishing touch to an album page.*

▲ *In heritage layouts it's often important to explain the historical background to the photographs as well as establishing identities and locations.*

◀ *On this layout for a new baby the words encapsulating the feelings of the proud parents are addressed to the little boy, who will read them in the future.*

▶ *Instead of providing a commentary on these pictures, the journaling here is a collection of single words conveying the character of the child and all the aspects of a day on the farm.*

▲ Beautifully formed lettering made with a calligraphy pen can become a focal point of a scrapbook design, or as here, the front of an album cover.

▲ Random words forming the background to this sequence of pictures convey ideas associated with the pleasures of travel, while a panel records the details.

My Great-Grandfathers
Fathers of the Bride and Groom

MY GRANDFATHERS

Two old men in sepia
Stand with flowers in hand
At my parents wedding
My god how proud they stand

My Victorian grand-pa-pa's
With shining boots and heads of grey
Caught in a moment from the past
Prepared for the wedding day

If only they could tell us
Of the places they had been
Of mining tales and sailing ships
And places we've never seen

Perhaps a tale of comrades gone
When a great war swept like a flood
To leave young Uncle Tom
In the Gallipoli mud

Of my loved Victorian gents
The memory still remains
What noble lineage are we now
With such blood in our veins

By Bob Dufty

◀ Writing in pen and ink takes time and practice to get right, but gives your work a beautiful hand-crafted, personal quality that cannot be replicated on a computer.

▲ If you have an aptitude for creative writing, an original poem can make a telling contribution. Or you could quote the work of others if the sentiments are appropriate.

Display and presentation

As well as making album pages for your scrapbook, you can also use your presentation skills to mount photographs and other family memorabilia for decorating album covers, memory boxes, memory quilts and even three-dimensional displays.

Archive albums in various formats and bindings are available from scrapbooking stores and other craft suppliers, but you can also buy all the fittings and materials you need to make your own. These unusual formats make particularly attractive gifts commemorating special occasions such as a wedding or the arrival of a baby.

ALBUM COVERS

Designing a special cover for each album gives you a wonderful opportunity to establish its theme and character, so that everyone who sees it will want to look inside and will know instantly what the subject of the chosen album is.

Baby girl album cover

This charming project provides an ideal way to display your favourite baby pictures, and the album will become a family heirloom to be treasured. Make one for each new child in the family, or give them as presents to parents or doting grandparents.

materials and equipment

- metal ruler
- craft knife
- cutting mat
- self-adhesive mount board
- pencil
- polyester wadding (batting), 35 x 33cm/14 x 13in
- scissors
- two pieces of fabric, 35 x 33cm/14 x 13in
- glue stick
- masking tape
- photograph, 15 x 10cm/ 6 x 4in
- watercolour paper, 3 x 30cm/ 1¼ x 12in
- stickers
- hole punch
- 20 sheets of watercolour paper, 29 x 27cm/11¾ x 10¾in
- ribbon

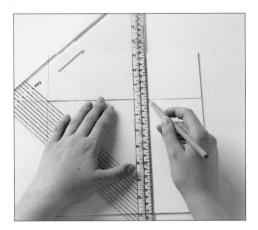

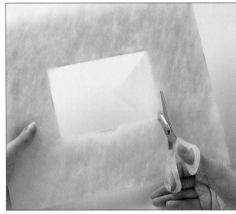

1 Using a metal ruler and craft knife and working on a cutting mat, cut three rectangles each 30 x 28cm/12 x 11¼in and one 30 x 25cm/12 x 10in from self-adhesive mount board. On the smaller rectangle, use a pencil and ruler or set square to draw lines 8cm/3¼in in from each edge to form the aperture for the picture.

2 To make the frame, use a craft knife to cut out the central rectangle and discard. Peel off the protective paper from the adhesive on the mount board and stick the piece of wadding, cut to size, over the frame. Using scissors, trim the wadding to the same size as the mount board.

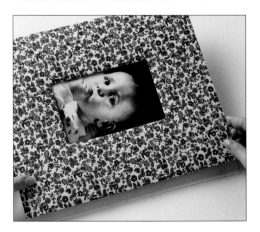

3 Place one rectangle of fabric right side down and lay the frame over it with the wadding underneath. Fold the surplus fabric to the wrong side of the mount board, mitring the corners carefully. Use a glue stick to secure the raw edges to the frame.

4 Cut two diagonal slits in the centre of the fabric, fold the surplus fabric to the back and glue down. Tape the photograph face down over the aperture so that the picture is visible from the padded fabric side. Cover one of the larger rectangles of mount board with the other piece of fabric.

5 Stick the narrow strip of watercolour paper down one long edge of a second large piece of mount board, then stick the frame in place over the rest of the board. Score along the line where the paper and frame join, so that the cover will open flat. Stick the remaining board to the wrong side of the fabric-covered board to form the back cover.

6 Position a coloured sticker at each corner of the photograph at the front of the album to disguise any raw edges of fabric. For extra security for the stickers, dab a tiny spot of glue from a glue stick on to the fabric as well.

7 Punch two holes centrally at the left edge of the front and back covers and the sheets of watercolour paper; the paper will form the album pages. Position the front and back covers on each side of the pages and lace them together with ribbon.

8 Tie the ribbon ends in a bow. Add a few more stickers above and below the bow along the strip of watercolour paper to complete the cover.

Christmas album cover

A pair of square cake boards in a seasonal design, joined together by simple metal screw posts, form the cover of this festive album. A pair of Scottie dogs, cut from sticky-backed felt, complement the plaid design used here and make a charming motif for the front cover. Use this book when planning your Christmas celebrations: there is plenty of room for guest lists, seating plans, special recipes and gift ideas, and after the festivities you can add Christmas memorabilia such as greetings cards and photos.

materials and equipment

- 2 foil cake boards, 25cm/10in square
- double-sided carpet tape
- scissors
- metallic red corrugated cardboard
- self-adhesive felt in green, black and white
- leather hole punch
- 2 screw posts
- black card (stock)
- pencil
- black cotton tape
- tracing paper
- narrow ribbon
- PVA (white) glue
- self-adhesive black cloth tape
- bradawl (awl)
- 4 split pins

1 Place the cake boards side by side, turning them to find the best position to join them (aiming to match the pattern). Stick a 2cm/¾in strip of double-sided carpet tape down each of the edges to be joined.

2 Cut a strip of corrugated cardboard measuring 10 × 25cm/4 × 10in. Stick this over the tape, joining the boards but leaving a 1cm/⅜in gap between them to accommodate the pages.

3 Turn the boards over and cut a rectangle of green self-adhesive felt large enough to cover the inside of the cover. Remove the backing paper and stick in place. Using a leather hole punch, make holes in the top and bottom of the back board, close to the edge of the corrugated cardboard strip. Push a screw post into each hole.

VARIATION: **Album cover with a window**

Although this album cover has a different subject matter, it is constructed in the same way as the Christmas album cover. The difference is that this album has a window cut in the front, and it has been covered with green felt.

4 From the black card cut 30 sheets 24cm/9½in square and 30 strips 4 × 24cm/ 1½ × 9½in. Make a hole gauge from a spare strip of card and punch out the holes in the card pages and strips. Slip them alternately on to the screw posts.

5 Poke two small holes in the front of the corrugated spine. Thread black tape through the holes and tie in a bow for decoration.

6 Draw a Scottie dog template and use it to cut out a black and a white felt dog. Cross a short length of narrow plaid ribbon at the neck of each dog and glue in position.

7 Remove the backing from each dog. Stick the dogs on to the lower right corner of the front cover, so that the white one slightly overlaps the black one.

8 Cut a rectangle of self-adhesive black felt to make a title plaque. At each corner, push a hole through the cloth, board and green felt using a bradawl. Insert a split pin in each hole and open it up on the inside.

Wedding album cover

The covers of this flamboyant album are made from sturdy silver cake boards, and the front cover is smothered in silk blooms that have been attached to a clear polypropylene sheet. Inside, the album is bound with screw posts, allowing you to add or remove pages as you wish.

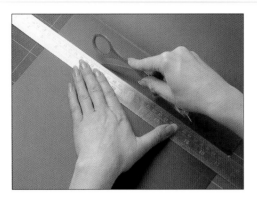

1 Using a craft knife and metal ruler on a cutting mat, cut a rectangle of polypropylene measuring 30 x 65cm/12 x 25½in. Score two parallel lines, 5cm/2in apart, across the mid-line, for the spine.

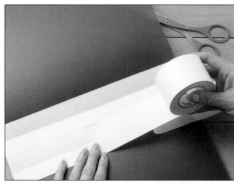

2 Reinforce the spine area on the inside with two lengths of self-adhesive cloth tape, positioning each one centrally over a scored line. Trim the ends flush with the cover.

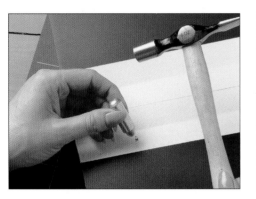

3 Using a punch and hammer, make two holes for the screw posts near the top and bottom of the back cover, in the area reinforced by the cloth tape.

4 Arrange the silk flowers on the front cover and mark the position of the centre of each large flower. Cut the bulbous end from the base of each flower using sturdy scissors. Press a split pin through the hole in the centre of each large flower.

5 Using a craft knife, make a small slit at one of the marks on the cover. (Start in the centre and work outwards.) Put your finger firmly on top of the split pin in a large flower and push the ends through the slit.

6 Open the ends of the split pin at the back. Repeat for the other large flowers. Once they are all in place, fill in any gaps by attaching single petals here and there using epoxy glue.

7 Use epoxy glue to attach smaller silk flowers and petals all around the edge of the cover, so that the plastic is completely hidden by them.

materials and equipment

- craft knife
- metal ruler
- cutting mat
- polypropylene sheet
- scissors
- self-adhesive cloth tape
- punch
- tack hammer
- assorted silk flowers, large and small
- split pins
- epoxy glue
- 2m/2¼yd wide satin ribbon
- double-sided carpet tape
- 3 silver cake boards, each 30cm/12in square
- weights
- 2 screw posts
- photographic refill pages

8 Cut a length of ribbon long enough to wrap around the book and tie in a bow. Cut another piece to wrap over the spine. With the cover open, lay the longer piece horizontally across the centre of the spine, then wrap the other piece around the spine. Stick both pieces of ribbon in place using double-sided carpet tape.

9 Punch holes in two of the cake boards to correspond with the holes made in the back cover for the screw posts. Sandwich the polypropylene cover, with the horizontal ribbon attached, between the boards, silver side out, and glue all the layers together. Leave the back boards under a weight until the glue is dry. Glue the front cover to the last cake board, with the ribbon sandwiched between and the silver facing out, so that the board forms the inside of the front cover.

10 Position the board so that a narrow silver border is left all around the edge. Leave the glue to harden with the back cover hanging over a table edge and weight the front cover with small weights. Insert the screw posts through the back cover, slip on the photographic refill pages and screw to secure. Tie the ribbon in a decorative bow to close the album.

Patchwork album cover

You do not need to be a skilled stitcher to accomplish a patchwork cover, as the patches are held securely in place with bonding web before sewing. Follow the patchwork pattern known as "Log Cabin" to arrange fabric strips around a central image or position patchwork squares in a random arrangement.

materials and equipment

- small album
- tape measure
- dressmaker's scissors
- extra-heavy non-woven interfacing
- fusible bonding web
- iron
- photograph printed on fabric using image transfer paper
- cotton print fabric in several colours
- pressing cloth
- sewing machine
- sewing thread
- dressmaker's pins

1 Measure the opened book and add 2cm/¾in to the height and 10cm/4in to the width measurements to allow for hems and side flaps. Following these measurements, cut out a piece of extra-heavy non-woven interfacing and a piece of fusible bonding web. Following the manufacturer's instructions, iron the bonding web to the interfacing. Peel off the backing paper.

2 Position your chosen image transfer so that it will appear centrally on the front cover. For the random arrangement, cut small squares of fabric and arrange them around the photo, overlapping them slightly.

3 When you have covered the front and back completely, place a pressing cloth over the patchwork and iron to fuse the scraps to the interfacing.

4 On a sewing machine, topstitch along all the joins between the patches with a satin stitch to cover the raw edges. Overcast around the the outer edges of the cover. With right sides together, turn in 5cm/2in down each short side and pin in place. Stitch along each end of these turnings with a 1cm/⅜in seam to make the side flaps, then turn right side out. Insert the album.

VARIATIONS: Cloth covers and books

For a fabric album cover, measure the opened book and add 2cm/¾in to the height and width measurements for seam allowances. Cut two flaps from contrasting fabric. Turn in and stitch narrow hems on each flap. Decorate the front cover with appliqué and beads, then pin on the flaps, right sides together, stitch with 1cm/⅜in seams and turn.

A cloth book makes a lovely personalized gift album for a baby, and can be filled with familiar images transferred on to fabric. Cut out double pages from sturdy wool fabric or felt and stitch a picture on each page, using images of special people or animals. Add a favourite motif to the front cover and stitch all the layers together at the spine.

ACCORDION ALBUMS

This ingenious and flexible format allows you to protect precious photographs and documents inside an album that closes between hard covers like a book, but can also be fully opened out to make a free-standing display on a table or mantelpiece.

Concertina book

Make this pretty accordion album to hold some of your favourite themed photographs. Choose a selection of luxurious decorative papers in similar shades of mauve for a really striking effect.

materials and equipment

- large rubber stamp in a leaf motif
- metallic ink stamp pad
- translucent paper
- craft knife
- metal ruler
- cutting mat
- thick cardboard
- decorative metallic paper
- glue stick
- bone folder
- handmade paper

1 Stamp the motif on to a selection of papers to choose the effects you like best. To do this, press the stamp into the ink pad to coat the surface with ink, then press the stamp on the paper. Lift it up carefully to avoid smudging. In this case, the motif was stamped on translucent paper using metallic ink. Take care when stamping on to tracing paper, as some stamping inks do not dry well on the resistant surface. If you have difficulty, stamp on a lightweight handmade paper instead. Cut out the motif using a craft knife and metal ruler and working on a cutting mat.

2 To make the front and back covers of the album, cut two pieces of thick cardboard to the required size using a craft knife and metal ruler, and working on a cutting mat. Then cut two pieces of decorative metallic paper 2.5cm/1in larger all round than the cardboard. Lay the paper right side down and glue one piece of cardboard to the centre of each piece. Cut across the corners of the paper, then glue the edges and carefully fold them over to stick them down securely on the cardboard. Turn the front cover over and glue the stamped leaf motif in the centre.

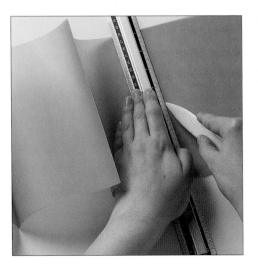

◀**3** Cut a long strip of translucent paper slightly narrower than the height of the cover boards. This will form the folded pages of the album. Measure the width of the album cover and make folds along the strip of paper to match. To do this, carefully and accurately measure the distance from one fold to another; use a metal ruler and bone folder to score and crease the paper to produce a succession of accordion folds. Trim off any excess paper at the end. When you have finished, ensure that the paper folds into a neat pile, and that it fits neatly inside the album.

4 Glue one end of the folded translucent paper on to the front cover of the album, then cover the whole with a sheet of handmade paper to coordinate with the rest of the album. Stick the other end of the translucent paper to the back cover and cover this with a second sheet of handmade paper. Fold up the book and place it under a heavy weight to prevent the papers from buckling as the glue dries.

Accordion wrap

This attractive book uses a folding technique developed in Japan to store long scrolls of paper. The paper used here for the covers contains fragments of coloured silk and threads, added to the paper pulp before forming the sheets.

materials and equipment

- 2 pieces of mounting board, 15 x 20cm/6 x 8in
- glue stick
- 2 sheets of handmade paper, 19 x 24cm/7½ x 9½in
- scissors
- craft knife
- metal ruler
- cutting mat
- narrow satin ribbon
- tapestry needle
- white cartridge (construction) paper 112 x 19cm/44 x 7½in
- bone folder

1 To make the covers, apply glue to one side of each piece of mounting board. Place the board centrally on the wrong side of each piece of handmade paper.

2 Cut diagonally across the corners of the two sheets of paper. Fold the excess paper over the boards and glue in place.

3 Using a craft knife, metal ruler and cutting mat, cut a 1cm/⅜in slit in the centre of each long side on both covers.

4 Cut four 25cm/10in lengths of ribbon. Using a tapestry needle, thread one through each slit and glue the end to the board.

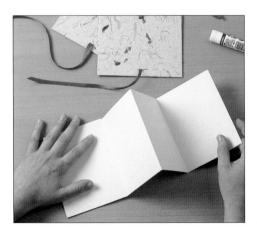

5 Using the bone folder, fold the cartridge paper into accordion pleats to form eight equal sections using accordion pleats.

6 Glue the end sections of the paper to the inside of the covers, positioning them centrally. Make sure the two covers line up.

7 Tie one pair of ribbons to create a book with turning pages.

VARIATION: Fan book

Fold a circle of paper into twelfths and cut down one fold to the centre. Trim the edge. Make two covers to fit the shape and glue to the end folds.

DISPLAY BOARDS

Rather than keeping all your creative ideas tucked away in albums, it can be fun to make scrapbook-style displays to go on the wall. Old prints fade easily, so it is a good idea to have copies made to use in this way and to keep the originals safely away from the light.

Seaside memory board

This collection of holiday memories serves both as a decorative feature for your wall and as a noticeboard to which other mementoes can be added from time to time. It could even be used as a memo board for day-to-day reminders. While you are on your trip, persuade the whole family to look for pretty souvenirs to remind them of your happy time on the beach together.

materials and equipment

- collection of seaside photographs
- pictures from printed sources of marine subjects such as sea, sand, sky, pebbles and shells
- old maps showing large areas of sea
- natural objects such as feathers and small shells
- scissors
- metal ruler
- craft knife
- cutting mat
- lightweight white board
- textured paper
- spray adhesive
- transparent photo corners

1 Spread out your family photographs, together with printed pictures from other sources, maps and seaside ephemera, to decide which to use. Cut out some of the background material with scissors, tear some pictures to give them ragged edges, and trim others with a metal ruler and craft knife so that you have a range of different textures and edges to the collection.

2 Assemble the larger, more abstract pictures of sky and sea on the board, overlapping them with areas of textured paper to make a background for the photographs. When you are happy with the arrangement, glue the background pictures down securely with spray adhesive. Arrange feathers and other pieces of seaside ephemera on the board.

◀ **3** Complete the memory board by adding your photographs to the arrangement, and secure them using transparent photo corners. If you are using duplicate prints you could stick them in position with glue once you have finalized the composition, but using photo corners enables you to place other mementoes behind the photos as your collection grows. Glue additional pieces of ephemera, such as small shells, around the photographs.

VARIATION: Seashore album

For a seaside-themed album, cover the boards with an enlarged detail of a photograph of sand and sea, and glue a real seashell to the front – look for flat shells when you're on the beach.

Pressed flower noticeboard

Natural linen and linen tape tone beautifully with the pressed flowers and leaves and the colour-washed wooden frame in this attractive design.

materials and equipment

- large, flat, rectangular wooden picture frame
- off-white emulsion (latex) paint
- medium-sized decorator's paintbrush
- pressed flowers and leaves
- measuring tape
- PVA (white) glue
- fine artist's paintbrush
- spray matt acrylic varnish
- natural linen or linen-look fabric
- scissors
- sheet of MDF (medium density fibreboard) cut to fit frame
- staple gun
- soft pencil
- linen dressmaking tape
- hammer
- decorative upholstery nails
- picture wire or cord for hanging

1 Paint the picture frame with a coat of off-white emulsion (latex) paint. Apply the paint in a thin wash, so that the texture of the wood shows through. Leave to dry.

2 Arrange the flowers and leaves with the help of a measuring tape. Starting in the centre of one short side of the frame and working outwards, apply a little PVA glue to the back of each flower and stick in place.

3 When the design is complete, leave until the glue is dry then spray the frame with matt acrylic varnish. Repeat if necessary but take care not to flatten the flowers.

4 Cut a piece of linen 5cm/2in larger all round than the MDF. Stretch the fabric over the board and secure it at the back with a staple gun, starting in the centre of each side and folding the corners neatly.

5 On the right side, mark out a large central diamond using a soft pencil. Cut four lengths of linen tape to fit and lay in place, stapling them together at the corners.

6 Arrange more lines of tape in a pleasing design, weaving them over and under each other. Trim the ends and secure at the back of the board with the staple gun.

7 On the right side, secure the linen tape with upholstery nails spaced at regular intervals. Fit the decorated board into the frame and attach picture wire or cord.

HERITAGE QUILTS

Traditional quilts have often been used to record special events or memories by applying embroidery or incorporating symbolic patchwork shapes. With the latest range of transfer papers you can now create a photographic quilt made up of family pictures for posterity too.

Memory quilt

This beautiful album quilt was made to commemorate the 70th birthday of the maker's mother. Some of the ivory silk fabric used was taken from a wedding dress, giving it particular sentimental value.

materials and equipment

- black and white photographs
- scraps of ivory silk in a variety of textures and shades
- image transfer paper
- iron
- paper
- pencil
- dressmaker's scissors
- calico
- measuring tape
- dressmaker's pins
- sewing machine
- ivory sewing thread
- ivory silk for the quilt backing
- quilt interlining
- tacking thread and needle
- coffee silk for binding the edges
- metallic sewing thread

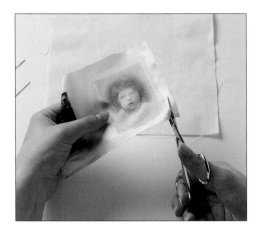

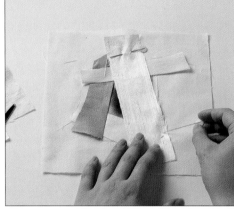

1 Transfer the photographs on to silk, using a transfer paper suitable for the fabric. Decide on the finished block size and estimate how many blocks you will need to make by working out a plan on paper. Cut the block squares from calico, adding a seam allowance all around of 2cm/¾in. Trim each transferred photograph and pin to the block through the border to avoid damaging the prints.

2 Cut random strips of different silks. Pin one strip right side down to one side of the photograph. Stitch the strip down, making sure the seam does not obscure the image, then flip the strip over to conceal the stitching and press lightly. Add the next strip at an angle, covering the end of the previous strip. Repeat, working clockwise round the image, and cut away excess fabric from each strip before adding the next.

3 Complete each calico block in the same way, mixing the colours and textures of silk randomly. When you have added all the strips, press each patch then trim away the excess fabric with scissors, leaving a 2cm/¾in seam allowance around the block.

4 Pin and stitch the blocks together in rows, adding extra strips of silk between them. Join the rows, then add a border. To assemble the quilt, place the backing right side down and the interlining on top. Finally place the quilt top right side up on top. Tack (baste) all three layers together.

5 Decorate the quilt with machine or hand quilting before binding the edges with coffee silk. Finish the design with machine embroidery using metallic thread in a zig-zag or other embroidery stitch.

Paper quilt wallhanging

In this exciting and original hanging, the images are not just framed but actually become part of the vibrantly coloured handmade paper squares. Paper pulp and pigments for dyeing it can be bought from craft suppliers.

materials and equipment

- collection of photographs or other souvenirs such as tickets, labels or press cuttings
- aluminium mesh
- strong scissors
- 2.5cm/1in-wide masking tape
- absorbent non-woven kitchen cloths
- recycled paper pulp
- paper dyes in 2–3 colours
- 2–3 large plastic bowls
- paper string or embroidery thread (floss)
- 60cm/24in dowelling, 6mm/¼in diameter

1 With your collection of materials in front of you, decide on a standard size for each patch and the number of patches that are required to make the hanging. In this case each patch will be 15cm/6in square.

2 To make the moulds for the paper, cut a 17.5cm/7in square of aluminium mesh, and a strip 15 × 4cm/6 × 1½in. Fold strips of masking tape over each edge of the mesh shapes to cover the sharp edges.

3 Cover a large board with several layers of non-woven kitchen cloth. Dye two or three batches of pulp following the manufacturer's instructions. Immerse the square mesh in the background colour pulp and lift the first square out of the bowl.

4 Turn the mesh carefully to deposit the square in the top corner of the couching cloth. Repeat to make a total of nine squares, laying them in three rows of three. Use the masking tape binding as a guide for the spacing between the squares.

5 Cut 36 lengths of paper string or embroidery thread 10cm/4in long, and lay them over the spaces to join the squares. Cut nine lengths 9cm/3½in long to make the hanging loops. Double these and arrange them along one side.

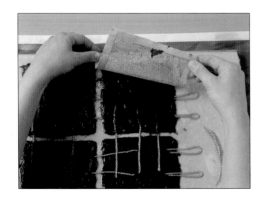

6 Couch nine more squares of the same coloured pulp on top of the first set, to hold the strings or threads in place.

7 Arrange your collection of images centrally on the squares of wet pulp.

8 Using different coloured pulp and the smaller mould, couch strips of pulp over the edges of the images to hold them in place. Leave for several days to dry naturally, then thread the dowelling rod through the loops.

KEEPSAKE BOXES

For small collections, or treasured three-dimensional objects that cannot be fitted into an album, a keepsake box is the answer. Look out for good quality packaging that can be recycled, or buy plain cardboard boxes from craft stores and decorate them to match the subject of your collection.

Découpage memory box

The art of decorating with paper scraps, which are overlaid and varnished to give the appearance of a hand-painted finish is known as découpage. This box is prettily decorated with pictures of coloured feathers, cats, flowers and fans, and finished with a pink ribbon border – every girl's ideal treasure box.

materials and equipment

- plain hexagonal cardboard box with lid
- acrylic or household emulsion (latex) paint in eau de Nil
- paintbrush
- scraps of old manuscript paper, or new paper aged by dyeing in tea
- glue stick
- selection of cut-out paper scraps printed with images of cats, fans, feathers and flowers
- acrylic matt varnish
- measuring tape
- scissors
- fabric ribbon
- fabric glue
- assorted buttons
- needle and thread

1 Paint the box inside and out with two coats of eau de Nil paint and leave to dry. Tear the manuscript paper into scraps and glue these to the sides and lid of the box. Cover with the printed scraps, overlapping them as desired. Apply two to three coats of acrylic varnish, leaving each coat to dry.

2 Measure the rim of the lid and cut a length of ribbon to this measurement. Using fabric glue, stick the ribbon around the rim. Using the same glue, stick a selection of buttons in assorted designs around the rim, on top of the ribbon.

3 Make a simple rosette shape with another length of ribbon and secure by stitching through the central folds. Stitch a button in to the centre, then glue the rosette to the centre of the box lid.

VARIATION: Travel memory box

To house a collection of holiday souvenirs, cover a travel-themed memory box with découpage using scraps of maps featuring appropriate destinations.

Fabric-covered box

Covering a box with a luxurious fabric such as linen, velvet or silk makes a very special setting for small treasures such as a collection of love letters and romantic trinkets. This box is cleverly constructed with ribbon ties so that it lies flat before assembly and could make a lovely surprise gift. If you are making the box as a memento of a family wedding you may even be able to obtain a little spare wedding dress fabric to make an extra-special reminder of the occasion for the bride.

materials and equipment

- craft knife
- metal ruler
- cutting mat
- strong cardboard
- squared pattern paper
- pencil
- scissors
- dressmaker's pins
- pale lilac linen
- dressmaker's scissors
- tacking (basting) thread
- needle
- narrow velvet ribbon
- grosgrain ribbon
- Ric-rac braid
- sewing machine
- sewing thread
- iron
- small embroidered motif
- fabric glue

1 Using a craft knife and metal ruler and working on a cutting mat, from strong cardboard cut out a base and a lid, each 19 x 15cm/7½ x 6in; two long sides each 19 x 7.5cm/7½ x 3in; and two short sides each 15 x 7.5cm/6 x 3in. These will be slipped inside the cover to make the box rigid.

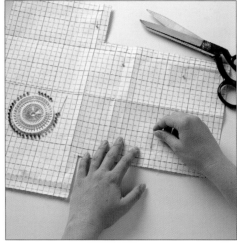

2 Make a paper pattern using the measurements on the template at the back of the book as a guide. Add a 1.5cm/⅝in seam allowance all around the pattern. Pin the pattern to a piece of lilac linen folded in half along the grain and cut out two matching pieces of fabric.

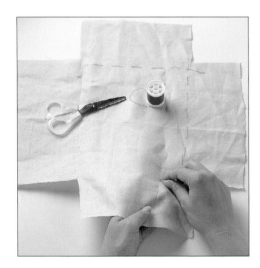

3 Using a contrasting coloured thread, and working on the piece of fabric intended for the right side of the cover, tack (baste) the fabric to mark out the stitching lines for the different sections of the box, following the guides on the template. Cut eight 15cm/6in lengths of narrow velvet ribbon for the corner ties and two 30cm/12in lengths of grosgrain ribbon for the front ties.

VARIATIONS: More fabric ideas

To memorialize a beloved pet, cover a box with fabric on to which you have transferred a favourite photograph.

Cover an old shoe box with decorative papers or fabrics appropriate for the occasion and add ribbons.

4 On the right side of the fabric, pin and tack a length of Ric-rac braid along the seam line around three sides of the box lid. Pin the ties in place at the corners and pin one piece of grosgrain ribbon to the lid.

5 Pin the last piece of grosgrain ribbon to the centre front section of the box base. Stitch the ribbon ties down with a straight machine stitch, turning the raw edges underneath to neaten.

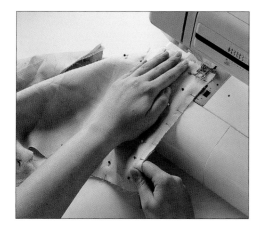

6 Pin the two pieces of fabric right sides together and stitch all around the edges of the box. Leave the long side at the front of the base open so that the cardboard sections can be slipped inside the cover. Clip the corners and trim the seam allowance, then turn the cover through to the right side and press.

7 Push the first piece of cardboard for the lid through the opening along the long side. Neatly stitch along the lid edge to enclose it using a zipper foot on the machine. Insert the cardboard for the long side at the back and enclose with another line of stitches, followed by the pieces for the short sides and the large piece for the base. Enclose each piece of cardboard with a line of stitches. Finally, insert the last piece for the long side at the front of the box.

8 When all the cardboard is in place, turn in the seam allowance of the opening and neatly slipstitch the seam. Glue an embroidered motif on to the box lid with fabric glue. Then tie the ribbon ties at each corner to assemble the box.

THREE-DIMENSIONS

The crafts of paper folding and paper sculpture open up many new avenues for creativity in scrapbooking. Here are two very simple ideas to start you thinking in three dimensions when devising themed settings for your photographs.

Our house

This fold-out display is an ideal showcase for photographs of a house renovation. Remember to preserve a piece of that ghastly old wallpaper that took you hours of work to remove.

materials and equipment

- three sheets of white cartridge (construction) paper, two measuring 38 x 60cm/15 x 24in and one 19 x 30cm/7½ x 12in
- bone folder
- pencil
- metal ruler
- craft knife
- cutting mat
- glue stick
- bulldog clips

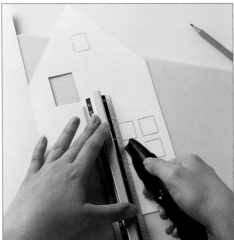

1 To make the accordion-style house on the right of the design, fold the small sheet of paper in half lengthwise, then fold the long ends back to align with the centre fold. Crease the folds sharply using a bone folder. Open the paper out, then fold it in half widthwise. Open out the sheet and mark in the pointed roofs on the two centre sections, following the template at the back of the book. Using a craft knife and a metal ruler and working on a cutting mat, cut out the roof sections and cut out two small windows under each pointed roof. Fold the design widthwise and glue the two sides of each outer section together so that the house will stand up.

2 To make the folded house at the left of the design, take a large sheet of paper and fold over a third of it at the right-hand side. On this third, lightly draw a pointed roof and windows. Cut out the roof and windows as before.

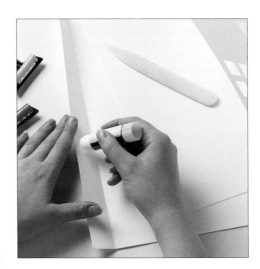

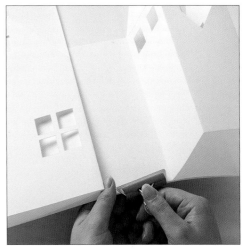

3 For the background, fold in 2cm/¾in down one short side of the last sheet of white paper. Crease the fold sharply using the bone folder. Glue the plain section of the larger house to this flap so that the house can be lifted and turned like the page of a book.

4 Glue one side of the smaller house to the right-hand side of the main album page. Secure the paper with bulldog clips while the glue dries. Arrange photographs and memorabilia on the background page and inside the left-hand house.

Butterfly bonanza

These two charming ideas for presenting a single photograph use matching butterfly motifs, which are folded and glued so that they appear to flutter around the picture. Punched holes give their wings a lacy appearance.

materials and equipment

- pencil
- paper
- scissors
- selection of pastel-coloured papers, including white
- cutting mat
- craft knife
- revolving leather punch
- fancy-edged scissors
- fine corrugated white cardboard
- glue stick
- heavy white paper
- coloured card (stock)
- photographs
- transparent photo corners

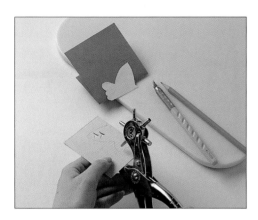

1 Enlarge the butterfly template at the back of the book in three different sizes and cut them out. Place a template on a piece of folded coloured paper and trace around it. Cut out the small angled shapes in the wings using a craft knife and working on a cutting mat, and make decorative round holes in various sizes using a leather punch.

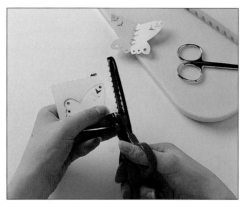

2 Keeping the paper folded, cut round the outline of the butterfly with fancy-edged scissors. Make a selection of butterfly motifs in different sizes and colours. Do not flatten out the central folds. To make winged cards, cut out one wing only, then cut out a rectangle around the wing using fancy-edged scissors. Fold the wing outwards.

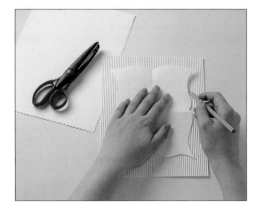

3 To make a foundation on which to mount the butterflies, enlarge the frame template so that it is about 2.5cm/1in larger all round than the photograph, then cut it out. Position it on a piece of white corrugated cardboard and draw round it lightly with a pencil. Cut out the shape, taking care not to crush the ridges of the cardboard. Glue the cut-out on to a slightly larger rectangle of heavy white paper and mount this on a larger piece of coloured card.

VARIATION: Butterfly theme

Butterflies are a perennially popular motif. They can be stencilled, stamped, cut out from paper and applied in different ways to album pages.

4 Carefully make four tiny marks at the corners where you intend to mount the photograph, then arrange the butterfly motifs around the frame, slotting some individual butterflies inside the winged cards. Glue them in place using a glue stick. Finally, attach the photograph to the mount using transparent photo corners.

5 To make the photo mailer, cut a long strip of heavy white paper slightly wider than the photograph and long enough to enclose it plus an overlap for the butterfly. Crease the vertical folds. Cut out one small and one large butterfly motif from coloured paper, then cut out a half large motif from the end flap. Using the photo as a guide, position and cut four diagonal slots to take the corners.

6 Assemble the photo mailer by sticking the large butterfly to the front of the card in such a position that the wings slot through the folded half motif cut in the flap. The action of slotting the wings together will keep the card closed. Stick a small motif on the front of the card and mount the photograph inside.

Children

Babies and children are of course among the most popular subjects for scrapbooking: all parents long to preserve their memories of their offspring as they grow up so quickly. For most people, it's also when they have their own children that they become most aware of the need to pass on the family history to future generations. There is nothing older children like more than revisiting their own earliest memories – seeing pictures of their former little selves and being reminded of special times they can just remember, or discovering what they were like as babies, before their memories begin. As well as photographs, of which you will have plenty to choose from, include some of the children's early works of art or attempts at writing.

Album page for a baby boy

Soft pastel shades dictate the look of this album page, which has a contemporary style. Keep a tiny but important memento, such as the baby's hospital identification tag, safely inside a small clear plastic envelope.

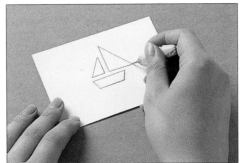

I Cut out rectangles of plain and printed paper, and arrange them on the heavy white paper. Use different-sized rectangles to make a pleasing layout. Glue in position. Arrange the collage items on the background. Small mementoes can be placed in clear plastic envelopes. Glue all the background items in place.

2 Take a small piece of white card and draw a simple motif, such as a toy boat, on the wrong side of it. Working on a cork mat or corrugated cardboard to protect the work surface, use a bodkin or paper piercer to make pinpricks at regular intervals along the outline of the design using the pencil line as a guide.

materials and equipment

- scissors
- plain paper in pastel colours
- striped printed paper, such as wallpaper
- heavy white paper
- glue stick
- baby mementoes
- small, clear plastic envelope
- white card (stock)
- pencil
- cork mat or corrugated cardboard
- bodkin or paper piercer
- fancy-edged scissors in wavy and postage stamp designs
- rotating leather hole punch
- lettering stencil
- craft knife
- cutting mat
- baby Ric-rac braid

3 Cut out a rectangle of blue paper using wavy-edged scissors. Then cut out the pinpricked motif with fancy-edged scissors in a postage stamp design and glue it on the blue paper.

VARIATION: A patchwork background

Simple photographs can be enhanced in many ways. Here a single photograph takes centre stage and the ephemera that is added is colour co-ordinated to hold the design idea together. The stripey pastel patchwork background is appropriately coloured for a baby boy and matches his clothing.

The zipper pocket at the bottom of the page is a good place to keep any small items of memorabilia, such as small cards expressing good wishes from friends and family. The cute faces are a fun addition to this light-hearted album page.

4 Make a mount for the photograph by cutting out a piece of white card larger all round than the photograph, using wavy-edged scissors. Pierce small decorative holes all around the edges of the card using a rotating leather hole punch.

5 Place a lettering stencil over a rectangular piece of blue paper and stencil the letter of your choice on the card. Cut the letter out carefully with a craft knife, working on a cutting mat. Trim the corners of the paper shape with scissors to round them gently.

6 Mount the cut-out letter on a rectangle of pale yellow paper, then on a larger fancy-edged rectangle of white card. Pierce a small hole in the centre top of the label and thread it with a short length of baby Ric-rac braid. Tie this in a bow. Carefully glue everything to the background.

Album page for a baby girl

Pages dedicated to baby girls don't always have to be pale pink and frilly. This cheeky picture called for a bolder treatment, so the page uses bright colours and a stitched paisley motif with the sparkle of tiny gems.

materials and equipment

- scraps of card (card stock)
- pencil
- felt squares in blue, lime green, light purple and dark purple
- scissors
- stranded embroidery thread (floss) in lime green, fuchsia and turquoise
- needle
- small self-adhesive gems
- tweezers
- 30cm/12in square sheet of bright pink card (card stock)
- glue stick
- small buckle
- self-adhesive foam pads
- photograph
- chipboard letters
- craft paint in purple
- artist's brush

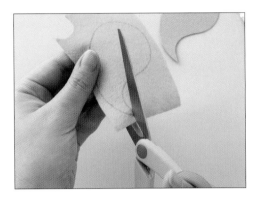

1 Draw three large and two small paisley shapes on card and cut them out. Use them as templates to cut out five felt shapes in assorted colours.

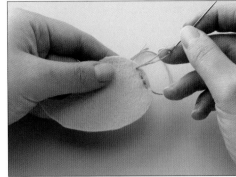

2 Work a row of backstitch around the edge of each felt shape using six strands of contrasting embroidery thread. Work three lazy daisy stitches in the centre of each large shape and one on each small shape.

3 Stick a small self-adhesive gem to the embroidery stitches in the centre of each paisley shape, grasping the gems with tweezers to make this easier.

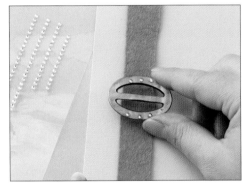

4 Cut a strip of purple felt 2cm/¾in wide and 30cm/12in long and glue it down the left side of the background card near the edge. Decorate a small buckle with more sticky gems and glue it to the felt belt.

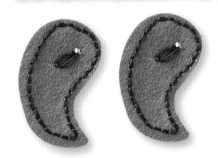

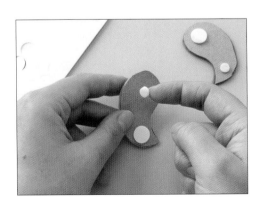

5 Glue the decorated felt shapes to the matching card shapes. Stick two foam pads on the back of each small paisley shape so that they will be slightly raised.

6 Position the photograph centrally in the area to the right of the felt strip and glue it to the background. Arrange the three large paisley shapes down the left side of the picture, then position the small shapes between them. Glue all the shapes in place.

7 Paint chipboard letters to spell the child's name in purple to match the felt shapes and leave to dry. Glue them in place at the bottom right of the layout.

{Lilly}

Schoolday memories

This memento of your schooldays will bring back memories of past escapades, glories and disasters. Indulge yourself and relive all those carefree times by making a schooldays album page.

materials and equipment

- brick-effect dolls' house paper
- sharp scissors
- glue stick
- envelope
- selection of school photographs
- transparent photo corners
- small labels
- black pen
- striped grosgrain ribbon
- metal badge
- embroidered pocket and cap badges
- school reports
- star stickers

1 Cut two sheets of brick-effect paper to match the size of your album pages and glue in position. Glue the envelope in one corner so that the flap faces upwards. Arrange the photographs on the page then secure with photo corners.

2 Next to each photograph, stick a handwritten label giving the year each picture was taken (or use computer-printed labels if you prefer). The album pages here show three generations of schoolchildren.

STARTING SCHOOL

Starting school is a major milestone for every child, but after just a few weeks they all seem to settle into their new life, making friends, learning new skills and starting on the path to independence. Mark the progress from the first uncertain day to being one of a trio of best friends with a special album page.

materials and equipment

- 30cm/12in square sheet of plain background paper
- brick-effect paper
- two or more photographs
- photo corners
- small labels
- alphabet fridge magnets
- photocopier
- scissors
- coloured pencils

3 Fold the grosgrain ribbon in half and attach the metal badge to the top of the ribbon near the fold. Trim the ribbon ends to create a V shape. Glue the ribbon to the flap of the envelope. (Always keep a sheet of paper between the two album pages when they are closed to prevent the badge damaging the pictures.)

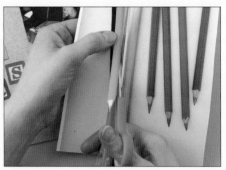

1 Cut two 2.5cm/1in strips of brick-effect paper and stick them along the top and bottom of the background paper. Mount the photographs in the centre with photo corners. Add a printed or handwritten date label under each.

2 Photocopy the fridge magnets and the pencils, reducing the size as necessary. Cut them out individually and arrange around the pictures. The letters can spell out a caption or be placed randomly. Glue everything in place.

4 Glue the embroidered badges to the pages, positioning the cap badge just above the envelope. Fill the envelope with extra pictures and school reports. Finally, arrange a sprinkling of star stickers over the pages.

Polka-dot mini-album

This handy-sized accordion album, in its own brightly decorated matching box, could be filled with a selection of photographs from every stage of a child's life, to make an enchanting gift for a proud grandparent.

materials and equipment

- rectangular cardboard box
- handmade paper in orange, pink, turquoise and green
- small coins
- pencil
- scissors
- hole punch
- glue stick
- thick card (stock)
- metal ruler
- craft knife and cutting mat
- paper parcel tape
- thin green card
- pair of compasses
- thin satin ribbon

1 Cover the box with orange handmade paper. Draw around small coins on to orange, pink, turquoise and green paper. Cut out all the circles. Punch small holes in the centre of some circles using a hole punch. Glue the circles to the top and sides of the box, overlapping some of them.

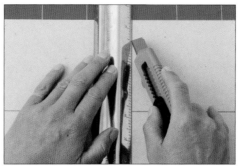

2 Measure and mark out four identical rectangles of thick card to a size that will fit neatly inside the box. Cut them out using a craft knife and a metal ruler and working on a cutting mat.

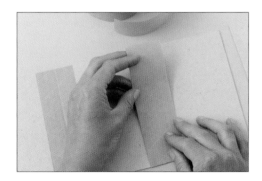

3 Place the rectangles side by side in a row, leaving gaps of about 3mm/⅛in between them. Cut six strips of paper tape, slightly longer than the card. Stick the tape to the cards, over the gaps, to join them together. Repeat on the other side. Leave to dry, then trim away the excess tape.

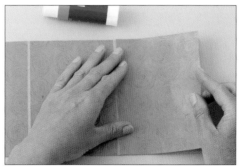

4 Fold along the joins to make an accordion album. Cut eight pieces of turquoise handmade paper to the same dimensions as the cards. Glue one piece to the front and one to the back of each page of the album.

5 Cut six strips of orange paper 2.5cm/1in wide to match the height of the pages. Glue a strip over the middle of each fold on the front and back.

6 Decorate the front of the album with small multicoloured circles of paper to match the box.

7 Draw a circle 6cm/2¼in in diameter on thin green card and cut it out. Trim a small photo into a slightly smaller circle and glue it to the green circle to make a tag.

8 Punch a hole in the top of the tag and add a length of thin satin ribbon as a tie. FIll the album with photographs. Tie the tag around the album to keep it closed, then place the album in the box.

VARIATION: Snow scene

Children playing in the snow are always full of fun and vitality, with bright smiles and rosy cheeks. Once the snow stops falling and the sun comes out, it's a great time to take photographs of them for your album, to store up memories of exciting days.

On this scrapbook page, blue and white spotted paper has been used to resemble a snowy sky, and the torn white edges and glittering stars, plus the pale colouring of all the elements, help to reinforce the cold, bright winter light in the photograph. You could create a similar snowy background for a winter page by sticking on individual self-adhesive dots in a random arrangement on plain paper.

Growing up together

Birthdays, Christmas and Easter holidays are family times that are especially important to grandparents, aunts, uncles and cousins. Keep a record of how the children are growing in the intervening months by collecting together pictures taken on these special occasions.

materials and equipment

- six photographs
- coloured paper
- corner punch
- 30cm/12in square of background paper
- tear-off calendar
- glue stick

1 Trim all the photographs to measure 7 × 9cm/2¾ × 3½in. Glue each on to a piece of coloured paper and trim the margins to 1cm/⅜in all around.

2 Trim the corners with a decorative punch to give the frames a pretty, lacy look.

VARIATION: Family secrets

Here's another idea for a family album page that shows all the children together yet allows each of them to make a personal contribution – if you can persuade them to take part.

Create matching mini-folders from thin card (stock), one for each child, and decorate the fronts with small photographs, each mounted on a torn square of handmade floral paper. Fasten each folder with a short loop of ribbon and a small button.

Inside the little folders you could insert a few folded pages of white paper and get each child to write something about themselves and what they have been doing, or make up a story or a poem, or draw some pictures. Alternatively, you could paste in more photographs or other memorabilia, or write your own account of your children's progress and achievements. Decorate the rest of the page with a few small embellishments and give it a title and a date.

You could make a page of this kind every year as an ongoing record of your growing offspring, with pictures shot specially for the album page. Both you and other family members, and the children themselves, will enjoy looking back over the years to see these snapshots of themselves as developing individuals within a family group.

3 Arrange the pictures in two scattered rows of three, in chronological order, on the background paper.

4 Add a few tear-off pages from the calendar, scattered over the page. Circle the dates when the pictures were taken on the calendar pages.

Special occasions

Many of our most memorable and enjoyable experiences occur on the important annual festivals such as Christmas, Easter and Thanksgiving, which give a regular rhythm to family life and are traditionally times when everyone wants to get together with relatives and friends for informal and joyful celebrations.

As well as these parties, there are the very special occasions that mark life's milestones, such as graduation, engagement, marriage and the birth of a baby, to name but a few. All these high days and holidays demand to be commemorated by special pages in your albums, and all make great themes for which a wealth of decorative material is available, as well as a good collection of photographs of the event. The following pages include ideas for pages based on both seasonal festivities and more personal celebrations.

Valentine's celebration

The traditional imagery of Valentine's Day is perfect for an album page expressing the way you feel about your partner. Use the phrases on this layout as inspiration for your own special messages to the one you love.

1 Cut a 12 × 4in/30 × 10cm rectangle of pearl white paper and glue it to the left-hand side of the red card background, aligning the edges, to make a wide border.

2 Print out all the words and phrases, except "Forever", on to white paper. Trim "I love you because…" and "…you're wonderful!" to thin white strips measuring 10 × 2cm/4 × ¾in. Glue to the top and bottom of the border.

3 Glue two swing tags on to the back of a sheet of silver paper, and one on to red paper. Cut the papers to shape by cutting around the edges of the tags. Re-punch the holes with an eyelet punch.

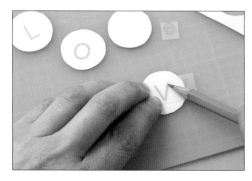

4 Cut out the three printed phrases and glue one to the front of each tag. Punch three small hearts from red vellum and glue these to the tags, over the text.

5 Position the tags on the border. Mark the positions of the holes for the elastic at the sides of the tags and punch the holes with an eyelet punch. Thread the elastic to make crosses and tie at the back. Insert the tags with the red tag in the centre.

6 To make the frame, draw a 12.5 × 15cm/ 5 × 6in rectangle on thick card. Draw a second rectangle inside it, 2cm/¾in smaller all round. Cut it out using a craft knife and metal ruler. Dry-brush a thin coat of parchment-coloured paint over the frame and leave it to dry.

7 Cut out four small discs of white card. Inscribe the letters L, O, V and E on the discs using rub-on letters.

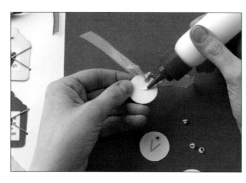

8 Punch a small hole in the top of each disc using an eyelet punch. Insert an eyelet into each, then a length of ribbon. Glue the four discs to the top of the page.

9 Cut out the printed words "you" and "me". Glue them to small heart-shaped tags. Attach the hearts to the page beside the border panel using white eyelets.

materials and equipment

- scissors
- pearl white paper
- metal ruler
- pencil
- craft knife
- cutting mat
- 30cm/12in square sheet of thin red card (stock)
- spray adhesive
- computer and printer
- thin white paper
- 3 small swing tags
- silver and red paper
- small eyelet punch
- tack hammer
- red vellum paper
- heart punch
- thin round elastic in silver
- thick card (stock)
- acrylic paint in parchment
- paintbrush
- white card
- gold rub-on letters
- 6 eyelets
- thin red and silver ribbon
- 2 small heart tags
- white vellum
- thin steel wire
- strong clear glue
- photograph
- masking tape
- 4 photo corners

10 Print the word "Forever" on to a sheet of white vellum. Trim closely, then glue with spray adhesive to a larger strip of white vellum. Attach the strip to the bottom of the page.

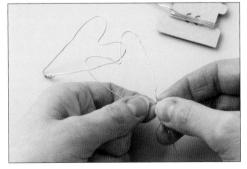

11 Cut two pieces of steel wire 15cm/6in long. Bend into two hearts. Twist the ends of one heart together and loop the second heart through the first before twisting the ends. Glue the entwined hearts over the vellum panel using strong clear glue.

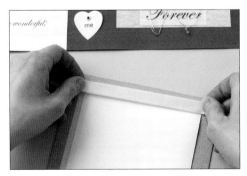

12 Attach the photo to the back of the painted frame with strips of masking tape. Position the framed picture in the centre of the red area of the page and attach it using photo corners.

An engagement

This simple and beautiful layout expresses a single idea very clearly: the love and happiness of the newly engaged couple. The use of translucent vellum for the heart shapes creates a pretty, layered look. It's essential to use spray adhesive for the vellum, as any other glue will show through.

materials and equipment

- polka-dot paper
- metal ruler
- pencil
- craft knife
- cutting mat
- 30cm/12in square sheet of thin cream card (card stock)
- spray adhesive
- gold paper
- scallop-edged scissors
- red vellum
- light pink vellum
- dark pink paper
- 1 large photograph and 3 small ones

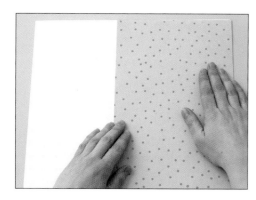

1 Cut a 30 x 18cm/12 x 7in rectangle of polka-dot paper using a craft knife and metal ruler and working on a cutting mat. Glue the paper to the right-hand side of the cream card, aligning the outer edges.

2 Cut three rectangles of gold paper 7 x 5cm/2¾ x 2in, and one 17 x 14.5cm/6¾ x 5¾in. Trim all the sides with scallop-edged scissors. Cut out the centres to make frames with narrow borders.

3 Glue the large frame to the lower part of the polka dot paper. Trace the heart templates at the back of the book. Cut out one large heart and one small heart from light pink vellum, and one medium heart and one small heart each from red vellum and dark pink paper. Glue the small hearts down the left-hand side and the medium hearts to the right above the large frame.

4 Glue the large pink heart to the middle of the page. Glue the small frames over the small hearts and glue the photographs in position in the frames.

VARIATION: Other special occasions

Right: This mosaic treatment is a good way to include plenty of individual shots of people who attend a farewell party. The scrapbook album page is a perfect record of those who attended as well as a good reminder of the occasion.

Far right: To mark the occasion of being voted lord mayor, this scrapbook album page is decorated with appropriately sombre colours.

Below: A handmade album cover for a special wedding anniversary is decorated with a ribbon of satin roses. The matt cream textured boards are appropriate for the subject.

Christmas celebrations

It's a treat to use the traditional festive colours of green and red for a Christmas layout, and deep red velvet-effect paper creates a fabulous rich background. Add plenty of gold and glitter for a thoroughly opulent look.

materials and equipment

- red velvet-effect paper
- ruler
- pencil
- scissors
- spray adhesive
- 30cm/12in square sheet of green card (stock)
- tartan border sticker
- sheet of gold glitter card (stock)
- Christmas photograph
- fancy-edged scissors
- glue dots
- star punch
- oval cutter
- gold paper ribbon

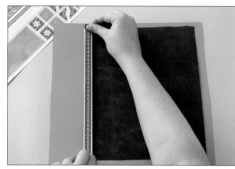

1 Cut a rectangle measuring 28 x 22.5cm/ 11 x 9in from the red velvet-effect paper and glue it to the green card, leaving a narrow border of green at the top, bottom and right-hand side.

2 Use a tartan border sticker to decorate the left-hand edge of the red velvet paper, sticking it centrally along the join.

VARIATION: Digital Christmas

Online scrapbooking stores offer a host of backgrounds and other ingredients for seasonally themed digital pages, so it's very easy to put together a page including pictures of your Christmas festivities. You could even add pictures of the children opening their presents and email it to friends and family on the big day itself.

3 Cut a piece of gold glitter card slightly larger all around than the photograph. Trim the edge using fancy-edged scissors. Glue the photograph to the gold card then glue in place on the background.

Nathan and Santa

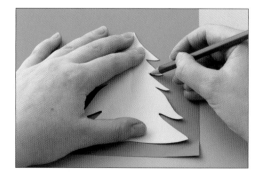

4 Using the tree template at the back of the book cut a Christmas tree out of green card. Punch some stars from gold card and glue in place. Glue the tree to the background. Cut three gold oval baubles and punch a hole near one end of each for threading a short length of paper ribbon through. Glue all the decorations in place.

Thanksgiving

A collection of vintage scraps and a row of patches cut from homespun fabrics embody the traditional values of American Thanksgiving celebrations, suggesting comfort and warmth. A brown paper background and manila photo corners add to the old-time feeling of this autumnal page.

materials and equipment

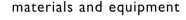

- spray adhesive
- 20 x 30cm/8 x 12in rectangle of blue craft paper
- 30cm/12in square sheet of brown card (stock)
- scissors
- narrow double-sided tape
- striped ribbon
- 4 shirt buttons
- red thread and needle
- 2 portrait format photographs
- 8 manila photo corners
- reproduction Thanksgiving scraps and photocopies
- glue stick
- skeleton leaves
- check cotton fabric scraps

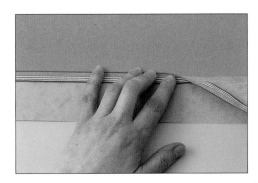

1 Glue the blue craft paper to the centre of the background card. Cut two strips of double-sided tape and stick them over the two joins. Peel the protective layer from the tape and stick down two 32cm/13in lengths of ribbon, overlapping 1cm/½in at each end.

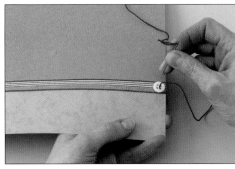

2 Turn the ends of ribbon to the wrong side and stick them down. Sew on a button at each end of the ribbons using red thread. Stitch through the card as well as the ribbon and fasten off securely on the back.

3 Arrange the two photographs on the blue section of the background, then attach them to the page with photo corners.

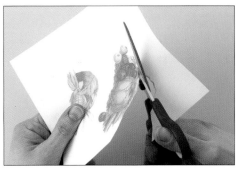

4 If you do not have enough original scraps, you can photocopy them, adjusting the sizes as necessary. Try reversing some copies to create a greater variety of images for the collage. Cut out the images accurately.

5 Arrange the scraps on the page and glue lightly in place with a glue stick. Don't stick down the edges at this stage.

6 Slip a few skeleton leaves in among the scraps. When you are happy with the arrangement, stick down both the leaves and the scraps securely.

7 Cut out several small fabric squares, following the grain of the fabric carefully to create an accurate shape. Gently pull away a few threads from each side to create fringed edges.

8 Arrange the fabric pieces evenly along the brown section at the lower edge of the page and stick down using a glue stick, leaving the fringed edges free.

Hannukah

The lighting of candles is an important part of the celebration of Hannukah, the Jewish festival of light. For impact, use one large photograph to fill one of the pages of this double-page spread. The title is arranged over both pages and uses a variety of letter styles. Metal embellishments with a Hannukah theme are available from scrapbooking suppliers.

materials and equipment

- 30cm/12in square sheet of pale blue card (stock)
- pencil
- scissors
- scrap paper
- patterned rubber stamp
- clear embossing stamp pad
- silver embossing powder
- heat tool
- 2 x 30cm/12in square sheets of navy blue card (stock)
- spray adhesive
- die-cut machine
- large label die
- 3 metal embellishments
- pale blue sheer ribbon
- assorted chipboard letters
- glue dots

1 Draw a capital "H" on pale blue card and cut it out. Rest it on a sheet of scrap paper and stamp it randomly using a patterned stamp and clear embossing fluid.

2 Place the pattern-stamped letter on a clean sheet of paper folded in the centre and sprinkle it liberally with silver embossing powder. (The paper will catch the excess powder and make it easier to pour back into the container.)

3 Using the heat tool, heat the embossing powder until it turns from powdery to shiny. Keep the tool moving to avoid scorching the card.

4 Glue the photograph in the centre of one of the navy blue sheets. Cut two 2.5cm/1in strips of pale blue card. Stick one down the left side of the page, centred in the margin. Trim the decorated initial and glue it at lower right, overlapping the photo.

5 Use a die-cut machine to cut out three labels from pale blue card. Alternatively, make a template and cut out three labels by hand.

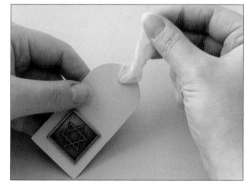

6 Attach the metal embellishments to the tags using glue dots. Cut three lengths of ribbon to loop through the top of each tag.

7 Arrange the remaining assorted letters along the bottom of the second page of the layout to finish the title. Make sure the heavy letters are firmly secured.

8 Stick the remaining pale blue strip acoss the top of the second page. Place the three decorated tags in a row below it and use glue dots to attach them firmly to the card.

Mum's birthday

If the children have made a special effort to surprise their mum on her birthday, that's definitely worth recording in style. The tiny envelopes on this layout can conceal a few mementoes or additional pictures of the day.

materials and equipment

- 30cm/12in square sheet of pale blue card (stock)
- pencil and metal ruler
- craft knife and cutting mat
- pink, white, lilac, light yellow and light green paper
- glue stick
- pair of compasses
- scissors
- flower punch
- tracing paper
- white, pink and lilac card (stock)
- small coin
- eyelet punch and eyelets
- photograph
- narrow organza ribbon

1 Draw a rectangle 15 × 10cm/6 × 4in on the blue card, 9.5cm/3¾in from the top and bottom edges, and 6cm/2½in in from the right edge. Cut out the rectangle using a craft knife and a metal ruler.

2 Cut a 20 × 15cm/8 × 6in rectangle of pale pink paper. Glue the paper to the back of the card, over the aperture.

3 Cut two 5cm/2in strips of white paper to fit across the page. Glue them in place, 2.5cm/1in in from the top and bottom edges, and trim any excess.

4 Draw and cut out eight 4cm/1¾in diameter circles of paper, two each in lilac, pink, light yellow and pale green. Glue the circles to the white strips. Punch eight flower shapes in the same colours and glue them in the centres of the circles.

5 Copy the envelope pattern at the back of the book on to thin white card and cut out to make a template. Draw around it once on pink and once on lilac card. Draw around a small coin twice on to pink card and twice on to lilac card. Cut them all out.

6 On the inside of the envelopes, score the fold lines and fold in the sides and flaps. Use an eyelet punch to make holes in the envelope flaps and the pink and lilac circles. Attach the circles to the flaps using eyelets.

7 Glue the photo in place inside the aperture, leaving equal amounts of pink border all round as a frame.

8 Glue the envelopes to the left side of the page, with the flaps to the front. Fill the envelopes, then fold in the sides and flaps and wrap a length of ribbon around the circles to keep the envelopes closed.

Father's Day

You could make this layout to honour your own or your children's father on Father's Day. The little pull-out book attached to the page means that the journaling can be kept for his eyes only: get the children to write in the book.

materials and equipment

- 3 x 30cm/12in square sheets of blue card (stock)
- 29cm/11½in square sheet of burgundy card (stock)
- tape runner
- 30 x 15cm/12 x 6in sheet of Argyll patterned paper
- photograph
- scissors
- silver embossing metal
- eyelet punch
- hammer
- screw brad
- metal ruler
- medium embossing tool
- pencil
- glue dots
- 30cm/12in burgundy ribbon
- 3 pale blue buttons

1 Glue the burgundy card on to a sheet of blue card, leaving an even margin all round. Attach the Argyll patterned paper across the top half of the page. Cut out a piece of blue card a little larger than the photograph and mat the picture with it. Mount the photo towards the top left corner of the album page so that there is room below it for further decoration.

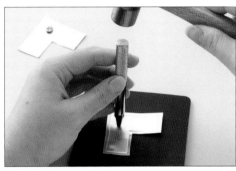

2 Cut out an L-shaped piece of silver embossing metal to make a photo corner. Use an eyelet punch to make a small hole in the centre. Push the screw brad through and bend open the fasteners. Place in the top right corner of the layout.

3 Cut a 9.5cm/3½in square of embossing metal. Lay it on top of a spare piece of patterned paper and emboss it by laying a ruler along the lines of the design and scoring with the embossing tool.

4 To make the book, lightly mark the remaining sheet of blue card at 10cm/4in intervals along each edge. Fold up the first third using the marked edge as a guide. Crease the fold.

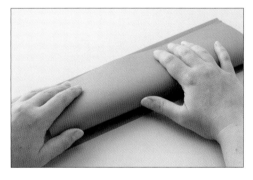

5 Fold the remaining third back the other way to make an accordion fold.

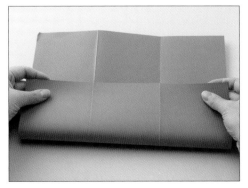

6 Unfold and turn the card through 90 degrees. Repeat the two folds in the other direction. Unfold again.

7 You should now have nine equal squares. Using scissors, cut out the top right square and the bottom left square.

8 Fold the top left corner square to cover the centre square and crease sharply.

9 Flip the card over and repeat with the opposite corner.

10 The sheet can now be folded naturally into a square book shape, opening from left to right.

11 Attach the embossed metal cover to the front of the book using glue dots.

12 Stick a length of ribbon across the back of the book. This will be used to tie the book shut. Attach the book to your page using glue dots.

13 To complete the layout, attach the three buttons using glue dots.

Weddings

The history of wedding photography is almost as long as that of photography itself, as couples began to visit the photographer's studio for a picture to commemorate their marriage as early as the 1840s. However, the limits of technology meant that the camera did not leave the studio to cover the whole affair until the boom in weddings almost a century later.

It was not until the 1970s that the formal posed photographic style gave way to a more relaxed approach. Since then, weddings have been portrayed in a much more journalistic style, and the traditional album of posed shots is also giving way to much freer treatments, for which the skills of scrapbooking are extremely well suited. Many small reminders of the big day, such as menus, confetti and flowers from the bouquet, can now take their place in an album that captures the whole atmosphere of the wedding in a unique way.

A traditional wedding

This lovely reminder of a special day, featuring the wedding photograph and invitation, and decorated with cut-out doves and hearts, is simple yet effective in black, white and gold. This page can be the first in a wedding album, to be followed by other pictures of the happy day.

materials and equipment

- spiral-bound album
- craft knife
- metal ruler
- cutting mat
- heavy white paper
- fancy-edged scissors
- translucent glassine paper
- glue stick
- wedding photograph
- transparent photo corners
- scissors
- pencil
- gold paper
- gold card (stock)
- translucent envelope
- wedding mementoes:
  invitation, pressed flowers,
  ribbon, confetti

1 Before starting work on the layout itself, make a protective page for the treasured photograph by cutting the preceding page out of the album to within about 2.5cm/1in of the spiral binding. Use a craft knife and a metal ruler, and work on a cutting mat.

2 Cut another strip of paper slightly wider than the first strip from a sheet of heavy white paper. Trim one long edge with fancy-edged scissors. Cut a sheet of glassine paper or other translucent paper the same size as the album pages to replace the page you have removed.

3 Glue the glassine paper to the tab in the album, then cover this with the single strip of paper with the decorative edge visible. The translucent protective sheet should now be sandwiched between the two tabs. Allow to dry.

4 Assemble the photograph display. Using fancy-edged scissors, cut around the edges of a piece of heavy white paper slightly larger than the photograph. Mount the photo on this using transparent photo corners.

VARIATION: Family weddings

Many family photograph collections include formal pictures of relatives' weddings, copies of which were usually ordered from the professional photographer and sent out to guests or to those unable to attend the wedding. Often these pictures are to be found, years later, tucked into a drawer or in a box of miscellaneous prints. Yet they are an important part of your family history, as well as being fascinating glimpses of the past, and deserve to be properly presented in your albums.

If old photographs include wedding guests unknown to you, try to find out who they are from older family members and gather all the information you can about the day. The page you design can include journaling to preserve all these memories. In the case of more recent events that you attended yourself, you can include souvenirs such as the invitation and order of service.

It's nice to design the page in a way that is appropriate to the period and the style of the wedding: you can usually get plenty of ideas from the clothes worn by the guests and the settings of the photographs. Many of these will be in black and white so will look best against subtly coloured backgrounds.

5 Copy the dove and heart templates at the back of the book and cut them out. Draw round them on the wrong side of gold paper and heavy white paper. Reverse the dove motif so that they face in different directions. Cut them out.

6 To assemble the album page, stick down a piece of gold card slightly larger than the mounted photo. Add a translucent envelope containing a memento of the occasion such as an invitation, together with any other small saved pressed flowers, ribbon, confetti or similar. Place some of the motifs you have cut out inside the envelope too. Glue down the mounted photograph. Stick the dove and heart cut-outs on to the page in a pleasing arrangement.

An Indian wedding

Traditional Indian weddings are celebrated on a huge scale, with a great deal of ritual, and hundreds of guests are often invited and lavishly entertained. The ceremony is full of vibrant colour and sparkle, with splendid clothes, flowers and food, and provides plenty of visual inspiration for a gorgeous album page ornamented in red and gold.

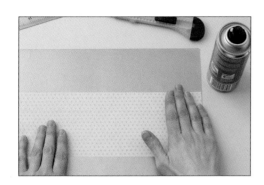

1 Cut a rectangle of starry tissue paper measuring 30 × 10cm/12 × 4in and use spray adhesive to stick it to the sheet of gold card 7.5cm/3in from the top edge.

2 Cut a 10cm/4in square of red embroidered paper. Glue it to the tissue paper panel on the left side of the page, matching the edges.

3 Cut a length of gold braid and another of sequins to fit along the top and bottom of the panel and glue them in place. Glue the photograph in the centre of the panel.

materials and equipment

- gold tissue with star pattern
- metal ruler and pencil
- craft knife and cutting mat
- 30cm/12in square sheet of thin gold card (stock)
- spray adhesive
- red embroidered paper
- fringed gold braid
- sequin strip
- PVA (white) glue
- 10cm/4in square photograph
- thin white card (stock)
- eyelet punch
- gold, red and green flower sequins
- star-shaped eyelets
- red and green shiny paper
- heart paper punch
- thin paper in gold and red
- small photos and mementoes
- gold marker pen
- thin gold ribbon

4 To make the folders, cut three rectangles of thin white card each 16 × 8cm/6 × 3in. Lightly score a line down the rectangles, 4cm/1½in from each side. Fold the scored lines to make flaps.

5 Punch a hole in the centre of each flap using an eyelet punch. Punch matching holes in two gold flower sequins. Attach the sequins to the flaps with star-shaped eyelets. Repeat for the other two folders.

6 Punch eight hearts for each folder from red or green shiny paper. Stick the hearts to the flaps of the folders, four on each door.

7 Cut two squares of red embroidered paper and one of thin gold paper to fit inside the folders and glue them in place. Draw a heart template to fit inside the squares and use it to cut out two gold and one red paper heart. Glue them into the folders and stick mementoes or photos of the bride and groom to the gold hearts.

8 Inscribe the names of the bride and groom in gold on the red heart. Glue the folders in position on the page, beneath the border, with the red heart in the centre. Cut three lengths of gold ribbon and tie the ribbon through the holes in the sequins to keep the flaps closed.

A contemporary wedding

Using computer-printed kisses and light, bright colours, this layout reflects a modern take on a timeless ceremony, inspired by the unconventional wedding group photograph that forms its centrepiece. You could add some text to some of the panels instead of the printed kisses if you prefer.

materials and equipment

- 30cm/12in square sheet of white card (stock)
- computer and printer
- tracing paper
- metal ruler
- pencil
- craft knife
- cutting mat
- spray adhesive
- lilac, turquoise, blue, green and cream paper
- scissors
- glue stick
- heart punch

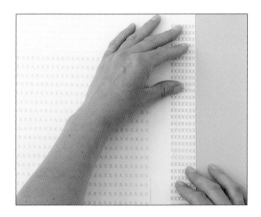

1 Print kisses on to two sheets of tracing paper. Trim the paper to size. Glue to the white card with spray adhesive to make decorative areas.

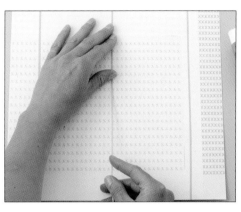

2 Cut three 30cm x 3mm/12 x ⅛in strips of lilac paper. Glue one strip down the middle of the card. Glue the remaining strips at each side of the card, 5cm/2in in from the edges.

3 Cut a selection of rectangles and ovals on to turquoise, lilac, blue and green paper. Cut them all out.

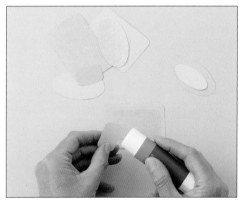

4 Assemble the layered shapes, gluing one colour on top of another.

5 Print the bride and groom's names and large kisses on to tracing paper. Trim them to size and glue them to the rectangles and ovals.

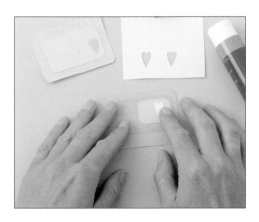

6 Punch hearts from cream, lilac and blue paper. Glue them to the rectangles.

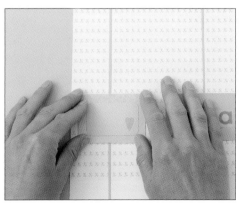

7 Arrange the rectangles down the lilac "strings", then glue them in place.

8 Trim the photo to size, rounding the corners. Glue it in place.

Heritage wedding

A heritage treatment for an old wedding photograph requires the use of colours and embellishments that are appropriate to the period of the picture. For this layout, fabrics and flowers in muted tones create a delicate background, and the look is subtle and stylish. Pieced calico was used here, but plain undyed fabric would be equally effective.

materials and equipment

- pieced natural calico fabric
- dressmaker's scissors
- 3 x 30cm/12in square sheets of kraft card (stock)
- spray adhesive
- large wedding photograph
- 30cm/12in square sheet of cream card (stock)
- craft knife and metal ruler
- cutting mat
- wide sheer cream ribbon
- jewelled stick pin
- pen and plain paper
- cork mat
- paper piercer or bodkin
- small pearl beads
- moulded paper flowers
- dimensional glaze
- stranded embroidery thread (floss) in cream
- needle
- sticky tabs

1 Cut two 32cm/12¾in squares of calico to create the backgrounds for the pages. Cover one sheet of kraft card completely with the fabric, attaching it with spray adhesive and turning the raw edges to the back of the sheet. Cut the second fabric square approximately in half, cutting in a gentle serpentine shape, then glue it to a second sheet of kraft card, leaving the right-hand side of the card bare.

2 Double-mat the wedding photograph on a sheet of kraft card and a larger sheet of cream card. Tie a loop of sheer cream ribbon to fit over the corner of the photograph and glue it at the back. Tie the ends into a bow at the front. Stick a jewelled stick pin through the knot of the ribbon bow. Attach the photograph to the centre of the left-hand page.

3 To create the title, write the word "Wedding" or the names of the bride and groom in a flowing script on a piece of plain paper. Place the uncovered area of the right-hand page on a cork mat with the inscribed paper on top and prick evenly through the paper and the card using a paper piercer or bodkin, following the written line.

4 Attach a pearl bead to the centre of each paper flower using dimensional glaze. Use a minimal amount of glaze, and leave it to dry thoroughly before attaching the flowers to the layout.

5 Glue individual flowers down the pages following the lines of the pieced fabric, and in a line following the curved side of the fabric to cover the raw edge. Attach three more flowers to the card at the foot of the right-hand page. Stitch the title with three strands of embroidery thread, using back stitch and following the pre-pricked holes.

6 On the back of the page, secure the ends of the thread with sticky tabs rather than tying knots, as these might create indentations visible from the front.

Our wedding day

A brightly coloured wedding dress and a fun photograph were the inspiration for this jolly layout, a radical departure from traditional wedding album pages. The red bodice of the dress was decorated with bold flowers and these motifs have been repeated in the page embellishments.

materials and equipment

- 2 x 30cm/12in square sheets white card (stock)
- craft knife and metal ruler
- cutting mat
- 2 x 30cm/12in square sheets red card (stock)
- spray adhesive
- large wedding photograph
- die-cut machine
- selection of flower dies
- large and extra large circle punches
- dark pink card (stock)
- medium pink card (stock)
- foam pads
- large and extra large daisy punches
- glue pen
- rub-on letters in pink
- embossing tool

1 To make the background, trim one sheet of white card and glue it to a red sheet to leave a narrow border of red all round. Mat the photograph on red card and attach to the background towards the top right. Die-cut a selection of flower shapes and circles in red, pink and white card. Mix and match the flowers, centres and circles and glue them together.

2 Attach foam pads to the backs of some of the completed embellishments to raise them on the page. Arrange all the flowers along the left side of the photograph so that they overlap. Stick in position.

3 Punch out a selection of daisies in two sizes and in different colours.

4 Using a glue pen, stick the small daisies to the centres of the large daisies, mixing the colours. Leave to dry.

5 Place the daisies around and between the other flower embellishments and glue in position on the page.

◀ **6** Apply the rub-on letters using an embossing tool, and position the title in the lower right area of the page below the photograph. Rub on the last letter first: this will ensure that you get the spacing correct and the word will not run off the page.

forever

BESSIE LOVE.

Family history

A heritage album is a delightful way to document your family's unique history and to preserve old photographs and mementoes for future generations. Most families have boxes of photographs just waiting to be unearthed and sorted out, and this in itself can be a fascinating journey back in time, particularly if you can ask your older relatives to help you identify the faces of long-lost family members and friends.

When you come to make selections of photographs for your pages, portraits and special occasions such as weddings and family parties will be central features, but try to include other shots that set them in context, such as pictures showing your forebears' houses or places of work, cars, gardens and home towns.

Family tree

This is a great way to record your family tree. Instead of drawing a diagram of names and dates, this family tree is decorated with pictures of each family member, glued on paper leaves with their details added alongside.

materials and equipment

- selection of family photographs or reprints
- scissors
- paper or card for template
- pencil
- paper in two shades of green
- glue stick
- sheet of marble-effect paper
- small labels
- pen
- green mount board (optional)

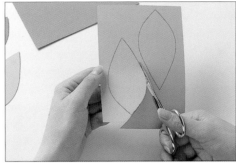

1 Re-photograph the pictures on sepia-effect or black and white film, or scan them and convert to monotone or duotone, ensuring that all the faces are a similar size. Cut out each portrait carefully.

2 Make a leaf template and draw around it on the wrong side of a piece of green paper. Cut around the outline. Repeat to make a leaf background for each picture, using paper in two shades of green.

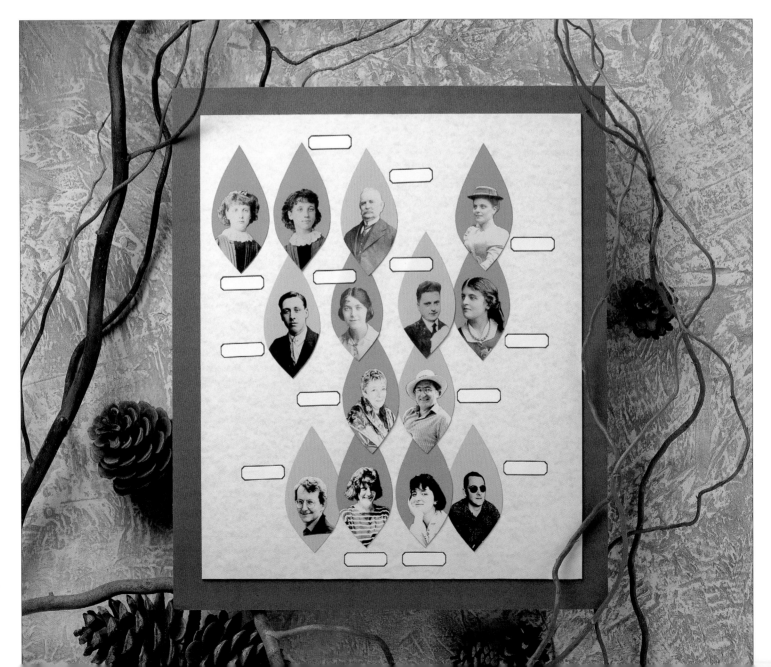

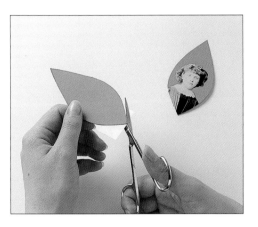

3 Glue a photograph on to each leaf and allow to dry. Trim away the excess photograph to fit the leaf shape.

4 Arrange the pictures on the marble paper background, with the youngest generation at the bottom. Glue in place. Next to each photograph stick a label on which to add names and dates. If desired, mount the family tree on green mount board to finish.

FAMILY CARS

Since the early days of the twentieth century, the car has been a prized family possession. Looking back through snapshots from holidays and outings over the years, you will find they crop up in pictures of your grandmother, father or aunt just as frequently as in those of younger relatives. Sort out all the photographs featuring cars, whether they are parked at picnics, driving along distant roads or being towed away on a breakdown truck, to make a record of your family motoring.

materials and equipment

- old road maps
- photocopier
- sheet of card (stock)
- glue stick
- driving handbooks
- scissors
- selection of photographs

1 Photocopy the maps on the lightest setting. Stick them to the card to make the background, overlapping them so that all the card is concealed. Copy images of road signs from old driving handbooks or maps and cut them out.

2 Arrange the pictures on the page, leaving space at the top and centre right. Glue lines of road sign cut-outs in these spaces, on bands of coloured paper if necessary so that they show up clearly. Stick down all the photographs using a glue stick.

Victorian scrap album page

Having a formal studio photograph taken was an important event for past generations, when cameras were prohibitively expensive and required the special skills of a professional photographer to operate them. The resulting portraits – like this charming oval picture – were framed and treasured. You can update an old family photograph in this way, or print out a contemporary picture in sepia to create a period-style picture.

materials and equipment

- original or reproduction sheet of coloured scraps
- photocopier
- scissors
- oval photograph
- 30cm/12in square sheet of coloured card (stock)
- paper glue
- paper doily
- coloured paper

1 Photocopy the sheet of scraps, enlarging them if you wish. Make a second copy, this time with the image reversed (use the "iron-on" paper setting on your printer or ask your local copy shop to do this for you). Cut out each image carefully around the outline with small scissors, taking care to cut away all the white background.

2 Cut out the photograph if necessary and glue it centrally to the background. Arrange the scraps around it, placing the mirror images on opposite sides. Overlap them to form a solid border, and glue them in place when you are pleased with the results. By adding a few that break out of the frame you will give movement to the design.

3 Choose a motif from the paper doily for the corner decoration. It should be a part of the design that is repeated so that you can use it four times, and should be about 5cm/2in high. Cut out the four motifs roughly and glue a piece of coloured paper to the wrong side of each. Cut out the paper following the outline of the motif.

4 Stick one motif down near each corner of the background, pointing the designs towards the centre. Cut out eight more small matching shapes from the paper doily and glue a pair to each side of each corner shape to finish the decoration.

VARIATION: Découpage boxes

If you have a collection of small trifles and keepsakes that have been handed down to you, give them safekeeping in a pretty box decorated with Victorian-style découpage. Plain cardboard boxes ideal for this purpose are available from craft suppliers in many shapes and sizes. Cut out small reproduction scraps of flowers, cherubs, butterflies and other pretty subjects, taking care to remove any white background, which would distract from the overall colourful effect, and glue them, overlapping, all over the base and lid. Apply several coats of glossy varnish to give a rich antique look.

Remember when...

This heritage layout has a homespun look to it that suits the rustic scene in the old photograph. It has been achieved by using neutral colours, fabric, hand-stitching and twill tape printed with a nostalgic message. Photographs showing relatives at work are usually rarer than those depicting family and friends, and a good subject to record for posterity.

1 Mat the photograph on cream card. Place it on a cork mat and pierce holes, evenly spaced, all round the mat. Work a running stitch through the holes to make a border.

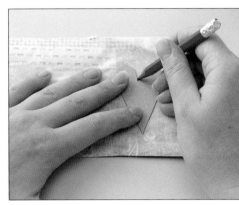

2 Cut a heart shape from scrap card to make a template. Iron fusible bonding web to the wrong side of the fabric. Draw round the template on the backing sheet and cut out five fabric hearts.

materials and equipment

- old photograph
- 30cm/12in square sheet of cream card (stock)
- craft knife
- metal ruler
- cutting mat
- spray adhesive
- cork mat
- paper piercer or bodkin
- stranded embroidery thread (floss) in cream
- needle
- scissors
- fusible bonding web
- patterned cotton fabric
- iron
- 30cm/12in square sheet of dark kraft card (stock)
- tape runner
- printed twill tape
- small brown buttons in two sizes
- glue dots

3 Arrange the hearts in a row across the bottom of the layout and use a tape runner to stick them in place.

4 Cut two lengths of printed twill tape and stick them to the layout, one 10cm/4in from the top and the other below the row of hearts. Attach the photograph to the layout, gluing it over the upper length of tape.

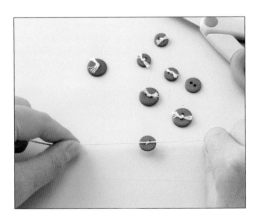

5 Tie stranded embroidery thread through the holes in the buttons. Trim to leave short ends and fluff out the strands.

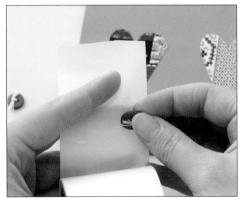

6 Attach the buttons to the tape between the printed words, using glue dots, and add more buttons beside the photograph.

7 Pierce two holes on each side of and through each heart and stitch with three strands of embroidery thread.

remember when...

remember when...

remember when...

remember when...

remember when...

Service To

IN

W.A. CULSHAW

BISTO
FOR ALL MEAT DISHES

Chocolat DE Provence

J. BERTRAND FRERES

Mother and child

This evocative sepia print of a serene mother and her robust baby boy, taken in 1909, is faded and fragile, and has to be stored carefully away from the light. To preserve the memory, it was copied and enlarged at a slightly darker setting, then cropped to remove the damaged area. The "shabby chic" style used for this layout is perfect for very old family photographs.

materials and equipment

- 35cm/14in length of fine lace, 10cm/4in wide
- scissors
- iron
- spray adhesive
- 30cm/12in square sheet of kraft card (stock)
- piece of floral-patterned fabric
- photocopier
- white A4 paper
- photograph
- glue stick
- tracing paper and pencil
- heavy pink paper
- letters and other ephemera
- 2 Victorian scraps or other pictures
- tiny paper flowers

1 Press the lace to remove any creases and trim the raw edge. Spray the wrong side with spray adhesive, and attach to the lower part of the background card with the scalloped edge facing downwards. Fold the ends of the lace to the back of the card and stick down.

2 Photocopy the fabric on to A4 paper, setting the printer to a lighter than normal setting to give a faded appearance to the design. Glue to the upper part of the background so that the lower edge lies along the top of the lace.

3 Enlarge the photograph so that it is about 17.5cm/7in high, trimming off any areas that were damaged in the original and darkening the print if necessary. Using spray adhesive, stick it down on the right-hand side of the floral paper.

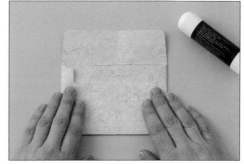

4 Trace the envelope template at the back of the book on to tracing paper and transfer it to heavy pink paper. Cut out, then fold all four flaps to the centre along the broken lines. Glue the bottom flap to the side flaps.

5 Stick the front of the envelope to the layout at the lower left. Fill the envelope with letters, postcards and other ephemera, displaying them so that the stamps and addresses face outwards.

6 Glue the two scraps in place, one on each side of the page.

7 Finish off the layout by gluing a scattering of tiny paper flowers across the page.

VARIATION: Family group

For this more recent photograph of a mother and her children, a more abstract setting has been chosen, using layers of torn paper in a subtle blend of buff and brick red inspired by the marbled paper used as the background. A black border around the picture adds definition to the rather soft grey tones of the photograph, and the assortment of letters in the title includes some black and white to match the central subject.

Edwardian childhood

The formal clothing of Edwardian childhood – bonnets, buttoned boots, frilly petticoats and fitted jackets – and the strict routine of the classroom were balanced by hours spent playing in the nursery with dolls, dolls' houses, toy cars and train sets. Record this lost era with a family photograph, pages from copy books and engravings from a contemporary shopping catalogue.

materials and equipment

- hand-marbled paper
- craft knife and metal ruler
- cutting mat
- 30cm/12in square sheet of white card (stock)
- spray adhesive
- photograph
- scanner and printer
- white paper
- scissors
- gummed black paper photo corners
- photocopier
- old copy book
- glue stick
- old engravings of toys

1 Cut a square of marbled paper to fit the background sheet, and stick in place with spray adhesive.

2 Enlarge the photograph so that it measures about 16cm/6½in high. Alter the brightness and colour balances if necessary to enhance the image if it is faded. Slip four old-fashioned paper photo corners on to the picture and place it in position on the left side of the layout.

3 Photocopy and cut out four pages from an old handwriting copy book. Cut two narrow strips from one of the pages.

4 Arrange the other three pages on the right side of the page so that they overlap each other and the edge of the layout.

5 Place one of the copy book strips at the top and one at the bottom of the left side and glue in place.

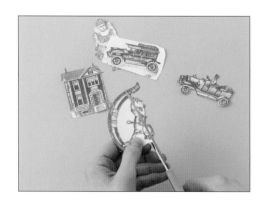

6 Cut out engraved images of dolls, train sets, rocking horses and other toys, cutting as close as possible to the outer edges.

7 Arrange all the toys on the layout over the background and the copy book pages.

8 Double check the position of all the various elements and when you are pleased with the design, glue everything securely in place.

University revue

Your pictures may not always be the perfect shape for square album pages. This production photograph from a student musical sums up all the glamour and excitement of amateur dramatics, but the upright, portrait format is not ideal. With a little photocopying and clever cutting, however, a single dancer can be turned into a chorus line that fills the stage.

materials and equipment

- theatrical photograph
- photocopier
- white paper
- scissors
- glue stick
- curtain from toy theatre kit
- heavy red paper
- wavy-edged scissors
- old sheet music
- 30cm/12in square sheet of gold card (stock)
- tracing paper
- pencil
- scraps of thin black and gold card (stock)

1 Photocopy the image five times, enlarging it if necessary. Cut around the figure to be reproduced on four of the copies. Glue the pictures together so that the figures overlap realistically.

2 Cut out the printed curtain from a toy theatre kit, or cut out a paper curtain shape, and glue it to the top of the picture. Mat the picture on a square of red paper trimmed with wavy-edged scissors.

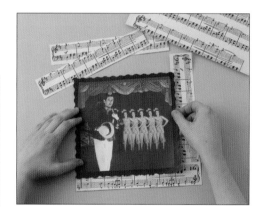

3 Cut four strips from a page of old sheet music and mount them on the back of the red paper to form a square frame. Glue to the centre of a sheet of gold card.

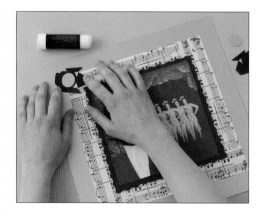

4 Trace the spotlight template at the back of the book and use it to cut out two spotlight silhouettes from black card and two oval discs from gold card. Glue the discs to the lights and fix in position at the top corners of the music.

VARIATION: **Period detail**

A page photocopied from an illustrated trade catalogue of the appropriate period makes a fascinating and evocative background for a heritage layout.

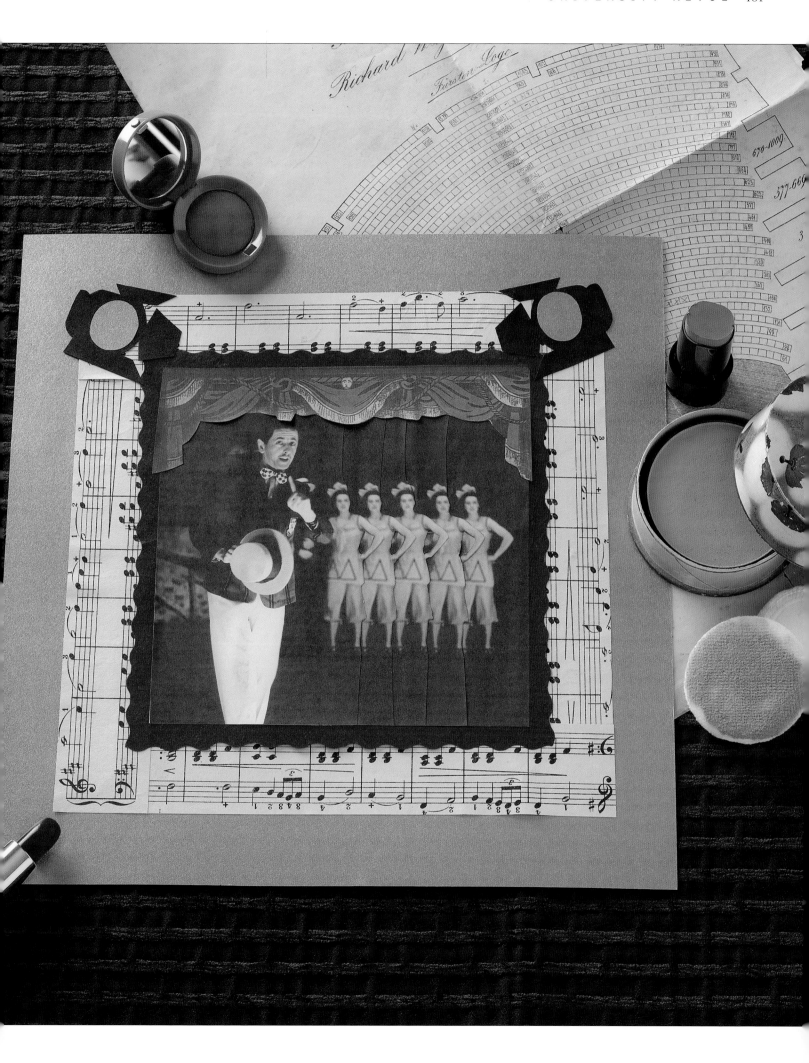

Family and friends

Happy times spent with your nearest and dearest are perfect subjects for your album pages, and you can include lots of informal snapshots of adults and children having fun and just being themselves – a world away from the formal posed photographs taken at special events such as weddings. For these pages you can go out armed with a camera with possible layouts already in mind, ready to look out for good subjects for backgrounds and embellishments as well as the focal points of the pages.

If you discuss your ideas with your friends and relatives you might also be able to get them to co-operate by posing together, larking about for action shots or even dressing up. If you have a digital camera you can easily take lots of pictures to give you plenty of choice at your next scrapbooking session. And if they know they've been involved, your friends will be eager to see themselves immortalized on the resulting pages.

Picnic in the park

This fun collage combines snapshots of an al fresco picnic with cut-outs of cutlery, wine bottles, plates and a picnic basket to tell the story of a good outing. This is a really enjoyable and simple way to record a memorable day; you could make similar pages about a trip to the zoo or a child's birthday party by creating collages in the same style. It's worth building up a stock of cuttings by saving promising pages from magazines with good colour photography. Alternatively, when you're snapping away during a picnic, take some pictures of small details such as the basket, rug, bottles and food, as well as general shots of your surroundings for the background.

materials and equipment

- magazine pages with pictures of picnic items
- scissors
- sheet of green paper
- glue stick
- snapshots of a family picnic
- transparent photo corners

1 Assemble the motifs for the design. Carefully and accurately cut out pictures of a picnic basket, picnic rug, plates, cutlery, glasses and food, using sharp scissors. Ensure there is no background showing once you have completed the cutting out.

2 Glue a picture of a travel rug down in one corner of the green background paper. Arrange photographs of the picnic on the paper, and when you are happy with the design, attach the pictures to the page with transparent photo corners.

3 Arrange the other cut-outs decoratively around the photographs to fill in the spaces. Some cut-outs can be placed on the rug, and others displayed in groups scattered around the picnic photographs. Glue them all in place.

VARIATIONS: Family outings

Below: Memories of childhood trips to the seaside invariably invoke pangs of nostalgia for traditional pleasures such as building sandcastles, eating ice creams and paddling in the sea, while the grown-ups looked on from their deck chairs. This digital album page captures the retro feel of those old memories by reproducing the photographs in a small square format with white borders like early colour prints. Behind them, an atmospheric photograph of a sandy beach is reproduced with a reduced opacity so that it fades into the background. A few marine embellishments complete the picture.

Above and Below: When you are portraying outings with children, include pictures of the animals or plants you saw as well as the children themselves, as reminders for them when they look at your album in future years.

Trip to the farm

In this small accordion album, photographs of a visit to a farm are mounted on tags slotted into pockets, and no child will be able to resist pulling them out to find his or her picture on each one. Close-up shots of crops and animals have been used to cover the pockets, conveying the flavour of the trip in near-abstract images that are all about texture and colour. A naive illustration created using rubber stamps provides the finishing touch.

materials and equipment

- 2 sheets of A4 card (stock) in lime green
- tracing paper
- pencil
- metal ruler
- craft knife
- cutting mat
- self-cling unmounted stamps
- clear acrylic block
- coloured ink pads
- gift wrap or magazine pages
- glue stick
- daisy punch
- white paper
- eyelet punch and eyelets
- thin card (stock) in pale blue, turquoise and lilac
- photographs
- narrow ribbon
- gift wrap

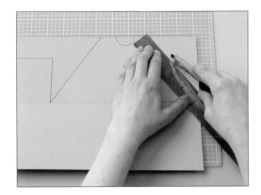

1 Fold one green card in half lengthwise. Press the fold firmly to make a sharp crease. Trace the album template at the back of the book and transfer the tracing to the green card, matching the central line to the crease. Cut out the album.

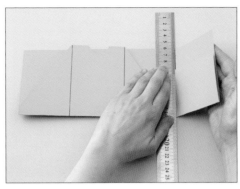

2 Fold the card where marked to create the album. Press all the folds firmly to make sharp creases.

3 Press the self-cling stamps one by one on to the acrylic block and stamp the flower and butterfly design on the large pocket.

4 Cut sections from gift wrap or pictures cut from magazines to fit the remaining pockets and glue in place.

5 Punch a small daisy from white paper.

6 Use an eyelet punch to make holes in the corners of the pockets, and in the daisy. Insert eyelets through the holes to fix the album together.

7 Trace the tag templates at the back of the book. Transfer the shapes to thin, coloured card and cut them out.

8 Punch four daisies from white paper. Glue one to the top of each tag.

9 Punch a hole through each daisy with an eyelet punch. Trim the photos to size and glue them to the tags.

10 Cut lengths of ribbon and tie one through the hole in the top of each tag.

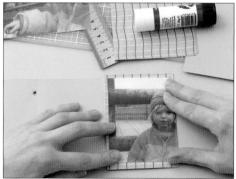

11 Cut two covers slightly larger than the album from the remaining sheet of card and cover them with gift wrap. Glue the covers to the front and back of the album. Trim and glue photos to the front and back covers. Cut a length of ribbon and tie it around the album to keep it closed.

A day in the garden

Summer days are often spent in the garden, having lunch or a drink and chatting with family and friends. Keep a record of this part of life by making a collage using photos of your loved ones relaxing outside, decorated with stamped garden designs and pressed flowers and leaves.

materials and equipment

- selection of rubber stamps with a garden theme: plant pots, flowers, garden tools
- selection of papers in shades of green, brown and off-white
- ink pads in black and dark green
- paper towels
- fancy-edged scissors
- scissors
- photographs
- sheet of brown paper
- glue stick
- gummed brown paper photo corners
- selection of pressed flowers and leaves

1 Stamp several versions of garden-themed designs on a selection of coloured and textured paper, using black and dark green ink. Clean the stamps between different colours with paper towels. Allow to dry.

2 Cut out some of the stamped motifs with fancy-edged scissors and others with ordinary scissors. Tear around some of the motifs to create rough edges.

VARIATION: Summer in the garden

For a digital scrapbook page, create the feel of a summer garden with a photographic montage in fresh greens and blues. You can find themed collections on scrapbooking websites offering suitable colourful borders and embellishments such as these jolly sunglasses, or make up your own borders and collage elements using the image-editing software on your computer. In the example on the right, all the images were cropped from one photograph, then enlarged and superimposed for a montage effect. The simpler treatment below could be achieved equally easily in digital or traditional form.

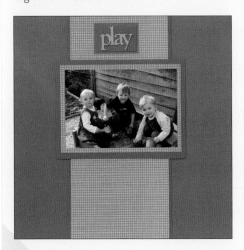

3 Arrange the photos on the foundation page. When you are happy with the arrangement, stick the pictures down with the photo corners.

4 Assemble the collage by adding the different stamped motifs, pressed flowers and leaves. Glue each item in position.

Gone fishing

Capture the magic of a long afternoon spent by the water's edge with this fun layout featuring a fond grandfather with his young grandson. Even if they didn't manage to hook anything with their makeshift rod, you can crop the photograph and add a catch consisting of a few embossed silver fish.

1 Cut a square of patterned paper to fit the background card and attach it with spray adhesive. Cut a 7.5cm/3in strip of dark blue paper to fit along the bottom of the page. Cut along the top edge with wavy-edged scissors and stick it in place.

2 Use the wavy-edged scissors to cut out a few "waves" from the pale blue paper and glue them at intervals across the "water".

materials and equipment

- patterned paper
- 30cm/12in square sheet of card (stock)
- spray adhesive
- craft knife
- metal ruler
- cutting mat
- thin paper in dark and pale blue
- wavy-edged scissors
- 2 photographs
- glue stick and sticky tape
- tracing paper
- fine waterproof pen
- silver embossing foil
- thick card or cork mat
- embossing tool or empty ballpoint pen
- old scissors
- large needle
- stranded embroidery thread (floss) in cream or fine string

3 Decide on the best position for the two photographs and stick them to the patterned background using a glue stick.

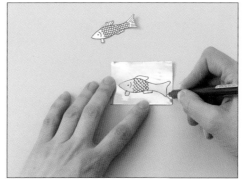

4 Trace the fish template at the back of the book and cut out around the outline. Cut a small rectangle of embossing foil and, using a fine waterproof pen, draw around the template, then fill in the detail.

5 Lay the foil on a piece of thick card or a cork mat and trace over the lines with a stylus or old ballpoint pen, pressing firmly.

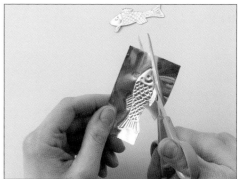

6 Use an old pair of scissors to cut out the fish. Make another three fish in the same way, reversing some of them so that they appear to swim in opposite directions.

7 Stick the fish to the dark blue paper with a glue stick, spacing them evenly between the waves.

8 Thread a large needle with thread or fine string. Bring the needle out at the tip of the fishing rod and take it back in close to the fish, allowing the thread to loop gently. Tape the ends to the wrong side.

Birthday party

Children's birthday parties are big events to organize so it's nice to have a record of the day, as well as of your children's favourite friends, so that you can see how the the celebrations and children change as the years pass.

materials and equipment

- selection of toning papers
- 6 photographs
- 30cm/12in square sheet of card (stock)
- cutting mat
- craft knife and metal ruler
- spray adhesive
- corner cutter
- purple metallic ink pad
- 5 tags
- glue dots
- stamp rubber stamp design
- flower and heart cutters
- brads
- sequins
- small floral stickers
- number template
- scissors

1 Choose a selection of toning papers in colours that match your photographs and the background card. Working on a cutting mat and using a craft knife and metal ruler, cut one 12.5cm/5in square and mat it to the top left-hand corner of the background.

2 Cut frames for your main photographs, 1cm/½in larger all around than the photographs. Use a corner cutter to trim the corners. Trim the photographs in the same way.

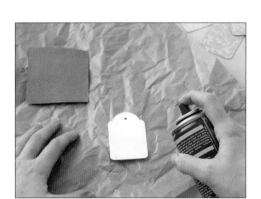

3 Tint the edge of the main photograph frame using a purple metallic ink pad. Allow to dry. Mat the photographs to the frames, then mat the frames in position on the background.

4 Choose different papers to cover each of the five gift tags. Working in a ventilated area and with scrap paper on the work surface, use spray adhesive to coat the tags and mat each to coloured paper. Allow to dry, then carefully cut each out.

5 Cut and trim three photographs and their corners to fit the tags. Cut slightly larger frames for each. Stick each of the three photographs to a frame, and a frame to a tag using glue dots or spray adhesive.

6 For a tag without a photograph, decorate a plain frame with a stamped design. Add stickers to decorate the other tag without a photograph.

7 Cut four flower motifs and one heart motif as additional decoration for the tags. Make a hole in the centre of each flower and in the top of four tags.

8 For the tags without photographs, thread a sequin on a brad, then a flower, a frame and a tag. Open out the wings of the brad. Stick the tag to the background.

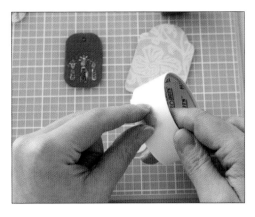

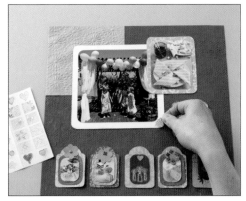

9 For the centre tag, stick a heart to the top of the frame. Decorate the remaining tags as you like.

10 Add small floral stickers to the background and the frames, as desired.

11 Cut out the child's age from coloured paper using a template. Decorate the edges with the ink pad as before. Stick in place.

Magic carpet

With a little imagination you can transform an ordinary afternoon in the garden into a fairytale fantasy. All you need is a photograph of your family or best friends sitting out in the sunshine and a picture of the hearthrug. When taking the photographs, get everyone to sit close together in a solid group, and photograph the rug from a low angle. Cut them out, mount them together on an idyllic blue sky and you have a magic carpet to take you all on a wonderful adventure.

materials and equipment

- group photograph
- computer and printer
- scissors
- photograph of rug
- hard and soft pencils
- tracing paper
- A4 sheet of thin silver card (stock)
- craft knife
- cutting mat
- scraps of coloured paper
- 60cm/24in metallic braid
- glue stick
- 30cm/12in square of sky-printed background paper
- tiny silver star stickers
- scrap of silver paper
- 4 small silver fabric motifs

1 Enlarge the group photograph so that it measures approximately 15cm/6in from side to side and cut it out, following the outline of the figures as closely as you can.

2 Enlarge the picture of the carpet to about 25cm/10in wide and cut out carefully, eliminating the original background.

3 Trace the template from the back of the book, enlarging it to 30cm/12in wide. Transfer the outline to silver card. Cut along the skyline with scissors and cut out the windows with a craft knife on a cutting mat.

4 Glue a small piece of coloured paper behind each window opening.

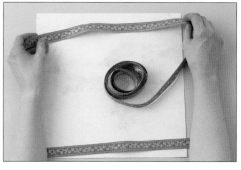

5 Cut two lengths of metallic braid and glue them along the top and bottom edges of the sky-printed background sheet.

6 Stick the silhouette to the background, just above the braid. Glue the family picture on to the carpet, then move it around the card until you are happy with its position. Stick it in place using a glue stick.

7 Scatter the silver star stickers across the sky. Cut out a small crescent moon from silver paper and stick it low down in the sky near the buildings.

8 Stick a silver motif on each corner, to cover the ends of the braid.

New Year's Eve

Beads, coiled wire and silver embellishments add a touch of sparkle to pictures of New Year's Eve celebrations. Lots of little ready-made ornaments are available to match this theme, so decorating the page is really easy. If the photographs are busy, keep the background simple so that there aren't too many things to distract the eye.

1 Cut a 30 x 15cm/12 x 6in rectangle of white card and mount all three photographs on it, cropping them a little if necessary to leave a narrow border of white between and around them.

2 Stick the panel of photographs in the centre of the black card. Punch four squares of black and white patterned papers and four squares of pale grey card and arrange them, alternating, down each side.

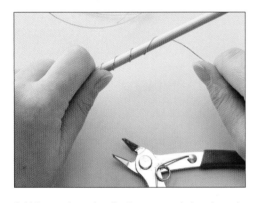

3 Wrap a length of wire around the dowel to form a coil. Stretch it to the length of the page, leaving 5cm/2in of straight wire at each end. Make a second coil to match.

4 Thread an assortment of small beads on to the wires. Use a generous amount as the wires are quite long.

5 Pierce holes at the the top and bottom of the layout where you wish to anchor the wires. Push the straight ends of the wires through the card and anchor them at the back of the layout with sticky tabs. Add the sticker embellishments to the plain grey squares.

6 Use a label maker to punch out a title for each photograph and the date on black tape. Stick the labels to the pictures and add the date in the corner of the layout.

materials and equipment

- craft knife
- metal ruler
- thin card (stock) in white and pale grey
- cutting mat
- 3 photographs, each 15 x 10cm/6 x 4in
- tape runner or glue stick
- 30cm/12in square sheet of black card (stock)
- black and white patterned papers
- 5cm/2in square punch
- fine silver wire
- thin dowel rod
- wire cutters
- small glass beads in assorted colours
- paper piercer or bodkin
- sticky tabs
- label maker
- black label tape

Sports

Whether your family members are active participants in sports, or fanatical supporters of a local team, sporting subjects make for rewarding layouts. This is a great theme for pages about children, where you can present them taking part in team games and school sports days, or showing off their daredevil skills on skateboards or bikes.

All kinds of games and sports make very satisfying subjects for scrapbooking pages, as they are all easily identified by the images and accessories associated with them, and there is plenty of strong colour in team strips, pitches and equipment. Add to these features the dramatic action shots you can capture in your photographs, and you can easily produce really eye-catching pages in this theme.

Cycling

This very simple double-page spread uses black ink trails to suggest the muddiness of a cycling trip in the countryside. Die-cut cog shapes and screw decorations reflect the mechanics of the bike.

materials and equipment

- black ink pad
- 2 x 30cm/12in square sheets of white card (stock)
- toy vehicle with rubber tyres
- sheet of metallic silver card (stock)
- craft knife and metal ruler
- cutting mat
- die-cut machine
- assorted cog dies
- matt silver paper
- 5cm/2in square punch
- photographs
- corner rounder
- glue stick
- paper piercer
- 5 screw brads

1 Brush the black ink pad around the edges of the sheets of white card to give the pages a "muddy" appearance.

2 Pat the ink pad on to the tread of a large wheel on a toy vehicle. Run the wheel across the card in different directions to create tyre tracks.

3 Cut two strips of metallic silver card 5cm/2in wide: these will form a band across the two pages. Using a die-cut machine, cut out a selection of cogs from the matt silver paper. Stick all the shapes to the strips, allowing some to overlap the edges and trimming them flush.

4 Punch details from photographs to create six square blocks. Round the two left-hand corners of the large photograph for the left-hand page, and the right-hand corners of a large photo for the right-hand page. Arrange all the pictures on the pages.

5 Position the silver strips under the photographs. Trim them so that the ends align with the pictures and round the corners. Glue everything in place. Pierce holes in the positions where you will insert the screw brads.

6 Push the brads into the holes and fold back the fasteners on the back of the pages to hold them in place.

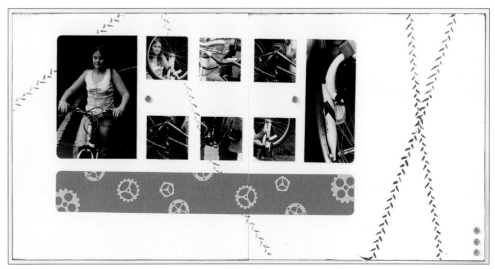

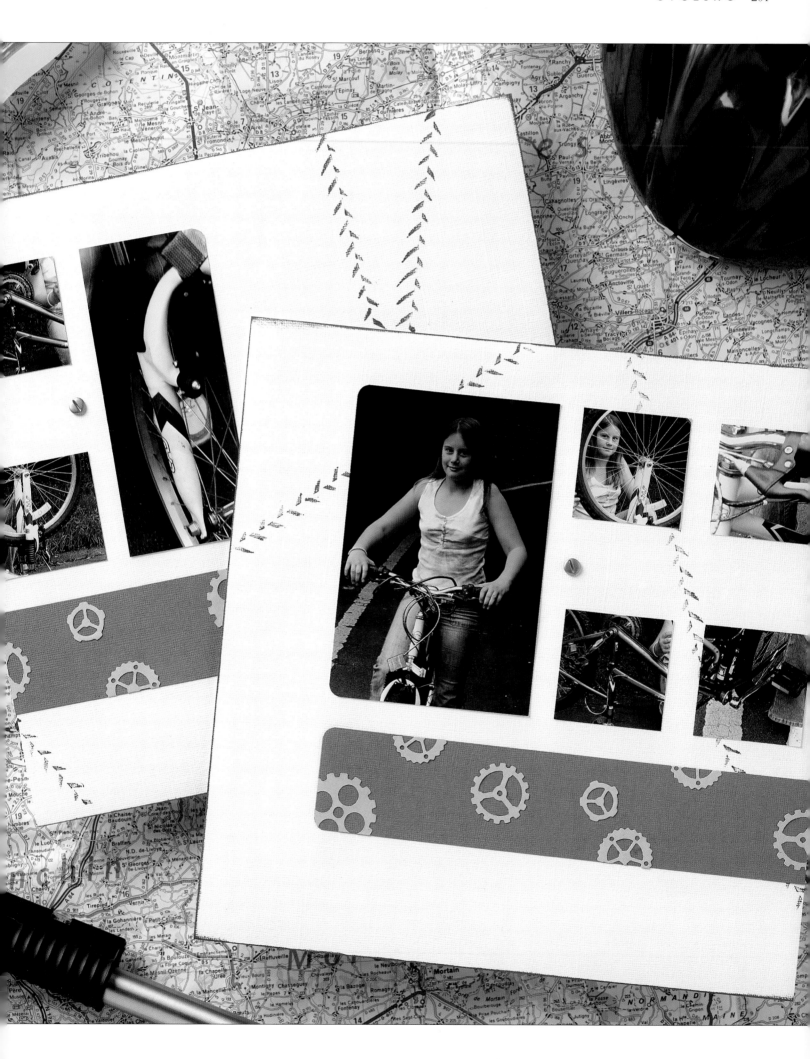

Basketball

The bright colours contrast with the black and white action photographs and the repeated circle motif clearly links with the ball game but also gives a sense of motion to the pages.

materials and equipment

- circle cutter
- thin card (stock) in lime green, turquoise and deep pink
- repositionable tape runner
- 2 x 30cm/12in square sheets of burnt orange card (stock)
- scissors
- eyelet tool kit
- letter stickers
- photographs
- 2 x 30cm/12in square sheets of chocolate brown card (stock)
- label maker
- black label tape

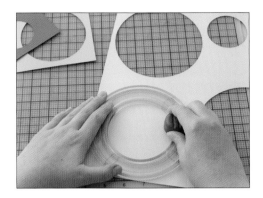

1 Cut out circles from the lime green, turquoise and deep pink card in assorted sizes. If you don't have a circle cutter to do this you can draw and cut out a number of templates or draw round plates and cups of various sizes.

2 Apply repositionable tape to the backs of the circles. This will allow you to move them around on the layout until you are happy with their positioning. Stick the circles to both sheets of burnt orange card in a random arrangement.

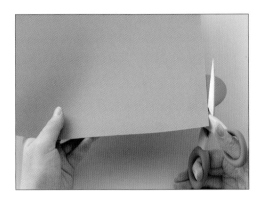

3 Allow some of the circles to overlap the edges of the sheets and trim off the excess with scissors. On the inner edges of the pages, stick the circles to one side and trim, then stick the remaining parts to the opposite page, aligning them accurately.

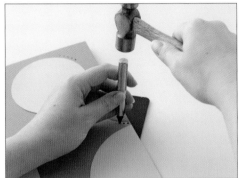

4 Use an eyelet tool to punch out small circles around parts of the large circles. If you have different sized punches try to use them all to add variety.

5 Create the title using letter stickers. When placing these, always work from the outer edge of the page towards the middle, which will sometimes mean spelling the word backwards, to ensure that each word is accurately positioned.

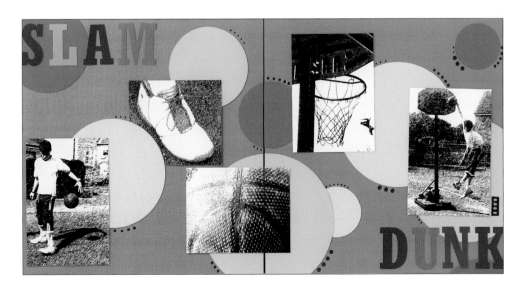

6 Position the photographs so that they overlap the card circles, taking care to avoid any of the punched circles.

7 Stick the finished pages to sheets of chocolate brown card, which will show through the punched holes.

8 Use a label maker and black tape to punch the date and stick the label beside one of the photographs.

Skateboarding

Grunge and funky colours go hand in hand with skateboarding, and this double page spread has plenty of both. Inks, fabric, curly paperclips and roughly torn paper combine to create a great background for these pictures.

materials and equipment

- 2 x 30cm/12in square sheets of turquoise card (stock)
- 2 x 30cm/12in square sheets of bright patterned paper
- thin lime card (stock)
- craft knife and metal ruler
- cutting mat
- ink pads in black and red
- hole punch
- roughly torn strips of woven cotton fabric
- "S" letter sticker
- die-cut "K"
- rub-on number "8"
- 4 round paperclips
- 4 photographs
- glue stick

1 Cut both sheets of turquoise card in half. Tear away a strip approximately 4cm/1½in wide from each side, tearing at a slight angle. Always tear towards yourself to expose the inner core of the card on the right side.

2 Moisten your finger and use it to roughen the torn edges of the card strips. Roll the edges back, without trying to do this too evenly. Stick the card strips on top of the squares of patterned paper.

3 Cut four strips of lime card 6mm/¼in wide and 30cm/12in long. Roughly ink the edges of each strip using the black ink pad, then glue to the turquoise cards, aligning the strips across the two pages. Punch pairs of holes to tie the fabric strips through.

4 To create the "S" for the title "skate", use the paper frame of a letter sticker as a template. Stick it gently to the layout (so that it can be peeled off later) and stipple through it using a red ink pad.

5 When the ink is dry, pull away the template. Add the die-cut "K" and rub on an "8" to complete the title.

6 Slide a paperclip on to the edge of each photograph. Arrange the photos at random angles across the centre of both pages and glue in position.

Skiing

Photographs of sunny days on the slopes demand pages with a touch of winter sparkle. This is a very simple layout, but the combination of snowflakes with silver patterned paper and an ice blue background gives a crisp, snowy look.

materials and equipment

- silver patterned paper
- guillotine (or craft knife, metal ruler and cutting mat)
- 2 x 30cm/12in square sheets of pale blue card (stock)
- eyelet punch
- tack hammer
- 24 silver eyelets
- foam brush
- acrylic paint in cobalt blue
- 6 sparkly snowflake buttons
- large white rub-on letters
- 4 photographs
- white card (stock), optional
- glue dots

1 Cut 12 strips of silver patterned paper measuring 2.5 x 18cm/1 x 7in. If you don't have a guillotine, mark out the strips and cut them using a craft knife and metal ruler and working on a cutting mat.

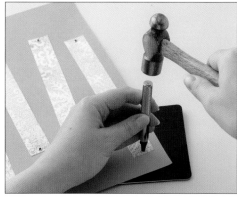

2 Lay the strips across the two sheets of blue card at uneven heights and angles. Use the eyelet tools and silver eyelets to attach them to the card at each end.

3 Using a foam brush, swipe a broad stripe of cobalt blue acrylic paint across the top left and bottom right corners of the layout. Leave to dry.

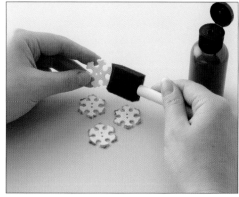

4 Dab the edges of the snowflake buttons with the blue paint to make them stand out more on the page.

5 When the paint is dry, rub on the white letters over it to create the titles.

6 Print the photographs with a white border or mat them on to white card. Glue them at angles across the pages and stick on the snowflake buttons using glue dots.

Tennis

If you or others in your family enjoy getting to grips with the game, make this tennis court layout to celebrate your skills. You could personalize the page by using your own club colours for the background.

materials and equipment

- 30cm/12in square sheet of green card (stock)
- 2 x 30cm/12in square sheets of purple card (stock)
- craft knife and metal ruler
- cutting mat
- spray adhesive
- photographs
- white acrylic paint
- paintbrush
- alphabet foam stamps
- 2 purple and 4 green photo turns
- paper piercer or bodkin
- 6 dark green brads
- date stamp
- black ink pad

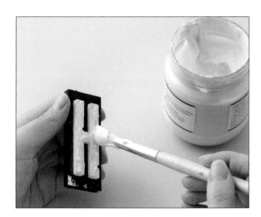

1 Cut two wide and one narrow strip of green card and glue them vertically to the purple sheets to make the background. Glue the photographs in position on both pages. Brush white acrylic paint on to foam stamps to print the titles.

2 On the right-hand page stamp the letters in reverse order from right to left so that you do not run out of space for the title. Take care not to overload the letters with paint or it will smudge. The words "game", "set" and "match" are used here.

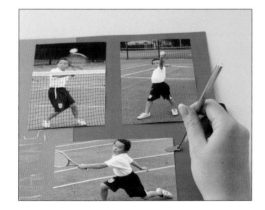

3 Lay a photo turn over the edge of each picture and pierce a hole in the card through the eye of the turn.

4 Push a brad through the hole and fold the fasteners down at the back of the card to anchor the turn to the page.

5 Add the date in the corner of the layout using a date stamp and a black ink pad.

School sports day

Make a first school sports day special for your child by creating a spread in your album to celebrate their determination, whether or not they managed to win any prizes. Your choice of photographs can emphasize what a good time everyone had taking part in the fun races.

materials and equipment

- large square punch
- photographs
- large dinner plate
- pencil
- 30cm/12in square sheet of patterned card (stock)
- scissors
- craft knife and metal ruler
- cutting mat
- 30cm/12in square sheets of cobalt and navy blue card (stock)
- glue stick
- computer and printer
- pale blue card (stock)
- 2 metal sports embellishments
- glue dots

1 Use a large square punch to cut out three interesting sections from your photographs. Move the photos around in the window of the punch until you find the area you want. (If you don't have a punch, cut out the details using a craft knife and metal ruler, working on a cutting mat.)

2 Draw round a large dinner plate on the patterned card and cut out the circle using scissors. Cut the circle in half and position each semicircle at the outside edge of the cobalt blue pages. Cut two wide strips of navy card and glue them next to the semicircles. Glue a strip of patterned paper at the inner edge of the right-hand page.

3 Print the title "determination" in reverse on pale blue card and cut out the individual letters using a craft knife. The letters are less likely to tear if you cut out the centres before the outlines. Take your time and make sure the blade is sharp.

4 Glue the letters up the right-hand side of the layout using a glue stick. Position the whole word first to help you space the letters evenly.

5 Mat all the photographs on pale blue card and arrange them on the layout. Print a caption on pale blue card and add it to the first page.

6 Tie the metal embellishments together with a thin strip of pale blue card and attach them to the layout using glue dots.

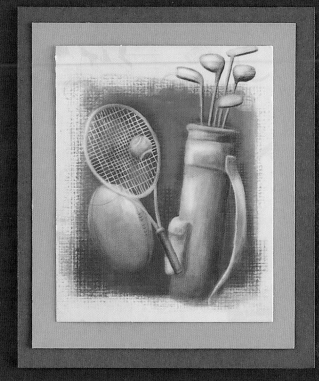

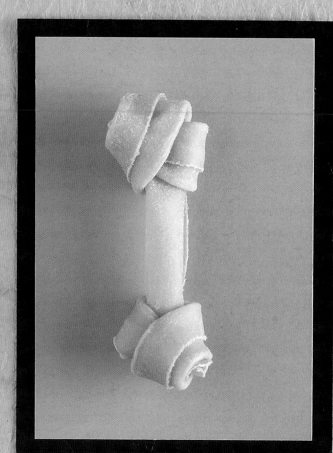

Family pets

Dogs, cats and other animals are important and much-loved members of many families. If you have pets, they're sure to feature often in your photographs of outings, celebrations at home, and fun and games in the garden, but it can also be rewarding to devote some special pages of your scrapbook to your animals, making them the stars rather than the supporting cast.

Animals' lives are far shorter than ours, and this is a lovely way to remember them in later years. Children usually have a special connection with their pets and love to look back at photographs of their antics, or to find out about pets that were around before they were born or when they were very small. Album pages can paint vivid pictures of your pets' lives if you include shots of them in youth and age, at play, at rest, enjoying their favourite toys and doing their party tricks.

My pet rabbit

Sometimes it's difficult to find the perfect ready-made embellishments for your pages, especially if you're working on an unusual subject. Why not make your own? Polymer clay is the ideal material with which to create easy small-scale pieces to decorate your album.

materials and equipment

- polymer clay in orange and green
- baking tray
- 2 rabbit photographs
- craft knife
- metal ruler
- cutting mat
- 30cm/12in square sheets of card (stock) in mid- green, dark green and lime
- spray adhesive
- large square punch
- green vellum
- tape runner
- rub-on faux stitches
- embossing tool
- wire cutters
- 3 rabbit buttons
- glue dots

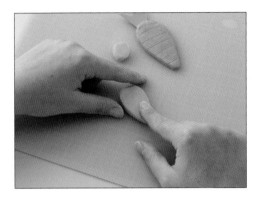

1 Mould a carrot shape in orange polymer clay and add some green leaves. Place the carrot on a baking tray and harden in an oven according to the manufacturer's instructions. Leave to cool.

2 Crop the photographs as necessary and mount on a large piece of mid-green card. Punch out three squares from dark green card and add them to the arrangement.

3 Create the left-hand border by layering a strip of torn green vellum with a narrower strip of torn dark green card. Glue the border to the background 2cm/¾in from the edge of the page.

4 In the 2cm/¾in gap use an embossing tool to rub on a line of faux stitches, taking care that they are straight.

5 Use wire cutters to snip the shanks off the backs of the rabbit buttons. Stick one to each dark green square using a glue dot.

6 Carefully tear green vellum into oval "lettuce leaves". Stick them overlapping at the bottom of the page.

7 Attach the polymer clay carrot near the lettuce leaves. Use a generous quantity of glue dots as it is quite heavy.

Folk art cat

The colours in these photographs of a favourite cat suggested they would work well with the natural blues, rusts and ochres characteristic of American folk art. This in turn inspired the simple embellishments of cut-out hearts and paper animal shapes, and the drawn "stitches" around the woodgrain panel, which are a reminder of traditional patchwork.

1 On a background sheet of off-white paper, assemble a background collage using woodgrain design and complementary coloured papers. Cut out four triangles of patterned paper to go across the corners. Copy the templates of the cat, heart and dove motifs at the back of the book and transfer them to the back of the patterned papers. Cut them out using scissors.

2 Glue the collage elements on to the background paper. Leave a narrow border around three sides and a wider strip down one side on which to place the cut-outs. Glue the cut-out motifs in position. Attach the photographs to the woodgrain panel using brown gummed photo corners. Finish the page by drawing "stitching" lines around the edges of the collage with a black marker pen.

materials and equipment

- off-white heavy paper
- patterned papers in woodgrain and check designs
- craft knife
- cutting mat
- tracing paper
- pencil
- scissors
- glue stick
- photographs
- brown paper photo corners
- black fine-tipped marker pen

Best friend

Create a pet montage with cut-out photographs and conventional snapshots, and decorate the whole thing with fun paw prints and cute stickers. Using a combination of rectangular snapshots and cut-outs adds interest to the overall page, while the paw prints and stickers provide extra colour.

materials and equipment

- photographs of dog
- scissors
- 2 sheets of white card (stock)
- glue stick
- selection of children's stickers of dogs and puppies
- thin card in blue and green
- craft knife
- metal ruler
- cutting mat
- rubber stamp with paw print motif
- coloured ink pads
- paper towel

1 Decide on the general layout of the album page, then work out which photographs you want to use. Either make extra colour copies or, if you have enough, cut around some of the dog images with scissors. Arrange the pictures on the plain paper then, when you are happy with the arrangement, glue all the pictures in position. Decorate with stickers of other breeds of dog.

2 For the second page, mount the two main photographs of the dog on different coloured pieces of card, then add stickers all around the photographs to frame them. If you prefer not to place stickers directly on the original photographs, use copies.

3 Decorate both pages with paw prints, either stamping a border design or making random prints at different angles. Wash the stamp between colours and pat dry with a paper towel.

Bill and Ben the goldfish

Pet fish are quiet and unassuming compared with larger animals, but are often valued family members, so give them their own moment of glory in your album with a special page dedicated to themselves. The background paper used for this layout had a squared design, making it very easy to create a scrapbook "aquarium" for this friendly pair.

materials and equipment

- craft knife
- 30cm/12in square sheet of scrapbook paper
- gold glitter paper
- bubble effect paper
- metal ruler
- cutting mat
- square patterned paper
- spray adhesive or paper glue
- pencil
- coin
- goldfish photographs
- scissors
- star tags
- printed names
- blue ribbon
- card tags
- self-adhesive shiny paper
- plain self-adhesive alphabet stickers
- patterned card alphabet stickers
- PVA (white) glue

1 Cut a panel of gold glitter paper to fit at the top of the scrapbook paper and a panel of bubble paper to fit at the bottom. Glue both of them in place.

2 Cut a thin band of square patterned paper to go on top of the bubble panel and glue in place.

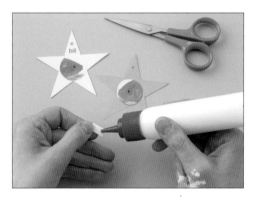

3 Draw around a coin on to the photos of your fishes, positioning it over their faces. Cut out the circles and glue one to each star tag. Print out the fishes' names, trim to size and glue one above each picture.

4 Trim the large photograph to fit the central panel, then glue it to the left side of the page.

5 Add short lengths of ribbon to the star tags and glue them in position on the right side of the page.

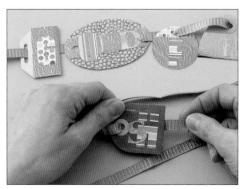

6 Decorate five tags in assorted shapes with pieces of self-adhesive shiny paper. Spell out the word "goldfish" on the tags with alphabet stickers. Thread all the tags in sequence on to a length of blue ribbon.

7 Position the ribbon across the top of the page then tuck the ends to the back of the page and glue them down with PVA glue.

GOLDFISH

bill

ben

Purry puss

This pampered fellow gets a very luxurious furry page to himself. If your cat is co-operative you should be able to get him to provide a paw print in paint with which to sign the page, but be sure to wipe the paint off his paw afterwards.

materials and equipment

- spray adhesive
- 30cm/12in square sheet of thin card (card stock)
- short pile fun fur or fleece
- scissors
- coin
- pencil
- thin card (stock) in red and green
- eyelet punch
- tack hammer
- gold rub-down letters
- 1cm/⅜in tartan ribbons
- PVA (white) glue
- 3 small swing tags
- gold paper
- glue stick
- photographs
- paw print
- narrow red ribbon
- collar bell
- 3 small gold safety pins
- thin red card
- metal ruler and pencil
- craft knife and cutting mat
- 4 photo corners

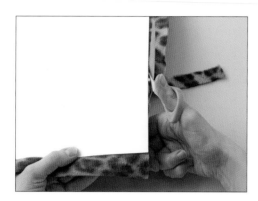

1 Spray adhesive on to one side of a sheet of card. Press the card firmly on to the wrong side of a piece of fun fur. Using scissors, trim the excess fabric from around the edges, as close to the card as possible.

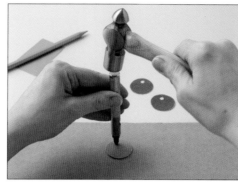

2 Draw around a coin on to red and green card to make discs, one for each letter of your pet's name. Cut them all out. Punch a large hole at the top of each disc with an eyelet punch.

3 Rub a letter on to each disc to spell your pet's name, alternating the colours of the discs as you go.

4 Tie each disc to a length of tartan ribbon. Use PVA glue to attach the ribbons to the right side of the page, turning the raw ends to the back.

5 Glue three tags to the wrong side of a piece of gold paper and trim away the excess paper. Re-punch the holes in the tags with an eyelet punch. Glue a small photo of your pet to one tag, and a paw print to a second. Tie a small collar bell to the third with thin red ribbon.

6 Pin the three gold tags to the bottom left corner of the page, attaching them with small gold safety pins.

7 Cut a rectangle of red card measuring 1cm/⅜in larger all round than the large photograph.

8 Attach photo corners to the picture and and stick it to the mount, leaving an even border all round. Glue the mount to the page.

Prize-winning pony

If you have ponies that win rosettes for you or your children you'll want to honour their achievements by creating a special page. This is a very simple design using brightly coloured paper, with no other embellishments.

materials and equipment

- craft knife
- 30cm/12in square sheets of card (stock) in green and orange
- metal ruler
- cutting mat
- glue stick
- red, blue and yellow paper
- circle cutter or circular templates and pencil
- scissors
- photographs

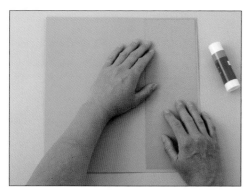

1 Cut a rectangle of orange card measuring 29 x 10cm/11½in x 4in and glue it to the right-hand side of the green card, leaving very narrow borders of green around three sides.

2 Cut three rectangles measuring 20 x 7cm/8 x 2¾in from red, blue and yellow paper. Glue them to the left side of the page, spacing them evenly, with the yellow at the top, then red, then blue.

3 Cut three triangles 20cm x 7cm/8in x 2¾in from red, blue and yellow paper. Glue them on top of the rectangles, placing red on yellow, blue on red and yellow on blue.

4 To make the rosettes, cut three large and three small circles of red, yellow and blue card. Glue the smaller circles on top of the large circles. Cut two thin rectangles in the same colours of each paper. Snip the ends diagonally to make ribbons. Glue the ribbons to the backs of the rosettes.

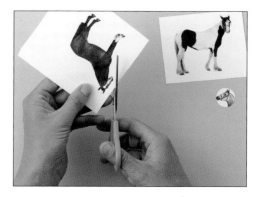

5 Draw a circle around each horse's head in a small photograph and cut it out.

6 Glue a horse's head in the centre of each rosette.

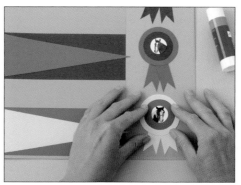

7 Glue the rosettes to the orange panel on the right of the page, with the red one at the top, blue in the middle and yellow at the bottom.

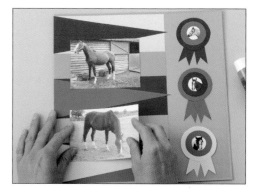

8 Glue two large horse photographs to the panel on the left side of the page, spacing the pictures evenly.

Travel

Trips and vacations are prime themes for scrapbooks: everyone's feeling relaxed, you have time to take lots of good pictures and – with luck – the weather's wonderful. If you're touring there will be new sights to see every day and new experiences to inspire you. Keeping your scrapbook in mind while you're away you'll remember to hoard lots of good-looking holiday ephemera, such as tickets, menus, hotel bills, little natural objects such as shells and pressed flowers, and maybe some exotic food packaging and foreign newspapers or magazines that you can take cuttings from.

Jot down plenty of notes so that you don't forget the name of that perfect beach or what you ate at your favourite restaurant. The more detailed your journaling the more memories you'll preserve, and the more fascinating your travel albums will be for you and your family in the years to come.

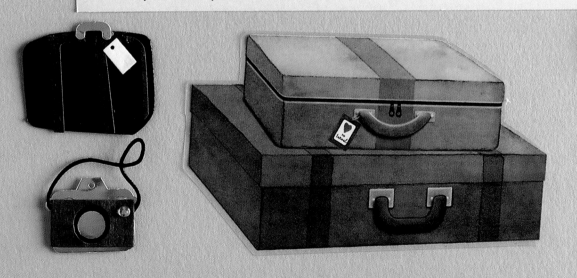

Beside the sea

A summer trip to the seaside is an intrinsic part of family life. The leisurely pastimes that make up a day's outing or a week's stay by the sea – paddling, swimming, beachcombing and building sandcastles – have remained unchanged over the years, and this album page brings together snaps of three generations of the same family having fun on the beach.

materials and equipment

- graph paper
- fine pen
- ruler
- A4 sheet of thin card (stock)
- craft knife
- cutting mat
- tracing paper
- selection of colour and black and white photographs and postcards
- watercolours
- fine paintbrush
- 30cm/12in square sheet of coloured card (stock)
- glue stick

1 Using the template at the back of the book as a guide, draw the postcard frame on graph paper, leaving margins of 5mm/¼in between all the shapes and 1cm/⅜in around the outside. Cut a rectangle of white card to the exact size of this rectangle.

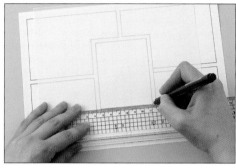

2 Trace each of the five segments on to a separate piece of tracing paper with a ruler and a fine pen. These templates will act as guides for selecting which images to use and where to crop them.

3 Place each tracing over your chosen pictures until you find a composition that will fit well within the outline. You may need to enlarge or reduce the photographs.

4 Black and white pictures can be hand-tinted with watercolour so that they blend in with the newer photographs. Use a fine brush to build up delicate layers of colour – without letting the paper become too wet.

5 Cut out the centre rectangle and one of the corner segments from the graph paper template. Draw around these segments on your chosen photographs and cut out around the outlines.

6 Glue the segments on to the white card rectangle, making light pencil guidelines to ensure that they are positioned correctly.

7 Photocopy and cut out other pictures that have not been used on the "postcard" then arrange these, along with the postcard itself, on the coloured card. Glue everything in place using a glue stick.

78342

Sightseeing in the States

The Stars and Stripes make a really colourful background, but this simple idea could easily be adapted using the flag of whichever country you have visited. The folded airmail envelope opens to reveal a mini-album of extra pictures.

materials and equipment

- dark blue paper
- craft knife
- metal ruler
- cutting mat
- 30cm/12in square sheet of white card (stock)
- silver star stickers
- pencil
- glue stick
- red paper
- 5 luggage labels
- photocopy of denim fabric
- hole punch
- photographs
- natural twine
- two airmail envelopes
- adhesive tape

1 To make the background flag, cut a 15cm/6in square of blue paper and glue it in the top left corner of the white card, matching the top and side edges exactly.

2 Stick 50 silver stars in nine rows to the blue square. For the first row space six stars evenly, starting 1.5cm/½in from the left-hand side, with their lower tips 2.5cm/1in below the top edge. For the second row position five stars between the stars of the first row.

3 Cut four strips of red paper 15 x 2cm/6 x ¾in, and three strips 30 x 2cm/12 x ¾in. Glue the strips to the white card to form the American flag, butting the short ones against the blue square, and leaving the same depth of white background between each horizontal strip.

4 To make the tags, remove the string from five luggage labels. Cover each label with denim paper and trim the paper to size. Make a new hole at the top of each label using a hole punch.

5 Trim a photograph to fit across the centre of each luggage label and glue in place. Tie a short length of twine through each hole.

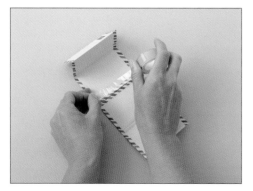

6 To make the mini-album, fold two airmail envelopes into three. Tape the ends together to make a six-page album.

7 Trim the remaining photographs to fit the pages of the mini-album and glue them in position.

8 Glue all the tags in place on the flag page, then stick the mini-album in the centre of the lower row.

Irish castles

Ireland is known as the Emerald Isle, but as well as being green and lush, the rolling hills are crammed with impressive old buildings. The heraldic imagery and clear colours used to embellish this page reflect the country's historic sites and beautiful unspoilt landscape.

materials and equipment

- 30cm/12in square sheet of pale blue mottled paper
- craft knife
- metal ruler
- cutting mat
- 30cm/12in square sheet of dark green paper
- spray adhesive
- three photographs printed with white borders
- wavy-edged scissors
- tracing paper and pencil
- scissors
- thin paper, such as origami paper, in blues and greens
- glue stick

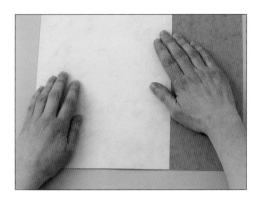

1 Cut a strip of pale blue mottled paper to fit across two-thirds of the green background paper. Glue it in place with spray adhesive, aligning the edges.

2 Trim the white borders of the photographs with wavy-edged scissors to give them a narrow decorative border.

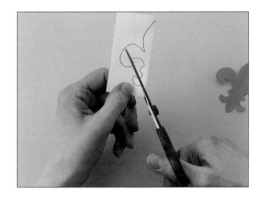

3 Trace the fleur-de-lys template at the back of the book. Fold a small square of blue paper in half, with right sides facing, and transfer one half of the outline on to the wrong side. Cut out the motif. Cut a second fleur-de-lys from green paper.

4 Glue two rectangles of different coloured paper together to make a small square, then stick the blue fleur-de-lys centrally along the join.

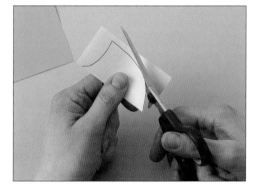

5 Use the shield template at the back of the book as a guide to cut out a small shield shape from pale blue paper.

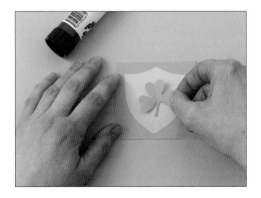

6 Following the template, cut out a green shamrock and glue it to the centre of the shield. Glue the shield on to a square of darker blue paper.

7 Glue the three photographs in position on the page, overlapping them slightly so that the join between the two background papers is concealed.

8 Stick the two decorated squares and the second fleur-de-lys into the spaces between the pictures.

Trip to Japan

There is always something exciting about discovering a new country and its culture. Record your journey by collecting interesting ephemera as you travel; when you get back home, display it on a series of luggage labels.

materials and equipment

- patterned origami paper
- 30cm/12in square sheet of deep red card (stock)
- scissors
- spray adhesive
- photocopier
- old atlas
- emphemera including tickets, bills and wrappers
- luggage labels
- photographs
- fine permanent marker pen
- hole punch
- narrow black ribbon
- self-adhesive foam pads

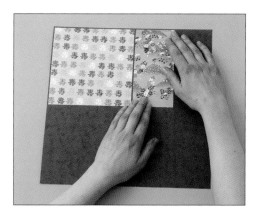

1 Cut one sheet of origami paper in half, then glue one and a half sheets to the top left corner of the background card with spray adhesive, leaving narrow margins between them and around the outer edges.

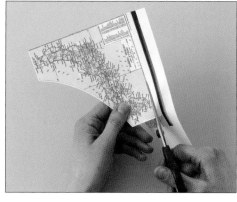

2 Photocopy a map of Japan from an atlas, reducing the size as necessary to fit into the bottom right-hand corner, and cut out, shaping the upper edge in a gentle curve. Glue in place using spray adhesive and add two tickets overlapping parts of the map.

3 Remove the string from a luggage label. Place it over a photograph and draw round the edge with a fine waterproof pen.

4 Mark the position of the hole, then cut out around the outline and punch a hole at the centre top.

5 Cut a 20cm/8in length of narrow ribbon and loop it through the hole. Make one or more additional labels in the same way.

6 Small items of memorabilia can be displayed by sticking them on to plain labels. Larger pieces, such as a calendar page, can be reduced in size on a photocopier.

7 Tie all the labels together loosely in a bunch. Attach the knot to the top left corner of the card and then anchor the labels on the page with foam pads.

Spanish memorabilia

This collection of memorabilia from a vacation in Spain is attractively displayed in a practical way, with functional pockets in which to slip airline tickets, restaurant bills, postcards and other bits and pieces picked up during the trip. A photo-montage of attractive places can be made from a duplicate set of pictures to fill another page of the album.

materials and equipment

- craft knife
- metal ruler
- cutting mat
- 4 x 30cm/12in square sheets of red card (card)
- masking tape
- pencil
- eyelet punch
- tack hammer
- small nickel eyelets
- scissors
- tickets, stamps and other travel memorabilia
- bone folder
- glue stick
- assorted paperclips
- photographs

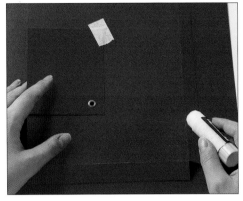

1 Using a craft knife and metal ruler and working on a cutting mat, cut out a 12.5cm/5in square from red card and tape it in the centre of one large square of card. Mark the positions for eyelets in each corner of the small square. Punch a hole at each marked point using an eyelet tool. Insert the eyelets through both layers of card. Tickets, pictures and travel memorabilia can be slipped under the small square.

2 To make a pocket, cut a larger square of red card and attach a smaller piece to it with an eyelet. Score around two adjacent edges of the square. Trim away the corner between the scored lines and fold in the edges sharply with a bone folder to make two flaps. Glue these to a large card square. Memorabilia, such as tickets, stamps and notes can be inserted in the flap pocket or attached to the pocket with paperclips.

3 For the photo-montage, use duplicate prints or make extra copies so that you can cut them up as necessary to make an effective composition. Arrange all the photographs and other pictures in a pleasing way on the last square of red card. Trim away any unnecessary parts of the photographs using a craft knife and a metal ruler, and working on a cutting mat. Once you are happy with your arrangement, glue all the pictures in place using a glue stick.

A day in the countryside

Machine stitching on card is a very quick way to add colour, pattern and texture to your page, and you can use a variety of stitches to real effect. This simple page uses fresh colours to echo the springlike tones of the photographs.

materials and equipment

- sewing machine
- light purple thread
- scrap card (stock)
- 2 x 30cm/12in square sheets of lilac card (stock)
- pencil
- scissors
- flower-shaped punches in two sizes
- light and dark purple card (stock)
- photographs
- glue dots
- pink rub-on letters
- embossing tool

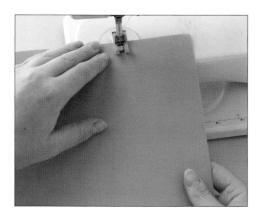

1 Thread the machine with light purple thread and do a test on spare card to get the tension right. Stitch slowly across the lower part of the page to create two gently waving lines. Align the starting points on the second page with the ends of the first lines.

2 Punch a selection of flowers from light and dark purple card using a large and a small punch.

3 Crumple the flowers to add texture. Flatten out and stick the smaller ones on top of the larger ones. Use glue dots to stick them along the lines of stitching.

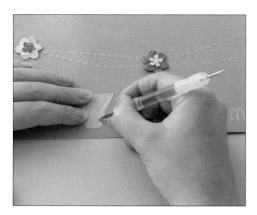

4 Double-mat the photographs on light and dark purple card and glue to the pages. Rub on the title lettering in one corner.

A weekend in Paris

This is an excellent way to combine a large number of photographs and your journaling on one page. The paper bag book contains pockets for mini-pages displaying more photographs as well as tickets, maps and other souvenirs.

materials and equipment

- guillotine
- photographs
- 30cm/12in square sheet of red card (stock)
- 3 flat-bottomed brown paper bags
- heavy-duty stapler
- selection of coloured card (stock)
- glue stick
- two-hole punch
- binder clip
- file tabs
- tickets, stamps and other travel memorabilia
- glue dots
- letter and number stickers

1 Using a guillotine, crop a selection of photographs into 6cm/2½in squares.

2 Arrange the photographs in a grid on the square card, using repositionable tape so that you can adjust them as necessary. Leave space for the title and the paper bag book on the right-hand side.

3 To make the book, stack the three bags together with the flat bottoms facing upwards and at alternate sides.

4 Fold the whole pile in half and make a crease at the fold. Staple along the fold to make the spine of the book.

5 Cut a piece of card to fit the height of the book and fold it over the spine. Glue in place using a glue stick. Punch two holes through the spine and insert the binder clip.

6 Cut out squares of card to fit the pockets created by the paper bags. Staple file tabs to the edges and fill the pages with pictures, ephemera and journaling.

7 Decorate the front of the book and place all the cards inside the pages.

8 Attach the book to the layout with a generous number of glue dots to support its weight. Use stickers to create the title and the date.

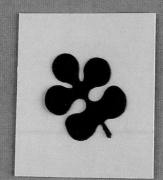

Celebrating the seasons

Though the seasons return to delight us year by year, no two days are ever truly alike, and nature is always ready to astonish us with its beauty. For photographers, the desire to capture fleeting effects of light and colour in the natural world is a powerful impulse, and successful attempts are well worth framing beautifully on your scrapbook layouts.

Pages with seasonal themes can make an album in themselves, perhaps highlighting your favourite landscapes or country walks, or tracing the annual round in your own garden. Or you can use them to punctuate more general collections of photographs, to place your family activities and celebrations in a seasonal context.

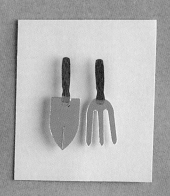
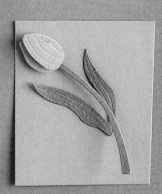

A seasonal mosaic

Photographic mosaic is a lot easier than it looks as long as you take your time and measure accurately before cutting up your pictures. Special sheets marked with a grid take care of all the spacing and lining up for you. This is a wonderful way to create an impressionistic image of seasonal flowers.

materials and equipment

- photographs
- repositionable tape runner
- cutting mat with printed grid
- craft knife
- metal ruler
- 30cm/12in square sheet white mosaic grid paper
- computer and printer
- thin card (stock) in white and mid-green
- scissors
- glue dots
- 5 metal charms with a garden theme

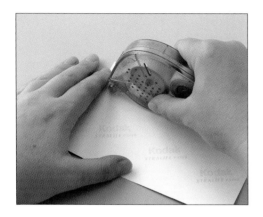

1 Cover the back of each photograph with repositionable adhesive. Be generous with this as it will make the cutting easier.

2 Stick each photograph to the cutting mat, aligning it carefully with the printed grid, and use a craft knife and metal ruler to cut it into 2.5cm/1in squares.

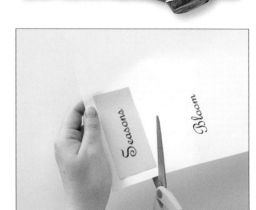

3 Reassemble the photographs on the mosaic grid. If you want any pictures to occupy blocks of squares, remember to allow for the spaces between the squares when calculating the size to cut.

4 Blend the edges of the photographs into each other a little, remembering to leave rectangular spaces for the titling as you arrange the pieces.

5 Print the titles on to white card. Carefully measure the spaces you need to fill on the grid and cut out the titles. Cut slightly larger rectangles from green card for the mats.

6 Mat the titles "bloom", "seasons" and "flower" and stick them in place in the spaces on the grid.

7 Use glue dots to attach the metal charms to the layout.

Spring in bloom

The bold colour scheme and geometric lines in this eye-catching picture of a tulip bed required an equally dramatic treatment. Red, green and white tracing papers, which have a translucent, matt finish, echo the colours of the flowers, and the spiral-petalled flower punch gives the finished page a strong, contemporary look. The white flower label bears the botanic name of the tulip species, but you could also use it to record the date or place where the picture was taken.

materials and equipment

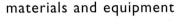

- A4 sheet of white tracing paper
- 30cm/12in square sheet of green card (stock)
- glue stick
- 2 A4 sheets of lime green tracing paper
- scissors
- flower picture
- glue dots
- flower-shaped punch
- thin white card (stock)
- A4 sheet of red tracing paper
- fine marker pen or computer and printer
- pencil

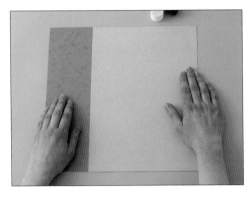

I Position the white tracing paper on the right-hand side of the green background card and glue it in place.

2 Position a sheet of green tracing paper so that it covers the lower part of the card and glue in place. Trim the edges as necessary so that they are all level.

3 Position the photograph centrally within the lime green square and stick in place with glue dots.

4 Using the flower-shaped punch, make five flowers from white card and stick them down with a glue stick to form an evenly spaced row down the centre of the green rectangle on the left.

5 Punch seven red and seven green flowers from the coloured tracing paper. Arrange them in two rows across the top rectangle, alternating the colours, and glue in place with the glue stick.

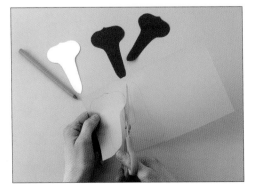

6 Copy the plant marker template at the back of the book and cut out two green and two red shapes from the remaining tracing paper.

7 For the named marker, either cut out a white label and write a name across the centre with a fine marker pen, or print the name on white paper. Place one of the tracing paper markers over it so that the name lies centrally in the top part, then draw round it and cut out the shape.

8 Arrange the coloured markers down the left side of the page and the named marker at the bottom right corner of the photograph, and glue in place.

Glorious summer

This bougainvillea-clad house, replete with peeling paintwork and faded wooden shutters, epitomizes the languid days of high summer and is a reminder of a happy holiday spent on the shores of an Italian lake. A photograph taken in the garden of the adjoining villa shared the same colour scheme: this was cut up into squares to make a mosaic-style frame, and the background was chosen to harmonize with the flowers.

materials and equipment

- transparent ruler
- pink mulberry paper
- glue stick
- A4 sheet of pale green paper
- spray adhesive
- 30cm/12in square sheet of purple card (stock)
- marbled paper in toning colours
- craft knife
- cutting mat
- main photograph, measuring 17.5 x 12.5cm/7 x 5in
- **two copies of a second photograph**

1 Using the edge of a ruler to give a deckle edge, tear two strips of mulberry paper each measuring about 2 x 30cm/¾ x 12in.

2 Glue one strip behind each long edge of the pale green paper so that about 8mm/⅓in is visible. Using spray adhesive, glue the paper to the centre of the purple background card and trim the ends.

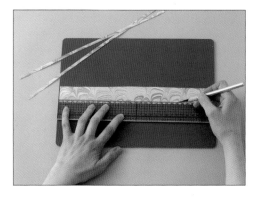

3 Using a craft knife and transparent ruler, cut four narrow strips of marbled paper, each measuring 6mm x 31cm/¼ x 12½in.

4 Glue two of the strips to the top and bottom edges of the card, to conceal the edges of the other papers. Glue the remaining strips to the side edges and mitre the corners neatly.

5 Glue the main photograph to the centre of the green paper, making sure that it lies completely flat.

6 Cut the other two photographs into 2.5cm/1in squares, using a craft knife and ruler and working on a cutting mat.

7 Glue these small squares around the main picture, alternating the light and dark tones to create a chequerboard effect.

Autumn colour

The fall in New England is world renowned for its glorious display of colour. Capture the hues of this "season of mists and mellow fruitfulness" with a special album page and make your own drift of dried leaves by using a special punch to cut shapes from duplicate pictures and toning card. As a finishing touch you could make a tiny luggage tag, using the leaf punch to make the hole and threading it with garden string, to record the date and location of your photographs.

materials and equipment

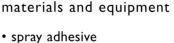

- spray adhesive
- 20 x 30cm/8 x 12in sheet of heavy cream tissue
- 30cm/12in square sheet of manila card (stock), plus extra for tag (optional)
- 3 autumnal photographs, plus an extra copy of each
- manila photo corners
- leaf-shaped punch
- glue stick
- coloured paper in matching autumnal shades
- self-adhesive foam pads
- garden string (optional)

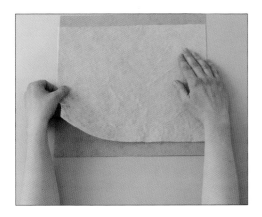

1 Spray the heavy tissue lightly with adhesive and smooth it down across the centre of the manila background card.

2 Position the three photographs on the central panel and secure them using manila photo corners.

3 Use the leaf-shaped punch to cut out a few leaf shapes from the duplicate copy of the topmost photograph.

4 Scatter these around the edges of the main picture so that they appear to be tumbling down through the sky and glue them in place using a glue stick.

5 Punch more leaves from the side and bottom edges of the other two photographs and stick them down randomly around the pictures, matching the colours.

6 Cut a few leaves from the remaining tissue paper and fix these along the bottom of the card.

7 Punch a selection of leaves from the coloured card and arrange them in a drift, with the darker colours towards the darker areas of the pictures.

8 Overlap the leaves for a naturalistic effect and use foam pads for some, to give a three-dimensional effect. Add a manila tag tied with string if you wish.

Winter wonderland

Though it may be the most monochromatic of the seasons, winter is rich in texture: dazzling icicles, the beauty of snowflakes and the dense whiteness of fallen snow. These three snow scenes are mounted on a background flecked with gold and silver leaf, and brought to life with golden snowflakes, some handmade and others from a peel-off sheet.

materials and equipment

- three wintry photographs printed with white borders
- crinkle-edged scissors
- 30cm/12in square sheet of mottled grey paper
- spray adhesive
- tissue paper flecked with gold and silver
- scissors
- glue stick
- 12 small white paper fasteners
- A4 sheet of pale blue tracing paper
- gold pen
- sharp pencil
- peel-off gold snowflake stickers

1 Trim the borders of each photograph using crinkle-edged scissors to create a decorative, frosted border.

2 Spray the background paper lightly with adhesive and cover it with metallic-flecked tissue. Trim the edges flush with the card.

3 Position the pictures on the background, overlapping and angling them if you wish to create an interesting arrangement. Glue in position with a glue stick.

4 Insert a small white paper fastener just inside each corner of the three pictures.

5 Photocopy the snowflake templates from the back of the book. Place a sheet of blue tracing paper over the first snowflake and draw in the details with a gold pen. Trace the outline with a pencil, then cut out. Make another two or three snowflakes in the same way.

6 Arrange the snowflakes in the largest space on the layout and stick them down using a glue stick.

7 Finish off the design by sprinkling a few golden peel-off snowflakes across the page.

The four seasons

These four shots of family and friends enjoying country walks reflect the changing moods and colours of the seasons. Choose papers that echo these hues for mounting and add a border of punched motifs – the simple square format pulls together the different compositions and styles of the pictures.

materials and equipment

- light green, dark green, brown and ice blue paper
- ruler
- craft knife
- cutting mat
- pencil
- 4 seasonal motif punches
- thin coloured paper
- glue stick
- photograph for each season
- 4 sheets of tracing paper to match coloured paper
- 16 small coloured paper fasteners
- 30cm/12in square sheet of card (card stock)

1 Cut a 6in/15cm square from each of the coloured papers. Pencil in five equally spaced marks along two adjacent sides of each square.

2 Using these marks as guides, punch motifs around the two sides. Choose designs that reflect the season or location of each picture – such as a snowflake for winter and a sun for summer.

3 Choose a complementary coloured paper for each main square and stick a small piece behind each cut-out motif.

4 Glue each photograph to a piece of toning tracing paper, leaving a margin of at least 3cm/1⅓in all round.

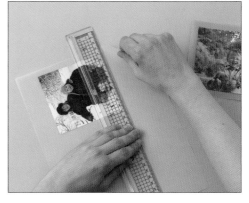

5 Tear the tracing paper against a ruler to create a narrow border with a deckle edge on all sides.

6 Glue the photographs to their respective backgrounds so that the innermost edges line up exactly.

7 As a decorative detail, attach a small coloured paper fastener to each corner of each picture.

8 Glue the four squares to the background paper, aligning them carefully.

TEMPLATES

Copy and enlarge the templates illustrated to complete your scrapbook album pages.

Stencilling p38

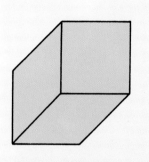

Making a kaleidoscope
p25

Decorating paper frames p28

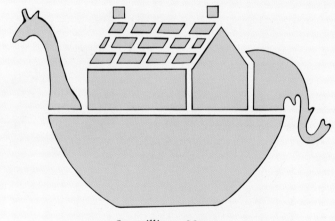

Stencilling p38

Paper appliqué p40

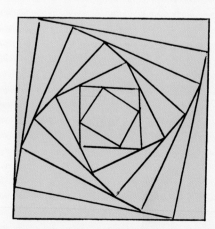

Iris-folding p48–9

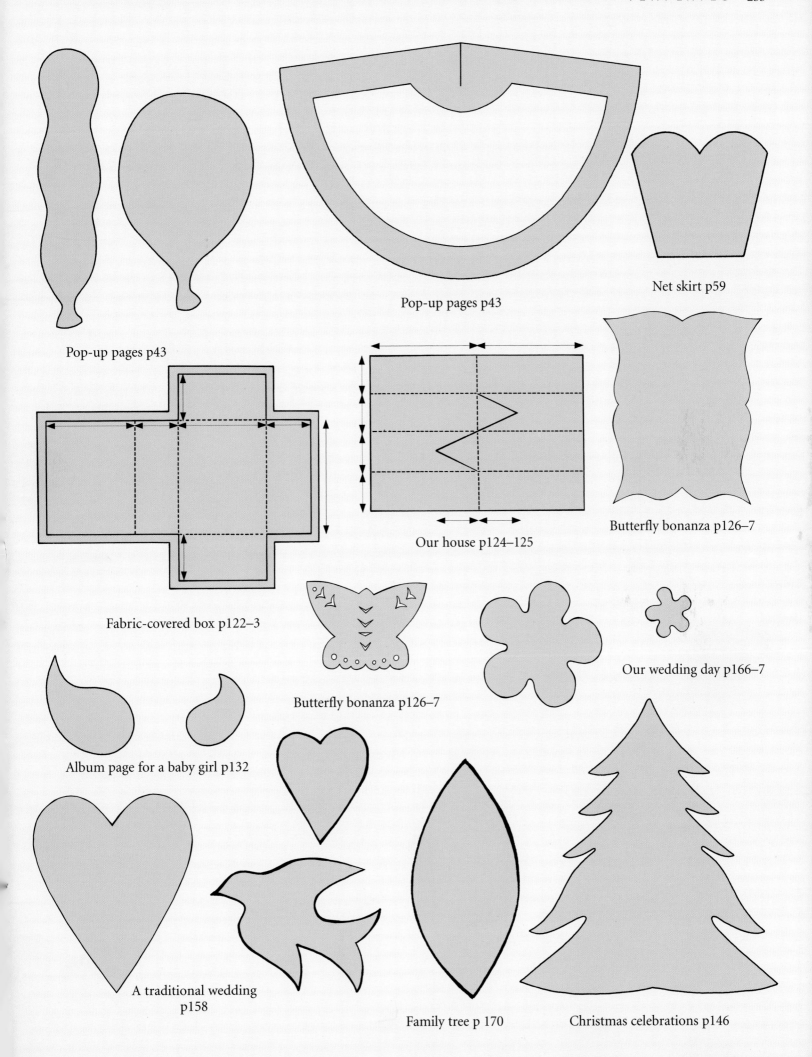

Pop-up pages p43

Net skirt p59

Pop-up pages p43

Butterfly bonanza p126–7

Our house p124–125

Fabric-covered box p122–3

Butterfly bonanza p126–7

Our wedding day p166–7

Album page for a baby girl p132

A traditional wedding p158

Family tree p 170

Christmas celebrations p146

101 *The All-Americans.* by Parish, James Robert; and Stanke, Don E. 448 p. illus. New Rochelle, N.Y.: Arlington House, 1977.

The subjects in this collective biography are Gary Cooper, Henry Fonda, William Holden, Rock Hudson, Fred MacMurray, Ronald Reagan, and James Stewart. Each is given a long biographical essay that concentrates on the film roles he has played. Information about the private lives of the men is limited to matters that have long been on public record. Predictably the strength of the text lies in the perceptive and intelligent treatment of the film performances by the experienced authors. They manage to capsulize the essence of a character, or a film, in a minimum of words. Since each of the subjects has appeared in a considerable number of films, it is possible to assess their individual talents and abilities from the comments offered by Parish and Stanke.

A filmography follows each essay and there is a final total index to the book. Pictures are plentiful but their reproduction is not up to Arlington House's usual high standards. The book adds substantial dimension to the constantly growing body of work pioneered by James Robert Parish. Recommended.

102 *All-in-One Movie Book.* by Petzold, Paul. 222 p. paper illus. New York: Amphoto, 1969.

All aspects and techniques of filmmaking are given along with many practical suggestions. Most suitable for the movie maker with some previous experience or background.

103 *All My Yesterdays.* by Robinson, Edward G.; and Spigelgass, Leonard. 344 p. illus. New York: Hawthorn Books, 1973.

The screen image of many film actors is an extension of their own personality. In the case of Edward G. Robinson, this was not true; off screen he was a cultivated, sensitive man who had a rare and unique appreciation of the arts. In this autobiography the reader comes to know the gentle man who not only amassed a famous collection of original paintings, but also was a political activist during the turbulent forties. Although the book was not completed when Robinson died at the age of 79 in early 1973, there is a fully dimensioned portrait presented. Filling in the spaces left vacant by the subject's death was the task of co-author Leonard Spigelgass, who was a close friend of Robinson's for over four decades.

The focus of the volume is sharply on Robinson and his career. His wives and his son are not ignored but the attention given them is that required to explain attitude and behavior. There is no vindictiveness or anger in the writing—perhaps the closest he comes is in discussing Miriam Hopkins, who he thought was most unprofessional and vain. Two picture sections, a list of his dramatic appearances and an index complete the book. The pictures are a mixture of film stills, candids, publicity shots, and news photos.

All the elements of this autobiography combine to offer an excellent book. Production, writing style, content and arrangement are most impressive. But the most important quality of the book is its ability to present the subject as a celebrated personality, a dedicated actor, a husband, a father, and finally as a human being experiencing the peaks and valleys of living. Recommended.

104 *All Star Cast—An Anecdotal History of Los Angeles.* by Longstreet, Stephen. illus. New York: Crowell, 1977.

Much of this volume deals with the film industry and Hollywood.

105 *All Talking, All Singing, All Dancing.* by Springer, John. 256 p. illus. New York: Citadel Press, 1966.

This is the definitive book about the movie musical to date. By using a handsome collection of his own stills, augmented by an affectionate but honest text, the author presents a history of the film genre for which American companies had practically no foreign competition, OLIVER (1968) and UMBRELLAS (1964) being exceptions. Divided loosely into periods influenced by a style or personality (Busby Berkeley, Fred Astaire), the book offers in addition a listing of film songs and composers from each period. A name and title index are also offered.

The only disagreement one might have is a minor one concerning the predictions in the "Looking Ahead" segment. Time has proven them to be incorrect or unfulfilled— "Jack Jones would be a best bet for movie musical stardom." This volume is infinitely preferable to McVay's *The Musical Film* and is recommended.

106 *All the Bright Young Men and Women.* by Skvorecky, Josef. 280 p. illus. Toronto: Peter Martin Associates, 1971.

This book was written as a personal memoir, yet it is much more. Using his own experiences, various research sources and several Czech film magazines, the author has created a critical history of Czech cinema, with a strong emphasis on the later years—those of his participation. Many familiar names appear—Hedy Lamarr, Hugh Haas, George Voskovec, Milos Forman, Jiri Menzel, Ivan Passer, etc. While the Czech film is not well known here, the coverage supplied by both text and visuals makes it seem more familiar. Most outstanding is his account of the Czech "New Wave," a dramatic, informative, and ironic story. Certainly the visuals selected here provide an introduction or review that equals anything else about Czech films in print. The text is chatty, sympathetic, informal and personalized, all adding to the book's readability. Typical of the author's sensitive approach is the chronological listing of films which he calls simply "The More Interesting." The list covers the individual years from 1898 to 1970. The director for each film is mentioned, as is the total number of films produced during that year. A detailed index concludes the book.

There are other volumes on Czech cinema, but not one has the overall impact of this one. What it may lack in historical structure, emphasis, or inclusion, it makes up for in style, selection, and warmth. Highly recommended.

107 *All the Stars in Heaven: The Story of Louis B. Mayer's Metro-Goldwyn-Mayer.* by Carey, Gary. 319 p. illus. New York: Dutton, 1981.

A biography of Louis B. Mayer that combines history, criticism and fact into a superb story. A much better book than either *Mayer and Thalberg* or *Hollywood Rajah.*

108 ALL THE WAY HOME. by Reisman, Philip, Jr. 365 p. paper illus. New York: Avon Books, 1963.

Script of the 1963 film, written by Philip Reisman, Jr. and directed by Alex Segal. Includes *All the Way Home,* the play by Tad Mosel.

109 *All Time Movie Favorites.* by Finler, Joel W. 189 p. illus. Norwalk, Conn: Longmeadow Press, 1976.

Dustin Hoffman introduces this survey of 200 films hits selected from the past seven decades of film history. For each film there is a short plot summary and some background information. Over 250 illustrations, some in color, accompany the text.

110 *Allan Dwan: The Last Pioneer.* by Bogdanovich, Peter. 200 p. illus. New York: Praeger, 1971.

After a short introduction, the major section of this volume is devoted to an interview with Dwan. Using some of his 400 films as a basis for questioning, the author succeeds not only in giving much information, description, and evaluation of a long career in Hollywood, but he manages to capture in print a pleasant, honest, and modest human being.

With a few exceptions (SUEZ (1938) and SANDS OF IWO JIMA (1949)) the Dwan sound films were mostly lower-rung B pictures—CATTLE QUEEN OF MONTANA (1954), PEARL OF THE SOUTH PACIFIC (1955), etc. His major creative period was during the silent era. Unfortunately, many of his more interesting films are lost. A lengthy filmography, not suprisingly, supplements the text nicely. The illustrations used are unfamiliar and quite pleasing. As a fascinating spotlight on an "unknown" director, this is an excellent volume.

111 *see 110*

112 *Alone With Me.* by Kitt, Eartha. 276 p. illus. Chicago: Henry Regency, 1976.

Although Eartha Kitt has appeared in such films as NEW FACES (1954), ST. LOUIS BLUES (1957), ANNA LUCASTA (1958), MARK OF THE HAWK (1958), THE SAINT OF DEVIL'S ISLAND (1961), and SYNANON (1965), she is known primarily as a night club and theatre performer. Her autobiography reflects this fact by the scant attention given to the films in a few short sentences. She does include, however, two chapters on Hollywood along with accounts of her friendships with James Dean and Marilyn Monroe.

Most of the volume deals with her rise from the cotton fields of South Carolina to the height of celebrity in the fifties. Details of her behavior at Lady Bird Johnson's White House luncheon and her CIA file are related along with other colorful incidents in her life. She is discreet about names, often using initials or blind items in her accounts. A few illustrations and an index complete the book.

It was always difficult to feel neutral about Eartha Kitt as a performer-singer. She displayed a love-me-or-leave-me attitude in much of her work. The same is true in her autobiography, which is acceptable for those who care.

113 *An Alphabetical Guide to Motion Pictures, Television, and Videotape Production.* by Levitan, Eli L. 797 p. illus. New York: McGraw-Hill, 1970.

A large, expensive book with contributions by experts in all aspects of visual production. Terms used in the industry are explained, sometimes with illustrations. Fields covered include equipment, filters, processing, lighting, etc. Primarily for the advanced filmmaker.

114 ALPHAVILLE. by Godard, Jean-Luc. 104 p. paper illus. New York:Simon & Schuster, 1966.

Script of the 1965 film written and directed by Jean-Luc Godard. Contains cast credits, filmography, and an introduction by Richard Roud. Original treatment: *A New Adventure of Lenny Caution*, by Godard.

115 *Alternatives.* compiled by Covert, Nadine; and Dick, Esme J. 12 p. paper New York: Educational Film Library Association, 1974.

Prepared for a 1974 workshop which explored alternatives in education, lifestyles, work, religion, crafts and politics, this filmography offers both description and evaluation of more than 150 titles. Arranged alphabetically, the films are further identified by their running time, year of release, director, color format, producer and distributor. The distributors' addresses and a subject index appear in the back pages. A short selected bioliography is also included. Film and print materials are suggested for use in the investigation of some of today's pertinent problems/topics. Recommended.

116 *Alternatives in Print: An International Catalog of Books, Pamphlets, Periodicals and Audiovisual Materials.* compiled by AIP Task Force. 668 p. New York: Neal-Schuman, 1980.

This bibliographic tool first appeared in 1971 and has since become a standard reference. It contains information on several thousand publishers which cannot be obtained through the usual references. A title index to the films listed is included.

117 AMARCORD. by Fellini, Federico; and Guerra, Tonino. 124 p. paper illus. New York: Berkley, 1975.

Script of the 1974 film directed by Fellini.

118 *Amateur Cinematography.* by Wheeler, Owen. 135 p. illus. London: Isaac Pitman & Sons, 1929.

An older volume on cinematography designed for nonprofessionals. Discusses topics such as persistence of vision, the nature of motion, early historical developments, projection, the kinetoscope, etc.

119 *The Amateur Filmmaker's Handbook of Sound Sync and Scoring.* by Collins, W. H. 210 p. illus. Blue Ridge Summit, Pa.: TAB Books, 1974.

The goal of the author is to offer information, advice and suggestions on providing commentary, background music and/or sound effects for amateur and semiprofessional filmmakers. The matching of sound and action by using a tape recorder, electronic synchronizer and projector is defined and discussed, as is the double system of post synchronization.

Introductory chapters consider the basic equipment, making slide presentations with sound, preparing films for sound addition, and simplified sound tracks. Techniques of sound recording, the use of the tape recorder, the projector and the synchronizer are discussed next. Attention is also given to lip-sync filming, commentary techniques, film presentation, and some alternate sync systems. Closing and appendix sections offer information on accessory equipment, some film totalizer tables, a glossary and a list of commercial companies which offer specialized services such as processing, vacuum treatment, waxing, slitting, striping, etc.

Written clearly with a minimum of technical jargon, the text is further clarified by an intelligent selection of photographs, drawings, charts and tables. The book should assist all filmmakers who wish to achieve intelligent and satisfying use of sound along with their visuals. Recommended.

120 *Amateur Film-Making.* by Sewell, George Harold. 114 p. illus. London: Blackie and Son, 1945.

An older volume on cinematography designed for the nonprofessional. *Making and Showing Your Own Films* by the same author was published in 1955.

121 *Amateur Movie Craft.* by Cameron, James R. 142 p. illus. Manhattan Beach, N.Y.: Cameron Publishing, 1928.

Another early volume by the prolific author of *Motion Picture Encyclopedia* and numerous other technical books on film.

122 *Amateur Movies and How to Make Them.* by Strasser, Alex. 80 p. illus. New York: Studio Publications, 1937.

This title in the *How to Do It* series deals with cinematography for the nonprofessional. Includes sections on the technical side; the artistic side; subjects; when the shooting is over, etc. A later edition appeared in 1949.

123 *The Amazing Careers of Bob Hope.* by Morella, Joe; and Epstein, Edward Z.; and Clark, Eleanor. 256 p. illus. New Rochelle, N.Y.: Arlington House, 1973.

What a pleasant surprise this book is—an account of Hope's professional life rather than a biography. While there are elements of biography included—an introductory chapter and a few other later references—they are minimal compared to the number of detailed critical annotations about his roles and performances. The careers in the title refer to vaudeville, the theatre, radio, films, television, USO tours and authorship.

The section on films is the most detailed, including as it does a complete filmography in addition to recreated scenes and dialogue, critical evaluation, popular reaction and author analysis of Hope's performances. There are more than 100 illustrations, all nicely reproduced and placed in appropriate positions throughout the book. The book is indexed.

Regardless of one's personal feeling about Bob Hope, this is a volume to be admired. In its presentation of the performer rather than the person, it is respectful and affectionate rather than saccharine. It is a good reference and an entertaining critical account of a man who seemingly cannot retire from the center stage. Recommended.

124 *The Ambiguous Image.* by Armes, Roy. 256 p. illus. Bloomington, Ind.: Indiana University Press, 1976.

Subtitled, "Narrative Style in Modern European Cinema," this volume explores selected films which contain a certain ambiguity of form, image and/or story and which are primarily concerned with the problems of modern man. Its period is the late fifties and the sixties during which such artists as Bergman, Resnais, and Antonioni emerged. Certain links with the past are noted in the work of Luis Bunuel, Jean-Pierre Melville, Michaelangelo Antonioni, Jacques Tati, Robert Bresson and Ingmar Bergman. Modernist films of the sixties are selected from the work of Alain Resnais, Alain Robbe-Grillet, Miklos Jansco, Pier Paolo Pasolini, and Walerian Borowczyk. In a final section the negation of the narrative is discussed using the works of Jean-Luc Godard, Dusan Makavejev and Jean-Marie Straub as models. A conclusion which links modernist cinema and contemporary culture is supplied along with an introductory chapter, illustrations, notes, a bibliography and an index.

Armes has created a series of individual director studies and then woven them into an important statement about a specific movement which he calls the Modernist Cinema. He is one of the first to define with clarity and to assess with sound critical judgement that group of recent European films which has created a renewed respect and awareness of film as an art form. Highly recommended.

125 AMERICA, AMERICA. by Kazan, Elia. 190 p. illus. New York: Stein & Day, 1962.

A novelized version of the screen play for the 1963 film.

126 *America at the Movies.* by Thorp, Margaret Farrand. 313 p. illus. New York: Arno Press, 1970 (1939).

This older volume is a general one that addresses itself to movie-going in the thirties. Because 85 million people attended films every week at that time, the motion picture industry was about to enter its most profitable decade. Subjects explored by the author include the audience, what they like in films, the effects of film, the industry, censorship, and movies as art and as propaganda. How the film industry tries to create demand for the productions is noted. The material in the volume is comprehensive but dated. In an attempt to review all of the facets of motion pictures, the author is forced to be quite general. The text is easy reading, and the author's style is chatty rather than pedantic. The original edition (1939) contained a collection of fine photographs and was indexed. Good for nostalgia lovers, historians, or researchers.

127 *America in the Dark: Hollywood and the Gift of Reality.* by Thomson, David. 288 p. New York: William Morrow, 1977.

This volume deals with the influence of Hollywood on American life. Many examples are used to show that films are the major source of today's stories/fiction, and, as such, have helped to shape our thoughts, feelings and attitudes.

Thomson's approach is a personal one that examines films and film genres as part of American cultural history rather than by a set of aesthetic standards. A filmography, a bibliography and an index are added.

128 *America in the Movies or "Santa Maria, It Had Slipped My Mind.* by Wood, Michael. 206 p. illus. New

York: Basic Books, 1975.

Michael Wood's study is concerned with recurring themes found in American films of the thirties and forties. His thesis is that only today can the full significance of these themes be appreciated. Chapter titles are indicative of the humor which accompanies the text. "The Blame on Mame" treats Rita Hayworth and other dangerous women while "Nice Guys Finish Last" talks about anti-heroes, lowliness, and the price of success. The subtitle, a line of dialogue from a Tyrone Power film, is used to indicate the refusal of Hollywood films to tackle in a direct manner the important social and moral issues of the period.

Wood's literary style tends toward being arty, verbose and a bit obscure at times. He is more concerned with style and fragmentary ideas than with a structured argument. A struggle to find topics for examination seems apparent, for much of what he offers is only partially true—or subjective—and ignores the laudable efforts of filmmakers to handle significant issues. For documentation see *Dialogue with the World*, which offers study guides based on themes and issues found in 100 films of the period that Wood considers. The few illustrations have been carefully selected and are well reproduced. An index is provided. In summary, the important questions raised by the author are buried by excess interpretation and a flashy literary style. Acceptable but ultimately disappointing.

129 *America's Mass Media Merchants.* by Read, William H. 209 p. Baltimore, Md.: Johns Hopkins University Press, 1976.

This volume is an examination of the expansion of America's mass media abroad. The foreign use of American newspapers, periodicals, films and TV programs is noted. Using both a historical and sociological approach, the author is concerned about the impact that these American exports have had and the emotions they have aroused.

A lengthy chapter entitled "America's Visual Media Merchants," deals with television and films. An economic history of the film industry is included along with an account of television's growth and development during the past three decades. What visual media are exported, to whom and with what results is discussed next. This topic is expanded further in a later chapter entitled "Influence and Ire." The author's personal view of the role of America's mass media merchants concludes the book. Chapter notes and an index are provided.

A topic seldom considered in film literature is treated here in a scholarly yet readable fashion. The text

is an ideal blend of research and interpretation that will appeal to any reader interested in national/international matters. Recommended.

130 *American Actors, 1861-1910: An Annotated Bibliography of Books Published in the United States in English from 1861 through 1976.* by Moyer, Ronald L. 268 p. Troy, N.Y.: Whitston, 1979.

Although this is a bibliography more pertinent to theatre studies than to film, some of the subjects did appear in silent films. Moyer offers an alphabetical-by-author listing of 363 books about American actors. His annotations are descriptive rather than evaluative and there is access to the material by several indexes.

131 *The American Animated Cartoon: A Critical Anthology.* edited by Peary, Gerald; and Peary, Danny. paper illus. New York: Dutton, 1980.

This anthology is divided into six major sections: Early History, Walt Disney, Warner Brothers, Other Studios, Cartoon Characters, and Cartoons Today. Six or seven articles by contributing authors appear under each heading. A bibliography, an index and some identification of the contributors concludes the book.

The editors announce early on that they intend to put to rest the idea that Disney was the only worthwhile producer of American film cartoons. Although some of the book might be considered anti-Disney (i.e., Disney's testimony before the HUAC), there is enough varied information and comment offered here to please anyone interested in the animated film.

132 *The American Cinema: Directors and Directions 1929-1968.* by Sarris, Andrew. 383 p. New York: Dutton, 1968.

After an introductory essay on a theory of film history, Sarris places his group of American directors into various categories. The arbitrary divisions, the assignment of the directors, and the discussions of their work may be arguable, but the quality and pertinence of the writing is unquestionable. A directorial chronology from 1915-1967 and a directorial index to the American cinema only enhance the reference value of this vital book. Beautifully done and highly recommended.

133 *The American Cinema and World War I.* by Isenberg, Michael T. 400 p.

illus. Madison, N.J.: Fairleigh Dickinson University Press, 1981.

134   *The American Cinema Editor's First Decade Anniversary Book.* by Smith, Frederick Y. 224 p. illus. Hollywood: American Cinema Editors, 1961.

The accomplishments of the cinema editors from 1950 to 1960 are noted. Volume II (301 pages), published in 1971, covers the sixties.

135   *American Cinematographer Hand Book and Reference Guide.* by Rose, Jackson J. 287 p. illus. Hollywood, Calif.: American Society of Cinematographers, 1947.

The 6th edition (1947) of this volume included some color illustrations. Improved, enlarged and revised from time to time, the book is concerned with cameras and cinematography.

136   *American Cinematographer Manual.* edited by Mascelli, Joseph; and Miller, Arthur C . 625 p. illus. Hollywood: American Society of Cinematographers, 1966.

An advanced work on motion picture techniques and technological advances in filmmaking which is designed for professionals. It has a possible reference value, but beginners are directed to author Mascelli's *The Five C's of Cinematography.*

137   *American Cinematographer Manual.* edited by Clarke, Charles G.; and Strenge, Walter. 669 p. illus. Hollywood, Calif.: American Society of Cinematographers, 1978.

The official publication of the American Society of Cinematographers, this comprehensive manual, in its fourth edition, covers virtually every phase of motion picture photography. Topics include photographic systems and equipment, film stock selection, lens angles, formulas, depth of field, special applications (helicopter, aerial, and underwater photography), special effects, lighting formulas, sound equipment, etc.

138   *An American Comedy: An Autobiography.* by Lloyd, Harold C.; and Stout, Wesley W. 204 p. illus. New York: Longmans, Green, 1928.

The early life of Harold Lloyd told with modesty and candor. The fashioning of Lloyd's screen character is a major theme. A good early film biography.

139   *An American Comedy.* by Lloyd, Harold. 138 p. paper illus. New York: Dover, 1971 (1928).

This autobiography was originally published by Longmans Green in 1928 with the title *An American Comedy: Acted by Harold Lloyd, Directed by Wesley W. Stout.* The current publishers are to be commended for reissuing the book (by arrangement with Lloyd) and for adding some pertinent material. Lloyd was one of the great silent screen comedians. He recalls his early life and career, giving much attention to the production of early silent films. New to this book are 67 illustrations, an interview with Lloyd called "The Serious Business of Being Funny," an introductory note by Richard Griffith, and a newly prepared index. Lloyd's story, related in a spare, factual style, was quite impressive and somewhat ahead of its time when it first appeared. The new material enhances the book's original quality, making it an outstanding example of early film biography. Recommended.

140   *American Entertainment.* by Csida, Joseph; and Csida, June Bundy. 448 p. illus. New York: Billboard (Watson Guptill), 1978.

This unusual survey of American show business divides the period from 1700 to 1977 into five eras: 1. The Show Business Pioneers, 1700-1893; 2. The Mad, Merry Mix of Live Show Business, 1894-1904; 3. Of Trusts and Stars, 1905-1918; 4. The Sound of a New Show Business, 1919-1946; 5. Technology, Conglomerates, and Superstars, 1947-1977. A sixth section called, "There Always Was Music," treats popular music over the entire period.

Each of the era sections offers a time chart, an introduction, an abundant sampling of original material taken from *Billboard* magazine, and a capsule history of show business during thatyear. More than 1000 illustrations are included along with an index.

Although the material has been selected and therefore presents a partial view of American entertainment history, the choices made by the Csidas seem representative. For example, the reader seeking a firsthand account of film history will find this book to be a rich source of information.

The potential audience for a volume such as this one is large; such diverse interests as nostalgia, history, reference, or reading pleasure can be nicely satisfied via its excellent text, materials, illustrations and arrangement. Recommended.

141 *American Family Life Films.* by Trojan, Judith. 425 p. illus. Metuchen, N.J.: Scarecrow, 1980.

Judith Trojan, who is associated with the Educational Film Library Association, has compiled a filmography "of 16mm films that cover the broad spectrum of family dynamics in America, past and present."

The films are divided into two groups: shorts and documentaries and selected dramatic features. In both sections the films are arranged alphabetically by title. Each entry gives the title, time, color format, date, director, distributor, a descriptive annotation and the suggested audience. No evaluations are provided. Access to the films is by a lengthy, detailed subject index. A bibliography, distributor list and a complete title index complete the book.

This is a useful reference for professionals concerned with American family life. The 2000 films listed here constitute a resource that can provide information on the many aspects of that subject.

142 *American Fashion.* by Lee, Sarah Tomerlin. illus. New York: Quadrangle.

This beautifully produced and illustrated volume is noted here because of its coverage of the Hollywood designer, Adrian. The clothes he created for movie stars, both on and off the screen, had an enormous influence on the styles that American women wanted and wore. The work of other, non-Hollywood fashion experts is also considered.

143 *The American Film.* by Rideout, Eric H. 163 p. illus. London: Mitre, 1937.

An overview of American film up to 1936.

The first four chapters of this survey of American Film (to 1936) are devoted to about 50 directors and their films. Other aspects—photography, art direction, sound, writing, acting, and exhibition—are discussed. A final chapter deals with the British film. Notes, an appendix, illustrations and an index complete the book.

144 *American Film Criticism.* edited by Kauffmann, Stanley. 443 p. New York: Liveright, 1972.

This fine anthology is subtitled, "From the Beginnings to CITIZEN KANE," and deals only with reviews of important films at the time they first appeared. No retrospective or current evaluations are used.

The forty-five year period is divided into three unequal parts. Some fifty pages of reviews are devoted to the beginnings—that early period of short films which lasted up to 1911. The next section of approximately 150 pages addresses itself to the longer silent films and includes reviews on such late twenties classics as THE CIRCUS (1928) and THE CROWD (1928).

The largest section deals with sound film reviews and takes the reader up to the early forties. The aim of the editor was to document the pre-Agee period of film reviewing, purportedly a wasteland in which no one was writing anything that could be considered serious criticism. The arrangement of the reviews is chronological by film, not by author. In certain cases—INTOLERANCE (1916), METROPOLIS (1928), LITTLE CAESAR (1930), etc.—more than one review is offered. Notes, a selected bibliography, and a long detailed index complete the book.

Writers represented include both familiar and unknown critics; it is in this selection that the editor has served the reader well. While some argument might be made about individual films—both those included and those missing—none can be made about the quality of the articles chosen for this entertaining, informative collection. Highly recommended.

145 *The American Film Directors.* by Lambray, Maureen. 179 p. illus. New York: Collier, 1976.

In what she calls "Volume I," Maureen Lambray has photographed 82 American film directors in informal poses. For each, she offers a listing of their film titles along with the date of release. Scattered throughout the book are 14 short quotations about directing. The book is published in a large-size format and each of the photos occupies a full page and often more. Subjects are a blend of the old breed, such as George Marshall and Alan Dwan, and the new wave—George Lucas and Steven Spielberg. An index is provided.

Since the photographs are the book's content, it should be noted that they are reproduced with care and presented in an attractive page layout. Certain pictures tell us some things about the directors that words alone could not. Other visuals communicate little.

This unique picture book will probably appeal to the knowledgeable filmgoer of today—the person who realizes the importance of the director in the filmmaking process. Acceptable.

146 *American Film Directors.* by Lloyd, Ronald. 143 p. paper illus. New York: New Viewpoints (Franklin Watts), 1976.

This volume, which is subtitled "The World As They See It," examines the work of six American film directors: John Ford, Orson Welles, Howard Hawks, Alfred Hitchcock, Arthur Penn and Stanley Kubrick. In addition, a few of the newer directors are discussed briefly in a final chapter; included in this group are Peter Bogdanovich, Francis Ford Coppola, and Robert Altman.

Although the book has been prepared for a juvenile audience, the text is honest and straightforward with no concession to a watered down or simplified approach. Vocabulary and content assume the young reader to be curious, informed and intellectually able. Well-selected illustrations and a good index add to the book's quality. Recommended.

147 *American Film Directors.* edited by Hochman, Stanley. 590 p. New York: Frederick Ungar, 1974.

In this first volume of a series entitled *A Library of Film Criticism*, a collection of short articles, excerpts, and comments has been selected for 65 American directors. More than 300 critics are represented. For example, on Fritz Lang there are critical statements from Kenneth Fearing (*New Masses*, 1936), John Marks (*Sight and Sound*, 1936), Robert Stebbins (*New Theatre*, 1937), *The National Board of Review* (1938), Alfred Eibel (*Fritz Lang*, 1964), Lewis Jacobs (*The Rise of the American Film*, 1939), Jacques Bourgeois (*Revue du Cinema*, 1946), Paul Rotha (*The Film Till Now*, 1949), Alton Cook (*New York World Telegram and Sun*, 1952), David Thompson (*Movie Man*, 1967), Peter Bogdanovich (*Fritz Lang in America*, 1967) and Paul M. Jensen (*The Cinema of Fritz Lang*, 1969). The comments are offered in an approximate chronological order, although the revisions and updating of certain books present some confusion in arrangement.

The task of locating and selecting the appropriate material for each director is formidable. In this Hochman has succeeded; he has provided an objective sampling of critical thought which facilitates an understanding of each man's work. Supplementing this wealth of material is a filmography for each director and a detailed index listing the critics and film titles. As a reference book or as a reader, this volume is most satisfying. Its scope is wide, its arrangement is efficient, and most of all, the selection of such consistently strong material is excellent. Highly recommended.

148 *American Film Exhibition and an Analysis of the Motion Picture Industry's Market Structure 1963-1980.* by Edgerton, Gary R. 235 p. New York: Garland, 1982.

A title in the *Dissertations on Film* series.

149 *American Film Genres.* by Kaminsky, Stuart M. 232 p. paper illus. Dayton, Ohio: Pflaum, 1974.

In this study the author suggests several approaches for use in analyzing American film genres. He employs individual films, comparisons between original sources and eventual film, groups of films, and individual directors in the exploration of his topic. The gangster film, the western, the film noir, the horror-science fiction film, the caper film, the musical, and the comedy film are among the genres he discusses. His argument is for analysis and understanding of a particular genre and then a consideration of any film within that genre. Evaluation is not his concern but relationship to the genre is.

The subtitle to the book, "Approaches to a Critical Theory of Film," states the author's purpose in another way. By giving serious study, analysis and consideration to popular but critically neglected films and the genres they represent, alternative avenues to film criticism and appreciation might emerge. A list of key films and a bibliography follow many of the chapters. The illustrations and a detailed index add to the book's quality.

Although genre study has been the subject of other volumes, none has approached the depth and persuasiveness of this one. Kaminsky's argument may be vulnerable and controversial but his attempt to explore and open new approaches to critical theory is to be appreciated.

150 *The American Film Heritage.* by Karr, Kathleen. 184 p. illus. Washington, D.C.: Acropolis Books, 1972.

Although the subtitle, "Impressions From the American Film Institute Archives," is appropriate, a more descriptive one might be "The American Film Institute Reader." The book is a collection of original articles which are connected in some way with the AFI collection, concern, or operation. "Lost" films which the AFI has rediscovered or reconstructed are described, e.g., THE MYSTERY OF THE WAX MUSEUM (1933), THE EMPEROR JONES (1933).

The work of neglected American directors—Michael Curtiz, William Beaudine, etc., is noted. Sections on film history relate accounts of early color attempts, the first animation films, comedy shorts, the B western, and vintage films from 1907-1914. Writers include Tom Shales, William Everson, Kevin Brownlow and others. In most instances the text is both factual and critical, attempting to give an honest evaluation of the importance of the subject at hand.

More impressive than the text are the visuals. Nearly 200 are supplied, and selection and reproduction are outstanding. The book is indexed. It has a certain reference value. This beautifully produced volume succeeds in all departments—text, visuals, format, subject matter, etc. One can find little fault with it and yet one expects a sturdier product from AFI. This is a sampling—and one to be admired—but AFI should be encouraging, producing, and facilitating major works in all areas of film literature rather than a pseudosouvenir book like this one. This is more a criticism of AFI than of this volume since its excellence is acknowledged. In any event, this book will please many readers and will delight anyone interested in film history. Recommended.

151 *The American Film Heritage.* by Ostrach, Herbert F.; and Hodgkinson, Anthony. paper Chelmsford, Mass.: Screen Studies, 1968.

This film study unit explores "a variety of film genres with emphasis on the particular contribution of each to our collective fantasy life." The first section introduces the unit and covers bits of the aesthetics, history, and social significance of films. In the second section, the genres and films mentioned are: Film Comedy—A NIGHT AT THE OPERA (1935); The Western—THE HORSE SOLDIERS (1959); The Spectacular—EL CID (1961); The Film of Ideas—CITIZEN KANE (1941); The Comedy of Social Realism—THE CATERED AFFAIR (1956); and The Musical—SEVEN BRIDES FOR SEVEN BROTHERS (1954).

Since this was one of the early film study units, it would be unreasonable at this time to fault the obvious structure and film choices in the unit. Suffice to say it is an admirable model for imitation and emulation. Using it along with the greater film resources we now have at our disposal, the reader can create excellent study guides. Recommended.

152 *American Film Index.* by Lauritzen, E.; and Lundquist, G. illus. Stockholm: Akademi Bokhandeln, University of Stockholm, 1977.

The credits, often including the casts, for 23,000 theatrical films (390 feet or more) released from July, 1908, to December, 1915, make up the major part of this large book. In addition there are over 100 full-page portraits and 135 short company histories.

Produced by two members of the Swedish Film Archive, this important reference supplements the work done thus far by the American Film Institute. This is an expensive volume but one that will provide data not available elsewhere.

153 *The American Film Industry.* edited by Balio, Tino. 499 p. illus. Madison, Wisc.: University of Wisconsin Press, 1976.

This anthology uses a chronological approach to explore the history and nature of the American film industry. It is divided into four major sections: 1. A Novelty Spawns Small Businesses (1894-1908); 2. Struggles for Control (1908-1930); 3. A Mature Oligopoly (1930-1948); and 4. Retrenchment, Reappraisal, and Reorganization (1948-). Under each heading there are four or more essays/articles pertinent to the period being considered.

Selection has been made with intelligence and skill, thus allowing the complicated story of an industry that gave birth to an art form to be comprehensible without being buried beneath figures, data, and legal terminology. Some visuals are included but many are too small for a complete understanding of their pictorial information. The book's final pages indentify the contributors and offer a bibliography, a title index, and a general index. Highly recommended.

154 *The American Film Institute Catalog of Motion Pictures: Feature Films 1961-1970.* edited by Krafsur, Richard P. 2 vols, 2244 p. New York: Bowker, 1976.

This catalog consists of two volumes which chronicle about 5800 feature films released in the United States from 1961 to 1970. Each film is described by title, cast, credits and a detailed plot synopsis in the first volume. Four indexes (subject, literary/dramatic source, filmmaker/corporate credits, and country of origin), which provide access to the long filmography, appear in the second volume.

This major reference was supported in part by the National Endowment for the Humanities and represents the second part of the ambitious AFI series. The earlier volumes published in 1971 covered the decade from 1921 to 1930.

Although the subject indexing may be a bit too detailed, the coverage provided here for the films of the sixties is as comprehensive as anyone could wish.

155   *The American Film Institute Catalog of Motion Pictures: Feature Films 1921-1930.* edited by Munden, Kenneth W. 2 vols, 1653 p. New York: Bowker, 1971.

This catalog, the first in a projected series, covers the feature films released in the United States from 1921 to 1930. In the first volume, each film is described by title, cast, credits, and a detailed plot synopsis. Access to the films is provided in the second volume by four indexes—subject, credit, source, and national origin.

As a record of the golden age of the silent film, this volume would be hard to equal. The factual information and its arrangement is most impressive. A notable achievement in film literature.

156   *The American Film Institute Catalog(s).* by American Film Institute, edited by Munden, Kenneth W. New York: Bowker, 1971.

Announced as an attempt to catalog in 19 volumes all the films made by American companies. Included will be feature films, short films, and newsreels. To date, the only volumes published are *Feature Films: 1921-1930* and *Feature Films: 1961-1970.* It is interesting to note that much assistance in compiling these volumes is being obtained from censorship records.

157   *The American Film Institute Guide to College Courses in Film and Television* edited by Granade, Charles, Jr. 334 p. paper Princeton, N.J.: Peterson's Guides, 1980.

This is the seventh edition of this guide which lists 7648 courses in film (3991), television (2532) and other media (1125). Since the information is based on responses from interested institutions, the above numbers represent a minimum.

The volume has a few introductory statements and then presents an arrangement of the states in alphabetical order with their colleges described in sufficient detail. Courses given by the colleges are listed in each entry. Also pertinent is the information presented here on foreign schools, grants, scholarships, festivals, awards, film-TV centers, media organizations, career descriptions, graduate degrees, and degrees by state. A general index of the colleges concludes the book.

Certainly each edition of this volume improves on the preceding ones. The seventh is no exception and would seem to be an essential reference-resource for anyone interested in or currently concerned with

film/TV education. Previous editions appeared under the title *Guide to College Courses in Film and Television* by the American Film Institute.

158   *American Film Institute Report.* edited by Kriegsman, Sali Ann. 52 p. paper illus. Washington, D.C.: American Film Institute, 1973.

This is number four of Volume 4 of the AFI Reports, whose formats are quite changeable. In this instance a group of five articles are accompanied by sections on directors, films, and books. The articles deal with Women's Image in Films (Molly Haskell), Cable TV (Russell Connor), New American Cinema (Ken Kelman), The Vietnam War on TV (Laurence W. Lichty) and D. W. Griffith (Stephen F. Zito).

159   *The American Film Institute Report, 1967-1971.* edited by Kriegsman, Sali Ann. 80 p. paper illus. Washington, D.C.: The American Film Institute, 1972.

This report of the first four years of the American Film Institute gives the reader some idea of the scope of the Institute's activities, from film preservation to publications, grants, and research. As with all reports, this one is self-congratulatory and some of the material sounds inflated beyond its actual importance; however, it is never dull.

Since the Institute is a controversial matter in many minds, this report may serve as an informational resource. It is nicely illustrated and appropriate for all collections.

160   *The American Film Institute Theatre Opening Series Program.* edited by American Film Institute. 16 p. paper illus. Washington, D.C.: American Film Institute, 1973.

The program for the initial series of films shown at the American Film Institute Theatre in Washington, D.C.

161   *American Film Institute Tribute Books.* edited by American Film Institute. paper illus. Washington, D.C.: American Film Institute, 1970.

Each year the American Film Institute pays tribute to an actor or director whose contribution to the American screen is recognized without question.

These books are the programs for the evening at which the honorees are paid homage by their fellow workers and by a compilation of film clips. The subjects include Fred Astaire (76 pages), Bette Davis (14 pages), William Wyler (52 pages), Orson Welles (36 pages), James Cagney (36 pages), John Ford (32 pages). Tribute books for Alfred Hitchcock, James Stewart, and Henry Fonda were also issued.

162 *American Film Now: The People, The Power, The Money, The Movies.* by Monaco, James. 540 p. illus. New York: Oxford University Press, 1979.

This volume, which might be termed a critical history of American film during the seventies, is certainly one of the most ambitious books of the decade. The author has provided a comprehensive detailed view of American filmmaking as it existed from 1968 to 1977 by examining the basic elements of the film industry: companies, filmmakers and products. He closes his lengthy survey with some recommendations for the eighties.

Written with a scholar's authority, the perceptive text is enriched by a diversity of elements that are uniformly rewarding. In addition to biographies, filmographies, charts, and critics' ten best lists, the reader will find an abundance of fine illustrations, a sound bibliography, a who's who for the seventies and a detailed index.

While there may be some quarrel with certain of Monaco's opinions and interpretations, there can be none with the intent of this volume and its satisfactory realization. The subject, scope, design, and style of the book make it essential reading for anyone interested in today's films. Highly recommended.

163 *American Folklore Films and Videotapes Index.* edited by Ferris, Bill; and Peiser, Judy. 338 p. paper illus. Memphis, Tenn.: Center for Southern Folklore, 1976.

In this index folklore is considered to have two major themes—experience (background, general history) and traditions (music, crafts, and tales). A long subject index, which lists film titles under appropriate subject headings, appears first. In the next section the films are listed alphabetically by title with both informational data and a brief descriptive annotation. These two divisions make up the major portion of the text. The few final sections include some videotape annotations, a list of special collections, a list of the films and videotapes arranged by distributor and, finally, the addresses of the distributors.

This is a most worthy reference in which the classification and description of over 1800 titles has been accomplished with clarity and efficiency. As a result use of the index is easy and access to many informational sources on American folklore is relatively simple. Highly recommended.

164 AMERICAN GRAFFITI. by Lucas, George; and Katz, Gloria; and Huyck, Willard. 189 p. paper illus. New York: Ballantine, 1973.

Script of the 1973 film directed by Lucas. Contains production notes and production credits including music used in the film.

165 *American History/American Film.* edited by O'Connor, John E.; and Jackson, Martin, A. 224 p. paper illus. New York: Ungar, 1979.

In this anthology, subtitled "Interpreting the American Image," fourteen historians each view a specific film as a reflection of the American past. Taken into account are the national climate and the stage of the development of the motion picture industry at the time of the film's release. The films analyzed include: WAY DOWN EAST (1920), THE BIG PARADE (1925), THE SCAR OF SHAME (1927), PUBLIC ENEMY (1931), STEAMBOAT ROUND THE BEND (1935), DRUMS ALONG THE MOHAWK (1939), MISSION TO MOSCOW (1943), THE BEST YEARS OF OUR LIVES (1946), RED RIVER (1948), VIVA ZAPATA (1951), INVASION OF THE BODY SNATCHERS (1956), DR. STRANGELOVE (1964), BONNIE AND CLYDE (1967), and ROCKY (1976).

The major point of the volume seems to be that selected films can be used by historians as a source of research. Each essay covers a different period or aspect of American life and is followed by extensive chapter notes and rental sources. A selected bibliography and an index are added.

This is an unusual approach and how effective the essays are without a viewing of the films will depend upon the reader's background and experience.

166 *American Issues Forum Film List.* edited by Covert, Nadine. 32 p. New York: Educational Film Library Association, 1975.

The American Issues Forum, a program designed for the national bicentennial, provides "a framework for the exploration of matters of common concern to all citizens." It consists of nine major issues— "Working in America," "American in the World," "Certain Unalienable Rights," etc. Scheduled for monthly consideration, each of the major issues is subdivided into weekly topics. For example, "Working in America" has four subheadings: (1) The American Work Ethic, (2) Organization of the Labor Force, (3) The Welfare State: Providing a Livelihood, and (4) Enjoying the Fruits of Labor.

The Educational Film Library Association, assisted by a grant from the National Endowment for the Humanities, has compiled a filmography that is correlated to the forum structure. Under "Working in America—The American Work Ethic" the following films are annotated: THE BLUE COLLAR TRAP (1972), CLERICAL WORKERS (1973), FACTORY (1970), THE FACTORY (1971), LOOSE BOLTS (1973), MODERN TIMES (1938), SALESMAN (1969), WHY MAN CREATES (1968) and WORK (1970). The annotations offer running time, color format, release date, producer, distributor, description, a partial evaluation and, at times, suggestions for use. An index of all the film titles arranged alphabetically and a list of distributors complete the book.

Not only was this a fine aid in planning bicentennial programs, but also it remains a reference book that has lasting value and pertinence for all users of film. Both film selection and annotation provide a superior resource that deserves wide notice and distribution.

167   *The American Movie.* by Everson, William K. 149 p. illus. New York: Atheneum, 1963.

A short survey of American film history highlighting some film pioneers, some classic films and a look at trends and patterns. The Everson text and full page illustrations are fine but some disappointment must be noted at the postage stamp illustrations that predominate. Ironically, Everson warns the reader not to judge films until they are seen on a large movie screen. Much excellence here along with a major production fault.

168   *The American Movie Goddess.* edited by McCreadie, Marsha. 92 p. paper illus. New York: John Wiley, 1973.

A new approach to the typical course in writing given to college freshmen or sophomores is offered in this volume, which is part of the *Perception in Communication* series. It uses photographs, essays, song lyrics, illustrations and other materials to recall three decades in recent American history, with a specific movie goddess selected as a symbol of each decade. The thirties section is named "Streamlined Austerity and the Glamorized No" and Greta Garbo is the representative figure. Rita Hayworth is selected for the forties section entitled "The Bad Girl—Pin-Ups, Mechanized Sex, Fun and War." The fifties are personified by Marilyn Monroe, with

this section called "Bringing It All Home with the Innocent Blonde, Synthetically Natural Sex Queen."

As indicated above, each section offers mixed media materials which appeared during the decade being described. The selection, of course, is an arbitrary one; other cases, symbols and collections could be formulated. However, in each instance here the materials are provocative enough to stimulate a written response, interpretation, or further investigation. As a further aid to use, some questions and suggested projects are also included.

The creation of posters, collages, poems, plays, sketches, songs, tapes, etc., are other possibilities for the use of the material. Correlating this text with the showing of representative films of the three stars would seem a certain method to gain student interest and participation. In summary this attempt to suggest new and better ways of teaching is creative, imaginative, and, most important, stimulating for both student and teacher. The implication for the development of similar units for the high school level is obvious. Recommended.

169   *The American Movies Reference Book: The Sound Era.* by Michael, Paul. 629 p. illus. Englewood Cliffs, N.J.: Prentice Hall, 1969.

A large and expensive reference book which is excellent for browsing. It is divided into six sections. 1. The History: each decade from the thirties through the sixties is reviewed separately. Film categories (the musical, the western, etc.) recall the films made during each 10-year period. 2. The Players: 600 film actors and actresses are listed in alphabetical order. For each, there is a brief biography, followed by a listing of his or her English language films and a still from one of the films. 3. The Films: more than 1000 films are arranged in alphabetical order. Cast credits, data, and background are given. 4. The Directors: 50 directors, along with their American sound films, are listed, accompanied by a single still. 5. The Producers: 50 producers are presented with credits and a still. 6. The Awards: includes Academy Awards (1927-1967), New York Critics Awards (1935-1967), National Board of Review Awards (1930-1967), the Patsy Awards (1951-1966), *Film Daily's* Ten Best Awards (1922-1967), *Photoplay* Gold Medal Awards (1920-1967), and a listing of the top grossing films (1930- 1966). A bibliography and an index conclude this oversized volume.

The book is a most commendable and impressive achievement. Any reservations one may have are minor, but for the record they should be noted.

Selection: can the omission of THE BANK DICK, Jimmy Durante, Joseph Von Sternberg, Slim Summerville, THE INVISIBLE MAN, Alan Jones, LADY FROM SHANGHAI, etc. be justified when we find included LIFE BEGINS FOR ANDY HARDY, MY SON JOHN, Alan Mara, Connie Gilchrist, Iris Adrian, and LASSIE COME HOME? Inaccuracies: the listing following THE ZIEGFELD FOLLIES may possibly be what was originally planned but the final released film differs greatly. Lucine Amara did not play the role of Blanche Thebom in THE GREAT CARUSO. Limitations: the book is based only on American sound films.

In spite of the above, the book is a fine reference volume. It is equally rewarding as browsing material.

170 *The American Museum of Natural History Catalog of Special Film Collections.* by Burns, Sheila; and Pollack, Beth and Mandl, Rita. 59 p. paper New York: American Museum of Natural History, 1974.

The special films described in this catalog were made by museum staff members, scientists, anthropologists and explorers. The time period covered is over 65 years. Arranged alphabetically by title, each entry includes a complete description of the film; there are entries of the producers, filmmakers, expeditions and expedition leaders, all of which refer back to the title entry. A subject index appears at the end of the catalog.

Noted here not only for its unique content, but also for the excellent access provided to the film information.

171 *The American Musical.* by Vallance, Tom. 192 p. paper illus. New York: A. S. Barnes, 1970.

An encyclopedia of the American film musical offering more than 500 entries. The major number are film personalities and artisans, for each of whom there is a capsule career description followed by the subject's major films. An index to 1750 musical films mentioned throughout the book is given. A few subject topics are also treated—band leaders, ballet in the musical, composers on the screen, etc. Although it is an interesting and well-produced reference work, the text accompanying each entry is flat and uninspired and many of the black and white stills cry out for color. Some of the entries cannot be found in other popular references.

172 *American Newsfilm 1914-1919, The Underexposed War.* by Mould, David

H. 320 p. New York: Garland, 1982.
A title in the *Dissertations on Film* series.

173 *The American Newsreel, 1911-1967.* by Fielding, Raymond. 392 p. illus. Norman, Okla.: University of Oklahoma Press, 1972.

Buried in the bibliography of this book is the information that Fielding wrote his Ph.D. thesis in 1961 on "A History of the American Motion Picture Newsreel," and in 1956 he wrote a Master's thesis on "The March of Time, 1935-42." Probably both studies were blended to form this volume, a detailed study of the rise and decline of the American newsreel.

Some interesting statements made by the author give an idea of the book's coverage. For example, many of the early newsreels used false restagings of events; newsreels did not deliver the news; newsreels were more entertainment than education or information; newsreels affected film booking to a large extent during the block-booking era; THE MARCH OF TIME, which was more a documentary than a newsreel, indicated some of the potential value of the form; newsreels failed because of a domination by newspapermen rather than filmmakers, and because of an inability or refusal to compete with television and newspapers.

These arguments and many more are woven into the factual history that Fielding has written from so much data. The notes, bibliography and index take up about 20 percent of the book. Some pictures are included but they are often too small and most are poorly reproduced.

As a detailed scholarly history of an extinct film form, this volume is impressive. The text is readable, and the author is not afraid to use gossip, emotion, opinion, and affection in telling his story. Recommended.

174 *The American Nightmare: Essays On The Horror Film.* by Britton, Andrew; and Lippe, Richard; and Williams, Tony; and Wood, Robin. 100 p. paper illus. Ottawa, Ontario: Canadian Film Institute, 1979.

This anthology on the American horror film consists of twelve essays, some of which have appeared earlier in other publications. They treat specific films—THE EXORCIST (1973), JAWS (1975), SISTERS (1973), FULL CIRCLE (1977), DEMON (1977), MARTIN (1977), and others—along with critical evaluations of directors who specialize in the horror genre—

Larry Cohen, George Romero, John Carpenter, et al. The volume is illustrated and indexed.

The common theme of the American horror film is well served by this volume. Written from several different critical perspectives, the articles offer a depth of analysis seldom encountered in genre examinations. Recommended.

175 *American Picture Palaces: The Architecture of Fantasy.* by Naylor, David. 210 p. illus. New York: Van Nostrand Reinhold, 1981.

An authoritative survey and history of movie palaces is offered in this handsome, oversized volume, architects, design, demolition, bastarization, conversions, etc are discussed. Naylor emphasizes the role of the movie theatre in creating glamor and excitement.

176 *American Politics: Sources of Print and Nonprint Materials.* edited by Stein, Susan R. 250 p. New York: Neal-Schuman, 1979.

This reference contains selected sources for films on American politics.

177 *American Screenwriters—One and Two.* edited by Morsberger, Robert; and Thompson, Tracy. 2 volumes Detroit, Mich.: Gale.

178 *American Silent Film.* by Everson, William K. 387 p. illus. New York: Oxford University Press, 1978.

This history is an example of William K. Everson's ability to make the people, events, and films of the silent era into a topic of interest and even fascination. His talent is a blend of scholarship, writing ability, enthusiasm, and affection. These qualities permeate the pages of this remarkable book.

In chronological fashion, he traces the development of the American film industry from its beginnings in the late 19th century to the introduction of sound films in the late nineteen twenties. Using the most recent research and film discoveries, he gives attention to film aesthetics, D. W. Griffith, subtitles, the female stars, genres, European influences, etc. Concluding sections include an essay on silent film scholarship and a chronology of highlights from the silent period. The book is indexed.

Adding to the quality of the book are the many carefully reproduced illustrations. They are presented with a black framing that simulates the silent screen image most effectively.

If there is a "star system" in film literature, then Everson is one of its leading examples. His books are eagerly awaited and, once in hand, read with enthusiasm and satisfaction. The present volume is no exception. A wide audience will read it, use it and enjoy it for many years to come. Highly recommended.

179 *American Standard Nomenclature for Motion Picture Film Used in Studios and Processing Labs.* compiled by American National Standards Institute. paper New York: American National Standards Institute, 1971.

This publication has the identification number ANSI PH 22.56-1971.

180 *The American Theatre and The Motion Picture in America.* by Anderson, John; and Fulop-Miller, Rene. illus. New York: Dial Press, 1938.

An out-of-print volume with the film portion (by Fulop-Miller) the smaller. Many illustrations, some in color.

181 *American Theatres of Today.* by Sexton, Randolph W.; and Betts, B. F. 175 p. illus. New York: Architectural Book Pub. Co., 1927.

Contains architectural drawings and sketches of motion picture theatres of the period. A second volume was published in 1930.

182 *American Theatrical Arts: A Guide to Manuscripts and Special Collections in the U.S. and Canada.* by Young, William C. 168 p. Chicago: American Library Association, 1971.

A survey of 138 theatrical arts collections, this guide is also useful for locating film items. The book lists the collections alphabetically by state, and then by the symbol used in the National Union Catalog. The second portion lists subjects and personalities covered by the various collections. A good reference tool.

183 *American Visions: The Films of Chaplin, Ford, Capra and Welles, 1936-1941.* by Maland, Charles J. 459 p. New York: Arno, 1977.

The films made between 1936 and 1941 by Charles

Chaplin, John Ford, Frank Capra, and Orson Welles are examined to show the relationship between a director and the national environment. This is a reprint of the author's doctoral dissertation.

184 *The American West on Film: Myth and Reality.* by Maynard, Richard A. 144 p. paper illus. Rochelle Park, N.J.: Hayden, 1974.

This anthology has as its goal an exploration of the American West legend, the films made about it, and the implications of both. After some factual material about the real West, the first appearances of the Western myth in literary works are noted. In the longest section there are materials on the myth as perpetuated by the motion picture. Here we find essays, script excerpts, promotional suggestions, discussion questions, and even Gene Autry's "Ten Commandments of the Cowboy." A final section discusses the emergence of the cowboy anti-hero in the post-sixties westerns—e.g., THE WILD BUNCH (1969) and DOC (1971). An excerpt from Arthur Kopit's stage play, "Indians," is also included.

Contributors include Pauline Kael, Robert Warshow, Peter Bogdanovich, and William Everson, among others. A filmography and distributor list are appended. A few illustrations appear in the latter pages. The selection and quality of the articles is to be appreciated, as is their arrangement into a provocative study. Not only is the volume useful for analyzing a specific film genre, but it also has broader implications for studies of the effects of mass media on American society. Recommended.

185 *The Americans.* by Frost, David. 250 p. New York: Stein & Day, 1970.

A collection of transcripts of David Frost's television programs. It is noted here since it contains interviews with Orson Welles, Jon Voight, Raquel Welch, Peter Fonda and Dennis Hopper.

186 AMERICATHON-1998. by Israel, Neil; and Mislove, Michael; and Johnson, Monica. unpaginated paper illus. Los Angeles: Fotonovel, 1979.

This *Fotonovel* (see series entry) contains 350 stills, some original film dialogue, song lyrics, and connecting narrative from the 1979 film, AMERICATHON-1998.

187 *Amphoto Books (A Series).* paper illus. New York: Amphoto, 1965 to 1973.

Amphoto is a publishing house which specializes in books on various aspects of photography, including cinematography.

Some titles are: *Better 8mm Home Movie Guide* (Murray Duitz); *Better Electric Eye Movies* (Myron Matzkin); *Better Super 8 Movie Making* (Myron Matzkin); *Camera Techniques for the Color Movie Maker* (Dick Ham); *Electric Eye Movie Manual* (Ira B. Current); *Family Movie Fun for All* (Myron Matzkin); *How to Animate Cut-Outs* (C. H. Barton); *How to Choose Music* (F. Rawlings); *How to Direct Your Own Home Movies* (Tony Rose); *How to Do Sound Films* (D. M. Neale); *How to Edit Your Own Home Movies* (H. Baddeley); *How to Film* (G. Wain); *How to Make 8mm Movies* (N. Bau); *How to Title Your Own Home Movies* (L. F. Minter); *Lens Techniques for Color Movie Magic* (Glen H. Turner); *Making Movies* (Carlton Wallace); *Movie and Videotape Special Effects* (Emil Brodbeck); *Photographer's Guide to Movie Making* (Edwin Gilmout); *Photographic Make-up for Still and Movie* (Vincent J. R. Kehoe); *Scenarios, Scenarios, Scenarios* (Donald Horn); *Sound for Your Color Movies* (G. W. Cushman); *Titling Your Color Movies* (James W. Moore).

The above represent a sampling of titles. They are included here since they deal with cinematography, but also because some of the titles offer inexpensive alternatives for certain areas of film information.

188 *An Analysis of* A DIARY FOR TIMOTHY. by Cameron, Evan. 68 p. paper Bridgewater, Mass.: The Experiment Press, 1967.

Directed by Humphrey Jennings and narrated by Michael Redgrave, A DIARY FOR TIMOTHY (1945) was a documentary film about the last days of World War II in Great Britain. Its subject was the future as it related to several men and a baby.

189 *An Analysis of Motion Pictures About War Released By The American Film Industry, 1939-1970.* by Shain, Russell Earl. 448 p. illus. New York: Arno Press, 1976.

Written in 1971 at the University of Illinois at Urbana-Champaign, this work is an examination of the use of war as the subject matter of films by the motion picture industry over a thirty year period. The author's analysis of the delicate role that the war movie has played in American society represents a different approach to the study of the motion picture industry's societal responsibilities in relation to nationalistic concerns. This title is included in the *Dissertations on Film* series.

190   *Anarchist Cinema.* by Lovell, Alan. 40 p. paper illus. London: Peace News, 1967.

Contains articles on three directors: Luis Bunuel, Georges Franju and Jean Vigo.

191   *Anatomy of a Motion Picture.* by Griffith, Richard. 119 p. illus. New York: St. Martin's Press, 1959.

As an exposition of all the facets of making the 1959 film, THE ANATOMY OF A MURDER, this volume is outstanding. It is a beautiful combination of candid photographs taken on actual location in Ishpeming, Michigan, by Gjon Mili and Al St. Hilaire and an illuminating, knowledgeable text by Richard Griffith. After a short introduction by Robert Traver, author of the novel upon which the film was based, the various film elements such as sound, music, photography, and publicity are considered. An index might have helped but this is a minor omission. The book is successful on all other counts.

192   *The Anatomy of Cinematic Humor.* by Jordan, Thomas H. 164 p. New York: Revisionist Press, 1975.

In the first section of this critical analysis, the author suggests several theories of comedy and notes some selected forms of humor. This introduces the second part of the book, a discussion of humor and the movies, wherein he cites many specific examples of comedy films, explaining at length the reason for their success or failure. The concluding chapter is an appreciation of the Marx Brothers who, the author states, embodied all the various forms of comedy in their films.

Footnotes, an index of film titles, and a general index conclude the volume. The book uses typewritten pages that have been photo-offset. This presentation should not deter readers from a readable, well-reasoned analysis of cinematic humor. Recommended.

193   *The Anatomy of Cinematic Humor— with an Analytic Essay on the Marx Brothers.* by Jordan, Thomas H. 164 p. illus. New York: Revisionist, 1975.

194   *Anatomy of Film.* by Dick, Bernard F. 211 p. illus. New York: St. Martin's Press, 1978.

In an effort to make a presentation of film aesthetics which is instructional as well as entertaining, the author uses examples of many films. Drawing from four groupings (film study war-horses, television

standards, films with published scripts, and recent critical/popular successes), he covers such topics as time, sound, color, lighting, shot, scene, sequence, cut, transition, editing, literary devices, film subtext, total film, film authorship and film criticism. Antonioni's THE PASSENGER (1975) receives detailed attention as an example of total film, while the section on film authorship contains an interview with Billy Wilder. The book is illustrated and indexed.

This pleasing introduction to film aesthetics has many virtues—an interesting, nontechnical text, many well-selected film examples, a structured comprehensive coverage of a wide subject area, and most important, an affection and respect for film that is apparent throughout. A fine film study text which will please a wide general audience. Recommended.

195   *Anatomy of Motion Picture Art.* by Eliott, Eric. 151 p. illus. Terriet, Switzerland: Pool, 1928.

An early examination of technique and aesthetics. The influence of the avant-garde filmmakers of the twenties is evident in the presentation. Attention is given to pictorial composition, camera technique, titling, close-ups, motion, continuity, etc. The contribution of D. W. Griffith to the art of the film is noted throughout.

196   *Anatomy of the Film.* by Wollenberg, H. H. 104 p. illus. London: Marsland, 1947.

A collection of several lectures made into a primer in film appreciation.

197   *Anatomy of the Movies.* by Pirie, David. 320 p. illus. New York: Macmillan, 1981.

198   *The Anatomy of the Movies.* by Prats, A. J. 192 p. illus. Lexington, Ky.: University Press of Kentucky, 1981.

199   *The Ancient World in the Cinema.* by Solomon, Jon. 210 p. illus. New York: A. S. Barnes, 1978.

How pleasing it is to find a film book written by a scholar from a discipline such as Greek and Classical Languages and Literature. Using his impressive background, Jon Solomon has assigned a selected group of about 400 films to various ancient historical periods or civilizations—Greek, Roman, biblical, Babylonian, Egyptian, et al. He discusses their validity in dress, manner, and setting based on the artifacts and historical writings available for comparison. Critical comment about the films is also given. He concludes that intensive research is partly responsible for the more successful films. Accompanying the text are film stills and illustrations of artifacts. Most impressive is a series of chronological charts which place the films in the time period they represent. The volume is indexed.

Solomon's treatment is both serious and fascinating, offering a blend of scholarship and pop culture that is rare in film books. Recommended.

200 *And The Envelope Please.* by Altman, Richard. 160 p. illus. New York: Lippincott, 1978.

Some 25 quizzes formulated around the Academy Awards are offered in this book which is appropriately subtitled, "A Quiz Book About the Academy Awards." Every quiz has a specific theme—a category, a personality, a year, etc. There are 20 questions in each, with certain questions having several parts so that, all-in-all, several thousand individual queries are made.

The questions are well formulated with generous memory-prodding hints sprinkled throughout. Answers are provided in the final pages. Illustrations consist mostly of awards being presented/accepted.

The volume is a pleasant recreation that will serve to broaden and sharpen the reader's knowledge of the Academy Awards. Acceptable.

201 *Andre Malraux's* ESPOIR: The Propaganda/Art Film and the Spanish Civil War. by Michalczyk, John J. 185 p. illus. University, Miss.: Romance Monographs, 1977.

A study of the 1945 film, which was begun in 1938 and completed when Franco's troops entered Barcelona in 1939. Little of Malraux's novel was used; instead there are mostly scenes of air raids, escapes, pilot comradery, and street fighting. All roles were played by non-actors. This volume, which resembles a carelessly written dissertation, is one of the few English language sources that treats Andre Malraux and his film.

202 *Andre Previn.* by Greenfield, Edward. 96 p. illus. New York: Drake, 1973.

A title in the *Record Masters* series, this biographical appreciation of Andre Previn gives some attention to his film work. Most of the volume is concerned with his later activities as classical composer and conductor. The text is quite detailed and manages to catch some of the many facets that make up this

talented, active musician. A discography notes his contributions to various film scores along with his recorded jazz and classical performances. Many excellent illustrations help to make this volume a most satisfying excursion into musical biography. Recommended.

203 *Andrzej Wajda: Polish Cinema.* edited by MacArthur, Colin. 60 p. paper illus. London: British Film Institute, 1970.

This anthology is an appreciation of the Polish filmmaker, Andrzej Wajda.

204 *Andy Warhol.* by Coplans, John. 160 p. illus. Greenwich, Conn.: New York Graphic Society, 1970.

A summary of Warhol's films and art, made up of three essays. The film section was written by Jonas Mekas, who offers an evaluation of Warhol's work that is worshipfully fanatic. The many illustrations, some in color, include film stills.

205 *Andy Warhol.* by Crone, Rainer. 331 p. illus. New York: Praeger, 1970.

A portion of this volume is devoted to Warhol's films. A biography, filmography, and bibliography are offered along with many illustrations.

206 *Andy Warhol.* by Gidal, Peter. 160 p. paper illus. New York: Dutton, 1970.

This volume is of interest because of Warhol's films, which constitute a portion of the book's total content. His biography and a consideration of his paintings share the spotlight.

207 *Anglo-American Cataloging Rules.* edited by Gorman, Michael; and Winkler, Paul W. 620 p. illus. Chicago: American Library Association, 1978.

The latest international standards of machine-readable cataloguing and bibliographical methods are contained in these suggestions for recording all print and nonprint materials (including films).

208 *Animals in Motion.* by Muybridge, Eadweard. 416 p. illus. New York: Dover, 1975.

A reference for animators and artists, this volume is also of interest to film historians. More than 4000 highspeed sequence shots show 34 different birds and animals in various motion activities—walking, running, leaping, flying, galloping, pacing. First published in 1887, some of the photos were taken at a speed of 1/2000th of a second. The volume contains an introduction by Lewis Brown.

209 *The Animated Cartoon Film in Belgium.* by Maelstaf, R. 100 p. paper illus. Brussels: Ministry of Foreign Affairs, 1970.

Although cartoon films were being produced in Belgium prior to World War I, no written record or history was kept. This publication attempts to remedy that neglect for the period since that time. A very short section notes the pioneers who were active in the twenties and thirties. The animated cartoon made in Belgium after 1940 is the major concern of the text. Biographical notes on 12 Belgian animators, along with descriptions of their films, are followed by detailed annotations of four full-length cartoons: PINOCCHIO IN SPACE (1964), ASTERIX THE GAUL (1968), ASTERIX AND CLEOPATRA (1969), TINTIN AND THE TEMPLE OF THE SUN (1969). Some film companies, a few film animation training schools, and a list of the Belgian animated films made since 1958 are given next. The closing section is devoted to the technique of the animated film from the idea to the production.

This is very specialized material that will be of moderate interest to most readers.

210 *Animated Cartoons: How They Are Made, Their Origin and Development.* by Lutz, Edwin George. 261 p. illus. New York: Scribner's 1926 (1920).

This account of animated cartoons was originally published in 1920 and includes material on technique, mechanics, after-image, perspective, trick effects, motion in animals, common movements, drawings, humorous effects, etc. Not only is the history of cartoons reviewed, but also some predictions are made for their future in entertainment and education. Numerous illustrations include stills, diagrams and drawings.

211 *The Animated Film.* by Manvell, Roger. 64 p. illus. New York: Hastings House, 1955.

In addition to giving a short history of the animated film, Manvell uses ANIMAL FARM (1955) as a major example to indicate the challenges of this film form. Divided into three major sections, evolution, craft, and future, the book is profusely illustrated and impressively produced. One of the better volumes on

animation.

212 *Animated Film: Concepts, Methods, Uses.* by Madsen, Roy. 235 p. illus. New York: Interland Pub. Co., 1969.

This is a definitive text on animation. All processes, terms, and techniques are covered, in addition to a short history. It has a bibliography, a filmography, a glossary and an index and is beautifully produced with diagrams, pictures, charts, and tables. The text is presented in an arrangement approaching programed material and is always comprehensible. This is a fine reference book that can also serve as a motivation, or a how-to-do-it source. Recommended.

213 *The Animated Film.* by Stephenson, Ralph. 206 p. paper illus. New York: A. S. Barnes, 1973.

This volume is an updating of Stephenson's earlier work, *Animation in the Cinema*, and includes revisions, new material, and several additional topics (e.g., computer animation). After anopening chapter which defines and describes animation, the author traces the history of this film form. Beginning with pre-twenties attempts, he quickly assesses Walt Disney, UPA and others in the United States. Other chapters look at animation films in Canada, Britain, France, Poland, Czechoslovakia, Yugoslavia, Italy, the Balkans, Russia, Germany, Japan and Scandinavia.

A final section on trends in animation concludes the text. A short bibliography is followed by a listing of selected animators along with their films. A detailed index completes the work. All visuals are reproduced in black and white but are still very effective. The earlier book was called an essential volume for all collections and this updated edition has improved on the original. It is a scholarly work that is not only informative but entertaining as well. Highly recommended.

214 *Animated Film Making.* by Kinsey, Anthony. 95 p. paper illus. London: Studio Vista, 1970.

A short volume on the techniques of animation aimed at the amateur filmmaker.

215 *Animated Photography: The ABC of the Cinematograph.* by Hepworth, Cecil M. 128 p. illus. New York: Arno Press, 1970.

An historical document, first published in 1900, that will be of interest primarily to scholars. It might be used with Hepworth's autobiography, *Came the Dawn.*

216 *Animated Pictures.* by Jenkins, Charles Francis. 118 p. illus. New York: Arno Press, 1970.

A reprint of a 1898 historical document which indicates the historical development of chronophotography along with its uses and potentials.

217 *The Animated* RAGGEDY ANN & ANDY. by Canemaker, John. 292 p. illus. Indianapolis: BobbsMerrill, 1977.

Although the title might suggest otherwise, this book is required reading for adults interested in the making of animated films. Using the feature, RAGGEDY ANN & ANDY (1976), as his skeletal core, John Canemaker offers "An Intimate Look at the Art of Animation: Its History, Techniques, and Artists."

Background to the production of the film considers the storyboard process, personality animation and the original source of the material—in this case the books written by Johnny Gruelle. A biographical portrait of Gruelle (1888-1938) is presented. The second section tells how the production was organized and proposed for financing. The director of the film, Richard Williams, is profiled. The third section, which deals with the making of the film, stresses the creative artists involved—Joseph Raposo (music), Tissa David, Art Babbitt, and Emery Hawkins (animators). A final section explains the work of the East and West Coast studios with emphasis again placed on the creative personnel involved. A selected bibliography and an index are included.

All the elements of this volume are first-rate—an impressive production, beautiful color illustrations and a logical, well-arranged text. The result is an entertaining exposition of the complexity and artistry found in animated filmmaking. Highly recommended.

218 *Animating Films without a Camera.* by Bourgeois, Jacques. 48 p. illus. New York: Sterling, 1974.

This is a title in the *Little Crafts* series of over 70 books dealing with creative hobbies and activities. Translated from an original French version, the short volume is surprisingly comprehensive in its treatment of a type of animation created by drawing directly on film. Introductory discussions of animation and film characteristics are followed by an exposition of the materials and techniques required to draw on film. Suggestions for practice projects precede a more complex activity—that of animation by a group of workers. The use of fogged film, scratching, splicing, editing and sound effects is described in final sections. The book contains many photographs, charts, diagrams, and drawings, some of which are in color. An index is provided.

The clearly written text and the splendid illustrations will provide the reader with a stimulus for experimentation in animation. In addition, the content (and its easily comprehensible presentation) is not readily available in most of the advanced technical books. Recommended.

219 *Animation.* by Elsas, Diane; and Laybourne, Kit. 26 p. Washington, D.C.: American Film Institute, 1977.

This collection of information and resources on animation includes organizations, training programs, courses, distributors, equipment, supplies, film festivals, books, and periodicals.

220 *Animation.* by Blair, Preston. 40 p. paper illus. Poster Art Service, 1975.

A how-to-do-it book for students of animation.

221 *Animation: Learn How to Draw Animated Cartoons.* by Blair, Preston. 40 p. paper illus. Laguna Beach, Calif.: Foster, 1949.

This volume, number 26 in the *How to Draw* series, was also published under the title *Advanced Animation.*

222 *Animation Art in the Commercial Film.* by Levitan, Eli L. 128 p. illus. New York: Reinhold, 1960.

Deals with the one-minute animated TV commercial rather than the theatrical cartoon. A General Electric commercial is used as the primary example. The nontechnical explanations, illustrations and glossary make it valuable for vocational guidance work.

223 *The Animation Book.* by Laybourne, Kit. 272 p. paper illus. New York: Crown, 1979.

Kit Laybourne correctly subtitles this book "A Complete Guide to Animated Filmmaking—From Flip-Books to Sound Cartoons." He offers a wide range of approaches to animation, stressing the work of the individual artist rather than the collaborative act. The book, directed at the young, new, adventurous animator is divided into four parts: fundamentals, techniques, tools and resources. It is copiously illustrated with photographs, drawings, sketches, stills, diagrams, and frame enlargements. An index is also provided.

Beautifully designed, the volume offers excellent explanations of various animation techniques in addition to providing inspiration and direction to the aspiring creator. Young adults will respond to Laybourne's sincere admiration and respect for the animator's art. His ability to communicate knowledge, technique and feeling to his reader is unique—especially in books about filmmaking. Highly recommended.

224 *Animation in the Cinema.* by Stephenson, Ralph. 176 p. paper illus. New York: Barnes, 1967.

After defining and describing the animated film, Stephenson points out the differences between animation and live action. Attention is given to the neglected and usually forgotten history of the early pre-1938 cartoon. The work of Disney, his competitors, UPA, and the rise of modern-TV-influenced animators are later topics. Other sections of the book consider the animated film of other nations (Canada, Britain, Poland, Czechoslovakia, Yugoslavia, Italy, USSR, Germany and Japan).

Especially valuable is the filmography which lists the animated films of many of the directors mentioned in the text. This is a scholarly book, but not pedantic, whose illustrations are few but well chosen. Recommended.

225 *see 226*

226 *Animation in 12 Hard Lessons.* by Heath, Bob. 142 p. paper illus. West Islip, N.Y.: Robert P. Heath Productions, 1972.

This oversized 11 inch x 14 inch course in animation is already in its third printing and deservedly so. Known for his short film THE CRITIC (1963), the author has drawn on his long experience as a professional animator in designing this volume. Using over 800 large-sized drawings, diagrams, charts and tables, along with a text that is always comprehensible, the book is aimed for the serious student who is willing to work (hard). As the title states, the approach is that of a programmed correspondence course. Each lesson is presented in a step-by-step exposition and is followed by some questions and assignments. Answers to the lessons are given at the back of the book. Some basic equipment is recommended—a drawing-animation desk, light box,

pegs, punches, cels, etc.—but the list seems modest. A glossary of terms completes the book.

A complex film technique has been simplified by a programmed approach, a well-written, interesting narrative and some fine visuals. As indicated above, the book is designed for individual use, and most aspiring animators will want a copy for personal use. Highly recommended.

227 *The Animation Stand.* by Perisic, Zoran. 168 p. paper illus. New York: Hastings House, 1976.

When a camera is placed on a stand, a number of specialized operations such as animation, titling, copying, optical effects, etc., can be performed. In this volume, one of *The Media Manuals* series, Zoran Perisic explores a wide range of activities possible with the animation stand. He coordinates many diagrams, line drawings, charts, and other visuals with a no-nonsense text that requires a high degree of concentration and effort from the reader. A helpful glossary and a short bibliography are added.

Although the volume is quite comprehensive, it does not require a sequential usage. Portions may be used without reference to all the sections which precede them. A manual that should satisfy both the amateur and the professional filmmaker. Recommended.

228 *Animations of Mortality.* by Gilliam, Terry; and Cowell, Lucinda. 96 p. paper illus. New York: Methuen, 1979.

Gilliam is the animator for several Monty Python films. In this oversized volume, he talks about his work and includes some full-color drawings.

229 *Ann-Margaret: A Dream Come True.* by Peters, Neal; and Smith, David. N.Y.: Delilah, 1981.

230 *Ann Miller: Tops in Taps: An Authorized Pictorial Biography.* by Connor, Jim. 224 p. illus. New York: Watts, 1981.

An instant book that offers nothing new about Ann Miller except a few illustrations. A more appropriate title is *The Films of Ann Miller.*

231 *Anna Neagle Says "There's Always Tomorrow.* by Neagle, Anna. 236 p. illus. London: W. H. Allen, 1974.

Anna Neagle has had a long career in films and on the British stage. From an early appearance as a child dancer in 1917 to her role in the 1974 London production of "No, No, Nanette," she has enjoyed a most active career. Married to producer Herbert Wilcox, she has been associated with films for more than three decades. She has appeared in over 35 films, usually as the star or leading lady, and has herself produced three films. At the height of her film popularity she appeared in several Hollywood movies—IRENE (1942), NO, NO, NANETTE (1940), SUNNY (1941) and FOREVER AND A DAY (1943).

In this rather sterile account of a long career, Dame Neagle writes with the refinement and dignity befitting her title. She is kind, forgiving, understanding and tolerant in recalling people and incidents. Several sections of illustrations indicate the richness of her roles and experiences, which she understates or de-emphasizes throughout. A film list (without dates!), a stage appearance list (with dates), a list of awards and an index complete the work. The author has been selective, careful and ladylike in this memoir. As a result, the book will appeal mostly to those who recall with nostalgic affection the charming film actress of the thirties and forties. Acceptable. See also *Dames of the Theatre, It's Been Fun,* and *Twenty-Five Thousand Sunsets.*

232   *Annals of the American Academy of Political and Social Science.* edited by King, Clyde L.; and Tichenor, Frank A; and Watkins, Gordon S. 236 p. New York: Arno Press, 1970.

Contains: 1) *The Motion Picture in Its Economic and Social Aspects,* edited by Clyde L. King and Frank A. Tichenor (1926) and 2) *The Motion Picture Industry,* edited by Gordon S. Watkins (1947).

233   ANNE OF THE THOUSAND DAYS. 24 p. paper illus. Hollywood: Universal Studios, 1970.

This small publication resembles a souvenir booklet but is was never sold at theatres. It was probably prepared for critics, reviewers, and publicists. The background of the film is given along with two letters—one written by Henry to Anne, and the second by Anne to Henry. Individual pages are devoted to Richard Burton, Genevieve Bujold, producer Hal Wallis and director Charles Jarrott. Supporting cast and technical credits are included.

234   *Annotated Bibliography of Films in Automation, Data Processing, and Computer Science.* by Solomon, Martin B., Jr.; and Lovan, Nora G. 38 p. paper Lexington, Ky.: University of Kentucky Press, 1967.

This short older paperback is noted here because of the difficulty in finding suitable films on automation, data processing, and computer science and because of its impressive arrangement of film information. How effective the book is can only be determined by teachers or specialists using it in the three areas.

An alphabetical list of the film titles is followed by a subject index to the films. In the next section each entry lists the film code, the year of production, the suggested audiences, and the film title. An annotation follows, which is mostly descriptive rather than critical or evaluative.

Film data—time, sound/silent, color/black and white, and film gauge-size—are listed, and the entry concludes with purchasing or rental information, along with the name of the organization distributing the film. A detailed directory of these distributors appears at the end of the book.

The need for frequent revision of such filmographies is dictated by changes in certain data (price, rental, distributorship) and the production of many new films in these three areas. A specialized reference that should still be regarded as a model for other filmographies.

235   *The Annotated Dracula.* by Stoker, Bram; and Wold, Leonard. 362 p. paper illus. New York: Crown Publishers, 1975.

More than you ever wanted to know about *Dracula* is contained in this carefully designed version of the Bram Stoker story. Thoroughly annotated, illustrated, analyzed and visualized, the story is presented as an authentic reproduction of the first edition. Visuals, maps, calendars, and charts are abundantly supplied.

It is noted here since the character of Count Dracula is such a staple of horror films; a short selected filmography is included. A long and comprehensive bibliography gives evidence of the public's enduring interest in vampirism and the Count. For all who make or enjoy vampire movies.

236   *The Annotated Frankenstein.* by Shelley, Mary. 356 p. paper illus. New York: Crown, 1977.

Some reference is made to the Frankenstein films. Notes are by Leonard Wolf.

237   *Annual Index to Motion Picture Credits 1978.* edited by Ramsey, Verna. 443 p. paper Westport, Conn.: Greenwood Press, 1979.

The Academy of Motion Picture Arts and Sciences has long gathered film credits and other industry information primarily for distribution to the motion picture community. Because of the demand by a wider audience, including buffs, writers, critics, and students, the Academy's publishing activities have recently expanded.

This particular volume offers complete film entries for the year 1978. Included is the title, production company, releasing company, completion date, running time, MPAA rating, producer, director, art director, cinematographer, film editor, costume designer, sound, music, writers, and cast.

In addition to the complete entry for each film, there are indexes for each of the ten major film crafts, another by releasing company and finally by individual name with a reference to craft and film. The information is similar to that contained in *Screen Achievement Record Bulletin*.

238   *Anthony Asquith.* by Noble, Peter. 44 p. paper illus. London: British Film Institute, 1951.

The early career of the British film director is reviewed in this short volume, which is number 5 in the *New Index* series. Asquith's first films appeared in the late twenties and were noticed because of their vitality and use of new techniques; later films substituted a slower pace and some glossiness for the earlier experimentation. Although Asquith was still active in the sixties (THE YELLOW ROLLS ROYCE, 1965), this volume deals with the first two decades of his career.

239   *Anthony Mann.* by Basinger, Jeanine. 230 p. illus. Boston: Twayne, 1979.

In addition to the helpful elements usually found in the *Twayne Theatrical Arts* series (chronology, notes, references, bibliography, filmography, illustrations and index), this volume consists of six chapters dealing with career, early films noir films, western films, epic films, and two films, MEN IN WAR (1957) and GOD'S LITTLE ACRE (1958), which are discussed at length.

The author has a strong affection and respect for her subject. Her long study, research and teaching of Mann's films result in a superior director study.

Although Mann's 26 years as a director result in a filmography that is relatively rich, only selected examples are treated in depth here. Basinger sees most of Mann's films as a journey taken by a hero which results in a new understanding of himself. She is able to make the reader share her appreciation of this neglected filmmaker.

240   *Anthropology-Reality-Cinema: The Films of Jean Rouch.* edited by Eaton, Mick. New York: Zoetrope, 1979.

Rouch is a French film director who has recorded his ethnological work on film. Later he made experimental films which dealt with the theme of reality vs. fiction.

241   *Antitrust in the Motion Picture Industry: Economic and Legal Analysis.* by Conant, Michael. 240 p. Berkeley: University of California Press, 1961.

A summary and analysis of the numerous antitrust cases involving the motion picture industry. Attention is given to conditions that caused the suits. Very specialized and of limited interest to most general readers, the work includes a list of cases, a bibliography, and an index.

242   *Antonioni.* by Cameron, Ian; and Wood, Robin. 144 p. paper illus. New York: Praeger, 1969.

This analysis of Antonioni's films is divided into two sections. The first, written by Cameron, treats the black and white films while Wood comments on the color films. BLOW-UP (1967) is included but ZABRISKIE POINT (1970) is not. Each of the chapters is as arresting as the films themselves, and may serve as an admirable guide for a new perspective with which to re-view the films. There are many fine illustrations and a good filmography. This small, nicely designed volume treats in a succinct and clear manner material that other sources labor over in endless chatter and conjecture.

243   *Antonioni.* by Strick, Philip. 58 p. paper illus. London: Motion Publications, 1965.

A short monograph on Antonioni's films.

244   *Antonioni, Bergman, Resnais.* by Cowie, Peter. 160 p. paper illus. New York: A. S. Barnes, 1963.

A collection of three early monographs by Cowie. Each has an introduction followed by an analysis of the director's films. Illustrations are fine and some references are given.

245 *Any Old Lion.* by Jay, John Mark. 138 p. illus. London: Leslie Frewin, 1966.

An account of the filming of BORN FREE (1966) in Africa.

246 *Anything for a Quiet Life; The Autobiography of Jack Hawkins.* by Hawkins, Jack. 180 p. illus. Briarcliff Manor, N.Y.: Stein & Day, 1974.

This autobiography reflects the professional image of Jack Hawkins—strong, competent restrained, and a bit disappointing after an initial acquaintance. Hawkins' personal life and career were not marked by any startling incidents until the last few years of his life. Beginning struggles, marriage and divorce from Jessica Tandy, early success on stage, a second marriage, and a long, impressive career in films are related in a rather bland fashion. The drama in his life came with the loss of his voice via cancer of the throat and a subsequent laryngectomy. He is the second noted actor to write about this experience—William Gargan told of a similar misfortune in *Why Me?*

Hawkins admits that films accounted for his celebrity but, like so many English actors, evidences much more affection and respect for the stage. A few of his films are given attention. BEN HUR, a major one, is not mentioned. No filmography or listing of his stage roles is provided. A short index is included and there is a postscript by his wife in which she describes his last few months. "Quiet" seems to describe the content and tone of this volume adequately.

247 THE APARTMENT and THE FORTUNE COOKIE: Two Screen Plays. by Wilder, Billy; and Diamond, I. A. L. 191 p. illus. New York: Praeger, 1971.

Script of the 1960 film directed by Billy Wilder. Contains cast credits and an introduction.

248 *Ape: Monster of the Movies.* by Annan, David. 95 p. illus. New York: Bounty, 1975.

The use of the ape in motion pictures has provided a continuing fascination for audiences for almost 80 years. This volume explores that use by examining KING KONG (1933) in great detail and giving some lesser attention to other selected films. Many illustrations accompany the historical overview which concludes with the PLANET OF THE APES film series. Some of the material presented is not suitable for youngsters but mature readers will enjoy the provocative analysis offered.

249 *Apes in Fact and Fiction.* by Berger, Gilda. 86 p. illus. New York: Franklin Watts, 1980.

Written for a juvenile audience, this volume from the *Fact and Fiction* series treats real and fictional apes in an attempt to separate truth from myth. The behavior and physical characteristics of apes are described in the wild, in the laboratory, in fiction and in film. A complete chapter is devoted to KING KONG (1933). Some other Kong movies which followed, along with selected examples of other film apes, are discussed in a final chapter.

Although the book offers a partial, surface treatment of its subject, the selection of material offered is quite good. The illustrations are well produced and the text offers information and stories that will fascinate young readers.

250 *An Appalling Talent: Ken Russell.* by Baxter, John. 240 p. illus. London: Michael Joseph, 1973.

An interesting account of Russell's career and films is given along with many anecdotes about his working relationships with Oliver Reed, Alan Bates, Glenda Jackson, Vanessa Redgrave, etc. Illustrations are good and the book is indexed.

251 *An Approach to Film Study: A Selected Booklist.* by Bowles, Stephen E. 108 p. New York: Revisionist Press, 1974.

Bowles is best known as the author of the impressive 2-volume *Index to Critical Film Reviews*.

252 *The Apu Trilogy.* by Wood, Robin. 96 p. paper illus. New York: Praeger, 1971.

Study of Satyajit Ray's famous films: PATHER PANCHALI; THE UNVANQUISHED, APARAJITO (1957), and THE WORLD OF APU (1959).

253 *The Apu Trilogy.* by Wood, Robin. 96 p. illus. New York: Praeger, 1971.

As the title indicates, this short book concentrates exclusively on the films which form Satyajit Ray's Apu trilogy: PATHER PANCHALI (1954), APARAJITO (1956), and THE WORLD OF APU (1959), each of which is given a separate chapter, following an introductory section which explores the overall qualities of the trilogy. The closing pages contain picture credits, a list of Ray's other films, and a selected bibliography. There are fewer illustrations than usual in this Praeger volume and their quality is no better than average. The book is not indexed. The acceptance or success of this volume will depend upon the reader's enthusiasm for Ray's work, and that appears to be minimal in America. Although Robin Wood tries to create admiration for Ray and his work, his task is somewhat akin to selling *Little Women* to readers of *The Godfather*.

254 *Arab Cinema and Culture.* 188 p. paper illus. Beirut: Arab Film and TV Centre, 1965.

Report of a conference held in cooperation with UNESCO.

255 *Archeology of the Cinema.* by Ceram, C.W. 264 p. illus. New York: Harcourt, Brace, 1965.

A history of the cinema prior to 1897. By the use of a scholarly, well-researched narrative complemented by almost 300 illustrations, the author makes a possibly dull subject come to life. The edition examined was produced in Germany and mention should be made of its high quality, distinct typography and the sharpness of its illustrations. It is excellent on all counts. Bibliography and general index.

256 *The Architectural Digest Book of Celebrity Homes.* edited by Rense, Paige. 256 p. illus. Los Angeles: Knapp Press, 1978.

Thirty heavily illustrated essay-interviews taken from the pages of *Architectural Digest* show us the homes of selected celebrities. Film personalities include Robert Redford, Merle Oberon, Joan Crawford, Delores Del Rio, Jean Arthur, Polly Bergen and Woody Allen. More than 250 full-color photographs are included.

257 *Are They Safe at the Cinema?* by Hills, Janet. 24 p. paper illus. London: British Film Institute, 1954.

A reply to the critics of the cinema who are concerned with its effect on children. Moral and religious aspects are considered.

258 *Are We Movie-Made?* by Moley, Raymond. 64 p. New York: Macy- Masius, 1938.

This is a companion volume to Adler's *Art and Prudence* and the Payne Fund Studies. It deals with the effect of movies on the minds of young people. Moley's conclusions are sound and much easier to take than Adler's.

259 *Are You Anybody? Conversations with Wives of Celebrities.* by Funt, Marilyn. 339 p. illus. New York: Dial Press, 1979.

A collection of 20 interviews with wives of celebrities which emphasizes the identity crisis they almost all have. The demands of celebrity are mentioned frequently as are their own careers. Most of the subjects are frank, articulate and seemingly honest in their answers. It is ironic that in the time since the book was published an appreciable number have been separated or divorced.

260 *Are You Now or Have You Ever Been.* by Bentley, Eric. 160 p. paper illus. New York: Harper and Row, 1972.

Bentley once again (see *Thirty Years of Treason*) uses the investigations of the House Un-American Activities Committee (HUAC) from 1947-1958 as a basis for these dialogues. Some 18 witnesses are represented, with varying space accorded to each. Representing only a tiny fraction of all the testimony taken during the hearings, this sample has been selected, abridged, edited, and arranged by Bentley for dramatic effect. Film names appearing in this collage are Sam G. Wood, Edward Dmytryk, Ring Lardner, Jr., Larry Parks, Sterling Hayden, Jose Ferrer, Marc Lawrence and Lionel Stander. Many full-page portraits of the witnesses taken at the hearings are used effectively throughout.

The shameful period of the HUAC hearings is recreated here in the actual words of the participants and a strong statement ensues. Whether the fact that the dialogue is selected will lessen the impact on the reader is an individual question. Acceptable.

261 ARIZONA: *The Winning of a Mighty Empire Inspires the Making of a Great Picture.* 36 p. illus. Hollywood: Columbia Pictures, 1940.

This impressive, oversized book has much to recommend it. The black and white illustrations, large in size and reproduced with great clarity, are outstanding. Twelve pages are devoted to a portion of the script which is illustrated directly. Some attention is paid to Director Wesley Ruggles, the writers, the cast, and other studio personnel. Statistics about the film are also offered. This book was not sold at theatres but was probably issued as a studio campaign book or souvenir.

262 *Arlene Francis, A Memoir.* by Francis, Arlene; and Rome, Florence. illus. New York: Simon and Schuster,

1978.

Arlene Francis is recognized as a television personality, although she has appeared intermittently in films since MURDERS IN THE RUE MORGUE (1932). Her other films include STAGE DOOR CANTEEN (1943), ALL MY SONS (1948), ONE, TWO, THREE (1961) and THE THRILL OF IT ALL (1963). In this carefully stated memoir Francis faces the sad fact that she is more successful at selling products than acting.

263 *The Armchair Odeon.* by Gifford, Denis. 299 p. paper Hertfordshire, England: Fountain Press, 1974.

An oversized paperback collector's guide to 8mm motion pictures. The 10-minute excerpt reels are emphasized, but feature films are also treated. An index is provided.

264 *The Arnhem Report.* by Johnstone, Iain. 173 p. paper illus. London: Star Books, 1977.

The story of the making of A BRIDGE TOO FAR (1977).

265 *Around Cinemas.* by Agate, James. 284 p. London: Home and Van Thal, 1946.

A two-volume work of Agate's film criticism, comments and articles that appeared in *The Tatler* from 1921 to 1946. Both volumes are indexed by films and players; directors, producers, and authors; and miscellaneous subjects. Film literature that is superior and readable.

266 AROUND THE WORLD IN 80 DAYS. edited by Cohn, Art. 72 p. illus. New York: Random House, 1956.

A program book designed to be sold at showings of the film, this volume also included a foreword by Mike Todd, a profile of Mike Todd, picture statistics, plot, cast, and production credits. The cast included many stars playing cameo roles and short biographies of each are here. Behind-the-scenes personnel get the biography treatment, too. The picture reproduction is poor, and stills lack definition and clarity. The text can be forgotten; it seems a filler here. The book's value is in those biographical sketches.

267 *Art and Animation: The Story of Halas and Batchelor Animation Studio, 1940-1980.* by Manvell, Roger. 128 p. illus. New York: Hastings House, 1980.

A history of the animation company responsible for many short films and a few features. Styles, techniques, finances, personnel, films etc. are discussed.

268 *Art and Design in the British Film.* by Carrick, Edward. 133 p. illus. London: Dobson, 1948.

A pictorial directory of British art directors and their work. It includes an introduction by Roger Manvell along with many beautiful black-and-white sketches and drawings. The book is essential reading for filmmakers and can also provide an aesthetically pleasing experience for the casual browser.

269 *Art and Prudence: A Study in Practical Philosophy.* by Adler, Mortimer. 700 p. New York: Longmans, Green & Co., 1937.

A partial rebuttal and criticism of the Payne Fund Studies, this volume is also a study of the motion picture as a moral problem. Adler leans heavily on Aristotle's views of the relationship of art and morals. Scholarly, substantial, philosophical, and pedantic.

270 *Art and Visual Perception.* by Arnheim, Rudolf. 485 p. illus. Berkeley, Calif.: University of California Press, 1969.

Denotes what takes place when an individual either creates or experiences a work of art. Nontechnical and readable, with many illustrations. Reprint of 1954 book.

271 *Art in Cinema: A Symposium on the Avant-Garde Film.* edited by Stauffacher, Frank. 104 p. illus. New York: Arno Press, 1947-1968.

In 1946 the San Francisco Museum of Art showed a series of film programs dealing with avant-garde art films. This volume was produced concurrently to complement the showings. Included are articles by such filmmakers as Hans Richter, Man Ray, Luis Bunuel, Erich Pommer and others. The latter section consists of program notes on the films shown in the first series. Many of these are taken from Iris Barry's *Film Notes.* A section on the music to accompany the silent films is included.

Nicely produced, the book deals with a very specialized small segment of film history. The underground film of today, which certainly is the offspring of the early avant-garde films, makes the subject somewhat dated. Nevertheless, the experimental art films considered herein are pre-1946 classics and most worthy of attention. Bibliography and index.

272   *Art in Movement: New Directions in Animation.* by Halas, John; and Manvell, Roger. 192 p. illus. New York: Hastings House, 1970.

The two major sections in this excellent book are outstanding. The first, dealing with new techniques in animation and visual effects, covers film stock, stop-motion camera, combined media, split screen, freeze frame, etc. The second surveys the animated film in the contemporary international scene. The book is generous in providing many excellent stills to accompany the informative and understandable text. An index is provided. Written and produced with care and expertise, this book is recommended.

273   *Art Index.* paper New York: H. W. Wilson, 1929.

This quarterly indexes more than 100 periodicals which are devoted to art, sculpture, painting, ceramics, etc. Cumulated indexes cover 2- or 3-year periods. Included in this index are several film periodicals.

274   *The Art of Alfred Hitchcock.* by Spoto, Donald. 525 p. illus. New York: Hopkinson and Blake, 1976.

Donald Spoto prepared himself well to write this critical study of Alfred Hitchcock's feature films. Not only did he view all but one—THE MOUNTAIN EAGLE (1926)—of the 53 features, but many were seen several times. Research, interviews and a visit to the FAMILY PLOT (1976) set provided the remaining material for the book.

In careful detail the author examines each film, noting plots, acting, technique, recurring themes, symbols, metaphors, etc. Quite often the subjective criticism and argument offered is strongly supported by the author's use of psychological or sociological concepts. His interpretations are consistently persuasive and convincing.

In addition to some well-selected illustrations, the volume contains a series of storyboards for two sequences in FAMILY PLOT. A lengthy index and a good filmography are also included. The bibliography notes only five books that the author used most frequently.

Here is an analytical study of a fascinating group of films, all characterized by the style, artistry, and intelligence of a legendary director. The book is certain to please a wide audience, with its most avid readers to be found among students and film enthusiasts. It should be required reading before viewing any Hitchcock film. Highly recommended.

275   *The Art of Animation.* by Walt Disney Studios. 24 p. paper illus. New York: American Federation of Arts, 1958.

A short explanation of the process of making animated motion pictures using SLEEPING BEAUTY (1959) as an example.

276   *The Art of Cinema: Selected Essays.* New York: Arno, 1972.

This original compilation consists of several well-known articles on film. Included are: 1) "The Ambivalence of Realism" by George Amberg; 2) "An Anagram of Ideas on Art, Form and Film" by Maya Deren; 3) "Cinematography: The Creative Use of Reality" by Maya Deren; 4) "Psychology of Film Experience" by Hugo Mauerhofer; 5) "Towards a Film Aesthetic" by Herbert Read; 6) "The Witness Point: Definitions of Film Art" by Vernon Young. These essays direct attention to the acceptance of film as an art form. A foreward by George Amberg is included.

277   *The Art of Cineplastics.* by Faure, Elie. 63 p. illus. Boston: Four Seas Co., 1923.

Translated from the French, this study originally appeared in the pages of *The Freeman*; only 1000 copies of the original book edition were printed. Its most recent reprinting is by Arno Press and appears in a book entitled, *Screen Monographs Number One.* With comments on silent films from France and Italy added to a long section on "The Art of Charlie Chaplin," this essay compares film to the plastic arts and concludes that it is a synthesis of all of them—cineplastic. Faure was one of the first to recognize the possibilities and potentials of film, and his essay is one of the earliest statements on film aesthetics.

278   *The Art of Interviewing for Television, Radio, and Film.* by Broughton, Irv. 266 p. illus. Blue Ridge Summit, Pa.: TAB, 1981.

This volume deals with the planning, preparation and conducting of interviews. It offers suggestions on questioning, action and reaction, legal aspects, technical limitations, etc. Some transcripts of actual interviews are included.

279 *The Art of Make-up for Stage and Screen.* by Holland, Cecil. 102 p. illus. Hollywood, Calif.: Cinematex Pub. Co., 1927.

This volume treats the subject of theatrical make-up as practiced in the twenties.

280 *The Art of Photoplay Making.* by Freeburg, Victor Oscar. 283 p. illus. New York: Arno Press, 1970.

Reprint of an early discussion of film aesthetics based on lectures given at Columbia University in 1915-16. It proposes standards for film that are applicable to any art form.

281 *The Art of Photoplay Writing.* by Barker, Ellen Frye. 100 p. St. Louis, Mo.: Colossus, 1919.

An early how-to-write-it book offering principles, terms, preparation, models, and suggestions.

282 *The Art of Photoplay Writing.* edited by Carr, Catherine. 119 p. New York: Hannis Jordan, 1914.

This early volume on scriptwriting offers advice and guidance from several authors, along with two examples of synopsis and story. General topics include the art of the photoplay, the making of a photoplay, feature films from fiction and plays, photoplay form, the vision scene, behind the scenes in a studio, why photoplays fail, motive in the photoplay, etc.

283 *The Art of* STAR WARS. edited by Titelman, Carol W. 176 p. paper illus. New York: Ballantine, 1979.

The various stages in the production of STAR WARS (1977), from the first rough concepts to Ralph McQuarrie's actual production paintings, are presented here. In addition there are costume sketches, storyboards, posters, and photographs. Also included is the complete script of the film by George Lucas.

284 *The Art of the American Film 1900-1971.* by Higham, Charles. 322 p. illus. New York: Anchor Press, 1973.

In his introduction, Higham announces many things this book will not treat—business, economics, industry, superstars, cult figures, contemporary directors, animated films, documentary films, etc. What he has included is a survey of selected creative figures along with directors who survived the silent to sound changeover. Thus, Griffith, DeMille, Lubitsch, von Stroheim, von Sternberg, Welles, Hitchcock, Wilder, etc., are given individual treatment. Other filmmakers are grouped in chapters such as "Major Figures of the Talkies," "Pictorialists," "New Directors, New Directions," etc.

What Higham has attempted is a concise critical history of the American film. His success is only partial and much of what he offers is familiar—found in many earlier volumes including the following by Higham: *The Celluloid Muse: Hollywood Directors Speak, The Films of Orson Welles, Hollywood Cameramen, Hollywood in the Forties,* and *Hollywood at Sunset.* Illustrations are nicely reproduced but the selection and placement are questionable. In the silent section a still from HUMORESQUE (1946) appears, the same visual from CLEOPATRA (1934) is used twice, and stills from lesser films are plentiful— THE STRANGER'S RETURN (1933), BRIGHT LEAF (1950), THE HELEN MORGAN STORY (1957), A WOMAN'S FACE (1941), RUTHLESS (1948), IN HARM'S WAY (1965), etc. An index is also provided.

The survey provided by Higham is selective and subjective. Although the reader may not agree with the critical appraisals, the subjects never lose appeal or interest. Acceptable.

285 *The Art of the Cinematographer.* by Maltin, Leonard. 144 p. paper illus. New York: Dover, 1978.

This is a reprint of *Behind the Camera: The Cinematographer's Art,* published in 1971. Some revision, a new preface and an enlarged format enhance this version.

286 *The Art of* THE EMPIRE STRIKES BACK. by Bulluck, Vic; and Hoffman, Valerie. 176 p. paper illus. New York: Ballantine, 1980.

A collection of production illustrations, matte paintings, costume sketches, storyboards, stills, etc., from THE EMPIRE STRIKES BACK (1980).

287 *The Art of the Film.* by Lindgren, Ernest. 258 p. illus. New York: Macmillan, 1963.

A revised edition of the 1949 volume. Lindgren, the former director of the British Film Institute, gives a clear, readable survey of film techniques including editing, sound, photography, music, and acting. Using examples from many classic films, the author shows how a film is constructed of these diverse elements. A final portion devoted to film criticism offers the standards of judgment based upon the techniques discussed earlier.

The outstanding quality of this book is the clarity of the author's style; avoiding pretentiousness or intellectualism, he offers a scholarly, enlightening experience. Supplementing the text are a bibliography, a glossary, and many beautifully reproduced stills from films mentioned in the text.

288   *The Art of the Great Hollywood Portrait Photographers, 1925-1940.* by Kobal, John. 292 p. illus. New York: Alfred A. Knopf, 1980.

This handsome collection of 150 studio portraits is accompanied by descriptions of the art of the famous star-photographers—Bull, Willinger, Hurrell, Engstead, etc.

The centerpiece, of course, is their glamor photography, which Kobal likens to an art form. He includes an introductory essay, and adds a list of later, lesser-known photographers. The quality evident in this small sampling of their work is exceptionally high.

289   *The Art of the Motion Picture.* by Benoit-Levy, Jean. 263 p. illus. New York: Coward McCann, 1946.

Translated from the French, this book covers what was relatively new ground in 1946. Discussions of the film in the classroom, the educational film, and other topics are all now dated. While many of the basic tenets of filmmaking are presented with intelligence and clarity, there is too much obsolete information surrounding the basics to make the search rewarding. The book may be of interest to scholars but most others will be impatient.

290   *The Art of the Moving Picture.* by Lindsay, Vachel. 324 p. New York: Liveright, 1970.

This is a reprint of one of the earliest books (1915) to appear on film aesthetics. Written by a poet who was fascinated by and opinionated about the motion picture, the book contains many prophecies which have come true—the auteur theory, film libraries, instructional film, and others. Some of his ideas are most erroneous, but his batting average is quite high. For example, his insistence in 1915 that film is an "Art," his suggestion of this book as a college text for serious study of film, and his division of motion pictures into three large categories; these are valid ideas.

291   *The Art of W. C. Fields.* by Everson, William K. 232 p. illus. Indianapolis: Bobbs-Merrill, 1967.

This is a triple decker book—part biography, part filmography and part picture book with emphasis on the films of Fields. Included is a discussion of several "lost" films. The author's ability and authority are such that he can editorialize about the careless treatment of historical films and make it seem right in context with his subject. His treatment of Fields, as both person and performer, is fair and objective. His assessment of Fields' place in screen comedy annals likewise seems accurate.

Each of the films is analyzed in a depth not usually found in this book genre, and the stills are unusual, interesting, and, in the case of the later, unretouched photos, somewhat startling. Highly recommended.

292   *The Art of Walt Disney.* by Feild, Robert D. 290 p. illus. New York: Macmillan, 1942.

This volume deals with the history, development, and operation of the Disney studios. It considers working conditions, problems of animation work, the many stages that occur between the original idea and the final film, and the thousands of drawings. The many color plates and illustrations are superior. Text, production and concept are all outstanding. Most fascinating when read with Richard Schickel's *The Disney Version* and *The Story of Walt Disney* by Diane Disney Miller.

293   *The Art of Walt Disney.* by Finch, Christopher. 458 p. illus. New York: Abrams, 1973.

This is a very expensive art book that boasts 763 illustrations, about half in full color. A dozen foldouts are also produced in color. The superb visual feast supports Finch's bland text which has apparently been approved by the Disney Studios. Much better is Peter Blake's essay on Disneyland (Cal.) and Disney World (Fla.) which appeared originally in an architectural journal. Finch considers animation techniques, filmmaking, Disney's career, the history of the Disney Studios and the Disney films. The volume is important for its visuals—beautifully reproduced, substantial in size, and varied in selection.

294   *The Art of Watching Films.* by Boggs, Joseph M. 291 p. paper illus. Menlo Park, Calif.: Benjamin/Cummings, 1978.

According to the author, the purpose of this volume is "to provide students with enough guidance so that they may discover some new insights into films (by) themselves..." Examples from current and classical films are avoided, and, instead, common techniques/practices are explained. What results is a book on film aesthetics—theme, purpose, dramatic elements, visual elements, sound, music, acting, and direction. Two final sections deal with film analysis and its special problems, along with offering some exercises and questions. The book is indexed and illustrated.

An interesting approach to teaching film appreciation is suggested here. Although it tends toward the theoretical rather than the concrete, it may appeal to some students and teachers if an appropriate group of films is used with it.

295 *Arthur Penn.* by Wood, Robin. 144 p. paper illus. New York: Praeger: 1970.

The films directed by Arthur Penn include THE LEFT-HANDED GUN (1958), THE MIRACLE WORKER (1962), MICKEY ONE (1965), THE CHASE (1966), BONNIE AND CLYDE (1967), ALICE'S RESTAURANT (1969), and LITTLE BIG MAN (1970). This volume examines each one in some depth. The last had not been completed at publication time, and its making is described.

Everything about this volume is first rate except the picture reproduction. The contrast is too accentuated and as a result, some of the pictorial values are lost in blackness. A filmography along with an account of Penn's stage and television work is included. An up-to-date look at one of the most competent American directors, this book will appeal to most readers. It is hoped there will be more production control in future editions of this volume. The pictures deserve better.

296 *Artificially Arranged Scenes: The Films of Georges Melies.* by Frazer, John. 269 p. illus. Boston: G. K. Hall, 1979.

Each volume in this excellent G. K. Hall series offers some surprises—an indication of flexibility in both the writing and arrangement. In this case, the usual annotated bibliography is missing and in its place there is an annotated filmography of the films of Georges Melies. It is partial since many of the original films are lost, but the numerous examples of Melies' genius that we still have aredescribed in words and pictures. Preceding the filmography is one section which discusses the creative-artistic world of 1900 and another which concentrates on the life/career of Melies himself. Concluding portions of the book include notes, a bibliography, filmographies for both George Melies and Gaston Melies, and an index.

The joy of this volume is to be found in the film annotations which are both descriptive and critical. For the person concerned with Georges Melies' monumental contribution to the art of film, there is no better starting place than this fine reference.

297 *The Arts and Their Interrelations.* edited by Garvin, Harry R. 187 p. Lewisburg, Pa.: Bucknell University Press, 1979.

Recent examples of the interrelationships between the arts are noted in the ten essays of this anthology. Several deal with film.

298 *Arts in America: A Bibliography.* edited by Karpel, Bernard. 4 vols. Washington, D.C.: Smithsonian, 1980.

Selected as one of the Outstanding References of 1980 by the American Library Association, this four-volume set contains 25,000 annotated entries.

The section on film (in vol. 3) consists of more than 1200 entries and was written by George P. Rehrauer, author of this book. An index to the total bibliography appears in the fourth volume.

299 *As I Remember Them.* by Cantor, Eddie. 144 p. illus. New York: Duell, Sloan & Pearce, 1963.

If the reader can overlook or ignore the inane and patronizing text, the pictures of Fields, Garbo, Garland, Cagney, Jolson, et al. may please. Otherwise, this assembly-line paste-up job is quite forgettable.

300 *As Time Goes By: Memoirs of a Writer.* by Koch, Howard. 220 p. illus. New York: Harcourt, Brace, Jovanovich, 1979.

Koch was a well-known screen writer whose credits include such films as CASABLANCA (1942), THE LETTER (1940), LETTER FROM AN UNKNOWN WOMAN (1948), THE FOX (1968), etc. His writing of MISSION TO MOSCOW (1943) was the major cause of his being blacklisted by Hollywood in the early fifties. Koch's personal story is fleshed out with personalities and incidents from Hollywood's golden era. Although his career ended unhappily, Koch still writes hoping for options on his work.

The tone of the book is accepting rather than angry. Koch's autobiography, which is introduced by John Houseman, offers an observation of Hollywood in both its prime and its decline. Some illustrations accompany this pleasant, amiable memoir.

301 *Asian Film Directory and Who's Who.* edited by Doraiswamy, V. 392 p. illus. Bombay, India, 1956.

First published in 1952, this is the second edition of a reference that offers data/information about the Asian film industry.

302 *Aspects of American Film History Prior to 1920.* by Slide, Anthony. 173 p. illus. Metuchen, N.J.: Scarecrow, 1978.

Anthony Slide, a noted film historian, provides a group of 13 essays on various aspects of the early American film industry. Film stardom, comediennes, child stars, directors, companies, and fan magazines from the early silent era are typical topics. Individual attention is given to actress Ethel Grandin and author Katherine Anne Porter. In a chapter entitled "The First Motion Picture Bibliography," he reprints a 1916 listing of film books compiled by S. Gershanek which appeared first in the periodical, *Motography.* He concludes with an essay whose title probably suggests his own approach to his work: "Film History Can Be Fun." Appendixes and an index are provided.

The author's enthusiasm for his subjects is apparent throughout. His only pitfall is an occasional inability to distinguish the trivial from the important. Most readers will find this historical potpourri both informative and entertaining.

303 THE ASPHALT JUNGLE. by Maddow, Ben; and Huston, John. 147 p. illus. Carbondale, Ill.: Southern Illinois University Press, 1980.

Script of the 1950 film directed by John Huston. Contains an afterword by W. R. Burnett, the author of the novel upon which the film was based.

304 *Astaire & Rogers.* by Topper, Susanne. 206 p. paper illus. New York: Leisure Books, 1976.

This dual biography interweaves the stories of Astaire and Rogers with the major emphasis on the thirties period when they made nine of their ten team films. Topper suggests that their personal feelings toward each other were much less than friendly or warm. In addition, the portrait of the mild-mannered perfectionist, Astaire, beleaguered by a group of strong-willed women (Ginger, her mother, Irene Castle, etc.) is amusing. Their contribution as a team to uplifting Depression America is noted again and again. Some illustrations and a team filmography complete this modest but entertaining book.

305 *The Attitude of High School Students Toward Motion Pictures.* by Perry, Clarence A. 55 p. paper illus. New York: National Board of Review of Motion Pictures, 1923.

An early study dealing with the relationship of motion pictures and youth. Includes tables and diagrams.

306 *Audio Brandon Films Collection of International Cinema.* 224 p. paper illus. Mount Vernon, N.Y.: Audio Brandon Films, 1975.

This is the second volume about the Audio Brandon library of films and, while not as voluminous as the first, it does contain much informative and entertaining material. The films are arranged under the country of origin and for each there is technical data, a synopsis, background information, review excerpts, and one or more stills. Reproduction of the visuals is consistently excellent and they have been selected to arouse reader interest. A final section, entitled "A Guide to the Audio Brandon International Cinema Collection," arranges the entire library (volumes one and two) under subject headings such as Social Issues, Literature, Religion, etc. Alphabetical title lists of feature films and short films complete the volume. For information, reference or simply enjoyment, it is hard to top this production. Highly recommended.

Macmillan Films, an associate company with Audio Brandon, has issued four film study extracts on films which appear in both catalogs: THE BATTLE OF ALGIERS (1966)—Three Women, Three Bombs; NOTORIOUS (1946)—the Key Sequence; SPELLBOUND (1945)—the Razor Sequence; and THE THRONE OF BLOOD (1961)—First Meeting with the Spirit. Each includes plot outlines, analysis of the film elements in the extract (image, photography, sound, editing), notes and recommended readings.

307 *Audio Visual Man.* edited by Babin, Pierre. 218 p. paper illus. Dayton, Ohio: Pflaum, 1970.

Media and religious education is the major theme of this volume, which has three parts. The first deals with audiovisual language and faith. Learning a new language is the second section, while projects and projections make up the final part. The understanding of visuals is emphasized and although film is not singled out, it is an essential part of this discussion. The plea for visual literacy is persuasively stated. Much of the argument can be applied to any visual medium—film, television, posters, slides, etc. The many visuals used are noteworthy and the entire production is exemplary. The book was written originally in French.

Of primary interest to religious educators, this volume has much pertinence for others—training directors, teachers, media designers, etc. Recommended.

308 *Audio Visual Materials on Drama.* by British University Film Council. 195 p. paper London: The Council, 1973.

This is a catalog of films, filmstrips, videotapes and audio tapes that can be used in the teaching of drama at the university level. Only data and description of the various media are offered; there is no evaluation. Documentary materials on such topics as costume, theory, mime, actors, etc., are listed. In addition a group of feature films pertinent to the study of drama is noted. A subject index, a title index, a bibliography and a list of distributors are provided.

309 *Audio Visual Resource Guide.* edited by Abrams, Nick. 477 p. paper New York: Friendship Press, 1972.

The ninth edition of this excellent reference book updates and replaces previous editions, the last of which appeared in 1966. Some of the previous evaluations reappear here but there are many new materials listed. Selection is made on the basis of pertinence to religious education but that does not limit the use of many of the materials in other fields. In addition to films, many slides, audio tapes, recordings, and other nonprint materials are listed. The structure of the evaluations is consistent: divided into thirds, each considers biographical data, a summary of the content, and an evaluation—either highly recommended, recommended, acceptable, or limited.

A subject area index along with an alphabetical guide to those areas will assist users searching for materials on specific topics rather than individual titles. The hundreds of evaluations which follow are arranged alphabetically by title. Suggestions for appropriate audiences are also given. The films considered in the main body of the guide are the short ones but a closing section does give attention to a large selection of feature films. The distributors of the materials listed in the guide are given, as are some recommended publications on media resources. In this edition, the publishers have improved on established excellence. The selection, evaluations, coverage and format of this volume make it an essential reference.

310 *Audio-Visual Resources for Population Education and Family Planning: An International Guide for Social Work Educators.* compiled by Atkins, Jacqueline Marx. paper New York: International Association of Schools of Social Work, 1975.

An annotated list of materials, including many films, accompanied by articles on resources, equipment, and materials.

311 *The Audio/Brandon 16mm Collections of International Cinema.* edited by Kerbel, Michael; and Edelstein, Robert. 532 p. paper illus. Mount Vernon, N. Y.: Audio/Brandon, 1971.

This oversized catalog offers many hours of browsing pleasure in addition to much information and reference. Films are grouped according to country of origin in the first and longest section of the book. Shorter sections are given to silent films, experimental films and short films. Each film is accompanied by production credits and data, one or more stills, a long and unusually intelligent annotation and some review or critical quotes.

The sampling of films is numerically and qualitatively impressive. An excellent, well-produced catalog with many photographs.

312 *Audiovisual Equipment and Materials.* by Schroeder, Don; and Lane, Gary. 172 p. paper illus. Metuchen, N.J.: Scarecrow, 1979.

The purpose of this manual is to provide suggestions for the basic repair and maintenance of all types of audiovisual hardware. Using text, drawings, and photographs, the authors offer four major topics: service concepts, equipment maintenance and repair, and appendices. A bibliography and an index complete the book.

With respect to motion picture projectors, most repairs must be done by a trained technician. However, there are enough helpful suggestions contained here for the layman projectionist to warrant an initial reading and constant referral.

313 *see 314*

314 *Audio-Visual Equipment Directory.* by National Audiovisual Association. paper illus. Fairfax, Va.: National Audiovisual Association, 1954-

45

This directory is an annual that lists the audio-visual hardware currently available. Arranged by specific item, the text includes a chapter of motion picture projectors "being manufactured" along with pictures, specifications, prices, etc. The information offered is descriptive, not evaluative or comparative.

315 *Audio Visual Equipment Self Instruction Manual.* by Oates, Stanton C. 226 p. paper illus. Dubuque, Iowa: Wm. C. Brown, 1971.

Contains directions and advice on the operation of audiovisual machines, including motion picture projectors.

316 *An Audio-Visual Guide to American Holidays.* edited by Emmens, Carol A.; and Maglione, Harry. 284 p. Metuchen, N.J.: Scarecrow, 1978.

Over 1200 entries provide descriptive annotations of nonprint media that can be used in the celebration of American holidays. The arrangement offers a grouping of various media forms under each holiday heading. For example, listed under Lincoln's Birthday, there are 16mm films, filmstrips/slides, records/ cassettes, transparencies and, prints. Other media considered include 8mm film, video, and realia. Descriptive data for each medium is provided along with grade levels. Entries suitable for more than one holiday are cross-referenced. A distributor list and a general title index complete the book.

This volume should be most valuable for those professionals who deal with young children and for teachers of American history.

317   *see 318*

318 *A-V Instruction.* by Brown, James; and Lewis, Richard; and Harcleroad, Fred. illus. New York: McGraw-Hill, 1979.

The fifth edition of this standard textbook discusses the technology, media and methods used by teachers, media specialists, librarians, etc. Much information on the motion picture film medium is offered.

319 *AV Instruction Technology Manual for Independent Study.* by Brown, James; and Lewis, Richard B. 256 p. paper illus. New York: McGraw-Hill, 1973.

This is the fourth edition of a standard self-instruction manual on audiovisual technology. Includes information on motion picture projector operation, etc.

320 *Audiovisual Machines.* by Davidson, Raymond L. 266 p. paper illus. Scranton, Pa.: International Text, 1969.

Explains the operation of audiovisual equipment including motion picture projectors.

321   *see 323*

322   *see 323*

323 *Audiovisual Market Place: A Multimedia Guide (1979).* edited by Barnes, James; and Weber, Olga. 434 p. paper New York: R. R. Bowker, 1969- .

This is the ninth edition of a standard reference tool that is devoted to audiovisual software, hardware, and related information. The software section lists audiovisual producers, distributors, companies, services, facilities, libraries, consultants, etc., while the hardware section notes equipment manufacturers and dealers. In the information section there are AV convention dates, awards, festivals, reference books, directors, periodicals, journals, associations, state AV administrators, funding sources, and a glossary. A total index is provided.

Since so much of the information found here pertains to film, it is often a basic source to consult. It is easy to use, comprehensive in covering its "marketplace" subject, and includes additional features that are of value to anyone concerned with film.

324 *AV Media and Libraries.* by Prostano, Emanuel T. 276 p. Littleton, Colo.: Libraries Unlimited, 1972.

A large collection of selected readings which includes only four on 16mm film. Found in a section entitled "An Old Standby," they are: "Feature Films in Your Library," by Paul Spehr; "The Entertainment Film in Education," by Bosley Crowther; "The Picture Book Projected," by Morton Shindell; and "Films on Demand," by Lynne Hofer.

325 *Audiovisual Production.* by Vance, Adrian. 192 p. illus. New York: Amphoto, 1979.

How to produce audiovisual projects for a profit is the theme of this volume. The term "audiovisual" includes sound films, slide shows, and filmstrips. Using a generalized approach, Vance considers the idea and creation of a project, the selling of it and its ultimate production. Economics, script, set, props, lighting, camera, film, performers, art, special effects and sound are among the topics he discusses. The advice offered, based on his impressive experience, is both comprehensive and practical. The attractive illustrations provided supplement the text nicely and the book is indexed.

For the person interested in the creation of audiovisuals for whatever purpose, this volume is a stimulating, helpful guide. Recommended.

326 *Audio Visual Resource Guide.* by Cox, Jr. Alva I. 597 p. paper New York: National Council of Churches of Christ in the U.S.A., 1966.

The eighth edition of this excellent reference contains more than 3000 evaluations of materials including films that can be used in churches, schools, and libraries. Also considered are theatrical films, books, periodicals and other materials. The book is oriented toward a church- religious usage. The evaluations are superior, and this volume should be useful to anyone dealing with films.

327 *Audio Visual Script Writing.* by Parker, Norton S. 330 p. illus. New Brunswick, N.J.: Rutgers University Press, 1968.

A "how-to-do-it" book that combines common sense, a down-to-earth approach, and much technical wisdom. The topic is how to write audiovisual scripts and the author describes what a script is and why it takes the form it does. He considers fundamental principles and techniques and avoids philosophical discussions. Although the emphasis is on writing scripts for the nontheatrical film, he discusses the entertainment film briefly. Good for all filmmakers but especially recommended for the beginner who wishes to learn script writing by individual study.

328 *Audio Visual Services in the Small Public Library.* by Anderson, Herschel V. 21 p. paper Chicago: American Library Association, 1969.

A short booklet describing nonprint services, including film in small public libararies.

329 *Audio-Visuals in the Church.* by Getz, Gene A. 256 p. paper Chicago: Moody Press, 1959.

An older volume that discusses the use of nonprint materials, including films, in a religious setting.

330 *Audition.* by Shurtleff, Michael. 187 p. New York: Walker, 1978.

Although Michael Shurtleff has been associated primarily with theatre projects, the advice he offers to aspiring actors is universal. His volume, subtitled "Everything an Actor Needs to Know to Get the Part," consists mostly of twelve "Guideposts" to auditions. Each of these deals with some aspect of an audition and is supported by practical comments and advice. Anecdotes about famous names are saved mostly for a section called "Observations From a Life in the Theatre. <

This is an essential volume for anyone who wants to act in any medium.

331 *The Australian Cinema.* by Baxter, John. 118 p. paper illus. Sydney, Australia: Pacific Books, 1970.

The purpose of this small volume is to acquaint readers with the Australian cinema via a bit of history, some discussion of the artists concerned, and a very partial survey of the films. Because of an initial native lack of interest in the Australian cinema, the reconstruction is sketchy and piecemeal. As a beginning step in the recording of a country's cinema, the book is admirable. While major names are not treated in depth, they are recognized, and a basis for further exploration is established. The photographs are provocative and a sturdy index is provided.

Worth the price of the book alone is the notation of two films which offer a sampling of Australian films and are available from Australian Consulates the world over. Recommended.

332 *Australian Film Posters 1906-1960.* edited by Adamson, Judith; and Beckett, Barbara. 56 p. paper illus. Sydney: Currency Press/Australian Film Institute, 1978.

A fine group of film posters selected from the National Film Archive and certain private collections is presented in this oversize book. A sense of Australian film history can be obtained from the well-reproduced visuals and the accompanying text.

333 *Australian Films—A Catalogue of Scientific, Educational and Cultural Films.* 121 p. paper Canberra: National Library of Australia, 1972.

This is the 12th yearly supplement to an original catalog which covered the period of 1940 to 1958. This annual treats those films produced in Australia during 1970 along with a few earlier omissions. The major section lists the films alphabetically by title, giving data and description but no evaluation. A subject list and the names of the producers and distributors are also provided.

334 *Australian Silent Films.* by Reade, Eric. 192 p. illus. Melbourne: Lansdowne Press, 1970.

Although there is as much text as visual material in this volume, it carries the subtitle, "A Pictorial History 1896-1929." Beginning with the film coverage of the Melbourne Cup meeting in 1896, it considers the films, the personalities, and the businessmen associated with the Australian film industry for the first three decades of this century. The silent film era ended in Australia with the banning of THE DEVIL'S PLAYGROUND (1929).

All types of films produced over the years are described—newsreels, features, comedies, travelogues, educational shorts, etc. The people associated with the Australian film industry are unfamiliar to American readers; many are identified here and certain individuals receive detailed attention. The poor quality of visual reproduction throughout the volume is puzzling. The availability of film stills seems to be a problem and some fuzzy enlargements of frames and photographs were apparently used.

An outstanding feature of the volume is a chronological filmography of all the Australian silent films. Information varies with each entry, but most list cast, credits, and theatres where the films played. A detailed index is also supplied. The national cinema of Australia has received scant attention from historians and scholars to date. This welcome volume satisfies the need for both a source of information about and an interpretation of the early Australian films. Recommended.

335 *Author's Photoplay Manual.* by Palmer, Frederick. 238 p. Hollywood Calif.: Palmer Institute of Authorship, 1924.

Frederick Palmer was the author of several books on screenwriting which were published by the Palmer Photoplay Corp. or the Palmer Institute of Authorship. Most of the volumes appeared in the early twenties and attempted to mass-produce screenplays by suggesting standard plots, devices, situations etc. Other titles include *The Essentials of Photoplay Writing* (1921), *Palmer Plan Handbook* (1921), *Photoplay Plot Encyclopedia* (1922), *Photoplay Writing* (1920), and *Technique of the Photoplay* (1924).

336 *The Authorized Biography of James Mason.* by Monaghan, John P. 78 p. paper illus. London: World Film Productions, 1947.

James Mason supplies the foreword to this early biography, written at a time when Mason was just starting to enjoy world celebrity.

337 *Authors on Film.* edited by Geduld, Harry M. 303 p. Bloomington, Ind.: Indiana Univ. Press, 1972.

An anthology designed to indicate the diverse interests and involvements of well-known writers in film. Five general categories indicate the organization of the material: 1) From Silence to Sound—Gorky, Tolstoy, Sandburg, Gide, Brecht, Hardy, etc.; 2) The Medium and its Messages—Wolf, Mencken, G. B. Shaw, Mann, etc.; 3) Authors on Screenwriting—T. S. Eliot, W. S. Maugham, Capote, etc.; The Hollywood Experience—Dreiser, F. Scott Fitzgerald, Faulkner; 5) Of Mice and Movie Stars—Cocteau, Dos Passos, Hemingway, Baldwin, etc.

Thirty-five authors are represented and all the articles offer interesting and worthwhile content. The selection, arrangement, and editing by Geduld are commendable, as is the original conception for the book. The interest evidenced by the appearance of several recent books about the relationship between literature and film is served well here. Some short notes on the authors are provided and there is an index—a thoughtful addition not usually found in books of this genre. Highly recommended.

338 *Authorship and Narrative in the Cinema.* by Luhr, William; and Lehman, Peter. 320 p. illus. New York: G.P. Putnam's, 1977.

The fact that this volume was created by combining the material of two doctoral dissertations is apparent throughout. In the first section the text argues the concept of auteurism by using John Ford as a model. THE SEARCHERS (1956) and THE MAN WHO SHOT LIBERTY VALANCE (1962) are analyzed in great detail to show that a film is indeed the creation of the director. In the second portion the intent is to prove that the story is only one element of several which make a film and it is the director's creative interpretation of the story which determines the film. Three versions of DR. JEKYLL AND MR. HYDE (1921, 1931, 1941) are used along with two other derivations of the Robert Louis Stevenson novel—THE HOUSE OF FRIGHT (1960) and THE NUTTY PROFESSOR (1963). Both sections support the auteur theory of film criticism.

The subtitle of the volume is "Issues in Contemporary Aesthetics and Criticism." While it may be a bit too broad for this volume's limited content, it does convey the authors' intent—to improve the quality of today's film criticism. Their discussion of the role of the narrative in film is made valid by appropriate examples and explanations. They show narrative as one part of many which the director must ultimately handle. To them considering him as the film's author is absolutely justifiable.

339 *An Autobiography.* by Rutherford, Margaret. 230 p. illus. London: H. W. Allen, 1972.

This autobiography, as told to Gwen Robyns, is about what you might expect from Dame Rutherford. She is frank, open, and amusing when she discusses herself. When speaking of her co-workers, she is kind, courteous, and always the lady. Her life was not without its deep sorrows, and she was rather late in reaching celebrity status. The sex-change of her adopted son must have caused her considerable anguish when the story was picked up by the press and published around the world, yet she handles this subject with dignity and sensitivity. Anyone who has enjoyed Margaret Rutherford on the screen will be pleased with this volume. Recommended.

340 *The Autobiography and Sex Life of Andy Warhol.* by Wilcock, John. unpaginated. paper illus. New York: Other Scenes (Hopkinson and Blake), 1971.

A series of interviews conducted by John Wilcock on the subject of Andy Warhol is offered in this book. Those interviewed include Charles Henri Ford, Nico, Eleanor Ward, Gerard Malanga, Naomi Levine, Paul Morrissey, Marisol, Taylor Mead, Ultra Violet, Buddy Wirtschafter, Ronnie Tavel, Brigid Polk, Fred Hughes, David Bourdon, Viva, Lou Reed, Gretchen Berg, Sam Green, Ivan Karp, Mario Amaya, Leo Castelli, Henry Geldzahler and John Wilcock. In addition to photographs of Warhol and some examples of his work, there are portraits of each of the interviewees. A few articles, "Andy as Movie Maker," "On the Road with the Exploding Plastic Inevitable," and "L.A. Weekend with Warhol," appear along with the interviews. His filmmaking is emphasized throughout.

Usually material on Warhol is controversial, provocative, shocking, rebellious, or a put-on. The text here is all of these and more—made even more fascinating by the passage of years since the book's original appearance. Recommended.

341 AUTOBIOGRAPHY OF A PRINCESS: *Also Being the Adventures of an American Film Director in the Land of the Maharajas.* by Ivory, James. 177 p. illus. New York: Harper, 1975.

This volume is a heavily illustrated memoir of Royal India from the mid-1800's to 1930. Included is Ruth Prawer Jhabvala's screenplay of Ivory's film, AUTOBIOGRAPHY OF A PRINCESS (1975), which combines fictional characters with scenes shot in Indian courts. The story is concerned with an exiled Indian Princess living in London.

342 *The Autobiography of Cecil B. DeMille,* by DeMille, Cecil B.; edited by Hayne, Donald. 465 p. illus. Englewood Cliffs, N.J.: Prentice-Hall, 1959.

This volume tells little about the inner man but a great deal about 70 motion pictures he directed. The style employed is a polite, noncontroversial recital of facts or memories. When opinion is offered, it is usually in refutation of some DeMille legend. Especially good if used with *The Films of Cecil B. DeMille.* Filmography and index.

343 *The Autobiography of Will Rogers.* edited by Day, Donald. 410 p. illus. Boston: Houghton Mifflin, 1949.

A selection of Rogers' writing taken mostly from pieces written between 1922 and 1935. Editing, arrangement, and linking narratives are by Donald Day, who has also written a separate biography. Unfortunately, because of the source material there is little about films here—in fact, only two humorous articles about the industry. Persons looking for information about Rogers' film career are advised to see the biographies by Donald Day, P. J. O'Brien and Betty Rogers.

344 *The Automonous Image: Cinematic Narration and Humanism.* by Prats, A. J. 192 p. Lexington, Ky.: University Press of Kentucky, 1981.

345 AUTUMN SONATA. by Bergman, Ingmar. 85 p. illus. New York: Pantheon, 1978.

Contains only the script, written and directed by Ingmar Bergman, of the 1978 film, which starred Ingrid Bergman and Liv Ullman.

346 *Ava: A Portrait of a Star.* by Hanna, David. 256 p. illus. New York: G. P. Putnam's, 1960.

Although it is biographical in part, this volume presents more of a character portrait than a life story. The author had a close associaton with his subject for more than seven years, serving her as publicist, personal manager and friend.

Written as a sort of expanded diary, the text follows Hanna's first employment as publicist for THE BAREFOOT CONTESSA (1954) and closes with the making of ON THE BEACH (1959). During that period he records the changes of the Gardner personality— the eventual emergence of the suspicious, hard, demanding and unhappy professional. Her romantic life is given minor attention, while her professional activities are noted in detail. In addition he describes, with clarity and authority, the personalities and the organizations that control the life of a film star. The portrait is an objective one, interesting for what is said and provocative for that which is implied. It is a superior character study of a female superstar.

347 *Ava.* by Higham, Charles. 281 p. illus. New York: Delacorte, 1974.

An unofficial biography based on interviews with persons who knew Ava Gardner socially or professionally. Considering the events, men and films in Gardner's life, the account here appears carefully diluted. Evidently the star's assistance and approval are essential if any worthwhile biography is to appear. Illustrations, a filmography and an index are of some help. Acceptable.

348 *Ava Gardner.* by Kass, Judith M. 159 p. paper illus. New York: Jove (Harcourt Brace Jovanovich), 1977.

To date Ava Gardner has been the subject of two unauthorized biographies, *Ava* by Charles Higham and *Ava: Portrait of a Star* by David Hanna. Both authors emphasized her colorful personal life and gave only partial attention to her films. The oversight is corrected in this fine appreciation by Judith M. Kass, who starts off by defining Gardner's screen image in succinct fashion. She was the woman who, on the way to the bedroom, made her man wonder if she was a good guy who could be trusted and if she had staying power. Forever searching for happiness, Gardner was alternately committed, retiring, aggressive, generous, self-hating, gutsy, long-suffering, and usually triumphant.

Gardner's films from WE WERE DANCING (1942) to THE SENTINEL (1977) are discussed in a four-decade arrangement—Starting Out (the 40s), The Top (the 50s), The Slope (the 60s), and Peace and Quiet (the 70s). A bibliography, a filmography, and an index complete the book. Illustrations are well selected but some of the more recent ones are less than flattering.

This evaluation of Ava Gardner's work by a female writer is most welcome, for she is able to interpret with sensitivity many of the individual bits and pieces of her subject's life. Ultimately the reasons for the misguided but enormously successful career of Ava Gardner become clear. Recommended.

349 *The Avant-Garde Film: A Reader of Theory and Criticism.* edited by Sitney, P. Adams. 295 p. paper illus. New York: New York University Press, 1978.

A title in the *Anthology Film Archives* series, this collection of articles is both history and theory. Using original articles, translations, and reprints, the text concentrates on the avant-garde filmmaker and his films.

Contributors include Vertov, Richter, Eisenstein, Dulac, Deren, Brakhage, Mekas, and many others. The book is illustrated and an index is provided.

350 L'AVVENTURA. by Antonioni, Michelangelo; and Bartolini, Eli; and Guerra, Tonino. 288 p. paper illus. New York: Grove Press, 1969.

Script of the 1959 film directed by Antonioni. Contains cast credits; introduction consists of two interviews with Antonioni. Included are nine critical articles by George Amberg, Dominique Fernandez, Penelope Huston, Penelope Gilliatt, Bosley Crowther, John Simon, Dwight McDonald, Joseph Bennett, and William S. Pechter.

351 *Awake in the Dark.* edited by Denby, David. 395 p. paper New York: Vintage, 1977.

This crackling anthology of American film criticism, ranging from 1915 to the present, is made up of seven sections: in defense of a popular new art form; film as high art; critical method; genres; directors; performers; and entertainment. The 20 contributors are well-known, outspoken critics who represent a wide range of independent views. They vary from Vachel Lindsay to John Simon and offer film reviews, essays, program notes, appreciations, and critical arguments.

The collection offers a fine sampling of film criticism, showing its variety, intelligence, and depth.

The book may be used in many ways—as entertaining reading, classroom study or reference. Recommended.

352 *The Award Movies: A Complete Guide from A to Z.* by Pickard, Roy. 294 p. illus. London: Frederick Muller, 1980.

This is an encyclopedia based upon the Academy Awards, the National Board of Review selections, the New York Film Critics awards, the British Academy awards, and film festival awards from Venice, Cannes, Berlin, Karlovy, Vary, and Moscow. A half- century coverage is provided and many obscure foreign films are described.

353 *Awards, Honors, and Prizes.* edited by Wasserman, Paul. 579 p. Detroit, Mich.: Gale Research, 1972.

Anyone searching for a directory of motion picture awards and their donors is advised to consult this volume. Divided into three sections, the material deals not only with motion picture awards, but also with art, business, government, literature, fashion, medicine, and other categories, professions, or industries in which awards are given.

The first section is a main listing arranged alphabetically by sponsoring organization. Here each award that the organization gives is noted (even discontinued ones) along with a full description that includes data such as purpose of the award, terms of eligibility, form of award, frequency, etc. Entries are quite thorough and explain the awards most satisfactorily. For example, American Association of University Professors Education Writers Award: "To recognize outstanding interpretive reporting of issues in higher education in the following media: radio, TV, film, or print. To the author. Certificate. Awarded annually. Established 1969."

A second section is an alphabetical arrangement of the individual awards by specific or distinctive name; for example, Jean Hersholt Humanitarian Award, Emily Award, Ralph H. Landes Award.

A subject index which contains headings for music, theatre, entertainment and television as well as motion pictures comprises the final section of the book. For ease of use, comprehensiveness and readability, this volume is excellent.

354 *Awards, Honors and Prizes—Volume I, United States and Canada.* edited by Wasserman, Paul; and McLean, Janice. 700 p. Detroit: Gale Research, 1978.

This fourth edition of a valuable and entertaining reference book has been enlarged, revised, and updated. It now contains information on more than 5000 prizes-awards given in the United States and Canada for personal or professional efforts in some 450 different subject areas. For this review the awards-prizes for film were used to examine the volume.

There are three sections in the book: a detailed listing of the sponsoring organizations arranged alphabetically, a list of subjects and cross references with a subject index of awards, and finally, an alphabetical index of the awards by name. To find what awards are given in the field of cinema, the subject index was consulted first. It noted headings for cinematography, film criticism, instructional films and motion pictures. The cinematography heading listed six awards, all administered by the Society of Motion Picture and Television Engineers. Film Criticism noted a single award given by The American Federation of Film Societies whose current address and status is unknown (they did not respond to two inquiries sent by the editors apparently). Instructional films listed five organizations giving awards while motion pictures showed 40 such sponsors. The detailed organizational listings give the full information about each award—name, address of sponsor, current status, purpose, terms of eligibility, form of award, frequency, date established and by whom, and dedication.

This is a unique reference book that provides information not readily available elsewhere. The arrangement is a logical one, easy to understand and use. Because of its wide range of subjects and the detail provided for each award, the book will appeal to a wide, varied audience—even to the casual browser. Volume II will deal with International and Foreign awards.

355 *"B" Movies.* by Miller, Don. 350 p. paper illus. New York: Curtis Books, 1973.

The first thing some will want to do with this book is to rip out the objectionable advertising bound to it. After that the book is certain to please and impress you. In a detailed narrative, the author provides a history of the "B" film from the early thirties until the close of World War II. The "B" product of the major studios, the independent studios, the poverty row group—Republic, Monogram, PRC—and others is described. A small collection of illustrations appears in the book's center. An almost necessary table of contents and an introduction are missing but there is a lengthy index to compensate in part for these omissions.

The author's style is informal, yet serious and respectful of his material. In a way this modest volume provides in textual material what other more expensive volumes provide only partially in visuals, e.g., *A Thousand and One Delights* or *The Thrill of It All*. This is another fine entry in a new paperback series.

356 BABY DOLL. by Williams, Tennessee. 140 p. illus. New York: NewDirections, 1956.

Script of the 1956 film directed by Elia Kazan. Also contains the two short playlets from which the film was derived.

357 THE BACHELOR PARTY. by Chayefsky, Paddy. 127 p. paper illus. New York: New American Library, 1957.

Script of the 1957 film directed by Delbert Mann.

358 *Back in the Saddle Again.* by Autry, Gene; and Herskowitz, Mickey. 252 p. illus. New York: Doubleday, 1978.

It is no surprise that Gene Autry's autobiography has many of the same qualities as his films. In an informal, folksy style that often digresses or stops for a anecdote (song), he recalls his rise from telegraph operator to multi-media celebrity with directness, a pleasing simplicity, and, apparently, a sharp memory. No shocks or secrets are revealed although he does give attention to his problem with drinking. Sufficient attention is given to his 93 films and his recordings. A filmography and a discography are included along with many illustrations. The volume is indexed.

A predictable performance designed to please Autry aficionados and the fans of the western film genre.

359 *The Back Lot.* by Levenson, Jordan. 79 p. paper illus. Los Angeles: Levenson Press, 1972.

An expensive paperback that details the craft of the laborer in both motion pictures and television. Activities on the set and on location are described by text and drawings. A good behind-the-scenes look at the practical side of filmmaking.

360 THE BACK OF BEYOND. by Else, Eric. 176 p. illus. London: Longmans Green, 1968.

This volume is described as "a compilation for use in studying John Heyer's film of inland Australia." It contains text, illustrations, maps, and a bibliography. Heyer, a documentarist with the Shell Film Unit in Australia, made THE BACK OF BEYOND in 1954.

361 *Backstage: TV/Film and Tape Directory—1980.* paper illus. New York: Backstage Publications, 1980.

A directory listing services and products needed by film and television producers.

362 *The Bad Guys; A Pictorial History of the Movie Villain.* by Everson, William K. 241 p. illus. New York: Citadel Press, 1964.

Everson displays his usual competence, taste, and respect for his subject—in this case, the movie villains. By arranging them in various categories, i.e., the western outlaw, the monsters, the foreigners, and so on, he manages to cover most of the familiar faces audiences have feared or sneered at. One chapter on bad girls is tacked on as a kind of afterthought.

The text is intelligent and written with style and enthusiasm. The stills are superior. Indexed.

363 *Ballet for Film and Television.* by Franks, Arthur Henry. 85 p. illus. London: Pitman, 1950.

This older volume treats both the potential and the actual results of putting ballet on film. Analyses of selected examples from famous ballets are offered, along with listings of books, periodicals and films dealing with this form of the dance.

364 THE BANK DICK. by Fields, W. C. 88 p. paper illus. New York: Simon & Schuster, 1973.

Script of the 1940 film directed by Edward Cline. Contains notes, contemporary reviews, and cast and credits.

365 BARABBAS: The Story of a Motion Picture. by Fry, Christopher; edited by Jones, Lon. 189 p. illus. Bologna, Italy: Capelli, 1962.

Script of the 1962 film directed by Richard Fleisher. Contains an introduction by Lon Jones. The book is in two parts: From Story to Script (various treatments, scripts) and From Script to Screen (articles by persons involved in making the film, i.e., cinematographer, costume designer, composer, publicity director, et al.).

366 BARABBAS. 20 p. paper illus. New York: Program Publishing Co., 1962.

Attention is given first to the novel by Par Lagerkvist on which the film was based and then to the actual production. Later, the final film story is outlined in detail. A single page is devoted to Anthony Quinn and some cast and production credits are indicated. Six paintings of Barabbas which were commissioned for the film are reproduced nicely.

367 *Barbara Stanwyck.* by Vermilye, Jerry. 159 p. paper illus. New York: Pyramid, 1975.

The life and career of Barbara Stanwyck has been treated before—notably in Ella Smith's excellent coffee-table volume—but Jerry Vermilye provides a most rewarding survey in this well-produced volume. Attention is focused on her many films, and both descriptive and critical analysis is offered. He divides the Stanwyck career into appropriate periods —Up from Brooklyn, The Depression Heroine, Light Comedy, Dark Drama, The Queen and The Grand Dame of Television. A bibliography, a filmography and an index complete the book.

The illustrations are quite good in both selection and reproduction; they show the growth of an actress over four decades, progressing from an ambitious ingenue to a respected professional. Stanwyck's status as a legend seems assured and the contribution she has made to the Hollywood films is immeasurable. The well-written volume is an indication and appreciation of the magnitude of her talent, her effort and her success. Recommended.

368 *Barbra Streisand.* by Eldred, Patricia M. paper illus. New York: Creative Education, 1975.

This is another short volume with original drawings designed for the very young reader. The subject is Streisand, whose life, career, and talent are made into a fairy story here.

369 *Barbra: The First Decade.* by Spada, James. 224 p. illus. Secaucus, N. J.: Citadel, 1974.

Barbra Streisand's achievements on stage, recordings, television, and in films are noted in this pictorial tribute. The text is adoring and the selection of narrative material—review excerpts, a *Mad* magazine comic strip, etc.—is questionable. Visuals, however, are quite pleasing as they show the development of the harried secretary, Miss Marmelstein, in the 1962 Broadway musical "I Can Get It for You Wholesale" to the glamorous heroine of THE WAY

WE WERE (1974). Acceptable.

370 *Barbra.: An Illustrated Biography.* by Brady, Frank. 160 p. paper illus. Today Press/Grosset & Dunlap, 1979.

Using over 100 illustrations the author reviews Barbra Striesand's life and career from April 24, 1942 to late 1978 in this over sized paper back.

371 *Bardot: Eternal Sex Goddess.* by Evans, Peter. 186 p. illus. London: Lester Frewin, 1972.

This biography of Bardot has more pertinence for European audiences than for Americans since Bardot never enjoyed a great popularity here. The usual and well-known factual material is here along with photographs, a filmography, and an index. Acceptable.

372 *Bardot: An Intimate Biography.* by Frischauer, Willi. 222 p. illus. London: Joseph, 1978.

This biography of the French film star includes text, illustrations, a filmography, and an index.

373 *The Bare Bones Camera Course for Film and Video.* by Schroeppel, Tom. paper illus. Miami: Schroeppel, 1980.

The author calls his book, "A Non-threatening, Yet Complete, Introduction to the Fundamentals of Television and Movie Camerawork."

374 *Barnes Museum—Catalogue of the Collection.* by Barnes, John. 69 p. paper illus. St. Ives, Cornwall, England: Barnes Museum of Cinematography, 1967.

The catalogue, titled "Precursors of the Cinema," deals with optical projection, peepshows, dioramas, shadowgraphy, etc.

375 *The Barrymores.* by Alpert, Hollis. 397 p. illus. New York: Dial Press, 1964.

Author Alpert is a film critic and the work of Ethel, Lionel and John Barrymore in motion pictures is given equal prominence with their careers in other media. The writing is objective, respectful and honest. Illustrations are outstanding. An excellent biography; beautifully written and produced.

376   *The Barrymores: The Royal Family In Hollywood.* by Kotsilibas-Davis, James. 384 p. illus. New York: Crown, 1981.

The Hollywood careers of John Lionel and Ethel are surveyed. Anecdotes are plentiful and there is a filmography, a bibliography and an index.

377   *Bashful Billionaire.* by Gerber, Albert B. 352 p. paper New York: Dell, 1968.

Written in a "Tom Swift" chapter heading style (i.e., "Howard Hughes and His Motion Picture Camera"), this unauthorized biography has some sections of interest to students of film history. Considerable attention is given to the making of the legendary HELL'S ANGELS (1927) while SCARFACE (1932) and THE FRONT PAGE (1931) are brushed over rather briefly. The making of THE OUTLAW (1943) and Hughes' purchase and subsequent sale of the RKO Studios are each treated in separate chapters. His relationships with female screen stars is noted with considerable detail. Because the book covers Hughes' activities in all fields, the cinema sections are comparatively limited.

378   *Basic All 8mm Movie Shooting Guide.* by Tydings, Kenneth S. 126 p. paper illus. Philadelphia: Chilton, 1961.

There are five major chapters in this older volume on 8mm filming: 1. Preparing the Basic Camera Shot; 2. Practicing the Basic Shooting Situations; 3. Telling a Story: Movie-Making Technique; 4. The Story; and 5. Practical Shooting Scripts. A final section called "The Factopedia," offers a miscellany of information ranging from harmonious colors to projection data. An excellent glossary of photographic terms appears here.

The models and the visuals are dated but the information about shooting 8mm film remains pertinent.

379   *Basic Animation Stand Techniques.* by Salt, Brian G. D. 239 p. illus. Elmsford, N.Y.: Pergamon, 1977.

A technical presentation of how to use an animation stand.

380   *Basic Books in the Mass Media.* by Blum, Eleanor. 252 p. Urbana, Ill.: University of Illinois Press, 1972.

The subtitle describes the general content of this reference book: "An Annotated, Selected Booklist (665 titles) Covering General Communications (104), Book Publishing (70), Broadcasting (124), Film (109), Magazines (33), Newspapers (99), Advertising (64), Indexes (13), and Scholarly and Professional Periodicals (49)." For obvious reasons, the film section was the one chosen for evaluation here. It is assumed that it is a representative sample.

The books are listed alphabetically by author, along with title, location, publisher and date. No mention is made of paperback formats; illustrations and the presence of an index in several of the books is not noted, e.g., *The Film Till Now, Movie Comedy Teams,* etc. The name of the author of this latter book is Maltin, not Malton as listed.

Blum states that her choices are subjective. Fine, but when a book uses the word "basic" in its title, there is a responsibility to exercise care in selection. Some of the inclusions are pleasant volumes but certainly not basic: e.g., Baxter's *The Gangster Film,* the Camerons' *Dames* and *The Heavies,* Lahue's *Clown Princes and Court Jesters,* Walker's *Stardom: The Hollywood Phenomena.* Where are the Blum volumes? Powdermaker? Bluestone? Arnheim? Bazin? Many other excellent books which are now basic staples of any film collection could be named.

Placement of the titles may be questionable. Should Stedman's *The Serials,* which deals with magazines, comic strips, films, radio and television, be listed in the film section? Especially since the film portion occupies about one-third of the text to the two-thirds assigned to Radio and TV? Some of the annotations are incorrect— *Variety* does not review underground or commercial (sponsored) films. The articles in *AV Communication Review* are not experimental.

No evaluations are offered, only descriptive annotation. However, the inclusion of a title in this "basic" listing would indicate approval or endorsement. What could have been an outstanding reference book is only an average one because of poor selection criteria, lack of evaluations, faulty descriptions, misspellings, and inaccuracies. If used with care and with an understanding of its weaknesses and limitations, it can be an aid.

381   *Basic Color Photography.* by Feininger, Andreas. 128 p. illus. Englewood Cliffs, N.J.: Prentice-Hall, 1972.

Although the text addresses itself to still photography, there is much that is pertinent for the cinematographer. Specifically, it is the latter two sections, dealing with techniques of color photography and the art of color photography, which are most applicable. The rationale for the last section is stated succinctly by the author: "It is an indisputable fact that successful color photography is impossible un-

less the know-how is guided by the know-why."
Acceptable.

382 *Basic 8mm Movie Reference Guide.*
by Pollock, Norman. 127 p. paper illus. Philadelphia: Chilton, 1960.

This older volume is a guide to making 8mm motion
pictures and treats such topics as the camera, lens,
film, exposure lighting, filters, shooting, editing, titling and projecting. A collection of short miscellaneous topics completes the book which is
illustrated but not indexed. Although the technology of the camera and the film have advanced during
the past 20 years, many of the basic ideas and
suggestions about 8mm filmmaking contained here
are still pertinent.

383 *Basic Filmmaking.* by Kamisky,
Stuart; and Hodgon, Dan. 256 p. illus. New York: Arco, 1981.

384 *Basic Magnetic Sound Recording for
Motion Pictures.* edited by Kodak
Staff. 41 p. paper illus. Rochester,
N.Y.: Kodak, 1969.

This booklet deals with magnetic sound recording
and its use on films instead of the usual optical
sound track. Combining a magnetic sound track
with a motion picture requires patience and an understanding of the requirements. This volume offers
techniques and suggestions on how to make creditable magnetic sound tracks for 8m and 16mm films.
Topics treated include equipment, script preparation, shooting, recording, narrating, editing, etc.

This is another in the valuable series of "how-to-
make-it" books that Kodak produces. As is usual
with the series, this book is attractive, reliable, and
comparatively inexpensive.

385 *Basic Motion Picture Technology.* by
Happe, L. Bernard. 362 p. illus. New
York: Hastings House, 1971.

A complete coverage of the history and development of motion picture technology, including current practice, innovations, and trends, with
emphasis on the practical and technical material.
Profusely illustrated with diagrams and pictures.

386 *Basic Motion Picture Technology.* by
Happe', L. Bernard. 371 p. illus. New
York: Hastings House, 1975.

This is the second edition of a work which was
originally published in 1971. It has been revised and
enlarged with greater attention given to production

methods, projection, and theatre practice. Recent
developments in all three areas are described.
Happe' confines his discussion to the technical aspects of professional cinematography and does not
consider such creative elements as the script, set
design, make-up, direction, and so forth.

A review of the history of film technology and principles is followed by a consideration of photography
and image characteristics. How sounds and images
are recorded leads to descriptions of studio production. Film processing and duplication methods are
considered and a chapter on presentation concludes
the main text. Appendixes, a bibliography, a glossary, and an index complete the book.

Many drawings which are nicely coordinated with
the text are featured. They are well-designed and of
enormous help in explaining certain complex processes.

This is a volume designed for the mature reader or
advanced student who wishes to gain a general understanding of the technology of motion pictures.
Mathematical and electronic details are minimal
with most attention given to a developmental exposition of the cinematographic process via the the
lean, exact text and the many fine visuals. Recommended.

387 *see 388*

388 *Basic Production Techniques for Motion Pictures.* edited by Kodak Staff.
60 p. paper illus. Rochester, N.Y.:
Eastman Kodak, 1976.

As Audiovisual Data Book P-18, this volume is addressed to those persons in business, industry, medicine, television, education, government and
elsewhere who wish to be informed about basic techniques in filmmaking. It deals with such topics as
planning, equipment, types of films, film language,
lighting, editing, titling, sound, storage, etc. A glossary and some references conclude the volume. This
is a comprehensive, well-illustrated volume on the
basics of filmmaking. Recommended.

389 *Basic Titling and Animation for Motion Pictures.* compiled by Eastman
Kodak. paper illus. New York: Amphoto, 1970.

This Kodak book is designed for the amateur rather
than the skilled professional. It describes techniques
for titling and animation that are appropriate for the
small-scale producer—the teacher, the media specialist, the librarian, etc.

390 *Basil Rathbone: His Life and His Films.* by Druxman, Michael B. 357 p. illus. New York: A.S. Barnes, 1975.

"He was a good actor and a nice guy" is the rather mild tribute from Fredric March that concludes this equally mild survey of Basil Rathbone's life and films. Written in a chronological, factual manner that avoids any controversy or interpretation in depth, the text is detailed with dates, names, play titles, etc. The major section is devoted to the filmography, which begins with INNOCENT (1921) and ends with HILLBILLYS IN A HAUNTED HOUSE (1967). Title, release date, cast and credits, a brief synopsis, some background material, and a one-sentence critical excerpt appear for each film. One, two, or three stills accompany each entry in the filmography. The book is not indexed. Acceptable.

391 *Bateman and I in Filmland.* by Clark, Dudley. 91 p. illus. London: T. F. Unwin, 1926.

This satire on the motion pictures was illustrated by Henry Mayo Bateman and employs fantasy, anecdotes, etc., in its unusual text.

392 THE BATTLE OF ALGIERS. by Solinas, Pier Nico; and Pontecorvo, Gillo. 288 p. illus. New York: Scribner's, 1973.

Script of the 1966 film directed by Pontecorvo. Includes interviews with Pontecorvo and Solinas, along with awards, cast and production credits.

393 THE BATTLE OF BRITAIN. edited by Tipthorp, Peter 32 p. paper illus. London: Sackville Publishing Ltd., 1967.

In this souvenir book, a foreword by the Duke of Edinburgh and an introduction by Lord Dowding are followed by the historical data and quotations that provide the basis for the film. In addition to the film story, there is biographical data on director Guy Hamilton and producers Harry Saltzman and Ben Fisz. Cast and production credits follow a long description of how the film was made. The concluding section is a tribute to the aces of the Battle in the form of a Roll of Honor.

394 THE BATTLE OF BRITAIN: The Making of A Film. by Mosley, Leonard. 207 p. illus. New York: Stein & Day, 1969.

Two stories are presented. The major one concerns the making of the film, THE BATTLE OF BRITAIN (1969); the second is a retelling of the story of that battle. Because of the author's wartime experience, both sections are informative, interesting, and well-written. However, since the subject film received such a limited exposure largely because of a lack of critical praise, the book itself is diminished in value. The illustrations in both black and white and color are excellent.

395 BATTLE OF THE BULGE. 28 p. paper illus. Hollywood: Warner Brothers, 1966.

The usual format is followed in this souvenir book: the story and production are discussed first, followed by page portraits of Henry Fonda, Robert Shaw, Robert Ryan and Dana Andrews. A map of the battle area precedes a plug for Jack Warner and William R. Forman of Cinerama. The director, Ken Annakin, and producers Milton Sperling and Philip Yordan get the largest share of attention in the supporting cast-and-credits section.

396 *Bazin.* by Dudley, Andrew. 273 p. illus. New York: Oxford, 1978.

Andre Bazin, often called "The Father of the New Wave," was a critic-theorist whose major theme was that of "auteurism." As founder of the periodical *Cahiers du Cinema,* he inspired a group of young French critics, resulting in a rebirth of the French cinema during the early sixties. In addition to his own extensive research, Andrew Dudley has used numerous excerpts from the writings of Bazin in this appreciation. There are also illustrations, a bibliography and an index. The result is a detailed account of a short but influential life dedicated to a greater understanding of film. Of interest primarily to the film scholars, the volume will be appreciated to a greater degree if the reader is familiar with Bazin's *What is Cinema?* and his studies, *Orson Welles,* and *Jean Renoir.*

397 THE BEACH AT FALESA. by Thomas, Dylan. 126 p. New York: Stein & Day, 1964.

An unfilmed screenplay by Dylan Thomas based on a story by Robert Louis Stevenson. An interesting reading experience.

398 *The Beatles—Books.*

Although the Beatles made only four films, they are known to millions because of these features. Information about the Beatles can be found in many books. When they first received international attention such titles as *All About the Beatles* by Edward De Balsio (Macfadden), *A Cellarful of Noise* by Brian Epstein (Doubleday), *Here Are the Beatles,* by Charles Hamblett (New English Library), *The Original Beatles Book* by Earl Leaf (Petersen), and

The Beatles Book by Norman Parkinson and Maureen Cleave (Hutchinson) appeared.

Later titles included *The Beatles: The Authorized Biography* by Hunter Davies (McGraw-Hill), *The Beatles: The Real Story* by Julius Fast (Putnam), *The Beatles Book* edited by Edward Davis (Cowles), *Apple to the Core* by Peter McCabe and Robert Schonfeld (Pocket Books), *The Beatles* by Geoffrey Stokes (Times), *The Beatles: An Illustrated Record* by Roy Carr and Tony Tyler (Harmony), *All Together Now: The First Complete Beatles Discography* by Harry Castleman and Walter Podrazik (Ballantine), *The Beatles A to Z* by Goldie Friede, Robin Titone, and Sue Weiner (Methuen), and *Shout! The Beatles in Their Generation* by Norman Philip (Simon and Schuster).

Just as Ringo and John Lennon appeared by themselves in some films, there are books devoted to the individual Beatles such as *Strawberry Fields Forever: John Lennon Remembered* by Vic Garbarini and Brian Cullman (Bantam).

399 *The Beatles in Richard Lester's* A HARD DAY'S NIGHT. edited by Difranco, J. Philip. 297 p. paper illus. New York: Penguin, 1977.

A recreation of the Beatles's first film, A HARD DAY'S NIGHT (1964), this volume is composed of the shooting script accompanied by more than 1100 frame enlargements. The goal of the editor was to relate the original shooting script to the final finished film. Material deleted from the original script is placed in brackets throughout. There is an introduction by Andrew Sarris and a lengthy interview with director Richard Lester.

The film deals with the imprisonment that fame brings to the four young musicians. Sometimes called a documentary, it offered a variety of camera styles and directorial techniques which were widely imitated in later films.

In the mode of Richard Anobile's *Classic Film* series, this volume offers much more to the reader. The effort to show the creative process in filmmaking—evolution from script to final edited film—is quite successful. When the basic material for this effort is the recreation of a much loved and critically praised movie, the combination is irresistible. This book will be treasured and admired. Highly recommended.

400 *The Beatles in the* THE YELLOW SUBMARINE. by Wilk, Max. 128 p. paper illus. New York: World, 1968.

This is not a script of the film but a book based on the song. Certain drawings seem to have been taken from the film but that is the only connection.

401 *The Beatles—Yesterday—Today—Tomorrow...* by Larkin, Rochelle. 108 p. paper illus. New York: Scholastic, 1974.

A rapid survey of the rise of the Beatles is offered in this short volume. Very little attention is given to their films and the book attaches an optimistic storybook ending which seems rather unlikely today. Very limited value.

402 *Beaton.* by Danziger, James. 256 p. illus. New York: Viking, 1980.

The attraction here is the collection of Cecil Beaton photographs that constitute the major portion of the book. A biographical sketch that attempts to relate Beaton's life and time to the visuals is included. Since the author was personally acquainted with Beaton and also had the photographer's published diaries to draw upon, the biographical portion seems accurate in its depiction of the artist.

Many celebrity portraits, along with war, travel, fashion, Hollywood, and other illustrations appear. The editing and writing supplied by Danziger serve these visuals extremely well. The combination is hard to resist. Recommended.

403 *The Beauties and the Beasts—The Mob in Show Business.* by Messick, Hank. 256 p. New York: David McKay, 1973.

Although it is written in a sensationalized, newspaper style, this volume explores some aspects of the motion picture industry and its personalities that are largely ignored in other film literature. Selected relationships between gangsters, studio heads and performers are related in a reportorial fashion that employs the who-what-where-when-why structure. The topic covers several areas of show business, but major attention is given to such Hollywood names as Jean Harlow, Louis B. Mayer, Marion Davies, George Raft, Frank Sinatra, Marilyn Monroe, Jill St. John, Joseph Schenck, Bugsy Siegel, Longie Zwillman, Willie Bioff, George Browne, and many others. The opening chapter on Fannie Brice and Nicky Arnstein will be of interest to those who enjoyed FUNNY GIRL (1968) and FUNNY LADY (1975), since it contradicts the romanticized accounts offered in those films. The volume is indexed but not illustrated.

The compromise between gossip-scandal retelling and straight investigation reportage can be accepted here because of the book's unique topic. It does suggest more than it reveals, but is still worthy of consideration.

404   *Beautiful Film Stories.* by Bakacs, Anna. New York: Vantage, 1978.

405   BEAUTY AND THE BEAST. by Cocteau, Jean; edited by Hammond, Robert M. 441 p. New York: New York University Press, 1970.

Script of the 1946 film directed by Cocteau. Contains cast credits an an introduction by Robert Hammond and two side-by-side versions of the script, one in English, the other in French.

406   *Bebe: The Films of Brigitte Bardot.* by Crawley, Tony. 256 p. illus. Secaucus, N.J.: Citadel, 1977.

Since the subject of this volume enjoyed international celebrity both off and on screen, the potential for an above-average *Citadel* book is obvious. It has been realized by author Crawley. In a long biographical essay, he divides Bardot's life into beginnings, the fifties, the sixties, and the seventies.

The filmography is quite good, giving the original film title along with the American and the British alternates. Along with credits, cast, stories, notes and reviews, there are many Bardot illustrations as her films from LE TROU NORMAND (1952) to THE GAY AND JOYOUS STORY OF COLINOT, THE SKIRT PULLER-UPPER (1973) are recalled. It is ironic that so many of her later films were never shown in America. A portrait gallery completes the book.

The volume communicates the essence of Bardot as both a public and a private figure. This is a worthy exception to the run-of-the-mill product.

407   BECKET. 32 p. paper illus. New York: National Publishers, 1964.

A section entitled "Footnotes to History," which details the story of Thomas Becket, opens this souvenir book. Two pages are given to each of the stars, Richard Burton and Peter O'Toole, while producer Hal Wallis and director Peter Glenville get a page. The rest of the cast and production crew members receive some small mention. An article by Stephen Watts entitled "The Mood of Becket" is followed by a section about the various stage versions of Jean Anouilh's play, "Becket," upon which the film was based.

408   *Bedfordshire Cinemas to 1980.* by Peck, G. C. Bedford, England: Bed-

fordshire County Library, 1981.

409   *Before I Forget.* by Mason, James. 384 p. illus. London: Hamish Hamilton, 1981.

410   *Before My Eyes: Film Criticism and Comment.* by Kauffmann, Stanley. 464 p. New York: Harper, 1980.

A collection of 140 film reviews written from 1974 to 1979 for *The New Republic*, this is the fourth such Kauffmann volume. The standards which characterized the earlier volumes—taste, intelligence, background, sophistication, and a skill at pleasing readers—are all in evidence again. A few essays are added to the reviews. For anyone seriously interested in film, Kauffmann is required reading.

411   *Before Your Very Eyes.* by Askey, Arthur. 191 p. illus. London: Woburn Press, 1975.

Arthur Askey is a British radio comedian who made some films during the forties and fifties, often appearing with Richard Murdoch.

412   *Beginner's Guide to Super 8 Filmmaking.* by Eagle, Arnold. paper illus. New York: David McKay, 1979.

Techniques, equipment, accessories, sound, and titling are among the topics considered in this step-by-step explanation of the Super 8 filmmaking system. The addition of sound after filming as well as the synchronous system is also discussed.

413   THE BEGINNING OR THE END: The Book of the Film. by Miller, Leslie. 90 p. paper illus. London: Hollywood Publishers, 1947.

In addition to the story of the film taken from the screenplay, this volume offers some information on the production of the film and its stars.

414   *Beginnings of the Biograph.* by Hendricks, Gordon. 78 p. illus. New York: Beginning of the American Film, 1964.

The account related here concerns itself with the period of 1896-1897 when motion picture pioneers developed the Biograph camera and projector, and the card-flipping Mutoscope. The first public showings of motion pictures projected on a screen are described, as are accounts of filmmaking and film production. The book is scholarly, well-documented research but will have limited appeal to all except the student and the historian. The illustrations are unfamiliar and very good.

415 *The Beginnings of the Cinema in England.* by Barnes, John. 240 p. illus. New York: Barnes and Noble, 1976.

This technical history resembles C.W. Ceram's *Archeology of the Cinema* in many ways. Using words, pictures, and diagrams, early cameras and projectors of the late 19th century are described. Such devices include the Kinetescope, the Theatograph, the Kinetic Camera, the Kineopticon, and the Cinematographe et al. Names such as Robert W. Paul, Birt Acres, the Lumieres, appear with frequency. Some attention is given to the socio-economic setting in which the first films were shown. Emphasis is on the 1892-1896 period. Appendixes include a filmography (1895-96), a chronology, notes, a film index and a general index. An admirable work, but very specialized.

416 *Behind Closed Dors.* by Dors, Diana. 208 p. illus. London: W. H. Allen, 1979.

417 *Behind the Camera.* by Kuhns, William; and Giardino, Thomas F. paper 178 p. illus. Dayton, Ohio: Pflaum, 1971.

Designed for beginners in filmmaking, this volume considers lighting, sound, camera, lenses, etc. A production log, kept by a group of young filmmakers during the making of a short film SPARROWS is included as are a few critical evaluations of this film. A print of the film may be rented or purchased to accompany the use of the text.

418 *Behind the Camera.* by Maltin, Leonard. 240 p. paper illus. New York: New American Library, 1971.

A volume about the artists behind the camera which contains a long introductory essay by Maltin and five interviews with noted American cameramen. Arthur C. Miller, Hal Mohr, Hal Rosson, Lucien Ballard, and Conrad Hall are representative of almost all the periods of American film history. After each interview, a listing of the films that each shot is given. The nominees for Academy Awards in cinematography are noted, with the winners indicated by an asterisk. The book is illustrated and indexed.

The Maltin essay is a historical survey and evaluation of the contribution that the camerman has

made to films. The article is well-researched and serves as a tribute to the neglected artist whose work can be crucial to the success or failure of a film. The interviews are interesting and indicate a sort of pioneer individuality in the subjects.

This is an unusual, illuminating volume that may need a little help in gaining reader attention. In this case, the effort is most worthwhile. Recommended.

419 *Behind the Camera.* by Barkas, Natalie. 237 p. illus. London: Geoffrey Bles, 1934.

Reminiscences of filmmaking in West Africa by the wife of Geoffrey Barkas, a director noted for making documentary, educational and nature films in the twenties. Acting as a script girl on this expedition, Mrs. Barkas relates the experiences of filming native actors, location sequences, bush warfare, etc. In addition to directing, Barkas also wrote, produced and was the cameraman for many of his films.

420 *Behind the Cinema Screen.* by Chesmore, Stuart. 100 p. illus. London: Thomas Nelson, 1934.

This volume, which was designed for younger readers, is a predecessor of the later *Behind the Scenes* series. Using photographs, diagrams, stills, and drawings by A. L. Stephens, it offers an account of filmmaking in a large studio. Starting with script preparation, it describes sets, make-up, camera work, editing, special effects, newsreels, cartoons, instructional films, and sound projection. Special attention is given to the story of Mickey Mouse and to a history of the film in England. The book was number five in the *Discovery* series.

421 *Behind the Motion-Picture Screen.* by Lescarboura, Austin Celestin. 420 p. illus. New York: B. Blom, 1971 (1921).

Originally published in 1921 by the Scientific American Publishing Company of New York, this volume on filmmaking in the early part of this century contains over 300 illustrations. Its long subtitle describes the content: "How the scenario writer, director, cameraman, scene painter and carpenter, laboratory man, art director, property man, electrician, projector operator and others contribute their share of work toward the realization of the wonderful photoplays of today; and how the motion picture is rapidly extending into many fields aside from that of entertainment."

422 *Behind the Motion Picture Screen.* by Lescarboura, Austin. 420 p. illus.

Darby, Pa.: Arden Library, 1978 (1919).

The text, with 300 illustrations, treats actors, craftsmen, artists, cameramen, reporters, etc. and their roles in bringing films to the screen. Published originally in 1919 by the Scientific American Publishing Company of New York.

423 *Behind the Scenes: Theatre and Film Interviews From Transatlantic Review.* by McCrindle, Joseph F. 341 p. paper New York: Holt, Rinehart & Winston, 1971.

The emphasis in this collection of interviews is on theatrical actors, directors and playwrights rather than film personalities. The film directors questioned are Philippe De Broca, Federico Fellini, John Schlesinger, Tony Richardson and Lindsay Anderson.

424 *Behind the Scenes in a Film Studio.* by Grey, Elizabeth. 102 p. illus. London: Phoenix House, 1967.

Following the usual large studio structure with intelligence and with respect for the young reader, this book also includes a diagrammatic plan of the studio (instead of the usual aerial shot), a sample of shooting script, an intricate shooting schedule or "cross plot," a call sheet, a production unit diagram, and a continuity report. Index and glossary.

425 *Behind the Scenes in Hollywood.* by Haskin, Dorothy. 77 p. illus. Grand Rapids, Mich.: Zondervan, 1951.

A critical look at Hollywood, from a religious viewpoint, by the author of *Twice-Born Stars You Would Like to Know* (1955).

426 *Behind the Scenes in Motion Pictures.* by Cooke, David C. 64 p. illus. New York: Dodd, Mead, 1960.

A short volume on how motion pictures are made. The studio used is Paramount. Obviously much of what is stated is either out-of-date or not pertinent today, but the book is saved somewhat by an intelligent selection of pictures to accompany each page of narrative.

427 *Behind the Scenes of Otto Preminger.* by Frischauer, Willi. 279 p. illus. New York: William Morrow, 1974.

The author has known Otto Preminger for more than 40 years, their acquaintanceship going back to Vienna in the twenties. In this unauthorized biography, he uses his observations and recollections along with much supplementary research to present a well-balanced portrait of the controversial director. Attention is paid to the personal, private Preminger; the acknowledgment and acceptance of his son, Eric, is described most touchingly. Some other rather important events are omitted—Preminger's relationship with Dorothy Dandridge is barely mentioned here, although Dandridge covers it in detail in her autobiography.

Preminger's filmmaking method is given more attention than the films. Unlike Gerald Pratley's study, little attempt is made here to examine Preminger's contribution to screen history. The best the author can manage is that it is "open to question." A bibliography, filmography, an index, and some production shots round out the biography. The innuendo in the title promises a bit more than the book eventually delivers. It is an acceptable but incomplete biography of a director whose work and career remain subjects for critical debate.

428 *Behind the Screen.* by Goldwyn, Samuel. 263 p. New York: George H. Doran, 1923.

Part autobiography, part observation, part name-dropping (e.g., Chaplin, Pickford, Fairbanks, Elinor Glyn). Goldwyn's literary style was called "unintentionally funny" back in 1923.

429 *Behind the Screen: How Films are Made.* edited by Watts, Stephen. 176 p. illus. New York: Dodge Pub. Co., 1938.

An anthology on the aspects of filmmaking. This book includes articles by: Hunt Stromberg, producer; George Cukor, director; Frances Marion, script; Adrian, costume design; Natalie Kalmus, color; Leslie Howard, acting; Lionel Barrymore, acting; Douglas Shearer, sound; and others. Sounds and reads like an MGM super-production.

430 *Behind the Screen: The History and the Techniques of the Motion Picture.* by MacGowan, Kenneth. 528 p. illus. New York: Delacorte Press, 1965.

As the subtitle indicates, this is a history of the motion picture related primarily by tracing technological invention and development. Much attention is given to pre-cinema history and the devices man used to give an illusion of motion. The contributions of major personalities such as Griffith, Chaplin and

Eisenstein, as well as those of certain behind-the-scenes personnel, are noted. The final portion is devoted to recent attempts at technical innovation designed to recapture lost audiences. A tight structure for the book is lacking and it rambles over its wide range of subject matter.

A veteran film producer, LIFEBOAT (1944), LITTLE WOMEN (1933), etc., the author is never hesitant to contradict some of the widely published myths and legends. In his writing he is dogmatic, cantankerous, opinionated, and controversial. Supporting his non-technical text are some of the best pictures and illustrations on cinema history to be found. In a laudable attempt to make the concept of the Mutoscope clear, he even includes an approximation of a riffle book featuring Mickey Mouse. The volume has much to recommend it.

431 *Belafonte: An Unauthorized Biography.* by Shaw, Arnold. 287 p. paper illus. New York: Pyramid Books, 1960.

The emphasis is on Belafonte the singer rather than the actor. Some brief mention is made of the subject's films: BRIGHT ROAD (1953), CARMEN JONES (1955), ISLAND IN THE SUN (1957), THE WORLD, THE FLESH AND THE DEVIL (1959) and ODDS AGAINST TOMORROW (1959).

432 BELLE DE JOUR. by Bunuel, Luis; and Carriere, Jean-Claude. 168 p. paper illus. New York: Simon and Schuster, 1971.

Script of the 1967 film directed by Bunuel. Contains: two interviews with Bunuel, an article by Andrew Sarris, and cast and production credits.

433 *The Bennett Playbill.* by Bennett, Joan; and Kibbee, Lois. 332 p. New York: Holt, Rinehart & Winston, 1970.

Contains a fairly brief but good section on Hollywood and the Joan Bennett films. It is mostly concerned with theater, with the first half concentrating on Richard Bennett and other theatrical ancestors. In the latter section, the Wanger-Lang shooting gets major coverage.

434 *Bergman:* PERSONA and SHAME. by Bergman, Ingmar. 191 p. paper illus. New York: Grossman, 1972.

Contains an introduction, "Snakeskin," by Ingmar Bergman; and cast and production credits for PER-

SONA (1966), and SHAME (1968).

435 *Bergman.* edited by Cooper, Geoffrey; and Warham, Christopher. 64 p. Beaverton, Ore.: International Scholarly Book Service, 1980.

This appreciation of Ingmar Bergman originated at the University of Western Australia.

436 *Bergman on Bergman: Interviews with Ingmar Bergman.* by Bjorkman, Stig; and Manns, Torsten; and Sima, Jonas. 288 p. illus. New York: Simon & Schuster, 1974.

The initial interview for this book took place in January, 1968. Thirteen more sessions were held, and from the more than 50 hours of conversation that resulted, this book was made. The three interviewers are film critics and editors of the film periodical, *Chaplin;* in addition, they enjoy separate careers in journalism, architecture and filmmaking.

Bergman discusses many aspects of his personal and professional life—his childhood, theatre work, his films and the company of actors associated with him. The tone of the conversation is relaxed, friendly, and happy—not the gloomy, pessimistic atmosphere that pervades most of Bergman's films. The questions and comments of the interviews provide the stimulus for Bergman to give a most intimate and complete self-portrait.

The many illustrations complement the text and are reproduced in acceptable fashion. There is an index to the interviews, and a Bergman filmography is also included. This is an essential major work on one of the most important figures in the history of the cinema. It is highly recommended.

437 *Bernadette Lafont: An Interview.* by Hughes, John. 56 p. paper illus. New York: Zoetrope, 1978.

This interview between underground filmmaker Bernadette Lafont and critic John Hughes is accompanied by illustrations and a filmography.

438 *Bertolt Brecht's Berlin.* by von Eckardt, Wolf.; and Gilman, Sander L. 170 p. illus. Garden City, N.Y.: Anchor/Doubleday, 1975.

This volume, subtitled "A Scrapbook of the Twenties," contains an informative chapter on the films of that decade. The illustrations are mostly unfamiliar, showing German performers, such as Henry Porten, Lilian Harvey, Dietrich, Riefenstahl, Luis

Trenker, Emil Jannings, Lotte Lenya, etc.

439   *see   440*

440   *Best Actress—Academy Awards.* by Osborne, Robert. 84 p. paper illus. La Habra, Calif.: E. E. Schworck, 1970

An excerpt from Osborne's *The Academy Awards Illustrated.*

441   *The Best Film Plays of 1945.* edited by Gassner, John; and Nichols, Dudley. 648 p. illus. New York: Crown, 1946.

Contains cast credits, an introduction "A Second Annual," by John Gassner, and an article, "The Machine from the God," by Dudley Nichols. Includes scripts of THE LOST WEEKEND, SPELL-BOUND, DOUBLE INDEMNITY, A TREE GROWS IN BROOKLYN, NONE BUT THE LONELY HEART, THE SOUTHERNER, THE STORY OF G.I. JOE, THIRTY SECONDS OVER TOKYO, OVER TWENTY ONE, and A MEDAL FOR BENNY.

442   *Best Film Plays 1943-44.* edited by Gassner, John; and Nichols, Dudley. 694 p. illus. New York: Crown, 1945.

Contains cast credits, and introduction, "Writer, Director and Film," by Dudley Nichols, and two articles, "The Motion Picture Industry and the War Effort," by Walter Wanger, and "Preface to WILSON," by Darryl Zanuck. Includes scripts of WILSON, THE PURPLE HEART, GOING MY WAY, THE MIRACLE OF MORGAN'S CREEK, WATCH ON THE RHINE, DRAGON SEED, THE MORE THE MERRIER, THE OX BOW INCIDENT, HAIL THE CONQUERING HERO, and CASABLANCA.

443   *The Best from Famous Monsters of Filmland.* edited by Ackerman, Forrest J. 162 p. paper illus. New York: Paperback Library, 1964.

A collection of more than 150 stills from horror movies—both silent and sound. There is some attempt to group pictures around a theme, but the important thing is the photographs.

444   *Best Moving Pictures—1922, 1923.* edited by Sherwood, Robert E. 346 p. illus. Brooklyn, N.Y.: Revisionist, 1981 (1923).

An early twenties yearbook that treats a wide range of topics—actors, films, awards, grosses, publicity, short films, censorship, etc. Originally published in

Boston by Small, Maynard.

445   *The Best of Buster.* edited by Anobile, Richard. 256 p. paper illus. New York: Crown (Darien House), 1976.

After an introduction by Raymond Rohauer and a preface by editor Anobile, more than 1000 frame blowups provide a sampling of Buster Keaton's creative genius. Short sequences are taken from THE GOAT (1921), SHERLOCK JR. (1924), THE NAVIGATOR (1924), GO WEST (1925), SEVEN CHANCES (1925), and THE GENERAL (1926). As usual with this series, the clarity of the visuals is most impressive. The films above are from the silent screen era and so there is no accompanying dialogue. Only a few titles are included and the volume is almost completely visual. Recommended.

446   *The Best of Groucho.* by Marx, Groucho. 3 volumes paper illus. New York: Manor, 1980.

A boxed set consisting of *Groucho and Me* (1959), *Memoirs of a Mangy Lover* (1963), and *The Groucho Letters* (1967).

447   *The Best of Life.* edited by Life Staff. 304 p. illus. New York: Time Life Books, 1973.

Among the 700 different visuals in this anthology of photographs from *Life* magazine, there are many which deal with Hollywood and film performers.

448   *The Best Pictures 1939-1940.* edited by Wald, Jerry; and Macaulay, Richard. 534 p. illus. New York: Dodd, Mead, 1940.

Contains an introduction by Jerry Wald and Richard Macaulay and a preface by Walter Wanger. Includes: 1) "The Production Season" ; 2) major films released from July, 1939 to July, 1940; 3) Academy Awards up to 1938; 4) N. Y. Film Critics' Circle Awards to 1938; 5) *Film Daily's*" 10 Best Pictures of the Year," 1922 to 1938; and 6) the condensed scripts of BACHELOR MOTHER, GOODBYE MR. CHIPS, NINOTCHKA, REBECCA, MR. SMITH GOES TO WASHINGTON, DR. ERLICH'S MAGIC BULLET, and DESTRY RIDES AGAIN.

449   *The Best Remaining Seats: The Story of the Golden Age of the Movie Palace.* by Hall, Ben M. 260 p. illus. New York: Bramhall House (Crown), 1961.

A sentimental tribute to the great movie palaces, this

book is both historical and nostalgic. By the use of many pictures and a thoughtful text, the era of large scale motion picture exhibition (1920-1960) is covered. The book officially ends at 1960 with the destruction of the New York Roxy. All facets of the large cinema cathedrals are covered—architecture, furnishings, great organs, orchestras, staff, usher corps, and stage shows. Indexed.

450 *Best TV Commercials of the Year.* edited by Ross, Wallace A. 191 p. illus. New York: Hastings House, 1967.

A pictorial record of the finalists in a TV commercial contest. These "Clio" awards are given yearly to commercials which are adventurous, creative, stimulating, and successful in their purpose—attracting viewer attention. A thin plastic recording of the best radio commercials is included.

Indicated here as a source of information, stimulation, and inspiration for young filmmakers—the newest trends and techniques can be found most readily in the film commercial and this book presents a concise, well-produced study of this film form.

451 *The Best Years of My Life.* by Russell, Harold; and Ferullo, Dan. 192 p. illus. Middlebury, Vt.: Eriksson, 1981.

Russell tells of his life before and after his war injury. His celebrity which resulted from THE BEST YEARS OF OUR LIVES (1946) is brought up to date.

452 *Bette: The Life of Bette Davis.* by Higham, Charles. 316 p. illus. New York: Macmillan, 1981.

A reheated version of an oft-told story. The reader should return to *The Lonely Life* as author Higham frequently does here.

453 *Bette Davis: A Biography.* by Noble, Peter. 231 p. illus. London: Skelton Robinson, 1948.

This spare biography is based on information and quotations found in film periodicals, books and newspapers. Although Miss Davis supplies a rather detached foreword, the book did not have the benefit of her cooperation as did the later *The Lonely Life.*

The time period covered is Miss Davis' "Golden Years," 1930-1947. Missing however, are discussions of such classic films as ALL ABOUT EVE (1950) and WHAT EVER HAPPENED TO BABY JANE? (1962). A partial filmography is offered at the book's conclusion. This volume may be used to supplement *The*

Lonely Life and *The Films of Bette Davis.* It is most acceptable for its sympathetic and affectionate coverage of this durable star's early career.

454 *Bette Davis.* by Vermilye, Jerry. 159 p. paper illus. New York: Pyramid, 1973.

A volume in a new series, *The Pyramid Illustrated History of the Movies,* the standard structure of which includes an introductory overview of the life-career of the subject, followed by the films, conveniently divided into appropriate periods. In this case, we have The Early Years, The First Triumphs, The Battle with Warners, The Vintage Years, Years of Decline, The See-Saw Years, and The Final Fright Films. Closing sections include a filmography, bibliography, and an index, all of which add to the reference value of the book.

This is another fine book in what promises to be an outstanding series. All elements are of high quality. Reproduction of the many photographs is good, the text is literate, spare, and critical, and there is enough unfamiliar material to intrigue most readers; for example, several illustrations are of Davis in scenes that the public never saw. Along with the Dody biography, *The Lonely Life,* this is a basic book on a legendary film actress.

455 *Better Motion Pictures.* by Eastman, Fred; and Ouellette, Edward. 60 p. Boston: Interdenominational Committee on Cooperative Publication of Adult Texts, 1936.

The moral and religious aspects of motion pictures are discussed in this title from the *Learning For Life* series.

456 *Better Movies in Minutes.* edited by Kodak Consumer Markets Div. 57 p. paper illus. Rochester, N.Y.: Eastman Kodak, 1974.

Here is another example of the high quality, low cost books that Eastman Kodak publishes. This book is numbered AD-4 and is aimed at the person who wishes to improve his film product. The text touches on many aspects of making motion pictures—cameras, motors, lenses, lighting, sound, titling, editing, exhibition, and maintenance. It is readable and comprehensive, supported throughout by a series of beautiful full-color illustrations. Readers will probably overlook the frequent Kodak commercials when they appear amidst such attractive visuals. Two other volumes worthy of attention are *Home Movies Made Easy* (AD-5) and *How to Make Good Sound*

Movies (AD-2). All are recommended.

457 *Better Super-8 Movie Making.* by Matzkin, Myron. 128 p. paper illus. Philadelphia: Chilton, 1967.

Designed for the beginning filmmaker, this basic volume deals only with super-8 cameras and the techniques for using them. Easy, practical, and helpful.

458 *Betty Boop.* by Fleisher, Max. unpaginated. paper illus. New York: Avon, 1975.

Austrian-born Max Fleisher was a cartoonist who enjoyed a long career in Hollywood as the creator of animated cartoon films with characters such as Popeye the Sailor, Koko the Clown, and Betty Boop. During the thirties, his only rival was Walt Disney. In addition to short cartoons, he produced two feature-length cartoon films—GULLIVER'S TRAVELS (1939) and MR. BUG GOES TO TOWN (1941). Betty Boop was the first animated cartoon vamp and the essence of her personality is caught in this collection of newspaper comic strips taken from the 1935-36 period. Most of the situations deal with Betty Boop's experiences as a film star. Acceptable.

459 *Betty Grable: The Reluctant Movie Queen.* by Warren, Doug. 288 p. illus. New York: St. Martin's, 1981.

A surface biography that deals primarily with facts rather than interpretation. Warren opts for nostalgia instead of understanding.

460 *Between Hell and Charing Cross.* by Wilcox, Pamela. illus. London: Allen and Unwin, 1977.

The author is the daughter of British film producer Herbert Wilcox, and has had careers in both film and television. She tells about some of her experiences in Hollywood and with John Grierson, but most of the story is personal soap opera.

461 *Between Ourselves.* by Hicks, Seymour. illus. London: Cassell, 1930.

Seymour Hicks was a character actor who appeared in British films during the thirties. He also wrote *Me and My Missus* in 1939.

462 *Between the Acts.* by Cantor, Eddie. 115 p. New York: Simon and Schuster, 1930.

This small book is noted here because it contains one article called "talkies." Not much, but someone may reassess Cantor's talent as a film performer one of these days and the information may help. For the record only.

463 BETWEEN TWO MOONS: An Unfilmed Screenplay. by Mungo, Raymond; and Bartlett, Richard. 223 p. paper illus. Boston: Beacon Press, 1972.

Using the screenplay form, this unique paperback has a text, many drawings and lots of murky symbolism. It is included here as an example of the influence of film on current literature. A case of the medium being far more important than the message.

464 *Beverly Hills: Portrait of a Fabled City.* by Basten, Fred E. 383 p. illus. Los Angeles, Calif.: Douglas-West, 1975.

Using more than 450 illustrations and an informative text, Fred Basten traces the history of Beverly Hills from the late 18th century to the present. Emphasis is on the current century when filmmakers built their homes in this ideal location. Using a decade-by-decade approach, the book shows residences, public buildings, churches, stores, schools, and libraries. Its value is twofold—as a record of the lifestyle of filmmakers during Hollywood's golden era and as an example of how an industry can create a community. The illustrations are well reproduced and an index is provided.

465 *Beverly Hills: The Golden Ghetto.* by Wagner, Walter. 288 p. illus. New York: Grosset & Dunlap, 1976.

A debunking of the myth of Beverly Hills, this rather nasty expose deals with police, schools, citizens, scandals, doctors, psychiatrists, and other small town elements. Life in Beverly Hills—both past and present—is described and the author argues that the motion picture industry is leaving this nontypical bedroom community. Illustrated and indexed, this is a downbeat volume that is peripheral to film literature.

466 *Beverly Hills Is My Beat.* by Anderson, Clinton. 218 p. illus. Englewood Cliffs, N. J.: Prentice-Hall, 1960.

An account of the activities of the Chief of Police in Beverly Hills and some of the cases in which he was involved. No shocking secrets are divulged, and with the exception of Chaplin, Stompanato-Turner, Walter Wanger, and few others, all famous names are changed or withheld. As a portrait of police work amidst the glamour of Hollywood, this volume is acceptable. It is not the expose that the title may suggest.

467 *Beyond Formula: American Film Genres.* by Solomon, Stanley J. 310 p. illus. New York: Harcourt Brace Jovanovich, 1976.

This study of American film genres treats the major classifications—the western, the musical, the horror film, the crime film, the detective film, and the war film. In each instance a few preliminary chapters identify the unique form and characteristics of the genre; the description is followed by discussions of several specific films which exemplify each genre. For example, the crime films section first discusses the categories of criminal films, the gangster mind, criminal values, and prisoners. Analyses are then offered of THE PUBLIC ENEMY (1931), FORCE OF EVIL (1949), WHITE HEAT (1949), RIOT IN CELL BLOCK 11 (1954), ON THE WATERFRONT (1954), BONNIE AND CLYDE (1967) and THE GODFATHER (1972).

Supporting the text are a fine selection of visuals, a bibliography, and index of films, a list of distributors, and a general index. These elements enrich a superior text that has been written in a logical, well-balanced style. This volume is an outstanding example of film criticism and comment based on the genre approach to film study. Highly recommended.

468 *Beyond the Image.* by Holloway, Ronald. paper New York: World Council of Churches, 1977.

Ronald Holloway provides an exploration of religious ideas as presented in films from Griffith to Bergman. Using a world history of cinema as his base, he identifies various attitudes toward religion as they were found in different periods. His approach is the scholarly one that such specialized and neglected material deserves. Recommended.

469 THE BIBLE. by Fry, Christopher. 175 p. paper illus. New York, Pocketbooks, 1966.

Script of the 1966 film directed by John Huston.

470 THE BIBLE. by Liebling, Howard; and Lubalin, Herb. 44 p. paper illus. New York: Alsid Distributors, 1966.

Beginning with some quotations from the screenplay by Christopher Fry, this souvenir book tells of the attempts of producer Dino De Laurentis and director John Huston to preserve fidelity to the text of the Bible. Using large illustrations by Ernst Haas, the cameraman who is probably better known for his still photography than for his motion picture work, the book gives evidence of an attempt to make a film on a grand scale. Only the last few pages are devoted to cast and production credits. An impressive effort that causes the reader to wonder what went wrong in making the film.

471 *Bibliographic Index.* New York: H. W. Wilson Co., 1938- .

This reference work indexes current bibliographies by subject. It is issued semi- annually with bound annuals and three-year cumulations availabe. Forty or more bibliographic citations are the standard for inclusion in this work. It includes bibliographies published as books or parts of books or in pamphlets. Some 1700 periodicals are examined for other bibliographic material. "Moving Pictures" is the entry to look at first.

472 *Bibliography of Film Librarianship.* by Kula, Sam. 68 p. paper London: The Library Association, 1967.

Using works published in English, this bibliography goes up to 1965. It employs the following subject headings: bibliographies—general, evolution of library film services, training for film librarianship, administration of film services (public), administration of film services (college, university), administration of film services (special libraries), administration of film services (television libraries), cooperative library film services, stock material libraries, film archives (film as history), film archives (administrative), cataloging rules, cataloging and classification, storage and presentation, copyright, glossaries of film terms. A combined author and title index completes this small but valuable book which is somewhat dated but still of value.

473 *Bibliography of Screen Celebrities: An A-Z Guide to over 500 Books Written about Individual Screen Actors and Actresses.* compiled by Skinner, J. W. 12 p. Worthing: International Film Collector, 1978.

474 *A Bibliography of Song Sheets.* by McDonald, Gerald D. 55 p. Rochester: Music Library Association, 1958.

Subtitled "Sports and Recreations in American Popular Songs," this volume devotes Part IV to "Songs of the Silent Film."

475 THE BICYCLE THIEF. by Zavattini, Cesare. 100 p. paper illus. New York: Simon & Schuster, 1968.

Script of the 1947 film directed by Vittorio DeSica. Contains cast credits and an introduction by Simon Hartog.

476 *Big Bad Wolves: Masculinity in the American Film.* by Mellen, Joan. 365 p. illus. New York: Pantheon, 1977.

Joan Mellen is a consistent writer whose books explore and explain aspects of the film that have been overlooked or taken for granted. Here she provides a historical overview of the male image reflected in American films from THE GREAT TRAIN ROBBERY (1903) to ONE ON ONE (1977). Her argument is that the myth of masculinity perpetuated by the screen has not only demeaned men but the total American culture.

The examples she chooses for her arguments vary from obvious to surprising to unfamiliar. Her remarkably persuasive text should convince most readers of the disservice done to American males by films.

Mellen's latest contribution to the sociology of the screen is most impressive. An educational entertainment, this volume will be embraced by the concerned militant and has the potential for affecting a change of attitude in the accepting general reader. Illustrations are well selected and the volume is indexed. Highly recommended.

477 THE BIG FISHERMAN. edited by Hardiman, James. 50 p. illus. New York: Random House, 1959.

A program book issued to accompany hard ticket showings of THE BIG FISHERMAN (1959). Outstanding color shots from the film contribute much to this account of one of the few super productions to be filmed entirely in the United States. An interesting memoir.

478 *The Big Love.* by Aadland, Florence; and Thomey, Tedd. 158 p. paper New York: Lancer Books, 1961.

More trash from the past. The opening sentence gives a preview of what is to follow: "There's one thing I want to make clear right off: my baby was a virgin the day she met Errol Flynn." This account of Beverly Aadland's relationship with Errol Flynn as interpreted by Beverly's mother is obviously suspect. An investigation of murder and prostitution several years after Flynn's death put Beverly in juve-

nile hall for a period. Mother Aadland was held on five charges of contributing to Beverly's delinquency. The book is dedicated to "The Swashbuckler, himself, with all our love." Depressing, sad, and an example of what many would consider obscene in publishing. Not recommended, but noted for the record.

479 *Big Media, Little Media: Tools and Technologies.* by Schramm, Wilbur. paper illus. Beverly Hills, Calif.: Sage, 1980.

A survey designed to aid educators in reviewing the existing information bearing on the choice between big media and little media for instruction. Film, of course, is one of the possible choices.

480 *Big Screen, Little Screen.* by Reed, Rex. 433 p. illus. New York: Macmillan, 1971.

In his third book, Rex Reed expands his coverage to television programs (including commercials), films, performers, and his own experiences in filming MYRA BRECKENRIDGE (1970). Still one of the best journalists appearing between covers today, Reed can attract and entertain most readers.

481 *The Big Swingers.* by Fenton, Robert W. 258 p. illus. Englewood Cliffs, N. J.: Prentice-Hall, 1967.

A biography of Edgar Rice Burroughs which traces the Tarzan character through books, films, and comics, giving plots, themes, and players.

482 *Big U: Universal in the Silent Days.* by Edmonds, I. G. 162 p. illus. New York: A.S. Barnes, 1977.

The early history of a still-functioning Hollywood studio is told in this volume. From its founding in 1912 to the present day, Universal studios has played an important role in motion picture history. Almost simultaneously with the publication of this book on the silent days of Universal, another volume by Michael G. Fitzgerald called *Universal Pictures* appeared which covers the sound era from 1928 to 1976. Since this volume is concerned with the period from 1912 to 1928, the two books are ideal for anyone interested in the history of Universal Studios.

The name of Carl Laemmle is synonymous with Universal Pictures since he was its president from 1912 to 1936. Under his guidance the studio became a business organization whose product was motion pictures—most of which were profitable. Many famous actors and directors received their early training and apprenticeship at the studio. The author covers all these aspects of the studio's operation and more in an interesting narrative that was based on personal interviews and research.

Supporting the text are 150 rare photographs. The book is indexed.

A unique contribution to film history is made by this volume. By using his personal resources in dealing with a subject that is specialized and rather factual, the author has made his work both entertaining and informative.

483 *The Big V: A History of the Vitagraph Company.* by Slide, Anthony. 232 p. illus. Metuchen, N.J.: Scarecrow, 1976.

Vitagraph, one of the most important silent film production companies, was founded in 1896 and remained active until its absorption by the Warner brothers in 1925. Founded by J. Stuart Blackton and Albert E. Smith, the studio established the star system, had a repertory group of actors and technicians, and was the forerunner of the larger studios of the thirties. In detailed fashion, Anthony Slide tells the story of the studio, its founders, actors, and films. Following the thoroughly researched text there are some excellent supporting elements: a bibliography (107 entries); a Vitagraph Who's Who (short biographical paragraphs of 50 of Viatagraph's most important personnel); a listing of Vitagraph films from 1910 to 1915; and an index to the text.

This is a delightful combination of entertainment, scholarship and reference. Although the films and the names will be largely unfamiliar to most readers, they will enjoy the story told by Slide. He has the uncommon ability to blend research and history into a readable account. Highly recommended.

484 *Bijou Kinema.* by Benfield, Robert. 62 p. paper illus. Sheffield City: Sheffield City Polytechnic, 1976.

A history of early cinema in Yorkshire.

485 *Bill Adler's Letters to Elvis.* by Adler, Bill. illus. New York: Grosset & Dunlap, 1978.

486 *Bill Collins' Book of Movies.* by Collins, Bill. illus. Australia: Cassell, 1978.

Bill Collins wears a number of professional hats in his native Australia—interviewer, TV host, college lecturer, film historian, archivist, etc. In a very sub-jective book, he discusses his enthusiasm for certain films, which he groups under headings such as Great Experiences, A World on Film, Neglected Master-pieces, etc. Australian films are considered,as is the author's fondness for film trivia. Illustrations are plentiful but selected with a personal bias. Ultimately, the book tells as much about the author as it does about the films he likes.

487 *Billy Bitzer: His Story.* by Bitzer, G. W. 266 p. illus. New York: Farrar Straus & Giroux, 1973.

What a satisfying autobiography this is! Although it was written around 1944 and covers only the period up to 1920, it does not have the flavor of memora-bilia. For the most part it is an honest, unpretentious account of the early and middle career of the most widely known cameraman in motion picture history. His images often had a simple beauty to them; that can be seem by the samples used in this book. His text has that same quality. In his descriptions of the personalities with whom he worked, he is generous, sensitive, and affectionate. His love of his profession is evident throughout.

Since he was inseparable from D. W. Griffith for so many years, it is not surprising that Griffith gets as much attention here as he did in Lillian Gish's au-tobiography. He co-stars once again.

As indicated above, the visuals provide pure pleas-ure and the publishers have watched their reproduc-tion carefully. A Bitzer filmography—probably the first complete one—and an index complete the book. Excellent on all counts and a fine contribution to American film history. Highly recommended.

488 BILLY JACK. by Christina, Frank; and Christina, Teresa. 124 p. paper illus. New York: Avon, 1973.

Script of the 1971 film directed by T. C. Frank. Con-tains cast, credits, and an introduction by Tom Laughlin and Delores Taylor.

489 *Billy Wilder.* by Madsen, Axel. 167 p. paper illus. Bloomington, Ind.: Indiana University Press, 1969.

Another excellent book in the *Cinema* series, this one contains a rather complete portrait of Wilder and a surface look at his films. Certain of his rela-tionships with people from his films are explored, but not in great depth. Most of the author's narra-tive is descriptive, the critical comments usually be-ing quotations from other sources. The book is valuable, if only to recall Wilder's films, DOUBLE INDEMNITY (1944), THE LOST WEEKEND (1945),

SUNSET BOULEVARD (1950), ACE IN THE HOLE (1951), SOME LIKE IT HOT (1959), and THE APARTMENT (1960). Illustrations used throughout are of high quality and are selected with intelligence. A filmography is included, too. Recommended for most readers.

490 *Billy Wilder.* by Dick, Bernard F. 168 p. illus. Boston: Twayne, 1980.

Billy Wilder gets the *Twayne Theatrical Arts* series treatment of text, illustrations, chronology, notes, references, bibliography, filmography, and index. Here, the text departs from a straight chronological presentation placing the films into similar groups instead—human comedies, September songs, dirty fairy tales, bosom buddies, sleuthing around, etc. The final chapter called "Down Among The Rotting Palms" deals with SUNSET BOULEVARD (1950) and FEDORA (1979).

Billy Wilder's work is very rich in material to write about and Bernard Dick uses this opportunity wisely. His analysis is more satisfying than that found in other books on Wilder but the feeling persists that the films contain more than what is offered here.

491 *Billy Wilder in Hollywood.* by Zolotow, Maurice. 364 p. illus. New York: G. P. Putman's, 1977.

In this remarkable biography, Maurice Zolotow has provided so many different views of Billy Wilder that, when the reader has finished the book, he will feel a personal acquaintance with the director. Such an accomplishment testifies to enormous research activity and a first-rate writing talent.

As in Zolotow's biographies of Marilyn Monroe and John Wayne, there is great detail provided. He never forgets that these are motion picture people, and as a result, the films get heavy attention. Beginning with Wilder's first American writing assignment on LOTTERY LOVER (1935), the text treats all the films that he helped to create over a forty-year period. Certain of Zolotow's conjectures regarding Wilder's recent succession of failures are quite provocative, as they are related to incidents in the director's private life.

The text is roughly chronological, although the author occasionally interrupts his time continuum to offer an interview comment, periodical quotations, a pertinent anecdote or simply someone's opinion of Wilder. As with all good biographers, Zolotow seems genuinely fond of Wilder, calling him on several occasions "the man you hate to love." Apparently not all of the people interviewed shared a similar feeling about Wilder.

The volume is indexed and there is a center section of visuals. The absence of a filmography is unexplainable—and almost unforgiveable.

This volume is an example of film biography at its very best. Not only is it richly entertaining, but it offers informational and critical substance instead of the customary froth. Highly recommended.

492 *Bing.* by Thompson, Charles, 249 p. illus. New York: David McKay, 1976.

Since this is an authorized biography, the portrait of the legendary Bing Crosby is very carefully presented. Although the book is crammed with information about Crosby's long productive life and career, the reader may sense that much material has been omitted, specifically in the area of personal relationships.

For more than five decades Crosby was an entertainer whose career covered most facets of show business. This aspect of his life is covered adequately. However, his relationships with Dixie Lee Crosby and his first four sons are given surface treatment while others, such as Joan Caulfield and Marion Talley, are simply ignored. Ethel Merman, Martha Raye, Bob Burns, Miriam Hopkins, Louise Campbell and Shirley Ross played prominent roles in his films but are not mentioned in the text. The book is heavy on certain names but they seem curiously selected.

A few illustrations are provided and the book is indexed. No attempt is made to provide a filmography, a discography or any other appearance record.

Serious factual errors occur on page 212. The author states that in 1963 Crosby failed to get the rights to THE RAINMAKER for which Burt Lancaster won an Oscar. THE RAINMAKER was released in 1956 and Lancaster won an Oscar for ELMER GANTRY in 1960.

This volume is another attempt to perpetuate the public image of Crosby. To the other cautious works such as *Call Me Lucky* and *Bing and Other Things* we may now add one more. The definitive biography-study-appreciation on Crosby has yet to appear. This volume is pleasant to read while we wait.

493 *Bing and Other Things.* by Crosby, Kathryn. 214 p. illus. New York: Meredith Press, 1967.

Other than the 1953 autobiography, *Call Me Lucky*, Bing Crosby has been a rather neglected subject for study-appreciation in film literature. The publication of an authorized biography, *Bing*, may suggest a long overdue critical study of this legendary performer.

This sixties volume was an interim attempt to keep the Crosby name professionally alive and to establish wife Kathryn as an entity with whom to reckon. Her life before and after meeting Bing Crosby is related in *Ladies Home Journal* style with mild noncontroversial accounts of Hollywood life and filmmaking. One would get the impression that the Crosby life is all peanut butter and jelly rather than champagne and caviar.

Some candid photographs support the just-plain-folk style of the text. Other than a smattering of factual information, there is not much to be learned about Bing Crosby here. Noted for the record.

494 *Bing Crosby.* edited by Marill, A. H. 64 p. paper illus. Kew Gardens, N.Y.: Cinefax, 1969.

Illustrations, stills,and candids visualize many of the films and events of Crosby's long career.

495 *Bing Crosby.* by Bauer, Barbara. 159 p. paper illus. New York: Pyramid, 1977.

This title in the *Pyramid Illustrated History of the Movies* series examines the life and career of Bing Crosby. The standard series format of blending many illustrations with a literate text works well, as usual. A bibliography, a filmography, and an index are included.

496 *Bing Crosby: The Hollow Man.* by Shepherd, Donald; and Slatzer, Robert F. 320 p. illus. New York: St. Martin's, 1981.

A hatchet job on Bing Crosby that stresses the the dark, negative side of the singer.

497 *Biograph Bulletins 1896-1908.* by Niver, Kemp R. 464 p. illus. Los Angeles: Locare Research, 1971.

This very specialized reference work is typical of Niver's continuing contribution to film history and literature. Using the Biograph Bulletins, those handbills which described individual films produced by the company, he provides reproductions of original source materials that may be used in many ways. The period covered is 1896 to 1908, when D. W. Griffith became a full-time director at Biograph. Some of the bulletins contain capsule annotations and reminders of other Biograph films in addition to the one being featured.

As an introduction, selected newspaper accounts of audience reaction to Biograph projectors, programs and films are reprinted. Niver supports all this material by personal notes where necessary, an alphabetical fimography with cameraman, filming date, copyright date, and page number reference, and finally a chronological filmography for each of Biograph's major cameraman.

Niver has once more created an example of research that should be studied by other historians and scholars. It is informative, entertaining, and above all, arranged for easy reference. Uses for the material seem unlimited and the volume has a curiosity-nostalgia quality that will appeal to many audiences. The volume is highly recommended.

498 *Biograph Bulletins 1908-1912.* 471 p. illus. New York: Octagon Books, 1973.

This volume contains Biograph Bullentins issued from 1908 to 1912, when they were discontinued. This period coincides with the early part of D. W. Griffith's tenure at the studio and the book begins with his first film, THE ADVENTURES OF DOLLY (1908). Many of his other short films are included, but the bulletins also contain the work of other directors of the period.

Each bulletin describes the film, has one or more stills, and gives some other data. This set has an introduction by Eileen Bowser and some of the bulletins have annotations by Billy Bitzer, who worked at the Museum of Modern Art during the thirties. It is the Museum's collection which is reproduced here.

The preservation of the bulletins in this edition and the earlier one is a commendable project. Material of interest to students, researchers, and historians has become accessible. The book is recommended.

499 *The Biograph in Battle.* by Dickson, William K. 295 p. illus. London: Fisher Unwin, 1901.

This scarce volume is a diary (1899-1900) kept by the author during the first month of the Boer War. Sent to Africa by the British War Office, Dickson tells of his early use of the motion picture camera to record both the actual and staged incidents.

500 *Biographical Books: 1950-1980.* 1557 p. New York: R. R. Bowker, 1980.

This volume lists biographical or autobiographical books published or distributed in the United States between 1950 and 1980. Drawn from databases, the directory is divided into an author and title index, a name and subject index, and a vocational index. Of course the volume lists many volumes that are pertinent to cinema literature. This reference is similar to the earlier *Biography Index* (Wilson), and the *Chicorel Index to Biographies.*

501 *A Biographical Dictionary of Film.* by Thompson, David. 629 p. paper New York: William Morrow, 1976.

More than 800 personalities are considered in this massive collective biography. In a strict sense the essays accorded each are not total biography; however, sufficient material from the lives of the subjects has been selected by David Thompson to provide both a mini-portrait and a framework for critical comment.

The careers and talents of many performers, directors, and producers are evaluated in an original style that may antagonize the loyal fan. For example, is THE PAJAMA GAME (1957) really Doris Day's best film? Many would argue for LOVE ME OR LEAVE ME (1955). Is MAME (1974) Lucille Ball's most successful film? Did Eleanor Parker grow quite crazy in IN-TERRUPTED MELODY (1955)? Isn't LITTLE BOY LOST (1953), which contained one of Bing Crosby's better performances, worthy of mention? Occasionally the author's statements reflect questionable judgement or subjective criticism rather than biographical fact. Embroidering them into one essay may possibly be a disservice to the subject since the reader may not be able to separate fact from opinion.

Aside from this one reservation, the book is not only a solid reading experience but also an excellent reference source. In each essay many films are mentioned along with their director and year of release. Selected biographical publications are noted and some cross-indexing is employed. For example, the reader will find the Stanley Donen entry cross-indexed to Norma Talmadge, the link being a comparison to the Jean Hagen character in SINGIN' IN THE RAIN (1952).

The enormity of Thompson's work and his ultimate achievement is evidenced by the attraction this volume will have for a wide audience. It is teasingly controversial, enormously informative, and fine reading entertainment. Recommended.

502 *The Biographical Encyclopedia and Who's Who of the American Theatre.* by Rigdon, Walter. 1100 p. New York: James H. Heineman, 1966.

Contains over 3000 entries of American stage performers, many of whom have also appeared in films.

503 *Biography Index.* New York: H. W. Wilson, 1946-.

This reference concerns itself with biographical material appearing in obituaries, books and some 1600 periodicals. It is issued quarterly with bound and permanent annual and three year cumulations available. Each volume has a list of professions and occupations. Thus under "Motion Pictures" we find authors, critics, directors, executives, photographers and producers. Motion picture performers are listed under "Actors and Actresses." This is an easy-to-use vital reference source for information about people concerned with film.

504 *Bioscope Shows and Their Engines.* by Fay, Arthur. 36 p. paper illus. Lingfield, England: Oakwood Press, 1966.

A historical account published to commemorate the 70th birthday of cinematography, this booklet also pays tribute to the early British film exhibitors.

505 *The Bioscope 1908-1932.* illus. London: World Micro Films, 1908-1932.

The Biscope was a weekly film journal that served as a primary source of information during the early years of film history. It noted major technical advances, descriptions of new inventions, world wide coverage of motion picture developments, fully annotated reviews of films, and many other items of importance in the film world. The microfilm edition of over 24 years of *The Bioscope* consists of 67 reels of 35mm positive roll microfilm. More than 100,000 pages are reproduced. The cooperation of the British Film Institute made this project possible. Recommended.

506 THE BIRTH OF A NATION. by Huff, Theodore; and Griffith, D. W. 69 p. paper illus. New York: The Museum of Modern Art, 1961.

A shot-by-shot analysis of Griffith's THE BIRTH OF A NATION (1915).

507 THE BIRTH OF A NATION. by Stern, Seymour. 39 p. paper illus. New York: Group for Film Study, 1955.

This special issue of *Cinemages* is devoted to a discussion of the famous film and its director. It is written by the most qualified and dedicated authority on all matters pertaining to D. W. Griffith.

508 THE BIRTH OF A NATION Story. by Aitken, Roy E.; and Nelson, Al P. 96

p. illus. Middleburg, Va.: Wm. Den-lingers, 1956.

With one of the legendary films as his topic, the film's producer, Roy E. Aitken, recalls its history from the signing of D. W. Griffith in 1913 to the consideration of a remake in 1954. Although much of the writing is quite subjective and contradicts other published accounts, the book is an absorbing account by one of the participants in the creation of a film milestone.

Attention and description are given to the motion picture industry and personalities of the 1915 era. The rarely seen stills are reproduced in a sepia tone which diminishes their effectiveness somewhat. The book is essential to the person studying any aspect of THE BIRTH OF A NATION (1915).

509 *The Birth of Photography: The Story of The Formative Years 1800-1900.* by Coe, Brian. 144 p. illus. New York: Taplinger, 1977.

The origins of the cinema during the 19th century are discussed in this attractive history.

510 *The Birth of the Movies.* by Wenden, D. J. 192 p. paper illus. New York: Dutton, 1975.

Rather than present new material or interpretation, the author has opted for a rearrangement of the first three decades of motion picture history. In the opening chapters he reviews the development of the film from a novelty into an art form. In succeeding chapters he indicates relationships between these developments and economics, society, and politics. The final portion of the book examines Hollywood as a film capital and the implications of the introduction of sound to films.

References, further reading, and an index complete the volume. Illustrations are well reproduced, with the majority chosen from the British Film Institute collection. For the novice, the volume provides a solid, well-researched review of the silent era. Others may find the material overly familiar and lacking any uniqueness. Acceptable.

511 *Birth of the Talkies: From Edison to Jolson.* by Geduld, Harry M. 337 p. Bloomington, Ind.: Indiana University Press, 1975.

This volume carefully traces and documents one of the most revolutionary discoveries in American history. Beginning with the early attempts to reproduce sound in the late 19th century, the author arranges

all the noteworthy progressions toward sound-plus-visual that were made in the first two decades of this century. Major attention is given to DON JUAN (1926) and THE JAZZ SINGER (1927), with detailed information about their genesis, making, reception and effect noted.

Closing portions indicate a sample of opinions from prominent personalities about talking pictures, a filmography—arranged by studio—of the Hollywood sound feature films produced in 1929, a listing of sound-on-disk patents and sound-on-film patents, the patent appeal docket from the case of Lee De Forest vs. Tri-Ergon, copious chapter notes, and an index.

Except for the most dedicated, readers will find most of this volume too factual, scholarly and pedantic. Geduld's descriptions of the two films are certainly interesting but the surrounding material on patents, inventions, etc., is quite specialized and of limited concern to the general reader. There is no quarrel with the historical account offered; it simply lacks reader appeal. The author and publisher, in this case, have opted for a straight text approach rather than a more popular, palatable, visualized account. Acceptable.

512 *Bittersweet.* by Strasberg, Susan. 285 p. illus. New York: G. P. Putnam's, 1980.

Strasberg's autobiography is rich in theatrical background—her parents, the Actor's Studio, early fame on the stage in "The Diary of Anne Frank" etc. Initial film work included PICNIC (1955) and THE COBWEB (1955). After that, she led a chaotic life which included a love affair with Richard Burton, an unhappy marriage, drugs, hallucinogens, and career troubles. Strasberg writes about herself without excessive pity; likewise, the many celebriies who were always part of her life are treated in a matter-of-fact manner. The result is an engrossing story of a survivor in the world of show business.

513 BLACK DOLL: A Silent Film Script. by Gorey, Edward. New York: Gotham, 1973.

An unfilmed script.

514 *Black Film as Genre.* by Cripps, Thomas. 184 p. illus. Bloomington, Ind.: Indiana University Press, 1978.

Thomas Cripps, the author of *Slow Fade to Black*, continues his examination of black films in this book. Beginning with some definitions (a black film is made by and with black artists primarily for showing to a black audience), he discusses and documents the evolution of black film. This overview ranges from UNCLE TOM'S CABIN (1903) to CLAUDINE (1974). Some slight attention is given to television.

Six black genre films—THE SCAR OF SHAME (1927), THE ST. LOUIS BLUES (1929), BLOOD OF JESUS (1941), THE NEGRO SOLDIER (1943), NOTHING BUT A MAN (1964), and SWEET SWEETBACK'S BAADASSSSS SONG (1971)—are analyzed in separate chapters. Finally there is a short section on criticism and scholarship which reviews several recent studies on blacks in film.

Supporting the text are some illustrations, a bibliography, cast and credits for the six analyzed films, a filmography-listing of black genre films, and an index.

This is a logical extension of the work that Mapp, Bogle, Leab, and others have done. It summarizes one aspect of the black image in films and makes some valid recommendations. Acceptable.

515   *Black Film Stars.* by Landay, Eileen. 194 p. illus. New York: Drake, 1973.

A fine book that covers most aspects of the black image in films, this volume offers several outstanding features. There are over 200 nicely reproduced illustrations which accompany a well-written critical text. The material is arranged chronologically and is divided between personalities and films. Thus, along with chapters on Stepin Fetchit, Lena Horne, Eartha Kitt, and Jim Brown, there are others on THE GREEN PASTURES (1936), CARMEN JONES (1955), and PORGY AND BESS (1959). The evolution of the black image in films is traced from Bert Williams to Cicely Tyson and from UNCLE TOM'S CABIN (1909) to SOUNDER (1972). A solid bibliography and a helpful index complete the book. This volume accomplishes much in an informative, entertaining manner. Its material is well selected and presented with intelligence and taste. Highly recommended.

516   *Black Films: A Selected List.* compiled by New York Public Library. 12 p. paper New York: New York Public Library, 1970.

A short 12-page filmography prepared for the Black Films Workshop given in June, 1970. In addition to providing release date, running time and credits, the entries are described. A list of distributors is appended.

517   *Black Films and Film-Makers.* edited by Patterson, Lindsay. 298 p. illus. New York: Dodd, Mead, 1975.

This anthology about black film consists of 30 articles arranged under six general headings: Nigger to Supernigger; Movie Milestones; The Black Actor: The Early Years; The Black Actor: A New Status; Establishing Your Own; and The Seventies: Only the Heroes Have Changed. Illustrations, a filmography, a bibliography, and an index complete the volume.

The articles, which have been chosen from a variety of sources, span a period from 1929 to 1975. Authors include Lena Horne, Thomas Cripps, Edward Mapp, Robert Benchley, Bosley Crowther, and James Baldwin, among others.

The diversity of writing styles and the lack of a strong unifying structure weakens the total impact of this volume. However, as a varied assortment of facts, ideas and opinions on black film, it does provide an engrossing reading experience.

518   THE BLACK HOLE. edited by Walt Disney Studios. 12 p. illus. New York:Harmony Books, 1979.

This "pop-up" book, designed for youngsters, is based on the Disney film, THE BLACK HOLE (1979). It consists of six settings constructed so that when the reader opens the volume flat, certain elements in the scene stand up to give a third-dimension effect. It is a typical example of the many pop-up books based on motion pictures that are currently being published for children.

519   THE BLACK HOLE Poster Book. by Walt Disney Productions. 23 p. paper illus. New York: Harmony, 1979.

Some 22 full-color posters and a blueprint of the explorer craft, "Palomino," comprise this book. The reverse side of each poster explains the visual. A most attractive presentation of film material for display.

520   *Black Hollywood.* by Null, Gary. 254 p. illus. Secaucus, N.J.: Citadel, 1975.

In seven chapters (decades) a selected history of blacks in Hollywood films is presented. More than 250 films which emphasized black actors/black themes are noted in text and illustrations. As in most *Citadel* publications, the visuals—over 400 in this case—predominate while the anemic text offers little analysis or interpretation. An index is provided.

521   *Black Images in the American Theatre.* by Archer, Leonard C. 351 p. illus. Brooklyn, N.Y.: Pageant-Poseidon, 1973.

The motives in publishing this volume are laudable, but in the face of other recent material on the same topic, one wonders why the material used here was not rewritten with much greater care. Using a 1956 doctoral dissertation as a base, this volume adds an epilogue covering 1956 to 1973. Thus the volume seems to be segmented rather than a totality.

Its relevance is negligible because of the careless researching done in its two sections on film. Errors abound. For example: ALL THE KING'S MEN is used for ALL THE YOUNG MEN (page 295); FATHER OF THE BLUES is used for ST. LOUIS BLUES (page 294); ONE POTATO, TWO POTATOS is used for ONE POTATO, TWO POTATO (page 297); PATCH 12 is used for DEATH OF A GUNFIGHTER (page 299); THE STORY OF BILLIE HOLIDAY is used for LADY SINGS THE BLUES (page 307); reference is made to John Ford's Irish play "The Informers" instead of John Ford's film, THE INFORMER (1935) (page 300); Paul Robeson played Othello on stage in 1942, not 1932 (page 98); correct film titles are used in footnotes but are not correlated with the text—thus the unknowing reader will assume two different films rather than one which had a title change (see page 307).

The subtitle speaks of "NAACP Protest Campaigns —Stage, Screen, Radio and Television." This topic gets lost time and time again amidst the short affectionate biographies inserted throughout the author's chronological account and argument. In a volume such as this, a bibliography would seem essential. There is none. Some random illustrations are appended and there is an index. The material on stage and radio may be stronger than that on film—but the reader interested in black images on the screen is advised to consult Peter Noble's *The Negro in Films,* Edward Mapp's *Blacks in American Films,* *Toms, Coons, Mulattos, Mammies and Bucks* by Bogle; or *Black Film Stars* by Landay. Not recommended.

522 *Black Magic: A Pictorial History of the Negro in American Entertainment.* by Hughes, Langston; and Meltzer, Milton. 375 p. illus. Englewood Cliffs, N. J.: Prentice-Hall, 1967.

Only 26 pages of this volume are devoted to the Negro in films. An earlier volume, Peter Noble's *The Negro in Films* covers most of the same topics as this book but in much greater depth. The volume is well-produced, and as a picture book it is excellent. It is in the scope and unbalanced emphasis that the book suffers. Index.

523 *The Black Man on Film: Racial Stereotyping.* edited by Maynard, Richard A. 134 p. paper illus. Rochelle Park, N.J.: Hayden, 1974.

Designed as a high school text on the treatment of blacks in films, this sourcebook/anthology is divided into six parts: A Historical Survey of the Black Stereotype on Film; THE BIRTH OF A NATION (1915); Some Samples of Opinion 1929-1955 (Stepin Fetchit to CARMEN JONES, 1954); A "New" Image for the Future (Sidney Poitier); Possible Solutions and Trends for the Future; and The Movie Indian and the Movie Jew—Parallel Studies in Stereotyping. Suggested questions for discussion follow each part. A filmography and distributor list complete the work.

While the intent of this volume is praiseworthy, the selection of its contents may raise certain questions. (1) Is the extended emphasis on THE BIRTH OF A NATION (1915) and on Sidney Poitier justified? (2) Doesn't listing RAISIN IN THE SUN (1961) under "The Sidney Poitier Stereotype" heading and then annotating the film with, "Lorraine Hansberry's classic drama adapted for the screen gave Poitier one of his most human roles," seem to be burying the whole film for the sake of a single character? (3) Doesn't the filmography and the text ignore the isolation of blacks in musical films? (4) Wouldn't an index to titles and names be very helpful? (5) Why is there no bibliography to encourage the reader toward pertinent volumes such as Bogle, Mapp, Noble, Wall, Silva, Rollins, Hughes and Meltzer?

As a sourcebook and an introduction to a major issue in our society, this volume has value. However, any study of the questions that this volume suggests would be unbalanced and partial without the addition of other pertinent films, books, and articles. Acceptable.

524 *Blacks in American Films: Today and Yesterday.* by Mapp, Edward. 278 p. illus. Metuchen, N. J.: Scarecrow Press, 1972.

An examination of the portrayal of the Negro in American motion pictures, focusing on the extent to which a changing society for blacks is reflected in American motion pictures. Old and new sterotypes are compared, and the emergence of black stars and changing screen images is noted. Recommended. Bibliography and index.

525 *Blacks in American Movies: A Selected Bibliography.* edited by Powers, Anne. 157 p. Metuchen, N.J.: Scarecrow Press, 1974.

This excellent guide to information about blacks in American films is well structured. A list of periodicals cited precedes the preface and introduction. Book and dissertation references are noted with annotations appearing for certain titles. The main section deals with 662 articles taken from periodicals. They are classified according to subject, periodical, and chronological appearance. Final sections include a filmography of feature films from 1904 to 1930 by and about blacks, and an author-subject index.

Although it is admittedly partial, the selection of material for inclusion is impressive. Arrangement of the material is good, but some time is needed to comprehend what is offered and where it is located. The patient user of this volume will ultimately discover the vast information resource that Powers has provided. Recommended.

526 *Blacks in Black and White: A Source Book on Black Films.* by Sampson, H. T. 343 p. illus. Metuchen, N.J.: Scarecrow, 1977.

The use of the word "source" in this book's title is very appropriate for it offers a diverse collection of information on all-black cast films that is rare and unusual.

Included is a historical overview of black-cast films from 1910 to 1950; an account of the production companies with special attention given to the Lincoln Motion Picture Company and the Micheaux Film Corporation; synopses and credits for 100 black-cast films from 1910 to 1950; and a collection of over 50 short biographical sketches of black performers. There are several appendixes: a list of all-black films produced by independent film producers 1904-1950; a partial list of film credits for featured players in black-cast films 1915-1950; and an index.

The scope of Sampson's work is awesome, as is the diligent research that is essential to produce an effort such as this. Certainly, he has performed a service in creating a reference that will become a standard. It can be viewed as a model for the presentation of specialized information in a coherent, useable, and readable form. Higly recommended.

527 *Blacks in Films.* by Pines, Jim. 143 p. illus. London: Studio Vista, 1975.

Pines is also the author of *Blacks in the Cinema: The Changing Image,* a 24-page booklet published by the British Film Institute in 1971. His books deal with racial themes and images in American films.

528 *Blacks in the Cinema—The Changing Image.* by Pines, Jim. 24 p. paper London: British Film Institute, 1971.

A short introduction precedes the title essay. Footnotes and a filmography are provided.

529 *Blake Edwards.* by Lehman, Peter; and Luhr, William. 301 p. illus. Athens, Ohio: Ohio University Press, 1981.

This appreciation consists of two sections: an analysis of the themes/content of Edward's films and then a review of the films by subgenre, i.e., Peter Sellers films, Julie Andrews films, etc.

530 *Blond Venus: A Life of Marlene Dietrich.* by Frewin, Leslie. 159 p. illus. London: MacGibbon and Kee, 1955.

This is the original British version of Frewin's biography of Marlene Dietrich. The later American edition published by Stein and Day as *Dietrich* is updated, has a few more pictures, and is still no better than this poor tribute.

531 *Blondes, Brunettes and Bullets.* by Granlund, Nils Thor; and Feder, Sid and and Hancock, Ralph. 300 p. New York: David McKay, 1957.

A publicity agent recalls how Clara Bow, Charlie Chaplin, Joan Crawford, William S. Hart, Mary Miles Minter, Ginger Rogers, and other got started in Hollywood.

532 *Blood, Brains and Beer: An Autobiography.* by Ogilvy, David. 181 p. illus. New York: Atheneum, 1978.

Ogilvy is an advertising executive who has written several books. This volume contains a chapter about doing research for the Hollywood film industry.

533 THE BLOOD OF A POET. by Cocteau, Jean. 53 p. illus. New York: Bodley Press, 1949.

The scenario of Cocteau's 1930 film translated by opera singer Lily Pons. Also includes some commentary by Cocteau.

534 *Bloody Wednesday: The True Story of the Ramon Novarro Murder.* by Harrison, Joel L. 335 p. paper illus. Chatsworth, Calif.: Major Books, 1978.

This original paperback is an illustrated account of the 1968 murder of silent movie star Ramon Novarro and the follow-up investigation.

535 BLOW-UP. by Antonioni, Michelangelo; and Guerra, Tonino. 119 p. paper illus. New York: Simon and Schuster, 1971.

Script of the 1966 film directed by Antonioni. Contains an interview with Antonioni; three articles written by Antonioni; cast and production credits; notes.

536 *see 537*

537 THE BLUE ANGEL. by Mann, Heinrich; and von Sternberg, Josef. 340 p. paper illus. New York: Ungar, 1979.

A combination of the 1905 novel by Heinrich Mann originally called *Professor Unrat* and the continuity film script of the 1929 film is offered in this volume. It includes cast credits, comments by von Sternberg, and a foreword by Stanely Hochman. Although the film is accepted largely as the creation of von Sternberg, he is not credited offically for the script. Carl Zuckmayer, Karl Vollmoeller, and Robert Liebman share that distinction, but von Sternberg insists that no comprehensive scenario was ever made and most of the film was improvised. The other men are given courtesy credits by the director here.

538 *The Blue Book of Hollywood Musicals.* by Burton, Jack. 296 p. illus. Watkins Glen, N. Y.: Century House, 1953.

A year-by-year recapitulation of Hollywood Musicals beginning with THE JAZZ SINGER (1927) and ending with WITH A SONG IN MY HEART (1952). This volume has a great subtitle: "Songs From the Sound Tracks and the Stars Who Sang Them Since the Birth of the Talkies a Quarter-Century Ago. <

Each year has an introductory survey followed by two classification: musical and feature films with songs (occasionally feature cartoons and western films with songs are listed). Most of the films list studio, director, and leading players. Index of film titles. Highly recommended.

539 *Blue Book of the Screen.* edited by Wing, Ruth. 415 p. illus. New York: Gordon Press, 1976 (1923).

A heavily illustrated collective biography that treats over 150 film personalities of the early twenties. Pub-

lished originally by the Blue Book of the Screen, Inc. Hollywood, Calif.

540 THE BLUE DAHLIA. by Chandler, Raymond. 139 p. illus. Carbondale, Ill.: Southern Illinois Univ. Press, 1976.

Script and cast credits of the 1946 film directed by George Marshall.

The volume also includes: "Lost Fortnight, a Memoir" by John Houseman and "Afterword: Raymond Chandler and Hollywood" by Matthew J. Bruccoli.

The appendix contains a Chandler filmography, and bibliographies of Chandler scripts and articles on Hollywood.

541 THE BLUE MAX. by Liebling, Howard. 32 p. paper illus. New York: Souvenir Programs, Inc., 1966.

As background for the reader of this souvenir book, there is a picture gallery of famous flyers, medals, and airplanes from World War I. Film stills used tend to resemble actual photographs of the period. The cast and technical credits are given and the final section deals with the making of the film.

542 *Blue Meridian: The Search for the Great White Shark.* by Mattheissen, Peter. 197 p. paper illus. New York: New American Library, 1971.

An account of the expedition that resulted in the film, BLUE WATER, WHITE DEATH (1971).

543 *Blue Money.* by See, Carolyn. 234 p. New York: David McKay, 1975.

The subtitle of this volume is "Pornography and the Pornographers—An Intimate Look at the Two-Billion Dollar Fantasy Industry." Using what she terms an "anthropological" approach, the author presents portraits of about eight personalities who are involved in some way with the pornography industry. They include Marvin Miller (publisher), Matt Cimber (film producer), Linda Lovelace (actress-performer), Jim Holland (theatre-chain operator and sexual device sales mogul), Raymond Gaver (crusader for decent literature), Phil and Gerri (two live-show performers) and Burton Marks (attorney). Other topics discussed are court decisions, the Legion of Decency and a pornography convention.

The difference between this volume and similar ones is the attitude-approach of the author. All of the usual sex book topics and activities are here in addition to a few new and rather unique ones. The author treats them as an investigator rather than a thrill-seeking participant; this is the book's major distinction. There are no illustrations and the book is not indexed. It is a candid, uncompromising look at the merchandising of a product along with some unflattering portraits of the entrepreneurs involved in this economically rewarding activity. Acceptable.

544 BLUE MOVIE. by Warhol, Andy. 126 p. paper illus. New York: Grove Press, 1970.

Script of the 1970 film directed by Warhol.

545 *The Bluffer's Guide to Cinema.* by Wlaschin, Ken. 64 p. paper New York: Crown, 1971.

This is one of those inexpensive novelty books designed to give to a friend in order to indicate your own sophistication. While it is meant to be sharp, devasting, and oh-so-clever, the material defeats the purpose. Much of it is too close to the truth to be either satire or humor and, therefore, will be read for information instead. For example: "Stanley Kubrick: It's OK to call Kubrick the best American director in some circles and 2001: A SPACE ODYSSEY (1968) has made science-fiction respectable (the hippies loved it). PATHS OF GLORY (1957) is perhaps his best."

The author is not David Frost, whose name appears in large letters on the cover. The inside title page indicates the author to be Ken Wlaschin and the American editor to be Leslie Elliott. Mr. Frost's rather small contribution is a page and a half introduction.

The major theme of the book is cults—those for directors, actors, supporting players, films, and genres. Sections on critics and on cinema jargon complete the book. This is a mixture that does not blend well. It may amuse and entertain the more knowledgeable reader but others may have some difficulty in differentiating valid information from some rather strained attempts at humor.

546 DON'T LOOK BACK. by Pennebaker, D. A. 159 p. paper illus. New York: Ballantine Books, 1968.

Script of the 1967 film directed by Pennebaker. This transcript of the cinema-verite film concentrates on the dialogue rather than the visuals. Since there was no prepared script, what is recorded here is simply what is said in the final print of the film.

547 *Bob Hope: Portrait of a Superstar.* by Thompson, Charles. New York: St. Martin's, 1981.

548 *Body and Soul: The Story of John Garfield.* by Swindell, Larry. 288 p. illus. New York: William Morrow, 1975.

John Garfield made about 30 feature films during a Hollywood career that spanned the years from 1938 to 1951. Only a few of his films are memorable but his performances in them remain unforgettable. In most of them he was the rebel hero—a kind of casting that had its roots in Garfield's personal history. His rise from a poor Jewish ghetto to a brilliant career which was sacrificed for principle is the stereotyped American story. What Garfield supplied to this often-told story was virility, charisma, impudence and talent.

In a thoroughly researched text, Swindell gives appropriate emphasis to all the prominent events in Garfield's meteoric life—theatre, politics, filmmaking, love affairs, marriage, societal concerns, etc. The author's expertise in blending fact, opinion, interpretation, and comment results in a portrait of an unusual actor-personality presented against a background of Hollywood and Broadway during two critical decades in American history—the thirties and forties. Two photographic sections, a filmography and an index are valuable additions to this biography of an original screen personality. Recommended.

549 *The Body Merchant: The Story of Earl Carroll* by Murray, Ken. 243 p. illus. New York: Ritchie, 1976.

Earl Carroll was a spin-off of Flo Ziegfeld and is most remembered for his shows which presented females in various stages of undress. When one of his shows, "Murder at the Vanities," was sold to Paramount, he came to Hollywood where he was publicist, producer, and finally restaurateur. In December of 1938 he opened Earl Carroll's Hollywood Theatre Restaurant. In 1948 he was killed in a plane crash.

A colorful story has been sacrificed because of the author-comedian's lack of confidence in a straightforward telling. Instead, he has embellished it with too many sexual anecdotes, digressions, suggestions, and approaches. Even these are acceptable when they are essential to the story line, but not when they are told with a leer and do not further the reader's understanding of the biographical subject.

550 *Bogart.* by Gehman, Richard. 159 p. paper illus. Greenwich, Conn: Gold Medal Books, 1965.

An interesting and honest view of Bogart as an actor and a human being. Gehman enjoyed a friendship with Bogart during his final years and much of his comment stems from reminiscenses of these times. Sections of the book are devoted to Bogart's stage roles and to his films. The comments offered by Bogart about individual films are penetrating, wise and humorous. His stage appearances are accompanied by some of the critics' views of his work. It is consistently entertaining and informative. One of the better Bogart biographies.

551 *Bogart.* by Hanna, David. 201 p. paper illus. New York: Leisure Books, 1976.

Written by a film publicist who knew and worked with Bogart, this book is a sensible, objective view of the actor, the man and his life. It was during the filming of THE BAREFOOT CONTESSA (1954) that Bogart and the author became personally acquainted, but since Hanna had been a Hollywood publicist for almost two decades prior, his knowledge of Bogart in Hollywood was extensive.

The text he offers is a combination of his actual experiences, quotations, factual matters of record, and his personal thoughts. The latter are most intriguing, as in the instance of comparing Bogart to the other male stars with whom he's worked. A center section of illustrations is included.

Anyone still interested in the Bogart legend should not overlook this modest gem. Recommended.

552 *Bogart.* by Eyles, Allen. 128 p. illus. Garden City, N.Y.: Doubleday, 1975.

A short biography that emphasizes Bogart's films, this volume is part of the *Movie Makers* series. Its outstanding feature is the collection of visuals, but content and treatment are inferior to the Bogart volumes by Benchley and Hyams.

553 *Bogart.* 82 p. illus. paper New York: Starlog, 1981.

554 *Bogart and Bacall.* by Hyams, Joe. 245 p. illus. New York: David McKay, 1975.

Joe Hyams is a much more effective writer when he concerns himself with biography rather than autobiography. In 1966 his book, *Bogie*, was an acceptable account of the actor's life with considerable attention given to Lauren Bacall's part in it. He has rearranged portions of his older material, and added some new sections on Bacall in this volume.

Emphasis here is on the pair rather than Bogart. Using a parallel structure, the author traces the lives of each until they merge into a professional and private pair in the early forties. Their films are given attention, as are the well-known public and private incidents of their marriage, the Committee for the First Amendment-HUAC Hearings, the Rat Pack, Bogart's last days, etc. Since Hyams was a personal friend of the pair, his writing reflects not only their constant cooperation through the years, but his ability to recall incident and anecdote which have grown richer in retrospect. Illustrations have been well selected, with informal candids and newsphotos predominating. An index is provided, but there are no filmographies. An admirable blending of the old (Bogart) with the new (Bacall), this volume should please many readers. Recommended.

555 *The Bogart File.* by Pettigrew, Terence. 213 p. illus. London: Golden Eagle Press, 1977.

Another volume on Bogart. Contains a filmography and an index.

556 *Bogart's Face.* paper illus. New York: Random House, 1970.

More than 50 close-ups of Bogart in a novelty book.

557 *Bogey: The Films of Humphrey Bogart.* by McCarty, Clifford. 190 p. illus. New York: Bonanza Books, 1965.

Seventy-five Bogart films are described by several illustrations, extended production and cast credits, and a plot synopsis. One wishes that more background data was given for each film—i.e., critical reception, quotes, awards, etc. In spite of a very brief text, this is one of the better books on Bogart. Highly recommended.

558 *Bogey: The Good-Bad Guy.* by Goodman, Ezra. 223 p. New York: Lyle Stuart, 1965.

This book is part biography, part character description and analysis, and part character assassination. The author knew Bogart as a subject for magazine articles and studio publicity releases. The view of Bogart presented here is bitter-sweet in keeping with the book's title. For example, the actor who alienates the "little people" at the studio is contrasted with the Bogart who cries at weddings and at repeated showings of the March-Gaynor A STAR IS BORN

(1938).

Not only is the author's cynical and predominantly negative view of Bogart (and others) given, but a cross section opinion of people who knew or worked with Bogart is also presented. The final portrait which emerges is not very flattering and summarizes Bogart as a conscientious actor who was not very much as a human being. The text has a tendency to become repetitious, giving an impression of padding. Biographical data is skipped over rapidly in favor of gossip, opinion, and self-serving anecdotes from the interviewees.

559 *Bogey: The Man, the Actor, the Legend.* by Ruddy, Jonah; and Hill, Jonathan. 248 p. paper New York: Tower Publications, 1965.

This biography is a departure from the usual format. Strict chronological fashion is avoided in favor of a series of back-and-forth time jumps. Thus many incidents occur out of order and this may prove a bit disconcerting to a reader who likes the linear narrative. Many opinions of Bogart are quoted—those of his friends, coworkers and directors.

The overall effect of the book is a very positive one. It is probably the broadest of all the biographies and yet one wishes that some of the material were anti-Bogart. The quoted comments about Bogart give the book its strength.

560 *Bogey's Baby.* by Greenberger, Howard. 216 p. illus. New York: St. Martin's Press, 1978.

The major subject of this biography is Bacall, with secondary prominence given to Bogart. Other than detailing many previously published incidents, this volume does not add much that is new to the Bogarts' story. In minimizing Bacall's early life and her post-Bogart experiences, the author seemingly relies on the Bogart presence to carry his story. Since the volume was written without his subjects' cooperation, the material obtained from secondary sources seems familiar.

Many of the illustrations taken from *Movie Life* are below average in clarity and are small in size. The book is not indexed and there is no filmography. At times the editing is careless, with misspellings of Molly Haskell, Las Vegas, etc.

This book offers little to anyone who has read one of the several earlier Bogart-Bacall volumes; for others it is acceptable.

561 *Bogie: The Biography of Humphrey Bogart.* by Hyams, Joe. 211 p. illus. New York: New American Library, 1966.

Although this is one of several Bogart biographies, this one has some distinguishing features. Included is an introduction by Lauren Bacall and certain candid shots that indicate an entree in Bogart's later personal life that other biographers did not enjoy.

There is much factual detail in this volume. Any attempt at critical or objective analysis of Bogart as a person and a performer is colored by the author's admiration for his subject. As a result, the book is an affectionate but not very penetrating view of a Hollywood legend. No index, filmography, bibliography, or the like is provided.

562 *Bolex 8 Guide.* by Sharp, Gerald Reynolds. 120 p. paper illus. London: Focal Press, 1966.

The volume examined was the 5th edition, and it dealt with using Bolex B-8, C-8, D-8, L-8, and Zoom Reflex P-1, P-2, P-3, P-4, S-1, K-1, and K-2 cameras. This manual on Bolex cinematography contains many illustrations, tables and diagrams.

563 *Bongo.* by Walt Disney Productions. 26 p. illus. New York: Simon & Schuster, 1947.

Adapted from the characters and backgrounds created by the Disney Studios for the film FUN AND FANCY FREE (1947), this volume was designed for children by Edgar Starr. The original "Bongo" story was adapted by Sinclair Lewis and that version was used for the film.

564 *The Bonnie and Clyde Book.* edited by Wake, Sandra; and Hayden, Nicola. 223 p. illus. New York: Simon and Schuster, 1972.

In this departure from the *Modern and Classic Film Script* series, the publishers have placed in hardcover material similar to that found in the series. In addition to the script which occupies more than one half of the book, there are several interviews with director Arthur Penn and Warren Beatty, some articles by the script writers, the consultant, and Pauline Kael, and finally a sampling of the critical reaction to the film.

With the exception of the script, all the material has appeared earlier elsewhere. The potential popularity of the script, its cost to the publisher and the hardcover format probably dictated the publication of this script outside the *Modern and Classic* series. The ultimate value of that decision is questionable. Certainly the acclaim and reputation of the paperback series is such that it seems discriminatory to exclude one fine script and roadshow it. The book is acceptable, of course, and will be very popular with a wide audience. Whether its minor differences merit individual and separate treatment is a question.

565 *Boo, to My Friends.* by Laye, Evelyn. illus. London: Hurst and Blackett, 1958.

Evelyn Laye was a star of the London stage since 1916. Her film work was mostly in early sound musicals during the thirties.

566 *A Book.* by Arnaz, Desi. 322 p. illus. New York: Morrow, 1976.

Arnaz is known chiefly as Ricky Ricardo in the "I Love Lucy" television show and as the one-time husband of star, Lucille Ball. Before the success of the TV series, he had been a Broadway, vaudeville, and film performer. His movie credits include: TOO MANY GIRLS (1940), FATHER TAKES A WIFE (1941), FOUR JACKS AND A JILL (1941), THE NAVY COMES THROUGH (1942), BATAAN (1943), CUBAN PETE (1946), and HOLIDAY IN HAVANA (1948). Two post "Lucy" films, THE LONG LONG TRAILER (1954) and FOREVER, DARLING (1956), attempted to capitalize on the Arnaz-Ball TV popularity.

In this frank, well-written and often vulgar account, Arnaz discusses his successes and failures with objectivity. There is no self-pity, only a nostalgic longing for the high times he had in his rise from Cuban exile to world celebrity. Success apparently turned his life into a nightmare, and he finally opted for a simple retirement—from Lucy and television.

The volume is illustrated but no index is provided. This is a story about a man who is familiar to the millions of viewers who watched and loved "I Love Lucy." They cannot help but be fascinated by his colorful but ultimately unhappy life. Recommended.

567 *The Book of* ALIEN. by Scanlon, Paul; and Gross, Michael. 112 p. paper illus. New York: Simon and Schuster, 1979.

An account of the production of ALIEN (1979) that includes designs, sketches, technical details, special effects, interviews, comments, and—most important —an abundance of visuals, many in full color.

568 *The Book of Hollywood Quotes.* compiled by Herman, Gary. 128 p. paper

illus. New York: Quick Fox, 1979.

This oversized original paperback book contains hundreds of quotations from Hollywood personalities along with many fine illustrations and an identification index. The statements range from classic lines of dialogue to insights and insults.

569 *The Book of Movie Photography.* by Cheshire, David. 287 p. illus. New York: Knopf, 1979.

The publisher calls this "The Complete Guide to Better Moviemaking," and that description is very accurate. Not only does the text offer a most comprehensive survey of filmmaking (history, camera, film, sound, production, special effects, processing, editing, projecting, references, terms) but the copious information is presented in concert with a superior group of illustrations, charts, diagrams, and drawings. The text avoids pedantic technical explanations and the visuals add considerably to the clarification of concepts and techniques of filmmaking.

The result is an attractive oversized volume whose text can be easily understood and whose pictures are a pleasure to view. Production values are impressive throughout, making it one of the outstanding books on this subject currently available. Highly recommended.

570 *The Book of Sleuths.* by Pate, Janet. 124 p. illus. London: New English Library, 1977.

Contains a filmography and a bibliography.

571 *A Bookless Curriculum.* by Brown, Roland G. 136 p. paper illus. Dayton, Ohio: Pflaum, 1972.

This is an account of an educational experiment conducted by the author, a senior high school teacher. An attempt was made to create a media-based curriculum for use with those high school students who cannot or will not read—the potential dropouts, failures, school-haters, etc. The initial design procedures, the objectives, the testing instruments and the curriculum—which consisted of film units, discussion units and project units—are all given, along with a final evaluation of the project. The appendix contains sample questionnaires, statistical analyses, student evaluation of the films, a bibliography and a film list with distributor's names and individual film rental costs. (Total cost was about $1000.)

Brown's account has several values. As an educational experiment, it has pertinence for curriculum change in the humanities. In addition, the plan can serve as a stimulus or model for other exploration, experimentation, study and research in changing curriculum. Finally, the study guide type units can be most helpful to teachers using any of the individual films. The book is highly recommended.

572 *Books About Film.* by Monaco, James; and Schenker, Susan. 48 p. paper illus. New York: Zoetrope, 1976.

Subtitled "A Bibliographical Checklist," this short booklet offers a selected list of film books arranged under 13 headings. Brief introductions appear for each heading followed by the books which are arranged alphabetically according to author surname. Occasionally a few words describe or evaluate a book, e.g.., *Spellbound in Darkness...* "early cinema" or *The Jaws Log...* "good journalism, recommended, "—but for most entries there is no annotation.

As a convenient guide to available books on current film topics, the checklist can be most helpful. Its concise, easy-to-use format can provide the reader with substantial initial bibliographic information that will make any literature search more direct and efficient. Recommended.

573 *Borinquen.* edited by New York Public Library, Office of Adult Services. 46 p. paper New York: New York Public Library, 1978.

A mediagraphy on the Puerto Rican experience, this short booklet lists films, records and books selected by seven Spanish-language authorities. Annotations are provided.

574 *Boris Karloff and His Films.* by Jensen, Paul M. 194 p. illus. New York: A. S. Barnes, 1974.

It is unfortunate that this workmanlike study of Boris Karloff arrives so late in the competition. In the last few years, no fewer than seven books have been devoted to the horror star and his films. Since this one cannot add much new material to what has already been reported, it must rely upon a retelling of the familiar; it does exactly that, employing an economical, factual style, punctuated with some sound critical judgments and evaluations. Emphasis is on the films of the thirties and early forties with plots, settings, characters, etc., described in detail. Silent films, later sound films and Karloff's excursions into other media are treated but briefly.

The author's thoroughness in researching his

material is evidenced by the long impressive bibliography. A filmography, a name index and a film index complete the book. Illustrations are well selected with stills, portraits and frame enlargements used. Reproduction is acceptable. This study is an admirable effort, for which appreciation may be diminished by some earlier treatments of the same material. Acceptable.

575 *Born To Lose: The Gangster Film in America.* by Rosow, Eugene. 422 p. illus. New York: Oxford University Press, 1978.

This genre study employs a historical base for its critical examination of the evolution and development ofb the gangster film. The first section explores such American phenomena and myths as robber barons, western outlaws, gangs, the concept of success, cities, immigrants, and the propitious arrival of the motion picture industry at the turn of the century. Early silents, such as Griffith's THE MUSKETEERS OF PIG ALLEY (1912), were followed by many gangster films, most of which reflected the lawlessness of the Roaring Twenties. The depression period, which spawned some of the classic films, LITTLE CAESAR (1930), THE PUBLIC ENEMY (1931), and SCARFACE (1932) saw the genre come to full development. The final section, which covers 1935 to 1976, indicates the plot embellishments, the careful detail, and the character refinements that audiences see in today's gangster films. WHITE HEAT (1949), ON THE WATERFRONT (1951), BONNIE AND CLYDE (1967), and THE GODFATHER I, II (1972, 1974) are among the many films examined. The major point made throughout is that the gangster films reflect the times in which they were made.

The book is well illustrated and supporting the text are notes, a lengthy biliography and an index. The critically annotated filmography and the chronological listing of selected gangster films from 1912 to 1976 summarize the author's coverage nicely.

This is an excellent example of genre study—carefully researched, well-written and produced with care. Recommended.

576 *Born to Star: The Lupino Lane Story.* by White, James Dillon. 304 p. illus. London: Heinemann, 1957.

A biography of the pint-sized acrobat-tumbler who had a career as an actor and director in films from 1915 to 1939. Some of his early films were made in Hollywood.

577 *Borrowed Time: The 37 Years of Bobby Darin.* by DiOrio, Al 250 p. illus. Philadelphia: Running Press, 1981.

Contains a filmography of the actor-singer who rose to fame quickly but died at an early age.

578 *Bosley Crowther: Social Critic of the Film, 1940-1967.* by Beaver, Frank Eugene. 187 p. New York: Arno, 1974.

This study was prepared in 1970 as a partial requirement for a doctoral degree at the University of Michigan and is reprinted as a part of Arno's *Dissertations on Film* series. Its subject is Bosley Crowther's film reviews, which appeared for almost three decades in the *New York Times.* Crowther's early insistence on the social-responsibility function of films and its effect on his criticism are noted along with his efforts to gain the right to free expression for filmmakers. How Crowther championed the cause of free, socially aware and responsible films is the concern of this study.

The data for the author's survey is taken from the reviews, and many films are cited. An appendix of Crowther's Ten Best Lists from 1940 to 1967 and a bibliography complete the work. A personal interview with Crowther is noted by the author. This is an interesting study of an important film critic and the possible effects his writing had upon the film industry in America. Since many films are cited, the addition of an index would have enhanced the value of the book for the user. Acceptable.

579 *Boston Public Library Film Catalog.* Boston: Boston Public Library, 1975 (Supplements in 1976 and 1978).

580 *Bound and Gagged: The Story of the Silent Serials.* by Lahue, Kalton C. 352 p. illus. New York: Barnes, 1968.

The history of the silent serial, its development, form, actors, directors, plots, and final demise, is described in this volume. The author considers the serial on the basis of the creative intent of the makers, which was to produce popular entertainment leading to economic gain.

The volume is handsomely produced with many rare illustrations. The detail with which the text is written is amazing and indicates extensive research and investigation into a neglected area of silent screen history. An added bonus is the inclusion of the original script of the first chapter of the 1920 Pathe serial, PIRATE GOLD. There is also a separate index of serials in addition to the general index. A fascinating excursion into one area of silent screen history, this

book is highly recommended.

581 *The Boy Who Dared to Rock: The Definitive Elvis.* by Lichter, Paul. 304 p. paper illus. New York: Doubleday (Dolphin), 1978.

Paul Lichter, the author of this volume and *Elvis in Hollywood,* owns and operates the Elvis Unique Record Club and the Memphis Flash (circulation: 128,-000). His is a household name among Presley fans. This information might suggest a fan-oriented, adoring biography—and that is what we get. Elvis's clothes, possessions, box office figures, records, concerts, films, etc., are all given much attention but little or nothing is told of the person behind the public idol. Anything negative—divorce, drugs, personal relationships, temperament—is overlooked in the reinforcement of the legend. Anyone with the background material that Lichter possesses should do much better.

There are some redeeming elements—a fine collection of visuals, some of which are in full-color; lists of his concert appearances and his recording sessions; a long discography; and a short filmography. The discography includes pictures of many record covers and also indicates the large number of bootleg discs in existence.

This is a much better reference book than a biography. However, the Presley fan will probably approve of it all.

582 *The Boy's and Girl's Book of Films and Television.* by Field, Mary; and Miller, Maud; and Manvell, Roger. 143 p. illus. New York: Roy Publishers, 1961.

An updating and revision of the earlier volume which dealt only with film.

583 *The Boy's and Girl's Film Book.* by Field, Mary; and Miller, Maud. 192 p. illus. London: Burke Pub. Co., 1947.

Survey of film history, trends, and children as filmmakers, etc., designed with many illustrations, specifically for younger children.

584 *Boys, Movies, and City Streets.* by Cressey, Paul G.; and Thrasher, Frederic M. New York: Macmillan, 1933.

This announced volume of the original Payne Fund Studies was not included in the Arno Press reprint of 1970. It was to be a survey of boy's movie attendance in the congested inner city areas. Certain of its conclusions are cited in the summary volume, *Our Movie-Made Children*. No certain evidence exists that this was published.

585   *Brakhage.* by Clark, Dan. 82 p. paper New York: Film-maker's Cinematheque, 1966.

This volume, which is number two in the *Film-maker's Cinematheque Monograph* series, is a collection of criticism, articles, essays, filmography, etc., on the noted experimental filmmaker. Some samples of Brakhage's writing are included.

586   *The Brakhage Lectures.* by Brakhage, Stan. 106 p. illus. Chicago: The Good Lion, 1972.

The author gave these four lectures at the Art Institute of Chicago in the winter of 1970-71. Each is devoted to a director-legend: Melies, Griffith, Dreyer, and Eisenstein. Brakhage's writing style is unusual—at times nonlinear, then narrative, followed by a stream of consciousness featuring digressions involving history, politics, semantics, etc. As with Brakhage's films, the patron should expect the unexpected. Each lecture is preceded by a small gallery of illustrations and portraits of the subject. They are from the collection of the Museum of Modern Art and their reproduction here is adequate.

For the reader familiar with the life and work of the four directors, the book will provide a new perspective on rather familiar material. The novice will find both the style and the content quite baffling. (It should be noted that the original presentation of this material was supplemented by showings of many of the directors' films.) Recommended.

587   *Brakhage Scrapbook: Collected Writings.* edited by Haller, Robert A.; and Haller, Robert S. 256 p. illus. Philadelphia: Treacle, 1981.

588   *Brando.* by Carey, Gary. 279 p. paper illus. New York: Pocket Books, 1973.

This is still another surprisingly good paperback original and, along with the Robert Taylor biography, suggests a possible trend in publishing. All of the well-known Brando stories, incidents, films and newspaper notoriety are related. His rebel image, STREETCAR NAMED DESIRE (1951), the marriages to oriental women, MUTINY ON THE BOUNTY (1962), the career decline, THE GODFATHER (1972) and LAST TANGO IN PARIS (1973) are all here, as is his April 1973 rejection of the Academy Award.

The book is mostly pro-Brando but occasionally the author presents a contrasting view. The text is both descriptive and critical when speaking of his screen performances. The off-screen personality is a bit harder to examine and evaluate. His LAST TANGO IN PARIS co-star's assertion about Brando's bisexuality, in a *New York Times* interview, is carefully avoided, as is any in-depth examination of his off-screen behavior. Missing too, is a final evaluation of his contribution to screen acting and film art. Many people regard Brando as a major force in bringing film to its wide acceptance as an art form today.

There is a collection of illustrations at the book's center but no index or filmography—serious omissions. This biography provides a full portrait of the professional side of Brando and a limited one of the personal. Much better than the Offen book, it is highly recommended.

589   *Brando.* by Offen, Ron. 222 p. illus. Chicago: Henry Regnery Co., 1973.

Brando is what you would expect to appear at this time. Apparently designed to capitalize on his GOD-FATHER (1972) comeback and a second Academy Award, the book has a deadline quality that allows for little more than a researching of the periodical literature and film references. Probably the best chapter is the concluding one in which Offen summarizes Brando's contributions to and effects on film acting and muses a bit about his professional future. Most of the preceding material is a chronological arrangement of previously printed material. The author has never met Brando.

There are numerous omissions and errors, e.g., Joan Tetzl is listed as Joan Teizel, Robert Keith is identified as J. C. Flippen, Vivien Leigh's Academy Award for STREETCAR NAMED DESIRE (1951) is not mentioned, nor is Brando's nonparticipation in World War II. Many sources claim Brando named his first son for his friend, Christian Marquand, but Offen makes no comment on this.

Some interesting visuals are gathered in a center arrangement and, although the book is not indexed, a filmography with cast listings is appended.

The final portrait that the book projects is that of a loner who has tried to be true to himself in all ways. In doing so, he has not sought public affection and there is little in this derivative account to make him a likeable person. While one can admire his performances and his dedication to causes, Brando does not seem, from the material in this book, to be a person you would like to know. The validity of this reaction can only be proven when Brando cooperates in a biographical venture.

For the immediate present, this volume will appease the curious and please most nondiscriminating readers. Its economy in recapping Brando's career makes it easy, noncontroversial reading.

590 *Brando: The Unauthorized Biography.* by Morella, Joe; and Epstein, Edward Z. 248 p. illus. New York: Crown, 1973.

It is surprising to find how much of the material in this biography is identical with that in Gary Carey's. The reason is that both are unauthorized and depend on secondary sources. This one is not as detailed and leans more toward the anecdote or the short moment. As an example, compare the treatment in both books of the 1947 Brando-Bankhead collision.

The first portion is the biography up to the release of LAST TANGO IN PARIS (1973) but it does not relate the Academy Award embarrassment. The account is rather straightforward and, for the most part, avoids the not-so-subtle innuendo that blemished the author's *Lana*. The reader will not learn much that is new about Brando for he has been the recipient of wide media coverage. The authors' attempt is to tie it all together in the hope that some defineable portrait emerges; unfortunately, it doesn't.

A definite plus for this volume is the second section called "Brando—His Careers to Date." Resembling a miniversion of the typical *Citadel* picture book this could easily be called, "The Films of Marlon Brando." Not surprisingly, a book with that exact title, written by Tony Thomas, has been published. Here some attention is given to his theatre appearances but the focus is his films. Cast and production credits, a few stills and some review excerpts are given for each. In this section the illustrations are fine but some of those used earlier (see Shelley Winters, page 44) are simply bad.

Since this volume is not as detailed as Carey's and cannot compete with the 400 photos in the Thomas book, its only potential is as a compromise.

591 *Brando.* by Shipman, David. 127 p. illus. London: Macmillan, 1974.

One of the *Movie Maker* series, this volume explores the films and career of Marlon Brando. Illustrations are attractive with some in color; an index and a filmography are also included.

592 *Brando For Breakfast.* by Kashfi, Anna; and Stein, E. P. 256 p. New York: Crown, 1979.

Life with Marlon Brando is described by his ex-wife, whose stormy relationship with him lasted for a much longer period than the two years (1957-1959) they were married. In this volume she tries to understand Brando; she admires his accomplishments as an actor but has many, many reservations about him as a person. It should be noted that she divulges some intimate things about Brando's sexual characteristics and behavior that are really cheap shots.

In trying to arouse sympathy for "a poor innocent girl betrayed by a giant male superstar," she creates an opposite reaction in the reader, suggesting that she may be trying with this book to regain the celebrity she once briefly enjoyed. The reader will probably be left with one thought: poor Marlon....

593 *Brando in the Camera Eye.* by Shaw, Stan. 160 p. illus. New York: Exeter, 1979.

Stan Shaw, a famous photojournalist, focuses on Marlon Brando in this words-and-pictures tribute. Using many newly published photographs and a terse commentary, the author concentrates on the period between VIVA ZAPATA (1952) and ONE EYED JACKS (1961). A biographical essay and a filmography round out the portrait.

The subject is fascinating, the visuals are adequately reproduced, and the visual tribute is appropriate. A pleasing volume.

594 *Bransby Williams by Himself.* by Williams, Bransby. 240 p. illus. London: Hutchinson, 1954.

This is the autobiography of a stage actor who has also appeared in British films.

595 *The Brave Ghouls.* by Reisner, Bob. 64 p. illus. New York: Bobbs-Merrill, 1960.

This is an older picture book composed of stills from horror films in which a supposedly humorous caption accompanies each visual. In any event, the stills are fun to look at.

596 *Bravo Maurice!* by Chevalier, Maurice. 240 p. illus. London: Allen and Unwin, Ltd., 1973.

A selection of short pieces taken from the copious autobiographical writings of Maurice Chevalier. Originally published in French, this translation is by Mary Fitton. The selection is good but the sources of the articles are not identified. This is unfortunate since the publishers claim that most of these sources have never been translated into English. Acceptable.

597 *Brazilian Cinema.* by Johnson, Randal; and Stam, Robert. 260 p. illus. Rutherford, N.J.: Fairleigh Dickinson University Press, 1981.

A collection of articles which offer a historical and critical overview of Brazilian cinema, especially that made after 1960.

598 *Breaking into the Movies.* by Emerson, John; and Loos, Anita. 115 p. illus. New York: James A. McCann Co., 1921.

In addition to reviewing their own careers in Hollywood, the authors offer advice and information on acting technique, film production, studio jobs, make-up, dress, salaries, etc. The complete continuity for RED HOT ROMANCE (1922) is included.

599 *Breaking into the Movies.* edited by Jones, Charles Reed. 215 p. New York: The Unicorn Press, 1927.

An all-star cast of contributors is represented in this volume of advice on how to crash the gates of Hollywood in the twenties. The contents include: "Breaking in as an Extra" by Laura La Plante; "Up from the Extra Ranks" by Colleen Moore; "Achieving Stardom" by Dolores Del Rio; "The Leading Man" by Ramon Navarro; "The Leading Woman" by Norma Shearer; "The Modern Westerner" by Ken Maynard; "Good Girls in Pictures" by Lois Wilson; "Bad Girls in Pictures" by Lya de Putti; "Physical Culture and Poise" by Billie Dove; "The Comedian" by Harry Langdon; "The Comedienne" by Louise Fazenda; "The Director" by Alan Dwan; "The Gag Man" by Frank Capra; and "Taking the Breaks" by Reginald Denny. There are other articles about athletics on the screen, animals in motion pictures, the casting director, the newsreel cameraman, costume design, and publicity.

600 *Breaking Through, Selling Out, Dropping Dead and Other Notes on Filmmaking.* by Bayer, William. 227 p. New York: Macmillan, 1971.

"In theory an agent is someone who admires your talent, gives you love, warmth, and protection, and develops your career. In practice you will find that the amount of admiration and love you receive is directly proportional to your income." The two sentences above introduce a much longer section, "Agents," which appears between "AFI" and "Audiences." Many other pertinent topics on filmmaking appear in this cynical, witty, and abrasive book. The alphabetical arrangement is arbitrary, since titles such as "Paying One's Dues," "Ego Trips," "Juggling," and "Hustling," are more entertaining than referential. It is the writing that counts here—a style and a statement that indicates wisdom, experience, and a survival instinct in the difficult field of filmmaking.

Since the book is really advice to the student, the novice, or the beginning director, some of it may have a cliche' sound to the more mature reader. But even familiar topics are treated with honesty, candor and clarity. The result is a book that is intelligent, valuable and entertaining. This unusual volume is highly recommended.

601 *The Brechtian Aspect of Radical Cinema.* by Walsh, Martin. 108 p. New York: Zoetrope, 1981.

A collection of essays suggesting the influence of Bertolt Brecht's works on filmmakers such as Godard, Medvedkin, Straub/Muillet, etc.

602 BRIAN'S SONG. by Blinn, William. 119 p. paper illus. New York: Bantam, 1972.

Script of the 1972 film directed by Buzz Kulick. This is a film made for television but eventually shown elsewhere. Includes production and cast credits, and a list of awards the film received.

603 THE BRIDGE ON THE RIVER KWAI. 16 p. paper illus. New York: Progressive Lithographers, Inc., 1957.

This short souvenir booklet has one section on making the 1957 film, full page photographs of William Holden, Jack Hawkins, and Alec Guinness, some misprinted color shots from the film, a few black and white scenes (which are better) and one half-page devoted to director David Lean.

604 A BRIDGE TOO FAR. by Levine, Joseph E. paper illus. New York: Joseph E. Levine Presents, Inc., 1977.

Subtitled "Notes of a Film Maker," this attractive book offers many visuals taken during the production of A BRIDGE TOO FAR (1977). Introduced by the director of the film, Sir Richard Attenborough, the book has a relatively short text by producer Joseph E. Levine.

605 *Bright Moments: A Black Media Guide and Reader.* edited by Bourne, St. Clair. 128 p. illus. New York: Zoetrope (Chamba Media Foundation),

1981.

A survey of 20 years of Black films and filmmaking is given via essays, articles, interviews, etc.

606 *The Bright Side of Billy Wilder, Primarily.* by Wood, Tom. 257 p. illus. New York: Doubleday, 1969.

Biographical closeup of director Wilder by film publicist Wood. Wilder's experiences with Monroe, Bogart, et al. are detailed. Many "Wilderisms" are recalled. Covers the period from Wilder's first important script MENSCHEN AM SONNTAG (1929) to THE PRIVATE LIFE OF SHERLOCK HOLMES (1970). includes a filmography.

607 *Brigitte: The Story of Brigitte Bardot.* by Reid, Gordon. 35 p. paper illus. London: Eurap, 1958.

A paperback biography written at the peak of Bardot's fame.

608 *Brigitte Bardot.* by De Laborderie, Renaud. 48 p. paper illus. Manchester, England: World Distributors, 1964.

This short booklet has the long subtitle, "Renaud de Laborderie Spotlights in Words and Pictures the Career of the Remarkable Brigitte Bardot."

609 *Brigitte Bardot.* by Sagan, Francoise. illus. New York: Delacorte, 1976.

This picture book has only one subject but it is a very fascinating one—Brigitte Bardot, the one-time sex kitten who is now a middle-aged, mature woman. The book offers a gallery of Bardot photographs by Ghislain Dussart, all of which are identified in detail in an appendix. The text, translated from the French by Judith Sachs, consists of a brief statement by Bardot and a short six-page essay by Sagan. Acceptable.

610 *Brigitte Bardot and the Lolita Syndrome.* by de Beauvoir, Simone. 88 p. illus. London: Reynal, 1961.

A serious essay on the effect of Bardot on society. The author, an existentialist philosopher, discussess the myth of Bardot as an imaginary creature, the eternal female, a child-woman. The role of Bardot's creator, Roger Vadim, is also noted.

611 *The Brigitte Bardot Story.* by Carpozi, Jr., George. 157 p. paper illus.

New York: Belmont Books, 1961.

A biography of Bardot written by the night city editor of the now defunct *New York Journal American.* Her marriage at age 15, Roger Vadim's Svengali act, AND GOD CREATED WOMAN (1956), the suicide attempt, and the world celebrity are all detailed in breezy, reporter-like prose.

612 *Bring On the Empty Horses.* by Niven, David. 369 p. illus. New York: G. P. Putnam's, 1975.

In his second book, David Niven relinquishes the center stage to the film superstars he knew as friends and fellow actors. Covering the period from the mid-thirties to the early sixties, this recollection of Hollywood's golden era has an all-star cast. Clark Gable, Errol Flynn, Constance Bennett, Greta Garbo, Ronald Colman, David Selznick, Douglas Fairbanks, Charlie Chaplin, Humphrey Bogart and Fred Astaire are chosen for single-chapter attention. Many other personalities figure prominently in the book. The structure that Niven employs is a personality parade rather than a chronological narrative. In addition he includes what appears to be a composite portrait of a fading Hollywood actress in a two-part fiction piece, "Out Little Girl." A center section of illustrations is composed mostly of candid shots taken by the author.

As with his autobiography, *The Moon's a Balloon,* Niven is good company as a raconteur who possesses impressive literary gifts. He recognizes life's joy and humor and is able to communicate his acceptance of it to the reader, even when retelling events that are basically ironic or unhappy. His wit almost always is in perfect balance with his good taste and the blend makes for some entertaining and informative recollections. The content is not new but Niven's retelling of it is delightful. Highly recommended.

613 *Britain Can Take It.* by Reynolds, Quentin. 321 p. illus. New York: Dutton, 1941.

This volume, which appeared before the United States entered World War II, was intended to warn and alert the American people. It was adapted from the film, LONDON CAN TAKE IT (1940), directed by Humphrey Jennings and Harry Watt, with a narration by Quentin Reynolds.

614 *British Cinema.* by Gifford, Denis. 176 p. paper illus. New York: Barnes, 1968.

A "who's who" of the British film world, this

volume contains biographical data for 546 actors and directors. The approach is a purely British one; only films and people having a predominant British origin are included. Thus, Rex Harrison's biographical sketch ends with THE YELLOW ROLLS ROYCE (1965) even though Mr. Harrison has been active with MY FAIR LADY (1964), DR. DOLITTLE (1967), THE HONEY POT (1967), STAIRCASE (1969), and A FLEA IN HER EAR (1968).

Certain British personalities are not included, probably because their total screen work was deemed not sufficient. Gertrude Lawrence REMBRANDT (1936) and MEN ARE NOT GODS (1937) is one such case. These are minor faults when the book's overall reference value is considered. The short capsule phrases that describe the entries are most amusing. Nine portraits are given on each page of illustrations and are quite good. The title index is lengthy and should be a most useful aid in tracking down the relatively unknown film. This is an essential reference book and casual readers will find it interesting.

615   *British Cinemas and Their Audiences.* by Mayer, J. P. 280 p. illus. London: Dobson, 1949.

A survey of British movie-goers giving quotes from 400 letters about film preference, reaction to films, and similar information.

616   *British Creators of Film Technique.* edited by Sadoul, Georges. 10 p. paper London: British Film Institute, 1948.

This pamphlet carries a subtitle, "British Scenario Writers, the Creators of the Language of D. W. Griffith, G. A. Smith, Alfred Collins, and Some Others."

617   *British Feature Directors: An Index to Their Work.* compiled by Cavander, Kenneth. 15 p. paper London: British Film Institute, 1958.

618   *The British Film Catalogue 1895-1970.* by Gifford, Denis. 1000 p. New York: McGraw-Hill, 1973.

This reference guide to British entertainment films is arranged chronologically from 1895 to 1970. For each year, the films are arranged in order of their exhibition date and given a catalog number. This number is used in the alphabetical title index which appears at the book's end. Where applicable each entry also indicates length, censor's certificate, silent or sound, color system, screen ratio, stereoscopy,

production company, distribution company, reissue, producer, director, story source, screenplay, narrator, cast and characters, subject (23 headings), plot summary, awards, additional information, series and serials. A bibliography is also included. This well-designed reference volume gives information on over 14,000 British films in a clear, concise manner. Its value is obvious. Recommended.

619   *The British Film Industry.* by Political and Economic Planning (P.E.P.) Staff. 307 p. London: P.E.P., 1952.

A report on the history and organization of the British film industry in the fifties. The economic problems of producing feature films are put forth and analyzed. The original report was updated in 1958.

620   *The British Film Institute Film Title Index 1908-1974.* paper London: World Microfilms, 1908-1974.

This microfilm set consists of a card index of more than 200,000 films produced worldwide since the early part of the century. Feature films, documentaries, and cartoons are considered; newsreels and TV films are not. There are 90 reels in this second edition, each containing about 2000 cards reproduced on 16mm positive microfilm. On each card the following information appears: original film title; producer, director, leading actors; production company data; country of production; running time, footage; synopsis; and reference to reviews and articles in the BFI library. Recommended.

621   *The BFI in the Regions.* compiled by British Film Institute. 32 p. paper illus. London: British Film Institute, 1973.

An account of the activities of the British Film Institute in encouraging film study and appreciation is given in this paperback. Some 36 film theatres in various outlying areas of Great Britain have been helped. Most of these are operated by local groups with the role of the BFI being that of advisor and source of information. Topics considered in this account include history, finance, membership, housing, film selection, film societies, film presentation, relationships with the commercial movie houses, etc.

622   *The British Film Institute "Little Magazines" Series 1889-1972.* paper illus. London: World Microfilms, 1889-1972.

This project is devoted to those film periodicals

which have had a relatively short run. Many periodicals announce publication, appear a few times and then vanish from public view. Invariably they contain articles of interest to the teacher, student, historian and researcher. The British Film Institute has a large collection of such short-lived small magazines and this set of 35mm positive roll microfilm reels contains many of them. Recommended.

623 *British Film Institute National Film Archive Catalogs.* by British Film Institute. London: the British Film Institute.

The British Film Institute publishes many small pamphlets and booklets, and, on occasion, larger volumes. Three of the BFI archive catalogs are: Catalog I: *Silent News Films From 1895 to 1934*— gives title, date, and short description; 1965, 308 pages. Catalog II: *Silent Non-Fiction Films From 1895-1934*—gives descriptive data, title, running time, director; 1960, 195 pages. Catalog III: *Science Fiction Films From 1895 to 1930*—gives data and short plot outlines; 1966, 326 pages.

624 *The British Film Institute; Personality and General Subject Index.* paper London: World Microfilms, 1935-1974.

This microfilm project is really an index to the BFI periodical holdings, which number about 250 titles to date. The index, which appears on 10 reels of 16mm positive roll microfilm, has two parts: first, a listing for prominent individuals (interviews, articles, filmographies and other substantive items are noted), and second, a general subjects listing. Recommended.

625 *BFI Production Board.* edited by Lovell, Alan. 68 p. paper London: British Film Institute (Zoetrope in U.S.), 1976.

This booklet begins with some background about the Production Board which began its life as The Experiment Film Fund in 1952. Its purpose is to provide financial support for the making of worthy films which probably could not be produced elsewhere, and to train personnel for the commerical film-TV industry. Funding procedures, interviews with board members, filmmaker comments, television activities and other topics are treated. After some conclusions, there is a listing of films and filmmakers supported, a financial accounting, and a listing of board members.

This volume is pertinent to the British film industry and probably of little interest to the general reader. The model described herein can be compared in some ways to the Filmmaker Grants Program funded by the American Film Institute. Acceptable.

626 *British Film Institute publications.* paper London: British Film Institute, 1945-.

The British Film Institute is very active in publishing specialized material of interest for all collections. A 1974 listing shows the following titles. They are listed under the BFI department responsible for their creation.

General: *Sight and Sound*, periodical, quarterly, 1932- ; *Monthly Film Bulletin*, periodical, monthly 1934- ; *Michael Powell*, Kevin Gough Yates, 1971; *The BFI in the Regions*, 1970; *Fifty Years of Soviet Cinema*, 1917-1967, stills; *Interim Distribution Catalog*, 1974, BFI, 1974; *Study Extract Catalogue Supplement*, BFI, 1971; *Films on Offer*, BFI, 1974; *Victor Saville*, Cyril B. Rollins and Robert Wareing, 1972; *The Films on Martin Ritt*, Sheila Whitaker, 1972; *Carl Dreyer*, Ebbe Neergaard, 1950; *Marcel Carne*, Jean Queval, 1950; *Frank Capra*, Richard Griffith, 1950; *Jean Vigo*, Harry Feldman and Joseph Feldman, 1951; *Anthony Asquith*, Peter Noble, 1951; *The Early Works of Charles Chaplin*, Theodore Huff; *Rene Clair*, Catherine de la Roche, 1958; *Humphrey Jennings*, Various, 1950; *Joseph L. Mankiewicz*, John Russell Taylor, 1960; *Richard Massingham*, Various, 1955; *Max Ophuls*, Richard Roud, 1958; *Federico Fellini*, Susanne Budgen, 1966; *To Encourage the Art of the Film*, Ivan Butler, 1972.

National Film Archive: *Film Preservation*, Herbert Volkman, 1965; *National Film Archive Catalogue, Part I: Silent News Films 1895-1933*, 1965; *National Film Archive Catalogue, Part II: Silent Non-Fiction Films 1895-1934*, 1960; *National Film Archive Catalogue, Part III: Silent Fiction Films 1895-1930*, 1966; *National Film Archive Catalogue of Viewing Copies*, 1971; *National Film Archive Catalogue of Viewing Copies, Supplement*, 1973; *Rules for Use in the Cataloging Department of the National Film Archive*, 1960.

Information and Documentation: *Periodical Holdings, 1974*, 1974; *British National Film Catalog*, quarterly with annual circulations, 1963-.

Educational Advisory Services: *Film Teaching*, Paddy Whannel, Peter Harcourt, eds., 1968; *Film Making in Schools and Colleges*, Peter Harcourt, Peter Theobald, eds., 1966; *Budd Boetticher*, Jim Kitses, ed., 1969; *Working Papers on the Cinema: Sociology and Semiology*, Peter Wollen, ed., 1969; *Violence on the Screen*, Andre Glucksmann, 1971; *Film and Television in Education for Teaching*, BFI, 1960;

Film in English Teaching, Roy Knight, ed. 1972; *Talking About the Cinema*, Jim Kitses, Ann Kaplan, 1966.

It should be noted that the *Cinema One* series is also produced in association withthe British Film Institute.

627   *British Film Music.* by Huntley, John. 247 p. illus. London: Skelton Robinson, 1947.

A general discussion of film music followed by a close look at British musical films produced from 1936 to 1946. Music composed for documentary films is also given attention. The appendices contain data about the composers and orchestras. Introduction by Muir Mathieson.

628   *The British Film Yearbook.* edited by Noble, Peter. illus. London: Skelton Robinson; British American Film Holding, 1946-.

From 1946 to date Peter Noble has edited this yearbook. Early volumes surveyed the major events of the year in film in addition to offering articles, illustrations, tables, indexes, the year's releases, awards, biographies, etc. In recent years its title was changed to the *British Film and Television Yearbook.* At present it is the British equivalent to *The International Motion Picture Almanac.*

In the 27th edition (1972-73) more than 400 of its 600 pages are devoted to a biographical section covering actors, directors, writers, designers, and others who are currently active in British films and television. There is also much additional information on equipment, supplies, film labs, studios, production companies, trade organizations, etc. Many illustrations are provided.

629   *British Film Yearbook 1947-1948.* edited by Noble, Peter. 381 p. illus. London: Skelton Robinson, 1948.

Outstanding articles on every aspect of films. Contributors include James Agate, C. A. Lejeune, Ernest Irving, Paul Rotha, Thorold Dickinson, Anthony Asquith, and others. Includes an A-to-Z "who's who" listing, other reference sections, complete indices, and statistics.

630   *The British National Film Catalog.* edited by Moulds, Michael. London: British Industrial and Scientific Film Association, annual.

Provides full information about all short films

released in Great Britian. It is published in quarterly issues, followed by a bound annual cumulated volume. The nonfiction films are arranged in subject order with full subject indexing. Titles, companies, and individuals associated with the films are also indexed.

631   *British National Film Catalogue.* by British Film Institute. paper London: British Film Institute, 1963-   .

This annual catalog offers details of worldwide nonfeature film production. It is organized according to subject and considers a wide range of films. Begun under the auspices of UNESCO in 1963, it is now published in quarterly issues with an annual cumulation.

632   *British Official Films in the Second World War: A Descriptive Catalog.* by Thorpe, Frances; and Pronay, Nicholas. 321 p. Santa Barbara, Calif.: American Bibliographical Center, Clio Press, 1980.

633   *British Screen Stars.* edited by Noble, Peter. 91 p. paper illus. London: Skelton Robinson, 1946.

An example of one of the fan "yearbooks" which appeared for several years in the late forties. Lots of pictures of British film actors along with information about their current activities.

634   *British Technicolor Films.* by Huntley, John. 224 p. illus. London: Robinson, Skelton, 1950.

A survey of color films in Britain from 1936 to 1948.

635   *British Transport Film Library Catalogue.* 36 p. London: Melbury House, 1973.

A catalog of films dealing with transportation, this book offers an alphabetical title index and an arrangement by subject, e.g., British railways, London transportation, waterways, docks, travel, national transportation, etc.

636   *Broadway and Hollywood: Costumes Designed By Irene Sharaff.* by Sharaff, Irene. 136 p. illus. New York: Van Nostrand, 1976.

Books on costume design for motion pictures are rare; when an attractive volume such as this one appears, the importance of the designer's work can be reassessed and totally appreciated.

Using an autobiographical framework, the author devotes most of the text to her work for the stage and films. She has costumed hundreds of celebrities and her anecdotes buzz with confidences, asides, opinions and reactions concerning them. Thus the text becomes a rich brew of some carefully selected memoirs, a review of her professional activities, and many short characterizations of well-known performers.

In any volume about costume design the visuals should predominate, and here they certainly do. Ranging from simple line drawings to full-color plates, they also include many photographs. Occasionally their size is too small for full study or appreciation; they are almost all deserving of full-page reproduction. An index completes the volume.

It is a difficult task to create an interesting book about a profession that demands so much artistry, talent, creativity, research ability, and hard work. Irene Sharaff has succeeded by combining a brisk colorful text with the appropriate visualization of her work. Production values are mostly impressive and the spice is supplied by her supporting cast of stars. A beautifully composed book of consistent high quality, this one will appeal to readers in search of something different in film literature. Recommended.

637 *Broadway and Hollywood.* by McLaughlin, Robert. 302 p. New York: Arno, 1974.

This volume, one in the *Dissertations on Film* series, was written in 1970 as one of the requirements for a doctoral degree at the University of Wisconsin. Its subtitle, "A History of Economic Interaction," indicates the focus and range of its content. Beginning with the economic impact that the first films had upon theatre at the turn of the century, the end of touring companies, the migration of actors and playwrights to film work, and the beginning of economic interrelationships are described.

During the period from 1927 to 1946, further economic adjustments were necessary and a state of peaceful coexistence took place. The advent of television, however, again necessitated further change and adjustment of the enterprises concerned. The continuing symbiotic relationship of the three is noted. Notes, tables, and a bibliography complete the work. As a historical survey of certain interrelationships of theatre, motion pictures and television, this study has pertinence mostly for scholars, historians and researchers. Acceptable.

638 *Broadway and Hollywood, Too.* by Aros, Andrew A. 60 p. paper Diamond Bar, Calif.: Applause, 1980.

639 *Bronson!* by Harbinson, W. A. 166 p. paper illus. New York: Pinnacle, 1975.

This original paperback is subtitled "A Biographical Portrait," while the author refers to it as "a speculative biography based on Bronson's own view of himself given to the media." "Speculative" is certainly the right word since much of the text assumes Bronson's thoughts, reactions, and emotions. Only in the factual recitations and the film criticism sections is the author convincing. He makes much of Bronson's early years as the coal-miner son of immigrant parents and his long struggle to achieve financial security. His evaluation of Bronson's screen image and attitude toward success provides the stronger portion of the book. A center section of small, crowded visuals surveys Bronson's career. A filmography, completes the biography which is the first one available on Bronson. It is acceptable primarily for that reason.

640 *The Brooke Book.* by Shields, Brooke. unpaginated paper illus. New York: Simon and Schuster, 1978.

An example of "too much, too soon" in print, this volume is supposedly the opinions and thoughts of the child actress.

641 BROTHER CARL. by Sontag, Susan. 176 p. paper illus. New York: Farrar, Straus & Giroux, 1974.

Script of the 1971 film directed by Sontag. Contains an introduction by Sontag, cast and credits.

642 *Bruce Lee: The Man Only I Knew.* Lee, Linda.

The story of how a five-foot seven-inch 135-pound weakling transformed himself into an international film star is related by his wife in this interesting book. Bruce Lee's fascination with gung-fu, karate, and kung fu enabled him to become the most widely known exponent of these martial arts. She tells of his rise to Oriental superstar after being a child movie actor, a juvenile delinquent, a teacher, and a student of philosophy. The portrait provided is what might be expected from a loving wife. It is both a tribute and a biography, concentrating on positive accomplishments while minimizing anything that might be unpleasant or tarnishing to the image she wishes to perpetuate. Therefore much attention is given to the training and discipline Lee needed to master the martial arts. Illustrations help the text somewhat and a series of flip-the-pages photos give the illusion of Bruce Lee in action. There is no index.

As objective biography this volume is no great shakes; but as an introduction to the world of kung fu and as a wife's memoir-tribute to her husband it is quite acceptable. See also *The Legend of Bruce Lee, Kung Fu: Cinema of Vengeance,* and *Bruce Lee—King of Kung Fu.*

643 *Bruce Lee: King of Kung Fu.* by Dennis, Felix; and Atyeo, Don. 96 p. paper illus. San Francisco: Straight Arrow Books, 1975.

This original biography paperback carries a subtitle, "The True Story of His Life, His Art, His Films, His Death," which sums up the content nicely. The oversized page format accommodates many large-sized illustrations whose reproduction ranges from sharp to murky. They have been well selected to complement the familiar story of Bruce Lee's rise to international fame as the "King of Kung Fu." Told in journalistic style and format, the narrative covers his early years in San Francisco, the introduction to martial arts, his years in Hong Kong, the first films, Hollywood's discovery of the Kung Fu films, and his Valentino-like death.

Taking a cue from its subject matter, the book moves quickly, gracefully, and with frequent excitement. It has been well researched and will add to the Bruce Lee legend. Since drugs and sex play a prominent role in the latter pages, the book is acceptable for mature adults.

644 *Bud: The Brando I Knew.* by Fiore, Carlo. 294 p. illus. New York: Delacorte, 1974.

Marlon Brando has always been a private person whose life away from the cameras is zealously hidden. This volume contains some interesting information about his early career on stage and in films. During the period of 1944 to 1960, Fiore was a friend, confidant, stand-in, and dialogue coach for Brando. More about the relationship between the two men is revealed than probably was intended. In portraying the unique lifestyle of this famous actor, the author emphasizes the sexual, the vulgar, and the neurotic. In doing so he diminishes himself rather than Brando and the reader can only wonder about this kiss-and-tell betrayal of a friendship. There are many photographs provided to support the intimate text. There is no index. The volume will fascinate readers familiar with Brando's work and those looking for sensationalized, selected confidences. Because of the emphasis on intimate personal matters, the book is acceptable for mature readers.

645 *Bud and Lou: The Abbott and Costello Story.* by Thomas, Bob. 224 illus. Philadelphia: J. B. Lippincott, 1977.

Although Bob Thomas had the assistance of many persons who knew the team of Abbott and Costello, his use of what he learned is disappointing. While the factual data is abundant, his critical evaluation of them as performers and his portrait of them as men is ultimately unsatisfying. The fact that in real life they were opposites of the characters they created on screen tells most of the story. Aggressive, determined, ambitious Lou Costello was the dominant personality while Bud Abbott was the relaxed, easy-going follower.

The technique of recreating many of their supposed conversations may appeal to the nondiscriminating reader but it weakens any serious attempt at biography. Some attractive elements are present however, such as a collection of well-selected photographs, a filmography, an index, and, for a select audience, excerpts from many of their routines, along with the complete script of "Who's on First?"

The drama that existed in the careers and the relationship of the two comedians has been suggested but not realized in this volume. What is offered is a popularized biographical review of a comedy team whose status as creative artists is still to be determined. Acceptable.

646 *Budd Boetticher: The Western.* edited by Kitses, Jim. 50 p. paper illus. London: British Film Intitute, 1969.

A collection of articles that includes interviews, a filmography, essays by Andre Bazin, Andrew Sarris, Peter Wollen, and Jim Kitses. The volume was prepared in conjunction with a showing of Boetticher's films at the National Film Theatre.

647 BUFFALO BILL AND THE INDIANS. by Altman, Robert; and Rudolph, Alan. 151 p. illus. New York: Bantam, 1976.

Script of the 1976 film directed by Robert Altman. Contains cast and credits.

648 *Bulgarian Cartoon Films.* unpaginated. paper illus. Sofia, Bulgaria: State Film Distributors, 1972.

A yearly account of cartoon films produced in Bulgaria, this catalog is written in four languages: English, French, Russian and Spanish. Each annual is a supplement to the original volume which covered cartoon films made in Bulgaria from 1955 to 1961.

649 *Bulgarian Short Films.* unpaginated. paper Sofia, Bulgaria: State Film Distributors, 1973.

A yearly catalog of short films produced in Bulgaria, this annual offers information and data in English, French, Russian and Spanish. Each annual is a supplement to the original one which covered those short films made in Bulgaria from the late fifties up to 1962.

650 *Bulls, Balls, Bicycles and Actors.* by Bickford, Charles. 336 p. New York: Eriksson, Paul S., 1965.

An autobiography of sorts, this book is rather lopsided in its consideration of what is interesting to the reading public. Since 1930 Charles Bickford has been a "film name" —yet only half of this book is devoted to those four decades in Hollywood (he died in 1967). Most of this section is devoted to his first four motion pictures. He avoids names using "Mr. X" etc. (Is "The Golem" really William Wyler?) His negative experiences with Cecil B. DeMille, Louis B. Mayer, Irving Thalberg and William Randolph Hearst are treated in some detail. Everything else concerning motion pictures is skipped over in favor of some uninteresting anecdotes about hunting, travel, and other pursuits. Mr. Bickford's regard for his own films and the motion picture industry is quite low. His contempt shows through, largely by his omissions. The book is a distinct disappointment.

651 *Bunch: A Biography of Nelson Keys.* by Carstairs, John Paddy. 255 p. illus. London: Hurst and Blackett, 1941.

An older biography of the British comedian, Nelson Keys, who appeared in silent films and the early talkies.

652 *Burke's Steerage.* by Burke, Tom. 379 p. New York: G.P. Putnam's, 1976.

Tom Burke, a graduate of the Rex Reed/John Simon school of journalism, offers a collection of celebrity "pieces" that he wrote originally for such periodicals as *Esquire, Rolling Stone, Cosmopolitan, Holiday,* etc. Based on interviews, the versions presented here eliminate the questions and have added the opinions and reactions of the interviewer. The questions would have been better.

Burke comes across as a biased egoist who is using his subjects rather than presenting them. Much of his sixties material is dated and some of the more recent material is simply dull. His ability to hide prejudice is minimal.

653 *Burt Lancaster: A Pictorial Treasury of His Films.* by Vermilye, J. 160 p. illus. New York: Crescent Books, 1970.

This inexpensive book is one of the first four picture volumes in *Hollywood's Magic People* series. Its format is similar to that used with Charles Laughton and John Huston—a continuous text accompanying many nicely reproduced pictures with a filmography at the book's conclusion.

654 *Burt Lancaster.* by Thomas, Tony. 160 p. paper illus. New York: Pyramid, 1975.

A portrait of an ambitious young actor who rose from one Broadway show to a cinema career covering over 50 films. In this volume Tony Thomas traces Lancaster's films from THE KILLERS (1946) to THE MIDNIGHT MAN (1974). Much is made of Lancaster's independence in choosing provocative material for filming during his later career. The general evaluation of his work by the author is objective and critically sound. Visuals are plentiful and are reproduced with clarity. A bibliography, filmography and an index complete the book. Burt Lancaster has been a film star for almost three decades. This volume offers justification in words and visuals for that longevity. Recommended.

655 *Burt Reynolds.* by Hurwood, Bernhardt J. 112 p. paper illus. New York: Quick Fox, 1979.

This is one of the first book-length biographies available on Burt Reynolds. It relies heavily on previously published materials and, even so, has difficulty filling a total book. Many full and double-page illustrations accompany the text. Because Reynolds has worked long and hard to reach his current celebrity status, he is guarded about unauthorized books and articles. Also, since the *Cosmopolitan* centerfold, the financial value of such material is not unknown to him.

What is provided here is a review of Reynold's life as reflected in the media. Critical attention to his performances is minimal in a text which concentrates on his personal and public behavior. A filmography lists 30 films from ANGEL BABY (1961) to HOOPER (1978).

656 *Burt Reynolds: Portrait of a Superstar.* by Whitley, Dianna. 112 p. paper illus. New York: Today Press (Grosset and Dunlap), 1979.

Just what you might expect in any appreciation of an actor-personality such as Burt Reynolds—illustrations, biography, a career review, and some attention to the Reynolds image. The oversized book format seems appropriate.

657   *The Busby Berkeley Book.* by Thomas, Tony; and Terry, Jim; and Berkeley, Busby. 192 p. illus. Greenwich, Conn.: New York Graphic Society, 1973.

What a beautiful book this is! It surveys the films of Busby Berkeley with a maximum of visuals and some appropriate narrative. What the reader will remember is the content of the pictures and the painstaking reproduction of them. Not only are there stills from the finished films, but many production or shooting pictures are included in order to show Berkeley's filmmaking methods. As expected, there are the geometrical groupings, military formations, and marching band designs here. The final film JUMBO (1962) and the stage revival of "No, No, Nanette" (1971) conclude this tribute to Berkeley. An index is provided.

The book is pure visual delight. Everything here helps to recreate with affectionate accuracy, an era of screen history that brought great pleasure to audiences. This book should repeat that action. Highly recommended.

658   *Business Films; How to Make and Use Them.* by Spooner, Peter. 360 p. illus. London: Business Publications, 1959.

A rather complete overview of the business film is offered in this volume. An introductory section examines the scope of this film genre, and more than two dozen companies describe their experiences in using such films. Other sections are concerned with film stocks, printing methods, cameras, projection, editing equipment, film construction, film records, adding sound, films for work study, films for research, sponsorship, potential audiences, films for advertising, films for training, films for communications, and finally, showmanship in films. A directory, a bibliography, and an index are added.

659   *Business Films Make Business Sense.* edited by Kodak Staff. 20 p. paper illus. Rochester N.Y.: Kodak, 1977.

A collection of ideas and suggestions on how to use business films to increase sales and profits. Some case histories are mentioned.

660   *The Business Man in the Amusement World: A Volume of Progress in the Field of the Theatre.* by Grau, Robert. 362 p. illus. New York: Ozer, 1972 (1910).

A reprint of the 1910 book originally published by the Broadway Publishing Company, this was one of the first volumes to note the rise of motion pictures as both entertainment and social force. Written by a booking agent, the text records the growth of the nickelodeons, the use of films with vaudeville, and the commercial importance of this early curiosity. Comment on theatre is intermingled with the information on motion pictures.

661   *The Business of Filmmaking.* by Pollock, Jeffrey J.; and da Silva, Paul; and Rogers, Richard H. 96 p. paper illus. Rochester, N.Y.: Kodak, 1978.

This book (Kodak publication number H-55) is devoted to the business of planning, producing and distributing nontheatrical films. Its comprehensive text consists of eight parts: marketing the film concept; the successful film proposal; production data post production; film distribution and promotion; daily business activities; references; and Kodak resources.

Easy to read and attractive in its layout, the book should serve a variety of readers. Filmmakers, students, teachers, and even general readers will find the material both interesting and valuable. A large amount of practical information is presented and a teaching guide is available. Recommended.

662   *Buster Keaton.* by Lebel, J. P. 180 p. paper illus. New York: A. S. Barnes, 1967.

A short biographical sketch followed by a critical analysis of Keaton's art, and a filmography. Although examples from his films are used throughout, the films themselves are not treated individually but only as a totality characterizing his art. Recommended.

663   *Buster Keaton.* by Robinson, David. 198 p. illus. Bloomington, Ind.: Indiana University Press, 1969.

Although it leans heavily for its biographical material on both the Blesh and Keaton volumes, this book devotes most of its pages to the films. Each of the silent feature films is described, and analyzed in depth; in the case of OUR HOSPITALITY (1923), the final reel is broken down into its component shots.

A filmography of both the silent shorts and features is given. The fine illustrations and the intelligent analysis offered make this book a worthwhile addition to the growing Keaton Story. Recommended for all readers. The production, as in all the *Cinema One* Series, is outstanding.

664 *Buster Keaton And the Dynamics of Visual Wit.* by Wead, George. 370 p. New York: Arno Press, 1976.

Written in 1973 at Northwestern University, in partial fulfillment of the Doctoral program, this study examines the theory of film comedy with particular emphasis on the enigmatic style of Buster Keaton. The comic style and film character of Keaton are thoroughly analyzed and placed in the context of a theory of film comedy. Keaton's portrayal of the hapless victim of fate and machines is described in detail. This title is included in the *Dissertations on Film* series.

665 *Buster Keaton's* THE GENERAL. edited by Anobile, Richard. 256 p. paperillus. New York: Flare (Avon), 1975.

This is the first silent film selected for the *Film Classics Library* Series. Instead of the usual dialogue, title cards are used to facilitate the visual narrative. The 2100 frame enlargements used in this presentation are necessitated by Keaton's reliance on sight gags and visual nuance. Most of the frames are clearly reproduced and Anobile's selection of them makes the story easy to follow. An introduction is provided by Raymond Rohauer along with a 1972 interview with Marion Mack, the female lead in THE GENERAL (1926).

This is another fine addition to the series. Recommended.

666 BUTCH CASSIDY AND THE SUNDANCE KID. by Goldman, William. 185 p. paper illus. New York: Bantam Books, 1969. Script of the 1969 film directed by George Roy Hill. Contains cast credits.

667 *Butter with My Bread: The Memoirs of Olga Petrova.* by Petrova, Olga. 371 p. New York: Bobbs Merrill, 1942.

Olga Petrova was an actress in silent films who specialized in portraying wicked women.

668 *By a Stroke of Luck!* by Stewart, Donald Ogden. 302 p. illus. New York: Paddington Press, 1975.

Stewart, a writer of plays, essays, articles, books and screenplays, enjoyed several decades of prominence until, as one of the "Unfriendly Ten," he became a blacklist victim of the McCarthy-HUAC witchhunts. In this sensitive, appealing autobiography Stewart recalls the rewarding years that preceded his voluntary exile to Europe in 1953. As the author of numerous screenplays written during Hollywood's golden era, Stewart worked with many film personalities. A large portion of this book deals with those Hollywood experiences, the climax of which was his Academy Award for the screenplay of THE PHILADELPHIA STORY (1941). Some visuals and an index accompany the text, but a filmography and a bibliography are conspicuously absent.

The author wrote this book as an octogenarian whose perceptive reflections about his earlier years indicate an acceptance of life's rewards and disappointments. It is difficult to resist the author's warmth, wit, intelligence and stylish maturity. These qualities blended with his social consciousness have provided a memorable reading experience. Recommended.

669 *By Emily Possessed.* by Thomas, Mona Burns. 165 p. illus. New York: Exposition Press, 1973.

Although this short biography deals mostly with theatre and television, it is noted here because the author is the mother of former child film actor, Frankie Thomas, and wife of character actor Frank Thomas. At one period in the thirties both father and son were popular performers in films, and it is the account of those times that gives the book some small pertinence for film collections. Frankie Thomas is now involved with teaching, writing and publishing materials on contract bridge. His father, Frank M. Thomas, still works in films occasionally. Acceptable.

670 CABARET. 24 p. paper illus. New York: Souvenir Book Publishers, 1972.

The emphasis in this souvenir book is on performers. Star Liza Minnelli receives six pages of attention via some general shots from the 1972 film. Joel Grey, Michael York, and supporting cast members, Helmut Griem and Marisa Berenson, are also spotlighted. The story, other cast members and technical credits are given, and there are longer profiles of producer Cy Feuer and director Bob Fosse.

671 *Cable Television.* edited by Henstell, Bruce. 26 p. paper Washington, D.C.: American Film Institute, 1972.

This discussion about cable TV (CATV) is only peripheral to film literature at this point but promises to become an important topic. The showing of films over cable TV is a major concern, mentioned only briefly here. Most attention is given to a description of cable TV and its ultimate effects. A bibliography is included. Acceptable.

672 *Cads and Cavaliers: The Film Adventurers.* by Thomas, Tony. 242 p. illus. New York: A. S. Barnes, 1973.

In this collective biography, the linking theme appears to be the swashbucklers—pirates, adventurers, rogues, cads and cavaliers. Seven chapters examine the careers of Douglas Fairbanks, Jr. and Sr., John Barrymore, George Sanders, Vincent Price, David Niven, Basil Rathbone, and Errol Flynn. Each is a miniature biography that is factual and critical. The concluding section is titled "A Gallery of Adventurers," and offers a very mixed selection of film characterizations which range from Bob Hope's MONSIEUR BEAUCAIRE (1946) to Laurence Olivier's HAMLET (1948), the criteria for inclusion apparently being at least one dueling scene.

There are book-biographies available for all eight major subjects, so one can question the need for further material. It is the approach here that matters. By emphasizing critical evaluations of each subject's films and using a plentiful collection of visuals to support his text, the author produces results that range from good to excellent. The section devoted to Flynn is particularly well written. An index is provided and there is an anemic foreword by Thaddeus Tuleja.

One may wish that author Thomas had applied his considerable talent to certain actors who appear briefly in the final section (e.g., Cornel Wilde, Stewart Granger, Ronald Colman) rather than the more familiar names; but that is quibbling since he does so well with those subjects he has selected. This is an entertaining, well-written book that is sure to please many readers. Recommended.

673 *Cagney.* by Offen, Ron. 217 p. illus. Chicago: Henry Regnery, 1972.

Using a fan magazine approach that includes "recreated" conversations, this unauthorized biography is not much of a compliment to Cagney. While it gives the external facts of his life and covers his films fairly comprehensively, it remains a restatement of what has already been published. Errors are made with names, studios and in the general text. The illustrations are average and the filmography is anemic. Forget this one and look at *The Films of James Cagney*, which has some production faults but a much better coverage of the subject.

674 *Cagney: The Actor as Auteur.* by McGilligan, Patrick. 240 p. illus. New York: A.S. Barnes, 1975.

In this appreciation of James Cagney, the author employs a useful arrangement of his material. Beginning with a biographical chapter on the actor's early theatrical years, he progresses quickly to Hollywood and the Cagney films. Elements of biography become peripheral as each of the films is described and evaluated. In concluding chapters, McGilligan tries to define Cagney's contribution to film history in terms of talent, charm, sex appeal, image, symbolism, etc., as evidenced in the films. A final section considers Cagney's own influences on his screen roles; hence the use of "auteur" in the book's title.

A filmography, a bibliography, a list of stage roles, his appearances on radio and television and an index are included. The visuals, which are nicely reproduced, consist mostly of film stills and portraits.

What sets this rewarding study apart from lesser volumes is the intelligent use the author makes of his material. The idea of the actor as auteur will undoubtedly become increasingly common in cinema literature and is encouraged by the successful argument presented here. The book shows that an appreciation written around a central theme can result in excellent film criticism. Recommended.

675 *Cagney.* by Freedland, Michael. 255 p. illus. New York: Stein and Day, 1975.

An unauthorized biography of James Cagney, this volume traces his career from a chorus boy on the New York stage to the American Film Institute tribute in 1974. The facts of Cagney's life are related in chronological order with some assistance given to the author by the actor's friends and co-workers, e.g., Pat O'Brien and Ralph Bellamy. Cagney's 62 films, from SINNER'S HOLIDAY (1930) to ONE, TWO, THREE (1961), are noted and there is a pictorial section provided. Acceptable.

676 *Cagney by Cagney.* by Cagney, James. 216 p. paper illus. New York: Pocket Books, 1976.

A modest collection of anecdotes, memoirs, poetry, acknowledgements, etc., that reads like transcribed and edited tape recordings. Cagney recalls in swift fashion his rise from vaudeville-Broadway-dancer to screen celebrity, giving some attention to his large catalog of films. Mostly the book recalls, in a polite, superficial way, the other actors and directors who worked with him. A center section of illustrations shows Cagney both on and off screen.

Here is a volume that should be much better than the unoffending, guarded success story that it is. Apparently the main idea of the work is to point out in both text and illustrations the great disparity between the screen image and the private person of James Cagney. Acceptable because of the source rather than the material provided.

677 *Cahiers Du Cinema.* 64 p. paper illus. New York: Thousand Eyes, 1978.

Includes a general introduction by T. L. French, a long interview with Serge Daney, "Les Cahiers du Cinema 1968-1977" and "The T(h)errorized" by Serge Daney. Notes and filmographies are added.

678 *Caligari's Cabinet and Other Grand Illusions: A History of Film Design.* by Barsacq, Leon. 264 p. illus. Boston: Little, Brown (New York Graphic Society), 1976.

This attractive volume is an English language version of *Le Decor de Film*, a 1970 book published in French by Editions Seghers. Michael Bullock's translation has been complemented by revisions and expansions supplied by Elliott Stern. The result is an authoritative historical survey of set and scenery design. Beginning with the painted sets used in early French films, the text progresses to constructed sets, integrated sets, natural scenery, realistic backgrounds and postwar scenic design. Final chapters are devoted to research, the use of color, set creation/construction and special effects. Filmographies of noted set designers are supplied along with a listing of the Academy Awards given for art decoration and set decoration (1927-1975). A fine bibliography, a title index and a name index complete the book.

The illustrations are plentiful and carefully reproduced. Their selection is impressive and they correlate nicely with the text material.

The volume has as its central theme the development of a film aesthetic that is often overlooked or taken for granted. In a well-researched and logically developed text, the author has provided a detailed survey that informs and entertains. Avoiding the pitfall of a pedantic treatment, Barsacq has combined fact, description, opinion, criticism, and visuals into a most pleasurable reading-viewing experience.

679 *Caligari's Children.* by Prawer, S. S. 307 p. illus. New York: Oxford University Press, 1980.

Subtitled "The Film as a Tale of Terror," this volume provides a structured examination of the enduring fascination of audiences for the horror film. After a detailed description of the genre, Prawer treats two cases of the transfer of book-into-film: DR. JEKYLL AND MR. HYDE (1932) and VAMPYRE (1932). He uses THE CABINET OF DR. CALIGARI (1919) as a model from the German silent film era which suggested the themes and iconography for hundreds of horror films which appeared over the next six decades. In addition to these major topics, he discusses many other films, noting the devices used by filmmakers to evoke terror and fear in the viewer. His conclusions flow in logical order from the text and will provide the careful reader with some provocative thoughts about the horror film. A lengthy bibliography, illustrations, a name index and a title index complete the books.

Prawer is competing in a field that has been used to excess by earlier writers—as witnessed in his own selected bibliography. Certainly Carlos Clarens, William Everson, Ivan Butler, Ed Naha and others have covered the genre more than adequately. Yet much of what the author offers here seems original and fresh—probably because of the respect, scholarship, and thought he provides for his subject.

680 *Call Me Lucky: Bing Crosby's Own Story.* by Martin, Pete; and Crosby, Bing. 228 p. paper New York: Simon & Schuster, 1953.

The small portion of this volume that deals with Crosby's films is written so well that it makes one wish that there were greater emphasis on this aspect of his career. Anecdotes about Carole Lombard, Marion Davies, Mack Sennett, W. C. Fields, and others, are just fine. The style is better than one usually finds in the "as told to" books. While the privacy of the real Crosby is never invaded, the public image is reinforced throughout. The lack of an index and illustrations lessens the value of the book.

681 *Call Them Irreplaceable.* by Fisher, John. 224 p. illus. New York: Stein and Day, 1976.

A series of tributes to a dozen legendary performers is the substance of this attractive book. In each instance elements of biographical data are blended with critical comment and analysis in an effort to explain "How and Why the Great Ones Soared." The subjects are Al Jolson, Maurice Chevalier, Jimmy Durante, Noel Coward, Jack Benny, Fred Astaire, Bing Crosby, Marlene Dietrich, Bob Hope, Judy Garland, Danny Kaye and Frank Sinatra. Framing the tributes are an introduction, a finale and a special lyric by Sammy Cahn. A bibliography and an index complete the work.

Illustrations consist of a full-page line caricature/drawing by Hirschfeld and a double-page montage of photographs for each performer. All elements of the book's production are outstanding.

It is the text, however, which is the determinant of this book's quality. Written with honesty, perception and knowledge, the tributes succeed for the most part in explaining each star's special qualities. Recommended.

682   *Came the Dawn: Memories of a Film Pioneer.* by Hepworth, Cecil M. 207 p. illus. New York: Phoenix House, 1951.

An autobiography of a British filmmaker who was active before the turn of the century. Born in 1874, Hepworth began making films which ran 40 seconds in 1898. He continued with films until 1923 when the last Hepworth Picture Play was made. The author is most qualified to report on this early period in British film history. This book will appeal primarily to scholars, researchers, and historians. Index and photographs.

683   CAMELOT. by Combs, Carl. 48 p. paper illus. New York: National Publishers, 1968.

Some small, unfocused, fuzzy photographs spoil this otherwise attractive souvenir book. Starting with the Arthurian legend, the text and photos describe the actors, costumes, sets, artifacts, armor, animals, makeup, and hairstyles. Richard Harris, Vanessa Redgrave, Franco Nero and David Hemmings receive individual attention, as do composers Alan Jay Lerner and Frederick Loewe, conductor Alfred Newman, director Joshua Logan and producer Jack Warner. Supporting cast and technical credits are also noted.

684   *Camera!*: Digest of the Motion Picture Industry Anthology. edited by Gordon, R. 6 volumes New York: Gordon Press, 1976.

A reprinting of material that originally appeared in *Camera!* from 1918 to 1924.

685   *The Camera and I* by Ivens, Joris 279 p. illus. New York: International Publishers, 1969.

This is the autobiography of a documentary filmmaker whose works include THE SPANISH EARTH (1937), FOUR HUNDRED MILLION (1938), THE STORY OF G. I. JOE (1945), POWER AND THE LAND (1940) and others. An interesting account of both the man and the documentary film movement.

686   *The Camera Man.* by Collins, Francis Arnold. 278 p. illus. New York: Century Co., 1916.

Subtitled "His Adventures in Many Fields, with Practical Suggestions for the Amateur," this volume tells of photographing news stories, sea adventures, government work, war battles, etc. Among the cameramen mentioned are Lawrence Darmour and L. M. Burrud. In discussing the work of the latter, mention is made of the contract between Pancho Villa and a film company to wage the Mexican insurrection only during those times when filming was possible.

687   *Camera Over Hollywood.* by Swope, John. 98 p. illus. New York: Random House, 1939.

A most attractive book of photographs designed to show the glamorous side of Hollywood in the thirties. Major studios, homes of the stars, extra players, and many famous film personalities are the subjects of the pictures. Short captions are provided for the attractive visuals.

688   *Camera Techniques For the Color Movie Maker.* by Ham, Dick. 96 p. paper illus. New York: Amphoto, 1959.

A method of making color movies explained for the beginner.

689   *Camerado: Hollywood and the American Male.* by Spoto, Donald. 238 p. paper illus. New York: New American Library, 1978.

The changing masculine image reflected on American screens over the past five decades is the subject of this investigation. Admitting to selectivity, the author examines characters, personalities, films and directors under general headings of ordinary, charming, funny, sad, lawless and strong. There are illustrations and an index to supplement the readable text.

Spoto combines the virtues of good writing and extensive background to provide a comprehensive study that is intelligent, thought-provoking, and, at times, debatable. In a sense, it is a popularized doctoral dissertation lacking only the pedantic framework found in such works. Recommended.

690 *Cameras West.* by Manchel, Frank. 150 p. illus. Englewood Cliffs, N.J.: Prentice-Hall, 1971.

The history of the western film, from THE GREAT TRAIN ROBBERY (1903) to TRUE GRIT (1969), is covered in this most welcome book. Aimed at a school audience, the volume has many attractive features. The text is factual, evaluative, and critical, with many films being described as "overlooked" or "underrated," for example, "one week later another low-budget screen masterpiece appeared and with just as little recognition as Peckinpah's RIDE THE HIGH COUNTRY (1962): David Miller's LONELY ARE THE BRAVE (1962)." The author justifies his opinion in the paragraph that follows.

Many film stills and some actual photographs—Doc Holliday, Wyatt Earp, the Long Branch Saloon in Dodge City, etc.—add interest and clarity. Unfortunately, since the visuals are presented in six groupings, they do not always coincide with the narrative, but this is a minor matter. A bibliography and an index complete the book. With nearly twice the number of pages of his previous books, the author has been able to develop his theme in a most satisfactory way. Treatment, selection, and total coverage are commendable. A highly recommended book.

691 *Cameron Technical Books (A Series).* by Cameron, James R. illus. Cameron Publishing Company, 1920- .

James Cameron was the author or coauthor of a number of titles dealing with the technical side of motion picture exhibition, projection and cinematography.

Some of his books are: *Amateur Movie Craft* (1928), *Cameron's Encyclopedia on Sound Motion Pictures* (1930), *Cinematography and Talkies* (1932), *Examination Questions and Answers* (1953), *Cameron's Fundamentals of Motion Picture Projection* (1950), *Motion Picture Projection* (1929, 1969), *Motion Pictures With Sound* (1929), *Servicing and Trouble-Shooting Charts* (1936), *Cameron's Theatre Television For Projectionists* (1965). The above is just a sampling of Cameron's publications, which appear in many updated editions, often with variations of their original title.

692 *Can You Hear Me Mother?* by Powell, Sandy. illus. London: Jupiter, 1975.

Powell was a music hall performer who starred in a series of British film comedies during the thirties. The title of this volume was his identifying phrase on radio.

693 *Can't Argue with a Sunrise: A Paper Movie.* by Stoumen, Lou. 192 p. paper illus. Millbrae, Calif.: Celestial Arts, 1975.

Lou Stoumen is a filmmaker—THE NAKED EYE (1957), THE BLACK FOX (1962), THE OTHER WORLD OF WINSTON CHURCHILL (1966), etc.—who has attempted a new media form, the paper movie, with this book. By arranging 95 photographs into six sequences and providing a short but appropriate voice-over narration, he takes the reader on a biographical and philosophical journey.

The photographs have been reproduced with care and the poetic narration is most satisfying. This volume should please a wide audience.

694 CAN'T STOP THE MUSIC. 144 p. paper illus. Los Angeles: Pinnacle, 1980.

A *Photonovel* containing more than 150 illustrations from the 1980 film, along with a full-color section devoted to the leading players. Enough dialogue and text are provided so that the slight story line is discernible. The film was written by Bronte Woodard and Allan Carr, and directed by Nancy Walker.

695 *Canadian Feature Films, Part I (1913-1940).* edited by Morris, Peter. Ottawa: Canadian Film Institue, 1970.

Some 60 Canadian films are arranged in chronological order, and 19 foreign films which were shot in Canada are listed. Volume II covers the period from the 1941 to 1969.

696 *Canadian Feature Films 1913-1969.: Part II: 1941-1963.* by Morris, Peter. 44 p. paper illus. Ottawa: Canadian Film Institute, 1974.

This volume continues the filmography previously published which covered the period 1913 to 1940. There are three parts: feature films produced in Canada 1941-1963; Non-Canadian films adapted from original Canadian sources or shot on location in Canada; and a selection of foreign produced features with "Canadian content."

A production index for Parts One and Two and a title index for the entire book are added. The films in Part One are nicely described by technical data and credits, a synopsis, comments, and references. Only film data and credits are noted in the other two parts. Illustrations are clearly reproduced and add dimension to the volume.

This is an excellent reference which has been carefully prepared and presented. Highly recommended.

697 *Canadian Feature Films 1964-1969.* by Handling, Piers. 64 p. paper illus. Ottawa: Canadian Film Institute, 1976.

A departure from the structure of the two earlier volumes can be noted here. After an introduction the films are grouped chronologically by year with six periods covered—1964-1969 inclusive. Each film is described by technical data, credits, shooting location, synopsis, comments, notes and references. Excellent illustrations from many of the films appear throughout. An index to the credits and a title index complete the volume.

The emergence of the Canadian National Cinema can be easily discerned in this volume. Content, financing, critical and public acceptance, etc.—all facets of large-scale filmmaking—are treated.

When this book is used with the earlier volumes, a thorough and valid coverage of feature film production in Canada can be obtained. Used alone, this volume documents a period of growth and expansion of national cinema. Highly recommended.

698 *Canadian Film Production Index.* edited by Veronneau, Pierre. 95 p. paper Quebec: Cinetheque Quebecoise, 1976.

A bilingual directory of film production information.

699 *Canadian Film Reader.* edited by Feldman, Seth; and Nelson, Joyce. New York: Zoetrope.

A collection of articles by more than forty Canadian critics, filmmakers, and scholars. The subjects range widely and in order to provide some continuity appear under five large headings: The Early Years of the National Film Board; Its Role and Contributions; Feature Filmmaking in Quebec and English Canada; Experimental Films and Filmmakers; and The Problems of the Past and the Outlook for the Future. Included are essays, interviews, historical accounts, and criticism.

700 *Canadian Government Motion Picture Bureau 1917-1941.* by Backhouse, Charles F. 44 p. paper Ottawa: Canadian Film Institute, 1978.

The Canadian Government Motion Picture Bureau was the forerunner of the National Film Board of Canada. Its major function was to inform the world via film of Canada's beauties and potentials.

A historical study of the Bureau is provided here in four parts: The Beginning (1918-1920); The Good Years (1920-1931); The Decline (1931-1939); and Under the National Film Board (1939-1941). Appendixes list the names of officials, votes, salaries, expenditures, revenues, original 1918 equipment purchases, and prints in circulation from 1929-1941.

701 *Canadian Women Film-Makers.: An Interim Filmography.* by Reid, Alison. 11 p. paper Ottawa: Canadian Film Institute, 1972.

This catalog is number 8 in the series titled *Canadian Filmography.*

702 *Cannon Fire! The Art of Making Award-Winning Amateur Movies.* by Satariano, Cecil. 74 p. paper illus. London: Bachman and Turner, 1973.

A how-to-do-it book on cinematography written for nonprofessionals by a well-known Italian cameraman, this volume emphasizes subject, location, acting, and audience.

703 *Capital and Culture: German Cinema, 1933-45.* by Petley, Julian. 162 p. illus. paper London: British Film Institute, 1979.

704 *Captioned Films for the Deaf—Catalog.* compiled by U.S. Office of Education. 29 p. paper Washington, D.C.: U.S. Government Printing Office, 1964.

A listing of those films which are a part of the program of captioned films for the deaf.

705 *Captioned Films for the Deaf—Hearings before Congressional Committees on Education and Labor.* 82 vols. 90 p. paper Washington, D.C.: U.S. Government Printing Office, 1962.

The following volumes are records of two hearings held on the Captioned Films for the Deaf Program in 1962: (1) August 7, 1962—Senate Committee on Labor and Public Welfare—hearing held on Bill S2511 which would provide an increased program; (2)September 5, 1962—House Committee on Education and Labor—hearing held on Bills S2511, HR 12979, and HR 13063 which would provide for the production and distribution of educational and training films for deaf persons.

706 *Captioned Films for the Deaf—Program.* compiled by U.S. Office of Education. 8 p. paper Washington, D.C.: U.S. Government Printing Office, 1961.

This short booklet describes the program of captioned films for the deaf which was authorized by Public Law 85-905. Revised at irregular intervals—usually when the Congress has approved some legislature affecting the program.

707 *Caravan of Love and Money.* by Forcade, Thomas King. 128 p. paper illus. New York: New American Library, 1972.

Warner Brothers decided to make a rock movie, a kind of sequel to WOODSTOCK (1970). They put together a caravan of far-out characters, hippies, freaks, a French director and some rock performers. This group was sent on a cross-country tour and eventually landed in England. The author accompanied much of the tour and describes the activities in this volume. Sex, music and drugs are given the most attention. The final film was to be called MEDICINE BALL CARAVAN or CARAVAN OF LOVE. Rumor has it that the crew was so high on drugs that no suitable footage was obtained. A finished film was shown for a very short period and was quickly withdrawn by Warners.

The book details some unattractive excesses of individuals, groups and institutions. Far from being a joyous experience, the trip reads like a come-together of some very sad human beings looking for the impossible. Its a real bummer. The language is coarse, the visuals are suggestive, and the personnel need washing.

708 THE CARDINAL. by Quint, Beverly. 48 p. paper illus. New York: Mar-King Publishing Corp., 1963.

Director Otto Preminger is really the star of this souvenir book. The story of the 1963 film is interwoven with anaccount of the making of the film. Cast and technical credits are given in the centerfold. Several fuzzy photographs are distracting.

709 *Careers in Film and Television.* by Elsas, Diana; and Kelso, Lulu. 10 p. paper Washington, D.C.: American Film Institute, 1977.

This *Factfile* offers information to anyone interested in seeking a job in film or television. In addition to some helpful suggestions, the pamphlet notes some publications which contain job listings, a number of available apprenticeship/training programs, and a bibliography of information sources. An excellent beginning point for the unknowing, bewildered, and perplexed.

710 *Caricature.* by Nerman, Einer. 80 p. illus. New York: American Studio Books, 1946.

A collection of drawings of stars of the forties, including West, Bankhead, Miranda, Astaire, Garbo, Dietrich, Gable, Crawford, Chevalier, and others.

711 *Carl Dreyer.* edited by Dyssegaard, Soren. 50 p. paper illus. Copenhagen: Danish Ministry of Foreign Affairs, 1969.

Much of the same material that appears in *Jesus* is contained in this paperback distributed by the Danish Ministry of Foreign Affairs. The Dreyer biography by Ib Monty; the article, "Working with Dreyer," by Preben Thomsen; and five scenes from *Jesus*, the last Dreyer script, are given, as is the tribute by Jean Renoir. The illustrations in this volume are beautifully reproduced and do not appear in *Jesus*. This is splendid film material.

712 *Carl Dreyer, A Film Director's Work.* by Neergaard, Ebbe. 42 p. paper illus. London: British Film Institute, London, 1950.

This booklet (BFI new index series no. 1) contains a biography and reviews of Dryer's films from THE PRESIDENT (1920) to TWO PEOPLE (1945). Additional short articles and a filmography add to the portrait.

713 *Carl Laemmle and Universal Pictures: A Tribute.* 204 p. illus. New York: Gordon Press, 1976 (1926).

On Feb 18, 1926 the entire issue of *Film Daily* was devoted to Carl Laemmle and Universal Studios. It contains biographical data on the Universal actors and on Laemmle.

714 CARNAL KNOWLEDGE. by Feiffer, Jules. 118 p. illus. New York: Farrar, Straus, and Giroux, 1971.

Script of the 1971 film directed by Mike Nichols. Contains cast and credits.

715 *Carol Burnett.* by Paige, David. 31 p. paper illus. Mankato, Minn.: Creative Education, 1977.

A superficial biography designed for very young readers.

716 *The Carol Burnett Story.* by Carpozi, George Jr. 206 p. paper illus. New York: Warner, 1975.

For many years Carol Burnett devoted all her energies to television. She did appear, not too impressively, in WHO'S BEEN SLEEPING IN MY BED? (1963). Lately she has been more successful in films such as PETE AND TILLIE (1972), THE FRONT PAGE (1974) and A WEDDING (1978). This volume is devoted mostly to Burnett's rise to become the best commedienne-actress we have today.

717 *Carole Lombard.* by Maltin, Leonard. 160 p. paper illus. New York: Pyramid, 1976.

In a text that has been well researched, Maltin gives major attention to a review of the Lombard films. Perhaps the off-screen life of the actress has been adequately covered in such volumes as *Gable and Lombard, Screwball: The Life of Carole Lombard,* and *Gable and Lombard and Powell and Harlow.* There does seem to be, however, a specific relationship between the roles on-screen and the affectionate, fun-loving female off-screen that merits a deeper consideration than that provided here. On this aspect of Lombard's artistry, Maltin seems content to report rather than analyze. With the films he is much more detailed, offering plots, background information, and critical evaluation.

Illustrations are excellent throughout and several portraits of Lombard are alone worth the price of the book. A bibliography, a filmography, and an index complete the volume. Acceptable.

718 *The* CARRY-ON Book. by Eastaugh, Kenneth. 160 p. paper illus. North Pomfret, Vt.: David and Charles, 1978.

The twenty-eight films made in the CARRY-ON Series between 1958 and 1978 testify to the popular success of these British comedies. This volume pays tribute to the films, their creators and the actors who populated them.

The first section is loosely historical and deals with production matters, grosses, critical reception, filmmakers, and so forth, while the second part recalls incidents and anecdotes relating to the films. The final section is a filmography that offers script excerpts, cast, and stills. The book is nicely illustrated throughout. No index is provided.

Using a most appropriate approach to its subject, the author is not above using puns, visual humor, bawdiness and vulgarity. At other times he mixes factual data with reminiscences and research to brew a suitably serious overview of this film phenomena.

Anyone who has ever laughed at a CARRY-ON film will appreciate this tribute. Newcomers are in for a valid introduction to some very funny films. Recommended.

719 *Cars of the Stars.* by Barris, George; and Scagnetti, Jack. 264 p. illus. New York: Jonathan David, 1974.

This specialized volume was designed to appeal to both the car and the movie buff. An earlier and much less expensive paperback volume by Barris covered part of the same material presented here. Barris is well known as the customizer of cars for the stars and for specific films. Using over 300 photographs, including several in color, the text covers Barris' designs for individuals (Wayne, Sinatra, Presley, et al.) and for films: THE LOVE BUG (1969), DIAMONDS ARE FOREVER (1972), CHITTY CHITTY BANG BANG (1968), Some classic star cars of yesterday (Mary Pickford, Clara Bow, Richard Dix, etc.), and finally the racing cars of James Garner, Steve McQueen, Paul Newman are described. Trivial information on topics such as James Dean's death car, the staging of movie chases and crashes, the Persian rugs in Efrem Zimbalist's Bentley and so on is added. Acceptable.

720 *Cars of the Stars and Movie Memories.* by Clymer, Floyd. 152 p. paper illus. Los Angeles: Floyd Clymer, 1954.

This unusual volume is devoted to pictures and stories about film personalities and/or their cars. Cecil B. DeMille provided the foreword to this historical collection of actor portraits and automobile pictures.

721 *Cartoon Animation for Everyone.* by Cleave, Alan. 132 p. illus. New York:

Morgan and Morgan, 1973.

Much of the material found in this volume originally appeared in *Movie Maker* magazine. In preparing it for book format the author has expanded his text and added many new illustrations. The result is a totally pleasing and useful volume.

The material is arranged into 12 chapters starting with the basic necessities for cartooning and concluding with the making of a fully synchronized sound cartoon. A glossary is appended.

All the topics pertinent to beginning animation are here—cels, cut-outs, cycles, timing, backgrounds, settings, and special effects. The narrative is clear, informal, and specific while the illustrations are simple and effective. Throughout the author has taken a complicated process and translated it into terms that the layman can comprehend.

Much hard work is usually required to gain the skills necessary for animation. This volume makes that effort much easier.

722 *Cartooning.* by Nelson, Roy P. paper illus. Chicago: Henry Regnery, 1975.

723 *Cary Grant.* by Govoni, Albert. 233 p. illus. Chicago: Henry Regnery Co., 1971.

Author Govoni has not succeeded in capturing the life, personality, and charisma of his subject. The phrase, "unauthorized biography," here means nearly complete reliance upon newspapers and periodicals for content. The attempts of the author to pad the book by providing either period description (the early Depression), or critical evaluation (INDISCREET) (1958), are ineffective and embarrassing. Inaccuracies and errors occur. GRAND HOTEL (1932) was not the Academy Award film for which Hepburn and Laughton received their first awards. There is no mention of relationships between Grant and his directors—Hitchcock, Donen, Capra, Hawks, Stevens, Cukor, McCarey, Kanin, etc.—an imposing roster if there ever was one.

No attempt is made to present a portrait of the human being, the author being content to offer an introductory apology followed by a recitation of chronological facts. Therefore, the text is unbalanced, with the earlier years getting minor attention and the later years—Grant with Betsy Drake and Grant with Dyan Cannon—getting excessive coverage. The photograph selection is also lopsided. INDISCREET gets 6 stills, WALK, DON'T RUN (1966), CHARADE (1963), and FATHER GOOSE (1964) each receive 5 stills, MR. LUCKY (1943) and OPERATION PETTICOAT (1959) get 2 apiece and there is one each

for TO CATCH A THIEF (1955), DREAM WIFE (1953), THAT TOUCH OF MINK (1962), and NORTH BY NORTHWEST (1959). There is nothing from Grant's first decade of filmmaking and a total of 62 films are not represented by stills. An unsatisfactory attempt is made to overcome the film omissions by including a critical filmography. The book is not indexed, probably because the text does not offer sufficient material. This disappointing volume is not recommended.

724 *Cary Grant.* by Vermilye, Jerry. 160 p. paper illus. New York: Pyramid, 1973.

Since Cary Grant made 72 feature films, the major portion of the text of this volume is devoted to recalling the films and Grant's roles in them. Minimal critical comment accompanies the many plot outlines and film descriptions. Very little of his personal life is disclosed, and that which is presented is a matter of public record.

The many film stills which appear are well reproduced, and two full-page portraits are most effective. A filmography, a bibliography and an index have been created with care and obvious effort. They, along with the visuals, bring some distinction to what is a pedestrian account of a long, durable career rather than a portrait of a film star. Albert Govoni had similar difficulty in his unauthorized biography, *Cary Grant*, as did Donald Deschner in *The Films of Cary Grant*. Perhaps any biography of the actor needs his cooperation or authorship. Biographical reservations aside, the detailed account of his films, the illustrations, and the supportive materials make this a worthwhile book.

725 *Cary Grant: The Light Touch.* by Godfrey, Lionel. New York: St. Martin's, 1981.

726 *Cary Grant Film Album.* compiled by Eyles, Allen. 52 p. illus Shepperton, Surrey, England: Ian Allan, Ltd., 1971.

This picture book, published originally in England, resembles a mini-version of the *Citadel* books. Using a chronological review of Grant's films, the book offers some comment about each. His first feature was THIS IS THE NIGHT in 1932, while his last film to date is WALK, DON'T RUN in 1966. One or more stills are provided for each film.

Reproduction quality is high, and several color visuals are most attractive. Because there is no index, the book has a limited reference value. It is, however, most informative and entertaining. Acceptable.

727 *Cary Grant—In the Spotlight.* edited by Galley Press. 160 p. illus. New York: Galley/Mayflower, 1980.

A generous assortment of illustrations accompanies a biographical essay in this appreciation of Cary Grant.

728 CASABLANCA: Script and Legend. by Koch, Howard. 223 p. illus. Woodstock, N.Y.: The Overlook Press, 1973.

In addition to the full script by Julius J. Epstein, Philip G. Epstein and Howard Koch, this volume contains some interesting background that is already causing controversy. In an article called, "The Making of CASABLANCA, author Koch suggests, not so subtly, that he was most responsible for the final script. This has been quickly refuted by Julius Epstein, who, with his brother, claims the major contribution. Be that as it may, the script reads almost as beautifully as the film plays; perhaps because of the film's familiarity, the reader's mind can envision each scene and almost hear the dialogue being recited. There are some original reviews, a few critical analyses of the film and a closing comment by Koch to complete the volume. The book is illustrated but not indexed.

For about five decades, CASABLANCA (1942) has been a most popular film and this volume can only help to solidify its position as a classic. Recommended.

729 *The Case Against Pornography.* by Holbrook, David. La Salle, Ill.: Open Court Pub. Co., 1974.

A prejudiced argument based on the supposition that most people are incompetent to judge and, therefore, need protection against pornography.

730 *Case History of a Movie.* by Schary, Dore; and Palmer, Charles. 242 p. illus. New York: Random House, 1950.

The movie described in this book is THE NEXT VOICE YOU HEAR (1950), one of the less successful pictures turned out by Dore Schary during his stay at MGM (1948-1956). It is a detailed account of the making of a film from idea to sneak preview.

While it is informative, the closeness of the author to the subject does not permit much critical objectivity. The few pictures are excellent; and perhaps this project would have made a better pictorial history. One also regrets that Schary did not write earlier with THE SPIRAL STAIRCASE (1946), THE SET-UP (1948), THE WINDOW (1949), BATTLEGROUND (1949), or later with BAD DAY AT BLACK ROCK (1954). In summary, this is an acceptable volume about a minor film written in a mild, noncontroversial style.

731 *A Casebook on Film.* by Samuels, Charles Thomas. 250 p. New York: Van Nostrand, 1970.

According to the author, the casebook is a single volume which contains "a collection of assorted essays on a single topic, together with suggestions for further work." In this case, the single topic of "film" is first divided into "The Theory of Film" and "Applied Theory." "Theory" is further divided into film aesthetics, filmmaking, and film criticism. "Applied Theory" consists of reviews and articles about three films, THE GRADUATE (1967), BONNIE AND CLYDE (1967), and BLOW UP (1967).

The title may be misleading to certain readers. The author's suggestion that the book provides a common experience for students would seem valid only if showings of the three films were arranged to follow the 12 essays on these films. In summary, the articles are interesting but the rationale for this collection would seem quite suspect. The *Focus Series* on CITIZEN KANE (1941) and D. W. Griffith are much better examples of casebooks. As an anthology, this voulme is lopsided, and as a text for a film course, it is incomplete.

732 *Cases on the Motion Picture Industry.* edited by Gragg, Charles I. 687 p. New York: McGraw-Hill, 1930.

Published as volume 8 of the *Harvard Business Reports*, this book contains commentaries on the cases by Howard Thompson Lewis, the author of the 1933 study entitled *The Motion Picture Industry.*

733 *A Cast of Lions.* by Foreman, Carl. 128 p. illus. London: Collins, 1966.

An account of the making of the film BORN FREE (1966), related by its producer. Aimed for the family audience, the book contains many candids and stills of the actors and lions.

734 *Cast of Thousands.* by Loos, Anita. 288 illus. New York: Grosset and Dunlap, 1977.

This memoir from Anita Loos may remind the reader of a pictorial version of her previous two, *A Girl Like I* and *Kiss Hollywood Goodbye.* Once again she recalls the many celebrities she has known in her long career as a writer. This time, however, she provides personal photographs, letters, drawings, correspondence and other memorabilia to complement her stories and anecdotes.

During her 80 years Ms. Loos learned the art of pleasing her public. This volume is no exception. Recommended.

735   *The Casting Couch and Me.* by Wood, Joan F.; and Bain, Donald S. 216 illus. New York: Sam Post (Walker), 1974.

Joan Wood, an actress who has appeared in British films, television, and theatre, describes her experiences in establishing her career. The volume is subtitled "The Uninhibited Memoirs of a Young Actress" and is in the tradition of *Coffee, Tea, or Me?*

736   *Castles in the Air.* by Castle, Irene. 204 p. illus. Garden City, N.Y.: Doubleday, 1958.

Not only was Irene Castle the subject and the original-story author of the Astaire-Rogers film, THE STORY OF VERNON AND IRENE CASTLE (1939), but she also appeared in more than 15 silent films and serials from 1915 to 1922.

737   *Catalog of Educational and Documentary Films.* by Stewart, William. 370 p. paper Glasgow: Scottish Film Office, 1972.

A large catalog of films available through the Scottish Film Office, this volume arranges its contents according to the Dewey Decimal System. A separate section identifies material suitable for film study. For each film there is a description along with a recommended audience level. A title index is also provided.

738   *Catalog of Holdings: The American Film Institute Collection and United Artists Collection at the Library of Congress.* compiled by American Film Institute Staff. 214 p. paper Washington, D.C.: American Film Institute, 1978.

Some 14,000 films officially acquisitioned by the American Film Institute up to 1977 are included in this catalog. The Film Collection at the Library of Congress is an archive and a study resource. Certain titles listed here are not yet available for viewing by

scholars, while many others are. It is even possible—but not easy—to purchase copies of certain films for study.

The films are listed alphabetically by title with the release year, producer, director and actor noted. A final column headed "Holdings" indicates whether the film is a short, a feature, a trailer, or a serial, if it is incomplete, if it is acetate or safety base preservation material and if it is available for viewing at the Library of Congress. Those films donated to the collection by United Artists are identifed by an asterick.

It should be noted that at this time the collections reflects AFI's major concern—film preservation—and the archives have concentrated on the "nitrate era" —when films where made on stock which ultimately decomposes.

This is a specialized reference that will facilitate the work of film scholars and historians.

739   *Catalog of Museum Publications and Media.: A Directory and Index of Publications and Audiovisuals Available from United States and Canadian Institutions.* edited by Wasserman, Paul; and Herman, Esther. 1044 p. Detroit: Gale Research, 1980.

Formerly called *Museum Media*, this volume lists difficult-to-find materials produced by museums, libraries, and historical societies. Almost 1000 institutions are represented and access to their products is provided by several indexes.

740   *Catalog of Shorts, Selected Features and Serial Films for Film Study.* 384 p. paper illus. New York: Contemporary Films, 1973.

McGraw-Hill Films and Contemporary Films are associated with the same parent company although each publishes a separate catalog. Contemporary offers the most interesting collection, although many of the same films are listed in both catalogs. Attractive stills taken from the films accompany the text, which is descriptive rather than evaluative. Varying in length and quality, the annotations offer technical data, credits, and, in some cases, critical quotes and prizes won. This is another example of an outstanding distributor catalog that will afford the user many pleasant hours of reading and browsing. It is also an excellent source of film information. Highly recommended.

741 *Catalog of the Book Library of the British Film Institute.* compiled by British Film Institute Staff. 3 vols. Boston: G. K. Hall, 1975.

This catalog is probably the most complete listing of film literature in the world. Nearly all the English-language books and pamphlets written on cinema are here and, in addition, there are the important film writings which have appeared in other languages. The three volumes consist of four parts: (1) author catalog, (2) title catalog, (3) script catalog, and (4) subject catalog. An estimated 53,700 cards are reproduced with 21 appearing on each page.

742 *Catalog of the Communications Library (University of Illinois).* 3 vols. Boston: G. K. Hall, 1975.

The catalog consists of almost 50,000 cards representing 10,500 monographs and continuations along with 200 periodicals. The communication subjects include journalism, radio, television, magazines, book publishing, censorship, copyright, etc. Film is covered with special attention given to motion picture history, theory and economics.

743 *A Catalog of United States Government Produced Audiovisual Materials.* compiled by National Audiovisual Center. 356 p. paper Washington, D.C.: General Services Administration, 1974.

Several indexes are in this large catalog to aid the user in location and retrieval of information on U.S. Government audiovisual material. They provide (1) an outline of major subject headings with subheads listed beneath; (2) a guide to the above subject section—topics, names, words which refer the reader back to the subject section; and (3) an expansion of the major subject by including appropriate film titles beneath each of the subheadings. In other words, the audiovisuals are listed according to subject. The major portion of the catalog is the title section, which lists all the audiovisuals alphabetically by title. Each entry here also indicates pertinent information on such items as running time, gauge, sound, color format, producer, title number, year of release, agency number, sale price, cassette, number of tracks, monaural or stereo, etc. A short description of the audiovisual follows.

The great majority of entries are 16mm films. A few cartridges, audio discs, audio tapes, slide sets, and filmstrips are listed. Buried within the catalog and available for sale are such classics as THE BATTLE OF SAN PIETRO (1945), WHY WE FIGHT series (1945), THE RIVER (1939), THE PLOW THAT BROKE THE PLAINS (1936), and ORIGINS OF THE MOTION PICTURE (1955).

744 *Catalogue of Yugoslav Documentary and Short Films (1967-68).* 192 p. paper Beograd: Festival Jugoslovenskog Filma, 1968.

A yearly catalog written in English, this volume lists 157 films produced between the 14th and 15th annual Film Festival held in Beograd. Also included in this annual are an index to the films and an index to the producers.

745 *The Cataloging and Classification of Cinema Literature.* by Steele, Robert. 133 p. Metuchen, N.J.: Scarecrow Press, 1967.

In this unusual and most competent technical book, the author discusses the problems and possibilities of cataloging cinema literature in libraries. Dealing mostly with the Dewey Decimal and the Library of Congress Systems, and some variations thereof, he also examines the classification schemes of a few larger libraries having extensive film collections. Included are the Academy of Motion Picture Arts and Sciences, the Canadian Film Institute Library, the Museum of Modern Art, and a few others. An expansion of the Library of Congress classification designed by the author and a final summary complete the short volume. A sound exploration and argument ending with a nod toward the Library of Congress System, the book is a valuable aid and has much pertinence for all librarians inundated by the flood of cinema books today.

746 *Cataloguing Audiovisual Materials.* by Fleisher, Eugene; and Goodman, Helen. 388 p. paper illus. New York: Neal-Schuman, 1979.

This helpful volume carries the subtitle, "A Manual Based on the Anglo-American Cataloguing Rules." Individual chapters deal with a specific medium—cartographic materials, sound recordings, motion pictures, video recordings, graphic materials, 3-D artifacts-realia, and kits. For each medium there is an introduction, several problems with solutions, sample entry cards, etc. Illustrations, a glossary, a bibliography, and a subject index accompany the text material.

Designed as a manual to be used in a teaching situation, this volume can also be used by individuals. The well-selected contents, and their arrangement and clarity, contribute to the manual's high potential for solving nonprint cataloguing problems.

747 *Cataloging of Audiovisual Materials.* edited by Olson, Nancy B. paper illus. Mankato, Minn.: Minnesota Scholarly Press, 1980.

This manual of cataloging instructions is based on the AACR 2 rules and includes illustrations, worksheets, and explanations for handling all types of audiovisual software, including films.

748 *Catalogue of Brazilian Films: Brasil Cinema, 1975, Number 10.* 185 p. paper illus. Rio de Janeiro: Embrafilme, 1977.

749 *Catalogue of Educational Motion Picture Films.* compiled by Kleine, George. 336 p. Chicago: George Kleine, 1910.

Here is one of the earliest published catalogs devoted to the short educational film. Over 1000 films are described but only as to content and length—other data is not given. Subjects include education, travel, newsreels, nature study, war, etc. A later catalog published in 1915 (162 p.) listed short films on agriculture, aviation, history, industries, public health, military science, zoology, etc.

750 *Catalogue of Films on Sports.* compiled by Council for Cultural Cooperation. 161 p. paper Strasbourg: Council of Europe, 1965.

The films in this catalog are arranged by subject using some 40 sports ranging from archery to wrestling. For each film the following information is given: title, country of origin, title translation in English, year, producer, distributor, running time, color or black and white, and a brief description. The films are indexed by title and by country of origin in the book's closing pages.

751 *Catalogue of Romanian Animation Films.* 67 p. paper illus. Bucharest: Romania Film, 1975.

752 *Catalogue of Romanian Short Films.* compiled by Romaniafilm. 130 p. paper illus. Bucharest: Romaniafilm, 1975.

This indexed annual contains a listing of short films, documentaries, and science films distributed by Romaniafilm.

753 *Catastrophe: The End of the Cinema?* by Annan, David. 111 p. paper illus. New York: Crown, 1975.

The greatest catastrophe to an individual is the loss of his life. This volume examines survival films—a genre in which the life of a hero or heroine is endangered by some enormous and/or unusual force or occurrence. These dangers include war, fire, sinkings, quakes, wind, drought, plague, invasion, space visitors, supernatural beings, and giant monsters.

Drawings, stills, posters and sketches accompany a sturdy text in which the author examines man's attitudes toward catastrophe as reflected in film.

This is a most unusual approach to a film genre which concentrates on the appeal of disaster films to the public. Unfortunately there are no supporting elements to the text and visuals. Acceptable.

754 *Catholic Viewpoint on Censorship.* by Gardiner, Harold Charles. 192 p. Garden City, N.Y.: Hanover House, 1958.

A title in the *Catholic Viewpoint* series, this volume was written by the coauthor of *Movies, Morals and Art.*

755 *Caught in the Act.* by Stuart, John. 32 p. paper illus. London: Silent Picture, 1971.

From a leading man in British silent films, John Stuart gradually assumed character parts and remains active today. His filmography numbers well over 100 films.

756 *Cecil B. DeMille.* by Higham, Charles. 335 p. illus. New York: Scribner's, 1973.

The life and career of Cecil B. DeMille has been related by DeMille himself, by his brother, his assistant, and by Ringgold and Bodeen in a picture book, *The Films of Cecil B. DeMille.* Can another volume add anything new to this available information? The answer here is a partial yes—for the book is a blending of the old and the new. Higham's approach emphasizes the silent films, which he considers the creations of a great film director. DeMille's tragedy was his evolution into the great mass entertainer. The sound films evidence this latter period.

With the cooperation of DeMille's daughter, the author had access to much original material. The many illustrations add strength to the text, and there is a filmography and an index that make the book suitable for reference. The ultimate portrait that emerges is a positive one, but one that is not too different from those already presented. Much of the anecdotal material is unfamiliar, and yet certain segments seem to be a retelling of well-known DeMille incidents. The approach, the research, and the total effort of the author are most commendable, but the ultimate question of whether it was worthwhile, needed, or illuminating to any degree may occur.

For the reader not already acquainted with DeMille, the book is most rewarding; for those who have gone through the above-mentioned volumes, this reading may seem more like a review than a fresh experience. In either case, the book can be recommended.

757 *Cecil B. DeMille.* edited by Wisdom Staff. illus. Beverly Hills: Wisdom, 1958.

Although *Wisdom* was a periodical, its format was that of a hardbound book. Volume 10 featured Cecil B. DeMille and THE TEN COMMANDMENTS (1956). In addition to some good illustrations, there was a tribute to DeMille, scenes from the film, and a section called "From the Wisdom of ..." by DeMille.

758 *Cecil B. DeMille, Young Dramatist.* by Myers, Hortense; and Burnett, Ruth. 200 p. illus. Indianapolis: Bobbs-Merrill, 1963.

A book written for children which tells of DeMille's youth and his early years in Hollywood.

759 *Cecil Beaton: Memoirs of the 40's.* by Beaton, Cecil. 310 p. illus. New York: McGraw-Hill, 1972.

In his memoir of the forties, Beaton divides the text geographically. London, Paris, New York and California are the settings against which he recalls his interactions with the famous and near-famous. Names, places, events, and comments are the substance of the book. Cocteau, Picasso, Churchill and, of course, Garbo are featured prominently and other film names of the period are given lesser attention. A look from on high at the beautiful people of the forties by an author who wears a very specialized kind of eyeglass. Not essential, but acceptable.

760 *Cecil Beaton: Stage and Film Designs.* by Spencer, Charles. 115 p. illus. New York: St. Martin's Press, 1975.

This attractive volume carries a somewhat misleading title. Cecil Beaton has probably spent as much time designing for films as he has for any other of the entertainment forms, but that work is treated in a brief chapter which merely mentions titles in pass-

ing. His work for MY FAIR LADY (1963) is recognized in a separate chapter but this material has been copiously covered elsewhere in both periodicals and books, e.g., Beaton's *Fair Lady.*

The text consists of biographical information and a survey of Beaton's work for the theatre, ballet, and opera. His ability at writing is also noted—*Cecil Beaton: Memoirs of the 40's.*

The visuals are superb, having been selected with intelligence and reproduced with care. Most are devoted to Beaton's designs but there are some early biographical photographs. A list of productions designed by Beaton underlines his long, successful record of achievement. Past exhibitions of his work are noted and a bibliography is included.

It is unfortunate that the film work of Cecil Beaton is given minor considerations in this volume. Nevertheless, the book still has much relevance and value.

761 *Celebrity.* edited by Monaco, James. 258 p. paper illus. New York: Delta, 1978.

James Monaco has compiled a series of articles—including several by himself—about the complex phenomena of celebrity. Grouped under general headings— "State of the Art," "Personas," "The Self as Art," "Gossip," etc.—the articles have been selected mostly from periodicals and books. An impressive author list, including Norman Mailer, Ingmar Bergman, Wilfrid Seed, Nora Ephron, Joan Didion, and others is presented. Reading these contemplations on celebrity provides a different subject analysis that is both thought-provoking and entertaining. Monaco has added personal touches throughout, not only with his own excellent pieces, but also by providing headnotes, photographs, and captions to accompany the other authors' articles. The book is indexed.

762 *Celebrity Circus.* by Higham, Charles. 322 p. illus. New York: Delacorte, 1979.

Higham's circus consists of interviews arranged in two categories: stardust and spangles (performers) and ringmasters (directors). Collected from several sources, the interviews are reprinted here with a short, new introduction provided for each. The subjects are also visualized via a center section of portraits and illustrations.

Although some of the material is dated, much of it still remains engrossing reading. Higham is an experienced Hollywood reporter who captures his subjects and their milieu with ease and apparent accuracy. It can be sensed that he is holding back much of what he might like to say because of either ethical, professional or moral reasons. What he does select for publication is both entertaining and informative. Recommended.

763 *Celebrity Homes II.* edited by Rense, Paige. 256 p. illus. Los Angeles: Knapp, 1981.

Among the celebrities showing their homes are Fred Astaire, Candice Bergen, James Caan, George Cukor, Kirk Douglas, Ali Macgraw, Mike Nichols, Marsha Mason, Barbra Streisand and John Wayne.

764 *Celebrity Register.* by Blackwell, Earl. 562 p. illus. New York: Simon & Schuster, 1975.

Everything you ever wanted to know about celebrities ranging from Hank Aaron to Adolph Zukor. Blackwell has a talent for confusing trivia, gossip, and name-dropping with biographical data. The book is well illustrated and covers the many fields—sports, arts, politics, etc.—which generate celebrities. A directory of addresses is included. This is the third edition, the previous ones in 1959 and 1963 having been edited by Cleveland Amory.

765 *Celluloid: The Film Today.* by Rotha, Paul. 259 p. illus. London: Longmans, Green, 1931.

This is early Rotha with essays and reviews. A look at the films of today (1930) is followed by reviews of eight films, an essay on the revival of naturalism, and finally a consideration of the films of Fritz Lang.

766 *Celluloid and Symbols.* edited by Cooper, John; and Skrade, Carl. 143 p. Philadelphia: Fortress, 1970.

A collection of nine statements which examine the relationship between films and the theology of today. Contributors are serious about the films' assumption of certain church responsibilities along with an ability to link religion and the various denominations. The writers are all quite positive, but of independent minds as to the particular films and the best methodology to employ in their usage.

767 *The Celluloid Closet: Homosexuality in the Movies.* by Russo, Vito. 288 p. illus. New York: Harper, 1981.

A history-survey of gay images in films, this well-written study also looks at societal framework in which the films were presented. Russo writes with

passion, humor and justifiable cynicism. He has produced an important volume that is also fine reading.

768 *The Celluloid Curriculum.* by Maynard, Richard A. 276 p. illus. New York: Hayden Book Co., 1971.

This is a book about using films in the classroom that should be a continual source of ideas and suggestions for teachers. It is composed of units which depend upon film for their execution. Unit subjects include power and revolution, Black America, crime and punishment, marriage, sex education, responsibility, ethics, social problems, and literature. In a second section, movies are used as reflections of a time, era, or stereotype; included here are the west, war, Africa, the Black in films, the Depression, McCarthyism, history, and violence. Annotations on films are plentiful, as are suggestions on how to use them. A filmography, bibliography, and a title index are supportive elements to the units. It is an essential resource for the modern teacher—at all levels.

769 *The Celluloid Empire: A History of the American Movie Industry.* by Stanley, Robert H. 328 p. illus. New York: Hastings House, 1978.

The concern of this volume is the business-economics of American motion pictures over the past 80 years. The text treats many of the people and films that were determinants of financial failures or fortunes. It is in this area that the volume is weakest, relying on an encyclopedic recital of factual information that often reads like a high school research report (e.g., see D. W. Griffith; ESCAPE (1940); Jean Harlow). Although the attempt to provide a survey of the economic history of Hollywood is laudable, the result here is a flat, unexciting recap of familiar facts, incidents and questionable legends (business dealings in Hollywood were never open knowledge). Illustrations, a selected bibliography, a reprint of the motion picture Production Code, and an index complete the book. Acceptable but rather dull.

770 *The Celluloid Literature: Film in the Humanities.* by Jinks, William. 164 p. paper illus. Beverly Hills, Calif.: Glencoe Press, 1971.

In this provocative book, the author provides an introduction to film art, and then attempts to show the similarities in form and content between literature and the narrative film. Topics such as language, point of view, sound, and structure are considered. Concluding the book are a summary chapter and one on film criticism. The volume is nicely illustrated and has a selected bibliography.

Although the "comparative" goal occasionally gets a bit lost in the author's enthusiasm for defining the elements of film art, the volume is most stimulating and worthwhile. It represents a modern, well-presented view of a relationship that has intrigued many early writers.

771   *The Celluloid Love Feast.* by Grove, Martin A.; and Ruben, William S. 174 p. paper illus. New York: Lancer Books, 1971.

This paperback is quite a mixture; a reasonable text combined with erotic photographs that are probably included to capture the browser's dollar. The subtitle, "The Story of Erotic Movies," is a valid one, since the book considers the history, directors, (Osco, De Renzy, Metzger, Meyer), censorship, the content, the audience, and a sampling of films. In addition, the attitudes of various nations towards pornographic films are explored and the landmark films, I AM CURIOUS (YELLOW) (1967) and CENSORSHIP IN DENMARK (1970), receive detailed treatment. An interview with Saul Shiffrin, a distributor of erotic films, and a prediction of the effect of videocassettes and cable television on the viewing of these films concludes the book.

Throughout, there are stills from the various films which are well reproduced. An extended bibliography is given. For anyone interested in the erotic film the book does present an overall survey that seems rather complete. The text is unexpectedly literate and elements of basic research are evident. The only other similar volume is *Contemporary Erotic Cinema.*

772   *The Celluloid Mistress or, The Custard Pie of Dr. Caligari.* by Ackland, Rodney; and Grant, Elspeth. 264 p. . illus. London: Allan Wingate, 1954.

Rodney Ackland is a British playwright and screen writer who has assembled a group of amusing recollections in this partial biography. Familiar British film names abound and there is no hesitancy to be waspish or sarcastic about these famous people. For example, director-producer Gabriel Pascal is given a most complete yet stylish and efficient put-down. American Director D. W. Griffith also gets the author's scalpel treatment.

The style is early Rex Reed, but the author endears himself by an introductory statement: "I looked upon the stage merely as a way of breaking into the film studios." Obviously, the book is enjoyable reading which contributes little to cinema literature.

There are some average illustrations and an index. This is a relaxing entertainment.

773   *The Celluloid Muse: Hollywood Directors Speak.* edited by Higham, Charles; and Greenberg, Joel. 268 p. illus. London: Angus and Robertson, 1969.

More interviews with some famous and other not-so-famous directors: Irving Rapper, Jean Negulesco, John Frankenheimer, Robert Aldrich, Curtis Bernhardt, George Cukor, Hitchcock, Lang, Mamoulian, Lewis .Milestone, Minnelli, Mark Robson, Jacques Tourneur, King Vidor, and Billy Wilder. The book contains illustrations an index and a filmography.

774   *The Celluloid Persuasion.* by Murray, Lawrence. 165 p. paper Grand Rapids, Mich.: William Eerdmans, 1979.

In this volume, which he subtitles "Movies and the Liberal Arts," Lawrence Murray argues for the proper use of motion pictures and television programs in education. In five challenging sections, he offers definitions, methodologies, suggestions, comments and pure information (bibliography, distributors, indexes, etc.) on how he perceives film as an educational medium. Possibilities for research are also noted.

As a guide to improving education with films, this volume is rich with ideas and information. The author's arguments and comments will be appreciated by the dedicated teacher, and, ultimately, his audience.

775   *Celluloid Rock: 20 Years of Movie Rock.* by Jenkinson, Philip; and Warner, Alan. 136 p. paper illus. New York: Warner Books, 1976.

The twenty years referred to in the title of this survey of popular rock music in films extend approximately from THE WILD ONE (1953) to WATTSTAX (1973). Celluloid rock is given a very broad interpretation with such mild practitioners as Paul Anka, Glen Campbell, Connie Francis, and Pat Boone included along with such unquestionable choices as Elvis Presley, the Beatles, the Rolling Stones, and Chuck Berry.

The text reflects the evolution of popular rock music as reflected in both American and British films over two decades. It should be noted that the films followed established musical trends rather than introducing new forms. A chronological approach is used and there are many visuals to remind us of how uninspired and banal most of the films were. A selected filmography and a general text complete the volume, which should have its greatest popularity with younger, less discriminating readers. Acceptable.

776 *The Celluloid Sacrifice: Aspects of Sex in the Movies.* by Walker, Alexander. 241 p. illus. New York: Hawthorn Books, 1967.

Republished in paperback as *Sex in the Movies* "Cinema...òisÖ a temple of sex with its goddesses, its guardians, and its victims," said Jean Cocteau. This volume used his statement as a framework—discussing Bara, Bow, Pickford, West, Dietrich, Garbo, Harlow, Monroe, and Taylor as the goddesses. The guardians are American and British censors while the victims are Mastroianni, Hudson, and the stable of leading-men opposites to Doris Day types. The purpose of the book is to examine female sexuality in motion pictures, to look at certain controls of the sex drive as it is expressed in films, and finally to give evidence of the victimization of screen heroes by female dominance.

The emphasis herein is on American films with only a cursory look at a few Italian sex comedies. Much of the content seems familiar and some of it approaches cliche through reappearance in so many other guises and forms. The total book is not, however, without appeal. The familiar portions are comfortable reminders, and the chapters on censorship are more readable than is usual with this topic. Pictures, a bibliography, and an index complete the book.

777 *The Celluloid South: Hollywood and the Southern Myth.* by Campbell, Edward D., Jr. 256 p. illus. Knoxville, Tenn.: University of Tennessee Press, 1981.

778 *The Celluloid Vampires.* by Murphy, Michael J. 351 p. illus. Ann Arbor, Mich.: Pierian, 1979.

The subtitle of this volume, "A History and a Filmography, 1879-1979," is appropriate since it consists of two almost equal parts. In seven chapters, the history of the vampire film is covered. Beginning with LE MANOIR DU DIABLE (1897), the text traces the evolution and growth of the genre up to Louis Jourdan's TV film, COUNT DRACULA (1978).

Although the detailed text rambles a bit and is overloaded with plot synopses, it is still enjoyable reading. What reader is not attracted by vampire stories and films? The filmography, which makes up the second part of the book, is arranged chronologically by year. Each entry offers title, country of origin, film company, director, screenplay, music, cast, other credits, and, at times, a short synopsis. Illustrations, a bibliography, notes and an index are added.

This volume has several strengths, the major ones being the selection and arrangement of the material. The international survey and the complementary items provided make this an excellent, though somewhat specialized, reference.

779 *The Celluloid Weapon.* by White, David M.; and Averson, Richard. 271 p. illus. Boston: Beacon Press, 1972.

The feature-length commercial film which contains a "message" or looks at a problem is the concern of this oversized book. Sometimes called "films of social consciousness," they indicate the potential of the motion picture to go beyond the entertainment function. Some of these films were obvious propaganda, others were more subtle versions of the celluloid weapon. The concern of the authors is to put forth a history of these films rather than a critical analysis.

With emphasis on the Griffith era, social comment made in silent films is covered in two early chapters. Themes found in the thirties films include prison reform, depression problems, war, criminals, mob action, corruption in politics. The forties added topics such as migrant workers, the Nazi threat, alcoholism, racial prejudice, the shame of our mental institutions, and anti-Communism. The fifties and sixties added films which reflected the social concerns of those decades. Some notes, additional bibliographic sources and two detailed indexes complete the book.

Richard Averson has selected many attractive stills which are reproduced with a consistent clarity. The type face (Melior) and the special paper used are pleasing to the eye. The scope of the work is so large that it limits the authors to a descriptive rather than an evaluative or analytical approach. Since an historical account, however, is their stated goal, the book is most successful in fulfilling it. It is carefully researched; it fills an obvious void in film literature and is written and produced with excellence. Highly recommended.

780 *Celluloid Wings: The Impact of the Movies on Aviation.* by Farmer, James H. 382 p. illus. San Diego, Calif.: A. S. Barnes, 1981.

781 *The Censor Marches On.* by Ernst, Morris L.; and Lindey, Alexander. 346 p. New York: Doubleday, 1940.

This is a continuation of Ernst's crusade against unfair censorship. A survey of the 1940 scene, this volume discusses recent milestones in the administration of obscenity laws in the United States. It covers not only film, but also literature, radio, art, etc. Some 50 pages of court decisions are included. Amusing, instructive and stimulating.

782 *The Censor, the Drama, and the Film, 1900-1934.* by Knowles, Dorothy. 294 p. London: G. Allen and Unwin, 1934.

The author considers the drama and the film in separate sections. In the second half of the book, she discusses the how-and-why of film censorship, the act of censorship, what film censorship really is, and finally, who the censor is. A bibliography and an index are included.

783 *Censored: The Private Life of the Movies.* by Ernst, Morris L.; and Lorentz, Pare. 199 p. illus. New York: Cape, 1930.

An early message regarding the development of movie censorship. Many examples of the silly, petty and harmful acts of censors are cited. The possible power of certain monopolies over film content is noted. A readable and informative history.

784 *Censorship: The Search For the Obscene.* by Ernst, Morris L.; and Schwartz, Alan U. 288 p. New York: Macmillan, 1964.

In this volume two attorneys discuss the history of censorship and the inhibiting action that it has on many creative artists. Starting with documentation showing the relationship between sexual mores and political-economic necessities, the authors mention many of the targets used in the hunt for obscenity during the last century or so. The motion picture industry is derided for its passive acceptance of much censorship. Court cases involving motion pictures such as THE MIRACLE (1948) are given attention but the most influential court decisions on films came after this book's publication.

Essential for anyone interested in censorship in any medium. The general reader will also find much information and argument in this book which says that "the best censorship is the least censorship."

785 *Censorship: For and Against.* edited by Hart, H. H. 255 p. illus. New York: Hart Publishing, 1972.

This original anthology includes twelve essays by critics, lawyers, and publicists arguing for or against censorship. Critics Hollis Alpert and Judith Crist focus their contributions on film, while others consider books, magazines, the stage, and government data as targets of censorship. The book is noted here for its concise summary of all aspects of censorship.

786 *Censorship: Government and Obscenity.* by Murphy, Terrence J. 294 p. Baltimore: Helicon, 1963.

Deals with definitions, laws, constitutionality, enforcement, conflicts, etc.

787 *Censorship Landmarks.* by De Grazia, Edward. 657 p. illus. New York: R. R. Bowker, 1969.

Many of the cases discussed in this volume are concerned with films.

788 *Censorship of the Movies: The Social and Political Control of a Mass Medium.* by Randall, Richard S. 280 p. Madison, Wisc.: University of Wisconsin Press, 1968.

A serious study of motion picture censorship and its many aspects. Deals with definitions, laws, history of film censorship, and groups practicing censorship. The role of governments and church groups in censorship is considered; self-regulation by the motion picture industry is also described. Recommended for the advanced film scholar and those readers with a specialized interest in censorship.

789 CHAFED ELBOWS. by Downey, Robert. 144 p. paper illus. New York: Lancer Books, Inc., 1967.

Script of the 1967 film directed by Downey. Also contains a foreword by Robert Downey, and two articles: "Backward," by Robery Downey; and critic's comments ON CHAFED ELBOWS.

790 *Chairman's Choice.* by Films, Inc. 162 p. paper illus. Wilmette, Ill.: Films, Inc., 1974.

Addressed to college film programmers, this attractive catalog describes recent films available for campus showings. Most of the rental rates are prohibitive for schools, museums, libraries. College showings recover rental costs by a modest admission charge. About 75 films are presented via a full-page still, price, credits (producer, director, cinematography, screenplay, music, studio, cast), rating, color, running time, synopsis, and critical excerpts. Still selection is excellent and the catalog is a good reference for recent films. Recommended.

791 THE CHAMP. by Newman, Walter. unpaginated paper illus. Los Angeles: Fotonovel 1979.

This *Fotonovel* (see series entry) contains over 350 stills, some original film dialogue, connecting narrative, and cast credits for the 1979 film, THE CHAMP, which was directed by Franco Zeffirelli.

792 *Champagne Before Breakfast.* edited by Gardner, Hy. 304 p. New York: Holt, 1954.

Throughout this compilation of anecdotes, column paragraphs and longer personality pieces, enough film personalities are mentioned to warrant its inclusion here. One chapter is entitled "So This Is Hollywood."

Most of the material is press agentry designed for a fan magazine audience. The accuracy of some of it is questionable: for example, on page 210, "W. C. Fields' feud with Ed Wynn was tame compared with the one he had around 1924 with a scene stealer then known as Baby LeRoy. Though highly publicized and good for a thousand laughs the feud was really on the level." Baby LeRoy was a gurgling infant who appeared in several films with Fields about 1934.

The book is not indexed, so it has no reference value, and scholars will have to wade through a lot of nonsense to find anything worthwhile. Noted here for the record.

793 *Champagne From My Slipper.* by Miller, Ruby. 192 p. illus. London: Herbert Jenkins, 1962.

An autobiography of British actress Ruby Miller—later known as Ruby Laura Rose Darewkski—who appeared in supporting roles in both silent and sound films, mostly between 1916 and 1941. Under the name of Mme. Max Darewski she wrote *Believe Me or Not* in 1933.

794 *Change Lobsters and Dance.* by Palmer, Lilli. 330 p. illus. New York: Macmillan, 1975.

Lilli Palmer was introduced to American audiences shortly after World War II when she appeared in CLOAK AND DAGGER (1946) with Gary Cooper. Her life up till then consisted of childhood years in Germany and an escape from Nazism to Paris and London during the thirties, followed by a successful stage career and marriage to Rex Harrison in 1943. Her later career as film and stage actress receives full attention along with the important events of her personal life.

An ability to handle delicate situations with tact and honesty is displayed in her discussion of the roles that Carole Landis and Kay Kendall played in her life. Her portraits of other celebrities, such as Noel Coward, Garbo, George Bernard Shaw, and others, are sharp, instinctive and revealing. The literary style used by the author is similar in many ways to her better screen characterizations—witty, sophisticated, and completely captivating, as in BUT NOT FOR ME (1959) and THE PLEASURE OF HIS COMPANY (1961). Attempts to be objective about herself and others are constantly evident and the reader will be persuaded by the combination of apparent honesty and literary skill.

Two photographic sections are valuable additions, but the omission of both a filmography and an index in such a quality volume is incomprehensible. Intelligent and readable, this autobiography is sure to please those readers who are aware of Lilli Palmer's abilities as an actress. Her skill as a writer will delight other discriminating readers of all ages. Highly recommended.

795 *A Change of Hearts.* by Koch, Kenneth. 257 p. paper illus. New York: Vintage, 1973.

A collection of plays, films, and other dramatic works by Kenneth Koch from 1951 to 1971. Included on pages 195-197 are ten suggested film scripts: 1) Because; 2) The Color Game; 3) Mountains and Electricity; 4) Sheep Harbor; 5) Oval Gold; 6) Moby Dick; 7) L'Ecole Normale; 8) The Cemetery; 9) The Scotty Dog; and 10) The Apple. Not essential in any way.

796 *Change of Socio-Economic Attitudes under Radical Motion Picture Propaganda.* by Rosenthal, Solomon P. 46 p. paper New York: Archives of Psychology, 1934.

This short volume, number 166 in the *Archives of Psychology* series, was based on the author's thesis at Columbia University. A bibliography is included.

797 *A Change of Tack: Making* THE SHADOW LINE. by Sulik, Boleslaw. 113 p. paper illus. London: British Film Institute (Zoetrope in U.S.), 1976.

THE SHADOW LINE (1976) is a film based on a semi-autobiographical work by Joseph Conrad. It was directed by Andrzej Wajda. A coproduction of the British Thames Television Company and the State Film Industry of Poland, the film was shown both on television and in theatres. In this account of the film's making, its script writer, Boleslaw Sulik, considers both technical production problems along with those created by the cultural differences between the two producing organizations. He includes script excerpts, stills, production shots, cast names and production credits.

Since Sulik worked so closely with Wajda, the account offers a detailed portrait of the well-known Polish director. In addition it provides insights into some of the complexities of coproduction. An account of a unique experience in filmmaking, this is a well-written and nicely produced booklet. It will have a special appeal for the academic audience. Recommended.

798 *Changing.* by Ullman, Liv. 244 p. New York: Alfred Knopf, 1977.

In this unique autobiographical reminiscence, Liv Ullman recalls selected moments in a busy and eventful life. In doing so she shares with the reader some philosophy, wisdom and questions about life and love. She touches briefly on her filmmaking experiences in Hollywood, preferring to emphasize her films with Ingmar Bergman — PERSONA (1967), THE PASSION OF ANNA (1970), SCENES FROM A MARRIAGE (1974) and FACE TO FACE (1976).

Because there are no illustrations, filmography, or index for this volume, its reference value is negligible. However, as a statement about what is to be a reknowned actress, a mother and a woman in today's world, it is superb. Recommended.

799 *Chaplin: Last of the Clowns.* by Tyler, Parker. 200 p. illus. New York: Vanguard Press, 1947.

A typical Tyler tribute to Chaplin: part biography, part description, and mostly analysis of Chaplin's techniques, themes, symbols, meanings, etc. Leans somewhat heavily on Theodore Huff's objective information. Nevertheless, this is a feast for lovers of Tyler's unique and singular brand of film comment and analysis.

800 *Chaplin: The Immortal Tramp.* by Minney, R. J. 170 p. illus. London: Newnes, 1955.

This warm biography written by a personal friend discusses Chaplin's life, art and personality.

801 *Chaplin: Genesis of a Clown.* by Sobel, Raoul; and Francis, David. 253 p. paper illus. New York: Horizon Press (Quartet Books), 1978.

This is another study of Chaplin based on the concept that he was a product of his early environment. The emphasis is on the short silents, with many examples of how the films reflect the experiences of an underprivileged childhood.

802 *Chaplin.* by Gifford, Denis. 128 p. illus. London: Macmillan, 1974.

One of the *Movie Maker* series, this volume considers the career and films of Charlie Chaplin. The text is indexed and there is a long filmography.

803 *Chaplin.* by Manvell, Roger. 240 p. illus. Boston: Little, Brown, 1974.

This title in the *Library of World Biography* series brings the story of the Little Fellow up to 1972, when he returned to the United States after a 20-year exile. Following a long introductory chapter, emphasis is given to Chaplin's life and career during the first four decades of this century. THE GREAT DICTATOR (1940), MONSIEUR VERDOUX (1947) and LIMELIGHT (1952) are treated with brevity, as are his two later failures, A KING IN NEW YORK (1954) and A COUNTESS FROM HONG KONG (1966). Chaplin seemed unable to function as a successful filmmaker outside the United States. His work here from 1914 to 1952 represents an unparalleled period of artistic creation.

A few illustrations appear near the book's center and an index is included. Especially noteworthy is a selected annotated bibliography, which lists most of the major books on Chaplin. Manvell continues to write with an informed confidence and relaxed style that again suggests long experience with his materials and craft. The early career of his hero will seem very familiar to many readers; thankfully, Manvell has brought the story up to the present. Acceptable.

804 *Chaplin: Clown and Genius.* 32 p. illus. Manchester England: World Distributors, 1978.

805 *Chaplin, the Movies and Charlie.* by Jacobs, David. 143 p. illus. New

ways the book is similar to her performances on screen—witty, dry, intelligent and unassuming.

818 *Charlie Chaplin.* by Delluc, Louis; and Miles, Hamish. 96 p. illus. London: John Lane, Bodley Head, 1922.

An early Chaplin biography that includes an analysis/assessment of his first comedies.

819 *Charlie Chaplin.* by Huff, Theodore. 354 p. illus. New York: Henry Schuman, 1951.

It has been said that the best that any volume on Chaplin can do is to describe his artistry. No words can reproduce it. Huff's biography succeeds nicely on this issue and several others. He is not blinded by the comic genius of his subject and objectivity is evident throughout.

Coverage of the private and public lives of Chaplin is given as straight reporting. There is no attempt at sensationalism or gossip repetition. It is in the plot analyses of Chaplin's important films that the author appears most comfortable and productive. He provides detailed plot outlines, background material, casts, and production credits. Short biographies of persons important to Chaplin and his work are also given. The many pictures are well selected but their reproduction is only average. Teddy Huff was a sensitive, conscientious man who approached life cautiously, but with a quiet competence. The book's text reflects these qualities. It is probably the best total view of Chaplin available. Highly recommended.

820 *Charlie Chaplin: Early Comedies.* by Quigly, Isabel. 159 p. paper illus. New York: Dutton, 1968.

This work concentrates on the early short films. An equal combination of pictures and text give the volume some individuality as do some of the Chaplin caricatures and advertisements taken from the newspapers of the period.

As usual with this series, the production is excellent. The abundant stills are well reproduced although some look as if they were taken directly from the films. The author's descriptive and critical comments are intelligent without becoming pedantic. Although the material has been covered before, the presentation here is of sufficient quality to warrant a recommendation.

821 *Charlie Chaplin: His Life and Art.* by Bowman, William Dodgson. 134 p. illus. New York: John Day, 1931.

In this naive, nonanalytical biography, the author follows a predictable course. After a short foreword by Douglas Fairbanks, Jr., there is a rather thin account of Chaplin's youth. The story of Chaplin's discovery of America and vice-versa is followed by sections on his work, his women, his friends, his talkies, etc. This is a supplementary biography that is suitable mostly for researchers.

822 *Charlie Chaplin: King of Tragedy.* by Von Ulm, Gerith. 403 p. illus. Idaho: Caxton, 1940.

A very good Chaplin biography which unfortunately covers his life only up to 1940. Much of it is based upon information supplied by (Toraichi) Kono who was Chaplin's chauffeur and general man Friday from 1916 to 1934. The result is a more frank, closer, more familiar view than in many of the other Chaplin biographies. The illustrations are quite unusual. Some of the personalities in Chaplin's life get a rough treatment, e.g., Paulette Goddard.

823 *Charlie Chaplin.* by McCabe, John. illus. New York: Doubleday, 1978.

John McCabe, who has written some excellent books about Laurel and Hardy, tackles a much more difficult, elusive subject here. His research, including some observations on the young Chaplin by Stan Laurel, has served him well and the final portrait is a reasoned, satisfactory one. It stresses the idea that Chaplin's childhood and early struggles had an enormous influence on his adult behavior and provided much of the material upon which he based his film incidents, themes, and backgrounds. McCabe is a sympathetic biographer who avoids passing judgments, a pitfall for anyone tackling Chaplin as a subject. This is one of the better Chaplin biographies. Recommended.

824 *Charlie Chaplin* THE GOLD RUSH by Magniaux, Phillippe. 50 p. illus. New York: Drake.

A cartoon version of Chaplin's classic film designed for children.

825 *Charlie Chaplin.* by Moss, Robert F. 158 p. paper illus. New York: Pyramid, 1975.

A most creditable study of Chaplin is presented here. Avoiding any detailed description of Chaplin's personal life, the author does use biographical information and incident to support his suggestions about the source of some of Chaplin's film material. Typical of the overall excellence of the text is the summary chapter which deals with Chaplin's occasional poor taste, his overpraised directorial ability, his lack of technical expertise, the failure to give any opportunity to supporting players, the misnomer "King of Tragedy," and so on. Complementing his literate text is a fine selection of well-reproduced visuals, including stills, portraits, and newspaper photographs. A bibliography, a filmography and an index are added.

Another volume on Chaplin might seem excessive at this point, but this one provides an objective critical assessment that earlier books do not. Adding the fine collection of visuals and the solid supporting material to the well-written review of Chaplin's career results in a most impressive book. Highly recommended.

826   *Charlie Chaplin.* by Sacranie, Raj. 64 p. illus. London: H. Hamilton, 1980.

A biography of Charlie Chaplin written for young readers.

827   *Charlie Chaplin* MODERN TIMES 50 p. illus. New York: Drake.

A cartoon version of Chaplin's classic film designed for children. A large-page format is employed and the 250 illustrations are in color.

828   *Charlie Chaplin's Own Story.* by Chaplin, Charlie. Indianapolis, Ind.: Bobbs-Merrill, 1916.

The first autobiography—perhaps a bit premature in 1916.

829   *Charlie—The Improbable Life and Time of Charles MacArthur.* by Hecht, Ben. 242 p. paper illus. New York: Harper, 1957.

Charles MacArthur functioned as a director, original author, producer and screenwriter in Hollywood during the thirties. He was married to Helen Hayes and was the father of actor James MacArthur. In this biography written by his friend and frequent collaborator, Ben Hecht, some attention is given to his years in Hollywood. The book is illustrated and indexed.

Written as the affectionate final tribute to a friend, the volume offers some short glimpses of life among certain rebel nonconformist celebrities of the thirties. As a biography it falls short, but as a collection of witty entertaining anecdotes, it is quite rewarding.

830   *Charlton Heston.* by Druxman, Michael B. 159 p. paper illus. New York: Pyramid, 1976.

A title in the *Pyramid Illustrated History of the Movies* series, this survey of the life and career of Charlton Heston includes the usual elements—text, illustrations, a filmography, a bibliography, and an index.

831   *Charlton Heston, Jack Nicholson.* edited by Henstell, Bruce. 31 p. paper Washington, D.C.: The Americam Film Institute, 1972.

These two individual pieces are part of the *Dialogue On Film* series. Heston talks about the directors he has worked for—Orson Welles, William Wyler, Sam Peckinpah, and Franklin Schaffner. Nicholson offers similar comments as he tells of his work with Roger Corman. The book concludes with selected bibliographies on both men.

832   *Charlton Heston: The Actor's Life— Journals 1956-1976.* by Heston, Charlton. 482 p. illus. New York: Dutton, 1978.

It is hard to dislike anything about Charlton Heston —his films, his performances in them, his television and stage appearances. It is also very difficult to get very enthusiastic. The same personal feeling applies to this volume. While it is never a poor book, it settles for a kind of mild, mediocre, middle-of-the-road recall when it should have been a stimulating review of 20 years in several exciting professions. Perhaps it is the reflection of a man who prefers to play it safe rather than to take any risks in his writing, performing, and working with fellow professionals.

The entries in this journal are fragments, edited by Hollis Alpert, from records kept by Heston of his professional activities. Other than a devotion to his family, much of his personal life remains quite private. He is overly careful in discussing his fellow workers. For example, in planning his portrayal of Ben Hur, how did he see the character of Messala (Steven Boyd)? Did Boyd concur? What contribution was made by William Wyler in evolving this relationship which is crucial to the film? These are valid questions a reader might wish answered. Heston writes that Boyd was companionable, a good choice for the part, had trouble with contact lenses, and other such surface observations, but nothing having any analytical depth or challenge. There are some illustrations but the book is not indexed.

It's easy to like Heston; he's a comfortable man to

spend a few reading hours with. If only he could manage, once in a while, to be exciting, or controversial, or colorful, or off-color, or offensive....

833 *Charmed Lives: A Family Romance.* by Korda, Michael. 498 p. illus. New York: Random House, 1979.

The author, Michael Korda, writes about his father, Vincent, and his two uncles, Alexander and Zoltan Korda, in this collective biography. In telling the story of three determined brothers who came from poverty in Hungary to riches in England, the author includes many personal anecdotes and private memories. The text mentions the personalities that were part of the Korda's British motion picture empire—Merle Oberon, Charles Laughton, Laurence Olivier, Vivien Leigh, etc. That the Kordas were a bit larger than life is emphasized, especially the leader of the family, Sir Alexander Korda, who eventually charmed his way into a position of world influence and importance.

The author does not analyze the Korda films (no filmography is given) and acknowledges his debt to Karol Kulik's *Alexander Korda* for factual material. What he does is to provide a personal memoir of his family and their associates that is most enjoyable. An index and some illustrations are added.

834 *Chekov's Enterprise.* by Koenig, Walter. 222 p. paper illus. New York: Pocket Books, 1980.

This volume, which is subtitled "A Personal Journal of the Making of STAR TREK, the Motion Picture," was written by the actor who plays the role of Russian lieutenant Pavel Chekov in the 1980 film. His diary covers several months of the production that failed so badly with theatre audiences. Likewise this volume will appeal to a vary limited audience since it deals with trivial matters and often seems like an ego trip for the author. The success of the original TV show, followed by 50 or more Star Trek conventions, may have lulled the filmmakers into thinking they were working on an infallible project. This attitude is conveyed by the author, whose saving grace is that he included the word "personal" in the book's subtitle. The few illustrations that appear in a center section are too small and have been poorly selected.

835 *Chestnuts in Her Lap 1936-1946.* by Lejeune, C. A. 192 p. London: Phoenix House, 1947.

This is a treasure of film criticism and comment, written by the author for *The Manchester Guardian* and *The Observer.* Obviously the films she considers

are old but a surprising majority are still prominent in film discussions and writings.

The style is typical British understatement coupled with wisdom, intelligence and a beautiful way with words. Two short examples: BRIEF ENCOUNTER (1946): "But for a very few people it will remain a bedside film, to be taken out and relished to one's heart's content; to be familiarized and loved; to be seen, and savoured, in quietness, over and over again." THE ADVENTURES OF ROBIN HOOD (1938): "This was a film that was half-made before a shot was in the camera. Tradition has been working on the script for seven hundred years."

The approach is a common-sense, nonpretentious one and is a refreshing change from some of today's in-depth analysis. Too much attention is given to plot but this is a minor flaw when it is possible to discover something memorable/quotable in each piece. No illustrations but a general index of names and titles. Highly recommended.

836 *Chevalier: The Films and Career of Maurice Chevalier.* by Ringgold, Gene; and Bodeen, DeWitt. 245 p. illus. Secaucus, N.J.: Citadel, 1973.

The biographical portion of this volume is longer and more detailed than most others in this series—mostly because of the longevity and international celebrity of Maurice Chevalier. The filmography notes silent films from TROP CREDULE (1908) to JIM BOUGNE BOXEUR (1924), compilation films, guest appearances, and finally sound feature films from INNOCENTS OF PARIS (1929) to MONKEYS, GO HOME (1967). For each, cast, credits, songs, story and critical comments are given.

Since the period of Chevalier's greatest fame was in the twenties and thirties, the volume emphasizes those periods. Unfortunately the reproduction quality of many of the illustrations is quite poor. The films, with a very few exceptions, are undistinguished and now dated. Chevalier's status as a film performer is still undecided. This volume may help to assess his contribution, but to younger readers he is probably best remembered as a supporting character actor in a series of Walt Disney films. Acceptable.

837 *Chicorel Index to Biographies.* edited by Chicorel, Marietta. 2 vols. New York: Chicorel, 1974.

838 *Chicorel Index to Film Literature.* edited by Chicorel, Marietta. 1500 p. New York: Chicorel, 1975.

This film bibliography offers some 3000 film books which are spread over two large volumes. The books, which are not annotated, are only listed under 150 subject headings. The user may question the efficient use of page space, especially since the cost of the two-volume set is so great.

Certain headings are questionable, such as "Film Classics" and "Celebrities and Personalities." In addition to being selective rather than comprehensive in her book choices, in the author index the editor omits the names of writers whose books are listed. Not acceptable.

839   *The Child Audience.* Bauchard, Philippe.

This is a report on "Press, Film, and Radio for Children." See also the other UNESCO publications, entitled *The Entertainment Film for Juvenile Audiences* (1950), *Films for Children and Adolescents* (1956), and *Film Programmes for the Young* (1959).

840   *A Child of the Century.* by Hecht, Ben 608 p. illus. New York: Signet Books, 1954.

Hecht's autobiography touches only briefly on his career as a screenwriter. It does have many anecdotes about film personalities—Selznick, Helen Hayes, John Barrymore, Harpo, etc.

841   *Child Star Dolls and Toys.* by Burdick, Loraine. 170 p. illus. New York: Macmillan (Quest), 1968.

More information about collectibles.

842   *The Child Stars.* by Zierold, Norman J. 250 p. illus. New York: Coward-McCann, 1965.

During the twenties and thirties a group of child movie stars enjoyed a national popularity never again duplicated. A description of the struggle to attain this prominence and what eventually happened to these child stars is the subject of this book.

Jackie Coogan, Baby LeRoy, Shirley Temple, Jane Withers, Judy Garland, Freddie Bartholomew, Deanna Durbin, Mickey Rooney and Jackie Cooper are the subjects each receiving an individual essay. The conclusion is a chapter on other child stars of lesser magnitude. The rarely seen photographs used throughout are amusing and nostalgic. Using a style that is reportorial rather than analytic, the author describes mostly externals and only hints at what must have been several most unusual childhoods. If common themes such as the perennial party, the

parent obsessed with show business, the mismanaged fortune, and the abnormal adolescence, had been woven together in a summary chapter, the volume may have had a more total effect rather than the scattered results it now has. A good book that could have been much better.

843   *Children and Film/Television.* by Elsas, Diana; and Kelso, Lulu. 8 p. paper Washington, D.C.: American Film Institute, 1977.

This title in the *Factfile* series offers annotated listings of organizations, books, pamphlets, periodicals, and filmographies, all of which deal with children and film/television. It is a very valuable resource for anyone dealing with young people from preschool through high school.

844   *Children and Movies.* by Mitchell, Alice Miller. 181 p. New York: Ozer, 1971 (1929).

Published originally by the University of Chicago in 1929, this study of children and movies appeared prior to the Payne Fund Studies, which treated some of the same topics. Supported by the Wiebolt Foundation, Ms. Mitchell examined the movie experience of 10,000 children—from public schools, from juvenile correction institutions, and from the Boy Scouts and Girl Scouts of America. The study investigated frequency and time of attendance, movie companions, reasons for choice of films, and a likening with other recreational forms. There is a fascinating comparison of film attendance and book reading. Many tables support the text of the study and the conclusions are interesting. The book is indexed.

Although this pioneer study is dated, and certain of its conclusions are questionable today, it can still serve as a guide and model for present-day studies. For that reason it is recommended.

845   *Children and Screen Violence.* by Edgar, Patricia. New York: University of Queensland Press, 1977.

846   *Children and the Cinema.* edited by British Film Institute. 31 p. illus. London: British Film Institute, 1946.

This is the report of a conference sponsored jointly by the National Council of Women and the BFI.

847   *Children Are Centers for Understanding Media.* edited by Rice, Susan; and Mukerji, Rose. 89 p. illus. Washington, D.C.: Association for Childhood

Education International, 1973.

848 *Children As Film Makers.* by Lidstone, John; and McIntosh, Don. III p. illus. New York: Van Nostrand, 1970.

This text is designed for the teacher who desires to use filmmaking in a classroom situation. It relates, in a detailed but simple fashion, much information on equipment, techniques, and class organization.

849 *Children in the Cinema.* by Ford, Richard. 232 p. London: Allen and Unwin, 1939.

A British version of the Payne Fund Studies that looks at the role that cinema plays in a child's life. Employs a practical, observational approach of listening to and observing children, rather than statistics.

850 CHILDREN OF PARADISE (LES ENFANTS DU PARADIS). by Prevert, Jacques. 218 p. paper illus. New York: Simon & Schuster, 1968.

Script of the 1944 film directed by Marcel Carne. Contains cast credits and short interviews with Carne and Prevert.

851 *Children's Attendance at Motion Pictures.* by Dale, Edgar. 81 p. New York: Macmillan, 1935.

Another Payne Fund Study which set out to discover the frequency of attendance of school children at commercial motion pictures. Done in 1929-30, the age, sex, and companions of the viewer were investigated as was the time and day of viewing and those programs most frequently viewed. Historically useful, the study can also serve as an early model of research.

852 *Children's Film Foundation Catalogue and Index of Films.* 44 p. paper illus. London: Children's Film Foundation, 1972.

This catalog is a filmography of the features, featurettes, serials, series, compilation films, shorts and cartoons that CFF distributes. Each entry contains title, running time, color format, synopsis, credits, cast, awards, and a still. An opening index lists the films alphabetically by title. Their appearance in the main body of the catalog is chronological by date of release and by film form. A short supplementary list was published in 1974. See also *Young Cinema* and

Saturday Morning Cinema.

853 *Children's Film Tastes.* by Barclay, John Bruce. 63 p. paper Edinburgh, Scotland: Scottish Educational Film Association, 1956.

A report on an experimental series of film programs given for children at the Gateway Theatre in Edinburgh, 1956.

854 *Children's Sleep.* by Renshaw, Samuel; and Miller, Vernon L.; and Marquis, Dorothy P. 242 p. New York: Arno Press, 1970 (1933).

A Payne Fund Study volume published in 1970 by Arno, this one considers the effect on the sleep of children that seeing motion pictures, as well as other unrelated factors, may have.

855 *The Children's Movie Quiz Book.* by Pickard, Roy. 64 p. London: Muller, 1979.

856 *Chilean Cinema.* edited by Chanan, Michael. 102 p. paper illus. London: British Film Institute (Zoetrope in N.Y.), 1976.

Includes a bibliography and filmography.

857 CHINA IS NEAR. by Tattoli, Elda; and Bellocchio, Marco. 160 p. illus. New York: Orion Press, 1969.

Script of the 1967 film directed by Bellocchio. Contains an introduction by Tommaso Chiaretti and "The Authors on Tape" —Chiaretti interviewing Bellocchio and Tattoli.

858 *The Chinese Silver Screen.* by Eberhard, Wolfram. 241 p. Taipei, Republic of China: Orient Cultural Service, 1972.

This is volume 23 in the series entitled *Asian Folklore and Social Life Monographs.* Dealing with Hong Kong and Taiwanese motion pictures produced in the sixties, the book contains plot outlines of 329 films. It is designed more for those interested in subject-content than in technique-aesthetics, e.g. the folklorist, the sociologist, or the student of Chinese opera and literature. The annotations are written in English with some Chinese words used to identify titles, names, etc. An index of themes and topics is provided. Acceptable.

859   *Chitra Bani.: A Book on Film Appreciation.* by Roberge, Gaston. 274 p. paper illus. Calcutta: Chitra Bani, 1974.

This admirable book was written, designed and produced for a specific audience—the average Indian reader. It had to be inexpensive, pertinent to Indian films, and relatively elementary in its approach. The Indian culture does not produce the experienced sophisticated filmgoer or student that many other countries do. The Indian portion of the book's title means "Image and Sound" ; the book, however, is written entirely in English.

A foreword by Satyajit Ray is followed by a general discussion of communication, the media environment, mass media in India, art, painting, theatre, and music. The social function of art is explored. The aesthetics and technical aspects of films are considered next. Film History, Film Criticism, and Film in a Contemporary Culture are the topics treated in the remaining sections. A glossary, Hollywood Academy Awards (1928-1970), a bibliography, and a list of film distributors in India conclude the book. A center section of illustrations is also provided. The blending of the national India cinema with an introduction to general world cinema and film appreciation creates an unusual but not incompatible mixture. In the context of the book's goal, it is excellent, unique and quite acceptable.

860   CHITTY CHITTY BANG BANG. by Newman, Jeffrey. 48 p. paper illus. New York: National Publishers, Inc., 1968.

An example of one of the better souvenir books. The text relates the synopsis of the 1968 film in a correlation with the songs. A second section deals with Dick Van Dyke, Sally Ann Howes and Lionel Jeffries in detail, and with the others in the cast to a lesser degree. Some behind-the-camera credits are given, with special attention to the production design. Photographs throughout are quite clear, a rarity for this kind of book.

861   *Christ and Celebrity Gods.* by Boyd, Malcolm. 145 p. Greenwich, Conn.: Seabury Press, 1958.

Subtitled "The Church in Mass Culture," this volume treats the relationship between religion and films.

862   *The Christian and the Movies.* by Paine, Stephen W. 79 p. illus. Grand Rapids, Mich.: Wm. B. Eerdmans,

1957.

863   *Christian Metz and the Reality of Film.* by Cozyris, George Agis. New York: Arno, 1979.

An assessment of the contribution made toward the understanding of film by semiologist Christian Metz is the topic of this title from the *Dissertations on Film* series. Limitations and weaknesses in Metz's work are indicated.

864   *The Christopher Reeves Scrapbook.* by Steinberg, Margery. paper illus. New York: Ace (Tempo), 1980.

A collection of photos and text about the young actor who has made three major films to date: SUPERMAN (1978), SOMEWHERE IN TIME (1980), and SUPERMAN II (1981).

865   *The Chronicles of Charlie Chaplin.* by Reed, Langford. 120 p. illus. London: Cassel, 1917.

Contains descriptive, fictionalized versions of Chaplin's Essanay films, including BY THE SEA (1915), SHANGHAIED (1915), THE TRAMP (1915), IN THE PARK (1915), THE CHAMPION (1915), A WOMAN (1915), A NIGHT OUT (1915), THE BANK (1915), CARMEN (1916), POLICE (1916), HIS NEW JOB (1915), A NIGHT AT THE SHOW (1915), THE JITNEY ELOPEMENT (1915), and WORK (1915).

866   *Church and Cinema: A Way of Viewing Film.* by Wall, James M. 135 p. illus. Grand Rapids: W. B. Eerdmans Publishing Co., 1971.

Author Wall, who is also the editor of *The Christian Advocate,* presents suggestions for viewing films designed to help the print-oriented person discover film as film.

After a treatment of the relationships of film and the church from both an historical and current perspective, an attempt is made to persuade the film viewer to abandon the plot pattern (What is it about?) in favor of the film-as-film approach (What is it trying to say?). Using many well-chosen examples, the author expands his argument in chapters dealing with blacks in film and sex in cinema. Concluding sections contain a history of censorship and some film reviews taken from *The Christian Advocate.*

Although the book seems to promise much more than it eventually delivers, its arguments/examples are so intelligently presented that the reader becomes absorbed despite the rather familiar territory. The author's stretching of a long article into a book can be forgiven because of his persuasiveness and sensitivity. Illustrations are rather good and the book is indexed.

867 *Cicely.* by Courtneidge, Cicely. 224 p. illus. London: Hutchinson, 1953.

This is the autobiography of the Australian comedienne who has been a favorite of British audiences for decades. After a long career on the stage, she began to appear in films in the early thirties and was still active in THE WRONG BOX (1966). She excelled in playing eccentric character roles, many of which relied on ridiculous disguises.

868 *Cine-Craft.* by Beal, J. David. 254 p. illus. London: Focal Press, 1974.

A handsomely produced volume on cinematography, this book features many attractive illustrations, a solid text and a helpful index.

869 *Cine-Photography.* by Paul, Norman. 92 p. paper illus. London: Foyle, 1965.

A title in the Foyles *Handbooks* series, this volume explains motion picture photography for the beginner.

870 *Cine Photography All the Year Round.* by Wallace, Carlton. paper illus. New York: Amphoto, 1965.

A basic book on cinematography that considers the problem of varied weather. Discusses techniques and the processing of film.

871 *Cine-Photography for Amateurs.* by Reyner, John Hereward. 180 p. illus. Boston: American Photographic Publishing Co., 1932.

An early text for beginning filmmakers that contains sections on both 9.5mm and 16mm film, along with such topics as color, equipment, titling, etc.

872 *Cine Titling.* by Daborn, John. 112 p. paper illus. London: Fountain Press, 1960.

A title in the Fountain *Moviebook* series, this typical how-to-do-it book contains illustrations, diagrams, etc.

873 *Cineliteracy: Film Among the Arts.* by Eidsuik, Charles. 303 p. illus. New York: Random House, 1978.

This volume has two goals—an overview of the languages of film, and the provision of a film aesthetic. There are three major sections: 1. How movies work (response, structure, artifice, convention, human dimension); 2. The cinema in cultural perspective (prefilm popular arts, antipopular arts, literature, the visual arts, theatre, fusions); and 3. Exploration (values, the future in film, film and theatre, the independent film). The outline above merely suggests the serious, intellectual approach taken in the text. To understand the many ideas, concepts, philosophies, and theories put forth by the author requires a diligent, careful study-reading by the user. Supplementing the text are chapter notes, a bibliography, and an index. The numerous illustrations are correlated with specific passages in the book. The advanced student of film study will find Eidsuik's presentation to be both enlightening and provocative. Others who lack a substantial base or experience in film matters may find this volume rather rough going.

874 *Cinema.* by Lejeune, Caroline A. 255 p. London: A. MacLehose, 1931.

Reviews and comments on performers and directors —Chaplin, Pickford, Sennett, Fairbanks, Lubitsch, von Stroheim, Nazimova, and others.

875 *The Cinema.* by Reed, Stanley William. 122 p. illus. London: London Educational Supply Assoc., 1959.

A history of the film from early biscuit box cinema to films of today. The Silent Era is emphasized.

876 *Cinema.* by Wiseman, Thomas. 181 p. illus. New York: A. S. Barnes, 1965.

Still another in the flow of text-plus-picture books on the history of the cinema. This one differs only by a few of the emphases. For example, more attention is given to von Stroheim than to Griffith. Also detailed is the work of the newer foreign directors who specialize in a more personal cinema; excluded is the new American Wave, as the author ends with Billy Wilder, Elia Kazan and Otto Preminger.

Four color pictures along with many black and white shots are assets to the book. However, while the theme of the book seems to be the conflict of business and art in cinema, it is only fitfully developed.

Certainly the book is interesting since its subject matter offers endless fascination. Perhaps if the comments and pictures did not seem rather familiar, one could be more enthusiastic. Acceptable as supplementary reading and reference.

877 *The Cinema: Its Present Position and Future Possibilities.* by Cinema Commision of Inquiry. 467 p. New York: Arno Press, 1970 (1917).

The report and the chief evidence taken by The Cinema Commission of Inquiry. The National Council of Public Morals initiated this investigation during World War I.

878 *The Cinema.* by Reed, Stanley. 122 p. illus. London: The Educational Supply Association, Ltd., 1952.

This nicely illustrated history of the cinema emphasizes the early years. Written by the Secretary of the British Film Institute, the book is aimed at the elementary school student and, in this context, is excellent. Not only is the text suitable, but the supporting illustrations and suggestions are also fine. For example, there are diagrams on how to make a thaumatrope, a flip book, and a phenakistiscope. Actual photographs are well selected but the reproduction is overly dark. The book is indexed. This volume is certainly worth revising, with some improvement in picture reproduction. It should find a warm welcome from many younger readers. Recommended.

879 *The Cinema: A History.* by Reader, Keith. 200 p. paper illus. New York: David McKay, 1979.

A title in the *Teach Yourself Books* series, this volume is an American reprint of the original British edition. Unfortunately, the production is extremely inexpensive and the book will not stand up under any heavy use. The paper is the pulp variety and the few poorly selected illustrations are limited to a center section.

Since a history of the cinema is being told in less than 200 pages, it must necessarily be an overview. As such the text provided here is adequate with a sentence or so given to certain films, directors, actors or events. Supporting the history is a glossary, a filmography, some notes on the text, and an index.

The author shows promise as a critical historian. What he needs is a production that will allow him fuller expression and an editor to advise him on selection and omission.

880 *The Cinema.* compiled by Child Welfare Committee. 34 p. paper Geneva: League of Nations, 1928.

The booklet relates the replies of governments to the questionnaire drawn up by the Child Welfare Committee in its 3rd session in May, 1927. The Committee is part of the Advisory Commission for the Protection and Welfare of Children and Young People.

881 *The Cinema.* by Jackson-Wrigley, M.; and Leyland, Eric. 195 p. London: Grafton, 1939.

This rare volume is accurately described by its subtitle, "Historical, Technical and Bibliographical. A Survey for Librarians and Students." It is divided into three parts: historical, technical, and educational and libraries. Each of these sections is terse and succinct. For example, "historical" treats invention and industry while "technical" treats production, technique, color film, and amateur cinematography. The third part, "educational and libraries" , predicts the large interest areas of the post-war period: film and school, film and library, and the British Film Institute. A long, early bibliography is followed by lists of cinema periodicals, outstanding films, and a historical chronology. The book is indexed.

This is certainly a pioneer volume that will delight historians, bibliographers, and scholars.

882 *The Cinema.* by Lindgren, Ernest. 23 p. paper London: English Universities Press, 1944.

A small booklet designed to promote discussion and produced with the cooperation of the Association for Education in Citizenship, this was a title in the *Unless We Plan Now* series. A pioneer attempt to improve motion picture literacy, it offered a good bibliography.

883 *Cinema.* by Leish, Kenneth W. 192 p. illus. New York: Newsweek Books, 1974.

As a part of the series entitled *World of Culture*, this volume had to conform to the standard structure and form used for all volumes. It employs a historical review, a selection of biographical excerpts and a chronology; these elements are combined well here. The survey of cinema provided is a brief overview which concentrates mostly on the rise of the Hollywood studios and their replacement in the last two decades by the independent filmmakers. The international scene is not ignored, however, in what amounts to a summary survey of film history highlights.

The biographical section is entitled "Making the Movies" and there are brief excerpts from books on or by Chaplin, Lillian Gish, D. W. Griffith, Kevin Brownlow, Lillian Hellman, John Houseman and George Cukor. The two-page chronology compares film events with world happenings in a highly selective fashion. Major Academy Award winners including Best Foreign Language Films are noted through 1973, along with a list of 20 top-grossing films up to then. A short bibliography and a good index complete the book. Over 200 illustrations are used and they are consistently well reproduced. A number appear in full color, adding a visual attractiveness seldom found in film books today.

The text is comprehensive, objective, and avoids excessive treatment of any particular topic. Adding the rich collection of visuals and the other supplementary features makes this volume especially welcome. It can be used with a wide range of audiences and is recommended. Mention should be made of its attractive price—unusual for a volume containing such an abundance of color work.

884 *Cinema: A Critical Dictionary.* edited by Roud, Richard. 2 vols. 1136 p. illus. New York: Viking, 1980.

For his book, Roud employed 41 writers in addition to himself to create 234 entries, most of which deal with film directors. In many instances the contributors are well-known film authorities—Robin Wood, John Russell Taylor, Tom Milne, James Monaco, Andrew Sarris, and others. Their subjective essays reflect their critical criteria and usually demand strong reader background. Roud includes 17 pieces of his own and provides some comments to the others.

The effort involved here and the outcome must be acknowledged as a notable contribution to film literature. Popular acceptance of the work may be limited by what appears to be a overly serious "highbrow" approach, designed to impress and awe the reader—terminology, balance, foreign language citations, selection and treatment of subjects, obscure films, etc. Therefore using this "Dictionary" as a reference may be somewhat disappointing; however, as an anthology offering a wide range of critical thinking and commentary on cinema, it is excellent.

885 *The Cinema.* by Ellis-Jones, Barrie. paper Exeter, N.H.: Heinemann, 1977.

886 *Cinema.* by Gomez, Mesa L. New York: Gordon Press, 1976.

887 *Cinema and History: British Newsreels and the Spanish Civil War.* by Aldgate, Anthony. New York: Zoetrope, 1980.

888 *Cinema and Society.* by Monaco, Paul. 194 p. New York: Elsevier, 1976.

Based on the author's thesis, written in 1973, this volume carries the subtitle, "France and Germany During the Twenties." It deals with the social aspects of the film in those countries during the decade which followed the First World War. Examined are the economics of the film industry, its relationship with government, and films' reflection of the thoughts, prejudices, actions and goals of the population's "group mind." Separate filmographies for each nation are appended and there is a very detailed bibliography. The book is indexed.

The volume's origin testifies to the careful research and presentation that is apparent throughout. Although there are copious chapter notes and references, the study is written in a logical, readable, almost narrative style. Its clearly stated conclusions will be intriguing to anyone interested in the relationship between film, society, and history. Those innovative instructors who use entertainment films as a reflection of a specific historical period will find the book quite valuable. Recommended.

889 *The Cinema and Television.* by Legg, Stuart; and Fairthorne, Robert. 96 p. illus. London: Longmans, Green, 1930.

An early volume which emphasizes the technical side of cinematography—how movement is reproduced, how still photography led to moving pictures, the movie camera, the film projector, the growth of the film industry, the discovery of sound and of color, what the camera can do, etc. Issued as part of the *March of Time* series edited by Arthur Elton, this volume was revised and updated in 1939.

890 *The Cinema and the Protection of Youth.* by European Committee on Crime Problems. 107 p. paper Strasbourg, France: Council of Europe, 1968.

A discussion of the effects of cinema and the means that some European countries have taken to protect their youth from certain films are the concerns of the book. In addition to an introductory title essay, there are sections on European censorship, the effects of film upon individuals and groups, and legislation relating to the cinema. The book provides a good summary of a difficult subject.

891   *see   890*

892   *The Cinema and the Public.* by Box, Kathleen. 17 p. paper London: Central Office of Information, 1946.

A short 1946 investigation of the filmgoers of that period made by The Social Survey. Inquiries such as frequency of attendance, money spent for film entertainment, etc. were used.

893   *The Cinema and the Public.* by Ashley, Walter. 44 p. London: I. Nicholson and Watson, 1934.

An older book which offers a critical analysis of the origin, constitution, and control of the British Film Institute during its early years.

894   *Cinema and the School.: A Guide to 101 Major American Films.* by Langman, Larry; and Fajans, Milt. 157 p. paper illus. Dayton, Ohio: Pflaum, 1975.

This filmography presents 101 entries suggested for possible use in secondary schools. Selection was made using four criteria: critical acclaim, classroom suitability, availability and literary origin. Given for each title is the year of release, running time, color format, plot, characterization, dramatic and literary techniques, and themes. A glossary, film distributor list, a chronological listing, a classification by genre, literary source and publisher list, and a name index complete the book. The few illustrations are acceptable but add little to the book.

The volume is a valuable resource for teachers of English and Humanities. Its impressive structure makes it convenient to use, the selection of film titles is faultless, and all of the supporting sections are helpful.

895   *Cinema and Theatre Organ: A Comprehensive Description of This Instrument, Its Constituent Part and Its Use.* by Whitworth, Reginald. 144 p. illus. Braintree, Mass.: Organ Literature, 1981.

896   *Cinema and Value Philosophy.* by McGuire, Jeremiah C. 91 p. New York: Philosophical Library, 1968.

This volume demands an extensive background, education and experience of its readers. It seemingly is an attempt to prove that value theory can provide a critical base for evaluating the worth of films. I must admit I had neither the time, patience nor inclination to wade through this one. To be fair, then, no evaluation is given here. The prospective reader is on his own.

897   *The Cinema as Art.* by Stephenson, Ralph; and Debrix, J. R. 268 p. paper illus. Baltimore, Md.: Penguin Books, 1967.

By the use of hundreds of examples, the authors show how the filmmaker uses cinematic techniques to capture the idea he wishes his audience to absorb. Included are chapters on those characteristics of film that make it a unique art—time, space, nonreality, etc.

An ideal blending of aesthetics, practice, example and illustration, the book is a major contribution to the small group of good volumes devoted to film appreciation as opposed to film reviewing. Stills are excellent as is an index of films and directors. Although this is a basic book for many readers, it is not a volume for all. Some will find it too difficult, abstract, or theoretical. However, it should be required reading in all college film courses. It offers a most rewarding experience.

898   *The Cinema as a Graphic Art.* by Nilsen, Vladimir. 227 p. illus. London: Newnes, 1959 (1937).

The cameraman as a creative artist rather than an automated technician is the theme of this early volume which is dedicated by the author to Sergei Eisenstein, his co-worker at the Russian State Institute of Cinematography.

Using many diagrams and pictures, the book is divided into two major sections, "The Compositional Construction of the Shot," and "Creative Problems of the Art of the Camera Man," with a very short section on "Methods of Working Out the Scenario." Because of the excellent combination of text and illustration, the book can be comprehended with relative ease and effort. Because of its advanced technical nature, however, beginning filmmakers will find it valuable as a later reading rather than a primary one.

899   *Cinema Beyond the Danube.: The Camera and Politics.* by Stoil, Michael Jon. 198 p. illus. Metuchen, N.J.: Scarecrow Press, 1974.

In this analysis of Eastern European cinema, Stoil combines a historical survey with social, political and aesthetic comment. After a general introduction to the socialist film industry, a history covering the years 1908 to 1973 is related. Emphasis is on the Soviet cinema, but attention is given to filmmaking in Poland, Hungary, Yugoslavia, Czechoslovakia, and Albania. One genre, Fantastic-Utopian films, is singled out for detailed examination, and the author provides a summary statement on cinema and ideology. The few illustrations are well selected and adequately reproduced. A bibliography, a filmography and a short index complete the book.

The author seems more confident with the social-political-historical aspects of his survey than with the subject of film. His use of film history and aesthetics is often murky and obscure rather than clearly structured and stated; his detailed analyses of some classic films seem familiar rather than original —see POTEMKIN (1925), STORM OVER ASIA (1928), and CLOSELY WATCHED TRAINS (1966). However, the scope of the volume, the almost personal interpretation provided, and the amount of detail and analysis supplied are the positive qualities of the book. Acceptable.

900 *Cinema Booklist: Supplememt 2.* by Rehrauer, George. 482 p. paper Metuchen, N.J.: Scarecrow, 1977.

This volume emphasizes film literature published in the period 1973-1975. It continues the approach and format of the two earlier volumes, offering about 1000 annotated entries, an author index, subject index, an interview index and a film script index.

901 *Cinema Booklist.* by Rehrauer, George. 473 p. Metuchen, N.J.: Scarecrow Press, 1972.

This volume provides a comprehensive reference guide to the film literature written between 1940 and 1970. All classifications of material (history, aesthetics, biographies, etc.) and all formats are covered in this bibliographic guide to the literature of the cinema. Complete citations and descriptive-evaluative annotations of more than 1600 film books and scripts will assist readers in their search for books on film topics. It was selected by the American Library Association as one of the outstanding reference books published in 1972. *Film News* stated in its review "This knowledgeable and perceptive selection, fully annotated, is of exceptional help as a reliable research tool for film study courses and an indispensable item on library reference shelves."

902 *Cinema Booklist: Supplement One.* by Rehrauer, George. 405 p. Metuchen, N.J.: Scarecrow Press, 1974.

This volume continues the work of the original volume, emphasizing here the film literature written between 1971 and 1973. It is comprehensive in its treatment of all classifications of material (criticism, film scripts, filmmaking, etc.) in all formats (hardbound, paperback, pamphlet, etc.). Some 900 titles are included with complete citations and a descriptive, evaluative annotation provided for each.

Arrangement of entries is alphabetical by title. Both author and subject indexes are cumulative, covering the main volume as well as Supplement One. An appendix listing of 270 full-length film scripts, both modern and classic, provides a summary of this literary form to date. More then 100 film souvenir books are treated in the text and indexed separately. Finally, an index to interviews with more than 400 filmmakers (directors, actors, writers, cameramen, etc.) provides a guide for locating this primary source.

This completely indexed work will assist readers in their search for books or information on film topics. Librarians and educators will find it valuable in building film-related collections, while the general audience, including film buffs, will find it an entertaining reader-reference tool. In its review, *Choice* magazine stated: "The descriptive entries are succinct and the criticism balanced and helpful. A necessary book for bibliography and film collections."

903 *Cinema Borealis: Ingmar Bergman and the Swedish Ethos.* by Young, Vernon. 331 p. illus. New York: David Lewis, 1971.

By the use of explanation, reason, documentation, and examination, the author attempts to prove that Bergman's themes reflect the Swedish temperament. Another worthwhile addition to the Bergman literature.

904 *Cinema Catalog.* by Lubovski, Git. 524 p. paper illus. Hollywood, Calif.: Larry Edmunds Bookshop, 1970.

This catalog of books, magazines, autographs, pictures, sheet music, lobby cards, posters, press books and programs is a solidly concentrated information source on cinema. Its use as a cinema literature reference is almost limitless. With annotations, authors and dates, the book section is quite valuable. Obviously no attempt at evaluation is made since the catalog is designed for sales purposes. For the same reason perhaps, the publishers are not listed.

905 *Cinema Cavalcade.* by Blyth, H. E. 124 p. illus. Johannesburg, South Africa: Max Virginia Cigarettes, 1938.

As a promotional device, the manufacturers of Max Virginia cigarettes enclosed small cards of movie stills and star portraits in their packages. Using these same cards as illustrations, a book about the history of film was prepared. The 250 card illustrations are pasted in this book, which deals with film history, films of fact, films of fun, and films of fiction. The text is enjoyable and the illustration-cards are most attractive. Alexander Korda supplies a foreword to this example of nostalgia from the thirties.

906 *Cinema Craftsmanship.: A Book for Photoplaywrights.* by Patterson, Frances Taylor. 277 p. illus. New York: Harcourt, Brace, 1921.

The complete process of screenwriting from idea-inception to final film is considered in this early volume. Attention is given to plot, characters, setting, adaptations, scenarios, technique, synopsis, markets, etc. An index and a bibliography are provided.

907 *Cinema Equipment You Can Build.* Holman, L. Bruce.

Using an informal, easy-to-understand text and some excellent drawings, L. Bruce Holman has created an unusual and valuable book. His goal is to suggest inexpensive ways to duplicate costly filmmaking apparatus. Some of the projects include rewinds, an editing bench, animation stands, a clap board, a microphone boom, rear projection screens, a shoulder brace, a tripod dolly and a projection booth. A total of more than 50 different topics are considered and described.

Both the professional and the amateur will be served by the suggestions and advice offered here. Supplier names and addresses are given throughout. This helpful do-it-yourself guide is recommended.

908 *Cinema Examined.* edited by Mac-Cann, Richard Dyer. paper New York: Dutton, 1978.

A selection of articles taken from *Cinema Journal* 1966-1976.

909 *Cinema Eye, Cinema Ear: Some Key Film-Makers of the Sixties.* by Taylor, John Russell. 294 p. paper New York: Hill and Wang, 1964.

Six master directors, artists who have refused to fit any particular pattern and who typify the trend of directing auteur films in the sixties, are the subjects in this book. The author, a film critic for the *London Times* and a writer for *Sight and Sound*, does not depend upon the tape recorder technique but offers instead a critical essay on the work and style of each director. The statement of film critic Alexandre Astruc in 1948 about "Camera-Stylo," (Camera as Fountain Pen) seems uncanny prediction.

The directors chosen are Fellini, Antonioni, Bunuel, Bresson, Bergman, and Hitchcock. One additional chapter looks at Truffaut, Godard, and Resnais as representative of Nouvelle Vogue (New Wave). Filmographies are given for each. With the great interest in directors today, this volume will certainly enjoy a deserved popularity. It is well-written and the critical comments are sound. One reservation: the subjects may seem very familiar because of over-exposure in print. As a small survey of the sixties, it is very good and recommended.

910 *Cinema Great Britain.* unpaginated. illus. London: Film Producers Association of Great Britain, 1970.

This survey of 75 years of British film is written in French and English, and covers the period from 1895 to 1970. Final sections list the awards received by British films and make some predictions about the films of the seventies.

911 *The Cinema Handbook.* by Lescarboura, Austin Celestin. 507 p. illus. New York: Scientific American Pub. Co., 1921.

The book describes its contents in a long subtitle: "A guide to practical motion picture work of the non-theatrical order, particularly as applied to the reporting of news, to industrial and educational purposes, to advertising, selling and general publicity, to the production of amateur photoplays and to entertainment in the school, church, club, community center, and home."

912 *Cinema in Britain.* by Butler, Ivan. 307 p. illus. New York: A. S. Barnes, 1973.

This is the long-needed British equivalent to the American Blum-Mayer-Griffith books. Using a chronological format, beginning with 1895 and ending with 1971, the author selects a few important films for each year, usually notes the credits for same, and gives an historical-critical rationale for their inclusion. A few "Facts of Interest" close each yearly section.

Because of unfamiliarity and a lack of any memorable achievement in silent films, the book comes alive in 1925 when Hitchcock directed PLEASURE GARDEN. Probably the most discernible fact about the films prior to that time is the early use of subject matter dear to the hearts of British filmmakers: ROMEO AND JULIET (1908), HENRY VIII (1911), SCOTT'S ANTARCTIC EXPEDITION (1911), HAMLET (1913), 60 YEARS A QUEEN (1913). The films from the next four decades are mostly familiar, although titles are listed that one does not usually think of as being British films: THE AFRICAN QUEEN (1952), MOBY DICK (1956), SUDDENLY LAST SUMMER (1959), THE HAUNTING (1963), REPULSION (1965), etc. Another apparent fact is that not all worthwhile British films find their way to American screens; PEEPING TOM (1960), and HOFFMAN, a 1970 Peter Sellers' vehicle, have not received any perceptible attention in the U.S., yet Butler endorses them as fine films.

The text is informed, readable, and objective in its evaluations. Picture reproduction is quite good and the selection of illustrations is outstanding, with rare stills taking priority over the frequently used ones. Up to this time, the reader had to look at many different books to survey the British film: Low, Larsen, Balcon, Powell, Manvell, Gifford and others. Butler has performed a service in creating a book that is excellent as entertainment, history, or reference. Highly recommended.

913 *The Cinema in Denmark.* by Peetz-Schou, Morten. 35 p. paper Copenhagen: The Danish Government Film Foundation, 1970.

The role that can be played by government in fostering, nurturing and encouraging the art of film is documented in this short, provocative book. In May 1964 a new law was passed that placed a 15 percent tax on every admission ticket and a sliding scale tax on the profits made by licensed films. These revenues were allocated to a film foundation whose purpose is "to promote the art of the film." Grants are made to scriptwriters, loans, festivals, workshops, a film school, production guarantees, and awards. A film museum and books on film are also the responsibility of the foundation. Short films as well as feature films are considered.

The clear, logical explanation offered by this book should serve as a stimulus to similar efforts by other countries. A longer book which would examine and evaluate the law and the foundation, and their effect on Danish film, would be most valuable.

914 *Cinema in Finland.* edited by Hillier, Jim. 67 p. paper London: British Film Institute (Zoetrope in U.S.), 1975.

This collection of essays has two purposes: the first is to introduce the reader to the world of Finnish films and filmmakers; a second is to identify and describe those Finnish films which are available for showing in noncommercial situations outside of Finland. Two directors, Nyrki Tapiovaara and Risto Jarva, receive individual attention in the essays, which also include a historical survey, a 1936 article by Tapiovaara on "Film in the Social Struggle," and a chronology. The filmography which closes the booklet offers notes on the directors, credits, and commentary for the currently available Finnish films.

In this booklet an unfamiliar national cinema receives attention and for this reason, the publication is important. In addition, however, the material chosen here is informative, readable and ultimately useful. Recommended.

915 *The Cinema in Pakistan.* by Kabir, Alamgir. 194 p. illus. Dacca: Sandhani Pub., 1969.

This survey covers production, criticism, exhibition, etc. of films made in Pakistan, including documentaries and features. The author is director of the Dacca Film Institute.

916 *Cinema in Revolution.* edited by Schnitzer, Luda; and Schnitzer, Jean; and Martin, Marcel; and Robinson, David. 208 p. illus. New York: Hill and Wang, 1973.

A collection of essays and reminiscences of filmmaking during the twenties is the substance of this volume. Translated from Russian into French and then from French into English, the essays depict the "Heroic Era of Soviet Film." The original authors include Sergei Yutkevitch, Sergei Eisenstein, Grigori Alexandrov, Lev Kuleshov, Dziga Vertov, Griogri Kozintsev, Sergei Gerasimov, Vsevolod Pudovkin, Anatoli Golovnya, Alexander Dovzhenko, Yevgeni Gabrilovitch and Mikhail Romm—certainly an adequate representation of the Soviet film artisans of the twenties.

The book emphasizes the period in which the new art of cinema emerged as a revolutionary weapon, and the specific role played in its formation by a theatrical director, Vsevolod Meyerhold. Illustrations are adequately reproduced and Robinson has added an introduction, a glossary of persons and an index for this English edition. This is excellent but very specialized material.

917 *Cinema in Rural Nigeria.* by Morton-Williams, P. 195 p. paper Lagos, Nigeria: Federal Information Service, 1952.

This study of the impact of educational films on rural audiences in Nigeria is organized in a logical manner. Described are the films used, the showings, the reactions of the audience, evaluation of those reactions, analysis of the audience, and finally, a conclusion about the impact of the films.

918 *The Cinema in the Arab Countries.* edited by Sadoul, Georges. Beirut: Arab Cine/TV Center.

Based on reports given between 1962 and 1965 at round table meetings held in Alexandria and Beirut, this survey of film activities in 17 Arab countries is quite unusual. Statistical data are given as to films produced, number of theatres, traveling units, imported films, etc. A good reference.

919 *Cinema in the Eighties.* edited by Apria, Adriano 109 p. illus. paper New York: Zoetrope, 1981.

A collection of essays by filmmakers and film scholars.

920 *Cinema in the U.A.R.* by El-Mazzaoui, Farid. Ministry of Culture, 1972.

Combines a history of the Egyptian cinema and a survey of the creative artists involved.

921 *Cinema Mexicain.* by Camp, A. New York: Gordon Press, 1976.

922 *The Cinema of Alain Resnais.* by Armes, Roy 175 p. paper illus. New York: A. S. Barnes, 1968.

After a discussion of Resnais' attitude and approach to film direction, a short biography is offered. The major portion of the book is devoted to his short documentary films (including NIGHT AND FOG (1955) and his important feature films: HIROSHIMA, MON AMOUR (1959); LAST YEAR AT MARIENBAD (1961), MURIEL (1963); and MLA GUERRE EST FINIE (1966). A filmography and bibliography complete the book.

Resnais' contribution to the New Wave and the

subsequent effect of his work on today's films is indisputable. His films lend themselves to many interpretations and the ones presented here make interesting and challenging reading. The book has the value of helping a reader understand what the artist-director may be stating in his films; it should be used concurrently with a viewing of any of the films. Reading the book without having seen the films will diminish its usefulness.

923 *The Cinema of Alfred Hitchcock.* by Bogdanovich, Peter. 48 p. paper illus. New York: Musuem of Modern Art, 1963.

A short MOMA booklet in which Hitchcock's films —up to THE BIRDS (1963)—are discussed via questions and answers from an interview, 12-14 February, 1963. The format is the same used by Truffaut much later in his *Hitchcock.*

924 *The Cinema of Andrzej Wajda.* by Michatek, Bolestaw. 175p. paper illus. New York: A. S. Barnes, 1973.

A monograph on Andrzej Wajda, the director of GENERATION (1954), ASHES AND DIAMONDS (1958), KANAL (1955), EVERYTHING FOR SALE (1967), and LANDSCAPE AFTER THE BATTLE (1972). Written by some of Poland's most prominent critics, the volume includes a full filmography and other reference material.

925 *The Cinema of Carl Dreyer.* by Milne, Tom. 240 p. paper illus. New York: A. S. Barnes, 1970.

A study of the Danish director whose films are outstanding examples of light and composition.

926 *The Cinema of David Lean.* by Pratley, Gerald. 256 p. illus. New York: A. S. Barnes, 1974.

This study of the films of David Lean begins with a short history and appreciation. Each of his 15 films from IN WHICH WE SERVE (1942) to RYAN'S DAUGHTER (1970) is analyzed in detail in the separate chapters which follow. Cast, credits, and synopses are given along with critical comments from both Lean and the author. Accompanying the text are more than 100 fine stills from the films, and a gallery of David Lean players completes the volume. A very short index seems to be an afterthought.

The text is sympathetic and appreciative, but not always accurate. (For example, a careless error exists in the BLITHE SPIRIT (1945) section, where Constance Cummings is incorrectly identified in both picture and text.) Lean's attention to detail combined with his efforts to make the camera's observations intimate and revealing are noted. His ability to inspire fine performances from his players is recalled by both text and illustrations. Recommended.

927 *The Cinema of Dirk Bogarde.* by Hinxman, Margaret; and d'Arcy, Susan. 200 p. illus. New York: A. S. Barnes, 1975.

Director Joseph Losey provides the introduction to this most welcome volume. A few brief sections which are mostly candid photographs suggest the early days, the fan idol, Bogarde off-the-set, and Bogarde as actor. The accompanying text is factual, favorable and fan-oriented. It is the long filmography section which follows that gives the book its quality. The actor's films from DANCING WITH CRIME (1947) to THE SERPENT (1973) are described with stills, portraits, candids, synopses and review excerpts. Occasionally Bogarde is quoted as critic of his own films. A portrait gallery called "The Changing Face of Bogarde" concludes the book. It is not indexed.

Picture quality is consistently above average, and, with the exception of the careful, rather prejudiced opening text, the book is a well-deserved tribute to a fine actor. Nearly all of his films are British, but since many are shown frequently on American television, Bogarde is a well-known subject. This volume will interest and appeal to many readers. Recommended.

928 *The Cinema of Edward G. Robinson.* by Parish, James Robert; and Marill, Alvin H. 270 p. illus. New York: A. S. Barnes, 1972.

This volume resembles the *Citadel* series in size, format, title and style. An introductory biographical essay is followed by a list of Robinson's stage appearances and a few selected photographs of him in various theatrical roles. The major section on his films begins with THE BRIGHT SHAWL (1923) and ends with SONG OF NORWAY (1970). For most, cast and production credits, a synopsis, and a few selected critical excerpts are given. Brief sections on radio, television and short film appearances complete the book.

Fortunately, the picture quality in this volume is much improved over other books in this series (on Swanson, DeMille, James Stewart), but there are still a few which are badly reproduced. While the opening essay is critical to a degree, it would have been a greater service to the reader to place the pertinent author comments with the individual films

and enlarge them. Selecting excerpts is no substitute for a well-organized total critique. The lack of an index is a major omission and seriously limits the book's reference value. Although this volume is an improvement over some earlier Barnes' efforts, it still has some flaws.

929 *The Cinema of Ernst Lubitsch.* by Poague, Leland A. 183 p. illus. New York: A. S. Barnes, 1978.

A different critical approach is attempted in this study of the films of Ernst Lubitsch. In his effort to go beyond citing various examples of "The Lubitsch Touch," Poague tries to validate a changing and deepening of Lubitsch's style by contrasting various films— often an early silent with a later sound film. In part, his conclusions center about the humanism of the films which he perceives as changing from stylishly superficial to meaningful and hopeful.

Lubitsch made 28 films in Hollywood; for this study the following 13 are used: THE MARRIAGE CIRCLE (1924), LADY WINDERMERE'S FAN (1925), SO THIS IS PARIS (1926), THE STUDENT PRINCE (1927), THE LOVE PARADE (1929), ONE HOUR WITH YOU (1932), TROUBLE IN PARADISE (1932), THE MERRY WIDOW (1934), NINOTCHKA (1939), THE SHOP AROUND THE CORNER (1940), TO BE OR NOT TO BE (1942), HEAVEN CAN WAIT (1943), and CLUNY BROWN (1946).

A short bibliography, a filmography and an index complete the volume. Illustrations are well selected and reproduced.

Because of the relative unavailability of most of the films above (only the last five are ever shown— infrequently to be sure—on television), it will be difficult for the reader to possess any personal base upon which to approach this critical study. Since he must rely on the author's interpretations and judgement, the reader becomes somewhat passive. If he is willing to accept that role, he will be rewarded by a provocative approach to film criticism. Recommended.

930 *The Cinema of Federico Fellini.* by Rosenthal, Stuart. 190 p. illus. New York: A. S. Barnes, 1976.

An analysis of Fellini's films provided in overview fashion. Characters are the subject of the first part; what they might mean to Fellini and to the film viewer is explored. The techniques used by Fellini to present his characters are treated next. Final chapters examine certain films in depth, continually emphasizing Fellini's identification with his characters along with his attempts to review and accept his personal past by film interpretations of it.

A detailed filmography, a lengthy bibliography and an index complete the work. Illustrations have been well selected and are clearly reproduced.

Several previous volumes have considered the Fellini films individually. Rosenthal's treatment of them as a total work results in some new ideas and valid interpretations. Acceptable.

931 *The Cinema of Francois Truffaut.* by Petrie, Graham. 224 p. paper illus. New York: A. S. Barnes, 1970.

This book uses common themes rather than a chronological approach to explore the work of this gifted director. Complete filmography, many illustrations, and a bibliography.

932 *The Cinema of Frank Capra.* by Poague, Leland A. 252 p. illus. New York: A. S. Barnes, 1975.

In this volume, which is subtitled "An Approach to Film Comedy," the author has used portions of a dissertation he wrote at the University of Oregon. The first part of the text, which tends toward theory, analyzes Capra with regard to his critics, his comic vision, his film romances, his characters, his style and the Comic Tradition. Later portions deal specifically with the following Capra films: THE STRONG MAN (1926), LONG PANTS (1927), THE BITTER TEA OF GENERAL YEN (1933), IT HAPPENED ONE NIGHT (1934), MR. DEEDS GOES TO TOWN (1936), MR. SMITH GOES TO WASHINGTON (1939), MEET JOHN DOE (1941), IT'S A WONDERFUL LIFE (1946) and POCKETFUL OF MIRACLES (1961). Chapter notes, a detailed filmography, a lengthy bibliography, and an index are added. The volume is generously illustrated with film stills whose reproduction quality is generally quite good.

This evaluative study of Capra's work has been carefully prepared and documented; however, the often pedantic analysis offered may remind readers of the book's origin as a university thesis. As references on Capra, the supporting materials are impressive. Recommended.

933 *The Cinema of Fritz Lang.* by Jensen, Paul M. 223 p. paper illus. New York: A. S. Barnes, 1969.

Although small portions of this volume could be considered biographical, the greater portion is devoted specifically to Lang's films. The surprising number that he directed are recalled, described, and analyzed in detail and depth. Starting as a scriptwriter in 1917 and concluding with a 1960 film, THE 1000 EYES OF DR. MABUSE, Lang had a long and productive career in motion pictures.

Films given extended attention by the author are METROPOLIS (1926), M (1931), FURY (1936), YOU ONLY LIVE ONCE (1937), WOMAN IN THE WINDOW (1944), SCARLET STREET (1945), THE BIG HEAT (1953), HUMAN DESIRE (1954) and others. Stills, filmography, bibliography are included although an index is missing, limiting somewhat the book's reference value.

934 *The Cinema of Gene Kelly.* by Griffith, Richard. 16 p. paper illus. New York: Museum of Modern Art, 1962.

A three-page biography, some stills and a filmography take Kelly's career from FOR ME AND MY GAL (1942) to GIGOT (1962), which he directed. Dance numbers from the films are listed. Acceptable.

935 *The Cinema of Howard Hawks.* by Bogdanovich, Peter. 38 p. paper illus. New York: Musuem of Modern Art, 1962.

Published originally with a retrospective showing of Hawks' films in 1962, this volume consists of an enlarged filmography accompanied by Hawks' comments on each film. The many well-known films that Hawks directed and the quality of his comments would warrant a much extended volume. Until such time, this and Robin Wood's book are adequate.

936 *The Cinema of John Ford.* by Baxter, John. 176 p. paper illus. New York: A. S. Barnes, 1971.

In this tribute to John Ford, the opening chapter considers certain factors which help to interpret Ford's success as a director. History, style, writers, Catholicism and the Ford hero are discussed. Selected films are used to illustrate recurring themes, consistency of style, and Ford's expansive artistry. For example, THE INFORMER (1935) uses much of Ford's Irish background and heritage, while THE FUGITIVE (1947) and MARY OF SCOTLAND (1936) indicate Catholic themes and influence. STAGECOACH (1939), FORT APACHE (1948), and SHE WORE A YELLOW RIBBON (1949) show his use of natural settings (Monument Valley, especially) as symbols which could be linked with dramatic situations. The family as the basic strength of society is examplified in THE GRAPES OF WRATH (1940), MY DARLING CLEMENTINE (1946), and HOW GREEN WAS MY VALLEY (1941). Other sections deal with the sea, war, pilgrims, and the aging hero. A total Ford filmography from 1917-1966 and a very short bibliography complete the book. Illustrations tend to be somewhat dark and the poor contrast values diminish their effectiveness.

Earlier interviews (Peter Bogdanovich's *John Ford* and *Interviews with Film Directors*, by Sarris) have considered some of the same Ford materials. Even so, the selection of films and the discussion-analysis of them here is different and quite admirable. Many of the arguments proposed by Baxter are extreme in their subjectivity, others illuminate areas formerly taken for granted or ignored. Baxter's work here is of the same high quality as in his previous books.

937 *The Cinema of John Frankenheimer.* by Pratley, Gerald. 240 p. paper illus. New York: A. S. Barnes, 1969.

This volume differs somewhat in its format. Each of Frankenheimer's films is given a synopsis which is followed by some author comment. The most interesting portion follows next when Frankenheimer is quoted on each film. In a few instances script excerpts are given. Finally there is a short chapter on the many television dramas that Frankenheimer directed with several philosophical and attitudinal sections by the director.

Several results accrue to the reader. The films are covered in detail, with more objectivity from the director than from the author. A full portrait of Frankenheimer as a professional emerges, with much more frankness and self-evaluation than is usual in these small volumes. The book is nicely illustrated with both stills and candids but there is no index. The filmography is scattered as chapter headings rather than a final summary. This is an excellent volume in concept and final product.

938 *The Cinema of John Huston.* by Pratley, Gerald. 223 p. illus. New York: A. S. Barnes, 1977.

In a modification of a book-length interview, the author surveys the films of John Huston and includes a few digressions about his life, career, and philosophy. Taken from some 14 hours of tape recordings, the text tells of Huston's pre-film careers, his entrance to Hollywood as a writer, the first films at Warners, the Army films, the final studio films and his recent work as an international filmmaker. A trio of short sections—Huston as Actor, Personal Reflections, and An Appreciation by Pratley—conclude the book which is adequately illustrated.

The main attraction here is Huston's comments on his own films. He is uniformly generous, kind and forgiving in his recall of experiences with filmmaking, performers, and studio executives. This mellow self-image is in some contradiction to the one presented in books such as *John Huston, King Rebel* and *Picture*. Pratley's contribution in distilling and arranging the material should not be overlooked. It makes possible a new appreciation of this exciting, dedicated filmmaker. Recommended.

939 *The Cinema of Josef von Sternberg.* by Baxter, John. 192 p. paper illus. New York: A. S. Barnes, 1971.

Another excellent Baxter book, this adds interpretation, critical comment, and personal reminiscence to some familiar material. Production quality of the volume is outstanding. A fine collection of visuals, a bibliography and a filmography add greatly to the readable text, which is footnoted. The enigma and charisma of von Sternberg are explored and his films are described and evaluated. The analysis of I, CLAUDIUS (1937) is noteworthy. Recommended.

940 *The Cinema of Josephy Losey.* by Leahy, James. 175 p. paper illus. New York: A. S. Barnes, 1967.

This is one of the more successful volumes in this series, probably because of the subject's cooperation with the author. Sections of Losey interviews are placed in appropriate chapters of the text. After a short introductory essay, his films are considered individually and in chronological order starting with THE BOY WITH GREEN HAIR (1948) and ending with ACCIDENT (1967). A filmography and a bibliography complete the book, which is nicely illustrated.

The personal life of the director is not explored; however, some interesting information about him is offered, e.g., Losey was one of the Hollywood exiles of 1951; his work in cinema is influenced by Brecht; and his films represent a continual probing and testing of philosophies and value systems. An above-average tribute to a director who is underrated in America, this volume is a step toward further recognition. Would that the early films were a bit more available. This is a fine volume and might be rewarding to read along with *Losey on Losey*.

941 *A Cinema of Loneliness.* by Kolker, Robert Phillip. 395. p. illus. New York: Oxford University Press, 1980.

Five filmmakers—Arthur Penn, Stanley Kubrick, Francis Ford Coppola, Martin Scorsese, and Robert Altman— are the subjects of this study of recent films made in isolation and about isolation. The influence of other directors, movements, Hollywood corporate structure, and other factors on the five is noted as the author critically examines a few films selected from the total output of each. For example, in the case of Stanley Kubrick, the author concentrates on PATHS OF GLORY (1957), DR. STRANGE-GLOVE (1963), A CLOCKWORK ORANGE (1971), and BARRY LYNDON (1975). Recurring elements in the films, such as isolation, helplessness, violence, passivity, solitude, doomed heroism, etc., are noted and an attempt to view them as reflection of the recent American condition is made. The volume is indexed and contains photographs, notes, and a filmography.

Some engrossing observations about the films of the sixties and seventies are made in Kolker's in-depth analyses. Intelligent and persuasive, he recognizes that his is not the final word on these still active filmmakers; for the present, however, what he says will be provocative and stimulating to the reader in search of a critic with an original viewpoint. Recommended.

942   *The Cinema of Luis Bunuel.* by Buache, Freddy. 207 p. paper illus. New York: A.S. Barnes, 1973.

From UN CHIEN ANDALOU (1928) to TRISTANA (1970), the author explores and examines all of Bunuel's films up to 1971. The individuality and often sacrilegious views that characterize Bunuel's films, and the varied audience reactions to them, are noted.

The book was translated from the French by Peter Graham and has acceptable illustrations and a filmography. An index is also provided.

943   *Cinema of Mystery.* by London, Rose. III p. paper illus. New York: Bounty (Crown), 1975.

A most interesting structure, which offers Edgar Allan Poe as the originator of the cinema of suspense, is employed here. After initial biographical chapter, Poe's themes, fears and obsessions are related to various films. Included are premature burial, return of the dead, omens of death (cats and ravens), blood, the heart, time ticking away, the worm, decay, the ape-beast, haunted palaces, and so forth. Obviously the Roger Corman—Vincent Price films of Poe's stories receive extended attention.

The many illustrations are excellent and the text is informative, and at times, provocative. The popularization of a subject that warrants serious treatment is somewhat disappointing. The reader may desire an expanded text that is more critical and less descriptive. An introduction and index would have added substantially to reader use and understanding.

In summary, the book offers an excellent subject handled in minimal fashion. Acceptable.

944   *The Cinema of Orson Welles.* by Bogdanovich, Peter. 16 p. paper illus. New York: Museum of Modern Art, 1961.

The major Welles' films are listed and analyzed.

945   *The Cinema of Orson Welles.* by Cowie, Peter. 207 p. paper illus. New York: A. S. Barnes, 1965.

The title refers to the films that Welles had directed, not the ones in which he acted under someone else's direction (COMPULSION (1959), THE VIP'S (1963), etc.). His films are few in number, only ten.

Each of his films is discussed, with major attention given to CITIZEN KANE (1941), THE MAGNIFICENT AMBERSONS (1942) and THE TRIAL (1963). One could argue with the author's almost complete dismissal of THE STRANGER (1946), or with his preference for THE TRIAL (1963) over THE LADY FROM SHANGHAI or TOUCH OF EVIL (1958). MACBETH (1948), OTHELLO (1951), MR. ARKADIN (1955), and CHIMES AT MIDNIGHT (1966) are the other films evaluated. Many illustrations show the range of Welles as an actor. The appendices include several articles by or about Welles, a filmography, listings of his other creative efforts, and a long bibliography. Although the reader may take issue with the evaluations, no objection should be raised about the book. It is excellent and recommended for all readers.

946   *The Cinema of Otto Preminger.* by Pratley, Gerald. 190 p. paper illus. New York: A. S. Barnes, 1971.

The first section of this book considers films made while Preminger was a contract director for various studios (1931-1952); films made by him as an independent filmmaker are examined in the second section (1953-1971). A large portion of the book is taken from interviews, press releases, and articles—all written by Preminger. Supporting the many Preminger statements are cast credits and a short synopsis for each of the films.

While Preminger does not remember every film, there is more than enough comment to give the reader a good idea of Preminger as director-producer. His ideas and methods are colorful, opinionated and stimulating. Pratley's task in preparing this volume seems to be primarily in selection, arrangement, and editing of Preminger's prose. This he has done with economy and style.

The illustrations are small but reproduction is better and sharper than is usual in these books. A final section offers data on Preminger's stage productions both here and in Europe. The format of the book, together with Preminger's open prose, will please most readers. Recommended.

947 *The Cinema of Roman Polanski.* by Butler, Ivan. 191 p. paper illus. New York: A. S. Barnes, 1970.

This volume pays tribute to the director of only five feature films, two of which were not successful with either the critics or the public. A brief biography is followed by a discussion of the short films, emphasizing TWO MEN AND A WARDROBE (1957), WHEN ANGELS FALL (1958), and MAMMALS (1959). Each of the five features is given a complete chapter of descriptive and critical analysis.

The illustrations are plentiful and clearly reproduced and a list of interviews and articles are included. Subjectively, this positive look at a young filmmaker is a tribute denied many older directors whose accomplishments are far greater. Objectively, the book is a nicely produced account of Polanski and his films to date (the Sharon Tate tragedy is not discussed).

948 *The Cinema of Satyajit Ray.* by Das Gupta, Chidinanda. illus. Bangalore, India: 1978.

A critical appreciation of Indian filmmaker Satyajit Ray by a professional contemporary, this survey presents its subject as a classicist who combines the traditions of India with some aspects of Western culture.

949 *The Cinema of Sidney Poitier.* by Keyser, Lester J.; and Ruszkowski, Andre H. 192 p. illus. New York: A. S. Barnes, 1980.

What a fine complement this volume is to Sidney Poitier's autobiography, *This Life.* Although some biographical background is provided, the emphasis is on the films. Using illustrations of remarkable clarity, the book covers Poitier's film career from NO WAY OUT (1950) to A PIECE OF THE ACTION (1977). The films are treated in chronological groupings: The Road to Stardom (1950-1957); Recognition and Success (1958-1966); The Three Top Vehicles (1967); Response to Public Challenge (1968-1971); and Director and Producer Poitier (1972-). The last category seems prophetic since Poitier directed the enormously popular comedy, STIR CRAZY, in 1980. A filmography, bibliography, and an index complete the book.

The authors have provided a critical examination of Poitier's films that never overlooks the changing image of the black in Hollywood films. Augmented

by a handsome physical production and some strong supporting elements, their appreciation of Poitier's work should please many readers.

950 *The Cinema of Stanley Kubrick.* by Kagan, Norman. 204 p. illus. New York: Holt, Rinehart and Winston, 1972.

Kagan's study of Kubrick's films employs a structured approach. For each film he gives a visual summary and also notes lines, plots, sound effects, music, etc. Kubrick's comments, if any, are quoted and there is a summarization of critical reaction. Kagan then offers his own analysis and evaluation of the film. All of the above procedure is explained in an introduction and there is one summary chapter on problems and prospects. Some notes and a filmography appear at the book's end.

Kagan's attempt to familiarize the reader with the film before discussing it critically is sound. Unfortunately, at times, the description takes up more space than the criticism. Acceptable.

951 *Cinema of the Fantastic.* by Steinbrunner, Chris; and Goldblatt, Burt. 282 p. illus. New York: Saturday Review Press, 1972.

In this collection of fifteen extended film reviews, some attempt is made to create a developmental history of the fantasy film by using a chronological arrangement: A TRIP TO THE MOON (1902); METROPOLIS (1927); FREAKS (1932); KING KONG (1933); THE BLACK CAT (1934); THE BRIDE OF FRANKENSTEIN (1935); MAD LOVE (1935); FLASH GORDON (1936); THINGS TO COME (1936); THE THIEF OF BAGDAD (1940); BEAUTY AND THE BEAST (1946); THE THING (1951); 20,000 LEAGUES UNDER THE SEA (1954); INVASION OF THE BODY SNATCHERS (1956); FORBIDDEN PLANET (1956).

Each film is described by cast and credit data, some introductory narrative, a lengthy plot description, and a few concluding statements. The illustrations accompanying each include stills and enlarged frames from the films. Reproduction is simply bad in several cases and in no case is it ever better than acceptable. The author's selection is mixed: a few films have not been considered in earlier books— MAD LOVE, FREAKS, THE BLACK CAT—while several others have been overly analyzed—KING KONG, FLASH GORDON, BEAUTY AND THE BEAST. The narrative is average and seems more at ease in description than in evaluation and criticism. What would have been a pleasant paperback original has been produced as an expensive hardcover edition.

952   *Cinema of the Maestros.* by Rondi, Gian Luigi. 455 p. illus. Rome: Rusconi, 1979.

A collection of interviews with 57 film directors and one film actress (Ingrid Bergman).

953   *Cinema of the Third World.* by Student Association of Auckland University. 78 p. paper illus. Auckland, N.Z.: The Association, 1972.

Thepolitical aspect of motion pictures was the general theme for a film festival held in conjunction with the 14th New Zealand Universities' Arts Festival in 1972. This volume contains notes, illustrations, and bibliographical references about the films that were shown.

954   *Cinema One* Books (A series). Various publishers beginning in the 1960s. Paperback and hardcover; illus.

This attractive and well-produced film series is concerned with directors, technicians, actors, genres, and aesthetics. The books in the *Cinema One* series are published in Britain by Secker and Warburg in association with the British Film Institute. They are edited either by *Sight and Sound* or by the Educational Advisory Service of BFI. In the U.S. they have been published by Indiana University Press, Doubleday, and Viking.

The volumes are consistent in the high quality of the text and the illustrations provided. They are usually available in both hardbound and paperback editions. Older titles are frequently revised and updated.

This excellent series includes the following titles (with authors): *Losey on Losey* (Tom Milne); *How it Happened Here* (Kevin Brownlow); *Godard* (Richard Roud); *The New Wave* (Peter Graham); *Signs and Meaning in the Cinema* (Peter Wollen); *Buster Keaton* (David Robinson); *Billy Wilder* (Axel Madsen); *Pasolini on Pasolini* (Oswald Stack); *Rouben Mamoulian* (Tom Milne); *Horizons West* (Jim Kitses); *Hollywood Cameramen: Sources of Light* (Charles Higham); *Samuel Fuller* (Nicholas Garnham); *Melville on Melville* (Rui Nogueira); *Jean-Marie Straub* (Richard Roud); *Sirk on Sirk* (John Halliday); *Studies in Documentary* (Alan Lovell & Jim Hillier); *Val Lewton: The Reality of Terror* (Joel E. Siegel); *Underworld USA* (Colin McArthur); *Orson Welles* (Joseph McBride); *Visconti* (Geoffrey Nowell-Smith); *Theories of Film* (Anthony Tudor); *Truffaut* (Don Allen); *Westerns* (Phillip French); *Kazan on Kazan* (Michael Ciment); *Resnais* (John Ward); *Howard Hawks* (Robin Wood).

955   *The Cinema Organ.* by Foort, Reginald. 199 p. illus. Vestal, N.Y.: Vestal Press, 1970 (1932).

This reprint of an early thirties' volume explores the pipe organ that was a typical fixture in the movie palaces of that time. Specific installations are described and some suggestions for playing the organ are given.

956   *Cinema Parade: Fifty Years of Film Shows.* by Bird, John H. 119 p. illus. Birmingham, England: Corners Brothers, 1947.

An early history of film exhibition in Great Britian.

957   *Cinema 79.* edited by Castell, David. 143 p. paper illus. England: BCW Publishing; U.S.: Two Continents, New York, 1978.

A collection of articles dealing mostly with current films such as SUPERMAN (1979), SATURDAY NIGHT FEVER (1978) and general topics such as animation, sci-fi films, the Oscars, etc. This annual has an asset in its copious illustrations. Many are full-page, some are in color, and nearly all are clearly reproduced.

Attractive in its production and often fun to read, this book is an unexpected pleasure.

958   *Cinema Sources: A Guide to the Film Reference Collection of Memorial Library.* by Richardson, Larry L. 65 p. paper Madison, Wisc.: Memorial Library, 1979.

This guide to reference sources on films is arranged in four sections: film reviews; plots, performers, filmmakers, scripts; film research; and odds, ends, oscars. Good annotations and a wide selection of titles make this a valuable tool.

959   *Cinema Star Albums (A Series).* paper illus. Seattle, Wash.: Cinema Books By Post.

The *Cinema Star Albums* are softcover books with glossy dust jackets that are written and published in Japan. Each volume contains from 100 to over 250 pages of high gloss photos, many a full page in size, in both black and white and in color. Most volumes have English captions in addition to Japanese. They are rather expensive when compared to their American counterparts.

Subjects are listed with the number of pages for each volume indicated: *Marilyn Monroe* (240) (160), *Bri-*

gitte Bardot (256), *Farrah Fawcett* (160), *Catherine Deneuve* (256), *Audrey Hepburn* (184) (112), *Alain Delon* (176) (172) (144), *James Dean* (168) (210), *Jane Fonda* (184), *Steve McQueen* (200), *Franco Nero* (176), *Garbo and Dietrich* (240), *Redford and Hoffman* (193), *Giuliano Gemma* (194), *Clint Eastwood* (176) (160), *Vivien Leigh* (168), *Elizabeth Taylor* (192), *Charlton Heston* (188), *Paul Newman* (178), *Nathalie Delon* (144), *Olivia Hussey* (160) (112), *Faye Dunaway* (170), *Katharine Ross* (158), *Bruce Lee* (212) (128), *Jacqueline Bisset* (176), *Sophia Loren* (190), *Clark Gable* (176), *Dominique Sanda* (150), *Jean Paul Belmondo* (214), *Candice Bergen* (176), *Julie Andrews* (184), *John Wayne* (224), *Claudia Cardinale* (109), *Barbra Streisand* (176), *Al Pacino* (158), *Robert Redford* (176), *Humphrey Bogart* (224), *Jack Nicholson* (176), *Sylvia Kristel* (152), *Sean Connery* (176), *Charles Bronson* (184), *Burt Reynolds* (176), *Tatum O'Neal* (168), *Marlon Brando* (192), *Ingrid Bergman* (160), *Peter Fonda* (160), *Elvis Presley* (192), *Grace Kelly* (184), *Romy Schneider* (176), *James Coburn* (176), *Gregory Peck* (194), *Roger Moore* (180), *Jodie Foster* (128), *Robert DeNiro* (160), *Charlie Chaplin* (192), *Brooke Shields* (104), *Jean Gabin* (192), *Dustin Hoffman* (168), *Cary Grant* (192).

In addition to the books on film stars there are such other titles available as: *Film Annual 1975* (276), *Film Annual 1976* (292), *Film Annual 1977* (282), *Film Annual 1978* (288), *Film Annual 1979* (276), *Actresses of the 1920's* (238), *50 Stars Pin Ups* (136), *Screen Lovers* (184), *Actresses of 1930's* (208), *Kung Fu!* (183), *The Western* (256), *Trains in the Movies* (200).

960 *Cinema Stunts.* by Cripwell, K. R. 64 p. illus. London: Collins English Library, 1977.

An explanation of film stunts aimed at the young reader.

961 *Cinema, the Magic Vehicle.: A Guide to Its Achievement—Journey Two: The Cinema in the Fifties.* by Garbicz, Adam; and Klinowski, Jacek. 551 p. illus. Metuchen, N.J.: Scarecrow, 1979.

In what is essentially a critically annotated filmography of films of the fifties, the authors continue the work begun in an earlier volume. That book covered 36 years and reviewed 447 films. Here we have a few more than 300 films, complete with credits, cast, synopsis and critical comment. Access to the films is by a chronological table of contents, a title index and a director index.

The book has a certain reference value, but the infor-

mation listed here can be found easily elsewhere. Thus, the value of the book depends primarily on the criticism offered. In most instances it is acceptable but rather uninvolving.

962 *Cinema, the Magic Vehicle.: A Guide to Its Achievement.* by Garbicz, Adam; and Klinowski, Jacek. 551 p. Metuchen, N.J.: Scarecrow Press, 1975.

Despite its awkward title, this volume offers much in its film-by-film approach to motion picture history and accomplishment. Subtitled "Journey One: The Cinema Through 1949," the book presents an annotated filmography of several hundred feature films selected because they are "good... exciting to watch...relatively little known...or of a certain aesthetic standard...."

Following a chronological title index, there is a short resume of important events in cinema history. The collection of mini-essays on specific films which follows is arranged chronologically from 1913 to 1949. Each entry contains the title, director, cast and production credits, country of origin, length in reels and feet, release date, plot description, historical placement, and critical comment. The extent of the latter three components varies with each film. The number of films considered for each year seems in direct proportion to the maturity of the film art, i.e., 1913 lists two titles while 1949 lists 23. Symbols are used to designate films of first, second and third rank. Separate indexes for directors and film titles are provided.

There are many strengths in this rather personal historical filmography. Selection is very good and includes many foreign films; information and annotation have been carefully checked for accuracy; the critical approach emphasizes sociology, history and aesthetics; the format of the book makes it both an easy-to-use reference and a collection of enjoyable film criticism for reading. Recommended.

963 *The Cinema Today.* by Spencer, Douglas A.; and Waley, Hubert D. 202 p. illus. New York: Oxford University Press, 1939.

This volume offers a general description of the film industry with attention given to (1) technical matters-cameras, projectors, sound recording devices, film processing, etc; (2) economic aspects—distribution, exhibition, projection etc.; and (3) sociological topics—film genres, social effects of films, use of educational films, etc. The book was revised and updated in 1946 and in 1956.

964 *Cinema Verite.* by Issari, M. Ali. 208 p. illus. East Lansing, Mich.: Michigan State University Press, 1971.

After presenting many conflicting statements about Cinema Verite, the first portion of this volume attempts to define it. The author then covers the history of Cinema Verite, the French (Jean Rouch) versus the American school (Richard Leacock), some brief biographies of Cinema Verite filmmakers —Mario Ruspoli, Jacques Rozier, Chris Marker, Albert Maysles, William C. Jersey, Jr., Frederick Wiseman—and the recent technological developments that facilitate Cinema Verite. Extended bio-filmographies of Dziga Vertov and Robert Flaherty are included in the appendices.

The book is indexed and a multilanguage bibliography is included. Illustrations are few for a book of this type and the selection is not impressive. Since this is one of the first books devoted to Cinema Verite, it deserves consideration. However, it seems to be more a "paste-up collection" of quotation data and opinions than an original work, and may leave the reader a bit disappointed.

965 *Cinema Verite in America.: Studies in Uncontrolled Documentary.* by Mamber, Stephen. 288 p. illus. Cambridge, Mass.: MIT Press, 1974.

Any volume dealing with cinema verite must define the term. Mamber calls for "a filming method employing hand-held cameras and live, synchronous sound." Recognizing the absence of a filmmaking philosophy in this statement, further clarification is offered by adding that its essential element is "the filming of real people in uncontrolled situations."

In this volume, the author concentrates on the work of American filmmakers—Robert Drew, Richard Leacock, D. A. Pennebaker, the Maysles brothers, and Frederick Wiseman. An opening background chapter makes note of the contributions of Dziga Vertov, Robert Flaherty and others to the cinema verite form. Following chapters discuss in detail the major films of the Americans listed above. There are notes, filmographies, a bibliography, and an index to support the text. Film rental sources are given and the films for a course are suggested. The volume is illustrated but reproduction has given a faded, light appearance to many of the visuals.

The selection of content and its subsequent treatment by the author is most satisfying. Treating in detail the work of filmmakers who are usually given a page or so in general survey books helps to correct the neglect of these artists by film bookers and audiences. A pertinent topic has been given careful scholarly attention and the result is an unusual and rewarding volume. Recommended.

966 *Cinema Yesterday and Today.* by Clair, Rene. 260 p. paper illus. New York: Dover Books, 1972.

Clair has written a revision of his earlier book, *Reflections on the Cinema*, adding material and comment reflecting a 1970 viewpoint. Thus, three periods predominate: the earlier two, when the Clair of 1950 "conversed" with the Clair of 1930, and now, the modern seventies. Clair's comments are wise, well-stated and of lasting pertinence. His range of topics is very wide, and all are handled with professional ease. The device of three "Clairs" who can exchange opinions works well; the resulting total statement is remarkably unified and evidences Clair's passionate involvement with film.

The translation by Stanley Appelbaum is graceful, and there is a short, appropriate introduction by R. C. Dale. Illustrations, and separate indexes for films and persons, have been supplied for this American edition. This is a welcome revision of an important early work with, now, an extra dimension. Recommended.

967 *The Cinema 1952.* edited by Manvell, Roger. New York: Arno, 1978.

A yearbook covering cinema in all its aspects with essays, reviews, illustrations, indexes, etc. Books for 1950 and 1951 are also available.

968 *Cinema '80.* edited by Castell, David. 160 p. illus. New York: Hippocrene, 1980.

The fifth annual in a series, this one contains seven articles and many illustrations, including some full color portraits.

969 *Cinemabilia: Catalogue of Film Literature.* 264 p. paper illus. New York: Cinemabilia, 1972.

This catalogue lists some 3500 entries, alphabetized by author, under 17 headings. There is no appreciable annotation and absolutely no evaluation. An index lists names of authors and selected personalities.

While this volume can be used with efficiency by persons familiar with film literature, the general reader and even the researcher will find the going a bit rough if they are looking for something which is rare, unusual, or unique. It is necessary to guess the subject category or to know the author. A reference book with limited potential.

970 *Cinemania: Aspects of Filmic Creation.* by Bennett, Alfred Gordon. 432 p. illus. London: Jarrolds, 1937.

This volume on film aesthetics was one of the earliest to make a plea for the recognition of the film director as an "auteur." Other topics include the art and mechanics of filmmaking, film criticism, production procedures, film rights, and selected examples of outstanding films. The past, the present (1937), and the future of films are discussed. A bibliography and an index complete the work.

971 *Cinematic Design.* by Hacker, Leonard. 193 p. illus. Boston: American Photographic Pub. Co., 1931.

The title in this case refers to the total design of a film rather than to specific forms of design such as set or costume design. The first rather short section considers theoretical concepts about form, rhythm, color, relativity, spatial relationships, pictorial composition and other similar topics. The second and longer section offers nine experimental scenarios for the reader-learner's possible use. Typical titles are a ferry tale, musical shoes, afternoon of a canoe, clock fantasy, symphony mechanique, and symphony natural and synthetic.

972 *The Cinematic Imagination.* by Murray, Edward. 330 p. New York: Frederick Ungar, 1972.

A specialized, scholarly exploration of the effect that film has had upon writers and their product. The works of modern playwrights are examined with a view toward discovering cinematic techniques—montage, parallel editing, dissolves, etc.—in the writings of O'Neill, Brecht, Tennessee Williams, Gertrude Stein, Arthur Miller and others. A second section attempts a similar study of novelists, including Dreiser, Joyce, Woolf, Dos Passos, Hemingway, Steinbeck and others.

Interrelationships between film and the two literary forms are suggested and a few large concepts are stated, such as: "The literary history of our times has to a large extent been that of the development of the cinematic imagination," and "Literary works based on cinematic technique often lose power when transferred to the screen."

The explorations of the novels and plays sometimes seem verbose and digressive. The analyses offered are likely to be at variance with those of the informed reader. The author rarely considers alternative interpretations, usually opting for the one that suits his argument. The book is documented, however, by copious footnotes and references. For a full

appreciation of this work, the reader must come to it with a wide experience in playgoing, film-viewing and novel-reading. A willingness to wade through a long and demanding argument is also required. The reader with these qualifications will be rewarded with a provocative, stimulating look at film's effect on other media.

Somewhat similar material appears in Richardson's *Literature and Film* and in Van Nostrand's *The Denatured Novel.*

973 *The Cinematic Muse: Critical Studies in the History of French Cinema.* by Thiher, Allen. 216 p. illus. Columbia, Mo.: University of Missouri Press, 1979.

A personal history of the French film, from UN CHIEN ANDALOU (1928) to TWO OR THREE THINGS I KNOW ABOUT HER (1966), this survey relates the films to other parts of the French culture.

The influential filmmakers such as Bunuel, Bresson, Clair, Vigo, etc., are evaluated critically. Illustrations, a bibliography, and an index accompany the text.

974 *Cinematics.* by Weiss, Paul. 227 p. Carbondale, Ill.: Southern Illinois University Press, 1975.

Paul Weiss is a professor of philosophy whose many books and articles have explored such diverse areas as sports, the arts, father-son relationships, and religion. In this volume he approaches the subject of film aesthetics from a philosophical viewpoint. His approach is traditional in the ordering of his topics: definition, script, performers, cinemakers, montagists, directors, five varieties of art films, elicited emotions, appearances and realism. Propaganda and educational films, disclosive and documentary films, Escapist and experimental films are discussed in that order. His departure from the traditional takes the form of an interrupted text. In preparing his final manuscript he has included the criticism and comments of five film scholars at the exact points where the questions arise. It is somewhat similar to reading a perfectly edited manuscript rather than a corrected final publication.

The quality of both Weiss' discourse and the interruptions is uniformly high. Most of the issues indigenous to film aesthetics are raised and explored on a nonobfuscating level. Only occasionally is there a slight tendency to be verbose or obscure. The temptation to be intellectually dazzling has been avoided in favor of a comprehensive, provocative exploratory approach. The book contains notes, references and an index. This volume is one of the most reward-ing treatises on film aesthetics to appear in years. It is readable, informative, stimulating, and sparkles with philosophical and intellectual challenges. Highly recommended.

975 *The Cinematograph and Natural Science.* by Donaldson, Leonard. 130 p. illus. London: Ganes, 1912.

This historical book deals with "the achievements and possibilities of cinematography as an aid to scientific research." A supplement taken from *The Bioscope* offers sidelights on scientific applications of cinematography.

976 *The Cinematograph Book.* edited by Jones, Bernard Edward. 216 p. illus. New York: Cassell, 1916.

Called "a complete practical guide to the taking and projecting of cinematograph pictures," this early volume also discusses combination printing, trick films, illusions of size, motion and distance, exhibi-tion, legal restrictions, etc.

977 *The Cinematograph Book.* edited by Jones, Bernard E. 215 p. illus. Lon-don: Cassell, 1925.

This early volume on filmmaking was called "a com-plete and practical guide to taking and projecting cinematograph pictures."

978 *Cinematographer's Field Guide: Mo-tion Picture Camera Films.* edited by Kodak Staff. 98 p. illus. Rochester, N.Y.: Kodak, 1980.

This is the third edition of a small, hardcover book that deals with the 15 types of motion picture film that Kodak produces. In addition there is an abun-dance of other information on shooting, equipment, accessories, packaging, etc.

979 *see 978*

980 *Cinematographers Laszlo Kovacs and Vilmos Zsigmond.* edited by Reed, Rochelle. 28 p. paper illus. Washing-ton, D.C.: American Film Institute, 1974.

This first issue of the fourth volume of the *Dialogue on Film* series contains interviews with two cinema-tographers who are currently very active on the Hol-lywood scene. The Kovacs transcript (April 27, 1974) has been printed in full, but the Zsigmond

section (March 3, 1974) is partial, with portions previously published. A filmography for both men is included.

981 *Cinematographic Annual, 1930, 1931.* edited by Hall, Hal. 606, 425 p. New York: Arno, 1972.

These yearbooks, published originally by The American Society of Cinematographers, contain over 70 articles. Among the titles in the 1930 volume (606 pages) are: "Cinematography As An Art Form" ; "Motion Pictures in Natural Color" ; "Architectural Acoustics" ; "Cinemachinery For the Personal Movie."

The 1931 volume (425 pages) includes: "Making Matte Shots" ; "Projection Arcs" ; "The Larger Screen" ; "Motion Pictures Must Move."

The range of subjects is broad, but they will be primarily of interest to researchers and historians.

982 *Cinematographic Institutions.* by In-ternational Film and Television Council. 100 p. paper illus. Paris: UNESCO, 1973.

This book, number 68 in the UNESCO *Reports and Papers on Mass Communication* series, examines ex-isting cinematographic institutions in the hope that they may serve as models for developing nations. The text notes three major classifications: institu-tions for particular categories of films, institutions for particular stages and functions, and overall insti-tutions. A large group of appendixes describes varia-tions on the above groups. The abundant information offered here can be used in a variety of ways. In addition to providing background, models, suggestions, advice, and possibilities, the text gives names, addresses, and locations of some important but little known institutions. Recommended.

983 *Cinematographic Techniques in Bi-ology and Medicine.* edited by Bur-ton, Alexis L. 512 p. illus. New York: Academic Press, 1971.

A collection of chapters by different authors about the techniques and equipment necessary for produc-ing films in biology and medicine. An open section deals with film—its properties, storage, processing, and handling. The next section deals with the hard-ware, cameras and projectors. Filmmaking is cov-ered with special chapters on time-lapse, X-ray and high speed cinematography, as well as on animation, microscope filming and oscilloscope cameras. Sec-tions on editing and projection are provided, and the book closes with four chapters on television, the TV camera, the film chain and the videotape machine.

The qualities found in the book are uniformly high: the text, visuals, charts, diagrams, plates, index, etc. all contribute to the book's excellence. Certain sections are technical and demand background in mathematics and science for full comprehension. The book may be useful as a model for future volumes dealing with filmmaking in other specific disciplines—chemistry, physics, dance, etc. It is comprehensive, thorough and structured.

With the growing interest of medical libraries in nonprint materials, this book is a natural for such institutions. It has much value, too, in colleges and universities for its valuable suggestions on making teaching films in biology and medicine. It is highly recommended.

984 *Cinematography: A Guide for Film Makers and Film Teachers.* by Malkiewicz, J. Kris.; and Rogers, Robert E. 216 p. illus. New York: Van Nostrand Reinhold, 1973.

An attractive volume intended for the person with some experience in filmmaking. It covers the same topics as many others in the field—cameras, filters, lights, techniques, etc.—but the production of this book is outstanding. Good visuals predominate, and both a bibliography and index are included. Acceptable.

985 *Cinematography and Talkies.* by Cameron, James Ross; and Dubray, Joseph Albert. 255 p. illus. Woodmont, Conn.: Cameron, 1932.

An early text which includes a survey of techniques and apparatus, a historical explanation of photography, early experiments, light, lenses, motion picture film, titles, cutting, trick photography, animation, etc. Some advertising material is added for good measure.

986 CINERAMA HOLIDAY. 20 p. paper illus. New York: Cinerama Publishers, 1954.

This 1954 Cinerama effort was the work of producer Louis de Rochemont and pictured the experiences of two couples as they visited various foreign locales. The production and the story are described, the musical numbers by Morton Gould are listed, and there is a diagram of the three-projector system of Cinerama. Photographic work is very poor and the booklet appears to have been assembled in haste.

987 CIRCUS WORLD. 32 p. paper illus. New York: National Publishers, 1964.

This souvenir book is divided into two parts: 1) the world of the circus, and 2) an inside view. Stars John Wayne, Claudia Cardinale, and Rita Hayworth receive full-page attention along with producer Samuel Bronston and director Henry Hathaway. Other cast and production credits for the 1964 film are indicated.

988 CISCO PIKE. by Norton, Bill L. 165 p. paper illus. New York: Bantam Books, 1971.

Script of the 1971 film directed by Norton. Contains cast credits and four articles: 1) CISCO PIKE and its parts (Gerald Ayres); 2) "The Cycle Becomes a Maze" (Jacoba Atlas); 3) "Kris Kristofferson: Lonely Sound From Nashville" (Edwin Miller); 4) "Did You Enjoy Working with the Actors?" "Oh, Yeah. Especially the Nonactors," an interview with Bill Norton conducted by Norma Whittaker.

989 *The* CITIZEN KANE *Book.* by Kael, Pauline. 440 p. illus. Boston:Little, Brown, 1971.

This is one of the most popular and widely known film books to appear in recent years. It combines Pauline Kael's brilliant long piece, "Raising Kane," with the shooting script of CITIZEN KANE (1941) by Herman J. Mankiewicz and Orson Welles. The cutting continuity, which is a record of the final film, is also included. Kael's position is that Mankiewicz is responsible for much of CITIZEN KANE, and has not received appropriate acknowledgement; accordingly, she offers a listing of his screenwriting credits, from THE ROAD TO MANDALAY in 1929 to THE PRIDE OF ST. LOUIS in 1952. An index to "Raising Kane" is also provided. In all her writing Kael combines scholarship, research, intelligence, wit and ability. "Raising Kane" is already recoginzed as a classic article.

The book has been produced in an oversized format with large type and sufficient space for the many frame enlargements from the film. Kael's contribution, added to the scripts of the film that many think is the greatest ever created, make this volume essential reading. Hopefully it will be a model for future books.

990 *The Civil War in Motion Pictures.* compiled by Spehr, Paul C. 109 p. paper Washington, D.C.: Library of Congress, 1961.

This listing of films produced in the United States since 1897 is arranged into theatrical films, educational films, and newsreels. An index and information about sources of the films are also included.

991   *The Civil War on the Screen and Other Essays.* by Spears, Jack. 240 p. illus. New York: A. S. Barnes, 1977.

A curious but appealing mixture of topics appears in this collection of four essays. The longest is devoted to a very detailed examination of films dealing with the Civil War, its period, or its effects. Beginning with UNCLE TOM'S CABIN (1903) to ALVAREZ KELLY (1966), the essay treats, in a general chronological fashion, hundreds of films which have Civil War themes. The silent screen is covered with a historian's enthusiasm and delight while the sound era gives most attention to GONE WITH THE WIND (1939). The essay form is most appropriate to the presentation which embroiders themes, characters, and incidents into an interpretation of the Civil War as reflected in films. It is unfortunate that no final total summary of all the aspects examined is offered.

The remaining three essays are devoted to biographical appreciations of Alla Nazimova, Edwin S. Porter, and Louis Wolheim. Selection of these neglected subjects is laudable, as is the treatment accorded them. A rare venture into film biography is presented by Spears. The essays are supported by appropriate visuals, filmographies (except for Porter), and an index.

This is material that has appeal for a potentially large audience. The Civil War section can be studied by students at any level or it can provide a variety of recollections to the general reader. The three biographies will be catnip to the film buff. All in all, this is a remarkable work.

992   *The Clapperboard Book of the Cinema.* by Halliwell, Leslie; and Murray, Graham. 1263 p. illus. London: Hart-Davis MacGibbon, 1975.

993   *The Clapperboard Film Quiz Book.* by Murray, Graham. 128 p. illus. London: Independent Television Books Arrow Books, 1978.

Based on the Granada Television series, "Clapperboard," this quiz book contains illustrations and answers.

994   *Clark Gable.* by Carpozi, George Jr. 160 p. paper illus. New York: Pyramid Books, 1961.

This biography is similar to the others in its surface coverage of the personality of Gable. It is largely a chronological recital of events. In its discussion of Gable's film roles and work, however, it is very good. The occasional padding (a chapter, midway, on the star system), and the careless contradictions (p. 70: "in 1936 Carole Lombard was just another of the many dozens of potentially great screen actresses" ; p. 99: "By the time she began dating Clark Gable, she was the top comedienne in Hollywood") detract from its effectiveness. The author's style is a bit soapsudsy at times ("they decided there was only one way out. DIVORCE!" and "What Gable had to say spelled out what Kay said she had a feeling would come... A PROPOSAL OF MARRIAGE!"). The illustrations are excellent and include most of Gable's leading ladies. Disappointing on some counts but superior on others, this volume mostly presents the same picture of Gable that the more expensive books do. Not essential but an adequate coverage.

995   *Clark Gable: A Personal Portrait.* by Gable, Kathleen. 153 p. illus. Englewood Clifs, N.J.: Prentice-Hall, 1961.

This warm intimate memoir is more an account of a marriage and a husband than of an actor and his profession. Mrs. Gable includes many pictures in this affectionate portrait.

996   *Clark Gable.* by Jordan, Rene. 159 p. paper illus. New York: Pyramid, 1973.

As one of the initial releases in a series called, *The Pyramid Illustrated History of the Movies*, this volume is consistent in quality with the others. A good opening section distills much of the copious material previously published on Gable into a succinct, perceptive overview of the man, the actor, and the legend. The title, "The Right Time for the Right Face," is a sample of the author's ability to be economical and still totally informative.

The films are placed in chronological divisions: the first dozen, the first Oscar, the star years, and the final post-war years. A bibliography, filmography and index conclude the book. The many illustrations are quite acceptable and complement the objective text nicely. Trying to define Gable's appeal is an impossible task, but the author makes a creditable, intelligent attempt. This is as good a book on Gable as any that have appeared thus far. Recommended.

997   *A Class Divided.* by Peters, William. illus. New York: Doubleday.

Filmmaker William Peters was responsible for the

television documentary, THE EYE OF THE STORM (1970), which concerned itself with a schoolroom experiment in discrimination. In this absorbing book, he gives the background of the film, the intent of the experiment, the actual filming, and the eventual effect all this had on both participants and viewers.

998 *The Classic American Novel and the Movies.* edited by Peary, Gerald; and Shatzkin; Roger. 356 p. paper illus. New York: Ungar, 1977.

The relationship between the novel and the film is explored in this anthology. It consists of thirty essays, of which more than half were written expressly for this volume. For the author's purpose, the "classic" American novel is one of lasting quality published before 1930. Thus we have the book titles dictating the essay arrangement from *The Last of the Mohicans* (1826) to *The Sound and the Fury* (1929). Film sources, contributor identifications, film credits, a filmography, a bibliography and an index complete the book. Illustrations are well selected and adequately reproduced.

The book's value is predominately as a text to accompany a film/literature course. Individual articles would be most appropriate for a reading and viewing of the topic film.

999 *The Classic Cinema.* by Solomon, Stanley J. 354 p. paper illus. New York: Harcourt, Brace, Jovanovich, 1973.

The fourteen films chosen for study in this volume are not "The Top 14," nor are they always examples of the best work of a specific director, e.g., Hitchcock's VERTIGO (1958). What they do try to represent is a varied sampling of great films that exemplify historical and stylistic developments in the narrative film.

The films are: INTOLERANCE (1916), THE CABINET OF DR. CALIGARI (1919), POTEMKIN (1925), THE GOLD RUSH (1925), THE PASSION OF JOAN OF ARC (1928), M (1931), RULES OF THE GAME (1939), CITIZEN KANE (1941), THE BICYCLE THIEF (1948), THE SEVENTH SEAL (1957), VERTIGO (1958), THE RED DESERT (1964), BELLE DE JOUR (1967), and SATYRICON (1969). For each, cast and production credits are given, plus an introductory statement and several critical articles. For VERTIGO the following articles are offered: "Narrative Viewpoint in VERTIGO," by David Thompson; "Thematic Structure in VERTIGO," by Robin Wood; and "VERTIGO: The Cure is Worse Than the Dis-Ease," by Donald M. Spoto. A single still is used as a title page for each film. Filmo-

graphies and selected bibliographies are supplied for the 14 directors, and the book has an index.

Of all the recent books designed to support introductory courses in film study or appreciation, this one seems most suitable. It treats the silent films that are usually shown and considers directors—if not the films—representing the sound era. No book will ever satisfy all teachers; some may prefer a Ford western, a Kelly-Donen musical; or a Truffaut, Godard or Resnais to certain of the directors represented here. The book's greatest potential is as a supporting text.

1000 *Classic Movie Monsters.* by Glut, Donald F. 442 p. illus. Metuchen, N.J.: Scarecrow, 1978.

An introduction by writer-director Kurt Siodmak addresses itself to a 1941 film, THE WOLF MAN, for which he provided the screenplay. The text which follows treats nine film monsters or fiends that have fascinated the author. Since he has written two earlier books, *The Frankenstein Legend* and *The Dracula Book*, he does not reexamine those characters here. Individual chapters are devoted to the Wolfman, Dr. Jekyll, the Invisible Man, the Mummy, the Hunchback of Notre Dame, the Phantom of the Opera, the Creature from the Black Lagoon, King Kong, and Godzilla.

For each character Glut offers a detailed account which includes illustrations, a review of the media in which the character has appeared, plot synopses, background information, critical comment and general appreciation. The volume is indexed.

Glut's interest, affection and knowledge of monsters serves the reader well. In what is really a lively entertainment, he provides a terse overview of nine unforgettable creations. How they have been interpreted by legend, literature and modern popular media—especially film—is emphasized.

1001 *Classics of Film Literature (A Series).* illus. New York: Garland, 1971- .

The Garland Publishing Company has reprinted 32 volumes for this series. They are expensive hardbound duplicates of the originals.

Titles include: *Making a Film* (Lindsay Anderson), *Shots in the Dark* (Edgar Anstey, editor), *Promised Land* (Cedric Belfrage), *The Private Life of Henry VIII* (Lajos Biro, and Arthur Wimperis), *The Two Hundred Days of 8-1/2* (Deena Boyer), *Twinkle Twinkle Movie Star* (Harry Brundidge), *Heil Hollywood* (Jack Preston, Buschlen), *Van Dyke and the Mythical City Hollywood* (Robert Cannom), *The*

Mighty Barnum (Gene Fowler and Bess Meredyth), *Our Lady Cinema* (Harry Furniss) *Best Film Plays, 1943-1944* (John Gassner and Dudley Nichols), *Best Film Plays, 1945* (John Gassner and Dudley Nichols), *Twenty Best Film Plays* (John Gassner and Dudley Nichols), *The Red Shoes Ballet* (Monk Gibbon), *The Tales of Hoffman* (Monk Gibbon), *Ten Million Photoplay Plots* (Wycliffe Aber Hill), *Souls for Sale* (Rupert Hughes), *Little Stores from the Screen* (William Addison Lathrop), *I Should Have Stayed Home* (Horace McCoy), *How to Write and Sell Film Scrips* (Frances Marion), *Four Star Scripts* (Lorraine Noble), *History of Hollywood* (Edwin O. Palmer), *A Violent Life* (Pier Paolo Pasolini), *Motion Picture Continuities* (Frances Patterson), *shoot! (si gura): The Notebooks of Serafino Gubbio, Cinematograph Operator* (Luigi Pirandello), *The Golden Egg* (James Pollak), *Jew Suss* (Arthur Rawlinson and Dorothy Farnum), *Rotha on the Film* (Paul Rotha), *Case History of a Movie* (Dore Schary), *A Generation of Motion Pictures* (William A. Short), *Thought Control in the U.S.A., A Tree is a Tree* (King Vidor).

1002 *Classics of the Film.* edited by Lennig, Arthur. 250 p. paper illus. Madison, Wisc.: Wisconsin Film Society Press, 1965.

Some 13 writers contribute articles about a group of well-known motion pictures both silent and sound. They include American, German, French and Scandinavian films. In addition, there are articles on the horror film, Lugosi, and von Stroheim. The material presented is interesting and would be quite useful in the selection and presentation of the films in a film society or classroom setting.

1003 *Classics of the Foreign Film.* by Tyler, Parker. 253 p. illus. New York: Bonanza Books, 1962.

An ultimate blend of picture and text can be found in this essential volume. Beginning with CALIGARI in 1919 and ending with LA NOTTE in 1961, the book arranges in chronological fashion by year of release the foreign films that the author considers to be classics. He includes 75 films, of which about a dozen are from the silent era.

The pictures are selected with care and discrimination. The text is quite subjective, and provocative enough to challenge most readers. This volume is outstanding for all purposes, reference, enjoyment, scholarship, and record. Highly recommended as a basic book.

1004 *Classics of the Horror Film.* by Everson, William K. 255 p. illus. Secaucus, N.J.: Citadel, 1974.

Everson's survey extends from THE CABINET OF DR. CALIGARI (1919) to THE EXORCIST (1973) and offers his selection of classics of the genre. Limiting himself to "pure horror films," he discusses in detail such predictable items as NOSFERATU (1922), PHANTOM OF THE OPERA (1925), DRACULA (1931), FRANKENSTEIN (1931), FREAKS (1932), and DR. JEKYLL AND MR. HYDE (1932), along with a few surprises such as SPARROWS (1926) and STRANGLER OF THE SWAMPS (1946).

Over 400 visuals complement the informed and often enthusiastic text. Unfortunately, even a scholar-teacher-critic with Everson's impressive credentials has difficulty bringing any freshness to this seemingly undying topic—too much of it reads and looks familiar. The lack of an index diminishes the book's quality still further. Carlos Claren's *An Illustrated History of the Horror Film* remains the definitive study of this genre. This volume is acceptable with the reservations noted above.

1005 *Classics of the Silent Screen: A Pictorial Treasury.* by Franklin, Joe. 255 p. illus. New York: Citadel Press, 1959.

Two major sections make up this indispensable book. The first is a review of 50 American silent film classics. Each is given at least one page and one still; many are given several pages and pictures. The second portion is devoted to pictures and biographies of 75 silent film stars. The appendix includes a section on the questions asked the author most frequently about the silent screen era. His answers are those of someone who is respectful of and informed about the period.

A latter section gives the director and cast of the 50 films in the first section. There is no general index. This volume succeeds in all areas and is a basic book for any collection of film literature. Proof of its popularity is its many reprintings and its almost permanent appearance in book stores.

1006 *A Classified Guide to Sources of Educational Film Material.* edited by Kingdon, John Michael. 48 p. paper London: The Educational Foundation for Visual Aids, 1972.

This is the second edition of the Guide which first appeared in 1968. The cosponsor is the National Committee for Visual Aids in Education.

1007 *A Classified Guide to Sources of Educational Material.* edited by Kingdon, J. M. 48 p. paper London: Educational Foundation for Visual Aids and National Committee for Audio-Visual Aids in Education, 1972.

Almost 400 British organizations and groups are listed alphabetically by name in this resource. An abundance of abbreviated information appears with each entry—sponsor, number of items available, producer, catalogue, distributor, film types, age levels, prices, loans, sales, etc. Certain materials listed here are unique and limited to British use.

1008 *Classroom Cinema.* by Maynard, Richard A. 218 p. illus. New York: Teachers College Press, 1977.

Maynard's concern here is identical with that presented in his earlier book, *The Celluloid Curriculum* —the use of film by classroom teachers. In addition to some material which originally appeared in *Scholastic* magazine, the author has drawn on his own classroom experiences. The result is an argument and a plan for using film as a motivation for acquiring language skills, discussion ability, and visual literacy.

The book consists of two major sections: a basic guide for the use of film by classroom teachers; and a collection of suggestions, strategies, and units for the classroom. A filmography, a bibliography, a distributor list, and a film title index complete the volume.

The publication of a book which addresses itself to the introduction /improvement of classroom teaching via films is unusual in the late seventies. A neglected area is well served by this volume, with its many film reviews, original ideas, and reinforcement of the rationale for intelligent film use. Recommended.

1009 *Claude Chabrol.* by Wood, Robin; and Walker, Michael. 144 p. illus. New York: Praeger, 1970.

A study of the nouvelle vague director among whose major films are LES COUNSINS (1959), LANDRU (1963), LES BICHES (1968), and LA FEMME INFIDELE (1968). Starting with the influence of Hitchcock on Chabrol, the book treats the films in chronological order. For the most part, each author worked separately and the sections they contributed are indicated in a forward.

While the description/analysis offered is fairly interesting, the reader may be disadvantaged by a non-familiarity with many of Chabrol's works. The few that have been available in America have passed by quickly, while many have not been shown here in commercial theatres. The production of the book is above average with good representative stills and a filmography contributing to its quality. There is no index.

1010 *Claudette Colbert.* by Everson, William K. 159 p. paper illus. New York: Pyramid, 1976.

The critical appreciation of Claudette Colbert's work in films—a study that is long overdue—has finally appeared in this book by historian William K. Everson. Combining such a knowledgeable, dedicated writer with a colorful film subject indicates good planning and judgement. The result is a most satisfying account of Colbert's long and successful career as a major Hollywood film star.

The author wisely concentrates on Colbert's films and gives little attention to the woman off-screen, except to state that she kept her personal life entirely private, avoiding any undue attention to it by skillfully employing tact, diplomacy, and discretion.

The introductory section, which deals with her screen image and her directors, is followed by a chronological examination of her 64 films, from FOR THE LOVE OF MIKE (1927), to PARRISH (1961). Illustrations, a bibliography, a filmography, and an index complete the volume.

The quality of the *Pyramid* series is again evidenced by the superior content and treatment found here. Everson's well-known abilities as critic and historian are put to excellent use in this rewarding study. Recommended.

1011 CLEOPATRA. 48 p. paper illus. New York: National Publishers, Inc., 1963.

"Cleopatra, Queen of Egypt, History and Legend" is the title of the introductory article in this souvenir book. How the final screen story was taken from historical accounts and then filmed is related in the next section. Double pages are given to each of the stars, Elizabeth Taylor, Richard Burton and Rex Harrison, and to director Joseph Mankiewicz. Other cast members and technical credits are noted. Unusual features include a section on the battles, and a chronology of the lives of Cleopatra, Ceasar and Anthony.

1012 *Cleopatra in Mink.* by Rice, Cy. 160 p. paper illus. New York: Paperback

Library, 1962.

An early unauthorized biography of Elizabeth Taylor.

1013 *The* CLEOPATRA Papers: A Private Correspondence. by Brodsky, Jack; and Weiss, Nathan. 175 p. New York: Simon & Schuster, 1963.

CLEOPATRA (1963) may have the distinction of being the film most "covered" by the mass media. Books, magazine articles, newspaper stories, and television interviews surrounded its making. This volume is one of several which mark the occasion. A series of letters, phone calls and cablegrams make up the body of the book. When read in order, they give one perspective about old-style filmmaking in general and CLEOPATRA specifically.

Since the film being considered was one of the last dinosaurs to be issued by a major studio, it undoubtedly has some importance in Hollywood history. Together with DR. DOLITTLE (1967), STAR (1968), DARLING LILI (1970), PAINT YOUR WAGON (1969), and CAMELOT (1967), this film contributed to the demise of Hollywood. As the period of peak interest in the film has passed, this book will have a very limited appeal to most readers. Historians may eventually use it for reference.

1014 *Cliffhanger.* by Barbour, Alan G. 248 p. illus. New York: A and W Publishers, 1977.

This volume, which carries the subtitle "A Pictorial History of the Motion Picture Serial," is an elaborate spinoff of Barbour's earlier book on the same subject, *Days of Thrills and Adventure*. In his introduction, the author states that his original purpose of presenting "an entertaining picture of the color and excitement the serials gave" is still valid for this book.

Rather than a historical framework, a genre or personality approach is used. Individual chapters are devoted to Dick Tracy serials, western serials, jungle serials, Buster Crabbe serials, etc. For each there is an introductory essay and many clearly reproduced stills. As in the first volume, a complete list of sound serials arranged chronologically by studio is appended. This book also contains an index.

A subject of wide appeal, an affectionate treatment, an intelligent selection and arrangement of materials, and finally, some impressive production values —all these elements are present in this volume. Highly recommended.

1015 *Clint Eastwood: All-American Anti-Hero.* by Downing, David; and Herman, Gary. 144 p. paper illus. New York: Quick Fox, 1977.

This rewarding biography is both critical and affectionate. Using stills, candids, portraits, and other visuals to complement a well-researched text, the authors tell the story of Eastwood's rise from a minor player in FRANCIS IN THE NAVY (1954) to superstar status in THE ENFORCER (1976). Each of his major films receives attention and critical appraisal, and the supporting text is rich with quotes from Eastwood and his professional associates.

A refreshing presentation of a reluctant superstar can be found in the pages of this original paperback. It is strong, sound, low-key entertainment, very much like the screen presence of its subject. Recommended.

1016 *Clint Eastwood.* by Kaminsky, Stuart M. 150 p. paper illus. New York: Signet, 1974.

This modest unauthorized biography emphasizes the career and films of Clint Eastwood; little attention is given to the personal-private life of the man who is currently one of the most popular film actors in the world. His progress from bit roles to the television series "Raw Hide" and then to the Sergio Leone films is described, as are all the major films he has made since. Quotations from co-workers, directors and by Eastwood himself are copious. An interview with the author is also included. A filmography completes the book. Some illustrations, which appear in a center section, are poorly reproduced.

Using a spare, brisk style, the author has provided an informative and absorbing review of the Eastwood career to date. Because the book helps to explain the appeal of the screen character that Eastwood has established, it should appeal to many readers. It is superior in many ways to the much more expensive biography written by Peter Douglas. Recommended.

1017 *Clint Eastwood.* by Agan, Patrick. 188 p. paper illus. New York: Pyramid, 1975.

1018 *see 1015*

1019 *Clint Eastwood: Movin' On.* by Douglas, Peter. 147 p. illus. Chicago: Henry Regnery, 1974.

This short unauthorized biography concentrates on

the professional work of its subject, Clint Eastwood. Little is written about the man himself, and much of what is offered seems like padding. Although no bibliography is given, acknowledgment is made to an article by DeWitt Bodeen, one chapter is made up of an article written by Eastwood for *Action Magazine*, and there is a 15-page filmography. In the text the plot outlines for the films are given in great detail, and there are unnecessary side excursions into mini-biographies of Eastwood's costars. All of these elements may be construed as stretching or padding.

The text is mostly factual and avoids any analysis, evaluation or interpretation of either Eastwood's ability or his films' content and quality. On occasion the text is difficult to decode. For example, in discussing THE WITCHES: "The film starts a steady and fatal final slump from the elegant and claustrophobic first Visconti sketch to the dismal pointless De Sica bit at the end....Eastwood starred in the fifth and final segment ...entitled 'A Night Like Any Other'.... 'A Night Like Any Other' in no way stands up to comparison with Visconti's later work ROCCO AND HIS BROTHERS." Part of the above is a quote from *Variety* on a film which has not been shown commercially. It is difficult to determine who directed Eastwood's sequence and when it appeared in this anthology film. ROCCO AND HIS BROTHERS was made in 1960, while THE WITCHES was made in 1966.

Inaccuracies and careless omissions can be found throughout the volume—for example, the section on Jean Seberg does not mention ST. JOAN (1957) and suggests she lived much of her early life in France. Pat Hingle did not come to public notice in SOL MADRID (1966)—his earlier performances in NO DOWN PAYMENT (1957) and in SPLENDOR IN THE GRASS (1961) were highly acclaimed.

A center section of photographs and an index are helpful but the text weaknesses are so strong that nothing can save the volume from being a disappointment. An argument can be made for an analysis of Eastwood's life and films. Unfortunately this volume seems like a rapidly prepared magazine sketch designed for nondiscriminating fans of Clint Eastwood. A more responsible work has appeared in *Clint Eastwood* by Stuart M. Kaminsky.

1020   A CLOCKWORK ORANGE. by Kubrick, Stanley. paper illus. New York: Ballantine Books, 1972.

This visualized script of the 1971 film directed by Kubrick is best described by Kubrick's introductory statement: "I have always wondered if there might be a more meaningful way to present a book about a film. To make, as it were, a complete, graphic representation of the film, cut by cut, with the dialogue printed in the proper place in relation to the cuts, so that within the limits of still photographs and words, an accurate (and I hope interesting) record of a film might be available." Right on. A most successful and fascinating screenplay book. The inclusion of the material which earned the film an X rating may bother some readers.

1021   CLOSE ENCOUNTERS OF THE THIRD KIND: *A Document of the Film.* edited by Durwood, Thomas. 144 p. paper illus. New York: Ballantine, 1978.

Quotations from many of the filmmakers who participated in the production of this 1977 film accompany over 150 full-color visuals taken from the film. Ray Bradbury provides an introduction and there is an epilogue by Carl Sagan.

1022   *see   1021*

1023   CLOSE ENCOUNTERS OF THE THIRD KIND *Diary.* by Balaban, Bob. 177 p. paper illus. New York: Paradise Press, 1978.

In the 1978 film, CLOSE ENCOUNTERS OF THE THIRD KIND, Bob Balaban played the role of Francois Truffaut's interpreter. During the making of the film in 1976-1977, he kept a diary as the crew travelled to such locations as Wyoming, Alabama, India and Hollywood. The result is a subjective, positive look at the process of major filmmaking. Balaban admires most of his coworkers—especially directors Spielberg and Truffaut and actor Richard Dreyfuss —and is able to convey his excitement at participating in such a large-scale adventure. He includes an extended list of credits and some on-set photographs.

1024   *see   1023*

1025   CLOSE ENCOUNTERS OF THE THIRD KIND *Portfolio.* edited by Columbia Pictures. 18 p. paper illus. New York: Ariel, 1977.

Eighteen full-color plates taken from scenes in the 1977 film comprise this portfolio. The visuals are printed on heavier paper stock and will recall many of the elements that contributed to the success of the film.

1026   *Close-up.* by Gruen, John. 206 p. illus. New York: Viking, 1968.

A collection of interviews with celebrities. Film personalities include Fellini, Bette Davis, Judy Garland, Shelley Winters, Candice Bergen, Mario Montez (an Andy Warhol personality), Simone Signoret, Vivien Leigh, Busby Berkeley, Joseph Losey, Ruby Keeler, and Alain Resnais.

1027 *Close-Up: A Critical Perspective on Films.* by Kinder, Marsha; and Houston, Beverle. 395 p. paper illus. New York: Harcourt, 1972.

An attempt to establish an aesthetic for the evaluation of films. This is not the usual pedantic, philosophical discourse but an excellent book which examines, in depth and detail, films which are accepted examples of the aesthetic being considered. For example, the qualities in the silent film that indicated film as an art form are noted in BIRTH OF A NATION (1915), POTEMKIN (1925), CALIGARI (1919), THE LAST LAUGH (1924), THE LOVE OF JEANNE NEY (1927), BALLET MECANIQUE (1924), UN CHIEN ANDALOU (1928) and THE PASSION OF JOAN OF ARC (1928).

A second section examines sound, depth focus, advanced technology (2001: A SPACE ODDSSEY 1968) and a few underground films. Three large categories of documentary films—ethnic, war and rock—are treated next, and there are chapters on neo-realism, the French New Wave, American humanistic realism, myth in movies, and politics in film.

As indicated, the scope is wide, but the material is presented in a sequential, hierarchical order that aids comprehension. Some of the discussions are engrossing. The authors have brought thought, intelligence and effort to a difficult task in film criticism and have succeeded admirably. Illustrations are fine, and are placed appropriately throughout the book. The films discussed in the text are listed along with distributor addresses and there is a most helpful index. Impressive as a college text. Highly recommended.

1028 *Close Up: The Contract Director.* edited by Tuska, Jon. 457 p. illus. Metuchen, N.J.: Scarecrow Press, 1976.

During Hollywood's Golden Era, the studios signed motion picture directors to long term contracts, under which they were required to handle any and all assignments. In this volume there are study-appreciations of ten such directors, each presented by a different author. The subjects are Walter Lang, H. Bruce Humberstone, William Dieterle, Joseph Kane, William Witney, Lesley Selander, Yakima Canutt, Lewis Milestone, Edward Dmytryk, and

Howard Hawks.

The articles employ research, an original interview, critical comment and other background material to describe and interpret each subject and his work. A portrait and a filmography appear for each director and a general name and title index to the entire book is provided.

Each author treats his assignment in a slightly different fashion and the result is a varied but fairly entertaining collection.

1029 *Close-Up: The Hollywood Director.* edited by Tuska, Jon. 444 p. illus. Metuchen, N.J.: Scarecrow, 1978.

This is the second of the *Close-Up* books and like the others, it is a collection of appreciations of Hollywood directors. In this case the subjects are Billy Wilder, Henry King, Frank Capra, Spencer Gordon Bennett, William Wyler, William Wellman, John Huston, Douglas Kirk, and Alfred Hitchcock. The essays are all newly written and accompanied by illustrations and short filmographies.

It should be noted that most of the directors have been subjects of earlier, more detailed biographies and career studies. To commission an essay on Hitchcock at this point seems to request the redundant. As part of the total three volumes, this book has more justification than as a single isolated volume which offers material that is quite familiar.

1030 *Close Up:* LAST TANGO IN PARIS. edited by Carroll, Kent E. 176 p. paper illus. New York: Grove Press, 1973.

This is an anthology of articles about the film, LAST TANGO IN PARIS, its stars, director and critical reception. Contributors include Norman Mailer, John Simon, Nat Hentoff, Parker Tyler, Alberto Moravia and others. Two interviews are included—director Bernardo Bertolucci and female lead Maria Schneider. The controversy that surrounded the film originally has diminished considerably and cooler heads now prevail. The film has now appeared on many "Best Film Lists" and has been consigned to double bills in neighborhood theatres.

This volume does summarize much of the critical thought and analysis that met the film upon its release. The articles chosen are representative although they tend slightly toward a negative view. The visuals used in the book are only fair in both reproduction and selection. Recommended for a mature audience.

1031 *Close-Up: The Contemporary Director.* edited by Tuska, Jon. 437 p. illus. Metuchen, N.J.: Scarecrow, 1980.

This anthology consists of career studies of ten film directors: Sidney Pollack, Sam Fuller, Sam Peckinpah, George Roy Hill, Robert Altman, Dick Richards, Hal Ashby, Peter Bogdanovich, Martin Scorsese, and Roman Polanski. Each study was written specifically for this book and there is no apparent connecting theme for the directors, chosen as contemporary. A short filmography (called a checklist here) is provided along with rental sources and an index.

This is the final volume of a trilogy, the earlier titles being *Close-Up: The Hollywood Director* and *Close-Up: The Contract Director.*

Anyone interested in today's films will find much of interest here. New interviews, excerpts from previous interviews, critical analyses, background information, plot synopses and other elements are offered in these enlightening studies.

1032 *Close Up (A Series).* by Bryher, Winifred. edited by MacPherson, Kenneth; illus. New York: Arno, 1973.

One of the first magazines devoted to the history, aesthetics, theory, and criticism of film, *Close Up* is reprinted in the following volumes: Vol. I, 1927; Vol. II and III, 1928; Vol. IV and V, 1929; Vol VI and VII, 1930; Vol. VIII, 1931; Vol. IX, 1932; Vol. X, 1933.

An introduction to the series was written by Herman Weinberg and there is a new three-part index in Volume X. One of the outstanding features of this magazine was its use of many stills. Acceptable.

1033 *Close-Ups: From the Golden Age of the Silent Cinema.* by Finch, John Richard; and Elby, Paul. 566 p. illus. New York: A.S. Barnes, 1979.

A collection of 484 full-page portraits of silent-screen actors is presented here. Taken from the Jorifin Collection, the visuals are divided into two groupings: the first, arranged chronologically, ranges from Broncho Billy Anderson to El Brendel; the second features personalities who made silent films but found greater success in sound films. Following each section are the selected biographical sketches of the subjects.

Placement of some of the actors may be questionable (Wallace Reid, Buela Bondi, the Marx Brothers, for example), as is some of the biographical comment

("Tallulah Bankhead made film history") and omissions (WATCH ON THE RHINE (1943)), which earned Paul Lukas an Oscar is not mentioned in his biography). Photographic quality is acceptable but not as impressive as that found in other similar collections such as *Grand Illusions, Image Makers, A World of Movies,* and *Hollywood Glamour Portraits.*

The volume is important for its pictorial coverage of faces from the silent screen. It is diminished somewhat by reproduction quality, biographical generalities, and inconsistent selection and arrangement.

1034 *Close-Ups: The Movie Star Book.* edited by Peary, Danny. 606 p. paper illus. New York: Workman, 1979.

This anthology is made up of both original and reprinted articles, essays, tributes, and reminiscenses —all of which are devoted to giving a portrait or profile of some famous movie star. The 140 subjects range from Joel McCrea to Sissy Spacek, and include both the popular (Burt Reynolds) and the legendary (Claude Rains).

Several appendixes are most helpful; they include subject filmographies, an index to movie titles mentioned in the text, and a general name index. The hundreds of illustrations which are well selected and nicely reproduced add greatly to the book.

Although treatment varies in approach, length, style, and objectivity, most of the articles are of more than passing interest. Coverage is impressive and the volume offers many hours of pleasant reading. Recommended.

1035 *Closely Watched Films: The Czechoslovak Experience.* by Liehm, Antonin J. 485 p. illus. White Plains, N.Y.: International Arts and Sciences Press, 1974.

According to the author, the Czech cinema had four generations of filmmakers: the pre-Nazi group who struggled against commercial studio productions, the post-World War II group who led to the formation of a public film industry, the fifties group who were born into public filmmaking, and finally, the New Wave of the sixties. Interviews are offered with 32 filmmakers representing the four generations. Since the author was a friend and contemporary of the directors, the introductory comments and the questions take on a particular pertinence. The framework supplied by the author adds considerably to the statements made by the directors.

A filmography is provided for each interviewee and there are separate indexes for names and film titles. A full-page photograph of each director introduces his interview. These illustrations comprise one more strong element of the book's quality. Although its material is specialized rather than popular, the production and content of this book are recommended to the serious student of film.

1036   CLOSELY WATCHED TRAINS. by Hrabal, Bohumil; and Menzel, Jiri. 144 p. paper illus. New York: Simon and Schuster, 1971.

Script of the 1967 film directed by Menzel. Contains: an introduction by Bohumil Hrabal; "Jiri Menzel" by Jan Zalman; "A Track All Its Own" by John Simon; cast and credits.

1037   *Clown Princes and Court Jesters: Some Great Comics of the Silent Screen.* by Lahue, Kalton C.; and Gill, Sam. 406 p. illus. New York: A. S. Barnes, 1970.

Some 50 comics, both male and female, are profiled in individual chapters in this book. The text consists of an attempt at detailed analysis of each player's artistry in addition to some biographical material. There are many pictures and their quality varies. The alphabetical arrangement will enhance the book's obvious value. This is one of the better productions from Barnes. Recommended.

1038   *Clozentropy: A Technique for Studying Audience Response to Films.* by Lynch, F. Dennis. 127 p. illus. New York: Arno Press, 1978.

Written in 1972 at the University of Iowa, in partial fulfillment of the doctoral program, this winner of the Speech Communication Association Research Board's Outstanding Doctoral Dissertation Award is a study in the analysis of audience response to films. The development of a testing methodology and its subsequent application to a subject group are discussed by the author, whose test instrument has been widely cited as a valid method for measuring film complexity and audience sophistication. This title appears in the *Dissertations on Film* series.

1039   *Cocktails For Two.* by Coslow, Sam. 304 p. illus. New Rochelle, N.Y.: Arlington House, 1977.

Subtitled, "The Many Lives of Giant Songwriter Sam Coslow," this autobiography recalls a life studded with incident and celebrity. From an early association with Thomas A. Edison through vaudeville, radio, films, and finally Wall Street, Coslow has worked with many of the famous names of this century. The dust jacket lists a sampling from what is called "a cast of thousands." While so many names may have an instantaneous appeal, the lasting result is a surface account that merely mentions many of these stars in a passing paragraph or two. Coslow also displays a tendency to use some tired material, e.g., Robert Young is known to TV fans today as Dr. Marcus Welby; Arline Judge and Johnny Downs are subjects for trivia contests today, and so forth. Nevertheless, Coslow's career was so varied and colorful that it is hard to resist his fast paced narrative. Perhaps what he needed most in the preparation of this book was a strong-willed collaborator.

Most of the illustrations show the book's hero in the company of famous names. Appendix I lists Coslow's personal favorites from his 500 published compositions, while the second appendix is a selected discography of Coslow songs. The book is indexed.

In this memoir, ego predominates while shyness and humility are conspicuously absent—and perhaps rightly so since so many of the author's accomplishments were impressively successful. What is lacking, however is the literary ability to raise this recall of a rich life above the level of a fan magazine confession. Acceptable.

1040   *Cocteau.* by Gilson, Rene Translated by Ciba Vaughn. 192 p. paper New York: Crown, 1969.

Jean Cocteau has written and directed some films. In others he has been responsible for the scenario or the dialogue, and finally his direct influence in yet others can be documented. All these aspects of the Cocteau cinema are examined in this book.

The opening essay by the author is remarkable for its clarity in dealing with the complex career of Cocteau. Other portions include a section of direct quotations by Cocteau, some excerpts from screen plays, a few critical appreciations and an attempt to describe Cocteau from personal association. Also included are a filmography, a bibliography, a discography, and a chronology. This book serves to remind us of the appreciable contribution of Cocteau to cinema. Well written, with a welcome difference in structure, the book makes some order out of the complexity that is characteristic of an artist such as Cocteau.

1041   *Cocteau.* by Steegmuller, Francis. 583 p. illus. Boston: Little, Brown, 1970.

This biography cover Cocteau's creative life from

about 1914 to the immediate post-World War II years. Heavy documentation gives the volume the appearance of a dissertation. Many papers and letters are quoted at great length and, while they add dimension to the characterizations, they slow up the pace of the narrative. Since Cocteau had so many interactions with famous names of the period, the biographical line gets a bit lost from time to time.

All the major films except THE TESTAMENT OF ORPHEUS (1959) receive attention but the reader will sense no great enthusiasm for this facet of Cocteau's art.

The book is supported by illustrations, an index, notes, a bibliography, and many appendices. This is a scholarly achievement in biography that will appeal to a small minority audience.

1042 *Cocteau.* by Fraigneau, Andre 192 p. illus. New York: Grove Press, 1961.

A translation from the French-language original by Donald Lehmkuhl. Includes a bibliography.

1043 *Cocteau on the Film.* by Cocteau, Jean. 140 p. New York: Roy Pub., 1954.

A conversation with Andre Fraigneau about Cocteau's films and what he attempted in them. As a poet, Cocteau presents his concept of film as a personal language.

1044 *Cocteau on the Film.* by Cocteau, Jean. 141 p. paper illus. New York: Dover, 1972.

An updating of the original 1954 English edition. Conversations between Cocteau and Andre Fraigneau were recorded by the latter and translated into English by Vera Traill. Cocteau talks about his films, the role of a poet, the nature of film, his actors, and many other topics. For this edition the publishers have added 30 stills from the films, most of which are adequately reproduced. A Cocteau filmography completes the book. Highly recommended.

1045 *Cole Porter: A Biography.* by Schwartz, Charles. 399 p. illus. New York: Dial, 1977.

Based on interviews, personal documents, and other research, this biography succeeds nicely in explaining both the person and the artist that was Cole Porter.

Schwartz traces the composer's life from Peru, Indiana, to Yale, Harvard, Broadway and ultimately Hollywood. Much attention is paid to the hundreds of sophisticated Porter songs, many of which are standards of popular music. Personal relationships are explored and the subject of Porter's homosexuality is handled with taste. Also included are illustrations, a songography, a discography, a bibliography, and an index.

1046 *The Collected Screenplays of Bernard Shaw.* by Shaw, George Bernard. edited by Dukore, F.; 487 p. illus. Athens, Ga.: University of Georgia Press, 1980.

A long essay introduces this collection of Bernard Shaw screenplays: SAINT JOAN (1927), Director: W. Newman; ARMS AND THE MAN (1932), Director: C. Lewis; PYGMALION (1938), Directors: A. Asquith and L. Howard; CAESAR AND CLEOPATRA (1945), Director: G. Pascal.

1047 *Collected Works (Vol. 3— Scenarios, On the Cinema, Interviews, Letters).* by Artaud, Antonin. 255 p. illus. London: Calder and Boyars, 1972.

1048 *Collectibles: The Nostalgia Collector's Bible.* by Sugar, Bert Randolph. 320 p. illus. New York: Quick Fox, 1980.

A price guide to buying, selling and trading collectibles, many of which pertain to film personalities or characters.

1049 *Collecting and Enjoying Old Movies.* by Munro, Fred F., Jr. 56 p. paper illus. Bellmore, N.Y.: Impact Promotion and Publishing, 1972.

This rather high-priced book covers much the same material that is treated in *Collecting Classic Films* and *The Armchair Odeon.* The difference is the treatment of the material—here, it is a bit breathless and often corny or hackneyed. Titles such as "Films You Can Get," "What They Are About," "Where to Get Them," "The Wonderful World of Silent Movies," etc., are used throughout. The topics considered include posters, technical problems, projectors, gauges, magnetic sound, vari-tint, the mystique of collecting, etc. Priority for purchase or use should be given to the other books mentioned above.

1050 *Collecting Classic Films.* by Lahue, Kalton C. 159 p. illus. New York: Hastings House, 1970.

This is an indispensable book for that small, select, and financially solvent audience of film collectors. All aspects of collecting films are taken into account —what to collect, where to find it, how to present it and how to care for it.

The classics considered are primarily silent films available on 8mm. The first few chapters survey the silent screen very nicely, indeed. Later chapters dealing with technical processes do not offer equal general interest. Has much value for schools offering film courses and showings. It is often less expensive to purchase a silent film on 8mm than to rent it on 16mm.

1051 *Collecting Movie Memorabilia.* by Chaneles, Sol. 176 p. illus. New York: Arco Publishing Co., 1977.

Among the types of movie memorabilia considered here are stills, color photographs, color negatives, posters, lobby cards, inserts, decorative realia, fan magazines, press books, movie books, and soundtrack recordings. For each of these an explanatory chapter is provided along with some illustrative material and a possible price list of a few selected specimens. The last chapter discusses sources of memorabilia such as stores, dealers, collectors, and archives. An index completes the volume.

Although some reservations may be expressed about the prices listed, the clarity of certain definitions, and the frequent intrusion of certain personal preferences, the book is to be praised for bringing together the fragmented elements of movie material collecting. Recommended.

1052 *A Collection of Great Science Fiction Films.* by Strickland, A. W.; and Ackerman, Forrest. 200 p. illus. Bloomington, Ind.: TIS, 1979.

1053 *Collective Bargaining in the Motion Picture Industry.* by Lovell, Hugh Gilbert; and Carter, Tasile. 54 p. paper Berkeley, Calif.: Institute of Industrial Relations, University of California, 1935.

An early survey study which describes "a struggle for stability" in the motion picture industry.

1054 *The Collector's Encyclopedia of Shirley Temple Dolls and Collectibles.* by Smith, Patricia. illus. New York: Crown, 1977.

More testimony to the popularity of Shirley Temple in the mid-thirties is given in this guide to dolls, dishes, clothes, etc., which offers identification information and suggests values. More than 500 illustrations in both color and black-and-white are included.

1055 *The College Film Library Collection.* edited by Jones, Emily. 154 p. paper Williamsport, Pa.: Bro-Dart, 1971.

A listing of films by subject area, with entries quite similar to the Educational Film Library Association (EFLA) evaluations with which Ms. Jones worked for so many years. They offer data, description, and evaluation. One section contains a listing of feature films that are described as classics; the final section lists film distributors. The subject index appears at the back (an unfortunate decision). Recommended.

1056 *Collette at the Movies.* by Collette. 213 p. paper illus. New York: Ungar, 1980.

This unusual compilation of Collette's film writing consists of scattered reviews, articles and two scripts, LAC-AUX-DANES (1933) and DIVINE (1935). Accompanying this selection are some photographs and a filmography. Collette also wrote several other scenarios, or assisted by supplying additional dialogue for films.

The scripts here hold minimal interest for most readers and the criticism is mostly on a few obscure silent films. Based on the evidence here, Collette's contribution to film literature was a negligible one.

1057 *Collura: Actor with a Gun.* by Davidson, Bill. 221 p. New York: Simon and Schuster, 1977.

The true story of a stage, film, and television actor who moonlighted as an undercover narcotics cop. After several close calls, show business wins out over law enforcement. Lots of action and profanity for gullible readers.

1058 *Colour Cinematography.* by Cornwell-Clyne, Adrian. 780 p. illus. London: Chapman and Hall, 1951.

A revised and updated version of a text originally published in the thirties. This third edition treats the history, development, and use of color cinematography.

1059 *Color in Motion Pictures and Television.* by Trimble, Lyne Starling. 267 p. Los Angeles: Optical Standards,

1969.

This is the second edition of a text that deals with color cinematography. A bibliography is included.

1060 *Colour Motion Picture Film Materials Especially Suited to Presentation by Colour Television.* compiled by European Broadcasting Union. 11 p. paper illus. Brussels: Albert Lancaster, 1968.

1061 *Combat Films: American Realism, 1945-1970.* by Rubin, Steven J. 245 p. illus. Jefferson, N.C.: McFarland, 1980.

1062 *"Come Up and See Me Sometime".* by Hanna, David. 223 p. paper illus. New York: Tower Publishers, 1976.

This original paperback notes that it is both a "confidential" and "uncensored" biography of Mae West. "Unauthorized" might have been more accurate for there is little in West's life that is shocking or scandalous today. She was a comedienne who was ahead of her time in using the topic of sex as a vehicle for humor.

Hanna, who has written for many periodicals including *Uncensored* and *Whisper*, knows how to tell a story quickly and still maintain reader interest. He uses a breezy, reportorial style in tracing West's rise from a vaudeville shimmy dancer to a screen legend. He borrows heavily on previously published interviews and other matters of public record. His ability at integrating the information into an entertaining humorous story is matched by the carefully planned material that his subject provided. A few illustrations appear in a center section.

1063 *The Comeback.* by Robinson, Jay; and Hardiman, Jim. illus. Lincoln, Va.: Chosen Books, 1979.

Jay Robinson achieved celebrity as a Broadway actor before he was twenty. His appearance as Caligula in THE ROBE (1953) and DEMETRIUS AND THE GLADIATORS (1954) indicated a promising future in films. However, his difficult early life plus an addiction to drugs caused him to throw away his career. A few minor film parts, a stay in prison, and a slow recovery made up his life for the next decade. His journey back was helped by his courage and determination, a devoted wife, and the born-again Christian Movement. Recently he has been active in television but he does occasionally appear in films—SHAMPOO (1975), BORN AGAIN (1978), etc.

Inspirational books occasionally are preachy, but such is not the case here as Robinson tells his personal story in a terse, objective way. There is no trace of self-pity, only, perhaps, a regret that he handled his original good fortunes so poorly. Illustrations, and a list of his stage, film, and television credits accompany this unique story of a remarkable comeback.

1064 *The Comedians.* by Thomey, Tedd; and Wilner, Norman. 208 p. paper New York: Pyramid Books, 1970.

Most of the subjects of this collective biography have appeared in films, and although that aspect of their career is not emphasized, this book still has pertinence for film collections. Some of the comedians are Red Skelton, Phyllis Diller, Oscar Levant, Phil Silvers, Laurel and Hardy, Martha Raye and Jackie Gleason. There is no index or illustrations, but the writing style is brisk, spare, and most enjoyable. Better than many more ambitious attempts.

1065 *Comedy Films.* by Montgomery, John. 337 p. illus. London: George Allen and Unwin, 1954.

A factual history of film comedy and comedians written by a British author, this book reflects it origin throughout. Many unfamiliar names and faces populate the book and much of the historical narrative concerns the British film industry. Then, too, the book does not stay with its topic exclusively—many other film genres are mentioned.

Much of the evaluation given is no longer valid. For example, time has not treated the films made by such popular comedians of the forties as Crosby, Hope, Kaye, and Abbott and Costello too kindly. They are more embarrassing than funny to today's sophisticated audiences. A book that concerns itself exclusively with screen comedy would be most welcome. This one does not begin to approach its title. Of minor interest except to scholars and historians, and even to them its inclusions and evaluations are questionable.

1066 *Comedy in Action.* by Blistein, E. M. 146 p. Durham, N.C.: Duke University Press, 1964.

An analysis of comedy and comedians in theatre, literature, radio and movies.

1067 *The Comedy World of Stan Laurel.* by McCabe, John. 221 p. illus. Garden City, N.Y.: Doubleday, 1974.

This volume is really a supplement to the author's

earlier dual biography *Mr. Laurel and Mr. Hardy.* Using material supplied by Laurel's third wife along with interviews of Laurel and his co-workers, the author has compiled a further tribute to the comedian. Bits of biography are intermingled with scripts of skits, reminiscences, and analysis of the performer's comic artistry. The approach is affectionate and admiring. Some illustrations are included and the book is indexed. Acceptable.

1068 *The Comic Image of the Jew.* by Altman, Sig. 234 p. Rutherford, N.J.: Fairleigh Dickinson University Press, 1971.

Subtitled, "Explorations of a Pop Culture Phenomenon," this study looks at American films, theatre, television, and books with two criteria: (1) the presence of a Jewish comic image, and (2) the prevalence of "arbitrariness" in the Jewish humor. The author found film is the only medium to meet both criteria almost perfectly.

The second section of the book outlines the historical background of the Jewish comic image in America. Topics include the humor of early times, emancipation, nonemancipation, cities and anti-Semites. A short look at the Jewish comedian in American society is followed by a summary-conclusion, a list of plays with Jewish characters, a bibliography, and an index.

The author's rationale and method for the study appear in the opening pages. His finding that "The Jew, compared to members of other groups, is currently the comic figure par excellence in films," should interest anyone concerned with the sociology of media. Here is an absorbing study that hopefully will inspire similar investigations. Recommended.

1069 *The Comic Mind: Comedy and the Movies.* by Mast, Gerald. 288 p. illus. Indianapolis, Ind.: Bobbs-Merrill, 1973.

Mast begins this study with some basic definitions and then analyzes many comedy films. The first section deals with the silent film and illuminates those qualities which were unique to its comedy form. Sound films are treated in the latter portion and the differences between them and the silents are described. The book treats international film, is illustrated, indexed and has a bibliography.

Mast's previous book indicated that he could write with style, economy and quality; this volume confirms that opinion. It is somewhat similar to but much better than *Comedy Films* by John Montgomery. Highly recommended.

1070 *Comics, Radio, Movies... and Children.* by Josette, Frank. 32 p. illus. New York: Public Affairs Committee, 1949.

1071 COMING APART. edited by Ginsberg, Milton M. 205 p. paper illus. New York: Lancer, 1970.

Script of the 1969 film written and directed by Milton Ginsberg.

1072 *Coming Next Week.: A Pictorial History of Film Advertising.* by Sweeney, Russell C. 303 p. illus. New York: A.S. Barnes, 1973.

This scrapbook of newspaper and magazine ads for films is arranged chronologically, covering the years from 1920 to 1940. No text is offered, and the only purpose of the book is to give the reader a nostalgic journey in motion picture history. The ads appear in their original size with extra local information added about prices, short subjects, etc. Reproduction gets better as the pen and ink drawings of the twenties are replaced by the halftones and photos of the thirties, but in no instance is it more than adequate. No index is offered.

This is specialized material for the film buff or a last-minute gift for an aging relative. No one can get too angry at a book that strives to entertain as this one does—but, it seems to be a frill rather than anything sturdy or essential. Acceptable.

1073 *The Command Is Forward.* by Harmon, Francis S. 56 p. New York: Richard R. Smith, 1944.

Selections from addresses on the role of the motion picture industry in war and peace are given in this book. Taken mostly from the World War II period, the excerpts give evidence of some of the actions of the industry. Obviously, its role was much larger, more influential, and certainly more complex than this historical curiosity would have the reader believe. Harmon was an executive vice chairman of the War Activities Committee of the Motion Picture Industry.

1074 *Committee: The Extraordinary Career of the House Committee on Un-American Activities.* by Goodman, Walter. 564 p. illus. New York: Farrar, Straus, & Giroux, 1968.

1075 *The Committee on Film Classification Hearing.* compiled by Committee on Communication, U.S. Senate. 58 p. paper illus. Washington, D.C.: U.S. Government Printing Office, 1969.

Transcript of the hearing on Senate Resolution 9, which took place during the 90th Congress, June 11, 1968.

1076 *The Common Good: New York State's Legislature in Action: A Film Teaching Guide.* edited by Bureau of Social Studies Education. 14 p. paper illus. Albany, N.Y.: State Education Dept., 1964.

A guide designed to accompany showings of the film, THE COMMON GOOD.

1077 *Communications Law—1975.* by Goodale, James C. 828 p. paper New York: Practising Law Institute, 1975.

This handbook, developed for a PLI course, examines such topics as privacy, the first amendment, advertising liability, free press, fair trial, etc.

1078 *The Communications Revolution.* by Gordon, George N. 338 p. illus. New York: Hastings House, 1977.

Using a personalized style, George N. Gordon has written a book the scope of which might intimidate a more cautious man. Subtitled, "A History of Mass Media in the United States," the volume traces print, radio, film and television from their invention/introduction to their present-day status.

By treating the media collectively rather than individually, the various independent segments which make up the text are blended into a historical continuum. Sprinkled throughout are the major events, personalities, controversies, and legal battles that characterize the mass media.

Supporting the detailed but always comprehensible text are a selected bibliography and an index.

The importance of this volume is two-fold: it presents a concise history of the motion picture in America, and also shows the relationship between film and other mass media through the years. The author has provided an intelligently integrated review of some of the important personalities and events that have shaped the communications revolution in America during the past two centuries. As

either a textbook, required reading, or simply as a weekend entertainment, this volume is a complete success. Recommended.

1079 *The Communicative Arts.* by Steinberg, Charles S. 371 p. New York: Hastings House, 1970.

As one of the titles in the *Studies in Public Communication* series, this volume provides an introduction to mass media. Individual chapters focus on books, newspapers, magazines, television and, of course, film. In a chapter entitled "The Motion Picture in Transition," the history, development, economics and sociology of the film are quickly reviewed. The short, strange bibliography which concludes the chapter is composed of selected titles, not at all representative of a basic list of books on film as a mass medium. In certain ways the text resembles the bibliography in the matter of choice and representation.

By trying to cover such a complex subject in a single chapter, the author is suspect in what he selects. His presentation of film as a mass medium is weakened by the absence of such topics as film research, the use of film as propaganda in World War II, the Payne Fund Studies, etc. Other chapters make short partial references to motion pictures and both the old motion picture code and the new codes of self-regulation appear in the appendix. As part of this total statement, the survey chapter on film is acceptable. However, those readers searching for a more balanced account might look at one of the recent histories such as Gerald Mast's *A Short History of the Movies* and Alan Casty's *Development of the Film.*

1080 *The Community and the Motion Picture.* by National Conference on Motion Pictures. 96 p. New York: Ozer, 1971 (1929).

This report of the National Conference on Motion Pictures held in New York City in 1929 was originally published by the Motion Picture Producers and Distributors of America. Representatives from 21 states met for four days to discuss motion picture production, distribution and exhibition. Speaker statements, questions, answers and comments make up the report. Three pages of motion picture definitions will cause the reader to smile—for example, "triangle" is defined as "two men and a woman story" —an interpretation not necessarily accurate today. The report is indexed.

As an example of the interaction between interested lay persons and the industry, this book has interest for the historian or researcher.

1081   *Community Media Handbook.* by Zelmer, A. C. Lynn. 241 p. Metuchen, N.J.: Scarecrow Press, 1973.

Film is only one of many types of media discussed in this provocative volume, but the importance of the total concept makes it worth noting. Zelmer is concerned with a new-breed institution—the Community Media Center, which offers a service to community groups and persons who cannot use professionals or experts, for whatever reason. He suggests simple and inexpensive ideas on media basics, low budget films, TV, photography, simulations, street theatre, cable TV and other community communication topics.

The question that should occur to specialists is to what extent they wish to provide the services suggestedhere. For other readers, the information has relevance in its suggestions of simple and economical media methods. Strongly recommended.

1082   *A Companion to the Movies.* by Pickard, Roy. 286 p. illus. Surrey: Lutterworth Press, 1972.

This volume calls itself "a guide to the leading players, directors, screenwriters, composers, cameramen and other artists who have worked in the English-speaking cinema over the last 70 years." Using a genre approach, the author further divides each genre chapter into a chronology of the famous films, and then a listing of personalities associated with the films. He has included several other bonus checklists and the entire effort is a very good reference book. Recommended.

1083   *A Companion to the Movies.: From 1903 to the Present Day.* by Pickard, Roy. 287 p. illus. New York: Hippocrene Books, 1974.

In this useful reference book, the author has distributed more than 1000 entries among a dozen film genres—comedy, fantasy, western, musical, romance, etc. For each genre he offers selected film reviews and mini-biographies. For example, under epics he reviews THE BIRTH OF A NATION (1915), INTOLERANCE (1916), SAMPSON AND DELILAH (1950), WAR AND PEACE (1956), THE TEN COMMANDMENTS (1956), BEN HUR (1959), SPARTACUS (1960), EL CID (1961), and CLEOPATRA (1963). Short biographical sketches are given for Stanley Baker, Anne Bauchens, Stephen Boyd, Yul Brynner, Richard Burton, Yakima Cannutt, Jack Cardiff, Finlay Currie, Tony Curtis, Dino De Laurentis, Cecil B. DeMille, Frederick M. Frank, D. W. Griffith, Susan Hayward, Charlton Heston, John Ireland, Rudolph

Kopp, Robert Krasker, Jesse Lasky, Jr., Herbert Lom, Sophia Loren, Jeanie MacPherson, Anthony Mann, Peverell Marley, Andrew Marton, Victor Mature, Victor Milner, Jack Palance, Miklos Rozsa, Leon Shamroy, Omar Sharif, Jean Simmons, Robert L. Surtees, Frank Thring, Dimitri Tiomkin, Peter Ustinov, Franz Waxman, Henry Wilcoxon, Philip Yordan and Waldemar Young. Appendixes for cameramen, famous film scores, original scripts, and Academy Awards are added. Most important of all is a name index which locates the personality entries in the book. A director or actor may be listed under several genres but the entry in each case is pertinent to that specific genre. A center section contains some well-reproduced stills from the films listed.

Several reservations can be noted: first, the subjectivity of the selection and its placement, always a topic for argument; secondly, there is no index provided for the film titles. Does one look for CASABLANCA (1943) under romance? thriller? plays into films? Finally, the critical evaluations are a bit shaky. Is SAMPSON AND DELILAH (1950) a milestone or classic film? Does THE GREAT ZIEGFELD (1935) deserve a place in the musicals? There is so much information offered in this volume along with an obvious devotion and dedication by the author that the few reservations noted become insignificant. The volume is highly recommended.

1084   *The Comparative Effectiveness of Sound Motion Pictures and Printed Communication For the Motivation of High School Students in Mathematics.* edited by Tiemens, Robert K. 72 p. paper Iowa City: State University of Iowa, 1962.

This research study includes diagrams, tables, etc.

1085   *A Comparative Study of Selected American Film Critics, 1958-1974.* by Blades, Joseph Dalton Jr. New York:

Written in 1974 at Bowling Green State University as partial fulfillment of the doctoral program, this title in the *Dissertations on Film* series describes six major film critics and their influence on the film industry: John Simon, Pauline Kael, Stanley Kauffman, Andrew Sarris, Judith Crist, and Vincent Canby. The author examines their contributions to the growth of an enlightened film public and also establishes their vital role as architects of film aesthetics.

1086 *A Comparison of Exhibitions and Distribution Patterns in Three Recent Feature Motion Pictures.* by Daly, David Anthony. New York: Arno, 1980.

How THE GREAT GATSBY, JAWS and THE STORY OF ADELE H. have been distributed and exhibited is the subject of this title in the *Dissertations in Film* series.

1087 *A Competitive Cinema.* by Kelly, Terence; and Norton, Graham; and Perry, George. 204 p. illus. London: Institute of Economic Affairs, 1966.

After a research period of two years, the authors issued this analysis of the British Film Industry. They cover the history, the background of the current economic problems, the conflicts of interest and the failure of the government to help. Their recommendations for improvement include a revamping of the existing booking structure, a more lenient censorship, a London showcase for all films, a requirement for theatre operators to indicate when a film has been altered or cut, etc. The exposition of the problems is comprehensive and clear while the proposals for correction are fresh and sensible.

1088 *The Compleat Guide to Film Study.* edited by Poteet, G. Howard. 242 p. paper illus. Urbana, Illinois: The National Council of English Teachers, 1972.

The stated purpose of this anthology is "to help teachers and students learn how to explore the art form of film and to help them derive some bases for understanding it." Using a traditional approach, the book considers rationale for teaching film, some past history, film language, film as literature, film composition, film and the curriculum, and the future of film study. Supporting these sections are a filmography about films and filmmaking, with rental sources, a list of published screenplays, a short selected bibliography from the films mentioned in the narrative. One puzzling characteristic of the book is its shape—six inches high and nine inches wide—which may create some problems in both handling and storage.

Since many of the articles have appeared previously in periodicals (*Media and Methods*, etc.) and brochures (*Films About Movies*, by Kodak), the quality is almost built-in. However, the editor's contribution in selection and arrangement is commendable: the book does provide a "compleat" guide to film study. Recommended.

1089 *The Compleat Sinatra.* by Lonstein, Albert I.; and Marino, Vito R. 388 p. illus. Monroe, N.Y.: Library Research Association, 1970.

This unusual reference book deals with the many show business careers of Frank Sinatra. A discography, filmography, TV, radio, film, concert and stage appearances are included. From his first short in 1935, MAJOR BOWES AMATEUR HOUR, to DIRTY DINGUS MAGEE in 1970, his films are noted. In each case, title, studio, release date, color or black and white, cast, production credits, running time and a synopsis are given. Cameos, guest appearances and unbilled walk-ons are listed, too.

The photographs used throughout the book are well reproduced, and include numerous candids and publicity shots in addition to movie stills. Many of the recordings are of movie songs and they are so indicated in the recording section.

This specialized reference book is admirable on many counts—content, photos, arrangement—and is an ideal supplement to the articles and books listed in a selected bibliography, and to the recent *Citadel* book, *The Films of Frank Sinatra.*

1090 *The Complete Book of Amateur Film Making.* by Grosset, Phillip. illus. New York: Amphoto, 1967.

The author discusses the problems he has encountered in making films, and offers much practical advice. Topics include equipment, techniques, and other aspects of compiling a film.

1091 *The Complete Book of 8mm Movie Making.* by Yulsman, Jerry. 224 p. illus. New York: Coward, McCann & Geoghegan, 1972.

The text of this valuable aid is divided into four major sections: equipment, film makings, in the can, and sound. Each provides a rather complete overview; for example, the first introduces the 8mm filmmaking world, then considers lenses, and finally suggests some 25 guidelines or criteria for the purchase of an 8mm camera. The other sections are equally comprehensive and include many correlated pictures and charts. Eleven appendices range from tables on running times to comparisons of footage on audio cassettes and 8mm film which may aid synchronization. A lengthy index is provided.

The author's style is practical-pedantic; the information is presented in a clear, straightforward manner and is arranged in a hierarchical fashion. For older students and adults, the book can provide valuable direction and insight into 8mm filmmaking. It is recommended for mature audiences.

1092 *The Complete Book of Movie Lists.* by Van Daalen, Nicholas. 288 p. paper illus. New York: Dutton, 1979.

A compilation of lists dealing with film topics—awards, actors, directors, films, etc. Photographs and drawings accompany the opinions, facts and statistics.

1093 *The Complete Book of Movie Making.* by Rose, Tony. 109 p. illus. New York: Morgan and Morgan, 1971.

This attractive book by the editor of *Movie Maker Magazine* deals with both 16mm and 8mm filmmaking. In 17 chapters, the basic elements such as camera, lens, lighting, editing, sound, etc., are presented in progressive fashion. Since the author is concerned with both the mechanics and the creativity of filming, several chapters are devoted to film language and aesthetics. The sections are brief but comprehensive, and each contains visuals which help explain and expand the text. Diagrams, script extracts, and some tables of data on gate sizes, running times, etc. are also helpful. The production qualities contained here are both unique and attractive. Arrangement of the material is quite pleasing, and the full color film frames on the cover will catch the reader's eye.

"Complete" is a word to use with caution, but in this case it is almost justified by the text. Rose's blending of mechanics and aesthetics succeeds very nicely. Recommended.

1094 *The Complete Crosby.* by Thompson, Charles. paper illus. London: Star Books, 1978.

A revision of *Bing: The Authorized Biography*, on the occasion of Crosby's death. The original book has been updated and includes a series of tributes.

1095 *The Complete Elvis Presley: An Illustrated Record.* by Carr, Roy; and Farren, Mick. illus. New York: Crown (Harmony), 1978.

Attention is focused on Elvis Presley's recordings in this complete discography. Many illustrations accompany the story of his recording activities, which includeall the soundtracks made from his films.

1096 *The Complete Encyclopedia of Popular Music and Jazz (1900-1950).* by

Kinkle, Roger D. 4 vols. New Rochelle, N.Y.: Arlington House, 1974.

A sizeable gap in reference books about popular arts and culture has been filled with the welcome appearance of this four-volume set. Volume 1 is devoted to a historical review of popular music and jazz arranged in a year-by-year chronology. For example, the year 1929 opens with an alphabetical listing of Broadway musicals noting opening date, number of performances, cast members, composer, lyricist, and the hit songs. An alphabetical list of popular songs follows, with composer and lyricist indicated. Next, movie musicals are listed alphabetically with cast members,songs, and composers shown. Finally, two lists of selected representative recordings are offered —one for popular music, and the second for jazz. These are arranged alphabetically by artist, each entry indicating the record company, number, and the two songs appearing on the disc. No listing of long-playing records appears here, since their acceptance by the public occurred after 1950.

Volumes 2 and 3 contain biographies of those personalities who were associated with popular music and jazz in some capacity—as performing artist, composer, arranger, band leader, instrumentalist, etc. Here we find names such as Ray Bolger, Fred Astaire, June Haver, Bob Hope, Howard Keel, Burl Ives, Ray Heindorf, Teddy Wilson, Franz Waxman, and Kate Smith. Each biography gives birthdate, birthplace, date and place of death, vocation, a narrative about the subject's professional work and career, and a listing of representative recordings and LPs.

Several long appendices follow. They include a listing of 33,000 recordings issued by the nine major record companies from mid-twenties to the early forties, the period of renaissance of the record industry; Academy Award winners and nominees for music, 1934-1973; *Down Beat* and *Metronome* poll winners, 1934-1973; a time chart of release dates for 19 major record labels, 1924-1945 (this locates the year of release by use of the record number); and a short section on record collecting. Four major indexes make up the final volume: song titles (over 28,000); personalities (over 11,500); movie musicals (over 1200); and Broadway musicals (over 1500). All are arranged alphabetically. This massive multi-faceted reference work is impressive in its scope, seemingly accurate in its data and pleasing in its appearance. Once its contents and their arrangement are known, it is an easy, convenient and efficient tool to use in locating information.

The value of this reference work is obvious. For the period it covers, it offers more information on film performers and film music than any other work. Of course, Limbacher's *Film Music*, Taylor and Jackson's *The Hollywood Musical*, and *Variety Music Calvacade* are more specialized references that can be used to supplement this work. However, for data on popular music and jazz during the first half of this century, the searcher will probably need go no further than this impressive compilation. Highly recommended.

1097 *The Complete Films of Eisenstein.* by Hetherington, John. 155 p. paper illus. New York: Dutton, 1974.

The first portion of this original paperback offers a heretofore unpublished essay by Eisenstein, followed by a short chronology of his life and career. His films are presented in chronological order, 1923 to 1945, using several stills with accompanying narrative to describe each. Since the visuals are the important element here, it must be noted that they vary in quality. Many of the full-page photographs have a fuzzy, unfocused, grainy appearance. While it is always possible to discern Eisenstein's composition of a shot, the clarity of the original is lost. Reproduction of the smaller illustrations is better, but what is gained in clarity is lost in detail. Reducing scenes involving masses of people to a 2 inch x 3-1/4 inch size does a disservice to the filmmaker who designed for a large screen.

The volume does offer some valuable information in its visuals and narrative; furthermore, it gives the unacquainted a valid idea of Eisenstein's work and artistry. There is still much excitement and reward in examining these stills and frames. Some mention should be made of the price, which seems quite high. When compared to the photo quality and cost of the picture paperbacks published by such companies as Pyramid, Pflaum, and Dover, it is hard to rationalize the high price and the questionable reproductions of this book. Acceptable.

1098 *The Complete Films of William S. Hart: A Pictorial Record.* by Koszarski, Diane Kaiser. 152 p. paper illus. New York: Dover, 1980.

This original paperback book covers both short films and feature films that William S. Hart made from 1914 to 1925. Each of the 69 films is treated individually with cast, credits, a synopsis, review excerpts and a few stills. The latter—over 200 in number—are reproduced with a clarity and sharpness that is typical of Dover's careful visual reproduction. The Hart filmography is introduced by a biographical essay which deals with both his private and public lives.

Not only does this attractive volume cover the ca-

reer of a legendary American actor, but it also illuminates silent screen history from the vantage point of the western film genre.

1099 *The Complete* GREED *of Erich von Stroheim.* by Weinberg, Herman G. illus. New York: Arno, 1972.

This oversized memorial to von Stroheim and his classic film is a very special publishing venture. With the careful reproduction of 348 stills and 52 production stills, Herman Weinberg has tried to reconstruct the original GREED (1923). Using the full script, he arranges the pictures in sequential order, and gives some dialogue or continuity. The concluding page of the novel and of the screenplay are reproduced. This beautiful book will appeal to anyone who knows the von Stroheim-GREED legend. Recommended.

1100 *The Complete Kinemanager.* by Hutchison, J. 253 p. London: Kinematograph Publications, 1937.

A review of the duties, responsibilities, and rights of the motion picture theatre manager and his staff, this is a companion volume to *The Complete Projectionist.*

1101 *The Complete Motion Picture Quiz Book.* by Trigg, Harry D.; and Trigg, Yolanda, L. 356 p. paper New York: Doubleday, 1975.

The alternate title for this entertainment is "60,000 Points About Motion Pictures," a reference to scoring the 130 quizzes provided here. Each game appears in two versions: one for the film buff and the second for "the Duffer," that person whose film experiences are limited. In the latter instance either the material is easier or more information is given. A cumulative score card, which has a possible high of 30,000 points for each type of quiz, is included. Not only do the quizzes contain well-selected, mindstretching questions, but also their formats are very imaginative and avoid the usual quiz cliches.

Users can sharpen their talent for retrieving trivial information and also pick up some new facts in the process. This is one of the better quiz books—a delightful film entertainment.

1102 *The Complete Movie Quiz-Book.* by Vance, Malcolm. 118 p. paper illus. New York: Drake, 1976.

An advanced quiz book that offers over 90 questions, most of which contain 20 parts. For example, under the title "Orientals on the Screen," the challenge reads: "Listed below are stars who have portrayed Orientals or Eurasians in films. Identify the films." Twenty performers including Ruby Keeler, Hurd Hatfield, Ona Munson, and Merle Oberon are listed and five points are awarded for a correct answer. Other questions are more difficult.

The book is unusual and quite challenging. For the film buff it would make an ideal gift or personal purchase.

1103 *The Complete 9.5mm Cinematographer.* by Abbott, Harold B. 200 p. illus. London: Iliffe & Sons, 1937.

An older British book on cinematography written for the amateur filmmaker. Illustrations and diagrams are plentiful. The book is noted here because of its treatment of an unfamiliar film gauge.

1104 *Complete Portrait Collection of Academy Award Winners.* by Volpe, Nicholas. 68 p. paper illus. Santa Monica, Calif.: International Sales Services, 1961.

Portraits of the best actors and actresses, as noted by the Academy Awards, taken from the Beverly Hills Brown Derby Collection.

1105 *The Complete Technique of Making Films.* by Monier, Pierre. 304 p. paper illus. New York: Ballantine Books, 1968 (1959).

A complete and detailed rundown on all the processes of filmmaking with much technical material presented in a clear and interesting manner. Aimed at all filmmakers, experienced or otherwise.

1106 *The Complete Technique of Making Films.* by Monier, Pierre Albert. 304 p. illus. London: Focal Press, 1959.

An older volume on filmmaking, this one was taken from the original French edition and supplemented with some material on special effects.

1107 *The Complete Unabridged Super Trivia Encyclopedia.* by Worth, Fred L. 798 p. paper New York: Warner, 1977.

So much of this encyclopedia is devoted to film topics that it deserves consideration as a limited, specialized reference book. Among the hundreds of entries the reader will find: marriages (3 pages listing famous film pairs), James Bond (2 pages of casts,

actors, songs), Ma and Pa Kettle (film titles, dates), Humphrey Bogart (complete filmography, etc.), Academy Awards (pictures, songs), pseudonyms (film actors' original names), etc.

Obviously, this is a mixed bag of information that is often inconsistent in its selection of trivia headings. However, it is fun to read and it may answer some difficult questions. It is certainly worth a look.

1108 *The Complete* WEDDING MARCH *of Erich von Stroheim.* by Weinberg, Herman G. 330 p. illus. Boston: Little, Brown, 1975.

Herman G. Weinberg adds to the work he began in his pictorial reconstruction of GREED and continued with *Stroheim—A Pictoral Record of His Nine Films.* In this handsomely produced volume, he has arranged 255 still photographs in accordance with the original screenplay of THE WEDDING MARCH (1927). Enough captions and titles are provided so that the reader can easily follow both the plot and the director's intent. A lengthy, highly detailed and documented explanatory essay introduces the pictorial section by providing background, interpretation and critical comment. Weinberg's almost compulsive interest in von Stroheim coupled with a Viennese background and temperament more than qualifies him for such an essay and reconstruction. It should be noted that the film was planned in two parts, the second of which is apparently lost. The author recreates both parts here.

All of the elements necessary for an outstanding film book are present here—an informed accurate text by a dedicated author, consistently fine photographic reproduction, and attractive arrangement, design and presentation of the material. It should also be noted that the price of this volume makes it much more suitable for acquisition than the GREED volume. This is very specialized material that is highly recommended.

1109 *The Complete Works of Akira Kurosawa.* by Kurosawa, Akira. illus. Tokyo: Kinema Jumpo Sho Company, 1971-72.

The scripts of Kurosawa's major films are presented in a multi-volume set. Printed in a bilingual format, with Japanese and English columns set side by side, the scripts are generously illustrated. There has been no American distribution of these volumes as yet and they are obtainable only from the Japanese publisher. The films include THE BAD SLEEP WELL (1960), DO-DES KA-DEN (1970), DRUNKEN ANGEL (1948), THE IDIOT (1951), IKURU (1952), NO REGRETS FOR OUR YOUTH (1946), ONE WONDERFUL SUNDAY

(1947), QUIET DUEL (1949), SANSHIRO SUGATA (1943), STRAY DOG (1949), and THREE BAD MEN IN A HIDDEN FORTRESS (1958).

1110 *The Complete Works of Sergei M. Eisenstein.* by Martin, Marcel; and Lecouvette, Guy; and Segal, Abraham. illus. New York: Grove Press, 1971.

The unusual aspect of this publication is the inclusion of 120 slides taken from Eisenstein's films. Each slide is annotated in a text which accompanies the package.

1111 *Composing for the Film.* by Eisler, Hans. 165 p. London: Oxford University Press, 1948.

In this look at film music, a leftist composer discusses challenges of writing cinematic music, with examples taken mostly from obscure German films. The writing style is as murky as some of those old impressionistic movies.

1112 *Composition: The Anatomy of Picture Making.* by Sternberg, Harry. illus. New York: Pitman Pub. Co., 1958.

Although this book addresses itself to composition in still pictures, so much of the content is applicable to filmmaking, it is considered here. Border, space, shapes, activity, values and communication through design are preliminary topics leading to a longer concluding section on analyzing pictures. Student exercises are suggested. This small concise volume covers picture aesthetics efficiently and clearly. The text avoids complex terminology and the visuals used as examples have been chosen wisely. It should prove valuable for beginning courses in filmmaking, and film aesthetics.

1113 *The Compound Cinema.* by Potamkin, Harry Alan. edited by Jacobs, Lewis. 640 p. illus. New York: Teachers College Press, 1977.

During the latter years of his short life (1900-1933), Harry Potamkin wrote extensively on the film. Although his articles appeared in many different periodicals of the late twenties and early thirties, his work is unfamiliar to most of today's film scholars. Lewis Jacobs has selected and arranged an abundant sampling in this volume; included are reviews of films and books, articles, essays, and appreciations.

Jacobs has arranged the material under the follow-

ing general headings: film theory, film technique, the director's medium, sociological considerations, national traits, the politics of film art, film reviews, book reviews, and other writings.

In addition to being a copius writer, Potamkin had an early vision of the film as both an art form and a political/sociological force. Much of his writing is based upon a Marxian philosophy; for example, his review of SHANGHAI EXPRESS (1932) rages against Hollywood, Paramount, and Von Sternberg, calling their treatment of the revolutionaries "a slanderous, baseless propaganda." He urges viewing of several "profound and convincing Soviet films."

The volume contains a Potamkin bibliography, several indexes, and a few illustrations. For students and scholars the discovery of Potamkin will be a rewarding and stimulating reading experience.

1114 *A Comprehensive Resource Guide to 16mm Mental Health Films.* by MHMEP Staff. 127 p. paper Springfield, Va.: The Mental Health Media Evaluation Project, 1977.

During 1976 and 1977 the Mental Health Media Evaluation Project searched the 16mm film industry for films pertinent to public mental health education. Criteria for inclusion in this final listing included: (1) 16mm format; (2) less than 60 minutes in length; (3) content applicable to public mental health education; (4) released since 1966 or considered a recognized classic; (5) available in U.S. for rental, lease or purchase. Films on alcoholism or drugs were not considered because of earlier publication in these areas. Finally, inclusion here does not imply recommendation; see instead *An Evaluative Guide to 16mm Mental Health Films.*

In essence, then, this is a carefully arranged filmography of relatively recent releases in the wide area of mental health. Entries are arranged alphabetically by title with time, color format, grade level, availability, release date and a short annotation given for each. Access to the films can also be made by a subject index, a key word index, and a subject heading outline. Closing the book are selected feature films and documentaries running longer than 60 minutes. A distributor list is added. Recommended for professionals who deal with mental health education.

1115 *Computer Animation.* edited by Halas, John. 176 p. illus. New York: Hastings House, 1974.

A subject as new and complex as computer animation requires the expertise of many individuals for full treatment. This attractive volume attempts to satisfy that requirement by collecting chapter-length statements on various aspects of filmmaking with a computer from some 25 experts. After some introductory pages which include an essential glossary, the articles address themselves to such topics as computer animation techniques, new forms, man and computer, FORTRAN in computer films, programming languages, geometrical animation, camp and camper on Atlas, Genesy's interactive animation, solids animation, the computer studio, the animation stand, and computer film as film art.

The text is characterized by technical depth and detail. Supporting the words are illustrations, diagrams, and charts, all of which are clearly reproduced and appropriately placed. A classified index and a general index complete the work. In order for the computer to be used in filmmaking, the cooperation of animators, designers, layout men and other creative artisans is needed. This volume explores the techniques, forms, uses and problems of computer films. It is addressed to the experienced professional, but this should not discourage the interested reader from exploring its provocative contents. Highly recommended.

1116   *Comstockery in America: Patterns of Censorship and Control.* by Haney, Robert W. 199 p. Boston: Beacon, 1960.

1117   *Contemporary Film and the New Generation.* edited by Savary, Louis M.; and Carrico, J. Paul. 160 p. paper illus. New York: Association Press, 1971.

A selection of stills, script excerpts, and comments from film personalities. The first section deals with the audience and the reasons they attend films. Some concerns about contemporary films—violence, insiders, outsiders, social change, religion, heroes—are stated, and predictions are made about directors, financing films, experimental films, and the film of the future.

The book was designed to appeal to the under-30's and it puts into words and reinforces what they already know or feel. Visuals are quite good and the selective format works nicely. The potential danger of a volume like this is that it may be accepted as gospel rather than as a basis for further discussion. Acceptable.

1118   *The Concept of Structuralism.* by Bettit, Philip. 118 p. paper illus. Los Angeles: University of California

Press, 1977.

Some of the theory contained in this small volume may be applied to film study.

1119   *A Concise History of the Cinema.* edited by Cowie, Peter. 473 p. paper illus. New York: A. S. Barnes, 1971.

Thirty writers contribute to this two volume history of international cinema. Volume I covers pre-screen to World War II. Volume II covers to 1970. In each the films, directors, technological developments, and other topics are noted.

1120   *Confessions of a Cultist: On the Cinema 1955-1969.* by Sarris, Andrew. 480 p. New York: Simon & Schuster, 1970.

In his introduction to this collection of film criticism and comments, Sarris defines a film cultist as "Someone who love movies beyond all reason." He qualifies. In spite of his dislike of some fine films (Fellini's 8-1/2 (1963)) and his championing of some lesser contributions to film art (THE CARDINAL (1963), he is honest and presents valid arguments to support his views.

Since he derives his auteur philosophy of film criticism from French critics Alexandre Astruc and Andre Bazin, his focus is on directors and their personal stamp or style. As one of the most respected influential film critics writing today, Andrew Sarris deserves the attention of any reader interested in current cinema. Recommended.

1121   *Confessions of a Hollywood Columnist.* by Graham, Sheilah 310 p. paper New York: Bantam Books, 1969.

In typically waspish fashion, the last of the Hollywood gossip queens writes of the film colony as she has known it for several decades. All the major stars are given attention, sometimes a complete chapter. "Barbra," "Cary," "Frankie," and "Marilyn" are the titles of some of the 21 chapters.

By the many small, off-hand comments, the reader may get the impression that Miss Graham has little respect for most actors and in some cases, complete contempt. To her many of them are insecure, brainless, egotistical children. She is practical about herself and her career. When she writes of a possible marriage: "I liked him, although I was not in love him, but I thought, with all that money I could easily make the transition; and I was oh, Lord, so weary of the agents and the actors and the prying into other people's lives." The book is similar to the

Rex Reed subject format, but not the style. Where Reed quides his subjects into giving a portrait of themselves, Miss Graham gives you her picture. The book is gossip, innuendo, tale-telling and edited, opinionated viewpoint. It is also entertaining and will be very popular with nondiscriminating readers.

1122 *Confessions of a Scoundrel.* by Orlando, Guido. 275 p. illus. Philadelphia: Winston, 1954.

The author claims to have appeared in silent films; he later became a publicity man.

1123 *Confessions of an Actor.* by Barrymore, John. 134 p. illus. New York: Blom, 1971 (1926).

Originally published in 1926 by Bobbs-Merrill, this memoir deals mostly with Barrymore's youth and his early stage performances. Some slight reference is made to his brother Lionel's career in films, and his own preparation for screen roles. Stills from a few of his films are included.

1124 *Confessions of an Ex-Fan Magazine Writer.* by Wilkie, Jane. New York: Doubleday, 1981.

The author has been a writer-editor of fan magazines for more than 30 years. In spite of this long experience, she divulges little of interest here.

1125 *Conflict and Control in the Cinema: A Reader in Film and Society.* edited by Tullock, John. 818 p. illus. South Melbourne: Macmillan, 1977.

1126 *Connections: Technology and Change.* by EFLA Staff. 27 p. paper New York: Educational Film Library Association, 1979.

This filmography was designed to accompany the Courses By Newspaper program on issues related to technology and change. The entries are arranged under 15 general headings and include the usual film data along with a useful annotation. Additional resources and a distributor list are added.

1127 *Conrad Hall.* edited by Reed, Rochelle. 24 p. paper illus. Washington, D.C.: American Film Institute, 1973.

Cinematographer Conrad Hall was invited by the AFI to a seminar in the spring of 1973. Discussion revolved around the film FAT CITY (1971), which was

shown prior to the interview conducted by Howard Schwartz. Hall's filmography from EDGE OF FURY (1958) to THE DAY OF THE LOCUST (1974) is given.

1128 *Constance Bennett.* by McBride, Mary M. 81 p. illus. New York: Gordon Press, 1976.

Published originally in 1932 as the life story of Constance Bennett by Star Library Publications of New York.

1129 *Construction of Research Films.* by Densham, D. H. 104 p. illus. New York: Pergamon Press, 1959.

Information on making short films—script, continuity, direction, light, color, editing, possible problems, etc.

1130 *Contemporary Authors.* edited by Locher, Frances Carol. 660 p. Detroit: Gale Research, 1978.

Recent volumes in the *Contemporary Authors* series offer about 2000 biographical sketches of writers in the fields of fiction, nonfiction, poetry, journalism, drama, motion pictures, television, and other fields. This review concerns itself with those who have written for films. A cursory examination of the book shows entries for director-writers Michelangelo Antonioni, Richard Brooks, Joseph Mankiewicz; for screenplay writers Stirling Silliphant, Henry Ephron, Larry Gelbart, Horton Foote, Norman Lear; for Hollywood spokesman Jack Valenti and for film book authors Jon Tuska and Roy Armes. Each sketch contains biographical information, a bibliography, work in progress, sidelight information, and sources for further research.

Access to the 54,000 biographies in the complete series is by a cumulative index.

The information provided by this impressive reference is unique since it blends a variety of sources (including the author himself) into one concentrated entry. The scope, format, and ease of accessibility of the information makes this series a primary source for film research.

1131 *The Contemporary Cinema.* by Houston, Penelope. 222 p. paper illus. Baltimore, Md.: Penguin Books, 1963.

This original paperback is a survey by the editor of *Sight and Sound* of recent international cinema. It addresses itself directly to the major important film developments that occurred in the two post-war decades (1945-1963). Artistic trends, new directors, important films, and the industry's economic struggles for survival are some of the topics.

The writing style is spare, intelligent, informed and readable. Author Houston is on target in nearly all of her text; her early critical judgement of some directors has proven accurate over the years. Added features include a director's filmography, a representative set of international film stills, a biography and an index. This is an excellent volume for the more mature film enthusiast. College students should enjoy it immensely since it summarizes so brilliantly the new cinema. Recommended.

1132 *Contemporary Erotic Cinema.* by Rotsler, William. 280 p. paper illus. New York: Ballantine, 1973.

The first of three major parts gives definitions, background, legal attitudes and critics' reactions, and reviews filmmaking activity on both coasts. Interviews with actors, actresses, producers, directors and distributors form the second section. The final portion offers interviews and articles about the standard ingredients of the erotic film. An appendix presents what the author calls "The Erotic Cinema Checklist." Films are evaluated as XXX - Hardcore, XX - Simulation, X - Relatively Cool. The author is looking for erotic content and reaction rather than artistic merit, and awards stars on that basis. Thus BEHIND THE GREEN DOOR, DEEP THROAT (1972), and HIGH RISE all get four stars and 3 Xs, meaning they are erotic hardcore. A section of softcore illustrations is included.

The subject matter, the interview dialogue, and the topic itself may be offensive to certain readers.

1133 *Contemporary Films/McGraw Hill Feature Film Collection.* 261 p. paper illus. New York: McGraw-Hill, 197-

This fine catalog offers a collection of international feature-length films that includes many longer documentaries. Arranged alphabetically by title under the country of their origin, the films are described by a still, partial cast and production credits, release date, alternate titles, a synopsis and short critical excerpts. In most cases a full page is devoted to a single film. There is a complete film title index provided in the book's final pages.

As a reference, as a rental-purchase-lease guide or simply as a browser's entertainment, this catalog is eminently worthwhile. The arrangement of films by country of origin also gives some insight into selected national cinemas. Highly recommended.

1134 *Contemporary Films' Mini Course on Film Study.* by Schillaci, Peter. 36 p. paper illus. New York: McGraw-Hill(Contemporary Films), 1973.

The mini-course is divided into four parts, each of which consists of an explanatory text and study guides for several short films. The four topics and the 14 films are arranged as follows: (1) The Language of Images—SKY (1962), GLASS (1958), OLYMPIA DIVING SEQUENCE (1936), and VERY NICE, VERY NICE (1961); (2) The Creative Use of Actuality—VIVRE (1959), GRANTON TRAWLER (1934), and THE SEASON (1966); (3) The Varieties of Film Experience—CLAY (1964), 6,5,4,3,2,1 (1970), TIME PIECE (1965), and DREAM OF THE WILD HORSES (1962); and (4) Narrative and Film—STRINGBEAN (1964), HANGMAN (1964), and MASQUE OF THE RED DEATH (1970). A selected bibliography of books and periodicals is included.

Although it is a commercially sponsored book that promotes a film distributor's product, there can be no reservation about the excellence of the text, the films selected, the study guides and the supporting material presented here. It is most valuable for anyone concerned with teaching film; those presenting or using films will also find it extremely helpful. Highly recommended.

1135 *The Contemporary Greek Cinema.* by Schuster, Mel. 360 p. illus. Metuchen, N.J.: Scarecrow, 1979.

In his attempt to show what has happened to Greek films since 1970, Mel Schuster has engaged in his usual diligent research, including, this time, a stay in Greece to study at firsthand the films and filmmakers. The result is a rich book that deserves much critical attention. Although written as a kind of personal exploration, it includes much specific information in the biographies, filmographies, addresses, index and coverage of the Thessaloniki Film Festival from 1960 to 1977.

In his writing Schuster is able to do two things that most academics wish they could. He selects important areas in film literature that are neglected or not covered and then gives them a written treatment that cannot be surpassed. A most impressive book.

1136 *Contemporary Japanese Literature.* edited by Hibbett, Howard. 512 p. paper illus. New York: Knopf, 1977.

This anthology, which represents a sampling from almost two dozen Japanese authors, contains two film scripts: IKIRU (1952) and TOKYO STORY (1953).

Illustrations from each of the films are included.

1137 *Contemporary Literary Criticism Number 16.* edited by Gunton, Sharon R. 690 p. Detroit: Gale Research, 1980.

The volumes in this series carry the subtitle, "Excerpts From Criticism of Works of Today's Novelists, Poets, Playwrights, Short Story Writers, Filmmakers and Other Creative Writers." Number 16 is devoted exclusively to 39 film directors, ranging from Woody Allen to Lina Wertmuller. For each there are portions of film criticism taken from either books or periodicals. For example, the entry for Francis Ford Coppola includes a short biographical sketch followed by comments about YOU'RE A BIG BOY NOW (1967), FINIAN'S RAINBOW (1968), THE RAIN PEOPLE (1969), THE GODFATHER (1972), THE CONVERSATION (1974), THE GODFATHER—PART II (1975), and APOCALYPSE NOW (1979).

The entire book contains 850 excerpts, a bibliography of the sources, a cumulative series index of authors, and a cumulative series index of critics.

The selection of the directors is in keeping with the series format—they are contemporary. A satisfying mixture of critical comment is offered for each, making the volume a good reference that may be read simply for pleasure.

1138 *Contemporary Polish Cinematography: A Collective Work.* 173 p. illus. Warsaw: Polonia Pub. House, 1962.

After a short introductory chapter on the pre-1939 history of the Polish film, the film industry, film clubs, amateur films, and the post-war (1946-1961) film press. A filmography of feature films and a listing of festival prize winners complete the volume.

Many fine illustrations complement the text which tends to be expositional rather than critical. Because of the unfamiliarity of the subject matter and the very limited exhibition of Polish films in the world market, this volume is probably most valuable as a reference work.

1139 *The Content of Motion Pictures.* by Dale, Edgar. 234 p. New York: Arno Press, 1970 (1935).

One of the 12 Payne Fund Studies done in the thirties, this example of media research has been largely neglected until Arno reprinted it in 1970. The subject here is the content of motion pictures and entails such topics as locales, themes, character description, sex and love-making, marriage, romantic love,

crime, etc. There is even a chapter devoted to the content of newsreels. This book has value for historical interest and as a model for future studies.

1140 *Contests, Festivals and Grants.* by Gadney, Alan. 578 p. paper Glendale, Calif.: Festival, 1978.

The full title to this handy reference book is, *Gadney's Guide to 1800 International Contests, Festivals and Grants in Film and Video, Photography, TV-Radio Broadcasting, Writing, Poetry, Playwrighting and Journalism.* Entries in the film section are arranged under 30 headings such as abstract, animated, short, grants, student filmmaker, etc. For each there is complete sponsor data, the date, a description of the event, the general rules, fees, awards, judging information and deadlines. Further access to the events/grants is provided by an alphabetical index and a subject/category index.

Anyone planning to participate in or attend film events or to seek grants can do no better than begin with this efficiently arranged volume. It is a concentrated, rich source of information.

1141 *Continental Film Review* Anthology, 1953-55. edited by Gordon, G. 2 volumes New York: Gordon Press, 1976.

Material taken from the London Magazine which was published from 1953 to 1972.

1142 *Continued Next Week: A History of the Moving Picture Serial.* by Lahue, Kalton C. 293 p. illus. Norman, Okla.: University of Oklahoma Press, 1964.

This is an earlier volume on the same topic by the same author as *Bound and Gagged.* The subtitle may be somewhat misleading in that only the silent serial is considered. Starting with 1914 and ending in 1930, the author looks at some of the representative serial products. The text, both descriptive and evaluative, has obviously been well-researched and written with a most affectionate bias.

The illustrations are adequate. One of the books's outstanding features is the 123-page appendix which lists serials from 1912 to 1930. Included are cast and production credits, release dates and companies, and chapter titles. The casual reader will find portions of the text rather heavy because of the unfamiliarity with the performers mentioned. Only the very dedicated will be able to digest this completely. It has certain value as a reference.

1143 *Continuity Girl, a Story of Film Production.* by Robinson, Martha. 181 p. illus. London: Oxford University Press, 1946.

A simplistic account of how motion pictures are made.

1144 *Continuous Performance.* by Balaban, Carrie. 240 p. illus. New York: Putnam, 1940.

A biography of a Chicago movie magnate, Abe J. Balaban, who rose from nickelodeon operation to theatre chain ownership. Written by an adoring wife, it is suspect.

1145 *Control Techniques in Film Processing.* edited by Society of Motion Picture and Television Engineers. paper illus. Scarsdale, N.Y.: SMPTE, 1975.

Noted here as an example of the technical depth that can be found in cinema literature, this volume was prepared by a subcommittee of the Lab Practice Committee of the SMPTE. It deals with general principles, mechanical evaluation, control instruments, sensitometric control, processing chemistry and analysis, and economic considerations in establishing a process control system.

1146 *A Conversation About Screenwriting with Joan Tewkesbury.* edited by Loeb, Anthony. 24 p. paper illus. Chicago: Columbia College Press, 1975.

This booklet is an edited record of an interview with screenwriter Joan Tewkesbury conducted by Anthony Loeb at Columbia College on November 5, 1975. It deals mostly with Tewkesbury's work with Robert Altman— NASHVILLE (1975) and THIEVES LIKE US (1974). Some illustrations are included.

1147 *A Conversation with John Cassavetes.* edited by Loeb, Anthony. 16 p. paper illus. Chicago: Columbia College Press, 1975.

A record of an interview with John Cassavetes conducted by Anthony Loeb at Columbia College on March 5, 1975, this booklet is nicely illustrated and contains a filmography.

1148 *Conversations.* by Shay, Don. illus. Albuquerque, N.M.: Kaleidoscope Press, 1969.

There are eight in-depth interviews conducted, with one exception (Crabbe), in the late sixties. The personalities interviewed are Buster Crabbe, Peter Falk, Henry Fonda, Charlton Heston, Karl Malden, Gregory Peck, Edward G. Robinson and Rod Steiger.

Each interview is reported in the tape recorder or dialogue fashion. The result is a more honest, candid view of the subject than that offered in other formats. In most instances, the questions posed concentrate on areas and issues of filmmaking. The responses give the reader much deeper insight into the person of the subject. Praise must be extended to the many illustrations used (some of which are not identified). Equally fine are the filmographies including cast credits for all eight men. An unusually good example of the interview volume.

1149 *Conversations in the Raw.* by Reed, Rex. 312 p. New York: World Pub. Co., 1969.

Rex Reed is to the film interview as Pauline Kael is to the film review. Along with John Simon they form the devilish triumvirate of current film writing.

Throughout all of Reed's interviews, there seems to run an underlying sensitivity to his subjects. It is only when they forget their manners, their good fortune, or the value of a moderate humility that Reed exposes them, in a rather ruthless fashion. He simply reports the conversation with deadly accuracy and gives a total observation of the setting. The result in such a case is often devastating, and, of course, totally entertaining. The subjects emerge as human beings rather than the mythical characters given us by the fan magazines.

1150 *Conversations with Joan Crawford.* by Newquist, Roy. illus. Secaucus, N.J.: Citadel, 1980.

In a series of interviews given a few months before her death, Joan Crawford addresses some of the gossip, rumor, and controversy that surrounded her life. She speaks of her brother, mother, children, coworkers, and other assorted Crawford concerns. She loved Clark Gable, disliked Bette Davis and Spencer Tracy, and admits she was too strict with her children at times. Some of her comments seem to anticipate *Mommie Dearest*.

1151 *Conversations with Marilyn.* by Weatherby, W. J. 229 p. New York: Mason/Charter, 1976.

The author first met Marilyn Monroe when he covered the making of THE MISFITS (1961) for *The Manchester Guardian.* They become better acquainted later in New York City when they met several times in a neighborhood bar. Both periods are recalled in this volume.

Although the author is skilled in presenting his subject rather than himself, one gets the feeling that his basic raw material—the actual conversations with Monroe—was insufficient for a full book and he has had to pad with some familiar peripheral material. This is expecially true with the portion that deals with THE MISFITS production. The New York bar conversations are far more interesting and offer a portrait of Monroe which is easy to accept—that of an intelligent actress who has a talent to become what people expect her to be.

The importance of this volume lies in the Monroe quotations and comments, which are entertaining and enlightening. If there still remains a fascination with the Monroe mystique, this volume will satisfy readers searching for another and somewhat different portrait of the actress. Acceptable.

1152 *Cooking with the Stars.* edited by Singer, Jane Sherrod. 432 p. illus. New York: A.S. Barnes, 1970.

This unusual volume carries subtitles such as "Hollywood's Favorite Recipes" and "A Collection of Recipes Tested in the Kitchens of Hollywood." The contributions are arranged in food category fashion: appetizers, beverages, soups, salads, seafoods, poultry, game, meat, vegtables, etc. Illustrations of the stars come from a variety of sources and some of the recipes are accompanied by autographs or explanations. The recipes are bound to interest most cooks and, for the reader who can believe that Frank Sinatra's favorite recipe is for meatballs, there may be some additional excitement.

1153 *Coop: The Life and Legend of Gary Cooper.* by Kaminsky, Stuart. 295 p. illus. New York: St. Martin's Press, 1980.

That the author had some difficulty in stretching his material might be seen in the scant 221 pages of text he offers. Although Gary Cooper may not offer the best biographical potential, his private life was not without incident, and certainly the enigma of the man offers challenge. Kaminsky relies on public record, film viewing, and interviews with Cooper's friends and coworkers. The latter are not especially informative and consist largely of short tributes about Cooper's skill as a film actor. Kaminsky's strength is in his explanation of how Cooper developed from a handsome supporting player into one of

the screen's legendary icons.

A bibliography, a detailed filmography, a few illustrations and an index occupy the final third of the book.

Occasionally interesting, this volume does suggest that Cooper, as both performer and person, may be an exciting subject. Unfortunately Kaminsky offers little more than a flat, meager partial portrait.

1154 *Cooperative Film Services in Public Libraries.* by Cody, Patricia Blair; and Myer, Violet F. 127 p. paper Chicago: American Library Association, 1956.

A look at the film services available at public libraries in the United States in the period which followed World War II.

1155 COPPERFIELD '70.: *The Story of the Making of the Omnibus-20th Century-Fox Film.* by Curry, George. 210 p. paper illus. New York: Ballantine, 1971.

Contains a script of the film along with the story of the production, divided into three periods — pre-shooting, actual photography, and post-shooting. Photographs.

1156 *Copyright.* by Hurst, Walter E. 284 p. paper illus. Hollywood, Calif.: Seven Arts Press, 1977.

This informational, how-to-do-it book has the lengthy subtitle, "How to Register Your Copyright and Introduction to New and Historical Copyright Law." It contains some historical background, a description of the 1976 Copyright Act, instructions for copyright application, Supreme Court interpretations, copyright exploitations, and other topics. Helpful illustrations have been provided by Don Rico and access to the many topics covered is by a detailed index.

A practical approach to a complex subject which should prove valuable to anyone concerned with copyright.

1157 *Copyrights, Trademarks, and Literary Property Course, 1978-1979.* New York: Practising Law Institute, 1979.

1158 *Core Media Collection for Secondary Schools.* by Brown, Lucy Gregor.

221 p. New York: Bowker, 1975.

The intention of this volume is to provide a qualitative selection guide to 2000 titles of nonprint media. It addresses itself to the curriculum needs of students in grades 7 to 12 and to other young adults. Criteria used in selection are authenticity, technical quality, appropriateness, student level, interest and motivation, accuracy in context, and validity in treatment. Sources used in selection are books, periodicals, services, school catalogs, journals, awards, and "author experience." The main body of the volume lists the titles in accordance with Sears list of subject headings. An alphabetical index of titles and a roster of producers/distributors concludes the book. A cursory inspection of the book suggests the following questions.

(1) Is ita true core collection or simply a listing of recommended titles? Placing only one performer (James Earl Jones) under Actors and Actresses is an example of core imbalance. Placing the original cast recordings of the songs from a musical adaptation (Oliver) under Drama is not only imbalance but possible misplacement. Omitting classic 16mm films such as WHY MAN CREATES or AN OCCURRENCE AT OWL CREEK BRIDGE from any secondary school core is incomprehensible, when lesser known titles are included.

(2) What was the author's role in selection? Sources are indicated, but her endorsement is not.

(3) Why do some entries contain a description while others do not? For example, what is the content of the filmstrip THE REVOLUTION: FRONTIERS AFLAME?

(4) Is the volume addressed only to those familiar with Sears? For example, where is the material on film study? Mass media? The communication heading does not list titles pertinent to these two vital areas.

(5) Why is 16mm film almost absent from the list? The explanation given is that most schools do not purchase short films. The fact that many belong to pools for which they provide selection input is ignored.

(6)Aren't the few 16mm films ultimately listed a poor, unbalanced selection for a core? Does the following list represent the best 16mm films for the given subjects? AMERICAN TIME CAPSULE (U.S.—History); THE BALLAD OF CROWFOOT (Indians of North America); BIG HORN (Bighorn Sheep); CASTLES MADE OF SAND (Humanities); CREATIVE HANDS (Folk Art, American); FIRE MOUNTAIN (Volcanoes); FLIGHT (Flight); FOG (Weather); FOR YOUNG PLEASURE (Art—Appreciation); HORSES (Horses); IS THERE A CAREER IN HEALTH SERVICES FOR YOU? (Career Guidance); KING OF THE HILL (Human Relations); POLLUTION: IT'S UP TO YOU (Pollution); PULSE OF LIFE (Health Education); THERE IS A LAW AGAINST IT (Consumer Education); and TOMMY'S FIRST CAR (Consumer Education).

(7) Why a film and a filmstrip with the same title on the same topic (Horses)?

(8) Since there is no listing by type of media, it is difficult to tell except by actual count, but isn't there a predominance of filmstrips in this collection? Are no simulation games suitable for a core collection?

(9) Was the book edited and proofread? Media and Method appears for Media and Methods; two source entries (ESL and GVL) are given for Gaver's Elementary School Library Collection without any further distinguishing identification; Miller, Inge and Albee are omitted under the Dramatist heading. Designation of sound or silent is omitted in the 8mm film loop of AN AMERICAN TIME CAPSULE.

In summary, this appears to be a random selection of recommended nonprint titles arranged under Sears headings. As such it is acceptable, but it is most vulnerable in calling itself a core collection and is not acceptable in that context.

1159   CORNER IN WHEAT. by Petric, Vlada. 31 p. paper illus. Cambridge, Mass.: University Film Study Center, 1975.

A shot-by-shot analysis of D.W. Griffith's film, A CORNER IN WHEAT (1910), is accompanied by a discussion of the filmmaker's structural and directorial techniques.

1160   *Costume Design in the Movies.* by Leese, Elizabeth. 168 p. illus. New York: Ungar, 1977.

This reference book devoted to costume design in films is an excellent one which combines information and illustrations in a most entertaining presentation. A short history of costume design introduces a biographical dictionary of the most famous names in the profession. For each there is a short biography, a list of Academy Award/ Society of Film and Television Arts nominations, and a filmography. Close by many of the entries are visual examples of the costumes and/or picture of the designer. The index provides access to all the titles listed in the designer filmographies. A list of Oscar and SFTA nominations (and winners) concludes the volume.

Used as a reference or a browsing experience, this book offers an abundance of pleasure and information. Topic, arrangement, production, presentation, support elements—all these are combined into an outstanding film book. Highly recommended.

1161 *Costumes by Nathan.* by Nathan, Archie. 207 p. illus. London: Newnes, 1960.

Autobiography of costume designer Archie Nathan which includes illustrations of the stars in Nathan designs.

1162 *Council of Europe Film Weeks.* 112 p. illus. Strasbourg: Council of Europe, 1966.

Arranged in a loose-leaf binder are one-page descriptions designed to acquaint the world with good European short films. This grouping was selected and shown in Paris (1964) and Edinburgh (1965). The information is directed at distributors who may wish to acquire the films. Contributing countries are Germany, Great Britian, Sweden, Denmark, Italy, Turkey, France, Switzerland, Austria, and the Netherlands.

1163 *Counseling Clients in the Entertainment Industry.* by Silfen, Martin E. 300 p. paper New York: Practising Law Institute, 1980.

This specialized volume examines contractual relations involving the performer. It is derived from a course given at the Practising Law Institute.

1164 *The Count: The Life and Films of Bela "Dracula" Lugosi.* by Lennig, Arthur. 347 p. illus. New York: G. P. Putnam's, 1974.

Arthur Lennig's long interest in Bela Lugosi has been combined with his ability to write critically about his enthusiasms in this volume. Although his affection for Lugosi is apparent throughout, Lennig is objective about the human qualities, mistakes and failings of his subject. He describes Lugosi's early career in the Hungarian theatre and his first Broadway roles in the twenties. It was his appearance in the Broadway play, "Dracula," that led to his most famous film. Lugosi began his film career in 1917 with A LEOPARD and made his last film, PLAN 9 FROM OUTER SPACE, in 1959. Lennig gives attention to the other films he made during his lifetime, offering both description and critical analysis for most.

The photographs have been carefully selected and reproduced, adding a visual dimension to the excellent text. The filmography is another asset, as is the detailed index. A fascinating study of a colorful actor and personality, this volume will attract and ultimately reward many readers. Recommended.

1165 *Course in Motion Picture Appreciation.* by Sterner, Alice Parvin; and Bowden, W. Paul. 61 p. paper Newark, N.J.: Educational and Recreational Guides, 1937.

This pioneering effort at introducing the serious study of motion pictures into the schools includes a short bibliography and was produced with the cooperation of the Finer Films Federation of New Jersey.

1166 *The Cowboy: Six Shooters, Songs and Sex.* edited by Harris, Charles W.; and Rainey, Buck. 167 p. illus. Norman, Oklahoma: University of Oklahoma Press, 1976.

The spring 1975 issue of *The Red River Valley Historical Review* was a special issue devoted to essays about the life and customs of the American cowboy. That anthology is reprinted in this attractively produced volume which attempts to separate fact from fiction and reality from myth. Treated are such topics as the cowboy's weapons, his sex life, and his music, as well as his image in literature, films and in myth.

Although many of the essays include references to films, it is the long article by Buck Rainey, entitled "The Reel Cowboy," which is of pertinence to film literature. The author rejects the major Hollywood westerns as insignificant in formulating the image of the cowboy and chooses instead to discuss the qualities, plots, characters, directors and stars of the B westerns. Using a historical approach, the narrative, which is both factual and critical, ends with the death of the genre in 1954. A pleasing collection of illustrations and drawings accompany the text along with many footnotes and a general index.

This study has the virtues and faults of most anthologies. It lacks cohesiveness as it attempts to integrate several disparate approaches to a general theme. What it does offer, however, is some freshness and vitality in its treatment of a topic that has long fascinated writers and readers. Acceptable.

1167 *Cowboy Heroes.* 82 p. illus. paper New York: Starlog, 1981.

A collective biography.

1168 *Craft Films: An Index of International Films on Crafts.* compiled by Salz, Kay. 156 p. New York: Neal-Schuman, 1979.

This attractive book was initiated by the New York State Craftsmen Inc., a nonprofit organization dedicated to furthering public interest in crafts. Included under this broad subject heading are such crafts as basketry, blacksmithing, bread baking, ceramics, glass, jewelery, kites, leatherwork, metalwork, printmaking, quilts, spinning, textiles, weaving, and woodworking.

Editor-compiler Kay Salz has arranged over 1000 films alphabetically by title. For each there is the usual film data and a short descriptive annotation. A detailed subject guide facilitates access to the individual films. A distributor index and an index of the artists and craftspeople appearing in the films are also included.

With the renewal of interest and enthusiasm for handicrafts, this volume is certainly most welcome. It is a quality production that can be used advantageously in a wide variety of situations by a diverse audience.

1169 *The Craft of Comedy.* by Seyler, Athene. illus. London: Muller, 1943.

The author is a comedy character actress who appeared in British films from the twenties to the sixties.

1170 *The Craft of Film.* edited by Fisher, David J. paper illus. London: Attic Pub., 1970.

This project consists of 22 oversized booklets collected in a binder. It addresses itself to technical matters such as lighting, cameras, film speeds and qualities rather than design, acting or production. A follow-up subscription service is provided.

1171 *The Craft of the Screenwriter.* by Brady, John. 488 p. New York: Simon and Schuster, 1981.

A collection of interviews with William Goldman, Ernest Lehman, Paul Schrader, Neil Simon, Robert Towne, and Paddy Chayefsky. How directors are often ruthless in their interpretation of a screenplay is mentioned frequently.

1172 *Crash Kavanagh.* by Kavanagh, Reginald. 256 p. illus. London: Parrish, 1953.

Reginald (Crash) Kavanagh was a stuntman who specialized in performing car crashes for films. He also did "air to ground" transfers and many other stunts for the cameras.

1173 *Crawford: The Last Years.* by Johnes, Carl. 172 p. paper New York: Dell, 1979.

Carl Johnes met Joan Crawford when he was sent by Columbia Pictures to perform a service for the actress. They remained friends for the five-year period preceding her death. With his almost eager approval, Crawford used him in a variety of roles—companion, confidante, messenger, errand boy, etc.

In this affectionate memoir, he gives a fully dimensioned portrait of the legendary actress in her twilight years.

The reader is left with a nice feeling about Crawford, very unlike the sour taste left by Christina Crawford in *Mommie Dearest*.

1174 *The Crazy Mirror: Hollywood Comedy and the American Image.* by Durgnat, Raymond. 280 p. illus. London: Faber & Faber, 1969.

The Crazy Mirror is an unfortunate title for so excellent a book. It is an analysis of American screen comedy with an attempt to relate the screen happenings in particular films to the American scene and personality of the period of the films. Much of the analysis is in-depth, subjective, and controversial.

As is usual with Durgnat's work, the book is scholarly but eminently readable. Because of the wide range of examples offered in the text and the fine filmography appended, this book is recommended.

1175 *Crazy Salad.* by Ephron, Nora. 201 p. New York: Random, 1975.

A collection of articles about women, some of whom have worked in films.

1176 *Crazy Sundays: F. Scott Fitzgerald in Hollywood.* by Latham, Aaron. 308 p. illus. New York: Viking Press, 1971.

As indicated in the subtitle, this volume by a young reporter addresses itself exclusively to Fitzgerald in Hollywood. In 1927, just as sound films became a reality, Fitzgerald was writing a script called "Lipstick" for Constance Talmadge. His work on other later films such as A YANK AT OXFORD (1938), THREE COMRADES (1938), and THE WOMEN (1939), is examined. WINTER CARNIVAL (1939) written along with Budd Schulberg was to be his last screen-writing effort.

The description of what screenplay writing was like in the heyday of the big studios is the book's strength. Impressive also is the apparent research done by the author in reviewing most of the Hollywood scriptwriting done by Fitzgerald. Recommended.

1177 *Creating Special Effects for TV and Films.* by Wilkie, Bernard. 158 p. paper illus. New York: Hastings House, 1977.

Special effects are used in film and television to enrich certain scenes by creating simple illusions which aim at approaching realism. They encompass a wide variety of techniques, many of which are discussed in this volume, which is one of the *Media Manuals* series. Included are such effects as matte shots, scenic projection, stopframe animation, mirrored effects, models, miniature, periscopes, etc. Specific attention is given to such on-screen simulations as fire, water, explosions, bullets, arrows, knives, break-away furniture, weather extremes, cobwebs, automobiles, etc. Although the text has been designed as a professional's guide to the design and use of special effects, the general reader will find much of the presentation informative and revealing.

The book is nicely illustrated and contains a glossary and a few suggestions for further reading. It continues the high quality characteristics of the *Media Manuals* series. Recommended.

1178 *The Creation of Dino De Laurentiis'* KING KONG. by Bahrenburg, Bruce. 273 p. paper illus. New York: Pocket Books, 1976.

Bruce Bahrenburg was the unit publicist for KING KONG (1976) and, following his recently acquired habit, he has written a book about the film's production. Ego evidently pervaded the entire effort, stretching from the arrogant producer to the inferior, rather stupid idea of remaking the classic 1933 film. Here we have another attempt to substitute publicity hype for creative talent. Early on, the informed reader will know he is in a publicity person's hands when THE GREAT GATSBY (1974) is identified as a blockbuster movie. Such statements do not inspire confidence. Some of the technical work and shooting described is slightly interesting but most of the reportage is trivial, resulting in a dull book about a dull movie.

1179 *Creative Differences: Profiles of Hollywood Dissidents.* by Zheutlin, Barbara; and Talbot, David. 370 p. paper illus. Boston: South End Press, 1978.

This collective biography, which concentrates on the Hollywood Left, includes 16 film workers representing a wide diversity of jobs within the film industry. They are writers Albert Maltz and Abraham Polonsky, cinematographer Haskell Wexler, actresses Jane Fonda and Hilda Haynes, executive Thom Mount, director Michael Schultz, studio office workers Carol Chaka, Lynda Calhoun and Patti Bereyso and political activists Mark Rosenberg, Bruce Green, Mike Gray, Jesus Salvador Trevino, and Lynn Phillips.

The biographies, which emphasize the political beliefs and activities of the subjects, provide a history of the Left in Hollywood from pre-blacklist days to the present. The authors and the subjects are committed to the vision of people working together for social change. Here they are concerned with how to use motion pictures to bring about desired changes.

This is a different kind of collective biography in that its major intent is to provide a historical survey of the Hollywood Left and its political influence. Mature readers will find a most provocative subject handled with intelligence, skill, and style.

1180 *Creative Film-Making.* by Smallman, Kirk. 245 p. illus. London: Collier-Macmillan, 1969.

This volume is an introduction to filmmaking and includes sections on films, cameras, lighting, lenses, editing, sound, etc. The large 8 inch x 11 inch pages give an impression of spaciousness since the large type used seldom fills more than 60 percent of the space available. The reader may wonder whether the white expanse on each printed page is for personal notes on the many topics.

Picture quality varies widely and some images are bled off the page making the message incomplete—for example, the comparison of film sizes. A few shots are too small for total effectiveness. Other pictures and diagrams are very good. The text, presented in a leisurely manner, is both chatty and informative. A sample script and an economy budget are included. This volume is designed primarily for individual personal use.

1181 *Creative Intention.* by Parker, Ben R.; and Drabnik, Patricia J. 292 p. New York: Law-Arts Publishers, 1974.

Subtitled "About Audio Visual Communication from Hollywood to John Doe," this volume offers a different approach to producing and directing for motion pictures and television. It employs a thoughtful, philosophical and theoretical exposition rather than the usual arrangement of production activities. Emphasizing creative self-expression and imagination, the authors have aimed the professional text at the "John Doe" reader.

Topics discussed in the first "Hollywood" section include interpretation, the director, story projection, the blending of visual and audio elements, the scenario, evaluation, creative intention, and live television. The second "John Doe" section defines and describes the work of the creative individuals involved in film and TV production—unit manager, art director, wardrobe supervisor, key grip, et al. Scripting, editing and composition sections precede the cinema techniques of lighting, casting, locations, sound rehearsals, blocking, etc. After some concluding suggestions, the authors add samples of basic schedule and budget forms and some further reference and resources. The volume has a good index. The drawings used throughout are simple, easy to understand, andcomplement the text nicely.

The possible audience for such a text as this is large. It deals with professional-advanced production and direction and will be appreciated by commercial producers, writers, directors, etc. However, so much of the material is applicable to any attempt at audiovisual creation that the book also has value for the beginner, the student, the advanced nonprofessional, and others. The clear exposition found in the text and visuals, supported by the underlying emphasis on creative self-expression, will make the book valuable and interesting to many readers. Recommended. Obviously it is also a strong candidate for a basic text in media design and filmmaking courses.

1182   *The Creative Teacher.* edited by Evans, William H. 164 p. paper New York: Bantam, 1971.

Some selected trends, developments and methodologies in teaching English on the secondary school level are discussed by 14 educators in this volume. The chapter entitled "Film Experience in the Literature Class" by H. James Crow is of specific interest. It is an informative, provocative challenge supplemented by notes, information sources and a short bibliography.

1183   *Creative Use of Films in Education.* by Beeler, Duane; and McCallister, Frank. 86 p. paper illus. Chicago: Labor Education Div., Roosevelt University, 1968.

Subtitled "A Case Study of an Adult Educational Program for Union Leaders," this volume makes suggestions for the use of film with a specific audience. Making no claims to be the definitive method, the text emphasizes the creativity of the teacher or leader as the major factor in film use. The philosophy of using film is established in two introductory chapters. Major sections are devoted to three film genres—the labor training film, the documentary film, and the entertainment feature film. An appendix contains a bibliography, and film sources and film distributors.

The text offers a well-written, no-nonsense approach to film use and it should be of value to anyone concerned with adult education. Illustrations are presented in a bluish monotone which diminishes their effectiveness; however, it is the text which gives this volume its quality. Recommended.

1184   *Creativity in the Communicative Arts: A Selective Bibliography 1960-1970.* edited by Ceynar, Marvin E. 134 p. Troy, N.Y.: Whitston, 1975.

Although there are many publications on the subject of creativity, this volume claims to be the only bibliography on the topic of creativity in the communicative arts. Limited to the 1960-70 decade, the selective listings emphasize periodical articles rather than books, theses, or dissertations. In the selection process, creativity was identified with "innovations of a valuable sort."

Eleven areas are identified in the text: advertising, art, education, fiction, films, group communication, mass media, music, poetry, speech communication, and theatre. An author index completes the book.

The film section covers pages 51 to 54 and lists a total of 36 entries. Arranged alphabetically in an intermix of both titles and author surnames, the entries seem to be concerned mostly with underground films and experimentation. Two paragraphs in the preface explain what the compilers attempted in this short film section and end with, "Hopefully, the persons using this bibliography will come up with a sound definition and understanding of creativity in films."

With the availability of so many periodical indexes and other reference tools, the small listing here might justify the use, but not the purchase of this volume.

1185   *Creators of Life: A History of Animation.* by Heraldson, Donald. 298 p. illus. New York: Drake, 1975.

The title of this book describes only a part of its contents. Much of the text is concerned with the many complex processes of animation.

It begins with a chronological history of the early "creators" and their work—Edison, Friese-Greene, Melies, Cohl, Blackton, McCay, and others.

The center section deals with the processes, including puppet animation. Then its back to biography with longer concluding chapters on John R. Bray, Paul Houghton Terry, Max Fleischer, Walt Disney and Richard Williams. Appendixes include a bibliography, directions for making an animated film, a timing/frames chart, Academy Awards for animated films, and a list of suppliers of animation materials. The volume is illustrated, but unfortunately, the reproduction of the visuals ranges from poor to fair at best.

In his attempt to cover the fields of history and production, the author has provided a detailed overview of both. The interested reader will be very satisfied. If the book is used as an introductory volume, it can provide a strong valuable base for further study. Recommended.

1186 *Crime and Justice in America.* by Dick, Esme. 15 p. paper New York: Educational Film Library Association, 1977.

This list of films correlates with the Courses By Newspaper program entitled "Crime and Justice in America." The entries are distributed under 15 general headings and include the usual data and a good annotation. Additional resources, films, and a distributor list complete the filmography.

1187 *Crime, Detective, Espionage, Mystery and Thriller Fiction & Film: A Comprehensive Bibliography of Critical Writing through 1979.* by Skene-Melvin, David; and Skene-Melvin, Ann. 367 p. Westport, Conn.: Greenwood, 1980.

1188 *Crime Movies.* by Clarens, Carlos. 351 p. paper illus. New York: W. W. Norton, 1980.

With the same meticulous care that he provided for *An Illustrated History of the Horror Film*, Carlos Clarens considers the gangster film "From Griffith to THE GODFATHER and Beyond." In addition to background, critical comment and overview, the author treats plots, actors, directors, political and social trends. He tries to relate the gangster films to the decade in which they appeared. Many fine illustra-

tions and a detailed index accompany this excellent original critical analysis of the genre.

1189 *The Crisis of the Film.* by Fletcher, John Gould. 35 p. paper Seattle: University of Washington, 1929.

An early argument concerning the motion pictures' failure to live up to its potential, this short monograph urged the creation of a film university. Reprinted in *Screen Monographs II*.

1190 *Critical Approaches to Federico Fellini's* 8-1/2. by Benderson, Albert Edward. 239 p. New York: Arno, 1974.

This volume receives the minimal production typical of the *Dissertations on Film* series. The typewritten pages of the original dissertation appear to have been used for this publication. Written at the State University of New York in Buffalo in 1973, the study offers both a contextual and an archetypal analysis along with chapters on "The Autobiographical Fallacy" and "The World of Fellini's Films." The appendixes offer a synopsis of 8-1/2 (1963) and a discussion of "The Pinocchio Motif" in 8-1/2. A lengthy bibliography concludes the study.

Although the ideas, analyses, and interpretations put forth by the author are stimulating, their presentation in an expensive hardbound volume that features typewritten print on low-quality paper and omits any illustrations, index, etc., may give purchasers pause. The material may be more appropriate for one of the serious film periodicals.

1191 *Critical Focus: An Introduction to Film.* by Blumenberg, Richard M. 315 p. paper illus. Belmont, Calif.: Wadsworth Publishing Co., 1975.

This text aims at a general introduction to film study by giving attention to history, aesthetics, theory, criticism, scripting, filmmaking, and censorship. After offering a rationale for studying film, the text relates it to other arts and discusses its unique qualities. In succeeding sections the narrative film, the documentary film, and the experimental film are explored, using the subdisciplines of film study listed above. A final section on filmmaking is followed by an epilogue, a discussion of careers in film, a bibliography, a glossary, and an index. Accompanying the text are many well-selected illustrations which are adequately reproduced.

The author has attempted a departure from the usual introductory text, and while some of his emphases may be debatable, by and large this is a most successful effort. It can be used in a variety of situations with a range of student audiences. Recommended.

1192 *A Critical History of the British Cinema.* by Armes, Roy. 374 p. illus. New York: Oxford University Press, 1978.

According to the author, "The primary aim of this present history—in addition to providing a synthesis of the available knowledge—is therefore to provide a genuinely critical perspective on eighty years of British filmmaking." Unfortunately, only a slight and partial success is achieved.

While an enormous quantity of factual data is presented, little of it is boiled down into readable/recognizable trends, concepts, or thoughts. Instead, film titles are grouped together in meaningless fashion in what seems to be an attempt to "get it all in." The critical function is often minimized in short, rather perfunctory plot analyses, accompanied by a few predictable, standard comments. Many important names or titles associated with British film are largely overlooked—STAGE FRIGHT (1950), ST. MARTIN'S LANE (1938), SAPPHIRE (1959), VICTIM (1961), Jack Hawkins, Joyce Grenfell, Rex Harrison, Glynis Johns—because of the auteur approach that has been used.

The volume is nicely illustrated and a bibliography, chapter notes, and an index are added.

Armes has attempted a formidable task and, because of either a wealth of material, an inappropriate arrangement, or simply being too close to his subject, has had difficulty in bringing a sense of order or joy to his account. It is difficult to feel any involvement or affection for the story as presented here.

1193 *The Critical Index.* by Gerlach, John C.; and Gerlach, Lana. 726 p. paper New York: Teachers College Press, 1973.

This bibliography of articles on film in English was generated by a computer. Its entries cover the period 1946 to 1973 and are arranged first by names and then by topics. Twenty-two periodicals were used and some 5000 items are listed.

In the names section the user will find articles on actors, cinematographers, critics, directors, films, novelists, producers and screenwriters. The topic section is arranged in hierarchical fashion and both a list of 175 topics and a corresponding dictionary of the topics are included to aid the user. Thus, in the name section under "Garland," we find two articles: "The Great Come-back" by Peter Brinson from *Films and Filming*, December 1954, pp. 4-5 and

"Judy Garland" also from *Films and Filming*, October 1961, pp. 10-11. Mel Schuster's bibliography *Motion Picture Performers* lists 100 periodical articles about Garland. The researcher will have to decide whether to limit his investigation to only the "primary" periodicals listed here or to the wide range offered by Schuster in his books.

The name index here occupies the first half of the book. In the second, topic, half we find under cinematographers some 18 pages of articles arranged alphabetically by subject name. Thus, for James Wong Howe there are six articles with author names used to determine their order. An author index, a title index and some rather surface coverage of supplementary materials complete the book. While there can be no argument about the intention of this reference volume, some reservation can be made about its limited coverage and its arrangement of material (alphabetically vs. chronologically). Acceptable.

1194 *Critical Index of Films on Man and His Environment.* by Conservation Education Association. 32 p. paper Danville, Ill.: Interstate, 1972.

1195 *Criticism and Censorship.* by Kerr, Walter. 86 p. paper Milwaukee: Bruce Publishing Co., 1954.

In this early publication, the eminent critic, Walter Kerr, discusses the relationship between criticism and censorship. The material was taken from a Gabriel Richard Lecture which was cosponsored by the National Catholic Educational Association and Trinity College of Washington, D.C.

1196 *Criticizing the Critics.* by English, John W. 240 p. New York: Hastings House, 1979.

An investigation into the practice of professional criticism is served in buffet style in this book. Using samples from the fields of film, art, dance, books, music and even restaurants, John English offers comments on the service that critics perform for the mass media audience. The goal is to educate and inform the reader in order that he may be able to understand and evaluate the work of the critic.

What the volume lacks is any clear direction or conclusion. Instead it offers bits and pieces about criticism, coming around finally to some general conclusions and recommendations.

The text does discuss the critical process, the multiple roles of critics, ethics, and effects, but saves its major space for "Random Notes on the State of the

Art." It may be disappointing to some that depth has been sacrificed for a breezy overview. This is not to say that the book is lacking in appeal or interest. It is constantly entertaining, and anyone who pays attention to critical evaluations will find it quite enjoyable.

1197 *A Critique of Film Theory.* by Henderson, Brian. 233 paper New York: Dutton, 1980.

Brian Henderson is concerned with film theory in this collection of nine essays, most of which were previously published in periodicals such as *Film Quarterly* and *Film Comment.* They are arranged in a form that considers and criticizes the film theories of Eisenstein, Bazin, and Godard first. Then there is an evaluation of Christian Metz's work with film semantics. Several conclusions are offered including the obvious one about the necessity for the continual critique of film theory.

The discussion offered here is an intensely intellectual one demanding continual rereading and rethinking for any degree of comprehension. It will be very heavy going for most readers and only those with an advanced background in the aesthetics of the arts and/or film theory will survive the many references, citations, concepts, doctrines, theories, models, structures, propositions, assumptions and words that Henderson uses for his complex critique.

1198 CROMWELL. by Ashley, Maurice. 40 p. paper illus. London: Juvenile Group, IPC Magazines, 1970.

A biography of Cromwell opens this souvenir book. Other names from the same period are noted and there is a historical essay entitled "The Man From Huntingdonshire." A diagram of the Battle of Naseby follows. The remainder of the book deals with the making of the 1970 film and with its stars, Richard Harris and Alec Guinness. Other cast and technical credits include director Ken Hughes.

1199 *The Crosby Years.* by Barnes, Ken. 216 p. illus. New York: St. Martin's Press, 1980.

Ken Barnes served as the producer of several Bing Crosby albums and capitalizes on that experience here. Sections dealing with Crosby's music are stonger than the surface coverage given to the other biographical elements. Included are a discography, a filmography, selected music and lyrics, and some fine illustrations.

1200 *Crossroads to the Cinema.* by Brode, Douglas. 480 p. paper Boston: Holbrook Press, 1975.

In this anthology-textbook there are 5 major headings: movie medium; makeup of the movies; film and the arts; film genres; and themes, trends, and transitions. Under each heading there are six or seven articles, essays, or lectures taken from a variety of recently published sources. Each article is preceded by a page of author comment/introduction and followed by some study questions. Additional readings are suggested in the book's final pages and a list of film distributors is appended.

The selection, arrangement and presentation of the articles is very good. Recommended.

1201 THE CROWNING EXPERIENCE. edited by Hardiman, James W. paper illus. New York: Random House, 1960.

A full-color souvenir book of the Moral Re-Armament film, THE CROWNING EXPERIENCE (1960).

1202 *Cubism and the Cinema.* by De Smit, David. 18 p. paper illus. Boston: Communication Arts Division, Boston University, 1964.

A short discussion that includes a bibliography.

1203 *The Cubist Cinema.* by Lawder, Standish D. 265 p. paper illus. New York: New York University Press, 1975.

An examination of the interrelationship of film and modern art is offered in this unusual volume. By examining the films of Hans Richter, Viking Eggeling, Walter Ruttman, Fernand Leger, La Rove, Blaise Cendrars, Abel Gance, Germaine Dulac, Guido Seeber, and others, the author suggests the contribution that these filmmakers have made to the early art of this century. Likewise, a fascination with film as an art form is attributed to such artists as Picasso, Kandinsky, Schonberg, and others. Emphasis is on the period from 1895 to 1925.

A short analysis of Leger's BALLET MECANIQUE (1924) is included along with 300 frame enlargements from the film. The many other illustrations that appear include stills, paintings, frame enlargements, sketches, and diagrams. An index and some notes to the text are provided.

The author concludes with, "The art of the film has rather little to do with the traditional world of aesthetic contemplation generated by static works of art. But modern art in general has been increasingly concerned with precisely those characteristics of filmic expression, most notably movement, the elimination of aesthetic distance between the art object and the direct experience of life itself."

This is a superb study that is recommended.

1204 *Cukor and Co.: The Films of George Cukor and His Collaborators.* by Carey, Gary. 167 p. paper illus. New York: Museum of Modern Art, 1970.

This is an illustrated Cukor filmography, complete with casts, plot outlines, critical comment, etc. Garbo, Bankhead and Hepburn are among the many ladies present.

1205 *Cult Movies: The Classics, The Sleepers, The Weird, and The Wonderful.* by Peary, Danny. 416 p. illus. paper New York: Dell, 1981.

One hundred films get individual treatment with an essay and pictures in this well-produced original paperback. A cult film is defined as one "worshipped" by its passionate fans as they view it again and again. Credits and a plot outline are also given for each film.

1206 *The Cultural-Political Traditions and Developments of the Soviet Cinema, 1917-1972.* by Cohen, Louis Harris. 727 p. illus. New York: Arno, 1974.

This volume is one in the *Dissertations on Film* series and was written as one of the requirements for an advanced degree at the University of Southern California in 1973. It is a historical survey of 55 years of Soviet cinema, beginning with the October Socialist Revolution of 1917 and ending with the 50th anniversary of the USSR in 1972. Significant developments, trends, political principles, effectiveness, studio facilities, supporting institutes, financing, and international cultural relations are among the topics explored with respect to the Soviet cinema.

The volume is massive and includes the detail and documentation that such studies demand. After a summary-conclusion, there are nine appendixes and a very lengthy bibliography. Tables and illustrations are also provided. The work done by the author in preparing this impressive study should be appreciated. He has researched a topic in film history which has received attention from only a few others, such as Jay Leyda in *Kino* and John David Rimberg in *The Motion Picture in the Soviet Union 1918-1952.* No

one has covered as long a historical period as Cohen has. Acceptable.

1207 *The Culture Barons.* by Levine, Fay. 312 p. illus. New York: Thomas Crowell, 1976.

Culture is defined by the author as any activities that go on at museums and performing arts centers. This includes opera, ballet, theater, painting, rock music, and film. A culture baron is a person who handles the money "that shapes the political economy of creativity."

The section on film includes background material about present day studio heads, a long interview with Robert Evans (Paramount studio head, independent producer), shorter ones with Mike Medavoy (United Artists vice president), Otto Preminger (independent producer), David R. Smith (Disney archivist), and reports of meetings with Larry Turman (independent producer) and Bert Schneider (independent producer).

The question raised by the author is whether the film fare seen by so many people in theaters and on television should be determined by a few powerful people. This perennial problem cannot be explored totally by a few interviews, but Levine does give the background and stimulus for a further continuing study of the question. Recommended.

1208 *Culture For the Millions.* edited by Jacobs, Norman. 200 p. paper Boston: Beacon Press, 1961.

Subtitled "Mass Media in Modern Society," this volume is based on papers presented and discussed at a seminar sponsored jointly by the Tamiment Institute and the Journal of the American Academy of Arts and Sciences. It was held at Tamiment-In-The-Poconos in June, 1960.

1209 *Current Film Periodicals in English.* compiled by Reilly, Adam. 25 p. paper New York: Educational Film Library Association, 1972.

A revised edition of Reilly's original work which has been impossible to obtain for several years. For each periodical, he gives subscription data, a description including size, content, themes, recent article titles, etc., and the policy of the periodical in publishing manuscripts.

A back page has a statistical breakdown of the periodicals by place of origin, along with two recommended lists of periodicals—one for large libraries (25 titles) and a second for the small library (7 titles).

An editorial slip seems to have placed the lists in the wrong position. "All of the above" apparently refers to the titles in the closing small library list.

The information, its arrangement, and the ease of use make this an outstanding reference work. It is not only a selection tool, but will serve as a guide to aspiring film critics and writers in search of a market for their efforts.

1210 *A Curriculum in Film.* by Katz, John Stuart. 130 p. paper illus. Ontario, Toronto: The Ontario Institute for Studies in Education, 1972.

This volume is a description of the OISE film-literature project; it is also a resource since it lists the collection of materials that were used. The approach to film study used by the project was thematic, with "Man and Machines" selected as the topic to be explored via film, readings, and discussions. Groups of short films, feature films, study guides, and recommended books used in the project are annotated. The latter section deals with film grammar and includes a glossary of basic film terms. Film distributors and a selected bibliography make up the appendix. Illustrations are provided but there is no index.

As a model of a film study project, this text suggests many ideas and materials that might be used effectively in a variety of situations. Recommended.

1211 *A Curriculum in Film.* by Katz, John Stuart; and Oliver, Curt; and Aird, Forbes. 130 p. paper illus. Toronto: Ontario Institute for Studies in Education, 1972.

Containing suggestions for the teaching and study of motion pictures, this book is number 13 in the *Curriculum* series. A lengthy bibliography is included.

1212 *The Curtain Rises: The Story of Ossie Davis.* by Funke, Lewis. 64 p. illus. New York: Grosset and Dunlap, 1971.

A biography of the black actor-writer-director written for young people. Indexed.

1213 *Curtains.* by Tynan, Kenneth. 495 p. New York: Atheneum, 1961.

Noted here because of three excellent short articles on Garbo, W. C. Fields, and James Cagney, this book is devoted almost exclusively to theatrical reviews and comment for the 1950-1960 period.

1214 CUSTER OF THE WEST. 20 p. paper illus. 1967.

This brief souvenir book contains mostly historical background on George Armstrong Custer along with shots from the 1967 film. Cast credits are noted in the centerfold and only star Robert Shaw receives extra attention throughout. Neither author nor publisher would own up to this one.

1215 *Cut: The Unseen Cinema.* by Philips, Baxter. 111 p. paper illus. New York: Bounty, 1975.

Some indication of the content of this volume can be sensed from its cover—a Lolita sucking a pair of scissors instead of the traditional lollipop. Employing a general chronological approach, the book traces by text and illustrations the patterns of censorship in films. Four sections cover silent films, political censorship, the death of the Hollywood Production Code, and today's film violence. The text is thorough, providing both description and interpretation of censorship. It is the visual collection that will attract readers for a variety of reasons. Certain examples are either shocking, sensationalized, provocative or erotic. Their selection may be justified by the topic but their inclusion will not diminish sales either. For mature adults this volume can be recommended as both informative and entertaining. It is not suitable for younger people.

1216 *"Cut! Print".* by Miller, Tony; and Miller, Patricia George. 188 p. paper illus. Los Angeles, Calif.: Ohara, 1972.

Subtitled "The Language and Structure of Filmmaking," this book is for the most part an illustrated glossary of film terms supported by some peripheral material on the studio complex, its departments, personnel, procedures, and budgets. A Film Industry Directory (for the west coast only) completes the book.

All of the elements, with the possible exception of the limited directory, are just fine. The glossary seems complete, nontechnical, tinged with some humor (e.g., for one-liner, see zinger), and is nicely illustrated with many line drawings. Film production procedures are shown in some of the best flow charts to be found in any volume.

Far superior to a similar volume, *Glossary of Motion Picture Terminology*, this excellent reference is highly recommended.

1217 *D. W. Griffith: American Film Master.* by Barry, Iris. 40 p. illus. New

York: Museum of Modern Art, 1965 (1940).

This short expensive volume was originally published in 1940 (8000 copies) and was recently reprinted. Included in its 40 pages are many illustrations which limit the amount of the text. The result is a short surface overview of Griffith's life and his major films. revised 1965 edition has an annotated filmography by Eileen Bowser.

1218 *D. W. Griffith: The Years at Biograph.* by Henderson, Robert M. 250 p. illus. New York: Farrar, Straus, & Giroux, 1970.

The five years that Griffith spent at Biograph (1908-1913) making hundreds of two-reelers set the stage for the development of film as an art. This original research covers that period. There is much supporting documentation, a lengthy bibliography, a film list, an actor list, and sources of the films. The few pictures used are poor but the text is scholarly, readable, and responsible. The in-depth treatment of a very specialized subject may limit its potential for the general reader.

1219 *D. W. Griffith: His Life and His Work.* by Henderson, Robert M. 326 p. illus. New York: Oxford University Press, 1972.

Before the appearance of this volume, the *Focus on* book, and the one edited by James Hart (*The Man Who Invented Hollywood*), the major work on Griffith was a special edition of *Film Culture* in 1965 compiled by Seymour Stern. Other available materials were either poor (Croy) or partial (Barry, Gish, Griffith, O'Dell, and Henderson).

Although this fussy account is heavily detailed and documented, it does present most of what is publicly known about Griffith. At this point it would be foolish to charge that "the real Griffith does not emerge...." Because of his guarded private life and the delayed recognition accorded him, that portrait will probably never be drawn. Why argue over his possible Jewish ancestry, the old-age decline into lechery, his secret mistress, etc? These matters do not help explain his importance to film history and art.

The visuals, reproduced nicely, are a joy, but they would have been more helpful to the text if they had been scattered rather than lumped together. An appendix lists all the Griffith films with cast and credits for the features. Notes and an index complete the book. This volume attempts the impossible and almost succeeds. Highly recommended.

1220 *D. W. Griffith.* by Stern, Seymour. New York: Gordon Press.

1221 *D. W. Griffith and His Films.* by Phillips, Leona; and Phillips, Jill. 416 p. illus. New York: Gordon Press, 1975.

1222 *D. W. Griffith: His Biograph Films in Perspective.* by Niver, Kemp R. 189 p. illus. Los Angeles: Historical Films, 1974.

In another successful attempt at film research, Kemp Niver examines some 50 films made by D. W. Griffith during his Biograph period. Niver's argument for trusting in original material rather than a secondary source is sound, as is his result. By his selections he shows how Griffith matured as a filmmaker. In the 1908 film ADVENTURES OF DOLLIE, he used 13 scenes and 12 camera positions, while five years later in THE GIRL AND HER TRUST (1912) he used 130 scenes photographed from 35 positions.

Griffith's growing familiarity, ease and sophistication with the new medium is shown by a carefully worded text and some nicely reproduced scenes from the films. Production data and credits are given for the films. The book is indexed.

Another contribution to screen history is made by Kemp Niver with this excellent volume. Its methodology and result are examples for aspiring film historians to follow. Highly recommended.

1223 *D. W. Griffith's* THE BATTLE AT EL-DERBUSH GULCH. by Niver, Kemp R. 65 p. illus. Los Angeles, Calif.: Locare Research Group, 1972.

Kemp R. Niver is a dedicated historian-researcher. Here, he offers a reconstruction of the film, using many of its frames and titles, and surrounds this with original Biograph materials. Using sources such as *The Bioscope, The Moving Picture World,* trade magazine summaries, and *The Biograph,* he recreates some of the beginnings of the industry that the film represented. He notes the many errors made by other authors concerning this film—Mrs. D.W. Griffith, Billy Bitzer, Kevin Brownlow, and Robert Henderson—and offers his recreation of it to set the record straight.

The illustrations are largely reproductions of frames taken directly from the paper prints on deposit with The Library of Congress. An index completes the volume. The scholarship evidenced here is gratifying; like Niver's previous works, this one is a contribution to film history. Recommended.

1224 *D. W. Griffith's* THE BIRTH OF A NATION.: *Controversy, Suppression and the First Amendment as it Applies to Filmic Expression, 1915-1973.* by Fleener, Nickieann. New York: Arno, 1980.

A very detailed examination of the attempts made to prevent the showing of THE BIRTH OF A NATION, 1915 to 1973. A title in the *Dissertations on Film* series.

1225 *Dada: Monography of a Movement.* edited by Verkauf, Willy. 109 p. paper illus. New York: St. Martin's Press, 1975.

This anthology of essays on the Dada movement contains some material on Dada in film. A few of the writers, such as film director Hans Richter, were active in the movement.

1226 *Daily Express Film Book.* edited by Betts, Ernest. 207 p. illus. London: Daily Express, 1935.

Over 200 short profiles of film actors are offered in this older collective biography.

1227 *David O. Selznick's Hollywood.* by Hauer, Ronald. 426 p. illus. New York: Alfred Knopf, 1980.

How can anyone resist a super production like this book? In an oversized coffee-table format (eight pounds in weight and 11 inches x 14 inches in size) crammed with both black and white and full-color illustrations, the golden age of Hollywood is described via David O. Selznick's career in the film business. Although his entire life is considered, the volume emphasizes the period from 1926 to 1957. The text is detailed, but the essence of this ornate scrapbook is the author's collection of Selznick memorabilia—posters, stills, designs, memos, advertisements, production shots, frame enlargements, product tie-ins, etc.

The result of all this is a dazzling, opulent production that is probably the most expensive film book ever published. As Selznick stated, "There are only two kinds of class: first class and no class."

Ronald Hauer's homage to David O. Selznick is first class more often than not.

1228 *Dale: My Personal Picture Album.* by Rogers, Dale Evans. 127 p. illus. Old Tappan, N.J.: Fleming H. Re-

vell Co., 1971.

The same material covered in *The Woman at the Well* is visualized in this autobiographical picture book. Some of the illustrations are of the professional appearances of the author and her husband but most are of family members, including about 14 grandchildren. The text is brief and with much less religious sermonizing than in *The Woman at the Well*. Much of the text is a verbatim duplication of the earlier book. Picture reproduction is average.

The book has little pertinence for film scholars. Admirers of Roy and Dale and their religious philosophy will enjoy this version of the Rogers-Evans saga. Others will only look and wonder.

1229 *Dalton Trumbo.* by Cook, Bruce. 343 p. illus. New York: Charles Scribner's 1977.

Dalton Trumbo is probably best known as the author of *Johnny Got His Gun* and as one of the "Hollywood Ten." This volume carries a jacket subtitle, "A Biography of the Oscar-Winning Screenwriter Who Broke the Hollywood Blacklist." It traces his life from his birth in 1905 in Colorado to his death in 1976. Major attention is given to his work as a Hollywood writer, a career which lasted from the mid-thirties to the seventies, when he rewrote the script for PAPILLON (1974).

The author has meticulously gathered his material from primary sources—including interviews, correspondence, papers, and most importantly, Trumbo himself. He has arranged and interpreted this information in a biography which is sympathetic and persuasive. In addition to Trumbo, there is much attention given to Hollywood personalities including the people involved in the HUAC hearings and the Hollywood Blacklist.

A few illustrations, a bibliography, and an index complete the volume. The absence of a filmography is unexplainable.

This volume adds some dimension to a subject already well covered in film literature—the Hollywood Ten and the HUAC hearings. More importantly it presents a detailed and affectionate portrait of a free spirit who was true to himself. Recommended.

1230 *Dame Edith Evans: Ned's Girl.* by Forbes, Bryan. 300 p. illus. New York: Little, Brown, 1978.

Based in part on interviews and unpublished correspondence, this is a loving appreciation of British actress Edith Evans who is known best for her stage work. Following World War II she created some memorable screen characters in WOMAN OF DOLWYN (1948), THE IMPORTANCE OF BEING EARNEST (1951), THE WHISPERERS (1967), and several other films.

This approved biography was written by film director Bryan Forbes who worked with Edith Evans in several films. Emphasis is on the performer's early years and her stage work; surprisingly little is recorded of her ventures into the film medium.

Forbes writes with an affection and respect befitting one of the most loved and admired British actresses of this century. What he does not emphasize is that we still can see examples of her artistry in films such as THE QUEEN OF SPADES (1948), THE CHALK GARDEN (1963), and TOM JONES (1962).

A career chronology and an index complete the book. Interested readers should also see *Edith Evans: A Personal Memoir* by Jean Batters.

1231 *Dames.* by Cameron, Ian; and Cameron, Elisabeth. 144 p. illus. New York: Praeger, 1969.

The criteria for inclusion of an actress in this volume is that she appeared in a post-1939 film as the companion of a "heavy," a moll, a tart, a night club singer, a saloon girl, or the like. The selection is quite subjective and arbitrary. Where are such as Davis, Crawford, Sondergaard, Moorehead, Emerson, Signoret, and Woodward?—the title and theme are somewhat misleading. However, as a collection of short biographies and stills of some of the more interesting film actresses, the book is fine. The sketches are well-written and each is accompanied by a filmography. The excellent stills identify many familiar faces whose names are unknown or forgotten to most viewers. A pleasant, enjoyable book for all; as a reference the omissions are serious.

1232 *Dames of the Theatre.* by Johns, Eric. 179 p. illus. New Rochelle, N.Y.: Arlington House, 1974.

A rewarding reading experience is contained in this modest collective biography. The subjects have in common the fact that they are actresses and have been given the title of "dame" by British Royalty. All have made great successes in the theatre and a few are well known to filmgoers. The latter include May Whitty, Sybil Thorndike, Edith Evans, Peggy Ashcroft, Flora Robson, Judith Anderson, Margaret Rutherford, Gladys Cooper, Anna Neagle and Cecily Courtneidge.

Each dame gets a short biographical sketch which reviews her professional career—both factually and critically. The author's style is informal but respectful of his subjects; his admiration for their strengths and accomplishments is evident throughout the book. Excellent portraits and some scene illustrations are included along with a short bibliography. The book is not indexed. Although the view of these artists is from a theatre seat, there is much here to please a film buff who can recognize superior acting no matter where it appears. Acceptable reading for all.

1233 *Damned in Paradise: The Life of John Barrymore.* by Kobler, John. 401 p. illus. New York: Atheneum, 1977.

Any volume dealing with John Barrymore holds a certain anticipatory fascination since the subject had such a long, colorful, and varied career in the mass media. This biography is not content to rest on the substance of Barrymore's life but makes an attempt to provide some reason and explanation for his drive toward self-destruction. Based in part on new material this account offers a different perspective on the actor than did Gene Fowler in *Good Night Sweet Prince*. It follows Barrymore from his childhood spent in a world of theatrical performers to a spectacular career on stage, screen, and radio. An alcoholic at age 14, seduced by his stepmother at 15, Barrymore was to participate in four unsuccessful marriages, numerous scandals, several well-reported escapades, and finally, in a series of self-degrading performances which demeaned the talents he once possessed.

This well-researched volume includes a lengthy bibliography, a detailed index, and pictorial section that complements the text nicely. A carefully prepared and planned account of a fascinating but ultimately tragic figure is presented. The volume helps to explain the enigma of John Barrymore and, for those readers familiar with his artistry, the book will be richly rewarding. Others will find it an absorbing dramatic biography. Recommended.

1234 *Dance and Its Creators: Choreographers At Work.* by Walker, Kathrine Sorley. 214 p. illus. New York: John Day Co., 1972.

One extremely short section is devoted to dance in films; this book is otherwise concerned almost exclusively with classical ballet, though modern dance gets some slight acknowledgment. A selected filmography lists mostly short films, along with three feature films: THE GOLDWYN FOLLIES (1938), OKLAHOMA (1955), and THE RED SHOES (1948). Even within the narrow definition of dance used here, the topic of ballet in films (e.g., THE TALES OF HOFFMAN (1951), THE GLASS SLIPPER (1955), HANS CHRISTIAN ANDERSEN (1952), LIMELIGHT (1952), THE UNFINISHED DANCE (1947), THE KING AND I (1957), ON YOUR TOES (1939), BLACK TIGHTS (1960), the Gene Kelly or Fred Astaire films) deserves more than just a passing mention of WEST SIDE STORY (1961) and OLIVER (1968).

It may be petty to care about this omission, since the author is obviously not concerned with any form other than the live classical ballet performance. But a more appropriate title is needed—this one is misleading.

1235 *Dance and Mime Film and Videotape Catalog.* edited by Kitching, Jessie; and Braun, Susan. New York: Dance Films, 1980.

1236 *The Dance Collection.* by N.Y. Public Library. 10 volumes Boston: G. K. Hall, 1977.

A massive bibliography of over 300,000 entries that includes many references on dance in films.

1237 *Dance in the Hollywood Musical.* by Delemater, Jerome. 324 p. illus. Ann Arbor, Mich.: University of Michigan Press, 1981.

1238 *Dancing in the Dark.* by Dietz, Howard. 370 p. illus. New York: Quadrangle, 1974.

Howard Dietz enjoyed careers as a lyricist, a writer and an MGM publicity chief. In his autobiography he recalls many of the personalities with whom he worked—Harlow, Garland, Astaire, Garbo, Gable, Tracy, et al. He writes with abundant humor and affection about a successful life that was interrupted in 1954 by a form of Parkinson's disease. Included are over 100 photographs, the lyrics to 30 of his songs, a list of his theatrical shows, etc. Acceptable.

1239 DANISH BLUE. by Axel, Gabriel. 126 p. paper illus. New York: Evergreen Press, 1970.

Script of the 1970 film written and directed by Gabriel Axel. Contains cast credits.

1240 *The Danny Kaye Story.* by Singer, Kurt D. 241 p. illus New York: Nelson, 1958.

This is a general biography for nondiscriminating audiences in which many cliche ploys are used: the poor boy's rise from poverty in Brooklyn, the Pagliacci complex, the work for UNICEF, and so on—sentimentality runs rampant.

1241 *Dark Dreams.* by Derry, Charles. 143 p. illus. New York: A. S. Barnes, 1977.

In this survey, which is subtitled "A Psychological History of the Modern Horror Film," the text covers a time period of 1943 (DAY OF WRATH) to 1976 (THE OMEN). Concentration is on the films of the last decade and the author finds three sub-genres of the horror film emerging— personality, Armageddon, and demonic. Each of these receives an individual section complete with numerous examples, extended analyses, and many stills. Final sections offer interviews with selected directors (Robert Aldrich, William Castle, Curtis Harrington, George Romero, William Friedkin), three separate filmographies, a bibliography, and an index.

Everything about this volume is first rate—especially the author's selection and analysis, the supporting interviews and filmographies, and the clearly reproduced visuals. Even John Russell Taylor's error in the foreword where he says, "....Gloria Grahame in a musical would be an unknown quantity," can be forgiven. Apparently he never saw OKLAHOMA (1955) in which she played Ado Annie.

This is a book that offers a refreshing approach to a well-worn genre. It is sure to please, delight and excite a wide audience. Highly recommended.

1242 *Dark Lady of the Silents.* by Cooper, Miriam; and Herndon, Bonnie. 256 p. illus. New York: Bobbs-Merrill, 1973.

What should have been an exciting reminiscence turns out to be a rather casual and extremely mild account of "My Life in Early Hollywood." The teller is Miriam Cooper, whose major distinctions are that she played leading roles in Griffith's THE BIRTH OF A NATION (1915) and INTOLERANCE (1916), and married Raoul Walsh before he became a famous director. The author promises much when she states she can "tell it the way it was" because "I was there." Reader confidence is immediately shaken when she identifies Mary Pickford as "The Biograph Girl" —that title refers to Florence Lawrence if we are to believe most film historians. Cooper pushes forward and retells so many familiar details, stories, and descriptions that the narrative reads like a parody of a term-paper biography. Of some interest is her personal opinion of the famous names of the period but most of these observations are noted on the book's dust jacket.

Three picture sections attempt visual support for the text and there is an index. A filmography indicates a very busy actress with some impressive credits. When one considers the rich period of film history, the personalities involved, and the author's in-depth involvement with the emergence of a new art form, her casual, vague and detached style does not seem to suit the material. Film history is a lot more important than she apparently believes it to be. Finally her self-portrait is not an attractive or complete one. The major portion of the book covers the decade from 1913 to 1923 and the years that followed are skipped over in a few of the book's final pages. The book is not impressive as biography or film history. However, the novice reader may enjoy a recapitulation of the period. On that basis the book is acceptable.

1243   *The Dark of the Screen.* by Peterson, Sidney. 220 p. illus. New York: New York University Press, 1980.

Five essays by an experimental filmmaker-teacher. This volume is number four in the *Anthology Film Archives* series.

1244   *The Dark Side of the Screen: Film Noir.* by Hirsch, Foster. 192 p. illus. San Diego, Calif.: A. S. Barnes, 1981.

A genre survey which gives attention to themes, patterns, characters, directors, actors, etc.

1245   DARLING LILI. 26 p. paper illus. London: National Publishers,1971.

The story of this underrated 1971 film is told via a collection of sepia-tinted photographs in this souvenir book. One specific section is devoted to "The German Ace" and attention is paid to historical background, the cars, and the Windsor's House. Cast and production credits are noted, with individual pages given to Julie Andrews, Rock Hudson, and director Blake Edwards.

1246   *David Bowie.* by Claire, Vivian. 80 p. paper illus. New York: Flash, 1977.

To date, David Bowie has appeared in one major film, THE MAN WHO FELL TO EARTH (1976).

1247   DAVID HOLZMAN'S DIARY. by Carson, L. M. Kit; and McBride, Jim. 126 p. paper illus. New York: Farrar, Straus & Giroux, 1970.

Script of 1970 film directed by Jim McBride. Cast credits and introduction by L. M. Kit Carson.

1248   *David Lean and His Films.* by Silver, Alain; and Ursini, James. 255 p. illus. London: Leslie Frewin, 1974.

David Lean's films—from IN WHICH WE SERVE (1942) to RYAN'S DAUGHTER (1970)—are the subject of this attractively produced volume. Using stills, text and script excerpts, each of the 15 films is discussed in a selected fragmented way that assumes a total reader familiarity with them. As a result, the text may seem puzzling, unclear, and unsatisfying to some. The excellent illustrations consist of frame blowups and stills. Other than the few sentences which precede the filmography, Lean's personal life is ignored. A bibliography and an index complete the volume.

Lean's work is so admirable that one wishes a better appreciation had resulted. While this volume offers some attractive supporting elements, its value must ultimately rest on the text which, in this case, is erratic.

1249   *David Sohn's Film Notes on Selected Short Films.* by Sohn, David. 113 p. paper illus. Fairfield, N.J.: Cebco-Pflaum, 1975.

Comments and suggestions from the reliable David Sohn on the use of more than 100 short films. Curriculum areas and grade levels are indicated. An essential for teachers, Sohn's notes are also extremely useful for many other film users.

1250   *David Wolper, Leni Riefenstahl.* edited by Reed, Rochelle. 24 p. paper illus. Washington, D.C.: American Film Institute, 1972.

The format change of this series presents a new problem in its indication of titles. One would expect this to be another double interview, but it is not. Only David Wolper is the subject and the title seems to refer to the cover illustration. Wolper's specific topic is the 1972 Olympic Games, although he deals more generally with the film of today—documentary, commercial, or television. Three staff members from his organization contribute to the discussion. Acceptable.

1251   A DAY AT THE RACES. by Pirosh, Robert; and Seaton, George; and Oppenheimer, George. 256 p. paper illus. New York: Viking Press, 1972.

Script of the 1937 film directed by Sam Wood. Contains cast and production credits.

180

1252 DAY FOR NIGHT. by Truffaut, Francois; and Richard, Jean-Louis; and Schiffman, Suzanne. 175 p. paper illus. New York: Grove, 1975.

Script of the 1973 film directed by Truffaut. Includes cast, credits, a description of the characters, a translator's note, and a foreword by Truffaut. More than 50 stills accompany the script.

1253 *The Day the Laughter Stopped.* by Yallop, David. 348 p. illus. New York: St. Martin's Press, 1976.

In what is obviously an assiduous effort, David Yallop has reconstructed the notorious 1921 Roscoe (Fatty) Arbuckle party and the trial that followed. He places the drama in a sociological context by arguing that the Arbuckle case is still having an effect on everyone in America today. Censorship, fear, repression, industry cowardice, self-appointed guardians of morality—all these deterrents to our freedom are still with us today.

Yallop's reconstruction is based largely upon the records of the trial and interviews with some actual participants/witnesses. Surrounding the courtroom section are the biographical elements that place the trial in context with the actor's life and a particular period of American history. An impressive filmography, a bibliography, an index, and some photographs complete the book.

In using an approach structured on research and interview, the author has created another variation of the American tragedy. Implications about celebrity, justice, opportunism, courage, and many other aspects of the American national character can be derived from this work. On a simpler level, it is the totally involving story of the rise and fall of a funny fat man. Recommended.

1254 *A Day with Our Gang.* by Parker, Eleanor Lewis; and Stax. 20 p. illus. Racine, Wisc.: Whitman, 1929.

The child actors who made up "Our Gang" in 1929 are seen in illustrations by Stax (some colored) and described in a brief text by Parker.

1255 *The Days Grow Short: The Life and Music of Kurt Weill.* by Sanders, Ronald. 469 p. illus. New York: Holt, Rinehart & Winston, 1980.

Although Kurt Weill is known mostly for his theatre work, some of his music and plays have made their way onto film—THE THREEPENNY OPERA (1931, 1963), KNICKERBOCKER HOLIDAY (1944), LADY IN THE DARK (1944) and ONE TOUCH OF VENUS (1948). This biography, written without the cooperation of Weill's widow, Lotte Lenya, traces his life from Dessau, Germany, in 1900, to his death in 1950. It is detailed in its analysis of Weill's work, but a bit lacking in its presentation of Weill as a person who could easily be interpreted as an Everyman symbol in the first half of this century.

1256 *Days of Thrills and Adventure.* by Barbour, Alan G. 168 p. illus. New York: Collier-Macmillian, 1970.

This is a definitive picture history of the sound serial. Covering the period from 1930 to 1956 by an affectionate, accurate text and many exciting stills, the book pays attention to a film genre often forgotten or overlooked.

A lengthy introduction by William Everson is followed by one short chapter on the silent film serial. Then, it's on to the serials of Mascot, Republic, Universal, Columbia, and the independent studios. The coverage appears most complete and a total listing is given in the appendix. Especially commendable are the reproductions. A quality book. Highly recommended.

1257 *Dear Boris.* by Lindsay, Cynthia. 273 p. illus. New York: Knopf, 1975.

A loving appreciation of Boris Karloff is presented here in a beautifully produced volume. The text is set in an attractive Dutch-style type on high quality paper and is accompanied by many clearly reproduced unfamiliar illustrations. Since the author was a friend of Karloff's for 36 years, the biography offered here is affectionate, full of personal memories, and carefully researched. For example, she includes a family tree which traces his roots back to the early 1800s.

Karloff emerges as a private, complex, friendly person whose success in horror films exacted a high personal and professional cost. The reader searching for scandal or gossip may be disappointed; nevertheless, this is the definitive biography of a great actor whose work affected us all. A splendid filmography concludes the book. There is no index.

1258 *Dear Hollywood.* by Lowell, Juliet. 96 p. illus. New York: Duell, Sloan and Pearce, 1950.

During the forties Juliet Lowell enjoyed considerable popular success by compiling short volumes containing well-edited letters to various groups of people—columnists, congressmen, etc. In this volume she treats letters written to Hollywood stars, producers, the mayor, the Chamber of Commerce, etc. Supposedly this is a collection of unintentionally funny letters. Sophisticated readers of today may find some nostalgic or sociological value here, but most will sense a manufactured, forced humor. A curiosity from the past, noted here for the record.

1259 *Dear Me.* by Ustinov, Peter. 348 p. paper illus. New York: Penguin Books, 1978.

Peter Ustinov is a Renaissance man, recognized as a playwright, novelist, actor, director, raconteur, lecturer, and frequent guest host on literate TV talk shows. He writes very much as he talks, with wit, intelligence, grace and sensitivity. In this biography he emphasizes his family roots and his early years with only a passing mention or so of the last two decades. Ustinov as writer is not afraid of digressions, conversations with himself, social issues, world problems and other topics unusual to an autobiography.

The volume avoids self-congratulation and offers instead some very funny anecdotes of Ustinov's fellow actors— Olivier, Richardson, Laughton, Gielgud, Edith Evans. Throughout, humor is balanced nicely with serious opinion, comment and meditation.

This autobiography is one of the best to appear during the seventies. It is hoped that another volume concentrating on Ustinov's later years will be forthcoming. An index and some illustrations are added.

1260 *Dear Mr. G: The Biography of Clark Gable.* by Garceau, Jean; and Cocke, Inez. 297 p. illus. Boston, Little, Brown, 1961.

This is a factual, anecdotal biography of Gable written by the woman who was his secretary for 21 years. The first half devotes equal attention to Carole Lombard. All the externals of the life and career of the most successful romantic film star are here; however, there is no attempt to reveal the off-stage personality. Everything related is most positive and flattering; the portrait is one dimensional.

Some pictures are included but no filmography, bibliography or index is at hand. As a gathering and recapitulation of the known events in a male star's life, this book is fine. As a biography it lacks depth and appropriate emphasis. For example, Gable's experiences and work on THE MISFITS (1961) is dismissed in a very few paragraphs.

1261 *Death: A Bibliographical Guide.* by Miller, Albert Jay; and Acri, Michael James. 375 p. Metuchen N.J.:

Scarecrow, 1977.

Noted here for the films under the "Audiovisual Media" section.

1262 *Death and Dying.* by Mason, Edward A. 16 p. paper New York: Educational Film Library Association, 1978.

This is a filmography to accompany the Courses By Newspaper program entitled "Death and Dying: Challenge and Change." The films appear under 14 headings and include the usual data along with a helpful annotation. A list of distributors and some audiovisual materials complete the pamphlet.

1263 *The Debonairs.* by Parish, James Robert; and Stanke, Don E. 511 p. illus. New Rochelle, N.Y.: Arlington House, 1975.

A debonair is described in this volume as an impeccably groomed actor possessed of wit, sophistication and taste who employed courage, style and intelligence in overcoming insuperable obstacles. He was most evident in the films of the thirties. The authors have chosen eight such actors for this collective biography: George Brent, Melvyn Douglas, Cary Grant, Rex Harrison, Ray Milland, Robert Montgomery, David Niven, and William Powell.

An introduction by Earl Anderson traces the development of the debonair acting style in the 19th century theatre. Its transference to films is noted. The biographies that follow consist of narrative, stills and a detailed filmography.

As with most of the Parish biographies, the narrative deals primarily with a review of the subject's films. Plots are recalled, critical reaction is noted and incidental information is offered. Observations about personal lives are minimal and based on public record. Picture quality is acceptable throughout and the book is indexed.

Biographies such as the ones offered here are sometimes more satisfying than autobiographies and to have neglected subjects like Brent, Montgomery, Powell and Douglas covered is most welcome. Niven, of course, is hard to top since he writes so well as both chronicler and autobiographer. Thus, as a totality, this book affords a well-researched coverage of the careers of eight male stars. As an entertainment or a reference, it typifies the care, thought, and hard work found in the recent Parish books.

1264 *Deborah Kerr.* by Braun, Eric. 264 p. illus. New York: St. Martin's

Press, 1977.

This is a straightforward approved biography of a film actress known predominately for portraying heroines who had dignity, manners, and behaved bravely through any and all crises. Although she tried to break the image several times, she was most successful in playing "the English Lady." Her many variations of this part give evidence of her talent for making it seem so effortless.

The author has been acquainted with his subject for more than three decades and traces her career from a 1938 ballet debut to THE ARRANGEMENT (1968), and her recent stage appearances. Since her rise to celebrity was swift and she has led a carefully guarded private life, there remains only a recital of the events that made up her life and career for the past 40 years. The author provides this information with such admiration and affection that the stereotype of "Lady Kerr" is reinforced.

The volume is illustrated and indexed and contains a bibliography, a filmography, a discography, and a listing of her stage appearances.

Those who have found the depth and discipline of a devoted professional in Kerr's film performances will enjoy this book. Others may be a bit bored as charm, good manners, and beauty alone do not generate terribly exciting biographies.

1265 *Decency in Motion Pictures.* by Quigley, Martin. 100 p. New York: Macmillan, 1937.

An analysis of Hollywood censorship and the production code.

1266 *The Decline and Fall of the Love Goddesses.* by Agan, Patrick. 286 p. paper illus. New York: Pinnacle, 1979.

Despite its provocative title, this volume is a collective biography which resembles in many ways the volumes written by James Parish. Subjects here are Frances Farmer, Betty Grable, Rita Hayworth, Linda Darnell, Veronica Lake, Betty Hutton, Susan Hayward, Dorothy Dandridge, Jayne Mansfield, and Marilyn Monroe. The author's criteria for selection is that they were all considered at one time to be love goddesses (Betty Hutton???).

Since most of the subjects lived rather melodramatic personal lives, any biographical recall is not without interest. Agan dwells on the sensational elements, emphasizing that the women were the winners and ultimately the losers in the rough game of Hollywood celebrity.

This volume is nicely illustrated and contains a filmography for each subject.

1267 *The Decline of the Cinema: An Economist's Report.* by Spraos, John. 168 p. London: Allen & Unwin, 1962.

A discussion of the changing patterns of motion picture economics in Great Britian, this report is an argument for subsidized exhibition designed to stop or diminish the closing of cinemas. The wisdom of a sound and simple observation such as "Film-going depends upon the availability of cinemas," has certainly escaped the American film industry. Topics such as the effect of TV, the shortage of films, and other factors contributing to the decline are mentioned. The book concludes with some suggestions and a prediction of a new but smaller dimension of movie-going in the future.

1268 *The* DEEP THROAT *Papers.* 191 p. paper illus. New York: Manor Books, 1973.

This anthology—which is intended "For sale to mature adults only" —contains illustrations, articles, interviews, testimony and a court decision about DEEP THROAT (1972). Included also is an abbreviated picture-text version of the film which conveys a very clear idea of the plot and the action. Nothing in the media during the past decade has created the furor that this film has. Social and legal questions concerning the film will be argued for years to come. The material in this volume, although selected and, at times, sensationalized, covers many elements of the controversy. The material can be of interest to anyone interested in film censorship, obscenity, or the sociological effects of the cinema.

1269 *Deeper Into Movies.* by Kael, Pauline. 458 p. Boston: Little Brown, 1973.

What more can be said about Ms. Kael? She writes film literature that can be re-read with profit and enjoyment by many audiences. In this latest collection of her reviews from *The New Yorker*, from September 1969 to March 1972, she starts with BUTCH CASSIDY (1969), considers 150 other films, and ends up with WHAT'S UP DOC? (1972) The book is indexed. Highly recommended.

1270 *Deerstalker: Holmes and Watson on Screen.* by Haydock, Ron. 313 p. illus. Metuchen, N.J.: Scarecrow, 1978.

A detailed history of the Sherlock Holmes character in over 400 film and television appearances forms the substance of this volume. Written in a dry, pedantic style, the text treats the films, plots, actors, TV programs, etc., in a chronological fashion. A bibliography, a few illustrations, and an index complete the volume.

Since the earlier books *The Sherlock Holmes File* and *Sherlock Holmes on the Screen* contain much of the same material, the reader has a choice. Haydock's study is more detailed but packaged in a bland, routine presentation. The other books are more fun.

1271   DELIVERANCE by Dickey, James. 184 p. illus. Carbondale, Ill.: Southern Illinois University Press, 1981.

A script of the 1975 film directed by John Boorman.

1272   *DeMille: The Man and His Pictures.* by Essoe, Gabe; and Lee, Raymond. 319 p. illus. New York: A. S. Barnes, 1970.

Included in this volume is a speech DeMille delivered to the Screen Producer's Guild, an excerpt from Charles Bickford's book, *Bulls, Balls, Bicycles and Actors*, five pages of vital statistics, 13 pages of tribute by Charlton Heston, a tribute of equal length from Henry Wilcoxon, and two shorter ones from Elmer Bernstein and Art Arthur.

If one adds to the above, numerous tiny illustrations (a large portion of which are poorly reproduced), some reconstructed dialogue, and many long quotations from other sources, one may understand why this book is not recommended. Readers are referred to *The Films of Cecil B. DeMille*, his *Autobiography*, and to Koury's *Yes, Mr. DeMille*.

1273   *The Denatured Novel.* by Van Nostrand, Albert. 224 p. Indianapolis: Bobbs-Merrill, 1960.

The novel written for economic gain rather than for creative expression is described as "denatured." This book is an argument that assigns much of the blame for the denatured novel on Hollywood and films.

1274   *Design in Motion.* by Halas, John; and Manvell, Roger. 160 p. illus. New York: Hastings House, 1962.

A world-wide look at animated films. Includes cartoons, experimental films, and those with serious themes. Wide coverage with many excellent illustra-

tions and a well correlated text.

1275   *Designers of Soviet Films.* by Silantieva, T. 216 p. illus. Chicago: Imported Publications, Moscow: Soviet Art Publishers, 1972.

With a text in both Russian and English, this volume, developed from a 1967 exhibition, explores Soviet film set and costume design. An introductory chapter of text precedes the main body of the book—a collection of almost 250 visuals in both color and black-and-white that illustrate set designs and costumes from selected films. The illustrations are arranged chronologically by decades, ranging from 1920 to 1960. Each visual is numbered and can be identified only if the reader can translate the designer's name, given in Russian, into English. This difficulty occurs because the English language list of illustrations given in the book's final pages is arranged alphabetically by the designer's name. Thus an attractive, helpful reference work is weakened by editorial carelessness. The book does offer a rich visual feast for the reader who is not in search of specific information.

1276   *Designing for Films.* by Carrick, Edward. 128 p. illus. London: Studio Pub., 1949.

A revised and expanded edition of the author's *Designing for Moving Pictures*.

1277   *Designing for Moving Pictures: How To Do It Series Number 27.* by Carrick, Edward. 104 p. illus. London: Studio Pub., 1941.

Explores the fundamentals of art direction, i.e., properties, designing and building sets, etc. Attention is given to theory and practice as well as to materials and methods. Many fine illustrations and diagrams accompany the text along with an appendix, glossary, and bibliography. The book was revised in 1949 in a better, slightly larger edition retitled *Designing for Films*.

1278   *Designing for Visual Aids.* by Wright, Andrew. 96 p. paper illus. New York: Van Nostrand Reinhold, 1970.

This useful volume considers all media including film. Intended for teachers who produce their own teaching aids, it offers principles, concepts, examples and advice on designing such aids. A bibliography is included.

1279 *Designing Male.* by Greer, Howard. 310 p. illus. New York: G. P. Putnam's, 1951.

The autobiography of a costume designer who came to Hollywood in 1923. After a period at Paramount, he opened his own dress shop and worked as a freelance artist for the studios. This volume includes illustrations of the costumes he designed for the stars (Loretta Young, Pola Negri, etc.).

1280 *Detectionary.* by Roseman, Mill. 299 p. illus. Woodstock, N.Y.: Overlook, 1977.

Called "A Biographical Dictionary of Leading Characters in Mystery Fiction," this reference-reader has four major sections. The first provides an annotated listing of detectives and villains by name. Next there is an annotated listing of cases, by book title. The third concerns itself with films. Again the detective names are used to recall the films. Finally, over 300 authors are identified by detective names and book titles. This wealth of information is accompanied by more than 100 film stills. Enthusiasts of the detective film will relish this volume.

1281 *The Detective in Film.* by Everson, William K. 247 p. illus. Secaucus, N.J.: Citadel, 1972.

The idea of a photo-text survey of the detective in films is provocative, but the resultant book is rather unsatisfying, especially from an author who is usually so reliable in blending scholarship and entertainment. Perhaps the investigation uncovered much less quality material than other genre studies.

Tribute is paid to the "Master," Sherlock Holmes, in the opening chapter, which is followed by an examination of the silent screen detective. An insertion of three classics—THE KENNEL MURDER CASE (1933), GREEN FOR DANGER (1947), and THE MALTESE FALCON (1941)—between silent films and talkies seems awkward. Bulldog Drummond, Charlie Chan, Mr. Moto, Philo Vance, Nick Charles, The Falcon and The Lone Wolf are among the familiar names treated here in varying detail. FBI agents, G-men, T-men, secret agents, district attorneys, inspectors, sheriffs, investigators are all mentioned as examples of the detective genre. European sleuths, with a separate section devoted to British detectives, are noted, as are the detective characters of some of Hitchcock's films. After a short chapter on comedy and camp, the private eye—from Marlowe to Klute—is recognized. A full index completes the book.

Picture quality is adequate but there has been a change in the paper used by *Citadel* for this series.

Instead of the former semigloss type, a kind of dull-matte paper now appears and the effect on the visuals is to diminish their sharpness. Compare this volume to *The Films of Clark Gable*, for example, and the difference is obvious.

Everson's research, experience, and verbal ability are still apparent, but he seems to have had difficulty in placing the material into an appropriate framework or format. The disparate, unconnected chapters lack unity. Acceptable but not essential.

1282 *The Detective in Hollywood.* by Tuska, Jon. 480 p. illus. New York: Doubleday, 1978.

The detective film has always been popular with audiences; in this survey which extends from SHERLOCK HOLMES BAFFLED (1900) to THE LATE SHOW (1977), Jon Tuska examines the detective characters, their author-creators, actor-creators, directors, scenarists, and others associated with the film genre. Much attention is given to series such as the low-budget Charlie Chan, Mr. Moto, and Boston Blackie films. Many of the titles he discusses are unfamiliar and rarely shown today. Added to this mixture are interviews, anecdotes, gossip, financial data, romantic digressions, a discussion of film noir, literary appreciations of Dashiell Hammett and Raymond Chandler, unusual trivia tid bits, etc.

With a voluminous text crammed with assorted features, many well-selected photographs, and an index, the volume is a strong reference work in the area of detective films. It's also fun to read.

1283 *Development of the Film.* by Casty, Alan. 425 p. paper illus. New York: Harcourt, Brace, Jovanovich, 1973.

Casty uses a tri-part structure to present his critical history of the development of film as an art. The first portion covers silent films, with emphasis on Griffith, the Russians and the Germans, and notes the approach toward realism as evidenced in von Stroheim's work. The second section describes the two decades following the introduction of sound films, with social concerns and the establishment of realism as the dominant themes. In the final section Casty considers the new consolidations and directions seen in the films of the Italian neo-realists, the French New Wave, and the individual master directors—Bergman, Fellini, Antonioni, etc.

The discussion is by no means limited to the three major themes. The author provides a review of many other films and genres. Emphasis throughout is on directors, and, in his attempt to cover as much as possible, the author sometimes mentions several films in one sentence. Those unfamiliar with the films will not find this especially informative. The many visuals are adequately reproduced. A lengthy index completes the book.

This is an excellent text for college courses and is equally effective as a book for individual reading or reference. Highly recommended.

1284   *The Devil Finds Work.* by Baldwin, James. 122 p. New York: Dial, 1976.

In what he calls an essay, James Baldwin discusses certain films and the effect they have had upon him. Beginning with a small black boy's fascination with Joan Crawford, he recalls such items as Bette Davis' pop eyes, the final shot in A TALE OF TWO CITIES (1936), Sylvia Sidney's need to escape, etc. In later sections he analyses films such as THE DEFIANT ONES (1958), IN THE HEAT OF THE NIGHT (1967), GUESS WHO'S COMING TO DINNER (1967), and THE EXORCIST (1974) from a personal view. Most of these films have meant little if anything to him and, in his explanations of their failure, the reader learns much about the author and his views. The image of the black in films is his predominant theme, and his conclusion seems to be that films have always reflected the attitudes and opinions of American society.

The essay is a personal statement which combines lucid observations about film with a valid questioning of the nature of our society.

Mature readers will find Baldwin's work both challenging and enlightening. The use of film analysis as a vehicle for personal expression is relatively rare in literature. James Baldwin justifies the methodology in this volume. Acceptable.

1285   *The Devil in the Book.* by Trumbo, Dalton. 42 p. paper Los Angeles: California   Emergency   Defense Committee, 1956.

Written by one of the "unfriendly 10," this booklet deals with Communism in California and theUnited States, the Alien Registration Act of 1940, and the blacklisting of entertainers. Reprinted in 1972 in *The Time of the Toad.*

1286   *The Devil's Camera.* by Burnett, Richard George; and Martell, Edward D. 130 p. London: Epworth, 1932.

Subtitled "Menace of a Film-Ridden World," this plea for censorship deals with moral and religious aspects of motion pictures.

1287   *Dialogue on Film.* by American Film Institute Staff. paper illus. Washington, D.C.: American Film Institute, 1970.

Interviews of filmmakers held by the AFI appear in a series entitled *Dialogue on Film.* The titles appearing in volumes 1 and 2 are noted in the entry for the *Dialogue on Film* series. Since August 1973 the following titles have been published: Rick Rosenberg and Robert Christiansen (television producers); Conrad Hall (cinematographer); Henry Fonda; Henry Mancini; William Friedkin; Fritz Lang and Bernardo Bertolucci; Lucille Ball; Spielberg, Barwood, Robbins, and Zsigmond on SUGARLAND EXPRESS; Roman Polanski; Robert Altman; Laszlo Kovacs and Vilmos Zsigmond (cinematographers); Paul Mazursky and Paul Morrissey; Olivia De Havilland ; George C. Scott and Trish Van Devere; Martin Scorsese; and Hal B. Wallis. The above are listed as separate entries under individual titles in this volume.

1288   *Dialogue on Film Series.* by American Film Institute Staff. paper illus. Washington D.C.: American Film Institute, 1970-73.

The dialogue series started with three small paperback books: *Federico Fellini*; *Rouben Mamoulian: Style is the Man*; and *Frank Capra: One Man-One Film.* A format change followed and the next group was issued as pages to be placed in a three-ring binder. They included: *Charlton Heston, Jack Nicholson, Robert Aldrich, Milos Forman, Ingrid Thulin, John Cassavetes, Peter Falk, Alfred Hitchcock, Paul Williams, Cable Television.* The most recent change is the reappearance of these publications as separate units resembling a periodical. Referred to as Volume 2 they include: *University Advisory Committee Seminar, David Wolper, Stan Brakhage and Ed Emshwiller, Richard Attenborough, Liv Ullman,* and *Television Seminar-NBC.*

1289   *Dialogue with the World: A Modern Approach to the Humanities.* edited by Jones, Rev. G. William. 206 p. paper illus. Wilmette, Ill.: Films, Inc., 1969.

Here is an essential reference book for anyone who plans to use feature films with discussion groups. Contains 100 discussion guides. Each individual guide gives a still from the film, a synopsis, some critical comments, a list of credits and awards, and a group of questions for discussion. Some introductory articles concerning the background and use of discussion methodology precede the collection.

The films are divided into the general categories of sex and marriage; like it is ...; prejudice; integrity vs. expediency; war: all kinds of problems; facing up to the truth; justice and mercy—the same?; death as an end; the meaning of existence: why?; and ethics and the organization man. Valuable and interesting in many different ways.

1290 *Diana Ross: Supreme Lady.* by Berman, Connie. 182 p. paper illus. New York: Popular, 1978.

An original paperback, this biography of singer Diana Ross traces her success story from ghetto to Motown to superstar. Illustrations and a discography are added.

1291 *Diana Ross.* by Eldred, Patricia M. 48 paper illus. Mankato, Minn: Creative Education, 1975.

A title in the *Rock and Pop Stars* series, this brief biography of singer Diana Ross was designed for younger readers.

1292 *The Diana Ross Scrapbook.* by Goldman, Jane. paper illus. Sunridge, 1978.

An illustrated biography that traces Diana Ross's rise from the Detroit slums to international celebrity.

1293 *The Diane Keaton Scrapbook.* by Munshower, Suzanne. 96 p. paper illus. New York: Grosset & Dunlap (Today), 1979.

A picture biography of the actress is one of the *Scrapbook* series of celebrity portraits, created this time by Suzanne Munshower. Others include John Travolta, Shaun Cassidy, and Dolly Parton. Apparently the goal of the series is to "write-'em-up while they're hot."

In this heavily illustrated paperback, Keaton's life is related in chronological chapters: Beginnings, The Big Break, Movies-Movies-Movies, Life with Woody, Growing, New Challenges, Offstage, and A New Romance. The premature coverage offered here will suffice as a temporary information source designed primarily for ardent fans of Ms. Keaton.

1294 *Dianying—Electric Shadows.* by Leyda, Jay. 515 p. illus. Cambridge, Mass.: MIT Press, 1972.

The title of this scholarly volume comes from the Chinese term for film and its literal translation—

Dian (Electric) and Ying (Shadows). Further description of the book is given in the subtitle, "An Account of Films and the Film Audience in China." It is much more, of course, since it also treats the history, the production, the industry, and the personnel involved in Chinese filmmaking. Many films are described and examined as reflectors of Chinese thought and political philosophy. Leyda worked in China from 1959 to 1964 and a portion of this book derives from his firsthand observations. Another major source is a two-volume work, *History of the Development of Chinese Cinema*, by Cheng Chi-Hua, but there are also many others given. In fact, the section on sources which follows the text is a bibliography of impressive proportions.

The single section of visuals is bland and somewhat disappointing, while the scattered line drawings, cartoons, and symbols throughout the text do not compensate for the lack of adequate visual sampling of films.

The unusual reference value of the book is evidenced not only by the text but by the appendix, which includes the above section on sources, in addition to a selected list of important Chinese films from 1897-1966 and a fine collection of mini-biographies of Chinese film artisans. There is a lengthy index. The book will be a delight to historians, scholars and researchers. Leyda has treated an unknown area of world film history with diligence, wit, firsthand observation and reportage, and intelligence. The subject matter is too specialized and remote for the general reader, who may balk at 500 pages of unfamiliar names and films. However, this one can be heartily endorsed and recommended for the scholar.

1295 *Diary of a Film* (LA BELLE ET LA BETE). by Cocteau, Jean. 216 p. illus. New York: Roy Pub., 1950.

This diary refers to nearly a year spent from mid-1945 to 1946 in making the French film, BEAUTY AND THE BEAST. The creator of the film, Jean Cocteau, offers a record of both personal and professional happenings during the film's production.

Although the diary illuminates the artist, Cocteau, the book needs to be used with the film to be totally effective. Illustrations consist mostly of a few stills from the picture—only one candid shot of Cocteau with the cast is offered. A specialized book for readers with a more than average interest in Cocteau and his most famous film.

1296 *Diary of a Lover of Marilyn Monroe.* by Lembourn, Hans Jorgen. 214 p. New York: Arbor House, 1979.

The question that lingers after reading this volume is whether it is fact, fiction, or a combination of the two. Purporting to be a diary-inspired account of a 40-day relationship between Monroe and Lembourn, the text consists of long reconstructed conversations and monologues along with some narrative-bridging sections. Monroe, as presented, is the same girl-woman detailed in earlier works. The difference is that here she becomes a character in a love story instead of being a biographical subject. Lembourn's memory of her is kind, affectionate and touched with sweet sadness.

In whatever way this work is categorized, there is still sufficient quality in the writing to interest most readers. Since it provides further reinforcement to the ever-growing legend of Marilyn Monroe, its truth probably doesn't matter much. Monroe remains a topic of interest to readers, regardless of the format in which she is remembered.

1297 *L136-Diary with Ingmar Bergman.* by Sjoman, Vilgot. 243 p. paper Ann Arbor, Mich.: Karoma, 1978.

The "L136" in the title refers to the production number of Ingmar Bergman's 1962 film, WINTER LIGHT. Sjoman, an aspiring author-critic-director, kept a record of Bergman at work noting the personalities, activities, and problems involved in the creation of a Bergman film. John Simon offers a lengthy preface which is followed by the 3-part diary: the screenplay; the shooting; and editing, mixing, and premiere. Sjoman's account, which runs from late 1960 to spring of 1963, is personal, subjective, and admiring. He has captured the thought, work and personal habits of Bergman in what might appear to be an unlikely vehicle— a personal diary. How successful he was can be seen in his own aquisition of film-directing skills as evidenced in the I AM CURIOUS films he created in 1963 and 1965.

This is an essential specialized volume for anyone interested in Bergman as a director. The reader who is unfamiliar with the director or his films will get impatient or lost—perhaps both.

1298 *Dickens and Film.* by Zambrano, A. L. 442 p. illus. New York: Gordon Press, 1977.

The intention of this volume is to show the influence that the writings of Charles Dickens had on films and film directors. Attention is given to D. W. Griffith's attempts to reproduce the Dickens literary style in film form.

Supporting the pedantic discussion is a filmography of screen adaptations of Dickens' stories.

It should be noted that this is a very expensive book, whose production values—offset printing of typed pages—do not justify its cost.

1299 *Dictionary of Cinematography and Sound Recording.* by Sharps, Wallace S. illus. 143 p. London: Fountain Press, 1959.

The book is divided into two sections. Part I consists of short concise explanations of cameras, film characteristics, lenses, sound, lighting, editing, splicing, etc.; Part II is a dictionary of terms used in the above processes. A good reference book.

1300 *see 1299*

1301 *Dictionary of Film Makers.* by Sadoul, Georges. 288 p. paper Berkeley, Calif.: University of California Press, 1972.

Translated, edited, and updated by Peter Morris, this reference work is quite special. "Film Makers" in the title refers to those persons "who have contributed something to the artistic industry of the cinema." Sadoul's original 1000 entries have been increased and expanded by about 15 percent by Morris.

Bibliographic information, a filmography with dates, and some critical comments make up most entries, which are arranged alphabetically. Directors, editors, writers, animators, composers, art directors and cameramen from more than 25 countries are represented. The emphasis is on international cinema rather than on any one particular country. As with any such compilation of artists, there are probably some omissions, but with the added new material it is hard to find them. Probably one of the most useful and valuable reference books to appear in the English language in years.

1302 *Dictionary of Films.* by Sadoul, Georges; and Morris, Peter. 432 p. Berkeley, Calif.: University of California Press, 1972.

In this dictionary there are 1200 films, of which the author claims to have seen 95 percent. He suggests that any inaccuracies in the listings are due to adaptations, wording, or memory—either his or the reader's. Peter Morris, the translator, has provided an introduction to this English language edition explaining some of the changes he made.

Each entry has title, country, date, cast and production credits, running time, and color or black and white. A short synopsis, some background information, and critical evaluation follow in most cases. An incomplete but quite valuable reference work.

1303 *A Dictionary of Literary, Dramatic and Cinematic Terms.* by Barnet, Sylvan; and Berman, Morton; and Burto, William. 124 p. paper Boston: Little, Brown, 1971.

Based on examination of this reference book, cinematic terms can apparently be covered by explanations of nine nouns: cuts, director, documentary, dubbing, film, new wave, sequence, shot, and soft focus. All other cinema terms are related to these nine, e.g., "auteur theory ... see director." The nine terms do not receive any lengthy consideration. The inclusion of "cinematic" in the title will mislead many readers. Such a small sampling does not represent film terminology and even the terms selected seem arbitrary; why, for example, use "soft focus" over "deep focus" or "wide angle" ? While this volume may be helpful in the study of literature and drama, it offers little to the student of cinema. Not recommended. Glossaries found in the back of many film books do a far better job.

1304 *The Dictionary of Marketing and Related Terms in the Motion Picture Industry.* by Delson, Donn. 70 p. paper New York: Bradson, 1978.

A collection of advertising, sales, production and financial terms arranged alphabetically and defined in clear, precise language, this modest glossary is designed for the novice more than for the professional. Some cross-referencing is provided making the volume efficient to use.

1305 *Dictionary of Motion Picture and Video Terms.* compiled by Quick, John; and LaBau, Tom; and Wolff, Herbert. 320 p. illus. Boston: Herman, 1978.

A dictionary that contains all the officially sanctioned terms of the Society of Motion Picture and Television Engineers, as well as the slang expressions of the profession.

1306 *Dictionary of 1,000 Best Films.* by Pickard, R. A. E. 496 p. illus. New York: Association Press, 1971.

One thousand sound and silent films representing the best in world cinema from 1903 to 1970 are presented alphabetically. Each entry has the country of origin, the year, a short plot synopsis, studio and production credits, and a few cast names. Suppor-

tive information is sometimes also offered.

The author's subjective selection includes such films as APACHE (1954), CAGED (1950), FATHER'S LITTLE DIVIDEND (1951), PLATINUM BLONDE (1931), and TAKE ME OUT TO THE BALL GAME (1949). Omitted, among others, are Kurosawa's IKIRU (1952), and YOJIMBO (1961), the emphasis falling on the American film. The treatment of short films is superficial —THE RED BALLOON (1956) and TIME OUT OF WAR (1954) are here but NIGHT AND FOG (1955) is missing.

Useful as a quick reference tool, but whether it offers much more than some far less expensive guides is for the prospective purchaser to decide. Recommmended, with the above stated reservation.

1307 *A Dictionary of the Cinema.* by Graham, Peter. 158 p. illus. New York: A. S. Barnes, 1964.

As stated on the end cover, "This dictionary of the cinema contains 628 entries and has an index to over 5,000 film titles mentioned in the text." Other than the 12 picture pages which uniformly feature a dozen small rectangular portraits of film personalities, the cover sentence describes this small volume. Some very brief words or phrases accompany the subject's biographies in addition to the dates of their birth (death) and their films.

The dictionary covers the world scene and certain entries may be unfamiliar. The inclusion of advertising material is distracting. Picture quality is only fair. Even with the reservations listed above, subsequent improved editions (with advertising dropped) could make this title essential.

1308 *Dietrich: The Story of a Star.* by Frewin, Leslie. 192 p. illus. New York: Stein & Day, 1967.

This biography promises a good deal more than it delivers. In a preface the author tells of repeated suggestions and threats he received, all discouraging this story. No one needed to be concerned. It is tepid, discloses nothing new, and quite frequently is inaccurate. Perhaps omissions are its greatest fault. Largely factual, the book follows Dietrich's career through all its periods and phases. The picture section and the filmography are very good. No index is provided.

Errors abound: the Mamoulian version of DR. JEKYLL AND MR. HYDE (1931) was not the first; John Gilbert was not at the height of his popularity when he died in 1936. Textual omissions include Hemingway (a brief mention), Bachrach, WITNESS FOR THE PROSECUTION (1957), TOUCH OF EVIL (1958), box office poison, etc. Little mention is made of her recordings whose popularity date back to pre-BLUE ANGEL (1929) years. Acceptable only for the general reader who wants a detailed external account of a star. This book was called *Blond Venus* in its original British version.

1309 *Dietrich Bonhoeffer: Memo for a Movie.* by Gill, Theodore H. 264 p. paper New York: Macmillan, 1970.

A bibliography of a religious leader written at the request of a film studio but never filmed.

1310 *Different Strokes.* by Wells, John Warren. 252 p. paper New York: Dell, 1974.

The subtitle of this original paperback is "Or How I (Gulp) Wrote, Directed, and Starred in an X-Rated Movie." Calling his effort "an expensively produced erotic film," the author also doubts that anyone will see it, because of the 1973 Supreme Court ruling on local community determination of obscenity. Included here are the screenplay, a diary of the making of the film and a short interview with the female star. According to Harry Reems in *Here Comes Harry Reems*, a film he made called SPIKEY'S MAGIC WAND was changed to DIFFERENT STROKES. It also starred Andrea True and Georgina Spelvin. Reems' description bears little resemblance to the film described here, but factual reliability is not a strong point with porno filmmakers, since few actual names are used because of possible prosecution. Noted here because of the first use of script-diary-interview book format with an erotic film—the same treatment accorded the "important" films in the past.

1311 *Differentiating the Media.* edited by Asheim, Lester; and Fenwick, Sara I. 74 p. Chicago: University of Chicago, 1975.

This record of the proceedings of the 37th annual Conference of the Graduate Library School, held on August 5-6, 1974, contains five presentations framed by an introduction (Asheim) and a summary (Fenwick). Topics dealt with include television (Ron Powers), print (Donald R. Gordon), administrative problems (Wesley Doak), literature into film (Virginia Wright Wexman) and content versus container (Frances Henne). The latter two sections are of interest since Henne considers film use in libraries while Wexman uses Dashiell Hammett's *The Maltese Faclon* as her example for a discussion of the transfer from one medium to another.

The book combines five different views and topics

into an exploration of the characteristics and uses of the several media, and will appeal to anyone concerned with nonprint. Recommended.

1312 *The Difficulty of Being.* by Cocteau, Jean. 160 p. New York: Coward-McCann, 1967.

1313 *Dinah! A Biography.* by Cassiday, Bruce. 212p. illus. New York: Franklin Watts, 1979.

This short biography is testimony to the drive, ambition, and determination of Frances Rose Shore, known usually as "Dinah." Her career has spanned some 40 years with success of a sort in most of the media. Perhaps films were the least of her accomplishments; her own evaluation was, "I bombed as a movie star." She did appear in THANK YOUR LUCKY STARS (1943), UP IN ARMS (1944), FOLLOW THE BOYS (1944), BELLE OF THE YUKON (1944), TILL THE CLOUDS ROLL BY (1946), and AARON SLICK FROM PUNKIN CRICK (1952). These films are mentioned incidentally in the story of how a young southern girl attained international celebrity at an early age and maintained it to date by flexibility, self-discipline, and high intelligence. A few illustrations accompany the rather bland, factual text.

People who still admire and enjoy Dinah Shore may appreciate this inspirational account. For those who remember her as an icon of World War II, the book may also have special significance. Younger readers, who know her as a TV person who sings poorly and talks to celebrities will find little excitement here.

1314 *The Dino de Laurentis Production of* KING KONG. by Guillermin, John; and Semple, Lorenzo, Jr. 179 p. illus. New York: Ace, 1977.

1315 *Directing Motion Pictures.* edited by Marner, Terence St. John. 158 p. paper illus. New York: A. S. Barnes, 1972.

This book, "compiled and edited" by Marner, uses material "collected" from John Schlesinger, Jim Clark, Charles Crichton, Sid Cole, Wolf Rilla, Jerzy Skolimowski, Tony Richardson, and Joseph Losey, but the original sources are not indentified; whether they are from previously published articles or from direct interviews is not divulged. The author supplies the connective narrative and the supplementary diagrams and illustrations.

The subject of directing is surveyed by attention to role, preparation, script, shot selection, visual continuity, composition, viewpoint, movement, acting, rehearsals, and improvisation. On each of the above areas there are comments from each participant. This scheme works surprisingly well, probably because of the editor's expertise in selection, arrangement and bridging. Visuals are plentiful and adequately reproduced. Two short script extracts appear in the appendix, and the book is indexed.

The diversity of opinion offered, the overall coverage of a difficult topic, and the common-sense selection of readable quotations all blend to make this a very entertaining, instructive and useful book. Recommended.

1316 *Directing the Film: Film Directors and Their Art.* compiled by Sherman, Eric. 352 p. illus. Boston: Little, Brown, 1976.

Eric Sherman has selected excerpts from the American Film Institute Series, *Interviews with Film Directors*, for this anthology.

Seventy-five directors, both American and European, are represented in the collection. The excerpts are arranged according to the many aspects of directing—script, casting, rehearsal, actors, camera, etc. Sherman provides the connecting narrative when necessary and there are also biographies of the 75 subjects included. The volume is indexed.

This is an example of how the wealth of material that the AFI has gathered can be made palatable and useful to the general reader. Sherman's ability in selecting and synthesizing the director comments makes this a most impressive volume.

1317 *The Director's Event: Interviews with Five American Film-Makers.* by Sherman, Eric; and Rubin, Martin. 200 p. illus. New York: Atheneum, 1970.

The five directors referred to in the subtitle are Budd Boetticher, Peter Bogdanovich, Samuel Fuller, Arthur Penn, and Abraham Polonsky. Most of the questioning in the interviews concentrates on specific emotions, effects, and moments created by these directors in their films. A filmography follows each interview and the appendix lists commercial distributors of the film discussed. Illustrations used are small in size and limited in their effectiveness. This is a top-notch book of its kind. Recommended.

1318 *Directors and Directions.: Cinema for the Seventies.* by Taylor, John Russell. 327 p. New York: Farrar, Straus & Giroux, 1975.

Following rather closely the structure he used in *Cinema Eye, Cinema Ear*, John Russell Taylor provides eight critical essays on film directors who have established their reputations as auteurs in the last 10 years. Selected for his analytical scrutiny and ultimate appreciation are Lindsay Anderson, Claude Chabrol, Miklos Jacso, Stanley Kubrick, Dusan Makavajev, Pier Paolo Pasolini, Satyajit Ray, and Andy Warhol-Paul Morrissey.

The essays emphasize the totality and uniqueness of the filmmaker's work rather than providing a chronological survey. Of course, specific examples from films are discussed at length, but primarily as evidence of recurring themes, developing techniques or directorial style. Filmographies and bibliographies for each subject are provided in the closing pages of the book. There are no illustrations or index. The selection of directors made by Taylor is an intelligent one, and his critical analysis of them is informed, provocative and enjoyable. Recommended.

1319 *Directors at Work.* by Kramer, Anne. edited by Kantor, Bernard R.; and Blacker, Irwin R.; 442 p. New York: Funk and Wagnalls, 1970.

The stated intent of this volume is "to show how a variety of directors have responded to the American system of film-making." The group interviewed by the authors consists of Richard Brooke, George Cukor, Norman Jewison, Elia Kazan, Stanley Kramer, Richard Lester, Jerry Lewis, Elliot Silverstein, Robert Wise and William Wyler.

In addition to knowing the filmmaking process thoroughly, the authors also indicate total familiarity with the films and careers of their subjects. The questions asked are penetrating; as the directors give information, opinion, and attitude, they also reveal their personality. A filmography and a description of setting and background precede each interview. With the current interest in directors, this book cannot fail to win admiration and popularity.

1320 *Directors Guild of America Directory of Members.* 369 p. paper illus. Hollywood, Calif.: Directors Guild of America, 1971.

The fifth annual edition of a reference book that has value both within the film industry and in many libraries. It records in an alphabetical roster the largest membership in Guild history, along with a greater listing of credits and other information than ever before. Individual entries vary considerably in length. Some simply give the director's name, his home city and his ranking—assistant, associate or (full) director. Others give an extended list of credits along with agency and home addresses. Many of the credits refer to television programs. The total membership is divided into geographical groupings, with New York City, Hollywood, Chicago, Boston, Cleveland, Detroit and Florida represented. The latter five areas have small representation. Awards made by the Guild are noted, along with an index of agents, attorneys and business managers.

The book is a worthy addition to any reference collection, and future editions, which will probably increase the information given with each entry, may make it much more widely known than it is now. Currently it is distributed to libraries and universities around the world.

1321 *Directors in Action.* edited by Thomas, Bob. 283 p. paper illus. Indianapolis: Bobbs-Merrill, 1973.

This anthology of articles taken from *Action*, the official magazine of the Directors Guild of America, has much to recommend it. Only the arrangement of the material seems puzzling, and there is no editor statement explaining the structure of the book. The focus is on directors, the act of direction, and on specific films. Section headings are: (1) Orson Welles and CITIZEN KANE, (2) Directors at Work, (3) The Director-Actor, (4) The Western, (5) John Ford and STAGECOACH, (6) Anatomy of a Chase: THE FRENCH CONNECTION, (7) The World of the Assistant Director, and (8) The First Feature.

Directors Guild award winners for both film and television are listed and there are indexes for titles and names. The visuals which appear throughout are well reproduced and are essential to many of the articles. Interest in the subject matter of this book should be uniformly high and ensure its popularity in all quarters. The articles and their authors are most impressive and the production is of high quality. The random arrangement of the material is a small disadvantage but will not limit reader enthusiasm. Highly recommended.

1322 *Directory of American Film Scholars.* by Phillips, Leona; and Phillips, Jill. 120 p. New York: Gordon Press, 1975.

Another expensive volume from Gordon Press, this directory lists many persons involved in the study and teaching of motion pictures.

1323   *see   1324*

1324 *Directory of Blacks in the Performing Arts.* by Mapp, Edward. 428 p. illus. Metuchen, N.J.: Scarecrow, 1978.

This directory provides biographical information on 850 blacks, living and deceased, who have been recognized for their work in film, television, theatre, opera, ballet, night clubs and/or classical concert work. Arranged alphabetically by performer surname, the entries include such headings as real name, profession, birth date and place, death date and place, education, special interests, address, honors, career data, clubs, films, memberships, compositions, recordings, publications, television, theatre, and relationships. Some of the information is selected or partial (records, clubs, theatre, etc.), but there is more than enough in each case for a very satisfactory identification.

1325 *Directory of Film Libraries in North America.* edited by Clark, Joan E. 87 p. paper New York: Film Library Information Council, 1971.

A listing of more than 1800 film libraries in North America, this somewhat specialized reference work is of great value to film distributors and salesmen.

1326 *Directory of Non-Royalty Films for Television.* edited by Williams, T. M. 108 p. paper Ames, Iowa: Iowa State, 1954.

Since this volume is almost thirty years old, it is of limited value today. However, its format and structure can serve as a model for similar books. A general introduction describes the organization of the material and discusses TV clearance problems. The latter topic consists of rights such as ownership, musical composition, musical performance, privacy, and other considerations. The films in the book are each given a clearance rating, on a scale of Class I (all risks in showing assumed by the producer) to Class V (all showings are made at the TV station's risk).

Films listed are largely the "free" films listed in other publications such as *The Educator's Guide to Free Films.* As noted in that annotation, the showing of commercially sponsored films without a preview is a risk. While many are entertaining, educational and technically excellent, others are simply one long hard-sell commercial. There is an alphabetical title listing, a subject listing, and a short listing of "Series" films. Information on obtaining government films is noted, along with the distribution sources.

This is more a model of the kind of reference material that will be needed in the era of Cable TV rather than a source of useable information. See also *TV "Free" Film Source Book, Vol. 12.*

1327 *A Directory of 16mm Film Collections in Colleges and Universities in the United States.* by Mirwis, Allan. 74 p. paper Bloomington, Ind.: Indiana University Press, 1972.

This listing of colleges and universities which maintain film collections, using questionnaire responses from the institutions, gives the following data arranged by state: institution name, address, name, title of person in charge, telephone number, free loan policy, rental policy, number of titles (and prints) catalog frequency and availability, and other comments. A time-saving section preceding the main body of the book lists all institutions which have out-of-state rental policies.

For anyone who uses film, this is a most helpful aid. It is arranged for easy use and will suggest possible sources of films that may not be noted elsewhere.

1328 *Directory of U.S. Government Audiovisual Personnel.* by National Audiovisual Center. paper Washington, D.C.: National Audiovisual Center, General Services Administration, 1976.

This directory, which has been published at irregular intervals, lists some 50 Federal agencies along with their personnel in its 5th edition. All these persons are involved in some way with the radio, TV, film, photography, recording and exhibit activities of the government.

1329 *Dirty Movies: An Illustrated History of the Stag Film 1915-1970.* by Di Lauro, Al; and Rabkin, Gerald. 160 p. illus. New York: Chelsea House, 1976.

To the authors, the stag film is the "illegal filmic depiction of actual, non-simulated sexual acts, produced for private viewing or for showing in officially decried but socially tolerated circumstances (the brothel, the smoker, etc.)." The X-rated films such as DEEP THROAT (1972) shown publicly since 1970 are referred to as "pornos. <

Following an introduction by Kenneth Tynan, various aspects of stag films are discussed—their attraction for the viewer, their history, actions, plots, performers, and national differences. A bibliography is introduced by the statement, "The literature on pornography exceeds the literature of pornography." A selected filmography concludes the volume. Illustrations are made from frame blowups and give evidence of the primitive filming techniques used to make stag films.

Any attempt at a serious treatment or study of stag films is both vulnerable and risky. Honest feeling and reaction to them is private and personal within each individual viewer. Without a large controlled interview situation, attempts to generalize may reflect author attitude more than anything else. Although this volume does offer some provocative thoughtful comment, much of its content appears to be narrowly selected—i.e., cited examples and illustrations seem to have been taken from only a few films out of the many thousands made over the 65 years covered. The total text appears on only 100 pages and much of their area is given to illustrations.

Since the topic and the visuals still remain suitable primarily for private adult reading and viewing, its success with certain readers seems assured. For serious readers it does offer an overview of a film genre that is not available elsewhere.

1330 *The Disciple and His Devil.* by Pascal, Valerie. 356 p. illus. New York: McGraw-Hill, 1970.

The title of the book refers primarily to the first section. The disciple was Gabriel Pascal, who produced film versions of devil George Bernard Shaw's "Pygmalion", "Major Barbara", and "Caesar and Cleopatra". The original idea to musicalize "Pygmalion" was supposedly Pascal's. Latter portions of the book deal with Pascal's decline as a producer and as a husband.

Written by Pascal's actress wife, this bitter-sweet book has correspondence, portraits, remembrances, and a once-devoted spouse's analysis of the Pascal-Shaw relationship. The final image given of Pascal is that of a very ambitious wheeler-dealer. Two picture sections show Pascal and Valerie with other celebrities, and a few stills from the films. Of moderate interest.

1331 *Discovering the Movies.* by Starr, Cecile. 144 p. illus. New York: Van Nostrand, 1972.

Imagine, if you can, a film study book that combines history, aesthetics, reference, criticism, and biography in 144 pages. Ms. Starr has designed such a text for a youth audience, and with considerable success. Beginning with pre-screen history, she quickly advances to Melies, Porter, Griffith, and Chaplin. Flaherty, Grierson, and McLaren occupy the second section of the book. A few available films supporting the text in each chapter are described and evaluated. Distributor-rental-sale information is given in the appendices along with some bibliography suggestions. One of the outstanding appendices is entitled "Film Study in the Classroom." A compilation of helpful suggestions on using/studying films in a classroom situation, these few pages seem to contain the distillation of the author's many years of experience in teaching film. Picture work throughout is superior and a short but adequate index is provided.

For the audience for which it is intended, this volume is a must. It cannot fail to excite, involve, and inspire any youngster toward further investigation of film. More mature readers can cover the familiar ground quickly but will find sufficient new material here to warrant attention. Recommended.

1332 *Discovery in Film.* by Heyer, Robert; and Meyer, Anthony. 220 p. paper illus. New York: Association Press; Paramus, N.J.: Paulist Press, 1969.

The introductory remarks are valid: "...explores the use of short, nonfeature films for educational purposes.... It has in mind educators who work with teenagers and adults in discussion situations..." The films are divided among five categories: communication, freedom, love, peace, and happiness, although several "underground" films are not given a classification. For each film, there is offered comment, discussion questions, resource material, and statistical data. Several appendixes on related subjects conclude the book. Many illustrations are included and they are technically excellent and highly motivating. Material is presented in a pertinent, useful style.

1333 *Discovery in Film—Book Two.* by Gordon, Malcolm. 162 p. paper illus. Paramus, N.J.: Paulist Press, 1973.

As the second volume in what is, hopefully, a series, this book describes 81 short films and offers suggestions for their use in a variety of educational settings. A thematic arrangement is used in which the films are placed under such headings as communications, freedom, peace, love, and happiness. All the headings are repeated from the first book with one omission—the underground. For each film there is a brief synopsis, data on running time, color, rental cost, purchase price, and distributor, and a few suggestions or questions for use with audiences. Illustrations are used effectively throughout and an alphabetical title index is included.

Subtitling the book "A Teacher Sourcebook" may justify the inclusion of some suggestions for a Super-8 filmmaking course, but may also lessen the book's potential audience. Although it is more modest in content and production than its predecessor, this volume, too, is an essential reference for librarians, educators, and clergy.

1334 *A Discovery of Cinema.* by Dickinson, Thorold. 164 p. paper illus. New York: Oxford University Press, 1971.

Dickinson provides a very structured overview of film, combining history, aesthetics, and criticism. Adapting George Huaco's model from *The Sociology of Film Art*, Dickinson delineates four factors which determine the history of film: climate (political, economic, etc.), technology, creativity, and audience. Using these factors, he examines three periods of cinema: The Silent Era (1895-1927), The Early Sound Era (1927-1947), and The Modern Sound Era. In his discussion, he gives attention to classic films, notable directors (mostly European), film technology, and the film industry. At times, he belabors a point, e.g., monochromatic film, but his encyclopedic knowledge and skill in structuring his information more than compensate.

The stills are well reproduced and add considerably to the book's effectiveness. A bibliography, an index and several appendixes complete the volume. This is an outstanding short volume that will appeal to a wide audience. Dickinsons's approach is scholarly but it is that of an experienced, secure teacher who guides his reader rather than overwhelms him. Highly recommended.

1335 *Disney Animation: The Illusion of Life.* by Thomas, Frank; and Johnston, Ollie. 575 p. illus. New York: Abbeville, 1981.

Everything about animation told by two Disney animators with full explanations and more than 2700 illustrations, many in full color. Walt Disney as studio head, as an inspiration and as a difficult man of varying moods is described.

1336 *Disney Classic Film Series.* paper illus. Moonachie, N.J.: Pyramid, 1975- .

A series of digest-sized paperbacks with full-color covers and containing illustrations from the Disney films and television movies.

Titles include *Snow White and the Seven Dwarfs, Sleeping Beauty, Robin Hood, Peter Pan, Dr. Syn Alias the Scarecrow, Tonka, Two Against the Arctic,* and *My Dog the Thief.*

1337 *The Disney Films.* by Maltin, Leonard. 312 p. illus. New York: Crown, 1973.

This well-researched book concentrates on the feature films of Walt Disney. After an overview of Disney's life and career, each of the feature films from SNOW WHITE AND THE SEVEN DWARFS (1937) to THE HAPPIEST MILLIONAIRE (1963) receives individual attention. Listings of cast, songs, and technical production credits are given along with a plot synopsis. Maltin offers not only his own evaluation of the film but tells the film's box office fate, its critical reception, and even describes the social climate of the country when the film appeared. A rather full account is thus rendered.

Final sections deal with the films made by the Disney Studios after Walt's death, Walt Disney on television, and most important of all, the Disney short films. In this latter section, an affectionate essay discusses the shorts and is followed by a chronological listing of them. Included are cartoons of Oswald, Mickey Mouse, Silly Symphonies, Donald Duck, Goofy, Pluto, and Chip and Dale. The *True-Life Adventures*, and *People and Places* series are here also. A detailed index completes the volume. Illustrations are adequately reproduced—but only in black and white. The absence of color diminishes their effectiveness —especially those taken from the animated features.

Maltin's style is mostly positive, admiring and noncritical—he is more a fan than a critic. The reader may easily become bored with the numerous Fred MacMurray films and wish that space had been given to some of the more provocative Disney work. However, with Disney there was always something for everyone in the family and this book is no exception. Acceptable.

1338 *The Disney Poster Book.* edited by Carvainis, Maria. 47 p. paper illus. New York: Harmony Books (Crown), 1977.

This collection of 24 full-color posters of Walt Disney characters is introduced by Maurice Sendak, who analyzes their appeal to youngsters. True, it is the posters which provide the attraction since they have been carefully selected and beautifully reproduced. Each begs to be taken from the book and hung up for all to enjoy. Highly recommended.

1339 *The Disney Version.* by Schickel, Richard. 384 p. New York: Simon & Schuster, 1968.

Subtitled "The Life, Times, Art and Commerce of Walt Disney," this biography is not a very complimentary one. It is rather a debunking of the Disney myth and an attempt to tell Disney's story objectively. The fact that all cooperation from Disney and his studio was denied the author may have had some effect on the author's presentation and selection of material.

Covering the early cartoons, the animated features, the nature studies and the family features, the narrative also tells of the many diverse financial interests such as Disneyland and merchandising that Disney developed. His relationships with the people he employed are explored in depth. There are no pictures (the studio holds copyrights) but there is a good bibliography. Certainly one of the better biographies of recent years, this volume should fascinate readers of all types except the very young. Valuable and highly recommended.

1340 *Disneyana: Walt Disney Collectibles.* by Munsey, Cecil. 385 p. illus. New York: Hawthorn, 1970.

This well-researched volume is a history of the collectibles and merchandising items that were inspired by Walt Disney films. Starting with Disney's pre-Mickey Mouse era, the text considers first his early cartoon character, Oswald the Rabbit. Others, such as Pinocchio or Snow White, are shown in original studio merchandising catalogs from the thirties to the present. All collectibles are dated by year of issue. Over 500 visuals of the collectibles are included, along with several appendixes listing prices, characters, comic book editions, etc. Recommended.

1341 *Dissertations on Film—A Series.* illus. New York: Arno, 1973- .

The titles in this series of dissertations on film were written in partial fulfillment of the requirements for a Ph.D. degree. Unfortunately the books offer minimum production quality at a maximum cost. While it is understandable that these volumes will have a limited sale, perhaps some other publishing format could make them available at a lower cost. They are deserving of a wide circulation and the present logistics may limit their availability. It should be noted that in the present versions, few or no changes seem to have been made between the original dissertation and its appearance as a publication.

Titles in the series include: *Bosley Crowther: Social Critic of the Film*, by Frank Eugene Beaver; *Critical Approaches to Federico Fellini's 8-1/2*, by Albert Edward Benderson; *The Cultural-Political Traditions and Developments of the Soviet Cinema: 1917-1972*, by Louis Harris Cohen; *Pudovkin's Films and Film Theory*, by Peter Dart; *The Legion of Decency: A*

Sociological Analysis of the Emergence and Development of a Social Pressure Group, by Paul W. Facey; *The Gangster Film: Emergence, Variation and Decay of a Genre, 1930-1940,* by Stephen L. Karpf; *The Origins of American Film Criticism,* by Myron O. Lounsbury; *The Silent Partner: The History of the American Film Manufacturing Company, 1910-1912,* by Timothy James Lyons; *Broadway and Hollywood: A History of Economic Interaction,* by Robert McLaughlin; *The Early Development of the Motion Picture, 1887-1909,* by Joseph H. North; *The Motion Picture in the Soviet Union,* by John Rimberg; *A Historical Study of the Academy of the Motion Picture Arts and Sciences (1927-1947),* by Pierre N. Sands; and *Vachel Lindsay: The Poet As Film Thinker,* by Glenn J. Wolfe;

In Its Own Image: The Cinematic Vision of Hollywood, by Patrick Donald Anderson; *The Mobile Mise En Scene: A Critical Analysis of the Theory and Practice of Long-Take Camera Movement in the Narrative Film,* by Lutz Bacher; *An Investigation of the Motives For and Realization of Music to Accompany the American Silent Film 1896-1927,* by Charles Merrell Berg; *A Comparative Study of Selected American Film Critics, 1958-1974,* by Joseph Dalton Blades, Jr.; *The Lutheran Milieu of the Films of Ingmar Bergman,* by Richard Aloysius Blake; *An Historical and Descriptive Analysis of the* WHY WE FIGHT *Series,* by Thomas William Bohn; *Response to Innovation: A Study of Popular Argument About New Mass Media,* by Robert Edward Davis; *Persistence of Vision: The Films of Robert Altman,* by Neil Feineman; *The National Board of Censorship (Review) of Motion Pictures, 1909-1922,* by Charles Matthew Feldman; *Evolution of Style in the Early Work of Dziga Vertov,* by Seth R. Feldman.

Film Theory of James Agee, by Mark Wilson Flanders; *The Aesthetic of Isolation in Film Theory: Hugo Munsterberg,* by Donald Laurence Fredericksen; *Selected Attempts at Stereoscopic Moving Pictures and Their Relationship to the Development of Motion Picture Technology, 1852-1903,* by H. Mark Gosser; *Gradients of Depth in the Cinema Image,* by Charles Henry Harpole; *Film As a National Art: NFB of Canada and the Film Board Idea,* by C. Rodney James; *Toward a Definition of the American Film Noir (1941-1949),* by A. M. Karimi; *Clozentropy: A Technique for Studying Audience Response to Films,* by F. Dennis Lynch; *Michelangelo Antonioni's Neo Realism: A World View,* by Robert Joseph Lyons; *American Visions: The Films of Chaplin, Ford, Capra, and Welles, 1936-1941,* by Charles John Maland; *The Identity Crisis Theme in American Feature*

Films, 1960-1969, by John Lenard Mason; *The Simplification of American Life: Hollywood Films of the 1930's,* by Jeffery Morton Paine;

Sources of Meaning in Motion Pictures and Television, by Calvin Pryluck; *A Historical Study of the Development of American Motion Picture Content and Techniques Prior to 1904,* by Richard Arlo Sanderson; *The Study of Film as An Art Form in the American Secondary Schools,* by Stuart Alan Selby; *An Analysis of Motion Pictures about War Released by the American Film Industry, 1939-1970,* James Agee: *A Study of His Film Criticism,* by John J. Snyder; *The Effects of Television on the Motion Picture and Radio Industries,* by Fredric Stuart; *The Theory and Practice of the Cine-Roman,* by William F. Van Wert; *Buster Keaton and the Dynamics of Visual Wit,* by George Wead; *Film Archetypes: Sisters, Mistresses, Mothers, and Daughters,* by Janice R. Welsch; *Ralph Steiner: Filmmaker and Still Photographer,* by Joel Steward Zuker.

1342   *Distinguished Company.* by Gielgud, John. illus. New York: Doubleday, 1972.

Sir John Gielgud recalls some "youthful enthusiasm" here, mostly stage actors that he knew early on in his career —Ellen Terry, John Barrymore, Charles Laughton, Cedric Hardwicke, Leslie Howard, etc. He pays tribute to their professional skill and spoken wit in the typical generous but reserved Gielgud style.

1343   *Diversion: Twenty-Two Authors on the Lively Arts.* edited by Sutro, John. 224 p. illus. London: Max Parrish, 1950.

Since the majority of the articles in this anthology are about films, the book is noted here. The following topics are covered: cinema houses ("Pleasured and Palaces," by John Betjeman), film music ("The Celluloid Plays a Tune," by Alan Rawsthorne), film publicity ("The Ballyhooly Truth," anonymous), film fans ("Frustrated, Lonely and Peculiar," by Norah Alexander), set design ("His Eyes Were Never Bloodshot," by Simon Harcourt-Smith), INTOLERANCE (1916)("The Greatest Movie Ever Made," by Rodney Ackland), cinema horror ("H for Horripilant," by Dilys Powell), the silent era ("The Twilight of the Silent Days," by Cecil Beaton), screenwriting ("Writing in Pictures," by Nigel Balchin, and "A Magnificent Pity for Camels," by Terence Rattigan), art vs. commerce in films ("The Third Eye," by Thorold Dickinson), and ballet in film ("The Orchestration of Movement," by Robert Helpmann). This is an above-average collection of interesting and amusing articles. Some fine rare illustrations accompany the text. Recommended.

1344 *The Divine Garbo.* by Sands, Frederick; and Broman, Sven. 243 p. illus. New York: Grosset, 1979.

In 1977 Frederick Sands spoke to Greta Garbo and it is those meetings that he uses for this volume. Nothing particularly new or startling is revealed, except, perhaps, the rather negative impression the author notes—an elderly woman who is self-interested to the exclusion of all else.

The volume appears in a superb, oversized production. Many illustrations accompany the text, which also includes some impressive research via interviews by Sven Broman.

For those who have not yet tired of the Garbo story and legend, this is an attractive addition. The blend of Garbo-now and Garbo-then packaged so handsomely qualifies it for reader consideration.

1345 *Do Films Teach World Understanding?* by British Parliamentary Group for World Government. 60 p. paper London: House of Commons, 1968.

This was a study of 19 selected films thought to be potentially useful in encouraging a sense of world community. The research was performed in various classroom situations; purpose, methods, results, and pupil/teacher responses are discussed. An appendix offers the forms used and tabulations of the findings.

Certain conclusions of the study are interesting: one theme or concept in a film is more effective than several; films with words/narration or with animation are not as effective as purely visual presentations; symbolism in films is not effective in the satisfaction of the particular goal of this study; film notes or study guides are essential; feature-length films are not so successful as shorter films; the optimum running time for the most effective films was found to be 15 to 30 minutes. This study is highly recommended. Its implications for research in film use and in teacher training are numerous.

1346 *Do You Sleep in the Nude?* by Reed, Rex. 255 p. paper New York: Signet Books, 1968.

Rex Reed is the interviewer-journalist who has the ability to get his subjects to say things that make vigorous and sometimes scandalous reading. In his reporting, he is alternately bitchy, sympathetic, gossipy, affectionate, cynical and humorous, but never

dull. Because this is his earliest collection, the pieces have an individuality that later ones do not possess. Here he is a master of interview technique and interpretation. A most satisfying entertainment.

1347 DOC. by Hamill, Pete. 202 p. paper illus. New York: Paperback Library, 1971.

Script of the 1971 film directed by Frank Perry. Contains cast credits.

1348 THE DOCTOR AND THE DEVILS *and Other Scripts.* by Thomas, Dylan. 229 p. New York: New Directions Pub. Corp., 1966.

Contains 1) THE DOCTOR AND THE DEVILS (not filmed), 2) TWENTY YEARS A-GROWING (not filmed), 3) A Dream of Winter (a poem), and 4) The Londoner (a radio script).

1349 DOCTOR DOLITTLE. by Stern, Harold. 48 p. paper illus. New York: National Publishers, 1967.

The first portion of this souvenir book contains the plot description, many fine stills, and the songs. Two articles, "Out of Dreams Comes Reality" and "Of Time and the Animals," provide background information about the 1967 film. Perhaps the outstanding feature included is the designer's sketchbook. The usual credits and individual biographies are also given. A most impressive example of what a souvenir book should be.

1350 DOCTOR ZHIVAGO. by Bolt, Robert. 224 p. color illus. New York:Random House, 1965.

Script of the 1964 film directed by David Lean. Introduction by Robert Bolt.

1351 DOCTOR ZHIVAGO. 32 p. paper illus. 1965.

The spotlight is given to author Boris Pasternak, director David Lean, and screenplay writer Robert Bolt in this souvenir book. Major cast members are given a single page, including a still from the 1965 film. Producer Carlo Ponti is profiled and other production credits are noted. Many of the photographs are quite fuzzy, and the entire book is unimpressive.

1352 *Documentary: A History of the Non-Fiction Film.* by Barnouw, Erik. 332 p. illus. New York: Oxford University Press, 1974.

The history of the documentary/nonfiction film is approached by Barnouw through its creators. Filmmakers such as Lumiere, Flaherty, Dziga-Vertov, Grierson, and Wright lead the way toward such creative artists of today as Wiseman, the Maysles brothers, Leacock, etc. Using section headings such as Images at Work, Sound and Fury, Clouded Lens, and Sharp Focus, the text further classifies the filmmakers as explorers, painters, poets, observers, catalysts, guerrillas, etc.

The approach is chronological and many films are described and critically evaluated. Source notes for each subheading are supplied and there is a lengthy bibliography provided. The book is indexed. Visuals include both portraits of the filmmakers and stills from their works. As a carefully researched and well-written history of the nonfiction film, this volume is excellent. Its appeal to readers may be lessened somewhat by the appearance of much of the material found in earlier publications and by the limited popular appeal of this film genre. Recommended.

1353 *Documentary and Educational Films.* 159 p. paper Warsaw: Film Polski, 1970.

This catalog of Polish films is published in four languages: Polish, English, French, and German. The films are listed both alphabetically by title and then by subject area—art, history, science, etc. Title, data, and a short description are given for each film.

1354 *Documentary and Educational Films of the 1930's.* by Low, Rachael. 244 p. illus. London: Allen & Unwin; New York: R.R. Bowker, 1979.

Rachael Low continues her monumental work, *The History of the British Film*, with this volume, the seventh in a series. Here she is concerned with two related film forms: the documentary and the educational film. The former is covered by a lengthy account of the documentary movement in Britain during the thirties. The growth of films designed for education is traced with relative brevity. Attention is given to the films, their production, and the use-acceptance of them.

Supporting the two major elements are a bibliography, a filmography, notes, an index, and a short account of the beginnings of the British Film Institute.

This volume continues the over-all excellence and quality that was found in the earlier volumes. Low writes a succint, no-nonsense historical reference

that is crammed with data, narrative and opinion. A valuable record that is also a pleasant reading experience.

1355 *The Documentary Conscience: A Casebook in Film Making.* by Rosenthal, Alan. 446 p. paper illus. Berkeley, Calif.: University of California Press, 1980.

Alan Rosenthal, the author of *The New Documentary in Action: A Casebook in Film Making*, uses the same format here. Some 29 filmmakers are interviewed about their commitment to this film genre. He talks with them about funding, public/critical indifference, distribution problems, etc. His subjects come from the various subheads of documentary film: political, television, personal, radical messages, social problems, history, investigations, straight documentary, etc.

The long introduction by Rosenthal again indicates the background which qualifies him to conduct his interviews. His questions and comments are intelligent and thought-provoking, providing an excellent state-of-the-art survey.

1356 *Documentary Explorations.* by Levin, G. Roy. 420 p. paper illus. Garden City, N.Y.: Doubleday, 1972.

A brief outline of the history of documentary film introduces this collection of interviews. The history considers the documentaries of various countries in separate short statements. Following this serviceable section are the author's interviews with Basil Wright, Lindsay Anderson, Richard Cawston, Tony Garnett and Kenneth Loach from Britain; Georges Franju and Jean Rouch from France; and Henri Storck from Belgium. The United States is represented by Willard Van Dyke, Richard Leacock, D. A. Pennebaker, Albert Maysles, David Maysles, Arthur Barron, Frederick Wiseman, Ed Pincus, Michael Shamberg, and David Cort. A short biographical sketch is provided for each.

Although all of the interviews express ideas, opinions, attitudes or prejudices about making documentary films, the maximum effect of each statement will depend upon the reader's knowledge of the films. Filmographies are provided at the conclusion of each interview. A collection of stills, a short bibliography, and a useful index complete the book.

The author's qualifications for this work are evidenced by the filmmakers selected, the questions asked, and the final choice and arrangement of material. Highly recommended.

1357 *Documentary Film.* by Rotha, Paul. This volume was done in collaboration with Sinclair Road and Richard Griffith. 3rd ed. rev., 412 p. illus. London: Faber & Faber, 1952.

"The use of the film medium to interpret creatively and in social terms the life of the people as it exists in reality" : with this phrase as a guide, this early classic on the documentary film considers ideas, information, history and other factors pertinent to this motion picture form. It was first published during the World War II era and much of its content indicates that time framework. Social issues are emphasized and are considered from the British point of view.

The third revision (1952) gives some attention to the American documentary and to the use of films by the U. S. Armed Forces. A listing of 100 important documentary films and a bibliography are given. Although much of the content is valid today, the book suffers somewhat from the dated references and the emphasis on past social issues. However, it is still a classic.

1358 *Documentary in Denmark.* by Neegaard, Ebbe. 89 p. Copenhagen: Statens Filmcentral, 1948.

A catalog of documentary films produced in Denmark from 1940 to 1948.

1359 *The Documentary Tradition, from* NANOOK to WOODSTOCK. by Jacobs, Lewis. 530 p. illus. New York: Hopkinson and Blake, 1971.

An illustrated anthology of the documentary film from 1920-1970.

1360 *Documentation of Red Stars in Hollywood.* by Fagan, Myron C. 110 p. illus. Hollywood: Cinema Education Guild, 1950.

The writer was deeply concerned about the communist influence in Hollywood and wrote several books on the subject.

1361 *The Dogs Bark: Public People and Private Places.* by Capote, Truman. 419 p. paper New York: New American Library, 1977.

A collection of previously published articles that includes profiles of Brando, Mae West, Bogart, Monroe, Cocteau, etc., along with an account of the filming of IN COLD BLOOD (1967).

1362 *Doing It Yourself.* by Reichert, Julia. 76 p. paper New York: Association of Independent Video and Film-makers, 1977.

Addressed primarily to independent filmmakers, this volume has the subtitle, "A Handbook on Independent Film Distribution." The emphasis is on self-distribution for nontheatrical showings of short films (those running less than 70 minutes.) Topics include self-distribution, advertising, promotion, costs, bookings, and office management. Final sections discuss European possibilities, speaking engagements, cooperatives, film festivals, business forms, etc.

Since the book comes from a productive independent filmmaker, it offers basic nuts-and-bolts information that is the result of experience. An invaluable book for the neophyte filmmaker, it also offers practical advice and professional wisdom for other readers.

1363 *Doing the Media.* edited by Laybourne, Kit; and Cianciolo, Pauline. 212 p. illus. Chicago: American Library Assoc., 1978.

Called "A Portfolio of Activities, Ideas, and Resources," this anthology originated at John Culkin's Center for Understanding Media in 1972. In this revised edition, there are seven general headings: introduction, photography, film, video, sound, other media, and curriculum design. A section listing media resources (books, periodicals, organizations, distributors) and an index complete the book.

The film section offers six articles which deal with student filmmaking, a film theatre, film discussions, and film showing follow-up activities.

The volume is generously illustrated and attractively produced. All the suggested activities have been tested and therefore offer interested professionals some creative ideas about using media with young people. Recommended.

1364 *The Dollars and Sense of Business Films.* by Film Steering Committee, A.N.A. 128 p. illus. New York: Association of National Advertisers, 1954.

One hundred fifty-seven films were studied in this early research project concerning the economics of producing and distributing advertising and public relations films, sometimes called "business" or "sponsored" films.

1365 *Don Siegel: American Cinema.* by Lovell, Alan. 81 p. paper London: British Film Institute; (Zoetrope in U.S.), 1975.

This appreciation of Don Siegel contains an introduction, and evaluative essay, a career sketch, some notes on DIRTY HARRY (1971), an interview, a filmography, and a bibliography. Since Siegel is one of the most colorful creative directors on the American scene, this small booklet is a total pleasure. In addition it is a valid reference on Siegel. Recommended.

1366 *see 1365*

1367 *Don Siegel: Director.* by Kaminsky, Stuart. 319 p. paper illus. New York: Curtis, 1974.

This appreciation of director Don Siegel has a foreword by Peter Bogdanovich and an afterword by Sam Peckinpah. A filmography is included.

1368 *Don't Fall Off the Mountain.* by MacLaine, Shirley. 270 p. New York: W. W. Norton, 1970.

An unusual film autobiography that has literary merit, charm, and wit. It covers Miss MacLaine's unique marriage arrangement, her enthusiasms and disillusionments, her travels overseas, and her philosophy about Hollywood, fame, and success. One of the best cinema autobiographies ever.

1369 *Don't Get Me Wrong — I Love Hollywood.* by Skolsky, Sidney. 250 p. illus. New York: G.P. Putnam's, 1975.

For more than 40 years Sidney Skolskyhas covered the Hollywood scene via newspapers and radio. In addition he served as a producer for THE JOLSON STORY (1946) and in various other professional capacities. In this slightly autobiographical account of his life and career, major space is devoted to recalling stories, information and anecdotes about Hollywood's golden years. An all-star cast populates the pages, yet there is none of the maliciousness, bitchery, or vendetta found in other gossip tomes. As indicated in the title, Skolsky loves Hollywood and its denizens.

A center section of photographs shows Skolsky as an intimate of the stars—playing cards, riding bikes, in conversational huddles, etc. Thankfully, the book is indexed which makes the concentration of original Skolsky material accessible.

Skolsky is a wise writer who uses selected portions of what he knows and allows the reader to fill in the spaces. This technique results in far more colorful reading than the simple truth. Acceptable.

1370 *Don't Look at the Camera.* by Watt, Harry. 194 p. illus. New York: St. Martin's, 1974.

An autobiography of British filmmaker Harry Watt, this book describes his work as a pioneer in the documentary film movement. His association with John Grierson, Basil Wright, Humphrey Jennings, Alberto Cavalcanti, Robert Flaherty and others is noted, as are his own accomplishments in film direction—notably in films such as NIGHT MAIL (1936), LONDON CAN TAKE IT (1940) and TARGET FOR TONIGHT (1941). An index and selected illustrations accompany this lighthearted memoir. Acceptable.

1371 *Don't Look at the Camera!* by Ewing, Sam; and Abolin, R. W. 224 p. illus. Blue Ridge Summit, Pa.: TAB Books, 1973.

Television photography and filmmaking are the subjects of this concise presentation. A bibliography is provided.

1372 *Don't Say Yes Until I Finish Talking: A Biography of Darryl F. Zanuck.* by Gussow, Mel. 318 p. illus. Garden City, N.Y.: Doubleday, 1971.

Biography of one of the most creative of the motion picture moguls. Zanuck learned the business by writing scripts. Eventually, with the help of Rin Tin Tin and others, he became the head of Warner Brothers. In the early thirties he left Warners to form 20th Century-Fox with Joseph Schenck. Until 1956, he ran that studio and was responsible in varying degrees for many of the film classics that were made there. After leaving in 1956, he returned in 1962—post-CLEOPATRA (1963)—with THE LONGEST DAY (1962) and rescued Fox. In 1971, he was still engaged in a boardroom power struggle for control of the company. This movie mogul was an energetic competitive scrapper who seemingly fought and loved quite the same way in private as he did professionally.

The book has some minor flaws, e.g., the roles of Schenck and Skouras in the studio story are minimized. The accusation of being a bought critic levelled against Frank Nugent seems unfair, and the assessment of several directors' abilities is questionable. In the author's favor is the fact that he does not avoid the private life of Zanuck but instead handles it with taste, never descending to gossip or innuendo. The accounts of their relationship with Zanuck by his four unsuccessful film proteges (Darvi, Greco, Demick, and Gilles) are frank yet sympathetic. An excellent filmography, some fine photographs, and an extended index. Recommended.

1373 *Donald Duck.* by Blitz, Marcia. 256 p. illus. New York: Harmony Books, 1979.

Donald Duck is given the same gala treatment that other film stars are accorded in this biographical appreciation. His creators, early supporting roles, merchandising, emergence as a star, role in the war, and his appearance in print and on TV are covered. Over 130 cartoon shorts from THE WISE LITTLE HEN (1934) to SCROOGE MCDUCK AND MONEY (1967) are described along with his five feature films made in the forties: THE RELUCTANT DRAGON (1941), SALUDOS AMIGOS (1943), THE THREE CABALLEROS (1945), FUN AND FANCY FREE (1947) and MELODY TIME (1948).

In addition to this detailed coverage, the book offers a section on animated filmmaking, one complete cartoon (DONALD'S NEPHEWS 1938), hundreds of illustrations (many in full color), a filmography, a trivia quiz, and a bibliography.

This is a beautifully composed tribute to a film superstar that is long overdue. Donald's appeal is international and this book explains his great popularity in a series of entertainingly written and produced chapters. Recommended.

1374 *Doris Day.* by Morris, George. 159 p. paper illus. New York: Pyramid, 1976.

George Morris' survey of Doris Day's life and career follows the established format of the *Illustrated History of the Movies* series, a brief appreciation followed by a review of the Day films. Her career can be divided into two major periods—the early Warner musicals and the later Universal romantic comedies. In between there were digressions with Hitchcock, Cagney, Gable, and a final sextet of films that were uniformly deplorable, although the author finds some slight quality in several. All of her films are discussed with intelligence, and the critical views offered are interesting, if not always convincing.

The illustrations are quite good, although they constantly emphasize the Day persona rather than the Day film. A bibliography, a filmography, and an index complete the book. Acceptable.

1375 *Doris Day: Her Own Story.* by Hotchner, A. E. 301 p. illus. New York: William Morrow, 1976.

Told in a frank, straightforward fashion, the story of the private Doris Day is at variance with her screen image. She has experienced three marriages that failed, a severe nervous breakdown and several bouts with depression. A. E. Hotchner, the author of *Papa Hemingway*, had the complete cooperation of the actress in preparing this biography. Two major themes dear to most fans emerge: Day in real life little resembles the virginal goody two-shoes screen image, and monied celebrity along with beauty doesn't guarantee happiness.

The book contains a few illustrations and a filmography placed vertically across the pages. Throughout the pages there are separate statements/interviews with Day's costars, relatives, business associates, etc.

The final portrait of the actress is an admirable one though different from her screen character. LOVE ME OR LEAVE ME (1955) could well be her autobiographical film statement.

1376 *Doris Day.* by Thomey, Tedd. 139 p. paper Derby, Conn.: Monarch Books, 1962.

Doris Day has had a career in films spanning two decades, and at one time was the nation's leading box office star. The absence of any important biography, appreciation, or filmography volume on her for so long was puzzling. The only available full-length biography for many years was this original paperback by Thomey. Unfortunately it uses recreated conversations, a fan-magazine style of writing, and a soap-opera format. In addition to the poor text, the volume lacks illustrations, an index and a filmography.

The need for a serious, well-researched biographical study of Doris Day and her films may be partially satisfied by her official biography, *Doris Day: Her Own Story*, which was coauthored by A. E. Hotchner and published by William Morrow in late 1975.

1377 *The Doris Day Scrapbook.* by Gelb, Alan. 159 p. paper illus. New York: Grosset and Dunlap, 1977.

This early title in the *Scrapbook Series* covers the life and career of Doris Day in both text and illustrations. In seven chapters— "Typical American Beauty," "Sentimental Journey," "The Golden Tonsil," "Day-Time," "The Great Years," "Super Doris," and "Whatever Will Be..." —Gelb emphasizes the films giving both plot summary and background information. A filmography and an index are included. The more than 150 visuals consist of stills, candids, and publicity shots. This appreciation of the actress is well-written and nicely produced.

1378 *Dorothy and Lillian Gish.* by Gish, Lillian. 312 p. illus. New York: Scribner's, 1973.

A pictorial record of the careers on stage and in films of the two Gish sisters, this volume includes over 800 visuals, including stills, portraits, playbills, candids, etc. Accompanying the photographs is a minimal, modest text that provides the framework and continuity to the book. The care given to the reproduction of the illustrations is exemplary, as is the selection—most of them are unfamiliar and published here for the first time.

This volume is a most attractive record of the professional activities of two determined actresses. It is also a reflection of the growth of motion pictures from a sideshow curiosity attraction to a major art form. Acceptable.

1379 *Dorothy Dandridge: A Portrait in Black.* by Mills, Earl. 250 p. paper illus. Los Angeles, Calif.: Holloway House, 1970.

A biography by the personal manager of Dorothy Dandridge. Readers familiar with her autobiography will find this modest paperback an interesting supplement. Some may be a bit shocked by the rawness and the compromise that characterized her life.

An outstanding element of this book is the number of beautifully reproduced photographs, probably, one would guess, from the author's collection.

This is a portrait of a black entertainer as envisioned by a personal friend and business associate. It is a modest, rewarding book. Recommended.

1380 *Double Exposure.* by McDowall, Roddy. 253 p. illus. New York: Delacorte, 1966.

An attractive collection of many full-page portraits with a short comment or sketch accompanying each. These mini-texts were written by celebrities, usually expressing admiration or affection for the pictured subject. Thus we find Simone Signoret described by Katherine Hepburn, Judy Holliday by George Cukor, Hedda Hopper by Mary Martin, Sidney Poitier by Harry Belafonte, and other tributes, all varying in length from one paragraph to several pages. The concept, the production, and the contents are simply excellent. Recommended.

1381 *Double Feature: Movies and Politics.* by Goodwin, Michael; and Marcus, Greil. 128 p. illus. New York: Outerbridge and Lazard, Inc., 1972.

The two major elements of this film program are an extended interview with Jean-Luc Godard and Jean-Pierre Gorin and the script of a-movie-to-be-read entitled "This Is It: The Marin Shoot Out." An introduction of sorts, "The Garbage Truck of the Proletariat," is the cartoon that precedes the two main features.

Subtitled "Movies and Politics," the book addresses itself to the assumptions and priorities of seeing and making films. Early Godard films were made with the idea that the film itself was more important than its effect on audiences. This priority was reversed in later films, when Godard joined with other French militants known as the Dziga Vertov Group. Jean-Pierre Gorin was a member of that group when the interview was given in New York City, 1970.

Like most double bills, the main feature is padded out by a lower-rung effort, the script. The provocative topic of politics and film is handled in a gimmicky, ineffective format and is only intermittently satisfying. A few photographs are of no great assistance but the filmography of Godard and the Dziga Vertov Group is a plus. Acceptable.

1382 *Double Takes.* by Walker, Alexander. 260 p. North Pomfret, Vt.: Hamish Hamilton, 1977.

Alexander Walker is the film critic for the London *Evening Standard* and the author of several books including *Rudolph Valentino, The Celluloid Sacrifice,* and *Stanley Kubrick Directs.* In this volume, which he has subtitled, "Notes and Afterthoughts on the Movies 1956-76," he offers original reviews along with newly written comments about his present evaluations of the films. Although Richard Schickel employed the same idea in *Second Sight,* Walker's reconsiderations are more informative and entertaining. They often tell us as much about Walker as they do about a particular film. The two decades of film reviews are arranged under general headings: "Ladies First," "The Lighter Side," "Blood and Guts," etc. An index is provided.

For an excellent study of ongoing film criticism, this is a hard book to beat. With intelligence, wit, and background, Walker is continually able to amuse, provoke, and entertain the reader. Recommended.

1383 *Doug & Mary.* by Carey, Gary. 248 p. illus. New York: E. P. Dutton, 1977.

Although Douglas Fairbanks and Mary Pickford have been the subjects of several earlier books, this is the first to treat them as a couple. The details of their romance and marriage are related against the background of an emerging motion picture industry. Sprinkled throughout are stories and observations from many persons who knew the famous pair. Supporting the text are illustrations, a filmography, and an index.

The author has provided a serious, carefully searched account of one of the most famous couples of the 20th century. Unfortunately, with fame goes familiarity, and much of what Carey includes we have heard/read before. The volume will please those readers unacquainted with the silent screen era in Hollywood or those who never tire of nostalgia. Acceptable.

1384 *Doug and Mary and Others.* by Talmey, Allene. 181 p. illus. New York: Macy-Masius, 1927.

Short bright biographies of stars, producers, directors of the twenties: Fairbanks, Pickford, Swanson, Talmadge, etc. Amusing, perceptive and witty, with woodcuts by Betrand Zadig.

1385 *Douglas Fairbanks: the Fourth Musketeer.* by Hancock, Ralph; and Fairbanks, Letitia. 276 p. illus. New York: Henry Holt & Co., 1953.

This is the biography of the silent screen superman who was one of the most popular Hollywood personalities of the twenties before he died in 1939, an almost forgotten man. Most of the first portion of this book is devoted to his 15 years as an actor on the New York stage. His entrance into motion pictures in 1915 was concurrent with meeting Mary Pickford and the premiere of Griffith's BIRTH OF A NATION. His films and his relationships with his wives, his son, his co-workers (e.g., Chaplin) make up the rest of the volume.

Since a major portion of this work deals with the Fairbanks' films, it has importance. The portrait that emerges is not always flattering but the authors try to present an honest picture of the subject with sympathy and understanding. Some pictures are included. There is no index or bibliography.

1386 *Douglas Fairbanks: The Making of a Screen Character.* by Cooke, Alistair. 36 p. illus. New York: The Museum of Modern Art, 1940.

Some years ago the Museum of Modern Art published 8000 copies of this small hardbound book on Fairbanks and his films. Obtaining it today at a resonable price might be both difficult and time-consuming. An opening essay discusses the studio's creation of a screen image (a "star" personality). Fairbanks' life is considered next, including the developmental years with Griffith, Anita Loos, and John Emerson. He is also discussed as a philosopher, athlete, and showman.

A chronology of important events and film releases is given in the book, which is illustrated and indexed. This interesting approach to biography is too short to be totally effective. Omitted, for instance is the story told by Anita Loos of the accidental success of HIS PICTURE IN THE PAPERS (1916) the film that made Fairbanks into an overnight screen star. Too limited in coverage.

1387 *Douglas Sirk.* edited by Mulvey, Laura; and Halliday, Jon. 120 p. paper Edinburgh: Film Festival; New York: Zoetrope, 1972.

This anthology of critical articles is devoted to the American film director, Douglas Sirk.

1388 *Douglas Sirk.* by Stern, Michael. 214 p. illus. Boston: Twayne, 1979.

Douglas Sirk is probably best known for the group of Universal melodramas he directed during the fifties. In this appreciation Michael Stern provides a background to Sirk's career and then analyzes some of his Universal features—MAGNIFICENT OBSESSION (1954), ALL THAT HEAVEN ALLOWS (1955), THERE'S ALWAYS TOMORROW (1965), WRITTEN ON THE WIND (1956), THE TARNISHED ANGELS (1957), A TIME TO LOVE AND A TIME TO DIE (1958) and IMITATION OF LIFE (1959).

Unfortunately the notes, references, bibliography, filmography, and index in the review copy examined pertained to Peter Watkins and not to Douglas Sirk. There was enough excellent material present, however, to indicate a first-rate study of a relatively unknown American director.

1389 *see 1387*

1390 *Down The Yellow Brick Road: The Making of* THE WIZARD OF OZ. by McClelland, Doug. 159 p. paper illus. New York: Pyramid, 1976.

Rather than the usual memoir, diary, or day-by-day recital of the production activities of a specific film, this volume is a well-researched collection of data, quotations, and descriptive information about THE WIZARD OF OZ (1939). It is divided into six major sections: the picture, the book, the casting, the production, the music, and the legend.

Much of the material is unfamiliar and the reader may be surprised at some of the original casting or at the costly musical deletions made after the first preview.

The volume includes production and picture stills, portraits, drawings, publicity cards, etc. Reproduction of these is quite good and they add considerable dimension to the text. For example, the tight close-ups of the scarecrow, the tin man and the lion show in detail how their makeup was created by Jack Dawn.

This is a book that will please a wide audience. Recommended.

1391   *A Dozen and One.* by Tully, Jim. 242 p. illus. Hollywood: Murray and Gee, 1943.

This collective biography treats Gable, Chaplin, and some others.

1392   *Dr. Jekyll and Mr. Hyde.* edited by Anobile, Richard. 256 p. paper illus. New York: Avon (A Flare Book), 1975.

Since most critics consider Rouben Mamoulian's 1931 film, DR. JEKYLL AND MR. HYDE, to be the definitive version of the famous story, its appearance in the *Film Classics Library* series is most welcome. Using more than 1500 frame enlargements and all of the original dialogue, Richard Anobile has reconstructed this famous film in a most satisfactory manner. All of the nuance suggested by director Mamoulian is recaptured in the frames selected. The theme of Victorian sexual repression and hypocrisy is easily discernible in this presentation.

The picture quality is quite good with the Jekyll-to-Hyde transformations presented most effectively. An introduction by Anobile provides the background for the film with appreciation expressed for the work of Mamoulian, Fredric March and Miriam Hopkins. Recommended.

1393   DR. JEKYLL AND MR. HYDE. by Stevenson, Robert Louis. 96 p. paper illus. New York: Harper and Row, 1976.

This paperback, designed for young readers, is adapted by Horace J. Elias from the film, DR. JE-KYLL AND MR. HYDE (1941), which starred Spencer Tracy. It is noted here as a forerunner of both the *Film Classics Library* and the *Fotonovel* series. Using

one page of frame enlargements for each page of text, it attempts to reproduce the film rather than Robert Louis Stevenson's classic novel. THE WIZARD OF OZ (1939) is also published in this series.

1394   *Dracula.* by Thorne, Ian. 47 p. illus. Mankato, Minn.: Crestwood House, 1977.

A review of Dracula films written for young readers.

1395   *The Dracula Book.* by Glut, Donald F. 388 p. illus. Metuchen, N.J.: Scarecrow Press, 1975.

Donald Glut has provided a study on the character, Dracula, that is similar to his earlier book, *The Frankenstein Legend.* His opening chapters explore the legends, myths, images and ancestors surrounding the vampire Dracula. Attention is given to the sadistic Vlad Dracula (1430-1476), a major source for the books and stories which appeared during the next five centuries. General information about vampires precedes a discussion of Bram Stoker's classic volume. Stage dramatizations, films, radio plays, television programs, other books (including comics), recordings, wax museum figures, etc., are described to prove the eternal fascination that the Dracula character has for audiences.

Four chapters—the silents, The Universal Studio films, The Hammer Studio films, and independently produced films—are devoted to the Dracula films. Thoroughly researched, these chapters cover the Dracula films with the emphasis on production information and plot description rather than critical evaluation. The films of Christopher Lee and William Marshall receive extended attention, a temptation the author should have resisted. Both actors have provided introductions and, in turn, Glut has dedicated the book to them.

The absence of a bibliography in a work such as this is a serious flaw. Glut mentions certain sources in his opening acknowledgment, but this presentation is of limited value to the researcher. An index is provided and there are some illustrations. In certain ways this volume resembles *In Search of Dracula.* However, its attention to the Dracula films is more extensive and it does offer a rather complete coverage of the Dracula character as represented in the mass media. Acceptable.

1396   *The Dragon Movie Quiz Book.* by Rickard, Roy. 80 p. illus. paper London: Muller, 1979.

1397 *The Drama Scholars' Index to Plays and Filmscripts.: A Guide to Plays and Filmscripts in Selected Anthologies, Series and Periodicals.* by Samples, Gordon. 448 p. Metuchen, N.J.: Scarecrow Press, 1974.

A careful reading of the above title will indicate the general content of this reference volume. Aimed at scholars, it offers selected references not found in other indexes. These include both foreign and English-language sources along with numerous anthologies. The volume adds to the existing indexes rather than duplicating them. The second volume was published in 1980.

It is noted here because of the inclusion of filmscripts. The source citation is noted under the author's name. Titles are cross-referenced to the author's name. For example, the reader wishing to locate the filmscript for THE SILENCE (1964) may first look under that title. There he will be told to look under "Bergman, Ingmar," where two sources are noted: (1) the periodical *L'Avant-Scene du Cinema*, no. 37, 1964, and (2) the book, *A Film Trilogy* (New York, Orion Press, 1967). Final pages indicate the anthologies and periodicals cited in the book.

The volume will be useful to film scholars searching for sources not usually given in most reference books. However, its emphasis on drama and its restrictive selection criteria make it a limited reference in the area of film study. Acceptable.

1398 *The Dramatic Art of the Film.* by Casty, Alan. 192 p. illus. New York: Harper, 1971.

1399 *Drat: Being the Encapsulated View of Life by W. C. Fields in His Own Words.* edited by Anobile, Richard J. 128 p. illus. New York: World Pub. Co., 1968.

Notable mostly for the collection of excellent stills used to accompany some of Fields' more famous comments, this book will have appeal to both the new and the older Fields cult. It is designed primarily for entertainment.

1400 *The Drawings of Norman McLaren.* by McLaren, Norman. 192 p. illus. Montreal, Quebec: Tundra Books, 1975.

Norman McLaren is one of the world's most honored filmmakers, having created more than 50 films that have been applauded by festivals, critics, and most importantly, an ever-increasing audience.

Since he began work in 1941 at the National Film Board of Canada, he has engaged in a recreation—the art of drawing. This volume shows more than 500 of the drawings from his private collection. Most are line drawings made with pencil, pen, and/or brush. Of course there are similarities to some of his film creations here. A sparse text taken from interviews with Michael White accompanies the collection of fantastic visuals.

This is a volume that is hard to classify—film book or art book? Whatever its category, it will provide many hours of pleasure to the reader with some background in either art, film animation, or McLaren. Recommended.

1401 *Drawn and Quartered.* by Winnington, Richard. 126 p. illus. London: Saturn Press, 1949.

Sophisticated film criticism from the mid-forties accompanied by film star sketches drawn by the author.

1402 *A Dreadful Man.* by Aherne, Brian. 242 p. illus. New York: Simon and Schuster, 1979.

This volume consists mostly of letters sent to Brian Aherne from Benita Hume, the actress and widow of Ronald Colman. She married George Sanders in 1958, only one month after Colman's death. Apparently Benita appreciated Sanders' eccentricities and lived happily with him until her death in 1968. Four years later Sanders took his own life, leaving a note which stated, "I am bored."

Essentially lazy and remote, Sanders chose a life of acting and marrying wealthy women. In telling Sanders' story, Aherne includes much information about his own career. Both men were members of the British Colony of actors in Hollywood during the thirties and forties. Aherne is unsparing in his recital on Sanders' faults, although other characters are treated with affection.

A prejudiced but nevertheless lively biography of a man who was bored but apparently never was boring. Some illustrations are included.

1403 *The Dream Beside Me.* by Williams, Carol Traynor. 304 p. Rutherford: Fairleigh Dickinson University Press, 1980.

In a smart, sharp style Carol Traynor Williams recalls the films of the forties and their implication for her generation. In this volume, which she subtitles

"The Movies and the Children of the Forties," she examines among other things films, rituals, effects, Hollywood beauty, history, working women in wartime and after, GONE WITH THE WIND (1939), and anti-feminist attitudes in films. Chapter notes, an appendix, a long bibliography, and a index complete the book.

Many of her observations are amusing, and most of the text is interesting when read as a personal review and reaction to a specific group of films. Only in a tedious appendix entitled "Subjective Typology" does Williams let the reader down a bit. Long lists of actors and actresses assigned to category headings add little to the text.

1404   *A Dream of Dracula: In Search of the Living Dead.* by Wolf, Leonard. 327 p. illus. Boston: Little, Brown, 1972.

Although this volume is supposedly an investigation into the role of the vampire in literature, culture, society, theatre, film, and in real life, it is more a rambling discourse on various topics dealing with vampirism. Missing is a discernible form or structure, and anyone searching for specific information on vampires will have to search with diligence and may still not find it. The book is not indexed but it does have drawings, maps and pictures. A bibliography and some chapter notes complete the volume.

The author includes a short interview with Christopher Lee, some analysis of the Lugosi-Browning DRACULA (1931), and brief mention of a few other vampire films. This material is rather erratic, with major omissions (there are more than 100 films about vampires, and a popular television film, THE NIGHT STALKER (1971), etc.) and some overemphasis (John Carradine, Christopher Lee). Persons interested in the topic "Vampires in Films" should see the McNally-Florescu volume. While this volume is a fascinating, well-written general reading experience, it is not pertinent for film information for the reasons indicated above.

1405   *Dream Palaces — Hollywood at Home.* by Lockwood, Charles. 320 p. illus. New York: Viking, 1981.

A social history based on the the magnificent estates and mansions owned by stars of the twenties— Swanson, Valentino, Chaplin, Keaton, Marion Davies, Pickford, Barrymore, etc. Stories and anecdotes about the occupants add to the appeal of this book.

1406   *Dream Street: The American Movies and the Popular Imagination 1889-1939.* by Iftovic, Edward. 2 volumes, 800 p. Brooklyn, N.Y.: Revisionist, 1977.

1407   *The Dream That Kicks: The Prehistory and Early Years of Cinema in Great Britain.* by Chanan, Michael. 353 p. Boston: Routledge and Kegan Paul, 1980.

The long, detailed, serious text of this history is divided into six sections: introduction, the dialectic of invention, music hall and pop culture, middle class culture and its influences, the early years, and the dream that kicks. A bibliography and an index are included.

1408   *Dreams and Dead Ends.* by Shadoian, Jack. 366 p. illus. Cambridge, Mass.: MIT Press, 1977.

Subtitled "The American Gangster/Crime Film," this study is composed of 18 lengthy critical analyses of specific films and a linking narrative. The author's interest is in the meaning of genre, and in those things that are uniquely indigenous to genre study and criticism. In a chronological fashion he arranges his 18 films under six general headings: The Classic Gangster Film—LITTLE CAESAR (1930), THE PUBLIC ENEMY (1931); The Descent into Noir—HIGH SIERRA (1941), THE KILLERS (1946); The Stress and Strain for Affirmation—KISS OF DEATH (1947), FORCE OF EVIL (1948), GUN CRAZY (1949); Disequilibrium and Change at Midcentury—D.O.A. (1949), WHITE HEAT (1949); "Seeing" Through the Fifties—PICKUP ON SOUTH STREET (1953), 99 RIVER STREET (1953), THE PHENIX CITY STORY (1955), THE BROTHERS RICO (1957), KISS ME DEADLY (1955); and The Modernist Perspective—BONNIE AND CLYDE (1967), POINT BLANK (1967), THE GODFATHER (1972), THE GODFATHER II (1975). Selected frame enlargements, a bibliography, chapter notes, and an index are provided.

The unusual depth and detail provided in the examination of each film provides rich material for reader thought and reaction. Arrangement of the study is logical and natural with justification provided for the author's selections. The volume is a model of genre study that helps to advance the art of film criticism. Highly recommended.

1409   *The Dreams and the Dreamers: Adventures of a Professional Movie Goer.* by Alpert, Hollis. 258 p. New

York: Macmillan, 1962.

Articles and essays about film topics originally written for magazines are collected in this volume. Actors and directors receive most of the attention with an occasional venture into such topics as censorship, aromatics (smell systems in theaters) and Hollywood cliches.

Author Alpert, well-known film critic, is informed, witty, and entertaining. What seems to be lacking is a strong discernible theme, credo, or rationale for the book. No index or illustrations are included. As pleasant reading, this volume is most satisfactory.

1410 *Dreams for Sale: The Rise and Fall of the Triangle Film Corporation.* by Lahue, Kalton C. 216 p. illus. New York: Barnes, 1971.

The Triangle Film Corporation was the dream of Harry Aitken who planned to use the talents of D. W. Griffith, Thomas Ince, and Mack Sennett as the three vertices. How the company came to be in the World War I period, its potential during its short existence, and the reasons for its collapse are covered in this well-researched account. The volume is profusely illustrated but the quality of picture reproduction varies greatly. Index.

1411 *The Dress Doctor.* by Head, Edith; and Ardmore, Jane Kesner. 249 p. illus. Boston: Little, Brown, 1959.

Although this volume is supposed to be an autobiography, it is more of a potpourri on designing clothes for celebrities. The portions about Miss Head's life are few and quite brief when they do appear. What we get is a series of consistently positive comments about the stars for whom she has designed clothes. Everybody is polite, glamorous, and cooperative, a chiffon never-never land. The last 60 pages are a guide for those who need help in selecting, wearing, and using clothing.

Obviously the book is designed primarily for a female audience whose interests are probably different from those of film enthusiasts. It should be noted that books on costume design for film are rare and this one may shed some light on the attendant problems of that profession. This is a disappointing book; instead of being an informative intelligent autobiography, it settles for commercial cliche.

1412 *Dreyer.* by Nash, Mark. 81 p. paper illus. London: British Film Institute; New York: Zoetrope, 1977.

1413 *Dreyer in Double Reflection.* by Dreyer, Carl; and Skoller, Donald. 205 p. illus. New York: Dutton, 1973.

A group of essays written by Carl Dreyer from 1920 to 1960 are arranged chronologically in this volume. Although the translations were not made by Skoller, he did edit them and he does provide introductory statements to each. In addition there are stills— supplied mostly by the Danish Film Museum— which are used to illustrate some of the concepts or ideas mentioned in Dreyer's essays. Reproduction of the visuals is adequate. Dreyer's writing on films, technological advances, personalities, aesthetics and other topics has a certain built-in appeal to those who are familiar with his films/reputation. Other readers may be introduced to this master director by this worthy book. Acceptable.

1414 *Drug Abuse Films.* by National Coordinating Council on Drug Education. 119 p. paper Chicago: American Library Assoc., 1972.

This third edition has much to offer in its consideration of about 200 films and audiovisuals about drug abuse. According to the president of the Drug Abuse Council, Dr. Thomas E. Bryant, all the titles reviewed were wanting to some degree. Thirty-one percent were classified "unacceptable" while another 53 percent were labeled "restricted." The remaining 16 percent were at least scientifically and conceptually "acceptable."

These evaluation headings—acceptable, restricted and unacceptable—are used to group the films. Arranged alphabetically by title under each heading, the information given is medium, year, audience, producer, source, rental cost, purchase price, running time, color format, gauge, sound and date of review. The main body of each entry consists of a synopsis and a detailed evaluation. The majority of the audiovisuals evaluated are 16mm films.

Supporting the well-written and useful information are introductory sections on use, evaluation procedures and forms, and selection. Credits are noted and a full index appears at the book's conclusion. As a reference and as a model of superior film evaluation, this excellent volume is highly recommended.

1415 *Duet.* by Ziegler, Anne; and Booth, Webster. 223 p. illus. London: Stanley Paul, 1951.

The memoirs of Booth and Ziegler, a pair of performers whose films include WALTZ TIME (1946) and THE LAUGHING LADY (1950).

1416 DUET FOR CANNIBALS. by Sontag, Susan. 129 p. paper illus. New York: Farrar, Straus, & Giroux, 1969.

Script of the 1970 film written and directed by Susan Sontag. Contains cast credits and an introduction by Sontag.

1417 *Duke: The Story of John Wayne.* by Tomkies, Mike. 149 p. illus. Chicago: H. Regnery, 1971.

John Wayne has enjoyed the status of super-star for more than 30 years. Since 1930 Wayne has appeared in more than 250 films (listed here in the appendix). The design of this biography is mostly anecdotal with attention given to many of the Wayne films. The resulting portrait is respectful and sincere. Wayne's politics are mostly ignored but his human qualities such as honesty, integrity, and sense of humor are stressed. The illustrations add to this short account of a long professional life; unfortunately, there is no index. Like Wayne's films, this biography is a crowd pleaser.

1418 *Duke: The John Wayne Album.* by Boswell, John; and David, Jay. 160 p. paper illus. New York: Ballantine, 1979.

Using a combination of more than 200 illustrations and an objective text, the authors review the life and career of John Wayne. A brisk reportorial style notes the successes and failures of a long career on the screen. Wayne is made to seem more the "man" and less the "legend" when his marital misfortunes and his early struggles are disclosed. The chronological narrative is occasionally interrupted by a topic or digression which is set off from the main text by special placement and darker print. Information about John Ford, Maureen O'Hara, Wayne's wives, certain films, Yakima Canut, etc., appears in this manner. The illustrations have been well chosen and are carefully reproduced. A filmography completes the volume.

This is one of the best books available on John Wayne. Text, photos, format, and production are all first-rate. Recommended.

1419 *Duke: The Real Story of John Wayne.* by Ramer, Jean. 187 p. paper New York: Award Books, 1973.

Written several years before his death, this unauthorized biography of John Wayne tells the familiar story from Iowa farm boy to California football hero, film player, superstar, and finally, legend. The section titles—Boyhood Days, The Boy Becomes a Man, His Loves, His Children, His Biggest Fight, etc.—reiterate the well-known events and persons in his life.

Throughout the text there are many Wayne quotations that are not acknowledged. In addition the author describes Wayne's thoughts and inner emotions, a practice that has no place in responsible biographical writing. Since no index, filmography or illustrations are provided, the value of the book is extremely limited. In its romanticized retelling of an American success story, it often resembles the fiction of Horatio Alger.

1420 *Durgnat on Film.* by Durgnat, Raymond. 238 p. paper illus. London: Faber and Faber, 1976.

This volume is made up of nine chapters from *The Crazy Mirror* and fourteen chapters from *Films and Feelings*, earlier books by Durgnat. The latter volume has as its major theme the contribution of aesthetic style, personal style, story structure, and symbols to the content of a film. Its original section on personal style has been replaced here with appropriate examples from *The Crazy Mirror*. Apparently a new book with a new title has been created from two older volumes for reasons which are not made clear.

1421 *Dutch Cinema.* by Cowie, Peter. 154 p. illus. New York: A.S. Barnes, 1979.

Critic-historian Peter Cowie, founder and editor of the annual *International Film Guide*, is also responsible for a number of critically applauded books about film. Here he tackles an area of motion picture history that has been largely neglected to date—the Dutch Cinema. With a carefully researched and written text, he traces the development of that nation's cinema over the past 80 years. The emphasis in the text is on the filmmakers rather than on factual narrative, with Joris Ivens, Bert Haanstra, and Fons Rademakers receiving special attention. Filmographies, illustrations, a bibliography and a film title index complete the book. Cowie has provided the reader with a most welcome history and appreciation of the Dutch Cinema. His analysis of numerous filmmakers and their work makes this volume a valuable reference reader.

1422 *Dutch Film 76/77.* edited by Wallagh, Constant. 47 p. illus. The Hague: Government Publishing Office, 1978.

An annual publication which surveys Dutch filmmaking activities. The 1975 edition, prepared by B. J. Bertina, contained more information in its 72 pages.

1423 *Dwight MacDonald on Movies.* by MacDonald, Dwight. 492 p. Englewood Cliffs, N.J.: Prentice-Hall, 1969.

To put the matter quickly, this feast of words, style, and authority is one of the finest collections of film criticism and writing ever published. Since MacDonald has been writing (not exclusively, however) about film for more than four decades, the maturity and wisdom are no surprise. His style of writing consists of wit, irreverence, and of course evidence of limitless knowledge and background. His range is wide as he considers many aspects of world cinema; films and book reviews along with essays and articles are offered.

1424 *Dynamics of the Film.* by Feldman, Jose; and Feldman, Harry. 255 p. illus. New York: Heritage House, 1952.

A consideration of photographic techniques that distinguish film from other arts. Much attention is given to the individual shot, but its reason for being in the total film is slighted.

1425 *Dynamite Kids Guide to the Movies.* by Ronan, Margaret. 80 p. illus. paper New York: School Book Service, 1980.

1426 *Dziga Vertov: A Guide to References and Resources.* by Feldman, Seth R. 232 p. Boston: G. K. Hall, 1979.

Although Dziga Vertov is a subject of concern mostly to film scholars, theorists, and historians, there is an enormous amount of literature available about him and his films. In this reference, Seth R. Feldman offers a listing of Vertov items that attempts to be comprehensive. Its scope is quite impressive. Adhering to the general format-structure of the series, he presents biographical background, critical survey, a filmography, bibliographies of primary and secondary sources, archives, distributors and indexes.

An outstanding feature of this book is the detail found in the filmography annotations. When the large number of films made by Vertov is considered, the coverage provided here is excellent. In addition, the bibliography and other supporting sections all add considerably to the careful treatment given to a specialized subject. Interested users will find this book an ideal place in which to begin their study or search.

1427 *Each Man in His Time—The Life Story of a Director.* by Walsh, Raoul. 385 p. paper illus. New York: Farrar, Straus and Giroux, 1974.

At the time he wrote this free-wheeling autobiography, the author was in his mid-eighties. Both the content and the style of this exciting book indicate no diminution of talent, imagination or wit. After a brief account of his formative years, Walsh gets quickly to Hollywood's beginning. By working with D. W. Griffith, he learned the film business at an early age. From his first experience as an actor in short silent films to his maturity as a noted craftsman, Walsh has lived a full life, some of which he recalls with apparent delight here.

The narrative is choppy as he jumps from one selected topic to the next. As a result, major gaps exist in this recital. The volume is strongest when he discusses his work—weakest when he relives romantic and sexual adventures. Perhaps the lapses into machismo are forgiveable in the recollections of an octogenarian, but one wishes he had used the space to discuss some of his unmentioned films.

The book suffers from an absence of dates—Walsh either dislikes exactness or is uncertain of his memory. A chronology or a filmography would have helped greatly. For example, in what year did he direct his first film, HOME FROM THE SEA? Other references do not list this film at all. They note his birth year as 1892, but try and find that information in this book. The visuals contained in the center section are good and a helpful index is provided. This is a rewarding reading experience that could have also been a fine reference with a bit more material added. Highly recommended.

1428 *Eadweard Muybridge: The Man Who Invented the Moving Picture.* by MacDonnell, Kevin. 158 p. illus. Boston: Little, Brown & Co., 1972.

Although Eadweard Muybridge was born and died in England, he accomplished much of his important work during the many years he spent in America. He achieved fame as a photographer, inventor, writer, speaker, and even as a defendant in a murder trial. His great contributions were the changing of scientific understanding of animal and human locomotion and the invention of their pictorial representation.

The biographical essay which opens this oversized volume concentrates on the professional accomplishments and only suggests bits of the personal life. Following, there are samples of Muybridge's photographic work grouped under specific periods or topics: Alaska, Yosemite Valley, the Modoc War, Central America, Palo Alto, and other travels. The two last sections describe his work at Pennsylvania University and his invention of the Zoo-praxiscope. In the appendix there are extracts from his trial and two articles: the first on Muybridge's technique, the second on the author's search for the material presented in the book. A bibliography is included but there is no index.

An exhibit of Muybridge's photographic work in New York City in 1973 was held in commemoration of Muybridge's collaboration in 1872 with Leland Stanford on horses in motion. That was the beginning of the studies that ultimately led to the projected motion picture. Visuals selected for this volume will give the reader a far greater understanding and appreciation of Muybridge's contribution to the art of motion pictures. They also stimulate the reader's desire to know more about the man himself. The small evidence presented here indicates that he was a unique personality and a creative artist of considerable dimension. This volume provides enlightenment about an era and a personality. The book is highly recommended.

1429 *Eadweard Muybridge: The Father of the Motion Picture.* by Hendricks, Gordon. 271 p. illus. New York: Grossman, 1975.

The appearance of any new work by Gordon Hendricks is reason for excitement, anticipation and, ultimately, satisfaction. In his latest and longest work on film history, Hendricks has chosen Eadweard Muybridge as the subject for his research and investigation. Following his usual procedure of examining many original sources in his search for material, the author has drawn a minutely detailed portrait of the man and his career.

In addition to his pioneer studies on human and animal motion, attention is given to such matters as his work as a photographer, the trial for murdering his wife's lover, and his final years. The selection, placement and reproduction of almost 200 visuals can serve as a model for other historians to emulate. Among the fascinating pictures, there are half-stereographs, line drawings, plates from the University of Pennsylvania series, periodical covers and lantern slides. This rich collection of visual material supplements the meticulously written text in creating an outstanding contribution to the literature on the history of film. Recommended.

It should be noted that another very good and often

similar volume, entitled *Eadweard Muybridge: The Man Who Invented the Moving Picture,* by Kevin MacDonnell, was published by Little, Brown in 1972.

1430 *Ealing Studios.* by Barr, Charles, 198 p. illus. Woodstock, N.Y.: Overlook, 1980.

For the twenty-year period from 1939 to 1958, a small British studio produced over 90 films, many of them memorable. In this history of the Ealing Studios, the author attempts to show the reflection of English events, issues, problems, stereotypes, attitudes, etc., in the films. In addition he pays tribute to the many creative artists and businessmen who were responsible for SCOTT OF THE ANTARCTIC (1948), KIND HEARTS AND CORONETS (1949), THE LAVENDER HILL MOB (1951), THE MAN IN THE WHITE SUIT (1951), THE LADYKILLERS (1955) and other films. The volume includes many illustrations, a filmography, and an index.

1431 *Early American Cinema.* by Slide, Anthony; and O'Dell, Paul. 192 p. paper illus. New York: A. S. Barnes, 1970.

This is a book about the first decade or so of motion picture production and exhibition. The early companies (Vitagraph, Kalem, Essanay, Biograph, and Keystone) are treated In addition the early comedies of Chaplin and the many short films that D. W. Griffith produced at Biograph are considered. Some attention is given to the first serials. Illustrations are quite good and while some of the material is familiar, the total treatment is more than acceptable.

1432 *The Early Development of the Motion Picture, 1887-1909.* by North, Joseph H. 313 p. New York: Arno Press, 1973.

One of the doctoral dissertations on film topics, reproduced by Arno exactly as submitted to the degree-granting school. The purpose of this study is to identify the accomplishments of film pioneers and indicate the relationship of their work to that of Griffith and those after. The period covered is 1887-1909, the scene mostly Europe and America. Some background is given about the inventors, the first exhibitions, the early road showings, and the problems faced by the exhibitors. The films of the period are reviewed, with several "longer" ones discussed in depth. Films made by scientists, business firms, The War Office, The Salvation Army and amateurs are noted. Lawsuits, and the change from episode films to narrative films are explained. Motion picture exchanges, the screen theatre, mass production of films and a chapter on Griffith complete the work. A bibliography supports the study.

1433 *Early Film Making in Los Angeles.* by Clarke, Charles E. 59 p. illus. Los Angeles: Dawson's Book Shop, 1976.

In 1903 the first motion picture camera arrived in Los Angeles. This volume, published in a limited edition of 300 copies, deals with those early days as recalled and researched by a cinematographer who was active at that time. The many illustrations add dimension to this short, perfunctory version of a familiar story.

1434 *Early Hollywood Crazy Quilt.* by Hungerford, Katherine L. 85 p. paper illus. Washington, D.C.: Katherine Hungerford, 1949.

A personal publication that deals with Hollywood and motion pictures.

1435 *Early Screenplays.* by Fellini, Federico. 198 p. paper illus. New York: Grossman, 1971.

Contains the scripts of: VARIETY LIGHTS (1950) and THE WHITE SHEIK (1952).

1436 *Early Stages: Scenes From a Life.* by Jackson, Anne. 220 p. illus. Boston: Little, Brown, 1979.

Anne Jackson, a stage actress who occasionally appears in films, recalls the early years of her life up to her marriage to Eli Wallach and the birth of her first child.

1437 *Early Women Directors.* by Slide, Anthony. 119 p. illus. New York: A.S. Barnes, 1977.

The subtitle of this book about female film directors is "Their Role in the Development of the Silent Cinema" and it sums up the content nicely. Separate chapters are devoted to Alice Guy Blache, Lois Weber, Margery Wilson, Mrs. Wallace Reid, Frances Marion, and Dorothy Arzner. Other women directors, including a group from the Universal Studios, are treated collectively. A bibliography completes the volume which contains more than 100 old stills, portraits, and production shots.

The author, a recognized authority on silent film history, continues to write specialized volumes designed to appeal to a limited audience. While buffs

and scholars will be quite fascinated by the abundance of unfamiliar names, dates, and film titles, the general reader will become bewildered and tired after the first few pages. The seeker of entertaining nostalgia will find this presentation too pedantic.

1438 *see 1439*

1439 *The Early Works of Charlie Chaplin.* by Huff, Theodore. 24 p. paper illus. London: British Film Institute, 1961.

A revised edition of a booklet that appeared in the *New Index* series published by the BFI in the early fifties and also as a special supplement in *Sight and Sound*; it was first published as *An Index to the Films of Charlie Chaplin*.

1440 *Earning Money with Your 8/16 mm Camera.* by Barleben, Karl. 127 p. paper illus. New York: Chilton, 1960.

A title in the *Modern Camera* Series, this older paperback deals with free-lance photography—making money with a camera. It assumes the reader is a competent filmmaker and concentrates on such topics as finding work, assignments vs. speculation, prices, television, weddings, press, home films, sports, etc. Much of the volume deals with equipment and these pages are dated. It is noted here because it was one of the first books to go into the business/economic use of 8/16 mm motion picture cameras.

1441 EARTHQUAKE.: The Story of a Movie. by Fox, George. 128 p. paper illus. New York: Signet, 1974.

There are two major sections in this book. First, the story of the 1974 film is told in a format that seems to combine script and novel. Short passages describe shots, while longer ones are devoted to character dialogue and action. In the second section there is Fox's rather selected general account of the making of the film—idea, research, development, first-draft screenplay, casting, and production. Most interesting are the brief explanations of the special effects used in the film. Many of the stills and production shots included in a center section are too small to be effective. The book has no index. Partial film credits appear on the outside back cover. Acceptable.

1442 *Eastern Europe.* by Hibbin, Nina. 239 p. paper illus. New York: Barnes, 1969.

A most interesting reference arrangement exists in this book. It considers the filmmakers of Albania, Bulgaria, Czechoslovakia, East Germany, Hungary, Poland, Romania, the USSR, and Yugoslavia categorically by country.

An alphabetical list of film directors, players and technicians of importance follows a brief survey of postwar production in each locale. The latter section of the book lists the titles of all films mentioned throughout the book in alphabetical fashion followed by a numerical cross-reference to the filmakers involved. There are many illustrations from the films included. The print used is a larger type than usual and the total production of the book is excellent.

1443   EASY RIDER. by Hopper, Dennis; and Fonda, Peter; and Southern, Terry. 191 p. paper illus. New York: New American Library, 1970.

Script of the 1969 film directed by Dennis Hopper. Contains cast credits and six articles: 1) Into the Issue of the Good Old Time Movie Versus The Good Old Time (Dennis Hopper); 2) Will EASY RIDER do it for Dennis Hopper? (Tom Burke); 3) Jack Nicholson: Talking and Talked About (Marjory Adams); 4) EASY RIDER Soundtrack (Robert Chistgau); 5) *Rolling Stone* Raps with Peter Fonda (Elizabeth Campbell); and 6) Introduction to EASY RIDER (Frederic Tuten).

1444   *Easy the Hard Way.* by Pasternak, Joe. 224 p. illus. London: W. H. Allen, 1956.

Pasternak describes his autobiography "as a major story with a happy ending." This phrase is apt not only for the book but for almost all of the films he produced. Although he had considerable experience in European filmmaking, he became known primarily because of his production of the early Durbin films which helped to save Universal Studios from bankruptcy. At Universal he worked with Dietrich on DESTRY RIDES AGAIN (1939) and the three follow-ups. After his relocation to Metro, he was responsible for the production of the many wartime musicals and comedies. Stars of these films included Garland, Lanza, and the Metro quartet of musical heroines, Grayson, Powell, Allyson, and Williams.

This impressive career is related with a modesty and humility that is not altogether believable. The approach is positive with the "happy ending" syndrome evident at all times. The illustrations are uninspired and a filmography and index would help. A career of such proportion as Pasternak's deserves a more detailed, documentary approach. This au-

tobiography is a *Silver Screen* feature when it should be a *New Yorker* profile.

1445   *Echoes—Memoirs of Andre Kostelanetz.* by Kostelanetz, Andre; and Hammond, Gloria. New York: Harcourt Brace Jovanovich, 1981.

Anecdotes and observations about an array of musical personalities, some of whom worked in films.

1446   *The Economic Aspects of the Film Industry in India.* by Jain, Rikhab Dass. 255 p. illus. Delhi: Atma Ram, 1960.

A survey of the Indian film industry based on the author's thesis done at Agra University. Includes a foreword by S. Radhakrishnan, illustrations, maps, diagrams, tables, and a bibliography.

1447   *Economic Control of the Motion Picture Industry.* by Huettig, Mae D. 163 p. illus. Philadelphia: University of Pennsylvania Press, 1944.

A study of the early development of motion pictures followed by a detailed account of economic conditions within the film industry in the forties. This is a research project with emphasis on intercorporate relationships, financial policies, etc.; serious, specialized, rewarding history.

1448   *The Economic Situation of the Cinema in Europe.* edited by Degand, Claude. 48 p. paper illus. Strasbourg: Council of Europe, 1978.

This report is derived from a symposium on "Cinema and the State" held in Lisbon, June 14-16, 1978.

1449   *The Economics of New Educational Media (Volume 2—Cost and Effectiveness).* 316 p. paper illus. New York: UNESCO, 1980.

Reports, case studies and abstracts of recent work done on new educational technology form the content of this volume. Some of the material is pertinent to film.

1450   ECSTASY *and Me: My Life as A Woman.* by Lamarr, Hedy. 256 p. paper illus. Greenwich, Conn.: Fawcett Pub., 1966.

This monumental example of bad taste probably had the desired result—much royalty money for Miss

Lamarr. The pursuit of the dollar seems to be the only explanation for the many shocking sexual confessions contained within. From the screen historian's viewpoint, the approach used is unfortunate. Miss Lamarr's movie career certainly was eventful and colorful enough to maintain a film-oriented reader's interest without resorting to the overabundant sexual emphasis, although general sales would probably have been much less.

She does describe the filming of ECSTASY (1933), her encounters with L. B. Mayer, Cecil B. DeMille, and various film personalities of the period. The test of the quality of an autobiography is whether the reader has any feeling for the subject at the book's end; Miss Lamarr arouses nothing, except slight contempt.

1451 *Ed Wynn's Son.* by Wynn, Keenan. 237 p. illus. Garden City, N.Y.: Doubleday, 1959.

This is the autobiography of an actor who appeared in more than 100 films and who was known as "the fellow who got splashed when Esther Williams jumped into the pool." As usual, the professional work is slighted and the emphasis is on emotional and social matters. Perhaps the frankest, most honest portion of the book is the detailed description of the father-son relationship. Wynn's comments seem to apply to all famous-father and not-so-famous-son relationships in show business.

The few excellent illustrations will make the reader wish there were more. Ironically, a greater number are of the father rather than of the son. As a sample of show business autobiography, the book is better than most.

1452 *Edgar Wallace.* by Wallace, Ethel V. illus. London: Hutchinson, 1932.

Edgar Wallace was the author of several books which were used as the basis for films, most of which were made in the thirties. They include KING KONG (1933), and SANDERS OF THE RIVER (1935).

1453 *Edgar Wallace: The Biography of a Phenomenon.* by Lane, Margaret. 423 p. illus. London: Heinemann, 1938.

Wallace is an author whose books were often adapted for films. Films such as KING KONG (1933), THE HUMAN MONSTER (1940), and COAST OF SKELETONS (1965) were based on his original stories.

1454 *Edinburgh '77.* edited by Johnston, Claire. paper illus. Edinburgh: Film Festival; New York: Zoetrope, 1977.

An annual which appears as part of the Edinburgh Film Festival. The 1977 issue had as its theme "History/Production/Memory" and included: "The Writing of the History of the Cinema" by Geoffrey Nowell-Smith, "Memory, Phantasy Identity" by Colin McCabe, "Film and Popular Memory" by *Cahiers du Cinema,* a symposium on Raymond William's *Marxism and Literature,* and other articles by Stephen Heath, Annette Kuhn, and John Ellis.

1455 *Edison: The Man Who Made the Future.* by Clark, Ronald W. 256 p. New York: G.P. Putnam's, 1977.

This volume is a fine example of scientific biography. It presents diverse views of the legendary American pioneer — inventor, developer, conspirator, business magnate, showman, devoted family man and determined patriot. Told in chronological fashion, Edison's life includes a rough, uneducated childhood, some early struggles as a telegraphist, and ultimately the establishment of the studios where his discoveries and developments took place. Major attention is given to his work at Menlo Park, New Jersey, with the electric light and the phonograph. One chapter entitled "In Search of the Talkies" deals with early motion picture camera and projector development.

Strong support is given to the concentrated text by a most impressive collection of illustrations. Edison is shown from age 14 to age 80, along with many of his inventions, in sepia-tinted photos that suggest antiquity. A lengthy bibliography, several hundred reference notes, illustration acknowledgments, and an index complete the book.

Here is a carefully researched biography that presents with clarity many of the facets of a complex genius. Clark presents Edison the man and his achievements in a readable, nonpedantic fashion. Most readers will be fascinated.

1456 *The Edison Motion Picture Myth.* by Hendricks, Gordon. 216 p. illust. Berkeley: University of California Press, 1961.

Discusses the work at Edison's West Orange Lab up to 1892.

1457 *Edith Evans: A Personal Memoir.* by Batters, Jean. 159 p. illus. London: Hart-Davis MacGibbon, 1977.

1458   *Edith Evans.* by Trewin, John Courtenay. 116 p. illus. London: Rockliff, 1954.

This illustrated study of Dame Edith Evan's work contains a list of her appearances on stage and screen. Since it covers her career only up to the mid-fifties, some of her more notable films are omitted—LOOK BACK IN ANGER (1959), TOM JONES (1962), THE CHALK GARDEN (1963), THE WHISPERERS (1967), etc. During her long career, Dame Edith has appeared in relatively few films; A WELSH SINGER (1915), EAST IS EAST (1916), THE QUEEN OF SPADES (1949), WOMAN OF DOLWYN (1949) and THE IMPORTANCE OF BEING EARNEST (1952) were her only five at the time of this book's publication.

1459   *see   1458*

1460   *Editing and Titling.* by Croydon, John. 44 p. paper illus. London: Fountain Press, 1950.

This early title is No. 6 in the *Cinefacts* series.

1461   *Editing and Titling Movies.* by Sprungman, Ormal I. 144 p. illus. Chicago: Ziff-Davis, 1947.

An early title from the *Little Technical Library* series.

1462   *Editing Super 8.* by Copestake, Tim. 237 p. illus. New York: Focal, 1980.

A detailed guide to the editing process written for the dedicated amateur filmmaker.

1463   *Education and Training for Film and Television.* by Fisher, David; and Tasker, John. 92 p. paper illus. London: Education and Training Committee, British Kinematograph Sound and TV Society, 1973.

This volume examines the subject of training for film careers. Articles on film education and television education are offered along with material on sound, design, training schemes, equipment for training, course revision, etc. A bibliography and a list of training organizations are included.

1464   *Education Index. (A partial film reference).* Paper; New York: H.W. Wilson Co., 1929-.

This index is published monthly (except June and August) and covers the educational scene—teaching, administration, research, trends, etc. From 1929 to 1961, the index considered books, pamphlets, USOE publications, and periodicals. Since 1961 its coverage is limited to about 200 periodicals and the USOE publications. The index lists references to film as applied or used in education. Subject headings are "Film" and "Moving Picture Plays." Cumulated each year.

1465   *The Education of the Film-Maker: An International View.* 182 p. paper illus. Paris: UNESCO Press (American Film Institute), 1975.

This anthology is devoted to an international overview of the trends, needs, and potentials found in the education of filmmakers. Based on papers and discussions presented at a meeting organized by UNESCO in 1972, the text deals with a variety of issues, topics, and challenges. An introduction summarizes the main points developed in detail by the chapters which follow. Contributing the chapter-statements are representatives from Africa, Belgium, France, India, Japan, Mexico, Sweden, Union of the Soviet Socialist Republics, United Kingdom, United States of America, and Yugoslavia. George Stevens, Jr., the Director of The American Film Institute, supplied the chapter on the education of filmmakers in the United States.

While this volume may hold some interest for educators, its theme and content are a bit too specialized for the general reader. Then, too, when representatives of national governments get together to compare notes, there may be a problem in reporting. Certain portions of the text suggest a difficulty in separating wishes from reality. Acceptable.

1466   *Educational and Cultural Films: Experiments in European Co-Production.* edited by Van Nooten, S. I. Strasbourg, France: Council of Europe.

This report gives data about the development of European coproduction in making educational and cultural films. It contains a list of 50 short films made thus far under this plan.

1467   *Educational Film Guide.* edited by Krahn, Frederick A. 1037 p. New York: H. W. Wilson, 1953.

In 1953, the 11th edition of this pioneer reference listed some 11,000 educational films. Two supplements were published later to cover 1954 to 1958 and 1959 to 1962. Publication was then discontinued. Most of the films considered here offer a historical rather than a current interest.

1468 *Educational Film Locator.* compiled by Consortium of University Film Centers, R.R. Bowker. 2178 p. New York: R.R. Bowker, 1979.

Here is a catalog of catalogs created with the cooperation of a consortium of 50 university film centers. The holdings of the centers have been combined into one massive volume that should please most film users. Access to the films is provided by a detailed subject index which notes headings along with a cross-index to subjects. Next, under each subject heading, there are listings of films arranged alphabetically by title. Running time and audience levels for each film are indicated. The main body of the book consists of a long filmography representing about 200,000 titles arranged alphabetically. Each entry offers such basic data as title, color format, running time, sound or silent, gauge, annotation, producer/distributor, year of release, subject, audience level, and the consortium centers which own the film. A series listing, a foreign film title index, and producer/ distributor lists complete the volume.

University origins are reflected in the total collection. Although many of the films may be used in K-12 situations, the majority are for the college level. For example, out of the 200,000 titles, only 44 appear under the heading, "Motion Pictures, Children's Films." About 300 different titles are listed under "Children's Literature." Apparently the categories are apparently exclusive here yet they are not cross-indexed. LOVE TO KILL, ME AND DAD'S NEW WIFE, and SKINNY AND FATTY, which have audience level designations of junior and senior high school, appear under "Children's Films."

The volume can be used to compile a filmography on any of several hundred subjects quickly. Although the annotations are descriptive and not evaluative, they are helpful to some extent in selection. Rental policies of the centers are noted in the front pages of the book.

This is a massive film reference that can be extremely valuable and useful if its many virtues and few limitations are understood. Because of the pragmatic nature of film use, some of its subject headings and title placements may be a bit misleading. Since it does provide substantial information about educational films in a quick efficient manner, it is a fine addition to any library concerned with film service. Recommended.

1469 *Educational Films: Writing, Directing, and Producing for Classroom Television, and Industry.* by Herman, Lewis. 338 p. New York: Crown, Pub., 1965.

The subtitle of this book accurately describes the content. Although the scope is quite wide, Mr. Herman has no difficulty in covering his many topics adequately, and usually with considerable depth. As with his classic *Manual of Screen Playwriting*, this book is clear and quite complete. In addition to being a how-to-do-it manual, it is a readable discussion of the factors affecting film aesthetics. An essential text for any course in filmmaking, it also will have appeal for the amateur, the professional and the curious general reader. Highly recommended.

1470 *Educational Films in Illinois.* edited by University of Illinois Library School. 203 p. paper Urbana, Ill.: Illinois Library Assoc., 1953.

A survey made by the Graduate School of Library Science of Illinois University which offers a partial listing of 16mm non-theatrical films found in Illinois film libraries during the period 1950 to 1952.

1471 *Educational Media Catalogs on Microfiche.* illus. New York: Olympic Media Information, 1975.

A collection of 300 educational media catalogs reproduced in the microfiche format. Devoted primarily to software, the catalogs describe many films. The collection is indexed by distributors' names and includes directions for use.

1472 *Educational Media Index.* compiled by Educational Media Council. 14 vols. New York: McGraw-Hill, 1964.

A misguided project that attempted to cover the entire field of audio-visual materials, including film. The complicated format employed, the many errors and omissions, and the over-extended attempt to cover everything, among other weaknesses, contributed to the unanimous lack of enthusiasm that greeted this reference work, supported by the U. S. Office of Education. It is primarily for historical use at this point.

1473 *Educational Media Organizations Directory 1974.* compiled by DCM Associates. 88 p. paper New York: Educational Film Library Association, 1974.

Listing in this directory was limited to those organizations primarily concerned with educational media. They had to be either national organizations or regional organizations with national programs open to qualified applicants from the United States or Canada. The work was accomplished by sending questionnaires to possible candidates for inclusion. Judgment was made in accordance with the criteria and three groups emerged: the organizations that qualified, those that didn't and those that did not respond to the questionnaire. The latter two groups appear in the appendixes which follow the main grouping. Each entry in the main grouping offers five sections: (1) personnel; (2) activities, services and periodicals; (3) permanent committees and Task Forces; (4) aims, purpose and objectives; and (5) membership requirements. Although it is only partial at this point, the information offered by this volume can be used in many ways. It is indispensable to media centers and to anyone concerned with educational media. Highly recommended.

1474   *Educational   Media   Yearbook— 1973.* edited by Brown, James W. 453 p. New York: R. R. Bowker Co., 1973.

The publication of this volume-series is one of the most cheering events of the years. A long absent but essential service has been performed by the editor in bringing together almost all of the elements of educational media in a single classified and useable arrangement. Brown's determination of the major content areas and the articles he has selected to support them are quite beyond criticism. In addition, the final reference sections provide information whose quantity would seem exhausting to collect and sometimes difficult to find. Not only are these challenges met, but solid annotations are offered. Another example of fine quality is the 100-plus page bibliography of media items, which is supplemented by both a subject and an author index. A final Publisher-Producer-Distributor index is evidence of the book's thoroughness. It must be emphasized that the scope of this volume is all media rather than film only. However, there is a wealth of film information contained in its many sections.

The volume can be used in several ways—reference, textbook, reader—by many audiences, including teachers, librarians, media specialists, students, and administrators. There is no other publication that approaches the range of this book's content. With added qualities such as intelligent material arrangement and attractive production, it is apparent that the book is one to appreciate.

The appearance of a volume such as this on a yearly basis should be encouraged. Emphasis in future volumes should be on what has occurred during the year of the book rather than the repetition of some

of the "historical" articles given this time. The value of "60 Years of Feature Films" warmed over each year is questionable. But to have a summary progress report of the organizations already listed here and any other new ones formed through the year would be a service. The reference sections could be alternated on a three-year basis with other topics— specific research summaries, periodicals, media schools, etc.—appearing in the years between.

In summary, this is a most welcome addition to the literature. For the most part the articles have avoided obfuscation and jargon and have opted instead for clarity, information, and use. Encouragement should be given for the publication of future volumes but care should be taken not to simply repeat this first volume. This book is "a tough act to follow." Highly recommended.

1475   *Educational Motion Pictures and Libraries.* by McDonald, Gerald D. 184 p. Chicago: American Library Association, 1942.

This was a pioneer work noting the different uses made of films in public school, college, and university libraries. Some recommendations regarding training, systems, research, etc. are made. An historical document with much that is still vital.

1476   *Educator's Guide to Free Films.* compiled by Horkheimer, Mary Foley; and Diffor, John W. 790 p. Randolph, Wisc.: Educators' Progress Service, 1970.

This is the 30th edition of this guide, in which over 5000 free films are listed under curriculum areas. In addition, there is a title index, a subject index, and a source index. Users of this guide indicate that success varies in obtaining the films and that the showing of commercially sponsored films to groups without a preview or prior evaluation is a risk. Nevertheless, this guide is a most valuable and concentrated reference source that illuminates a major area in film that is still unfamiliar to many users.

1477   *Educator's Guide to Free Guidance Materials.* edited by Saterstrom, Mary. 526 p. paper Randolph, Wisc.: Educator's Progress Service, 1980.

The materials described in the title include films, filmstrips, slides, tapes, scripts, transcriptions and printed materials. Each medium is treated separately with the film section listing 1321 titles, arranged alphabetically under a few general headings. A general title index, a detailed subject index and a source-availability index complete the book.

This is the 19th edition of this annual reference, which can be used in a variety of ways by educators. Although most of the film titles appear in *Educator's Guide to Free Films*, the other media listings and the specialization that this book offers make it a valuable reference.

1478 *Educator's Guide to Free Health, Physical Education and Recreational Materials.* edited by Horkheimer, Foley A. 575 p. paper Randolph, Wisc.: Educator's Progress Service, 1980.

This is the 13th edition of this annual which was inspired by the older parent volume, *Educator's Guide to Free Films*. The arrangement differs in that this volume includes other materials such as filmstrips (81 titles), slides (103 sets), audio tapes (135), audio discs (18), videotapes (146) and print, along with the films (1565 titles).

The book is arranged by medium, with the films appearing first under three title headings—health, physical education, and recreation. Further classification is offered by subheadings under which the films are arranged alphabetically by title. A title index, a subject index and a source-availability index complete the volume.

Since most of the films listed here appear in the *Educator's Guide to Free Films*, the rationale for purchasing this volume might be to furnish a subject area film list to a specific school department or to locate free materials other than films.

1479 *Educator's Guide to Free Materials (A Series).* paper Randolph, Wisc.: Educator's Progress Service.

For several decades the Educator's Progress Service has been publishing annual guides to free materials, the most widely known being *The Educator's Guide to Free Films*.

Other titles developed by them over the years include: *Educator's Guide to Free Filmstrips, Educator's Guide to Free Guidance Materials, Educator's Guide to Free Health, Physical Education and Recreational Materials, Educator's Guide to Free Social Studies Materials, Educator's Guide to Free Science Materials, Educator's Guide to Free Tapes, Scripts, and Transcriptions, Educator's Grade Guide to Free Teaching Aids, Educator's Index of Free Materials,* and *Educator's Guide to Free Audio and Video Materials.*

The above guides which deal with films are treated with individual entries in this volume. It should be noted that the basic data is often repeated for several volumes, e.g., the listing in the free films guide will also appear in the subject area guides. The books, which are revised and updated each year with considerable care, are modestly priced and worthy of inclusion in media centers.

1480 *Educator's Guide to Free Science Materials.* edited by Saterstrom, Mary H. 372 p. paper Randolph, Wisc.: Educator's Progress Service, 1980.

The 21st edition of this reference lists 1125 films, 35 filmstrips, 31 slides, 49 audio tapes, 161 videotapes, 1 script, 5 transcriptions, and 519 printed materials, all pertaining, of course, to science. The media are listed separately with the films appearing first, grouped under six general headings: aerospace, biology, chemistry, environment, general science, and physics. Each entry gives the film title, date, gauge, sound, running time, annotation and sponsor. Availability and the issuing agencies are listed in the book's final pages along with a general title index and a detailed subject list. The volume should be a part of all media center collections. Although the film titles appear in *Educator's Guide to Free Films*, the additional materials listed here and the collecting of the science films in a separate volume make this a worthwhile reference tool.

1481 *Educator's Guide to Free Social Studies Materials.* by Suttles, Patricia H.; and Suttles, Steven A. 596 p. paper Randolph, Wisc.: Educator's Progress Service, 1980.

The 20th edition of this title in the *Educator's Progress* series contains a listing of 1803 films, 65 filmstrips, 160 slide sets, 1 set of transparencies, 105 audio tapes, 53 videotapes, 32 scripts, 109 audio discs, and 572 printed materials. The entries are arranged according to medium with the films appearing first. For each film the authors note the title, gauge, sound, running time, a descriptive annotation and the sponsor. The issuing agency and the film's availability are noted in the final pages, which also contain a general title index and a detailed subject index.

For social studies teachers and media specialists, the identification and separation of the films from the master listing, *Educator's Guide to Free Films*, will be a welcome convenience. The addition of the other media will also be of interest and value. Recommended.

1482   *Edward G. Robinson.* by Hirsh, Foster. 160 p. paper illus. New York: Pyramind, 1975.

The 87 roles that Edward G. Robinson played are emphasized in this account of his film career. Short opening sections are devoted to a general analysis of his screen characters and to his work in the theatre during the twenties. His first seven films are largely unfamiliar today; it was his eighth film, LITTLE CAESAR (1931), that brought him public recognition and a stardom which lasted over 40 years. Hirsch divides the films into four decades, with the final two films, SONG OF NORWAY (1970) and SOYLENT GREEN (1973) added to his sixties' work. A bibliography, a filmography, and an index are added. Illustrations, consisting mostly of portraits and stills, have been well chosen and are reproduced nicely.

The analysis that Hirsch provides concentrates on Robinson's characterizations rather than on the films. As a result, a different and far more interesting study emerges. The work of a devoted professional film actor is given a critical examination and appreciation not often found in today's literature. Recommended.

1483   *Edward S. Curtis in the Land of The War Canoes: A Pioneer Cinematographer in the Pacific Northwest.* by Holm, Gill; and Quimby, George. 128 p. illus. Seattle, Wash.: University of Washington Press, 1980.

1484   *The Effects of Mass Communication.* by Klapper, Joseph T. 302 p. Glencoe, Ill.: Free Press, 1960.

This volume deals primarily with mass media other than film—TV, radio, comic books, and newspapers. However, references to research done in the motion picture field are mentioned both in the text and the excellent bibliography.

1485   *The Effects of Television On the Motion Picture and Radio Industries.* by Stuart, Fredric. 213 p. illus. New York: Arno Press, 1976.

Written in 1960 at Columbia University, in partial fulfillment of the doctoral program, this study is an analysis of the interrelationships among the television, radio and movie industries. The author presents an extensive argument that identifies the appearance of the television industry as the major cause of the decline of the 1950 film industry in the United States. This title appears in the *Dissertations on Film* series.

1486   *The Effects of Two Types of Sound Motion Pictures on Attitudes of Adults Toward Minority Groups.* by Goldberg, Albert L. Palo Alto, Calif.: R & E Research Associates, 1974 (1956).

Done originally as a Doctoral dissertation at Indiana University in 1956.

1487   *EFLA Service supplements.* paper New York: Educational Film Library Association, 1959- .

EFLA has published a number of short annotated filmographies on a variety of topics. Some titles are: *Films and Filmstrips for the Space Age* (1967), *Films for Now* (1971) by Abigail M. Bishop, *Films on War and Peace* (1971) by Nadine Covert, *Minority Films in New York* (1971) by Abby Mason, *Movies About Movies* (1971) by James Limbacher, *Man and His Environment* (1972) by Hannah C. Williams, and *Death and Dying* (1973) by Edward A. Mason.

Other EFLA publications include: *Film Evaluation —Why and How* (1963), *EFLA's Film Library Administration Workshop* (1967), *A Guide for Film Teachers* (1968) by Roger Larson Jr., *American Film Festival Guides* (1959 to 1973), *Cumulative Index to Festival Guides* (1959 to 1963), and *Film As Art Program Notes* (1974). All of the above are good examples of the specialized services offered by EFLA. The quality and content in these publications is consistently high, and they are useful in a wide range of situations.

1488   *The Egotists.* by Fellaci, Oriana. 256 p. illus. Chicago: Regnery, 1968.

Within the "16 Surprising Interviews" in this book, there are eight which are pertinent to film. Sean Connery, Ingrid Bergman, Geraldine Chaplin, Fellini, Magnani, Moreau, Dean Martin, and Hitchcock are the subjects. Each interview is preceded by several pages of narrative framework. There are also a few unimpressive photographs.

The actual interviews are uninspired rather than "surprising". Apparently Miss Fallaci has more success with the ladies (Magnani, Moreau) than with the extrovert directors (Fellini, Hitchcock). The questions proposed lack depth, and reflect a fan magazine mentality and approach. Is anyone really interested in Hitchcock's sex life? This is fodder for the nondiscriminating reader. Note: with one or two exceptions, the same interviews appear in *Limelighters,* London: Michael Joseph, 1967.

1489 *800 Films for Film Study.* edited by Turner, D. John. 112 p. Ottawa: Canadian Film Institute, 1970.

A catalogue of films available in Canada that are recommended for film study.

1490 *8mm Film for Adult Audiences.* by Bell, Geoffrey. 40 p. paper Paris: UNESCO, 1968.

This book, number 54 in the UNESCO *Reports and Papers in Mass Communication* series, deals with 8mm film as a medium of instruction and information. Written at the time when single concept loop films were gaining acceptance, the text covers all the aspects of 8mm film usage—formats, hardware, methodology, production costs, administration, etc. The goal of the volume was to alert developing nations to the potential of 8mm film in education. Some of the material seems either obvious or dated today. However, enough valuable information remains to warrant attention.

1491 *8mm Sound Film and Education.* edited by Forsdale, Louis. 100 p. paper New York: Teachers College Press, 1962.

Proceedings of a conference held at Teachers College on November 8, 9, and 10, 1961. Forsdale was leading proponent of the use of 8mm film in education, and at the time of this conference, the narrow gauge film was predicted to become one of the major educational communication media.

1492 *8mm Film Directory.* edited by Kone, Grace Ann. 532 p. New York: Educational Film Library Association, 1969-70.

Descriptive annotations are given for all 8mm films (loops, reels, sound, silent, super 8, standard 8). The main section lists categories such as arts, education, fiction, language, recreation, religion, sciences, society and environment, and technology. Descriptions and pictures of hardware for 8mm projection are also included, as are producer addresses, a Dewey decimal index, and finally an alphabetical index of films and subjects.

1493 *8mm/16mm Movie-Making.* by Provisor, Henry. 272 p. illus. New York: Chilton Book Co., 1970.

A more advanced guide to filmmaking, this volume covers the subject in considerable detail. More than 100 illustrations, tables, and diagrams reinforce the author's clean crisp text. The advice given on selection procedures for both hardware and software seems both valid and valuable. An excellent book of its type.

1494 *The Eighth Veil—Ann Todd.* by Todd, Ann. 173 p. illus. London: Kimber, 1980.

An autobiography of the British actress who appeared in films from 1931 to 1980. Married to David Lean, she has also made documentary films.

1495 *Eighty Years of Cinema.* by Cowie, Peter. 323 p. illus. New York: A.S. Barnes, 1977.

The original edition of this title has been revised and updated to 1975. Arranged chronologically, the text offers reviews of a few outstanding films of each year. Full credits are given for these entries, followed by a list of other important films of the year and, here only, the country of origin and the director are noted along with a capsule comment. A final index helps to provide easy access to all the films discussed.

Cowie remains his own critic and often selects films that have been dismissed by others such as TOPAZ (1969), COOGAN'S BLUFF (1969), and BARRY LYNDON (1975). Visuals have been well selected and reproduced. Other production values are also superior to those of the original volume.

Cowie has the uncommon ability to provide information, education and entertainment simultaneously. This is a superb volume.

1496 *Eisenstaedt's Album.* by Eisenstaedt, Alfred. 224 p. illus. New York: Viking, 1980.

In this collection of more than 400 black-and-white photographs, the reader will find many film personalities: Chaplin, Monroe, Dietrich, Hepburn, Disney, Groucho, etc. The photojournalist, who worked for *Life* magazine from 1936 to 1972, calls his album, "Fifty Years of Friends and Acquaintances," and includes signatures, sayings, sketches, and personal photos. Other books of photographs by Eisenstaedt include *People, Witness to Our Time,* and *The Eye of Eisenstaedt,*—all published by Viking Press.

1497 *Eisenstein: A Documentary Portrait.* by Swallow, Norman. 155 p. paper illus. New York: Dutton, 1976.

Documentary, as used in this book's title, refers to the arrangement of many statements about Sergei

Eisenstein by persons who knew him. Interwoven with these recollections is a commentary derived from a television script about Eisenstein which also included the main body of quotations.

Among the people offering views of the famous Russian director are Basil Wright, Lewis Milestone, Marie Seton, Victor Shlovsky, Lazar Wechsler, John Grierson, Lev Kuleshov, Mikhail Romm and Grigori Kozinstev. Supporting the quotations are a good collection of visuals, a biographical note, a filmography, and an index.

This is a careful biography that, for the most part, presents affection, admiration and/or acknowledgment along with factual information, some of which is of debatable importance. Interpretation of the personal life of Eisenstein is minimized and, as a result, we have a rather external, sterile portrait.

Students and historians will appreciate this unusual presentation of film biography.

1498 *Eisenstein.* by Barna, Yon. 287 p. illus. Bloomington, Ind.: Indiana University Press, 1973.

This biography, first published in Rumania in 1966, has been revised by the author for the English-language edition. A foreword by Jay Leyda emphasizes that although Eisenstein completed only seven films, his unrealized plans, efforts, attempts and dreams have had an equally important effect on filmmaking. Barna has used such source materials as the films, their scripts, preparatory materials, drawings made for the films, sketches, notes, articles, film analyses, stenographic records, and personal drawings. A film made by Jay Leyda of the unsold portions of QUE VIVA MEXICO (1932) was also examined.

The account of Eisenstein's life and career which results from these researches is rich in detail and evaluation. If the personal portrait seems minimized and the professional-public image appears greatly enlarged, it is probably because of the author's decision as to importance and value in a national sense. Barna is a film director, writer and researcher for the television industry in Bucharest. The many illustrations are well reproduced and complement the text nicely. Notes, references, and a short bibliographic section are added along with a good index.

The approach here differs greatly from that used in previous English-language volumes on Eisenstein—the other major biography by Marie Seton, the partial biography by Leon Moussinac, accounts of his experiences in Hollywood and in Mexico, his essays, his lecture-lessons, and his articles and notes. This book synthesizes all these into an informative, readable account of a legendary filmmaker. Recom-

mended.

1499 *Eisenstein—Three Films.* edited by Leyda, Jay. 189 p. paper illus. New York: Harper and Row, 1974.

Contains an introduction by Jay Leyda and scripts of BATTLESHIP POTEMKIN, (1925); OCTOBER, (1928); and ALEXANDER NEVSKY, (1938), with cast and credits given for each.

1500 *Eisenstein's* POTEMKIN. by Mayer, David. illus. New York: Grossman, 1971.

The script along with a recreation and analysis.

1501 *Eisenstein's* IVAN THE TERRIBLE: A Neoformalist Analysis. by Thompson, Kristin. 320 p. illus. Princeton, N.J.: Princeton University Press, 1981.

Eisenstein's film is analyzed according to the laws for the structure of narrative literature developed by Russian formalists early in this century.

1502 EL CID. by Lamb, Harold. 26 p. illus. 1961.

The opening section of this souvenir book is devoted to supplying the history and background for the 1961 film. The two stars, Charlton Heston and Sophia Loren, are given individual attention and the major sequences of the production are described. They include: "The Tournament at Calahorra", "The Coronation at Burgos", and "The Siege and Battle of Valencia". Other cast and production credits are given and the entire book is characterized by some interesting and nicely reproduced photographs.

1503 EL TOPO: A Book of the Film. by Jodorowsky, Alexandro. 172 p. paper illus. New York: Douglas Book Corp., 1971.

Script of the 1970 film directed by Jodorowsky. Contains the script and an extended interview/conversation with Jodorowsky in which he talks about the making and the meaning of his film, among other things. Both film and conversation are designed to denigrate, attack, and upset traditional values. Jodorowsky's unique style depends rather heavily on surprise-shock.

1504 THE ELEANOR ROOSEVELT STORY. by MacLeish, Archibald. 101 p. illus. New York: Houghton, 1965.

This biography used stills and the narration of the 1965 film directed by Richard Kaplan, to tell its story.

1505 *Electric Eye Movie Manual.* by Current, Ira B. 123 p. illus. New York: Amphoto, 1961.

An older volume on motion picture cameras which incorporate an exposure meter system connected directly to the lens diaphragm. The text provides information on how such cameras work, their qualities, care, film uses, and terms.

Although many of the models are now obsolete, the suggestions and other information are not. The text, which is easily understood, is supplemented by photographs, charts, diagrams and tables.

1506 *The Electric Humanities.* by Allen, Don. 276 p. paper illus. Dayton, Ohio: Pflaum, 1971.

McLuhan's influence is evident throughout this volume—spiritually in the text and physically in the nonlinear layout. For most of the book, the author's words appear on the right-hand page while the opposite contains visuals, cartoons, quotes and quips. These elements are intermingled to provide suggestions and encouragement for teaching mass media and popular culture, which the author terms "the Electric Humanities." He describes the "Electric Environment" as consisting in part of the Drugstore Library (popular literature), the Picture Show (popular theatre-movies-TV), and the AM/FM—LP (popular music). For each medium he suggests items for teaching.

The book will reinforce, support, and assist the instructor interested in these areas, but as a recruiting device to gather the older or squarer teacher into the electronic fold, it will probably discourage as much as attract. As a plea for changing curriculum, methodology, content, and teacher attitude, the book is provocative.

1507 *Electronic Drama.: TV Plays of the Sixties.* compiled by Averson, Richard; and White, David Manning. 355 p. Boston: Beacon Press, 1971.

Contains the script of MY SWEET CHARLIE (1970), originally presented on NBC-TV on January 20, 1970, and after critical acclaim subsequently shown in movie theatres.

1508 *Electronic Imaging Techniques.* by Levitan, Eli L. 195 p. illus. New York: Van Nostrand Reinhold, 1977.

This source book, which carries a subtitle "A Handbook of Conventional and Computer-Controlled Animation, Optical, and Editing Processes," surveys the materials, tools, machines and methods concerned with animation and electronic imaging. The first section deals with conventional processes —animation, optical effects and editing. A detailed glossary is provided for each of these topics. The second part of the book is devoted to computer-controlled techniques of animation and electronics imaging—beflix, caesar, explor, GT40, synthavision, etc. Editing, processing and recent technological advances in the field are discussed and there is a computer glossary. The book is illustrated and indexed. Levitan is a respected authority with impressive experience as a practitioner and an author.

As a reference for the professional, this book should be invaluable. It offers practical scholarship in an attractively produced setting. For these reasons it should also be considered as a textbook for advanced college-level courses in filmmaking.

1509 *Elements of Color in Profesional Motion Pictures.* 104 p. illus. New York: Society of Motion Picture and Television Engineers, 1957.

This is a small compact book about color in motion pictures that can be understood by any mature reader. The many illustrative color photographs assist in the explanations of this complex subject.

1510 *Elements of Film.* by Bobker, Lee R. 303 p. illus. New York: Harcourt, Brace & World, 1969.

An unusual attempt to describe the combination of the two major aspects of film—the technical process and the creative process—is made in this volume. The entire filmmaking process, ranging through story-script, camera, sound, editing, direction and acting, are given proper attention. Chapters on present-day directors and film critics conclude the volume.

Bobker's total approach is modern. His frame of reference is "What's Happening Now." The structure, organization, and production of the book is commendable. Many excellent stills accompany the readable text. Recommended.

1511 *The Elements of Film Criticism.* by British Film Institute. 27 p. paper London: British Film Institute, 1944.

1512 *Elephant Dance.* by Flaherty, Frances Hubbard. 138 p. illus. London: Faber & Faber, 1937.

An account of the making of ELEPHANT BOY, a 1937 Korda film, is told here largely in terms of visuals and letters between members of the Flaherty family and others. Mrs. Flaherty's reporting is interesting, intelligent and sensitive. The pictures selected (many of them include the very young Sabu) are beautiful. This volume is another in the well-documented Flaherty saga. Well-written but of limited interest today.

1513 *Elia Kazan on What Makes a Director.* by Kazan, Elia. 22 p. paper New York: Directors Guild of America, 1973.

In 1973, at the conclusion of a retrospective of his films held at Wesleyan University, Elia Kazan spoke to the students. His talk was first published in *Action* and is reprinted in this booklet. Much of the wisdom Kazan accumulated as a film director for over two decades is in evidence here. He is practical, witty, sophisticated and, most important, honest. His words should be read by every aspiring filmmaker at the earliest possible moment. Recommended.

1514 *Elinor Glyn.* by Glyn, Anthony. 356 p. illus. London: Hutchinson, 1968 (1955).

The biography of the English novelist and screenwriter who created the concept of "It" during the twenties. In this volume the silent-film days of the twenties in Hollywood are described along with impressions of Chaplin, Fairbanks, Pickford, et al. Some sources list Anthony Glyn as a pseudonym for Elinor Glyn.

1515 *Elvis: What Happened?* by Dunleavy, Steve. 332 p. paper illus. New York: Ballantine, 1977.

This is the story told by three of Elvis Presley's former bodyguards to Steve Dunleavy. A story that sold more than five million books and was excerpted in periodicals around the world. Written before the singer's death, it was the first book to suggest the sour underside of success. Drugs, guns, death, sheriff's badges, mother-love, outbursts of temper, self-indulgence, etc., are the topics of this expose. The anecdotes and recollections seem basically true in the light of information made public after Presley died.

Of the flood of Elvis books that appeared in the late seventies this is probably the one to consider. The difference between Elvis' public and private image is its focus and reading it is a shattering experience.

1516 *Elizabeth Taylor.* by Waterbury, Ruth. 255 p. paper New York: Popular Library, 1964.

Written by the founder of *Silver Screen* magazine and a former editor of *Photoplay* magazine, this biography is characterized by fairness and objectivity. It is the Taylor story told up to the 1964 marriage to Burton, some three years after the romance began. Much attention is given to Taylor's relationships and marriages, while most of her films are treated casually. A glimpse into a most extravagant life style with its accompanying pleasures and sorrows is delineated. The Taylor personality and character emerge with clarity and apparent honesty.

There are no illustrations or index. Several of her films are not mentioned and there are some minor inaccuracies. The major source of information for this book seems to be publicity stories, and thus the account differs considerably from the Taylor memoir. This is an interesting biography of a film actress who continues to live in the superstar fashion of the twenties and thirties. Acceptable for nondiscriminating fans of Miss Taylor.

1517 *Elizabeth Taylor: An Informal Memoir.* by Taylor, Elizabeth. 177 p. illus. New York: Harper & Row, 1964.

In this short volume, Elizabeth Taylor has written a disarming memoir rather than an autobiography. Some of it is factual but the greater portion is philosophical reflection upon her actions, her career, and her personality. There are some appropriate illustrations by Roddy McDowall. No index is provided. Her opinion of most of her films is low and she is not hesitant to evaluate them as such. She refrains from gossip, innuendo, bitchery, and emerges as a rather positive character. It is interesting to read this book concurrently with the Waterbury biography and to note the great differences. Not a vital contribution to film literature, it is an absorbing look at herself by one of the screen superstars.

1518 *Elizabeth Taylor.* by Allan, John B. 139 p. paper Derby, Conn.: Monarch Books, 1961.

An early biography that covers Elizabeth Taylor's life and career up to 1961. Emphasis is placed on the childhood years and the marriages to Nicky Hilton, Michael Wilding, Mike Todd, and Eddie Fisher. Richrd Burton is not mentioned since they made their CLEOPATRA (1963) headlines a year or so after the publication of this volume. Time and the publication of so many books about Elizabeth Taylor have almost eliminated any value this biography may have had originally. Although it has no index or illustrations, it may be of interest to researchers and is noted for the record.

1519 *Elizabeth Taylor.* by Hirsch, Foster. 156 p. paper illus. New York: Pyramid, 1973.

A persuasive summary argument concerning women that Elizabeth Taylor has played on the screen begins this study. "The Lady's Not a Tramp" is the provocative title of the short biographical section which follows and introduces the chronological survey of her films. Starting with THERE'S ONE BORN EVERY MINUTE (1942), the films are placed in appropriately titled periods: Horses and Dogs, Puppy Love, The Wrong Man, The Cat, The Queen, and The Shrew. A bibliography, a filmography and an index complete the volume.

The strength of the author's text lies in his ability to differentiate the many characters Elizabeth Taylor has played both on screen and off. His evaluations of her performances are subjective and vulnerable at times, but he has put her career in perspective with greater skill than other Taylor authors. The illustrations are well chosen and clearly reproduced. Recommended.

1520 *Elizabeth Taylor: The Last Star.* by Kelley, Kitty. 439 p. illus. New York: Simon and Schuster, 1981.

An excellent retelling of a very familiar story. Kelley's expertise is her blending of anecdote, fact, gossip, and her avoidance of complex psychological interpretation.

1521 *The Elizabeth Taylor Story.* by Levy, Alan. 176 p. paper illus. New York: Hillman Books, 1961.

An original paperback, this early biography of Elizabeth Taylor contains 16 pages of illustrations.

1522 *The Elizabeth Taylor Story.* by Levy, Alan. 176 p. illus. New York: Hillman, 1961.

1523 *Elizabeth.: The Life and Career of Elizabeth Taylor.* by Sheppard, Dick. 607 p. paper illus. New York: Warner Books, 1974.

Detail is the outstanding characteristic of this lengthy biography. Since Elizabeth Taylor's life and career have been more than adequately covered in the media and in several earlier books, much of what is offered here is familiar. What makes this volume impressive is the obvious labor-of-love approach employed by the author. Treating his subject with tact, sensitivity, and affection, he has noted all of the major incidents of a most eventful life. In addition he has provided background, critical opinion, and interpretation to flesh out the basic narrative structure. The result is a study in depth of a fascinating screen personality.

A center section of photographs, a detailed filmography, and a long index add to the book's overall quality. This is one of the best biographies of Elizabeth Taylor.

1524 *Elsevier's Dictionary of Cinema, Sound and Music.* by Clason, W. E. 948 p. New York: Elsevier Pub. Co., 1956.

A most unusual reference book, this listing of over 3200 words in three major fields (cinema, acoustics, and music) gives the following information: 1) the American/British word—each given a number; 2) the field; 3) the definition; 4) the equivalent word in French, Spanish, Italian, Dutch, and German; and 5) a final section consisting of the words alphabetized in each foreign language with a corresponding English number. Should the foreign word be encountered in reading, its English equivalent and meaning could be easily obtained.

Certainly the book would be of great value to any professional concerned with the making of films in foreign countries. For the general reader, its major use might well be its definition of the technical terms.

1525 *Elvis.* by Hopkins, Jerry. 448 p illus. New York: Simon & Schuster, 1971.

The well-known externals are covered in a detailed fan magazine style. The real Elvis is still under wraps, in this unauthorized biography.

1526 *Elvis.* by Harbinson, W. A. 64 p. paper illus. New York: Dell, 1977.

A small purse-sized book derived from *The Illustrated Elvis* containing 40 photos of Presley.

1527 *Elvis.* by Mann, Richard. 186 p. paper illus. Van Nuys, Ca.: Bible Voice, 1977.

An acceptable retelling of the rise and fall of an American pop idol, this volume emphasizes the religious beliefs, actions and statements attributed to Presley.

The author is sympathetic rather than critical, emotional rather than objective. There is much conjecture on what Elvis might say, think or feel. Written for a specific audience, the volume explores Elvis from the religious viewpoint that his life should be a reminder, a warning and an encouragement to us all.

1528 *Elvis: Newly Discovered Drawings of Elvis Presley.* by Harper, Betty. paper illus. New York: Bantam, 1979.

Forty pencil drawings of Elvis Presley, made over a 20-year period by a Nashville portrait artist, make up this volume.

1529 *Elvis: Portrait of a Friend.* by Lacker, Marty; and Lacker, Patsy; and Smith, Leslie S. 320 p. illus. Memphis: Wimmer Brothers, 1978.

1530 *Elvis: The Films and Career of Elvis Presley.* by Zmijewsky, Steven; and Zmijewsky, Boris. 224 p. illus. Secaucus, N.J.: Citadel, 1976.

The reader will find little that is new in this synthesis of Presley biography, films, records and appearances. Almost half of the book is devoted to the 33 films with illustrations, synopsis, cast, credits, notes, etc. The 400 or so illustrations that appear throughout show Elvis mostly with female costars or fans. What is lacking in this volume is any attempt at interpretation of the information gathered. The volume is expensive and much more insight into the films and career of Elvis Presley can be obtained elsewhere at a much more reasonable price.

1531 *Elvis: The Final Years.* by Hopkins, Jerry. 260 p. illus. New York: St. Martin's Press, 1980.

Jerry Hopkins wrote an earlier volume entitled *Elvis: A Biography* which took his subject up to 1970. Based mostly on interviews and research, his new book covers the last years of Presley's life in a breezy, reportorial fashion. The singer's preoccupations with drugs, women, guns, extravagance, jewels, etc., are noted in this account of his decline. Much of the material is now familiar, but Hopkins' handling of it makes it palatable for those who still are fascinated by the legendary singer.

1532 *Elvis.* by Jones, Peter. illus. London: Octopus, 1976.

1533 *Elvis: His Life and Times in Poetry and Lines.* by West, Joan Buchanan. illus. Hicksville, N.Y.: Exposition, 1979.

1534 *Elvis: Images and Fancies.* by Tharpe, Jac. illus. Jackson: University Press of Mississippi, 1979.

1535 *Elvis: Lonely Star at the Top.* by Hanna, David. illus. New York: Nordon, 1977.

1536 *Elvis: The Legend Lives.* by Grove, Martin A. illus. New York: Manor, 1978.

1537 *Elvis.* by Goldman, Albert. 598 p. illus. New York: McGraw Hill, 1981.

Elvis Presley gets an intense "Mommie Dearest" treatment by Goldman in this biographical expose. Nothing escapes the author's scorn and ridicule—food, sex, recreation, relationships, cars, money, etc.

1538 *Elvis and His Friends.* by Gripe, Maria. illus. New York: Delacorte, 1976.

1539 *Elvis and His Secret.* by Gripe, Maria. illus. New York: Delacorte, 1976.

1540 *Elvis and the Colonel.* by Mann, May. 294 p. paper illus. New York: Pocket, 1976.

Written before his death, this biography of Elvis Presley avoids the sensationalism that surrounded his rapid decline and sudden demise. It is a Hollywood reporter's romantic version of the Presley legend—boyhood, poverty, parents, first performances, Colonel Parker, the army, Priscilla Beaulieu, wealth, and divorce.

The author knew Elvis and her account is based on interviews with him and many others who were part of his life. What results is the positive-American-legend portrait of Elvis that was prevalent before the exposure of his addiction to drugs. Several of the few illustrations show the author in Presley's company, mostly in the few years from 1957 to 1961.

Shortly after the singer's death, this volume was reprinted with the title, *The Private Elvis.*

1541 *Elvis '56—The Birth of a Legend.* by Wertheimer, Alfred. and A group of photographs taken of Elvis Presley at age 21 is the substance of this volume. Taken for RCA records, most of the illustrations have not been published before. paper illus. New York: Macmillan, 1979.

1542 *Elvis in Concert.* by Reggero, John. paper illus. New York: Delta, 1978.

A visual record of selected Presley concerts, this volume attempts to recall what it was like to attend such events. Over 100 illustrations accompany the text of this oversized paperback.

1543 *Elvis in His Own Words.* edited by Farren, Mick; and Marchbank, Pearce. 128 p. paper illus. New York: Omnibus (Quick Fox), 1977.

From a group of printed and recorded interviews, the editors have selected portions and arranged them under topic headings. These include girls, movies, Uncle Sam, critics, recordings, childhood, etc. Accompanying the quotations are related photographs, film stills, candids, publicity shots, newspaper photos, etc. The result is rather like one long illustrated interview which is carefully designed to perpetuate an image. The reader will discover nothing new or startling—Elvis as a performer is quite clear but Elvis as a person remains a mystery. Acceptable.

1544 *Elvis in Hollywood.* by Lichter, Paul. 188 p. paper illus. New York: Simon & Schuster, 1975.

This volume might easily be titled "The Films of Elvis Presley," since it is primarily a chronological presentation of his 33 films preceded by a short biographical chapter. For each film there are major cast names and production credits, a long synopsis, and most importantly, selected visuals pertinent to the film or its period. The photographs include stills, portraits, news photos, candids, production shots, posters, etc.

Very little effort is made to offer any critical evaluation of Presley's work, except through broad generalizations about his appearance or his songs. The light approach can also be detected in the chapter headings—The Early Years, The Growing Years, The Lazy Years, Something Different, and The Im-

age. A discography of Presley's film music is added. As a selected visual documentation of a lengthy film career, this volume is fine. But as an examination of a superstar's Hollywood experience, it lacks depth, objectivity and critical perception. Acceptable.

1545 *Elvis Lives!* illus. London: Galaxy, 1978.

1546 *The Elvis Picture Book.* paper illus. Tiburon, Calif.: Personality Editions, 1977.

A collection of photos and a bland text retell the story of Elvis Presley in this oversized paperback.

1547 *Elvis Presley: An Illustrated Biography.* by Wallraf, Rainer; and Plehn, Heinz 120 p. paper illus. New York: Quick Fox, 1978.

Although this volume is called a biography, it is more a representative scrapbook of Elvis Presley. In addition to the widely known and reported factual information about Elvis, this volume offers visual intepretation of what it was like to be Elvis. Personal photos range from a thin boy of six to the bloated performer some 36 years later. Record covers, movie posters, periodical front pages—are all offered in abundance. They help to describe his life.

This volume was translated from a German original and some of the material, recordings for example, might be confusing since no attempt is made to adapt it for American readers; it is, however, one of the best Elvis memorial books currently available.

1548 *Elvis Presley.* by Kling, Bernard; and Plehn, Heintz. illus. New York: Music Sales, 1979.

1549 *Elvis Presley.* by Slaughter, Todd. illus. London: Manda Brook, 1977.

1550 *Elvis Presley.* by Taylor, Paula. 31 p. illus. Mankato, Minn.: Creative Education, 1974.

Written for very young readers, this is a title in the *Rock and Pop Stars* series.

1551 *Elvis Presley: A Biography.* by Wallraf, Ranier. illus. Munich: Nuctern, 1977.

1552 *Elvis Presley: An Illustrated Biography.* by Harbison, William Allen. illus. London: Joseph, 1975.

1553   *Elvis Presley: An Illustrated Record.* by Carr, Roy. illus. New York: Harmony, 1980.

1554   *Elvis Presley: A Photoplay Tribute.* illus. New York: Cadrant, 1977.

1555   *Elvis Presley: A Study in Music.* by Matthew-Walker, Robert. illus. Tunbridge Wells, England: MIDAS, 1979.

1556   *Elvis Presley.* by Farren, Mick; and Marchbank, Pearce. New York: (Omnibus) Music Sales, 1978.

1557   *The Elvis Presley Encyclopedia.* compiled by Barlow, Roy. illus. Heanor, England: Albert Hand Pubs., 1964.

1558   *Elvis Presley, King of Kings.* by Panta, Ilona. illus. Hicksville, N.Y.: Exposition, 1979.

1559   *Elvis Presley Poster Book.* edited by Gelman, Woody. illus. New York: Crown.

1560   *The Elvis Presley Quizbook.* by Nash, Bruce M. 213 p. paper illus. New York: Warner Books, 1978.

Fifty quizzes based on the life and career of Elvis Presley are contained in this illustrated paperback. Topics include records and films, of course.

1561   *The Elvis Presley Scrapbook.* by Parish, James Robert. 185 p. paper illus. New York: Ballantine Books, 1975.

The term "scrapbook," as used here, means about 60 percent film survey, 20 percent text and 20 percent candid photographs. After brief coverage of the early years, Elvis makes his first film—LOVE ME TENDER (1956)—on page 24. The remainder of the book covers his films up to CHANGE OF HABIT (1969) with stills, posters, production shots, etc. No casts or credits are given and there is no summary filmography. Instead there is a discography covering both his singles and his albums. Attention is given throughout to his appearances in nightclubs, on TV, and in concerts. The text vacillates between offering a trib-

ute and an objective portrait. Only in the final pages is there a hint of the husband-wife relationship, the Colonel Parker personality and the ultimate Presley deterioration. Photo reproduction is adequate.

Those looking for a deep critical analysis of the phenomenon called Elvis Presley will not find it here. However, as general coverage of Elvis' life and career, this is a most acceptable volume.

1562   *Elvis Presley Souvenir Photo Album.* by Parker, Tom. illus. Madison, Tenn.: Elvis Presley Enterprises, 1956.

1563   *Elvis Presley Speaks.* by Holzer, Han. illus. New York: Manor, 1978.

1564   *The Elvis Presley Story.* edited by Gregory, James. illus. London: Thorpe & Porter, 1960.

1565   *Elvis Presley—The Beatles.* by Alico, Stella H. illus. West Haven, Conn.: Pendulum Press, 1979.

1566   *The Elvis Presley Trivia Quiz Book.* by Rosenbaum, Helen. 154 p. paper illus. New York: National American Library, 1978.

A series of 99 quizzes based on the life and career of Elvis Presley. Childhood, army, songs, costars, romances, and recordings are among the many topics covered. Also included are individual tests on each of his films and a photo quiz. Answers are given in the book's final pages.

1567   *The Elvis Presley Trivia Quiz Book.* by Rosenbaum, Helen. 154 p. paper illus. New York: Signet, 1978.

This concentrated volume contains 100 quizzes with over 1000 questions about Elvis Presley—his songs, movies, friends, family, producers, etc. There is one specific quiz with ten questions for each of his films.

A photo-quiz occupies the center section of the book. Answers are given at the back.

A detailed, trivia-approach to the life and career of an American legend, this volume offers a very different review than that found in most of the other recent Elvis books. A more appropriate title might have been "A Thousand Questions and Answers about Elvis."

1568 *Elvis Presley—1935-1977: A Tribute to the King.* illus. Wednesbury, England: Bavie, 1977.

1569 *Elvis Special.* by Hand, Albert. illus. Manchester, Mass.: World, 1962.

1570 *Elvis We Love You Tender.* by Presley, Dee; and Stanley, Billy; and Stanley, Rick; and Stanley, David. 395 p. illus. New York: Delacorte, 1979.

Read literally, this memoir tells of a heroine who married the father of a public idol and sacrificed herself and her three sons in serving the cause of commercialized celebrity. Reading between the lines the story might be that of a bored housewife who tries for a young celebrity but settles for his father. In doing so she and her sons enjoy the comforts and exotic pleasure that wealth and celebrity bring, turning bitter only when they are suddenly excluded by death. The truth probably lies somewhere between.

Devoted admirers of Elvis Presley will be excited by the insider's view provided by Dee Presley and her three sons. Others may find the memoir too intimate or too self-serving—and who's left to argue? Both of the heroes in her life—Vernon and Elvis Presley—are dead and there seems to be no existing relationship with Priscilla Presley. Therefore, the reader is left to evaluate the credulity of the memoirs by the evidence presented. Verdicts will undoubtedly vary.

A few pictures and an abbreviated index are also a part of this questionable memorial to Elvis Presley.

1571 *Elvis Yearbook.* paper illus. Tiburon, Calif.: Personality Editions, 1977.

Originally published in 1960, this oversized paperback contains pictures of Elvis Presley during his prime performing period.

1572 *Embattled Shadows: A History of Canadian Cinema 1895-1939.* by Morris, Peter. 350 p. paper illus. Montreal: McGill–Queen's University, 1978.

The author's worthy goal here is to fill in the literature gap that exists in pre-1939 Canadian film history. Although there are other publications in this area, such as *Canadian Government Motion Picture Bureau 1917-1941*, none is as comprehensive as the account Morris offers here. Unfortunately, with the attention given to detail, there comes a kind of pedantic recital of facts that makes for an unexciting survey rather than a colorful story.

The text is embellished with a good collection of illustrations, some very detailed chapter notes, and indexes. In addition there is a chronology (1894-1913) and a selected filmography (1913-1939).

For anyone concerned with the Canadian film, this volume is essential. It covers a neglected area of film history with the care and thoroughness that are typical of a dedicated scholar.

1573 *The Emergence of Film Art: (the Evolution and Development of the Motion Picture as an Art from 1900 to Present).* by Jacobs, Lewis. 453 p. illus. New York: Hopkinson & Blake, 1969.

Lewis Jacobs gives us another well-arranged historical anthology in this volume. His personal role as contributor and editor here seems greater than in his previous collection. The selections are all worthy of inclusion and, when taken together, they do satisfy Jacob's goals of "providing insight into creative film expression and presenting a historical overview of the medium's artistic development."

One minor comment: no argument can be raised about these goals but they do not seem terribly challenging to a man with Jacob's qualifications and experience. One continues to hope that he will do a second volume updating *The Rise of the American Film* which would be "pure" Jacobs. As a reading experience, the book is quite rewarding and is recommended.

1574 *Emil Jannings.* by Ihering, Herbert. 248 p. illus. New York: Gordon Press, 1976 (1942).

A biography of the German film actor first published in Heidelberg, 1942.

1575 *Emlyn Williams.* by Findlater, Richard. 112 p. illus. London: Rockliff, 1957.

A biography of the actor-director-playwright that is primarily an illustrated study of his work with a list of his appearances on stage and screen. His film career began in the early thirties with films such as SALLY BISHOP (1932) and was still flourishing in the seventies. His early life is also covered in two recent autobiographical volumes.

1576 *The Emotional Responses of Children to the Motion Picture Situation.*

by Dysinger, Wendell S.; and Rucknick, Christian A. 122 p. New York: Arno Press, 1970 (1933).

A Payne Fund Study which used the galvanometer to measure the emotional responses of children to film situations. Measurements were made in both the theatre and the laboratory. Scenes of danger, conflict, horror, love, eroticism, etc. were used. Interesting and scientific, with valuable results.

1577 *Empire: The Life, Legend and Madness of Howard Hughes.* by Barlett, Donald L.; and Steele, James B. 687 p. illus. New York: Norton, 1979.

A long, detailed biography of Howard Hughes, this volume includes material on the Hollywood years. The authors, investigative reporters who have a Pulitzer, picture Hughes as "an obsessive compulsive neurotic...a hopeless psychotic...an inept businessman...who lusted for fame and was ambivalent toward women..."

Obviously, the subject is too complex to capture in a completely dimensioned portrait but this volume comes close. Illustrations, an index and a bibliography support the carefully researched text.

1578 THE EMPIRE STRIKES BACK Notebook. by Smith, Lindsay. edited by Attias, Diana; 128 p. paper illus. New York: Ballantine, 1980.

Contains the final shooting script of THE EMPIRE STRIKES BACK (1980) along with interviews with director Irvin Kershner and screenwriter Lawrence Kasdan. Storyboards are positioned alongside the script to indicate the visual development of the film.

1579 THE EMPIRE STRIKES BACK Portfolio. by McQuarrie, Ralph. 24 p. paper illus. New York: Ballantine, 1980.

This volume contains 24 unbound full-color production paintings from THE EMPIRE STRIKES BACK (1980). Each of the 10 inch x 24 inch paintings by Ralph McQuarrie is numbered and captioned.

1580 THE EMPIRE STRIKES BACK Sketchbook. by Johnston, Joe; and Rodis-Jamero, Nilo. 128 p. paper illus. New York: Ballantine, 1980.

Created by the men who worked on the set designs, this oversized original paperback contains many of the production sketches for THE EMPIRE STRIKES BACK (1980).

1581 *Enchained in Film.* by Mayakovsky, Vladimir; and Brik, Lily. Ann Arbor, Mich.: Translation Press, 1981.

1582 ENCORE. by Clarke, T.; and Ambler, Eric; and Macrae, Arthur. 156 p. illus. Garden City, N. Y.: Doubleday, 1952.

Script of the 1951 film. Contains the Somerset Maugham short stories and the screenplays made from them: "The Ant and the Grasshopper" (director: Jackson, script: Clarke). "Gigolo and Gigolette" (director: French, script: Ambler). and "Winter Cruise" (director: Pelissier, script: Macrae).

1583 *Encountering Directors.* by Samuels, Charles Thomas. 255 p. illus. New York: G. P. Putnam's, 1972.

This collection of interviews is unusual in several respects. All interviews were conducted by Samuels within a three-year period, 1969-1972. To prepare himself, the author acquainted himself with all the films and with many of the published interviews of each director. Thus his questioning represents a knowledgeable, structured inquiry. Perhaps the only quality missing is a little lightness or humor, but since he was conducting many of these sessions through language translators, that lack is understandable. But the book is a bit heavy at times, and if the reader is not totally familiar with the films of a specific director, much of the interview's meaning may be lost. Directors questioned included Michelangelo Antonioni, Francois Truffaut, Robert Bresson, Rene Clair, Ermanno Olmi, Federico Fellini, Vittorio De Sica, Carol Reed, Ingmar Bergman, Jean Renoir and Alfred Hitchcock.

Each interview is preceded by a description of the emotional and physical surroundings in which it was given. A filmography is placed at the head of each unit. Illustrations abound but there is no identification for many of them and the reader (other than the film buff) can only guess as to the identity of the persons shown and to which films they refer.

The book has an extended index which will be of considerable reference value. Produced in an oversized coffee-table format, the book has attractive inside cover portraits of the subjects and the author. Since the interviews are comprehensive and well planned, the directors are current legends, and the production is outstanding, the book is highly recommended.

1584 *The Encyclopedia of Animated Cartoon Series, 1909-1979.* by Lenburg, Jeff. 190 p. illus. Westport, Conn.: Arlington House, 1981.

Over 300 cartoon series are described. For each there is the creator, director, studio, episode titles, voices, date of release, characters, running-time, plot summary, character description, background information, etc. Heavily illustrated.

1585 *Encyclopedia of Associations (Vol. 1).* edited by Fisk, Margaret. Detroit: Gale Research Co., 1968.

A partial film reference this is a specialized but useful publication that lists associations along with their addresses, directors, membership, number, and their goals, activities and publications. The associations are placed in categories such as "Trade, Business, and Commercial," "Educational and Cultural," etc. There is also a section devoted to inactive, defunct, or name-changed associations. The index lists the associations alphabetically and according to key word. The key words "Motion Pictures" and "Film" will provide most of the associations that film researchers will need.

1586 *Encyclopedia of Comedians.* by Franklin, Joe. 347 p. illus. Secaucus, N.J.: Citadel, 1979.

Comedians of the current century are listed along with short biographies and selected examples of their work. Along with film, the subjects come from vaudeville, the stage, radio and television.

1587 *Encyclopedia of Music for Pictures.* by Rapee, Erno. 510 p. New York: Arno Press, 1970 (1925).

Silent film music arranged by the mood desired.

1588 *Encyclopedia of Mystery and Detection.* by Steinbrunner, Chris; and Penzler, Otto. 436 p. illus. New York: McGraw-Hill, 1976.

The base of this attractive reference work is a group of 500 writers who have specialized in the mystery/detective genre. For each a biography which is factual, evaluative, and critical is presented. . The famous fictional characters who appear in their stories are given similar entries. Thus not only do we find an entry for "Conan Doyle, Sir Arthur" but also ones for "Holmes, Sherlock," "Moriarity, Professor James," and "Watson, Dr." Wherever pertinent, the entries contain a filmography which gives general comment, year of release, a few cast names, director, and a brief plot outline. Television, plays, and radio presentations are also noted.

Supporting the collective biography portions are some general entries — "Dime Novels," "Collecting Detective Fiction" — an introduction; a short selective bibliography; and many illustrations. Included among the latter are hundreds of film stills which have been well selected, intelligently placed, and carefully reproduced.

This is not a pure film reference but it is an essential aid in any study or investigation of the detective/mystery film genre. Recommended.

1589 *Encyclopedia of Practical Photography.* edited by Uslan, Seymour; and Lassiter, Kenneth. 14 vols. illus. New York: Scribners, 1979.

The forces at Amphoto and Kodak combined to produce this 14 volume encyclopedia. Since much of the information pertains to motion pictures, the project is noted here.

The scope is very wide and comprehensive. Using some previous material from Kodak publications, including the usual superb color visuals, the editors have also included new writing. Entries are classified by a system of 21 symbols (chemical, theory, lighting, optics, biography, etc.). A detailed index will accompany the set of books.

1590 *Encyclopedia of the Musical Film.* by Green, Stanley. 344 p. illus. New York: Oxford University Press, 1981.

This encyclopedia of the screen musical's most prominent individual's, songs, and films was written by the capable and always reliable Stanley Green.

1591 *Encyclopedia of the Third Reich.* by Snyder, Louis L. 410 p. illus. New York: McGraw-Hill, 1976.

This volume contains considerable material on the films, filmmakers and film production of the Third Reich.

1592 *Energy.* by Higgins, Judith H. 195 p. Santa Barbara, Calif: American Bibliographic Center, 1979.

This is the second title in the *Multimedia Guide for Children and Young Adults* series. The major section lists multimedia materials (print, films, filmstrips, videotapes, slides, audiotapes, charts, posters, and kits) under some twenty energy headings: coal, electric, gas, oil, solar energy, etc. Each entry offers complete data and an annotation that is largely descriptive. Usually some recommendations, reservations, and/or suggestions for use are mentioned, but only briefly. A second shorter but similar section lists curriculum materials (guides, courses, units, manuals, modules, or activity packages). Other sources of information on energy, along with databases, are noted next. Closing sections include a publisher/distributor list, an author index, a title index, and a subject index.

This book differs from the first publication, *Latino Materials*, in several respects. Not only has the scope of materials considered been appreciably widened, but access to the materials has been made more efficient by the additional indexes and appendixes provided. The volume should be extremely helpful to anyone concerned with energy education. Recommended.

1593   *Energy and the Way We Live.* by Dick, Esme. 20 p. paper New York: Educational Film Library Association, 1979.

This is a filmography designed to be used with Courses By Newspapers program, "Energy and the Way We Live." Titles are arranged under 15 general course headings and include the usual data and a helpful annotation. Distributors and additional resources are listed in the final pages.

1594   *Enjoying the Arts/Film.* by Newton, Sandra Salinas. 176 p. illus. New York: Richards Rosen, 1978.

As an introduction to the art of the film, this volume is excellent. In six carefully composed chapters, the author presents overviews of history, aesthetics, filmmaking, film genres, directors, and national cinemas. A few illustrations and an index accompany the text.

The accomplishment here is one of distillation. In less than 200 pages, Newton has selected most of the important events, concepts and practices associated with film. When used as a beginning text or reader in film study, this volume should be most successful. Recommended.

1595   *Enjoyment of Laughter.* by Eastman, Max. London: Hamish Hamilton, 1937.

Contains an impression of Chaplin by one of his close friends. Chaplin's personal assessment of humor is discussed. See also Eastman's *Great Companions.*

1596   *Enough, No More.* by Wells, Ingeborg. translated by Sudley, Lord. 294 p. illus. London: Herbert Joseph, 1948.

An autobiography of the German actress written before her appearances in CAPTAIN HORATIO HORNBLOWER (1951) and ACROSS THE BRIDGE (1957).

1597   *Enriching the Curriculum through Motion Pictures: Final Report.* by Meierhenry, Wesley C. 255 p. illus. Lincoln, Nebr.: University of NebraskaPress, 1953.

1598   *Enter—The Comics.* by Topffer, Rudolphe; edited by Wiese, E. 80 p. illus. Lincoln, Nebr.: University of Nebraska Press, 1965.

Rudolphe Topffer (1799-1846), a lecturer on classical rhetoric at the Academy of Geneva, liked to draw faces. He noted that two faces could converse, and if the conversation were preceded and followed by other drawings, a story could be told by pictures. Thus in the mid-1800s, he created a base for the eventual development of both comics and the cinema.

This volume contains two different examples of his work. The first, a long piece called "Essay on Physiognomy," written in 1845, is an attempt to find a language for facial expressions. Many line drawings accompany the text which considers faces of all shapes, sizes, and with varying features. His faces are satirical and exaggerated. The second offering is an early picture story. "The True Story of Monsieur Crepin," told in comic strip fashion, circa 1837.

The editor has not only translated and edited the original works but has written a fine introduction and supplied many explanatory notes and references to supplement the two major pieces. Pre-screen history is a specialized subject of limited appeal, but it is gratifying to discover a scholarly research work in this area that is readable, entertaining and informative. It represents a fine contribution to a neglected area of film history.

1599   *The Entertainers as Seen by Hirschfeld.* by Hirschfeld, Al. illus. London: Elm Tree, 1977.

Hirschfeld is the artist who hides the name of his daughter, Nina, in all his drawings of performers. His work appears frequently in the theatrical section of *The New York Sunday Times.* This volume offers a collection of his caricatures of such stars as Tallulah Bankhead, Charles Laughton, and many others.

1600 *Entertainment: A Cross-Cultural Examination.* edited by Fischer, Heinz-Dietrich; and Melnik, Stefan R. 352 p. illus. New York: Hastings House, 1980.

Twenty seven experts on mass communication offer essays which argue the presence of messages and values in all entertainments.

1601 *The Entertainment Film for Juvenile Audiences.* by Storck, Henri. 240 p. New York: UNESCO/Columbia University Press, 1950.

An investigation into many factors (effects, censorship, reactions, etc.) connected with motion pictures and youth.

1602 ENTRACTE. by Clair, Rene. 140 p. paper illus. New York: Simon & Schuster, 1970.

Script of the 1924 film directed by Rene Clair. Contained in the same volume as A NOUS LA LIBERTE (1931). Articles: "Picabia, Satie, and the First Night of ENTR'ACTE and "Pciabia's Original Notes for ENTR'ACTE.

1603 *The Environment Film Review.* by Kurtz, Alice S.; and Kelley, Kevin J. 155 p. paper New York: Environment Information Center, 1972.

This annual guide to films on environment appeared first in 1972, and one hopes for its continued publication. It begins with a list of film distributors and then proceeds to its two major divisions. The first review section is the longer and more interesting. Under each of 21 major environmental categories (air pollution, land use and misuse, wildlife, etc.), appropriate films are arranged alphabetically. Reviews provide most or all of the following: critical rating, length, color or black and white, purchase/rental price, release date, sponsor, producer, distributor, director, writer, narrator and possible audiences, with some cross referencing to other reviews.

The second section contains an alphabetical index, a keyword list, a subject index, an industry index, a sponsor index, and a list of acronyms for agencies, terms, and materials.

The reviews are originals, not excerpted quotes, and offer both descriptive and critical annotations. The length is usually several hundred words and one can only admire the thoroughness of the reviewers. The several reference elements offered here blend well to make an easy-to-use, valuable aid. The resulting filmographies would fill an existing need for improved selection tools for the purchase or rental of films. Highly recommended.

1604 *Eric Portman.* by Tynan, Kenneth. illus London: Rockliff, 1955.

Portman was a much admired stage actor whose work in films was also of constant high quality. He appeared in British films from the mid-thirties until his death in the late sixties.

1605 *Eric Rohmer.* by Rohmer, Eric. paper illus. London: Lorrimer, 1972.

Contains script, cast and production credits for: CLAIRE'S KNEE, (1972); MY NIGHT AT MAUD'S (1970); LA COLLECTIONEUSE (1968).

1606 *(hommage a) Erich von Stroheim.* by Gobeil, Charlotte. 54 p. paper illus. Ottawa: Canadian Film Institute, 1966.

This short anthology on von Stroheim includes articles by Iris Barry, Herman O. Weinberg, Lotte H. Eisner, Gloria Swanson and others. In addition, there are two synopses and one film introduction as originally written/spoken by von Stroheim. Most of the book is written in English but there are three articles in French. A filmography and a bibliography complete the tribute.

Rather special material that may be difficult to obtain, this volume is noted here for students, historians and others who have an in-depth interest in von Stroheim.

1607 *Ernest Hemingway: A Life Story.* by Baker, Carlos. 978 p. paper illus. New York: Bantam, 1969.

The definitive biography of Hemingway is noted here, since so much of his work was used for films and some of his friends were filmmakers. This intensively researched and documented volume also contains a lengthy index and some illustrations.

1608 *Ernst Lubitsch: A Guide to References and Resources.* by Carringer, Robert; and Sabath, Barry. 262 p. Boston: G.K. Hall, 1978.

Since Ernst Lubitsch had a career that included filmmaking in Europe and in America, the amount of reference and resource available is comparatively

231

large. Following a biography and a critical survey, a filmography divides his films into four periods: Early German (1913-1918), German Features (1918-1923), American Silent (1923-1929), and American Sound (1929-1948). For each film, cast credits, synopsis, notes and references are given. The selected bibliography which follows is arranged with helpful annotations for many of the entries. Writings, performances, and other film-related activities are noted along with archival sources and film distributors. Both an author index and film title index are provided.

Care has been taken in presenting a maximum amount of reference material in a most efficient manner. The number of cross- and sub-references used will aid any scholar in the quick location of specific information. For example, there are 13 review sources preceding the author's annotation for Herman Weinberg's *The Lubitsch Touch.*

In certain ways this is a model reference book. While one may quarrel with the many long plot outlines offered, there can be nothing but praise for the bibliography.

1609 *Ernst Lubitsch's* NINOTCHKA. edited by Anobile, Richard 256 p. paper illus. New York: Avon, 1975.

Once it has been stated that this series is the next best thing to owning a print of the film, there remains only the responsibility of explaining why. Using original negative material supplied by MGM, Richard Anobile has recreated a visual record of NINOTCHKA (1939). Some 1500 frame blow-ups have been carefully reproduced and arranged with anywhere from two to nine visuals per page. The complete dialogue has been inserted at appropriate places.

The clarity of the visuals along with the careful production the book has received enable the reader to approximate the experience of seeing the film. Anobile's format allows the viewer-reader to proceed at his own pace—a decided advantage for anyone who wishes to study this classic film. Those who are meeting NINOTCHKA for the first time will be as entertained and delighted as her older admirers have been for more than three decades. Recommended.

1610 *Eros in the Cinema.* by Durgnat, Raymond. 207 p. illus. London: Calder & Boyars, 1966.

This volume is a consideration of erotic content in certain films. Although it is no longer necessary to disguise sexual connotation in motion pictures, there is still a strong argument to be made for subtlety in

erotic suggestion. Many films are considered from different viewpoints. The interpretation offered is the author's and, although allowing for much disagreement by the reader, is entertaining and informative. Some of the provocative illustrations that accompany the text are poorly reproduced. Excellent material for more mature readers.

1611 *Erotic Movies.* by Wortley, Richard. 140 p. illus. New York: Cresent, 1975.

A quick overview of movies that deal with erotic or sexually arousing themes/incidents is provided here. Using more than 200 stills — mostly female nudes — Wortley tries to trace the evolution of this film genre from Melies' films to the soft porn of the seventies. What results is a sketchy, patchwork text which serves mostly as an accompaniment to the pictures.

1612 *Erotica for the Millions (Love in the Movies).* by Brusendorff, Ove; and Henningsen, Paul. 147 p. illus. London: The Rodney Book, 1960..

The title and the fact that this book is translated from the Danish may tell enough.

1613 *Errol and Me.* by Haymes, Nora Eddington Flynn. 176 p. paper illus. New York: Signet Books, 1960.

Although it is a sensationalized confessional of seven years of marriage to Errol Flynn, this paperpack does offer a closeup of what celebrity, drugs, and alcohol can do to a human being and the people around him. Admittedly aimed at those who enjoy gossip and scandal, the book presents a portrait in depth. If the excesses can be mentally excised by the reader, the final impression is quite affecting. Illustrations are incorporated with the text. This volume has some value for special readers.

1614 *Errol Flynn.* edited by Parish, James Robert paper illus. Kew Gardens, N.Y.: Cinefax, 1969.

An oversized pictorial paperback with a complete filmography and some biographical data. It is the unusual collection of stills and candids that makes the book a pleasant surprise.

1615 *Errol Flynn.* by Morris, George. 160 p. paper illus. New York: Pyramid, 1975.

The life and career of Errol Flynn are reviewed in

this title from *The Illustrated History of the Movies* series. After a brief appreciation, the author gets quickly to Flynn's first film experience, IN THE WAKE OF THE BOUNTY (1933), in which he portrayed Fletcher Christian. The narrative moves almost directly to Flynn's signing by Warner Brothers and CAPTAIN BLOOD (1935). This film brought instant stardom to Flynn and was followed by a long series of successful films, all of which are described and illustrated here. The final half of the book is devoted to the dramatic decline of this superstar, which began with SAN ANTONIO (1945) and ended with CUBAN REBEL GIRLS (1959).

The book contains many well-selected visuals which have been clearly reproduced. A bibliography, a filmography, and an index complete the volume.

To millions of people Errol Flynn on screen was a fascinating actor-personality; to those who knew him off screen, he was in many ways a reflection of his screen image. In a tight, largely factual narrative, George Morris has caught the essence of this Hollywood legend. Recommended.

1616   *Errol Flynn: A Memoir.* by Conrad, Earl. 222 p. illus. New York: Dodd Mead, 1978.

In the late fifties, Earl Conrad worked with Errol Flynn in writing *My Wicked, Wicked Ways.* It is the memory of that experience which forms the base of this memoir. Although it is punctuated with bits of biographical material, the text is largely an account of Flynn's behavior and observations during their time together. The actor was nearing the end of his life and the portrait presented here is not an attractive one.

A center section of illustrations provides some rare visuals from Flynn's early years. His films are listed in an appendix. No index is provided.

In his attempt to discover the "enigma" of Flynn, Conrad makes much of the actor's relationship with his mother. It is suggested that the treatment accorded women by Flynn had its roots in this maternal conflict.

If there are still readers hungry for information about the late actor, this volume will provide some slight nourishment. Others will find the earlier Flynn autobiography to be the definitive statement about the rise and fall of a beautiful hedonist who also happened to be an actor, writer, and adventurer.

1617   *Errol Flynn: The Untold Story.* by Higham, Charles. illus. New York: Doubleday, 1980.

What Charles Higham offers here as an untold story is some government documentation linking Errol Flynn to a known German agent. The evidence is circumstantial and hardly worth the attention the author gives it. With the rest of its pages devoted to Flynn's hedonism, the book offers a totally unattractive portrait of the actor. Too bad he's not around to defend himself.

1618   *ESP and the Stars.* by Kleiner, Dick. 209 p. New York: Grosset and Dunlap, 1970.

Psychic experiences related by 71 film celebrities. The author's paperback, *The Ghosts Who Danced With Kim Novak*, covers the same ground.

1619   *Essay and General Literature Index.* edited by Sears, M. E.; and Shaw, M. Paper and hardbound. New York: H. W. Wilson Co., 1900-

A partial film reference, this guide indexes authors, subjects, and titles of articles or essays found in collections or anthologies. The basic index (1900-1933) has been updated to the present by supplements published on a nonregular basis. Since much of the film literature of late has been either collections (the interview books by Sarris, Geduld, Gelmis) or anthologies (Jacobs, Talbot, MacCann), this index can help in the location of shorter pieces. Look under the subject heading of "Moving Picture"

1620   *The Essential Cinema.* edited by Sitney, P. Adams. 380 p. illus. New York: Anthology Film Archives, New York University Press, 1975.

Subtitled "Essays on Films in the Collection of Anthology Film Archives," this volume consists of both commissioned articles and previously published pieces. A filmography entitled, "The Essential Works of the Art of the Cinema," introduces the 14 essays which make up the text. Supporting elements include a very lengthy bibliography arranged alphabetically by filmmaker, and a list of distributors of the films within the collection of the Anthology Film Archives. Highly recommended.

1621   *The Esthetic of Jean Cocteau.* by Crowson, Lydia. 206 p. Hanover, N.H.: University Press of New England, 1978.

An evaluation of Cocteau's work using structuralism and analytic philosophy.

1622 *Esthetics Contemporary.* edited by Kostelanetz, Richard. 444 p. paper New York: Prometheus, 1978.

A chapter on film by Paul Sharits is included in this volume about avant-garde aesthetic principles.

1623 *The Eternal Male.* by Sharif, Omar; and Guinchard, Marie-Therese. 184 p. illus. New York: Doubleday, 1977.

Omar Sharif's description of himself, "a Europeanized Middle Easterner," is called most accurate by his coauthor. She describes him as physically handsome, intelligent, off-handed, professionally committed and yet an antistar who is very much alone in life. In a largely factual recall, Sharif tells about himself in careful, restrained fashion revealing little of the inner man.

Some controversial views on the role of women are offered along with his impressions of such costars as Streisand, Loren, Bergman, and Gardner.

The book is nicely illustrated, but there is no index or filmography. Omar Sharif has never been a generator of American enthusiasm. This rambling autobiography will help to maintain his "so what" status.

1624 *Ethnic American Minorities.* edited by Johnson, Harry A. 304 p. New York: R. R. Bowker, 1976.

This volume is an efficiently arranged mediagraphy thatdeals with four ethnic groups: the Afro-American; the Asian American, the Native Indian American, and the Spanish-speaking American. Each section is introduced by an essay which describes the group and its role in America. Bibliographies are provided for the Afro, Asian and Indian sections while notes are given for all except the Indian chapter.

The final portion of the book deals with other ethnic minorities in America's history—American Jews, migrant Americans, Eskimos, European immigrants, etc. No notes or bibliography are offered here.

The nonprint listing which follows each section is arranged by medium: films, filmstrips, slides, transparencies, audio recordings, video cassettes, and finally, study prints/pictures /posters/graphics. The annotations provided for each title listed are largely descriptive although some judgmental words/phrases appear occasionally. At least one distributor or producer is noted in each case and an address directory is appended.

A listing of all the media mentioned throughout the book is arranged alphabetically by title, and a general subject index concludes the book.

The volume can be appreciated for two strong reasons—its choice of subjects that have not had published mediagraphy attention heretofore, and its intelligent arrangement which affords easy efficient retrieval of information. This is a valuable and pertinent reference. Highly recommended.

1625 *Ethnic Film and Filmstrip Guide for Libraries and Media Centers.* by Wynar, Lubomyr R.; and Buttlar, Lois. 277 p. Littleton, Colo.: Libraries Unlimited, 1980.

This guide is made up of five parts: an introductory essay that treats the problems of bibliographic control selection and evaluation; a listing (140 entries) of multi-ethnic films and filmstrips; a listing (1252 entries) of ethnic films and filmstrips arranged by ethnic group; a producer/distributor list; and a general title index. Entries were obtained from 504 questionnaires sent to producers, distributors, libraries, archives, ethnic periodicals, etc., and from standard audiovisual reference sources—NICEM, EFLA, *Educational Film Locator*, Library of Congress catalogs, etc. Annotations were derived by actual viewing or from published reviews in journals such as *Previews, Booklist, Film News*, etc. The result of this extensive search is a valuable collection of titles arranged under about 46 different ethnic groups—Armenian Americans, Eskimos, Irish Americans, Polish Americans, etc. The films (features and short films) are noted first, followed by the filmstrips (sound and silent). A large number of the films and filmstrips are about five American ethnic groups—Blacks, Indians, Jews, Asians and Hispanics. Individual entries consists of the standard data—format, time, sound, color, distributor, release date, price, recommended audience, and a short descriptive annotation.

The authors have performed a worthwhile service in collecting, arranging, and describing selected ethnic materials that are pertinent for educational use.

1626 *Ethnographic Film.* by Heider, Karl G. 166 p. Austin, Tex.: University of Texas Press, 1977.

Although the author prefers to describe ethnographic films rather than define them, he does state "...ethnographic films unite the art and skills of the filmmaker with the trained intellect and insights of the ethnographer." Well-known examples of the genre include NANOOK OF THE NORTH (1922), SONG OF CEYLON (1934), LOUISIANA STORY (1948), DEAD BIRDS (1963), and DESERT PEOPLE (1969). After the descriptive introductory section, Heider's text offers a history. Following are a discussion of the attributes of ethnographic film, a section on making the films, and a final statement on how the films may be used in teaching. A filmography, a bibliography and an index complete the volume. A few diagrams appear but there are no illustrations in the book.

For specialists and scholars, the volume will offer information and insight on a film genre that is almost unidentified in the literature. Teachers will find the suggestions for use to be particularly valuable. Recommended.

1627 *Evaluating Motion Pictures.* edited by Greater Hartford Forum. 65 p. paper Hartford, Conn.: Greater Hartford Forum, 1967.

A report of the 7th annual Forum, the theme of which was "Evaluating Motion Pictures."

1628 *An Evaluative Guide to 16mm Mental Health Films.* compiled by MHMEP Staff. 71 p. paper Springfield, Va.: The Mental Health Media Evaluation Project, 1977.

During 1976 and 1977 the Mental Health Media Evaluation Project searched the 16mm film industry for films pertinent to public mental health education. Criteria for inclusion in this final listing included: (1) 16mm format; (2) less then 60 minutes in length; (3) content applicable to public mental health education; (4) released since 1966 or considered a recognized classic; (5) available in U.S. for rental, lease or purchase. Films on alcoholism or drugs were not considered because of earlier publications in these areas.

Approximately 500 titles were viewed and evaluated. Those films with a rating of "good" or above are included here. Entries are arranged alphabetically by title and offer running time, color, grade level, availability, release date, descriptive annotation, suggestions for use and evaluator's comments. Access is by several subject indexes and a list of distributors in included.

This is an excellent reference volume that can be used in a wide variety of institutional settings. Recommended.

1629 *Eve's Hollywood.* by Babitz, Eve. 271 p. paper New York: Dell, 1975.

Eve's Hollywood is quite different from the mythical studio setting in most people's imagination. Her father was a studio musician, her classmates were fu-

ture stars (Yvette Mimieux), her dates were notorious figures (Johnny Stompanato, Bobby Beausoleil of the Manson Family), she swam in Bernard Herrmann's pool, and became disenchanted after meeting Tony Curtis in person. It is difficult to determine whether this is a biography or a novel which uses real people and locations. In any event, its pertinence to film history is minimal.

1630 *Even Elvis.* by Thornton, Mary Ann. illus. Harrison, Ark.: New Leaf, 1979.

1631 EVENTS. by Baker, Fred. 128 p. paper illus. New York: Grove Press, 1970.

Script of the 1970 film directed by Baker.

1632 *Every Day's a Matinee.* by Wilk, Max. 288 p. illus. New York: W. W.Norton, 1975.

Although the emphasis is on television and the theatre, there is enough attention given to films and film performers in this book to warrant its consideration here. In autobiographical order, Wilk recalls incidents and anecdotes about the famous folk he has met during his career as a writer for the several media. He claims responsibility for scouting the original Maltese Falcon and Perry Mason stories. As a young man he was with the show, "This is the Army," on tour and in Hollywood. Later he was assigned to an Air Force motion picture unit. A final chapter is devoted to Leland Hayward with whom Wilk had a long professional association.

Probably the volume is exactly what the author intended — a light, entertaining memoir by a fellow who is anxious to share his enjoyment of show business with the reader. Acceptable.

1633 *Every Frenchman Has One.* by De Havilland, Olivia. 202 p. paper New York: Random House, 1962.

With little emphasis on her films, the only reason for listing this volume is that it does reflect the wit and charm of its authoress. If Miss De Havilland ever decides to write about her professional career, the resulting book should be something quite special.

1634 *Every Other Inch a Lady.* by Lillie, Beatrice; and Philip, John; and Brough, James. 360 p. illus. Garden City, N.Y.: Doubleday, 1972.

There is little mention of her films in this disappointing autobiography of Beatrice Lillie. Although she mentions EXIT SMILING (1926) and DR. RHYTHM (1938) briefly, she neglects ARE YOU THERE? (1930), ON APPROVAL (1943), AROUND THE WORLD IN 80 DAYS (1956), and THOROUGHLY MODERN MILLIE (1967). Nor does the book make up in biographical excellence what it lacks in coverage of her career. No valid picture of a woman or a personality emerges and a series of thinly connected stories and anecdotes is offered as a life story. Further evidence of the lack of concern in creating the book is its lack of an index. Over a period of years Miss Lillie was reported from time to time as accepting royalty advances from her publishers, but not writing much. Two co-authors and a dull book are further evidence of her disinterest. Not recommended.

1635 *Everybody Loves Somebody Sometime (Especially Himself).: The Story of Dean Martin and Jerry Lewis.* by Marx, Arthur. 320 p. illus. New York: Hawthorn, 1974.

This dual biography of Martin and Lewis treats their careers as individuals and as team members. It tells how each man began, how they met, their first night club act, the synthesis of the successful team, their breakup, and the subsequent careers that each had. The author emphasizes the team period and blames Lewis' ego for the separation. Their films are recalled along with the antics that were part of their stage and television appearances. Illustrations, a bibliography, and an index complete the volume. Acceptable.

1636 *Everyone's Gone to the Movies.* by Ingham, Gordon. 46 p. paper illus. Auckland, New Zealand: Minerva, 1973.

Deals with the 60 cinemas of Auckland and some others.

1637 *Everything and Nothing: The Dorothy Dandridge Tragedy.* by Dandridge, Dorothy; and Conrad, Earl. 215 p. illus. New York: Abelard-Schulman, 1970.

This autobiography completed by Earl Conrad details the conflicts of a black actress who was successful in the white entertainment world. The early racial battles and problems, the distinction of the Academy Award nomination in 1954, and the subsequent decline are covered. Miss Dandridge writes quite frankly about herself, naming her lovers, and trying to understand what happened to her and why.

The Nicholas Brothers, Phil Moore, Harry Belafonte, Harry Cohn, and Otto Preminger are some of the men who figure prominently in this star's life. The dramatic ingredients included in this autobiography deserve a better treatment. In spite of an attempt as sensationalism via shocking confessions, the final picture of Miss Dandridge is a rather sympathetic one. Recommended.

1638 *The Evolution of Character Portrayals in the Films of Sidney Poitier: 1950-1978.* by Kelley, Samuel L. 286 p. New York: Garland, 1982.

1639 *Evolution of Style in the Early Work on Dziga Vertov.* by Feldman, Seth R. New York: Arno, 1977.

Written in 1975 at the State University of New York at Buffalo in partial fulfillment of the doctoral program, this study explores the film work of Dziga Vertov, centering on the period from 1917 to 1925. Through a detailed examination of his films and writings, the author analyzes Vertov's contributions to the growth of the nonfiction film in light of his political stand during post-revolutionary Russia. An appendix provides the reader with selected shot lists from the "Kinonedelia" newsreels. This title is included in the *Dissertations on Film* series.

1640 *Exam Questions and Answers on Sound Motion Picture Projection.* by Cameron, James R. paper illus. Coral Gables, Fla.: Cameron Pub. Co.

Contains examples of questions asked by various examining boards for a projectionist's operating license, and answers to them. National Learning Publishers in New York City distributes two volumes in a Civil Service Exam Passbook Series: *Motion Picture Operator* and *Film Editor*, both written by Jack Rudman.

1641 *An Examination of Narrative Structure in Four Films By Frank Capra.* by Rose, Brian Geoffrey. New York: Arno, 1980.

The four films examined in this title from the *Dissertations on Film* series are MR DEEDS GOES TO TOWN (1936), MR. SMITH GOES TO WASHINGTON (1939), MEET JOHN DOE (1941), and IT'S A WONDERFUL LIFE (1946).

1642 *Existential Errands.* by Mailer, Norman. 365 p. Boston: Little, Brown, 1972.

This collection of Mailer's writings contains two articles on film: "Some Dirt in the Talk" and "A Course in Film-Making."

1643 EXODUS. by Ryan, Tom. 64 p. paper illus. New York: Random House, 1960.

The subtitle of this souvenir book is "A Report by Tom Ryan" and it gives the first portion a distinctive newspaper format. Each page has a typical headline such as "Exodus Location Search to Begin," or "Preminger Finds His Karen." Cast and production credits form the centerpiece of the book and precede a photo preview of the 1960 film itself. An admirable attempt to do something different; it succeeds rather well.

1644 THE EXORCIST—The Strange Story Behind the Film. by Newman, Howard. illus. New York: Pinnacle, 1974.

Newman was the unit publicist for THE EXORCIST (1973), and a devotion to his craft shows here as he converts routine mishaps into diabolical occult curses—which always make better copy. By far the more interesting sections of this book tell how the special effects, make-up, camerawork, etc., were achieved for the film. Much of this material was covered in far more satisfactory accounts by Blatty and Travers and Reiff. Acceptable.

1645 *Expanded Cinema.* by Youngblood, Gene. 432 p. paper illus. New York: Dutton, 1970.

Take an exciting topic, and 60 full-color pictures among the 284 illustrations provided, and the potential for creating a major contribution to film study is present. The author's text more than meets the challenge. Exploring new forms of cinema such as computer films, laser movies, and multi-screen shows, the author looks at not only the technology of the expanded cinema, but also the thinking and creativity that goes into these messages.

The book includes some interviews and many analyses which are not always written within a layman's comprehension; terms such as "synaesthetic cinema," "cybernetic cinema," and "intermedia and holographic cinema" are chapter topics. This is a most important volume in film literature and is a candidate for classic status. It is difficult reading but nevertheless essential.

1646 *Expanding Media.* edited by Boyle, Deirdre. 343 p. Phoenix, Ariz.: Oryx, 1977.

Using only post-1969 articles, Deirdre Boyle has designed this anthology to answer some of the philosophical and practical questions raised by and about media. She has arranged her material under eight headings: why media?, selection and evaluation, programming, production, audiovisual equipment, standards and cataloging, education, and media politics. Several articles deal specifically with film.

As promised in the introduction, many of the issues, problems, and concerns of the media professional are addressed in the articles. Selection of them is impressive, resulting in an outstanding anthology. For anyone concerned with media, this volume is required reading. Highly recommended.

1647 *Experiment in the Film.* edited by Manvell, Roger. 285 p. illus. New York: Arno Press, 1970 (1949).

A series of articles on experimental or avant-garde films in France, America, Russia, Germany, and England. Contributors include Manvell, Lewis Jacobs, Hans Richter, Edgar Anstey and others. An index of experimental films is given.

1648 *Experiment in Totality.* by Moholy-Nagy, Sibyl. 259 p. paper illus. Cambridge, Mass.: M.I.T. Press, 1969.

1649 *Experimental Animation.* by Russett, Robert; and Starr, Cecile. 224 p. paper illus. New York: Van Nostrand Reinhold, 1976.

Subtitled "A Visual Anthology," this book offers articles, interviews, and statements concerning 38 filmmakers who are noted for their achievement in the experimental animation film genre. Arranged in groups under such headings as pioneers, independent animators, contemporary imagists, experiments in sound, etc. the articles are preceded by an introduction in each case. Supporting the collection are a glossary, notes, a bibliography, a recommended filmography, film distribution sources, a film title-filmmaker index, and almost 300 illustrations. The latter have been carefully reproduced and placed throughout the book. They include portraits, stills, frames, strips, and pictures of animation equipment.

The success of any anthology depends largely on the careful selection of content. In this instance both the text and the visuals have been chosen with intelligence, taste, and sound critical judgment. Quality film periodicals and original writing provide the text while the listed picture credits and sources number several hundred.

The book is a multi-purpose volume that can serve

as a reader, a manual of suggested animation techniques, collective biography, or reference. Highly recommended.

1650   *Experimental Cinema.* by Curtis, David. 168 p. illus. New York: Universe Books, 1971.

This volume on the avant-garde film gives an overview of the history and development of this particular film form. The author treats the silent films of the twenties (Surrealism, Dadaism), Hollywood films of the thirties and forties, the "underground films" of the fifties and sixties, and the current "expanded cinema" movements.

1651   *Experimental Cinema 1930-1934.* by Amberg, Dr. George. New York, Arno Press, 1970.

Experimental Cinema was the name of a film journal published in the early thirties. Its subtitle was "A Monthly Projecting Important International Film Manifestations." After a few issues its publication became erratic and over four years, five issues were produced. Lewis Jacobs was one of the editors throughout. This volume reproduces the 5 issues with good technical quality. Primarily of interest to the dedicated cinema enthusiast, student or historian.

1652   *Experiments on Comprehension and Impact of Movies among Children and Young People.* by Minkkinen, Sirkka. 37 p. paper Helsinki: OY Yliesradio AB, 1969.

A research report from the Section for Long-Range Planning of the Finnish Broadcasting Company. Includes some tables.

1653   *Explorations in National Cinemas.* edited by Lawton, Ben; and Staiger, Janet. 160 p. paper Pleasantville, N.Y.: Redgrave, 1977.

This is part one of the *1977 Film Studies Annual.* The second part is entitled, *Film: Historical-Theoretical Speculations.* Both are intended "to reflect a serious, scholarly, nonpartisan approach to film studies."

As a product of an annual conference, this anthology contains the typical articles. Analyses of THE LAST MOVIE (1971), MEDIUM COOL (1969), FORT APACHE (1948), BARRY LYNDON (1975), CLOSELY WATCHED TRAINS (1967), IVAN THE TERRIBLE (1943), LA SALAMANDRE (1971), THE WHITE SHEIK

(1952), TOBY DAMMIT (1967), and THE CLOWNS (1971) are included. It should be noted that not all the articles are a direct result of the conference.

A previous annual (1976) emphasized film theory along with the French, German, and Italian film. These volumes are written and designed for a small audience of film scholars. In this respect they are quite successful.

1654   *Exploring the Film.* by Kuhns, William; and Stanley, Robert. 190 p. paper illus. Dayton, Ohio: George A. Pflaum, 1968.

One of the newer film text books designed for today's students, this one should serve as a model for other publications to emulate. It is dedicated to the serious study of motion pictures, and by discussing all the elements and aspects of film in an informative, enthusiastic, and intelligent manner, it will persuade and reinforce its readers in their attitude towards film. Illustrations are used with wisdom and taste, and a pop-art McLuhan approach is evident throughout. Highly recommended.

1655   *Expo 67 Films.* by Siskind, Jacob. 40 p. paper illus. Montreal: Tundra, 1967.

Films shown at Expo 67 are noted.

1656   *Exposing Cine Film.* by Smethurst, Philip C. 84 p. illus. London: Link House, 1938.

This older manual on cinematography carried the subtitle "Exposure Difficulties Solved." Smethurst was a very active technical writer during the thirties and this particular book was already in its 9th edition.

1657   *Exposure to Films and School Adjustment.* by Sennton, Olena. 287 p. illus. Stockholm: Almqvist and Wiksell, 1965.

A set of studies in educational psychology dealing with cinema attendance and film violence preference as related to emotional adjustment and school achievement. Includes diagrams and tables.

1658   *Express to Hollywood.* by McLaglen, Victor. 287 p. illus. London: Jarrolds, 1934.

An autobiography in which the last two short chapters are devoted to films.

1659 THE EXTERMINATING ANGEL, NAZARIN, LOS OLVIDADOS. by Bunuel, Luis. 299 p. paper illus. New York: Simon and Schuster, 1972.

Contains scripts, articles, cast and production credits for: THE EXTERMINATING ANGEL (1962); NAZARIN (1959); and LOS OLVIDADOS (1950).

1660 *Eye, Film, and Camera in Color Photography.* by Evans, Ralph M. 410 p. illus. New York: John Wiley, 1959.

The theme of this volume is that the camera does not always record reality. Therefore, the photographer must understand the vagaries of photography and the psychology of vision. Written by a Kodak specialist, the book addresses itself to this problem and is both informative and provocative.

1661 *The Eye of History.* by Pfragner, Julius. 240 p. New York: Rand McNally, 1964.

This is a translation from German, and is intended for secondary school collections. A blend of fact and fiction is used to relate the development of motion photography from magic lantern to the sound film. An index is offered to help identify the actual persons from the fictional. The work betrays its European origin but still offers technical and historical data of value.

1662 *F. Scott Fitzgerald and the American Dream.* by Fahey, William A. illus. New York: Crowell, 1973.

Noted here as only one of many available volumes on F. Scott Fitzgerald which deal with his Hollywood experiences and his relationship with Sheila Graham.

1663 *The Fabulous Fanny.* by Katkov, Norman. 337 p. illus. New York: Knopf, 1953.

Although Fanny Brice was known mostly for her stage appearances in many editions of the Ziegfeld Follies and for her later work as Baby Snooks on radio, she did appear in several films. They include, not surprisingly, THE GREAT ZIEGFELD (1935) and THE ZIEGFELD FOLLIES (1945). Her other films were MY MAN (1929), NIGHT CLUB (1929), BE YOURSELF (1930), and EVERYBODY SING (1938). The films get almost no attention here.

Readers of this rather bland biography of a most unique personality will inevitably compare it with the story related in FUNNY GIRL (1968) and FUNNY LADY (1975)—in addition to noting some rather strong similarities in the life, career and temperament of Barbra Streisand.

1664 *The Fabulous Fantasy Films.* by Rovin, Jeff. 271 p. illus. New York: A. S. Barnes, 1977.

For this volume specific distinction is made in the separation of fantasy films from horror and science fiction films. To the author "fantasy" implies man's imagination unrestrained. Although he does include a few borderline cases, Rovin remains relatively true to his selection criteria and describes over 6000 films in which common sense is ignored while the viewer's imagination is expanded. The films are arranged under 17 general headings such as the ghost, angels and death, witchcraft and voodoo, the devil, mythology, etc. The cast and credits for 500 fantasy films are appended, as are a series of short interviews (George Pal, Tony Randall, Robert Wise, Ray Harryhausen, William Castle, and Ricou Browning). An index and more than 400 illustrations complete the volume.

The text is skillfully written with critical comment and descriptive narrative nicely balanced. Selection of the films and their accompanying stills is excellent.Although much of this material has been covered in earlier books, the blending of subject, style and scholarship makes this a notable volume. Recommended.

1665 *The Fabulous Fifties.* edited by New York Times Staff. illus. New York: Arno.

The era of Presley, Monroe, Dean and GREASE (1978) as reflected in selected front pages of *The New York Times*. Over 300 illustrations appear in this oversized volume.

1666 *The Fabulous Fondas.* by Brough, James. 296 p. illus. New York: David McKay, 1973.

Depending to a rather large degree on previously published material about the Fondas, author Brough has synthesized an integrated biography of the trio. Since this is an unofficial biography, he has had to rely on the previous published material and some interviews with persons acquainted with the subjects.

The private life of the Fondas is complex in many ways. Marriages, suicides, accidents, deaths, and divorces seem to have been companions to the families that are related and interrelated in this account. At times the reader may yearn for a genealogy chart.

The final portraits which emerge are predictable, with Henry as a private man hiding behind the actor mask of a solid, strong American male; Jane as the sexually liberated woman who fights for unpopular causes; and Peter as the drug-using rebel who is often a combination of the other two. A small number of illustrations are offered in one section and the volume is indexed.

Some errors in the book are evident. The dust cover mentions THE CAINE MUTINY (1954) as one of Henry Fonda's films—it was not. WELCOME TO HARD TIMES (1967) is listed in the text and the index as WELCOME TO HOUND TIME. Brough states Mike Nichols became a "hot ticket" director because of CATCH 22 (1970) and CARNAL KNOWLEDGE (1971)—try THE GRADUATE (1967) and WHO'S AFRAID OF VIRGINIA WOOLF? (1966) instead. A much more satisfying total view of the Fondas can be found in John Springer's picture book. However, for those readers who prefer a greater emphasis on their complex private lives than on their films, this volume will be satisfying. Acceptable.

1667   *The Fabulous Life of Bing Crosby.* by Carpozi, George, Jr. 217 p. paper illus. New York: Manor Books, 1977.

The reader should get some warning when the table of contents lists chapter titles such as "Enter Old Ski Nose," "Going My Way—to an Academy Award," "Brando K.O.'s Bing," and "A Girl At Last," among others. This biography was written for those middle-Americans who loved Bing Crosby. Using numerous quotes from a wide variety of sources, the author has reconstructed Crosby's life and career. The rift between the first four sons and Crosby is emphasized along with the dramatic marriage to Dixie Lee. Some illustrations are added but are not correlated to the text.

This is a typical Carpozi work, put together following the subject's death. For the nondiscriminating reader.

1668   *The Fabulous Orson Welles.* by Noble, Peter. 276 p. illus. London: Hutchinson, 1956.

Here is a full length biography of Welles written in the mid-fifties that presents a challenge to the many current and announced books on Welles. Written by Peter Noble in a frankly affectionate style rich in anecdotes, the book presents a most positive view of Welles (concentrating on his professional life), and forgiving him continually, blaming others for many unfulfilled projects.

It should be noted that major films such as TOUCH OF EVIL (1958) and THE TRIAL (1962), were made by Welles after this book was published. The illustrations are exceptional—beautifully reproduced, intelligently selected, and wisely placed to complement the text. There is an index. This is an admirable biography of a most unique artist and self-creation that is highly recommended.

1669   *The Fabulous Thirties: Italian Cinema 1929-1944.* by Apra, Adriano; and Pistagnesi, Patricia. 115 p. paper illus. New York: Rizzoli International (Electra), 1979.

This oversized critical review of Italian films from 1929-1944 also contains short biographies of 15 Italian filmmakers.

1670   *The Fabulous Tom Mix.* by Mix, Olive Stokes; and Heath, Eric 177 p. illus. Englewood Cliffs, N. J.: Prentice-Hall, 1957.

A partial biography of Tom Mix by his widow containing good descriptions of horse riding, cowboy stunts and circuses. Attention is given to the making of Westerns during the silent film era.

1671   A FACE IN THE CROWD. by Schulberg, Budd. 172 p. New York: Random House, 1957.

Script of 1957 film directed by Kazan. Contains cast credits with an introduction by Elia Kazan and a preface by Budd Schulberg.

1672   *The Face on the Cutting Room Floor: The Story of Movie and Television Censorship.* by Schumach, Murray. 305 p. illus. New York: William Morrow & Co., 1964.

By detailing the various factors that cause, surround, and interpret film censorship, Schumach provides an informal, nonchronological history. Using many actual instances of films whose final form was changed because of censorship, the book divulges much data that is relatively unknown. Topics such as the scandals, the code, the pressure groups including the federal government, and the blacklists are treated. There is only one short chapter on television censorship. Included are some comments on how foreign countries handle the question of censorship, along with a reprinting of the complete motion picture code.

The author relates his material in a light style. The

illustrations are selected with taste and are clearly reproduced. Reading the many abuses committed in the name of censorship will make the reader feel glad about the demise of the code. This book may be read as entertainment or as history—either way, it is excellent and highly recommended.

1673 FACE TO FACE. by Bergman, Ingmar. 118 p. paper illus. New York: Pantheon, 1976.

Script of the 1976 film written and directed by Ingmar Bergman.

1674 FACES. by Cassavetes, John. 319 p. paper illus. New York: New American Library, 1970.

Script of 1968 film directed by Cassavetes. Contains cast credits and three atrticles: 1) "FACES from My Point of View" (Al Ruban), 2) "Equipment Used," and 3) "Editing Notes."

1675 *Faces, Forms, Films: The Artistry of Lon Chaney.* by Anderson, Robert G. 216 p. illus. New York: A. S. Barnes, 1971.

Since there is very little about Lon Chaney available in books, any new volume should be happily anticipated. While there are reservations about the totality of this effort, it is rewarding in many ways.

First, it is profusely illustrated with examples of Chaney's many film roles and his various makeups in them. It also has a detailed filmography, and indexes to both text and illustrations.

A biographical sketch of sorts begins the volume, but it can scarcely be called a biography. The author's approach throughout is uniformly positive and noncritical. The life story is related in factual terms and there is little attempt to explain the "person" of Chaney. The films and film roles receive the greatest attention. At times the text seems extremely repetitive, with explanations of the same characters and the same films given in several different sections of the book. The frequent comments about the perfection of Chaney's makeup raise questions about the author's bias. As an attempt to describe the work of Lon Chaney, though, it is interesting and enjoyable. Recommended.

1676 *The Faces of Hollywood.* by Bull, Clarence; and Lee, Raymond. 256 p. illus. New York: A. S. Barnes, 1968.

For several decades Clarence Bull was the photographer in charge of portraits at the Metro-Goldwyn-Mayer studio. This volume is a collection of some of his portrait work. Consisting mostly of famous and familiar faces, the photographic artistry is so great that one wishes he had included many more. Where, for example, are Astaire, Nat Pendelton, the Marx Brothers, Van Johnson, Peter Lawford and other who had long tenure at Metro? But this is minor quibbling. The gallery of portraits provided is so rewarding that no objection can be made.

Reproduction of the photos is excellent in most cases. Some are printed a bit darkly and the viewer may wonder if this was the photographer's intent or careless quality control in the printing. Some short narrative consisting of memoirs and reminiscences accompanies a few chapters at the book's beginning. This text is forgettable but the pictures throughout the book are not. Not an essential book, but highly recommended for most reader-viewers.

1677 *Faces on Film.: Newcomers and Old Timers on the Big Screen.* by Ronan, Margaret. 144 p. illus. New York: Scholastic Book Services, 1970.

In this gallery of verbal and visual portraits the author has selected "Outstanding Screen Personalities" and arranged them categorically. For example, "The Good Guys" section consists of John Wayne, Gregory Peck, Charlton Heston, Anthony Quinn and Jim Brown. Other section titles are Superstars, Anti-Heroes, Merchants of Menace, New Faces, The British Are Coming, Tried and True, and It's A Family Affair. A narrative links the few short paragraphs that each performer receives. More fan magazine blurb than biography; the text mentions hobbies, a few film titles, wive's names, quotations, etc. An illustration has been selected for each performer and the quality of reproduction is acceptable.

The challenge for a volume such as this is, first, with the selection of material, and, next, with the treatment of it. In both instances this volume is wanting. Selection includes Bela Lugosi (no films at all since 1959—and no major one since THE BODY SNATCHERS in 1945), the Sinatras (who else but Frank?), the Dean Martins (who else but Dean?), Tommy Steele, Kyle Johnson and Christopher Jones (who?), etc. Treatment includes placing Patty Duke along with Doris Day, Robert Mitchum, Kirk Douglas as "Tried and True," listing Karloff's films as "over 30" in number—he made more than 150 films, etc. The final attempt to introduce material on "How to Evaluate Films" seems like atonement for what has preceded it. Some strong material has been weakened by a sugarized approach and a careless selection and presentation. Not acceptable.

1678   *Fact and Fiction (A Series).* 86 p. illus. New York: Franklin Watts, 1980.

This series of books, written for a juvenile audience, uses the difference between fact and fiction as its overall theme. Titles include: *Apes in Fact and Fiction* by Gilda Berger, *Mad Scientists in Fact and Fiction* by Melvin Berger, *Mummies in Fact and Fiction* by Arnold Madison, *Robots in Fact and Fiction* by Melvin Berger and *Space Travel in Fact and Fiction* by Keith Deutsch.

The fiction in the title includes films, and although the scope is limited, there is enough coverage in each instance to suggest the general film treatment of the title subject. Many stills from films are used to illustrate the ideas of the text. When used in the proper context with a knowledgeable leader, the books can encourage some intelligent young adult discussions about the interrelationships between science, film, and literature.

1679   *Factfiles — A Series.* Washington, D.C.: American Film Institute, 1978- .

The American Film Institute publishes a series of short documents on a variety of topics in film and television. Intended as references, they offer factual information. Titles include: *Film and Television Periodicals in English; Careers in Film and Television; Student Film Festivals and Awards; Guide to Classroom Use of Film; Women and Film/ Television; Children and Film/Television; Movie and TV Nostalgia; Film Music; Animation; Third World Cinema; Film/TV: A Research Guide; Film/TV: Grants, Scholarships, Special Programs.*

1680   *Facts on File.* New York: Facts on File, Inc., 1940-.

A partial film reference, this index to world events is published weekly, and digests the news reports from several metropolitan daily newspapers. An annual bound volume is published as is a cumulated five-year index. Look under the subject heading of "Motion Pictures" for reports on such film topics as censorship, obituaries, releases, etc.

1681   *The Factual Film, An Arts Inquiry Report.* 295 p. London: Oxford University Press, 1947.

The uses, recommendations, and policies for the nontheatrical film in London (documentary, educational, news and other types of films) are treated in this work. In addition to a glossary, bibliography and an index, there is an appendix which includes:

1) the British film industry; 2) censorship; 3) the film in Scotland; and 4) the Film Board of Canada.

1682   *Fair Lady.* by Beaton, Cecil 128 p. illus. New York: Holt, Rinehart & Winston, 1964.

In 1962, when Cecil Beaton was hired as costume and set designer for the film of MY FAIR LADY, he began a diary. This book includes portions of the diary text, along with line sketches and photographs of the actors, and relates all of the tedious work, the constant corrections, and the tensions that are indigenous to making film musicals.

The author's style is martini-dry, and there is sophistication, wit, and intelligence in the comments. The author favors certain personalities and devotes a major share of the book to them. Others receive limited attention. No index is offered. A designer's view of filmmaking, this volume conveys to the reader the tremendous effort and detail necessary to create certain moods and effects in films via costuming.

1683   *The Fairbanks Album.* by Fairbanks, Jr., Douglas; and Schickel, Richard. 287 p. illus. Boston: Little Brown (A New York Graphic Society Book), 1975.

Douglas Fairbanks and his son, Douglas Fairbanks, Jr., are the subjects of this pictorial dual-biography. The photographs are taken mostly from the Fairbanks' private collection, but other sources contributed stills, newsphotos, etc. A connecting narrative is provided by Richard Schickel, who authored an earlier book on Fairbanks, Sr.

Both the public and the private persons are shown with much attention given to the father-son relationship. The approach is so careful that the book becomes a positive, loving, and forgiving memoir rather than any objective or critical assessment of the two colorful subjects.

The volume has been attractively produced with noticeable care given to the reproduction of the photographs. Many are models of clarity while others are simply beautiful to look at. There is no index but a chronology provides a career review and a filmography of sorts.

Schickel's skill in assessing the celebrity of Fairbanks, Sr. is used once again to good advantage; in addition it is extended to the son whose personality is apparently quite unlike his father's. The text combines with the 360 well-selected Fairbanks' photographs to form a tasteful and rewarding memoir. Recommended.

1684 *The Fairy Tale in Film.* edited by Green Tiger Press Staff. 16 p. paper illus. La Jolla, Calif.: Green Tiger Press, 1977.

This is the program for a film series presented in La Jolla, California in 1977. Some 15 films, derived from fairy tales, are described by illustration, cast, synopsis, etc.

1685 *The Fall Guy by the Duke's Double.* by Roberson, "Bad Chuck" ; and Thoene, Brodie. 352 p. illus. Seattle, Wash.: Hancock House, 1979.

John Wayne provides the foreword to this account of a stuntman who worked with the superstar for 30 years. The book is similar to *Stunt Man* in that it describes many of the choreographed stunts designed for films. Written in the rough language of the stunting profession, the text is rich in anecdotes and provides a view of the world of filmmaking that is largely unfamiliar.

1686 THE FALL OF THE ROMAN EMPIRE. by Durant, Will. 36 p. paper illus. New York: National Publishers, 1964.

Will Durant provides the prologue to this souvenir book. Each of the major cast members, producer Samuel Bronston and director Anthony Mann are spotlighted. One special section focuses on the Roman Forum, its ruins today and how it was recreated for the film. Another is immodestly titled, "Profile of an Epic." Other cast and production credits are given. Like the 1964 film, this book is rather dull and uninspired.

1687 *Falling for Stars.* by Hagner, John G. 126 p. illus. Hollywood: El Jon, 1965.

A Hollywood stuntman's account of his film work.

1688 *Fame: Portraits of Celebrated People.* by Benedict, Brad. paper illus. New York: Harmony/Crown, 1980.

A collection of 330 color portraits and caricatures by 50 different artists. The subjects include movie stars, political figures, rock singers, etc.

1689 *The Family Movie-Making Book.* by Garon, Jay; and Wilson, Morgan. 249 p. illus. Indianapolis: Bobbs Merrill, 1977.

This beginner's guide to the making of short films about the family is presented in attractive fashion. The text is divided into two general topics: a relatively short section entitled, "Getting Ready For the Camera," which discusses equipment, lighting, editing, titling, sound, and film terminology; a length-section which offers sample shooting scripts for films about holidays, short stories, family incidents, talkies, and historic days. A total of 34 scripts is offered in this section.

The volume is illustrated by both drawings and photographs. Since the explanations are clear and the directions are easy to follow, the beginning filmmaker will find the book a helpful aid in making his first visual stories and statements. Acceptable.

1690 *Famous Black Entertainers of Today.* by Abdul, Raoul. 159 p. illus. New York: Dodd, Mead & Co., 1974.

A collective biography written for young people, this volume profiles 18 personalities. Those who have appeared in films include Cicely Tyson, James Earl Jones, Diana Ross, Ben Vereen, Flip Wilson, Ron O'Neal and Melvin Van Peebles.

In most cases the story of the performer is told via a short interview. The content of the sketches is simple, noncontroversial, and inspirational. An attractive studio portrait of each subject appears in the center section and the volume is indexed. The selection of subjects is an excellent one and the appreciative treatment accorded each is appropriate. Acceptable for young people.

1691 *Famous Faces — A Photograph Album of Personal Reminiscences.* by Weissberger, L. Arnold. 443 p. illus. New York: Harry N. Abrams, 1977.

Looking through this volume will require considerable time, but the rewards are many if the reader is interested in or fascinated by the personalities who have dominated the arts since the end of World War II. The format is a deceptively simple one: Arnold Weissberger, a theatrical attorney, is allowing us to look at his personal photograph album, assembled from 1946 to 1971. He has included some 1500 informal pictures (some 642 are in full color) of people who have enjoyed celebrity status for varying periods of time — some for decades, others for a brief minute. The author has arranged his visuals chronologically and, for each period, a renowned personality makes some introductory comment. Beginning with Noel Coward, those providing such appreciations include Igor Stravinsky, Sir John Gielgud, Douglas Fairbanks, Jr., Dame Rebecca West, Anita

Loos, and Orson Welles. Each contributor is represented and rewarded with a special colored paper section upon which his or her photographs are mounted individually. A final biographical section not only identifies the many subjects but provides an index to the photographs. Thus, the faces that belong to such names as Ross Hunter, Paul Zindel, John Schlesinger, Sir Carol Reed, Alan Pakula, Anna Massey, Sidney Lumet, can easily be located.

Aside from satisfying the reader's curiosity about famous people, the volume can be enjoyed in a variety of other ways. It examines fame and its cost, in addition to providing a record of changing fashions, hair styles, and even social mores. An unusual visual treat enriched by a most appropriate commentary and a luxurious production. Recommended.

1692 *Famous Film Folk.* by Fox, Charles Donald. 256 p. illus. New York: George H. Doran, 1925.

Silent screen stars are shown in this "gallery of life." More than 242 illustrations along with half-page biographies are offered.

1693 *Famous Monsters of Filmland Strike Back.* by Ackerman, Forrest J. 162 p. (paper) illus. New York: Paperback Library, 1965.

A third collection that is even more irreverent than the first two, this paperback again offers over 150 stills from horror movies. A bit of repetition is noticeable but not enough to diminish reader enjoyment of this nonessential frivolity. Students and adults alike will delight in browsing over the stills. Note: see *The Best from Famous Monsters of Filmland* and *Son of Famous Monsters of Filmland.*

1694 *Famous Movie Detectives.* by Pitts, Michael R. 357 p. illus. Metuchen, N.J.: Scarecrow, 1979.

Michael Pitts deals with movie detectives and their films in this recall of some 24 celluloid sleuths. Each receives a critical review and description followed by a filmography. A bibliography of original detective novels/stories, an index, and some illustrations complete the book. Most of the characters treated are predictable, but Pitt does include Hildegarde Withers, Torchy Blane, Bill Crane, Craig Kennedy, J. G. Reeder, and Lemmy Caution.

Sherlock Holmes and Philip Marlowe are omitted since they are treated in other volumes by the same publisher. Certain materials similar to what is offered here appeared in a 1971 volume by Pitts' occasional coauthor, James Parish, called *The Great*

Movie Series.

1695 *Famous Names in Film.* by Robertson, Sheila. 48 p. illus. Hove England: Wayland, 1980.

A collective biography written for young readers.

1696 *Famous Negro Entertainers of Stage Screen and TV.* by Rollins, Charlemae. 122 p. illus. New York: Dodd, 1967.

These are short biographies designed for youthful readers. Although most of the subjects have appeared in films, only Poitier has achieved his fame via the film medium. Others such as Nat King Cole, Louis Armstrong, Eartha Kitt, Duke Ellington, etc. are stars in other areas of the entertainment world.

1697   *see 1696*

1698 *Famous People on Film.* by Emmens, Carol A. 365 p. illus. Metuchen, N.J.: Scarecrow, 1977.

A filmography of non-theatrical films which have famous people as their subject, this volume synthesizes much useful information. Arranged alphabetically by personality surname, the entries offer the usual data including a descriptive annotation and, when appropriate, a recommended grade level. Illustrations, a title index, a subject index, and a list of biographical feature films are included.

1699 *Famous Stars of Filmdom (Men).* by Hughes, Elinor. 342 p. illus. Freeport, N. Y.: Books for Libraries Press, 1970 (1932).

Biographies of some leading male stars of the twenties and thirties including Arliss, John Barrymore, Richard Barthelmess, Warner Baxter, Chaplin, Chevalier, Colman, Cooper, Fairbanks Sr. and Jr., Walter Houston, Jannings, Mix, William Powell, and Will Rogers. The text is pedantic and factual. The photograph reproduction is poor, and the reader may wonder why this one was given a new life.

1700 *Famous Stars of Filmdom(Women).* by Hughes, Elinor. 341 p. illus. Freeport, N. Y.: Books for Libraries Press, 1970 (1931).

Biographies of some leading female stars of the twenties and thirties including Constance Bennett, Ruth Chatterton, Claudette Colbert, Dolores Costello, Joan Crawford, Bebe Daniels, Marlene Dietrich, Marie Dressler, Kay Francis, Greta Garbo, Janet Gaynor, Ann Harding, Mary Pickford, Norma Sherer, and Gloria Swanson. The text is inane, romantic, and external and the photographs are poorly reproduced. If this one can be resurrected, anything is possible.

1701 *Fanfare: The Confessions of a Press Agent.* by Maney, Richard. 374 p. paper New York: Harper, 1957.

Maney's clients and associates included Tallulah Bankhead, Laurence Olivier, Billy Rose and other colorful show business folk.

1702 FANTASTIC VOYAGE. 18 p. paper illus. Hollywood: 20th Century Fox, 1966.

A souvenir book which should be much better than it is when one considers the possibilities offered by the 1966 film it describes. After the story outline there are accounts of the preparation made for the filming and an article about "The Incredible World of Inner Space." Some of the pages are arranged in a fold-out format which offers no great advantage to the reader, merely awkwardness in handling. Color photographs are carelessly reproduced. Cast and production credits are noted. The neglect that characterized the handling of the film is repeated here.

1703 *Fantasy Films and Their Fiends.* by Jones, Jack Ray. 131 p. paper illus. Oklahoma City,1964.

Called a "Collector's Edition," this volume deals with films of the supernatural.

1704 *FAO Film Loan Catalogue.* 277 p. New York: Unipub, 1980.

A UNESCO catalog from the Food and Agriculture Organization (FAO).

1705 FAR FROM THE MADDING CROWD. by Freiman, Ray. 32 p. paper illus. New York: National Publishers, 1967.

Bergen Evans provides the introductory essay, entitled "About Far From the Madding Crowd," in this souvenir book. A map of Essex during Thomas Hardy's time is reproduced. The remainder of the book is devoted to cast and film shots, many of which show director John Schlesinger in action. Cast and production credits are given.

1706 *Farrah.* by Burstein, Patricia. 160 p. paper illus. New York: Signet, 1977.

An unauthorized biography which appeared at the height of Farrah Fawcett-Major's popularity as one of "Charlie's Angels" on TV, this volume does not deal with her films. Recent starring roles in SOMEBODY KILLED HER HUSBAND (1979), SUNBURN (1980), and SATURN 3 (1980), have not added to her popularity. This biography will not help much either.

1707 *Farrah and Lee.* by Berman, Connie. 151 p. paper illus. New York: Ace, 1977.

An original paperback designed to capitalize on the fleeting popularity of two television personalities who have not succeeded nearly so well in films — Farrah Fawcett and Lee Majors.

1708 *Fassbinder.* by Rayns, Tony. 62 p. paper London: British Film Institute (Zoetrope in U.S.), 1976.

This anthology examines selected works of the controversial German director, Rainer Werner Fassbinder, as it also presents a short survey of the postwar German cinema. Fassbinder's work in the theatre is discussed, and there are notes on form and syntax in his films. Closing sections are devoted to a 1974 interview, a filmography, and a bibliography.

The impressive creative output of Fassbinder has dwarfed the few English language evaluations of his work currently available. This volume helps to even that discrepancy and serves to introduce the reader to the most widely known German film director since Leni Riefenstahl. Recommended.

1709 *Father Goose: The Story of Mack Sennett.* by Fowler, Gene. 407 p. illus. New York: Covici-Friede, 1934.

This older biography of Mack Sennett is a literary heritage from a writer of talent and experience. Although it is flawed by some imaginary conversations, much of it has a style, wit and compassion absent from recent biographies. It seems a safe assumption that Fowler knew Sennett, for he presents him here as a human being with many faults and a few virtues. Figuring largely in the man's history are Griffith, Chaplin, Arbuckle, and Mable Normand.

The illustrations are old-fashioned, rather unusual, and reproduced with the clarity one associates with certain silent films. There is no index. This is a totally enjoyable biography.

1710 *Fatty.* by Fine, Gerald. 224 p. paper illus. Los Angeles: Gerald Fine Productions, 1971.

This sensationalized biography was written with the aid of Minta Durfee Arbuckle, Fatty's widow. Many fascinating illustrations accompany the popularized account of the comedian's life and career.

1711 *The Fatty Arbuckle Case.* by Guild, Leo. 156 p. paper New York: Paperback Library, 1962.

An account of the sensational happenings and the subsequent trial that ended the silent comedian's acting career. After 1921 he directed a few comedies under another name but never appeared before the cameras again.

1712 *Faulkner: A Biography.* by Blotner, Joseph. 2 vols. illus. New York: Random House, 1977.

A massive two-volume authorized biography of William Faulkner that deals with his experiences in Hollywood.

1713 *Faulkner and Film.* by Kawin, Bruce F. 192 p. paper illus. New York: Frederick Ungar, 1977.

The relationship between Faulkner and film exists on two levels. The first is the influence of a novelist on filmmakers; the second, and more apparent, is the use of his novels as film material and the fact that he himself worked sporadically as a script consultant/screenwriter from 1932 to 1954. Using interviews, script analyses, original material from studio vaults, and other research, Bruce Kawin concludes that Faulkner's importance to film history is assured by the influence of his fiction rather than by the quality of the Faulkner films.

The author has composed a scholarly essay that combines biography and criticism to explore another aspect of the relationship between film and literature. His thoroughness is evidenced not only in the carefully prepared text but by the inclusion of meticulous chapter notes, a detailed Faulkner filmography, a center pictorial section, and an index. Two unknown and unproduced scripts written by Faulkner, REVOLT IN THE EARTH (based on *Absalom, Absalom*) and DREADFUL HOLLOW, are also discussed.

This book is another outstanding title in the impressive *Ungar Film Library Series* edited by Stanley Hochman. Its scholarly investigation of American literature and film history is informative, exciting,

and entertaining. Highly recommended.

1714 *Faulkner's Intruder In The Dust: Novel Into Film.* by Fadiman, Regina K. 330 p. illus. Knoxville, Tenn: University of Tennessee Press, 1978.

This volume consists of two parts: a discussion of adapting Faulkner's novel into a film; and the screenplay written by Ben Maddow. Appendixes include pages from both the continuity script and the director's shooting script, along with a filmography for director Clarence Brown and a bibliography-filmography for scriptwriter Maddow. Illustrations and an index accompany the text.

In the introductory section, Fadiman discusses in detail the complex process of translating a novel into a film. She considers the time period, the shooting location, the filmmakers, the studio hierarchy, and critical reception. Each of her five chapters is supplemented by notes which suggest a depth of research uncommon to books of film scripts.

A rewarding combination of essay and script, this volume should interest anyone concerned with the process of making films from novels. Although book, topic, and film belong to another era, the discussion has validity for today.

1715 *Favorite Movies.* by Nobile, Philip. 301 p. New York: Macmillan, 1973.

The question "What is your favorite movie?" is asked of 27 film critics in this unique volume. After some discussion of the meaning of "favorite," the contributors settle down to answer the question in individualistic styles. Some select one film while others offer "favorites." Although most of the critics are well known, they are identified in the closing sections of the text. The volume is indexed.

The choices and the justifications for them are quite interesting. Among the more surprising selections are CASABLANCA (1942), THE THIRD MAN (1950), THE SEARCHERS (1956), LAWRENCE OF ARABIA (1962), DOCKS OF NEW YORK (1945), and FAHRENHEIT 451 (1966). Certain critics tend to apologize for their choices while others digress widely on directors, periods, and genres. The framework of this volume has a built-in appeal and the group of writers asked to fill it in is most satisfying. Recommended.

1716 *Feature Film Finance Seminar.* paper Toronto: Motion Picture Institute of Canada, 1978.

Contains transcripts from The First Annual Seminar on Financing Canadian Features. The meeting was cosponsored by the Canadian Film Development Council and included speakers/panelists from banks, production companies, government agencies, unions, etc.

1717 *Feature Films As History.* by Short, Kenneth. 192 p. Knoxville, Tenn.: University of Tennessee Press, 1981.

1718 *Feature Films on 8mm and 16mm.* by Limbacher, James. 368 p. New York: Bowker, 1974.

The fourth edition of this reference work has the following subtitle: "A Directory of Feature Films Available for Rental, Sale and Lease in the United States ... With Serials and Director's Indexes." More than 15,000 feature titles are listed; the definition of a feature is: (1) a film 48 minutes or more in length, or (2) a film more than one reel in length (a most vulnerable statement). A short section lists serial titles such as BUCK ROGERS (12 episodes, 1939), CAPTAIN VIDEO (15 episodes, 1951), ZORRO RIDES AGAIN (12 episodes, 1937), etc. The addresses of film companies and distributors are given alphabetically and by geographical area. A selected list of film reference works precedes the index of directors, which was prepared by Charles G. Banciu.

Updating this reference work is a continuing process and supplements to the book appear five times a year in *Sightlines*, a magazine published by the Educational Film Library Association. Obviously the kinetic nature of the film business makes some omissions and errors inevitable.

The fourth edition of this valuable reference is most welcome, and if used as a means rather than the final word, it can be very helpful in the location of feature films. Recommended.

1719 *Feature Films on 8mm, 16mm and Videotape.* compiled by Limbacher, James. 447 p. New York: R.R. Bowker, 1979.

The sixth edition of this standard reference work incorporates the new medium of videotapes into the current pool of 8mm and 16mm films that are available for rental, sale and/or lease. More than 20,000 titles are listed in this long filmography, and, of this number, some 1500 are now available on videotape. Limbacher's easy-to-use format lends itself to the inclusion of videodiscs in future editions.

Entries are arranged alphabetically by title and offer the following information: releasing company (country of origin for foreign films), release date, running time, color format, sound or silent, a few cast names, director, selected distributors, and avail-

ability via rental, sale, or lease. Supporting the main section is a short listing of serials, an index of directors with individual filmographies provided, and film company-distributor data.

Aside from its primary purpose of locating rental-lease-sale sources, this volume also offers film information not easily available elsewhere. For example, Leonard Maltin's *TV Movies*, a fine reference with 12,000 entries, does not include certain titles that Limbacher does—e.g. THE CALLING OF DAN MATHEWS (1936), HAND OF DEATH (1962), OLIVER TWIST (1922, 1933), RADIO CITY REVELS (1938). Of course, the goal of each volume differs, but to the person simply seeking basic film information, Limbacher is undoubtedly the richer source.

In summary this volume improves with age and with each edition. In addition to providing an abundance of film information that is easy to retrieve, the book is fine for reading or browsing. Anyone who watches films on television or goes to the movies cannot help but be attracted by the scope of Limbacher's work. Recommended.

1720 *Federico Fellini.* by Salachas, Gilbert. 224 p. paper illus. New York: Crown, 1969 (1963).

This concise book is divided into four major sections: 1) an essay by Salachas that is both biographical and critical in considering Fellini and his films; 2) a selection of statements written or spoken by Fellini; 3) exerpts from the scripts of several Fellini films; and 4) a collection of short critical articles and tributes about Fellini.

The book is illustrated and has a bibliography, a filmography and an index. The quality of the writing throughout is exeptionally high. The long essay is quite objective, but most respectful. The subject's writings reflect the showman-artist and the final short pieces are well-chosen.

1721 *Federico Fellini.* edited by Silke, James R. 15 p. paper Washington, D.C.: The American Film Institute, 1970.

In January 1970, Federico Fellini, his wife, actress Giulietta Masina, actor Anthony Quinn, and director Sam Fuller held a discussion at the AFI Center in Beverly Hills. This short book is a transcription of the discussion which centered about Fellini and FELLINI SATYRICON (1969). A bibliography, a filmography, and an index to the topics discussed are included. Acceptable.

1722 *Federico Fellini: A Guide to References and Resources.* by Stubbs, John C. 346 p. Boston: G.K. Hall, 1978.

This is another excellent addition to the *Guide to References and Resources* series. It follows the general structure, with sections devoted to biographical background, a critical survey, the films, the bibliography, Fellini writings, archival sources, distributors, film title index and an author index.

The research, writing and arrangement all indicate care and intelligence. The text is not only informative but critical in many instances. As a general guide to the work of Federico Fellini, it would be hard to beat this impressive reference book.

1723 *Federico Fellini: An Annotated International Bibliography.* by Price, Barbara Anne; and Price, Theodore. 282 p. Metuchen, N.J.: Scarecrow, 1978.

This bibliography is the work of a husband-and-wife team whose affection for their subject and each other is acknowledged early on. They have divided their references into primary sources (screenplays, essays, drawings, interviews, etc.), and secondary sources (books, dissertations, articles, and reviews.) A few appendices and an author/editor index complete the book.

Two things distinguish the bibliography. First, the number (1652) and scope of the entries indicates exhaustive searching. Second, the quality of the annotations is high — they are readable, informative and often entertaining. This is a good place to start in any serious study of Federico Fellini.

1724 *Federico Fellini.* edited by Bondanella, Peter. 314 p. paper illus. New York: Oxford University Press, 1978.

This anthology includes articles on Fellini by various authors along with interviews and statements on the subject of film art by Fellini himself. The articles offer not only critical evaluations of specific films, but also general analyses of the themes and techniques found in Fellini films. A bibliography, a few illustrations, and a filmography accompany the text.

Some 22 authors from five nations are represented in a collection that covers a time period of almost three decades. The world and work of Fellini lends itself to analysis, discussion, and interpretation. Evidence of the lasting artistry of his visual statements can be found in this collection. Recommended.

1725 *Federico Fellini: The Search for a New Mythology.* by Ketcham, Charles B. 94 p. paper New York: Paulist Press, 1976.

The author states in his introduction that Fellini seems to feel "the shaking of the foundations" of western culture and is concerned in his films with redefinition of the old symbols and discovery of the new. Using an auteur approach which correlates the author's life experience with his films, Ketcham divides his study of Fellini into two parts: the cinema artist and the films. The latter section concentrates on LA STRADA (1954), LA DOLCE VITA (1959) and 8 1/2 (1962). In both sections wide use is made of quotations by Fellini. A strong bibliography and some detailed chapter notes complete the volume.

On one level the volume presents an interesting analysis of Fellini and his films while on another it shows how films can contribute to man's understanding of the human condition. Since Fellini gives constant attention to the church and Catholicism in his films, the author, a professor of religion, has an abundant supply of examples for analysis. The volume thus becomes an excellent exploration of the relationship between religion and film art. Recommended.

1726 *Federico Fellini: A Poet of Reality.* by Goldberg, Toby. 115 p. paper Boston: Broadcasting and Film Division, Boston University, 1965.

A survey of Fellini's films from VARIETY LIGHTS (1950) to 8-1/2 (1963). Some critical comments and biographical data are included.

1727 *Feet First.* by Finney, Ben. 255 p. illus. New York: Crown, 1971.

Ben Finney has enjoyed careers as a film actor, a marine, and a commissioner of sports. During his lifetime he has met many celebrated people and he tells about them in this autobiography. Personalities include Humphrey Bogart, Harpo Marx, Charles MacArthur, Lauren Bacall, Scott Fitzgerald, Ernest Hemingway and Marilyn Miller. Many other names are dropped in this harmless ego excursion which does contain a chapter on making silent films with Betty Compson and Barbara LaMarr.

1728 *Fellini.* by Budgen, Susanne. 128 p. paper illus. London: British Film Institute, 1966.

This is not a biography but a study of Fellini-as-artist as evidenced in his films. The author is concerned with the elements in the films that are obviously autobiographical and yet universally applicable. She believes that by looking into himself, Fellini has discovered the world.

In addition to the major films (up to JULIETTE OF THE SPIRITS (1965), there is also an edited interview from Belgian TV, a discussion (with Marcello Mastroianni as another participant), a script exerpt from LA STRADA (1954), a filmography, and a section of footnotes to the text. The book is indexed. The illustrations are small and murky but with the execllence of everything else offered here, this is a minor matter.

1729 *Fellini.* by Solmi, Angelo. 183 p. illus. New York: Humanities Press, 1968.

The first portion of this volume is a review of the key themes that reapear in Fellini's films; in the latter section, the Fellini biography and films are discussed. Along with a small collection of candid shots which cover Fellini's life up to 1962, the text offers an absorbing portrait of this controversial director.

The biographical portion of the text is affectionate, respectful and tends to be factual rather than analytical. The making of the films is detailed as is the plot synopsis offered for each. A short bibliography completes the volume. An acceptable account of Fellini, this book seems to lack the excitement of its subject.

1730 *Fellini: An Intimate Portrait.* by Betti, Liliana. 256 p. New York: Little, Brown 1979.

For almost 20 years Liliana Betti has held the exhausting position of personal assistant to Federico Fellini. In this memoir, she presents the director as she perceives him — a genius who has given himself completely to his art. He is in constant movement — racing, roaming, talking, creating, conceptualizing. That he can be ruthless, untruthful, overly impatient and yet sensitive is noted. Like many artists, he sees things as larger than they actually are — an enlargement or distortion technique that serves him professionally and personally.

Make no mistake, Betti likes her employer and forgives all in the cause of artistry. She treats three films in some detail: FELLINI ROMA (1972), AMARCORD (1974) and CASANOVA (1977). Illustrations are included.

1731 *Fellini on Fellini.* by Fellini, Federico. 180 p. illus. New York: Delacorte/Seymour Lawrence, 1976.

This anthology of articles, interviews, letters, and other Fellini papers is arranged chronologically. His

hometown of Rimini, the Rossellini association with OPEN CITY (1945) and PAISAN (1946), letters defending LA STRADA (1954) and other films, the conception of LA DOLCE VITA (1959), the showing of 8 1/2 (1962) in Russia, the presence of clowns in his films, the birth of a film — these topics are presented in approximately that order. A filmography, a list of the sources used for the text, and an index to the stills and film titles in the text complete the book.

The material provided here has importance for several reasons. Although it is fragmented, it can serve until a structured autobiography appears. In addition, it provides insight into the interpretation and appreciation of Fellini's films. Finally, it is simply a fine reading experience; Fellini is often as provocative in print as he is on film. Highly recommended.

1732 FELLINI SATYRICON. by Fellini, Federico; and Zapponi, Bernardino. 280 p. paper illus. New York: Ballantine Books, 1970.

Script of the 1970 film directed by Fellini. Contains cast credits and four articles: 1) "From the Planet Rome" (Dario Zanelli); 2) "Documentary of a Dream; A Dialogue Between Alberto Moravia and Federico Fellini" ; 3) "The Strange Journey" (Bernardino Zapponi); and 4) "The Treatment."

1733 *Fellini the Artist.* by Murray, Edward. 256 p. illus. New York: Frederick Ungar, 1976.

Another fine book has been written by the author of *Nine American Film Critics* and *The Cinematic Imagination.* In this case it is a four-part study of Federico Fellini which includes a biography, a survey of his filmmaking methods, a dozen film analyses, and a concluding assessment of Fellini's contribution to film history to date.

In a well-researched text Murray has blended factual information, Fellini quotes, subjective interpretation and many other elements including a few illustrations. A filmography, a bibliography, and an index complete the book.

The structure used serves the reader well. Short essays on biography and directorial technique provide the base for a "reviewing" of Fellini's films through the author's eyes and mind. This section forms the body and the major portion of the book. The critical analyses of the films are clearly presented, imaginative, and provocative. Murray, who is not afraid of subjective appraisal, is capable of intellectual prodding without alienating reader interest.

For Fellini admirers, this is a volume to treasure. For other readers, it is a brilliant, clearly stated evaluation-study of Fellini that informs and entertains most effectively. Recommended.

1734 *Fellini's Films.* edited by Strich, Christian. 344 p. illus. New York: G.P. Putnams, 1977.

The possibility that a picture book can be an overwhelming emotional experience is totally substantiated by this superb volume. Using careful selection criteria, the editor has assembled 400 stills from Federico Fellini's 15 1/2 films and presented them with a plot synopsis, production and cast credits. Beginning with JULIET OF THE SPIRITS (1965) many of the visuals appear in full color.

Fascination with this large, oversized volume can occur on several levels. First, and most simply, the pictures by themselves are a visual feast, blending a high standard of technical aesthetics with absorbing subject matter. On another level the reader who is familiar with the director's life and career can correlate the stills with his previous viewing and reading experiences of Fellini's work. Here are the reminders of how a filmmaker has placed many elements of his personal life into the fabric of his films. The themes, methods, and people that fascinate Fellini are here to perform a similar function for the reader.

Occasionally a book can cause an inner excitement equivalent to that often enjoyed in dance, music, art, theatre, or film. Here is such a book. It is highly recommended.

1735 *Fellini's Penance: The Meaning of* AMARCORD. by Price, Theodore. 35 p. paper Old Bridge, N.J.: Boethius Press, 1977.

This pamphlet on AMARCORD (1974) provides a critical commentary written by a Fellini authority-enthusiast. Theodore Price not only reviews the film in detail, but also points out the director's recurrent themes and techniques. Short but solid in all respects.

1736 *Festivals Sourcebook.* by Wassermann, Paul. 656 p. Detroit: Gale, 1977.

This volume carries a long subtitle: "A Reference Guide to Fairs, Festivals, and Celebrations in Agriculture, Antiques, the Arts, Theater and Drama, Arts and Crafts, Community, Dance, Ethnic Events, Film, Folk, Food and Drink, History, Indians, Marine, Music, Seasons and Wildlife." About 50 film events can be found among the 3800 festivals listed.

1737 *FIAF Directory of Film and TV Documentation Sources.* by Davies, Brenda; and Luijckx, John. 70 p. paper Amsterdam: Netherlands Filmmuseum, 1976.

A publication by The Federation Internationale des Archives du Film whose cataloging procedures for film and television vary from the Anglo-American Cataloguing Rules (AACR2).

1738 *Fiction and the Camera Eye: Visual Consciousness in Film and the Modern Novel.* by Spiegel, Alan. 203 p. Charlottesville, Va.: University Press of Virginia, 1976.

Emphasis here is on the "cinematic" fiction of authors such as Faulkner, Conrad, Dickens, Joyce, Zola, Hemingway, etc. Some attention is given to filmmakers Griffith, Eisenstein, Keaton, Renoir, Rossellini, Antonioni, Truffaut and Godard. The author is on stronger ground with fiction than with film and some of his arguments concerning the motion picture are either vulnerable or unsupported in his text.

1739 *Fiction and the Screen.* by Ortman, Marguerite G. 148 p. illus. Boston: Marshall Jones Co., 1935.

This is an attempt to look at all sources of screen plays—the short story, novel, play, orginal, etc.—to determine their relative value for the screen.

1740 *Fiction Into Film*—A WALK IN THE SPRING RAIN. by Maddux, Rachel; and Silliphant, Stirling; and Isaacs, Neil D. 240 p. illus. Knoxville, Tenn.: University of Tennessee Press, 1970.

This book is a combination of the original novella (Maddux), the screenplay (Silliphant), and the chronological account of the film's development, production and presentation (Isaacs). The 100 pages by Issacs constitute the original text material and are devoted to an exposition of the problems and procedures necessary to turn a work of fiction into a finished film. It is unfortunate that the final product was not successful. The importance of the book is diminished somewhat by the film's failure. Its high price will not help either. The book does have some interest for students and aspiring writers.

1741 FIDDLER ON THE ROOF. 32 p. paper illus. Englewood Cliffs, N.J.: Charnell Theatrical Enterprises, 1971.

The major portion of this souvenir book is devoted to a telling of the story by the use of narrative and stills taken from the 1971 film. One small portion details how the film was made, with appropriate attention given to director Norman Jewison and star Topol. Small capsule biographies of other cast members and some production credits are given.

1742 *Field's Day.* by Fields, W. C. 32 p. paper illus. Kansas City, Mo.: Hallmark (Attic), 1970.

A collection of photographs and comments by W. C. Fields.

1743 *Fields for President.* by Fields, W. C. 163p. illus. New York: Dodd Mead, 1971 (1939).

A reprint of some Fieldsian wisdom and philosophy. It may be surprising to some readers that Fields was the author of a number of magazine articles and essays.

1744 *50 Classic Motion Pictures: The Stuff That Dreams Are Made of.* by Zinman, David. 311 p. illus. New York: Crown, 1970.

An arbitrary selection of well-known and loved motion pictures, this volume applies the word "classic" in a broad sense. Divided into categories such as dames, he-men, monsters, funny men, directors, intrigue, etc., the book includes such critically ignored films as CHARLIE CHAN AT THE OPERA (1936), MAYTIME (1937), NIGHTMARE ALLEY (1947), SHE (1935), FLASH GORDON (1936), etc.

Picture reproduction and selection are excellent in most cases with only a few illustrations tending toward darkness. The text is another matter, resembling a printed version of the affectionate spoken commentary which usually accompanies intimate showings of "Golden Age" films. It is gushy, lacks critical depth, and largely retells the content of the film. In each case some background material is offered before the film is discussed. The book will provide may hours of enjoyable browsing.

1745 *Fifty Famous Faces in Transition.* edited by Berliner, Burt. 96 p. paper illus. New York: Fireside (Simon and Schuster), 1980.

The purpose of this collection of photographs is to show a selected group of celebrities at different periods of their lives. Many film personalities are included.

1746 *Fifty Famous Films 1915-1945.* by British Film Institute 106 p. London: British Film Institute, 1945.

The film notes, written by members of the National Film Theater, are given here for 50 famous films. Although the emphasis is on the silent classics, some sound films are included, the last being BRIEF ENCOUNTER (1946) and CITIZEN KANE (1941). The notes are well-written and should be of interest to most readers. They offer invaluable background for showings of the films.

1747 55 DAYS AT PEKING. 20 p. paper illus. New York: Program Publishing Co., 1963.

A historical essay entitled "China, During the Siege at Peking" open this souvenir book. The re-creation of Peking in Madrid, where this 1963 film was made, is described next. Stars Charlton Heston, Ava Gardner, and David Niven are given individual pages, as is producer Samuel Bronston. The final section is devoted to "The Men Who Made 55 Days at Peking."

1748 *50 from the 50's.* by Zinman, David. 418 p. illus. New Rochelle, N.Y.: Arlington House, 1979.

With this elaborate filmography, which is subtitled "Vintage Films From America's Mid-century," David Zinman offers 50 examples to show that the underrated decade contained enough quality movies to compare with other similar periods. The selection is subjective; therefore, the questions of inclusion and omission do arise. For example, Zinman is light on classic musicals — GIGI (1958), THE BANDWAGON (1953), and FUNNY FACE (1957), are missing. Inother genres, some weak films are included such as TEA AND SYMPATHY (1956), THAT'S MY BOY (1951), PEYTON PLACE (1957), and PILLOW TALK (1959). For each film, a detailed retelling of the plot is offered along with other comment that varies from a valid analysis and production description (THE INCREDIBLE SHRINKING MAN 1957) to simple biographical information (Kirk Douglas in DETECTIVE STORY 1951). The production of the book is impressive, with clear sharp illustrations and attractive layouts predominating. A lengthy index and a bibliography are provided.

Certainly the modest goal of the author has been achieved in this handsome book. He does show that the fifties offered some fine films. One wishes, however, that in making his case, he had minimized plot retelling in favor of expanded comments and background information. The potential audience for this book is probably quite familiar with the stories and a short paragraph or so would suffice. Enrichment should take priority over reminder.

1749 *Fifty Golden Years of Oscar.* by Osborne, Robert. illus. La Harba, Calif.: ESE California, 1979.

Subtitled "The Official History of The Academy of Motion Picture Arts and Sciences," this volume presents the winners, nominations, ceremonies, special awards, etc., of the period 1927 to 1977. In more than 300 large-sized pages, the book uses many fine illustrations, an interesting narrative and an abundance of factual information to document the history of the Academy Awards. Quotations from selected winners appear throughout and, most important of all, there is a detailed index that makes this attractive, well-produced volume into a fine reference book. Highly recommended.

1750 *Fifty Great American Silent films, 1912-1920: A Pictorial Survey.* by Slide, Anthony; and Wagenknecht, Edward. 176 p. illus. paper New York: Dover, 1981.

An attractive, beautifully illustrated selection of silent films complete with credits and critical text. Recommended.

1751 *Fifty Major Film-Makers.* edited by Cowie, Peter. 287 p. illus. New York: Barnes, 1975.

One of the features of *International Film Guide* is the annual selection of five "Directors of the Year." Those filmmakers honored over the period 1964-1973 appear in this volume, with the original essays updated and additional stills added. A filmography appears at the conclusion of each article. The final index is devoted to the film titles mentioned in the 50 essays.

The collection of outstanding filmmakers present in this volume represents only a sampling of the currently active directorial talent. Written by Cowie and others, the essays are thorough in their description and evaluation of each subject's work. The stills and the filmographies provide excellent supportive material to the main text.

In summary this is a compilation to be appreciated. Its range of subjects is impressive and the treatment accorded them is most appropriate. Recommended.

1752 *50 Super Stars.* by Kobal, John. 160 p. paper illus. New York: Bounty Books, 1974.

Who could help but be attracted and ultimately absorbed by such a production as this volume? Using oversized, spiral-bound 12 inch x 17 inch pages, the author has provided a mini-biography, a filmography and several pages of illustrations for each of the 50 super stars. An introductory essay by John Russell Taylor sets limits on the concept of stardom. Then the parade of personalities from Fred Astaire to Mae West begins. The short biographies are largely factual, although a critical statement appears now and again. Illustrations include stills, portraits, song sheet covers, posters, newspaper shots, etc. Many are in full color and the quality of reproduction is consistently above average.

A volume so rich in visual attractions which also offers some basic biographical data cannot help but delight most readers. Libraries and schools concerned with using feature films should consider the purchase of two volumes so that the attractive material can be separated and used in film/book publicity. Highly recommended.

1753 *The Fifty Worst Films of All Time (and How They Got That Way).* by Medved, Harry; and Dreyfuss, Randy. 288 p. paper illus. New York: Popular Library, 1978.

Another clever idea similar to the Turkey Awards is presented in print here. Using an oversized book format, the authors select, describe and analyze 50 films in a mocking text. Illustrations, review excerpts, and bits of dialogue are used to strengthen the author's argument.

If the reader can overcome the cheap shot approach at what is admittedly a most difficult form of storytelling, he may find this attack on films amusing. Others may classify the young authors as sophomoric opportunists.

1754 *The Fifty-Year Decline and Fall of Hollywood.* by Goodman, Ezra. 465 p. New York: Simon & Shuster, 1961.

The general theme of this book seems to be that with the passing of the founders and pioneers of the film industry, there is an accompanying methodical death of Hollywood. Support for this theory is given by chapters devoted to old-timers (Griffith, Porter, Bronco Billy, etc.), the gossip business, reviewers, studio heads, publicity departments, and off-screen creative artists. Extended attention is given to

Monroe, Bogart, and Novak.

The author is cynical, bitter, sarcastic, and disappointed in the failure of Hollywood influentials to recognize the importance of film as an art. He uses names and writes with truth, candor and perception. There are no illustrations but an index is provided. Although this is an opinionated and singular view of Hollywood, the abundance of anecdote, fact, and comment make it pertinent for all.

1755 *Fifty Years of American Comedy.* by Treadwell, Bill. 241 p. New York: Exposition, 1951.

Treats many comedians who have appeared in films.

1756 *Fifty Years of German Film.* by Wollenberg, Hans H. 48 p. illus. London: Falcon Press, 1948.

Stills and text combined to indicate the development of the German Film up to the mid-forties.

1757 *Fifty Years of Italian Cinema.* by Palmieri, E. Ferdinando; and Margadonna, Ettore M.; and Egromo, Mario. 319 p. illus. Rome: Carlo Besetti, Edizioni d'Arte, 1954.

Each author is responsible for one period of Italian cinema coverage in this volume; Beginnings (1904-1930); Transition Period (1930-1942); and Post-War Period (1942-1954). In each case, an introductory essay is followed by many superb stills taken from the films of that particular period. This is an essential, beautifully illustrated survey. Highly recommended.

1758 *Fifty Years of Movie Posters.* edited by Kobal, John. 176 p. paper illus. New York: Crown, 1973.

In this oversized spiral-bound volume there are 275 movie posters along with lobby cards, music sheets and other advertising materials. Many of the posters, which cover a half-century of filmmaking (1910-1960), are in full color. This is a special volume that will please a wide range of readers and browsers. Recommended.

1759 *Fifty Years of Peter Pan.* by Green, Roger Lancelyn. 250 p. illus. London: Peter Davis, 1954.

This book is devoted mostly to the numerous productions of the play; however, it does contain an unfilmed script of PETER PAN.

1760 *Fifty Years of Soviet Cinema, 1917-1967.* 29 p. paper illus. London: British Film Institute, 1967.

This oversized volume from the *Folio* series contains only reproductions from classic Russian films—there is no text. It was prepared by the British Film Institute and Sovexportfilm to commemorate the 50th anniversary of the October Revolution.

1761 *Fifty Years on Theatre Row.* by Ackery, Ivan. 253 p. illus. Vancouver: Hancock, 1980.

The autobiography of a Canadian theatre man who was involved in vaudeville, silent films, and sound films.

1762 *The Figure in Film.* by Clifton, N. Roy. 580 p. Newark, Del.: University of Delaware, 1981.

1763 *Figures of Light: Film Criticism and Comment.* by Kauffmann, Stanley 296 p. New York: Harper and Row, 1971.

The film reviews of Stanley Kauffmann from the 1967-70 period (written mostly for *The New Republic*) are assembled here. Reviews are arranged chronologically but the table of contents lists the films alphabetically, and the book is indexed. Mr. Kauffmann is a serious, literate, and readable critic who writes, in a noncompromising style, about films from aesthetic standards rather than as a guide for mass audiences. Therefore most of his attention is directed to "important" or "influential" films rather than toward entertainments. He does consider FUNNY GIRL (1968), THE ODD COUPLE (1968), TRUE GRIT (1969), and a few other popular films but the majority of the reviews are of the art theatre films—those potential classics enjoyed by a smaller but more discerning audience. Recommended.

1764 *Filling the Gap.* by Terry-Thomas. 168 p. illus. London: Parrish, 1959.

The epitome of the British "Silly Ass," Terry-Thomas has appeared in many films, from THE LUCKY MASCOT (1948) to THE TEMPEST (1979). This autobiography may have been somewhat premature.

1765 FILM. by Beckett, Samuel. 95 p. paper illus. New York: Grove 1969.

Script of the 1964 film directed by Alan Schneider, Contains an article on directing FILM by Schneider.

1766 *Film.* by Manvell, Roger. 240 p. paper illus. Baltimore, Md.: Penguin Books, 1950.

One of the early classics of film literature, this paperback first appeared in 1944 and was revised once in 1946, and again in 1950. Major additions and deletions occured each time. The author describes it as "a survey of the affairs of cinema to promote discussion." In the opening section the essentials of film art are considered, while the second considers the effect of film on society. Several other short pieces are included.

There are many illustrations, all small in size but adequately reproduced. A representative directors' filmography, a bibliography, a name index and a title index are included. As a pioneer work of high quality in its field, this book deserves reprinting. Statistical information aside, much of its content is still applicable today. Its influence is obvious on the many similar but less worthy volumes that have appeared since. Highly recommended.

1767 *Film.* by Museum of Modern Art. 64 p. paper illus. New York: 1969.

This gem of a circulating catalog apparently gets smaller with each edition (the rewards of commercial distribution have induced many producers to withdraw films from the Museum's circulating collection). What remains in this edition is primarily silent films and specialized films which have little commercial potential. The films are arranged historically by the country of their origin. As always, the annotations are appreciative, respectful, and informative. Much can be learned from a reading of this catalog. The catalog's index to many films that are not annotated elsewhere makes it highly recommended.

1768 *The Film.* edited by Sarris, Andrew. 64 p. Indianapolis; Bobbs-Merrill, 1968.

This short volume comes from a series of secondary school booklets entitled "The Bobbs-Merrill Series in Composition and Rhetoric." Articles besides Sarris' are by critics such as Kael, Archer, Alpert, Simon, MacDonald, etc. The booklet approaches its topic, film, via the criticism of three groups of directors—American (Kubrick, Kazan and Lewis), French (Truffaut, Bresson, and New Wave), and Italian (Antonioni and Fellni). This collection has more structure than usual and it should appeal to most readers. Since it was designed as a text, interesting questions follow each article. Nicely done and recommended in spite of no illustrations, index, bibliography, etc.

1769 *Film: A Montage of Theories.* edited by MacCann, Richard Dyer. 384 p. paper illus. New York: Dutton, 1966.

In this book containing many well-known writings the selection of the articles is intelligent and sequential and the author list most impressive. Full appreciation of the book requires considerable background and sophistication regarding film and, therefore, the book may be somewhat difficult for the beginner or the younger reader, although it is essential for the serious student of film.

1770 *Film: An Anthology.* edited by Talbot, Daniel. 650 p. New York: Simon & Schuster, 1959.

Three major divisions are used to group articles in this anthology: 1) aesthetics, social commentary, and analysis; 2) theory and technique; and 3) history and personal. Dating as far back as 1923, the articles (and the authors) are familiar, accepted, and worthy of attention. In all cases, they were selected with the discrimination that comes with a wide knowledge of cinema literature.

The book provides some excellent general or random reading for the advanced cinema devotee. Since the collection covers Melies, Griffith, Chaplin, Caligari, Agee's "Comedy's Greatest Era," directors of the thirties, etc. the book will "fit" most survey, appreciation, or history courses on film given in colleges today.

1771 *The Film: A Psychological Study— The Silent Photoplay in 1916.* by Munsterberg, Hugo. 100 p. paper New York: Dover, 1970.

The author of this neglected treatise was a Harvard psychologist who numbered among his friends William James, Theodore Roosevelt, Woodrow Wilson, and Andrew Carnegie. Written in 1916, this study was originally called *The Photoplay: A Psychological Study.* The book explores such topics as: 1) viewer perception of depth; 2) conditions necessary for the illusion of motion; and 3) the correspondence of the fade-out, the close-up, and the dissolve with attention, memory, and imagination. A second part is a general discussion of film aesthetics which justifies the recognition of film as a new art form. Recommended for historians and advanced students.

1772 *Film: Dutch Art Today.* by Boost, C. 100 p. illus. Amsterdam: Netherland Information Service, 1958.

A survey of filmmaking in Holland—mostly short

films and documentaries. The role of government support is stressed.

1773 *The Film: Its Economic, Social, and Artistic Problems.* by Schmidt, Georg; and Schmalenbach, Werner; and Bachlin, Peter. 140 p. illus. London: Falcon Press, 1948.

Translated from the German with Manvell's supervision. Contains many stills, diagrams, etc.

1774 *Film: The Creative Eye.* by Sohn, David. 176 p. paper illus. Dayton, Ohio : Pflaum, 1970.

Divided into four major sections, this volume discusses 17 short films and their creators. The sections are: I. The Searching Eye: The Observer and the Creative Spirit (the films of Saul Bass along with an interveiw); II. The Precise Eye: A Sharper Vision (four films by Fred Hudson discussed); III. The Inventive Eye: Impression and Compression (films by Dan McLaughlin, Charles Braverman and David Adams used to illustrate kinestasis, the animation of still photographs through fast cutting ; and IV. The Sensitive Eye: The Poetry of Awareness (seven films by Greg MacGillivray, Jim Freeman, David Adams and others indicate physical exhilaration). A welcome addition to the literature surrounding the short film.

1775 *Film: The Creative Process.* by Lawson, John Howard. 380 p. illus. New York: Hill and Wang, 1964.

Opinionated, Marxist values applied in an attempt to develop an aesthetic of the film, this effort is about 30 years late. Forget this one unless you wish to use it as an example of biased, prejudiced writing designed to persuade rather than educate. Not recommended.

1776 *Film: How and Where to Find Out What You Want to Know.* by Monaco, James. 9 p. paper New York: Zoetrope, 1975.

This short pamphlet covers the basic reference tools with brief no-nonsense annotations. In addition, more than 75 film periodicals are listed.

1777 *Film: An Introduction.* by Fell, John L. 274 p. paper illus. New York: Praeger, 1975.

The title of this volume is quite appropriate—its contents do provide an introduction to the serious consideration of film. In logical sequence Fell considers the viewer, film elements, filmmaking, film theory and criticism, ending with some predictions about film forms of the future. Appendixes are concerned with film reference publications, film periodicals, film study in United States, film distribution sources and distributors. An index of film titles and a general index complete the work. Illustrations used throughout the book are adequate. Acceptable.

1778 *Film: The Democratic Art.* by Jowett, Garth. 482 p. Boston: Little, Brown, 1976.

Jowett spent more than six years in the preparation and writing of this volume. His labors are evident throughout and he is to be complimented on total achievement in a formidable area of film literature. He is offering a sociological history of the film in America and his concern is with "movie-going" in this country during the past 75 years.

Beginning with the first audiences at the turn of the century, he discusses the development of the motion picture industry, content of the early films, moral and social issues, effects on children, health, morals, manners, censorship and many other topics pertinent to sociology. The text is presented in chronological form, using period divisions such as America the Movies (1930-1941), Hollywood Goes to War (1939-1945), The Meaning of Hollywood (1946-1960), The Decline of Control (1947-1970), and The Uncertain Future (1960-1975). More than two dozen tables appear throughout the book. Copious references and footnotes are included with each chapter and a lengthy bibliography is appended.

At a time when so many people are interested in reviewing and re-examining American films of the past, the appearance of Jowett's research is most welcome. He has presented in this readable, efficiently organized survey a key to the intelligent understanding of those films and the circumstances under which they were made and shown. This volume is highly recommended. Its publication is an important event for all persons seriously concerned with the study of American films.

1779 *Film—The Medium and the Maker.* by Scott, James F. 340 p. paper illus. New York: Holt, Rinehart & Winston, 1975.

This volume deals with film aesthetics, recognizing throughout the necessary relationship between art and technology. After differentiating between the auteur and the cooperative theories of filmmaking, the author devotes sections to composition, lighting, sound, story and script, acting and staging, editing and assembly, etc. A summary conclusion is also presented. In addition to many well-selected illustrations, the book contains a bibliography, a fine list of short films that can be used to illustrate one or more aesthetic elements, a distributor roster, and an index.

Especially commendable is the solid framework or structure provided by the author. The consistent clarity of his explanations of the various aesthetics is enchanced by the use of practical examples and illustrations. He has successfully avoided the murky obfuscation that one finds too frequently in books on aesthetics. The supplementary suggestions for reading and viewing are as solid and substantial as the text. Recommended and deserving of consideration as a basic text for introductory film courses on the college level.

1780 *Film—A Reference Guide.* by Armour, Robert A. 251 p. Westport, Conn.: Greenwood, 1980.

In what seems to be another spinoff from existing film-book bibliographies, Robert Armour has rearranged several thousand book titles under major headings: History, Production, Criticism, Genres, Geography, etc. His comments, which are mostly descriptive, appear in narrative form and are followed by the bibliographic data on the books mentioned. Since so much of the information offered is available in earlier bibliographies, the rationale for the writing and publishing of such a volume as this is questionable.

1781 *Film: Historical-Theoretical Speculations.* edited by Lawton, Ben; and Staiger, Janet. 81 p. paper Pleasantville, N.Y.: Redgrave, 1977.

This is part two of the 1977 Film Studies Annual. The first part is entitled *Exploration in National Cinemas.* Both are intended "to reflect a serious, scholarly nonpartisan approach to film studies. <

This particular volume is the typical anthology product that follows a conference, even though not all of the articles stem directly from the annual meeting. It does represent material of a very specialized nature that should satisfy its intended audience.

1782 *Film: Form and Function.* by Wead, George; and Lellis, George. 512 p. illus. New YorK: Houghton Mifflin, 1981.

1783 *Film.* by Willink, E. New York: Gordon Press, 1976.

1784 *Film Acting as a Career.* by Bamburg, Lilian. 154 p. illus. London: Foulsham, 1929.

The emphasis is on voice in this volume which appeared around the birth of talking pictures. There are also sections on history, production, make-up, dress, movement, etc.

1785 *The Film Acting of John Barrymore.* by Garton, Joseph W. New York: Arno, 1980.

This title in the *Dissertations on Film* series describes Barrymore's approach to acting as a blending of styles. The 19th century with the 20th. Many films are discussed in an attempt to assess his contribution to film acting.

1786 *The Film Actor.* by Pate, Michael. 245 p. New York: A. S. Barnes, 1970.

A how-to-do-it book by an actor-teacher that features a broad introduction to the field, a glossary of terms, the blocking-out and staging of a film scene, some practice exercises, and diagrams of camera movement.

1787 *Film Actor's Guide: Western Europe.* by Parish, James Robert. 606 p. illus. Metuchen, N.J.: Scarecrow, 1977.

As the first in a projected series that will eventually include Eastern Europe, Asia, Africa and Australia, this volume lists filmographies/credits for almost 600 performers who made their major reputation in Western Europe. Scandinavia and certain Middle European countries are not covered.

Entries are alphabetical by surname and consist of biographical data and name-date-company listings of their feature films up to 1975. Over 100 illustrations of the performers appear throughout. For example, the reader will find that Tommy Steele's real name is Thomas Hicks and he was born on Dec. 17, 1936, in Bermondsey, London. In his first film, THE SHIRALEE (1957), he sang the title song, and then made ten other films, the last being WHERE'S JACK (1968). A photograph of Steele unexpectedly appears on a later page.

This is a solid reference book that offers a great amount of information that is not easy to obtain elsewhere. The arrangement is excellent and the content seems very reliable.

1788 *The Film Addict's Archive: Poetry and Prose of the Cinema.* by Oakes, Phillip. London: Elm Tree Books, 1977.

A selection of prose and poetry by noted writers, all relating in one way or another to the cinema.

1789 *Film Against the State.* by Ealler, Robert. paper illus. Cambridge Springs, Pa.: Alliance College Polish Club, 1966.

Deals with Polish motion pictures from 1956 to 1961.

1790 *Film and Cinema Statistics.: A Preliminary Report on Methodology with Tables Giving Current Statistics.* compiled by UNESCO. 111 p. paper Paris: UNESCO, 1955.

International in scope, this compilation offers data on such industry items as box office income, production, exhibition outlets, imported films, etc. Summaries are provided in French and German.

1791 *Film and Education: A Symposium on the Role of Film in the Field of Education.* edited by Elliott, Godfrey. 597 p. New York: Philosophical Library, 1948.

This volume deals with the educational film, a category much easier to define in 1948 than in the eighties. There are sections on the psychology of viewing film, research in films, techniques of use, applications in subject fields, films for training, libraries, churches, societies, forums, etc. The last section is on principles and practices and concludes with a chapter on selection and evaluation. Although a certain amount of the material is dated, (and current revision of the material may be difficult because of the many authors represented in the text) there is sufficient information to warrant consideration of the book by schools and colleges. It is not recommended for general readers.

1792 *Film and Effect.* by Chittock, John. 28 p. paper illus. London: Financial Times, 1967.

This booklet carries the cover subtitle, "A Pilot Experiment to Assess the Effectiveness of Sponsored Documentary Films in Changing Public Attitudes."

1793 *Film and Fiction: The Dynamics of Exchange.* by Cohen, Keith. 228 p. illus. New Haven, Conn.: Yale University Press, 1979.

An examination of the relationship between film and fiction, this volume shows the effects that each have had on the other. Beginning with the late 1800s, Cohen traces developments in the arts which led ultimately to the cinematic form of narrative. Several modern novels are then examined for their cinematic form. Illustrations and an index complete the study.

1794 *Film and Its Techniques.* by Spottiswoode, Raymond. 516 p. illus. Berkeley, Calif.: University of California Press, 1965 (1951).

This is a basic book, a classic in its field, on the technology of creating a motion picture. Using a group of appealing cartoons and diagrams (by Jean-Paul Ladouceur) and a detailed but always comprehensible text, the book explains in depth all of the techniques and practices which underlie filmmaking. Emphasis is placed on documentary filming, probably because of the author's association with the National Film Board of Canada. The same high standards of that organization have been carried over into book authorship by Spottiswoode. An extended glossary and a bibliography of technical books (all pre-1950) are also given.

1795 *Film and Literature: Contrasts in Media.* edited by Marcus, Fred H. 283 p. paper Scranton, Pa.: Chandler, 1971.

After an opening section on the art of the film, this anthology addresses itself to the differences and similarities between films and their literary sources. A few of the examples used are from novels (*Catch 22, Hud, Lord of the Flies, The Grapes of Wrath, Tom Jones, Oliver Twist, Midnight Cowboy*), plays ("Romeo and Juliet" , "Pygmalion") and the short story ("An Occurrence at Owl Creek Bridge"). Lists of films, distributors, and some films made from notable novels, stories, and plays appear as appendixes.

No argument can be made about the selection of the authors or their specific articles. They are of varied opinions and are representative of different time periods in film history. The emphasis on the novel as a film source is heavy, while the short story and play are given much less attention. This may be statistically valid but it unbalances the discussion. Illustrations are acceptable but only seven films are represented. The volume is a good compilation that should satisfy the reader interested in the relationship of literature and film. Acceptable.

1796 *Film and Literature.* by Beja, Morris. 335 p. illus. New York: Longman, 1979.

The goal of this textbook is to explore both film and literature, and to examine the relationship existing between them. Stressed is the value and advantage of looking at these two art forms together.

Following four chapters of exposition on the above theme, some 25 films derived from novels, stories, plays or original screenplays are critically discussed. For each there is background for the film and its source, some "Topics to Think About" and some suggested reading. Illustrations, a glossary of film and literary terms, a list of distributors, a bibliography, and an index complete the book.

This is a carefully prepared textbook that sets a standard for use in film study. With the increased availability of films via the new technologies, courses using books such as this one should proliferate.

1797 *Film and Reality.* by Armes, Roy. 254 p. paper Baltimore: Penguin, 1974.

The text of this absorbing survey considers three "strands of development" in its examination of film and reality. First, realism in film is traced from Lumiere to the Cinema Verite of the sixties and certain television films of today. The next topic, film illusion, begins with Edison's films and leads to the large studios, the star system, and ultimately to the work done during Hollywood's golden years. The final section, devoted to film modernism, examines the work of filmmakers such as Bunuel, Resnais, Godard, Anger, etc. The author has tried to indicate the relationship between artistic accomplishment and historical context throughout.

The goal of the book is stated succinctly in the opening pages: "A triadic model of this kind lets us see clearly the range of the cinema as an art form. We are concerned with three major cinematic approaches to reality: the uncovering of the real, the imitating of the real and the questioning of the real." A fine annotated bibliography offered in three sections which correspond to the text is included along with a useful index.

The study presented by Armes is an impressive one which will both challenge and enlighten the reader. Few statements made in recent years have had the intellectual quality and historical accuracy displayed here. In searching for an aesthetic applicable to all films, the author has offered a tri-part structure that is deserving of serious consideration. Highly recommended.

1798 *Film and Revolution.* by MacBean, James Roy. 339 p. illus. Bloomington, Ind.: Indiana University Press, 1975.

MacBean is a film critic who has formulated a theory of film aesthetics which has its roots in Marxist teachings. In this volume he attempts to justify his theory in three ways: by reviewing the work of Jean-Luc Godard as an example of revolutionary cinema which validates his theory; by examining the work of other filmmakers to determine the universality of the theory; and by denying the work of Christian Metz on the semiology of the cinema and proposing instead his own cinema aesthetic which is correlated to our changing political ideology. Supporting his argument are illustrations, chapter notes, and an index.

Anyone interested in the serious study of cinema will be fascinated by the suggestions, observations, and analyses that MacBean offers. He is a most informed and persuasive advocate of cinema-as-revolution. Since the material he presents is very specialized and almost demands an acquaintance with the films he describes, the book will appeal to a limited audience. It is ideal for use in certain college courses, and film intellectuals will be delighted with the challenges it offers. Highly recommended.

1799 *The Film and Ron Kelly.* edited by Gobeil, Charlotte. 22 p. paper illus. Ottawa: Canadian Film Institute, 1965.

This appreciation of the Canadian filmmaker, Ron Kelly, includes illustrations and a filmography.

1800 *Film and School: A Handbook in Motion Picture Evaluation.* by Rand, Helene; and Lewis, Richard. 182 p. New York: Appleton, 1937.

This volume is based on the results of a study made by the National Council of English Teachers on the evaluation of motion pictures. It is a handbook giving suggestions, methods, sources, and plans and it contains an annotated list of materials.

1801 *Film and School.* by Miller, Helen M.; and Lewis, Richard. 181 p. illus. New York: Appleton-Century, 1937.

The authors, with the help of Edgar Dale and Sarah Mullen, have compiled a handbook in moving picture evaluation. The publication was sponsored by the National Council of Teachers of English as part of its effort to establish standards for motion pictures and newspapers. The book includes illustrations, forms, diagrams, and a section on source materials.

1802 *Film and Society.* by MacCann, Richard Dyer. 182 p. New York: Scribners, 1964.

Designed as a research anthology, this book has pertinence for the general reader and student. The focus here is on censorship and control vs. complete freedom. Section titles reflect various aspects: 1. Films: Past, Present, and Future; 2. What Does the Audience Want?; 3. Does the Screen Reflect Society?; 4. Can the Screen Influence Society?; 5. Should the Screen Be Controlled? 6. Should Film Distribution Overseas Be Restricted?; and 7. Should Films for Television be Controlled? Discounting the few pages devoted to research techniques, most readers will find much of general sociological interest here. The articles are well selected and present a range of opinion. Recommended.

1803 *Film and Suspense.* by Loker, Altan. 231 p. paper Istanbul: Altan Loker, 1976.

1804 *Film and Television: Basic Principles and Definitions.* by International Edinburgh Film Festival, 1963. 47 p. paper Edinburgh: Edinburgh Contrast, 1964.

A report of a conference held in Edinburgh, August 23 and 24, 1963, with a general theme of "What is a Television Film?" Organized and presented by Contrast and the International Film and Television Council.

1805 *Film and Television As An Aspect of European Culture.* by Quinn, James. 168 p. illus. Leyden, Netherlands: A. W. Sijthoff, 1968.

A survey of the educational and cultural effects of television and films on the United Kingdom and other European countries. The period covered is the decade between 1955 and 1965. The attitudes of the British Film Institute, the teaching profession, the TV and film industries and the public are noted. The book closes with a series of recommendations based on the findings.

1806 *Film & TV Festival Directory.* edited by Zwerdling, Shirley. 174 p. New York: Back Stage Publications, 1970.

This compilation of information about film (and TV) festivals is divided into three large classifications: U.S. festivals, international festivals, and amateur film festivals, worldwide. Other features include a list of awards, a monthly calendar and a cross-index of categories. A final index emphasizes countries, with a listing of all festivals held within their borders.

While some of the data seem repetitious, anyone seeking information on festivals will find this a useful reference aid. With a reservation noted concerning the temporary status of some of the festivals, the book should serve as a valuable guide.

1807 *Film and TV Graphics.* edited by Herdeg, Walter; and Halas, John. 119 p. illus. Zurich: The Graphis Press, 1967.

This interesting book, presented in three languages —English, German and French—examines the graphics found in recent films of all types: the entertainment film, the sponsored film, the commercial, and the experimental film. The text begins with the visual revolution and ends with a prediction about film and TV graphics in the future. Illustrations and text are outstanding. Although its topic is specialized, it will offer the general reader who can get beyond the title several hours of unusual reading and entertainment.

1808 *Film and Television in Education for Teaching.* 66 p. paper London: British Film Institute, 1960.

This report was made by a joint working party made up of representatives of the Association of Teachers in Colleges and Departments of Education, along with representatives from the British Film Institute. Its goal was to explore ways and means of introducing the study of film and television into teacher education. After some background which describes public concern about TV and film, the situation prevalent at most teacher training colleges is examined. Suggested ways of introducing film/TV study include (1) as a main course, (2) as part of a wider course, (3) in curriculum courses and (4) by college film societies. Appendixes follow a summary-conclusion chapter.

The material here indicates an early interest and awareness of the importance of the serious study of film and television in teacher training institutions.

Many years later, much of what was expressed here still remains valid. Acceptable.

1809   *Film and Television in Poland.* by Fuksiewicz, Jacek. 295 p. paper illus. Chicago: Imported Publications, 1978.

In addition to material on Polish features and short films, such subjects as cinematography, film culture, and the film industry in Poland are treated here. Other sections identify Polish films which have won awards and filmmakers who are currently active. Illustrations, some in color, are plentiful.

1810   *Film and Television in the Service of Opera and Ballet and of Museums.* by UNESCO. 55 p. paper Paris: UNESCO, 1961.

A title in the UNESCO series, *Reports and Papers on Mass Communications*, this paper (number 32) consists of reports on two meetings: the International Congress on Opera and Ballet in Television and Film, Salzburg, 1959, and the Conference of Museum, Film and Television Experts, Brussels, 1958.

1811   *Film and Television Makeup.* by Buchman, Herman. 223 p. illus. New York: Watson Guptill, 1973.

Although intended for a specialized audience, this volume on makeup techniques is so clear and comprehensive that it will fascinate many a reader. By the use of illustrations and a modest text, the author outlines procedures for all types of makeup. Beginning with a description of tools and materials, he indicates basic techniques for black and white film and for color film. There are chapters on Aging, The Bald Cap, Latex Rubber Face Pieces, Wigs, and Beards. One section is devoted to ways of obtaining special effects—blood, bruises, scars, tattoos, burns, etc. How to provide makeup for the black performer is also indicated.

Most of the book is devoted to film makeup; only one short chapter on television requirements is provided. The final rewarding section, a gallery of great makeup achievements, features Olivier, Guinness, Muni, Chaney, Laughton, Karloff, Barrymore and others. Very few females appear except under a subheading entitled "Their Individual Looks Became Their Trademark," which may be a bit of a cop-out by the author. Where, for example, is Crawford in A WOMAN'S FACE (1941), Dietrich in WITNESS FOR THE PROSECUTION (1957), etc.?

A list of suppliers and a general index conclude the book. Picture quality is uniformly excellent with both color photos and black and white illustrations reproduced with a care essential for this type of book. Anyone concerned with film makeup will find this book to be an essential.

1812   *Film and Television Materials for Politics.* by British Universities Film Council. 92 p. paper London: British Universities Film Council, 1976.

1813   *Film and Television Periodicals in English.* by Elsas, Diana; and Kelso, Lulu. 9 p. paper Washington, D.C.: American Film Institute, 1977.

A title in the *Factfile* series, this pamphlet first lists film periodicals and then the various indexes that can be used to locate periodical information.

1814   *Film and the Critical Eye.* by De Nitto, Dennis; and Herman, William. 543 p. paper illus. New York: Macmillan, 1975.

The major section of this volume consists of essays on 14 classic films along with much shorter comments on six others. Selected for a detailed critical analysis are THE LAST LAUGH (Murnau, 1924), THE GOLD RUSH (Chaplin, 1925), M (Lang, 1931), GRAND ILLUSION (Renoir, 1938), THE RULES OF THE GAME (Renoir, 1939), BEAUTY AND THE BEAST (Cocteau, 1945), RASHOMON (Kurosawa, 1950), LA RONDE (Ophuls, 1950), THE SEVENTH SEAL (Bergman, 1956), WILD STRAWBERRIES (Bergman, 1957), ASHES AND DIAMONDS (Wajda, 1958), L'AVVENTURA (Antonioni, 1960), IL POSTO (Olmi, 1961), JULES AND JIM (Truffaut, 1961).

In most cases the perspective, the story, characterization and themes, an analysis of major sequences, and the style/approach of the film are discussed. Two introductory sections are concerned with viewing and interpreting a film, and with the language and rhetoric of film. Closing sections include director biographies and filmographies, bibliographies and an index. The illustrations are mostly stills from the films and are used effectively throughout the book.

As a text for use in film courses, the volume consolidates well-selected and well-written information on 14 classic films in one volume. The lack of flexibility in choosing films may be a disadvantage to the book's use, however. Many film courses can only accommodate 14 feature film showings. Therefore the content of this volume must be in almost complete accord with the instructor's wishes in order to qualify as a student text. The book is excellent as a resource for the teacher of film courses, and, of course, will attract many individual readers who are interested in one or more of the films. Recommended for careful consideration as a text, but recommended without reservation as a reference reader.

1815 *Film and the Director.* by Livingston, Don. 209 p. paper illus. New York: Capricorn Books, 1969 (1953).

This is a reprint of a 1953 handbook whose title is misleading today. The book is a guide to all of the techniques and principles that are essential for filmmaking. Chapter titles such as the screen technique, the cut, movement, about camera, about sound, etc. indicate the coverage. Written before many of the new technological developments freed the filmmaker from the studio, the book still contains much valuable information. Outstanding diagrams on camera placement, composition, the process screen, and dubbing, along with charts, forms, schedules and illustrations add immeasurably to the book.

1816 *Film and the Future.* by Buchanan, Andrew. 104 p. illus. London: Allen & Unwin, 1945.

Various types of films are examined to provide some suggestions and direction for the future.

1817 *Film and the Historian.* by British Universities Film Council 50 p. paper London: British Universities Film Council, 1968.

1818 *Film and the Liberal Arts.* by Ross, T.J. 419 p. paper New York: Holt, Rinehart and Winston, 1970.

This textbook-anthology uses as a theme film and its relationships to certain liberal arts, such as rhetoric, literature, music, visual arts, society, and aesthetics. Several well-selected articles make up each section with many authorities represented. Under "Film and Society," for example, we have contributions by David Riesman, William Everson, Robert Warshow, Susan Sontag, Pauline Kael, Kingsley Amis, and Marshall McLuhan. A series of discussion and exercise questions follow each article.

For each major division, a group of films is recommended. The annotations for these films are included in the appendix along with distributors. A short bibliography is also offered. The book is indexed.

Although the book is designed as a text, its use is not limited to that function. It offers fascinating reading, and some pertinent articles on film for general educational use. Recommended.

1819 *Film and the Narrative Tradition.* by Fell, John L. 284 p. illus. Norman, Okla.: University of Oklahoma Press, 1974.

The author's goal in this volume is to trace the influence of several 19th-century entertainment forms on the art form of the 20th century, motion pictures. He explores novels, comic strips, magazine illustrations, art movements, popular literature, theatre, fairground and parlor entertainments. Their determination of the narrative form that films would eventually take is his general theme. His method is to describe the age-period-societal framework, to discuss the various media emphasizing their use of time-space-movement, and finally to analyze some early films in order to trace their derivation from the other media forms.

Supporting this original unique study are some well-selected illustrations, a Kemp Niver filmography, a bibliography, a name index and a general index. This is a scholarly volume that deserves a wider audience and circulation than it will probably receive. Fell's formulation of a provocative thesis and his investigation of it using a historical research methodology makes for some fascinating moments of reader stimulation and discovery. Highly recommended.

1820 *The Film and the Public.* by Manvell, Roger. 352 p. paper illus. Baltimore: Penguin Books, 1955.

This perhaps hard-to-find paperback is a successor to the author's *Film* but is, for all practical purposes, a different volume. Major sections here are The Silent Film, The Sound Film, The Film and Industry, The Cinema and Society, and Television and the Film. A middle section studies some 23 classic films as models of the different form and styles of filmmaking which reveal the development of the art.

As in the earlier volume, there is an extended bibliography. A brilliant listing of directors and their films follows. Divided into five historical periods, this director's filmography covers the art up to 1954, and its quality and uniqueness alone can justify acquiring the book. The illustrations are beautiful. Highly recommended.

1821 *Film and Theatre.* by Nicoll, Allardyce. 255 p. New York: Thomas Y. Crowell, 1936.

The author's purpose in this older volume is to present the basic principles underlying cinematic art and then to relate these principles to the art of the stage. While it is scholarly and well-documented, the writing has a seeming acceptance of stage-theatre drama but a hesitating and questioning approach to cinema. The relative age of each of these arts in 1936 probably explains this attitude. Then, too, the author's field of specialization is drama, not film. One might wonder what he would say today with quality theatre offerings becoming fewer while motion picture masterpieces appear with greater frequency than ever. This book is interesting historically and one of its assets is an extended bibliography on cinema.

1822 *Film and/as Literature.* by Harrington, John. 364 p. paper illus. Englewood Cliffs, N.J.: Prentice Hall, 1977.

Certain relationships which exist between film and literature are the concern of this anthology. Divided into seven major sections, the text explores adaptation, theatre, novels, poetry, authorship-auteurship, message-medium, and the common concerns of film and literature. Each of the sections contains several articles which are rather standard pieces of cinema literature, usually written by well-known authors. Harrington's major contribution to the book seems to have been the selection and arrangement of the pieces. He does provide a short introduction to each section. The Library of Congress Cataloging in Publication Data provided indicates both a bibliography and an index, but neither were present in the paperback editon examined.

What has been provided is a theoretical discussion of certain major issues existing in/between film and literature; it is advanced, specialized material that demands considerable reader background. Recommended.

1823 *Film Animation: A Simplified Approach.* by Halas, John. 93 p. paper illus. New York: Unipub, 1976.

This book is part of the series, *Monographs on Communication Technology and Utilization.* It is concerned with film animation, presenting some basic techniques for the experienced filmmaker. Its intention is to suggest short-cuts in time, material and facilities in order that more animated films may be produced by units with modest budgets. Six detailed chapters cover basic principles, techniques, mechanics, preproduction, production, and economy.

The book is indexed and well illustrated. The author, who is also known as the director of ANIMAL FARM (1955), has put forth a practical and readable text that will serve the interested filmmaker in many ways. The quality of production and the reasonable price are additional reasons for it to be recommended.

1824 *Film Animation as a Hobby.* by Hobson, Andrew; and Hobson, Mark. 46 p. illus. New York: Sterling, 1975.

A delightful how-to-do-it book designed for young people but valuable to aspiring filmmakers of all ages. Opening sections offer suggestions on the making of short animated films by using the single (or few) frame release method. Equipment, speeds, timing, cutouts, planning and shooting are discussed. A visual script for a 5 minute film, DEAR OLD DAD, is presented. Closing sections treat other types of animation, special effects, and editing. The book is beautifully illustrated and is indexed.

In a clear logical progression the steps in simple film animation are outlined. The reader will be attracted, challenged, and rewarded by this book. Highly recommended.

1825 *The Film Answers Back: An Historical Appreciation of the Cinema.* by Robson, E. W.; and Robson, M. M. 336 p. illus. London: John Lane, The Bodley Head, 1939.

Interwoven through this history of the cinema are several major themes, three of which are 1) the power of the box office to determine film content, 2) the cultures of various nations as reflected in their films, and 3) the potential of film as a force for world good. The use of a historical approach combined with sociological argument is not a new form but it does serve well in this instance. The volume is dated, going only to the mid-thirties in its film survey. There are many illustrations and an index. A stimulating, scholarly book that will appeal to all those interested in total cinema. The short analyses of many memorable films will delight readers.

This volume was reprinted in 1972 by Arno.

1826 *Film Appreciation.* by Casebier, Allan. 207 p. paper illus. New York: Harcourt, Brace, Jovanovich, 1976.

An introductory textbook designed for film appreciation courses, this volume uses analysis of conventional filmmaking techniques and devices to help students understand and evaluate what they see on the screen. Many examples from well-known films are offered along with illustrations, a filmography, a bibliography, and an index.

1827 *Film Appreciation: A Creative Look at Film Arts.* by Abi-Nader, Sister Jeanette. 96 p. paper Glassboro, N.J.: Educational Impact, 1979.

A mini-course containing student-oriented information and assignments. This introduction to film is accompanied by a filmography and a bibliography.

1828 *Film Appreciation: The Art of Five Directors.* by Seton, Marie. 70 p. paper illus. New Delhi: National Institute of Audio Visual Education, 1965.

1829 *Film Appreciation: An Outline and Study Guide for Colleges and Universities.* by Phillips, Leona; and Phillips, Jill. New York: Gordon Press, 1978.

1830 *Film Archetypes: Sisters, Mistresses, Mothers, Daughters.* by Welsh, Janice R. 371 p. New York: Arno, 1978.

The original title of this study, written at Northwestern University in 1975, was *An Analysis of the Female: Images of Hollywood's Most Popular Post World War II Female Stars.* It deals with a topic not usually found in the *Dissertations on Film* series — that of the female star image. Welsh uses Doris Day, Debbie Reynolds, Marilyn Monroe, Kim Novak, Elizabeth Taylor, Audrey Hepburn and Grace Kelly for her investigation. Their film roles are examined for content, age, economic/social status, marital status, family visibility, nationality, locale, era, studio, director, male lead, genre, and structure. Each star is first treated separately and then in concert in the summary section.

The conclusions are numerous, with the stars assigned to predictable image categories: sisters (Day, Reynolds); mistresses (Monroe, Novak); daughters (Hepburn, Kelly) and mother (Taylor). An appendix and a bibliography are added.

1831 *Film Art: An Introduction.* by Bordwell, David; and Thompson, Kristin. 339 p. paper illus. Reading,

Mass.: Addison-Wesley, 1979.

The purpose of this book is to provide an introduction to the aesthetics of film by emphasizing the whole film. It treats film production, form, function, style, techniques, critical analysis, and history; and employs frame enlargements, notes, queries, an index, and suggestions for reading and research to enrich the text. Concentration is on those elements that enable us to experience film as an art form rather than as an educational, propaganda, or social history medium.

Choice, arrangement, and presentation of the material is uniformly excellent. The approach here is more pedantic than entertaining and a serious study of the text will provide most readers with a solid base in film aesthetics. Recommended.

1832 *Film as a National Art: NFB of Canada and the Film Board Idea.* by James, C. Rodney. New York: Arno, 1977.

This massive volume contains adetailed history of The National Film Board of Canada and its predecessor, an overview of the 8000 films it has produced, a discussion of its relationship with the Canadian government, and, finally, an account of the contribution/role played by John Grierson in establishing the Board.

This is a specialized history whose reference value is enhanced by the inclusion of a 40-page index.

1833 *Film As a Subversive Art.* by Vogel, Amos. 336 p. illus. New York: Random House, 1974.

The subversion of existing values, institutions, mores, and taboos by the film art is the subject of this volume. The titles of its three major divisions can only suggest the detailed content: the subversion of form (time, space, plot, narrative, montage, movement, etc.); the subversion of content (godard, Nazi cinema, Third World cinema, etc.); forbidden subjects of the cinema (visual taboos, nudity, homosexuality, blasphemy, anti-clericalism, witchcraft, etc.) A final part entitled "Towards a New Consciousness" provides an overview and summary with emphasis on recent films. Each chapter contains text material, an annotated filmography, and many illustrations. A solid, compact bibliography, employs three subject headings: cinema, art, and general. Indexes for English language films, foreign language films and directors are provided.

This is a fascinating book to read, to look at and to explore. Its consideration of forbidden, controversial, and taboo topics is handled in both an intellectual and popular fashion. Many readers will find using it a most provocative experience because of its subject matter and its illustrations. Recommended for mature individuals.

1834 *Film as Art.* by Arnheim, Rudolf. 230 p. Berkeley, Calif.: University of California Press, 1966.

The writings contained in this volume stem from the thirties. Arnheim's theory is that the restrictions of film are the very factors which make it an art. His enthusiasms for sound, color and third dimension in film are minimal. Using many examples the book describes the basic elements of the film medium and compares them with their counterparts "in reality." The differences provide the film medium with its artistic resource.

The volume contains such a wealth of comment and theory that it can provide a continual intellectual delight to the devotee or student. Consider this statement written by Arnheim during the twenties: "Artistic and scientific descriptions of reality are cast in molds that derive not so much from the subject matter itself as from the properties of the medium employed."

1835 *Film as Film.* by Perkins, V. F. 198 p. paper Baltimore, Md.: Penguin Books, 1972.

As indicated in his subtitle, "Understanding and Judging Movies," Perkins attempts to define what makes a good movie and to establish criteria for evaluating films. The films used for examples are popular ones rather than art films or critics' choices. An overview of critical theories from Vachel Lindsay in 1922 through Arnheim, Balazs, Kracauer, Rotha, Manvell and others follows. He concludes that their theories emphasized creation rather than perception. For a better definition of film, it is necessary to concentrate on the screen. He considers, in turn, the photograph, technology, technique, form, discipline,world image, participation, direction and authorship. His final definition of fiction film is "A synthetic process whose conventions allow the creation of forms in which thought and feeling are continually related to our common experience in the world."

What Perkins is proposing is a spectator-based aesthetic rather than one determined by imposed conventions and nonapplicable criteria. "A theory of film is a theory of film criticism—not of film making." This volume can be read for the author's provocative and well-argued statement or for a review of some aesthetic theories advanced during the past 60 years. Recommended.

1836 *Film as Film: Critical Responses to Film Art.* by Boyum, Joy Gould; and Scott, Adrienne. 397 p. paper illus. Boston: Allyn and Bacon, 1971.

This exploration of the criteria for modern film criticism uses more than 100 examples of film criticism as they apply to 25 films. A short introductory portion entitled "Theory" talks of film as art, some inherent personal problems in the critical act, and other problems of criticism whichstem from the nature of film itself. The major portion, logically called "Practice," gives several critical evaluations or reviews for each film. The number of reviews or criticisms varies: for example, 8-1/2 (1963) has three while BLOW-UP (1967) has eight.

A listing of ten books the authors recommend as being helpful in a study of film is offered. Included are Arnheim, Bluestone, Eisenstein, Huss-Silverstein, Kracauer, Lindgren, Manvell, Montagu, Pudovkin, and Stephenson-Debrix—a rather heavy serving of film aesthetics.

The book can be used as a text, as a reference for the 25 classic films, or simply for reading pleasure. It brings together some provocative arguments on film criticism, but the meat of the book is the collection of reviews. Acceptable.

1837 *Film As History: The Nature of Film Evidence.* by Grenville, J. A. S. 24 p. paper illus. Birmingham, England.: University of Birmingham, 1971.

A printing of an inaugural lecture delivered at the University of Birmingham in 1970 by John Ashley Soames Grenville.

1838 *Film As Insight.* by Fischer, Edward. 208 p. paper illus. Notre Dame, Ind.: Fides, 1971.

The theme of this excellent book is insight into the human condition via films. In the first section, Fischer examines the techniques that filmmakers use to create this insight. The second longer section looks at certain films that explore what it's like to be human. Films mentioned in the text are arranged alphabetically in a final index and the distributors of the films are noted. A few illustrations appear in a center section. The strength of this volume comes from Fischer's ability to write with clarity and intelligence about his particular way of approaching films. Without becoming pedantic or overly philosophical, he makes a valid statement that offers an aesthetic for consideration: the finest films are mirrors of man.

His selection of films for use as examples and for discussion is defensible and will create a desire in the reader to see many of them once again. This is an excellent volume that will appeal to and ultimately please a wide range of readers. Highly recommended.

1839 *Film as Investment.* by Madden, Paul M. 45 p. paper London: Pursuit Productions, 1977.

This short presentation on the economics of film production includes several tables of data.

1840 *Film Biographies.* by Brakhage, Stan. 295 p. paper illus. Berkeley, Calif.: Turtle Island, 1979.

An unusual collection of subjects is presented by Stan Brakhage in this collective biography. In conversational essays which combine biographical data, critical appreciation and interpretation, he discusses Melies, Griffith, Dreyer, Eisenstein, Chaplin, Keaton, Vigo, Laurel & Hardy, Lang, Murnau, and Dovzhenko. One additional piece deals with the initial conception of THE CABINET OF DR. CALIGARI (1919) by Hans Janowitz and Carl Mayer.

Using the techniques of a practiced lecturer, Brakhage brings to his subjects a familiarity and an understanding of what it is to be a filmmaker. While some of his statements are pure suppositions, he provides enough supporting fact, argument, and data so that these conjectures seem both possible and likely. A portrait introduces each section.

It should be noted that the essays on Melies, Griffith, Dreyer and Eisenstein appeared in an earlier volume, *The Brakhage Lectures.* The author has enlarged his group of subjects and provided a rich critical and biographical analysis of some legendary filmmakers. Recommended.

1841 *The Film Book for Business, Education, and Industry.* by Wilson, William H.; and Haas, Kenneth B. 259 p. illus. Englewood Cliffs, N.J.: Prentice-Hall, 1950.

After a few chapters explaining the use of films in marketing, industry, public relations, medicine, religion, and education, the volume discusses film production: script preparation, filming techniques, costs, and personnel. A few chapters on distribution and projection conclude the text.

A glossary, a list of film sources, and an index are added; the illustrations throughout are excellent. The statistical and source material is obsolete, but there is pictorial material and information that is still pertinent. Considerable borrowing of much of the presentation has taken place since 1950. The original remains quite valuable and should be updated.

1842 *The Film Book of J. R. R. Tolkien.* by Bakshi, Ralph; and Tolkien, J. R. R. 82 p. illus. New York: Ballantine, 1978.

This volume combines a text, based on the script of Ralph Bakshi's THE LORD OF THE RINGS (1978), with more than 150 color illustrations from the animated film. Bakshi's technique involved filming costumed actors first and using those frames to guide the animator's drawings.

1843 *Film: Book I—The Audience and the Filmmaker.* edited by Hughes, Robert 170 p. illus. New York: Grove Press, 1959.

The audience indicated in the subtitle receives attention from Siegfried Kracauer who describes the effects and gratifications offered to it via film, and by Arthur Knight who discusses the conflict of film art and commerce and the effect of that conflict on audiences. The remainder of the volume examines some of the problems of a few dedicated creative directors. The responses by 11 directors to a questionnaire, sections from two film scripts which were never made, and articles on Fellini, Flaherty, Stoney, and Mekas complete the work. Satisfying for the advanced reader.

1844 *Film: Book II—Films of Peace and War.* edited by Hughes, Robert. 255 p. illus. New York: Grove Press, 1962.

An in-depth examination of the issues, problems, and difficulties which arise when the film artist attempts to create an honest anti-war film. Articles, interviews, and a question-and-answer section form the first part of the text. The most valuable latter portions are perhaps the scripts of Renais' NIGHT AND FOG (1955), and Huston's LET THERE BE LIGHT (1945).

Since this volume was written before MASH (1970), CATCH-22 (1970) and PATTON (1970) appeared on screens, it is interesting to re-read the article entitled "Nobody Dies—Shades of Patriotism in the Hollywood War and Anti-War Film" by Colin Young. Other articles by such as Herbert Gold, Norman McLaren and Donald Richie are equally stimulating. This volume combines three topics (war, peace, and films) of intense concern to today's youth.

1845 *The Film Buff's Bible of Motion Pictures (1915-1972)*. edited by Baer, D. Richard. Hollywood, Calif.: Hollywood Film Archive, 1972.

In this reference book more than 13,000 films are listed along with ratings supplied by Baer/Hollywood Film Archive placed alongside the ratings of Steven Scheuer (*Movies on TV*) and Leonard Maltin (*TV Movies*). In addition, the year of release, the running time, the distributor, and occasional comments are noted. Each listing is given one line resulting in small type and very brief comments. A final section lists about 1000 alternate titles for some selected films. See *The Film Buff's Checklist*.

1846 *The Film Buff's Catalog*. by Meyer, William R. 432 p. New Rochelle, N.Y.: Arlington House, 1979.

This book offers a collection of film topics handled in a partial and rather casual fashion. It contains a book bibliography, a list of periodicals, a guide to selected film directors, a set of annotated genre/topic filmographies, and lists of film distributors, schools, instructors, bookshops, photo sources, research facilities, repertory cinema, soundtracks and fan clubs.

Much of this information has been offered for many years by annuals (*The International Film Guide, The International Motion Picture Almanac*), by series (*Cinema Booklist I, II, III*), and by books (*The American Cinema, Film Music*). The major contribution of the author seems to be the selection and assembling of material.

Each of the selected topics deserves consideration with detail and depth provided. The surface coverage given here constitutes a mere sampling. The "Buff" mentioned in the title will probably find many of Meyer's choices familiar and not particularly useful. Other than a beginner or novice, it is difficult to think of any potential reader-audience for this volume.

1847 *The Film Buff's Bible of Motion Pictures (1915-1972)*. edited by Baer, D. Richard. 171 p. Hollywood: Calif.: Hollywood Film Archive, 1972.

In this reference book more than 13,000 films are listed along with ratings supplied by Baer/Hollywood Film Archive, placed alongside the ratings of Steven Scheuer (*Movies on TV*) and Leonard Maltin (*TV Movies*). In addition the year of release, the running time, the distributor, and occasional com-

ments are noted. Each listing is given one line, resulting in small type and very brief comments. A final section lists about 1000 alternate titles for some selected films.

There is very little reason for this book when the reader can obtain more information at a much lower cost in either Scheuer or Maltin.

1848 *The Film Business.: A History of British Cinema, 1896-1972*. by Betts, Ernest. 349 p. illus. New York: Pitman Pub. Co., 1973.

The qualifications of author Ernest Betts to write a book on such a broad topic as the history of British cinema are impressive. He has been a scenario writer, film critic and a public relations representative for major studios for more than 40 years. In a previous volume, *Inside Pictures*, he offered a large helping of personal trivia. In this newer and far superior book, Betts is concerned with providing factual information and interpretation about an industry. Not only are many films considered, but also attention is given to the social and political framework in which they first appeared. Betts divides his account into the silent era, the early transition to sound films, the emergence of the creative artisans of the thirties, war-time films and documentaries, the post-war period, transition in the fifties, and the emergence of new talents and products in the sixties and early seventies.

Although there is some lack of consistency in the form of the presentation, the overall range of material and its efficient, no-nonsense exposition minimize this fault. Some nicely reproduced illustrations are grouped in a center section, which weakens their contribution to the book. More visuals placed to correlate with the text sections would add to the book's quality. As a valid historical survey that can stand by itself, or as a short alternative to Rachel Low's epic series, this volume can be recommended.

1849 *Film Canadiana.: The Canadian Film Institute Yearbook of Canadian Cinema, 1972-1973*. edited by Chenier, Louise. 238 p. paper illus. Ottawa: Canadian Film Institute, 1973.

Written in English and French, this yearbook for 1972-1973 offers a filmography of Canadian films; a bibliography of books and periodical articles on Canadian film; a listing of Canadian film organizations, festivals, awards, statistics; and a general index. Volume 2 covered 1970-1971 in 144 pages while Volume 3 covering 1971-1972 appeared in two parts

—a bilingual filmography listing fiction and nonfiction films in the first part, and a group of indexes in the second. Quarterly issues of Film Canadiana are available along with a yearly cumulation volume from the Canadian Film Institute.

1850 *Film Canadiana 1978-79.* edited by Reid, Alison. 335 p. paper illus. Ottawa: Canadian Film Institute, 1979.

In four major sections — filmography, bibliography, organizations, festivals and awards — this annual covers the Canadian film scene. The volume has been enlarged and now includes five introductory articles, a film production services list, and an expanded subject index for the films. The text is bilingual and contains a few illustrations. This is a fine, one-volume reference that will answer most questions on contemporary Canadian filmmaking.

1851 *The Film Career of Alain Robbe-Grillet.* by Van Wert, William F. 208 p. Boston: G.K. Hall, 1977.

In this study-resource on Alain Robbe-Grillet, the established format for the *Film Career* series is repeated— biography, critical evaluation, filmography, annotated bibliography, archival sources, film distributors, and index. Robbe-Grillet's films are few (only eight) but his influence as a novelist and filmmaker has been enormous — a fact evidenced by nearly 600 articles mentioned in the bibliography. Since Robbe-Grillet and his work are known only to a small audience in this country, the book is most suitable for film students and scholars.

1852 *The Film Career of Billy Wilder.* by Seidman, Steve. 175 p. Boston: G.K. Hall, 1977.

There are several parts to this reference-source book on Billy Wilder. The first two are biographical and deal with Wilder's career in Europe and Hollywood. A long detailed filmography, an annotated bibliography, a list of projects based on Wilder's work, archival sources, a distributor list, and title and author indexes are also provided.

Wilder's films have been the subject of several other volumes. The combination of biographical text, critical analysis, and reference material make this book one of the better ones.

1853 *The Film Career of Buster Keaton.* by Wead, George; and Lellis, George. 174 p. Boston: G.K. Hall, 1977.

Here is a reference-source book about Buster Kea-

ton and his films. It includes: a biography; a critical survey of his work; an annotated, detailed filmography; a lengthy bibliography; archival sources; and a distributor's list. Although Keaton's work looked spontaneous, it was the result of careful, patient planning and hard work. Themes, structures, techniques and perspectives found in the films are noted with an emphasis on their contradictory comic-versus- serious nature.

1854 *Film Cataloguing Handbook.* by Smither, Roger B.; and Penn, David J. 58 p. paper illus. London: Imperial War Museum, Department of Information Retrieval, 1976.

1855 *Film Catalogue.* 761 p. Toronto, Ontario: College Biblio. Centre, 1973.

This loose-leaf catalog of films, videotapes, and loops used in Ontario colleges is computer-generated. Monthly updates are provided and there are half-year cumulations. Films are placed in a subject arrangement with data and description provided. There are name, title, and subject indexes given along with the various college codes. This latter information is used to indicate custody of a particular film.

1856 *Film Cataloguing Rules.* edited by Film Production Librarians Group, Cataloguing Committee. 71 p. paper illus. London: ASLIB, 1963.

In addition to noting the rules for cataloguing fiction and nonfiction films, attention is also given to compilation films, news films, pictorial material other than films, sound material, added entries, capitalization, punctuation, figures, etc. A section of the book is devoted to definitions, abbreviations, and sample entries.

1857 *Film Censors and the Law.* by Hunnings, Neville March. 474 p. illus. London: Allen & Unwin, 1967.

A study of comparative law in the field of film censorship. The first section is devoted to England and examines four periods: 1896 to 1909, 1910 to 1924, 1925 to 1955, and 1956 to 1967. In the following section four Federal countries (United States, India, Canada, and Australia) and three European countries (Denmark, France, and the Soviet Union) are treated. A concluding section is supplemented by several appendixes which list court cases, x-rated films, films involved in censorship, statutes in various countries, etc. There is also an impressive bibliography and an index.

1858   *Film Censorship.* by Phelps, Guy. 319 London: Victor Gollancz, 1975.

This volume is concerned with recent censorship activities in Great Britain. The author includes sections on background history, boards of censors, political censorship, pressure groups, research, etc. Following a short chapter which considers censorship around the world, a summary of the problem is offered along with some speculation about the future. Numerous chapter notes and an index conclude the volume.

While the account offered here may be of interest to some researchers or students, the text will be of minor concern to most readers since it deals with persons, organizations, and situations that are largely unfamiliar to Americans. However, since the book has been well researched and carefully structured, it does offer some general ideas, thoughts, and concepts that are applicable anywhere. Acceptable.

1859   *Film Censorship in Australia.* by Bertrand, Ina. 227 p. illus. St. Lucia, Queensland: University of Queensland Press, 1978.

A chronological history of film censorship in Australia is provided here. From the initial primitive showings of the late 1800s to the permissive programs of today, the film medium has always been a target for censorship. Dr. Bertrand reviews the laws, persons, social attitudes and group pressures that have operated in the area of film censorship. Because this is a scholarly study that treats many unfamiliar films, its appeal to the American reader may be limited. On the other hand, the text, which at times deals with sex, violence, horror, blasphemy, drugs, low habits of life and assorted vices, is never without interest.

The volume is illustrated and contains chapter notes, a filmography of censored films, a list of governmental acts affecting films, a bibliography, and an index.

1860   *The Film Classic Library Series.* edited by Anobile, Richard. paper illus. New York: Avon, 1974- .

Using the technique that he introduced in the comedy volumes of the series *The Visual and Verbal Gems of ...*, which included *A Flask of Fields, Who's on First?, Hooray for Captain Spaulding, Why a Duck?,* and *A Fine Mess,* Anobile has created a fine series of film reconstructions or recreations using frame enlargements (usually 1000 to 1500 in number)

and all the original dialogue. This method allows the reader-viewer access to shot setups, camera angles, frame composition, and dialogue. Missing, of course, is movement and sound.

Presentation of the film in this form can satisfy many needs. Not only will the nostalgia buff be pleased, but the student-researcher- historian-writer has reliable source material to use at his convenience. The filmmaking techniques mentioned above can be studied and a detailed, individually paced analysis of the film is possible. In schools the books can be used with nonreaders since their format resembles a comic book with minimal dialogue. The possibilities of using this series in connection with reading problem groups seem great. To create readiness for film study or for book analysis is another potential for the series. Films appearing in the series include FRANKENSTEIN (1931), CASABLANCA (1942), PSYCHO (1960), THE MALTESE FALCON (1941), NINOTCHKA (1939), and STAGECOACH (1939). These titles show the same judicious selection evident in the choice of film frames. The series should be very popular; it represents the intelligent adaptation of an older technique to produce a new type of film book.

1861   *Film Classification: The Bishop Speaks Again.* by Kennedy, John E. 23 p. paper Notre Dame, Ind.: Our Sunday Visitor Press, 1966.

1862   *Film Collecting.* by McKee, Gerald. 224 p. illus. New York: A. S. Barnes, 1978.

The world of film collecting is described in this volume that is handicapped by its British origin. Copyright laws differ considerably in various countries, and as a result the availablity of films to collectors is directly proportional to the length of the copyright laws of each country. If a film falls into public domain, it is available to all. There are many such films in that category in the U.S. today. As a result the collection of 16mm prints is more prevalent here than in England where the collector's gauge seems to be super 8. The format there is usually 20 minute condensations of feature films available for sale from film companies. Since McKee emphasizes the narrow gauge collecting, his text is somewhat limited for the American reader/collector. He does offer some facts of historical interest, helpful hints on collecting in general, and some sources of information. Perhaps the most pertinent chapter is on 16mm collecting, in which there are listed many films which are in public domain in the United States. It might be noted that the cost of the super 8 copies often approaches that of the 16mm prints. The volume is illustrated and indexed.

In summary there is some information here to interest the experienced film collector in America. The beginner will find much of it to be theoretical and of limited practical value. Acceptable.

1863 *Film Composers in America: A Check List of Their Work.* edited by McCarthy, Clifford. 193 p. Hollywood: Oxford Press, 1953.

Supposedly, this basic reference tool was limited to a printing of 400 copies. If true, this was remedied by an updating and reprinting in 1972 by DaCapo Press.

Listing approximately 165 composers alphabetically, the book arranges the film compostitions of each in chronological fashion, going back in certain cases to scores for silent films. The latter part of the book is an alphabetical arrangement of film titles with the numerical composer reference given. Highly recommended.

1864 *Film Costume: An Annotated Bibliography.* by Prichard, Susan P. 577 p. Metuchen, N.J.: Scarecrow, 1981.

Almost 4000 citations are listed and described. The period covered is the silents to 1980 and designers, their costumes and the stars who wore them are treated.

1865 *A Film Course Manual.* edited by Sweeting, Charles. 60 p. paper Berkeley, Calif.: McCutchan Pub. Co., 1971.

Areas of film treated in this brief paperback include: film literature, history, reviewing, exhibiting, acting, writing, directing, aesthetics, research, and factual films. Each chapter is written by or devoted to an authority in that particular field. Designed by a teacher, the book is useful for most film courses either as the text for the course or as supplementary reading.

1866 *Film Course Study Guides.* by Kernan, Margot. paper illus. New York: Grove Press Films, 1973.

Three course outlines are available in this series: the politics of revolution, racism, and radical voices. Each includes a short introduction and a series of suggested films for the course. The film is outlined, some information offered about its director, and the credits are listed. Naturally, many of the films are distributed by Grove Press. Additional features appear in the individual volumes. In politics, for example, there is a chronology of how film began; in racism there is a chronology on civil rights and the law. All three have suggested reading lists.

The outlines provide good starting points for building film courses, but it would be naive to think that they are sufficient by themselves. Much more film material is available on these subjects than is indicated here, and a more balanced program would probably result from its inclusion. Acceptable.

1867 *Film Craft: The Art of Picture Production.* by Brunel, Adrian. 238 p. London: Newnes, 1935.

A collection of comments which divides the phases of making films into pre-scenario, production, and editing. This book also offers two shooting scripts, one silent and one sound. A glossary and an appendix are included.

1868 *Film Criticism.: An Index to Critics' Anthologies.* by Heinzkill, Richard. 151 p. Metuchen, N.J.: Scarecrow Press, 1975.

This short index facilitates the location of selected reviews and essays of some 27 film critics that have been published in 40 anthologies. Most of the index headings are film titles, with occasional listings of actors, directors, and authors whose work has been discussed by a particular critic. It is possible to find that reviews of LA GUERRE EST FINIE (1966) by Crist, Kael, Kauffmann, Reed, Sarris, Schickel, Sheed and Simon are available in specific books. Frank Capra is discussed by Farber, Kael, Pechter and Sarris, while Mel Torme's book on Judy Garland, *The Other Side of the Rainbow* is discussed by Sarris.

Of course the value of the index volume depends upon the availability of the 40 primary volumes.

1869 *Film Criticism and Caricatures — 1943-1953.* by Winnington, Richard. 196 p. illus. London: Paul Elek, 1975.

In 1948 critic Richard Winnington (1905-1953) published a selection of his work and caricatures taken from the *News Chronicle* and entitled *Drawn and Quartered.* Paul Rotha has made a new selection from the period 1943-53 for this book. A short biographical sketch introduces the drawings and reviews, most of which are brief but effective. The caricatures are delightful and express a type of visual comment that is rare in film criticism. A few longer articles conclude the book. There is an index.

This is rich entertainment that proves film criticism

can be both light and perceptive. Highly recommended.

1870   *Film Criticism in Popular American Periodicals 1933-1967.* by Poteet, George H. III p. New York: Revisionist Press, 1977.

Although unidentified, this volume seems to be a dissertation done in 1971 at Teachers College, Columbia University. It is "a computer-assisted content analysis" of selected film criticism found in *Christian Century, Commonweal, The New Republic, Newsweek,* and *The New Yorker.* The text is presented in the typewritten page format of dissertations.

The study established 13 themes (audience reaction, plot description, writer, genre, technical comment etc), and some 5536 sentences composed of 131,066 words were examined. Shifts in the emphases of the critical writings over certain periods were noted, and the changing face of film criticism from 1933 to 1967 was suggested.

Certainly the methodology used in this study would be a most provocative topic for discussion by some film study authorities. The volume itself should be of some interest to doctoral candidates and committee members. Others will find it to be much ado about relatively little.

1871   *The Film Criticism of Otis Ferguson.* edited by Wilson, Robert. 475 p. Philadelphia: Temple University Press, 1971.

A forgotten film critic for *The New Republic,* Otis Ferguson wrote during the years from 1934 to 1942. He was killed in World War II at the age of 36. A few essays accompany the hundreds of film reviews which are said to represent about 80 percent of all his writing.

The reviews and articles are enjoyable, informative, perceptive, and timeless—an indication of a critic writing not only for his time but well ahead of it. A name index and a title index complete the book. As excellent reading, as a sample of exemplary film criticism and as a reference work, this book is simply outstanding.

1872   *Film, Culture, and the Black Filmmaker A Study of Functional Relationships and Parallel Developments.* by Diakite, Madubuko. New York: Arno Press, 1980.

This volume examines how black filmmakers reflect

their perceptions of the world via the film medium. A title in the *Dissertations on Film* series.

1873   *Film Culture Reader.* edited by Sitney, P. Adams 438 p. illus. New York: Praeger, 1970.

A collection of articles taken from *Film Culture,* the independent filmmakers' magazine. Presenting avant-garde views, principles, and beliefs for more than 15 years, the magazine is an American equivalent to several of the European film journals. The articles are representative and include contributions by nearly all the celebrities of the underground film movement. The book should be of great interest to college students and those engaged in making experimental films.

1874   *Film Cutting.* by Burder, John. 158 p. paper illus. New York: Hastings House, 1975.

This is one of a new series called *Media Manuals* which deal with film and TV production and are from the same publisher as *The Technique of ...* and *The Work of ...* series. In this instance the subject is film editing and it is covered in admirable fashion by text, illustrations, and diagram. The visuals are most impressive, often showing complex ideas with clarity. Basic techniques are presented along with practical tips and economical shortcuts. A bibliography and a glossary are included.

The idea of publishing *Media Manuals* is to be applauded. This one is an example of combining high quality production, useful material, and an excellent arrangement. Highly recommended.

1875   *Film Daily* Directors Annual and Production Guide of 1931. edited by Alicoate, J. New York: Gordon Press, 1976.

This usual content of these yearbooks deals with directors, editors, writers, their films, the studios, statistics, biographies, the code, releases, etc. Also reprinted by this publisher are the annuals for 1929, 1930, 1932, 1934, 1935, 1936 and 1937.

1876   *Film Daily Yearbook.* edited by Fordin, Hugh. 52 ed. 1074 p. illus. New York: Arno Press, 1970.

For many years this annual has been an essential reference for professionals. With the emergence of film as an art, the use of this volume by many others is assured. It contains statistical information and articles about the motion picture industry that are current, vital and obtainable nowhere else.

Current personnel, businesses, organizations, and services are noted, feature release credits for the year are listed, and one section gives the titles, release dates and studios of all feature films since 1915 (!). In another section, filmed books and plays with their original titles are named of this reference, making all 51 previous volumes (1918-1969) available. An essential film reference.

1877 *Film Daily* Yearbook (s), 1918-1941. 20 volumes New York: Gordon Press, 1976.

Reprinting of a series of valuable film reference books. Each contains an abundance of information and statistics on all phases of Hollywood film production.

1878 *Film Daily Yearbooks, 1918-1922.* illus. New York: Arno, 1973.

These are the first volumes of *Film Daily Yearbook*, known then as *Wid's Year Book*. This series includes: Volume 1, 1918; Volume 2, 1919-1920; Volume 3, 1920-1921; Volume 4, 1921-1922. The first two are a larger page size than the latter pair. Interesting for historians and researchers, but users should note the availability of the *Film Daily Yearbooks* from 1918 to 1969 on microfilm.

1879 *Film Daily Yearbooks, 1918-1969.* illus. New York: Arno, 1972.

These volumes have been available previously as a set or individually. Now they have been published on 18 reels of microfilm, 35mm format, at about 25 percent of the cost of the printed volumes. The amount and extent of information in these volumes is enormous and encompasses all aspects of the film industry. Highly recommended.

1880 *Film Design.* edited by Marner, Terence John. 165 p. paper illus. New York: A. S. Barnes, 1974.

This is the fourth volume in a series on professional motion picture techniques prepared in association with the London Film School. Twelve professional production designers and/or art directors are the major contributors to the text, which has been compiled, arranged and edited by Marner. The visual background of a film is the responsibility of the art director and he makes certain that each film shot is designed with care, accuracy, and intelligence. Obviously he works in very close concert with the director.

Topics discussed here include the production unit, design and preparation of locations, manipulation of space, studio-set design and special effects. Some outstanding examples of costume and film design are recommended for further study at the book's conclusion. Short biographies of the contributors to this volume are added and the book is indexed. The visuals used are most impressive and helpful. They consist of sketches, diagrams, color plates, and black and white photographs. Care has been exercised in their accurate reproduction. This is a fine technical volume that is highly recommended for the clarity of its presentation.

1881 *The Film Director: A Practical Guide to Motion Picture and Television Techniques.* by Bare, Richard L. 243 p. illus. New York: Macmillan, 1971.

This practical and readable guide to filmmaking techniques deals with topics such as how to direct, treatment of actors, use of film and camera, how to get a job directing, etc. Much of the general information offered is interesting and presented with intelligence and taste. The book is illustrated, indexed and includes a bibliography.

1882 *The Film Director as Superstar.* by Gelmis, Joseph. 316 p. Garden City, N. Y.: Doubleday, 1970.

After an introductory chapter on the role of directors in films, 16 directors are asked questions about film aesthetics and techniques, their personal backgrounds and opinions, and their advice to movie moviemakers. A short biography-and-filmography introduction precedes each interview and a picture of each director (except Bernardo Bertolucci) is also included. The interviews are moderately interesting. One quotable remark from Norman Mailer lingers: "Moviemaking is like sex ... you start doing it, and then you get interested in getting better at it."

1883 *Film Directors Guide: Western Europe.* by Parish, James Robert. 292 p. illus. Metuchen, N.J.: Scarecrow, 1976.

This is the second volume of a contemplated series that will ultimately consider film directors from Eastern Europe, Asia, Africa, and Australia. It is a filmography of directors who first gained prominence in Western Europe. The user should consult the list of countries represented to prevent possible confusion; for example Sweden, Norway, and Denmark are not included but certain credits for Hungarian and Czech directors do appear. The directors are arranged alphabetically by surname and, following a few bits of biographicalinformation, their films are listed in chronological order with the releasing company, the date, and other contributions of the subject noted (co-scripting, titling, editing, acting, etc.). James Robert Parish and his associates are profiled in the book's final pages.

1884   *Film Directors—A Guide to Their American Films.* by Parish, James Robert; and Pitts, Michael R. 436 p. illus. Metuchen, N.J.: Scarecrow Press, 1974.

Criteria for inclusion in this collection of 520 director filmographies include the following: national and international directors of American films were eligible; their films had to be considered as part of the American cinema; only films running more than four reels/40 minutes were included; serials and documentaries were included; entries were taken from both the silent and the sound eras of the American cinema. In providing this extensive group of filmographies, the authors hope that they will suggest some director studies to writers and researchers.

Each filmography lists the director's name, birthplace, and date of death, where applicable. Films are arranged chronologically by year of release. A few illustrations are sprinkled throughout the book. This is a valuable reference book.

1885   *Film Editing Handbook: Technique of 16mm Film Cutting.* by Churchill, Hugh B. 198 p. paper illus. Belmont, Cal.: Wadsworth Publishing, 1972.

This handbook was designed as a guide for students who are relatively inexperienced in film editing. It does not treat creative "editing" but addresses itself exclusively to "physical" editing. Based on the author's teaching experiences, the material is divided into two major sections: "Picture Cutting" and "Sound Cutting." In the opening silent film portion, the basic cutting techniques are introduced, and ultimately serve as a preparation for cutting the sound track. Each of the techniques is given separate attention with a purpose stated, followed by a step-by-step explanation. Drawings, charts, sample forms, and tables appear as supplementary material throughout the book.

The appendices, especially valuable, contain more sample forms and charts, a survey of editing equipment, a list of editing tools, and some manufacturer-supplier-dealer information. A short bibliography lists only four books devoted totally to film editing. Other references contain only individual chapters on either creative or physical editing. A detailed glossary and an index complete the book.

The book was designed to be read once and then used simultaneously with the physical act of editing, as a sort of lab manual or guide. Its effectiveness in actual use is not evaluated here. It does appear to have the potential for making a complex technical task much easier for the novice. Recommended.

1886   *Film Education: A Collection of Experiences and Ideas.* edited by Gidley, M.; and Wicks, Stephen. 96 p. Ontario: School of Education, University of Exeter, 1975.

This volume is number 36 in the *Themes in Education* series.

1887   *see   1886*

1888   *Film Education in Secondary Schools: A Study of Film Use and Teaching in Selected English and Film Courses.* by Lynch, Joan Driscoll. 297 p. New York: Garland, 1982.

A title in the *Dissertations on Film* series.

1889   *Film—Encounter.* by Currie, Hector; and Staples, Donald. 272 p. paper illus. Dayton, Ohio: Pflaum, 1973.

This collection of 248 full-page stills from classic films is divided into five parts, all of which have "Encounter" as a connecting theme. The Immediate Encounter, which opens the book, treats gesture and space among other philosophical concepts of film. On each page a still is offered with a quotation beneath it—the combination designed to prod and provoke reader thought rather than to explain. The Decisive Encounter, the Thematic, the Formal, and the Essential follow in the same pattern.

The book can be used on several levels. Simply as a collection of stills, it is quite beautiful. On another level, as an exercise in film aesthetics and theory, it takes on added value and fascination. In advanced classes, the book should generate unlimited discussion. The visual richness of the volume suggests many other uses, e.g., dismantling the book and using the visuals as illustrations of themes used in films, or as illustrations of filmmaking techniques. It will be a great aid to the teacher with imagination. The stills will suggest films for initial viewing or re-showing. Even the credits for the quotations provide a bibliography of sorts.

In summary, this is a volume which will appeal to

many different audiences. It is enthusiastically recommended as one of the finest film books to appear in the seventies.

1890 *The Film Encyclopedia.* by Katz, Ephraim. 1280 p. New York: Thomas Y. Crowell, 1979.

From AAAA (Associated Actors and Artists of America) to Zurlini, Valerio, this encyclopedia contains over 7000 entries. Its strongest offerings are the thousands of biographies of Hollywood filmmakers, with many entries being very detailed and including complete filmographies. The user will find entries for studios, history, technical terms, awards, film organizations, etc. In its subtitle, the claim is made that this is "The Most Comprehensive Encyclopedia of World Cinema in a Single Volume." If the word biographical could be inserted, the title might be valid. As a total encyclopedia, this volume suffers a bit in comparison with the technical entries of *The International Encyclopedia of Film.* Halliwell's *The Filmgoer's Companion* also may have some champions since it offers over 10,000 entries—though not in as detailed a fashion as Katz does here.

1891 *Film Essays and a Lecture.* by Eisenstein, Sergei; edited by Leyda, Jay 220 p. llus. London: Dobson Books, 1968.

This volume has several unusual examples of Eisenstein's writings. There is an estimate of the work of Charlie Chaplin, a tribute to John Ford and his film, YOUNG MR. LINCOLN (1939), and a lecture to his students on "Problems of Compostition." A listing of the published writings of Eisenstein with notations about their English translations is included. Certain of the essays are not easy to read, but the theory proposed makes the effort worthwhile. Recommended for serious students.

1892 *Film Evaluation: Why and How??* edited by Zeitlan, Susan C. 32 p. paper New York: Educational Film Libraries Association, 1963.

A report on the EFLA workshop held on January 24 and 25, 1963, in Chicago.

1893 *Film Evaluation Guide: Supplement Two.* edited by Dick, Esme J. 131 p. New York: Educational Film Library Association, 1972.

The first *Film Evaluation Guide* covered the period 1946-1965, while Supplement One dealt with 1965-67. This current compilation is made from the film

evaluation cards issued between September 1967 and August 1971. The films are arranged alphabetically by title and give a critical comment and a rating along with the usual data. Especially helpful is the subject index which directs the user to films which deal with a specific area—Asia, botany, city planning, sports, women, etc.

1894 *Film Evaluation Guide 1946-1965.* 526 p. New York: Educational Film Library Association, 1965.

This is the first compilation of the EFLA reviews of 4500 short films from 1946 to 1965 Available separately are two supplements covering 1965-1967 and 1967-1970. Since 1946 approximately 7000 films have been reviewed. Under the EFLA plan a subscriber receives about 36 film evaluation cards each month. The cards list subject area, running time, price, date, technical rating, critical comment, and a final rating. Evaluations of the films are done by committees made up of individuals from schools, colleges, libraries, etc. Cumulations of the cards are published in bound volumes as described above.

This is one of the few reference sources available for collected film evaluations. It should be noted that many of the short films reviewed are recognized classics and do not resemble the old-fashioned "Educational" motion picture.

1895 *The Film Experience: Elements of Motion Picture Art.* by Huss, Roy; and Silverstein, Nathan. 172 p. illus. New York: Harper & Row. 1968.

The purpose of this fine volume is "the expansion of perception and of the capacity to taste fully of tne film experience." The authors will probably be quite successful in this aim. By attention to such elements as continuity, visual rhythm within the shot, structural rhythm, imagery, tone, point of view and theme, an argument is presented. The work never falls into the trap of becoming pretentious or pedantic, but is always readable and interesting. Illustrations and diagrams are commendable and a good bibliography and an index are included. Highly recommended for any serious filmgoer.

1896 *Film Facts.* by Steinberg, Corbett S. 350 p. New York: Facts on File, 1980.

A potpourri of information about film topics is offered here. The material is arranged under seven large headings: The Market Place, The Stars, The Studios, The Festivals, The "Ten Best" Lists, The Awards, and The Codes and Regulations. Coverage includes financial successes, critical awards, movie "worsts," attendance, salaries, etc. This volume was published in 1978 as a much less expensive paperback entitled *Reel Facts*.

1897 *Film Fame.* by Robinson, Gerda. 210 p. paper illus. Beverly Hills, Calif.: Fame Pub. Co., 1966.

This paperback contains 100 star portraits (in an 8 inch x 10 inch close-up format) along with a full-page biographical essay for each portrait. Picture reproduction is excellent and the text is surprisingly literate. A good reference book with possible other uses. Recommended.

1898 *The Film Fan's Bedside Book (No. 1 and No. 2).* edited by Lynx, J. J. 144 & 136 p. illus. London: Coordination Press, 1948, 1949.

The outstanding feature of these volumes is the illustrations, many of which are in full color. Articles are arranged in a fan magazine anthology form and are only slightly better than those found in the pulps.

1899 *Film Fantasy Scrapbook.* by Harryhausen, Ray. 118 p. illus. New York: A. S. Barnes, 1972.

Author Harryhausen began his film career with George Pal and Willis O'Brien. Since then he has served as associate producer, special visual effects creator, or animator on many films. In this volume he is concerned with his specialty, the three-dimensional animated film. Using stills, sketches and diagrams from his personal collection, he has attempted to describe such special effects as front projection, traveling matte, sodium backing process, perspective photography, and the Dynamation Process.

The author considers individual films chronologically from KING KONG (1933) to THE VALLEY OF GWANGI (1969). For each he gives some short production background and then explains in detail some of the major challenges in visualizing the script. The sketches and stills are selected to correlate with specific sections of the text. An added bonus is the inclusion of advertisements for several of the later films.

There can be no quarrel with the author's credentials, the appeal of his topic, or the large number of effective visuals. However, there seems to be an editor-publisher willingness to settle for something less than excellence. Where, for example are the following. 1) A filmography for Harryhausen, O'Brien, or of those films which belong to this genre? 2) The

year of release for each film in the text? Trying to find the year for THE VALLEY OF GWANGI can be a research challenge. 3) An index to the specific techniques, names, titles, etc. in the text? Certainly this book has reference value. 4) Production control on certain reproductions? (Pages 33, 41, 63, etc., are badly reproduced). If film frames must be used, why not with the care noted elsewhere in the book? The use of greyish-colored pages throughout gives a drab appearance to the book. 5) Production control on the book's binding? After approximately three weeks, the covers on one edition began to buckle noticeably. 6) The editor expertise in selecting an appropriate title? This one does not indicate the richness of information within the book.

As implied above, the total effectiveness of this book is diminished by the absence of several simple components.

1900 *Film Festival.* by Scherer, Kees. 142 p. paper illus. London: Andre Deutsch, 1962.

This volume gives a short history of the Cannes Film Festival, a description of the personalities, starlets and happenings that characterize such events, and 95 photographs taken during the 13th Annual Festival. While the technical quality of the reproduction is high, the paper for the printed text resembles newsprint. Over all, of low quality and eminently forgettable unless you have a film competing in such an event. Not recommended.

1901 *The Film Finds Its Tongue.* by Green, Fitzhugh. 316 p. illus. New York: Benjamin Blom, 1971 (1929).

This book has the usual faults of a specialized reprint: an exhorbitant price, poorly reproduced photographs, and no introduction or preface to the edition. The emphasis in the rather patronizing text is on Warner Brothers and will remind readers of a literary style long in disuse.

1902 *Film Flam.* by Paul, Elliot. 160 p. London: Frederick Muller, 1956.

The comments of a writer in Hollywood.

1903 *Film Flashes.* 2 vols. illus. New York: Leslie-Judge, 1916.

Two older volumes, subtitled "The Wit and Humor of a Nation in Pictures," which contain anecdotes, satires, etc., about moving pictures.

1904 *Film Folk*. by Wagner, Rob. 356 p. illus. New York: The Century Co., 1918.

In this book the close-ups of the men, women and children who make the movies are fictional characters designed by the author to amuse and inform. By pretending to be a film favorite, a movie queen, a cameraman, a director, a male extra, a publicity man and a scenario writer, Wagner gives an informative portrait of motion picture making during the early days of the large studios. The original approach was quite satirical and the book today seems even more amusing. The few pictures blend nicely with the author's style and intent.

1905 *Film Form*. by Eisenstein, Sergei M. 279 p. paper illus. New York: Harcourt, 1949.

This is a collection of essays translated by Jay Leyda which put forth Eisenstein's theory of film. Included is an analysis of the Odessa Steps sequence from POTEMKIN (1925) and an essay entitled "Dickens, Griffith, and the Film Today" that points up the cinematic qualities in Dickens works. One of the early classics of film literature, this book is not always easy to read or to comprehend. For the dedicated historian or scholar.

1906 *Film Form and The Film Sense*. by Eisenstein, Sergei M. paper illus. New York: World, 1957.

Two Eisenstein classics combined in one inexpensive paperback.

1907   *see   1908*

1908 *The Film Game*. by Warren, Low. 236 p. illus. New York: Gordon Press, 1976 (1937).

Originally published in London by T. Werner Laurie, this overview of the film industry combined history, personality, production, appreciation, etc.

1909 *Film Genre: Theory & Criticism*. edited by Grant, Barry K. 249 p. Metuchen, N.J.: Scarecrow, 1977.

This anthology has as its theme the genre approach to film; it consists of 15 essays arranged in two sections. The first deals with the theory of genre while the second treats nine specific genres: screwball, disaster, epic, gangster, horror, musical, monster, sports, and the western. A lengthy bibliography is also arranged according to genre. The book is indexed.

The essays, all of which have been previously published, vary in approach, style, and quality. There is sufficient information, critical comment and original opinion here to warrant reader attention. However, the beginner is referred to *American Film Genres* for a stronger, more unified statement on the subject.

1910 *Film Goers Annual of 1932*. edited by Mutch, William A. 176 p. illus. New York: Gordon Press, 1976 (1932).

A profusely illustrated year book that waoriginally published in London.

1911 *Film Guide—Psychology Today Films*. 160 p. paper illus. Del Mar, Calif.: CRM Books, 1971.

This volume offers correlated reading to a series of eight films in the *Psychology Today* series. Titles of the films (and their chapter counterparts) are: (1) ASPECTS OF BEHAVIOR; (2) THE SENSORY WORLD; (3) INFORMATION PROCESSING; (4) LEARNING; (5) DEVELOPMENT; (6) SOCIAL PSYCHOLOGY; (7) PERSONALITY; (8) ABNORMAL BEHAVIOR. Evaluation forms for each of the films are added. Noted here as an example of the intelligent correlation of print and film in the learning-teaching process.

1912 *Film Guide's Handbook: Cartoon Production*. by Turney, Harold M. 96 p. paper illus. Hollywood: Film Guide.

A title in the *Film Guide* series devoted to the production of animated cartoons.

1913 *The Film HAMLET* edited by Cross, Brenda. 76 p. illus. London: Saturn Press, 1948.

Stills and articles on the prodution of HAMLET. Most of the usual craftsmen-artists are represented as is Laurence Olivier who tells of adapting the play to the screen.

1914 *The Film Idea*. by Solomon, Stanely J. 403 p. paper illus. New York: Harcourt, Brace, Jovanovich, 1972.

A textbook on the narrative film, composed of three major sections. The first examines the elements of the film medium—time, space, motion, shots, editing, dimension, color, the craftsman and the artist. Part two is concerned with the historical development of the narrative film, from Melies and Porter to Bergman. Theory and aesthetics are the concern of the last part in which there is further exploration of shots, movement, editing, verbal-visual interactions and structure. The appendix contains a glossary, a filmography of selected directors and a bibliography. Illustrations are plentiful and their reproduction is uniformly excellent. A few pages of color illustrations have received the same care and are quite attractive. The quality and arrangement of the content is impressive, as is the production. As a textbook for college courses in film study, the book is outstanding. Highly recommended.

1915   *The Film in Colonial Development.* by Conference on The Film in Colonial Development. 52 p. paper London: British Film Institute, 1948.

A report of a conference which dealt with films in education.

1916   *The Film in Education.* by Buchanan, Andrew. 256 p. illus. London: Phoenix House, 1951.

A definition of the educational film begins this survey of the film in education, which deals with its history in England and its development in specific academic fields. Planning, production, and distribution are considered, with much attention paid to two British national organizations: The National Committee for Visual Aids and The Educational Foundation for Visual Aids.

Presentation, with its elements of introduction, projection, and discussion, is treated; a symposium of teachers offer opinions and the author analyzes their conclusions; and the final topic is the effect of entertainment films on children. A closing summary statement is made by the author.

The author attempts too much, but this older volume includes sufficient useful information, valuable comment and good suggestions to warrant attention. The book is indexed and has a bibliography that is of historical interest.

1917   *Film in English Teaching.* edited by Knight, Roy. 248 p. London: British Film Institute, 1972.

A collection of articles and advice by teachers on using films in those courses dealing with the English language. Films mentioned are not always familiar or accessible in the U.S. A bibliography, course outlines, material sources, and other appendixes are included.

1918   *The Film in France.* by Fowler, Roy. 56 p. paper illus. London: Pendulum Pub., 1946.

This small book, an examination of the films made in France during the German occupation (approximately 1940 to 1945) was designed to acquaint the British public with a body of films that had not been shown outside France. A short but interesting study.

1919   *Film in Higher Education and Research.* edited by Groves, Peter D. 332 p. paper illus. New York: Pergamon Press, 1966.

This is the printed version of a conference entitled "The Use of Film in Higher Education and Research" held at the College of Advanced Technology, Birmingham, England, in September 1964. Major topics include the film and the university, the supply of films, films in teaching, films in research, and the production of films. Several articles or addresses are given under each topic. Also printed is a panel discussion on "The Future of the Film in Higher Education."

While the theme is undeniably valid and imposing, certain of the articles appear either too elementary or too contrived. Reference names and organizations mentioned in the appendices are almost exclusively British.

1920   *The Film in History: Restaging the Past.* by Sorlin, Pierre. 226 p. illus. Oxford, England: Blackwell, 1980.

1921   *Film in India, 1963.* by India Ministry of Information and Broadcasting. 28 p. paper Delhi: India Ministry of Information and Broadcasting, 1964.

1922   *The Film in Industrial Safety Training.* by Ignatius, Paul R. 119 p. paper Boston: Harvard Graduate School of Business Administration, 1949.

This paper, which deals with industrial accidents and the use of films in training personnel in safety procedures, was part of an audiovisual aids research project which was begun at the Harvard Graduate School of Business Administration in 1946. It includes bibliographical footnotes.

1923   *The Film in National Life.* by Commission on Educational and Cultural Films. 204 p. London: Allen and

Unwin, 1932.

A report of an enquiry conducted by the Commission on Educational and Cultural Films into the service which the motion picture may render to education and social progress. Includes a bibliography, and a preface by the chairman of the committee, Sir Benjamin Gott.

1924 *Film in Society.* edited by Berger, Arthur A. 151 p. New York: Transaction Books, 1980.

An anthology of articles, reviews, etc. taken from *Society* from 1967 to 1976.

1925 *Film in Sweden: Ingmar Bergman and Society.* by Bergom-Larsson, Maria. 127 p. illus. New York: A.S. Barnes, 1979.

The third volume in the *Film in Sweden* series, this work concentrates on Bergman's attitudes toward the social framework in which he grew up and how his background influenced his films. The text is divided into three parts, each representing a theme the author finds in the films: The Patriarchal Structure; From Clown to Parasite: The Artist and Society; and Inner and Outer Violence: In Here—Out There. A summary, notes, a filmography, a bibliography, and a film title index complete the book. Films selected for detailed analysis include FRENZY (1944), WILD STRAWBERRIES (1957), SAWDUST AND TINSEL (1953), THE SILENCE (1963), PERSONA (1966), THE SHAME (1968), THE PASSION OF ANNA (1969), THE MAGICIAN (1958), and HOUR OF THE WOLF (1968). The volume is illustrated.

This study offers further testimony to the stature and importance of Bergman's films. Although more has been written about them than about any other body of films, they still can withstand variations in their analysis without becoming familiar, over-used, or tiresome. The treatment here is clear, intriguing, and informative; it helps the reader to understand in part the richness of content to be found in Bergman's films. Recommended.

1926 *Film in Sweden: Stars and Players.* by Cowie, Peter. 128 p. illus. New York: A.S. Barnes, 1978.

According to Peter Cowie, there are no stars in Swedish cinema, only players. Yet he acknowledges Garbo, Bergman and Ullmann. This collective biography treats both players and stars but emphasizes the former. Critical appreciations are provided for Maj-Britt Nilsson, Bibi Andersson, Liv Ullmann, Harriet Andersson, Ingrid Thulin, Eva Dahl Beck,

Agneta Ekmanner, Lena Nyman, Anita Ekstrom, Gunnar Bjornstrand, Max von Sydow, Birger Malm Sten, Stig Olin, Erland Josephson, and Per Oscarsson. Filmographies are provided for each subject and there is a final film title index.

The provision of information and comment on this important group of performers is to be commended. Cowie, an experienced critic-author-editor, offers his usual excellent text along with a fine selection of visuals and supporting elements. Recommended.

1927 *Film in Sweden: The New Directors.* by Bjorkman, Stig. 127 p. illus. New York: A. S. Barnes, 1977.

The works of ten Swedish film directors who have gained prominence since 1968 are discussed in this volume. Included are filmmakers Bo Widerberg, Vilgot Sjoman, Kjell Grede, Jan Troell, Jonas Cornell, Jan Halldoff, Mai Zetterling, Johan Bergenstrahle, Roy Andersson, and Lasse Forsberg. The time limitation was set approximately by the Swedish Film Reform Act of 1963 which established several funds to encourage filmmaking.

A separate chapter is devoted to each director, in which his films are described and critically evaluated. Selected stills accompany the text and the final pages offer a filmography for each of the directors.

In this up-to-date assessment of filmmaking and filmmakers in Sweden, Stig Bjorkman has provided information and detail not easily available elsewhere. The volume should please film scholars and students by its thoughtful presentation of the most recent decade in the Swedish cinema. Recommended.

1928 *Film in the Battle of Ideas.* by Lawson, John Howard. 126 p. paper New York: Masses and Mainstream, 1953.

The author, one of the "Unfriendly Ten" who was indicted by the House Un-American Committee in Washington in 1947, presents a plea for overhauling the American film. Since films are a major source of information about America to the rest of the world, should they present ideas, propaganda, human values, or should they be entertainment devoid of ideological lecturing or sermonizing? Can they do both? By examining a sampling of Hollywood films from the forties, the author underlines their negative values. His final section is a proposal for change.

As we've seen, films do tackle the themes that Lawson desires and television has replaced motion pictures as the popular mass medium. How valid is the argument for today's film and TV content? The book is slanted but also exciting and provocative. Not for the casual reader but for the serious student or scholar.

1929 *Film in the Classroom: Why Use It— How to Use It.* by Amelio, Ralph J. 208 P. paper Dayton, Ohio: Pflaum, 1971.

A further discussion of The Willowbrook Cinema Study Project, this volume explains the goals and structure of the program. In addition to units of study, it also offers material on evaluation, organization, and operation of the project.

1930 *Film in the Language Arts Class.* by Aquino, John. 56 p. paper Washington, D.C.: National Education Association, 1976.

1931 *Film in the Life of the School.* by Mallery, David. 53 p. paper Boston: National Association of Independent Schools, 1968.

1932 *A Film In the Making.* by Collier, John W. 95 p. illus. London: World Film Publications, 1947.

The film being made in this case is IT ALWAYS RAINS ON SUNDAY (1947), which was adapted from the novel by Arthur J. La Bern. Googie Withers, John McCallum, Jack Warner and Edward Chapman were the actors in this Ealing Studios production.

1933 *Film in the Third Reich.: A Study of the German Cinema 1933-1945.* by Hull, David Stewart. 291 p. illus. Berkeley, Calif.: University of California Press, 1969.

A brilliant, well-researched study of the German film from 1933 to 1945, this volume will be of interest and value to many readers. The correlation between the films produced and the events in Hitler's Germany is a fascinating topic that is treated with respect, talent and scholarship here. This book, together with *From Caligari to Hitler,* covers an essential chapter of film history.

The text is presented in intelligent straightfoward fashion. The stills are excellent and provide stimulus to see the films, or at least more stills from these films. A model of scholarship in film history. Highly recommended.

1934 *The Film Index: A Bibliography; Vol. I—The Film Art.* edited by Leonard, Harold. 723 p. illus. New York: Arno Press, 1966 (1941).

Originally published in 1941 by the Museum of Modern Art, this massive bibliography of more than 8000 entries was the result of government sponsorship (WPA) during the Depression years. It covers the film up to 1941 and contains digests of 700 books, 3000 articles from magazines and periodicals (excluding newspapers), and 4000 film reviews. Several thousand films are listed, some with full descriptive paragraphs. An essential reference volume.

1935 *Film-Index 1929.* by Lauritzen, Einar; and Lundquist, Gunnar. 190 p. Stockholm: Solna, 1973.

A catalog of the feature films shown in Stockholm in 1929, with additional selected features and shorts also noted.

1936 *The Film Industries.* by Mayer, Michael F. 212 p. New York: Hastings House, 1973, 1978.

This volume, which is part of the *Studies in Media Management* series, has for its subtitle, "Practical Business/Legal Problems in Production, Distribution, and Exhibition." The author, a practicing theatrical attorney, identifies three large problem areas for his text: production, distribution-exhibition, and content. A short section on the future of the film industries concludes the book. Specific problems discussed include contracts, options, finance, subsidies, agreements, licensing, non-theatrical marketing, piracy, defamation, privacy, and copyright.

Mayer's consideration of the problems provides information, advice, and in certain instances, entertaining anecdotes. He avoids legal jargon and speaks with familiarity and clarity about the many cases taken from his own experiences.

For certain courses offered in programs leading to a film degree, the book is a most suitable text. It will also interest those readers who wish to know more about the operation of the film industry. Acceptable for all film collections. Enlarged and updated in 1978.

1937 *The Film Industry.* by Boughey, Davidson. 110 p. illus. London: Pitman, 1921.

This older book, which deals with British film production, is a title in the series Pitman's *Common Commodities and Industries.* Illustrated with technical material, its eleven chapters cover raw film manufacture, cameras, perforation, developing, printing, toning, studio operation, film types, personnel, fiction and nonfiction films, distribution, projections, and exhibition.

1938 *The Film Industry in Six European Countries.* by London Film Center. 156 p. New York: UNESCO Columbia University Press, 1950.

A detailed study of the film industry in Denmark as compared with that in Norway, Sweden, Italy, France and the United Kingdom.

1939 *A Film Is Born.* by Lee, Norran. 127 p. illus. London: Jordan, 1945.

This volume on studio film production carries the subtitle, "How 40 Film Fathers Bring a Modern Talking Picture Into Being."

1940 *Film Is—The International Free Cinema.* by Dwoskin, Stephen. 268 p. illus. Woodstock, N.Y.: Overlook Press, 1975.

In this book "free cinema," sometimes called "underground," "experimental" or "avant-garde," means the independently made film that represents a personal creative expression. The genre includes a wide range of forms, methods, and themes. The history of the independent film from the twenties to today is recalled, along with descriptions of the work and techniques of hundreds of filmmakers. Over 700 films are discussed in some detail. A film title index, a bibliography, a pictorial section, and a lengthy general index complete the work.

International in scope, the survey is the work of a dedicated enthusiast. The author's experience and success as an independent filmmaker qualify him for this role. His comment, criticism, and recollections are interesting, provocative reading and may be helpful in suggesting new approaches to creative filmmaking. Information on many obscure films and filmmakers is easily obtained by using the detailed indexes; thus the book can serve also as a useful reference. Recommended.

1941 *Film Language.: A Semiotics of the Cinema.* by Metz, Christian. 268 p. New York: Oxford University Press, 1974.

A collection of previously published articles, this volume uses the techniques, terms, and methods of semiotics and structural linguistics to see if they

have pertinence for developing a film language. Employing an impressive knowledge of film language, the author tries to superimpose it on the aesthetic framework of linguistics theory. In the process, many unfamiliar words, terms, concepts, etc., are brought to the text.

A sense of frustration may result for all except the most informed/determined reader. Those who stay to the end will be rewarded with an intellectual exercise in film aesthetics and language that is rare in film study. Since this is a translation from the French, most of the references are unfamiliar and difficult to obtain. Two films, 8-1/2 (1963) and ADIEU PHILLIPPINE (1962), are analyzed in some detail. Unfortunately, the latter is almost unknown in the United States. Because of the reservations indicated above, the volume is suitable only for a select few.

1942 *Film Library Administration Bibliography.* edited by Chach, Maryann; and Emmens, Carol A. 30 p. paper New York: Educational Film Library Association, 1978.

This bibliography arranges its titles under nine general headings: libraries, feature films, film periodicals, nonnarrative films, children's media, film utilization, copyright, mass media, and the arts. Annotations provided are mostly descriptive, with an evaluative word or so given for some entries. It is unfortunate that no introduction is provided. Persons other than film librarians may not be attracted by the title of this fine bibliography. It certainly has pertinence for media centers, media specialists, and academic and public libraries.

1943 *Film Library Techniques.* by Harrison, Helen P. 277 p. New York: Hastings House, 1973.

This title, which is part of the *Studies in Media Management* series, is most welcome. British in origin, it is concerned with the administration of all types of film libraries, distribution, production, government, research, archives, newsreel, television and education. After discussing their function along with their history and development, the text examines procedures common to all libraries: selection, handling, retrieval, listing, documentation, cataloging, storage, etc. Since the approach to the subject is an administrative one, staffing, layout, planning and economics are stressed. Two final sections give attention to copyright and possible future developments.

Anyone who is not British and an experienced film librarian may have some difficulty in interpreting certain entries in the bibliography. They lack complete data as to publisher location, etc., and the many acronyms are sure to confuse the novice. A useful index is provided. No illustrations are used, but some diagrams of flow charts and staffing appear.

This is a unique and helpful book that will be of value to most film librarians. Although it deals with specialized material and probably goes into greater depth and detail than required by most professionals, the book offers a concentration of film information not available elsewhere. Highly recommended.

1944   *Film Literature Index—1973.* by Aceto, Vincent J.; and Silva, Fred; and Graves, Jane. paper Albany, N.Y.: Filmdex, 1400 Washington Ave., Albany, N.Y. 12222, 1975.

A subscription to this bibliographic tool consists of four quarterly issues (paperback) and a clothbound cumulation. Film periodicals (125) are indexed along with subjective selections from about 150 other non-film periodicals (*Variety, Village Voice, Media and Methods*). Access to the periodical titles is provided by both identification acronym used in the text and by an alphabetical listing containing address, subscription rates, etc. Subject headings are well selected and offer easy access to certain summary information which heretofore has been difficult to locate, e.g., book reviews, festivals, awards, and women filmmakers.

The first issues of *Film Literature Index* are exciting to discover, fascinating to explore and most gratifying to use. When the enormous amount of work, devotion and expense that such a work demands is measured against the quality of the final product, the implications are for a standard, accepted reference work to emerge. This volume certainly has that potential. It is deserving of strong support from librarians, educators, and film scholars. Recommended.

1945   *The Film Maker and His World: A Young Person's Guide.* by Minney, R. J. 160 p. London: Victor Gollancz, Ltd., 1964.

Aimed at a young audience, this volume surveys the usual topics in filmmaking. Starting with a short account of early films, the text concentrates on the roles of various participants in the filmmaking process—the producer, director, actor, art director, etc. Other topics such as casting, trick photography, film schools, and art vs. industry are discussed. Somewhat dated and rather uninspired to start with, this volume has been surpassed by many later ones on the same topic.

1946   *A Film Maker's Guide to Planning, Directing and Shooting Films for Pleasure and Profit.* by Branston, Brian. 205 p. illus. London: Allen and Unwin, 1967.

A handbook on cinematography designed for the amateur.

1947   *The Film Maker's Guide to Pornography.* by Ziplow, Steven. 160 p. paper illus. New York: Drake, 1977.

The use of porno filmmaking as a stepping stone to commercial film production is suggested in this rather unusual guide. In practical terms the author offers advice on direction, actors, scripts, sets, equipment, sound, distribution, legal risks, and other elements of filming pornographic motion pictures. Since the text is based on the author's personal experiences with the genre, the guidance offered seems sound and knowledgeable.

1948   *Film Maker's Guide to Super 8.* compiled by *Super 8 Filmmaker* Editors. 357 p. illus. New York: Van Nostrand Reinhold, 1980.

This anthology is packed with helpful, well-written, easy-to-understand articles about super 8 filmmaking. Designed for both the beginner and the advanced filmmaker, the volume arranges its articles under the predictable headings: equipment, sound, script, filming techniques, processing, printing, editing, special effects and situations, documentary film, economics, education, and home construction of equipment. A glossary, index, author biographies, and a resource directory conclude the book. Photographs, drawings, tables, and diagrams supplement the text strongly throughout.

There is a wealth of advice, suggestion, and direction given in these articles selected from the first five years of *Super 8 Filmmaker* magazine. It should be hard to go wrong with this guide at hand. Recommended.

1949   *Film Makers on Filmmaking.* edited by Geduld, Harry M. 302 p. Bloomington, Ind.: Indiana University Press, 1967.

The subtitle of the book, "Statements on Their Art by Thirty Directors," adequately describes the content. The articles are difficult to evaluate, ranging from excellent to poor, from rare to familiar. Many are excerpts from books—Sennett, Chaplin, Hitchcock, von Sternberg—while others are mostly from periodicals—*Sight and Sound, Films and Filmmaking, Film Culture*, etc. Two groupings are presented: "Pioneers and Prophets" and "Film Masters and Film Mentors." As general reading about film direction, the book is acceptable—what anthology is not? —but this one lacks cohesiveness and a specific central theme, and has no illustrations or index.

1950 *Film Making.* by Derks, Mik; and Poster, Steve. 80 p. paper illus. Los Angeles: Peterson, 1977.

Here is an attractive volume that appears in a magazine format, which may cause it to be overlooked. This would be unfortunate, since it contains an abundance of information presented in an excellent, well-illustrated production. Pictures, charts, diagrams and drawings complement a readable, practical text. There are sections devoted to script, budget, direction, camera, lighting, sound, and post-production. Additional topics include Hollywood techniques for home movies, the documentary film, and film festivals. Recommended especially for the beginning filmmaker.

1951 *Film Making in Creative Teaching.* by Kennedy, Keith. 128 p. illus. New York: Watson-Guptill, 1972.

This British book was designed for use by teachers of junior high students. Its primary concern is communication, with film regarded as one method of communication. Suggested ways of using film in the learning process are supplemented by explanations of the equipment needed and an emphasis on the use of imagination and creativity. The hardware includes not only motion picture cameras, but still cameras, polaroids, tape recorders, and loop projectors. The latter portions of the book suggest projects such as camera adventures, photopoems, photo hunts, collages, montages and improvisations. A list of suppliers, a bibliography, and an index complete the book.

The admirable intentions of this volume are larger than the achievements. Some of this may be due to its British origin, for there are wide differences in the respective curricula of England and America, and in the structure for teaching and methodologies. Some of the suggestions seem awkward to implement, others seem dated. Whenever a book employs illustrations of technology, the risk of their being quickly out-of-date is great. Some of the illustrations are of older machines (page 43) and are of brands more familiar to European purchasers (Philips, Rank Aldis, Eumig Mark, etc.) Certain references are out-

dated; for example, Limbacher's *Guide to 8mm and 16mm Films* is now published by Bowker and has a new title.

These reservations are minor when one considers the total effort. The rationale for the book's dominant theme—using film to communicate—is presented with intelligence and argument based upon teaching experience. Some adjustment and compromise will be required before full communication can take place.

1952 *Film Making On a Low Budget.* by Winter, Myrtle; and Spurr, Norman F. 31 p. paper illus. Paris: UNESCO, 1960.

This title is number 29 of a series, *Reports and Papers on Mass Communications,* and deals with the making of documentary films as developed by the UNESCO-UNRWA project.

1953 *Film Music.* by London, Kurt. 280 p. illus. New York: Arno Press, 1970 (1936).

An advanced, though dated (1936), discussion of the film music—its history, development, aesthetics and possibilities.

1954 *Film Music.* by Elsas, Diana; and Sharples, Win, Jr. 24 p. paper Washington, D.C.: American Film Institute, 1977.

This title in the AFI *Factfile* series deals with several aspects of film music: organizations, schools, sources, films on film music, oral history programs, a bibliography, and a periodical list.

1955 *Film Music—From Violins to Video.* edited by Limbacher, James. 835 p. Metuchen, N.J.: Scarecrow Press, 1974.

There are really two books here. The first is an anthology of articles on film music written mostly by composers and critics. The articles are placed under seven headings: I. The Early Days, II. Theories and Comments, III. Techniques, IV. Scoring the Dramatic Film, V. The Film Spectacle, VI. Classical Music on the Screen, and VII. Animated Films and Comedies. A short bibliography concludes this part.

The second is a reference section consisting of four parts: I. Film Titles and Dates (an alphabetical listing of all film titles considered in this volume); II. Films and Their Composers (a chronological year-by-year listing of film titles with composer/musical director noted); III. Composers and Their Films (filmographies are given for composers/musical directors, listing films in yearly chronological order, then by alphabetical order within each year); IV. Recorded Musical Scores (a selected listing by title of those films whose scores have been recorded on discs/tape). Films that have a vocal score—MY FAIR LADY (1965), SINGING IN THE RAIN (1952), etc.—are not included.

While the anthology portion of the volume provides some fascinating background and insight into the world of film music, it is the latter reference section which makes this volume outstanding. One might argue about the arrangement of the material. Why the duplication of titles and dates in the first two sections when a consolidation of the material would serve the same purpose? Is the chronology important enough to merit more than 220 pages? If so, couldn't a simpler, more concise format be evolved for showing what it is that Limbacher has in mind with the chronology? These are simply minor disappointments in a major reference work. A wealth of information is presented and once the user comprehends the arrangement, he should find the book to be an invaluable source of information on film music. It is highly recommended.

1956   *Film Narratives of Alain Resnais.* by Sweet, Freddy. Ann Arbor, Mich.: University of Michigan Press, 1981.

1957   *Film News Omnibus Volume 2.* edited by Lee, Rohama. 288 p. paper illus. New York: Film News, 1979.

Reviews of 16mm films from the pages of *Film News* form the content of this volume, the second to be published. Volume One concentrated on reviews published from 1970 to 1972, while this book deals mostly with those which appeared from 1973 to 1975. Treated are feature films, documentaries and short films. A subject index, alphabetical index, distributor lists, and short identifications of the reviewers represented conclude the book. Although more than 400 16mm films are considered, the selection is still a subjective one since it derives from the reviewing policies of *Film News*. Nevertheless the book should be helpful to anyone who uses 16mm film.

1958   *Film News Omnibus, Volume I.* edited by Lee, Rohama. 270 p. paper illus. New York: Film News, 1973.

This collection of film reviews originally published in the periodical *Film News* is presented in an unusual way. Feature films are considered in a first short section, while documentaries and short subjects are treated in a longer second section. Individual films are arranged alphabetically by title in both sections, but groups of films are also considered. The alphabetical index of all the films at the back of the book provides a tool for locating those appearing in groups. There is a subject listing, some distributor names and addresses, and finally, a rundown of the reviewers' names and credentials.

The reviews seem to be uniformly positive, but they do vary in length, quality and approach—a result of being written by a range of personalities. It is difficult to locate criteria for inclusion, other than the original review having appeared in *Film News*. Release dates go back as far as 1955 for NIGHT AND FOG, but the emphasis is on recent films. While such a reference tool as this is most welcome, it must be noted that it is a partial work which considers only a small sampling of the many 16mm films available at present. Acceptable.

1959   *Film Noir.* edited by Silver, Alain; and Ward, Elizabeth. 393 p. illus. Woodstock, N.Y.: Overlook Press, 1979.

A long annotated filmography constitutes the major portion of this encyclopedic reference. After the genre has been described and discussed in a terse introduction, several hundred films are listed alphabetically by title. Information given for each film includes full cast and production credits, dates, title(s), shooting location, and running time. The substance of each entry is the original annotation supplied by one of 17 contributing authors to this volume. These annotations usually consist of two paragraphs—a plot synopsis, and a critical analysis/comment which sometimes includes background information on the film. Illustrations are provided along with a detailed index, a bibliography and several appendixes, a film noir chronology, directors of the genre, writers, cinematographers, producers, performers, and releasing companies.

To date, this volume is the definitive study and resource for the film noir genre. It can be used by a large audience in a variety of ways, almost always with rewarding pleasure. Recommended.

1960   *Film Noir.* by Andrews, Bruce. Providence, R.I.: Burning Deck, 1978.

1961   *Film Notes.* edited by Bowser, Eileen 128 p. paper New York: Museum of Modern Art, 1969.

This is the most recent revision of the film notes that

were written by members of the Museum of Modern Art staff. Designed to be used with the films of the circulating collection of the Museum of Modern Art, they are not comprehensive. However, they do cover many of the classic films of both the sound and silent eras. The film notes are preceded by cast and production credits. An index of films, another of the filmmakers, and a bibliography are included. This is an essential reference volume that would be of great assistance to anyone engaged in showing classic films. Highly recommended.

1962 *Film Notes.* edited by Lenning, A. 150 p. paper illus. Madison, Wisc.: Wisconsin Film Society, 1960.

A series of film notes for use by film societies and other organizations, this volume offers material on films from Germany, the USSR, Scandinavia and America. In addition a chapter on the great comedians is included. Approximately two dozen films are discussed with a background, analysis, and credits offered. The notes make interesting reading even by themselves and should prove most valuable when used in conjunction with the film showings. This is a very good source book, a model, a reader and a reference.

1963 *Film Notes for Reel People.* edited by Kodak Staff. paper illus. Rochester, N.J.: Kodak, 1977- .

A series of pamphlets on film topics designed to improve skills and knowledge of the film as a communication medium. Topics include film handling, projection practices and techniques, troubleshooting and prevention of damage, showmanship and the theatre, the intermittent movement, the case for test films, some notes on tape splicing 35mm films, a checklist for maintaining quality presentations, cleaning release prints, and newfangled 35mm platter transports.

1964 *Film Odyssey.* by Ferlita, Ernest; and May, John R. 163 p. paper New York: Paulist Press, 1976.

Subtitled "The Art of Film As Search For Meaning," this volume examines 21 films that address themselves to three basic questions: Where do I come from? What am I? Where am I going? Under the heading of the personal dimension, films such as EAST OF EDEN (1954), LA STRADA (1954), and IKURU (1952) appear. The social dimension treats films such as EASY RIDER (1969), MIDNIGHT COWBOY (1969), THE GODFATHER (1972). The religious dimension explores FELLINI SATYRICON (1970), THE SEVENTH SEAL (1956), LA DOLCE VITA (1961), 2001: A SPACE

ODYSSEY (1968) and other films.

Surrounding the film analyses are bibliographic footnotes, an introduction, and a conclusion. An appendix expands the list of films under the three headings and offers distributor addresses. There are no illustrations or index.

The author's methodology suggests the use of films as vehicles for the discovery of self. Thus as the protagonists in each film search for a meaning to their existence, so does the viewer reexamine his own life. Of course, reading and discussion should accompany the viewing of the films.

Although the book was designed for religious groups and institutions, it is by no means limited; it is a valuable resource ideally suited for use with all mature audiences. Recommended.

1965 *The Film of* MURDER IN THE CATHEDRAL. by Eliot, T. S.; and Hoellering, George. 171 p. illus. London: Faber & Faber, 1952.

In addition to separate prefaces by author Eliot and director Hoellering, the other sections of this volume are the screenplay and 48 pages of stills from the film. It is the group of photographs that give added distinction to this volume. They are beautifully reproduced and include both full-page portraits and filmstrip pages, each of which has 28 small stills from the film. Although the film has been ignored and nearly forgotten, the format of this book should be used as a mode for film book production.

1966 *Film on the Left: American Documentary Film from 1931-1942.* by Alexander, William 364 p. illus. Princeton, N.J.: Princeton University Press, 1981.

1967 *Film Periodicals.*

A primary source of information about films is the periodical, sometimes known as a quarterly, a magazine, a journal, etc. Several excellent indexes to periodicals are: *Film Literature Index (Aneceto), Retrospective Index To Film Periodicals, 1930-1971* (Batty), *Index To Critical Film Reviews* (Bowles), *The Critical Index* (Gerlach), *International Index To Film Periodicals* (Jones), *The Film Index* (Leonard), *The New Film Index* (MacCann), *Motion Picture Directors* (Schuster), and *Motion Picture Performers* (Schuster).

Periodicals lead a precarious existence because of the economics of publishing. Some appear for a brief time, while a few others last for decades. Few people other than film enthusiasts are fully aware of the number of periodicals devoted to film which are published all over the world. The general public is more conscious of the fan magazine, which they might regard as aimed at the teenager and not worthy of serious consideration. This genus of literature mostly finds its way into the waste basket. Today many older magazines of this type do have a scarcity value. Few issues contain anything of lasting value; however, as documents of contemporary taste and interest, they should not be overlooked.

The intellectual recognition of the film trailed by many years the flourishing of popular and trade writing, but it did come. The medium of film is no longer considered to be solely a popular entertainment; it has intruded into the world of art and culture and is an expression or form of intellectual communication. Film publications have reflected this change. It is the more serious film literature that is of concern here.

Below is a selected list of periodicals, past and present; it is not meant to be total or comprehensive. For further information the reader is directed to the *Standard Periodical Dictionary, Ulrich's International Periodical Directory,* or Bill Katz's *Magazines for Libraries.*

Action! Los Angeles, *AC Movie News* Newton, Mass., *Adam Film World* Los Angeles, *After Dark* New York, *Afterimage* Rochester, N.Y., *American Cinematographer* Hollywood, *American Cinemeditor* Los Angeles, *American Classic Screen* Lawrence, Kans., *American Film* New York, *Art and Cinema* New York, *Audio-Visual Communications* New York, *The Big Reel* Summerfield, N.C., *Bright Lights* Los Angeles, *Camera Obscura* Berkeley, *Canadian Cinematography* Toronto, *Canyon Cinema News* Berkeley, *Center for Southern Folklore Newsletter* Memphis, Tenn., *Cine-Tracts—A Journal of Film and Cultural Studies* Montreal, *Cineaste* New York, *Cinefantastique* Oak Park, Ill., *Cinegram Magazine* Ann Arbor, *Cinema* Beverly Hills, *Cinema Canada* Toronto, *The Cinemeditor* Los Angeles, *Cinema Journal* Iowa City, *Cinema Magazine* Kansas City, *Cinemagic* Warren, Mich., *Cineworld* Toronto, *Classic Film Collector* Davenport, Iowa, *Communication Arts* Washington, D.C., *Continental Film Review* London,

Daily Variety Hollywood, *Fantastic Films Magazine* Chicago, *Film* London, *Film and Broadcasting Review* New York, *Film and History.* Newark, N.J., *Film Collector's World* Rapid City, Ill., *Film Comment* New York, *Film Criticism* Edinboro, Pa., *Film Culture* New York, *Film Facts* New York, *Film Fan Monthly* Teaneck, N.J., *Film Heritage* Dayton, Ohio, *Film Journal* New York, *Film Library Quarterly* New York, *Film News* New York, *Film Quar-*

terly Berkeley, *The Film Reader* Evanston, Ill., *Film Review Digest* Millwood, N.Y., *Filmmakers Film and Video Monthly* Ward Hill, Mass., *Filmmaker's Newsletter* New York, *Filmmusic Notebook* Los Angeles, *Films and Filming* London, *Film in Reviews* New York, *Film Society Review* New York, *Film World* Washington, D.C., *The Films of Yesteryear* Clearwater, Fla., *Focus on Film* London, *Funnyworld Magazine* New York, *The Hollywood Reporter* Hollywood, *Hollywood Studio Magazine* Sherman Oaks, Calif.,

Image Rochester, N. Y., *Independent Film Journal* New York, *International Film Collector* Lawrence, Mass., *Inter/view* New York, *Journal of Popular Film and Television* Bowling Green, Ohio, *Journal of the SMPTE* New York, *Journal of the University Film Association* Philadelphia, *Jump Cut* Berkeley, *Landers Film Reviews* Los Angeles, *Literature/Film Quarterly.* Salisbury, Md., *Media and Methods* Philadelphia, *Millimeter* New York, *Millennium Film Journal* New York, *Mindrot* Minneapolis, *Motion Picture Daily* New York, *Moviegoer* New York, *New Cinema Review* New York, *Newsreel Magazine* Indian Rocks Beach, Fla., *On Location* Hollywood, *Photon* Brooklyn, *Popular Photography* New York, *Pratfall* Universal City, Calif., *Quarterly Review of Film Studies* Pleasantville, N.Y.,

Screen London, *Screen Actor* Los Angeles, *Screen Facts* Kew Gardens, N.Y., *Screen Thrills* Raleigh, N.C., *Shakespeare on Film Newsletter* Glen Head, N.Y., *Show* New York, *Show Business* New York, *Shooting* Passaic, N.J., *Sight and Sound* London, *Sightlines* New York, *The Silent Picture* London, *Super-8 Filmmaker* Palo Alto, Calif., *Take One* Montreal, *Today's Filmmaker* Hempstead, N.Y., *Training in Business and Industry* New York, *Under Western Skies* Clearwater, Fla., *University Film Association Journal* Columbus, Ohio, *Variety* New York, *Velvet Light Trap* Madison, Wis., *Wide Angle* Athens, Ohio, *The World of Yesterday* Clearwater, Fla.

1968   *Film-Play Production for Amateurs.* by Sewell, George H. 164 p. illus. New York: Pitman, 1939.

A guide to amateur filmmaking with sections on story, continuity, preparation, personnel, equipment, actors, scenery, props, make-up, editing, titling, etc.

1969   *Film Preservation.* by Volkman, Herbert. 60 p. paper illus. London: British Film Institute, 1965.

This is a report of the Preservation Committee of the International Federation of Film Archives (FIAF), the group responsible for *The International Index to Film Periodicals.* Originally published in 1963, the report considers several aspects of preserving film. Properties of optical cinematograph films, along with magnetic films and tapes, are described. Storage problems, conditions, procedures and buildings are emphasized; attention is given to the processes involved in film restoration. Closing sections discuss the qualifications of personnel involved with film preservation. A bibliography and key to the text sections complete the book.

The specialized material presented here is essential to any person, group or institution involved in film service. Schools, museums, colleges, and libraries that maintain film collections will find the information valuable from both the custodial and economic viewpoint.

1970 *see 1971*

1971 *Film Problems of Soviet Russia.* by Bryher, Winifred. 140 p. illus. Territet, Switzerland: Riant Chateau, Pool, 1929.

A comprehensive survey of the Russian film industry in the twenties which emphasizes history and directors. It includes a general index, a film title index, and some rare stills and portraits.

1972 *Film Production.* by Brunel, Adrian. 184 p. illus. London: Newnes, 1936.

An anthology that explores the studio production of motion pictures. Following an introduction by Alexander Korda, the text treats such topics as art direction, the assistant director, the associate producer, casting, the continuity girl, dialogue, editing, hairdressing, make-up, screen treatment, sound, etc.

1973 *Film Production and Management.* by Balcon, Michael. 20 p. paper London: British Institute of Management, 1950.

A short essay which explains film production and points out its differences from other businesses.

1974 *Film Production by International Cooperation.* by Jongbloed, H. 35 p. paper Paris: UNESCO, 1961.

This paper is number 34 in the series, *Reports and Papers on Mass Communication,* and carries the subtitle, "A Report on Various Methods of Co-Production in the Field of Educational and Cultural Films."

1975 *Film Production Directory, Ontario/ Canada.* by Ministry of Industry and Tourism. 169 p. paper illus. Ontario: Ministry of Industry and Tourism, 1976.

This volume is a collection of information on the production of features, commercials, and films for television in Canada.

1976 *Film Programmer's Guide to 16mm Rentals.* edited by Artel, Linda J.; and Weaver, Kathleen. 164 p. paper Albany, Calif.: Reel Research, 1973.

It is imperative that the user become acquainted with the format of this concentrated reference book before venturing into its main body of 8000 films. The major section contains selected feature films and short films. Following is a smaller section on documentary films. All 8000 films—both feature and short—are classified under these two headings. Educational films are not considered and for these, the reader is referred to NICEM or the Indiana University Film Catalog. Each listing gives some or all of the following information: title; director; release date; running time; color; distributor; rental cost. A selected director's listing (which also includes some personalities e.g., W. C. Fields, Abbott and Costello, etc.) and some distributor-rental information conclude the book.

The limitations of the volume are soon apparent: the contents are selected and constitute a sampling; the format for use requires some time to decipher; the distributor information noted for each film is partial in many cases; other distributors than those named handle the film in these cases; the director listings get confused at times e.g., the Marx Brothers get director credit for AT THE CIRCUS, instead of Edward Buzzell; the information given for films is incomplete in many cases with release date, director, etc., missing; since there are no subject headings and no annotations, the book assumes the reader knows the film he wants, and is seeking further information about it.

Even with these reservations, there is much to admire in the book. It is so tightly packed with information that one can easily understand the omissions and inconsistencies. It does have the potential for helping the user locate films and film information. Its modest price when compared to other similar volumes is another positive factor. This is a valuable reference that can be used to advantage by film users. Recommended.

1977   *Film Programmes for the Young.* compiled by UNESCO 30 p. paper Paris: UNESCO, 1959.

This title is number 28 in the series, *Reports and Papers on Mass Communications*, and carries the subtitle, "A Report on a Presentation of Children's Films Organized by the International Centre of Films for Children, Brussels, September 19-23, 1958."

1978   *Film Projecting without Tears or Technicalities.* by Simpson, Margaret. 51 p. paper illus. London: National Committee for Audiovisual Aids in Education, 1966.

A useful volume on motion picture projection that includes diagrams, suggestions, general information on lamps, maintenance, etc., and a final section on "the unexpected."

1979   *Film Propaganda.* by Taylor, Richard. illus. New York: Barnes and Noble, 1979.

An examination of the use of film by the Soviet Union and Nazi Germany to solidify public opinion about the goals and aspirations of each ideology. The role of the audience in determining the effectiveness of the film messages is noted.

1980   *Film Publicity: A Handbook on the Production and Distribution of Propaganda Films.* by Box, Sidney. 142 p. illus. London: L. Dickson, 1937.

The sponsored film is the concern of this book. It offers advice and information on the production and distribution of "publicity" films. Several scripts/synopses are included along with a glossary and illustrations.

1981   *Film Reader 1.* 144 p. paper Evanston, Ill.: Northwestern University.

This journal, dedicated to the application of current theories in film scholarship, focuses in its first number on semiology and auteurism. A collection of articles deals with the semiological codes operating in CITIZEN KANE (1941).

The second section deals with auteurism in modern Hollywood. Noted here because the first journal is really a book worthy of both hardback rebinding and circulation.

1982   *Film—Readings in the Mass Media.* by Kirschner, Allen; and Kirschner, Linda. 315 p. paper New York: Odyssey Press, 1971.

Perhaps the rationale for this anthology is explicit in its title, but one wishes the introduction offered some further elucidation. We are given instead a capsule history of film in four parts: One Minute Please (1896-1912), You Are Living the Story (1912-1927), You Ain't Heard Nothin' Yet (1927-1950), and Movies Are Better than Ever (1950 on).

The body of the book consists of three major divisions with appropriate reprintings under each. Section I, "Form and Technique," features personalities such as McLuhan, Agee, Griffith, Hitchcock, Antonioni and Mekas. Persons familiar with film literature anthologies can probably guess the titles of the articles. Section II is entitled "Audience and Effect," the majority of authors here being critics—Schickel, Kerr, Kauffmann, Knight, Crist, etc. Critics are also heavily represented in the last section, titled "Critics and Criticism." Kael, Adler, Tyler, Alpert, Crowther, Morgenstern and others appear. A further section reproduces statements on "The Future of the Film" by members of the National Society of Film Critics. A selected bibliography completes the volume.

As a text for a film or communications course, the book may offer a service to the student by bringing together a collection of well-known articles, but since many of the articles appear elsewhere in film collections, the volume may be redundant. Its rather high price and the absence of a unifying statement by the authors are other negative factors.

1983   *Film—Real to Reel.* by Coynik, David. 274 p. paper illus. Dayton, Ohio: Pflaum, 1972.

The author denies this is a textbook, preferring to call it a companion to film study. And he is quite right, for the style, approach and tone all suggest informality and exchange of ideas rather than pure exposition.

Film aesthetics is the first major topic considered. Starting with a discussion of the shot, Coynik proceeds to editing, rhythm, sound, motion, light, and color. Film forms and genres appear next and they include feature films, documentaries, animation films, and experimental or "now" films, as the author calls them. A final chapter suggests that the reader make his own film and offers encouragement and advice.

The numerous visuals used are well reproduced and supplement the text in excellent fashion. Some small reservation may be expressed at the absence of color illustrations in the section which deals with color.- Some of the captions on the photographs seem a bit calculated—a shot of Orson Welles splattered with mud has a sentence underneath telling of his difficulties with the studios. Many of the stills and the examples cited in the text are taken from the classic films that usually appear in film study courses.

As a book for individual or group reading, this volume is excellent. The examples used are clearly explained, no attempt is made at verbal acrobatics, and the experience of reading it is both comfortable and rewarding. It can be used with equal effectiveness by young adults or more mature readers. Highly recommended.

1984 *Film Research*. compiled by Bukalski, Peter J. 215 p. Boston, Mass.: G. K. Hall, 1972.

The title of this book may be somewhat misleading, for the topic is not film research but suggested aids for doing film research. It is largely a bibliography of film books. An introductory essay provides a general overview of film study and film literature. Fifty books are listed in the next section, "Essential Works," with a brief annotation for each title. Short chapters listing film rental and film sales agencies are followed by a listing of periodicals. The bibliography, the major portion of the text, divides film books into the usual categories: 1) film history, theory, criticism, and introductory works; 2) film production and technology; 3) film genre; 4) sociology and economics of film; 5) national cinemas; 6) film scripts; 7) particular films; 8) personalities, biographies, filmographies; 9) film education; 10) film related works; 11) careers in film; 12) bibliographies, guides and indexes; 13) selected works in foreign languages. Book titles listed under these categories are not annotated; only author, title, publisher and date are given.

Since the material used in this volume so closely parallels that of *Cinema Booklist* and this book, the following comments may not be impartial or objective.

A listing of book titles without evaluation or even description is of limited value. The *Larry Edmund's Cinema Catalog* gives many more titles and annotations than Bukalski does here and at far lower cost.

The fifty annotations that are given vary in quality: e.g., on MacGowan's *Behind the Screen*, < ... it is best in its accounts of technological developments of film but less than inadequate in its discussion of many historical films." Why include it as an essential work? Why not include Jacobs' *The Rise of the American Film* instead? This latter book is recog-

nized by most film scholars as one of the classics in film literature. Incidentally, Jacobs wrote this book; he did not edit it, as indicated in Bukalski's nonannotated bibliography.

The arrangement of the books is questionable. To place introductory books in one listing along with history, theory, and criticism may not offer the best service to the researcher. For example, into what categories do the following fall: *Contemporary Film, Movie Reader, Black Magic, Image Maker,* or *The New Spirit in the Cinema*? The absence of an annotation for this last title can be misleading, since it is a reprint of a 1930 book. The arrangement assumes that the searcher will know the author's specialty. No index is given to overcome these important limitations for reference use.

The script section lists books which are not scripts; they merely contain visuals from the films, e.g., *Yellow Submarine* or *Zuckerkland* or *Young Aphrodites.*

There are other disturbing features—omissions, incorrect placement, and poor arrangement—that diminish the value of this volume to a considerable degree. It cannot be recommended, other than as a checklist.

1985 *Film Resource Centers in New York City*. compiled by Emmens, Carol A. 28 p. paper New York: Educational Film Library Association, 1976.

The aim of this short directory is to list 25 film resource centers in New York City that are open to the public. Information was obtained from questionnaires and includes institution data, aims, services, facilities, publications and special features.

A valuable reference for those in the New York metropolitan area concerned with film study.

1986 *Film Resources For Sex Education*. by Burleson, Derek L.; and Barbash, Gary. 52 p. paper New York: Sex Information and Educational Council of the U.S., 1976.

The films, filmstrips, slides, cassettes and transparencies listed in this mediagraphy have been reviewed. Due to the sensitive nature of the subjects, inclusion does not imply recommendation, but may suggest consideration for use. Topics include reproduction, sexual development, emotional and social behavior, premarital sex, teenage marriage, pregnancy, childbirth, and venereal disease. The materials, mostly 16mm films, are arranged alphabetically by title and access is aided by a subject heading index. Each entry contains the product information, an annotation, and the suggested grade level. Producer-distributor addresses are noted in the rear pages.

An essential volume for anyone dealing with sex education, the volume will also help institutions such as social agencies.

1987   *Film Review.* edited by Speed, F. Maurice. 225 p. illus. New York: A. S. Barnes, 1944-.

The theme is a survey of world cinema for the years listed and includes sections such as "The Releases of the Year," "In Memoriam," "The Year's Awards," etc. However, each volume in this annual series differs slightly from the earlier one. The latter books include pertinent articles which are not always directly related to the yearly theme. The quality of writing in these articles is usually high. Perhaps the most intriguing section of the later books is entitled "Releases of the Year in Pictures." The black and white illustrations used in the section are plentiful and reproduced with excellent technical quality. The filmography ("Releases of the Year in Detail") includes synopsis, some evaluation, cast, behind-camera credits, and other data. As a reference or for pleasurable looking and reading, this series is recommended.

1988   *Film Review Digest 1977.* edited by Brownstone, David M.; and Frank, Irene M. 438 p. New York: KTO Press, 1978.

Feature films released from the fall of 1976 to the summer of 1977 are treated in this reference volume. The films are arranged alphabetically by title, with each entry offering cast, credits, producer, time, classification and several excerpts from published reviews. The latter are taken from some 28 different periodicals, with about ten excerpts being offered for each film. The excerpts are usually a paragraph in length, averaging about 100 words or so. A list of the periodicals is given along with a title listing. Awards given out during the year are noted. They include the following: Academy Awards, The National Society of Film Critics, The New York Film Critics, National Board of Review, Writer's Guild of America, The Cannes Film Festival, and The Berlin Film Festival. In addition to a general index, there is an index to the reviewers cited.

While it is interesting to read short critical comments about films, several reservations about excerpts should be noted. How is the selection made? Can the entire sense of a long critical review be distilled in a short paragraph? How much more does

this format do for the reader than that of the short capsule reviews of Leonard Maltin (*TV Movies*) or Steven Scheuer (*Movies on TV*)? Other than the dedicated filmgoer, it is difficult to determine who might use and read this type of volume. Its most valuable feature is the newness of the information it offers.

1989   *Film Review Index.* edited by Doak, Wesley A.; and Speed, William J. Pasadena, Cal.: Audio-Visual Associates, 1972.

This annual index to film reviews offers a unique service. Available in several formats, including loose-leaf and microfilm, the index is published in quarterly cumulative installments with volume four being the compilation for the entire year. More than 90 publications are indexed and they are listed at the front with complete data on publication schedule, address, subscription price, etc. The films are first arranged alphabetically by title, with a separate line for each review. Since several film formats are included, differentiation is made by symbols: M for 16mm films, FF for feature film, F for filmstrip, E for 8mm, L for film loop, C for cartridge, S for slide, T for transparency, K for kit, VT for video tapes. The type of entry—review, annotation or mention—is noted, and the source volume, issue date, page and reviewer's name are listed. The format makes it relatively easy to trace a review.

The films are then rearranged under subject headings in a separate guide following the alphabetical listing. A list of distributor names and addresses completes the book. An abbreviation list for the periodicals is given but there is none for the distributors. Appreciation must be expressed for the intent of this service. To bring some order to the chaotic world of film evaluation, selection, purchase and rental is an accomplishment indeed. Highly recommended.

1990   *Film Reviews in Psychiatry, Psychology and Mental Health.: A Descriptive and Evaluative Listing of Educational and Instructional Films.* edited by Froelich, Robert E. Ann Arbor, Mich.: Pierian, 1974.

1991   *Film Score: The View from the Podium.* by Thomas, Tony. 266 p. illus. New York: A.S. Barnes, 1979.

Twenty major composers are the subjects in this volume whose general purpose is to explore the craft of writing film music. Each man receives a single chapter which contains a portrait, a biographical essay by author Thomas, and a statement on film music by the subject himself. Arrangement is in a loose chronological fashion—Copland, Rozsa, Waxman, Steiner and others from Hollywood's golden age, followed eventually by Jerry Fielding, Jerry Goldsmith and Leonard Rosenman. A post-1970 discography and a bibliography complete the volume.

Tony Thomas has written previously about film music in his books on Busby Berkeley, Gene Kelly, Harry Warren, and in a 1972 publication, *Music for the Movies*. His crusade for a greater appreciation of the film composer continues with this specialized collection of composer statements. An admirable addition to cinema literature.

1992 *The Film Script: The Technique of Writing for the Screen.* by Brunel, Adrian. 192 p. illus. London: Burke, 1948.

A rather complete coverage of film script writing is given in this book. Starting with advice on a choice of subject, factors such as originality, attitude, and treatment are also discussed. The creation of the script, with examination of such elements as sequences and dialogue, is treated next and the latter portions deal with the marketing of the final script, title, script conferences, and revisions. The illustrations used to visualize terms such as close-up, focus, tank shots, angle shots, etc. The book concludes with a dictionary of terms and four script extracts from ANNA KARENINA (1948), BROKEN JOURNEY (1948), IS THIS PARIS? (1948) and THE CAPTIVE HEART (1946). One of the better books on scriptwriting.

1993 *The Film Script.* by Thompson, Charles V. 93 p. illus. London: Fountain Press, 1962.

An easy-to-read how-to-do-it book that includes certain advice not found in other expensive volumes. Starting with the suggestion of news items as a source of ideas for scripts, the author treats the rhetoric of the film in some detail. Later he explores possible ways of incorporating suspense or laughter into a script. The book is a simple, useful tool containing many sketches and much valuable information. Highly recommended.

1994 *The Film Script: A Guide for Writers.* by Giustini, Rolando. 224 p. illus. Englewood Cliffs, N.J.: Prentice Hall, 1980.

1995 *Film Scripts (A Series).* New York: Simon & Schuster; London. Lorrimer, 1968- .

Since 1968 Simon and Schuster has published a series of scripts in two categories: modern film scripts and classic film scripts. The dividing date between the two categories seems to be World War II. The scripts seem to appear first under the Lorrimer banner in London. The time- lag in publication sometimes is a matter of more than a year, and it is not unusual for a title to appear in London long before it is seen here. Occasionally the title is changed.

The following is a partial list of the scripts that Simon and Schuster has published: Modern Film Scripts: ALPHAVILLE (Godard); ASHES AND DIAMONDS (Wajda); BELLE DE JOUR (Bunuel); THE BICYCLE THIEF (De Sica); A BLOND IN LOVE (Forman); BLOW-UP (Antonioni); CLAIRE'S KNEE (Rohmer); CLOSELY WATCHED TRAINS (Menzel); LA COLLECTIONEUSE (Rohmer); THE FIREMAN'S BALL (Forman); GENERATION (Wajda); IF (Anderson); IKURU (Kurosawa); JULES AND JIM (Truffaut); KANAL (Wajda); LOVES OF A BLOND (Forman); A MAN AND A WOMAN (Lelouche); MY NIGHT AT MAUD'S (Rohmer); OEDIPUS REX (Pasolini); LE PETIT SOLDAT (Godard); PIERROT LE FOU (Godard); THE SEVEN SAMURAI (Kurosawa); THE SEVENTH SEAL (Bergman); THE THIRD MAN (Reed); THE TRIAL (Welles); TRISTANA (Bunuel); WILD STRAWBERRIES (Bergman).

Classic Film Scripts: L'AGE D'OR (Bunuel); THE BLUE ANGEL (von Sternberg); THE CABINET OF DR. CALIGARI (Wiene); UN CHIEN ANDALOU (Bunuel); CHILDREN OF PARADISE (Carne); DUCK SOUP (McCarey); EARTH (Dovzhenko); ENTR'ACTE (Clair); GRAND ILLUSION (Renoir); GREED (von Stroheim); IVAN THE TERRIBLE (Eisenstein); LE JOUR SE LEVE (Carne); M (Lang); METROPOLIS (Lang); MONKEY BUSINESS (McLeod); MOROCCO (von Sternberg); MOTHER (Pudovkin); NEVER GIVE A SUCKER AN EVEN BREAK (Cline); A NOUS LA LIBERTE (Clair); PANDORA'S BOX (Pabst); POTEMKIN (Eisenstein); RULES OF THE GAME (Renoir); SHANGHAI EXPRESS (von Sternberg); STAGECOACH (Ford); TILLIE AND GUS (Martin).

1996 *Film Scripts Four.* edited by Garrett, George P.; and Hardison, O. B., Jr.; and Gelfman, Jane R. 500 p. paper New York: Appleton-Century-Crofts, 1972.

Contains: introduction (same as *Film Scripts One*); A HARD DAY'S NIGHT, (1964); THE BEST MAN (1964); DARLING (1965). Appendix: initial and closing pages of final shooting schedule of THE BEST MAN (1963);

glossary (changed somewhat from Volumes *Film Scripts One and Two*); bibliography (updated since *Film Scripts One and Two*).

1997   *Film Scripts One.* by Gelfman, Jane R. edited by Garrett, George P.; and Hardison, O. B., Jr.; 544 p. paper New York: Appleton-Century-Crofts, 1971.

Contains: introduction; HENRY V (1944); THE BIG SLEEP (1946); A STREETCAR NAMED DESIRE, (1951) and appendix which has the initial and closing pages of final shooting schedule of THE BEST MAN (1963); a glossary; and bibliography.

1998   *Film Scripts Three.* edited by Garrett, George P.; and Hardison, O. B., Jr.; and Gelfman, Jane R. 618 p. paper New York: Appleton-Century-Crofts, 1972.

Contains introduction (same as *Film Scripts Two*); THE APARTMENT (1960); THE MISFITS, (1961); CHARADE (1963). Appendix contains initial and closing pages of final shooting schedule of THE BEST MAN, (1963); glossary (changed somewhat from *Film Scripts One and Two*); bibliography (updated since *Film Scripts One and Two*).

1999   *Film Scripts Two.* edited by Garrett, George P.; and Hardison, O. B. Jr.; and Gelfman, Jane R. 548 p. paper New York: Appleton-Century-Crofts, 1971.

Contains: introduction (same as *Film Scripts One*); HIGH NOON (1952); TWELVE ANGRY MEN, (1957); THE DEFIANT ONES, (1958). Appendix: and an appendix with the initial and closing pages of final shooting schedule of THE BEST MAN, (1963); a glossary; and bibliography. Appendix is the same as in *Film Scripts Two.*

2000   *Film Scriptwriting.* by Swain, Dwight V. 373 p. New York: Hastings House, 1976.

This volume is about scriptwriting tools and how to use them. In his foreword the author states, "...writing a successful film script is not one thing, but many; for writing is a process made up of an infinity of sub-processes. 'Learning to write' means learning how to go through the steps involved in such sub-processes with facility, and how to relate these various sub-processes to each other and to incorporate them into an integrated whole."

In the pages of information, advice, and example which follow, Swain first explores the factual film by discussing the proposal outline, film treatment, sequence outline, shooting script, and narration. Next is his detailed consideration of the feature film, including such topics as story, characters, dialogue, master scenes, and adaptations. An appendix contains a bibliography, a glossary, and short sections on the storyboard and the judgment of screen time.

The book's subtitle, "A Practical Manual," is most appropriate, for the author's approach is informal and emphasizes talent at work rather than theoretical analysis. More important, perhaps, is his avoidance of a pedagogical exposition in favor of a readable, stimulating personal statement. Highly recommended.

2001   *Film Semiotics, Metz, and Leone's Trilogy.* by Roth, Lane. 231 p. New York: Garland, 1982.

2002   *The Film Sense.* by Eisenstein, Sergei M. paper illus. New York: Harcourt, 1947.

This translation by Jay Leyda finds Eisenstein at his most theoretical—again exploring, thinking, and investigating. These mental exercise essays were attempts to develop and explain his theory of film. The results are erratic, stimulating, frustrating, and challenging. For historians and scholars. See *Film Form and The Film Sense.*

2003   *Film Service Profiles.* compiled by Salz, Kay. 56 p. New York: Center for Cultural Resources (Center for Arts Information), 1980.

2004   *Film 71-72.* edited by Denby, David. 299 p. paper New York: Simon & Schuster, 1972.

2005   *Film 70-71.* edited by Denby, David. 319 p. paper New York: Simon and Schuster, 1971.

The fourth yearly anthology by the National Society of Film Critics. The editor this time is David Denby, film critic for *The Atlantic*, and the usual representation can be noted—Kael, Simon, Knight, Alpert, Gilliatt, Schickel, Sarris, Kauffmann, Morgenstern, etc. There are 22 members in the group. An account of the voting for the 1970 awards, some short critic identifications and an index complete the book. Another fine collection of film criticism, this volume is highly recommended.

2006 *Film 73/74.* edited by Cocks, Jay; and Denby, David. 369 p. Indianapolis, Ind.: Bobbs-Merrill, 1974.

An annual publication, this seventh anthology of film criticism by 22 members of the National Society of Film Critics covers about one-fifth of the films released in 1973. Expertly chosen reviews are arranged under general thematic categories such as young American directors, politics, comedy, cops and quarry, women: the missing presence, etc. A detailed report of the voting by the Circle for the "Bests" of 1973 is included, as is a listing of the awards given in previous years (1966 to 1972). The contributors are identified briefly at the book's conclusion and there are title and name indexes provided. This collection of the finest current film criticism is not only a source of reading pleasure but also a valuable reference. Highly recommended.

2007 *Film 68/69.* edited by Alpert, Hollis; and Sarris, Andrew. 281 p. New York: Simon & Schuster, 1969.

The second of a series this volume is a stimulating anthology of reviews of the more important films released in 1968-1969. The contributors to this volume read like a "Who's Who" in film criticism and authorship. Highly recommended.

2008 *Film 69/70.* edited by Morgenstern, Joseph; and Kanfer, Stefan. 286 p. New York: Simon & Schuster, 1970.

This is the third book is a series that is recommended reading for all.

2009 *Film 67/68.* edited by Schickel, Richard; and Simon, John. 320 p. (paper) New York: Simon & Schuster, 1968.

A provacative and entertaining anthology of writings by members of the National Society of Film Critics, this book has as it subject the most important films released in the United States in 1967. Representative reviews of the films are grouped according to genre—adolescents, westerns, social questions, etc. Longer articles on the effect of BLOW-UP (1967) on college audiences, the underground film, EXPO 67 (1968), and a symposium on "The Future of the Film" complete the book. Recommended for most readers; might be considered as a text in many college courses.

2010 *Film Sneaks Annual, 1972.* Ann Arbor, Mich.: Pierian Press, 1972.

Announced as a guide to 4500 nontheatrical films which cumulates ratings of these films by librarians from 40 major libraries over the last seven years. The sample page shows title, distributor, and a rating scale of six values: excellent, very good, good, average, fair, and poor. The film ANYONE FOR DIVING? (1968) had the score, VG—2; G—1; A—2, which would seem to indicate that five reviewers thought the film to be somewhere between average and very good.

2011 *A Film Society Handbook.* edited by Vannoey, R. C. 56 p. paper illus. London: Society for Education in Film and Television, 1966.

One section of this handbook offers practical advice on organizing a film society for young people; the other relates some actual experiences, problems, successes, and failures that established societies have had. The British ads and letters to the editor are amusing and helpful.

2012 *Film Society Primer.* edited by Starr, Cecile. 84 p. paper New York: American Federation of Film Societies, 1956.

A compilation of 22 articles about and for film societies.

2013 *Film Society Programmes, 1925-1939.* by London Film Society. 456 p. illus. New York: Arno, 1972.

These are the programs for 108 showings organized by the London Film Society during the years 1925 to 1939. Approximately 900 films were shown and notes about them appeared in the programs. Directors, players, production facts, casts, credits and other data are given. The programs indicate certain movements and trends in the history of motion pictures. Of interest primarily to researchers and historians.

2014 *Film—Space, Time, Light and Sound.* by Johnson, Lincoln F. 340 p. paper illus. New York: Holt, Rinehart & Winston, 1974.

The author's stated purpose is "to make you see" — as he believes the art of seeing can be learned. Not only is his goal praiseworthy but the material he has written, gathered and arranged here is of a consistent high order. He is dealing, of course, with those film aesthetics mentioned in his title—but he has included much more. After discussing the uniqueness of film, he treats movement through space and time, principles of continuity, harmony and contrast, color and tone, and sound. Latter chapters are devoted to tenses in film, film structure, style, genre and, finally, filmmakers.

In addition to the literate, knowledgeable text, there are hundreds of illustrations placed appropriately to correlate with the text. A filmography of the films in the text, a bibliography, notes, a glossary and an index complete the work. All are quite impressive in content and coverage. As a textbook for certain college courses, this volume is enthusiastically recommended.

2015   *A Film Star in Belgrave Square*. by Henrey, Robert. 186 p. illus. London: Peter Davies, 1948.

Written by the father of the eight-year-old boy who had a major role in Carol Reed's THE FALLEN IDOL (1948), this book tells some of the experiences in making the film. The boy is used as the focal point of the account. Because of the subjective approach used, the material is rather prosaic and written in a tourist style. The stills are rather uninspired. The book can be of use in background study of Carol Reed or the film.

2016   *Film Stars of History*. by Baily, F. E. 167 p. illus. London: MacDonald, 1944.

A comparison of real historical personages — Henry VIII, Queen Christina, Catherine The Great, Lord Nelson, Disraeli, Lincoln, etc.— with their screen representation. Both a real life portrait and a film still portrait are shown.

2017   *A Film Student's Index to the National Board of Review Magazine* 1926-1948. by Warfield, Nancy D. 93 p. paper New York: Little Film Gazette, 1974.

Although this book is not an index in the reference or research sense, it is a tool designed for film scholars. What Ms. Warfield has done is: (1) arrange the contents of each year's issues of *The National Board of Review Magazine* under four major headings (signed feature articles, unsigned feature articles, book reviews, and film Reviews); (2) rearrange the film reviews into a total listing by title and once again by director; and (3) rearrange the signed feature articles into a total listing arranged alphabetically by author surname.

The book will provide assistance to anyone searching for information on a specific film or director. Its use in locating a specific article by the author's sur-

name is peripheral and would probably not be utilized with any great frequency. What is missing, of course, is the arrangement of the articles—both signed and unsigned—under suitable film-study headings. The absence of these necessary aids to information retrieval makes the book not an index but more an "aid" or a "guide." Acceptable as such.

2018   *Film Study: A Resource Guide*. by Manchel, Frank. 422 p. Cranbury, N.J.: Fairleigh Dickinson University Press, 1973.

Frank Manchel is the author of a most successful series of film books for young readers. He has given his attention here to a reference work designed to assist those involved in film study—either teacher or student. The plan is a logical one and arranges the study materials into the following categories: (1) Introductory Works, Aesthetics, Techniques, Student Filmmaking; (2) Film Genres; (3) Film Stereotypes; (4) Film Themes; (5) Film Sources; (6) Film History; and (7) Film Study. Under these sections there are listed pertinent books, periodical articles, and films, with short descriptive-critical annotations given for each. Each large section is introduced by an explanatory essay.

Appendices and indexes are plentiful and include a glossary; a list of film critics and periodicals; a list of film distributors; the motion picture code and rating program; sources for further study; selected dissertations on film; an article title index; an author-article index; an author-book index; a book title index; a film personality index; a film title index; and a subject index. There is an overwhelming amount of valuable information in this impressive reference. It certainly will assist anyone concerned with film study and is highly recommended.

2019   *Film Study Collections*. by Allen, Nancy. 194 p. New York: Ungar, 1979.

Nancy Allen, a communications librarian, has assembled a guide to the materials associated with film studies. In 14 terse chapters she covers such topics as definitions, history, collection development, periodicals, evaluation, nonprint material, scripts, dealers, bookstores, archives, reference services, cataloging, and film study libraries. Appendixes offer lists of publishers' addresses and libraries holding screenplays. A topic index, a collections index, and a list of the works cited in the text complete the book.

This is a comprehensive survey of film study materials that should be of interest/value to a wide audience — scholars, historians, teachers, writers, librarians, etc. Hundreds of useful sources are noted and most include descriptive annotations. In addition, the linking narrative portions are clearly written and explain the various procedures necessary to locate the various kinds of information indigenous to film study.

2020 *Film Study Guides.* by Carringer, Robert. Champaign, Illinois: Stipes, 1977.

2021 *Film Study in Higher Education.* edited by Stewart, David C. 174 p. paper illus. Washington, D.C.: American Council on Education, 1966.

For anyone concerned with the serious study of films, this book is essential. It is pertinent not only for higher education, but for the secondary school as well. The selections are stimulating, informative, and full of suggestions and resource data. The detailed descriptions by different authors of the film courses that they give is valuable. In most cases, the missionary zeal that they feel for their topic percolates through the description. The appendices of film distributors, archives, libraries and societies are excellent. A short bibliography of books and periodicals is included. A required book for the professional, interesting for the advanced enthusiast.

2022 *Film Study in the High School.* by Culkin, John M. 35 p. paper illus. New York: Fordham Film Study Center, Fordham University, 1965.

An important statement about film education by one of its best known advocates, this text has been reprinted in the *Catholic High School Quarterly Bulletin* of Oct., 1965, and by the National Catholic Education Association.

2023 *Film Superlist: 20,000 Motion Pictures in the Public Domain (1894-1939).* compiled by Minus, Johnny; and Hale, William Storm. 1300 p. paper Hollywood: Seven Arts, 1973.

This volume is available in two formats: as a complete book or in ten separate booklets. For this review, booklet 2, which consists of films made between 1912 and 1939 with titles beginning with A, B, or CA, was used. The source is a public domain government document *Motion Pictures 1912-1939* on which the compilers have indicated copyright renewals in handwritten notations. The service performed here is the location of copyright renewals

and the posting of them onto the master list contained in *Motion Pictures 1912-1939*.

Once films fall into public domain, they belong to anyone and can be used for any purpose. Since the copyright law is complex, the authors suggest checking with the copyright office for final decision. Recent revisions of the copyright law are not discussed. A valuable reference volume.

2024 *Film Teaching.* by British Film Institute. 107 p. paper illus. London: British Film Institute, 1967.

A Full description of film courses operating in four major areas of education: 1) liberal studies; 2) teacher training; 3) adult education; and 4) university extramural courses.

2025 *Film Technique and Film Acting.* by Pudovkin, Vladimir I. 388 p. paper illus. New York: Grove, 1960.

Devoted to an explanation of editing as the foundation of film art, the first book was originally published in 1929. It has remained a classic work on early Russian montage theory. The second volume appeared first in 1935 and relates the Stanislavsky method of stage acting to performing for the motion picutre. As pioneer examples of serious writing in the field of cinema literature, both volumes are historically important and will appeal to historians and scholars. Others may become impatient with the detailed exposition.

2026 *Film Theory and Criticism.* edited by Mast, Gerald; and Cohen, Marshall. 639 p. paper illus. New York: Oxford University Press, 1974.

A collection of 54 articles taken from books and periodicals published during the past three decades. Author representation is predictable and impressive —Eisenstein, Pudovkin, Bazin, Arnheim, Balazs, Tyler, Youngblood, etc. The articles are divided into seven categories: film and reality; film image and film language; the film medium; film, theater and literature; kinds of film; the film artist; and the film audience. A bibliography and a few film stills are added.

The selection of articles seems a bit unbalanced. Why, for example, devote five articles out of 11 in the film, theater and literature section to Shakespearean films? Why limit film performers to two articles on Garbo in the film artist section? Although these are representative articles that contribute to the author's total statement, one wonders whether a more varied selection might have provided a more rounded result.

There can be no quarrel with the concept of the total book. The articles are a sampling of classic statements on film theory and criticism, and presenting them in one volume is a praiseworthy effort. The need for a book of this kind has been evident for a long time, and its appearance merits applause. As an introduction to film theory this volume is highly recommended for mature readers.

2027   *Film Theory of James Agee.* by Flanders, Mark Wilson. New York: Arno, 1977.

Written in 1971 at the University of Iowa in partial fulfillment of the doctoral program, this study examines the work and influence of the American film critic, James Agee. The author analyzes Agee's role in the field of film criticism by structuring his film critiques according to their aesthetic emphasis and examining their broader relationship to the film industry. This title appears in the *Dissertationson Film* series.

2028   *The Film Till Now.* by Rotha, Paul; and Griffith, Richard. 755 p. illus. New York: Funk and Wagnalls, 1949.

This 1930 classic which is constantly being up-dated (in 1949 and in 1967) is still a vital book. Although it is no longer a world film survey, it has enough superior poritions in its original material to warrant its longevity. The book gets weaker as it approaches the present.

2029   *Film Tricks.* by Schechter, Harold; and Everitt, David. paper illus. New York: Harlin Quist, 1980.

A survey of special effects in films from the turn of the century to METEOR (1979), this volume uses text and illustrations to explain the "tricks" of its title. Several hundred films are mentioned.

2030   *A Film Trilogy: Scripts of Three Films.* by Bergman, Imgmar. 143 p. illus. New York: Orion Press, 1968.

Contains: THROUGH A GLASS DARKLY (1961), WINTER LIGHT (1962), and THE SILENCE (1963).

2031   *Film-TV Law.* by Minus, Johnny; and Hale, William Storm. 232 p. illus. Hollywood, Calif.: Seven Arts Press, 1973.

The full title of this volume is *Your Introduction to Film-TV Copyright, Contracts and Other Law.* Its authors were responsible for the earlier handbook, *The Movie Industry Book.* Here, once again, they demonstrate their ability to be informative, instructional and nonpedantic in the presentation of an essentially technical-legal text. Using cartoons, forms, charts, outlines, exercises, etc., they attempt to give the reader a solid base in film-TV law. Topics discussed include contracts, torts, law suits, obscenity, pornography, finance, privacy, libel, unions, labor laws, insurance, taxes, copyright, piracy, etc. A useful glossary, an annotated bibliography, and an index complete the work.

The information presented here and its arrangement are sure to reward any reader seeking knowledge about the laws pertinent to films and TV. The book is essential for all institutions which offer degree programs in film study or filmmaking.

2032   *The Film User's Handbook.* by Rehrauer, George. 301 p. illus. New York: R. R. Bowker, 1975.

The goal of this volume is to provide a guide for acquiring, using, and controlling films—and for helping people to enjoy them. It answers questions that range from aesthetics and film history to selection procedures for films and equipment. Part One is devoted to a background for film service, while the second part deals with developing film programs in institutions. Supporting these major sections are illustrations, an introduction, several appendixes, a long bibliography, a glossary and an index.

In a review of this book for *Mass Media Booknotes,* it was called "definitive." Don Roberts in his review for *Library Journal* said, "... a mind boggling compendium of information ... I suspect it will become a classic.... The book doesn't miss a thing and is interesting reading.... I recommend this very highly to specialists, film programmers, students of film (including of course, the public), and library school collections."

2033   *Film Vocabulary.* by Van Nooten, S. I. 223 p. The Hague: Netherlands Government Information, 1970.

Some 900 film terms are listed here, in French, English, Dutch, Italian, German, Spanish, and Danish equivalents. A handy aid for anyone involved in international film matters.

2034   *Film World: A Guide to Cinema.* by Montagu, Ivor. 327 p. paper illus. Baltimore: Penguin Books, 1967.

This volume might stand as a model to others of its

type. In his attempt to cover all aspects of the cinema, the author is unusually successful. He discusses each topic with ease, competence, intelligence and a feeling for teaching his audience rather than befuddling them . The major divisions of the book are film as science, film as art, film as commodity, and film as vehicle. These four categories serve as an umbrella covering all facets of film.

The book is British and may cause some slight reader discomfort with the statistics and the exhibition problems which are unique to Britain. The center picture section is average in reproduction quality . It is the high quality of the writing and the comprehensiveness of the text that warrant recommendation. Some readers may have to read it slowly or re-read certain sections, but the effort will be rewarding.

2035 *Film Writing Forms: Methods of Preparing a Story for the Screen.* edited by Jacobs, Lewis. 61 p. paper illus. New York: Gotham Book Mart, 1934.

Some samples of a synopsis, an original, an adaptation, a scenario, a treatment, and a shooting scrip are included. This work is dated, with little current value . Other volumes cover the topic with far greater success.

2036 *Film/Cinema/Movie.* by Mast, Gerald. 299 p. illus. New York: Harper and Row, 1977.

This volume on film theory is divided into two parts, the first of which is an examination-evaluation of current film theories. In the second section, the author discusses the ways in which the viewer receives, perceives, understands, and feels the effects of cinema. The book's subtitle, "A Theory of Experience," is quite appropriate for this portion of the text. However, the title given is "An Integrated Succession of Projected Images and (Recorded) Sound," and it supplies the subject areas for the remaining section of the book — succession, projection, classification, and sound. A final chapter deals with the integration of three cinema languages — succession (time), image (space), and sound.

Throughout the text examples from many films are cited. The illustrations are frame enlargements which offer direct evidence rather than questionable visual information often contained in film stills. Notes, a bibliography, and an index complete the volume.

For the scholar or the academician, this book offers an abundance of ideas, suggestions, examples and questions. For them and for students, the book will be a strong catalyst for thought and discussion. Less dedicated readers may find the material presented here a bit too pedantic. Recommended.

2037 *Film/TV Graphics 2.* edited by Herdeg, Walter. 211 p. illus. New York: Hastings House, 1976.

This is an enlarged and updated edition of the volume first published in 1967. Subtitled "An International Survey of the Art of Film Animation," the book examines entertainment films, television films, sponsored films, commercial films, film titles and captions, and experiments. The text appears in English, German, and French but the attraction here is the universally understood visuals. They are superb, ranging from simple line cartoons to beautifully colored pictures.

For anyone interested in film animation, this volume is the one to seek out and treasure. It has been given a careful, precise production with each page offering some example of visual pleasure or joy. The text and the arrangement of the material provide substantial support to the illustrations. Highly recommended.

2038 *Filmarama.* compiled by Stewart, John. 394 p. Metuchen, N.J.: Scarecrow Press, 1975.

Subtitled "The Formidable Years, 1893-1919," this listing of film actor credits is admittedly partial since more than 150,000 films were made in the above stated period. An attempt is made to offer the subject's film name, real name, birthdate, death date, film titles, and stage play titles. However, complete data are not given for many entries andthe stage appearance listings are representative rather than complete. Occasionally the author will indicate direction credits (D. W. Griffith) but more often will not (Chaplin, Ford, von Stroheim, Donald Crisp, Van Dyke). A few attempts at character identification also appear—von Stroheim: INTOLERANCE (Second Pharisee). An alphabetical title index which notes release date, production company, and two or three player number references completes the volume; a sample index entry is MILLS OF THE GODS, THE (1909), Biograph, Linda Arvidson 79, Arthur V. Johnson 1363, Marion Leonard 1542.

It is difficult to ascertain the extent of international coverage; the content seems predominantly American. Then, too, the volume is not as complete as it might be—surely the birth and death dates for W. S. Van Dyke are easily available. It does offer, however, a wealth of information about some of the films and players of the early period of motion pictures. Acceptable.

2039 *Filmarama, Volume 2: The Flaming Years, 1920-1929.* by Stewart, John. 738 p. Metuchen, N.J.: Scarecrow, 1977.

This is the second volume of a contemplated series of six that will cover the period of 1893 to 1969. It provides screen, stage, radio and recording credits and, occasionally, bits of biographical information for actors and actresses of the twenties. The first section arranges the performers alphabetically by surname. Film titles referred to in section one are listed alphabetically in the index, which occupies the second part of the book. Using the first part the reader can learn that Jean Arthur was born Gladys Georgianna Greene in 1908 and appeared in almost 50 films during the twenties. The second section will indicate that FLAME OF THE YUKON was released in 1926 by Producer's Distributing Company and had Matthew Betz, Arnold Gray, Kenneth Harlan, and Seena Owen in its cast. Scholars, historians, researchers and buffs will delight in this series, a treasury of hard-to-find information.

2040 *Filmed Books and Plays, 1928-1974* by Enser, A. G. S. 549 p. New York: Academic Press 1975.

This is a new edition of a standard film reference which updates its content—a list of books and plays from which films have been made—to 1974. The book consists of three parts: (1) A film title index, which matches a film title (with author name, studio and year), publisher, form (play or novel), and the original title of the work, if changed; (2) an author index which matches the author names, written works, and publishers with the film stars, release dates, and changed titles where applicable and (3) a final section which lists the original title and author with the changed film title, release date and studio.

It should be noted that the film titles considered are British, thus the film we know as AMERICA, AMERICA (1963) is known here as the ANATOLIAN SMILE, while AN AMERICAN DREAM (1966) becomes SEE YOU IN HELL, DARLING. No key is provided for American-British film title changes.

As indicated above, this is an accepted standard reference whose pertinence increases with each edition. Highly recommended.

2041 *The Filmgoer's Book of Quotes.* by Halliwell, Leslie. 222 p. illus. New Rochelle, N.Y.: Arlington House, 1973.

Quotes, anecdotes, maxims, proverbs, definitions, ad-libs and other spoken forms abound in this volume aimed at the movie buff or nostalgia lover. The remarks are humorous and many have an intelligence or wit that makes them candidates for repetition. The entries are arranged in an unusual, almost random fashion. Certain personalities have a section devoted to them, while others are arranged under collective titles such as "Glamour Girls," "Critics" or "Stars." There are quizzes offered along with the quotations and an index identifies many of the speakers and their targets.

This is a pleasant entertainment that is strongest in its selection of quotations and weakest in the quizzes, which offer little to support the title. Much of the material here is reminiscent of Max Wilk's *The Wit and Wisdom of Hollywood*. Wilk offers his punch lines at the conclusion of paragraph settings; Halliwell is much briefer, identifying only the speaker and occasion. Acceptable.

2042 *see* *2043*

2043 *The Filmgoer's Companion.* by Halliwell, Leslie. 825 p. illus. New York: Hill and Wang, 1977.

Since its modest initial appearance in 1965, this film encyclopedia has appeared in five further editions, each one enlarging and improving upon its predecessor. The sixth edition now contains more than 10,000 varied entries (names, titles, topics, themes etc), which are supplemented by separate indexes for film titles, screen characters, film series, film themes, and title changes. A selected filmography and bibliography are added along with many illustrations.

Stated simply this is the best single volume reference on film available today. It becomes more valuable with each edition and the sixth continues its tradition of intelligent, thoughtful selection and preparation. It is an essential reference book.

2044 *Filmguide to ... (A Series).* edited by Geduld, Harry; and Gottesman, Ronald. paper Bloomington, Ind.: Indiana University Press, 1973- .

This series of film guides appears most promising in its initial releases. Included are the following titles which are treated individually elsewhere in this book: THE GENERAL (1925); THE GRAPES OF WRATH (1940); LA PASSION DE JEANNE D'ARC (1929); PSYCHO (1960); 2001: A SPACE ODYSSEY (1968).

The format for each is similar and includes the following elements: film credits, plot outline, a director profile, some production history, a long analysis, and a summary critique. Sections concluding the books are filmographies (usually simple title listings with director and studio notes), bibliographies (sometimes nicely annotated), rental sources, and notes to the text.

The series is designed to introduce the viewer to the film, give background information for its viewing, examine its techniques and message, and encourage discussion and further study. The series should be greeted with enthusiasm by teachers, students, and individual readers.

2045 *Filmguide to* HENRY V. by Geduld, Harry M. 82 p. paper Bloomington, Ind.: Indiana University Press, 1973.

The structure of this *Filmguide* is similar to the others in the series. Beginning with a synopsis, the book devotes short sections to director Laurence Olivier and to the production itself. It is the analysis and the summary critique that form the major content of the book. Closing sections include a director filmography and a bibliography.

The innovative use of color, music, verse dialogue and the Elizabethan theatre in the film are noted. Since HENRY V (1945) was the first Shakespearean film to gain both critical and audience approval, it had influence on later films. Viewed today, it still combines the beauty of Shakespeare's words with the visuals supplied by Olivier. This volume will intensify the appreciation of any viewer of the film, and for those students and scholars concerned with Shakespeare and film, it is an invaluable aid. Highly recommended.

2046 *Filmguide to* ODD MAN OUT. by De Felice, James. 85 p. paper Bloomington, Ind.: Indiana University Press, 1975.

The usual elements of credits, outline, director, production, analysis, summary critique, filmography, bibliography, rental sources and notes are retained in this volume of the *Filmguide* series. The subject is Carol Reed's classic film ODD MAN OUT (1947), made during the period of his greatest creativity. In the lengthy analysis of the film, author De Felice has missed little of the richness in detail that Reed provided. Theme, symbolism, allegory, directorial technique, acting, editing and the changes made from novel to film are some of the topics considered. When used with a viewing or study of the film, the volume is a valuable reference guide. Used alone, it offers some useful general information on Reed—his career, methods, films, etc. Recommended.

2047 *Filmguide to* THE BATTLE OF ALGIERS. by Mellen, Joan. 82 p. paper Bloomington, Ind.: Indiana University Press, 1973.

The form of this *Filmguide* is similar to the others: the plot outline, the director, and the production are introductory topics which lead to the major analysis and summary critique. A director filmography, a long annotated bibliography, and some chapter notes complete the book. The documentary effect that director Gillo Pontecorvo achieved in a fictional film is only one of several aspects considered here. Political and ideological factors, sound, music, images, and the work of an artist in recreating history are noted.

The guide offers much explanation, interpretation and appreciation of the film and is a most valuable aid to anyone who is planning to study/view it. Highly recommended.

2048 *Filmguide to* THE RULES OF THE GAME. by Mast, Gerald. 85 p. paper Bloomington, Ind.: Indiana University Press, 1973.

Here is another of the valuable resource books in the *Filmguide* series. In considering Renoir'sclassic film, Mast devotes introductory sections to a synopsis, the director, and the production. The major section of the guide offers an analysis which is then followed by a summary critique. A Renoir filmography and a bibliography conclude the book.

The number of approaches to and interpretations of THE RULES OF THE GAME is not limited. In his analysis Mast suggests some possibilities as he treats the film as a combination of comedy and tragedy, murder and farce. Failure is the key theme, and the major positive note that Mast sees in the film is the effort that the characters put forth. The film has never been an easy one for audiences to comprehend and accept. This volume can be most helpful to anyone approaching the film. Highly recommended.

2049 *Filmguide to* TRIUMPH OF THE WILL. by Barsam, Richard Meran. 82p. paper Bloomington: Indiana University Press, 1975.

The structure of the useful *Filmguide* series is maintained in this guide to a controversial, important film. After the credits and an outline of the film, detailed attention is given to both the director, Leni Riefenstahl, and the making of the film. The heart of the guide is a lengthy analysis of the film and a shorter summary critique. A Riefenstahl filmography, a bibliography, rental sources, and notes appear in the book's closing pages.

The volume is an important one for several reasons: its careful, intelligent treatment of a controversial director, based in part on author interviews; its astute analysis of the film including translations of certain speeches; and finally, its attention to film as propaganda. This volume is invaluable to any study/ showing of the film; but even without the film, the book contains rich, unique material on Riefenstahl, Germany and propaganda films that is not available elsewhere. Highly recommended.

2050 *Filmguide to* 8-1/2. by Perry, Ted. 89 p. Bloomington, Ind.: Indiana University Press, 1975.

A welcome addition to the *Filmguide* series, this volume includes the standard components: credits, outline, the director, the production, the analysis and a summary critique. Supporting the above are a Fellini filmography, a discography, a bibliography, some notes and a list of rental sources. Although all the elements in the book contribute to its high quality, it is the analysis that contains the most creative writing. Perry's detailed dissection of the film, and his interpretation of possible meanings, suggestions or rationales is stimulating and enlightening.

The film has the power to remain fascinating after repeated viewings; Perry's analysis offers fresh insight to either the first or the 21st experience of seeing 8-1/2 (1963). Highly recommended.

2051 *The Filmic Moment.* by Amelio, Ralph J. 164 p. paper illus. Dayton, Ohio: Pflaum, 1976.

Subtitled "Teaching American Genre Film Through Extracts," this volume depends upon the availability of certain films. A very limited series of extract-films available from only one distributor is the basis for the text, and although substitutions could be made, the book deals directly with these specific films. For example, to teach the horror genre, a 15-minute section of DR. JEKYLL AND MR. HYDE (1932) is used along with 18 minutes of KING KONG (1933). The text describes the plot of the film and the extract to be shown. Background and suggestions for discussion are followed by a bibliography.

The shaky premise upon which the book rests can be evidenced by the withdrawal of two films from the group after the text had been prepared. Although an appendix offers substitutions, the reader will sense an insecurity in the availability of specific excerpts. In a sense the volume becomes somewhat like the study guides distributed with films. Take away the film and the value of the guide becomes quite limit-

ed.

Illustrations, distributor information, suggested techniques for film study, recommended periodicals, and an index complete the book.

There is no quarrel with the concept of using film extracts in film study. Reservation results from the limitation imposed by designating specific extracts rather than treating in a general fashion the entire range of extract material mentioned in an early chapter. Acceptable.

2052 *Filming Assassinations.* by Kelly, Dave. 80 p. paper Berkeley, Calif.: Ithaca House, 1979.

2053 *Filming for Amateurs.* by Burnford, Paul. 107 p. paper illus. New York: Pitman, 1940.

A title in the *Pitman* series, this volume on cinematography for the beginner contains a foreword by Paul Rotha.

2054 *Filming For Television.* by Englander, A. Arthur; and Petzold, Paul. 266 p. illus. New York: Hastings House, 1976.

A. Arthur Englander, the senior film cameraman at BBC, was acclaimed for his work on many television series, including "Civilization." Paul Petzold is a writer-editor and coauthor of *The Technique of the Motion Picture Cameraman.* In this volume they have combined their talents to produce an explanation of how film is made for and used by television. After a short historical account, the authors progress quickly to TV studios, locations, drama production, the director, equipment, and materials. Attention is given to such technical topics as processing, rushes, movement, composition, exposure, control, contrast, lighting, filters, and certain effects, including composite photography. Specialized topics, such as chase sequences, interviews, the filming of works of art, and poetry readings, conclude the main text. The appendix contains examples of a filming diary, a shot list, a shooting schedule, and a filming schedule. A substantial glossary and an index conclude the book. A series of illustrations and drawings are correlated with the text.

This volume continues the quality and distinction that has characterized the *Communcation Arts Series.* Written for the serious, experienced reader, this text offers a straight forward exposition of fact, description, opinion and advice, always emphasizing the practical and useful rather than the theoretical. The active television cameraman should delight in the treasury of information offered; however, any aspiring filmmaker can also learn a great deal about filming for television here. Highly recommended.

2055 *The Filming of the West.* by Tuska, Jon. 618 p. illus. New York: Double-day, 1976.

Using 100 western films as the basic material for this study, Jon Tuska arranges and discusses them in chronological order. Thus each film is viewed not only as a model of its time but also as an element which contributed to this American film genre. He has further divided the text into appropriate periods: The Early Years; The Glittering Twenties; A Time of Darkness and Light; The Decline and Fall of the "B" Western; The Post War Years; Perpetuation of a Tradition; and Contemporary Trends in the Modern Western. An appendix notes rental sources for most of the 100 films and a very detailed index is included.

More than 200 illustrations not only support the text admirably but relate a pictorial history by themselves. They have been selected with intelligence and discrimination and their reproduction is above average. The author states that his preparation took a decade and included screening 8000 westerns, interviewing 600 people, and other assorted research tasks. This effort is evident when the purpose of the book is contrasted with its achievement. Tuska set out to tell the history of the western by concentrating on the filmmaking techniques, the filmmakers, and the social frames of his selected sampling of 100 western films. The result is this massive, detailed survey which is not only enjoyable reading, but also is an information source that will bring cheer to researchers.

Occasionally the author's affection for and involvement with his topic seems to blur his objectivity, but these same human qualities also communicate his unwavering respect and enthusiasm for the genre. A big book about a large subject that deserves wide attention.

2056 *Filming Sports.* edited by Kodak Staff. 288 p. illus. Rochester, N.Y.: Kodak, 1980.

Subtitled "The How-to Book for Coaches, Sports Information Directors, and Motion Picture/Still Sports Photographers," this oversized publication covers equipment, techniques, films, and methods for photographing action. Over 250 fine illustrations support the comprehensive text.

2057 *Filming TV News and Documentaries.* by Atkins, Jim, Jr.; and Willette, Leo. 158 p. illus. Philadelphia: Chilton, 1965.

Covers filmmaking, documentary films, and newsreels.

2058 *Filming* THE CANDIDATE. by Bahrenburg, Bruce. 254 p. paper illus. New York: Warner Paperback Library, 1972.

THE CANDIDATE (1972) was a film about a young California lawyer who runs for the U.S. Senate. In this behind-the-scenes account of the making of that film, Bruce Bahrenburg gives a detailed view of cast behavior, production activities, economics, compromises and other aspects of filmmaking. The material is arranged in chronological fashion with individual chapters emphasizing the star, the director, supporting actors, and some of the production personnel. A series of candid photos in the center section supplement the narrative nicely.

The author's approach is interesting, honest, and sympathetic to the filmmaking process. His coverage is quite complete and the reader will have a good comprehension of both process and people. For example, he writes of Natalie Wood who played a cameo role in the film: "As unobtrusively as she had appeared on the set, Natalie was gone, back to Los Angeles and her child. She brought to the set of THE CANDIDATE the presence of a movie star. She was one of the last, and there would always be those eyes pleading for affection."

Entertaining, informative and well-written, this book is one of the better accounts of the creation of a specific film. Recommended.

2059 *Filming the Family.* by Wain, George. 112 p. paper illus. London: Fountain, 1962.

This older volume on amateur filmmaking concentrates on recording such events as weddings, parties, and other family events. Cameras, filming techniques, titling, editing, sound and other topics are considered. Drawings, diagrams, and illustrations are plentiful.

2060 *Filming* THE GREAT GATSBY. by Bahrenburg, Bruce. 255 p. paper illus. New York: Berkley Medallion, 1974.

Bruce Bahrenburg covered the making of THE CANDIDATE (1972) with a quality of observation and writing that is unusual in these diary books. Since THE GREAT GATSBY was a film involving a much higher budget, more controversy, many colorful personalities and a publicity campaign unequalled in recent years, the author had more to work with in this instance. His selection from the abundant material combined with his ability to organize and present it without succumbing to a fan magazine level make this volume a better one than his first.

Arranged in a chronological format from the first shot made in Newport on June 11, 1973, to the wrap party on September 24, 1973, at Pinewood Studios in England, the book describes some of the pleasures and problems of filmmaking; star temperament, labor troubles, personality conflicts, etc., are contrasted with accomplishment, professional pride and human sensitivity. The few illustrations, which appear in a center section, add little to the book. There is no index. The volume takes on added interest since the reader probably knows the negative critical and popular reception given the picture. This is one of the better books about making a specific film. Recommended.

2061   *Filming Works Like This.* by Bendick, Jeanne; and Bendick, Robert. 95 p. illus. New York: McGraw Hill, 1970.

An earlier volume by the Bendicks, *Making the Movies,* was a pioneer in the field of film books for young readers, and its excellence is continued here. Using a combination of supportive text, line drawings and sketches, the authors consider all facets of student filmmaking. Design of the volume is so attractive that even the most reluctant student will be encouraged to try.

There is little need to analyze content; it is all here—cameras, lenses, film, lights, sound, scripts, budgets, schedules, editing, titles, animation, processing, projectors and sources. These and many other topics are presented in a usable and concise arrangement. The suitability and appeal of the visuals is undeniable; even a short index is provided. For the young person who may not or cannot respond to the professional books usually provided, this one will be attractive. The temptation to overpraise occurs when books such as this are published; it is so completely right in all its qualities—its knowledge of subject, treatment, and intended goals. Recommended.

2062   *Filmland in Ferment.* by Cousins, E. G. 304 p. illus. London: Denis Archer, 1932.

This early argument for the British Film Industry to take a world leadership role in motion picture pro-

duction is presented in three parts: film, actor, and audience. A preface is given by Jack Hulbert.

2063   *The Filmmaker's Art.* by Manoogian, Haig. 340 p. New York: Basic Books, 1966.

A readable discussion of the processes involved in making a film, why filmmaking is an art, a classification of films, and a brief history. Discussed in detail are such topics as the structure of films, the craft of film, planning, production, and editing. Most valuable is a sample short story, some suggested film treatments of it, and several shooting scripts. Also included are an outline of the steps in the production of films, a glossary of motion picture terms, and a very short annotated bibliography of books relevant to filmmaking. The book is a scholarly how-to-do-it. Interesting to the general reader and most valuable to the beginning filmmaker.

2064   *A Film Maker's Guide.* by Branston, Brian. 205 p. illus. London: Allen and Unwin, 1967.

This volume is aimed at the advanced filmmaker and includes information and suggestions on such topics as films, cameras, lenses, lighting, editing, etc. Some attention is given to the merchandising of the final film. A film entitled ADVENTURE—BALLOON TO SERENGETI is analyzed, and a glossary, appendices, and an index are included, in addition to many illustrations and diagrams.

2065   *Film-Making: From Script to Screen.* by Buchanan, Andrew 154 p. illus. London: Phoenix House, 1951 (1937).

As a book designed to 1) provide a guide to film production, 2) enumerate the departments of filmmaking, and 3) encourage future filmmakers, this reprinted volume is successful, tracing in simple, nontechnical language the act of making a film. The result is a series of basic statements or rules such as "A well-constructed scenario begins as a treatment and ends in the form of a shooting script." The latter portion of the book is devoted to the application of these basics to locational situations such as a village, town, factory, hospital, etc.

A few illustrations are included. The honesty and clarity of the book is admirable but it is disadvantaged by its dated (1937) illustration and examples. The newer books on the subject lack the simplicity of this approach but they offer, in turn, much more detail.

2066 *Filmmaking.* by Vendetti, James. 124 p. illus. New York: Richards Rosen Press, 1978.

2067 *Filmmaking: A Practical Guide.* by Linder, Carl. 304 p. illus. Englewood Cliffs, N.J.: Prentice-Hall, 1976.

The author calls the first section of this volume "The Tools of Filmmaking." Separate chapters are devoted to cameras, looking at the camera's subjects, planning, shooting, and putting the film together. The next three sections deal with broad film genres: the documentary; the fictional narrative; and the expressionistic film. Appendixes are devoted to suggested projects, recommended reading and a glossary. The book is indexed.

Unfortunately there are only eight pages of illustrations, all concentrated in one center section. In a book that purports to explain a visual art, such an economy in production tends to weaken any exposition provided by the author, no matter how strong. In choosing to use his bibliography of recommended periodical reading as a commercial for a magazine he edits, the author also does little to widen the range of his own work. The book list and the glossary are far more impressive. Although the text is clearly written and well organized, its presentation as an almost total reading experience rather than a balanced visual one, may deter persons who lack the necessary concentration for full comprehension and use. Acceptable.

2068 *Filmmaking: The Collaborative Art.* by Chase, Donald. 314 p. illus. Boston: Little, Brown, 1975.

In recent years there have been many books about the process of making the studio or commercial film. This is one of the best. Using excerpts from seminars and discussions sponsored by the American Film Institute, the author has selected, edited and arranged his material under the ten major creative roles necessary for any major motion picture: producer, screenwriter, actor, photography director, production designer, costume designer, script supervisor, editor, composer, and special effects man. Each of the sections is a composite of opinion and statement; for example, in "The Actor" there are comments from Charlton Heston, Leslie Caron, Lynn Carlin, Jon Voight, Henry Fonda, Nina Foch, Ingrid Thulin, Liv Ullman, Jack Benny, Peter Falk and others. The illusion which results because of the skillful editing is that of a round-table discussion on acting.

The volume is illustrated and mini-biographies of the participants appear in the book's final pages. Readers of the American Film Institute's monthly publication *Dialogue on Film* may recognize some of the material, but the author's expertise in reassembling it here makes re-reading it a pleasure. Recommended.

2069 *Filmmaking for Beginners.* by Horvath, Joan. 162 p. illus. New York: Thomas A. Nelson, 1974.

This volume on cinematography was designed for young people. It discusses equipment, technology and techniques for beginning filmmakers. After an opening section which documents the great interest that boys and girls have in filmmaking, the author devotes individual chapters to film types and gauges, cameras, photographic expression, scripts, shooting, special effects, editing, sound and animation. An index completes the book.

The text is written in an informal, nontechnical style which is supportive rather than challenging. Illustrations have been well selected with many providing identification figures of young people. Although it is a late entry in the filmmaking-for-children category, it is a good one and should satisfy its youthful readers. Recommended.

2070 *Filmmaking for Children.* by Rynew, Arden. 144 p. paper illus. Dayton, Ohio: Pflaum, 1971.

One of the most frequently voiced needs has been an adequate book on filmmaking for elementary school students. Rynew's book may satisfy that need, although most of the book is for teachers. Only the last section, the handbook, is suggested as a student text. The book is divided into four large divisions: "Background," "The Implementation of a Filmmaking Program", "Additional Filmmaking Information" and "Motion Picture Production Handbook (the student text). The accompanying text is informative, somewhat technical, and practical when appropriate. Rynew is a practicing art teacher in an elementary school and much of what he suggests seems based on his own experience. All the sections are valuable, but the "Handbook" portion will probably get the greatest teacher use.

It may be indelicate to indict an art teacher for his illustrations, but they are quite unimpressive. The drawings seem amateurish. Line drawings are cluttered with too much information, and the full-page blowups of 8mm film are murky and hard to interpret. However, there is enough valuable information, suggestion, and direction in the text to justify recommending this volume.

2071   *Filmmaking in Developing Countries.* edited by Fuglesang, Andreas. 123 p. illus. Uppsala, Sweden: Dag Hammarskjold Foundation, 1975.

This volume is a report of the Applied Communication Workshop, "The Function of Film as an Educational Medium in Development Work," that was held in Uppsala, Sweden in October, 1974. It is an anthology consisting of presentations and edited discussions on such topics as the functions of film, film research, animation, color, film music, training by films, film use, film evaluation, sociology of film, etc. The total program, personnel and the films screened during the workshop are noted in the appendices.

2072   *Film Making in Schools.* by Lowndes, Douglas. 128 p. illus. New York: Watson-Guptill, 1968.

After a discussion of the role that film can play in a school curriculum, the author surveys the basic hardware, both 8mm and 16 mm. No product evaluation is offered; only desired characteristics are stated. A number of projects designed to introduce students to film grammar are suggested. A technical notes section which expands the earlier material and considers additional aids in filmmaking concludes the book. Of British origin, this volume has valuable suggestions to offer anyone teaching students filmmaking. In this context it is especially recommended as a teacher's guide and reference. It is not suitable for individual study or general browsing.

2073   *see   2074*

2074   *Film Making in Schools and Colleges.* edited by Harcourt, Peter; and Theobald, Peter. 80 p. paper illus. London: British Film Institute, 1966.

After a short introduction, some advice on methods, techniques, film gauges, camera, editors, etc., is offered. Descriptions of filmmaking as practiced on seven different educational levels follow. Included are infant's school, junior school, comprehensive school, grammar school, technical college, art school, and teacher training school. A final page describes the services available from the British Film Institute and the Society for Education in Film and Television. The illustrations of students at work are reassuring but add little to the text.

This is an older volume that contains much helpful information for those about to use filmmaking in an educational setting. Acceptable.

2075   *Filmographic Dictionary of World Literature (Volume I—A to K).* by Daisne, Johan. 681 p. illus. New York: Humanities Press, 1972.

That the judgment of a book by its cover and appearance is inadvisable is demonstrated by this attractive looking volume. The cover, printed in four languages, catches the eye and the explanation of the contents in the introduction is impressive. Paper used is of very high quality and it all looks very promising.

Written in English, German, Dutch, and French, the book has three major parts. First, there is a list of certain selected authors, arranged alphabetically with a filmography supplied for each. Volume I begins with French writer Charles Abadie and ends with American Peter B. Kyne. The Kyne entry lists *Cappy Ricks, Cappy Ricks Returns,* and *Three Godfathers* as the source literature for several films which are noted beneath the appropriate book title. Any differences between film title and book title are indicated along with the country and year of production, and the name of the director. A few cast players are noted, sometimes with the name of the character they portray in the film.

The second section is a gallery of stills which covers approximately 340 pages and is an almost complete waste of space in a reference book. Pictures are poorly selected, badly reproduced, and presented unattractively. Some take up less than half a page, leaving large empty areas of white space. The illustrations are also arranged by literary author name.

The final section is a combined alphabetical index of all the films and literary sources noted in Section I. The reader is referred to the author name rather than to a specific page.

If the book is to have any reference value, it must be in the content of its first section, which runs about 240 pages. Reservations about these pages appear quickly. 1) Authors have been chosen in a selective fashion. Missing are Cervantes, Clark, Kazantzakis, Heller, etc. 2) Listings beneath each author are partial—under Raymond Chandler only THE BIG SLEEP (1946) is noted. No distinction is made between literary source genre—novel, short story, play, musical comedy, TV script, etc. 3) Some annotations seem incomplete, erroneous, or misleading—under Noel Coward we find him credited with STAR (1968). Most sources indicate that he contributed some uncredited dialogue for the Coward character but the film was based on a screenplay derived from the two Lawrence biographies and other sources. Then, too, BRIEF ENCOUNTER (1946) is taken from the short play, "Still Life," a part of the Coward "Tonight at 8:30" series. Here it is indicated as the original title of a literary work. 4) There are omissions within filmographies—Dashiel Hammett's *The Maltese Falcon* was also made under the title of SATAN MET A LADY in 1936. The author notes only the 1931 and the 1941 versions. 5) Certain credits are distorted. Here Kathryn Forbes is given credit for I REMEMBER MAMA, said to be taken from her novel, *Mama's Bank Account*. Most sources indicated the film was based primarily on John Van Druten's play taken from the novel.

The above reservations and comments are based on only a partial and cursory examination. When the author states he has worked with "scientific accuracy" and that the material is "the work of a lifetime," the reader/user may feel a bit intimidated. Another statement, "We want this book to illustrate how the whole of literature forms the basis of the seventh art," is simply irritating in its bias and partial ignorance.

The high price, the low level of a concentrated content and the vulnerability of some entries make this a most questionable source. Consider instead Dimmitt's *A Title Guide to the Talkies* and Enser's *Filmed Books and Plays*.

2076 *Filmography: Catalogue of Jewish Films.* edited by Cohen, E. M. 217 p. paper Jerusalem: Institute of Contemporary Jewry, 1969.

This is the first draft of a book that was not published or sold. However, it should be made available in some format, since it contains information not found elsewhere. A short introduction and a section on the use of the films precedes the detailed listing of the films. Some 1077 titles are arranged simply by accession number. An index of the titles and a second index according to subject enable the user to locate a desired film. Information about the distributors is also given.

2077 *A Filmography of Films About Movies and Moviemaking.* by Parker, David L. 15 p. paper Rochester, N.Y.: Eastman Kodak, 1971.

This 1971 filmography (Kodak number T-26) contains a total of 233 titles, an increase of 63 over the earlier edition. Entries are arranged alphabetically by title and offer basic data including a descriptive annotation. A distributor list is added. The films noted here are concerned with "many aspects of motion picture production, the history of cinema, general facts about movie film, and the nature of the film medium."

2078 *A Filmography of the Third World.* by Cyr, Helen W. 320 p. Metuchen, N.J.: Scarecrow, 1976.

In this filmography, Helen Cyr defines Third World as consisting of Africa, Asia, The Pacific, Latin America, and selected groups in North America (Afro-Americans, Asian Americans, Latinos, Native Americans). A few films noting the European view of Third World people or Third World experiences in Europe are included.

More than 2000 films are arranged geographically with the usual data (producer, date, time, color, format, distributor, descriptive annotation) given. Distributor addresses, a filmmaker list, and a title index conclude the volume.

Films chosen for inclusion cover a wide range of form (features, shorts, fiction, documentary, etc.) and content (history, art, religion, sports, travel, geography, politics). The list of directors, cinematographers, scenarists and composers includes many famous names.

This is a valuable reference book that brings together non-typical film information in an easy-to-use arrangement. For anyone concerned with interpretation of the Third World countries and their people, this volume would be essential.

2079 *Filmrow Film Index.* edited by Zucker, Ralph. 100 p. Los Angeles: Filmrow, 1981.

2080 *Filmrow Motion Picture Marketing BlackBook, Part I.* by Zucker, Ralph. 350 p. Los Angeles: Filmrow, 1981.

2081 *Filmrow Updata.* edited by Zucker, Ralph. 75 p. Los Angeles: Filmrow, 1981.

2082 *Films: A Quarterly of Discussions and Analysis (nos. 1-4, 1939-40).* by Kirstein, Lincoln; and Leyda, Jay; and Losey, Mary; and Stebbins, Robert; and Strasberg, Lee. New York: Arno Press, 1968.

This book consists of reprints of the quarterly magazine, *Films,* for November 1939, Spring 1940, Summer 1940, and Winter 1940. There is much to interest the sophisticated cinema reader in this volume, but the material is rather difficult to locate. No introduction or index is provided other than the front page of each issue. A short preface describing the genesis and demise of the magazine would also have been helpful.

2083   *Films: The Way of the Cinema.* by Buchanan, Andrew. 235 p. illus. London: Pitman & Sons, 1932.

This is an overview of many topics connected with filmmaking techniques, content, and criticism. A discussion of attitudes toward the cinema is followed by chapters on silent film, sound film, film story and production. A list of interesting films is offered, as are some comments on the cinema of the period (1932). Of greatest interest to historians or researchers.

2084   *Films—Subject and Exposure.* edited by Mannheim, L. A.; and Spencer, D. A. 132 p. illus. Englewood Cliffs, N.J.: Prentice-Hall (Amphoto), 1970.

Louis Philippe Clerc's *La Technique Photographique* was originally published in 1926. The sixth edition appeared just after the author's death in 1959. English editions from 1930 to 1954 were titled *Photography Theory and Practice.* After that date the volume's various topics were assigned to different experts who brought their specialized knowledge to updating, revising and rewriting the book. This volume contains the fourth section of the original and deals with the picture-taking techniques of focusing and exposure, and with the properties of sensitized film materials. Lighting and light sources are also considered.

The text is very technical and demands some background and experience in photography from the reader. Illustrations, diagrams, tables, graphs and formulas appear in abundance. The book is indexed.

This is a specialized volume for the professional photographer that derives from a classic work. Acceptable.

2085   *see   2083*

2086   *Films about the Film.* edited by Luttor, Marta; and Molnar, Istvan. 76 p. Budapest: Hungarian Research Institute of Cinematography and Film Archives, 1971.

Printed in English, this filmography is divided into five sections: 1. Character sketches of creative artists; 2. Analyses of films, special films; 3. Film histories and film anthologies; 4. Techniques and technology of the film; 5. Feature films about filmmaking.

2087   *Films and Broadcasts Demeaning Ethnic, Racial or Religious Groups.* by Subcommittee on Communications and Power. 97, 67 p. paper Washington, D.C.: U.S. Government Printing Office, 1970, 1971.

The reports of two hearings by the Subcommittee on Communications and Power of the Committee on Interstate and Foreign Commerce of the House of Representatives, the first on September 21, 1970, the second April 27-28, 1971. The rationale for the hearings was more than 70 similar resolutions which suggested that "Congress finds ethnic, racial or religious defamation or ridicule existing in motion pictures ... and that the producers ... should develop and adhere to a code of ethics that would rule such material out-of-bounds." The testimony of various witnesses, along with letters, exhibits, and appendices, all speak to the perpetuation of stereotypes by the media. The victim most often cited is the Mexican-American, although other nationalities are represented.

Noted here as a source of information about film, censorship, pressure groups, governmental regulation of media and other aspects of film history. Government documents can provide a rich source of such information.

2088   *Films and Children, the Positive Approach.* by Hills, Janet. 59 p. paper London: British Film Institute, 1951.

2089   *Films and Dreams: An Approach to Bergman.* edited by Petric, Vlada. Pleasantville, N.Y.: Redgrave, 1980.

2090   *Films and Feelings.* by Durgnat, Raymond. 288 p. illus. Cambridge, Mass.: MIT Press, 1967.

An attempt is made in this volume to point out some factors that will help to clarify the existing confusions of film criticism. By analyzing specific films, the difference between style and content is discussed, as is the reflection of certain sociological concepts in film content. The many discrepancies between the film critic and the viewing public are also considered.

Intelligence, perception, and a wide familiarity with films characterize the writing and the book may also be enjoyed simply as a collection of articles on various films and filmmakers. Several pages of illustrations are included. As a serious, thoughtful statement on film criticism, this book is most impressive. It is worthy of inclusion with the writings of the major critics. Somewhat advanced for the general reader.

2091 *Films and Film-Makers.* by Zalman, Jan. 99 p. illus. Prague: Orbis, 1968.

A perceptive, informative account of Czech cinema, with filmographies.

2092 *Films and Filmstrips for Language Arts: An Annotated Bibliography.* by May, Jill P. Urbana, Ill.: National Council of the Teachers of English, 1981.

2093 *Films and People.* edited by Jones, Emily S. 31 p. paper New York: Educational Film Library Association, 1952.

This descriptive catalog of selected films on the United Nations and UNESCO topics was compiled in connection with the Third National Conference of the U.S. National Commission on UNESCO. Purchase and rental sources of the films are included.

2094 *Films and the Second World War.* by Manvell, Roger. 388 p. illus. New York: A. S. Barnes, 1974.

This volume by Roger Manvell would seem to be the definitive book on war films so far. It is difficult to see how it could be bettered. Manvell is not only exploring the role of films in wartime, but also the way films reflect the emotions, attitudes, and reactions of the people involved. Starting with those films that predicted the Second World War, Manvell quickly progresses to the war years.

First there is Britain's lone stand against Germany, followed by the middle phase which involved Italy, Russia, France, the United States, Japan and several smaller nations. The victory in 1944-1945 and the post-war years of 1945-1950 are treated separately. A final consideration of the last two decades of films that have examined World War II in retrospect closes the volume. The scope of this study is international and films from many countries are described. Illustrations are selected and used with intelligence throughout. Reproduction of them is more than adequate. A bibliography along with separate indexes for film titles and for names support the comprehensive text.

Many of the films described in the text will be unfamiliar to most readers since they are of foreign origin and have had little or no showing in English-speaking countries. Then, too, attention is given not only to the entertainment film but also to the documentary. This latter category includes the propaganda films which were considered essential weapons during the war. Manvell's ability to gather this wide range of material and present it in a coherent, logical continuum is most impressive. The book is a model of popular research that will continue to inform and entertain readers for many years to come. Highly recommended.

2095 *Films Beget Films: Compilation Films from Propaganda to Drama* by Leyda, Jay. 176 p. London: George & Allen & Unwin, 1964.

The compilation film referred to in the subtitle begins its life in the cutting room and is made up of existing film shots. Examples of such films are HOLLYWOOD: THE GOLDEN YEARS (1964), THE TRUE GLORY (1945), and the WHY WE FIGHT (1942-1945) series of World War II. With the enormous appetites of TV, the growing prominence of educational groups, and the rise of video cassettes, compilation films will undoubtedly increase in number and popularity. This volume is not only a history of the form, but a discussion, with many examples, of its characteristics and influences. The volume is a bit of a surprise in that it delivers much more interesting information than its title would indicate. It is essential for film study courses and colleges.

2096 *Films by and or about Women 1972.* 72 p. paper Berkeley, Calif.: Women's History Research Center, 1972.

This directory of filmmakers, films and distributors is international in scope and covers both the present and the past. Films are noted with descriptive annotations and data under various categories—marriage, career, child care, biography, etc. Another section lists the films made by female filmmakers. Distributor information for the films mentioned in the book is also given.

2097 *Films by the Thousand.* by Scottish Central Film Library, Glasgow. 19 p. paper Glasgow: Scottish Film Office, 1964.

The story of the Scottish Central Film Library's first 25 years, 1939-1964.

2098 *Films Deliver.* edited by Schillaci, Anthony; and Culkin, John M. 348 p. paper illus. Englewood Cliffs, N.J.: Citation Press, 1970.

The purpose of this rather expensive paperback is to

show teachers how to use film and TV in their teaching. A collection of articles on various elements of TV and film study in the schools, the book includes topics such as methodology, sources, student filmmaking, and possible tie-ins with the local theatreowner. Perhaps the strongest section is the appendix which contains filmographies of recommended feature and short films, a bibliography, and an index.

Much of the material is similar to that found in the earlier *Screen Experience*, published by Pflaum. For the most part the prohibitive rental cost of classic, especially foreign, films is ignored in the text but mentioned extensively in the appendix.

2099   *Films Ex Libris: Literature in 16mm and Video.* by Parlato, Salvatore J., Jr. 261 p. Jefferson, N.C.: McFarland, 1980.

2100   *Films—Facts and Forecasts.* by Fawcett, L'Estrange. 277 p. illus. London: Geoffrey Bles, 1927.

This early analysis of the world film industry considers its potential, its problems, and its future.

2101   *Films for Anthropological Teaching.* by Heider, Karl G. paper Washington, D.C.: American Anthropological Association, 1977.

This is the Sixth edition of this particular reference work. The main portion of the book is an alphabetical arrangement of the films with a descriptive annotation of each. Further access is provided by a topic index and a geographical area index. Other information includes the identification of authors and researchers, film distributors, addresses, etc.

2102   *Films For, By, and About Women.* by Sullivan, Kaye. 552 p. Metuchen, N.J.: Scarecrow, 1980.

Sullivan provides an annotated (descriptive only) guide to films for, by and about women, which includes hundreds of rather broadly selected films. For example, HOW TO MARRY A MILLIONAIRE (1953) and HUD (1963) appear on the same page as HOW TO MAKE POTATO PRINTS (1955) and HOW TO SAY NO TO A RAPIST AND SURVIVE (1974). A list of decoded acronyms, a directory of film sources, a bibliography, an index of women filmmakers, and a subject index complete this useful filmography.

2103   *Films for Children.* 98 p. paper illus. Moscow: Sovexport.

Written in English, French and Spanish, this catalog offers credits and descriptions of selected Russian films for children. A long essay on films for children praises the Russian efforts in this area.

2104   *Films for Children.* 59 p. paper illus. New York: Educational Film Library Association, 1961, 1972.

A catalog of recommended films for children.

2105   *Films For Children Ages 3 to 5.* by Colliew, Marilyn; Almy, Millie; and Keller, Barbara. 82 p. paper illus. Berkeley: Instructional Laboratories, Dept. of Education, UCLA, 1977.

This filmography was formulated after a testing period that involved nursery school children, teachers, and educational consultants. Some 57 films are described by title, type, color format, running time, and distributors. There are also several paragraphs of descriptive-critical annotation, and a few suggested preparation or follow-up activities. The booklet uses an attractive light blue color which works well for the printed words, but tends to make the illustrations rather blurred. An essential volume for professionals who deal with nursery school children.

2106   *Films for Children and Adolescents.* edited by Barrot, Jean Pierre; and Billaaru, Ginette. 118 p. paper Paris: UNESCO, 1956.

2107   *Films for Classroom Teaching.* by Olsen, Leonard J. 53 p. paper illus. Baton Rouge, La.: State Dept. of Public Education, 1966.

2108   *Films for Education in New York State.* compiled by Division of Educational Communications. 80 p. paper Albany, N.Y.: State Education Department, 1963.

Prepared by David Rees, this is a survey and plan for the improved utilization of the educational film in the schools of New York State.

2109   *Films for General Studies.* compiled by Association for Liberal Education. 137 p. paper London: National Committee for AV Aids in Education, 1971.

An excellent catalog of films arranged alphabetically by title and offering long critical annotations along with film data. A subject index is included. In 1973 a supplement to this volume containing 131 pages was published.

2110 *Films for General Studies.* edited by Thole, John. 137 p. paper London: National Committee for Audiovisual Aids in Education, 1971.

A collection of 300 annotated appraisals of both short and feature films is offered here. The films are arranged alphabetically by title and for each is noted the distributor, running time, country of origin, date of release and color format. The long annotations are both descriptive and evaluative. Supporting the evaluations are an introduction, suggestions for using the films, a subject index, a distributor list, film rental costs, and some appraisal (evaluation) forms. Since most of the titles are internationally available, the evaluations have value for all film users. A 1973 supplement is similar and evaluates 200 more films. Both volumes are recommended.

2111 *Films for Humane Education.* paper New York: Argus Archives, 1979.

A filmography of recommended titles dealing with the oppression, use, and abuse of animals. Suggestions on the use of the films are included.

2112 *Films for Industry.* compiled by Central Film Library. 237 p. paper London: Central Film Library, Central Office of Information, 1972.

A catalog of 898 films for industrial users arranged under subject areas such as aircraft, ceramics, electronics, hotel industries, etc. An alphabetical list of film titles is added.

2113 *Films for Korean Studies.* by Butler, Lucius A.; and Youngs, Chaesoon T. 167 p. paper Honolulu: Center for Korean Studies, Univ. of Hawaii.

This unusual volume was compiled to provide information concerning the existence and availability of films about Korea. The 333 films listed are limited to the English language and have been selected from a variety of sources. They are arranged alphabetically by title, with film data, a descriptive annotation, and sources noted for each. Further access to the films is provided by a lengthy subject index. Producer/distributor addresses are appended.

This filmography could easily serve as a model for similar volumes dealing with unusual subjects. Its

contents are well designed, clearly described and intelligently cross-referenced. The book should be very helpful to those who deal with the subject of Korea in any manner.

2114 *Films for Labor.* paper illus. Washington, D.C.: American Federation of Labor and Congress of Industrial Organizations (AFL-CIO), 1969.

The films listed in this catalog are organized under nine headings: building unionism, political education, automation, civil rights and civil liberties, better schools, national issues and the legislative process, training films, international affairs, and films produced by AFL-CIO affiliates. A title index and a more detailed subject index are also provided. The introduction gives valuable suggestions on planning and conducting film showings, ordering films, posters, equipment, etc. Each film entry indicates title, running time, year of release, rental cost, producer and purchase price, if applicable. A detailed description of the film follows. Little evaluation or critical comment is attempted. This is a valuable reference-catalogue that can be useful in a wide variety of situations. Recommended.

2115 *Films for Libraries.* compiled by ALA Audiovisual Subcommittee. 81 p. paper Chicago: American Library Assoc., 1962.

Titles selected as appropriate for inclusion in public library collections by a subcommittee of the ALA Audiovisual Committee.

2116 *Films for Music Education and Opera Films.* by International Music Centre, Vienna. 114 p. paper New York: Unipub, 1962.

This filmography consists of two separate lists—one for music education films and a second for opera films. In the first the music education films are arranged under seven large categories (history, instruments, musicians, etc.) while the opera films are listed chronologically by opera premiere date (from "Il Combattimento di Tancredi e Clorinda" in 1624 to "The Medium" in 1954). Each film entry lists the title, country, producer, date, language, running time, a synopsis, and the distributor. Further access to the films is provided by alphabetical, country, and composer indexes.

Although this filmography does not cover recent years, it does describe many films which are still available, useful, and valuable for study and enjoyment.

2117 *Films for Personnel Management.* by Goodman, Louis. 116 p. paper New York: Educational Film Library Association, 1969.

An annotated filmography of more than 300 titles is presented in this book. The films are arranged by subject, and there is a title index and a source index provided to aid the user.

2118 *Films for the Community in Wartime.* compiled by Losey, Mary. 78 p. paper New York: National Board of Review of Motion Pictures, 1943.

A catalog of films recommended for use during World War II. Contains film information and distributor names.

2119 *Films for Universities.* by British Universities Film Council. 292 p. paper London: British Universities Film Council, 1968.

This is a list of films found to be useful in some aspects of university work. Since the origin of the book is British, the films and the distributors are out of England rather than America. It is noted here since some of the films are available worldwide and others may be obtained if they are special enough and have no counterpart elsewhere. The entries are arranged under the Universal Decimal Classification system.

2120 *Films for Universities.* compiled by British Universities Film Council. 292 p. paper London: British Universities Film Council, 1968.

A filmography arranged by Dewey classification. The entries give data and description but no evaluation. A final index lists the films alphabetically by title.

2121 *Films For Young Adults.* compiled by New York Library Association. 54 p. paper New York: Educational Film Library Association, 1970.

There is much to recommend in this brief list of annotated short films. Descriptions of certain films are concise and accurate. There is a bibliography, a subject index, a list of filmmakers and a list of distributors. Most of this information is useful and pertinent.

Some reservations must be noted. Admittedly this is a selected list, but certain films are shortchanged by being included within the description of another film. For EYE OF THE BEHOLDER (1958) the reader is referred to THE SWORD (1967) where the annotation reads: "With EYE OF THE BEHOLDER (Stuart Reynolds) and 12-12-41 (Xanadu), it evokes an extraordinary comment on perception and sensitivity." Good programming perhaps, but poor annotation for a film in the list. The user would have to use another source for full information.

Another selected list of feature films for young adults is given that should send the knowledgeable librarian scurrying to *Media and Methods* for suggestions. Finally, certain of the distributors seem to be rather high in their film prices.

2122 *Films from Britain.* compiled by British Film Institute. 158 p. paper London: H.M. Stationery Office, 1952.

A catalog of 1000 films on educational, scientific and cultural subjects available for sale abroad, compiled for the United Kingdom National Commission for UNESCO.

2123 *Films from Ghana.* compiled by Ghana Film Unit. 20 p. paper illus. Acers: Government Printer, 1958.

A catalog of films available from Ghana.

2124 *Films from the Netherlands.* compiled by Regeeringsvoorlichtingsdienst. 116 p. paper Netherlands: The Hague, 1956.

A catalog of 1000 Dutch films produced between 1944 and 1956.

2125 *Films in America 1929-1969.* by Quigley Jr., Martin; and Gertner, Richard; and Gipson, Henry Clay 319 p. illus. New York: Golden Press, 1970.

All aspects of the American motion picture industry are examined over a 40-year period. Nearly 400 films are given individual attention and there are more than 400 illustrations.

The emphasis in this volume is on the industrial/business film. When and how to use films is the opening topic, followed by an overview of film grammar. Film costs, uses, and distribution are considered next. Production is covered by chapters on selecting a producer, costs, script, photography, animation and sound. Final chapters concern themselves with foreign use of films and films on TV.

Much of the material in this very specialized book is dated.

2126 *Films in Business and Industry.* by Gipson, Henry Clay. 291 p. illus. New York: McGraw-Hill, 1947.

The emphasis in this volume is on the industrial/business film. When and how to use films is the opening topic, followed by an overview of film grammar. Film costs, uses, and distribution are considered next. Production is covered by chapters on selecting a producer, costs, script, photography, animation and sound. Final chapters concern themselves with foreign use of films and films on TV. Much of the material in this very specialized book is dated.

2127 *Films in Children's Programs.* compiled by Film Committee of the Children's and Young People's Services. 39 p. paper illus. Madison, Wisc.: Wisconsin Library Assoc., 1972.

A catalog of films recommended for showing to children.

2128 *Films in Depth.* by Schreivogel, Paul A. paper illus. Dayton, Ohio: Pflaum, 1970.

This unusual package of film study materials contains 13 booklets. The first is an introduction and overview of the series; each of the others addresses itself to a specific short film. Titles of the films are: FLAVIO (1964), THE LANGUAGE OF FACES (1961), THE LITTLE ISLAND (1958), NIGHT AND FOG (1955), NO REASON TO STAY (1965), AN OCCURRENCE AT OWL CREEK BRIDGE (1962), ORANGE AND BLUE (1962), OVERTURE—OVERTURE/NYITANY (1965), A STAIN ON HIS CONSCIENCE (1968), SUNDAY LARK (1964), TIME PIECE (1956), TOYS (1966). For information on each film, see individual entries as noted.

Each study guide offers an analysis of the film and attempts to relate it to some aspect of film technique or appreciation. The latter part of each guide suggests questions, offers background, script excerpts and other materials designed to stimulate thought and discussion. The guides are available separately. This elaboration of what Kuhns and others have done is an improvement over such sturdy, proven material since each title provides more background and greater depth to the analyses of the films.

2129 *Films in Focus.* by Reille, Louis. 128 p. paper illus. St. Meinrad, Ind.: Ab-

bey Press, 1970.

A Catholic priest gives an overview of film background, selection, censorship, morality, criticism, and even rental information.

2130 *The Films in My Life.* by Truffaut, Francois. 358 p. New York: Simon and Schuster, 1978.

The contents of this book consist of articles written by Francois Truffaut for various newspapers and periodicals. From 1954, when he was a journalist, to his later years as a film director, he has never lost his passion for films. The sampling of articles here—about one sixth of all his writing—gives ample evidence of his ardor.

The articles are divided into six groups: silent-sound directors; American film reviews; French film reviews; Japanese directors and their films; foreign film directors; and French New Wave directors. The book is indexed.

Since Truffaut's love affair with films has been carried on from childhood to the present, he has the informational background and experience to cover the wide variety of subjects offered here. As viewer, writer, and filmmaker, he has a clear vision of film—what it is and what it should be. He communicates his opinions and emotions about film to the reader with persuasive charm and logical argument. As with his earlier volume on Hitchcock, this is a book to be used again and again by anyone who shares Truffaut's feeling for film. Highly recommended.

2131 *Films in 1951.* compiled by British Film Institute. 72 p. paper illus. London: Sight and Sound, 1952.

A volume on British films and filmmakers prepared for the Festival of Britain.

2132 *Films in Our Lives: An Approach to Film Appreciation.* by Rosenthal, Newman H. 68 p. paper Melbourne: Cheshire, 1953.

2133 *Films in Review, 1950-1953.* edited by Hart, Henry. illus. New York: Arno, 1973.

A compilation of the first four years of *Films in Review*, a publication of the National Board of Review. Begun in 1950, the periodical is concerned primarily with film history, aesthetics and criticism, although it deals with all aspects of the motion picture. The first series consists of four volumes, one for each year from 1950 through 1953.

2134 *Films in the Classroom.* by Miller, Hannah Elsas. 313 p. Metuchen, N.J.: Scarecrow, 1979.

This "Practical Guide" is a collection of very familiar material freshened a bit by some references to video and a few good source lists. Chapters are devoted to equipment, film techniques, types of films, selecting, securing, showing, using, and making films. In many instances the content is similar to that presented in *The Film User's Handbook* (1975).

2135 *Film Study in the Elementary School.* by Sohn, David A.; and Stucker, Melinda. 281 p. paper Washington, D.C.: American Film Institute, 1968-69.

This is the report of a study made in the elementary grades (kindergarten through eight) of four schools in the Community Consolidated School District No. 65 in Cook County, Evanston, Ill. Sponsored by a grant from the American Film Institute, the study had as its goal the development of a curriculum for using quality films in the elementary schools that would apply to subject matter areas. After using pre-selected films, teachers reported on their own responses, the reactions of their students, and the follow-up activities employed. At the conclusion of the program, all teachers and a sampling of students were surveyed. The results are appended to the teacher reports on the film use.

The films selected for the study are, for the most part, accepted classics e.g., CORRAL (1954), DREAM OF THE WILD HORSES (1962), GLASS (1958), THE GOLDEN FISH (1959), PADDLE TO THE SEA (1966), etc. A few features were also used—THE GOLDEN AGE OF COMEDY (1958), WHISTLE DOWN THE WIND (1962), ANIMAL FARM (1955), NICHOLAS NICKLEBY (1947), THE SILENT WORLD (1956). Some general comments are made, but no conclusions are offered. The report is weak in rationale-explanation-conclusion, and in its puzzling arrangement of the teacher reports on film use. Variation in length and quality of those reports is also a negative factor.

For elementary school personnel willing to dig a bit, however, there are some rich rewards here. Many of the suggested activities are creative and imaginative, and the student-teacher evaluations of these well-known films are valuable guides. A report on work as important as this deserves two priority operations —first, some prepublication editing to create a tighter presentation and, ultimately, a wider distribution than this report apparently received.

2136 *Films Kids Like.* by Rice, Susan. 128 p. paper illus. Chicago: American Library Association, 1973.

Ms. Rice's book is an annotated listing of 229 short films that were tested by the Center for Understanding Media with children from ages three to twelve. Readiness and follow-up activities were included in making the determination of each film's effectiveness. Several grants aided the investigation.

The results are presented in a most attractive and usable form. An introductory essay discusses The Children's Film Theater and offers some practical advice on showing films for children in libraries, schools, and elsewhere. The main body of the work consists of the film listings, which include the film title; an annotation which tends to be mostly descriptive, with some helpful hints on use; running time; color or black and white; animation or live action; narration or no narration; the distributor; and the country of origin. Missing is the release date of the films. A key to the distributors concludes the book. Visuals used throughout are either stills from the films or candid shots of the youngsters enjoying the films. They are reproduced nicely and add variety to the listing. The book will be of great assistance to all professionals dealing with young children.

2137 *Films, 1945-1950.* by Forman, Denis. 64 p. paper illus. London: Longmans Green, 1952.

One of the titles in the *Arts in Britain* series, this volume was prepared for the British Council.

2138 *The Films of ... (A Series).* illus. New York: Citadel Press, 1963- .

A series of oversized volumes, most of which are devoted to individual film personalities, with a few about character-types in films— the rebel, the detective, the bad guys, etc.—or about a genre, such as the musical. The personality format is fairly standard, consisting of an introductory essay section, the films arranged in chronological order, and a short account of other show business appearances, if pertinent. The section devoted to the films is the major emphasis and follows a predictable structure: stills, cast and production credits, a plot outline, review excerpts, and occasionally some background information. Although similar in structure, the books vary greatly in quality.

When the volumes first appeared in the early sixties the words "The Films of" were given equal prominence with the subject. Recent volumes in the series minimize "The Films of" and maximize the subject name. However, rather than depart from the procedure established earlier, the books will continue to be treated as "The Films of ..." with the hope that this entry and the subject index will facilitate any necessary searching.

Titles in the series include: *All Talking! All Singing! All Dancing!; The Bad Guys; Bogey; The Detective in Films; The Films of Ingrid Bergman; The Films of Marlon Brando; The Films of James Cagney; The Films of Charlie Chaplin; The Films of Gary Cooper; The Films of Joan Crawford; The Films of Bette Davis; The Films of Cecil B. DeMille; The Films of Marlene Dietrich; The Films of Kirk Douglas; The Films of W. C. Fields; The Films of Errol Flynn; The Films of Clark Gable; The Films of Greta Garbo; The Films of Jean Harlow; The Films of Katharine Hepburn; The Films of Laurel and Hardy; The Films of Carole Lombard; The Films of Fredric March; The Films of Marilyn Monroe; The Films of Paul Newman; The Films of Frank Sinatra; The Films of Spencer Tracy; The Films of John Wayne; The Fondas; Judy; A Pictorial History of the Western Film; Rebels: The Rebel Hero in Films; Tarzan of the Movies.*

The titles in this series are shuffled around quite a bit between subsidiary companies, book clubs and paperback reprints. Names such as Bonanza Books, Cadillac Publishing, Lyle Stuart, Movie Book Club, and others are associated at times with Citadel Books. The editions put out by the several companies vary greatly in the quality of paper used, photo reproduction and binding.

2139 *The Films of... (A Series).* paper illus. London: Barnden Castell Williams, 1974- .

This modest series imitates some of the older, more established ones such as those published by Citadel, A. S. Barnes, Zemmer, Praeger, Pyramid, etc. A short biography of each subject is followed by an equally short appreciation, and a filmography completes the book. Illustrations—mostly stills from the subject's films—are adequately reproduced. The books, made from inexpensive paper stock, look fragile, and will probably not stand up to any hard or frequent use.

2140 *Films of a Changing World: Volume II.* edited by Ackerman, Jean Marie. 73 p. paper illus. Washington, D.C.: Society for International Development, 1976.

This anthology of essays/reviews continues the work of editor Ackerman which first appeared in 1975. Selected from *The International Development Review* from 1972 to 1976, each article is fashioned around a topic of international concern and suggests media which may serve to illuminate thinking on the topic. The media is examined critically and includes films, filmstrips, print, and slides.

Supporting the text is an alphabetical index, a subject index, a geographical index, a filmmaker's index and several bibliographies. The book is illustrated.

This guide is an excellent example of the type of film reference that is always needed but rarely found. It is a critical approach to media that the user will find rewarding and satisfying. Highly recommended.

2141 *Films of a Changing World: Volume 2.* by Ackermann, Jean Maire. 106 p. paper Washington, D.C.: Society for International Development, 1972.

In the constant search for evaluations of short films, the user occasionally finds an intelligent, reliable source of unique reviews. This volume is that kind of discovery. The guide has as its goals the encouragement of international exchange of good films and the production of better films by developing countries. Since such films are usually ignored, the notes on them offered here are most welcome. Reprinted directly as they appeared in *International Development Review*, each commentary usually deals with several films and offers data on the films in a separate section called "References." The reprints date from March, 1963 to December, 1971. An alphabetical title index, a geographical index and a subject index help the user in retrieving information. A bibliography of lists, catalogs, periodicals, readings, and references is added.

Here is a volume that makes a relatively unknown genre of short films available for consideration. The value of the book to a wide audience is undeniable. Highly recommended.

2142 *The Films of Akira Kurosawa.* by Richie, Donald. 218 p. illus. Berkeley, Calif.: University of California Press, 1965.

This is a beautifully written and produced book by one of the foremost authorities on Japanese films. Two dozen films are discussed in detail. All sections of the book have been done with great care. The text, illustrations, filmography, and bibliography are all impressive. The technical reproduction of the stills is outstanding and gives the reader's an accurate idea of the film images. The volume is highly recommended.

2143   *The Films of Alan Ladd.* by Henry, Marily; and DeSourdis, Ron. 256 p. illus. Secaucus, N.J.: Citadel, 1981.

2144   *The Films of Alfred Hitchcock.* by Perry, George. 160 p. paper illus. New York: Dutton, 1965.

This impressively produced *Pictureback* consists mostly of stills from Hitchcock's films ranging from the silents of the early twenties to MARNIE (1964). As usual with this series, there is an admirable blend of pictures and text. The text is both descriptive and critical. No filmography is given but a brief chronology of films is included. A welcome addition to the several Hitchcock books.

2145   *The Films of Alfred Hitchcock.* by Harris, Robert A.; and Lasky, Michael S. 256 p. illus. Secaucus, N.J.: Citadel, 1976.

In this *Citadel* series volume there are the predicatable elements—an introductory biographical essay and a lengthy filmography. In Hitchcock's case, the latter takes the reader from NUMBER THIRTEEN (1922) up to FAMILY PLOT (1976). For each film there are illustrations, cast, credits, plot outline, production notes and review excerpts. Attention is given to the director's methods and the reasons he chose certain stories for his films. As always, the illustrations are a major attraction. Hitchcock's appearances in his own films are identified.

2146   *The Films of Alice Faye.* by Moshier, W. Franklyn. 182 p. paper illus. San Francisco: Moshier, 1971.

This personally produced tribute contains a biographical essay, complete credits, and notes on each of Alice Faye's films. Most impressive is the disclosure of the songs and scenes which were omitted from the final versions of the films.

This edition is available only from the author, who is probably more of an authority on Alice Faye than she is herself—which may suggest a combined effort toward an autobiography. Acceptable. Reprinted as *The Alice Faye Movie Book* by Stackpole.

2147   *The Films of Anthony Asquith.* by Minney, R. J. 284 p. illus. New York: A.S.Barnes, 1976.

Anthony Asquith was a British film director whose career spanned almost four decades. From BOADICEA (1926) to THE YELLOW ROLLS ROYCE (1964), he was active in making films, most of which are relatively unknown in America. The account of Asquith's life provided here is uniformly positive and sometimes a bit too saccharine in its admiration. Stronger by far are those portions which discuss the films, but even here a positive prejudice shows, e.g. was THE MILLIONAIRESS (1960) "an enormous success both with press and public" ? In America it certainly wasn't.

The title of the volume is a bit misleading since the films are integrated into the text rather than being treated separately. A filmography which notes cast, credits, and a plot outline is added in the book's final pages. The book is indexed and nicely illustrated.

Based on the numerous quotes provided by those who worked with Asquith, he was respected, revered and loved; anyone who carried the nickname "Puffin" throughout his entire life with dignity must inspire a certain amount of awe and admiration. The biography presented here is pleasant reading, with the film descriptions providing the excitement that apparently was lacking in Asquith's personal story. Acceptable.

2148   *The Films of Anthony Quinn.* by Marill, Alvin H. 255 illus. Secaucus, N.J.: Citadel, 1975.

After a short introduction by Arthur Kennedy, the usual elements of the *Citadel* series follow—a biographical essay ("Quinn—the Man From Chihuahua"), and a filmography of 109 films from PAROLE (1936) to THE DESTRUCTORS (1974). The performer remains very active professionally and has portrayed several important film roles since 1974.

Each film entry consists of illustrations, cast, credits, a plot summary and slight background information. Quinn's stage and television appearances are also noted.

2149   *The Films of Barbra Streisand.* by Castell, David. 47 p. paper illus. London: Barnden Castell Williams, 1974.

This original paperback contains a biography, summaries of the reviews of her films from FUNNY GIRL (1969) to FUNNY LADY (1975), a filmography listing casts and credits, and many illustrations. The reproduction quality of the visuals varies considerably. Acceptable.

2150   *The Films of Bela Lugosi.* by Bojarsky, Richard. 256 p. illus. Secaucus, N.J.: Citadel, 1980.

2151 *The Films of Bette Davis.* by Ringgold, Gene. 191 p. illus. New York: Bonanza Books, 1965.

This star's films are divided into three periods— apprenticeship, acclaim, and admiration—and besides the cast and production credits, a plot summary and a few critical quotes are given. Missing are Miss Davis' post 1965 films. Picture selection and quality are above average. There is no index.

While this is a pleasurable book to read or to browse, one cannot help wishing for more critical evaluation of the films in general and Miss Davis' work in particular. (For example, Miss Davis in interviews thinks of THE CATERED AFFAIR as one of her most underrated and ignored performances. The book tells little of what the critical concensus actually was.)

2152 *The Films of Bing Crosby.* by Bookbinder, Robert. 255 p. illus. Secaucus, N.J.: Citadel, 1977.

Since Bing Crosby enjoyed success in so many different media, it is not surprising to find a group of diverse elements in this volume devoted mostly to his 54 feature films. Film songs recognized by the Academy Awards, big box office films, cameo roles, short subjects, his television film, DR. COOK'S GARDEN (1970), and other show business activities are noted. Casts, credits, stills, synopses, songs, and comments are offered for each of the features from THE BIG BROADCAST (1932) to STAGECOACH (1966). The usual biographical essay precedes the filmography.

The lengthy career of a popular American idol is recalled in a rather unexciting, pedantic presentation. Reading about Crosby's post World War II films and activities suggests a story about a cast-iron, folk-hero image and public fickleness that has yet to be written.

2153 *The Films of Boris Karloff.* by Bojarski, Richard; and Deals, Kenneth. 287 p. illus. Secaucus, N.J.: Citadel, 1974.

Since Karloff depended upon make-up for many of his roles, this volume provides not only the usual biography and filmography but also a fine portrait gallery of the actor. The biography covers the career in films, on stage, radio and TV. A simple listing of his early silent and sound films introduces the filmography. From GRAFT (1931) to CAULDRON OF BLOOD (1971), each film is given the full treatment with stills, cast, credits, synopsis, notes and review excerpts.

The final section notes the television programs on which Karloff appeared from a 1949 "Chevrolet on Broadway" to a 1968 "The Name of the Game." The photographs, reproduced with above-average fidelity here, coupled with an admirable subject, many of whose appearances were in horror films, make a volume that will appeal to readers. Although it is a relative latecomer in Karloff coverage, this is one of the most rewarding volumes. Recommended.

2154 *The Films of Burt Reynolds.* by Whitman, Mark. 60 p. paper illus. Bembridge, Isle of Wight, Barnden Castell Williams, 1975.

Using a mostly factual text interlaced with some interview quotes, this short review of Burt Reynolds' life and career emphasizes the machismo which has been identified with the star's public image. Illustrations are clearly reproduced and the filmography, which covers from ANGEL BABY (1960) to W. W. AND THE DIXIE DANCEKINGS (1975), gives full cast and production credits. Acceptable.

2155 *The Films of Burt Reynolds.* by Streebeck, Nancy. 256 p. illus. Secaucus, N.J.: Citadel, 1981.

2156 *The Films of Carl-Theodor Dreyer.* by Bordwell, David. 251 p. illus. Berkeley, Calif.: University of California Press, 1981.

Formalist criticism applied to the complex films of Dreyer, this volume is heavy going for all except the most dedicated.

2157 *The Films of Carole Lombard.* by Ott, Frederick W. 192 p. illus. Secaucus, N.J.: Citadel, 1972.

The usual format of this series is applied to Carole Lombard. Picture quality is good. Acceptable.

2158 *see 2159*

2159 *The Films of Cary Grant.* by Deschner, Donald. 276 p. paper illus. Secaucus, N.J.: Citadel, 1973.

Originally announced for publication in 1971, this volume finally appeared in 1973. It contains the usual *Citadel* material—an opening biographical essay, the films chronologically arranged, and a final list of short films, radio and television appearances. The special Academy Award that Grant received in 1970 is noted. Picture quality is adequate and the selection of review quotes is an improvement over those found in other similar volumes. Acceptable.

2160 *The Films of Cecil B. DeMille.* by Ringgold, Gene; and Bodeen, De-Witt. 377 p. illus. New York: Citadel Press, 1969.

This picture book has a brief biographical sketch, followed by presentations of each of the 52 silent and 18 sound films that DeMille directed. An interesting addenda is the account of DeMille's association with the "Lux Radio Theatre." A listing of the titles and casts will recall the magnitude and popularity of this legendary radio series. Production and cast credits for each film are given as is a short synopsis and some excerpts from original reviews. Highly recommended.

2161 *The Films of Charles Bronson.* by Andrews, Emma. 60 p. paper illus. Bembridge, Isle of Wight: Barnden Castell Williams, 1975.

The long career of Charles Bronson from U.S.S. TEA-KETTLE (1950) to BREAKOUT (1975) is traced in this booklet by both text and illustration. Some attention is given to the actor's personal life via factual data and many interview quotations.

Picture reproduction is excellent and often unflattering to the mature Bronson. A solid filmography is included. Acceptable.

2162 *The Films of Charles Bronson.* by Vermilye, Jerry. 256 p. illus. Secaucus, N.J.: Citadel, 1981.

2163 *The Films of Charlie Chaplin.* edited by McDonald, Gerald D.; and Conway, Michael; and Ricci, Mark. 224 p. illus. New York: Bonanza Books, 1965.

The 80 films that Chaplin has made, excluding THE COUNTESS FROM HONG KONG (1967), are represented here by stills, cast lists, plot outlines, and short excerpts from reviews. The reproduction of the stills, many of which are unfamiliar, is quite good, and along with the introductory essays, help to present the evolution of an unknown comedian into possibly the greatest film artist of the 20th Century. Recommended.

2164 *The Films of Charlton Heston.* by Rovin, Jeff. 224 p. illus. Secaucus, N.J.: Citadel, 1977.

A review of the films that Charlton Heston has made from DARK CITY (1950) to TWO MINUTE WARNING (1976) indicates a lot of average-competent performances in many quite ordinary vehicles. After an initial biographical essay, the films are recalled by cast, credits, stills, synopses, and comment. Heston's stage work is also noted.

The same comment can be applied to this book as to Heston's *The Actor's Life*—it is bland and uninteresting when one considers his longevity and experience as a major Hollywood star. For the dedicated only.

2165 *The Films of Charlton Heston.* by Williams, John. 47 p. paper illus. London: Barnden Castell Williams, 1974.

The text of this original paperback consists of a short biography and a longer appreciation. A filmography traces Heston's film work from PEER GYNT (1941) to AIRPORT 1975 (1975). The photographs are well selected and visualize the survival of a Hollywood actor for more than 30 years. Acceptable.

2166 *The Films of Clark Gable.* by Essoe, Gabe. 255 p. illus. New York: Citadel Press, 1970.

The first 100 pages are devoted to a long illustrated biography and many tributes, primarily from females. A short section deals with Gable's stage appearances and his bit roles in silent films. The 67 films in which he had important or leading roles are then noted with casts, credits, synopses and review quotes. This book contains many more illustrations than is usual in this series and the quality is outstanding, almost without exception. The concentrated text of the first portion is at least equivalent to any of the several biographies (excepting Charles Sammuels' fine book, *The King*). This outstanding volume is recommended for all.

2167 *The Films of Clint Eastwood.* by Zmijewsky, Boris; and Pfeiffer, Lee. 256 p. illus. Secaucus, N.J.: Citadel, 1981.

2168 *Films of Comment and Persuasion of the 30's.* by Low, Rachael. illus. New York: Bowker, 1979.

Rachael Low continues her monumental history of the British film with this volume, the sixth in a series. Here she examines films which deal with the problems and issues that characterized the thirties.

2169 *The Films of David Niven.* by Garrett, Gerard. 256 p. illus. Secaucus, N.J.: Citadel, 1976.

Citadel is apparently running out of superstars upon which to base their expensive coffee table volumes. David Niven has appeared in more than 75 films, most of them now forgotten. Each is recalled here via stills, cast, credits, plot outline, review excerpts and comment. Some attention is given to his television work.

Admirers of the actor will be pleased, but to many others, Garrett's forced appreciation, like Niven's films, is not very memorable.

2170 *The Films of Dolores Del Rio.* by Woll, Allen L. New York: Gordon Press, 1979.

2171 *The Films of Don Shebib.* by Handling, Piers. 148 p. paper illus. Ottawa: Canadian Film Institute, 1978.

Here is another volume in a *CFI* series that attempts to make the reader more aware of a neglected or relatively unknown yet promising filmmaker. Most of Don Shebib's work has been with short films but he has made four impressive feature films— GOIN' DOWN THE ROAD (1970), RIP-OFF (1971), BETWEEN FRIENDS (1973), and SECOND WIND (1976). His career to date is covered by the usual elements in this series—an essay, an interview, a filmography, and a bibliography. The essay is a lengthy one (six chapters) and provides a critical review of Shebib's films. Some illustrations, mostly of Shebib, complete the study. Certainly the role of the CFI in providing information about promising Canadian filmmakers is completely fulfilled in this appreciation. The ultimate effect on the reader is a sensitivity to Shebib's work and a desire to examine as many of his films as possible.

2172 *The Films of Doris Day.* by Young, Christopher. 253 p. illus. Secaucus, N.J.: Citadel, 1977.

The films and career of Doris Day receive a perfunctory treatment in this volume. Beginning with RO-MANCE ON THE HIGH SEAS (1948), the text offers cast, credits, stills, songs, synopses, and review quotes for all her films up to WITH SIX YOU GET EGGROLL (1968). In addition to a mediocre biographical essay, there is one section devoted to "Doris Day on Television." There appear to be hundreds of Day portraits scattered throughout the book. Of course, Doris Day admirers will be pleased. Others may find that, like some of her films, the book is often a bit much.

2173 *The Films of D.W. Griffith.* by Wagenknecht, Edward; and Slide, Anthony. 276 p. illus. New York: Crown, 1975.

A long-existing gap in film literature has been filled with the appearance of this volume. It is a factual, critical and pictorial survey of D.W. Griffith's feature films.

Arranged in chronological sequence from JUDITH OF BETHULIA (1914) to THE STRUGGLE (1931), the 33 films are described by cast-credit data, the story, a set of captioned stills, and a critical essay. The authors have apportioned the work with each taking responsibility for a portion of the critical pieces. A few films have been evaluated by Arthur Lennig.

There is also an introduction by Lillian Gish, a long chapter on Griffith's Biograph period with a full title listing, a bibliography, and an index.

When two authorities combine their knowledge and skills in a quality volume that is carefully designed and produced, the result is an exceptional volume— as this one is. It is one of the definitive volumes on Griffith and deserves attention from readers of all ages and interests. Highly recommended.,

2174 *The Films of Elizabeth Taylor.* by Vermilye, Jerry; and Ricci, Mark. 256 p. illus. Secaucus, N.J.: Citadel, 1978.

The usual bland biographical essay introduces this volume in the *Citadel* series. Each of Elizabeth Taylor's films from THERE'S ONE BORN EVERY MINUTE (1942) to THE DRIVER'S SEAT (1974) is described by stills, cast, credits, a plot outline, comments and review excerpts. As usual with this series, the photographs are the main attraction.

2175 *The Films of Elizabeth Taylor.* by d'Arcy, Susan. 47 p. paper illus. London: Barnden Castell Williams, 1974.

A biography of Elizabeth Taylor occupies almost half of this original paperback. Remaining sections are devoted to an appreciation and a filmography— from MAN OR MOUSE (1942) to THE BLUEBIRD OF HAPPINESS (1975). Reproduction quality of the illustrations ranges from very light underexposure to darkened overexposure. Acceptable.

2176 *The Films of Errol Flynn.* by Thomas, Tony; and Behlmer, Rudy;

and McCarty, Clifford. 224 p. illus. New York: Citadel Press, 1969.

After an unexpected tribute by Greer Garson, this book further surprises the reader by including several pre-CAPTAIN BLOOD (1935) films in which Flynn played minor roles. The major films include nicely reproduced stills, production credits, casts and background notes. No reviews are quoted. The book is divided into four sections, each introduced by a continuation of Flynn's biography. Very nicely done.

2177 *The Films of Frank Capra.* by Scherle, Victor; and Turner, William. 278 p. illus. Secaucus, N.J.: Citadel, 1977.

The typical *Citadel* series format is adhered to in this volume. Each of Frank Capra's 40 films are described by visuals, plot synopsis, and cast credits. Critical material is scarce; the pages are filled, however, with appreciations from Capra's coworkers, actors, directors, etc., and Capra, himself, comments on his career and his films.

This is an appreciation of Capra rather than a critical analysis of his work. Those desiring more depth are directed to *The Cinema of Frank Capra, The Films of Frank Capra* by Donald Willis or *Frank Capra: The Man And His Films.* Even Capra's autobiography, *The Name Above the Title,* has more substance.

2178 *The Films of Frank Capra.* by Willis, Donald C. 214 p. illus. Metuchen, N.J.: Scarecrow Press, 1974.

A fresh view of Frank Capra's accomplishments is provided by Donald C. Willis. While Capra's autobiography tells about making the films, Willis is concerned with critical analyses of them. Placing the films under appropriate headings such as "Capra's American Hero," "Adaptations East and West," "Early Columbia, Late Paramount Comedies" and "Harry Langdon," he presents information, data, analyses and personal comment about each. Contrary to most critical opinion, he dislikes LOST HORIZON (1937) but favors ARSENIC AND OLD LACE (1944).

Certain performers, such as Cary Grant in the above film, get a page or two of appreciation, while Sinatra, Eleanor Parker, Thelma Ritter, and Edward G. Robinson are not even mentioned in the discussion of A HOLE IN THE HEAD (1959). Many chapter notes add dimension to the strong personal opinions that are offered. Appendixes note Capra's other films, his early screenwriting efforts, a few Capra-inspired films, Oscar nominations and awards given to Capra films, and a review of Capra's autobiography. An index is included.

Willis' subjective approach to his topic is stimulating, intelligent, and always justified in a readable text. Factual information is sound and the copious footnotes add dimension and scope to this rewarding critical study. Recommended.

2179 *The Films of Frank Sinatra.* by Ringgold, Gene; and McCarty, Clifford. 249 p. illus. New York: Citadel, 1971.

The opening biographical sketch is factual rather than analytical and is followed by the films—from LAS VEGAS NIGHTS (1941) to DIRTY DINGUS MAGEE (1969). The text states that many of the films are poor but appropriately commercial in nature. Examination verifies this statement—especially with such examples as THE KISSING BANDIT (1947), DOUBLE DYNAMITE (1950), 4 FOR TEXAS, and the above DIRTY DINGUS MAGEE. The authors are careful to include some kind words about each in their selection of review excerpts.

The photographic reproduction and the selection of illustrations are remarkably fine. One exception is THE LIST OF ADRIAN MESSENGER (1963), where Sinatra is not shown in his gypsy stable-boy makeup. There is an index and some miscellaneous short film appearances are noted at the end. The photographs and the reference data are the important contribution here. Other than the opening essay, there is no critical contribution from the authors, merely the assembling of material. Acceptable.

2180 *see* *2181*

2181 *The Films of Fredric March.* by Quirk, Lawrence J. 255 p. illus. New York: Citadel, 1971.

The format is consistent with previous publications in the *Citadel* series. A long biographical essay is followed by a chronological recall of March's films. Starting with THE DUMMY (1929) and finishing with TICK...TICK...TICK (1970), each film has a player listing, production credits, a descriptive narrative that includes both supportive information and plot description, and finally some review excerpts. This data surrounds the many illustrations which are the strength and richness of the book. A final section gives a chronological listing of the 18 Broadway plays in which March appeared from 1920 to 1961.

March's career has covered the entire Hollywood era of sound films and his performances have been consistently excellent. This tribute to him is not only justified but the execution and quality of the work is most appropriate for the subject and his career. This is one of the better *Citadel* volumes and is recommended.

2182 *The Films of Fritz Lang.* by Ott, Frederick W. 287 p. illus. Secaucus, N.J.: Citadel, 1979.

Now that the personality list has been somewhat covered in the *Citadel* series, they have looked at directors as possible subjects for their coffee table volumes. Hitchcock and Ford have already appeared and now we have Fritz Lang, a surprising choice. Perhaps it is because of the personal acquaintance of the author with Lang. In any event this is one of the better volumes in the series. It covers Lang's career from 1919 to 1961 and offers both biography and filmography. Each of Lang's films is described by stills, cast, credit, plot outline, review excerpts, and comments. Over 500 visuals appear in the volume and, with the literate text, help to make this an impressive appreciation of the director.

2183 *The Films of Gary Cooper.* by Dickens, Homer. 280 p. illus. New York: Citadel Press, 1970.

Another fine picture book by Dickens which follows the usual structure for each film—stills, cast, credits, synopsis, and notes including review excerpts. A short biography and a separate section for Cooper's short films are included. Picture reproduction is excellent. Recommended.

2184 *The Films of Gene Kelly.* by Thomas, Tony. 243 p. illus. Secaucus, N.J.: Citadel, 1974.

Another in the long list of titles found in the *Citadel* series, this volume conforms to the pattern. Each one of more than 40 Kelly films is described by illustrations, casts, credits, critical comment, review excerpts, and plot synopses. Fred Astaire provides an introduction and there is a biographical chapter entitled "The Loneliness of the Long-Distance Dancer."

This appreciation covers Kelly's work only up to 1973; it should be noted that he remains active in films — THAT'S ENTERTAINMENT II (1976), XANADU (1980), etc. For greater depth and coverage, the reader is referred to Hirschorn's *Gene Kelly.*

2185 *The Films of George Pal.* by Hickman, Gail Morgan. 177 p. illus. New York: A.S. Barnes, 1977.

A long overdue tribute to George Pal is expressed in this well-researched volume. Beginning with THE PUPPETOONS, those short animated films which appeared on theatre screens in the early forties, the text next considers each of the 14 feature films that George Pal directed/produced. Attention is given to the special effects which were an integral part of such Pal films as DESTINATION MOON (1950), THE WAR OF THE WORLDS (1953), TOM THUMB (1958), THE TIME MACHINE (1959), THE WONDERFUL WORLD OF THE BROTHERS GRIMM (1962) and SEVEN FACES OF DR. LAO (1964). Especially impressive in this regard are the many visuals which illustrate the special effects and their creation. The volume is indexed.

The author has wisely opted for a consideration of George Pal's films rather than the usual biography-filmography. As a result this volume will hold the interest of a large audience on a number of levels. It is certain that young people familiar with the films from their television showings will respond enthusiastically. Recommended.

2186 *The Films of Ginger Rogers.* by Dickens, Homer. 256 p. illus. Secaucus, N.J.: Citadel, 1975.

All of Ginger Roger's 73 films together with her short films and stage appearances are noted in this *Citadel* series volume. The filmography occupies the major portion of the text with each entry noting cast, credits, plot, review excerpts, and background information. Over 400 illustrations appear throughout. In addition there is the usual biographical chapter and a photo section dealing with the team of Fred Astaire and Ginger Rogers. Homer Dickens is one of the dependable authors in the *Citadel* series. In this instance he does quite well by Ginger Rogers.

2187 *The Films of Greta Garbo.* by Conway, Michael; and McGregor, Dion; and Ricci, Mark. 155 p. illus. New York: Bonanza Books, 1963.

In this book an essay entitled "The Garbo Image," by Parker Tyler, introduces the 27 films of Garbo. Cast, production credits, a synopsis, and critic's comments are given for each. Author comments included with the synopses are on the dull side ("This was Garbo's twelfth film and the last with Nils Asther and John Mack Brown"). The picture reproduction in this edition is only adequate, with some illustrations looking fuzzy, unfocused or underexposed. Garbo deserves better.

2188   *The Films of Hal Roach.* by Everson, William K. 96 p. paper illus. New York: Museum of Modern Art, 1970.

Roach was responsible in some capacity for more than 2000 films, both shorts and features. This critical biographical sketch attempts to explain his approach to comedy. There are more than 40 illustrations. A highlight is a 1969 interview with Roach.

2189   *The Films of Hedy Lamarr.* Young, Christopher.

Remember Hedy Lamarr, "The Most Beautiful Woman in the World" ? Christopher Young has in this *Citadel* series volume that includes the usual biographical essay and the detailed filmography. Each of her films is identified by stills, cast, credits, plot outline, production notes, and review excerpts. The beauty of Hedy Lamarr is evidenced in the hundreds of portraits, candids, and other pictures that are presented. Attention is also given to her appearances on television.

2190   *The Films of Hellmuch Costard.* edited by Dawson, Jan. New York: Zeotrope, 1979.

Costard is a director in the new German cinema who has been called "the protagonist of the underground."

2191   *The Films of Howard Hawks.* by Willis, Donald C. 235 p. illus. Metuchen, N.J.: Scarecrow, 1975.

The author regards Howard Hawks as his favorite American film director, and, in this well-written study, justifies his opinion. Arranging about 35 of Hawk's films under genre headings, he presents arguments that Hawk's reputation as a superb auteurist is deserved. In the appendix there is a discussion of auteurs and auteurists, an interview with Howard Hawks, a filmography, and an index. A few illustrations appear throughout the book.

Because of its range and longevity, the work of Howard Hawks provides a rich, fertile ground for critics and authors. Donald Willis has provided a readable, enlightening appreciation.

2192   *The Films of Ingmar Bergman.* by Donner, Jorn. 276 p. paper illus. New York: Dover, 1972.

This is the same book as *The Personal Vision of Ingmar Bergman*, published in 1964 by Indiana University Press. For this edition some new illustrations have been provided and the entire production is more impressive than the original.

2193   *The Films of Ingrid Bergman.* by Quirk, Lawrence J. 224 p. illus. New York: Citadel, 1970.

Stage and television appearances are added to the films of Bergman in this volume. The films are divided into chronological groups (e.g., "The Rossellini Period") with casts, review quotes, etc.

2194   *The Films of Jack Lemmon.* by Baltake, Joe. 255 p. illus. Secaucus, N.J.: Citadel, 1977.

Comments by Walter Matthau, Judith Crist, and Billy Wilder are included in this appreciation of Jack Lemmon. Following the introductory biographical essay, Lemmon's films, from IT SHOULD HAPPEN TO YOU (1954) to AIRPORT 77 (1977), are described by stills, cast, credits, notes, and review excerpts. A final section is devoted to his leading ladies. Added pluses are the comments by Lemmon on some of his roles, the many unfamiliar visuals, and the coverage of the actor in theatre and on television. This is one of the better *Citadel* volumes.

2195   *The Films of Jacques Tati.* by Maddock, Brent. 179 p. illus. Metuchen, N.J.: Scarecrow, 1977.

Jacques Tati has made only five feature films, yet he is often compared to Chaplin, Keaton, Lloyd and other great visual comedians. Since he wrote, directed and starred in his speechless comedies, the comparison is quite warranted. Brent Haddock analyzes each of the films, adding much background information and comment. A filmography, a bibliography, illustrations and chapter notes are included.

This is a most welcome study of a superb filmmaker whose work is largely unrecognized in America. Maddock's authority on his subject is substantiated by careful research, study and consideration accompanied by affection and appreciation.

2196   *The Films of James Caan.* by d'Arcy, Susan. unpaginated. paper illus. London: Barnden Castell Williams, 1975.

The material on Caan represents another first for this enterprising series of paperback originals. A long biographical essay opens this survey of his life and career. Appended is a relatively short filmography—from LADY IN A CAGE (1964) to ROLLERBALL (1975). Visuals are mostly portraits or Caan close-ups. Acceptable.

2197 *The Films of James Cagney.* by Dickens, Homer. 249 p. illus. Secaucus, N.J.: Citadel, 1972.

Since this volume was obtained through the Movie Book Club at a reduced price, it may be a special cheaper edition. This information is given because the immediate observation is that the paper is a less expensive kind and the reproduction quality of the photographs extremely variable. Because James Cagney is such an ideal subject and because Homer Dickens is one of the more dependable authors in the *Citadel* series—Dietrich, Cooper and Hepburn—the negative production factors are most unfortunate.

A short essay, "The Anti-Hero," is followed by a gallery of Cagney portraits. The long filmography has stills, credits, synopses, critical excerpts, and notes. It is in this last section that Dickens demonstrates his knowledge and understanding of the subject's career. A theatre chronicle of the plays that Cagney did before Hollywood (1920-1930) closes the book, which is not indexed. Acceptable, but Cagney has been shortchanged by Citadel (or Cadillac, as printed on the binding).

2198 *The Films of James Dean.* by Whittman, Mark. 47 p. paper illus. London: Barnden Castell Williams, 1974.

James Dean appeared in a total of seven films—three as an unbilled extra, three as a star, and one as the subject of a compilation film. These films are noted in the filmography and appreciation offered by this original paperback. A longer biographical section and more illustrations are included to compensate for the short film career. Picture reproduction is below average, but the selection is good. Acceptable.

2199 *The Films of James Mason.* by Hirschhorn, Clive. 256 p. illus. Secaucus, N.J.: Citadel, 1977.

This volume in the *Citadel* series departs slightly from standard format in that it offers James Mason's "Second Thoughts" on his films. They appear occasionally, following the credits, cast, synopses, stills, and comments/review excerpts of his 92 films. Brief in length, they tend to be socially informal rather than deeply critical. Mason's career has spanned more than four decades—this volume covers from

LATE EXTRA (1935) to MANDINGO (1975)—and he is still very active in films at this writing. A long impressive career is documented here and the result is an above-average book.

2200 *The Films of James Stewart.* by Jones, Ken D.; and McClure, Arthur F.; and Twomey, Alfred E. 256 p. illus. New York: A.S. Barnes, 1970.

This book contains a foreword by Henry Fonda, a very short biography, and the films. Unlike other volumes of this type, the films are placed in continuous succession instead of on separate pages. Pictures are small and are barely acceptable reproductions. The synopsis given for each film is minimal and so are the review quotes. This book represents poor production and inadequate treatment of a major screen personality and his work.

2201 *The Films of Jane Fonda.* by Haddad-Garcia, George. 256 p. illus. Secaucus, N.J.: Citadel, 1981.

The *Citadel* format applied to Jane Fonda. Biography followed by detailed filmography. Fonda is well served by the author's objectivity.

2202 *The Films of Jean Harlow.* by Conway, Michael; and Ricci, Mark. 159 p. illus. New York: Citadel Press, 1965.

Here is the usual formula of stills, casts, credits, synopses and critical excerpts. Her 25 films indicate not only her right to be called sex goddess but also her due to be recognized as a gifted comedienne. The book never quite captures the Harlow charisma but it does address itself briefly to the attacks on her reputation by fast-buck writers.

2203 *The Films of Jean-Luc Godard.* edited by Cameron, Ian, 192 p. paper illus. New York: Praeger, 1970.

A group of critics offering both analysis and evaluation write articles on the films of Godard (BREATHLESS (1960), ALPHAVILLE (1965), WEEKEND (1967), etc.)

2204 *Films of Jean Vigo.* by Simon, William G. Ann Arbor, Mich.: University of Michigan Press, 1981.

2205 *The Films of Jeanette MacDonald and Nelson Eddy.* by Castanza, Philip. illus. Secaucus, N.J.: Citadel,

1978.

Another *Citadel* volume which is in the nature of a tribute rather than a critical survey, this book deals with the team of Jeanette MacDonald and Nelson Eddy. Casts, credits, plots, illustrations, notes, etc., are given for each of their eight team films as well as for the films they made individually. Tributes by a few MGM contemporaries and biographical profiles are included.

For a much better survey of the films, a book with the same title, by Eleanor Knowles, *The Films of Jeanette MacDonald and Nelson Eddy* is suggested.

2206   *The Films of Jeanette MacDonald and Nelson Eddy.* by Knowles, Eleanor. 469 p. illus. New York:A. S. Barnes, 1976.

This oversized volume is true to its title since it deals almost exclusively with the films of its two subjects. Although some biographical information is offered, it is mostly factual rather than critical or interpretive. The richness of the book lies in the abundance of fascinating detail offered in describing the films. In addition to the usual elements such as plot outlines, cast and production credits, stills, and review excerpts, there is a wealth of background information provided for each film. Jeanette MacDonald's film career is carefully traced from THE LOVE PARADE (1930) to THE SUN COMES UP (1949) while Nelson Eddy's films from BROADWAY TO HOLLYWOOD (1933) to NORTHWEST OUTPOST (1947) are recalled. Predictably the eight films they made together receive major attention. A rather complete discography and a selected radio index are added along with a detailed index.

The visuals have been well selected and include some fascinating material from the early years of each star. The research necessary to produce a volume such as this is enormous. When diligence, affection, admiration and intelligence are applied to the organization and interpretation of that basic data, the result is a richly satisfying volume. Older admirers and recent discoverers of the singing team will be completely delighted. The book is a definitive and appropriate tribute to their musical talent and personal appeal. Highly recommended.

2207   *The Films of Joan Crawford.* by Quirk, Lawrence J. 222 p. illus. New York: Citadel Press, 1968.

More than 80 motion pictures detail the career of one of the screen's indestructible ladies in this volume. After a short biographical sketch, the films from PRETTY LADIES (1925) to BERSERK (1968) are

examined. In addition to stills, the cast, production credits, a synopsis and some review quotes are given.

The stills are quite good but the accompanying materials are rather ordinary. Do the plot outlines of the films warrant so much textual space at the expense of evaluation of the films or the leading lady in them? Aside from Crawford fans, most readers will not find in these pages the excitement or the treatment that Crawford deserves.

2208   *The Films of John Garfield.* by Gelman, Howard. 224 p. illus. Secaucus, N.J.: Citadel, 1975.

The *Citadel* series assembly line offers a slight departure with this book. While it contains the usual cast, credits, plot, illustrations and background for each of Garfield's 33 films, it also offers a better biographical section than that which is usually found in this series. Not only in Abraham Polonsky's introduction, but also in Gelman's analysis of Garfield's career and persona, the text provides some thoughtful material. A section on politics, Garfield's involvement with the House Un-American Activities Committee and his blacklisting by Hollywood is unusual.

2209   *The Films of John Wayne.* by Ricci, Mark; and Zmijewsky, Boris; and Zmijewsky, Steve. 288 p. illus. New York: Citadel, 1970. .

This large film book presents the 144 films that John Wayne has appeared in, ending with RIO LOBO (1969). Wayne, of course, has made several since then. For each film there usually are several stills, cast and production credits, and a plot synopsis. Over 400 illustrations fill the book. One of the more interesting features of the book is the biographical section at the beginning of the volume. Several portraits of Wayne accompany each page and are arranged in chronological order. It is possible to watch Wayne age within a dozen or so pages.

Other portions of the book are rather uninspired. There is no critical comment of the films. Rather than the synopses, some evaluation might have been welcome. (Neither the cinematic nor the private Wayne is clearly identifiable from this book.) An acceptable work that could have and should have been much better.

2210   *The Films of Josef von Sternberg.* by Andrew Sarris. 56 p. illus. New York: Museum of Modern Art, 1966.

After a brief biographical account, Sarris launches into an analysis and critical evaluation of the 18 films of von Sternberg. Chronological arrangement is from SALVATION HUNTERS (1925) to ANATAHAN (1953). As usual Sarris is perceptive, informed, and fair to this neglected director. Recommended for most readers. (Reading pleasure is increased if read with the subject's autobiography, *Fun In A Chinese Laundry.*)

2211 *The Films of Judy Garland.* by Baxter, Brian. 47 p. paper illus. London: Barnden Castell Williams, 1974.

The dark, murky photography that occasionally diminishes this series appears in this volume. Although the illustrations are representative of Garland's long career, their effect is minimized by poor reproduction. A biography, appreciation, a short bibliography and a selected discography are presented along with a filmography which covers from EVERY SUNDAY (1936) to I COULD GO ON SINGING (1962). Acceptable.

2212 *The Films of Katharine Hepburn.* by Dickens, Homer 244 p. illus. New York: Citadel Press, 1971.

Homer Dickens is an author to be applauded. Here is another outstanding picture-text-reference similar to his previous ones on Dietrich and Gary Cooper. Avoiding the usual pattern, he gives an impressive biographical sketch which avoids all the noncorroborated guessing about Hepburn's personal life and simply states facts (e.g., her marriage and divorce to Ludlow Ogden Smith are mentioned without comment). Each film has cast and promotion credits, a thankfully short synopsis, several well-selected critical quotes, and finally some interesting background notes. Final sections include similar material about Hepburn's stage roles and a gallery of portraits. There is no index. The book is a nearly "pure" Hepburn tribute and allows few others to share her spotlight. Highly recommended.

2213 *The Films of Kirk Douglas.* by Thomas, Tony. 256 p. illus. Secaucus, N.J.: Citadel, 1972.

A better book than most of the newer titles in this series. Starting with a biography, it is primarily a record of the 54 films that Douglas had made up to the book's publication. It contains casts, credits, and synopses as well as the author's own evaluations. Other data are also noted. Photographs in this book are adequately reproduced and some come from Douglas' private collection. Acceptable.

2214 *The Films of Lana Turner.* by Valentino, Lou. 288 p. illus. Secaucus, N.J.: Citadel, 1976.

Mervyn LeRoy provides the foreword to this appreciation of Lana Turner and her 52 films. The biographical sketch which introduces the text is more detailed than usual in the *Citadel* series. It is followed by a filmography that describes each entry from A STAR IS BORN (1937) to BITTERSWEET LOVE (1975) with illustrations, cast, credits, plot summary, comment, review excerpts, etc. Turner's appearances in other media are noted.

This volume is several notches above the level of the usual books in this series, the reason being that the author is an ardent fan of Lana Turner. He has lavished obvious care, affection, good taste and discretion on this subjective tribute to his favorite star.

2215 *The Films of Laurel and Hardy.* by Everson, William K. 223 p. paper illus. New York: Citadel Press, 1967.

A sales figure of over 30,000 copies has been quoted for this volume. This is not at all surprising, considering its overall excellence, its subjects, and the obvious affection of the author for the pair. The stills are models of clarity and reproduction. As is usual with all of Everson's writing, the text complements the visuals but can also stand by itself. Each of the team's films is discussed as are the individual films made by each before their fortuitous merger. A brief plot outline is presented for each film followed by a detailed and thoughtful analysis of the work of the team. The text is not the usual review excerpts, cast credits and extended plot descriptions found in other volumes—it is a full measure of high quality film literature. Recommended.

2216 *The Films of Laurence Olivier.* by Morley, Margaret. illus. Secaucus, N.J.: Citadel, 1978.

2217 *The Films of Leni Riefenstahl.* by Hinton, David B. 168 p. illus. Metuchen, N.J.: Scarecrow, 1978.

The debate about art and politics as exemplified by the work of Leni Riefenstahl is continued in this book. David Hinton interviewed his subject, had access to her archives, and spoke to others who had worked with her. The result is a largely favorable portrait.

Each of her films is analyzed along with some discussion of uncompleted or current projects. In her seventies, the filmmaker remains very active. Photographs, an index, a selected bibliography, chapter notes, a list of awards, a short essay on writing the music for TIEFLAND (1954) by Herbert Windt, and the decision of the Baden State Commission for Political Cleansing complete the study.

The sympathetic appreciation offered here adds more argument and opinion to the Riefenstahl controversy. It should be read along with other less positive viewpoints.

2218   *The Films of Liza Minnelli.* by d'Arcy, Susan. 47 p. paper illus. London: Barnden Castell Williams, 1973.

At the time of this publication, Liza Minnelli had made only four major films. (Her one-shot appearance from IN THE GOOD OLD SUMMERTIME (1949) at age three surely doesn't count.) Therefore this volume must lean heavily on illustrations, personality portraits, awards and a discography. The illustrations are interesting and show a gradual metamorphosis from ugly ducking to well-groomed lady. The filmography lists CHARLIE BUBBLES (1967), THE STERILE CUCKOO (1969), TELL ME THAT YOU LOVE ME, JUNIE MOON (1969) and CABARET (1972). Acceptable.

2219   *The Films of Mae West.* by Tuska, Jon. 191 p. illus. Secaucus, N.J.: Citadel, 1973.

Since the films of Mae West from NIGHT AFTER NIGHT (1932) to MYRA BRECKINRIDGE (1970) are so few, this volume has been enlarged by giving a longer treatment to each film. Using more illustrations—many of them full page—and providing a lengthy introduction, Tuska reviews Mae West's career. Her stage appearances are also covered in both text and photographs, as are her excursions into television and radio. The filmography gives cast, credits, stills, background information and even dialogue excerpts. Picture quality is above average throughout. There is no index. Acceptable.

2220   *The Films of Marilyn Monroe.* by Conway, Michael; and Ricci, Mark. 160 p. illus. New York: Citadel Press, 1964.

From SCUDDA HOO! SCUDDA HAY! in 1948 to THE MISFITS in 1961, Marilyn Monroe became a film legend. In this volume, the almost 30 films that she made are considered separately. Each has cast and production credits, a plot synopsis, some short comment, and some excerpts from the film's reviews. The pictures are as familiar as the text and neither captures the excitement of the subject.

2221   *The Films of Marlene Dietrich.* by Dickens, Homer. 223 p. illus. New York: Citadel Press, 1968.

Probably the most surprising information in this exciting volume is that Dietrich appeared in some 17 motion pictures before BLUE ANGEL (1929)—even as an extra in Garbo's THE JOYLESS STREET (1925). All these films have an accompanying synopsis and some film notes. A biographical account introduces the book. The text is excellent, the pictures are well-chosen and well-reproduced, and the subject is magical, mysterious, and seemingly eternal. Who could ask for more? Recommended.,

2222   *The Films of Marlon Brando.* by Thomas, Tony. 246 p. illus. Secaucus, N.J.: Citadel Press, 1973.

A most satisfying account of Marlon Brando, told through his films. While much of the personal life story is omitted, the professional life is covered completely. Starting with a biographical essay that emphasizes the pre-Hollywood life and career, the book departs from the usual Citadel format in the main film section. A descriptive evaluation of each film is given instead of the standard synopsis plus critical excerpts. Cast and production credits are listed as always. LAST TANGO IN PARIS (1972) is the final film discussed. Pauline Kael contributes a foreword and there is an afterword about Brando's refusal of the Oscar.

The substitution of critical narrative for factual rehash is commendable. However, in the rush to cash in on the Brando revival, the editors were most lax in proofreading; spelling, grammatical, and name errors abound and certain sentences lack meaning because of word omissions. Picture quality is acceptable in the film section but poor in the biographical portion. There is no index.

Tony Thomas has written a fine, biased, evaluation of the film work of Brando. It is a better total book than any of the biographies.

2223   *The Films of Martin Ritt.* by Whitaker, Sheila. 24 p. illus. London: British Film Institute, 1972.

Inexpensive production characterizes this booklet prepared for the Martin Ritt retrospective held at the National Film Theatre in 1972. According to the author, Ritt is a director neglected by both critics and audiences. Her intention here is to provide correction to unfair treatment. A biographical chronology and a filmography with major cast and production credits introduce the text, which deals with recurring themes and motifs. A short section on Ritt's directorial style and a bibliography conclude the booklet. The filmography treats Ritt's work from EDGE OF THE CITY (1957) to PETE 'N' TILLIE (1972). Some very perceptive analysis, along with well-selected supportive material, is weakened by the faded mimeographed appearance of the pages and visuals. Acceptable.

2224 *The Films of Mary Pickford.* by Lee, Raymond. 175 p. illus. New York: A.S. Barnes, 1970.

They have "done wrong" by America's sweetheart in this volume. The production, picture selection, text and overall organization are all mediocre at best and usually worse than that. Beginning with a short biographical introduction by Edward Wagenknecht, the book consists of portraits, stills from pictures, studio publicity shots, and candids. Actually only the latter half of the book is about her 125 short films and 52 full-length features. Small size, space-wasting placement, and dark and unclear reproduction mark the pictures throughout. This volume can be considered as usable only until an appropriate picture volume of Pickford is produced.

2225 *The Films of Michael Caine.* by Andrews, Emma. 47 p. paper illus. London: Barnden Castell Williams, 1974.

Modest biography and appreciation sections accompany a large collection of interesting Caine photographs. In addition there is a filmography that covers from A HILL IN KOREA (1956) to THE MAN WHO WOULD BE KING (1975). Reproduction of the illustrations is above average. Acceptable.

2226 *The Films of Michael Winner.* by Harding, Bill. 224 p. illus. London: Muller, 1978.

2227 *The Films of Montgomery Clift.* by Kass, Judith M. 223 p. illus. Secaucus, N.J.: Citadel, 1979.

This volume in the *Citadel* series concentrates on Montgomery Clift's films and stage work. Since two strong biographies of Clift have preceded this volume, the emphasis is wise. The films are described by stills, plot synopses, casts, credits, review excerpts, and background information. Clift's brother has supplied a foreword.

2228 *The Films of Myrna Loy.* by Quirk, Lawrence J. 256 p. illus. Secaucus, N.J.: Citadel, 1980.

2229 *The Films of Nancy Carroll: A Charmer's Almanac.* by Nemcek, Paul L. 223 p. illus. New York: Lyle Stuart, 1969.

A chronological biography opens the book, followed by the films arranged in the usual cast-credits-song-synopsis-criticism fashion. Picture quality is excellent. An interesting pictorial account of a rather short but vibrant film career.

2230 *The Films of 1974.* by Castell, David; and Williams, John. 94 p. paper illus. London: Barnden Castell Williams, 1975.

This volume is a lengthy filmography that gives casts and credits for films shown in London's West End during 1974. Containing many portrait stills, the volume also offers a personality index which refers actor names to the filmography. A distributor index completes the volume. Acceptable.

2231 *The Films of Norma Shearer.* by Jacobs, Jack; and Braum, Myron. 250 p. illus. New York: A.S. Barnes, 1976.

Norma Shearer was once the reigning queen of the MGM studios. After a long apprenticeship in silent films, she married Irving Thalberg in 1927 and usually had her choice of material, leading men, writers, and directors until his death in 1936. She continued to make films until the early forties. This volume covers her biography in an opening section and then recalls each of her films in chronological order. Credits, the cast, a plot outline, selected critical excerpts, and a few illustrations are given for all films except those in which she had a bit part.

The biographical portion suffers from the fan-like adoration of the authors, the relating of film plots which are repeated later, and some lengthy digressions which are not 'essential to the Shearer story (e.g.,the career of Bob Evans). In the films section the photographs are the attraction, showing the evolution of the beautiful girl in THE FLAPPER (1920) into the mature, sophisticated woman of HER CARDBOARD LOVER (1942). Reproduction is good and many unfamiliar stills have been selected.

The poise, grace, and cool charm that Norma Shearer had on screen is reflected in the pages of this volume. It should please anyone who is acquainted with her film performances. Acceptable.

2232 *The Films of Oliver Reed.* by d'Arcy, Susan. 47 p. paper illus. London:

Barnden Castell Williams, 1974.

This original paperback contains the standard elements of the series: a biography, an appreciation, a filmography, and selected illustrations. The filmography covers from BEAT GIRL (1959) to TOMMY (1974). Illustrations are interesting, but reproduction quality is not consistent. Acceptable.

2233   *The Films of Orson Welles.* by Highman, Charles. 210 p. illus. Berkeley, Calif.: University of California Press, 1970.

This is the work of an Australian scholar-aficionado dedicating his energies to a fascinating and controversial topic. Not a biography of Welles, the book devotes an individual analytic chapter to each of Welles' films. Included are such rarities as his television films, the legendary South American footage for IT'S ALL TRUE (1942), and the contribution to JOURNEY INTO FEAR (1942). The examination is supplemented and supported by interviews with many individuals who worked with Welles on the films. Ironically, or intentionally, the author did not use Welles himself as a resource.

The material of the book is excellent; the narrative is intelligent, controversial, and frank, while the stills are examples of the picture clarity and composition that characterize Welles' films. There is no scarcity of printed material on Welles or the few films he directed. This is one of the better volumes and is recommended.

2234   *The Films of Paul Newman.* by Quirk, Lawrence. 224 p. illus. New York: Citadel, 1971.

The record of the films and life of a unique actor and a potentially fine director.

2235   *The Films of Paul Newman.* by Thompson, Kenneth. 47 p. paper illus. London: Barnden Castell Williams, 1973.

A short biography introduces a longer appreciation of Newman's films. The filmography which ends the book gives casts and credits for his films from THE SILVER CHALICE (1954) to THE STING (1973). Illustrations mostly consist of Newman in his various roles. Acceptable.

2236   *The Films of Rita Hayworth.* by Ringgold, Gene. 256 p. illus. Secaucus, N.J.: Citadel, 1975.

Subtitled, "The Legend and Career of a Love Goddess," this *Citadel* volume covers Hayworth's films from UNDER THE PAMPAS MOON (1935) to THE WRATH OF GOD (1972). For each there are credits, cast, notes, stills, and review excerpts. The films are arranged chronologically under headings of Rita Casino, starlet, love goddess, and superstar. Framing the filmography are the usual biographical essay, a section noting television appearances, unrealized projects, etc. A pleasant, predictable, and expensive book.

2237   *The Films of Robert Altman.* by Karp, Alan. 171 p. illus. Metuchen, N.J.: Scarecrow, 1981.

A critical appreciation of an auteur who insists on involving his audience in his films. Themes such as dreamer vs. realist, the illusion of personal direction of life, etc. are examined.

2238   *The Films of Robert Bresson.* 144 p. illus. New York: Praeger, 1969.

This volume is a compilation of articles about Bresson and his films written by five critics. Following the introductory overview, each film is given a separate chapter of extended analysis and comment. The book is well produced, with interesting visuals to accompany the challenging text, and constitutes a persuasive argument for wider exhibition of the films in the United States, where they are relatively unknown. A thoughtful tribute to a respected director.

2239   *The Films of Robert Redford.* by Spada, James. 256 p. illus. Secaucus, N.J.: Citadel, 1977.

A slight departure from the established *Citadel* format and order can be found here. The text is arranged into four sections: Growing Up Redford; Robert Redford on Broadway; Robert Redford on Television; and Robert Redford on the Big Screen. This latter section reviews Redford's films from WARHUNT (1962) to ALL THE PRESIDENT'S MEN (1976) using casts, credits, stills, synposes, notes, and review excerpts. Concluding the book are A Candid Gallery, A Look into the Future, and A Portrait Gallery.

By the intelligent use of many visuals and an above-average text, the Redford mystique-charisma is partially explained. Certainly the book testifies that the actor has paid his dues. Admirers will be very satisfied but those curious about his tremendous popularity will have to remain so until a more definitive study appears.

2240 *The Films of Robert Redford.* by Castell, David. 47 p. paper illus. London: Barnden Castell Williams, 1974.

In addition to the usual biography, appreciation and filmography, this volume contains sections entitled "Between Takes" (candids), "Leading Ladies" (only five shown), "Redford Talking" (short quotes), and "About Redford" (personality profile). The filmography covers WAR HUNT (1961) to THE GREAT GATSBY (1974). Illustrations are well selected and reproduced. Acceptable.

2241 *The Films of Robert Rossen.* by Casty, Alan. 95 p. illus. New York: Museum of Modern Art, 1969.

The subject of Robert Rossen and his films would seem to deserve a larger treatment than the brief but excellent one offered here. Two sections which make up the book include 1) the usual biographical sketch coupled with an analysis of the films, and 2) a chronological (one film per page) catalog of Rossen's work. Included for each film is a still, and cast and production credits.

The essay portion is well written, but the early Warner's screenplays are given little attention, the emphasis being placed on the later pictures that Rossen directed. Rossen's life, both as an artist and as a man, makes a fascinating story. The treatment offered here is appreciative, understanding and affectionate. Recommended.

2242 *The Films of Robert Taylor.* by Quirk, Lawrence J. 223 p. illus. Secaucus, N.J.: Citadel, 1975.

Robert Taylor died in 1969 after a 35-year career that included 75 films. In this typical *Citadel* series volume, each Taylor film is described by illustrations, cast, credits, plot, review excerpts, etc. The usual biographical sketch precedes the filmography and attention is paid to a few documentary films and some of Taylor's leading ladies.

2243 *The Films of Roddy McDowall.* by Castell, David. unpaginated. paper illus. London: Barnden Castell Williams, 1975.

Here is an unusual paperback devoted to a consistently fine actor whose film work has spanned four decades. His life and career are reviewed in a long essay which is supplemented by an abbreviated filmography—from SCRUFFY (1938) to FUNNY LADY (1975). The many visuals are well selected and adequately reproduced. Acceptable.

2244 *The Films of Roger Corman: Brilliance on a Budget.* by Naha, Ed. 224 p. illus. New York: Arco, 1981.

The first half of this appreciation deals with Corman's life, and contains quotes from his associates. Each of Corman's films is described in the second part. Over 100 illustrations are included.

2245 *The Films of Roger Moore.* by Williams, John. 47 p. paper illus. London: Barnden Castell Williams, 1973.

Roger Moore is known in America primarily as a television actor ("The Persuaders," "Maverick," "The Saint," etc.). He made a few films here in the fifties and then moved into overseas productions. The filmography notes his work from THE LAST TIME I SAW PARIS (1954) to WHO NEEDS FRIENDS? (1975). A biography and an appreciation accompany the many illustrations, all of which appear rather dark and murky. Acceptable.

2246 *The Films of Ronald Colman.* by Quirk, Lawrence J. 255 p. illus. Secaucus, N.J.: Citadel, 1977.

As of the date of this volume, there has been no large scale revival, reevaluation, or retrospective for Ronald Colman's films. It is surprising to find such an above-average tribute appearing in the expensive *Citadel* series. A biographical essay entitled "Ronald Colman: The Man and the Artist" is followed by a listing of his films. The first grouping is his British silents from THE LIVE WIRE (1917) to THE BLACK SPIDER (1920); the second group consists of his American films, HANDCUFFS OR KISSES? (1921) to THE STORY OF MANKIND (1957). For each film there are stills, casts, credits, and comments. A portrait gallery concludes the book.

Readers will be reminded of the distinguished career of an almost forgotten actor by this carefully prepared and well-written tribute.

2247 *The Films of Ronald Reagan.* by Thomas, Tony. 224 p. illus. Secaucus, N.J.: Citadel, 1980.

Ronald Reagan gets the *Citadel* series treatment in this survey of his film career. Each of his films is described by illustrations, credits, casts, plot outlines, review excerpts, etc. Also mentioned is Reagan's work in radio and television. The author is sympathetic and suggests that Reagan's ability as an actor is underrated.

2248   *The Films of Sean Connery.* by Andrews, Emma. 47 p. paper illus. London: Barnden Castell Williams, 1974.

The biography of Sean Connery offered here is quite brief, probably because of his insistence on a private, personal life. An appreciation and a filmography from NO ROAD BACK (1956) to THE MAN WHO WOULD BE KING (1975) complete the short volume. Visuals show the change from a typical film juvenile into a mature character actor. Acceptable.

2249   *The Films of Sherlock Holmes.* by Steinbrunner, Chris; and Michaels, Norman. 253 p. illus. Secaucus, N.J.: Citadel, 1978.

This entry in the *Citadel* series is a bit late in treating its subject, the Sherlock Holmes films. Previously published titles which cover the same material include *Deerstalker, Sherlock Holmes on the Screen,* and *Holmes of the Movies.*

It should be noted that the volume offers a selection and omits many films mentioned in the other books. Illustrations are plentiful and the over-all treatment is diverting.

2250   *The Films of Shirley MacLaine.* by Denis, Christopher. 256 p. illus. Secaucus, N.J.: Citadel, 1981.

2251   *The Films of Shirley Temple.* by Windeler, Robert. 256 p. illus. Secaucus, N.J.: Citadel, 1978.

A very long biographical essay introduces the Temple filmography which begins with a short, WAR BABIES (1932), and ends with A KISS FOR CORLISS (1949). Cast, credits, stills, and comments are given for each film. Her television series, "The Shirley Temple Story Book," also receives attention.

Temple was an American phenomena of the early thirties Depression period, and most of her films have lost their initial charm and interest. The volume will certainly appeal to the Temple buffs and collectors but sociologists and historians might also take a look.

2252   *The Films of Shirley MacLaine.* by Erens, Patricia. 202 p. illus. New York: A.S. Barnes, 1978.

To date Shirley MacLaine has appeared in 29 films and directed one. This volume reviews her work with a particularly appropriate feminist viewpoint. Using both her off-screen activities and her film

roles, the author traces her career from THE TROUBLE WITH HARRY (1955) to THE TURNING POINT (1977). Each film is discussed with elements of plot, background, characterization, critical reception, the MacLaine persona etc. included. A group of well-selected illustrations accompanies the text. Cast and credits for the films are given in an appendix. Chapter notes, a bibliography, and an index are also added.

In attempting something beyond the usual *Films of...* book, Ms. Erens has been quite successful. The concept of paralleling MacLaine's screen image with her public and private life works well. MacLaine is, after all, a colorful and unique female who has proved repeatedly that she is more than a movie star. The book is a fresh look at what has been a remarkable life and career. It will appeal to a wide audience. Acceptable.

2253   *The Films of Sidney Poitier.* by Marill, Alvin H. 224 p. illus. Secaucus, N. J.: Citadel, 1978.

This appreciation of Sidney Poitier runs true to the *Citadel* series. Using stills, casts, credits, synopses, comments and review excerpts, Poitier's feature films are recalled from NO WAY OUT (1950) to A PIECE OF THE ACTION (1978). Other film appearances are noted along with sections about his work in television and the theatre. A biographical essay which introduces the filmography is called "Sidney Poitier: Long Journey From Cat."

The visuals are pleasant but the complex critical evaluation that Poitier's work demands is missing.

2254   *Films of Social Comment.* edited by Graf, Herbert. paper Bonn, Germany: Cultural Program Office of the American Embassy, 1973.

This background material was assembled for a study seminar on social realism and criticism in the American cinema. Films treated include GREED (1923), THE CROWD (1928), MR. SMITH GOES TO WASHINGTON (1939), THE GRAPES OF WRATH (1940), CITIZEN KANE (1941), THE OX BOW INCIDENT (1943), BOOMERANG (1947), REBEL WITHOUT A CAUSE (1955), SHADOWS (1961), etc.

2255   *The Films of Sophia Loren.* by Crawley, Tony. 256 p. illus. Secaucus, N.J.: Citadel, 1976.

This volume in the *Citadel* series is devoted to the films of Sophia Loren from AIDA (1953) to VERDICT (1974). For each film there are stills, cast, credits, plot outline, review excerpts, and selected comments by both the author and Miss Loren. The mandatory biographical essay is included along with many candid photos, portraits, and other visuals.

2256 *The Films of Spencer Tracy.* by Deschner, Donald 255 p. illus. New York: Citadel, 1968.

From apprentice film actor appearing in short subjects in 1930 to a "living legend" status in 1967, Spencer Tracy is described by friends, coworkers, reviewers, and by his own films in this disappointing volume. After approximately 66 pages of redundant tribute, appreciation and textual biography, the films are presented, with little or no consistency. Credits and a short narrative plot synopsis are given for each. Some have articles relating to the film ("My Favorite Movie Scene," by Linda Darnell) others have reprinted reviews. Many of the important films have nothing but plot outline and credits STATE OF THE UNION (1948); ADAMS'S RIB (1949); EDWARD, MY SON (1949), etc.

The reviews and articles are dated; there is no retrospective look at the films and no evaluation or critical discussion by the author is given. Pictures are poorly chosen (where is a shot of Tracy as Mr. Hyde?) and some lack obvious player identification. Production credits are questionable (Fryer and Carr produced THE DESK SET (1957)—it was William Marchant who wrote it). Spencer Tracy and his films deserve better.

2257 *The Films of Stanley Kubrick.* by Devries, Daniel. 75 p. paper Grand Rapids, Mich.: Wm. B. Eerdmans, 1973.

This collection of essays about Kubrick's films notes some common characteristics of his work. The thematic use of visual image, a consistent anti-humanism, and a preference for the stylized rather than the realistic are found in most of his films. However, the films are quite different from each other and the essays deal with that uniqueness. A bibliography and a filmography complete the book. This is interesting, provocative film criticism.

2258 *The Films of Steve McQueen.* by Campbell, Joanna. 47 p. paper illus. London: Barnden Castell Williams, 1973.

The McQueen biography which begins this story is a bit longer than others in the series. It is followed by an appreciation and a filmography—from NEVER LOVE A STRANGER (1957) to PAPILLON (1973). Picture reproduction is mostly above average with only

a few dark, murky shots. Acceptable.

2259 *The Films of Susan Hayward.* by Moreno, Eduardo. 286 p. illus. Secaucus, N.J.: Citadel, 1979.

This title in the *Citadel* series is devoted to the life and career of Susan Hayward. Following a biographical essay, each of her films is described by stills, a plot outline, cast, credits, review excerpts, and comments by Moreno. In addition, other facets of her career—television, stage and modeling—are noted. As usual, the photographs are numerous and add considerably to the quality of the survey.

2260 *The Films of Tennessee Williams.* by Phillips, Gene D. 336 p. illus. Cranbury, N.J.: Art Alliance, 1980.

2261 *The Films of the Fifties.* by Brode, Douglas. 288 p. illus. Secaucus, N.J.: Citadel, 1976.

Although this book is a departure from the usual performer tribute found in the *Citadel* series, it remains essentially a picture book. For the most part the text misses the opportunity to show the reflection of the fifties in films; it rests instead on the casts, credits, plots, illustrations, etc., of 100 films selected by the author. His choices are not always predictable but even the obscure films get a relatively superficial treatment. Other studies of the fifties' films have done it better.

2262 *The Films of the Forties.* by Thomas, Tony. 287 p. illus. Secaucus, N.J.: Citadel, 1975.

In choosing the 100 films for this *Citadel* series book, the author has employed a rigid numerical method: picking ten "most important" films for each year of the decade. As usual, there are casts, credits, plot outlines, comments, illustrations, etc., for each of the 100 films. As a nostalgia picture book, this volume provides a pleasant reminder of the quality of films from that decade.

2263 *Films of the Year, 1927-1928.* by Herring, Robert. 40 p. illus. London: The Studio, 1928.

A review of the year which includes many attractive illustrations.

2264 *Films of the Year 1927-1928.* by Herring, Robert. 40 p. illus. New York: Gordon Press, 1976 (1928).

A record of the year via full page stills, company, cast, director, etc. Along with an introductory essay. Published originally in London by The Studio, Ltd.

2265   *The Films of 20th Century Fox: A Pictorial History.* by Thomas, Tony; and Solomon, Aubrey. 463 p. illus. Secaucus, N.J.: Citadel, 1979.

In what represents a radical departure for the *Citadel* series, a valuable reference book has been produced. Almost double the size of the usual volume, this one is a filmography of the 20th Century Fox Studios from THE LITTLEST REBEL (1935) to THE ROSE (1979). For each title, there is cast, credits, synopsis and historical background given.

Sections on the films produced separately by Fox films and by 20th Century Pictures are also included. Almost 800 illustrations show film scenes, studio sets, actors, etc.

2266   *Films of Tyranny.* by Byrne, Richard B. 152 p. paper illus. Madison, Wisc.: College Printing and Typing Co., 1966.

In this analysis of THE CABINET OF DR. CALIGARI (1919), THE GOLEM (1920), and NOSFERATU (1922), the shots from each film are numbered and named, their lengths are given and their composition is described. The book is illustrated and comes in a looseleaf binder. Most unusual and quite valuable for film study courses.

2267   *The Films of Tyrone Power.* by Belafonte, Dennis; and Marill, Alvin H. 224 p. illus. Secaucus, N.J.: Citadel, 1979.

Director Henry King introduces this volume in the *Citadel* series. Each film is identified by stills, cast, credits, plot synopsis, comments and review excerpts. In addition Power's work in other media is noted. The more than 400 illustrations add more to this film survey than the long introductory biographical chapter.

2268   *The Films of Vincent Price.* by McAsh, Ian F. 47 p. paper illus. London: Barnden Castell Williams, 1974.

The filmography furnished here gives selected credits and casts for Price's films from SERVICE DE LUXE (1938) to PERCY'S PROGRESS (1974). In addition there is the short biographical section and a longer appreciation. Illustrations are mostly of a mature Price in his horror roles—conspicuously missing are any visuals from his early films. Reproduction is adequate. Acceptable.

2269   *The Films of Vincente Minnelli.* edited by Yates, Penny. 40 p. paper New York: Zoetrope.

An anthology with contributions from George Morris, Joel E. Siegel, T.L. French and Penny Yates, this appreciation-evaluation of Vincente Minnelli's career also includes a bibliography and a filmography.

2270   *The Films of W. C. Fields.* by Deschner, Donald. 192 p. illus. New York: Citadel Press, 1966.

In addition to the popularity of its subject, the care and imagination that have gone into the creation of this book are reasons for its best-seller status. It is an excellent example of the picture-text.

Surrounding the films are a short biography, appreciations, articles, and some writings by Fields himself. Each film lists cast, production credits, synopsis and review excerpts. Happily, the emphasis is on the reviews, which have been selected with discrimination. Picture quality is high throughout. The surprising element in this volume is the number of silent films that Fields made. One wishes also that 20th Century Fox would make the deleted sequence from TALES OF MANHATTAN (1942) available for viewing, if only as a TV program.

2271   *The Films of Warren Beatty.* by Quirk, Lawrence J. 222 p. illus. Secaucus, N.J.: Citadel, 1979.

Although Warren Beatty has made only 15 films in the period from 1961 to 1979, he enjoys the status of a major film star. In this typical *Citadel* series survey, each of the films is described by stills, plot synopsis, cast, credits, review excerpts, and background information. Preceding the filmography is a biographical section. Illustrations are plentiful but the text lacks any in-depth critical analysis of the films or any new information about Beatty.

2272   *The Films of William Holden.* by Quirk, Lawrence J. 255 p. illus. Secaucus, N.J.: Citadel, 1973.

A heavily illustrated essay opens this volume; it is entitled "William Holden: His Life and Work," and the emphasis is on the work. Immediately following is the filmography of almost 60 films from GOLDEN BOY (1939) to BREEZY (1973). For each, cast, credits, some critical notes and review excerpts are given, along with representative stills. Picture reproduction is acceptable and the background material supplied by author Quirk is above the average found in this series. Acceptable.

2273 *The Films of World War II.* by Morella, Joe; and Epstein, Edward Z.; and Griggs, John. 254 p. illus. Secaucus, N.J.: Citadel, 1973.

A collection of nearly 100 feature films made from 1937 to 1946 is given the *Citadel* treatment here—cast, credits, synopsis, critical comments, and stills. After a brief introduction by Judith Crist, a few pre-war films are noted—CONFESSIONS OF A NAZI SPY (1939), FOREIGN CORRESPONDENT (1940), THE GREAT DICTATOR (1940), MAN HUNT (1941), etc. The remaining films deal more directly with American participation in World War II. It should be emphasized that the films are selected rather than all-inclusive and it is not surprising to find some unexpected appearances—THANK YOUR LUCKY STARS (1943), THE DOUGH GIRLS (1944), YANKEE DOODLE DANDY (1942), and some strange absences, e.g., THIS ABOVE ALL (1942).

Picture quality is acceptable and the book has some nostalgia value. However, the subject of war films has been handled in greater depth in less expensive volumes. Acceptable.

2274 *Films on Art.* compiled by The Canadian Centre for Films on Art for the American Federation of Arts. 220 p. New York: Watson-Guptill, 1977.

Over 450 short films on the arts of painting, sculpture, prints, drawing, photography, architecture and archeology are described in this update of an original 1952 publication. For each film, the title, running time, color, guage, country of origin, date, producer, credits, summary and distribution data are given. Films are arranged alphabetically by title and additional access is provided by a subject index, an artist index, and an expanded title index which includes individual titles from series entries. Inclusion in this list was determined by a film's quality and suitability so that, in a sense, these are "recommended" films. No individual evaluations are given.

Since the criteria of access, need, presentation and selection are met so thoroughly by this excellent volume, it is highly recommended for reference and for those who are concerned with education in any of the arts noted above.

2275 *Films on Art.* edited by Eaton, Katherine. 62 p., 84 p. paper illus. Ottawa: Canadian Centre for Films on Art, 1968, 1973.

Two catalogs (numbers 8 and 10, which are revisions of numbers 1 and 3) that contain some 1154 films on art found in film collections of the Canadian Film Institute, the National Film Board of Canada and the Canadian Diplomatic Mission. Films are arranged by title, by subject (leather, painting, drawing, sculpture, etc.), and by artist name.

2276 *Films on Art—Panorama 1953.* by Bolen, Francis. 80 p. paper illus. Paris: UNESCO, 1953.

2277 *Films on Death and Dying.* by Mason, Edward. unpaginated. paper New York: Educational Film Library Association, 1973.

This EFLA Supplement is a filmography about death and dying prepared by Doctor Edward Mason. In addition to a critical discussion of 40 films, the usual descriptive data, running time, date, distributor, etc., is included. Other Supplements treat War and Peace, Minority Films in New York, Movies about Movies, Films for Now, Man and His Environment, and Alternatives. All are valuable aids for institutions offering film programs.

2278 *Films on Film History.* by Slide, Anthony. 234 p. Metuchen, N.J.: Scarecrow, 1979.

This filmography deals with the history of the cinema and includes all film forms: documentaries, features, shorts, compilations, etc. It excludes films on the creation of a specific production or filmmaking in general.

The films are arranged alphabetically by title, with each entry offering the usual data (producer, date, time, format, etc.) and, thankfully, an original annotation by Slide. The author is a highly regarded film historian and his assessments of the films are both informative and entertaining. A subject index and a distributor list complete the book. It should be noted that many of the films are listed as "not available." The use of some others in film study courses is debatable; romanticizing, fictionalizing, distorting, and minimizing the historical truth in them was a usual procedure. However, Slide's treatment makes this volume as much an entertainment as a reference.

2279 *Films on Music.* compiled by Canadian Film Institute. 33 p. paper Ottawa: Canadian Film Institute, 1960.

2280 *Films on Offer.* paper London: British Film Institute, 1970- .

An annual catalog containing a selection of rental films available from the Central Booking Agency of the BFI. Contains distributor information.

2281 *Films on the Campus: Cinema Production in Colleges and Universities.* by Fensch, Thomas. 534 p. illus. New York: A. S. Barnes, 1970.

This book surveys campus filmmaking by looking at representative programs given by colleges in three regions of the United States—east coast, west coast, and midwest. Described are the courses, professors, philosophies, and films that are part of each university's program. Several sample scripts are reprinted.

The text and the many fine illustrations present to the reader a cross-section of student filmmaking. It should serve as a guide and an inspiration for those institutions which are beginning film studies or even considering them. In addition, the book is most valuable for students looking for a college which offers programs in films.

In spite of all its virtues and possible uses, the book is not totally satisfying. At times it reads like a precis of college catalogs; at other times it is most critical in its evaluations and comments. This book is not the last word on this subject, but presently the only one. Recommended on that basis.

2282 *Films on the Earth Sciences.* compiled by Canadian Film Institute. 153 p. paper Ottawa: The National Science Film Library, 1971.

A catalog that uses the Dewey classification to arrange its films under headings such as astronomy, physics, chemistry, geology, health, engineering, mining, hydraulics, public health, transportation, etc. For each there is a description and the suggested audience. Films are also listed under a title index.

2283 *Films on the Performing Arts.* 24 p. paper Ottawa: National Arts Centre, 1968.

This example of a Canadian bilingual film catalog offers a subject listing of titles followed by the main entries arranged alphabetically by title. There is also an alphabetical listing of titles available from di-

plomatic missions in Canada. A combined title index concludes the catalog. Reversed and starting from the back cover, the identical material is presented in the French language.

The listing is an older one, but does include many films still in print. Major subjects include dance, drama, music, opera, festivals, marionettes, puppets, community arts, community cultural centers, and National Film Board of Canada films.

2284 *Films on Traditional Music and Dance: A First International Catalogue.* edited by Kennedy, Peter. 261 p. paper illus. New York: Unipub, 1970.

One hundred countries are represented in this filmography which covers folk dance, song, and instrumental music. Films arc arranged under the country of origin and are described by title, type of film, time, characteristics, producer, director, distributor, and synopsis. Selection of the films was made by The International Folk Music Council.

2285 *Films on TV.* by Buscombe, Edward. 64 p. paper London: Society for Education in Film and Television.

Called "Screen Pamphlet 1," this is a UNESCO report that deals with (1) The Transmission of Cinematographic Films on TV, and (2) TV Programmes About the Cinema in the United Kingdom and Eire. Conclusions, a summary of the recommendations, and an appendix are included.

2286 *Films on War and American Policy.* by Cochran, Blake. 63 p. paper Washington, D.C.: American Council on Education, 1940.

A filmography designed for wartime's eve in the United States.

2287 *Films Relating to Communism.* edited by Cook, James A. 418 p. paper Los Angeles: Research Institute on Communist Strategy and Propaganda, University of Southern California, 1965.

This is an annotated survey of 1000 films relating to Communism. Film data is given, but no critical evaluations are provided. Also included are a subject index, an alphabetical title index, and a directory of sources.

2288 *Films since 1939.* by Powell, Dilys. 40 p. paper illus. London: Longmans Green & Co., (The British Council), 1947.

This short essay is an account of all the important film work, both documentary and feature, done in Britain from 1939 to 1945. Attention is given to the filmmakers rising to prominence at this time—David Lean, Carol Reed, etc. This small volume has importance since it covers the opening chapter of a golden period of motion-picture making in Britain. Not for the casual reader but a fine reference for the scholar or historian.

2289 *Films Suitable for Children.* compiled by National Library of Australia. 41 p. paper Canberra, Australia: National Library, 1965.

2290 *Films—Too Good for Words.* by Parlato, Salvatore J., Jr. 209 p. New York: R. R. Bowker, 1973.

The subtitle to this reference book is "A Directory of Non-Narrated 16mm Films." Using a broad classification scheme involving 13 categories, the author has described nearly 1000 films. For example, the 150 titles placed under "The Arts" are listed alphabetically by title. A description of the film follows, but there is no evaluation and the author warns that inclusion in this book is not to be interpreted as endorsement. Distributor name, running time, color or black and white, and release date are given. A few silent films are noted, but most are sound. A second section indexes all the films alphabetically by title, while the next section attempts a subject index. Finally a producer/distributor directory is offered.

While this reference has some small value in the selection of films for possible use, much of the same information can be obtained with evaluations elsewhere. A film user glancing at the total group will wonder about the criteria for inclusion in this book. Is it nonnarration? If so, one could probably compile any number of similar groupings from a collection of producer catalogs. A limited reference that is acceptable only when the reservations above are noted.

2291 *The Films You Don't See on Television.* by Schlossheimer, Michael. 177 p. New York: Vantage Press, 1979.

Many fondly remembered films have never been shown on television. The many diverse reasons for this are discussed in this unusual volume. By devoting a chapter to each of the major studios, along with one for the independent studios, the author discusses specific films and tells why they have never appeared on television. Usually the reason has to do with author rights, remakes, copyright, personal ownership, censorship, "lost" films, etc. A selected filmography and a general index complete the book.

Here is a new topic in film literature — important and in need of some attention. The author provides an overview that is a bit simplistic at times but never less than interesting. Film buffs and collectors will find it most rewarding reading.

2292 *The Filmviewer's Handbook.* by McAnany, Emile G.; and Williams, Robert. 208 p. paper Glen Rock, N.J.: Paulist Press, 1965.

A compilation of topics for those interested in film showing in schools, libraries, churches, etc. Contains a short history of film, the language of film, the film society, the film series or program, organization of a film society, important directors and their films, and a bibliography. Although the book tries to cover too much, there is still a great amount of valuable information offered to the reader.

2293 *Final Cut—The Making and Breaking of a Film.* by Sylbert, Paul. 243 p. New York: Seabury Press, 1974.

The film referred to in the subtitle of this book is THE STEAGLE (1971) and its creation is described and deplored herein by its director. During a two-year period, the difficulties, problems and successes in the production of a film are noted. The author has written a cynical, blistering, negative account which he admits is a catharsis. As presented, his case is as sympathetic and persuasive as it is devastating, witty and sharp-edged. Other than himself and star Richard Benjamin, there are mostly villains in this recital —Embassy-Avco mogul Joseph E. Levine and Executive Producer Frank P. Rosenberg are the major ones with some unnamed assistant directors, actresses, editors, and others rounding out the enemy forces.

The disillusionment inherent in not having the right of final cut and the constant humiliating compromises necessary to make the film are emphasized. The final film was quickly dismissed by press and public after emasculation by the studio. The account of its creation and ultimate destruction is one of the best reports on the making of a specific film that have been published. Highly recommended.

2294 *Financial Characteristics of Selected "B" Film Productions of Albert J. Cohen, 1951-1957.* by Vincent, Richard. New York: Arno, 1980.

Using the files of Albert J. Cohen, the volume examines the background, preparation, financing and final cost of ten films. A title in the *Dissertations on Film* series.

2295 *Finch, Bloody Finch: A Life of Peter Finch.* by Dundy, Elaine. 352 p. illus. New York: Holt, Rinehart & Winston, 1980.

This is a workmanlike biography of Peter Finch written by the author of *The Dud Avocado*. Carefully researched, Finch's life from a difficult childhood and adolescence in Australia to world celebrity is told in an unobtrusive style that easily accommodates the moods, vagaries, and fortunes of the subject. Peter Finch was brilliant, erratic, talented and troubled—a man of dedication, passion and ambition who, at times, was irritatingly self-indulgent and weak. Dundy catches all this and much more in her sensitive depiction of this fine actor. Photographs, a filmography, and an index round out the book.

Because of the high level of research, interpretation, and writing found here, this volume provides a very satisfying study of Peter Finch. It will please the large audience who appreciated the actor's film performances.

2296 *Finchy.* by Finch, Yolande. 224 p. illus. New York: Simon and Schuster, 1981.

An acid portrait of Peter Finch by an ex-wife is subordinated to a boring autobiographical recall of the author's love affairs.

2297 *Finding Marilyn: A Romance.* by Conover, David. 200 p. illus. New York: Grosset and Dunlap, 1981.

An illustrated account of a long friendship between the author and Marilyn Monroe. He believes she was murdered and argues to reopen the case of her death.

2298 *A Fine Mess!* edited by Anobile, Richard. 256 p. illus. New York: Crown, 1975.

This is the sixth volume in a successful series, *The Visual Gems of...*, edited by Anobile, who is the pioneer in the frame-enlargement technique for reproducing films in book form. In this instance he has provided over 1000 frame blowups from a compilation film, THE CRAZY WORLD OF LAUREL AND HARDY (1965), which in turn was composed of moments from more than 50 original Laurel and Hardy films. Although the compilation used many silent films, only sound films appear here. They include: GOING BYE BYE (1934), SWISS MISS (1938), THE MUSIC BOX (1932), TOWED IN A HOLE (1932) and BUSY BODIES (1933). The original dialogue, which was minimal, has been placed with the appropriate frames. Picture reproduction is acceptable and often impressive, when the amount of physicalaction involved in these excerpts is considered. This is another series volume which will please a wide range of readers. It is highly recommended.

2299 FINIAN'S RAINBOW. by Sloane, Burt. 48 p. paper illus. New York: National Publishers, 1968.

Two background articles introduce this souvenir book: "The Fanciful Joy of Finian's World: How It All Came to Be," and "Touching Finian's Magic to the Screen." Small illustrations from the 1968 film are used rather ineffectively throughout. Single pages are given to Fred Astaire, Petula Clark and Tommy Steele, with similar attention to producer Joseph Landon and director Francis Ford Coppola. Flat and unsatisfying—just like the film.

2300 *Finnish Cinema.* by Cowie, Peter. 128 p. illus. New York: A.S. Barnes, 1976.

This survey, sponsored by the Finnish Film Foundation, is concerned mostly with trends and achievements. Since 1907 only a few hundred films have been made in Finland and only a fraction of those survive. This volume is based upon research, interviews and a viewing of 60 or so films. Cowie begins historically, then devotes a chapter to Nyrki Tapiovaara, an early director whose limited work has had a great influence on current filmmakers. Recurring themes such as the memories of war and the pastoral tradition are discussed. Later sections of the book are concerned with both the older directors and the new wave. Filmographies, a bibliography, and a title index complete the survey. Illustrations in a volume such as this are most important since they give the reader visual clues to the films being discussed. In this book they have been well selected and clearly reproduced.

An important though specialized volume. Recommended.

2301 *Fire from the Flint: The Amazing Careers of Thomas Dixon.* by Cook, Raymond Allen. 255 p. illus. Winston-Salem, N.C.: John F. Blair,

1968.

This is a biography of the author of *The Clansman* the book upon which THE BIRTH OF A NATION (1915) was based. Scant attention is given to D. W. Griffith here. Other than for some slight background history, this volume has little cinema study value.

2302   *The First Colour Motion Pictures.* by Thomas, David B. 44 p. paper illus. London: H. M. Stationery Office, 1969.

This Science Museum monograph deals with the history of color cinematography, and includes a bibliography.

2303   *see   2302*

2304   *The First Freedom.* by Ernst, Morris L. 316 p. New York: Macmillan, 1946.

This Ernst volume on censorship has one section on film in addition to those on radio, press, etc. Its theme is the impending loss of freedom of expression in the mass media and it is loaded with statistics, arguments, warnings and sound advice.

2305   *The First One Hundred Noted Men and Women of the Screen.* by Lowrey, Carolyn. 201 p. illus. New York: Moffat, Yard, 1920.

Included among the 100 subjects are performers, directors and writers who were famous during the early silent screen days. Each is given a page of biography and a full-page portrait.

2306   *The First Quarter Century of the Motion Picture Theatre.* by Kerr, Eleanor. 11 p. paper New York: Potter, 1940.

2307   *The First Time.* by Fleming, Karl; and Fleming, Anne Taylor. 288 p. paper New York: Berkley, 1975.

This anthology of confessions deals with sex initiation and deflowering. Twenty-eight male and female celebrities recall their first sexual experiences in short memoirs that are alternately humorous, touching, frank and intimate. The film personalities include Dyan Cannon, Joseph Cotten, Sally Kellerman, Jack Lemmon, Debbie Reynolds, Rudy Vallee, and Mae West.

This report on American sexual behavior is unusual.

Other than some four letter words which are used with regularity, the text is not as scandalous as the description above might suggest.

2308   *The First Twenty Years: A Segment of Film History.* by Niver, Kemp R. 176 p. illus. Los Angeles: Locare Research Group, 1968.

Another outstanding contribution to film history by Niver, this is a consideration of over 100 short films made between 1894 FRED OTT'S SNEEZE and 1913 Griffith's WAR OF THE PRIMAL TRIBES. Selected because of their uniqueness in theme or technique, the films provide much to attract the historian, the student, and others.

2309   *The First Whole Library Catalog.* edited by Films, Inc. Staff. 96 p. paper illus. Wilmette, Ind.: Films, Inc., 1973.

The stated purpose of this book is "to function as a source of films, film presentation equipment, and film books and magazines for libraries." For the first time a major film distributor has noted in this mass-produced catalog certain feature films available on a five-year lease. Titles such as CITIZEN KANE (1941), KING KONG (1933), FUNNY FACE (1957), and THE GRAPES OF WRATH (1940) are among those available under this arrangement. Other films are described by words and visuals and there are valuable suggestions for programming and use. The books mentioned tend to reflect one distributor and are limited to popular titles.

This oversized volume, patterned after *The Whole Earth Catalog*, will have a wide appeal; there is something for teachers, librarians, film buffs, browsers, etc., in this well-produced catalog. Its visuals have been carefully selected with a variety of stills, sketches, drawings, cartoons, etc., placed appropriately throughout. A programming index and a title index are also supplied. Highly recommended.

2310   *Fit for the Chase.* by Lee, Raymond. 237 p. illus. New York: A. S. Barnes, 1969.

A chronicle of the automobiles that have figured in the plots of many films. This book is obviously quite specialized.

2311   *Five Ages of the Cinema.* by Tarbox, Charles H. 90 p. Smithtown, N.Y.: Exposition, 1980.

A comprehensive overview of the motion picture

industry with a center section of rare photographs. The author is a veteran in the distribution of films.

2312   *The Five C's of Cinematography.* by Mascelli, Joseph E. 250 p. illus. Hollywood: Cine/Graphics Publications, 1965.

If there is a classic volume on motion picutre filming techniques, this is probably it. By using five headings— camera angles, continuity, cutting, close-ups, and composition—the author covers the basic information that any moviemaker needs. It is concise, informative, well-illustrated, and offers many placement diagrams. The approach is practical and down-to-earth, which makes possible the understanding of a technical-artistc process. The edition examined was in its fourth printing and indicates 20,000 copies within five years. This may be interpreted as rare popularity for a not-inexpensive technical volume.

2313   *The Five Lives of Ben Hecht.* by Fetherling, Doug. 228 p. New York :Zoetrope, 1977.

In this terse, almost short, biography, Doug Fetherling gives the reader a full portrait of Ben Hecht. Not only do Hecht's personality, appearance, attitudes, and habits come under scrutiny, but examples from his body of work (more than 30 books and 70 films) are critically examined. Supporting this thoughtful study are a bibliography and a filmography along with a list of sources and an index.

2314   *Five Screenplays.* by Pinter, Harold. 367 p. London: Methuen & Co. Ltd., 1971.

Contains scripts of THE SERVANT (1963), THE PUMP-KIN EATER (1964), THE QUILLER MEMORANDUM (1966), ACCIDENT (1967), THE GO-BETWEEN (1971). Only casts and director are given.

2315   *Flashback: An Autobiography of a British Film Maker.* by Pearson, George. 236 p. illus. London: Allen & Unwin, 1957.

This autobiography tells of an educator who became a filmmaker and eventually combined the two vocations in his final years. During the period from 1912 to 1937, Pearson was engaged largely in directing silent and sound feature pictures. His later work was in the short documentary field. His last responsiblity was the training of technicians from all parts of the British Commonwealth.

The interest that this book has for the modern reader stems from its portrait of the infant film industry in Britain. Written with affection and respect, the book is a serious attempt to describe and evaluate a career in filmmaking. The author's style is persuasive and the illustrations are fine. This volume will probably be of very limited interest to most.

2316   *Flashback: Nora Johnson on Nunnally Johnson.* by Johnson, Nora. 407p. illus. New York: Doubleday, 1979.

In one sense this is a dual biography; telling about her screenwriter father has provided the author with a vehicle for her own memoirs. Nunnally Johnson had an eventful life with three wives, five children, a long tenure at 20th Century Fox as writer-producer-director, and painful oblivion brought on by the new Hollywood breeds. Any portrait of a father by a daughter is inevitably bittersweet. The pair's letters, meetings, family life, working arrangements all serve to underline this precarious and complex relationship.

Nora Johnson's portrait of her father and his milieu is emotional and hardly objective, but it does present another view of the creative artist in Hollywood. It is a valuable addition to that body of film literature written by the children of filmmakers.

Illustrations and an index accompany the text. It might be noted that Nora Johnson also wrote *The World of Henry Orient* and collaborated with her father on the screenplay of her book. He later produced a stage musical of the same story.

2317   *Flashbacks.* by Tobias, Mel C. illus. Hong Kong: Gulliver, 1980.

An outsized book that deals in detail with the film industry of Hong Kong, this volume is heavily illustrated. Much attention is given to Bruce Lee and the many spin-offs of his Kung Fu films.

2318   *A Flask of Fields.* edited by Anobile, Richard J. 272 p. illus. New York: Norton (Darien House), 1972.

The format of this volume is the same as that of Anobile's *Why A Duck?* and *Who's on First?*. Frames from 10 films made for Paramount and Universal are used along with script dialogue to provide the "verbal and visual gems of W. C. Fields." An introduction by Judith Crist sets the stage for the print recreation of some of Fields' better film moments. The illustrations are acceptable and help to recapture some of the special quality of Fields' humor. Not essential but a pleasant entertainment.

2319 FLAVIO. by Schreivogel, Paul A. 20 p. paper illus. Dayton, Ohio: Pflaum, 1970.

A study guide for the 1964 film directed by Gordon Parks.

2320 *The Fleisher Story.* by Cabarga, Leslie. 184 p. illus. New York: Nostalgia Press, 1976.

The Fleisher brothers, Max and Dave, founded an animation studio from which came the cartoons of Koko, The Bouncing Ball, Betty Boop, Popeye, and Superman, among others. In addition to the hundreds of short animated films they produced, the Fleisher brothers made two features—GULLIVER'S TRAVELS (1939) and MR. BUG GOES TO TOWN (1941). Their invention of several devices used in the animation process was almost inevitable since they were pioneers already at work in 1915. This volume details their personal and professional history including their long relationship with Paramount Pictures.

The volume has as its outstanding feature over 300 illustrations which include a wide range of visual material—drawings, frame enlargements, photographs, advertisements, background drawings, model charts, a flip book, diagrams, and comic strips. Although reproduction quality varies considerably, the visuals are totally fascinating and complement the author's detailed narrative in excellent fashion. The absence of an index is a disservice to this carefully prepared text-and-picture book. A filmography is included.

More than just a nostalgia trip, this eye-catching volume combines history, technology, personal drama and visual delights to provide a rich entertainment. Young people will love this one and so will their elders. Recommended.

2321 *Flesh and Fantasy.* by Stallings, Penny; and Mandelbaum, Howard. 288 p. illus. New York: St. Martins, 1978.

The Old Hollywood is revived with illustrations, innuendo, gossip, rumor, scandal and, on occasion, truth in this glorified trip down memory lane. Typical topics include multi-marriage, facial surgery, toupees, bosoms (real and false), film roman-a-clefs, original castings that did not materialize, quizzes, games, feuds, etc. More than 1000 photographs supplement the text, which includes most of the names associated with Hollywood's Golden Years.

2322 *The Flick and I.* by Batschelet, Ralph J. 176 p. Hicksville, N.Y.: Ex-

position, 1981.

2323 *The Flicks or Whatever Became of Andy Hardy.* by Champlin, Charles. 277 p. illus. Pasadena, Calif.: Ward Ritchie, 1977.

Charles Champlin is a well-known and highly respected film writer who is quite unlike most of his critic contemporaries. He writes with concern and objectivity, avoiding excesses in both words and feelings. Here he is concerned with the recent evolution of movies as reflected by their content, audiences, stars, and directors.

Following a short history, the text concentrates on the last three decades of film production. With the help of many well-chosen illustrations, Champlin identifies those films which are reflections of the changing society and times during which they were made. Reading the text is a pleasurable experience that will recall the many fine films that have appeared in the last 30 years. A bibliography and an index are provided. Highly recommended.

2324 *Flight 777.* by Colvin, Ian G. 212 p. illus. London: Evans, 1957.

This volume concerns itself with the death of Leslie Howard. A plane in which he was traveling was shot down on a flight from Lisbon to London during World War II. The rumor exists that Howard's flight was used as a blind for Winston Churchill who was also flying that day.

2325 *Flora Robson.* by Dunbar, Janet. 276 p. illus. London: George G. Harrap, 1960.

Although many of her films are mentioned in this authorized biography of the English actress, the emphasis is on theatrical roles that she created on the London stage. The text is affectionate, respectful, and rather mild. A helpful index is included in which the Robson films are differentiated from the plays.

2326 *Florence Desmond by Herself.* by Desmond, Florence. 303 p. illus. London: George G. Harrap, 1953.

Florence Desmond was an actress-impressionist-impersonator who appeared in many revues on the London stage. Her work in motion pictures is confined to a few British films made from the thirties to the fifties. She can be seen in THREE CAME HOME (1950), made by a Hollywood studio.

2327 *Florida and the American Motion Picture Industry, 1898-1980.* by Nelson, Richard Alan. 2 volumes, 798 p. New York: Garland, 1982.

A title in the *Dissertations on Film* series.

2328 *Focal Cinebooks (A Series).* paper illus. London and New York: Focal Press, 1950- .

This series of books is devoted to amateur filmmaking and covers a range of activities. Many of the books first appeared in the early fifties and have been reprinted since in newer, revised editions, as many as ten times.

Titles include: *How to Act, How to Add Sound, How to Animate Cut-Outs, How to Cartoon, How to Choose Music, How to Direct, How to Do Tricks, How to Do the Simpler Tricks, How to Edit, How to Film, How to Film Children, How to Film Indoors, How to Make Cine Gadgets, How to Make 8mm Films, How to Make Films at School, How to Make Holiday Films, How to Plan Your 8mm Films, How to Process Substandard Film, How to Produce Magnetic Sound, How to Project Substandard Film, How to Title, How to Use Colour, How to Use 8mm at Work, How to Write Film Stories.*

2329 *The Focal Encyclopedia of Film and Television Techniques.* edited by Spottiswoode, Raymond. 1124 p. illus. New York: Hastings House, 1969.

This is the giant of all books on film and television technique—its size, wide range, and high price qualify it for the title. With Spottiswoode as general editor, its excellence is no surprise. Divided into a preface, some 1600 entries, and a survey-guide to the entries, this book is the result of the efforts of approximately 100 authors . For persons who deal with the technical portions of filmmaking or TV, this book is an essential.

2330 *The Focal Encyclopedia of Photography.* 1696 p. illus. New York: McGraw-Hill, 1969.

There are 2400 separate entries in the 11th edition of this reference work. More than 1700 illustrations help to make this volume an essential in any collection.

2331 *The Focalguide to Editing Super 8.* by Copestake, Tim. 192 p. paper illus. New York: Focal.

A title in the *Focalguide* series, this book describes the equipment and techniques the amateur filmmaker can use in editing Super 8 film. The book contains a clear, terse text along with many diagrams and illustrations.

2332 *The Focalguide to Movie Titling.* by Jenkins, Philip. 216 p. paper illus. New York: Focal.

The high level of production and writing found in the *Focalguide* series is continued here. Using a clearly written text along with many helpful diagrams and illustrations, the volume guides the reader through techniques of movie titling. Fades, dissolves, superimpositions, animation, lighting, etc., are discussed.

2333 *The Focalguide to Moviemaking.* by Petzold, Paul. 224 p. paper illus. New York: Focal.

All of the stages of amateur filmmaking—scripting, equipment, shooting, editing, exhibiting, etc.—are treated in this volume, a title in the excellent *Focalguide* series. As usual the text, diagrams and illustrations are outstanding.

2334 *The Focalguide to Shooting Animation.* by Perisic, Zoran. 224 p. paper illus. New York: Focal, 1978.

Various techniques for creating animated films are explained in this concise, impressive volume. Using a clear text and lots of helpful diagrams, the book leads the reader through such topics as registration, pegbar use, strobing, polarizing, etc. The vocabulary of animation is introduced and there are many photographs to supplement the text. A welcome addition to the *Focalguide* series.

2335 *Focus on ... (A Series).* edited by Gottesman, Ronald; and Geduld, Harry. paper illus. Englewood Cliffs, N.J.: Prentice-Hall, 1972- .

This fine series of books concentrates predominately on individual films, directors and genres. Usually there are an introduction, essays, reviews, script excerpts, illustrations, a filmography and a bibliography, but individual books may vary somewhat. When used in connection with film showings or film study, they can serve as enrichment, reference, and recreational reading.

The titles include *Focus on* THE BIRTH OF A NATION; *Focus on* BLOW-UP; *Focus on* BONNIE AND CLYDE; *Focus on Chaplin; Focus on* CITIZEN KANE; *Focus on Godard; Focus on D. W. Griffith; Focus on Howard*

Hawks; Focus on Hitchcock; Focus on The Horror Film; Focus on RASHOMON; *Focus on The Science Fiction Film; Focus on* THE SEVENTH SEAL; *Focus on Shakespearean Films; Focus on* SHOOT THE PIANO PLAYER.

2336 *Focus on* BLOW-UP. edited by Huss, Roy. 171 p. paper illus. Englewood Cliffs, N.J.: Prentice-Hall, 1971.

There are three introductory pieces about Antonioni and BLOW-UP (1966) that provide a base for the material that follows. Six original reviews are followed by seven essays which interpret, evaluate, and discuss this controversial film. A synopsis and outline, a shot analysis of three important sequences, a filmography and a bibliography complete the book. In the appendix one finds the short story by Julio Cortazar upon which the film was based and an article telling of its adaptation. There is one center section containing a few stills which are nicely reproduced.

Since BLOW-UP received a mixed critical reaction on its first appearance, it is not surprising to find some of the contributors here addressing themselves to the topic of critical responsibility. Other aspects of the film, its reception, its importance and its director are treated. Selection of the articles is fine and the format of this series applies beautifully to this particular film. Highly recommended.

2337 *Focus on* BONNIE AND CLYDE. edited by Cawelti, John G. 176 p. paper illus. Englewood Cliffs, N.J.: Prentice-Hall, 1973.

This anthology has more to recommend it than does the higher priced *The Bonnie and Clyde Book*. It includes an interview with director Arthur Penn, original reviews, essays, some original articles by the real life participants, a script extract, and some changes and revisions of the original script. Supporting these elements are a Penn filmography, a bibliography, an index and a few illustrations.

While all the materials are worthy of inclusion, the outstanding article is the anlysis by the author entitled "The Artistic Power of BONNIE AND CLYDE." Since he had access to Penn's script and obviously studied it in detail, his understanding and interpretation of the film is impressive. The section on changes and revisions is a result of access to the script. This volume on BONNIE AND CLYDE (1967) is the superior, and less expensive one, and is highly recommended.

2338 *Focus on Chaplin.* edited by McCaffrey, Donald W. 174 p. paper illus. Englewood Cliffs, N.J.: Prentice-Hall, 1971.

After a short introduction, the editor divides his selections into four groups: career, working method, essays, and reviews. Five articles in the career-method sections are by Chaplin himself. The reviews range from the early films to the mini-features, THE KID (1920), THE PILGRIM (1923), and to the classic features, THE GOLD RUSH (1924), THE CIRCUS (1928), CITY LIGHTS (1931), MODERN TIMES (1936), THE GREAT DICTATOR (1940), MONSIEUR VERDOUX (1947), and LIMELIGHT (1952). Short excerpts from THE KID, SHOULDER ARMS (1918), and MODERN TIMES are included, with a Chaplin filmography, a bibliography and an index. The illustrations used in the centerfold are familiar and not reproduced well.

Since there is so much material available on Chaplin, any new volume must offer something not easily available elsewhere. By its inclusion of the reviews, the original Chaplin articles, and the script excerpts, this book merits attention. Recommended.

2339 *Focus on* CITIZEN KANE. edited by Gottesman, Ronald. 178 p. paper illus. Englewood Cliffs, N.J.: Prentice-Hall, 1971.

This is a new volume in the *Spectrum* Series that is quite unique in its design. The subject is CITIZEN KANE (1941) and logically much of the book is by and about Welles—including interviews, essays, and commentaries. There are also original reviews of thefilm, as well as statements by the film's composer and its cameraman. Further commentaries are given by Bazin, Truffaut, Higham and others. The final section contains a plot outline, a content outline, a script excerpt, a filmography, a bibliography and an index. The illustrations are fine. The concept, design, selection, and execution by the editor and by the publisher of this volume are totally commendable. At last here is concrete evidence at least one motion picture is recognized as being equal in importance to a classic of the written word.

2340 *Focus on D. W. Griffith.* edited by Geduld, Harry. 182 p. paper illus. Englewood Cliffs, N.J.: Prentice-Hall, 1971.

A major portion of this book is devoted to the writings of D. W. Griffith. Essays on his films and his artistry provide the remainder. A filmography, bibliography, an index, and a few stills complete the book.

Geduld has performed a service for the reader in gathering the original Griffith pieces. Together with the biographical articles that introduce the book, and the critical essay that completes it, they contribute much to solving the enigma that was Griffith. Perhaps the weakest portion is the collection of visuals. They are all familiar, the reproduction is only fair, and they are too few in number to add any great dimension to the portrait. Contributing authors, other than Griffith, include Lillian Gish, Linda Arvidson, A. Nicholas Vardac, Lewis Jacobs, Jay Leyda, and Erich von Stroheim. The bibliography is lengthy and annotated.

With all the recent print attention directed toward Griffith, it is rewarding to discover a fine volume such as this in the group. Whether for film study, research, general reading, or simple entertainment, this book can be highly recommended.

2341   *Focus on Film and Theatre.* edited by Hurt, James. 188 p. paper illus. Englewood Cliffs, N.J.: Prentice-Hall, 1974.

The relationships of film and theatre are explored in this excellent anthology. Following an introduction by Hurt, the articles are divided into two categories. In the first part, five critics, from Vachel Lindsay in 1915 to Stanley Kauffmann in 1972, provide a historical coverage of the topic. The second section contains articles by actors, directors, and playwrights who have worked in both media. The relationships of theatre and film are not fixed but constantly changing. This collection describes their evolution.

A small collection of photographs attempts an impossible task—to contrast visually stage and screen productions of the same vehicle. Both the filmography and the bibliography provided are selective. The book is indexed. Recommended.

2342   *Focus on Films.* by Le Harivel, J. P. 90 p. paper London: C. A. Watts & Co ., 1952.

A series of short chapters written by a British filmmaker about various aspects of the medium and the industry, this volume is quite dated in many instances. Some history, sociology, commerce, aesthetics, and prognostication are offered. The paperback examined was a rather poor physical production. There are no illustrations and no index. A short bibliography is given.

Many of the author's predictions on such topics as motion picture attendance, television competition, and the future of the musical film have not come true. Yet, other observations made about two

decades ago are quite valid. It should be emphasized that most of the material is based on the film in Britain.

2343   *Focus on Godard.* edited by Brown, Royal S. 190 p. paper illus. Englewood Cliffs, N.J.: Prentice-Hall, 1972.

A series of interviews with Godard, accompanied by one with a continuity girl and another with the Dziga-Vertov Group and followed by reviews, essays, and commentaries. Of all the New Wave directors, probably Godard has received the most attention,both in print and out. This collection of articles is sufficiently wide so that the reader will receive a sound introduction to this important New Wave director, his films and the controversy they have caused.

An unusually detailed filmography, a bibliography, and an index support the articles. The few illustrations used in the centerfold are well selected and reproduced. As an introductory study of Godard and his films, this volume is quite good. The collection of interviews alone is a unique feature; when added to the other elements, it contributes much to the picture of Godard. Recommended.

2344   *Focus on Hitchcock.* edited by LaValley, Albert J. 186 p. paper illus. Englewood Cliffs, N.J.: Prentice-Hall, 1972.

How much more there is to say about Hitchcock is debatable, but this fine collection does gather together some opinions about him that have been offered in the past. It begins with two interviews and two articles by Hitchcock himself. The next section contains evaluations of Hitchcock and his films by Lindsay Anderson, Andre Bazin, Robin Wood, Andrew Sarris, and Raymond Durgnat. The remaining articles address themselves to specific films: NOTORIOUS (1946), STRANGERS ON A TRAIN (1951), THE WRONG MAN (1957), PSYCHO (1960), and the television series.

An unusual and surprisingly good analysis of the plane-cornfield sequence from NORTH BY NORTHWEST (1959) appears next. Utilizing some 30 pages, the sequence is analyzed shot-by-shot, using story boards to suggest the frame composition. A filmography, a bibliography, an index and a few stills complete the book. As a survey of Hitchcock's work and his contribution to film, this volume would be hard to beat. It is excellent in all ways and that shot-by-shot analysis is worth the price alone. This is another superior title in the *Focus on* series and is highly recommended.

2345 *Focus on Howard Hawks.* edited by McBride, Joseph. 178 p. paper illus. Englewood Cliffs, N.J.: Prentice-Hall, 1972.

Two short articles are followed by an audience interview of Hawks which took place in Chicago, 1970. The essays, which are the bulk of the text, are fewer than usual with this series, but in greater depth. One by Andrew Sarris, for example, runs 30 pages. Mostly, the essays explore Hawks' methods, themes, films, and his place among major American directors. A few of his films receive individual notice: RIO BRAVO (1958), MAN'S FAVORITE SPORT (1964), EL DORADO (1966) and RIO LOBO (1970). The filmography offers a short plot outline in addition to the usual information, while the bibliography refers mostly to French publications. An index and a few stills complete the book.

Hawks is probably one of the least known American directors. His work has been shown continuously for almost 50 years and shows no sign of subsiding on the TV screen. This book remedies some of the neglect, as did an earlier one by Robin Wood. Recommended.

2346 *Focus on Learning: Motion Pictures in the School.* by Hoban, Charles F., Jr. 172 p. Washington, D.C.: American Council on Education, 1942.

2347 *Focus on Orson Welles.* edited by Gottesman, Ronald. 218 p. illus. Englewood Cliffs, N.J.: Prentice-Hall, 1975.

Another fine group of articles, essays and interviews has been put together for this volume in the *Focus On...* series. They are divided into three sections: The Man (pieces by Kenneth Tynan, Peter Bogdanovich, and Charlton Heston), The Techniques (Richard T. Jameson and Phyllis Goldfarb) and The Films (Joseph McBride, Peter Cowie, John Russell Taylor, Charles Champlin, and seven others).

The selection and commission of the articles make for a rather detailed portrait of the subject, his methods, and his accomplishments. Further support is given by a detailed filmography, a selected and annotated bibliography, and an index. A center section of illustrations is also added.

The care and effort that is characteristic of this series is evidenced once more in this volume. Gottesman's admiration and knowledge of his subject has resulted in his assembling a richly satisfying collection that ultimately seems more a total appreciation than several disparate pieces. Highly recommended.

2348 *Focus on* RASHOMON. edited by Richie, Donald. 185 p. paper illus. Englewood Cliffs, N.J.: Prentice-Hall, 1972.

After an introduction to Kurosawa and the film, eight reviews are reprinted. Commentaries and essays on the Japanese film in general and RASHOMON (1950) in particular complete the text. Plot outline and synopsis, a script extract, a filmography, a bibliography, and an index support the text articles. The two short stories upon which the film was based are included and there is a good sampling of illustrations in the centerfold. There can be no argument with the material offered. The consistent excellence of this series is further reinforced by this fine volume. Highly recommended.

2349 *Focus on Shakespearean films.* by Eckert, Charles W. 184 p. paper illus. Englewood Cliffs, N.J.: Prentice-Hall, 1972.

An unusual approach is used by Eckert in this survey of Shakespearean films. After a section of introductory articles, he selects certain films made from the plays, arranges them chronologically, and gives one or two reviews under each. Thus we have Dierterle's A MIDSUMMER NIGHT'S DREAM (1935); Olivier's HENRY V (1944) and HAMLET (1948); Welles' MACBETH (1948) and OTHELLO (1951); Mankiewicz's JULIUS CAESAR (1953); Castellani's ROMEO AND JULIET (1954); the Russian ROMEO AND JULIET BALLET (1954) and OTHELLO (1955); Olivier's RICHARD III (1955); the Russian HAMLET (1964); Burge's OTHELLO (1965); Zeffirelli's THE TAMING OF THE SHREW (1966); and, finally, Welles' CHIMES AT MIDNIGHT (1966). The reviewers include Allardyce Nicoll, James Agee, Bosley Crowther, Mary McCarthy, Dwight MacDonald, John Simon, and others. A filmography, a bibliography, an index, and a few stills complete the book. The filmography indicates many other Shakespearean films that are not mentioned in the text. The question of selection arises again: why, for example, the seldom seen Russian films instead of Cukor's ROMEO AND JULIET (1936) or Zeffirelli's in 1968?

For anyone interested in the topic of "From Shakespearean Play to Film," the book will be most valuable. If used together with Manvell and Ball, the subject can be covered in considerable depth. Recommended.

2350 *Focus on* SHOOT THE PIANO PLAYER. edited by Braudy, Leo. 182 p. paper illus. Englewood Cliffs, N.J.: Prentice-Hall, 1972.

The same format used with the other *Focus on* books is employed here. An introductory section deals with Truffaut and SHOOT THE PIANO PLAYER (1960). Five reprinted reviews are followed by 13 essays and commentaries. The final portion of the book contains a synopsis and outline, three scenes not used in the final film, an excerpt from the script, a filmography, a bibliography and an index. A few illustrations are included in a center section. The book can be used in a variety of ways and should be helpful in most. It adds to the literature on Truffaut and offers a study guide for viewing the film. Recommended.

2351 *Focus on* THE BIRTH OF A NATION. edited by Silva, Fred. 184 p. paper illus. Englewood Cliffs, N.J.: Prentice-Hall, 1971.

The content of this *Focus on* volume is divided among D. W. Griffith, the film, and its effect. Introductory chapters on the director and his film are followed by six original reviews. The commentaries address themselves to the making of the film, newspaper editorials and replies, and several articles by Griffith. Writers like Sarris, Jacobs and Noble try to assess the impact of the film, its effect on the black struggle for equality, and its importance in film and national history. The usual plot synopsis and outline are given, as are a Griffith filmography, a bibliography and an index. A few illustrations are not impressive. This collection of articles covers both the immediate (1915) response to the film and some latter assessments which are cooler and more objective. It is important to note that the selections in the book indicate a wide range of opinion. This is another fine contribution from this consistently excellent series. Highly recommended.

2352 *Focus on The Horror Film.* by Huss, Roy; and Ross, T. J. 186 p. paper illus. Englewood Cliffs, N.J.: Prentice-Hall, 1972.

The three dozen articles in this compilation are arranged in four groups: the horror domain, gothic horror, monster terror, and psychological thriller. Under this last category, for example, there are essays on Val Lewton, THE BIRDS (1963), ROSEMARY'S BABY (1968), REPULSION (1965) and TARGETS (1968). In addition there are a chronology, filmography, a bibliography, an index, and a few stills. Excerpts from the scripts of a 1910 version of FRANKENSTEIN and from THE BRIDE OF FRANKENSTEIN (1935) appear in two of the articles.

There is enough here to satisfy most horror-film buffs. While one might question the absence of certain films—THE HAUNTING (1963) and THE INNOCENTS (1961)—the presence in the text of so many classic films of this genre more than compensates. This volume is a natural audience pleaser and can be recommended.

2353 *Focus on The Science Fiction Film.* edited by Johnson, William. 182 p. paper illus. Englewood Cliffs, N.J.: Prentice-Hall, 1972.

This anthology might also serve as a general history of the science fiction genre since it is arranged chronologically. Following an introduction and a chronology, the book is divided into four sections: Beginnings (1895-1949), The Popular Years (1950-59), Moving On (1960-70), and Taking Stock: Some Issues and Answers. A filmography, bibliography, index and a few stills complete the volume.

The articles vary in their subject matter, dealing with trends, techniques, directors, scripts, diaries of filmmaking, etc. The filmography is a short one for a major genre and suggests a scarcity of classic science fiction films. The absence of THE DEVIL DOLL (1936), BARBARELLA (1968), THE BLOB (1958), BUCK ROGERS (1939), THE FLY (1958), and many others makes the reader wonder what the qualifications were for inclusion. The definition offered in the introduction does not cover the omissions. But this is a very minor matter. The concern should be the quality of the material offered, and it is first-rate here. From Melies to 2001 (1969) the subject is handled in an informative, exciting manner that should please most readers. Recommended.

2354 *Focus on* THE SEVENTH SEAL. edited by Steene, Birgitta. 182 p. paper illus. Englewood Cliffs, N.J.: Prentice-Hall, 1972.

This compilation of articles about Ingmar Bergman and THE SEVENTH SEAL (1956) continues the excellent *Focus on* series. Ingmar Bergman is described in the introductory articles, interviews and analyses. Eight reviews of the film are followed by 17 more essays and commentaries. The original play, "Wood Painting," which served as the inspiration for the film, is reprinted. A plot synopsis, an outline, a script excerpt, a filmography, a bibliography and an index complete the book. This wealth of material will assist anyone studying Bergman, THE SEVENTH SEAL, or both, and a viewing of the film will be more rewarding after the use of this resource. The selection, arrangement and concept of this volume is excellent. Highly recommended.

2355 *Focus on the Western.* edited by Nachbar, Jack. 150 p. illus. Englewood Cliffs, N.J.: Prentice-Hall, 1974.

A fine survey of the western film genre is offered in this anthology. Attention is given to the history, form, structure, characters, and settings of the western. Its place in our culture is noted and finally, the contemporary western is described. Strong support for this wide overview is provided by a chronology, a bibliography and an index. The six pages of photographs placed in a center section unfortunately add little.

The arrangement of the materials in the book is logical and useful. Articles chosen are illustrative of the fine writing and criticism available on the western. Kitses, Warsaw and Cawelti are among the contributors. In summary this volume continues the excellence of the *Focus on...* series. It is highly recommended.

2356 *Folger Shakespeare Filmography: A Directory of Feature Films Based on the Works of Shakespeare.* by Parker, Barry M. Washington, D.C.: Folger Books, 1979.

2357 *Fonda: My Life.* by Fonda, Henry; and Teichmann, Howard. 327 p. illus. New York: NAL, 1981.

A tape-recorded autobiography shaped by Teichmann into a readable portrait of a complex, difficult perfectionist. The five marriages, the poor relationships with Jane and Peter, the suicides and the always present self-doubt are treated.

2358 *The Fondas: The Films and the Careers of Henry, Jane, and Peter Fonda.* by Springer, John. 279 p. illus. New York: Citadel, 1970.

After a rather long introduction of appreciations by John Steinbeck, Joshua Logan, and Robert Ryan, and a coverage of the Fondas' careers in the theatre and television, this volume considers the films of all three in chronological order. Obviously, the lion's share of the book goes to the father.

Each film is covered by a few stills, partial credits, a short background section and some comments from critics. Stills are from the author's collection and are further evidence of its excellence.

2359 *Fonzie.* by Grove, Martin A. 170 p. paper illus. New York: Zebra, 1976.

An original paperback biography of the television personality Henry Winkler, whose first few films were notably unsuccessful.

2360 *Footnotes to the Film.* edited by Davy, Charles. 334 p. illus. New York: Arno Press, 1970 (1938).

Articles (first printed in 1938) on the making of films by such people as Forsyth Hardy, Elizabeth Bowen, Alberto Cavalcanti, Robert Donat, Basil Wright, Graham Greene, Alexander Korda, Alfred Hitchcock, Alistair Cooke, and John Grierson.

2361 *For Adults Only.* by Dors, Diana; and Hobbs, Jack. 256 p. illus. London: W. H. Allen, 1978.

Diana Dors' second volume in her autobiographical saga. See also *Swingin' Dors.*

2362 *For Filmgoers Only: The Intelligent Filmgoer's Guide to the Film.* edited by Lambert, R. S. 98 p. London: Faber & Faber, 1934.

Five lectures from a 1933 gathering are printed here: "An Introduction" (R. S. Lambert); "The Development of Cinema" (Paul Rotha); "Axes to Grind: The Film As Propaganda" (Andrew Buchanan); "Can the Film Educate?" (Mary Field); "Why We Get the Films We Do" (R.S. Lambert); and "Eyes & No Eyes: What to Look for in Films" (C. A. Lejeune).

2363 *For Love of Liz.* by Joseph, Joan. 202 p. paper illus. New York: Manor Books, 1976.

An original paperback biography of Elizabeth Taylor that includes a filmography.

2364 *For Special Occasions.* by Schary, Dore. 200 p. New York: Random House, 1962.

This memoir deals with the boyhood of Dore Schary.

2365 *For the Sake of Shadows.* by Miller, Max. 200 p. New York: Dutton, 1936.

The impressions of a writer (I COVER THE WATERFRONT, 1933) in Hollywood. Negative and critical, the book becomes a therapeutic confession of his disturbing experiences in the film industry.

2366 FORCE MAJEURE; THE DISPOSSESSED; HASTA LUEGO. by John, Errol. 145 p. London: Faber and Faber, 1967.

Three unfilmed scripts.

2367 *Forces of Power.* by Taub, William L. illus. New York: Grosset and Dunlap, 1979.

Sections of this expose deal with the motion picture industry. Taub was a behind-the-scenes operator who moved in the worlds of politics, finance, trade unions, and the movies.

2368 *Foreign Films on American Screens.* by Mayer, Michael F. 119 p. paper illus. New York: Arco Pub. Co., 1965.

This book provides a most informative and entertaining survey of the post-war foreign film in America. The directors, the actors, the economics, and the censorship of the foreign film are discussed. The appendices list awards, foreign festivals, distributors, theatres, and samples of ratings from *Green Sheet, Parent's Magazine, Christian Science Monitor,* and the Legion of Decency. With the new freedom of the screen and the rating system, some of the comments are outdated and certain rating organizations are now defunct.

Much of the first section is a picture-text format. Illustrations are excellent, especially the director pages. Both the introduction by Arthur Knight and the author's text are intelligent and informed. The book fills a gap between Parker Tyler's *Classics Of The Foreign Film* and the many paperbacks on foreign film devoted to a single theme. Highly recommended.

2369 *The Foremost Films of 1938: A Yearbook of the American Screen.* by Vreeland, Frank. 347 p. illus. New York: Pitman, 1939.

A praiseworthy attempt to establish an annual series that failed. It reviews the film year and selects 10 films for individual treatment giving the plot and key scenes for WELLS FARGO; IN OLD CHICAGO; THE BUCCANEER; MALGIERS; SNOW WHITE AND THE SEVEN DWARFS ; LOVE FINDS ANDY HARDY; YOU CAN'T TAKE IT WITH YOU; THE YOUNG IN HEART; THE CERTAIN AGE; and THE CITADEL. There are resumes of several hundred other films and the volume is indexed.

2370 *Forever Is a Hell of a Long Time.* by Stauffer, Teddy. 309 p. illus. Chicago: Henry Regnery, 1976.

Translated from the German, this autobiography traces the life and career of Teddy Stauffer—also known as "Mr. Acapulco." Beginning as a Swiss student violinist, Stauffer ultimately became the official host for one of Acapulco's most famous hotels. In between were periods as a famous European bandleader, a Sun Valley ski instructor, a Mexican drifter, and a hotel manager.

At various times in his life, Stauffer has been friendly with Hollywood personalities. Married to both Hedy Lamarr and Faith Domergue, he also notes relationships with Maria Montez, Rita Hayworth, Linda Christian, Errol Flynn, Maurice Chevalier, and others.

A center section of illustrations deals mostly with Stauffer and his celebrity acquaintances. The book is indexed.

The final impression given is that of an opportunist-survivor who, more than once, was at the right place at the right time. However, a claim to importance based upon casual acquaintance with celebrities is suspect, while name-dropping and braggadocio are not likely to endear the author to his readers. Since most of Stauffer's actions and accomplishments were self-serving, there is a slightly sourish aftertaste to these recollections of a colorful but unimportant life. Acceptable.

2371 *Forever Sophia: An Intimate Portrait.* by Levy, Alan. 227 p. paper illus. New York: Baronet, 1979.

The background of this publication is almost as interesting as its content. Levy had visited and interviewed Sophia Loren extensively over a ten-year period and expected the autobiographical assignment, which went instead to A. E. Hotchner. Levy used his Loren files and his firsthand observations to produce this book which competes with the "official" Hotchner biography. This one is better.

Told in terse reportorial fashion, the story follows Loren's rise from Sofia Scicolone, an illegitimate, deprived child of Naples, to Sophia Loren, the international film beauty. In telling his story Levy makes good use of his previous articles, interviews, and research. The portrait which emerges is affectionate and admiring, but lacking the detail of the other book. Some good illustrations accompany the text. No index is provided. Acceptable.

2372 *Forgotten Films to Remember.* by Springer, John. 256 p. illus. Secaucus, N.J.: Citadel, 1970.

In his never-ending attempt to share his love of films with a wide audience, John Springer gives attention here to those films which may be termed "underrated," "lost," "forgotten," or "overlooked." He describes his survey as "a brief history of 50 years of the American talking picture." Using hundreds of attractive stills, he recalls in words and images selected films of quality from 1928 to 1959. The sixties and seventies are covered by a brief filmography.

As always, Springer's work deserves better production from his publisher. There are no indexes nor a table of contents; as a result, access to information about a specific film is difficult if the reader does not know the year of release.

Although the book falls below its potential, Springer's critical comments and historical interpretations, along with the many fine illustrations, make the book essential for anyone who, like Springer, has an affection and appreciation of the American sound film.

2373   *Forgotten Horrors.* by Turner, George E.; and Price, Michael H. 216 p. illus. New York: A.S. Barnes, 1980.

The subtitle, "Early Talkie Chillers from Poverty Row," describes the content of this volume. It is a chronological (1929 to 1937) filmography of rather unfamiliar motion pictures that have theme/genre and low cost in common. Each film is described by credits, cast, a synopsis, a few illustrations and some critical background notes. The volume is indexed.

Here is a specialized volume that will excite older film buffs and also appeal to younger film enthusiasts. The outrageous plots, tacky productions, and extreme overacting that characterized these films are recalled in fine style by the text and illustrations.

This book not only can be read with much pleasure but also can be used as a valuable reference source. Where else can you find as much information on DRUMS O' VOODOO (1934) more quickly?

2374   THE FORGOTTEN VILLAGE. by Steinbeck, John. 143 p. illus. New York: Viking Press, 1941.

Script of the 1941 film directed by Herbert Kline. Contains cast credits and an introduction by Steinbeck.

2375   *Forming and Running a Film Society.* edited by Evans, Jon; and Han-

cock, Margaret. 24 p. paper London: British Film Institute, 1961.

This small book, a joint venture of the British Film Institute and the Federation of Film Societies, treats the past history of film societies, their aims, how to form one, budgeting, rules and regulations. Advice is given on launching a society, planning programs, booking, operation, insurance, royalties, etc. Final sections discuss the work of the two sponsoring organizations. Here is sound practical advice that has been hard to come by in the U.S. until recently.

2376   *Formula For Stardom.* by Gillette, Don Carle. Los Angeles: Beacon, 1979.

Gillette was once editor of *Billboard* and *The Hollywood Reporter*. In that capacity he met many of the legends of show business—Jolson, Gable, Cohan, Chaplin, Gish, etc. In this volume, which is more a memoir than a guide to a film career, he recalls the rise of many major personalities. His advice can be summarized by two concepts: self-discipline and live performance with an audience.

2377   *The Forties Gals.* by Parish, James Robert; and Stanke, Don E. 465 p. illus. Westport, Conn: Arlington House, 1980.

For this latest collective biography James Parish has selected seven actresses whose fame peaked in the forties: Lauren Bacall, Susan Hayward, Ida Lupino, Virginia Mayo, Ann Sheridan, Esther Williams and Jane Wyman. Except for Bacall and Hayward, there are no full-length biographies available on the subjects to date. For each actress there is a biographical essay, many illustrations and a complete detailed filmography.

As usual with the Parish biographies, the text contains mostly factual material with a sprinkling of critical comment and a tidbit or so of gossip. The approach is more that of a fan than that of a critic.

2378   THE FORTUNE COOKIE. by Diamond, I. A. L. illus. 191 p. New York: Praeger, 1971.

Script of the 1966 film directed by Billy Wilder.

2379   *Fortune in Films.* by Moszynski, Andrzej B.; and Nicol, Robert C. 56 p. paper New York: Film Finance Publications, 1977.

This volume on the independent production of films consists of two major sections—project framework, and investment presentation. Topics considered under the framework portion include the role of independent production, competition, finance options, packaging, legalities, and presentation. The second part on the financing presentation discusses cover, index, illustration, synopsis, status, financing, marketing, development, biographies and appendices. All of the above is supplemented by a short bibliography and a ten-page summary of a 1975 speech by Jack Valenti.

The material offered here may serve nicely as an outline or guide for the knowledgeable fledglingproducer. Those needing detailed narrative or information should look elsewhere.

2380 42ND STREET. by James, Rian; and Seymour, James. paper illus. Madison, Wisc.: University of Wisconsin Press.

Script of the 1933 film directed by Lloyd Bacon. This volume was edited by Rocco Fumento.

2381 *Forty Years in Hollywood.* by Freulich, Roman; and Abramson, Joan. 201 p. illus. New York: A. S. Barnes, 1971.

The title suggests biography but the data furnished about the author-photographer of this book is so brief as to be almost unnoticeable. He worked first at Universal and later at Republic, where he was head of the photographic department. The book is primarily a collection of photographs. Two sections of illustrations of Universal films and stars are offered, and a third one is of Republic films and stars. A final section is a mixture of United Artist and independent productions, a few afterthoughts, some second chancers, and a number of fillers. Introducing each of the four pictorial sections is a collection of hoary stories, tired anecdotes, and some rather flat narratives about unrelated subjects. An index is provided.

The pity is that the book constantly indicates how good it might have been. Nearly all the visuals are very clearly reproduced and many are examples of memorable photography. Others, such as the early Universal groups, have a nostalgic interest. Occasionally the text goes beyond blandness to discuss the directorial methods of Welles, Whale, Ford, etc. But ultimately the book is defeated by poor organization, faulty selection of text and visuals, and inadequate development of what was used. Freulich received four Academy Awards but specific mention of these honors is almost impossible to find in this book.

The photographic work is of high quality and is well reproduced. Perhaps the author's long experience with Universal and Republic has conditioned him to a world of "B" efforts—good visuals but no story.

2382 *Forty Years of Film History (1895-1935): Notes on the Films.* by Lindgren, Ernest. 108 p. paper London: British Film Institute, 1952.

Another hard-to-find survey by the well-known film historian.

2383 *Forty Years of Screen Credits.* by Weaver, John T. 1458 p. (2 vols.) illus. Metuchen, N.J.: Scarecrow Press, 1970.

This reference guide lists several thousand actors in alphabetical order and follows each with a filmography including release dates. The period covered is 1920-1969. This is an excellent reference volume that is relatively easy to use. Some material—Academy Award data, etc.—is expendable but the major body of this reference is admirable. In addition to well-known names, many minor players are listed.

2384 *40 Years with Oscar at the Academy Awards.* by Osborne, Robert. 84 p. paper illus. Le Habra, Calif.: E. E. Schworck, 1970.

A paperback excerpt from Osborne's *The Academy Awards Illustrated.*

2385 *Fotokino Worterbuch.* edited by Wolter, Wilhelm F. 4 vol. Halle (Saale): Fotokinoverlag Halle, 1960.

A dictionary consisting of 4 volumes that covers photography and allied subjects in German, English, Russian and French. Includes material on the cinema and motion picture photography, along with bibliographies.

2386 *Fotonovel-(A Series).* paper illus. Los Angeles: Fotonovel, 1978-.

A welcome addition to film literature, this series of books recreates popular films by providing more than 350 visuals taken directly from the film. Accompanying dialogue appears in comic book balloon style along with some sparse connecting narrative. Between 100,000 and 200,000 copies of each of these paperback film recreations are published. They will be viewed, read and enjoyed by a large audience.

Titles published include: THE CHAMP (1979); LOVE AT FIRST BITE (1980); INVASION OF THE BODY

SNATCHERS (1978); ICE CASTLES (1978); GREASE (1978); HAIR (1979); BUCK ROGERS (1979); NIGHTWING (1979); ROCKY II (1979); HEAVEN CAN WAIT (1978); REVENGE OF THE PINK PANTHER (1978); LORD OF THE RINGS (1979); AMERICATHON—1998 (1979).

2387 *Four Aspects of the Film.* by Limbacher, James L. 386 p. illus. New York: Brussel & Brussel, Inc. 1969.

The four aspects are color, width, depth, and sound. Certain avant-grade aspects such as variable screen size for a single film, multiple screens, live action combined with film, subliminal films, and smells to accompany film are also considered. Each of the four divisions is approached historically and the innovations in that area are noted in a chronological fashion. References are given after each chapter and there is a small section of diagrams and illustrations. A bibliography of books and periodicals is offered.

Appendices make up a large portion of the book, including listings of natural color and tinted films, widescreen films, 3-dimensional films, and pioneer sound films. Although the book is technical, it will have some interest for the scholar and the historian.

2388 *Four Fabulous Faces: Garbo, Swanson, Crawford, Dietrich.* by Carr, Larry. 492 p. illus. New Rochelle, N.Y.: Arlington House, 1970.

A history, a fashion show, a mirror of popular taste, and an example of superior photographic portraiture; this volume may be considered all of these. A thousand photographs, some in color, include the work of photographers such as Cecil Beaton and Richard Avedon. This handsome, well-produced book apparently was designed for gift-giving or for ownership by devotees of the quartet of legends.

2389 *Four Giants of the West.* by Hanna, David. 223 p. paper illus. New York: Belmont Tower, 1976.

The four actors profiled in this collective biography —James Stewart, Henry Fonda, John Wayne, Gary Cooper—may be "Giants of the West," but that is incidental to the life stories told by David Hanna. Certainly his interpretation of familiar facts and material provides interesting accounts of these American legends. Hanna, in a succinct, rather terse style, conveys the essence of each man. In a relatively few pages he does as much in providing a dimensioned portrait as many of the full-length biographies do. An excellent starting point for anyone interested in these four American "originals."

2390 *Four Great Comedians: Chaplin, Lloyd, Keaton, Langdon.* by McCaffrey, Donald W. 175 p. paper illus. New York: A. S. Barnes, 1968.

The emphasis in this volume is on technique and style rather than biography. Major attention is given to the four named, although some other silent screen comedians are mentioned. Some shot-by-shot analysis of the films is included in an attempt to analyze the success of these artists in making audiences laugh for these many years. Even allowing that the approach is a bit different, the subject material seems a bit exhausted and overly familiar. Stills are adequate—in some cases cropped off rather unevenly. A bibliography is included but there is no index. For the novice and the casual reader, this book will be informative and entertaining. The advanced student and the sophisticated reader may think they've read it before.

2391 THE 400 BLOWS. by Truffaut, Francois; and Moussy, Marcel. 256 p.paper illus. New York: Grove Press, 1969.

Script of the 1959 film directed by Truffaut. Contains cast credits, an introduction by Robert Hughes, and these features: a collage from *Cahiers du Cinema* (5 articles); two interviews with Truffaut; and four critics on THE 400 BLOWS.

2392 *Four Screenplays.* by Clair, Rene. 439 p. illus. New York: Orion Press, 1970.

Scripts of four films. Contains cast credits, a foreword and a commentary for each film. The screenplays are LE SILENCE EST D'OR (1946), LA BEAUTE DU DIABLE (1949), LES BELLES DE NUIT (1952), and LES GRANDES MANOEUVRES (1955).

2393 *Four Screenplays.* by Dreyer, Carl. 296 p. illus. Bloomington, Ind.: Indiana University Press, 1970.

Scripts of four films. Contains cast credits, an introduction by Ole Storm, a foreword by Carl Dreyer, and a filmography. The screenplays are LA PASSION DE JEANNE D'ARC (1927), VAMPYR (1931), VREDENS DAG, (DAY OF WRATH) (1943), and THE WORD (1954).

2394 *Four Screenplays of Ingmar Bergman.* by Bergman, Ingmar. 384 p. illus. New York: Simon & Schuster, 1960.

Scripts of four films. Includes SMILES OF A SUMMER NIGHT (1955), THE SEVENTH SEAL (1956), WILD STRAWBERRIES (1958), and THE MAGICIAN (1959).

2395 *The Four Seasons of Success.* by Schulberg, Budd. 203 p. New York: Doubleday, 1972.

Schulberg relates the experiences of six famous writers who journeyed to Hollywood to improve their fortunes: Scott Fitzgerald, Dorothy Parker, William Saroyan, Nathaniel West, Thomas Heggen and John Steinbeck. Since he knew all the subjects, Schulberg's story is personal, intimate and goes beyond the usual factual accounts. This is an unusually rewarding book that tells what happens to writers when critics, institutions and audiences cool in admiration for them. Recommended.

2396 *Four Star Scripts: Actual Shooting Scripts and How They are Written.* edited by Noble, Loraine. 392 p. Garden City, N.Y.: Doubleday, Doran & Co., 1936.

Contains an introduction by Lorriane Noble, two articles— "Back of the Scenes in a Talking Picture Script" and "How Scripts Are Written" — and the scripts of LADY FOR A DAY (1933), IT HAPPENED ONE NIGHT (1934), LITTLE WOMEN (1933), and THE STORY OF LOUIS PASTEUR (1936).

2397 *The Fox Girls.* by Parish, James Robert. 722 p. illus. New Rochelle, N.Y.: Arlington House, 1971.

This detailed look at "15 Beautiful Vixens and One Adorable Cub" gives a possible clue to the master plan of author Parish. *The Paramount Pretties* followed this volume and used an identical format. Are we to expect "The MGM Ladies" and "The Warner's Liberated Women" as upcoming volumes? Let us hope so, for there are some nice things about this book. It provides a light, entertaining and up-to-date look at the careers of some screen ladies and legends.

Each subject in this collective biography is given a chapter-essay, with the emphasis placed on career and films rather than on personal life. A gallery of photographs, mainly stills from films, accompanies each narrative portrait. Concluding each section is a filmography listing major cast and production credits for each of the star's films.

The fifteen ladies are: Theda Bara, Anne Baxter, Jeanne Crain, Linda Darnell, Alice Faye, Janet Gaynor, Betty Grable, June Haver, Sonja Henie, Carmen Miranda, Marilyn Monroe, Sheree North, Gene Tierney, Raquel Welch, and Loretta Young. The "cub" is Shirley Temple. The biographies are descriptive rather than critical, and the reader will have the "public image" reinforced rather than gain any privileged insight into a human personality.

One major reservation concerns picture quality, which is only average. A questionable decision to use more photographs but to reduce their size results in a disservice to the illustrations. Their impact is diminished considerably. The book will probably have a wide and deserved success, however. Its likely popularity and its reference value make it acceptable.

2398 *Fox Talbot and the Invention of Photography.* by Buckland, Gail. illus. Boston: David R. Godine, 1980.

Early in the 19th century William Henry Fox Talbot produced photographs using the sun's light. These were the forefathers of today's photographic processes. Talbot did not make his discoveries known until after Daguerre announced his images on metal plates. In this biography, Buckland shows the many sides of Talbot along with his appreciable number of discoveries and inventions. Her research is accompanied by more than 250 illustrations, all of which are quite rare and fascinating to view.

2399 *Frame by Frame: A Black Filmography.* by Klotman, Phyllis Rauch. 700 p. Bloomington, Ind.: Indiana University Press, 1979.

More than 3000 films having either black themes and/or subject matter, or the participation of blacks as filmmakers or actors are listed here. Black is given a broad definition encompassing persons from America, Latin America, the Caribbean, and Africa. For each film entry there is the usual descriptive data and technical information. Most important, however, is the annotation which emphasizes the presence and participation of blacks, although many films of various types including features, short films, and documentaries are considered. The filmography is nevertheless a selected one with the author indicating her criteria and omissions in the introduction.

Supplementing the 600-page filmography are a distributor list, a bibliography, and indexes for black performers, authors, screenwriters, producers, and directors.

This is a major reference book which adds to the work done in the *Scarecrow* series by Edward Mapp, Anne Powers, Helen Cyr, and Henry Sampson. Although the typewriter print used does not make for an impressive physical production, the scope, organization and treatment of the material is uniformly excellent. The indexes and the annotations deserve special attention and commendation. Recommended.

2400   *Frames.* compiled by Griffin, George. 96 p. paper illus. New York: G. Griffin, 1978.

For this unusual book 70 artists have contributed drawings, cut-outs, and photographs in an effort to show the diversity of the American independent animated film. The samples come mostly from film frames and vary from groups of numbers to abstracts to comic characters. All have the artist's name affixed and there is occasionally some explanatory statement. The contributors' addresses are given in the final pages. This is an attractive book of animation art that will serve as inspiration, model, source, and guide for anyone interested in this particular film genre. Recommended.

2401   *Frames of Reference—Essays on the Rhetoric of Film.* edited by Walz, Eugene P.; and Harrington, John; and Di Marco, Vincent. 145 p. Dubuque, Iowa: Kendall/Hunt Pub. Co., 1972.

The stated purpose of this volume is to encourage an "active" viewing of film—a participation that will bring both critical judgment and imagination to the experience. To that end, it offers 13 essays on specific films, one on film comedy and one on Ingmar Bergman. The selection of titles is a mixture with no discernible connection. The content of the essays varies, with some discussing critical response, while others analyze script excerpts. Cast and credits are given along with some questions for discussion in most cases.

Although it is difficult to discern the structure of this collection, the essays offer interesting reading. They can be used as study guides for viewing and discussion of the films. Acceptable.

2402   *France.* by Martin, Marcel. 191 p. paper illus. New York: A. S. Barnes, 1971.

One of the *Screen Series* books about the cinema of a special country. This one is a guide to the directors, actors and technicians of France. An index with several thousand titles mentioned in the text is provided.

2403   *Francesco Rosi.* by Gibson, Roma. 25 p. paper illus. London: British Film Institute, 1977.

A publication in the *Film Availability* series (Documentation Film No. 3), this appreciation of the Italian film director, Francesco Rosi, contains text and a filmography.

His films, which are characterized by social and political concerns, include SALVATORE GIULIANO (1961), HANDS OVER THE CITY (1963), and MORE THAN A MIRACLE (1968).

2404   *Francis Ford Coppola.* by Johnson, Robert K. 199 p. illus. Boston: Twayne, 1977.

It may be a bit premature to write an appreciation of Francis Ford Coppola since he has been concerned with relatively few films to date. However, this title in the *Twayne Theatrical Arts Series* offers a rewarding look at these films. The films he has directed which receive individual analysis and comment are: YOU'RE A BIG BOY NOW (1967), THE RAIN PEOPLE (1969), FINIAN'S RAINBOW (1968), THE GODFATHER (1972), THE CONVERSATION (1974), and THE GODFATHER II (1975). Some biographical information and Coppola's other film activities (writing, producing, etc.) are also noted. The book concludes with chapter notes/references, a filmography, a selected bibliography and an index. A few illustrations are provided.

Most readers are familiar with the GODFATHER films and the comment-analysis offered here will be very welcome. The other films are discussed with such skill and critical insight that the reader will be encouraged to see them with the new perspective supplied by the author. Recommended.

2405 *Francois Truffaut*. by Insdorf, Annette. 250 p. illus. Boston: Twayne, 1978.

Truffaut considers this critical appreciation of his work to be the "most sensitive and intelligent" one available in English. The author's total knowledge and sharp interpretation of the Truffaut films is strongly supported by footnotes, an index, a bibliography, and a filmography. She examines the recurrent themes (friendship, women, language as communication, children, etc.) along with his new wave association and the influences of Hitchcock and Jean Renoir. This title in the Twayne *Theatrical Arts* series is indicative of the continuing excellence of the series.

2406 *Francois Truffaut*. by Crisp, C. G. 144 p. illus. New York: Praeger, 1972.

Basing his book on interviews given by Truffaut over the last decade, Crisp has two goals in mind: to note the creative activities of Truffaut and to indicate the motives that shaped them. Thus the films are discussed with a sensitivity to Truffaut's background and life, and an awareness of the framework in which the films were conceived and ultimately made. The introduction is biographical and much attention is paid to Truffaut's role as a critic for *Cahiers*. In chronological order, each of the films is described and analyzed. Few in number, they include THE 400 BLOWS (1959), SHOOT THE PIANO PLAYER (1960), JULES AND JIM (1961), LOVE AT TWENTY (1962) (one episode), THE SOFT SKIN (1964), FAHRENHEIT 451 (1966), THE BRIDE WORE BLACK (1967), STOLEN KISSES (1968), THE SIREN OF THE MISSISSIPPI (1969), THE WILD CHILD (1969), and BED AND BOARD (1970). Autobiographical elements which run through the films are pointed out.

Illustration quality is above average and the credits for all the films are given. The bibliography indicates published screenplays, the major interviews, and some of Truffaut's writing for *Cahiers*.

Like most of the *Praeger Film Library* Series, this one is impressive. The writing is authoritative, readable and informative. Crisp's detection approach is most valid with Truffaut and worthy of consideration with other auteur directors. An excellent study of a craftsman-artist. Recommended.

2407 *Franju*. by Durgnat, Raymond. 144 p. illus. Berkeley, Calif.: University of California Press, 1968.

Georges Franju is a French film director who is probably best known in the United States for a film shown on television as THE HORROR CHAMBER OF DR. FAUSTUS (1960) (LES YEUX SANS VISAGE in France). This book pays tribute to many of his other films in addition. After a too brief biography and a rather intellectualized discussion of Franju's directorial style, his films are described and analyzed. Some 15 shorter films and seven longer ones are considered.

Much attention is given to comparision of Franju's films with earlier ones in an attempt to show possible origins of his style. The author's approach is typical "Cahiers" —and may be a bit too much in depth for the general reader. Certainly the book would be more meaningful if Franju's films were more familiar. For example, the section on THE HORROR CHAMBER OF DR. FAUSTUS is the most interesting, probably due to the visual knowledge acquired from its TV showings. A filmography and a bibliography are included. Recommended for the advance student/reader.

2408 *Frank Capra*. by Griffith, Richard. 38 p. paper illus. London: British Film Institute, 1950.

This BFI booklet (index series no. 3) covers Capra's films individually from the Langdon era of THE STRONG MAN (1926) to RIDING HIGH (1949). The films are preceded by a short analysis of his total work. An interesting prologue to Capra's autobiography.

2409 *Frank Capra: The Name Above the Title*. by Capra, Frank 513 p. illus. New York: Macmillan, 1971.

"There are no rules in filmmaking, only sins. . . and the cardinal sin is dullness." This statement opens the autobiography of this famous American director and seems to be his guiding principle. He may be an opinionated, corny, flag-waving, aggressive individualist but he is never dull—at least not in these pages. The book divides itself into logical sequences —the silent comedy days with Sennett and Langdon, the formative golden years at Columbia with Harry Cohn, the war years, and the bitter-sad years of Hollywood's decline. His career closely parallels the rise and fall of Hollywood.

The accounts of himself, his films, and his associates appear to be objective. Although humility is not one of his strong points, he seems honest and fair in retelling the many events and anecdotes of his lifetime. A nicely balanced portrait of Hollywood filmmaking emerges as a result. The photographs are superior, the book is indexed, and only the absence of a filmography keeps it from being an absolute success.

2410 *Frank Capra: One Man—One Film.* edited by Silke, James R. 27 p. paper illus. Washington, D.C.: The American Film Institute, 1971.

The discussion published here was held in May 1971 at the AFI Center in Beverly Hills. Capra's autobiography had just been published and there was a renewal of interest in the man and his films. In addition to the interview there is a filmography, a bibliography and an index to the topics covered in the discussion. A few illustrations are also included. Acceptable.

2411 *Frank Capra.* by Maland, Charles J. 218 p. illus. Boston: Twayne, 1980.

Charles J. Maland believes IT'S A WONDERFUL LIFE (1946) is Frank Capra's masterpiece and devotes a long chapter to its analysis in this study. The text is arranged into seven chronological chapters—Early Life (1897-1926), Entry into Film (1927-1930), First Success (1931-1935), The Peak Years (1936-1941), World War II (1942-1945), The Masterpiece (1945-1946), and Declining Fortunes (1947 to date). A summary chapter ends the text.

As usual with the *Twayne Theatrical Arts* series, the standard elements (chronology, notes, references, illustrations, bibliography, filmography and index) support the text strongly. The fact that Capra has already had several books devoted to his career and his films takes a bit of the edge off this appreciation. However, fitting the subject into the series format provides a tight, readable assessment of a noted American director.

2412 *Frank Capra.: The Man and His Films.* edited by Glatzer, Richard; and Raeburn, John. 190 p. paper illus. Ann Arbor, Mich.: Univeristy of Michigan Press, 1975.

The collection of articles, essays, reviews, and interviews contained in this volume is divided in accordance with the title, with five about "The Man" and 17 devoted to "His Films" . Author representation is impressive, with names such as James Agee, Lewis Jacobs, Otis Ferguson, Graham Greene, and Richard Griffith among the contributors. The articles are arranged in a chronological fashion with the Langdon silents first and the post-war films last. Attention accorded the films is uneven; several are merely mentioned while others, e.g., IT'S A WONDERFUL LIFE (1946), receive extended coverage. An introductory chapter, a center gallery of selected stills, a spare filmography offering only title and date, and a short bibliography complete the volume.

There can be little quarrel with the main content—it certainly satisfies the book's goal of providing a biographical perspective and varying critical interpretations of Capra's work. However, an index, a more detailed, informative filmography, and a longer annotated bibliography would have added considerably to the book's total impact and eventual value. To locate information on a specific Capra film is not easy. Although this is a more detailed study, *American Film Directors* offers a similar but shorter evaluation of Capra's work. Since 64 other American directors are also considered, it provides considerable economic and functional competition to volumes such as this one. Acceptable.

2413 *Frank Sinatra.* by Scaduto, Tony. 159 p. illus. London: Michael Joseph.

2414 *Frank Sinatra.* by Taylor, Paula. illus. Mankato, Minn.: Creative Education, 1976.

Designed for the very young reader, this title in the *Rock and Pop Stars* series offers a brief account of the phenomenal life and career of Frank Sinatra. Illustrations are by John Keely.

2415 *Frank Sinatra: The Man, the Myth and the Music.* by Goddard, Peter. 154 p. paper illus. Don Mills, Ont., Canada: Greywood Publishing, 1973.

Here is a modest account of Frank Sinatra's life and career. Although the author is plainly a devotee of his subject, he provides a coverage which is not always complete or complimentary. In addition, his critical judgment is often vulnerable, e.g., his use of TAKE ME OUT TO THE BALLGAME (1949) as an example of Sinatra's film decline—a much stronger case can be made by citing THE KISSING BANDIT (1948). No mention is made of two major Sinatra films—ANCHORS AWEIGH (1944) and ON THE TOWN (1949).

Goddard is strongest in his ability to place a perspective on Sinatra's many public feuds, battles and outbursts. The singer's private life is also handled with a compassionate understanding absent in other accounts. The book contains no discography, filmography or index. The reproduction quality of its illustrations is above average. Although the book is flawed in several important areas, it is still one of the better accounts of a talented, troubled showbusiness legend who still creates excitement and controversy whenever he appears in public. Recommended.

2416 *Frank Sinatra.* by Howlett, John. paper illus. New York: Wallaby, 1980.

2417 *Frank Sinatra—Is This Man Mafia?* by Carpozi, George, Jr. 376 p. paper New York: Manor Books, 1979.

The title of this original unauthorized biography must be misleading, since what is offered is a redistillation of all the public records involving Sinatra rather than any new disclosures. Carpozi specializes in this type of biographical synthesis, usually prepared at a time of high public interest.

His copious flow has produced individual biographies of Bing Crosby, Andrew Young, Anwar Sadat, Jackie Kennedy, the Son of Sam, Alice Crimmins, Brigitte Bardot, Gary Cooper, Cher, Clark Gable, Carol Burnett, Marilyn Monroe, John Wayne and five volumes of collective biographies entitled *That's Hollywood.*

This review of Sinatra's life and career is fast-paced, easy reading. It does cover most of the highs and lows in his long career. For those unacquainted with the Sinatra story, this is as good an introduction as any.

2418 *Frank Tashlin.* edited by Johnston, Claire; and Willemen, Paul. 149 p. paper illus. London: Journal of the Society for Education in Film and Television, 1973.

Prepared for the Edinburgh Film Festival, this anthology contains tributes, interviews, appreciations, etc., along with a chronology and a filmography. Tashlin has enjoyed several careers, including those of animator, cartoon director, author, scriptwriter and director of feature films (mostly comedies).

2419 *The Frankenscience Monster.* by Ackerman, Forrest J. 191 p. paper illus. New York: Ace, 1969.

The author of this unusual book is known for his creation of "Film Monster" magazines and many other activities which derive from his interest in horror and fantasy films. In this volume he has assembled a tribute to Boris Karloff which consists of articles, interviews, biographies and appreciations. Most of the items are quite enjoyable and a few have a value beyond casual reading. For example, a tribute to Jack Pierce, the makeup artist who created the Frankenstein monster, would have pleased Karloff, who acknowledged his debt to Pierce many times. Several long articles on Karloff, two filmographies— one alphabetical, the second chronological

—and a reading version of Frankenstein based on the film are all quality elements in this rewarding book. Almost as good are a long picture section and listings of his television and stage appearances. With this excellent volume and the later one by Denis Gifford, *A Pictorial History of Horror Movies,* readers will have access to a richness of materials on Karloff.

2420 FRANKENSTEIN—THE TRUE STORY. by Isherwood, Christopher; and Bachardy, Don. 222 p. paper New York: Avon, 1973.

Script of the 1973 film directed by Jack Smight. It was made for television but will probably appear in 16mm film rental libraries.

2421 *Frankenstein.* by Thorne, Ian. 47 p. illus. Mankato, Minn.: Crestwood House, 1977.

A review of Frankenstein films written for young readers.

2422 *The Frankenstein Legend.* by Glut, Donald Frank. 398 p. illus. Metuchen, N.J.: Scarecrow Press, 1973.

The complete story of Frankenstein's monster—in legend, literature, theatre, motion pictures, radio, television, comic books, toys, and other forms. The illustrated volume's subtitle is "A Tribute to Mary Shelley and Boris Karloff."

The major portion of the book is concerned with films, dividing them roughly into the silent films, the Karloff-Universal films, and the Hammer films of the sixties. Much of the information is quite detailed and deals with all aspects of the films—stars, scores, stories, etc. Picture quality is acceptable, and the book is indexed.

The book is unique, specialized, and impressive in the range of its coverage. It's a real treat for the many devotees of horror films and books.

2423 *Frankie—The Life and Loves of Frank Sinatra.* by Dwiggins, Don. 156 p. paper New York: Paperback Library, 1961.

The top of page 32 reads, "Other newsmen made Sinatra see red. They angered him by being inaccurate, slovenly, often dishonest." One can only imagine Sinatra's feeling if he ever read this unauthorized and quite irresponsible biography, written by a Hollywood newsman of more than 25 years of experience. It abounds in errors and misleading phrases or descriptions; numbers and dates are manipulated with no apparent checking. Examples of the carelessness include: 1) "Bunny Barrigan" for "Bunny Berigan" 2) Bob Eberle identified as a band leader; 3) Sinatra hired by Dorsey to be one of the Pied Pipers; 4) Gene Kelly appearing in STEP LIVELY (1944); 5) Juliet Prowse assigned to the chorus line in CAN-CAN (1960); 6) 1300 seats sold at $100 each, netting more than a million; and 7) many and constant references to Sinatra singing "That Old Black Magic" long before it was written (1942). For trivia detectives the book is a constant challenge. For all other readers, and for its subject, it is a disservice.

2424 *Freaks: Cinema of the Bizarre.* by Adrian, Werner. 111 p. paper illus. New York: Warner Books, 1976.

This volume provides an exploration of the way in which freaks—the ugly, the deformed, the grotesque—have been used in motion pictures. Reference is made to legends, sideshows, midways, and exhibitions but the major portion of the text is concerned with film monsters. Chapters have typical titles such as freaks, beast people, mutation freaks, big people—little people, horrors from beyond.

Although the topic apparently has a lasting interest for readers, it is carelessly treated in this volume. On page 28 Henry Hull is identified as Werner (misspelled) Oland. Page 12 states "A film was made, LUST FOR LIFE, in which Mel Ferrer played the painter (Toulouse-Lautrec)..." The film was MOULIN ROUGE (1952) and its star was Jose Ferrer. On page 60 a caption states "Maureen O'Sullivan plays the lethal lady in THE DEVIL DOLL (1936)..." This is incorrect: she played the innocent daughter-heroine. There are also many omissions: on page 41 Michael Redgrave is not identified in the well-known still from DEAD OF NIGHT (1943), nor is Jean Marais on page 70; there is no caption at all for page 81.

Despite some good visuals and an impressive coverage, the numerous errors and omissions make this volume unacceptable.

2425 *Fred Astaire: A Pictorial Treasury of His Films.* by Thompson, H. 160 p. illus. New York: Crescent Books, 1970.

Using stills and a continuous text, the book details Astaire's career from DANCING LADY (1933) to FINIAN'S RAINBOW (1968). Filmography.

2426 *Fred Astaire.* by Freedland, Michael. 277 p. paper illus. New York: Grosset & Dunlap, 1976.

Fred Astaire's rise from child vaudeville performer to his "living legend" status of today is related in a fan magazine writer's style, giving too much attention to factual details and not enough to interpretation. This unauthorized biography is helped by almost 200 illustrations, many of which seem unfamiliar. The volume is indexed.

Apparently an artist's attempts at perfection can be caught with ease by the camera but not by the typewriter.

2427 *Fred Astaire.* by Harvey, Stephen. 158 p. paper illus. New York: Pyramid, 1975.

A general appreciation introduces this review of Fred Astaire's life and career. His early theatrical appearances with his sister Adele are recalled as a preparation for a long film career. The musicals with Ginger Rogers and a series of other partners are reviewed, as are his nonmusical films. Harvey offers some plot description, background information and critical evaluation of each.

The illustrations are appropriate choices and are nicely reproduced. A bibliography, a filmography and an index complete the book.

This is another title in the impressive *Pyramid* series which continues to offer more quality, content and critical thought than other higher priced series. Recommended.

2428 *Fred Astaire.* by Green, Benny. 176 p. illus. New York: Exeter (Bookthrift), 1979.

Another review of Astaire's long career on stage and in films, this volume includes a filmography, a discography and an index. The result is illustrated, surface biography which is redeemed a bit by the choice of visuals.

2429 *Fred Astaire and His Work.* by Hackl, Alfons. 122 p. illus. Vienna: Edition Austria International, 1970.

Astaire's work on stage, screen, television and recordings is the concern of this nicely produced volume. Each aspect is treated separately with cast credits, illustrations, dates, and indexed.

2430 *The Fred Astaire/Ginger Rogers Movie Book.* by Croce, Arlene. 192 p. illus. New York: Outerbridge and Lazard, 1972.

2431   *The Fred Astaire Story: His Life, His Films, His Friends.* compiled by British Broadcasting Corporation. 68 p. illus. London: British Broadcasting Corporation, 1975.

This souvenir guide to the Radio 2 biography and the BBC television Astaire-Rogers film season includes a bibliography and a filmography.

2432   *The Fred Emney Story.* by Fairlie, Gerard. 190 p. illus. London: Hutchinson, 1960.

A biography of the stocky British comedian whose trademarks were a growl, a cigar, and a top hat. Emney appeared in a few films such as BREWSTER'S MILLIONS (1935) and THE SANDWICH MAN (1966).

2433   *Fred Zinnemann.* by Griffith, Richard. 20 p. paper illus. New York: Museum of Modern Art, 1958.

A short filmography prepared for a showing of Zinnemann's films at the Museum.

2434   *Frederick Wiseman.* by Atkins, Thomas R. 134 p. paper illus. New York: Monarch Press (Simon and Schuster), 1976.

This appreciation of filmmaker Frederick Wiseman takes the form of an anthology. An introductory essay by Atkins is followed by two interviews. Next Elliot Richardson argues about TITICUT FOLLIES (1967) and then Atkins interviews Wiseman about PRIMATE (1974). Single reviews of TITICUT FOLLIES (1967), HIGH SCHOOL (1968), BASIC TRAINING (1971), ESSENE (1972), along with a few review excerpts follow. A biography, a filmography, a bibliography and a list of rental sources complete the book.

Although he has been well covered by the periodicals, this is the first book to appear on Wiseman. The material that Atkins has written and gathered provides a fine introduction to the work of this unique filmmaker. Highly recommended.

2435   *Frederick Wiseman: A Guide to References and Resources.* by Ellsworth, Liz. 212 p. Boston: G. K. Hall, 1979.

Until the publication of this volume, the only book devoted to the filmmaker was *Frederick Wiseman*, published in 1976. This new volume not only supplements the above but greatly exceeds its coverage by the large amount of diverse information offered. It begins with short biographical and critical survey sections which are followed by detailed descriptions of eleven films, giving synopses, credits, notes, and most importantly, shot lists for some of the films. In a sense, the scripts (shot-lists) for TITICUT FOLLIES (1967), HIGH SCHOOL (1968), HOSPITAL (1970) and PRIMATE (1974) are presented here.

The bibliography consists of 212 annotated items, including reviews arranged chronologically by year from 1963 to 1978. Awards, festival screenings, archival sources, film distributors, a film title index and an author index complete the volume.

The emphasis here is on the films, and the inclusion of the four shot lists is to be applauded. Anyone seriously interested in studying the work of this pioneering filmmaker is advised to begin with this volume; it is so much more than the reference indicated in its title.

2436   *Freedom of the Movies.* by Inglis, Ruth, A. 241 p. Chicago: University of Chicago Press, 1947.

This report on self-regulation of films is from the Commission of Freedom of the Press. It is no longer pertinent to today's films but it can offer a historical background to the censorship of films during the first half of this century. Since patterns of exhibition and distribution have changed along with audiences, much material appears old-fashioned and quaint. Topics treated are social role, history, economics, early attempts at control, and self-regulation of the screen. The book may be of some interest to those concerned with censorship .

2437   FREEDOM TO LOVE. by Kronhausen, Phyllis; and Kronhausen, Eberhard. 191 p. paper illus. New York: Grove, 1970.

Script of the 1970 film directed by the Kronhausens. Contains cast and credits. Also has interviews with Hugh Hefner, Kenneth Tynan, Michael McClure (author of the play, "Beard"), a Danish porno shop owner, "swingers," and Daughters of Bilitis.

2438   *French Cinema of the Occupation and Resistance: The Birth of a Critical Esthetic.* by Bazin, Andre. 256 p. illus. New York: Ungar, 1981.

A collection of early essays by Andre Bazin from the period 1943-1946 with some annotations by Francois Truffaut. The 30 studies are characterized by some elements that are missing in Bazin's later writing—simplicity, fervor, directness, etc.

2439 *French Cinema Since 1946: Vol. 1—The Great Tradition.* by Armes, Roy. 208 p. paper illus. New York: A. S. Barnes, 1970 (1960).

Following a brief introductory chapter, this volume (first published in 1960) considers individually the most important French film directors of the early post-World War II years. Listed as veteran directors are Rene Clair, Jean Renoir, Marcel Carne, Max Ophuls, and Jean Cocteau. In the next grouping, Henri-Georges Clouzot, Rene Clement, Jacques Becker and Claude Autant-Lara are classified as traditionalists. Innovators and independents are Robert Bresson, Jacques Tati, Jean Gremillon, Georges Rouquier, and Roger Leenhardt. Filmographies for each director are given. There are illustrations throughout. Although it treats a somewhat specialized topic, this is a volume of high quality.

2440 *French Cinema Since 1946: Vol. 2—the Personal Style.* by Armes, Roy. 175 p. illus. New York: A. S. Barnes, 1966.

An account of French cinema from the close of World War II to the mid-sixties, this book considers the personal style of a group of "New Wave" directors. Included for consideration are Franju, Melville, Chabrol, Godard, Truffaut, Varda, Resnais, Marker, Astruc, Malle, Vadim, Rouch, Demy, Etaix, Robbe-Grillet, Lelouch, and Rivette. A filmography and short biography is included for each.

Following a short general description of the film trends of the 20 post-World War II years, the book considers the style and some of the works of each director listed above. Because of the range covered, the discussions are brief. However, as an introduction to one of the most creative and influential periods of cinema history, this book is most valuable. Well written, concise, efficient, and a bit prejudiced, it is recommended as a primer for those interested in studying the work of the French New Wave directors in depth. For the general reader it is equally valuable and entertaining.

2441 *French Film.* by Armes, Roy. 160 p. paper illus. New York: Dutton, 1970.

This is a survey of 40 major French directors who have made films over the first 75 years of the motion picture—in other words, from Lumiere to Lelouch. Each is given a short critical and biographical sketch along with at least one related film still. The result is another outstanding *Dutton Pictureback* book. Highly recommended.

2442 *French Film.* by Sadoul, Georges. 131 p. illus. London: Falcon Press, 1953.

Written by a French film historian for British readers, this book is a history of French film from 1890 to 1950. It offers a fine balance of text and illustrations and once more underlines the significant and major contribution that French filmmakers have made to the art. It may be hard to find.

2443 *French Impressionist Cinema: Film Culture, Film Theory, and Film Style.* by Bordwell, David. New York: Arno, 1980.

The nature and development of the "French Impressionist" cinema (1918-1928) is examined including analyses of 36 films of the period. A title in the *Dissertations on Film* series.

2444 THE FRENCH LIEUTENANT'S WOMAN: *A Screenplay.* by Pinter, Harold. Boston, Mass.: Little, Brown, 1981.

The script of the 1981 film directed by Karel Reisz.

2445 *The French Literary Filmmakers.* by Michalczyk, John J. 187 p. illus. East Brunswick, N.J.: Art Alliance Press, 1980.

The dovetailing of the two arts, literature and cinema, in France is the subject of this study. Selected for analysis are such writer-filmmakers as Jean Cocteau, Sacha Guitry, Marcel Pagnol, Jean Giono, Andre Malraux, Alain Robbe-Grillet, and Marguerite Duras. The author suggests that although the literary intellectuals may lose their innocence upon becoming involved with film, they will gain a greater awareness of their own aesthetic talents and limitations.

Supporting the well-researched text are many film analyses, numerous chapter notes, a filmography and a bibliography for each subject, and an index. A few rather murky illustrations are added.

Certainly an examination of the literature-cinema relationship as it occurs in France is unusual. In a readable text that is detailed without becoming heavy, the author offers a scholarly investigation that is both fresh and creative.

2446 *French Social Cinema of the Nineteen Thirties.: A Cinematographic Expression of Popular Front Consciousness.* by Strebel, Elizabeth G.

New York: Arno, 1980.

This study examines why the French social film arose in 1935, and discusses the interaction between film and French society at that time. It considers film as an agent of historical change. A title in the *Dissertations on Film* series.

2447 *Friese-Greene: Close-Up of an Inventor.* by Allister, Ray. 192 p. illus. London: Marsland Publications, 1949.

The absorbing and tragic story of Britain's pioneer film inventor.

2448 *Fritz Lang.* by Eisner, Lotte H. 416 p. illus. New York: Oxford University Press, 1977.

The title of this volume may suggest a biography of Fritz Lang. Although a short autobiographical sketch does appear in the early pages, the greatest part of this book is devoted to a critical account of Lang's films beginning with TOTENTANZ (1919) and ending with DIE TAUSEND AUGEN DES DR. MABUSE (1960). In her examination of the films, Eisner relies on conversations, scripts, reviews, personal observations, and many other sources of information. The result is an in-depth study of the work of a legendary director that will serve as a standard interpretation. The care and thoroughness of the author is always apparent. Supporting her main text are a group of clearly reproduced stills, a bibliography, a detailed filmography, and a discussion of some unrealized Lang projects. The volume is not indexed.

The high quality of the Eisner text merits a superior production and the publishers have provided it. All of the elements of this book are blended into one of the most rewarding and satisfying director appreciations to appear in years. Highly recommended.

2449 *Fritz Lang.* by Armour, Robert A. illus. Boston: Twayne, 1978.

This early title in the *Theatrical Arts* series offers a critical appreciation of Fritz Lang. In addition to biographical information, the text discusses Lang's use of various plot devices, themes, and directorial techniques. For purposes of comparison, Armour divides the Lang films into genres: war, western, gangster, social protest, etc. For each film there is a plot synopsis, background information and comment. Notes, references, a filmography, a bibliography, and an index accompany this attractively produced appreciation.

2450 *Fritz Lang: The Image and the Look.* edited by Jenkins, Stephen. 168 p. illus. London: British Film Institute, 1981.

A re-evaluation of Lang's films with an emphasis on the female roles. An annotated filmography is included.

2451 *Fritz Lang in America.* by Bogdanovich, Peter. 144 p. paper illus. New York: Praeger, 1967.

In this printed interview, Fritz Lang looks at his American films made during the period 1936 to 1956. The interview is preceded by a short critical article on Lang and his work. Questions to Lang by the author are well-chosen and some represent issues that film buffs have discussed for years. For example: What was the reason for the "cop-out" finale for WOMAN IN THE WINDOW? (1944) or What was Lang's role in the 1951 remake of M?

The illustrations are plentiful, beautifully reproduced, and intelligently selected. Topic, treatment, format and production combine to make this an outstanding volume. One very minor negative point in the book design is the use of oversize solid black letters for chapter headings and title pages. But, no matter, this volume is highly recommended.

2452 *Fritz Lang/Bernardo Bertolucci.* edited by Reed, Rochelle. 28 p. paper illus. Washington, D.C.: American Film Institute, 1974.

The interview with Fritz Lang contained here was made in May, 1973, with James Powers, RochelleReed and Donald Chase. Bertolucci and actress Argentina Brunetti spoke at a seminar held on January 16, 1974. Filmographies for both directors are included.

2453 *From Caligari to Hitler: A Psychological History of the German Film.* by Kracauer, Siegfried. 361 p. illus. Princeton, N.J.: Princeton University Press, 1947.

This book is an attempt to use film as a medium of research. Analyzing the German films from 1918 to 1933 can provide predictive evidence of the events that took place during the Hitler era. Kracauer deals with popular pictorial and narrative motifs, and with psychological dispositions as reflected in films. The book is a classic of its kind—brilliant, intellectual, probing, and intuitive. Advanced readers will savor its many outstanding qualities. The stills are beautifully reproduced. A valuable structural analysis and an excellent bibliography are included. Highly recommended.

2454 *From Enchantment to Rage.* by Kovacs, Steven. 297 p. illus. East Brunswick, N.J.: Fairleigh Dickinson University Press, 1980.

Kovac's study, which is subtitled "The Story of Surrealist Cinema," has two aims: an examination of the Surrealists' interest in films, and the reflection of the movement's aims and concerns in selected films. Certain limitations are imposed: the period is 1923 to 1930, the time of the original Surrealist movement in Paris; the films are limited to those made by members of the movement and accepted by them as being surrealistic.

In a detailed, documented text the author discusses the poets, their films, and the limited realization of their goals in using film as a medium for surrealism.

Some poorly produced frame enlargements, copious chapter notes, scenarios of several Man Ray films, a bibliography and an index complete the work.

Here is a work of dedication that has been thoroughly researched and carefully presented. However, since the films are not easily available for study or viewing, the result is a pedantic reading exercise that will delight a small scholarly audience.

2455 *From Fiction to Film:* THE ROCKING HORSE WINNER. by Barrett, Gerald R.; and Erskine, Thomas L. 238 p. paper illus. Encino, Calif.: Dickenson Pub Co., 1974.

As the third volume in the valuable *From Fiction to Film* series, this one uses the same structure as the earlier books. The D. H. Lawrence short story is followed by three critical articles. Appearing next is the entire script of the feature film along with three essays about that film. Some suggestions for papers and an annotated bibliography complete the book. The few illustrations are poorly reproduced and seem unnecessary. This volume is a welcome addition to an impressive, continuing effort by the authors. The inclusion of a detailed shot-numbered script of a feature film adds a wider dimension to the series. Recommended.

2456 *From Fiction to Film... (A Series).* by Barrett, Gerald R.; and Erskine, Thomas L. paper illus. Encino, Calif.: Dickenson, 1972- .

This series is concerned with the teaching of short stories, films, and the art of adaptation. For each, Barrett provides the same introduction, which considers the problems of changing material from one medium to another. The original short story is reprinted with selected critical essays appended. The film section contains the script with correlated visuals. Selected critical essays are also given for the film, as are some suggestions for student papers on both the short story and the film.

The first two releases, treated individually elsewhere in this book, are AN OCCURRENCE AT OWL CREEK BRIDGE (1956) and SILENT SNOW, SECRET SNOW (1966). The third in the series is D. H. Lawrence's THE ROCKING HORSE WINNER (1949). Increasing interest in literary adaptations and the quality of the first two releases more than justify this series.

2457 *From Hollywood.* by Bodeen, DeWitt. 352 p. illus. New York: A.S. Barnes, 1976.

The subtitle of this collective biography, "The Careers of 15 American Stars," is not exact since the volume treats 17 performers. Of these, eight were known only for their work in silent films: Theda Bara, Marguerite Clark, Geraldine Farrar, Harold Lockwood, May Allison, Wallace Reid, Anita Stewart, and Constance Talmadge. The remaining nine who made the transition from silent to sound films are: John Barrymore, Delores Costello, Alice Brady, Lon Chaney, Betty Compson, Bebe Daniels, Delores Del Rio, Richard Dix, and Douglas Fairbanks, Sr.

The career of each subject is described by text, a full-page portrait, several nicely reproduced stills, and a filmography. Since the text material has been taken mostly from previously published sources, it is factual and descriptive rather than critical. Bodeen's selection and treatment of these legendary film performers is most satisfactory. For the audience who remembers them, the book will be a nostalgic treat. Acceptable.

2458 *From Hollywood with Love.* by Love, Bessie. 160p. illus. North Pomfret, Vermont: Hamish Hamilton (David & Charles), 1977.

Bessie Love has had a long career in films, starting with THE FLYING TORPEDO (1916) and continuing for six decades through THE RITZ (1976). At this writing she remains active as a featured player. Her autobiography tells mostly of her early days and her experiences with Griffith, Fairbanks, THE BROADWAY MELODY (1929), and other Hollywood personalities, films, and activities. The book's final pages tell how, after World War II, she busied herself with British radio, plays, television, and films.

There are some illustrations, a filmography, and an index.

Aside from a firsthand recall of Hollywood during its most important developmental period, Besie Love has provided an admirable self-portrait. She is objective, and uses the same no-nonsense approach that one can witness in her work over the last 60 years. A strong, talented, and likeable woman is presented in these pages. Recommended.

2459 *From Jules Verne to* STAR TREK. by Rovin, Jeff. 147 p. paper illus. New York: Drake, 1977.

A survey of science fiction movies is the substance of this volume. With many illustrations, the author identifies his selection of films by casts, credits, plot synopses, general comments, etc.

Rovin is becoming an old hand at this kind of book. His selection here is fairly interesting and his critical treatment is reasonable. A few television series are also noted.

2460 *From Reverence to Rape.* by Haskell, Molly. 388 p. paper illus. New York: Holt, Rinehart and Winston, 1973.

The subtitle, "The Treatment of Women in the Movies," describes the concern of this stimulating volume. An introductory overview position of how women have been presented, portrayed, or visualized in film is followed by a historical review divided into decades. Special sections are devoted to the woman's film and to the European films and directors. The author believes the director to be an important element in the creation of the female roles in films. She discusses many of them, and cites numerous examples of films which present different views of women. Her major argument is that women have lost much ground from the twenties to the sixties. In recent years they seem to be an "endangered species."

Several groups of well-reproduced illustrations are offered, but they are too few and too selective for such an encompassing topic. In one illustration Madge Evans is identified as Constance Cummings, a surprising error since Ms. Haskell is so accurate in text and other visuals. A detailed index adds value and dimension to the book. This volume is a most welcome review of a neglected topic in film history. The author's development and original treatment of the material is outstanding. Highly recommended for mature readers.

2461 *From Sambo to Superspade: The Black Experience in Motion Pictures.* by Leab, Daniel J. 301 p. paper illus. Boston: Houghton Mifflin, 1975.

It is unfortunate that this volume is such a late entry among the several surveys of the black image in films that have appeared recently. Although the production values of the book are excellent, the very detailed text covers material very similar to that found in Noble, Mapp, Bogle and other books. This may be another instance of the occupational hazards of disparate authors preparing manuscripts on the same topic simultaneously.

Leab covers the first films, THE BIRTH OF A NATION (1914), later silents, early sound films, the pioneering portraits of the forties, Horne, Poitier, Belafonte, Dandridge, and the black box-office hits of the seventies. The text tends toward the factual or descriptive narrative and avoids any original critical analyses. As a result much of it is familiar.

Picture selection and reproduction are excellent. Notes, a bibliography and an index complete the work. The book has been well researched and is comprehensive in its coverage. However, the omission of William Hoffman's biography of Sidney Poitier, Wall's chapter on Blacks in Film and Newquist's interview with Poitier in *A Special Kind of Magic* is a bit puzzling. Acceptable.

2462 *From Scarface to Scarlett: American Films in the 1930's.* by Dooley, Roger. 704 p. illus. New York: Harcourt Brace Jovanovich, 1981.

A survey of films from Hollywood, 1930 to 1939, this history emphasizes the factual rather than the critical. The arrangement is by genre, an improvement over the typical chronology.

2463 *From Script to Screen.* by Woodhouse, Bruce. 192 p. illus. London: Winchester, 1948.

Following an introduction by Alexander Korda, this volume follows the production of a film by describing such things as how a film is planned, a day in the studio, the formation of a team, actors, studio personnel, location shooting, advertising, etc. Includes property dope sheet, studio call sheet, a script extract, etc.

2464 *From* THE BLOB to STAR WARS— The Science Fiction Movie Quiz Book. by Andrews, Bart; and

Davenport, Howard. 154 p. paper illus. New York: Signet, 1977.

This paperback consists of 101 quizzes on science fiction films. The usual format—questions and matching, appear along with one quiz based on the 24 illustrations in the center section. Answers are provided in the rear pages. The subtitle, "1001 Trivia Teasers for Sci-Fi Fans," sums it all up nicely.

2465 *From the Land Beyond Beyond.* by Rovin, Jeff. 277 p. paper illus. New York: Berkley, 1977.

This volume, which is subtitled "The Films of Willis O'Brien and Ray Harryhausen," is not only a tribute to the technical artistry of both men but is also a review of their film careers. After an introductory chapter dealing with Melies and his early screen effects, the text traces Willis O'Brien's work from a first stop-motion film, THE DINOSAUR AND THE MISSING LINK (1917), to KING KONG (1933), followed by relative oblivion until his death in 1962. This short section devoted to O'Brien suggests that he was not aware of the classic status of KING KONG and of his reputation as a special effects pioneer. The major portion of the volume concerns Ray Harryhausen, who was inspired by the work of O'Brien. Working initially with O'Brien on MIGHTY JOE YOUNG (1949), he progressed rapidly to independent production on THE BEAST FROM TWENTY THOUSAND FATHOMS (1953). His few films are detailed and the text ends with a chapter on other animators such as George Pal, Jim Danforth, and Eiji Tsuburaya. The volume is indexed and well illustrated. Unfortunately there is no filmography; as a result, to ascertain dates, credits, or a concentrated total view of the work of each man, it is necessary to search the text (which does not always provide the information.)

The outstanding feature of the book is its attention to the special effects provided for each film. It will inspire a respect and admiration for such dedicated animators as O'Brien and Harryhausen. Recommended.

2466 FROM THE LIFE OF THE MARIONETTES. by Bergman, Ingmar. 99 p. paper illus. New York: Pantheon, 1980.

Script of the 1980 film directed by Bergman.

2467 *From the Stocks to the Stars.* by Lupino, Stanley. 288 p. illus. London: Hutchinson, 1934.

Subtitled "An Unconventional Autobiography," this book is the story of the musical comedy actor who made many films during the thirties. He also wrote for both stage and screen, and was a theatrical producer. His daughter is Ida Lupino.

2468 *From Under My Hat.* by Hopper, Hedda. 311 p. Garden City, N.Y.: Doubleday & Co., 1952.

The obligation of writing a Hollywood gossip column on a regular schedule had a debilitating effect on this autobiography. Portions of it are perceptive, well-written, and absorbing. Other sections are gossipy anecdotes spiced with innuendo and suggestion. Most of the time Miss Hopper names names, only occasionally resorting to the libel-suit protection of anonymity.

Early portions of the book are devoted to the author's life in the theatre as Mrs. DeWolf Hopper. Her first visit to Hollywood in 1915 begins a long association with the motion picture industry and its personalities. Only the last few pages are devoted to her career as a columnist with the 1920-1940 period receiving greatest attention. There is no index or illustration. Not very important in film literature the book is still fun and will please most readers. Film buffs will enjoy many of the anecdotes and nonperceptive opinions, e.g., CITIZEN KANE (1941) was praised out of proportion to its merit.

2469 *Front and Center.* by Houseman, John. 512 p. illus. New York: Simon & Schuster, 1979.

John Houseman is a dependable professional who has proven his talent and ability as producer, director, actor and author. It is in the latter capacity that he continues the autobiography he began in *Runthrough.* A short recap of the earlier volume is followed by accounts of his experiences with "The Voice of America (1942-43)," "Hollywood as Producer (1943-1946)," "The Theatre (1947-1950)," and "Once Again, Hollywood (1951-1955)."

The sections dealing with film production in the 40's and 50's are totally absorbing as they evidence a dedicated professional in action. His portrait of the worlds of film and theatre includes many character sketches of the inhabitants therein. In this book Houseman does not dwell on himself but on that which was to be accomplished. The result is fascinating reading. Highly recommended.

2470 *Full Length Animated Feature Films.* by Edera, Bruno. 198 p. illus. New York: Hastings House, 1977.

The title and the cover of this volume suggest a potential that is not easy to satisfy. Fortunately, this book delivers more than is expected and does it in a way that is visually, intellectually, and aesthetically satisfying. The text is divided into two sections, the first of which deals with the history and aesthetics of the animated feature film. How this form developed in America, Europe, the Middle East, Asia, and Australasia is related. Modern developments including some new directions for the animated feature are noted. The second part of the book is an extended filmography that lists many animated feature films alphabetically by country of origin—from Argentina to the U.S.A. Each entry contains the title, technical data, extensive credits, and a story outline. Critical evaluation is not provided. Final pages note works in progress, uncompleted works, films with insufficient information, and films with animation inserts—e.g., ANCHORS AWEIGH (1945), MARY POPPINS (1964). A bibliography and an index complete the volume. Throughout the book there are many well-reproduced illustrations, some in color.

This volume can be enthusiastically recommended for a number of reasons. Primarily it is an enormously satisfying reading experience that can be enjoyed by a wide audience range. Some reservation might be noted about the story descriptions of recent animated films such as FRITZ THE CAT (1972) and HEAVY TRAFFIC (1973) but taste and discrimination prevail. As a reference the volume fills a void in cinema literature by providing easy access to information about a neglected film genre. The international coverage is very impressive in both sections. Finally, the appreciation and affection that the author feels for his subject is communicated clearly to the reader. For the most part the text avoids explanations of technical processes, opting instead to relate an account of the historical development of the form. The many films described in detail complement the factual narrative in excellent fashion.

As usual the production values supplied by the publishers are outstanding in today's marketplace of cinema books. Highly recommended.

2471   *Fun and Games with* JESSIE JAMES. by Walker, Don. 74 p. paper illus. Pineville, Mo.: McDonald County News Gazette, 1976.

In 1938 the lives of the inhabitants of McDonald County in Missouri were shaken when a 20th Century Fox troupe arrived to film JESSE JAMES (1939). At that time the author was a police reporter and feature writer for *The Joplin Globe*. In covering the filming he wrote many articles and it is this source material he has used for this volume. Since he has opted for an emphasis on pleasant nostalgia rather than stark realism, the book is a sunny, affectionate

memoir of location shooting during Hollywood's golden era. Some line drawings have been provided by Michael Keefe.

This enjoyable look at the past tells us almost as much about the author as it does about filming JESSE JAMES. Both are pleasant subjects. Acceptable.

2472   *Fun in a Chinese Laundry.* by von Sternberg, Josef. 348 p. illus. New York: Macmillan, 1965.

More a collection of anecdotes and memoirs than a linear autobiography, this book does present a rather full portrait of this controversial artist-con man-director. Written with a cynical, sophisticated, biting, literate and sometimes persuasive style, von Sternberg continually announces that his only interest is to present material which will clarify his complex personality to the reader. Perhaps. In his zealousness to reveal the real von Sternberg, many other persons receive his scornful eye. Laughton, Jennings, DeMille, and even Dietrich, among others, do not fare well at all. Any young person interested in film directing will find this account inspirational. Others will find it completely entertaining. There are a few pictures and an index. Very highly recommended.

2473   FUNNY GIRL. by Brodsky, Jack. 48 p. paper illus. New York: National Publishers, 1968.

Stars Barbra Streisand and Omar Sharif and director William Wyler are introduced in the opening sections of this souvenir book. "Behind the Cameras of FUNNY GIRL" includes producer Ray Stark, dance director Herb Ross, and scriptwriter Isobel Lennart. "Presenting Miss Fanny Brice" pays tribute to the original subject, while "Words and Music" discusses the musical portions of the 1968 film. Supporting players Walter Pidgeon, Kay Medford, and Ann Francis are each given one biographical page, along with listings of the cast and production credits.

2474   *Funny Men of the Movies.* by Edelson, Edward. 128 p. illus. New York: Doubleday, 1976.

Written for a juvenile audience, this volume is concerned with comedy in movies. Its approach is through the men—actors, producers, and directors —whose forte was comedy and their films. Individual chapters are given to Mack Sennett, Chaplin, Keaton, Laurel and Hardy, the Marx Brothers, and W. C. Fields. Many other performers who appeared in such comedy genres as screwball comedies or short subjects share the remaining pages.

A few reservations must be stated. The Library of Congress Cataloging in Publication Data given in the book's opening pages states: "...discusses comedy in movies and television and such funny men as...the Hardys...." With the exception of a few lines on pages 116-117 television is hardly mentioned in the text. The Sons of the Desert might sue if they discovered their idols called "the Hardys." Certain portions involving critical judgment seem vulnerable. For example, in discussing Danny Kaye, only THE COURT JESTER (1956) and THE INSPECTOR GENERAL (1949) are treated. With Preston Sturges no mention is made of THE MIRACLE OF MORGAN'S CREEK (1944). Is Bob Hope really "as big a hit in the 1970s as he was in the 1930s" and was Mae West "a female W. C. Fields" ?

Although much of his text has been selected with perception and stated with skill, there are a number of disturbing evaluations and omissions. For the knowledgeable, mature reader this is no problem for he understands the fallibility of writing about films. However, for the young person who is seeking information is there not a disservice in presenting questionable critical judgment as fact or data? In addition to the text there are some rather good illustrations provided along with a useful index.

Perhaps better editorial advice might have minimized the debatable portions of the text. The volume is acceptable with the reservation noted above.

2475 *The Funsters.* by Parish, James Robert; and Leonard, William T. 752 p. illus. New Rochelle, N.Y.: Arlington House, 1979.

This massive volume offers biographies of 62 film comedians, ranging in length from nine pages (Arthur Lake) to 15 pages (Eve Arden). Most of the pieces, however, occupy about ten pages which include text, illustrations, and a filmography. The subjects are arranged alphabetically and probably the only major film comics missing from this imposing roster are Hugh Herbert, Edgar Kennedy, and Andy Clyde. As usual with Parish volumes, the selection and the reproduction of the numerous illustrations are outstanding. The text is largely factual, although occasional criticism/evaluation is offered and even some gossip or trivia materials pop up now and again. The result is a series of short, terse biographical sketches that serve to remind the reader of the artistry of these unique comic actors. Parish has served up another fine smorgasbord of biography. There's something here for everyone and no one goes away hungry. Recommended.

2476 *Future Indefinite: An Autobiography, 1939-45.* by Coward, Noel. 336 p. illus. London: William Heinemann, 1954.

Another installment of Coward's autobiography. See also *Present Indicative.*

2477 *Future of the British Film Industry.* edited by Prime Minister's Working Party. 33 p. paper London: Her Majesty's Stationery Office, 1976.

A report of the Prime Minister's Working Party chaired by John Terry.

2478 *Future Tense: The Cinema of Science Fiction.* by Brosnan, John. 320 p. paper illus. New York: St. Martin's Press, 1978.

Brosnan begins his chronological survey of science fiction films with a strong criterion: they must involve some aspect of science (in a very broad sense) as the reason for the story. He then proceeds to examine, in both a critical and descriptive fashion, almost 400 films from A TRIP TO THE MOON (1903) to STAR WARS (1977). Emphasis is on the more recent films; the 1977-78 period receives almost twice the number of pages that the 30-year silent film era does. Brosnan's selection and treatment may be very subjective (where is 2001: A SPACE ODYSSEY?) but he does include many fascinating films. His personal comments are balanced with background material, quotes, and plot summaries, all of which combine to provide an above average survey of a film genre.

Illustrations are provided along with a filmography of science fiction TV movies, references, and indexes.

2479 *G. W. Pabst.* by Atwell, Lee. 184 p. illus. Boston: Twayne, 1977.

Geog Wilhelm Pabst, the noted German film director, is the subject of this volume in the Twayne *Theatrical Arts* series. The chapters of the text are arranged chronologically—The Early Years, The Silent Period, The Louise Brooks Years, The French Period, The Nazi Period, etc. A summary, chapter notes-references, a bibliography, a filmography, and an index complete the book. A few illustrations are included.

Known in America for films such as THE JOYLESS STREET (1925), THE LOVE OF JEANNE NEY (1927), PANDORA'S BOX (1928), THE WHITE HELL OF PITZ-PALU (1929), THE THREEPENNY OPERA (1931), and KAMERADSCHAFT (1931), Pabst has been a rare subject for English language cinema literature. This well-written appreciation should remedy that neglect and bring renewed attention to a pioneer artist-auteur-director. Recommended.

2480 *Gable.* by Williams, Chester. 154 p. illus. New York: Fleet Press Corp., 1968.

This short, expensive volume adds nothing to the Gable story. Some hints, a little innuendo, and a great deal of repetition of oft-told anecdotes are its substance. Two picture sections are poor in both selection and reproduction. There is a listing of his films but no index is provided. Interested readers should be sent to *The Films Of Clark Gable* or to *The King.* Not recommended.

2481 *Gable: A Complete Gallery of His Screen Portraits.* edited by Essoe, Gabe; and Lee, Ray. 144 p. paper illus. Los Angeles: Price, Stern, Sloan, 1967.

Following an author's introduction, a foreword by Joan Crawford, and a short chapter of biography, this volume considers all of Gable's films in chronological order. Publicity stills, film credits, the cast, a brief plot synopsis and an excerpt from a review are included for each film. This small, unassuming volume is better in many ways than some larger ones on the films of other stars. Picture reproduction is sharp and distinct. The unfamiliarity of many of the stills is a delight. Most of the review quotes are well selected. The size of the volume may make it an orphan when it is compared to the *Citadel* Series.

2482 *Gable and Lombard.* by Harris, Warren G. 189 p. illus. New York: Simon & Schuster, 1974.

Since Clark Gable's death in 1960 there have been several full-length biographies and at least three volumes about his films. Lombard has been the subject of one *Citadel* collection and of large sections of the Gable biographies, and has been included in several collective biographies such as *The Paramount Pretties.* After this heavy coverage, what is left to say about these two? Fortunately, Warren Harris not only has uncovered some original material, but also retells the well-known factual portions with a fresh and breezy approach that makes the familiar seem new.

Sufficient attention is paid to their early careers but the author has wisely concentrated on the period of their romance and marriage. Anecdotes, interpretations and characterizations are abundantly sprinkled throughout the narrative, which is pleasantly objective. Faults and virtues are given equal coverage and the subjects are portrayed as two fortunate human beings who enjoyed each other. A few illustrations and an index support this entertaining biography. Since some of Lombard's quotations are full of colorful obscenities, this volume is recommended primarily for mature readers.

2483 *Gable and Lombard and Powell and Harlow.* by Morella, Joe; and Epstein, Edward Z. 272 p. paper illus. New York: Dell, 1975.

To attempt a collective biography on a quartet of film stars when three of them have already been the subjects of many books and articles takes courage. Not only have the authors succeeded in retelling some familiar material, but they also have provided a biographical interweaving of the lives that is both fascinating and imaginative. Improving on a structure used by Garson Kanin in *Tracy and Hepburn* and borrowing the form and suggestion implicit in the film title, BOB AND CAROL AND TED AND ALICE (1969), they have fashioned a book which will attract and please a wide range of readers.

Well-researched and written with honesty, style and frankness, the book covers the Hollywood careers of four major personalities. William Powell has not been the subject of any previous books—and he gets the least attention here—probably because of the rather sedate private life he has always chosen for himself. The other three are part of the flamboyance that characterized Hollywood in the thirties. Illustrations, which are placed throughout the book, are adequately reproduced. Unfortunately no filmographies are provided and the book is not indexed.

The authors have a list of film books to their credit and they have apparently honed their biographical skills to a high degree of craftsmanship. This entertaining volume blends research, a terse literary style, a sense of popular appeal, and four legendary film personalities into one of the best collective biographies to appear in a long while. Recommended.

2484 *Gadney's Guide to 1800 International Contests, Festivals and Grants...* by Gadney, Alan. 518 p. paper Glendale, Calif.: Festival, 1978.

The full title of this handy reference book is *Gadney's Guide to 1800 International Contests, Festivals, and Grants in Film and Video, Photography, TV-Radio Broadcasting, Writing, Poetry, Playwriting and Journalism.* Entries in the film section are arranged under 30 headings such as abstract, animated, short, grants, student filmmaker, etc. For each there is complete sponsor data, the date, a description of the event, the general rules, fees, awards, judging information and deadlines. Further access to the events/grants is provided by a alphabetical index and a subject/category index.

Anyone planning to participate in or attend film events or to seek grants can do no better than begin with this efficiently arranged volume. It is a concentrated, rich source of information.

2485 *The Gangster Film.* by Baxter, John. 160 p. paper illus. New York: A. S. Barnes, 1970.

A historical essay on the gangster film followed by a mini- dictionary of 220 entries—directors, actors, real gangsters, etc.

2486 *The Gangster Film, 1930-1940.* by Karpf, Stephen Louis. 299 p. illus. New York: Arno, 1973.

This is one of the doctoral dissertations on film topics which are reproduced exactly as submitted to the degree-granting school. An introduction which explains the study is followed by an analysis of some archetypical films—LITTLE CAESAR (1930), THE PUBLIC ENEMY (1931), SCARFACE (1932) and THE PETRIFIED FOREST (1936). The decay of the gangster film, and how and why it occurred, is explored by the examples of Robinson, Muni, Cagney and Bogart. A concluding section tries to isolate the positive contributions made by the genre to later films. Some other pertinent films are examined by script excerpts, synopses, cast and production credits. A bibliography completes the study. Acceptable.

2487 *Gangster Movies.* by Hossent, Harry. 160 p. illus. London: Octopus Books, 1974.

Excellent visuals are the outstanding feature of this book. Using over 200 illustrations, including 26 color pages, the volume surveys "The Gangsters, Hoodlums and Tough Guys of the Screen." The structure of the narrative is thematic rather than chronological, with the author employing the chatty fan magazine style of a tour guide rather than the serious approach of a teacher-critic. As a result the book's appeal rests largely on the visuals and they are quite good, indeed. A title index and a general index complete this satisfying pictorial exploration of a film genre. Recommended.

2488 *Gangsters.* by Gabree, John. 156 p. paper illus. New York: Pyramid, 1973.

The subtitle of this genre study is "From LITTLE CAESAR to THE GODFATHER," indicating coverage of the era of sound films. After some genre generalization and an examination of the biographical gangster film, a chronological approach is employed. Separate chapters are devoted to the thirties, the early forties, the post-war films, and to the violent years of the early fifties and sixties. BONNIE AND CLYDE (1967) and THE GODFATHER (1972) rate special attention as the next-to-closing topics. The concluding section examines the gangster films of today. A selected filmography for this genre is arranged alphabetically by title and gives some cast and credit names. A short bibliography and an index complete the book. Illustrations have been well selected and placed. With the exception of a few dark ones, they are well reproduced.

It is the text here that deserves praise. It is clearly written, with a respect for the genre and a clear goal constantly in evidence. Comprehensive in scope, it is consistent in both entertaining and informing the reader. Recommended.

2489 *Gangsters and Hoodlums: The Underworld in the Cinema.* by Lee, Raymond; and Van Hecke, B. C. illus. 264 p. New York: A. S. Barnes, 1971.

The title notwithstanding, this book is really a random collection of stills. Some are related to the theme while others are not—FURY (1936), THE YOUNG STRANGER (1957), DOUBLE INDEMINITY (1944), for example, are all out of place. Under a chapter head, "Hoods Down Through the Years..." one finds Robert Montgomery, John Barrymore, Clark Gable, Gene Kelly, James Mason, Ray Milland, etc. There are four pages of "The Faces of Rod Steiger" which include stills from THE LOVED ONE (1964) and THE MARK (1961). In many cases either a still is not identified or a well-known performer is ignored while lesser names are mentioned. Certain photographic sequences begin in the middle of a page and extend to the middle of the next one. A large picture of Lyle Bettger appears on page 217 that is almost identical with the one on page 140. The choice of stills is poor, the arrangement of the book is careless and haphazard, the text is intellectually insulting and the entire result is disastrous. Readers are referred to the less expensive and far superior *The Heavies.*

2490 *Gangsters From* LITTLE CAESAR *to* THE GODFATHER. by Gabree, John. Farmingdale, N.Y.: Brown, 1980.

2491 *Garbo.* by Bainbridge, John. 256 p. illus. Garden City, N.Y.: Doubleday, 1955.

Of all the Garbo biographies, this one is probably the most satisfying. It includes all of the factual material of other books, and then supplements it with critical analysis of her professional career and some personal supposition based on her history and her behavioral patterns. A filmography and an index complete the portrait. An excellent biography.

2492 *Garbo.* by Zierold, Norman. 196 p. illus. New York: Stein and Day, 1969.

Another biography of the screen's foremost legend, this book adds little that is new. Some interviews, several anecdotes, a half dozen or so unfamiliar pictures added to a well-known story. The real mystique never emerges. Dedicated fans of Garbo may enjoy this book, but others are advised to look at the other materials available.

2493 *Garbo: A Biography.* by Billquist, Fritiof. 255 p. illus. New York: G. P. Putman's, 1960.

Translated from the Swedish, this biography was written by a friend and fellow actor. Much of the volume consists of reconstructed conversations, early letters, quotes from periodicals, etc. All these are linked together by a chatty, story-telling narrative. Easy to read and with much entertainment value, the book is a pleasant nondefintive retelling of a familiar story. Pictures, a filmography, and an index are included. Not a major contribution to film literature.

2494 *Garbo.* by Sjolander, Ture. 139 p. illus. New York: Harper and Row, 1971.

This attempt at Garbo's biography is told largely via oversized photographs, a brief text, and supporting evidence such as horoscope, handwriting analysis, and caricatures. Photographs used in the major portion of the book are family snaps, publicity pictures, candids, and newspaper shots. The film stills are located on the last four pages. Thus we have many portraits of Garbo off-screen which can be interpreted to a large extent by the viewer. The text supplied by the author supplements but never dictates interpretation of the Garbo charisma or mystery. Quality of photo reproduction is unusually good with a few exceptions. Several double-page illustrations place the subject near the centerfold, thus limiting their effectiveness. The nature of the volume does not suggest an index.

This is a specialized, high-priced volume that will enrapture a small audience, generally please a larger audience, and probably mystify the youth audience. The amount of knowledge this book adds to the Garbo legend is debatable and it is a rather costly entertainment.

2495 *Garbo: A Portrait.* by Walker, Alexander. 191 p. illus. New York: Macmillan, 1980.

The majority of the photographs in this volume are the copyright of Metro-Goldwyn-Mayer, who authorized this biography of Garbo. In addition to the visuals they allowed film historian Alexander Walker unlimited access to the studio files. Unfortunately the promise of such a collaboration is unfulfilled, as this biography adds little to what is already public knowledge of Garbo. Some business and professional matters are disclosed, but these tend to reinforce the established persona of the actress rather than enlarge it.

The fact that Garbo has been the subject of many book-length studies for almost 50 years, and that, in addition, there are hundreds of shorter articles available may account for the familiarity of this portrait. However, Walker is a meticulous writer and he has used his resources with intelligence and skill. Although the partnership with MGM may have limited certain aspects, the visuals with which they have supplied him add newness. Some of the interpretation about Garbo's studio life is fresh, and the amount of factual information offered is enormous. For the reader seeking Garbo's story for the first time, this volume would seem to be a good choice. Others will find enough to keep them deeply interested.

2496 *Garbo and the Night Watchman: A Selection from the Writings of British and American Film Critics.* edited by Cooke, Alistair. 352 p. London: Cape, 1937.

This classic anthology of critical writings from America and Britain has been long out of print and is very hard to find. Nine critics are involved and they all consider one picture, MODERN TIMES (1931), in the book's concluding section. The participants are Robert Herring, Don Herold, John Marks, Meyer Levin, Alistair Cooke, Robert Forsythe, Graham Greene, Otis Ferguson, and Cecilia Ager.

2497 *The Garden of Allah.* by Graham, Sheilah. 256 p. illus. New York:

Crown, 1970.

In 1927 Alla Nazimova converted her Hollywood mansion into a bungalow hotel called, logically, The Garden of Allah. During its three decades of existence, it was famous as a haven where Hollywood's personalities could play, fight and cavort without worrying about the public eye. The hotel was closed in 1959 and the hottest items at auction were Errol Flynn's beds. Considering the richness of material upon which she could draw, Miss Graham's book is quite bad. For the undiscriminating reader.

2498 *Gary Cooper.* by Arce, Hector. 260 p. paper illus. New York: Bantam, 1980.

In this well-researched biography, which is described as "intimate," Hector Arce traces the event-filled life of Gary Cooper. From the ambitious young actor who apparently used sex to advance his career to the icon of the screen who exemplified the strong silent American hero, Cooper enjoyed a long stay as a Hollywood star. Arce covers his story in lively detail emphasizing the early uninhibited sexual behavior and the later maturity that enabled Cooper to be kind to those who worked with him.

Although there is no filmography, most of Cooper's films are discussed in the text. A bibliography and a center section of illustrations are included. Of the three Cooper biographies which appeared almost simultaneously around 1979-1980, Arce's is the most gossipy/popularized. Larry Swindell's *The Last Hero* has more over-all quality as serious biography, while Stuart Kaminsky's *Coop* is overly pedantic.

2499 *Gary Cooper.* by Jordan, Rene. 160 p. paper illus. New York: Pyramid, 1974.

A general description of the typical character that Gary Cooper played on the screen introduces this review of his films. Some early biographical data leads to Cooper's film debut as a stuntman, extra, and bit player in the mid-twenties. From the first major film, THE WINNING OF BARBARA WORTH (1926) to THE NAKED EDGE (1961), his 85 films are recalled here with both a descriptive and critical narrative. A filmography, a bibliography and an index complete the volume. The illustrations, which are mostly stills and portraits, are well reproduced and provide a record of Cooper's maturing as a film performer. The volume is a well-written and fitting tribute to an actor whose art was often misunderstood or underrated. Jordan has captured the essence of the screen Gary Cooper. Recommended.

2500 *The Gary Cooper Story.* by Carpozi, George, Jr. 263 p. illus. New Rochelle, N.Y.: Arlington House, 1970.

A biography along with many photographs and a filmography of Cooper's 95 films.

2501 *The Gay Illiterate.* by Parsons, Louella O. 194 p. Garden City, N.Y.: Garden City Pub. Co., 1944.

This autobiography of the most famous Hollywood columnist covers her career from a Dixon, Illinois, schoolgirl working summers as a reporter to the most powerful gossip goddess of the forties. As she recalls her personal story, she seasons it with saccharine accounts of her favorite celebrities and some vinegary observations about others. None of this is offered with any depth or great perception. It is opinionated reporting in the journalistic tradition of "names make news." Written during World War II years, some of the material is a bit embarrassing (Japanese-Americans are called vermin). No index or illustrations are provided. There is inevitable interest in the story of such a powerful woman. Along with Walter Winchell, she was one of a kind and we will probably not see her like again. Some historical value but the modern cinema buff will find little attraction.

2502 *Gays and Films.* edited by Dyer, Richard. 78 p. paper illus. London: British Films Institute; New York: Zoetrope, 1977.

An unusual anthology is presented in this original paperback. Three essays dealing in detail with gay topics are included along with a lengthy filmography and bibliography. The first article by Caroline Sheldon offers some thoughts about lesbians and films. Stereotyping in films is discussed next by Richard Dyer and the final essay by Jack Babuscio deals with camp and the gay sensibility. The long filmography by Dyer is not annotated, but offers many surprising titles—GILDA (1946), THERE WAS A CROOKED MAN (1969), etc.

Exploitation and sensationalism are absent here. This is a volume that is sensitive, intelligent, and serious in its intent—the examination in depth of a few aspects of gayness in films.

2503 *Gene Kelly.* by Burrows, Michael. paper illus. Cornwall, England: Primestyle, 1971.

Pictures, films, discussion about Kelly in the usual Burrows-Primestyle fashion.

2504   *Gene Kelly.* by Basinger, Jeanine. 160 p. paper illus. New York: Pyramid. 1976.

This title in the *Pyramid Illustrated History of the Movies* series assesses the life and films of Gene Kelly. In the usual terse style of the series, the author provides a critical appreciation that includes text, illustrations, a filmography, a bibliography, and an index.

2505   *Gene Kelly.* by Hirschhorn, Clive. 335 p. illus. Chicago: Henry Regnery, 1975.

With the cooperation of the subject and many people who have known or worked with him, Clive Hirschhorn has written a substantial biography of a very private man, Gene Kelly. Generous coverage is provided for his pre-Hollywood years; an account of the mounting of the stage musical, "Pal Joey," is especially absorbing and informative. The Hollywood years are described in detail, with more than usual attention given to the personal and professional aspects of Kelly's personality.

With only a few exceptions, the author writes with respect, objectivity and a security based on strong research. One can take exception to his omission of the Garland-Kelly "Be a Clown" finale to THE PIRATE (1948), his inference that KIND LADY (1951) starred Angela Lansbury and Betsy Blair, his assertion that HELLO DOLLY (1969) was the best film musical of the sixties, etc. But this emphasis on Kelly's creativity and ultimate success in liberating the Hollywood film musical more than compensates for the few vulnerable portions. Accompanying the unusually honest and forthright text (see, for examples, sections on Lorenz Hart, Michael Kidd, Louis B. Mayer, Barbra Streisand, Walter Matthau) are two photographic sections, a filmography, an index, and a short introduction-tribute by Frank Sinatra.

The author's evaluation of Kelly's contribution to film history is well documented in this fascinating and informative book. It is one of the better male-star biographies to appear in recent years and is recommended.

2506   THE GENERAL. by Rubinstein, E. 83 p. paper Bloomington, Ind.: Indiana University Press, 1973.

This *Filmguide* gives equal attention to THE GENERAL (1925) and its creator, Buster Keaton. After a few pages of credits and plot outline, the author summarizes the Keaton career, with emphasis on the production of THE GENERAL. In the next section, an in-depth analysis of the film is offered. Not only are the film's scenes described in detail but much description and evaluation of Keaton's technique is included. The summary critique is largely the author's rather than other critics. A partial filmography, a bibliography with some annotations, rental and purchase sources and some notes to the text complete the book.

The biographical sections are somewhat familiar, probably because of the earlier biographies and books, but the analysis section is new and provocative. Visual comedy cannot be described in print; thus, the author's aim here is not to make you laugh but to facilitate your understanding and appreciation of Keaton's artistry. In this endeavor, he succeeds. Since the film is easily available for detailed study, this volume can enrich that study experience to a great degree. Recommended.

2507   *General Bibliography of Motion Pictures.* edited by Vincent, Carl; and Redi, Riccardo; and Venturini, Franco. 252 p. New York: Arno, 1972.

This bibliography is presented in three languages—Italian, French and English—and includes both books and selected articles from periodicals. The classifications used are: general works; history; aesthetics, criticism; techniques; social, moral problems; legal, economic; cinema and science; 16mm and amateur Films; documentation, anthologies; subject, screenplays; unclassified books. The titles are arranged by author, and the annotations vary considerably. In some entries a complete table of contents is given, in others only a few words.

Use of this reference is not easy and some of the materials listed are too obscure for anyone except the most dedicated researcher. Acceptable.

2508   *A Generation of Motion Pictures.* by Short, William A. 402 p. New York: Garland, 1928.

This title in the *Garland Reprint* series is a collection of negative comments on motion pictures that led to the formation of Payne Fund Studies. The Reverend Short was untiring in his efforts to condemn the movies and to establish strong censorship.

2509   *The Genius: A Memoir of Max Reinhardt.* by Reinhardt, Gottfried. 420 p. illus. New York: Knopf, 1979.

Max Reinhardt was the producer-director of such stage spectacles as "The Miracle," "The Eternal Road," and "Die Fledermaus." The only existing example we have of his work is the 1935 film, A

MIDSUMMER NIGHT'S DREAM, which was an adaptation of his stage production. This memoir mentions the film only briefly and uses the director's last days, as recorded in his son's 1943 diary, as the inspiration for examining his legendary stage career.

2510 *The Genius of Busby Berkeley.* by Pike, Bob; and Martin, Dave. 194 p. paper illus. Reseda, Calif.: Creative Film Society, 1973.

This tribute to Busby Berkeley has much to recommend it. A long interview done in 1963 with Dave Martin is supplemented by appropriate correlated visuals. The biography by Bob Pike which follows is largely factual and avoids any critical interpretation of the influence of Berkeley's private life on his work. A pleasant pictorial section follows and the book ends with a detailed filmography which includes lengthy review excerpts.

The contributions in camera technique that Berkeley made to the art of the motion picture are often overlooked or demeaned because his genre was the musical—a case of content obscuring technique. This volume with the fine interview and the other supporting sections should do much to dispel any doubts about Berkeley's importance in film history. Though not as luxuriously produced as *The Busby Berkeley Book*, this volume is sure to please many readers. Recommended.

2511 *Genre.* by Neale, Stephen. New York: Zoetrope, 1980.

2512 *Genre: The Musical.* by Altman, Rick. 180 p. illus. Boston: Routledge and Kegan Paul, 1981.

2513 *Gentlemen to the Rescue: The Heroes of the Silent Screen.* by Lahue, Kalton C. 244 p. illus. New York: A. S. Barnes, 1972.

Another in the series of books ground out by the same author and publisher. Someone, somewhere, must be buying them, but this one is as bad as the others. Purportedly a collective biography of silent screen male stars, it has the predictable format. Two or three pages of narrative for each, followed by four or five pages of stills. A lifetime compressed into a few pages usually deteriorates into a series of factual sentences, and the bland recitals here are no exception. In most cases the picture quality is poor, with dark hues predominating to such an extent that the visual becomes murky and indistinct. A few stills are reproduced adequately.

Perhaps the greatest service this book can offer is the biography that is scarce or unavailable. To aid the searcher the list of players treated includes King Baggot, John Barrymore, Richard Barthelmess, Carlyle Blackwell, Francis X. Bushman, Lon Chaney, Ronald Colman, Maurice Costello, Richard Dix, Douglas Fairbanks, William Farnum, John Gilbert, Sessue Hayakawa, Johnny Hines, Jack Holt, Houdini, Rod LaRocque, Elmo Lincoln, Tommy Meighan, Tony Moreno, Ramon Novarro, Herbert Rawlinson, Charles Ray, Wallace Reid, Will Rogers, Milton Sills, Rudolph Valentino, Henry B. Walthall, Bryant Washburn, Ben Wilson. This book should be considered only when other sources are not available. It is not recommended.

2514 *George C. Scott: The Man, the Actor, the Legend.* by Harbinson, W. A. 243 p. paper illus. New York: Pinnacle, 1977.

An unauthorized biography of George C. Scott, this original paperback was researched via some interview transcripts, material found in newspapers and periodicals, and a few interviews. The result is a predictable surface portrait of the colorful actor, held together by many previous published Scott quotations. Illustrations, a filmography, and a record of his stage work are included. A freelance British writer, W.A. Harbison is also the author of *The Illustrated Elvis Presley* and *Bronson*.

2515 *George C. Scott/Trish Van DeVere.* edited by Reed, Rochelle. 24 p. paper illus. Washington, D.C.: American Film Institute, 1975.

During a publicity tour for his film, THE SAVAGE IS LOOSE (1974), George C. Scott along with his wife and costar, Trish Van DeVere, appeared for an interview at the AFI Center for Advanced Film Studies in October, 1974. A transcript of that discussion, which centered around the film, is reprinted here. Two short biographies, a long Scott filmography, a shorter one (six films) for Van DeVere, and Scott's television credits are added.

2516 *George Eastman.* by Ackerman, Carl William. 522 p. illus. New York: Houghton Mifflin, 1930.

A biography of George Eastman (1854-1942), the American pioneer in cinematography; it tells how his production of roll film made him a millionaire.

2517   *George Formby.* by Fisher, John. 96 p. illus. London: Woburn Press, 1975.

This title in the *Entertainer* Series deals with George Formby, a music hall comedian identified by a toothy grin and a ukelele. He appeared in films during the thirties and forties and, at one time, was Britain's top box-office star. Another biography, *George Formby*, by Alan Randal and Ray Seaton was published by W. H. Allen in 1974.

2518   *George Formby.* by Randal, Alan; and Seaton, Ray. 192 p. illus. London: W. H. Allen, 1974.

Formby is a toothy music hall entertainer who made most of his films during the World War II period. Another biography, *George Formby* by John Fisher, appeared in 1975.

2519   *The George Kleine Collection of Early Motion Pictures in The Library of Congress.* edited by Horwitz, Rita; and Harrison, Harriet. 270 p. illus. Washington, D.C.: Library of Congress, 1980.

The George Kleine Collection of 456 titles (900 reels) is an important part of the National Film Collection of the Library of Congress. This catalog identifies and describes the films, in addition to offering background on George Kleine, directions for use, a general index, a chronological index and some illustrations.

George Kleine (1864-1931) gained his knowledge of films via his father's optical equipment business. He was quick to recognize the potential of the film business and became involved with many different aspects of exhibition and production.

2520   *George Kleine's Cycle of Film Classics.* by Kleine, George. 62 p. illus. New York: George C. Kleine, 1916.

Kleine was a distributor of films in the early silent days and this catalog includes such pre-1916 films as SPARTACUS, JULIUS CAESAR, ANTONY AND CLEOPATRA, QUO VADIS?, THE LAST DAYS OF POMPEII, OTHELLO, VANITY FAIR, etc.

2521   *George Raft.* by Yablonsky, Lewis. 289 p. illus. New York: McGraw-Hill, 1974.

The rise and fall of a nice guy whose screen image was a tough, masculine Latin lover is related in this official biography. Raft is portrayed as an easy, pleasant naive man who would have preferred love and marriage to the fame and countless one-night stands he experienced. His early years with Valentino as a dance-hall gigolo, the mob associations, screen fame and, finally, the last two decades of decline are described. Yablonsky writes with objectivity and sprinkles his narrative with quotes from people who knew and worked with Raft. Some illustrations are provided in a center section and a filmography, bibliography and index are added.

George Raft's life was like his films—crammed with action, romance and excitement. However, the book suggests that the actor was never able to interpret fully what was happening. When his innocence and good nature is contrasted with the strength of his screen image, a fascinating study results. Recommended for mature readers.

2522   *The George Raft File: The Unauthorized Biography.* by Parish, James Robert; and Whitney, Steven. 288 p. illus. New York: Drake, 1974.

The most impressive portions of this volume are those dealing with George Raft's film career. More than 80 of his films are described with casts, credits, synopses, review excerpts and critical comment. In telling the personal side of Raft's life, the authors are not so successful. Raft's cooperation with Lewis Jablonsky in writing *George Raft* probably did not allow for his participation in this volume. The illustrations provided are adequate, and a list of radio and television appearances is added. Joan Bennett supplies the foreword. Acceptable.

2523   *George S. Kaufman: An Intimate Biography.* by Teichman, Howard. 333 p. paper illus. New York: Dell, 1972.

Although George S. Kaufman is remembered primarily as a playwright and a Broadway theatre personality, he had some association with Hollywood films—most of it apparently unpleasant. A few of his experiences in the film industry appear here; one chapter is even called "The Man Who Hated Hollywood." It should also be noted that many of the stage personalities mentioned in the text were active in films. This is an excellent biography that has a limited pertinence for film reference.

2524   *George Stevens, An American Romantic.* by Richie, Donald. 104 p. paper illus. New York: Museum of Modern Art, 1970.

This small booklet contains a monograph followed by a filmography, and many illustrations. A needed tribute to one of America's finest artist-directors. An enlarged full-scale treatment would be welcome.

2525 *The German Cinema.* by Manvell, Roger; and Fraenkel, Heinrich. 159 p. illus. New York: Praeger, 1971.

Until the appearance of this volume, the books by Eisner, Hull, Kracauer, and Wollenberg were the principal sources of information on the German film. Each deals with only a portion of German film history, but Manvell and Fraenkel have attempted to survey the entire history in this fine overview. They divide the history into eight eras: pioneer films, the twenties, sound films before Hitler, early Nazi films, later Nazi films, aftermath films, decline in the fifties, and the new German cinema of the sixties. The text is supported by many notes and sources; it departs somewhat from Kracauer and is in greater agreement with Eisner on the Expressionist films and Hull on the Nazi films. It stands alone on the German films made after World War II.

A bibliography, an index of names and a separate one for selected films end the book. Many illustrations are used and they are mostly effective. Since this volume is unique in its coverage of an important national cinema, and because it is uniformly excellent in text, photographs, production, and supporting material, it has value.

2526 *Germany.* by Bucher, Felix. 298 p. paper illus. New York: A. S. Barnes, 1970.

This is an illustrated guide to more than 400 film personalities and artisans of the German cinema arranged alphabetically. An index of names and more than 6000 film titles further enhance the book's value. Although picture quality is only acceptable, many of the illustrations are unusual and rarely seen,e.g., Ernst Lubitsch playing a silent comedy role.

2527 *The Gershwin Years.* by Jablonski, Edward; and Stewart, Lawrence D. 416 p. illus. New York: Doubleday, 1973.

This biography of George and Ira Gershwin, an update of the critically applauded 1958 volume, adds some new biographical material, an expanded bibliography, a new discography, a show chronology, and a song list. Illustrations remain impressive and the total production is excellent. Listed here because of the extensive use of the Gershwin music made by Hollywood.

It should be noted that several other Gershwin bio-graphies have been written. They include *George Gershwin: Man and Legend* and *George Gershwin,* both by Merle Armitage; *The Story of George Gershwin* and *George Gershwin: His Journey to Greatness,* both by David Ewen; *George Gershwin* by Isaac Goldberg; *Gershwin* by Robert Payne; and *The Life of George Gershwin* by Robert Rushmore.

2528 *The Gershwins.* by Kimball, Robert; and Simon, Alfred. 234 p. illus. New York: Atheneum, 1973.

This is a beautiful, oversized coffee-table book that is packed with miscellaneous items relating to George and Ira Gershwin—music, lyrics, photographs, drawings, sheet music covers, song lists, a discography, a bibliography, a piano rollography, anecdotes, memoirs, etc. It is a combination scrapbook, journal, photo album, and pictorial biography that is noted here since so much of the Gershwins' music has been used in Hollywood films. In addition, the films for which they wrote original scores—SHALL WE DANCE (1937), A DAMSEL IN DISTRESS (1937), and GOLDWYN FOLLIES (1938)—are treated in individual sections. Ira's film work after George's death in 1937 is also noted.

2529 *Gertrude Lawrence.* by Morley, Sheridan. illus. New York: McGraw-Hill, 1980.

2530 *Gertrude Lawrence As Mrs. A.* by Aldrich, Richard Stoddard. 414 p. illus. New York: Greystone Press, 1954.

An intimate biography of the stage star written by her husband soon after her death in 1952. Lawrence appeared in only a few films but was the subject of a super-musical, STAR (1968). See also her autobiography, *A Star Danced.*

2531 *Get Me Geisler.* by Roeburt, John. 191 p. paper New York: Belmont Books, 1962.

After a short biographical chapter, the author writes of the famous Geisler cases—those involving Errol Flynn, Robert Mitchum, Edward G. Robinson, Jr., Charlie Chaplin, Alexander Pantages and Cheryl Crane. There is some editorial comment by the author, but most of the volume is a retelling of the familiar scandals along with excerpts from the testimony during the trials. An unsuccessful attempt to sensationalize some dated material.

2532 *Getting Ideas from the Movies.* by Holoday, Perry W.; and Stoddard, George P. 102 p. New York: Arno Press, 1970 (1933).

One of the Payne Fund Studies of Motion Pictures and Social Values, this one first appeared in 1933. The question investigated here was how much children remember of the films they see. The findings indicated that children retain about 60 percent of what an adult would retain. Various differences between age groups and the types of items retained are noted. This early research will be of interest to students; it is too specialized and dated for the general reader.

2533 *Getting into* DEEP THROAT. by Smith, Richard N. 286 p. paper illus. New York: Berkley, 1973.

Using the notoriety surrounding DEEP THROAT (1972) as his topic, the author has put together chapters on performers Linda Lovelace and Harry Reems, director Gerard Damiano, and publisher Al Goldstein. In the second portion of the book, transcripts of the testimony given at the obscenity trial of the film are presented. The trial lasted from December 19, 1972, through January 3, 1973, and heard witnesses such as Arthur Knight, Ernest Van den Haag, Max Levin, Edward J. Hornick, and John Money. All of the above supposedly have expertise in matters concerning sex and their opinions are repeated here.

The few illustrations in the centerfold are designed to capture the drugstore paperback buyer who will be more than disappointed with the legal matters—if he ever gets to read the entire book. Those opening chapters are another matter, as they are outspoken about acting in and making hardcore pornographic films. Obviously this is not a volume for general circulation. However, the record of the testimony may have some value to those readers interested in obscenity and the law.

2534 *Getting into Film.* by London, Mel. 178 p. paper illus. New York: Ballantine, 1977.

Subtitled "The First Complete Career Guide to the Film Industry," this volume attempts to provide job descriptions for technical and creative positions. Not only are the many different film products of the industry identified, but the various departments responsible for their creation are also described—production, writing, cinematography, editing, music, sound, animation, art, graphics, actors, directors, etc. In addition, London offers sections on advertising agencies, film unions, schools, training programs, grants, festivals, etc. The volume, which is copiously illustrated, offers some practical advice on job hunting, interviews, follow-ups, reading, etc.

How helpful volumes such as this one are in obtaining jobs is difficult to ascertain. A friend or relative already in the industry/union is probably a better potential avenue. Nevertheless, the book is useful in providing an overview of the diverse jobs in filmmaking.

2535 THE GETTING OF WISDOM. by Witcombe, Eleanor. 94 p. paper illus. Richmond, Victoria: Heinemann Educational Australian Pty. Ltd., 1978.

Script of the 1977 film directed by Bruce Beresford.

2536 *Getting Started in Filmmaking.* by Schiff, Lillian. 96 p. illus. New York: Sterling, 1978.

Sterling Publishers are responsible for an admirable series of film books designed for young people. Previous titles have been *Animating Films Without a Camera*, *Film Animation as a Hobby*, and *Pictures Without a Camera*. This particular volume deals with the basic elements of filmmaking—the camera, film, equipment, shots, camera angles, editing, splicing, personnel, script, costumes, make-up, props, sets, lighting. These topics are treated in a brief but adequate text which is supplemented by many well-selected visuals. The volume is indexed.

The need for an up-to-date book on filmmaking for young people is filled nicely by this publication. It is comprehensive, readable, and to-the-point. Recommended.

2537 *Getting to Know Him: A Biography of Oscar Hammerstein II.* by Fordin, Hugh. 383 p. illus. New York: Random House, 1977.

An illustrated biography of the lyricist for many stage and film musicals. From THE DESERT SONG (1929) to THE SOUND OF MUSIC (1965) he worked with various composers, achieving his greatest success with Jerome Kern and Richard Rodgers.

2538 *The Ghosts Who Danced with Kim Novak.* by Kleiner, Dick. 160 p. paper New York: Ace, 1970.

See *ESP and the Stars.*

2539 *The Ghouls.* edited by Haining, Peter. 383 p. illus. Stein & Day, 1971.

This volume is an unusual anthology of 18 short stories which were the source material for a like number of horror films. Included are the original stories which inspired THE PHANTOM OF THE OPERA (1925), FREAKS (1932), THE MOST DANGEROUS GAME (1932), DRACULA'S DAUGHTER (1936), THE BEAST WITH 5 FINGERS (1946), THE FLY (1958), and other films. Abbreviated cast and production credits are given for each film in the appendix. Vincent Price introduces the book and Christopher Lee contributes an afterword. With only a limited value, the book is noted here because of its unique format.

2540 *Gielgud: An Actor and His Time.* by Gielgud, John; and Miller, John; and Powell, John. 255 p. illus. New York: Clarkson N. Potter, 1980.

This volume resulted from a reconstruction, rewriting and reediting of a series of BBC radio interviews that Sir John Gielgud gave about his life and career in the theatre. In a series of interviews with Dick Cavett for PBS television in America, Gielgud repeated many parts of this volume almost verbatim—using it almost as a prepared script. He is apparently pleased with this unintended autobiography, and the reader will be too.

There are no secrets, scandals or revelations here. It is a recall of many years in the theatre along with impersonal character sketches of the actors he has known. Slight attention is given to his relatively recent activity in films—JULIUS CAESAR (1952), BECKET (1964), THE LOVED ONE (1965), THE CHARGE OF THE LIGHT BRIGADE (1967), CHIMES AT MIDNIGHT (1964), GOLD (1974), MURDER ON THE ORIENT EXPRESS (1974), PROVIDENCE (1976). He had made some films earlier that he apparently prefers to forget—a matter of vanity about his young image on film—INSULT (1932), THE GOOD COMPANIONS (1933), SECRET AGENT (1935), THE PRIME MINISTER (1941), etc. Many fine illustrations and an index are provided, but the essential career chronology is unfortunately missing.

In any event, this is a rich memoir that will appeal to anyone who loves acting raised to an art by a witty, wise, dedicated professional. Recommended. Interested readers may also see Gielgud's *Early Stages* and *John Gielgud* by Ronald Hayman.

2541 *The Gift Horse.* by Knef, Hildegard. 384 p. illus. New York: McGraw-Hill, 1971.

An autobiography of an international stage and screen star along with her impressions of the people and places she encountered in the film industry. Enough dramatic material for several films. Ironic, cynical, powerful, emotional, and ultmately rewarding.

2542 GIGI. 13 p. paper illus. New York: Al Greenstone Co., 1957.

This small souvenir book does not reflect the quality of the 1958 film it attempts to describe. Most of the illustrations are selected poorly and printed in either black and white or with a color tint. The story is related, with the songs noted at the point in the narrative in which they are sung or performed. One section indicates that Paris is really the star of the film. Producer Arthur Freed, director Vincente Minnelli, and designer Cecil Beaton along with Alan Jay Lerner and Frederic Loewe are the creative people profiled.

2543 *Gina Lollobrigida: Her Life and Films.* by Reid, Gordon. 64 p. paper illus. London: EURAP, 1956.

This title in the *Film Star Biographies* series includes a filmography.

2544 *Ginger: Salute to a Star.* by Richards, Dick. 192 p. illus. Brighton, England: Clifton Books, 1969.

An unauthorized biorgraphy of one of the durable ladies of the screen, this book is characterized by a blinding adoration of the subject by the author. It reads like a rather long testimonial. Carelessness and errors abound. For example: 1) Dick Powell and Ruby Keeler did not sing a duet of "Shuffle Off to Buffalo" in 42ND STREET (1932); 2) Busby Berkeley was not a set designer; 3) John Held, Jr. (the famous cartoonist, illustrator and writer) was not "A mystery man who had a transient reputation on the American stage in the twenties"; and 4) Patricia Ellis and Lona Andre were not "unknowns" in the thirties.

The style is treacle fan magazine and Miss Rogers emerges as a superwoman in all of the aspects of her life. Any errors in judgement (and there were so many) are excused or rationalized with rapidity, while much is made of her financial ability, her professional approach to her work, and her devotion to physical fitness. The book is a bit of a bore. There is an index and a group of ordinary illustrations. Perhaps the Rogers filmography is the most valuable portion of the volume. One suspects a tie-in with this volume and Miss Rogers's appearance in the London "Mame." The subject deserves a more dispassionate, careful biographer.

2545 *Ginger, Loretta and Irene Who?* by Eels, George. 393 p. illus. New York: G. P. Putnam's, 1976.

The subjects in this collective biography include Ginger Rogers, Miriam Hopkins, Ruth Etting, Kay Francis, Loretta Young, and Irene Bentley. The apposition provided for each gives some clue as to the author's opinion of his subject. For example, the career longevity of Rogers, whom he names "The Survivor," is looked upon with awe rather than admiration. Hopkins (The Maverick), Etting (The Box Office Bait), and Kay Francis (The Sell-Out) are viewed sympathetically. Loretta Young (The Manipulator) gets a complete going-over in an almost totally negative essay. The Who of the book's title is Irene Bentley (The Dropout) who sought oblivion rather than a film career.

Eels sets the stage by recalling the New Year's Eve of 1933 when all six women were on the brink of fame. Filmographies are provided for each actress and there are stage listings for Rogers, Hopkins, Etting, and Francis. A long discography for Etting is also included and the book is indexed.

Not only has the author been thorough in searching out the enormous amount of information required for this volume, but he has been able to apply a style that combines research, criticism, evaluation, interpretation, and even gossip. This is solid biography that is certain to please many readers. The book's reference potential is high, too. Recommended.

2546 *Ginger Rogers.* by McGilligan, Patrick. 159 p. paper illus. New York: Pyramid, 1975.

Here at last is a book devoted to a durable screen star who was still an active TV-stage performer in the seventies. From YOUNG MAN OF MANHATTAN (1930) to HARLOW (1965), Ginger Rogers was a film personality and star. The 73 films she made during her career are reviewed and evaluated in this attractive book. Accompanied by some very well reproduced visuals, the text is also supported by a bibliography, a filmography and an index.

Although she is most remembered for the musicals she made with Astaire, her career had a much wider range of roles, most of which she performed with sensitivity and skill. Her artistry rescues a minor film such as TEENAGE REBEL (1956) from being pure soap opera.

This is a most rewarding evaluation of a long career, and its appearance is welcome since the only other volume on Rogers is *Ginger*, a rather poor biography published in England. This one sets the record straight.

2547 *The Girl in the Hairy Paw.* edited by Gottesman, Ron; and Geduld, Harry. 285 p. paper illus. New York: Avon (Flare), 1976.

This original paperback anthology, described as a "documentary study," is also a fine source book for the classic film, KING KONG (1933). Subtitled "King Kong as Myth, Movie and Monster," the volume divides its contents into five parts: 1. Born: The Eighth Wonder of the World; 2. Hail to the King; 3. The Beast in the Critical Jungle; 4. Artists and Models; and 5. Incongruities. In these sections attention is given to the origins of the giant ape legends, their appearance in art, literature, and early motion pictures, the making of the 1933 film, critical reviews and essays and some spin-offs of the original film. The latter include film sequels, magazine covers, advertisements, and comic books.

The fascination with the original film increases yearly. This book will attract and please a wide audience of youngsters, old timers, students, and scholars. All will find an admirable collection of mostly unfamiliar material arranged in an intelligent, affectionate tribute. Highly recommended.

2548 *A Girl Like I.* by Loos, Anita. 275 p. illus. New York: Viking 1966.

The author presents a partial autobiography here, ending her account quite early. Certain anecdotes do take place in later years, but the narrative ceases with the publication of *Gentleman Prefer Blondes* in 1926. A large portion of the book is devoted to Hollywood during its formative years, 1912 to 1920. Miss Loos worked as a script writer for D. W. Griffith and Douglas Fairbanks, Sr.

Personalities play a large part in the story—von Stroheim, the Talmadge sisters, Marion Davies, Mabel Normand, Jack Pickford, and many others appear. Vachel Lindsay was one of the author's early infatuations. The illustrations are excellent on all counts. The book inspires the hope that Miss Loos will relate more of her fascinating screenwriting career. This is excellent biography, written in a clever yet sensitive style. A readable, enjoyable and informative portrait of early filmmaking, the book is a distinct contribution to film history. Highly recommended.

2549 *The Girl Who Had Everything: The Story of "The Fire and Ice Girl."* by Leigh, Dorian; and Hobe, Laura. illus. New York: Doubleday, 1980.

The author was a well-known model and agent during the fifties. In this autobiography she includes material about her sister, Suzy Parker, who had a brief career as a film actress.

2550 *Girls Who Do Stag Movies.* by Square, Melrose. Los Angeles: Holloway.

2551 *Giving Up the Ghost.* by Dody, Sanford. 334 p. New York: M. Evans, 1980.

Sanford Dody has served as ghost writer, coauthor, and confidant for several celebrities—Bette Davis, Helen Hayes, Robert Merrill, Elaine Barrymore, and Dagmar Godowsky. In this volume he recalls the joys and sorrows of being an anonymous writer who sees his creative work published as the autobiography of a famous star.

With a bittersweet humor, Dody writes of what it is to become close to the famous "off stage." Readers familiar with *The Lonely Life, First Person Plural,* or *On Reflection: An Autobiography* know the quality that Dody brings to each assignment. Here he discloses his experiences along with lots of gossipy observations and comments. He also speaks of three possible biographical collaborations which never worked out—Garland, Hepburn and Elsa Lanchester.

Dody's account here suggests that he is first of all a star-struck fan of "show business" people and matters. Thankfully, he also possesses a sophisticated wit and an effervescent writing style that deserve the single billing that this volume at last provides.

2552 *Glad You Asked That.* by Gardner, Marilyn; and Gardner, Hy. 182 p. paper illus. New York: Ace, 1976.

This is a quickly assembled volume that uses gossip column items and interviews as a base. The questions are either inane or uninteresting, exceeded only by the insignificance of the answers. For example—Question: "Was Mary Tyler Moore really born in New York?" Answer: "Yes, Mary Tyler Moore was born in Brooklyn. Close to what was once known as Ebbets Field, home of "Dem Bums" The Dodgers." Literary expertise here apparently lies in generalizing and padding by providing unasked-for information.

Since no index or subject divisions are used, the volume must be considered a reading experience. As such it is bland and absolutely nonessential. Does anyone really care "What Zsa Zsa Gabor says about getting presents from men" ????

2553 *Gladys Cooper.* by Morley, Sheridan. 336 p. illus. New York: McGraw Hill, 1979.

This biography of Gladys Cooper, a performer familiar to both film and theatre audiences, was written by her grandson. As a result the volume is more a detailed tribute than a critical biography. The many roles Gladys Cooper has undertaken in the various media are noted in the text and in listings. In addition there is a bibliography, an index, and many illustrations.

Who can argue with a biographical valentine to an actress who has been as admired as frequently and as long as Gladys Cooper?

2554 *Gladys Cooper.* by Cooper, Gladys. 288 p. illus. London: Hutchinson, 1931.

An autobiography of the distinguished British stage and screen star who began a Hollywood career much after this early memoir was written. A later autobiography, *Without Veils,* continues her story. Her screen image was that of the sympathetic, aristocratic parent—as exemplified by her role as Rex Harrison's mother in MY FAIR LADY (1964).

2555 *Glamorous Movie Stars of the Thirties Paper Dolls.* by Tierney, Tom. 32 p. paper illus. New York: Dover, 1978.

This is a very different kind of film book. Eight famous actresses are represented in full-color paper-doll format—Judy Garland, Greta Garbo, Carole Lombard, Joan Crawford, Nancy Carroll, Jean Harlow, Constance Bennett, and Jeanette MacDonald. Each doll is provided with several costume changes, all reproductions of clothes made by Hollywood's top costume designers to be worn in specific films. For example, Crawford's selection comes from DANCING LADY (1933), RAIN (1932), MANNEQUIN (1938), GRAND HOTEL (1932), THE WOMEN (1939) and THE GORGEOUS HUSSY (1936).

2556 *Glamour: Film Fashion and Beauty.* edited by Noble, Peter; and Saxon, Yvonne. 72 p. illus. London: Burke, 1953.

Contains advice on dress, make-up, behavior, etc., from stars of the late forties and early fifties.

2557 *The Glamour Girls.* by Parish, James Robert; and Stanke, Don E. 752 p. illus. Rochelle, N.Y.: Arlington House, 1975.

The collective biographies authored and coauthored by Parish—*Hollywood's Great Love Teams, The RKO Gals, The Fox Girls, The Paramount Pretties, The MGM Stock Company, The Slapstick Queens,* etc.—run counter to tradition and practice. Each new one improves somewhat upon those which have preceded it.

Nine glamorous film stars from the thirties, forties and fifties are profiled here: Joan Bennett, Yvonne De Carlo, Rita Hayworth, Audrey Hepburn, Jennifer Jones, Maria Montez, Kim Novak, Merle Oberon, and Vera Ralston. A portrait of each subject introduces the essay, stills, candids and a filmography. Since the text dwells primarily on the films of the subject, the number of pages devoted to each lady varies. The more famous and durable actresses such as Joan Bennett and Rita Hayworth get approximately 100 pages apiece, while Maria Montez and Vera Ralston get about half that number. A foreword by Rona Barrett and an introduction by Rene Jordan seem unnecessary. A word from the authors about their intent, rationale, selection, etc., would have been preferable.

The book's value and strength is found in the biographies and illustrations. The style of the text suggests different authorship of various sections; it is often more relaxed and amusing than in previous books. Slight elements of humor are present, especially in the opening paragraphs of each biography. Descriptions of the films are uniformly good and more critical comment appears throughout the text than ever before. Finally, picture selection and reproduction are well above average. All the essential elements of a good collective biography are to be found in a satisfying blend here. This volume should satisfy the needs of several different audiences—nostalgia, reference, information, or entertainment. Recommended.

2558   *Glauber Rocha and the Cinema Novo in Brazil.: A Study of His Films and Critical Writing.* by Hollyman, Burns Saint Patrick. 220 p. New York: Garland, 1982.

A title in the *Dissertations on Film* series.

2559   *The Glen Campbell Story.* by Kramer, Freda. 125 p. paper illus. New York: Pyramid, 1970.

Written when Glen Campbell was at the peak of his popularity via recordings and TV, this book notes that he was signed for a six-picture film contract by producer Hal Wallis. He was a hot property and

Wallis was hoping to repeat the success he had with Elvis Presley. Some attention is given to making TRUE GRIT (1969) with John Wayne, and his second film, NORWOOD (1970), is mentioned. What is not noted in this volume is Campbell's rather rapid fall from the popularity charts and his failure to make any other films to date. Written for Campbell's fans and illustrated with some folksy pictures selected to reinforce the public image, this account is of very limited value.

2560   *Glenn Ford: R.F.D. Beverly Hills.* by Ford, Glenn; and Redfield, Margaret. 185 p. . illus. Old Tappan, N.J.: Hewitt House, 1970.

2561   *Glenn Miller and His Orchestra.* by Simon, George T. 473 p. illus. New York: Thomas Y. Crowell, 1974.

This excellent biography is noted here since it contains short sections on the two films made by the Glenn Miller Orchestra—SUN VALLEY SERENADE (1941) and ORCHESTRA WIVES (1942). The early forties witnessed the use of big bands in films and the experiences noted here are typical. This volume is acceptable to film readers, but it is an outstanding music/biography reference.

2562   *Gloria Swanson.* by Hudson, Richard; and Lee, Raymond. 269 p. illus. New York: A. S. Barnes, 1970.

This is another poorly produced Barnes volume which seems to exemplify a frightening trend. The book is padded with small photographs using approximately one-half of a page, leaving vast areas of white paper. Photo reproduction is of varying quality—some appear underexposed while others look slightly out of focus. Since the text is minimal and not impressive, the book must rely on the photographs for its appeal and importance. Unfortunately it does not make the grade. Not recommended.

2563   *Glorious Technicolor: The Movies' Magic Rainbow.* by Basten, Fred E. 320 p. illus. New York: A. S. Barnes, 1979.

The development of the Technicolor process is traced using material from the Technicolor Corporation files. Linked closely is the story of Natalie and Herbert Kalmus and their efforts, problems, and hurdles in bringing color to the screen. Historic Technicolor films are treated along with those actors whose careers were greatly advanced by the color process. A Technicolor filmography, a bibliography, illustrations, and an index complete the book. This is a welcome addition to the small number of books that deal with technical matters in an entertaining yet informative way.

2564 *Glossary of Film Terms.* compiled by Mercer, John. 92 p. paper Houston, Texas: University Film Association, University of Houston, 1979.

The work of compiling this glossary was begun in 1973 and it includes many of the entries from the 1955 publication, *Terms Used in the Production of 16mm Non-Theatrical Motion Pictures* The final group of terms was reviewed by a panel of five persons, with all copyrighted/ASA/ANSI terms eliminated. The result, called *University Film Association Monograph No. 2,* is an impressive collection of film terms accompanied by readable, easy-to- understand definitions. A basic reference.

2565 *Glossary of Motion Picture Terminology.* edited by Jordan, Thurston, C., Jr. 64 p. paper illus. Menlo Park, Calif.: Pacific Coast Pub., 1968.

This is a small technical volume of words which are arranged alphabetically, defined, and sometimes illustrated by pictures. Its probable use is as a personal reference book although there are several other volumes which have similar glossaries as appendices. A luxury item.

2566 *God in Hollywood.* by Canfield, Alyce. 160 p. paper New York: Wisdom House, 1961.

This paperback inspirational sermon uses screen personalities as persuasion. Jane Russell is the first subject and her story is followed by descriptions of the various church groups in Hollywood, the stars who turn to Judaism, off-beat religions, June Haver, Hollywood failures, and finally, Pat Boone. Throughout, an attempt is made to link career and/ or personal misfortunes to a lack of faith in religion. Examples of success are cited for those who are openly religious. It is ironic that many of the positive examples cited by the author have turned into negative failures since this book appeared. Ms. Canfield is on shaky ground in her attempt to prove a relationship between success, happiness and religion.

2567 *Godard.* by Roud, Richard. 192 p. illus. Bloomington, Ind.: Indiana University Press, 1970.

This revised and updated version of the 1967 work

remains the definitive analysis of Godard's work. The use of contradictions, both in the cinematic medium itself and in the content of his films is discussed, as are his subjects, themes, alternations and methods. The approach is serious and demands much intellectual background for full appreciation. Great familiarity with Godard's films is also essential. Illustrations are well-chosen and the filmography is given in detail. Not for the casual, general reader.

2568 *Godard: Images, Sounds, Politics.* by MacGabe, Colin. 175 p. illus. Bloomington, Ind.: Indiana University Press, 1980.

This critical appreciation of Jean-Luc Godard is concerned with his post—1968 career and films. There are sections dealing with money, politics, images of women and sexuality, television, etc. At the end of each there is an interview excerpt with Godard which addresses itself to the topic of the section. A bibliography, illustrations, and a filmography complete the book.

Excellent for those familiar with Godard, the study is a bit heavy for the uninitiated.

2569 *Godard and Others—Essays on Film Form.* by Giannetti, Louis D. 184 p. illus. Rutherford, N.J.: Fairleigh Dickinson University Press, 1975.

Four long essays make up the content of this volume, which deals with two selected film aesthetics—film structure and film texture. The first examines Godard's MASCULINE-FEMININE (1965) as an example of a new film genre, the dramatic essay. After comparisons with the literary essay form, Giannetti points out Godard's attempt to blend the characteristics of narrative film, documentary film, and avant-garde film into a personal statement about contemporary French youth. The aesthetic of the mobile camera is the second topic and cinematic metaphors are treated in the third essay.

Two films are examined in detail here—Hitchcock's PSYCHO (1960) and Bergman's PERSONA (1965). In the last section, the tradition of the plotless film is explored, using ALICE'S RESTAURANT (1969) as the major example. Many other films are referred to in the text in less detail than the four mentioned above. The book is illustrated with well-selected film stills, but their reproduction quality is only fair. An index is provided.

Apparently the four essays were written separately and not as elements of the same work. Evaluated as a collection of disparate essays, they are quite impressive. Many of the ideas or possibilities that the author points out are provocative and stimulating. At times, especially in the metaphors essay, he has a tendency to overanalyze certain elements of specific films, giving them a meaning or interpretation that the filmmaker probably did not intend. But even this slight excess is rather enjoyable to read, since it suggests a very fertile imagination in the author. The book is recommended.

2570   *Godard on Godard.* by Godard, Jean-Luc. 292 p. paper illus. New York: Viking, 1972.

Tom Milne has translated and edited this collection of selected writings by Jean-Luc Godard. The early pieces are film criticism; the later essays and interviews deal with Godard's experiences as a filmmaker. The period from 1950 to 1967, which includes his participation in *La Gazette du Cinema* and *Cahiers du Cinema*, is covered. Milne offers comment on each of the Godard articles in a lengthy section following the main text. There is an index of names and a separate index of films. Richard Roud, the author of *Godard*, provides an introduction.

A good number of visuals adds dimension to the articles, though reproduction of them is only average. In some ways this collection of writing resembles his films and will affect readers as the films affect viewers. Godard fans will find it rich, others will wonder what all the shouting has been about. Recommended.

2571   *Godard: Three Films.* by Godard, Jean-Luc. 192 p. paper illus. New York: Harper and Row, 1975.

This volume contains scripts of the following films: A WOMAN IS A WOMAN (1961); A MARRIED WOMAN (1964); TWO OR THREE THINGS I KNOW ABOUT HER (1965). Also includes an introduction by Alistair Whyte, a review of each film and a short interview with Anna Karina.

2572   THE GODDESS. by Chayefsky, Paddy. 167 p. illus. New York: Simon & Schuster, 1958.

Script of the 1958 film directed by John Cromwell.

2573   THE GODFATHER. 24 p. paper illus. New York: Souvenir Book Publishers, 1972.

This souvenir book is almost too concise in dealing with its important subject. Opening pages describing the making of the 1972 film are followed by short biographies of the cast members. Production credits

complete the book. Perhaps the several extended acounts written about making the film intimidated the creators of this book.

2574   THE GODFATHER Journal. by Zuckerman, Ira. 143 p. paper New York: Manor Books, 1972.

Ira Zuckerman was given a grant from the American Film Institute which enabled him to serve as an assistant to director Francis Ford Coppola during the filming of THE GODFATHER (1972) in New York City. He created this informative paperback from the journal he kept during the 70 days. The reader is treated to a partial look at the problems, procedures, and pleasures of making a high budget film. The views of the participants are clearer and in greater depth than in some total biographies. Brando, Coppola, Albert Ruddy, Robert Evans, and others are seen in a working situation rather than posing for a verbal portrait.

Only the journal is offered; there are no illustrations. The quality of the observations—factual, objective, avoiding sensation—and the author's experience and intelligence in selecting those matters which describe the totality of filmmaking are the book's strong points. This modest effort is an unexpectedly good look at filmmaking.

2575   THE GODFATHER Papers and Other Confessions. by Puzo, Mario. 252 p. New York: G. P. Putnam's, 1972.

THE GODFATHER *Papers* is a misnomer for this book since only one short article, "The Making of THE GODFATHER," is about the 1972 film. The bulk of the book is "other confessions" —a compilation of reviews, interviews, stories, articles, etc., written by Puzo in pre-GODFATHER days. The one article is acceptable but the rest of the book is rubbish. It may be wiser to wait until a reprint of THE GODFATHER article appears in a film anthology. See also THE GODFATHER *Journal*

2576   *Godfrey Daniels!* by Anobile, Richard 224 p. illus. New York: Crown, 1975.

Anobile, the enterprising young author who pioneered the frame-blowup book, continues his *Verbal and Visual Gems* series with this new title. This volume recreates scenes from four of W. C. Fields' classic short films—THE FATAL GLASS OF BEER (1933), THE DENTIST (1932), THE PHARMACIST (1933), and THE BARBER SHOP (1933). The shorts represent the Fields career at mid-point. A decade earlier he had discovered the character of Eustace

McGargle in the stage musical "Poppy." Refining and sharpening the persona of McGargle over the years, Fields had, by 1932-33, just about perfected the character he would play in films for the next 10 or 12 years. These shorts show all the Fields attitudes, prejudices, traits, etc., which typified his later roles. The title is a typical example of a Fields expletive.

Reproduction of the blowups is acceptable. A well-written, succinct summary of Fields' career and artistry serves as an introduction to this fine Anobile volume. Like the others in the series, this one will please a wide range of reader. Recommended.

2577 *Gods and Goddesses of the Movies.* by Kobal, John. 152 p. illus. New York: Crescent Books, 1973.

A survey of the romantic film and the stars who appeared in this rather broad genre is presented in this volume. For the first 50 years of film history, an imitation of life and love was offered to moviegoers. Nearly all of the films considered here are from that earlier period rather than the realistic sixties and seventies. Kobal examines screen personalities and their films in both text and visual. Mixing biographical data and some subjective but hardly controversial opinions, Kobal is more satisfying in dealing with performers than with directors.

The visuals are adequate. Most are well-reproduced, but some have a dulling monochrome wash or are too dark and too small in size (pp. 23, 135, 137). Accuracy in titling the visuals is an occasional problem: June Duprez is not identified in a full-page color portrait on page 14; a still from BACK STREET (1941) is mislabeled on page 73; Greer Garson was not a favorite of the thirties—she was introduced in 1938 but was most popular during the forties. An index is provided. In summary this is an adequate treatment in text and visuals of a generalized topic in cinema history. Acceptable.

2578 *God's Works Through Elvis.* by Long, Rev. Marvin R. illus. Hicksville, N.Y.: Exposition Press, 1979.

2579 *Godzilla.* by Thorne, Ian. 47 p. illus. Mankato, Minn.: Crestwood House, 1977.

A review of Godzilla movies written for young readers.

2580 *Going Hollywood.* by Brenner, Marie. 214 p. illus New York: Delacorte, 1977.

Marie Brenner uses a group of articles written previously for periodical publication as the main body of her cynical dissection of today's Hollywood film business. She has arranged them in typical show biz story fashion: On the Way Up (Robert De Niro, Marthe Keller); At the Top (Barbra Streisand, Sue Mengers, Dino De Laurentis, Lester Persky); and On the Way Down (Tom Laughlin, Cher, Ali MacGraw). Introductory and concluding essays unify the disparate pieces so that the book possesses a central motif identified in its subtitle, "An Insider's Look at Power and Pretense in the Movie Business."

What makes this volume superior to others on the same theme is the author's ability to differentiate reality from the fantasy—hype—illusion that characterizes the film industry and its denizens.Since Hollywood operates almost exclusively on this latter level, it is no small accomplishment for a reporter to resist even the tiniest seduction by this expensive make-believe. Brenner writes clearly and coldly about what she sees and senses while recording with disbelief much of what she is told. A few portrait drawings are included. The volume is not indexed. Recommended.

2581 *Going Steady.* by Kael, Pauline. 304 p. Boston: Little, Brown & Co., 1970.

In January 1968, Pauline Kael began writing a regular column for the *New Yorker* magazine. This book is a collection of some of her pieces since then. With the exception of one longer essay entitled, "Trash, Art and the Movies," all are film reviews. A subdued, mature Kael appears in these pages. The criticism is as intelligent and well-stated as always but there seems to be a more discernible structure and set of standards to her reviewing than previously noted. A joy for everyone.

2582 *Going to the Cinema.* by Buchanan, Andrew. 160 p. illus. London: Phoenix House, 1947.

A title in the *Excursions Series For Young People,* this volume considers such topics as Why go to the cinema? What is a film? Also considered are documentary films, cartoons, newsreels, films for young people, film criticism, films that everyone should see, etc. An index is provided.

2583 GOLD DIGGERS OF 1933. by Gelsey, Erwin; and Seymour, James. paper illus. Madison, Wisc.: University of Wisconsin Press.

Script of the 1933 film directed by Mervyn LeRoy. This volume was edited by Arthur Houe.

2584 *The Golden Age of "B" Movies.* by McClelland, Doug. 216 p. paper illus. Nashville, Tenn.: Charter House, 1978.

Evelyn Ankers, called the "Queen of the 'B's," introduces this filmography devoted to 50 inexpensive films that were made to occupy the bottom portion of a double feature film program. Arranged alphabetically, each entry includes detailed cast and credits, illustrations, plot outlines, personal comments, dialogue quotes, etc. McClelland's choices are mostly forgotten or unfamiliar titles such as DESTINY (1944), MY BUDDY (1944), HIT THE ROAD (1941) and such.

For the film buff or the "over 50" viewer, the volume will be pure delight. It recalls a time in American history that was filled with visual pleasures such as those recalled by McClelland here.

2585 *The Golden Age of Serials.* 69 p. paper illus. New York: Ivy Film, 1975.

This catalog (No. 474) lists over 60 sound serials which Ivy Film rents. It is noted here because of the detailed full-page description provided for each. Given are title, number of chapters, titles of individual chapters, date of release, genre, running times, a long cast list, another long production credit list, and a detailed plot outline. A small still is provided for each serial but poor photographic reproduction limits their effectiveness. Feature length versions of some of the serials are available and their alternate titles are indicated in a separate listing.

In addition to this catalog, Ivy Films publishes three others: *Directory of Feature Films, Ivy Directors Catalog,* and *Ivy's Shorts Catalog.* The serials catalog has a cover price, but most similar rental catalogs are available free of charge to the serious user. A unique volume.

2586 *The Golden Age of Sound Comedy.* by McCaffrey, Donald W. 208 p. illus. New York: A. S. Barnes, 1973.

Whenever an attempt is made to delineate "comic films and comedians of the thirties," the result is somewhat predictable. The reader expects the Marx Brothers, Laurel and Hardy, Fields, and Chaplin. In this respect, McCaffrey continues his earlier work, *Four Great Comedians* and *Focus on Chaplin,* by following the careers of his subjects into the thirties. In addition he adds chapters on Joe E. Brown, musicals, the sophisticated comedy, and another genre he calls the middle class comedy. Each chapter is accompanied by a collection of appropriate stills which are well selected and nicely reproduced. A bibliography, a name index, and a title index complete the book.

As indicated above, the personalities that a thirties' survey requires are represented. Unfortunately these same personalities have been the subjects of so many books recently that not much can be added to the material already published. McCaffrey does not choose to do an in-depth critical analysis but opts instead for a general survey. In the less familiar portions of the book, McCaffrey includes films which may have elements of comedy but belong mostly to other genres—musicals, mysteries, drama. Certain personalities who seem natural to the topic are missing in the text Martha Raye, Robert Benchley, Polly Moran, Jean Harlow, etc. Short films and animated cartoons are not covered.

What could have been a provocative study of the comedy films of the thirties becomes instead a survey of the work of some overused performer-subjects accompanied by an occasional debatable choice, e.g., is THE WIZARD OF OZ (1939) really a comedy and do its comic elements rate the extended coverage given here? There are sections in which McCaffrey is effective and impressive—the chapter on Joe E. Brown, for example. But for the most part, the book offers material that is not always well chosen nor organized and examined in a structured way. The challenge set by the book's title is not met.

2587 *The Golden Age of the Movie Palace.* by Hall, Ben M. 262 p. paper illus. New York: Clarkson N. Potter (Crown), 1975 (1961).

This is the paperback edition of *The Best Remaining Seats* which was published in 1961.

2588 *The Golden Days at San Simeon.* by Murray, Ken. 163 p. illus. Garden City, N.Y.: Doubleday, 1971.

This book contains a collection of photographs of many Hollywood personalities enjoying the hospitality of William Randolph Hearst and Marion Davies at San Simeon and at the beach house in Santa Monica. It tells of the construction of San Simeon, and a good part of the book provides a tour of it as it appears today. There is some discussion of Hearst's involvement with films.

The book may be of interest for several reasons: Davies, Hearst as film producer, CITIZEN KANE (1941) analogies, or simply because of some of the persons in the photographs. As in most of Ken Murray's efforts, the subjects are far more interesting than the treatment provided. Murray appears to be a writer-producer-actor-speaker who succeeds not on his ability but through his acquaintance with the important people of Hollywood. Ronald Reagan has written the foreword to this particular volume. Acceptable.

2589 *The Golden Ham: A Candid Biography of Jackie Gleason.* by Bishop, Jim. 298 p. paper illus. New York: Simon and Schuster, 1956.

Jackie Gleason and his careers in the various media (including film) are treated in this objective biography. Since the volume appeared, Gleason has worked in films from time to time—THE HUSTLER (1961), HOW TO COMMIT MARRIAGE (1969), DON'T DRINK THE WATER (1969), SMOKEY AND THE BANDIT (1977), etc.

2590 *The Golden Harvest of the Silver Screen.* compiled by Hunter, Dulin and Company. 31 p. paper illus. Los Angeles: Hunter, Dulin and Company, 1927.

An early example of film industry information provided by a brokerage house, this booklet carries the subtitle, "Compiled from Reliable Sources as a Basis for Evaluating Motion Picture Securities." There have been many other such publications, but they are difficult to locate since they are considered to be advertisements more than literature, and are not collected, cataloged, reviewed, etc., by the usual bibliographic procedures.

2591 *The Golden Turkey Awards: Nominees and Winners—The Worst Achievements in Hollywood History.* by Medved, Harry; and Medved, Michael. 274 p. paper illus. New York: Putnam (Perigee), 1980.

Give the brothers a high mark for imagination and concept; however, given the idea of picking out the worst of Hollywood products, it's hard to go wrong with any personal listings. Anyway, they have gathered a group of films, mostly those with outrageous titles, from the horror-sci-fi genre and given them some fanciful awards. All of this resembles the Harvard Lampoon awards that have been around for years.

2592 GOLDFINGER. 16 p. paper illus. New York: Program Publishing Co., 1965.

A fan magazine approach is used in this brief souvenir book. Close-up pictures of star Sean Connery and supporting players Gert Frobe, Honor Blackman, Shirley Eaton, and Harold Sakata accompany the usual studio-created biographies. One interesting page is devoted to the devices used in the 1964 picture but it is not enough to redeem the rest of this book.

2593 *Goldwyn.* by Marx, Arthur. 376 p. illus. New York: W.W. Norton, 1976.

This volume, which is subtitled "A Biography of the Man Behind the Myth," is a variation of the rags-to-riches story—but with a difference. The subject in this a case is colorful rogue who had a talent for confusing and misusing words or phrases with devastating effect. The resultant expressions called "Goldwynisms" are sprinkled generously throughout the book. Goldwyn was an original—a self-creation that is captured with clarity in this instance.

Marx is a facile author, supplying an in-depth narrative that is breezy, entertaining, and objective. Two possible weaknesses about the book should be noted. First, confidence in the author's research is shaken by a few factual errors such as: page 172, when Lucille Ball's contract with Goldwyn expired, she joined RKO—not Columbia as stated; page 150, Joan Evans was a film actress during the fifties—not the thirties as stated. Second, a Goldwyn filmography, which would seem essential for a study such as this, is missing. A few illustrations do appear in a center section and the book is nicely indexed.

Read as biography, entertainment or history, this is a most satisfying book. Its detailed description of a unique and memorable mogul is sure to please and amuse a wide audience. Recommended.

2594 *Gone Hollywood.* by Finch, Christopher; and Rosenkranz, Linda. 300 p. illus. New York: Doubleday, 1979.

The movie colony in the golden age of films, 1920-1940, is recalled in a series of alphabetically arranged topics here. Subjects include agents, cars, coaches, discoveries, dressing rooms, extras, love, marriage, divorce, new names, parties, phobias, salaries, sneak previews and a week in the life of a Hollywood bachelor. Interwoven in the essays are many anecdotes, legends, and informational bits, some of which are familiar, e.g., the evaluation of Fred Astaire's screen test.

The attempt to recall the Hollywood community prior to World War II in this unusual way is mostly successful, for the authors write with style and a sense of humor. There are many illustrations, a bibliography, and an index.

2595 *Gone With the Ape.* by Anglund, Dale; and Hirsch, Janis. New York: Berkley, 1977.

2596 GONE WITH THE WIND. by Thomas, Bob. 32 p. illus. New York: National Publishers, 1967.

This is not the original 6-page program book from 1939 but the souvenir book printed for the 1967 revival. In addition to "The Story of GONE WITH THE WIND," it contains full-page portraits of Clark Gable, Vivien Leigh, Leslie Howard, and Olivia de Havilland. Other impressive visuals include the burning of Atlanta and the railway station hospital scene. The original world premiere in Atlanta is recalled and cast and production credits are given.

2597 GONE WITH THE WIND. by Howard, Sidney. 416 p. illus. New York:Macmillan, 1980.

Screenplay of the 1939 film directed by Victor Fleming. Contains cast, credits and a long introductory essay by Richard Harwell, who prepared this version of the script and was also editor of *Margaret Mitchell's "Gone With the Wind" Letters: 1936-1949.* The volume is heavily illustrated with stills, publicity shots, candids, etc.

2598 *GWTW/1939.* by Warfield, Nancy D. 56 p. paper illus. New York: The Little Film Gazette of Nancy D. Warfield, 1978.

Nancy Warfield employs her critical abilities by analyzing selected aspects of GONE WITH THE WIND (1939) in this essay. She considers such matters as the period of the film's release, its literary and film forerunners, production problems, similarities with *THE BIRTH OF A NATION (1914), treatment of blacks, etc. Excerpts from a 1940 review by Lincoln Kirstein are appended along with notes and a bibliography. The oversized paperback is nicely illustrated.

Warfield's original and unusual publications have often provided intellectually stimulating comments on film topics. This one is no exception.

2599 *Good-Bye, Baby, and Amen.* by Bailey, David; and Evans, Peter. 239 p. illus. New York: Coward-McCann, 1969.

Subtitled "A Saraband For the Sixties," this oversized picture book has as its subjects many persons concerned with film. Actors, actresses, directors, writers and producers populate its pages. Some of the subjects receive a double treatment—usually a full page photo and a full page of text; others are represented only via visuals. While the text is entertaining, it is the visuals that give the book its great appeal. Highly recommended for a mature audience. The nudity may limit its use.

2600 *Good Company.* by Field, Mary. 192 p. illus. New York: Longman's, Green, 1952.

Here is the story of Child's Entertainment Film Movement in Great Britain during the period from 1943 to 1950. It is an account of how both the film industry and the public were convinced that the production of films designed specifically for child audiences was feasible and desirable. The films that resulted are listed and evaluated. The book has great usefulness at present for those who argue for the same cause in both motion picture and television programming.

2601 *Good Company: A Memoir Mostly Theatrical.* by Drutman, Irving. 274 p. illus. Boston: Little, Brown, 1976.

Irving Drutman, who has edited two collections of Janet Flanner's reports from Europe, here provides a theatrical memoir. His good company includes Mae West, Oscar Levant, Tallulah Bankhead, and others. One chapter is devoted to Drutman's publicity work for the film industry. Goldwyn, Lillian Hellman, Anna Magnani, and other film personalities are discussed.

2602 *Good Dames.* by Parish, James Robert. 277 p. illus. New York: A. S. Barnes, 1974.

Author Parish continues what appears to be an ambitious project—to provide readers with biographies of all the important Hollywood film actresses. With *The Fox Girls, The Slapstick Queens, The Paramount Pretties* and *The RKO Gals* already published, he adds this collective biography of five well-known supporting players—Eve Arden, Agnes Moorehead, Angela Lansbury, Thelma Ritter, and Eileen Heckart. Each receives a lengthy biography that is factual and admiring rather than critical and interpretative. Taken largely from public sources, the accounts avoid anything negative or controversial and settle instead for a recapitulation of the subject's career. Personal incident is glossed over quickly. Many nicely reproduced photographs and a detailed filmography accompany each biography.

When offering the amount of factual material that Parish and his staff do here, some errors or misjudgments are likely, e.g., Columbia Records released the original cast album of "Dear World," not Capital; the picture captions on page 184 are apparently reversed; Lansbury's first entrance in "Anyone Can Whistle" was of such show-stopping proportions that the remainder of the musical couldn't sustain the impact of those few minutes.

The title is an uneasy one—even the subtitle, "Virtue in the Cinema," listed on the dust jacket is omitted in the book. Whether Lansbury and Moorehead should be called good dames on the basis of their screen roles is questionable, as is the inclusion of Heckart with so few films to her credit. Parish has not covered Claire Trevor, Joan Blondell, Gloria Grahame, Ann Sothern, Audrey Totter, Shelley Winters, et al., all of whom have longer film careers and would seem more suitable than Heckart.

Those are minor reservations when the amount of information offered about these five fine performers is considered. The tributes paid to them here are entertaining, informative, and often nostalgic. Recommended.

2603 *Good Looking: Film Studies, Short Films and Filmmaking.* by Sohn, David. paper Philadelphia: North American Publishing Co., 1976.

This anthology, composed of articles that have appeared in the periodical *Media and Methods*, is divided into the three areas indicated in its title. All three are of interest but the section on short films has added value, in that it contains many evaluations.

Most of the information contained here reflects the policy of the parent periodical; it is practical and useable rather than theoretical. The book is an excellent resource for anyone who uses film in a nontheatrical setting.

2604 *Good Morning Boys.* by Seaton, Ray. illus. London: Barrie and Jenkins, 1978.

A biography of Will Hay, a British actor who appeared on the screen in adaptations of his stage schoolmaster character from 1933 to 1944.

2605 *Good Night Mrs. Calabash: The Secret of Jimmy Durante.* by Cahn, William. illus. 191 p. New York: Duell, Sloan & Pearce, 1963.

In this picture book with minimum text, the Durante career in motion pictures is largely ignored.

2606 *Good Night Sweet Prince: The Life and Times of John Barrymore.* by Fowler, Gene. 477 p. illus. New York: Viking Press, 1944.

The fact that John Barrymore appeared in more than 70 motion pictures may not be apparent to the casual reader of this excellent biography. Some attention is given to this facet of Barrymore's career but most of the films are not even mentioned. Barrymore will certainly be remembered more for his performances in A BILL OF DIVORCEMENT (1932), ROMEO AND JULIET (1936), TOPAZE (1933), GRAND HOTEL (1932) and other films than by his stage performances, including "Hamlet" . The biography is candid, honest, affectionate. A beautiful tribute to a man who was an actor in every sense of the word.

2607 *The Goodbye Book.* by Ramsay, Robert; and Toye, Randall. 155 p. illus. New York: Van Nostrand, 1979.

A collection of "goodbyes" from movies, literature, and life is offered here. The first part is devoted to lover's farewells, the second to politician's goodbyes, and the final to last words. An index of names completes the volume, which is illustrated by some line drawings. Only a few film references are included, and since they are intermixed with the text, they are not easily accessible.

2608 GOODBYE, MR. CHIPS. 20 p. paper illus. New York: National Publishers, 1969.

A photo-postcard-album format is used in this short souvenir book but as a compensation there is a large poster inside. In addition to the cast and the production credits, there is a section devoted to the making of the 1969 film.

2609 *Goodness Had Nothing to Do with It.* by West, Mae. 223 p. paper illus. New York: Avon Books, 1959.

Written in typical Westian dialogue, the story related here is the author's fiction about her life. Miss West has always been careful about her public image and this book was designed to reinforce her attempts. She presents herself as a racy, clever, romantic who behaves at times with surprising naivete and innocence. All accounts described herein are external and designed for laughs or self-promotion. Taken with the above reservations, the book is fun to read, and certainly is more palatable than her recently published interviews, which were monuments of bad taste, sexual fantasy, and senility. The volume originally ended in the late fifties. A recent revision has MYRA BRECKINRIDGE (1970) and other material added; the newer material is short and indicates the hand of a strong editor.

2610   *Gordon Parks.* by Turk, Midge. 33 p. illus. New York: Crowell, 1971.

Written for young readers, this is the biography of the black American film director and still photographer.

2611   *Gotta Sing, Gotta Dance: A Pictorial History of Film Musicals.* by Kobal, John. 320 p. illus. New York: Hamlyn, 1970.

This volume seems like a Monogram remake of John Springer's *All Talking, All Singing, All Dancing,* even to its catchy title. With the exception of a chapter on the foreign film musical, it covers the same ground, although in a somewhat different order and arrangement. Apparently, an effort has been made to make this material seem different from Springer's. The lengthy test is acceptable and the pictures are well chosen although the reproduction of them is only fair. An acceptable book that suffers somewhat by comparison and its late arrival.

2612   *Grace Kelly.* by Katz, Marjorie. 96 p. illus. New York: Coward-McCann, 1971.

A biography of the actress-princess written for young people.

2613   *see   2612*

2614   *The Graceland Gates.* by Loyd, Harold. illus. Memphis: Modern Age, 1978.

Graceland is, of course, the name of Elvis Presley's home in Tennessee.

2615   *Gradients of Depth in the Cinema Image.* by Harpole, Charles Henry. 293 p. New York: Arno, 1976.

This unique investigation, written at New York University in 1976 and published as a title in the *Dissertations on Film* series, deals with that single characteristic of film aesthetics called depth perception. Harpole discusses such aspects of cinematographic depth as theory, heritage from other arts, position, light, optics, chemistry, sharp focus, diagonal depth, and two-plane depths. German expressionist films and Soviet montage films are used for examples, as are CITIZEN KANE (1941) and other films. In his conclusion Harpole identifies seven gradients of depth he has found in the cinema image and indicates both their past use and their future potential. The text is accompanied by an appendix, a bibliography, and an index.

2616   *Grafilm: An Approach to a New Medium.* by Byrne-Daniel, J. 96 p. illus. New York: Van Nostrand-Reinhold, 1970.

In an attempt to present a new plan for introducing students to film, the author obfuscates just a bit. Using a project plan, six ideas are suggested: 1) a film outlined by story boards; 2) a film made by drawing on clear leader; 3) a film made by moving a camera over a large art print; 4) a film made from 72 pieces of art; 5) a film made of simple animation; and 6) a final film which combines all of the above techniques. These projects are presented logically and sequentially. There is nothing new suggested except perhaps the structured arrangement of simple filming techniques.

2617   *Graham Greene: The Films of His Fiction.* by Phillips, Gene D. 203 p. illus. New York: Teachers College Press, 1974.

Several interesting corollaries to the major topic, Graham Greene's films, are explored in this provocative book. Are films scripted by the original book's author preferable to those written by a second party? Does a familiarity with film aesthetics and criticism influence an author's literary style? Or his ability to translate his own work into cinematic terms? These questions and others are raised by the author. His main effort is devoted, however, to a detailed critical examination of nearly all of the 25 films made from Graham Greene's books. For clarity he divides Greene's stories into "Entertainments" and "Serious Fiction," with separate sections of the book devoted to each category. Under each he first considers those adaptations done by other screenwriters and, then, those done by Greene himself. Stills from each film are provided and they are reproduced with admirable clarity. A bibliography, a filmography and an index complete the book.

The author has chosen a pertinent subject for research, study and interpretation. His selection and treatment of the material is impressive, informative and even challenging at times. The production given this book is outstanding.

2618 *Graham Greene on Film.* by Greene, Graham. 284 p. illus. New York: Simon and Schuster, 1972.

This volume of collected film criticism from the years 1935-1939 has several virtues and one severe fault. Any collection of reviews of classic, forgotten, neglected and unknown films from the Golden Thirties has a lot going for it initially. Add many nicely reproduced stills from the films discussed and you've strengthened the brew. If the subjects include many unknown British features and a few documentaries along with a sprinkling of other European films, the appeal is further increased. If all of the above is placed in an attractively produced book, a success seems assured. However...

Styles in film criticism change and Greene as film critic is much different from Greene as story teller, novelist or screenplay writer. A definite aesthetic seems lacking and his reliance on emotional reaction to personality rather than evaluation of an individual performance is indicative of a kind of intellectual fan dance. He is never at a loss in sounding informed, witty, and sophisticated but the passage of some 30 years shows the evaluations to be incorrect more often than not, e.g., WUTHERING HEIGHTS (1939) "The whole picture is keepsake stuff" ; LITTLE TOUGH GUY (1938) "One of the best melodramas in recent years;" SARATOGA (1937) "One of Miss Harlow's better films" ; FOLLOW THE FLEET (1936) "Miss Harriet Hilliard...is infinitely to be preferred to Miss Irene Dunne" ; and so on. The comments read today as if they were written by a cynical scholar with an entertaining literary style but with only a meager background in films, their history and evolution.

As an exercise in recreating a bygone period of film history, and as a reminder of a large sampling of the films of that period, the book is pure pleasure, but it cannot be considered as serious film criticism. As nostalgia, it is recommended.

2619 *A Grammar of the Film.* by Spottiswoode, Raymond. 328 p. Berkeley, Calif.: University of California Press, 1950 (1935).

An attempt to explain the entire mystique of motion pictures, this book treats film language, film sound, history, categories, film analysis and film synthesis. The newer preface written some 16 years after the original publication in 1935 is mature, wry, and quite critical of the original text. Still valuable and informative.

2620 *Grammar of the Film Language.* by Arijon, Daniel. 624 p. illus. New York: Hastings House, 1976.

Here is a practical book on filmmaking that has been designed for the reader who has already acquired some background information/experience on the subject. Its introductory material covers a range of subjects that include editing, types of films, and film grammar. Complete chapters are concerned with the triangle principle, dialogues between two, three, four and more players, editing static dialogue scenes, the nature of screen motion, master shots, movement of players, the panning camera, the travelling camera, the camera crane, and many other topics. The final section deals with film punctuation and describes methods of connecting and visually sharpening the filmmaker's final shots and sequences.

The volume can be a most helpful reference for the filmmaker-at-work. Problems discussed are typical ones encountered in most filmmaking experiences. To help explain their nature and suggest possible solutions, the author has provided over 1500 cartoon-like drawings to supplement his text. The volume is indexed.

This is a most impressive attempt at providing a comprehensive guide to filmmaking techniques. It avoids complex technical explanations by combining a clear, easy-to-read text with some simplified illustrations. Recommended for filmmaking courses and to all practicing filmmakers.

2621 GRAND ILLUSION. by Renoir, Jean; and Spaak, Charles. paper 108 p. illus. New York: Simon & Schuster, 1968.

Script of the 1937 film directed by Renoir. Contains cast credits, an introduction "A Note from Jean Renoir" ; and an article, "My First Meeting with Jean Renoir," by Eric von Stroheim.

2622 *Grand Illusions.* by Lawton, Richard; and Leckey, Hugo. 255 p. illus. New York: McGraw-Hill, 1973.

Here is a collection of 260 duotone photographs concentrating on the Hollywood period of 1920-1950. Accompanying the visuals is an essay, "Grand Illusions," by Hugo Leckey, which traces his relationship with the cinema from a boyhood in Ireland to the fringe areas of Hollywood. Its presence is a mystery, since it is a verbose reminiscence that adds nothing to the heart of the book—the photographs.

Studio portraits and performer stills make up most of the illustrations, which are divided by decade. Selection was based upon both subject and quality of each photograph. Responsible coverage of the prominent personalities of the period has been provided with only a few slips—i.e., ten Dietrichs and seven Swansons compared with one each of West, Garland, Dunne, etc. A final index facilitates location of specific photographs. This is a second volume of what appears to be a series. Lawton is to be commended for his continuing and successful efforts in providing these aesthetic experiences in visual beauty. Highly recommended.

2623 GRAND PRIX. by Arnell, Gordon. 32 p. paper illus. New York: National Publishers, 1966.

A most interesting approach to a souvenir book; many of the pages have a montage of shots from the 1966 film bordered by a descriptive narrative. Some short actor biographies are followed by the professional racers who appeared in the film. Ten of the most famous racing tracks in the world are noted, as are the world champion drivers from 1950 to 1966. Even a vocabulary of circuit sayings is offered. Cast and production credits complete this fascinating and specialized program book. A noteworthy attempt to do something different.

2624 *Grandma's Scrapbook of Silent Movie Stars.* by Kaduck, John M. 116 p. illus. Des Moines, Iowa: Wallace-Homestead, 1976.

A collection of illustrations along with a bibliography and an index.

2625 THE GRAPES OF WRATH. by French, Warren. 87 p. paper Bloomington, Ind.: Indiana University Press, 1973.

Appreciation must be expressed to Warren French for his approach to this volume, one of the initial *Filmguides.* Although he covers some familiar ground—Bluestone's, and Asheim's pioneer works on novels into film—he does it with the eye of the seventies critic. Dividing the film into 15 sequences and 50 scenes, he establishes a structure which serves him (and the reader) well. The outline and the analysis make use of these divisions, as does the film-novel comparison given in the appendix.

Other elements are not neglected—the credits, a short Ford biography and appreciation, the production history and a summary critique are given. The Ford filmography is a listing of titles along with studio origin. Much more valuable is an annotated bibliography describing materials about Ford and THE GRAPES OF WRATH (1940). The design of this volume and the noteworthy selection of material are both excellent. Highly recommended.

2626 *Graphic Violence on the Screen.* edited by Atkins, Thomas R. 96 p. paper illus. New York: Monarch, 1976.

Several aspects of screen violence are explored in this anthology. Its five essays deal with such topics as film noir, the Italian western, the kung fu films, the drive-in meat movie, the Hammer horror films, etc. A personal statement by Vivian C. Sobchack on death in the movies concludes the volume. The illustrations have been well chosen, and there is a selected filmography on screen violence added.

This volume, an overview of a current controversial topic, avoids taking any strong position other than to insist that audiences love and apparently need screen violence. It does offer a base for further investigation, analysis, and debate. Acceptable.

2627 GREASE. by Woodard, Bronte. unpaginated paper illus. Los Angeles: Fotonovel, 1978.

This *Fotonovel* (see series entry) contains over 350 stills, some original film dialogue, song lyrics by Jim Jacobs and Warren Casey, connecting narrative and cast credits of the 1978 film, GREASE, which was directed by Randal Kleiser.

2628 *The* GREASE *Album.* by Sollars, Michael. paper illus. New York: Ariel Books, 1978.

Complete coverage of the 1978 film GREASE is provided in this beautifully produced souvenir book. Cast, story, stars, supporting players, and guest artists are shown in full-color photographs and are profiled in the text. Stills from the film and production candids complete the book. Anyone who liked the film will be delighted with this attractive album.

2629 *The Great Adventure Films.* by Thomas, Tony. 282 p. illus. Secaucus, N.J.: Citadel, 1976.

This heavily visualized filmography represents the author's personal choice of 50 adventure films. Using the *Citadel* series format, each entry consists of illustrations, cast, credits, synopsis, background, and critical excerpts. Thomas's selection consists mostly of films from the swashbuckler, literature classic, and epic genres. Since the text lacks any critical depth, and the selection is ego-based, the volume is mildly interesting, at best.

2630 *The Great American Comedy Scene.* by Cahn, William; and Cahn, Rhoda. 190 p. paper illus. New York: Simon and Schuster (Monarch), 1979.

A new version of *The Laugh-Makers: A Pictorial History of American Comedians* (1957).

2631 *The Great American Movie Book.* edited by Michael, Paul. 342 p. illus. Englewood Cliffs, N.J.: Prentice-Hall, 1980.

An updating of Michael's earlier volume, *The American Movies Reference Book: The Sound Era* (1969), this new book covers films through 1978. Some features of the earlier volume have been omitted.

2632 *Great Animals of the Movies.* by Edelson, Edward. 135 p. illus. Garden City, N.Y.: Doubleday, 1980

In a continuing series of film books designed for the young reader, Edward Edelson chooses topics that have a special appeal for that particular audience. In other volumes he has treated monsters, science fiction, funny men, film spectaculars, kids, and tough gals and guys of films. His subject here is film animals, and he profiles some of the most famous: Lassie, Francis, Cheetah, Rin Tin Tin, Benji, Tony, Trigger, Elsa, and even Clint Eastwood's Clyde. In seven taut chapters, many other film creatures are reviewed. The final chapter is devoted to television animals: Mr. Ed, J. Fred Muggs, Morris the Cat, etc. Illustrations are clearly reproduced and there is a useful index.

This is an excellent volume for the youth audience. Older readers will enjoy it, too.

2633 *The Great Audience.* by Seldes, Gilbert. 239 p. New York: Viking Press, 1951.

Three popular arts—motion pictures, radio, and television— are examined to determine their effect on the tastes, standards, and environments of the great audience.

More than one third of the volume is devoted to films. Nearly all of Seldes' writings were ahead of their time; even today his work remains current, readable and prophetic. The section included here is a broad overview of film topics given as a base on which he builds his argument about the lost audience for films.

2634 *The Great British Films.* by Vermilye, Jerry. 255 p. illus. Secaucus, N.J.: Citadel, 1978.

Since Citadel seems to be running out of saleable subjects for their *Films of...* series, they apparently have turned to specific topical filmographies such as this one. Some 75 British films from THE PRIVATE LIFE OF HENRY VIII (1933) to THE GO-BETWEEN (1971) are recalled by credits, cast, comments, stills, and synopses. Critical evaluation is somewhat predictable and limited, because of the word "great" in the book's title.

The saving grace here is not the production or the treatment but the actual content—those 75 British classics. When so many beloved films are presented to the reader in one package, it is hard to find too much fault.

2635 *The Great British Picture Show.* by Perry, George. 367 p. illus. New York: Hill and Wang, 1974.

This history of the British cinema is subtitled "From the '90s to the '70s." Three decades of silent films are treated in rapid fashion within the first 60 pages. The remaining portions deal with the sound films, a collection of mini-biographies, a bibliography and an index. Because of the enormous number of names and titles mentioned, the text tends to be a factual exposition rather than a critical analysis. Supporting materials are uniformly excellent. The illustrations are well reproduced and nicely integrated. Individual filmographies appear as part of the short biographies. The bibliography and the index will be most useful to the reader who wishes further or specific information. In summary, this volume is a complete general survey of British film history. Surrounding the text are some very good reference sections and illustrations. Acceptable.

2636 *The Great Cartoon Stars: A Who's Who.* compiled by Gifford, Denis. 128 p. illus. London: Jupiter Books, 1979.

2637 *The Great Charlie.* by Payne, Robert. 287 p. illus. London: Andre Deutsch, 1952.

More an exploration of the roots and predecessors of Chaplin's comedy style than a biography, this volume considers such early clowns as Deburau and Grimaldi, Marionettes, Punch, Pan, and Pierrot. The comic styles of certain contemporaries of Chaplin such as W. C. Fields are also examined. However, most of the text is devoted to a detailed examination of Chaplin's screen personality. Accompanied by a group of excellent stills, the critical analysis offered here is unusual and stimulating. For the person familiar with Chaplin's art, this is an excellent analysis; beginners are advised to read other biographical appreciations first. Note: other titles for this book have been *Charlie Chaplin* and *The Great God Pan*.

2638 *Great Child Stars*. by Parish, James Robert. 206 p. paper illus. New York: Ace, 1976.

James Robert Parish has furnished a copious output of biographical information in his many books. Here, in a collective biography that he dedicates to "show business mothers everywhere," he provides capsule profiles of 24 child film stars. Arranged alphabetically by surname, each short chapter offers text, a picture and a film chronology.

Selection is excellent, Parish remains Parish, and the entire work is totally commendable.

2639 *The Great Comedians Talk About Comedy*. by Wilde, Larry. 382 p. illus. New York: Citadel, 1968.

This collection of interviews has a certain importance since many of the subjects have made films. However, comedy is defined throughout in a very broad sense, covering much more than film comedy. Those interviewed are Woody Allen, Milton Berle, Shelley Berman, Jack Benny, Joey Bishop, George Burns, Johnny Carson, Maurice Chevalier, Phyllis Diller, Jimmy Durante, Dick Gregory, Bob Hope, George Jessel, Jerry Lewis, Danny Thomas, Larry Wilde, and Ed Wynn. All comedy resists analysis and that is evident in the interviews. But the book will interest readers and the Jerry Lewis interview is reason enough to consider the volume. Acceptable.

2640 *Great Companions: Critical Memoirs of Some Famous Friends*. by Eastman, Max. 312 p. illus. New York: Farrar, Straus and Cudahy, 1959.

Eastman devotes one chapter to Chaplin. See also *Enjoyment of Laughter*.

2641 *The Great Cowboy Stars of Movies and Television*. by Miller, Leo O. 384 p. illus. New Rochelle, N.Y.: Arlington House, 1979.

In this collective biography, which resembles the volumes done by Parish. Author Leo Miller presents 43 cowboy stars. He has divided his subjects into three groups: Living Legends, New Breed, and Ghost Riders in the Sky. For each there is biographical information, much subject quotation and hardly any critical evaluation. A photograph and a filmography listing round out the entries. Those portions of the text which reflect the opinion of the author are uniformly admiring, to the point of becoming fan magazine prose. In keeping with the film cowboy "image," positive virtues are mentioned constantly, while personal character flaws or negatives are passed over quickly or else omitted. Everyone's a hero here.

Since there are other earlier books which cover the same ground more thoroughly (e.g. *The Western* by Allen Eyles), the value and appeal of this volume may be limited to the undiscriminating devotee of film and television westerns.

2642 *The Great Dane and The Great Northern Film Company*. by Bergsten, Bebe. 116 p. illus. Los Angeles: Locare Research Group, 1973.

The Dane referred to in the title is Ole Olsen, a pioneer who began making films in 1906. In middle age, after careers as a carnival barker and peep show owner, he arrived in Copenhagen and opened a motion picture theatre. To obtain product, he produced his own films, via the Nordisk Film Company. More than 100 films were produced in 1906. He continued to expand his activities to the point where he had branches in Berlin, London, Vienna, Genoa and New York City. In 1912 and 1913 the company made films of two or three reels, thus preparing the way for the feature film. Sixteen Nordisk films are described in the latter section of the book by cast and production data, a synopsis, some frame reproductions and a beautifully reproduced publicity still. The book is indexed.

Some unfamiliar subjects are treated with respect, scholarship and intelligence. The research necessary to produce the quality seen here is obvious. In addition, production values—the binding, print, layout, and photo reproduction—are superior. The book is highly recommended.

2643 *The Great Fear*. by Cautie, David. 697 p. New York: Simon and Schuster, 1978.

A study of the anti-communist witch hunts, this volume gives some attention to the investigation of Hollywood and its "subversive" films, people, and activities.

2644 *Great Film Directors: A Critical Anthology.* edited by Braudy, Leo; and Dickstein, Morris. 778 p. paper New York: Oxford University Press, 1978.

In this anthology there are 80 articles devoted to critical discussions of some 23 directors: Antonioni, Bergman, Bresson, Bunuel, Capra, Chaplin, Dreyer, Eisenstein, Fellini, Flaherty, Ford, Godard, Griffith, Hawks, Hitchcock, Keaton, Kurosawa, Lang, Renoir, Rossellini, von Sternberg, Truffaut, and Welles.

The contributors to the anthology are primarily critics or filmmakers. Selection was made with an attempt to define the work of each director. Indirectly many theoretical or aesthetic theories of film criticism are also presented. The volume will appeal largely to persons studying the work of the 23 directors. Others will welcome the opportunity to pick and choose those articles which fit their current interest. Acceptable.

2645 *Great Film Plays: Vol. 1—Scripts of Six Classic films.* edited by Gassner, John. 334 p. paper New York: Crown, 1959.

A paperback made from *Twenty Best Film Plays* and containing IT HAPPENED ONE NIGHT (1934); REBECCA (1940); THE LIFE OF EMILE ZOLA (1937); THE GOOD EARTH (1937); ALL THAT MONEY CAN BUY (1941); and STAGECOACH (1939).

2646 *The Great Films: Fifty Golden Years of Motion Pictures.* by Crowther, Bosley. 258 p. illus. New York: G. P. Putnam's 1967.

A group of 50 films are given speical attention in this volume by former *New York Times* film critic, Bosley Crowther. Whether these represent the 50 greatest films of all time, as suggested, is debatable. No argument can be made about the quality; they are all classic films for one reason or another. Some were popular successes, and others were failures. A second list of 100 distinguished films is appended—still no mention of GIGI (1958), A STAR IS BORN (1954), HAMLET (1948), etc. If one can overlook the selection aspect, then the book is immensely satisfying. Several pages of stills, plot description, analysis, and background material are devoted to each film. The selection of stills is superior and the narrative is of uniform high quality. A film index, a bibliography and a name index are included. Recommended highly.

2647 *The Great Funnies: A History of Film Comedy.* by Robinson, David. 160 p. paper illus. New York: Dutton, 1969.

This analysis of film comedy extends from 1898 to 1968 and, as usual with this *Pictureback* series, is admirable. There are many illustrations.

2648 *The Great Gangster Pictures.* by Parish, James Robert; and Pitts, Michael R. 431 p. illus. Metuchen, N.J.: Scarecrow, 1976.

Another selected genre filmography is offered by Parish and Pitts. Arranged alphabetically by title, hundreds of gangster films from 1912 to 1974 are described by data, casts, credits, plot synopsis, and most importantly, critical comment and background information. By addressing film quality and period importance, the latter two features give the filmography its major distinction. American films get the major attention with only a sprinkling of foreign titles presented. Illustrations give the reader some idea of the characters and locales indigenous to this genre, as does an introductory essay by Edward Connor. Appended is a list of gangster programs from radio and television.

2649 *The Great Garbo.* by Payne, Robert. 297 p. illus. New York: Praeger, 1976.

In this critical appreciation of Garbo's career as a motion picture actress, Robert Payne concentrates on a detailed study of her relatively few films. Biographical information is limited, with greatest attention given to her early pre-Hollywood years. In chronological order each of her films from THE SAGA OF GOSTA BERLING (1923) to TWO FACED WOMAN (1941) is described and critically evaluated. The author's opinions are original, unique and often controversial. To him Garbo was the "stella assoluta, the star above all other stars," and much of his text reflects a prejudice based on infatuation. Flaws are noted in the work of the professionals surrounding Garbo but she emerges as a model of near perfection. Objectivity seems to be a missing quality in many critical portions of the text.

The illustrations provided, however, are almost faultless in both selection and reproduction. Here the reader will find many diverse and beautiful portraits of Garbo that may explain her legend more persuasively than pages of text. A chronology, a bibliography, and an index complete the volume.

If the reader shares or accepts Payne's evaluations of Garbo's work, he will be delighted with this volume. The detailed text and the attractive illustrations provide a feast for Garbo devotees. Others who are more restrained in their appreciation of the actress will have to take their pleasure mostly in the visuals and try applying some objectivity to the adoring text. Acceptable.

2650 *The Great Goldwyn.* by Johnston, Alva. 99 p. illus. New York: Random House, 1937.

This is a short, dated biography of Samuel Goldwyn that resembles a *New Yorker* profile minus the in-depth personality analysis. While much attention is given to externals such as Goldwyn's need for absolute authority, his impatience with his underlings, his inability to be a good loser, etc., little is said about the human side of the man. We are shown the performer on stage, but never the human being offstage. The book is well written and the author does try to be objective in his writing. A few pictures are included.

2651 *Great Horror Movies.* by Friedman, Favius. 160 p. paper illus. New York: Scholastic Book Services, 1974.

There are some things to admire in this collection of annotations for 70 horror movies. For each, abbreviated cast and production credits are given with a short synopsis following. Some factual or background material concludes the description. The presentations are uniformly interesting and will excite reader curiosity.

However, some reservations about arrangement and approach should be mentioned. Does the teen-aged audience really appreciate the cuteness implicit in terms such as "Real Cool Ghouls," "Creepy-Crawlies," "Eerie-Weirdies," etc.? Would a table of contents indicating chapter headings have been of value? Should the introduction inform the reader about the author's arrangement of his material? Much is made of the illustrations on the back cover and in a title page subheading. They are termed "marvelous," and undeniably the originals were. However, the reproduction and reduction employed here does not warrant the adjective.

In summary, some proven material has been diminished by poor arrangement, a mediocre production and by an under-estimation of audience intelligence. The information and description offered in the 70 annotations make the book acceptable.

2652 *Great Ideas in Cinema.* by Armes, Roy. London: Robert Maxwell, 1971.

A general book of film history designed for young readers.

2653 *Great Kids of the Movies.* by Edelson, Edward. 128 p. illus. New York: Doubleday, 1979.

This survey of Hollywood child actors covers the five-decade period from 1920 to 1970. Written for young readers, the volume is nicely illustrated and contains an index. Since so many subjects are included in a relatively short text, the coverage is very general, sacrificing detail for scope.

2654 *The Great Little Movie Quiz Book.* by McDermott, John. 71 p. Philadelphia: Franklin, 1975.

The 30 separate quizzes offered in this small volume cover topics that include the Academy Awards, musicals, directors, gangsters, famous pairs, and detectives. Methodologies employed are straight answer, matching, and multiple choice. Answers are noted in the final pages.

The questions, most of which are in the mid-range of difficulty, are entertaining and thoughtfully arranged. Buffs will find the volume to be a pleasant stimulation that offers a few hours of fun. Acceptable.

2655 *Great Lives of the Century.* by New York Times. illus. New York: New York Times Press, 1977.

An oversized necrology taken directly from the *New York Times* pages, this volume treats 104 personalities whose lives and careers are described in detail. Film personalities include Bing Crosby, Walt Disney, Clark Gable, Judy Garland, Marilyn Monroe, Elvis Presley, Will Rogers, and others.

2656 *Great Lovers of the Movies.* by Mercer, Jane. 176 p. illus. New York: Crescent (Crown), 1975.

This collective biography consists of 23 male film stars arranged in the approximate chronological order of their celebrity. Beginning with Douglas Fairbanks, probably the first great male superstar, the volume ends with Clint Eastwood. Dustin Hoffman, Al Pacino, and Robert DeNiro are probably not included because they are more closely identified with anti-heroes and character portrayals than with romantic roles. For each star there is an essay, a filmography, a bibliography, and selected stills. At least one portrait is provided for each and some of these are in full color.

All the elements in this volume are quite good. The essays are carefully formulated and emphasize roles rather than personal incidents. Picture reproduction is clear and the color work is most attractive. Each filmography is concentrated on one page but film title, year, company and a few cast names are given for every entry.

The reference value of this volume is high and, of course, it has definite audience appeal. Recommended.

2657 *Great Moments From the Films of Walt Disney.* 96 p. illus. New York: Smith (Rutledge Press), 1981.

2658 *Great Monsters of the Movies.* by Edelson, Edward. 101 p. illus. Garden City, N.Y.: Doubleday, 1973.

This is written for a juvenile audience. Edelson divides his book into sections such as legends, pioneers, frightening men, big beasts, and a miscellany of monsters. Melies, Chaney, Karloff, Lugosi and Chaney, Jr. receive individual attention. The illustrations are passable at best, and the approach, content, format, and design are overly familiar. With the experience most kids have had with horror films on TV, they could probably come up with a better book than this. Manchel's volume, *Terrors of the Screen*, is still the one to choose for children to read.

2659 *Great Monsters of the Movies.* by Davidson, Robert K. 128 p. paper illus. New York: Jove (Pyramid), 1977.

Designed for the young nondiscriminating reader, this paperback reviews the movie monsters in four genres: the Frankenstein Monster; Creatures of the Night; Man into Monster; and Creatures From Other Worlds. Illustrations, a bibliography, and an index complete the book. Selection and arrangement of the material is good, but the text is elemental in its combination of fact, anecdote and comment-opinion. Reproduction of the visuals varies from very fuzzy to sharp. In other words, this is a mediocre production of material that has a lasting and proven appeal to young audiences.

2660 *Great Mother of Pearl.* by Fields, W. C. illus. Los Angeles: Stanyan, 1970.

Another collection of photos and sayings of W. C. Fields, this volume falls somewhere between a very short book and an elaborate greeting card.

2661 *The Great Motion Picture Soundtrack Robbery.* by Sutak, Ken. 111 p. Hamden, Conn.: Shoe String (Archon), 1976.

The author's concern here is with the problem of copyright infringement as it specifically applies to film soundtrack recordings. Since the film soundtrack is the small thin portion of the film located opposite the visual, it is not copyrighted separately. The track itself is made up of separate elements—(music, voice, effects, etc.)—which are mixed or combined to create the final total sound. These individual elements are not copyrighted either. The question considered is whether the soundtrack receives the protection of copyright when it is granted to the film as a totality. The operation of several small manufacturers who market disc recordings of soundtracks has raised the issue: are they legal entities or are they pirates? The author's argument is that these men are indeed violators of copyright.

Many other aspects of the problem are explored in rather technical legal language. A short glossary helps somewhat, as does a valuable index. In his lengthy introduction the author discusses copyright in general terms. Throughout he includes documentation by footnotes and case identifications. Much of this specialized material was published originally in *The Bulletin of the Copyright Society of the U.S.A.*

2662 *The Great Movie Cartoon Parade.* by Rider, David. 120 p. paper illus. New York: Bounty (Crown), 1976.

John Halas has provided a critical history and appreciation of animated cartoons in his introduction to his attractive volume. A biographical parade of more than 60 cartoon characters from Asterix to Yogi Bear is presented via text and visuals in the main section of the book. Included are the most well-known—Mr. Magoo, Popeye, Bugs Bunny, etc. —and such lesser-known ones as Foo Foo, Lucky Luke, Milo, and Pepe le Pew.

The visuals, which are the book's main attraction, range from black-and-white drawings to full-color stills. Their variety and arrangement are most impressive. Reproduction is generally very good, with only the early cartoon characters such as Koko the Clown (1917) or Krazy Kat (1916) looking rather primitive—which they obviously were.

A welcome appendix lists 16 major cartoon producers from the United States and Great Britain along with short company histories, their directors, and the cartoon characters they developed. The volume is indexed.

This book will appeal to a very wide audience ranging from children to senior citizens. Its content has been selected and arranged with affection and its production is admirable. Recommended.

2663 *The Great Movie Comedians.* by Maltin, Leonard. 238 p. illus. New York: Crown, 1978.

This volume of collective critical biography evolved from the author's direction of a bicentennial salute to American film comedy at the Museum of Modern Art. He has chosen 18 individual comedians and four teams for evaluation, appreciation, and biographical exposition. Most of the subjects are predictable, but the inclusion of Mable Normand, Charley Chase, Raymond Griffith, and Marie Dressler is a pleasant surprise. In addition to the text, there are numerous illustrations and a filmography for each subject. The book is indexed.

Maltin's approach is that of an emotional enthusiast rather than a critical intellectual, but his sincere effort in sharing his film-viewing experiences and research will be appreciated by most readers.

2664 *Great Movie Heroes.* by Parish, James Robert. 115 p. paper illus. New York: Harper and Row, 1975.

In this collective biography, some 22 male film personalities are profiled. Each is given a few pages of tightly packed factual information, a few illustrations, and a filmography consisting only of title and date. Sujects include Bogart, Brando, Cooper, Dean, Eastwood, Flynn, Fonda, Gable, Gould, Grant, Hoffman, Ladd, McQueen, Newman, Poitier, Power, Redford, Reynolds, Segal, Stewart, Tracy and Wayne.

With most of the names there can be no quarrel, but the inclusion of Gould, Segal, and Hoffman may be a bit premature. Since the volume seems designed for young adults, the selection is probably quite appropriate.

As with most of Parish's collective biographies the text is compact, economical, and altogether efficient. While little evaluation or interpretation is offered, there are enough critical-value words in the factual text so that a sense of the actor's public and private persona can be obtained. The book also has value as a quick reference source.

2665 *Great Movie Quiz Book.* by Worth, Fred. illus. Chatsworth, Calif.: Brooke House.

One hundred classic films are used to offer more than 2000 questions for film buffs in this volume. Arrangement is alphabetical and answers are prov-

ided.

2666 *The Great Movie Serials.* by Harmon, Jim; and Glut, Donald F. 384 p. illus. New York: Doubleday and Co., 1972.

In an introductory note, the authors state that the one essential element of the film serial was action. This may be the reason for the lack of excitement in this book: action is hard to describe, tedious to read in words and needs to be visualized. The first illustrations follow page 171 and use only eight pages; another eight-page section appears after page 194. The visuals are mostly half-page and the selection is poor. Thus an essential element of a book such as this is damagingly weak.

The well-researched text divided the serials (mostly sound) into types or categories: the girls, science fiction, the westerns, the boys, real life heroes, the jungle, aviator, detectives, super-heroes, etc. This latter group includes Superman and Captain Marvel, while the girls considers Pearl White, the Jungle Queens, the Tiger Woman, the Female Zorro, Linda Stirling, Phylis Coates, and others. In addition to much factual information about production, special effects, and casts, there are plot outlines, script excerpts, and evaluative comments. A general index completes the book.

Unless one is an afficionado of the serial, the book will have a limited appeal. A far more effective treatment of the subject is available in books such as *To Be Continued* and *Days of Thrills and Adventure.* One positive quality about the book is its potential for reference, via the copious text and detailed index. Acceptable.

2667 *The Great Movie Series.* edited by Parish, James Robert. 333 p. illus. New York: A. S. Barnes, 1971.

This impressive oversized volume reviews 25 of the sound motion picture series made by Hollywood from 1930 to 1968. One non-Hollywood series, the James Bond films, completes the group. Each series has an introductory essay—more descriptive than critical—followed by selected stills and a filmography of the entire series. A seemingly complete cast listing, along with studio, date, running time, director, author, screen play, art direction, music direction, camera, and editing credits are noted in most instances.

The series considered include: Andy Hardy, Blondie, Bomba, Boston Blackie, Bowery Boys, Charlie Chan, Crime Doctor, Dr. Christian, Dr. Kildare, Ellery Queen, The Falcon, Francis the talking mule,

Hopalong Cassidy, James Bond, Jungle Jim, The Lone Wolf, Ma and Pa Kettle, Maisie, Matt Helm, Mr. Moto, Philo Vance, The Saint, Sherlock Holmes, Tarzan, The Thin Man.

Since this is a rather ambitious reference attempt, one is tempted to forgive errors in spelling, e.g., Adele Jerkins for Adele Jergens; confusion in story plots, e.g., Smersh or Spectre in the Bond outlines, and other small slips. Although, with an editorship consisting of one chief, one associate and three contributors, perhaps a higher degree of accuracy might be expected. The numerous stills are nicely reproduced and the total text is more than acceptable. As either a reference book or an entertainment, the volume is acceptable.

2668 *The Great Movie Shorts.* by Maltin, Leonard. 236 p. illus. New York: Crown, 1972.

Anyone who regards this volume as "a coffee table book" does it and its potential audience a great disservice; it is much more than the usual book in that genre. Providing a broad survey of the one-and two-reel short films (taken mostly from the thirties and forties), the author has researched his work with such diligence that he establishes a standard that will be difficult for most writers to meet. Some indication of his potential for writing this book can be noted by examining his earlier book, *Movie Comedy Teams,* which treated some of the same material.

Starting with the studios, he progresses quickly to the film series, where he gives extended attention to Our Gang, Laurel and Hardy, Charley Chase, Harry Langdon, W. C. Fields, Thelma Todd, Zasu Pitts, Patsy Kelly, Andy Clyde, Edgar Kennedy, Leon Errol, The Three Stooges, Pete Smith, Buster Keaton, Robert Benchley and Joe McDoakes. The short films of other comedians are also described. Filmographies listing cast, director, date, studio, and a short synopsis follow each performer's section. The work is not limited to comedy shorts. Series such as "Crime Does Not Pay," "Screen Snapshots," "John Nesbitt's Passing Parade," and newsreels, travelogues, musicals, documentaries and sport shorts are also included. Cartoons and World War II shorts are not considered. More than 200 rather special illustrations supplement the text. Reproduction quality is above average and the selection is unique, nostalgic, and frequently exciting. An extended index further enhances the book's reference value.

The book will appeal to a wide range of audiences—scholars, buffs, historians, nostalgia lovers, the curious, and the library browsers—and all will be well rewarded by Maltin's affection for his topic, his impressive research, and the total production of what

can only be called a fine contribution to cinema literature. Highly recommended.

2669 *Great Movie Spectaculars.* by Edelson, Edward. 149 p. paper illus. New York: Archway, 1976.

In other volumes specifically designed for the young readers, Edward Edelson has treated movie monsters and science fiction movies. Here he is concerned with another large film genre, the spectacular. His approach is partly historical (DeMille, Griffith), partly sub-genre (swashbucklers, westerns, disasters, musicals), and partly how-did-they-do-it? Some adequate illustrations and an index are added.

As usual with Edelson's books, this one combines responsible writing with intelligent arrangement and presentation. He and Frank Manchel are among the most impressive writers of film books for young readers.

2670 *The Great Movie Stars: The Golden Years.* by Shipman, David. 576 p. illus. New York: Crown, 1970.

There are two possible reservations about this volume that may occur to the reader. In giving some 160 stars attention, he is certain to be vulnerable in the selection process. By limiting his field to a closing date of 1945, he also limits the use of the volume. A summary of each personality is given along with photos, critical quotes, gossip, opinions and statistical data. An interesting feature is a listing of title changes between English and American films. Picture quality varies but the text is straightforward and frank. A bibliography and an index are given. This is a good browser's book. Recommended.

2671 *The Great Movie Stars.* by Shipman, David. 568 p. illus. New York: St. Martin's Press, 1972.

Written as the follow-up or sequel to his earlier book, this volume surpasses that effort. Subtitled "The International Years," the book covers film performers active in the period following World War II to the present. More than 220 mini-biographies are offered and some tell more about the subject than full-length life stories elsewhere. Shipman not only offers the factual information, but is critical about the films, gossipy about the private lives and temperaments, and extremely biased in his treatment of a few favorites. (For a typical example of Shipman at his best, try "Susan Hayward.")

Reading this book recalls the pleasurable experience of discovering the Blum pictorial books: it is addictive, charmingly prejudiced, enormously entertaining; its picture selection criteria are similar to Blum's and it is a book that can be re-read and re-used many times. The many illustrations have been reproduced with care, a brief bibliography is given, and there is a listing of film title changes.

With a book of this size and scope, some errors and omissions are a certainty, e.g., isn't the still on page 214 from DEADLINE AT DAWN (1946) rather than from THE HAIRY APE? Is Goldie Hawn with her one Academy Award (included) more a star than Jack Hawkins (excluded)? This last situation is even more puzzling in view of Shipman's rather British viewpoint. Perhaps his introductory explanation on criteria for selection explains it, but it still seems quite subjective.

These are strictly minor matters, for this book is a most welcome arrival. It is an ideal reference and a rich entertainment. Highly recommended.

2672 *The Great Movies.* by Bayer, William. 252 p. illus. New York: Grosset and Dunlap, 1973.

What an irresistible combination of elements are combined in this volume! Take 60 films that deserve to be called "Great Movies." Add some of the most attractive visuals to be published in a long time and a provocative text by the witty author of *Breaking Through,* ... etc. and it's a sure winner—as this volume certainly is.

Bayer divides his choices into 12 major genre categories—Westerns, musicals, comedies, etc. After an introductory statement, the five films treated under each classification are discussed. Some plot elements are mentioned, but the essay for each film is largely expository and critical with the stress placed on why it was chosen rather than what it is about. Data on all five films is presented at the end of each section.

Anyone making a best films list will include personal favorites. This author does, but there are few surprises here—except perhaps CONTEMPT (1964), THE MANCHURIAN CANDIDATE (1962), THE SEARCHERS (1956), and THE BAD AND THE BEAUTIFUL (1952). Many readers could suggest valid replacements for these. Some of the author's dogmatic statements are vulnerable too; e.g., on Bogart: "For 10 years he played minor parts, until in 1941 he appeared as Sam Spade in THE MALTESE FALCON (1941)." His roles in HIGH SIERRA (1941), MARKED WOMAN (1937), and THE PETRIFIED FOREST (1936) were certainly not "minor." These are tiny flaws, however, in the frisky, entertaining commentary that Bayer provides.

As indicated above, the visuals are consistently fine,

with many color photos and some attractive portraits. Aside from excellent reproduction, many of the visuals are rare since they come from private collections. An index adds value to the book. Here then is another fine visual experience enhanced by a literate entertaining text. Highly recommended.

2673 *Great Movies on TV.* by Friedman, Favius. 127 p. paper illus. New York: Scholastic Book Services, 1972.

Some 60 films are treated in this pleasant volume. Arranged alphabetically from THE AFRICAN QUEEN (1952) to YOUNG CASSIDY (1965), each entry gives cast and credits, a brief synopsis, and a short background information feature called "Behind the Scenes." Selection in accordance with the book's title is a problem. Some of the films are in fact "good" or "very good," but not "great." To mislead a juvenile audience into thinking that ARSENIC AND OLD LACE (1944), THE BLACK ARROW (1948), GREEN MANSIONS (1959), HOUND OF THE BASKERVILLES (1939), THE 39 STEPS (the 1960 remake) and THREE CAME HOME (1950) are "great" films is a disservice. They are competent examples of studio filmmaking. Television offers many accepted classics which need identification and endorsement from repsonsible adults; care must be taken to avoid the indiscriminate use of value words in describing lesser films. The stills which accompany each entry are adequate but often give little indication of the film's content or theme.

To some immature reader the presence of a statement in a book or newspaper signifies absolute truth. For that reason this volume is not acceptable.

2674 THE GREAT MUPPET CAPER—*The Making of a Masterpiece.* by Weiner, Ellis. 96 p. illus. paper New York: Bantam (Muppet Press), 1981.

An illustrated account of making the 1981 film which was directed Jim Henson and D. Lazer.

2675 *Great Names and How They are Made.* by Cocroft, Thoda. 270 p. illus. New York: Dartnell, 1941.

Cocroft is a graphologist who analyzes the signatures of film celebrities (Gish, Hepburn, Hayes, Olivier, Leigh, etc.) in this unusual volume.

2676 THE GREAT RACE. 33 p. paper illus. Hollywood: Warner Brothers, 1965.

Some familiar faces appear in this attractive souvenir book. After the plot is related in great detail, there are individual sections devoted to Jack L. Warner, the producer, and to Blake Edwards, the director. Each of the three stars gets a double page consisting of a center narrative and a perimeter of photographs. Although some attempt at quality can be detected, many of the photographs are only average in color fidelity and focus. An amusing section on the devices that were used and the supporting cast and production credits of this 1965 film complete the book.

2677 *The Great Romantic Films.* by Quirk, Lawrence J. 224 p. illus. Secaucus, N.J.: Citadel, 1974.

Fifty films have been selected as landmark films which exemplify the romantic mystique. Obviously such a choice is personal and author Quirk has included some surprises, e.g., THE HOUSE ON 56TH STREET (1933), KINGS ROW (1942), TEOREMA (1969), DEATH IN VENICE (1971) and A SEPARATE PEACE (1972).

The films are arranged in order of their release date. Cast credits, stills, and a critical essay accompany each. It is the essay that provides whatever intellectual nourishment there is here; not only does the author recall plot and background, but he also offers both a personal and critical appraisal of the films. By both text and selection, the author has left himself vulnerable to a charge of loving "camp" movies— HUMORESQUE, MADAME X, MY REPUTATION, BACK STREET, ALL THAT HEAVEN ALLOWS—and others that do not have a reputation as "great" films no matter what genre. Their lasting appeal to mass audiences, however, may certify them for the more serious consideration that Quirk offers here. Acceptable.

2678 *Great Science Fiction from the Movies.* by Edelson, Edward. 149 p. paper illus.. New York: Archway (Pocket Books), 1976.

When this volume originally appeared in a hardcover edition, it was called *Visions of Tomorrow: Great Science Fiction From the Movies.* Designed for young readers, the text provides an overview of about 60 films and TV programs in the science fiction genre. The approach is roughly chronological, discussing in order Melies' A TRIP TO THE MOON (1902), METROPOLIS (1928), Jules Verne, H. G. Wells, serials, Invaders From Space, The End of the World, To the Moon, Strange Places and Odd Beings. A final chapter is devoted to television programs. The volume is indexed and contains a few illustrations.

Edelson's text is quite acceptable as both a description and an argument for improved quality in the genre. Unfortunately, the production quality of the paperback examined was inferior and its poor binding indicated a short life.

2679 *The Great Science Fiction Pictures.* by Parish, James Robert; and Pitts, Michael R. 382 p. illus. Metuchen, N.J.: Scarecrow, 1977.

Several hundred science fiction films are described by data, cast, credits, synopsis, review excerpts, critical comment and background information in this filmography. Illustrations help to identify some of the unique characteristics of this genre. A list of science fiction shows on radio and television along with a bibliography complete the book.

While the pure information provided by the authors makes this a good reference source, it is the critical comment that will delight most readers. The authors are able to draw on their apparently unlimited knowledge of films in this survey of the science fiction film genre.

2680 *Great Serial Ads.* compiled by Barbour, Alan. 64 p. paper illus. New York: Screen Facts Press, 1965.

A collection of advertisements for the movie serials, selected and arranged by specialist Barbour. No text —just illustrations.

2681 *The Great Show Business Animals.* by Rothel, David. 292 p. illus. San Diego: A. S. Barnes, 1980.

With care and dedication, David Rothel presents an unusual collective biography of show business animals. Both individual animals (Trigger) and master characters played by several animals (Lassie) are treated.

The volume divides its subjects into animal categories—monkeys, dogs, horses etc.—and coverage of each animal varies, with items of background, history, interviews with filmmakers and trainers, film plots, etc., making up the content. Certain of the animals are known only from television (Fred the Cockatoo).

Almost 200 illustrations, a bibliography, and an index complete the book.

This is a nicely prepared but specialized volume that will be enjoyed primarily by younger readers. It also provides a good reference for trivia buffs.

2682 *The Great Songwriters of Hollywood.* by Craig, Warren. 287 p. illus. San Diego: A. S. Barnes, 1980.

Warren Craig, who also wrote a book on American popular songwriters called *Sweet and Lowdown*, is apparently fascinated by songwriters; in this collective biography he profiles 32 composers and lyricists who have written for Hollywood films. Each receives a short biographical page or so and a chronological filmography which lists the songs for each film. For example, in 1941 Mack Gordon wrote the words for four songs in SUN VALLEY SERENADE: "Chattanooga Choo Choo," "I Know Why," "It Happened in Sun Valley," and "The Kiss Polka." A song title index, a people index, and some illustrations complete the book. The subject portraits and song sheet covers add much to the book's quality.

This is an ideal reference for anyone interested in the musical film. Most of the Hollywood's best songs and songwriters are identified in an easy-to-use arrangement.

2683 *Great Sports Movies.* by Manchel, Frank. 116 p. illus. New York: Franklin Watts, 1980.

In this volume, designed for younger readers, Frank Manchel provides a survey of a neglected film genre, the sports film. Until recently, movies about sports were commercially risky ventures. Whether competitive sports help or hurt American society is a continuing question reflected in these films.

In his usual competent fashion, Manchel provides much content and coverage in his survey. Elements of history, biography, comment, analysis, and pure information are expertly blended with some carefully selected illustrations. An index and a bibliography are provided.

Once again Manchel is making film study attractive to younger readers by intelligent selection, arrangement, and presentation. Other readers will also be pleased by this volume.

2684 *The Great Spy Films.* by Rubenstein, Leonard. 223 p. illus. Secaucus, N.J.: Citadel, 1979.

A personal selection of 50 spy films by the author is the content of this volume in the *Citadel* series. The typical pattern of providing cast, credits, illustrations, background, comment, etc., for each film is followed. Selection is acceptable as are the comments of the author. Readers interested in the genre should note that Parish and Pitts treat 463 spy films in their book, *The Great Spy Pictures.*

2685 *The Great Spy Pictures.* by Parish, James Robert; and Pitts, Michael R. 585 p. illus. Metuchen, N.J.: Scare-

crow Press, 1974.

Excellent and generous coverage of a film genre is provided in this survey. Using "A History of the Spy Film (1914-1973)" as an introduction, the text describes and often critically evaluates 463 selected spy films. Arranged alphabetically by title, the entries list title, studio, year of release, running time, full cast and production credits and a precis. This latter section is more than a plot summary and often includes critical comment, trivia material, and pure subjective statement. Closing sections include a listing of radio and TV spy shows, a selected bibliography by T. Allan Taylor of spy movies and finally, a listing of spy novel series with individual titles noted. Illustrations are well selected and placed throughout the book.

While one can argue about the use of the word "great" in the title, nothing can be said about the respectful treatment accorded the films here. The text is witty, informative, and entertaining. In its stated attempt to be representative rather than all-encompassing, it is highly successful. Supporting materials also help to identify the appeal, longevity, and popularity of the genre. Recommended.

2686 *Great Stars of Hollywood's Golden Age.* edited by Platt, Frank C. 214 p. paper illus. New York: Signet Books, 1966.

Most of the articles appearing in this compilation were apparently taken from issues of *Liberty Magazine* (1929-1942). The articles on Valentino, Garbo and Lombard were written by Adela Rogers St. Johns while Harlow, Chaplin, and John Barrymore are described by the other authors. The style is "thirties" fan-magazine but there is a nostalgic interest and curiosity fanned by the subsequent and franker biographies which are available today. While this is no great reading adventure, the articles are selected with more editorial taste than those appearing in similar hardbound volumes.

2687 *Great Times Good Times: The Odyssey of Maurice Barrymore.* by Kotsilibas-Davis, James. 538 p. illus. Garden City, N.Y.: Doubleday, 1977.

This lengthy, detailed biography traces the life of Maurice Barrymore from his birth in 1849 in India to his death in 1905. It has been meticulously researched and offers a fascinating reconstruction of a life that combines triumph and tragedy.

Maurice Barrymore's life was over before movies became a mass medium or a modern art. A single mention of motion pictures—as a challenge to the legitimate theatre—appears on page 394. Other than that singular instance, the book's importance to film collections is the voluminous background information it offers about John, Ethel and Lionel Barrymore, the children of Maurice and Georgie Drew. Each of the Barrymore offsprings went on to become legendary performers on both stage and screen.

The carefully written text is supported by some fascinating visuals, a long bibliography and a detailed index. Recommended.

2688 *The Great TV and Movie Quiz.* 256 p. illus. paper New York: Playmore and Prestige, 1981.

2689 *The Great Villains.* by Pate, Janet. 120 p. illus. New York: Bobbs-Merrill, 1975.

An unusual and fascinating collection of villains is offered in this volume designed for young readers. Using 40 nasty characters taken from stage, screen, literature, myth, and the comics, the author outlines their story, offers background information, and notes films, plays, and selected print materials about each. For example: Mr. Edward Hyde is described by an excerpt and an outline of the story plot from Stevenson's *The Strange Case of Dr. Jekyll and Mr. Hyde,* some background information and listings of 16 films, four plays and ten editions of the famous story are noted. Illustrations taken from a wide range of sources including the films accompany each entry. No index is provided.

Although it is a rich and rewarding entertainment in itself, the book will create an appetite within the reader for the original story, the films, or the plays. An intelligent and creative treatment of a fascinating subject. Recommended.

2690 THE GREAT WALDO PEPPER. by Goldman, William. 224 p. paper illus. New York: Dell, 1975.

Script of the 1975 film directed by George Roy Hill. Includes cast, credits, an introduction and an afterword-interview by George Roy Hill.

2691 *The Great Western Pictures.* by Parish, James Robert; and Pitts, Michael R. 457 p. illus. Metuchen, N.J.: Scarecrow Press, 1976.

This selected filmography is the third in a genre series; having previously treated spy films and gangster films, the authors have given their attention to westerns here.

Arranged alphabetically by title, the book begins with ADVENTURES OF RED RYDER (1940) and ends with ZORRO'S FIGHTING LEGION (1939). In between there are hundreds of entries, many of which contain cast, credits, a plot synopsis, background material, and an occasional critical quote or comment. Others simply list credits and chapter titles. The 135 stills used throughout are clearly reproduced and there are television, radio, and book lists offered to supplement the filmography.

The use of the word "great" in the book's title is an exaggeration, of course. What we find here is a mixed collection of western films recalled in print. For the western buff it may be a volume to admire and treasure. Other readers will find it an acceptable entertainment and perhaps a useful film title reference.

2692 *Great Western Stars.* by Parish, James Robert. 256 p. paper illus. New York: Ace Books, 1976.

Parish offers a collective biography of 25 male western stars in this original paperback. For each there is a short essay, which combines selected career and private life information, together with a still and a filmography. The subjects range from superstars (John Wayne, Clint Eastwood) to lesser lights (Don Barry, Allen Lane, Charles Starrett, Bob Steele). As usual with the Parish biographies, the material is well selected and presented in a pleasant, if unexciting, text.

2693 *The Greatest Fox of Them All.* by Allvine, Glendon. 244 p. illus. New York: Lyle Stuart, 1969.

This is the story of another film mogul, William Fox, which details his early meteoric rise to Hollywood heights, his equally fast fall to prison in the forties, and his death in 1952. This saga is related in an uneven style with some anecdotes expanded far beyond their worth. Important events are sometimes glossed over in a short sentence. In one instance an entire chapter is given to a court petition by Demetrius Skouras.

The author's style is waspish and cynical—his view of Fox is one of amused fascination rather than admiration. Accuracy is not one of the book's strong points, e.g., Jacqueline Susann did not respond to public demand with *Beyond the Valley of the Dolls.* A few pictures accompany the latter portion of the text. The book looks at the Fox Studio when it was controlled by Sidney Kent, Joseph Schenck, Spyros Skouras, Darryl Zanuck and Richard Zanuck. The later dethroning of Richard adds still another unwritten chapter to the story.

2694 *The Greatest Star.* by Jordan, Rene. 253 p. New York: G. P. Putnam's, 1975.

Subtitled, "The Barbra Streisand Story," this unauthorized biography is an absorbing study of an ambitious, talented female whose rapid rise to superstar status was a show business phenomenon of the sixties. The author traces Streisand's private and professional lives with a dispassionate text and, as a result, the portrait which emerges is a nonflattering, rather disillusioning one. The performer seemingly is so involved with the goals of success-achievement-career that it is difficult for her to sustain any lengthy personal relationships. Apparently Streisand is fun to visit but not to live with.

Detailed attention is given to her few films and to her recordings. Unfortunately all supporting elements—index, discography, filmography, illustrations—are missing. However, in this instance the strong text almost obscures their absence. Jordan is a writer who can exercise objectivity in both narrative and criticism. His well-researched coverage of the complex child-girl-woman is continually involving. Readers will find this book to be one of the best female performer biographies written in years. Recommended.

2695 THE GREATEST STORY EVER TOLD. 34 p. illus. New York: Ivy Hill Lithograph, 1965.

Oversized stills from the 1965 film are used to illustrate an essay on religion and film in this unusual souvenir book. The latter section is devoted to portraits of the various characters in the film, nearly all of whom are portrayed by noted actors. The same concept which was distracting in the film is again at work here—a guessing game as to which actor is playing what role. The book clarifies it all on the last pages by indicating all cast credits along with other technical and production credits. The producer-director is identified only in the subtitle, "A Film by George Stevens."

2696 *The Greatest Stunts Ever.* by Hagner, John G. 30 p. paper illus. Hollywood: El Jon Publications, 1967.

A short volume about stuntmen, the films for which they create their stunts, and the stars for whom they double.

2697 GREED. by von Stroheim, Erich. 352 p. paper illus. New York: Simon and Schuster, 1972.

In addition to reprinting von Stroheim's original 10-hour shooting script, a comparison is made between the release version of the 1923 film and the original script. Scenes contained in the original script but missing from the film are bracketed. Entire sequences which were deleted are indicated by footnotes.

Supporting articles include the following: "Dreams of Realism" by Erich von Stroheim; "Introducing GREED" by Joel W. Finler; "Stroheim's GREED" by Herman G. Weinberg; "My Experience With Stroheim During the Making of GREED" by Jean Hersholt; "Shooting GREED" by William Daniels; "The Making of GREED" by Erich von Stroheim; two contemporary reviews of GREED (1924, 1925); and cast credits. Readers are directed to this excellent book, which is much less expensive than the Weinberg reconstruction of GREED for Arno Press.

2698 THE GREEN PASTURES. by Connelly, Marc. 208 p. paper illus. Madison, Wisc.: University of Wisconsin Press, 1979.

Script of the 1936 film directed by William Kieghley. This volume was edited by Thomas Cripps and contains an introduction, a bibliography, cast, and credits.

2699 *Gregory Peck.* by Thomas, Tony. 160 p. paper illus. New York: Pyramid, 1977.

Tony Thomas has written critical appreciations of such colorful performers as Errol Flynn and Marlon Brando. In this volume he tackles what has probably been his most challenging subject, Gregory Peck. While it is possible to describe a typical Peck role/performance, it is difficult to offer much variety in critical reactions since Peck's roles were relatively similar. Thomas notes his few departures from the standard image of an ideal American man of strength and integrity.

A review of Peck's early stage career introduces the film section, beginning with DAYS OF GLORY (1944) and ending with MACARTHUR (1977). A brief bibliography notes six periodical sources while the filmography lists Peck's 47 films to date. An index completes the volume. The many visuals which complement the text are clearly reproduced.

Explaining and evaluating the film career of Gregory Peck is not an easy assignment. Tony Thomas has succeeded not only in suggesting the reasons for Peck's longevity as a screen performer, but also has given the reader some insight into the man himself. Recommended.

2700 *Gregory Peck: The Man Behind the Legend.* by Freedland, Michael. 250 p. illus New York: Morrow, 1980.

This is an unauthorized biography, and although the author tries hard to create some excitement in his portrait, he is less than successful. Peck is a very private individual whose life is void of controversy, scandal, gossip, rumor, etc. The lack of Peck's cooperation has left Freedland only matters of public record upon which to base his story. A few poorly reproduced illustrations and a filmography accompany the bland text.

2701 *Greta Garbo.* by Durgnat, Raymond; and Kobal, John. 160 p. paper illus. New York: Dutton, 1965.

Another impressive *Dutton Vista* book delineating the life and career of a motion picture legend. Again, the text and pictures are excellent throughout. The filmography gives a short synopsis followed by critical comments about each film. The fine bibliography offered is a bit longer than usual in this series. Produced with taste and talent, the book is enthusiastically recommended to all readers interested in perhaps the strongest example of Hollywood's star system.

2702 *see 2704*

2703 *Greta Garbo.* by Corliss, Richard. 157 p. paper illus. New York: Pyramid, 1974.

In the first pages of this volume the author states that it is to be "a study of her beauty and talent as it shone through her 25 extant feature films." After acknowledgment of the role that Irving Thalberg played in her career, directors and leading men are examined with respect to the rapport they were able to create with her. THE SAGA OF GOSTA BERLING (1924), her first feature of note, begins the section on her silent films. Another chapter is devoted to the sound films, of which TWO -FACED WOMAN (1941) was the last. A short statement on "Garbo-as-Legend," along with a bibliography, filmography and index, completes the book

Some interesting illustrations have been selected to complement the text, but the general quality of their reproduction is below average. The text supplied by Corliss is rich in ideas and opinions and offers a view of Garbo that is often individual and unusual. This is no small accomplishment when the large amount of literature already available on Garbo is considered. Recommended.

2704 *Greta Garbo: The Story of a Specialist.* by Laing, E. E. 244 p. illus. London: J. Gifford, 1946.

A biography that divides Garbo's life into three periods: schoolgirl, actress, movie star.

2705 *Grierson on Documentary.* by Grierson, John; edited by Hardy, Forsyth. 411 p. Berkeley, Calif.: University of California Press, 1966.

Here is a collection of the writings of John Grierson, mostly pertaining to documentary film. Included are some reviews and critical writings about early sound motion pictures and directors, a speech given to the American Library Association in 1946 on the library in an international world, and an analysis of television. The introduction by Forsyth Hardy furnishes a biographical sketch of Grierson that makes the articles which follow much more meaningful. In his writings, Grierson is, among other things, intelligent, opinionated, angry, agile and witty, but never dull. Recommended for most readers.

2706 *Grierson on the Movies.* by Grierson, John. 200 p. London: Faber and Faber, 1981.

A collection of film reviews by John Grierson from the period 1925 to 1959. Forsyth Hardy edited and supplies an introduction.

2707 *Griffith: First Artist of the Movies.* by Williams, Martin. 171 p. illus. New York: Oxford University Press, 1980.

Using previously published materials, Martin Williams has attempted to "synthesize" a critical biography of D. W. Griffith in this volume. He includes bits of history, descriptions of the Griffith films, quotes from other sources, some illustrations, a bibliography, and an index.

As an introduction to Griffith and his work, the volume is rather bland and uninteresting. The drama and the excitement of the silent film period, much of which can be related to Griffith, is missing.

2708 *The Griffith Actresses.* by Slide, Anthony. 181 p. illus. New York: A. S. Barnes, 1973.

Anthony Slide has written a collective biography using research libraries, films, books, periodicals and interviews as the major information sources. His connecting theme is D. W. Griffith and his purpose is to show the mutual advantage of the various actresses' association with the great director. An opening section describes a "Griffith Girl" in general terms and is followed by individual chapters about Blanche Sweet, Mary Pickford, Dorothy Gish, Lillian Gish, Mae Marsh, Miriam Cooper, Clarine Seymour and Carol Dempster. A final chapter considers the actresses that Griffith employed during his declining years—Lupe Velez, Zita Johann, Betty Jewel and Riza Royce. A brief list of the British names of American Biograph players and a much longer list of actresses who worked for Griffith make up the appendix. A selected bibliography completes the book. Visuals used throughout are taken from stills and frame enlargement. Reproduction is adequate and the selection is rather good, with only a few familiar visuals used.

Several of the actresses have been subjects of full-length biographies—the Gish sisters, Mary Pickford, and Miriam Cooper—and this may diminish the appeal of the book. The less familiar portions are absorbing and the entire text is written with style and intelligence. The subject matter is rather specialized with an appeal for the film buff, historian and scholar. Recommended.

2709 *Griffith and the Rise of Hollywood.* by O'Dell, Paul; and Slide, Anthony. 163 p. paper illus. New York: A. S. Barnes, 1970.

Not unexpectedly, the emphasis here is on THE BIRTH OF A NATION (1915) and INTOLERANCE (1916). In addition to Griffith, Thomas Ince is given some attention as is the rise of the star system with Pickford, etc. The photographs are unusual and the book is a welcome addition. Recommended.

2710 *Grigori Kozintsev.* by Leaming, Barbara. 154 p. illus. Boston: Twayne, 1980.

Grigori Kozintsev was a Russian film director whose career spanned almost five decades (1924-1973). In addition to supplying the usual elements (chronology, epilogue, notes, bibliography, filmography) of the *Twayne Theatrical Arts* series, this study singles out three films from the filmmaker's mature period—DON QUIXOTE (1957), HAMLET (1963) and KING LEAR (1971)—for detailed attention. Bibliographical and career coverage is provided along with information on Kozintsev's other films. The total result is another fine Twayne volume, this time on a relatively unknown subject.

2711 *Groucho.* by Arce, Hector. 541 p. illus. New York: G. P. Putnam's, 1979.

Hector Arce is the author of two earlier books about Groucho Marx, *The Secret Word is Groucho* and *The Grouchophile.* Because of the relationship he had established with Groucho, he was asked to write an authorized biography. The result is a predictable portrait of a self-doubting man who was witty, romantic and most unpleasant to live with. Groucho's inability to relate to his wives, his children and people in general is discussed along with the background story of the Marx Brothers and their rise to fame. The text focuses on Groucho after the last Marx Brothers films of the forties. There are anecdotes, illustrations, a bibliography and an index to accompany the story.

Readers of previous Marx Brothers books will find a minimum of new material here, but may enjoy the detailed portrait of Groucho in his declining years that Arce depicts with sympathy and understanding.

2712 *Groucho and Me.* by Marx, Groucho. 256 p. paper New York: Dell, 1959.

Written in typical Groucho style, this autobiography has Marxian comments on everything from sex to fishing. Starting at the turn of the century, the book traces Groucho's career through vaudeville, the theatre, films, and, finally, television. The section on film is quite short and is devoted mostly to an argument between the Marx Brothers and Warner Brothers concerning the title, A NIGHT IN CASABLANCA (1946). Although it is fun to read, the book probably can be best used to supplement the more critical volumes on the Marx Brothers films. No index or pictures are included.

2713 *Groucho, Chico, Harpo and Sometimes Zeppo.* by Adamson, Joe. 512 p. illus. New York: Simon & Schuster, 1973.

Although a late entry in the Marx Brothers-in-print-sweepstakes, this is one of the better ones. Blending history, biography, criticism, analysis, and dialogue excerpts, the author indicates the factors involved in the rise and fall of the Marx teams. A biography and some illustrations support the text. The popularity of this book with audiences is assured. Recommended.

2714 *The Groucho Letters, To and From Groucho Marx.* by Marx, Groucho. 319 p. New York: Simon & Schuster, 1967.

The letters are arranged in categories—two of these,

titled "Movie Business" and "Broadway and Hollywood," are pertinent enough for inclusion in this list. The major portion of the book, however, deals with noncinematic matter—television, politics, etc. Groucho seldom fails to be entertaining and this book is no exception.

2715 *The Grouchophile.* by Marx, Groucho. 384 p. illus. New York: Bobbs-Merrill, 1976.

The life of Groucho Marx has been adequately covered in earlier individual and group biographies of the Marx Brothers. What makes this volume unique is the more than 700 illustrations which range from stills and candids to posters, line drawings and cartoons.

Following a short introduction by Hector Arce, the pictorial reminiscence begins with Minnie and her boys about 1900 and ends with tributes given to Groucho during 1975-76. In addition to the visual material which is specifically identified and described by Groucho via a numbering system, there are excerpts from previous books, scripts, and songs. A final index provides access to this rich material. Most importantly, all the films that Groucho has made get individual attention.

Not only is this a visual summary of Groucho material to date, it is also his personal presentation of those incidents, things, and people he considers important in his life. It will delight Groucho devotees and please almost everyone else. Recommended.

2716 *Growing Up in Hollywood.* by Parrish, Robert. 229 p. illus. New York: Harcourt Brace Jovanovich, 1976.

The unusual format for the type, style, and layout of this autobiography is reminiscent of the old-fashioned Horatio Alger books published early in this century. Since the author's story is concerned with how to strive and succeed in Hollywood, the design choice is most appropriate. Parrish started as an actor, learned cutting and film direction along the way and ended up as a recipient of the Academy Award for the editing of BODY AND SOUL (1947). Made up largely of short anecdotal chapters, the author presents vivid portraits of John Ford and Harry Cohn. Unfortunately the story ends around 1950 with an account of Parrish's first attendance at a Screen Director's Guild meeting.

A few illustrations and an index are included in this pleasant memoir of Hollywood's golden years. Acceptable.

2717 *Growing Up With Chico.* by Marx, Maxine. 200 p. illus. Englewood Cliffs, N.J.: Prentice-Hall, 1980.

A portrait of Chico Marx by his eldest daughter reveals little that is new about the piano-playing member of the comedy team. That he loved gambling and women obsessively has been documented in many of the earlier studies of the Marx Brothers. In this affectionate memoir of her father, the author does offer some first-rate observations about the relationships between the brothers.

2718 THE GUEST. by Fugard, Athol; and Devenish, Ross. 84 p. paper illus. London: Wildwood House, 1977.

Script of the 1978 film, directed by Devenish, that deals with "an episode in the life of Eugene Marais."

2719 *Guidance in Aesthetic Appreciation: The Film in the United Kingdom.* by Reed, Stanley. 15 p. paper London: British Film Institute, 1955.

An early publication in the area of film appreciation.

2720 *Guide Book to Film.* by Gottesman, Ronald; and Geduld, Harry M. 220 p. paper New York: Holt, Rinehart, Winston, 1972.

Called an eleven-in-one reference, this book contains: 1) an annotated list of books and periodicals, 2) theses and dissertations about film, 3) museums and archives, 4) film schools, 5) equipment and supplies, 6) distributors, 7) bookstores, publishers, etc., 8) film organizations and services, 9) festivals and contests, 10) awards, 11) terminology.

Like any other volume which attempts such broad reference coverage in so relatively few pages, this one has serious drawbacks. Much of the material appears to be a condensation or extract from more detailed sources. The annotations in the book section range from a single phrase to a few sentences. To some readers the most interesting section will be the theses and dissertations (taken from *Journal of the University Film Association* by Raymond Fielding).

2721 *A Guide for Film Teachers to Filmmaking by Teenagers.* by Larson, Rodger, Jr. 48 p. paper illus. New York: Dept. of Cultural Affairs, 1968.

Worthwhile, practical, and inexpensive. Tells how to operate a film club with teenagers.

2722   *Guide to... (A Series).* paper illus. Alexandria, Va.: Serina Press.

Serina Press publishes a series of rather expensive guides to films about selected topics. The filmographies include descriptions rather than evaluations. Among the titles are: *Guide to Films about Famous People, ... Foreign Loan Film, ... Government Loan Film,* and *... Military Loan Film.*

Additional titles announced include: *Guide to Films about the Use of Dangerous Drugs, Narcotics, Alcohol and Tobacco; ... Films about Ecology, Adaptation and Pollution; ... Films about Negroes; ... Free Loan Films about Foreign Lands; ... Free Loan Films for Entertainment; ... Free Loan Sports Films; ... Free Loan Training Films;* and *... Personal Guidance Films for Elementary Schools.* It should be noted that much of the information provided by these guides can be located in other sources at much less expense.

2723   *Guide to Classroom Use of Film/ Television.* by Elsas, Diana; and Kelso, Lulu. 13 p. paper Washington, D.C.: American Film Institute, 1977.

This title in the *Factfile* series lists a variety of resources—books, pamphlets, articles, periodicals, organizations, distributors, etc.—which pertain to using film and television in the classroom. Descriptive annotations are provided for many of the entries.

2724   *A Guide to Critical Reviews—Part IV: The Screenplay from* THE JAZZ SINGER *to* DR. STRANGELOVE. by Salem, James M. 2 vols. Metuchen, N.J.: Scarecrow Press, 1971.

Provides a bibliography of critical reviews of feature-length motion pictures released from October, 1927 through the end of 1963. Approximately 12,000 American and foreign screenplays are included, with cross references liberally provided to assist the reader in tracking down titles and to indicate films released under more than one title. The reviews cited in this volume appeared in American or Canadian periodicals and *The New York Times.* Highly recommended.

2725   *Guide to Dance in Film.* by Parker, David L.; and Siegel, Esther. 220 p. Detroit: Gale Research, 1978.

This unusual reference offers a listing of 1750 films containing dance performances. The dances range from complete ballets, THE MOOR'S PAVANNE (1950), to Fred Astaire's several contributions to a single film, SWINGTIME (1936). Entries are arranged alphabetically by film title, and include videotape availability, year, country of origin, production company, running time, silent or sound, color format, director, choreographer, music, dancers, and, occasionally, genre. Short descriptive annotations accompany some of the entries. Three indexes—name, production company, and country of origin—complete the book.

With any such work there are predictable reviewer reservations—in this case, the definitions of "dance" and "dancers" as used herein. For example: the Crosby-Hope dances from the "Road" pictures are not listed, while many lesser dance efforts, such as Hope's in HERE COME THE GIRLS (1953), are. Many other memorable dance performances are omitted: Jack Buchanan in THE BAND WAGON (1953), Cyd Charisse in THE HARVEY GIRLS (1946), Debbie Reynolds in PEPE (1960), Betty Garrett in ON THE TOWN (1949).

Selection, for the most part, is not a matter for prolonged argument. It has been done with uniform care and diligence here. This commendable reference does provide access to many dance performances that can be found in films. The amount of information and its arrangement is most impressive. Recommended.

2726   *A Guide to Film and Television Courses in Canada 1978-1979.* by Hecquet, Marie-Claude; and McNicoll, David. 167 p. paper Ottawa: Canadian Film Institute, 1978.

This is a reference for persons who are interested in post-secondary study in the related areas of film and television. No evaluations are offered, simply information about more than 70 colleges, universities and schools. Arranged alphabetically by Canadian province, the entries are rather complete, listing course descriptions, programs, names, etc. In addition to its primary purpose, the book can be used to gain insight, ideas, and perceptions about film study programs and courses.

2727   *Guide to Filmmaking.* by Pincus, Edward. 256 p. paper illus. New York: New American Library, 1969.

"From Choosing a Camera to Screening the Movie" is the subtitle, accurately describing this handbook of filmmaking. Topics include 8mm versus 16mm, the camera, the lens, exposure, film stock, filming, lighting, the lab, color, filters, editing, printing, and sound. The book has photographs, diagrams, tables, appendices, and an index. For anyone at any stage of sophistication in filmmaking, this excellent paperback has much to offer. Its concentration and presentation of information in a clear, logical, and sequential book is admirable. Highly recommended.

2728 *Guide to Films about Famous People.* 206 p. paper Alexandria, Va.: Serina Press, 1969.

An annotated listing of nearly 1500 films that concern themselves in whole or part with famous people. There is also an index of names and a list of sources. Most of the films are not free, but are available via rentals. Limited.

2729 *Guide to Films on Education.* edited by British Industrial and Scientific Film Association 88 p. paper London: BISFA, 1971.

This is the first supplement to the original volume published in 1969. The films listed deal with teacher training and the study of education. An index is included.

2730 *Guide to Films on Education.* by British Industrial and Scientific Film Association. 120 p. paper London: British Industrial and Scientific Film Association, 1969.

After an introduction, foreword, and explanation of use of this catalog, the films are offered according to suggested audience: primary, secondary, tertiary, special schools, out of school, etc. Accompanying each entry is a description of content, an appraisal, and further clarification of the intended audience. A distributor list and a total title index complete this volume.

2731 *A Guide to Films on First Aid, Nursing and Allied Topics.* compiled by St. John Ambulance Association and Brigade. 72 p. paper London: St. John Ambulance Association and Brigade, 1972.

Approximately 150 films are arranged in alphabetical order in this catalog. For each entry there is the film data, the content, an appraisal, and the rental information. A subject index completes the work.

2732 *Guide to Films on Psychology and Psychiatry.* compiled by British Industrial and Scientific Film Associa-

tion. 138 p. paper London: British Industrial and Scientific Film Association, 1968.

The films in this catalog are grouped into two title areas: Psychology including child, experimental, social, industrial, etc.; and Psychiatry including child, handicapped, diagnostic, treatment, nursing, voluntary service, psycho-pathology, psychoses, addiction, etc. A distributor list and a title index complete the catalog.

2733 *Guide to Films on the Construction Industry.* compiled by British Industrial and Scientific Film Association. 77 p. paper London: British Industrial and Scientific Film Association, 1968.

After an explanation on the use of this catalog, the films are listed under a Dewey classification and include such headings as civil engineering, buildings, physical planning, architecture, etc. Each entry offers film data, content description, appraisal, and recommended audience. A list of distributors, a subject index, and a title index complete the catalog.

2734 *Guide to Foreign-Government Loan Film.* 136 p. paper Alexandria, Va.: Serina Press, 1969.

This guide contains a listing by country of more than 3000 films sponsored by foreign governments. Some have narration or dialogue in the language of the sponsor. About 1800 are loaned free while the rest require a nominal fee. Most interesting.

2735 *Guide to Free-Loan Training Films.* 205 p. paper Alexandria, Va.: Serina Press, 1970.

This guide contains annotations of nearly 2000 training films which are available on a free-loan basis. The films are grouped under various subject areas—electronics, metals, plumbing, etc. An alphabetical listing of the films and a source directory conclude the volume.

2736 *A Guide to Good Viewing.* by Reed, Stanley. 122 p. illus. London: Ward Lock, 1961.

A discussion and analysis of the many genres of film.

2737 *Guide to Government-Loan Film.* 130 p. paper Alexandria, Va.: Serina Press, 1969.

In this small expensive volume, some 900 motion pictures produced or sponsored by various government agencies are briefly described. Among other sections are an alphabetical listing of some 2000 government films, including the original 900, and a subject index which applies only to the first 900. The 900-films section consists of an alphabetical listing of the agencies with the films sponsored by each following. The criteria used for inclusion in the 900 films is general interest, as contrasted with technical or professional topics. Since the body of reference books in the area of film is so small, it is disheartening to note that this book is not very necessary. The films listed require a strong selection-preview policy before exhibition.

2738 *A Guide to Independent Film and Video.* edited by Melton, Hollis. 87 p. paper New York: Anthology Film Archives, 1976.

This guide is organized to offer information in five areas of concern to the independent artist: film and video making; distribution; programming and exhibition; study; and funding. The numerous entries which appear under each heading are fully annotated. Included are persons, organizations, books, periodicals, foundations, libraries, museums, and galleries. It should be stressed that the focus of the volume is on independent creative activity in film and video. However, much of the information is useful and pertinent for other areas. This is a vital reference that is highly recommended.

2739 *The Guide to Kinematography.* by Bennett, Colin N. 277 p. illus. London: Heron, 1917.

This early volume carries the subtitle, "...For Camera Men, Operators and All Who 'Want to Know'."

2740 *A Guide to Kinematography (Projection Action).* by Bennett, Colin N. 194 p. illus. London: Pitman, 1923.

This early volume carries the subtitle, "...for Managers, Manager Operators, and Operators of Kinema Theatres, Containing Valuable Information on the Technical, Human, and Legal Aspects of the Industry."

2741 *Guide to Location Information, 1977-78.* by Pavlick, John M. 337 p. paper Los Angeles: Association of Motion Picture and Television Producers, 1977.

This volume, which is updated at irregular intervals, is a compilation of data on permits, regulations, contracts, procedures, etc., for shooting films "on location" in the United States.

2742 *Guide to Military-Loan Film.* 148 p. paper Alexandria, Va.: Serina Press, 1969.

The synopses of nearly 1500 films available on free loan from the U.S. Army, Air Force, Navy, Marines, and Corps of Engineers are given. In addition there is a consolidated, alphabetical title listing, and a source directory.

2743 *A Guide to Processing Black-and-White Motion Picture Films.* edited by Kodak Staff. 60 p. paper illus. Rochester, N.Y.: Kodak, 1979.

This book is designed to help the reader understand the range of black and white films available today and the handling of these films in terms of exposure, processing, and storage. Processing cycles, techniques for processing by hand and by machine, control methods, analytical procedures, silver recovery, and waste disposal are among the other topics treated.

2744 *A Guide to Publications and Films on Fire.* compiled by Fire Protection Association. 51 p. paper London: Fire Prevention Information and Public Centre, 1973.

In addition to a short section of films which gives the usual data, description and distributor, this volume also treats slides, filmstrips, publications, posters and other visual aids.

2745 *A Guide to References and Resources (A Series).* edited by Gottesman, Ronald. Boston: G. K. Hall, 1977- .

This useful series on film directors, written by teachers, scholars and historians and edited by the reliable Ronald Gottesman, is a most impressive addition to the film reference literature. A blue binding identifies the books, which are all structured in similar fashion. For each subject there are sections dealing with a biography, a critical survey of his work, a filmography, a bibliography of criticism, a bibliography of the subject's writing and other professional credits, archival sources and film distributors. Two indexes—film titles and authors—provide further access to the information sources. The series is essential to the writer or scholar concerned with the serious study of the directors. Among the subjects treated are Robert Aldrich, Lindsay Anderson,

Charles Chaplin, Walt Disney, Federico Fellini, Robert Flaherty, Jean-Luc Godard, Stanley Kubrick, Akira Kurosawa, David Lean, Richard Lester, Ernst Lubitsch, Sidney Lumet, Arthur Penn, Roman Polanski, Ken Russell, John Schlesinger, and Frederick Wiseman. Other volumes which have the same format but different series titles include *The Film Career of Alain Robbe-Grillet, The Film Career of Buster Keaton, The Film Career of Billy Wilder*, and *Artificially Arranged Scenes: The Films of Georges Melies.*

2746 *Guide To Short Films.* by Schrank, Jeffrey. 197 p. paper illus. Rochelle Park, N.J.: Hayden, 1979.

Jeffrey Schrank once again provides assistance to users of short films in an entertaining, informative filmography. He annotates, in both descriptive and evaluative terms, more than 220 short films. Arranged alphabetically by title, each entry offers Schrank's subjective comments along with running time, color format, producer, and distributor. In most cases the date of release is also indicated. A few illustrations, a distributor address list, and a subject index complete the volume.

Schrank's earlier volumes established him as an authority on the use of various nonprint media in teaching situations. For almost a decade, books on the evaluation and suggested uses of the short film have been missing from publishers' lists, and since there is no one more competent to fill this existing void than Jeffrey Schrank, the appearance of this volume is most welcome. An excellent addition to the literature, it is highly recommended for anyone who uses short films.

2747 *A Guide to Short Films for Religious Education (Volume II).* by McCaffrey, Patrick J. 108 p. paper illus. South Bend, Ind: Fides Press, 1968.

This is another short book designed primarily for religious education that can be used profitably in many other situations. In addition to evaluating many well-known short films, the author discusses some of his experiences in using films with various audiences. A list of film distributors concludes the book. Each film evaluation includes a rating, synopsis, discussion questions, recommended age level, technical rating, physical description and qualifying remarks. This book treats films such as NIGHT AND FOG (1955), PHOEBE (1965), THE QUIET ONE (1948), TWO MEN AND A WARDROBE (1957), A DANCER'S WORLD (1965), etc. Volume I of this series by the same author and publisher describes 70 other short films.

2748 *Guide to the Ford Film Collection.* by National Archives and Records Service. 118 p. illus. Washington, D.C.: General Services Administration, 1970.

The film records described in this guide are the more than one million feet of motion pictures contained in the Ford Historical Film Collection.

2749 *A Guide to the Literature of the Motion Picture.* by Christeson, Frances Mary. 76 p. paper Los Angeles: University of Southern California, 1938.

An early bibliography that appeared before *The Film Index.*

2750 *Guidelines for Audiovisual Materials and Services for Public Libraries.* by Public Library Association. 33 p. paper Chicago: American Library Association, 1970.

Suggested standards on personnel, services, space, equipment, storage, maintenance, materials, etc., for libraries serving 150,000 or more persons. Standards for film collections are included. It should be noted that the PLA standards are changed from time to time and are noted in updated revisions of this publication.

2751 *Guidelines For Audio-Visual Services in Academic Libraries.* by Association of College and Research Libraries. paper Chicago: American Library Association, 1968.

Suggested standards concerning personnel, services, space, equipment, storage, maintenance, materials, etc., for college and research libraries are noted. Included are standards for film services and collections. It should be noted that these standards are changed from time to time and are noted in updated revisions of this publication.

2752 *Guides to Educational Media.* by Rufsvold, Margaret. 168 p. paper Chicago: American Library Association, 1977.

This is the 4th edition of a standard reference in the nonprint area. It offers a listing of educational media books, references, and catalogs, each of which has a detailed annotation. Many of the entries deal with films and are not found in most bibliographies. A rich source of film information.

2753 GUILTY OF TREASON. by Lavery, Emmet. 126 p. illus. St. Paul, Minn.: Catholic Digest, 1949.

The shooting script of the film which was directed by Felix Feist.

2754 *The Guinness Book of Film Facts and Feats.* by Robertson, Patrick. 280 p. illus. New York: Sterling, 1980.

As the title implies, this is a collection of firsts, greatests, mosts, biggests, and other superlatives. There are 19 chapters of such assorted information along with several indexes for access. How much of this is trivia, how accurate the statements are, what coverage is provided—these questions fade with the attraction of so much diverse and unusual information.

2755 THE GUNS OF NAVARONE. 20 p. paper illus. New York: Program Publishing Co., 1961.

This souvenir book is below average in appearance and content. By the use of much portrait art work, the stars and cast of the 1961 film are shown. Production and technical credits are also listed, and a map is reproduced on the back cover. Everyone concerned deserves better treatment.

2756 *Guru Dutt, 1925-1965.* by Rangoonwalla, Firoze. 133 p. Poona: National Film Archive of India, 1973.

2757 *Guts and Glory.* by Suid, Lawrence H. 357 p. paper illus. Reading, Mass.: Addison-Wesley, 1978.

The basic source material for this survey of war films was the more than 300 interviews the author conducted—primarily with media, military and film people. An examination of the military image in Hollywood films is the author's primary goal, although several other important aspects of war-in-film are raised, i.e., U.S. military assistance, propaganda, social impact, antiwar statements, etc.

After an introductory overview, Suid divides his films into groupings: World Wars I and II, John Wayne, Vietnam, biography, etc. His text is well researched and presented in a logical fashion—from the glorification of war to dedicated opposition. Much background material on the making of the films is offered. Illustrations, a filmography, a list of the interview subjects, chapter notes, and an index complete the book.

Anyone contemplating a book on a major film genre might use this one as model. Suid proves that scholarship and entertainment can be compatible.

2758 *GWTW: The Making of* GONE WITH THE WIND. by Lambert, Gavin. 238p. illus. Boston: Little, Brown, 1973.

Gavin Lambert has written several novels about Hollywood, along with one outstanding volume on director George Cukor. This latter work was an ideal predecessor to this most recent work about GONE WITH THE WIND (1939). Cukor was the original director who worked for two years in preparing the film and then was suddenly dismissed after a few weeks of shooting. Unofficially he continued to help Vivien Leigh and Olivia De Havilland for the remainder of the filming. Lambert discusses the Cukor incident along with many other behind-the-scenes conflicts, maneuvers, and intrigues. The final impression left with the reader is amazement that the film ever got made at all.

Many illustrations of the participants, along with stills from the film, are carefully reproduced and visualize much of the text. A short bibliography and an index are provided. As a study of Hollywood filmmaking during the studio days of the thirties, this volume is one of the best yet written. Lambert is knowledgeable, affectionate, objective, and compassionate toward the characters concerned and the industry as it was. His meticulously detailed account should please all readers—especially the many millions who have seen and re-seen GONE WITH THE WIND. Highly recommended.

2759 *The Gypsy in My Soul.* by Greco, Jose. 279 p. illus. New York: Doubleday, 1977.

Here are the memoirs of Jose Greco, who was best known for his flamenco dancing. He appeared in a few films: SOMBRERO (1953), AROUND THE WORLD IN 80 DAYS (1956), HOLIDAY FOR LOVERS (1959), THE PLEASURE SEEKERS (1964), SHIP OF FOOLS (1965), etc.

2760 *H. G. Wells in the Cinema.* by Wykes, Alan. 176 p. illus. London: Jupiter, 1977.

Consisting mostly of visuals, this overview of films based on the writing of H. G. Wells contains a lengthy filmography.

2761 *Hadn't We the Gaiety?* by Carstairs, John Paddy. 107 p. illus. London:

Hurst and Blackett, 1945.

During the years he served as a film director from the thirties to the sixties, Carstairs was responsible for many films—mostly light-hearted comedies. This volume of "autobiographical reminiscences" recalls many of the personalities he worked with during that period. In addition to his film career, Carstairs is also known as a writer, painter and novelist. See also *Honest Injun* and *Movie Merry-Go-Round*. In 1941 he wrote *Bunch: A Biography of Nelson Keys by His Son* (a stage and screen actor, Keys had appeared in a few films from 1927 to 1936).

2762 *Haiku and the Film.* by Hemenway, David R. 11 p. paper Boston: Broadcasting and Film Division, Boston University, 1964.

2763 *Hail Columbia.* by Larkin, Rochelle. 445 p. illus. New Rochelle, N.Y.: Arlington House, 1975.

Some excellent material receives poor treatment in this account of the Columbia Pictures studio. The consistent quality of its "A" product, the performances of its actors, and the colorful directors and moguls constitute a richness that should facilitate an author's work. Larkin's effort here is careless, routine and uninspired.

Using the Columbia films as a nucleus around which she builds the history is an acceptable approach, but the division of the films into genres weakens the structure. What emerges is a series of genre filmographies which only occasionally recall that the volume is supposedly a history. Even the genre designations lack consistency and common acceptance, e.g., Capra Years, Screwball Comedies, The Stars (?), Musicals, The Oscars (?), The Road Pictures (?), Great Movies, etc. From time to time, the text departs from this genre approach and considers the personalities that worked for Columbia. Too often dates are omitted in discussing a performer'sfilms and the reader is at a loss to determine the time period being discussed, e.g., see pp. 332-335 on Cary Grant.

The most disturbing aspect of this work is the carelessness and inaccuracy of the text. For example, page 94, concerning Women's Lib: "Except for Rosalind Russell and maybe Joan Crawford, nobody in the thirties heard of it;" a strong case can be made for Katharine Hepburn, Bette Davis, Glenda Farrell, and others. Page 127, concerning Rita Hayworth: "....and the brightest one (musical) that she made came along soon after THE LADY FROM SHANGHAI. It was the sparkling COVER GIRL..."; in fact, THE LADY FROM SHANGHAI was made in 1948,

while COVER GIRL was made four years earlier in 1944. Page 189, concerning JOLSON SINGS AGAIN (1949): "Columbia squeezed out a sequel the following year;" JOLSON SINGS AGAIN appeared three years after THE JOLSON STORY (1946). (In both the Hayworth and Jolson cases, Larkin has the correct data in her chapter and film credits.) Page 109, caption is incorrect—Claude Rains is also invisible. Page 206, caption is incorrect—the picture is not of Streisand as Baby Snooks but as the Eva character in an "Uncle Tom's Cabin" parody. Page 208, caption is incorrect—in the film Streisand has met Billy Rose long before this scene. Page 203, Streisand's role in THE OWL AND THE PUSSYCAT (1970) is one of comedy rather than drama. Page 195, BYE BYE BIRDIE (1963) did not bring star status to Dick Van Dyke—he has often deplored the cutting of his and Janet Leigh's parts to supporting roles for Ann-Margret. Page 197, "The Most Happy Fella" is mentioned as a film casualty—in fact, the stage play was never made into a film. Pages 195-196, two illustrations imply that PORGY AND BESS (1959) was a Columbia film; the picture is regarded as a Samuel Goldwyn production that was distributed by Columbia; this important distinction is not noted in the text. Page 178, why are the FUNNY LADY (1975) credits placed with the 1940-50 "Star" films of Hayworth, Novak, Holliday, Lemmon, Ford and Holden? The movie certainly belongs with the "Musicals" chapter.

Illustrations are plentiful and are well reproduced. In fact the Arlington House production work is once again exemplary throughout. In addition to a selected cast and production-credit appendix to each chapter, there is a long final appendix which lists more than 1600 films made by Columbia Studios since 1922. Unfortunately the author has decided to indicate the writers here rather than cast names and directors. As a result, it would be difficult to find Fritz Lang's films for Columbia in this volume—or William Castle's or Henry Levin's, each of whom directed more than 30 features for Columbia from 1944 to 1969.

As indicated above, the wealth of material available on the Columbia Studios has been poorly chosen, arranged, and treated. Because the production values are high the volume will afford some readers pleasure and reference use; ultimately, however, it is a major disappointment. Not acceptable.

2764 HAIR. by Weller, Michael. unpaginated paper illus. Los Angeles: Fotonovel, 1979.

This *Fotonovel* (see series entry) contains over 350 stills, some original film dialogue, the song lyrics by Gerome Ragni and James Rado, some connecting narrative, and the cast credits for the 1979 film, HAIR, which was directed by Milos Forman.

2765 *Hair on a Cue Ball.* by Monett, Negley. 213 p. New York: Exposition Press, 1955.

Subtitled "The Hair-raising Adventures of a Hollywood Writer."

2766 *Hal B. Wallis.* edited by Reed, Rochelle. 24 p. illus. Washington, D.C.: American Film Institute, 1975.

Hal Wallis has served as producer, co-producer or executive producer on more than 190 films. A transcript of a 1974 interview with him at the AFI Center for Advanced Studies is presented here along with a filmography. Mr. Wallis suggested the viewing of three of his films as a preparation for this session: BECKET (1964), ANNE OF THE THOUSAND DAYS (1969), and TRUE GRIT (1969).

2767 *Hal in the Classroom—Science Fiction Films.* by Amelio, Ralph J. 153 p. paper illus. Dayton, Ohio: Pflaum, 1974.

This anthology of nine essays on science fiction films considers both the genre and certain specific films. For example, Dennis Peary writes on "Political Attitudes in American Science Fiction Films," while R. C. Dale considers "Narrative, Fable and Dream in KING KONG." The annotated filmography of both short films and features which follows the essays is largely descriptive. However, the outstanding elements of the films are noted. Annotations in the lengthy bibliography are also noncritical. A list of film distributors concludes the volume.

Although the volume is devoted to a specialized film topic, acceptance of the book by the interested reader seems assured. Certainly the articles, the filmography and bibliography make it an ideal resource-reference reader for educators. Acceptable.

2768 *Hal Wallis, Film Producer.* edited by Mancia, Adrienne. 12 p. paper illus. New York: Museum of Modern Art, 1970.

This short booklet was written to accompany a retrospective of Wallis' films given at the Museum during 1970-71. It consists of an introduction, an interview, a filmography, and the detailed listing of the Wallis films. This latter section consists of a single illustration from each film along with the cast

and production credits. It covers the films from DAWN PATROL in 1930 to ANNE OF THE THOUSAND DAYS in 1969.

2769 HALF A SIXPENCE. 32 p. paper illus. New York: National Publishers, 1968.

The story of the 1968 film is told with a minimum of narrative and a maximum of illustration in this souvenir book. In addition to a page devoted to H. G. Wells, the author of the original work on which the film was based, there are several pages devoted to the cast and production crew. Here is one case where the book is probably better than the final film.

2770 *A Half Century of American Film.* 160 p. paper illus. New York: Films, Inc.

A catalog of films available from Films Incorporated. Each of some 500 lists production data and credits, a synopsis and selected (carefully!) critical comments. The films are grouped into five decades ending with the sixties. At the book's end, some suggestions for programming films are offered. This is a treasure that might easily be overlooked. It is a most enjoyable reading experience, a partial history, and a valuable reference.

2771 *Halfway Through the Door: An Actor's Journey Toward the Self.* by Arkin, Alan. 85 p. New York: Harper and Row, 1979.

This is not a typical show business book but one that is very different in tone and content. In less than 100 pages, Alan Arkin describes his progress from moodiness, semi-depression and weariness to some small success at self-knowledge, joy, freedom, energy and power. The method he used was that of the transcendent spirit, involving a guru, meditation, psychic experiences, reincarnation, etc.

There are no jokes, no illustrations, no biographical memoirs here. What is offered is a persuasive, clearly written account of how an unhappy actor has begun to find peace and pleasure.

2772 *The Hall of Fame of Western Film Stars.* by Corneau, Ernest N. 307 p. illus. North Quincy, Mass.: Christopher Pub. House, 1969.

Approximately 150 short biographies of western film stars are offered in this volume. Supplemented by montage pages of photos from the author's private collection, they include performers who are "known primarily for their work in westerns." Why James Stewart is included and Henry Fonda is omitted, for example, is not clearly explained. Both a general index and an alphabetical index are provided. The arrangement of the biographies is difficult to ascertain and one has to refer to the index.

2773 THE HALLELUJAH TRAIL. 20 p. paper illus. New York: Alsid Distributors, 1965.

This oversized souvenir book reflects the concept employed in making the 1965 film—everything much larger than life and told with a tongue-in-cheek style. Some cartoon art is intermixed with the illustrations from the film and the portraits of the cast. Both production and cast credits are noted. The book, like the film, should be more clever and wittier than it is.

2774 *Halliwell's Film Guide.* by Halliwell, Leslie. 897 p. illus. New York: Charles Scribner, 1978.

In his usual thorough and entertaining fashion, Halliwell presents reviews and recollections of some 8000 feature films. For each he offers the following information: title, rating, country of origin, year of release, running time, color format, distributor, producer, alternative title, synopsis, assessment, writer, director, photographer, music credit, cast, and brief critical quotes. The result is a reference-reader that is sure to bring hours of pleasure to most users.

As always Halliwell is unique in his enthusiasms and displeasures. Never concerned with the majority critical opinion, he will endorse certain works and then add a devastating negative comment from another critic.

To make the information more accessible some explanatory notes and an alphabetical index of alternative titles are included. There is also an essay entitled, "The Decline And Fall Of The Movie."

Leslie Halliwell should be considered as one of Great Britain's national assets. His work in providing film information that is carefully researched, stylishly presented, and artfully arranged is second to none. This latest reference book reinforces his position as a master of film reference writing. Highly recommended.

2775 *Halliwell's Movie Quiz.* by Halliwell, Leslie. 304 p. paper illus. New York: Penguin, 1978.

Picture problems and film poster tests are included along with the more than 3500 questions offered by Leslie Halliwell in this quiz book about the movies.

The degree of difficulty is higher here, and films considered are international in scope, from the silent period to the present. Halliwell's high level of presentation is maintained here.

2776 *Halo Over Hollywood.* by Jessel, George. 176 p. illus. Van Nuys, Calif.: Toastmaster, 1963.

More in the long, eventful life of performer-producer-speaker, George Jessel.

2777 *Hamilton's Movie:* BILITIS. by Hamilton, David. 109 p. illus. New York: Camera Graphic, 1977.

Over 100 illustrations taken from David Hamilton's film, BILITIS (1976), are the attraction in this book. The movie was based on Pierre Louys' erotic poems.

2778 HAMLET: *The Film and the Play.* edited by Dent, Alan. illus. London: World Film Publications, 1948.

The main portion of this volume is devoted to the text of Shakespeare's play. Film directions and omissions are indicated. Supporting the play/script are a foreword by Laurence Olivier, an essay on the design of the film by Roger Furse, and a chapter on text-editing Shakespeare by Alan Dent.

2779 *The Hamlyn History of the Movies.* by Davies, Mary; and Anderson, Janice; and Arnold, Peter. 224 p. illus. London: Hamlyn, 1975.

A typical Hamlyn survey, this volume contains many full-color illustrations and a bibliography.

2780 *Hancock.* by Hancock, Freddie; and Nathan, David. illus. London: William Kinber, 1969.

A biography of Tony Hancock, best known as a radio and television comedian. His efforts at film comedy have been mostly unsuccessful, as can be seen in ORDERS ARE ORDERS (1954), THE REBEL (1960), CALL ME GENIUS (1961), THE PUNCH AND JUDY MAN (1962), THOSE MAGNIFICENT MEN IN THEIR FLYING MACHINES (1965), and THE WRONG BOX (1966).

2781 HAND IN HAND. by Morgan, Diana. 57 p. illus. Surrey: The World's Work, 1963.

This children's book is based upon the 1961 film. Since the book consists almost entirely of stills from the films, linked by the barest of narrative, it is noted here as a film book rather than a novel. Credits are complex, reading as follows: HAND IN HAND, a screen play by Diana Morgan, based on an adaptation by Leopold Atlas of a story by Sidney Harmon. The film is shown frequently on television and this pictorial-print version of the material should delight youngsters.

2782   *Handbook for Canadian Film Societies.* by Beauvais, Jean; and La Cote, Guy. 116 p. illus. Ottawa: Canadian Federation of Film Societies, 1959.

2783   *Handbook of Animation Techniques.* by Levitan, Eli L. 318 p. illus. New York: Van Nostrand Reinhold, 1979.

That reliable authority on motion picture techniques, Eli Levitan, has written a comprehensive survey on the art of animation using his long experience with television commercials. In the first section, devoted to the state of the art, he discusses in detail the processes involved in making animated films. Beginning with such basic elements as characters, backgrounds, cels, animation boards, cycles, effects, etc., he progesses to animation and live action, computer-generated techniques and other advanced topics. The second section, which deals specifically with commercial film production, treats aerial image photography, computerized animation, the recording, optical printer, the matte and other recent technological developments in this field.

Most helpful to the reader are the hundreds of illustrations which accompany Levitan's carefully prepared text. A glossary and an index complete the book.

The processes involved in making animated commercial films are complex and to understand them requires some effort or study by the reader. Eli Levitan has eased that task by providing a lucid text and some fine illustrations. His work has been given a fine production by his publishers. This attractive, useful handbook is highly recommended.

2784   *Handbook of Basic Motion Picture Techniques.* by Brodbeck, E. E. 224 p. illus. Philadelphia: American Photographic Pub., Chilton Co., 1966.

This is another acceptable book for the beginner in filmmaking. All aspects of the process are treated in a nontechnical manner that reassures rather than discourages. The analyses follow a methodical step-by-step exposition that will enable the reader to profit from the useful information offered.

2785   *A Handbook of Canadian Film.* by Beattie, Eleanor. 280 p. paper illus. Toronto: Peter Martin Associates, 1973.

Facts and information about the field of film in Canada are plentiful in this handbook. Following an introduction to Canadian film, there are 27 sections on various related topics. The longest section, accounting for more than half the volume, is a listing of Canadian filmmakers. Each entry has a short biographical sketch, a filmography and a bibliography. Shorter sections, which make up the remaining portion of the book, deal with animation, film music, actors, associations, children's films, festivals, collections, addresses, etc. Especially valuable for Canadian schools, the volume can also be used effectively by persons located elsewhere. An acceptable reference.

2786   *Handbook of Film Production.* by Quick, John; and La Bau, Tom. 304 p. illus. New York: Macmillan, 1972.

The title of this valuable resource has been well selected. Covering the many phases of filmmaking with thoroughness, the authors make extensive use of illustrations, charts, and diagrams to supplement a well-written text. Though the book is technical at times, it will probably be comprehensible to most readers. Outstanding among the 26 chapters are unique ones on screen history, the definition of a film, direction, special effects, editing and storage-care of films. The remaining sections are almost as impressive, and it is difficult to find a weak portion of the text.

In keeping with the consistent quality of the book, the authors include a bibliography listing most of the film production volumes of recent years. A list of equipment suppliers and dealers and a lengthy index complete the book. Because of the excellence of all aspects of this book—coverage, style, production values—it can be enthusiastically recommended. It is one of the best books on filmmaking to be published in the last decade.

2787   *A Handbook of Film, Theater and Television Music on Record 1948-1969.* compiled by Smolian, Steven. paper New York: Record Undertaker, 1970.

This portfolio-discography consists of two parts: an

alphabetical listing and an index.

2788 *The Handbook of Motion Picture Photography.* edited by McKay, Herbert C. 293 p. illus. New York: Falk, 1927.

Designed as a text on cinematography for use at the New York Institute of Photography, this handbook contains illustrations, tables, diagrams, etc. See also the earlier volume, *A Condensed Course in Motion Picture Photography*, edited by Carl L. Gregory and published by the Institute in 1920.

2789 *Handbook of Motion Picture Production.* by Adams, William D. 352 p. illus. New York: John Wiley, 1977.

This how-to-do-it volume on motion picture production departs from the usual presentation, opting instead for a synthesized approach rather that one which considers each element in chronological isolation. The point is made early that the various techniques of filmmaking occur simultaneously and in unison. Although individual chapters are devoted to production, script, shooting, sound, editing, etc., the total process of filmmaking is always an overriding concern.

The volume is filled with practical information that is presented in a readable, easy-to-understand text. There are many drawings, diagrams, and illustrations that will also assist the reader in comprehending the filmmaking process. A bibliography and an index complete the volume.

Because of the author's ability to take familiar material, embellish it with information from his own experience, and then organize it with style, this volume is one of the best expositions of filmmaking to be published recently. It is ideal for both personal and class use. Highly recommended.

2790 *Handbook of Recommended Standards and Procedures for Motion Picture Laboratory Services.* compiled by Association of Cinema Labs. 50 p. paper illus. Washington, D.C.: Association of Cinema Laboratories, 1966.

This is the second edition of a technical handbook.

2791 *A Handbook of Sound Recording.* by Honore, Paul M. 213 p. illus. New York: A. S. Barnes, 1980.

This volume, which is subtitled "A Text for Motion Picture and General Sound Recording," describes the domain of the professional sound engineer. The intent of the author is to enable the filmmaker to do it himself or at least communicate in a meaningful manner with a sound engineer who can do it for the filmmaker. His approach is a sequential one—the construction of a sound track—rather than a discussion of the isolated elements of sound recording. Some technical jargon and mathematical matters appear where necessary, along with much practical guidance and troubleshooting advice. Almost 200 line drawings help to simplify the explanations offered in the text. The book is indexed.

The complex world of the sound engineer is clarified to a large extent here, by constant use of simplified language and diagrams. Honore has put together a helpful, practical guide to sound production. Anyone concerned with the creation of audiovisuals will be delighted with this excellent text.

2792 *Handbook of Super 8 Production.* by Mikolas, Mark; and Hoos, Gunther. 314 p. paper illus. New York: United Business Pub., 1976.

Apparently the authors of this very comprehensive handbook on super-8 filmmaking are nonconformists. Much about the format of this superb volume is a departure from the usual. True, there are sections on the various processes in super-8 filmmaking —systems, budgets, cinematography, sound, editing, etc. However, the authors have also included information on optical printing, front projection, rear screen transfer to videotape and many other unusual topics. They are not hesitant to spotlight articles by other filmmakers, advertisements, summaries, highlights, etc. Much of what is presented is fresh, new, and not available elsewhere. The illustrations and diagrams are most helpful. Unfortunately, there is no index, but one is tempted to overlook that omission in light of the excellence present throughout. Recommended.

2793 *The Handbook of TV and Film Technique.* by Curran, Charles. 120 p. paper illus. New York: Pellegrini and Cudahy, 1953.

A title in the *VisualArts* series, this volume has the subtitle "A Non-Technical Production Guide for Executives." It was originally published as *The Handbook of Motion Picture Techniques for Business Men* in 1952.

2794 *Handbook of the Indian Film Industry.* compiled by Motion Picture Society of India. 483 p. paper illus.

Bombay: Motion Picture Society of India, 1949.

2795 *Handbook of the North Carolina Adult Film Project.* compiled by North Carolina Library Association. 171 p. paper illus. Raleigh: North Carolina State Library, 1962.

The Project was sponsored by the Public Libraries Section of the North Carolina Library Association, the North Carolina State Library, the Bureau of Audio-Visual Education, and the University of North Carolina. A second, shorter handbook appeared in 1966.

2796 *Handbook on Soviet Drama.* by Dana, H. W. L. 158 p. New York: The American-Russian Institute, 1938.

This volume contains a bibliography, with one section devoted to the Russian cinema.

2797 *Handley's Pages.* by Handley, Tommy. illus. London: Stanley Paul, 1938.

During the World War II era Tommy Handley made a few films, but he is known mostly for his radio work. Other biographies are *Tommy Handley* by Ted Kavanaugh and *That Man* by Bill Grundy.

2798 *Hanging In With the Holy Grail.* by Warfield, Nancy. 28 p. paper illus. New York: The Little Film Gazette of Nancy D. Warfield, 1976.

A conference entitled "Western Movies: Myths and Images" was held at Sun Valley, Idaho from June 29 to July 4, 1976. This volume is "an affectionate memoir" of that meeting.

In addition to reviewing some of the substance of the conference, the author also notes her personal thoughts and reactions to events and personalities. The names of the participants are noted, as well as the films which were shown. Four illustrations are provided.

The volume will have special interest for writers and devotees of the western film. Others may find it a bit special. For greater effect it might be read with *The Structure of John Ford's* STAGECOACH also written by Ms. Warfield.

2799 *Hanging On in Paradise.* by Guiles, Fred Lawrence. 412 p. illus. New York: McGraw-Hill, 1975.

Using the many brilliant and famous literary figures who were employed by the Hollywood studios as his major characters, Fred Guiles has fashioned a rather unfocused portrait of Hollywood during its golden years. He relates some of the typical experiences that Dorothy Parker, Robert Sherwood, Aldous Huxley, Lillian Hellman, Ben Hecht, Charles MacArthur and other well-known authors had at the major film studios. In addition many stars of the past are recalled via anecdotes, film plot outlines, or personality asides. Anna Sten, Kay Francis, Dorothy Mackail, Norma Shearer, and Alice White are examples.

Several photographic sections offer some well-selected visuals which are adequately reproduced. The captions beneath them, however, seem to have been written by a fan-magazine apprentice copy boy. Selected filmographies by John E. Schultheiss are provided for many of the authors mentioned in the text. A bibliography, source notes, and an index complete the book. The production given this volume is deserving of praise. The dust jacket offers a sketched group portrait of 13 authors. The front cover of the book has an attractive gold design imprinted on a black background. Type style and arrangement of the material are impressive.

The book's weakness lies in the author's almost haphazard treatment of what is rather strong subject matter. The book ultimately furnishes both a period portrait of Hollywood and a study of the famous writers' roles in that period; however, the many digressions by the author, along with no clearly discernible structure, may suggest to the reader a collection of disassociated bits rather than a cohesive whole made up of essential elements. Acceptable.

2800 *Hans Richter.* by Richter, Hans. 191 p. illus. New York: Holt, Rinehart & Winston, 1971.

Hans Richter is known as a filmmaker, a writer, a sculptor and a painter. This appreciation shows his growth and achievements in each area. Attention is given to the abstract films for which he is known. Illustrations, a glossary, notes, and a list of his works complete the book.

2801 THE HAPPIEST MILLIONAIRE. by Carothers, A. J. 142 p. paper illus. New York: Scholastic Book Services, 1967. Script of the 1967 film directed by Norman Tokar.

Script of the 1967 film directed by Norman Tokar.

408

2802 THE HAPPIEST MILLIONAIRE. 32 p. paper illus. New York: National Publishers, 1967.

This souvenir book begins with "The Story Behind the Story", that of Anthony J. Drexel Biddle. It continues with pages devoted to the cast, which includes Fred McMurray, Tommy Steele, Greer Garson, Geraldine Page, Gladys Cooper and even George, the alligator. Some attention is paid to the design of the sets and costumes, and supporting cast and production credits are noted.

2803 *Happy Birthday, Charlie Brown.* by Schulz, Charles M.; and Mendelson, Lee. 160 p. paper illus. New York: Ballantine, 1980.

A scrapbook of diverse Charlie Brown items, including some discussion of the Charlie Brown movies.

2804 *Happy Go Lucky.: My Life.* by More, Kenneth. 192 p. illus. London: Robert Hale, 1959.

Kenneth More was a leading man in many British films from 1948 to the sixties. Specializing in lighter roles, he appeared in such films as BRANDY FOR THE PARSON (1951), GENEVIEVE (1953), and DOCTOR IN THE HOUSE (1954).

2805 *see 2804*

2806 *Happy Times.* by Zerbe, Jerome; and Gill, Brendan. 288 p. illus. New York: Harcourt Brace Jovanovich, 1973.

In what might be called a social history, photographer Jerome Zerbe and writer Brendan Gill have reviewed life among the rich, the celebrated, and the beautiful for the past four decades. Emphasizing the thirties and the forties, they have provided illustrations, text and captions to a brisk examination of life among the celebrity gods. Of course, film personalities predominate.

Zerbe's photographs deserve extended study. Carefully composed and lighted, they often reveal more about the cameraman than the subject. The words supplied by Gill are witty, cynical, biting—the kind of observations one overhears at a show business cocktail party. The volume is indexed.

The elements of an outstanding picture book are present here—concept, selection, arrangement, continuity, and production quality. Mature persons may find values and attractions that will differ from those discovered by younger readers, but the book will certainly reward both groups with several hours of pure visual and literary pleasure. Recommended.

2807 *Happy Trails: The Story of Roy Rogers and Dale Evans.* by Rogers, Roy; and Evans, Dale; and Stowers, Carlton. 213 p. illus. Waco, Texas: Word Books, 1979.

Another account of how the singing cowboy met, romanced, and married the queen of the west. Contains illustrations and a filmography.

2808 A HARD DAY'S NIGHT. 12 p. paper illus. New York: Program Publishing Co., 1964.

This poorly produced souvenir book features only a dozen pages and has practically no color photography. The black and white illustrations are from the 1964 film and of The Beatles in off-screen activities. Some small attention is paid to the songs featured in the film and to the supporting cast and production crew. An easy day's labor to earn a fast dollar.

2809 *Harlequin's Stick, Charlie's Cane.* by Madden, David. 174 p. illus. Bowling Green, Ky.: Bowling Green University, 1975.

The subtitle of this book, "A Comparative Study of Commedia Dell' Arte and Silent Slapstick Comedy," summarizes its topic in succinct fashion. Citing common elements such as icons, scenarios, improvisations, slapstick-force, sound, silence, gesture, and costume, the author shows the many similarities between the two once-popular folk art forms.

Sharing equal prominence with the surprisingly brief text are many illustrations and drawings. They are placed so that they correlate directly with the text. Their reproduction is adequate, with only a few being too dark for full comprehension. Some notes and a bibliography conclude the volume.

Madden's study is an interesting one that shows some of the roots of silent screen comedy. Both the Commedia Dell' Arte and the silent screen are gone, but their legacy to us is noted by this unusual and well-researched study. Acceptable.

2810 *Harlow: An Intimate Biography.* by Shulman, Irving. illus. New York: Bernard Geis Associates, 1964.

A sensational but rather fictional account of Harlow's life, this book is an example of defamation of character without the possibility of rebuttal. Based upon what appears to be the flimsiest sources and documentation, the book accents sexual matters above all else. Her film work is almost ignored. The volume is monumentally unfair to a fine screen comedienne. Try *The Films of Jean Harlow* and ignore this one.

2811   *Harold Lloyd: The Shape of Laughter.* by Schickel, Richard. 218 p. illus. Greenwich, Conn.: New York Graphic Society, 1974.

Richard Schickel has provided both a critical biography and a review of Lloyd's films in this handsome volume. Beginning with an assessment of Lloyd's current position among the great silent film stars, the author traces his career from birth (1893) in Buchard, Nebraska, to his death in a fabulous Hollywood mansion (1971). Lloyd's attainment of the American Dream and his ultimate disillusionment seems to be a dominant theme. Attention is also given to Lloyd's comic methods and techniques, the major influences and the repetition of American values in his films and his life.

A second section is similar to one of *The Films of...* series. Most of his early short films have been lost, but the features from A SAILOR-MADE MAN (1921) to MAD WEDNESDAY (1947) are recalled via text and stills. A filmography by Eileen Bowser identifies the titles of the early shorts and the material used in the two final compilation features produced and edited by Lloyd. There is no index. More than 200 photographs are well reproduced and the entire production is typical of the excellence usually found in New York Graphic's books.

Schickel's narrative is quite detailed, critically sharp, and often adventurous in its attempt to evaluate Lloyd's artistry. He is always fair to his subject; personal and private failures are retold without sensationalizing them. Throughout, the author never loses his objectivity. This is a major study that brings new light to a neglected American film artist. It will help in a reconsideration of Lloyd's contribution to screen history. Recommended.

2812   *Harold Lloyd: The King of Daredevil Comedy.* by Reilly, Adam. 240 p. illus. New York: Macmillan, 1977.

An appreciation of Harold Lloyd is provided in several ways here—in a brief biography, a filmography of his short films (1915-1921), a very detailed filmography of his feature films, and a five-part anthology of articles about the comedian. Most of the 180 short films in which Lloyd appeared are briefly annotated; several are described in some detail. It is the feature films that get full treatment. From A SAILOR-MADE MAN (1921) to THE SIN OF HAROLD DIDDLEBOCK

(1947) (retitled MAD WEDNESDAY when re-released in 1950), each feature is described by cast, credits, synopsis, critical comment, background data, illustrations and review excerpts. The five essays are by Andrew Sarris, William K. Everson, Leonard Maltin, Len Borger, and John Belton. A collective biography called "Lloyd's Film Family," a short bibliography, a distributor list and an index complete the book.

The attractions here are the more than 300 illustrations and the efficient synthesis of many Lloyd elements into a single volume. While the book adds little that is unfamiliar, it does arrange what is known and felt into a readable, entertaining appreciation.

2813   *Harold Lloyd's World of Comedy.* by Cahn, William. 208 p. illus. New York: Duell, Sloan & Pearce, 1964.

This book is only a partial biography. Unfortunately the book is padded with extraneous material that exists in superior form in other volumes. Pictures of audiences, photographers, letters, contracts and preview cards are not essential or primary material. Nor does it seem necessary to survey the comedians of the screen once again. One suspects that much of this padding consists of outtakes from Cahn's *The Laugh Makers.*

Thankfully there is enough of Lloyd and his films to warrant a reluctant approval. The stills from the films are just fine as are the photos of Lloyd in his "Lonesome Luke" days. The book is indexed, but alas!, the essential filmography is missing. This dilution of the career of a major silent screen comedian will have to suffice until a defintive volume is written.

2814   *Harpo Speaks.* by Marx, Harpo; and Barber, Rowland. 384 p. paper illus. New York: Avon Books, 1961.

Harpo's autobiography emphasizes people and incidents that made him unique and different from his brothers. His friendships with Woolcott, Levant, Parker, and other denizens of the Algonquin Set are detailed. His films are not considered except for the noting of a few titles. There is no index. Most modern readers will appreciate the humor of the book but will grow somewhat impatient with the incessant name-dropping. The volume has a limited use in giving an individual off-screen portrait of one member of the Marx brothers.

2815   *Harry Warren and the Hollywood Musical.* by Thomas, Tony. 344 p.

illus. Secaucus, N.J.: Citadel, 1975.

Harry Warren is a retired song composer. For more than three decades he wrote songs for Hollywood musicals made at Warners, Fox, MGM and Paramount. His career is reviewed by Thomas in an unexciting, perfunctory style. Even though Warren cooperated, there is little use made of the experiences that he had as a highly productive songwriter (250 songs in 25 years) whose work was extremely popular: top ten lists, Academy Awards, etc. His contribution to American culture during the Depression, World War II, and the recovery period and after is enormous but largely unrecognized. This volume is a disappointing tribute to such a man. What it offers is the usual collection of nearly 300 visuals which tell little about the man. Actors bring parts of themselves to a role, but what can you tell about Harry Warren by looking at a still from TIN PAN ALLEY (1940)? A filmography, a songography and original sheet music for 25 songs complete the book.

2816 HARTARI! 42 p. illus. Japan: Arthur L. Wilde Co., 1962.

This souvenir book is excellent on all counts—color, content, photography, and format are uniformly impressive. Opening with an article by the Chief Game Warden of Tanganyika, Major Bruce Kinloch, the book contains a plot summary, production stories and articles, biographies of director Howard Hawks, stars John Wayne and Hardy Kruger, and others. Other supplemental features include "Delinquents of the Animal World" and "Catcher in the Veldt." In addition to stills from the 1962 film, there are candids and some original art work including a large double page map of Tanganyika. Composer Henry Mancini also is alloted one complete page of biographical data. An outstanding example of what a souvenir book should be.

2817 *Hastings House Books (A Series).* New York: Hastings House.

This publishing house offers several series of books under a general heading of *Communications Arts* books. Included are: *Humanistic Studies in the Communication Arts; The Library of Animation Technology; The Library of Communication Techniques; The Library of Film and Television Practice; The Library of Image and Sound Technology; Media Manuals* (see separate entry); *Studies in Media Management; Studies in Public Communication.*

The individual volumes, many of which deal with film topics, are uniformly well produced and offer an abundance of specialized information. Most are beautifully illustrated and contain clear, concise ex-

planations of topics, techniques, principles, etc., not available elsewhere.

2818 *Haunted Hollywood.* by Holzer, Hans. 133 p. illus. New York: Bobbs-Merrill, 1974.

Hans Holzer is a psychic investigator who has written ten books about such things as ghosts, life after death, hypnosis, and prophecy. In this volume he reports his investigations of some haunted Hollywood homes such as those that belonged to Jean Harlow, Carole Lombard, John Barrymore, Clifton Webb and Harry Houdini. In addition, he tells of the experiences certain psychics have had in seeing or communicating with deceased persons.

Ghost stories have an enduring popularity and Holzer has had much experience in relating them. The combination of medium and message works well here.

A few line drawings are included but the main attraction here is the all-star cast of ghosts and the haunting of their former Hollywood homes. This volume will have a decided fascination for many readers. Acceptable.

2819 *The Haunted Screen.* by Eisner, Lotte H. 360 p. illus. Berkeley, Calif.: University of California Press, 1969.

The theme of this large volume is Expressionism in the German cinema. It concentrates on the twenties and spotlights such film directors as Lubitsch, Murnau, and Lang. THE CABINET OF DR. CALIGARI (1919), WAXWORKS (1924), METROPOLIS (1928), and THE LAST LAUGH (1924) are among the films discussed. Stimulated by two dissimilar factors—the theatre of Max Reinhardt and the Expressionist movement in art, the German cinema approached an excellence in this period never again equalled. Many illustrations complement the scholarly text.

2820 *Have Tux, Will Travel, Bob Hope's Own Story.* by Martin, Pete. 308 p. paper New York: Simon & Schuster, 1954.

Approximately 30 pages are devoted to Hope's films in this predictable autobiography. The rest is stage, vaudeville, wartime tours, radio, etc. Written in a forties style, the attempts at wit may put off today's reader. The paperback version has an index but no illustrations. For the devoted only.

2821 *Haven't I Seen You Somewhere Before?* edited by Limbacher, James. 279 p. Ann Arbor, Mich.: Pierian, 1979.

When it originally appeared as a mimeographed listing, this reference was called "a valuable contribution to film reference materials." Updated, expanded and attractively published, the new volume carries the subtitle, "Remakes, Sequels, and Series in Motion Pictures and Television 1896-1978." Entries are arranged alphabetically by the first production of a work. Thus, under DARK VICTORY the reader will find the first 1939 Warner Brothers' version was based on a play by George Brewer, Jr. and Bertram Bloch. There were TV versions using the same title in 1951, 1954, 1955, 1957 and 1976. Another film version called STOLEN HOURS appeared in 1963. Looking at the entry STOLEN HOURS, the reader is directed to DARK VICTORY.

The sequels section lists the original film first and then the sequels in chronological order. In the series section, names, titles, and characters are used to identify the film groupings. Examples of series include Tarzan, Gene Autry, Gidget, Mr. Moto, Wheeler and Woolsey, The Hit Parade, etc.

Although Limbacher admits to certain limitations, he maintains that this is the only book that brings all this material together, and how very right he is! The new production values and the updating make it an essential reference volume.

2822 HAVOC IN HEAVEN: *Pictures and Text From the Cartoon Film.* San Francisco: China Books, 1979.

2823 HAWAII. 32 p. illus. New York: National Publishers, 1966.

With a few fuzzy exceptions, the illustrations in this souvenir book are so impressive that the reader will wonder why the 1967 film was so dull and unmoving. Using scenery, portraits, film stills, and even tintypes, the story and the background of the film are related. Stars, supporting cast, director George Roy Hill, producer Walter Mirisch, composer Elmer Bernstein, and costume designer Dorothy Jenkins are all given special attention. Based upon the evidence here, one suspects there may have been too much material for one film.

2824 *The Hays Office.* by Moley, Raymond. 266 p. illus. Indianapolis: Bobbs-Merrill, 1945.

An account of the motion picture industry's attempt to govern and regulate itself. "When a business falls into practices which endanger the public interest, there is an irrestible drift toward governmental control or regulation of that business"; it was this axiom that led to the formation of the Hays Office, an agency designed to avoid outside regulation of the industry. Starting with a short account of the economic and organizational development of motion pictures, the author describes Will Hays, the office, and the code. The book will have a limited appeal to most readers. Scholars interested in film history or censorship studies will find it valuable.

2825 *Haywire.* by Hayward, Brooke. 325 p. illus. New York: Alfred Knopf, 1977.

The story of a rich and privileged American family and its gradual disintegration is told in this autobiography. Author Brooke Hayward is the daughter of film agent Leland Hayward and film actress Margaret Sullavan, who at one time was married to Henry Fonda. Brooke grew up in Hollywood and included among her associates Jane and Peter Fonda, Johanna Mankiewicz, Dennis Hopper, James Stewart, and hundreds of other film personalities. It is the immediate family, however, that is her concern as she traces her parents' addiction to show business, her sister's withdrawal and suicide, her brother's interrment in a mental hospital, and her own survival. The history of the Hayward family is told with detail, affection, and understanding. The individuals who made up the quintet are clearly defined and at times the motivation for their behavior is suggested. However, the question which lingers is "What went wrong (haywire)"?

The book is appealing on several levels. It offers a fully dimensioned portrait of a film actress-mother-woman that has no equal, except perhaps that of Laurette Taylor. Each of the other elements here is strong enough to warrant the individual attention given. Weaving them together into a recognizable American tragedy is the author's achievement. A few portraits of the leading characters are included, but in this case they are hardly necessary. Highly recommended.

2826 *Health: A Multimedia Source Guide.* by Ash, Joan; and Stevenson, Michael. 185 p. New York: Bowker, 1976.

The key word in the title of this volume is "source." It is not a listing of multimedia per se, but an arrangement of 700 sources that produce/distribute health materials. Distinction is made, via chapter division, between associations, societies, foundations, book dealers, governmental agencies, libraries, commercial companies, publishers, research institutes, etc. Each entry under these chapter headings indicates the organization name, address, telephone number, the official in charge, the purpose, special services, and publications. An alphabetical listing of all 700 sources, a subject index and an index to free or inexpensive material conclude the volume.

The location of print material sources is relatively easy. Retrieval of the information by individual non-print medium is more difficult. For example, if a film on venereal disease is desired, the user would have to look at 30 entries to find who has films available and then write for catalogs. Upon searching he is liable to encounter such general terms as "educational materials," "other materials," "various media," etc.

In summary this reference has brought together the sources of information on health, saving the user much effort. However, the user may have to perform further retrieval activities to obtain the material that he desires. Acceptable.

2827 *The Heart of Hollywood.* by Cairn, James. 224 p. London: David Smith, 1945.

Articles on film actors, along with film criticism and reviews.

2828 *The Heart of Hollywood.* by Thomas, Bob. 112 p. illus. New York: Price, Stern, Sloan, 1971.

A pictorial history of the Motion Picture and Television Relief Fund and the service it has provided to the film industry.

2829 *Heart-Throbs.* by Tresidder, Jack. 121 p. illus. New York: Crescent (Crown), 1974.

"The Magnetic Moody Males of Your Dreams" mentioned in this book's subtitle refers to the 106 men described within by text and illustration. Most are film stars and the author attempts to explain their magnetism and attraction. The theme is another excuse to publish a lot of illustrations and call it a survey.

2830 HEAVEN CAN WAIT. by May, Elaine; and Beatty, Warren. unpaginated paper illus. Los Angeles: Fotonovel, 1978.

This *Fotonovel* (see series entry) contains over 400 stills, some original film dialogue, connecting narra-

tive, and cast credits for the 1978 film, HEAVEN CAN WAIT, which was directed by Beatty and Buck Henry.

2831 *The Heavies.* by Cameron, Ian; and Cameron, Elizabeth. 144 p. illus. New York: Praeger, 1969.

A collection of cinematic bad men chosen by appearance, talent, or role, this book is companion to *Dames.* A short biography and filmography is given for each actor. The pictures are fair to good, the comments interesting and opinionated, the selection quite arbitrary. However, the book still offers a partial reference, some enjoyable reading, and an opportunity to label by name some familiar faces. With the reservations listed above, the book is good for most readers.

2832 *Hedda   and   Louella.* by Eels, George. 360 p. illus. New York: G. P. Putnam's, 1972.

Dual biography is a rarity and George Eels, who impressed so with his work on Cole Porter, succeeds once more with this volume. Tracing the careers of each of his subjects in alternate chapters, he manages to capture not only their disparities and similarities but also the absurdity of the society in which they lived and worked.

Both women have written several books, including autobiographies, so the basic information about their careers is known. The challenge to Eels was not only to purify their accounts but to interpret and assess their importance to Hollywood and filmmaking. He does this with clarity and ease, yet remains objective and readable. Illustrations, grouped together in the center of the book, are quite good; in fact, more would be welcome. An index is also provided. This volume will be popular with mature readers and is recommended.

2833 HELEN OF TROY. 12 p. paper illus. Hollywood: Warner Brothers, 1956.

The production of this short souvenir book is unusual and rather attractive. The text is centered on the pages, with a border of illustrations. The pictures are tinted in a pleasing monochrome. Some description of "The World's Largest Prop" is given and the two stars—Rossana Podesta (Helen) and Jack Sernas (Paris)—are profiled. Supporting cast members and production personnel are noted. Brigitte Bardot played a minor role as one of Helen's handmaidens.

2834   *A Hell of a Life*. by Richman, Harry; and Gehman, Richard. 242 p. illus. Des Moines, Iowa: Meredith, 1966.

A racy, ribald autobiography of the singer-entertainer who appeared in only a few films—PUTTIN' ON THE RITZ (1930) and THE MUSIC GOES 'ROUND (1936), for example.

2835   HELLO DOLLY. by Hirschberg, Jack. 48 p. paper illus. New York:20th Century Fox Film Corp., 1969.

Photographs are outstanding in this souvenir book and include not only the stars, Barbra Streisand and Walter Matthau, but director Gene Kelly and other production personnel. The songs used in the 1969 film are given special attention and there are listings of the supporting cast and backstage technicians.

2836   *Hello Hollywood*. by Rivkin, Allen; and Kerr, Laura. 571 p. New York: Doubleday & Co., 1962.

With the general theme of "The Story of the Movies by the People Who Make Them," this anthology is presented in the form of a movie. After a series of credit titles, the articles are connected by dialogues that attempt to weld the many parts into a single whole. Periodicals such as *Screen Writer, Daily Variety*, and *Hollywood Reporter* provide much of the material. Chapter excerpts from books such as *Case History of a Movie, Marilyn Monroe, Garbo, Father Goose, Agee on Film, Dress Doctor, Mr. Laurel and Mr. Hardy*, and *Seen Any Good Movies Lately?* are included. There is no table of contents and the readers will have no idea of the contents and authors unless he consults the opening index, which may or may not help. The book-as-movie gimmick is unwieldy and forced. A straight introductory paragraph would have been much better. This is a fine anthology seriously flawed by an artificial, silly format. Revision and elimination, are needed. Meanwhile, recommended only with great reservation.

2837   *Hello, I Must Be Going*. by Chandler, Charlotte. 568 p. paper illus. Garden City, N.Y.: Doubleday, 1978.

This long volume is devoted to an account of Groucho Marx in his last, declining years. Depicted as an obnoxious, almost senile person, the Groucho persona is completely lost with old age. What charm and interest the book possesses lies in the recalling of Groucho gems from the past. This is mostly through interviews with "Groucho and His Friends," the latter consisting of Woody Allen, George Burns, Bill Cosby, Billy Wilder, and many others. This volume was a result of an earlier *Playboy* interview which pleased Groucho. The author was apparently made welcome in the Marx household. Her description of life there is very kind to Erin Fleming, Groucho's companion.

Some illustrations are included along with a short chronology, but there is no index. The omission is a serious one since the text contains so many names; even the names of those interviewed are not listed anywhere. The book is a case of more being less.

2838   HELL'S ANGELS *Movie Program*. Tuscon, Ariz.: Beachcomber.

2839   HELP. by Behm, Marc. 28 p. illus. New York: Random House, 1965.

This souvenir book is an improvement over the one issued for the first Beatles film. Containing both color and black and white photographs, the format is similar: the story, the songs and lyrics, and some behind-the-scenes candid shots. The hardcover production supplied by publisher seemingly makes the difference.

2840   *see* *2839*

2841   *Help Wanted, Male and Female*. by Momand, A. B. 73 p. Shawnee, Okla.: Oklahoma Baptist University Press, 1940.

This volume carries an alternate title, "The Great Motion Picture Conspiracy, Condensed....An Exhibitor's Story..." and deals with the distribution practices of the motion picture industry during the thirties.

2842   *Hemingway and Film*. by Phillips, Gene D. 192 p. paper illus. New York: Ungar, 1980.

The films that have been made from Ernest Hemingway's novels and short stories are analyzed in this volume, which is similar to the previous ones on Faulkner and Tennessee Williams. Gene Phillips groups the films under general theme headings—war, growing pains, a man alone, etc.—and provides comparisons between film and source, along with occasional background information about the film productions. His general conclusion is that the films often reflect Hemingway's original work, and are not Hollywood distortions as Hemingway suggested. Introductory sections, a Hemingway chronology, a filmography, a bibliography, film sources, chapter notes, an index, and illustrations support the analysis. Readers interested in the relationship between film and literature will appreciate Phillip's work with a rather difficult subject.

2843 *Hemingway and the Movies.* by Laurence, Frank M. 336 p. illus. Jackson, Miss.: University of Mississippi, 1980.

This volume, which deals with the transfer of Ernest Hemingway's novels and stories to the screen, is similar to Gene D. Phillips' *Hemingway and Film.* In a stronger, more convincing text, Laurence explains how Hollywood diluted the themes and made the stories conform to industry needs. The analyses he provides for the films are very good.

2844 *Henry Fonda.* by Kerbel, Michael. 160 p. paper illus. New York: Pyramid, 1975.

The long screen career of Henry Fonda is reviewed in this volume, a title in *The Illustrated History of the Movies* Series. After an introductory appreciation, along with a brief biographical sketch, the text examines some 79 films beginning with THE FARMER TAKES A WIFE (1935) and ending with ASH WEDNESDAY (1973). Fonda is still active in films, having appeared in several other films after ASH WEDNESDAY, and winning an Oscar for ON GOLDEN POND (1981). Some attention is given to his stage and television appearances and to his relationships with his children, Jane and Peter.

To encompass a long and active career and a colorful, dramatic private life in the requisite 160 pages of this series necessitates a spare, economical text. This is what has been provided, along with some good illustrations, a bibliography, a list of Broadway stage appearances, and a filmography. The book is indexed.

As evidenced in the several biographies published previously, the Fonda screen image is easier to capture, explore, and explain than that of the private man. This volume wisely concentrates on his career and offers an entertaining overview and appreciation of Fonda's four decades of fine film acting.

2845 *Henry Fonda.* edited by Reed, Rochelle. 24 p. paper illus. Washington, D.C.: American Film Institute, 1973.

Henry Fonda and director Robert Totten were interviewed by AFI members upon completion of a film made for television, THE RED PONY (1973). Questions were general, covering Fonda's long career

rather than concentrating on the new film. A filmography, videography and a bibliography are included.

2846 *Henry, Jane and Peter: The Fabulous Fondas.* by Stewart, Jack. 208 p. paper New York: Tower, 1976.

A collective biography of the acting Fonda family, this original paperback leans heavily on previously published material and matters of public record. As a result it is a largely factual recount of three lives, punctuated occasionally by quotes taken from unacknowledged sources. Selected films are discussed and some slight critical comment is offered. A center section of photographs adds little to the biographies. The Fondas are probably "larger than life" and do not fit comfortably into such a cramped format as this volume. The view is partial and ultimately unsatisfying.

2847 *Henry King: Filmography.* compiled by Canham, Kingsley. 17 p. paper London: British Film Institute, 1977.

2848 *Henry Mancini.* edited by Reed, Rochelle. 24 p. paper illus. Washington, D.C.: American Film Institute, 1974.

In this interview conducted in late 1973 at the AFI Center in Beverly Hills, composer Henry Mancini discusses his career and the elements of writing and scoring music for films. A complete filmography of Mancini's scores, songs, and partial scores is appended to the interview, which was conducted by James Powers.

2849 *Heraclitus or the Future of Films.* by Betts, E. 96 p. New York: Dutton, 1928.

This argument about accepting film as art considers the economic and industry factors as limitations. The author describes the film world of the late twenties and gives attention to such aesthetics as image, narrative, music and mood. Some theoretical predictions about the future of the film are made.

2850 *Here Comes Harry Reems!* by Reems, Harry. 209 p. paper illus. New York: Pinnacle Books, 1975.

In this X-rated memoir, male porno star Harry Reems joins the other would-be authors like Linda Lovelace, Marilyn Chambers, et al., in trying to cash in before the market collapses. The 1973 Supreme Court decision placing obscenity decisions in the hands of local communities has greatly reduced the number of film theatres showing erotic films. Reems makes some small attempt at biography and he does strive for a light approach. However, in order to accumulate any text of interest, he is forced to recount many of his experiences as a sexual athlete. The inevitable description of the porno film industry and its denizens is also used.

There is some slight evidence that with proper editorial guidance Reems could have written a ribald, rather funny account of his career. He has opted instead for a vulgar, pornographic exercise in bad taste that will undoubtedly sell many thousands of copies. Noted for the record.

2851 *Here Lies the Heart.* by de Acosta, Mercedes. 372 p. illus. New York: Reynal, 1960.

A script writer fashions a portrait of Hollywood in an autobiography that touches on her friendships with Garbo, Dietrich, and others.

2852 *Here Today.* by Tanner, Louise. 320 p. paper New York: Delta, 1963.

Each of the 14 subjects in this collective biography contributed something to America's cultural history while they were young. From Hollywood the author has selected Shirley Temple and James Dean. Harold Russell, who appeared in THE BEST YEARS OF OUR LIVES (1946), is also one of Tanner's subjects.

2853 *Here's Looking at You, Kid.* by Silke, James R. 317 p. illus. Boston: Little, Brown, 1976.

A history of the Warner Brothers studio is presented here in text and nearly 500 illustrations. The author, a former screenwriter, uses personnel (writers, musicians, directors, etc.) for chapter headings, thereby avoiding a straight chronological narrative. The copious text at times resembles a publicity release and may disappoint those who expect something comparable in quality to the illustrations, which are superbly reproduced and include such visuals as candids, stills, portraits, and studio cards.

The second disappointment the reader may encounter is the lack of an index. With such an enormous amount of information, some access other than chapter headings should have been provided. Recommended for the visuals.

2854 *Here's to the Friars: The Heart of Show Business.* by Adams, Joey. illus. New York: Crown, 1976.

A history of the Friars is offered by Joey Adams in this volume which includes routines, quips, one-liners, and anecdotes about selected members of the show business group. Material from the Friars' Roasts is included. The membership of the organization boasts many film personalities.

2855 *Here's to the Next Time.* by Hall, Henry. 240 p. illus. London: Odhams Press, 1955.

The autobiography of a musician-composer-actor whose professional career encompasses films, theatre, and television.

2856 *Heretic: A Partisan Autobiography.* by Fitchman, Stephen H. 362 p. paper Kansas City, Mo.: Beacon Hill, 1977.

The author is a Unitarian minister who is a dedicated fighter for civil liberties. This autobiography includes material on the House Un-American Activities Committee and the Hollywood Ten.

2857 *A Heritage of Horror.* by Pirie, David. 192 p. paper illus. New York: Avon (Equinox), 1973.

This volume, which is subtitled "The English Gothic Cinema 1946-1972," combines illustrative, text, and reference material in a most satisfactory manner. The author seeks to prove that the horror film is the singular genre that Britain can claim as its own. In his survey of several hundred films made in or by British studios, the author is both descriptive and critical. To complement his study he includes film checklists for the Hammer Studios, Terence Fisher, John Gilling, Vernon Sewell, and Don Sharp. The combination filmography and index for all British horror films made between 1945 and 1972 is a fitting conclusion to the book. It is quite detailed noting release date, studio, producer, director, scriptwriter, cast, etc. The illustrations are mostly unfamiliar and have been well selected and reproduced.

In a genre field which is currently overburdened by too many books, the appearance of this one is most welcome. In approach, style, and overall content it is consistently absorbing and enlightening. The author's thesis about British domination in the production of horror films during the past few decades is well substantiated here. Recommended.

2858 *The Hero.* by Babcock, David. 52 p. paper illus. Waltham, Mass.: Film Study Programs, 1968.

An attempt to analyze eight contemporary film heroes is made in this study unit. To sharpen film appreciation it is designed as a study of genres, as an examination of Hollywood's dream-factory product, and as a stimulus to reading. Six feature films are used: SHANE (1953), HUD (1963), STALAG 17 (1953), THE MALTESE FALCON (1941), ALL THE WAY HOME (1963), and SEVEN DAYS IN MAY (1964). Since all of these films were suggested by novels or plays, the unit can be used in a study of literature and films. Each film is treated in a separate chapter with a plot summary; discussions of theme, character and technique; a discussion guide; and some suggested activities. To provide flexibility some related or alternate films are listed. A short bibliography on heroes is given.

While the user may have some reservation about the lack of flexibility in a unit such as this, he cannot help but be impressed by its detail and construction. It can easily serve as a model for similar locally designed units. Highly recommended.

2859 *Heroes, Heavies and Sagebrush: A Pictorial History of the "B" Western Player.* by McClure, Arthur F.; and Jones, Ken D. 350 p. illus. New York: A. S. Barnes, 1972.

Here is a more ambitious and more successful book than the other volumes in what is apparently a series. An earlier effort by McClure treated the minor film players whose faces were familiar although their names were not. In this volume it is the player in the "B" western film who is considered. Subjects range from "Superstars" John Wayne, Tom Mix, Buck Jones, and Gene Autry to such unknowns as Syd Saylor, Nacho Galindo, and Iron Eyes Cody. The oversized book is divided into five sections: heroes, sidekicks, heavies, Indians, and assorted players. A short biographical sketch is given for each subject, with one or two stills which identify him facially. Films mentioned in the biography are selected and are limited to westerns. Obviously, certain faces and names keep reappearing throughout the various sections and in the many illustrations.

The reference value of the book could have been increased greatly by a single-page alphabetical listing of all the subjects. Under the present format, a reader might have to check five sections to locate the desired biography. Fortunately the notoriously bad picture reproduction that characterizes many Barnes volumes is not present in this one. Nearly all the pictures are well printed and they include many full-page portraits. This volume represents a step forward for publisher and author. Most qualities are improved but there is still a way to go. The material

should be designed with more than the casual browser in mind and the biographies could be extended by using consistent abbreviations for statistical data.

2860 *Heroes of Eros: Male Sexuality in the Movies.* by Malone, Michael. 181 p. paper illus. New York: Dutton, 1979.

If one approaches this survey of male sexuality in films as an essay expressing a singular point of view, he will be able to accept this well-illustrated review. However, the placement or assignment of various actors into specific categories—lovers, pinups, pectorals, heroes, rebels—with accompanying analysis as to their sexual appeal for audiences, may raise a few questions. The author acknowledges the difficulty of his task, and tries to see a wide diversity of elements that make up sexuality.

Selection of the all-important visuals is excellent; they supplement Malone's discussion by providing evidence of the actors' visual appeal. No index is provided.

The change in the character and thus the sexuality of the Hollywood hero over the years is noted as are the leading box office stars from 1932 (Farrell, Gable) to 1976 (Redford, Nicholson, Eastwood, Reynolds, Pacino, Bronson, Hoffman).

If the limitations of this exercise are understood and accepted by the reader, a provocative reading experience is provided. The nondiscriminating reader will probably enjoy the pictures-with-text for other, more personal reasons.

2861 *Heroes of the Horrors.* by Beck, Calvin Thomas. 353 p. paper illus. New York: Collier (Macmillan), 1975.

In this collective biography, the subjects are Lon Chaney, Sr., Bela Lugosi, Boris Karloff, Peter Lorre, Lon Chaney, Jr., and Vincent Price. For each a long biography and appreciation is offered. Included are film synopses, evaluations, portraits, film stills, script excerpts, filmography, and quotes. In short, a combination of elements that succeeds very well in describing the unique talent of each performer.

The text has been carefully researched and is beautifully complemented by the richness, unfamiliarity and variety of the visuals. Reproduction quality is especially noteworthy.

Here is an impressive volume that has been painstakingly created. Selection, production, and literary quality are all well above the usual found in books devoted to the horror film or its personalities. This one is a winner in all respects. Highly recommended.

2862   *The Heroine or The Horse.* by Swann, Thomas Burnett. 134 p. illus. New York: A. S. Barnes, 1977.

It is difficult to determine what this volume is really about. Subtitled "Leading Ladies in Republic's Films," it might be collective biography; however, it offers such an unbalanced, poorly selected collection of biographical snippets, it cannot qualify for that designation. Could it be a history of the Republic Studios shown through its leading female players? A tracing on the LC Cataloging Publication Data indicates such a heading. Again, the approach is too oblique to warrant such an assignment. It seems more accurate to call this a collection of widely assorted biographical bits, most of which have two common elements hidden within then—the subjects were female and at one time or another they happened to appear in at least one Republic film.

Editing and proofreading are poor. A quick scan discloses "Kurk" for "Kurt" (page 69), "Carpos" for "Carpozi" (page 130), "Farnett" for "Fernett" (page 130), etc. On page 29 Helen Westley is identified as Ona Munson while Binnie Barnes is called "a mulefaced curmudgeon." Stills are poorly selected, incorrectly assigned (page 67) and unbalanced in number—25 stills are devoted to Adele Jergens while Vera Hruba Ralston, a name synonomous with Republic Pictures, is represented by only six. Padding is evident throughout with most attention given to accomplishments at other studios, a few full-page male portraits, unnecessary trivia such as the physical measurements of Ivan Kirov, quotations from letters to the author, etc. A bibliography and an index are provided but a filmography, which might have helped to unify the material, is absent.

The individual chapters devoted to Judy Canova, Vera Hruba Ralston and Adele Mara may please some readers but most others will be quite disappointed. Unacceptable.

2863   *Heyday: An Autobiography.* by Schary, Dore. 341 p. illus. Boston: Little, Brown, 1980.

The thoroughness that characterized Dore Schary's work as screenwriter, producer, studio head, and playwright is evident in this autobiography. His rise from a New Jersey boyhood to head of MGM is meticulously related with a final quarter of the book devoted to the Broadway production of his play, *Sunrise at Campobello.* Unfortunately with all the attention to detail provided, dramatic structure is weakened and the reader is given a self-congratulating super-hero. Schary's devotion to his faith, the Jewish community, his family, friends, and associates is repeatedly stressed. There are tangents, digressions and political philosophies intermixed with the narrative line, and the result is a generally disappointing recall of the 27 years Schary spent in the film industry.

2864   HIGH SIERRA. by Huston, John; and Burnett, W. R. 192 p. paper illus. Madison, Wisc.: University of Wisconsin Press, 1979.

Script of the 1941 film directed by Raoul Walsh.

This volume has been edited by Douglas Gomery, who also provides an introductory essay. Cast and credits are included.

2865   *High Speed Photography.* by Saxe, Raymond F. illus. New York: Amphoto, 1966.

A section of this book deals with high-speed cine cameras. Other topics include streak and framing cameras, short exposure picture-taking devices, flash X-rays, and other electronic techniques.

2866   THE HILL. by Fast, Howard. 123 p. Garden City, N.Y.: Doubleday, 1964.

In this modern version of Christ's Passion, Calvary is Harlem's Mount Morris Park, and Pontius Pilate operates out of a steel-and-glass office tower. The script remains unfilmed.

2867   *Hints on Photoplay Writing.* by Peacocke, Leslie T. 146 p. illus. Chicago: Photoplay Publishing, 1916.

The "hints" are compiled from a series of articles written by Peacocke for *Photoplay* magazine which were published in 1915-1916.

2868   HIROSHIMA MON AMOUR. by Duras, Marguerite. 112 p. paper illus. New York: Grove Press, 1961.

Script of the 1959 film directed by Alain Resnais. Contains cast credits, an introduction by Marguerite Duras, a synopsis, and four appendices (notes, Nevers, portrait of the Japanese man, and portrait of the French woman).

2869   HIROSHIMA MON AMOUR and UNE AUSSI LONGUE ABSENCE. by Duras, Marguerite. 191 p. illus. London: Calder and Boyars, 1966.

Scripts of the 1959-60 films directed by Alain Resnais and Henri Colpi. Contains an introduction by Duras.

2870 *His Eye Is on the Sparrow.* by Waters, Ethel; and Samuels, Charles. 278 p. paper New York: Pyramid, 1967 (1950).

The autobiography of the black singer-actress who has had careers in vaudeville, cabarets, radio, stage, television and films. Her screen debut was in ON WITH THE SHOW (1929) and has included leading roles in such films as TALES OF MANHATTAN (1942), CABIN IN THE SKY (1943), PINKY (1949) and MEMBER OF THE WEDDING (1952).

2871 *His Majesty the American: The Films of Douglas Fairbanks, Sr.* by Tibbets, John C.; and Welsh, James M. 223 p. illus. New York: A. S. Barnes, 1977.

This volume is successful in its treatment of certain aspects of the unusual life and career of Douglas Fairbanks, Sr. The major concern of the text is the 43 films that Fairbanks made from 1915 to 1934. Biographical coverage is also provided in sufficient amount and, finally, there is a continual attempt to define Fairbanks and his films in relation to their period in American history.

The text is written with an appropriate blend of factual information, quotation, and interpretation. Analysis is provided in depth and the similarity of Fairbanks' screen character and his personal self-image is often noted. Many fine illustrations support the thoughtful appreciation that the authors have provided. A filmography, a bibliography, and an index complete the work. There is a consistent quality in all the elements of this volume that will appeal to all types of readers. Recommended.

2872 *His Picture in the Papers.* by Schickel, Richard. 171 p. illus. New York: Charterhouse, 1973.

What Schickel has done in this well-written volume is to attempt an examination of American film stardom in the twenties. He discusses the rewards, demands, and dangers that the celebrity star system provides. Using the career of Douglas Fairbanks, Sr., as a case study, the biographical content of this volume rests primarily on two previous studies of Fairbanks by Hancock and Fairbanks, and by Alistair Cooke, while those portions which deal with celebrity were suggested in part by Walker and Mankiewicz. While the life of Fairbanks is familiar

from the above books and from the biographies of his contemporaries—Pickford, Chaplin, and son, Fairbanks, Jr.—it is the interpretations, conjecture, and supposition about celebrity that the author applies to the facts which makes this volume provocative and fascinating. An adequate center section of photographs and an index support this long essay.

Mature readers cannot help but delight in this serious and rewarding volume. Younger readers may be too unfamiliar with Fairbanks' artistry, the twenties and the psychology involved in creating overnight heroes. Acceptable.

2873 *His Weird and Wanton Ways.* by Mathison, Richard. 249 p. New York: William Morrow, 1977.

Subtitled "The Secret Life of Howard Hughes," this volume consists of short anecdotes or incidents, most of which involve Jeff Chouinard, the head of security for Hughes for 18 years, 1949 to 1968. The period represents the latter portion of Hughes' life and does not include much material about Hollywood, film studios, or filmmaking. Actress Jean Peters, who married Hughes, is mentioned frequently.

The use of this volume is limited by the absence of illustrations and an index.

2874 *The Historian and the Film.* edited by Smith, Paul. 208 p. New York: Cambridge University Press, 1976.

This collection of articles explores the use of film by historians as direct evidence about or as a recreation of times past. The potentials and the dangers of employing film material to teach history are considered along with other pertinent topics such as content, interpretation, and social effect.

Eleven articles appear under the major subject headings: the raw materials, film as historical evidence, film as historical factor, and film in the interpretation and teaching of history.

A lengthy bibliography and a list of organizations concerned with film and history are added. The book is indexed.

This is the first important volume to address itself to the vital relationship between film and history. The implications set forth by this excellent collection of articles cannot help but affect the attitude toward and use of film by historians. Highly recommended.

2875 *An Historical and Descriptive Analysis of the* WHY WE FIGHT *series.* by Bohn, Thomas William. New York:

Arno, 1977.

Written in 1968 at the University of Wisconsin as partial fulfillment of the doctoral program, this study examines the World War II soldier orientation films known as the WHY WE FIGHT series. Bohn analyzes their production, content, purpose and contribution to our history. Although the films might be dismissed as wartime propaganda, the author believes that a thorough exploration and analysis is appropriate. This title appears in the *Dissertations on Film* series.

2876 *A Historical Study of the Academy of Motion Picture Arts and Sciences (1927-1947).* by Sands, Pierre Norman. 262 p. New York: Arno, 1973.

This is one of six doctoral dissertations on film topics reproduced by Arno exactly as they were submitted to the degree-granting school. This study is a historical investigation of the Academy of Motion Picture Arts and Sciences and its contribution to education and the Industry during the years, 1927-1947. The historical portion covers the founding period, the first banquet, constitution, by-laws, boards, facilities, publications, membership, officers, awards, etc.

The Academy's contributions to education are more provocative and include: institutions, the commerical community, and the military—all covered in a rather short section. Its service to the film industry itself is much larger.

A summary and conclusions are presented. A bibliography and some appendixes support the rather weak argument. The study seems to lack objectivity and was based on what the Academy said or wrote rather than an evaluation by disinterested parties. Acceptable.

2877 *A Historical Study of the Development of American Motion Picture Content and Techniques Prior to 1904.* by Sanderson, Richard Arlo. 251 p. illus. New York: Arno Press, 1977.

Written in 1961 at the University of Southern California, in partial fulfillment of the Doctoral program, this historical record relies upon original materials and research to survey pre-1904 film activities in America. The author discusses in detail what types of films were produced prior to what are now considered the early American film classics. Film subjects, trends, and techniques are the primary topics considered by the author in his investigation. This title is included in the *Dissertations on Film*

series.

2878 *History and Heartburn: The Saga of Australian Film 1896-1978.* by Reade, Eric. 353 p. illus. Rutherford, N.J.: Fairleigh Dickinson University Press, 1979.

In this attractive, oversized book, Eric Reade tells the story of the Australian film, employing a carefully researched text and hundreds of rare illustrations. Because of his earlier volume, *Australian Silent Films,* Reade covers the silent film era in a single chapter; the sound films, however, receive detailed attention. Along with historical incidents, many filmmakers who have worked in Australian films are identified, as are those films which were exported to foreign markets. The final impression left by the book is that the Australian film industry has all the requisites for becoming a major source of fine films that can be appreciated by many different world audiences.

The illustrations are outstanding and support the text superbly. An index is provided to this most welcome history of a national cinema of promise and potential.

2879 *The History and Social Significance of Motion Pictures in South Africa, 1895-1940.* by Gutshe, Thelma. 404 p. illus. Cape Town: Howard Timmins, 1972.

Originally written as a thesis at the University of Cape Town, South Africa, this survey of motion pictures includes bibliographical references.

2880 *A History of Film.* by Ellis, Jack C. 452 p. paper illus. Englewood Cliffs, N.J.: Prentice Hall, 1979.

Jack Ellis approaches a history of film on a national cinema basis—that is, he isolates, identifies, and discusses movements and contributions made by nations or countries to the film art. Thus the Scandinavian, German, Soviet, French, British, Asian, Italian, and Third World cinemas figure importantly, while American film, of course, is given major attention throughout his survey. Each of 22 chapters contains textual material and illustrations followed by a chronological listing of selected "films of the period" and a bibliography, "books on the period." The book is illustrated and indexed.

In the writing of any film history, selection is probably the most important factor. Ellis has been intelligent, discriminating, and balanced in his choices. As a result, the final text, its arrangement and presentation make this an ideal basic book for courses on the history of world cinema. Most helpful to students will be the numerous bibliographies and filmographies Ellis has provided. Recommended.

2881 *A History of Films.* by Fell, John L. 588 p. paper illus. New York: Holt, Rinehart, and Winston, 1979.

In 21 chapters, each with its own bibliography, John Fell offers a history that is acceptable but not outstanding. Designed as a college text, the volume surveys film history with attention to essential elements—inventions, directors, classic films, industry, animation, world cinema, etc. The volume is illustrated and contains separate indexes for names, film titles and general topics.

2882 *History of Hollywood.* by Palmer, Edwin O. 294 p. illus. New York: Garland, 1978 (1937).

This is a reprint of a volume that was originally published in 1937, then revised and extended in 1938. It is the latter version that Garland Publishing presents here. Long out-of-print, the books have commanded high prices in specialized bookstores.

It is the story of the geographical area that came to be known as "Hollywood." Starting with a geological history, the author delves into anthropology, 16th century history, the presence of the Spaniards, Mexicans, and, finally, the arrival of the white race.

All of this information is documented by pictures, tables of data, and references to businesses, churches, schools, libraries, banks, hotels, hospitals, etc. The history is carried up to 1938 and ends with the statement, "Hollywood 'Marches On'." A detailed index accompanies this unusual text, which describes Hollywood in a way that the reader might not expect.

2883 *A History of Motion Picture Color Technology.* by Ryan, Roderick T. 278 p. illus. New York: Focal Press, 1977.

This is a technical book that uses history as a structure upon which to describe the various processes introduced from 1900 to 1975 to reproduce color on film. From more than 100 possible methods, the important ones are selected and grouped under two broad categories: additive and subtractive. Under the additive heading, there are discussions of optical, mechanical and shared area image processes while the subtractive systems include optical separation, mechanical separation, bi-pack photography, and multi-layer materials. Processing procedures are de-

scribed and chemical formulas are noted. The volume contains a glossary, chapter references, a bibliography, tables, diagrams, and two indexes.

This is a book that will be appreciated primarily by the professional cinematographer. The film scholar will also find sections of it quite pertinent to any discussion of the role of technology in motion picture history.

2884 *The History of Motion Pictures.* by Bardeche, Maurice; and Brasillach, Robert. 412 p. New York: Arno Press, 1970 (1938).

See *History of the Film.*

2885 *A History of Narrative Film, 1889-1979.* compiled by Cook, David. New York: Norton, 1981.

2886 *History of Taiwanese Film, 1921-1950.* by Lu Su-Shang. Pasadena, Calif.: E. Langstaff.

2887 *A History of the American Avant-Garde Cinema.* edited by Singer, Marilyn. 176 p. paper illus. New York: American Federation of Arts, 1970.

This is a catalog designed to accompany an exhibition of avant-garde films, and also to be used as a resource-text. It is an anthology of seven articles by different authors, each of whom deals with a different chronological period. For example, Lucy Fischer discusses the period 1943 to 1948 which saw such avant-garde films as MESHES OF THE AFTERNOON (1943), FIREWORKS (1947), MOTHER'S DAY (1948) appear. In addition to the essays there is an introduction, an opening chapter, footnotes, many illustrations, a list of film sources, filmographies, and bibliographies.

Much more than a catalog, this attractively produced volume deserves recognition as one of the better texts on the American avant-garde film.

2888 *A History of the American Film.* by Durang, Christopher. 160 p. paper New York: Avon, 1978.

This is a play that had a very short run on Broadway but is enjoying great popularity with community and college theatre groups. It is noted here since it leans so heavily on motion picture history, legend and cliche. Film genres, songs, characters, situations, and techniques are parodied.

2889 *History of the American Film Industry From its Beginnings to 1931.* by Hampton, Benjamin B. 456 p. paper illus. New York: Dover Pub., 1970.

This is one of the few classic books written on the history of the American film industry. The period covered is from infancy to 1931, the beginning of the sound era. The approach is more a business and a finance one rather than how motion pictures became an art form. Many celebrated film names are mentioned in its pages, and accounts of financial battles, law suits, and distribution practices are plentiful. Thus, a fully detailed account of the early growth of an industry is realized.

Four sections of pictures are included and they are quite rare. It is sad that the reproduction of them is so poor; it does them a disservice. The book is indexed and there is a nice introduction by Richard Griffith. Unfortunately, the publishers have seen fit to include 14 pages of advertising. A bibliography would have been much more valuable to the reader/purchaser. The book is highly recommended. Enthusiasm for the publishers is not nearly so high.

2890 *The History of the British Film (Three Volumes).: 1. 1896-1906; 2. 1906-1914; and 3. 1914-1918.* by Low, Rachel. illus. London: Allen & Unwin, 1950.

This series of three volumes was written by the librarian of the British Film Academy as a doctoral study and published under the auspices of the British Film Institute. It is an exhaustive research and compilation of findings on British films from 1896 to 1918. Volume 1 covers 1896 to 1906, Volume 2 covers 1906 through 1914, and Volume 3 covers 1914 through 1918.

The three volumes are similar in structure. In the first section of each, topics such as audience, economics, organization, regulation, and film personalities are considered. The second section is concerned with an analysis of the films of the period—their content, source, technique, appeal, etc. Each volume contains a small amount of pictorial material, and several appendices, usually a listing of the films of the period, a sample script, and a description of the studio of that time. Very specialized material.

2891 *The History of the British Film, 1918-1929.* by Low, Rachel. 544 p. illus. London: George Allen & Unwin, 1971.

This, the fourth volume in Ms. Low's monumental survey of British film history, covers the period of the twenties. Topics considered include the emergence of film as an art form, the formation of the British Board of Censors, foreign competition, and the Quota Act of 1927-28. Names of films, directors, actors, and producers are scattered throughout the book, as are quotes and interviews with pioneers of the period.

Perhaps the most impressive feature is the list of feature films of the twenties. Using more than a third of the book, the author gives an alphabetical arrangement with title, producer, length, trade showing date, director, cast, screenwriter, art director, film editor, and other data indicated. A bibliography, a long index and many well-reproduced illustrations add to the overall impressiveness of this work.

2892 *The History of the Cannes Film Festival 1946-1979.* by Sarris, Andrew. 450 p. New York: Chelsea House, 1981.

2893 *A History of the Cinema From Its Origins to 1970.* by Rhode, Eric. 674 p. illus. New York: Hill and Wang, 1976.

In 15 chapters Eric Rhode traces the history of motion pictures from the inventions and discoveries of the late 19th century to the decade (1960-70) of filmmaking which he describes as "radical compromise." The well-written narrative emphasizes the countries and the socioeconomic conditions that brought forth movements and advances in cinema art. Soviet montage, French avant-garde, Italian neo-realism, the New Wave—all these and other numerous influences on today's films are discussed at length. Throughout the text many directors and their classic films are considered and evaluated from both a historical and a critical perspective. The result is an overwhelmingly detailed account that demands background, attention, and effort from the reader for full appreciation.

The comprehensive text is supplemented by more than 300 photographs which have been well selected and reproduced with adequate clarity. Some of them, however, are too small for full comprehension or effect. Copious chapter notes are supplied and there is a long bibliography and an equally lengthy index.

The impressive scholarship found in this volume qualifies it as one of the outstanding histories of film to appear during the last decade. Highly recommended.

2894 *History of the Film (The History of Motion Pictures).* by Bardeche, Maurice; and Brasillach, Robert; edited by Barry, Iris. 412 p. illus. London: Allen & Unwin, 1938.

Another of the classic histories of the film, this volume covers the period from 1895 to 1935. Written originally in French (*Histoire du Cinema*), the English translation was done by Iris Barry who also provides a postscript for the years 1935-1938. Although the viewpoint of the authors is international rather than provincial, many of their comments and critiques are suspect today, e.g., is the Mamoulian DR. JEKYLL AND MR. HYDE (1931) absurd? Are all the Dietrich—von Sternberg films which followed MOROCCO (1930) deplorable? Is the section on W. C. Fields, the Marx brothers, and Laurel and Hardy valid? Today's audiences and critics would disagree.

The strength of the volume lies in its factual and documented narrative. Its second strength is the work of translator Barry who does not hesitate to disagree with and correct the authors. She provides needed balance for the work. An index of film titles and a general index are included. This is an important volume that belongs with the Ramsaye and Jacobs histories. Its occasional weaknesses are overshadowed by its still excellent reportage of the early years of film history.

2895 *History of the Kinetograph, Kinetoscope and Kinetophonograph.* by Dickson, W. K. L.; and Dickson, Antonia. 65 p. illus. New York: Arno Press, 1970 (1895).

A short historical document which has original film frames of Carmencita, the Spanish dancer; Sandow, the strong man; Fred Ott's record of a sneeze, etc. More interesting than most of these primary source materials, this quick historical journey into the past will appeal to certain readers. High school students may find it especially intriguing.

2896 *A History of the Movies.* by Hampton, Benjamin B. 456 p. illus. New York: Arno Press, 1970 (1931).

See *A History of the American Film Industry.*

2897 *History of the National Film Board of Canada.* by McKay, Marjorie. 147 p. paper National Film Board of Canada, 1964.

Commissioned in 1964, this study provides a carefully researched history of the Board. See also *A Brief History: The National Film Board of Canada* by James Lysyshyn.

2898 *The History of the South African Film Industry, 1940-71: A Bibliography.* compiled by Udeman, Adrienne. 48 p. paper Johannesburg: University of Witwatersrand, 1972.

2899 *The History of World Cinema.* by Robinson, David. 440 p. illus. New York: Stein & Day, 1973.

Using a similar structure to that of Thorold Dickinson, who acknowledged George Huaco, Robinson states that those films which appear on the screen during a specific time and at a particular place are determined by four factors: an esthetic, a technology, an economy and an audience.

With that approach in mind he examines world cinema from the pre-screen era to the seventies. His divisions of this continuum are named with imagination: heritage (pre-1895), discovery (1895-1908), metamorphosis (1908-18), apogee (1918-27), revolution (1927-30), on the eve (1930-39), realities (1939-46), survival (1946-56), revival (1956-72) and legacy. A most pleasing and comprehensive outline told in a few words and dates. The text is both factual and critical and covers many facets of film's history. The one area that seems minimized is the American film. For example, the 1946-56 period gives one short paragraph to the American musical and two sentences to the western. The author neglects A STAR IS BORN (1954), AN AMERICAN IN PARIS (1951), SINGIN' IN THE RAIN (1952), FUNNY FACE (1957), THE BAND WAGON (1953), SHANE (1953), etc. He makes an error in this same section when he says Ford's THE SUN SHINES BRIGHT (1954) contributes to the western legend, naming it along with MY DARLING CLEMENTINE (1946), WAGONMASTER (1950), and SHE WORE A YELLOW RIBBON (1949). It was a rework of the Judge Priest stories by Irvin S. Cobb in which Will Rogers had starred back in 1934. In any event, the coverage is worldwide and arguments over emphasis and selection are subjective. Robinson's attempt to describe the whole of film history is admirable if not always successful.

A final short article on animated film is followed by selected or complete filmographies for many of the directors named in the text. A rather cramped bibliography and three separate indexes (general, films, names) complete the book. There are more than 100 photographs, most of which are nicely reproduced; these appear throughout the book rather than in one or two concentrated sections.

Since this is the first "longer" general history of world cinema in about 30 years—if one omits Dickinson, Mast and Casty—it is welcome in spite of its omissions, emphases, and mistakes. It attempts an almost impossible task and succeeds much of the time. Highly recommended.

2900 *Hitch: The Life and Times of Alfred Hitchcock.* by Taylor, John Russell. 321 p. illus. New York: Pantheon, 1978.

This volume on Alfred Hitchcock has the distinction of having been written with the full cooperation of the subject. As a result the reader is privy to many things not available in the numerous other volumes on the director. For example, we are told such things as the inspiration of the Grant-Bergman kissing scene in NOTORIOUS (1946), the complex relationship between Hitchcock and Tippi Hedren, the adolescent behavior of Paul Newman at his first Hitchcock dinner, etc. Other aspects have been carefully researched, especially the early years. The critical comment on the films is brief but valid and the overall portrait of Hitchcock reflects a determined effort at sincerity and objectivity on the part of the author. A few illustrations and an index complete the volume. The absence of a filmography is puzzling.

This study approaches its subject in several ways: through personal knowledge, biographical research, critical analyses of films, and by contributions from Hitchcock's relatives, friends, and coworkers. A pleasing blend is achieved and the book is certainly one to read or use more than once. Since Taylor emphasizes the man/artist rather than the films, this book is unique among the many which exist on Hitchcock. Highly recommended.

2901 *Hitchcock.* by Truffaut, Francois. 256 p. illus. New York: Simon & Schuster, 1967.

By the use of about 500 carefully prepared questions and with the help of nearly the same number of illustrations, Truffaut interviews and pays homage in print to his idol. His film tribute was THE BRIDE WORE BLACK (1968) but this book succeeds much more than the film.

Since the Hitchcock films are treated in a somewhat chronological order, there are elements of biography present. However, the main goal of the volume is to validate the high position the author assigns to Hitchcock by duo-analysis of his films. The author's detailed knowledge of his subject's work along with Hitchcock's apparent ease in conversing with such a celebrated disciple has resulted in an outstanding

film book. In all aspects this is a model. Author intelligence and preparation, skillful editing, adroit selection of illustrations and fine production values combine to make this an essential and vital book. Highly recommended for all.

2902 *Hitchcock.* by Perry, George. 126 p. illus. New York: Doubleday, 1975.

A title in *The Movie Makers* series, this volume adds little to the already existing literature on Hitchcock. Its outstanding feature is the collection of visuals featured throughout the book. They include portraits, production shots, and stills, with several appearing in full color. Arrangement of the text is chronologically by period, beginning with Hitchcock's birth in 1899 and ending with FRENZY (1972).

The text, which is both descriptive and critical, is further supported by a filmography and an index. Acceptable.

2903 *Hitchcock: The First Forty-Four Films.* by Rohmer, Eric; and Chabrol, Claude. 178 p. paper illus. New York: Ungar, 1979.

An appreciation by two New Wave directors, this volume was originally published in Paris in 1957. The analysis extends chronologically from THE PLEASURE GARDEN (1925) to THE WRONG MAN (1957) and emphasizes the recurrent themes of the films. A filmography, illustrations, and an index complete the book.

Acknowledged by most critics to be the first serious study of Hitchcock's films, this volume is slightly diminished by the many subsequent writers who borrowed heavily from it and wrote Hitchcock criticism in English language books first. Nevertheless, this is a pioneer volume of film criticism whose English translation and publication is a welcome event.

2904 *Hitchcock's British Films.* by Yacowar, Maurice. 314 p. illus. Hamden, Conn.: Archon Books, 1977.

This volume offers a provocative analysis of each of the 23 feature films that Alfred Hitchcock made prior to his arrival in America in 1939 to direct REBECCA (1940). Beginning with THE PLEASURE GARDEN (1925), each of the films receives a detailed description and analysis. By the time the final British film, JAMAICA INN (1939), is reached, the author has traced many of the themes, techniques, characters, and plot structures that recur in the later Hitchcock films. A final chapter summarizes the author's findings, observations, and conclusions while the appendix offers some possible interpretations of Hitchcock's well-known appearances in his own films. Some notes, selected film stills, and an index support the text.

Since most of the other Hitchcock volumes emphasize his later films, it is rewarding to find a volume which deals effectively with the artist's formative years. Yacowar has provided some unique and often vulnerable readings of the films; as a result, anyone familiar with the post-40s Hitchcock films will be stimulated and ultimately enriched by reading this work. Recommended.

2905 *Hitchcock's Films.* by Wood, Robin. 204 p. paper illus. New York: A. S. Barnes, 1969.

After an introduction in which many of Hitchcock's films are discussed, the author offers one chapter of very detailed analysis for each of the following films STRANGERS ON A TRAIN (1951), REAR WINDOW (1954), VERTIGO (1958), NORTH BY NORTHWEST (1959), PSYCHO (1960), THE BIRDS (1963), MARNIE (1964), and TORN CURTAIN (1966).

Some of the opinions/analysis presented are not found in other volumes on Hitchcock. For example, the author's argument that VERTIGO is Hitchcock's masterpiece to date, or MARNIE is "one of Hitchcock's richest, most fully achieved and mature masterpieces" may surprise readers. The arguments offered to back up such statements are very stimulating. There is more text than pictures in this book and the edition examined had many of the picture captions cut off. The book is an interesting, valid addition to the number of volumes on Hitchcock, and, as such, is recommended.

2906 *Holly-Would!* by Hagen, John Milton. 254 p. illus. New Rochelle, N.Y.: Arlington, 1974.

The old-style gossip columns are recalled by the collection of over 2500 short paragraphs or single sentences about Hollywood and its personalities offered in this volume. Most of these were the exaggerations or fabrications of studio publicity departments or press agents and had little to do with reality. They were trivial but seemed to satisfy the continual need of their readers for information about Hollywood and its stars. For example, "Genevieve Tobin designs her own gowns—except those she wears in pictures." "Spencer Tracy ran out of the theater when he saw himself for the first time on the screen. Lucky his audiences don't do it!" More than 100 full-page line illustrations and portraits drawn by Frederic (Feg) Murray are added as visualizations of the same type of material.

A few of the blurbs are fun to read, but after several pages they soon become tiresome, predictable and redundant. The visuals provide some variation, but an entire meal of verbal appetizers is not all-satisfying. Acceptable.

2907 *Hollywood: The Movie Colony; The Movie Makers.* by Rosten, Leo C. 436 p. New York: Harcourt Brace, 1941.

A serious sociological study of pre-1940 Hollywood, this book consists of two major sections and a concluding chapter about Hollywood's effect on the world's people and countries. The first section, entitled "The Movie Colony," examines the life of Hollywood—its activities, goals, values, social structure, and attitudes. In the second section, "The Movie Makers," four creative groups are examined —producers, directors, actors, and writers.

The sophisticated film buff of today will probably be familiar with the external coverage provided here. By reading many of the more recent biographies and studies, a reader would be much more acquainted with the actual inner workings of the Hollywood of the twenties and thirties. There is a certain nostalgic value along with some still pertinent sociological/anthropological truths that may interest some readers. Much of the factual data, of course, is no longer valid. A book for screen historians and other specialized audiences.

2908 *Hollywood: The Golden Era.* by Spears, Jack. 440 p. illus. New York: A. S. Barnes, 1971.

The title of this fine volume may be misleading to some readers. A collection of 12 articles which originally appeared in *Films in Review* has been updated and revised with impressive results. Chapters are devoted to surveys of films dealing with World War I, comic strips, baseball, doctors, and the Indian. Other chapters deal with the work of Max Linder, Norma Talmadge, Colleen Moore, Marshall Neilan and Robert Florey. Other sections deal with Mary Pickford's directors and Chaplin's collaborators.

The book has separate indexes for films and subjects and offers filmographies for Talmadge, Florey, Neilan and Moore. Illustrations are fascinating in content but small in size and only fairly reproduced. The care with which the author has selected his subjects and the thoroughness of his work are evident throughout. Here is a fine example of scholarly writing/research made into fascinating reading by the ability of the author. Highly recommended.

2909 *Hollywood.* by Kanin, Garson. 401 p. New York: Viking, 1974.

In 1937 at the age of 24, Garson Kanin was brought to Hollywood by Samuel Goldwyn "to learn the business." In this volume he recalls his experiences with diverse industry personalities listed in the subtitle as "Stars and Starlets, Tycoons and Flesh Peddlers, Movie-Makers and Money-Makers, Frauds and Geniuses, Hopefuls and Has-beens, Great Lovers and Sex Symbols."

Kanin is known as a Broadway playwright, a film director, a writer of screenplays and a book author. His ability to recall the past combined with his considerable literary skill results in an entertaining, gossipy collection of anecdotes about Hollywood's Golden Era and its personalities. Although most of the content seems familiar, the style of the storyteller makes it worthwhile reading. Acceptable.

2910 *Hollywood: Land and Legend.* by Cini, Zelda; and Crane, Bob; and Brown, Peter. 192 p. illus. Westport, Conn.: Arlington House, 1980.

In a sense this is a companion volume to Edwin Palmer's *History of Hollywood*. Both trace the history of that geographical area in California called "Hollywood." Palmer's book, which ends in 1938, is more academically detailed, while this attractive study is primarily visual. In a terse text, the authors trace the rise and fall of this community from the turn of the century to its present status as a pop music center. The land is used differently today, but the legend formulated during the first half of this century persists. It is to that legend that this book addresses itself, as it reviews the silent era, the golden era, and the war years. Bittersweet in its content and tone, the volume should have enormous appeal to those who "grew up" with the Hollywood of legend.

2911 *Hollywood: The First 100 Years.* by Torrence, Bruce. 288 p. illus. New York: Zoetrope, 1981.

A collection of 300 photographs taken from the author's private collection which detail the history of the city of Hollywood.

2912 *Hollywood According to Hollywood.* by Barris, Alex. 212 p. illus. New York: A.S. Barnes, 1978.

To begin this survey of films about Hollywood, Jim Backus in HOLLYWOOD STORY (1951) is quoted: "Backstage stories are okay but back-camera stories are absolutely no good." The author then goes on to describe hundreds of films which disprove the Backus statement. An attempt to separate the films into nine thematic groups—dream machine, expose, satire, recycles, biography, etc.—is only partially successful. A chronological history which offered some observation on the changing self-image of Hollywood and its people might have been more appropriate. The detailed index provided is most helpful in locating titles and names.

The selection of films and the accompanying critical comment is rich in nostalgia, offering evidence of Hollywood's frequent self-interest. The many clearly reproduced stills add to the enjoyment most readers will find here. Alex Barris proves that back-camera stories are indeed okay.

2913 *Hollywood Album.* illus. London: Sampson Low Marston, 1947- .

An annual that deals with "the wonderful city and its famous inhabitants." The 14th volume (1960) contained articles such as: "The Great Challenge" (Tony Curtis), "Things I Do for Fun" (Robert Taylor), "Trips and Treasures" (Ann Baxter), "What Next?" (Troy Donahue), etc. There are many full-page portraits, some of which are in color.

2914 *Hollywood Album.* edited by Keylin, Arleen; and Fleischer, Suri. 312 p. illus. New York: Arno, 1977.

As indicated in its subtitle, "Lives and Deaths of Hollywood Stars from the Pages of the *New York Times*," this volume is a combination of necrology and collective biography. The *New York Times* usually publishes the equivalent of a feature article upon the death of a well-known or important personage, and more than 200 such obituary articles are included in this unusual collection.

Arranged alphabetically by subject surname, they cover the period from 1926 (Valentino) to 1977 (Crawford). Each article consists of one or more illustrations and a mostly factual biographical essay that still manages to convey the subject's special appeal for audiences. Total filmographies taken from *The New York Times Film Review Index* for each subject appear in a final section.

Aside from the nostalgic appeal of these biographies, the book offers a wealth of factual data that cannot be found elsewhere. For example, the user will find extensive biographical information on Claude Rains, Edward Everett Horton, Brian Donlevy, Jeff Chandler and others who have not yet been subjects for book biographies.

Although the name does not adequately convey the content, this is a fine volume for both the reader and the reference shelf. Recommended.

2915 *Hollywood Album Two.* edited by New York Times. illus. New York: Times Books, 1978.

The follow-up to the original necrology made up of *New York Times* obituaries, this volume adds over 150 more film personalities to the collection.

2916 *Hollywood and After.* by Toeplitz, Jerzy. 288 p. paper illus. Chicago: Henry Regnery, 1975.

Subtitled "The Changing Face of Movies in America," this volume is a translation of the original, which was published in Polish as *Nowy Film Amerykanski.* It is concerned with the changes that have occurred lately in both the American film industry and in its product. The disappearance of the major studios, the replacement of moguls by corporate boards, the marriage between television and the film industry—all these factors have led to a hybrid product that shows some new characteristics and some traces of the old. That the dream has been overhauled, revitalized, reduced and redesigned is the author's theme. Emphasis is given to today's creative actors, directors, writers and to some of the possible trends and omens for the future.

The book contains a good collection of film stills in a center section and there are three separate indexes (film, name and general) along with bibliographic notes at the book's end. The volume has been well researched and is written with a rather serious, pedantic style. While the reader may not always agree with Toeplitz, it is fascinating to read and consider comment and criticism on American films by a qualified European film historian. Although the author has made two short visits to Hollywood, he is essentially an outside observer. Recommended.

2917 *Hollywood and Moving Pictures for Those Planning a Film Career.* by Reimherr, Herbert. 84 p. paper illus. Los Angeles: David Graham Fischer, 1932.

Depression-period advice on how to break into the movies. Includes photos of thirties film stars and treats topics such as qualifications, abilities, acting, studio politics, rackets, etc.

2918 *Hollywood and the Academy Awards.* by Fredrik, Nathalie. 203 p. illus. Los Angeles: Award Publications, 1968.

After a thankfully short foreword by Bob Hope, a description of the Academy Awards is given. A chart showing the major category winners (excluding directors) serves as a table of contents. For each year from 1927 to 1967, the best film and the four acting awards are listed along with a paragraph of comment on each. (From 1927 to 1935 no awards were given for supporting players.) Winners in other categories are listed in tabular form after each 10 year period.

The omission of the direction awards in the text is a major flaw; not as serious but also diminishing the book's value is the lack of foreign picture awards, documentary awards, short subject awards, etc. Written in fan magazine style, the text is more bland than critical. Pictures used are acceptable but very familiar. The volume seems to aim at both popular appeal and reference and does not really succeed either way. Recommended as a partial reference. Certain readers may enjoy it too.

2919 *Hollywood and the American Image.* by Thomas, Tony. 192 p. illus. Westport, Conn.: Arlington House, 1981.

2920 *Hollywood and the Great Fan Magazines.* edited by Levin, Martin. 224 p. illus. New York: Arbor House, 1970.

This book is a collection of movie star articles taken from fan magazines such as *Photoplay, Motion Picture, Silver Screen, Screenland, Screen Book* and *Modern Screen.* It resembles an oversize anniversary issue of any of the above. The major portion of the inane "camp" articles stems from the thirties, with some small samplings from the twenties and forties and they read like the product of studio publicity departments. In most cases the content is predictable, dull, and noncontroversial.

Reproduction of the photographs is below average and there is no index. An unnecessary emphasis on text is evidenced by the last 50 pages, which consist totally of print— no illustrations, titles, etc. As a sociological document, this book may have some slight value. It fails badly as nostalgia. Other than a very rapid browsing, most readers won't bother with the silly text. A fine book about fan magazines is possible but this is not it.

2921 *Hollywood and the Great Stars.* edited by Pascall, Jeremy. 256 p. illus. London: Phoebus, 1976.

This historical survey, which was taken from previously published material, deals with "The Stars, The

Sex Symbols, The Legend, The Movies, and How It All Began." Some of the illustrations are in full color.

2922   *Hollywood and the Movies.* by Lane, Tamer; and Lane, Anabel. 98 p. paper illus. Hollywood: Mercury, 1930.

A collection of miscellaneous writings about the Hollywood film colony, its people and its pictures. Includes many full-page drawings and portraits of film stars and directors of the early thirties—Garbo, Barrymore, Griffith, Swanson, etc.

2923   *Hollywood As a World Center.* by Sheehen, Perley P. 115 p. paper Hollywood: Hollywood Citizen Press, 1924.

2924   *Hollywood As It Really Is.* by Debries, Erwin. illus. London: Routledge, 1930.

Contains 60 pictures with an introduction and explanation. A title in the *Seen by the Camera* series.

2925   *Hollywood at Sunset.* by Higham, Charles. 181 p. illus. New York: Saturday Review Press, 1972.

The reference in Higham's title is to the period from 1946 to 1971, a sunset lasting a quarter century and not altogether invisible even now. In 1946 the highest yearly attendance at films in the United States was recorded. Immediately thereafter a series of events occurred which contributed to the demise of a business system that had been enormously successful for nearly three decades. A temporary loss of the European market, govenment actions which ended block booking and theatre ownership by distributors/producers, and the investigations of Communism in Hollywood Studios by the House Un-American Activities Committee are cited as destructive factors appearing in the late forties. Television and post-war leisure habit changes were felt in the early fifties. Experiments in wide screen, 3-D, or Cinerama processes did not bring the lost audiences back. Blockbuster films such as CLEOPARTRA (1963) and MUTINY ON THE BOUNTY (1962) debilitated the studios even more, making them easy acquisitions for agencies, conglomerates and other Wall Street tenacles. The auctions at the MGM and Fox Studios close the book on a sad and melancholy note.

Short biographical sketches of the men behind the scenes—studio heads, 3-D inventors, agency presidents, etc.—are placed in the appropriate chronology of the story and these brief portraits give the book its strength. Higham is not nearly so effective when he evaluates films since he offers only subjective opinion without corroborating argument: "Jerry Lewis' THE NUTTY PROFESSOR (1963)—an inspired comedy that was a witty exception to such inane films as BREAKFAST AT TIFFANYS (1961)."

A short center pictorial section shows a few of the major characters discussed in the text. Why the book is without a table of contents and an index is a mystery. Segments of Higham's material are certainly most pertinent to students and scholars and their retrieval from the book in its present form is quite difficult. There is much to appreciate here but one wishes there had been a firmer editorial hand; the book could have and should have been better.

2926   *Hollywood at the Crossroads.* by Bernstein, Irving. 78 p. paper Hollywood, 1957.

An economic study of the motion picture industry prepared for the Hollywood American Federation of Labor Film Council.

2927   *Hollywood at War.* by Jones, Ken D.; and McClure, Authur F. 320 p. illus. New York: A. S. Barnes, 1973.

According to the authors, one third of all Hollywood features produced between 1942 and 1945 could be termed war films. It is that period which receives major attention in this book. Over 400 war films—including a few pre-1942 ones—are covered by giving complete casts, studio, director, and release date, in addition to a still from each. The films are introduced by a rather perfunctory essay on Hollywood and the war effort.

It is difficult to find a rationale for the final form of this volume. Certainly the subject is a valid, exciting one around which to build a narrative-pictorial essay; to cover the period and some 400 examples in a 10-page introduction devoted mostly to a retelling of plots is a disservice. Space used for cast listings could have been used for critical comment, evaluation, observation, etc. The visuals are effective and deserve stronger support from the text. The book's reference value is minimal since there is no index or listing of the films. A potentially good book has been made ineffective and almost valueless by the treatment accorded it. Of limited interest.

2928   *Hollywood Babylon.* by Anger, Kenneth. 271 p. paper illus. Phoenix, Ariz.: Assoc. Professional Services, 1965.

Scandal, gossip, innuendo, *Confidential* magazine material, shock words, pornography, depths of bad taste, depravity, sin, shock. All of these terms apply to this book. Published before our current era of freedom, this volume has been an "underground" bestseller. Its subject is the public and private scandals of Hollywood. In most cases names are used and, where they are not, a picture of the probable subject appears on the following page, with some innocuous caption.

Although it is enormously popular with a portion of the general audience, the book certainly should also be known to historians, films students, and sociologists. All prospective readers should receive some warning about the content. The author is a filmmaker, best known for SCORPIO RISING (1963).

2929 *Hollywood Babylon.* by Anger, Kenneth. 305 p. illus. San Francisco: Straight Arrow, 1975.

More than a decade ago, Kenneth Anger, the underground filmmaker known for films such as FIREWORKS (1947) and SCORPIO RISING (1963), wrote *Hollywood Babylon* for a French publisher, Jean Jacques Pauvert. According to Anger it was pirated by an American porno publisher, Marvin Miller, and subsequently became a paperback bestseller. The author received no royalties from the tremendous sale of the pirated version. For several years now, an authorized edition in English has been promised. The difficulties in adapting the original work into a book acceptable for mass distribution and advertising were probably extensive.

The basic text remains the same, but many additions, deletions and word changes are obvious. Anger is concerned with a history of Hollywood's public and private scandals. In addition to reviewing those of public record, he employs hint, innuendo, rumor and suggestion to indicate some possible private scandals. His text is arranged chronologically, and covers the silent screen era first. New material on Garland, Turner, Mansfield, and others is included in the closing sections. As indicated above, much of the earlier sensationalized shocking material has been eliminated. Substituted is a more careful, very considered text and a fascinating collection of photographs which indicate diligent searching and wary selection. The care taken in their sharp reproduction is most commendable. Although they supplement the text, their presentation and use are major contributions to the book.

In summary, *Hollywood Babylon* is no longer what it used to be. In an apparent move away from pseudo-porno toward respectable gossip mongering, the sensationalism has been severely toned down.

Thankfully, it has been replaced by an intelligent text that deals in surprises and titillations rather than shock. The set of illustrations used this time around more than justifies the acquisition of this book. Recommended.

2930 *The Hollywood Beauties.* by Parish, James Robert; and Mank, Gregory W.; and Stanke, Don E. 476 p. illus. New Rochelle, N.Y.: Arlington House, 1978.

It is hard to resist the work of Parish and his cohorts. They select the most popular/legendary screen personalities, and then with some in-depth research and analysis, come up with biographies that present a mostly factual, nonsensationalized portrait of the public and private life of each subject. Here they are concerned with Delores Del Rio, Kay Francis, Ava Gardner, Jean Harlow, Grace Kelly, Elizabeth Taylor, and Lana Turner.

In each case a long biographical portrait is supplemented by many visuals and a detailed filmography. Selection of information and pictures is done with taste and discrimination, with much additional care apparently given to factual accuracy and name-spelling. As a reliable reference or simply as a rewarding recall of some fascinating females and their lives, this volume is most satisfying. As with the other books in this series, it should please a wide audience.

2931 *Hollywood by Starlight.* by Minney, R. J. 260 p. illus. London: Chapman and Hall, 1935.

A writer's experiences in Hollywood with such personalities as Chaplin, Zanuck, Disney, Shirley Temple, etc.

2932 *The Hollywood Cage.* by Hamblett, Charles. 450 p. illus. New York: Hart Pub. Co., 1969.

An attempt to give a sensationalized portrait of "the Hollywood that killed Marilyn Monroe," this volume resembles one of those terrible films that everyone enjoys. Based on interviews and observations made when he was a Hollywood correspondent for London newspapers, the total image presented is negative, jaded, corrupt, and rather sick. The validity of this one-sided view is suspect—wasn't there anyone to qualify as a nice, pleasant human being?

The major interest rests in the informal portraits of the personalities; some are very brief while others are given much coverage—Monroe and Novak have the last 100 pages devoted almost exclusively to them. Appropriately, many candid photographs accompany the text. There is an index. The book is a mixture of good and bad. Some of it is superior writing while other portions are trash. As a gossip-scandal book, this volume would enjoy much reader popularity. Serious readers will have to sift a lot of dross to find the nuggets.

2933   *Hollywood Cameramen.* by Higham, Charles. 176 p. illus. Bloomington, Ind.: Indiana University Press, 1970.

A collection of interviews with cameramen, this unusual volume spotlights their contribution to filmmaking. The subjects are Stanley Cortez, William Daniels, Lee Garmes, James Wong Howe, Arthur Miller, Leon Shamroy and Karl Struss. The interviews are in the form of statements rather than questions and answers. Illustrations and a filmography for each are included. Another superior contribution from Higham.

2934   *Hollywood Cesspool: A Startling Survey of Movieland Lives and Morals, Pictures and Results.* by Sumner, Robert L. 284 p. illus. Wheaton, Ill.: Sword of the Lord, 1955.

The author is an evangelist who gives a picture of Hollywood as he sees it—a community of loose-living, morally decadent citizens. Predictably, he rages against smoking, drinking, divorce, dope, etc. An index of personalities is provided.

2935   *Hollywood Character Actors.* by Parish, James Robert. 542 p. illus. New Rochelle, N.Y.: Arlington House, 1978.

The problem of where to locate a biography-filmography for character actors such as Abner Biberman, Samuel S. Hinds, or Maude Eburne has been resolved nicely with the publication of this large collective biography. Performers (372) are arranged in alphabetical order and for each there is a photograph, their original name, a short biographical section (dates, marriages, divorces, children, character type), a classic line of dialogue from one of their films, and a complete filmography of feature films made (title, date, and studio are given).

There is much to be appreciated about this book—its comprehensiveness, the obvious affection for the players that is reflected in the short biographical comments, and the quality production given the book by the publisher. A few reservations must be noted, however. Instead of emphasizing portraits of

the players as was done in *Who Is That?*, *The Versatiles*, and *Character People*, the authors have made frequent use of stills showing several actors with the subject not being especially prominent. For example, recognition of Alan Dinehart, Regis Toomey, Torin Thatcher, Clarence Muse, Una Merkel, Vladimir Sokoloff, etc., may be difficult for the person who is not a film buff or a trivia expert. In this same vein, selection of the visuals is not consistently strong, with a mixture of good portraits, some fine stills and some others in which the faces are too small or nontypical of the character subject.

The inclusion of a "classic" line of dialogue for each actor may be questionable. For whom is this information intended, how much does it add to the biography, and what is the criteria for a "classic" line? To be so named, shouldn't the dialogue bring an instant mental picture of the actor who said it originally—i.e. "Nobody's perfect...," "I steal...," "Peel me a grape...," "My little chickadee...," "Who's on first?..," "This is Mrs. Norman Maine...."

The reader who is searching for information on Hollywood character actors will find an abundance in this volume. It is a most useful reference tool and is recommended.

2936   *Hollywood Collects.* by Otis Art Institute. pages unnumbered. paper illus. Los Angeles: Otis Art Institute 1970.

This volume is a catalog of an exhibition entitled "Hollywood Collects" sponsored by the Otis Art Institute in early 1970. An excellent introduction by Henry J. Seldis discusses the activities, philosophies and attitudes of various film personalities toward art collection. The book itself contains both plates of the works exhibited and photographs of the homes of the collectors. Beautifully produced, the book is a visual delight. It is a most pleasurable look at a side of Hollywood life that is relatively unknown.

2937   *Hollywood Color Portraits.* edited by Kobal, John. 157 p. illus. New York: William Morrow, 1981.

Seventy-four, full-page, full-color photographs from late 1930's to late 1950's. Kobal supplies comments to the portraits and Carlos Clarens provides an unrelated history of color motion picture film. The visuals provide the pleasure here.

2938   *Hollywood Confidential.* edited by Hirsch, Phil 222 p. paper New York: Pyramid Books, 1967.

A series of articles on Hollywood stars reprinted

from *Man's Magazine* this collection has chapters on Robert Mitchum, Lee Marvin, Alan Ladd, Jack Carter, Jack Palance, Marlon Brando, David Niven, George C. Scott, and Peter O'Toole. Two ladies, Judy Garland and Barbara Payton, share this company. The article on Payton is an extended one—55 pages.

Each article tries to use sensationalism for a teaser, but inevitably becomes biographical. Written for a nondemanding audience, the style is spare and nonintellectual. Since biographical or background data is not easily available on some of the above personalities, the book may be of interest. In summary, a book designed for one audience which ultimately has some pertinence for another.

2939 *Hollywood Confidential.* by Feinman, Jeffrey. 205 p. paper illus. Chicago: Playboy Press, 1976.

A summary of well publicized Hollywood scandals is presented under headings such as: drugs (Garland, Wally Reid, Jeanne Eagels, Robert Walker), suicide (Paul Bern, Lupe Velez, Monroe, Dorothy Dandridge), gangsters (Bugsy Siegel, Mickey Cohen), murder (Fatty Arbuckle, William Desmond Taylor, Thomas Ince, Ramon Novarro), lovers (Valentino, Chaplin, Clara Bow, Marion Davies), marriage (Clark Gable, Lana Turner), gossip (Louella Parsons, Hedda Hopper) and others. Since so much is covered and all of it depends upon previous books and public record, the volume reads like a tired rehash of the overly familiar. The author owes a debt to Kenneth Anger whose book, *Hollywood Babylon*, is quoted frequently.

Interested readers are referred to the latter volume for the final word in Hollywood scandal mongering.

2940 *Hollywood Corral.* by Miller, Don. 255 p. paper illus. New York: Popular Library, 1976.

The concern of this volume is the low budget or "B" western that was the staple of movie house matinees during the thirties and forties and of television later on. Starting in 1929 with Hoot Gibson, Ken Maynard, and Tom Mix, the author traces the history of this sub-genre via descriptions of films and personalities. The appearance of "Gunsmoke" on television in 1955 signaled the end of the "B" western. Among the many stars who played roles in these films were Randolph Scott, Robert Mitchum, John Wayne, Buster Crabbe, and William Boyd, and they, along with hundreds of other actors, are discussed in the text.

The nostalgic journey provided is accompanied by many well-reproduced stills. Unfortunately the book is not indexed so its reference value is limited. Acceptable.

2941 *Hollywood Costume.* by McConathy, Dale; and Vreeland, Diana. 317 p. illus. New York: Harry N. Abrams, 1976.

There is a richness and opulence about this volume that will remind readers of the elegance and taste once found in many Hollywood movies. Using as a base the costumes assembled for the Metropolitan Museum of Art's show, "Romantic and Glamorous Hollywood Design," the authors have created a historical survey of a relatively unappreciated aesthetic of filmmaking. They have divided their book into seven decade chapters, using examples of costume design to explain the art as evidenced in the films of each period. Much more is offered, however, than the book's title would indicate. The films and personalities indigenous to each period define the societal setting of our recent past. Biographical data, critical comment, quotations from interviews, background information, and a supporting bibliography are also included.

Excellent as all these text elements are, it will be the illustrations that most readers will cherish. Carefully selected to correlate with the text, the visuals are uniformly excellent in content and reproduction. Especially beautiful are the color plates made from the Museum's show by fashion photographer Keith Trumbo. They are carefully identified and present a version of that exhibition which probably has some advantage over personal attendance because of proximity, eye location, emphasis, etc. Other visuals include portraits, stills, and publicity shots. Biographical notes on the designers represented and an index complete the book.

The subtitle, "Glamour! Glitter! Romance!," is certainly appropriate, but the book is a great deal more. Within its eye-catching brocaded cloth covers, there is an adroit blending of intelligent text with attractive photographs; it is a multifaceted survey that offers a superb description of the art of costume design set against a background of films, performers, history, and societal effects. The result is a volume that is certain to attract and please a large audience. Highly recommended.

2942 *Hollywood Costume Design.* by Chierichetti, David. 192 p. illus. New York: Harmony, 1977.

A somewhat different approach than that used in *Hollywood Costume* is employed in this tribute to the world of Hollywood film fashion. After a brief introduction, the major Hollywood studios—MGM, Paramount, Warners, Fox, RKO, Columbia, Universal—and the independents—receive individual attention. The stars, designers, and the fashions that emanated from each studio are discussed and often shown.

The text is interesting and often enlightening but most readers will be more attracted by the abundant supply of beautiful visuals that the author uses to illustrate his words. Selected with care and discrimination, they are clearly reproduced in adequate size. Some appear in color. The reference value of the book is increased by filmographies for the major designers and a detailed index.

Here we have a visually exciting book that is enhanced by an informed text and several good reference features. It should appeal to a wide audience on levels such as art, fashion, memorabilia, history, buff, and photography. Highly recommended.

2943 *Hollywood Director.* by Chierichetti, David. 398 p. paper illus. New York: Curtis, 1973.

Mitchell Leisen is the subject of this exploration of a major Hollywood director. Starting as a costume designer for Cecil B. DeMille in 1919, Leisen became a set designer, art director and finally assistant director. By 1932 he was ready to assume the responsibility of a film director. His career is traced by examining all his films up to 1957 in depth. A few final pages are devoted to his television work. The emphasis in this volume is on the career rather than the personal life of the subject, although there is enough biography given to satisfy most readers. It is the detail and the in-depth explorations of the films that are remarkable. Done as oral history under a grant from the American Film Institute, the material comes mostly from Leisen himself, with short contributions from many creative people who were involved in his films, his career or his life.

A fine collection of visuals supports this oral history, as does a rather detailed filmography. The book is not indexed. Because there is so much original data, information, and opinion offered, this omission is unfortunate, for it weakens the book's reference value. The lack of an index, however, should not deter anyone from acquiring the book. As a study of both a man and a period, it is highly successful, and is unique for this genre of film book. Most of it has the ring of truth and is told with sensitivity; when its detail and depth are considered, that is no small achievement. A volume as professionally and emotionally rewarding as this one is not only a tribute to Leisen, but should also be a great satisfaction to the author and the AFI. Highly recommended.

2944 *Hollywood Directors: 1914-1940.* edited by Koszarski, Richard. 364 p. paper illus. New York: Oxford University Press, 1976.

This anthology contains 50 articles written by American film directors during the period 1914 to 1939. Arranged in chronological order, they appear under four headings: Pioneers, 1914-1920; Silent Age, 1921-1927; Transition to Sound, 1928-1933; and The Dream Factory, 1934-1940. In addition to an opening statement, the author has provided a full-page introduction to each essay. Some illustrations, an index, and a foreword by Francois Truffaut complete the book.

A reading of this volume may serve well in studying any of the general areas of motion pictures—history, aesthetics, theory, filmmaking, and personalities. The selection of the contents has been made with care and the introductions provide a helpful frame for greater appreciation of the articles. Acceptable.

2945 *Hollywood Directors: 1941-1976.* edited by Koszarski, Richard. 426 p. illus. New York: Oxford University Press, 1977.

Richard Koszarski continues the work of his previous volume, which covered the 1914-1940 period. It again consists of articles written by directors about themselves, their views, and one or more of their films. A short page of background information introduces each piece. The 50 subjects range from Orson Welles to Michael Ritchie. Photographs and a detailed index are added.

As with most anthologies, the appeal of the articles varies. Writing style, subject, articulation, self-perception, and wit are some of the factors that affect the quality of the essays.

2946 *The Hollywood Epic.* by Hirsch, Foster. 129 p. illus. New York: A.S. Barnes, 1978.

In this genre study, Foster Hirsch first discusses the history and style of epic films. He describes their vastness, scale, heroism, emphasis on action and movement, and external characterization. Then he subdivides the genre into foreign, moral, religious, national and historical epics. Final chapters are devoted to the epic hero and to some films that do not qualify as epics. The book is heavily illustrated and offers a bibliography, a filmography, and an index.

Hirsch's approach to this Hollywood staple is sensible, selective, and objective. He has chosen some fine examples of the genre and analyzed them with critical skill. This is a rewarding study.

2947 *The Hollywood Exiles.* by Baxter, John. 242 p. illus. New York: Taplinger, 1976.

Employing his fine critical perception, a definitive writing skill, and his wide knowledge of film, John Baxter has created an unusual book about the foreign filmmakers who came to Hollywood during its golden years of 1930-1950. With diverse backgrounds and experiences obtained in their native European countries, these artists arrived in America seeking fortune and fame. Their effect on Hollywood and its impact on them is related in a detailed, absorbing narrative. Prominent among the many personalities discussed are Bertholt Brecht, Chaplin, Dietrich, Garbo, Emil Jannings, Fritz Lang, Stan Laurel, Ernst Lubitsch, Pola Negri, Max Reinhardt, Josef von Sternberg, Karl Zuckmayer, and Adolph Zukor.

The author is quite thorough in his research of the period and he has provided a fine collection of rare photographs to support his text. Source notes, a name index, and a title index complete the book.

A different and rather unique exploration of one facet of Hollywood during its heyday is provided here. The book, which has been carefully written and beautifully produced, warrants the attention of film buffs, historians, scholars, and students. It will also delight and please the general reader. Recommended.

2948 *Hollywood Film Acting.* by Noose, Theodore, 176 p. New York: A.S. Barnes, 1979.

With this work Theodore Noose has written an acting guidebook for the beginner in motion pictures and television. He divides his text into the craft (characterization, physical senses, moods and emotions, dialogue, delivery, auditions) and the business (agents, casting directors, studios, production houses, the average workday). All of this is preceded by a lengthy introduction which offers a generalized description of the Hollywood acting business. A summary, a glossary, and an index conclude the book.

The text the author provides is written largely from his own impressive experience as an actor along with suggestions made to him by others in the business. The result is an economical distillation of facts, practical advice, and guidance that will inform and may inspire the novice.

2949 *Hollywood Film Production Manual.* paper Burbank, Calif.: Arejay Sales, 1972.

Originally published in 1954, this loose-leaf binder contains a wide variey of information about the preparation of production budgets. Included are labor contracts, rate schedules for equipment, wages, transportation, etc. Locales covered are Hollywood, New York City, and Mexico. Supplements noting changes are available on an annual basis by subscription.

2950 *Hollywood Genres: Formulas, Filmmaking and the Studio System.* by Schatz, Thomas. 297 p. illus. Philadelphia: Temple University Press, 1981.

Genre films made from 1930 to 1960 are examined. The author concludes the studio's need for box-office films perpetuated genre films—imitations of previous successes. Audiences, too, learned to compare the films with their predecessors. This is a very good explanation and exploration of genre films.

2951 *Hollywood Glamor Portraits.* edited by Kobal, John. 144 p. paper illus. New York: Dover, 1976.

The subtitle of this volume explains it nicely: "145 Photos of Stars 1926-1949." An introduction and statements by five photographers about their careers introduce the gallery of portraits. Arranged in a somewhat chronological fashion, the visuals are all carefully reproduced and provide a reminder of the artistry of studio photographers and the beauty of their subjects. A handsomely produced book that can be recommended.

2952 *Hollywood Goes to War—Films and American Society 1939-1952.* by Shinder, Colin. 152 p. illus. Boston: Routledge and Kegan Paul, 1979.

The role of films in an American society before, during and after World War II is the announced topic of this book. Once again the question of movies as a reflection or as a shaper of society is raised. With noble goals such as these, it is unfortunate that the author was not able to discipline his approach to such a serious study by eliminating attempts at humor and nonpertinent, pro-British critical asides. Debating the contributions of each nation to the winning of World War II belongs in another volume, and belittling with a 1980 film sophistication some forties' films which were made for a specific wartime purpose seems like taking cheap shots.

The book has received a superior production exemplified by many clearly reproduced illustrations, a high quality paper and an attractive cover. There are notes, a bibliography, and an index to support the subjective text.

Although Shindler's text is weakened by the above-mentioned personal indulgences, the attempt to analyze a specific period of American history through its films provides some provocative if vulnerable arguments. The author gives his interpretations based on secondary sources. Those who were here will probably recall the period quite differently.

2953 *Hollywood Gold: The Award Winning Movies.* by Pickard, Roy. 252 p. paper illus. New York: Taplinger, 1979.

A paperback version of *The Oscar Movies From A-Z,* this volume differs only in the addition of the 1977 winners.

2954 *The Hollywood Greats.* by Horman, Barry. 272 p. illus. New York: Franklin Watts, 1980.

This collective biography derives from scripts of a BBC television series, "The Hollywood Greats." In addition to a retelling of the lives of its ten subjects, the volume gives attention to the Hollywood background in which the stars existed. Based in part on interviews, the text treats the eccentricities and behavior of its subjects objectively but with a sensitivity based on admiration and affection. Each profile runs 25 pages and includes some full-page photographs. The stars selected for this volume are Clark Gable, Spencer Tracy, Gary Cooper, Humphrey Bogart, Joan Crawford, Ronald Colman, Jean Harlow, Judy Garland, and Charles Laughton. Detailed individual biographies have already been published for each of these actors, and since nothing new is offered here, the reader may question the publication of more of the same.

2955 *The Hollywood Hallucination.* by Tyler, Parker. 246 p. New York: Creative Age Press, 1944.

Parker Tyler, one of the first film writers to consider motion pictures as an art form, voices strong opinions in this series of essays. Written in the forties, much of what he writes is still provocative and interesting. He chooses as topics most of the classic films of the period. Not always logical and at times lacking clarity, Tyler is still a master critic of the film art. Recommended as film criticism written well ahead of its time.

2956 *Hollywood Hussar: The Life and Times of John Loder.* by Loder, John. 178 p. illus. London: Howard Baker, 1977.

John Loder appeared in many British and American films from THE FIRSTBORN (1928) to THE FIRECHASERS (1970). During the thirties, at the peak of his popularity, he usually played the handsome hero role. His Hollywood films include HOW GREEN WAS MY VALLEY (1941), DARK VICTORY (1942), and DISHONORED LADY (1947). After his career faded, he retired to Argentina. This autobiography is illustrated and indexed.

2957 *Hollywood in a Suitcase.* by Davis, Sammy, Jr. 254 p. illus. New York: William Morrow, 1980.

In this collection of anecdotes about his "close personal friends," Sammy Davis, Jr. takes on the role of a friendly gossip columnist. Garland, Bogart, Burton, Taylor, and Presley are subjects, along with Sinatra, Wayne, Lawford, Goldwyn, Martin, Eastwood, Monroe and many others. If you care about the author's personal feelings, attitudes, opinions and comments, the book will have appeal. It does reveal a lot about Sammy Davis, Jr.

2958 *Hollywood in Fiction: Some Versions of the American Myth.* by Spatz, Jonas. 148 p. paper The Hague: Mouton, 1969.

A title in the *Studies in American Literature* series, this volume deals historically and critically with the portrait of Hollywood presented in selected American fiction. A bibliography is included.

2959 *Hollywood in the Forties.* by Higham, Charles; and Greenberg, Joel. 192 p. paper illus. New York: A. S. Barnes, 1968.

A review of many films of the forties, this book groups the films by genre—war, comedy, musical, etc. The evaluations of certain films—VICTORY (1940), THE SEA WOLF (1941), THE WOMAN IN WHITE (1948), etc.—are surprising and may whet the reader's appetite for a re-viewing, and reconsideration. Because many of the films appear on TV, the book is current, stimulating reading and can serve as a partial reference. Illustrations are interesting but it is the text that is the book's major asset. Highly recommended for all readers.

2960 *Hollywood in the Seventies.* by Keyser, Les. 176 p. illus. San Diego, Calif.: A. S. Barnes, 1981.

A fine addition to the series, Keyser's history emphasizes the super-productions, the remakes and sequels which dominated the seventies. Actors, directors, finance, distribution, trends, etc.—all receive attention.

2961 *Hollywood in the Sixties.* by Baxter, John. 172 p. illus. New York: A. S. Barnes, 1972.

This volume covers some of the same ground as Higham's *Hollywood At Sunset* but the emphasis is quite different. Baxter explores films rather than individuals and studios. The first two chapters outline the decline of the studios and the disappointing efforts of some of the outstanding directors of earlier years—Zinnemann, Kramer, Preminger, Kazan, Rossen, Minnelli, etc. Contrasted with these are newer directors such as Mike Nichols, Sidney Lumet, Frank Perry and Arthur Penn. Remaining chapters are devoted to film genres—the musical, the mystery, the western, the sex comedy, etc. A lengthy index is provided, and the illustrations are mostly above average.

The book's weakness is the interjection of personal bias as accepted truth. Baxter is most vulnerable when he states: 1) Rosalind Russell gave a performance of wit and animation in GYPSY (1962). (Most critics thought she watered down so much of the character of Rose that the motivation for the story was lost. The rest of Baxter's comments about GYPSY are equally unfounded. It was a poor movie-based upon a great musical.) 2) Debbie Reynolds gave a "spirited performance" in THE UNSINKABLE MOLLY BROWN (1964). (Her distasteful shrieking put the entire film out of perspective.) 3) The score to SWEET CHARITY (1969) is called "routine." (Yet he singles out three songs for individual positive comment in the paragraph that follows.) 4) Of all Billy Wilder's parodies, KISS ME STUPID (1964) is both the funniest and most accurate. (Most critics thought otherwise.)

Since much of the volume consists of film criticism, there has to be reservation about such solo opinions, lacking any stated corroboration or evidence. Presented as film history, the book is suspect. As a personal overview of the films of the sixties, it will please and entertain the noncritical reader. Because of its broad coverage and the fine index, it also has some reference value.

2962 *Hollywood in the Thirties.* by Baxter, John. 160 p. paper illus. New York: A.S. Barnes, 1968.

A critical account of many Hollywood films produced in the thirties linked by an examination of the major studios and the directors working for them. Informative and comprehensive, the book is excellent for both reading and reference. A very broad topic is handled with efficiency, respect, and style. Highly recommended for most readers.

2963 *Hollywood in the Twenties.* by Robinson, David. 176 p. paper illus. New York: A. S. Barnes, 1968.

This is a view of American films and filmmaking in the last years of the silent era. Using a base of historical and sociological description, the author considers the pioneer directors from the teens (Griffith, etc.), the imported foreign directors (Lubitsch, Murnau, etc.), the directors who came from within the industry, and finally, six master directors—Chaplin, Keaton, von Stroheim, von Sternberg, Ford and Flaherty. In the closing section, various personalities of the twenties are reviewed. The book has structure, intelligence and style. The scope of the book allows only a passing mention of some artists who deserve greater attention. Illustrations are excellent and the book is indexed. Recommended highly for all.

2964 *Hollywood in the 1940's: The Star's Own Stories.* edited by Wilson, Ivy Crane. 160 p. paper illus. New York: Ungar, 1980.

Hollywood Album, an annual published in London from 1947 to 1960, is the source of the articles found in this anthology. Edited by Ivy Crane Wilson, almost three dozen essays purportedly authored by such film stars as Ronald Reagan, Shirley Temple, Evelyn Keyes, Irene Dunne, and Joan Bennett detail the stars' hobbies, concerns, families, etc. Publicity departments of the studios undoubtedly had much to do with the final essays. Lots of illustrations accompany the fan magazine nostalgia presented here.

2965 *Hollywood in Transition.* by MacCann, Richard Dyer. 208 p. Boston: Houghton, Mifflin Co., 1962.

The beginning of the end of Hollywood is the subject of this book. Freedom from four restrictive influences—censorship, studio control, domestic market demands, and assembly line production—has followed the television revolution of the fifties. The causes and effects of these new freedoms on production are considered in the first section while the latter portion looks at producers, directors, writers and stars as they now function in the changing Hollywood.

Since the material was adapted from magazine articles published over a period of ten years, the book appears fragmented rather than unified. The latter section especially seems contrived of leftover bits and pieces. Much of its is dated. Of limited interest and value.

2966   *The Hollywood Indian: Stereotypes of Native Americans in Films.* by New Jersey State Museum. 80 p. illus. Trenton, N.J.: New Jersey State Museum, 1981.

2967   *Hollywood is a Four Letter Town.* by Bacon, James. 324 p. illus. Chicago: Henry Regnery, 1975.

For 18 years James Bacon has been a Hollywood correspondent for Associated Press; currently he writes a widely syndicated column that appears in almost 500 newspapers around the world. In addition to his writing he has appeared in several hundred movie and television films. These impressive credentials serve him well in providing material for this volume of gossip, anecdote, and opinion. The selection and treatment of his raw material is not as good.

Some of what he relates is old familiar material—Mae West's "goodness" line, her selection of Cary Grant as her leading man, Tony Curtis comparing Marilyn Monroe to Hitler, Joe E. Lewis quotes, Desi Arnaz's comment on Lucille Ball as communist. More interesting are his impressions of personalities and the stories he uses to substantiate his opinions. Some of the anecdotes are fresh, ribald, and quotable —i.e., Betsy Drake's comment on Ari Onassis' bar stools. At times he lapses into bad taste, in what seems to be a pursuit of literary notoriety leading to increased sales. In rating terms, this is a soft-core text.

The book contains a few illustrations of the author and his chapter subjects. It is also indexed.

2968   *Hollywood Kids.* edited by Maltin, Leonard. 256 p. paper illus. New York: Popular Library, 1978.

This collective biography boasts a well-known group of authors—Mel Schuster, James Limbacher, David Chierichetti, Jerry Vermilye, and others. The subjects they write about are Jackie Cooper, Scotty Beckett, Jane Withers, Dickie Moore, Bonita Gran-

ville, Terry Kilburn, Margaret Kerry, Roddy McDowall, Gloria Jean, Darryl Hickman, Dean Stockwell, Russ Tamblyn, Brandon de Wilde and Mark Lester. Included in addition to the biographical essay for each are illustrations and a filmography that provides year, director, and cast.

Since the essays come from a variety of sources, they vary from the terse to the verbose. The illustrations, although poorly reproduced, give the reader some idea of the child star's appeal. Unfortunately, the small type used may cause some readers discomfort.

A potpourri of interesting material that deserves a more careful production.

2969   *Hollywood Lawyer.* by Golden, Milton M. 192 p. paper New York: Signet Books, 1960.

The cover blurb and picture should be warning enough. The book purports to be the autobiographical revelations of a prominent attorney about his scorching cases. It is nothing more than a series of composite cases designed to titillate but also disguised to prevent any possible identification. With two exceptions no real names are used in the more than 20 cases related. The recurrent motive or theme of each case is sex/love. Designed for the fast buck trade.

2970   *Hollywood Lawyer: The Jerry Geisler Story.* by Geisler, Jerry; and Martin, Pete. 342 p. paper illus. New York: Pocket Books, 1962.

This is a recollection of some legal battles in which Geisler acted as defense attorney. Cases involving Flynn, Chaplin, Mitchum, Busby Berkeley, Edward G. Robinson, Ruth Etting, and others are discussed. The book is indexed and has some unusual candid photographs. Not essential by any means, it is nevertheless an absorbing view of famous people in trouble with the law.

2971   *Hollywood Leg Man.* by Rosenstein, Jaik. 212 p. Los Angeles : Madison Press, 1950.

A collection of short pieces about Hollywood by a man who was a press agent and a legman for Hedda Hopper. His responsibility in this latter job was to hunt up or check out items for Hopper's column. The proximity to Hopper had its effect, for the text reads like old-fashioned Hollywood gossip. Many blind items are used and the wholebook promises to divulge much but delivers little. Of very limited interest today.

2972 *Hollywood Looks at Its Audience: A Report of Film Audience Research.* by Handel, Leo A. 240 p. Urbana, Ill.: University of Illinois Press, 1950.

This volume presents a summary of the film audience research procedures used by the American film industry up to the late forties. It is somewhat dated today but still has pertinence for those interested in media research. After certain fundamental facts of audience research are introduced, some studies of individual productions are examined. Topics such as the audience—its composition, attendance habits, story preference, censorship attitudes, and its player likes and dislikes—are considered next. Content analysis and social effects are the final topics discussed. The text is written in clear layman's language and is accompanied by many charts, graphs and tables of data. An index is provided. A basic work with limited value and appeal.

2973 *Hollywood, Mayfair and All That Jazz: The Roy Fox Story.* by Fox, Roy. 248 p. illus. London: Leslie Frewin, 1975.

2974 *Hollywood Merry-Go-Round.* by Hecht, Andrew. 212 p. illus. New York: Grosset and Dunlap, 1947.

A facetious, satirical look at Hollywood, complete with many anecdotes, some illustrations by Leo Hershfeld, and an introduction by Bob Hope.

2975 *The Hollywood Musical.* by Taylor, John Russell; and Jackson, Arthur. 278 p. illus. New York: McGraw-Hill, 1971.

Five related essays consider various aspects of the musical film in this handsome book's opening pages. Among the topics are the translation of stage musicals into film, the composers, the performers, the directors, and an evaluation of the genre. Linking these chapters is a sort of critical history. The two main sections follow, the first being a selected filmography listing 1443 pictures with the usual data—title, year, running time, cast credits, and production credits. The bonus here is the inclusion of the songs from each, with a key to the actor(s) who performed them. The filmography is flawed by inconsistency in selection. For example: THE COUNTRY GIRL (1954) is included but GOOD NEWS (1947) is not; A DAY AT THE RACES (1937) is in, but A NIGHT AT THE OPERA (1935) is not; ONE NIGHT OF LOVE (1934) is in, but THE GREAT CARUSO (1951) is

not; THE GLENN MILLER STORY (1954) is in, but THE BENNY GOODMAN STORY (1955) is not.

The second section is an index of names, which gives some bits of biographical data and a listing of credits—but only in relation to musical films. Those films listed in the filmography appear here in bold print. Again, some inconsistency occurs. IN OLD CHICAGO (1938) (Ameche), LITTLE BOY LOST (1953) (Crosby), LOVE AFFAIR (1939) (Dunne), JUKE GIRL (1942) (Sheridan) may have a song hidden somewhere but are not musicals in any way. There are alphabetical indexes for the songs and for the film titles at the book's end. Many fine illustrations appear and several in color are most pleasing.

In spite of the inconsistency and the assignment of some titles, the book has a fine reference potential. It seems limited to that use since the opening essays are not strong enough to attract reader interest and the indexes and filmography are not reading material except for the dedicated musical buff.

2976 *The Hollywood Musical: A Picture Quiz Book.* by Appelbaum, Stanley. 221 p. paper illus. New York: Dover Publications, 1974.

Thankfully, the third volume in this series duplicates the excellence of the others. Using 215 stills from musical films, the authors have provided an informative visual survey of the Hollywood musical. The stills have been arranged according to personality (e.g., Garland), composer (e.g., Jerome Kern) or topic (e.g., biographies). Some questions are proposed for each, with the answers supplied at the back of the book. The important element here is the visual, supported nicely by indexes to the performers and film titles. The production, selection and arrangement of its material recommend this book to all.

2977 *The Hollywood Musical.* by Mordden, Ethan. 256 p. illus. New York: St. Martin's, 1981.

A terse, selective review that offers some questionable critical evaluations. He is strong on interpreting history but a bit weak on assessing individual films and performers.

2978 *The Hollywood Musical.* by Hirschhorn, Clive. 456 p. illus. New York: Crown, 1981.

A large reference volume that tries to be comprehensive about a subject that defies exact dimension. 1344 films are described by plot, cast, song numbers, personnel credits, background, critical opinion, illustration, etc. Errors are numerous and some of the pictures are too small or difficult to identify.

2979 *Hollywood Musicals.* by Sennett, Ted. 384 p. illus. New York: Abrams, 1981.

A coffee table book that combines intelligent text with attractive illustrations. Sennett provides a history—not a filmography—that is selective, critical and most enjoyable.

2980 *Hollywood Now.* by Fadiman, William. 174 p. New York: Liveright, 1972.

The author has had an impressive career in films, having been a producer, a vice president, and an executive literary advisor in Hollywood. He is certainly qualified to write this volume, a view of Hollywood today, which contains elements of filmmaking, industry organization, history, and sociology. It is an honest, absorbing and useful book. Key topics considered by Fadiman are the industry, the agent, the director, the star, the writer, the producer, and the future. The book is not illustrated but it has a short bibliography and an index.

The text is informed, witty, sometimes cynical, practical, and, most of all, respectful. It avoids that common practice of today, taking potshots at the remains of Hollywood. Fadiman reminds us of what failed in the past but also of what is still valuable or functional today. In general, his attitude is cautiously pessimistic; he sees subsidization and a change in film content as two possible remedies for Hollywood's ills. A concise, intelligent view of Hollywood, past and present, this volume is recommended.

2981 *Hollywood on Hollywood.* by Parish, James Robert; and Pitts, Michael R. 431 p. illus. Metuchen, N.J.: Scarecrow, 1978.

In this survey of what might be called a minor film genre, the authors offer an annotated filmography of about 300 films on Hollywood. No specific definition is offered and selection is very broad: it includes such peripheral "Hollywood" titles as CITIZEN KANE (1941), 'TILL THE CLOUDS ROLL BY (1946) and SWEET BIRD OF YOUTH (1962). The films are arranged alphabetically by title and offer casts, credits, plots and commentaries, along with some illustrations and an introduction by De Witt Bodeen added for support. What is needed is an author's explanation and some concluding remarks about the films comprising this questionable genre.

2982 *Hollywood on Record: The Film Stars' Discography.* by Pitts, Michael R.; and Harrison, Louis H. 411 p. illus. Metuchen, N.J.: Scarecrow, 1978.

This is a fascinating discography that offers surprises with almost every entry. From Bud Abbott to Vera Zorina, there are listings of the LP, original cast, soundtrack, compilation and 45rpm recordings made by Hollywood personalities. Of course, some came to films already established as recording stars (Crosby, Andrews Sisters, Burl Ives, etc.). In any event, for the collector or the devoted fan, there are riches to discover (e.g., Judy Garland in "Lady in the The Dark" taken from a radio broadcast). This volume is an essential film reference.

2983 *Hollywood on Trial.* by Kahn, Gordon. 229 p. paper New York: Boni and Gaer, 1948.

In 1947, the House Un-American Activities Committee subpoenaed 45 persons, all employed in some craft of the motion picture industry. The purpose was to reveal subversive, Communist, and un-American influences in motion pictures. This volume is an account of the hearings which led to the indictment of the Unfriendly Ten for contempt of Congress and their subsequent blacklisting in Hollywood.

The account given here is prejudiced and bitter. Its purpose is not so much to inform as to persuade. While the reader will deeply deplore the methods used by the congressional committee and the abuse of personal freedom that was evidenced, he may long for a less hysterical, more objective account. An interesting historical document in the area of motion pictures and society that will have its major appeal to students and scholars.

2984 *Hollywood Panorama.* by Harmon, Bob. 95 p. paper illus. New York: Dutton, 1971.

This delightful book consists of 30 full-color panels of caricatures of movie stars—past and present—all drawn by Bob Harmon. Some are costumed for their most famous roles: Garbo in CAMILLE (1936), Leslie Caron in GIGI (1958), W. C. Fields as Mr. Micawber, etc. Others are portrayed in various activities: swimming, tennis, socializing, etc. Identification is the game and most buffs will find it easy, for Harmon has been highly successful in capturing the uniqueness of his many, many subjects. The nonbuff will find it more challenging but will be helped by the reverse side of each plate, on which there appears an indentification diagram, the names, and the film role, if applicable.

The publisher suggests a mural made by combining all 30 plates. Projection via the opaque projector is possible; a contest could be held prior to film showings; and simply as pictorial aids for display, the plates are fine. Different and highly recommended.

2985 *Hollywood Pilot: The Biography of Paul Mantz.* by Dwiggins, Don. 249 p. illus. New York: Doubleday & Co., 1967.

This is the life of Paul Mantz, the well-publicized stunt man who was killed during the making of THE FLIGHT OF THE PHOENIX (1966). Employed by Hollywood for many years, Mantz was at one time a technical advisor for Amelia Earhart. The emphasis in the volume is on aeronautics and not much insight will be gained about Hollywood or filmmaking.

2986 *Hollywood Players: The Forties.* by Parish, James Robert; and DeCarl, Lennard. 544 p. illus. New Rochelle, N.Y.: Arlington House, 1975.

This collective biography treats familiar screen personalities of the forties who were less than star attractions. Although they played both leading and supporting roles, they did not develop sufficient charisma, good fortune or longevity to survive the next two decades as film actors. Many came to tragic ends—(Gig Young, Gail Russell, Bobby Driscoll, Tom Neal, Carol Landis)—while others accepted fading careers with grace, often pursuing careers in other media—(Teresa Wright, Geraldine Fitzgerald, Patricia Morison, Macdonald Carey). A few are still active today in films.

The 83 biographies are arranged alphabetically, with a portrait, several stills, and a filmography accompanying each. Most of the text is a factual recital of career data and personal incident. Occasional brief critical comments add a seasoning to the well-researched narrative, while certain other assessments of the subjects are sharp, succinct, and penetrating. A detailed title-name index completes the book. Photographic reproduction is above average throughout.

As a reference, a nostalgia trip, or factual biography, this volume is most rewarding. The careful reviews and assessments provided by the authors are impressive and satisfying. Recommended.

2987 *Hollywood Players: The Thirties.* by Parish, James Robert; and Leonard, William T. 576 p. illus. New Ro-

chelle, N.Y.: Arlington House, 1976.

The indefatigable James Robert Parish is with us once again with another fine collective biography. This time he, along with coauthor William Leonard, is concentrating on 71 well-known performers from the thirties who never quite achieved international stardom and celebrity. Included are such stalwarts as Brian Donlevy, Preston Foster, Victor Jory, Margaret Lindsay, Gilbert Roland, and Fay Wray. For each there are several pages of biographical information which emphasize screen performances, a few illustrations, and a filmography. A comprehensive index to the book is also provided.

As usual, the reading of unfamiliar material about film actors who are old acquaintances is a delightful experience. Parish has perfected the technique of locating and selecting biographical material, blending it with some subtle critical comment and adding a few nostalgic illustrations. The publishers have supported him admirably by providing superior production. Type style, paper quality, illustration reproduction, and clarity are all excellent.

This is a welcome addition to a most valuable and distinguished series. Recommended.

2988 *The Hollywood Posse.* by Cary, Diana Serra. 268 p. paper illus. Boston: Houghton Mifflin, 1975.

This is the story of a group of authentic but unemployed cowboys who arrived in Hollywood concurrently with D.W. Griffith, around 1912. They survived the next five decades by bringing their skill and knowledge to many Hollywood films in which they rode, did stunts, and doubled for stars. The book is romantically subtitled "The Story of a Gallant Band of Horsemen Who Made Movie History."

Anecdotal in form, the text recalls incidents with Cecil B. DeMille, John Ford, Tom Mix and others. At the book's end several of the group have taken jobs at Disneyland driving stagecoaches and training mules for a live trail ride.

The author, whose father was one of the group, grew up with these men and her memory of them is emotional, personal and admiring. She had a film career of her own as the child star, Baby Peggy.

The accounts of filmmaking are almost buried by the multitude of personal incidents and relationships. The lack of an index eliminates any reference value the book may have. Acceptable.

2989 *The Hollywood Professionals.* by Canham, Kingsley. paper illus. New

York: A. S. Barnes, 1973.

The first book in a series, this one discusses the film careers of three Hollywood directors who have been somewhat neglected by today's critics: Michael Curtiz, Raoul Walsh, and Henry Hathaway. The full filmography for Curtiz alone justifies the book.

2990 *The Hollywood Professionals (Volume 2): Henry King, Lewis Milestone, Sam Wood.* by Denton, Clive; and Canham, Kingsley; and Thomas, Tony. 192 p. paper illus. New York: A. S. Barnes, 1974.

This volume emphasizes the goal of the series—to spotlight the work of Hollywood directors who are usually ignored by students, teachers and authors. These were the men whose films were crafted with a care, competence, and creativity rarely seen in today's films.

The three subjects—King, Milestone and Wood—receive separate consideration via a monograph and a detailed filmography. Since the essays are written by different authors, the style and content of each varies. Denton emphasizes a few selected films—STATE FAIR (1933), JESSE JAMES (1939), TWELVE O'CLOCK HIGH (1949)—while Canham and Thomas are more concerned with a total overview of their subjects' lives and careers. In all three instances the narratives are largely factual, with some small amount of critical interpretation and evaluation added. The filmographies for King and Milestone have short annotations; there are none in the filmography for Wood. Illustrations are adequate and the book is indexed. A rewarding reminder of the impressive contribution made by three master craftsmen, this volume is recommended.

2991 *The Hollywood Professionals (Volume 3): Howard Hawks, Frank Borzage, Edgar G. Ulmer.* by Belton, John. 182 p paper illus. New York: A. S. Barnes, 1974.

The third volume in this most welcome series is up to the standard of the earlier ones. The criterion for inclusion in the series is a career as a Hollywood director whose films were characterized by a competence, proficiency and gloss not seen in today's films. A critical essay on the films of each man explores themes, techniques, approaches, and other aspects of his films. The annotated filmography which follows gives film data, cast, credits, and a one-sentence plot outline in most cases.

Although Hawks has been covered in other volumes, neither Borzage nor Ulmer has received

the tribute of a published book study of their work. This volume helps to fill that gap. Many illustrations including some frame enlargements are used throughout the book to complement the text. An index of names is also provided. This is another admirable volume in a series designed to remind readers of the talented men who were responsible for the quality that identified so many Hollywood films. Recommended.

2992 *The Hollywood Professionals: Tod Browning, Don Siegel.* by Rosenthal, Stuart; and Kass, Judith M. 207 p. paper illus. New York: A. S.Barnes, 1975.

The fourth volume in a fine series which spotlights the work of Hollywood directors. Both Siegel and Browning have been relatively ignored in cinema literature to date, a situation that makes this volume most welcome.

Rosenthal's monograph on Browning considers the patterns, plots, and casts, of his films, along with his long relationship with Lon Chaney. Frustration, the dominant theme found in most of Browning's work, is subdivided into four variations, and the films are grouped under the appropriate headings. A detailed filmography concludes this rewarding tribute to a neglected artist.

The study on Don Siegel comprises the greater portion of the book. After identifying eight major elements in Siegel's work, Judith Kass notes their presence in individual films. Included are such elements as the anti-hero, pessimism, the damaged-vulnerable hero, time limitation, the strong-fatal woman, etc.

Many rewarding illustrations appear throughout the book which also contains a name index. A detailed filmography is included.

The combination of two fascinating director subjects, along with rewarding critical essays, fine visuals, and good supportive material makes this volume worth recommending.

2993 *The Hollywood Professionals: King Vidor, John Cromwell, Mervyn LeRoy.* by Denton, Clive; and Canham, Kingsley. 192 p. paper illus. A.S. Barnes, 1976.

The fifth volume in a series devoted to Hollywood directors who have been neglected and ignored in the film literature. Vidor and LeRoy have both written books about themselves, but material on Cromwell is somewhat scarce. Each man is given a critical essay, some illustrations, and a filmogrpahy. The result is a review and reminder of the appreciable contribution that each man made to film history. Cromwell's work is probably less familiar than that of the other two and the reader may be pleasantly surprised to find it includes OF HUMAN BONDAGE (1934), THE PRISONER OF ZENDA (1937), ALGIERS (1938), ANNA AND THE KING OF SIAM (1944), CAGED (1950) and THE GODDESS (1958).

This volume and the series in general are a delight to read. The books serve several purposes, not the least of which is to recall many fine films and the men who directed them.

2994 *The Hollywood Professionals: Frank Capra, George Cukor, Clarence Brown.* by Estrin, Allen. 192 p. paper illus. New York: A.S. Barnes, 1978.

Studies of Frank Capra, George Cukor, and Clarence Brown are offered in this volume of *The Hollywood Professionals* series. There have been other books on Capra and Cukor but Brown certainly qualifies as a neglected subject. Comment and criticism offered by Estrin is supported by detailed filmographies and many illustrations.

2995 *The Hollywood Professionals: Billy Wilder, Leo McCarey.* by Poague, Leland A. 319 p. illus. New York: A.S. Barnes, 1980.

This fine series continues with almost book-length appreciations of Billy Wilder and Leo McCarey. In Wilder's case, biographical material has been available in earlier books; here, the author wisely devotes his essay to a critical examination of Wilder's films. Leo McCarey's life and career have been ignored for the most part by authors. Poague offers little biographical background but does treat selected McCarey films. His analyses and critical evaluations for certain films of both directors are certainly provocative. Sometimes they are also far fetched, (SOME LIKE IT HOT (1959)—as a study of capitalism and sex?) or poorly researched (THE LOST WEEKEND (1945)—look at Jackson's novel for Birnham's motivation) or overly detailed (THE AWFUL TRUTH (1937)—did McCarey really consider all the nuance that Poague finds in this last film? Most directors of McCarey's era were simply making comedy films). Nevertheless, the two essays do provide an enjoyable reading experience. Illustrations, filmographies, and an index complete this welcome addition to the series.

2996 *Hollywood Rajah: The Life and Times of Louis B. Mayer.* by Crowther, Bosley. 339 p. illus. New York: Holt, Rinehart, & Winston, 1960.

As the second MGM-based volume by the author of *The Lion's Share*, this one necessarily duplicates some of the material found in the earlier book. Using the life of Louis B. Mayer (1882-1957), the most powerful studio head in film history, as his theme, Crowther also gives a peripheral view of the entire industry during that period. Once more the famous MGM personalities stud the pages as they relate to and react against Mayer.

Quite factual and analytical, this biography contains less of the gossip-anecdote-legend of the earlier book and readers may not find it as enjoyable. Illustrations are fine and there is detailed index. Recommended for historians and scholars as a worthwhile example of film biography. General readers are referred to *The Lion's Share.*

2997 *Hollywood Red: The Autobiography of Lester Cole.* by Cole, Lester. 450 p. illus. Palo Alto, Calif.: Ramparts, 1981.

Lester Cole who wrote many screenplays in the thirties and forties, was also one of the Hollywood ten.

2998 *The Hollywood Reliables.* by Parish, James Robert; and Mank, Gregory W. 313 p. illus. Westport, Conn.: Arlington House, 1980.

The Parish collective biography series continue to grow, not only in number but also in book size. Here, in an attractive coffee table volume, the lives and careers of six male actors are presented with text, illustration and filmography. This time the subjects are Dana Andrews, Wallace Beery, Pat O'Brien, Walter Pidgeon, Spencer Tracy and Robert Young. Although they lack the depth and interpretation possible with investigative reporting via interviews and subject cooperation, the essays seem to improve with each volume and the more than 200 illustrations provided are superb. The volume is indexed.

Many books ago, James Parish discovered that the public has an insatiable appetite for biographical stories and pictures of people from Hollywood's golden age. Once again he satisfies that need nicely with his portraits of six Hollywood icons.

2999 *Hollywood Renaissance.* by Jacobs, Diane. 192 p. illus. New York: A.S. Barnes, 1977.

Diane Jacobs identifies a Hollywood renaissance

with the emergence of a small group of American directors during the 1960s. They include John Cassavetes, Robert Altman, Francis Ford Coppola, Martin Scorsese, and Paul Mazursky.

For each she has provided an appreciation which includes general background, critical comment, stills, and an individual consideration of each film the man has directed to date. Full filmographies offering technical data, cast, and production credits appear for each in the book's final pages.

The author's ability to communicate her understanding of and enthusiasm for the work of these directors is appreciable. Her judgments are sound and her writing is always interesting, never pedantic. She gives every evidence of being a fine film critic.

Anyone interested in today's film will welcome this volume. Highly recommended.

3000   *Hollywood R.I.P.* by Edmonds, I. G. 158 p. paper Evanston, Ill.: Regency, 1963.

The infamous scandals of Hollywood are reviewed again in this uninspired paperback. Fatty Arbuckle, Lupe Velez, Mable Normand, William Desmond Taylor, Alexander Pantages, Lana Turner, Mary Nolan, Errol Flynn, Charles Chaplin, Mary Astor, Wallace Reid, Clara Bow, Taylor-Burton, and Marilyn Monroe are all given attention. It is difficult to make scandal dull but the author succeeds in this unimaginative reprise of well-worn material.

3001   *Hollywood Saga.* by DeMille, W. C. 319 p. illus. New York: Dutton, 1939.

This is the story of playwright-director William C. DeMille, the brother of Cecil, and his years in Hollywood. He came for a short visit in 1914 and stayed some 20 years. Those early years of silent films are described in a mild quiet narrative.

3002   *Hollywood Scapegoat: Erich von Stroheim.* by Noble, Peter. 246 p. illus. London: Fortune, 1950.

A hard-to-find biography of the famed director which should be reprinted. Although there are other current books on von Stroheim, this one offers many rewards. The biographical portions are well written with attention given to detail and incident. The subject's work as both director and actor has been thoroughly researched and documented. There is an index to the creative work of Stroheim as an actor, writer, and director from 1914 to 1950.

The appendix is almost another book by itself since it is a collection of articles on von Stroheim by noted film writers, critics, and historians. The book is indexed and the photographs are rare and have been selected with an eye for the accompanying text. This is an almost perfect tribute to a perfectionist director. Most highly recommended.

3003   *Hollywood Screen Stars.* by Noble, Peter. 86 p. illus. London: British Yearbooks, 1946.

One of the several yearbooks created by Peter Noble, this one was devoted to American performers. In 1947 it was published by Skelton Robinson of London and contained 20 full-page illustrations in its presentation of over 500 film actors.

3004   *The Hollywood Screen-Writers.* edited by Corliss, Richard. 328 p. paper New York: Avon, 1972.

This original paperback anthology focuses attention on a neglected and misunderstood area in filmaking: the creation of a script. By a judicious choice of articles and interviews about screenwriters, the editor has managed an eloquent arrangement for the re-evaluation of their role. A chronological arrangement of the material presents Anita Loos as an early representative of the craft. The Golden Years feature Jules Furthman, Ben Hecht, Preston Sturges, Dudley Nichols and Howard Koch. During the House Un-American Committee Hearings and the McCarthy Era, the intent of the screenwriter was questioned by the Government. Ring Lardner, Jr., Bordon Chase, Dalton Trumbo, and James Poe were names familiar during this period. Writer rebirth is indicated by Eleanor Perry, Penelope Gilliatt, Jules Feiffer and others. A symposium section which records the responses of 12 noted writers to the same questionnaire precedes the final section, fifty filmographies of perhaps the best known screenwriters in the American cinema. Each article or interview has a filmography appended.

The book, which derives much of its material from the periodical, *Film Comment,* is promised as the first of a series, which is good news. The description of the screenwriting craft along with individual portraits of noted writers makes informative, vital, and enjoyable reading. The editor can be criticized on one major count. The reference value is less than adequate. The provision of a simple index of writer names would have helped immeasurably. With so many filmographies in the book, it could have approximated a poor-man's version of *Who Wrote the Movie and What Else Did He Write?.* The table of contents is of some assistance, but two poor reference situations exist: first, with the writers who are "buried" within a general article—Paul Mazursky, Larry Tucker, David Newman, Robert Benton, etc. —and secondly, with the 50 names included in the final filmography. A single-page index to the names would have made the book much more useful. Even with this large reservation, the quality of the book is such that is is enthusiastically recommended.

3005 *Hollywood '70.* by Cosulich, Callisto. 175 p. illus. Florence: Vallecci, 1978.

3006 *Hollywood Short Cuts to Glamour.* by Parker, Ruth. 88 p. illus. Culver City, Calif.: Murray and Gee, 1949.

Hints on how to achieve personal beauty.

3007 *Hollywood Shorts.* by Ray, Charles. 177 p. illus. Los Angeles: California Graphic Press, 1935.

Carries the subtitle, "Compiled from Incidents in the Everday Life of Men and Women Who Entertain in Pictures." The author was a leading man in silent films who specialized in playing country boys.

3008 *The Hollywood Social Problem Film: From the Depression to the Fifties.* by Roffman, Peter; and Purdy, Jim. 365 p. illus. Bloomington, Ind.: Indiana University Press, 1981.

Films from 1930 to 1950 which deal with crime, politics, social conditions etc. are analyzed in an attempt to define a genre. The effort is not very successful.

3009 *Hollywood Speaks.: An Oral History.* by Steen, Mike. 379 p. New York: G. P. Putnam's, 1974.

An oral historian is a person who gathers and preserves spontaneous conversations with people who have significance to the subject being investigated. The portable audio-cassette recorder has made this type of interview possible. The conversations with Hollywood professionals contained in this book are presented to help the reader "understand, appreciate and enjoy the history of the motion picture. <

Perhaps history is a bit misleading in its titular use here; certainly oral history is offered, but the book is not a history of Hollywood. It is more a collection of interviews with "the people who make the movies." Represented are leading man (Henry Fonda), leading lady (Rosalind Russell), character player (Agnes Moorehead), young actor (David Cannon), screenwriter (Stewart Stern), director (William A.

Wellman) and some 19 others. Each interview gives an autobiographical opening, discusses the subject's training and how he began in the film industry. His specific job is explained and the remainder of the conversation deals with reminiscences, opinions, and general thoughts about personalities, films, and the motion picture business.

Steen is an adroit interviewer, his subjects are well chosen and the oral histories he presents make absorbing reading; anyone familiar with his interviewees will be fascinated. Unfortunately there are no photographs or filmographies offered. They would have added more to an already fine accomplishment. Highly recommended.

3010 *Hollywood Star Reporter.* by Franklin, Lindy. 158 p. paper illus. New York: Popular Library, 1975.

The author is Film Library Institute Publications' Hollywood editor and her text in this volume consists of interviews and articles about teenage idols. Only a few of the 17 chapters deal with film personalities. The volume is designed to appeal to nondiscriminating pre-adolescent fans and has no pertinence for film study.

3011 *Hollywood Starlet: The Career of Barbara Lawrence.* by Connor, Jim. 152 p. illus. Brooklyn: SLP Publications, 1977.

Barbara Lawrence made some 23 films in the period from 1944 to 1958. Her role was usually that of a young, attractive blonde 'Tootsie' who provided the contrast, counter-attraction or romantic threat to the leading lady. Her tenure with the Hollywood studio coincided approximately with that of Marilyn Monroe, and Lawrence lost out in any competition which may have existed.

The author, who is a devoted fan, arranged private publication of this volume. He sees Lawrence as the prototype of the Hollywood starlet who almost succeeded. Each of her films is described with cast credits, synopsis, critical excerpts, advertisements, illustrations, songs, etc. There is also a biographical essay and an introduction by Robert Horton. Barbara Lawrence, who retired to become a wife and mother, should be grateful to the author for such a detailed, affectionate tribute.

3012 *The Hollywood Studios.* by Pickard, Roy. 392 p. illus. London: Muller, 1978.

3013   *Hollywood Studio Musicians.* by Faulkner, Robert R. 218 p. Chicago: Aldine Atherton, 1971.

Described as a "sociological" analysis of the work, careers, and roles of creative artists in an industry devoted to mass culture, this volume carries the subtitle, "Their Work and Careers in the Recording Industry." It is a serious research supported by a grant from UCLA and reads like a popularized doctoral dissertation. It is heavily referenced, footnoted, and contains several charts. The appendix notes the methodological approaches and offers some personal reflections on the research. An index is provided. Since it deals with a specific type of creative artist within the film studios, it is of importance to this bibliography. It is very specialized, and will interest few readers.

3014   *The Hollywood Style.* by Knight, Arthur; and Elisofon, Eliot. 219 p. illus. New York: Macmillan, 1969.

If the reader agrees with the author's premise that Hollywood has housed the American equivalent of European royalty, this volume may provide a quite unusual experience. With Knight supplying the text and Elisofon the pictures, this expensive volume describes homes built by motion picture personalities over a 40-year period. The theory is advanced that the homes reflect the personalities of the inhabitants and the book therefore is a record of a life style made possible by the motion picture. The accumulation of art is noted. The original features of the homes are attributed to their design by noted architectural artists such as Wright, Neutra, Beckett and Pereira.

Many of the beautiful illustrations are in color and are double-paged. The text is up to Knight's usual standard of excellence. If the possible criticism of ostentatiousness can be overlooked, the book may provide a richly rewarding trip through wonderland. Not essential but a pleasure for those who can afford it.

3015   *The Hollywood TV Producer.: His Work and His Audience.* by Cantor, Muriel G. 256 p. New York: Basic Books, 1971.

This is a book about the producer of films for television. Its content comes from 59 tape-recorded interviews with producers, direct observation, and researching the literature of the field. Since the producer usually determines the content of his show, his influence on a particular audience is great. This volume examines the men, their work setting, training, commitment, and associates. The relationships between a producer, a network and an audience are examined. The appendixes, a lengthy bibliography and an index contribute to the impressive study made by the author. Although its emphasis is on television, there is valuable content for anyone interested in the portrait of a producer. Acceptable.

3016   *The Hollywood that Was.* by Marlowe, Don. 192 p. illus Fort Worth, Texas: Branch-Smith, 1969.

A potpourri of pictures, anecdotes, brief biographies, and sentimental reminiscences. The author, one of the original Our Gang child actors, certainly has the experience and background to recall better material than this. The pictures are rare and include many then-and-now shots. To add to the mixture, the book concludes with a nine-page listing of movie personalities with their given names, e.g., Barbara Stanwyck: Ruby Stevens. The book's potential is not fully realized. No index or table of contents is offered. This might be appropriate as a gift to the film buff who has everything, but its use for most readers is minimal.

3017   *Hollywood, The Dream Factory.* by Powdermaker, Hortense. 342 p. Boston: Little, Brown, 1951.

With the recent demise of Hollywood, the book becomes somewhat schizophrenic—portions are lasting truths applicable to filmmaking anywhere, while other sections are myths, tribal customs, and rituals native to that late and largely imaginary area. The book is still a most stimulating superimposition of a professional study methodology on a pragmatic volatile commercial industry. Most valuable.

3018   *Hollywood, the Haunted House.* by Mayersberg, Paul. 211 p. paper New York: Ballantine Books, 1967.

Business versus art in the making of motion pictures in America is the theme of this book. By skillfully using quotes from directors, writers, producers and studio heads, the author of this provocatively up-to-date book explores the techniques, systems, studio politics and intrigues that have characterized the making of American films. Each major category of the creative artist receives a chapter of attention. Most fascinating is the blend of the numerous quotations into a statement. No index or illustrations are offered but there is an unusual bibliography which includes novels about Hollywood. Although some of the text is open to question, most of it is informative and thoughtful. Recommended for all readers.

3019 *Hollywood: The Movie Factory.* edited by Maltin, Leonard. 284 p. paper illus. New York: Popular Library, 1976.

In an effort to recall and describe Hollywood during its Golden Age from 1920 to 1950, Leonard Maltin has selected a series of interviews and articles from *Film Fan Monthly* and *Movie Star News* for this interesting volume. Interviewed are Ralph Bellamy, Joan Blondell, Frances Mercer, Henry Wilcoxon, Elliott Nugent, Anita Loos, Burgess Meredith and Ruth Waterbury. In addition there are articles on Johnny Mack Brown, Torchy Blane, Tom and Jerry, John Ford, the MGM studios, and others.

The many illustrations which appear throughout the book are well reproduced and nicely integrated into the content.

The care and affection-for-subject which characterize Maltin's books are once more evident here. Not only will this anthology please nostalgia/film buffs but it can serve as a reference reader for the generation which is currently discovering the artistry of the Hollywood film. Recommended.

3020 *Hollywood: The Pioneers.* by Brownlow, Kevin; and Kobal, John. 272 p.illus. New York: Alfred Knopf, 1979.

This is a volume to treasure, to retain in a personal library, and to re-read at frequent intervals. By its tasteful combination of prose and picture, it recaptures the essence of the American silent film era that is almost always absent in the flood of recently published film histories. One has to return to Bardeche, Ramsaye, Jacobs, Hampton, Niver, or to even to Brownlow himself for similar treatments.

Prepared in connection with a BBC television series, the volume boasts a superb collection of photographs assembled by John Kobal, with an explanatory critical text provided by Kevin Brownlow. Based in part on interviews and research, the text is arranged into 24 chapters/topics which provide a chronological survey of the first three decades of film history. Brownlow's expertise as an author-historian was quickly established with his earlier volumes and this one will increase his prestige.

The superb reproduction of Kobal's illustrations is unusual in books today and gives evidence of the care and clarity the early filmmakers took in still photography. As a record of a legendary era that uses both words and pictures for a maximum effect, this book is hard to beat. Highly recommended.

3021 *Hollywood through the Back Door.* by Holstius, Nils E. 319 p. New York: Longman's, 1937.

A disgruntled account of an honest man who tries to crash the Hollywood of the thirties and fails. Hollywood is described as a system (stars, executives, work, homes) with rigid rules of operation. The author seems foolish and quite naive at times.

3022 *Hollywood Today.* by Eyles, Allen; and Billings, Pat. 192p. paper illus. New York: A.S. Barnes, 1971.

A dictionary of 370 talents active in Hollywood during the past decade. Includes directors, stars, producers.

3023 *Hollywood Tragedy—From Fatty Arbuckle to Marilyn Monroe.* by Carr, William H. A. 159 p. paper New York: Lancer Books, 1962.

According to the author, this book is about scandals. It is also a tract "against the injustice and cruelty of leaping to conclusions and hounding the unfortunate." Perhaps, but this latter element is forgotten as the classic scandals of Hollywood are again recited. Monroe, Arbuckle, William Desmond Taylor, Harlow and Paul Bern, Thelma Todd, Flynn, Chaplin, Lupe Velez, Bergman, Turner, and Taylor each receive a chapter of attention focused upon a major scandal in their career. Some get extended coverage while other receive a surface recital of newspaper accounts.

Obviously this is fan magazine material which many readers will label trash. However, for the interested scholar (censorship, sociology, mass media, etc.) whose reference sources are meager, the book can provide a rapid review of this byproduct of the star system. Noted here for reference purposes as indicated above. If it were re-edited with a sociological approach, updated,and published in hardback, one suspects it might be a popular book.

3024 *Hollywood U.K.* by Walker, Alexander. 493 p. illus. New York: Stein & Day, 1974.

The subject of this impressive survey is the British film industry of the sixties. Affluence, youth, satire and permissiveness were some of the trends that were reflected in a decade of British films financed largely by American dollars. Using a chronological framework, the author has considered films, finance, filmmakers, distributors, trends, forms, social concerns, escapism, and other pertinent topics. The account is detailed and factual but never overly statistical. Much of the book's quality derives from the critical analysis offered by Walker. As a practicing London film critic, he has witnessed much of the change he describes firsthand. His knowledge and understanding of the British film industry is apparent on every page—from behind-the-scenes accounts of making BLOW-UP (1967) to the withdrawal of American finance in the seventies.

An industry chronology (1959-1970) summarizes each year and includes a listing of British films released. The few illustrations are satisfying, but the richness and scope of the material would seem to dictate more. An index completes the work. A rich, fascinating period in film history is covered with intelligence, perception and firsthand observation. Highly recommended.

3025 *Hollywood Uncensored: The Stars— Their Secrets and Their Scandals.* by Hirsch, Phil. 188 p. paper illus. New York: Pyramid books, 1965.

Fan magazine articles on Rory Calhoun, Tony Curtis, Jimmy Durante, Jerry Lewis, George Maharis, Jayne Mansfield, Dean Martin, Steve McQueen, Mickey Rooney, Robert Vaughn, John Wayne, Tuesday Weld, and Keenan Wynn.

3026 *Hollywood Undressed.* by Ullback, Sylvia. 250 p. New York: Brentano's, 1931.

"Observations of Sylvia as Noted by Her Secretary" on such subjects as Hollywood, actors, actresses, beauty, diet, etc.

3027 *Hollywood, U.S.A.: From Script to Screen.* by Field, Alice Evans. 256 illus. New York: Vantage, 1952.

The making of a film from producer's blueprint to writing, casting, producing. Contains a list of films made from plays and novels. A very general treatment.

3028 *Hollywood Voices.* edited by Sarris, Andrew. 180 p. illus. New York: Bobbs-Merrill, 1971.

This volume is a bit of a puzzle. Directors Cukor, Preminger, Huston, Losey, Welles, Ray, Polonsky, Mamoulian and Sturges are represented by interviews taken from the total of 40 that appeared in Sarris' *Interviews With Film Directors.* The only discernible changes here seem to occur in the filmographies, and they are minimal indeed. A few acceptable illustrations that are not found in the paperback version of the longer work accompany the text here. Although the format and production quality on this "spin-off" are quite high, so is the price. Nowhere, except in the book's title, is there any mention that this is about 20 percent of the content of the earlier book, and it suggests the possibility of that total content appearing now in five volumes at nearly five times the original price. There is no quarrel with the excellence of the material, but prospective purchasers should be completely aware of what they are buying.

3029 *Hollywood When Silents Were Golden.* by Scott, Evelyn F. 223 p. illus. New York: McGraw-Hill, 1972.

The author's mother, Beulah Dix Flebbe, came for a short visit with the DeMille family in Hollywood and remained 50 years. As description of life in Hollywood from 1916 to about 1930, the book is an affectionate tribute. Names and nostalgia for the period abound. The view is antiseptic and will scandalize or offend no one. A picture section is disappointing in both selection and size. The volume seems like an afterthought attempt to capitalize on the current popularity of Hollywood nostalgia.

3030 *Hollywood Without Makeup.* by Martin, Pete. 255 p. Philadelphia: J.P. Lippincott Co., 1948.

A rearrangement of articles originally written for *The Saturday Evening Post.* Each chapter appears to be an edited composite of several Post articles. For example, in a chapter entitled, "Upper Cruster," biographical sketches of producers Nunnally Johnson, Mark Hellinger, and Leo McCarey are linked. Other subjects included actresses (Garson, Gardner, Montez), a director (Mike Curtiz), producers (King brothers), actors (Duryea, Carradine, Bushman, Peck, Harrison, Lancaster), backstage technicians and pianists (Carmichael, Iturbi).

The articles are linked together in a contrived manner with an apparent effort to diguise their origin. Taken singly, they offer varying degrss of interest since they view their subjects at different phases of their careers, e.g., mature Curtiz and McCarey, young Gardner and Lancaster. No index, photos, references are given. Interesting to read from today's vantage point, the book has limited value. However, the section on Curtiz merits attention.

3031 *The Hollywood Writers' War.* by Schwartz, Nancy; and Schwartz, Sheila. 448 p. illus. New York: Knopf, 1981.

3032 *Hollywood 1920-1970.* edited by Cowie, Peter. 186 p. illus. New York: A.S. Barnes, 1977.

This oversized volume is a compilation of five previously published books: *Hollywood in the Twenties* by David Robinson, *Hollywood in the Thirties* by John Baxter, *Hollywood in the Forties* by Charles Higham and Joel Greenberg, *Hollywood in the Fifties* by Gordon Gow, and *Hollywood in the Sixties* by John Baxter. These titles were published in the late sixties and early seventies by A.S. Barnes. Reprinted here on 10 1/2" by 13" pages, the text appears more voluminous than in the original smaller books but is apparently unchanged. Many new larger-sized visuals have been added to the original group of illustrations. In addition there is a helpful cumulative total index to the five books.

Although the approach, format, style, and writing quality varies with each book, their compilation is praiseworthy. The detailed record of American filmmaking, films and filmmakers presented here will please a wide range of readers and scholars. Film history becomes available as reading pleasure, nostalgia, or simply information in this creative publishing venture. Recommended.

3033 *Hollywood's Canada.* by Berton, Pierre. 303 p. illus. Toronto: McClelland and Stewart, 1975.

The concern of this volume is clearly stated in its subtitle, "The Americanization of Our National Image." By an examination of almost 600 films made by Hollywood which used a Canadian setting, Berton shows the errors, falsifications, exaggerations, and untruths perpetuated about Canada and its people. Few of the films were actually shot in Canada, and those that were concentrated on only one or two general geographical locations.

The people, including mounted police, Canadian Indians, explorers, and pioneers were transformed into Hollywood character stereotypes bearing little resemblance to the originals. As a result, the image of Canada presented to the world via Hollywood films is erroneous, misleading, and a disservice in many ways.

In addition to a well-prepared and strongly stated text, there are more than 100 film stills illustrating many of the points made in the text. Other supporting materials include a filmography of Hollywood movies about Canada, some chapter notes and an index.

For Canadians this volume should excite a variety of emotions from humor to anger. Other readers will appreciate the scope of the study and its execution.

Recommended.

3034 *Hollywood's Children.* by Cary, Diana Serra. 290 p. illus. Boston: Houghton Mifflin, 1979.

Subtitled "An Inside Account of the Child Star Era," this group portrait covers a period from the Gold Rush (Lotta Crabtree) to the fifties (Mickey Rooney, Judy Garland, etc.). The concentration is on the twenties, when the author was known as Baby Peggy. She recalls her silent moviemaking days along with what happens when growth toward adolescence brings on instant obscurity. Similarities between the private lives of child stars (stage mothers, unsuccessful adult relationships, mismanaged funds, psychological traumas) are noted.

Illustrations, a bibliography, and an index supplement this often sad survey based to a large extent on personal experience and observation. All the aspects of Hollywood child stardom are covered with sympathy and understanding. The volume should be required study for all mothers who have theatrical ambitions for their offspring. Other readers will be entertained, enriched, and ultimately moved by this fine book.

3035 *Hollywood's Famous Recipes of the Movie Stars.* by Knight, Midgie. 96 p. illus. Los Angeles: Goodan-Jenkins Furniture Company, 1932.

An early example of the premium gift—this time a book in which 100 film actors offer their favorite recipes. The portraits and the recipes are from the author's private collection.

3036 *Hollywood's Great Love Teams.* by Parish, James Robert. 828 p. illus. New Rochelle, N.Y.: Arlington House, 1974.

It is getting more and more difficult to resist the appeal of the Parish books. They really are a series, although they have never been identified as such— probably because of their appearance through different publishing houses. The formula seen in *The Fox Girls*, *The Paramount Pretties*, *The RKO Gals*, *The Slapstick Queens*, *Good Dames*, and *The MGM Stock Company* is apparently enduring and popular. Each subject is described by biographical data, career information and film annotation. In most instances the material uses a narrative factual approach, avoiding both critical interpretation and a retelling of personal/private events. With some minor variation, this format is used again in this volume. Each of 28 teams is introduced in male-then-female order with biographical data and filmography given for each. A few pages of well-reproduced stills follow as an introduction to the films that starred the pair. A synopsis, background material, critical quotes and evaluation accompany each film. A final portion follows the pair's careers after their film partnership ended. The volume is fully indexed.

Selection is always controversial in a volume such as this, e.g., is the Leslie Howard-Bette Davis team with three films more deserving of inclusion than George Brent-Bette Davis, with 11? The author faces this inevitable question in his introduction. His explanation of the absence of Astaire-Rogers—that they are already well covered in other books—is contradicted by the inclusion of Tracy-Hepburn, a team that is certainly represented in other volumes. However, a majority of the selections are valid and will please most readers. In summary, this is a volume that contains the ingredients of popular success—appealing subjects, information, nostalgia, visuals, and some light critical analysis. Recommended.

3037 *Hollywood's Greatest Love Stories.* by Kleiner, Dick. 277 p. paper New York: Pocket Books, 1976.

This original paperback designed for romantics is subtitled, "How and Why the Stars Fell in Love." In twelve separate chapters, the relationship of a dozen well-known couples is recalled. Only three, June Haver—Fred MacMurray, Grace Kelly—Prince Rainier, and Sophia Loren—Carlo Ponti, still exist. The other pairs, Bacall-Bogart, Bergman-Rossellini, Gardener-Sinatra, Hayworth-Aly Kahn, Hepburn-Tracy, Lombard-Gable, Monroe-DiMaggio, Taylor-Todd, and Ullmann—Bergman have ceased due to death or personal choice.

The coverage here is on an external, surface level based largely on publicity, image, and the romantic imagination of the author. Any Hollywood love relationship is so complex that even the participants would be unable to describe it. What is offered here then is a kind of romantic fiction based mostly on legends created for publicity purposes.

3038 *Hollywood's Hollywood.* by Behlmer, Rudy; and Thomas, Tony. 345 p. illus. Secaucus, N.J.: Citadel, 1975.

In its apparent effort to broaden its film coverage, Citadel has published this volume, subtitled "The Movies About the Movies." Another departure is the use of a chapter-essay form rather than the usual individual film treatment. Some 200 films are grouped into thematic categories—biographies,

murders, big knives, star-spangled rhythms, bombshells, goddesses, etc. There are over 400 visuals and an index.

The buff or the browser may enjoy this presentation but the serious reader will deplore the lack of any attempt to make a historical correlation.

3039 *Hollywood's Hottest Secrets.* by Ramer, Jean. 188 p. paper New York: Award Books, 1974.

Hollywood scandals are resurrected once again in this sensationalized book that promises much more than it ultimately divulges. The subjects are predictable: Lana Turner, Ingrid Bergman, Elizabeth Taylor, Sharon Tate, Monroe, Sinatra, Brando, Garland, Flynn, Harlow and Valentino. There is nothing presented here that is not already a matter of public or published record. The only service the book offers is to summarize the individual troubles, difficulties and fates that have haunted some of Hollywood's most famous personalities. Acceptable on this basis.

3040 *Hollywood's Movie Commandments.* by Martin, Olga J. 301 p. New York: Arno Press, 1970 (1937).

This book was an analysis of the Production Code designed to acquaint readers with the purpose and operation of the code. The first portion offers a historical and social background, followed by sections on moral values, crime and sex. Some general censorable topics such as profanity, suicide, vulgarity, etc. are also considered. The closing chapters devote themselves to the problems of screen writing and compliance with the code. The code is reprinted in the appendix along with some amendments to it. Useful for historians and researchers.

3041 *Hollywood's Other Men.* by Barris, Alex. 223 p. paper illus. New York: A. S. Barnes, 1975.

The subject of this volume is the male performer who provided contrast to the male star or lead in Hollywood films. They played the roles of friends, buddies, pals, rivals, villains, etc., and were usually presented via script, costume, and direction as inferior in some way to the hero. Examples given in the volume range from the thirties to thesixties with a decided emphasis on the early decades.

Although the theme is a provocative one, it is developed carelessly here. Examples cited under some of the headings—funny friend, nice friend, rival, lucky friend—seem arbitrary and forced, as is the extended attention given to Bing Crosby and Ralph Bellamy. Illustrations show not only the "other man" roles but parts played by the actors which do not fall into the topic stereotype (heroes, character parts, protagonists, etc.). The presence of these stills without a sufficiently clear statement explaining their inclusion may be both confusing and misleading to some readers. For example, from the caption on page 27 for a still from TEA AND SYMPATHY (1956), one might infer that Leif Erikson was "the other man." Based on the definition established by the author, this is a very debatable use of still and caption.

Outright errors exist, to wit: the still on page 56 is from THE HOODLUM SAINT (1946) and not ZIEGFELD FOLLIES (1946); William Powell had the lead and did not make a guest appearance, as stated in the citation. On page 84: in HOLIDAY (1938), Lew Ayres should be identified as Katharine (misspelled in the book as Katherine) Hepburn's brother, rather than a nice tipsy friend. On page 108: Frank Sinatra did lose Kathryn Grayson to Peter Lawford in IT HAPPENED IN BROOKLYN (1947). On page 165: Barry Nelson was Spencer Tracy's ghostly friend from heaven in A GUY NAMED JOE (1943) and not one of the cadets that Tracy coaches.

The major asset in the volume is the fine collection of stills, most of which are unfamiliar. They are acceptably reproduced and will offer pleasure to the reader who appreciates nostalgia, trivia, or film lore. The index provided is a name index, although it is not so titled. A second index of film titles would have added considerable dimension to the volume. Although the treatment is disappointing and careless, the stills are most appealing. Acceptable.

3042 *Hollywood's Other Women.* by Barris, Alex. 212 p. illus. New York: A. S. Barnes, 1975.

If one looks at this volume simply as a collection of stills linked together by a colorless text about female film characters, it is acceptable. It becomes vulnerable when it claims to be anything more than that. Female film performances have been grouped into categories such as mothers, bitches, vamps, witches, harlots, etc. Examples of these roles are then described and illustrated. A final chapter pays tribute to Bette Davis as "The All-Around Broad." Little distinction is made between a "typed" performer and one fortunate or young enough to play a wide variety of roles.

Assignment is arbitrary and many actresses appear in several categories (e.g., Angela Lansbury and Joan Crawford). The text is often too general or misleading; for example, should Margaret Dumont be included as "a classic Bitch?" Ida Lupino's bet-

ter performances—THE HARD WAY (1942), WHILE THE CITY SLEEPS (1956), etc.—are ignored; likewise Virginia Bruce in THE GREAT ZIEGFELD (1935). Did Ina Claire make a career out of playing classic bitches? Eight films in a variety of parts make up her total filmography. The title under the illustration of THE RELUCTANT DEBUTANTE (1958) on page 35 is misleading—there is no romantic triangle situation in the film. Can BELL, BOOK AND CANDLE (1959) really be called "a spooky movie?"

For the nondiscriminating browser, this volume may offer a pleasurable hour or so. The serious film reader will be disappointed with both the selection and the treatment of the material. Picture reproduction is good but selection is only average, with many of thechoices containing several characters rather than simply one or two for easy identification. An index of names helps somewhat. Acceptable with the reservations noted above.

3043 *Hollywood's Poverty Row, 1930-1950.* by Fernett, Gene. 163 p. illus. Satellite Beach, Fla.: Coral Reef Publications, 1973.

Poverty Row was not a geographical location in Hollywood, but rather a group of motion picture studios. They operated from approximately 1930 to 1950 and produced films with very low budgets. Many Hollywood personalities began their careers in such films—Rita Hayworth, Gene Autry, and Roy Rogers were three—while others spent their declining professional years appearing in these productions. This volume provides a historical overview of the two decades of production of these studios—Monogram, Republic, Mascot, Grand National, Tiffany, Lippert, and others.

The text is a result of research, interviews, interest and energy generated by the author. Occasionally, some interesting digressions appear, but they are indicative of the writer-buff who is anxious to share his enthusiasms with the reader. Most of the presentation is structured, factual and critical; it represents a thoughtful exposition of a rather neglected aspect of Hollywood history. The visuals supplied are of consistent interest. Reproduction quality is mostly above average, with only a few underexposed photographs included. Although the topic is somewhat unusual, it will have appeal for those readers interested in history, nostalgia, or the forgotten films of Poverty Row. Acceptable.

3044 *Hollywood's Unsolved Mysteries.* by Austin, John. 190 p. paper New York: Ace Books, 1970.

This is yet another re-telling of the sensational Hollywood scandals. Film personalities such as William Desmond Taylor, Thelma Todd, Jean Harlow, Marilyn Monroe, Fatty Arbuckle, et al. are among the unfortunate ones involved. An attempt is made to introduce some stories that are not so familiar but these concern minor or unknown names such as Jean Spangler or Marina Habe.

The author's style is dull and factual except for the introduction where he is both opinionated and incorrect. For example: "All B movies were 60 minutes in length" and "90 percent of the people working in Hollywood earn a great deal of money." Irresponsible statements such as these will not reassure the reader. This book is a failure—even for its intended market. Forget it.

3045 *Holmes of the Movies.* by Davies, David Stuart. 175 p. illus. New York: Bramhall House, 1976.

Subtitled "The Screen Career of Sherlock Holmes," this survey not only considers the many films made about the famous detective but also treats the actors who interpreted the character. Using a chronological approach, Davies recalls the silent films, the Basil Rathbone series (three chapters), and the recent variations on the Holmes stories—THE PRIVATE LIFE OF SHERLOCK HOLMES (1970), THEY MIGHT BE GIANTS (1972), THE ADVENTURE OF SHERLOCK HOLMES' SMARTER BROTHER (1975), and THE SEVEN PER CENT SOLUTION (1976). A few foreign language films are also discussed. Since the volume is nicely illustrated, the reader can compare the physical qualities that the various actors brought to the role. A selected filmography is included but no index is provided.

There are several other volumes which treat the same subject in a more comprehensive fashion: *Sherlock Holmes on the Screen, Deerstalker,* and *The Sherlock Holmes File.* While this volume is an adequate survey, its limited selection from the nearly 300 Holmes films places it at a comparative disadvantage. Acceptable.

3046 *Homage to Georges Melies.* edited by Davis, Myrna M. paper New York: Push Pin Studios, 1967.

3047 *Homage to John Grierson.* by Cinematheque Canadienne. 13 p. paper illus. Montreal: Cinematheque Canadienne, 1964.

Published on the occasion of the National Film Board's 25th anniversary, December, 1964.

3048 *The Home Movie Scenario Book.* by Ryskind, Morrie; and Stevens, C. F.; and Englander, James. 174 p. New York: Richard Manson, 1927.

This historical curio consists mostly of 20 scenarios designed for the amateur to film. Titles will give the reader a clue to the content and quality: "The Golf Widow," "The Way of a Transgressor," "What to Do With Chaperones," "A Modern John Alden," etc. The second section deals with the elements of amateur filmmaking, starting with the establishment of the home movie company—a director, cameraman, technical helpers, players, etc. Directing, acting, sets, lighting, makeup and editing are treated next. A glossary of terms completes the book. Commerical sound films appeared almost simultaneously with this book. No mention is made of sound, however. The book is an attractive piece of memorabilia that may have historical interest but is of little practical value today. Noted for the record.

3049 *Home Movies.* by Fellow, Malcolm Stuart. 144 p. illus. New York: Drake, 1974.

A glossary of terms used in making films opens this volume, which is then arranged in standard fashion. Equipment purchase, principles of photography, color, light, planning, titling, tricks, editing, sound, commentary and finally exhibition are considered sequentially. A final chapter suggests sources for ideas for home movies. A short index completes the work. The quality of the illustrations is variable. Diagrams and sketches are excellent. A number of the black-and-white illustrations are too dark (e.g., pages 65, 67), while the color illustrations are rather one-note in continually picturing overly made-up models wearing mini-skirts.

The text provided is clear and comprehensive in its coverage, with the author tending toward the informal-practical approach rather than the technical. Unfortunately the volume lacks any outstanding element or quality which might separate it from the many other volumes which exist on the same subject. Acceptable.

3050 *Home Movies Made Easy.* by Knight, Frank R. 96 p. illus. New York: Doubleday, 1960.

A beginner's guide to motion picture photography, this book covers camera selection, production, editing and exhibition. Drawings and pictures, some in color, help a great deal.

3051 *Home Movies Made Easy.* edited by Kodak Staff. 148 p. paper illus. Rochester, N.Y.: Eastman Kodak, 1974.

Glossy production of attractive illustrations accompanied by a clear expository text characterize this Kodak standard which is devoted to amateur 8mm filmmaking. As usual with the *Kodak* publications, the content is excellent and the price is right.

3052 *Home Videotape-Disc Guide: Movies and Entertainment.* New York: NAL (Plume), 1980.

3053 *Hommage to the Vancouver CBC Film Unit.* by Cinematheque Canadienne. paper illus. Montreal: Cinematheque Canadienne, 1964.

Published on the occasion of the 25th anniversary of the Canadian Broadcasting Corporation Vancouver Film Unit, August, 1964.

3054 *Honest Injun.* by Carstairs, John Paddy. 168 p. illus. London: Hurst and Blackett, 1942.

This "light-hearted autobiography" contains photos of many of the leading players of the period who were friends, workers and acquaintances of the author. Carstairs was a man of many talents, having had careers as a film and television director, novelist, painter, writer, and naval officer. In this volume he offers portraits of many celebrities. See also *Hadn't We the Gaiety?* and *Movie Merry-Go-Round.*

3055 AN HONEST MAN. (un Honnete Homme). by Kyrou, Ado. 39 p. paper London: Rodney, 1964.

3056 *The Honeycomb.* by St. John, Adela Rogers. 700 p. illus. Garden City, N.Y.: Doubleday, 1969.

Adela Rogers St. John is best known as a reporter and feature writer for the Hearst newspapers. During her 50-year career as a newswoman, she has written much about Hollywood and its personalities. In this second volume of autobiography she is concerned mostly with the period of 1920 to 1950. Although the text is concerned with legendary news stories such as the Lindbergh kidnapping and the Edward VIII abdication, there is some material about Hollywood in the twenties and thirties. The author was confidante and friend to Mary Pickford, Marion Davies, William Randolph Hearst, Rudolph

Valentino, Clark Gable, Mabel Normand and many others. Peripheral film material but interesting.

3057 *Hooray for Captain Spaulding!* by Anobile, Richard 224 p. illus. New York: Darien House, 1974.

Anobile is the enterprising producer of books which reproduce whole films or sequences by using numerous frame blow-ups and the original dialogue, e.g., WHY A DUCK?, A FLASH OF FIELDS, WHO'S ON FIRST?, FRANKENSTEIN, THE MALTESE FALCON, CASABLANCA, PSYCHO, etc. He is also the coauthor of *The Marx Brothers Scrapbook.*

Part of his activity to reproduce ANIMAL CRACKERS (1930) for this volume necessitated acquiring permission from the copyright owners to reproduce the visuals (Universal) and the dialogue (George S. Kaufman Estate and Morrie Ryskind). Once obtained, he selected the frames to be enlarged and the words to accompany them. Over 800 visuals are used in the volume and a remarkable reconstruction of ANIMAL CRACKERS emerges. Although the enlargements never possess the clarity of a production still, they are adequate in quality for the purpose intended here. The dialogue is printed both as captions to the frames and in comic-strip balloon style. The title is taken from the song which celebrates Groucho's first entrance in the film.

To be able to have a Marx Brothers' film available for leisurely viewing or studying would excite many people anticipating the reliving of some treasured moments from the far past. This volume is the next best thing. Recommended.

3058 *Horizons West.* by Kitses, Jim. 176 p. paper illus. Bloomington, Ind.: Indiana University Press, 1969.

An analysis of the westerns made by three film directors—Anthony Mann, Budd Boetticher, and Sam Peckinpah. An opening chapter discusses general elements of this Hollywood genre. A list of other films is given along with the filmography of the westerns for each director. The illustrations are exceptionally good. Since the directors are men whose creative work is only now being recognized to any great extent, this volume performs a service in considering overlooked, forgotten or ignored films, e.g., THE LAST FRONTIER (1955) or DEVIL'S DOORWAY (1950). A scholarly, interesting book that is highly recommended for all.

3059 *The Horrific World of Monsters.* by Barber, Dulan. 121 p. illus. London: Marshal Cavendish, 1974.

Real and unreal monsters arranged alphabetically. Some films are mentioned and there are a few color illustrations. Indexed.

3060   *Horror and Fantasy in the Movies.* by Hutchinson, Tom. 156 p. illus. New York: Crescent (Crown), 1974.

Three film genres—Horror, Fantasy, and Science Fiction— are surveyed in six chapters in this attractively illustrated volume. Written by the film critic for the *London Sunday Telegraph*, the text is above average for a book whose major attraction is its visuals—stills, lobby cards, posters, etc.

3061   *Horror and Science Fiction Films: A Checklist.* by Willis, Donald C. 612 p. Metuchen, N.J.: Scarecrow, 1972.

As the title indicates, this reference book is a listing of 4400 titles in the film genres of horror and science fiction. For each entry, the following information is given: title, country of origin, studio, production credits, cast credits, synopsis and comment. Some of the data indicated above were not available on early silent films. Four addenda complete the book: "Titles Announced for 1971-72," "Shorts, Animated, Puppet Films," "Out List," and "References."

Some attempt is made to define the criteria for the placement of a film in the main listing or the out list, but decisions seem more subjective than objective. Annotations are short, prejudiced, elementary, and even poor at times, appearing as if they are condensations of the outlines appearing in TV movie guides or other film listings. For example: JUST IMAGINE (1930) is described as a "S-F musical set in New York in 1980." The annotation on DOCTOR X (1932) reads: "Synthetic flesh! silly; once in a while silly enough to be some fun; at any rate better than Curtiz's other early thirties horror hit, MYSTERY OF THE WAX MUSEUM (1933)." On DR. JEKYLL AND MR. HYDE (1932): "This may or may not be the best verison of the tired old story (which wasn't much to begin with) but good it isn't. There are some impressive touches, mainly in the treatment of Hyde, but Hopkins is dull, and there are the usual obligatory time-filling scenes with Jekyll. Better then Mamoulian's early 'Classics'." These words seem self-contradictory and unfair to the films.

Perhaps the most important service provided is the almost all-inclusive main listing. Nearly any horror film or science fiction film that one can recall is there. The coverage is impressive. As a specialized reference tool, the book is suitable. As a recreation or pleasure book, it would have been much better if the annotations had reflected general critical consensus rather than the author's personal bias.

3062   *The Horror Factory.* by Dettman, Bruce; and Bedford, Michael. 193 p. illus. New York: Gordon Press, 1976.

In a series of short essays, the authors review "The Horror Films of Universal, 1931-1955." They have divided the films into appropriate groupings: The Classics, Karloff and Lugosi, The Continuing Story of Famous Monsters, etc. A filmography and a bibliography complete the volume. A few illustrations appear in a center section.

The essays include critical comment, background information, and plot synopsis. Although some films found here are rarely treated in film literature, the reader may still question the reason for this volume which repeats much of what has already been written about horror films. Had the authors concentrated on the studio and the filmmakers rather than the films, the title would be more precise than it is.

Production consists of reproducing typewritten copy, and this has been done poorly. Inked-in corrections are very visible, errata is noted, and the care given to editing and preparing the manuscript seems minimal. Since the price of this volume seems excessive for a mediocre text poorly produced, the volume is not acceptable.

3063   *The Horror Film.* by Butler, Ivan. 176 p. paper illus. New York: Barnes, 1967.

Included in this fine small volume is a brief survey of the horror film including a recapitulation of the screen careers of Dracula and Frankenstein. Some films, e.g., FREAKS (1932), VAMPYR (1931), and some directors, e.g., Clouzot, Hitchcock, Corman and Polanski, get special attention. The latter portion consists of a chronology (title-date -director) of horror films. Descriptive and evaluative annotations along with cast listings are offered for certain films. When you take a topic with proven popularity and endurance and treat it with intelligence, admiration and respect, the result is an excellent volume such as this. Highly recommended to all readers.

3064   *Horror Film Album.* by Eyles, Allen. 52 p. paper illus. London: Ian Allen, 1971.

Almost 200 photographs provide a chronological survey of the horror film in this volume. The author supplies captions for the visuals.

3065   *Horror Film Stars.* by Pitts, Michael R. 324 p. illus. Jefferson, N.C.: McFarland, 1981.

A collective biography of fifteen major stars and twenty-two featured players.

3066 *Horror Films.* by Dillard, R. H. W. 129 p. paper illus. New York: Monarch, 1976.

This volume is an argument for the acceptance of the horror film as "a valid and meaningful artistic genre directly related to our direct experience." The author uses detailed analyses of four films as his major text: FRANKENSTEIN (1931), THE WOLF MAN (1941), NIGHT OF THE LIVING DEAD (1968) and SATYRICON (1969). Introductory and summary chapters are included along with a lengthy bibliography, a filmography, and an interesting collection of photographs.

The critical treatment afforded the films is both informative and stimulating; it will probably encourage the reader to seek another viewing of the films. In other words, the author's argument is successful. Recommended.

3067 *Horror in Film and Literature.* by Zambrano, A. L. New York: Gordon, 1976.

3068 *Horror Movies.* by Frank, Alan G. 160 p. illus. Secaucus, N.J.: Octopus, 1974.

Published in England as a title in the *Movie Treasury* series, this volume is another survey of horror and terror films. The predictable Dracula-Frankenstein-Monster-Mad Scientist films are covered by text and by 200 illustrations, of which 40 are in color. Designed for mass-market appeal, the book will surely please the naive or nondiscriminating patron. The more sophisticated reader will find some solace in certain nicely reproduced visuals. Acceptable.

3069 *The Horror People.* by Brosnan, John. 304 p. illus. New York: St. Martin's Press, 1976.

After dealing successfully in his first book with the artists responsible for special effects, Brosnan now gives his attention to a collective biographical appreciation of filmmakers associated with horror films. Included are Lon Chaney, Boris Karloff, Bela Lugosi, Vincent Price, Lon Chaney, Jr., Peter Cushing, Christopher Lee, James Whale, Val Lewton, Robert Bloch, Terence Fisher, William Castle, Richard Matheson, Karl Freund, Tod Browning, Jack Arnold, Roger Corman, Freddie Francis, Roy Baker, Milton Subotsky, Kevin Francis and others.

The subjects named above receive extended attention along with Hammer films, American International films, etc. Shorter profiles are provided for many other personalities in both the text and in an appendix entitled "More Horror People." References are noted and a very detailed index is provided. Most of the illustrations have been carefully reproduced and complement the text nicely.

Many interview quotations are interwoven with the author's biographical narrative and critical evaluations. The richness of the author's material, his skill in presenting it and the excellent production given to this volume make it stand out among the many books available on the subject. Recommended.

3070 *Horror!* by Douglas, Drake. 309 p. illus. New York: Macmillan, 1966.

Both print and film examples are used in this book which deals with the subject of horror. Each horror character genre, such as werewolf, vampire, monster, mummy, etc., is given a chapter of description, analysis, and example. Plot outlines of the original novels, short stories, or films are included. Photographs are few and overly familiar. Some interesting opinions and comments are offered but much of the book seems padded with material that is well known. This book should be given a rather low priority. Other books on the same topic are available and should take precedence.

3071 *Horrors: From Screen to Scream.* by Naha, Ed. 306 p. paper illus. New York: Flare (Avon), 1975.

The appeal of the horror film appears permanent if one is to judge by the number of books published on the subject. In this volume, which is subtitled "An Encyclopedic Guide to the Greatest Horror and Fantasy Films of All Time," the author has provided factual and critical annotations for many films and some selected filmmakers (Boris Karloff, Peter Lorre, Claude Rains, Basil Rathbone, Arthur P. Jacobs, Willis O'Brien, Val Lewton, Herbert Lom, etc.). Intermixed with the entries are hundreds of illustrations, most of which are clearly reproduced.

Some slight reservation might be had about the author's critical judgment and his memory of film plots. The total accomplishment is most impressive. Although this book is designed primarily as an entertainment, it also has a high reference value. In addition to studio, year of release, plot outlines, background information, and critical evaluation, most of the film entries indicate a few cast names and the director. Recommended.

3072 *Horses in the Movies.* by Hintz, H. F. 146 p. illus. New York: A.S. Barnes, 1979.

In his introduction, the author states, "The horse has been and will continue to be a very important part of the movie industry and American culture." He employs eight chapters to substantiate his claim and the result is a unique book that is quite comprehensive. The text consists largely of a collective biography of famous horse stars along with shorter background sections, a horse filmography, a Disney horse filmography, a bibliography, and many illustrations. The book is indexed. Hintz' approach to a film topic that is seldom treated in books is factual, serious, and respectful. This is not surprising, since he is a professor of animal nutrition at Cornell. His book should surprise and please a large audience of young readers.

3073 *Hot Line! The Letters I Get and Write.* by Reynolds, Burt. 128 p. paper illus. New York: Signet Books, 1972,

"When you're hot, you're hot" —thus, this snickering, leering appeal to prurient curiosity is a product of the Reynolds' centerfold celebrity. The visuals and the text in this example of publishing garbage are dirty, simple-minded, and ultimately insulting. Noted here as an example of the length to which ambitious performers will go to promote themselves. Devices such as hair pieces, retouching, and padding are obvious in the visuals and the letters seem to be the product of an overstimulated but underexercised ghost-editor.

3074 *Hound and Horn: Essays on Cinema.* New York: Arno, 1972.

The *Hound and Horn* was a little magazine which appeared in the late twenties and the early thirties. Devoted to all the arts, it was one of the first to carry critical reviews and essays on film.

This compilation includes the following: "Eisenstein's New York" by Jere Abbott; "In Memory of Harry Alan Potamkin, 1900-1933," Anonymous; "Nationalism in German Films" by Alfred H. Barr, Jr.; "Spoilation of QUE VIVA MEXICO" by Kirk Bond; "The Art of Kipps" by Grant Code; "The Dynamic Square" by Sergei Eisenstein; "Periodical Reviews: Movie Magazines" by Henry-Russell Hitchcock Jr.; "James Cagney and the American Hero" by Lincoln Kirstein; "Eisenstein and the Theory of Cinema," by Harry Alan Potamkin; "A Proposal for a School of the Motion Picture," by Harry Alan Potamkin; "Pabst and the Social Film," by Harry Alan Potamkin; "Pudovkin and the Revolutionary Film," by Harry Alan Potamkin; "Animated Cartoons" by Kenneth White; "F. W. Murnau" by Kenneth White; "Garbo and Dietrich" by Kenneth White; "The Style of Ernst Lubitsch" by Kenneth White; "Movie Chronicle" by Kenneth White.

3075 *An Hour with the Movies and the Talkies.* by Seldes, Gilbert. 156 p. Philadelphia: J. P. Lippincott, 1929.

The title stems from the fact that the book was designed for one hour's reading time. After a brief, rather compact history of films, two questions are raised by discussion: 1) why no other performer in films has attained the stature of Chaplin, and 2) whether films have reached their ultimate form with the arrival of the talkies. Early, excellent Seldes; recommended.

3076 *The House of Horror.: The Story of the Hammer Films.* edited by Eyles, Allen; and Adkinson, Robert; and Fry, Nicholas. 127 p. paper illus. New York: Third Press, 1974.

Most filmgoers associate Hammer films with the Frankenstein-Dracula-Mummy updates that appeared during the fifties. Surprisingly, the history of the Hammer organization goes back to THE PUBLIC LIFE OF HENRY THE NINTH (1935) and includes comedies (FURTHER UP THE CREEK, 1958), adventures (THE VIKING QUEEN, 1967), melodrama (HELL IS A CITY, 1960) and contemporary problem films (ON THE BUSES, 1971). This volume surveys the total output of the Hammer studios by first paying biographical tribute to Michael Carreras, Terence Fisher, Christopher Lee and Peter Cushing. Described next is the period from 1935 to the early fifties. The resurrection of the famous monsters occurred during the fifties and the sixties. A final section discusses other nonhorror films that Hammer has produced. A total filmography completes the volume. Picture quality and selection are very good, reflecting in no small way the sensationalism of the Hammer product. Blood, sex, and gore are constant elements in the visuals. A colored section of publicity handouts emphasizes the same qualities.

This is an entertaining, informative account of a studio that has brought thrills and chills to audiences for nearly four decades. The pictorial sex and nudity may limit the book's use but it does provide very popular reading. Recommended.

3077 *The House of Van Du: A Biography of the Stage and Screen Actor, Grant Mitchell.* by DuBois, Aaron. 126 p. illus. New York: William-Frederick, 1962.

Grant Mitchell was a character actor who specialized in playing mature American males prominent in small towns—politicians, lawyers, bankers, etc.

3078 *The House that Shadows Built.* by Irwin, Will. 293 p. illus Garden City, N.Y.: Doubleday, 1928.

A period piece which seems to be a written-to-order biography of Adolph Zukor, this book is nevertheless often quoted as a reference. It is a Horatio Alger version of Zukor's career written in the romantic style of the twenties with all uncomplimentary views of the subject omitted. In spite of this subjective approach, there are some interesting accounts and personalities in the book, e.g., Hale's tours, Bernhardt's QUEEN ELIZABETH (1912), Mary Pickford, etc. Although it is primarily about the competition to survive, the book gives the impression that there was little tension or struggle involved. Mr. Zukor apparently was God-like and possessed no vices or faults. A bit hard to take. Of interest only to historians and scholars. Not recommended.

3079 THE HOUSEHOLDER. by Jhabvala, Ruth Prawer. 219 p. illus. Delhi: Ramlochan, 1965.

The screenplay of the 1963 film, adapted from Jhabvala's novel, directed by James Ivory.

3080 *How Films Are Made.* by Reed, Stanley; and Huntley, John. 90 p. illus. London: The Educational Supply Association Ltd., 1955.

An older volume designed for educational use, this book covers the making of a film from script to screen. The contribution made by each artisan is explained, sometimes by the use of invented dialogue. Some of the illustrations are excellent in content but poor in reproduction. The book is indexed. Since much of the material is either out-of-date or seems to "talk down" to the reader, the book is only of minor historical interest.

3081 *How Hollywood Rates.* by Raborn, George. 64 p. Los Altos, Calif.: B. Nelson, 1955.

Subtitled "27 Years of Rating 700 Stars and 1500 Movies," the text employs a rating system apparently devised by the author who rates people, genres, songs, kisses, pairings, figures, worst performances, etc. This is camp fun, not to be taken seriously.

3082 *How I Filmed the War.* by Malins, Geoffrey H; and Warren, Low. 307 p. illus. London: Herbert Jenkins, 1919.

Malins was a director of silent short and feature films who also served as a cinematographer for the British War Office during the First World War. In this volume he tells about filming amidst the battlefront areas, editing, censorship problems, and the effect his films had upon recruiting.

3083 *How it Happened Here—the Making of a Film.* by Brownlow, Kevin. 184 p. illus Garden City, Doubleday N.Y.: 1968.

Here is the story of Brownlow's efforts to make the 1963 film, IT HAPPENED HERE. At the age of 18 with a borrowed camera and no funds, he began a project which was completed 8 years later. His co-director was 16-year-old Andrew Mollo. The efforts, errors, and disillusionments of the pair are related in a way that will be inspirational to the novice filmmaker. Since this is a British story and the subject film received scant attention in the United States, reader interest may be diminished. The book is interesting as an earlier writing effort of Brownlow who later produced the excellent book *The Parade's Gone By.* Limited interest to the general reader.

3084 *How Motion Pictures Are Made.* by Croy, Homer. 371 p. illus New York: Harper, 1918.

A very early history of the development of motion pictures—descriptions of inventions, trick photography, special uses of motion pictures, early animation, etc.

3085 *How the Great Comedy Writers Create Laughter.* by Wilde, Larry. 285 p. Chicago: Nelson Hall, 1976.

This collection of interviews has as its general theme the work of the comedy writer. Asked how they make people laugh are Mel Brooks, Goodman Ace, Art Buchwald, Abe Burrows, Bill Dana, Selma Diamond, Jack Douglas, Hal Kanter, Norman Lear, Carl Reiner and Neil Simon.

The comment, advice, and reflection offered in each interview make for entertaining yet informative reading. Since many of the subjects have had experience in film writing, the book has pertinence for film collections. Unfortunately no credit listings are offered so, aside from what is mentioned in the conversation, it is impossible to determine the writer's participation in the various entertainment media. Acceptable.

3086   HOW THE WEST WAS WON. 36 p. illus. New York: Random House, 1963.

Since there were so many stars and co-stars in this Cinerama-MGM production, each receives only a small portrait and a paragraph of biography. The central section contains a collection of photographs from the 1963 film, arranged to approximate the continuity of the film. Directors Henry Hathaway, John Ford, and George Marshall, along with other production personnel, are given special attention, and there is a rather good diagram of the Cinerama process included. The care that the publisher takes in producing these program books is again evident.

3087   *How They Made* SONS OF MATTHEW. by Dunn, Maxwell. 210 p.illus. London: Angus and Robertson, 1949.

The making of the film SONS OF MATTHEW (1949) is recounted in this book. Produced and directed by Charles Chauvel, the film was made in Queensland, Australia.

3088   *How They Make a Motion Picture.* by Hoadley, Ray. 119 p. illus. New York: Crowell, 1939.

Clear, readable descriptions of sets, wardrobe, makeup, lighting, sound, props, etc. Many photographs. Aimed at young adults.

3089   *How to Add Sound to Amateur Films.* by Neale, D. M. 160 p. paper illus. London: Focal Press, 1961.

The 3rd edition of a title in the *Focal Cinebook* series.

3090   *How to Animate Cut-Outs for Amateur Films.* by Barton, Cyril H. 119 p. paper illus. New York: Focal Press, 1960.

A title in the *Focal Cinebook* series that discusses a type of motion picture animation for beginning filmmakers.

3091   *How to Appreciate Motion Pictures.* by Dale, Edgar. 243 p. New York: Arno Press, 1970 (1937).

One of the original Payne Fund "Studies of Motion Pictures and Social Values" published in 1937, this one is a manual on motion picture criticism prepared for high school students.

3092   *How to Audition for TV, Movies, Commercials, Plays, Musicals.* by Hunt, Gordon. 333 p. illus. New York: Harper and Row, 1977.

Subtitled "Advice from a Casting Director," this volume contains two main parts, the advice and the interviews. In the first, Gordon Hunt offers the wisdom gained by long experience as both a director and a casting director on both coasts. He speaks in general terms of such matters as pictures, resumes, interviews, call-backs, etc. Only two of the interviews deal specifically with film auditions (James Bridges and Milton Katselas), although the others contain pertinent information for anyone seeking a chance.

The text by Hunt is knowing, sympathetic and encouraging while the interviews are surprisingly frank and honest. As a result this handbook is well worth the attention of anyone trying to break into show business.

3093   *How to Be a Movie Star or A Terrible Beauty Is Born.* by Chase, Chris. 208 p. New York: Harper and Row, 1974.

This collection of humorous articles has the connecting theme of getting ahead in show business. Told with a delightful light style, the accounts of the efforts made by a young actress to succeed are often hilarious—yet depend on truth for their substance. The book's attraction is the way the author looks at her varied experiences.

Two short chapters deal with film experiences—the first tells of making KILLER'S KISS (1955) with the then novice director Stanley Kubrick. Preston Sturges was eager to have Ms. Chase participate in his comeback attempt that never materialized. Throughout the book other film actors are quoted and discussed, but the emphasis is mostly on the theatrical failures in which the author appeared. This volume is not pertinent for film students but is does offer some witty, entertaining, and perceptive comments about show business. Acceptable for mature readers.

3094   *How to Become a Film Artiste.* by Dangerfield, Fred; and Howard, Norman. 99 p. London: Odhams Press, 1921.

Early advice on the art of photoplay acting.

3095 *How to Become a Movie Star.* by Klaw, Irving. 126 p. illus. New York: Klaw, 1946.

Advice on the art of acting for motion pictures.

3096 *How to Break into Motion Pictures, Television, Commercials and Modeling.* by Blanchard, Nina. 240 p. illus. New York: Doubleday, 1978.

Eileen Ford provides the foreword for this career manual which was written by the director of a West Coast talent/model agency. The usual predictable elements are present: types of work, training necessary, interviews, agents, etc. Informational sections are intermixed with anecdotes, illustrations and advice. The appendixes offer many lists—drama schools, actors' workshops, coaches, agencies, unions—along with a glossary and a bibliography.

3097 *How to Break Into the Movies.* by Zugsmith, Albert. 173 p. paper New York: Macfadden, 1963.

Remember Phillipa Fallon? She had roles in Producer Zugsmith's GIRL IN THE KREMLIN (1957), HIGH SCHOOL CONFIDENTIAL (1960), and PRIVATE LIVES OF ADAM AND EVE (1961). With his success in guiding Miss Fallon in films as an impetus, Zugsmith offers his rules for film fame, punctuated by tidbits of information, e.g., Doris Day sang with a band, John Wayne was a stuntman, etc. The text is always predictable. There are also chapters on writing, producing, direction and other behind-the-camera careers. Zugsmith's films and the book are consistent: the films are obvious, cheap, intellectually insulting, and promise more than they deliver. So does the book. The strongest portion is the appendix, which offers job descriptions along with some union-guild names and addresses. The remaining information is obsolete today. Noted for the record.

3098 *How to Cartoon (For Amateur Films).* by Halas, John; and Privett, Bob. 132 p. paper illus. London: Focal Press, 1955.

This excellent small paperback is crammed with information about making cartoon/animated films. It is aimed at the student or amateur and does not consider the elaborate processes used by studios. Script, materials for animation, speed and timing, principles of movement, and cartoon photography are some of the topics discussed. An indexed glossary is given for reference. The publishers list these other titles in the same *Focal Cinebook* Series: *How to Film* by G. Wain; *How to Script* by Oswell Blakes-

ton; *How to Direct* by Tony Rose; *How to Project* by Norman Jenkins; *How to Title* by Leslie Wheeler; *How to Use Colour* by C. L. Thompson; *How to Edit* by H. Baddeley; *How to Make 8MM Films* by N. Bau; *How to Write Film Stories* by D. M. Neale; *How to Produce Effects* by Julien Caunter; *How to Film Children* by M. Natkin; *How to Make Commentaries* by M. Kirsch; *How to Choose Music* by F. Rawlings.

The above titles are noted here to indicate the range and coverage of filmmaking topics available in print and usually found in the larger photographic shops. Many other similar series are available.

3099 *How to Choose Music for Amateur Films.* by Rawlings, F. 128 p. paper illus. London: Focal Press, 1961.

A title in the *Focal Cinebook* series.

3100 *How to Direct as an Amateur.* by Rose, Tony. 152 p. paper illus. London: Focal Press, 1958.

The 3rd edition of a title in the *Focal Cinebook* series, this volume is introduced by Roy Boulting.

3101 *How to Do Sound Films.* by Neale, Denis M. 155 p. paper illus. London: Focal Press, 1969.

The 4th revised edition of this volume treats the many ways in which a filmmaker can produced a good quality sound film or add sound to an existing silent one. All gauges of amateur film—8mm, super 8mm, and 16mm—are considered.

3102 *How to Edit.* by Baddeley, Hugh. 144 p. paper illus. New York: Focal Press, 1968.

This title from the *Focal Cinebook* Series was first published in 1951 and by 1968 was in its seventh edition. Among the topics covered are splices, assembling shots, adding fades/dissolves, editing principles, shot duration, assembly of complete scenes, and relational editing. Final chapters deal with film space, time, and sound editing. A glossary is added.

3103 *How to Enter and Win Film Contests.* by Gadney, Alan. 195 p. New York: Facts on File, 1981.

3104 *How to Film as an Amateur.* by Wain, G. 150 p. paper illus. London: Focal Press, 1960.

A title in the *Focal Cinebook* series, this volume on

amateur cinematography was in its ninth edition in this 1960 printing.

3105   *How to Film Indoors as an Amateur.* by Minter, L. F. 144 p. paper illus. London: Focal Press, 1957.

A title in the *Focal Cinebook* series.

3106   *How to Get into Show Business.* by Joels, Merrill E. 157 p. New York: Hastings House, 1969.

Practical advice for aspiring actors in fields of radio, television, theatre and films. Describes agents, auditions, unions, etc. An updated enlarged edition of *Acting is a Business.*

3107   *How to Judge Motion Pictures.* by Mullen, Sarah F. 60 p. paper illus. New York: Scholastic, 1934.

This pamphlet, whose text consists of two sections—seeing the picture and evaluating the picture—was designed for high school students. It also contains a separate section on "How to Organize a Photoplay Club."

3108   *How to Locate Reviews of Plays and Films.* by Samples, Gordon. 114 p. Metuchen, N.J.: Scarecrow, 1976.

The contents of this guide are divided into two sections: plays and films. Under films there are group listings for study guides, indexing services, newspaper indexes, criticism checklists, review collections, film periodicals, film genre guides, catalogs, and sources of film memorabilia. Each entry is accompanied by a short descriptive annotation and a notation of the period covered. The lists are subjective and, as such, quite acceptable. They should facilitate the search for film information.

3109   *How to Make a Jewish Movie.* by Shavelson, Melville. 244 p. illus. Englewood Cliffs, N. J.: Prentice-Hall, 1971.

The problems of creating the film CAST A GIANT SHADOW (1966) is the major topic of this volume. Written by a former gag-man and script writer, portions are autobiographical, i.e., recollections of work at Paramount, Warner Brothers, etc. The film, a biography of David Marcus, employed an all-star cast and was a gigantic failure both critically and at the box office. An ability to relate what must have been a disillusioning experience with humor, understanding and maturity is the author's outstanding

quality.

3110   *How to Make and Operate Moving Pictures.* edited by Jones, Bernard E. 216 p. illus. New York: Funk and Wagnalls, 1917.

"A practical guide to taking and projecting cinematograph pictures," this early volume contains numerous line drawings and half-tone plates. There are sections on making trick films, holding exhibitions of films at home, the laws governing the use of cinematograph pictures, etc.

3111   *How to Make Animated Cartoons: The History and Technique.* by Falk, Nat. 79 p. illus. New York: Foundation Books, 1941.

3112   *How to Make Animated Movies.* by Kinsey, Anthony. 95 p. illus. New York: Viking Press, 1970.

The subject of animated films that can be made by amateurs is well-handled in this compact primer. Beautifully illustrated in a manner which makes many animation processes seem easy, the book also contains clear and concise textual material. Topics include equipment, timing sequences, cels, animation without a camera, etc. Even a section on the history of the animated film is given. The book has a short bibliography and an index. Highly recommended.

3113   *How to Make Cine Gadgets for Amateur Camerawork.* by Walden, Harry. 120 p. paper illus. London: Focal Press, 1959.

A book on cinematography from the *Focal Cinebook* series.

3114   *How to Make 8mm Films.* by Bau, N. 183 p. paper illus. New York: Focal Press, 1967.

A title in the *Focal Cinebook* series, this book deals with all aspects of 8mm filmmaking. The films, the cameras, apertures, filters and accessories are treated prior to a discussion of shooting the film. Subjects, tricks, special effects and titling methods are suggested. Editing and sound addition are discussed along with projectors and final presentation to an audience. Many drawings help to explain the text and a glossary is appended.

3115 *How to Make 8mm Movies.* by Bau, Nicolas. 180 p. paper illus. London: Focal Press, 1966.

This is the 8th edition of a book from the *Focal Cinebook* series that has had the earlier title, *How to Make 8mm Films as an Amateur.*

3116 *How to Make Exciting Home Movies and Stop Boring Your Friends and Relatives.* by Schultz, Dodi; and Schultz, Ed. 152 p. illus. Garden City, N.Y.: Doubleday, 1973.

This volume has an imaginative title but a rather predictable and pedestrian text. The usual topics are covered, with a disappointing difference; instead of having visuals appear throughout the book, they are grouped into two sections. There are 35 color visuals and 38 black and white—which sounds bountiful—but many of these are grouped two to a page. The book is unrelieved text for the most part, and a better presentation of the identical material can be obtained at a much lower price at most photography stores.

3117 *How to Make Films at School.* by Beal, J. D. 147 p. illus. London: Focal Press, 1968.

The first section of this book makes a strong argument for filmmaking in schools, and notes some educational trends and aims in support. The central portion of the book is a broad general discussion of the techniques, processes, and problems of filmmaking. Final pages make a plea for school cooperation in filmmaking and offer some suggestions toward achieving such cooperation. A good glossary and an appendix complete the book.

This volume is unusual in its attempt to relate and correlate filmmking with the schools. It is of British origin and some of the academic approach may differ from that of other countries, but there is enough valid information and suggestion here to merit recommendation.

3118 *How to Make Good Home Movies.* by Kodak Staff 174 p. paper illus. Rochester, N.Y.: Kodak, 1966.

A small concise guide that is of value to all beginning filmmakers. The first of two parts deals with the process of movie making, while the second concerns itself primarily with technical data, material description, and special techniques. Many diagrams and colored pictures help to explain and illustrate ideas in the text. The book is indexed. This is a basic book—an ideal text, a good reference, and a bargain

to boot.

3119 *How to Make Good Sound Movies.* edited by Eastman Kodak Co. 98 p. paper illus. Rochester, N.Y.: Kodak, 1973.

Here is another of the books that Kodak publishes for the nonprofessional filmmaker. Supplemented by dozens of beautiful color illustrations, the text discusses the problems that occur when the dimension of sound is added to films. Microphones, their placement and handling, editing, splicing, prerecorded sound, live recording, etc.—all these and many other topics relating to sound are examined. It must be emphasized that the book was designed to promote the sale of noncompatible projectors, cameras and film; there is enough general information and advice offered, however, to warrant some reader interest. Acceptable.

3120 *How to Make It In Hollywood.* by Hyland, Wende; and Hayens, Roberta. 237 p. illus. Chicago: Nelson-Hall, 1975.

Advice on how to succeed and survive as a motion picture actor is offered in this collection of interviews. The subjects are successful professionals and include actors (Jack Lemmon, Walter Matthau, Susan Aspach, Telly Savalas), directors (Daniel Mann, Michael Campus, Milton Katselas), producers (Tony Spinner, Albert S. Ruddy, Aaron Spelling, David Dortort), casting directors (Renee Valente, Ethel Winant), and a talent agent (Meyer Mishkin).

The questions are pertinent and the responses are candid, brisk, and practical. For anyone interested in acting for films, the volume will be most useful and rewarding. Acceptable.

3121 *How to Make Money in Motion Pictures.* by Kozak, Yitka. paper Long Beach, N.Y.: Josephine Company, 1979.

3122 *How to Make Movie Magic.* by Caunter, Julien. 348 p. illus. Philadelphia: Chilton Book Co., 1971.

Originally published in two volumes titled *How to Do the Simpler Tricks* and *How to Do Tricks*, this book is a revised and combined edition. The book is addressed to the amateur filmmaker and offers suggestions on camera magic via exposure, focus, lens, speeds, distortions, reflection, filters, and chemicals. Fades, wipes, dissolves, the special effects box, reverse action, stop-motion, superimposition, ghosts, masks and post-filming treatments are described in the second half. An indexed glossary completes the book. Visuals and diagrams throughout are quite helpful.

Here is a small book that can be used by the non-professional filmmaker or by the reader interested in knowing how some film effects are obtained. Recommended.

3123 *How to Make Movies—A Practical Guide to Group Film-Making.* by Ferguson, Robert. 88 p. illus. New York: Viking, 1969.

The important word in the subtitle is "Group." Since this excellent book is based on the film work experience the author has had in schools, colleges, etc., attention is given to such topics as forming groups, equipment, scripts, editing, etc. All of the major aspects of filming are covered by individual chapters. There is a richness of illustration and example. The text is readable and effective. A bibliography and an index are included. Highly recommended.

3124 *How to Make or Not to Make a Canadian Film.* edited by Paquet, Andre. 21 p. paper illus. Montreal: Cinematheque Canadienne, 1967.

3125 *How To Make Your Own Movies.* by Weiss, Harvey. 96 p. illus. Reading, Mass.: Addison-Wesley, 1973.

A guide to filmmaking designed for younger readers.

3126 *How to Organize and Run a Film Society.* by Weiner, Janet. 210 p. paper illus. New York: Collier Books, 1973.

This valuable book has some outstanding features and a few unnecessary ones. Stronger sections appear at the beginning where organization, selection of films, and publicity are treated. Whether listing 900 films and indicating the distributors for them is necessary is debatable, especially when it takes up half of the book. The inclusion of some film bookstores is also an isolated resource; certainly the prices for posters and stills from these sources are rather prohibitive, and most film books today can be found in libraries, discount stores or on paperback racks. The discussion on programming is quite good, as is the chapter on publicity which contains some practical suggestions. There are diagrams, drawings, and some poster reproductions. The book is indexed.

A surface coverage of what usually turns out to be a complex operation, but a starting point, nevertheless.

3127 *How to Plan Your Super 8mm Movies.* by Willson, Clifford V. 130 p. paper illus. Garden City, N.Y.: Amphoto, 1973 (1964).

This is the second revised edition of *How to Plan Your 8mm Films.* The text takes into account the popularity of super 8mm film and stresses those preparations necessary for satisfactory amateur filmmaking.

3128 *How to Prepare a Production Budget for Film and Video Tape.* by Costa, Sylvia Allen. 190 p. Blue Ridge Summit, Pa.: TAB Books, 1973.

This guide to the preparation of budgets will impress upon the reader-user the enormity of detail connected with filmmaking. After establishing a rationale for budgets, the author discusses the elements which must be considered—studios, locations, equipment, film stock, lab charges, sound costs, personnel, editing, special effects, overhead, etc. In the individual chapters devoted to each item, there are charts, diagrams, forms and other supplements to the detailed narrative. The text is written with unusual clarity and the author provides copious background information and explanation for the novice filmmaker. A glossary of terms concludes the volume. Schools which offer filmmaking courses will find the book to be a valuable reference. Acceptable.

3129 *How to Process Substandard Film.* by Wheeler, Leslie J. 117 p. paper illus. London: Focal Press, 1960.

A title in the *Focal Cinebook* series which deals with cinematography—specifically the developing process and the use of developers.

3130 *How to Produce Magnetic Sound for Films.* by Chittock, John. 152 p. paper illus. London: Focal Press, 1962.

A title in the *Focal Cinebook* series that deals with the recording and reproducing of sound by the use of magnetic recorders/recordings.

3131 *How to Project Substandard Films.* by Jenkins, Norman. 152 p. paper illus. London: Focal Press, 1955.

A title in the *Focal Cinebook* series that deals with film projection.

3132 *How To Read A Film.* by Monaco, James. 502 p. illus. New York: Oxford University Press, 1977.

This superb volume has at its subtitle "The Art, Technology, Language, History, and Theory of Film and Media." Employing a structure that reflects the subtitle, the text offers six major sections, each devoted to an exposition of one specific area of film study and appreciation. Three very helpful appendixes complete the volume—a glossary, a bibliography, and a film-media chronology.

Each of the components of the book has been given a detailed presentation and has been prepared with constant attention to its contribution to the theme of the total work. For example, the section on technology begins with a linking with the previous section on art. The text then deals with lens, camera, film stock, soundtrack and post-production activities. In logical sequence, the chapter which follows discusses the language of film.

Nicely integrated with the text is a wide variety of stills, charts, and diagrams, all of which are clearly reproduced. The volume is indexed.

No short review can adequately convey the richness of information and detail found in this volume. For most college courses in film study or appreciation, this is a definitive text. Highly recommended.

3133 *How to Read Donald Duck.* by Dorfman, Ariel; and Mattelart, Armand. 112 p. illus. New York: International General, 1975.

The subtitle of this unusual volume is "Imperialist Ideology in the Disney Comic." First published in Chile in 1971, it has been banned and burned since. It was also restricted in the United States for over a year. Its aim is to show how the Disney fantasy world reproduces the American dream world, producing a disastrous effect on the development of the third world nations.

It is, of course, a Marxist attack on American imperialism, using the Disney content as ammunition.

A most unique volume that deserves to be studied, explained, discussed, and challenged. The opening pages recognize the copyrighted materials and announce that these are used without authorization or consent of Walt Disney Productions. In fact, the authors-in-exile end their introduction with "Donald go home!"

3134 *How to Repair Movie and Slide Projectors.* by Villastrigo, Robert. 303 p. illus. Blue Ridge Summit, Penn.: Tab Books, 1978.

In this how-to-do-it repair handbook, individual chapters are devoted to the repair of 16mm and 8mm motion picture projectors. Other chapters deal with slide, filmstrip, overhead, and opaque projectors. A special section on lamps and another on accessories conclude the volume, which is indexed.

For the adventurous, economy-minded film projectionist, this volume will be invaluable. Although some of the repairs discussed are quite technical, others are rather simple if the clear directions provided are followed. Institutions and individuals owning projectors should also own this volume. Recommended.

3135 *How to Run a Picture Theatre.* edited by Staff of Kinematograph and Lantern Weekly. 127 p. illus. London: Baron, 1914.

A handbook for proprietors, managers, and exhibitors.

3136 *How to Script Amateur Films.* by Blakeston, Oswell. 152 p. paper illus. London: Focal Press, 1956.

First published in 1953, this title in the *Focal Cinebooks* series contains an introduction by Paul Rotha.

3137 *How To Sell Your Film Project.* by Beckman, Henry. 312 p. paper illus. New York: Pinnacle, 1979.

The complexity of breaking into commercial film production is exemplified by this original volume, which is a guide for the preparation of a motion picture presentation for prospective investors. From copyright through corporate structure, financial structure, pre-production, previews, and post-production, the steps are described with an emphasis on the forms, charts, budgets, and contracts that are necessary. Although there is an initial disclaimer about dispensing legal, accounting, or other professional services, the text is often very technical in the advice and information it offers. The experienced professional who wishes to enter the competitive field of film production will find this volume quite helpful in many ways, but others may be turned off by the abundance of noncreative activities required.

3138 *How to Shoot a Movie Story: The Technique of Pictorial Continuity.* by Gaskill, Arthur; and Englander, David. 135 p. paper illus. Hastings-on-Hudson, N.Y.: Morgan & Morgan, 1965.

In 1947 the authors' *Pictorial Continuity* was published. This paperback appears to be derived from that volume. It offers professional guidance and explanation on techniques for assembling shots in such a manner that the films which result are coherent and interesting. Invaluable for both beginners and advanced film makers.

3139   *How to Shoot Home Movies.* by Ney, Uwe. 299 p. illus. New York: Crown, 1978.

This beautifully produced volume, which was translated from the German language, includes all of the standard topics one usually finds in amateur filmmaking books. It is the presentation and selection of the material here that is outstanding. Using a clearly written text and many helpful illustrations, the author covers film types, cameras, accessories, filming, titles, editing, scoring, presentation, and equipment care. A long glossary and some tables complete the book.

This volume resembles a "class" production of the material one finds in the *Kodak* paperback manuals. Much more detail is included here however, and the production elements—binding, large print, clear illustrations—enhance the book's value and appeal. Among the many books currently available on home moviemaking, this is one of the best.

3140   *How to Start an Audiovisual Collection.* edited by Nadler, Myra. 165 p. Metuchen, N.J.: Scarecrow, 1978.

This volume consists of seven chapters, each devoted to a basic element of collection development: the collection, hardware, services, space and facilities, personnel, publicity, and public relations. A final section offers a lengthy glossary. This is essential reading for anyone dealing with nonprint services for the first time.

3141   *How to Title Amateur Films.* by Minter, L. F. 131 p. paper illus. London: Focal Press, 1962.

This is the 7th revised edition of a title in the *Focal Cinebooks* series. The 8th edition, which appeared in 1970, is called *How To Title Your Own Home Movies.*

3142   *How to Title Home Movies.* by Cushman, George W. 85 p. paper illus. Hollywood: Ver Halen, 1943.

3143   *How to Use a Motion Picture.* by Hartley, William H. 8 p. paper Washington, D.C.: National Council for the Social Studies, 1965.

This pamphlet is included here as an example of the kind of information on films and film use that is available from many national associations. In a very few pages, this publication gives a rationale for film use, suggestions on use, an overview of what is available in classroom, government, theatrical, and commercial films, and several pages on the steps necessary for effective use of the film. A selected bibliography is offered, too. Excellent material is available in this format but it takes some digging to discover titles and organizations.

3144   *How to Use 8mm,* by Grosset, Philip. 94 p. paper illus. London: Fountain, 1961.

This volume offers both essential technical information and practical advice on how to make films with 8mm film. Emphasis is on how to use the 8mm equipment rather than how it works. Suggested subjects include family, friends, and locations.

3145   *How to Use 9.5mm.* by Neale, Denis M. 168 p. paper illus. London: Focal Press, 1955.

A title in the *Focal Cinebook* series, this volume deals with a film gauge that is used in Europe but seldom in United States.

3146   *How to Win Stage and Screen Roles for Your Child.* by Shallenberger, John B. Connellsville, Penn.: Shallway Foundation.

3147   *How to Write a Film Story.* by Allen, G. M. 100 p. illus. London: Allen and Unwin, 1926.

Advice on writing silent film scripts. Topics include: inside a film studio; on choosing plots; principles of construction; titles; the close-up; description of scenes and effects; behind the camera; stars? or companies?; and how and where to send your scenario. Some specimen pages of a script are presented and an analysis is offered.

3148   *How to Write a Movie.* by Gale, Arthur L. 199 p. New York: Brick Row Book Shop, 1936.

Continuity and scenario principles are put forth in a no-nonsense fashion—sound advice and instruction for the beginner— including a sample script and a glossary of terms.

3149 *How to Write a Photoplay.* by Hoagland, Herbert C. 78 p. New York: Magazine Maker Publishing Co., 1912.

In addition to a model scenario, this early advice on writing for the screen includes information on how photoplays are produced, what will be accepted and what won't, possible markets, etc.

3150 *How to Write and Sell Film Stories.* by Marion, Frances. 365 p. New York: Covici-Friede, 1937.

This older volume on screenplay writing is by a well-known author who recently wrote her autobiography. The first section deals with characters, plot, motivation, theme, dialogue, emotions, etc.; the second section presents the script of THE ADVENTURES OF MARCO POLO (1938).

3151 *How to Write Commentaries for Films.* by Kirsch, Maurice. 120 p. paper illus. London: Focal Press, 1966.

This title in the *Focal Cinebook* series contains an introduction by Eamonn Andrews.

3152 *How to Write, Direct, and Produce Effective Business Films and Documentaries.* by McGuire, Jerry. 292 p. Blue Ridge Summit, Pa.: Tab Books, 1978.

Written in an informal chatty style, this how-to-do-it book is an impressive blend of information and advice. Dealing with such topics as scripts, clients, videotape, direction, production, unions, and agents, the text covers the basic necessities for short film production. The author does not hesitate to include personal anecdotes or opinions. He believes the heart of the process is the script, but he gives sufficient attention to the other activities so that a broad base is provided. Sample forms, agent addresses, lab prices, production agreements, etc., appear in the appendix. The book is indexed.

The excellent presentation found in this modest volume will provide both motivation and direction for the making of business and documentary films. Highly recommended.

3153 *How to Write Educational and Technical Films.* by Hoyt, Robert. Lawrence, Kansas: Big Morning Press, 1978.

3154 *How to Write Film Stories for Amateur Films.* by Harrison, Richard. 144 p. paper illus. London: Focal Press, 1954.

A title in the *Focal Cinebook* series.

3155 *How to Write for Moving Pictures.* by Bertsch, Marguerite. 275 p. illus. New York: George H. Doran, 1917.

Author Bertsch subtitles her book "A Manual of Instruction and Information" and bases her offering on her experience as director and editor for the Vitagraph Company and the Famous Players Film Company. Written in 1917, the book's seven major divisions are: writing, production, hackneyed themes, themes based on conflict, themes based on social conflict, divided interest and censorship. Since this was the era of BIRTH OF A NATION (1915) and INTOLERANCE (1916), it is a bit surprising to find chapters on the dissolve, double exposure, the cutback, and the close-up. There are 14 illustrations to help explain the text. This book for historians and researchers is noted here for the record.

3156 *How to Write for the Movies.* by Parsons, Louella 202 p. Chicago: A.C. McClurg, 1915.

A rather complete survey of film writing by the woman who was to become famous as a gossip columnist. Here she discusses the birth of the motion picture story, the tools of the trade, the market, continuity, scenic action, the flashback, copyright, plagiarism, and many other topics. Included is a sample scenario and a glossary.

3157 *How to Write Photoplays.* by Caine, Clarence J. 269 p. Philadelphia: David McKay, 1916.

A reproduction of a series of articles on the subject of film writing as they appeared in the "Hints For Scenario Writers" department of *Picture-Play* weekly and *Picture-Play* magazine.

3158 *How to Write Photoplays.* by Emerson, John; and Loos, Anita. 154 p. illus. New York: James A. McCann, 1920.

In addition to a complete scenario entitled "The Love Expert," the authors offer an abundance of information on such topics as tools of the trade, writing a movie, terminology, star sympathy, title, markets, characterization, censorship, etc.

3159 *How to Write Plots That Sell* by Rockwell, F. A. 279 p. paper Chicago: Henry Regnery, 1975.

The focus of this volume is a paraphrase of its title: where do you find plots that you can write about and then sell. After two introductory chapters, plot sources such as jokes, the daily news, quotations, irritations, values, the Bible, Cinderella, Faust, goals, and classics are considered in detail. The author's concluding advice is to crisscross the plot lines during the use of either of three major methods of structure: The Blueprint, The Actor-Goal Plot Chart, or The Actor-Ideal Desire Plot Chart. The book is indexed.

Within the text the author analyses many well-known plots taken from novels, films, and plays. She discusses their sources, construction, and resolution with such skill, intelligence, and clarity that she makes the task of writing stories seem easy—almost a recreation.

Although writing for motion pictures requires other skills not mentioned here, the basics are present. As a starting point for any aspiring writer, this volume can be most helpful. Recommended.

3160 *Howard Hawks.* by Wood, Robin. 200 p. illus. New York: Doubleday & Co., 1968.

This "auteur" analysis of the films of Howard Hawks is a bit different in structure. It places the films in groups which represent the major themes or attitudes that author Wood finds recurrent in Hawks' work. Thus chapters have headings such as "Self-Respect and Responsibility," The Lure of Irresponsibility," "Male Relationships," etc. There is even a group entitled "Failures and Marginal Works." The analysis is well presented by argument, example and explanation. Whether GENTLEMEN PREFER BLONDES (1953) and THE BIG SLEEP (1946) are failure's while MAN'S FAVORITE SPORT (1964) is a success is a debatable but interesting assertion. Picture quality is excellent and there is a filmography but no index. This is another in the impressive *Cinema One* series. While some of the text may be questionable, the quality of production and effort are not. Recommended.

3161 *Howard Hughes.* by Keats, John. 304 p. illus. London: Macgibbon & Kee, 1967.

Although this well-written unauthorized biography

treats all of his business activities, enough attention is given to the motion pictures that Howard Hughes masterminded to warrant its inclusion in this list. Starting with some silents, there then followed HELL'S ANGELS (1930), THE FRONT PAGE (1931), SCARFACE (1932), and THE OUTLAW (1943). His purchase of the RKO Studio in the late forties is also detailed. Illustrations are included but there is no index.

3162 *Howard Hughes: The Hidden Years.* by Phelan, James. 301 p. paper illus. New York: Warner, 1977.

This Howard Hughes biography was written by an investigative journalist who used the accounts of two Hughes' associates as basic source material. All the eccentricities of Hughes' later years involving such matters as secrecy, eating habits, cleanliness, drugs, phobias, business methods, etc., are revealed.

3163 *Howard, The Amazing Mr. Hughes.* by Dietrich, Noah; and Thomas, Bob. 303 p. paper illus. Greenwich, Conn.: Fawcett Publications, 1972.

For 32 years, Noah Dietrich was a close associate of Howard Hughes, acting as business associate and confidante. Bob Thomas is the experienced biographer of Irving Thalberg, Walt Disney, Harry Cohn, David Selznick, and others. This combination of experiences applied to a subject like Howard Hughes seems sure-fire. For the most part it does work well in this volume.

The familiar Hollywood stories—Jean Harlow, Billie Dove, HELL'S ANGELS (1930), COCK OF THE AIR (1932), Multicolor, RKO, Jane Russell, Jean Peters —all receive attention. The personal side of Hughes is emphasized throughout, getting as detailed at times as a discussion of his chronic constipation. While the writing style is a bit naive and amateurish —unlike Thomas' *King Cohn*—it is bearable, and the content and the visuals compensate for the lack in literary quality. The book is not indexed.

3164 *Hughes.* by Mathison, Richard. illus. New York: Morrow, 1977.

Another Howard Hughes biography, this one is based to a large extent upon the recollections of his security chief. Mostly anecdotal, the volume concentrates on the last half of Hughes' life, which was spent mostly in Hollywood and Las Vegas. His erratic and unusual behavior is emphasized.

3165 *The Human Figure in Motion.* by Muybridge, Eadweard. 400 p. illus.

New York: Dover, 1955.

This is a recent printing of a book originally published in 1955. It contains a selection of 195 plates taken from the eleven-volume work, *Animal Locomotion*, which first appeared in 1887. The plates, consisting of a number of pictures on each, appear here in the same size format as in the original work. They show 163 types of human action via 4789 separate photographs. Taken at speeds up to 1/6000th of a second, the photographs have been stopped in series, with each plate collection defining one specific action—i.e., a man throwing a baseball.

An introduction provides historical information about the origin of Muybridge's investigations. The photographs have been reproduced with consistent clarity and provide a useful resource for photographers, sculptors, artists, and others.

The book has pertinence for film collections since Muybridge's work led directly to the invention of the motion picture. Another similar volume containing about 4000 photographs is entitled *Animals in Motion* and shows 34 animals and birds in 123 different types of action. Acceptable.

3166 *Humphrey Bogart: The Man and His Films.* by Michael, Paul. 191 p. illus. Indianapolis: Bobbs-Merrill, 1965.

A chapter of biographical text introduces this picture book. Bogart's films are presented in chronological order. Nearly all of the films are accompanied by one or two stills, a credit and cast listing, and a rather lengthy plot outline.

The text is above average and the illustrations have been selected with discrimination. Some critical evaluation of the films or of Bogart's performances, rather than the long plot outlines, might have been preferred.

3167 *Humphrey Bogart.* by Barbour, Alan G. 160 p. paper illus. New York: Pyramid, 1973.

This is one of a quartet of initial releases in the series *Pyramind Illustrated History of the Movies.* Congratulations seem to be in order on all counts—writing, selection, production and value.

The book is logically arranged—an opening section on Bogart's personal and professional life is followed by a detailed discussion of his films. A final evaluation, a filmography, bibliography and an index complete the book. The films are divided into appropriate periods: the early years, the Warner Repertory Company, the peak years— THE MAL-

TESE FALCON (1941) to THE AFRICAN QUEEN (1952), and the final films.

Although Bogart has been more than adequately covered in the literature, this small volume combines the best elements of the older, more expensive books. It is decidedly visual, with many stills, all clearly reproduced. It is a well arranged reference tool, with the filmography and index as supports to the film chronology. Finally, it covers in a most acceptable prose style all of the elements that make up the Bogart legend, without resorting to innuendo or gossip. The films are not only described but also evaluated. In summary, this seems to be a basic volume on Bogart and is highly recommended.

3168 *Humphrey Bogart.* by Benchley, Nathaniel. 242 p. illus. Boston: Little, Brown, 1975.

Created by a long-time friend and admirer, this biography on Bogart is the best to appear so far. It combines a well-written, intelligent narrative with many sharply reproduced visuals—a pairing which gives the reader an in-depth portrait of a complex actor. The many faces of Bogart are recalled with varying emotions by the author. Bogart was not always easy, charming, intelligent, or sensitive; much about him seems contradictory, in both his public and private image.

Many recreated conversations appear, and they are acceptable in this instance because of Benchley's seemingly valid memory and his skillful integration of them in the story. Throughout there is affectionate objectivity that only a very close acquaintance and observation would permit. The book has no filmography or index and this is unquestionably a weakness. However, the two major elements—words and pictures—are so strong in this instance that the reader will probably not notice the absence. Recommended.

3169 *Humphrey Jennings: A Tribute.* 18 p. paper illus. London: British Film Institute, 1950.

A tribute to Jennings, a distinguished documentarist, by John Grierson, Kathleen Raine, Basil Wright, Ian Dalrymple, Dilys Powell, John Greenwood. One of the *BFI Index* series.

3170 *Humphrey Jennings: Filmmaker—Painter—Poet.* edited by Jennings, Mary-Lou. 72 p. New York: Zoetrope, 1981.

3171 *A Hundred Different Lives: An Autobiography.* by Massey, Raymond. 447 p. illus. Boston: Little, Brown, 1979.

In an earlier autobiography entitled *When I Was Young*, Raymond Massey recalled his first twenty-five years, up to the time he decided to become an actor. This second volume is devoted almost exclusively to his career as an actor on stage, screen, and television. From the mid-twenties until his retirement because of arthritis in 1976, he recalls the celebrated persons with whom he worked and played. On Broadway, in Hollywood or London, Raymond Massey has always been considered a dedicated professional. Certain of the roles he created are legendary—Abraham Lincoln, Ethan Frome, Oswald Cabal (THINGS TO COME, 1935), Adam Trask (EAST OF EDEN, 1954), Dr. Gillespie, etc.—while even a miscasting such as Jonathan Brewster (ARSENIC AND OLD LACE 1942), remains an interesting though unsuccessful performance. A preference for working in the theatre can be discerned but Massey does give attention to certain of his films. He is selective about his private life as well, giving the reader merely hints and suggestions about what life with Massey might be. Illustrations and an index accompany the text. What is missing is a list of Massey's performances in the various media. Such an omission for a long, active career such as Massey's is incomprehensible and unforgiveable.

The persona that characterized Raymond Massey's performances on screen is reflected here—stern, matter-of-fact, formal, a stickler for detail—all these adjectives come to mind. Perhaps this is to be expected from an autobiography. It would have been more pleasant, however, to meet the man that Christopher Plummer calls "a hell of a lot of fun" in his introduction to this book.

3172 *A Hundred Million Moviegoers Must Be Right.* by Price, Ira. 179 p. illus. Cleveland, Ohio: Movie Appreciation Press, 1938.

An early volume devoted to film criticism and appreciation.

3173 *Hungarian Cinema Today: History Must Answer to Man.* by Petrie, Graham. 284 p. illus. New York: Zoetrope, 1978.

In his effort to introduce readers to the Hungarian cinema, Graham Petrie concentrates on the work of three directors: Miklos Janesco, Istvan Szabo, and Istvan Gaal. A brief historical survey introduces the study which is concluded by sections dealing with the sixties and the early seventies. Other directors and their films are mentioned in this latter part. A bibliography, a selected filmography (1932-1977), illustrations, and an index complete the work.

Although most of the material in this volume is unfamiliar to American readers, it does provide an excellent introduction to a film form that is devoted largely to the exploration of both social and political problems.

3174 *The Hurrell Style.* by Hurrell, George; and Stine, Whitney. 218 p. illus. New York: John Day, 1976.

George Hurrell, one of the foremost portrait photographers in America, began his career in 1926. In addition to working for film and TV studios, he is a free-lance photographer whose work has appeared in many major magazines. The collection offered here is subtitled "50 Years of Photographing Hollywood."

It is, of course, the visuals which give the book its substance. They are exquisitely beautiful examples of an art form that seems almost extinct today. Reproduction has been meticulous and placement-layout is quite attractive. Technical data has been provided for each photograph.

Supporting the visuals is a bland derivative text supplied by Whitney Stine, which is relieved only by Hurrell's comments about the stars he photographed. Recommended.

3175 HUSBANDS. 30 p. paper illus. 1970.

This is not the typical souvenir book but an attempt to present mostly oversized visuals of shots from the 1970 film. There is little text aside from the usual cast and production credits. All the performers are pictured and identified. A beautiful presentation and production.

3176 *I Ain't Down Yet.* by Storm, Gale. Indianapolis, Ind.: Bobbs-Merrill, 1981.

3177 *I Am a Cinema.* by Calatayud, Miguel. 36 p. illus. Oxford, England: Blackwell, 1977.

This short volume, originally published in Spanish and designed for young readers, is part of the *Who Am I?* series. The illustrations provided by the author are the outstanding feature of the book.

3178 I AM A FUGITIVE FROM A CHAIN GANG. by Gibney, Sheridan; and Holmes, Brown; and Burns, Robert E. 224 p. illus. Madison, Wisc.: University of Wisconsin Press, 1981.

The script of the 1932 film directed by Mervyn LeRoy.

3179 I AM CURIOUS (BLUE). by Sjoman, Vilgot; and Minow, Martin and and Bohman, Jenny 219 p. paper illus. New York: Grove Press, 1970.

Script of the 1970 film directed by Vilgot Sjoman. Contains cast credits.

3180 I AM CURIOUS (YELLOW). by Sjoman, Vilgot. 254 p. paper illus. New York: Grove Press, 1968.

Script of the 1968 film directed by Sjoman. Contains cast credits and excerpts from the obscenity trial.

3181 *I Am Gazing into My 8-Ball.* by Wilson, Earl. 182 p. Garden City, N.Y.: Doubleday, 1945.

A World War II book that offered escapism via gossip column nonsense and press agentry. Names like Lana Turner, Carol Landis, Ann Sheridan, Howard Dietz, Tallulah Bankhead (on LIFEBOAT, 1944), Jimmy Durante, Garbo, Nunnally Johnson, Betty Hutton, Gregory Ratoff, Dorothy Lamour, Charles Boyer, Veronica Lake, Katharine Hepburn, and Rags Ragland are featured in the short anecdotes and paragraphs that make up the book. The book has some value as an indication of the public's interest four decades ago. It hasn't changed much since then. Noted for the record.

3182 *I Am Not An Island: An Experiment in Autobiography.* by Abbas, Khwaja Ahmed. 551 p. illus. New Delhi: Vikas, 1977.

Abbas is an influential director and writer of Indian films who is known primarily for CHILDREN OF THE EARTH (1946) and THE DREAM (1963).

3183 *I Am Still Alive.* by Grace, Dick. 255 p. illus. New York: Rand McNally, 1931.

The author was a stunt flyer who appeared in WINGS (1927), HELL'S ANGELS (1930) and other films. In this autobiography, he discusses his unique occupation and gives some attention to his contemporaries in the field. See also *Squadron of Death: The True Adventures of a Movie Plane-Crasher* by the same author published in 1929 by Doubleday, and reissued under their Sun Dial imprint in 1937.

3184 *I Blow My Own Horn.* by Lasky, Jesse L.; and Weldon, Don. 284 p. Garden City, N.Y.: Doubleday & Co., 1957.

Approximately one third of this autobiography is devoted to Lasky's early days as vaudeville performer, producer and booking agent. The remainder is about his career in motion pictures with the emphasis on the silent film era. As the title indicates, modesty is not one of Lasky's virtues. Never hesitant to take credit, some of his claims are nevertheless a bit suspect. (For example, his account of OLD IRONSIDES (1926) and Lorenzo del Riccio's Magnescope Lens differs completely from Glendon Allwine's *The Greatest Fox of Them All.*)

If the reader accepts the subjectivity, this book is one of the better film autobiographies. Its real value is in the many film anecdotes. Of major interest to historians and to mature readers.

3185 *I Called Him Babe.* by Cocke, Marian J. illus. Memphis, Tenn.: Memphis State University Press, 1979.

3186 *I Couldn't Smoke the Grass on My Father's Lawn.* by Chaplin, Michael. 171 p. paper illus. New York: Ballantine Books, 1966.

Still another view of Chaplin is offered in this book by his son, Michael, whose maternal grandfather was Eugene O'Neill. He likens being the son of a great man to living next to a huge monument where a person must decide whether to remain in its shade or run to avoid its shadow. Although much of the volume is devoted to Michael's immature behavior and rebellion, there are sections devoted to the father-son relationship that are revealing and quite sad.

Michael played an important role in Chaplin's film A KING IN NEW YORK (1957). The experience is only briefly mentioned here. The book includes some family pictures. There is no index. Both major characters as presented here will arouse little reader sympathy or admiration. The book is listed since it presents a view of Chaplin from a different time and position than the others.

3187 *I Don't Mind the Sex, It's the Violence: Film Censorship Explained.*

by Wistrich, Enid. 160 p. paper London: Marion Boyars, 1978.

The author served as chairman of the film viewing board of the Greater London Film Council from 1973 to 1975. This volume tells of her attempts to abolish prior censorship of movies for adults and her reasons for recommending this action. She cites paternalism, irrational fear, and a lack of positive evidence about effect as major arguments. Appendixes offer a list of controversial films from the past two decades and a list of films inspected by the Film Council from 1967 to 1977. A very short bibliography (for this topic) is added along with an index.

The arguments presented here are not new. It is the author's practical experiences with film censorship, told with taste and serious dedication, that qualify the book for attention.

Incidentally, the publishers seem to be working against the author via their lurid cover and the identification of controversial films.

3188   *I Found It At the Movies.* by Yacowar, Maurice. 153 p. New York: Revisionist Press, 1977.

A collection of essays, articles and reviews by Maurice Yacowar comprise the content of this book. The author, a teacher at Brock University in Ontario, has a unique style of writing film reviews. He offers a few short succinct paragraphs that usually convey the essence of the film and his own reaction to it. Longer articles which appear in the first portion of the book are well structured and researched.

The production given this volume—(reproduced typewritten pages with noticeable corrections)—is an inferior one. With the exception of the pun-title, Yacowar's work deserves a better presentation than the one provided by Revisionist Press.

3189   *I Had to Be "Wee."* by Wood, Georgie. 196 p. illus. London: Hutchinson, 1948.

An autobiography of Wee Georgie Wood, a midget comedian who appeared in silent films during the twenties.

3190   *I, James Dean: The Real Story behind America's Most Popular Idol.* by Thomas T. T. 128 p. illus. New York: Popular Library, 1957.

3191   *I Know It When I See It.* by Leach, Michael. 153 p. Philadelphia: Westminster, 1975.

In his attempt to provide a perspective on pornography, the author has used films as his major source of examples. Subtitled "Pornography, Violence, and Public Sensitivity," the book is divided into five chapters (reels) with an introduction (preview) and an annotated bibliography (trailer). After the formulation of a definition of pornography, the text considers sex, violence, and censorship with respect to films. In the concluding chapter Leach suggests that the last frontier is the one within us and hopes for a sexually mature and religiously open society.

The author writes in a pleasant informal style and makes his statement about pornography with intelligence, taste, and wit. Since he is a former Roman Catholic priest, it is probable that his religious and humanistic beliefs shaped most of the arguments presented here. Acceptable.

3192   *I Know the Face but....* by Bull, Peter Cecil. 219 p. illus. London: Peter Davies, 1959.

An account of the author's experiences as a stage and screen actor. Peter Bull's career in films began with AS YOU LIKE IT (1936) and includes SARABAND (1949), OLIVER TWIST (1951), THE LAVENDER HILL MOB (1951), and TOM THUMB (1958). Later films such as TOM JONES (1963), DR. STRANGELOVE (1964) and DOCTOR DOLITTLE (1967) are not treated in this volume.

3193   *I Like What I Know: A Visual Autobiography.* by Price, Vincent. 313 p. illus. New York: Doubleday, 1959.

The emphasis is on art—appreciation, evaluation, and collection. Illustrations are art works from his own collection. Mr. Price's debt to films is still to be paid.

3194   *I Lost it at the Movies.* by Kael, Pauline. 365 p. Boston: Little, Brown, 1965.

Is there anyone who does not know about this brilliant, emotional, witty, sarcastic lady? If not, they have an exhilarating experience reading this book of film criticism. The articles and reviews are from a variety of periodicals of the years 1953-63. They evidence a coming-of-age of film criticism. It should be noted that many readers feel that her writing is weakened by her bitter attacks on other film critics. Miss Kael should not be explained or analyzed —she should be experienced. As an example of a particular genre of film criticism, this volume is essential and can easily serve as a model for aspiring critics.

3195 *I Love You, Clark Gable, etc.* by Tashman, George. 159 p. paper illus. Richmond, Calif.: Brombacher, 1977.

Subtitled "Male Sex Symbols of the Silver Screen," this collective biography offers 22 profiles.

3196 *I Never Met a Kid I Liked.* by Fields, W.C. edited by Mason, Paul. 58p. illus. New York: Random House, 1970.

More Fieldsian comment and wisdom with pictures.

3197 I NEVER SANG FOR MY FATHER. by Anderson, Robert. 159 p. paper illus. New York: Signet Books, 1970.

Script of the 1970 film directed by Gilberg Cates. Contains cast credits, an introduction by Robert Anderson, and "Notes on Making the Film," by Gilbert Cates.

3198 *I Remember It Well.* by Chevalier, Maurice. 221 p. illus. New York: Macmillan, 1970.

This is an account of Chevalier's farewell tour and his first months of retirement. Little reference is made to his films. There is no index. Little pertinence for film scholars.

3199 *I Remember It Well.* by Minnelli, Vincente; and Arce, Hector. 391 p. illus. New York: Doubleday, 1974.

Vincente Minnelli's films are characterized by both style and good taste. His autobiography has those same qualities. From an account of his theatrical work in the early thirties to the Academy Award ceremonies in 1973, he recalls a career containing triumphs, disappointments and disasters. His 35 films make up most of this memoir, but he does discuss one of his three marriages in some detail, expressing pride and affection for the women concerned, Judy Garland, and their daughter, Liza Minnelli.

Portraits of other show business personalities are sprinkled throughout his narrative. To almost all, he is understanding and kind. Modest about his own films, he describes their creation in detail with the enthusiasm and respect of an artist devoted to his craft. The many fine illustrations seem to be taken from his private collection. A lengthy index is most helpful, but a badly needed filmography is missing,

replaced by a listing of his film titles and their year of release. This rewarding volume is one of the best director autobiographies to appear in recent years. It is highly recommended.

3200 *I Remember Jimmy: The Life and Times of Jimmy Durante.* by Adler, Irene. 191 p. paper illus. Westport, Conn.: Arlington House, 1980.

This affectionate tribute to Jimmy Durante consists mostly of clearly reproduced visuals, along with some introductory text. The rare photographs, most of which are candids rather than studio stills, indicate a warm, fun-loving professional who made friends and fans without effort. "Beloved" can be applied to Durante without sounding like a cliche. His filmography indicates almost 40 films from ROADHOUSE NIGHTS (1929) to IT'S A MAD, MAD, MAD, MAD WORLD (1963).

For those who remember Durante, this is a very special book. Those who never saw him perform missed one of the most endearing comic characters of this century; a book can only suggest the rich genius of his self-creation.

3201 *I Remember Romano's.* by Kendall, Henry. 224 p. illus. London: MacDonald, 1960.

Kendall was a London revue actor who was popular during the thirties and forties. Noted mostly for comedy roles, he played a variety of parts in films from 1921 to 1961. This volume was published shortly before his death in 1962.

3202 *I Say, Look Here.* by Bull, Peter. 200 p. illus London: Peter Davies, 1965.

Further autobiographical recollections of the British actor who has appeared in films from the thirties to the sixties.

3203 *I Should Care—The Sammy Cahn Story.* by Cahn, Sammy. 318 p. illus. New York: Arbor House, 1974.

Sammy Cahn's show business career began with the writing lyrics to "Bei Mir Bist Du Schon" in 1933. For more than four decades he has continued to write song lyrics for films, Broadway shows, television and for his own pleasure. In addition to initial awards, many of his songs also have the status of "standards" —which means they are continually performed years after their creation. This autobiography recounts his early years on New York's Lower East Side and later adventures in vaudeville, radio, the big band era, films, shows and finally his own show on Broadway, "Words and Music." In addition to talking about his career, he shows no hesitation in discussing his private life—his two marriages and his feelings about the men with whom he has worked so closely, Jule Styne and Jimmy Van Heusen.

Celebrities have always been an important element in Cahn's life. He appreciates most of them, but Doris Day, Artie Shaw, Frank Sinatra, Julie Harris, and Al Freeman, Jr., are not among Cahn's great enthusiasms. Many other famous names are generously sprinkled throughout the text, which is always entertaining and doggedly optimistic. Illustrations are well chosen and an index is provided along with a songography. In addition, the lyrics of 30 of his most famous songs are included. Although it may be a bit too reminiscent of a modern Horatio Alger story, this portrait of a popular songwriter who has been successful in several media will please most readers. Acceptable.

3204   *I Swore I Never Would.* by French, Harold. 206 p. illus. London: Secker and Warburg, 1970.

Harold French is a noted British actor-writer-director-producer. In this early autobiography, he tells of his early years as a child actor in the period prior to World War I.

3205   *I Wanna Tell You a Story.* by Bygraves, Max. illus. London: W. H. Allen, 1976.

Bygraves is a theatre comedian who has appeared in a few films.

3206   *I Was a Hollywood Stunt Girl.* by Scott, Audrey. 119 p. Philadelphia: Dorrance, 1969.

In this short autobiography of a Hollywood stunt actress, it is surprising to note how many times the reader has seen Miss Scott on screen—unknowingly. She has doubled for nearly every major female star in Hollywood from 1928 to the early sixties. It is this career of performing dangerous stunts that she describes in the book. In addition there is much extraneous material about horses, clubs, and athletics. The text is straightforward narrative with little editorial comment, except that which is most favorable. There are neither illustrations nor an index. Interesting as a look at the more dangerous aspects of filmmaking, the book is disappointing in its treatment of the cinema personalities and productions which populate its pages.

3207   *I Was Born Greek.* by Mercouri, Melina. 253 p. illus. Garden City, N.Y.: Doubleday, 1971.

Much of this autobiography is political but some attention is given to Mercouri's film work. Starting with her film with Michael Cacoyannis, STELLA (1954), she tells about her initial meeting with Jules Dassin, their first film, HE WHO MUST DIE (1956), and making THE LAW (1959), PHAEDRA (1961), NEVER ON SUNDAY (1960), TOPKAPI (1964) and other films. A short collection of photographs appears in the mid-section. The book is not indexed.

An attempt has been made by the author to duplicate in words the Mercouri personality, which depends upon so many diverse physical, emotional and mental elements. The result is only partially successful. She is at her best when she is the light comedienne, at her tedious worst when she is the militant authoress. The autobiography has sufficient pleasurable moments to make it acceptable.

3208   *I Was Curious: Diary of the Making of a Film.* by Sjoman, Vilgot 217 p. illus. New York: Grove Press, 1968.

This diary follows a small group of Swedish moviemakers through the process of making both parts of the I AM CURIOUS film, the YELLOW (1968) and the BLUE (1970). In addition to the preparation for the film and the actual filming, some of the post-filming reactions are given. Flashbacks are used throughout and the account is not chronological. The illustrations are few and only average in interest or pertinence to the text. (Grove's later books on Scandinavian films are more erotic in both text and illustrations.) The film was an important one primarmly because of the controversy that surrounded the showing of the first portion, I AM CURIOUS (YELLOW) (1968) in America. At this point the interest in it is largely historical.

3209   *I'll Cry Tomorrow.* by Roth, Lillian. 347 p. illus. New York: Frederic Fell, 1954.

This is the well-known biography which traces Lillian Roth's career from child vaudeville performer to leading Broadway and Hollywood actress. Her long battle with alcoholism provides the drama.

3210   *I'm Gonna Make You Love Me: The Story of Diana Ross.* by Haskins, James. 154 p. illus. New York: Dial, 1980.

Written for young adults, this unauthorized biography of Diana Ross traces her life story from background singer to media superstar. Individual chapters are devoted to her films, LADY SINGS THE BLUES (1972) and MAHOGANY (1975), with some mention of her disasterous performance in THE WIZ (1978) in the closing pages. A discography and some illustrations are included. This is a fan-level biography that is acceptable only to fill a temporary void. A critical biography of Diana Ross at this time in her career may be premature; there are undoubtedly many fine things still to come.

3211 ICE CASTLES. by Wrye, Donald; and Baim, Gary L. unpaginated paper illus. Los Angeles: Fotonovel, 1978.

This *Fotonovel* (see series entry)contains over 350 stills, some original film dialogue, connecting narrative, and cast credits for the 1978 film, ICE CASTLES, which was directed by Wrye.

3212 ICE STATION ZEBRA. by Tobias, John. 32 p. paper illus. New York: National Publishers, 1968.

The format of this souvenir book makes it a bit more difficult to follow since the content is spread over two pages at times and is visualized with rather small photographs. Included are a diagram of a nuclear submarine, some explanation of the special effects used in this 1969 film, and the usual cast, director, and producer credits. The photographs tend to resemble those found in *National Geographic* rather than stills from a film.

3213 *Icy Hell.* by Hudson, Will E. 308 p. illus. New York: Stokes, 1937.

This volume relates "the experiences of a newsreel cameraman in the Aleutian Islands, Eastern Siberia and the Arctic fringe of Alaska."

3214 *Ida Lupino.* by Vermilye, Jerry. 160 p. paper illus. New York: Pyramid, 1977.

A title in the *Illustrated History of The Movies* series, this volume pays tribute to actress-filmmaker Ida Lupino. Using numerous illustrations and an informed text, her life and career up to 1975 is presented. A filmography, a bibliography, and an index accompany the survey.

3215 *Ida Lupino as Film Director, 1949-1953: An Auteur Approach.* by Stewart, Lucy Ann Ligett. New York: Arno Press, 1980.

A study of the content and perspective of the films

directed by actress Ida Lupino. Stewart also investigates the validity of the auteur approach. This is a title in the *Dissertations on Film* series.

3216 *Ideas for Short Films.* by Strasser, Alexander. 80 p. London: Link House, 1937.

This title in the *Amateur Cine World* series offers a group of simple scripts for beginning filmmakers.

3217 *Ideas of Order in Literature and Film.: Selected Papers From the Fourth Annual Florida State University Conference on Literature and Film.* 136 p. paper Gainsville, Florida: University Presses of Florida, 1981.

3218 *Ideas on Film.* edited by Starr, Cecile. 251 p. illus. New York: Funk & Wagnalls, 1951.

Subtitled "A Handbook For the 16mm Film User," this anthology contains some items that are valuable and still pertinent, but it also has much deadwood. The over 100 pages devoted to reviews of pre-1951 films are of questionable use. Industrial films, film sources, and film libraries have changed greatly in 20 years, and the information herein is not applicable today. The format of such a book is good but it needs constant updating. Not recommended.

3219 *Identity.* edited by Maynard, Richard A. 192 p. paper illus. New York: Scholastic Book Services, 1974.

This volume contains scripts of the following films: THAT'S ME (1961), Walker Stuart; THE LONELINESS OF THE LONG-DISTANCE RUNNER (1962), Tony Richardson; COOL HAND LUKE (1967), Stuart Rosenberg; and UP THE DOWN STAIRCASE (1967), Robert Mulligan.

3220 *The Identity Crisis Theme in American Feature Films, 1960-1969.* by Mason, John L. 384 p. New York: Arno Press, 1977.

Written in 1973 at Ohio State University, in partial fulfillment of the doctoral program, this sociological study of feature films of the sixties classifies topical trends in the cinema during this period. The author's analysis is supported by several interviews with notable directors and producers of the era. By combining techniques from several disciplines, the author has produced a work which is unusual in both its subject matter and the approach used. This title is included in the *Dissertations on Film* series.

3221 *Ideology and the Image.: Social Representation in the Cinema and Other Media.* by Nichols, Bill. 456 p. illus. Bloomington, Ind.: Indiana University Press, 1981.

An exploration of representation in feature films, documentaries, and ethnographic films that employs current theories, concepts, and principles. The illustrations are frame enlargements.

3222 *The Idols of Silence.* by Slide, Anthony. 207 p. illus. New York: A.S. Barnes, 1976.

Assorted elements are combined in this appreciation which is subtitled "Stars of the Cinema Before the Talkies." The first section is a collective biography that is divided into three parts: The Trailblazers (Mignon Anderson, Hobart Bosworth, Billie Rhodes, Kathlyn Williams), The Idols of the Teens (Elmer Clifton, Olga Petrova, Henry B. Walthall), and Stars of the Twenties (Priscilla Bonner, Bebe Daniels, Ben Lyon, Jetta Goudal, Ralph Graves, Alice Terry). Two fan magazine writers, Adele Whitely Fletcher and Ruth Waterbury, are also profiled. The biographical sections take the form of either an interview or a factual narrative often augmented by quotations from books or periodicals.

The second section is a collection of selected bibliographies for more than 100 silent film performers. Arranged alphabetically by author the entries range in number from three for Syd Chaplin to 116 for Charles Chaplin. Accompanying this varied material are over 200 visuals, most of which are unfamiliar. Their reproduction is uniformly good.

For the silent film buff or the film historian this assortment is rich with pleasures and informational treasures. For the general reader the material is too fragmented and rather specialized.

3223 *I.E.: The Autobiography of Mickey Rooney.* by Rooney, Mickey. 249 p. illus. New York: G. P. Putnam's, 1965.

This autobiography is a frank, open confessional in which the subject avoids both apology and self-pity. The many mistakes—social, emotional, and economic—are readily admitted with accompanying rationale wherever possible. Readers may gain a greater understanding of Rooney's well-chronicled behavior but their opinions about him are not likely to change.

In his account of the motion picture industry and personalities of the early forties, Rooney is not always kind. Much of what was probably eliminated because of potential lawsuits is hinted at in a carefully worded narrative. The pictures are few and forgettable and there is no index. This is one of the stronger Hollywood attempts at autobiography. For the most part, Rooney avoids bad taste and still manages to appear naughty, surprising, and honest about himself. Good for mature readers who grew up with Andy Hardy.

3224 IF. by Sherwin, David. 167 p. paper illus. New York: Simon & Schuster, 1969.

Script of the 1969 film directed by Lindsay Anderson. Contains a preface by Anderson.

3225 IKIRU. by Kurosawa, Akira; and Hashinoto, Shinobu; and Oguni, Hideo. 88 p. paper illus. New York: Simon & Schuster, 1968.

Script of the 1952 film directed by Kurosawa. Contains cast credits, a filmography, and an introduction by Donald Richie.

3226 *Il Film e la Sua Storia.* by Turconi, Davide; and Bassotto, Camillo 255 p. illus. Venice: Capelli Editore, 1965.

This Italian book is included here because its goals are similar in part to those of this volume. It is an extended bibliography of film history books arranged by country of origin. The time period covered is from approximately 1900 to 1963. Primary interest for most users will be in the section devoted to publications originating in the United States and Great Britain. Titles and publishing information are in English but all annotations are in Italian.

A surprising number of excellent illustrations supplement the text. Anyone who reads Italian will find this a most valuable source book. Its use with others will vary. Perhaps a translation is in order. Note also that film biography, criticism, techniques, and certain other categories are omitted: for the most part, only the general historical category is considered.

3227 *The Illustrated Disney Songbook.* compiled by Disney Studios. illus. New York: Random House, 1979.

This oversized volume begins with a history of Disney films which includes the selection and use of the songs. On the following pages 80 songs are presented, scored for piano and arranged for guitar. Throughout the book there are many illustrations taken from the Disney films.

3228 *The Illustrated Elvis.* by Harbinson, W. A. illus. New York: Grosset and Dunlap, 1976.

Published shortly before Elvis' death in 1977, this volume was ready for reprints, memorial editions and spin-offs in the financial rush to memorialize the singer. Not only did it appear in several hardback and paperback versions, but it was also abridged by Ace publishers.

More than 400 photographs, arranged in chronological fashion, with accompanying text tell the Presley story. From a poor-white-trash beginning to super stardom is Horatio Alger narrative material, but the illustrations bring a realism to the legend.

3229 *The Illustrated Encyclopedia of the World's Great Movie Stars and Their Films.* by Wlaschin, Ken. 235 p. illus. New York: Harmony (Crown), 1979.

This attractive book has been written and designed to appeal on several levels: reference, nostalgia, film buff material, and critical review. Happily, it succeeds nicely in all categories. A differentiation is made between a star and an actor as the author introduces his selection of 400 stars (those performers who have created an enduring screen personality). They are presented in three groups: silent movie stars, classic movie stars, and modern movie stars. The typical entry includes a critique, biographical information, one or more illustrations, and a list of the subject's best films. A general index concludes the book.

If there is such a book genre as a subjectively personal reference book, this is it. Wlaschin's choices, prejudices, and favorites define the book. Since he is apparently a movie critic of taste and conviction, this is all to the good. The text he provides is often great fun to read. In addition the illustrations are nicely selected and clearly reproduced. This is a unique book that can be used by diverse audiences for a variety of reasons. Highly recommended.

3230 *The Illustrated Frankenstein.* by Stoker, John. 128 p. illus. paper Newton Abbot, England: Westridge Books, 1980.

3231 *An Illustrated Glossary of Film Terms.* by Geduld, Harry M.; and

Gottesman, Ronald. 179 p. paper illus. New York: Holt, Rinehart & Winston, 1973.

This glossary has two major qualities that contribute to its overall excellence: a careful selection of many stills and diagrams and a concise, easy-to-understand text. As complementary factors, the text and illustrations blend to make clear in nontechnical language most of the terms one might encounter in film study.

Three pages of abbreviations precede the glossary, which extends from "A and B printing" to "Zoom lens." Definitions are accurate, literate and often mention specific films, books, personalities, etc., to help interpret their meaning. Many of the terms are cross-referenced and certain other terms are clustered under major headings. In this latter instance the reader will find under "Angles" definitions for dutch, eye level, high, low, reverse, side, and subjective angles. Reproduction of the many helpful illustrations is very good and, as indicated above, the selection is admirable. A mark of distinction for a reference book is its suitability for reading or browsing. Not only can this glossary be read for pleasure, but it efficiently satisfies its major function—that of providing clear, comprehensive definitions of film terms. An essential reference.

3232 *An Illustrated History of the Horror Film.* by Clarens, Carlos 256 p. illus. New York: G. P. Putnam's, 1967.

Starting with the films of Melies and working up to ALPHAVILLE (1965), historical acounts and critical evaluations of certain horror films are intermingled. While an attempt to categorize the excellent photographs is only partly successful, the pictures are so good that they can withstand any arrangement. A final section gives the cast and credits for over 300 horror films. A book such as this has a built-in success factor—it treats a popular cinematic subject with print and pictures and does it well. Highly recommended for all.

3233 *The Illustrated Movie Quiz Book.* by Burt, Rob. 96 p. illus. paper London: Severn House, 1981.

3234 *The Illustrated Who's Who in British Films.* by Gifford, Dennis. 334 p. illus. Detroit: Gale, 1978.

This straightforward reference book is an alphabetical listing of over 1000 British filmmakers. Covering the period 1895 to 1977, the text offers basic information for each individual: names, titles, honors, film

473

activities, birth place, date, marriages, etc., along with a filmography limited to British productions. Almost 300 illustrations accompany the entries. Concluding the volume is a biographical bibliography, also arranged alphabetically by subject surname.

As he did in *The British Film Catalogue 1895-1970*, Dennis Gifford has assembled a valuable reference tool for anyone seeking information about British filmmakers. In his short biographical comments, he has tried to relieve the monotony of 1000 or so similar entries by offering occasional critical assessments of the subjects. The illustrations Gifford has chosen also add variety to the book. All in all, this is a solid, well-assembled reference book.

3235 *The Image.* by Boorstin, Daniel J. 315 p. New York: Atheneum, 1962.

The role of films in creating "images" which substitute for reality is explored. The question proposed is, "Do we like the image so much we cannot recognize/accept reality?"

3236 *Image and Influence.* by Tudor, Andrew. 260 p. New York: St. Martin's Press, 1975.

The overview provided by this book, which is subtitled "Studies in the Sociology of Film," considers such topics as patterns of communication, film communicators, movie audiences, movie languages, patterns of culture, sociological movements in film, popular genres, and patterns of change. A bibliography and an index are also included.

The author's goal is to provide a general review of his subject along with selected critical evaluations of what has been done/written and what remains to be accomplished. Varying his styles and approaches, the author balances the conceptual with the empirical, the process with the audience, and the macroscopic with the microscopic.

Here is a carefully formulated state-of-the-art book that has as its base the research and thought in three fields: sociology, film, and mass communications. It deserves a place among those few volumes in film literature which are called classic. Highly recommended.

3237 *The Image Industries.* by Lynch, William F. 159 p. New York: Sheed & Ward, 1959.

A religious educator's original, intellectual views about certain problems of the mass media, this book urges the creation of competent critics for our mass culture. Other topics considered are the failure of

mass media to differentiate between fantasy and reality, the weakening of the public's feeling and sensibility, the restriction of the freedom of imagination, and the characteristic "bigness" of many ideas and actions, as presented by the media. Obviously the viewpoint is that of a Catholic theologian; by the use of examples from the media—mostly films—his argument is made most persuasively. A stimulating book for the advanced reader.

3238 *The Image Maker.* edited by Henderson, Ron. 96 p. paper illus. Richmond, Va.: John Knox Press, 1971.

Six interviews with directors Miklos Jansco, Abraham Polonsky, Jaromil Jires, Jean Renoir, Ingmar Bergman, and Peter Fonda make up the first part of this book. An introduction is provided to each interview except Fonda's. The second section is a collection of six essays on various topics. According to Henderson, their commonality is that they all point to film as image maker. Perhaps. Some rather good visuals are included.

The interviews are the major attraction here and one suspects the essays were fillers. Were they written for this book? No sources are given for the essays, but Schillaci's "Film As Environment" appeared earlier in *Films Deliver*.

3239 *Image Maker: Will Rogers and the American Dream.* by Brown, William. 304 p. illus. Columbia, Mo.: University of Missouri Press, 1970.

Brown attempts to explain and analyze Will Rogers as a national idol with four faces: the American Adam, the American Democrat, the Self-Made Man, and the American Prometheus. The book concentrates on the public image rather than the private man. It emphasizes the comments and writings of Rogers but ignores Rogers as a screen performer both in silents and in the sound era. Even as supporting material to a study of Rogers, the book is limited. The approach is worshipful and prejudiced, extolling Rogers' virtues and minimizing his faults or omissions. Not recommended.

3240 *The Image Makers: 60 Years of Hollywood Glamour.* by Trent, Paul; and Lawton, Richard. 327 p. illus. New York: McGraw-Hill, 1972.

This book is aptly subtitled because everything about it indicates glamour: visuals, layout, dust jacket, type style, paper quality, etc., are all above the ordinary. An introductory essay discusses those stars who had a public image, usually created and prized above all else by the studio masterminds. Some were able to change this image, others could not, e.g., Mary Pickford, Garbo. The studio photographers are named and an informal history of the film star photo is delineated.

The substance of the book is the pictures, which are of two major types—the gallery portrait and the candid. Concentration is on the former; only a very few candids are included. Presented in a chronological fashion by decades, the visuals are consistently breathtaking. When the charisma of these unique people was exposed by the photographer, you have the almost perfect blending of subject and artist. Selection is wide, with Barbara Stanwyck, Bette Davis and Marlene Dietrich, with six pictures each, among those most represented. A few of the later photographs are in full color. In the book's closing pages the subjects are indexed by year, photographer, film studio, film title, and page reference.

This is a visual experience and feast that will please many readers and lookers. With few words and much beauty, it indicates that quality of the Hollywood movie star that is sadly missing in today's acting professionals.

3241 *The Image of the Artist in Fictional Cinema.* by Lanier, Vincent. Eugene, Ore.: University of Oregon, 1969.

An investigation to ascertain the image of the artist (painter, sculptor, etc.) as reflected in feature films. The conclusions of this research are surprising.

3242 *Image* on the Art and Evolution of the Film. edited by Deutelbaum, Marshall. 248 p. paper illus. New York: Dover, 1979.

A collection of photographs and articles from the magazine, *Image*, of the International Museum of Photography, this anthology emphasizes the history of the silent screen. It reflects the interests, activities, and goals of the museum which is located in the George Eastman House at Rochester, N.Y. Some 38 articles are arranged under seven general headings: prehistory (1827-1893); pioneering age (1894-1906); heroic age (1906-1913); classic age (1914-1928); studies of individual films; interviews; and the film still. Although the content goes back to the early nineteenth century, the earliest article source is an April 1952 issue of *Image*. Most of the material comes from issues printed in the seventies.

Sharing equal prominence with the many specialized topics treated in the articles are the 263 illustrations. They include frame enlargements, stills, production shots, etc., all of which have been newly prepared. A detailed index has been included.

This is a volume to excite film historians, buffs, and many general readers. It offers some unique material, well selected and reproduced. The combination of text, visuals, and outstanding production makes this one of the best film history anthologies to come along in years. Highly recommended.

3243 *Image/Music/Text.* by Barthes, Roland. 222 p. illus. New York: Hill and Wang, 1977.

The author of *Elements of Semiology* examines structuralist philosophy as applied to film semiotics.

3244 *Images and the Imageless.: A Study in Religious Consciousness and Film.* by Martin, Thomas M. 200 p. Lewisburg, Penn.: Bucknell University Press, 1981.

An attempt to relate the film medium to religious studies by means of the spatial interpretation and orientation that is common to both forms of reflection.

3245 *Images at the Horizon: A Workship with Werner Herzog.* edited by Walsh, Gene. New York: Zoetrope, 1980.

Includes an interview with Herzog.

3246 *Images of Alcoholism.* edited by Cook, Jim; and Lewington, Mike. New York: Zoetrope, 1980.

3247 *Images of Man.* by Drew, Donald J. 121 p. paper illus. Downers Grove, Ill.: InterVarsity Press, 1974.

InterVarsity Press is a publisher of religious materials. In the preface to this book, which is subtitled "A Critique of the Contemporary Cinema," the author states that each art or cultural activity within a society both reflects and promotes its own thought-forms and lifestyles. He believes the cinema to be the leader in this cultural consensus and attempts to explore the questions and answers supplied by film to man's current search for meaning. As a summary he offers some criteria for judging films.

Opening chapters justify the cultural consensus idea, while sections on violence, sex, tripping, working,- playing, and religion relate those topics to man's search for meaning. Final portions of the book consider censorship, criticism, and developing a Christian perspective. There are some appropriate illustrations and chapter notes. The volume is not indexed.

The question of whether film reflects "who and what man is" has been explored in a structured persuasive text. Since the author's viewpoint, criteria, and argument have been determined by his religion, readers should be aware of his emphasis on Christianity, scripture, God, and religion. Acceptable.

3248   *Images of Violence.* by Faure, William. 128 p. paper illus. London: Studio Vista, 1973.

A survey of violence in films, whose contents include: milestones, violence in art, violence—illusory and real, choreographed killing, action shock, wild west, and violence endorsed.

3249   *The Imaginary Signifier: Psychoanalysis and the Cinema.* by Metz, Christian. Bloomington, Ind.: Indiana University Press, 1981.

Metz explores aspects of the psychological anchoring of cinema as a social institution and looks at the operations of meaning in the film text.

3250   *The Immediate Experience.* by Warshow, Robert. 282 p. Garden City, N.Y.: Doubleday, 1962.

" Movies, Comics, Theatre, and Other Aspects of Popular Culture" is the subtitle of this volume. The major portion, however, is devoted to film reviews and essays by a former writer for *Commentary Magazine* and *Partisan Review* (1946-1955). Charles Chaplin, the art film, and American movies are the major categories examined. An intelligent, readable sample of responsible film criticism. (The author died in 1955.)

3251   *The Immortal Jolson, His Life and Times.* by Sieben, Pearl. 231 p. illus. New York: Fell, 1962.

3252   THE IMMORTAL ONE. by Robbe-Grillet, Alain. 173 p. illus. London: Calder and Boyars, 1971.

Script of the 1963 film directed by Alain Robbe-Grillet. Includes preliminary notes; cast and production credits; a shot-by-shot description of the film which the author calls "a Cine-Novel."

3253   *Immortals of the Screen.* edited by Stuart, Ray. 224 p. illus. Los Angeles: Sherbourne Press, 1965.

This subjective selection of more than 100 "immortals" is quite fascinating. Subjects range from superstars (Monroe) to supporting players (Alan Hale) to bit players (Henry Armetta). The emphasis is slightly on the nonstars but all are familiar and welcome. The usual format for each is a brief biography, a studio portrait and a few stills from the subject's films. Beneath each still is some character identification and comment. Picture selection is excellent, the reproduction is acceptable, and the text is informative, critical, and straightforward. Highly recommended, either as a partial reference or a book for browsing.

3254   *The Impact of Film.* by Madsen, Roy Paul. 571 p. illus. New York: Macmillan, 1973.

This volume is about cinema-television—the fusion of two media—and its variety of forms and concepts. The subtitle used is "How Ideas Are Communicated through Cinema and Television." A first section dealing with the viewer and his characteristics is followed by explanations of film language, editing, sound, animation and special effects. Some of the various genres of film are described next—drama, comedy, musical, documentaries, commercials, propaganda, etc. The closing sections are devoted to teaching via film-television and the research pertinent to this methodology. A bibliography, a title index, and a general index conclude the volume. Illustrations are effectively used throughout the book.

Combining many separate elements to make a specific total statement about the impact of film-television, this volume succeeds most effectively. It blends aesthetics, sociology, film forms, education, research and other topics into a logical, coherent exposition. Its potential for many readers seems unlimited and it is highly recommended.

3255   *An Impersonation of Angels: a Biography of Jean Cocteau.* by Brown, Frederick. 438 p. illus. New York: Viking, 1968.

Another fine biography of Jean Cocteau which gives brief accounts of the films and their making. The book is absorbing and compassionate, yet objective. Film stills are not used in the illustrations; these are mostly informal poses of Cocteau and his friends. The book has a detailed index, a bibliography of French and English books, and many explanatory notes. Acceptable.

3256 *The Intimate Journal of Rudolph Valentino.* by Valentino, Rudolph. 256 p. New York: Wm. Faro, 1931.

Although it claims Valentino as its author, this volume was written anonymously after his death. It is a biography that emphasizes the more sensational events in his well-publicized personal life, including his last illness. His films and film roles are discussed.

3257 *In a Glamorous Fashion: The Fabulous Years of Hollywood Costume Design.* by La Vine, Robert W. 224 p. illus. New York: Scribner's, 1980.

This intriguing oversized volume consists of two sections. First, there is a historical survey of costume design in films from the twenties to date. Blending fact with anecdote, critical opinion and memoirs, the author describes the evolution of his profession as a reflection of Hollywood filmmaking trends and economic conditions. In the second section, La Vine offers biographical appreciations of ten designers—Edith Head, Cecil Beaton, Adrian, Travis Banton, Orry-Kelly, etc.

Illustrations are an integral part of this kind of book, and more than 200 are provided. Cecil Beaton provides a foreword, Diana Vreeland an introduction, and Anita Loos an afterword.

This is information, film history, visual art, and nostalgia served in a most attractive package.

3258 *In and Out of Character.* by Rathbone, Basil. 278 p. illus. Garden City, N.Y.: Doubleday, 1962.

This is another of the many autobiographies which extoll the legitimate theatre over all other media. Although Rathbone owes his celebrity and much more to the modest Sherlock Holmes films he made in the forties, he blithely states "the whole procedure of making a moving picture from its inception to its final screening before the public is a series of purely technological and mechanical devices." Nowhere does he recognize film as an art—only as a source of creature comfort.

His attitude toward the character of Holmes is, therefore, not surprising. He came to hate Sherlock Holmes. This feeling and his opinion of films makes this a rather disillusioning reading experience. There are a few bland pictures, but no index or filmography is given.

3259 *In Focus.* by Murray, John A.; and Murray, Janette. 74 p. illus. Melbourne: Georgian House, 1972.

A short volume concentrating on three basics of motion pictures—production, direction and cinematography. A bibliography and some illustrations are included.

3260 see *3259*

3261 *In Focus: A Guide to Using Films.* by Blackaby, Linda; and Georgakas, Dan; and Margolis, Barbara. 206 p. paper illus. New York: Zoetrope, 1980.

This handbook deals with the various elements associated with the intelligent use of film with an audience. Topics include goals, selection, planning, space, time, publicity, discussion, projection, sound, evaluation and follow-up. Sources for films and information for other helpful aids/resources are noted.

Much of the information given here can also be found in the earlier volume, *The Film Users's Handbook.*

3262 *In Front of the Camera.: How to Make It and Survive in Movies and Television.* by Sandler, Bernard; and Posner, Steve. 192 p. illus. New York: Dutton, 1981.

Advice on how to get yourself noticed, an agent, a set of professional photographs, etc. Sound advice from the operator of a talent agency.

3263 *In Hollywood Tonight.* by Duncan, Peter. 192 p. illus. London: W. Laurie, 1951.

Duncan was a British radio personality who played host to celebrities. Additions to this collection of interveiws can be found in a later volume entitled *In Show Business Tonight.*

3264 see *3263*

3265 *In Its Own Image: The Cinematic Vision of Hollywood.* by Anderson, Patrick Donald. 365 p. New York: Arno, 1978.

It is surprising to find a subject that has been used several times for commercial publication—(*Hollywood on Hollywood, Hollywood According to Hollywood, Hollywood's Hollywood, Movies on Movies*, etc.)—appearing in the *Dissertations on Film* series. Written at the University of Michigan in 1976, this critical exploration of a film genre is divided into four chapters: I. Conventions of the Genre; II. Early Success in the Movies; III. The Dark Side of the Dream; IV. In America's Image.

A selected bibliography and a filmography complete the book.

3266 IN OLD CHICAGO. by Trotti, Lamar; and Levien, Sonya. 263 p. illus. Beverly Hills: Twentieth Century Fox Film Corp., 1937.

Script of the 1938 film, which was directed by Henry King.

3267 *In Old Hollywood: The Movies During Their Golden Years.* by Jackson, Clyde O. Hicksville, N.Y.: Exposition, 1977.

3268 *In Person, Lena Horne.* by Horne, Lena; and Arstein, Helen; and Moss, Carlton. 249 p. paper New York: Greenberg, 1950.

3269 *In Search of Dracula.* by McNally, Raymond; and Florescu, Radu. 225 p. illus. Greenwich, Conn.: New York Graphic Society, 1972.

In this overview of all the aspects of the Dracula legend, one chapter is devoted to "Bram Stoker and the Vampire in Fiction and Film." More important, perhaps, is the filmography given at the book's conclusion which lists silent and sound films from 1896 to 1971 that dealt with vampires. Melies' THE HAUNTED CASTLE (1897) begins the list and THE RETURN OF COUNT YORGA (1971) is the last film noted. Noted here for the record.

3270 *In the Beginning.* by Niver, Kemp R. 60 p. paper illus. New York: Brandon Books, 1967.

This small booklet is subtitled "Program Notes to Accompany One Hundred Early Motion Pictures." The films were selected from the photographic conversion project that the Library of Congress initiated to preserve the early paper rolls and make them available for study and research. The 100 films, available on 26 reels, are grouped according to the copyright applicant or country of origin. Making such films available is most commendable. To that specialized small group interested in early screen history, this little booklet is a gem; there is much useful and interesting historical information to warrant the scholar's attention. Others may not find it

very pertinent.

3271 *In the Bigtime.* by Bakeless, Katherine. 208 p. illus. Philadelphia: J. P. Lippincott, 1953.

A collection of short biographies of personalities from the world of entertainment and art. Film actors profiled are Fred Astaire, James Stewart, and Bing Crosby. Aimed at the young adolescent.

3272 *In The Dark: A Primer For The Movies.* by Barsam, Richard M. 216 p. paper illus. New York: Viking, 1977.

This primer on film, which was designed for young adults, consists of three parts: history, production, and criticism. Events and filmmakers from both the silent and the sound eras are recalled in the history section. Film is a collaborative art that often includes a production unit with a diversity of creative artists, a studio, equipment, etc.; that is the theme of the production section. Under criticism, certain basic elements are stated with an emphasis on the contributions of the director. Two films—LOUISIANA STORY (1948) and THE GRAPES OF WRATH (1940)—are analyzed in detail. Illustrations, suggested viewing and reading, and an index complete the book.

The creation of a terse, succinct primer from the vast amount of film information and history available is no small challenge. Barsam's choices and his treatment of them are well suited for his intended audience. In addition, production quality is high with many visuals nicely reproduced. The book should capture the attention and enthusiasm of the young reader with no difficulty.

3273 IN THE FRENCH STYLE. by Shaw, Irwin. 208 p. paper illus. New York: Macfadden-Bartell, 1963.

Script of the 1963 film directed by Robert Parrish. Contains cast credits, an introduction by Shaw; two articles by Shaw: "Paris! Paris!" and "A Year to Learn the Language" and two short stories also by Shaw: "In the French Style" and "The Winter City."

3274 IN THE MESH (L'ENGRENAGE). by Sartre, Jean-Paul. 128 p. London: Andrew Dakers Limited, 1954.

An unfilmed script.

3275 *In Vogue.* by Howell, Georgina. 344 p. illus. New York: Schocken Books, 1975.

In 1892 *Vogue* was founded in New York as a society magazine. Conde Nast bought it in 1909 and turned it into America's leading fashion periodical. British *Vogue* was begun in 1916 and it is the source from which this book was derived. Subtitled "Sixty Years of International Celebrities and Fashion From British Vogue," the book identifies seven eras: The Great Escape (1916-1929); The Reckless Twenties (1924-1929); The Threadbare Thirties (1930-1939); Fashion by Government Order (1940-1947); The Fashion-Conscious Fifties (1948-1959); The Revolutionary Sixties (1960-1969); and The Uncertain Seventies (1970-1975). Some attention is given to the influence of film costume design on fashion but the emphasis is mostly on the styles created by the famous names—Chanel, Schiaparelli, Dior, Saint Laurent, etc.

Although the illustrations are plentiful, those showing film personalities are surprisingly few and rather predictable—(Garbo, Dietrich, Crawford, Audrey Hepburn etc.). The text alternates fact and description with chatter and gossip, providing a most entertaining mixture. An index is included.

While this volume is not directly concerned with film, there is enough related material to make it acceptable.

3276 *Independent Filmmaking.* by Lipton, Lenny. 432 p. paper illus. San Francisco: Straight Arrow Books, 1972.

Subtitled "A Complete Guide to 8mm, Super 8, Single 8 and 16mm Moviemaking," this is an encyclopedia for the nonprofessional filmmaker. Each of its ten chapters is crammed with information, opinion, charts, diagrams, tables and visuals. Chapter titles encompass the totality of independent filmmaking—the format, the film, the camera, the lens, shooting, splicing and editing, sound and magnetic recording, preparing the sound track, the laboratory's role, and a final mixed bag of topics.

In addition to the detailed text, the visuals, which are chosen wisely and reproduced beautifully, add to the clarity of the book. Understanding the technical portions should be no great problem for most readers, since Lipton uses an easy informal personal style. An index enhances the reference value of the book and a second index of the illustrations should satisfy the curious. Stan Brakhage supplies a well-written, witty introduction. This is one of the best books on independent filmmaking to appear in some

time. It can be used effectively by anyone who needs a comprehensive guide to filmmaking. Highly recommended.

3277 *Index to Critical Film Reviews.* edited by Bowles, Stephen E. 2 vols.: 782 p. New York: Burt Franklin, 1975.

Although it is divided into two books, this index has several components. Volume I begins an index to certain reviews of films arranged alphabetically by film title; it covers film titles from A to M; the second volume covers film titles from N to Z. In addition, the second book contains an index to reviews of certain film books, again arranged alphabetically by book title. Supporting these two major elements are indexes for directors, film reviewers, authors, and book reviewers. A subject index to books about film and a union list of film periodical locations conclude the second book.

The books, which cover the period 1930 to 1972, index some 20,000 reviews of 600 films and 6000 reviews of 1200 books. The film periodicals chosen for this index were limited to 29 scholarly, English-language publications that are not indexed by other references such as *Readers' Guide to Periodical Literature*. In the first section each entry gives the film title, director, periodical, volume, number, date, pages, author, and number of words, along with certain bibliographical abbreviations. The number of periodicals under each film title ranges from one to about 10 with one and two source listings predominating. Other than substituting author for director, the book review entries are similar.

As a result of the limited sources, the films and books treated in this index are selected titles and do not approach a comprehensive selection. For example, there are no reviews for such films as ALEXANDER NEVSKY (1939), MR. SMITH GOES TO WASHINGTON (1939), NINOTCHKA (1939), THE LONG VOYAGE HOME (1940), MY SISTER EILEEN (1942), DOUBLE INDEMNITY (1944), etc. Remakes of films, such as M (1951) or MY SISTER EILEEN (1955), are listed but not identified as second versions; only the date indicates which film is being reviewed. This may be confusing to some users who are unaware of a particular film's history. Since most of the periodicals used are of current vintage, newer films get more attention than do the older, more classic films, e.g., THREE ON A COUCH (1966) has four entries, while THE MALTESE FALCON (1941) has only one retrospective review written in 1966.

The subject index to the books employs only 11 large categories, which limits its usefulness to some degree, depending upon the user's need. In the checklist of library abbreviations, the unknowing reader may question the arrangement of the state names which is based on the alphabetical symbols for the institutions within that state rather than the state name itself. This is not explained anywhere in the text.

Detailed attention has been given to this reference work because it is an important one. Wide in scope and requiring much author effort, it should be considered as a valuable and useful tool. It treats a partial group of books and films, but it does offer information not available in such other film indexes as *The New Film Index*, *The Critical Index*, and *Guide to Critical Reviews*. Once the purpose and coverage of the book are understood, it can be a decided asset. Its value will depend upon one's access to the periodicals indexed.

3278   *Index to 8mm Educational Motion Cartridges.* by The National Information Center for Educational Media (NICEM). 402 p. New York: Bowker, 1969.

This index lists over 9000 films in the cartridged format. For each the following information is given: 1) title, 2) running time, 3) year of release, 4) audience level, 5) producer, distributor, 6) color, sound, sound system data, 7) a brief description, and 8) series title, if any. It should be noted that all the information is descriptive, not evaluative. All 8mm cartridged films require a special projector for showing.

3279   *Index to Film Culture.* paper New York: Film Culture, 1968.

This is not an index in the usual reference sense. It is simply a listing of the tables of contents of the periodical, *Film Culture*, from volume 1 to volume 46. This short work should be of some assistance but one wishes that a more usable index had been produced.

3280   *Index to Films in Review*, 1950-1959. by Fawcett, Marion. 105 p. New York: National Board of Review of Motion Pictures, 1961.

This valuable index to an important film periodical first lists all of the article titles from 1950 to 1959 alphabetically, then by subject, using headings such as arts, biography, interviews, aesthetics, film music, etc. Other sections are devoted to book reviews, film titles, illustrations, author names, directors, actors, actresses, etc. The index is quite easy to use and the cross listings will be of great assistance to the searcher who has meager information to begin with.

3281   *Index to Films in Review*, 1960-1964. by Fawcett, Marion. 196 p. New York: National Board of Review, 1966.

This second index to *Films in Review*, covering the years 1960 to 1964, differs from the earlier index; a straight alphabetical arrangement is used here rather than the earlier section/division format. The claim that this is more efficient is debatable, but the ultimate value of this research tool is not. A valuable reference work.

3282   *Index to Films in Review*, 1965-1969. by Lester, Sandra. 234 p. New York: National Board of Review, 1973.

3283   *Index to Instructional Media Catalogs.* edited by Weber, Olga S. 272 p. New York: R. R. Bowker, 1974.

In this guide to the catalogs of suppliers of specific instructional materials, there are many elements applicable to motion pictures. It is arranged in three parts: a subject/media index, a product and services index, and a directory of companies. In the subject/media index, the major headings are language arts; mathematics; science; social studies; business, vocational and professional training; early childhood materials; the arts; and health and safety. An example of its usefulness can be illustrated by looking at the literature (American) subheadings under language arts. Listed here are the names of film distributors with the grade levels of their films indicated. Under 8mm loops there are five entries, under super 8mm Loops there are eight entries, and under 16mm reel there are 87 entries. The specific subheading of cinematography and TV found under the arts heading also lists over 100 entries for 16mm reel film distributors.

In the product and services index section the following headings are pertinent: film cartridges, film cartridge projectors, film loop projectors, film maintenance equipment, film reel accessories, motion picture cameras, motion picture 8mm loops, motion picture projectors 8mm and 16mm, and motion pictures 16mm. This latter category lists about 200 entries. The final directory is an alphabetical listing of the names and addresses of the companies named in the first two sections.

3284   *Index to Sixteen mm Educational Films.* by The National Information Center for Educational Media (NICEM). 1111 p. New York: Bowker, 1969.

This is an index derived from the NICEM data bank and contains more than 30,000 entries for commercially available films. The main alphabetical listing of films includes: 1) the complete title, 2) edition, 3) running time, 4) whether black & white or color, 5) description, 6) series title, if any, 7) audience level, 8) producer, 9) distributor, 10) production code, and 11) year of release on 16mm. The films are not evaluated, only described. Access to the list is by title or by a subject guide which contains major subject headings to facilitate location. A major subject heading outline is also given. Finally, an alphabetical directory of producers & distributors is provided. A major reference work.

3285 *An Index to the Creative Work of Alexander Dovzhenko.* by Leyda, Jay. New York: Gordon Press, 1980 (1947).

Published originally in 1947 by the British Film Institute as a special supplement to *Sight and Sound* Index Series No. 12.

3286 *An Index to the Creative Work of David Wark Griffith.* by Stern, Seymour. 2 vols. London: British Film Institute, 1944, 1946.

Prepared as a special supplement to *Sight and Sound,* the index deals with Griffith from 1908 to 1916 and with three of his feature films, THE BIRTH OF A NATION (1915), INTOLERANCE (1916), and HEARTS OF THE WORLD (1918).

3287 *An Index to the Creative Work of V.I. Pudovkin.* by Leyda, Jay. New York: Gordon Press, 1980 (1948).

Published originally in 1948 by the British Film Institute as a special supplement to *Sight and Sound* Index Series No. 16.

3288 *Index To The New York Times* Film Reviews. 1142 p. illus. New York: Arno, 1970.

This valuable reference source has other uses in addition to being a guide to the five volumes in the original set. For those libraries which have the *Times* on microfilm, or for the small library that simply wants the name index with the accompanying film titles, the citations to the *Times* reviews, the title index, the corporate index, the awards section, or the picture collection of 2000 performers, this single volume may suffice.

3289 INDIA SONG. by Duras, Marguerite. 146 p. paper illus. New York: Grove, 1976.

A script of the 1976 French film, directed by Duras, which starred Delphine Seyrig.

3290 *Indian Cinema Today.* by Sarkar, Kobita. 167 p. illus. New Delhi: Sterling (Columbus: South Asia), 1975.

Kobita Sarkar is an Indian film critic who also has served as a censor, a festival judge, a magazine correspondent, and a commentator on films. In this collection of essays, she explores the modern Indian cinema, noting the elements which have influenced and shaped it. Discussed are such topics as directors, the star system, film characters, censorship, violence, humor, sex, romance, song, dance, audience, regional film, experimental films, film societies, art theatres, and national awards. A few faded illustrations and an index complete the book.

So little is available in English about the Indian cinema that the interested reader is usually grateful for information in any form. Sarkar's analytical essays are much more than the filling of a historical/literary void. She is a perceptive, knowledgeable critic who can make the completely unfamiliar seem almost comprehensible. Although an actual viewing is preferable, at this point reading Sarkar seems the next best thing.

3291 *Indian Film.* by Barnouw, Erik; and Krishnaswamy, S. 301 p. illus. New York: Columbia University Press, 1963.

Many people may think that Indian films are mostly those of Satyajit Ray, such as the APU Trilogy. This book corrects this misconception, providing a history of the Indian film industry and the great quantity of feature films it has produced. It may be difficult for the general reader to relate to this somewhat obscure topic in cinema since few Indian films have been shown outside of India. Some fair but small illustrations are included as is a bibliography citing several Indian periodicals and books. The book is a scholarly effort to make better known a certain body of cinematic effort and is praiseworthy for this goal. Interesting to scholars and historians but with little potential for the general reader.

3292 *The Indian Film.* by Shah, Panna. 290 p. Illus. Bombay: The Motion Picture Society of India, 1950.

This book provides a historical, sociological, and

481

economic survey of the Indian motion picture industry. Although much of the material is dated, the topic is so specialized that this book still is quite pertinent for students, scholars, and historians. The writing is somewhat naive as is the format and topic arrangement of the book. Illustrations are few but effective. A bibliography and index are included. Invaluable for research, this book is not for the general reader.

3293   *Indian Film.* by Shah, Panna. 290 p. illus. Westport, Conn.: Greenwood, 1981.

3294   *Indian Filmography: Silent and Hindi Films (1897-1969).* by Rangoonwalla, Firoze. 471 p. Bombay: J. Udeshi, 1970.

See also *Indian Films Index* by the same author.

3295   *Indian Films Index (1912-1967).* by Rangoonwalla, Firoze. 130 p. Bombay: J. Udeshi, 1968.

See also *Indian Filmography: Silent and Hindi Films 1897-1969* by the same author.

3296   *Indian Films—An Annual.* by Dharap, B. V. 500 p. paper illus. Poona, India: Motion Picture Enterprises, 1972- .

In 1976 the Indian film industry made 507 feature films and over 1000 shorts. Accordingly, B.V. Dharap's annual survey of that industry grows with each edition. The fifth, which covers 1976, offers sections on production, distribution, exhibition, foreign markets, import of films and machinery, motion pictures and government, screen organizations, a title index, film facts, etc. Under these headings the user will find credits, casts, box office hits, awards, studios, actors, directors, distributors, labs, etc.

3297   *Industrial and Business Films.* by Stork, Leopold. 180 p. illus. London: Phoenix House, 1962.

Suggestions for making and using films in business and industry.

3298   *The Industrial Film Guide.* edited by Steadman, Helen. 219 p. London: Kogan Page, 1974.

Although the use of this volume in America may be limited by the British origin of and references given for many of the films, it can still serve as a valuable

selection tool.

It is a filmography arranged by industrial subject area—accounting, building, engineering, food, hotel, printing etc.—under each classification. The films are arranged alphabetically by title. Each entry offers title, distributor, date, time, rental source, charge, color, and a descriptive annotation. Distributor and source addresses are given elsewhere in the book. There is also a master title index and a detailed subject index.

Since there is such a great deal that is common to industrial problems or processes in America and Britain, the book may suggest valuable audiovisual information sources that are not widely known in America. It is certainly worthy of the attention of anyone concerned with industrial training.

3299   *Industrial Film Maker.* edited by Ferris, Theodore N.; and Marchak, John P. St. Paul, Minn.: Changing Times, 1976.

3300   *Industrial Motion Pictures.* by Kodak Staff. 76 p. paper illus. Rochester, N.Y.: Kodak.

The concern here is with the service film rather than with the promotional one. Its aim is to show how good service films can be produced simply and inexpensively.

3301   *The Industry: Life in the Hollywood Fast Lane.* by David, Saul. 288 p. New York: Times Books, 1981.

David, a producer, offers memoirs of a career that began in the sixties. Some attention is given to VON RYAN'S EXPRESS (1965) and its star, Frank Sinatra. Like his films, the book varies in quality and interest.

3302   *The Influence of the Cinema on Contemporary Auditoria Design.* by Worthington, Clifford. 123 p. illus. London: Pitman, 1952.

3303   *The Influence of Subliminal Suggestion on the Response to Two Films.* by Veeder, Gerry K. New York: Arno, 1980.

A study on the measurement of response to a subliminal stimulus, especially its effect on film or television viewing. A title in the *Dissertations on Film* series.

3304 *The Influence of the Cinema on Children and Adolescents.* edited by UNESCO. 106 p. paper New York: UNESCO, 1961.

This annotated international bibliography is number 31 of the UNESCO *Reports and Papers on Mass Communications*. Titles are assigned to the following categories: (1) general works, (2) attitudes of youth toward the cinema, (3) analysis of film content, (4) process of seeing a film, (5) influence and after-effect of films, (6) educational aspects and practical measures, and (7) miscellaneous. An index of authors concludes the work.

3305 *The Information Film: A Report of the Public Library Inquiry.* by Waldron, Gloria. 281 p. New York: Columbia University Press, 1949.

This book is one of the studies made by the Public Library Inquiry group back in the late forties. The aim of this organization was to examine the evident alteration of the original concept of the free public library through a series of studies. Some 60 public libraries were surveyed and studied as to their use of film back in 1948-1949. At that time such topics as: "Film: A New Dimension to Education," "Film and the Public Library," and "Problems and Prospects in 16mm," seemed quite new. Although this book has some historial interest, the vast growth of film use and understanding in our public libraries has made much of it sound very naive and quite cliche. Recommended only to the research scholar—too dated to be of interest to most readers.

3306 *Informational Film Year Book 1947.* 175 p. illus. Edinburgh: Albyn Press, 1947.

This was the forerunner of *International Film Guide*. Emphasis at this point was on the nontheatrical film. Historical interest only.

3307 *Ingmar Bergman.* by Steene, Birgitta. 158 p. New York: Twayne, 1968.

The inclusion of a filmmaker in the Twayne series of books devoted to major writers of the world is unusual. However, it is more than justified by the exposition of author Steene. Starting with an evaluation of Bergman's early plays, the author next analyzes Bergman's films using a literary approach. The rationale for this type of analysis is threefold: 1) The recurrence of certain motifs in the films; 2) a dependence upon a dramatic story; and 3) the fact that published screen plays of the films resemble literary works rather than instructional guides for shooting

a film. The analyses offered are uniformly excellent and will be of great value to anyone interested in the art of Ingmar Bergman. The references and bibliography are also outstanding. A book for all serious students of cinema.

3308 *Ingmar Bergman.* by Wood, Robin. 192 p. paper illus. New York: Praeger, 1969.

The films of Bergman are studied and analyzed in this remarkable book. After discussing some recurrent themes (the absence of the permanent home, the journey used as a structure), the films are grouped in rough subject areas. For example, THE SEVENTH SEAL (1957), THE MAGICIAN (1958) and THE DEVIL'S EYE (1960), are in a category labeled "doubts and Fears" while "Lessons In Love" includes A LESSON IN LOVE (1954), SMILES OF A SUMMER NIGHT (1955), and WILD STRAWBERRIES (1957).

The analyses and interpretations of the films are at times brilliant, although they probably will not convince all students of Bergman's work. A necessity for anyone sincerely interested in the film as an art form. Filmography and short bibliography.

3309 *Ingmar Bergman: Essays in Criticism.* by Kaminsky, Stuart M.; and Hill, Joseph F. 340 p. paper illus. New York: Oxford, 1975.

Author representation is international in this anthology which offers 25 critical essays on Bergman and his films. Since the approach is analytical rather than factual, a previous acquaintance with the films is helpful. Also included is an interview with Bergman, some illustrations, and a filmography.

3310 *Ingmar Bergman: The Cinema as Mistress.* by Moseley, Philip. 192 p. London: Marion Boyars, 1981.

A critical survey of Bergman's films stressing recurring themes, questions, etc. Bergman's post-1972 films are largely ignored.

3311 *Ingmar Bergman: Four Decades in the Theatre.* by Marker, Lise-Lone; and Marker, Frederick J. 320 p. illus. New York: Cambridge University Press, 1981.

A detailed study of Ingmar Bergman's most important stage productions. Works by Strindberg, Ibsen and Moliere are emphasized.

3312 *Ingmar Bergman and the Search for Meaning.* by Gill, Jerry 32 p. paper Grand Rapids, Mich.: Wm. B. Eerdmans Pub. Co., 1969.

Five Bergman films—THE SEVENTH SEAL (1957), WILD STRAWBERRIES (1957), THROUGH A GLASS DARKLY (1961), WINTER LIGHT (1963), and THE SILENCE (1963) are analyzed from the perspective of Christian ethics.

3313 *Ingmar Bergman Directs.* by Simon, John. 315 p. illus. New York: Harcourt Brace Jovanovich, 1972.

A lengthy interview begins this latest Simon venture into film literature. In the short introduction which follows, he disposes of fellow critics Andrew Sarris, Richard Schickel, and Parker Tyler in short order and goes on to assess the work and artistry of Bergman. To prove his point that Bergman is the greatest filmmaker in the world today, he examines four films in detail: THE CLOWN'S EVENING (NAKED NIGHT) (1953), SMILES OF A SUMMER NIGHT (1955), WINTER LIGHT (1962) and PERSONA (1966). The filmography at the book's end gives cast and production credits for only this quartet of films.

The analyses of the films, which deal with themes, symbols, relationships, are in depth—with Simon's faults as a critic-writer less apparent than usual. As expected, he writes with style, discrimination and intellect. His appreciation of Bergman and his efforts seems sincere and almost affectionate. Absent are the Simon smugness, self-satisfaction and intolerance that appear in other writings.

The visuals, attributed to Halcyon Enterprises, are an asset to the book. They provide an analysis which attempts to run concurrently with the Simon narrative, and most of them appear to be taken directly from the films. Their reproduction is much better than usual for this type of photograph.

The fact that Simon treats only four Bergman films may disappoint those who have personal favorites. Incidentally, one might suspect, on the basis of the interview, that these four would be Bergman's choices also. The sampling offered does give enough evidence of Bergman's style, recurrent themes, artistic growth, and overall virtuosity to satisfy most readers.

The few films treated here may limit the book's value. For fuller coverage, see Steene's *Ingmar Bergman*, Wood's *Ingmar Bergman*, Young's *Cinema Borealis*, Gibson's *The Silence of God*, or Donner's *The Personal Vision of Ingmar Bergman*.

3314 *Ingrid Bergman: An Intimate Portrait.* by Steele, Joseph Henry. 332 p. paper illus. New York: Popular Library, 1959.

Based on notes, letters, recollections, and confidences, this biography of Bergman was written by a former publicity director of the Selznick Studios who later became Bergman's press agent and friend. The emphasis is on the Rossellini period of Miss Bergman's career. Also covered fully is Bergman's New York stage appearance in Maxwell Anderson's *Joan of Lorraine*.

A clear picture is given of the Bergman personality and charisma. The weakness and strength of the lady are presented in what seems to be honest and objective writing. A fascinating biography of one of the screens female superstars, this volume suffers from disproportionate attention to the various elements of Bergman's life.

3315 *Ingrid Bergman: My Story.* by Bergman, Ingrid; and Burgess, Alan. 494 p. illus. New York: Delacorte, 1980.

Does Ingrid Bergman offer anything more in this disjointed autobiography than can be found in previously published works? The answer is not very much. She is content to review the factual portions of her life and disregard the personal thoughts and feelings about the major events in her long, colorful career. Everything is in very good taste, but it is also rather dull. Some illustrations and a filmography along with the comments of those around her—directors, costars, husbands, children, etc.—complete the portrait.

3316 *Ingrid Bergman.* by Brown, Curtis F. 157 p. paper illus. New York: Pyramid, 1973.

The Bergman biography written by Joseph Steele was published in 1959 and gave little attention to her films. Lawrence Quirk's *The Films of Ingrid Bergman* addressed itself primarily to Bergman's career. This new volume is a combination of the above two and in many ways is more satisfying. Brown makes a valid point about the chemistry between Bergman and her leading men in his introduction and returns to it constantly as he discusses each of her films. Her stage work is acknowledged, and there is some attention given to her private life. A bibliography, filmography and an index complete the book. Reproduction of the visuals is very good and all elements of the production are impressive. Highly recommended.

3317 *Inner Views.* by Hofsess, John. 171 p. illus. Scarborough, Ontario: McGraw-Hill Ryerson, 1975.

Ten interviews with Canadian filmmakers comprise the content of this book. The subjects are Claude Jutra, Alan King, Don Shebib, Jack Darcus, Graeme Gerguson, Frank Vitale, William Fruet, Paul Almond, Denys Arcand, and Pierre Berton.

In his introduction the author discusses Canadian film from the economic, historical, and aesthetic viewpoints. The interviews are presented within a narrative framework rather than as a question-and-answer transcript. While some of the material may be known to U.S. readers, much of it deals with unfamiliar topics and titles. However, given the introductory base, the reader's interest will be maintained.

This is a satisfying visit with Canadian filmmakers that cannot help but develop a greater appreciation and understanding of their work. Recommended.

3318 *The Innocent Eye: The Life of Robert J. Flaherty.* by Calder-Marshall, Arthur. 304 p. illus. New York: Harcourt, Brace and World, 1963.

Based largely on material gathered by Paul Rotha and Basil Wright, this biography succeeds in giving the reader an objective view of the personality of the artist Flaherty, as well as the making of the classic films, NANOOK OF THE NORTH (1920), MOANA (1926), MAN OF ARAN (1934), THE LAND (1941), and LOUISIANA STORY (1948). The many illustrations are first rate and there are outlines of the above films included in the appendix. An index, a filmography, and a bibliography complete the book. An excellent biography of a pioneer filmmaker whose influence is evident in today's films, this book deserves a wide audience, although the limited availability of the films and the remoteness of the subject to today's readers will probably limit its popularity.

3319 *An Innocent in Hollywood.* by Winchester, Clarence. 140 p. illus. London: Cassell, 1934.

Hollywood in the early thirties as refelected by advice, gossip, information about such as Mae West, Lupe Velez, Bebe Daniels, Leslie Howard, etc.

3320 *Innovators of the French Cinema.* by Reif, Tony. 25 p. paper Ottawa: Canadian Film Institute, 1965.

An introducion to a series of programs presented by the National Film Theatre in Ottawa. Emphasis is on the directors/producers.

3321 *Inquisition in Eden.* by Bessie, Alvah. 268 p. New York: Macmillan Co., 1965.

This is another account of the confrontation between "The Hollywood Ten" and the House Un-American Activities Committee. Written by the author of such forties' screenplays as NORTHERN PURSUIT (1943) and HOTEL BERLIN (1945), the book offers considerable detail and much attention to the personalities involved. Quite specialized.

3322 *The Inquisition in Hollywood: Politics in the Film Community, 1930-1960.* by Ceplair, Larry; and Englund, Steven. 336 p. illus. New York: Doubleday (Anchor), 1980.

The House Un-American Activities Committee investigations had their roots in the 1930s. In this detailed study, the authors trace the history and note the factors that brought about the period that Lillian Hellman called "scoundrel time." The hysteria in the film community, the jailing of the Hollywood Ten, the blacklisting—all the events of that infamous time are reviewed here with total concern and objectivity. The authors assess, interpret, and clarify many of the complex issues of the period in this well-written political history of the Hollywood Studio era.

3323 *The Inquisition in Hollywood: Politics in the Film Community 1930-1960.* by Ceplair, Larry; and Englund, Steven. 536 p. illus. Garden City, N.Y.: Anchor/Doubleday, 1980.

A meticulously researched account with over 100 pages devoted to appendixes. Notes, a bibliography, and an index.

3324 *Inside Black Hollywood.* by Speed, Carol. 256 p. illus. paper Los Angeles: Holloway, 1980.

3325 *Inside Elvis.* by Parker, Ed. Rampert House.

The author of this profile of Elvis Presley served as security advisor and personal bodyguard to the star during his final years. Parker remains loyal to Elvis and gives rational explanations for Presley's bizarre behavior. It seems Elvis had a wild sense of humor, was fun-loving, and not a drug addict. He hints that

Elvis was kept in a drugged state so that those around him could enjoy the booze, pills and sex milieu described in the other Elvis exposes. Another Elvis book written for the nondiscriminating fan.

3326 *Inside Linda Lovelace.* by Lovelace, Linda. 184 p. paper illus. New York: Pinnacle Books, 1973.

For the few who may not have heard about or seen Linda Lovelace, she is the star of DEEP THROAT (1972). In a book that is supposedly an autobiography, the author tells of her early life, the making of the film, and then offers some sexual advice. A group of pictures of the author from the age of one to the present make up a centerfold gallery. No one else intrudes on these photographs, which are of the early Playboy variety. The text, however, is something else and deserves an X rating—only for adults over 21. Ms. Lovelace not only believes in sexual freedom but also in sexual excess.

There is some information about the making of the film but it is surrounded by sexual escapades and other fantasies. Most readers will be turned off after a few pages by the uninspired pornography and the author's apparently insatiable appetite for sexual adventure. Noted here for the record. In 1980 she disclaimed authorship. Tina Russell, another porno film actress, covers the same ground and the same people in her book, *Porno Star.*

3327 *Inside Pictures.* by Betts, Ernest. 161 p. illus. London: Cresset Press, 1960.

This is a chatty, but flat reminiscence based on a lengthy career in the British film industry. Beginning in the thirties as a scenario writer and a public relations man, Mr. Betts has most recently been a film critic for several British newspapers. Filled with anecdotes about British and American film names, it has a typical British reserve about all it discusses —nothing unkind or ungentlemanly is said or indicated. Much of it is trivial. Do we really care today that Ann Miller bought Irish linen instead of brandy? Or that Cyd Charisse is only happy when she is working in the studio? Illustrations and an index complete the book.

3328 *Inside Secrets of Photoplay Writing.* by Bradley, Willard King. 187 p. New York: Funk and Wagnalls, 1926.

Suggestions and advice on preparing scripts for the silent screen. Sources of inspiration, thinking in visual terms, titles, continuity, and other topics are discussed. A model synopsis ("The Beloved Imp") and some helpful hints conclude the work.

3329 *The Inside Story of the Hollywood Christian Group.* by Orr, Edwin J. 134 p. illus. Grand Rapids, Mich.: Zondervan, 1955.

3330 *Inside* THE DEEP. by Guber, Peter. 182 p. paper illus. New York: Bantam, 1977.

An account of the filming of THE DEEP (1977) is given by its producer, Peter Guber, in this original paperback. The film, based on a novel by Peter Benchley, starred Robert Shaw, Jacqueline Bissett, and Nick Nolte and was directed by Peter Yates. A large part of the shooting was devoted to underwater scenes, and Guber relates many of the difficulties involved in such photography. The general tone of the book resembles that of a long publicity piece— everyone is serious, hard working, and lovable. A list of credits and some excellent location shots are included.

3331 *Instructional Film Research 1918-1950 (Rapid Mass Learning).* by Hoban, Charles; and Van Ormer, Edward. Pages not numbered. New York: Arno Press, 1970 (1950).

A reprint of the summary and evaluation of three decades of research on instructional film. Done originally in 1950 at Penn State and sponsored by the Army and the Navy.

3332 *Instructions in Filming.* by Bateman, Robert. 124 p. illus. London:- Museum Press, 1967.

A guide designed for young people who are interested in making films and have only limited resources at their disposal. Indexed.

3333 *Interim Distribution Catalog: The Art and History of Film and TV.* ritish Film Institute Staff.

This catalog of films available for rental from the British Film Institute is published at irregular intervals. The feature film section is arranged chronologically and treats both silent and sound titles. Notes given beneath each are descriptive and critical. Other sections treat short films and documentaries, film study material, film study extracts, and film study units. A section on television material is also included. Indexed.

3334 *Intermission: A True Story.* by Baxter, Anne. 384 p. New York: Putnam, 1976.

A movie star gives up fame, career and a life of luxurious ease to live primitively in the Australian outback country. This may sound like fiction but it is Anne Baxter's true story set against a pioneer wilderness background. Interspersed are flashbacks of her Hollywood experiences. In a few words Baxter can convey the bittersweet glitter of Hollywood life better than most writers. In both the flashbacks and in her current story, she interprets her experiences with the intelligence of a skilled writer and actress. This is a fine book but one hopes that Baxter will eventually concentrate on her Hollywood years.

3335 *International Congress of Libraries and Museums of the Performing Arts.* edited by International Federation of Library Associations. 95 p. paper The Hague, Netherlands: Centre of the International Theatre Institute, 1965.

Prepared in French, English and German, the reports of the annual meetings (congress) of the special section of the Theatrical Libraries and Museums of the International Federation of Library Associations appear in varied lengths from different publishers. This one is concerned with the 7th congress, which was held in Amsterdam, September 6-9, 1965; included are the speeches, essays and lectures of the meeting. Other sessions were held in Munich (1963), Budapest (1968), etc.

3336 *International Directory of 16mm Film Collectors.* edited by Forman, Evan. 69 p. paper Mobile, Alabama: E. Forman, 1973.

Mr. Forman publishes this directory from time to time. His information is obtained by requesting any collector who wishes to be listed to send him the particulars—name, address, types of films desired, gauge, etc. The listing is without cost but the catalog has a printed price of $15. In this recent issue, there are 5000 names arranged by state. Unfortunately, they are not arranged in any fashion under each state. Some entries do list the special interests of the collector, but most are simply names and addresses. A very specialized reference.

3337 *International Elvis Presley Appreciation Society Handbook.* compiled by Saville, Tim. illus. Heanor, England: Albert Hand, 1970.

3338 *The International Encyclopedia of Film.* edited by Manvell, Roger. 574 p. illus. New York: Crown, 1972.

This reference concentrates on the world history of film as an art and as an industry. It avoids film technology and all other complex facets of film production. Between general terms (animation, censorship, documentary, screen writing) and the national cinemas of countries (Canada, India, Japan, Spain, etc.) are placed individual biographies (Brooks, Louise; Lupino, Ida; Hunter, Ross; etc.) and definitions (bridge, dubbing, pre-release, etc.) In addition, there is 1) a chronological outline of film history with the major events of each year indicated; 2) a lengthy bibliography; 3) an index of principal title changes; 4) an index of films; and 5) an index of names.

Both color and black and white illustrations are used with considerable success. They support the text immeasurably and are reproduced with a clarity that is unusual today. The efforts of everyone concerned here should be applauded. It is an ideal reference book.

3339 *International Film Annual.* edited by Dixon, Campbell. London: John Calder, Vol. 1: 1957 (167 p.); Vol. 2: 1958 (181 p); Vol. 3: 1959 (165 p.)

A collection of both black and white and color stills, articles and data concerning films and events from the years indicated in the titles. The articles are broad in scope, usually written by celebrities who are not necessarily authors. While having some items of interest for readers, most of the material here is too fragmentary and broad to warrant attention.

3340 *International Film Guide—1974.* edited by Cowie, Peter. 608 p. paper illus. New York: A. S. Barnes, 1973.

This annual reference seems to improve with each edition. For 1974 all of the usual features appear—the directors of the year, the choice of films, the film soundtracks, the world survey, film festivals, film books, etc.—but the coverage seems more in-depth than in earlier volumes. The world survey which occupies approximately half the book offers reports from more than 50 countries. Included here are statistics, reviews, announcements, summaries of industry and filmmaker activity, and local advertisements. Use of the book is facilitated by indexes and by the indication of the topic at the page bottom.

Although some of the information is familiar from the preceding volumes, there is so much that is new that the book can be considered as a fresh publication each year. The book is illustrated and the many advertisements are a fascinating source of information. Because of its quality, content, reference value and entertainment potential, the book is highly recommended. The reasonable price is no handicap either.

3341 *International Film Guide 1977.* edited by Cowie, Peter. 504 p. paper illus. New York: A. S. Barnes, 1977.

This indispensible reference seems to improve with each yearly edition. The book for 1975-1976 includes the standard sections (directors of the year, the world survey) and the shorter sections devoted to awards, schools, television, nontheatrical films, archives, film books, etc. Many advertisements are intermixed with the text pages but since the volume is international in scope, they often offer information not easily available elsewhere. For example, film books originating in Europe are described long before their appearance in American editions/translations. The illustrations are equally important since they convey a sense of international filmmaking to the reader.

In summary this annual continues to be an exciting, essential reference volume. Highly recommended.

3342 *The International Film Industry: Western Europe and America since 1945.* by Guback, Thomas H. 244 p. illus. Bloomington, Ind.: Indiana University Press, 1969.

The international co-production of motion pictures is the subject treated here. Aspects discussed include dollar investments, financial assistance, quotas, tariffs, government protection, etc. The film which results from international cooperation is also considered. The acceptance of American films in Europe and the fate of European films in America are treated in some depth. Well written, factual, and scholarly in approach, the book contains many tables of data. Although not for recreational reading, it has pertinence for anyone involved with the film industry and for the film scholar.

3343 *International Film Necrology.* by Stewart, William T.; and McClure, Arthur F.; and Jones, Ken D. 342 p. illus. New York: Garland, 1981.

3344 *International Index to Film Periodicals 1972.* edited by Jones, Karen. 344 p. New York: R. R. Bowker,

1973.

This book is a result of a cooperative plan by the 24 members of the International Federation of Film Archives. Coordinating their documentation efforts by indexing periodicals was the goal of this first project. Using about 60 selected periodicals which deal exclusively with film, the contributors came up with a total of 7000 entries for the year 1972. Selected from many countries, the sources included numerous foreign language periodicals. Translations of titles are not given, but all annotations are in English.

The entries are classified into the following categories: (1) general reference material, (2) institutions, festivals, conferences, (3) film industry: economics, production, (4) distribution, exhibition, (5) society and cinema, (6) film education, (7) aesthetics, theory, criticism, (8) history of the cinema, (9) individual films, (10) biography, and (11) miscellaneous. Annotations vary in length but most are satisfactory in describing the article content. Some effort must be made to understand the different arrangements of the material under each classification. Retrieval of a source is made easier by an index of subject headings which concludes the book.

A needed reference work has made its appearance in this fine volume. Coverage, arrangement and treatment of the material is most satisfying, and subsequent editions should improve on this initial prototype.

The 1973 edition of the *International Index to Film Periodicals* (395 pp.) was edited by Michael Moulds and follows the format of the initial volume. An author index has been added to facilitate retrieval. With the continued publication of these volumes, their value increases.

3345 *International Index to Multi-Media Information.* edited by Doak, Wesley A.; and Speed, William J. 462 p. Pasadena, Calif.: Audio-Visual Association, 1975.

This volume, which is distributed by R. R. Bowker, is a three-year cumulation (1970 to 1972) of the formerly titled *Film Review Index.* The original material has been altered somewhat to conform to the change of title and approach that the editors adopted in 1973. Now called *The International Index to Multi-Media Information,* the quarterly service usescomputer-based data. It is also probable that three-year cumulations such as this one will continue to be issued.

The initial cumulation lists all types of nonprint media, with films predominating. More than 60 periodicals are indexed and the entries for films contain much concentrated information. Sought for each citation are the following elements: title, series title, production company, production date, distribution company, release date, format(s), sound indicator, color indicator, length, price, LC number, suggested classification, ISBN (number), order number, citation source, volume number, issue number, date of issue, page, citation indicator, reviewer, quotation, audience level, subject-author headings, see reference, and distributor address. Obviously each entry does not contain all of these elements—only those pertinent to a full description. Subject-Author headings and Distributor Addresses appear as separate sections which follow the main text. The names and addresses of the 64 periodicals indexed are placed in the book's opening pages.

The convenience of having this vital reference material in one volume cannot be overestimated. The quarterly volumes have been impressive since their original issue in 1970 and the availability of three-year cumulations enhances the service they provide. The index, in any format, is essential; it offers enormous assistance to teachers, administrators, librarians and others who wish to make intelligent, accountable selections of useful nonprint materials.

3346 *International Motion Picture Almanac.* edited by Aaronson, Charles. 844 p. illus. New York: Quigley Publications, 1963.

The 1963 volume examined was the 34th edition of this reference work, which is designed primarily for those concerned with the commercial aspects of the feature film. (The 41st edition, 1970, had the same editor, the same publisher and almost the same number of pages: 848.) Major sections include 1) over 300 pages of short biographies of people concerned with the film industry; 2) a listing of features released between 1944 and 1962; 3) names and addresses of groups, companies and organizations concerned with film production, distribution and exhibition; 4) censorship, and codes; 5) award and poll winners, and 6) names and addresss of newspapers, magazines and journals concerned with films.

In addition there are many other features and quite a few advertisements. Amidst these ads there is a list of "The Great Hundred" films which can provide discussion material for several hours.

3347 *International Portrait Gallery—Volume Ten.: Film Directors and Producers Supplement.* 64 p. illus. Detroit, Mich.: Gale, 1981.

3348 *Interviews with Film Directors.* by Sarris, Andrew. 557 p. paper New York: Avon Books, 1967.

After an introductory essay entitled, "The Fall and Rise of the Film Director," which inevitably drifts to Bazin and auteur theory, the author presents edited interveiws with 40 directors. It should be noted that these are interviews gathered from magazines and film journals. The questioners range from Jean-Luc Godard to Penelope Houston. Each interview is preceded by an introduction or background and is followed by a filmography. The hardbound edition also contains pictures of the 40 directors. The selection is excellent, the supporting material is very strong and the paperback price is right. This is simply one of the most vital, basic compilations now in print.

3349 *Intimacies—Stars Share Their Confidences and Feelings.* by Ebert, Alan. 384 p. paper New York: Dell, 1980.

About two dozen female celebrities talk about fear, ageing, loneliness, insecurity, etc.

3350 *The Intimate Diary of Linda Lovelace.* by Lovelace, Linda; and Wallin, Carl. 141 p. paper illus. New York: Pinnacle, 1974.

Linda Lovelace continues the story of her life and career in this X-rated paperback. Included are some "blind" names which will be easily identifiable for many readers—a Las Vegas superstar, a magazine publisher, a famous football player, a father-son film duo, etc. Most of the untidy text is pseudo-erotic, indicative of the consistent bad taste of the authoress. Noted for the record.

3351 *The Intimate Life of Rudolph Valentino.* by Scagnetti, Jack. 160 p. illus. Middle Village, N.Y.: Jonathan David, 1975.

In this biography the author seems content to retell the familiar rather than offer any new insight into the Valentino legend. He makes good use of both a recorded memoir by Luther Mahoney, a close friend and employee of Valentino, and a collection of photographs obtained from Mahoney and Raymond Lee, a film historian. These illustrations help somewhat, but the relatively high price of the book and the uninspired treatment of the subject will limit its acceptance.

3352 *The Intimate Sex Lives of Famous People.* by Wallace, Irving. 640 p. illus. New York: Delacorte, 1981.

250 sketches that suggest more than they reveal. Many of the subjects appeared in films.

3353 *Intimate Talks with Movie Stars.* by Weitzel, Edward. 124 p. illus. New York: Dale, 1921.

The author was a writer for *Moving Picture World*.

3354 *Into Film.* by Goldstein, Lawrence; and Kaufman, Jay. 607 p. illus. New York: E.P. Dutton, 1976.

An explanation of the art of filmmaking is offered in this volume by using a frame-by-frame analysis technique. The authors have selected key moments from many classic films—represented by selected frames and an explanatory text—and have used them to describe both aesthetics (time, image, sound) and techniques (editing, camera, lighting). Two longer examples from POTEMKIN (1925) and BREATHLESS (1961) appear at the lower right of the book's pages and can be viewed in flip card fashion to create an illusion of motion. Several appendixes, a glossary, and a bibliography complete the volume.

The investigation of the filmmaking process by a frame-by-frame analysis is most fascinating. Although the volume is rather technical and demands some background for full reader comprehension, it offers a most rewarding discourse. Production values are excellent; the consistent clarity of the thousands of visuals and their intelligent integration into the author's carefully prepared text make this an outstanding volume on film aesthetics and mechanics. Highly recommended.

3355 INTOLERANCE. by Huff, Theodore. 155 p. paper New York: Museum of Modern Art, 1966.

Reconstructed script of the 1916 film directed by D.W. Griffith. Contains cast credits.

3356 *An Introduction to American Movies.* by Earley, Steven C. 337 p. paper illus. New York: New American Library (Mentor), 1978.

This original paperback consists of two major sections—a history and a genre survey of American films. Since the history is limited to 123 pages, most of the material is selected and treated in brief rapid-fire fashion. Some deserve greater depth and detail —i.e. "William Friedkin's SORCERER (1977) is an oustanding remake...." The same quality of brevity applies to the second longer section where 13 different genres of film are explored.

To supplement the two overviews, there are illustrations, a glossary, a bibliography in an academic rather than literary format, a distributor list, and an index.

While it is easy to find errors of judgment in the placement and evaluation of films and filmmakers, the total enterprise is surprisingly fresh in its view of overworked material. What Earley has provided is an appetizer or trailer to whet your appetite for more. Read in this context, the book is very successful.

3357 *An Introduction to Cinematography.* by Mercer, John. 198 p. paper illus. Champaign, Ill.: Stipes Pub. Co., 1968.

Apparently designed as a textbook for introductory courses in filmmaking, this book has much to interest both the student and the general reader. Divided into two major sections, silent cinematography and producing sound films, the book explains in simple terms and pictures many of the technical and creative operations of filmmaking. A final section is a short discussion of films for television.

A down-to-earth approach accompanied by useful suggestions and practice exercises enables the reader to use the volume as individual self-instruction. Although the book addresses itself to 16mm filming, some transfer of learning to the 8mm format is possible. The drawings and the diagrams are commendable.

3358 *An Introduction to Film.* by Sobchack, Vivian; and Sobchack, Thomas. illus. Boston: Little, Brown.

This textbook on the history and aesthetics of film was designed for the beginning student.

3359 *An Introduction to the American Underground Film.* by Renan, Sheldon. 318 p. paper illus. New York: Dutton, 1967.

The world of the underground film is covered expertly by this definitive primer. It includes a general description and history of the genre and a collection of biographical sketches of filmmakers and performers involved with the underground movement in films. The distribution, exhibition, and critical evaluation procedures for the films are also noted.

One final chapter on expanded cinema is an early and very successful summary of that spirit of cinematic inquiry. The appendix lists the major underground films mentioned in the text along with the following rental data: filmmaker, length, color, gauge(s), sound or silent, and distributor. A complete index is given. The book is thorough, clear, and respectful to its topic. Pictures taken from film frames are more than adequate. Recommended.

3360 *Introduction to the Art of the Movies.* by Jacobs, Lewis. 302 p. paper illus. New York: Noonday Press (Farrar, Straus & Giroux), 1960.

This collection of articles on cinema purports to "heighten the reader's understanding of the movie at its best." Every book on cinema should have this as a primary goal but should also have additional aims. While these articles are typical of such anthologies —many excellent, some average, —it would have been a service to the reader to provide a linking theme. A chronological arrangement of the articles by publishing dates simulates an historical approach to film, but it seems a weak format in this instance.

Some of the articles will have great reader appeal— for instance, there is a 1933 article by Dwight MacDonald on Hollywood directors with a correction letter by Ted Huff that almost justifies the entire book. The illustrations are few and somewhat below average in clarity of reproduction.

3361 *An Introduction to the Egyptian Cinema.* by Khan, M. 93 p. paper illus. London: Information, 1969.

After a history which traces Egyptian film from an 1863 magic lantern showing to 1969, three important filmmakers and their works are discussed. They are Salah Abu Saif, Youssef Shahin, and Hussein Kamal. A filmography for each is provided. Other industry personalities are treated in less detail. The career of Omar El-Sharif is considered separately and concludes with a negative comment about his non- Egyptian films of the past ten years. A filmography for Sharif is also given. This is an interesting account for the specialized reader somewhat unbalanced by the major emphasis on four individuals. There is no index and the illustration quality varies considerably.

3362 *Introduction to the Photoplay.* edited by Tibbetts, John C. 383 p. illus. Shawnee-Mission, Kansas: National Film Society, 1977 (1929).

This limited boxed edition of a 1929 anthology is impressive in several ways. The production is outstanding and the content is historically pertinent. The 15 articles are derived from a lecture course given in 1929, "The Dawn of the Talkies." Although put into manuscript form, the lectures were never published until now. Film topics addressed include scientific foundations, history, theory, writing, acting, criticism, commerce, aesthetics, control and predictions. More than 70 clearly reproduced photographs accompany the lectures along with an introduction, annotations, a bibliography, film title index and a general index.

Anyone interested in the development of the film industry in America will find a rich source of information here. Historians, of course, will be overjoyed at having such primary source material at hand.

3363 *Introduction to 3-D.* by Dewhurst, H. 152 p. illus. London: Chapman, 1954.

Written at the time when several new ideas in motion picture projection were introduced, this volume deals with three-dimensional photography in motion pictures, wide-screen cinemascope, cinerama and stereo television. A bibliography is included.

3364 INVASION OF THE BODY SNATCHERS. by Richter, W. D. unpaginated paper illus. Los Angeles: Fotonovel, 1979.

This *Fotonovel* (see series entry) contains 350 stills, some original film dialogue, connecting narrations and cast credits for the 1978 film, INVASION OF THE BODY SNATCHERS, which was directed by Philip Kaufman.

3365 *Investigation Hollywood!* by Otash, Fred. 252 p. Chicago: Henry Regnery, 1976.

Fred Otash was a cop with the Los Angeles Police Department for ten years. After he resigned, he became a private detective and for this book recalls various cases from his files. They involve such personalities as Frank Sinatra, Errol Flynn, Vic Damone, Scott Brady, Jeffrey Hunter, and Judy Garland. Much of what he relates is a matter of public record and the small human interest material he is able to provide is offset by bad judgment and poor taste. He lapses frequently into sexual vulgarities and pseudo-macho prose, and uses the literary style of Mickey Spillane, who has supplied an introduction of sorts to the book. The result is often awkward and embarrassing.

To some it may seem that the author is engaged in

a sleazy business and therefore the book has some slight value in its unintentional reflection of the dreariness in spying on other people's activities. It should be a bestseller in paperback.

3366   *Investigation of So-Called "Blacklisting" in the Entertainment Industry.* edited by House Committee on Un-American Activities (HUAC). 244 p. paper Washington, D.C.: U.S. Government Printing Office, 1956.

A transcript of the hearings held before the Committee on Un-American Activities of the House of Representatives, during the second session of the 84th Congress from July 10 to July 18, 1956. Includes a report of the Fund for the Republic, Inc.

3367   *An Investigation of the Improvement of Educational Motion Pictures: and a Derivation of Principles Relating to the Effectiveness of These Media.* by Vander Meer, Abram; and Morrison, Jack; and Smith, Philip. 93 p. paper illus. University Park, Pa.: College of Education, Pennsylvania State University, 1965.

3368   *An Investigation of the Motives For and Realization of Music to Accompany the American Silent Film, 1896-1927.* by Berg, Charles Merrell. New York: Arno, 1976.

Written in 1973 at the University of Iowa in partial fulfillment of the doctoral program, this study examines silent film music and its relationship to the emotional and aesthetic attraction of the silent film. A thorough investigation by the author not only offers explanations for the purpose of music in the silent film but also examines the implementation of its usage and its service to the silent film industry. This title appears in the *Dissertations on Film* series.

3369   *Invitation to the Film.* by O'Laoghaire, Liam. 203 p. illus. Tralee, Ireland: Merryman, 1945.

Deals with the film in Ireland, its problems, and potentials (1940's). Includes a general survey, some fine illustrations, a filmography and a glossary.

3370   *Invitation to the Theatre.* by Kernodle, George R. 677 p. illus. New York: Harcourt, 1967.

Here is a buried treasure. This book contains nearly 100 pages on film which the author calls an art for the large minority. Scholarship and sound critical judgment are combined in a compact, excellent overview of film, although the emphasis is on recent examples. The long bibliography is descriptive but not at all discriminating.

3371   *The Irish Peacock.* by Grady, Billy. 288 p. illus. New Rochelle, N.Y.: Arlington House, 1972.

Billy Grady was born in 1890 and by 1917 was involved in New York City show business. Engaged by MGM in 1931 as a talent representative, he dealt with many Hollywood personalities. He has selected incidents, anecdotes, and details for retelling in this volume, which he subtitles "The Confessions of a Legendary Talent Agent." In most of his writing he is complimentary about the performers he knew. The closest he comes to being somewhat testy is in calling Rock Hudson an ingrate for failing to sign with MGM. His role in "discovering" Van Johnson, Dan Dailey, Howard Keel, Donna Reed and others is noted. Events in the text appear in a random, nonchronological order, and any mention of dates is carefully avoided.

Although the story is sprinkled with some of the brightest names in show business, the dull recall of trivial matters negates the potential impact of such an all-star cast. A center section of illustrations and a rather detailed index cannot save these bland and seemingly pointless memoirs. It is hard to believe that a long career in dealing with the famous could yield so little of interest. Merely acceptable, at best.

3372   IRMA LA DOUCE. by Wilder, Billy; and Diamond, I.A.L. 127 p. paper illus. New York: Tower, 1963.

Script of the 1963 film directed by Wilder.

3373   *Irving Berlin.* by Freedland, Michael. 224 p. paper illus. New York: Stein and Day, 1974.

This volume seems more a review of Irving Berlin's life and songs than a biography. Although the author provides the factual information and often places it in the context of recreated dialogue, the text never rises above the level of an expanded biographical index entry.

Freedland's style is not always helpful or accurate— " It was the year that Robert Donat walked off with all the movie honors for GOODBYE, MR. CHIPS ..." (only one award was given); after the sneak preview of TOP HAT (1935): "MGM was distraught, the

Rogers and Astaire films containing Berlin scores—TOP HAT (1935), FOLLOW THE FLEET (1936) and CAREFREE (1938)—were all made by RKO.

Illustrations, a song title index, and a general index are provided. The excitement inherent in Irving Berlin's life, career and times is not captured in this modest biographical review. While the nondiscriminating younger person may enjoy the rapid coverage, the informed reader will miss the analysis and detail that are characteristic of a good biography.

3374 IS PARIS BURNING?. by Weiss, Nathan. 32 p. paper illus. New York, 1966.

This souvenir book is sprinkled liberally with quotations from persons who played major roles in the liberation of Paris from the Nazis. Historic background is provided and there is some discussion of the making of the 1966 film. The many stars are noted along with the production people and supporting cast. The book is almost as confusing as the film.

3375 *Is That Who I Think It Is?* by Agan, Patrick. 201 p. paper illus. New York: Ace, 1975.

This volume not only is similar in format to the Lamparski *Whatever Became of...* series, but also shares the same paperback publisher. One hundred personalities are each profiled in a two-page review of career and life. Accompanying the short biographies are two small, poorly reproduced pictures—the subject then and the subject today. Many of the persons in this first volume had screen careers and it is sad to see the glamour of yesterday replaced with the realism of today. The author's style and approach equals in every way that of Lamparski's; what is lacking here are production values—especially in picture clarity and size. A forthcoming Volume II is announced on the final page. Acceptable.

3376 *Is That Who I Think It Is? Volume 2.* by Agan, Patrick. 201 p. paper illus. New York: Ace Books, 1976.

3377 *Is That Who I Think It Is? Volume 3.* by Agan, Patrick. 201 p. paper illus. New York: Ace Books, 1976.

3378 *Is There Life After High School?* by Keyes, Ralph. 256 p. paper illus. New York: Warner, 1977.

An exploration of the effect that the American secondary school has on its graduates is the topic of this light hearted survey. The high school experiences of some film stars and other celebrities are briefly recalled in the text and the notes.

3379 ISADORA. 48 p. paper illus. New York: Universal Picture Corp., 1968.

The story of Isadora Duncan is told in this souvenir book both by narrative and photographs. There is also a section on the making of the 1969 film. Individual attention is accorded stars Vanessa Redgrave, James Fox, and Jason Robards. Production, direction, and supporting cast credits are also given.

3380 *Israel Films 1973.* compiled by Israel Film Centre. 26 p. paper illus. Jerusalem: The Israel Film Centre, 1974.

A catalog of Israeli films.

3381 *The Israeli Film: Social and Cultural Influences 1912-1972.* by Arzooni, O. Gloria J. 387 p. New York: Garland, 1982.

A title in the *Dissertations on Film* series.

3382 *The "IT" Girl: The Incredible Story of Clara Bow.* by Morella, Joe; and Epstein, Edward Z. 284 p. illus. New York: Delacorte Press, 1976.

Authors Morella and Epstein are at it again. After writing popular biographies of Lucille Ball, Lana Turner, Marlon Brando, and Judy Garland, they have turned their attention to the emancipated notorious flapper of the silent screen, Clara Bow. In a breezy novelized text, they follow their subject from Brooklyn poverty to Hollywood fame.

The total result is quite mixed. Outstanding are those sections of the text which examine, describe, and evaluate the twenties, Clara Bow as a personality, and her effect on people—both on screen and in her personal life. Less effective and often simply embarrassing are the created conversations, unsubtle innuendos, sexual dimensions, and careless conjectures which are rather prevalent throughout the book. A few illustrations indicate the unique appeal of the "It" girl.

That the volume is designed primarily for a mass audience of nondiscriminating readers is evidenced by the absence of a filmography, a bibliography, and an index. It is the student, historian or film buff who will be disappointed with the style, content and treatment accorded such a colorful subject. Acceptable.

3383 *It Takes More Than Talent.* by LeRoy, Mervyn; and Canfield, Alyce. 300 p. New York: Alfred Knopf, 1953.

Within the first few pages, the reader learns that Mervyn LeRoy was married to Doris Warner, daughter of one of The Warner Brothers, and that his cousin was Jesse Lasky. He announces his first rule in trying "to crack Hollywood" : never ask relatives or friends in the business for a job. The remainder of the book is full of such suspect advice. Interwoven with the phoney, fan magazine inspirational pitch, are some short external accounts of his experiences in the motion picture industry. Even within these brief sentences, there are errors: Lana Turner, e.g., did not star in THE GREAT ZIEGFELD (1935). The advice, format and approach are dated and insulting to today's readers. There are no pictures and no index. Forget this one.

3384 *It Took Nine Tailors.* by Menjou, Adolphe; and Musselman, M.M. 238 p. illus. New York: McGraw, 1948.

An autobiography, tracing Menjou's rise from restaurant cashier to movie actor, that is packed with interesting detail on films and film history. Unfortunately, the author-subject is never quite as fascinating as his profession. Note: there is one chapter on Chaplin's A WOMAN OF PARIS (1923).

3385 *It Was Fun While It Lasted.* by Lewis, Arthur H. 320 p. illus. New York: Trident Press, 1973.

This lament for "the Hollywood that was" consists mostly of observations and comments by the author supplemented by interviews with Mae West, Glenn Ford, Zsa Zsa Gabor, Ida Lupino, Joan Blondell, Barbara Stanwyck, Betty Blythe, Lewis Milestone, Dore Schary and John Wayne. No connecting theme other than the general topic exists, and the pieces bear little relationship to each other. However, they are entertaining and they generate a range of emotions, from sadness to hilarity. The book has been carelessly prepared and errors—factual, grammatical, and spelling—abound.

3386 *It's a Hell of a Life But Not a Bad Living: A Hollywood Memoir.* by Dmytryk, Edward. 310 p. illus. New York: Times Books, 1978.

This autobiography is crammed with information, opinions, comments, and interpretations about life in Hollywood. Dmytryk is perhaps best known as a forties Hollywood director—(MURDER MY SWEET (1944), CROSSFIRE (1947))—who was one of the "Unfriendly Ten." After penance and punishment, he returned to direct such films as THE CAINE MUTINY (1954), THE YOUNG LIONS (1958), MIRAGE (1965) etc. In this honest memoir he traces his career from messenger boy at Famous Players-Lasky to director of 51 films. In spite of a 50-year career, Dmytryk will probably be remembered most for his confrontations with the HUAC in the fifties. Sections dealing with this time in his life are the book's strongest parts, but the rest is rather good too. His portraits of Brando, Clift, Burton, Menjou, Tracy, Gable, Mitchum, and others are enjoyable to read. The book is nicely illustrated and contains both a filmography and an index.

Here is one of the better director autobiographies of the decade. It is honest, witty and to the point; most importantly, it offers a subjective evaluation of a long Hollywood career that enables the reader to "meet" Edward Dmytryk.

3387 *It's Been Fun.* by Neagle, Anna. 78 p. illus. London: World Film Publications, 1949.

An early autobiography of a dancer who became a famous film actress specializing in costume and historical dramas. Known as "The First Lady of the British Films," Anna Neagle made her first motion picture, SHOULD A DOCTOR TELL?, in 1930 and has appeared in many others since then.

3388 *It's Good to Know.* by Bullock, Randy; and Balsiger, Dave. 233 p. paper illus. Milford, Mich.: Mott Media, 1975.

Randy Bullock has appeared in two films produced by Billy Graham's company—TIME TO RUN (1972) and ISN'T IT GOOD TO KNOW (1973). His life before a conversion to Christianity is told in graphic detail and includes radicalism, drugs, sex, romance, gangsters, hippies, demonstrations, etc. In the last short chapters his brief career as a film actor is described. There are a few center illustrations but there is no index. The volume should be popular with the religious book audience and is acceptable for others.

3389 *It's Not Enough To Be Hungarian.* by Varconi, Victor; and Honeck, Ed. 192 p. illus. Denver: Graphic Impressions, 1976.

Victor Varconi was a character actor who appeared in many Hollywood films from POISONED PARADISE (1924) to THE ATOMIC SUBMARINE (1959). In addition, he made silent films in Europe from 1913 to 1914.

Born in Hungary in 1891, Varconi lovingly recalls his life which includes the first Hungarian motion picture ever made—CSIKOS (1913)—World War I, Austria, Pola Negri, Hollywood, Cecil B. DeMille, theatre, and television.

Recent conversations between Varconi and Honeck appear throughout the book as pauses in the biographical narrative. The small group of visuals which occupies a center section is fascinating and correlates nicely with the text. More pictures should have been added. No index is provided but a film list appears in the book's opening pages.

This is a warm, joyous memoir, and for many readers, that will be enough to please. However, a few more illustrations and an index would have made it a much better book.

3390 *It's Only a Movie.* by McKowen, Clark; and Sparke, William; and Byars, Mel. 188 p. illus. Englewood Cliffs, N.J.: Prentice-Hall, 1972.

Using quotations, visuals, interviews, quizzes, words, titles, advice, criticism, and many other print devices, the authors have put together a labyrinth on films and filmmaking. All of these items are put into Madison Avenue ad montages by Mel Byars. The appeal of this type of volume is dissipated quickly by the continual cuteness and the exhausting fragmentation of material. If experienced in small doses, like a book of crossword puzzles, it may be more rewarding. The list of literary and photo-art permissions runs two tightly spaced, small-print pages, and indicates the number of participants in this McLuhan stew. The college student with some film background may be enthusiastic about the book, as will the film buff, but the general reader may well wonder what it is.

3391 *The Italian Cinema.* by Jarratt, Vernon. 115 p. illus. New York: Falcon Press, 1951.

An important book which presents a historical review of Italian film from 1907 to the late forties. Greater understanding of the origins of some of the classic Italian films which followed World War II can be gained from the volume. The pre-1950 works of directors such as Blasetti, Camerini, Castellani, Costa, De Robertis, De Santis, De Sica, Freda, Lattuada, Rossellini, Soldati, Visconti, and Zampa are discussed.

The reader is cautioned on two counts: first, the book is an older one and covers the long period preceding the Golden period of Italian moviemaking; and then, some of the financial statistics are a bit difficult to comprehend since they are given in Italian lira and translated at times to English pounds. The illustrations are beautiful and the text is written with an intelligent brevity. This is a solid reference which needs updating or perhaps a second volume to complete its coverage. For the most part, the films that are discussed here are not the ones that we see.

3392 *The Italian Cinema.* by Leprohon, Pierre. 256 p. illus. New York: Praeger, 1972.

An enormous amount of detailed information appears in this most welcome critical history of the Italian film, which is divided into seven periods: The Early Years (1895-1908), The Golden Age (1909-1916), The Period of Decline (1917-1929), The Cinema Under Fascism (1930-1943), The Period of Neo-Realism (1943-1950), The Difficult Decade (1951-1959), and New and Young Cinema (1960-1969). Each is surveyed in depth and data on names, dates, locations, etc. are given along with critical comment, historical analyses, and trend indentifications. The author uses a serious, rather determined approach that is compatible with the scholarly tone of the work. His evaluations of the classic Italian films are enlightening, balanced, and most valid. The frequent provision of background information about the making of the films is laudable.

Picture quality is acceptable, as are the notes, references, bibliography and the index. An added feature to be appreciated is a biographical dictionary of 150 people who have contributed to the shaping of the Italian cinema. This extended section (25 pages) is a reference work in itself. The quality of the content, its arrangement for reference use, and the production values all qualify this book as a study that enriches film literature. Highly recommended.

3393 *Italian Cinema Today.* by Rondi, Gian Luigi. 279 p. illus. New York: Hill & Wang, 1966.

The period covered in this pictorial book is from 1952 to 1965. A longer first section is devoted to the work of the established leading directors, Antonioni, Rossellini, Fellini, and others. the second portion of the book looks at the films of the young directors who were establishing reputations during this period: Olmi and Pasolini, for example. Directors are discussed individually with some text and illustrations given for each. Only the major films of each are covered. Bosley Crowther supplied a short foreword to the work. The reproduction of stills is excellent; add to this a valid, perceptive text. Recommended for all readers.

3394   *Italian Cinema, 1945-51.* edited by Malerba, Luigi. 99 p. illus. New York: Gordon Press, 1976 (1952).

An overview of Italian cinema during the post World War II period. Originally published in Rome by Bestetti.

3395   IT'S A MAD, MAD, MAD, MAD, WORLD. 36 p. paper illus. New York: Mar-King Publishing Co., 1963.

An account of the making of this challenging film opens this souvenir book. Its conception and the problem of using so many comedians to full advantage are discussed. Other interesting features of the book include a centerfold cartoon of all the performers, a two-page montage, and individual biographies of the stars, each written by one of the other performers in the 1963 film. Supporting players, director and producer are noted. A most satisfying program book.

3396   *It's Alive!: The Classic Cinema Saga of Frankenstein.* by Mank, Gregory William. 193 p. illus. San Diego, Calif.: A. S. Barnes, 1981.

A survey of the Universal Studio's cycle of eight Frankenstein films from FRANKENSTEIN (1931) to ABBOTT AND COSTELLO MEET FRANKENSTEIN (1948). Included are plot outlines, filmmaker quotes, background material, credits, biographies, illustrations, etc. Horror film buffs will be delighted.

3397   IVAN THE TERRIBLE. by Eisenstein, Sergei M. 319 p. paper illus. New York: Simon & Schuster, 1962.

Script of the 1942-1946 films directed by Eisenstein. Translated by Herbert Marshall. Contains cast credits; an introduction by Ivor Montagu; four articles: "Notes on the Translation" (Ivor Montagu), "Notes on the Film Transcripts" (Ivor Montagu), "My Drawings" (Sergei Eisenstein), and "Sketches on Margins" (V. Nikolskaya); and a bibliography.

3398   IVAN THE TERRIBLE. by Eisenstein, Sergei M. 264 p. paper illus. New York: Simon & Schuster, 1970.

Script of the 1944-1958 films directed by Eisenstein. Includes: IVAN THE TERRIBLE (1944), THE BOYAR'S PLOT (1958), and IVAN'S STRUGGLE (taken from unfilmed script). Also contains cast credits and three acticles: "From History to the Film" (Postislav Yurenyev), "The Second Summit" (Mikhail Romm), and "Interview with Stalin" (Nikolai Cherkasov).

3399   *Ivor: The Story of an Achievement.* by McQueen-Pope, Walter J. 550 p. illus. London: W. H. Allen, 1952.

Ivor Novello was a composer-playwright-actor who appeared in both silent and sound films. Known mostly for his stage musicals in the thirties, he also wrote scripts for a few sound films after he found his personality and style unsuited to the talkies.

3400   *Ivor.* by Wilson, Sandy. illus. London: Michael Joseph, 1975.

Sandy Wilson, who has written several musical comedies including "The Boy Friend," gives his attention to Ivor Novello in this biography. He traces Novello's diversified career from a Valentino-look-alike of the silent screen to the matinee idol and playwright he became later. Over 300 illustrations are included.

3401   *Ivor Novello: Man of the Theatre.* by Noble, Peter. 306 p. illus. London: Falcon Press, 1951.

Novello was a romantic matinee idol during the twenties and thirties on both stage and screen. In addition to acting, he was also a playwright and a musician. In this latter capacity, he is remembered as the composer of "Keep the Home Fires Burning." This volume is an authorized biography.

3402   *Ivor, the Story of an Achievement: A Biography of Ivor Novello.* by MacQueen-Pope, Walter. 550 p. London: W. H. Allen, 1951.

3403   *Jack Benny.* by Benny, Mary Livingstone; and Marks, Hilliard; and Borie, Marcia. 322 p. illus. New York: Doubleday, 1978.

The edge on biographies of Jack Benny belongs to Irving Fein, whose book appeared two years earlier. This memoir, written by Benny's widow, is a warm-hearted, detailed view of the performer from his first stage appearance in 1911 to his death in 1974. It is more of a tribute than a biography, with friends of Benny also recalling incidents in the comic's life.

Benny was a kind, generous man who could be a driving perfectionist when performing. His art, of course, was that he made performing look so easy.

3404 *Jack Benny: An Intimate Biography.* by Fein, Irving A. 319 p. illus. New York: G. P. Putnam's, 1976.

The author of this biography was Jack Benny's personal manager and producer for 28 years. Even with so close an association, the subject seems to have escaped the author. Possessed of admirable recall, Fein offers hundreds of stories, anecdotes, and scenes which amuse but do not divulge much about feeling or character. Benny emerges as a basically likeable, generous superstar who was remarkably private and "in control" at all times. Most of his life was void of any great problems and was spent doing what he enjoyed most—entertaining.

3405 *The Jack Benny Show.* by Josefsberg, Milt. 496 p. illus. New Rochelle, N.Y.: Arlington House, 1977.

If you were not an admirer of Jack Benny up to now, this volume may cause you to change your mind. More an affectionate tribute than a biography, the book is packed with incident, anecdote, and script excerpt rather than any critical analysis of the man or his work. The approach is a logical one since the author's profession is writing, supervising and producing comedy shows.

Attention is given to biographical matters but they are reported with little or no interpretation. Missing also is a balanced portrait of the subject; what we are told is that Benny was a nice warm man who overreacted to other comics' material. His relationships with others are described but only superficially. The reader wonders whether Benny ever had any human failings, temptations or mistakes.

The treasure of the book is the Benny anecdotes, of which the author has an encyclopedic knowledge. They are delightful to read and perhaps they explain Benny better than a narrative text could. Some illustrations are included, and best of all, there is a filmography, a radio-TV chronology, and a detailed index.

Because of its determined positive approach to its subject, the volume is not a very exciting biography. It is, however, a rich, entertaining tribute to an American entertainer, embellished by hundreds of little stories and memories that will cheer most readers. Recommended.

3406 *Jack Lemmon.* by Holtzman, Will. 160 p. paper illus. New York: Pyra-

mid, 1977.

Jack Lemmon's career as a film actor has lasted over 25 years and at this writing is still going strong. While the roles have changed from romantic juvenile leads to character parts the integrity of the acting has been constant. The survey provided by Holtzman here covers Lemmon's impressive career with considerable detail. From IT SHOULD HAPPEN TO YOU (1954) to AIRPORT 1977 (1977), each of Lemmon's 34 films are described in words and pictures. In addition there are biographical sections, a bibliography, a filmography, and an index.

The quality of the series is maintained in this volume. Jack Lemmon is an interesting subject and some of his films are classics. Holtzman's appreciation is worthy of an actor who has given so many fine performances.

3407 *Jack Nicholson: Face to Face.* by Crane, Robert David; and Fryer, Christopher. 192 p. illus. New York: M. Evans and Co., 1975.

A wise course has been followed by the authors in this biography-appreciation of Jack Nicholson. Because of a relatively short career in films, which consisted mostly of low-budget quickies, "The Films of" approach would have not only been awkward but premature. Instead they have opted for a portrait of their subject provided by interviews with his fellow actors, directors, producers, and two with Nicholson himself. Even the author's summary-commentary is presented in a dialogue format. A filmography that offers cast, credits, and a synopsis is appended along with an index. Among those interviewed are Roger Corman, Karen Black, Bruce Dern, Ann-Margret, Robert Evans and Dennis Hopper.

Many posters, stills and informal production shots contribute visual support to the portrait. As a different kind of biography-appreciation, this volume deserves attention. An unusually colorful subject is presented with objectivity, detail, and frankness in a nicely produced book. Recommended for mature adults.

3408 *Jack Nicholson: The Search for a Superstar.* by Dickens, Norman. 182 p. paper illus. New York: Signet, 1975.

Although it was written without Jack Nicholson's cooperation and against his wishes, this original paperback biography has much to recommend it. The author has reserached his subject quite thoroughly and has spoken with many of Nicholson's friends and acquaintants. He has selected and

497

organized his findings in a highly readable and entertaining fashion. Although the persona of his subject is obviously quite elusive and often contradictory, Dickens has caught many of the character facets that make up this actor's complex personality. Thus, the book's subtitle, "The Search for a Superstar," seems most appropriate. A picture section and a filmography add to the well-written text.

It is both surprising and pleasing to find a book of this quality appearing as an original paperback biography. Since the book deals rather frankly with Nicholson's opinions about sex and drugs, it is recommended for mature adults.

3409 *Jack Oakie's Double Takes.* by Oakie, Jack. 217 p. paper illus. San Francisco: Strawberry Hill, 1980.

Jack Oakie died in 1978 after a long show business career that included over one hundred films from FINDERS KEEPERS (1927) to LOVER COME BACK (1962). This volume is not an autobiography but a collection of anecdotal memoirs featuring his coworkers from Hollywood's Golden Age—Garbo, Crawford, Chaplin, Shirley Temple, Crosby, Clara Bow, etc. Oakie is true to character here as the loveable rascal who has a soft heart for everyone. An index, illustrations, and listings of Oakie's show business appearances complete the book.

3410 *Jack of All Trades.* by Warner, Jack. illus. London: W. H. Allen, 1975.

Jack Warner is a light comedy performer known mostly for his film appearances in the post-World War II decade.

3411 *The Jacqueline Susann Story.* by Ventura, Jeffrey. 170 p. paper illus. Happauge, N.Y.: Award Books, 1976.

Jacqueline Susann was the author of several novels which were made into films: THE VALLEY OF THE DOLLS (1967), THE LOVE MACHINE (1971), and ONCE IS NOT ENOUGH (1974). Much of this volume is concerned with the books, the films, and the Hollywood personalities who were part of Susann's life and career. A few illustrations are offered in a center section.

3412 *Jacques Tati.* by Gilliatt, Penelope. 96 p. illus. London: Woburn Press, 1976.

A title from The *Entertainers* series, this appreciation of Jacques Tati is made up of biography, interview quotations, and critical comment. Tati has

directed only six feature films and is known to American audiences primarily for MR. HULOT'S HOLIDAY (1953) and MON ONCLE (1958).

The author is quite successful in presenting a fully dimensioned portrait of this unusual artist. His attitudes toward his work, his comedy techniques and his personal life are considered. Supplementing the text are many illustrations and a detailed filmography.

Tati has been compared with Keaton, Lloyd and other great film comedians. Gilliatt's book gives substantial justification for the comparisons. Recommended.

3413 *Jacques Tourneur.* edited by Johnston, Claire; and Willemen, Paul. 67 p. paper Edinburgh: Film Festival, 1975.

This short anthology devoted to Jacques Tourneur consists of five articles, an interview, a bio-filmography, and a selected bibliography. It was prepared for the 1975 Edinburgh Film Festival, where a retrospective showing of Tourneur's films was held.

The director's career began in the early twenties and he was still actively making films for American television in the late sixties.

This modest volume serves as an introductory appreciation of Tourneur and his work. An in-depth study would seem most appropriate. Acceptable.

3414 *James Agee: A Study of His Film Criticism.* by Snyder, John J. 229 p. New York: Arno Press, 1977.

Written in 1969 at St. John's University, in partial fulfillment of the doctoral program, this work examines James Agee's role as film critic. Since Pulitzer Prize winner Agee is best known for his books, his writings as a film critic have previously received little attention. They spanned many years, appeared in several different publications and are basic to the field of film criticism. The author places Agee's reviews in context by discussing the developments in film theory and practice concurrent with his work, as well as contrasting the reviews with Agee's other writings. This comprehensive title appears in the *Dissertations on Film* series.

3415 *The James Bond Films.* by Rubin, Steven J. 224 p. illus. Westport, Conn.: Arlington House, 1981.

3416 *James Bond in the Cinema.* by Brosnan, John. 176 p. illus. New York:

A. S. Barnes, 1972.

With the exception of the Bond fanatics, most readers will find this book to be too much of a good thing. Beginning with an appreciation, the book covers the first seven James Bond films with individual chapters devoted to each. Using the film or film script as the structure, the author describes the action, quotes a bit of dialogue and adds production information, novel-film comparisons, etc. The films are: DR. NO (1962), FROM RUSSIA WITH LOVE (1963), GOLDFINGER (1964), THUNDERBALL (1965), YOU ONLY LIVE TWICE (1967), ON HER MAJESTY'S SECRET SERVICE (1969), DIAMONDS ARE FOREVER (1971).

The book is adequately illustrated and there are full credit listings for the films in the appendix. One other appendix considers the offshoots of the Bond series—Matt Helm, Derek Flint, Modesty Blaise, etc. For the devotees and aficionados of Bond, the book will be a delight; others will find it of moderate interest at best. For them, the James Bond section found in series collections (*The Great Movie Series* and *Saturday Afternoon at the Bijou*) would probably serve better.

3417 *James Cagney.* by Bergman, Andrew. 156 p. paper illus. New York: Pyramid, 1973.

Here is another outstanding volume in the consistently impressive *Pyramid* series. Combining literate critical text with sharply reproduced visuals, the book compares most favorably with much higher priced publications. Cagney is a fascinating film character and the appraisal of his work here is satisfactory. While the reader may not agree with all of Bergman's judgments—is THE BRIDE CAME C.O.D. really all that bad?—enough provocative argument is offered to justify most of his statements.

The nine chapters of the book deal with the Cagney career, not with the man. The author states early on that Cagney is a private person and he does not pursue the biographical aspect. A bibliography, a filmography and an index complete the volume. This book is outstanding in almost every way and is highly recommended.

3418 *James Cagney—In the Spotlight.* edited by Galley Press. 160 p. illus. New York: Galley/Mayflower, 1980.

A biographical essay and a collection of illustrations (stills, candids, studio publicity shots, etc.) comprise this appreciation of James Cagney.

3419 *James Dean: A Biography.* by Bast, William. 149 p. paper New York: Ballantine Books, 1956.

This posthumous biography of James Dean was written by his most intimate friend. Author Bast shared many of Dean's early struggles to achieve celebrity status, and his proximity to his subject colors his portrait. Since Dean became a film legend from appearances in three films, REBEL WITHOUT A CAUSE (1955), EAST OF EDEN (1955), and GIANT (1956), the account is a fascinating one. It may surprise some that Dean played bits in SAILOR BEWARE (1951), FIXED BAYONETS (1951) and HAS ANYBODY SEEN MY GAL? (1952).

3420 *James Dean: A Biography.* by Howlett, John. 191 p. paper illus. New York: Simon and Schuster, 1976.

In oversized book format John Howlett presents, in objective fashion, the story of James Dean's life and career. The three major films are described and there are some attempts made at analyzing the sociology of the 1950s, that period in which the James Dean cult appeared. Illustrations are very good and a bibliography is included.

3421 *James Dean: A Biography.* by Howlett, John. 190 p. illus. London: Plexus, 1974.

A large format biography of James Dean including more than 130 illustrations.

3422 *James Dean: A Short Life.* by Herndon, Venable. 288 p. illus. New York: Doubleday, 1974.

This better-than-average biography was the third on Dean. An earlier one by William Bast appeared in 1956 and one by David Dalton appeared almost simultaneously with this one. Using the Bast book and an unpublished doctoral thesis by Robert Wayne Tysl as primary sources, the author also interviewed people who knew Dean. Many articles in periodicals were also consulted. The result is a well-balanced portrait of a complex performer. The author is sympathetic and forgiving of Dean's offscreen behavior as he writes a dramatic biography rather than a critical one.

Photographs appear in two sections and there is an astrological reading by John Beck added. An index completes the book. Although some of the material is identical with that appearing in other volumes, the treatment of it is different here. The intimate storytelling approach employed makes for pleasurable entertainment rather than serious examination of an

American tragedy. Acceptable.

3423 *James Dean: The Mutant King.* by Dalton, David. 356 p. illus. San Francisco: Straight Arrow Books, 1974.

With only three major films to his credit, James Dean became one of Hollywood's legends. This, the third book-length biography, is the best and most comprehensive. The earliest by Bast is mostly a memoir by a friend, while another one by Herndon lacks the detail offered here. The research performed in locating photographs, documents and interviewing people who knew Dean is evident throughout. Factual data about Dean's television work and the shooting of his three films—EAST OF EDEN (1955), REBEL WITHOUT A CAUSE (1955) and GIANT (1956) —is provided within the detailed biographical section. An evaluation of Dean as a person, performer, and cult hero in mid-fifties America concludes the book.

Visuals used throughout are well chosen—their content is strong and most are unfamiliar. Reproduction of them is adequate. There is a long bibliography and a good index to support the colorful text. This volume is highly recommended. It is not only a solid biography but it is a frightening comment on America in mid-century.

3424 *James Dean Revisited.* by Stock, Dennis. 128 p. paper illus. New York: Penguin, 1978.

The author is a photojournalist who first met James Dean in 1953. Here he offers text and photos taken in three locations: Dean's hometown of Fairmount (Indiana), New York City, and Hollywood. The photos, which are largely unfamiliar, give this book its distinction; they are carefully reproduced and tell a great deal about the subject. The text, however, once again reinforces the image of Dean as a restless creative artist. His three films are treated in the closing pages.

3425 *The James Dean Story.* by Martinetti, Ronald. 185 p. paper illus. New York: Pinnacle, 1975.

This late entry in the James Dean biography sweepstakes adds little that was not already disclosed in the volumes by Bast, Herndon and Dalton. It has a few elements not usually found in an original paperback—a noncritical narrative, some good photographs, a bibliography and an index. The author has researched his subject in considerable depth, but, although different sources are cited throughout, the portrait of Dean that emerges is familiar. It is that of an ambitious actor who manipulated people to attain success. Standards of behavior and loyalty were practically nonexistent to Dean, as was the ability to experience any empathy with others. Acceptable.

3426 *James Dean—special issues of various periodicals.* paper illus.

After James Dean's death, several fan magazine tribute-memorial-biographies appeared. They included the following titles: *I, James Dean*, by T. T. Thomas, 128 p. illus., paper, N.Y.: Popular Library 1957; *James Dean Album*, no author noted, 68 p. illus., paper, N.Y.: Ideal Pub. Corp., 1956; *The Official James Dean Anniversary Book*, Peter Meyerson, ed., 74 p. illus., paper, N.Y.: Dell, 1956; *Jimmy Dean Returns*, no author noted, 66 p. illus., paper, N.Y.: Rave Pub. Corp., 1956; *The Real James Dean Story*, no authornoted, 64 p. illus., paper, N.Y.: Fawcett, 1956.

3427 *James Stewart.* by Thompson, Howard. 160 p. paper illus. New York: Pyramid, 1974.

As film and TV critic for *The New York Times*, Howard Thompson is well qualified to write this review of the life and career of James Stewart. For more than three decades, Stewart was known for a warm and sincere personality. Thompson traces the development of that image from THE MURDER MAN (1935) to FOOL'S PARADE (1971). Accompanying the text is a filmography, a bibliography, an index and many illustrations. Recommended.

3428 *James Whale's* FRANKENSTEIN. edited by Anobile, Richard. 256 p. paper illus. New York: Avon, 1974.

Although one might disagree with certain introductory statements made by Anobile about director James Whale, there can be little disagreement with this presentation of FRANKENSTEIN (1931). Using more than 1000 frame blowups and all the original dialogue, the book recreates the famous horror film. Picture reproduction is quite good and all the memorable sequences have been well assembled by Anobile's selection of frames. His explanation of the missing footage from the monster-little girl scene is especially fascinating. Since it was present in the initial theatrical release and in the first revivals, it can be recalled in detail by many persons.

In any event, this will be a popular book. It can satisfy the needs of many different audiences, just as its source has done for almost half a century. Highly recommended. See also the *Classic Film* series.

3429 *James Wong Howe: Cinematographer.* by Rainsberger, Todd. 224 p. illus. San Diego, Calif.: A. S. Barnes, 1981.

A combination of biography and cinematography text. James Wong Howe was a cameraman in Hollywood from 1922 to 1970, and many of his professional techniques are discussed.

3430 JAN HUSS. by Kratochvil, Miles V.; and Vavra, Otakar. 173 p. illus. Prague: Artia, 1957.

Script of the 1954 film which was directed by Otakar Vavra.

3431 *Jane: An Intimate Biography.* by Kiernan, Thomas. 358 p. New York: G. P. Putnam's, 1973.

Although the author knew Jane Fonda for a short period at the start of her acting career, he was not able to secure her cooperation in preparing this biography. Perhaps this was a fortunate circumstance, since the result is a hard, objective and revealing portrait of this controversial female. The eras in Jane's life are roughly divided into child, student, actress, hedonist, radical, and activist. Emphasis is placed on the latter four periods, with detail and documentation offered along with some conjecture and suggestion.

There was apparently enough public material and inside privileged information available to the author for him to assemble what seems to be an accurate portrait of this complex woman. Since her father's and her brother's lives are interwoven with hers, they too receive adequate attention. For Roger Vadim, a most unusual man who fascinated the author, a provocative description is provided.

The book lacks illustrations and an index, which may indicate a lack of faith by the publisher in the book's quality. True, it is the last of three recent books on the Fondas, Springer's and Brough's having come out earlier. The concentration on Jane in this volume may, however, give it an appeal to certain readers that the others lacked. The author states that Jane's life has been a mirror of our times, and her reactions are those shared by all of us. For the audience who accepts this premise, the book will be an emotional reading experience. Others will remain unconvinced and will continue to dislike Ms. Fonda. Recommended for mature readers.

3432 *Jane Fonda: All American Anti-Heroine.* by Herman, Gary; and Downing, David. 144 p. paper illus. New York: Quick Fox, 1980.

Jane Fonda is a survivor. Despite some poor films, a negative press, and a hostile public, she has become a respected film actress and a leader in the American feminist and social change movements. This heavily illustrated biography traces her life and career from 1937 to 1980. It is quite detailed and provides critical comment on her films and plays along with numerous quotes from interviews. A filmography is included.

The result is a total portrait of a strong, talented, intelligent actress who has learned enough from her experiences to take a place as one of the outstanding females of the 20th century. Recommended.

3433 *Janet Flanner's World: Uncollected Writings, 1932-1975.* by Flanner, Janet. New York: Harcourt Brace Jovanovich, 1979.

As a European correspondent for *The New Yorker* for almost 50 years, Janet Flanner wrote many pieces she called "Letters From...." In this, her ninth book, there are 76 such pieces, some of which deal with film topics. Among her subjects are Bette Davis, Ingrid Bergman, the post-war Italian cinema, and Thomas Mann as "Goethe in Hollywood."

3434 *Japan.* by Svensson, Arne. 188 p. paper illus. New York: A. S. Barnes, 1971.

One of the *Screen Series* books about the cinema of a specific country, this one is a guide to the major directors, actors, and technicians of Japan. Credits and plot outlines are given for the important films and there is an index of the films mentioned in the text.

3435 *Japan: Film Image.* by Tucker, Richard. 144 p. illus. London: Studio Vista, 1973.

This overview of the Japanese film includes a historical survey, a discussion of the works of the major Japanese filmmakers, and notation of the changes that have taken place within the film industry.

3436 *Japanese Cinema: Film Style and National Character.* by Richie, Donald. 261 p. paper illus. Garden City, N.Y.: Doubleday, 1971.

An updating of Richie's early works (*The Japanese Movie* and *The Japanese Film*), emphasizing themes, directors, and films of Japan. The volume is illustrated, indexed, and contains a list of Japanese films available in the United States. Recommended.

3437 *Japanese Film Directors*. by Bock, Audie. 370 p. illus. New York: Kodansha International, 1978.

This collective biography/appreciation discusses the life, style, and best films of ten Japanese film directors. Included are Kenji Mizoguchi, Yasujiro Ozu, Mikio Naruse, Akira Kurosawa, Keisuke Kinoshita, Kon Ichikawa, Masaki Kobayashi, Shohei Imamura, Nagisa Oshima, and Masahiro Shinoda. In addition to an essay on each, there are also individual filmographies, chapter notes, and annotations. A final index and a bibliography complete the book. The essays are arranged in a chronological fashion with the early masters first and the new wave directors last. Interviews that the author had with many of her subjects are incorporated into the text. Donald Richie has supplied an introduction.

In addition to being a fine reference, this volume helps to extend and expand our knowledge and appreciation of the Japanese film. It is well written and nicely organized. Recommended.

3438 *The Japanese Film—Art and Industry*. by Anderson, Joseph L.; and Richie, Donald. 496 p. illus. Rutland, Vt.: Charles E. Tuttle Co., 1959.

To many people, the cinema of Japan means Akira Kurosawa, for it is his films that are shown at colleges and festivals. While giving full acknowledgment to Kurosawa, the authors present a historical and critical account of the Japanese film from 1898 to 1959. Their aim is to make known the general excellence of Japanese films which are not usually shown outside of Japan. The book includes many unfamiliar but interesting stills, discussions of Japanese actors and directors, and finally the Japanese audience. An excellent but very specialized book of interest primarily to to the scholar. Because of its extended name and title index, it can be used as a partial reference.

3439 *The Japanese Movie: An Illustrated History*. by Richie, Donald. 200 p. illus. Rutland, Vt.: Japan Publications Trading Co., 1966.

As a survey of Japanese films from their beginning until the mid-sixties, this volume is a companion to the other writings by Richie (and Anderson) on the same topic. Discussions include the themes (usually tragic) and the repeated technique of placing current problems in the context of the past. Attention is given to the manner in which the films reflect Japa-

nese character, philosophy and history. The book is nicely illustrated.

3440 *Japanese Movies*. by Richie, Donald. 198 p. illus. Rutland, Vt.: Charles E. Tuttle, 1961.

An early Richie survey of the Japanese film that deals with content, recurring themes, etc., this book was originally published by the Japan Travel Bureau. The Japanese sees his suroundings as an extension of himself. That attitude is documented in the films considered. In this volume, the emphasis on film history is small; it can be found, however, in the other books on Japanese film by Richie.

3441 *The* JAWS *Log*. by Gottlieb, Carl. 221 p. paper illus. New York: Dell, 1975.

Written as an afterthought when the critical and popular acceptance of the film seemed assured, this book is not a diary kept during production. It is a collection of selected recollections of the film's production written by the coauthor of the screenplay, Carl Gottlieb. Using memory, gossip and opinion along with production reports, memos, and factual data, he has provided an account of the making of one of the most popular films ever. The extreme fascination of audiences with the subject of killer sharks was unpredictable and ultimately quite surprising to all concerned. The author's style is chatty-informal and avoids the usual public relations cliches. His treatment of filmmakers involved with local personalities is amusing sociology. Of greater interest to film students are his accounts of how the special effects involving the shark were obtained.

Illustrations are exceptionally strong in both selection and reproduction. A few help to personalize the text by showing the author as actor and scriptwriter on the set. Further audience interest can be seen by Dell's printing and placing of 850,000 copies of this title. The 8,650,000 copies of the original novel (*Jaws*), the 225,000 copies of *On Location: The Making of the Movie Jaws* and the box-office records the 1975 film has established offer solid statistical evidence of the topic's popular appeal. This volume enhances that appeal rather than capitalizing upon it. Recommended.

3442 *The* JAWS 2 *Log*. by Loynd, Ray. 219 p. paper illus. New York: Dell, 1978.

Observations, interviews, memos, and opinions are a few of the sources used in writing this account of major studio filmmaking. During 1977-78, the author visited Martha's Vineyard and Florida in the filming of JAWS 2. His account is supplemented by candid shots, drawings, stills, etc. The book concludes with the film's cast and credits.

This is an account of making a film that ultimately failed at the box office, proving once again "the curse of the sequel."

3443 *Jayne Mansfield.* by Mann, May. 277 p. illus. New York: Drake 1973.

A biography that emphasizes the sensational rather than the professional, this book by a Hollywood columnist who was a friend of Ms. Mansfield is never dull—just badly written. When you consider that the subject was a Philadelphia Main Liner with an I.Q. of 163, a Hollywood sex symbol, and a sympathetic, warm female who had continual trouble with men, it's hard to be uninteresting. The author tells of Mansfield's struggle to achieve stardom, her marriages, and the sad events that led up to the final tragic automobile accident.

The weakness of this book lies not with the subject but with the author. She never seems to present a heroine the audience can admire. Instead, she settles for mysticism, spiritualism, and the influence of the devil, and indicates that Jayne Mansfield came back from beyond to tell her to write this book. Some private photographs are among the 60 illustrations. Not a very good biography, this volume will still be popular with the general audience.

3444 *Jayne Mansfield and the American Fifties.* by Saxton, Martha. 256 p. illus. New York: Houghton, 1975.

Jayne Mansfield's pursuit of the questionable status of super sex symbol is related as an object lesson in this biography. How she sacrifices husbands, children, dignity, values and, ultimately, her life is related with cynicism and occasional bitterness. Written from a feminist viewpoint, the text considers Mansfield's ideals as typical of those prevalent in American society during the 1950s. Saxton provides sensationalized detail and interpretation but her efforts to integrate Mansfield and the Women's Lib Movement are not successful. It would appear that Mansfield's life needs little interpretation or explanation as an American tragedy; it speaks for itself. Acceptable for adults.

3445 *Jayne Mansfield's Wild, Wild, World.* by Mansfield, Jayne. 128 p. paper illus. Los Angeles: Holloway, 1963.

3446 *Jazz in the Movies.* by Meeker, David. illus. New Rochelle, N.Y.: Arlington House, 1977.

Subtitled "A Guide to Jazz Musicians 1917-1977," this volume offers 2239 film titles arranged alphabetically. Each film noted contains some contribution by one or more jazz musicians or singers. An index of the jazz musicians named in the entries completes the volume.

There can be little quarrel with the intent or need for a reference work of this kind. For the most part it is a successful, though admittedly partial, account of jazz musicians in films. As such, it is most welcome; however, a few general reservations should be expressed.

There is apparent confusion between the terms "straight musician" and "jazz musician." The author excludes the "straight" film scores of Andre Previn, Michel LeGrand and Elmer Bernstein but includes the work of such "straight" performers as Glenn Miller, the Mills Brothers, Les Brown, Skinnay Ennis, Pearl Bailey, Claude Thornhill and Ina Ray Hutton. Can this latter group be considered jazz performers?

No clear distinction is made between swing music, rock music, and jazz. As a result there are some important omissions and questionable inclusions. For example, Fats Domino is listed for several films, but in the entry for THE BLACKBOARD JUNGLE (1955), no mention is made of Bill Haley and the Comets or the theme song of the film, "Rock Around the Clock."

Proofreading seems a bit careless throughout. In entry No. 440 Edmond O'Brien is spelled "O'Brian"; in No. 448 DANCING COED (1939), a feature film with Lana Turner and Artie Shaw, is listed as running 4 minutes; in No. 822 WHITE CHRISTMAS (1954) is called, incorrectly, a remake of HOLIDAY INN (1942); in No. 1175 THE HANDS OF ORLAC (1935) is listed as THE HANDS OR ORLAC.

The capsule criticisms supplied for many of the films are often critically vulnerable since they evaluate dogmatically without any substantiation. Comments about the jazz work of the performers would be far more welcome than suspect judgment about the entire film and would be much more in keeping with the intention of the book.

The amount of the contribution made by the jazz artist varies widely. In many entries a performer is singled out as a member of a large studio orchestra; this may cause the reader to wonder, for example, how many jazz musicians were used in recording the lively Girl Hunt Ballet from THE BAND WAGON (1953), a film that is not mentioned here.

Within the limitations expressed above, the volume appears to be a useful reference. With it, it is possible to retrieve information about jazz musicians, films, and music with comparative ease. Acceptable.

3447 *Jazz in the Movies.* by Meeker, David. 90 p. paper illus. London: British Film Institute, 1972.

This filmography lists the titles of films that have jazz backgrounds, plots, scores, etc. Arranged alphabetically by title, each entry indicates the country of origin, the release date, the director, running time, and a short annotation. An index of jazz names and some late additions complete the book.

3448 THE JAZZ SINGER. by Cohn, Alfred A. 188 p. paper illus. Madison, Wisc.: University of Wisconsin Press, 1979.

Script of the 1927 film which was directed by Alan Crosland. Also included is a long introduction entitled, "History of a Popular Culture Classic," by Robert L. Carringer and "The Day of Atonement," a short story by Sampson Raphaelson upon which both the stage play and the film were based. There are descriptions of the eight sound sequences, a breakdown of the musical score, and four articles about Warner Brothers and the development of the sound film. Annotations, notes, cast and production credits complete the volume.

3449 *Jean Cocteau: The History of a Poet's Age.* by Fowlie, Wallace. 181 p. illus. Bloomington, Ind.: Indiana University Press, 1968.

Considers various aspects of Cocteau's artistry in individual chapters on his novels, plays, art, films, and other writings. Three very spare biographical chapters open the book.

The interest here is in the work rather than the person. Cocteau's exotic, flamboyant life is related only when and if it helps to explain the many examples of his poetic genius. The chapter on films is very good, and mention is made of his films in several other parts of the book. Illustrations are few and unimpressive, but a chronology, a bibliography, and an index add to the book. Acceptable.

3450 *Jean Cocteau: The Man and the Mirror.* by Sprigge, Elizabeth; and Kihm, Jean-Jacques. 286 p. illus. New York: Coward-McCann, 1968.

Enough attention is given to Cocteau's films in this complex biography to warrant its inclusion here. Starting with a 16mm amateur film called JEAN COCTEAU TAIT DU CINEMA, the text describes Cocteau's contribution to BLOOD OF A POET (1930), THE ETERNAL RETURN (1943), BEAUTY AND THE BEAST (1946), RUY BLAS (1947), THE EAGLE WITH TWO HEADS (1948), LES PARENTS TERRIBLES (1948), ORPHEUS (1950), LES ENFANTS TERRIBLES (1950), THE TESTAMENT OF ORPHEUS (1959), among other films.

Cocteau's life is heavily punctuated by interactions with the creative artists of his period and this volume tries to mention them all; as a result, everything gets a rather short description rather than the scholarly detail supplied by Francis Steegmuller in his Cocteau biography.

The book is illustrated, indexed, and includes a chronological bibliography. A fascinating subject is given a quality biography here. The book should please the more sophisticated and is recommended for mature readers.

3451 *Jean Cocteau: Three Screenplays.* by Cocteau, Jean. 250 p. paper illus. New York: Grossman, 1972.

Contains scripts and cast credits for: THE ETERNAL RETURN (1943); BEAUTY AND THE BEAST (1946); ORPHEUS (1950).

3452 *Jean Cocteau.* by Crosland, Margaret. 206 p. illus. London: Nevill, 1955.

3453 *Jean Cocteau.* by Fowlie, Wallace. 181 p. Bloomington: Indiana University Press, 1966.

3454 *Jean Cocteau and His Films of Orphic Identity.* by Evans, Arthur B. 174 p. illus. Philadelphia: Art Alliance Press, 1977.

A logical development is offered by the author as he attempts to show Jean Cocteau's self-identification with the Greek God, Orpheus, in three separate films. An introductory section differentiates the poetic from the narrative film. In the next section recurrent themes found in Cocteau's work are related to the Orpheus legend. The remainder of the book is devoted to analyses of BLOOD OF A POET (1932), ORPHEUS (1950) and THE TESTAMENT OF ORPHEUS (1960). Some concluding statements, a bibliography, and an index complete the volume. Selected stills from the three films accompany the text.

Evans uses material suggested by Cocteau's writing, contemporary film and literary criticism, Cocteau biographies, and other varied sources. He blends his research with some personal thought and observation to present a clarification of Cocteau's three poetic films. As a result, a most original and intelligent approach to scholarly film appreciation is offered here. Highly recommended.

3455 *Jean Harlow.* by Brown, Curtis F. 160 p. paper illus. New York: Pyramid, 1977.

Although this volume has many of the consistently excellent *Pyramid* elements—beautiful illustrations, a bibliography, a filmography, an index—it is weakened by its text. Since the life story of Jean Harlow has been told in print numerous times and has been the subject of at least two films, it would seem acceptable to concentrate on an evaluation of her screen work at this time. Author Brown apparently found that difficult to do. He pads his one-note text with partial filmographies of other performers (Lana Turner, Marilyn Monroe, Jeanette MacDonald), far too many dialogue quotations and lots of extraneous material—the Cagney-Clarke grapefruit scene, Frank Capra's themes, a trivia reference to "Mary Hartman, Mary Hartman," a review of the year 1936, and finally, overly detailed plot summaries of the films.

The visuals, as usual, are a prime feature. In this case there are many attractive portraits which help to explain the Harlow persona more effectively and efficiently than does the author. Acceptable.

3456 *Jean Harlow, Hollywood Comet.* by Davies, Dentner. 153 p. illus. London: Constable, 1937.

A biography of the Hollywood star published shortly after her death in 1937.

3457 *The Jean Harlow Story.* by Pascal, John. 158 p. paper illus. New York: Popular Library, 1964.

Here's the familiar story told without any special distinction from other accounts—except perhaps its good taste in avoiding sensationalism. There is however, a fine middle section of photographs which are well-selected and nicely reprinted. An abbreviated filmography completes the volume.

3458 *Jean Harlow's Life Story.* by Parsons, Louella. 32 p. paper illus. New York: Dell, 1937.

Published originally after Harlow's death in 1937, this volume was expanded and reissued in 1964 following the publication of Irving Shulman's *Harlow.*

3459 *Jean-Luc Godard.* by Kreidl, John. 273 p. illus. Boston: Twayne, 1980.

Jean-Luc Godard's films are so rich in their narrative form, subject matter and filmic structure that many volumes have been written about them. This one, by John Kreidl, appears in the *Twayne Theatrical Arts* series and incorporates the usual elements with the text-illustrations, a chronology, notes, references, a bibliography, a filmography, and an index.

Most of the text is a critical review in which Godard's films and career are treated together. His "breakthrough" film, BREATHLESS (1960), does receive a long separate analysis. Other films, themes, metaphors, politics, and assorted Godardian topics are handled in the remaining chapters.

For anyone studying Godard, this volume will be quite rewarding. However, like his films, it may not be pleasing to everyone.

3460 *Jean-Luc Godard: A Guide to References and Resources.* by Lesage, Julia. 438 p. Boston: G. K. Hall, 1979.

Two challenging tasks faced the author of this reference book: supplying order to the many printed pieces about (and by) director Jean-Luc Godard, and providing explanations /synopses of his films. Julia Lesage has been successful in both. Using a professional's approach, she explains her methodology and proceeds to the biographical sketch and critical survey. The latter is an essay worthy of attention by itself. In the filmography which follows, full credits, notes, and a synopsis for each of Godard's 44 films, from OPERATION BETON (1958) to SUR ET SOUS LA COMMUNICATION (1977), are given. More than 2000 items are noted in the chronological bibliography which follows. Descriptive annotations are provided here, as they are for the group of almost 200 articles authored by Godard which are given next. Screenplays, photo essays, scripts, etc., of Godard's films are then listed. Archives, distributor names, a film title index and an author index complete the book.

The monumental task of organizing all the Godard literature into usable, understandable fashion has been accomplished nicely in this reference book. It is the essential starting point for anyone concerned with an in-depth investigation/study of the controversial film director.

3461 *Jean-Luc Godard, A Critical Anthology.* edited by Mussman, Toby. 319 p. paper illus. New York: Dutton, 1968.

Eighteen essays and reviews along with three interviews, five Godard-written articles, two scenarios, a chronology and a filmography make up this compact, detailed examination of Godard and his films. The scenarios are A WOMAN IS A WOMAN (1932) and MY LIFE TO LIVE (1962). The contents will be uniformly interesting to any reader wishing to ascertain the reasons for Godard's prominence as a film director. Illustrations are adequate and the detailed chronology- filmography is helpful. Recommended.

3462 *Jean-Luc Godard: An Investigation into His Films and His Philosophy.* by Collet, Jean. 219 p. paper illus. New York: Crown, 1970.

Several different sections comprise this intellectually stimulating study-in-depth of the work of Godard. There is a long introductory essay which looks at Godard's films as pieces contributing to a whole. Attention is given to the development of Godard as the philosopher of cinematography. Several interviews, a few articles authored by Godard, and excerpts from his screen plays follow. Comments from critics on individual films, a bio-filmography (plot summaries, credits, festival honors, English language titles) and a bibliography conclude the work. This is an excellent volume on a controversial, stimulating and exasperating filmmaker.

3463 *Jean Renoir: Films 1924-1939.* edited by Beylie, Claude. illus. New York: Grove Press, 1971.

Similar to the Eisenstein set, this is another Grove publication that includes 120 slides taken from Renoir's films. Each slide is annotated in the text. Similar slide sets on Welles, Godard, Bunuel and others are available.

3464 *Jean Renoir.* by Bazin, Andre. 320 p. illus. New York: Simon and Schuster, 1973.

This translated work of Andre Bazin is one of the better books on Renoir. It is affectionate and admires Renoir's technical brilliance and compassionate view of his fellow men. Bazin died before the completion of the biography, but several of his disciples such as Truffaut, Godard and Rohmer offer some help. The book is illustrated, indexed, and contains a filmography. Recommended.

3465 *Jean Renoir.* by Leprohon, Pierre. 256 p. illus. New York: Crown, 1971.

This translation of the original French volume published in 1967 by Editions Seghers has much to recommend it. A long enthusiastic essay by Leprohon is followed by some short selections from Renoir's writings on film. Five excerpts from Renoir screenplays and a wide sampling of critics' evaluations of Renoir complete the text. There is a filmography, a bibliography, and an index.

Although the seventies saw the almost simultaneous appearance of several books on Renoir, this compact volume is one of the best. The author's rather one-sided essay is balanced by his perceptive selection of Renoir material. The illustrations are acceptable, although some are rather dark. This book provides a portrait of the director, a description of his films, and an evaluation of his place in film history. Recommended.

3466 *Jean Renoir: The World of His Films.* by Braudy, Leo. 286 p. illus. Garden City, N.Y.: Doubleday & Co., 1971.

The 50-year career of Jean Renoir is documented in this thorough, careful and interesting study. All of Renoir's 36 films are examined to determine relationships that pervade the entire body of his work. The two major motifs of nature and theatre are related to both society and to the actor-heroes who must link them. The text is largely critical and saves the usual biographical sketch for a closing chapter. The appendix has a filmography, a bibliography and an index. Illustrations are plentiful and adequately reproduced. They are mostly one-half page in size which diminishes their effectiveness somewhat. The volume has much to recommend it.

3467 *Jean Renoir: A Guide to References and Resources.* by Faulkner, Christopher. 356 p. Boston: G.K. Hall, 1979.

An excellent approach to the life and career of Jean Renoir is provided here by biographical, filmographical, and bibliographical elements. Since the French filmmaker enjoyed activity and prominence for more than 40 years, a considerable body of material is treated. A lengthy biographical chronicle replaces the usual essay and is followed by "A New Introduction to His Work." The filmography which appears next is detailed, descriptive and critical, offering notes, credits, synopses, and comment. Primary sources are then noted and include Renoir's film appearances, along with his books, screenplays, and articles. A chronological structure is used here and with the secondary sources that follow. Books, pamphlets, articles, recordings, and slides dealing with Renoir are identified and described. Numerous archives and libraries which contain Renoir materials are named next, along with the distributors of his films. A title index and an author index complete the work.

The critical comments which permeate most of the material offered in this reference are most pertinent and should be appreciated. Christopher Faulkner has served his subject well by providing an enormous amount of information written with style and intelligence.

3468 *Jean Renoir: Essays, Conversations, Reviews.* by Gilliatt, Penelope. 136 p. paper illus. New York: McGraw-Hill, 1975.

Two essays introduce the eleven film reviews provided in this volume on Jean Renoir. Supporting the above are a filmography, a section of stills and an index.

The introductory essay (1974) dwells on GRAND IL-LUSION (1938) while the second and longer one (1968) is more general and includes many Renoir comments and quotations. The reviews have apparently also been adapted from Gilliatt's earlier writing.

There is no quarrel with the author's ability as a writer-critic; she is among the best around today. Combining previously written pieces about a specific filmmaker is a legitimate but usually lifeless creative activity. The brevity of the text (83 pages) combined with the waste of space in the visual section (16 half-filled pages) and the expanded filmography (44 pages) may cause some questioning by the economy-minded reader. Acceptable.

3469 *Jean Renoir.* by Durgnat, Raymond. 429 p. illus. Berkeley, Calif.: University of California Press, 1974.

Any new book by Raymond Durgnat arouses expectations of a rewarding experience. This volume is yet another example of the time, care, knowledge and intelligence that Durgnat supplies to his books. Jean Renoir has already been the subject of other critics in books, periodicals, interviews; Renoir's recent memoir seemed to cover all the unfilled biographical spaces. However, Durgnat's study wisely concentrates on the films and offers biographical information only where it is pertinent or helpful in explaining a particular film or its creation.

The films, presented in chronological order, provide the structure about which Durgnat embroiders his film criticism, appreciation and biography. The volume is profusely illustrated, although many of the stills are too small in size to offer the novice

reader any idea of the quality of Renoir's images. A solid bibliography and a helpful index conclude the book. Durgnat is a reliable film critic who gives attention to both the individual details and the totality of a film. His comments are supported by rationale, argument, and fact. The creative accomplishments of Jean Renoir as described by Raymond Durgnat offer the discriminating reader a unique model of film criticism. Highly recommended.

3470 *Jean Renoir: My Life and My Films.* by Renoir, Jean. 287 p. illus. New York: Atheneum, 1974.

This memoir is one to be admired and treasured. The reader will sense its richness in the very first paragraph when the author states "Louis Lumiere was another Gutenberg. His invention has caused as many disasters as the dissemination of thought through books." Renoir does not attempt a review of his films, since he thinks Andre Bazin has done this brilliantly. Instead he recalls the people and events that have made him what he is. Using anecdotes and character sketches, he covers almost 50 years of film history—from his silent film, CATHE-RINE (1923) to the thirties' sound films, Hollywood, color films, television and finally LE PETIT THEATRE DE JEAN RENOIR (1974). He is generous in acknowledging the influence of von Stroheim, Griffith, Chaplin and others on his work. The illustrations that accompany the text are personal shots of family and friends rather than professional stills from films. An index is provided.

Renoir has worked hard in his creative life producing a body of classic films that are characterized by a poetic humanitarianism; the memoirs he offers here have the same qualities of his films: the thoughts, reminiscences, and opinions of this octagenarian artist are intelligent, disarming and consistently pleasant to share. (Critical evaluations of his work can be found in the aforementioned volume by Bazin and in books by Leprohon, Braudy and Durgnat.) Highly recommended.

3471 *Jean Renoir: The French Films 1924-1939.* by Sesonske, Alexander. 463 p. paper illus. Cambridge, Mass.: Harvard University Press, 1980.

After a short introduction and a biographical sketch, each of 24 Renoir films from CATHERINE (1923) to THE RULES OF THE GAME (1939) are critically examined and discussed. The author's structure is to offer some general comments, then to proceed with details, using three general headings: characterization, narrative and treatment, and style and form. Certain films get more attention than others in Sesonske's totally subjective approach to his subject. However, the book does provide a perceptive, informative and pleasurable survey.

An epilogue, notes, a bibliography, an index and many frame enlargements round out the book. Recommended.

3472 *Jean Vigo.* by Smith, John. 96 p. paper illus. New York: Praeger, 1971.

The influential French director and his three classic films are discussed: A PROPOS DE NICE (1930), ZERO DE CONDUITE (1932), and L'ATALANTE (1934).

3473 *Jean Vigo.* by Gomes, P. E. Salles. 256 p. illus. Los Angeles: University of California Press, 1971.

Jean Vigo's total work—three shorter films and one feature—can be viewed in a single evening. To understand the critical success and the impact of the films may require a more prolonged and deeper examination. This volume will aid greatly in that endeavor. Written with the cooperation of Vigo's family, the original edition of this book appeared in France in 1957. Consisting of five logical sections, it provides a detailed coverage of Vigo's life and work.

The first section tells about his father, Miguel Alemeyda, an anarchist whose influence on Vigo's films can be traced. Vigo's early life up to the making of A PROPOS DE NICE (1930) and TARIS (1931) are considered next. Following are lengthy chapters on both ZERO DE CONDUITE (1932) and L'ATLANTE (1934). The content and the making of the films is told with much detail.

Vigo's early death at the age of 29 is described in the closing pages. A summarization and analysis of Vigo's influence on later films and directors is made in a final impressive statement. Notes, references, a filmography, and an index are offered. Some of the illustrations are quite rare, coming as they do from Mme. Luce Vigo, while others are stills and frames from the films. Unfortunately, reproduction of the photographs is on the dark and murky side.

The scholarship, effort, and admiration of the author is apparent throughout. The importance of Vigo is proposed, argued and finally justified in this fine tribute. Recommended.

3474 *Jean Vigo.* by Smith, John M. 144 p. paper illus. New York: Praeger, 1972.

The films of Jean Vigo are given individual attention in this rather special volume. Emphasis is on ZERO DE CONDUITE (1932) and L'ATALANTE (1934), but attention is also given to A PROPOS DE NICE (1930) and TARIS (1931). The introductory chapter deals whth those contributing factors that Vigo used in creating his films. Biographical data is covered in a chronology given at the book's end, along with a bibliography and additional data on the two major films. Many illustrations are murky, probably because they are enlargements of film frames. A viewing of the Vigo films is almost demanded by this volume.

3475 *Jean Vigo.* by Feldman, Harry; and Feldman, Joseph. 28 p. paper illus. London: British Film Institute, 1951.

An out-of-print booklet that was number 4 in the *New Index* series published by BFI in the early fifties. Known also as *An Index to the Creative Work of Jean Vigo.* It appeared as a special supplement in *Sight and Sound.*

3476 *Jeanette MacDonald.* by Stern, Lee Edward. 159 p. paper illus. New York: Jove, 1977.

Jeanette MacDonald is the subject of this appreciation, a title in the *Illustrated History Of the Movies* series. Her career and films are recalled via text, illustrations, a bibliography, a filmography and an index.

3477 *Jeanette MacDonald: A Pictorial Treasury.* by Rich, Sharon. 253 p. illus. Los Angeles: Times Mirror Press, 1973.

3478 *The Jeanette MacDonald Story.* by Parish, James Robert. 181 p. illus. New York: Mason/Charter, 1976.

Jeanette MacDonald did not drink, smoke or enjoy risque stories told at parties. Her only bad habit was constant lateness. Other than these traits, we learn much more about the professional than the person in this biography. She was ambitious, determined, exacting and hard-working with respect to her career. Other than matters of public record, her private life remains privileged information. Gene Raymond, her husband and the person most qualified to define her personal qualities, did not participate in the creation of this book.

Largely a positive tribute to the singing actress, the text carefully traces her appearances in many facets of show business—theatre, films, concerts, opera, recordings, television, and summer stock. Two sections of visuals are included, but no index, bibliography, or career chronology is provided.

In this instance, author Parish competes with himself and others to his disadvantage. His own *Hollywood's Great Love Teams* and *The MGM Stock Company* offer much of the same material arranged more efficiently for reference. More formidable competition is provided by Knowles' *The Films of Jeanette MacDonald and Nelson Eddy*, which offers both biographical coverage and a very fine film review. This volume will appeal mostly to the fans and admirers of Jeanette MacDonald. Acceptable.

3479 THE JERK. by Martin, Steve; and Gottlieb, Carl; and Elias, Michael. 144 p. paper illus. New York: Warner, 1979.

A photonovel of THE JERK (1979) which includes many frame enlargements from the film, connecting narrative, cast and production credits. Carl Gottlieb is responsible for the introduction and the text adaptation of the original film script. The movie was directed by Carl Reiner.

3480 *Jerome Kern: His Life and Music.* by Bordman, Gerald. 544 p. illus. New York: Oxford University Press, 1980.

A scholarly review of Jerome Kern's contribution to the American musical stage is offered in this book. Emphasis is on Kern's career, which is traced from high school in Newark, New Jersey in 1902 to his death in 1945. Since many of Kern's stage musicals were adapted for the screen and since he also wrote several original scores for films, this volume is noted here. Among his films are SWINGTIME (1936), HIGH, WIDE AND HANDSOME (1937), YOU WERE NEVER LOVELIER (1942), COVER GIRL (1944) and CENTENNIAL SUMMER (1946). Of course his music was also used in a highly fictionalized film biography, TILL THE CLOUDS ROLL BY (1946).

3481 *Jessie Matthews: A Biography.* by Thornton, Michael. 359 p. illus. London: Hart, Davis, MacGibbon, 1974.

Known primarily as a dancer-singer in British musicals of the thirties, Jessie Mathews had a relatively short film career. She retired from motion picture work at the beginning of World War II and appeared only in one major film, TOM THUMB (1958), after that. For many years she played a leading role in a daytime radio serial. Her performances is such films as EVERGREEN (1934), GANGWAY (1937), SAILING ALONG (1938), and CLIMBING HIGH (1939) are recalled with admiration.

3482 *see 3481*

3483 JESUS. by Dreyer, Carl Theodore. 312 p. illus. New York: Dial Press, 1972.

There is much more in this volume than the script of Dreyer's planned film on the life of Jesus. Three essays by Dreyer about the film and why he wanted to make it, along with tributes to Dreyer from Renoir, Fellini, and Truffaut, are included. An essay entitled "Working with Dreyer" by Preben Thomsen and a short review of his career by Ib Monty also supplement the main text—the script of JESUS, which is quite detailed, with many explanatory paragraphs describing the shots and scenes. A fine collection of illustrations of stills from Dreyer's films introduces the book in appropriate fashion.

The quality of this volume is high in all respects—content, selection, arrangement and production. While a script that was never filmed may have a limited appeal, the remaining materials serve a double purpose: they enhance the reading of JESUS and give background for the appreciation of Dreyer's other film classics. This is a beautifully produced book that is recommended.

3484 JESUS CHRIST SUPERSTAR. by James, David; and Sanders, John. 112 p. paper illus. New York: Dell, 1973.

This is a souvenir book designed by John Sanders, with photographs by David James showing scenes in color and inblack and white from the motion picture version of the Tim Rice/Andrew Lloyd Webber rock musical. Selections from the lyrics caption many of the photographs. There is a short text about the making of the film, and complete cast and production credits are included.

3485 JEW SUSS. by Rawlinson, Arthur; and Farnum, Dorothy. 174 p. illus. London: Methuen, 1935.

Script of the 1934 film directed by Lothar Mendes. In addition to the script, Ernest Betts gives the background, history, glossary, etc. concerning this controversial film. Also made in Germany in 1940 and directed by Viet Harlan.

3486 *Jewish Films in the United States: A Comprehensive and Descriptive Filmography.* compiled by Fox, Stuart. 359 p. Boston: G.K. Hall, 1976.

This is a companion volume to the one published in 1972 entitled *Catalogue of Jewish Films in Israel*, and is the result of cooperation between the Hebrew University of Jerusalem and the University of Southern California. Here a wider interpretation of "Jewish Film" is used, and since this listing was derived from printed material such as magazines and catalogs, it contains some films which may be "lost." The approximately 4000 titles noted include all types of films which are grouped under general form headings: features, documentaries, newsreels, television shows etc. Most entries provide technical data, credits, and a description of subject content. A title index and a subject index are provided.

The book is a specialized reference. In addition to its informational content, it offers a model for film research that can be used in a wide variety of circumstances.

3487   *Jim: The Author's Self-Centered Memoir on the Great Jim Brown.* by Toback, James. 133 p. illus. New York: Doubleday, 1971.

The author had a compulsion to know Brown. In this relating of his reasons and his eventual interaction with Brown, the reader learns intimate details about both author and subject. The emphasis here is on sports and sex, with Brown's films given little attention.

3488   *Jiri Trnka: Artist and Puppet Master.* by Bocek, Jaroslav. 272 p. illus. Prague: Artia, 1965

A biography and appreciation of Czech animator Jiri Trnka, whose short films have enjoyed international critical and popular success. Full-color illustrations and a filmography are included.

3489   *Joan Crawford.* by Thomas, Bob. 382 p. paper illus. New York: Bantam, 1979.

A softening counter-balance to *Mommie Dearest* is provided by Bob Thomas here. He uses in a somewhat perfunctory way his personal knowledge of Joan Crawford along with research that included coworkers, acquaintances, movie magazine articles and other sources. The resultant portrait that surfaces is that of an ambitious, hardworking female who fought hard to attain celebrity and to keep it. Her triumphs (stardom and survival) and her failures (marriage and motherhood) are noted as well as the miserable early background which apparently shaped her adult life to a great extent. While the paradoxical person depicted here is not admirable,

the reader will have a respect for some of her characteristics— determination, strength, courage and survival instinct. Apparently Crawford was a human contradiction.

Accompanying the detailed reprise of Crawford's life and career are illustrations, a filmography, a bibliography, a videography, and an index. Recommended to counteract the sour bias found in Christina Crawford's account of her mother.

3490   *Joan Crawford: The Raging Star.* by Castle, Charles. 207 p. illus. London: New English Library, 1977.

Called an "authorised" biography, this account of Joan Crawford's life and career includes a bibliography, a detailed filmography and an index.

3491   *Joan Crawford.* by Harvey, Stephen. 159 p. paper illus. New York: Pyramid, 1974.

This tribute to Joan Crawford examines her screen performances, with unusual attention given to her twenties "Flapper" period, during which she made 22 silent films. The periods which followed are easy to identify—a MGM fashion plate in the thirties, a dramatic long-suffering female in the forties and fifties, and finally a horror-thriller grand dame of the sixties.

In good films or bad films, Crawford's work was always interesting; the text reflects that star quality which had sufficient flexibility and intelligence to blend with the times. The illustrations provided are very good and they are nicely reproduced. The filmography, bibliography and index also add quality to this rewarding book. Recommended.

3492   JOAN OF ARC. by Anderson, Maxwell; and Solt, Andrew. 171 p. illus. New York: Sloane, 1948.

The text is excerpted from the screenplay and accompanies many full-page stills from the 1948 film, which was directed by Victor Fleming.

3493   *see 3492*

3494   *A Job for Superman.* by Alyn, Kirk. 118 p. illus. Los Angeles: Kirk Alyn, 1971.

Alyn was one of the first actors to portray Superman in motion pictures.

3495   JOE. by Wexler, Norman. 128 p. paper illus. New York: Avon Books,

1970.

Script of the 1970 film directed by John G. Avildsen. Contains cast credits, an introduction by Judith Christ, and production notes.

3496 *Joe Franklin's Encyclopedia of Comedians.* by Franklin, Joe. 349 p. illus. Secaucus, N.J.: Citadel, 1979.

The selection of comedians here is made from various media—radio, television, screen, vaudeville, nightclubs, etc. Those who have appeared in films are numerous since Hollywood has always used the other media as a training ground and a source of talent. Illustrations are plentiful and the biographical data is concise but adequate.

3497 *John and Diana: A Love Story.* by Norbom, Mary Ann. 205 p. paper illus. New York: Bantam, 1979.

Based on interviews, articles, and other research, Mary Ann Norbom speculates on the relationship of John Travolta and Diana Hyland in this volume. Her taste is questionable in almost every aspect of this ghoulish book. To guess what Hyland's death meant to Travolta without talking to him seems a writer's conceit and an insensitive invasion of privacy.

3498 *John Barrymore: The Legend and the Man.* by Power-Waters, Alma. 282 p. illus. New York: Messner, 1941.

An authorized biography of Barrymore written shortly before his death in 1942.

3499 *John Cassavetes, Peter Falk.* edited by Henstell, Bruce. 23 p. paper Washington, D.C.: American Film Institute, 1972.

In January 1971 this interview with Cassavetes and Falk was held at the AFI Center in Beverly Hills. Both had worked together in HUSBANDS (1970) and Cassavetes had just completed MINNIE AND MOSKOWITZ (1971). A bibliography and a filmography for Cassavetes is included. Acceptable.

3500 *John Cromwell.* by Davies, Brenda. 40 p. paper illus. London: British Film Institute, 1974.

In this booklet a short biography of the American director is followed by a detailed listing of his films.

3501 *John Ford.* by Bogdanovich, Peter. 144 p. illus. Berkeley, Calif.: University of California, 1968.

The physical arrangement of this book differs from most. In four sections, the reader is given 1) a view of Ford at work on CHEYENNE AUTUMN (1964); 2) a discussion by the author of Ford's films; 3) an interview in which Ford discusses some of his films, and 4) a filmography. This format succeeds in both informing the novice reader and reminding the movie buff of Ford's gigantic contribution to cinema. Ford's own comments on his films (1918 to 1966) give fascinating side lights and background to some of the screen's classics (e.g., THE INFORMER (1935)). Illustrations are fine and capsule summaries and comments are included in the filmography. The book is to be treasured. Essential reading for anyone interested in film.

3502 *John Ford.* by McBride, Joseph; and Wilmington, Michael. 234 p. illus. New York: Da Capo, 1975.

This analysis of director John Ford and his films begins with an emotional chapter about his death and burial followed by a summary of the themes, attitudes, and techniques found in his work. A 1970 interview with Ford leads to a discussion of selected films, which are divided by theme/concept/subject. Outlaws, Men At War, Ireland, Rebels, Western Myth vs. Reality, and Women are the broad headings that are considered. The filmography lists only the films considered in the text. A long impressive bibliography completes the book.

Because this is a rather late entry on Ford and it resembles the structural approach of John Baxter's study, *The Cinema of John Ford,* some problems in material selection may be present. For example, one may wish for the use of different films from Ford's rich output—half of them here repeat Baxter's selection, and STAGECOACH (1939) has been the subject of many essays and articles. However, there is enough that is new in the analysis and comment to warrant reader interest and attention. Acceptable.

3503 *John Ford.* by Sinclair, Andrew. 284 p. illus. New York: Dial, 1979.

John Ford's life was a busy one. Between 1917 and 1971, he directed over 100 films, served as unofficial American spy, OSS member and naval officer, and exercised profound effect on American life through the romanticizing of liberty, justice and democracy in his films. In a relatively short text, Sinclair covers the career high spots, but slights some essential personal matters such as Ford's failure as a husband and father. Since a recurrent theme in his films is the

511

importance of family, this dark side of his personal life is an enigma worthy of exploration.

Illustrations, a very long filmography, an index and notes areincluded. The strength of this volume lies in the sections devoted to Ford's military activities. Ford, the patriot, is a lot clearer than Ford, the family man.

3504   *John Ford and Andrew V. McLaglen.* by Burrows, Michael. 32 p. paper illus. Cornwall, England: Primestyle Ltd, 1970.

This second *Formative Film* booklet uses quotations from interviews, letters and reviews, straight narrative, critical and analytical interpretation, and photographs in describing John Ford and his disciple, Andrew McLaglen. The text is a potpourri of material used to create overall impressions of the two subjects. Some of it is chatty, informal and unfocused. A structured formal approach may have served better. A filmography and several full-page illustrations conclude the booklet. Picture reproduction is only average. This volume is inexpensive, unassuming and pleasant but adds little to the material already available on Ford.

3505   *John Ford and the Traditional Moral Order.* by Stavig, Mark. 225 p. illus. Madison, Wisc.: University of Wisconsin Press, 1968.

3506   *The John Ford Movie Mystery.* by Sarris, Andrew. 192 p. illus. Bloomington, Ind.: Indiana University Press, 1976.

In a chronological examination of John Ford's career, Andrew Sarris identifies four periods of creativity: The Early Silent Days (1917-1930); The Story Teller (1930-1939); The Poet Laureate (1940-1947); and The Poet and Rememberer of Things Past (1948-1966). Ford was an elusive, private person and gave scant information about his goals, themes, and methods to students and critics of his work. The title is appropriate since Sarris traces the vacillating critical opinion of Ford's work from 1917 to 1966. Calling Ford "an American Renoir," Sarris points out his strengths and weaknesses, successes and failures, as he surveys many of the Ford films in detail.

The text is supported by some rather small illustrations, a filmography, and a selected bibliography.

Sarris' typical thoroughness is evident not only in the delineation of Ford and his work, but also in the presentation of the different critical climates during which the Ford films appeared. His appreciation of

Ford is presented with a persuasive argument and example that will encourage further study and consideration of Ford's rich film legacy. Recommended.

3507   *John Ford's* STAGECOACH. edited by Anobile, Richard. 256 p. paper illus. New York: Avon, 1975.

This book re-creation of STAGECOACH (1939) in the *Film Classics Library* series is a welcome addition. It may have presented some problems because of the abundance of action in the film. Certain of the 1200 visuals presented here are a bit fuzzy, and since they have been created by blow-ups of selected original film frames, this is understandable. Furthermore, Anobile points out that the quality of his negatives was another variable.

The complete dialogue has been placed under the appropriate shots. Thus the persons who wish to analyze or study the film, John Ford's direction, or Dudley Nichol's script may do so at their leisure. Orson Welles has admitted to using this film as his primer for learning filmmaking. He viewed it more than 40 times as a preparation for CITIZEN KANE (1941). Anobile has also included John Ford's remarks on STAGECOACH as they appeared in *Action* magazine. They provide the ideal introduction to the film reconstruction. This is another fine book in what promises to be an outstanding series. Recommended.

3508   *John Garfield.* by Morris, George. 160 p. paper illus. New York: Harcourt, Brace, Jovanovich, 1977.

This title in the *Illustrated History of the Movies* series covers the stormy personal life and the relatively brief film career of John Garfield. It includes many illustrations, a filmography, a bibliography, and an index. Another fine addition to the series.

3509   *John Garfield: His Life and Films.* by Beaver, James N., Jr. 204 p. illus. New York: A. S. Barnes, 1978.

John Garfield made only 35 films, none of which is considered a classic today. His contribution was to bring to the screen the image of a hero-rebel, a realistic man whose faults and virtues were related to the society in which he functioned. Many actors were to take inspiration from Garfield's creation and add their own refinements to the rebel character—Brando, Dean, Clift, Pacino, DeNiro, and others.

In this volume the author provides a straightforward biographical chapter and a rundown of the 35 films. Credits, a synopsis, review excerpts, and a few stills are offered for each film. Visual evidence that Garfield did not appear in FOOTLIGHT PARADE (1933) is offered in an appendix along with lists of his stage and radio appearances. The book ends with Clifford Odets' tribute to Garfield at the time of his death in 1952. An index is provided. The illustrations are well selected and reproduced, with the exception of a few from Garfield's early theatre days. These appear to be composites or recreations.

As indicated, this is a factual recall of the life and career of a colorful actor. What is missing is the in-depth critical evaluation of Garfield's individual characterizations and the exploration of his effect on audiences and on those actors who so closely followed his original creation. Acceptable.

3510 *John Gielgud.* by Hayman, Ronald. 276 p. illus. New York: Random House, 1972.

Although this sterile biography is largely a recital of theatrical triumphs and disasters, a few films are mentioned in passing: SECRET AGENT (1936), THE PRIME MINISTER (1940), JULIUS CAESAR (1953), THE LOVED ONE (1965), and THE CHARGE OF THE LIGHT BRIGADE (1968)—each acknowledged with a paragraph or two. See also *John Gielgud: An Actor's Biography in Pictures*, by Hallam Fordham.

3511 *John Gielgud: An Actor's Biography in Pictures.* by Fordham, Hallam. 128 p. illus. London: John Lehmann, 1952.

John Gielgud is a noted British stage and screen performer and a record of his career from the twenties to 1950 has been compiled and described pictorially by Fordham in this volume. Gielgud has contributed a personal statement also.

3512 *John Grierson: A Documentary Biography.* by Hardy, Forsyth. 298 p. illus. Salem, N.H.: Faber and Faber, 1979.

This biography was not only written by a life-long associate of John Grierson but was enriched by the almost unanimous cooperation of family, friends, associates, and institutions. In 1946 Forsyth Hardy edited a collection of Grierson's writings in *Grierson on Documentary*. Here, more than three decades later, he tells the filmmaker's personal story and assesses Grierson's importance in the history of motion pictures. Painstakingly researched, the text is rich with observation and recollection. The accomplishments of Grierson as producer, idea man, teacher, film theorist, developer of talent, and general "father" of the documentary film are described and discussed. Because of his apparently unlimited energy, the range and number of Grierson's activities was enormous. His dedication and devotion to the documentary film form is emphasized while his mistakes, prejudices, and poor judgments are minimized.

Several sections of illustrations, extensive chapter notes, and an index complete the book. Time has not always been kind to Grierson's films and philosophies, but Forsyth Hardy remembers him here with affection and appreciation.

3513 *John Grierson: Film Master.* by Beveridge, James. 361 p. illus. N.Y.: Macmillan, 1978.

The author worked with John Grierson for a time, and was preparing a film biography when the documentary filmmaker died in 1972. Using his personal knowledge and the resource he gathered for the film, Beveridge provides a kind of anthology-source book of interviews, speeches, statements, articles, etc., rather than a linear, narrative biography. The material is arranged chronologically from Grierson's youth in Scotland to his teaching at McGill University in Montreal, but it is presented in "pure" form rather than interpreted. As a result, some of it is rather reverential and adoring, since it was written in retrospect. Grierson's comments and speeches remain superb examples of the filmmaker who can best interpret his own thought and work.

The volume is nicely illustrated, but alas, there is no index. This is a volume whose individual parts are more valuable than the whole.

3514 *John Huston: A Pictorial Treasury of His Films.* by Tozzi, Romano. 160 p. illus. New York: Crescent (Crown), 1970.

There is much to recommend in this economy picture book. The photographs are well selected in most cases, beautifully reproduced, and show Huston as a writer, director, and actor. The Huston filmography is listed at the end of the book which may be a reference convenience. Some other features are not so positive. The rather bland noncritical text runs nonstop throughout the book and sometimes does not relate to the adjacent photographs. The poor policy of placing a still on the left-hand page and then using an enlargement from or near-duplicate of that still on the right-hand page (pp. 34-35, 76-77, 82-83, 88-89, 96-97, 104-105) seems to be picture padding. A most acceptable record of his many accomplishments.

3515 *John Huston.* by Madsen, Axel. 280 p. illus. Garden City, N.Y.: Doubleday, 1978.

After an introductory chapter which sets forth the colorful characteristics and behavioral patterns of director John Huston, the text of this volume offers a chronological recital of the events in Huston's life. Picture follows picture, relationship follows relationship, late decline follows early success. To enliven the often told story, Madsen has included some gossip, speculation, and a galaxy of film stars.

Supporting the fast-paced but superficial biography are illustrations, a filmography, a bibliography, and an index. The book is acceptable for the nondiscriminating movie fan, but the serious reader will be disappointed.

3516 *John Huston, King Rebel.* by Nolan, William F. 247 p. illus. Los Angeles: Sherbourne Press, 1965.

An unusual kind of biography, this volume thankfully concentrates on the films of John Huston. The book begins with a full chapter of varied quotes about Huston made by his famous friends, acquaintances and co-workers. A very brief account of his early years is followed by a longer account of the making of THE MALTESE FALCON (1941). Chapters devoted to each of his films follow his career up to 1965 and his completion of THE BIBLE (1966). Interwoven between the accounts of the filmmaking is sufficient anecdotal material about Huston to allow a full portrait to emerge.

A few pictures are offered along with a filmography and a bibliography. The author's style is reportorial rather than literary. Some errors exist (Marilyn Monroe's role in THE ASPHALT JUNGLE (1950) was not her first speaking role). The emphasis on Huston's work makes this an outstanding biography. Recommended for all.

3517 *John Huston: Maker of Magic.* by Kaminsky, Stuart. 237 p. illus. Boston: Houghton Mifflin, 1978.

Other than the author's admiration for John Huston's films, the reason for this volume is difficult to ascertain. Most of what is related has appeared in previous volumes—*John Huston, King Rebel; John Huston: A Pictorial Treasury of His Films;* and *The Cinema of John Huston.* The latter title is a lengthy interview with Huston about his films, an opportunity which was apparently denied Kaminsky. His disenchantment with his subject as a person is indicated in the book's opening pages.

What the author presents is biography combined with a review of the Huston films. The latter is cursory while the former consists mostly of references, quotes, and citations of previously published material. The bibliography, filmography, and index provided are detailed. A center section offers a few illustrations. The production quality of the book is excellent.

For readers unfamiliar with John Huston and his films, this volume is an acceptable introduction. Those looking for a substantial in-depth critical evaluation of the filmmaker or his work will have to seek elsewhere.

3518 *John Huston's* THE MALTESE FALCON. edited by Anobile, Richard. 256 p. paper illus. New York: Avon Books, 1974.

As Anobile points out in his introduction, THE MALTESE FALCON (1941) is largely devoid of any action. Its appeal rests with director John Huston's use of the camera and with the performances. The first element is most apparent in this re-creation of the film by more than 1400 frame enlargements. All the original dialogue appears beneath the appropriate visuals and certain readers will be able to imagine the Bogart snarl, the Astor seductiveness, the Peter Lorre purr, and the Greenstreet growl. Reproduction of the frames is very good and the student can examine in minute detail the camera set-ups that Huston employed.

THE MALTESE FALCON is a legendary film for a number of reasons and most of them can be easily discovered in this excellent reconstruction. Highly recommended. See also the *Film Classic Library* series.

3519 *John Neville.* by Trewin, John C. 136 p. illus. London: Rockliff, 1961.

John Neville is a stage actor who has appeared in a few films—most of which were made after this book was published. Titles includes OSCAR WILDE (1960), MR. TOPAZE (1962), BILLY BUDD (1962) and A STUDY IN TERROR (1965), in which he played Sherlock Holmes.

3520 *John Schlesinger: A Guide to References and Resources.* by Brooker, Nancy J. 132 p. Boston: G.K. Hall, 1978.

After an opening biographical chapter, a critical survey examines each of Schlesinger's major films. The filmography which follows gives full credits, detailed synopses, and notes for the films. A bibliography, arranged annually from 1962 to 1977, appears next. Activities in theatre, television and advertising are noted. The book concludes with a film distributor list and an index.

This modestly produced volume is ideal for anyone wishing to locate information about John Schlesinger.

3521 *John Schlesinger.* by Phillips, Gene D. 199 p. illus. Boston: Twayne, 1981.

3522 *John Steinbeck and His Films.* by Burrows, Michael. 36 p. paper illus. London: Primestyle Ltd., 1970.

Using plot outlines, critical blurbs and visuals, the author gives a chronological history of Steinbeck and the filming of his novels. Readers may also refer to Schulberg's account of the writer's career in Hollywood.

3523 *The John Travolta Scrapbook.* by Munshower, Suzanne. 121 p. paper illus. New York: Grosset & Dunlap, 1978.

This illustrated biography is one of the *Scrapbook* series prepared by Ms. Munshower and combines text and visuals nicely. Adapted from a 1976 publication, *Meet John Travolta*, this volume traces his career from high school drop-out to Broadway performer and then on to television celebrity and finally films.

The volume is well produced but perhaps a bit premature since its subject is a bit young for a serious biography. However, his fans, for whom the book was created, will be enthralled.

3524 *John Wayne: The Actor, the Man.* by Bishop, George. 254 p. illus. Thornwood, N.Y.: Caroline House, 1979.

Among George Bishop's credentials for authorship of a John Wayne biography are a long period as a "Wayne watcher" and writing credits that include books on sex offenders, booze, executions, clowns, and Frank Sinatra. What he offers here is an often gushy fan magazine tribute that seems to be based on the huge amount of material already published on Wayne—books, periodicals, interviews, films, etc. To this he adds personal interpretations such as suggesting Wayne's thoughts, reasoning, and behavior. There is an abundance of conjecture based upon recent information (i.e. Montgomery Clift) rather than direct confirmation from a biographical subject. Although quotations are numerous, as are plot synopses and illustrations, the actual text runs less than 200 pages. The filmography, which offers mini-

mal information, is stretched to 27 pages. An index is provided.

In a rather florid style, the text blends factual data and subjectivity. Rather than a critical biography, an affectionate tribute is offered here. As such, it is acceptable for admirers of John Wayne.

3525 *John Wayne.* by Barbour, Alan G. 160 p. paper illus. New York: Pyramid, 1974.

Although the production values of the *Pyramid* series areapparently diminishing, the quality of the content remains high. In this well-written study, Wayne is described by his screen image and his off-stage personality in the opening sections. Some interesting contrasts emerge. Wayne at 67 years of age is the father of seven, and the grandfather of twenty—no screen role has ever suggested such patriarchal activity. Ten of his major films are described in detail in a chapter titled "The Essential Wayne." Individual chapters are devoted to each decade in his career from the thirties to the seventies. A bibliography, filmography, and an index complete the book. The visuals are well selected but suffer from occasional poor reproduction. This is another fine title in the *Pyramid* series. One can only hope that the hardbound editions which appear are of a higher paper and reproduction quality than the paperback examined. Recommended.

3526 *John Wayne.* by Paige, David. 31 p. paper illus. Mankato, Minn.: Creative Education, 1974.

A title in the *Stars of Stage & Screen* series, this biography was designed for younger readers. It contains original illustrations rather than stills.

3527 *John Wayne and the Movies.* by Eyles, Allen. 320 p. illus. New York: A. S. Barnes, 1976.

A critical study of John Wayne's films is provided in this book. It is a late entry, having been preceded by more than six earlier volumes which also treat the Wayne career in varying depths; however, the care, detail, and evaluation found here surpass the film coverage found in the others.

Eyles is concerned with the development of Wayne's screen image. Starting with a frame enlargement from HANGMAN'S HOUSE (1928), he traces the actor's progress through more than 100 motion pictures to ROOSTER COGBURN (1975). The early films are treated in groupings, but from STAGECOACH (1939) on, each is given a descriptive-critical essay and one or more stills. Detailed casts and credits are noted in a concluding filmography and there is an index which lists title changes. The many illustrations have been well selected and reproduced; they provide a visual counterpart to the text's study of Wayne's changing image.

Regardless of the reader's feeling about Wayne as a performer or a person, his long career must be acknowledged as a superior accomplishment. Allen Eyles justifies the "living legend" status of Wayne in this most satisfying study. Recommended.

3528 *John Wayne in the Camera's Eye.* by Shaw, Stan. 160 p. illus. New York: Exeter.

Another volume from the *In the Camera's Eye* series. This one, again, consists mostly of candid shots of John Wayne.

3529 *The John Wayne Story.* by Carpozi, George. 279 p. illus. New Rochelle: Arlington House, 1972.

"... I'd like to predict regarding this book—my fifteenth—that some reviewers will be as critical as they were about each of my other fourteen tomes, saying that I 'failed to capture the real'... John Wayne, that this biography is only a 'superficial study' and perhaps even an injustice to the most imposing movie actor of our time." This is from George Carpozi in a forewarning to this volume. Right on, Mr. Carpozi.

There are inconsistencies between the closing filmography and the text. For example: 1) The text states HANGMAN'S HOUSE (1928) was Wayne's first film; the filmography lists MOTHER MACHREE (1928) and FOUR SONS (1928) as earlier films. A direct quote in Ricci: "The first picture I worked on I remember was MOTHER MACHREE..." 2) No other sources list FOUR SONS as a Wayne film—Weaver, Michaels, Ricci, or Tomkies. If true, Carpozi should elaborate in the text. He does not. 3) Ricci lists, with a still and cast credits, WORDS AND MUSIC (1929) and CHEER UP AND SMILE (1930) as Wayne films. Carpozi omits these. Photographic work is only fair, and the overall selection is poor. An index is provided.

Author Carpozi wrote certain of his other books as paperback originals. This volume seems more appropriate to that format rather than a costly hardbound book. The drugstore audience may be more appreciative and less critical. Not recommended. Interested parties should look at *The Films of John Wayne* by Mark Ricci.

3530 *Jolie Gabor.* by Gabor, Jolie; and Adams, Cindy. 315 p. illus. New York: Mason/Charter, 1975.

This Hungarian success story "as told to Cindy Adams" is about how Jansci Tilleman became Jolie Gabor, owner of a famous jewelry store, media celebrity, and outspoken mentor of three daughters, Zsa Zsa, Eva, and Magda. With this kind of plot and cast, the results are predictable. Jolie's account of her struggles and triumphs is sprinkled with anecdotes, gossip, and innuendo—all seasoned with a generous amount of sex talk and name dropping— i.e., Elizabeth Taylor, Clark Gable, James Mason, Tyrone Power, etc. Since George Sanders was married to two of the daughters, he receives special, and mostly negative, attention from Mama Gabor. A few photographs are included but the book is not indexed.

This biography provides light enjoyable reading for those who appreciate stories based on the strive-and-succeed ethic. It is a mixture of calculated frankness, the romantic recollections of old age, some obvious exaggerations and a middle European philosophy of life that is distinctly unique in our American culture.

3531 *Jolson.* by Freedland, Michael. 256 p. illus. New York: Stein and Day, 1972.

This affectionate retelling of Jolson's life offers much new information, with attention focused primarily on the performing aspects—minstrels, theatre, recording, film, radio and entertaining GIs. Apparently Jolson was an egomaniac who only came completely alive when appearing before an audience. Much of the book describes his live performances. His career in films never equalled his stage triumphs in the World War I period. The only exception is the most famous Jolson film, THE JOLSON STORY (1946)— an irony because he is portrayed by another actor, Larry Parks. According to the author, Jolson does play himself in one blackface number, "Swanee," in that film.

The attention to his film appearances from an abortive attempt with D. W. Griffith to RHAPSODY IN BLUE in 1943 is gratifying. The two biographical films, THE JOLSON STORY and JOLSON SINGS AGAIN (1949) get major attention, but adequate mention is made of the others. There are some things, however, that diminish the book's total effectiveness. Time periods are treated casually by Freedland, e.g., did Rudy Keeler sign for 42ND STREET in 1929? The portrait of Ruby Keeler is altogether rather phantomlike and unsatisfactory. This is unfortunate since the Keeler-Jolson relationship is so important to the story. Perhaps the book is at its best when persons who knew Jolson reminisce via anecdotes and professional put-downs. George Jessel's statement,

"He was a no-good son of a bitch but he was the greatest entertainer I've ever seen," tells the reader a great deal in a few words. The author, for all his prose, fails to provide such succinct clarity in his portrait.

Other weaknesses are the absence of a filmography, a discography, a bibliography, and a list of theatrical appearances. Some photographs are included but they seem carelessly chosen and they are poorly reproduced. The book is indexed. *Jolson* is a blend of strong and weak (or absent) components that will bring mixed reactions from readers. With more attention to the research and listing of specific performances, better illustrations, and a more extensive use of the resource people, the book could have been excellent. It can certainly be recommended for its intelligent treatment of the Jolson films.

3532 *Joris Ivens.* by Delmar, Rosalind. New York: Zoetrope, 1980.

3533 *Josef von Sternberg: A Critical Study of the Great Film Director.* by Weinberg, Herman G. 255 p. paper illus. New York: Dutton, 1967.

A scholarly examination of von Sternberg and his films by a dedicated writer, this volume includes an interview, some correspondence, two scenario excerpts, some critical reviews, a filmography and a biography. The thoroughness and perception of the author is admirable. This portrait of the colorful director should be read along with his autobiography. A fine achievement.

3534 *Joseph L. Mankiewicz: An Index to His Work.* by Taylor, John Russel 24 p. paper illus. London: British Film Institute, 1960.

One of the *FI Index* series, this time on the multitalented writer-director responsible for such films as CLEOPATRA (1963), ALL ABOUT EVE (1950), and A LETTER TO THREE WIVES (1948).

3535 *Joseph L. Mankiewicz: An Index to His Work.* by Taylor, John Russell. paper illus. London: British Film Institute, 1960.

3536 *Joseph Losey.* by Hirsch, Foster. 256 p. illus. Boston: Twayne, 1980.

Joseph Losey gained prominence as the director of THE SERVANT (1963), a dozen years after he had been blacklisted in the United States. Since then he has made his films in England. This appreciation updates two earlier works, *Losey on Losey* and *The Cinema of Joseph Losey,* by giving full attention not only to the early films but also to those he made in the late sixties and the seventies.

Hirsch regards Losey as an auteur director and gives sufficient argument to support his opinion. This well-researched, detailed study is enriched by a bibliography, a filmography, notes, references, an index and some illustrations. There is also a long note on Losey's filmed opera, DON GIOVANNI (1979).

3537 *Josh.* by Logan, Joshua. 408 p. illus. New York: Delacorte, 1976.

This revealing autobiography, subtitled "My Up and Down, In and Out Life," traces Joshua Logan's career to the time when he accepted Harry Cohn's offer to direct the film PICNIC (1956). At that point he announces, "...the future is another story," indicating that his experiences as a film director are to appear in a sequel to this book. The chronology offered here does indicate his direction of the films PICNIC, BUS STOP (1956), SAYONARA (1957), SOUTH PACIFIC (1958), TALL STORY (1960), FANNY (1961), ENSIGN PULVER (1964), CAMELOT (1967) and PAINT YOUR WAGON (1969).

One chapter does deal with his early Hollywood experiences as a dialogue director for THE GARDEN OF ALLAH (1936) and HISTORY IS MADE AT NIGHT (1937) and as codirector of I MET MY LOVE AGAIN (1938). His characterizations of Dietrich, Boyer, Joseph Schildkraut, David O. Selznick, and Walter Wanger are devastating. It should be noted that although the author is unsparing with himself, he speaks kindly about most of his professional associates. A follow-up to this well-written account of a busy life will be welcome. This volume is illustrated and indexed.

3538 *The Journal of* THE LOVED ONE. by Southern, Terry. 116 p. paper illus. New York: Random House, 1965.

The advertising slogan used to publicize THE LOVED ONE when it appeared in 1965 was "The picture that has something to offend everyone." This book is like that, too. If you look closely at the many pictures (by William Claxton) you will probably discover something offensive, distasteful and/or sickening.

Meant as some sort of high camp or put-on, the movie misfired completely according to its critics, and disappeared overnight. This volume gives some clues concerning its failure. Perhaps it was a practical joke that told well but was unfunny when executed. The quality of the candids is high. They are quite good. The text, however, is dotted with "inside" humor and gets cute or coy at times. There is no index. If the picture is ever "found" again (uncut), it might be interesting to use this volume as a readiness material before viewing.

3539 *A Journal of the Plague Years.* by Kanfer, Stefan. 306 p. illus. New York: Atheneum, 1973.

Another book about those years from 1947 to 1962 when the HUAC, the blacklist, *Red Channels*, and J. Parnell Thomas were familiar and frightening names to many persons in show business. Kanfer takes to task all those who capitulated in one form or another to the pressure; he is unforgiving of Elia Kazan and Larry Parks for having "sung" to the HUAC, of talent agencies for having used the blacklist, and of film studios for their purges.

Although Robert Vaughn's book *Only Victims* is superior in all respects, this volume indicates enough passionate anger on the part of the author to make the reader forgive some rather poor writing and organization. The conclusion of both books is similar. Tracking down and punishing persons whose political views differ from those in power is not a new governmental activity. The warning is implicit throughout—to guard against a repetition of these events today. Acceptable.

3540 *The Journal of The Society for Education in Film and Television, Autumn 1972.* edited by Rohdie, Sam. 136 p. paper London: The Society for Education in Film and Television, 1972.

Although this is a journal available by subscription, its appearance is similar to many paperback books, and it is sold in individual issues in bookstores. For those reasons it is noted here. The Autumn 1972 issue is an anthology containing articles on John Ford's YOUNG MR. LINCOLN (1939), Hitchcock's British films, cinema verite in America, and an interview with Ivor Montagu. The material is specialized.

3541 *The Journals of Jean Cocteau.* by Cocteau, Jean. 250 p. illus. Bloomington, Ind.: Indiana University Press, 1964.

The journals containing memoirs, correspondence, reminiscences, etc. were edited and translated by Wallace Fowlie and are illustrated with drawings by Cocteau. A selected bibliography is included.

3542 *Journey Down Sunset Boulevard: The Films of Billy Wilder.* by Sinyard, Neil; and Turner, Adrian. 366 p. illus. Ryde, England: BCW Publishing, 1979.

3543 *A Journey Into Darkness: The Art of James Whale's Horror Films.* by Ellis, Reed. New York: Arno, 1980.

A study of director James Whale's influence on contemporary films. Emphasis is placed on Whale's four principal films. A title in the *Dissertations on Film* series.

3544 *Journey to a Legend and Back: The British Realistic Film.* by Orbanz, Eva. 213 p. New York: Zoetrope, 1981.

Interviews with Paul Rotha, Lindsay Anderson, Karel Reisz, Tony Garnett, Basil Wright and others. In addition, forty-six selected filmmakers receive attention via biographies, filmographies and bibliographies.

3545 *The Joy of Hustling.* by Tyler, Gregg. 286 p. paper illus. New York: Manor Books, 1976.

The author has had a wide variety of experiences—social, professional and sexual—on the fringes of show business. With little regard for his self-image or reputation, he tells about many of his relationships with celebrities of both sexes. Names mentioned include Jayne Mansfield, Judy Garland, Liza Minelli, the Kennedys, and numerous others. The juiciest anecdotes are about the stars who have died. Occasionally, he resorts to a pseudonym for a living personality but always provides enough clues for the reader to guess the identity. Some illustrations appear in a center section.

This is kiss-and-tell writing at a rather base level. However, since the appetite of the reading audience for celebrity scandal and innuendo seems insatiable, this volume will be devoured by a wide audience.

3546 *The Joy of Marilyn in the Camera Eye.* by Shaw, Sam. 160 p. illus. New York: Exeter, 1979.

Sam Shaw is a professional photojournalist who has worked with many film stars. For this volume he has combined a spare commentary with over 100 photographs he took of Marilyn Monroe. Many have never been published before and most of them receive adequate reproduction here. A short biographical essay and an abbreviated filmography complete the volume.

Shaw's personal appreciation of Monroe via his text and photos is most pleasing.

3547 *Joyce Grenfell Requests The Pleasure.* by Grenfell, Joyce. 295 p. illus. New York: St. Martin's, 1977.

For those who have been exposed to the artistry of Joyce Grenfell, this volume will be most pleasing. Written with the wit, intelligence and style that characterized her work, the text traces her life from childhood to a modest celebrity as a multi-talented entertainer and writer. Although her story is not a dramatic tell-all confession, she does recall her American mother, the celebrities who were part of her life, her drift into show business, wartime service, revues, films, and finally, a one-woman show called "Joyce Grenfell Requests the Pleasure," the source of the book's title. Illustrations and an index accompany this autobiography.

For most people, to have seen Grenfell was to have loved her. Her work in the St. Trinians comedies, in Hitchcock's STAGE FRIGHT (1950) selling "ducks, lovely ducks," or as Julie Andrews' mother in THE AMERICANIZATION OF EMILY (1964) are just a few examples of her talent. She was in the tradition of Beatrice Lillie and Margaret Rutherford, but was also able to bring tears to the eyes of her audience. Her autobiography will be welcomed by her admirers, but the proper appreciation of this great performer is yet to be written.

3548 JUDGMENT AT NUREMBERG. by Kaplan, Mike. 32 p. paper illus. New York: Souvenir Program Co., 1961.

Black and white photography is used exclusively in this souvenir book, probably because of the nature of the 1961 film rather than for economic measures. The portraits of Tracy, Lancaster, Widmark, Dietrich, Schell, Garland and Clift are quite impressive. Writer Abby Mann and director-producer Stanley Kramer are also given attention. The story of the film is told largely by visuals and the supporting cast and production credits are given.

3549 JUDGMENT AT NUREMBERG. by Mann, Abby. 182 p. illus. London: Cassell, 1961.

Script of the 1961 film directed by Stanley Kramer. Contains cast and production credits.

3550 *Judith Crist's TV Guide to the Movies.* by Crist, Judith. 415 p. paper New York: Popular Library, 1974.

If the reader expects a volume similar to the TV movies books by Scheuer and Maltin, he may be surprised and perhaps disappointed in this one. Ms. Crist's selection of 1500 titles apparently is a personal one, since no criteria are noted. The films she has chosen are given mini-reviews ranging in length from a sentence to a full paragraph. As usual she is clear, witty and decisive in her evaluations. As a TV guide the book is limited. Although it contains reviews of many films made for television, it is weak in its scant coverage of older, pre-1960 theatrical films. Choice, too, is questionable. Included are such titles as THE BLACK SCORPION (1957) and ROGUE'S MARCH (1953), but such Academy Award nominees as ALL ABOUT EVE (1950), DECISION BEFORE DAWN (1951), THE QUIET MAN (1952), WITNESS FOR THE PROSECUTION (1957), ALFIE (1966), etc., are not reviewed. The films from the thirties, forties and fifties that make up much of TV film programming are practically absent.

If the book does not serve as a satisfactory guide to movies on TV, it is still a satisfying and refreshing browsing experience. It is rewarding to have Crist recall the films to mind by her usually sound criticism. The book is sure to please many readers. However, the title may be misleading and cause some frustration in the search for evaluations. Recommended.

3551 *Judy: The Films and Career of Judy Garland.* by Morella, Joe; and Epstein, Edward. 217 p. illus. New York: Citadel Press, 1969.

Published before her death in 1969, this volume covers Garland's life up to her last marriage to Mickey Deans. An introduction by Judith Crist, tributes by Arthur Freed, E. Y. Harburg, Gene Kelly, George Murphy, and Joe Pasternak, and a surface biography precede the main section of films. Short chapters on the concerts, television, and the Garland cult conclude the book. An unusual chapter showing her life in headlines also appears.

Each of the films has credits, comments and excerpts from reviews accompanying the stills. The text of the biographical chapter is external and cautious. While the "tributes" are typically dull, Crist's introduction is most worthwhile. The pictures are fine, the text is average or less, and the book should be used with a better biography if one is to understand this legend. Essential for the Garland cult.

3552 *Judy.* by Frank, Gerold. 638 p. illus. New York: Harper and Row, 1975.

Is it possible to know more than you want to about Judy Garland? This massive volume may suggest a positive answer to some readers. Prepared with the cooperation of Garland's ex-husbands, relatives, friends and professional associates, the book presents a very detailed review of a predominantly unhappy life. Those events and incidents that the author was privy to are described in great detail. However, comparisons with *Young Judy, Weep No More My Lady, Judy Garland* and *Rainbow* indicate gaps, omissions, and prejudices in this work. For example, all of the cooperating interviewees emerge as rather positive characters while Garland appears as an anti-heroine; the question of Frank Gumm's homosexuality, which might provide a rationale for the behavior for both Ethel Gumm and her daughter, Judy, is barely mentioned; and Garland's radio and TV appearances are given only passing notice. The copy examined was a prepublication version. Accompanying material indicated that the published edition would be hardbound, illustrated and indexed.

Despite its inflated coverage and its other weaknesses, the book will satisfy Garland's cult and the reader masochistic enough to stay with more than 600 pages of unhappiness. This biography once again proves that "more is often less." Suitable for adults.

3553 *Judy: A Remembrance.* by Melton, David. illus. Hollywood: Stanyan Books, 1972.

In many ways, this small novelty book about Judy Garland is more satisfying than some of the full-blown biographies. Using original drawings based on Garland stills and portraits, the author has provided a two-track narrative. On page tops there is a poetic tribute, while biographical facts appear at the page bottom. All elements combine in a fitting emotional remembrance—the author's stated purpose. A most pleasant tribute that will please many readers.

3554 *Judy Garland.* by Steiger, Brad. 190 p. paper illus. New York: Ace, 1969.

With some reservations, this paperback by Brad Steiger is not bad at all. Starting with a biography that is nonromanticized and factual in the telling, this small volume includes a filmography with excerpts from reviews added. These review quotes are nearly the same as those in *Judy*, by Morella and Epstein.

An extended horoscope, Garland's portrait via numerology, a handwriting analysis and a biorhythm chart are also offered to those readers interested in that sort of thing. A section of illustrations is quite good. Some of the fragmented text is repetitious and engenders suspicion that the volume was produced hurriedly after Garland's death. With the elimination of the occult material and a bit more care in the text, a really fine biography might have resulted.

3555 *Judy Garland.* by Edwards, Anne. 349 p. illus. New York: Simon & Schuster, 1974.

When several biographies appear on the same personality within a year, comparisons are necessary, since only the most dedicated admirer will wade through them all. Published almost concurrently are *Weep No More My Lady, Judy, Young Judy, Little Girl Lost,* and *Rainbow.* In Edwards' account, Garland is a victim—used by her mother, the studio, Louis B. Mayer, her husbands and others. While this makes for dramatic interest and audience sympathy-identification, it is in direct contradiction of others who knew her in either a professional or private capacity. One example is Mel Torme, whose book, *The Other Side of the Rainbow,* presents a completely different view of Garland. There are too many others to disregard if we are to accept the one-sided version furnished by Edwards.

The appendixes provide strong support to the otherwise suspect biography. Original poems, a videography, and selected radio, concert and vaudeville appearances are offered. Some fine illustrations are clustered together in a center section. The book is indexed. The approach taken by the author was probably determined by her sources. Since Garland was often irresponsible, careless and even dishonest in many of the statements she made to the press and during interviews, the use of such source material must be balanced with more objective research. This version of Garland's life resembles prejudiced autobiography rather than responsible biography. Acceptable.

3556 *Judy Garland.* by Juneau, James. 157 p. paper illus. New York: Pyramid, 1974.

Combining both biography and a critical review of her films, this fine tribute manages to give some rationale for Garland's status as a legend. The incidents in her private life are stated rather factually without comment or interpretation, e.g., "She was married twice in the sixties.... In 1965 she and her daughter Liza did a concert together at the London Palladium." Treatment of her films is much more detailed and critical, e.g., regarding ZIEGFELD FOLLIES (1946), "It is one of the few times Garland has had to perform material so blatantly unsuitable to her.... Garland's interpretation is more suggestive of Bette Davis putting on airs.... Garland and her feather boa make a fine fluttery entrance but the rest of it is labored clumsy satire."

All her films are evaluated but major attention is paid to THE WIZARD OF OZ (1939) and A STAR IS BORN (1955). A bibliography, filmography and index complete the volume. Illustrations are plentiful and reproduced with care. Mostly stills and portraits are used, but some candids are included. The book furnishes an excellent review of Garland's career and there is sufficient background information offered to give the reader some insight into the personal problems of this legendary entertainer. Recommended.

3557 *The Judy Garland Souvenir Songbook.* compiled by Harnne, Howard; and Rickman, Charles. 298 p. illus. New York: Chappell Music Co.-Barnes & Noble, 1976.

This music collection of 68 songs identified with Judy Garland is noted here since it contains 80 illustrations (stills, posters, candids), a filmography and a discography.

3558 *Judy, With Love.* by Smith, Lorna. 208 p. illus. London: Hale, 1975.

This biography of Judy Garand, subtitled "The Story of Miss Show Business," includes text, illustrations, a filmography, and an index.

3559 *Jule: The Story of Composer Jule Styne.* by Taylor, Theodore. 293 p. illus. New York: Random House, 1979.

Since this volume contains many direct quotes of its subject, Jule Styne, and the copyright belongs to Styne, it may have been a commissioned biography. Its hero emerges as a super-professional from whom music has flowed copiously for over 60 years. He has been associated with top performers and classic stage musicals, and throughout his career, he has played, composed, coached and conducted music. As a person, apparently his only major flaw was an addiction to gambling. In brief fashion, his associations with Sammy Cahn, Frank Sinatra, Comden and Green, Stephen Sondheim, Ethel Merman and many others are noted. Most of the story is told in a "and-then-I-wrote" framework. Since his output (1400 songs) has been so large and so successful for so many years, the reader will be familiar with the films, shows and songs mentioned. The section about his Hollywood activities is particularly well written.

Some errors in the text indicate weak research/editing. For example: it was Bob Crosby, not Bing, in SIS HOPKINS (1941); THE GRAPES OF WRATH (1940) was not a mid-thirties production; it was Kay Kyser, not Kaiser; STEP LIVELY (1944) was based on the play, "Room Service," and the script cannot be called "a screen story of no importance"; the Styne stage musical was "Walking Happy," a film released in 1973 was called WALKING TALL.

A few carefully selected illustrations and an index are included. Unfortunately, there is no career chronology or listing of his music, an omission which, along with the careless editing, weakens the story of a living legend.

3560 JULES AND JIM. by Truffaut, Francois; and Gruault, Jean. 100 p. paper illus. New York: Simon & Schuster, 1968.

Script of the 1962 film directed by Truffaut.

3561 *Julie: The Life and Times of John Garfield.* by Wolfe, Bernard; and Medard, Edward. illus. Los Angeles: Wollstonecraft, 1976.

The rise of John Garfield from a tough Bronx kid to a Hollywood star is retold in this biography. His fall from grace via the HUAC hearings during the McCarthy era is discussed, as are some of the questionable circumstances surrounding his death.

3562 *Julie Andrews: A Biography.* by Windeler, Robert. 253 p. illus. New York: Putnam, 1970.

An affectionate rather than an objective biography. The story covers the early years very quickly and, fortunately, emphasizes the Broadway and Hollywood periods. Whether the reader will finish with a strong impression of what Miss Andrews "is really like" is doubtful, for the personal side is largely omitted in favor of the professional, public image. The stills used are excellent. Light, non-controversial reading for the Julie Andrews fan.

3563 *Julie Andrews: The Unauthorized Life Story of a Super-Star.* by Cottrell, John. 212 p. paper New York: Dell, 1968.

This inexpensive book covers the same material (early life and successes and late triumphs on Broadway and in films) that the Windeler biography does. Only the external personality of the subject emerges.

Some critical analysis of her talent and her performances is made.

3564 *Julien Bryan and His Documentary Motion Pictures.* by Bryan, Julien. paper illus. New York: International Film Foundation, 1950.

A short essay by and about the famed documentary filmmaker, produced and published by Bryan's distributor.

3565 JULIET OF THE SPIRITS. by Fellini, Federico; and Pinelli, Tullio; and Rondi, Brunello. 118 p. paper illus. New York: Ballantine Books, 1966.

Two scripts of the 1965 film directed by Fellini. Contains cast credits, an introduction by Tullio Kezich and "The Long Interview" by Federico Fellini and Tullio Kezich.

3566 JULIUS CAESAR. 24 p. paper illus. New York: Al Greenstone Co., 1953.

After the players, director, and producer are introduced in this souvenir book, the task of filming Shakespeare's play is discussed. Many stills from the 1953 picture and quotations from the play are used throughout. For the uninitiated, a synopsis is also provided.

3567 *Jungle Tales of the Cinema.* by Behlmer, Rudy. 37 p. paper illus. Hollywood: publisher not given, 1960.

A quick survey of jungle films (Tarzan, King Kong, Simba, etc.).

3568 *Just Me.* by White, Pearl. 179 p. illus. New York: George H. Doran, 1919.

Describes her early life and her rise to film popularity in THE PERILS OF PAULINE (1914). Does not cover the later years as does *Pearl White, The Peerless Fearless Girl,* which also has many illustrations. Only one portrait is provided here by Ms. White.

3569 *The Kaleidoscopic Lens: How Hollywood Views Ethnic Groups.* edited by Miller, Randall M. 222 p. illus. Englewood, N.J.: Ozer, 1981.

A collection of essays dealing with the way Hollywood has shown nine ethnic groups.

3570 *Karel Reisz.* by Gaston, George. 166 p. illus. Boston: Twayne, 1980.

Karel Reisz's number of feature films is only six—and they are each given a separate chapter of analysis in this title from the *Twayne Theatrical Arts* series. After an introduction which describes his first short films, the text treats SATURDAY NIGHT AND SUNDAY MORNING (1960), NIGHT MUST FALL (1964), MORGAN! (1966), ISADORA (1968), THE GAMBLER (1974) and WHO'LL STOP THE RAIN (1978) in detail. A concluding chapter along with illustrations, a chronology, notes, references, a bibliography, a filmography and index complete the book.

This well-written appreciation/study of a slow-working director will bring attention to his underrated group of films. The analyses provided by Gaston are well researched, written with clarity, and are stimulating to read.

3571 *Karloff.* by Barbour, Alan; and Marill, Alvin; and Parish, James Robert. 64 p. paper illus. Kew Gardens, N.Y.: Cinefax, 1969.

The film career of Boris Karloff told in stills and publicity shots is the substance of this volume. A short biographical introduction and a list of his films frame the illustrations. The pictures are not intended to be comprehensive, and some of his films, mostly silents, do not have pictures to represent them. An entertaining book.

3572 *Karloff.* by Underwood, Peter. 238 p. illus. New York: Drake Publishers, 1972.

It is difficult to believe that a man who created so much excitement for so many audiences in several media should be the victim of such a dull, uninspired biography. The reason may be that only a few major sources—two previously published interviews and one actual meeting with Karloff—are relied upon heavily. Other snippets of interviews, newspaper and magazine comments are used so frequently as to create an impression of padding. Another indication of stretching is the inclusion of several pages devoted exclusively to Lon Chaney. The narrative section of the book, then, is a recital of factual information dressed up to resemble a biography written with the complete cooperation of the subject.

The other sections of the book are more valuable since they are straightforward reference—a bibliography, a discography, and an annotated filmography. A detailed index and a gallery of photographs are also assets. In summary, the book is a mixed bag of the good, bad and indifferent. It may do as a temporary source, enriched by its reference sections, but readers are advised to look at Gifford (*Karloff, the Man, the Monster, the Movies*) and Ackerman (*The Frankenscience Monster*).

3573 *Karloff and Company: The Horror Film.* by Moss, Robert F. 158 p. paper illus. New York: Pyramid, 1974.

The horror film holds a continuing fascination for readers and audiences. After so many books on the genre it is difficult to conceive a new approach. That predicament can be discerned in the title to the present work, which suggests a survey of both Karloff's films and horror films in general. Unfortunately the final choice and arrangement of material is not totally satisfying.

A chronological scheme introduces some silent horror film classics—THE CABINET OF DR. CALIGARI (1919), THE GOLEM (1920), NOSFERATU (1922) and others. Karloff as the Frankenstein monster appeared in 1931 and the volume departs here for two chapters to examine his career up to TARGETS (1968). Karloff made over 150 films but only a sampling is examined here. The text returns to DRACULA (1931) and employs a type-of-monster approach, i.e., vampires, devils, demons, crazy ladies, ghosts, and finally Gothic horrors. Vincent Price is predominant in this latter section. Two full-page shots of Karloff conclude the narrative portion. A selected filmography, a short bibliography and an index complete the work.

Stills from horror films are always fascinating and those contained here are no exception. In most cases they are clearly reproduced. This entertaining volume is weakened somewhat by an attempt to cover two separate large subjects. Nevertheless, its appeal to a wide audience is undeniable. Acceptable.

3574 *Karloff, The Man, The Monster, The Movies.* by Gifford, Denis. 352 p. paper illus. New York: Curtis Books, 1973.

Everything you've ever wanted to know about Boris Karloff is probably contained in this volume. Starting with a factual biography that is liberally sprinkled with quotes from previously published articles and interviews, the book's major section examines the Karloff films. He started his screen career as an extra in Fairbank's HIS MAJESTY THE AMERICAN in 1919 and was still active in HOUSE OF EVIL, a film made for a Mexican company in 1968. For most of the films, extended cast and production credits are given, along with a detailed synopsis and some critical comment. Occasionally an excerpt from a review is included. Closing pages list his recordings, his

writings, and a list of unfilmed productions that were announced as "vehicles" for him. A small pictorial section suggests that, from the large number of films made by Karloff, a very fine pictorial account could be created. One did appear in the sixties but it was only 64 pages in length: *Karloff*, by Barbour et al. The task of indexing this volume would have been enormous but it would have added greatly to the reference value.

There is little comparison between this excellent book, which appears in a modest production, and the more elaborate Underwood biography (*Karloff*). This one wins on nearly all criteria except size, visuals, and paper quality. Highly recommended.

3575 *Kate: The Life of Katharine Hepburn.* by Higham, Charles. 244 p. illus. New York: W. W. Norton, 1975.

A biography written with the cooperation of the subject usually results in a rewarding, full portrait. This account of one of the most famous and durable actresses of this century is no exception. Within the bounds of good taste and privacy, the "Kate" described by Higham appears to be quite faithful to the original. The author has based his detailed text not only on interviews with Hepburn but with many of her friends and professional associates as well. Of course the interviews were used in addition to the usual reference sources of information—books, articles, reviews, newspaper items, etc. There are a few unimpressive photographs gathered in a center section, and the volume is indexed. The lack of a bibliography is puzzling.

The strength of the book comes from the entertaining recollections of Hepburn's personal and professional acquaintances, which are nicely integrated into the well-researched chronological narrative. Each person saw Hepburn with different eyes, yet there is a certain agreement about her strength, determination, talent and individuality. At the conclusion, readers will feel they have met an exceptional female who has been true to herself, while becoming a legend on stage, in films, and on television. Recommended.

3576 *Katharine Hepburn.* by Marill, Alvin H. 160 p. paper illus. New York: Pyramid, 1973.

Since there are only about three previous books on Hepburn, this volume in *The Pyramid Illustrated History of the Movies* series is most welcome. Although some of the illustrations are not reproduced as well as those in other series volumes, remaining aspects are of equal quality.

Probably because of the nonexistence of a full-length biography, no opening overview of the star's personal-professional life is given here. Instead the book is divided into four major divisions: the stage years, the RKO years, the MGM years, and the independent years—into which the biographical elements and the films are interwoven. Throughout her long career, Hepburn has returned often to the stage, and her appearances in that medium are noted also. A filmography, a bibliography, a list of radio appearances, and an index complete the book.

As indicated, the book's strength is its review of the Hepburn films and the notation of her appearances on stage and radio. The missing ingredient is the personal-biographical one. The quality, content, and reference material in this volume are most impressive.A recommended book.

3577 *Katharine Hepburn.* by Carey, Gary. 238 p. paper illus. New York: Pocket Books, 1975.

Although this unofficial biography offers little that is new in either fact or appreciation, it does provide as much insight into its subject as the approved biography written by Charles Higham. Since Hepburn is labeled an elusive, enigmatic, private individual, any attempt at analyzing her must rely on public records, interview quotations from others, and critical comments. Carey has employed these sources with intelligence and added a rapid reportorial style. The result is a descriptive study of a legendary film actress that emphasizes her career rather than her personal life.

A few illustrations appear in the book's center. No index or filmography is provided, which is a serious omission in any modern film biography. The volume does provide a serviceable portrait of Hepburn and will please most readers. Acceptable.

3578 *Katharine Hepburn—In the Spotlight.* edited by Galley Press. 160 p. illus. New York: Galley/Mayflower, 1980.

Two major sections make up this appreciation of Katharine Hepburn—a long biographical essay and a collection of illustrations.

3579 *Kazan on Kazan.* by Ciment, Michel. 199 p. illus. New York: Viking, 1974.

Most of the material used in this extended interview was taped in 1971. The long and varied Kazan career in motion pictures, the theatre, and radio is noted, with the emphasis lying on his film work. Each of

his films is discussed, with the author providing adequate springboard questions. Kazan is at no loss for words or recollections and he is unusually frank in his evaluation of himself and others. Mistakes, poor judgment, and simple ignorance on his part are noted along with justifiable pride about some things in his films. His comments are surprisingly candid: Bankhead: "a monster, an ossified professional" ; James Dean, " a cocker "; Jeanne Crain: "the blandest person I ever worked with" ; John Garfield: "I really loved him" ; Spencer Tracy: "plump, lazy, inert, Irish, sly" ; Katharine Hepburn: "if the eggs are cold, she cries."

Blending the observations and experiences of an artist like Kazan with a well-prepared interviewer, some fine photographs, and a good bio-filmography has resulted in an excellent volume. Highly recommended.

3580 *Keaton.* by Blesh, Rudi. 395 p. illus. New York: Macmillan, 1966.

A beautiful volume that combines biography, analysis, and evaluation, this book appeared around the time of Keaton's death and is an appropriate tribute to him. It covers the same ground as the 1960 autobiography, but the emphasis here is on the films. Most of them are described in detail and it is sad to note how few have been shown lately. Included is a welcome listing of all the Keaton films with partial credits given in most cases. The author's style, the illustrations, the production of the book and the obvious care that went into its creation make this book an essential for all readers.

3581 *Keaton: The Man Who Wouldn't Lie Down.* by Dardis, Tom. 340 p. illus. New York: Charles Scribner's, 1979.

To write about a comedian whose life has already been covered in an autobiography, *My Wonderful World of Slapstick*, and several biography/appreciations (written by such authors as Rudi Blesh, Jean-Patrick Lebel, Donald W. McCaffrey, and David Robinson), a person should have something new to say or add to the existing literature. Happily, in addition to the cooperation of Keaton's wife, sister, and friends, Tom Dardis has had access to certain materials (taped interviews, business files) that were not used by earlier writers. The result justifies this latest Keaton biography.

The author is sympathetic, understanding, and ultimately forgiving in his recital of the events in Keaton's colorful life. Of unusual interest is Dardis' account of Keaton's early life as the child star of a vaudeville act, "The Three Keatons." In addition, the comedian's alcoholism, womanizing, and general irresponsible behavior are discussed fully. The text is detailed with a carefully researched historical subplot about the motion picture industry underlining the main Keaton story. Other personalities who receive attention include Fatty Arbuckle, the Talmadge sisters, Chaplin, the Keaton family, and Joseph Schenck. Many of Keaton's films are described and analyzed critically.

Supporting the warm, admiring portrait are notes, a bibliography, a filmography, some fine illustrations, and an index. This volume should help to bring about the long delayed reevaluation of Keaton as one of this century's major artists. Recommended.

3582 *Keaton: The Silent Features Close Up.* by Moews, Daniel. 337 p. paper Berkeley, Calif.: University of California Press, 1977.

Daniel Moews accomplishes many things in this volume dealing with nine silent Buster Keaton films. He recalls and reconstructs each film, explaining why they are comedy classics, how they reflect their times, and how they lend themselves to different forms of analysis. In addition to biographical information on Keaton, the enormous personal contribution made to the films by him is noted. A final section offers lengthy bibliographical and filmographical comments which help to make this volume required reading for anyone studying Keaton. The book is indexed and the nine films examined are OUR HOSPITALITY (1923), SHERLOCK JUNIOR (1924), THE NAVIGATOR (1924), SEVEN CHANCES (1925), GO WEST (1925), BATTLING BUTLER (1926), THE GENERAL (1927), COLLEGE (1927) and STEAMBOAT BILL, JR. (1928).

3583 *Keeping Score: Film Music 1972-1979.* by Limbacher, James. 519 p. Metuchen, N.J.: Scarecrow, 1981.

A follow-up to his earlier *Film Music*, this volume by James Limbacher concentrates on the period from 1973 to 1979. It includes some earlier music, a discography, a bibliography, in addition to the basic material on film music and composers.

3584 *Kemps Film and Television Yearbook.* edited by Goodliffe, F. J. 1029 p. paper illus. London: Kemps Group, 1979.

This British yearbook has grown in size from 369 pages in its first edition to over a thousand pages in this one. Divided into two parts, the British and the International Industry, it offers information on a wide range of services and persons. Included are

agents, aviation, broadcasting, car hire, editing, engineers, equipment, facilities, labs, libraries, location, music, production companies, properties, radio, services, sound, special effects, studios, technicians, and television.

As indicated above, the first section deals with Britain while the second part covers 30 countries from Australia to the United States. Advertisements appear throughout the book and there are several indexes to the contents.

3585 *Ken Russell.* edited by Atkins, Thomas R. 132 p. paper illus. New York: Monarch, 1976.

This anthology consists of five essays entitled: Introduction, The Early Films, The Television Films, Three Masterpieces of Sexuality—WOMEN IN LOVE (1969), THE MUSIC LOVERS (1970), and THE DEVILS (1971)—and Methods of Adaptation. Script excerpts from MAHLER (1974) and TOMMY (1975) along with a short biographical sketch, a filmography, and a selected bibliography complete the volume.

Although the anthology form may lack the unified approach of a critical study by one author, this volume does present a most satisfying overview of Ken Russell's films. The excellent selection of clearly reproduced stills further enriches the reader's experience. Recommended.

3586 *Ken Russell: A Director in Search of a Hero.* by Wilson, Colin. 71 p. illus. London: Intergroup Publishing, 1974.

A short biography and appreciation of Ken Russell based on a BBC interview. Wilson's comments are often unique.

3587 *Ken Russell: A Guide to References and Resources.* by Rosenfeldt, Diane. 140 p. Boston: G.K. Hall, 1978.

The elements in this resource book about Ken Russell include a short biography, a critical evaluation, a filmography with full credits and detailed synopses, a long annotated bibliography (1964 to 1977), a section on other film activities and writings, three archival sources, a film distributor list, and an author index. The production of the book is modest but the material is clearly presented. Certainly anyone interested in locating information about Russell would do well to start here with this well-prepared reference book.

3588 *Ken Russell: The Adaptor As Creator.* by Gomez, Joseph A. 223 p. illus. London: Frederick Muller, 1976.

An examination of Russell's films from his early amateur attempts—PEEPSHOW (1956), AMELIA AND THE ANGELS (1957), LOURDES (1958)—to LISZTOMANIA (1975) is offered by Gomez. The major features each receive a separate chapter of comment and analysis. Concluding the volume are a filmography and a bibliogrpahy. The volume is not indexed. Some excellent illustrations accompany the thoughtful text.

Russell's films are not readily assimilated by critics and audiences; the same may be true of this appreciation. Admirers of Russell will find the book to be a confirmation. Scoffers will not be converted.

3589 *Kenji Mizoguchi.* by Morris, Peter. 48 p. paper illus. Ottawa: Canadian Film Institute, 1967.

One of the first appreciations of the Japanese director to appear in English. This booklet consists of two articles and some comments by Mizoguchi.

3590 *The Keystone Movie Guide.* by Tydings, Kenneth S. 128 p. paper illus. New York: Greenberg, 1954.

A title in the *Modern Camera Guide* series, this volume deals with cameras and cinematography.

3591 KHARTOUM. 32 p. paper illus. New York: Alsid Distributors, 1966.

Many of the pictures in this unusual souvenir book extend over two pages, across the width of the book. A comparison is made between the typical studio portrait and the actor made-up for his role in this film. Attention is also given to research, costume design, action sequences, and the encampments used in the film. The usual cast and technical credits are noted. The book is as pleasantly surprising as was the 1966 film.

3592 *Kilgallen.* by Israel, Lee. paper illus. New York: Dell, 1980.

Although Dorothy Kilgallen was known primarily as a radio-television personality, she rose to prominence as a Broadway gossip columnist. Lee Israel relates her story in this sensationalized, snappy biography. Many Hollywood names appear throughout the well-researched text. Columnist Kilgallen would probably have been envious of Israel's reportorial skill.

3593 *Kim Novak: Goddess of Love.* by Fritch, Charles E. paper illus. Derby, Conn: Monarch.

3594 *Kim Novak On Camera.* by Kleno, Larry. 320 p. illus New York: A. S.Barnes, 1980.

What a pleasant surprise this volume is! Combining the qualities of *The Cinema of...* series with a biographical portrait, the text offers so much more than just a recall of Kim Novak's films. Not only are there many illustrations, script excerpts, and backstage anecdotes, but the book also contains an abundance of tributes from Novak's coworkers. That she was capable of fine acting is documented by the author several times. It is true that most of her performances have stood up well over the years and her filmography is an impressive one. The author displays a talent for letting the reader sense the kind of person Novak is: "She has survived by knowing when to turn it off... a person who remains true to herself."

This is a rich, detailed appreciation of an actress whose reputation and legend have grown over the years—a Hollywood Cinderella story with a happy ending. Recommended.

3595 *The Kindergarten of the Movies: A History of The Fine Arts Company.* by Slide, Anthony. 236 p. illus. Metuchen, N.J.: Scarecrow, 1980.

The Fine Arts Company, headed by D. W. Griffith, existed from 1915 to 1917, and in that short period introduced Douglas Fairbanks and Erich von Stroheim to film audiences. Several feature films were produced with celebrated names such as De Wolf Hopper, Sir Herbert Beerbohm Tree, Lillian Gish, Norma Talmadge, and Mae Marsh. A year-by-year account of the studio's activities is given by historian Anthony Slide, along with full chapters on Griffith, Hopper, Fairbanks and Tree. Almost half of the book is devoted to appendixes: a Fine Arts Who's Who, a complete filmography, MACBETH (1916) credits, and selected commentary on INTOLERANCE (1916). A bibliography and an index complete the study.

Slide's admirable work in providing order, accuracy, and understanding to film history is continued here. His in-depth description of a film company and the period in which it functioned adds another dimension to his nine previously published books.

3596 *Kindly Leave the Stage.* by More, Kenneth. 128 p. illus. London: Michael Joseph, 1965.

Kenneth More, a British star of stage and screen, describes the pleasures and pitfalls of being a celebrity.

3597 *The Kindness of Strangers.* by Viertel, Salka. 338 p. New York: Holt, Rinehart & Winston, 1969.

Most of this autobiography is devoted to an unusual life in Hollywood. The author arrived there in 1929 and had a close acquaintance with not only the artists, musicians and writers but also the studios in which they labored. She worked on all of Garbo's films, and came to know not only Garbo but Brecht, Zinnemann, Thalberg, Lubitsch, etc. The book concludes with her involvement with the Hollywood Ten and the hearings in the early fifties. Intelligent, emotional, warm and quite middle-European in style.

3598 *Kinematograph Studio Technique.* by Macbean, L. C. III p. illus. London: Pitman, 1922.

This is "a practical outline of the artistic and technical work in the production of film plays, for producers, camera-men, artistes, and others engaged in or desirous of entering the kinematograph industry." Topics include production, types of studios, methods of production, the scenario, art direction, locations, lenses, camera, cinematography, and lighting.

3599 *Kinetic Art: Theory and Practice.* edited by Malina, Frank J. 244 p. paper illus. New York: Dover, 1974.

This anthology of 44 articles taken from the quarterly journal, *Leonardo*, also includes an introduction, a glossary and an index. The editor defines kinetic art to include "visual experiences provided by slide projection, cinema, and television techniques." Suggestions for the incorporation of new techniques into films appear throughout. Examples of article titles are "Animation of Color for Cinema Film," "Images of Trajectories of Mobiles by Means of Photographs" and "Cinema: Metaforms." The volume is not for the casual reader, but rather for the inquisitive film avant-gardist.

3600 *The Kinetoscope.* by Hendricks, Gordon. 182 p. illus. New York: Beginnings of the American Film, 1966.

This is historian-researcher Hendrick's impressive account of America's first commercially successful motion picture exhibitor. This work, the third of series that he is writing "to set history straight," is characterized by rare illustrations, painstaking research, and the scholar's approach of using primary sources. (His comments about microfilm are quite negative.) Starting with the Black Maria and the first motion pictures, he discusses the Columbian Exhibition, the Broadway showings, and the kinetoscope parlors which followed. Other devices similar to the kinetoscope are mentioned. The appendix is devoted to biographies of William Kennedy, Laurie Dickson and the Lathams. An impressive, scholarly research.

3601 *The King: A Biography of Clark Gable.* by Samuels, Charles. 262 p. paper New York: Popular Library, 1963.

On the third page of this biography the following appears: "Yet Gable was no saint, no matter what people heard. He was tight with money, quite rough on many of the women who loved him, and seldom, if ever, let anyone, man or woman, get really close to him" and on the fourth page: "He was a gentleman; a breed not often found in any branch of the theatrical world. It never seemed to occur to him to exploit the men and women who worshipped him. He was not too good with words nor too bright. But his ability to use everything he had in his work showed the gift for utter concentration...." These two samples indicate the tone of this biography. They probably tell more than the other Gable biographies do en toto. The entire book has the quality of candor. This is a fascinating, well-written biography that gives a full portrait of a subject seemingly difficult for other writers to capture.

3602 *King Cohn: The Life and Times of Harry Cohn.* by Thomas, Bob. 344 p. illus. New York: G. P. Putnam's, 1967.

Frank, revealing, accurate, brilliant, powerful—all these adjectives and many more describe this eminently readable biography of mogul Cohn. As head of Columbia Pictures, he was responsible for classic films and classic hatreds. Although the author tries to present an objective portrait, he is at his best in recounting Cohn's clashes with his underlings—stars, directors, and others. The volume is an amazing collection of legend, lore, and anecdotes, and has become a minor classic in film biography. There are some good illustrations and an index in the hardbound edition which are eliminated from the Bantam paperback. A superior book.

3603 *The King is Dead: Elvis Presley.* by Grove, Martin A. 252 p. paper illus. New York: Manor House, 1977.

This original paperback is a potpourri of Presley material that includes biographical information, critical comment, quotes, a few photos, an interview with radio programming executive Rick Sklar, a discography, a detailed filmography, and conjecture about Elvis' last years. The author is the editor of *T.V. Stars Today* and has written biographies of Henry Winkler, John Travolta, and Donny and Marie. His book is addressed to the nondiscriminating fan who prefers a surface review of the familiar Presley legend.

3604 *King Kong.* by Thorne, Ian. 47 p. illus. Mankato, Minn.: Crestwood House, 1977.

A review of King Kong movies written for young readers.

3605 *The* KING KONG *Story.* by Pascall, Jeremy. 64 p. illus. Secaucus, N.J.: Chartwell, 1977.

A review of KING KONG (1933) including its plot, making and sequels constitutes the greater portion of this book. A final chapter is devoted to the dismal remake of KING KONG in 1977. Using text, stills and posters, the author provides a pleasant summary designed for young, nondiscriminating readers.

3606 KING LEAR: The Space of Tragedy. by Kozintsev, Grigori. 260 p.illus. Berkeley, Calif.: University of California Press, 1977.

Subtitled "The Diary of a Film Director," this volume tells of filming Shakespeare's play, "King Lear," from 1968 to 1972. Director Kozintsev offers thoughts on Shakespeare's characters, memoirs of early days in Russian filmmaking, and an account of the actual production of the film.

What distinguishes the diary is the richness of thought and imagination the director brought to his project. Although his mind darts from topic to topic, everything seems essential to the creative process. The reader is privy to a mind at work. A few illustrations and an index accompany this remarkable work.

3607 *King of Comedy—Mack Sennett.* by Sennett, Mack; and Shipp, Cameron. 284 p. illus. London: Peter Davies, 1965.

The life of Mack Sennett is much more factually detailed here than in the incomplete 1934 biography, *Father Goose.* In addition there is the philosophy, comment, and opinion typical of a man in the twilight of his life. According to the appendix, the book is based on interviews with Sennett and his associates, and on other references. It may be assumed that Shipp's contribution to the final product was very great.

A distinct disappointment is the pictorial section. Photographs have been overly reduced—sometimes there are three on a page. It is stated that Sennett donated nearly 150,000 pictures to the Motion Picture Academy; the selection in this book is certainly a poor sample. The value of this volume lies in retelling the facts and events of a master filmmaker.

3608 KING OF KINGS. 32 p. illus. 1961.

The usual format is followed in this souvenir book. Beginning with a prologue, the book offers the cast and the production in words and photographs. Closing sections are devoted to remaining cast and production credits. It should be emphasized that this is the book for the 1961 production which starred Jeffrey Hunter. A souvenir book was also produced for the 1927 silent version which starred H. B. Warner.

3609 *King Twist: A Portrait of Frank Randle.* by Nuttall, Jeff. 139 p. illus. London: Routledge and Kegan Paul, 1978.

Frank Randle was a British music hall comedian who made a series of low-budget film comedies in the forties.

3610 *King Vidor.* by Baxter, John. 94 p. paper illus. New York: Monarch, 1976.

This appreciation and review of King Vidor's films has two outstanding qualities—a concise yet satisfying text and a collection of clearly reproduced stills. Baxter's criticism is subjective and often at odds with majority opinion, but it is usually stated with rationale. A filmography and a bibliography complete the book.

A reminder of the quality and number of memorable Vidor films, this volume also summarizes the themes and motivations found in them. Baxter's skill in considering both the elements of a career and its totality make this a superior study. Highly recommended.

3611 *King Vidor on Film Making.* by Vidor, King. 239 p. illus. New York: David McKay Co., 1972.

Combining approximately equal parts of autobiography, common sense, and how-its-done advice, Vidor has written a second successful book. (See *A Tree is a Tree.*) His linking theme, film direction, is also his major topic. All of the elements he believes to be part of that creative process—acting, lighting, editing, special effects, etc.—are described in the context of his own experience and observation. Probably the most unusual aspect of his discussion is the appreciation and faith he has about 16mm filmmaking. He sees much similarity in its use today to the methods employed in the early silent days when creative improvisation by directors was usual and necessary.

Vidor's style is both informal and informative. Although the book is crammed with famous names, the author is never anything but gentlemanly in their treatment. Illustrations are reproduced acceptably, but poorly selected. They should have complemented the text to a much greater degree. An index is provided.

3612 *Kings of the B's.* edited by McCarthy, Todd; and Flynn, Charles. 561 p. paper illus. New York: Dutton, 1975.

This anthology of film history and criticism, which has as its subtitle "Working Within the Hollywood System," is a survey of "B" movies and their makers. After the introductory section on "Approaches," the text is made up of four units: people, films, interviews, and filmographies.

Using essays, articles, appreciations, reviews, and interviews, the book examines those filmmakers who aspired to commercial success rather than critical-artistic recognition. A historical chart, illustrations, filmographies for 325 directors, and an index support the main text.

Author representation is impressive, with names like Sarris, Farber, and Bogdanovich among the contributors. Subjects for the interviews include Samuel Z. Arkoff, Steve Broidy, William Castle, Roger Corman, Joseph Kane, Phil Carson, Herschell Gordon Lewis, Arthur Lubin, Edgar G. Ulmer, and Albert Zugsmith. The topic chosen for the book does not lend itself to an easy treatment. However McCarthy and Flynn have provided a rich, detailed presentation that satisfies the demands of the subject. Their written contributions, along with the intelligent selection and arrangement of the other materials, are consistently impressive. The book will delight the film buff, inform the novice, and entertain the general reader. Recommended.

3613 *Kings of Tragedy.* by Wayne, Jane Ellen. 246 p. paper illus. New York: Manor House, 1976.

The subjects in this collective biography are, with the single exception of Aly Kahn, all deceased male film stars: John Barrymore, Fatty Arbuckle, Errol Flynn, Rudolph Valentino, Spencer Tracy, Clark Gable, John Garfield and John Gilbert. For each there is a separate chapter of text and a portrait. No index is provided.

The coverage for each is a superficial review of the well-known events and people who made up the lives of these famous men. Although all were blessed with luck, none apparently had the intelligence or courage to handle celebrity successfully. Much more could have been of the tragic elements that were common to their lives; instead, the author settles for a set of quickly prepared summaries.

Although the cover page claims the book was "brilliantly researched," there are basic errors throughout, such as calling Leatrice Joy "Beatrice" constantly or claiming Valentino was cast opposite Natacha Rambova in CAMILLE (1921) when she was the set designer for that film.

3614 *Kino: A History of the Russian and Soviet Film.* by Leyda, Jay. 525 p. illus. London: Allen and Unwin, 1960.

This massive history of the Russian-Soviet film indicates scholarship, devotion and hard work on the part of the author. The result justifies this commendable effort. This history is divided into 17 "periods" extending from 1896 to 1947. A short postscript chapter covers the 1948-1958 decade. In the appendices there are a few articles, a bibliography, and a filmography. It is this last section which is quite impressive, listing selected films with credits from 1907 to 1958. Thirty-two pages of photographs and an index are included. Since we see so few of the Russian films, this book would seem to be primarily of academic interest.

3615 *Kirk Douglas.* by McBride, Joseph. 160 p. paper illus. New York: Pyramid, 1976.

Joseph McBride has accomplished an enormous task in this volume, a title in *The Illustrated History of the Movies* series. He has taken an underrated, hard-to-like screen personality and given his subject depth, perception and fair critical judgment. The solid appreciation which opens the volume gives some indication of the quality which is to follow. Using the resources of a dedicated writer, McBride has covered Douglas' career from THE STRANGE LOVE OF MARTHA IVERS (1946) to ONCE IS NOT ENOUGH (1975). Douglas, still quite active in films, has made several films since this latter one.

The volume has many fine illustrations which not only define the Douglas screen image but also visually describe the films that he has made. A bibliography, a filmography and an index complete the book.

A noncompromising actor capable of arousing a variety of strong emotions in his audiences is given a superb review here. Recommended.

3616   *Kiss Hollywood Goodbye.* by Loos, Anita. 216 p. paper illus. New York: Ballantine Books, 1975.

In 1975 Anita Loos was a spry octogenarian who appeared at publisher's parties, retrospective film showings, Broadway revivals, etc. Known primarily as the author of *Gentlemen Prefer Blondes*, she enjoyed a long Hollywood career as a scriptwriter. Her early days with D. W. Griffith and Douglas Fairbanks were covered in her first autobiography, *A Girl Like I*. She continues her story here in a nonlinear narrative that covers the late twenties to the early forties. Responsible for the screenplays of GENTLEMEN PREFER BLONDES (1928), RED HEADED WOMAN (1932), SAN FRANCISCO (1936), THE WOMEN (1939) and other films, Miss Loos worked with many famous personalities. Her portraits of them and of herself make this autobiography one of the most rewarding memoirs about the golden age of Hollywood to appear yet. Although the author is often overly subjective in discussing her acquaintances, lovers and friends, she views herself quite objectively and with a delightful sense of humor. A center section of photographs helps to identify many of her characters, and a list of her screenplays is added. The book is not indexed. Recommended.

3617   *Kiss Kiss Bang Bang.* by Kael, Pauline. 498 p. paper New York: Bantam Books, 1969.

The always fascinating, ever entertaining Miss Kael is at it again in this second collection of her writings. In addition to film reviews, this one includes a long article on the making of THE GROUP (1966), in which she operates with a rusty razor blade on Director Sidney Lumet. There are profiles on Brando, Welles, and Kramer, but best of all, some 280 short capsule recollections/reviews of films from the past. Anyone who deals with repertory films (schools, libraries, museums) will find this section a wonderful resource for film collections, film notes, and discussion. All of the accolades, tributes, and compliments, spewed over the covers of this paperback are deserved. Miss Kael is a joy.

3618   *Kit Parker Films Catalog.* edited by Parker, Kit. 351 p. paper illus. Carmel Valley, Calif.: Kit Parker, 1980.

What a busy person this Kit Parker must be! Not only does the company bear his name but he is responsible for this superb catalog which is a treasury of reference, information visuals, criticism, background, etc.

Hundreds of films appear under a dozen headings: USA, silent era, Russia, animation, serials, etc. Retrieval of individual titles is facilitated by the final indexes provided. Many illustrations and drawings appear all through the book.

A sample quote from the annotation on THEY MADE ME A CRIMINAL (1939) indicates the light but informed approach of the writer: "Although the title might imply this is one of Warner Brothers' social message films of the 30s, the worst thing Garfield encounters is the Dead End Kids. Come to think of it, that could have been deadly."

Fun to read, easy to use and a pleasure to look at—what higher accolade can a film catalog earn? Supplements appear at irregular intervals.

3619   *Kitsch.* by Dorfles, Gillo. 313 p. illus. New York: Universe, 1969.

This volume about the world of bad taste has a selection by Lotte Eisner on films.

3620   *Klaw & Erlanger Present Famous Plays in Pictures.* by Niver, Kemp R.; edited by Bergsten, Bebe. 178 p. illus. Los Angeles: Locare, 1977.

Marc Klaw and Abraham Erlanger are best known as the founders of a theatrical booking company that was prosperous around the turn of the century. Their two unsuccessful ventures into the world of early motion picture production are recalled in this historical research by Kemp R. Niver.

In 1897 they invested an enormous amount of money to film THE PASSION PLAY, which was based upon the European stage presentation given at Horitz, Bohemia. The film had 50 scenes, introduced the leading actors at the start, and told a story that ran for 50 minutes. Because of the cut-throat competition of the period, the copyright legalities, and the limited duplication processes, the venture was not a success. In 1914 once again the team produced 26 films, all of which were characterized by a costly, careful production that was unusual for the time. Again, they failed.

Both attempts at film production are discussed here with text, newspaper ads, frame enlargements, and advertisements. Each of the 26 films made in 1914 receives detailed attention.

The volume is another impressive performance by Niver and illuminates an unfamiliar portion of early motion picture history. As always his work is characterized by affection, dedication, and intelligence. Recommended.

3621 *Knight Errant.* by Connell, Brian. 255 p. illus. Garden City, N.Y.: Doubleday, 1955.

This is the biography of Douglas Fairbanks, Jr., whose career spanned three decades (1923-1953), who married Joan Crawford, and who spent a part of his youth with his father, Douglas Fairbanks, Sr., and his stepmother, Mary Pickford, at their home, Pickfair. His public, social, and romantic activities are emphasized while the film work is mentioned in passing. The early portions do give the reader some insight into the problems of being the son of a Hollywood legend. The author's style is adequate. Some photographs (none from the films) are included but there is no filmography or index.

3622 KNIGHTS OF THE ROUND TABLE. 14 p. paper illus. New York: Al Greenstone Co., 1954.

This modest souvenir book opens with the legend and the story followed by the cast and production credits. The photographs are rather unattractive; a color process was used that results in exaggerated hues rather than soft natural colors. Some attention is given to Cinemascope and how it differs from the normal ratio.

3623 *Know Your Movies.* by Beaton, Welford. 192 p. Hollywood: Howard Hill, 1932.

Using many examples and a good deal of analysis, the theory and practice of motion picture production are discussed. Cecil B. DeMille provides the foreword.

3624 *Know Your Movies: The Theory and Practice of Motion Picture Production.* by Beaton, Welford. 192 p. New York: Gordon Press, 1976 (1932).

Cecil B. DeMille provides a foreword to this discussion of film aesthetics circa 1931. Originally published by Howard Hill in Hollywood, 1932.

3625 *Knowing the Score: Notes on Film Music.* by Bazelon, Irwin. 432 p. illus. New York: Arco, 1981.

3626 *Knowing the Score: Notes on Film Music.* by Bazelon, Irwin. 352 p. illus. New York: Van Nostrand, Reinhold, 1976.

Superb coverage of the topic, film music, is provided in this book. Beginning with a short history, the author later considers the contemporary composer, film scoring techniques, and specific examples that he calls "film moments." A series of interviews with film composers follows. The subjects are: Elmer Bernstein, Leonard Rosenman, Jerry Goldsmith, John Williams, Richard Rodney Bennett, Alex North, Lalo Schifrin, Bernard Herrmann, David Raskin, Bernardo Segall, Laurence Rosenthal, Johnny Mandel, Paul Glass, John Barry, and Gail Kubik. Sample pages from the musical scores to several films complete the volume. An index is provided and the book is nicely illustrated.

Much of book's quality apparently derives from the author's experience as a practicing musician-composer. Introduction, explanation, examination, comment, criticism, example—all these facets of film music and more are covered by Bazelon with perception, scholarship, and style in this well-produced volume. Although some of the content demands formal musical training or education, there is enough solid material to warrant the attention of the general audience. Recommended.

3627 *Kodak pamphlets.* paper illus. Rochester, N.Y.: Kodak Consumer Markets Division, 1970- .

The Eastman Kodak Company has a Photo Information Department which publishes a series of pamphlets/booklets concerned with filmmaking. Printed on high quality paper, they contain a succinct, readable text and fine illustrations—usually in color. Their cost is modest and they provide information obtainable only in more expensive volumes. Titles include: *Care of Your Processed Kodak Movie Films* (AD-29); *Easy Ways to Make Still and Movie Titles* (AC-60); *How Your Pictures Are Processed at Kodak* (AI-117); *Editing Your Movies* (AD-26); *Getting the Most Out of Your 8mm Film* (AD-21); *A Glossary of Photographic Terms* (AA-9); *Indoor Movie-Making* (AD-11); *Kodak 16mm Movie Films* (AD-22); *Making a Movie* (AD-10); *Maintaining Your Still and Movie Camera and Projector* (AA-1); *Movies on the Move-Your Vacation* (AD-13); *Tips on Using Kodak Super 8 Movie Film* (AD-28); *Showmanship in Home-Movie Projection* (AD-43); *A Stu-*

dent's Guide to Careers in Motion Picture Production (C3-87); and *What Happened to My Movies?* (AD-6).

3628 *Kops and Custards: The Legend of Keystone Films.* by Lahue, Kalton C.; and Brewer, Terry. 177 p. illus. Norman, Okla.: University of Oklahoma Press, 1968.

A history of the Keystone Film Company from 1912 until 1920. The role of Mack Sennett as the power behind the company is discussed, as are the Keystone personalities and the films in which they appeared. The historical aspects are intelligently covered although there may be an over familiarity with some of the material. The stills are poorly reproduced. An appendix of the Keystone comedies, a title index, and a general index add to the book's value. Useful as a reference and guide.

3629 KRAKATOA EAST OF JAVA. 32 p. paper illus. 1969.

A souvenir book which contains many shots from the 1969 film, a synopsis, cast and production credits, and one section on the new single-projector Cinerama process. The use of one projector rather than three narrows the field of vision from 146 degrees to 120 degrees. This change hastened the demise of the Cinerama process.

3630 *Kris Kristofferson.* by Kalet, Beth. 96 p. paper illus. New York: Quick Fox, 1979.

Since Kris Kristofferson is a relatively recent arrival to films, most of this volume concentrates on his earlier careers as Phi Beta Kappa student, Rhodes scholar, army captain, poet, songwriter and rock star. One short chapter is devoted to his films. The 50 or so illustrations are quite limited, with a few recent events and films overly represented while other important events have no pictorial representations. Most of the sparse text seems a blend of factual information and fan magazine hype; it never comes close to giving a portrait of this complex, talented, tormented man.

3631 *Kuleshov on Film.* by Kuleshov, Lev; edited by Levaco, Ronald. 226 p. paper Berkeley: University of California Press, 1974.

Lev Kuleshov (1899-1970) was a Russian film director who also taught at the Soviet Film School. He was a key influence on Sergei Eisenstein and Valdimir Pudovkin. This collection of his writings which was translated and edited by Ronald Levaco, contains one short book, "The Art of the Cinema," and 12 selected essays on filmmaking that are both practical and theoretical. Supporting the texts are a lengthy introduction, a bibliography of Kuleshov's articles and books, a filmography, and an index. Acceptable.

3632 *Kung Fu—Cinema of Vengeance.* by Glaessner, Verina. 134 p. paper illus. New York: Bounty/Crown, 1974.

The phenomenon of the Kung Fu motion picture genre is covered very well in this unusual volume. A brief description of the genre introduces a text concerned primarily with the Kung Fu industry of Hong Kong, its players, directors, and producers. Some attention is also given to the effect of the Kung Fu films in Western countries. A chapter on Bruce Lee will undoubtedly interest American readers. Whether they recognize other spotlighted performers such as Angelo Mao, Wany Yu, David Chiang and Ti Lung will depend upon their previous viewing of this film genre. The stills are well selected from a limited number of films and there is a title index provided. The use of a different, rather nervous typeface for the chapter headings makes for confusion rather than comprehension and the binding on the paperback examined split upon the book's first opening.

A current topic of interest has been handled by the author with obvious care and intelligent selection of material. A far greater understanding—and perhaps appreciation—for this film genre will result after reading this book. Recommended.

3633 *Kurt Weill In Europe.* by Kowalke, Kim H. 589 p. Ann Arbor, Mich.: University Research Press, 1980.

Although Kurt Weill's work was predominately for the theatre, it had both a direct and indirect influence on film and film music. This is a doctoral thesis complete with footnotes, charts, examples of music, etc.

The Days Grow Short by Ronald Sanders is less pedantic and probably more pleasing to most readers.

3634 *L. J. M. Daguerre.* by Gernsheim, Helmut; and Gernsheim, Alison. 216 p. illus. London: Secker; Cleveland: World, 1956.

A biography of "the first photographer" which carries the subtitle, "The History of the Diorama and the Daguerreotype." Includes illustrations and a bibliography.

3635 L'AGE D'OR. by Bunuel, Luis; and Dali, Salvador. 71 p. paper illus. New York: Simon & Schuster, 1968.

Script of the 1930 film, directed by Luis Bunuel. Includes cast credits and a filmography. Introduction is entitled "Surrealists" ; also included are 1) "L'Age d'Or" (Ado Kyrou); 2) two notes for Luis Bunuel; and 3) a note on the script. (In the same volume is the script of UN CHIEN ANDALOU (1929).)

3636 LA DOLCE VITA. by Fellini, Federico; and Pinelli, Tullio; Flaiano, Ennio; and Rondi, Brunello. 276 p. paper illus. New York: Ballantine Books, 1961.

Script of the 1959 film directed by Fellini. Contains cast credits and an article entitled "Adventures of a Journalist," by Hollis Alpert.

3637 LA DOLCE VITA. by de Vecchi, Mario. 24 p. paper illus. New York: National Publishers, 1961.

A synopsis of the film is given in both text and stills in this souvenir book. The cast is listed in the centerfold, in the chronological sequence in which they appear. Technical credits are also given. Fellini and the major cast names are given some special attention and there is an article entitled, "The Sweet Life's Hard Knocks" by Mario de Vecchi.

3638 LA GUERRE EST FINIE. by Semprun, Jorge. 192 p. paper illus. New York: Grove Press, 1967.

Script of the 1966 film directed by Alain Resnais. Contains cast credits.

3639 *Labour Power in the British Film Industry.* by Chanan, Michael. 57 p. paper London: British Film Institute (Zoetrope in U.S.), 1976.

The topic of this booklet is labor and trade union struggle in the British film industry. The author's purpose is to indicate a neglected area of British film history and to suggest some problems within that area which deserve further examination.

An introductory section deals with the division of labor in film production and with the concept of aesthetic labor. Following is a survey of cinema unions in Britain prior to 1930 and an account of the early years of ACT (The Association of Cinematograph Technicians). A widespread projectionists' strike in 1938 is described and some brief mention is made of post World War II union activities.

The author presents his labor history with the viewpoint of Marxian philosophy and teaching. As a result his essay becomes a mixture of selected information, biased interpretations and obvious Marxist preaching. An unfamiliar topic of limited interest receives questionable treatment here. Acceptable with reservations noted.

3640 *Labor Relations in the Performing Arts.* by Moscow, Michael H. 218 p. New York: Associated Councils of the Arts, 1969.

An introductory survey with a foreword by John T. Dunlop. Some bibliographical references are given.

3641 LACOMBE, LUCIEN. by Malle, Louis; and Modiano, Patrick. 122 p. paper illus. New York: Viking, 1975.

Script of the 1974 film directed by Malle. Contains script and cast credits.

3642 *Ladd: The Life, The Legend, The Legacy of Alan Ladd.* by Linet, Beverly. 294 p. illus. New York: Arbor House, 1979.

Called "a lost talent" by Geraldine Fitzgerald, Alan Ladd desperately craved critical approval throughout his two decades as a major film star (1942-1964). His second wife and Svengali, Sue Carol, desired celebrity. Apparently this conflict, coupled with a poor personal self-image, led first to chronicinsecurity and ultimately to self-destruction.

The Ladd tragedy is told in details obtained mostly from previously published materials and interviews. Since "The Ladd Legacy" —Alan Ladd, Jr., David Ladd, and Cheryl Ladd, is currently rather powerful in Hollywood, it is not surprising to find this book to be positive, sympathetic, and understanding. It even suggests that Ladd's films are worthy of a cult appreciation.

Illustrations, a filmography, and an index supplement Linet's rather factual story. The reader may sense that much remains untold about this short man who underplayed his roles and apparently his personal life. What has been presented here is a carefully scripted melodrama that is reminiscent of the more obvious cliches of A STAR IS BORN (1935, 1955).

3643 *Ladies in Distress.* by Lahue, Kalton C. 334 p. illus. New York: A. S. Barnes, 1971.

A pictorial account of silent screen heroines in danger.

3644   *The Lady and the Law.* by Berkman, Edward O. 403 p. illus. Boston: Little, Brown, 1976.

Fanny Ellen Holtzmann was a lawyer who specialized in motion picture and copyright cases. In this biography, written by her nephew, her career is traced from Brooklyn to the capitals of the world and the United Nations. Her clients and friends included Edmund Goulding, John Gilbert, Garbo, Gertrude Lawrence, Clifton Webb, Irving Thalberg, Fred Astaire, and others. In London she won a libel case against MGM for their film, RASPUTIN AND THE EMPRESS (1934), and as a result, became a sought-after lawyer in Hollywood. This is a remarkable story, told here with many anecdotes about show business and its characters.

3645   *A Lady Goes to Hollywood.* by Partridge, Helen (Phoebe Sheldon). 259 p. New York: Macmillan, 1941.

In this book, the wife of Bellamy Partridge visits Hollywood with her husband when one of his novels is adapted for the screen. She decides that Connecticut is better. Told in a folksy, cutesy style most suited to genteel lady readers of the twenties.

3646   *Lamparski's Hidden Hollywood: Where Stars Lived, Loved and Died.* by Lamparski, Richard. 128 p. illus. paper New York: Simon and Schuster (Fireside), 1981.

3647   *Lana: The Public and Private Lives of Miss Turner.* by Morella, Joe; and Epstein, Edward Z. 297 p. illus. New York: Citadel Press, 1971.

Based for the most part on public documents, previously published news releases, and private interviews, this unauthorized biography is an exercise for imaginative minds. Much of what is said is familiar but the chronological arrangement of the material and the carefully phrased innuendo suggest much more than is stated. As a result, a rather unhappy and at times lurid biography unfolds. The story of Lana Turner is told in terms of her films, her affairs, seven marriages, one sensational courtroom trial, a successful screen comeback, and a theatrical tour in "Forty Carats."

The care that was necessary to avoid legal action is reflected continually by the text. The illustrations seem chosen with greater freedom. A center picture section covers almost all the personalities who played a role in Miss Turner's professional/private life. Index and filmography are omitted, probably because they would be of slight interest to the audience for whom this book was designed.

The book has value only in its depiction of the minimal difference between Miss Turner's screen life and her personal life. The volume should enjoy great popularity with the nondiscriminating general reader.

3648   *Lana Turner.* by Basinger, Jeanine. 160 p. paper illus. New York: Pyramid, 1976.

The life and career of Lana Turner are covered in this title from the Pyramid *Illustrated History of the Movies* series. In addition to many illustrations, a filmography, a bibliography, and an index accompany the text.

3649   *Landers Film Reviews.* Los Angeles: Landers Associates, 1956- .

Published monthly except June, July and August, this service supplies reviews of 16mm educational and documentary films. The individual reviews contain data such as the date of release, price, running time, preview, purchase or rental source, production credits, audience level, subject area, and purpose in addition to the text. Each issue has a subject index and a title index which are cumulated in the May publication. Certain yearly volumes from the past are available as is a cumulated title index covering June 1961 to May 1968.

3650   *Landing Rightside Up in TV and Film.* by Jones, G. William. 128 p. paper illus. Nashville: Abingdon Press, 1973.

G. William Jones has given us another valuable little book in this attempt to offer some new advice on the problems of communicating with young people via television and films. Using a semi-serious programmed approach, the book consists of double-paged units, each having a cartoon on the left page and approximately one-half page of narrative on the right. The reader supposedly can read only those units which are pertinent to his need, but the book is so knowledgeable and entertaining that most users will probably read it all. Since Mr. Jones is not one to labor his points, the book is also concise, yet it does cover the major problems that film users encounter. For example: What do you say before a film showing? How do you capture the greatest benefit of a film or program in a follow-up discussion? How do you find appropriate material?

The cartoon style may not please all readers—a tendency to overdraw seems evident. A simpler, uncluttered format would have been more in keeping with the text. A good bibliography is given. For anyone communicating with audiences of any age via films or television, the book is a most helpful aid. Recommended.

3651 *Landmark Films: The Cinema and Our Century.* by Wolf, William; and Wolf, Lillian Kramer. 429 p. illus. New York: Paddington Press, 1979.

In this carefully prepared buffet of 38 films, critic William Wolf does several things with his offerings. Not only does he offer a critical summary-recapitulation of each film, but he also relates them to a historical time. This perspective is established both within the essay and by a group of headlines which introduce, recall, and identify each decade. In addition, the place in film history of each of his "landmarks" is indicated by relating it to other films of the genre.

Interwoven into the text is interview/conversational material that the author has gathered—probably in his position of film critic for *Cue* magazine for more than 15 years. An illustration, the cast, and credits are included for each film. A bibliography and an index complete the book.

The analogy to a well-prepared meal that began this review can be repeated. Wolf has prepared a rich banquet of many different films using a variety of seasoned critical and historical approaches. The result should be extremely satisfying to a wide audience. Recommended.

3652 *Landscape of Contemporary Cinema.* by Lewis, Leon.; and Sherman, William David. 97 p. Buffalo, N.Y.: Buffalo Spectrum Press, 1967.

A series of short, intellectual and common-sense essays on various film topics, this collection is much more satisfying and enjoyable than some of the "headier" cinema tomes. The aim of the authors is to present a view of modern cinema and to communicate their excitement about it. They succeed nicely.

The book has three general sections: directors, Hollywood in the sixties, and films around the world. Several of the articles are outstanding, such as those on Welles, Preminger's BUNNY LAKE IS MISSING (1965), Natalie Wood, and Tuesday Weld. The final list of things which "turn us on" is sophomoric and not in keeping with the high calibre of the essays. No illustrations, index, etc. are included. This small

volume is an ideal balance to other modern film criticism. The writing style will remind some readers of James Agee. Highly recommended.

3653 *Language and Cinema.* by Metz, Christian. 304 p. illus. The Hague: Mouton, 1974.

One of the standard references in film semiotics, this volume treats cinematic language, codes, textual systems, etc. It is very technical and quite demanding. There are numerous references and an index of films, names, and subjects.

3654 *The Language and Technique of the Film.* by Bettetini, Gian Franco. 202 p. illus. The Hague: Mouton, 1973.

In this attempt to intellectualize film, the author divides his content into three major sections. The first deals with the film and its signs, codes, communications, etc. A theory of filmmaking which emphasizes the semiological approach and point of view is offered next. Finally the importance of film editing or cutting is treated. Antonioni, Bergman, and Godard are mentioned in many of the author's examples. References, an index of film titles, and an index of names make up the appendixes.

3655 *Language of Change: Moving Images of Man.* by Slade, Mark. 186 p. illus. Toronto: Holt, Rinehart and Winston of Canada, 1970.

The impact of moving images on social, scientific and philosophical structures is explored in this volume. Includes references and a list of film titles.

3656 THE LANGUAGE OF FACES. by Schreivogel, Paul A. 20 p. paper illus. Dayton, Ohio: Pflaum, 1970.

A study guide for the 1961 film directed by John Korty. Found in *Films in Depth* and also available separately.

3657 *The Language of Film.* by Whitaker, Rod. 178 p. illus. Englewood Cliffs, N.J.: Prentice-Hall, 1970.

This book attempts to explore the language of film from both the technical and the aesthetic point of view. It treats such topics as plot, theme, narrative organization, actor's contribution, meaning in films, etc. Whether the author's assignment of names to intuitive processes is efficiency or obfuscation is a question still open. The volume adds little that is new to the aesthetics or grammar of film.

3658   *The Language of Show Biz.* edited by Sergel, Sherman L. 254 p. illus. Chicago: Dramatic Pub. Co., 1973.

The attractive oversized dictionary unfortunately pays no attention to motion picture language. Most of the items defined belong in realm of theatre, circus, and other live performances. Television, film, recordings—the most popular elements of today's mass entertainments are not treated and thus there are no definitions of "sneak preview," "pilot," "dubbing," and other basic show biz words. True, the introduction does say it is "the private language of theatre," but isn't that a bit after the fact? The name given to the book is a misnomer. Show biz today encompasses much more than theatre, circus, vaudeville, burlesque, carnival and toby shows! Not pertinent for film study.

3659   *Language of Vision.* by Kepes, Gyorgy. 228 p. illus. Chicago: Paul Theobald, 1964.

Visual language explained and explored. Mostly illustrations.

3660   *Lanza: His Tragic Life.* by Strait, Raymond; and Robinson, Terry. 181 p. illus. Englewood Cliffs, N.J.: Prentice-Hall, 1980.

Terry Robinson was the physical therapist selected by Louis B. Mayer to keep Mario Lanza in condition. His coauthor, Raymond Strait, has written biographies of Jayne Mansfield, Jean Peters, Rosemary Clooney and other celebrities. With the implied approval of the four Lanza children, the men relate the story of the singer and his wife with rather indifferent results. Much of the text is a factual recall of events already on public record. Here the familiar story is mixed with recreated conversations and a few private, intimate anecdotes. What gives this volume some distinction is the treatment of the relationship between Betty and Mario Lanza. It suggests that a stronger partner might have brought some order and discipline to the tenor's turbulent, tragic life.

Included are a few carefully selected illustrations, a discography, and an index. Although films brought Lanza world fame, there is no filmography.

The portrait here is a predictable one: that of a gifted singer whose personal life and career are flawed by obsessive self-indulgence.

3661   *The Lardners: My Family Remembered.* by Lardner, Ring, Jr. 371 p. paper illus. New York: Harper and Row, 1976.

Screenwriter Ring Lardner, Jr. was the winner of two Oscars and was also a member of the Hollywood Ten in the 1950s. In this affectionate memoir he dwells on his parents, brothers, and friends. His remarkable family is recalled with a simple, genuine feeling that avoids mawkishness in favor of sensitivity, taste, and discretion.

3662   *Las Vegas is My Beat.* by Pearl, Ralph. 251 p. illus. Secaucus, N.J.: Lyle Stuart, 1973.

A history of Las Vegas from the forties to the present, along with short vignettes of the artists who have worked there. Since many film personalities have appeared on the stages of Las Vegas, their respective fates there make interesting reading. Tony Curtis, Susan Hayward, Mario Lanza, Elvis Presley, Judy Garland, Jayne Mansfield, Marlene Dietrich and others are discussed. The author is a Las Vegas columnist and his writing style, his concept of humor, and his sense of proportion are all deficient. Only his subjects matter, and he succeeds in making them seem deficient, too. The book is noted for the record.

3663   *The Last Days of Elvis.* paper illus. Tiburon, Calif.: Personality Editions, 1977.

An oversize quickie paperback that combines text and illustrations to expose "the events that led up to Elvis' death and the bizarre aftermath."

3664   *The Last Hero: A Biography of Gary Cooper.* by Swindell, Larry. 360 p. illus. New York: Doubleday, 1980.

The Gary Cooper story is told once again in effortless fashion by Larry Swindell in this book. From his birth in 1901 to his death in 1961, Cooper lived an almost "charmed" life. Not overly intelligent nor particularly talented, he was compensated by having an imposing physique and unusually handsome facial features. In addition to being in the right place at the right time, Cooper learned quickly how to use his physical qualities to his greatest advantage. After that, everything, including stardom, came naturally.

The author tells all this in a breezy, straightforward manner that is appropriate to such success stories. Swindell sees Cooper and his Hollywood surroundings clearly and apparently understands the changes in Cooper that took place as he became a screen legend. Illustrations, a filmography, and an index accompany this comprehensive, entertaining biography.

3665 *The Last New Wave: The Australian Film Revival.* by Stratton, David. 356 p. illus. New York: Ungar, 1981.

3666 *The Last of the Novelists.* by Bruccoli, Matthew J. 163 p. Carbondale, Ill.: Southern Illinois University Press, 1977.

A study of F. Scott Fitzgerald's *The Last Tycoon*, a novel drawn from the author's experiences and observations in Hollywood.

3667 LAST TANGO IN PARIS. by Bertolucci, Bernardo; and Arcalli, Franco. 224 p. illus. New York: Delacorte, 1972.

Script of the 1972 film directed by Bertolucci. Contains the script plus cast names, 50 stills, an introductory essay by Pauline Kael, and "A Transit to Narcissus" by Norman Mailer.

3668 *The Last Whole Film Catalog.* edited by Bender, Vivian. 164 p. paper illus. Wilmette, Ill.: Films, Inc. 1976.

As the title indicates, this is a film catalog, but with a noticeable difference. Using the same format as its predecessors, *The First Whole Library Catalog* and *The Second Whole Library Catalog*, this volume employs thousands of drawings, sketches, diagrams, photographs, and other assorted visuals to complement a text that is both interesting and informative. Not only are there more than a thousand films from the Films Incorporated library presented, but attention is also given to selected books and periodicals. A typical entry might include a descriptive paragraph, critical quotes, awards, technical data, costs, and distributor-publisher information. The films and books are divided into four large categories: humanities, social science, science, and feature films. A title index and a subject index make the book easy to use in the location of specific films.

This volume is an outstanding example of combining business with pleasure. The unusual approach is creative, informative and addictive, since unwary browsers are sure to become hooked once they open this attractive eye-catching catalog. Highly recommended.

3669 LAST YEAR AT MARIENBAD. by Robbe-Grillet, Alain. 168 p. paper illus. New York: Grove Press, 1962.

Script of the 1961 film directed by Alan Resnais. Contains cast credits, a filmography, and an introduction by Alain Robbe-Grillet.

3670 *Latin America Cinema: Film and History.* edited by Burns, E. Bradford. 137 p. paper illus. Los Angeles: UCLA Latin American Center, 1975.

This volume is concerned with the use of film in teaching history. It employs the anthology form with sections by the author, and by Eugene C. McCreary, Joan Mellen, and several students from the author's school. An opening section considers the use of films in studying Latin America's past. Further support to the idea of film as history is offered in two articles which deal with theory, interrelationships, style, and the fictional documentary. The students' contribution focuses on specific examples, e.g., Bolivia and the film BLOOD OF THE CONDOR (1969). Film sources and two bibliographies complete the volume. A center section of stills from pertinent films is included.

This is very specialized material that should be of interest primarily to educators on the secondary and college levels. Students and researchers may find the bibliographies especially helpful. Acceptable.

3671 *The Latin Image in American Films.* by Woll, Allen L. 126 p. paper illus. Los Angeles: Latin American Center, UCLA, 1977.

The image of the Latin American is the subject of this study. The historical survey which is used begins with those silent films which portrayed the Latin as a "greaser." The myth of the Latin lover is discussed with Ramon Novarro and Douglas Fairbanks (in THE AMERICANO) as early examples. The first decade of sound films, 1928-1939, includes Delores Del Rio and Wallace Beery (VIVA VILLA, 1933) among many others. RKO Studio's film, HI, GAUCHO (1936) is analyzed. With World War II, the nation (and the studios) embarked on a good neighbor policy. In films, a new sensitivity emerged only to be lost again at the war's end. Carmen Miranda and Lupe Velez are discussed in this section.

Final sections deal with the Latin American film industry, post-war realistic films (VIVA ZAPATA, 1952, and SALT OF THE EARTH, 1954), and the return of the "greaser" stereotype (CHE, 1969 and BANANAS, 1971). A filmography, bibliography, illustrations, and an index supplement the text.

The book's goals are "to reveal the continuance of misconceptions" about the Latin image in American films, and, of course, to encourage correction. Both goals are nicely realized.

3672   *Latino Materials.* by Duran, Daniel Flores. 249 p. Santa Barbara, Calif.: American Bibliograph Press, 1979.

This is the first title in a proposed series of selection guides that are subtitled "A Multimedia Guide for Children and Young Adults." The book begins with four essays which introduce the general areas of literature and library service for Latinos (Spanish-speaking Americans). Following, there are three large sections devoted to general, Mexican-American and Puerto Rican resources. In each section the resources (books, journals, and films) are arranged under the following subheadings: elementary, secondary, and professional. A glossary, a publisher/distributor list, a subject index, and an author/title index complete the book.

Each film entry gives complete data and a helpful evaluative annotation. It is unfortunate that only films were considered, for surely there are captioned filmstrips, audio cassettes, and other materials which might have been included.

With the increasing interest in providing services for Latinos, the filmography contained within this volume certainly is valuable now and for the future. It is hoped that other nonprint materials can be considered in future editions. Acceptable.

3673   *Laugh, Clown, Cry: The Story of Charlie Chaplin.* by Olesky, Walter G. illus. Milwaukee, Wisc.: Raintree, 1976.

A biography of Charlie Chaplin designed for junior high school students.

3674   *The Laugh Makers: A Pictorial History of American Comedians.* by Cahn, William. 192 p. illus. New York: G. P. Pubnam's, 1957.

A picture and text book that traces American comedy from 1787 to 1957, this volume is considered here because of the prevalence of screen personalities in the latter half of the book. Separate sections are devoted to silent screen comedians and to those of the sound era. The photographs are fascinating but there is little depth to the writing. One might also quarrel with the emphasis (why Judy Holliday and not Joan Davis or Judy Canova?), the omissions (Harry Langdon is hidden in a list of names, Abbott and Costello are pictured but not discussed), and finally, the titling of the photographs. Any attempt at a topic of this scope deserves some appreciation. Revised, updated, and retitled in 1970 as *A Pictorial History of the Great Comedians.*

3675   *Laugh with Lucy: The Story of Lucille Ball.* by Cohen, Joel H. 92 p. paper illus. New York: Scholastic Book Service, 1974.

The emphasis in this biography of Lucille Ball is on her television work, but there is one chapter entitled "In the Movies." The material is a harmless, noncritical review of Ball's life, consisting largely of anecdotes and quotes from previously published material.

3676   *Laughter Is a Wonderful Thing.* by Brown, Joe E.; and Hancock, Ralph 312 p. illus. New York: Barnes, 1956.

In a motion picture career that spanned nearly 40 years, Joe E. Brown made more than 45 films, most of them with star billing. This autobiography does not indicate this vast cinema experience to the reader. Instead it is devoted to early vaudeville/stage days, wartime tours and horse racing. Perhaps the book will cause the reader to wonder why there has been no revival of the films of this popular comedian of the thirties. Little evidence or description is offered of Brown's technique or style. The pictures included are largely of the family album type. Another disappointing autobiography, not recommended except "for the record."

3677   *The Laughton Story.* by Singer, Kurt. 308 p. illus. Philadelphia: John C. Winston, 1954.

Charles Laughton was a film personality whose early performances are classic models of screen acting. His later roles were mostly overacted but his final screen efforts indicated a regained artistry. It is unfortunate that this book which has all the construction elements of a superior cinema biography should be so seriously flawed by errors and inaccuracies in the text. To illustrate: 1) Maureen O'Hara is credited on p. 85 to the 1932 PAYMENT DEFERRED instead of Maureen O'Sullivan; 2) DeMille did not direct QUO VADIS in 1951, Mervyn LeRoy did. Nor did he direct an early silent version. More than a page of text is based on this erroneous data (pp. 96-97); 3)The text reads "after I, CLAUDIUS (1938) was finished...." This film has become legendary largely because it was unfinished; 4) THE SIDEWALKS OF LONDON (1938) is not cited by most film authorities as one of the great pictures in all of film history; and 5) SALOME (1953) was made by Columbia and not MGM.

Despite these errors, the book has value in its extended consideration of Laughton's film career.

Then, too, the personality of the subject emerges, which is a rarity in film biography. Much of the latter portion is devoted to Laughton's reading tours and his presentations of plays which were mostly spoken or read. This book was published before Laughton's masterful direction of an underrated film, THE NIGHT OF THE HUNTER (1955) and his improved performances in WITNESS FOR THE PROSECUTION (1957), SPARTACUS (1960), and ADVISE AND CONSENT (1962). Because of the carelessness of the text, this volume cannot be recommended without some reservation.

3678 *Launder and Gilliat.* by Brown, Geoff. 159 p. paper London: British Film Institute; (N.Y.: Zoetrope), 1977.

Sidney Gilliat and Frank Launder are a team of British filmmakers who have written, directed, and produced their own films since the late thirties. This volume is an overview of their impressive careers and includes many comments by the subjects themselves.

3679 *Laurel and Hardy.* by Barr, Charles. 144 p. illus Berkeley, Calif.:University of California Press, 1968 .

After a short appreciation and some brief biography, this book uses PUTTING PANTS ON PHILIP (1927), to begin its analytic history of this team's work. Examples from their silent and sound short films and from their longer sound features are used to explain their techniques, structure, and gags. Some of the pictorial illustration exists in a filmstrip format in order that the development of a gag may be easily followed. Other larger stills are reproduced with commendable fidelity. An evaluative filmography includes a brief plot outline, date, director, etc. Since many of the short silent comedies are available for outright purchase, this book is an excellent guide for the neophyte Laurel and Hardy devotee and collector. For others it is an admirable analysis of the durable art of this comedy team. Recommended.

3680 *Laurel and Hardy.* by McCabe, John; and Kilgore, Al. 400 p. illus. New York: E.P. Dutton, 1975.

Although this volume resembles Everson's *The Films of Laurel and Hardy*, it improves and surpasses the many excellent elements of the earlier book. Its basic structure is a pictorial filmography with narrative, interpretation, comment, criticism, and appreciation supplied by Laurel and Hardy's Boswell, John McCabe. The many stills taken from the films place this volume between the Richard

Anobile *Classic Film* series and the *Citadel/Pyramid* series. It is an excellent combination of the structural strengths of these series.

It is important to emphasize that, although the volume resembles others, it stands alone in the quality of its tribute to Laurel and Hardy. Production values are outstanding and include a most attractive dust jacket, a rarity these days. Pictorial reproduction is uniformly excellent. The McCabe text approaches a kind of perfection in its care and accuracy, and the filmography material supplied by Richard W. Bann is impressively detailed. The tributes to Laurel and Hardy by filmmakers and the preview essay by McCabe also contribute to the book's quality.

In addition to the many film stills, the book contains production shots, candids, publicity shots, and newspaper pictures. The constitution and the activities of "The Sons of the Desert," a society devoted to the appreciation of Laurel and Hardy, concludes the book. Highly recommended.

3681 *The Laurel and Hardy Book.* edited by Maltin, Leonard. 301 p. paper illus. New York: Curtis, 1973.

This modest volume does not compete with the biography, *Mr. Laurel and Mr. Hardy*, nor *The Films of Laurel and Hardy*, but offers instead some fine supplementary material to both those volumes. Much of this material comes from the newsletter of The Sons of the Desert, the organization devoted "to the loving study of the persons and films of Stan Laurel and Oliver Hardy." In addition to selected articles on the team, a section is devoted to eight members of their stock company: James Finlayson, Mae Busch, Charlie Hall, Walter Long, Anita Garvin, Richard Cramer, Arthur Housman and Tiny Sanford. There is also one index to Laurel's films, another for Hardy's films, and a separate filmography for the team films. This latter reference gives detailed attention to the supporting players who appeared with the team. Many interesting visuals appear throughout the book.

While this volume is supplementary rather than basic, there is enough new detail and data given to warrant recommendation. Although some of the material may be a bit familiar, general reader reponse will still be most positive—and certain patrons will be ecstatic.

3682 *The Laurel and Hardy Scrapbook.* by Scagnetti, Jack. 160 p. illus. Middle Village, N.Y.: Jonathan David, 1976.

539

It is hard to resist any material about these two beloved comics. Although what is presented here is familiar, it is still pleasing to read about their early years as individual actors and their long tenure as a team. Using hundreds of visuals, their films from 45 MINUTES FROM HOLLYWOOD (1926) to ATOLL K (1951) are recalled. A long picture section concludes the book. Loyal fans of the team will enjoy this book.

3683 *Lauren Bacall By Myself.* by Bacall, Lauren. 377 p. illus. New York: Alfred Knopf, 1978.

After being the supporting subject in several biographies of Humphrey Bogart, Lauren Bacall decided to tell her own story. The result is one of the best film autobiographies of the decade. With good taste she avoids sensationalism and tells what seems to be an honest story with objectivity and integrity. Her ambitious rise from a theatre usher to a world celebrity is a Cinderella variation but as Bacall recalls it, the story is refreshing, exciting and involving. Although many famous names have been a part of her life, she recognizes them primarily as human beings who possess varying blends of virtues and faults. The men in her life, Bogart, Sinatra, and Jason Robards, are treated with the understanding, emotion, and sensitivity that results from a deep personal relationship.

The book is handsomely produced and a fine selection of visuals accompanies the text. Its only flaw is the absence of both an index and a filmography.

In summary this is a brisk, no-nonsense story that reflects the warmth, charm and wit of a dedicated actress who is professional about all she does. Recommended.

3684 *Laurence Olivier.* by Cottrell, John. 416 p. illus. Englewood Cliffs, N. J.: Prentice Hall, 1975.

This is probably the most carefully researched and detailed biography of Laurence Olivier as an actor that is available. Although major events of his life from a stage debut as a child to his knighthood are mentioned, his professional life is the major theme. Those qualities of dedication and determination that have made him this century's foremost actor are emphasized. In a sense, he has willed his own prominence by having the courage to take risks and to do the unexpected. Cottrell does not tell the reader the reason or source of Olivier's ambition, or very much about his private life. He concentrates instead on Olivier's career, which probably reflects the man behind it. The text suggests that Olivier's acting genius was made, not born. Illustrations and a bibliography are included.

3685 *Laurence Olivier.* by Darlington, W. A. 92 p. illus. Whickham, England: Morgan Grampian, 1968.

A review of Olivier's life and career; includes some illustrations in color.

3686   *see   3685*

3687 *Laurence Olivier.* edited by Wisdom Staff. illus. Beverly Hills: Wisdom, 1957.

Although *Wisdom* was a periodical, its format was that of a hardbound book. Volume 7 featured Laurence Olivier and Shakespeare; it included some fine illustrations and articles, such as "Shakespeare in Films," "On Shakespeare," and "His Life on Film."

3688 *Laurence Olivier: Theater and Cinema.* by Daniels, Robert L. 317 p. illus. New York: A. S. Barnes, 1980.

This is really a version of *The Cinema of...* series since the book is almost exclusively concerned with the films of Laurence Olivier. There is some mention of his theater and television performances, along with a few snippets of biographical information—but the concern here is his films. They are discussed in chronological order from TOO MANY CROOKS (1930) to DRACULA (1979). At this writing Olivier is still making films: THE JAZZ SINGER (1980), CLASH OF THE TITANS (1981), INCHON (1981), etc.

Each of his films is described by cast and production credits, illustrations, a synopsis, review excerpts, and comment/background information. The overview of his film work is enlightening, for many unfamiliar English films are included along with a few forgotten titles.

A book such as this one depends for its quality more on selection and arrangement than on the brief critical writings supplied. However, in both areas the author has been quite successful. For the worldwide audience that has enjoyed and appreciated Laurence Olivier's work, reading this volume will be a most rewarding experience.

3689 *Laurette.* by Courtney, Marguerite. 445 p. illus. New York: Atheneum, 1968 (1955).

A biography of the noted stage actress, Laurette Taylor, written by her daughter, this volume contains some material on the silent film made from her stage success, PEG O' MY HEART (1923). HAPPINESS (1924) and ONE NIGHT IN ROME (1924) were Taylor's other films. Two chapters are devoted to her filmmaking— "Hollywood and Peg" and "Hollywood, 1924." The book is nicely illustrated and contains a useful index.

3690 *Law and the Entertainment Industry.* 218 p. paper Berkeley, Calif.: School of Law, University of California, 1954.

This symposium on legal problems of actors, writers, motion picture producers, broadcasters, and telecasters appeared in the *California Law Review*, volume 42, number 1, in the spring of 1954.

3691 *Law and the Publishing and Entertainment Media.* by Joint Committee on Continuing Legal Education. 230 p. Philadelphia: American Law Institute and American Bar Association, 1973.

The study materials containedhere were prepared for an ALI-ABA course of study and deal with legal problems affecting the media such as copyright. Attention is given to both press and motion pictures.

3692 *The Law of Motion Pictures.* by Frohlich, Louis D; and Schwartz, Charles. 943 p. New York: Backer, Voorhis, 1918.

Treats the various rights of the author, actor, professional scenario writer, director, producer, distributor, exhibitor, and the public. Contains chapters on unfair competition and copyright protection in the United States and Great Britain.

3693 *Law of the Stage, Screen and Radio.* by Marchetti, Roger. 476 p. San Francisco: Suttonhouse, 1936.

Includes authors' literary property and copyright in photoplays, censorship of films, defamation through the screen, etc.

3694 LAWRENCE OF ARABIA. by Woolfenden, John R. 32 p. paper illus. New York: Richard Davis & Co., 1962.

One of the better examples of a souvenir book. An excellent section entitled "The Legend of Lawrence" is followed by some fold-out visuals and historical maps. Cast and production names are treated in some detail, and there is a Lawrence chronology plus a bibliography.

3695 LE JOUR SE LEVE. by Prevert, Jacques. 128 p. paper illus. New York: Simon & Schuster, 1970.

Script of the 1939 film directed by Marcel Carne. Contains cast credits and "LE JOUR SE LEVE—Poetic Realism," by Andre Bazin.

3696 LE PETIT SOLDAT. by Godard, Jean-Luc. 95 p. paper illus. London: Lorrimer; New York: Simon & Schuster, 1967.

Script of the 1960 film directed by Godard.

3697 *Leading Film Discussions.* by Friedlander, Madeline S. 42 p. paper New York: League of Women Voters, 1972.

This valuable little book is divided into four main sections: planning a program, conducting a discussion, training leaders via workshops, and making arrangements for the program. The final section is devoted to films and film sources. Each section is a small treasure by itself. Together they form a vital reference for anyone who uses film with an audience. Most of the suggestions and advice are first rate, practical, and pertinent. The list of recommended films reflects the interests of the League and deals mostly with environment, government, urban problems, racial problems and the United Nations. A bibliography and a directory of film sources conclude the volume.

The material offered here is unique and should suggest to both the beginner and the experienced professional many new ways in which a film-discussion program can be improved. An essential book for this purpose.

3698 *The Leading Ladies.* by Parish, James Robert; and Stanke, Don E. 526 p. illus. New Rochelle, N.Y.: Arlington House, 1977.

In this collective biography Parish and Stanke have tackled six rather formidable subjects: Joan Crawford, Bette Davis, Olivia de Havilland, Rosalind Russell, Joan Blondell and Barbara Stanwyck. Aside from talent and personality, the one quality common to the sextet was an ability to survive. Each was a major star for almost four decades. The treatment accorded each consists of a long biographical essay enhanced by carefully selected stills and a detailed filmography. The essays consist mostly of film synopses, factual information and quotes, but, in a subtle way, the authors do include commentand criticism. Of course, the selection and placement of the material also constitutes editorializing. Picture reproduction is excellent throughout and there is a master index for all six biographies.

The continuing success of the Parish collective biographies is testimony enough to their quality and appeal. They express with intelligence and dignity the affection and admiration that many readers feel for the star subjects. Recommended.

3699 *Leading Ladies.* by Clark, Electa. 252 p. New York: Stein and Day, 1976.

Subtitled "An Affectionate Look at American Women of the Twentieth Century," this book is divided into eight chapters/decades. It is an attempt to combine elements of collective biography with American history and the women's liberation movement. Some attention is given to selected film actresses—Mary Pickford, Lillian Gish, Greta Garbo, Katharine Hepburn, Judy Garland—but is a minimal sampling when the effect of films and film performers on the American public is considered.

Theme here is stronger than treatment; the biographical material is general rather than concisely selected and the historical thread is interrupted continually for personality descriptions. This is acceptable reading but it should have and could have been much better.

3700 *Learning from Films.* by Lumsdaine, Arthur A.; and May, Mark A. 357 p. illus. New Haven, Conn: Yale University Press, 1958.

Films used in teaching is the subject of this book. Portions are devoted to film as an educational tool, film and other learning activities, film evaluation, film use, and film potential.

3701 *Learning the Liveliest Arts: The Critical Enjoyment of Film and Television.* by Perkins, William Herbert. 319 p. illus. Sydney: Angus and Robertson, 1972.

This guide to the appreciation of film and television includes diagrams, tables and bibliographic references in addition to many illustrations.

3702 *Lee Strasberg: The Imperfect Genius of the Actor's Studio.* by Adams, Cindy. 398 p. illus. New York: Doubleday, 1980.

Cindy Adams has popularized what should have been a scholarly biography in her treatment of Lee Strasberg. Dropping the names of Monroe, Dean, Brando, Winters, Pacino, etc., she recalls Strasberg's life with gossip and anecdote rather than solid research. Strasberg was such an influential and colorful character that the result is readable entertainment despite the approach. Not only did Strasberg influence many film actors, but also he appeared in films such as THE GODFATHER (1972) and GOING IN SYTLE (1980).

3703 *Leg Art: Sixty Years of Hollywood Cheesecake.* by Lacy, Madison S.; and Morgan, Don. 256 p. illus. Secaucus, N.J.: Citadel, 1981.

3704 *Legal and Business Problems of the Motion Picture Industry.* by Baumgarten, Paul A. 616 p. paper illus. New York: Practising Law Institute, 1973.

Prepared for distribution at the Legal and Business Problems of the Motion Picture Industry Workshop, February 1973, this handbook considers such topics as patents, copyrights, trademarks, literary properties, etc.

3705 *The Legend of Bruce Lee.* by Block, Alex Ben. 171 p. paper illus. New York: Dell, 1974.

A more objective and critical biography of Bruce Lee is offered here than in his wife's tribute, *Bruce Lee: The Man Only I Knew*. His life as a child living in two cultures, his discovery of the martial arts, his rise to worldwide celebrity as an Oriental film star, and his sudden shocking death are all treated. In the latter instance, an attempt is made to separate truth from rumor by using factual report, testimony, and interviews.

Photographs appearing in a center section are well selected, although their reproduction is below average. A short bibliography indicates some unique titles which encompass the martial arts along with Chinese wisdom, history, religion and philosophy. There is no index. For those readers interested in kung fu, gung-fu, or karate, this book is recommended. As a biography of the "King of Kung Fu," it is most acceptable.

3706 *Legendary Ladies.* 82 p. illus. paper New York: Starlog, 1981.

A heavily illustrated collective biography.

3707 *The Legion of Decency.* by Facey, Paul W. 206 p. New York: Arno, 1974.

This volume is one in the *Dissertations on Film* series and was written as one of the requirements for an advanced degree at Fordham University in 1945. The Legion of Decency was a Catholic organization formed to protect people (especially children) against the influence of immoral films. The book's subtitle is "A Sociological Analysis of the Emergence and Development of a Social Pressure Group." An introductory chapter considers the sociological problem of the motion picture along with early attempts at control. The Legion of Decency became a permanent group in 1934 after several years of planning. Its structure, its goals and its methods are detailed in separate chapters. A concluding section explores the relationship between the Legion and other groups in society. A bibliography is appended.

This is a facsimile of Lacey's doctoral dissertation; many footnotes, tables, and a bibliography support the text. What must be noted is that the author was a Catholic father writing about a Catholic organization at a Catholic university. Then, too, the world of 1945 had not been exposed to the sophisticating influence of 25 years of television. For these reasons, the study must be considered with a historical perspective. The description of a social pressure group and its methods contains some powerful lessons; however, both the interpretation and evaluation of the Legion lack complete objectivity. Acceptable.

3708 *Legislation for Film, Press and Radio.* by Terrou, Fernand; and Solal, Lucien. 420 p. New York: Arno Press, 1972 (1951).

Originally issued in 1951 as number 607 of the UNESCO series, *Press, Film and Radio in the World Today,* this volume deals with the laws and regulations which applied then to moving pictures, radio and the press. A bibliography is included.

3709 *Lemmon: A Biography.* by Widener, Don. 247 p. illus. New York: Macmillan, 1975.

This biography can serve as a model for other authors planning books on film personalities. With the cooperation of Jack Lemmon himself, and the help of actors, directors, producers, and others, Don Widener has created a portrait that is both appealing and revealing. Although he is most positive about and sympathetic toward his subject, the author does not hesitate in pointing out the actor's faults and imperfections. His drinking, his fear of confrontation, his lack of self-protection in accepting film roles—these weaknesses are related along with others. However, what remains with the reader is the positive qualities that have made Lemmon's long and successful career possible. He is characterized as a kind, thoughtful man who has achieved film stardom without stepping on anyone.

The material gathered and selected by the author is top-notch, with much attention given to Lemmon's films. Also helpful are some illustrations and an index. The absence of a filmography is puzzling.

This biography is as hard to resist as the on-screen personality of its subject. It should be embraced by the wide audience who recognize Jack Lemmon as one of the foremost screen actors of our time. Recommended.

3710 *Lena.* by Horne, Lena; and Schickel, Richard. 224 p. paper illus. New York: Signet Books, 1966.

This is a superior autobiography that has a most interesting section on Hollywood and some of its personalities. For a long period, Lena Horne's film career consisted mostly of standing in front of a huge pillar as she sang a song. These short musical sequences were not integrated into the story line, so that they could be deleted without destroying the continuity, and thus make the film acceptable in certain markets. Many other problems that this fine artist faced are discussed with intelligence, wit, and taste.

3711 *Leni Riefenstahl: The Fallen Film Goddess.* by Infield, Glenn B. 278 p. illus. New York: Thomas Y. Crowell, 1976.

Although this volume has a subtitle on its dust cover which reads "The Intimate and Shocking Story of Adolf Hitler and Leni Riefenstahl," it states in its foreword that it is not a biography. Instead it claims to be a study of the fusion of filmmaking and politics.

Actually it is a little of each of these several themes. While Riefenstahl's life and career during the thirties are emphasized, other periods are also discussed. Her associations with Hitler are both documented and suggested. The relationship between politics and art is considered at length.

Major attention is given to two films, TRIUMPH OF THE WILL (1935) and OLYMPIA (1938). There are a few illustrations, notes, a filmography, a bibliography, and an index.

This well-researched investigation concludes that it was the artist's association with Hitler and a decision to use her genius to glorify his cause that brought about her ultimate tragedy. A fundamental question about the use and function of film is handled with skill and intelligence here. Recommended.

3712   *Leni Riefenstahl.* by Berg-Pan, Renata. 222 p. illus. Boston: Twayne, 1980.

Leni Riefenstahl's small number of films are covered in detail in this title from the Twayne's *Theatrical Arts* series. Since so much controversy exists about her activities during the Third Reich, a chapter is devoted to her life and times. In the preface, the author acknowledges the difficulty of writing about her. Most of the remaining text deals with the Mountain films, THE BLUE LIGHT (1932), TRIUMPH OF THE WILL (1935), OLYMPIA (1938) and TIEFLAND (1954). Illustrations, notes, references, a chronology, a bibliography, a filmography, and an index complete the book.

Berg-Pan's accomplishment is in her handling of a "touchy" subject and producing a valid study/appreciation. She has tried to avoid getting stuck in the political opinions and arguments, opting instead for the tangible films to analyze. This she does with notable success.

3713   *The Lens and All Its Jobs.* by Ray, Sidney. 158 p. paper illus. New York: Focal, 1977.

This title in the *Media Manuals* series is a companion to the author's *The Lens in Action.* In a text which is somewhat less technical than the previous book, Ray describes the procedures used in the design, production, and testing of lenses. The variety of types available and their use by the media is noted. Selected optical systems and opto-electronic devices are also described. Excellent illustrations, drawings, and diagrams appear in abundance to assist the reader in understanding basic optical principles and the use of lenses. A glossary and a bibliography are included.

3714   *The Lens in Action.* by Ray, Sidney. 201 p. paper illus. New York: Hastings House, 1976.

More than 100 topics relating to lenses are discussed in some detail in this volume, a title in the *Media Manuals* series. The main purpose of the volume is to provide an overview of the basic characteristics of image formation via lenses, and, in addition, to give attention to human vision and camera viewfinders.

As indicated above, the approach is wide, and the coverage appears quite comprehensive. Illustrative material is limited to diagrams. A glossary and a bibliography are appended.

Certainly some background in optics will be helpful in using this volume. Effort has been made to avoid too much technical detail and explanation, but the subject demands the use of some rather complex diagrams, formulas, and descriptions.

For the person working in still photography, motion pictures, or television, the volume will be most helpful and rewarding. The amateur will derive some idea of the facility and utility of lenses. Recommended.

3715   *Lens Techniques for Color Movie Magic.* by Turner, Glen H. 96 p. paper illus. San Francisco: Camera Craft, 1958.

3716   *Leo McCarey and the Comic Anti-Hero in American Film.* by Gehring, Wes D. New York: Arno, 1980.

The relationship between the career of film director Leo McCarey and the emergence of the comic anti-hero in films is examined in this title from the *Dissertations On Film* series.

3717   *see 3718*

3718   *Leopold Stokowski: A Profile.* by Chasins, Abram. 313 p. illus. New York: Hawthorn, 1979.

In this straightforward biography of the famed, forceful conductor, Leopold Stokowski, attention is given to his work in FANTASIA (1940). His early recognition of film (along with radio and recordings) as a medium of musical importance is noted. The author, a music critic, knew Stokowski for 50 years and therefore much of this volume deals with musical matters and questions. Illustrations, a bibliography, a discography, and an index supplement the text.

3719   LES LIAISONS DANGEREUSES. by Vailland, Roger; and Brule, Claude; and Vadim, Roger. 256 p. paper illus. New York: Ballantine, 1962.

Script of 1959 film directed by Roger Vadim. Contains cast credits and an introduction by Vadim.

3720   *Lessons with Eisenstein.* by Nizhny, Vladimir. 182 p. illus. New York:

Hill and Wang, 1962.

The re-creation of four lessons as they were original-ly taught by Eisenstein are presented here by one of his pupils. "Directorial Solution," "Mise-en-Scene," "Break-up into Shots," and "Mise-en-Shot" are the lesson titles. Illustrations for the lessons are black-board-type sketches. Appended is Eisenstein's teaching program, which was designed to cover four years of training at the State Institute of Cinematog-raphy in Moscow.

This book will have much interest for the advanced student but the average reader will have difficulty with the depth and complexity of the subjects pre-sented in the lessons. Recommended with en-thusiasm for students and filmmakers.

3721 *Let the Chips Fall.* by Vallee, Rudy. 320 p. illus. Harrisburg, Pa.: Stack-pole, 1975.

Rudy Vallee has been performing professionally in different media since the twenties. For example, over a period of four decades he has appeared in about 40 films. However, the reader would not sense this rather extensive film experience from this me-moir. Rather than a career review or an autobiogra-phy, Vallee has chosen to use this volume as a vehicle by which he evens the score with those who have done him wrong over the years. Recipients of his wrath include George White, Milton Berle, Vic-tor Borge, Robert Morse, Walter Winchell, and quite a few others. There is no denying the fascina-tion of attack-via-print. It is exactly those portions of the memoir which offer the most insight into the vitriolic character of the subject. In other instances when he boasts of his irresistible appeal, his sexual prowess, his oversized talent and his unending kind-nesses to others, the text is not nearly so convincing. A few candid photos and portraits accompany the text, and an index is provided.

Although portions of this volume are entertaining and amusing, most of it seems a catharsis for Vallee. His selection of those portions of his life and career he thinks will interest readers is questionable. His story requires the services of an objective biographer who is able to resist the problems of ego, prejudice and temperament that apparently plague the sub-ject. Acceptable.

3722 *Let's Go to the Movies.* by Barry, Iris. 293 p. illus. New York: Payson and Clarke, 1926.

Silent film criticism from an English film reviewer who later came to the Museum of Modern Art. Sharp insight, some compromise with commercial-

ism, and an obvious love for her subject. An early Kael or Crist, and yet neither of these.

3723 *Let's Make Movies.* by Simon, Sam-uel. 112 p paper illus. New York: French, 1940.

3724 *Let's See It Again: Free Films for Elementary Schools.* by Kislia, J. A. 126 p. paper Dayton, Ohio: Pflaum, 1975.

More than 200 films are treated in this evaluative filmography. Each entry contains title, color format, running time, rating, audience, subject, producer/ distributor, and the year of release. Annotations are descriptive and critical. Beneath some of the entries are selected teacher and student comments. The rat-ings are a bit complex: Poor-Fair—films disliked by children on a first viewing, whether partial or com-plete, or films unsuitable for grades K-8; Good— films containing useful subject matter; Very Good-Excellent—those films which appeal to children and adults on different levels—film art combined with education.

Several reservations should be noted about the mis-leading title, which seems to suggest a group of recommended see-it-again free films. This is only partially true, since a number of poor-fair films are included and indexed. Also given are "free" sources which serve rather specific areas. What is free and available to citizens of Southern California may not be easy to obtain in the New England area. The author dismisses this problem by generalizing about the inevitable presence of the films in various types of libraries—public, state, college, commercial com-pany, etc. Finally, the films are evaluated with re-spect to the K-8 audience and its subsets; thus the value of the book to those who serve a wider range of audiences is reduced.

No quarrel can be raised with the idea of evaluating free films for use with different audiences. In this instance, however, an attempt to attract sales via a provocative title and some questionable selection-treatment-arrangement of content diminishes that worthy idea. Acceptable with the reservations noted above.

3725 *Let'Em Eat Cheesecake.* by Wilson, Earl. 302 p. illus. Garden City, N.Y.: Doubleday, 1949.

Earl Wilson is a New York columnist who writes about show business personalities. In this generous sampling of 1940s gossip column writing, there are stories, jokes, witty sayings, anecdotes, insults, etc.

—all dealing with the famous folk of that era. Humorous line drawings are in keeping with the very light text and there is an index to help locate Wilson's subjects. Movie personalities are mentioned throughout.

3726 *The Letters of Nunnally Johnson.* edited by Johnson, Doris; and Leventhal, Ellen. 288 p. illus. New York: Knopf, 1981.

A collection of letters sent to fellow professionals as commentary on Hollywood from 1944 to 1976. Fun to read, the letters are impersonal and only indirectly acquaint the reader with the writer.

3727 *Lewis Milestone.* by Millichap, Joseph R. Boston: Twayne, 1981.

3728 *Liberty and License in the Indian Cinema.* by Vasudev, Aruna. 221 p. New Delhi: Vikas (Columbus: South Asia), 1978.

The author obtained her doctorate at the University of Paris with a thesis on censorship in the Indian cinema. This volume is an expansion of that thesis.

From July 7, 1896 to date, the cinema has been a part of Indian life. In 1976 there were 507 features films made in India—a number unchallenged by any other country in the world. The author traces the growth of the film industry, emphasizing the controls, restrictions, and limitations put upon it both officially and indirectly. Informally, the text mentions laws, acts, censor boards, editorials, committees, statutes, resolutions—anything that attempted to regulate Indian film. A final chapter suggests a rational, workable balance between liberty and license, freedom and responsibility. Included are a select bibliography and an index. Unfortunately, there are no illustrations.

In tracing censorship in the Indian film, the author also offers a history of sorts. Both aspects of this study are interesting and will appeal to the scholar/historian.

3729 *The Library of Communication Techniques (A Series).* illus. New York: Hastings House, 1973.

This excellent series is published by Hastings House in cooperation with Focal Press of London. The titles provide a complete basic library in the techniques of filmmaking. Each volume is handsomely produced with many illustrations, diagrams, charts and other visuals. While the texts tend to range from basic introduction to more complex technical mat-

ters, they are usually comprehensible to most readers. The books are constantly revised and updated to keep pace with technological change and innovations in practice.

The titles include: *The Technique of Documentary Film Production; The Technique of Editing 16mm Films; The Technique of Film Animations; The Technique of Film Cutting Room; The Technique of Film Editing; The Technique of Film and Television Makeup; The Technique of Film Music; The Technique of Lighting for Television and Motion Pictures; The Technique of Motion Picture Camera; The Technique of Sound Studio; The Technique of Special Effects Cinematography.*

3730 *The Library of Congress Author Catalog: Vol. 24—Films, 1948-1952.* Ann Arbor, Mich.: 1953.

This is the first separate volume on films to be published by the Library of Congress. It is based on the cards for films that were issued for the first time in 1951.

3731 *The Library of Congress Catalog of Motion Pictures and Filmstrips: Vol. 28—1953-1957.* 1088 p. Ann Arbor, Mich.: 1958.

This is a continuation of the listing of films from the cards printed by the Library of Congress, which in turn were based on copyright applications. The following volumes are sequential to the above: vol. 53 and 54—1958-1962, pub. 1963; vols. 71 and 72—1963-1967. There are omissions, a lack of consistent format, and certain changes occur from volume to volume. Nevertheless, the total work has merit.

3732 THE LICKERISH QUARTET. by DeForrest, Michael. paper New York: Audobox, 1970.

Script of the 1970 film directed by Radley Metzger.

3733 *The Life and Adventures of Carl Laemmle.* by Drinkwater, John. 288 p. illus. New York: G. P. Putnam's, 1931.

When this verbose, factual, and stiff biography appeared in 1931, Carl Laemmle was already well into his sixties. He had handed control of Universal Studios over to his son, and his power and prestige were diminishing. This volume reads like a long eulogy prepared much ahead of the event it commemorates. Nowhere is there much evidence of the human being —the man whose studio was the epitome of Hollywood nepotism. His relationships with Pickford, Thalberg, von Stroheim and others are mentioned very briefly.

The photographs resemble samples from the Laemmle family album. There is no index. One would suspect that the writing of this biography was subsidized. It will have appeal only to historians and researchers. Others interested in Carl Laemmle are referred to the brief (and probably best-written) chapter in Zierold's *The Moguls.*

3734 *The Life and Crimes of Errol Flynn.* by Godfrey, Lionel. 176 p. illus. New York: St. Martin's Press, 1977.

The use of the word "crimes" in the title of this biography is ironic, according to the author. Within the numerous books previously published about Errol Flynn, the author feels there has been an imbalance which has emphasized the sensational events of Flynn's life and career to the near exclusion of other aspects. An exposition of all of the complex qualities that finally led Flynn to tragedy is the goal of the book.

Although the author has reconstructed certain thoughts and events, he thankfully depends upon quotations for the dialogue which appears. He has borrowed generously from other sources, including Flynn's autobiography, *My Wicked, Wicked Ways.* The illustrations, obtained from a private collection, are unusual and adequately reproduced. A bibliography, a filmography, a discography, and an index complete the book.

For the reader unfamiliar with the life and career of Errol Flynn, this volume will provide an entertaining overview. Others will find it an acceptable reminder of much of what they have read elsewhere.

3735 *The Life and Curious Death of Marilyn Monroe.* by Slatzer, Robert F. 256 p. illus. New York: Pinnacle—Two Continents, 1975.

Robert Slatzer was friend, lover, and secret husband of Marilyn Monroe. He recalls their time together at the start of her career with affection and respect. His main purpose in writing the volume is to raise questions about her death. With documentation ranging from birth certificates to phone bills, he argues that Robert Kennedy was involved somehow in her last hours. If a new inquest were held, he believes it would show that the actress did not die by her own hand. Another interesting view of Monroe and some disturbing questions are presented by this volume. Acceptable for mature adults.

3736 *Life and Death in Hollywood.* paper illus. Cincinnati, Ohio: Zebra Picture Books, 1950.

This small photograph collection covers familiar ground, mostly the Hollywood scandals, but with visuals rather than text. Divided into chapters, the predictable subjects appear in chronological order: D. W. Griffith, Mack Sennett, Mary Pickford, Fatty Arbuckle, Wally Reid, William Desmond Taylor, Chaplin, Valentino, Garbo, Clara Bow, Harlow, and Hayworth. Noted here as one of the early picture books—a preview of the genre that was to appear in the sixties via Citadel, Crown and other publishers.

3737 *The Life and Death of Elvis Presley.* by Harbison, William Allen. illus. London: Joseph, 1977.

3738 *The Life and Invention of Thomas Alva Edison.* by Dickson, W. K. L. 362 p. illus. London: Chatto and Windus, 1894.

This is a volume of historical interest. During the period when he worked for Edison, the author invented the Kinetograph and the Kinetoscope. One chapter of this total biography is devoted to these devices. The author's name, incidentally, is William Kennedy Laurie Dickson.

3739 *The Life and Legend of Gene Fowler.* by Smith, H. Allen. 320 p. illus. New York: Morrow, 1977.

Gene Fowler, the author of numerous screenplays and such memorable biographies as *Good Night, Sweet Prince* (John Barrymore) and *Father Goose* (Mack Sennett), is recalled in this memoir by his friend, H. Allen Smith. Using Fowler's rich, colorful life (1907-1960) as his basic story, Smith has added important elements of style and form to the telling. Recalling many anecdotes, incidents, and legends, the author is able to bring authenticity, humor and intelligence to material that might have seemed foolish or juvenile in other hands. Often Fowler's escapades defy analysis; they are the stuff that rejected scripts are made of—improbable and unreal. Yet, not only does Smith tell his small stories well, but, in his large one, creates a portrait of a truly unique American original. The text also gives attention to some other originals, all friends of Fowler: John Barrymore, W. C. Fields, Ben Hecht, Charles MacArthur, and Red Skelton. Some illustrations and an index are provided. Most needed but missing here is a bibliography/filmography of Fowler's work that could explain or describe the range and diversity of his writing. That omission is a major flaw in a major work. Otherwise the book is one to treasure. Recommended.

3740   *The Life and Legend of Tom Mix.* by Mix, Paul E. 206 p. illus. New York: A. S. Barnes, 1972.

The author, who is not directly related to Tom Mix, has done an enormous amount of investigation in preparing this biography. Unfortunately, its base of research-data shows continually through the narrative which, instead of inviting reader involvement, becomes largely a recital of facts, quotes, and historical references. Its intention and its thoroughness must be admired, but it is not much fun to read.

The pedantic-statistical text might have been more palatable if greater care had been taken with the numerous illustrations. The selection shows depth (the home of the employer of Tom's father), originality (the highway marker denoting Mix's fatal accident) and variety (stills, frames, posters, ads and candids), but all of these qualities are defeated by murky production, overexposure and fuzzy printing. Granted that some of the original material has deteriorated, it should still be possible to obtain better quality control over the illustrations.

The impressive research carries over to the appendix which lists the museums, libraries, and companies that provided materials on Mix. A good filmography is given and some microfilm records are described but their location is not noted. Had the author been able to apply some critical, analytical and narrative style to his talent for research, this would be a far more entertaining book. Devotees of western films will probably find the book quite satisfying and it does provide much reference material on Mix.

3741   *Life and Lillian Gish.* by Paine, Albert B. 303 p. illus. New York: Macmillan, 1932.

This early biography discusses Lillian Gish's work in films and on stage.

3742   *The Life and Loves of Cary Grant.* by Guthrie, Lee. 239 p. illus. New York: Drake, 1977.

This unauthorized biography is a weak attempt to relate what is promised in its title. Since Grant is an intensely private person, what appears here is material based on either public records or the author's conjecture. Major themes such as failure in marriage, drug experimentation, etc., are treated superficially as is the personality of the actor off-screen. Illustrations, a filmography, and an index help to pad out this disappointing biography.

3743   *The Life and Loves of Gable.* by Scagnetti, Jack. 160 p. illus. Middle Village, N.J.: Jonathan David, 1976.

In this straightforward account of the life and career of Clark Gable, some attention is given to his wives and lovers. However, the star of the book is Gable and most of the volume is a retelling of his well-known story. Although the text is presented in an efficient, newspaper-like prose, there is little critical depth or analysis offered. In fact we learn nothing more than that which has already been related by Jean Garceau, Gabe Essoe, George Carpozi, Chester Williams, Kathleen Gable, Charles Samuels, Rene Jordan, Warren Harris, and Joe Morella-Edward Epstein. To compete with this already published group, a new book on Gable should offer something unique, unusual, or new. Unfortunately this volume does not.

The illustrations are stronger than the text, as they show the evolution of a gawky, unattractive teenager into a handsome mature male. The omission of a filmography and an index, combined with the blandness that results from reading an overly familiar story, weakens the book's appeal and usefulness.

3744   *The Life and Loves of Lana Turner.* by Wright, Jacqueline. 160 p. paper New York: Wisdom House, 1961.

3745   *The Life and Times of John Wayne.* 79 p. illus. New York: Hamison House, 1979.

A heavily illustrated biography of John Wayne presented in a large oversized format. In addition to the usual biographical elements, attention is given to the international reaction to his death.

3746   THE LIFE AND TIMES OF JUDGE ROY BEAN. by Milius, John. 180 p. paper illus. New York: Bantam, 1973.

Script of the 1972 film directed by John Huston. Contains cast and production credits.

3747   *Life Goes to the Movies.* edited by Scherman, David. 304 p. illus. New York: Time-Life Books, 1975.

In addition to offering over 700 fascinating black-and-white and color photographs, this volume aims at some textual significance. It attempts to explore the symbiotic relationship that existed between the film industry and the magazine. How each needed and served the other is delineated in an above average text.

The volume is not a history of the movies. Instead it is a sampling made over the 36 years of *Life*'s existence which shows the changing styles, attitudes, and mores of the film industry for that period.

Picture reproduction is most satisfactory and the accompanying text/captions are surprisingly good. The volume is certain to be very popular and deservedly so. It can be enthusiastically recommended.

3748   *see 3747*

3749   *Life in a Movie Club.* by Cappello, Patrick H. 127 p. paper illus. New York: Vantage, 1970.

Deals with filmmaking.

3750   *Life is a Banquet.* by Russell, Rosalind; and Chase, Chris. 260 p. illus. New York: Random House, 1977.

It is amazing how this volume reflects the same woman that filmgoers remember from a film career that lasted almost four decades. During that time we had Russell as the young ingenue, the snappy sophisticated heroine, the other woman, the independent female, and finally the older family relative. Her private life as reported here was remarkably similar. A warm acceptance of life's pleasures and disappointments pervades the text, but, as in AUNTIE MAME (1958), the downs constitute a few short moments as compared to the many joys.

The style used by the author is chatty and much of the humor is derived by looking back at the young innocent actress ambitiously making her way in wicked Hollywood.

Supporting this pleasing memoir are a filmography, an index and a collection of carefully selected visuals.

Rosalind Russell was always concerned about her public image, and she continues that personal policy here. The portrait presented is that of a positive, loving woman who acquired success in several very competitive fields with little effort. Most readers will enjoy this version of Cinderella Russell as recalled by Auntie Mame. Acceptable.

3751   *The Life of Elvis Presley.* by Shaver, Sean; and Holand, Hal. illus. Kansas City: Timor, 1979.

3752   THE LIFE OF EMILE ZOLA: *The Authorized Story of the Film.* by Fielding, Hubert. 128 p. illus. London: Joseph, 1938.

An early example of a movie tie-in, this volume was derived from the 1937 Warner Brothers film which starred Paul Muni.

3753   *The Life of Raymond Chandler.* by MacShane, Frank. 306 p. illus. New York: Dutton, 1976.

Raymond Chandler is best known as the creator of Philip Marlowe, the private detective and hero of such novels as *The Big Sleep, Farewell, My Lovely, The Lady in the Lake, The High Window, The Little Sister* and *The Long Goodbye.* All eventually appeared as films with some being remade several times. It was inevitable that Chandler's literary reputation should lead him to Hollywood, where he worked as a screenwriter on such films as DOUBLE INDEMNITY (1943), AND NOW TOMORROW (1944), THE UNSEEN (1945), THE BLUE DAHLIA (1946) and STRANGERS ON A TRAIN (1951).

In this well-written and thoroughly researched biography, the author gives detailed attention to Chandler's experiences with such filmmakers as Billy Wilder, Alfred Hitchcock, and Ray Stark. The films adapted from his novels by other writers are also discussed.

The book contains a center section of illustrations, many pages of carefully arranged source notes, a selected list of Chandler's publications, and an index.

For those who have enjoyed the Philip Marlowe novels or the films generated from them, MacShane offers an objective, entertaining biography of Marlowe's creator. His portrait of Hollywood in the forties and several of its unique personalities is an additional reward.

The revival of interest in Chandler is evidenced by books such as *The Blue Dahlia* and *Raymond Chandler on Screen.* This fine volume presents the strongest justification so far for a reassessment of Chandler's work. Recommended.

3754   *The Life of Robert Taylor.* by Wayne, Jane Ellen. 349 p. paper illus. New York: Warner Books, 1973.

Biographies of screen personalities range widely in quality and it is unusual for one as good as this to be published as an original paperback. It exhibits some interesting features, including the author's access to many letters written by Taylor and the cooperation of many persons close to him. While outside sources and references are few, the privileged inside information seems plentiful.

The portrait that emerges is not one of charisma or

strength. Taylor was a beautiful male who lacked aggressiveness. For much of his life he was a puppet dominated by his mother, by his wife (Barbara Stanwyck), and by Louis B. Mayer. His ever-present concern about his masculine image would obviously make an interesting psychoanalytical study. Even toward his life's end, he seemed content to relinquish his role as master in favor of fussiness, penny-pinching and image-worry. The portrait of Stanwyck presented here is fascinating: constantly sedated, hard, foul-mouthed, and money-hungry—another meaty role, but this time self-created.

A few pictures show Taylor with his more famous leading ladies. There is no index but a rather good filmography completes the volume. Only infrequently does the book lapse into questionable taste, and that mostly when sex is the topic. The recreated dialogue may bother some purists, too, but, all in all, this is a better-than-average biography. The book can be highly recommended.

3755   *A Life on Film.* by Astor, Mary. 245 p. paper illus. New York: Dell, 1972.

The genre of film biography goes forward a few steps with this fascinating, absorbing life story. Miss Astor's first volume, *Mary Astor, My Story*, emphasized her personal life, with little attention given to her many films. The situation is reversed here and the bulk of this volume tells about the films, her co-workers, and the industry. The privileges, responsibilities and the disadvantages of being the "total professional" are fully delineated. In her writing, as on the screen, Miss Astor has the ability of the true artist—that of being able to command the sympathy and respect of an audience without apparently trying for it. In turn, she can be intellectual, witty, compassionate, and even bitchy, but she always appears totally honest. At the book's conclusion, she emerges with stature, not only as a consistently fine actress but as a strong human being.

The photographs in the paperback edition are only fair. The book does contain a filmography, listing rather complete credits for 109 feature films in which she appeared. There is also an index which is quite helpful. It is pleasure to give high recommendation to a film star autobiography. This one is in the same thoroughbred class as Bette Davis' *The Lonely Life.* Miss Astor obviously deserves one more award.

3756   *Life Stories of the Movie Stars.* by Tinee, Mae. 64 p. illus. Hamilton, Ohio: Presto, 1916.

Photos and short biographical sketches of many of the silent screen stars and directors—Sennett, Griffith, Chaplin, Arbuckle, and others.

3757   *Life Stories of the Stars.* by Wood, Leslie. 144 p. illus. London: Burke Pub. Co., 1946.

A collective biography that treats 23 subjects and includes over 90 stills-portraits, some of which are in color. Included are such Hollywood names as Cary Grant, Joan Fontaine, Ingrid Bergman, Gary Cooper, Bette Davis, and Greer Garson.

3758   *The Life Story of an Ugly Duckling.* by Dressler, Marie. 234 p. illus. New York: Robert McBride, 1924.

This earlier autobiography of Dressler is as informal and amusing as is her *My Own Story.* This consumate actress knows exactly how far she can go in her performing and her writing—never too sentimental, never overly mawkish. In a phrase, "just right."

3759   *The Life Story of Clark Gable: The Child, the Trouper, the Screen Sensation.* by McBride, Mary Margaret. 61 p. illus. New York: Star Library, 1932.

3760   *The Life Story of Constance Bennett.* by McBride, Mary Margaret. 61 p. illus. New York: Star Library, 1932.

3761   *The Life Story of Danny Kaye.* by Richards, Dick. 70 p. paper illus. London: Convoy, 1949.

3762   *The Life That Late He Led.* by Eels, George. 447 p. paper illus. New York: Berkley Publishing, 1967.

Most people associate Cole Porter with Broadway theatre, and rightfully so. What they may not be aware of is his long and prolific musical contribution to motion pictures. Not only were many of his stage musicals translated into film, but he wrote several memorable original scores for films. His filmography is fascinating: BATTLE OF PARIS (1929); 50 MILLION FRENCHMEN (1930); WAKE UP AND DREAM and THE GAY DIVORCEE (1934); ADIOS, ARGENTINA (1935); BORN TO DANCE and ANYTHING GOES (1936); ROSALIE (1937); BREAK THE NEWS (1938); THE SUN NEVER SETS (1939); BROADWAY MELODY OF 1940 (1940); YOU'LL NEVER GET RICH (1941); SOMETHING TO SHOUT ABOUT and PANAMA HATTIE (1942); DUBARRY WAS A LADY and LET'S FACE IT (1943); HOLLYWOOD CANTEEN and MISSISSIPPI BLUE (1944); NIGHT AND DAY (1945); THE PIRATE (1946);

MADAM'S RIB (1949); KISS ME KATE (1953); HIGH SOCIETY (1956); SILK STOCKINGS and LES GIRLS (1957); and CAN-CAN (1960).

The volume also contains a 1936 diary of his days in Hollywood, preparing his first full score for the film BORN TO DANCE. Names of film celebrities proliferate in this detailed and factual book. Porter's wit, talent, courage, and sophistication are made known in an affectionate but objective text by Eels. For those who were adults during Porter's reign as one of America's top composers, the book is a total pleasure.

The book is indexed, contains a few illustrations and a chronological listing of all Porter's musical activities. Although only partially concerned with film composing, this volume can be recommended.

3763 *Life with Googie.* by McCallum, John. illus. London: Heinemann.

Googie is, of course, Googie Withers, a British stage and screen star best known in America for her work in ON APPROVAL (1944), DEAD OF NIGHT (1945), IT ALWAYS RAINS ON SUNDAY (1947), THE MAGIC BOX (1951) and other films. Written by her husband, this dual biography is mostly a memoir of their life and activities together. The McCallum's story is flavored with show business stories and anecdotes.

3764 *Life with Groucho.* by Marx, Arthur. 310 p. New York: Simon & Schuster, 1954.

A profile of Groucho both on and off stage written by his son. Entertaining, affectionate, and a bit imitative of Dad's style. A good addition to the literature about the Marxes.

3765 *Life with the Lyons: The Autobiography of Bebe Daniels and Ben Lyon.* by Daniels, Bebe; and Lyon, Ben. 256 p. illus. London: Odhams, 1953.

Ben Lyon was a leading man in films (HELL'S ANGELS 1930), during the twenties and thirties. In the post-war years he served as a casting director for 20th Century Fox. Bebe Daniels appeared in American films from 1908 (as a child) to 1939, reaching stardom in the late twenties. Before World War II the Lyons moved to London, where they became popular performers in radio, television and films. Among their British films were HI GANG (1940), LIFE WITH THE LYONS (1953), and THE LYONS IN PARIS (1955). Bebe died in 1971. Interested readers should also refer to *Bebe and Ben* written by Jill Allgood and published by Robert Hale in 1975.

3766 *Life's Little Dramas.* by Hodges, Bart. 173 p. illus. New York: Duell, Sloan & Pearce, 1948.

Selected Hollywood personalities tell their stories to the author, who has also provided the illustrations for this volume. The many subjects range from Basil Rathbone to Mary Pickford.

3767 *Light and Shadows: A History of Motion Pictures.* by Bohn, Thomas W.; and Stromgren, Richard L. 537 p. paper illus. Port Washington, N.Y.: Alfred Publishing, 1976.

The appearance of a new book on the history of the motion picture may be a cause for apprehension since the subject has been well-covered by earlier publications. No such feeling is necessary here since the authors have provided a fresh structure and approach to their material. Relating the development of motion pictures to commerce, technology, culture, art, and sociology, they have avoided a tendency of most writers to recall films and plots in one long filmography. Instead they have offered three general sections: The Emergence of an Industry; The Addition of Sound to Films; and Motion Pictures after World War II. The text is quite detailed, nicely illustrated, and adequately supported by a bibliography, a name index, a title index, and a general index.

Any history of film must be selective, and in this respect the authors have provided most satisfactory coverage. Proper attention is paid here to the important events, personalities, trends, and developments that have characterized motion pictures for eight decades. Because of the intelligent selection of its materials and the readable style used in presenting them, the book is a major addition to that small body of cinema literature dealing with the history of the film. Recommended.

3768 *Light of a Star.* by Robyns, Gwen. 256 p. illus. New York: A. S. Barnes, 1970.

The American edition of the Vivien Leigh biography that appeared in England two years earlier. It is surprisingly good and many of the usual criticisms of star biography cannot be applied here. A rather clear portrait of the complex person that Vivien Leigh was does emerge by the book's end. According to the author, Miss Leigh was a total professional and a perfectionist, always working to improve her performances—with only one notable exception, her role as wife to Laurence Olivier. She seems to have taken that part for granted and the discovery of the marriage's failure was a principal cause of her early death. The text notes her positive qualities such as thoughtfulness, humility, and emotional control, and balances them against her overambition, vanity, and a candor that could be mistaken for spitefulness.

Some attention is given to her major films—GONE WITH THE WIND (1939), A STREETCAR NAMED DESIRE (1951), THE ROMAN SPRING OF MRS. STONE (1961) and SHIP OF FOOLS (1965). The important film neglected is CAESAR AND CLEOPATRA (1945); other than noting friction between Gabriel Pascal and Leigh, not much is said about her fine performance. Ironically, all her theatrical appearances, including out-of-town failures, are described in detail. The author handles discreetly and sensitively the nervous breakdowns, sicknesses, emotional relationships, and other happenings in the star's personal life. There are some illustrations, but they fail completely to capture the physical beauty of this fine actress. The book is indexed but a listing of the plays and films, which would seem essential, is not given.

The total portrait given here is affectionate yet objective, probably because much of the author's material came from persons who knew Vivien Leigh. The book is a deserved tribute to a fine actress and a complex human being. Recommended.

3769 *Light Up Your Torches and Pull Up Your Tights.* by Garnett, Tay. 416 p. illus. New Rochelle, N.Y.: Arlington House, 1973.

Tay Garnett had a variety of careers before he became a writer for Mack Sennett in the twenties. Since that time he has been writing and directing films and in recent years has been most active in television. The richness of his experience should have resulted in a far better autobiography than this. But his films leave one with the feeling that they could have been much better in most instances if Garnett had greater control and discipline, and the book reads the same way. Narrative and interest are sacrificed in favor of a gag, a wisecrack, or an unimportant anecdote.

Often he refuses to state the reasons why a film did not succeed, sometimes using courtesy as his out: "As a kindness to many people, I shall forgo a recital of most of the tragedies of that misbegotten film." The personalities who populate his little stories are presented in sugarcoated prose: "gallant Gable ... utterly lovely Martha Scott ... serious-minded Robert Taylor ... multitalented Gene Kelly ... wise Walter Pidgeon ... " etc. A fear of becoming too serious seems to hover over the narrative which loses reader involvement by using many unrelated shots rather than settling for a well-defined scene.

Illustrations are quite small and mounted several to a page. This is acceptable for portraits but the reader will have to squint to see some of the actors mentioned in the captions. An index, a filmography and a listing of TV and radio credits are added values.

3770 *Lighting For Location Motion Pictures.* by Ritsko, Alan J. 224 p. illus. New York: Van Nostrand, 1979.

This specialized volume by Alan Ritsko covers the typical lighting problems encountered in making motion pictures outide of the studio environment. Using examples and visual illustrations, he shows relative positions of lights, actors, cameras, settings, etc., in making various types of films—features, documentaries, commercials, etc. Topics such as color, intensity, quality, exposure, light-metering, temperature, balance, and electricity are treated. A helpful index is provided. The author has taken a technical subject and simplified it via text and illustrations. Although it requires some study and concentration for total comprehension, the interested nonprofessional can certainly profit from the reading and use of this helpful guide.

3771 LIMELIGHT *and After*: The Education of an Actress. by Bloom, Claire. New York: Harper and Row, 1981.

3772 *The Limits of Infinity.* by Sobchack, Vivian Carol. 246 p. illus. New York: A.S. Barnes, 1980.

Subtitled "The American Science Fiction Film," this volume surveys the period from 1950 to 1975 in an attempt to fill the lack of aesthetic criticism currently available on this particular genre. After establishing some definitions and themes indigenous to science fiction, the author examines in detail the images (iconography) and the sounds of the science fiction film. Notes, a bibliography, and an index complete the book.

In a short statement Sobchack concludes that the tension between the visual depiction of the unknown future and the verbal dependence on the known present is a quality unique to this genre. Tension is the basic aesthetic of the science fiction films that Sobchack considers in this unusual study. While it is possible to have some reservation about the limitations she imposes on the study, her debt to similar essays and studies appearing in periodical, and her omission of a filmography, there can be little quarrel with her result: a logical synthesis of research, experience and critical opinion blended into a provocative statement about an American film genre.

3773 *Lindsay Anderson.* by Sussex, Elizabeth. 96 p. paper illus. New York: Praeger, 1970.

Best known in America as the director of THIS SPORTING LIFE (1963) and IF (1969), Lindsay Anderson has also been an author, critic, and publisher. In addition to films, he has directed for the theatre and television. Much of this volume is devoted to an analysis of his two feature films; a dozen of his short films are also considered. Included are some interesting illustrations and a filmography. The text is formal and intellectual and overlooks some obvious strengths of the features. Reader reaction to this volume will depend largely upon knowledge of the two feature films. Otherwise the material is much more pertinent for British audiences. Recommended.

3774 THE LION IN WINTER. 32 p. paper illus. New York: Ronark Program Co., 1968.

A map of the domains which provide the motivation for the story is given at the beginning of this souvenir book. Some historical background precedes a discussion of the making of the 1968 film. Tribute is paid to the cast and production personnel in the final sections of this impressive book. Production values here are much above the average.

3775 THE LION IN WINTER. by Goldman, James. 139 p. paper illus. New York: Dell Publishing Co., 1968.

Script of the 1968 film directed by Anthony Harvey.

3776 *The Lion's Share.* by Crowther, Bosley. 320 p. illus. New York: Dutton, 1957.

Using the MGM studios as the framework, Crowther provides a history of the American film from the Vitascope at Herald Square to the departure of studio heads Loew and Schary in 1956. Much of the anecdotal material involves familiar names since MGM was "the Studio of the Stars." The combination of gossip, scholarship, writing ability, and famous names makes for an absorbing and entertaining book. Anyone interested in a case study of a major film studio could not be better served than by this volume. The illustrations are most appropriate and reproduced with clarity. Highly recommended.

3777 *The Lions of* LIVING FREE. by Couffer, Jack. 96 p. illus. New York: E. P. Dutton, 1972.

Jack Couffer's career as a naturalist photographer, which began with Walt Disney, was described in his book, *Song of Wild Laughter.* Since then, Couffer directed two films for other studios—RING OF BRIGHT WATER (1969) and LIVING FREE (1972). It is the making of the latter film that is related in this book. Attention is given to the actors—Susan Hampshire and Nigel Davenport—the lions, the territory of East Africa and its people. The film was an unsuccessful attempt to duplicate the success of the original, BORN FREE (1966). Just as audiences felt that one film about a mature woman's "attraction" to lions was quite enough, the reader will find most of this account familiar and predictable. The book *On Playing With Lions*, which accompanied the original film, covered some of the same material presented here.

There are some illustrations which are consistent with the total effort—flat, unimaginative, and repetitive. No index is provided. Chalk this book up as a sequel which depended upon another sequel. A case of too much inbreeding resulting in an anemic offspring. Young readers may have some interest in this book but it is not generally recommended.

3778 *Lipton on Filmmaking.* by Lipton, Lenny. 223 p. paper illus. New York: Simon and Schuster, 1979.

In addition to composing the lyrics to "Puff The Magic Dragon," Lenny Lipton has established a reputation as an authority on the super-8 medium. A frequent contributor to filmmaking periodicals, he is also the author of *Independent Filmmaking* and *The Super-8 Book.* For this volume he has selected and revised periodical articles which have appeared in *Super-8 Filmmaker* and *American Cinematographer.* Arranged under five general headings—polavision, tools for making the image, recording the image, after image, and the shape of images to come—they offer the reader a survey/overview of nonprofessional filmmaking. Lipton writes an informal practical prose which avoids technical jargon and favors simple, clear description and explanation. Lipton's personalized advice and guidance is abundant. Many illustrations and charts, along with an index, complete the book. Anyone interested in personal filmmaking should find this anthology most helpful and rewarding.

3779 *A List of Films on Africa.* by Moyne, Claudia W. paper Brookline, Mass.: African Studies Center Boston University, 1966.

3780 *List of Films Recommended for Children and Adolescents.* compiled by Department of Mass Communication, UNESCO. 118 p. paper Paris: UNESCO, 1956.

A list of films based on selections made in 22 countries. This is *Report and Papers on Mass Communication No. 19,* written in French and English.

3781 *Literary and Socio-Political Trends in Italian Cinema.* edited by Lawton, Benjamin Ray, Jr. 297 p. paper Los Angeles: Center for Italian Studies, UCLA, 1973.

Designed as a text to accompany a UCLA course with the same title, this anthology consists of three major divisions. The first reflects the title by offering five articles on poetry, politics, sociology, and other influences on the recent Italian film. "A History of Italian Cinema" comprises the second, with the text broken into five periods—the silent, pre-war sound, late forties neo-realism, the fifties, and the last two decades. An appendix offers separate sections on Fellini, Visconti, two lists of film periodicals, and a bibliography on political overtones of Italian Cinema. An unusual timeline chart of the Italian Cinema from 1905 to 1975 concludes the book.

As with most anthologies, the quality of the elements varies. In its present form, this seems to be a book-in-the-making. With some additional material and professional editing, the volume would be a fine addition to the literature on Italian film.

3782 *Literary Market Place.* New York: Bowker, 1940- .

This annual (1940 to date) directory lists the names and addresses of a few educational film producers, associations, and periodicals.

3783 *Literary Property.* by Wincor, Richard. 154 p. paper New York: Potter, 1970.

The relationships between an author and the agencies which use his original work are the substance of this book. It is a guide for those involved with contracts, subsidiary rights, remakes, etc. Much emphasis is on the film industry and its use of literary properties. Some samples of author contracts are given. Essential for anyone who plans to write for films. It is quite specialized but noted here for its pertinence for filmmaking.

3784 *Literature and Film.* by Richardson, Robert. 150 p. Bloomington, Ind.: Indiana University Press, 1969.

The author's theses seem to be as follows: 1) literature and film are similar in many ways; 2) during the infancy of motion pictures, literature had an effect on film form and structure; 3) in recent years, film has had an effect on modern literary forms; 4) film criticism and literary criticism can influence and learn from each other; and 5) poetry, literature, and film, at their best, have similar goals. By using examples from literature, poetry, films, etc., the author presents an unusual, thoughtful and serious discussion. Resembling a doctoral dissertaion, the book is highly recommended for advanced students. The general reader looking for intellectual stimulation may be rewarded also. The casual browser and the cinema buff may be bewildered or bored or both.

3785 *Literature and Film: An Annotated Bibliography, 1900-1977.* by Welch, Jeffery. 328 p. New York: Garland, 1979.

3786 *The Literature of Cinema (A Series).* edited by Amberg, George; and Dworkin, Martin S. New York: Arno Press, 1972.

This ambitious and commendable publishing series has made another 36 books on film available. The first grouping in 1970 included 48 titles. The volumes in this series vary in audience appeal.

Titles in the second series, selected by George Amberg, include: *Friese-Green: Close-Up of an Inventor; Theory of the Film; Let's Go to the Movies; Brigitte Bardot and the Lolita Syndrome; Art and Design in the British Film; Report on Blacklisting, Part I; Que Viva Mexico; Dynamics of the Film; The Odyssey of a Film-Maker; Charlie Chaplin; Hollywood on Trial; Hollywood Scapegoat; The Film Answers Back; Anatomy of the Film; The Use of the Film.*

Three original compilation volumes complete the Amberg selections: *The Art of the Cinema; Origins of the American Film; Hound and Horn.*

The Complete GREED *of Erich von Stroheim* is a separate Arno publication edited by Herman Weinberg that can be considered as part of the series.

Martin S. Dworkin selected titles for this series which include: *Around Cinemas, 2 Volumes; Cinematographic Annual, 2 Volumes; Scrutiny of Cinema; British Film Music; The Motion-Picture Cameraman; Movement; Sociology of Film; Film and Theatre; 20 Years of British Film, 1925-1945;*

Soviet Cinema; Scandinavian Film; The Italian Cinema; French Film; 50 Years of German Film.

3787 *The Literature of Cinema: 48 Books About Cinema.* edited by Dworkin, Martin S. illus. New York: Arno Press, 1970.

This ambitious and commendable publishing project has made available some 48 volumes on cinema. Many of these books were out of print, rare, forgotten, etc. Others were still available in editions from various publishers. Depending upon the audience served, this collection will have different values. Its emphasis is on the historical/sociological/technical side of films with serveral of the books dating back to the 1900s and earlier.

The titles in the collection are considered individually in this book. They include: *America at the Movies* (1939), *Animated Pictures* (1898), *Animated Photography: the ABC of the Cinematography* (1900), *L' Arte Cinematographique No. 1-8* (1926-1931), *Art of Photoplay Making* (1918), *Art of the Motion Picture* (1946), *Cildren's Attendance at Motion Pictures* (1935), *Children's Sleep* (1933), *Cinema: Its Present Position and Future Possibilities* (1917), *Content of Motion Pictures* (1935), *Emotional Responses of Children to the Motion Picture Situation* (1933), *Encyclopedia of Music For Pictures* (1925), *Experiment in the Film* (1949), *Film Music* (1936), *Footnotes to the Film* (1938), *Getting Ideas from the Movies* (1933), *History of Motion Pictures* (1938), *History of the Kinetograph, Kinetascope, and Kinetophonograph* (1895), *History of the Movies* (1931), *Hollywood* (1941), *Hollywood's Movie Commandments* (1937), *House that Shadows Built* (1928), *How to Appreciate Motion Pictures* (1937), *Instructional Film Research 1918-1950 (Rapid Mass Learning)* (1950), *Living Pictures: Their History, Photo Reproduction and Practical Working* (1899), *Mind and the Film* (1926), *Motion Picture Industry* (1947), *Motion Picture in its Economic and Social Aspects* (1947), *Motion Picture Moods for Pianists and Organists* (1924), *Motion Pictures and Standards of Morality* (1933), *Motion Pictures and the Social Attitudes of Children* (1933), *Motion Pictures and Youth* (1933), *Motion Pictures in Education: A Summary of the Literature* (1938), *Motion Picture Work* (1915), *Movies and Conduct* (1933), *Movies, Delinquency, and Crime* (1933), *Moving Pictures* (1912), *Musical Accompaniment of Moving Pictures* (1920), *Negro, in Films* (1949), *New Spirit in the Cinema* (1930), *New Spirit in the Russian Theatre 1917-1928* (1929), *New Theatre and Cinema Of Soviet Russia* (1924), *Opportunities in the Motion Picture Industry* (1922), *Our Movie Made Children* (1935), *Photo Drama* (1914), *Photo Play* (1916), *Pictorial Beauty on the Screen* (1923), *Screen Monographs - I*

(1923, 1928, 1937), *Screen Monographs - II* (1915, 1929, 1929, 1930), and *Upton Sinclair Presents William Fox* (1933).

3788 *The Literature of the Film.* by Dyment, Alan R. 398 p. London: Whitelion Publishers (Gale Research-U.S. Distrib.), 1975.

This volume is subtitled "A Bibliographical Guide to the Film as Art and Entertainment, 1936-1970." It is an oversized book that offers a selected listing of 1303 entries, most of which are English language books. Periodicals, publicity materials, unpublished studies, pamphlets of less than 30 pages, and highly technical works are among the items not treated here.

The book distributes its titles among the usual film subject headings: history, personalities, film and society, etc. Entries are arranged under certain headings according to author's surname while others are placed alphabetically by either subject (personalities) or film title (screenplays). A very short annotation, usually a simple sentence, accompanies some of the entries. The table of contents lists the major headings and there is an author-film title-personality name index which follows the text.

An examination of the book discloses some major weaknesses: inconsistency, poor arrangement, inferior production, and a rather high price. Inconsistency can be noted in the annotations. For *Happy Go Lucky: My Life* by Kenneth More we find: "An autobiography by the British Comedy Actors." Kenneth More is quite well known and the title is self-explanatory. However, for *Reflected Glory: An Autobiographical Sketch* by Peter Noble there is no annotation. Most users do not know who Noble is and an annotation would help in this instance. In certain entries mention is made of either "an index" or "no index" ; yet others ignore the question of an index altogether. For example, neither *Easy the Hard Way* by Joe Pasternack or Cecil Beaton's *Fair Lady* contains an index but no mention of the absence is made. For *Dear Mr. G., Zen Showed Me the Way, The Danny Kaye Story,* and *John Huston—King Rebel,* the phrase "no index" appears in the annotation. With regard to dates the volume is inconsistent. The subtitle limits the books to 1970 but many 1971 publications are noted. Then, too, a five-year gap between cut-off date and publication is a serious handicap to the user searching for current information.

Many of the titles listed here were reissued early in the seventies by such publishers as Arno, Ozer, and others. Also, in what is probably a typographical error, the publication date for *Claude Chabrol* is noted as 1870.

The arrangement takes some study to comprehend. Without a subject index of topics, the reader may have some difficulty finding books that deal with such film literature topics as film study, film research, New Wave directors, film series, reference books, interviews, copyright, Hollywood, anthologies, etc. The book suffers from several poor production factors. The printed material is spaced very widely and spread out over each page in what seems a most inefficient use of available page space in a reference book. The material seems "stretched" to 400 pages. Further evidence of this can be noted by the absence of cross-references and the repetition of complete entries when a particular book appears under more than one subject heading. The pages resemble typewritten manuscript and often paragraphs are blurred or murky.

Exception must be made to the distributor's claim that this is the first major guide to film literature since *The Film Index*. Similar works by Limbacher, Bukalsi, and Manchel appeared several years ago; there is a two-volume guide to film literature by Chicorel and three volumes of what many critics have named the standard work in the field of film literature, *Cinema Booklist*.

In view of its late appearance and older material, its high price, and the many weaknesses noted above, the volume must be considered as unacceptable.

3789   LITTLE CAESAR. by Faragoh, Francis. 200 p. illus. Madison, Wisc.: University of Wisconsin Press, 1981.

The script of the 1930 film, directed by Mervyn LeRoy.

3790   LITTLE FAUSS AND BIG HALSY. by Eastman, Charles. 160 p. paper illus. New York: Pocket Books, 1970.

Script of 1970 film directed by Sidney J. Furie.

3791   *The Little Fellow: The Life and Work of Charles Spencer Chaplin.* by Cotes, Peter; and Niklaus, Thelma. 181 p. illus. New York: Citadel Press, 1965.

This compact volume is divided into two major sections—the biographical and the critical analysis of Chaplin's film art. The biographical portion is straightforward, inclusive and sympathetic. It is the analysis of the artist-poet-comedian that is the great strength of the book. The Chaplin films are annotated and there are some excerpts from his writings. A

review of the Chaplin autobiography, a bibliography, and an index conclude the volume.

The many photographs add much to the book. At times the text has difficulty in keeping its chronology straight. Portions of it seem to have been written over a span of years—and, yet, no attempt is made to unify the time periods of the various sections. Another adequate addition to the numerous books on Chaplin, this one covers no new ground but is as good as most of the others. Preference for basic Chaplin still goes to the combination of the autobiography and Huff's unauthorized biography.

3792   *The Little Film Gazette of Nancy D. Warfield.* by Warfield, Nancy D. paper illus. New York: Little Film Gazette, 1973-1975.

The above title covers a series of monographs on selected film topics written and published by Nancy D. Warfield. They included: *Notes on* LES ENFANTS DU PARADIS, *Alain Delon and* BORSALINO, *The Structure of John Ford's* STAGECOACH, *A Film Student's Index to the National Board of Review Magazine 1926-1948*, and THE MAN WHO SHOT LIBERTY VALANCE (*A Study of John Ford's Films*).

3793   *Little Girl Lost: The Life and Hard Times of Judy Garland.* by Di Orio, Jr., Al 298 p. illus. New Rochelle, N.Y.: Arlington House, 1973.

A sympathetic retelling of the Garland life—or is it legend?—is presented here by a worshipping author who became a fan at the age of 13. A collector who owns thousands of articles, recordings and photographs, he knows the external facts of Garland's life and career. He succeeds admirably in giving data, statistics and other information. Where he fails is in giving an objective, full-dimensioned portrait of his subject. As a reference work on Garland, this is a very good book. As biography, it is the stuff of second-rate fan magazines.

Among the strong points are some well-selected illustrations which are nicely reproduced, a long detailed discography, a filmography, and a videography. An index is also provided. For Garland fans, the book will be most attractive, even though the material is overly familiar from the earlier books by Torme, Deans, Morella and Steiger. Acceptable.

3794   THE LITTLE ISLAND. by Schreivogel, Paul A. 20 p. paper illus. Dayton, Ohio: Pflaum, 1970.

A study guide for the 1958 film directed by Richard

Williams. Found in *Films in Depth* and also available separately.

3795 *A Little Love and Good Company.* by Nesbitt, Cathleen. 262 p. illus. Owens Mills, Md.: Stemmer House, 1977.

The face of Cathleen Nesbitt is so well-known to most filmgoers that it is surprising to find her filmography numbers only 22 films, most of which were made after she passed her fiftieth birthday. This may be due to a confusion with another aged contemporary, Gladys Cooper, or to a familiarity with her television appearances.

In this autobiography author Nesbitt is concerned primarily with her theatrical career. With ladylike accuracy she recalls the roles, the actors, and the incidents which have been a part of her long, busy life. Familiar show business names abound in her recollections, which are uniformly positive, affectionate, and respectful. Apparently there are some persons she prefers not to mention. Otherwise, how can one account for the fact that she includes eleven references to the stage version of "My Fair Lady" and six to Rex Harrison, but none to Julie Andrews? For all we are told, the latter lady could have been elsewhere during the long run of that hit show. No reference is made to her effective work with Cary Grant in AN AFFAIR TO REMEMBER (1957) either. In general the film and TV work which has made her so familiar to viewers is glossed over quickly.

Illustrations and an index are provided to this pleasant autobiography. Acceptable.

3796 LITTLE MURDERS. by Feiffer, Jules. 144 p. paper illus. New York: Paperback Library, 1968.

Script of the 1968 film directed by Alan Arkin.

3797 *Little Stories from the Screen.* by Lathrop, William A. 324 p. illus. New York: Britton, 1917.

Contains 25 scenarios as they were submitted to the studios for filming. Accompanied by stills from the films.

3798 *Liv Ullman.* edited by Reed, Rochelle. 24 p. paper illus. Washington, DC: American Film Institute, 1973.

While she was making LOST HORIZON (1973) in Hollywood, Liv Ullman gave this interview in March, 1972. Much audience interest was expressed about her philosophy of acting and about Ingmar Bergman. The responses are as cool as her performances.

3799 *Liv Ullman.* by Garfinkel, Bernie. illus. New York: Drake, 1975.

3800 *The Liveliest Art.* by Knight, Arthur. 352 p. paper illus. New York: New American Library, 1959.

This popularized history of the motion picture has probably enjoyed the largest reader audience of all film books. Appearing first in 1957, it has been reissued several times in paperback format and is still widely used as a text-reader in schools and colleges. When one considers the range of the book—world cinema from 1895 to 1955—any carping with the lack of depth seems a petty complaint. The author's style is literate, amusing, and informed.

Included are appropriate stills, a bibliography of 100 recommended books on film, a film distributor list, a film title index, and a general index. Add to this some 300 pages of interesting narrative and comment on film and it is easy to explain the volume's enduring popularity. The attractive low price of the paperback is another contributing factor.

As an example that film history can be both entertaining and informative, this book stands tall. Highly recommended.

3801 *Living Cinema: New Directions in Contemporary Film-Making.* by Marcorelles, Louis. 155 p. illus. New York: Praeger, 1973.

This volume is the result of several meetings sponsored by UNESCO over the period of 1963 to 1968 and originally published as *Elements pour un Nouveau Cinema.* The theme of the conferences was "the cultural value of the cinema, radio and television in contemporary society." The topic of this book is cinema verite, living cinema, or, to use the author's term, "direct cinema." He also mentions a minor, unexplored genre of documentary films, concrete cinema.

With the new technology that provides lightweight cameras, fast-speed film and portable recording devices, the author argues that the production crew becomes a participant in any filmmaking. Pure sound, unadulterated by studio technicians, is possible along with a freedom to match the visual with this sound. Using the work of Richard Leacock, Pierre Perrault, Jean Rouch and others as examples, Marcorelles reexamines the role of cinema in today's society and suggests potentials for this new direct cinema that have not been recognized as yet. Concrete cinema, however, leaves nothing to chance; everything is deliberate, as in an animated cartoon. Using existing proven elements, this film form would complement the direct cinema. The author has little faith in or encouragement for Hollywood films, Bergman/Fellini films, or any standard cinema. The future, he pontificates, belongs to the direct cinema.

This book is presented as an argument and offers provocative reading for the advanced reader or filmmaker. Acceptable.

3802   LIVING FREE. by Reeves, Leonard. 14 p. paper illus. London: Sackville Smeets, 1972.

The 1972 film that this souvenir book honors, a spinoff of *BORN FREE* (1966), did not fare nearly as well as its predecessor. The few pages are devoted to articles with such titles as: "The Men Who Took Lions to Kenya," "The Film That Couldn't Be Made," "Facts About Lions," etc. Carl Foreman, the producer, is the only human to receive individual attention.

3803   *Living Images.* by Kauffmann, Stanley. 404 p. paper New York: Harper and Row, 1975.

In his third collection of film criticism, Stanley Kauffmann offers 131 reviews written originally for *The New Republic* during the years 1970-1974. In addition there are eight essays on specific films taken from *Horizon*, 1972-1974. He concludes with an essay that he calls the introduction to this volume.

Put simply, Kauffmann is one of the finest film critics we have. He is consistent, responsible, and, most of all, enlightening in his approach to films. His three volumes represent American film criticism at its peak. Highly recommended.

3804   *Living in Fear.* by Daniels, Les. 248 p. illus. New York: Scribner's, 1975.

Subtitled "A History of Horror in the Mass Media," this volume deals with the horror narrative from the play *Oresteia* (458 B.C.) to the film THE EXORCIST (1974). Interspersed with the author's study are complete short stories by authors such as Poe, Bierce, Lovecraft, and James.

Since this is a chronological study, attention is given to films in the latter chapters. Beginning with Edison's version of the Frankenstein story in 1910, the text traces the horror film through its many variations and cycles over the next six decades. Stills from classic films support the survey. An index completes the work.

In addition to its appeal as a sound critical work, a major value of this volume is its placement of the horror film in a context with other forms of the horror narrative—literature, television, radio and comics. The fascination of the genre is enhanced by the appearance of this fascinating work. Recommended.

3805   *Living It Up, or They Still Love Me in Altoona.* by Burns, George. 251 p. illus. New York: G. P. Putnam's, 1976.

If the reader likes George Burns' standard routine of mixing rambling anecdotes, one-liners, philosophy, and show biz comment into a funny monologue, he will appreciate this venture by Burns into biographical reminiscence. He gets serious about wife Gracie Allen and friend Jack Benny, but never about himself. Generous in his praise of others, Burns is a master at interpreting the many lives he has enjoyed during his more than eight decades. He also includes script excerpts, speeches, and other samples of his on-stage material.

The volume is not indexed but it does contain a collection of illustrations. An amusing performance that reinforces the public image but does not reveal much about George Burns when he is without an audience.

3806   *Living Pictures: Their History, Photo-Production and Practical Working.* by Hopwood, Henry V. 377 p. illus. New York: Arno Press, 1970 (1899).

First published in 1899, this is a detailed survey (1830-1897) of the inventions and discoveries that led to the invention of the motion picture. A digest of British patents and an annotated bibliography are also given.

3807   *Living Pictures.* by Hopwood, Henry V. 377 p. illus. London: The Hatton Press, 1915.

Treats history, production, and practical working of motion pictures. Contains classified lists of British patents and a bibliography by Robert B. Foster.

3808   *The Living Screen: What Goes on in Films and Television.* by Manvell, Roger. 192 p. illus. London: George G. Harrad & Co., 1961.

This volume has Manvell traveling over familiar roads. Topics such as: What Is a Film?, How Does a Film Get Made?, How Does a Film Get Shown?, Was the Film Good of its Kind?, How the Film has Developed, The Main Kinds of Film, The Stars, The Art of the Film—all these repeat much of what Manvell has written before. Of course, this volume includes some exploration of TV and contains short script extracts from the film THE LADY KILLERS (1955) and the television play "Roundabout." Anything written by Manvell is characterized by experience, maturity, and intelligence. This volume resembles a *Reader's Digest* version of some previous efforts. Of minimum value.

3809 *Liza Minnelli.* by Paige, David. 31 p. paper illus. Mankato, Minn.: Creative Education, 1977.

A superficial biography designed for very young readers.

3810 *Liza!* by Parish, James Robert; and Ano, Jack. 176 p. paper illus. New York: Pocket Books, 1975.

A more appropriate title for this unauthorized biography might have been "Liza and Judy," since so much of it involves an unusual mother-daughter relationship. An attempt is made to present an objective portrait of Liza Minnelli as an aggressive, ambitious, hard-working, competitive, determined, talented woman. Both the professional and personal sides of her life are examined, sometimes with devastating results. Thankfully the authors try to avoid a fan magazine expose in favor of a detailed character delineation. They are successful much of the time.

A center section of visuals is adequate and four appendixes note Liza Minnelli's career to date: a filmography, a list of stage appearances, a discography, and a list of television appearances. The filmography lists a total of seven films, of which only four are important: CHARLIE BUBBLES (1968), THE STERILE CUCKOO (1969), TELL ME THAT YOU LOVE ME, JUNIE MOON (1970), and CABARET (1972). Unfortunately the book has no index. It is both surprising and pleasing to find objectivity, quality and style in an original paperback such as this one. Recommended.

3811 *Locklear: The Man Who Walked on Wings.* by Ronnie, Art. 333 p. illus. New York: A. S. Barnes, 1973.

Ormer Leslie Locklear had a short professional career as a flying daredevil, stunt pilot, and silent movie star. It lasted only 16 months. He became famous because of his ability to walk on the wings of planes in flight, and, in 1919, he appeared in fairs and exhibitions across the country at very expensive fees. Much of his activity during this period was in Hollywood—a young town just entering its second decade of existence.

Author Ronnie has researched this period of Locklear's life with diligence and admiration. He tells of Locklear's years in the Army Air Corps during World War I, of his development of the various stunts such as changing planes, hanging upside down in flight, etc., and of his spectacular but short career in Hollywood. Two films—THE GREAT AIR ROBBERY and THE SKYWAYMAN—are described in detail. Locklear was killed in a crash on August 2, 1920, just prior to the release of this latter film. The visuals which accompany the text are unfamiliar and representative of the pre-twenties period. Reproduction is acceptable. A lengthy bibliography and an index complete the volume.

Although this material is quite specialized, the author has recreated a period in film history and a personality attuned to those times. The potential adult audience of this book will be mostly nostalgia buffs and aviation devotees. It will be popular with young adult audiences.

3812 *Log of a Film Director.* by Lee, Norman H. 156 p. illus. London: Quality Press, 1949.

This is the autobiography of Norman H. Lee, a writer-director of more than 50 British films from 1928 to 1950. Most of his efforts were minor "B" type films made under the British quota system, and therefore, unknown in America. He wrote about films, filmmaking and film personalities in four other books: *Money for Film Stories* (1937), *A Film Is Born* (1945), *Land Lubber's Log* (1945) and *My Personal Log* (1947).

3813 *Lolita*: A Screenplay. by Nabokov, Vladimir. 213 p. New York: McGraw-Hill, 1974.

This is not the screenplay of the 1962 film directed by Stanley Kubrick—it is the script that Nabokov wrote in 1960 for a film version. According to the author, the final version of the film LOLITA (1962) bears little resemblance to his original script, which he offers here as "a vivacious variation of an old novel."

3814 *The Lonely Artist.* by Coorey, Philip. 118 p. illus. Colombo, Ceylon: Lake House Investments, 1970.

This book is subtitled "A Critical Introduction to

the Films of Lester James Peries," and concerns itself not only with Peries but also with the film industry in Ceylon and with the Sinhala film. In three sections, the book deals with Peries' films, their analysis, and his personal comments and philosophies about filmmaking. A bibliography and an index are somewhat helpful but nonfamiliarity with the films, the historical framework surrounding their production, and the culture for which they are primarily designed will limit reader interest. Illustrations are adequate.

3815 *The Lonely Beauties.* edited by Hill, Norman. 239 p. paper New York: Popular Library, 1971.

The ladies mentioned in the title are Jean Harlow, Marilyn Monroe, Diana Barrymore, Carole Landis, Judy Garland, Inger Stevens, and Linda Darnell. Linking them together in this paperback are the tragic themes of unhappy lives and early deaths. The book is a rather sad attempt to sensationalize the misfortunes of past screen royalty.

3816 *The Lonely Life: An Autobiography.* by Davis, Bette. 254 p. illus. New York: G. P. Putnam's, 1962.

In the past decade, this autobiography has become a sort of model to emulate. Although Sanford Dody is ackowledged as her "collaborator in every sense of the word," Miss Davis has apparently forgotten his contribution in recent interviews.

Dody's writing ability was first apparent in the Dagmar Godowsky biography and later in Helen Hayes' *On Reflection.* This book, too, has his unique style, a quiet wit, and unusual intelligence. One might surmise that his participation in this volume was not a small one.

The book is an excellent example of film star biography. Certain portions are near classic; for instance, the section on the vanity of male actors deserves a place of honor in any acting anthology. Although the Davis films are given moderate attention, the Hollywood life of the thirties and forties is fully described. The personal and emotional problems of being a superstar are handled quite objectively and with minimal self-pity. The photographs in the edition examined are interesting but are poorly reproduced with a noticeable lack of contrast and definition. Unfortunately there is no index. In this case, however, it is the text that counts. Readers will not be disappointed. Highly recommended.

3817 *Long Live the King: A Biography of Clark Gable.* by Tornabene, Lyn.

396 p. illus. New York: G. P. Putnam's, 1976.

There were several biographies of Clark Gable published during the sixties. What makes this one a bit different is the enormous amount of detail. Based on interviews and other primary source material, the text covers the events of Gable's life in a slow, methodical fashion. Efficient use is made of Tornabene's intensive research, which in this case includes many quotations from other writings on Gable.

The reader will discover little that is new here but may find some questions raised about accepted stories in the Gable legend, i.e., Did Gable really make his first screen test in a loin cloth?; Did Harlow and Gable have an affair?; Was the macho rivalry between John Huston and Gable during the filming of THE MISFITS (1961) the major cause of Gable's death?

A fine set of photographs accompanies the carefully written text. The appendixes include Gable's will, a handwriting analysis, a 1935 MGM movie contract, and selected remarks about Gable from a psychologist. The book is indexed.

Very familiar material is reviewed and expanded in this admirable work. Most readers will be pleased with the larger portrait furnished here. Recommended.

3818 *A Long Look at Short Films.* by Knight, Derrick; and Porter, Vincent. 185 p. paper New York: Pergamon Press, 1967.

This book is an argument for the survival and preservation of the short film in Great Britian. The opening discusssion of the entertainment film and the factual film has interesting and pertinent material. The rest of the book is too specialized to be of interest to most readers. Lists of short films in the appendices are offered as samplings, e.g., Short Films Registered in 1964," "Successful Short Films from Selected Film Festivals, 1960-65," etc. These lists have limited value. The book is too remote, too specialized in its specific argument, and too British to be recommended to the vast majority of readers.

3819 *The Long View.* by Wright, Basil. 731 p. New York: Knopf, 1974.

Best known as the filmmaker responsible for SONG OF CEYLON (1934), THE IMMORTAL LAND (1958), and other classic documentaries, Basil Wright is also a gifted writer and critic. He thinks of this book as a record of a love affair with the film medium. What he really offers here is a personalized survey of the history of world cinema. Using THE LUMIERE

BROTHERS (1895), THE BIRTH OF A NATION (1915), THE JAZZ SINGER (1927), GONE WITH THE WIND (1939), OPEN CITY (1945), PATHER PANCHALI (1956), A BOUT DE SOUFFLE (1960) and WOODSTOCK (1970) as "sign posts," he fleshes out the different eras of film history with asides, opinions, analyses and comments. The result is a very long volume that is alternately brilliant and dull. Those readers whose interests and enthusiasms coincide with Wright's will have a joyous time. Others will find the reading quite tedious.

An extended bibliography and a very detailed index accompany more than 700 pages of heavy text. It is true that Basil Wright can write with sophistication and erudition. In this case, however, he did not write with economy. Acceptable.

3820 THE LONGEST DAY. by Hift, Fred. 40 p. paper illus. New York: Program Publishing Company, 1962.

The profile of producer Darryl F. Zanuck which opens this souvenir book is followed by a section entitled "Making THE LONGEST DAY Come True—Again." Many of the visuals are candid shots taken during the making of the 1962 film. There are also shots from the film, maps, line drawings, and small photographs of the cast members. The official cast credits are divided into four sections: who's who in the American cast, the British cast, the French cast, and the German cast.

3821 *Look Back in Love.* by Elliot and Edith Farmer. Sequim, Wash.: Gemaia Press, 1979.

More about Frances Farmer from a member of the Farmer family.

3822 *The Look* Book. edited by Rosten, Leo. 400 p. illus. New York: Harry N. Abrams, 1975.

The magazine *Look* appeared in 1937 and lasted until 1971. Modeled after *Life* and the rotogravure sections of newspapers, it emphasized the visual. This heavy, oversized, expensive volume is a selection from the biweekly that featured movie stars, politicians, entertainers, athletes and an occasional intellectual in its pages.

Nostalgia furnished here is very, very glamorous but a distortion—the American experience really wasn't always as beautiful as suggested here.

3823 *Looking Away: Hollywood and Vietnam.* by Smith, Julian. 236 p. illus. New York: Scribner's, 1975.

Several hundred war films from 1941 (SERGEANT YORK) to 1968 (THE GREEN BERETS) provide the evidence for the statements that Julian Smith wishes to make about Hollywood and the Vietnam war. His general argument is that Hollywood ignored the war. It is in his exploration of the possible reasons for this rejection that the author makes most of his disturbing, provocative and well-reasoned arguments.

Although films did not deal directly with the Vietnam war, its effect on both film content and film viewers was enormous. Attitudes toward the government and the military changed considerably. The patriotic hero films of the forties vanished and were replaced by DR. STRANGELOVE (1964), FAIL SAFE (1964), CATCH 22 (1970), PATTON (1970), SLAUGHTERHOUSE-FIVE (1972), etc. The predictable role of the Department of Defense in supplying assistance to producers is shown in a list of films made with their cooperation—the provision of men, machines and material. A few illustrations appear strategically placed for purposes of irony. There is a bibliography, an extract from the Department of Defense policy on cooperation with nongovernmental agencies, and a good index.

In his attempt to show some of the effects of the Vietnam war on the U.S., Smith has used the medium of a specific film genre along with its makers and viewers. His text is written in a unique personal style, and few readers will be unchallenged by his total statement. Most younger readers do not possess sufficient background or experience to appreciate the author's ability to synthesize research, opinion, observation and original thought into a coherent whole. The book can be recommended without hesitation, however, for a mature audience.

3824 *Looking Back.* by Schmidt, Thomas. 36 p. paper illus. Mount Vernon, N.Y.: Audio Brandon Films, 1975.

Subtitled "A Motion Picture View of the American Past," this annotated filmography of over 100 motion pictures is divided into six major chapters, each of which covers a period in recent American history. An appendix of other films, a bibliography, a topic index and a film index follow the main text. Rather than treating the films separately, the author has woven them into his narrative, which often suggests the value of the film in interpreting or reflecting its particular time. Illustrations are fine and the entire catalog is a most commendable effort. Highly recommended.

3825 *Looking Back on Life, etc.* by Robey, Sir George. 318 p. illus. London:

Constable and Co., 1933.

Known as the "Prime Minister of Mirth," this music hall performer made his first film in 1914 when he was well into middle age. He had appeared in several silent comedies and a few sound films when this volume was published. Until his death in 1954, he remained active in films, radio and television. An account of Robey's early life and career can be found in another autobiography called *My Life up till Now*, published in 1908 by Greening and Co., in London.

3826 *The* LOONEY TUNES *Poster Book.* edited by Jones, Chuck. paper illus. New York: Harmony (Crown), 1979.

This volume offers 11-inch by 15-inch posters of such LOONEY TUNES characters as Bugs Bunny, Honey Bunny, Sylvester, Tweety, Speedy Gonzales, Porky Pig, Petunia Pig, Elmer Fudd, Daffy Duck, Henry Hawk, Yosemite Sam, Beaky Buzzard, Foghorn Leghorn, Road Runner, Wile E. Coyote, Pepe Le Pew, and Tasmanian Devil. Mel Blanc supplies an introduction to this unusual and attractive poster collection.

3827 *Loose in the Kitchen.* by Hunter, Kim. 394 p. illus. North Hollywood, Calif.: Domina, 1975.

3828 LORD JIM. 28 p. paper illus. New York: Mar-King Publishing, 1964.

Perhaps the outstanding feature of this souvenir book is the use of large stills from the 1964 film. Richard Brooks, the writer-director of the film, gets attention, as do the major cast members. One page is given to Joseph Conrad, author of the book upon which the film is based. Other cast and production credits are noted.

3829 *Lorentz on Film: Movies—1927 to 1941.* by Lorentz, Pare. 228 p. paper illus. New York: Hopkinson and Blake, 1975.

Pare Lorentz is known primarily as the filmmaker responsible for THE PLOW THAT BROKE THE PLAINS (1937) and THE RIVER (1937). That he was the first head of the U.S. Film Service and that he wrote about films from the late twenties to the seventies are lesser known aspects of his career as filmmaker, film critic and film enthusiast. This volume contains samples of his film criticism and writing from 1927 to 1941—Hollywood's golden era. The reader will find such remarks as "Sternberg dramatizes Miss Dietrich with lights and music until, if she were a semi-invalid, she nevertheless would appear exotic and powerful" ; "The biggest mistake anyone could make about Hollywood is in expecting to meet someone in Hollywood who is interested in motion pictures" ; and "Like Chaplin, Disney is his own author, director and actor; like Chaplin he lives, eats, and sleeps work."

Contradictions, an awkward writing style, wit, perception, early recognition of the auteur theory and a determination to raise the quality of films—all these qualities can be detected in the few quotes above. Throughout the book those same qualities and concepts are constantly in evidence. A few illustrations and an index are provided. The book will certainly delight film students and buffs. Older readers will enjoy rediscovering some forgotten films, people and moments. Nostalgia served with intelligence cannot help but win new admirers for Lorentz —an accepted legend as a documentary filmmaker but revealed here for the first time as an astute film critic. Recommended.

3830 *Lorenzo Goes to Hollywood.* by Arnold, Edward. 282 p. illus. New York: Liveright Pub. Co., 1940.

This is a moderately interesting autobiography that goes only up to the making of MR. SMITH GOES TO WASHINGTON in 1939. Little attention is given to Arnold's film work. The emphasis is on stage appearances and personalities. The insufficient detail in the book limits its value.

3831 *Los Angeles: City of Dreams.* by St. George, Mark. 152 p. illus. New York: Crown, 1975.

A portrait of Los Angeles in pictures and verse is presented in this book, which has the subtitle "Up the Mellow Yellow Brick Road." Divided into five sections—places, people, action, ritual, and vision— the volume describes the unique environment in which the major film and television studios exist.

The illustrations, most of which are the work of the author, are excellent, but the verse tries too hard at what is basically simple communication.

Perhaps this volume offers a clue to the many misjudgments made by filmmakers in both the selection and treatment of their material. Certainly the rest of the world is not at all like the Los Angeles presented here. Acceptable.

3832 *Loser Take All: The Comic Art of Woody Allen.* by Yacowar, Maurice. 243 p. illus. New York: Ungar, 1979.

A study of Woody Allen's creative work as playwright, actor, nightclub monologuist, filmmaker, and author is undertaken by Maurice Yacowar. Using recordings, films, and printed pieces, he reviews the comedian's use of a carefully prepared image— that of the little neurotic Jewish man who operates under such burdens as self-doubts, lust, guilt, sexual inadequacy, and high intelligence. Each of Allen's nine films from WHAT'S UP, TIGER LILY? (1966), to MANHATTAN (1979), is analyzed in a separate chapter. A summary, a center pictorial section, chapter notes, a filmography, a bibliography, and an index complete the book.

Allen is beginning to attract the same type of serious critical attention that has been accorded to the major film comedian-auteur of this century, Charlie Chaplin. Yacowar does full justice to both Allen's abilities and his body of work, treating each with scholarly respect and admiration. He has carefully summarized the Allen persona that so many modern audiences identify with and find hilarious; this book should enjoy an enormous success with those same groups. Highly recommended.

3833 *Losey on Losey.* by Milne, Tom. 192 p. illus. London: Secker & Warburg, 1967.

The text of this book was taken from a series of interviews done shortly after Losey's film, ACCIDENT, was completed in 1967. Losey's opinions of his work, his career,and his co-workers are elicited by the author. Losey's films are certainly controversial. Beginning with THE BOY WITH GREEN HAIR in 1948, most of the films have had delayed recognition. When McCarthyism forced his departure from Hollywood after directing only a few films, he settled in England where most of his later films were made. His comments on EVA (1962), THE SERVANT (1963), MODESTY BLAISE (1966), and ACCIDENT (1967), make absorbing reading. Stills used are faithfully reproduced. A filmography is given. This volume is another welcome addition in the *Cinema One* Series.

3834 *Lost Films.* by Carey, Gary. 91 p. paper illus. New York: Museum of Modern Art, 1970.

This attractive but expensive paperback pleads the worthy cause of film preservation. By detailing with pictures, plot synopses, and casts, some 30 films thought to be lost from the late silent era, the argument is strengthened. Because of the chemical decomposition of the original negatives of these films, the only hope for their reappearance is the eventual discovery of good prints in some vault or some fan's private collection.

3835 *The Loudest Screen Kiss and Other Little-Known Facts About the Movies.* by Seuling, Barbara. 95 p. illus. New York: Doubleday, 1976.

This collection of trivia has apparently been designed for the nondiscriminating, unknowing reader. Most of the "facts" offered are so familiar that they border on cliche, i.e., Doris Day's real name, Grace Kelly being called Princess Grace, birds being strapped to the backs of children for THE BIRDS (1963), Bob Hope traveling all over the world to entertain servicemen. Other facts are either historically vulnerable or unprovable, e.g. the earliest film record of a news event, the longest running movie, John Wayne cooking for his film crews, the world's largest movie screen.

Illustrations are line drawings done by the author. The volume is not indexed. Since the author is responsible for two earlier and similar volumes, one on sports and another on obscure laws, it would seem that there may be an impulse-buyer market for books such as this one. It is a harmless work; acceptable with the above reservations.

3836 *Louis Jouvet: Man of the Theatre.* by Knapp, Bettina L. 345 p. New York: Columbia University Press, 1957.

3837 *Lou's on First: A Biography.* by Costello, Chris; and Strait, Raymond. 384 p. illus. New York: St. Martin's, 1981.

A biography of Lou Costello written by his daughter which once more describes the comedian's aggressive, dominant personality off screen. His treatment of his wife and his partner, Bud Abbott, seems like material for a psychiatrist.

3838 *Love and Death: A Study in Censorship.* by Legman, Gershon 95 p. paper New York: Hacker Art, 1963.

Deals with censorship and the screen's treatment of women, social injustice, mature themes, etc.

3839 *Love Goddesses of the Movies.* by Manvell, Roger. 176 p. illus. New York: Crescent, 1975.

Roger Manvell's concern is women film stars in this collective biography-appreciation, arranged in chronological order from 1910 to the sixties and after. He singles out 19 famous screen actresses for critical attention. In his introduction Manvell sets forth criteria, but his choices for Love Goddesses of the Movies are predictable—Swanson, Garbo, Harlow, Dietrich, Hayworth, Grable, Bardot, Monroe, Taylor, etc. The choice of Arletty, Vivien Leigh, and Jeanne Moreau may represent a subjective application of his criteria.

The stars are placed within a decade (Ingrid Bergman in the fifties?) and for each there are illustrations, biographical information and a review of her screen performances. An introduction to each decade is supplied along with a filmography and a bibliography.

It is surprising to find Roger Manvell, who has written so many serious studies of film topics, lending his talent to such a commercially designed project as this. He tries to bring some class and erudition to it, but it still resembles the many potboilers one finds in quantity in the remainder bookstores.

3840   *Love Honor and Dismay.* by Harrison, Elizabeth. 202 p. Garden City, N.Y.: Doubleday, 1977.

In this enjoyable memoir the author gets down to business rather quickly when she meets Richard Harris for the first time on page eleven. She devotes the remainder of the book to witty and sensitive observations about marriage to actors, initial career struggles, early recognition, final celebrity, and the high life of film superstars. After a dozen years of turbulent marriage, she divorces the flamboyant Harris and marries the debonair Rex Harrison. By 1975, she has divorced him and concluded that in order to survive as an individual, it was inevitable that she leave two such strong personalities.

The book is a quick read, sprinkled with many harmless anecdotes about the famous. The author doesn't bother with dates or other specific information but tries to convey to the reader what it's like to be the wife of two famous but quite different and difficult men. Her portrait of Harris is most detailed, and since there is no book biography available at this time, it is most welcome. Harrison has already been profiled by his first wife, Lilli Palmer, and by himself; here the author wisely devotes only a small portion of the book to her life with him. No index or illustrations are provided. Acceptable.

3841   *Love in the Film.* by Everson, William K. 251 p. illus. Secaucus, N.J.: Citadel, 1979.

Fifty films about love are arranged in chronological order and discussed by the eminent film historian, William K. Everson. Introductory sections describe the various periods in which the films appeared, a most helpful aid since the scope of the films is inter-

national and they range from silents to sound features.

As usual with this series, the illustrations are the main attraction. Here, they have to share costar billing with Everson's always dependable informative text.

3842   *see 3841*

3843   *Love Laughter and Tears: My Hollywood Story.* by St. Johns, Adela Rogers. 326 p. paper illus. New York: Signet, 1978.

Adela Rogers St. Johns has been around Hollywood almost from its beginning. She has written copiously and emotionally for decades about the film industry and its people. Here she offers memories of the golden years of Hollywood. Included are selected scandals, tragedies, love affairs, and intrigues that she covered during her career. Apparently she, as "custodian of the legends," perceived herself as a parental mother figure who has the responsibility of dispensing love, advice, direction, guidance, verbal spankings, etc., to the Hollywood community.

Her writing is gushy, cliche-ridden, fan magazine gossip that is difficult to wade through. The "legends" involve Garbo, Gilbert, Chaplin, Wallace Reid, Harlow, Arbuckle, Clara Bow, Gable, Bergman, Crawford, Sennett, Griffin, etc. A few illustrations are included.

3844   *Love Scene: The Story of Laurence Olivier and Vivien Leigh.* by Lasky, Jesse, Jr.; and Silver, Pat. 256 p. illus. New York: Thomas Crowell, 1978.

The title of this volume is appropriate since it deals almost exclusively with the tragic relationship of two people, largely ignoring the years preceding their meeting and following their parting, It is told from an insider's vantage point, since the author has lived, worked and socialized with many persons who knew the pair. Rich in names, anecdotes, gossip and description, the text recalls the years from 1937 to 1967 in the lives of the legendary actors. A bibliography, some good illustrations, and an index are included.

There have been several books written about the pair previously but none has concentrated so intensely on the joys and difficulties of their relationship. This is an intimate portrait of two major personalities of this century during the peak of their powers. It would be a loss if the book were buried in the surfeit of Leigh-Olivier material being published. As one of the more fully dimensioned portraits of this mercurial pair now available, the book should not be missed by anyone interested in the dramatic performing arts.

3845 *Love, Sex, Death, and the Meaning of Life: Woody Allen's Comedy.* by Hirsch, Foster. 231 p. New York: McGraw-Hill, 1981.

An appraisal of Woody Allen's films, this volume indicates the comedian's sources and inspirations. Biography and criticism are nicely combined.

3846 LOVE STORY. by Saunders, Marvin. 28 p. paper illus. New York: National Publishers Inc., 1970.

Consisting mostly of stills from the 1970 film, this souvenir book is rather unimpressive. Brief biographies of Ali McGraw, Ryan O'Neal, Ray Milland, John Marley, producer Howard G. Minsky, director Arthur Hiller and author Erich Segal are given. Perhaps the most interesting feature is an advertisement from the publishers for 32 other titles in the souvenir book series that they publish. This is the first such instance noted.

3847 *The* LOVE STORY *Story.* by Meyer, Nicholas. 224 p. paper illus. New York: Avon, 1971.

Meyer was the unit publicist on LOVE STORY, which meant that all material about the making of the film had to go through his hands. Much of it is repeated here. In an introduction, he promises to be honest rather than protective. To a degree he succeeds, but nearly all the participants emerge as rather saintly figures and one assumes that, if honest, he also does not tell all. The account is nevertheless quite detailed, although much of it is trivial. It does give the reader a final impression of having "been with" the film from beginning to end.

There are portraits of Ali McGraw, Ryan O'Neal, Arthur Hiller, Howard Minsky, Erich Segal and others. The similarity of LOVE STORY to CAMILLE is noted also. The book is nicely illustrated but there is no index. This is an interesting account of present-day filmmaking that is sure to please those readers who know LOVE STORY as a film, a book, or both. Recommended.

3848 *A Loving Gentleman.* by Carpenter, Meta; and Borsten, Orin. 352 p. paper illus. New York: Harcourt Brace Jovanovich, 1977.

Meta Carpenter met William Faulkner in the thirties when both worked for Howard Hawks in Hollywood. Her version of their subsequent love affair is related against the background of Hollywood's golden years.

As in many such stories, the characters meet and fall in love, but cannot marry. Because he will not divorce his wife, they part, see each other occasionally, correspond, and live out a bittersweet relationship until 1962 when Faulkner dies. Although the above sounds cliche, the authors are able to provide the tact, sensitivity, feeling and taste necessary for such a tale.

A beautiful relationship is given appropriate respect and care in this interpretation.

3849 *Loving Lucy.* by Andrews, Bart; and Watson, Thomas J. 224 p. illus. New York: St. Martin's Press, 1980.

Called "An Illustrated Tribute to Lucille Ball," this volume covers the actress' career on stage, screen and television for more than 45 years. The almost 400 illustrations are the main attraction here, although the admiring text was written by two "Lucy" experts—the author of *Lucy & Ricky & Fred & Ethel* and the codirector of the CBS research department.

3850 *Low Budget Features.* by Brown, William O. 240 p. paper illus. Hollywood, Calif.: W. O. Brown, 1971.

This volume is available only from its author. Most of the elements involved in making low-budget films are discussed: finance, budget, schedules, etc. Charts and forms are pictured, and other data is presented. The approach is a no-nonsense straightforward one that emphasizes spareness and efficiency, which are essential to anyone interested in low-budget features.

3851 *see 3850*

3852 *The Lubitsch Touch: A Critical Study.* by Weinberg, Herman G. 344 p. paper illus. New York: Dutton, 1968.

Opening with a well-researched account of the life and work of Ernst Lubitsch, this volume also includes an excerpt from the screenplay of NINOTCHKA (1939), interviews with and tributes from some associates of Lubitsch, and an annotated filmography. The biographical portion emphasizes the early silent screen years with only the briefest consideration of some of the Lubitsch sound films —DESIRE

(1936), ANGEL (1937), BLUEBEARD'S EIGHTH WIFE (1938), SHOP AROUND THE CORNER (1940), etc. Some illustrations and a chronological bibliography are also offered. This is an important book for those interested in the film history of the silent screen. Lubitsch's sound films are slighted and perhaps need a volume of their own.

3853 *Luchino Visconti: Three Screenplays.* 313 p. illus. New York: Orion Press, 1970.

Contains WHITE NIGHTS (1957), ROCCO AND HIS BROTHERS (1960), and THE JOB (1962) (from BOCCACCIO '70), and cast credits.

3854 *Lucille Ball.* edited by Reed, Rochelle. 24 p. paper illus. Washington, D .C.: American Film Institute, 1974.

Lucille Ball spoke with the students of the American Film Institute in January, 1974. The transcript of the interview is printed here along with a filmography and a videography.

3855 *Lucille Ball.* by Paige, David. 31 p. paper illus. Mankato, Minn.: Creative Education, 1977.

A superficial biography written for very young readers.

3856 *The Lucille Ball Story.* by Gregory, James. 210 p. paper illus. New York: Signet, 1974.

The genesis for this original paperback was an interview prepared for *Movie Digest*, a short-lived magazine which was discontinued before the interview could be published. In an economical move, author Gregory found another use for his original material. Using it in a skeletal fashion, he has added other interviews, research, data and information to it in order to present a full-length portrait of "a legend who makes us laugh."

The original interview has been segmented, and around each short fragment, the author has written a chapter. Ball's story is told in chronological order from her birth (1911) and childhood in Jamestown, N.Y., to her movie set activities in MAME (1973). Two words apply to most of her life—ambitious and employed. The woman described here is the public legend—not the strong, tough power boss who occasionally emerges on TV talk shows. A center section contains eight pages of photographs which are well selected and reproduced. The book is not indexed and there is no filmography. Acceptable.

3857 *Lucky Star.: The Autobiography of Margaret Lockwood.* by Lockwood, Margaret. 191 p. illus. London: Odhams Press, 1955.

The heroine of such film classics as THE LADY VANISHES (1938) and NIGHT TRAIN (1940) began her film career in 1935 with LORNA DOONE. Since 1955 she has appeared mostly on stage and television. See also *My Life and Films.*

3858 *Lucy: The Bitter Sweet Life of Lucille Ball.* by Morella, Joe; and Epstein, Edward Z. 281 p. illus. Secaucus, N.J.: Lyle Stuart, 1973.

Lucille Ball has been a performer for more than 40 years. This unauthorized biography describes both her personal and professional life, with the emphasis on the years following the early fifties. It was then, with the enormous success of "I Love Lucy," that she was able to synthesize all her previous experiences as a chorus girl, extra, dramatic actress, comedienne, singer, dancer and general all-around performer. The book skips over the early film years and concentrates on the relationship with Desi Arnaz, their children, Luci and Desi, Jr., and finally her second marriage to Gary Morton. Some attention is given the accusation that she had "communist ties" during the witchhunt years of Joe McCarthy.

Two sections of photographs are average in quality, but there is no index or filmography. Acceptable until a fully documented biography appears.

3859 *Lugosi: The Man Behind the Cape.* by Cremer, Robert. 307 p. illus. Chicago: Henry Regnery, 1976.

This is an authorized biography that presents a fully dimensioned portrait of a fine actor trapped by the success of a single role. With the assistance of Bela Lugosi's wife and son, the author has provided a detailed account of a fascinating man. Starting with Lugosi's self-commitment for drug addiction, the volume recalls his life from his birth in Transylvania on October 20, 1882 to his death in Hollywood on August 16, 1956. The account tells of his early successes, the stage roles, the films, his personal and romantic relationships, and his final tragic misfortunes. In general Lugosi is portrayed as a kind, dedicated professional whose attitudes and behavior mirrored his middle-European origins. Chapter notes, a stageography, a filmography, some visuals, and an index complete the book.

After Arthur Lennig's book, *The Count*, it would seem unnecessary to have another study of Lugosi;

however, this book offers insights on Lugosi's personal life not available heretofore. In addition Cremer has carefully researched his subject, uncovering material which adds to a better understanding of both the man and the actor. Cremer has done admirably in gathering his material and treating it with style and compassion. Recommended.

3860 *Luis Bunuel.* by Durgnat, Raymond. 152 p. illus. paper Berkeley, Calif.: University of California Press, 1968.

This volume considers the Bunuel films from UN CHIEN ANDALOU (1928) TO BELLE DE JOUR (1968). Emphasizing the themes, plots, and influences of the film more than biographical detail, the book also explores the complex symbolism which is characteristic of all his work. Many film stills are offered as is a filmography and a bibliography. The reading is not easy but neither is the subject.

3861 *Luis Bunuel.* by Kyrou, Ado. 208 p. illus. New York: Simon & Schuster 1963.

A varied view of the perennial avant-garde director by both himself and others. Includes reviews, interviews, and script excerpts. The author contributes a very subjective but boring tribute in the introductory essay. A good bibliography is provided.

3862 *Luis Bunuel: A Critical Biography.* by Aranda, J. Francisco. 327 p. paper illus. New York: Da Capo 1976.

Translated from the original Spanish-language volume and edited by David Robinson, this detailed volume offers a critical examination of Luis Bunuel's life and career. His films are covered in a lengthy biographical essay which contains narrative text, factual information, opinion, script excerpts, quotations, and synopses. In the latter section of the book, an anthology of Bunuel's literary texts written from 1922 to 1933 is followed by a few of his critical essays. Scenarios for "The Duchess of Alba and Goya" and "Ilegible, Son of Flauta" appear next. A filmography, a bibliography, and an index complete the volume. The illustrations which appear throughout the book are well chosen and adequately reproduced.

The elements listed above have been combined and correlated in a most impressive fashion, giving the reader one of the best and most detailed evaluations of Bunuel currently available. Recommended.

3863 *Lunatics and Lovers.* by Sennett, Ted. 368 p. illus. New Rochelle, N.Y.: Arlington House, 1973.

The author calls this volume a tribute to the screen's "screwball" and romantic comedies. By taking selected films of the thirties and early forties, placing them in general groups, and describing many of their plots, he has surveyed two sub-genres of film comedy. Using categories dealing with the Cinderella syndrome, the poor little rich girl, boss ladies, lambs and wolves, wives, husbands, friends and secretaries, etc., Sennett has established a structure in which he can retell plots, discuss performers, and recall the golden days of Hollywood. Very little is offered in the way of introducion, critical analysis, or summary, and definition of his two film genres is difficult to obtain either in the text or in the selection of films. For example, is MR. SMITH GOES TO WASHINGTON (1939) a screwball comedy? a romantic comedy?

The weakness of the text is the absence of any interpretation of the sampling of films. Information is given but not analyzed. Much stronger is the provision of reference elements—a long filmography, a bibliography, and short capsule biographies of the players, writers and directors of these films. Illustrations are very good and the book has a detailed index. The book is sure to please many readers and is recommended.

3864 *The Lutheran Milieu of the Films of Ingmar Bergman.* by Blake, Richard Aloysius. 333 p. New York: Arno, 1978.

Written originally at Northwestern University in 1972, this title in the *Dissertations on Film* series examines the work of Ingmar Bergman in relation to Martin Luther. An introduction notes various influences on Bergman—the church, Sweden, history, literature, philosophy, etc. The five chapters which follow—on sin and guilt, silence and wrath, faith and reconciliation, love and sexuality, society and institutions—consider the major questions, themes, structures, philosophies and ideas found in Bergman's films. The final chapter summarizes Blake's findings and concludes that the films are products of the Lutheran tradition since there are so many similar concepts in Bergman's films and in Luther's works.

Supporting the text are a filmography, an appendix and a list of sources.

3865 M. by Von Harbou, Thea. 112 p. paper illus. New York: Simon &

Schuster, 1968.

Script of the 1931 film directed by Fritz Lang. Contains cast credits and an introduction by Nicholas Garnham.

3866 *M.* by Lee, Raymond. 64 p. paper illus. Encino, Ca.: Defilee, 1958.

A reminiscence about the author's days as a child actor in silent films. The text mentions many cinema personalities of that period.

3867 MACBETH: The Making of a Film. by Hutton, Clayton. 68 p. illus. London: Max Parrish, 1960.

Treats the historic background of the play, initiation of the film project, financing, casting, shooting and the final film story. A superficial coverage that might supplement a showing of the film which starred Maurice Evans and Judith Anderson. Some small historical interest.

3868 *Mack Sennett's Keystone: The Man, the Myth, and the Comedies.* by Lahue, Kalton C. 315 p. illus. New York: A. S. Barnes, 1971.

In his ninth trip to the mines of silent film, author Lahue purports to set the record straight on Mack Sennett and the Keystone Film Company. He discounts Sennett's autobiography and several other books and uses instead films made available by both Paul Killiam and Blackhawk Films and a series of interviews with Sennett's business manager, George B. Stout. The opening section on Sennett is followed by chapters dealing with Keystone Players. Mabel Normand, Fred Mace, Ford Sterling, Roscoe "Fatty" Arbuckle, Chester Conklin, Mack Swain, and Charlie Chaplin are given individual attention, and the careers of many lesser known personalities are described. Certain of the Keystone films are described and illustrated by the use of frame enlargements from the films. Many of the illustrations lack total focus and look rather fuzzy. Others do not have a balanced contrast, with black predominating.

The appendixes include a list of the Keystone films indicating the length, working title, final title, director, and the date finished. Three Keystone scripts are reprinted and there is an index of titles and one of names. While one may have some reservation about the author's announced goal and his success in reaching it, the obvious effort spent in creating this volume is laudable.

3869 MACKENNA'S GOLD. 32 p. paper illus. 1969.

Gold is the major motivation in the 1969 film upon which this souvenir book is based. Beginning with a map, the book identifies gold with the land, the people, and their quest for same. The usual cast and production credits are given.

3870 *Macmillan Audio-Brandon Films.* edited by Kerbel, Michael; and Edelstein, Robert. 630 p. Mount Vernon, N.Y.: Macmillan Audio-Brandon, 1973.

This beautiful catalog, subtitled "16mm Collection of International Cinema, 1974-75," resembles a Sears Roebuck catalog in size and shape. The book is divided into three major sections: feature films, experimental films and short films. The sound feature, the silent feature and the silent short categories are subdivided by country of origin. Experimental films are placed into the classic period, American, foreign, and miscellaneous. The sound short films are arranged according to subject area (art, music, etc.), with special listings accorded Robert Benchley, W. C. Fields, Laurel and Hardy, and Mack Sennett.

The sound feature films are the major product, and the greatest attention is given to them, with representation of some 30 countries in 448 pages. Additional features include an index of selected directors with a filmography beneath each, and an alphabetical title list. The majority of films are treated individually with many occupying a complete page. For example, the entry for GIANT (1956) gives the year of release, running time, color, rental schedule, and rather complete cast and production credits. A short plot outline is followed by background information, interpretation, and a listing of awards or recognition the film received. A few critical excerpts, some of which are a paragraph or more, are also given. Four stills from the picture are placed around the side and bottom of the page.

The book is a browser's delight, but its reference value cannot be overemphasized. Information on many of the foreign films is not easy to retrieve elsewhere, but locating it here is a simple operation. How easy is it, for example, to find information on a film called A WORKER'S DIARY (1966)? It happens to be one of the six films described quite satisfactorily on pages 206-207 in a section entitled "Films From Finland."

Obviously the purpose of the catalog is to promote, encourage and facilitate the rental of films. The by-product of good will engendered by making such a fine book available can only be an eventual source of satisfaction (and profit) to Macmillan Audio-Brandon. Simply stated, this book is a blend of commerce, publishing, and film art that is highly recommended.

3871 *Mad Scientists.* by Thorn, Ian. 47 p. illus. Mankato, Minn.: Crestwood House, 1977.

A review of "mad scientist" films, written for very young readers.

3872 *Made in Heaven, Settled in Court.* by Mitchelson, Marvin. paper New York: Warner Books, 1980.

The memoirs of a man who started out as a process server and became one of Hollywood's top divorce attorneys. Cases involving Brando, Loren, James Mason, Groucho Marx, Lee Marvin, Tony Curtis and other Hollywood personalities are recalled.

3873 *Made in Hollywood.* by Bacon, James. 318 p. paper illus. New York: Warner, 1977.

James Bacon, a gossip columnist who has been around Hollywood for more than 20 years, offers a selection of anecdotes, stories, memoirs and conversations from that time period. Most of Bacon's concerns are with sexual matters, and, to the careful reader, he will probably seem a prejudiced writer.

3874 MADE IN U.S.A. by Godard, Jean-Luc. 87 p. paper illus. London:Lorrimer, 1967.

Script of the 1967 film directed by Godard.

3875 *Mae West.* by Bavar, Michael. 159 p. paper illus. New York: Pyramid, 1975.

Although Mae West made only eleven films, she is known mostly for those few appearances. This volume reviews those films, offering many snippets of the original dialogue. Plots are retold and the effect that West had upon her leading men and ultimately upon her audiences is considered. The illustrations, consisting mostly of stills from the films, are nicely reproduced. A bibliography, a filmography and an index are added.

This is a fine evaluation of the films of a show business legend. Recommended for mature adults—young people may wonder what "all the shouting was about."

3876 *Mae West: A Biography.* by Eells, George; and Musgrove, Stanley. 351 p. New York: William Morrow, 1982.

A biography of the self-created legend who took infinite pains to prolong her life and image.

3877 *Magic and Myth of the Movies.* by Tyler, Parker. 283 p. illus. New York: Holt, 1947.

In his second book, Tyler looks at the meanings, myths, and symbols found in films of the forties. Usually his interpretations and analyses tend toward the Freudian, and many of them will cause the reader some bewilderment. For example, quite a case is made that Mortimer Brewster's (Cary Grant's) frantic behavior in ARSENIC AND OLD LACE (1944) is based on his fear of sexual impotence. The bodies in the cellar symbolize his failure to consumate sexual affairs, etc. Anyone familiar with the film might allow this interpretation, but feel it is stretching things far beyond what was intended by the director or author. Still Tyler's point may be that the symbols are not present by deliberate design.

When film criticism ceases to be fun to write or to read and becomes, instead, an exercise in obfuscation, far-fetched analogies and murky symbolism, the reader is liable to become either frustrated or annoyed. Illustrations are good and the book is certainly different. Readers will probably loathe it or love it.

3878 *The Magic Factory: How MGM Made* AN AMERICAN IN PARIS. by Knox, Donald. 217 p. illus. New York: Praeger, 1973.

Called an oral history by the author, this volume is really a group of interviews, broken apart and re-set as a mosaic on a specific example of filmmaking. In addition, the working of a major studio during the declining years of Hollywood is exemplified. The quotes are from a wide variety of personalities—director, stars, prop men, and other studio workers, including an office boy. The statements were made in 1970, some two decades after the film's release. Supporting this unusual text, there are illustrations, sketches, diagrams, script excerpts, budget forms, and advertising posters. All of these are clearly reproduced, although the color of the film is missing. Musical numbers are noted in the appendix, along with the staff list and the cast. Andrew Sarris has written a foreword and there is a preface by the author.

With this provocative manner of recreating a specific experience and a general era, the author has acted unobtrusively; but one senses that the interviews, their rearrangement, and the background research were not small challenges. This is a fine reading experience that can be recommended. Using it before a viewing of the film would seem to be a prime example of what film study is all about.

3879   *The Magic Lantern: How Movies Got to Move.* by Thurman, Judith; and David, Jonathan. New York: Atheneum, 1976.

A history designed for the young reader.

3880   *Magic Methods of Screenwriting.* by Lee, Donna. Tarzana, Calif.: Del Oeste, 1978.

3881   *Magic Moments from the Movies.* by Yost, Elwy. 290 p. illus. Garden City, N.Y.: Doubleday, 1978.

A recollection of favorite scenes from almost 150 films forms the content of this book. Written by a Canadian television executive who was once a film critic, the text is very subjective with the author writing as if the films belonged to him and he has deigned to share them. His selection is lopsided and indicates a preference for lightweight adventure and fantasy films.

Choices are arranged chronologically with each decade described by a short introductory essay. A complete title index is added, as are about 50 illustrations. And how many people do you know who could talk/record a similar book in one evening?

3882   *The Magic Moving Picture Book.* compiled by Bliss, Sands and Co. 29 p. paper illus. New York: Dover, 1975 (1898).

This book was first published in 1898 by Bliss, Sands, and Company of London under the title, *The Motograph Moving Picture Book.* It consists of 13 illustrations and an acetate transparency, which is stored in an inside cover pocket. By placing the transparency over the illustrations and moving it up and down, an illusion of motion is created. Smoke, flames, water flow, and turning wheels are among the subjects.

This novelty appeared concurrently with the earliest projected motion pictures. It may be of interest to film historians as an example of man's attempt to reproduce motion in still pictures. Acceptable.

3883   *The Magic of Rudolph Valentino.* by Mackenzie, Norman A. 210 p. illus. New York: International Publications Service, 1974.

Originally published in London by the Research Pub. Co., this biography uses as primary sources *Valentino As I Knew Him, Rudy, An Intimate Portrait of Rudolph Valentino, My Private Diary, The Intimate Journal of Rudolph Valentino,* and *Remember Valentino.* Although the author claims to have done extensive research, his efforts have produced a cleansed, sterile, expurgated synthesis of the well-known facts of Valentino's life and career.

The book is further flawed by the author's gushy, infatuated school-girl approach, which may have been suitable to Valentino's Roaring Twenties but is not proper for the seventies. The recreation of misspelled dialogue ("Just Pierre, I think your swell" —p. 32) severely weakens any faith the reader may have in the book's integrity. The supposed communication at the Italian consulate when Valentino tried to enlist is another example. Much more useful are the illustrations, the detailed filmography and the index.

Someone should have advised the author to present his research material in an objective narrative and to offer as his original contribution an analysis of his subject—as public idol and private person. Today we are mature enough to handle the probability that Valentino's wives were lesbians and that his private sexual behavior may have had some effect upon his screen performance. Acceptable for the useful reference sections and the illustrations.

3884   *Magic Shadows: The Story of the Origin of Motion Pictures.* by Quigley, Martin. 191 p. illus. New York: Quigley Publishing Co., 1960 (1948).

Published first in 1948, this book was used as a basis for *The Origins of the Motion Picture* (1955). Its subject is the pre-screen history of man's attempt to create the illusion of motion in his pictures and drawings. The various devices along with the men who designed them are discussed. Good background material but Ceram's *Archeology of the Cinema* is still the better one.

3885   *The Magic World of Orson Welles.* by Naremore, James. 339 p. New York: Oxford University Press, 1978.

The goal of this volume is to scrutinize the political and psychological implications of the films that Orson Welles has directed. Since Welles has always been concerned with politics, society, and social issues, the historical context in which his films were created is considered by the author. All his films are discussed, but CITIZEN KANE (1941), THE MAGNIFICENT AMBERSONS (1942), TOUCH OF EVIL (1958), THE TRIAL (1962), and CHIMES AT MIDNIGHT (1966) receive lengthy detailed attention. Bibliographic notes, a filmography, and an index complete the study. The illustrations are frames from the films which, in a few cases, have not been enlarged enough to have much value.

The attempt of the author to provide a new and different look at Welles' films is praiseworthy. By attempting to show the influence of Welles' life and times on his work, Naremore has given the reader another perspective on a remarkable group of films. The fascination that Welles has for scholars, students, critics and aspiring filmmakers will be reinforced with this thoughtful, well-written study. Recommended.

3886 *The Magician and the Cinema.* by Barnouw, Erik. 144 p. illus. New York: Oxford University Press, 1981.

The influence that stage magicians had on the early films is Barnouw's topic. Magicians discussed include Melies, Trewey, Hertz, Blackton and Houdini.

3887 *The Magician of Sunset Boulevard.* by Kohner, Frederick. 198 p. illus. Palos Verdes, Calif.: Morgan, 1977.

First published in German in 1974, this biography carries the subtitle "The Improbable Life of Paul Kohner, Hollywood Agent." Introduced by Charles Chaplin, the story traces Paul Kohner's rise from an ambitious youth in pre-Nazi Europe to Hollywood's most important independent international talent agent. Of course many film members are mentioned (Ingram Ullmann, Liv Ullmann, Charles Bronson, John Huston, Albert Basserman, Maurice Chevalier, Lana Turner, etc.) in this success story—written by Kohner's brother. The text is mostly an affectionate memoir that employs a sugary style more suited to fiction. It is accompanied by illustrations and an index.

3888 *Magill's Survey of Cinema.* edited by Magill, Frank. 4 Vols. 2200 p. Englewood Cliffs, N.J.: Salem, 1980.

Each of 515 English language films from 1927 to 1980 is described by an essay-review in this four-volume set. Written by a staff of 125 professionals, the essays vary in length from 1000 to 2500 words. For example, THE JAZZ SINGER (1927), reviewed by Anthony Slide, runs about three pages while KRAMER VS. KRAMER (1979) by Robert Mitchell is covered in five. The films are arranged alphabetically by title with cast, credits and technical data provided for each. Several indexes in volume four provide further access to the information—directors, screenwriters, cinematographers, editors, performers, a chronological title list. A list of the contributors and a glossary of film terms appear in the first volume.

This is an expensive but valuable reference work. Selection, writing, arrangement, and reference-access are uniformly excellent. In some ways the work resembles *Cinema, the Magic Vehicle* by Adam Garbicz and Jacek Klinowski, but the treatment and quality of Magill's four volumes dwarfs the former.

3889 MAIDSTONE, A Mystery. by Mailer, Norman. 191 p. paper illus. New York: Signet, 1971.

Script of the 1968 film directed by Mailer. Includes: "A Combined Account of the Filming of MAIDSTONE," by Sally Beauman, J. Anthony Lukas and James Toback; "A Course in Filmmaking," by Norman Mailer; "A Numbered Listing of the Shots/Cuts in the Dream Sequence;" foreword, notes, cast, production credits by Norman Mailer.

3890 MAJOR BARBARA. by Shaw, Bernard. 160 p. paper illus. Baltimore: Penguin Books, 1951.

Script of the 1941 film directed by Gabriel Pascal.

3891 *The Major Film Theories: an Introduction.* by Andrew, J. Dudley. 278 p. paper illus. New York: Oxford University Press, 1976.

This volume was designed as an aid to the reading of those major film theorists whose work is available in English. Discussed are the theories set forth by Hugo Munsterberg, Rudolf Arnheim, Sergei Eisenstein, Bela Balazs, Siegfried Kracauer, Andre Bazin, Jean Mitry, and Christian Metz. A short closing section deals with Amedee Ayfre and Henri Angel. An introduction, notes, a bibliography and an index complete the book, which also contains a few illustrations.

The task of putting order to the many complex film theories treated here is not an easy one. Andrew succeeds quite well in clarifying the work of the theorists and placing it in a historical perspective. Acceptable.

3892 *Make 'Em Laugh.* by Fry, William F., Jr.; and Allen, Melanie. 203 p. illus. Palo Alto, Calif.: Science and Behavior Books, 1975.

This volume contains interviews with seven Hollywood comedy writers—Norman Lear, Jack Elinson, Ruth Brooks Flippen, Billy Barnes, Herbie Baker, Arnie Rosen, and Bob Henry. Emphasis is placed on a review of their lives to show how they have developed their present methodology in creating comedy. Most of the writing by the subjects is done for television, films or theatre. Only partial credits are noted and the text tends toward the general subject of comedy rather than specific incidents.

In addition to a murky candid shot of the subject, an introduction and a summary support the interview. In these sections the authors attempt to provide the framework that surrounds the creation of comedy by the individual subject—his family, background, experience, goals, philosophy, preferences, and attitudes.

Humor is always a difficult subject to write about or to discuss. This volume offers many provocative suggestions about what comedy is and how it is created. It is a stimulating, intelligent study that deserves serious attention. Recommended.

3893 *Make It Again, Sam.* by Druxman, Michael R. 285 p. illus. New York: Barnes, 1975.

Since this volume deals primarily with 33 literary works and the films derived from them, its subtitle, "A Survey of Movie Remakes," may be somewhat misleading to readers. It is more applicable to the concluding quarter of the book which is titled "A Compendium of Film Remakes." Here we have a partial listing of some 500 literary properties that have been filmed more than once. But use of the word "selected" might have been appropriate along with elimination of "survey" since this volume makes no attempt at being comprehensive. In the main body of the book, each of the 33 literary properties, which were selected because of "illustrative value," has a plot outline, comparisons between the film versions, critical reaction, background information and a few stills, Author comment or criticism is omitted for the most part.

The author's intended audience is the buff rather than the scholar. Any reservations about selection, scope and treatment therefore become secondary to illustrations, nostalgia and the overall theme of remakes. With regard to these latter three qualities, the book is acceptable.

3894 *Make Your Own Animated Movies: Yellow Ball Workshop Film Techniques.* 102 p. illus. Boston: Little, Brown, 1970.

This small volume contains a wealth of information on the creation of animated motion pictures. Aimed primarily at the amateur filmmaker of any age, it discusses techniques such as flip cards, clay, drawing on film, cutouts, etc. The work at the Yellow Ball Workshop is done on 16mm; therefore, one drawback may be the relative difficulty of using some of these techniques with 8mm film and cameras. The small size of 8mm film certainly makes drawing on it more difficult. Then, too, most student cameras do not have single frame action. To overcome this handicap, a suggestion is offered by the author to touch the advance button lightly and expose a few frames. This is an approximate method that does not offer the accuracy that the single frame control does. The book is readable, nicely illustrated, and well-organized.

3895 *Make Your Own Professional Movies.* by Goodwin, Nancy; and Manilla, James N. 209 p. New York: Macmillan, 1971.

This book on filmmaking describes the act rather than giving "how-to" instruction. Relying completely on words to express the art of filmmaking is a courageous act but in this case not an especially successful or rewarding one. Most of the book is pure exposition—first a glossary, then the role of the crew, sample scripts to shoot, movie festivals and contests to enter, etc.

Emphasis on the different topics is puzzling. The instruction on editing and splicing is given in a total of six pages. The suggested scripts use more than 113 pages. Although there is a "helpful hints" approach to the material that some readers may appreciate, most will be disappointed by the imbalance in the text. The word "professional" in the title is certainly a misnomer. With no index and no illustrations to support the questionable text, the book cannot be recommended for any perceivable situation. The quality of other available volumes—Bobker's *Making Movies*, for example—is much superior to that of this book.

3896 *Make 'em Laugh: Life Studies of Comedy Writers.* by Fry, William F.; and Allen, Melanie. 202 p. illus. Palo Alto, Calif.: Science & Behavior Books, 1975.

3897 *Making a Film.* by Anderson, Lindsay. 223 p. illus. London: Allen & Unwin, 1952.

The process of making the film SECRET PEOPLE (1952), is the topic of this older volume. Balancing the creative and the technical portions, Anderson personalizes each of the crafts involved in filmmaking. The importance of personalities and temperaments is indicated. An interesting nonacademic approach to an overworked topic.

3898 *Making a Monster.* by Taylor, Al; and Roy, Sue. 278 p. illus. New York: Crown, 1980.

Actor Christopher Lee introduces this collective biography and appreciation which carries the subtitle "The Creation of Screen Characters by the Great Make-up Artists." Individual chapters are devoted to 30 men who were responsible for designing the make-up for hundreds of unusual or grotesque film characters. The methods used to create various effects, such as aging, scars, distortions, disfigurations, period hairpieces, mutations, etc., are detailed. Most fascinating are the more than 400 illustrations which accompany this behind-the-scenes look. The volume is indexed.

Although the craftsmen discussed here are probably unfamiliar names, most of their creations are not. Finding out how they came into being is a totally absorbing experience that will delight a wide range of readers.

3899 *Making and Showing Your Own Films.* by Sewell, George H. 311 p. illus. New York: Pitman, 1955.

3900 *Making 8mm Movies.* by Grosset, Philip. 232 p. paper illus. London: Fountain, 1959.

3901 *Making Films in Super Eight.* by Huxley, D. New York: Cambridge University Press, 1978.

3902 *Making Films Work For Your Community.* by Committee on Community Use of Film. 71 p. paper illus. New York: Educational Film Library Association, 1946.

This short anthology treats topics such as community film problems, managing a film forum, film aesthetics, film sources and the use of equipment. Later sections are devoted to film programs in small communities, public libraries, museums, churches, and young people's groups. Much of the material is still valid and, of course, the general topic is more important than ever. However, the anthology approach to this vital community service is too fragmented to be effective or useful. An updating by a single author might provide the unifying quality that this volume lacks.

3903 *Making Films Your Business.* by Gregory, Mollie. 256 p. New York: Schocken Books, 1979.

This volume is a treasury of practical information about the business of filmmaking by the smaller entrepreneur rather than large studios. The same rules apply, of course, in most areas—copyright, piracy, rights, partnerships etc. But the discussion provided here is applicable to simple film production. In ten concentrated chapters, the author covers requisite talents, writing, selling, financing, costs, distribution laws and video liberation. Information films, features and documentaries are given individual attention. Appendixes include information on grants, contracts, budgets, proposals, organizations, and other reference sources. An index is provided.

In a guide that can be used by both amateur and professional, Mollie Gregory has gathered together the basics of the film business and presented them in a readable, practical text. A most impressive work.

3904 *Making For the Falcon: Studies in Recent Film.* by Holt, Jerry. Lanham, Md.: University Press of America, 1976.

3905 *Making Home Movies.* by Bowler, Stanley W.; and Wigens, Tony; and Grosset, Philip. 16 p. paper illus. London: B.B.C. Publications, 1967.

Encased in a plastic holder, these 16 cards contain instructions on filmmaking for beginners. Half of the cards contain information on filming, editing, etc., while the other eight can be used to provide storyboards for creating scenarios.

3906 *Making Home Video.: How to Get the Most From Your Video Cassette Recording Equipment.* by Bishop, John Melville; and Bishop, Naomi Hawes. 200 p. illus. New York: Wideview, 1981.

One of the best manuals on VCR operation. Expect many others to appear.

3907 *Making It Big.* by Stevens, Marc; and Clapton, Diana. 219 p. paper New York: Zebra, 1977.

Another soft-core attempt at print pornography, this purported biography tells us more about Marc Stevens' adventures after his retirement from the world of porn movies. In his previous similar volume, *10-1/2*, the more "exciting" filmmaking adventures were related. Here, he seems to be scraping the bottom, as he describes drug addiction, hustling and other depravities.

3908 *Making It Move.* by Trojanski, John; and Rockwood, Louis. 151 p. paper illus. Dayton, Ohio: Pflaum, 1973.

This primer on animation has several goals—it aims at definition and appreciation but concentrates on technique. Readers are told and shown how to create animated films. Among the topics considered are handmade films, puppets, objects, cut-outs, cels, kinestasis, pixillation, and motion distortion. An early chapter discusses flipbooks and zoetropes. Explanations offered are clear, easy to follow, and complemented by many clearly reproduced illustrations and sketches. An index completes the book.

Although its intended audience is in the junior-senior high school age range, the book will have appeal and value to both a younger and older audience. It is an ideal introduction to animation techniques for those readers who would like to try but do not know where to begin. Highly recommended.

3909 *Making* LEGEND OF THE WEREWOLF. by Buscombe, Edward. 121 p. paper illus. London: British Film Institute (Zoetrope in U.S.), 1976.

This is a record of the production of a horror film, LEGEND OF THE WEREWOLF. Initial scripting began in April 1974 and the completed film had its premiere in October 1975. The text divides itself into three phases: pre-production (the production company, the script, the star, the budget, the schedule, the sets, casting, the unions, etc.), shooting (assignments, a typical day, stunts, special effects, etc.), and post production (editing, sound, music, dubbing, publicity, distribution etc.). Supporting the text are photographs, charts, diagrams, schedules, posters, call sheets, advertisements, and other visuals. Several short interviews appear throughout the text.

As both entertainment and education, this lively account of filmmaking is successful. The author has been comprehensive in his coverage, his subject matter is fascinating, and his arrangement of material is

logical. The book will please most readers. Recommended.

3910 *Making Money Making Movies: The Independent Movie-Maker's Handbook.* by Tromberg, Sheldon. 204 p. paper New York: Vision (Watts), 1979.

A no-nonsense approach to professional filmmaking is given in this handbook which covers planning, production, contracts, budgets, etc. All phases of independent filmmaking are treated. The emphasis on the practical rather than the aesthetic is exemplified by the practice exercises offered in the writing and analysis of scripts, proposals, treatments, etc.

3911 *Making Motion Pictures.* by Hauenstein, A. Dean; and Bachmeyer, Steven A. 80 p. paper illus. Bloomington, Ill.: McKnight, 1975.

This is an activity manual designed to accompany the secondary school text, *The World of Communications: Audiovisual Media.* Although it correlates with the text and other supporting materials, it does offer many suggestions and activities on filmmaking that can be used in a variety of situations outside the classroom. Anyone concerned with student filmmaking should consider this manual and the text as part of their program.

3912 *Making Movies: Student Films to Features.* by Colman, Hila. 192 p. illus. New York: World Pub. Co., 1969.

As part of the *Careers in the Making* series, this volume has much to recommend it for a youthful audience. All other groups may find it a bit basic and somewhat naive. Using ALICE'S RESTAURANT (1969), as a filmmaking case study, the author interviews the various workers, technicians and artists involved in the film. Other chapters are devoted to documentaries, TV commercials, the short film, student films, etc. The appendices contain a listing of colleges offering courses and degree programs in film. A listing of the many unions involved in filmmaking is also included as are some sample training programs of the unions.

There is much of value here for the interested young reader. The pictorial sketches by George Guzzi are modern and youth-oriented. No photographs or stills are used. Perhaps the author has de-emphasized the powerful role of the unions in determining employment but she states that conditions are changing and one hopes that she is correct. It is ironic that ALICE'S RESTAURANT received an "R" rating which means that this book's potential audience could not see it unless accompanied by their parents.

3913   *Making Movies: From Script to Screen.* by Bobker, Lee R.; and Marinis, Louise. 304 p. paper illus. New York: Harcourt, Brace, Jovanovich, 1973.

As the title indicates, this volume attempts to explain the filmmaking process from script to screen. Attention is paid to both the technical and creative aspects: scripts, budgets and schedules are considered first, with cinematography, sound recording, and editing following as the major emphases of the book. Some shorter final sections deal with film distribution and careers. Suggested reading and viewing lists follow many of the sections.

The description above cannot convey in any way the quality, depth and inclusiveness of the book. Readers familiar with Bobker's *Elements of Film* will have some idea of what to expect, but even they will be surprised at the excellence here. The structure is linear—pre-film, filming, and post-filming—and logical. The content is comprehensive, not overly technical, and supported by a very fine collection of visuals. All are beautifully reproduced, with several in full color, and in addition, there are charts, diagrams and contractual forms.

The book may be used by many audiences—filmmakers, students, general readers, etc. Since it is indexed, it can answer many questions about filmmaking that arise in classrooms and libraries. This is the best book on filmmaking to appear in the seventies. It is enthusiastically recommended. Teachers of filmmaking should consider it as a text for their courses.

3914   *Making Movies.* by Wallace, Carlton. 143 p. illus. New York: Evans, 1965.

All aspects of filmmaking are considered in this volume designed for the beginner. A glossary and some sample scripts accompany the usual topics—camera, techniques, editing, etc.

3915   *The Making of* EL CID. by Guber, Peter. 134 p. illus. Madrid: Campeador, 1962.

3916   *The Making of* EXORCIST II: THE HERETIC. by Pallenberg, Barbara. 208 p. paper illus. New York: Warner Books, 1977.

Corrado Pallenberg is a Vatican specialist who acted as a guide for the director of EXORCIST II: THE HERETIC (1977), John Boormman. Pallenberg's son, Rospo, had worked with Boorman on other films and was hired as creative associate and second unit director. Barbara Pallenberg, the author of this account, apparently had a kind of inside access to the production that few writers enjoy. She follows the making of the film from the initial troubled casting to the first rough cut. The film, which was unsuccessful critically and commercially, would be much more interesting to watch after reading this insider's account. Unfortunately, she provides full production credits but neglects to include cast credits, an index, and an explanation of her own relationship to the project and this book.

3917   *The Making of Feature Films—A Guide.* by Butler, Ivan. 191 p. paper illus. Baltimore: Penguin Books, 1970.

This is a late arrival to the list of books that tell how feature films are made. Single chapters are devoted to certain of the creative people involved in filmmaking such as the producer, the actor, the scriptwriter, the composer, the editor and cameraman. The book is as good as any other on this topic and since it is an original paperback the price is right. There is no index.

3918   *The Making of* HENRY V. by Hutton, C. Clayton. 72 p. illus. London: Eagle Lion Film Distributors, E. J. Day, 1944.

This account of the production of Olivier's HENRY V (1944) includes maps, plans, coats of arms and other illustrations, some of which are in color.

3919   *see 3918*

3920   *The Making of* KING KONG. by Goldner, Orville; and Turner, George E. 271 p. illus. New York: A. S. Barnes, 1975.

An indicated in the book's subtitle, this is "The Story Behind a Film Classic." Divided into three parts—genesis, making, and postlude—the text is supplemented by no less than 10 appendixes and an index. For those who have enjoyed and admired this film classic since its original appearance in 1933, accounts of how individual scenes and effects were created will be completely fascinating. The text is relatively clear in its description and avoids technical jargon for the most part. It parallels the script of the film, starting with Denham's Bowery search for a heroine and then progressing to the voyage to Skull Island, the chase, and finally, Kong in New York. Since one of the authors—Orville Goldner—worked as a technician on the film, the account of the making of KING KONG should be honest and reliable. It certainly reads that way.

Illustrations provide a range in quality and pertinence, with drawings used to supplement stills and production shots. Selected frame enlargements from the film would have strengthened the visual portions. KING KONG has been around for so long it has become a personal possession to many viewers and tampering with it is cause for outcry. Fortunately the authors have treated the film, its story, and its classic status with respect and affection. Recommended.

3921   *The Making of Kubrick's* 2001. edited by Agel, Jerome. 368 p. paper illus. New York: New American Library, 1970.

Author Agel edited several McLuhan books and certain production effects are repeated in this anthology about the making of one of the most important films of the last decade. There are nonlinear quotations, partial pictures, nearly blank pages, cartoons, lists, etc. Surprise and unpredictability abound. The collection includes: 1) "The Sentinel," by Arthur C. Clarke—the story upon which the film was based; 2) several *New Yorker* articles on Kubrick, Clarke and the film; 3) deleted interviews with scientists which originally opened the film; 4) a 96-page photo section; 5) professional and lay audience response to the film; and 6) a *Playboy* interview with Kubrick. Many other shorter articles and quotations are presented.

Anyone interested in superior attempts in communication and expression cannot help but be impressed by this volume, as they probably were by the film. It is a satisfying collection on both the intellectual and the aesthetic levels. This is one volume that should have been published as an oversized hardbound book. Highly recommended.

3922   *The Making of "No, No, Nanette."* by Dunn, Don. 350 p. paper illus. New York: Dell, 1972.

The participation of such film luminaries as director Busby Berkeley and performers Ruby Keeler, Patsy Kelly, Bobby Van, and Frank McHugh in the turbulent preparation of the Broadway hit enables the author to provide much biographical background. Extensive in the case of Berkeley and Keeler, the sympathetic text makes much of the inactive personality who is rediscovered in his old age. Acceptable.

3923   *The Making of* ONE DAY IN THE LIFE OF IVAN DENISOVICH. by Solzhenitsyn, Alexander; and Harwood, Ronald. 271 p. paper illus. New York: Ballantine, 1971.

This volume contains: 1) an introduction by Ronald Harwood which tells how the film was made; 2) the original story by Alexander Solzhenitsyn, translated by Gillon Aitken; 3) the screenplay by Ronald Harwood; 4) cast and production credits.

3924   *The Making of* RAIDERS OF THE LOST ARK. by Taylor, Derek. 192 p. illus. New York: Ballantine, 1981.

3925   *The Making of* STAR TREK—THE MOTION PICTURE. by Sackett, Susan; and Roddenberry, Gene. 221 paper illus. New York: Pocket Books, 1980.

Gene Roddenberry, the creator of the "Star Trek" television series, and Susan Sackett, his secretary-assistant, combine to give a behind-the-scenes account of making STAR TREK—THE MOTION PICTURE (1980). Sackett had written two previous volumes on the TV programs and had the title of assistant to the producer during the filming. Obviously, the book is a rah! rah! promotion piece that is hardly objective. It contains text, illustrations, memos, production report pages, script excerpts, and full, detailed credits.

Fans of "Star Trek," known as "trekkies," may enjoy this account. Others will find it as dull as the film that resulted from all the effort.

3926   *The Making of* SUPERMAN. by Petrou, David Michael. 224 p. paper illus. New York: Warner, 1978.

A brief history of the Superman character in radio, comics, and films precedes an account of how the 1978 film was made. Told in narrative rather than diary style, the text discusses the cast members, special effects, production difficulties and other events that were part of the 350-day shooting schedule.

The long list of credits as they appear in the film are given the book's final pages. Illustrations are limited to a few center pages.

3927   *The Making of* THE ADVENTURERS. by Wolfe, Maynard Frank. 239 p.

paper illus. New York: Paperback Library, 1970.

In addition to telling the story of THE ADVENTUR-ERS (1970), via many pictures and abbreviated text, this volume features an extended interview with the producer-director, Lewis Gilbert. The title is a bit of a misnomer, since other than the interview, the "making" aspect is limited to a few pages and pictures; the book is primarily a photo-story of publicity fodder using both color and black and white stills, and featuring much nudity. Any permanent interest is diminished by the critical reception given the picture.

3928 *The Making of the Great Westerns.* by Meyer, William R. 464 p. illus. New Rochelle, N.Y.: Arlington House, 1979.

Thirty western films are examined by William Meyer in an attempt to show the realization of a film from its "inception to release and beyond." What is provided is mostly background materials concerning the productions along with any public arguments that may have occurred. The only mention of Meyer's sources is a list of acknowledgements; he does not state in his introduction whether his text is based on interviews or original sources. Most of it appears to come from previously published materials. What he has gathered here is some interesting supporting information about his selected examples of the western film genre. Supplementing this are such elements as cast, credits, review excerpts, and illustrations.

Thankfully, plot synopses are limited to a paragraph or so, and the selection of films includes a few rarities as examples or models: TUMBLEWEEDS (1925), HIT THE SADDLE (1937), THE TALL T (1957), and even THE MISFITS (1961). A bibliography and an index complete the book.

Although this is a volume that will be enthusiastically received by the western film aficionados, there is also a sufficient concentration of production background information to interest most readers.

3929 *The Making of* THE HAPPY HOOK-ER. by Moore, R. paper illus. 1975.

An account of the making of THE HAPPY HOOKER (1975), accompanied by illustrations of the production.

3930 *The Making of the Movie,* JAWS. by Blake, Edith. 181 p. paper illus. New York: Ballantine, 1975.

Except for production quality, this volume is identical with *On Location...On Martha's Vineyard*. With the success of the film JAWS (1975), Ballantine Books secured the rights to Edith Blake's account of the film's production and gave the book mass distribution.

3931 *The Making of* THE OTHER SIDE OF MIDNIGHT. by Bahrenburg, Bruce. 254 p. paper illus. New York: Dell, 1977.

Bruce Bahrenberg, the publicist for the film, writes about the production of THE OTHER SIDE OF MIDNIGHT (1977) in such locales as Paris, Washington, and Hollywood. Characters include actors John Beck, Susan Sarandon, Raf Vallone, Marie-France Disier, and filmmakers Frank Vablans, Irene Sharaff, Sydney Guilaroff among others. His diary begins on Nov. 2, 1976 and concludes with the wrap party on Feb. 15, 1977.

As a publicist, the author's primary responsibility is to make his film known to a potential audience. With that goal in mind, he has written a chatty, inoffensive account of the problems, relationships, and rewards found in multi-million dollar independent film production in the seventies.

Some illustrations appear in a center section. A list of cast and production credits would have added appreciably.

3932 *The Making of* THE SPY WHO LOVED ME. by Bennett, Tony. 47 p. illus. Milton Keynes, England: Open University Press, 1979.

This volume was prepared for the communication and society course given by the Open University.

3933 *The Making of* THE WIZARD OF OZ. by Harmetz, Aljean. 329 p. illus. New York: Alfred Knopf, 1977.

A very detailed description of moviemaking during the golden years at MGM is provided by this unusual book. Its subject is Production No. 1060, the now classic THE WIZARD OF OZ (1939), and its method is to investigate the various contributions made to the film by its artisans—the studio heads, the scriptwriters, the musicians, the actors, the directors, the designers, the special effects men, etc.

In addition to an abundance of unfamiliar information, the reader will also be impressed by the enormity of making such a studio production. The number of choices, decisions and compromises were innumerable and continued up to the final previews. The author has concluded her study of this production by noting the perennial television showings, the fate of the film's participants, the MGM auction of Dorothy's slippers, and a short biography of the original story author, L. Frank Baum. Final production credits, a bibliography and an index are provided. Illustrative material consists not only of many clearly reproduced photographs, but also of sections of charts, musical scores, memos, lists, and camera records.

This is a thoroughly researched study that is not only informative but enjoyable to read as well. It is an ideal blend of education and entertainment rarely found in film books. Highly recommended.

3934 *Making the Movies.* by Bendick, Jeanne. 190 p. illus. New York: McGraw-Hill, 1945.

Prepared for young people, this guide to studio film production is compact and simple. It traces the film from script to finished form, discussing the various professions, crafts, and techniques needed along the way. Some attention is given to Army and Navy cameramen. The cartoon illustrations done by the author are most effective and a glossary and a bibliography are added. The book is indexed. One of the best of its type; highly recommended.

3935 *Making the Movies.* by Dench, Ernest A. 177 p. illus. New York: Macmillan, 1915.

Reprinted in part from the *Motion Picture Magazine* and the *Picture Play Weekly*, this volume is a survey of motion picture production as practiced in 1915. In its 40 chapters there is a wide range of topics— from child actors to biblical motion pictures.

3936 *Making Wildlife Movies: A Beginner's Guide.* by Parsons, Christopher. 224 p. illus. Harrisburg, Pa.: Stackpole, 1971.

Expert advice from an experienced professional who enjoys his work and is able to communicate his enthusiasm to his audience. Acceptable.

3937 *Making Your Own Movies.* by Helfman, Harry. 95 p. illus. New York: Morrow, 1970.

After a brief historical introduction, the emphasis in this volume is on script writing. The other procedures of filmmaking are given adequate attention and are supported by sequential photographs. Both live action and animation films are explained. Most appropriate for the advanced amateur.

3938   *see 3937*

3939 *Mamoulian.* by Milne, Tom. 176 p. paper illus. Bloomington, Ind.: Indiana University Press, 1969.

A welcome addition to this excellent series, this volume concerns itself with the films of Mamoulian from APPLAUSE in 1929 to SILK STOCKINGS in 1957. The many innovative practices, the early combination of sight and sound LOVE ME TONIGHT (1932), the use of sexual frustration as motivation DR. JEKYLL AND MR. HYDE (1931), the emergence as a ladies director (Dietrich, Garbo, Sten)—all of these aspects and many others which characterize his work are detailed here.

Text, illustrations and filmography are uniformly above average. For the reader unfamiliar with this director's work and his total contribution to film, this book is a treasure that fills in a missing portion of Hollywood film history. To the cinema buff, it is advantageous to have this material collected in one small attractive volume. Recommended for all.

3940 A MAN AND A WOMAN. by Lelouch, Claude; and Uytterhoeven, Pierre 116 p. paper illus. New York: Simon & Schuster, 1971.

Script of the 1966 film directed by Lelouch. Contains cast credits, an introduction and articles, including "A Conversation Between Lelouch and Uytterhoeven."

3941 *Man and the Movies.* edited by Robinson, W. R. 371 p. illus. Baton Rouge, La.: Louisiana State University Press, 1967.

A most interesting collection of articles but the main theme, the impact of movies on American culture, is somewhat elusive in this book. The other stated purpose—arguments that motion pictures should receive the serious consideration given other arts—is much better served. The first section deals with motion picture genres (westerns, horror, etc.). The second considers Hitchcock, Griffith, Bergman, Antonioni, Fellini, Visconti, etc. The final section deals primarily with writers (Faulkner in Hollywood) and critics. A few of the articles are excellent and most are worthy of some attention. Be aware, however, that this is not a sociological report, but primarily a collection of readings. The title does the book a disservice.

3942 A MAN FOR ALL SEASONS. 31 p. paper illus. Englewood Cliffs, N.J.:

Ronark Program Co., 1966.

This souvenir book is made up mostly of stills from the 1966 film. Some attention is given to the cast members and production personnel, but director Fred Zinnemann and playwright Robert Bolt—who was responsible for the script taken from his original play—are the special subjects of this interesting volume.

3943 *Man From Krypton: The Gospel According to Superman.* by White, John Wesley. Minneapolis, Minn.: Bethany House, 1978.

3944 *The Man in the Straw Hat: My Story.* by Chevalier, Maurice. 245 p. illus. New York: Thomas Crowell Co., 1949.

Covers the author's life prior to World War II in some detail but Chevalier ignores the war years, using the same nonchalance with which he views his early films. They are ignored while Chevalier pays lasting tribute to Chevalier. A disappointing autobiography.

3945 MAN OF ARAN. by Mullen, Pat. 288 p. paper illus. Cambridge, Mass.: MIT Press, 1970 (1935).

First published in 1935, the first and shorter portion of this captivating book is autobiographical, detailing a man's life on the Aran Islands. Documentary filmmaker Robert Flaherty came to shoot MAN OF ARAN on the island in 1934. It is the account of his stay on the island that provides the second and major portion of the book. Although the author appeared in the film, his more important role was that of liason between Flaherty and the islanders. As a result of this interaction, a portrait of Flaherty also emerges in the book.

The style is simple, honest, and quite disarming. Some of the passages approach a kind of natural beauty. Illustrations are taken from the completed film and there are two maps given. A bit specialized and of limited interest to today's audiences, the book can still appeal on two levels. Historically, it presents a factual record of the making of a motion picture classic. As literature, it is first rate biography and a fine example of documentary reporting.

3946 MAN OF LA MANCHA. 30 p. paper illus. Englewood Cliffs, N.J.: Charnell Theatrical Ent., 1972.

Dale Wasserman, the author of the original play, contributes an opening article entitled "A Long Time in La Mancha." The remainder of this souvenir book is devoted to telling the story with illustrations and narrative. Photographic quality is extremely variable. Individual pages are given to Peter O'Toole, Sophia Loren, James Coco, and director Arthur Hiller. Other cast and production credits are listed.

3947 *Man Ray: The Rigor of Imagination.* by Schwartz, Arturo. 384 p. illus. New York: Rizzoli, 1978.

Man Ray is probably best known as the leader of the Dada and Surrealism movements in America. The author, a personal friend of Ray, has provided a rich, fully detailed biography that devotes one complete section to the artist's early Surrealistic films. Attention is also given to Ray's experiences in Hollywood in an appendix by Henry Miller.

An index, a long bibliography, and hundreds of illustrations accompany this comprehensive portrait of the painter-photographer-writer-filmmaker.

3948 THE MAN WHO COULD WORK MIRACLES. by Wells, H. G. 109 p. illus. New York: Macmillan, 1936.

Script of the 1936 film directed by Lothar Mendes. A screen treatment by the author of an original story he wrote long before 1936.

3949 *The Man Who Invented Hollywood.* edited by Hart, James. 170 p. illus. Louisville, Ky.: Touchstone Publishing. Co., 1972.

The major portion of this book is an autobiography of D. W. Griffith, written in a predictable romantic, southern-Victorian style. Supporting the autobiography are an introduction by Frank Capra, some interview notes taken by Hart, many illustrations, and some concluding information. The latter is necessary since the autobiography was unfinished. With the interest in and constant reevaluation of Griffith's work, a book such as this becomes important source material. If the reader is willing to penetrate the old-fashioned prose, there is much rewarding information and observation.

Picture quality is quite good for the most part and James Hart's attempts to add more pertinent information to the Griffith life story must be appreciated. There is a Grifith chronology but no index. Recommended.

3950   THE MAN WHO LOVED WOMEN. by Truffaut, Francois; and Fermaud, Michael; and Schiffman, Suzanne. paper illus. New York: Grove, 1977.

A script of the 1977 film directed by Francois Truffaut. Contains over 120 illustrations from the film.

3951   *The Man Who Photographed the World: Burton Holmes—Travelogues, 1892-1938.* by Holmes, Burton; edited by Caldwell, Genoa. 319 p. illus. New York: Harry N. Abrams, 1977.

Burton Holmes was a well-known lecturer during the early decades of the twentieth century. His subject was travel and his scope was the entire world. He journeyed to many countries using both still and motion picture cameras to record sights and impressions. He was the first to present pictures of Italy, Hawaii, Japan, and China to American audiences at a time when travel was indeed a luxury reserved for the affluent. From 1915 to 1921 he produced silent travelogue films for Paramount. To most moviegoers he is best remembered for the short sound films that he made for MGM during the thirties and forties.

This volume contains words and still pictures selected from his in-person lectures which represent the period from 1892 to 1938. Many of the early photographs were glass slides which Holmes had hand-painted in order to present color pictures to his audiences. The samples reproduced here compare favorably to the best in today's color photography. All of the visuals, however, are fascinating examples of Holmes' ability to combine technique and content. They are presented in chronological fashion and constitute a guided tour to the world during the early years of this century. This is a book that will fascinate readers of all ages. Recommended.

3952   THE MAN WHO SHOT LIBERTY VALANCE. by Warfield, Nancy D. 28 p. paper illus. New York: Little Film Gazette, 1975.

This monograph addresses itself broadly to the question of why John Ford made THE MAN WHO SHOT LIBERTY VALANCE (1962). Using the examples of STAGECOACH (1939), MY DARLING CLEMENTINE (1946), and this film, the author attempts to show this trilogy as Ford's manipulation of Plato's man-emerging-from-the-cave simile. Warfield has used information, research, quotations, opinion and a few portraits, and the result is a stimulating, well-written monograph that helps with the interpretation of

Ford's work. Acceptable.

3953   *The Man With No Name: Clint Eastwood.* by Johnstone, Iain. 144 p. illus. Santa Barbara, Calif.: Quill, 1981.

Based on a BBC television program, this biography of Clint Eastwood is both informative and entertaining.

3954   *Man's Creative Imagination.* by Barry, Gerald; and Bronowski, J.; and Huxley, Julian. 347 p. illus. Garden City, N.Y.: Doubleday, 1965. (The Doubleday Pictorial Library of the Arts.)

Basil Wright has created the section on motion pictures included in this volume. Students and teachers may find it quite valuable.

3955   *The Management of Motion Picture Theatres.* by Ricketson, Frank H., Jr. 376 p. illus. New York: McGraw-Hill, 1938.

Includes the usual topics in theatre management: personnel, operation, policy, advertising, physical plant, financial structure, booking attractions, etc. The volume is indexed.

3956   *The Manipulators.* by Sobel, Robert. 458 p. Garden City, N.Y.: Doubleday, 1976.

The theme here is the power of media to manipulate, and film is one of the media considered.

3957   *Mank: The Wit, World and Life of Herman Mankiewicz.* by Meryman, Richard. 351 p. illus. New York: Morrow, 1978.

Best known for his scriptwriting contribution to CITIZEN KANE (1941), Herman Mankiewicz was an "in" celebrity writer during Hollywood's golden years. For over 30 years he knew everyone of importance in the world of show business. In turn, he was known for his talent, wit, intellect and an addiction for drink and gambling. His parental relationship was a factor but his self-destruction seemed to be his own grand design.

This well-researched biography is packed with Hollywood narrative, anecdotes, and details, all woven together in a terse style that alternates laughs with tears. Illustrations, a lengthy filmography from THE

ROAD TO MANDALAY (1926) to THE PRIDE OF ST. LOUIS (1952), an index, and some illustrations accompany Mank's story. The book appeared about the same time as a biography of his brother, Joseph, *Pictures Will Talk*.

3958 *The Mansions of Beverly Hills.* by Regan, Michael. 80 p. illus. Los Angeles: Regan, 1966.

An illustrated tour of the homes of yesterday's stars and moguls—Pickfair, Lloyd, Keaton, Goldwyn, Cohn, Selznick, etc.

3959 *A Manual for Evaluators of Films and Filmstrips.* by Allison, Mary L.; and Jones, Emily S.; and Schofield, Edward T. 23 p. paper Paris: UNESCO, 1956.

3960 *A Manual of Film Cataloging.* by International Federation of Film Cataloging Commission. illus. New York: Burt Franklin (Lenox Hill), 1978.

Prepared under the direction of The International Federation of Film Archives (FIAF), this volume describes a variety of cataloging procedures for films.

3961 *Manual of Narrow-Gauge Cinematography.* edited by Pereira, Arthur. 514 p. illus. London: Fountain, 1952.

The first edition of this work was published in 1949 with the title *Manual of Sub-Standard Cinematography.*

3962 *Manual on Film Evaluation.* by Jones, Emily S. 32 p. paper New York: Educational Film Library Association, 1974.

Jones' newest volume on film evaluation had a few predecessors: Allison, Jones and Schofield's *A Manual for Evaluators of Films and Filmstrips* (UNESCO, 1959), Jones' *Brief Guide for Film Evaluators* (196?), and the first edition of her *Manual on Film Evaluation* (1967). The revised edition provides advice, direction, and information about this all-important procedure. Topics considered include definitions, rationale, attitude, committees, forms, synopses, audience, ratings, and workshops. There is so little available in the literature on the vital process of film evaluation that the reappearance and improvement of a standard work on the subject is an

event to applaud. Stated simply, the manual is basic and essential for anyone who evaluates film—librarians, media specialists, administrators, teachers, etc. It endows the evaluation activity with such practical qualities as approach, procedure, and structure—and then describes them with clarity and intelligence.

3963 *Marcel Carne.* by Queval, Jean. 27 p. paper illus. London: British Film Institute, 1950.

The films and career of the brilliant French director are discussed in this short volume, which covers his earliest and most productive period, 1936 to 1948. This title is number 2 in the *New Index* series.

3964 *The March of the Movies.* by Towers, Harry A.; and Mitchell, Leslie. 88 p. illus. London: S. Low, Marston, 1947.

Heavily illustrated, this volume deals with a variety of subjects—history, finance, scripts, film as art, direction, music, photography, etc.—as well as personalities: Hitchcock, Rank, DeMille, Disney, Lloyd, etc.

3965 *The March of Time, 1935-1951.* by Fielding, Raymond. 359 p. illus. New York: Oxford University Press, 1978.

Once again Raymond Fielding combines research and interviews to provide a survey of the almost 300 films that were known as THE MARCH OF TIME. From the Depression through World War II and after, these pseudo-documentary films were an anticipated part of neighborhood movie programs. They dealt with controversial social issues, people, the economy, institutions, etc. Sponsored by *Time* magazine, the films were made by a dedicated group of men presided over by Louis De Rochemont. The voice-over narration of the films ("Time Marches On") was done by Westbrook Van Voorhis in a heavy, somber, serious manner that seemed to defy anyone to question the validity of the films. Ironically much of the visual material was not original footage but carefully staged reconstructions.

The story of the films, their production, and the men who made them—especially Roy Larsen, Lothar Wolff, Tom Orchard, Jack Glenn, and Richard De Rochemont—is told in this colorful account. Supplements to the text include biographical notes, a bibliography, a list of research resources, a filmography, and an index.

A most impressive work that should especially

please those who recall the films, this study shows Fielding's continuing accomplishment in providing scholarly yet readable records of film journalism. See also *The American Newsreel 1911-1967*.

3966   *Margaret Mitchell's Gone with the Wind Letters, 1936-1949.* edited by Harwell, Richard. 441 p. illus. New York: Macmillan, 1976.

The letters in this volume were selected from the Margaret Mitchell Marsh Collection located in the University of Georgia libraries. From over 12,000 letters that she wrote, several hundred are included here. Since they were generated by both her book and the film made from it, the letters are pertinent to film collections. For example, in the year 1939, there are letters to David O. Selznick, Vivien Leigh, Leslie Howard, and Olivia de Havilland. Many of the other letters are also about the film.

Margaret Mitchell's correspondence is a joy to read. The expression of her personality and intelligence in these letters has wit, style, and care. She provides the reader with a self-portrait that is totally detailed and ultimately charming.

Some illustrations and an index are provided. This book should appeal to the many millions who have loved the novel and the film for so many years. Highly recommended.

3967   *Margaret Rutherford.* by Keown, Eric. 94 p. illus. London: Rockliff, 1956.

This is an illustrated study of Miss Rutherford's work for stage and screen with a list of her appearances. It was No. 7 in a series of *Theatre World* monographs. The photographs which accompany the text are beautifully reproduced. Although this book is dated, the text is commendable and the production is superior. Be aware that the emphasis is on theatre rather than film. Also in the *Theatre World* monograph series are similar monographs on Alec Guiness (by Kenneth Tynan); Dame Edith Evans (J. C. Trewin); Peggy Ashcroft (Eric Keown); Dame Sybil Thorndike (J. C. Trewin); Paul Rogers (Audrey Williamson); Paul Scofield (J. C. Trewin); Emlyn Williams (Richard Findlater); Gladys Cooper (A. V. Cookman); and Sir Ralph Richardson Harold Hobson).

3968   *Marilyn: The Tragic Venus.* by Hoyt, Edwin P. 279 p. illus. New York: Duell, 1965.

By interviewing persons who knew Monroe, the author has created a biography, but one with limita-

tions. Certain key personalities did not participate and when he began, the author was not acquainted with her films. What has resulted is a sympathetic portrait which offers no new information or analysis.

3969   *Marilyn: A Biography.* by Mailer, Norman. 270 p. illus. New York: Grosset and Dunlap, 1973.

One of the big events in publishing circles in 1973 was the first printing of 400,000 copies of this Marilyn Monroe biography. The original intent was to have Norman Mailer write a preface of 10,000 words to a coffee table book of Monroe photographs. It didn't quite work out that way; he wrote some 90,000 words and the photographs now supplement his biographical essay.

Mailer's writing has been called "novelistic biography," "a meditation," "inaccurate," "careless," and "plagiarism." The last charge stems from Mailer's reliance on two earlier Monroe biographies by Maurice Zolotow and Fred Lawrence Guiles. Not noted by the critics was the duplication of much material that appeared in a 1968 paperback by James A. Hudson, *The Mysterious Death of Marilyn Monroe*.

Monroe's lust for fame and her self-destruction wish seem familiar to Mailer. He wrote this material in 60 days, inventing scenes, checking only 14 persons who knew Monroe (he didn't), and ultimately denying the book was a biography (why, then, the final title?). What is offered is Mailer's stylistically brilliant interpretation of two major biographical sources on Monroe, accompanied by his personal speculations about her sex life, her death, and her real self. Style not withstanding, the book is unfair to everyone except Mailer, who seems to believe he can write it all ways—part novel, part biography, part interpretation, and part conjecture. He can't.

The photographs are varied, fascinating and ultimately relate a better biography than Mailer does. The book is an assured success because of the controversy, publicity, subject matter, author personality and other factors that have surrounded its publication. It is an acceptable although disappointing essay.

3970   *Marilyn: An Untold Story.* by Rosten, Norman. 125 p. paper illus. New York: Signet, 1973.

This memoir was written by author-poet Norman Rosten who was a friend of Marilyn Monroe during the last seven years of her life. His portrait is loving, compassionate and tender—that of a person who values and respects the trust of a friendship. While the framework of his recollections is familiar, the detail is not. Emphasis is on positive qualities; Monroe's negative behaviors are noted but usually excused or rationalized. Some candid photos are included with the short text.

Although this material is prejudiced, it does add dimension to the total Monroe portrait. Many of Monroe's simple, honest qualities, overlooked by other biographers, are noted and interpreted with affection here. They help to give the reader a close-up not available heretofore. Acceptable.

3971 *Marilyn: The Last Months.* by Murray, Eunice; and Shade, Rose. 157 p. paper illus. New York: Pyramid, 1975.

Eunice Murray acted as companion-housekeeper for Marilyn Monroe during the final eight months of the star's life. In this volume, written with Rose Shade, she recalls that dramatic period in 1962. Fired by her studio after making only a few shots of the film SOMETHING'S GOT TO GIVE, Monroe had already been through a dynamic but fading screen career, three ill-fated marriages, innumerable emotional liaisons, drug withdrawal, and a lifetime of other traumatic experiences crowded into a decade or so.

The author does not think that Monroe intended suicide—there were too many career plans and possibilities being considered. It is suggested that an initial sedation produced "an automatic physical reaction that kept her downing pills in semi-stupor." The author does not fulfill the book cover's promise of providing "intimate facts" or "answers to whispered questions." She gives the reader one more positive view of a child-woman seemingly destined for tragedy. Acceptable.

3972 *see* 3971

3973 *Marilyn Beck's Hollywood.* by Beck, Marilyn. 258 p. illus. New York: Hawthorn, 1973.

The author has become a widely syndicated columnist within the past six years. For those readers interested in who will show up for the Academy Awards, whatever happened to Elliott Gould in 1972, the new morality of Hollywood and other gossip column topics, the book may have some appeal. Some of the illustrations show the author socializing with the stars. For the curious an index is provided. In no way essential but acceptable as reader entertainment.

3974 *Marilyn Chambers: My Story.* by Chambers, Marilyn. 232 p. paper illus. New York: Warner, 1975.

An original paperback autobiography of the porno film actress who achieved some degree of celebrity by appearing on Ivory Snow boxes and in BEHIND THE GREEN DOOR (1973). There is a similarity to the lives and careers of the porno stars who enjoyed a short-lived vogue during the early seventies. This volume is no better or worse than the others by Linda Lovelace, Harry Reems, et al. It is acceptable only for adults and noted here for the record.

3975 *Marilyn Lives!* by Oppenheimer, Joel. New York: G. P. Putnam's, 1981.

3976 *Marilyn Monroe.* by Zolotow, Maurice. 340 p. illus. New York: Harcourt, Brace & Co., 1960.

This is an excellent biography of Marilyn Monroe, written with her partial cooperation. It ends with her work on LET'S MAKE LOVE (1960) and does not include THE MISFITS (1961) and her death shortly thereafter. The author has not been afraid to offer comment and criticism about his subject's life and films. Much of the material reads as fresh and unhackneyed. The book is entertaining, and yet somewhat sad since the reader is aware of the unwritten finale. Much research and interviewing are indicated by the quality of the writing. Another positive feature is the detailed critical explanation and analysis of the films. Some unusual photographs are included but there is no index, filmography, or bibliography. One of the better biographies on a Hollywood legend, this book is recommended.

3977 *Marilyn Monroe: A Composite View.* edited by Wagenknecht, Edward. 200 p. illus. New York: Chilton Book Co., 1969.

By using a collection of personal interviews, recollections, and analyses from books and periodicals, the author attempts to give a character portrait rather than a biography of Marilyn Monroe. The selection of articles is good, but in some cases, rather familiar. Other articles seem chosen because of the author name rather than the contribution to the portrait. Pictures are few and rather routine. There is no index. Anyone familiar with the Monroe legend will not find much of this material either new or startling. The book may appeal to the fan magazine reader. Not recommended.

3978 *Marilyn Monroe.* by Mellen, Joan. 157 p. paper illus. New York: Pyramid, 1973.

This volume is a departure from the usual format of the *Pyramid* series. Instead of the major interest being a focus on the films, Ms. Mellen devotes much of her text to an examination of Monroe's private life and film image. When the films are considered, it is not in the usual plot-synopsis and critical-quote fashion, but as an analysis of the Monroe role in each and its relationship to the other characters in the film. Most of the films she dismisses as unworthy, saving praise mostly for BUS STOP (1956) and THE MISFITS (1961). Those films showed elements of the real Marilyn Monroe that were not evident in her usual role of the empty-headed blonde victimized by men or society. The visuals, which are well reproduced and nicely selected, include stills, candids, and studio portraits. A bibliography, filmography and an index complete the book.

One can question the value of yet another book on Monroe, but in this case it is more than justified. The fascinating insight that the author brings to her in-depth analysis of both Monroe and her screen roles will appeal to many readers much more than the widely sold and publicized Mailer book. This volume is another outstanding contribution from Pyramid and is highly recommended.

3979 *Marilyn Monroe: A Life on Film.* by Kobal, John. 176 p. illus. New York: Hamlyn, 1974.

This volume was probably designed as an inexpensive "cover" for the Mailer volume. An introductory essay by David Robinson introduces a collection of Monroe photographs arranged in an approximate chronological fashion. Using mostly studio publicity shots and production and film stills along with some candid shots, John Kobal adds a connecting text. Picture reproduction is above average and the love affair between Monroe and the camera is in constant evidence. A good filmography, a bibliography, a discography, and an index complete the volume. This is a most acceptable and attractive volume, diminished only by the many similar volumes which preceded it and the overexposure of all aspects of Marilyn Monroe's life and career.

3980 *Marilyn Monroe Confidential.* by Pepitone, Lena; and Stasien, William. 251 p. illus. New York: Simon & Schuster, 1979.

Lena Pepitone acted as personal maid and wardrobe mistress for Marilyn Monroe during the last six years of the actress' life. She calls this memoir of Monroe, "an intimate, personal account." Claiming that Monroe told her things that she told no one before, Pepitone has set down the recollections of the actress, along with her own observations and interpretations.

No opportunity for sensationalism is overlooked—rape, an illegitimate child, prostitution, lesbianism, sex, drugs, alcohol, breakdowns, etc.

Perhaps to compensate for divulging Monroe's sleazy personal history, the author also speaks of her finer qualities—generosity, naivete, kindness, etc. Pepitone's acutely accurate recollection of Monroe's habits, behavior, and conversation seems very questionable, but who can argue with an "only remaining witness"? Sleazy and seamy, the volume will probably be very popular.

3981 *Marilyn Monroe; Her Own Story.* by Carpozi, George Jr. 222 p. paper illus. New York: Belmont Books, 1961.

3982 *Marilyn Monroe Paper Dolls.* by Tierney, Tom. 32 p. paper illus. New York: Dover, 1979.

In this original booklet, made of heavy stock paper, Tom Tierney furnishes a Marilyn Monroe paper doll, 31 costumes to put on the doll, and a very brief survey of the actress' life and career. The dresses are taken from 24 of Monroe's films—from LADIES OF THE CHORUS (1948) TO SOMETHING'S GOT TO GIVE (1962).

3983 *The Marilyn Monroe Story.* by Franklin, Joe; and Palmer, Laurie. 80 p. paper illus. New York: Rudolph Field Co., 1953.

An early paperback biography of Monroe.

3984 *see 3983*

3985 *Marinetti.* edited by Flint, R. W. 363 p. New York: Farrar, Straus & Giroux, 1972.

A compilation from the writings of Filippo Tommaso Marinetti (1876-1944), one of the major personalities in the Italian avant-garde movement during the early years of this century. His predictions about the cinema, much ahead of their time, were quite accurate. Acceptable.

3986 *Mario Lanza.* by Bernard, Matt. 224 p. paper New York: Macfadden-Bartell, 1971.

This sensationalized biography emphasizes the excesses of Mario Lanza rather than his accomplishments. As a result, a most unflattering portrait of a gifted artist is presented. Many reconstructed conversations and some rather personal information cause the reader to wonder what Bernard's sources were. The book is nevertheless a fascinating curiosity, since Lanza was always bigger than life, on screen and off. This melange of gossip, innuendo, and sensationalism is a disservice to his memory.

3987 *Mario Lanza and Max Steiner.* by Burrows, Michael. paper illus. Cornwall, England: Primestyle, 1971.

Another dual presentation—this time Mario Lanza and Max Steiner. Typical Burrows-Primestyle approach with illustrations, filmographies, comments, quotations, etc.

3988 *Marion Davies.* by Guiles, Fred Lawrence. 419 p. illus. New York: McGraw-Hill, 1972.

Not only was Marion Davies a movie performer for a long period of time but, in the minds of many people, she also served as the inspiration for the character of Susan Alexander in CITIZEN KANE (1941). Author Guiles documents the first association and disproves the second. Marion Davies had few of the personal qualities ascribed to Susan Alexander and was a talented performer to boot. In this detailed and well-researched biography, the author traces Davies' rise from Follies girl in 1916 to film actress of reknown in the late twenties and early thirties. During this time and for many years after (a total of some 35 years), she was William Randolph Hearst's mistress.

The experiences with filmmaking—both silent and sound—are given much attention, as are the later years when the visitors to San Simeon included many film personalities. There is also an account of the making of CITIZEN KANE, the contribution of Herman Mankiewicz, and the resultant furor that the film caused in the Hearst menage. World War II prevented the film from having great impact in 1941 and its subsequent emergence as a classic in 1950 had little effect on Davies and Hearst.

Three picture sections illustrate various periods of Davies' life clearly and objectively. This is a fine biographical portrait of an underrated film actress who was the victim of an untruth promoted by a classic film. Highly recommended.

3989 *Marjoe.* by Gaines, Steven S. 236 p. paper New York: Dell, 1973.

Combining elements of sex, religion, drugs, con games and much more, this biography of an evangelical superstar has no reference to the recent film work of its subject. Although it will please most readers, it is not pertinent for film study.

3990 *The Mark Hellinger Story: A Biography of Broadway and Hollywood.* by Bishop, Jim. 367 p. illus. New York: Appleton, 1952.

The biography of the New York columnist who became a motion picture writer, THE ROARING TWENTIES (1939), and a producer, THE KILLERS (1946), BRUTE FORCE (1947), NAKED CITY (1947). The book resembles his films—fast, vivid, evocative and violent. Hellinger died in 1947 at the age of 44.

3991 *Mark Lester: The Boy, His Life and His Films.* by Kidd, Paul. 81 p. illus. Ilfracombe, England: Stockwell, 1975.

A biography of the British child star who appeared in such films as OLIVER (1968), RUN WILD, RUN FREE (1969), and BLACK BEAUTY (1971).

3992 *The Marketing of Films.* by Goyal, Trishla. 545 p. Calcutta: Intertrade, 1966.

3993 *The Marketing of Motion Pictures.* by Musun, Chris Dr. 336 p. Los Angeles: Chris Musun, 1969.

This is a privately printed volume (a dissertation) which covers the following topics: 1) the consumer; 2) markets for films; 3) channels of distribution; 4) trade practices and government regulations; 5) promotion of films; 6) financing; 7) key variables affecting box office; 8) prediction of grosses. Obviously, this is a business volume that stresses the use of market research.

3994 *Marlene.* by Higham, Charles. 319 p. illus. New York: W. W. Norton, 1977.

Charles Higham is one of the best show business biographers now practicing. After considerable success with a difficult subject, Katharine Hepburn, he takes on a far more complex woman, Marlene Dietrich, in this volume. Other biographies have preceded his, but none has presented so complete a portrait. He follows Dietrich from her cabaret appearances in Berlin during the twenties to her public appearances during the early seventies. In between, of course, is the long, varied, and colorful screen career that enabled Dietrich to become the living legend we know today. In tracing her climb to this rarified status Higham tells us much about the woman and her philosophy of life. Although a great deal of this material might lend itself toward a sensationalistic approach, the author presents a low key, honest exposition characterized by sensitivity and taste. A short photo section is included along with lists offilm and theatre appearances. The volume is indexed.

The most severe test of any biography is the final feeling of "knowing" the subject. Higham has accomplished the formidable task of letting us "know" Dietrich in intimate detail and yet has still preserved her charismatic mystery, appeal, and excitement. This book should enjoy a lengthy success with audiences weaned on the television showings of Dietrich's films. It certainly sets a high standard for future celebrity biographies. Recommended.

3995 *Marlene Dietrich.* by Kobal, John. 160 p. paper illus. New York: Dutton, 1968.

The career of Dietrich beautifully told in words and pictures. Included are a filmography and discography. The technical quality of the pictures (many are non-Dietrich photos) and their use to complement the text might serve as a model to other publishers and authors. Highly recommended.

3996 *Marlene Dietrich: Image and Legend.* by Griffith, Richard. 32 p. paper illus. New York: Museum of Modern Art Film Library, 1959.

This booklet was used as a program for a retrospective showing of some of Dietrich's films at the museum in 1959. After an opening essay on Dietrich, there are some stills—mostly studio but some candids—and finally, a listing of her film roles. The three-part list (extra player, featured player and star) takes the reader up to TOUCH OF EVIL in 1958. Interesting, quick reading but not essential.

3997 *Marlene Dietrich.* by Morley, Sheridan. 128 p. illus. New York: McGraw Hill, 1977.

Sheridan Morley reviews the life and career of Marlene Dietrich in what turns out to be an appreciation rather than a critical biography. Relying quite heavily on unacknowledged quotations from previously published works and a fine collection of photographs, the author contributes little more than a skill at assembling selected materials. At times he is inaccurate, e.g., Dietrich's role in NO HIGHWAY IN THE SKY (1951) was not as a "guest star," she was one of three leading players; furthermore, to call RANCHO NOTORIOUS (1952) "...at best a very poor man's DESTRY (1939)" seems to indicate an unfamiliarity with Dietrich's films.

A filmography, a bibliography, and an index add a needed dimension to the narrative which lacks critical insight. As a nicely illustrated appreciation of a legendary actress, this volume is acceptable. It should please a general, nondiscriminating audience.

3998 *Marlene Dietrich.* by Silver, Charles. 160 p. paper illus. New York: Pyramid, 1974.

The approach that Charles Silver employs in describing Dietrich's career is a departure from the usual chronological review. He begins with Germany and the early von Sternberg period, which leads eventually to roles as salon ladies and saloon girls. After World War II, Dietrich's roles were mostly reprises of those she played earlier. The author entitles his closing nonchronological sections "Return(s) to Germany", "To the Salon", and "To the Saloon." Such a structure lends variety to the interpretation of the Dietrich career and persona.

Visuals are outstanding and indicate the care always taken in photographing Dietrich throughout the years. A bibliography, a filmography, and an index complete the volume. Although Dietrich has been the subject of many previous volumes, this one summarizes her career quite nicely with an objective text and many well-selected photographs. Recommended.

3999 *Marlene Dietrich's ABC.* by Dietrich, Marlene. 160 p. paper New York: Avon Books, 1962.

A dictionary of selected words and phrases defined in the light of Dietrich's experience, enthusiasm, sentiment, and commercial know-how. She dishes out advice, recipes, tributes and fragments of autobiography and for the most part avoids the pitfall of being cute or coy. Contains many references to filmmaking and film personalities and is a warm, amusing and rewarding book.

4000 *Marlon Brando.* by Jordan, Rene. 157 p. paper illus. New York: Pyramid, 1973.

The recent spate of books on Brando is increased by one more—but this late entry is one of the better ones. Although some attention is given to Brando's off-screen personality and behavior, the major portion of the book is concerned with his films. Each of the 27 films is described and evaluated critically. In a few instances some analysis of character and plot is offered.

Most of the visuals are up to the usual *Pyramid* reproduction standards and add much to Jordan's text. A bibliography, filmography and an index are also included. This is a fine volume that is well written and nicely reproduced. When this book is combined with the Gary Carey biography on Brando, the total result of two inexpensive paperbacks is far more impressive than any of the higher-priced volumes. Highly recommended.

4001   *Marlon Brando.* by Paige, David. 39 p.   paper   illus.   Mankato, Minn.:Creative Education, 1971.

A superficial biography designed for very young readers.

4002   *Marlon: Portrait of the Rebel as an Artist.* by Thomas, Bob. 296 p. paper illus. New York: Ballantine Books, 1975.

The biographical skills that were evident in the author's earlier studies of Harry Cohn, David Selznick, and Irving Thalberg are once again used to good effect in this volume. Many different evaluations of Brando as both person and performer are interwoven with anecdotes and factual data to produce a fascinating portrait of the nonconformist actor. Supporting the strong text are some well-selected illustrations and an index.

The reader in search of material from which to formulate a personal opinion about Brando can hardly do better than this volume. Thomas has managed to combine all the pertinent matters concerning Brando into a fast-moving, readable account. Recommended.

4003   MAROONED. by Stern, Harold. 24 p. paper. illus. New York: National Publishers, 1969.

A space glossary and a section entitled "Tomorrow Is Now" are the unusual features of this souvenir book. The visuals concentrate on the space flight and space activities. Gregory Peck gets the most attention as star, and producer Mike Frankovich and director John Sturges are also spotlighted. Other cast members and production personnel are noted.

4004   *Marquee Ministry.* by Konzelman, Robert G. 123 p. illus. New York: Harper and Row, 1972.

Does the idea of transforming your local theatre into a community forum seem radical? Can there be cooperation between the film industry, the local theatre manager, and the members of the community? Konzelman, a Director of Educational Research for the American Lutheran Church, believes in both ideas and discusses the power of the church in determining future films. He opts for cooperation, understanding, and interaction between the church and the film industry rather than censure, threats, and control. A dialogical film study which considers motion pictures as a communication both to and from our culture is recommended. Some evaluation criteria for the selection of those films which might be used in such a study are suggested. Final chapters offer advice on leading discussions, the role of the church pastor, organizing film festivals, and other matters which might help to bring about the effective use of secular films. A short bibliography is appended.

In theory, the ideas proposed certainly are stimulating and workable; in practice, some of them may be defeated by economic, political, or self-serving motivations. Many people consider the motion picture theatre as a doomed or dying institution. (Statistical and observational evidence supports this view.) Reasons for this belief are many but foremost is the reluctance of people to leave the house. The attraction outside must be strong, indeed. In other words, people should do the things suggested by Konzelman, but will they?

In any event, the comments, advice, and suggestions for using films have much general application and will interest those who teach film. Recommended.

4005   THE MARRIED WOMAN by Godard, Jean-Luc. unnumbered paper illus. New York: Berkley, 1965.

Fragments of a film shot in 1964, written and directed by Jean-Luc Godard. Contains an introduction: "Jean-Luc Godard cou La Raison Ardente." This is a picture book with a text based upon the English subtitles; it is not a film script.

4006   *Marshall Delaney at the Movies.* by Fulford, Robert. 244 p. Toronto, Ontario: Peter Martin, 1974.

A Canadian critic unfamiliar to most readers in the U.S. makes his print debut in this collection of film reviews—with rather pleasing results. In the book there are innumerable instances of unique critical perception; only occasionally is Mulford's writing weakened by attitudes and prejudices that may alienate readers, e.g., the use of such terms as "My hairy young friends," "a retarded youngish adult" (Sidney Poitier), "a faggot's nightmare," etc. He is enthusiastic and informed about Canadian cinema, which is treated in the first group of reviews. Hollywood film reviews appear in a center section, while international films are considered in the final pages of the book.

Subtitled "The Contemporary World as Seen on Film," the collection contains reviews that originally appeared in a Canadian periodical *Saturday Night*, from 1965 to 1974. Marshall Delaney is an alias created by Fulford as an alter ego in order to gain freedom from personal restraints. In the latter instance he has been quite successful. In summary the criticism presented here is fresh, stimulating and even irritating at times. The ability of Fulford to provoke emotion is unquestionable, as is his ability to write entertaining film criticism. Recommended.

4007 *The Martial Arts Film.* by Mintz, Marilyn D. 243 p. illus. New York: A. S. Barnes, 1978.

According to the author: "A film is considered a martial arts film if competence as a martial arts performer, making use of personal strength, determines role and behavior in plot," and "The essential aspect...is the emphasis on fighting ability. The individual against great odds, having to rely on his own spiritual and physical capabilities to survive and endure."

In the very broad context of these statements, Marilyn Mintz offers little more than a review of Kung Fu cinema. Using broad dimensions such as comedy, violence, tragedy, concept, application, culture, image, sound and sense, she tries to define a film genre. Unfortunately she goes little further than providing an overview of selected Kung Fu and Samurai films. Her efforts are not helped by the illustrations—many of which are so dark they cannot be understood. The filmography provided is narrow, consisting only of Chinese and Japanese films, while the bibliography is extensive but not clearly discernible in the text. An index is provided.

The volume appears to be an attempt to broaden what was originally a study of Kung Fu films. Its goals as stated are not realized and any merit that the original material may have had has been weakened by the poor illustrations and weak supporting

elements. A disappointing effort, characterized by an incorrect titling on the dust cover provided.

4008 *Martin Scorsese.* edited by Reed, Rochelle. 24 p. paper illus. Washington, D.C.: American Film Institute, 1975.

With only three major films to his credit, Martin Scorsese impressed many critics with his directorial skill. His films, ALICE DOESN'T LIVE HERE ANYMORE (1974), MEAN STREETS (1973) and BOX CAR BERTHA (1972) and an earlier short film, THE BIG SHAVE (1967) were shown prior to an AFI seminar. A transcript of that meeting in February, 1975, is reprinted here. A short biography and a filmography are included.

4009 *Martin Scorsese: The First Decade.* by Kelly, Mary Pat. 206 p. paper illus. Pleasantville, N.Y.: Redgrave, 1980.

This study/appreciation of film director Martin Scorsese has a short opening statement by Michael Powell, followed by biographical chapters dealing with his youth, the New York University years, his first films, his actors, his family, etc. The book concludes with selected reviews of Scorsese's films, a filmography and a chronology.

The author has known her subject since 1965, and he has cooperated to some extent with this book—an interview, quotes, pictures, etc. The result is an admirable survey of Scorsese's career to date.

The illustrations are excellent and the book serves as a fine introduction to the work of one of America's most promising film directors.

4010 *Marvellous Melies.* by Hammond, Paul. 159 p. illus. New York: St. Martin's, 1975.

The text and the supporting material in this appreciation of Georges Melies are very impressive. Carefully researched and documented, the book consists of two major sections: the first on his life from 1861 to 1938; the second devoted to critical analyses of his film styles and content. Brief introductory and final chapters provide a framework for these two main portions. Appendixes include chapter references, a trickography and a long filmography for Melies. A detailed index is also provided.

All of the material above has been researched and prepared with apparent care and concern. Unfortunately, production decisions concerning book and illustration size negate much of the impact of the text and appendixes. Using many tiny, postage-stamp-size visuals may lower costs but provides nothing more than severe eye-strain and frustration in the reader. Melies dealt exclusively with the visual sense and to minimize pictorial examples of his genius-artistry is to denegrate any appreciation of his invaluable contribution to the art of film. The superb text and reference materials are highly recommended but the thoughtless presentation of the illustrations make this volume merely acceptable.

4011 *Marvin: The Story of Lee Marvin.* by Zec, Donald. 252 p. illus. New York: St. Martin's Press, 1980.

A biography written with the subject's cooperation, this volume captures the public persona of Lee Marvin—a concentration of macho characteristics covering an almost peace-loving inner man. Illustrations, a filmography and an index are helpful.

4012 *The Marx Bros. Scrapbook.* by Marx, Groucho; and Anobile, Richard 256 p. illus. New York: Darien House, 1973.

Is there such a thing as sour autobiography? Is it possible to learn so much about a performer's off-stage life that appreciation of his professional work begins to diminish? This book along with *Son of Groucho* suggests that such may be the case with the mustachioed Marx Brother. While none of the five Marx Brothers emerges as a likeable human being, it is the fully detailed portrait of Groucho—given directly and indirectly via interview in his own words—which is most disillusioning. At age 83, he seems a foul-mouthed, impotent lecher, who is living on past accomplishments. In this long memoir, he is most reluctant to give anyone else credit for any contribution to the Marx Brothers legend.

The book treats the other brothers to a lesser degree —Chico as a gambler and a woman chaser, Harpo as a mild, passive man whose best friend was Alexander Woolcott, Gummo as a paternal-maternal figure and finally, Zeppo as an aggressive, arrogant wheeler-dealer. There was a kind of loyalty among the brothers based on family ties, but they apparently did not like each other very much. The book contains some very fine things, including many illustrations of pictures and memorabilia—song sheets, posters, music, programs, etc. Spaced between the major Groucho interview, there are shorter, more positive interviews with Gummo, Zeppo, and with directors, writers, and others who helped create the Marx Brothers' celebrity. These balance the biased recollections of Groucho. A final index is another asset.

If the reader can tolerate the nasty, negative insults of Groucho, the book does offer an abundance of information and visuals that will please admirers. Because of Groucho's uninhibited language, the book can only be recommended for mature audiences.

4013 *The Marx Brothers.* by Crichton, Kyle. 310 p. illus. Garden City, N.Y.: Doubleday, 1950.

This collective biography about the five Marx Brothers has a heroine, Minnie Marx, their mother. By her persistence and determination, she pushed, coaxed, argued and yanked her sons onto the vaudeville stage. The volume covers the early period of the Marxes' career quite thoroughly, and it is easy to see how their motion picture comedy technique developed. However, the book, written with wit, style, and affection, does not consider their films at all. It ends about 1928 with their musical comedy successes on Broadway. There are some early nontheatrical illustrations but there is no index. As background material, this book is quite informative, but the reader interested primarily in their films will be disappointed.

4014 *The Marx Brothers: Their World of Comedy.* by Eyles, Allen. 175 p. paper illus. New York: A. S. Barnes, 1966.

In an interview, Groucho made a typically scathing comment. "Ten books have been written about the Marxes," he said, "and most of them are nothing more than a retelling of the screenplays of their films." Perhaps this was one of the books he had in mind. Each of the Marx Brothers' films is described in rather detailed fashion with a minimum of interpretation, criticism, or evaluation. Much of the movie dialogue is quoted. Surrounding the film descriptions are a few short sections concerning their early stage careers, their post-film careers and their place in motion picture history. Perhaps one of the nicest portions of this book is the two page autobiography of Margaret Dumont, the dignified dowager of their films. A filmography and a bibliography are given. This is a rather uninspired treatement of a major cinema subject.

4015 *The Marx Brothers.* by Wolf, William. 157 p. paper illus. New York: Pyramid, 1975.

An opening chapter of this delightful volume on the Marx Brothers tells "How They Got That Way."

Later sections deal with the stage, the Paramount years, the Metro years, the decline, and the ultimate acclaim. Although they made only 13 films as a team, they have become a legend in cinema history. Wolf's comprehensive review and evaluation of their films helps to explain why.

Supporting the text are some fine illustrations, a bibliography, a filmography, and an index. Films in which members of the team appeared separately are also noted.

This is a well-researched review of the Marx Brothers' films that should please a wide range of readers. Recommended.

4016   *The Marx Brothers.* by Durgnat, Raymond. 88 p. paper illus. Vienna: Osterreichisches Filmmuseum, 1966.

Contains illustrations, a filmography, and a bibliography.

4017   *The Marx Brothers at the Movies.* by Zimmerman, Paul D.; and Goldblatt, Burt. 224 p. illus. New York: G. P. Putnam's, 1968.

The 13 films that the Marx Brothers made as a team from 1929 to 1949 are the subject of this picture-text. After a brief introduction, each film is discussed with much of the original dialogue and "business" included. Critical evaluation and some factual material about the films is also given. There is no index. The illustrations are taken from stills and from actual film frames. The picture quality therefore varies greatly. The text is entertaining and written with care. While not a major contribution to screen literature, the book is certain to have a wide general appeal. Recommended.

4018   *Mary Pickford and Douglas Fairbanks.* by Herndon, Booton. 324 p. illus. New York: W.W. Norton, 1977.

Subtitled "The Most Popular Couple the World Has Known," this illustrated dual biography offers a thoroughly researched account of the pair. With appropriate psychological insight, Herndon concerns himself not only with the events in their lives, but why things happened as they did. Their relationships as lovers, husband and wife, business partners, and superstars are related. The films of both are examined, as is their rich contribution to the art of film, and their influence on the film industry.

The author lists his sources (Fairbanks family members, friends, etc.) with some commentary, and provides both a bibliography and an index.

Pickford has the major role here with much attention given to her public role as a worldwide superstar. A sympathetic in-depth portrait of the actress is presented, while that of Fairbanks is somewhat less detailed and distinct.

4019   *Mary Pickford, Comedienne.* by Niver, Kemp R. 156 p. illus. Los Angeles: Locare Research, 1969.

A pictorial record of Mary Pickford at the Biograph Studios from 1909 to 1912, this book provides a good period description along with some very rare illustrations. Plot outlines are given for each film (not all of them were comedies). Exceptional in all ways.

4020   MARY POPPINS. 16 p. paper illus. New York: National Publishers, 1964.

In a straightforward fashion this souvenir book treats author, cast, music, animation and production of the 1964 film. Stars Julie Andrews and Dick Van Dyke are singled out for special treatment.

4021   *Mary Shelley's Monster: The Story of Frankenstein.* by Tropp, Martin. 192 p. illus. Boston: Houghton Mifflin, 1976.

Mary Shelley's novel, *Frankenstein*, has not only been a popular success since its publication in 1818 but has greatly influenced subsequent horror stories. In this volume Martin Tropp explores the factors and influences that may have contributed to Mary Shelley's creation. In addition he gives critical attention to many of the films which have used Shelley's novel as source material.

The text is well researched and arranged, with a survey of the stories, books, tales, myths and people that may have been used by the authoress in writing her book. A final portion deals with the films and provides a valid balance of factual information and critical analysis.

A helpful selection of illustrations is provided along with chapter notes, a filmography, a bibliography, and an index.

Tropp's scholarly approach along with his provision of copious detail gives the book distinction. His detailed study of the authoress and her monster creation offers a rewarding reading experience that will especially please devotees of the horror genre. Recommended.

4022 *Mary Tyler Moore*. by Paige, David. 31 p. paper illus. Mankato, Minn.: Creative Education, 1977.

A superficial biography designed for very young readers.

4023 *Mascelli's Cine Workbook*. by Mascelli, Joseph V. 144 p. paper illus. Hollywood, Calif.: Cine/Graphic Publications, 1973.

The reliable Mr.Mascelli has succeeded one again. Not only is he responsible for what many consider the best book on cinematography, but he has now also produced a multi-media kit that will impress all advanced filmmakers with its contents, arrangement and thoroughness. There are two books in the package—one serves as a text while the other contains the "tools." The text offers concentrated information on many filmmaking topics, while the second volume includes grids, tables, charts, rulers, targets, filters, color samples, and calculators for exposures, lights, etc. The end pockets contain rulers, tissues, a magnifying glass, and a marking pencil among other items. All of these are noted here to give some idea of the possible range, scope and use of this package. The accompanying narrative explains the use of the materials.

It must be emphasized that this kit is most appropriate for the filmmaker who has had experience, since it demands some background for reasonable comprehension. Obviously it has its greatest potential for professionals and in advanced filmmaking courses. However, there is enough basic information contained within the kit to make it valuable for any interested reader. Recommended and essential for those schools and colleges which teach filmmaking.

4024 MASCULINE FEMININE. by Godard, Jean-Luc. 288 p. paper illus. New York: Grove Press, 1969.

Script of the 1965 film directed by Godard. Contains cast credits and seven extra parts: 1) a Robert Hughes article, 2) a Pierre Billard article, 3) Guy de Maupassant Stories, 4) "Chronicle of a Winter," by Jean-Luc Godard, 5) interviews with Godard, 6) criticism and reviews, and 7) excerpts from Michel Vianey's "En Attendant Godard," and Philippe Labro's "Le Nouveau Candide."

4025 *Mask or Face: Reflections in an Actor's Mirror*. by Redgrave, Michael. 188 p. illus. London: Heinemann, 1958.

A statement on acting that contains sections such as mask or face, to be me or not to be me, Shakespeare and the actors, actors and audiences, notes on direction, etc. A chapter entitled, "I Am Not a Camera," is based on a lecture that Redgrave delivered to the British Film Institute Summer School in 1954. The book contains illustrations of Redgrave in both stage and screen roles, but there is no index.

4026 *Mass Communication: A Sociological Perspective*. by Wright, Charles R. 124 paper New York: Random House, 1959.

Contains a section on Soviet film.

4027 *Mass Communication: Television, Radio, Film, Press; The Media and Their Practice in the United States of America*. by Barnouw, Erik. 280 p. illus. New York: Rinehart, 1956.

A general survey on communication with attention given to motion pictures. Contains bibliographies.

4028 *Mass Culture: The Popular Arts in America*. by White, David M. edited by Rosenberg, Bernard; 561 p. Glencoe, Ill.: Free Press, 1957.

An anthology with several articles on films.

4029 *Mass Means of Communication*. edited by Daughters of St. Paul. 202 p. illus. Boston: St. Paul Editions, 1967.

Includes statements by several popes on the subject of motion pictures.

4030 *The Mass Media: Their Impact on Children and Family Life*. by Klineberg, Otto; and Klapper, Joseph T. 48 p. paper New York: Television Information Office, 1960.

4031 *Mass Media: The Invisible Environment Revisited*. by Glessing, Robert J.; and White, William P. 277 p. paper illus. Chicago: Science Research Associates, 1976.

Prepared as a secondary school text, this anthology treats broad topics pertinent to mass media by offering a few selected articles for each. In the case of film, there are three: "On the Future of Movies" by Pauline Kael, "The Docudramatelementary" by Norman Corwin, and "Films, Movies, and Audiences" by Penelope Huston.

In addition to the above, there are more than 60 other articles on topics ranging from print, music, comics, to advertising, minorities, sports, and TV violence.

Peripheral to film collections, this volume deserves consideration by secondary schools and junior colleges as one of the better texts currently available on mass communication.

4032   *Mass Media and Children: A Study of Exposure Habits and Cognitive Efforts.* by Bailyn, Lotte. 48 paper Washington, D.C.: American Psychological Association, 1959.

4033   *Mass Media and Communication.* by Steinberg, Charles. 700 p. paper illus. New York: Hastings, 1972.

This anthology provides a survey of the impact of mass media on society. Commentaries, a bibliography and appendices accompany the text.

4034   *Mass Media and Mass Man.* by Casty, Alan. 260 p. paper illus. New York: Holt, Rinehart & Winston, 1968.

This collection of articles focuses on media "as processors and conveyors of culture and information." It is noted here since it contains seven articles that deal specifically with films and certain others that make some reference to the film medium.

4035   *The Mass Media and Modern Society.* by Peterson, Theodore B; and Jensen, Jay W.; and Rivers, William L. 259 p. New York: Holt, Rinehart, Winston, 1965.

4036   *Mass Media and Violence.* by Lange, David L.; and Baker, Robert K.; and Ball, Sandra J. 614 p. paper Washington, D.C.: U.S. Government Printing Office, 1969.

A report to the National Commission on the Causes and Prevention of Violence, from the Task Force on Mass Media and Violence. Bibliographical sources are included.

4037   *Mass Media and You.* by Repath, Austin. 217 p. illus. Ontario: Longmans, 1966.

4038   *Mass Media in a Free Society.* edited by Agee, Warren K. 96 p. paper Lawrence, Kansas: The University Press of Kansas, 1969.

This book consists of six presentations which were originally made at the William Allen White Centennial Seminar at the University of Kansas in 1968. The general theme was the challenges to be met today and in the future by newspapers, TV, motion pictures and magazines. Bosley Crowther gave the presentation on films, entitled "Magic, Myth and Monotony: A Measure of the Role of Movies in a Free State."

What was acceptable writing on film in the thirties and forties now seems naive, uptight, and senile. Crowther should have quit when he was ahead. Acceptable for the rest of the book—especially Stan Freberg on TV—but the film article is a disservice.

4039   *Mass Media in America.* by Pember, Don R. 380 p. paper illus. Chicago: Science Research Associates, 1974.

In this attractive text, there is one chapter, "Movies and the Dream Factory," that has special pertinence for film collections. It is a very general historical overview of Hollywood filmmaking over the past 60 years.

Much of the information contained in the surrounding chapters is also pertinent to films. A short bibliography is provided. Acceptable.

4040   *Mass Media in the Soviet Union.* by Hopkins, Mark W. 384 p. illus. New York: Pegasus, 1970.

4041   *The Master Handbook of Still and Movie Titling for Amateur and Professional.* by Stecker, Elinor H. 463 p. Blue Ridge Summit, Pa.: Tab Books, 1979.

The goal of this volume is the production of professional-looking titles for slides and films. In nine chapters crammed with information, instruction, advice, illustrations, diagrams, charts, etc., the author presents the basics of titling. She discusses what, when, where, equipment, layout, color, light, exposure, backgrounds, and lettering. A glossary, appendixes, a bibliography, and an index complete the handbook.

This is another impressive Tab production that addresses its subject with efficiency, clarity and practical know-how. Recommended.

4042 *Master of None.* by Pertwee, Roland. 309 p. illus. London: Peter Davis, 1940.

Roland Pertwee was a scriptwriter whose work for British films extended over the three decades, 1920-50. One of his sons, Michael, is also a screenwriter and author of *Name Dropping*; his other son, Jon, is an actor.

4043 *Mastering the Film and Other Essays.* by Samuels, Charles Thomas. 228 p. Knoxville, Tenn.: University of Tennessee Press, 1977.

Charles Thomas Samuels was a teacher, author, and critic whose reputation has grown since his death, by his own hand, in 1974. A sampling of his essays and reviews on film appears in this volume.

At the time of his death, he was preparing a volume, *Mastering the Film*, which examined film aesthetics by using the work of a dozen noted film directors. Four chapters (Carol Reed, Jean Renoir, Alfred Hitchcock, and Federico Fellini) and some notes for an introduction to the intended volume make up the first section. The latter portion is devoted to a selection of his film reviews and essays which originally appeared in such periodicals as *The American Scholar* and *Hudson Review*. Some chapter notes and an index are included.

The depth and clarity of Samuels' writing make it essential reading for anyone concerned with film criticism. He has the ability to differentiate the various elements of filmmaking and discuss them with attention given to their pertinence for a specific film. The natural intelligence and precision of his writing make his arguments most convincing. This is a rich, rewarding reading experience. Highly recommended.

4044 *Masters and Masterpieces of the Screen.* by Taylor, Cora W. 112 p. illus. New York: Collier, 1927.

A comprehensive survey of the motion pictures from the early development to 1927. Considers the dramatic, artistic, and educational phases; the outstanding successes and leading personalities. Presented for the most part pictorially, the book has an introduction by Will B. Hays.

4045 *Masters and Masterpieces of the Screen.* by Taylor, Cora W. 112 p. illus. New York: Gordon Press, 1976 (1927).

Heavily illustrated survey of motion pictures, 1900-

1927, with brief biographies of many actors. Originally published in 1927 by Collier, N.Y.

4046 *Masters of Menace: Greenstreet and Lorre.* by Sennett, Ted. 228 p. paper illus. New York: Dutton, 1979.

What we have here resembles a double volume of the *Illustrated History of the Movies* series. Since the author, Ted Sennett, was the general editor of that fine series, the similarity is not surprising. The arrangement is a bit different; the early separate careers for both men are noted first, then an account of the films they made together is given, and finally, there is a presentation of the films they made apart from each other. Accompanying the many synopses, descriptions, and comments are some attractive visuals, filmographies, and an index.

Although the book does not delve too deeply into the personal lives of these two fine actors, their film careers are covered thoroughly. This is a volume that will delight everyone who admires the artistry that Lorre and Greenstreet brought to many of their screen roles.

4047 *Masters of Stage and Screen.* by Lipovsky, Alexander. 367 p. illus. Moscow: Progress, 1969.

Soviet film actors who were winners of the Lenin prize for performing arts are noted in this collective biography.

4048 *Masters of the American Cinema.* by Giannetti, Louis D. 466 p. illus. Englewood Cliffs, N.J.: Prentice Hall, 1981.

The first section introduces American cinema via studios, stars, genres, industry, aesthetics, etc. In the second part 18 American directors are discussed. Illustrations and bibliographies are plentiful.

4049 *Masterworks of the British Cinema.* by 352 p. illus. New York: Harper and Row, 1974.

An introduction by John Russell Taylor precedes the scripts of the following films: BRIEF ENCOUNTER (1945), David Lean; THE THIRD MAN (1950), Carol Reed; KIND HEARTS AND CORONETS (1950), Robert Hamer; and SATURDAY NIGHT AND SUNDAY MORNING (1960), Karel Reisz. Casts and credits are given for each of the films and a collection of critical comments is appended.

4050   *Masterworks of the French Cinema.*
350 p. paper illus. New York: Harper and Row, 1974.

This collection of scripts of classic French films includes: THE ITALIAN STRAW HAT (1927), Rene Clair; GRAND ILLUSION (1937), Jean Renoir; LA RONDE (1950), Max Ophuls; and THE WAGES OF FEAR (1953), Henri-Georges Clouzot. It also contains an introduction by John Weightman and a critical appendix with the following articles: "THE ITALIAN STRAW HAT", by Roger Manvell; "GRAND ILLUSION—A Note from Jean Renoir"; "My First Meeting with Jean Renoir," by Erich von Stroheim; GRAND ILLUSION, by Joel Finler; "LA RONDE—Interview with Ophuls," by Francis Koval; and "WAGES OF FEAR—A Review" (1954), by Karel Reisz.

4051   *Masterworks of the German Cinema.*
300 p. paper illus. New York: Harper and Row, 1974.

This collection of scripts of classic German films includes: THE GOLEM (1920), Paul Wegener and Carl Boese; NOSFERATU (1922), F. W. Murnau; M (1931), Fritz Lang; and THE THREE PENNY OPERA (1931), G. W. Pabst. Notes, cast, and credits accompany the scripts, and there are critiques of the films by Lotte Eisner, Paul Rotha, and Paul M. Jensen. Roger Manvell provides the introduction.

4052   *Materials for Occupational Education: An Annotated Source Guide.*
edited by Schuman, Patricia Glass; and Crowley, Maureen. 300 p. New York: Neal-Schuman, 1979.

Contains selected sources of films dealing with occupations.

4053   *The Matinee Idols.* by Carroll, David. 159 p. illus. New York: Arbor House, 1972.

Divided into two portions, the theatre and the film, this collective biography of male performers who appealed primarily to the female audience is a fascinating sample of memorabilia. Each biography is accompanied by several varied illustrations—portraits, stills, candids, sketches, etc.—and sometimes reprints of articles by the subject. Film stars include Francis X. Bushman, Lou Tellegen, Douglas Fairbanks, William S. Hart, Tom Mix, Wallace Reid, Rudolph Valentino, Ramon Novarro, John Gilbert, and John Barrymore; some others—Antonio Moreno, Ricardo Cortez, Jack Holt, Charles Ray, Richard Barthelmess—are pictured but not discussed in the text. Picture quality is acceptable and the book is indexed.

Interesting but hardly essential material, this volume will have a curiosity appeal for the general reader. The material presented lacks depth, and other books, like Blum's *A Pictorial History of the Silent Screen,* supply more and better visuals.

4054   *Matty.* by Matthews, A. E. 232 p. illus. London: Hutchinson, 1952.

Alfred Edward Matthews was a stage actor who made films from the late thirties until his death in 1960. Since his motion picture career began rather late in his life, he usually portrayed crotchety, cranky old men.

4055   *see   4054*

4056   MAURIE. by Morrow, Douglas. 180 p. paper illus. New York: Grosset & Dunlap, 1973.

Script of the 1973 film directed by Daniel Mann. Contains script, cast and credits.

4057   *Max Miller.* by East, John M. illus. London: W. H. Allen, 1977.

Miller is a British music hall comedian who starred in a series of films during the thirties.

4058   *Max Ophuls.* by Roud, Richard. 44 p. paper illus. London: British Film Institute, 1958.

A *BFI Index* series booklet on the director of LOLA MONTES (1955) and LETTER FROM AN UNKNOWN WOMAN (1948). Illustrations and a filmography accompany the text.

4059   *Max Ophuls and The Cinema of Desire.* by Williams, Alan Larson. New York: Arno, 1980.

An examination of the artistry of Max Ophuls using four films: LETTER FROM AN UNKNOWN WOMAN (1948), MADAME DE (1953), LA RONDE (1950), LOLA MONTES (1955). This is a title in the *Dissertations on Film* series.

4060   *May '68 and Film Culture.* by Harvey, Sylvia. 169 p. paper London: British Film Institute (Zoetrope in U.S.), 1980.

The unusual title of this volume derives from Sylvia Harvey's argument that "the landscape of film studies has been transformed by post-'68 developments in Marxist French film theory." After discussing the 1968 events, she makes reference to earlier arguments about the materialist view of cultural productions and then extends her analysis to recent theories about ideology and culture.

Appendixes and a bibliograpy complete the original, stimulating position taken by the author. For those scholars engaged in debate on film theory, she offers a persuasive argument.

4061 MAYA. 14 p. paper illus. 1966.

The souvenir book of MAYA is like the 1966 film—small, unassuming, and pleasant. Stars Clint Walker and young Jay North are given some attention but the backgrounds shot in India and the elephants steal it all.

4062 *Mayer and Thalberg: The Make-Believe Saints.* by Marx, Samuel. 273 p. illus. New York: Random House, 1975.

Samuel Marx began his Hollywood career as the story editor for MGM in 1930, and stayed at that studio during the next two decades. A portion of his tenure coincided with the productive Mayer-Thalberg period that established the studio as the world's greatest. In this volume he briefly reviews the early life of both men before beginning the detailed account of the pair's 13-year association, which ended with Thalberg's death in 1936. It is at this point that Marx concludes his volume, although both he and Mayer continued to work at MGM for many more years.

Both men have been the subjects of earlier biographies—Thalberg by Bob Thomas and Mayer by Bosley Crowther—and have figured prominently in other volumes. However, this is the first that considers the relationship between them in detail. By drawing on both his own experience and that of others, the author has formulated favorable portraits of both men. Of course, the MGM studios and its personalities become essential elements of his narrative. The few illustrations included serve primarily to show the physical appearance of the two subjects. A filmography of selected Mayer-Thalberg productions and an index are added.

Sam Marx has written a fine dual biography that further illuminates an important period in Hollywood history. It is hoped that he uses his vast repository of memories and experiences at MGM in future volumes. This one is an excellent beginning. Recommended.

4063 ME AND MY BIKE. by Thomas, Dylan. 53 p. illus. New York: McGraw-Hill, 1965.

This unfilmed screenplay is an operetta combining fantasy with social comment. Contains an introduction by Sydney Box.

4064 *Measurement and Analysis of Psychological Response to Film.* by Case, Harry W.; and Levonian, Edward. 70 p. paper illus. Los Angeles: University of California, 1962.

A report (number 62-66) on Title VII project number 458 of the National Defense Education Act of 1958. Includes a bibliography.

4065 *The Measurement of the Effectiveness of the Documentary Sound Film: as a Supplement in the Teaching of Methods to College Students Being Prepared to Teach in the Secondary Schools.* edited by Department of Secondary Education, Pennsylvania State University. 115 p. paper illus. University Park, Pa.: Pennsylvania State University, 1962.

The report of project number 217 of the National Defense Act of 1958. Robert B. Patrick was the director.

4066 *Measuring the Effectiveness of Sound Pictures as Teaching Aids.* by Arnspiger, Varney Clyde. 156 p. New York: AMS Press, 1972 (1933).

Originally published in 1933 by Teachers College of Columbia University as number 565 of the series, *Contributions to Education*, this study deals with moving pictures and their use in education, natural history, music, etc.

4067 *The Mechanized Muse.* by Kennedy, Margaret. 52 p. London: Allen and Unwin, 1942.

A discussion of film—its development, aesthetics, limitations, problems, etc.—told in a pleasant, easy text.

4068 *Media: The Compleat Guide.* by Monaco, James. 300 p. illus. New York: Zoetrope, 1981.

Comments on that "old" medium, film, and all the new ones.

4069 *Media and Kids.* by Morrow, James; and Suid, Murray. 144 p. paper illus. Rochelle Park, N.J.: Hayden Books, 1977.

This volume carries the subtitle "Real-World Learning in the Schools," and is addressed to teachers. It proposes a series of activities involving media such as stage performing, design-making and drawing, photography, radio, movies, and television. Individual chapters present the concept of each medium with an emphasis on its grammar. This is followed by some suggested activities. Selected standards along with a few sources/resource conclude the sections.

The chapter that deals with movies discusses scripting, shooting, cutting, recording and acting under the concepts heading. Suggested activities include making a one-reeler, a documentary, an instructional film, a genre film, a cut-out animation film, or a table-top animation film. Under standards, there are discussions of technical difficulties, vagueness, shotless thinking, insufficient coverage, and squeamish cutting. The sources/resources listed are mostly standard texts which correlate nicely with the chapter content.

4070 *Media Culture.* by Monaco, James. 335 p. paper illus. New York: Delta, 1978.

In this anthology, James Monaco is dealing with mass media: television, radio, records, books, magazines, newspapers, and movies. The articles dealing with films are "Politics Under the Palms" by Bo Burlingham and "Harry Makes A Movie" by Robert Alan Arthur. The first deals with Hollywood people, while the second discusses how a producer initiates a new film. Some of the material in other sections is also pertinent to film and attention is given in the appendix to film company ownership and the twenty-five top-grossing films to date. A bibliography and an index complete the book.

4071 *The Media Environment.* by Stanley, Robert H.; and Steinberg, Charles S. 306 p. New York: Hastings House, 1976.

This volume is subtitled "Mass Communications in American Society," and considers print, films, radio, and television separately. Problems and topics common to the above media are also treated—censorship, right of access, defamation, minority representation, public relations, and new technologies. A bibliography and an index complete the work.

In addition to the general sections on mass media, there are three chapters on motion pictures. The first deals with early motion picture history, the second with the Hollywood hierarchy, and the final one with Hollywood's attempts at self-regulation.

The consideration of motion pictures as a mass communication medium gives the book its importance for film collections. When compared and/or treated with other media, motion pictures take on a significance that is often minimized in volumes devoted to film history. This volume places film in a proper sociological perspective.

4072 *The Media Equipment Resource Center Directory.* compiled by Young Film Makers Foundation. 96 p. paper illus. New York: Media Equipment Resource Center, 1977.

This is really a catalog of new films and video programs that were independently produced with the assistance of the Center. 16mm films, super 8mm films, videotapes, and other media works are listed along with distributor, length, plot outline, and rental/sale price.

4073 *Media for Christian Formation.* by Dalglish, William A. 393 p. paper illus. Dayton, Ohio: Pflaum, 1969.

The first volume of what has become a series contains more than 150 evaluations of short films in addition to other reviews of filmscripts, recordings, etc. The selection of media is a general one that has application in a variety of situations including, of course, religious instruction. The media is arranged alphabetically by title. Lengthy annotations describe, suggest uses and possible audiences, and give technical data. A subject index and a distributor list are added. Essential.

4074 *Media in Value Education: A Critical Guide.* by Schrank, Jeffrey. 168 p. paper illus. Chicago: Argus Communications, 1970.

Written as an aid to teachers of religious education, this paperback offers much that will be of value to others. The major portion of the volume is devoted to reviews of 75 short films. Distributor information is given along with a comparison chart on film rental costs. Each film annotation includes several questions that can be used as a discussion guide. There are short chapters on recordings, tapes and other media. An annotated guide to suppliers of media and pertinent material concludes the book. There is a short title index. This is a most valuable reference book; enthusiastically recommended.

4075 *Media-Made Dixie.* by Kirby, Jack Temple. 203 p. illus. Baton Rouge: Louisiana State University Press, 1978.

The ability of the American mass media to introduce, perpetuate, and integrate ideas and perceptions into the national consciousness is reexamined in this volume. Not only is the author concerned with the stereotyped images of the South, but he suggests that there may have been a major change from the period of THE BIRTH OF A NATION (1914) to ROOTS (1977). Using selected examples of media, Kirby identifies the various views of the South and concludes by predicting an end to the separateness of the South.

The text is relatively short and rushes past many provocative areas, giving a surface coverage rather than a penetrating examination. Plays, radio, minstrels, vaudeville, and television are largely ignored in favor of the more accessible book and film media. As a result, the material presented is similar at times to that found in several of the recently published studies about the image of the black in films. The volume contains a list of sources, chapter notes, and an index.

Although a great deal of research is indicated, the reader may have some reservations about its interpretation. Errors noted include: "Tobacco Road" played to rave notices for seven and a half years... The play was denounced unanimously by the critics. Of "Suddenly Last Summer": Sebastian marries Catherine Holly... In both play and film, Catherine was Sebastian's cousin, not his wife. To suggest also that Sebastian's mother, Violet, considers Catherine a love rival is to misinterpret a large part of the play.

In summary, this volume seems lacking in depth and often familiar in content, giving an overview rather than an analysis.

4076 *Media Made in California: Hollywood, Politics and the News.* by Tunstall, Jeremy; and Walker, David. 224 p. illus. New York: Oxford University Press, 1981.

A study written by two British authors during a one year stay (1978-79) at the University of California. The effect of California's mass media on state and nation is their concern.

4077 *Media Manuals (A Series).* 128-208 p. paper illus. New York: Hastings House.

Published by Hastings House, in association with Focal Press of London, these manuals provide introductions to the basic production elements of the audiovisual media.

Titles include: *The Animation Stand; Creating Special Effects for TV and Films; The Lens and All Its Jobs; The Lens in Action; Motion Picture Camera and Lighting Equipment Motion Picture Camera Techniques; Script Continuity and the Production Secretary ; 16mm Film Cutting; Your Film and the Lab; Script Writing for Animation.*

This excellent series treats background, techniques, and equipment in addition to offering discussions by experts on practical application to professional tasks. Most titles are copiously illustrated and offer a glossary and a bibliography.

4078 *The Media Reader.* by Valdes, Joan; and Crow, Jeanne. 390 p. paper illus. Dayton, Ohio: Pflaum, 1975.

Although this anthology was designed to complement the author's text, *The Media Works*, it can also be considered independently. A collection of articles on newspapers, magazines, comics, radio, television, advertising and movies, the book is arranged according to the text's three major headings: The Workings, The Mass Message, and The Personal Message. The articles pertaining to film include: "Right on with Rugoff," by Hollis Alpert; "How Films Are Made," by Rene Clair; "On Location in Hays, Kansas," by Peter Bogdanovich; "The Sneak Preview," by Lillian Ross; CASABLANCA and Bogie," by Ralph J. Gleason; "Notes on Black Movies," by Pauline Kael; "Reel One," by Adrien Stoutenberg; "Going to the Movies," by Pauline Kael; "Rhythm," by Ivor Montagu; and "Film Negatives," by Stanley Kauffmann. In addition, there are excerpts from interviews with film directors Kubrick, Coppola, Bergman, Penn and Truffaut.

The quality of these 10 pieces added to the many other fine articles included which have implication for the film medium make this volume a most appropriate candidate for acquisition. Recommended. For those using the author's text, it would seem to be a welcome essential.

4079 *Media Review Digest—An Annual.* edited by Wall, C. Edward. Ann Arbor, Mich.: Pierian, 1970.

The successor to *Multi Media Reviews Index*, this invaluable resource indexed a total of 171 periodicals in its ninth volume, *Media Review Digest 1979*.

This edition contained 40,000 citations and cross-references to reviews and descriptions of all types of non-print media. Films appear in the first section and include both features and shorts. In a typical feature entry the user will find that JULIA (1978) runs 118 minutes in sound and color and received mostly but not all, positive reviews from 16periodicals cited. Oscar and Golden Globe nominations are also noted. Some review excerpts are given along with the reviewer's name (if identifiable) and other citation information—date, volume, page, etc. A shorter documentary film, MEN OF BRONZE (1977), runs 60 minutes in sound and color. Purchase and rental prices are given. It is the story of a combat regiment of U.S. blacks in World War I. The four periodicals cited rate it "good to excellent" and it won both a Red Ribbon and a Cine Golden Eagle Award. Final sections include selected film awards and prizes, mediagraphies, a bibliography, general subject indicator, a classified subject index, an alphabetical subject index, a reviewer index, a geographical index, and a producer-distributor address list.

The production of such a total reference as this must be formidable. Its appearance in a logical, understandable, easy-to-use format is a small miracle to those of us who have tried to search for this information simply summarized. It is absolutely essential for all film users.

4080 *Media Sexploitation.* by Key, Wilson Bryan. 234 p. illus. Englewood Cliffs, N.J.: Prentice-Hall, 1976.

The subtitle on the dust jacket of this book proclaims "The Hidden Implants in America's Mass Media and How They Program and Condition Your Subconscious Mind." Areas considered include periodicals (*Playboy*, etc.), fashion advertising (*Vogue*, etc.), product advertising (*Ladies Home Journal*, etc.), rock music ("Tommy," "Hey, Jude," etc.), and television. One chapter is devoted to THE EXORCIST (1975), with an extended analysis of the many factors used in the film to create the sensationalism which accompanied its showings. Some of these were hidden, subliminal or symbolic. The author shows how the director was able to obtain the effects and reactions he wanted.

Anyone who is concerned with media will appreciate this study. It identifies with clarity and precision those techniques which manipulate and condition us without our knowledge. Recommended.

4081 *Media Three for Christian Formation.* edited by Dalglish, William A. 372 p. paper illus. Dayton, Ohio: Pflaum, 1973.

This is the third volume in a series which evaluates audiovisual resources suitable for programs of Christian formation. A majority of the items have use and purpose in many nonreligious programs. Over 400 media reviews are provided along with distributor information, lists of film/filmstrip/tape libraries, and a detailed subject index. Preceding the lengthy, thorough evaluations is a listing of titles according to medium. The film list here accounts for more than half of the 400 evaluations. Selection of the films for evaluation is outstanding, with many recognized classic short films represented. A typical entry includes a description of plot-content-approach-style along with a critical evaluation and some possibilities for use. Audience level is suggested and technical data about the films is noted. A few visuals appear throughout the book. An excellent reference-resource-aid, this volume is essential for all institutions that offer film service or film information.

4082 *Media Two: For Christian Formation.* edited by Dalglish, William A. 502 p. paper illus. Dayton, Ohio: Pflaum, 1970.

Although this is a guide to all media forms, it does contain descriptive evaluations of more than 200 short films. Written for religious groups, the material covered is not at all exclusive. Many short art films and documentaries are evaluated. Materials are arranged alphabetically by title. There is a subject index and a compilation of library and source addresses. This is one of the better reference works and should be included in all collections. The compactness and efficiency of this effort should make some of the other film evaluation services blush.

4083 *The Media Works.* by Valdes, Joan; and Crow, Jeanne. 282 p. paper illus. Dayton, Ohio: Pflaum, 1973.

Although concerned with the broad field of media and mass communication, there is sufficient attention given to motion pictures in this volume to warrant its inclusion here. An up-to-the-minute textbook designed for young adults, this outstanding compilation of narrative, suggestions, questions, problems, bibliographies, filmographies and visuals should find rapid acceptance in schools. It would be unfortunate if its readership was limited to the student, for there is much to stimulate, provoke and even excite all readers. There are three major sections: the workings; the mass message; and the personal message. In addition to films, other mass media examined are television, advertising, magazines, comics, radio and newspapers.

Format, presentation, organization, style and content are top grade, as are the production values.

Illustrations, drawings, and cartoons are abundant and appropriate. There is much creativity, intelligence, and obvious effort apparent in this quality text, which may initiate much needed courses in mass media in our schools. It is enthusiastically recommended.

4084   *Mediaware: Selection, Operation, and Maintenance.* by Wyman, Raymond. 188 p. paper illus. Dubuque, Iowa: William C. Brown, 1969.

Information and suggestions are offered on the selections, operation, and maintenance of motion picture projectors.

4085   *Medical Films Available in Great Britain.* by British Industrial and Scientific Films Association 114p. paper London: British Industrial and Scientific Films Association, 1971.

Offering data and description only, this catalog arranges the films under appropriate medical headings, e.g., dentistry; dermatology; eye, ear, nose and throat; pediatrics; and surgery. In addition, an alphabetical title list, a distributor list, a subject index, and suggestions for use are offered.

4086   *Medical Photography in Practice—A Symposium.* edited by Linssen, Eugene F. 343 p. illus. London: Foundation Press, 1961.

Designed for physicans and technicians in all branches of medical photography, this volume includes chapters on motion pictures along with explanations of other types of medical illustration.

4087   *Meet Elvis Presley.* by Friedman, Favius. 128 p. illus. New York: Scholastic Book Services, 1971.

By 1973 this modest biography of Elvis Presley was in its fifth printing. Since it is aimed at a teen-aged audience, its sales offer testimony to the continuing popularity of its subject. The biography is a popularized, noncontroversial account of his rise from Memphis teenager to show-business legend. Quotations from fans, acquaintances and co-workers are intermingled with recalled and reconstructed personal Elvis dialogue.

Production values are below average. Although the book is hardbound, the inexpensive paper used will probably not stand up to any heavy use. Picture quality is acceptable. As a low-cost book designed for the mass teenaged audience, this volume can be unhesitatingly endorsed. Otherwise, it is only acceptable.

4088   *Meeting at the Sphinx.* by Deans, Marjorie. 146 p. illus. London: McDonald, 1946.

The book tells of the making of CAESAR AND CLEOPATRA, the 1945 film directed by Gabriel Pascal which starred Vivien Leigh and Claude Rains. With introductions by both George Bernard Shaw and Pascal, the volume resembles a publicity book in its explanation of the components of the film. Discussed are the players, the music, the costumes, the sets, etc. The photographs from the film are most attractive but the text approaches press agentry. In retrospect it is interesting to note that the film was unsuccessful financially. Its critical reception was mixed upon initial release but it gained respect and admiration after the appearance of the Taylor-Burton CLEOPATRA (1963).

4089   *Meeting Mrs. Jenkins.* by Burton, Richard. 24 p. illus. New York: William Morrow & Co., 1966.

Originally written for *Vogue*, the Burton text has been embellished here by some color portraits of Elizabeth Taylor. Three scenes—a home in Bel Air, a restaurant five years later, and Paris—provide the physical settings for this portrait of Taylor. The book is trivial, but Burton writes well and the visuals are beautiful. Noted here for the record.

4090   *Mel Brooks: The Irreverent Funny Man.* by Adler, Bill; and Feinman, Jeffrey. 190 p. Chicago: Playboy Press, 1976.

Perhaps this biography-appreciation of Mel Brooks is a bit premature since it only covers THE PRODUCERS (1968), THE 12 CHAIRS (1970), BLAZING SADDLES (1974) and YOUNG FRANKENSTEIN (1975). It does relate how he began his career as a stagehand in Red Bank, New Jersey, wrote for Sid Caeser's "Show of Shows," recorded the "2000-Year-Old-Man" routines with Carl Reiner, and finally became a filmmaker. His marriage to Anne Bancroft is noted although little is said of his first marriage and three children.

Since Brooks is currently one of our most successful actor-writer-producer-directors, this appreciation of him is most welcome. It does give some insight into his background and its influence on the outrageous, offbeat comedies he creates. Unfortunately, the volume lacks a filmography, a bibliography, illustrations, and an index. These items would have improved the book immeasurably.

4091   *Mel Brook's* HISTORY OF THE WORLD PART I. by Brooks, Mel. unpag. illus. paper New York: Warner Books, 1981.

An instant book about the 1981 film directed by Mel Brooks.

4092   *Mel Brooks'* HIGH ANXIETY. by Brooks, Mel; and Clark, Ron; and DeLuca, Rudy; and Levinson, Barry. 151 p. paper illus. New York: Grosset and Dunlap, 1977.

This novelization of the script of HIGH ANXIETY (1977) was done by Robert Pilpel. It is noted here because of the large number of stills used as illustrations. Mel Brooks supplies a short introduction.

4093   *Melville on Melville.* edited by Nogueira, Rui. 176 p. illus. New York: Viking Press, 1971.

Jean-Pierre Melville, a French filmmaker, is unknown to most Americans; his eleven feature films have had few showings in this country. An individualist who usually writes his own scripts and has assumed many other roles in filmmaking, he prefers the thriller genre. He frequently voices his admiration for American films and directors of the thirties, and their influence can be detected in his films, most of which were made in the sixties.

This volume is structured like Truffaut's *Hitchcock* —a series of questions proposed to Melville which lead him to review his films in chronological order. While the quality and value of Melville's responses are unquestionably high, the reader who has not seen his films is at a disadvantage. The familiarity factor was certainly important in the success of Truffaut's book.

Illustrations are adequate and there is a detailed filmography. Since Melville is an important French filmmaker of the sixties, this specialized volume may serve to acquaint readers with his work. Acceptable.

4094   *Memo from David O. Selznick.* edited by Behlmer, Rudy. 518 p. illus. Viking Press, 1972.

A different approach to film literature is used in this collection of memoranda written by David O. Selznick over the period 1926 to 1962. Selected from a reservoir of two-thousand file boxes, the memos have been edited and arranged to give the book a narrative framework. Major attention, as might be expected, is given to the memos issued during the GONE WITH THE WIND era (1936-1941). REBECCA (1938-1941) is also singled out for an extended chapter. Since Selznick worked at Paramount, RKO, and Metro before forming his own company in 1935, the memos of those early years indicate his influence and effect on the careers of many famous actors— Hepburn, Astaire, Crawford, etc. The decline which coincided with his almost total devotion to the career of Jennifer Jones is indicated in the latter sections. One senses that the author is not sympathetic to the actress. Although she was a major focus of Selznick's activities from 1942 to 1963, the memos indicate that any achievement by Jones was due largely to Selznick's perseverance and backstage savvy. It should also be noted that Val Lewton— THE CAT PEOPLE (1942), THE BODY SNATCHER (1945), ISLE OF THE DEAD (1945), etc.—served as story editor to Selznick in the thirties.

Introducing each section is a montage of Selznick's statements, and these give a certain coherence to the material that follows. The appendix contains an edited Selznick lecture on the producer's function and the making of feature films. Another section called "Cast of Characters" identifies many of the names mentioned in the memos. An index is included, as are several groupings of illustrations. Photographic reproduction and selection are uniformly excellent.

This is a rich book about a larger-than-life personality, written in his own words. Not a biography, the volume will probably give the reader a more valid portrait of the real Selznick than any of the other biographical materials. Certain memos reveal him as uncertain, insecure, and annoying—a man who interfered, nagged and needled when he should have been occupied by other matters. They show his errors in judgment were as numerous as his correct decisions. Reading the memos concurrently with the Thomas biography is a most rewarding excursion. The work of a dedicated editor is obvious throughout and his shaping of the voluminous material into this fascinating collection is impressive. Highly recommended.

4095   *Memoirs of a Mangy Lover.* by Marx, Groucho. 214 p. illus. New York: Bernard Geis Assoc., 1963.

The substance of this book is a series of humorous essays on a wide range of topics. It is not autobiographical, except in the wildest, far-out Groucho manner. Drawings for the book are by Leo Hershfeld. File this one under "Humor" and forget it for cinema value.

4096 *Memoirs of a Moviegoer.* by Random, Henry. 144 p. San Francisco: Editorial Service Bureau, 1975.

In his definition of a moviegoer, the author uses a comparison with the avid reader—the person who reads books, reads about books and loves everything connected with them. The moviegoer is more than a fan and closer to an aficionado or informed enthusiast. The memoirs of author-moviegoer Henry Random are concerned with films of the thirties and forties. He recalls what film-going was like during those years—the films, stars, coming attractions, posters, store window display cards, the local theatre, the movie cathedrals, etc. The role of films —especially screwball comedies and musicals—during the depression is discussed and separate chapters offer tributes to John Garfield in FOUR DAUGHTERS (1938), and Humphrey Bogart in HIGH SIERRA (1939) and THE MALTESE FALCON (1941). Appreciation for several other selected private- eye films is expressed and the final chapter offers a rationale for being a moviegoer.

Although the book rambles about, approaching a stream-of-consciousness technique at times, it is difficult to resist the affection, respect and enthusiasm the author has for certain film experiences from his past. The volume is inexpensively produced with typed manuscript pages, no illustrations and no index. In production quality it resembles the self-published volumes one sees with increasing frequency today. If this is the case, one can only applaud Random's determination to make an entertaining statement on movie-going nostalgia available to a reading public. Acceptable.

4097 *Memoirs of a Professional Cad.* by Sanders, George. 192 p. illus. New York: G. P. Putnam's, 1960.

Only occasionally and incidentally is this book a biography. It is a series of wry, witty and wise comments on a performer's life, his profession, his acquaintances, and most of all himself. It is so enjoyable that one is tempted to overlook the major faults. It is not well-balanced, a large portion is devoted to the shooting of SOLOMON AND SHEBA (1959) and there is nothing about DORIAN GRAY (1944), REBECCA (1940), FOREIGN CORRESPONDENT (1940), or THE MOON AND SIXPENCE (1942). One questions Sander's memory or his seriousness when he calls Ann Baxter "the nearest thing to a heroine" in ALL ABOUT EVE (1950). The illustrations are few and poorly chosen; they look as if they were gathered in a great hurry from what was lying around the house. This could have been an outstanding example of film actor biography. Instead, the author has set-

tled for a few sophisticated laughs that are quickly forgotten. The book will please most readers, but the serious film student and the admirer of Sander's many fine performances will be disappointed.

4098 *Memoirs of a Star.* by Negri, Pola. 453 p. illus. Garden City, N.Y.: Doubleday, 1970.

This is an autobiography that is fun to read if you don't take it too seriously. In style, it resembles a straight version of Patrick Dennis' *Little Me*; when accounts in this book are compared with other sources, the divergence of viewpoint is enormous. The relationships with Lubitsch, Chaplin, Valentino, and others are all given attention, with Miss Negri emerging as a superheroine every time—silent screen style, of course.

What importance the book has is in its description of the motion picture industry and its people during the twenties. The illustrations are good. The author can apply the put-down with efficiency, ease, and seeming innocence. ("Those evenings always took the same form. Mary would sit at one end of the table, with Doug beside her, so they could hold hands as they told us the grosses of their respective films.") Knowledgeable readers may enjoy this self-tribute. Others may be somewhat mislead.

4099 *The Memoirs of An Amnesiac.* by Levant, Oscar. 312 p. paper New York: Bantam Books, 1965.

If Oscar Levant practiced an economy of words, he might have become the master of the epigram as his namesake was many decades ago. Although his book is verbose and sometimes cynical, his reminiscences are told with hilarity. It is listed here since it contains Oscar's observations on movie making and on personalities concerned with film. Like Oscar's pills, the book is addictive and hard to resist. Not essential but sure to please and amuse all.

4100 *Memoirs of the Devil.* by Vadim, Roger. 192 p. illus. London: Hutchinson and Company, 1976.

Roger Vadim is known as much for the actresses he has loved/married as for the films he has directed. In this memoir the emphasis is rightly placed on the females. Included are Brigitte Bardot, Annette Stroyberg, Anouk Aimee, Catherine Deneuve, and, of course, Jane Fonda. Vadim's filmography is not as impressive, including as it does such films as AND GOD CREATED WOMAN (1957), LES LIAISONS DANGEREUSES(1961) and PRETTY MAIDS ALL IN A ROW (1971).

A few visuals show the principal characters in this somewhat premature autobiography. The book is indexed. Acceptable.

4101   *The Memoirs of Will Hays.* by Hays, Will. 600 p. New York: Doubleday, 1955.

The last half of this autobiography is devoted to Hays' career in motion pictures, which covered the years from 1922 to 1945. An account of his early experiences practicing law and politics and becoming Postmaster General of the United States is related. His two decades in Hollywood consisted of being administrator, a moral guardian, an ambassador and a diplomat involved with governments, industries and personalities. The story is often fascinating, although it is told in the factual, formal manner that seems indicative of Hays' postion vis-a-vis the motion picture industry. This large volume will have little interest for today's general reader but it does offer the scholar and historian much information about censorship and Hollywood's attempts at self-regulation.

4102   *Memories: An Autobiography.* by Barrymore, Ethel. 310 p. illus. New York: Harper, 1955.

Ms. Barrymore makes mention of her latter-day career in films only in the concluding chapter, indicating that she loved living in Hollywood but not her films. "I have never seen any of the motion pictures in which I have appeared. When people ask me why, I laugh and say, 'Oh let me have my dream." Earlier in the book she discusses briefly the experience she had in making RASPUTIN AND THE EMPRESS (1932) with her brothers, John and Lionel. The rest of the volume is devoted exclusively to her career on the stage. Illustrations are good and there is a useful index.

4103   MEMORIES OF UNDERDEVELOPMENT. edited by Myerson, Michael. 214 p. paper illus. New York: Grossman, 1973.

The subtitle of this book is "The Revolutionary Films of Cuba," and its goal is to describe contemporary Cuban cinema. By giving the complete screenplay of MEMORIES OF UNDERDEVELOPMENT (1968) along with a script excerpt from LUCIA (1969), descriptions of other Cuban films, a film poster section and a lengthy introduction, Myerson has compiled a persuasive argument. Part of his narrative deals with the suppression of Cuban films in the United States. The book is nicely illustrated with stills from the films. Color would have helped the poster section, but the designs are still effective in black and white. While some readers may consider the content of this volume to be biased and controversial, there is a need for information on the Cuban cinema. Recommended.

4104   *Memory Book of Elvis.* 40 p. paper illus. Memphis, Tenn.: Memory Books, 1977.

This instant book is made up of newspaper clippings, 8 x 10 pictures of Elvis, his home, his airplane, etc., along with his life story. A limited edition (!), the book was "published in Memphis by some of his friends who knew him best."

4105   *Memos on the Movies: War Propaganda, 1914-1939.* by Johnston, Winifred. 68 p. paper Norman, Okla.: Cooperative Books, 1939.

A short but brilliant analysis of the role that films can play in the preparation of a people for war. Four conditions necessary to create a climate of opinion favoring war are noted and then traced in the World War I era. Since this is a 1939 publication, it stops short of World War II, but it does predict U.S. entry into that war by analyzing those films of the late thirties which fulfilled the first two conditions. For the researcher or the serious student, this volume is essential. It deserves inclusion in one of the many anthologies or reprints currently being issued.

4106   *Men and Ideas in Engineering.* by Kingery, R. A.; and Berg, R. D.; and Shillinger, E. H. 164 p. illus. Urbana, Ill.: University of Illinois Press, 1967.

Noted here because of a section which states that Professor Joseph Tykocinsky invented sound film in 1922. A cinema scholar (such as Gordon Hendricks) might make capital out of such a claim.

4107   *Men and Women.* edited by Maynard, Richard A. 204 p. illus. New York: Scholastic Book Services, 1974.

This volume contains scripts of the following films: SPLENDOR IN THE GRASS (1961), Elia Kazan; THE FAMILY WAY (1967), Roy Boulting; and NOTHING BUT A MAN (1964), Michael Roemer.

4108   *The Men Who Made the Movies.* by Schickel, Richard. 308 p. illus. New York: Atheneum, 1975.

This volume is derived from Schickel's television series on the PBS network. Fragments of longer interviews with eight Hollywood directors were integrated with film clips from their work for each of the programs. The subjects were Raoul Walsh, Alfred Hitchcock, King Vidor, Frank Capra, William Wellman, Howard Hawks, George Cukor and Vincente Minnelli. For this volume Schickel uses the longer, prefilming interviews and provides biographical sketches, notes and illustrations to support them. Highly recommended.

4109 *Menace of the Religious Movie.* by Tozer, A. H. Wisconsin Rapids, Wisconsin: Rapids Christian, 1974.

4110 *Merely Colossal.* by Mayer, Arthur. 264 p. illus. New York: Simon & Schuster, 1953.

This is a partial autobiography coupled with pseudo-historical accounts of various phases of the film business. The story is told in a slightly exaggerated, humorous manner underlined by many George Price cartoons which illustrate the book.

4111 *Merman.* by Merman, Ethel; and Eells, George. 325 p. illus. New York: Simon & Schuster, 1978.

In her usual outspoken fashion, Merman announces she will reveal no intimacies, but will concentrate on the ups and downs of her long career in show business.

For the most part, she drops names of songs, plays, people, etc., who were part of her climb from secretary to media star. Mistakes in marriage and career are noted, but quickly dismissed to get "on with the show."

With regard to her films, Merman was probably "too much" for the camera. The loud, brash, boisterous quality which made her stage shows successful do not stand the further enlargement of the screen.

The reader may be entertained with this recall of a "brassy dame," but Merman keeps a close guard up between the real person and the reader.

4112 MERRIE MELODIES *and* LOONEY TUNES: *A Critical History of Warner Brothers Cartoons.* by Putterman, Barry. 284 p. illus. New York: A.S. Barnes, 1979.

The animated cartoons put out by Warner Brothers are the subject of this volume. In addition to describing the rise and fall (1930-1964) of animation at Warners, Putterman gives the reader some critical evaluation of major cartoon directors—Tex Avery, Bob Clampett, Chuck Jones, and Frank Tashlin. Descriptive filmographies are provided for the directors and there is an annotated listing of nearly all the Warner cartoons. A lengthy index and over 140 illustrations are included.

4113 *Merv.* by Griffin, Merv; and Barsocchini, Peter. 288 p. illus. New York: Simon and Schuster, 1980.

Merv Grifffin is known primarily as the host of a syndicated television talk show. Privately he is a modern business mogul who owns and produces radio and television shows, and is active in building a sort of show business empire. This autobiography traces his rise from an overweight teenager to big band vocalist to film actor and finally to TV personality. Along the way Griffin has known many celebrities as friends, coworkers or guests on his show. Since he is a good story-teller, his memoirs of himself and his associates make for pleasant reading. But what is Merv Griffin really like?

4114 *Mervyn LeRoy: Take One.* by LeRoy, Mervyn; and Kleiner, Dick. 244 p. illus. New York: Hawthorn Books, 1974.

Modesty is not Mervyn LeRoy's long suit—within pages 122 to 125 we find: "It was another triumph for me..."; "Shakespeare agrees with me—the plays the thing"; "I never made a picture I didn't like"; "It was endlessly thrilling to stare at that tiny being (hisson) and to realize that I created him—with Doris' help, of course." His accuracy or memory is often suspect, too. On page 104 he incorrectly assigns a starring role to Lana Turner in the film WITHOUT RESERVATIONS (1946). On page 116 he says Ava Gardner played a bit part in BIG CITY BLUES (1932) —according to Gardner biography birthdates she would have been 10 years old; also her first trip to the coast was in the early forties. In the filmography he assigns starring roles to feature or bit players— Ginger Rogers in GOLD DIGGERS OF 1933, Bogart in BIG CITY BLUES (1932).

LeRoy traces his long career from San Francisco newsboy to Hollywood director-producer with unconvincing humility and whitewashed recollections. Nobody in the narrative is mean, unkind or cruel for long. Even those who transgress do so only momentarily, e.g., Wallace Beery on page 120, Hedda Hopper on page 168. An exception exists in the concluding chapter when LeRoy bemoans the death of his Hollywood and the new breed that has taken over. Two picture sections, a filmography and an index help somewhat, but the inherent phoniness found in the earlier autobiography, *It Takes More Than Talent*, apparently doesn't die easily. Acceptable because of LeRoy's screen credits, rather than his ability as a biographer.

4115   *The* METEOR *Scrapbook.* by Hurwood, Bernardt J. 127 p. paper illus. New York: Ace, 1979.

4116   *Method to the Madness: Hollywood Explained.* edited by Atkins, Dick. 207 p. illus. Livingston, N.J.: Prince Publishers, 1975.

This anthology consists of articles about today's Hollywood written by the editor and six contributors. Included are: "The Major Film Studios," by Arthur Knight; "The TV Networks," by James Hall; "The (Film) Independents," by John H. Dorr; "The (TV) Independents," by Cynthia Kirk; "The People," by Stephen Farber; and "Future Vision," by William M. Jackson.

Atkins has supplemented the articles with a linking screenplay, some definitions, a chronological explanation of production, and descriptive annotations of three trade papers. The book is illustrated but not indexed.

Older, sophisticated readers will be disappointed in the gimmicky structure and the lack of critical insight, but young people will find this a most interesting and informative volume. Its consideration of today's activities in Hollywood and the future media of cable and videodisc are undeniably attractive topics. Acceptable.

4117   METROPOLIS. by Von Harbou, Thea. paper illus. London: Lorrimer, 1972.

Script of the 1927 film directed by Fritz Lang. Published in the U.S., by Simon and Schuster (1973).

4118   METROPOLIS. by Lang, Fritz; and von Harbou, Thea. 131 p. paper illus. New York: Simon and Schuster, 1973.

This American publication of the script of Lang's 1927 film first appeared under the Lorrimer imprint. It contains cast, credits, and *Metropolis: The Film and the Book* by Paul M. Jensen and *Industrialism and Totalitarianism* by Siegfried Kracauer.

4119   *The Mexican Cinema: Interviews with Thirteen Directors.* by Nevares, Beatriz Reyes. 176 p. illus. Albuquerque: University of New Mexico Press, 1976.

The directors mentioned in the title are Emilio Fernandez, Alejandro Galindo, Ismael Rodriguez, Luis Bunuel, Luis Alcoriza, Felipe Cazals, Salomon Laiter, Juan Lopez Moctezuma, Jorge Fons, Jose Estrada, Sergio Olhovich, Arturo Ripstein, and Alberto Isaac. In selecting these filmmakers, the author has attempted to provide a sampling of talented men whose experience and success in the Mexican Cinema allow them to speak knowingly about it. Their common problems include small budgets, lack of equipment, rushed schedules, commercialized restriction to popular topics, lack of recognition, and so forth.

Illustrations include portraits and stills. The book also contains an introduction, an index, and a few suggested readings. The text has been translated from Spanish. This volume provides some needed information about a national cinema and its artists.

4120   *MGM.* edited by Buscombe, Edward. 88 p. New York: Zoetrope, 1981.

A collection of articles dealing with the question "what is an MGM film?" A bibliography is added.

4121   *The MGM Auction Catalog.* edited by David Weiss Company. 5 vols. paper illus. Los Angeles: David Weiss Company, 1970.

These are the five catalogs that accompanied the auction of many items owned by the Metro-Goldwyn-Mayer Studio. The sale was held from May 3 to May 20, 1970, at the studio in Culver City, California. The catalogs describe antiques, furniture, trucks, automobiles, statuary, steam locomotives, coaches, a paddle-wheel steamer, harbor and nautical equipment, wardrobes, miniatures, weaponry, vintage cars, etc.

4122   *MGM Library of Film Script (A Series).* paper illus. New York: Viking Press, 1972.

This attractive series supplies the original script with notations indicating how the script was changed into the final film. Illustrations are plentiful, clearly reproduced and well selected. Occasionally there are introductory pieces by persons concerned with making the film. Cast and production credits are noted.

The first six titles include: NINOTCHKA (1939); NORTH BY NORTHWEST (1959); ADAM'S RIB (1949); A NIGHT AT THE OPERA (1935); A DAY AT THE RACES (1937); SINGING IN THE RAIN (1952).

4123   *The MGM Stock Company: The Golden Era.* by Parish, James Robert; and Bowers, Ronald L. 862 p. illus. New Rochelle, N.Y.: Arlington House, 1973.

This volume proves that an exciting book can also be a fine reference work or vice versa. Almost 150 personalities who were part of the MGM studios during the legendary golden years are profiled here. Ranging from featured players such as Rags Raglund and Connie Gilchrist to superstars like Gable, Harlow, and Tracy, each biography is both descriptive and critical. Several illustrations and a filmography add dimension to the portraits. Other elements include a short history of MGM, a few capsule biographies of MGM executives, a listing of MGM Academy Award nominations and winners and a lengthy index.

It is difficult to find any major fault or flaw in this work. True, there is the question of selection—why include Richard Hart with four films and omit Nat Pendleton with almost 100? The filmography for the Marx Brothers lists YOURS FOR THE ASKING as a 1936 Paramount Picture in which Chico, Groucho and Harpo appeared. No explanation is given in the text and the film is not mentioned in other reference sources—Michaels or Weaver. But as indicated above, these are minor issues in a book that is excellent in so many ways. Production values are outstanding, with the reproduction of the many illustrations being particularly effective in most cases. In summary, this is one of the most outstanding collective biography volumes to appear thus far. It is a valuable reference that affords hours of rewarding reading for the film buff or scholar. Highly recommended.

4124   *The MGM Story.* by Eames, John Douglas. 400 p. illus. New York: Crown, 1975.

A splendid filmography of the 1705 films made by the Metro-Goldwyn-Mayer studio in its 50 years of existence is provided in this oversized book. Beginning with HE WHO GETS SLAPPED (1924) and ending with THAT'S ENTERTAINMENT (1974), the volume combines data, background information and visuals in describing the films and, indirectly, the studio. A section on famous MGM musicals and a very detailed index complete the volume. One of the most attractive features of the book is its use of many full-page stills; these have been selected with consistent taste and intelligence and are beautifully reproduced. Less effective are the hundreds of smaller 1-1/2 inch by 2 inch visuals which are often difficult to interpret.

For the researcher, reference librarian, historian or scholar, the book is an informational and visual treasure. Film buffs, readers, and casual browsers will be delighted when they discover the quality and range of the book's content. This volume should be considered as a model for other major studio filmographies. Highly recommended.

4125   *The MGM Years.* by Thomas, Lawrence B. 138 p. illus. New Rochelle, N.Y.: Arlington House, 1972.

This oversized book deals primarily with 40 MGM musicals which are each given several pages of stills, cast and production credits, plot outlines, etc. In addition to the selected musicals, more than 160 others are mentioned. Sections on dubbing, soundtrack recording, songs from nonmusical films, awards, and rental films are also given. Several indexes, a bibliography and a discography complete the volume. This is specialized material that is given affectionate treatment. The selection of visuals is rather good, although many of them require color for full appreciation. Acceptable.

4126   *Michael Balcon Presents A Lifetime of Films.* by Balcon, Michael. 239 p. illus. London: Hutchinson, 1969.

This book details the long career of one of the most influential men in British cinema; Balcon has been involved with the production of over 350 motion pictures during the period from 1922 to 1968. It is a fascinating account, flavored throughout with anecdotes about the many names with whom he worked. Hitchcock, Goldwyn, Louis B. Mayer, Jessie Matthews and many other cinema personalities are discussed in polite but personal terms.

Although the book is very chauvinistic, it still is essential for anyone who admires the large body of excellent cinema that Britain has given us. The style is very readable, the illustrations are good, and the emphasis, thank goodness, is on cinema. Familiarity with British cinema will help immeasurably, but the anecdotes, alone, make the reading of the book an enjoyable experience. A filmography is lacking, but with 350 films, this might be the substance for a separate volume.

4127 *Michael Balcon's 25 Years in Films.* edited by Danischewsky, M. 112 p. illus. London: World Film Publications, 1947.

In 1947 Michael Balcon had already spent more than 25 years in film studios and produced more than 300 films. This anthology is a tribute to this leader in British films. A profile-biography by Danischewsky begins the book, followed by memoir-appreciations from Michael Redgrave, Francoise Rosay, A. de Cavalcanti and others. One pictorial section shows portraits of Balcon stars with a capsule comment beneath each, while the second section concerns itself with his films. Scenes from some of the 300 films he produced from 1922 to 1947 are nicely reproduced here. Other short sections deal with his home, his family, and his associates.

The opening essay along with the film stills are the stronger attractions in the book. A total filmography would have added dimension to the profile. Specialized material that provides only partial coverage, this book could be of interest to students, historians, and researchers. Acceptable.

4128 *Michael Curtiz's* CASABLANCA. edited by Anobile, Richard. 256 p. paperillus. New York: Avon, 1975.

This title in the *Film Classics Library* series has the distinction of beginning with an Ingrid Bergman interview. It introduces the frame blowup recreation of CASABLANCA (1943), a film about which much has been written. Using over 1500 visuals taken directly from the film, along with all the spoken dialogue, the book enables the reader to experience many of the emotions engendered by a viewing of the actual film. Picture clarity is particularly good in this instance and the volume will please those millions who love and treasure this film. Highly recommended.

4129 *Michael Powell.* by Gough-Yates, Kevin. 16 p. paper London: British Film Institute, 1971.

Subtitled "In Collaboration with Emeric Pressburger," this booklet was written in conjunction with Michael Powell's 1971 appearance in the John Player Lecture Series. It consists of an introduction, a filmography, two interviews with Powell, one with Pressburger, and an article by Powell on the use of color in films. The filmography notes Powell's career as a film director from TWO CROWDED HOURS (1931) to AGE OF CONSENT (1968). He is also known as a producer of plays, films, and television, and as the author of two books. Acceptable.

4130 *Michael Redgrave, Actor.* by Findlater, Richard. 170 p. illus. London: William Heinemann, 1956.

To the author, the word "actor" is synonymous with "theatre performer"; as a result, unfortunately, the large number of screen performances given by this "controversial" actor is given short shrift in this biography. The book is flawed by this outdated attitude. A few film illustrations are included along with many theatre portraits. The book is indexed, footnoted and contains a chronological listing of all performances on stage and screen up to 1956.

4131 *Michael Snow: A Survey.* by Snow, Michael. 128 p. paper illus. Toronto: Art Gallery of Ontario, 1970.

Michael Snow is a Canadian painter, sculptor, musician and filmmaker. This volume gives attention to his achievements in these fields.

4132 *Michael Winner: Director.* by Gough-Yates, Kevin. London: British Film Institute, 1970.

4133 *Michelangelo Antonioni: An Introduction.* by Leprohon, Pierre. 207 p. illus. New York: Simon & Schuster, 1963.

There are four major sections in this book. The first is a biographical and critical account of Antonioni, the man and his work. In the second part, a selection of Antonioni's writings on the cinema are reprinted. Samples from three of his scripts and a story treatment of one film make up the third portion. The final section consists of criticism and commentary on the artist and his films. A filmography and a selected English bibliography are included along with many pertinent illustrations.

4134 *Michelangelo Antonioni's Neo-Realism: A World View.* by Lyons, Robert J. 207 p. New York: Arno, 1976.

This doctoral dissertation was done at Bowling Green State University in 1973 and deals with an analysis of Antonioni's directorial approaches to realism. Lyons establishes such concepts as identity-reality motifs, visual restatement, circular composition, inward character reality, role reversal, and barrier motifs. The afterword deals with THE PASSENGER (1975) and is followed by a bibliography.

Anyone who has been fascinated by Antonioni's films will find this approach to his work helpful and stimulating.

4135 *Mickey Mouse: Fifty Happy Years.* edited by Bain, David; and Harris, Bruce. 255 p. illus. New York: Harmony Books, 1977.

Mickey Mouse was created by Walt Disney in 1928 and this volume traces the many careers that the mouse enjoyed over his first half-century. Besides the films, there were newspaper strips, books, collectibles such as watches, games, and dolls, television and personal appearances, including hosting the two Disney Worlds. This survey begins with a history of both Disney and his mouse creation. Then a selected sampling of Mickey Mouse appearances is presented. Films covered in detail include PLANE CRAZY (1928), MICKEY'S RIVAL (1936), THE BRAVE LITTLE TAILOR (1938), the "Sorcerer's Apprentice" sequence from FANTASIA (1940) and the "Mickey and the Beanstalk" sequence from FUN AND FANCY FREE (1947). Lesser attention is given to a few other films with the coverage ranging from a single drawing to three or four. Reproduction of the many visuals is outstanding, with the color work being most impressive. A filmography and a bibliography conclude the book.

By careful selection, the editors have provided representative examples from the appearances of Mickey Mouse during the last 50 years. Although a few are overlong, these samplings succeed in showing the evolution of a cartoon character into a national symbol. More mature readers will probably appreciate most of the coverage with the possible exception of the long newspaper and book pieces. The book is a special treat for readers of all ages. Highly recommended.

4136 *Mickey Mouse Movie Stories.* edited by Walt Disney Studio Staff. 190 p. illus. Philadelphia: David McKay, 1931.

4137 *Microforms.*

Whether a roll of microfilm or a microfiche is a book is not the concern here. What is important is to note that many periodicals and other sources not considered by this bibliography are available in this format.

Titles include: *Audiovisual Instruction* (1956-), *Audiovisual Journal* (1968), *Cinema Quarterly* (1932-35), *Cinema Rising* (1972), *Cinema Studies* (1960-67), *Cinema-TV Today*, *Cinemantics* (1970), *Cinematography and Bioscope Magazine* (1906-07), *Film* (1933), *Film (Journal of BFFS)* (1954-1977), *Film Art* (1933-37), *Film Art* (1934-36), *Film Comment* (1962-77), *Film Daily* (1915-41), *Film Daily Yearbook* (1918-69), *Film Miscellany* (1946-47), *Movie Weekly* (1921-26), *Moving Picture Stories* (1913-29), *Moving Picture World* (1907-27), *National Film Archive* (BFI index) 1933, *Oral History Collection* (AFI), *Screen International, Sight and Sound* (1932), *Variety* (1905-).

The above is a sampling of titles listed in *Guide to Microforms in Print 1978.* Later editions of this reference will contain updates, additions, and may also indicate other sources such as newspapers, dissertations, occasional papers, etc.

4138 *Microscopes and Megaloscopes.* by Sibley, Brian. 14 p. paper London: Lewis Carroll Society, 1974.

This transcript of an address made to the Lewis Carroll Society on November 8, 1974, deals in part with films based on *Alice in Wonderland* and *Through the Looking Glass.* Its subtitle is "Alice in Pictures-that-Move and Pictures-that-Stand-Still." This limited edition of 100 signed and numbered copies contains a biography.

4139 *Midnight on the Desert: A Chapter of Autobiography.* by Priestley, J. B. 312 p. London: Heinemann, 1937.

This autobiography describes Priestley's 1935-1936 trip to America, which included a visit to Hollywood.

4140 THE MIGHTY BARNUM. by Fowler, Gene and Meredyth, Bess. 240 p. illus. New York: Covici Friede, 1934.

Script of the 1935 film directed by Walter Lang. Contains cast credits and an introduction by Gene Fowler.

4141 *Mike Nichols.* by Schuth, H. Wayne. 177 p. illus. Boston: Twayne, 1978.

This title in Twayne's *Theatrical Arts* series examines the six films Mike Nichols has made to date. Author Schuth begins with a short factual biographical sketch and then devotes individual chapters to WHO'S AFRAID OF VIRGINIA WOLF (1966), THE GRADUATE (1967), CATCH 22 (1970), CARNAL KNOWLEDGE (1971), THE DAY OF THE DOLPHIN (1973), and THE FORTUNE (1975). "Family," the television series which Nichols produced, is also discussed. Illustrations, notes, a bibliography, a filmography, and an index are added.

The analyses offered in critical detail here will help the reader to understand and appreciate Nichols' few films. His singular point of view, along with sophisticated, recurring themes and motifs, underline the alienated modernist sensibility that Nichols had presented in his work. Schuth admires his subject and with this fine critical study he should convert the unacquainted. Recommended.

4142   *Mike Wallace Asks!* edited by Preston, Charles; and Hamilton, Edward A. 128 p. paper illus. New York: Simon & Schuster, 1958.

This collection of 46 edited interviews from Mike Wallace's "Night Beat" television show includes such subjects as Jayne Mansfield, Tennessee Williams, Diana Barrymore, Ben Hecht, Tallulah Bankhead, Zsa Zsa Gabor, Rudy Vallee, George Jessell, Tony Perkins, Peter Ustinov, and Gloria Swanson. An identification paragraph and some illustrations accompany each interview.

4143   *Mikis Theodorakis: Musical and Social Change.* by Giannaris, George. 320 p. illus. New York: Praeger, 1973.

The biography of the composer of the scores for ZORBA THE GREEK (1964) and Z (1969) shows that his ideas about music and social change are compatible. This is specialized material.

4144   *Miklos Rozsa: A Sketch of His Life and Work.* by Palmer, Christopher. 78 p. paper illus. London: Breitkopf and Hartel, 1975.

This appreciation of film music composer Miklos Rozsa includes text, a musicography, a filmography and an index.

4145   MILDRED PIERCE. by MacDougall, Ranald; and Turney, Catherine. 259 p. illus. Madison, Wisc.: University of Wisconsin Press, 1980.

The script of the 1945 film directed by Michael Curtiz.

4146   *Miller's High Life.* by Miller, Ann; and Browning, Norma Lee. 283 p. illus. Garden City, N.Y.: Doubleday, 1972.

The durable Ann Miller tells about her life as a tap dancer, from the age of five to her TV success dancing on the giant soup can for a commerical. It's fan magazine material blown up to book size with little apparent help by Ms. Browning. Acceptable.

4147   *A Million and One Nights.* by Ramsaye, Terry. 868 p. paper illus. New York: Simon & Schuster, 1964 (1926).

This is the legendary classic book on the history of the film. Originally published in 1926 in two volumes, it was for many years a collector's item. In 1964 Simon & Schuster revived it in both hardbound and paperback formats, a publishing act to be thankful for. Starting with the prehistory of film, Ramsaye covers the early years of film history with depth, intelligence and scholarship. Inventions, patents, early films, distribution and exhibition practices and other related topics are all treated in this massive paperback.

Personalities such as Griffith, Pickford, Chaplin and the movie moguls receive appropriate attention. The book has become a standard history-reference for the period of the beginnings of film to 1925. The writing style is relaxed and respectful while the content is accurate and objective. A word is necessary about the outstanding production of this volume. The type is large and easy on the eyes while the many photographs are impressively reproduced. The book has a long detailed index.

4148   *The Million Dollar Studs.* by Moats, Alice-Leone. 282 p. illus. New York: Delacorte, 1977.

A few case studies of an almost extinct species, the fortune hunter, are offered here. Dealing primarily with Porfirio Rubirosa and the three Mdivani brothers (Serge, Alexis, and David), the text tells of their marriages/associations with heiresses, widows, and with film personalities such as Pola Negri, Mae Murray, Danielle Darrieux, and Zsa Zsa Gabor.

Of peripheral interest to film collections, the volume should fascinate the reader old enough to recall the decades when these European and Latin lotharios operated. A few illustrations and an index are included. Acceptable for mature readers.

4149   *Milos Forman.* by Forman, Milos. paper illus. London: Lorrimer, 1972.

Contains script, cast and production credits for: THE FIREMAN'S BALL (1967); A BLOND IN LOVE (LOVES OF A BLOND), (1965).

4150   *Milos Forman, Ingrid Thulin.* edited by Henstell, Bruce. 27 p. paper Washington, D.C.: American Film Institute, 1972.

The seminar session recorded here took place with

Forman at the AFI Center in Beverly Hills. The occasion was the release of TAKING OFF (1971). Lynn Carlin, Ultra Violet and John Klein were also present at this interview conducted by Frank Daniel. The Thulin interview coincided with the release of THE DAMNED (1970) and the interest of the participants is evident from the transcription. She also discusses acting for Pasolini, Fellini, Bergman and Visconti. A filmography is given for both but only the Forman piece has a bibliography. Acceptable.

4151 *The Milos Forman Stories.* by Liehm, Antonin J. 191 p. illus. White Plains, N.Y.: International Arts & Sciences Press, 1975.

The appearance of this volume coincided with Milos Forman's Academy Award as the best director of 1975 for ONE FLEW OVER THE CUCKOO'S NEST (1975). Although this film is not discussed, all his others to date are.

The author is a personal friend of the director and arranges his material as a series of Forman's conversations, memories, and recollections. According to the author, Milos Forman does not write stories—he lives them. Punctuating Forman's stream-of-consciousness account of his life are reviews of his films by Liehm, who also provides some supplementary material to Forman's stories. The illustrations, which are mostly informal personal shots or production stills, are most appropriate to the text. An index and a filmography are also provided.

Although Forman has functioned in various aspects of filmmaking, his directorial efforts are limited to only three short films and five features. His brief but impressive career is recalled here with the wit, style, and intelligence that characterize his films. This is a most pleasant introduction to a creative filmmaker whose artistry is just being recognized.

4152 *Milton Berle—An Autobiography.* by Berle, Milton; and Frankel, Haskel. 337 p. illus. New York: Delacorte Press, 1974.

A serious, often sad man is the subject of this unusual autobiography, written apparently as a therapeutic recall of a frantic, hurried life. Berle finally has found time to assess his life, and his evaluation of it is honest, frank and surprisingly humble at times. In his recital, he describes his career from child performer, through the famous television years, and up to the infrequent night club, film and television appearances he makes today. The films that he has appeared in receive minimal attention; Berle is more noted for his other show business appearances and the text reflects this. However, many film perform-

ers are mentioned often in a context that is more sensationalized than sensitive, (Monroe, Bankhead, etc).

Berle's romantic liaison with an unidentified movie queen of the thirties, which resulted in the birth of his unacknowledged son, is mentioned throughout the book. The soap opera dramatics of the resultant incidents may strain reader credulity and arouse suspicion that there is less here than the author indicates. Some photographs and an index are given. However, one essential element is missing—there is no chronology of Berle's show business appearances. This autobiography reinforces the same general impression about comic men that the earlier books on Bert Lahr and Phil Silvers did—funny men are rather sad offstage. Acceptable.

4153 *Milton's Paradise Mislaid.* by Milton, Billy. illus. London: Jupiter, 1976.

Billy Milton is a piano-playing performer who has appeared occasionally in British films from 1930 to 1970.

4154 *Milton's* PARADISE LOST.: *A Screenplay for the Cinema of the Mind.* by Collier, John. 144 p. paper New York: Alfred Knopf, 1973.

John Collier has written "Paradise Lost" as a screenplay with interesting results. Called "a screenplay for the cinema of the mind," it offers teachers of English and creative writing an example of what might be done as a student exercise. An article, "The Apology," precedes the script.

4155 *The Mind and the Film: A Treatise on the Psychological Factors in the Film.* by Buckle, Fort Gerard. 119 p. New York: Arno Press, 1970 (1926).

First published in 1926, this short book considers the fade, dissolve, iris, lighting, soft focus, etc. as photographic aids to the mind. Of interest to scholars and advanced students.

4156 *Mind's Eye.* by Dean, Basil. illus. London: Hutchinson, 1973.

Dean was a director/producer of British films during the thirties.

4157 *Mindscreen: Bergman, Godard and the Language of First-Person Film.* by Kawin, Bruce F. 240 p. illus. Princeton, N.J.: Princeton University Press, 1978.

Can film dream? After stating that film can represent both the creator's dream and the viewer's dream (and who can argue with that speculation?), the author also suggests that film itself can appear to think or dream (mindscreen). The major portion of the volume is devoted to a development of that idea. Films used in Kawin's discussion include SHERLOCK JR. (1924), CITIZEN KANE (1941), COMING APART (1969), RASHOMON (1950), LAST YEAR AT MARIENBAD (1961), PERSONA (1965), SHANE (1968), TWO OR THREE THINGS I KNOW ABOUT HER (1966) and others. Notes, including a Bugs Bunny cartoon, illustrations, a bibliography, and an index are added.

This volume is the work of a theorist and will appeal mostly to the advanced student concerned with film aesthetics. Ideas derived from theatre and literature are applied to film in a demanding and ultimately rewarding exploration.

4158 *The Mini-Documentary: Serializing TV News.* by Field, Stanley. 249 p. illus. Blue Ridge Summit, Pa.: Tab Books, 1975.

The mini-documentary, a form unique to local, non-network television, deals with the reporting/investigating of community issues. Shown during newscasts, it is an audiovisual statement about a social topic that can be exploratory, informative, and/or prescriptive.

This volume explores this form, considering in turn its structure, the interview, and the approaches of four local TV stations: WMAL, WRC, WTOP, and WTTG. Three of the stations are network affiliates while the latter one is an independent. Topics include equipment, techniques, film vs. tape, editing, etc. Scripts for eight mini-documentaries are provided. A summary survey of the form, a bibliography, and an index complete the book. There are a few illustrations which are not reproduced well.

The volume has pertinence for its consideration of a new film genre, the mini-documentary. Its potential use both in TV and other situations (school, college, cable, etc.) has yet to be recognized. Not only is this the only treatment of the genre so far, it is an impressive one. Recommended.

4159 MINNIE AND MOSKOWITZ. by Cassavetes, John. 116 p. illus. Los Angeles: Black Sparrow Press, 1973.

Script of the 1972 film directed by Cassavetes. Includes an introduction by the writer/director. Along with production and cast credits.

4160 MIRACLE IN MILAN. by de Sica, Vittorio; and Zavattini, Cesare. 121 p. illus. New York: Orion Press, 1968.

Script of the 1951 film directed by de Sica. Contains cast credits, a filmography (a list only), and two articles by de Sica: "How I Direct My Films" and "What I Wanted to Say in MIRACLE IN MILAN."

4161 *The Miracle of the Movies.* by Wood, Leslie. 352 p. illus. London: Burke Pub. Co., 1947.

This is one of the better histories of the cinema, illustrated with 120 very unusual photographs. It tells how films came into being, how theatres sprang up, and how the major motion picture production centers of the world emerged from early attempts at making films. The British and American film industries are given the most attention. While the major emphasis is on technical, economic, or factual data, there is much critical evaluation given to the people, films, and the events described in the book. Unfortunately there is no index.

The scope of this book is wide but the coverage is thorough. American readers may be puzzled somewhat at the English references and names but this is a minor inconvenience in a major book. Why this volume is not more widely known (quoted) is a mystery. Perhaps its British bias is the cause.

4162 *A Mirror for England: British Movies from Austerity to Affluence.* by Durgnat, Raymond. 336 p. illus. New York: Praeger, 1971.

This volume offers an analysis of the British life as reflected in the films of that nation. The attitudes, problems, and conflicts native to the various classes of British society are noted in the films, most of which are from the decade following World War II. A scholarly, pedantic work which may fascinate a few readers but will probably be of little interest to the large general audience.

4163 *Mirrors of Hollywood.* by Fox, Charles D. 143 p. illus. New York: Charles Renard, 1925.

What Hollywood was like in the twenties is shown in many illustrations, along with short biographical pieces on more than 400 film performers of the period. See also the author's *Famous Film Folk*, published by Doran in 1925.

4164 *Mirrors of Hollywood: Hollywood Studios of 1925.* by Fox, Charles D.

143 p. illus. New York: Gordon Press, 1976 (1925).

Published originally by Charles Renard, N.Y., this volume includes a section of brief biographies of film folk of 1925.

4165 THE MISFITS. by Miller, Arthur. 132 p. illus. New York: Viking Press, 1961.

Script of the 1961 film directed by John Huston.

4166 *Mis-Laid in Hollywood.* by Hyams, Joe. 224 p. New York: Peter H. Wyden, 1973.

If anyone is interested in the life of a disillusioned Hollywood columnist who has difficulty in differentiating between license and taste, he may enjoy this autobiography. For others it will be a series of anecdotes and reminiscences written to give importance to an apparently unhappy and insecure man. Chapters are devoted to Bogart, James Dean, Ava Gardner, Cary Grant, Gary Cooper, Brando, Diane Varsi, Sharon Tate, Marilyn Monroe, and Hyams' current wife, Elke Sommer. The writing is gossip-column style and enables any willing participant to breeze through this memoir. No pictures are provided and there is no index. Acceptable because of what it represents rather than what it is.

4167 *Miss Rona: An Autobiography.* by Barrett, Rona. 281 p. illus. Los Angeles: Nash Pub. Co., 1974.

A modern Cinderella story is told in this autobiography of an overweight, partially disabled loner who becomes the beautiful queen of Hollywood gossip by age 35. Like a bad-good movie, it is filled with sex, drama, love, success, high life and beautiful people. What it lacks is any quality—both in subject and writing—that will make the reader care. Expectation that the author may reveal some scandalous or shocking tidbits about Hollywood and its denizens will be unfulfilled; the author uses mostly "blind items" in her more juicy tales, while most of the others are rehashes of older public notoriety. Her own personal story indicates what aggressiveness combined with a bright mind can bring to a girl these days—three monthly movie magazines, a syndicated television newscast, several books in print, and a loving husband. Some illustrations are provided but they do not correlate with the text.

When you read Rona Barrett's columns or listen to her TV newscasts, you are not always convinced that she's telling you the entire story. The same is true of this book—its carefully selected bits and pieces will leave the reader wondering, "What is Rona Barrett really like?" Acceptable.

4168 *Miss Tallulah Bankhead.* by Israel, Lee. 384 p. illus. New York: G. P. Putnam's, 1972.

This fascinating biography contains short accounts of the few films that Bankhead made. Emphasis is on LIFEBOAT (1943), A ROYAL SCANDAL (1945), DIE DIE MY DARLING (1965) and THE DEVIL AND THE DEEP (1932). Although she was not primarily a film actress, the legacy of LIFEBOAT offers sufficient proof of Bankhead's artistry.

4169 MISSION TO MOSCOW. by Koch, Howard. paper illus. Madison, Wisc.: University of Wisconsin Press.

Script of the 1943 film directed by Michael Curtiz. This volume was edited by David Culbert.

4170 THE MISSOURI BREAKS. by McGuane, Thomas. 131 p. paper illus. New York: Ballantine, 1976.

Script of the 1976 film directed by Arthur Penn. Contains "Candid Conversations With The Leading Man," by Bruce Cook and short biographies of Marlon Brando, Jack Nicholson, Kathleen Lloyd, Arthur Penn, Elliott Kastner, Robert M. Sherman, and Thomas McGuane. Cast credits and partial production credits are given.

4171 *Mistah Jolson.* by Jolson, Harry; and Emley, Alban. 257 p. Hollywood: House-Wavren, 1951.

4172 *The Mob in Show Business.* by Messick, Hank. 272 p. paper illus. New York: Pyramid, 1975.

A paperback version of *The Beauties and the Beasts: The Mob in Show Business.*

4173 *The Mobile Image: Film as Environment.* by Lignell, E. E. 30 p. paper illus. New York: Herder & Herder, 1970.

4174 *The Mobile Mise En Scene.: A Critical Analysis of the Theory and Practice of Long-Take Camera Movement in the Narrative Film.* by Bacher, Lutz. New York: Arno, 1978.

Written in 1976 at Wayne State University as part of the Masters program, this study explores the development of the long-take camera movement and its historical influence on the growth of the cinema. Included is a detailed list of directors who frequently employ long-take camera movements in their films. The author provides the reader with comprehensive analyses of the work of Renoir, Rossellini, Dreyer, Ophuls, and others. This title is included in the *Dissertations on Film* series.

4175   *Modern Acting: A Guide for Stage, Screen and Radio.* by Gable, Josephine Dillion. 313 p. New York: Prentice-Hall, 1940.

Tips by the woman who married Clark Gable and taught him everything there is to know about acting.

4176   *The Modern American Novel and the Movies.* edited by Peary, Gerald; and Shatzkin, Roger. 461 p. paper illus. New York: Ungar, 1978.

The Frederick Ungar Company continues its investigations into the relationship between literature and film with this anthology. A previous anthology by the same editors explored the classic American novel and film. Here the classification "modern" includes 32 novels written between 1930 and 1970. For each there is an essay which addresses itself to the novel and the film it inspired. Contributing authors include William Everson, Norman Mailer, Robin Wood, Molly Haskell and two dozen others.

Articles in the collection vary in approach and appeal but the overall impression given to the reader is that of a complex relationship between literature and film. Certainly the enormous number of decisions which are necessary in the translation of one medium to another are indicative of this complexity. The understandable reluctance of the novelist to allow his work to be interpreted by a director is another factor in this relationship. Questions such as these are examined by the text. In addition there are two lengthy sections devoted to a bibliography and a filmography. A distributor list, contributor identification, and an index complete the book.

The selection, scope and presentation of the articles is excellent. The book should have several levels of appeal to a diversity of audiences.

4177   *Modern European Filmmakers and the Art of Adaptation.* edited by Horton, Andrew S.; and Magretta, Joan. 383 p. paper New York: Ungar, 1981.

A study of film adaptations made from novels and stories by European filmmakers. Each of 23 film adaptations is treated seperately by a different author. Another fine addition to the subject of literature and film.

4178   *The Modern Goliath.* by Soderberg, Milton A. 91 p. illus. Los Angeles: David Press, 1935.

...A study of talking pictures with a treatment of nontheatrical talking pictures, especially talking pictures forschools and churches, and some chapters on character education and values.

4179   *Modern Photoplay Writing, Its Craftsmanship.* by Dimick, Howard T. 392 p. Franklin, Ohio: J. K. Reeve, 1922.

A manual demonstrating the structural and dramatic principles of the new art as practiced by the modern playwright.

4180   *Modern Picture Houses and Theaters.* by Shand, Philip M. 39 p. illus. Philadelphia: J. B. Lippincott, 1930.

Aspects of theatre design and construction are considered in this heavily illustrated volume. Facades, foyers, auditoriums, social function, and the movie house as a building are among the topics considered.

4181   *Modernism in the Narrative Cinema: The Art Film as a Genre.* by Siska, William Charles. New York: Arno, 1980.

Siska studies the influence of the art film on the narrative cinema in this volume from the *Dissertations on Film* series. Detailed analyses of MICKEY ONE (1964), 8-1/2 (1963), THE LAST MOVIE (1973) and PIEPROT LE FOU (1965) are included.

4182   *Moe Howard and the Three Stooges.* by Howard, Moe. 208 p. illus. Secaucus, N.J.: Citadel, 1977.

In the thirties and forties, one of the most popular comedy teams in films was The Three Stooges—Larry, Curly and Moe. This volume, authored via tape by the leader, Moe Howard, recalls the history of the team from Howard's days as a single act to the team's beginning as a support to Ted Healy. There followed a succession of almost 200 features and short films made mostly for Harry Cohn at Columbia Studios. All of this is related in the text, stills, photos, a filmography, and an index. Moe Howard died shortly before publication of this volume but the violent slapstick of The Stooges lives on by the endless showing of their films on television.

4183 *The Moguls.* by Zierold, Norman. 354 p. illus. New York: Coward-Mc Cann, 1969.

The "moguls" are the group of Jewish refugees who came to America to escape foreign oppression and were ultimately responsible for the establishment of a new art form. With the passing of their era, the story of their ascent to power, their struggle to stay on top, and their ultimate retirement from the battle is told with a clarity and objectivity that is missing in earlier accounts. Each legend is given his own sequence, and little attempt is made to interweave the accounts except where the personalities all operated within the same studio.

Included are Selznick, Laemmle, Goldwyn, Zukor, B. P. Schulberg, Jesse Lasky, Cohn, Fox, the Warner Brothers, Zanuck, Schenck, and Mayer. (Zanuck is the non-Jewish exception pointed out by the author.) There is not much new here since most of the men are already subjects of individual biographies. As an introductory background reading, the book has merit. The more sophisticated readers are referred to the in-depth accounts of the moguls such as *King Cohn, Hollywood Rajah,* etc.

4184 *Moguls; Inside the Business of Show Business.* by Pye, Michael. 241 p. illus. New York: Holt, Rinehart, Winston, 1980.

A collective biography which combines factual information with interviews, this volume has as it subjects Jules Stein, William Paley, David Merrick, Peter Gruber, Trevor Nunn and Robert Stigwood. The association of these men with film is somewhat peripheral, since show business today is usually governed by complex arrangements called corporate empires.

4185 *Moholy-Nagy.* edited by Kostelanetz, Richard. 238 p. illus. New York: Praeger, 1970.

Known for his experiments with film, Laszlo Moholy-Nagy was concerned with aesthetics of light and space. In addition to being a filmmaker, he was also a painter, writer, and teacher.

See also *Experiments in Totality.* by Sybyl Moholy-Nagy and two books by Moholy-Nagy himself: *Vision in Motion* (1956, Theobald) and *Painting, Photography, Film* (1969, MIT Press).

4186 *Molly! An Autobiography.* by Picon, Molly; and Grillo, Jean Bergantini. 320 p. illus. New York: Simon and Schuster, 1980.

Molly Picon is known primarily as a star of the Yiddish theatre, but she has appeared on Broadway and in films. In this autobiography, she tells of her very busy career which has spanned 75 years. Her style is in keeping with her image—folksy, informal, confiding, affectionate. Picon's films include YIDDLE WITH HIS FIDDLE (1937), MAMELE: LITTLE MOTHERS (1938) and COME BLOW YOUR HORN (1963).

4187 *Moments With Chaplin.* by Ross, Lillian. 64 p. illus. New York: Dodd, Mead, 1980.

A slight, almost-padded memoir of the times that *New Yorker* staff writer Lillian Ross spent with Charlie Chaplin. The incidents take place in diverse geographical areas (New York City, Hollywood, Switzerland), but the "moments" are extended anecdotes and do not offer a satisfying profile of the artist.

4188 *Mommie Dearest.* by Crawford, Christina. 286 p. illus. New York: William Morrow, 1978.

So much has been written about this sensationalized account of a mother-adopted daughter relationship that readers feel familiar with the story without having read the book. It is a largely negative portrait of an ambitious, hard-working woman who believed that success, image, celebrity, and employment were the major goals of her life. In pursuit of these, Crawford apparently used, abused, neglected, and emotionally damaged her daughter. There are some illustrations provided—nearly all of Christina and Chris with almost none of Cindy and Cathy—but there is no index.

If the volume is read as the author's view of a traumatic, crippling relationship, then it has some value other than simply shock and sensation. After all, to isolate incidents from any child-parent relationship, distort them to a degree with literary license, and then ultimately forgive the sinner-parent is an exercise that many persons could accomplish. Christina Crawford has done exactly this with her maternal parent, who just happened to be a celebrity about whom there is enormous interest. A final regret is that the accused is not able to respond to the charges. The strength and style of the reply would certainly have made exciting reading. Acceptable.

4189 *Money and Finance.* by Ladley, Barbara; and Wilford, Jane. 208 p. New York: Neal-Schuman, 1980.

This reference is a title in the *Source Book* series that has previously considered such topics as energy, occupational education, and women. In this annotated listing of sources of print and nonprint materials, the user will find individual chapters devoted to consumer information, consumer agencies, consumer education, banking, business, employment, health, housing, home insurance, investments, legal services, retirement, social welfare, taxes, transportation, etc.

Under each topic the sources are arranged alphabetically, giving name, address, phone number and a descriptive annotation. The latter tells the kinds of information available, e.g., Consumers Union of the U.S. publishes books, films, cassettes, periodicals, etc. Appendixes include a list of nonprint distributors, a source index, a title index, and a subject index.

The scope, structure, and organization of this book can easily serve as a model for future books. The information given for the annotations seems valid and current. All in all, an excellent reference.

4190 *Money Behind the Screen.* by Klingender, F. D.; and Legg, Stuart. 79 p. London: Lawrence & Wishart, 1937.

Explores financial foundations of the film industry in both Britain and the United States.

4191 MONKEY BUSINESS. by Perelman, S. J.; and Johnstone, Will B; and Sheekman, Arthur. 183 p. paper illus. New York: Simon and Schuster, 1972.

Script of the 1931 film directed by Norman McLeod. Contains MONKEY BUSINESS (1931); DUCK SOUP (1933); Casts and credits.

4192 *Monopoly in Motion Picture Production and Distribution: 1908-1915.* by Cassady, Ralph Jr. 66 p. Los Angeles: University of Southern California Press, 1959.

A short account of monopoly featuring the Motion Picture Patents Company and the General Film Company.

4193 MONSIEUR HULOT'S HOLIDAY. by Carriere, Jeane-Claude. 198 p. illus. New York: Crowell, 1959.

A book which attempts the impossible—to put the visual artistry of Jacques Tati into words. Surprisingly, this libretto of Tati's classic 1951 film almost makes it.

4194   *see   4195*

4195 *Monster Movie Game.* by Stanley, John; and Whyte, Mal. unpaginated. paper illus. San Francisco: Troubador Press, 1974.

Two hundred questions about film monsters are proposed in this volume, and are placed under the predictable categories of Werewolf, Dracula, The Mummy, Apes, The Phantom, etc. Answers are given in the book's final pages. The illustrations used throughout are above average. Typical of the questions is: "What 1957 low budget horror film sported a younger wolf man in the form of Michael Landon?" There are also matching questions, fill-in-the-blanks, and multiple choice. Just like school. How much real information or trivia can be acquired is questionable, but to most movie buffs the questions will be fun. Acceptable.

4196 *Monsters.* by Wolf, Leonard. 128 p. illus. New York: Straight Arrow, 1974.

A review of 20 monsters and beasts, this volume treats Godzilla, King Kong, and Dracula, along with mythical, literary legends such as dragons, minotaurs, and unicorns.

4197 *Monsters.* by Price, Vincent; and Price, V.B. 182 p. illus. paper New York: Grosset and Dunlap (Today Press), 1981.

4198 *Monsters and Vampires.* by Frank, Alan. 160 p. illus. London: Octopus, 1976.

This book, subtitled "Spine-chilling Creatures of the Cinema," was written by Alan Frank who also authored *Horror Movies* for the same *Movie Treasury* series. Initial emphasis is on vampires with the first three chapters given to early vampires Bela Lugosi and Christopher Lee. Other vampire characters are noted along with monsters (The Golem, Frankenstein), beasts (The Mummy, Mr. Hyde, The Werewolf), mutations (Kong, The Creature), and outer space creatures. The volume is indexed.

Another excuse to publish 160 illustrations is provided here by the arbitrary structure and the very general textual treatment.

The journey through the horror film genre is harmless but adds little that is new or stimulating. As indicated above, it is the visual component that will attract and please readers.

4199 *Monsters from the Movies.* by Aylesworth, Thomas G. 160 p. illus. Philadelphia: J. B. Lippincott, 1972.

This book for children is part of a series called "The Weird and Horrible Library." Two other subjects, mummies and poltergeists, will give some idea of the range of the series. The first chapter combines film showings with a recap of Melies' career. The remaining chapters categorize the monsters into man-made, self-made, human fiends, the living dead, and creatures from another world. An appendix of some selected horror films and an index complete the book.

4200 *Monsters Who's Who.* 121 p. illus. New York: Crescent, 1974.

This is a dictionary of about 150 monsters—Achelous to Zombies—accompanied by a wide range of illustrations including movie stills, comic strips, and works of art. Many of the monsters have been the subjects of motion pictures: Dracula, Frankenstein, Godzilla, the Invisible Man, King Kong, the Wolfman. In addition, the text includes monsters from myth, legend, and literature. The coverage provided for each is elemental, being mostly a basic description. The 116 pictures are the book's main attraction.

4201 *Montgomery Clift: A Biography.* by Bosworth, Patricia. 437 p. illus. New York: Harcourt Brace Jovanovich, 1978.

Although Robert LaGuardia's *Monty* appeared some time before Bosworth's biography, the later book is by far the better. The same elements are treated but Bosworth blends them into a fully dimensioned portrait while LaGuardia opts mostly for shock and sensationalism.

The story of Montgomery Clift is a tragic one, destroyed as he was by family, easy success, homosexuality, and drugs. His destruction, however dramatic it was, is presented objectively by Bosworth, who allows the reader to judge the actor and the person. Illustrations, a career chronology, and an index complete the book.

This is an example of a well-researched, ultimately moving biography that is made richer by the creative interpretation of the author. Highly recommended.

4202 *Monty: A Biography of Montgomery Clift.* by LaGuardia, Robert. 304 p. illus. New York: Arbor House, 1977.

The entire field of film biography takes a major step forward with the publication of this superb biography. Montgomery Clift's tragic life story has an undeniable fascination; however, it is the treatment provided by Robert LaGuardia that sets this book above most celebrity biographies. Although he is sensitive and sympathetic to his subject, the author describes Clift's nasty, irrational nature with frightening objectivity.

There is much detail given about Clift's films. How he prepared for a role, his relationships with directors and other actors, his ability to perform while in a state of near emotional and physical collapse—all these facets of Clift's professional life are discussed. His private life is not neglected either, with attention paid to his homosexuality, drug addiction, and his uncontrolled talent for alienating those who cared about him. The volume also provides some appropriate visuals, a filmography, and an index.

Tragedy is one of the most difficult forms that a young author can attempt. For those readers who enjoyed and appreciated the actor's work, this brilliant character depiction of Montgomery Clift will be a shocking and ultimately cathartic reading experience. It is one of the best examples of "An American Tragedy" to appear in this decade. Highly recommended.

4203 MONTY PYTHON AND THE HOLY GRAIL. by Gilliam, Terry. 284 p. paper illus. New York: Methuen, 1977.

In addition to the script, this unusual volume includes a first draft, a financial statement, posters, stills, drawings, and other material.

4204 MONTY PYTHON'S THE LIFE OF BRIAN. by Monty Phython Group. 128 p. paper illus. New York: Grosset & Dunlap, 1979.

This is the complete script of the controversial Python film. Cast, credits, and stills are included. Reversing the book provides the reader with a scrapbook (photos, letters, sketches, ideas, diary jottings, etc.) about the production of the film.

4205 *The Moon's a Balloon.* by Niven, David. 380 p. illus. New York: G. P. Putnam's, 1972.

This has been one of the most popular film autobiographies ever published and the reason may be Niven's refusal to be terribly serious about it all. The light touch is applied constantly, whether to career, love, or philosophy of life. Only in a few spots is the book sombre or sad—and one senses that these were traumatic moments in Niven's life.

In the second half of the book Niven gets around to his career as an actor. His near appearance with Mae West in GOING TO TOWN (1935), and his screen test for Edmund Goulding were among his first experiences in Hollywood. The signing with Goldwyn, the acceptance by the Hollywood "British Colony," the small parts which led up to "Edgar" in WUTHERING HEIGHTS (1939) and other major roles are described. World War II, the accidental death of his first wife, career renewal, and his second marriage complete the story. Several illustrations from Niven's own private collection are used and these are snapshots rather than studio stills. The book is indexed.

There is a slight overbalance in space given to the early years and a shortchanging of the film years, but that is Niven's prerogative. His view of himself is charming, witty, and quite objective. Recommended, but with a warning—Niven is casual about his sexual experiences and short of naming names, tells all.

4206 *Morality and the Mass Media.* by Haselden, Kyle. 192 p. Nashville, Tenn.: Broadman, 1968.

4207 *The Morals of the Movie.* by Oberholtzer, Ellis Paxson. 251 p. New York: Ozer, 1971 (1922).

This book by a member of the Pennsylvania State Board of Censors appeared first in 1922 under the banner of the Penn Publishing Company of Philadelphia. It is currently reprinted by Ozer as part of the *Moving Pictures—Their Impact on Society* series. It purports to be a record of the author's experiences during a six-year period of operating the Censor's office. His philosophy is expressed by "Not many of us wish to violate correct standards of deportment in other departments of life. But we are not unmindful of our duty to our fellows, and we make rules to hinder and prevent that little part of the population which now or at some future time, shall stand ready to do damage to society. The laws which we would enact are not for those who direct their courses rightly; they are meant for and will only touch and restrict those who on some account are minded to

act in another sense. <

Examined are sex films, melodramas, serials, and comedies; and child audiences, censor boards, the industry, and politics. In the appendix there are several examples of censorship laws from locations such as Chicago; Portland, Oregon; Missouri; Massachusetts; and Quebec. The author does not quite follow his original premise—that of a record of experiences. What he offers is a rather long inspirational essay and justification for his activity. Of interest mostly to historians.

4208 *More About* ALL ABOUT EVE. by Mankiewicz, Joseph L.; and Carey, Gary. 357 p. New York: Random House, 1972.

A lengthy interview-article called "A Colloquy" introduces this volume. In it Mankiewicz speaks of the creation of the film with emphasis on the script and the characterization. Carey's role is to add pertinent background and detail. The script of the film follows. (It was printed separately in 1951.)

4209 *More Fabulous Faces.* by Carr, Larry. illus. Garden City, N. Y.: Doubleday.

The careers of five famous film actresses—Delores Del Rio, Myrna Loy, Carole Lombard, Bette Davis, and Katharine Hepburn—are traced from starlet to superstar. Using almost 850 pictures and an expository text, Carr examines, in chronological fashion, their evolution via lighting, makeup, dress, hair, camera placement, etc. This attractive volume is a sequel to Carr's popular *Four Fabulous Faces*.

4210 *More Films Kids Like.* by Gaffney, Maureen. 159 p. paper illus. Chicago: American Library Association, 1977.

Although this is a follow-up to Susan Rice's *Films Kids Like*, there is no overlap. It is a continuation which offers annotations on 200 additional films that have been tested with children. Both books, then, offer a total of 419 films from the period of the late sixties to the mid-seventies. Selection involved prescreening and adult testing in accordance with predetermined criteria. This was followed by testing with various children's groups in schools, where the showings involved teachers, prescreening, evaluations, etc. The final 200 films are a result of that lengthy testing period.

Each entry offers film data—title, running time, distributor, film type, country of origin—and a paragraph of descriptive-critical annotation. A section on activities to accompany film showings, a distributor list, a filmography for the very young (3 to 6 yrs.), and a subject index conclude the volume, which is illustrated with film stills and shots of children reacting to the films. Essential for persons and institutions engaged with the education and growth of children.

4211 *More From Hollywood.* by Bodeen, DeWitt. 356 p. illus. New York: A. S. Barnes, 1977.

In this volume DeWitt Bodeen continues his coverage of Hollywood personalities via mini-biographies, a project he began with *From Hollywood*. Although the subtitle reads, "The Careers of 15 Great American Stars," the subjects include director Val Lewton and writer Frances Marion. Others profiled include Elsie Ferguson, Pauline Frederick, Greta Garbo, Dorothy Gish, May McAvoy, Antonio Moreno, Nazimova, Ramon Novarro, Charles Ray, Blanche Sweet, Florence Bates, Clint Eastwood, and Jeanette MacDonald.

For each there is a largely factual biographical essay, some clearly reproduced illustrations and a filmography. An index is also provided.

Aside from the diversity of subjects, the reader may question the need of an additional noncritical essay on Garbo or Gish at this time. Most of Bodeen's other choices are much less familiar in the literature.

The essays which provide the major substance of the book are polite, admiring and lacking in depth. For example, Novarro's homosexuality and Nazimova's lesbianism are completely ignored, even though their life styles may help to interpret their work. Many quotations from previously published sources, along with a few personal anecdotes, appear throughout the text. This is a collective biography that makes some potentially exciting subjects appear either mild, bland, or colorless. Acceptable.

4212 *More Havoc.* by Havoc, June. 288 p. illus. New York: Harper, 1980.

The story of June Havoc, a show business star for over five decades, is continued here. In her first autobiography *Early Havoc* (1959), she told of her vaudeville fame as "Baby June." Much of that material has been popularized in GYPSY (1962). In this volume she tells mostly of her later years when she appeared in "Pal Joey" and other shows on Broadway, and also made films in Hollywood.

There are flashbacks to the early years and to her mother (Rose) and sister (Gypsy Rose Lee).

The memoir ends in 1954 and Havoc's story will probably be continued in a future book. Her style is

like her public persona: lively, witty, painfully honest, and emotional-at-will. Illustrations are included in this entertaining recall of a time when show business seemed much simpler and more glamorous than today.

4213 *More or Less.* by More, Kenneth. 286 p. paper illus. London: Hodder & Stoughton, 1978.

In a brisk breezy fashion Kenneth More recalls a career that has included success in the theatre, films, and television. Known in America mostly for his portrayal of Jolyon in "The Forsythe Saga" series on television, he has appeared in many films which are still seen with regularity—GENEVIEVE (1953), DOCTOR IN THE HOUSE (1954), REACH FOR THE SKY (1956), etc. In a positive, up-beat narrative that includes many anecdotes and recollections of other British performers, More tells of a rather easy rise from young stagehand to mature star. The same quality of relaxed strength and good humor that characterizes his performances is evident in these pages. This is a light, pleasant, ingratiating autobiography.

Some illustrations and an index are provided; however, a much-needed career chronology is missing.

4214 *The Morning After.* by Sheed, Wilfred. 304 p. New York: Farrar, Straus and Giroux, 1971.

Wilfred Sheed is a versatile writer who is equally at ease in judging books, films, theatre, sports or politics. A sampling of his critical essays is offered in this book. The film section has an even dozen reviews written originally for *Esquire*; they deal mostly with the foreign or the specialized film: THE HIPPIE REVOLT (1968), GREETINGS (1969), etc. Sheed's style is a mixture of intelligence, wit, and sophistication. The sampling here is too small to discern any unique aesthetic other than his apparent preference for the imported or important film. His subjects are chosen according to his own taste rather than as a sampling of what's available. Sheed is a critic whose film reviews make rewarding reading. This sampling suggests the publication of a book devoted solely to his essays and reviews about films.

4215 MOROCCO, SHANGHAI EXPRESS. by von Sternberg, Josef. 136 p. paper illus. New York: Simon and Schuster, 1973.

Contains scripts for: MOROCCO, (1930); SHANGHAI EXPRESS, (1932).

4216   *Moscow over Hollywood.* by Fagan, Myron C. 107 p. illus. Los Angeles: Cary, 1948.

Fagan's concern is Communism in Hollywood, and this is one of several books he wrote on the subject.

4217   *Moses and Egypt.* by Noerdlinger, Henry S. 202 p. paper illus. Los Angeles: University of Southern California Press, 1956.

The use of 1900 books, 3000 photographs, and the resources of 30 libraries in America, Europe, and Africa in the preparation of a film is related here. It is the documentation of the 1956 film version of THE TEN COMMANDMENTS which was directed by Cecil B. DeMille, who provides an introduction to this book. The subjects researched include the period, the army, transportation, buildings, costumes, hair styles, jewelry, food, etc. A list of the libraries and museums consulted is given. Most unusual and worthwhile.

4218   *The Most Important and Misappreciated American Films Since the Beginning of the Cinema.* by Ledoux, Jacques. paper Brussels: Royal Film Archive of Belgium, 1978.

The results of a survey which asked selected critics, directors, writers, archivists, teachers, historians, ètc., to list "30 most important American Films" and "any number of misappreciated American Films" are given here. Designed for the Bicentennial, the book covers only up to 1976. About 203 responses were collated with the following films identified most frequently as "important": CITIZEN KANE (1941)—156 votes; SUNRISE (1927)—114 votes; GREED (1923)—106 votes; INTOLERANCE (1916)—105 votes.

There are comments and observations describing the methods and results of the survey.

4219   *The Most Important Art: East European Film After 1945.* by Liehm, Mira; and Liehm, Antonin J. 467 p. illus. Berkeley, Calif.: University of California Press, 1977.

This volume is a critical history of Eastern European filmmaking over the three decades which followed the end of World War II. An introductory chapter provides a preface which gives a pre-1945 background and overview. The first decade is covered in a section called, "Hope and Reality," which discusses the recovery of the nationalized film industry in each country in spite of the ever-present bureaucratic control. The next section, "Degrees of Dissent," indicates the growth and development of the revitalized filmmakers which in turn leads to revolts in several countries. A final section entitled, "The Possibilities of Art and the Art of the Possible," explores the most recent developments and innovations of nationalized filmmaking in Eastern Europe. Countries considered in all sections include the Soviet Union, the German Democratic Republic, Czechoslovakia, Poland, Yugoslavia, Bulgaria, Romania, and Hungary.

The many stills which accompany the text give the reader visual evidence and example about the films. A strong bibliography, an index of film titles and an index of names also make the book a valuable reference work.

In the hundreds of films and directors discussed here, there is a richness of information not available elsewhere. Happily the indexes provide quick access to this extensive material. In addition the interpretation and critical comment provide a historical development of several nationalized cinemas that is rare in film books. The earlier volumes on *Eastern European Filmmaking* by Nina Hibbins, and *New Cinema in Eastern Europe*, by Alistair Whyte do not offer the depth and detail found here. This unique example of scholarship, research and interpretation is highly recommended.

4220   *Mother Climbed Trees.* by Lindsay, Cynthia. 236 p. illus. New York: Simon & Schuster, 1958.

From Long Island to Connecticut and on to Hollywood, the author had an unpredictable existence because of a rather zany mother. Eventually father was a director in Hollywood, brother was killed in the war, the author was doing stunt work in films and mother remained an "Auntie Mame" character. The author's emotions toward her mother are quite mixed. Readers will feel the same way about the book.

4221   *Mother Goddam: The Story of the Career of Bette Davis.* by Stine, Whitney. 374 p. illus. New York: Hawthorn Books, 1974.

Is there really a need for yet another book on Bette Davis? Her life and career has been covered from as far back as 1948 in Peter Noble's biography. Sandford Dody's excellent biography, *The Films of Bette Davis,* and Jerry Vermilye's fine career study have appeared since. This volume is written by an adoring fan and as a result suffers from too many gushy passages and a lack of critical objectivity. It's as though Miss Moffatt-Davis was looking over Morgan Evans-Stine's shoulder as he wrote, and perhaps she was, since this volume contains her running comments—printed in red ink, yet—on the author's narrative. The Davis contributions are predictably self-serving but offer stronger content than the author's loving recital of the familiar.

Some excellent photographs are included and there is a good filmography appended along with a list of her stage appearances. A detailed index is provided here, which is most helpful. The earlier volumes lacked this essential feature. This is a book that is strong in production values, reference potential and in the new original Davis material. The author has failed his subject by providing affection instead of evaluation. Acceptable.

4222 *Motion Picture Acting.* by Albertson, Lillian. 135 p. New York: Funk & Wagnalls, 1947.

Lillian Albertson was a dramatic coach at Paramount and RKO studios during the thirties and forties. In this book she treats rudiments of acting such as poise, speech, movement, etc. A comparison of acting techniques for various media is made and some suggestions are offered about the mental preparation for a role. The celebrity testimonials which preface the book give it a nostalgic quality. Most of what Miss Albertson says is still valuable.

4223 *Motion Picture Acting.* by Agnew, Frances (Frances Scheuing). 101 p. illus. New York: Reliance Newspaper Syndicate, 1913.

How to prepare for photoplaying, what qualifications are necessary, how to secure an engagement, salaries paid to photoplayers, etc., are some of the concerns ofthis early compendium of advice for would-be actors. Closing the volume are statements from some of the leading film actors of the period.

4224 *Motion Picture Almanac (1929-1941).* edited by Ramsaye, Terry. 12 volumes New York: Gordon Press, 1976.

Reprintings of one of the most valuable references in film literature.

4225 *Motion Picture and AV Publications.* compiled by Kodak Editors. 26 p. paper illus. Rochester, N. Y.: Eastman Kodak, 1972.

This is an out-of-date bibliography that organizes its entries under eight general headings—general, reference, production, history-aesthetics, business-industry, education, religion, and television. About 200 books and periodicals are given descriptive annotations along with complete citations. The selection, which is poor, lacks both scope and balance and isindicative of that usually found in film bibliographies of the early seventies.

4226 *Motion Picture and Television Film Image Control and Processing Techniques.* by Corbett, D. J. 231 p. illus. New York: Amphoto, 1968.

This volume provides detailed coverage of motion picture laboratory work. It covers the elements of film processing and some theoretical aspects of photometry. For the professional engineer, cameraman, or technician.

4227 *The Motion Picture and the Teaching of English.* by Sheridan, Marion; and Owens, Harold; and MacRorie, Ken; and Marcus, Fred. 168 p. paper illus. New York: Appleton-Century-Crofts, 1965.

The National Council of Teachers of English working in association with Teaching Film Custodians developed this paperback. It was designed to indicate the unique characteristics of film and to show how films can be used in the teaching of English. CITIZEN KANE (1941) is used as a sample film for study, and one complete chapter is devoted to its analysis. A comparison of the book and the film of the GRAPES OF WRATH (1940) is made in another chapter. Attention is also given to film criticism, film genres, censorship and other topics related to film.

A bibliography and some distribution sources complete the book. It is indexed and there are a few illustrations. And a few errors, too. William Wyler did not direct THE LOST WEEKEND (1945) (p.40). Did Delbert Mann direct THE MARK? (1961) (p. 120). Or was it Guy Green? As an introduction to teaching and using films in a classroom, this volume has much value. It tackles the complex topic of film aesthetics in a manner that makes it comprehensible to the novice. While it resembles at times a *Reader's Digest* condensation of the classics on film aesthetics, it may lead teachers eventually to those primary sources. Recommended.

4228 *Motion Picture Camera and Lighting Equipment.* by Samuelson, David W. 220 p. paper illus. New York:

Hastings House, 1977.

Two aspects of the process of selecting motion picture hardware are treated in this title in the *Media Manual* series. Addressing itself to equipment choice and technique, it offers a discussion of the many characteristics of cameras along with their accessories—tripods, dollys, cranes, exposure meters, filters, etc. In addition, the lighting equipment used in most professional filmmaking is described. Beginning with sunlight, this latter section treats fresnels, carbon arcs, battery portables, fluorescents, halides, strobes, and other forms of illumination.

The author's intent is to provide information and, ultimately, criteria upon which an intelligent selection of equipment can be based. Since description of the hardware usually entails some consideration of how it can be used, the text also serves as a technique manual.

This excellent volume is a bit more technical than some others in the series but is still a rewarding source book for both the professional and the general reader. Recommended.

4229 *Motion Picture Camera Data.* by Samuelson, David. 172 p. paper illus. New York: Hastings House, 1979.

This volume gives specifications and operating instructions for many models of professional motion picture cameras. Topics treated include lenses, shutters, filters, viewfinders, batteries, etc. Some information on trouble-shooting is offered along with a bibliography and a listing of the manufacturers. The illustrations, including some diagrams and drawings, are plentiful.

4230 *Motion Picture Camera Techniques.* by Samuelson, David W. 200 p. paper illus. New York: Focal/Hastings House 1978.

This title in the uniformly excellent *Media Manuals* series is a guide for cinematographers that stresses commercial viability. In its coverage of a wide range of topics, the text is comprehensive, clear and practical. Samuelson begins with the script and proceeds through almost 100 individual chapters, each of which deals with some aspect of the craft. Advice, description, direction, aesthetics, diagrams, boards, graphs, line drawings, tables, and a bibliography are included in this concentration of information.

The expertise of the author is apparent throughout this clearly stated and illustrated review of motion picture camera techniques. An essential tool for all aspiring cinematographers, the manual also offers much to others in the field of film production.

4231 *The Motion-Picture Cameraman.* by Lutz, Edwin George. 248 p. illus. New York: Arno, 1972 (1927).

Originally published by Scribner in 1927, this book describes the cinematographic techniques of that period. There are chapters on cameras, lenses, locations, trick photography, development of film and other topics. Many illustrations and diagrams help to explain the text. Of interest to historians, researchers, and scholars.

4232 *Motion Picture Continuities.* edited by Patterson, Frances Taylor. 246 p. illus. New York: Columbia University Press, 1929.

Contains three complete scripts/continuities illustrating adaptations from different sources: A KISS FOR CINDERELLA (1926) from a play, THE SCARLET LETTER (1926) from a novel, and finally an original screen story, THE LAST COMMAND (1928). Differences between the originals and the adaptations are noted, together with other analysis and comment. Credits are given for the films along with some stills.

4233 *Motion Picture Directing: The Facts and Theories of the Newest Art.* by Milne, Peter. 234 p. illus. New York: Falk Pub. Co., 1922.

This volume about silent film directing not only discusses continuity, editing, photography, etc., but also considers the directorial methods of famous directors of the mid-silent period: Griffith, Ince, DeMille, Sennett, Lubitsch, etc. The art of directing is described by DeMille, Rex Ingram, Frank Borzage, and Marshall Neilan. An outstanding collection of stills, diagrams and portraits supplements the excellent text.

4234 *Motion Picture Directors.* by Schuster, Mel. 418 p. Metuchen, N.J.: Scarecrow Press, 1973.

The very prolific Mr. Schuster has done it again. After providing an essential reference book, *Motion Picture Performers*, he has repeated the format, this time with directors. The result is a bibliography of articles on directors which have appeared in 340 periodicals from 1900 to 1972. More than 2300 directors, filmmakers, and animators are listed.

Directors are arranged alphabetically by surname, making the volume very easy to use. Articles are listed under each chronologically. For example, the first entry for Cecil B. DeMille is from *Photoplay*, June 1915 while the last is from the May 1970 issue of *After Dark*. A total of 110 articles are listed in all. While DeMille is admittedly a unique entry, many others have equally exhaustive periodical coverage, e.g., Disney, Chaplin, Godard, Hitchcock, Welles, etc. The introduction contains a valid explanation of the criteria for selecting the directors for inclusion. Directors for whom no articles were found are listed. The 340 periodicals which were researched are named in the appendix.

The effort required to compile this thorough reference is obvious throughout. Recommended.

4235 *Motion Picture Discrimination: An Annotated Bibliography.* by Dale, Edward; and Morrison, John. 41 p. paper Columbus, Ohio: Bureau of Educational Research, Ohio State University, 1951.

Two major areas are considered: motion picture appreciation and motion pictures in education.

4236 *Motion Picture Distribution: An Accountant's Perspective.* by Leedy, David J. 73 p. Thousand Oaks, Calif.: Bradson, 1980.

4237 *Motion Picture Distribution Handbook.* by Robertson, Joseph F. 252 p. illus. Blue Ridge Summit, Pa.: TAB, 1979.

This guide, designed for both the professional and the amateur, deals with how motion pictures are sold and distributed. Among the topics discussed are booking schedules, rental fees, copyrights, promotion campaigns, foreign distribution, release prints, etc. Samples of contracts, schedules, and promotion campaigns are included along with a glossary and an index.

4238 *Motion Picture Distribution Trade Practices.* edited by Committee on Small Businesses, U.S. Senate. 952 p. paper Washington, D.C.: U.S. Government Printing Office, 1953.

A report of the hearings held in Los Angeles and Washington in 1953 by a subcommittee of the Committee on Small Businesses of the United States Senate, the 83rd Congress, the first session. The subject was the problems of independent motion picture exhibitors in regard to distribution trade practices.

4239 *Motion Picture Distribution—Business or Racket?* by Hurst, Walter E.; and Hale, William Storm. 159 p. illus. Hollywood, Calif.: Seven Arts Press, 1975.

A book that considers the practical and theoretical aspects of film distribution is a rarity. Not only does this volume offer a solid text, but it also includes cartoon drawings of distribution rackets, sample forms, an annotated bibliography, a short glossary and an index. The approach is very much the same as that used in the author's excellent *The Movie Industry Book* and *Film-TV Law*. It consists of down-to-earth, practical advice and suggestions on such distribution topics as contracts, financial terms, franchises, passes, advertising, pornography, expenses, ratios and even popcorn. Although the text is most serious, it employs a smartly sophisticated style which is delightful to discover in a technical book such as this.

This would seem to be an absolutely essential volume for anyone concerned with the distribution business, past, present or future. For those schools which offer a full degree program in film study, the book is highly recommended as a reference and as a possible text for certain specific courses.

4240 *Motion Picture Empire.* by Jobes, Gertrude. 398 p. illus. Hamden, Conn.: Archon Books, 1966.

A study of the business and financial aspects of the film industry during its formative years. Based in part on the author's personal recollections, this book considers the early inventions, the formation of the trusts, filmmaking as big business and similar topics. The emphasis is on the early years, and the later period of 1945 to 1970 is given scant attention. Some historical interest for the film scholar but this book is not recommended for the general reader.

4241 *Motion Picture Encyclopedia.* by Cifre, Joseph S. edited by Cameron, James R.; illus. Coral Gables, Fla.: Cameron Pub. Co., 1959.

A technical encyclopedia which should have pertinence for professionals. The first entry is "Absorption, Dieletric"; the final one, "Zoomer Lens." A 25-page entry on studio slang is amusing to read, but most of the book is quite technical. The issue examined is the 6th Edition and the volume is in its 26th year of publication.

4242 *The Motion Picture Film Editor.* by Ash, Rene L. 171 p. illus. Metuchen,

N.J.: Scarecrow Press, 1974.

After a brief introduction, two articles, "On Editing" by Jerry Greenberg and "The Functions of the Film Editor" by Jack W. Ogilvie, discuss the technique-art of editing films. The main body of the text is devoted to filmographies for some 652 editors. Television shows, TV movies, and documentaries are included with theatrical features. The film index which follows refers the reader back to the editors in the main section. Closing portions of the book indicate Oscar Awards, Emmy Awards and Eddie Awards. A few illustrations are included. This is a specialized reference book that is well arranged and convenient to use. It is recommended.

4243 *Motion Picture Films (Compulsory Block Booking and Blind Selling).* compiled by Committee on Interstate and Foreign Commerce of the House. 688 p. paper Washington, D.C.: U.S. Government Printing Office, 1940.

A transcript of the hearings held before the Committee on Interstate and Foreign Commerce of the House of Representatives, the 76th Congress, third session on S-280, a bill to prohibit and prevent the trade practices known as compulsory block booking and blind selling in the leasing of motion picture films in interstate and foreign commerce.

4244 *Motion Picture Handbook.* by Richardson, Frank H. 432 p. illus. New York: Moving Picture World, 1912.

This guide for managers and operators of motion picture theatres was entitled *Richardson's Handbook of Projection for Theatre Managers and Motion Picture Projectionists* when it appeared in its fourth edition in 1922.

4245 *The Motion Picture in America.* by Fulop-Miller, Rene. 200 of 430 total p. illus. New York: Dial Press, 1938.

An older history of films found in *The American Theatre and The Motion Picture in America*. A fine section of photographs are part of this rare volume.

4246 *The Motion Picture in the Soviet Union 1918-1952: A Sociological Analysis.* by Rimberg, John David. 238 p. New York: Arno, 1973.

This is one of the doctoral dissertations of film topics reproduced by Arno exactly as they were submitted to the degree-granting school. The thesis of this study is that the content and volume of film production in the Soviet Union are determined by compromise between three groups—government officials (propaganda), creative artists (works of art), and audiences (entertainment).

After a review of previous research studies of Soviet Union, the content desired by each group and their power potential are examined. Using the three areas of content, films from various periods of Soviet film history are examined. A summary seems to confirm Rimberg's main thesis. A bibliography and an appendix complete the work. Acceptable.

4247 *The Motion Picture Industry.* by Lewis, Howard T. 454 p. New York: Van Nostrand, 1933.

A comprehensive and thorough study of the motion picture industry (thirties) from three aspects—production, distribution, and exhibition.

4248 *Motion Picture Industry: Business and Legal Problems.* compiled by Practising Law Institute. 424 p. paper illus. New York: Practising Law Institute, 1972.

Prepared for distribution at the Motion Picture Industry Workshop, February, 1972, this handbook considers patents, trademarks, literary properties, etc.

4249 *The Motion Picture Industry: A Pattern of Control.* by Bertrand, Daniel; and Evans, W. Duane; and Blanchard, E. L. 92 p. paper Washington, D.C.: U.S. Government Printing Office, 1941.

A report that looks at patterns of monopoly in both motion picture distribution and exhibition. The unsurprising conclusion is that monopolies are designed to eliminate competition.

4250 *The Motion Picture, Its Making and Its Theater.* by Hulfish, David S. 144 p. illus. Chicago: Electricity Magazine, 1909.

A look at cinematography and theatres in the early days of the motion picture industry.

4251 *Motion Picture Making and Exhibiting.* by Rathbun, John B. 236 p. illus. Los Angeles: Holmes Book Company, 1914.

A comprehensive volume treating the principles of motography, the making of motion pictures, the scenario, censorship, the motion picture theater, the projector, the conduct of film exhibiting, methods of coloring films, talking pictures, etc."

4252 *Motion Picture Market Place.* compiled by Costner, Tom. 513 p. paper Boston: Little, Brown, 1976.

Designed as an annual, this directory consists of more than 70 separate categories of people, service, and equipment used in both television and film production. Typical categories include film repair, food services, equipment rental, advertising agencies, screening rooms, wardrobe, etc. Brief explanations precede the state-by-state alphabetically arranged entries which offer name, address, and telephone number. The enormous amount of information that has been gathered into this one volume, should be of interest and value to the professional. Aspiring filmmakers might study it as evidence that filmmaking is indeed a collaborative art.

4253 *Motion Picture Moods for Pianists and Organists.* by Rapee, Erno. 678 p. New York: Arno Press, 1970 (1924).

Selected piano music scores to accompany silent films.

4254 *Motion Picture Operation, Stage Electrics and Illusions.* by Horstmann, Henry C.; and Tousley, Victor H. 393 p. illus. Chicago: Drake, 1917.

A practical handbook and guide for theater electricians, motion picture operators, and managers of theaters and productions.

4255 *Motion Picture Performers: A Bibliography of Magazine and Periodical Articles, 1900-1969.* by Schuster, Mel. 702 p.Metuchen, N.J.: Scarecrow Press, 1971.

This book is an ideal research tool. Using the collection of the Library and Museum of Performing Arts at Lincoln Center, N.Y., the author has compiled a bibliography of articles appearing in several hundred magazines and periodicals from 1900 to 1969. The several thousand performers are arranged alphabetically, and the citations under each performer are listed chronologically. For example, the earliest article on Doris Day is from the *American Magazine*, May 1949. Fifty-five other articles are then list-

ed, the last one being from *TV Guide* of December 6, 1969.

The introduction explains the selection process and gives a list of the magazines and periodicals used. The names of several hundred performers for whom no articles were found (e.g. Ben Blue, Andrea Leeds, Laura La Plante) are also given. Impressive in scope and design, this reference book can be used for a variety of purposes, the major one of which is to furnish the historian or the researcher with an impressive head start of several hours or days.

4256 *Motion Picture Performers: A Bibliography of Magazine & Periodical Articles, Supplement Number One.* edited by Schuster, Mel. 783 p. Metuchen, N. J.: Scarecrow, 1976.

Mel Schuster has performed an almost impossible task—that of improving an outstanding original reference. He has increased the number of performers treated from 2900 to 5500, and the periodicals indexed from about 150 to 300. The original volume covered the period from 1900 to 1970—here about one-third of the entries deal with 1970 to 1974, the remainder being devoted to the name and periodical additions.

This is an absolutely unique reference that is a basic tool for any teacher, student, writer or scholar working in film studies. As a guide for finding periodical information on film performers, there is simply nothing like it. The field of cinema literature needs more devoted scholars like Schuster, for whom this volume is probably a labor of love, rather than a source of any appreciable income. Highly recommended.

4257 *Motion Picture Photography.* by Gregory, Carl Louis. 435 p. illus. New York: Falk Publishing, 1927.

This is now a historical curiosity rather than the how-to-do-it volume it was back in 1927. Several things make it unusual. Through its text and the photographs of filmmaking in the twenties, the reader can gain insight into the technology of the period. Certain chapters are especially interesting—animated cartoons, airplane photography, trick work, double exposure, submarine photography, etc. There is even a chapter on "The History of Cinematography." Noted here for the record.

4258 *Motion Picture Pioneer: The Selig Polyscore Company.* edited by Lahue, Kalton C. 224 p. illus. New York: A. S. Barnes, 1973.

This account of one of the first motion picture companies in America is told by photographs, bulletins, advertisements, film stills, editorials, articles, reviews and a narrative by Lahue. This unusual approach works well here. The specialized material has been organized most impressively by Lahue. Picture reproduction is variable but probably forgivable when one considers the rarity and age of some of the photographs. The book is not indexed. This is a good book that will appeal to a small, enthusiastic audience—buffs, historians, scholars, etc. The general reader will probably pass it by. Acceptable.

4259 *Motion Picture Prints from Color Originals.* edited by Kodak Staff. paper illus. Rochester, N.Y.: Kodak, 1977.

A guide that tells how to make super 8 color prints from 16mm and 35mm originals, 16mm color prints from 16mm camera originals, and 35mm and 16mm color prints from 35mm negatives.

4260 *Motion Picture Problems: The Cinema and the League of Nations.* by Seabury, William M. 426 p. New York: Avondale, 1929.

4261 *Motion Picture Production Facilities of Selected Colleges and Universities.* edited by Williams, Don G.; and Snyder, Luella V. 345 p. paper illus. Washington, D. C.: Government Printing Office, 1963.

The results of a survey commissioned by the U. S. Office of Education to the University Film Foundation of Ames, Iowa, are reported in USOE Bulletin 3963, Number 15.

4262 *Motion Picture Production Facilities of Selected Colleges and Universities.* compiled by University Film Foundation. 345 p. paper illus. Washington, D.C.: U.S. Government Printing Office, 1963.

Also known as Bulletin 1963, number 15 of the Office of Education, this survey was reported by Don G. Williams and Luella V. Snyder.

4263 *Motion Picture Production For Industry.* by Gordon, Jay E. 352 p. illus. New York: Macmillan, 1961.

A practical, professional guide to the production of industrial films written by an experienced filmmaker.

4264 *Motion Picture Production in British Columbia (1898-1940).* compiled by Browne, Colin. 389 p. paper illus. Vancouver: British Columbia Provincial Museum, 1978.

An attractive catalog that lists over 1000 films made in or about British Columbia up to World War II, this volume also includes some stills and a lengthy historical essay. Notes on about two dozen feature films, some of which were made as part of Britain's "quota quickie" ruling, are added.

4265 *Motion Picture Projection.* by Cameron, James R. 1010 p. illus. Coral Gables, Fla.: Cameron Publishing.

This is the 14th edition of this standard book designed for operators of projection and sound systems. Includes data on Cinemascope, Vistavision, Todd AO, Cinerama, Superscope, Perspecta Sound, etc.

4266 *Motion Picture Projection.* by Sloane, Thomas O'Conor. 303 p. illus. New York: Falk, 1922.

Along with projection and cinematography, this volume treats the history of motion pictures—toys, early attempts at projection, persistence of vision, etc.

4267 *Motion Picture Projection and Theatre Presentation Manual.* edited by Kloepfel, Don V. 178 p. illus. New York: Society of Motion Picture and Television Engineers, 1969 (1961).

Contains technical information on the care of films, splicing, care of projectors, area recommendations, ventilation, lighting, wall construction, screens, sound systems, theatre design. There are sections on drive-in theatres and on projection problems. A specialized book.

4268 *Motion Picture Sound Engineering.* compiled by Academy of Motion Picture Arts and Sciences. 547 p. illus. New York: D. Van Nostrand, 1938.

A series of lectures given in the early days of sound recording for films. Augmented by added chapters, illustrations, diagrams, bibliographies, etc.

4269 *Motion Picture Stills*. New York: Museum of Modern Art.

The Museum of Modern Art publishes collections of 8 inch x 10 inch glossy stills in connection with certain film showings held there. Some short text accompanies each packet. Available are: The Horror Film, Marlene Dietrich, D. W. Griffith, Josef von Sternberg, Sophia Loren, Katherine Hepburn, and Greta Garbo. There are usually ten pictures in each packet. Picture quality varies greatly, with the Dietrich collection being superior to the others.

4270 *Motion Picture Studio Campaign Books (1920-1940)*. by 20 volumes New York: Gordon Press, 1976.

4271 *Motion Picture Studio Directory and Trade Annual 1919-1920*. edited by Gordon, R. F. New York: Gordon Press, 1976 (1920).

A reprint of material originally published by *Motion Picture News* in Chicago and New York.

4272 *Motion Picture Technical Dictionary (English-French, French-English)*. by Gibbs, Charles R. 223 p. paper Paris: Nouvelle Editions, 1959.

4273 *Motion Picture, TV and Theatre Directory*. by Low, John B. 148 p. paper illus. Tarrytown, N.Y.: Motion Picture Enterprises Public, 1972.

This guide to commercial services and products appears semiannually in the spring and the fall. While it contains large amounts of commercial advertising, it also gives information that may not be easily available through other sources. It resembles *Audio Visual Market Place* somewhat, but each has unique offerings. A very long index lists well over 100 services or products for the AV field—including basics such as motion picture labs by state, film treatment, film schools, etc., and such rarities as animals for rent (trained), helicopters, underwater filming, etc. The directory posts a price, but is sent free once your name is on the mailing list. A good reference item.

4274 *Motion Picture Testing and Research*. edited by Gibson, James J. 267 p. illus. Washington, D.C.: U. S. Government Printing Office, 1947.

4275 *Motion Picture Theater Management*. by Franklin, Harold B. 365 p. illus. New York: George H. Doran, 1927.

A text on theater management that covers such topics as plant, personnel, finance, music, accidents, structure, legal considerations, etc.

4276 *The Motion Picture Theatre*. edited by Stote, Helen M. 429 p. illus. New York: Society of Motion Picture Engineers, 1948.

A collection of 38 articles prepared for presentation to the Society. Topics include construction, maintenance, modernization, acoustics, ventilation, lighting, floor coverings, etc.

4277 *The Motion Picture Trade Directory of 1928*. edited by Gordon, R. F. New York: Gordon Press, 1976 (1928).

A reprint of *The Reference Book of the Picture Trade: A Classified Quarterly of the Motion Picture and Allied Industries.*

4278 *Motion Picture, TV and Theatre Directory*. compiled by Pilzer, Herbert R. 192 p. paper illus. New York: Motion Picture Enterprises, 1979.

Published twice each year, this guide lists many services and products used by motion picture producers—advertising, animals, animation, audio, camera, costume, distribution, editing, processing, insurance, lighting, make-up, hair, music, sound, payroll, scenery, script, special effects, union, guilds, voice-overs, equipment rentals, etc.

4279 *Motion-Picture Work*. by Hulfish, David Sherill. 297 pages. illus. New York: Arno Press, 1970 (1913).

First published in 1913, motion pictures, motion picture photography, theatre management and operation along with the industry activities of the first film decade or so are described via text and stills, diagrams, drawings, etc.

4280 *Motion Pictures*. by Beckoff, Samuel. 114 p. paper illus. New York: Oxford Book Co., 1953.

An early textbook designed for high school students, this volume was part of the Oxford *Communication Arts* series. The topic of film appreciation for secondary school English classes was divided into 15 units, which included such headings as genres, critics, film problems, foreign films, literature and film, the director's role, etc. Throughout the volume, film is considered as a medium of entertainment/communication and as an industry. This is an overlooked pioneer volume that was a model for several of the texts that appeared in the late sixties and early seventies.

4281 *Motion Pictures: A Catalog of Books, Screenplays, Television Scripts and Production Stills.* compiled by Theatre Arts Library, Univ. of California. 775 p. Boston: G. K. Hall, 1976.

This is a revised, second edition of a bibliography which was first published in 1973. Certain ephemeral material has been eliminated while new material and acquisitions up to March 1976 have been included.

The catalog now has five sections, two of which appear for the first time: (1). Books, Periodicals and Journals—a collection of several thousand titles, mostly in English, arranged by author surname only. (2). Published Screenplays—taken from Section I, several hundred screenplays are arranged here by film title. (3). Unpublished Screenplays—several thousand American and British screenplays are noted along with a few in other languages. The screenplays are arranged by film title. (4). Television Scripts—several hundred television scripts are included. They are arranged alphabetically by individual program title or by series name. (5). Production Stills—sets of stills from several thousand films are noted. Arrangement is by film title.

The entire bibliography is composed of catalog cards which are arranged in three columns with seven cards in each, making a total of 21 entries per page. This format facilitates information retrieval and, although much of the material noted here is from a noncirculating special collection, it is available for reference or research purposes.

Even though the film material is represented only by catalog card information, this bibliography offers a much larger collection than that available in the more expensive bibliographies such as *The Chicorel Guide to Film Literature.* A valuable reference tool.

4282 *Motion Pictures.* by Beatty, LaMond F. 112 p. illus. Englewood Cliffs, N.J.: Educational Technology Pub., 1981.

This is volume 8 in the *Instructional Media Library* series.

4283 *Motion Pictures: Laws, Ordinances, and Regulations on Censorship, Minors, and Other Related Subjects.* by Cannon, Lucius H. 168 p. St. Louis: Public Library, 1920.

4284 *Motion Pictures: A Catalog of Books, Periodicals, Screen Plays and Production Stills.* 1169 p. Boston, Mass.: G. K. Hall, 1973.

A guide to the collection at the Theatre Arts Library, University of California at Los Angeles. This valuable reference tool is divided into three sections:

Section I (books and periodicals) includes the research collection of books on all aspects of film and the film industry, personal papers of film personalities (Stanley Kramer, Jack Benny, Charles Laughton, King Vidor, etc.), clippings, records, screenplays from Republic Studios.

Section II. (production stills) includes 87,000 stills from American and foreign films as far back as 1905. Jessen Collection, Richard Dix Collection, and the Columbia Pictures Stills Collection are represented.

Section III (screenplays) includes more than 3000 unpublished American, British, and foreign scripts.

4285 *Motion Pictures: A Study in Social Legislation.* by Young, Donald Ramsey. 109 p. New York: Ozer, 1971 (1922).

A reprint of the 1922 edition, now part of the series, "Moving Pictures: Their Impact on Society," this volume is an examination of the problem of moral standards in motion pictures. The author is a reformer who argues for state censorship as the only way of controlling film content to make it acceptable to local audiences. Any film which does not "uplift" an audience should be either censored or eliminated, according to Young. If the reader can overcome annoyance at the narrow viewpoint presented, the book may have some historical value. Acceptable.

4286 *Motion Pictures and Juvenile Delinquency.* compiled by U. S. Senate Committee on the Judiciary. 122 p. paper Washington, D. C.: U. S. Government Printing Office, 1956.

A report (number 2065) of the committee assigned to investigate juvenile delinquency in the United States by Senate resolution number 173 passed during the 2nd session of the 84th Congress. A bibliography and an interim report from the subcommittee are also included.

4287 *Motion Pictures and Social Attitudes of Children.* by Peterson, Ruth C.; and Thurstone, L. L. 75 p. New York: Arno Press, 1970 (1933).

This Payne Fund Study indicated that social attitudes such as race prejudice, views on capital punishment, etc., can be affected and changed by motion pictures. *The Social Conduct and Attitudes of Movie Fans* is bound with this volume.

4288 *Motion Pictures and Standards of Morality.* by Peters, Charles C. 285 p. New York: Arno Press, 1970 (1933).

To what extent do current (i.e., 1933) movies either comply or conflict with the standards of morality? This is the question governing the research done by author Peters (Penn State) in this Payne Fund Study. The methods used in this research areespecially noteworthy. Certain scenes were shown to various groups who were then asked to evaluate them. Each group was relatively homogeneous within itself but the totality represented a good cross-section sampling of American society. One of the more stimulating Payne Fund Studies.

4289 *Motion Pictures and the Arts in Canada.* by Drabinsky, Garth H. 201 p. Scarborough, Ontario: McGraw Hill-Ryerson, 1976.

Written by a lawyer, this specialized volume deals with the business and legal aspects of the film industry in Canada. Topics discussed include copyright, slander, libel, insurance, contracts, acquisition of film and subsidiary rights, financing, film music, obscenity and censorship, right of privacy, guilds, unions, and coproductions.

An unusual bibliography lists not only books and periodicals, but also treaties, agreements, statutes, and specific court cases involving motion pictures. The volume is indexed.

For anyone who is an active or budding participant in the Canadian film industry, this volume is essential reading and a necessary reference. By an acquaintance with the agreements, interpretations and rulings that have governed the Canadian film business, others will become sensitive to those matters which are part of the legal province in any country.

4290 *Motion Pictures and the Film Industry in Yugoslavia.* edited by Yugoslavia Information Center. 15 p. paper illus. Beograd, Yugoslavia:

Yugoslavia Information Center, 1960.

This pamphlet carries the publication number, 1008.

4291 *Motion Pictures and Youth.* by Charters, W. W. 66 p. New York: Arno Press, 1970 (1933).

First published in 1933, this is an introduction and summary of the Payne Fund Studies on the influence of motion pictures on youth. The many conclusions of the entire study were cautious, conservative, and open- minded. In general, this volume should be read first for a general overview of the several studies.

4292 *Motion Pictures as a Phase of Commercialized Amusement in Toledo, Ohio.* by Phelan, John Joseph. 292 p. Toledo, Ohio: Little Book Press, 1919.

This historical document is a title in the *Social Surveys* series and includes tables and a bibliography.

4293 *Motion Pictures as Test Stimuli.* by Schalock, Henry D.; and Beaird, James H.; and Simmons, Helen. 465 p. illus. Monmouth, Oregon: Teaching Research Div., Oregon State System of Higher Education, 1964.

An application of new media to the prediction of complex behavior.

4294 *Motion Pictures—Copyright Catalogs.* by prepared by the U.S. Copyright Office, Library of Congress. Washington, D.C.: Gov. Printing Office.

The following is a summary of the film reference volumes published by the U.S. government that are based on the records of the copyright office and the catalog cards of the Library of Congress (these volumes are annotated separately in this book): *Motion Pictures 1894-1912*; *Motion Pictures 1912-1939*; *Motion Pictures 1940-1949*; *Motion Pictures 1950-1959*; *The Library of Congress Author Catalog: Vol. 24—Films, Catalog of Motion Pictures and Filmstrips*; and *The Library of Congress Vol. 28—1953-1957*; *Vols. 53 & 54—1958-1962*; and *Vols. 71 & 72—1963-1967* .

4295 *Motion Pictures for Community Needs.* by Bollman, Gladys; and

Bollman, Henry. 296 p. illus. New York: Holt, 1922.

A practical manual of information and suggestion for educational, religious and social work, this volume treats distribution, exhibition, finance, programming, equipment, installations, mechanical and legal problems, etc.

4296   *Motion Pictures from the Library of Congress Print Collection 1894-1912.* by Niver, Kemp R. edited by Bergsten, Bebe. 402 p. Berkeley, Calif.: University of California Press, 1967.

This is an index of some 3000 films made from 1894 to 1912 in all parts of the world. The information about them comes from the paper positive prints that were deposited with the Library of Congress for copyright purposes. In 1953 the author began the project of transferring these paper prints onto modern film bases. The possibility of studying the modern reprintings of these old paper films is a thought to delight any film historian. Eventually much effect on the recorded accounts of early screen history should be noted.

In this index, the author gives 3000 titles, producers, copyright dates, lengths, contents, and sometimes casts, directors, and other pertinent information. He has divided the films into such major categories as comedy, documentary, drama, newsreels, and vaudeville acts. A subject index, and an alphabetical index complete the work. This major piece of research is an essential reference tool. It should be placed with the reference volumes on motion pictures published by the Copyright Office of the Library of Congress.

4297   *Motion Pictures in a Modern Curriculum.* by Bell, Reginald; and Cain, Leo; and Lamoreaux, Lillian. 179 p. illus. Washington, D.C.: American Council on Education, 1941.

4298   *Motion Pictures in Adult Education.* by Adam, T.R. 94 p. New York: American Association for Adult Education, 1940.

4299   *Motion Pictures in Education: A Summary of the Literature.* by Dale, Edgar; and Dunn, Fannie W.; and Hoban, Charles F.; and Schneider, Etta. 472 p. New York: Arno Press, 1970 (1938).

This is a reprint of a source book prepared for teachers, administrators, and others back in 1938. Areas covered are: the administration of visual aids, teaching with motion pictures and other visual aids, selecting instructional materials, film production in the schools, experimental research, and teacher preparation in visual education.

4300   *Motion Pictures in the Classroom.* by Wood, Ben D.; and Freeman, Frank W. 392 p. illus. Boston: Houghton Mifflin, 1929.

The results of an investigation made to determine the value of films in a regular classroom instruction are reported in this volume. The method, results, analysis and conclusions are noted.

4301   *Motion Pictures in the Philippines.* by Salumbides, Vicente. 237 p. illus. Manila: no publisher noted, 1952.

4302   *Motion Pictures Not Guilty.* edited by National Board of Review. 20 p. paper New York: National Board of Review, 1920.

The verdict is based on reports from chief probation officers of juvenile courts throughout the United States on the relationship of motion pictures to juvenile delinquency.

4303   *Motion Pictures, Television and Radio.* edited by Mehr, Linda Harris. 201 p. Boston: G.K. Hall, 1977.

Sponsored by the Film and Television Study Center Incorporated, this book is subtitled "A Union Catalogue of Manuscript and Special Collections in the Western United States." It is an alphabetical listing of those institutions in the states of Arizona, California, Colorado, Idaho, Montana, Nevada, New Mexico, Oregon, Utah, Washington and Wyoming which have film/television resources. Each entry offers institutional information (name, address, phone number, etc.) and collection description (size, type of items, usage restrictions, etc.). Information about materials in the collections is also provided by a general index. How to use the volume is clearly explained in the opening pages.

4304   *Motion Pictures: The Development of an Art from Silent Pictures to the Age of Television.* by Fulton, A. R. 320 p. illus. Norman, Okla.: University of Oklahoma Press, 1960.

This volume is a distillation of many of the classic books, films, and scripts that are part of screen history. It covers once again material that is overly familiar. Starting with invention, the author progresses to artist-director Melies, arranged scenes, arranged shots, and famous plays. By the time editing is discussed, the book is considering Griffith in 1915. The narrative continues through the coming of sound and concludes with source material for films, e.g., plays, novels, and short stories.

As a textbook, this volume has much to recommend it. It is a gathering together of vital information and historical accounts. For general reading it is too pedantic and too selective in its examples to have great appeal. The few photographs used are negligible. A bibliography, a glossary, and an index are included, as is a filmography of the few films explored in detail in the text. This volume has limited potential for reference.

4305 *Motion Pictures 1894-1912 (: Identified from the records of the U.S. Copyright Office).* by Walls, Howard Lamarr. 92 p. Washington, D.C.: U. S. Government Printing Office, 1953.

In the first section of this work prepared by the Copyright Office is an alphabetical list of all those films registered for copyright for the period 1894-1912. Indicated are the title, the claimant date and number of the copyright. The second part is an alphabetized claimant index in which all copyrights granted are listed in two ways: chronologically and alphabetically by title. An essential reference work.

4306 *Motion Pictures 1912-1939 (: Identified from the records of the U.S. Copyright Office).* 1256 p. Washington, D.C.: U. S. Government Printing Office, 1951.

This reference work lists over 35,000 photoplays and almost 16,000 films other than photoplays such as cartoons, newsreels, etc., all of which were registered with the Copyright Ofice from 1912-1939. The first section lists the titles with the usual accompanying data—running time, format, date of copyright, etc. The next section lists the claimants of the copyrights, and the final section lists series titles along with the claimant and the titles within the series. An essential reference.

4307 *Motion Picture 1940-1949 (: Identified from the records of the U.S. Copyright Office).* 599 p. Washington, D.C.: U. S. Government Printing Office, 1953.

This reference work lists over 7000 photoplays and almost 12,000 films other than photoplays, all of which were registered with the Copyright Office from 1940-1949. It is similar in format to the earlier volumes. The first section lists titles and data, the second lists claimant names while the final section is devoted to series. An essential reference.

4308 *Motion Pictures 1950-1959 (: Identified from the records of the U.S. Copyright Office).* 494 p. Washington, D.C.: Gov. Printing Office, 1960.

In general, the same format is used here as for the preceding volumes: title list, name index, and series list. For films after 1959 the *Library of Congress Catalog of Motion Pictures and Filmstrips* should be used. This reference is published as part of the *National Union Catalog* and is also sold separately. There are quarterly issues and/or an annual cumulation.

4309 *Motion Pictures 1960-1969: Catalog of Copyright Entries Cumulative Series. (Identified from the records of the U.S. Copyright Office.)* 744 p. paper Washington, D.C.: Government Printing Office, 1971.

This is the latest volume in the series, and the format employed for this volume is lessinformative than the ones used previously. Producer, director, and certain writing credits are omitted. Remains a necessary reference work.

4310 *Motors and Generators.* by Cameron, James R. 98 p. illus. Coral Gables, Fla.: Cameron, 1945.

The cover title reads *Motors and Motor-Generators for Projectionists.*

4311 *Mountains of Dreams: The Golden Years of Paramount Pictures.* by Halliwell, Leslie. 196 p. illus. New York: Stonehill, 1976.

Here is a disappointing account of Paramount Pictures and its founders, stars, and product. Using a chronological approach, the author devotes chapters to the stars and directors associated with Paramount —Zukor, Swanson, Crosby, Hope, Chevalier, Lubitsch, DeMille, Wilder, Sturges, Ladd, and others. The visuals, which are black-and-white line reproductions of newspaper advertisements, are initially fascinating but get monotonous quickly. The same might be said of the text.

There are some good things to be found here, but the volume is an overall failure when the wealth of material available to the author is considered. The definitive Paramount study/survey is yet to come.

4312   *Movement.* by Marey, Etienne Jules. 323 p. illus. New York: Arno, 1972 (1895).

Marey was a French scientist who was interested in the analysis of motion back in the mid-1880's. He was the first to "shoot" motion pictures with a single camera. This book, originally published in 1895, summarizes his work and thought on the subject. It has chapters on measuring time and space by photography, chronophotography, and locomotion—of man, of quadrupeds, in water and in air. A chapter on comparative locomotion also appears. Many photographs and charts help the text. Historically important.

4313   *Movement in Two Dimensions.* by Cook, Olive. 142 p. illus. London: Hutchinson, 1963.

The hundreds of years that preceded the first projected motion picture images had within them many attempts by man to create the illusion of motion. This book is an account of some of the toys, machines, gimmicks, gadgets, and attempts made prior to 1900. Amusing, informative, and clearly presented, the book also contains some very excellent illustrations. If it is used with the U.S. Navy film, THE ORIGINS OF THE MOTION PICTURE (1955), the book can be most effective. However, this book is valuable by itself. Recommended for readers interested in pre-screen history.

4314   *Movements in Animation (2 Volumes).* by Salt, Brian G. D. 535 p. illus. Elmsford, N. Y.: Pergamon, 1976.

This two-volume reference work designed for animators treats almost every form of movement. Diagrams, technical calculations, and tables abound in the set, which is intended for the professional and is quite expensive.

4315   *The Movie Ad Book.* by Vance, Malcolm. 160 p. illus. paper Minneapolis, Minn.: Control Data Publishing, 1981.

4316   *Movie and Videotape Special Effects.* by Brodbeck, Emil. 192 p. illus. Philadelphia: Chilton Books, 1968.

This work considers the entire range of special effects explaining what is possible and what is not. Equipment such as time-lapse gear units and animation machines is discussed. Special attention is given to such items as the matte box, filters, prisms, lens attachments, mirors, fog, heat, double exposures, backgrounds, animation, titles, sound, telephoto and zoom lenses, etc. A final chapter is devoted to videotape. The book is indexed. Mostly for the curious reader and the advanced or professional filmmaker.

4317   *The Movie Book.* by Jennings, Gary. 227 p. illus. New York: Dial Press, 1963.

This book is another attempt to cover the entire field of motion pictures. The range of topics is so wide that only surface attention can be given. Although the material is largely factual, an attempt at interpretation and evaluation is made. Some information is either incorrect or no longer valid and the author's opinions and emphases are often very questionable. The book is aimed at young people and, as such, is a disservice to them and to the motion picture art. Not recommended.

4318   *The Movie Book.* by Scheuer, Steven H. 384 p. illus. Chicago: Ridge/ Playboy, 1974.

Perhaps the title *The Movie Book* is an apt one, for what is offered here is a potpourri of many movie elements—history, star actors, genres, censors, production, directors, etc., with a text that is overflowing with film titles and actor names. The author manages to provide narrative linkage to the more than 400 illustrations, which are the book's major attraction.

These visuals have been selected with taste and reproduced with remarkable clarity. They constitute a truly fascinating recall of American films up to the seventies. Although the emphasis on selected genres (western, fantasy, comedy, war, musical, gangster, black) and race in films throws the over all survey a bit off balance, the production given the book compensates for the ommission of other essential elements, i.e., horror films, epic films, the film industry, etc. An index is added to what is a kind of "condensed survey" of motion pictures.

4319   *The Movie Brats.* by Pye, Michael; and Miles, Lynda. 273 p. illus. New York: Holt, Rinehart, Winston,

1979.

Subtitled "How the Film Generation Took Over Hollywood," this analysis concentrates on six new filmmakers—Francis Coppola, George Lucas, Brian De Palma, John Milius, Martin Scorsese and Steven Spielberg. The six have several common characteristics—age, a "movies" frame of reference, a Roger Corman type of training, an ability to judge the interests of today's audiences, and a sense of collaboration. The films, careers, and philosophies of each man are examined in detail and an attempt is made to explain his success.

This is one of the best written, most pertinent books on the film industry to appear in years. Its logical exposition and argument illuminates American history in general and film history specifically. The authors weave threads of art, commerce, ambition, talent, and sociology into a cohesive statement that has a discernible point of view. Changes in American sociology following World War II brought about the transfer of power from the studio moguls to the new breed of filmmaker.

4320 *The Movie Buff's Book.* edited by Sennett, Ted. 192 p. paper illus. New York: Pyramid, 1975.

Ted Sennett calls this book "An Entertainment" and that description is fitting. Divided into four general sections dealing with actors, films, theatres, and filmmakers, it includes articles ("Forgotten Movies"), quizzes, comments, biographical sketches (Margaret Hamilton), director tributes (Gregory LaCava), and many other attractions. Outstanding as always in the *Pyramid* series are the illustrations. Many are full page, most are sharply reproduced and all have been selected with intelligence and care. Answers to the quizzes appear in the back pages along with some short paragraphs about the contributing authors. In summary, this is an entertainment which educates and informs. Anyone exploring this volume will find their knowledge and understanding of films enriched to some degree. Recommended.

4321 *The Movie Buff's Book 2.* edited by Sennett, Ted. 160 p. paper illus. New York: Pyramid, 1977.

More quizzes, nostalgia, etc., in this sequel by Ted Sennett, who is the editor of the *Pyramid Illustrated History of the Movies* series.

4322 *The Movie Business: American Film Industry Practice.* edited by Bluem, A. William; and Squire, Jason E.

368 p. New York: Hastings House, 1972.

This anthology addresses itself to film considered as "a vast economic enterprise." The feature motion picture made for theatrical release is the ultimate concern of all the articles. There are sections on developing the story and screenplay, finance and budget, company management, production, distribution, and exhibition. Two concluding sections discuss the audience and the new technology.

The several articles that appear in each section have either been written specifically for this volume or adapted from previously published works. Author names are interesting and impressive: Charlton Heston, Russ Meyer, Stanley Kramer, Stirling Silliphant, Walter Reade, Jr., etc. The appendix contains excerpts from contracts of the major creative guilds (writers, directors, actors) and the craft unions (stage employees, moving picture operators). An index is also provided.

The intention of the authors is to fill the gap that exists in most college filmmaking curricula, and their selection and arrangement of material is commendable. As a text the book is a good addition to the literature and certainly belongs in university and college collections. At this point, however, it is almost the only recent volume that looks at the total industry (circa 1972) in a competent, professional manner.

4323 *The Movie Business.* by Lees, David; and Berkowitz, N. 189 p. paper New York: Vintage (Random House), 1981.

A layman's guide to the motion picture industry which explains production, finance, budgets, distribution, exhibition, etc. With its few hits and many misses, the movie business is compared to gambling.

4324 *Movie Cavalcade: the Story of the Cinema, Its Stars, Studios and Producers.* by Speed, Maurice F. 112 p. illus. London: Raven Books, 1944.

A four-part history of the cinema up to the early forties.

4325 *The Movie Collector's Catalog.* by Weiss, Ken. 160 p. paper illus. New Rochelle, N. Y.: Cummington Publishing, 1977.

Designed for film buffs and collectors, this catalog contains an abundance of information in both print and visual form. Eight general headings are offered:

Where to Buy Films, Movies Available, Publications, Projectors, Film Care, Accessories, Names of Collectors, and Rental Sources. Information given under each is representative rather than comprehensive.

Although the catalog is printed on pulp paper, the illustrations are well reproduced. Their selection is excellent, with many rare, almost forgotten performers and films shown. Prices are noted but should be used with some caution in these inflationary times.

As an introduction to all phases of film collecting, this is an admirable book. It will direct the interested reader to some of the most prominent sources that are concerned with this fascinating hobby. A most acceptable volume.

4326   *Movie Comedy.* edited by National Society of Film Critics. 308 p. New York: Grossman, 1977.

Selected, arranged, and edited by Stuart Byron and Elisabeth Weis, this anthology is concerned with film comedy. Some 25 critics offer reviews, articles, and appreciations, ranging from Mack Sennett to ONE FLEW OVER THE CUCKOO'S NEST (1976) and SEVEN BEAUTIES (1976). Their contributions are arranged under three large headings: Classical Traditions; Contemporary Trends; and European Comedy. Subheadings are also used and for each an introduction has been supplied by either Byron or Weis. Thus the Traditions section treats the silent and early sound eras, the Contemporary Trends section gives attention to spoofing, sex and marriage, and social satire, and the European section treats France, Britain, Italy, Yugoslavia, Czechoslovakia, Luis Bunuel, and Ingmar Bergman.

Because the articles have not been written specifically for this volume, there is the inevitable difficulty in mixing the styles and philosophies of 25 opinionated writers. The diverse elements do not blend into a unified statement on movie comedy. However, approached as a collection of responsible criticism dealing with a major film genre, the book has much merit. The quality of writing, the scope, the selection and the arrangement are impressive and ultimately rewarding. Recommended.

4327   *Movie Comedy Teams.* by Maltin, Leonard. 352 p. paper illus. New York: Signet, 1970.

Chapters about the famous comedy teams of motion pictures are followed by filmographies in this unusual book. Laurel and Hardy, Abbott and Costello, the Marx Brothers, Martin and Lewis, and the Ritz Brothers receive affectionate attention as do many other teams. Young author Maltin has obviously worked hard at the research and the location of stills needed for this fine paperback. Short biographies, anecdotes, plot outlines and cast listings abound.

4328   *The Movie Entertainment Industry: An Economic, Marketing, and Financial Study of the Motion Picture and Movie Theatre Market.* by Hirschhorn, S. 127 p. paper illus. New York: Morton Research, 1976.

A stock research report prepared for potential investors.

4329   *Movie Fact and Feats.* by Robertson, Patrick. 272 p. New York: Sterling, 1980.

4330   *Movie Fantastic: Beyond the Dream Machine.* by Annan, David. 132 p. paper illus. New York: Bounty/Crown, 1975.

This exploration of selected horror and science fiction films differs from other volumes in that it pays appropriate attention to historical backgrounds. The myths and legendary monsters that constitute the base on which the horror-science fiction genre rests are described with reference to cave drawings, early Indian civilizations, the Egyptian, Greek, Roman, and Oriental cultures, etc. The author employs four major headings for the discussion of the genre examples: Myths; THE CAT PEOPLE (1942), HERCULES UNCHAINED (1960), THE GOLEM (1920), etc. Machines METROPOLIS (1926), A TRIP TO THE MOON (1920), FANTASTIC VOYAGE (1966), etc. Visions; THE CABINET OF DR. CALIGARI (1919), NOSFERATU (1922), UN CHIEN ANDALOU (1929), FREAKS (1932), etc. and Nightmares; BEAUTY AND THE BEAST (1946), THE TOMB OF LIGEIA (1964), BLOOD AND ROSES (1960), THE INCREDIBLE SHRINKING MAN (1957), etc.

The titles of several thousand films in this genre can be found in the books by Donald C. Willis *Horror and Science Fiction Films,* Walt Lee's *Reference Guide to Fantastic Films,* and others. Thus the selection of films for evidence, corroboration, or analysis is wide, with many of them assignable to more than one of Annan's headings. The criteria for judging this volume rests with treatment rather than selection. Much of what the author states is subjective, debatable and often provocative, but his historical approach is different and informative. When supplemented by more than 300 illustrations which include stills, drawings, posters, museum photographs, frontispieces, postcards, etc., the total effort becomes quite impressive. Readers seemingly never tire of horror/science fiction material. The quality of this volume puts it in the acceptable category.

4331 *Movie Gallery.* compiled by Noah, Emil T., Jr. 400 p. illus. Fort Lauderdale, Fla.: Movie Ad Service, 1979.

A collection of over 1000 movie ads taken from original movie pressbooks issued by the major studios from the twenties to the seventies, this oversized volume was privately printed. Academy Award winners, collages, posters, and text accompany the illustrations.

4332 *Movie Horses: Their Treatment and Training.* by Amaral, Anthony. 160 p. illus. Indianapolis: Bobbs Merrill, 1967.

The author, a professional horse trainer, tells how horses are prepared for film work. Differentiating between horse extras, stunt horses, and horse stars, he notes the detailed training and treatment required. The work of the American Humane Society in protecting animals is applauded. Among the star animals mentioned and pictured are Misty, Rex, Francis, Tony (Tom Mix), Champion (Gene Autry), Trigger (Roy Rogers), Fritz (William S. Hart), and Mr. Ed of television.

4333 *Movie Humor Anthology.* edited by Gordon, R. F. 2 volumes New York: Gordon Press, 1976.

4334 *The Movie Industry Book: How Others Made and Lost Money in the Movie Industry.* by Minus, Johnny; and Hale, William Storm. 601 p. illus. Hollywood, Calif.: Seven Arts Press, 1970.

This cynical, tongue-in-cheek book designed for industry professionals includes material on putting a picture together; partnership; contracts—with samples reproduced; financing; budgets; censorship; distribution practices; and copyright. In addition there is a long facetious section of book reviews unlike any you've read before. The trade press and magazines receive a share of attention also. Even sections of Robert Osborne's *Academy Awards* are reprinted again. (Could Osborne be one of the authors?) There is much inside information given here—and after the reader adjusts to the sometimes outrageous style and format, the book is surprisingly rewarding.

4335 *Movie Journal: The Rise of the American Cinema,* 1959-1971. by Mekas, Jonas. 434 p. New York: Macmillan, 1972.

When Mekas began writing his weekly columns for *The Village Voice*, he considered both the commercial film and the experimental film. Since his passion was for the latter film form, he relinquished the commercial film assignments to Andrew Sarris and concentrated on the New American Cinema. This anthology consists of about one-third of the *Voice* columns from the period 1959-1971.

Mekas is a beautiful self-creation. An individual who writes in a conversational style flavored with charm, anger, pity and rage, he is opinionated and defensive at times, openminded and receptive at others. He is never dull. Readers unfamiliar with the American Experimental film may find some of the topics remote and of little interest, but anyone who has followed the growth and development of this film movement will be fascinated.

A fine collection of film writing that will have much appeal for a special audience. The index is a decided asset.

4336 *Movie Lot to Beachhead.* edited by *Look* Magazine Staff. 292 p. illus. Garden City, N.Y.: Doubleday, Doran, 1945.

The various activities of the American motion picture industry during World War II are detailed in this picture book. Some attempt to treat film as a social weapon or document is made but only superficially. It is the photographs rather than the text which provide interest here. Feature films, documentaries and newsreels are mentioned, and a final section deals with films for classroom use. Past history but still absorbing material for many readers.

4337 *Movie Mad America.* by Harding, Ulla E. 55 p. paper Grand Rapids, Mich.: Zondervan, 1942.

An indictment of the movies that uses predictable topics for argument—sex, crime, delinquency, morals, alcohol, film quality, lack of social responsibility, etc.

4338 *Movie-Made America: A Cultural History of American Movies.* by Sklar, Robert. 341 p. paper illus. New York: Vintage, 1975.

Another retelling of the history of the motion pictures in America, this solid scholarly volume differs in its approach and style. The author is interested in showing the effect of film on audiences, and conversely the shaping of films by audience taste and interest. Acknowledging film to be a popular art that was first designed by non-elitist moguls for a blue-collar mass audience, Sklar traces the rise of American film from the nickelodeon to the golden era, and then to the eventual dissolution of Hollywood.

The serious, almost pedantic, text is a combination of sociology, economics and film criticism, with the latter being the most impressive element of the three. Illustrations, a bibliography, and an index are added.

A worthwhile historical survey that describes both America and its films.

4339 *Movie Magic: The Story of Special Effects in the Cinema.* by Bosnan, John. 285 p. illus. New York: St. Martin's Press, 1974.

Other volumes have treated the topic of special effects—but this book combines a historical narrative survey along with some clear non-technical explanations not found in the other books. The men who created past screen miracles are noted throughout. An introductory section defines special effects and is followed by a chapter dealing with pioneers such as Melies, G. A. Smith, Edwin Porter, Norman Dawn, Charles Rosher, Eugene Shuftan and others. The sound period which followed is surveyed next, with particular attention given to the fifties and sixties. Later chapters consider cartoons with live action, war films, model animation, science fiction films, space trip films, etc.

In closing chapters the state of the art today is discussed along with predictions for the future. Supplementing this rich survey are some notes on the creative filmmakers mentioned in the text, a listing of Academy Award nominations and winners for special effects from 1939 to 1973, a short bibliography and an index. The selection of the many illustrations is fine but their reproduction is often disappointing.

A fascinating subject has been handled with careful competence in this volume. The scope, treatment and arrangement of the material are of a calibre that makes the volume enormously entertaining and informative. Highly recommended.

4340 *Movie Make-Up Manual.* by Oldridge, Harry B. 45 p. illus. New York: Sorg, 1927.

4341 *Movie Makers.* by Floherty, John J. 100 p. illus. Garden City, N.Y.:

Doubleday, 1935.

A gee-whiz account of moviemaking (in the thirties) designed for young readers. The text and illustrations make the industry seem quite glamorous.

4342 *The Movie Makers.* by Chaneles, Sol; and Wolsky, Albert. 544 p. illus. Secaucus, N.J.: Derbibooks, 1974.

More than 1000 photographs, including 16 pages of color portraits, accompany this biographical dictionary of over 2500 cinema personalities. About 500 pages are devoted to performers, while the remainder of the book is given to directors and a name index, provided presumably for cross-listing. Each entry gives performer name, birth date, death date where applicable, a paragraph or two of capsulized biography and a listing of selected films. This latter feature is called by various names: films, distinguished films, some of her films, his films include, highlights, credits include, notable credits, major credits, etc. The variety of titles gives evidence of the subjectivity and lack of completeness of the film titles listed.

A reading of the first section of the book uncovers various errors. On page 14—on Broadway, June Allyson was Betty Hutton's understudy in "Panama Hattie" not in "Best Foot Forward"; Allyson did not play the star role in "Best Foot Forward," but was only a featured player. Page 9—the musical "Wonderful Town" was based primarily on the play "My Sister Eileen" and it was not a revival. Page 12—Robert Alda was famous for his portrayal of George Gershwin in RHAPSODY IN BLUE (1944) long before "he became known to the public" in the stage musical, "Guys and Dolls" (1950), a vehicle which provided employment for a fading film actor. Later portions are equally suspect. On page 484—Erich von Stroheim first worked in Hollywood as an extra in THE BIRTH OF A NATION (1914)—not in the "long gone 20s." Page 507—Ingmar Bergman's pictures "have just one element in common: the camera work is invariably dazzling"; the camera work in most of Bergman's films is unobtrusive and anything but "dazzling."

It is unfortunate that such an attractive book did not receive more careful editing by competent historians. Although it presents an abundance of information in both text and visuals, the editing and selectivity weaken any great enthusiasm one might feel for it. Acceptable.

4343 *The Movie Makers: Artists in an Industry.* by Phillips, Rev. Gene D. 249 p. illus. Chicago: Nelson-Hall, Co., 1973.

This handsomely produced volume explores the work of a dozen directors and one cameraman, all of whom have received attention in earlier books. The author discusses James Wong Howe, Charlie Chaplin, Howard Hawks, George Cukor, George Stevens, Fred Zinnemann, and Stanley Kubrick in the American section. Carol Reed, David Lean, Joseph Losey, Bryan Forbes, John Schlesinger and Ken Russell are treated in the second section, "Movie Makers in Britain."

Each essay gives some career history, cites a few recurring themes, and devotes major attention to a discussion of the subject's films. In almost every case, the author has had personal contact with his subjects and this material along with his research has served him well. A simple filmography concludes each section. Many fine illustrations, including both stills and candids, appear throughout. Notes, a selected bibliography, and an index conclude the book.

Combining scholarship, personal experience and an ability to write in an entertaining, nonpedantic manner, the author has provided a fresh look at some familiar material. In addition, the production provided is most handsome, indicating a care and control lacking in many of today's publications. These factors combined with the appeal of the subjects to most readers give this book a highly recommended status.

4344 *Movie Makers (A Series).* illus. London: Macmillan, 1974- .

This series deals with some legendary film names. Published thus far are: Marlon Brando, Humphrey Bogart, and Charlie Chaplin. Announced for publication are: Alfred Hitchcock and Laurence Olivier.

4345 *Movie Making.* by Coynik, David. 240 p. paper illus. Chicago: Loyola University Press, 1974.

This "Student Work Text for Super 8 Film Production" contains units on equipment, planning, shooting, lighting, editing, sound and special effects. A glossary and a bibliography are also included. Each unit is subdivided into smaller subtopics. For example, the unit on shooting is divided into using the camera, moving the camera, and titles and fades. In addition to the units which comprise the text, five types of suggested activities appear throughout the book. They deal with visual perception, recall, investigation, experimentation and filmmaking.

Many visuals are used to explain, interpret or expand the text. All are well selected and have been reproduced with adequate size and clarity. A teacher's guide is available to accompany the student work text. It offers suggestions; exercises; information on materials, films, equipment, etc., that might be used in the course. The volume continually evidences an educator's concern for providing information, activities and encouragement to his pupil. This is not surprising since it is based on the author's experience in teaching filmmaking to a wide range of students.

It contains well-selected material arranged in a logical way and presented with interest and intelligence. Production quality is well above average and the supporting teacher's guide is most helpful. This volume on amateur super 8 filmmaking is one of the best to appear so far. Highly recommended.

4346 *Movie Making: A Guide to Film Production.* by Glimcher, Sumner; and Johnson, Warren. 288 p. paper illus. New York: Pocket Books, 1975.

An exposition of the basic procedures necessary to make films is offered by this volume. Basic principles of cinematography, planning, the camera, the lens, light shooting, animation, editing, and projection are among the topics treated in individual chapters. An appendix on preparing material for the sound mix, a glossary and an index complete the volume. More than 100 illustrations and diagrams are used to complement the narrative. Reproduction in most cases is adequate.

The text is written in comprehensible, businesslike fashion and offers a large quantity of information, advice, and example. In addition to all its other virtues, the book has a very modest price. Not only will it serve the individual reader, but also it can be used effectively as a class text for filmmaking and film study courses. Recommended.

4347 *Movie-Making As a Pastime.* by Bateman, Robert. 128 p. paper illus. London: Souvenir, 1960.

This volume on cinematography includes a bibliography.

4348 *Movie Making for the Beginner.* by McKay, Herbert C. 96 p. paper illus. Chicago: Ziff-Davis, 1939.

A title on cinematography from the *Little Technical Library* series that was revised and updated several times.

4349 *Movie Making for the Young Cameraman.* by Catling, Gordon; and Serjeant, Richard. 128 p. illus. New

Rochelle, N.Y.: Leisure Time, 1965.

Information for beginning filmmakers on equipment, scenarios, lighting, exposures, projection, titling, etc. Indexed.

4350 *Movie Making in 18 Lessons.* by Cushman, George. 128 p. paper illus. New York: Amphoto, 1971.

Each of these 18 lessons is composed of several paragraphs following an opening explanatory statement. The paragraphs, which are alphabetically numbered, present a single concept, idea, or technique that can be understood when taken out of context. The format resembles an outline that has been filled in.

When it is expanded to a narrative form in the book, it takes almost five pages. Lesson titles are standard —lenses, titles, lighting, editing, sound, etc. The illustrations, charts, and diagrams are most helpful. This is a sort of programmed approach that simplifies the process of filmmaking. It is readable, helpful, and informative. Recommended.

4351 *Movie Man.* by Thomson, David. 233 p. illus. New York: Stein & Day, 1967.

The man of the title is possibly the person who directs, acts in, is a character from, and/or is influenced by movies. These roles are considered by the author who suggests that just as there was a Stone Age Man or a Renaissance Man, today's individual can be called a Movie Man. Using elements of film—cinematography, screen, location, character, and narrative—the title theme is developed.

Most challenging and unusual, this book makes a valid argument concerning the effect of film on the individual and society. The examples used are well-selected and persuasive. Photographs are interesting and reproduced with care. A filmography of directors mentioned in the text is also included. This is somewhat advanced material, but because of the high quailty of the presentation, the book is recommended for most readers.

4352 *Movie Merry-Go-Round.* by Carstairs, John Paddy. 240 p. illus. London: Newnes, 1937.

Introduced by Madeleine Carroll, this volume is a general discussion of studio filmmaking. It includes sections on directing, editing, photography, costumes, animation, writing, etc. Besides the author, there are contributions by Adrian (costumes), Hans Dreier (art direction), Percy Westmore (makeup),

Jessie Matthews (acting), Joan Crawford(acting), Douglas Shearer (sound), Ivor Montagu (German film industry), and Adrian Brunel (general summary).

4353 *The Movie Moguls.* by French, Philip. 170 p. illus. Chicago: Regnery. 1969.

Many of the same subjects that appear in Zierold's book *The Moguls* are profiled in this volume—Cohn, DeMille, Disney, Goldwyn, Hughes, Mayer, Selznik, Wanger, Warner Bros., Zanuck. They are generalized as early victims who suffered discrimination all of their lives. The image given of them is largely negative. They contributed little to the art of film with the exception of their ability to gauge mass taste and to sense talent in performers. A well-written, sharp, fascinating look at some unattractive lengends.

4354 *Movie Monsters.* by Gifford, Denis. 159 p. paper illus. New York: Dutton, 1969.

Another fine contribution to film books, this one explores the monsters of film—vampires, golems, mummies, werewolves, etc. Each category is given special attention via text and illustrations. While the coverage may not be as complete as that in other similar volumes, the quality of both the narrative and the pictures make this small volume one of the best. The reader will be well acquainted with the monster genre after reading it.

The production is excellent and imaginative, at times using a process which creates a black and white drawing from a photograph. A filmography for each type of monster is appended. There is no index. Anyone interested in film will find this book entertaining, fascinating, and rewarding to read. Its popularity with the general audience is quite predictable. Highly recommended.

4355 *Movie Monsters.* by Aylesworth, Thomas G. 79 p. paper illus. Philadelphia: J. B. Lippincott, 1975.

Designed for the juvenile audience, this volume is composed of individual chapters devoted to selected movie monsters—King Kong, Godzilla, Frankenstein's Creature, the Wolf Man, the Mummy, the Fly, Dracula, the Bride of Frankenstein, Mr. Hyde, the Invisible Man, and Doctor Moreau's Creatures. Final chapters consider "copycat" versions of famous mosters along with some actors famous for their portrayal of monsters. A short filmography and an index complete the book. The many visuals which appear throughout the book are well selected and clearly reproduced.

Aylesworth is on sure ground by calling the monsters from classic films "The Greatest..." and the text he supplies to justify the billing is most appropriate. However, the question must be raised about the exhaustion of material in the horror film genre. Is there nothing else about classic films or film genres that might appeal to a juvenile audience? There must be something somewhere. Acceptable for young people.

4356 *Movie Monsters and their Masters: The Birth of the Horror Film.* by Quackenbush, Robert. Chicago: Albert Whitman, 1980.

A slight overview of the horror film genre designed for young readers.

4357 *The Movie Murder Mystery Quiz Book—Fifty Years /of /Whodunits.* by Howard, John M. 160 p. illus. paper San Diego, Calif.: A. S. Barnes, 1981.

4358 *The Movie Musical.* by Stern, Lee Edward. 160 p. paper illus. New York: Pyramid, 1974.

A chronological survey of the musical film genre is provided in this attractive volume. Using the twenties as a preview, the author singles out the two decades from 1930 to 1950 as the major period of the musical. The fifties signalled the end of the Hollywood musical; those that have appeared during the last 15 years were too large in size and too small in creative expression. Much of the content here is predictable, but Stern's handling of the familiar material is intelligent and, at times, quite subjective. Illustrations have been selected to show the evolution of style in the Hollywood musical and to recall many performers in famous singing/dancing roles. A bibliography (how could the author fail to include John Springer's *All Talking, All Singing, All Dancing!*) a filmography, and an index complete this pleasant volume. Acceptable.

4359 *The Movie Musical from Vitaphone to* 42ND STREET. edited by Kreuger, Miles. 367 p. paper illus. New York: Dover, 1975.

After several years of announcements of a book on the Hollywood musical by Miles Kreuger, one has finally appeared. Although it apparently is not the long-awaited work mentioned above, it is a most welcome addition to the literature on this film genre. Covering only a very short period (1926 to 1933) the text consists of articles, reviews, and illustrations taken from *Photoplay* magazine. All the musical films produced during this period are covered in chronological fashion with detailed cast listings and selected production credits. In addition, the author has selected articles about performers, the sound process, dubbing voices, and other topics pertinent to the early sound period.

Aside from a short introduction, Kreuger's responsibility has been one of selection; he has performed this function with distinction. Nostalgia predominates and the many familiar names active during this period, almost half a century ago, will please most readers or browsers. The researcher will discover an abundance of information conveniently arranged for retrieval by the chronological structure and two indexes—one for film titles, the second for personalities. The hundreds of visuals, including illustrations, portraits, publicity layouts, etc., are all well chosen and nicely reproduced. Film music is given special attention via the reproduction of a year (1929-1930) of record reviews. Every element of this volume is rewarding and all concerned with its production are to be applauded; it is a fine book. Highly recommended.

4360 *Movie Palaces: Survivors of an Elegant Era.* by Smith, Lucinda. illus: New York: Crown, 1979.

Affection for a disappearing form of architecture, the movie palace, is expressed via 181 color photographs by Ave Pildas and a text by Lucinda Smith. The latter provides an anecdotal history while Pildas attempts to photograph many of the still existing film temples before they become victims of a wrecking crew. The lobbies, ornamentation, organs, lounges, and much of the lush grandeur of a doomed architectural species is recalled.

4361 *Movie Parade: A Pictorial Survey of the World Cinema (1888-1949).* by Rotha, Paul; and Manvell, Roger. 160 p. illus. London: Studio Pub., 1950.

A revised edition of an earlier picture book by Rotha, this one includes an exceptional colletion of stills.

4362 *Movie People.* edited by Baker, Fred; and Firestone, Rose. 193 p. illus. New York: Douglas Book Corp., 1972.

Each chapter in this volume represents one step in the total process of making a feature film. The pre-production section deals with the producer (Roger Lewis) and the distributor (David Picker). Production chores are divided between the director (Sidney Lumet, Frances Ford Coppola), the screen writer (Terry Southern, James Salter), the actor (Rod Steiger), the editor (Aram Avakian) and the composer (Quincy Jones). After the film is released, the exhibitor (Walter Reade, Jr.) and the critic (Andrew Sarris) begin their work.

Inspired by a series of lectures, the individual presentations were edited, updated and augmented by adding some missing elements. For each of the contributors there is an introductory page which contains a small picture, some biographical data and a filmography. The articles are uniformly interesting, but because of the disparate experiences, the book does not have the unity it might have had if all had been working together on the same film. Taken as an anthology rather than a unified work, the book is more than satisfying.

4363   *The Movie Poster Book.* by Shapiro, Steve; and Chierichetti, David. 95 p. paper illus. New York: Dutton.

More than 100 movie posters, covering the period 1896-1955, are presented in this attractive book. An historical essay about posters introduces the collection, which is arranged almost chronologically. All the posters are in full color and have been reproduced with care. The selection is a fascinating one, offering both pop art and film information to the reader. A great deal of visual pleasure and nostalgia is offered. Recommended.

4364   *The Movie Quiz Book.* by Vance, Malcolm Frederick. 240 p. paper illus. New York: Paperback Library, 1970.

This book 1500 questions about films, actors, awards, songs and other film topics. Fun and games with film trivia, this volume is not essential in any way, but is still quite entertaining.

4365   *The Movie Quote Book.* compiled by Haun, Harry. 432 p. New York: Lippincott and Crowell, 1980.

This is collection of thousands of movie "quotes" arranged under several hundred subject headings. The number of "quotes" under each head ranges from about 5 to 25, and some cross-referencing is provided.

4366   *The Movie Rating Game.* by Farber, Stephen. 128 p. Washington, D. C.: Public Affairs Press, 1972.

An examination and critique of the movie rating system that came into being after the abolishment of the Code. A brief opening traces the history from censorship to code to the current rating or classification system. The thin line between a GP and an R rating is discussed. Other aspects of the system are evaluated and the total result is quite negative. Some appendixes are included. Most persons concerned with film are aware of the message of this book, but for the uninformed it may be useful.

4367   *Movie Reader.* edited by Cameron, Ian. 120 p. illus. New York: Praeger, 1972.

The first item of interest in this book appears opposite the title page: a summary chart by the editorial board of *Movie* evaluating directors. Since all the articles in this reader are from the magazine, the chart gives some indication of the content to follow.

The principles of the "auteur" theory are evident in the selection and content of the articles. Alfred Hitchcock and Howard Hawks (chart rating: great) are recognized by several articles, as are Otto Preminger, Nicholas Ray, Joseph Losey (brilliant). Appreciated but rated lower are Michael Powell (competent or ambitious), Frank Tashlin (very talented). Two directors—von Sternberg and Chabrol—do not appear on the chart but are given article treatment. Reviews and discussions of some specific films close the book.

The periodical *Movie* was initiated to offer some balance to the one-sided bias of the French Cahiers school of film criticism. Its aim was the critical recognition of underrated American and British directors and their films. The above rational explains most satisfactorily this book and its organization and content. Since writers such as Ian Cameron, Paul Mayersberg, Robin Wood, and Raymond Durgnant are each represented by several pieces, the high quality of the writing will be obvious to anyone familiar with cinema literature. Picture quality varies from excellent to some poorly reproduced illustrations that are far too dark and murky. Although the emphasis is on directors who are already well represented in print analyses, the freshness of approach here is sufficient to invite reader attention. Recommended.

4368   *Movie Special Effects.* by Rovin, Jeff. 171 p. illus. New York: A. S. Barnes, 1977.

Jeff Rovin continues the investigation into special effects that he began in *Those Fabulous Fantasy Films, From The Land Beyond Beyond*, and *A Pictorial History of Science Fiction Films*. Since these three earlier books were done for different publishers, there is some slight evidence of recycling the same material—Willis O'Brien, KING KONG (1933), the films of Ray Harryhausen, Melies, George Pal, etc. The avid buff will have encountered some of this text before.

The author's approach here is chronological, beginning with Melies and ending with the films of the present space age, 1960-75. A very short section on television films, a few chapter notes, and an index complete the book. Illustrations include both stills and production shots showing the special effects methods.

Rovin attempts to balance some of the technical detail involved in special effects with recollections of the films' contents. The result is an informative, readable explanation that will satisfy a wide audience. Acceptable.

4369   *Movie-Star Portraits of the Forties.* edited by Kobal, John. 162 p. paper illus. New York: Dover, 1977.

With this volume the publishers, assisted by John Kobal, present a beautifully selected and reproduced collection of 163 studio portraits. Limiting the subjects to the forties, Kobal provides a colorful recollection of that decade—the end of Hollywood's Golden Age. Arranged in a rough chronological order, the pictures begin with the famous Betty Grable over-the-shoulder pin-up pose of 1941 to a belligerent smouldering Marlon Brando in 1950.

As indicated, the reproduction of the portraits has been done with loving attention and care. Noted beneath each is the subject's name, the date, the photographer and the studio.

This volume can be considered a multi-purpose one; it can be used as a gift, as publicity material for film showings, as a still photography manual, as display material, or simply as a visual feast that will attract a variety of audiences. Hightly recommended.

4370   *The Movie Stars.* by Griffith, Richard. 512 p. illus. New York: Doubleday, 1970.

Here is another massive Griffith collection of pictures, history, observation, comment, and gossip, this time devoted to stars and the rise and fall of the system in which they functioned. Since celebrities/stars are an essential part of our culture, this detailed study of the qualities, the makers, and the personali-

ties who comprise the star system can be accepted as much more than a mere picture book.

Exciting material is present in abundance, and the book is indexed. Almost 600 illustrations taken mostly from the Museum of Modern Art collection of stills, posters, and candids, a joyous text written with affection by Griffith, and a nicely designed production all blend to make this an outstanding volume.

4371   *Movie Stars in Bathtubs.* compiled by Scagnetti, Jack. 160 p. illus. Middle Village, N.Y.: Jonathan David, 1975.

This volume is a collection of performer stills which has as its unifying theme bathing and the bathtub. Scagnetti has provided a short introduction which indicates the rationale for this book to be "good clean fun." Any sexual connotation between the bath and its associated nudity is avoided although bathtub scenes were almost always used for sexual titillation or comedy based upon exposure of the naked person.

For convenience the visuals are divided into chapters featuring females, males, males and females together, comics, and finally, children and animals. An index is provided. Picture reproduction is acceptable but selection and identification are often weak.

This volume is for the impulse reader-viewer who may be snared by its title or a rapid browsing of its contents. Considered as such, it is acceptable.

4372   *Movie Stars, Real People and Me.* by Logan, Joshua. 368 p. illus. New York: Delacorte, 1978.

One of the most rewarding discoveries for a reader is the author who is not only a great storyteller, but also has an abundant supply of personal experiences to relate. Joshua Logan is a superb raconteur whose life has been filled with the matters of Broadway and Hollywood. Along the way he has known/worked with many famous personalities including Garbo, Brando, Monroe, Bette Davis, Vanessa Redgrave, and Kim Novak. His first volume, *Josh*, was straightforward autobiography and took the reader up to an invitation to direct PICNIC in 1956. This book covers the period that follows and, rather than narrative autobiography, offers a joyous mixture of anecdotes, opinions, facts, gossip and memories. Logan is lavish with his praise and affection for actors, but he is also not at all hesitant to discuss in detail those personalities with whom he had difficulty: Bette Davis, Alan Jay Lerner, Paddy Chayefsky, Al

Freeman, Jr., etc. Illustrations, a Logan chronology, and an index are included in this entertainment, which should be irresistible to anyone interested in Broadway and Hollywood stories. Recommended.

4373 *Movie Stunts and the People Who Do Them.* by Miklowitz, Gloria D. 64 p. paper illus. New York: Harcourt, Brace, Jovanovich, 1980.

An account of that group of daring people whose profession consists of designing and performing stunts for films is given here. Designed for young readers, the text discusses the people, their preparations for a stunt, specific stunts, the annual stunt competition, how stunts are done, getting started, and some questions and answers about stunting. An index and some illustrations support the text.

The subject is fascinating for readers of any age, and the production treatment found here is above average.

4374 *Movie Techniques for the Advanced Amateur.* by Regnier, George; and Matzkin, Myron. 160 p. illus. New York: Amphoto, 1959.

The usual steps in filmmaking are described: shooting, scripting, lighting, direction, etc. Aimed at the more experienced or serious amateur.

4375 *Movie Trivia! Everything You Always Knew About Movies But Thought You Forgot.* by Andree, Mary. 72 p. paper Bellvue, Penn.: Pohl Associates, 1977.

4376 *Movie Workers.* edited by Keliher, Alice. 56 p. illus. New York: Harper, 1939.

A children's picture book about movie-making presented in a rather elementary fashion. The photographs make it worthwhile.

4377 *Movie World Almanac 1982-83.* by Baer, D. Richard. 360 p. illus. Hollywood, Calif.: Hollywood Film Archives, 1981.

4378 *The Movie World of Roger Corman.* edited by di Franco, J. Phillip. 269 p. illus. New York: Chelsea House, 1980.

An oversized scrapbook devoted to the life and ca-

reer of Roger Corman. Included are comments by Corman, his co-workers, posters, reviews, stills, a filmography, script excerpts, and other material pertinent to an appreciation of this unusual filmmaker, who has served as director, producer, distributor and teacher.

4379 *Movieland.* by Gomez de la Serna, Ramon. 273 p. New York: Macaulay, 1930.

A translation by Angel Flores of the Spanish book, *Cinelandia.*

4380 *The Moviemaker's Handbook.* edited by Wordsworth, Christopher. 320 p. illus. New York: Ziff-Davis, 1979.

This handsome, well-organized volume carries the subtitle "The Professional Guide to Making Perfect Home Movies." Divided into two parts, the text first considers the materials (films, camera, accessories, etc.) and then the processes of filmmaking (script, direction, production, sound, effects, etc.). Using nontechnical explanations along with hundreds of correlated illustrations, the authors provide a solid base for the amateur filmmaker. Practical advice such as the use of a medical wheelchair to make tracking shots is included throughout. A glossary and an index complete the book.

The superb production given this volume is compatible with its contents. Presented in a variety of attractive type styles, the text is informative, practical and comprehensive. Visuals appear in both color and black and white along with easy-to-read charts, diagrams, and schematics. All these elements combine to make this an outstanding book on filmmaking.

4381 *The Moviemakers.* by Fleming, Alice. 184 p. illus. New York: St. Martin's Press, 1973.

Here is a collective biography written for young people which carries the subtitle, "A History of American Movies Through the Lives of The Great Directors." However, there are really eleven subjects; presented in chronological fashion, they are: Edwin S. Porter, D. W. Griffith, Mack Sennett, Cecil B. DeMille, Robert Flaherty, Ernst Lubitsch, Frank Capra, John Ford, Walt Disney, Alfred Hitchcock, and Stanley Kubrick. Each is represented by a single chapter and a few illustrations. A bibliography and an index are included.

Several reservations about the volume should be noted. Other than the chronological arrangement, there is little connecting narrative provided and the historical aspect is minimized in the life stories presented. However, even these sketches are very partial and fragmented—i.e., the periods in the Lubitsch section jump from 1923 to 1933 to 1938 then back to 1931. Since no filmographies are included, it is difficult to comprehend the filmmaker's career/contribution with clarity. For example, a comparison of Ford's copious output with Kubrick's few films is impossible without filmographies.

The volume provides interesting but selected coverage of a representative group of American directors. Although it does little to depict any "history" of American film, it may serve as a motivation for young readers to seek out more detailed comprehensive accounts. Acceptable.

4382 *Moviemaking: A Guide for Beginners.* by Levine, Michael L. paper illus. New York: Charles Scribner's, 1980.

An illustrated guide designed for the young reader, this volume describes the amateur filmmaking process from story planning and rehearsal through the filming, editing and sound addition.

4383 *Moviemaking: A guide for Beginners.* by Levine, Michael L. 48 p. illus. New York: Scribner's, 1980.

A guide to filmmaking designed for youngreaders.

4384 *Moviemaking Illustrated: The Comic Book Filmbook.* by Morrow, James; and Suid, Murray. 150 p. paper illus. Rochelle Park, N.J.: Hayden, 1973.

An unusual approach to explaining filmmaking terms is employed in this volume. Names, procedures and techniques are described by both words and pictures—the pictures in this instance being frames or panels of selected comic strips. Each frame indicates a different camera setup and the reader is advised to "watch the book" rather than read it. Sections are devoted to stories, shots, cuts, sound and actors. Several practice exercises are suggested and some common errors are noted at the book's conclusion. A sample shooting script entitled "Robot on the Range" is added and the volume is indexed.

Although the idea of using comic strips to explain filmmaking terms appeared in Kuhn's *Exploring the Film* and probably earlier, there is no current text that develops the analogy with the clarity and efficiency evident here. Major points are covered most adequately and the reader can obtain a basic knowl-

edge of filmmaking terms with ease and pleasure. Although is was designed as a high school text, the range of appeal for this volume is wide and it can be recommended for others.

4385 *The Movies.* by Griffith, Richard; and Mayer, Arthur. 442 p. illus. New York: Simon & Schuster, 1957.

What starts out as a usual history of motion pictures changes at times into a series of topics relating to film which are treated historically. For example, in the section on "The Fight," stills from many sound motion pictures are combined with silent film illustrations; thus we have an interrupted time continuum, bouncing among four decades. In the section which follows, the historical narrative line is picked up again and carried forth. While this is a unique approach, it may be a bit confusing for the novice reader interested in screen history.

The selection of stills in the book is not beyond criticism. Many famous films and personalities are omitted. However, many of the ones that are used are quite rare, while others seemingly were taken directly from film frames. The text is intelligent and readable although there is more apparent scholarship in the silent era sections than with the more recent films. Sections on Tab Hunter and Kim Novak seem relatively unimportant today. In spite of these reservations, the book offers many rewards. It is not a basic book, but it has a reference value. Note: a revised, updated edition appeared in 1970. A few deletions (e.g., Tab Hunter) and some additions (Bogart, Monroe, Hepburn, a second preface) cover the sixties.

4386 *The Movies: An American Idiom; Readings in the Social History of the American Motion Picture.* edited by McClure, Arthur F. 440 p. Cranbury, N.J.: Fairleigh Dickinson University Press, 1971.

The editor has taken this collection of essays from many unusual and different sources. Authorship includes historians (Ramsaye), critics (Alpert), film stars (DeHavilland), humorists (Newhart), novelists (Markfield) and others. It is an expensive book and examination is suggested before purchase. The quality of the author's earlier film volumes offers little reassurance for this anthology.

4387 *Movies: A Psychological Study.* by Wolfenstein, Martha; and Leites, Nathan. 316 p. illus. Glencoe, Ill.: The Free Press, 1950.

The authors look at certain American films (up to 1950) to determine the "recurrent day-dreams" presented to the minds of the viewers. Recurring patterns in the categories of love, violence, and family relationships are discerned and comparisons with British and French films are made. The concluding attempt to summarize the findings is not totally successful.

4388 *Movies: The Universal Language.* by Sullivan, Sister Bede. 160 p. paper South Bend, Ind.: Fides Press, 1967.

Based on a program offered in a Kansas City High School where the author is Head of the English Department, this book outlines an 18 session course of about 36 total hours. In addition, a semester course of short films, film festivals, and movie production is discussed. Along with providing the rationale and procedure for a film study course, the author relates some of her experiences in teaching film to students of all ages.

4389 *The Movies: A Picture Quiz Book.* by Appelbaum, Stanley; and Cirker, Hayward. 244 p. paper illus. New York: Dover Publications, 1972.

Here is a sleeper of a film book. Intended for a specialized audience, it has value and pleasure for a much larger group. The reader who ignores the quiz format and simply browses through the admirable collection of stills will be exposed to a short, selected pictorial chronology of outstanding films from the period of 1900 to 1960. The quality of picture reproduction here puts many higher priced volumes to shame. Selection is thorough and covers all genres and major personalities. In addition, the book has two indexes, one for performers and one for film titles.

The quiz format may result in greater sales but it is an added attraction, not the main feature. Questions are posed in a serious but provocative paragraph or so. Answers are found in an informative listing near the book's closing pages. Highly recommended.

4390 *The Movies.* by Marshall Cavendish Editorial Advisory Board. 64 p. illus. London: Marshall Cavendish, 1970.

This short historical survey of film is divided into the following chapters: 1. Introduction, 2. Film for Art's Sake, 3. Hollywood's First Boom, 4. Hollywood's Heyday, 5. Life on the Screen, 6. Cinema Comes of Age, and 7. Script to Screen.

4391 *The Movies.* by Myers, Bernard L. 64 p. paper illus. London: Marshall Cavendish, 1970.

A short discussion of how movies are made, along with a brief history of the medium. Some of the illustrations are in color and the book is indexed.

4392 *Movies and Censorship.* by Crowther, Bosley. 28 p. paper New York: Public Affairs Committee, 1962.

The then film critic of the *New York Times* offers some comments on the question of censorship.

4393 *Movies and Conduct.* by Blumer, Herbert. 257 p. New York: Arno Press, 1970 (1933).

This Payne Study first published in 1933 concerns itself with the influence of film on the conduct of youth (excluding sex life). Children were asked to describe certain experiences connected with the viewing of films. The statements were interpreted and some generalizations were made. The techniques of this study are questionable.

4394 *Movies and How They Are Made.* by Manchel, Frank. 71 p. illus. Englewood Cliffs, N.J.: Prentice-Hall, 1968.

This delightful book is designed for students in grades three to seven but many readers beyond those grades will enjoy it. Using a blend of line drawings and an intelligent text which is never condescending, Manchel manages to inform, teach, and entertain. Such terms as "mass entertainment," "treatment," "associate producer," "unit manager," and so on are defined and explained with economy and clarity. The book treats all of the elements of filmmaking—budgets, scripts, schedules, shooting, locations, music and preview. A glossary and an index complete the volume. The line drawings by Kelly Mark throughout are most appropriate for the intended audience, relying on subtlety rather than exaggeration. Highly recommended for intermediate and junior high grades, and others may want to consider it, too.

4395 *Movies and Methods.* edited by Nichols, Bill. 640p. paper illus. Berkeley: University of California Press, 1977.

This anthology has been designed as a text for film study and treats its subject by presenting newer approaches to film analysis. Sections on political, genre, feminist, auteur and mis-en-scene criticism are followed by concluding sections on film theory and structuralism-semiology. Each section offers six or more articles which have been taken mostly from recent periodicals. They are well selected and arranged in the semiology section, they build sequentially, with each article enlarging some idea previously presented. A short introduction is provided to each of the major sections; a glossary and an index are also included.

The volume is an excellent collection for the reader/student with a background of film experience and study. It is not for the general or casual reader, since many of the films, terms, and ideas demand a strong basic familiarity for full comprehension of the articles in which they appear. Recommended.

4396 *Movies and Monasteries in U.S.A.* by Upson, Wilfrid. 91 p. illus. Glouster: Prink Nash Abbey, 1950.

The author is an English reverend who spent a short period in the United States visiting monasteries and Hollywood. His observations about the film studios and some film personalities are noted.

4397 *Movies and Morals.* by Schillaci, Anthony. 181 p. paper Notre Dame, Ind.: Fides, 1970.

The main thesis of this small but vital book is "that motion pictures, rather than being an object of fear and suspicion as far as morals are concerned, are in fact a vital source of emotional maturity and moral sensitivity." Using topics such as a new kind of cinema, art and morality, film as modern man's morality play, religion and film, and cultural exorcism, the author argues for a knowledgeable use of films rather than their dismissal as entertainment or depravity. The author's style is persuasive, personal, and dedicated. His belief in his cause is evident, yet the pitfall of sermonizing has been avoided.

The appendices are commendable, too. There are some examples of workshops on the use of film; a paperback bibliography; a few sample film series; and a filmography for religious topics, moral problems, and the human condition. A final section lists the major distributors of films. Although the book has a religious origin, there is so much of value and quality here that the book has pertinence for anyone who uses films. Many other readers will enjoy its arguments, too. Highly recommended.

4398 *Movies and Morals.* by Miles, Herbert J. 121 p. illus. Grand Rapids, Mich.: Zondervan, 1947.

Another book from Zondervan that raises religious and moral questions about the movies.

4399 *Movies and Sexuality.* edited by Atkins, Thomas R. 31 p. paper illus. Hollins College, Va.: Film Journal, 1973.

An anthology of five articles dealing with sexuality in films.

4400 *Movies and Society.* by Jarvie, I. C. 394 p. illus. New York: Basic Books, 1970.

Jarvie is a Canadian professor of sociology who has sound qualifications for such a work as this. He uses as his base three broad areas: The Film Industry—who makes films and why?; The Film Audience—who sees films and why?; and Film Criticism—how do we learn about and appraise films? By the use of anecdote, and brilliant, terse, or vitriolic comment, all related with enthusiasm and affection, the author covers his topic accurately. Occasionally, there is a conflict between the two roles that Jarvie enjoys—movie buff and crochety professor. For example, one's faith begins to falter a bit when he calls JOHN GOLDFARB PLEASE COME HOME (1964) a neglected satire. The book is one of the better sociological analyses of films and film audiences to be published recently. The long, long annotated bibliography is most impressive. This is enjoyment at the academic level. Highly recommended.

4401 *Movies Are Better Than Ever.* by Dowdy, Andrew. 242 p. illus. New York: William Morrow, 1973.

Here is a model that almost anyone can use to create a film book of their own. Choose a time period, re-screen, review and research as many films as possible from that period, write capsule annotations on each, assign them to genres and correlate the groups to incidents and movements in our national history. Yet to be written are such titles as: The Films of the McCarthy Era, ...the Nixon Years, ...the Teapot Dome Years, etc. Dowdy has followed the above plan and subtitled his work "Wide Screen Memories of the Fifties." The illustrations, the bibliography and the index cannot do much to rescue what is essentially a categorized descriptive filmography of fifties films. More critical insight can be obtained from one of the guides to movies on TV. A minor work. Acceptable.

4402 *Movies as Mass Communication.* by Jowett, Garth. 149 p. illus. Beverly

Hills: Sage, 1980.

This text book by the dependable Garth Jowett includes a bibliography and an index.

4403   *The Movies as Medium.* by Jacobs, Lewis. 335 p. illus. New York: Farrar, Straus & Giroux, 1970.

Twenty-two film makers discuss the nature of film art in this anthology of essays collected and introduced by Lewis Jacobs. Among the contributors are such talents as Bela Balazs, Carl Dreyer, Ivor Montagu, Robert Gessner, Jonas Mekas, and Sergei Eisenstein. Kurt Weill is the author of one essay called "Music in the Movies." Time, space, color, image, movement and sound are some of the aesthetics considered. This is another superior group of articles. It represents a modern statement on film aesthetics which has roots in the past but recognizes the important contribution of today's filmmakers.

4404   *Movies as Social Criticism: Aspects of Their Social Psychology.* by Jarvie, I. C. 207 p. illus. Metuchen, N.J.: Scarecrow, 1980.

Jarvie's argument in this volume is that movies are more than simple popular entertainments. In a complex way, films have a cause-and-effect relationship with society. That relationship vacillates constantly, with films taking a variety of postures: conformity, expose, criticism, protest, propaganda, conservationist, reflection, etc. In five chapters Jarvie considers the theoretical questions, the history, the reflection of reality, and film as a vehicle of social criticism and protest.

A long bibliography, a name index, a subject index and a filmography complete the statement.

Jarvie may be controversial, stubborn and opinionated, but he's not dull. His book is a fine example of film criticism in the area of film sociology.

4405   *The Movies Begin.* by Spehr, Paul C. 191 p. paper illus. Newark, N.J.: The Newark Museum; Dobbs Ferry, N.Y.: Morgan and Morgan, 1977.

This volume, which is subtitled "Making Movies in New Jersey 1887-1920," was published by the Newark Museum as part of its bicentennial celebration. Written as a complement to an exhibition which reviewed New Jersey's role in the early development of the motion picture, the book validates New Jersey's claim as the first movie capital of the world.

The text begins with some early film history, inventions, technological developments, and an account of pioneer filmmaking in the state. It is the next two chapters which hold the greatest pleasures. The first deals with the studios that made films in New Jersey. For each a narrative is supplied along with location, officers, directors, performers, and representative films. Next mini-biographies of the personalities who appeared in films made in New Jersey are offered. With both the studios and the filmmakers, the reader will be surprised by the names and the number involved.

Adding to the excellent research and writing is a collection of stills, portraits and production shots which are meticulously reproduced. A bibliography, a general index, and an index to film titles complete the book.

Here is an example of historical research that brings distinction to the author and to the museum. Production values supplied by the publisher are consistent with the content quality.

4406   *Movies, Censorship and the Law.* by Carmen, Ira H. 339 p. Ann Arbor, Mich.: University of Michigan Press, 1966.

The history of movie censorship is divided into early (1915-1952) and modern (1953-1965) periods. Federal actions involving censorship are examined therein. Other sections look at censorship by states and local communities. A chapter of conclusions and a long appendix consisting of questionnaires and interviews complete the book.

The recent trend in motion picture freedom relegates this volume to an historical status, and non-scholar interest in it will be relatively small. It is written in a pedantic style and is not easily read. A decided asset is the discussion of each of the important court cases pertinent to film censorship and obscenity.

4407   *The Movies Come from America.* by Seldes, Gilbert. 120 p. illus. New York: Scribner, 1937.

The title of this book is somewhat misleading. Using the history of motion pictures as his framework, Seldes relates, analyzes, and comments about films from their invention to about 1937. Surprisingly, the book is not outdated; certain statistics and a few time-related comments are the only indicators of the book's age.

This volume is a suitable companion to Knight's *The Liveliest Art* and Jacob's *The Rise of the American Film.* There is a short introduction by Chaplin which is provocative in the light of later events. The text is informative and, as are all Seldes books, well-written. Illustrations are excellent and the index seems helpful. This small volume should be republished since so much of what Seldes was saying in 1937 is still current. Highly recommended for all readers (if you can locate a copy). Published in England as *Movies for the Millions*.

4408 *Movies, Delinquency and Crime.* by Blumer, Herbert; and Hauser, Philip M. 233 p. New York: Arno Press, 1970 (1933).

This Payne Fund Study, first published in 1933, used a sampling of 300 young criminals, 55 ex-convicts, 300 delinquent girls and 1000 children from high delinquency areas and neighborhoods. Reports and questionnaires were employed. One final conclusion of this study: motion picture influence is directly proportional to the weaknesses of the family, school, church, and neighborhood that support the child.

4409 *Movies for Kids.* by Zornow, Edith; and Goldstein, Ruth M. 224 p. paper illus. New York: Avon, 1973.

Subtitled "A Guide for Parents and Teachers on the Entertainment Film for Children 9 to 13," this helpful aid identifies 125 feature films and 75 short films. In addition, it offers information on film distributors, organizations, books, periodicals and a few illustrations. The feature films are annotated in some detail and the usual credits and technical data are given. The short films get much briefer attention with a sentence or so of comment added to the technical data. An introduction and an essay on how to look at a movie precede the two filmographies.

4410 *Movies for the Millions.* by Seldes, Gilbert. 120 p. illus. London: B. T. Batsford, 1937.

This is the British title for *The Movies Come From America*.

4411 *Movies for TV.* by Battison, John. 376 p. illus. New York: Macmillan, 1950.

Although some of the factual material in this book is obsolete, there is still enough pertinent information to warrant the book's consideration here. As a discussion of how motion pictures are used for television broadcasting, the book explores many areas. Because of constant technological change and improvement, the book needs updating or replacement. However it may answer some questions that cannot be satisfied elsewhere.

4412 *Movies for TV: 21 Years of Ratings.* by Donchin, Fannie. 48 p. paper Mount Vernon, N.Y.: Consumers Union, 1968.

This booklet is an alphabetical listing of over 5600 films with ratings first by certain subscribers of Consumers Union and second by a consensus of critics. The time period covered is 1947 to 1968. Films are rated as excellent, good, fair, or poor. Where opinion is divided, two ratings are given (such as "fair-poor"), the first evaluation reflecting the majority opinion. In addition each film gives the year of its original review, and one or two of the actors appearing in it.

The number of responses or reviews upon which the ratings are based is not given or approximated. Some ratings may cause the reader to wonder—Antonioni films (mostly G), Bergman films (mostly G) etc. It is surprising to find such uniformity of ratings between the two groups and yet note that in several thousand samples, it is difficult to find a film that both groups agreed upon as being uniformly excellent. Updated in 1978.

4413 *Movies from the Mansion: A History of Pinewood Studios.* by Perry, George. 191 p. illus. London: Elm Tree Books/Hamish Hamilton, 1976.

In his introduction, Trevor Howard calls Pinewood the "best run" studio and one which offers a "personal touch." In this well-illustrated history provided by George Perry, these qualities can be sensed. Built in the thirties by Charles Boot on an estate some 20 miles from London, the studio quickly became a center of filmmaking in 1937-38. The war put a stop to activities until 1946-47 when such classic films as GREEN FOR DANGER, BLACK NARCISSUS, THE RED SHOES and OLIVER TWIST were made there. Since then the studio has continued to operate, always reflecting the peaks and valleys of British film production.

This volume reviews the films and filmmakers who were part of Pinewood's first 40 years. Illustrations have been carefully selected and reproduced. A chronological filmography of the films made at Pinewood and an index complete the book.

A delightful experience in reading and viewing, this history will increase the appreciation that already exists for many of the Pinewood studio's films. Recommended.

4414 *The Movies Grow Up, 1940-1981.* by Champlin, Charles. 284 p. illus.

Chicago: Swallow, 1981.

4415 *Movies in America.* by Kuhns, William. 248 p. paper illus. Dayton, Ohio: Pflaum, 1972.

One of the first books used widely as a text in film study courses was Kuhns' *Exploring the Film.* Since the qualities that distinguished that earlier volume are present to a greater degree in this volume, an even wider success is indicated. The title refers to movies in America, not the American Movie. The emphasis, however, is almost exclusively on American films, directors, columnists, and performers. A historical account provides the general framework but there are entertaining digressions and time-period juxtapositions of material. Kuhns' intention is to present an account of the film in America by tracing its development from a novelty to an art form and by examining the relationship between certain short periods of post-1900 American history and the films that appeared within them. He is mostly successful in this endeavor.

The creativity evident throughout this volume makes it unique among film books. Production quality is outstanding, with hundreds of unusual stills carefully arranged and reproduced. The book is a visual feast, a stimulating arrangement of what could easily be too-familiar material, and it has an intelligent text to cement the elements of the book. Because of the large number of pages, the oblong book format may be awkward to handle. There is a short bibliography and an index. Highly recommended.

4416 *Movies in Society: Sex, Crime and Censorship.* by Koenigil, Mark. 214 p. illus. New York: Robert Speller and Sons, 1962.

A translation from the Portugese, this volume is a collection of facts, generalizations, ambiguities, opinions, and quotations, all directed to the influence that films may have on the viewer. The author's approach is naive, idealistic and rather romantic. Even his stated purposes seem at variance with what is presented. There certainly is too much chauvinism in the presentation of the Brazilian motion picture industry as a major case study or example.

Production is poor and proofreading seems nonexistent. Captions under pictures are totally confusing, either being in error or giving one name for a picture of four people, all of whom are equally prominent in the still. This book is one to avoid. Not recommended.

4417 *The Movies in the Age of Innocence.* by Wagenknecht, Edward. 280 p. illus. Norman, Okla.: University of Oklahoma Press, 1962.

Divided into five general sections, this book is a subjective look at the era of the silent film. Based on the author's early movie-going and on research done in preparing this volume, the material is concise, interesting, and unique. Many of the motion pictures mentioned are usually overlooked in other historical accounts.

The titles of the five sections indicate the content: 1) "Came the Dawn," 2) "D. W. Griffith Presents," 3) "America's Sweetheart," 4) "Famous Players in Famous Plays," and 5) "The Ladies—God Bless Them." A tribute to Lillian Gish completes the volume.

Especially useful are the separate indexes of the titles and names. Picture selection and reproduction are adequate, but the number is relatively small. An excellent contribution to the early history of the cinema, this book is recommended for all readers.

4418 *Movies Into Film.* by Simon, John. 448 New York: Dial Press, 1971.

"Vicious, vicious, vicious" could easily be applied to Simon. He spares no one and is especially hard on females. His comments on Streisand ("a repellent, egomaniacal female impersonator"), Brenda Vaccaro ("a 'Dikey' kewpie doll"), Sandy Dennis ("walking catarrh") and others are devastating. His main obsession seems to be sex—with an emphasis on homosexual-lesbian relationships, which are plentiful in the films he reviews. These approaches to film criticism—bitchiness and sex—are not likely to limit a critic's celebrity. Add constant appearances on TV talk shows, on-going feuds with fellow critics, and some occasional fireworks in the Sunday *New York Times* and you have a recipe for certain success.

Simon has a background of knowledge and information about all the arts that serves him well in his film criticism. He can write in a style that informs, challenges, entertains, and shocks, but he is often guilty of monumental bad taste in speaking of other human beings.

The essays in this volume are mostly from *The New Leader* and take up where *Private Screenings* left off. They cover a period of about four years, from 1967 to 1970, and are arranged under subject headings rather than chronologically, e.g., adaptations, the youth film, young directors, musicals, etc. The introduction, which takes on both Pauline Kael and Andrew Sarris, should be required reading for anyone interested in film criticism. The book is indexed. John Simon is probably the most controversial critic writing today. He enjoys a love-hate relationship with his readers, his professional contemporaries, and his critics. Highly recommended.

4419 *Movies Made for Television.* edited by Marill, Alvin H. 399 p. illus. Westport, Conn.: Arlington House, 1980.

A void in film literature is filled with the publication of this attractive reference book, which deals with the telefeature and the mini-series films that appeared on TV screens from 1964-1979. Since many of these productions also enjoy circulation as 16mm films, the book is pertinent for this bibliography.

The films appear chronologically by TV season. Each entry notes the title, its initial showing date, producer, running time, credits, cast and an annotation consisting mostly of a plot description. The mini-series appear next and are followed by an alphabetical title list, an actor filmography and a director filmography. The hundreds of illustrations provided are clearly reproduced and add greatly to the book's impressive production.

Access to that increasing reservoir of films that will ultimately appear in other formats (video cassettes, discs, etc.) is provided in this efficient, attractive volume. Recommended.

4420 *Movies, Morals and Art.* by Getlein, Frank; and Gardiner, Harold C. 179 p. New York: Sheed & Ward, 1961.

This book consists of two sections written independently: "The Art of the Movie," by Frank Getlein, and "Moral Evaluations of the Films," by Harold Gardiner, S. J. As "an effort to approach the film arts in a positive fashion and make them the object of serious study," the book is vulnerable. Written for the most part in a naive, autocratic manner, the book opts to give interpretations and information rather than raise questions in the reader's mind. Largely it is a case of being told what to feel and how to react.

Some provocative, thoughtful points are made at times, but most of the first section lacks structure while the second does not seem to have a large sampling upon which to base its conclusions. The book may be valuable under very special circumstances such as discussions of censorship, pressure groups, morals in film, etc. For most readers, this book is not recommended.

4421 *The Movies, Mr. Griffith, and Me.* by Gish, Lillian; and Pinchot, Ann. 388 p. illus. Englewood Cliffs, N.J.: Prentice-Hall, 1969.

This fascinating duo-biography has given Miss Gish another outlet for her performing talents. She travels about the country appearing in an illustrated lecture based primarily on material in this book. Her presentation is undoubtedly an exciting event, as is this book. Artfully subordinating her life to the productive segment of Griffith's, she also gives a portrait of silent movie making that is technical, factual, and yet personal.

The early years are skipped over until the first appearances with Griffith in Biograph films and in the Griffith masterpieces (1908-1920). A detailed account of the industry and the personalities of the twenties follows. The last four decades of her career are skipped over quite rapidly. As indicated above, the lady is still quite active and probably has material for several more books. The author is quite selective in what she reveals. However, since her charisma—that of an intelligent, sensitive lady—is communicated so effortlessly to the reader, one cannot help but be enchanted. Add to this the richness of her material and experience, and you have a major contribution to film biography. Illustrations are uniformly excellent and the book is indexed. Recommended with enthusiasm.

4422 *Movies on Movies: How Hollywood Sees Itself.* by Meyers, Richard. 159 p. paper illus. New York: Drake, 1978.

Hollywood as reflected in films is the topic of this mediocre survey. The text arranges the films under genre-topic headings such as biographies, comedies, musicals, mysteries, westerns, silents, etc. The only access to the films discussed is a listing which appears at each chapter's beginning; there is no index. The book's quality is further diminished by the poor reproduction of the visuals.

After assigning the films to their particular chapter, the author seems content to relate plots and other buff-trivia information rather than attempt some correlation with actual film history. In *Hollywood's Hollywood* the identical topic is treated in much the same manner but it includes a larger and more impressive group of visuals.

4423 *The Movies on Trial.* by Perlman, William J. 254 p. New York: Macmillan, 1936.

This symposium in print on the topic of movie censorship was published at the time when the potency of film was beginning to be recognized nationally. Its subtitle, "The Views and Opinions of Outstanding Personalities Anent Screen Entertainment Past and Present," sums up the content nicely. Nearly all the articles are pro-movies and anti-censorship. Some of those represented are William Allen White, Upton Sinclair, Don Marquis, William Lyon Phelps, and Edward G. Robinson.

4424 *Movies on TV.* edited by Scheuer, Steven H. 404 p. paper New York: Bantam Books, 1969.

This is a recent edition of this low-priced reference volume. It has appeared with other titles but the original format is still the same. Given with each film is its title, its original release date, its foreign origin if pertinent, a rating of from one to four stars, a few cast names, a short synopsis and a few words of evaluation. This edition contains the above information on more than 7000 films arranged alphabetically. Although it was not designed for that purpose, the book is an essential reference tool. Easy to use, fun to read, and usually reliable in its ratings, the book is also quite accurate factually.

Earlier editions covered fewer films and sometimes different ones. Certain of the films in those editions are not currently available for TV showings. The volume in its other editions was called: *TV Movie Almanac and Ratings* (1958-1959), *TV Key Movie Reviews and Ratings* (1961), and *TV Key Movie Guide* (1966). For more than a decade, this series had the field to itself. Now it has some competition from Maltin's *TV Movies.* This book covers the thirties and the forties in addition to the last two decades.

4425 *The Movies On Your Mind.* by Greenberg, Harvey R. 273 p. paper New York: Saturday Review Press-Dutton, 1975.

This volume, which has the provocative subtitle "Film Classics On the Couch, From Fellini to Frankenstein," is an attempt to seek out the unconscious movie hidden within the cinema. The author likens film attendance to a session with an analyst, in that both can generate basic emotions and hidden traumas.

Although he considers many films, Greenberg concentrates on THE WIZARD OF OZ (1939), THE TREASURE OF SIERRA MADRE (1946), THE MALTESE FALCON (1941), CASABLANCA (1943), PSYCHO (1960), 8-1/2 (1963), WILD STRAWBERRIES (1958), KING KONG (1933) and 2001: A SPACE ODYSSEY (1968).

Psychoanalytical examinations of films have been

rare—Munsterberg's and Tyler's books are among the few that come to mind. Greenberg's explorations here are colorful, exciting, amusing and, at times, frightening. While the reader may not agree with the possible interpretations offered, he certainly will be stimulated and challenged. Short bibliographies appear throughout the book and it is indexed. There are no illustrations.

This volume will be most popular with mature adults and those who are familiar with the classic films named above. Recommended.

4426 *Movies Plus One: Seven Years of Film Reviewing.* by Pechter, William. 380 p. New York: Horizon, 1981.

4427 *Movies That Teach.* by Hoban, Charles F. 189 p. illus. New York: Dryden Press, 1946.

This was an analytical report to schools and colleges on the use of motion pictures for educational purposes. Experiences with service personnel in World War II served as the research base. Many charts, tables, etc.

4428 *Movies: The History of an Art and an Institution.* by Schickel, Richard. 208 p. illus. London: Macgibbon and Kee, 1965.

Here is still another visit to the mines of motion picture history but the discoveries are few. For the most part it is a rehash of material that has been covered by others in earlier and better books. Since this is a critical history, the author offers personal views along with the factual narrative but some of these limit the book even more. For example, in speaking of LA DOLCE VITA (1961) he says, "The whole exercise is vulgar, witless, and intellectually bankrupt." Many other recent films are considered by Schickel in the same irresponsible manner. There is always the danger that what is questionable subjective judgment may be considered by some readers as history. This is reading to make you angry.

Picture reproduction is only fair and the book contains a curious bibliography. In 1965 was it possible to say that there is no first class biography of Chaplin (Huff 1951?), DeMille (DeMille 1959?) or Eisenstein (Seton 1952?) Or of William Fox, can it be said that there are no works at all? ("Upton Sinclair presents William Fox" 1933?).

4429 *Movies with a Purpose.* 27 p. paper illus. Rochester, N.Y.: Eastman

Kodak, 1972.

This booklet is a guide to planning and producing super 8 motion pictures for instructional use. It deals with making the short, single-concept film and offers information and suggestion on cameras, storyboards, lighting, film speeds, lenses, editing, etc. Final pages deal with the language of filmmaking—closeup, medium shot, camera angle, telephoto lens, panning, titling, zooming, etc. Text and visuals are of the usual high quality found in other helpful Kodak booklets. Recommended.

4430 *Movietone Presents the 20th Century.* by Cohn, Lawrence. 379 p. illus. New York: St. Martin's Press, 1976.

Movietone newsreels were a familiar part of motion picture theatre programs from 1919 to 1963. This volume offers a collection of over 800 frame enlargements taken from the series. Since the goal of the newsreels was entertainment, rather than information or education, the selection includes fashions, sports, fads, parades, stunts, politicians campaigning, celebrities waving, etc. Remember Lew Lehr and "monkies is de cwaziest people"?

Some words are offered by Lowell Thomas (the voice of Movietone News) and there is a history of newscreens by Cohn. The illustrations comprise almost all of the book.

Although the book suggests that a Herculean task was performed by Cohn in selecting the illustrations from the millions of feet of newsreel film in the archives, the final result does little to recall the uniqueness of the newsreel itself, or a sense of the historical period it covered.

4431 *The Moving Image: A Guide to Cinematic Literacy.* by Gessner, Robert. 444 p. illus. New York: Dutton, 1968.

By considering the shooting script as the major ingredient of a film, the author analyzes elements of mechanics (scenes, shots, sequences, etc.), dramaturgy (characterization, conflict, action, and climax), and cinematic production (time, plasticity, sound and light). These elements in various combinations are shown by examples from many famous screenplays. Gessner develops his theme of cinematic literacy—to make the viewer aware of the patterns and structures that make motion pictures an art form—in an informative, efficient, nontechnical manner.

Other admirable features are fine illustrations, a lengthy bibliography, a glossary, a series of cinema literacy tests, a recommended film list, sources of film rentals, and an evaluation chart. There is a detailed index too. The overall excellence of the entire volume makes it highly recommended for the advanced student or writer.

4432 *The Moving Picture Book.* by Kuhns, William. 292 p. paper illus. Dayton, Ohio: Pflaum, 1975.

This introductory textbook, designed for high school and early college students, has two purposes. The first is to help the reader understand the terms, techniques and possibilities of films. Second is the encouragement for viewing more films, older films and unfamiliar films.

To accomplish these goals Kuhns has used visuals most generously. Accompanying the explanatory critical text are stills, frame enlargements, diagrams, drawings, etc. A sequence from a film is described by the shot-by-shot progression used so effectively in Richard Anobile's *Film Classic Library* series. The arrangement of the material employs general headings such as A Visual Dictionary, Sound, The Director, Animation, etc. Notes on the films mentioned most prominently in the text are added along with a distributor list. A detailed index completes the book.

As with an earlier text, *Exploring the Film,* Kuhns has provided an abundance of quality material upon which a fine film appreciation course can be structured. In addition, the book is eminently suitable for individual reading pleasure. Highly recommended.

4433 *Moving Pictures: How They are Made and Worked.* by Talbot, Frederick A. 340 p. illus. New York: Arno Press, 1970 (1912).

A very early discussion of various technical elements of motion pictures such as the celluloid film, the camera, the developing process, the projection, etc. There are also chapters devoted to "Moving Pictures of Microbes," "Trick Pictures," "Electric Spark Cinematography," and "Animation in Natural Colors." For the historian and the curious.

4434 *Moving Pictures: Their Impact on Society (A Series).* edited by Jowett, Garth S. New York: Ozer, 1972.

The intent of this collection is to provide reprints, for scholars and students, of books long out of print and difficult to obtain in the used book market. The books examined in this reprint edition are bound in silver cloth and are facsimile reproductions of the original editions. Charts, illustrations, indexes, and bibliographies have been retained.

Titles in the series are: *The Business Man in the Amusement World*, by Robert Grau; *Censored: The Private Life of the Movies*, by Morris Ernst and Pare Lorentz; *Children and Movies*, by Alice Miller Mitchell; *Children in the Cinema*, by Richard Ford; *The Community and the Motion Picture*, by the Hays Office; *Decency in Motion Pictures*, by Martin Quigley; *Economic Control of the Motion Picture Industry*, by Mae Dena Huettig; *The Hays Office*, by Raymond Moley; *The Morals of the Movie*, by Ellis P. Oberholtzer; *The Motion Picture Industry*, by Howard Thompson Lewis; *Motion Pictures: A Study in Social Legislation*, by Donald Ramsey Young; *The Movies on Trial*, by William J. Perlman; *New Courts of Industry*, by Louis Nizer; *The Public and the Motion Picture Industry*, by William Marston Seabury; *The Public Relations of the Motion Picture Industry*, by The Federal Council of Churches of Christ in America; *Selected Articles on Censorship of the Theater and Moving Pictures*, by Lamar Taney Beman; *Sociology of Film*, by Jakob Peter Mayer; *The Story of Films*, by Joseph Patrick Kennedy; *What's Wrong With the Movies?*, by Tamar Lane; *World Wide Influences of the Cinema*, by John Eugene Harley.

4435 *Moving Pictures.* by Sheahan, Eileen. 146 p. paper New York: A. S. Barnes, 1979.

This modest paperback carries the subtitle "An Annotated Guide to Selected Film Literature with Suggestions for the Study of Film." It is a bibliography of selected film literature—mostly reference works, with entries listed by form or topic, i.e., dictionaries, catalogs, histories, biography, periodicals, dissertations, etc. The annotations provided are descriptive and unfortunately do not offer critical judgments. A subject index and an author/title index are provided.

Although the listing is quite comprehensive, the failure to evaluate may be a disservice to the user who does not have the time or patience to search several sources in order to find the information he seeks.

4436 *Moving Pictures: Memoirs of a Hollywood Prince.* by Schulberg, Budd. 515 p. illus. New York: Stein and Day, 1981.

What it is like to grow up as a son of a Hollywood mogul is described by Schulberg. He mixes motion picture history with the story of rise and fall of his father. The account, which covers only the author's first seventeen years, contains a bitter portrait of actress Sylvia Sidney.

4437 *Moving Places: A Life at the Movies.* by Rosenbaum, Jonathan. 288 p. illus. New York: Harper, 1980.

This volume is an attempt to explain one's life in terms of the films seen during it. Since the author is relatively young, perhaps his endeavor should have been postponed until he had accumulated richer source material. In any event, he spends much time analyzing ON MOONLIGHT BAY (1951) as he recalls his own patterns of maturation. This is a new form of self-therapy we might all try.

4438 *Mr. Laurel & Mr. Hardy.* by McCabe, John. 175 p. paper illus. New York: New American Library, 1966.

This book is called an affectionate biography of Laurel and Hardy—a rather exact description. Disarming in its simple admiration for the subjects, the book is not quite a biography in the usual sense. Certainly the biographical portion is not critical in nature, based as it is on personal data, printed interviews, and personal letters. As a result the reader is not privileged to know in any depth the off-screen personalities of the two. What is given in good measure is an appreciation and analysis of their films and comedy techniques.

The picture quality in the paperback edition is quite poor. A film listing and an index conclude the book. When someone shares his enthusiasms and writes about them, it is difficult to dislike his literary effort: fans of Laurel and Hardy will love this book while others may not—it will tend to reinforce opinions rather than change them.

4439 *Mr. Rank: A Study of J. Arthur Rank and British Films.* by Wood, Alan. 288 p. London: Hodder & Stoughton, 1952.

Much of this biography addresses itself to the economics and finance of the British Film industry during the thirties and the forties. Certain portions of the volume are excellent while others are too specialized to be of concern to most readers. Certainly the chapter on British films before Rank is a fascinating summary. Later chapters about films made during Rank's regime are also quite good. The surrounding framework of financial competition, monopoly, government interference, etc. limits the general appeal of this book. the book is indexed but there are no pictures. A book of mixed blessings.

4440 *Mr. Showbusiness.* by Oliver, Vic. illus. London: Harrap, 1964.

Vic Oliver was a comedian, pianist, violinist, conductor, and businessman who also married Sarah Churchill. His popularity on radio led to his appearance in ten or so motion pictures from RHYTHM IN THE AIR (1936) to FOR OLD TIMES SAKE (1948). This autobiography was completed shortly before his death in 1964.

4441 *Mr. Wu Looks Back... Thoughts and Memories.* by Lang, A. Matheson. 224 p. paper illus. London: Stanley Paul and Co., 1941.

This is the autobiography of Lang, a Scottish-Canadian actor noted for his rather exaggerated theatrical style. From a successful career on the stage, he became a most popular star in both silent and early sound films. He was active in British motion picures from 1916 to 1936.

4442 *Mrs. Howard Hughes.* by Strait, Raymond. 244 p. paper illus. Los Angeles: Holloway House, 1970.

Although the title is correct, it is misleading. This book really is a biography of Jean Peters as an actress rather than as Mrs. Howard Hughes. The Hollywood years before her marriage are covered in great detail while the Hughes' years are barely mentioned. Jean Peters emerges as a super-heroine who survived the Hollywood mills virtually intact. The text leans heavily on previously published interviews and goes so far as to give the Peters' recipe for Caesar salad. There are many nicely produced illustrations. This is a book with a mixture of virtues and faults.

4443 *Multi-Media Materials for Afro-American Studies.* by Johnson, Harry A. 353 p. New York: Bowker, 1971.

An annotated mediagraphy that includes a number of films, this guide also has four articles by black educators and an index.

4444 *Multi-Media Reviews Index.* edited by Wall, C. Edward. Ann Arbor, Mich.: Pierian Press, 1970- .

An annual index to reviews of films, filmstrips, non-classical records, tapes, slides, transparencies, and other media. In addition to being a guide to the reviews, MMRI offers information about the films: title, distributor, date of release, gauge, running time, silent or sound, color or black and white, etc. The tone of the reviews is indicated by a plus or minus sign. A much needed reference. Recommended.

4445 *The Multilateral Exchange of Educational Audio-Visual Materials: Existing Mechanisms and Suggestions for the Future.* 117 p. paper New York: UNESCO, 1980.

A study of national and multilateral organizations, producers, and distributors of AV materials that considers how these organizations deal with the questions of exchange. Discussed are strategy, linguistic, economic and legal problems; four possible exchange models are presented.

4446 *A Multimedia Approach to Children's Literature.* by Greene, Ellin; and Schoenfeld, Madalynne. 262 p. paper illus. Chicago: American Library Association, 1972.

Films which are based on children's literature are noted in this volume. The 175 films which appear include both feature films and short films. Annotations are brief and tend to be descriptive rather than critical.

4447 *Multivision.* by Lewell, John. 269 p. illus. New York: Focal, 1980.

The subjects treated here are the production, creative techniques and technology involved in multivision presentations. Multivision is a general term used to describe techniques ranging from two projector, single-screen programs to multimedia extravaganzas. Topics covered include photography, animation, sound, graphics, etc.

4448 THE MUPPET MOVIE. by Juhl, Jerry; and Burns, Jack. 118 p. paper illus. New York: Peacock/Bantam, 1979.

Designed for young readers, this handsome book is a novelization taken from the film script by Juhl and Burns. It is noted here because of the numerous illustrations of scenes from the film. It also contains a final section called "The Muppet Movie Shooting Script" which is a misleading exaggeration. Only a few shots are described. Ultimately, it is the color illustrations of Kermit, Miss Piggy, other Muppets, and the assorted celebrities who appear in the film that constitute the book's major appeal. Anyway, at this time, is there anyone who can resist the Muppets in any form? Recommended.

4449 *Muray's Celebrity Portraits of the Twenties and Thirties.* by Muray,

Nickolas. 144 p. paper illus. New York: Dover, 1978.

Among the 135 attractive portraits so clearly reproduced here, there are many film personalities. Unfortunately there is no index and the reader will have to search to see if specific persons are included. Portraits are arranged alphabetically by subject surname and include such stars as Astaire, Bow, Chaplin, Colbert, Dietrich, Garbo, Harlow, Hayes, Jolson, Loos, Loy, Robeson, Robinson, Swanson, the Talmadge sisters, and Weissmuller. A visual feast for those acquainted with the period.

4450 *Murnau.* by Eisner, Lotte. 287 p. illus. Berkeley, Calif.: University of California Press, 1973.

First published in French in 1964, this revised and enlarged critical biography gives evidence of Lotte Eisner's ability to bring scholarly distinction and understanding to a challenging subject. Only 12 of F. W. Murnau's 21 films survive, and several of those are incomplete. Thus, the task of the historian-analyst becomes more difficult. In this case, Eisner has done a remarkable job in recreating an image of Murnau and his films. She includes reminiscences by Murnau's friends, his scriptwriters, his sets, camera work, lighting, and analyses of his films. Even the details of his accidental death are researched to set the record straight. Murnau's personal annotated copy of the script of NOSFERATU (1921) is added along with a filmography, a bibliography, and an index.

This is film scholarship to admire—a rich, satisfying evocation of a legendary director.

4451 *Museums with Film Programs.* compiled by Melton, Hollis. 20 p. paper New York: Educational Film Library Association, 1974.

Those museums in North America that have film programs are named here. Taken from the 1973 edition of *The Official Museum Directory*, the list is selective and incomplete but does offer specific information on film usage in a concise, economical way.

4452 *Music Editing for Motion Pictures.* by Lustig, Milton. 182 p. illus. New York: Hastings House, 1980.

The topic of this volume is the music editor and his functions and responsibilities in the production of a film. Although the composer writes the music, it is the editor who integrates it into the motion picture. In 36 separate sections, Lustig describes this incor-

poration as he discusses such topics as the spotting session, timing on the movieola, clicks, the coding machine, bar charts, the Newman system, scoring, tracking, dubbing, etc.

Diagrams, graphs, charts, a glossary, seven appendixes, and an index are added for reader assistance.

This is a specialized book that will appeal primarily to film musicians. However, the lay person can learn much about film music from the clear, linear exposition presented here.

4453 *Music Face to Face.* by Previn, Andre; and Hopkins, Antony. 132 p. London: Hamish Hamilton, 1971.

This conversation between critic-writer Antony Hopkins and musician Andre Previn is dual autobiography presented in a different format. Much of the dialogue deals, of course, with music, but film scores, names, and experiences crop up with some regularity. Acceptable.

4454 *Music for the Films.* by Sabaneev, Leonid L. 128 p. illus. London: Pitman, 1935.

This "handbook for composers and conductors" emphasizes the technical side of film music. It discusses systems of sound recording, principles of music montage, aesthetics, composition, conducting, synchronizing, etc.

4455 *Music for the Movies.* by Thomas, Tony. 270 p. illus. New York: A. S. Barnes, 1973.

A welcome survey of movie music. After a general introduction, the influence of European composers on film music is noted, along with the eventual emergence of the American composer. Mancini and others are given some special attention. An attempt is made to note recordings of film scores, but, as usual, there is confusion between record labels and record numbers here and in Europe. Recommended.

4456 *Music for the Movies.* by Levy, Louis. 182 p. illus. London: Low, 1948.

The author was a musical director and composer for many of the films at Gaumont and Gainsborough Studios until 1947. In this volume he discusses such topics as musical beginnings in films, music and mood, fitting music to image, the conductor, copyright, etc.

4457 *Music in Film and Television.* compiled by International Music Centre, Vienna. 197 p. paper Paris: UNESCO Press, 1975.

Using the previous UNESCO catalogs on opera, dance, ballet and traditional music in films as guides, the authors have produced "an international selective catalogue 1964-1974" of operas (78), concerts (47), educational programs (80), and experimental programs (14) that appear on film/TV. Each of the 223 entries contains the following when pertinent: title, music, libretto, production, distribution, adaptation, script, producer, technical data, date, language, cast, subject.

Ten separate indexes for titles, composers, authors, producers, directors, conductors, performing artists, orchestras, originations, abbreviations and addresses are provided. This is an essential reference for anyone dealing with education or film programming. In addition, many other film users will be pleased to discover the concentration of hard-to-find information contained here.

4458 *Music Scoring for TV and Motion Pictures.* by Skiles, Marlin. 266 p. illus. Blue Ridge Summit, Pa.: Tab Books, 1976.

This rather detailed discussion of the preparation of music to accompany films and television programs demands some background, training, or education in music for full reader appreciation. In his text Skiles offers many excerpts from printed musical scores along with charts, tables, and a technical vocabulary that may puzzle the non-musical user. The author has apparently tried to simplify his explanations as much as possible in order that the book can be used by a wide audience.

Individual chapters are devoted to the mechanics of scoring, the functional elements of scoring, instruments and their character, constructing the music score, and relating the score to the story. The text is frequently enriched by quotations from composers and critics of film music. Appendixes contain post-production logistics and a few short interviews with Quincy Jones, Hugo Friedhofer, David Grusin, John Green, Alex North, and Arthur Morton. The volume is indexed.

It is possible to gain much insight into the profession of film music composition from a reading/study of this book. The author's experience as a composer along with his ability in selecting and presenting complex material has enabled him to produce a most impressive volume on a specialized subject. Recommended.

4459 *The Musical: Notes.* by Dyer, Richard. 56 p. paper London: British Film Institute, 1975.

4460 *Musical Accompaniment of Moving Pictures.* by Lang, Edith; and West, George. 64 p. illus. New York: Arno Press, 1970 (1920).

A manual for film pianists and organists first published in 1920 which gives principles for the musical interpretation of films.

4461 *The Musical Film.* by McVay, Douglas. 175 p. paper illus. New York: A. S. Barnes, 1967.

Would you agree that: 1) WEST SIDE STORY (1961) is equalled and surpassed by GYPSY? (1962); that 2) the Curtis-Leigh sequence in PEPE (1960) is something to cherish?; that 3) IT'S ALWAYS FAIR WEATHER was the big letdown of 1955?; or that 4) A STAR IS BORN (1954) is the greatest picture ever seen? If you do, then this may be the musical film book for you, since these statements are typical of those made throughout.

The volume is a year-by-year comment on musicals that the author has seen. He seems to have missed most of Betty Grable, Alice Faye, the Paramount college musicals of the early thirties, and many others. Therefore, the title is a misnomer. These are really very personal opinions about a selected group of musical films. Taken as such, the book has some small merit. Certain of the comments, although eminently vulnerable, are quite amusing. Attention to the films is unbalanced with several pages devoted to some, e.g., ZIEGFELD FOLLIES (1946), and a short paragraph to others, GIGI (1958). The stills are acceptable as are the modest title index and a bibliography. In summary, this is a carelessly done book, saved only by the appeal of its subject matter and a few pictures.

4462 *The Musical from Broadway to Hollywood.* by Druxman, Michael B. 202 p. illus. New York: A. S. Barnes, 1980.

The transfer of a musical from the Broadway theatre to the movie screen is not always successful. Using 25 selected examples, Druxman discusses problems, pitfalls, successes and failures of such adaptations. More than 200 illustrations are included in the book, which is also indexed.

4463 *Musical Stages: An Autobiography.* by Rodgers, Richard. 384 p. paper illus. New York: Jove/Harcourt, Brace, Jovanovich, 1975.

Known mostly as a composer for the musical stage, Richard Rodgers did compose occasionally for films, i.e.: LOVE ME TONIGHT (1931), HALLELUJAH, I'M A BUM (1933), EVERGREEN (1935), STATE FAIR (1945), VICTORY AT SEA (1954), and others. In addition, many of his stage successes were transferred to films. In this autobiography, some attention is given to film matters. The volume is illustrated and indexed but lacks a career chronology, which would seem mandatory in Rodger's case. Since he accomplished so much in his lifetime, the account given here is tightly packed with incident, anecdote and fact, rather than letting anyone know the thoughts and emotions of the man behind all of the familiar, unforgettable music. His memoirs of the theatre legends who were associated with him provide some warm, happy moments for anyone who knows/loves his work.

4464 MUTINY ON THE BOUNTY. by Hudgins, Morgan. 36 p. illus. New York: Random House, 1962.

This souvenir book of the 1962 film furnishes much background material. In addition to the inevitable credits for cast and production, this volume has features on the ship, its sail plan, and a portion of its log. Tahiti yields many fine illustrations and other features include a map of the Bounty's journey, some historical notes, and an account of what happened to both the mutineers and the faithful members of the crew. This is one of the more interesting and admirable books made to accompany a film.

4465 *Muybridge, Man in Motion.* by Haas, Robert B. 300 p. illus. Berkeley, Calif.: University of California Press, 1975.

The long, colorful life of the pioneer photographer, Eadweard Muybridge, is related in this illustrated biography. His work, experiments, and studies of locomotion, all of which contributed to the discovery of motion pictures, are described along with the rather sensational events of his private life which includes a murder trial. Haas, an art authority, presents a fully dimensioned portrait of a complex and mysterious man.

4466 *Muybridge's Complete Human and Animal Locomotion.* by Muybridge, Eadweard. 1597 p. illus. New York: Dover, 1979.

This is a reproduction of Muybridge's 3 volume

photographic work that he published in 1887 under the title of *Animal Locomotion.* An encyclopedic record that consists of 781 plates and 25,000 stop-motion photographs, it has as its subjects humans, birds, snakes, and animals of all kinds. As an anticipation of motion picture cameras and projectors, this is a pioneer historical work that can still command the interest of the viewer. Its reproduction by Dover is superb.

4467 *My Autobiography.* by Chaplin, Charles. 512 p. illus. New York: Simon & Schuster, 1964.

Taking a very subjective look at himself and his career, Chaplin writes an essential autobiography but a flawed one. His selection and evaluation of what is important in his life is in marked contrast with the observations of his many unofficial biographers. Certainly this is his prerogative, but it results in unsatisfying, incomplete biography.

The stronger portions of this story occur before he becomes world famous. Early struggles, the evolution of the tramp character, descriptions of early motion picture techniques—all these make fascinating reading. Latter portions have a tendency toward name-dropping. Very little of his private life is related; he excuses these omissions by saying they are too painful to recall. Other omissions are not explained: for example, his 1957 film, A KING IN NEW YORK, is not mentioned by him except in the index and by the indentification of two stills. In spite of these weaknesses, the book is essential in that it represents what Chaplin wishes his audience and history to think of him. The book is profusely illustrated.

4468 *My Crazy Life.* by Flanagan, Bud. 160 p. paper illus. London: New English Library, 1962.

Bud Flanagan is best known as a member of the Crazy Gang, six men who were originally music hall duos—Bud Flanagan and Chesney Allen, Charlie Naughton and Jimmy Gold, and Jimmy Nervo and Teddy Knox. They made films as a gang and as individual teams. In 1963 Flanagan appeared by himself in THE WILD AFFAIR. This volume covers the most popular period of his professional life.

4469 *My Diary.* by O'Brien, Margaret. 117 p. illus. Philadelphia: Lippincott, 1943.

4470 *My Eskimo Friends*—NANOOK OF THE NORTH. by Flaherty, Robert; and Flaherty, Frances. 170 p. illus.

New York: Doubleday, Page, 1924.

A description of the people and experiences encountered while filming the classic documentary film, NANOOK OF THE NORTH (1924).

4471 MY FAIR LADY. 44 p. illus. New York: Warner Brothers, 1964.

Using a chronological arrangement of the songs as they appear in the film as the structure for the many visuals, this attractive souvenir book also describes the making of the 1964 film, its stars, and all the major names involved in the production. Included are director George Cukor, composer Frederick Loewe, author-lyricist Alan Jay Lerner, designer Cecil Beaton, musical supervisor Andre Previn, and producer Jack Warner. The author who started it all, George Bernard Shaw, is acknowledged only briefly. Supporting cast and other production credits are noted.

4472 *My Father and I.* by Schildkraut, Joseph; and Lania, Leo. 246 p. paper illus. New York: Viking, 1959.

Joseph Schildkraut was an Austrian actor who appeared in many important films from ORPHANS OF THE STORM (1921) to THE DIARY OF ANNE FRANK (1959). He came from a distinguished theatrical family and enjoyed great popularity as a actor on both stage and screen.

4473 *My Father, Charlie Chaplin.* by Chaplin, Charles Jr.; and Rau, N.; and Rau, M. 287 p. paper New York: Popular Library, 1960.

This respectful portrait of Chaplin is told with awe and admiration by his oldest son, Charles (who later took his own life). The offspring of Chaplin's second marriage were Charles, Jr., and Sydney, and this book tells of the boys' experiences with their father from childhood through adolescence and as adults.

Chaplin's work, his films, his personality, and his relationships with Lita Grey, Paulette Goddard, Joan Barry, and Oona O'Neill are discussed frankly. The book seems honest and fair in its account. The question that remains largely unanswered—in this book at least—is what it is like to be the son of a legend. Sympathy will be felt for the author although he never requests it. An admirable, interesting book that reveals a different portrait of Chaplin as a person. Recommended as supplementary

material to any serious study of Chaplin. The general reader will probably enjoy it, too.

4474 *My Father—My Son.* by Robinson, Edward G. Jr.; and Dufty, William. 237 p. paper New York: Popular Library, 1958.

Growing up in Hollywood and the temptations and pitfalls that such a life entails is the subject matter of this frank and raw autobiography. Written in the vein of *I'll Cry Tomorrow* and *Too Much, Too Soon,* it is a companion piece to complete this trilogy of youthful rebellion and ultimate failure. Its pertinence to a cinema collection is as supplementary or peripheral material. No index or illustrations are given.

4475 *My First Hundred Years in Hollywood.* by Warner, Jack L.; and Jennings, Dean. 331 p. illus. New York: Random House, 1965.

The subtitle of this autobiography might have been "From THE GREAT TRAIN ROBBERY (1903) to MY FAIR LADY (1964)," for those pictures form the filmends to Warner's career. From early exhibition, distribution, and production through silent film experience with Rin Tin Tin and John Barrymore, the Warner Brothers emerged with the first successful talking picture and founded a major studio that lasted several decades. Thankfully, the book is crammed with many anecdotes about the personalities and activities associated with the Warner Studio.

Written with a venomous wit at times, Warner's text is not too concerned about feelings and reputations. Sections on Bogart, Flynn, Davis, Garland, Curtiz, and Cagney are most enjoyable to read. More importantly, the reader gets a portrait of the subject that does not usually come through in biographies of studio chiefs. Enjoyable reading, written with humor and maturity, this is one of the better autobiographies of studio chiefs. Recommended for general audiences.

4476 *My Heart and I.* by Tauber, Diana Napier. 208 p. paper illus. London: Evans Brothers, 1959.

A biography of the film star of the thirties who married the famous tenor, Richard Tauber, retired temporarily, and resumed her film career after World War II.

4477 *My Heart Belongs.* by Martin, Mary. 320 p. illus. New York: William Morrow, 1976.

When an actress has established identities such as Venus, Peter Pan, Nellie Forbush, Maria Von Trapp and Flaming Agnes, it is difficult to separate the public image from the private person. As a result, when Mary Martin describes a negative action or emotion, the reader is likely to dimiss it as an external misfortune rather than a personality trait or problem. Martin would have a difficult time convincing anyone that she is anything but a warm, sweet, lovable, talented, feminine woman. For the most part she avoids that challenge and settles for the positive storybook heroine image.

Her Hollywood experiences are covered quickly in a short chapter in which she states that her filmmaking period is almost nonexistent in her memory. Records indicate that she appeared in almost a dozen motion pictures.

Emphasis is on her stage work where she originated what are now classic leading roles in American musical theatre. Her appetite for adding solid characters to her repertoire can be evidenced by her willingness to play parts created and individualized by other actresses—Dolly Levi, Annie Oakley, Sabina, etc. In keeping with the positive approach, she omits any mention of her portrayal of Billie Dawn in "Born Yesterday" on television. Audiences reacted most negatively to "our" Mary Martin playing the vulgar, uneducated brassy mistress of a junk tycoon.

Illustrations appear throughout the book and an index is added; unfortunately there are no listings of her stage, film, or television appearances. This is a major omission which lessens the book's reference value considerably.

Although the author has tried to present an objective portrait of herself and her career, one suspects that she has become too sensitive to audience demand. In her continual effort to please, she has given her admirers what they want and expect from Nellie, Peter, Maria and that crowd. Acceptable.

4478 *My Hollywood Diary.* by Wallace, Edgar. 259 p. illus. London: Hutchinson, 1932.

The last work of Edgar Wallace, with illustrations of stars such as Garbo, Shearer, Constance Bennett, etc.

4479 *My Ivory Cellar: The Story of Time Lapse Photography.* by Ott, John. 157 p. illus. Old Greenwich, Conn.: Devin.

An account of the author's experiences with time lapse photography. This is not a how-to-do-it book.

4480 *My Laugh Story.* by Henson, Leslie L. 293 p. paper illus. London: Hodder and Stoughton, 1926.

An early autobiography of a British actor who appeared infrequently in films from 1916 to 1956. See also *Yours Faithfully* (London: John Long, 1948).

4481 *My Life and Films.* by Lockwood, Margaret; edited by Warman, Eric. 78 p. paper illus. London: World Film Publications, 1948.

An early autobiographical effort by the heroine of many British World War II films. See also *Lucky Star.*

4482 *My Life East and West.* by Hart, William S. 346 p. illus. New York: Benjamin Blom, 1968 (1929).

After approximately 200 pages of autobiography dealing with his early life and experiences on the stage, author Hart gets to his career in films. The remaining portion of the volume has sufficient value to warrant its consideration here. Written in 1929 fan magazine style, the text describes the filming of westerns during the silent era. Photographs are below par but the index is more detailed than usual. This is an antique from the past that has value for historians and scholars. The general reader will pass it by.

4483 *My Life in Court.* by Nizer, Louis. 524 p. Garden City, N.Y.: Doubleday, 1962.

Noted here for the lengthy account of the proxy battle for control of MGM and Loew's as Louis B. Mayer tried to regain his position as studio head.

4484 *My Life in Pictures.* by Chaplin, Charles. 320 p. illus. New York: Grosset and Dunlap, 1975.

In many ways this pictorial autobiography is more satisfying than the earlier verbal attempt by Chaplin. Since he is a visual artist, it is appropriate for him to use photographs to recall his colorful life and career. The collection presented here is made up of stills, posters, announcements, candids, newspaper shots, frame enlargements, theatre programs, production stills and other pictorial memorabilia. Arranged in a general chronological fashion, the materials document Chaplin's rise from an obscure English stage performer to the international celebrity who many believe to be the greatest film artist ever. Emphasis is on the early silent years, with the sound films receiving some brief attention in the book's final pages. Photograph reproduction is acceptable. Sepia tones are used occasionally and 16 of the pages are in color. Instead of a final index, a "Guide to Illustrations" precedes the visuals.

The worth of one picture is again established in this superb collection. Although Chaplin has received more attention in print than any other film artist, it is impossible to recall any better interpretation of the performer and the man than that the presented here. Highly recommended.

4485 *My Life in the Wild.* by Tors, Ivan. 209 p. illus. Boston: Houghton Mifflin, 1979.

Ivan Tors, a Hungarian who came to Hollywood in the early forties as a writer, worked with Hepburn, Garland, Garson, Flynn and others at MGM. In 1950 he began to produce his own films, such as FLIPPER (1963), RHINO (1964), ZEBRA IN THE KITCHEN (1965), CLARENCE THE CROSS-EYED LION (1965), NAMU THE KILLER WHALE (1966), and GENTLE GIANT (1968). In recent years he has specialized in making animal series for television: "Gentle Ben," "Daktari," "Flipper," etc.

This illustrated volume tells of his adventures in filming all kinds of wild animals. While his writing style is often florid and excessive, the stories he tells are very entertaining. Those who enjoy animal stories and films will find this an absorbing book.

4486 *My Life, My Loves.* by Fisher, Eddie. New York: Harper and Row, 1981.

4487 *My Life on Trial.* Belli, Melvin M.

This autobiography of a well-known attorney includes some references to Hollywood performers.

4488 *My Life With...* by Carroll, Carroll. 288 p. paper illus. Canoga Park: Calif.: Major Books, 1970.

Carroll Carroll is a humorist whose experience as a reporter, a radio writer, and a columnist for *Variety* has brought him into close contact with many performers. In this collection of extended anecdotes, he recalls selected experiences with Crosby, Hope, Jolson, Dietrich, Zanuck and many others. Although the book is not concerned with motion pictures, some interesting views of celebrities are offered with a distinctive style and wit.

4489 *My Life with Chaplin.* by Chaplin, Lita Grey; and Cooper, Morton. 284 p. paper New York: Dell Pub., 1966.

A sensationalized, subjective account of a relationship between a 15-year-old girl and a 35-year-old legend. Intimate experiences with Chaplin are related as are social meetings with many of the personalities of the silent screen era. The final impression given is that of a rather sad and tragic life. Many will find the book in questionable taste but the reader/scholar who wishes another view of Chaplin may find something of interest here.

4490 *My Life With* CLEOPATRA. by Wanger, Walter; and Hyams, Joe. 182 p. paper New York: Bantam Books, 1963.

This is a fan magazine account of the making of CLEOPATRA (1963) and the more interesting activities that went on behind the cameras. Since the book is co-authored by a producer with impressive credits, portions of the volume give some insight into the problems of making motion pictures—in this case a most expensive and spectacular one. Unfortunately, the book is more Hyams than Wanger. Cold mashed potatoes left over from yesterday's feast. Of interest primarily to historians.

4491 *My Life With Elvis.* by Yancey, Becky; and Linedecker, Cliff. 360 p. illus. New York: St. Martin's Press, 1978.

This is the memoir you would expect from "A Fan Who Became Elvis' Private Secretary." Loyalty is the watchword and Becky Yancey betrays few confidences or secrets that would not have been approved by Elvis himself. She is more severe on the peripheral people—Elvis' father, wife, manager, guards, companions—than she is on her boss. As a result the portrait is at strong variance with the one presented in *Elvis: What Happened?* A few illustrations are included but there is no index or other supporting material.

This is a volume designed to perpetuate the legend. Written by an incurable fan, it will please similar Elvis devotees. Others will find its material overly familiar and its presentation too biased to be of much interest. Acceptable.

4492 *My Own Story.* by Dressler, Marie; and Harrington, Mildred. 290 p. illus. Boston: Little, Brown, 1934.

In this autobiography, written when she was 63, Marie Dressler relates a very surface account of her motion picture career. Very little is told of TILLIE'S PUNCTURED ROMANCE (1914) (Chaplin, Normand) ANNA CHRISTIE (1930) (Garbo), DINNER AT EIGHT (1933) (Harlow, Beery), etc. The comedies with Polly Moran and Wallace Beery are mentioned briefly. More attention is given to her philosophy of life, her advice, her creation of a public image, etc. Seemingly she was a vocal Senior Citizen before they became a recognized group. Her discussion of other personalities is uniformly positive. A good word is given for all. A few oversized pictures are poorly integrated into the text. There is not much here even for the scholar.

4493 *My Own Unaided Work.* by Gingold, Hermione. illus. London: Werner Laurie, 1952.

This volume was written before her success in America. Gingold had appeared in a few British films from 1936 to 1953, but it was GIGI (1958) that gave her film celebrity. She also wrote *The World is Square* (1958) and *Sirens Should Be Seen and Not Heard* (1963).

4494 *My Private Diary.* by Valentino, Rudolph. 312 p. illus. Chicago: Occult Pub. Co., 1929.

Michael A. Romano provides the introduction to this memoir. Published as autobiography after Valentino's death, its authenticity is suspect. Illustrations accompany the reminiscences, correspondence, etc.

4495 *My Rendezvous With Life.* by Pickford, Mary. 37 p. illus. New York:H. C. Kinsey, 1935.

America's sweetheart speculates on such heavy topics as immortality, consolation, and faith. She authored two similar books—*Why Not Look Beyond?* and *Why Not Try God?* (1934).

4496 *My Side: The Autobiography of Ruth Gordon.* by Gordon, Ruth. 502 p. illus. New York: Harper and Row, 1976.

Although Ruth Gordon has had a long, distinguished career in the theatre and as an author, it is her relatively few film performances that have given her the greatest celebrity. INSIDE DAISY CLOVER (1966), ROSEMARY'S BABY (1968), WHATEVER HAPPENED TO AUNT ALICE? (1969), WHERE'S POPPA? (1970) and HAROLD AND MAUDE (1971) have made

her known to millions of viewers. Unfortunately in this autobiography she gives a brief sentence or so to most of her films; only HAROLD AND MAUDE gets any appreciable coverage. It should be noted that certain material she has written, either directly for the screen—ADAM'S RIB (1949), A DOUBLE LIFE (1948), PAT AND MIKE (1952), THE MARRYING KIND (1952)—or as original plays bought later for the screen—OVER 21 (1945), THE ACTRESS (1953)—gets equally brief attention.

Apparently theatre is her first love and she is most adept at recalling her stage experiences. The volume is written in Gordon's unique style, with the many colorful characters which she has met in 60 years of constant professional activity appearing throughout.

A few illustrations and an index are helpful, but a career chronology is badly needed in Gordon's case. Acceptable.

4497 *My Side by King Kong.* by Wager, Walter. 119 p. paper New York: Collier, 1976.

This is an "autobiography" of Stanley Harold (King) Kong that might amuse unsophisticated fans of the 132-foot ape. Telling Kong's story allows Walter Wager, who wrote the impressive spy novel, *Telefon*, to use pseudo-comic routines, puns, inside-jokes, wild footnotes and assorted other sophomoric indulgences. Predictably Kong has strong opinions about a wide range of topics from Ann Darrow to RKO.

Humor is difficult subject to judge—some readers may indeed find this account funny. Anyway, its certainly different.

4498 *My Side of the Road.* by Lamour, Dorothy; and McInnes, Dick. 244 p. illus. Englewood Cliffs, N.J.: Prentice—Hall, 1980.

One's reaction to this autobiography will probably be similar to the prior feeling one has about the subject. Few minds will be changed by the story offered here. It is a mild memoir of the life and career of a modestly talented woman who was fortunate to be at the right studio at the right time—Paramount during the World War II years.

The anecdotes are harmless, the heroine is a hard-working performer-wife-mother and the story is mostly a "and then I made/appeared/sang" recital. Lamour takes care not to make too much of her bitterness toward Hope and Crosby for not giving her the lead in THE ROAD TO HONG KONG (1961), recognizing that her claim to celebrity rests largely on the "Road" films and the sarong she wore in several of them.

Illustrations, a filmography, and an index accompany this bland, disappointing recollection of a life crammed with the celebrities and films of Hollywood's golden era.

4499 *My Story: An Autobiography.* by Astor, Mary. 332 p. Garden City, N.Y.: Doubleday, 1959.

Miss Astor describes this book as an autobiographical analysis because the original material was written for a psychologist-priest. As a result, the book is a revealing and honest portrait of a life devoted to performing. Miss Astor's work extends from stage to screen and television. It is unfortunate that Miss Astor seemingly regards so much of her work in films as unworthy of mention and in some cases, does not bother to identify titles.

However, there is much included here about film personalities, backstage Hollywood and performer problems. Her ability to discuss with honest clarity her alcoholism, her many romances, and the famous Kaufman diary adds immeasurably to the book. A few illustrations are on the inside covers. One of the better film biographies.

4500 *My Story.* by Monroe, Marilyn. 143 p. illus. Briarcliff Manor, N.Y.: Stein and Day, 1974.

Although this volume lacks any introduction, the dust jacket and the final page assert that it is a manuscript given by Marilyn Monroe to her business partner, Milton Green, in whose name the copyright exists. It contains 35 short chapters, arranged in chronological order, from her traumatic childhood to her marriage to Joe DiMaggio. The writing reflects the screen image—a vulnerable, sexy woman wandering through the dangerous demanding pathway to Hollywood celebrity without notice or attention to the numerous flesh peddlers who populate the route.

Much contradiction exists between this story and the one told by others. Then, too, knowing the tragic conclusion does not lend conviction to the personal fairy tale related here. The reader will learn little that has not already appeared in earlier volumes. However, if the retelling of a studio-release-type biography in Monroe's unique style is desired, this volume is satisfactory. Acceptable.

4501 *My Ten Years in the Studios.* by Arliss, George. 349 p. illus. Boston: Little, Brown, 1941.

The transition of a stage performer into a motion picture actor is detailed in this volume. The period covered is approximately the first decade of sound films. Arliss originally was signed to make film versions of his stage successes. Later he created several original screen characters. The book is told in a leisurely, polite fashion. It is dignified, literate, intelligent, a bit pedantic, and it lacks any trace of humor. (When this book was written, Arliss was approximately 70 years old.)

From a performer noted for theatricalism in his portrayals, the book is a bit surprising in its serenity. It is pleasing, nevertheless. A good gallery of photographs is included as are the cast and credits of his films. Unfortunately the latter are not dated and are scattered throughout the book. Reading this volume may arouse a desire to see some of the films. (Is THE MILLIONAIRE (1931) with Cagney in a bit role a "lost" film?) Recommended for special interest readers.

4502 *My Time Is Your Time.* by Vallee, Rudy; and McKean, Gil. 244 p. paper illus. Stamford, Conn.: Astor-Honor, 1962.

Rudy Vallee was one of the original bandleader-crooners of the late twenties who went on to careers on stage, radio, television and films. From THE VAGABOND LOVER (1929) to HOW TO SUCCEED IN BUSINESS WITHOUT REALLY TRYING (1967), he appeared in leading roles in more than 35 films.

4503 *My Trip Abroad.* by Chaplin, Charles. 155 p. illus. New York: Harper, 1922.

An account of Chaplin's trip to Europe in the early twenties. Serious and thoughtful, the "little fellow" is replaced by the new world celebrity who is interested in things and persons of consequence.

4504 *My Victims.* by Berger, Oscar. 128 p. illus. New York: Harper, 1952.

A collection of caricatures of the stars of Hollywood's golden era, along with many other personalities.

4505 *My Way of Life.* by Crawford, Joan. 224 p. illus. New York: Simon and Schuster, 1971.

Although the book claims to be "autobiography and more," it is mostly "more." Ms. Crawford offers copious advice on dress, figure, face, hair, and other personal grooming matters. In addition she gives hints on travel, holding a job, keeping a man, entertaining, decoration, solitude, competing in a man's world, and many other such topics. These helpful hints for the incompetent have little place in film history.

4506 *My Wicked, Wicked Ways.* by Flynn, Errol. 512 p. paper New York: Dell, 1959.

This autobiography is a candid, colorful, well-written, and shocking. Flynn's adventurous life ended shortly after publication of this book, and it may be considered a typical Flynn legacy—a tongue-in-cheek adventure related with style. Those who scoff at Flynn's book or his films are not paying close attention. (Note: Earl Conrad is mentioned by his current publishers as having written this book for Flynn.)

Flynn's comments about his wives, co-stars, and directors are as unsparing as his statements about himself. Perhaps the one quality about the man that comes through consistently is the complete absence of self-pity. It is unfortunate that the book is not illustrated or indexed. Highly recommended, as entertainment, information, and a model of stylish film-star autobiography.

4507 *My Wild Love Experiences.* by Van Doren, Mamie. 128 p. paper illus.Chicago: Speciality Books, 1965.

A sad example of what aging sex kittens do with their extended leisure: they write (or have ghostwritten) books such as this one. Van Doren is also listed as author of *My Naughty, Naughty Life*, published in 1964.

4508 *My Wonderful World of Slapstick.* by Keaton, Buster; and Samuels, Charles. 282 p. illus. Garden City, N.Y. Doubleday, 1960.

The bittersweet career of one of the greatest silent screen comics is related in this autobiography. From early vaudeville days when he was five years old and became a case for the Society for the Prevention of Cruelty to Children (SPCC), the book traces his growth via vaudeville and early films toward his eventual world celebrity in the twenties. The last four decades of his life are a bit sad for the usual reasons—meaningless assignments, little recognition of his artistry until the last years, and financial troubles.

The emphasis here is on that golden period of silent film comedy, the twenties. His accounts of filmmaking are most satisfying. The book has little documentation of his films but does offer a few illustrations. No index is provided. A most valuable contribution

to screen history and literature. When his films become more available (through Raymond Rohauer), the book will serve as an admirable complement to them. Recommended.

4509 *My Young Life.* by Temple, Shirley; edited by Look Magazine Editors. 253 p. illus. Garden City, N.Y.: Garden City Publishing, 1945.

Lots of illustrations appear in this autobiography which takes Shirley Temple (born 1928) up to mid-adolescence.

4510 *The Myra Breckinridge Cookbook.* by Peper, Beverly; and Austen, Howard. 344 p. paper illus. Boston: Little, Brown, 1970.

If the reader is not already turned off by the title association, this paperback cookbook is unusual and may bring a smile. There are 300 recipes linked to films of the thirties and the forties. The quality of the food which results is uncertain, but the stills from the films will please most readers. Indexed.

4511 *Myrna Loy.* by Kay, Karyn. 160 p. paper illus. New York: Pyramid, 1977.

A title in the *Illustrated History Of the Movies* series, this volume surveys the life and films of Myrna Loy who is still active as a film performer. Her films are covered here from the mid-twenties to 1975. The text is accompanied by many photographs, a filmography, a bibliography, and an index.

4512 *Myself Among Others.* by Gordon, Ruth. 389 p. New York: Atheneum, 1971.

This series of character observations of varying lengths—one paragraph to a chapter—has a rambling, unstructured quality. Opinions, reminiscences, and recreated dialogues are given in a "Dear Diary" fashion. The book is noted here since Miss Gordon's life has included many film personalities and experiences. While some film personalities are mentioned, the legitimate stage supplies the setting for the largest number of anecdotes.

4513 *Myself and Some Others, etc.* by Nares, Owen. 204 p. paper illus. London: Duckworth, 1925.

The autobiography of a matinee idol who had a long career in films—from 1914 until 1941. Although he was very popular in the silents, he continued to appear with regularity on the London stage as a form of security.

4514 *The Mysterious Death of Marilyn Monroe.* by Hudson, James A. 112 p. paper illus. New York: Volitant Publishing Co., 1968.

This paperback quickie raises the following questions: What was Monroe's place in the "White House Set"? Who started the rumors about Monroe and Bobby Kennedy? Who talked to her on the last night of her life? Who was she telephoning as she died? How sure are authorities that Monroe was not murdered? Was vital evidence destroyed? Was Monroe a lesbian? Was Monroe a nymphomaniac?

It answers none of them. Noted here for the record.

4515 MYSTERY OF THE WAX MUSEUM. by Mullaly, Don; and Erickson, Carl. 163 p. paper illus. Madison, Wisc.: University of Wisconsin Press, 1979.

Script of the 1933 film directed by Michael Curtiz. Also contains: an introduction, "The Wax Museum Mystery," by Richard Koszarski, and cast, production credits and inventory.

4516 *Nabokov's Dark Cinema.* by Appel, Alfred, Jr. 324 p. illus. New York: Oxford University Press, 1974.

The argument put forth in this provocative volume is that Vladimir Nabokov's writing has been influenced to a great degree by film. Using *Lolita* as the primary case study, the author describes Nabokov's preparations for writing that novel. Other fiction written by Nabokov is discussed as is the work of other authors. Elements in their work are derived from film sources. Although Appel attributes a wide acquaintance with film to his authors, it is he who possesses the great knowledge of the medium. His ability to trace literary devices to their origins or use in motion pictures is continually impressive.

Attractive visuals are used intelligently throughout; they consist not only of film stills but also of personal photographs of Nabokov, cartoon frames, advertisements, etc. A detailed index and copious chapter notes complete the work. This volume is an example of outstanding scholarship. Presented in an attractive, well-produced format, it is sure to please the reader in search of a thoughtful intellectual exploration of the relationship between literature and film. Highly recommended.

4517 *The Naked and the Nude: Hollywood and Beyond.* by McConnachie, Brian. 152 p. paper illus. New York: Harmony, 1976.

The movie industry is satirized by the staff of *National Lampoon* in this paperback. There are illustrations, a fold-out map, and all the outrageous gags and comments one expects from the Lampoon writers.

4518 THE NAKED CITY. by Wald, Malvin; and Maltz, Albert. 148 p. illus. Carbondale, Ill.: Southern Illinois University Press, 1979.

Script of the 1948 film, which was directed by Jules Dassin. Also contains an afterword, "The Anatomy of a Hit," by Malvin Wald, and film credits.

4519 *Naked Hollywood.* by Weegee (Arthur Fellig); and Harris, Mel. illus. New York: Pellegrini & Cudahy, 1953.

The pictures in this collection were taken by Arthur Fellig (Weegee) during a four-year stay in Hollywood. Text and layout are by Mel Harris. Both men attempted to "define" Hollywood but admit to failure in the foreword. Nevertheless, the book does give a rather disillusioning portrait of Hollywood at the start of its demise. Its four acts are titled: dream factory; the people; private lives; and street scene. Noted here as one of the early picture books about film topics. A new addition was published in 1975 by Da Cabo.

4520 *Name Dropping.* by Pertwee, Michael. 213 p. paper illus. London: Leslie Frewin, 1974.

Michael Pertwee is a British writer known for his work in films, theatre and television. In this autobiography, he traces his life from World War I to the seventies. His career as a promising writer was interrupted by World War II, where he ended up as a major in the British Intelligence Corps. After demobilization, he resumed as "a highly professional hack" writing 37 films, 200 TV programs, six plays, two novels and this autobiography.

In accordance with the title, all the chapter heads include the word "dropping," and a selection of alphabetically dropped names preceeds the text. A few illustrations are added.

Pertwee's screen plays include LAUGHTER IN PARADISE (1951), TOP SECRET (1952), THE NAKED TRUTH (1958), THE MOUSE ON THE MOON (1962), A FUNNY

THING HAPPENED ON THE WAY TO THE FORUM (1966), SALT AND PEPPER (1963), etc. His accomplishments as a writer deserve more serious consideration. The frame that he has given his story is a bit too gimmicky.

4521 *Name That Movie: A Test Yourself Humor Book.* by Avallone, Michael. New York: School Book Service, 1978.

A quiz book designed for young adolescents.

4522 *Naming Names.* by Navasky, Victor S. 482 p. New York: Viking, 1980.

This examination of the McCarthy/Red-Scare era notes the focus of the House Un-American Activities Committee (HUAC) on Hollywood. Attention is given to the Hollywood Ten and the 1947 HUAC hearings. The resultant blacklists are described. In the spring of 1951, HUAC resumed hearings with Larry Parks "naming names," followed by many other informers.

In this meticulously researched volume, the author is concerned with differentiating between informers and resisters—both were victims of a great wrong, but it is the difference between the two that fascinates Navasky. What makes a person become an informer is a major theme of this "moral detective story."

4523 *Nancy.* by Reagan, Nancy; and Libby, Bill. 219 p. illus. New York: William Morrow, 1979.

An autobiography of film actress Nancy Davis who married Ronald Reagan and gave up her career for his. Much of this volume is devoted to persuading the reader that her husband is a wonderful, fine, decent human being. She is thankful she met such a man and feels he gave meaning to her life.

4524 *Nancy Reagan: A Special Kind of Love.* by Elwood, Roger. 159 p. paper illus. New York: Pocket Books, 1976.

The presidential primaries were held in the summer of 1976. This volume appeared earlier that year and its timing and content were probably dictated by that contest.

While some scant attention is given to background biography, including their film careers, the major portion of this text dealt with the recent life of the Reagans. Both are completely aware of mass media and its uses. This volume is a case in point. Acceptable only as an example of political campaign literature.

4525 NANOOK OF THE NORTH. by Kraus, Robert; and Flaherty, Robert. 32 p. illus. New York: Windmill Press, 1972.

Using Flaherty's classic, the author has selected pictures and captions to give young people an idea of Eskimo life.

4526 NASHVILLE. by Tewkesbury, Joan. paper illus. New York: Bantam, 1976.

Script of the 1975 film directed by Robert Altman. Also contains an introduction by Joan Tewkesbury, Hal Phillip Walker's platform, "New Roots For The Nation," lyrics to the songs, and complete cast and production credits.

4527 *Nathanael West: A Comprehensive Bibliography.* by White, William. 209 p. Kent, Ohio: Kent State University Press, 1975.

Nathanael West's books, plays, and periodical writings, along with biographical and critical material, are treated in this bibliography. Because of the increasing recognition and admiration of West's work, the volume will help to satisfy the many questions that arise about him. Of primary concern to film scholars is the list of filmscripts that he wrote. No mention is made of the two major films based on his novels—LONELYHEARTS (1958) and THE DAY OF THE LOCUST (1975)—although ADVICE TO THE LOVELORN (1932), the first adaptation of *Miss Lonelyhearts*, is noted.

The volume is designed for literature study rather than for film study.

4528 *The National Board of Censorship (Review) of Motion Pictures, 1909-1922.* by Feldman, Charles Matthew. New York: Arno, 1977.

Written in 1975 at the University of Michigan in partial fulfillment of the doctoral program, this study examines the historical growth of the National Board of Censorship from its initial conception in 1909 as a civic-oriented agency to its development as a national organization concerned with the self-regulation of the film industry. This comprehensive study, covering the legal and social transformation of this important and influential body, appears in the *Dissertations on Film* series.

4529 *National Directory of Arts Support by Business Corporations.* by Millsars, Daniel. 221 p. paper Washington D.C.: Washington International Arts Letter, 1979.

This is a title in *Arts Patronage* series. A long explanation on the title page reads, "listing some 700 of the many corporations along with 2800 of their subsidiaries, divisions, and affiliates, and a separate office locator; includes areas of corporate interest in arts/humanities and education in these fields."

The first section is an alphabetical listing of the corporations, consisting of the name, address, officers, the area of support, divisions and subsidiaries. References to film appear in some of the areas of interest, but inquiry would be necessary for full comprehension of type and amount of support provided. The closing section is an alphabetical "cream" list of patrons of the arts—those persons/officers most closely associated with providing grants.

The arrangement here necessitates a search through the first section to determine possible support for a specific medium or art. Once located, the minimal information given here necessitates further inquiry for any satisfactory information. Other titles in the *Arts Patronage* series are *Grants and Aid to Individuals in the Arts*, and *Arts Support by Private Foundations*.

4530 *National Film Archive Catalogue of Viewing Copies.* compiled by British Film Institute. paper London: British Film Institute, 1971.

A catalogue which lists 3000 duplicate prints available for student or researcher use on the Archive's premises. In the catalogue, films are classified as fiction, nonfiction or newsreel. Indexes to subjects, personalities and directors are included. A supplement to the above listing is also available.

4531 *National Film School.* compiled by Committee to Consider the Need for a National Film School. 49 p. paper London: Her Majesty's Stationery Office (HMSO), 1967.

A report from a committee established out of Britain's concern for its national film industry.

4532 *The National Film Theatre of London.* by Steele, Robert. 12 p. paper Boston: Communication Arts Division, Boston University, 1964.

4533 *National Organization for Audio-Visual Aids—Publications.* paper illus. London: The National Organization for Audio-Visual Aids (NOAVA), 1970-.

A proliferation of audiovisual organizations (NCAVAE, EFVA, NAVEX, etc.) is located at a single London address (33 Queene Anne St., London WIM OAL) and is housed under one umbrella title: The National Organization for Audio-Visual Aids. Each publishes materials that deal in part with film and its uses. A sampling of titles includes: *Visual Education*, Chris Webb, ed., periodical, 10 issues per year; *Lights Please—Using Projectors in the Classroom*, Robert Leggat, 1972; *Audio-Visual Aids—Films, Filmstrips, Transparencies, Wallsheets, Recorded Sound*, which is composed of seven volumes (in nine parts): Vol. 1 *Religious Education, English, Modern Languages*, 1971; Vol. 2 *History, Social History, Social Studies*, 1971; Vol. 3 *Economics, General, Physical and Economic Geography*, 1971; Vol. 4A *Regional Geography; General and Europe*, 1971; Vol. 4B *Regional Geography; The Americas, Africa, Asia, Australia*, 1971; Vol. 5 *Mathematics, Astronomy, Physics, Chemistry*, 1973; Vol. 6A *Palaentology, Biology, Botany, Zoology*, 1973; Vol. 6B *Human Biology, Hygiene, Health, Teacher Education*, 1973; and Vol. 7 *Engineering and Technology, Agriculture, Business Studies*, 1973.

Other titles include *Films for General Studies*, John Thole, ed., 1971; *Films or General Studies* 1973 Supplement, John Thole, ed., 1973; *A Classified Guide to Sources of Educational Film Material*, J. M. Kingdon, ed., 1972; *(A Survey of) British Research in Audio-Visual Aids, 1945-1971*, Helen Coppen, 1972; *(A Survey of) British Research in Audio-Visual Aids, 1972-1973*, Susie Rodwell, 1974; *The Audio-Visual Approach to Modern Language Teaching*, Peter J. Vernon, ed., 1973; *Audio-Visual Aids: An Introduction*, Tom Evans, ed., 1973; *A Report on 16mm Sound Film Projectors*, Experimental Development Unit Report, 1970.

4534 *The National Society of Film Critics on the Movie Star.* edited by Weis, Elisabeth. 390 p. illus. New York: Penguin, 1981.

A collection of essays, reviews, and personal interviews devoted to the star phenomena and the individuals who comprise it. Profiles for many stars are given in the material supplied by 26 contributing authors.

4535 *National Survey of Film and Television Higher Education Findings.*

compiled by Grogg, Sam. 26 p. paper Washington D.C.: American Film Institute, 1976.

This booklet presents the results of a questionnaire survey sent to over 3000 film/TV educators in the United States. About 24 percent, or 784, responded, and it is that data which is tabulated here. Questions included academic rank, years of experience, degrees, organizational membership, school goals, admission policies, teaching materials, teaching methods, periodicals used, texts, needed resources, etc. It is interesting to note the low priority consistently given to library books and periodicals.

4536 *The Natives Are Restless.* by Lindsay, Cynthia. 223 p. New York: Lippincott, 1960.

Short glimpses which indicate Hollywood was more straightlaced and conformist than surrounding Southern California communities.

4537 *The Nature and Art of Motion.* edited by Kepes, Gyorgy. 195 p. illus. New York: Braziller, 1964.

Theoretical principles and ideas expressed in articles by Gessner, Richter, etc. Many illustrations.

4538 *Nazi Cinema.* by Leiser, Erwin. 179 p. illus. New York: Macmillan, 1975.

A translation of the 1968 book, *Deutschland Erwache*, this volume considers the use of film by the Nazi party as an integral part of their plan for world domination. Analyzed in depth are films glorifying Hitler, Germany, and the Nazi party while others showed Russia, Poland, and England to be threatening evil neighbors. Jews as criminals deserving of extermination was a common theme, as was the glory of dying for the Fatherland.

How the party abolished critics, prepared special newsreels, and operated the Ministry of Popular Enlightenment as a war weapon is described. Every film had the same function: "to educate the people." Supporting this absorbing and sobering study are stills from the films, several appendixes, a bibliography, a filmography, and an index. These elements combine with the well-researched and written text to give the reader the best account of film as propaganda to date. Highly recommended.

4539 *'Neath the Mask: The Story of the East Family.* by East, John M. 356 p. illus. London: Allen and Unwin, 1967.

The author was a silent screen actor who appeared from 1914 in LITTLE LORD FAUNTLEROY to OWD BOB (1924).

4540 *Necrology of the Cinema.* by Stuckey, Frank. 161 p. New York: Gordon, 1977.

In the introduction to this volume, published in 1977, the author states, "...I was not able to find a book with the complete story of their deaths, so I wrote this book." Either he or his editors should have located Truitt's *Who Was Who on Screen*, originally published in 1974 with a second edition appearing in 1977. Also in 1977 the *New York Times* published *Hollywood Album*, a collection of obituaries from that newspaper. The duplication of effort could be forgiven if there was some quality to be found here. However, with such brief entries, and a typewritten offset production, the only thing this book has to offer is a provocative title.

4541 *The Need for Competent Film Music Criticism.* by Keller, Hans H. 22 p. paper London: British Film Institute, 1947.

A valid argument appears in an older pamphlet designed "for those who care for film as art, with a final section for those who do not."

4542 *Need Johnny Read?* by Goldman, Frederick; and Burnett, Linda R. 238 p. paper illus. Dayton, Ohio: Pflaum, 1971.

The question proposed by the title of this book challenges the position of print literacy in the educational experience. The authors present abundant evidence to identify their position in the first section. In the remaining portion they offer positive suggestions for enriching humanities courses, mostly by the use of films and by film study. Using six components of film—visuals, sound, editing, acting, narrative, symbolism and metaphor—is recommended as a base for film study. Other suggestions are intriguing—the use of short films only, a plea for teachers rather than pedantic scholars, etc.

The book is a strong argument for introducing courses in visual literacy into our schools. Reasons put forth are not only emotionally persuasive but are supported by citations, quotes, and references from authoritative sources. Highly recommended.

4543 *Negative Space: Manny Farber on the Movies.* by Farber, Manny. 288 p. New York: Praeger, 1971.

Manny Farber is a painter who obviously loves movies. This anthology of Farber's film criticism covers approximately 25 years and is indexed. Mr. Farber may not be a copious writer but he is one of high quality. Original in his approach and in his thinking, he is less the "arty" critic and more the searching entertaining analyst. His knowledge and background provide impressive corroboration for his arguments and opinions. Included here are articles on directors and producers Hawks, Huston, Val Lewton, Capra, Sturges, Seigel, Fuller, Godard and Bunuel. Other articles are on specific films, screen acting and the New York Film Festival.

Farber's style is on target and funny. He says 1) Jean Moreau's acting consists of two expressions— starved and half-starved; 2) Samuel Fuller's scripts might have been written by the bus driver of the "Honeymooners"; 3) Rosalind Russell in HIS GIRL FRIDAY (1940) plays a female Jimmy Breslin. He also has talent for inventing appropriate phrases and puns to describe qualities of film: "The Gimp," "Termite Art," "Nearer My Agee to Thee." "The Cold That Came into the Spy," "The Wizard of Gauze," "Day of the Lesteroid." Appreciation should be given to Praeger for collecting these pleasures. Highly recommended.

4544 *A Neglected Art.* by Prendergast, Roy M. 268 p. illus. New York: New York University Press, 1977.

Roy Prendergast divided his book, which is subtitled "A Critical Study of Music in Films," into three parts—history, aesthetics, and technique. In the first and longest section, he reviews the music in silent films, the early sound films, the golden age films (1935-50), recent films (1950-present) and animated/experimental films. The section on aesthetics treats the contribution of music to films, while the last section deals with the creative process of supplying music for films. The illustrations consist mostly of musical excerpts from famous film scores. A bibliography and an index conclude the study.

Although the ability to read/play music is almost essential for a full appreciation of the volume, there is enough textual information and critical comment to warrant general reader attention. Since Prendergast is working in a relatively undocumented film area, his opinions are quite original and often stimulating. He writes with clarity and his affectionate respect for his subject is apparent throughout. Recommended.

4545 *The Negro in Films.* by Noble, Peter. 288 p. illus. New York: Arno Press, 1970 (1948).

This pioneer volume had pertinence when it was first issued in 1948 and seems more important now. A reminder of the many ways in which blacks were used and misused in films, the book surveys both silent films and sound films for the first half of this century. Biographical sketches of leading players are included.

The book ends at the period when the films began to change in their portrayal of blacks; it becomes openended and proposes the question of what has happened since—which is dealt with in Mapp's *Blacks in American Films.* However, many of the older films appear with regularity on TV. Illustrations used are thoughtful and complement the text effectively. The appendices include a partially annotated bibliography and a list of films which featured blacks or contained racial themes.

4546 *The Negro in Hollywood Films.* by Jerome, Victor J. 64 p. paper New York: Masses and Mainstream, 1950.

An expansion of a lecture delivered at a public forum held under the auspices of the Marxist cultural magazine, *Masses and Mainstream,* on February 3, 1950.

4547 NEVER GIVE A SUCKER AN EVEN BREAK. by Niville, John T.; and Chaplin, Prescott; and Fields, W. C. 124 p. paper illus. New York: Simon and Schuster, 1973.

Script of the 1941 film directed by Edward Cline. Contains: NEVER GIVE A SUCKER AN EVEN BREAK (1941); TILLIE AND GUS (1933); an introduction by Andrew Sinclair; casts and credits.

4548 *Never Trust a Man Who Doesn't Drink.* by Fields, W. C. unpaginated. illus. Hollywood, Calif.: Stanyan Books, 1971.

The *Stanyan* series of books is distributed by Random House and has included *Bogart's Face, I Never Met a Kid I Liked, Actors About Acting, Loving, Living, Life* and *Judy—A Remembrance.* This collection of W. C. Fields' quotes, comments and wisdom, originally published in 1971, has had four printings up to 1975. Compiled by Paul Mason and illustrated by original art work, the short volume is a novelty book that will please admirers of Fields.

Acceptable.

4549   *The New American Cinema: A Critical Anthology.* edited by Battcock, Gregory. 256 p. paper illus. New York: Dutton, 1967.

The new American cinema of the title is sometimes known as the underground film. This anthology looks at some of the films and filmmakers associated with the movement which had its greatest impact in the sixties and spearheaded, in part, the new screen freedom. Today the use of the term "underground" might be replaced by either "experimental" or "avant-garde."

Considered in the volume are such filmmakers as Warhol, Mekas, Anger, Smith, Brakhage, the Kuchars, Markopoulous, and others. The format consists of a general survey, some explanation and theory and then a critical look at certain films and their creators. The quality of the articles varies greatly. Persons who have never seen the films may find the going a bit rough. For others, the anthology resembles the subject material. At times, you have to wade through a mass of material to get a few moments of complete artistry. Illustrations are few and poor in quality. Suggested primarily for special tastes and for scholars.

4550   *The New Australian Cinema.* edited by Murray, Scott. 207 p. illus. London: Elm Tree (Zoetrope in U.S.), 1980.

This profusely illustrated survey looks at the new wave of Australian films which began appearing on world screens in the seventies. Includes full color illustrations and a filmography.

4551   *The New Bohemia.* by Gruen, John. 180 p. illus. New York: Shorecrest, 1966.

This volume deals with the avant-garde, including those working with film. Gruen feels that filmmakers like Warhol or the Kuchar brothers will bring about an artistic renaissance by their irrationality. The volume also deals with musicians, playwrights, actors, etc.

4552   *The New Breed of Performer.* by Gemme, Leila. 189 p. paper illus. New York: Pocket Books, 1970.

To qualify for inclusion in this collective biography, a subject must have defied convention because of his or her convictions. Some have refused to be subservi-

ent to organizations while others are political/social activists. Film subjects include Liza Minnelli, Shirley MacLaine, George C. Scott, Bette Midler, Jon Voight, Bill Cosby, Jane Fonda, Barbra Streisand, and Marlon Brando. Each is given a capsule biography based on public records. Even such a simplistic approach is flawed here—dates are constantly confused, and the chronology of events is erroneous, i.e., screwball comedies come from the thirties, not the forties, and Streisand's first album in 1963 was largely responsible for her early fame.

The material presented is selected and noncritical. It will serve the casual reader looking for general information.

4553   *New Cinema in Britain.* by Manvell, Roger. 160 p. paper illus. New York: Dutton, 1969.

A picture-text history of the post-war British feature film, this book reminds one of the large and impressive contribtuion of English filmmakers to the cinema art. Here, in skillfully selected stills and intelligent narrative, is a recapitulation of what might be termed a Golden Age of British cinema. The author, a legendary name in film literature, adds still another achievement to his active career. The reproduction of the pictorial material is superior to that appearing in most books today. Very highly recommended for all readers.

4554   *New Cinema in Eastern Europe.* by Whyte, Alistair. 159 p. paper illus. New York: Dutton, 1971.

For the purposes of this book, Eastern Europe consists of Poland, Hungary, Czechoslovakia, Yugoslavia, Bulgaria, Albania, Romania and East Germany. As usual with the *Studio Vista* series, the many visuals are superbly reproduced. Nearly every page contains a visual large enough to reinforce the ideas of the accompanying text. Emphasis is on the new directors appearing in these countries. The recurrent theme in many of the films seems to be the role of the individual in society. The book has a short bibliography and an index. Beautifully done and highly recommended.

4555   *New Cinema in Europe.* by Manvell, Roger. 106 p. paper illus. New York: Dutton, 1966.

After an introduction which notes recent changes in the European film and the trend towards realism, Manvell groups the films by their country of origin —Italian, French, Swedish, British, Soviet, and Polish. As usual with this pictureback series, both text

666

and illustrations are excellent.

4556 *New Cinema in Finland.* edited by Hillier, Jim. 43 p. paper illus. London: British Film Institute, 1972.

4557 *New Cinema In Spain.* by Molin-Foix, Vincente. 55 p. paper London: BFT; New York: Zoetrope, 1977.

4558 *New Cinema in the USA.* by Manvell, Roger. 160 p. paper illus. New York: Dutton, 1968.

A survey of American feature films since 1946, this is another quality paperback from *Studio Vista/Dutton*. In this one the arrangement of films is by topic or category rather than chronological. The usual well-written Manvell text supported by a generous collection of nicely reproduced film stills earn more kudos for the author.

4559 *New Courts of Industry: Self Regulation Under the Motion Picture Code.* by Nizer, Louis. 344 p. New York: J. S. Ozer, 1971 (1935).

One of the series entitled, "Motion Pictures: Their Impact on Society," this 1935 volume was originally published by Longacre Press. It is a detailed analysis of the operation of the Hays Office and the administration of the Production Code. Problems, solutions, and the explanation of specific actions by the Office are discussed. The use of members of the industry to act as a court to settle disputes was a valid method then and remains so today. This volume is of historical interest only.

4560 *New Directions in Documentary.* compiled by International Edinburgh Film Festival. 41 p. paper illus. Edinburgh: Film House, 1952.

A report of the international conference held at Edinburgh, August 25-26, 1952.

4561 *The New Documentary in Action: A Casebook in Film-Making.* by Rosenthal, Alan. 320 p. illus. Berkeley, Calif.: University of California Press, 1971.

A collection of 17 interviews with leading directors from all film genres is recorded in this volume. Seven examples: "Direct Cinema (Frederick Wiseman); "TV Journalism" (Arthur Barron); "Re-Enactments" (Peter Watkins); "Specials" (Don Pen-

nebaker); "Sponsored Films" (George Stoney); "Candid Camera" (Allen Funt); and "Animation" (Norman McLaren). With participants of this calibre and an ability on the part of interviewer Rosenthal to question with honesty, intelligence and understanding, the book is almost certain to please most readers.

4562 *The New Film Index.* by MacCann, Richard Dyer; and Perry, Edward S. 522 p. New York: E. P. Dutton, 1975.

The long wait for this volume has been justified by its excellent content, format and production. As a supplement to the original classic volume, the book makes a few major departures or changes that are suggested by its subtitle, "A Bibliography of Magazine Articles in English 1930-1970." It eliminates illustrations and the treatment of books, film reviews, and book reviews—all of which were major elements of the original. Many of the entries in the first book also referred to chapters or parts of books, and that feature is also missing here. The category arrangement is quite different, with MacCann-Perry's being far more useful, efficient, and pertinent than the original's.

In the new work the articles are arranged under the following headings (which are further subdivided): 1. Introduction and Reference, 2. Motion-Picture Arts and Crafts, 3. Film Theory and Criticism, 4. Film History, 5. Biography, 6. Motion Picture Industry, 7. Film and Society, 8. Non-fiction Films, and 9. Case Histories of Film Making. A final section is a lengthy, detailed "Index to the Index," which will facilitate location and retrieval of any information contained in this massive, complex reference work.

The film periodicals indexed are noted and are approximately 40 in number. Many other general magazines are cited but no listing or count is furnished for this latter group. The book is essentially a subject index with the entries arranged chronologically by publication date. Author, title, source, date, volume, page, etc., are noted and a short descriptive annotation is offered for most entries. According to the authors, the annotations were supplied by students. About 10 percent of the entries are cross-indexed.

Since the differences between this book and its original inspiration are considerable, one might have some reservation about the title. There can be none, however, about the content, its arrangement, and the production care given it by the authors and publishers. These elements are consistently high in quality. Here, then, is an essential reference book.

4563 *The New German Cinema.* by Sandford, John. 180 p. illus. New York: Barnes and Noble (Harper), 1980.

This volume on the history of German film since World War II has been given a very fine production. This is in keeping with the high quality of the text, which presents sections on the background of West German cinema, seven directors (Alexander Kluge, Jean-Marie Straub, Volker Schlondorff, Werner Herzog, Rainer Werner Fassbinder, Wim Wenders, and Hans Jurgen Syberberg), other directors, the outlook, the problems and the prospect. Accompanying this material are notes, a glossary, a filmography, a bibliography, an index and some excellent illustrations. Recommended.

4564 *New Hollywood.* by Blumenberg, Hans C. 184 p. illus. Munich: Carl Hanser Verlag, 1976.

Contains a bibliography and a filmography.

4565 *The New Hollywood.* by Madsen, Axel. 183 p. illus. New York: Thomas Y. Crowell, 1975.

This volume explores the 20-year change in the American motion picture industry, from mogul domination through the money manager era and finally up to the seventies. In this latter section Peter Bogdanovich and Francis Ford Coppola are singled out for individual attention. Emphasis on the present can be noted in chapters devoted to studio heads, nonconformist directors, superstars, scripts, producer packaging, liberated directors, camera use, visual impact, finance, advertising-selling, mature themes, pornography, violence, audiences, film cycles, and future trends. Accompanying this survey are two sets of illustrations and an index.

The two elements that contribute most to the quality of the book are Madsen's encyclopedic knowledge of today's Hollywood and his ability to write witty, sophisticated paragraphs which enhance rather than weaken his narrative. He is critical without being destructive, objective without being bland, and erudite without being overconfident. The result is a well-written, informative and entertaining book. Recommended.

4566 *The New Hollywood and the Academy Awards.* by Fredrik, Nathalie. 208 p. paper illus. Beverly Hills, Calif.: Hollywood Awards Publ., 1971.

An updated paperback, see *Hollywood and the Academy Awards.*

4567 *New Jersey In the Classroom.* edited by Brainard, Elsie. 37 p. paper New Jersey: Educational Media Association, 1978.

A pioneer publication that can serve as an example for other states, this booklet lists all types of media currently available about New Jersey. In addition to much print material, the booklet also includes such films as CRANBERRY INDUSTRY OF NEW JERSEY, HERE IS NEW JERSEY, MOSQUITO STORY, etc. A title index and an index by media would have helped.

4568 *A New Joy.* by Evans, Colleen Townsend. 124 p. Old Tappan, N.J.: Fleming H. Revell, 1973.

Colleen Townsend was a film actress under contract to 20th-Century Fox whose films include JANIE (1944), THE WALLS OF JERICHO (1948), CHICKEN EVERY SUNDAY (1949) and WHEN WILLIE COMES MARCHING HOME (1950). With her marriage to a minister, she gave up her career to engage in religious activities such as speaking to groups, writing, and committee work. This volume is her interpretation of the beatitudes. It is not pertinent for film history but is noted for the record.

4569 *The New Latin American Cinema.* by Burton, Julianne. 29 p. paper New York: Cineaste, 1976.

An annotated bibliography (pamphlet No. 4) of English language sources of information on Latin American cinema from 1960 to 1976.

4570 *The New Literacy: The Language of Film and Television.* by Foster, Harold M. 72 p. paper Urbana, Ill.: National Council of the Teachers of English, 1979.

4571 *The New Media.* by Schramm, W.; and Coombs, P. H.; and Kahnert, F.; and Lyle, J. 175 p. New York: Columbia University Press, 1968.

Addressed to educators, this report is concerned with instructional television, radio, and films. It stresses such factors as cost, efficiency, and effectiveness. All levels of education are considered in studies conducted in 18 countries.

4572 *A New Note on the Film.: A Theory Of Film Criticism Derived from Susanne K Langer's Philosophy of Art.* by Curran, Trisha. New York:

Arno, 1980.

The author adapts Susan Langer's philosophy to an investigation of the mode, the primary illusion, the form of the film, and the critique of the form. This is a title in the *Dissertations on Film* series.

4573 *A New Pictorial History of the Talkies.* by Blum, Daniel; and Kobal, John. 392 p. illus. New York: G. P. Putnam's, 1973.

One of the classic volumes in film literature reappears here in a new updated edition. Enthusiasm for the original volume was great and still applies. However, some major reservations must be stated about the new material supplied by Kobal—which covers 1958 to 1973. First, his selection is simply not as good as Blum's. Examination of certain visuals Kobal uses shows them to be too small to interpret, e.g., THE SEAGULL (1968), THE RAILWAY CHILDREN (1971), THE TROJAN WOMEN (1972), or poorly chosen, e.g., MY FAIR LADY (1964), PRETTY MAIDS ALL IN A ROW (1971), THE BOYFRIEND (1971), and the unidentified picture on the bottom of page 329, etc. Other visuals are simply dull and not at all representative of their parent film. Picture reproduction in the Kobal section varies a great deal. Some visuals are so black as to defy immediate interpretation—WILLARD (1971), ROMA (1972), DR. FAUSTUS (1968), etc., while others are chopped off the page with an appreciable portion missing—ACCIDENT (1967), KES (1970), THE ABOMINABLE DR. PHIBES (1971), etc. The book has a detailed index. This volume is a cherished one for information/reference and for pure entertainment. The carelessness in the production and selection of new material detracts from Daniel Blum's original fine work and diminishes a popular book in film literature. Recommended with above reservations.

4574 *New Screen Techniques.* edited by Quigley, Martin. 208 p. illus. New York: Quigley Publ. Co., 1953.

An anthology that concerns itself with wide screen, 3-D, etc. Addressed mostly to industry professionals, the articles will have slight interest for the general audience.

4575 *New Singer New Song.* by Winter, David. 160 p. illus. Waco, Texas: Word Books, 1967.

The name of Cliff Richard is relatively unknown in this country. In England, during the early sixties, he was a top recording personality who also made several successful films. American audiences saw him in only one or two; the others were never given any distribution here. The best known is EXPRESSO BONGO (1959), in which he played the title role, a rock singer who achieves a sudden celebrity. Richard's life story does not present an especially flattering or inspiring example. He appears to be a determined, disciplined, ambitious, rather cold person who had more than a usual share of good luck. In the last chapter, Richard finds religious salvation via Billy Graham, the Christian Youth Crusade, and other Christian endeavors.

A filmography (six films) and a complete discography are included, as are several good illustrations. Whenever a book appears to have the sponsorship of a religious group, one suspects persuasion, propaganda and a hard sell for conversion—see Dale Evans, *Dale* and *The Woman at the Well.* While there are such elements in this book, they are minimal. The biography itself is unintentionally revealing, as much by its omissions as by its statements.

4576 *A New Song.* by Boone, Pat. 200 p. illus. Coral Stream, Ill.: Creation House, 1970.

In discussing his search and discovery of Jesus Christ, Pat Boone relates a few of his filmmaking experiences. His biographical references are selected by their pertinence to his religious beliefs. Following the same publishing example of Dale Evans, Anita Bryant, Colleen Townsend and others, Boone has apparently attracted a sufficient readership to warrant seven hardcover printings and an additional sale of 625,000 copies in five paperback printings up to 1973. That evidence suggests a quality that will escape those critics eager to dismiss this volume for all the easy reasons. Although religion is the major topic, Boone's honest, open style of talking about himself, his career and his family is often interesting and disarming. This is not a book for film study, but it does offer some insight into the topic of celebrities and religion.

4577 *The New Spirit in the Cinema.* by Carter, Huntly. 403 p. illus. New York: Arno Press, 1970 (1930).

A windy, overblown presentation about the state of cinema in 1930, this book has as its subtitle: "An analysis and interpretation of the parallel paths of the cinema, which have led to the present revolutionary crisis forming a study of the cinema as an instrument of sociological humanism." Sound like a put-on? Consider that the author also wrote *The New Spirit in Drama and Art*, *The New Spirit in European Drama*, *The New Spirit in the Russian Theatre*, etc. All this makes the reader wish for "The

New Spirit in Meaningful Communication."

The author's style is opinionated, unfocused, verbose, and quite offensive. He is not above intimidating the reader, the reviewer, or anyone who may not share his dubious opinions. A few pictures are included. Should this one ever come your way, consider it only as an early sample of the obfuscation and perversion of film literature. Decidedly not recommended.

4578   *The New Spirit in the Russian Theatre 1917-1928.* by Carter, Huntly. 348 p. illus. New York: Arno Press, 1970 (1929).

Relationships between film, radio and the theatre in Russia from 1917 to 1928 are studied.

4579   *New Star Over Hollywood.* by Anderson, Nancy. 191 p. illus. Van Nuys, Calif.: Bible Voice, 1975.

Nancy Anderson, a West Coast editor of *Photoplay*, records a spiritual, religious revival in Hollywood that has attracted certain celebrities. Here 20 of them go on public record as having committed their lives to Jesus. Separate treatments consisting mostly of a blend of biographical information and religious quotation are offered for each of the subjects. Those known for film work include Dean Jones, Jane Withers, James Fox, James Hampton, and Jack Cassidy. A portrait of each is provided.

4580   *The New Swedish Cinema.* by Sundgren, Nils Petter. 57 p. paper illus. Stockholm: The Swedish Institute, 1970.

Sundgren is a film critic and educator who addresses himself here to the rebirth of Swedish cinema in the sixties. The topics discussed are the Swedish Film Institute, the new directors, and the veterans. Bo Widerberg, Jan Troell, Jorn Donner, Vilgot Sjoman are among the former group, Ingmar Bergman, Alf Sjoberg and Arne Sucksdorff in the latter. The book is illustrated with pictures of most of the directors, and offers a short bibliography which separates its listings by language—English, French, Hungarian, Italian and Portuguese. As a short surface assessment of Swedish cinema during the sixties, this book is acceptable.

4581   *The New Technique of Screen Writing.* by Lane, Tamar. 342 p. New York: Whittlesey House, 1936.

The first section of this volume is concerned with technique, theory and other problems of screen writing. The book is quite dated in the second section which deals with the marketing of the finished script. The specimen manuscripts appended are still interesting. Contains the script of TRANSATLANTIC MERRY-GO-ROUND (1934).

4582   *The New Theatre and Cinema of Soviet Russia.* by Carter, Huntly. 277 p. illus. New York: Arno Press, 1970 (1924).

4583   *The New Wave.* by Graham, Peter. 184 p. illus. Garden City, N.Y.: Doubleday, 1968.

An anthology of writings by both directors and critics, this book attempts to describe the "New Wave" phenomena, the changing of the theoretical critic to the practicing director to the artist. Several of the New Wave directors were critics for *Cahiers du Cinema* and a small sampling of their writing is given. Two articles by Andre Bazin along with an appreciation of his contribution to film criticism are included. Most of the articles are serious, intellectual analyses that typify the influential *Cahiers* content. An attempt to unite the writings with the general theme is made. The book is specialized and will be of interest primarily to New Wave director devotees. Illustrations are good and a short bibliography is appended.

4584   *The New Wave.* by Monaco, James. 372 p. illus. New York: Oxford University Press, 1976.

The New Wave is defined by James Monaco in this detailed study as "simply Truffaut, Godard, Chabrol, Rohmer, and Rivette." In addition to presenting individual studies of these men, the author also develops a theory of the New Wave. Although the men are basically different, some common characteristics are noted: professional background as film critics, an intellectual attitude toward film art, a strong curiosity, etc. Each director is considered separately, with major attention given to Truffaut and Godard. Using the films of each director as a central focus, the author notes plots, directorial methods, actor performances, themes, and filmmaking techniques. Supplementing the film analysis is information about the director's political activities, their personal lives, and the possible meanings, interpretations or implications of their work. The book contains many illustrations, most of which are well reproduced. Some chapter notes and an impressive bibliography conclude the volume. An index is provided.

The analyses of the films of the five directors are impressive in scope, detail, and treatment. Monaco's carefully prepared text provides an intelligent explanation of and an excellent guide to the New Wave movement. Recommended.

4585 *New Women in Entertainment.* by Bowman, Kathleen. 47 p. paper illus. Mankato, Minn.: Creative Education, 1976.

Designed for a juvenile audience, this original paperback is a collective biography of seven female performers. Treated very briefly are Lily Tomlin, Diana Ross, Cicely Tyson, Valerie Harper and three pop music singers.

4586 *New York Film Festival Programs (1963-1975).* edited by Film Society of Lincoln Center. unpaginated illus. New York: Arno, 1976.

The programs distributed at the first 13 New York Film Festivals (1963-1975) are accumulated in this interesting book.

Arranged in chronological fashion, they usually provide casts, credits, an illustration, running time, previous awards and some background information. Since they are reproduced from originals, the reader is also provided with advertisements, acknowledgements, and announcements that are of little concern. The film information is important, however, as it provides a record of those films recognized by the festival.

4587 *New York Production Manual, 1979/1980.* by Bension, Shmuel. 600 p. paper illus. New York: Production Manual Inc., 1979.

This manual is a compilation of information designed to assist anyone engaged in the production of films or television in the New York area. Included are sections on production logistics (permits, insurance, major contacts, etc.), unions and guilds (wages, working conditions), and miscellaneous production services (10,000 entries listed under more than 100 different classifications).

4588 *New York Production Manual, 1981: The Producer's Masterguide for Motion Picture, Television Commercials and Videotape Industries.* by Bension, Shmuel. 1000 p. New York: N.Y. Production Manual, 1981.

4589 *The New York Times at the Movies.* compiled by New York Times Critics. illus. New York: New York Times Books, 1979.

A selection of film reviews from *The New York Times* are reproduced here along with stills, photos, original ads, posters, etc. Bosley Crowther supplies an introduction to the reviews, which span the period from BIRTH OF A NATION (1914) to SUPERMAN (1978).

4590 *The New York Times Biographical Edition.* edited by New York Times Editors. paper illus. New York: Arno, 1971- .

This compilation of "current biographical information of general interest" consists of two loose-leaf binders holding a total of some 3200 pages. The material is taken from the pages of the *New York Times* (features, articles, obits, etc.). Many persons who have appeared in films are included. Note: this reference is available only by subscription.

4591 *The New York Times Directory of the Film.* by New York Times Staff. 1243 p. illus. New York: Arno, 1971.

An introduction by Arthur Knight begins this spin-off from the massive six-volume set, *The New York Times Film Reviews, 1913-1968.* The contents include: 2000 small photos of actors and actresses; nearly 900 pages of credits (covers all 18,000 films of the large set); awards section, including Academy (from 1927), New York Film Critics (from 1935), and New York Times Ten Best (from 1924); 500 reviews, with selection based on awards listed above, arranged chronologically; a listing of 1500 film companies and their product. Much of the material here is selected from the key or index volume to the large set. This does not in any way diminish its value or potential. The vast amount of film information in this single volume makes it a "must" for those who cannot afford the larger set.

4592 *The New York Times* Film Reviews. 4961 p. (6 volumes) illus. New York: The Times, 1913-1968.

This massive reference work includes six volumes of 17,000 original film reviews as published in *The New York Times* arranged chronologically 1913-1968. The sixth volume is the key and guide to the other five, in addition to being an encyclopedia itself. In this 1300-page volume there are more than 250,000 entries arranged according to the personality, the film title, or the production company. More than 2000 small photographs comprise a section aptly called "The Portrait Gallery," and there is a summarized year-by-year award section. Its research value is apparent, and in addition it is not complicated to use and can answer many questions about film with both efficiency and accuracy.

4593   *The New York Times Film Reviews, 1913-1970: A One-Volume Selection.* by Amberg, George. 495 p. illus. New York: Quadrangle Books, 1971.

The blurb on the dust jacket says it right off: "For people who really deserve the enormous 7-volume set of the *New York Times Film Reviews* but just can't spare $425."

George Amberg has done a brilliant job in his one-volume selection of 400 reviews. This testimonial is based upon the experience of using the volume for several years and not finding it lacking more than once or twice. Reviews of nearly all of the critical and popular film classics seem to be here. In addition, there are six essays which divide the reviews into general eras, and an introduction, all by Amberg. A portrait section of the stars is unnecessary and the title index would be more functional if it were placed up front, rather than with those portraits. All of this is unimportant compared with the reference value of this book for the smaller library, or even its appeal to the individual who wants a basic reference work on film.

4594   *The New York Times Film Reviews, 1969-1970 .* 333 p. illus. New York: The New York Times, 1971.

This is the seventh volume in the set of *New York Times Film Reviews* and it now extends the collection from 1913 to 1970. Some 809 films are considered with illustrations and an index of over 10,000 entries. The volume is available by itself or as part of the complete set.

4595   *The New York Times Guide to Movies on TV.* edited by Thompson, Howard. 223 p. paper illus. Chicago, Quadrangle Books, 1970.

This indispensable guide may be used as a partial and abbreviated paperback version of the later volumes of the more expensive *New York Times Film Reviews.* Most of the more than 2000 films listed alphabetically here were made between 1950 and 1969. A few earlier films are considered. For each film the following data are given: a photograph, a one-line capsule comment (sometimes funny but often coy or cute), color or black & white, release

date, credits (usually scriptwriter, director, producer, and studio), cast (usually six or seven names), synopsis and evaluation (usually about 100 words and sometimes much more). Excepting certain flat one-liners, everything about the volume including the price is commendable. Recommended.

4596   *New Zealand Films.* compiled by High Commissioner for New Zealand in Canada. 62 p. paper illus. Ottawa: Office of the High Commissioner for New Zealand, 1961.

4597   *Newsreel: Documentary Filmmaking on the American Left.* by Nichols, William James. New York: Arno, 1980.

A study of the political filmmaking collective, Newsreel, from 1971 to 1975. Interviews, screenings, research, etc. lead to an analysis that combines Marxian philosophy, semiology, systems theory, and structuralism. This is a title in the *Dissertations on Film* series.

4598   *Newsreel Man.* by Peden, Charles. 126 p. illus. New York: Doubleday, Doran, 1932.

A general overview of the profession of making newsreel and travel films the world over. A bit of newsreel history is offered along with some impressions of world celebrities. Contains many illustrations.

4599   *Newsreels Across the World.* by Baechlin, Peter. 100 p. illus. New York: Columbia Univ. Press, 1952.

An international survey of newsreels—their costs, problems, coverage, etc.

4600   *Next Time Drive Off the Cliff!.* by Fernett, Gene. 205 p. illus. Cocoa, Fla.: Cinememories Pub. Co., 1968.

This text-picture book, from a limited edition of 1500 copies, is the study of one of the "Poverty Row" film studios that blossomed in Hollywood around 1930 and were out of business by the forties. In this case, Mascot Pictures Studio under the direction of its president, Nat Levine, turned out silent and sound serials and a few sound features. John Wayne, Boris Karloff, George Brent, Bela Lugosi and others appeared in Mascot films early in their careers.

The volume has many rare photographs and these cannot fail to interest the mature reader who will recall many faces and films. The younger reader might be a bit puzzled. Production quality of the book varies greatly. There is extensive page-padding of cast and credits in the appendix. (The information could fit in one quarter of the space it occupies.) Occasionally the text is fragmented and repetitious. The nostalgic, older movie buff will overlook these faults and enjoy this book immensely, if copies are still available.

4601 *Nice Work.* by Brunel, Adrian. 217 p. illus. London: Forbes Robertson, 1949.

Brunel was a filmmaker whose career in British films spans more than 30 years. The emphasis in this autobiography is on the silent picture era. He held many postions within the industry and knew many famous persons during his career. Most are indicated here. Primarily of interest to historians.

4602 NICHOLAS AND ALEXANDRA. 28 p. paper illus. Englewood Cliffs, N.J.: Charnell Theatrical Enterpr., 1971.

The emphasis is on history in this oversized souvenir book which includes several double-paged illustrations. In addition to the interesting historical background material, a diagram showing the royal line of Russian nobility is included. Cast and production credits are noted.

4603 *Nicholas Ray.* by Kreidl, John Francis. 230 p. illus. Boston, Mass.: Twayne, 1977.

This appreciation of Nicholas Ray, a volume in the Twayne *Theatrical Arts* series, concentrates on RE-BEL WITHOUT A CAUSE (1955). After a short biographical sketch, a few early Ray films are discussed briefly. JOHNNY GUITAR (1954) is given extended treatment as the archetypal Ray film. Following are five chapters which analyze REBEL WITHOUT A CAUSE from its original idea/script to its impact in America and Europe. Final chapters deal with a few of Ray's later films and his legacies to younger filmmakers. The text is illustrated and chapter notes/references are provided. An index and a filmography conclude the book.

The quality of the analysis provided, along with the supporting critical comment, make this a provocative, informative study of a neglected American director. Recommended.

4604 *Nicolas Roeg.* by Feineman, Neil. 153 p. illus. Boston: Twayne, 1978.

According to Warren French, the editor of the Twayne *Theatrical Arts* series, the purpose of the books is "to recognize and call attention" to unrecognized or neglected filmmakers "so that their audiences may be expanded and the opportunities to forward their work increased." This study of director Nicolas Roeg should help to make his four films —PERFORMANCE (1970), WALKABOUT (1971), DON'T LOOK NOW (1973), and THE MAN WHO FELL TO EARTH (1976)—more appreciated. After a distinguished career as a cinematographer, Roeg directed his first film at age 40.

His methods, style, and techniques are examined in detail. A major common theme to be discerned in all four films is the effect of dislocation—a placing of characters in a new, disturbing or threatening environment. It is unfortunate that the commercial weakness of the films has limited his output.

Completing the book are notes, a bibliography, a filmography, and an index. Illustrations are also provided. This is a first-rate critical study of a gifted filmmaker.

4605 NIGHT AND FOG. by Schreivogel, Paul A. 20 p. paper illus. Dayton, Ohio: Pflaum, 1970.

A study guide for the 1955 film directed by Alain Resnais.

4606 A NIGHT AT THE OPERA. by Kaufman, George S.; and Ryskind, Morrie; and McGuiness, James. 256 p. paper illus. New York: Viking, 1972.

Script of the 1935 film directed by Sam Wood. Contains cast and production credits.

4607 A NIGHT TO REMEMBER. 16 p. paper illus. New York: Program Publishing Co., 1958.

There is very little narrative in this souvenir book but some of the other features are quite unusual: for example, a diagram of the damage done by the iceberg to the Titanic, shown in a cross-section view, and a reproduction of a newspaper report of the disaster. Also included are the usual cast and production credits.

4608 NIGHTWING. by Shagan, Steve; and Shrake, Bud; and Smith, Martin Cruz. unpaginated paper illus. Los Angeles: Fotonovel, 1979.

This *Fotonovel* (see series entry) contains 350 stills, some original film dialogue, connecting narrative and cast credits for the 1979 film, NIGHTWING, which was directed by Arthur Hiller.

4609 NIJINSKY—The Film. by Gelatt, Roland. 128 p. paper illus. New York: Ballantine, 1980.

This heavily illustrated volume not only discusses the content of the 1980 film NIJINSKY, but also provides an account of its production. Sixty pages of full-color illustrations and more than 100 black and white photographs accompany the text provided by Roland Gellatt. Attention is given to the restaging of Nijinsky's most famous roles using duplicates of the original costumes and settings.

4610 *Nine American Film Critics.* by Murray, Edward. 248 p. illus. New York: Frederick Ungar, 1975.

As he indicates in his subtitle, Edward Murray offers "A Study of Theory and Practice" based on the work of nine leading film critics. Selecting only American writers, he devotes separate chapters to James Agee, Robert Warshow, Andrew Sarris, Parker Tyler, John Simon, Pauline Kael, Stanley Kauffmann, Vernon Young, and Dwight Mac-Donald. In each instance he is interested in deciding the principles or theories that guide the writer, in discovering how well these are employed, and in noting any individual strengths or weaknesses that affect critical judgments.

The career and background of the critic introduces each essay. An examination and exploration of the subject's writings follow, with many specific examples being cited as part of the argument. Book and article titles appear in the main body of the work rather than in footnotes. In his closing paragraphs, the author names Agee, Kauffmann, Young, and MacDonald as our finest movie critics—a rather safe, noncontroversial selection. An appendix in which filmmakers give short opinions of film critics and an index of film titles and directors complete the book.

"Criticizing the critics" is not a new occupation—it is an activity that appears soon after any criticism is offered. What distinguishes this presentation is the substance and logic of the author's investigation. Since he is persuasive without being pedantic, his text holds the reader's interest continually. In this volume, a neglected activity, that of evaluating critics, has been revived in a superior treatment which merits attention. Recommended.

4611 *The Nine Lives of Michael Todd.* by Cohn, Art. 344 p. paper New York: Pocket Books, 1959.

A fascinating biography with some Hollywood film backgrounds at the end of Todd's flamboyant career. Todd courted several film stars (Evelyn Keyes, Dietrich), worked with some others (Mae West, Shirley MacLaine), and married two (Joan Blondell, Elizabeth Taylor). His involvements with the studios, with the wide-screen Todd-AO process, and finally with his film, AROUND THE WORLD IN 80 DAYS (1956) make up most of the concluding portion of the book. It is a fine biography that captures an elusive subject. In 1958 both author and subject were killed in a plane crash and this book was completed by the author's widow.

4612 *The (1980)* STAR WARS *Poster Art Calendar.* edited by 20th Century Fox Studios. paper illus. New York: Ballantine, 1979.

A collection of movie posters from France, Hong Kong, Sweden, Italy, Japan, Israel, Spain and Norway depicting scenes and characters from STAR WARS (1977).

4613 *The 1978 Annual Index of Motion Picture Credits.* edited by Academy of Motion Picture Arts and Sciences. 443 p. Westport, Conn.: Greenwood, 1979- .

Since 1934 the Academy of Motion Picture Arts and Sciences has supplied information on motion picture credits as indicated in *The Screen Achievement Records Bulletin.* Greenwood Press will now publish that information, edited by Verna Ramsey, on an annual basis. The format remains constant: film titles, credits arranged by ten major film crafts, releasing companies, and individual credits with film and craft noted.

4614 *1976 Film Studies Annual.* by Staiger, Janet. edited by Lawton, Ben.; 319 p. West Lafayette, Ind.: Purdue University, 1976.

This anthology, divided into four parts—theory, German film, French film, and Italian film—results from a conference held at Purdue University, March 18-20, 1976. The volume is not intended as a record of the proceedings, but rather as a sampling of the film scholarship which characterized the conference.

The topics in the articles are not unusual—Fellini, Surrealism in Film, Fassbinder, Pasolini, Wertmuller, etc. Most of the essays are followed by notes. The typewritten pages which suggest minimal production values are counterbalanced by the high quality of the paper used.

This is an unusual, rather specialized book that will be enjoyed mostly by the serious film student.

4615 *99 Films on Drugs.* edited by Weber, David O. 68 p. paper New York: Educational Film Library Association, 1970.

Here is a filmography which must be approached with caution and additional information. Originally published by the University of California with a grant from the Maurice Falk Medical Fund, the book lists more than 99 films that deal with some aspect of drugs. Each entry begins with the title, year of release, time, color or black and white, distributor and producer. A lengthy descriptive annotation is followed by an evaluation. There is a final rating (Poor, Fair, Average, Good, Very Good, Excellent) and a recommendation for appropriate audiences (primary, intermediate, junior high, high school, college, adult, professional). For convenience there is a rating summary of all the films (only two are rated as excellent), and a classified index which groups films into areas of interest such as community action, rehabilitation, research, history, etc. Some drug films not reviewed are named, along with some titles that are currently unavailable. A distributor directory completes the volume.

The caution indicated in the opening sentence is occasioned by a report by the National Coordinating Council on Drug Education, a consortium of 133 organizations. In a publication entitled *Drug Abuse Films—An Evaluation Report*, they state that the majority of drug abuse films available today are "unacceptable." Of the 220 films reviewed, only 35 (166 percent) were approved "scientifically and conceptually acceptable." Thirty-one percent were totally unacceptable and 53 percent were considered "restricted" since they require special care in presentation. There are precautions urged in this volume but one wonders how many of the 99 films fit into the categories of the NCCDE report. The filmography is therefore a reference to be used with an awareness of its potential for good—or possible harm.

4616 NINOTCHKA. by Brackett, Charles; and Wilder, Billy; and Reisch, Walter. 114 p. paper illus. New York: Viking Press, 1972.

Script of the 1939 film directed by Ernst Lubitsch. Contains cast credits and production credits.

4617 *No Bed of Roses.* by Fontaine, Joan. 319 p. illus. New York: William Morrow, 1978.

This autobiography will bring mixed reactions from readers. They will enjoy the author's recollections of the many films, actors, directors, and scenes that were a part of her Hollywood career. However, there is a tone of bitterness and self-pity (no bed of roses) that pervades much of her story that is disappointing and disillusioning. On occasion even Fontaine seems to sense her self-indulgence and tries to counterbalance it with forgiveness and understanding for those who wronged her. The book is illustrated and indexed but has no filmography.

How much sympathy the reader will feel for Ms. Fontaine's troubles when contrasted with her amazing good fortune (a pretty girl with an average talent in the right place at the right time) is questionable. An interesting but ultimately negative reading experience.

4618 *No Case For Compulsion.* edited by The Rank Organization. 20 p. paper London: The Rank Organization, 1967.

A comment by the Rank Organization on the Association of Cinematograph, Television and Allied Technicians' report, *A Long Look at Short Films*, written by Derrick Knight and Vincent Porter.

4619 *No Chip on My Shoulder.* by Maschwitz, Eric. 208 p. illus. London: Herbert Jenkins, 1957.

Maschwitz has had a career as a lyricist-writer in Hollywood and as a director of the BBC in London. Many anecdotes about the celebrities he has known and worked with are related in this memoir. His scriptwriting credits include GOODBYE MR. CHIPS (1939) and BALALAIKA (1939); he also composed the music for SHOWTIME (1948).

4620 NO REASON TO STAY. by Schreivogel, Paul A. 19 p. paper illus. Dayton, Ohio: Pflaum, 1970.

A study guide for the 1966 film directed by Mort Ransen.

4621 *No Royal Road.* by Farrar, David. 171 p. illus. Eastbourne, England: Mortimer Publications, 1947.

Farrar is a British actor who appeared in films from the late thirties until the sixties, enjoying his greatest popularity immediately after World War II. He usually portrayed the rugged, good-looking, very masculine hero in adventure films.

4622 NOBODY WAVED GOOD-BYE. by Hermon, Voaden. 120 p. illus. Toronto: Macmillan, 1971.

The script of the 1964 film directed by Don Owen is accompanied by some background information and a few review excerpts.

4623 *Nobs and Nosh: Eating with the Beautiful People.* by Warren, Allan. 192 p. illus. London: Leslie Frewin, 1974.

An expensive coffee-table book that combines rather exotic recipes and elegant photographs, many of which are of film performers. Indexed.

4624 *Noel.* by Castle, Charles. illus. New York: Doubleday, 1973.

Using words and pictures, Noel Coward is recalled by such friends as John Gielgud, Richard Burton, David Niven and others.

4625 *Noel.* by Castle, Charles. 272 p. illus. London: W.H. Allen, 1972.

4626 *Noel Coward and His Friends.* by Lesley, Cole; and Payne, Graham; and and Morley, Sheridan. 215 p. illus. New York: Morrow, 1979.

A collection of Noel Coward memorabilia is offered here—sketches, paintings, music, manuscript pages, letters, photos, and theatre programs. The author compilers are the executors of Coward's estate and the volume is designed to be an appreciation of Coward's achievements rather than a revealing biography. Stories, anecdotes, sketches are plentiful in the retelling of the high points of Coward's life that accompanies the memorabilia. The book is a strong supplement to some of the previously published biographies and reinforces Coward's reputation as one of the wittiest, most elegant talents of this century.

4627 *Noel Coward.* by Levin, Milton. 158 p. New York: Twayne, 1968.

A biography of Noel Coward that includes a chronology, a bibliography and an index.

4628 *Non-Fiction Film: A Critical History.* by Barsam, Richard Meran. 332 p. paper illus. New York: Dutton, 1973.

This new critical history has much to recommend it. In considering the major periods and creators of documentary-factual films, it discusses the early films of Russia and America, the British school led by John Grierson, films surrounding the decade of World War II, the contribution of Robert Flaherty, the new documentaries of the sixties, and much more. The author describes a large number of films and provides political and sociological background to explain their origin and importance. The narrative is lively, respectful and objective.

Supporting sections are equally fine. Illustrations abound and they are well selected and nicely placed throughout the book. Films discussed in detail are listed in the appendix along with distributor information. An awards section, a strong bibliography and a lengthy index complete the book. While nonfiction films have been neglected in the past, there is evidence of an awakening interest and enthusiasm for them today. This volume will reinforce, encourage and expand that interest. Highly recommended.

4629 *Non-Book Materials and the Librarian: A Select Bibliography.* compiled by Andrew, Janet R. 21 p. paper London: Association of Special Libraries and Information Bureau (ASLIB), 1971.

4630 *Nonfiction Film Theory and Criticism.* edited by Barsam, Richard Meran. 382 p. paper New York: Dutton, 1976.

This anthology on the nonfiction film offers 26 articles/essays written by well-known filmmakers or critics of the genre. Included are such names as Leni Riefenstahl, John Grierson, Paul Rotha, Lindsay Anderson, Philip Dunne, Willard Van Dyke and Joris Ivens. A selected bibliography completes the book.

The editor's goal is simply to "offer some of the most significant writing on the subject of nonfiction film," and in his selection and arrangement of material, he has been completely successful. Recommended.

4631 *Nonprint Materials on Communications.: An Annotated Directory of Select Films, Videotapes, Video Cassettes, Simulations and Games.* by Buteau, June D. 444 p. Metuchen, N.J.: Scarecrow, 1976.

This mediagraphy is unique in that it sets criteria for inclusion. In addition to the release date, a helpful annotation is offered. Anyone searching for films on communication will find this a very helpful source of information.

4632 *Nonprint Media in Academic Libraries.* edited by Grove, Pearce S. 239 p. paper Chicago: American Library Assoc., 1975.

In this anthology there are the predictable articles dealing with bibliographic organization, selection, acquisition, standards, and the individual media: recordings, slides, films, filmstrips, maps, and still pictures. The chapter on film by Dwight F. Burlingame offers sections on film history, films in academic libraries, film holdings, forms, selection and acquisition, cataloging and processing, etc. The presentation is somewhat basic and not very inspiring.

4633 *Non-Theatrical Film Distributors: Sales-Service-Policies.* compiled by Emmens, Carol A. 66 p. paper New York: Educational Film Library Association, 1974.

This is a revised and expanded edition of a volume first published by the University of Michigan A-V Education Center. Using 137 replies to questionnaires sent to film distributors, data on the following headings was obtained: chief executive, types of films handled, extent of distribution, information sources available, distribution method, preview policy, discounts, footage replacement policy, print replacement policy, category of films handled, specialized subjects, seeking to distribute, and unique features. The distributors are arranged alphabetically by name with replies to the above information given in varying lengths from one word to complete paragraphs. It is hoped that in future editions the volume will expand its coverage. The present edition, however, is a most useful aid that can be recommended for all concerned with film service.

4634 *The Non-Western Films of John Ford.* by Place, J. A. 287 p. illus. Secaucus, N.J.: Citadel, 1979.

John Ford's filmography is so large that the editors of the *Citadel* series have devoted two volumes to it—the westerns and the non-westerns. In the typical format of this series, some 39 films are described by illustrations, cast, credits, plot outline, etc. Since the volume has been adapted from a doctoral dissertation, much analysis of the films is offered.

The author divides them into American films, Celtic films, Political films and War-military films.

Those searching for a deeper, more satisfying review of the Ford films may find it in *The John Ford Movie*

Mystery by Andrew Sarris, *John Ford* by Joseph McBride, *The Cinema of John Ford* by John Baxter, or Peter Bogdanovich's long interview, *John Ford.*

4635 *Norma Jean: The Life of Marilyn Monroe.* by Guiles, Fred Lawrence. 341 p. illus. New York: McGraw-Hill, 1969.

A detailed biography told in documentary style, this book is based on research and on interviews with people who knew Marilyn Monroe. Although he does not succeed in complete objectivity towards his subject, the author tries to present a balanced portrait. The account is absorbing and the detail fascinating. Pictures are minimal and standard. An index is provided. For readers interested in the Monroe legend or in good personality-biography, this book is recommended.

4636 *see 4638*

4637 *Norman McLaren.* by Collins, Maynard. 119 p. paper illus. Ottawa, Ontario: Canadian Film Institute, 1976.

The publication of this volume fills a need in film literature. It is a study of that prolific filmmaker, Norman McLaren, which brings together all the information that heretofore existed in scattered, fragmented forms. It begins with a short biography followed by a critical analysis of his work. The largest sections are an annotated filmography that is arranged chronologically and an interview that is undated. Closing sections include a list of awards received, a bibliography, a guide for film study, and an index.

McLaren's films are found in most collections which serve schools, colleges, museums, and libraries. At last supporting information has been made available in order that a full appreciation of the man and his films is possible. This volume is as carefully and efficiently designed as one of McLaren's films and is highly recommended.

4638 *Norman McLaren.* by Phillipe, Pierre. paper illus. Montreal: Cinematheque Canadienne, 1965.

This is the catalog of an exhibition presented at the Journee Internationales du Cinema d'Animation, Annecy, in 1965.

4639 *North American Film and Video Directory.* compiled by Weber, Olga S. 284 p. New York: R. R. Bowker, 1976.

Although this useful reference had some roots in an earlier volume, *Directory of Film Libraries in North America*, its scope and coverage have been greatly expanded. The information offered was obtained by questionnaires sent out in 1975 and 1976. A total of 1273 libraries and media centers responded with information about their film and video services. The data has been carefully edited and efficiently presented by Olga Weber. Arranged alphabetically, first by state and then by city/town, the entries note addresses, personnel, selection procedure, along with other pertinent items such as free loan film service, film collection size, other film service, other media collections, budget, video service, video equipment/facilities, videotape loan, video collection, cable TV, closed circuit TV, etc. An alphabetized index of the libraries, an index of special collections and a list of some film circuits/cooperatives conclude the volume.

This excellent reference source can be used in a wide variety of ways. An enormous amount of data is presented in a form that is easy and pleasant to handle. Recommended.

4640 NORTH BY NORTHWEST. by Lehman, Ernest. 148 p. paper illus. NewYork: Viking, 1972.

Script of the 1959 suspense film directed by Hitchcock. Contains cast and production credits.

4641 THE NORTH STAR. by Hellman, Lillian. 118 p. New York: Viking, 1943.

Script of the 1943 film directed by Lewis Milestone. Contains cast credits and an introduction by Louis Kronenberger. Note: the film is also titled ARMORED ATTACK.

4642 *Norwegian Films 1978.* 63 p. paper illus. Oslo: Norsk Filminstitutt, 1978.

A catalog of films produced in Norway.

4643 *Nostalgia Isn't What It Used to Be.* by Signoret, Simone. 416 p. illus. New York: Harper & Row, 1978.

In her autobiography, Simone Signoret emerges much the same as her general screen persona—strong, independent, worldy, spirited, intelligent and, most importantly, warm. She gives only brief attention to her film roles, and concentrates on those events that she wishes to place on public record—her political activities, her life during World War II, her long delayed visit to the United States, the Algerian war, etc.

She speaks as a show business survivor of such concerns as aging, acting techniques, the demands of celebrity. All of these self-selected topics of her life are related with discretion and occasional exuberance. Also included is Signoret's portrait of Marilyn Monroe, an example of how able she is in combining experience, wisdom, and dramatic sense in her writing (and acting). By selecting what to tell and what to retain as personal, Signoret comes out as the noble wife in the Monroe-Montand-Signoret affair, just as she comes out as the noble activist in this memoir.

4644 *The Nostalgia Quiz Book.* by Gross, Martin A. 240 p. paper New York: Signet, 1971.

This paperback reprint of the original 1969 Arlington House edition contains 1555 questions distributed over 150 separate quizzes. Topics covered are movies, music, personalities, science and industry, comics, sports, stage, print, radio and television. Answers are given in the back of the book. Examination of a few of the 34 quizzes on films indicates such topics as "Hollywood at War," "Gable Television," and "Hollywood Revival." Methodology used in the quizzes includes questioning, matching, filling in blanks, selecting from multiple choices, etc. The book offers a high quota of amusement, information and nostalgia.

4645 *The Nostalgia Quiz Book 2.* by Gross, Martin A. 272 p. New Rochelle, N.Y.: Arlington House, 1974.

Volumes dealing with the nostalgia-trivia of our recent past obviously have great appeal to readers. The first volume bearing this title sold more than 75,000 copies and this one should do as well or better. More than 150 quizzes with over 1500 questions are here to challenge the reader-buff. The quizzes are arranged in either the short-answer question, matching, multiple choice, or fill-in-the-blank formats. Answers are given in the book's final pages.

Some reservations should be noted. Certain questions are poorly worded, e.g., "name the two great comediennes who appeared in the Thelma Todd comedy shorts." The answers given are Patsy Kelly and Zazu Pitts, but Thelma Todd is a defensible reply to the question as posed.

Certain answers are partial and could be unfair to those without film reference books at hand, e.g., "Name three Abbott and Costello 'military' movies." The answers given: BUCK PRIVATES (1941), IN THE NAVY (1941), and ABBOTT AND COSTELLO IN THE FOREIGN LEGION (1950). Not noted: KEEP EM' FLYING (1941). Again, with the question, "Where did JOURNEY INTO FEAR (1942) take place?," the answer offered is Constantinople. Since the film moves from location to location via ship, a better and more comprehensive answer might have been either Constantinople, Turkey, or Batum.

Misspellings are evident, e.g., Yank Lausen for Yank Lawson, Tonelayo for Tondelayo, etc.

The importance of complete accuracy in any book dealing with trivia is essential—as anyone who has ever played competitively in these quizzes will testify. The number and range of the questions in the volume are sure to please most reader-users; attention to the fine details, however, would have made it a better volume. Acceptable.

4646 *The Nostalgia Quiz Book 3.* by Gross, Martin A. 352 p. New Rochelle, N.Y.: Arlington House, 1975.

The popularity of the first two *Nostalgia Quiz* volumes cannot be denied. They seem to be appearing on an annual basis, approaching the regularity of Lamparski's nostalgia series, *Whatever Became of...?* Nostalgia, trivia and escapism are the three major factors in the appeal of these volumes.

On this occasion, Gross has supplemented his basic 140 quizzes (over 1425 questions) with 10 crossword puzzles and a nostalgia diary of 365 memory questions. Not all the questions deal with movies and film stars; politics, history, sports, literature, etc., are other areas used for framing questions. Formats include direct questions, fill-in-the-blanks, multiple choice, matching, etc. Production accorded the volume is excellent and the book will please many readers. Recommended.

4647 *Not by a Long Shot: Adventures of a Documentary Film Producer.* by Cussler, Margaret. 200 p. illus. New York: Exposition, 1952.

A personal memoir with much material on the making of documentaries. In this case the film producer is a lady. Amusing, different, effective, and nicely illustrated.

4648 *Not for Publication.* by Lloyd, Peter. 80 p. London: Bow. 1968

This pamphlet which deals with censorship in Great Britain contains a section on motion pictures.

4649 *Not So Dumb (Animals in the Movies).* by Lee, Raymond. 380 p. illus. New York: A. S. Barnes, 1970.

Teddy, Tony, Rin-Tin-Tin, Trigger, Lassie, Leo and Cheetah along with other film animals are the subjects of this book. The vital contributions made by animals to many films are noted. Zoological coverage is quite complete and forgotten film moments will be restored to reader memories. The numerous photographs help immensely. Not an essential by any means, this volume is amusing and will appeal to most ages.

4650 *Not So Long Ago.* by Morris, Lloyd. 504 p. illus. New York: Random House, 1949.

A pre-McLuhan book, this is a study of how the motion pictures, the automobile, and the radio act as instruments of social power. Approximately the first 200 pages concern themselves exclusively with motion pictures. It is largely an account of early screen history with the emphasis on the early silent screen era (1895-1920) and it differs in its attempt to indicate certain social effects of the motion picture. The perspective is that of the sociologist-historian.

Much of the text is provocative and informative. Some excellent pictures are reproduced in a sepia tint that does them a disservice. With some revision, the section on motion picures could be extracted and published as a volume by itself. It has more merit than certain other pieces that are being reprinted today.

4651 *Not This Time, Cary Grant.* by Eder, Shirley. 277 p. paper illus. New York: Bantam, 1974.

This collection contains short pieces on such selected subject as "Oscar Memories", "Visiting Mae West", "A First Ocean Voyage", "Red Skelton's Farewell", "The GODFATHER Premiere", etc. The style of the author is to suggest that she is the ordinary, everyday fan suddenly pushed up against celebrities with assorted desires and drives. She makes much of being placed in embarrassing predicaments such as being scolded by Harry Truman, fighting off Vic Damone, and inviting Ethel Merman to a dinner only to have the food stolen. A center section shows the author with her celebrity friends. Although this volume is about Hollywood personalities, the material is so bland, trivial, and lacking in depth that it is hard to think of the book as anything but a time-killer —the kind of reading material found in the waiting rooms of doctors and dentists. Acceptable but lacking any importance.

4652 *Notable American Women.* by Sicherman, Barbara; and Green, Carol H. 773 p. Cambridge, Mass: Harvard University Press, 1980.

Inclusion in this collective biography was limited to notable women who had died between 1951 and 1975. Called "a biographical dictionary" for "the modern period," it supplements three earlier similar volumes. Many film personalities are included — Judy Garland, Marilyn Monroe, Ethel Barrymore, Louella Parsons, Gypsy Rose Lee—along with women from many other occupations and dedications.

4653   *The Notebooks of Raymond Chandler and English Summer.* by Chandler, Raymond. 113 p. illus. New York: Ecco Press, 1976.

In his novels Raymond Chandler created Philip Marlowe, the quintessential private detective. Chandler's stories served as material for the screen and he himself wrote the screenplays for such films as DOUBLE INDEMNITY (1944), THE BLUE DAHLIA (1946), and STRANGERS ON A TRAIN (1951). Frank Mac-Shane, who served as editor of this volume, has selected material from two surviving notebooks kept by Raymond Chandler for over 20 years. Included is an essay specifically on Hollywood, "A Qualified Farewell," along with a few other peripheral references to motion pictures. "English Summer," referred to in the book's title, is a short story that Chandler was planning to expand into a novel.

4654   *Notes.* by Coppola, Eleanor. 270 p. paper illus. New York: Pocket Books, 1980.

This is one of the best behind-the-scenes accounts of the making of a motion picture. The film in this case is APOCALYPSE NOW (1980), a very personal venture of director-writer-producer Francis Ford Coppola. His wife, the author, kept these notes from 1975 to 1978 during the location shooting in the Philippines and during the final stages of production in the United States. Along the way, she treats, in painfully honest fashion, such personal subjects as the deterioration of her marriage, her feelings toward her husband, the identification of Coppola with his characters, the extreme pressures that big budget filmmaking places on its participants, etc.

Her account of the making of a film takes this particular form of cinema literature away from the public relations flacks who have monopolized it so long. She provides some standards by which any future accounts of specific filmmaking should be judged.

4655   *Notes for a Life.* by Forbes, Bryan. 384 p. illus. London: Collins, 1974.

Bryan Forbes is a total filmmaker (actor-writer-di-

rector) who has been active in British films since the late forties. His films include: KING RAT (1965), THE L-SHAPED ROOM (1962), SEANCE ON A WET AFTERNOON (1964), THE WRONG BOX (1966), THE WHISPERERS (1967) and THE MAD WOMAN OF CHAILLOT (1969).

4656   *Notes of a Film Director.* by Eisenstein, Sergei. 207 p. paper illus. New York: Dover Pub., 1970.

These are translated articles written by Eisenstein which help to fill out a portrait of this director. The essays are grouped in three categories: "About Myself and My Films," "Problems of Film Direction," and "Portraits of Artists." An epilogue is entitled "Always Forward." Drawings by Eisenstein are an asset to the book. As additional material on the great director, this book is valuable, but it is rather specialized for the general reader.

4657   *Notes of a Soviet Actor.* by Cherkasov, Nikolai. 227 p. illus. Moscow: Foreign Languages Publishing House, 1957.

A discussion of acting techniques and methods for both stage and screen. The author is known for his work in such films as BALTIC DEPUTY (1937), PETER THE GREAT (1937), ALEXANDER NEVSKY (1938), IVAN THE TERRIBLE (1942), and DON QUIXOTE (1953).

4658   *Notes on Cinematography.* by Bresson, Robert. 72 p. paper New York: Urizen Books (Dutton), 1977.

This volume is a collection of memos or reminders that Robert Bresson has created for his own use. They reflect the filmmaking philosophies and techniques evident in his films. As with the films, they require considerable effort from the reader for full comprehension and understanding, i.e., "Your camera passes through faces, provided no mimicry (intentional or not intentional) gets in between. Cinematographic films are made of inner movements which are seen."

The books should be used concurrently with a viewing-study of Bresson's work. Acceptable.

4659   *Notes on* LES ENFANTS DU PARADIS. by Warfield, Nancy D. 19 p. paper illus. New York: Little Film Gazette, 1967.

This set of detailed, scholarly notes to LES ENFANTS DU PARADIS (1944) contains cast and production credits, a synopsis, background material, interpretation and critical analysis of the film. Illustrations of the film's leading characters are also provided. The author is a dedicated admirer of the film and offers an enrichment to its viewing here. This is specialized material, almost totally dependent upon one or more viewings of the film. Acceptable

4660 *Notes on Women's Cinema.* edited by Johnson, Claire. 40 p. paper London: Society for Education in Film and TV, 1973.

Also known as *Screen Pamphlet Two,* this anthology contains articles by Claire Johnson, Naome Gilburt, and Barbara Halpern Martineau. Its theme is stated thus: "The image of women in the cinema has been created by men. The emergent women's cinema has begun the transformation of that image. These notes explore ideas and strategies developed in women's films." The works of Agnes Varda, Susan Sontag, Ida Lupino and Dorothy Arzner are used for examples.

4661 *Nothing in Moderation: A Biography of Ernie Kovacs.* by Walley, David G. 225 p. illus. New York: Drake, 1975.

Here is a biography which follows Ernie Kovacs' career from early radio days in Trenton, N.J., to his final days as a film performer in Hollywood. Although he is best remembered as a television personality, he appeared in almost a dozen feature films during the late fifties and early sixties. Much of his inspired TV humor is recalled along with details of his chaotic private lifestyle—cigars, poker games, steam baths, tax liens, etc. Script excerpts, a list of radio and television appearances and a filmography are included. The volume is not well written, but its intention of honoring an American original must be applauded. Kovacs was planning to direct his own films and his accidental death was everyone's loss. Acceptable.

4662 A NOUS LA LIBERTE. by Clair, Rene. 140 p. paper illus. New York: Simon & Schuster, 1970.

Script of the 1931 film directed by Clair. Contains cast credits and three articles: 1) "To Fight the Machine" (by Georges Charensol); 2) "Picabia, Satie, and the First Night of ENTR'ACTE"; and 3) "Picabia's Original Notes for ENTR'ACTE. " Bound in the samevolume: ENTR'ACTE.

4663 *Nouvelle Vague: The First Decade.* by Durgnat, Raymond. 90 p. illus. Loughton, England: Motion Pub., 1966.

One of the first books on the New Wave and considered by many to be the best.

4664 *The Novel and the Cinema.* by Wagner, Geoffrey. 394 p. illus. Rutherford, N.J.: Fairleigh Dickinson University Press, 1975.

The first section of this volume discusses films and novels as popular art forms. How the words of novels are translated into visual images is the author's next concern. The relationship between art and photography is investigated along with the grammar and psychology of the film. Three ways in which novels have been adapted for the screen—transposition, commentary, analogy—are discussed in the closing pages. A few illustrations, a bibliography and an index are included.

Although this volume has been diligently researched and written with a scholar's thoroughness, it lacks warmth, enthusiasm, and a discernible point of view. The synthesis of Wagner's investigation and thought has resulted in a cold exposition of diverse facts, theories, concepts, interpretations and opinions. Some of the latter are quite vulnerable, e.g., was Kael's *The Citizen Kane Book* "instantly remaindered"? Occasionally intellectual showing-off is present in the form of name-dropping, and the reader may suspect the application of the John Simon syndrome of dazzling the reader with classic study references and phrases in several foreign languages. Several films are analyzed in support of the author's arguments and it is on this common ground that reader and writer can meet more readily. The success of that meeting will be determined by the reader's acceptance of the unusual subjective interpretations of the sample films.

In summary, the author's intelligence, background and effort are constantly evident and not at issue here. It is his literary style and his synthesis of the work that will influence reader acceptance and use of the volume. Acceptable.

4665 *Novels into Film: The Metamorphosis of Fiction into Cinema.* by Bluestone, George. 237 p. paper Berkeley, Calif.: University of California Press, 1957.

In this original study, Bluestone looks at the basic differences between the novel and the film as media forms. After analyzing six sample films made from classic novels, the author concludes that the inevitable change that occurs in a transfer from one medium to another causes a new autonomous form to be created. The films-novels used in the study are THE INFORMER (1935), WUTHERING HEIGHTS (1939), PRIDE AND PREJUDICE (1940), THE GRAPES OF WRATH (1940), THE OX-BOW INCIDENT (1943), and MADAME BOVARY (1949).

This is a serious study of the relationship between films and the novel. The research indicated in the analysis is impressive as are the author's critical approaches. A bibliography and an index are added. Recommended.

4666 *Nuclear War Films.* edited by Shaheen, Jack G. 193 p. illus. Carbondale, Ill.: Southern Illinois University Press, 1978.

This anthology, written by 21 film authorities, consists of 25 articles, each of which deals with a specific nuclear war film, or films. The period covered is 1946 to 1975, and feature films, documentaries and short films are included.

The essays on the 11 feature films are chronological, starting with THE BEGINNING OR THE END (1946) and concluding with THE BEDFORD INCIDENT (1965). Consideration of 21 shorter films follows. A few illustrations, a filmography, a distributor list, chapter notes and an index complete the volume.

The reader will probably draw several conclusions from these well-intentioned, thoughtful statements: (1) the nuclear war film genre reflects society's intense concern; (2) the number of films appear in inverse ration to the proliferation of nuclear weapons; (3) technology is inherently evil in the films and (4) the short films treat the subject more intelligently and creatively than do the features.

4667 *The Nureyev* VALENTINO. by Bland, Alexander. 128 p. paper illus. New York: Dell, 1977.

Subtitled "Portrait of a Film," this original paperback covers several aspects of the making of the 1977 film, VALENTINO. Opening pages contrast pictures of the real Valentino with Rudolf Nureyev's recreation. The directorial treatment provided by Ken Russell is discussed along with the contributions of other actors and filmmakers. The latter half of the book relates the story of the film in text and stills. The narrative provided by Alexander Bland is descriptive and factual rather than critical. Most readers will find the many illustrations to be the book's major attraction. They have been selected for interest and visual information. The clarity of their re-

production is impressive.

The kind of creative talent responsible for this volume was apparently absent from the film production. It is quite possible to enjoy this background preview more than the film itself. Acceptable.

4668 *The Nutcracker Suite.* edited by Walt Disney Productions. 72 p. illus. Boston: Little, Brown, 1941.

Tchaikovsky's music arranged for piano by Frederick Stark and accompanied by illustrations, some in color, from Disney's FANTASIA (1941).

4669 O LUCKY MAN!. by Sherwin, David. 192 p. paper illus. New York:Evergreen, 1973.

Script of the 1972 film directed by Lindsay Anderson. Contains a preface by Lindsay Anderson, and "Diary of a Script", by David Sherwin.

4670 *O'Grady: The Life and Times of Hollywood's No. 1 Private Eye.* by O'Grady, John; and Davis, Nolan. 238 p. Los Angeles: J. P. Tarcher, 1974.

In this self-tribute, John O'Grady describes the life of a private detective in Hollywood. The narrative often resembles a proposal for an action television series with a male lead who finds himself irresistible.

Very few actual names are mentioned (Rita Moreno, Errol Flynn, etc.) and the book's best feature is the description it offers of a rather sleazy profession. The author's brassy ego may be due to the 20 years he served with the Los Angeles Police Department before going into business for himself. No index or illustrations are offered.

4671 *The O'Hara Concern: A Biography of John O'Hara.* by Bruccoli, Matthew J. 416 p. illus. New York: Random House, 1975.

Since so many of John O'Hara's stories and novels were used for motion pictures, this excellent autobiography is noted here. Anecdotes of his life in Hollywood are included along with a chronology, index, illustrations, etc.

4672 *Obituaries on File.* by Levy, Felice. 2 vols. New York: Facts on File, 1979.

These two volumes contain a compilation of the obituaries which appeared in *Facts on File* from 1940 to 1978. Entries give the date of death, the age, and a few words of identification. Volume two contains a chronology index and a subject index.

4673 *The Object of My Affection.* by Tomlin, Pinky. 208 p. illus. Norman, Oklahoma: University of Oklahoma Press, 1981.

A biography of the Oklahoma farm boy whose songs and music made him famous in the early thirties. Tomlin appeared in 14 films before retiring to become a successful oilman.

4674 *Obscenity.* edited by Friedman, Leon. 342 p. New York: Chelsea House, 1970.

The introduction to this book describes the "Warren Court" at work during the decade from the mid-fifties to the mid-sixties when great changes were made in either interpretation or invocation of the Bill of Rights with regard to obscenity questions. The complete oral arguments before the Supreme Court in the major obscenity cases are presented in the body of the volume. Editorial notes accompany each case.

The book is listed here because of three cases involving films: 1) Kingsley International Pictures Corporation v. Regents (LADY CHATTERLY'S LOVER—1955); 2) Jacobellis v. Ohio (THE LOVERS —1958); and 3) Freedman v. Maryland (Film Censorship). The seven remaining cases have pertinence in explaining the freedom of expression in the arts that is enjoyed today.

4675 AN OCCURRENCE AT OWL CREEK BRIDGE. by Schreivogel, Paul A. 28 p. paper illus. Dayton, Ohio: Pflaum, 1970.

A study guide to the 1956 film directed by Robert Enrico.

4676 AN OCCURRENCE AT OWL CREEK BRIDGE. by Barrett, Gerald R.; and Erskine, Thomas L. 216 p. paper illus. Encino, Cal.: Dickenson Publishing Co., 1973.

This second title of the *From Fiction to Film* series is consistent in quality with the first. An introduction is followed by the original short story, "An Occurrence at Owl Creek Bridge," by Ambrose Bierce. Six short articles of criticism about the story conclude the fiction section. The section devoted to the film is unique. A shot analysis approach to the scripts is employed. Explanations of shots, transitions, camera movement, camera angles and sound precede the presentation of two scripts derived from Bierce's original story. The first is THE BRIDGE (or THE SPY), an 11-minute film directed in 1931 by King Vidor and notable for the use of Soviet editing techniques. More famous is Robert Enrico's short film, AN OCCURRENCE AT OWL CREEK BRIDGE (1956) which is presented next. Five critical articles on the films complete the film section. A list of questions leading to the writing of papers completes the book.

The concept, design, and selection of materials in the book is laudable. In secondary schools and colleges, the potential for use is enormous. For this audience the book is highly recommended.

4677 *Odd Woman Out: An Autobiography.* by Box, Muriel. 272 p. illus. London: Leslie Frewin, 1974.

An autobiography of film writer-producer-director Muriel Box, who began her career as a scriptgirl for British Instructional Films in the late twenties. She married Sydney Fox and with him founded London Independent Producers in 1946. Her many films include THE SEVENTH VEIL (1945), DEAR MURDERER (1948), THE BEACHCOMBER (1954), SIMON AND LAURA (1955), A NOVEL AFFAIR (1957), and RATTLE OF A SIMPLE MAN (1964).

4678 *Odham's Picturegoer Film Annual.* edited by Wall, Guy. illus. London: Odhams Press, 1949-1962.

This annual appeared from 1949 until 1962. Many attractive full-page portraits appeared within its pages, along with typical fan magazine articles, e.g., "The Prince of Beefcake" (Rock Hudson), "Every Actor Needs a Sideline" (Cliff Robertson), "Scenes We'll Always Remember," etc. Some of the illustrations were in color.

4679 *The Odyssey of a Film-Maker: Robert Flaherty's Story.* by Flaherty, Frances Hubbard. 45 p. illus. Urbana, Ill.: Phi Beta Mu, 1960.

This is a small book published by an international library science honorary society in an edition of 2000 copies. Written by his wife, the book concerns itself with Robert Flaherty's four great documentaries: NANOOK OF THE NORTH (1920), MOANA (1926), MAN OF ARAN (1934), and LOUISIANA STORY (1948). The account is largely factual and offers little insight into the person of Flaherty. It is a formal, public testimonial to a professional, in this case, the "Father of the Documentary Film." She has written two other books, *Samoa* and *Elephant Dance*, both about

Flaherty. The illustrations taken from the films are a magnificent testimony to the art of Flaherty. A good addition to the books on Flaherty and the documentary motion picture but not an essential.

4680 OEDIPUS REX. by Pasolini, Pier Paolo. 150 p. paper illus. New York: Simon and Schuster, 1971.

Script of the 1970 film directed by Pasolini. Contains: "Why That of Oedipus is a Story" by Pier Paolo Pasolini; cast and credits; "Cutting Continuity."

4681 OEDIPUS THE KING. translated by Roche, Paul. 92 p. paper illus. New York: New American Library, 1971.

The text used in the film OEDIPUS THE KING (1967) directed by Philip Saville. Illustrated with 12 pages of movie stills, the book includes a special introduction by Raymond Palmer outlining the problems involved in bringing a classic play to the motion picture screen.

4682 *Of Mice and Magic.* by Maltin, Leonard. 480 p. illus. New York: McGraw-Hill, 1980.

In this book Leonard Maltin gives his attention to a subgenre of his favorite topic, comedy films. Calling this volume, "A History of American Animated Cartoons," he traces their story from pioneer attempts around 1900 to the Ralph Bakshi features of the seventies. Each major American animation department is treated—Disney, Warners, MGM, etc.—by analysis of their cartoons and interviews of their chief animators. Filmographies of the studios are included along with Academy Award nominations/winners and a distributor list. Many illustrations accompany Maltin's survey.

4683 *Of Women and Their Elegance.* by Mailer, Norman. 288 p. illus. New York: Simon & Schuster, 1980.

Some illustrations by Milton H. Greene and an "imaginary memoir" by Marilyn Monroe make up this strange volume. Mailer's fascination with Monroe as a character continues as he tries to write a text that complements the pictures by Greene, a man who was Monroe's friend in the early sixties. The result is another dismal and disappointing one-sided attack on the Monroe persona.

4684 *Off Camera.* by Probst, Leonard. 269 p. illus. New York: Stein and Day, 1975.

Most of the 17 interviews contained in this volume were recorded during public sessions held at the New School from April, 1974, to June, 1975. A few were conducted in homes, offices or backstage at theatres.Subjects are Al Pacino, Paul Newman, Diana Rigg, George C. Scott, Dustin Hoffman, Mike Nichols, Elaine May, Lynn Redgrave, Shirley MacLaine, Angela Lansbury, Gwen Verdon, Woody Allen, and others.

The interviews indicate the author's detailed preparation along with the subjects' intelligence and skill in answering pertinent questions. In an opening chapter the author presents a few generalizations about super-stardom; full-page photographs of his subjects appear throughtout the book.

Each of the sessions is entertaining and informative. The moods range from confidential to comic but each star apparently knows himself, his capacities, and his goals; the opportunity for them to speak openly in a conversational format is used to advantage in most cases.

This is a delightful collection that should please many readers. Quotations from this volume are certain to be used in books yet to be written. Recommended.

4685 *Off-Guard.* by Galella, Ron. 192 p. illus. New York: McGraw-Hill, 1976.

Subtitled, "A Paparazzi Look at the Beautiful People," this collection of candid shots of celebrities has an introduction by Bruce Jay Friedman. Galella's chutzpah in obtaining these unusual unposed photos seems enormous. Subjects caught include Robert Redford, Sophia Loren, Marlon Brando, Elizabeth Taylor, Richard Burton, Frank Sinatra, Dustin Hoffman, Liza Minnelli, Brigette Bardot, Barbra Streisand and many others.

4686 *Off to the Pictures.* by Reynolds, Frank. 168 p. illus. London: Collins, 1937.

Using words and pictures the author, who was an artist for *Punch*, offers his comments and criticism of both films and film personalities from the thirties.

4687 *Off With Their Heads.* by Marion, Frances. 356 p. illus. New York: Macmillan, 1972.

Frances Marion enjoyed a career in Hollywood for more than 50 years, working as actress, writer, director and producer. Her greatest renown came as the author of screenplays for films such as THE WIND (1928), ANNA CHRISTIE (1930), DINNER AT

EIGHT (1933), and CAMILLE (1936). The story she relates is only coincidentally autobiography—in fact, she tells little of her personal life, preferring to relate the story of Hollywood with an emphasis on the personalities. The pages are strewn with all the famous names but there is always a rationale for inclusion; the author is never guilty of name-dropping. Her style is that of a screenplay writer who likes "scenes" rather than gossipy sensationalism. Thus the effect on some readers may be one of historical distrust but the book is interesting in spite of a few slight inaccuracies. Because it lacks the "best-seller" elements of wit, expose, cynicism, and bitchiness, it may not reach a wide audience, but it is a memoir that many would appreciate and enjoy.

Supporting the warm, engrossing narrative is a fine collection of photographs that are accurately reproduced. In addition there is a detailed index and a filmography which lists 137 entries from A GIRL OF YESTERDAY (1915) to THE CLOWN (1953). Similar in certain ways to Anita Loos' *A Girl Like I*, this volume covers a longer period of Hollywood history and offers a broader but gentler view. Recommended.

4688 *The Official* SGT. PEPPER'S LONELY HEARTS CLUB BAND *Scrapbook*. by Stigewood, Robert; and Anthony, Dee. paper illus. New York: Wallaby, 1980.

A behind-the-scenes look at the production of SGT. PEPPER'S LONELY HEARTS CLUB BAND (1980). Heavily illustrated, the book contains short biographies of the musicians and actors who appear in the film.

4689 *The Official* ROCKY *Scrapbook*. by Stallone, Sylvester. 96 p. paper illus. New York: Grosset and Dunlap, 1977.

This book in the *Scrapbook* series consists of two parts—a biography of the author with emphasis on how ROCKY (1976) was made; and a condensation of the film in captioned photographs. The more than 100 illustrations offered include candids, stills and publicity shots. A bit of ego inflation may be detected in the use of the author's name in the title. When it was reprinted as an Ace paperback—it was then called *Sylvester Stallone's Offical "Rocky" Scrapbook*.

4690 *Official Blueprints from* STAR TREK. by Kimble, David. 14 p. illus. New York: Wallaby/Pocket, 1980.

Fourteen blueprints in a plastic pouch show the various structures used in STAR TREK - THE MOTION PICTURE (1980).

4691 *The Official Book of Movie Lists*. by Essoe, Gabe. 256 p. illus. Westport, Conn.: Arlington House, 1981.

More than 100 Hollywood personalities give their lists of everything from "most exciting car chases" to "my favorite directors" and "10 most sexy actors" the volume was designed for fun, and for the most part that is exactly what it is.

4692 *The Official FBI File on Elvis A. Presley*. illus. Chicago: MEM, 1978.

4693 *The Official Fonzie Scrapbook*. by Davidson, Ben. 112 p. paper illus. New York: Grosset & Dunlap, 1977.

This appreciation of Henry Winkler deals predominantly with television and the "Happy Days" series in which he plays "the Fonz."

Heavily illustrated, as per usual in the *Scrapbook Series*, the book includes candids, publicity shots, etc. It does not deal with Winkler's two films to date.

4694 *The Official Movie Trivia Quiz Book*. by Andrews, Bart. 153 p. paper illus. New York: Signet, 1976.

Subtitled, "1,001 Questions for 'Late Show' Lovers," this collection of 99 quizzes deals with many diverse film topics. Different quiz formats are alternated and answers are given in the final pages. What makes this "official" is not clear, but the success of thebook is. In 1978 a sequel appeared, called, logically, *The Official Movie Trivia Quiz Book No. 2*. This time out the author was Martin A. Gross.

4695 *Oh, Lord, What Next?* by Russell, Geraldine Jacobi. 174 p. illus. New York: Vantage, 1960.

Jane Russell's mother tells about herself and her famous daughter in this autobiography.

4696 *Okay for Sound: How the Screen Found Its Voice*. edited by Thrasher, Frederick. 303 p. illus. New York: Duell, Sloan, and Pearce, 1946.

Viewed in retrospect, the title (and topic) of this book is an ideal framework (or excuse) for the presentation of many excellent stills. It is really a short multi-illustrated history of American motion pictures. There is some adequate text material that provides an introduction to the sections. However, the photos give the book its value. Unfortunately, there is no index. In spite of its misleading title, and the lack of reference sections, the volume is still one of the best picture books about American films. Highly recommended for all.

4697   THE OLD MAN AND THE SEA. 14 p. paper illus. New York: Souvenir Program, Inc., 1958.

The focus is on people in this souvenir book. It shows a few highlight scenes and then spotlights author Ernest Hemingway, star Spencer Tracy, producer Leland Hayward, director John Sturges, composer Dimitri Tiomkin, and cameraman James Wong Howe. Even Jack Warner gets into the act by furnishing an introduction to the book.

4698   OLIVER. by Weiss, Nathan. 48 p. paper illus. New York: National Publishers, 1968.

The attractive color photography in this souvenir book is its outstanding feature. Following an exposition of the story and an account of the making of the 1968 film, the large cast of featured players is given special atention. Other supporting cast members are noted, as are many of the behind-the-camera people including director Carol Reed and dance director Oona White.

4699   *Olivier.* edited by Gourlay, Logan. 208 p. illus. New York: Stein and Day,1974.

A most interesting form of biography-appreciation is used for this portrait of Laurence Olivier. He is described and evaluated by almost 30 personalities who know him and have worked with him in some professional capacity during his long career—either as fellow actors, directors, or writers.

It would be a mistake to assume that there is a unanimity of opinion regarding Olivier. Occasionally the reader receives the impression that the interviewee is restrained by factors of politeness, professional ethics, or simply libel from stating what he really thinks. The larger portion of the text, however, applauds Olivier as a person and as an achiever.

The illustrations provided show both his maturation as an actor and the range of his work. Some reviews, a theatre chronology, and a filmography complete the book.

The combination of a stimulating approach and a fascinating subject makes for a most pleasurable

reading experience. Much attention is given to his film work. The book can be enthusiastically recommended.

4700   *Olivia de Havilland.* by Kass, Judith M. 160 p. paper illus. New York: Pyramid, 1976.

Using the standard Pyramid format, the career of Olivia de Havilland is presented in words and pictures. From ALIBI IKE (1935) to AIRPORT 1977 (1977), each of her 46 films is described. Some biographical information is offered along with a bibliography, a filmography, and an index.

The author is impressive when describing the image and appeal that de Havilland projected on the screen. In addition, her comments on the films are satisfying and valid. She regrets that de Havilland had so little time "at the top"—that period of TO EACH HIS OWN (1946), THE SNAKE PIT (1948) and THE HEIRESS (1949).

The appreciation that Kass offers is a well-deserved one; her subject is a Hollywood survivor with many fine performances that give evidence of her talent. The fact that de Havilland never fulfilled her complete potential provides the bitter strain to the sweet tribute that Kass provides.

4701   *Olivia De Havilland.* edited by Reed, Rochelle. 24 p. paper illus. Washington, D.C.: American Film Institute, 1974.

On October 23, 1974, Olivia De Havilland was interviewed at the AFI Center for Advanced Film Studies. The text of the informal session is reprinted here. Added is a filmography which covers her long career from 1935 to 1972. Since much of the discussion referred to her directors, their names are indicated on the filmography.

4702   *Olivier: An Informal Portrait.* by Fairweather, Virginia. 183 p. illus. New York: Coward-McCann, 1969.

This is Olivier on stage only; his films are not mentioned.

4703   *Olivier-Shakespeare.* by Whitehead, Peter. 40 p. paper illus. London: Lorimer, 1966.

A short biography that includes a filmography and stills from Olivier's Shakespearean films.

4704   *The Oliviers.* by Barker, Felix. 371 p. illus. Philadelphia: J. B. Lippincott,

1953.

This early partial biography of the famous acting team takes the reader up to early 1953. Viewed today, the story is quite incomplete. Vivien Leigh had an active career up to the time of her death in 1967 and, at this writing, Lord Olivier is still very busy professionally. Ironically, the book ends with the leading characters happily married. The divorce of the Oliviers took place in 1960.

The part of their lives that is related here is fully detailed; this is an "authorized" biography. During its writing the author had access to the subjects, their friends, letters, documents, and diaries. The accent is on a recounting of professional matters rather than personal relationships. The filmmaking of both actors receives an adequate coverage. Olivier's early disasters with Garbo, WUTHERING HEIGHTS (1939), HAMLET (1948), and his other films are all described, as are Leigh's GONE WITH THE WIND (1939), CAESAR AND CLEOPATRA (1945), and A STREETCAR NAMED DESIRE (1951). The book is a prime source of biographical information about two of the most famous film actors of this century. Many illustrations and a good index add to the book's reference value. A chronology of their appearances in plays and films would have helped considerably.

4705 *Olympic's Film Finder.* by Carroll, Walter J. New York: Olympic Media Information, 1981.

4706 *On Being Funny: Woody Allen and Comedy.* by Lax, Eric. 243 p. illus. New York: Charterhouse, 1975.

Although this volume is purportedly an attempt to analyze the comedy of Woody Allen, it is much more than just that. There are large chunks of biographical material and incident; many critical judgments about his work as a writer, as a performer on television, in night clubs, in films and on stage; anecdotes; script excerpts; plot outlines; etc. Happily, much of the volume focuses on Allen's films and filmmaking methods. A few photographs appear in a center section, and the book is indexed. Why a chronology (or filmography) of Allen's work is not included is incomprehensible and almost unforgivable since it would add so much to an already fine work.

In addition to the observation of Woody Allen at close hand over a period of time, the author has used his other researches intelligently in formulating this portrait of one of the most talented and creative comedians currently active. The portrait of Allen presented is a positive one, due in part to his kindness and cooperation with the author. The millions

of Woody Allen fans will delight in reading this volume. In addition, it may hasten the inevitable discovery of his comic genius by those other millions who are currently missing something rare and special. Recommended.

4707 *On Cukor.* by Lambert, Gavin. 276 p. illus. New York: G. P. Putnam's, 1972.

When one examines the Cukor filmography, it appears that he has directed almost every other well-known film—and probably every major star.

This book is taken from oral history tapes sponsored by The American Film Institute and is a long edited interview with Cukor. An introduction, an index, and the filmography support the text which resembles the Truffaut-Hitchcock collaboration. In a loose chronological order, films or groups of films are used as chapter bases for discussion. A few general observations on persons, ideas, and techniques called "Interludes" punctuate the chapters. Lambert seems a superior interviewer for he does not display the awe and hero-worship that flawed the earlier model. He has obviously done his planning for this project extremely well, and his knowledge of the Cukor films is encyclopedic. Highly appreciative and respectful of Cukor's artistry, he does not hesitate, however, to express a difference of opinion. All this makes for fascinating reading.

A full portrait of the professional Cukor emerges, but the personal is never considered. His memory is not infallible—for example, he forgets Minnelli's THE CLOCK (1945) when he states that Garland had not played a serious role before A STAR IS BORN (1954) He offers some obvious truths that have gone relatively unnoticed till now—e.g., the similarity between the Harlow-Beery pairing in DINNER AT EIGHT (1933) and the Holliday-Crawford duo in BORN YESTERDAY (1950). In all of his responses Cukor seems honest, open, and relaxed, and most sensitive to the memory of the persons he has worked with. It is difficult to find any malice or bitterness, except toward those unnamed persons who cut several of his films into unrecognizable forms.

All of the illustrations—and there are many—are first-rate in selection, correlation, content and reproduction. The book is an example of successful chemistry between interviewer and subject, recorded in a nicely produced book that warrants hardcover format. Highly recommended.

4708 *On Film.* by Young, Vernon. 428 p. Chicago: Quadrangle Books, 1972.

Vernon Young is an international film critic whose work appears regularly in *The Hudson Review*. The author may be correct in his subtitle, "Unpopular Essays on a Popular Art," but only partially. Many of these witty and learned pieces will please enormously. A strong point of view coupled with the exposition of a knowing teacher characterizes the writing. He is never afraid to champion a minority film cause or to search diligently to locate a forgotten film in order to reassure the correctness of his memory. The entertaining attacks he makes on other film critics, directors, etc., are never as devastating as he believes they are. Mr. Youngis an eclectic writer whose statements indicate sensitivity, wit and experience.

The range of his topics is quite wide, taking in Nazi, Danish, Japanese, and Italian films; directors such as John Ford, Kurosawa, Eisenstein, Arne Sucksdorff; and re-evaluation of individual films such as THE THIRD MAN (1949) and THE LONG VOYAGE HOME (1940). The reader who can come to these essays with a film aesthetic background, some open-mindedness, and initial patience will be rewarded immeasurably. The book is indexed. Highly recommended. Younger readers may find it a bit too demanding.

4709   *...On Film.* 24 p. paper illus. Rochester, N.Y.: Eastman Kodak, 1975.

Several years ago the Eastman Kodak Co. initiated a publicity campaign based on statements by professionals. Ten such statements are presented in this beautifully produced booklet which features attractive portraits and interesting comments. Those pictured and quoted are Francis Ford Coppola, William Friedkin, Ken Mason, John Korty, Jay Sandrich, Steve Horn, Walt Topel, Rollin Binzer, Steve Spielberg, and John Hancock. An intelligent form of advertising, this attractive booklet combined information and visuals in a most impressive manner. Recommended.

4710   *On Location...On Martha's Vineyard.* by Blake, Edith. 133 p. paper illus. Orleans, Mass.: Lower Cape Publishing, 1975.

During the spring of 1974 the cast and production crew of the film, JAWS (1975), journeyed to Edgartown on Martha's Vineyard, Massachusetts, for location shooting. Edith Blake, a resident author of Edgartown, kept a record of the filmmaking in which she emphasized the confrontations between the locals and the Hollywood contingent. Although she acts as an objective eyewitness to the activities and reports in a chatty informal style, her sharp narrative is perceptive, detailed, and often witty. Her observations about the filmmaking process and its practitioners are those of an intelligent outsider and they provide a viewpoint that most records of this type do not have.

The illustrations have also been supplied by the author along with a few line drawings. They supplement the text nicely.

What started out as a completely individual project by Ms. Blake apparently was picked up by Ballantine Books and republished using the subtitle "The Making of the Movie, JAWS." Although the contents are identical, the original edition is preferable because of paper quality, picture reproduction, and other production factors. Recommended.

4711   *On Making a Movie:* BREWSTER MCCLOUD. by McClelland, C. Kirk. 359 p. paper illus. New York: Signet Books, 1971.

A record of the production of BREWSTER MCCLOUD (1970). Includes the script of the film.

4712   *On My Way to the Theatre.* by Kraft, Hy. 216 p. illus. New York: Macmillan, 1971.

In this memoir the author recalls his associations with many Hollywood and Broadway personalities. An account of Hollywood during the McCarthy era is included.

4713   *On Photography.* by Sontag, Susan. 207 p. New York: Farrar, Strauss, Giroux, 1977.

Much in Sontag's discussion of photography and the way in which it affects our perception of reality can also be applied to cinematography.

4714   *On Picture-Play Writing: A Handbook of Workmanship.* by Slevin, James. 92 p. Cedar Grove, N.J.: Farmer Smith, 1912.

4715   *On Playing with Lions.* by McKenna, Virginia; and Travers, Bill. 124 p. illus. New York: Harcourt, Brace, & World, 1966.

With the popular success of BORN FREE (1966), it was inevitable that a book be produced about the animals used in that film. Aimed at young audiences, there is a moderate text accompanied by many illustrations. A most appropriate and appealing book for young readers.

4716 *On Set: A Personal Story in Photographs and Words.* by Alda, Arlene. 128 p. illus. New York: Simon and Schuster, 1981.

Arlene Alda follows her husband, Alan, as he directs the film he wrote and starred in, THE FOUR SEASONS (1981). The result is a harmless scrapbook and diary that should please nondiscriminating fans.

4717 *On Stage Barbra Streisand.* by Keenan, Deborah. 48 p. paper illus. Mankato, Minn: Creative Education, 1976.

Streisand in a nutshell is presented in this economical review of her life and career. It should be appreciated by all unattractive little persons in the fifth grade.

4718 *On Stage Elvis Presley.* by Bowman, Kathleen. 48 p. paper illus. Mankato, Minn: Creative Education, 1976.

A short biography designed for nondiscriminating children, this volume evidences minimal production throughout.

4719 *On Stage Frank Sinatra.* by Lake, Harriet. 47 p. paper illus. Mankato, Minn: Creative Education, 1976.

Costs were cut everywhere in producing this biography for young readers. Frank Sinatra was never seen through more loving eyes than these.

4720 *On the Set of* FELLINI SATYRICON: *A Behind-the-Scenes Diary.* by Hughes, Eileen Lanouette. 248 p. illus. New York: Morrow, 1971.

This is a book similar to the diary kept on 8-1/2 (1963) using day-by-day observations made from quite a great distance, along with some very good illustrations. As a record of the making of an important motion picture (1968-69), it has value. In addition, Fellini cult members will be very pleased. However, for readers who have not seen or liked the film, the book will be a bit tedious to follow.

4721 *On the Verge of Revolt.* by French, Brandon. 194 p. paper illus. New York: Ungar, 1978.

The decade of the fifties as reflected in American films is the material of this volume. According to the author, the feminist revolution of the sixties had its roots in the fifties when women were "on the verge of revolt." Separate chapters are devoted to SUNSET BOULEVARD (1950), THE QUIET MAN (1952), THE MARRYING KIND (1952), SHANE (1953), FROM HERE TO ETERNITY (1953), THE COUNTRY GIRL (1955), THE TENDER TRAP (1955), MARTY (1955), ALL THAT HEAVEN ALLOWS (1956), PICNIC (1956), HEAVEN KNOWS, MR. ALLISON (1957), THE NUN'S STORY (1958), and SOME LIKE IT HOT (1959). Illustrations, a bibliography, a distributor list, and an index complete the book.

Since the analyses of the films emphasize such feminist concerns as sex, motherhood, marriage, ambition, loneliness, etc., the titles selected are appropriate. Some questionable interpretations and a tendency to examine isolated parts rather than the total film tend to dilute the author's argument. The volume does offer a base for further study.

4722 ON THE WATERFRONT. by Schulberg, Budd. 153 p. illus. Carbondale, Ill.: Southern Illinois University Press, 1980.

The final shooting script of the 1954 film which was directed by Elia Kazan. The volume also contains cast credits and an afterword by Budd Schulberg.

4723 *On the Way I Lost It: An Autobiography.* by Howerd, Frankie. 288 p. illus. London: W. H. Allen, 1976.

Frankie Howerd is best known for his work on the British radio and stage. Since THE RUNAWAY BUS (1954) he has appeared in about 15 comedy films, the last to date being HOUSE IN NIGHTMARE PARK (1973).

4724 *On Writing Quality Scripts for TV and Movies.: An Advanced Manual for Professional Scriptwriters.* Long Beach, N.Y.: Sunshine Books, 1981.

4725 *Once a Clown, Always a Clown: Reminiscences of DeWolf Hopper.* by Hopper, DeWolf. 238 p. illus. Boston: Little, Brown, 1927.

Written in collaboration with Wesley Winans Stout, these are selected memoirs of the actor who changed Elda Furry's name to Hedda Hopper. He enjoyed a long career in the theatre and made several silent films from 1915-1919. He is perhaps best remembered for his recitations of "Casey at the Bat."

Here, he devotes a long chapter called "Came Dawn at Hollywood" to his filming experiences.

4726 *Once Upon a Galaxy: A Journal of the Making of* THE EMPIRE STRIKESBACK. by Arnold, Alan. 288 p. paper illus. New York: Ballantine, 1980.

Ajournal that includes a day-by-day account of the making of THE EMPIRE STRIKES BACK (1980), this volume also contains interviews (cast members, George Lucas, special effects technicians, etc.) and several pages of illustrations.

4727 *The One and Only Bing.* by Thomas, Bob. 160 p. paper illus. New York: Grosset and Dunlap, 1977.

Although Bob Thomas is listed as author, this volume contains a long, illustrated filmography by Norm Goldstein and a detailed songography by Mary Campbell. All three sections combine to present selected aspects of Crosby's life and career. Much of Thomas' contribution is based on the interviews he did with Crosby for the Associated Press. As a result there is little that is new or enlightening about Crosby to be found here. The other two sections offer very good presentations of Crosby as a film performer and as a singer of popular songs. Supporting all three sections is a varied collection of visuals that span Crosby's career from Gonzaga College in 1917 to his last stage appearances in 1977.

En toto, this volume provides a competent but partial review of Crosby on and off stage.

4728 ONE DAY, WHEN I WAS LOST. by Baldwin, James. 167 p. illus. London: Michael Joseph, 1972.

This scenario, based on Alex Haley's *The Autobiography of Malcolm X*, was not filmed.

4729 *One Good Film Deserves Another.* by Druxman, Michael. 175 p. illus. New York: A. S. Barnes, 1977.

Subtitled "A Pictorial Survey of Film Sequels," this volume examines 25 selected films and their sequels. The author acknowledges all the pitfalls and reservations that a work such as this brings to mind, and states that his goal is to "amuse and inform the 'light' reader of movie memorabilia." In that particular limited purpose he is successful.

Following a short introductory chapter are the films and their sequels: BOYS TOWN (1938) and MEN OF BOYS TOWN (1941); TOPPER (1938), TOPPER TAKES A TRIP (1939) and TOPPER RETURNS (1941), etc. A compendium of films and sequels not related in the text is appended. Visuals provided adequately suggest the similarities and differences between the original film and its sequel(s).

While some question may be raised about the all-inclusiveness of the title and the subtitle, the book is acceptable in the light of the author's purpose—to entertain.

4730 *101 Films for Character Growth.* by Cushing, Jane. 110 p. paper Notre Dame, Ind.: Fides Pub., 1969.

This is a list of more than 100 short films along with a rating, topic designation, synopsis, age-level, and question set for each. The length of the films varies from 4 minutes, THE WALL (1965), to 58 minutes, MEMORANDUM (1966), with the majority running less than 30 minutes each. An introductory outline denotes various goals and attitudes to which certain films are assigned. For example, under "Man's Inhumanity to Man" one of the goals cited is a realization of prejudice. Six films are mentioned as aids in reaching that particular goal: ALL THE WAY HOME (1958), AN AMERICAN GIRL (1958), BOUNDARY LINES (1947), BROTHERHOOD OF MAN (1946), BURDEN OF TRUTH (1957), and THE SIT-IN (1961).

In the text the films are arranged according to the attitude-goal index. An alphabetical listing with descriptive data is offered at the end of the book. Since most of the films mentioned are the kind found in many library collections, this small book is invaluable for selecting films, conducting discussions, etc. Highly recommended.

4731 *100 Films For Juniors.* compiled by Alexander, S. G. P. 24 p. paper London: Society For Education in Film and Television.

4732 *One in a Thousand.* by Robertson, Marian. 64 p. illus. Evanston, Ill.: Row Peterson, 1941.

A title in *The Way of Life* series, this volume deals with seeking a career in Hollywood. It carries the subtitle, "The Way of Life on the Road to Hollywood."

4733 *One Naked Individual.* by Crawford, Cheryl. illus. Indianapolis: Bobbs-Merrill, 1976.

Cheryl Crawford's adult life was spent in the theatre as a producer and director. However, she has worked with so many film actors at the start of their careers that her effect, however peripheral to films, was a tangible one.

Her autobiography is filled with memories and anecdotes about movie stars who were part of her 50-year run in the theatre.

4734 *One Reel a Week.* by Balshofer, Fred J.; and Miller, Arthur C. 218 p. illus. Berkeley, Calif.: University of California Press, 1967.

This is a dual biography of two pioneer technicians, Balshofer, who started a motion picture company in Philadelphia in 1905, and Miller, hired at the age of fourteen to help him. Years later, while Balshofer was establishing and operating the New York Motion Picture Company (which included the subsidiary Keystone Company), Miller worked with Edwin S. Porter, reached Hollywood in the twenties, and became a popular cameraman. In the years that followed he was nominated seven times for Academy Awards and received three Oscars for his photographic skill.

With obvious respect and affection for their profession, the authors have written a valuable memoir in a straightforward, simple style. Both have contributed personal insights into major areas of motion picture history. The stills are so excellent that one wishes for more. This is one of the better books on early motion picture history. Readers unfamiliar with the names and the particular period of development may find the book a bit dull. To the historian, it will be quite exciting.

4735 *One Tear is Enough.* by Stone, Paulene; and Evans, Peter. 192 p. illus. London: Michael Joseph, 1975.

An account of Stone's life with Laurence Harvey, this volume covers their six-year relationship and short marriage. Harvey died of cancer less than a year after they were wed.

4736 *1000 and One; The Blue Book of Nontheatrical Films.* edited by Greene, Nelson L. Chicago: Educational Screen, 1920- .

There were several editions of this catalog of educational films from 1920 to 1954. In the years that followed, its name was changed to *The Blue Book of 16mm Films* and *The Blue Book of Audio-Visual Materials.* The fourth through the thirteenth editions were edited by Nelson L. Greene.

4737 ONE-TRICK PONY. by Simon, Paul. 224 p. illus. New York: Knopf, 1980.

A script of the 1980 film directed by R. Young.

4738 *The One with the Moustache is Costello.* by Frazier, George. 275 p. illus. New York: Random House, 1947.

This collective biography deals with subjects from films, sports and popular music. There are short, chatty, entertaining portraits of Bogart, Flynn and Lorre. There is no index.

4739 *The Only Good Indian.* by Friar, Ralph; and Friar, Natasha. 332 p. illus. New York: Drama Book Specialists, 1972.

This unusual book explores the portrait of the Indian as reflected in both silent and sound films. Some attention is also paid to the image presented by literature. Final sections of the book include a listing of actors who frequently played Indians and a long filmography that lists both sound and silent films. The films in this listing are arranged by subject category. There are some interesing visuals and the book is indexed. This is a definitive study of the Indian's portrayal in films. Perhaps more attention will be paid to the problem of the image of the American Indian, and this volume should aid in any discussion which may ensue. Recommended.

4740 *Only Victims.* by Vaughn, Robert. 355 p. New York: G. P. Putnam's, 1972.

The original source for this book was Vaughn's doctoral dissertation, done at the University of Southern California. It quotes Dalton Trumbo's trenchant comment about there being no heroes, villains, saints or devils but only victims in that dark time of 1938 to 1958. This was the period when investigations by the House Committee on Un-American Activities (HUAC) were prevalent. The study concerns itself with five different HUAC hearings: Martin Dies (1938), J. Parnell Thomas (1947), John Woods (1951-52), Harold Velde-Francis Walters (1953-55), and the Passport Hearings (1958). Vaughn tries to examine the effects of HUAC by considering three possibilities: actual effects (theatre closings, jobs lost, etc.), probable effects (moral, personal, and procedural), and possible effects (constructive, evolutionary, unapparent as yet). His conclusions are twofold: first, that the major goal of the Committee was punishment; and second, that the stifling of creative artists who lived in fear of the Committee is an incalculable loss. There are, of course, implications for us today and Vaughn notes these.

Senator George McGovern introduces the book; it has several appendices, a detailed bibliography and an index. While the book will appeal to a limited audience, its sound argument deserves a wider one. This book is one of the best of several ones on the hearings. All deserve the attention of anyone concerned with misuse of power, governmental or otherwise. Highly recommended.

4741 *An Open Book.* by Gordon, Ruth. 200 p. New York: Doubleday, 1980.

Here is another Gordon autobiographical grab bag consisting of portraits, vignettes, advice, comment and fact. The octogenarian actress writes of her career struggles from Boston to Hollywood in her own unique, conversational style. Certainly no one can project and interpret the Ruth Gordon image better than Ruth Gordon the writer.

4742 *An Open Book: John Huston.* by Huston, John. 389 p. illus. New York: Alfred A. Knopf, 1980.

The autobiography that John Huston provides here is similar to his creative endeavors as a film director. Most of the book is absorbing in its terse retelling of a very rich and eventful life; however, some parts seem self-indulgent in their insistence on relating at length tiresome stories of animals, macho activities, parrots, boxing, racing, Ireland, hunting, etc. These are obviously very important to Huston, but they make for dull stretches in what is a fairly interesting book. It is when Huston recalls his early film work or writes lovingly of his father that the reader meets a multi-talented, highly literate, sometimes eccentric man. Again, as in his films, the reader may not respond to it all but won't be bored. An index and illustrations are provided, but there is no filmography.

Huston apparently has a somewhat disassociated attitude about his film work, considering it almost as a minor distraction in a life full of major enthusiasms. He has had his own way once again, and maybe that's what good autobiography should be.

4743 *Operating Audiovisual Equipment.* by Eboch, Sidney; and Cochern, George W. 75 p. paper illus. San Francisco: Chandler, 1968.

This manual includes directions for the operation of a motion picture projector.

4744 *Operation Elvis.* by Levy, Alan. 117 p. illus. New York: Holt, 1960.

Elvis' career both before and during his army service is described here, comically, factually, and with sociological overtones. Cartoon illustrations by Dedini.

4745 *Opportunities in Acting: Stage, Motion Pictures, Television.* by Moore, Dick. 128 p. paper New York: Vocational Guidance Manuals, 1963.

Written by a former child movie actor, Dickie Moore, this discussion of acting as a profession has an introduction by Ralph Bellamy. It is a title in the *Vocational Guidance Manuals Career* series.

4746 *Opportunities in the Motion Picture Industry.* by Photoplay Research Society. 117 p. illus. New York: Arno Press, 1970 (1922).

How to qualify for positions in the motion picture industry in 1922.

4747 *The Oral Tradition: The Written Work and the Screen Image.* by Riesman, David. 40 p. illus. Yellow Springs, Ohio: Antioch Press, 1956.

A booklet based on a speech given by Riesman on October 5, 1955, in which he discussed the influence of film on society.

4748 ORANGE AND BLUE. by Schreivogel, Paul A. 20 p. paper illus. Dayton, Ohio: Pflaum, 1970.

A study guide for the 1962 film directed by Peter Chermayeff and Clare Chermayeff.

4749 *Ordeal: An Autobiography.* by Lovelace, Linda; and McGrady, Mike. 242 p. Secaucus, N.J.: Citadel, 1980.

The rationale for this autobiography is to set the record straight after the publication of two earlier ghosted books about her life. Lovelace, now living a "normal" life with husband, children and welfare, tells how Chuck Traynor held her prisoner and forced her into prostitution and pornography. She was paid very little for her appearance in DEEP THROAT (1972), a film that made millions for its producers. In this rather unique confession, the reader will find accounts of hypnotism, perversion, bestiality, rape, masochism, and other assorted diversions. All of this is too much to swallow.

4750 *Organizing a School Projectionist Club.* by Mannino, Philip. State College, Penn.: School Projectionists Club of America.

4751 *Orient: A Survey of Films Produced in Countries of Arab and Asian Culture.* by Holmes, Winifred. unpaginated UNESCO, 1959.

This survey of Asian films was prepared for the British Film Institute.

4752 *An Original Dead End Kid Presents.: Dead End Yells, Wedding Bells, Cockle Shells, and Dizzy Spells.* by Gorcey, Leo. III p. illus. New York: Vantage, 1967.

An autobiography of Leo Gorcey, who began his career as one of the DEAD END (1937) kids, and had a long career in films including a stretch as one of the Bowery Boys. He died shortly after the publication of this volume.

4753 *The Original Sin.* by Quinn, Anthony. 311 p. Boston: Little, Brown, 1972.

This is at best a partial autobiography, emphasizing the pre-screen years. Using psychiatric sessions and the literary metaphor of an 11-year-old boy to represent his immaturity, Quinn resorts to shock words and situations, frank descriptions of sexual encounters, and mental flagellation to interest the reader. It doesn't work too well.

The first third of the book tells of his parents and his life as a chicano in the slums of Los Angeles during the twenties. Later, encounters with Aimee Semple McPherson, Mae West, John Barrymore, Carole Lombard, Gary Cooper and Cecil B. DeMille are described. The book concludes with his discovery of his ability to love and the inevitable banishment of the "boy" Quinn. The two short sections that deal with his film career are fine. His experience as a beginning film actor in DeMille's THE PLAINSMAN (1936) is a fascinating reminiscence while the early contract negotiations will give the reader some insight into the operations of film studios of the thirties. The writing style is compounded of egotism, confession, sex and search. There are no illustrations, nor is an index provided. It is simply not "that kind of a book."

Admirers of Quinn will appreciate the exposure of self and others. Those who are less enthusiastic about his abilities will be bored by the heavy priority given to personal problems over professional matters.

4754 *Original Skin.* by Hanson, Gillian. 171 p. paper illus. New York: Tower Publications, 1970.

Subtitled "Nudity and Sex in Film and Theatre," this paperback is a reprint of a serious study originally published in England. The author traces the sexual revolution during the last four decades, as it first appeared in literature, then in experimental theatre and the avant-garde film, and finally in the mainstream of popular art. The question of liberty versus obscenity is considered along with that of realism versus sexploitation.

This background and history provides an introduction to the two major sections on cinema and the theatre. Various examples from recent films along with the opinions of filmmakers and authors are used in an examination of the trend to deal with sex in the open. Final sections deal with the relationships between life, art and entertainment. Although there have been changes since this book's appearance, the author has formulated an excellent summary of eroticism in films and theatre. No index is provided, but a few stills have been added—probably to increase the drugstore sales of an intelligent, nonerotic survey of a current trend in film and theatre. Acceptable for others.

4755 *The Origins of American Film Criticism.* by Lounsbury, Myron Osborn. 547 p. New York: Arno, 1973.

This is one of the doctoral dissertations reproduced by Arno exactly as they were submitted to the degree-granting school. Keeping in mind Ernest Callenbach's appraisal of American film literature as mostly a debate between form and content, an examination of the film literature preceding the Second World War is attempted here. The purpose is to offer an account of the evolution and growth of serious film criticism from 1909 to 1939, and its effect on the development and improvement of film techniques. *The Film Index* was used as a major source in this study, which spotlights Vachel Lindsay, Hugo Munsterberg, Gilbert Seldes, Victor Freeburg, and other early writers. Publication in 1939 of Lewis Jacobs' *The Rise of the American Film* provides the cut-off point of the study.

A conclusion suggests the existence of six basic types of critical opinion: Liberal Patrician, Modern Liberal, Social Radical, Popular Cultist, Aesthetic Idealist, and Modern Aesthete. The film critics of the pre-1939 period did not achieve a blend of form and content to any extent. A bibliography and an index complete the book.

4756 *Origins of the American Film.* by Hendricks, Gordon. 592 p. illus. New York: Arno, 1972.

Arno has performed a public service in gathering three books by Gordon Hendricks and publishing them in one volume. A new introduction by Hendricks sets the stage for these remarkale researches. Titles are: *The Edison Motion Picture Myth*; *Beginnings of the Biograph*; and *The Kinetoscope*.

4757 *The Origins of the Motion Picture.* by Thomas, David B. 32 p. paper illus. London: H. M. Stationery Office, 1964.

An introductory bookleton the pre-history of the screen, which includes a bibliography. It is a title in the *Science Museum* series.

4758 "Orphee": *The Play and the Film.* by Cocteau, Jean. 129 p. paper illus. Oxford: Basil Blackwell, 1976.

Contains the script of the film.

4759 *Orson Welles.* by Fowler, Roy Alexander. 100 p. illus. London: Pendulum Publications, 1946.

4760 *Orson Welles.* by Bessy, Maurice. 195 p. paper illus. New York: Crown, 1971.

Another book on Welles may seem superfluous or redundant but, thank goodness, this one is different. Rather than analyzing the films one-by-one, Bessy is content to offer his own critical-biographical essay and then follow it up with some articles and documents relating to Welles. Interviews, quotations, an unpublished screenplay on Salome, film reviews and appreciations are some of the forms in this section. The book is completed by a filmography, a bibliography and an index. Visuals used are selected with intelligence and reproduced with care.

The volume more than justifies its subtitle, "An Investigation into His Films and Philosophy." While the author essay tends to get heavy at times, it is nevertheless a satisfying blend of information, opinion, and analysis. The volume is a translation from *The Cinema d'Aujourd'hui Directors* Series. Highly recommeneded.

4761 *Orson Welles.* by McBride, Joseph. 192 p. paper illus. New York: Viking, 1972.

Another book on Welles? While it may seen unnecessary, McBride does offer some new material. He discusses the "Raising Kane" issue and describes an interview with Welles that took place while they filmed test shots for a proposed film. Several times he mentions the cooperation of Peter Bogdanovich, whose long-promised book with Welles is now called *This is Orson Welles.* When he comes to the critical evaluations of the films, he treats them all except THE STRANGER (1941). Several short pre-CITIZEN KANE (1941) films made by Welles in the 30's are described in much detail. A print of one, THE HEARTS OF AGE, exists and several frame enlargements are shown.

The careers of Orson Welles—as director, actor, radio performer, writer, and recording artist—are catalogued in the appendix. The book is not indexed and the visuals are quite disappointing, being mostly too small and/or too dark. Because of the charisma or mystique of the subject, no book about him can be without some interest. Much of what is related here is familiar but there are some new insights and information offered. Acceptable.

4762 *Orson Welles.* by McBride, Joseph. 159 p. paper illus. New York: Jove (Harcourt, Brace, Jovanovich), 1977.

This appreciation of Orson Welles is a title in the *Illustrated History of the Movies* series, which originated with Pyramid publishers in 1973. Fortunately there has been no change in the basic format of the series, which employs competent qualified writers to present a critical survey of the subject's career.

In the case of Welles, McBride has used many quotations from interviews, a fine selection of visuals, and most importantly, a serious consideration of those films in which Welles appeared but did not direct. Most books on Welles have emphasized his achievements as a director but few treat his work as an actor. A bibliography, a filmography, and an index complete the volume.

This account of one of cinema's living legends is impressive. McBride presents a detailed objective portrait of a multi-talented man who is presently occupied in many trivial television assignments, all accepted in order to raise money for the completion of his film THE OTHER SIDE OF THE WIND. This volume is a most welcome addition to the series. Recommended.

4763 *Orson Welles: A Critical View.* by Bazin, Andre. 138 p. paper illus. New York: Harper, 1978 (1972).

A classic of film criticism has been translated from the French language in this short book. Bazin, the influential film critic, discusses Welles as the influential filmmaker in a critical biofilmography that stands as a model to emulate. His text, divided into six chronological periods, gives attention to both Welles' life and his films. Supporting Bazin's essay are a profile of Welles by Jean Cocteau and a foreword by Francois Truffaut. This latter piece is as rich as the essay it introduces. In this volume an all-star cast collaborates beautifully to produce an achievement in film criticism. Highly recommended.

4764 *Orson Welles: A Prodigious Life.* by Brady, Frank. Englewood Cliffs, N.J.: Prentice-Hall, 1981.

4765 *Oscar at the Academy Awards.* by Osborne, Robert. 84 p. paper illus. Hollywood, Calif.: Osborne, 1968.

An abbreviated paperback spinoff of *Academy Awards Illustrated.*

4766 *The Oscar Directors.* by Edmonds, I. G.; and Mimura, Reiko. 253 p. paper illus. New York: A. S. Barnes, 1980.

An interesting approach to collective director appreciation is offered here. Fifty-three Academy Award-winning directors, from Frank Borzage (1928) to Robert Benton (1979), are presented in chronological order. For each man there is some biographical information and critical comment along with a recap of the film which earned the director his award. Special attention is given to the illustrations which come mostly from the authors' own collections. They are listed in the only index provided here.

While the attempt to do something unique is recognized, there are, perhaps, a few missed opportunities apparent. For example, director filmographies, a general index, a listing of the other directors nominated each year—any of these might have made the book more useful than the index to the visuals or the frequent lengthy plot synopses.

This is a pleasant volume that does not quite live up to its reference and resource potential.

4767 *The Oscar Movies From A-Z.* by Pickard, Roy. 247 p. illus. New York: Taplinger, 1977.

Roy Pickard apparently has an affection for dictionaries of motion picture topics. His previous volumes, *A Companion to the Movies* (1972) and *A Dictionary of 1000 Best Films* (1971) offered general selected film titles in an alphabetical arrangement. His newest work is much more specific, using only those films which have received Academy Award recognition in any category except two. Unfortunately the two he has chosen to exclude are short films and documentaries.

The period covered is 1927 to 1976 and each entry lists the film title, the year, the specific award(s), the person(s) responsible, an explanatory paragraph and a partial list of film credits along with color data and running time. Supporting the 500 or so entries are several appendixes: (1) a listing of the yearly awards in the four major categories: (film, director, actor, actress); (2) a yearly listing of the nominees in the four major categories; (3) a Pickard selection of 100 famous films that received no nominations whatsoever; (4) a list of films that received one or more nominations but won nothing; and finally, (5) a listing of the special awards made by the Academy. The index which concludes the book lists only winning films and people.

Pickard's expertise lies in the arrangement of the factual material rather than in the short synopsis accompanying each entry. His selection of material is satisfactory with one exception—the omission of material on the short films and documentaries. Since TV, schools and libraries make frequent and constant use of these film forms, their absence in this volume is a serious flaw. Otherwise, Pickard has created a useful guide that offers quick and easy access to information that will answer most questions about the Academy Awards.

4768 *The Oscar People* by Likeness, George. 432 p. illus. West Menota, Ill.: Wayside Press 1965.

As indicated in the title, this book concerns itself primarily with the actors and actresses who have been honored with an Oscar. A list of their other performances follows a biographical sketch. The award-winning pictures are also discussed in some depth. The history, background, and certain other categories of the awards are treated rather briefly. The statistical analysis that precedes the best picture and the best actor sections is most unusual and rather disconcerting. Very little mention is made of the much-reported politics, rivalries, vote-trading, and sentimentality that has characterized some of the ceremonies.

The book's shortcomings reflect those of the awards. Is there such a thing as the best picture of any year? If so, can it be recognized immediately? Does it matter that Clark Gable appeared in 3 top award films? Is color a deterrent to the best picture award? One is forced to wonder if the author's conclusions are justified by the Oscar evidence. This interesting account of certain aspects of the awards is recommended as a general reading and a secondary reference. Illustrations are distracting; they are presented with a single color tone (red or blue) over the black and white originals.

4769 *Oscar Quiz Book.* by Hopman, Stanley. paper illus. Waterbury, Conn.: Dale, 1978.

4770 *The Other Hollywood.* by Thorpe, Edward. 174 p. London: Michael Joseph, 1970.

Another nail in Hollywood's coffin! It purports to examine Hollywood today, and some idea of the approach can be seen by the chapter titles: Hideous Hollywood; Hi-Life Hollywood; Has-Been Hollywood; Housewives' Hollywood; High School Hollywood; Hustler's Hollywood; Homosexual's Hollywood; Hard Core Hollywood; Hybrid Hollywood; Hopeful Hollywood. The book is an example of sensationalized sociology.

4771 *The Other Side of Henry Winkler: My Story.* by Winkler, Henry. 160 p. paper illus. New York: Warner, 1976.

4772 *Other Side of the Coin: An Intimate Study of the Indian Film Industry.* by Gaur, Madan. 347 p. illus. Bombay: Vinod Billa, 1973.

4773 *The Other Side of the Rainbow.* by Torme, Mel. 241 p. illus. New York: Morrow, 1970.

This account of Judy Garland and her ill-fated TV series is noted here only as supplementary biographical material. The book is powerful, revealing, and a jolt to the stomach of the Garland legend.

4774 *The Other Side of the Screen: The Story of the Filming of* RAINTREE COUNTY. by Fenderson, Julia; and Fenderson, Bill. 63 p. paper Culver City, Calif.: Kerr, 1957.

4775 *Our Gang.* by Maltin, Leonard; and Bann, Richard W. 288 p. illus. New York: Crown, 1977.

In 1922 the first Our Gang comedy was made, and for the next 23 years there were 220 more films created in the series. Performers, directors, writers, and even studios changed but the Our Gang short films remained popular. They have enjoyed continuing acceptance since they were revived on television as "The Little Rascals."

This volume goes into great detail about the films, the actors, and the history of the series. Most of the book is a carefully prepared filmography. Each of the films is described by production data, cast, a synopsis, comment and evaluation. One or more stills appear for each film. Appendixes include biographies of the regular members and brief mention of others who were associated with the series briefly. The book is indexed.

As a record of an enduring film series, the volume is a splendid achievement. It has been carefully researched, intelligently arranged and, most importantly, approached with affection. It is a worthy model for other writers of film literature to consider. Recommended.

4776 *Our Lady Cinema.* by Furniss, Harry. 208 p. illus. Bristol: J. W. Arrowsmith, 1914.

The subtitle summarizes this volume: "How and Why I Went into the Photoplay World and What I Found There." A description of early filmmaking in British and American studios is given, along with many peripheral comments about writing, casting, direction, censorship, etc. The illustrations were drawn by the author.

4777 *Our Modern Art: The Movies.* by Callenbach, Ernest. 116 p. paper Chicago: Center for the Study of Liberal Education for Adults, 1955.

A suggested course outline with a chapter and discussion guide for each large area of film study is the content of this curriculum guide. Chapter subjects include westerns, animation, syntax, montage, experiment, etc. Suggested readings are given for each section. The outline is valid and would serve as a structure for a film course. The questions are thought-provoking and should stimulate discussion. For anyone who is involved in teaching or using film, this small volume should help immeasurably.

4778 *Our Movie-Made Children.* by Forman, Henry James. 288 p. New York: Macmillan, 1933.

From 1929 to 1933 the Payne Fund supported 12 independent research investigations concerning motion pictures in relation to children and youth. This volume is a popular summary of the studies. As one of the first inquiries made concerning the effects of media upon a specific audience, the studies are historically important. Since they were done 40 years ago, the findings are no longer all pertinent but the scholar will find that a surprising amount is. This summary is taken mostly from the following studies: 1) *Getting Ideas From Movies*. 2) *The Content of Motion Pictures*; 3) *Children's Attendance at Motion Pictures*; 4) *The Emotional Responses of Children to the Motion Picture*; 5) *Motion Pictures and Standards of Morality*; 6) *Motion Pictures and Social Attitudes of Children*; 7) *Relationship of Motion Pictures to the Character and Attitudes of Children*; 8) *Children's Sleep*; 9) *Movies and Conduct*; 10) *Movies, Delinquency, and Crime*; 11) *Boys, Movies, and City Streets*; 12) *How to Appreciate Motion Pictures*.

In addition to this popular summary, most of these important historical studies were published in separate volumes.

4779 *Our Movie Makers*. by Grump, Irving. 231 p. illus. New York: Dodd Mead, 1940.

Commercial motion picture production is described in detail here, with individual chapters devoted to specific activities, makeup, cutting room, shooting, etc.

4780 *Our Will Rogers*. by Croy, Homer. 377 p. New York: Duell Sloane Pearce, 1953.

Homer Croy was the author of *They Had to See Paris*, a novel upon which Will Rogers' first sound film was based. The men became friends in 1930, at the beginning of Rogers' second career in films. This is evident in the attention given by Croy to Rogers in the Hollywood of the 30's. The early chapter on the silent films is also well written. In fact, the book is surprising when one recall's Croy's disastrous biography of D. W. Griffith. The sources for the text are listed in a long appendix and the book is indexed. Since there is more attention to the films in this volume, it is acceptable.

4781 *Out of My Mind*. by Danischewsky, Monja. 176 p. illus. London: Michael Joseph, 1972.

Danischewsky, who also wrote *White Russian, Red Face*, was a producer-writer at Ealing Studios. The book includes memoirs and anecdotes about the people with whom she worked.

4782 OUTLAND. by Anobile, Richard. unpag. illus. paper New York: Warner Books, 1981.

A reconstruction of the 1981 film directed and written by Peter Hyams via frame enlargements and dialogue.

4783 *Outline for Teaching a Course in Basic Movie-Making*. 23 p. paper illus. Rochester, N.Y.: Eastman Kodak, 1973.

Prepared for the teacher about to present a first course in student filmmaking, this outline (AT-106) offers plans for 12 meetings. Supporting the lesson plans are some information sources, including a short bibliography. The course leans rather heavily on other Kodak publications, (see Kodak Pamphlets), but the structure is sound, flexible and adaptable to many situations. Most valuable in school situations, the outline can also be used with adult students quite effectively. Recommended.

4784 *Outline of Czechoslovakian Cinema*. by Dewey, Langdon. 122 p. illus. London: Informatics, 1971.

Czech cinema is historically divided into four periods: 1)1898-1918, 2) 1918-1930, 3) 1930-1945, and 4) 1945-1970. A bibliography and an index are added.

4785 *Outside London*. by Quinn, James. 47 p. paper illus. London: British Film Institute, 1965.

A report on motion picture theatres in Great Britain, prepared for the British Film Institute.

4786 *Over My Shoulder*. by Matthews, Jessie. 240 p. illus. New Rochelle, N.Y.: Arlington House, 1975.

Jessie Matthews is as charming in print as she was in those British musicals of the thirties. In this autobiography she recalls in a frank, nonsensationalized narrative her rapid rise to celebrity. Born in poverty into a large family, she was pushed toward a dancing career; the stress that sudden fame, several failed marriages, newspaper notoriety, personal insecurity and overwork can cause culminated in a series of breakdowns and a suicide attempt.

Considerable attention is given to her experiences in making films, and her story is sprinkled with celebrity names: Carol Reed, Anna Neagle, Michael Redgrave, Victor Saville, Noel Coward, etc. In describing herself and her supporting cast of actors, family members, husbands and acquaintances, the author is honest and tactful. The book is nicely illustrated and a short index is provided. While its greatest appeal will probably be to those who remember her performances with nostalgic affection, the book will also create a desire in younger readers to see the neglected Jessie Matthews films of the thirties. Recommended.

4787 *Overexposures: The Crisis in American Filmmaking.* by Thomson, David. 33 p. New York: William Morrow, 1981.

A series of essays in which the author chastises the Hollywood film industry for its current dull, depressed state. Full of stimulating ideas and opinions, the author provides some much needed critical comment.

4788 *Overture and Beginners.* by Denison, Michael. illus. London: Victor Gollancz, 1973.

Michael Denison was a leading man in British films during the forties and the fifties, often appearing opposite his wife, Dulcie Gray.

4789 OVERTURE, OVERTURE/NYITANY. by Schreivogel, Paul A. 20 p. paper illus. Dayton, Ohio: Pflaum, 1970.

A study guide for the 1958 film, OVERTURE, and the 1965 film, OVERTURE/NYITANY, directed by Janos Vadasz.

4790 *The Oxford Companion to Film.* edited by Bawden, Liz-Anne. 767 p. illus. New York: Oxford University Press, 1976.

This encyclopedia of film includes entries on specific films and filmmakers, production companies, national cinemas, genres, critics, movements, technical processes, etc. As in any such compendium, the treatment given each topic varies in length. Director biographies are usually much longer than those for actors, writers, etc.

The aim of the volume is to provide information and to suggest related topics to the reader. The volume is illustrated mostly by frame enlargements which have been well-selected and adequately reproduced. Since the focus of the volume is international, unfamiliar names and films appear with regularity. This most satisfactory reference book is characterized by a wide range of topics which have been intelligently selected and given accurate, well-written annotations. Recommended.

4791 *The Oz Scrapbook.* by Green, David L.; and Martin, Dick,. 182 p. illus. New York: Random House, 1977.

A book called *The Wonderful Wizard of Oz* was published in 1900 and America has not been the same since. There have been 39 more books, some stage plays, many radio stories, several motion pictures, and a few television presentations since then. This volume touches on all these versions of the land of Oz and its inhabitants.

One chapter is devoted to Oz on stage and screen. Many early silent films are noted along with the 1939 MGM sound classic now shown annually on television.

The text is complemented by many fascinating illustrations, some of which are in full color. In an appendix the 40 Oz books are listed along with some other Oz publications and a selected list of Oz information sources. No index is provided.

This book will have a definite appeal for young readers who want further background about Oz. Seekers of information about the films may be disappointed since they are mentioned only briefly with little detail or critical evaluation given. The absence of a filmography or a mediagraphy is unexplainable since so many of today's young people became acquainted with Oz through media presentations. Acceptable.

4792 *Ozu.* by Ritchie, Donald. 275 p. paper illus. Berkeley, Calif.: University of California Press, 1974.

An analysis of the methods used by Yasujiro Ozu in making his films is offered in this volume. Donald Ritchie, the author of several books on Japanese film, once again demonstrates his understanding of that national cinema, and, in this instance, the place of Ozu's 53 films within it. After an introduction of the subjects, themes, patterns, similarities, etc., of the films, Ritchie considers the script (construction, dialogue, characterization, motif, ethical climate, etc.), the shooting (visual style, grammatical devices, composition, camera position, etc.) and editing (circular form, transitions, length, tempo, order, time, etc.). A final summary chapter is followed by a lengthy biographical filmography, chapter notes, a bibliography, and an index. There are many illustrations throughout the book; unfortunately, some are too small to be effective. As in Ritchie's previous volumes, a devotion and dedication to Japanese film is immediately obvious. Here it is coupled with research and scholarship to produce a superb study of a neglected filmmaker. Highly recommended.

4793 *Ozu.* edited by Gillett, John; and Wilson, David. 42 p. paper London: British Film Institute; New York: Zoetrope.

An appreciation of Japanese director Yasujiro Ozu, this anthology of critical articles is accompanied by a filmography and a bibliography.

4794 *Packaging for Television and Motion Pictures.* by Barovick, Richard L. 320 p. illus. New York: Practising Law Institute, 1973.

Prepared for the 1973 Packaging for Television and Motion Pictures Workshop, this handbook deals with legislation, contracts, and forms encountered in putting together the elements of a production.

4795 *Paddy Chayefsky.* by Clum, John M. 149 p. Boston: Twayne (G. K. Hall), 1976.

Paddy Chayefsky is a writer who has been acclaimed for his work in television, theatre, and motion pictures. In this biographical appreciation, John Clum arranges his text into logical career divisions — Learning the Trade, The Bard of the Small Screen, The Dramatist of Disillusionment, The Oscar Winner, and the Activist as Playwright. A chronology, notes, references, a selected bibliography and an index complete the work.

It is the chapter on Chayefsky's screen work which has pertinence for film enthusiasts. He is the original author of AS YOUNG AS YOU FEEL (1951), MARTY (1955), THE CATERED AFFAIR (1956), THE BACHELOR PARTY (1957), THE GODDESS (1958), and MIDDLE OF THE NIGHT (1959). Not only did he write film scripts for most of the above, but he also adapted two works of other authors for the screen— THE AMERICANIZATION OF EMILY (1964) and PAINT YOUR WAGON (1970). He received Academy Awards for his original screenplays for THE HOSPITAL (1972) and NETWORK (1976).

Selected for discussion here are the early translations from TV to screen—MARTY, THE BACHELOR PARTY, and MIDDLE OF THE NIGHT—along with THE GODDESS, THE AMERICANIZATION OF EMILY, and THE HOSPITAL.

Some exception must be taken to Clum's failure to provide a filmography. In certain cases it is extremely difficult to ascertain Chayefsky's exact contribution from the chronology. Selection, too, is suspect with no treatment offered of PAINT YOUR WAGON, the only failure in Chayefsky's screenwriting career.

The volume has been carefully researched and Chayefsky's cooperation with the author is evident throughout. As a result the study is a valid one that furnishes sufficient evidence and argument for Chayefsky's position as one of America's leading writers. Recommended.

4796 PAINT YOUR WAGON. 32 p. paper illus. New York: National Publishers, 1969.

Peter Max's influence is apparent in the graphics work for this souvenir book. Cover designs and titling are unusual for the subject matter and probably reflect the lack of faith the producers had in their original material. All the songs used in the 1969 film are listed, along with other cast and production credits. Stars Lee Marvin, Clint Eastwood, and Jean Seberg share the spotlight with director Joshua Logan, composer Frederick Loewe, and author-lyricist Alan Jay Lerner.

4797 *Painting Photography Film.* by Moholy-Nagy, Laszlo. 150 p. illus. Cambridge, Mass.: MIT Press, 1969.

Treats such topics as "static-kinetic-optical-composition," "photography without a camera," "simultaneous or poly cinema," "type photo," etc.

4798 *Painting with Light.* by Alton, John. 191 p. illus. New York: Macmillan, 1962 (1949).

A leading Hollywood cameraman discusses motion picture lighting. About 300 illustrations complement the text beautifully. First published in 1949.

4799 *Palestine on Film.* by Downing, Taylor. 17 p. London: Council for the Advancement of Arab-British Understanding, 1979.

The Palestinian Arabs as portrayed in documentary films and newsreels 1930-1950.

4800 *Palmer Plan Handbook: Photoplay Writing, Simplified and Explained.* by Palmer, Frederick. 165 p. Los Angeles: Palmer Photoplay Corp., 1920.

"...a practical treatise on scenario writing as practiced at leading motion picture studios, with cross-references to successful examples including a current glossary of technical and semi-technical words and phrases, copyright laws, rules of the National Board of Censors, etc."

4801 PALS. by Homoki-Nagy, Istvan. 137 p. paper illus. Budapest: Corvina, 1961.

This record of the making of the film PALS (1958) was written by the film's director and translated by Istvan Farkas and Jozsef Hatvany.

4802 PANDORA'S BOX. by Pabst, G. W. 136 p. paper illus. New York: Simon and Schuster, 1971.

Script of the 1928 film directed by Pabst. Contains: "Pabst and Lulu" by Louise Brooks; "Pabst and the Miracle of Louise Brooks" by Lotte Eisner; cast and credits.

4803 *Paper Movie Machines.* by Wentz, Budd. 32 p. paper illus. San Franciso: Troubador Press, 1975.

Although this is an expendable volume designed for individual use, it can also serve many purposes in film study. Presented here are motion machine cutouts and instructions for their assembly using simple materials—tape, pencils, glue, tacks, cork, spools, toothpicks, etc. Students of film history will recognize very simplified models of the Kinematoscope, the Thaumatrope, the Phenakistoscope, the Zoetrope, the Kineograph, the Rolloscope, the Slideoscope, and the Praxinoscope. A more advanced project, the Kinora, capable of showing one minute of animation, concludes the volume.

For schools offering courses in film study and appreciation, this volume would be ideal for use with the short film, THE ORIGINS OF THE MOTION PICTURE (1951). Its appeal to creative young filmmakers is undeniable. Highly recommended.

4804 *Pappy: The Life of John Ford.* by Ford, Dan. 324 p. illus. Englewood Cliffs, N.J.: Prentice-Hall, 1979.

In writing this biography, Dan Ford, the grandson of John Ford, had access to information, documents and other materials that have not been available to other writers as yet. This advantage has served him well, for he has written a biography that is critical, personal, selected and, most of all, understanding. Blending his research with personal recollections and anecdotes, he recreates the fascinating story of a man who was easy to admire professionally but hard to like personally.

The many successes and few failures of Ford's life are included along with informal portraits of some of Ford's actors (John Wayne, Ward Bond, Henry Fonda, Victor McLaglen, George O'Brien, etc.) and

associates (Merian C. Cooper, Dudley Nichols, Darryl F. Zanuck, etc.).

A most successful excursion in biography can be found in this compassionate and moving portrait. Recommended.

4805 *The Parables of Lina Wertmuller.* by Ferlita, Ernest; and May, John R. 112 p. paper illus. Ramsey, N. J.: Paulist Press, 1977.

A short biographical sketch of Italian film director Lina Wertmuller introduces this lively analysis of her first films. Since the authors are of the opinion that Wertmuller's films (parables) are primarily concerned with the dilemma of the Macho Male with a cause, much of the text discusses man-woman relationships and their political overtones. Included in the book are illustrations, an interview with Wertmuller, a filmography, notes, and an index.

4806 *The Parade's Gone By.* by Brownlow, Kevin. 590 p. illus. New York: Knopf, 1968.

The author of this recent classic is modest about his work when he says he has attempted to recreate a period rather than write a history. He has succeeded in his aim. But, more than this, he has managed to show an affection, respect, and dedication to those persons who were developing an art from what was essentialiy a curiosity or side-show gimmick. The book is entertaining, informative, and quite nostalgic.

Using the loose framework of the various personnel involved in filmmaking (director, cameraman, stunt man, editor, stars, etc.), he provides his own analysis of the period along with conversations, interviews, and quotes from many people who were a part of it. Statements from legendary names of cinema history are here in abundance. A major asset of the book is the collection of unique photographs beautifully reproduced. An index of names and titles is also given. The volume is a triumph of style, organization, content, and good taste. This is one of the best books ever written on film.

4807 *Paramount Pictures and the People Who Made Them.* by Edmonds, I. G.; and Mimura, Reiko. 272 p. illus. San Diego: A. S. Barnes, 1980.

This volume's title suggests a lot more than what is actually offered—a selected overview of the history of Paramount Pictures from 1914 to 1966. Treatment of the silent era and the early sound years constitutes most of the text, with only a few pages devoted to the films of the forties and fifties. Balance is uneven with later stars, directors, and films treated superficially.

For example, Billy Wilder is not listed in the index and has a few lines of identification on pages 227 and 228. Cecil B. DeMille, whose name was almost synonomous with Paramount's, has two index citations. MAKE WAY FOR TOMORROW (1937) is not mentioned nor is Von Sternberg's THE SCARLET EMPRESS (1934).

The result is a partial sampling of the riches that make up the history of Paramount Pictures.

4808 *Paramount Pictures Collection.* 2 vols. paper illus. Beverly Hills: Academy of Motion Picture Arts and Sciences, 1980.

An inventory of the Paramount Pictures Collection, which is housed at the Academy, consisting of 200,000 photographs, scripts, press books, etc.

4809 *The Paramount Pretties.* by Parish, James Robert. 587 p. illus. New Rochelle, N.Y.: Arlington House, 1972.

The ladies have an exclusive spotlight in this collective biography. The subjects have been selected from the Paramount Studio contract list but the text considers films made for other studios as well. In approximately chronological order, according to their tenure at Paramount, the "Pretties" are: Gloria Swanson, Clara Bow, Claudette Colbert, Carole Lombard, Marlene Dietrich, Miriam Hopkins, Sylvia Sidney, Mae West, Dorothy Lamour, Paulette Goddard, Veronica Lake, Diana Lynn, Betty Hutton, Joan Caulfield, Lizabeth Scott, and Shirley MacLaine.

A short biographical overview introduces the detailed account of each subject's professional life, and only minor attention is paid to the personal side. Each portrait closes with a filmography containing technical and cast credits and a picture collection of about two dozen stills, portraits, and candids squeezed into 5 or 6 pages. The appendix has brief biographical sketches of the producers who furthered the careers of the main subjects: Jesse Lasky, Emanuel Cohen, William Le Baron, Ernst Lubitsch, B. P. Schulberg, Hal Wallis, and Adolph Zukor.

Most of the narrative is informational—a recital of facts, film plots, quotations, etc. When a negative criticism is offered, it is softened so that all the subjects emerge as rather nice ladies. That the author apparently loves 'em all is reflected in the star-worship approach used throughout. Male actors on the Paramount list do not fare nearly as well: "The rare exception of virile sexuality was Alan Ladd—the rest were as bland as could be: Fred MacMurray, Joel McCrea, Ray Milland, William Holden, Brian Donlevy, Sonny Tufts, and Robert Preston." Similar barbed comments appear about performances in films mostly forgotten.

Although there is much familiar material in the book (several of the ladies have individual biographies in print at this time), the reading is still entertaining, informative, and memory-prodding. Filmographies appear rather complete and are a fine supplement to the text. The pictures seem to be an afterthought and their small size and poor reproduction lessen their effectiveness. No index is provided and the only introduction is that which appears on the book's dust jacket. Although there are minor faults with this volume, the abundance of data presented in a readable, entertaining way should insure its appeal to a wide range of readers.

4810 *Pare Lorentz and the Documentary Film.* by Snyder, Robt. L. 232 p. illus. Norman, Okla.: University of Oklahoma Press, 1968.

In the thirties, Pare Lorentz produced several classic documentary films for the U.S. Government . They include THE PLOW THAT BROKE THE PLAINS (1936), THE RIVER (1937), and THE FIGHT FOR LIFE (1940); a major portion of this volume is devoted to a discussion of these three. Also included is a detailed explanation of the struggles to retain government support for Lorentz's filmmaking.

The illustrations give evidence of the director's artistry. Appendices include documents, a filmography, and a bibliography, and there is an index. When used with a viewing of the films, the book is most valuable. For readers unfamiliar with Lorentz's work, it may be remote. Recommended, then, for students, historians, and organizations using the films.

4811 *Pasolini on Pasolini: Interviews with Oswald Stack.* by Stack, Oswald. 176 p. illus. paper Bloomington, Ind.: Indiana University Press, 1969.

This well done, scholarly book is an extended interview with Pasolini using each of his major films as a key topic. Pasolini is an author, poet, scholar, artist, and critic; each of these interests has had an effect on his films. By adroit questioning, the influences on his films are summoned forth and discussed. It is unfortunate that only his film THE GOSPEL ACCORDING TO ST. MATTHEW (1964) has had any appreciable exhibition here. Since the text depends largely on the reader's familiarity with the creative work in all fields of Pasolini, who is not widely known in the U.S., most readers will be at a disadvantage. There is a filmography and a bibliography included. Chapter footnotes are used throughout.

4812   THE PASSENGER. by Peploe, Mark; and Wollen, Peter; and Antonioni, Michelangelo. 192 p. paper illus. New York: Grove, 1975.

Script of the 1975 film directed by Antonioni.

4813   THE PASSENGER. by Peploe, Mark; and Wollen, Peter; and Antonioni, Michelangelo. 192 p. paper illus. New York: Grove, 1975.

Includes full script, cast credits and "Antonioni's Haunting Vision" by Vincent Canby, "About Reprieve" by Penelope Gilliat, and "Antonioni Pauses Here in his Search" by Richard F. Shepard.

4814   LA PASSION DE JEANNE D'ARC (PASSION OF JOAN OF ARC). by Bordwell, David. 83 p. paper Bloomington, Ind.: Indiana University Press, 1973.

This *Filmguide* takes on a most demanding task: that of providing an analysis of a film that consists of many titles, a minimum of action, and a maximum of facial closeups. David Bordwell, a young author and obvious admirer of Carl Dreyer, is more than able to meet the challenge .

The book provides the usual credits, plot outlines, and production details. It is in the section on director Carl Dreyer and in the long analysis of the film that the quality is apparent. Both sections indicate a scholarship and drive not unlike the determination the author attributes to Dreyer. The summary critique is also a model for future authors to emulate. A filmography-listing, a fine annotated bibliography, two rental sources and some notes to the text complete the book.

One minor reservation concerns the author's limited attention to the sound version of the film which is a desecration of Dreyer's original. The potential user of this film should be warned that the sound version is to be avoided if at all possible. Turning off the sound, as Bordwell suggests, is only a minimum help. The removal of titles in favor of narration and the third-rate dramatic reading alter the pace of the original film completely. The above notwithstanding, the book is admirable on all counts and is highly recommended.

4815   *The Passionate Years.* by Crosby, Caresse. New York: Ecco Press.

The years before World War II in Paris are described here. Various film personalities (Chaplin, Dietrich, etc.) are mentioned.

4816   *Passport to Hollywood.* by Whittemore, Don; and Cecchettini, Philip Alan. 558 p. illus. New York: McGraw-Hill, 1976.

This unusual book, subtitled "Film Immigrants Anthology," deals with 13 European directors who were able to separate our national myth from reality and show Americans as they appear to the rest of the world. Included are Charles Chaplin, Erich von Stroheim, Ernst Lubitsch, Michael Curtiz, Victor Seastrom, James Whale, Alfred Hitchcock, F. W. Murnau, Paul Fejos, Slavko Vorkapich, Fritz Lang, Otto Preminger, and Milos Forman. For each there is an introductory essay which describes the director's career and some representative films. Following are reviews, essays, evaluations, etc., of the director/specific films. For example, the orientation essay on Hitchcock is followed by "Hitchcock and the Mechanics of Suspense" by Ian Cameron, "Hitchcock 2: Suspense and Meaning" again by Cameron, "A Long Rope" by Irving Pichel, four reviews of ROPE (1948), and "Alfred Hitchcock: Lost in the Wood" by George Kaplan.

An introduction by Charles Higham and some well-selected visuals complete the book, which was apparently written as a text to accompany a Public Broadcasting System film series which has not been shown at this time.

The inclusion of neglected artists such as Curtiz and Whale is almost sufficient rationale for any book at this point. Add to this the unique treatment afforded the more familiar names and you have a fine reading experience which would be even richer if complemented by a viewing of appropriate films. Recommended.

4817   *Past Imperfect: An Autobiography.* by Collins, Joan. 252 p. illus. London: W. H. Allen, 1978.

Joan Collins made her first screen appearance in I BELIEVE IN YOU (1952) and has had a continuing film career to date. She has appeared in British and American films, usually portraying a smouldering femme fatale. This autobiography is illustrated and contains a filmography.

4818   *Pat and Roald.* by Farrell, Barry. 241 p. illus. New York: Random

House, 1969.

This is the story of actress Patricia Neal's recovery from a series of strokes. Ending with her return to motion pictures in THE SUBJECT WAS ROSES (1968), the book details the efforts of both Miss Neal and her husband, author Roald Dahl, to overcome the many hardships that befell them. Inspirational in theme and approach, the volume has little to do with cinema and filmmaking. It can be used as a supplementary material. There are some pictures but no index.

4819 PAT GARRETT AND BILLY THE KID. by Wurlitzer, Rudolph. 130 p. paper illus. New York: New American Library, 1973.

Script of the 1973 film directed by Sam Peckinpah. Contains an introduction by Rudolph Wurlitzer, cast and credits.

4820 *The Path of Fame of the Czechoslovak Film.* by Broz, Jaroslav. 112 p. paper illus. Prague: Ceskoslovensky Filmexport, 1967.

Produced in rather primitive fashion, this short paperback is a history of Czech film. While the many illustrations are uniformly excellent, the text is somewhat pedantic and plodding. The typewritten pages do not add to the book's values. It is, however, indexed, and includes a listing of prize-winning films. Since so many of the films are obscure to American audiences, the book offers most to the researcher or the historian.

4821 *Patricia Neal and Margaret Sullavan.* by Burrows, Michael. 42 p. paper illus. London: Primestyle Ltd., 1971.

The Burrows-Primestyle books resemble magazines or periodicals devoted to a pair of subjects—in this case, Patricia Neal and Margaret Sullavan. The treatment consists of biographical bits, quotes, comments by the subject, and a critical appreciation. Stills from films and some portrait shots are usually included. A simple listing of the stars' films closes the book.

Other volumes in this series include: *Mario Lanza and Max Steiner*;

4822 *Pattern of Leisure.* by Blackburn, John D. 33 p. paper Glasgow: Scottish Educational Film Association and Scottish Film Council, 1961.

A study made to determine the importance of film and television among leisure activities in the Scottish Highlands and islands.

4823 *Patterns of Realism.* by Armes, Roy. 226 p. illus. New York: A. S. Barnes, 1972.

This study of the Italian Neo-Realist cinema begins with a discussion of realism and an attempt to describe the roots and origins of this movement in the pre-World War II cinema and literature of Italy. Visconti's OSSESSIONE (1942) is the link between the past and the Neo-Realist years (1945 to 1953) of the Italian cinema. Roberto Rossellini, Luchino Visconti and Vittorio De Sica (with writer Cesare Zavattini) are given major attention, and the works of Aldo Vergano, Giuseppe De Santis, Alberto Lattuada, Pietro Germi, Luigi Zampa, Luciano Emmer and Renato Castellani are also noted. Films which are analyzed in depth include OSSESSIONE, ROME OPEN CITY (1945), PAISAN (1946), GERMANY YEAR ZERO (1948), LA TERRA TREMA (1948) SHOESHINE (1946), BICYCLE THIEF (1948), UMBERTO D (1952), and MIRACLE IN MILAN (1950). A final evaluative section summarizes the Italian Neo-Realist movement and denotes its contribution to films and directors who followed.

A filmography arranged in chronological order is given of the films mentioned in the text, and there is a lengthy bibliography. The book is indexed and illustrated with many excellent photographs. This serious study is impressive for several reasons: the importance of the topic, the scholarly but unstuffy treatment, the excellence of the supporting illustrations and documentation, and the willingness of author Armes to take a frequently vulnerable position with confidence.

4824 *Paul Almond: The Flame Within.* by Edsforth, Janet. 56 p. paper illus. Ottawa, Ontario: Canadian Film Institute, 1972.

An appreciation of the Canadian film and television director whose initial feature films have been favorably received by critics. The first two, ISABEL (1968) and THE ACT OF THE HEART (1970), are covered in detail here. A complete Almond filmography is added.

4825 *Paul Mazursky—Paul Morrissey.* edited by Reed, Rochelle. 32 p. paper illus. Washington, D.C.: American Film Institute, 1974.

Transcripts of interviews held with Paul Mazursky

on February 19, 1974, and with Paul Morrissey on April 24, 1974, are printed here. Both men are filmmakers who write and direct their own films. They specialize somewhat, in that they make costly comedy films which are independent of Hollywood influences. Although their films are mentioned in the text, no final filmographies are included.

4826 *Paul Muni: His Life and His Films.* by Druxman, Michael B. 227 p. illus. New York: A. S. Barnes, 1974.

It may be true that Paul Muni was a private person with few friends, that he was stubbornly preoccupied with perfectionism in creating his characters, and that he made poor choices in selecting most of his total of 23 films; but is this enough upon which to build four introductory chapters? Michael Druxman has tried in this story of the life and films of Paul Muni. After an inane foreword by Mervyn LeRoy, the life of Muni as star, actor, and man is related in factual fashion. An overview of his career in the theatre, films, and on television follows. The second half of the book looks at Muni's films with some detail. For each, the cast, production credits, a plot outline, background data, some stills and a few critical excerpts are offered.

Lacking depth in both the biographical and filmography sections, the book provides only a distant look at the actor and his films. Quotes provided by people who worked with Muni run one or two sentences and the general critical analysis or evaluation offered by the author runs to statements such as "although the completed film left much to be desired, he had fun making it." The illustrations are adequately reproduced and help to nourish the somewhat anemic text. Muni was an enigma as an actor, a husband, and a person. This volume succeeds only intermittently in solving the mystery of Muni. Acceptable.

4827 *Paul Newman.* by Hamblett, Charles. 232 p. illus. Chicago: Henry Regnery, 1975.

Both the author and the subject agree that it is too early for a definitive biography; therefore this volume is more of an appreciation, although the structure is undeniably that of a biography. "Appreciation" is perhaps not quite the word—the book is flawed by Hamblett's continual flattery, adoration, and applause for Newman, who apparently can do no wrong. Objectivity toward the book's subject is conspicuously absent. The author's point of view is more one of a fan than of a responsible investigator or reporter. For example, on page 150: "Paul sent Joanne flowers and sherry, her favorite drink, to

London. Married eleven years, the reporter marvels, and still acting this way! Put that in your hubble-bubble, Hedda, and choke on the smoke."

The author employs so many peripheral digressions and so much nonpertinent material that the book seems padded with material accumulated for other projects—perhaps his book, *The Hollywood Cage*? Examples of this excess are the portions dealing with James Dean, Kirk Douglas, Clive Barnes, Hedda Hopper, Louella Parsons, and others. Supporting materials are weak. A center section of illustrations does not show Newman's development as a screen actor. Instead we are offered an unbalanced collection consisting of three photos of THE STING (1973), three of THE MACINTOSH MAN (1974), three of BUTCH CASSIDY AND THE SUNDANCE KID (1969), two of WUSA (1970), one of HOMBRE (1967) and one of SOMETIMES A GREAT NOTION (1971). The absence of an index is a major flaw. A filmography helps somewhat and Newman's four stage appearances are noted. Here then is a biased biographical portrait lacking any compensating support material. It may appeal to admirers of Paul Newman, but to others it will seem mythical and unconvincing. Acceptable with the reservations noted above.

4828 *Paul Newman.* by Kerbel, Michael. 158 p. paper illus. New York: Pyramid, 1974.

A good critical account of Paul Newman's career is given in this well-written book. After a succinct personality sketch, a biographical account of his early years leads to his first film, THE SILVER CHALICE (1954). Early comparisons with Marlon Brando and James Dean were overcome by stronger performances in later films. His recent success in teaming with Robert Redford for THE STING (1973) along with their earlier film, BUTCH CASSIDY AND THE SUNDANCE KID (1969), has elevated him to superstar status. Other recent films he has made have been disappointing. His ability as a film director is discussed in a final chapter. A bibliography, filmography, a list of stage appearances, and an index appear in the book's final pages. Illustrations are of consistent high quality in both selection and reproduction. The three full-page portraits taken at different ages offer attractive evidence of his maturation as an actor.

Although the criticism-evaluation of Newman's acting and directing is almost always uniformly favorable, the author does try to justify his favorable bias. Thankfully he has attempted more than a chronological recital of plots, stories, statistics, etc., and this effort makes for an entertaining text. Recommended.

4829 *Paul Newman.* by Paige, David. 31 p. paper illus. Mankato, Minn.: Creative Education, 1977.

A superficial biography designed for very young readers.

4830 *Paul Newman, Superstar: A Critical Biography.* by Godfrey, Lionel. 208 p. illus. New York: St. Martin's Press, 1978.

This well-intentioned book devotes itself to three facets of its subject—his life, his wife and his films. Since this is an unauthorized biography, those sections dealing with Newman's life are limited largely to matters of public record, previously published articles, interviews, studies, etc. The same is true of those portions devoted to Joanne Woodward. In discussing Newman's films the author is able to exercise more of his analytical and critical skills. Disturbing similarities to Brando, the enduring popularity in spite of unsuccessful films, and the opposing/contradictory facets of Newman's screen persona are discussed. Two sections of illustrations, two Newman filmographies (director and actor), a Woodward filmography and an index complete the volume.

Godfrey is a British film critic whose admiration for his subject is evident throughout. The book will please Newman's fans but other readers will find it rather humdrum and flat.

4831 *Paul Robeson.* by Greenfield, Eloise. illus. New York: T.Y. Crowell, 1975.

The life of the black singer-actor is told for young readers, in this title from the *Biography* series.

Illustrations are by George Ford. Some other Robeson biographies written for youngsters include *Paul Robeson: Citizen of the World* by Shirley Graham, *Paul Robeson: Mini Play*, and *Paul Robeson: The Life and Times of a Free Black Man* by Virginia Hamilton.

4832 *Paul Robeson: All American.* by Gilliam, Dorothy Butler. 216 p. illus. Washington, D.C.: New Republic, 1976.

This unauthorized biography draws upon interviews, original research and previous Robeson biographies. It tells of the rise of a gifted scholar, athlete and performer and the political controversy that led to a self-imposed exile, a physical breakdown, and virtual seclusion until his death early in 1976.

Since Robeson's varied talents and numerous interests were always utilized by active performance or participation, his story does not lack incident. Much of the text presented here recalls in detail the colorful and exciting life that Robeson created for himself. Discussion of his films is unfortunately brief; perhaps they were not viewed by the author as part of her research. The text is supported by some helpful illustrations, chapter notes, a bibliography, a list of his plays and films, and an index.

In a subtle and unobtrusive way, the author, who is a black woman, brings understanding, affection and compassion to an American who was "a product of his times." Acceptable.

4833 *Paul Robeson: The Great Forerunner.* edited by Freedomways Staff. 383 p. illus. New York: Dodd Mead, 1978.

The editors of *Freedomways*, a quarterly review of black writing, have created a portrait of Paul Robeson, made up mostly of articles from the magazine. The many aspects of his colorful life—politics, stage, music, film, philosophy, writings, etc.—are covered along with four original Robeson articles and some selections from his speeches and other writings. The final portions of the book consist of tributes to Robeson in both prose and poetry.

One article, "Paul Robeson in Film: An Iconoclast's Quest for a Role" by Anatol L. Schosser, presents a critical review of his film performances. It has been carefully researched and gives the reader a short but apparently accurate account of Robeson's career in that medium.

A center section of illustrations, a chronology, a lengthy bibliography, and an index all add to the comprehensiveness of the Robeson profile. By intelligent selection from the writings of Robeson and others, the editors have assembled a rich, provocative collection of material about a controversial artist. Recommended.

4834 *Paul Robeson.* by Seton, Marie. 254 p. illus. London: Dennis Dobson, 1958.

Paul Robeson is the black actor-singer who appeared on stage, in concerts, and in films during the thirties and forties. Remembered mostly for his performances in THE EMPEROR JONES (1933) and SHOWBOAT (1936), he also appeared in BODY AND SOUL (1924), BORDERLINE (1930), SANDERS OF THE RIVER (1935), KING SOLOMON'S MINES (1937), BIG FELLA (1937), THE SONG OF FREEDOM (1938), JERICHO (1938), DARK SANDS (1938), PROUD VALLEY (1941), NATIVE LAND (1942) and TALES OF MANHAT-

TAN (1942).

4835 *Paul Robeson: Citizen of the World.* by Graham, Shirley. 264 p. illus. New York: J. Messner, Inc., 1946.

A biography of the black actor-singer who appeared in films during the thirties and forties. See also *Paul Robeson* and *Paul Robeson: The American Othello.*

4836 *Paul Robeson: The American Othello.* by Hoyt, Edwin P. 228 p. New York: World, 1967.

A biography of the black actor-singer whose outspoken views on Communism during the thirties incurred popular disfavor. He appeared in several films during the thirties and forties. See also *Paul Robeson* and *Paul Robeson: Citizen of the World.*

4837 *Paul Robeson: The Life and Times of A Free Black Man.* by Hamilton, Virginia. illus. New York: Harper & Row, 1974.

Written for young readers, this biography covers Robeson's college days, his show business career and the difficulties he met because of his political beliefs.

4838 *Paul Rogers.* by Williamson, Audrey. and 125 p. illus. London: Barrie and Rockliff, 1956.

A study of the work and career of Paul Rogers which includes a chronology of his appearances on stage and screen up to 1956.

4839 *see 4838*

4840 *Paul Rotha: Documentary Diary.* by Rotha, Paul. 305 p. illus. New York: Hill and Wang, 1973.

Paul Rotha has written his account of the British documentary film movement that took place from about 1928 to 1939. His method is somewhat unique, as he alternates objective informational chapters with subjective accounts of his own career. A center section offers some visuals to support the text but they serve only to make the reader wish there were many more. They suggest that a picturebook exclusively on documentary films would be most welcome.

Rotha's style and content are compatible with his age and experience. He is dogmatic, opinionated, wise, and practical. Much of what he says can be construed as a teacher talking to learners and Rotha adapts to this role-playing with great ease. With the short film getting a wider acceptance than ever before, Rotha's words for aspiring filmmakers are valuable indeed. General readers may find the historical chapters a bit heavy. Recommended.

4841 *Paul Scofield.* by Trewin, John C. 101 p. illus. London: Rockliff, 1956.

When this volume first appeared, Paul Scofield had made one important film, THAT LADY (1955). Later he won an Academy Award for A MAN FOR ALL SEASONS (1966). Since he works primarily in the theatre, his filmography is short, consisting of about a dozen films.

4842 *Paul Williams.* edited by Henstell, Bruce. 31 p. paper Washington, D.C.: American Film Institute, 1972.

Paul Williams is the director of OUT OF IT, THE REVOLUTIONARY, and DEALING: OR THE BERKELEY-TO-BOSTON FORTY BRICK LOST-BAG BLUES. The first two films had been made and he was preparing the third when this interview was held in November of 1970. The focus is filmmaking and how one gets into it. A bibliography and a three-item filmography are included. Acceptable.

4843 *Pauline Frederick, On and Off the Stage.* by Elwood, Muriel. 225 p. Chicago: A. Kroch, 1940.

A poorly written biography of stage and screen actress Pauline Frederick. From 1915 to the time of her death she appeared in both silent and sound films, the last of which was THE BUCCANEER (1938). A filmography and an index are included.

4844 *Pearl White: The Peerless Fearless Girl.* by Weltman, Manuel; and Lee, Raymond. 226 p. illus. New York: A. S. Barnes, 1969.

Presented as a picture book with dialogue, this biography of Pearl White is fascinating to look at but a chore to read. The use of a novelized biography is a disservice to the subject and the reader. A filmography is included. Probably because of the format, no index is offered. A disappointment.

4845 *Peckinpah: The Western Films.* by Seydor, Paul. 301 p. illus. Urbana, Ill.: University of Illinois Press, 1980.

In this critical appreciation of director Sam Peckinpah, Paul Seydor considers only six western films, each of which was given a final cut by persons other than Peckinpah. The films are described in detail with attention given to the masculine tradition often found in literary works. The author finds much similarity between Norman Mailer and his subject. Illustrations, a filmography, and an index complete this scholarly study.

4846 *Peggy Ashcroft.* by Keown, Eric. 102 p. illus. London: Rockliff, 1955.

This volume is subtitled "An Illustrated Study of Her Work, with a List of Her Appearances on Stage and Screen." Known primarily as a stage actress, her films are few. They include THE WANDERING JEW (1933), THE 39 STEPS (1935), RHODES OF AFRICA (1936) and QUIET WEDDING (1940). Not noted in this volume—monograph number 3 in the *Theatre World* series—are her later appearances in THE NUN'S STORY (1958) and SECRET CEREMONY (1968).

4847 *Pen to Silversheet.* by Riddle, Melvin M. 140 p. paper illus. Los Angeles: White, 1922.

"...a comprehensive digest of the many arts and crafts involved in the fascinating industry—motion picture production."

4848 *The Penguin Film Review 1946-1949.* edited by Manvell, Roger. 2 vols., 960 p. illus. Totowa, N.J.: Rowman and Littlefield, 1977.

Scholars, historians and lay readers should be most grateful for the reappearance of the nine volumes of *The Penguin Film Review* in two bound volumes. The originals were high quality, attractive anthologies on film topics that convinced an international audience to treat film as a serious art form. Many of the excellent original articles have been quoted often throughout the years and it is rewarding to have the original sources accessible once again.

The production given the books is well above average, with only the illustrations lacking some of the clarity and tone of the original. A total index is added.

4849 *Penny Marshall and Cindy Williams.* by Berman, Connie. 154 p. paper illus. New York: Tempo 1977.

Designed to capitalize on the TV series "Laverne and Shirley," this dual biography may be somewhat premature, since its subjects—Penny Marshall and Cindy Williams—are relatively young performers. To date, Marshall has made no films, but Williams

has appeared in several, including TRAVELS WITH MY AUNT (1972), AMERICAN GRAFFITI (1973) and THE CONVERSATION (1974).

The book offers a factual fan magazine coverage which seldom captures anything except a carefully calculated public image. Acceptable for nondiscriminating fans of the girls.

4850 *Pentimento: A Book of Portraits.* by Hellman, Lillian. 297 p. Boston: Little, Brown, 1973.

Included in the seven separate sections or portraits is one entitled "Theatre," in which the author recalls some of her experiences as a screenwriter for Samuel Goldwyn. Noted for the record.

4851 *People Are Crazy Here.* by Reed, Rex. 306 p. illus. New York: Delacorte, 1974.

In this fourth collection of his articles, Rex Reed continues to expand his field of coverage. The Hollywood people are still given major attention, but he also includes interviews with such celebrities as Tennessee Williams, the Cockettes, Joe Namath, Grace Slick and others. The style and format are consistent with Reed's past writing. Observations are sharp, witty, bitchy, sarcastic, sympathetic and/or loving—usually depending upon the author's personal response to his subject. He is apparently mellowing with age, as most of the 48 articles reprinted here are positive. The interviews are light, breezy reading that offer entertaining detail about some well-known personalities. Reed's strength as a reporter is in describing what his mind sees and his heart feels. The volume is a rewarding collection of his work. Recommended.

4852 *People Who Make Movies.* by Taylor, Theodore. 158 p. illus. Garden City, N.Y.: Doubleday, 1967.

The personnel of a motion picture production company are described in this volume. Producer, director writer, film editor, and so on—each is given one of the 16 chapters. A generalized description of their contribution to the film is offered along with cited examples from various films. The book is aimed at a juvenile audience and uses, at times, a Hollywood fan magazine approach. Some of the activity described is applicable to the older methods of film production done under the aegis of the large studios and is no longer applicable. A glossary of terms and a few illustrations add little to the book. The book may appeal to the very young but has limited value for most of today's readers.

4853 *The People's Films.* by MacCann, Richard Dyer. 238 p. illus. New York: Hastings House, 1973.

This history of the films made by the U.S. Government is based on the author's doctoral dissertation, written in 1951. New material has been added, and certain sections have been updated. Some reference is made to the British-Canadian Documentary School of John Grierson but only as it affected the U.S. filmmakers.

The text covers the early period of the thirties, the work of Pare Lorentz, the U.S. Film Service, World War II films, and films made for foreign policy. A final section considers television as it applies to the presidency and Congress today. Probably because of its origin, the text is more informational than analytical or expository. It is unlikely that many will read it for pleasure, but it does serve as a reference source for a topic that has been rather neglected in film literature. A few illustrations are used, but they do not seem indicative of the attractive visuals that we associate with documentary films. The book is indexed.

The treatment and the nature of the subject suggest that this volume can be appreciated primarily as a reference work about a rather unknown area of filmmaking. Acceptable.

4854 PEPE. by Wilson, Harold. 36 p. illus. New York: Columbia Pictures, Inc., 1960.

Supposedly written as a diary by Cantinflas, this souvenir book describes the making of the 1960 film in studio press-release fashion. The latter sections are devoted to full page biographies of the other two major stars, Dan Dailey and Shirley Jones, and director-producer George Sidney. Cameo stars are grouped in page quartets and major production personnel get individual attention. The complete cast and production credits are given on the inside back cover pages, along with a listing of the musical numbers used in the film.

4855 *Perchance to Dream: The World of Ivor Novello.* by Rose, Richard. 199 p. illus. London: Frewin, 1974.

4856 *Performance and Politics in Popular Drama.* edited by Bradby, David; and James, Louis, and Sharratt, Bernard. 343 p. New York: Cambridge University Press, 1980.

An anthology of papers submitted for a conference on "popular" theatre, film, and television. Only two of the three sections deal with film: "Politics and Performance," and "Problems and Prospects."

4857 *The Performer in Mass Media.* by Hawes, William. 350 p. paper illus. New York: Hastings House, 1978.

This useful volume deals with appearing in the mass media, whether it be on a national level or within the local community. In two parts, the book deals with The Performer (appearance, voice, movement, etc.) and The Performer's Environment (studio, preparation, rehearsals, performance, evaluation etc.). Supporting the text is a glossary, notes, selected resources and an index. Illustrations provided are line drawings and diagrams.

Since it employs a broad approach to all mass media, this volume can be most helpful to those new to media—i.e., the persons appearing on local cable TV for the first time, students in communications courses, etc. Its information and suggestions are valuable, practical and pertinent. Acceptable.

4858 *Performing Arts: Books in Print.* by Schoolcraft, Ralph Newman. 761 p. New York: Drama Book Specialists, 1973.

This large annotated bibliography is an updating of *Theatre Books in Print*, which appeared originally in 1963 and was revised in 1966. For this edition there are two main sections: the first and longer part covers books published prior to 1971, while the second section considers those volumes published during the calendar year of 1971. In each there are four major categories: books on theatre and drama; books on the technical arts of the theatre; books on motion pictures, television and radio; and books on the mass media and the popular arts. Each of these is subdivided further.

The motion picture section lists several hundred volumes arranged under the categories of world cinema, films of particular countries, techniques of production, biographies and appreciations, and screenplays. Under these categories, there are further subcategories. For example, under world cinema there are sections for histories, for collected film reviews, and for annuals. In most instances, the books are listed alphabetically by author surname under these subcategories. An author index and a title index are provided to facilitate use, and there is a directory of book publishers appended. Each entry gives the author, title, publisher, year, pages, hardbound/paperback, price, annotation, and notes the presence of any or all of the following: bibliography, appendix, filmography, chronology, notes, index, illustrations.

Three reservations should be noted: (1) the titles are selected; many pertinent books in print are not listed; (2) the annotations are descriptive, not evaluative; thus, all volumes seem worthwhile based on the information furnished; (3) the arrangement of the materials may make the book's use by persons with limited information rather difficult. However, the amount and the reliability of the information offered are impressive. In checking the film sections, only a few minor discrepancies, e.g., number of pages, dates, were found. The annotations are uniformly concise, informative, and indicative of the title's contents. In summary this is a most valuable reference that is highly recommended.

4859 *Performing Arts Collections: An International Handbook.* edited by Veinstein, Andre; and Christout, Marie and and Bablet, Denis. 761 p. Paris: National Center of Scientific Research, 1960.

Prepared under the sponsorship of the International Federation of Library Associations and its Section for Performing Arts Libraries and Museums, this volume has its text in both French and English. A revised edition was published in 1967 with the title *Performing Arts Libraries and Museums of the World.*

4860 *Performing Arts Management and Law.* by Taubman, Joseph. 6 Vols. illus. New York: Law-Arts, 1973.

This six-volume set was written and compiled by a theatrical attorney. It consists of two volumes of text and four loose-leaf volumes of sample forms (film, television, theatre-dance, live performance). Made up of decisions, precedents and case histories, the text volumes include commentary and interpretation by the author. The set is an impressive compilation of materials that should be of great assistance to attorneys.

4861 *Performing Arts Research.* by Whalon, Marion K. 280 p. Detroit: Gale Research, 1976.

This bibliography, subtitled "A Guide to Information Sources," is divided into seven parts: (1) guides; (2) dictionaries, encyclopedias, and handbooks; (3) directories; (4) play indexes and finding lists; (5) sources for reviews of plays and motion pictures; (6) bibliographies, indexes and abstracts; and (7) illustrative and audiovisual sources. A combination index which lists authors, subjects and titles completes the book.

The entries are annotated offering mostly descriptive comment; a number of cross references are also provided.

A few inconsistencies are immediately apparent. Certain annotations do not indicate "a close examination" as claimed by the author, i.e. *A Reference Guide to Audio-Visual Information, Cinema Booklist, Guide Book to Film,* and *Film Research,* differ widely in many respects, but here they are similarly described with short, rather surface observations which do not indicate careful scrutiny. More serious perhaps is the omission from the index of the first three titles noted above. Cross indexing lacks consistency. For example, a title may direct the user to several other sources; those entries however will not always show a reference back to the first item. If the user chooses the entry which is not cross-indexed, he may miss a valuable source.

The arrangement of the material by type of reference work may be quite efficient for the professional researcher but it may also be somewhat difficult for the novice to use. An arrangement by the individual performing art, such as employed by Schoolcraft in *Performing Arts Books in Print,* might have been preferable.

The volume does provide a major service in its presentation of hundreds of titles for reference use. Acceptable.

4862 *Performing Arts Resource—Vol. 3.* edited by Perry, Ted. 144 p. illus. New York: Drama Book, 1977.

Both volume two and volume three in this series are anthologies dealing primarily with theatre and film. Volume three contains articles dealing with unpublished scripts, film preservation, reference works for film study, film collections, etc.

4863 *Periodical Holdings.* edited by Barrett, Gillian. 80 p. paper London: British Film Institute, 1974.

A listing of all periodicals held in the Information Department of the British Film Institute as of January 1, 1974. Not included are yearbooks, annuals, special issues of periodicals, some TV periodicals, newspapers, and nonfilm periodicals. Entries are arranged alphabetically by title, with each containing the country of origin, the language, the text, and the date. For example: "*Film Polski* (Poland: English/French text) 1963-68 Continued as *Polish Film.*" A specialized source of information on film periodicals that will be most valuable to writers, researchers and/or historians.

4864 PERRI. edited by Walt Disney Productions. 80 p. illus. London: Barrap, 1958.

Adapted from the Disney film, PERRI (1958), this volume has a text by Roy Disney and illustrations by the studio artists. The script of the film, written by Winston Hibler and Ralph Wright, was based on a Felix Salten story.

4865 *Persistence of Vision.* edited by McBride, Joseph. 222 p. Madison, Wisc.: Wisconsin Film Society Press, 1968.

Another collection of film notes, comments, and articles on both silent and sound films—somewhat similar to the Society's earlier *Classics of the Film.* THE NAVIGATOR (1924) and TRUE HEART SUSIE (1919), along with KING KONG (1933), CASABLANCA (1942), and THE STRANGER (1946) are representative examples of the films considered. There are several articles on Orson Welles and one written by Andrew Sarris. As a source book for film showings, it is excellent.

4866 *Persistence of Vision: The Films of Robert Altman.* by Feinman, Neil. 222 p. New York: Arno, 1978.

Written at the University of Florida in 1976, this title in the *Dissertations on Film* series is a critical appreciation/evaluation of Robert Altman's films. After an introductory section called "Altman on Altman," each of eight major films, from THAT COLD DAY IN THE PARK (1968) to NASHVILLE (1975), is treated in a separate chapter. Brief attention is given to BUFFALO BILL AND THE INDIANS (1976) in a final summary chapter which concludes that Altman is a true auteur. Each of his films is a personal statement formed by recurring identifiable intellectual and artistic structures.

Much of this material is also covered in popular fashion in *Robert Altman: American Innovator.*

4867 PERSONA and SHAME. by Bergman, Ingmar. 191 p. illus. Salem, N.H.: Merrimack Book Service, 1980.

Scripts of the 1967 and 1969 films directed by Ingmar Bergman. Illustrations and a 1965 address by Bergman are included.

4868 *Personal Filmmaking.* by Piper, James. 269 p. illus. Reston, Va.: Reston Pub. Co., 1975.

This volume offers an explanation of amateur film production using low-cost, accessible 8mm equipment along with ordinary recording machines. Attention is given to scripting, shooting, and editing the visuals and to the preparation of sound tracks. Designed for use in secondary schools and colleges, the volume emphasizes individual filmmaking rather than a group effort. Narrative films are recommended for the beginner rather than the documentary or experimental. A linear exposition beginning with equipment selection and ending with the first screenings is used. Three screenplays are offered in the appendix and the volume is indexed.

In his introduction the author makes apology for the economic necessity of eliminating much illustration and graphic material. Rightly so, for the illustrations that are used are few for a filmmaking text and are extremely small in size. The text is thorough and written in a comprehensible, nontechnical style. Many of the author's suggestions are both practical and inventive and make the book quite suitable for its intended audience, the beginning or amateur filmmaker. Acceptable.

4869 *Personal Views: Explorations in Films.* by Wood, Robin. 255 p. illus. London: Gordon Fraser, 1976.

A noted British critic writes on a series of film topics in this volume which contains illustrations, a bibliography, and an index.

4870 *The Personal Vision of Ingmar Bergman.* by Donner, Jorn. 276 p. illus. Bloomington, Ind.: Indiana University Press, 1966.

Still another collection of analyses of Bergman's films, this time by a Swedish filmmaker and critic. The examinations include factors such as content, technique, comparison with other filmmakers, and relationships with the existentialists. A bibliography and a film index are appended. Quite philosophical and specialized, the book is suitable only in conjunction with a showing of Bergman's films.

4871 *Personality Parade.* by Scott, Walter. 90 p. paper illus. New York: Grosset and Dunlap, 1971.

In 1958 Walter Scott's "Personality Parade" appeared for the first time in the roto-gravure supplement called *Parade* which accompanies many Sunday newspapers in the United States. It is a page which features questions about celebrities furnished by readers with responses supplied by Scott. In this collection there are over 350 items, many of which are about film personalities.

Typical are such questions as: How many times has Lana Turner been married? How old is she? What is the famous story about the Marx Brothers setting fire to MGM studios? How come Doris Day, Ava Gardner, Kim Novak and other Hollywood stars have never acted on the stage? Most of the queries are on this fan magazine gossip level but the replies are surprisingly sarcastic, witty or biting. For example, the response to the last question above is that stage acting demands talent while screen acting does not.

There are some illustrations scattered throughout the book but there is no index. The book is designed as a recreation or an entertainment and as such is acceptable.

4872 *Perspective.* by Rembar, Charles. New York: Arbor House, 1975.

The author of this volume is an attorney who has fought long for civil liberties. Here he describes his legal battles concerning censorship of films and literature.

4873 *Perspectives on the Study of Film.* edited by Katz, John Stuart. 339 p. illus. Boston: Little, Brown & Co., 1971.

The aim of editor Katz in this anthology is to offer the educator some suggestions for approaching film or film study. Four major sections indicate the large areas of concern: 1. Film Study and Education; 2. The Film As Art and Humanities; 3. The Film As Communications, Environment, Politics; and 4. Curriculum Design and Evaluation in Film Study. The range of authors represented is very wide and many impressive names are included: Huxley, McLuhan, Balazs, Sontag, Bluestone, Sarris, Kael, Mekas, etc.

This is not a textbook but a collection of writings designed to encourage a philosophy about film study. The articles are well selected, a few illustrations are provided, and a bibliography completes the book. As with any compilation, certain of the articles are familiar, but the majority offer new insights and ideas that will stimulate anyone concerned with teaching film. A specialized book that will have a limited appeal to the general reader.

4874 *Pete Martin Calls on...* by Martin, Pete. 510 p. New York: Simon & Schuster, 1962.

Some 40 interviews which originally appeared in the *Saturday Evening Post* make up this volume. Most of the subjects are film personalities. Here they are grouped in categories such as comics, sexpots, off-beats, etc. The long article "Did Acting Spoil Marilyn Monroe?" is reprinted here. Most of the interviews seem old-fashioned and lacking in depth. They represent a style of journalism prevalent in the forties and fifties. While much factual information is given and some opinion is offered, most of this content is "guarded" and "safe." There is no index or illustration. The book offers the general reader some nostalgia and portions will interest historians, writers, and researchers.

4875 *Peter Brook.* by Trewin, John C. illus. London: Macdonald, 1971.

Peter Brook is the noted stage director whose ventures into filmmaking were largely unsuccessful. His films include: THE BEGGAR'S OPERA (1952), LORD OF THE FILES (1963), MARAT/SADE (1966), and KING LEAR (1970).

4876 *Peter Finch: A Biography.* by Faulkner, Trader. 312 p. New York: Taplinger, 1979.

Trader Faulkner is well qualified to write a biography of Peter Finch. He met Finch in 1946 and became a life-long friend of the actor. Not content to rely solely on his memory of personal experiences, the author engaged in extensive research, interviewing hundreds of persons who also knew Finch. The result is a fully dimensioned biography that describes, with understanding and objectivity, the private and professional sides of Peter Finch. His one-line summary of Finch as "a child-man who never grew up but remained an incomparable actor" is consistent with the long, detailed text he provides.

Support is given to the narrative by some good illustrations, which show Finch's maturation from juvenile to character actor, and a filmography and an index.

A responsible biography that will fascinate anyone interested in acting in general or Peter Finch in particular. It deserves a large audience.

4877 *Peter Noble's Illustrated Film Quiz.* by Noble, Peter. paper illus. London: Pendulum Publications, 1946.

The energetic Peter Noble was usually ahead of the crowd. Here he offers 300 questions and answers about British and Hollywood films, directors and stars.

4878 *Peter Sellers: The Mask Behind the Face.* by Evans, Peter. 249 p. illus. Englewood Cliffs, N.J.: Prentice-

Hall, 1968.

Beginning with his near death in California in 1964, this biography traces Sellers' rise from vaudeville through the famous Goon shows on radio to his success in films. The accent is on people and psychological motivation with very little attention given to the films or their making. The illustrations from the films are excellent but the text is more an attempt at a personality probe than the account of a man who is known the world over for his films.

No index or filmography is given. The author is quoted as saying that, althoughhe knew Sellers for 15 years, he found when he began his research for this book that he did not know Sellers at all. One might suspect that the same situation still prevails. The book may please Sellers' fans.

4879   *see   4880*

4880   *Peter Ustinov.* by Willans, Geoffrey. 180 p. illus. London: Peter Owen, 1957.

A premature biography that covers Ustinov's life and career up to the mid-fifties. This volume is noted here since it treats Ustinov's experiences in making QUO VADIS (1951) and THE EGYPTIAN (1954) in some detail. The volume is not indexed, but Ustinov's films, plays, and publications to 1955 are listed.

4881   *Peter Watkins.* by Gomez, Joseph A. 214 p. illus. Boston: Twayne, 1979.

Peter Watkins is a British director whose films are usually securely based on reality, fact, and/or research. He employs a realistic, documentary style, with traces of social philosophy constantly in evidence. Here, Joseph Gomez provides an appreciation that covers Watkins' career chronologically—amateur films, BBC work, features, and recent projects. Notes, references, a bibliography, a filmography, an index and some illustrations complete the study.

This is another carefully researched and written volume in the excellent *Theatrical Arts* series. Gomez has used his personal skills most effectively in giving us a portrait of a dedicated filmmaker.

4882   *The Philosophy of Andy Warhol (From A to B and Back Again).* by Warhol, Andy. 241 p. New York: Harcourt, Brace, Jovanovich, 1975.

A collection of comments on topics such as death, art, success, economics, etc., this volume pays little attention to Warhol's career as a filmmaker. It appears to be an attempt by Warhol to find success in yet another medium. Warhol's philosophy is mostly on the cocktail party level—amusing at first but quickly perishable. The approach is that of a celebrity trying to tackle what he assumes are modern concerns with a light, faintly cynical style. There are no illustrations or index.

The philosophy espoused here may reflect the persona of Warhol, but a suspicious reader will have some doubts. In any event, most of the volume is entertaining chatter that will please Warhol admirers. Peripheral.

4883   *Photo and Scene Machines.* by Wentz, Budd. 32 p. paper illus. San Francisco: Troubador, 1977.

Printed on heavy stock paper, this booklet offers ten workable models of antique optical inventions. With the aid of a few basic materials (tape, glue, plastic wrap, flashlight, etc.), the user can create homemade versions of anamorphic pictures, a camera obscura, a photographic view camera, a magic lantern, a zoetrope, a diorama, a kaleidoscope, a bisceneorama, a stereoscope, a tin-can camera and a home darkroom.

Designed for young people, the activities contained here would benefit anyone engaged in the study of film.

4884   *The Photodrama.* by Phillips, Henry A. 221 p. New York: Arno Press, 1970 (1914).

This Arno reprint is a treatise on the photodrama (1914) that includes philosophy, censorship, dramatic construction and technique. The appendix contains the photoplay of THE SALT OF VENGEANCE (1912) and a glossary.

4885   *Photographer's Guide to Movie Making.* by Gilmour, Edwyn. 68 p. paper illus. New York: Amphoto, 1969.

This title in the Amphoto *Viewfinder* series describes the working of a movie camera, gives advice on purchasing a camera and discusses interchangeable lenses. Both silent and sound projectors are treated and there is an abbreviated section on filmmaking. A glossary is appended.

4886   *Photographers' Guide to Movie Making.* by Gilmour, Edwyn. 68 p. paper illus. New York: A. S. Barnes, 1963.

A basic guide for the amateur filmmaker that discusses films, cameras, lenses, projectors, etc.

4887 *Photographic Facts and Figures for the Amateur Cinematographer.* by Kendall, Geoffrey P. 55 p. paper London: Newnes, 1936.

4888 *The Photographic Study of Rapid Events.* by Chesterman, William D. 167 p. illus. Oxford: Clarendon, 1951.

A title in the series *Monographson the Physics and Chemistry of Materials*, this discussion of the scientific applications of cinematography is supplemented by text, plates, diagrams, and a bibliography.

4889 *Photographic Theory for the Motion Picture Cameraman.* edited by Campbell, Russell. 160 p. paper illus. New York: A. S. Barnes, 1971.

An introduction to photographic theory as applied to motion pictures, containing an analysis of inanimate factors which affect film. Includes diagrams, illustrations, color plates, etc. For the advanced filmmaker.

4890 *The Photographs of Chachaji: The Making of a Documentary Film.* by Mehta, Ved. 239 p. illus. New York: Oxford University Press, 1980.

This is the diary kept by a documentary filmmaker as he prepared a film about his elderly cousin. How Mehta chose his subject, collected his crew, got financial backing, and overcame the inevitable red tape are discussed. The final film was titled CHACHAJI: MY POOR RELATION (1980).

4891 *Photography and Cinematography: A Four-Language Illustrated Dictionary and Glossary of Terms.* by Townsend, Derek. 178 p. illus. London: Redman, 1964.

The four languages are English, French, German and Spanish.

4892 *Photography in Commerce and Industry.* by Faulkner-Taylor, A. 416 p. illus. London: Fountain Press, 1962.

A manual for the apprentice or professional covering training, equipment, systems, techniques, studio, factory, architecture, color, and motion pictures.

4893 *The Photoguide to Moviemaking.* by Petzold, Paul. 224 p. paper illus. New York: Amphoto, 1975.

A title in the *Photoguide* series, this heavily illustrated volume deals with basic topics: cameras, lenses, lighting, filming techniques, special effects, sound, editing, projectors, etc.

An index is provided along with many full-color illustrations. (Although the *Photoguide* series deals primarily with still photography, certain information contained in its volumes is applicable to cinematography.)

4894 *The Photoplay: A Psychological Study.* by Munsterberg, Hugo. 232 p. New York: Arno, 1970 (1916).

See: *The Film: A Psychological Study—The Silent Photoplay in 1916.*

4895 *The Photo-Play—How to Write; How to Sell.* by Nelson, John A. 232 p. paper Los Angeles: Photoplay Publishing, 1913.

A practical treatise on the form, structure and technique of the motion picture play of 1913, together with an analytical comparison of contra-literary forms and structures, an investigation of themes, and their sources. Contains suggestions on how to sell to the best advantage.

4896 *Photoplay Appreciation in American High Schools.* by Lewin, William. 122 p. New York: National Council of English Teachers/Appleton-Century, 1935.

This experiment, which involved 68 groups made up of some 36 teachers and 1851 students, indicated rather early the potential of film in the classroom. It concluded that film appreciation can be taught and that taste can be improved. Some promising methods of using films are indicated along with an acceptance of film as an art form and as a comment upon social experience. A bibliography is offered and the experiment's questionnaire is appended.

4897 *Photoplay Edition.* by Petaja, Emil. 211 p. paper illus. San Francisco: Sisu Publishers, 1975.

Years ago a photoplay edition of a book was one published to coincide with the release of a film based on a book, play, short story, etc. Its aim was to increase book sales and motion picture attendance. Aimed at the mass audience, the older volumes were hardbound but inexpensively produced and featured stills from the film both in the book and on its dust jacket. Today they are still produced—usually as paperbacks—and called "Tie-ins." Sometimes the original process is reversed and a novel is generated from an original film script. The stills from the film remain an essential feature and are often used on the cover design.

In this index the author is mostly concerned with hardcover books published from 1914 through 1974. After a few short introductory chapters, the films are listed alphabetically by title starting with the first entry: "ABE LINCOLN IN ILLINOIS by Robert E. Sherwood, 37 pictures, 1940, RKO—Raymond Massey, Ruth Gordon" and ending with: "YELLOW MEN AND GOLD by Gouverneur Morris, 1922, Goldwyn—Richard Dix, Helene Chadwick." The addition of an inadequate short section entitled "Soft Cover Edition Supplement" only weakens the book.

A very good sampling of illustrations and dust covers accompanies the bibliography, which the author claims makes no pretense at being complete. However, it is also inconsistent, with the basic information format varying with each entry. One wonders about selection also. For example, the entry for *Susannah of the Mounties* lists Grosset and Dunlap as publisher but gives no original author and number of stills. Not listed is the Random House edition, which credits Muriel Denison as author and contains over 25 full pages of stills and a montage of 16 Shirley Temple photographs on both endpapers. On page 107 *Lorna Doone* appears after *Love* and *Lost Lady*, but before *Long Live the King*, causing some bewilderment about the alphabetizing. This seems true throughout, with only the first letter of the title indicating placement. The final section is a listing of paperbacks that makes no differentiation between scripts, novelized versions of scripts, adaptations and diarylike accounts of making a particular film. In summary this is a somewhat unusual reference, weakened by arrangement and selection. Acceptable.

4898 *Photoplay Film Annual 1975.* edited by Ferguson, Ken. 1975 p. illus. London: Argus Press, 1974.

This annual contains fan magazine material which emphasizes personalities rather than films. Many articles and illustrations, some of which are in color, are offered.

4899 *Photoplay Plot Encyclopedia.* by Palmer, Frederick; and Howard, Eric. 165 p. Los Angeles: Palmer Photoplay Corp., 1920.

An analysis of the use in photoplays of the 36 basic dramatic situations and their subdivisions. Contains a list of all the fundamental dramatic material to be found in human experience, including the synopses of 100 produced representative photoplays, with a detailed analysis of the situations used in each. Practical suggestions are given for combining situations, for testing the strength and novelty of plots, and for building plots. An index to all the above is included.

Frederick Palmer is the author of several other books on scriptwriting which were published in the early twenties. Titles include: *Palmer Course and Service* (1922), *Author's Photoplay Manual* (1924), *The Essentials of Photoplay Writing* (1921), *Palmer Handbook of Scenario Construction* (1922), *Palmer Plan Handbook* (1921), *Reference Scenarios and Continuity* (1924), and *Technique of the Photoplay* (1924).

4900 *Photoplay Scenarios: How to Write and Sell Them.* by Ball, Eustace Hale. 186 p. New York: Hearst's International Library, 1915.

This manual of direction and advice includes such topics as the basis of the photoplay, technical preparation, what is dramatic principle, practical authorship methods, the story and its people, problems of censorship, the manuscript and its sale, sample scenarios, and informal suggestions.

4901 *The Photoplay Synopsis.* by Powell, Ardon Van Buren. 307 p. Springfield, Mass.: The Home Correspondence School, 1919.

An analysis of the art of synopsis writing which includes such topics as preparation, plot, caption, synopsis, examples, etc.

4902 *see 4903*

4903 *Photoplay* Treasury. edited by Gelman, Barbara. 373 p. illus. New York: Crown, 1972.

If a reader is told that an oversized coffee-table book containing "nostalgic picture-and-word stories" from *Photoplay* Magazine from the teen years through the forties is due, he anticipates something quite special. The anticipations are not fulfilled in this case; the book is a disappointment.

Very little quarrel can be made with the selection—there was a sameness about the fan-magazine articles of the period; only the names of the subjects were changed. The objection here is to the poor, indistinct, murky and sometimes nearly black reproduction of the illustrations. Examples are abundant but pages 52, 60, 69, 75, 115, 116, 131, 214, 215, 227, 273, 327, 366, 367 are especially bad. Where was production control on this vital element of the book? Today's reader will not have the patience to wade through too many pages of studio press agentry verbiage; visual nostalgia is the primary interest. There are some fine visuals in the book (pages 165, 308), which suggests that the poor reproduction of many of the others was avoidable. Stronger proof is available in a similar volume, *The Talkies*, which also used *Photoplay* articles but much more satisfactorily.

There is so much potential enjoyment in this book that it is disheartening to see it undermined by the careless production. Not recommended; instead, the reader is referred to the above-mentioned book by Richard Griffith, *The Talkies*.

4904 *Photoplay Writing*. by Wright, William Lord. 228 p. illus. New York: Falk, 1922.

A text used at the New York Institute of Photography which includes such topics as: can you write for the screen? what scenario editors want; where to begin; plot construction; writing for a star; studying the screen; titles; continuity; censorship; screen language; etc;

4905 *Photoplays*. by Spivey, Thomas S. 376 p. New York: Scenario Supply Corp., 1924.

This volume contains 14 film scripts (synopses and continuities), all of which were unproduced.

4906 *Pictorial Beauty on the Screen*. by Freeburg, Victor Oscar. 191 p. illus. New York: Arno Press, 1970 (1923).

This Arno reprint is an early volume on cinema composition. In 1923 Freeburg argued that films must have qualities of form, composition, light and shade. He offered principles which govern the creation of physical beauty on the screen.

4907 *Pictorial Cavalcade of Motion Pictures*. edited by Alicoate, Jack. 224 p. illus. New York: Film Daily, 1938.

The subtitle of this pictorial history reads, "Reflecting the Romantic and Colorful Days in which Motion Pictures Were Pioneered." A volume with the same title and editor was published in 1958, commemorating the 40th anniversary of *Film Daily* (1918-1958).

4908 *Pictorial Continuity*. by Gaskill, Arthur L.; and Englander, David A. 149p. New York: Duell, Sloan &

Pearce, 1947.

See *How to Shoot a Movie Story* .

4909 *A Pictorial History of Crime Films*. by Cameron, Ian. 221 p. illus. London: Hamlyn, 1975.

A pictorial survey of crime films, this volume contains section headings such as suspense, crime-and-punishment, violence, criminals, the organization, and the right side of the law. Emphasis is on American films and there is an attempt made to relate the film to the period of its first release. The more than 350 illustrations are the major attraction. An index is provided.

4910 *A Pictorial History of Hollywood Nudity*. by Lee, Raymond. 127 p. illus. Chicago: Camerarts, 1964.

4911 *A Pictorial History of Horror Movies*. by Gifford, Denis. 216 p. illus. New York: Hamlyn, 1973.

Any book that extolls the fascination of the horror movie can't be all bad; the trouble with this one is that it could have been a lot better. The author has a fine Dutton-Vista book called *Movie Monsters* to his credit. Expanding on that spare volume, he has produced an oversized book which is very much like one of his topics, Jekyll and Hyde. It was written and printed in London, and some of its attempts to appeal may be hard to comprehend here. For example, the chapter headings and the text often strain for humor where none is needed. Do headings like "Dr. Jekyll is Not Himself," "A Chip Off the Old Hump," and "How Grand Was My Guignol" help? Another reservation concerns the identification of the stills. In most cases all stills on a two-page spread are identified in a paragraph placed strategically on the page. The reader will become impatient rather quickly with uppers, lowers, lefts, rights, opposites, and bottoms.

The book does have some fine visuals. One of Claude Rains as the Phantom is almost worth the price alone, and there are many others of almost equal fascination. Reproduction ranges from good to excellent. An appendix contains a filmography for collectors, one bibliography for books and another for magazines, and a list of "H" certificate films ("H" meant "Horrific" in England, and no one under 16 was admitted to films marked as such). A rather complete index follows.

When the author is serious in his text, the material offered is very good. Visuals are mostly superior if the reader can bear the identification handicap mentioned above. To all these qualities, add an inexpensive price and the book can be recommended. It will certainly appeal to a large audience.

4912   *A Pictorial History of Indian Cinema.* by Rangoonwalla, Firoze. 125 p. illus. London: Hamlyn, 1979.

4913   *A Pictorial History of Science Fiction Films.* by Rovin, Jeff. 240 p. illus. Secaucus, N.J.: Citadel, 1975.

A pictorial survey of science fiction films is provided by specialist Jeff Rovin, who has written several other volumes on the subject. Using almost 450 illustrations, Rovin explores such sci-fi sub-genres as man in space, monsters, the end of the world, invaders from outer space, robots, etc.

The idea that science fiction lends itself well to visualization can be confirmed by the visuals offered here.

4914   *A Pictorial History of Sex in Films.* by Tyler, Parker. 256 p. illus. Secaucus, N.J.: Citadel, 1974.

Lyle Stuart, Inc., publisher of the *Citadel* series, is known for its selection of sensationalized sexual topics and stories. Here they have combined the offbeat critic, Parker Tyler, with one of his favorite topics and added several hundred provocative stills.

Tyler is always interesting, even when he is a bit hysterical about the symbols he sees in films. In his examination of films from THE KISS (1896) to LUDWIG (1973), he discusses forms of sexual activity and expression as they appear on screen. Heavy dependence is made upon films with limited circulation—the underground film, the obscure foreign film, etc.—for the more blatant examples. Unfortunately there is no index, an indication of the lack of scholarly and serious intent of the editors and publishers.

A typical *Citadel* volume it is not—it is instead a heavily illustrated Parker Tyler discourse, and that is just fine!

4915   *A Pictorial History of Sex in the Movies.* by Pascall, Jeremy; and Jeavons, Clyde. 217 p. illus. London: Hamlyn, 1975.

In this volume, whose title and content bear a close resemblance to a book by Parker Tyler, the authors provide a chronological review of sex in movies. Each of the decades, from the twenties to the seventies, receives a separate chapter of analysis and comment. Happily, some of the many illustrations are in color, but others are a bit too small for full comprehension. In general, the photo collection is much milder than Tyler's. Likewise, the text is more literal than Tyler's imaginative assignments of ideas sexual.

With the total freedom currently enjoyed by films, the content here is mild, notable primarily for the ways in which filmmakers suggested rather than showed sex. There are those who think it was better that way.

4916   *A Pictorial History of the Great Comedians.* by Cahn, William. 221p. illus. New York: Grosset & Dunlap, 1970.

Revised and retitled version of *The Laughmakers* .

4917   *A Pictorial History of the Movies.* by Taylor, Deems; and Peterson, Marcelene; and Hale, Bryant. 376 p. illus. New York: Simon & Schuster, 1950 (1943).

Originally published in 1943 and then revised in 1950, this pictorial history is the grandparent of the later volumes by Blum, Griffith, and others. It was, and is, a worthy model to emulate. The emphasis is on the illustrations, and they are plentiful. Photo reproduction in the revised edition is better than in the original—probably because of the wartime restrictions existing during the book's initial appearance. Text throughout is succinct, witty, and quite informative.

There is a short introduction by Taylor and a general index. It should be noted that the emphasis is on American films. As a pictorial history of the first half century of motion pictures, this book is hard to beat. Why it is not constantly revised and updated must be one of the publishing world's mysteries. Excellent.

4918   *A Pictorial History of the Movies.* by Davies, Mary; and Anderson, Janic; and Arnold, Peter. 224 p. illus. Northbrook, Ill.: Domus (Quality Books), 1976.

In this volume the history of the movies is told using a most unusual structure. The first half of the book considers the more common film genres—epics, horror, musical, crime, etc.—and offers a mini-history of each. The next quarter of the book is devoted to national cinemas—German, Soviet, Indian, etc.—and the last quarter deals with a mixture of film-related topics—directors, stars, studios, censorship, awards, etc. Obviously in trying to cover such a wide range of subjects with minimum narrative and maximum visual material, the authors have had to provide summaries rather than detailed presentations. The results here, however, are most pleasant. There is an abundance of attractive, clearly reproduced illustrations, some of which are in full color. The text covers many historical highlights and is not hesitant in offering both original criticism and interpretation.

This is an attractive volume that will entertain and inform its audience. The high quality of selection and treatment used in its preparation has resulted in an outstanding collection of visuals explained and interpreted most effectively by a carefully written text. Highly recommended.

4919 *A Pictorial History of the Silent Screen.* by Blum, Daniel. 334 p. illus. New York: Grosset & Dunlap, 1953.

The period of the silent screen from the early years to 1930 is covered in this book by a collection of over 3000 photographs accompanied by a very brief narrative. Arranged chronologically, the pictures tell the history of that special art, the silent screen, much more eloquently than certain other windy narratives. The pictures are fascinating, and in many cases unique. They are reproduced with high quality in most instances—the only exceptions being some photos of rare and forgotten subjects. The personalities appearing in the photographs are usually identified. In addition there is a detailed index of names and picture titles.

This book will capture most readers for hours at a time. At home, for example, the quickest way to lose the attention of a guest is to place this book on the coffee table. It is informative, entertaining, and a beautiful tribute to the silent era. Highly recommended.

4920 *A Pictorial History of the Talkies.* by Blum, Daniel. 318 p. illus. New York: G. P. Putnam Sons, 1958.

By using the same format as in his volume on the silent screen, author Blum again produces an essential volume for all collections. Arranged chronologically from 1927 to 1958, the several thousand pictures are well-chosen and nicely reproduced. Identifications and a full index make the book an idela reference. The book is basic and classic and a necessity for any film collection.

4921 *A Pictorial History of the Tarzan Movies.* by Lee, Raymond; and Co-

riell, Vernell. 82 p. paper illus. Los Angeles: Golden State News, 1966.

This visual survey includes a filmography.

4922 *A Pictorial History of the Western Film.* by Everson, William K. 246 p. illus. New York: Citadel Press, 1969.

Seventy years of the western film are presented in this book. It is all here—the actors, the directors, the films—and much incidental information pertinent to the topic. The title may be a bit misleading since there is a rather large proportion of text to accompany the many excellent stills. These illustrations include such rarities as Lugosi as Uncas in a 1922 German version of LAST OF THE MOHICANS, and Gable and Karloff as western villains in early sound films.

Certain important westerns are missing—RED GARTERS (1954), RANCHO NOTORIOUS (1952), CHEYENNE AUTUMN (1964), for example—while others are dismissed with a passing, even negative mention—WILL PENNY (1968) and the 1939 DESTRY. Considering the scope of the subject, however, the author has taken a rather comprehensive look. In summary, this is an important book and is highly recommended.

4923 *A Pictorial History of War Films.* by Jeavons, Clyde. 253 p. illus. Secaucus, N.J.: Citadel, 1974.

More than 350 illustrations appear in this survey of 75 years of war film production. International in coverage, the text emphasizes 20th century wars and conflicts. The author includes documentaries, TV series, and certain films which comment on war. His arrangement is chronological by date of the films. The illustrations used are nicely reproduced and captioned. An index is provided.

4924 *A Pictorial History of Westerns.* by Parkinson, Michael; and Jeavons, Clyde. 217 p. illus. New York: Hamlyn, 1973.

Similar to Gifford's *A Pictorial History of Horror Movies*, this book has some of the same virtues and faults. The text is divided into sections on the films, the stars, the stalwarts, the directors and two sub-genres: the spaghetti westerns and the TV westerns.

Visuals again play a vital part and their quality ranges from exceptional to poor. The latter include poorly contrasted shots which obliterate faces while the former are some full-page portraits and several beautiful color stills. Fitting the scope of the western outdoor scene to a small illustration seems to be a problem. Many of the pictures are hard to interpret, with tiny figures seen against an enormous landscape. Identification is also a problem here, with one explanatory paragraph for all the visuals on one or a double page. The reader again encounters the upper, lower, right, left, top, bottom, opposite, across syndrome. A lengthy index completes the book. The text is above average, the visuals satisfactory for the most part, and the arrangement a valid one for such a survey. Acceptable.

4925   *Picture.* by Ross, Lillian. 258 p. New York: Rinehart & Co., 1952.

Written originally as a multi-part profile for the *New Yorker* magazine, *Picture* is an account of the making of THE RED BADGE OF COURAGE (1951). Beginning with the enthusiasm of director John Huston and producer Gottfried Reinhardt, aided by the encouragement of Dore Schary, and hampered by the negativism of Louis B. Mayer, the project was finally completed. Critical response was very good but the picture was a commercial failure.

It is this evolution of idea into film that author Ross uses as subject matter. To it she adds a penetrating look at a large organization and the effect if can have on a creative work. The eternal Hollywood dilemma of art versus money underlies much of the account. From its first appearance this work has been considered as superior film literature. The years since have provided no reason to alter this evaluation. Recommended.

4926   *The Picture History of Charlie Chaplin.* by McDonald, Gerald.. 64 p. illus. New York: Nostalgia Press, 1965.

A collection of rare pictures and interesting text make up this small volume issued by an appropriately named publisher. Included are Chaplin comic strips, cartoons, posters, stills, advertisements, cutouts, etc. Film stills and candids are also used. This is an unusual and different book. There is no index and pages are not numbered. As pure entertainment, the book will please most readers.

4927   *A Picture History of the Cinema.* by Lindgren, Ernest. 160 p. illus. New York: Macmillan, 1960.

The point of view in this excellent book is to examine films as art rather than entertainment. Selection is wide, balanced equally between American film and foreign film. The book divides itself into predicatable periods of film history such as pioneers, growth

of an industry, World War I, sound, World War II, etc. A short text introduces each section. The text is well-written in a scholarly fashion and the accompanying black-and-white illustrations have been chosen with intelligence and discrimination. One drawback however, is the lack of identification of known actors in many of the illustrations. This is a most valuable book. Highly recommended.

4928   *The Picture House in East Anglia (to 1979).* by Peart, Stephen. 180 p. illus. Lavenham, Manitoba: Dalton, 1980.

4929   *Picture Palace: A Social History of the Cinema.* by Field, Aubrey. 160 p. illus. London: Gentry, 1974.

4930   *The Picture Palace (and Other Buildings for the Movies).* by Sharp, Dennis. 224 p. illus. New York: Praeger, 1969.

Intended primarily for architects, designers, and builders, this volume still may have interest for other readers. Using a historical development, the author examines the buildings that housed motion pictures from the magic lantern of Robertons's Exhibition Room in 1868 to the Curzon Cinema which opened in London in 1966. The illustrations, pictures, plans, etc. are all beautifully reproduced. Much information regarding the exhibition phase of films is contained in the text. This is not a basic or essential volume.

4931   *Picture Parade: Films and Stars of the Year.* by Noble, Peter. 160 p. illus. London: Burke, 1949.

A collection of portraits and stills mostly from English and American films produced in the late forties. Usually there is a short descriptive paragraph accompanying each picture and in a few cases, a longer text is given. A few pictures are in color, but the reproduction of all the illustrations ranges from poor to only fair. This is a nostalgia item.

4932   *Picture Pioneers.* by Mellor, G. J. 96 p. paper illus. Newcastle-upon-Tyne, England: Frank Graham, 1971.

Subtitled "The Story of the Northern Cinema, 1896-1971," this short book was prepared as a tribute to the 75th anniversary of the first film showing in England. Its aim is to acknowledge the role played by the North of England in the development of cinema. Since much of the information was provided by the pioneers of the title, the emphasis is on the early years. Hundreds of unfamiliar names stud this factual account, along with brief descriptions of the technology, the theatres, and the films of the time. The narrative works its way up to the introduction of sound films and concludes with a short chapter on the 1930-1971 period. An interesting finale is provided by the statements of more than 30 pioneers, who are each allotted a few paragraphs for a flashback.

Picture quality is only fair because of the age of the photographs used. An index of names and theatres is provided. The local accounts may be correct but the author's general knowledge of cinema history is suspect; for example, he overlooks DON JUAN (1926) completely in the account of sound films. This is very specialized history.

4933   *Picture Plays and How to Write Them.* by Muddle, E. 87 p. London: Picture Play Agency/Cinemato-Graph Press, 1911.

4934   *Picture Plays and How to Write Them.* by Farquharson, J. 166 p. New York: Hodder and Stoughton, 1916.

This volume not only offers suggestions and advice on how to write film scripts for silent movies, but also contains the complete scenario for THE SECOND MRS. TANQUERAY (1916), based on the play by Sir Arthur Pinero.

4935   *Picture Show Annual.* illus. London: Fleetway, Amalgamated, 1929- .

The 32nd volume published in 1960 contained some full-page portraits, and articles that tended to be general-collective rather than devoted to individuals, as indicated by the following titles: "X For Horror," "Love Scenes to Remember," "Stars Behind the Scenes," "How We Love to Hate Them," etc.

4936   *The Picture Show Annual.* 160 p. illus. London: Amalgamated Press, 1926- .

Boasting that it offered "The World's Best in Pictures," this annual was published from 1926 to 1937. It was a heavily illustrated fan book, typical of its time.

4937   *The Picture Story of Leo Tolstoy's War and Peace.*: An adaption from the novel and the film. by Geis, Bernard. 120 p. illus. New York: Frederick Fell, 1956.

An abridgement of Tolstoy's novel based on the 1956 film and illustrated with many photographs taken from that version. The cast credits are given.

4938   *Picture Theatre Advertising.* by Sargent, Epes W. 302 p. illus. New York: The Moving Picture World, 1915.

An early manual for theatre owners and managers that covers advertising in the lobby, on billboards, on the screen, in papers, etc. Tells how to prepare copy, run contests, find information, etc.

4939   *The Picturegoer's Who's Who and Encyclopedia of the Screen Today.* edited by Picturegoer Weekly. 608 p. illus. London: Odhams, 1933.

4940   *Pictures of Reality: Aesthetics, Politics and Pleasure.* by Lovell, Terry. III p. paper London: British Film Institute; (N.Y.: Zoetrope), 1980.

This "heavy" book has two aims: (1) to assess Althusserian Marxism and its impact on cultural studies, and (2) to adumbrate a Marxist theory of mass culture. After arguing that Marxism has a realist theory of knowledge and society, the author offers a critique of Louis Althusser and others, along with their theories of science and ideology. From this material implications are derived for the development of a concept and theory of ideology. Final sections look at Marxist theories of art.

That all the theory presented can be applied to film may explain why the British Film Institute published this atypical volume.

4941   *Pictures Will Talk: The Life and Films of Joseph L. Mankiewicz.* by Geist, Kenneth L. 443 p. illus. New York: Scribners, 1978.

Newspapers noted director Joseph L. Mankiewicz's change of mind in cooperating with Kenneth L. Geist in the preparation of this book. Despite the fact that this is now an unauthorized biography, it is a very, very good one. Using his own exhaustive research, Geist has put together a detailed yet very readable portrait of a creative man who can be sensitive yet shrewd, arrogant yet friendly. Crammed with anecdotes and personalities, the text covers Mankiewicz's personal life and productive film career with the same care, wit, and sophistication that the filmmaker invests in many of his productions.

An illustrated filmography, an index and over 60 photographs are included. This volume is one of the few Hollywood biographies that might be termed "excellent."

4942   *Pictures With a Purpose.* by Kidd, James R. 72 p. paper illus. Toronto: Canadian Association for Adult Education, 1953.

This title, number 7 in the *Learning for Living* series, deals with the distribution of nontheatrical films in Canada.

4943   *Pieces of Time.* by Bogdanovich, Peter. 269 p. New York: Arbor House, 1973.

It is easy to admire and like Peter Bogdanovich—admiration, for his achievements in writing film books and articles and for directing some important films; liking, for the man who is still star-struck, respectful, and appreciative of all those who went before him in films. In the pieces in this book, the image of the author that emerges is as strongly positive as the subjects he selects.

The book is a collection of reflections and comments upon films rather than critical analyses. The articles are taken from *Esquire* magazine, and the author has supplied a headnote for each, a device which adds to their effectiveness. They are divided into five groups: first impressions, actors, preferences, directors, and recent impressions. A helpful index is provided. Bogdanovich is ardent in expressing his movie affections and he usually convinces the reader of the truth, worth, and validity of his feelings. This informative, entertaining, and rather seductive book is recommended.

4944   *Pier Paolo Pasolini.* edited by Willemen, Paul. 88 p. paper illus. London: British Film Institute; New York: Zoetrope, 1977.

An appreciation of Italian film director Pier Paolo Pasolini, this anthology of critical essays also offers a bibliography and a filmography. Among the contributors are Geoffrey Nowell-Smith (Political-Ideological Sources), Roland Barthes and Richard Dyer (Homosexuality), Antonio Costa (Semiotics), and Don Ranvaud (Salo). An interview with Pasolini is added.

4945   *Pier Paolo Pasolini.* by Snyder, Stephen. 199 p. illus. Boston: Twayne, 1980.

In this critical appreciation of the films of Pier Paolo Pasolini, Stephen Snyder has tried to relate the films to the director's life and views. An introductory chapter deals with Pasolini's biography; then his films from ACCATONE (1961) to SALO (1975) are critically examined. As usual with Twayne's *Theatrical Arts* series, the text is complemented by illustrations, a chronology, notes, references, a bibliography, a filmography, and an index.

This volume is a study more than an appreciation; the author attempts to supply comment and analysis in order that the reader may determine the importance of Pasolini's works in film history. Anyone interested in this controversial director could do no better than to begin with this volume.

4946   PIERROT LE FOU. by Godard, Jean-Luc. 104 p. paper illus. New York: Simon & Schuster, 1969.

Script of the 1965 film directed by Godard. Contains cast credits and "Let's Talk About Pierrot," an interview with Jean-Luc Godard.

4947   *The Pin-Up: A Modest History.* by Gabor, Mark. 271 p. illus. New York: Universe Books, 1972.

This oversized coffee-table book traces the history of those visuals which offer sex appeal as their primary communication. Starting with the 1480 detail of Botticelli's "Birth of Venus," it covers the evolution of the pin-up through its heyday in World War II to the anything-goes centerfolds we have today. Much nudity is featured throughout. Two specific sections examine heroes and heroines of the screen. In addition there are chapters devoted to pinups found in calendars, magazines, posters, sex periodicals, and in publications aimed at sexual minorities. Of course, the visuals are the attraction here and there are hundreds of them. Most are well reproduced and many appear in full color.

The sections on film stars may have some pertinence for film historians but the other, more abundant material does not. In addition, the full nudity—much of it frontal—may eliminate the volume from consideration by many readers. However, the book does live up to its title and offers a diverting, if modest, history of the pin-up. A large number of mature readers will enjoy Gabor's collection of visuals and his illuminating text. Even the dust jacket is a famous pin-up—the 12 inch x 63 inch poster of the female model decorated in body paint, entitled "Exhibition."

4948 *The Pink Palace.* by Stuart, Sandra Lee. 224 p. paper illus. New York: Pocket Books, 1978.

Subtitled "Behind Closed Doors at the Beverly Hills Hotel," this compilation of gossip deals with many film celebrities. Apparently, staff members of the hotel, which was built in 1912, supplied the author with some of her material. None of it is especially shocking and since most of it is presented out of context, it has little meaning.

How exciting is the information that Sidney Poitier danced barefoot through the lobby after winning his Oscar?

An index and some illustrations accompany this expose which promises much more than it delivers.

4949 *Plan for Cinema.* by Bower, Dallas. 147 p. London: Dent & Sons, 1936.

The major thesis of this book is that films of outstanding merit must necessarily be rare, just as novels, paintings, symphonies, etc. of outstanding merit are rare. The question of "highbrow or lowbrow" or "Should films be entertainment, a social instrument, or art?" is proposed. The author argues for film as an art form by exploring topics such as opera in cinema. Here is an interesting early argument about a question which is still debated by the critics of today.

4950 *Plan for Film Studios: A Plea for Reform.* by Junge, Helmut. 64 p. paper illus. London: Focal, 1945.

Sir Patrick Abercrombie supplies a preface to this brief argument concerning the motion picture studios of Great Britain.

4951 *Planning and Producing Audio-Visual Materials.* by Kemp, Jerrold. 169 p. paper illus. San Francisco: Chandler, 1967.

Includes a section on motion pictures and much peripheral material that can be applied to film production.

4952 *Planning and Scripting Amateur Movies.* by Grosset, Philip. 127 p. illus. London: Fountain Press, 1963.

Divided into three parts—before filming, actual filming, and post-filming—this volume emphasizes the development of ideas into scenarios.

4953 *Planning Films for Schools.* compiled by Commission on Motion Pictures. 34 p. paper Washington, D.C.: American Council on Education, 1949.

This was final report number 36 in the series entitled *Reports of Committees and Conferences,* issued by the American Council on Education.

4954 *The Platinum Years.* by Willoughby, Bob; and Schickel, Richard. 271 p. illus. New York: Random House, 1974.

Bob Willoughby is an on-the-set photographer whose work on 22 films is sampled in this volume. Included are more than 200 photographs, many of which are in full color. They show the details of making such films as FROM HERE TO ETERNITY (1953), A STAR IS BORN (1955), MY FAIR LADY (1964), THE GREAT RACE (1965), THE GRADUATE (1967), THE COWBOYS (1971), etc. Richard Schickel's commentary on the films accompanies the fine collection of visuals. An outstanding example of the film photographer's art, this volume will fascinate a wide range of reader-viewers. Recommended.

4955 *The Playboy Interview.* edited by Golson, G. Barry. 722 p. paper illus. Chicago: Playboy Press, 1980.

This collection of 30 interviews taken from *Playboy* magazine includes ones with Mel Brooks, John Wayne, and Marlon Brando.

4956 *Playboy Interviews Peter Fonda and Joan Baez.* 144 p. paper illus. Chicago: Playboy Press, 1971.

The interview with Fonda gives his predictions about film, his attitudes toward life, and a filmography.

4957 *Playboy Sex in Cinema, Number Two.* by Alpert, Hollis; and Knight, Arthur. 144 p. paper illus. Chicago: Playboy Press, 1972.

The usual three parts appear in this annual: the films of 1971, a photo section, and the stars of the films. Acceptable for mature audiences. The sections by Alpert and Knight are, of course, quite good, but one wonders how many will read them.

4958 *Playboy's Sex in Cinema (A Series).* edited by Knight, Arthur. paper illus. Chicago: Playboy Press, 1970- .

By appealing to several senses or emotions simultaneously, the *Playboy* editors have developed an attractive and successful annual dealing with sex in cinema.

The format is consistent: an essay on the films of the year by Arthur Knight, a large center section of visuals, and a final essay on sex stars. The latter chapter was written by Hollis Alpert in the first three volumes and by Arthur Knight in the next three.

The editors have succeeded in supplying something for almost everyone. The many visuals have been expertly selected to include females, males, superstars, unknowns, porno performers, cartoons, etc. All are carefully and clearly reproduced and those in color are quite attractive. Knight's critical credentials are well established, as are Alpert's, and their essays are stimulating, tittilating and even informative.

Sex appears in films in an infinite variety; the view presented in these volumes tends to be narrow and in keeping with the established attitudes of Playboy Enterprises. Therefore, the books will be very popular with large segments of the reader audience for a variety of reasons.

4959 *Playboy's Sex in Cinema 1970.* by Knight, Arthur; and Alpert, Hollis. 144 p. paper illus. Chicago: Playboy Press, 1970.

This paperback is divided into three sections: the first is a narrative entitled "Films," the center section (as usual) is devoted to 107 pictures (16 in color), and the final text is called "Stars." The topic of concern is "Sex as Reflected in the Films of 1970." Expect that it will be popular for a variety of reasons.

4960 *Played Out: The Jean Seberg Story.* 381 p. illus. New York: Random House, 1981.

An absorbing story of a minor film actress whose life could be a metaphor for a segment of American youth during the fifties and sixties.

4961 *The Player: A Profile of an Art.* by Ross, Lillian; and Ross, Helen. 459 p. illus. New York: Simon & Schuster, 1962.

The 55 short biographies of players that make up this volume are based on interviews done from 1958-1962. Each is presented in autobiographical format,

preceded by a small photograph of the subject. Background for the articles was obtained not only from the subject but also from co-workers, friends, etc. The attempt is to give "A balanced and definitive picture of the art of acting."

Mention is made of acting on stage, in television, for films, etc., since most of the personalities considered are active in more than one medium. However, the emphasis is definitely on theatrical or stage performing. Twenty-one of the articles appeared originally in the *New Yorker.* Most of the photographs were taken by Lillian Ross (see *Picture*). Absorbing reading is provided by a most worthwhile collection of articles. The fact that film acting is not the primary consideration lessens the book's pertinence to film scholars.

4962 *A Player's Place: The Story of the Actors Studio.* by Garfield, David. 308 p. illus. New York: Macmillan, 1980.

The list of film performers who have studied at the Actors Studio, a theatre workshop located in New York City, is a long one. It includes such names as Anne Bancroft, Marlon Brando, Ellen Burstyn, Montgomery Clift, James Dean, Robert DeNiro, Jane Fonda, Dustin Hoffman, Steve McQueen, Paul Newman, Al Pacino, Shelley Winters, and many others. This volume tells the story of that workshop from its parent groups (The Moscow Art Theater, The Group Theater, etc.) and its official founding in October, 1947, to date. Prominent in the organization and operation of the studio were such names as Elia Kazan, Cheryl Crawford, Robert Lewis, and, of course, Lee Strasberg.

Illustrations, a list of Studio Life Members as of 1980, chapter notes, a bibliography, and an index accompany this account.

Anyone interested in today's actors and their methods will find this account both informative and entertaining. It suggests once again that artistry is the ability to make a difficult task look easy.

4963 *Please Don't Hate Me.* by Tiomkin, Dimitri; and Buranelli, Prosper. 261 p. Garden City, N.Y.: Doubelday, 1961.

The celebrated composer of many original motion picture scores and winner of seven Oscars discusses his life and film music. Lightweight, but witty and unusual.

4964 *Please Don't Shoot My Dog: The Autobiography of Jackie Cooper.* by

Cooper, Jackie; and Kleiner, Dick. 351 p. illus. New York: William Morrow,1981.

In certain ways, Jackie Cooper was a continual loser —his childhood, his father, his virginity etc. All this is told along with many other details, anecdotes, and musings about a career that has lasted over 50 years.

4965 *Poetry and Film.* compiled by Vogel, Amos. 28 p. paper New York: Gotham Book Mart, 1972.

A booklet that considers aesthetics, motion pictures and literature, experimental films and the work of Dylan Thomas and others.

4966 POINT OF ORDER. by DeAntonio, Emile; and Talbot, Daniel. 108 p. illus. New York: Norton, 1964.

Transcript of the television documentary film.

4967 *Polanski: Three Film Scripts.* by Polanski, Roman. 214 p. paper illus. New York: Harper and Row, 1975.

This volume contains scripts of the following films: KNIFE IN THE WATER (1961), REPULSION (1965), and CUL-DE-SAC (1966).

Also included is an introduction by Boleslaw Sulik, a single review of each film, and an interview with Polanski.

4968 *Polemics for a New Cinema.* by Thoms, Albie. 427 p. Sydney, Australia: Wild and Wooley, 1978.

This survey of experimental films and filmmakers from America, Europe and Australia devotes large sections to specific films—MARINETTI (1969), NED KELLY (1970), WOODSTOCK (1970), MORNING OF THE EARTH (1972), THE INNERMOST LIMITS OF PURE FUN (1971), etc. Attention is also given to avant-garde film festivals, aesthetics, politics, and video.

4969 *Polish Animated Films '71.* compiled by Film Polski. 140 p. paper illus. Warsaw: Film Polski, 1972.

Published yearly since 1966, this catalog has its films arranged under headings of cartoon, puppet, and combination techniques. A title index is provided and the text is in English, French and German.

4970 *Polish Cinema.* by Fuksiewicz, Jacek. 166 p. paper illus. Warsaw:

Interpress, 1973.

This brief survey of Polish cinema covers a wide range of topics: origins, history, features, shorts, documentaries, animated films, educational films, the "Polish School," cinematography in Poland, awards, etc. A large section is devoted to 55 Polish filmmakers who are currently active. The many illustrations which appear throughout the book are carefully reproduced and suggest a high quality of cinematography in Polish films. This modest book provides an excellent introduction to a national cinema whose product is almost unknown in America. Excellent.

4971 *Polish Cinema Publications.* paper illus. Warsaw: Film Polski, 1965- .

For many years Film Polski has published several major catalogs on Polish cinema. Written in several languages and beautifully illustrated, they provide yearly summaries of film production in Poland. *Polish Film Production* (in English, French, and German) gives credits, casts, illustrations, plot outlines and brief commentaries on feature films. Some illustrations are in color. (After 1968 this volume appears as the *Catalogue of Polish Feature Films.*) *Polish Animated Films* (in English, French, and German) gives credits, film data, and a short description of each film. Several small stills are also provided. Film titles are noted in the original Polish and the three featured languages, e.g., WIATR—THE WIND—LE VENT—DER WIND.

Also, *Documentary and Educational Films* (in English, French, and German) supplies credits, film data, stills and short descriptions. Films are arranged under subject headings, e.g., art, history, science, social problems, sport, children, touring, industry, and agriculture. A bimothly periodical in English and French, *Polish Film Polonais,* provides information about films, filmmakers, festivals, awards, studios, etc. The many illustrations are nicely reproduced and a soft-sell approach is used to promote Polish cinema. Titles mentioned above may be obtained from Film Polski, 00-48 Warsaw, Mazowiecka, 6/8.

4972 *The Political Censorship of Films.* by Montagu, Ivor. 44 p. paper London: Gollancz, 1929.

This short booklet includes both text and appendixes.

4973 *Political Change: A Film Guide.* by Morrison, James; and Blue, Richard. 87 p. paper Minneapolis, Minn.:

University of Minnesota, AV Library Service, 1975.

4974 *Politics and Cinema.* by Sarris, Andrew. 215 p. New York: Columbia University Press, 1978.

A collection of essays and reviews having a common theme of "Political Reality vs. Film Illusion" forms the content of this volume. Most of the pieces are reprinted from *The Village Voice* with only three taken from other sources. Films reviewed include: THE CANDIDATE (1972), THE MAN (1972), THE FRONT (1976), THE SORROW AND THE PITY (1971), HEARTS AND MINDS (1974), etc. An index is provided.

The appearance of Sarris' criticism in book form is always welcome. This anthology of disparate reviews having a central theme is unusual since it emphasizes the consistency of his critical criteria. The book offers further proof that Sarris' reputation as one of our most influential and respected critics is a deserved one. Highly recommended.

4975 *Politics and Film.* by Furhammer, Leif; and Isaksson, Folke. 257 p. illus. New York: Praeger, 1971.

The authors attempt to show the political content or purpose of some films made during or about the wars of the last 60 years. Attention is also given to some of the newer revolutionary films. After the historical framework has been established, certain individual films are described: TRIUMPH OF THE WILL (1935), MRS. MINIVER (1942), THE HITLER GANG (1944), TORN CURTAIN (1966), THE GREEN BERETS (1968), CHE (1969), etc. The concluding section summarizes the aesthetics of propaganda, the development of leader by film image (Churchill, Kennedy, Hitler, etc.), the unification of a diverse population into a "We," and finally the image of the enemy. Some conclusions complete the text which is supplemented by an extensive bibliography, an index and many fine illustrations.

Although the text is lacking in definition and an overall structure, it is still an intelligent introduction to a neglected topic in film literature. Written with clarity, the book often indicates scholarship and background. For many it will be provocative and exciting; others will take issue with its lack of focus and viewpoint. Recommended.

4976 *Politics and the Media.* edited by Clark, M. J. Elmsford, N.Y.: Pergamon, 1979.

This anthology, which carries the subtitle "Film and

Television for the Political Scientist and Historian," treats four general areas: the production context, relationships between the academic user and producer, the message received—a user perspective, and sources. Under each of these headings there are several essays which deal with the use of television or film in historiography—the study and writing of political science and history.

The text considers the context within which the media are produced along with the analytical and teaching framework in which the media can be used. The sources section notes institutions, archives, etc., where the films or television materials can be obtained.

The use of films as evidence in teaching history is a relatively new trend in educational methodology. This volume is a valuable sourcebook for teachers, researchers and scholars involved in higher education.

4977 *The Politics of the Soviet Cinema 1917-1929.* by Taylor, Richard. 230 p. New York: Cambridge University Press, 1979.

How the Soviet cinema became an instrument of propaganda instead of a creative, artistic medium is the subject of this study. The text traces the history of the medium from the Revolution to the close of the twenties, showing the many attempts made over the years to transform the film medium into an instrument of the state. A bibliography, notes, and an index accompany this view of politics and film.

4978 *Poor Me.* by Faith, Adam. 95 p. paper illus. London: Four Square Books, 1961.

The biography of a pop singer who made a few films in the early sixties including MIX ME A PERSON (1962) and NEVER LET GO (1963). See also *Adam, His Fabulous Year.*

4979 *Pop Culture in America.* edited by White, David Manning. 279 p. paper Chicago: Quadrangle Books, 1970.

An anthology designed to inform the reader about what's going on in radio, television, film, theatre, art, music, and books. Articles on film include the fine debate between Carl Foreman and Tyrone Guthrie on film vs. theatre (Foreman wins easily); "The Movies are Now High Art," by Richard Schickel; "Biggest Money-Making Movie of All Time—How Come?" by Joan Barthel; and "The Bard Competes with The Body" by C. A. LeJeune.

The Foreman-Guthrie debate alone is worth the price of the book. Recommended.

4980   *The "Pop-Up" Silly Symphonies.* edited by Walt Disney Productions. 45 p. illus. New York: Blue Ribbon, 1933.

Contains illustrations from BABES IN THE WOODS (1932) and KING NEPTUNE (1932).

4981   *Popcorn and Parable: A New Look at the Movies.* by Kahle, Roger; and Lee, Robert E.A. 128 p. illus. Minneapolis: Augsburg Publishing House, 1971.

As stated in the preface to this compact volume, its purpose is "to find in feature films a resource of our own faith and for our communication of religious truths to others." The authors urge the reader to study, to understand, and then to use films rather than think of them as a threat.

After an initial overview of the feature film of today, attention is given to topics such as film communication, fads, exploitation, sex, violence, etc. Many constructive suggestions are given in the closing sections which deal with film criticism and film festivals. A short bibliography and some explanatory notes are appended.

This is another volume in the growing list of books addressed to church workers. It is sound enough in its argument to merit consideration by many lay readers. Points are made with clarity and succinctness, the style is readable and the content is impressive. In summary, a fine small volume.

4982   *Popcorn in Paradise: The Wit and Wisdom of Hollywood.* edited by Colombo, John Robert. New York: Holt, Rinehart and Winston, 1979.

A collection of more than 3000 quotations from Hollywood personalities accompanied by some caricatures of the speakers.

4983   *Popcorn Venus.* by Rosen, Marjorie. 416 p. illus. New York: Coward, McCann & Geoghegan, 1973.

It is somewhat difficult to pinpoint the rationale for this volume. Is it an exploration of trends in depicting women in films? A study of the way women have been encouraged to view themselves? An analysis of the societal image of women? A review of woman's role in cinema? A study of the women behind the camera? A look at the on-and-off screen lives of film personalities (both female and male)? A selected history of the American film? The author attempts to satisfy all of these reasons for writing the volume and comes up with a mixed, variable result. Much of the volume shows a promise never fulfilled or realized. In the short sections devoted to Garbo, West, Gish, Dietrich, etc., there is evidence that a strong, stimulating statement about women's image in film could be formulated by Ms. Rosen. Instead she opts for a survey that attempts too much and deals largely in surface generalizations.

Several unfortunate paths are pursued. (1) It is a risky business to compare screen image with private image when the latter is largely a mystery. Who knew Kay Francis off screen? Even official biographers have difficulty pinning their subjects down. (2) When the text deals to a large extent with data and information rather than analysis, the material ought to be factual but sometimes is not, e.g., the 1936 version of THE CHILDREN'S HOUR did not deal at all with lesbianism, as is suggested; Rita Hayworth was an important screen personality (see BLOOD AND SAND (1941), STRAWBERRY BLONDE (1941) before the Astaire-Hayworth films; Carmen Miranda was not known for singing "Manana." (3) When critical opinion is offered, it should be indicated as subjective and individual when it differs from the general consensus, e.g., is von Stroheim's incomplete QUEEN KELLY (1928) really "magnificent and memorable"? Are Rosalind Russell's films from 1955 to 1971 proof of "incredible durability and pertinence"?

Two portrait galleries, a detailed index, some references and a lengthy bibliography accompany the text. The strength of this volume rests in the analysis of women's image in film. One wishes that the author had concentrated on this aspect of her topic rather than offering the potpourri that we find here. The volume may please readers hungry for information pertinent to women's liberation and is acceptable.

4984   *Popeye: The First Fifty Years.* by Sagendorf, Bud. 143 p. paper illus. New York: Workman, 1979.

This history of Popeye and his creator, Elzie Crisler Segar, was written by the cartoonist's only assistant, Bud Sagendorf.

Everything of interest to Popeye devotees is offered here—sample strips, profiles, statistics, maps, characters, collectibles, etc. Emphasis throughout is almost totally on Popeye in print. The film shorts which began in 1932 and are still seen with regularity on television receive minimal attention. The feature film POPEYE (1981), starring Robin Williams, is mentioned.

Good background information is provided by Sagendorf, but a book on the films is still needed.

4985 *Popism: The Warhol '6os.* by Warhol, Andy; and Hackett, Pat. 336 p. illus. New York: Harcourt, Brace, Jovanovich, 1980.

Andy Warhol was a central figure in the Pop movement which existed during the sixties. Similar to the earlier Dada movement, Popism expressed a rebellion against the status quo via art, film, music, clothing, behavior, etc. Here Warhol recalls his role as a cult figure who painted soup cans and Marilyn Monroe, in addition to making many experimental films. His studio, called The Factory, was a center of the movement.

4986 *The Popular Arts.* by Hall, Stuart; and Whannel, Paddy. 480 p. paper illus. New York: Pantheon Books, 1965.

Much attention is given to film as one of the popular arts.

4987 *The Popular Arts: A Critical Reader.* edited by Deer, Irving; and Deer, Harriet A. 356 p. paper New York: Charles Scribner's Sons, 1967.

A few of the more familiar articles on film appear in this anthology: "The Gangster As Tragic Hero" by Robert Warshow; "History on the Silver Screen" by Gilbert Highet; "From the Film" by Albert Hunt; "The Witness Point" by Vernon Young; and "Comedy's Greatest Era" by James Agee. A group of study questions follows each article. These five excellent articles listed are surrounded by several general articles on popular art topics—Kitsch, pornography, aesthetics, etc.—and a few specific ones on architecture, jazz, literature, television, still photography, the Western novel, science fiction, detective stories, American musicals, comic strips and best sellers; the appeal of the book is apparent. For anyone looking for a broad exploration and discussion of the popular arts with an emphasis on films, this volume will be quite satisfying.

Another book with the same major title exists, written by Stuart Hall and Paddy Whannel. It is a detailed presentation of the popular arts as the authors perceive them rather than an anthology. The approach is an integrated one with film examples and references used throughout the text. The effort, scholarship, and originality found here makes for the difference between a good book (the Deers' volume) and an excellent one (the Hall-Whannel volume).

4988 *Popular Cinematography.* by Langlands, Thomas F. 95 p. illus. London: Foyle, 1926.

4989 *Popular Culture.* edited by Educational Film Library Association. 17 p. paper New York: Educational Film Library Association, 1977.

This filmography is related to the program presented by Courses By Newspapers entitled "Popular Culture: Mirror of American Life." Selected films that discuss television, Hollywood, TV commercials, news, music, sports, politics, women, lifestyles, mass media and other topics relating to pop culture are described. Some additional filmographies and six television archives are noted along with the distributors of the film.

4990 *Popular Culture.* by White, David Manning; and Pendleton, John. 300 p. Delmar, Calif.: Publishers, Inc., 1978.

This anthology includes several articles on film.

4991 *Popular Television and Film.* edited by Bennett, Tony; and Boyd-Bowman, Susan; and Mercer, Colin; and Woollacott, Janet. 320 p. London: British Film Institute (Zoetrope in U.S.), 1981.

The emphasis in this anthology prepared for an Open University course on popular culture is on television. There are five essays devoted to film.

4992 PORGY AND BESS. by Freiman, Ray. 36 p. illus. New York: Random-House, 1959.

This souvenir book published by Random House is a model for other publishers to emulate; photography, arrangement, art work, and content are all outstanding. Beginning with a tribute to producer Sam Goldwyn, who gets more acknowledgement than anyone else, the book uses stills from the 1959 film to outline the story. A biography of George Gershwin is followed by Deems Taylor's account of the creation of the opera, "Porgy and Bess." Leo Lerman provides additional information on changing DuBose Heyward's story from a book into a play and then into the Gershwin opera. Major cast members are given short biographical sketches; the production personnel fare somewhat better. Closing pages list the songs and complete cast and production credits.

4993 *Porno Star.* by Russell, Tina. 224 p. paper New York: Lancer Books, 1973.

The author has appeared in more than 75 full-length pornography films and is obviously well qualified to discuss the porno film business. Real names have been changed in the text and, since there are no pictures in the book, the question of authenticity arises. If porno filmmaking is really as the author describes it here, that any film ever gets made is amazing. The performers never seem to tire of sexual activity with other actors, crew members, and themselves.

4994 *Pornography: The Sexual Mirage.* by Drakeford, John W.; and Hamm, Jack. 189 p. illus. Nashville: Thomas Nelson, 1973.

Prepared for a religious audience, this volume calls for action against pornography and obscenity. The argument presented is weak, ineffectual, and vulnerable. A chapter entitled "Skin Flicks, Roughies, Kinkies, and Ghoulies—the Movie Mess" is an example of the unconvincing text. It begins with a recall of the golden age of films (1930-1950), and traces the changes within the industry through the next two decades. The death of the code, the rating system, an analysis of 37 films, and the eventual appearance of films on the TV screen are other concerns. All of the generalizations, the selected quotations, and the cliches are supported by cartoons which often contain biblical proverbs.

Instead of a discussion based upon the unbiased presentation of evidence, research, and contrasting opinion, the authors have opted for scare tactics, emotional appeal, and exaggeration. Much of what they present is either questionable, incorrect, or only partially revealed. The book becomes a disservice to intelligent discussion of what is admittedly a problem—but certainly not the one described herein. Not recommended.

4995 *Portrait of a Director.* by Seton, Marie. 350 p. illus. Bloomington, Ind.: Indiana University Press, 1970.

Indian director, musician and scenarist Satyajit Ray took five years to complete PATHER PANCHALI (1954). The dedicated efforts of Ray, himself, along with a history of the Ray family is offered in this biography. Many of the films mentioned are unknown in America and the unfamiliarity may limit the book's appeal.

4996 *Portrait of a Flying Yorkshireman.* by Knight, Eric M. 231 p. illus. London: Chapman and Hall, 1952.

A collection of letters from Eric Knight in the United States to Paul Rotha in England, edited by Rotha.

4997 *A Portrait of* ALL THE PRESIDENT'S MEN. by Hirshberg, Jack. 170 p. paper illus. New York: Warner Books, 1976.

This volume on the making of ALL THE PRESIDENT'S MEN (1976) correctly gives most of its attention to the pre-filming activities. Beginning with the actual Watergate incident, it traces the work of Bob Woodward and Carl Bernstein, the involvement of Robert Redford, the signing of Dustin Hoffman and the appointment of Alan Pakula as director. It is not until the tenth chapter that the actual filming is described. The concluding section tells of the post-filming activities and gives final statistics on the film.

Supporting the text are many full-color production stills taken by Stanley Tretick.

In this volume the reader is provided with an absorbing account of how a film is created. The thousands of decisions and compromises necessary are suggested,as well as the economic realities of film production. The superb visuals stress the intensity of effort given to such a project by the participants. Recommended.

4998 *A Portrait of Joan: The Autobiography of Joan Crawford.* by Crawford, Joan; and Ardmore, Jane Kesner. 239 p. illus. Garden City, N.Y.:Doubleday, 1962.

This autobiography of a very durable lady who rose from Cinderella to queen is a very careful account. The subject is always sympathetic, always working, and always the star of the story. Much attention is given to her films. Her comments about the people in her life are fascinating; those who have wronged her are inevitably given understanding and a royal pardon. The photographs are exceptional—the inclusion of the Wampus Baby Stars of 1926 is an act of courage. A filmography is given but there is no index. This is superstar autobiography written in a fan magazine manner. Joan Crawford, the creation of both the studio and herself, seems to have taken over the entire person of Lucille Le Sueur, and pretending has replaced living. Interesting.

4999   *A Portrait of the Artist: The Plays of Tennessee Williams.* by Hirsch, Foster. 121 p. Port Washington, N.Y.: Kennikat, 1978.

A title in the *Literary Criticism* series, this combination of biography and critical comment emphasizes Williams' plays. Film actors and adaptations are mentioned. The author has also written *Elizabeth Taylor, Edward G. Robinson,* and *The Hollywood Epic.*

5000   *Portraits.* by Avedon, Richard. illus. New York: Farrar, Straus, & Giroux, 1976.

A luxurious picture book that contains many full-size photographs, four fold-outs, and an essay by Harold Rosenberg.

5001   *The Portrayal of China and India on the American Screen, 1896-1955.* by Jones, Dorothy B. 129 p. Cambridge, Mass.: Center for International Studies, MIT, 1955.

This study deals with the evolution of Chinese and Indian themes, locales, and characters as portrayed on American screens during the first half of this century.

5002   *Positive Images.* by Wengraf, Susan; and Artel, Linda. 167 p. paper illus. San Francisco: Bootlegger Press, 1976.

This volume has as its subtitle "A Guide to Non-Sexist Films for Young People." Criteria for inclusion is based on one or more of the following feminist perspectives: (1) avoidance of stereotyped male/female behavior, attitudes, work, leisure, etc.; (2) recognition of women's achievements and contributions; (3) consideration of women's problems such as pregnancy, abortion, rape, etc.

The text is divided into four sections: films, video,-filmstrips and slide shows, and photographs. The first section on several hundred films constitutes the major portion of the book. Arranged alphabetically by film title, each entry contains running time, color format, distributor, rental/sale costs, date of release, suggested audience and a paragraph of annotation. Although the comments are mostly descriptive, some evaluation of the individual films is made occasionally. Distributor addresses, a bibliography for non-sexist education and a subject index complete the work. The book is illustrated with stills from the films.

This is a resource that has much value in planning film programs. The information has been well written and is conveniently arranged for easy use. Recommended.

5003   *Post Literate Man and Film Editing: An Application of the Theories of Marshall McLuhan.* by Underhill, Frederic. paper illus. Boston: School of Public Communication, Boston University, 1964.

5004   *A Postillion Struck By Lightning.* by Bogarde, Dirk. 268 p. illus. New York: Holt, Rinehart and Winston, 1977.

In most of his later films, it seemed Dirk Bogarde sought unusual/intellectual material rather than simply accepting commercial potboiler assignments. That predilection coupled with the fact that he has recognized talents as a poet, writer and artist may help to explain this memoir.

Bogarde has recalled his early life, relating many detailed incidents and anecdotes that are of slight interest. Can it be assumed that the literary form he has provided will make them appealing to the reader? Perhaps so. However, Bogarde is an actor known best for his films and it is this portion of his life that has the most fascination for readers. In this initial biographical volume he takes us only as far as World War II when he began his acting career on the British stage. He has provided some original drawings for the book which is partially indexed.

His determined literary style is overly apparent throughout. He is also very reticent and far too selective in choosing his material; a private person, he intends to remain so. What the reader gets is a kind of fictionalized biography written so that style smothers content. Perhaps the next volume will be more rewarding for those of us who have admired his film acting.

5005   POTEMKIN. by Eisenstein, Sergei M. 104 p. paper illus. New York: Simon & Schuster, 1968.

Script of the 1926 film directed by Eisenstein. Contains cast credits, an introduction by Eisenstein, and an historical article by Andrew Sinclair.

5006   THE BATTLESHIP POTEMKIN. edited by Marshall, Herbert. 385 p. illus. New York: Avon, 1978.

This anthology is devoted to Eisenstein's classic

film, POTEMKIN (1925). In an attempt to tell the story of the film, the editor has selected a group of international authors who have written articles which deal with such matters as the film's creation, its artistry, its social and political effects, and the varying critical reception accorded it. Illustrations include many frame enlargements from the film.

5007 *Powell, Pressburger and Others.* edited by Christie, Ian. 124 p. paper illus. London: British Film Institute, 1978.

Michael Powell and Emeric Pressburger are the major subjects of this anthology-appreciation.

5008 *Power.* edited by Maynard, Richard A. 224 p. paper illus. New York: Scholastic Book Services, 1974.

This volume contains scripts of the following films: MR. SMITH GOES TO WASHINGTON (1939), Frank Capra; A FACE IN THE CROWD (1957), Elia Kazan; and THE CANDIDATE (1972), Michael Ritchie.

5009 *Practical Cinematography and its Applications.* by Talbot, Frederick A. 282 p. illus. Philadelphia: J. B. Lippincott, 1913.

5010 *Practical Guide to Classroom Media.* by Linton, Dolores; and Linton, David. 118 p. paper illus. Dayton, Ohio: Pflaum, 1971.

Another attractive volume designed to stimulate teachers in the use of media for the classroom. One chapter deals with film and discusses how film works, choosing a projector, the nature of film, film criticism, film language, selecting filmmaking equipment, and student filmmaking. A list of publishers and distributors completes the chapter. Other sections of the book deal with radio, recordings, still photography and television. In addition, there are suggested procedures for selection, evaluation and administration of media for the classroom.

The chapter on film provides a good overview of film in the classroom. While other books in the *Pflaum* series cover the subject in much greater depth, this book can serve as an introduction for the new teacher. Highly recommended.

5011 *The Practical Guide to Holiday and Family Movies.* by Townsend, Derek. 174 p. paper illus. London: St. Paul, 1961.

5012 *Practical Hints on Acting for the Cinema.* by Platt, Agnes. 160 p. illus. London: Paul, 1921.

A detailed early guide on how to achieve success in film acting. Attention is given to peripheral areas such as film as art, an actor's point of view, acting as a profession, in addition to the usual topics of movement, gesture, make-up, dress, facial expression, etc.

5013 *A Practical Manual of Screen Playwriting.* by Herman, Lewis. 294 p. paper illus. Cleveland: World Pub. Co., 1951.

This is one of the classic books in film literature. Not only is it a literate, informed how-to-do-it guide, but it also contains some subtle comments on the professions of filmmaking and film-writing. It is also a book on the components of film art. Eminently readable, it is characterized by a common sense approach. Its three large headings will give an idea of the scope of the book: 1) dramaturgy, 2) the filmic components, and 3) writing the screenplay. An index and illustrations are included. Since its appearance in the early fifties, this volume has been consistently popular with the novice and the professional. Unhesitatingly recommended.

5014 *Practical Motion Picture Photography.* edited by Campbell, Russell. 160 p. paper illus. New York: A. S. Barnes, 1970.

A series of interviews with 16 professional cinematographers that results in a detailed discussion of the practical problems—film stocks, labs, filters, etc.—which face the cameraman. Many diagrams and photos.

5015 *Practically True.* by Thesiger, Ernest. illus. London: Heinemann, 1927.

This character actor with the chiseled, angular face was a bit premature in writing this autobiography in 1927, since he created many memorable roles in sound films for the next 35 years.

5016 *Practically True (Reminiscences).* by Thesiger, Ernest. 191 p. illus. London: William Heinmann, 1927.

An early autobiography written before Thesiger's debut as a film actor. On the stage since 1909, he began his film career in THE OLD DARK HOUSE (1932) and is probably best known as the tall, thin, angular man in the dark cloak in THE BRIDE OF FRANKENSTEIN (1935). Thesiger was still appearing in films up to the time of his death—his last was THE ROMAN SPRING OF MRS. STONE (1961).

5017   *Practising Law Institute Books (A Series).* paper New York: Practicsing Law Institute, 1973- .

Most of these volumes are derived from courses given to practicing attorneys. They contain legal information on motion pictures which is difficult to find elsewhere. The content is a mixture of comments, pertinent periodical articles, records of court cases, sample forms, etc. Among the titles published are *Legal and Business Problems of the Motion Picture Industry* (1973), *Legal and Business Problems of Financing Motion Pictures* (1976), *Packaging for Television and Motion Pictures* (1973), *Obscenity and the Law* (1974) and *Tax Sheltered Investments* (1973).

5018   *Preface to Film.* by Williams, Raymond; and Orrom, Michael. 129 p. London: Film Drama, 1954.

The relationship between films and the dramatic tradition is explored and some predictions are made.

5019   *Preliminary List of Educational, Scientific and Cultural Films Produced in Australia from 1940 to 1953.* compiled by National Library of Australia. 86 p. paper Canberra, Australia: National Library, 1954.

5020   *Preminger: An Autobiography.* by Preminger, Otto. 208 p. illus. Garden City, N.Y.: Doubleday, 1977.

One of Otto Preminger's theatrical talents is to say and do things which are controversial. His autobiography is an exception to this well-documented behavioral pattern, for it is a straightforward, factual narrative that avoids extremes in both opinion and emotion.

Preminger traces his career from birth in Vienna about 1906 to the making of his film, ROSEBUD, in 1975. Along the way he tells of his stage work, his acting roles, his films and his relationships with other show business personalities. Although the text is personal and opinionated, he is modest about his own accomplishments, saving most of his enthusiasm for other people and their talents.

The volume contains a few illustrations, a list of his stage productions, a filmography, and an index. It is a welcome addition to the appreciations of Preming-

er already written by Gerald Pratley, *The Cinema of Otto Preminger,* and Willi Frischauer's *Behind the Scenes of Otto Preminger.* With most of his films, Preminger's primary goal was to present an entertaining story told with careful craftsmanship. This volume follows that tradition. Recommended.

5021   *Preparation and Evaluation in the Use of a Series of Brief Films of Selected Demonstrations from the Introductory College Physics Course.* edited by Purdue Research Foundation. 40 p. paper illus. Lafayette, Ind.: Purdue Research Foundation, 1961.

5022   *Present Day Bulgarian Cinema.* by Racheva, Maria. 152 p. illus. Sofia, Bulgaria: Sofia Press, 1968.

This small volume traces the history of the Bulgarian cinema starting with KALIN THE EAGLE (1950) and concluding with A TASTE OF ALMONDS (1967). Themes, genres, and artists are considered and a few predictions are made. A filmography is included but there is no index. Picture quality and production values are poor.

5023   *Present Indicative: An Autobiography.* by Coward, Noel. 371 p. illus. London: William Heinemann, 1937.

5024   *Presenting Entertainment Arts: Stage, Film, Television.* 192 p. illus. Dubuque, Iowa: Kendall-Hunt, 1980.

5025   *Preserving the Moving Image.* by Sargent, Ralph W. 152 p. paper illus. Washington, D.C.: Corporation for Public Broadcasting, 1974.

Preserving and storing films and videotapes are the concerns of this handsome, informative volume. Nitrate-base film (in use until 1951) is known to decay after a period of storage. The failure to safeguard early films has resulted in a loss of over 60 percent of the theatrical films made in this country. This statistic is also applicable to early TV shows, newsreels, and documentaries.

After noting the restoration work of the major American film archives, this volume discusses how to keep film, its treatment and storage, conditions in the field and recommendations. In a second section new approaches and technologies for preservation are described. The final section deals with videotape.

Although much of the text demands some technical knowledge, the person who is familiar with film use and storage problems will have little difficulty in comprehension. This is a specialized book but one of great value to those concerned with custody and protection of a national treasure/resource/art—the American film. Recommended.

5026 *Presley: Entertainer of the Century.* by Anthony, James. illus. New York: Belmont-Tower, 1976.

5027 *A Presley Speaks.* by Presley, Vester. paper illus. Memphis: Wimmer, 1977.

Vester Presley was Elvis' uncle and keeper of the Gate at Graceland. His memoir comes in the plain paperback edition or, "For Those Who Really Care," in a deluxe version which is boxed, has an engraved cover, and is wrapped in a white satin scarf.

5028 *Preston Sturges: An American Dreamer.* by Ursini, James. 240 p. paper illus. New York: Curtis Books, 1973.

The full title of this book is *The Fabulous Life and Times of Preston Sturges, An American Dreamer.* That's a lot of words but in this case they are all appropriate. He wrote successful plays and film scripts, and later directed a series of films which were recognized almost immediately as minor film classics. In an attempt to explain the mystery of Sturges and what made him run, author Ursini has made use of interviews, Sturges memorabilia, the films, and persons who knew and wrote about Sturges. What emerges from this research is a much better than usual biography and a critical appreciation of the films.

Each major film is treated separately and is followed by reference notes. In addition, there is a filmography and a bibliography at the book's end which enhance the book's reference value. A short pictorial section makes the reader wish for more, since some of the films are not represented at all. The book, based on work done at UCLA, is readable, enjoyable, and rewarding. The text is respectful and the ultimate portrait of Sturges comes as much from his films as from his actual experiences. What he believed is expressed by his characters, and the Sturges blend of American Horatio Algerism with European cynicism is usually evident.

A fine book which is recommended.

5029 *The Pretend Indians: Images of Native Americans in the Movies.* by Bataille, Gretchen; and Silet, Charles L. P. paper illus. Ames, Iowa: Iowa State University Press, 1980.

5030 *Preview.* edited by Warman, Eric. illus. London: Andrew Dakers, 1946-

An annual which features portraits, articles, photobiographies, etc. The articles are fan magazine level, with titles such as "Who Says You Have To Be Handsome?" (Kirk Douglas), "Cars of the Stars," "Being a Film Star is a Problem" (Robert Walker), etc. The books are hardbound and many of the illustrations are in full color.

5031 *The Primal Screen.* by Sarris, Andrew. 337 p. New York: Simon and Schuster, 1973.

Sarris writes with style, wit, intelligence and a known viewpoint—all of which give him a kind of star quality. You know well ahead of time what the performance will be. In this collection, he has gathered writings from *Film Culture, Film Comment, The New York Times, Princeton Alumni Weekly, Columbia University Forum Moviegoer, The Drama Review, Mid-Century Arts Magazine, Sight and Sound* and, of course, *The Village Voice.* He tackles causes (answering Kael and "Raising Kane"), styles (Keaton, James Stewart, Max Ophuls), genres (The Musical, The Spectacular), politics (Z (1969) THE-BIRTH OF A NATION (1915)), tributes (von Sternberg, Garland, Lloyd), and literary authors (Kerouac, Orwell). There are nearly 50 articles in all. The book is indexed. Anyone who enjoys and admires Sarris will delight in this collection. Since that potential audience is quite large, the book can be enthusiastically recommended.

5032 *Primary Cinema Resources: An Index to Screen Plays, Interviews, and Special Collections at the University of Southern California.* compiled by Wheaton, Christopher D.; and Jewell, Richard B. 312 p. Boston: G.K. Hall, 1975.

This is an initial attempt to index some of the archival material on motion pictures held by the Cinema Library, Department of Special Collections at the University of Southern California. Obtained from film studios, performers and teachers, the material noted here consists mostly of scripts, taped interviews and special collections.

The first portion of the book is a listing of film script titles with release date, studio and writer indicated. If the script is part of a special collection, the key number of the individual who donated the material is noted. Numbers with corresponding names are provided in a preface page. In a later section the contents of each of these individual collections are described in varying detail.

Middle sections include a screen writer's index which indicates the author's name along with those scripts to be found in the USC Library, and a listing of the tape interviews alphabetically arranged by interviewee surname.

The type of materials found in each section is not strictly exclusive—for example, under interviews we find tapes of radio programs, panels, etc.; under screen writers we find an interview, etc. However, all the material is arranged to provide maximum access to the elements found in the many collections which make up the library.

The volume indicates the wealth of research material available at (and through) the University of Southern California Library. Here is a welcome reference volume that is highly recommended.

5033   *A Primer for Film-Making.* by Roberts, Kenneth H.; and Sharples, Win Jr. 546 p. paper illus. Indianapolis, Inc.: Bobbs-Merrill, 1971.

The subtitle, "A Complete Guide to 16 and 35mm Film Production," is modest for this oversized volume. Not only are all the elements of filmmaking covered thoroughly, but there are several outstanding supporting sections. Beginning with a discussion of budgets, the authors cover in succession the following topics: camera, lens, film, lighting, script, lab development, editing, cutting room, opticals, titles, sound, sound cutting room, sound mix, and printing the film.

A long list of recommended films, arranged chronologically by periods and listed under various countries, is the first appendix. An outline of the items to consider in preparing a budget follows. A most valuable glossary based on American standard nomenclature and a short bibliography complete the text. A detailed index to all the material is provided.

The authors' approach to their subject is broad and one applauds their inclusion and attention to theory, practice, creativity, technology, and human frailty. They are interested in telling you "how" but suggest that creativity, imagination and experience must be added to technical proficiency in order to become a true filmmaker. Evidence of this attitude can be found in the bibliography, which lists no technical books but mostly titles that deal with film aesthetics and theory. The recommended films again underline this view.

By reason of its comprehensive content, treatment, approach, and arrangement, this volume can be enthusiastically recommended. The serious filmmaker will probably want to own a personal copy, more as a continuing reference than as a reading experience.

5034   *A Primer for Playgoers.* by Wright, Edward A. 270 p. illus. Englewood Cliffs, N.J.: Prentice-Hall, 1958.

To the author, theatre includes cinema and television as well as "the living theatre." Although the major emphasis is on the legitimate stage, much of what is said can be applied to film. One chapter points out the differences between the two. Many of the illustrations are of film directors. A glossary and an index are included. Readable, interesting and informative.

5035   *A Primer of Visual Literacy.* by Dondis, Donis A. 180 p. illus. Cambridge, Mass.: MIT Press, 1973.

According to Ms. Dondis, the invention of the camera has brought about a dramatic new view of communication and education. This primer is designed to teach students the interconnected arts of visual communication. The ability to see and read visual data is one broad definition of visual literacy. One method of increasing that ability is to make and design visual messages—art works, craftwork, graphics, photographs, films, and television programs. The book gives attention to all these areas in a sound text and, of course, many visual examples.

5036   *The Prince: The Public and Private Life of Laurence Harvey.* by Hickey, Des; and Smith, Gus. 296 p. illus. London: Leslie Frewin, 1975.

This biography, based on interviews with relatives, coworkers, etc., is illustrated and indexed. Its original title was *The Prince: Being The Public and Private Life of Larushka Mischa Skikne, A Jewish Lithuanian Vagabond Player, Otherwise Known as Laurence Harvey.*

5037   THE PRINCE AND THE SHOWGIRL. by Rattigan, Terence. 127 p. paper illus. New York: New American Library, 1957.

Script of the 1957 film directed by Lawrence Olivier.

5038 *Princess Grace.* by Bobyns, Gwen. 276 p. illus. New York: David McKay, 1976.

Although Grace Kelly had a short career spanning six years in Hollywood, it was by no means a minor one. In eleven films she played mostly leading roles opposite established male stars (Gable, Cooper, Stewart, Crosby, Grant, etc.), and was guided by such directors as Hitchcock, Ford, and Zinneman. An Academy Award for COUNTRY GIRL (1954) adds to this fairy tale experience.

The other parts of her life are similarly romantic. Born to a wealthy Philadelphia family, she went to study modeling in New York, and then went on to Hollywood. After that she married Prince Rainier of Monaco and has devoted herself to the role of Princess ever since.

This unauthorized biography leans heavily on previously published materials and upon interviews with persons who have known or worked with Grace Kelly. Two other biographies appeared about the time of her marriage, McCallum's *That Kelly Family*, and Gant Gaither's *Princess of Monaco*. This nicely illustrated volume covers her life up to the early seventies. The book also contains a useful index.

The author's theme seems to be that Grace Kelly, the woman of fire and ice, was created solely by Grace Kelly and no one else. Her detailed substantiation of this theory will be of interest to certain readers. Acceptable.

5039 *Princess Grace Kelly.* by Newman, Robert. 138 p. paper Derby, Conn.: Monarch, 1962.

An early, unauthorized biography of Grace Kelly, this original paperback is based largely on matters of public record.

5040 *see 5039*

5041 *Princess of Monaco: The Story of Grace Kelly.* by Gaither, Gant. 176 p. illus. New York: Holt, 1957.

For approximately 70 pages this book relates Grace Kelly's early life and Hollywood career. The remaining sections are devoted to her life as a princess. Even the short account of her film work consists mostly of brief mentions or surface anecdotes. The Academy Award gets two paragraphs, in which the author explains why she won. It seems she never missed a cue or a day of shooting, indicating a responsibility to her profession. She was cooperative and well liked. Anyone interested in the validity of the Awards should watch Garland in A STAR IS BORN (1954) and Kelly in THE COUNTRY GIRL (1954) for a comparison of excellence with competence.

A positive feature of the book is the three picture sections which total up to 48 pages. There is no index. The content is a surface recital of facts and trivia that sounds all too sticky to believe. Add to that a bland, worshipful writing style and all that is left are the illustrations. They alone make the book merely acceptable.

5042 *Principles of Cinematography.* by Wheeler, Leslie James. 440 p. illus. London: Fountain Press, 1963.

A popular motion picture handbook that has gone through several editions. Deals with equipment, principles, special effects, processing, etc.

5043 *Principles of Cinematography.* by Wheeler, Leslie. 440 p. illus. Hastings-On-Hudson, N.Y.: Morgan, 1969.

A standard work which covers the field of cinematography with remarkable thoroughness. The processes and the apparatus for the production and exhibition of motion pictures are explained, along with a short history of each subject. Chapter topics include: general principles, cameras, emulsions, processing equipment, quality control, sensitometry, printing film, reduction process, special effects, editing, projectors, sound, processing sound film, and sound reproduction. A bibliography of more than 1000 entries is especially valuable. One of the outstanding books on cinematography, this volume is highly recommended.

5044 *Principles of Visual Anthropology.* edited by Hochings, Paul. 521 p. illus. Chicago: Aldine-Atherton, 1975.

Ethnography, the use of motion pictures in anthropological study, is advocated in this book. A special section is devoted to this effective tool for ethnological investigation and teaching.

5045 *Print, Image and Sound: Essays on Media.* edited by Burke, John Gordon. 181 p. Chicago, Ill.: American Library Association, 1973.

A review of five areas of media in the sixties: journalism, educational television, rock music, little magazines, and cinema. A bibliography follows each.

Charles T. Samuels is the author of the article on film, "Cinema in the Sixties." This was the decade of "The Director" and Samuels emphasizes that in both the text and the filmography; the latter is arranged by director rather than by national cinema, genre, or film title. As with any such survey, there are omissions (Visconti, Rossen, Frankenheimer, Rohmer) and questionable inclusions (Jessua, Heifetz, Carlsen, Troell). His strong preference for Kubrick's STRANGELOVE (1963) over 2001 (1969) is never justified in the text, nor is the inclusion of Truffaut's THE BRIDE WORE BLACK (1967) with his three early classics (and wasn't THE 400 BLOWS (1959) a film of the late fifties?). In any event, the purpose of the articles is to give an overview of film in the sixties, and this it accomplishes. Acceptable.

5046   *The Private Antitrust Suit in American Business Competition: A Motion Picture Industry Case Analysis.* by Cassady, Ralph, Jr.; and Cassady, Ralph. 66 p. paper Los Angeles: Bureau of Business and Economic Research, Univ. of California, 1964.

5047   *Private Elvis.* edited by Cortez, Diego. 200 p. paper illus. Edison, N. J.: Two Continents, 1978.

A collection of 130 pictures, most of which show Elvis Presley during his Army service in Germany.

5048   *The Private Eye, the Cowboy, and the Very Naked Girl.* by Crist, Judith. 292 p. New York: Holt, Rinehart & Winston, 1968.

This volume is subtitled "Movies from CLEO to CLYDE", and samples five years of Judith Crist's outstandingly excellent film criticism. CLEOPATRA (1963) and BONNIE AND CLYDE (1967) are the representations of the change in films over that period —from empty spectacle to artistic achievement. Author Crist writes in a sharp, clear, sometimes severe style. Whatever her opinion happens to be, she is always able to offer intelligent justification for it. She is entertaining and, at the same time, quite true to herself and her values. In certain ways, her work resembles that of James Agee. A general index is provided. Highly recommended.

5049   *The Private Life of Greta Garbo.* by Palmborg, Rilla Page. 282 p. illus. Garden City, N.Y.: Doubleday, 1931.

In the introduction of this 1931 biography, the author writes: "This story will reveal the real Greta Garbo, the poor little Greta Garbo in Sweden, the Great Greta Garbo in Hollywood, Greta Garbo as her few intimate friends know her, Greta Garbo in her own home, a most amazing life of a great and most amazing person." The author had some moments with Garbo on a few occasions but the major sources of material are Garbo's cook and butler of this period, Gustaf and Sigrid Norin. John Loder and Wilhelm Sorensen tell a bit more but the rest of the material apparently comes from studio biographies, press releases, and newspaper reports.

For such an early biography, this one has some virtues. It is flawed by its style and the elusiveness of its subject. Acceptable as supplementary material.

5050   THE PRIVATE LIFE OF HENRY VIII. by Biro, Lajos; and Wimperis, Arthur. 108 p. illus. London: Methuen, 1934.

Script of the 1933 film directed by Alexander Korda.

5051   *Private Lives of Movie Stars.* edited by Paige, Ethel. 48 p. illus. New York: Arco, 1945.

Five subjects—Hedy Lamarr, James Cagney, Barbara Stanwyck, Red Skelton, and Lucille Ball—are treated in this collective biography.

5052   *The Private Reader: Selected Articles and Reviews.* by Van Doren, Mark. 416 p. New York: Holt, 1942.

Contains several film reviews.

5053   *Private Screenings.* by Simon, John. 316 p. New York: Macmillan, 1967.

Savage, unsparing, vitriolic, intelligent, witty, passionate—all these words describe the critical writings of John Simon. He is also an excellent teacher in that he will irritate, provoke, and finally please; reading him seriously will probably cause a change in anyone's behavior. Sample comment: "THE CHELSEA GIRLS (1966) is a testimonial to what happens when a camera falls into the hands of an aesthetic, moral, and intellectual bankrupt." These reviews are of films released during the sixties (1963-1966). Essays on criticism, Godard and the "cinematic non-woman" are included, as is a most useful index. For anyone interested in film criticism, this book is essential. Highly recommended for all readers.

5054   *The Privilege of His Company: Noel Coward Remembered.* by Marchant,

William. 276 p. illus. New York: Bobbs-Merrill, 1975.

Although there are only a few paragraphs pertaining to his film appearances, this volume is noted here because of the portrait of Noel Coward it presents. Rather than a biography, it is simply a personal portrait painted by detailed descriptions of Coward in a few selected situations. For example, his handling of a boorish actor, Laurence Harvey, tells more about the man's nature and true personality than any listing of his many accomplishments.

Marchant's adroit and sympathetic treatment of what is really a series of relatively brief encounters with Coward once again shows his skill as a sensitive, perceptive dramatist. The illustrations consist mostly of Coward posed either alone or with celebrity friends. Reproduction quality is adequate. The absence of an index detracts from the overall value of the book. Marchant's memoir deals with both the public and private faces of Noel Coward. It adds a considerable dimension to the picture already established by other writers and by Coward himself. Acceptable.

5055 *The Producer of the Motion Picture.* by Shah, L. P. 78 p. paper Bombay: Roopak Publications, 1951.

Originally written for the film department of the University of Southern California, this text deals with the producer and his role in the motion picture industry. Topics include production problems, the star system, publicity, salaries, sociological problems, censorship, legal matters, stages of production, etc.

5056 *Producing, Financing, and Distributing Film.* by Baumgarten, Paul A.; and Farber, Donald C. 198 p. New York: Drama Book Specialists, 1973.

Nearly everything you always wanted to know about the legal side of producing, financing and distributing films is considered in this most practical book. Early on, the authors state the impossibility of covering everything and opt to present a base upon which the concerned individual can build. A sampling of chapter headings indicates the range of the material—acquisition of a literary property; the screenplay agreement; the agent; production-distribution agreement; gross and net receipts; other forms of financing; production agreements with talent; director's agreement; music; etc.

The presentation is completely straightforward and avoids any intrusion of narrative or anecdote. Al-

though many unfamiliar terms are used, the author's text is comprehensible and relatively easy to follow. The book is not illustrated or indexed. For anyone interested in commercial filmmaking, the book is essential. It should be required reading in all the colleges which grant degrees in film. Acceptable.

5057 *Producing Industrial Films.* by De-Witt, Jack. 148 p. illus. New York: A. S. Barnes, 1968.

Another volume on filmmaking, this one differs somewhat in emphasizing the industrial film. Although the claim is made by the publisher that there is much for the home-movie maker in the book, this is not evident. It is for the serious businessman who has a responsibility for representing some aspect of his company through film. Since the book has an easy-to-read narrative, many good illustrations, a glossary of terms, and a reprinting of the standards used by film studios and labs, it has much value for the advanced filmmaker.

5058 *Producing School Movies.* by Child, Eleanor; and Finch, Hardy. 151 p. illus. New York: Appleton, 1941.

A manual on producing amateur films, designed for students and teachers.

5059 *Production and Use of Classrooms on Film Versus Traditional Observation in Teacher Education.* by Painter, William I. 16 p. paper Akron, Ohio: University of Akron, 1961.

5060 *Professional Association in the Mass Media.* compiled by Division of Free Flow of Information, UNESCO. 206 p. paper Paris: UNESCO, 1959.

A handbook listing press, film, radio and television organizations.

5061 *The Professional Cine Photographer.* by Clairmont, Leonard. 154 p. paper illus. Hollywood: Ver Halen, 1956.

Written for the professional, this volume treats such topics as cameras, lenses, filters, lighting, composition, special effects, titles, etc. A glossary is included.

5062 *Professional Cinematography.* by Clarke, Charles G. 183 p. illus. Hollywood, Calif.: American Society of Cinematographers, 1968 (1964).

Author Clarke had a long career as a cameraman in the Hollywood studios and his experience, sensitivity, and maturity serve him well in this book. The coverage is broad, including topics such as equipment, special effects, lighting, composition, and, surprisingly, personal relationships. The many diagrams and illustrations add much to this superior volume. The content may be somewhat advanced for the beginner but it will serve the advanced student admirably.

5063 *Professional Filmmaking.* by Ewing, Sam; and Abolin, R. W. 251 p. illus. Blue Ridge Summit, Pa.: TAB Books, 1974.

The first impression of this volume is not at all positive. An inexpensive brown binding encloses a text and illustrations printed on a cheap pulpy paper. Further examination shows that many of the photographs are poorly reproduced. However, a reading of the text will tend to minimize the economical production and poor visuals. Written in an informal, chatty fashion, the content covers the field of filmmaking in a casual but comprehensive fashion. Practical advice, sensible opinion and non-technical instruction are offered along with occasional anecdotes, stories or maxims. A glossary and an index support this most readable text. In summary, this is an above-average text on filmmaking weakened by the production given it. Perhaps subsequent editions can be upgraded so that the book can be recommended rather then being called only acceptable.

5064 *Professional Quality on Amateur Reversal Film.* by Smethurst, Phillip C. 104 p. illus. London: Link House, 1939.

A guide to exposing motion picture film.

5065 *Professional Secrets: An Autobiography of Jean Cocteau.* by Cocteau, Jean. 331 p. illus. New York: Farrar, Straus & Giroux, 1970.

Drawn from Cocteau's writings by Robert Phelps, this volume was translated from the French by Richard Howard and includes bibliographical references.

5066 *Professional 16/35MM Cameraman's Handbook.* by Carlson, Verne; Carlson, Sylvia. 383 p. illus. New York: American Photographic Book Pub. Co., 1970.

As the title suggests, this volume is written primarily for the professional cinematographer. After six concise chapters on field and set operations, the major section considers the currently available camera systems in both gauges. In addition to describing many characteristics and features of each camera, the loading and threading operation for every one is also shown. The final chapter looks at lenses and, as an appendix, there is a three-page glossary. Good illustrations are placed throughout the volume. This is an excellent reference book for all filmmakers justified by the wealth of information, advice, and problem-shooting offered. Highly recommended.

5067 *Professional Training of Film Technicians.* by Lods, Jean. 155 p. paper New York: UNESCO, 1951.

A survey of the education of film technicians in 1951. It includes the history, background, schools, institutes available, etc.

5068 *Professional Writer's Teleplay/ Screenplay Format.* by Coopersmith, Jerome. 25 p. paper New York: Writer's Guild of America (East), 1978.

Succinct advice and guidance on how to prepare a professional script.

5069 *Profiles and Personalities.* by Noble, Peter. 124 p. illus. London: Brownlee, 1946.

A collection of 30 character sketches of British performers and directors. Written immediately after World War II, the book features such names as Noel Coward, Carol Reed, Laurence Olivier, Vivien Leigh, J. Arthur Rank, etc.

5070 *Projecting Sound Pictures.* by Nadell, Aaron. 265 p. illus. New York: McGraw-Hill, 1931.

A practical textbook for projectionists and managers. Deals with sound motion pictures—the apparatus needed and how it works. Published at the time when sound-on-film became the accepted standard.

5071 *The Projection of England.* by Tallents, Stephen. 46 p. paper London: Olen Press, 1955 (1932).

This is a plea for the study of the national projection —image, public relations, good will, etc.—of Great Britain via film, print, cable, etc. The author cites the Russian's use of film as a model to follow using POTEMKIN (1925), SOIL (1930), STORM OVER ASIA (1928) and other films as examples. Originally published in 1932 by Faber and Faber.

5072 *Projectionist's Manual.* compiled by Bureau of Naval Personnel. 96 p. paper illus. Washington, D.C.: U.S. Government Printing Office, 1964.

Published for service personnel, this handy book offers much practical information and several diagrams on 16mm projection.

5073 *Projectionists' Programmed Primer.* by Yeamans, George T. paper illus. Muncie, Ind.: Ball State Bookstore, 1969.

Since its publication in 1969, this self-instructional program has been used with thousands of students throughout the United States and Canada. Its goal is to teach the basic principles of using the opaque, overhead, slide, filmstrip and motion picture projectors. Screens for projection are also discussed. By constant trial and revision of the program the average error rate found in testing has been minimized to less than five percent.

The program consists of nine sections—five of which are pertinent to motion picture projection. Titles and usual completion times are: projection systems (11 minutes); motion pictures (19 minutes); projection lamps (6 minutes); lenses (8 minutes) and projection screens (16 minutes).

Appendices include a 16mm projector check list, a 16mm projector trouble analyzer, a maintenance check list, a film damage check list, and a glossary of projection terms. Frames are clearly printed and the drawings are easy to comprehend.

This is a tested self-instructional program that is invaluable for the training of personnel who deal with motion picture film. Highly recommended.

5074 *Propaganda.* by Rhodes, Anthony. 319 p. illus. New York: Chelsea House, 1976.

This study of the methods used to persuade mass audiences during World War II includes motion pictures.

5075 *Propaganda and the Nazi War Film.* by Kracauer, Siegfried. 90 p. paper New York: Museum of Modern Art Film Library, 1942.

Kracauer later used this material as a supplement in his volume, *From Caligari to Hitler.*

5076 *Propaganda on Film: A Nation at War.* by Maynard, Richard A. 147 p. paper illus. Rochelle Park, N.J.: Hayden, 1975.

This anthology, a title in the *Film Attitudes and Issues* series, is an exploration of the relationships between theatrical films and political propaganda, specifically during periods of war. An introduction discusses propaganda characteristics and how film can be adapted for political use. POTEMKIN (1925) and TRIUMPH OF THE WILL (1935) are noted as early uses of cinematic propaganda. Selected American propaganda films from both World Wars are reviewed and a section on films made during cold wars concludes the volume. A short filmography and few rental sources are appended.

Some good materials have been selected to provide background, example, and information on a topic vital to our times. The study and subsequent recognition of propaganda should be a part of the secondary school curriculum. This volume will assist any such study by its intelligently structured examination of propaganda in the theatrical film. Highly recommended.

5077 *A Proper Job.* by Aherne, Brian. 355 p. illus. Boston: Houghton, Mifflin, 1969.

A well-written autobiography with the emphasis on theatre rather than films, this volume is a bit more philosophical than most. Public fickleness, fading fame, enforced idleness, loneliness, etc., are all given some attention. The illustrations are very good. It is a bit surprising to note the many mediocre films in which Aherne appeared. His quality films were few and this may explain his emphasis on theatre. His celebrity, however, rests upon his films. Not much has been added to cinema literature with this book.

5078 *Proposals for the Setting Up of a British Film Authority.* edited by Interim Action Committee on the Film Industry. 14 p. paper London: Her Majesty's Stationery Office, 1978.

A report from the committee chaired by Sir Harold Wilson.

5079 *The Proust Screenplay.* by Pinter, Harold; and Losey, Joseph; and Bray, Barbara. 177 p. paper New

York: Grove Press, 1977.

An unfilmed script of Marcel Proust's *A La Recherche Du Temps Perdu* (*Remembrance of Things Past*) is presented here along with a short introduction by Pinter.

5080 *P.S. I Love You.* by Sellers, Michael; and Sellers, Sarah; and Sellers, Victoria. 238 p. illus. New York: Dutton, 1981.

A prejudiced biography of a mean, neurotic actor written by his son who claims to have loved him. Seller's estate of several millions provides the sub text which has his widow, Lynne Frederick, as villainess who manipulated Sellers into making a codicil to his will.

5081 PSYCHO. by Naremore, James. 87 p. paper Bloomington, Ind.: Indiana University Press, 1973.

One of a new series of *Filmguides*, this short volume is not as immediately impressive as the others. If the reader is willing to accept PSYCHO (1960) as "a study of smalltown repression that includes cinematic comments on the latent violence and prurience in the viewer himself," the book will be pleasing to him. If this attributing of values and messages to a film statement seems writer-originated rather than director-planned, one may have reservations. Just as there are unsatisfactory portions of the film—the final explanatory scenes which should belong to Norman (Anthony Perkins) but which are given to an unfamiliar psychiatrist—there are some analyses and critical judgements here that will suggest more questions than they answer.

The volume contains the usual elements of this series —cast credits, a plot outline, a short section on Hitchcock, some production notes, an analysis, and a summary critique. The Hitchcock filmography is a selected listing of titles and the bibliography includes reviews, books, interviews and articles from periodicals. The analysis, which is the author's major contribution, leans heavily on the filmscript and the book by Robert Bloch. This section is a combination of straightforward exposition and unconvincing critical comment. Since so much has been written about PSYCHO previously, it may be difficult to do anything except provide a broad overview and summary. The author does this in adequate fashion.

Since the film is quite available via rentals and TV showings, the book should be popular with readers and viewers. It does bring together enough pertinent material to make viewing or re-viewing the film an exciting experience. Acceptable.

5082 *The Public and the Motion Picture Industry.* by Seabury, William Marston. 340 p. New York: Jerome S. Ozer, 1971 (1926).

Originally published in 1926 by the Macmillan Company, this book is part of a reprint series *Moving Pictures—Their Impact on Society*, In his preface, Seabury states "The purpose of this work is to initiate ... an international movement to fix and establish the status of the motion picture in every nation of the world as a new public utility, and to require the industry without diminishing the popularity of its entertainment, to consecrate its service to the cultivation and preservation of the world's peace and the moral, intellectual and cultural development of all people." Quite an order!

To accomplish this, the author sets out to educate and familiarize the reader with film industry terms, vernacular, and practices. Topics explained include exhibition, first run, block booking, circuit booking, trade associations, film clubs, blacklists, boycotts, credit ratings, raw stock, Federal and State statutes, censorship, etc. The motion picture industry in England, France and other countries is described and the volume ends with a summary of a proposed law reflecting his purpose stated above. Much of the material discussed is obsolete and of interest only to the historian or scholar.

5083 *The Public Appreciates Movies.* compiled by Opinion Research Corporation. 23 p. paper illus. Princeton, N.J.: Opinion Research, 1957.

Highlights of a survey conducted in June and July of 1957 for the Motion Pictures Association of America.

5084 *The Public Arts.* by Seldes, Gilbert. 303 p. paper New York: Simon & Schuster, 1956.

The main theme of this book is consideration of the effects brought about by the introduction of television into American society. Radio and motion pictures are used as earlier examples of the communications revolution. The first 60 pages devoted to film are of interest to cinema scholars since they deal with film aesthetics such as movement, sound, magic and space.

5085 THE PUBLIC ENEMY. by Glasmon, Kubec; and Bright, John. 224 p. illus. Madison, Wisc.: University of Wisconsin Press, 1981.

The script of the 1931 film directed by William Wellman.

5086 *The Public Is Never Wrong: The Autobiography of Adolph Zukor.* by Zukor, Adolph; and Kramer, Dale. 310 p. illus. New York: G. P. Putnam's, 1953.

This motion picture pioneer recounts his life rather blandly. Written when he was an octogenarian, the book resembles the musings of an ancient one who remembers the pleasant things of life but is inclined to forget or minimize the negatives. The era emphasized is roughly the silent screen period from 1912 to 1928. Zukor's dealings with Pickford, Fairbanks, Swanson, DeMille, Valentino, Negri, etc. are described in some detail.

As head of Paramount Pictures, he knew the stars of that company intimately. He has chosen to be positive, kind, and sometimes saccharine about them in this book. His comments about the Paramount stars of the thirties and forties are thankfully brief but still embarrassing. This book, which could have and should have been a fine book, is a mediocrity. The content, style and illustrations are all "second feature" quality.

5087 *Public Library Subject Headings for 16mm Motion Pictures.* compiled by California Library Association. 49 p. paper Sacramento: California Library Association, 1974.

This is a revised edition of a subject headings list for 16mm motion pictures that was first published in 1970. It was prepared by the Subject Headings Committee (Audio Visual Chapter) of the California Library Association. In addition to helping professional catalogers, its other major purpose is to provide librarians with a resource that will aid in the creation of printed film catalogs. The listing was compiled by examining large numbers of printed catalogs in order to locate accepted general headings. Certain headings were included from *Sears List of Subject Headings* and others because of public familiarity and understanding. The information provided here has pertinence to the increasing numbers of film specialists and AV catalogers appearing on library staffs. It is a most useful tool that belongs in every library concerned with film service.

5088 *The Public Life of Sherlock Holmes.* by Pointer, Michael. illus. New York: Drake, 1975.

Here is another survey of the Sherlock Holmes character as he appeared in film, television, theatre, and radio.

Somewhat stronger in its coverage of foreign films than in its scope, the text omits quite a few American films.

5089 *The Public Relations of the Motion Picture Industry.* by Federal Council of Churches of Christ in America. 155 p. New York: Jerome S. Ozer, 1971 (1931).

When this report first appeared, its price was fifty cents and it was published by the Federal Council of Churches of Christ in America. It considers the organized relations of the industry to the public, those maintained largely by the Hays Office, circa 1931. Data for the report was obtained by interviews and correspondence. The Hays Office cooperated with the researchers and the study, which was begun in 1930, appeared in 1931. The topic headings indicate the range of the investigation: The General Situation ... in the Industry; The Corporate Structure... in the Industry; Trade Organizations ... in the Industry; Production Process and the Public Interest; Distribution Process and the Public Interest; Exhibition and the Public Interest; The National Board of Review; Legal Censorship; The Committee on Public Relations; The Open Door Policy; Publicity Methods; Organizations Cooperating with the Industry; Organizations Advocating Legal Regulation; Self Regulation in the Industry.

A short chapter indicating conclusions is offered and there is an index to complete the report. Of interest primarily to researchers and historians.

5090 *Published Radio, Television and Film Scripts: A Bibliography.* by Poteet, G. Howard. 245 p. Troy, N.Y.: Whitston, 1975.

As indicated in its title, this reference work deals only with published works. Both complete scripts and excerpts/fragments are considered. There are over 650 entries in the film section, arranged alphabetically by title from A NOUS LA LIBERTE (1931) to YOU ONLY LIVE ONCE (1937). Excerpts are identified by the inclusion of page numbers; the complete scripts are listed without pagination. An author index completes the book.

The book probably has more value for general communications collections than for film collections, since so much of the material presented here has appeared earlier in books devoted exclusively to film, i.e., McCarty (*Published Screenplays*), Gottesman and Geduld (*Guide Book to Film*), Bukalski

(*Film Research*), Rehrauer (*Cinema Booklist*), etc.

5091 *Published Screenplays: A Checklist.* by McCarty, Clifford. 127 p. Kent, Ohio: Kent State University Press, 1971.

In this reference book, there are 388 entries listing published screenplays, the definition of which encompasses both complete scripts and excerpts. Arranged alphabetically by title, each entry gives: title of script, production company and date, director, script authorship, original source, and title of book containing script or excerpt, author, publisher, year, and pages. For anyone interested in excerpts, the book has some value. The complete script information is available in other reference works along with much other material.

5092 *Pudovkin's Films and Film Theory.* by Dart, Peter. 237 p. illus. New York: Arno Press, 1974.

Intended as a source book or a compilation of materials on Pudovkin, this volume contains a section on Pudovkin's creative life, including synopses of his films, an article by Pudovkin on his early films, and a filmography. The second section includes two more articles by Pudovkin and some analyses of his montage theory. The group of illustrations which follows is poorly reproduced and, along with the typewritten pages of the text, gives evidence of minimum production expenditure by the publishers. An index is provided. Since this is a title in the *Dissertations on Film* series, there are also copious footnotes. Acceptable.

5093 *Puffin Asquith.* by Minney, R. J. 273 p. illus. London: Leslie Frewin, 1973.

This book carries the subtitle, "The Biography of the Honourable Anthony Asquith—Aristocrat, Aesthete, Prime Minister's Son and Brilliant Film-Maker." Other material on Asquith can be found in *Anthony Asquith* by Peter Noble (BFI, 1950) and *Anthony Asquith—A Tribute* by George Elvin (BFI, 1968).

5094 PULL MY DAISY. by Kerouac, Jack. 38 p. paper illus. New York: Grove Press, 1961.

A partial screenplay of the 1958 film directed by Al Leslie and Robert Frank. Stills and text-commentary from the film.

5095 *Puppet Animation in the Cinema: History and Technique.* by Holman, Bruce L. 120 p. illus. New York: A. S. Barnes, 1975.

Although there have been portions of other volumes on animation devoted to the subject, this is the only one in recent years to deal exclusively with puppet animation. Beginning with some definitions, clarifications and limitations of the genre, the author divides his text into separate sections on history and technique. The short history section presents a chronological survey of the filmmakers and films representative of this form. Emphasis is on the work during the last few decades of such European artists as Jiri Trnka, Karel Zeman, Zenon Wasilewski, Hermina Tyrlova, Ladislas Starevitch, Bretislav Pojar, Wlodzimierz Haupe, etc. But certain Western filmmakers such as George Pal are also mentioned.

The technique section offers separate treatment for each of the elements necessary for an animated puppetfilm: production, construction, forms, sets, scenery, props, camera, lighting, sound, context, character, and aesthetics. Important reference sources are provided in three filmography sections —the first being an alphabetical listing by title of the world's puppet films and the second, titles arranged chronologically by years, 1907-1970; the filmographies of eight leading puppet animators are given in the last section. A bibliography and an index complete the book.

An important, neglected subject in film study has been given an admirable and thorough treatment here. Presented in an easy, usable arrangement, the fascinating material cannot help but increase knowledge and appreciation of the animated puppet film. Illustrations in the book range from stills to storyboards and filmmaker portraits. All are acceptably reproduced. Highly recommended.

5096 *Puppets and People.* by Wilson, S. S. 170 p. illus. San Diego, Calif. :A. S. Barnes, 1980.

Jim Danforth describes this volume as "an accurate, concise, and objective explanation of the methods used to create model-animation effects." A subtitle, "Dimensional Animation Combined With Live Action in the Cinema," appears on the title page. Both refer to the technique by which films such as KING KONG (1933) are made. The technique, which has been used in only 50 or so feature films to date, is described in detail in discussions of the construction of the puppets, the measure and control of each movement, and the combination of the puppet animation with live action. Explanations are given of such cinematic processes as rear projection, front projection, static matte, traveling matte, the electronic printer, etc. Finally, the author argues for story quality and puppet personality. A filmography and a bibliography are included with many illustrations and sketches.

The discussion by Wilson of this particular special effect is fascinating throughout. Although he is dealing with a complex technical process, his text is remarkably clear. The attention given to film history and aesthetics with regard to puppet animation-live action adds further distinction to his impressive exposition.

5097 *Pure Cinema.* by Park, William. 16 p. paper Bronxville, N.Y.: Sarah Lawrence College, 1972.

This short essay is noted here for two reasons. Primarily, it is an interesting statement on types of film—the movie, the documentary and the avant-garde. The latter genre receives the most attention, but the concluding paragraph predicts the persistence of all three by stating, "Pure cinema is any well-made and thoughtful film, regardless of the quarter from which it appears." Secondly, the publication is the first in a series of occasional pieces designed to communicate Sarah Lawrence faculty thinking to alumnae, parents and friends—an idea to be applauded.

5098 *Pursuits of Happiness: The Hollywood Comedy of Remarriage.* by Cavell, Stanley. illus. Cambridge, Mass.: Harvard University Press, 1981.

Seven classic films of the thirties and forties dealing with remarriage are examined for cinematic techniques and the themes of masculiniy, feminism, interdependence, liberty, etc. Katharine Hepburn appears frequently.

5099 *Put Money in Thy Purse.* by MacLiammoir, Michael. 258 p. illus. London: Methuen, 1952.

A diary made while filming the Orson Welles' version of OTHELLO (1951). The author played Iago in the film. Contains a preface by Welles.

5100 PYGMALION. by Shaw, Bernard. 125 p. paper illus. Baltimore, Md.: Penguin Books, 1951.

Script of the 1938 film which was directed by Anthony Asquith and Leslie Howard.

5101 *The Illustrated History of the Movies (A Series).* paper illus. New York: Pyramid, Harcourt Brace Jovanovich.

This impressive series or original paperbacks resembles and rivals the much more expensive *Citadel—The Films of...* series. Written with a sharp critical approach by film experts, the texts deals with the lives and careers of Hollywood actors and are superior to the Citadels. Picture quality varies a bit but is usually above average. Subjects include: Fred Astair, Ingrid Bergman, Humphrey Bogart, Marlon Brando, James Cagney, Charlie Chaplin, Claudette Colbert, Gary Cooper, Joan Crawford, Bing Crosby, Bette Davis, Doris Day, Olivia De Havilland, Marlene Dietrich, Kirk Douglas, W. C. Fields, Errol Flynn, Henry Fonda, Clark Gable, Greta Garbo, Ava Gardner, John Garfield, Judy Garland, Cary Grant, Jean Harlow, Rita Hayworth, Katharine Hepburn, Charlton Heston, William Holden, Karloff and Company, Gene Kelly, Burt Lancaster, Jack Lemmon, Carole Lombard, Myrna Loy, Ida Lupino, the Marx Brothers, Jeanette McDonald, Robert Mitchum, Marilyn Monroe, Paul Newman, Gregory Peck, Edward G. Robinson, Ginger Rogers, Rosalind Russell, Barbara Stanwyck, James Stewart, Elizabeth Taylor, Shirley Temple, Spencer Tracy, Lana Turner, John Wayne, Orson Welles and Mae West.

5102 *The Quality of Mercy: An Autobiography.* by McCambridge, Mercedes. 245 p. illus. New York: Times Books, 1981.

The author, who is in a constant state of anger, is still able to relate a quantity of entertaining anecdotes about her career and her personal problems. A tormented person who is a recovering alcoholic and a survivor of suicide, McCambridge once again provides a memorable performance.

5103 *The Quarterly Journal of The Library of Congress—Volume 37.* 503 p. paper Washington, D.C.: Government Printing Office, 1980.

Although the Journal is a periodical, established in 1943, the Summer-Fall issue of 1980 numbers 3-4, volume 37 is noted here. It resembles today's typical paperback book and deals mostly with film. It is an anthology of articles that have pertinence to the activities of the Library of Congress in the area of nonprint media. Motion picture topics include authenticating films, music for animated films, Scandinavian film reconstruction, the American Film Institute and the Library of Congress, opera singers as movie stars, voices from the silents, and filmmaking at Mutoscope and Biograph, 1900-1906

The remaining articles deal with recordings, the Armed Forces, radio service, and television programs in the Library of Congress. A plastic recording is enclosed which accompanies the article on music for animated films. An index is also provided.

Production is superb with a high quality paper used and excellent reproduction of the visuals provided. This volume is superior to most of the original film paperbacks published today.

5104   QUARTET. by Sherriff, R.C. 189 p. illus. Garden City, N.Y.: Doubleday, 1949.

Contains the following original short stories by Somerset Maugham and the screenplays made from them by R.C. Sherriff: "The Facts of Life," (Smart); "The Alien Corn," (French); "The Kite," (Crabtree); and "The Colonel's Lady," (Annakin).

5105   QUE VIVA MEXICO. by Eisenstein, Sergi M. 89 p. illus. London: Vision Press, 1951.

Script of the uncompleted 1933 film directed by Eisenstein. With an introduction by Ernest Lindgren.

5106   QUE VIVA MEXICO. by Eisenstein, Sergi 89 p. illus. New York: Arno, 1972.

An introduction by Ernest Lindgren and a brief biographical sketch open this outline of the script for QUE VIVA MEXICO (1932). The script outline consists of six parts: a prologue, four novels, and an epilogue. The conclusion tells what happened after the filming was discontinued. Most of the script portion is devoted to visuals which are very poorly reproduced. Acceptable.

5107   *Quest for Serenity.* by Markopoulos, Gregory J. 79 p. paper New York: Film-Maker's Cinematheque, 1965.

A diary-type account of the life and times of an artist making an underground film. It is short, subjective, and passionate; as film literature, it is an unusual document although it is not for all readers.

5108   *Questions of Cinema.* by Heath, Stephen. 272 p. illus. Bloomington, Indiana: Indiana University Press, 1981.

Using psychoanalysis, semiotics and Marxism, Heath offers an analysis of film as a signifying practice. Using many film examples, the author discusses the Lacanian concept of suture and its importance to cinematic discourse.

5109   *Quick and Easy Guide to Making Home Movies.* by Knight, Bob. 98 p. paper illus. New York: Collier, 1965.

Directed at the beginning filmmaker, this volume considers techniques, effects, and equipment. Super 8 film equipment receives special attention.

5110   *Quintana and Friends.* by Dunne, John Gregory. New York: Dutton, 1979.

Dunne, the author of *The Studio*, here offers a collection of articles, some of which deal with cinema topics such as life in Hollywood, Pauline Kael, movie people, stuntmen, film scriptwriting, etc.

5111   *A Quite Remarkable Father.* by Howard, Leslie Ruth. 307 p. illus. New York: Harcourt, Brace & Co., 1959.

The importance of Leslie Howard as a film actor and his kindness in helping William Gargan, Bette Davis, Humphrey Bogart, Ingrid Bergman, and many others during their early careers are mentioned only briefly here. His superior films OF HUMAN BONDAGE (1934), THE PETRIFIED FOREST (1936), GONE WITH THE WIND (1939), INTERMEZZO (1939), and PYGMALION (1938) also receive scant attention. Instead, the emphasis again is on stage performance with liberal doses of social and family life added. A few adequate pictures and an index which mixes film and play titles without category identification completes this biography. Limited interest because of the inappropriate treatment of such an important subject.

5112   QUO VADIS. 18 p. paper illus. New York: Al Greenstone, 1951.

This older example of a souvenir book is characterized by the unnatural color process used in reproducing the photographs. Attention is given to the story, the filmmaking, the cast, the production personnel, the novel, and the music. One of the titles used in the book describes it best— "Rome Burns Again."

5113   *The Quotations of W. C. Fields.* compiled by Lewis, Martin. 160 p. paper illus. New York: Drake Publishers, 1976.

This collection of quotations is arranged topically under such headings as money, dogs, children, drinking, etc. A short introduction to each section gives background or biographical information that serves to explain in part the origin of Fields' attitudes and philosophies on a particular subject.

Supporting the collection is a fine assortment of visuals and a short bibliography.

This volume is an exception to the usual Fields' publications; by its structure, selection, supporting text and excellent visuals, it offers the reader a valid suggestion of Fields' unique personality. Readers will not only be pleased by the overall quality of the book, but will also be entertained by its content. Recommended.

5114 *Radie's World.* by Harris, Radie. 288 p. illus. New York: G. P. Putnams, 1975.

Radie Harris is known, primarily, as the writer responsible for "Broadway Ballyhoo," a gossip column which has appeared in *The Hollywood Reporter* for many years. In this memoir, she combines autobiography with anecdote, the latter involving legendary stars and personalities. As her story progresses, she devotes individual sections to Garbo, Tyrone Power, Crawford, Garland and Minnelli, Audrey Hepburn, Rex Harrison and Kay Kendall, Elizabeth and Richard, Tallulah, Streisand, Bogart and Bacall, Ingrid Bergman, Mike Todd, Monroe, Katharine Hepburn, George Bernard Shaw, Vivien Leigh, Noel Coward, and Gertrude Lawrence. Many other celebrities are mentioned.

The book's illustrations show the author in the company of the stars, and an index is provided.

Since Harris has written the type of material found here for so long, she is quite good at it. Most readers will find her entertaining, honest and loyal in the reporting of her relationships with the stars.

5115 *Radio and Movie Productions.* by Yerian, John Cameron. 45 p. paper illus. Chicago: Children's Press, 1975.

This volume, designed for younger readers, contains illustrated instructions for choosing equipment and producing a radio broadcast and a motion picture. A shooting script is included along with a radio script.

5116 *The Radio City Music Hall.* by Francisco, Charles. 208 p. illus.

New York: E. P. Dutton, 1979.

In this oversized history of the "world's greatest theater," Charles Francisco traces his story from idea to building to success, decline and possible demolition. Much attention is given to the films which have played the Hall—the hits and the flops. An appendix lists all the films shown. Anecdotes, factual information, comment and almost 150 illustrations help the author in his attempt to capture the essence of this magnificent showplace. The volume is indexed.

5117 *Radio, Motion Picture and Reading Interests: A Study of High School Pupils.* by Sterner, Alice P. 102 p. paper illus. New York: Bureau of Publications, Teachers College, Columbia University, 1947.

5118 *Radiomovies, Radiovision, Television.* by Jenkins, Charles F. 143 p. illus. Washington, D.C.: National Capital Press, 1929.

A hard-to-find volume by one of the pioneers in motion picture cinematography, this volume deals with possibilities in the transmission of visual images through the air.

5119 RAIDERS OF THE LOST ARK: The Illustrated Screenplay. edited by Kasdan, Lawrence. 128 p. illus. New York: Ballantine, 1981.

A script of the 1981 film directed by Steven Spielberg.

5120 *Railways in the Cinema.* by Huntley, John. 168 p. illus. London: Ian Allan, 1969.

This is a detailed survey of films which contain scenes of railways. Silent films (1895-1928), sound films (1929-1969), short films, newsreels, and television are considered. An annotated index of films is appended. This is a very specialized topic treated in a superior manner.

5121 *The Rain Girl: The Tragic Story of Jeanne Eagels.* by Doherty, Edward J. 313 p. illus. Philadelphia: Macrae Smith, 1930.

5122 *Rainbow: The Stormy Life of Judy Garland.* by Finch, Christopher. 255 p. paper illus. New York: Grosset and Dunlap, 1975.

It is difficult to approach another book about Judy Garland since her life and career have already been treated in detailed fashion by Anne Edwards, James Juneau, Gerold Frank, Al Di Orio, Brad Steiger, Joe Morella, and others. This volume, late as it may be, is probably the most satisfying. Garland as performer and as person are the themes, with equal attention given to both. The book's strength are the author's analytical accounts of Garland's experiences and an impressive collection of photographs that practically tells the Garland legend without words. The impressive selection of visuals includes many rare candids and informal shots, all of which are sharply reproduced. Their intelligent placement throughout the book correlates them effectively with the text.

Supporting his analyses, the author has included a wide range of references and quotations which gives the book the quality of validity based on research. His personal evaluations of films and performances are occasionally vulnerable, e.g., A STAR IS BORN (1955) is called "a disappointing movie, full of marvelous things but fatally flawed." All in all, the volume supplies about the best Garland coverage to date. The well-balanced use of word and picture presents an objective portrait of the legendary performer devoid of the sensationalism and sentimentality that marred earlier volumes. Recommended.

5123   *Ralph Richardson.* by Hobson, Harold. 98 p. paper illus. London: Rockliff, 1958.

An illustrated study of Richardson's work, with a list of his appearances on stage and film.

5124   *Ralph Richardson.* by Hobson, Harold. 98 p. illus. New York: Macmillan, 1958.

5125   *Ralph Steiner: Filmmaker and Still Photographer.* by Zuker, Joel Stewart. 453 p. illus. New York: Arno, 1978.

It is unusual to find a critical biography such as this one in the *Dissertations on Film* series. Written at New York University in 1976, the study is based on interviews, correspondence, actual lectures, and print research. Known primarily as one of the photographers of THE PLOW THAT BROKE THE PLAINS (1936) and THE CITY (1939), Steiner was a founder in 1936 of Frontier Films along with Pare Lorentz, Willard Van Dyke, Jay Leyda and others. Earlier he directed Elia Kazan in a short film, PIE IN THE SKY (1934), which is reconstructed here by frame enlargements and a shot-by-shot study.

After a biographical chapter, the story is logically divided into separate sections which treat his work as a still photographer, an experimental filmmaker, a political filmmaker, and a documentary filmmaker. A summary and some conclusions are added.

A generous number of appendixes offer information on collections and exhibitions of his work. A reconstruction of CAFE UNIVERSAL (1934), a chronology, a filmography, and a bibliography complete the book.

5126   *Raoul Walsh.* edited by Hardy, Phil. 155 p. paper illus. Edinburgh: Edinburgh Film Festival, 1974.

A study of Walsh that includes several articles, an interview, a filmography and a bibliography. The articles deal with Walsh and Warner Bros., Walsh's film, PURSUED (1947), and the place of women in Walsh's films. There are similar volumes published by the Edinburgh Film Festival on Frank Tashlin and Douglas Sirk.

5127   *Raoul Walsh.* edited by Hardy, Phil. New York: Zoetrope, 1980.

5128   RASHOMON. by Kurosawa, Akira; and Hashimoto, Shinobu. 256 p. paper illus. New York: Grove Press, 1969.

Script of the 1950 film directed by Kurosawa. Contains cast credits; an introduction by Robert Hughes; two short stories, "Rashomon" and "In a Grove"; and four articles: 1) "RASHOMON as Modern Art" (Parker Tyler); 2) "Memory of Defeat in Japan: A Reappraisal of RASHOMON" (James F. Davidson); 3) "RASHOMON and Kurosawa" (Donald Richie); and 4) "THE OUTRAGE—An Excerpt from the Screenplay" (Michael Kanin).

5129   *Raymond Chandler On Screen: His Novels on Film.* by Pendo, Stephen. 240 p. illus. Metuchen, N.J.: Scarecrow, 1976.

There are several books which deal with the translation of novels into film form. None succeeds better than this literature-film analysis by Stephen Pendo. Raymond Chandler's six Philip Marlowe detective novels are each treated extensively in a separate essay here. In the case of FAREWELL MY LOVELY, the 1975 remake is also analyzed. (A remake of THE BIG SLEEP appeared in 1978.)

By the use of comparison charts, some of the differences between the two forms are clarified. Other points of departure including the Marlowe characterization are also noted in the interesting text. Full credits are given for all the films and many chapter notes are appended; illustrations and an index complete the book.

There are several ways of examining novels-and-film —by author, genre, period, or topic. Pendo makes a strong case for the "author" approach in this critical study. In emphasizing literary origins, however, he has a tendency to overlook the unique contribution of a strong film director in any translation.

5130 *Raymond Chandler Speaking.* edited by Gardiner, Dorothy; and Walker, K. S. 271 p. paper New York: Houghton Mifflin, 1977.

A collection of Chandler's letters which help to explain his work as novelist and screenwriter.

5131 *The Reader's Advisor: Volume Two.* edited by Courtney, Winifred F. New York: Bowker, 1969.

This guide to books includes a section on film literature. There is an introductory essay followed by a recommended basic collection of books which are annotated and placed in categories. In the edition examined, the film biography was found on pages 729 to 744 and listed books in reference, history, criticism and people in film. The annotations are carelessly done, completely erroneous in a few cases, and in others do not describe the contents of the book at all.

5132 *Reader's Guide to Periodical Literature.* New York: H. W. Wilson Co., 1900- .

This is an index to articles which appear in about 160 popular non-technical periodicals. It is published bi-monthly except during July and August when it appears monthly. Cumulated indexes are issued frequently. Look under the subject heading of "Moving Picture."

5133 *Reading, Film and Radio Tastes of High School Boys and Girls.* by Scott, Walter J. 207 p. illus. London: Oxford University Press, 1947.

5134 *Reagan: A Political Biography.* by Edwards, Lee. 252 p. San Diego, Calif.: Viewpoint Books, 1967.

Written as a "political biography," this paperback reads as campaign material for Reagan and the political conservative. The author was active in the Goldwater campaigns of the early sixties. One third of the volume is devoted to biographical data—covered more successfully in other volumes. The remaining portion is concerned with Reagan in politics (1965-1968).

The volume is indexed but there are no illustrations. A 1964 TV speech is included in the appendix. While the volume has little pertinence for film collections, it may have a place in American problems of democracy. Readers may wonder who inspired or commissioned the writing of this biography. Not recommended.

5135 *The Real and the Unreal.* by Davidson, Bill. 275 p. New York: Harper & Brothers, 1961.

A collection of articles about Hollywood in the fifties with chapter portraits of Kim Novak, Elizabeth Taylor, Gable, Ingrid Bergman, Sinatra, Astaire, Joshua Logan and Dick Clark, this volume offers some cynical and shrewd observations on a time and place now vanished. The recent past seems so old fashioned. The writing is crisp although somewhat fan magazine in nature, understandable since many of these articles originally appeared in mass circulation magazines. Interesting general reading but certainly not essential.

5136 *The Real F. Scott Fitzgerald.* by Graham, Sheilah. 287 p. illus. New York: Grosset & Dunlap, 1976.

Sheilah Graham provides more variations about her long love affair with F. Scott Fitzgerald in this volume which emphasizes the Hollywood years. In addition to describing their life together, she talks about the writer's relationships with others, his work, and his weaknesses. Included are letters, an unfinished play, notes on *The Last Tycoon*, etc. The volume is illustrated and indexed.

5137 *The Real Elvis: Good Old Boy.* by Staten, Vince. illus. Dayton, Ohio: Media Ventures, 1978.

5138 *The Real Howard Hughes Story.* by O'Keefe, Stanton. 251 p. illus. New York: American Affairs Press, 1972.

This paperback was designed to capitalize on the Clifford Irving-Howard Hughes biography fraud. It has one chapter on Hughes' Hollywood activities which reads like an outline rather than a narrative. One surprising element in this quickie book is the quality of the photo reproduction. Printed on pulp paper, the many visuals nevertheless have a clarity lacking in more expensive books. Many of the female film stars who knew Hughes in one way or another are shown. Sexual innuendo and contrived dramatics abound in the rickety narrative. Noted here for the record and for the historian who may write "Howard Hughes in Hollywood."

5139 *The Real James Dean.* by Gilmore, John. 168 p. paper illus. New York: Pyramid, 1975.

James Dean as recalled by his friend, John Gilmore, is the substance of this original paperback. Accompanying the memoir are contributions by Natalie Wood, Rock Hudson, Elia Kazan and others. Illustrations, a Dean chronology, and review excerpts complete the book.

5140   *see 5139*

5141 *The Real Mary Tyler Moore.* by Bryars, Chris. 188 p. paper illus. New York: Pinnacle, 1977.

Although she is known primarily as a television actress, Mary Tyler Moore has appeared in films such as X-15 (1961), THOROUGHLY MODERN MILLIE (1967), JUST DON'T STAND THERE (1968), WHAT'S SO BAD ABOUT FEELING GOOD? (1968), CHANGE OF HABIT (1970) and ORDINARY PEOPLE (1980). This unauthorized biography contains several pages of illustrations.

5142 *The Real Oscar: The Story Behind the Academy Awards.* 256 p. illus. Westport, Conn.: Arlington House, 1981.

Working on the premise that the Oscar Awards are sometimes given to the undeserving, the author tries to explain who, how, and why. An obvious truth is given an obvious treatment here.

5143 *The Real Stars.* edited by Maltin, Leonard. 320 p. paper illus. New York: Curtis Books, 1973.

As one of the first titles in a paperback series, this collection of articles about and interviews with character actors is most pleasurable. The book pays tribute to those supporting players whose faces are usually more familiar than their names. The selection includes Sara Allgood, Edgar Buchanan, Joyce Compton, Hans Conried, Bess Flowers, Gladys George, Billy Gilbert, Dorothy Granger, Rex Ingram, Rosiland Ivan, Patsy Kelly, Una Merkel, Mabel Paige, Gale Sondergaard, Hope Summers, Grady Sutton, and Blanche Yurka.

Each performer article is accompanied by several illustrations which are reproduced with consistent clarity and contrast. A filmography that gives title, studio, date, director and cast for each film follows the textual portion. In the case of Una Merkel, 94 films are listed, while Grady Sutton has appeared in more than 118.

Whether for nostalgia, entertainment or reference, this book has much merit. Many of the articles have appeared earlier in periodical format and are written by several authors with Maltin as a major contributor. Consistent in quality with the other books Maltin has brought into being, this one can be highly recommended.

5144 *The Real Stars III.* edited by Maltin, Leonard. 320 p. paper illus. New York: Popular Library, 1979.

Another anthology taken from Maltin's periodical, *Film Fan Monthly*, this volume profiles 14 character actors. The quality of the articles is variable but the subjects are admirable: Binnie Barnes, John Carradine, Virginia Christine, Ellen Corby, Laird Cregar, Maude Eburne, Mary Field, Dwight Frye, Richard Haydn, George O'Hanlon, Lee Patrick, Norma Varden, Mary Wickes and George Zucco.

5145 *The Real Stars—II.* edited by Maltin, Leonard. 285 p. paper illus. New York: Curtis, 1974.

A collective biography taken from the pages of *Film Fan Monthly*, this book offers as subjects such film actors as Iris Adrian, Lionel Atwill, Roy Barcroft, Cecil Cunningham, Cass Daley, Virginia Field, Sydney Greenstreet, Keye Luke, Bernard Nedell, Virginia O'Brien, Edna May Oliver, Maria Ouspenskaya, Almira Sessions, Raymond Walburn, Max Terhune, Gabby Hayes, Smiley Burnette, Gino Corrado, Lucien Littlefield and Nat Pendleton. The biographies are from a variety of authors including the editor. All are accompanied by illustrations and a filmography.

This collection pays tribute to a few of the outstanding featured players from Hollywood's golden years. Excellent for nostalgia, buff and reference use.

5146 *The Real Story of Al Jolson.* by Abramson, Martin. 48 p. paper illus. New York: Spectrolux, 1950.

5147 *The Real Story of Lucille Ball.* by Harris, Eleanor. 119 p. paper illus. New York: Farrar, Straus and Young, 1954.

5148 *The Real Tinsel.* by Rosenberg, Bernard; and Silverstein, Harry. 436 p. illus. New York: Macmillan, 1970.

A collection of edited interviews with senior citizens who were part of Hollywood's early history. Questions are removed and each article reads like a personal statement. Executives Hal Roach, Sr., Sol Lesser, Adolph Zukor, Walter Wanger and Dore Schary share the major spotlight with performers such as Conrad Nagel, Blanche Sweet, Mae Marsh, and Edward Everett Horton. In addition, the stuntman, director, cameraman, writer, critic, sound director and the voice animator are also represented.

Certain sections are quite familiar since the subjects are already represented by previously published biographies and books (Anita Loos, Dagmar Godowsky, Fritz Lang, Adolph Zukor, Arthur Mayer, et al.). The others are welcome additions to Hollywood history and myth. Each article has some unusual and rare photographs which add immeasurably to the book's appeal. There is a detailed index, too. This is a delightful book that will please most readers. Some of the reminiscences suggest a rather unreliable or perhaps romantic memory, but if the book is taken on the personal level and not the factual-historical one, it will offer a rewarding experience. Highly recommended.

5149 *The Real World of the Surrealists.* by Haslam, Malcolm. 272 p. illus. New York: Rizzoli, 1978.

Contains information on Surrealist films.

5150 *Realism and the Cinema.* by Williams, Christopher. 320 p. paper Boston: Routledge and Kegan Paul, 1980.

A reader designed to present the principal arguments about realism in the cinema. Abundant supplementary material supports the various articles and essays.

5151 *Reality on Reels: A Handbook on Radio-TV-Film Documentaries.* by Wolverton, Mike. 200 p. Houston, Texas: Gulf, 1981.

5152 REBECCA'S DAUGHTERS. by Thomas, Dylan. 144 p. paper Boston: Little, Brown, 1966.

An unfilmed script.

5153 *Rebel.* by Ellis, Royston. 157 p. paper illus. London: World, 1962.

A James Dean biography.

5154 *Rebels: The Rebel Hero in Films.* by Morella, Joe; and Epstein, Edward Z. 210 p. illus. New York: Citadel, 1971.

The careers and private lives of a group of actors who represent the rebel hero on film are depicted in this picture book. John Garfield, Marlon Brando, Montgomery Clift, James Dean, Paul Newman, Warren Beatty, Steve McQueen, Dustin Hoffman, and Peter Fonda are included.

5155 *Recording Sound for Motion Pictures.* edited by Cowan, Lester. 404 p. illus. New York: McGraw-Hill, 1931.

This early volume on sound recording was produced by the Academy of Motion Picture Arts and Sciences and treated such topics as equipment, studios, techniques, acoustics, etc.

5156 *The Recreational Cinema and the Young.* edited by Advisory Committee on Social Questions. 31 p. paper Geneva: League of Nations, 1938.

5157 THE RED BALLOON. by LaMorisse, Albert. 48 p. illus. New York: Doubleday, 1957.

This picture book, designed for children, is based on LaMorisse's classic short film, THE RED BALLOON (1956).

5158 *Red Roses Every Night: An Account of London Cinemas Under Fire.* by Morgan, Guy. 127 p. illus. London: Quality Press, 1948.

As suggested by the subtitle, this book covers the wartime period of 1939 to 1945.

5159 THE RED SHOES Ballet: A Critical Study. by Gibbon, Monk. 95 p.illus. London: Saturn Press, 1948.

Analysis of the elements of the ballet from the 1948 film, THE RED SHOES. Many fine illustrations.

5160 *Red Skelton.* by Marx, Arthur. 327 p. illus. New York: Dutton, 1979.

Arthur Marx is sympathetic yet objective in this unauthorized, somewhat sour biography of Red Skelton. A fully dimensioned portrait is provided, complete with detailed documentation of the comedian's virtues and flaws.

From an impoverished background, Skelton fought constantly and worked hard for his success. Natural gifts and the good fortune to marry Edna Stillwell carried him to fame. Then, comedy and tragedy became the governing forces in his life. Skelton's handling of his personal life and talents have not always been admirable. A final, almost passive, acceptance of old age is also not in the tradition of America's media heroes.

Marx covers all this and much more in this absorbing story. His material indicates effort in research, judgment in selection, and taste in presentation. This is one of the better biographies to appear lately; Red Skelton may not be pleased, but most readers will.

Unfortunately, the illustrations are meager and hardly representative of Skelton's long career. No filmography is provided, but the book is indexed.

5161 *Red Stars over Hollywood.* by O'Tuathail, Michael. 81 p. Tipperary: Tipperary Star, 1949.

A hysterical warning against Communism in Hollywood and in Hollywood films. Lists of names are included.

5162 *Red Treason in Hollywood.* by Fagan, Myron C. 121 p. illus. Hollywood: Cinema Education Guild, 1949.

Once again Fagan writes on the subject of Communism in Hollywood.

5163 *Rediscovering the American Cinema.* by Routt, William D.; and Leahy, James. 112 p. paper illus. Wilmette, Ill.: Films, Inc., 1970.

Another superior Films, Inc. catalog which divides its product into these general categories: "Towards an Aesthetic: Style and Influence in the American Cinema;" "Approaching the Auteur;" "Personalities: Stars, Producers, and Studio;" "Genres and Themes;" and "The World—British, French, Italian Cinema." Crammed with factual information and critical comment, the book is unusual in that it offers many short supportive bibliographies for the subjects treated. Illustrations are top notch and the entire catalog is a joy. The many uses to which this book may be put—reference reader, selection aid, bibliography source, etc.—qualify it as an essential. A shorter 25-page addendum is also available.

5164 *Rediscovering the American Cinema.* edited by Lemza, Douglas J. 224 p. paper illus. Wilmette, Ill.: Films Inc., 1977.

This catalog carries the same title as one issued in 1970. When Films, Inc. calls it a second edition, they may be performing a disservice to users of the volume, since it is almost a completely different book. In this instance a genre arrangement of the films is used rather than the auteur approach of the earlier book. Furthermore, this is a more professional glossy film book that almost eliminates commercialism. Many films have been added and some eliminated, while each genre has a prestigious introduction written by a film authority.

Individual film entries consist of technical data, production credits, selected cast names, a plot summary, one or more stills, and some critical excerpts. Major genre titles include western, horror, musical, crime, comedy, science fiction, social drama, drama, and women. Less attention is given to jungle, fight, costume, prison, religious, survival and war films. An alphabetical title index concludes the book.

Like its predecessor, this book satisfies in two ways: as a nostalgic reminder of the high quality of many American films and as a useful reference.

5165 *Reed All About Me.* by Reed, Oliver. illus. London: W.H. Allen, 1980.

5166 *The "Reel" Benchly.* by Hornby, George. 96 p. paper illus. New York: A.A. Wyn, 1950.

After a short foreword by Howard Dietz, six of the Robert Benchly short subjects receive attention. The MGM shorts from the thirties are: HOW TO SLEEP (1935), THE ROMANCE OF DIGESTION (1937), HOW TO TRAIN A DOG (1936), NO NEWS IS GOOD NEWS (1943), HOW TO BE A DETECTIVE (1936), and THE COURTSHIP OF THE NEWT (1938). For each, the narration and a few nicely reproduced stills are given. Very specialized.

5167 *Reel Change: A Guide to Social Issue Films.* edited by Peyton, Patricia. 140 p. paper illus. San Francisco: The Film Fund, 1979.

This reference is a listing of more than 3000 social issue media titles gathered from a variety of sources. Most of the items are 16mm films with only a small number of videotapes and slide presentations included. In the first section they are listed under ten large categories—aging, energy, ethnic issues, social concerns, etc.—with subheads provided where necessary. Each entry includes title, director, date, running time, color format, distributor, fee, and a descriptive annotation which varies from a single sentence to two paragraphs.

The second section, which deals with materials designed for children, lists media which offer positive ethnic images along with challenges to traditional roles and power relationships. The films cover social issues and avoid stereotypes of all kinds—ethnic, male, female, etc.

The final section lists classic international films which deal with social issues of a specific time period—World War I, urban problems, rural problems, work-labor movements, etc. A list of distributor addresses, some suggested resources, periodicals, hints for showing films, and a title index complete the volume. Attractive illustrations appear throughout.

Here is a resource that is impressive in content and presentation; it should be appreciated by a wide audience.

5168   *Reel Facts: The Moviebook of Records.* by Steinberg, Cobbett. 495 p. paper New York: Vintage, 1978.

This specialized reference book deals with film information such as box office receipts, Academy Award winners, film festival showings, "ten best" lists, most popular movies on TV, etc. Material from *Variety, The New York Times, Time,* and other publications is reprinted.

The section headings used are the awards, the "Ten Best" lists, the marketplace, the studios, the stars, the festivals, and the codes and regulations.

Familiarity with the contents and the arrangement will facilitate the book's use as a reference. Parts of it (i.e., the Harvard Lampoon Movie Worsts Awards) are fun to read, but much of the book is dull narrative (the codes), columns of numbers, or endless lists of film titles. The volume is also available in hardcover under another title, *Film Facts.*

5169   *Reel People, 1981.* edited by Fannas, Peggy. New York: Peter Glenn, 1981.

5170   *Reel Plastic Magic.* by Kardish, Laurence. 297 p. illus. Boston: Little, Brown, 1972.

The subtitle of this book, "A History of Films and Filmmaking in America," lacks a few adjectives such as "short," "repetitive," "flat," or several others. Purporting to be "addressed to the young who are without the background information to ponder more academic texts," the book ignores any new approach and opts for an old-fashioned textbook format.

Emphasis in the text falls on the silent film and the early sound films. Some attention is paid to such current "in" topics as underground avant-garde films, blacks in films, video cassettes, etc., but they are not woven into the text with naturalness or ease. The book closes with some suggested programs, distributor addresses, and a poorly selected bibliography. Several of those more "academic texts" referred to in the book's rationale are recommended here: the volumes of Jacobs, McCann, Ramsaye, Powdermaker, Lillian Ross, Renan, and Sarris, to name a few. Picture selection seems to have depended upon the collection at the Museum of Modern Art, where the author was employed. This photo availability may have determined the emphasis on the early years of film history.

Some of the information in the film program section is already obsolete (e.g., availability of certain films) and one questions its value to a young reader, or to anyone else. Much of the material is obvious, condescending, and unnecessary. This is a book surrounded by inconsistencies of approach, rationale, coverage, and style; an inferior re-telling of material that appears in many other more appropriate volumes. Not recommended.

For excellent presentations of similar material, look at Cecile Starr's *Discovering the Movies,* or Gerald Mast's *A Short History of the Movies,* or, best of all, William Kuhns' *Movies in America.*

5171   *The Reel Revolution.* by Hurley, Neil P. 175 p. paper Maryknoll, N.Y.: Orbis, 1978.

Neil Hurley, the author of *Toward A Film Humanism,* discusses film as a liberating force in this volume. Defined in a broad sense, "liberation" here takes on aspects of self, people, countries, violence, and revolution. That film can help people to realize their oppression and to seek their freedom is Hurley's main argument. By analysis he shows that themes of conformity, acceptance, frustration, protest, rebellion, and the appetite for justice are prevalent in films. They are there because of most filmmakers' "irrepressible urge to make enduring statements of universal and profound significance on the human condition."

The text deals with topics such as peaceful liberation, consciousness-raising, violence, and exploitation. Separate chapters are devoted to Chaplin's philosophy of liberation and to the Latin American cinema. Hurley's final pages look to the future and make some suggestions for additional film studies. The book is indexed.

This is an important book that suggests a different way of perceiving films. It is written in simple yet persuasive terms, and its use of film examples is most effective. Highly recommended.

5172   *Reeling.* by Kael, Pauline. 497 p. Boston: Little, Brown, 1976.

Like so many other good things in life, Pauline Kael seems to improve with the passage of time. This latest collection of her writing, which covers the period from September, 1972, to May, 1975, is a most satisfying reading experience. Since this is her fifth volume of film criticism, her literary talent and style hold little surprise; she remains sharp, appropriate, logical and even comfortable. More noticeable this time is the continuing refinement of her ability to observe and interpret films for the reader who has not seen them. Coupled with her intense enthusiasm for her subject, this talent enables her to capture the reader's attention and admiration with ease.

The articles appear in chronological order with each having a title and usually containing comment on more than one film. Since Kael wrote for *The New Yorker* from October to May, the book consists of three partial-year assignments and one longer piece called "On the Future of Movies." A helpful index to names and titles is added.

Kael is probably the most widely read and respected film critic currently active. This volume will serve to reinforce that reputation and to win new admirers. It is highly recommended.

5173   *A Reference Guide to Audiovisual Information.* by Limbacher, James. 197 p. New York: Bowker, 1972.

Audiovisual in the context of this book means mostly motion pictures, some music, and very little else. Transparencies, filmstrips, study prints, slides, posters, and the many other items that usually are associated with the term are barely mentioned, if at all. A helpful-hints kind of chapter called "The Ready Reference File" opens the book. What follows is a bibliography of reference books with short descriptive annotations; 325 books deal solely or primarily with film and about 60 others are concerned mostly with either recordings, television, or cataloging rules. The books are arranged alphabetically by title.

The periodical section which follows is only slightly more diversified. The books and the periodicals are indexed by subject in the next section. A glossary of audiovisual terms, a listing of publisher addresses and a long "selected" bibliography complete the book. This last section is arranged by subject heading: moving pictures—history, moving pictures—editing, etc. So much is attempted here that some major flaws within this overwhelming accumulation of data may be overlooked. But the reader should be concerned about the following items.

The imbalance of film titles over other titles.

The placement of so many titles in the reference category—*The New Wave, New Cinema in the U.S. A., Movies and Censorship, Mr. Laurel and Mr. Hardy, How to Make Animated Movies.* What book about film, then, is not a reference book?

The placement of certain titles in the second selected bibliography which certainly have more reference value than some of those chosen—*101 Films for Character Growth, The Rise of the American Film,* etc.

The appearance of certain titles in both sections: *Cinema, A Pictorial History of the Western Film,* etc.

The criteria for placement:

The listing of titles that were not yet published: *The Films of Cary Grant, Best Film Plays 1970-1971.*

The incorrect titles for books: *Lana Turner* for *Lana; Classical Movie Shorts* for *The Great Movie Shorts; Homosexuality in the Movies* for screening the sexes, etc.

The Placement of titles under inappropriate headings: *Film Scripts One* and *Film Scripts Two* belong under Moving Picture Plays rather than under Moving Pictures—Production and Direction.

Careless proofreading and annotation.

With all these reservations this volume cannot be recommended. The fact that some reference questions may be answered with its use qualifies it as merely acceptable. It is, indeed, a disappointing book.

5174   *Reference Guide to Fantastic Films.* compiled by Lee, Walt. 2d & 3d of 3 volumes, 406 & 613 pp. paper illus. Los Angeles: Chelsea Lee Books, Los Angeles, Calif. 90066, 1973, 1974.

The final two volumes in this ambitious reference work continue the features that make Volume I so acceptable. Volume II covers film titles G to O, while Volume III treats P to Z. Information about each film is presented in an efficient, concise fashion, and the synopses are still wonderfully succinct and entertaining, e.g., on THE NAKED JUNGLE (1953):

"South American plantation threatened by soldier or army ants, which eat all in their path, including people." Each volume contains a section on films which are difficult to classify and another on those candidates which had to be excluded. The visuals used throughout will increase the reader's curiosity and fascination. Volume III offers some closing comments on the entire work.

In all three volumes, the effort and the result are commendable. Recommended.

5175   *Reference Guide to Fantastic Films.: Volume I, A-F.* compiled by Lee, Walt. 189 p. paper illus. Los Angeles: Chelsea-Lee Books, 1972.

This guide to fantastic films covers only titles beginning with A to F, and groups the films into three categories: the largest group which are completely described, a small group of exclusions, and some films which are termed "problems," since they conflict in some way with the defined criteria for a fantastic film. The main section gives much data. A typical entry shows title, date, company, running time, producer, director, story, screenplay, art director, cameraman, editor, music, cast, plot, and some sources of reviews. The plot outline for FINGERS AT THE WINDOW (1942) gives some idea of the tight but valid annotation: "Evil psychiatrist Rathbone uses hypnotized lunatics to murder others with axes." There is so much potential reference value in this first book that one hopes the remaining volumes are issued quickly. Recommended.

5176   *Reference Guide to Reviews: A Checklist of Sources in the Humanities, Social Sciences, and Fine Arts.* edited by Gallup, Jennifer. 38 p. paper Vancouver, Canada: University of British Columbia Library, 1970.

5177   *A Reference Guide to the American Film Noir: 1940-1958.* by Ottoson, Robert. 290 p. illus. Metuchen, N.J.: Scarecrow, 1981.

An annotated filmography of over 250 examples of the film noir genre is followed by end notes, a selected bibliography, and an index. The annotations are a combination plot, author comment, and background material.

5178   *A Reference List of Audio-visual Materials.* edited by National Audio-visual Center. 390 p. paper Washington, D.C.: General Services Administration, 1978.

Produced by the United States Government, this is a catalog that is published at irregular intervals and lists selected U.S. Government audiovisuals that can be purchased. Some of the classic documentaries, such as the WHY WE FIGHT series and a few Pare Lorenz films, along with some outstanding training films are available. Unless a title is known, access to the films is difficult, even though there is a detailed subject list. For example, if one did not recall a title such as THE RIVER (1939), its annotation might be difficult to locate using the subject headings provided.

5179   *Reflected Glory.* by Noble, Peter. 235 p. illus. London: Jarrolds, 1958.

An autobiographical sketch by the author of several books on such film subjects as Bette Davis, Orson Welles, Erich von Stroheim, and the negro in films, in addition to yearbooks and picture collections.

5180   *Reflections: A Life In Two Worlds.* by Montalban, Ricardo; and Thomas, Bob. 164 p. illus. Garden City, N.Y.: Doubleday, 1980.

Ricardo Montalban has tried to depart from the usual autobiographical format in this volume. While attending a three-day religious retreat, the actor recalls his life and career. Much emphasis is given to his Mexican-Hispanic background, religion, prejudice, marriage, family life, and other virtues or convictions. His films and other activities receive minimal attention in what is a short book. No index or filmography is provided. A few illustrations are included.

Montalban's greatest success apparently is in his current role as Mr. Roarke in the television series, "Fantasy Island." While it is possible to appreciate the actor's standards of spirit and character, the espousal of them does not make especially interesting reading. Those in search of reaffirmation or inspiration may be pleased, but most readers will be bored or disappointed.

5181   *Reflections on the Cinema.* by Clair, Rene. 160 p. London: Kimber, 1953.

An out-of-print volume in which the author talks to himself. Two ages of Clair, youth and maturity, engage in a discussion on cinema.

5182   *Reflections on the Screen.* by Linden, George W. 297 p. illus. Los Angeles: Wadsworth, 1970.

A recent volume on film aesthetics that emphasizes form and function.

5183 *Regression Analysis of Prior Experiences of Key Production Personnel as Predictors of Revenues: from High-Grossing Motion Pictures in American Release.* by Simonet, Thomas Solon New York: Arno, 1980.

Using an investigation of motion picture revenue using a multiple linear regression technique, Simonet develops data about those factors which predict the success or failure of a film. Practices, myths and beliefs about predicting success are challenged. This is a title in the *Dissertations on Film* series.

5184 *Regulation Respecting Moving-Picture Theatres, Kinematograph, and Projectionists, and the Storage and Use of Nitrocellulose X-Ray Films.* 27 p. paper Victoria, British Columbia: K. M. MacDonald, 1970.

5185 *The Relation between Universities and Film, Radio and Television.* edited by Wickham, Glynne W. 55 p. paper London: Butterworth, 1956.

This title from the series *Publications of the University of Bristol* includes an address by Kenneth Macgowan on the modern media of communication.

5186 *Religion in the Cinema.* by Butler, Ivan. 208 p. paper illus. New York: A. S. Barnes, 1969.

This book tackles a very broad topic and covers the ground fairly well, if quite subjectively. The classifications for the films considered include Bible stories, crusades, Christ in cinema, churches, monks and nuns, etc. There are some instances where it is obvious that the author has not seen the film and is quoting another source who is more familiar with it. And some treatments lack balance; for example, John Ford's SEVEN WOMEN (1966) gets several pages while Zinnemann's THE NUN'S STORY (1959) gets a paragraph. There are omissions of films on witchcraft that received critical approval—BURN, WITCH, BURN (1962), HORROR HOTEL (1963) and THE DEVIL'S OWN (1966). The above reservations are minor when one considers the uniqueness of the subject and the scope of the work. A short index and a brief bibliography are included as is a collection of pertinent stills. Should be of interest to most readers.

5187 *Remakes, Series, and Sequels on Film and Television.* by Limbacher, James L. 87 p. Dearborn, Mich.: Public Library, 1970.

This valuable mimeographed reference lists a primary source (story, play, book, poem, etc.) followed by its first adaptation into either films or television. Subsequent uses of the same primary material are noted. For example, the first film based on Dickens' novel *Great Expectations* was made by Paramount in 1917. Subsequent versions were made in Denmark, 1921; the United States, 1934; Great Britain, 1947; and on NBC-TV in 1953. A listing of sequels and film series titles conclude the book. Under the MR. BELEDERE series, we find that its source was a book and the films in the series were: SITTING PRETTY (1948), MR. BELVEDERE GOES TO COLLEGE, (1949), and MR. BELVEDERE RINGS THE BELL, (1951). Another valuable contribution by Limbacher.

5188 *Remember Fred Karno? The Life of a Great Showman.* by Adeler, Edwin. ; and West, Con. 256 p. paper illus. London: John Long, 1939.

Karno was an acrobat who, along with three other knockabout performers, became famous for his comedy pantomime sketches on the stage during the early part of this century. At one time he sponsored five companies on the road. It was with Karno that Charlie Chaplin received his early training and it was from the American tour of that company that Chaplin came to the film studios of Hollywood. Fred Karno and his company were filmed in EARLY BIRDS (1923), a three-reel silent comedy.

5189 *Remember? Remember?* by Beaumont, Charles. 248 p. New York: Macmillan, 1963.

A tribute to nostalgia, this book recalls Chaplin, movie serials, horror films, movie palaces, Sennett comedies and Bela Lugosi. There are also chapters on radio, comic strips, pulp magazines and railroads. Amusing, light, memory-jogging material that was written ahead of the current wave of thirties nostalgia.

5190 *Remembered Laughter: The Life of Noel Coward.* by Lesley, Cole. 501 p. illus. New York: Knopf, 1976.

With the exception of his film work, there is not much more to say about Noel Coward's career after the appearance of this massive biographical overview. Detailed accounts of his activities from his childhood to his death are provided, along with many Coward quotations, letters and diary entries.

The private man was a generous, loveable, theatrical character who was also a homosexual. That part of Coward's life is covered, briefly, and with a discretion that he would have approved.

Since the author was secretary-confidant to Coward from 1936 until his death in 1973, the information provided is first hand, although a bit long-winded. As indicated above, Coward's film career is largely ignored. The volume is illustrated and indexed.

Coward, himself, covered Coward in two autobiographies, and there are other appreciations/studies available. This book is a witty, affectionate tribute to "the master" by an old friend.

5191 *Remembering James Agee.* edited by Madden, David. 172 p. illus. Baton Rouge: Louisiana State University Press, 1974.

A portrait of James Agee as a creative artist and as a person is offered in this compilation of articles. Written by people who knew him—wife, friend, editor, teacher, et al.—they cover various periods and major events in his life. Taken collectively they present an affectionate yet objective appreciation of Agee as writer, critic and poet. (They also recall him as husband, friend, and co-worker.) A final chronology provides a framework for the articles. His contributions to film were as a critic and as a scriptwriter.

The material offered in this volume helps to illuminate Agee's film criticism by suggesting a rationale for the critical aesthetic he eventually employed. The illustrations—like the memoirs—are personal and are placed in appropriate order for full effectivensess. Combining them with the humanized text enbales a reader to feel he has been allowed the privilege of an intimate glimpse into the life of an American artist. Acceptable.

5192 *Reminiscences of the Cinema in Bournemouth.* by George, Eric A. 14 p. paper Bournemouth, England: Bournemouth Local Studies Publications, 1978.

This short local publication on film history is apparently unique to England. With only a few exceptions, it is hard to recall anything similar in American film literature.

5193 *The Reminiscing Champ.* by Froboess, Harry. 141 p. illus. New York: Pageant, 1953.

Subtitled "A World Famous Stunt Man Tells His Story," this autobiography concentrates mostly on film stunts.

5194 *Renaissance of the Film.* edited by Bellone, Julius. 366 p. paper illus. New York: Collier Books, 1970.

Yet another compilation of film reviews by some 33 critics and writers. Most of the films covered are well-known modern classics, usually of foreign origin. Ironically the few American films are BONNIE AND CLYDE (1967) (the only recent American classic), MARNIE (1964) (a classic?), CITIZEN KANE (1941) (forties vintage), DR. STRANGELOVE (1964) (A British co-production), and MONSIEUR VERDOUX (1947) (another forties film). The book seems designed both for reading and as a text for modern film courses. The alignment of film critic with film, the illustrations, and the total production are all commendable. The book also offers a director's bibliography and an index.

5195 *Rene Clair.* by La Roche, Catherine De. 44 p. paper illus. London: British Film Institute, 1958.

This small booklet provides compact coverage of Clair's films from the 1923 PARIS QUI DORT to the 1957 PORTE DES LILAS. A bibliography and an introductory essay are also included.

5196 *Rene Clair.* by McGerr, Celia. 239 p. illus. Boston: Twayne, 1980.

Rene Clair's long association with the film extends from acting in LE LYS DE LA VIE (1920) to directing LES FETE GALANTES (1965). Actually he has made only 28 films. In this study/appreciation his life and career are treated in chronological fashion with special detailed attention given to LE MILLION (1931) and LES BELLES-DE-NUIT (1952). The usual chronology, illustrations, notes, references, bibliography, filmography and index found in the *Twayne Theatrical Arts* series are present.

McGerr conceived this appreciation as an aesthetic review of the films, and, because of her research and her use of Clair's own opinions about his films, the book is largely successful. The readers will undoubtedly be imbued with a desire to see more of Rene Clair's films.

5197 *The Report of The Commission on Obscentiy and Pornography.* 700 p paper New York: Bantam, 1970.

The authoritative study by government-appointed experts on the effects of pornography and obscenity on American society is reprinted here. It includes: 1) Overview of the Findings; 2) Recommendations of the Commission; 3) Reports of the Panels; and 4) Separate Statements by Commission Members.

There is no index and the user will have to search for the sections dealing with films. Much of this material has implications for education, law, film-making, codes, censorship, etc. It is an essential source study that can be used for reference and citation over and over again.

5198 *Report of the Commission on Technical Needs.* edited by Commission on Technical Needs, UNESCO. paper Paris: UNESCO, 1947.

Based on surveys of countries and territories, this report covers journalism, motion pictures, and radio. Similar reports and supplements followed, sometimes with slight title changes.

5199 *Report of the Departmental Committee on Children and the Cinema.* 109 p. paper London: H. M. Stationery Office, 1950.

5200 *Report of the Departmental Committee on the Employment of Children as Film Actors, in Theatrical Work and in Ballet.* 119 p. paper London: H.M. Stationery Office, 1950.

A detailed survey of the laws, restrictions, licenses, etc., that operate in the employment of British children. Covers night work, education, health, welfare, danger, penalties, medical exams, protection of earnings, etc.

5201 *Report of the Mission.* edited by Indian Film Industry's Mission to Europe and America. 84 p. paper illus. Bombay: Hirlekar, 1946.

The mission was sent to Europe and America with the support and approval of the Indian government to study the latest developments in the application and manufacturing sides of the film industry abroad. The investigation took place from July to December of 1945, and this volume is the report that followed.

5202 *Report on Blacklisting: Volume I. Movies.* by Cogley, John. 312 p. New York: Fund for the Republic, 1956.

This report embodies the results of a study of blacklisting practices made in 1954. Some 500 interested

people were interviewed, and the results were interpreted by John Cogley, then the Executive Director of *The Commonweal.* Typical questions used as guides for the interviews were: 1) Does blacklisting exist? 2) How did it develop ? 3) Is "clearance" possible? 4) What is the position of theatrical unions? the motion picture industry? advertising agencies? sponsors? 5) Did the "Hollywood Ten" use films for Communist propaganda?

The body of the book is a chronological arrangement of the 1947 hearings, the labor strikes, the 1951 hearings, the American Legion magazine letter list, Red Channels, etc. The appendix contains two major contributions: "The Legal Aspects," by Harold W. Horowitz, and "Communism and the Movies," by Dorothy B. Jones. The latter is an examination of the content of the films of the Unfriendly Ten. It is a model of organization and clarity for anyone interested in content analysis. The book is indexed. In summary, this excellent survey on blacklisting should be read as background before the other books of the Unfriendly Ten. It can also stand by itself as fascinating film history.

5203 *Report of the Film Industry Committee.* edited by Film Industry Committee. 61 p. paper Dublin: Stationery Office, Government Publications, 1968.

5204 *Report on the Motion Picture Distribution Industry in Canada.* compiled by Canadian Motion Picture Distributor's Assoc. 44 p. paper Toronto: Canadian Motion Picture Distributor's Association, 1978.

This report contains information about the Association (CMPDA), film industry economics, film distribution in Canada and its current status, and some observations and conclusions. Members of the Association are noted in the final pages.

5205 *A Report on the Outlook for the Profitable Production of Documentary Films for the Non-Theatrical Market.* by Losey, Mary. 50 p. paper New York: Film Program Services, 1948.

A survey conducted for the Sugar Research Foundation in April, 1948.

5206 *Report on the Work of the Child Welfare Committee on the Cinematograph.* compiled by Child

Welfare Committee. 13 p. paper Geneva: League of Nations, 1928.

5207 *Representative Photoplays Analyzed.* by O'Dell, Scott. 493 p. Hollywood: Palmer Institute of Authorship, 1924.

Over 100 representative silent photoplays are analyzed here with comments on the stories, actors, directors, production, etc. The selection is diverse with respect to the original source materials— books, plays, originals, and other forms. Synopses, analyses, credits, dramatic classifications, and an index make up this unusual casebook.

5208 *The Reproduction of Colour in Photography, Printing, and Television.* by Hunt, R. W. G. 500 p. illus. New York: John Wiley, 1967.

Addressed to anyone dealing with color pictures. The technical chapters are separated from the general text.

5209 *Republic Studios: Between Poverty Row and the Majors.* by Hurst, Richard Maurice. 262 p. Metuchen, N.J.: Scarecrow, 1979.

In seven chapters Richard Hurst covers some aspects of Republic Studios—its history, influence/ effect, the serials, the western stars, other films and the Republic legacy. Several appendixes, a bibliography and an index conclude the study.

Hurst's major thesis seems to be that Republic, with its basic, simple, straightforward product, did exert a strong influence on the film audience that was deeper and lasted longer than some major studio product. The conservative messages and the traditional themes of the films are identified and their effect on audiences in the South and Midwest is discussed. Although his text is too wordy to be totally persuasive, Hurst's unusual approach to a studio history is admirable.

5210 *Reruns: Fifty Memorable Films.* by Crowther, Bosley. 256 p. illus. New York: G. P. Putnam's, 1978.

In this volume Bosley Crowther employs the format that he used successfully in two earlier volumes, *The Great Films* and *Vintage Films.* He has selected 50 films, arranged them chronologically, and offers a critical appraisal of each. Excellent illustrations are provided and a foreword introduces his selection. His choices for his earlier books are listed and two indexes are added.

It is hard to go wrong with this type of presentation. Crowther conveys his affection for films by knowing how to supply the correct mixture of information, critical comment and visuals to the reader. A most satisfying volume.

5211 *Research Films in Biology, Anthropology, Psychology, and Medicine.* by Michaelis, Anthony R. 490 p. illus. New York: Academic Press, 1955.

Discusses cinematography in the experimental sciences, describing past methods and indicating possibilities. Describes use in biology, animal behavior, human record films, anthropology, psychology, psychiatry, X-ray, surgery, and medicine.

5212 *Research in Instructional Television and Film.* by Reid, Christopher J.; and MacLennan, Donald W. 216 p. paper Washington, D.C.: U.S. Government Printing Office, 1967.

5213 *The Resource Guide: For Adult Religious Education.* by Newland, Mary Reed. 196 p. paper Kansas City, Mo.: National Catholic Reporter Pub. Co., 1974.

In this volume a religious educator has compiled a group of recommended multi-media resources for use with adults. Using a diversity of topics as her subject headings, she has suggested possible books, pamphlets, cassettes, films, filmstrips, magazines, newspapers, radio programs, TV programs and vacation seminars for consideration. While not all of the topics and resources are suited for nonreligious use, many of them are. The sections on war, poverty, racism, ecology, consumerism, etc., can be of value in many institutional settings. Several films are suggested under each subject heading. A short annotation of each is given along with running time, color or black and white, and distributor.

The arrangement of the book limits its use somewhat. An index to the titles discussed in the text would have increased its value greatly. As an aid to religious educators, this volume can be highly recommended. For other users it is an acceptable reference.

5214 *Response to Innovation: A Study of Popular Argument About New Mass Media.* by Davis, Robert Edward.

New York: Arno, 1976.

Written in 1965 at the University of Iowa in partial fullfillment of the doctoral program, this title in the *Dissertations on Film* series examines film as a medium of mass communication. Viewed in a historical perspective, the medium of film is examined for its social and emotional effects on the public. Attitudinal responses to the initial entrance of film to the field of mass media are cited.

5215   *Responses to Drama: An Introduction to Plays and Movies.* by Altshuler, Thelma C.; and Janaro, Richard P. 351 p. illus. Boston: Houghton Mifflin, 1967.

5216   *The Rest of the Story.* by Graham, Sheilah. 317 p. paper illus. New York: Coward-McCann, 1964.

After F. Scott Fitzgerald died in the early forties, Miss Graham had to decide the course her life would take. Her career as a Hollywood columnist is the topic of most of this book. There is little depth in the writing as most of it reads like an extended gossip column with Graham admirers and enemies as topics. Everyone is made to revolve about the heroine, her ego and her children. Unexciting and unimportant.

5217   *The Restless Journey of James Agee.* by Moreau, Genevieve. 320 p. New York: William Morrow, 1977.

In addition to being a poet, novelist and journalist, James Agee was also a film critic and screenwriter. In this biography, attention is given to his Hollywood experiences, although the major emphasis is on other biographical and literary matters.

The two volumes called *Agee on Film* contain his criticism and his scripts. This well-researched biography provides the framework in which those film materials were created. A bibliography, some chapter notes, and an index are included.

5218   *The Restless Years: Diaries 1955-1963.* by Beaton, Cecil. 190 p. illus. London: Weidenfeld and Nicolson, 1976.

Designer Cecil Beaton continues his autobiography which takes him through GIGI (1958) and up to the film version of MY FAIR LADY (1964).

5219   *The Resurrection in Cannes: The Making of* THE PICASSO SUMMER.

by Herschensohn, Wes. 376 p. illus. New York: A. S. Barnes, 1979.

THE PICASSO SUMMER (1969) is a feature film based on a Ray Bradbury story and stars Albert Finney and Yvette Mimieux. Part of the film was to be animated and the author hoped to work with Pablo Picasso in creating a new form of animation. His meeting in 1964 with Picasso is related, along with later anecdotes about other film names concerned with making the film. The illustrations include some of the animated drawings. The volume is indexed.

5220   *Retrospective Index to Film Periodicals: 1930 to 1971.* by Batty, Linda. 425 p. New York: Bowker, 1975.

A most useful contribution to film research has been made by Linda Batty in compiling this index. Using as her base the entire contents of 14 English-language film periodicals, she has enhanced the book by adding articles and reviews from the *Village Voice*. The periodicals were selected in accordance with three criteria: excellence, coverage, and lasting interest. Adding the *Village Voice* material seems a most laudable idea; its staff has included such writers as Andrew Sarris, Jonas Mekas and Molly Haskell.

The index is divided into three separate but interrelated sections: film titles, film subjects, and film book review citations. The first section is a lengthy filmography arranged alphabetically by title. Each entry notes the country of origin and the director before listing the review citations, which are arranged alphabetically by author surname. Thus, for OH! WHAT A LOVELY WAR (1969) (UK, Richard Attenborough) we find: "French, Philip (from *Sight and Sound*); Gow, Gordon (from *Films and Filming*); Hart, Henry (from *Films in Review*); Sarris, Andrew (from *The Village Voice*); Spartacus (from *Cinema*)." Curiously, the film's release date is not given here, but quite often it can be determined by examining the dates of the reviews.

Two types of film subject headings appear in the second section: general headings, such as neo-realism, politics and film, Polish Cinema, etc., and personal names such as Henry Mancini, George Pal, Anthony Quinn, Phyllis Thaxter, et al. Many of the personality entries are cross-indexed to titles in the preceding film section. The book review citations which appear in the third and final section are arranged alphabetically according to the book author's surname. For example, to find a review of *Freedom of the Movies*, the searcher must know that Ruth A. Inglis wrote it. Many readers know the title *King Cohn* but would be at a loss to name the author.

The first two sections are easy to use and offer an

efficient guide to selected periodical information about films and filmmakers. Arrangement of the material in section three weakens its usefulness. The book contains some of the material found in the indexes of Gerlach, MacCann, Manchel, Bowles, and Salem. It also complements the FIAF volumes for 1972 and 1973. Recommended.

5221 *The Return of Rudolph Valentino.* by McKinstry, Carol. 193 p. illus. Los Angeles: Kirby and Gee, 1952.

Supposedly supplied by Rudolph Valentino after his death, the message is transmitted to the reader by the spiritualist-psychic author.

5222 *The Revealing Eye: Personalities of the 1920s.* by Muray, Nickolas. 307 p. illus. New York: Atheneum, 1967.

This coffee-table book has many beautiful full-sized portraits, faithfully reproduced in black-and-white, and a pedestrian text by Paul Gallico. It is not a film star collection, but since it includes so many persons who had a career of one kind or another in films, the book is noted here. The outstanding photographic work consistently captures much more of the subject than does the text. Not essential in any way.

5223 *The Reverend Goes to Hollywood.* by Evans, Charles. 222 p. New York: Crowell-Collier, 1962.

A folksy reminiscence by a minister who decided to become a motion picture actor, this volume is less autobiographical and more inspirational. The reader will find nothing negative or evil—only kindness, goodness, acceptance, and inspiration. If that sounds a bit dull, that is the way the book reads. High spots are a wink from Rosalind Russell and the loss of a role in THE CAINE MUTINY (1954). Unsophisticated readers may enjoy this one. Others are warned. Not recommended.

5224 *Reviewing for the Mass Media.* by Hunt, Todd. 190 p. paper Philadelphia: Chilton, 1972.

5225 *Revolutionary Soviet Film Posters.* by Constantine, Mildred; and Fern, Alan. 97 p. illus. Baltimore, Md.: Johns Hopkins University Press, 1974.

As an interdisciplinary volume which contains elements of art, history and film, this attractive book is unique. Using the film posters created mostly during the age of Soviet expressive realism, 1925-1930, the authors are concerned with the relationship between the filmmakers and the graphic arts following the revolution. The avant-garde artists were devoted to spreading the educational, political, and cultural messages to the new Russia. The film posters they created offer evidence of their remarkable talent and artistry.

Intelligent selection and careful attention to reproduction quality are evident in the 56 posters in black and white and the 16 posters in full color. Each poster occupies a full page. Some smaller stills, illustrations and other posters are also included along with an index, some notes and bibliographic information. The short essay which precedes the poster display is informative and sets the stage nicely for the exhibit. This is a different kind of film book that may serve as a model. It suggests new approaches to the study of film, art and society. Highly recommended.

5226 *Rex: An Autobiography.* by Harrison, Rex. 256 p. New York: William Morrow, 1974.

Here is an autobiography which charts "a pursuit of happiness" that includes five marriages, innumerable love affairs, several memorable stage and screen performances, and a few children. Because of his sense of privacy, very little human quality or warmth shows through. Most of the anecdotes are hollow and his recollection of his marriage to Lilli Palmer is at variance with her account. It is when he speaks of Kay Kendall that the reader will perceive some idea of what this autobiography might have been.

As he neared the end of his romances, marriages and long stage runs, Harrison often became impatient and desirous of escape. That syndrome percolates through much of this volume. It should have, and could have, been a much warmer and richer book. Acceptable.

5227 *Rex Ingram: Master of the Silent Cinema.* by O'Leary, Liam. 224 p. illus. New York: Barnes and Noble (Harper), 1980.

This well-intentioned biography deals with Rex Ingram, a director of silent films whose stars were rather colorful (Valentino, Alice Terry, Ramon Novarro, etc.). Using interviews of Ingram's associates, the author describes Ingram's directorial methods but offers little critical evaluation of the final films.

It is a challenge for any writer to attempt a rediscovery of a neglected filmmaker. Unfortunately

O'Leary isn't quite up to this difficult task.

5228 *The Rhetoric of Film.* by Harrington, John. 175 p. illus. New York: Holt, Rinehart and Winston, 1973.

The goal of this volume is to provide an understanding of the rhetoric of film in order that the viewer can perceive the persuasive aspects of film as well as its artistry. Carefully avoiding an over-use of film examples, the author discusses such aesthetics as film grammar, composition, visual reality, sound terminology, point of view, theme and unity, structure and organization, rhythm and continuity, and extended rhetoric. A glossary of film terms along with suggestions for further reading, a list of film distributors, and an index complete the volume.

Much of the obfuscation and mystery surrounding film rhetoric has been eliminated in this sensible, clearly written volume. The development is a logical one and the reader is encouraged to progress from basic considerations to the more sophisticated concepts by the carefully formulated text.

The volume should be a basic one for all college courses on film appreciation. It is recommended.

5229 *A Ribbon of Dreams.* by Cowie, Peter. 262 p. illus. New York: Barnes, 1973.

Comparing this "revision" with Cowie's earlier work, *The Cinema of Orson Welles,* we find: 1) it has been retitled, with the original title relegated to sub-status; 2) it is updated to include Welles' most recent films, CHIMES AT MIDNIGHT (1966) and THE IMMORTAL STORY (1968); 3) corrections ("sunrise" for "sunset," 1937 for 1938, etc.), rearrangements, and deletions have been made; 4) bibliographic citations have increased from 120 to 152; 5) it is now indexed; 6) visual content has increased but is not reproduced as well as in the earlier book; 7) new text material amounting to approximately 15 percent of the original text has been added; 8) the original retail price of the softcover edition has been multiplied about six times for this hardcover revision.

Much of the newer text material was probably suggested by writings on Welles by authors such as Kael, Higham, Bessy, McBride, and others. Since the original annotation of the book called the book "excellent and recommended for all readers," most of the changes above may be assumed as added values to an already acceptable volume. The high price and poor photo reproduction will give pause.

5230 *Richard and Elizabeth.* by David, Lester; and Robbin, Jhan. 242 p. illus. New York: Funk and Wagnalls, 1978.

It is unfortunate that the subject matter of this biography is not only familiar but of little current interest to most readers. Having reached middle age, both Richard Burton and Elizabeth Taylor have now adopted lifestyles that are related to the rapidly decreasing demand for their professional services. This volume reviews their early lives and their heyday—that period when they were the most publicized couple in the world.

Each is given a background biographical section, with the final three portions of the book concentrating on the rise and fall of a famous personal and professional partnership. Some clearly reproduced illustrations and an index are also included.

The style and the methodology of the authors is most suitable. From interviews with contemporaries of the Burtons, they have gathered some fresh anecdotes, insights and observations but even this new material cannot disguise the familiar story and a sense of reader overexposure to it. This volume is a case of the message slowly but certainly smothering the medium. Acceptable primarily for those who slept through the sixties.

5231 *Richard Attenborough.* edited by Reed, Rochelle. 24 p. paper illus. Washington, D.C.: American Film Institute, 1973.

Richard Attenborough was on a publicity tour for YOUNG WINSTON (1972) when this discussion took place in November, 1972. Most of the interview pertains to the new film, with occasional references to OH, WHAT A LOVELY WAR (1969), another directorial attempt. He talks of films in which he has acted and of people with whom he has worked. One of the better books in this series.

5232 *Richard Burton.* by Waterbury, Ruth. 171 p. paper illus. New York : Pyramid Books, 1965.

Written at the height of Burton's celebrity in 1965, this volume concentrates mostly on the CLEOPATRA (1963) scandal. Burton's life, however, is outlined with moderate attention to his films. The author's style is pulp magazine yet she is rather successful in giving a portrait of a talented, restless actor. A few candid shots are used for centerfold. There is no index. The book has little value to the serious reader.

5233 *Richard Burton: Very Close Up.* by Cottrell, John; and Cashin, Fergus. 385 p. illus. Englewood Cliffs, N.J.:

Prentice-Hall, 1971.

This unofficial biography is arranged as a predictable trilogy—Richie Jenkins, Richard Burton, and Richard and Elizabeth. Its outstanding quality is its detail. Using sources ranging from some close gushing friends to critical newspaper reviews, the authors have reconstructed Burton's career from South Wales to London and Hollywood, and from Philip Burton to Sybil to Elizabeth. (It is the last lady to whom the authors seem devoted.) Conversations, quotes, facts, and opinions are all blended into an interesting portrait which surpasses Waterbury's fan magazine biography written in the sixties.

One tends to forget Burton's long involvement with both stage and films. His pre-CLEOPATRA (1963) films are numerous and, as a group, show the same inconsistent performer that the later films do. The text is disproportionate in its attention to individual films; WHO'S AFRAID OF VIRGINIA WOOLF? (1966) gets a short two pages which tell nothing of the filmmaking, while THE VIPS (1963) and THE NIGHT OF THE IGUANA (1964) get whole chapters. A final section attempts to separate Burton, the man, from Burton, the myth, and to assess his work as an actor in several media. Burton's contribution to this biography was apparently minimal.

A picture gallery presented in the book's center is merely adequate. More photographs should have been selected and with greater care. Many of Burton's career highlights are missing: "The Lady's Not For Burning," "Time Remembered," LOOK BACK IN ANGER (1959), ANNE OF THE THOUSAND DAYS (1970), THE ROBE (1953), etc. The greatest lack is an index. There are certainly sufficient names and titles in the text to warrant one. A filmography, a discography, and a listing of the plays and television appearances would also enchance the book.

In summary, Burton's life is related in a detailed, documented fashion that is rather flat and devoid of emotion—a style that seems to be a contrast and an ultimate disservice to the man. The book will please readers who want a reminder of the well-publicized facts and can read between the lines of this rather formal presentation. A few additions—more pictures, an index, etc.—could make this merely acceptable book one that could be recommended.

5234 *Richard Burton.* by Ferris, Paul. 320 p. illus. New York: Coward, 1981.

An unauthorized biography based on previously published Burton interviews and some new interviews with a few of Burton's friends and relatives. Well-intentioned but medium nevertheless.

5235 *Richard Leiterman.* by Reid, Alison; and Evanchuck, P. M. 120 p. paper illus. Ottawa: Canadian Film Institute, 1978.

Richard Leiterman is a Canadian cinematographer who began working on documentary films in the early sixties. Among the many films he photographed is HIGH SCHOOL (1968). In the seventies he enlarged his activities to include other film forms, and also came into conflict with the IATSE, a cinematographer's union. He has continued making films, many of which have won recognition for outstanding photography.

This paperback consists of an essay which critically examines Leiterman's work, an interview, a filmography with credits noted, and a bibliography. In summary, the book is a welcome appreciation of a filmmaker who deserves wider recognition.

5236 *Richard Lester: A Guide to References and Resources.* by Rosenfeldt, Diane. 152 p. Boston: G.K. Hall, 1978.

This volume follows the basic structure of the series —a biography, a critical survey, a filmography, a bibliography, other film work and writing, archives, distributors, an author index, and a film title index.

It is the bibliography which is of major interest here. Many of the entries have only brief one-line annotations. The longer ones are much more helpful in determining which sources to use.

Although the volume certainly would be helpful in research dealing with Lester, it seems to lack the detail, sparkle, and the subject appreciation found in the other titles of the *Guide to References and Resources* series.

5237 *Richard Massingham.* by British Film Institute. 20 p. paper illus. London: British Film Institute 1955.

A tribute by his friends to a filmmaker who specialized in British government propaganda films of World War II and after. Illustrations and a filmography are a part of this *BFI Index* series booklet.

5238 *Richard Tauber.* by Tauber, Diana Napier. 237 p. illus. London: Art and Educational Publishers, 1949.

Written by his wife and published soon after his death, this is the biography of the Austrian opera singer who also enjoyed success as a songwriter, composer and film actor. His first films were done in Germany during the early thirties and were followed by several English productions in the late thirties. In the forties he appeared in THE LISBON STORY (1945) and WALTZ TIME (1948).

5239   *Rick Rosenberg and Robert Christiansen.* edited by Reed, Rochelle. 24 p. paper illus. Washington, D.C.: American Film Institute, 1973.

On December 13, 1972, filmmakers Rosenberg and Christiansen were interviewed by James Powers at an AFI seminar. Their remarks are recorded here. As producers of feature films for television they were responsible for ADAM AT SIX A.M. (1971), THE GLASS HOUSE (1972), GARGOYLES (1972), A BRAND NEW LIFE (1973), THE AUTOBIOGRAPHY OF MISS JANE PITTMAN (1973) and others.

5240   *Riders of the Range: The Sage Brush Heroes of the Sound Screen.* by La Hue, Kalton C. 259 p. illus. New York: A. S. Barnes, 1973.

A typical La Hue collective biography, this one offers 28 cowboy heroes in words and pictures. Each subject receives an individual noncritical section, with a catch-all chapter of also-rans closing the book. The words are bland and the illustrations are plentiful.

5241   *The Right Way to Write for Films.* by White, Moresby; and Stock, Freda. 117 p. Kingswood, Surrey: A. G. Elliot, 1948.

A title in the *Right Way* series.

5242   *The Rin Tin Tin Story.* by English, James W. 247 p. illus. New York: Dodd Mead, 1949.

One of the silent screen's most popular attractions, Rin Tin Tin, a German shepherd dog, appeared in films from WHERE THE NORTH BEGINS (1923) up to ROUGH WATERS (1930).

After the original died in 1932, there were five successors to the name Rin Tin Tin. Other books include *Little Folk's Story of Rin Tin Tin* (1927).

5243   *Ring Up the Curtain.* by Maltby, Henry F. 232 p. illus. London: Hutchinson and Company, 1950.

The subtitle, "Being the Stage and Film Memoirs of H. F. Maltby," indicates a autobiography of the actor-screenwriter-playwright who was active in Britain during the thirties and forties. He appeared in JACK OF ALL TRADES (1935), TROUBLE AHEAD (1936), PYGMALION (1938), THE GIRL WAS YOUNG (1938), TO THE VICTOR (1938), A CANTERBURY TALE (1944), etc.

5244   *The Rise and Fall of British Documentary.* by Sussex, Elizabeth. 219 p. illus. Berkeley, Calif.: University of California Press, 1975.

To relate this account of the film movement founded by John Grierson, the author has employed a film editing technique. Using a group of diverse interviews as her raw material, she has fragmented them and then rearranged the pieces into a chronological account. Interviewed were John Grierson, Basil Wright, John Taylor, Paul Rotha, Edgar Anstey, Sir Arthur Elton, Stuart Legg, Henry Watt, Alberto Cavalcanti, Pat Jackson, W. H. Auden and Ian Dalrymple. Connecting the reassembled segments is a narrative supplied by the author. Illustrations and an index are added.

The British documentary movement began in the early thirties, reached its peak in wartime and was ended by the fifties. Attempts to replace it by other movements such as the Free Cinema were unsuccessful and its lasting influence on international cinema is undeniable.

This volume not only reconstructs its history from primary sources, but also provides a critical evaluation of its contribution to world cinema. Much attention is also given to descriptions of the documentary film genre.

An important topic has been treated in a lively manner that makes for an informative and interesting reading experience. Recommended.

5245   *The Rise and Fall of Free Speech in America.* by Griffith, D. W. 58p. paper illus. Hollywood, Calif.: Larry Edmunds Bookshop, 1967 (1915).

A pamphlet published originally by Griffith in 1915 containing editorial excerpts from newspapers and periodicals upholding the right of BIRTH OF A NATION (1915) to be shown. Illustrated by editorial cartoons.

5246   *The Rise and Fall of the Horror Film: An Art History Approach to Fantasy Cinema.* by Soren, David. 172 p. paper illus. Columbia. Mo.: Lucas Brothers, 1977.

In his introduction David Soren admits to an exceedingly broad definition of the horror film. He includes fantasy cinema, and under that subcategory, adds some thirties musicals. What he has attempted is a historical survey of the influence of various art movements on selected films—usually those which lend themselves to disorientation, exaggeration, accented lighting variations, etc. This leads inevitably to the horror-fantasy genre.

The text, based on lectures given in the author's film courses, points out specific art influences in the films of Melies, Vigo, Cocteau, Lang, Berkely, Argento, Fisher, Dreyer, Murnau and others. Underlying his survey of films and filmmakers is the regret that today's film product relies on sex, sadism, and gratuitous violence rather than atmosphere, setting, and suggestion.

A folio of murky illustrations which appears at the book's end diminishes rather than helps the effectiveness of Soren's presentation. A bibliography is included, but unfortunately the book does not have an index.

Soren's work has been given less-than-average support via production, but the quality and uniqueness of his text make thisbook a rewarding reading experience. Recommended.

5247 *The Rise and Fall of the Matinee Idol.* edited by Curtis, Anthony. 215 p. illus. New York: St. Martin's Press, 1974.

This anthology pays tribute to the matinee idol— that male performer whose presence in a play or film insures audience attendance. Covering those performers of stage and screen who possessed this somewhat mysterious romantic/sexual attraction, the text identifies certain stars who can be called "idols." For example, Clark Gable qualifies, while Gary Cooper and Spencer Tracy do not. The first and longer section deals with theatrical personalities. Some of them also had film careers, but their appeal to an audience was an "in-person" one. Others, such as Valentino, were images loved by the camera. Seen in real life they would have been less than captivating to audiences.

The contributors to this intriguing analysis include many well-known authors, critics, and actors, e.g., Sandy Wilson, Dilys Powell, George Axelrod, and Cecil Beaton. They are identified more fully at the book's conclusion. A most attractive collection of visuals shows many of the actors mentioned in the text. The book is indexed. "Idol" seems to be a subheading of that actor genre, "star." This volume offers an analysis of that subgenre which is penetrating, informative, and best of all, entertaining. The nostalgia is plentiful and most readers will enjoy this imaginative study. Recommended.

5248 *The Rise of Ronald Reagan.* by Boyarsky, Bill. 269 p. illus. New York: Random House, 1968.

The emphasis in this biography is on the political years of the sixties. Approximately the first third is devoted to the material covered in Reagan's autobiography. This portion reinforces the impression which most readers of the latter book receive—that no one really is close to Reagan and any portrait is a partial and inconclusive one. As a quick summary or companion book to the autobiography, this one has some merit. Material on the films is minimal.

5249 *The Rise of the American Film: A Critical History.* by Jacobs, Lewis. 631 p. paper illus. New York: Columbia University Teachers College Press, 1968 (1939).

One of the four classic histories of film (Ramsaye, Bardeche and Brasillach, and Hampton are the others), this book is probably the most valuable for several reasons. Jacobs was one of the first to recognize and write about the film as an art form; the volume seems to have been a model for those histories which followed. Finally, his scholarship and research have not been equalled.

The history covers the American film only to 1939 and one wishes that Jacobs had continued this masterwork rather than devoted himself to editing anthologies. His literary style avoids the pedantic, professional approach, concentrating instead on being readable and critical. The collection of stills used is most impressive. Included is one of the most detailed bibliographies published as an appendix (covering the periods up to 1939). Separate indices are provided for film titles, names, and general topics. An essay on experimental cinema in America (1921-1947) is included in this edition. A monumental and classic achievement.

5250 *Risks and Rights in Publishing, Television, Radio, Motion Pictures, Advertising and the Theater.* by Spring, Samuel. 365 p. New York: W. W. Norton, 1956.

Deals with such topics as copyright, right of privacy, libel, slander, unfair competition, obscenity, etc., along with the laws pertaining to same.

5251 *Rita Hayworth.* by Peary, Gerald. 160 p. paper illus. New York: Pyramid, 1976.

A review of the life and career of Rita Hayworth,

this volume has several unusual elements. The visuals, which include some rare early photographs of Hayworth, show the evolution of a rather ordinary looking dancer into America's most popular love goddess of the forties. Her rapid descent from box office popularity to occasional small roles in obscure films is noted in this story which holds little promise of a happy ending.

Hayworth's 61 films from UNDER THE PAMPAS MOON (1935) to CIRCLE (1976) are covered, as are the externals of her personal life. A bibliography, a filmography, and an index complete the volume.

Peary's critical analysis of the films is sound and his account of her rise and fall is sympathetically objective. Illustrations are well chosen and reproduced. This is another fine volume in the *Pyramid* series. Recommended.

5252 *Rita Hayworth.* by Kobal, John. 328 p. illus. New York: W.W. Norton, 1978.

This disappointing biography apparently needed the cooperation of its subject, although an addenda entitled "Epilogue—A Meeting," does tell of the author's one encounter with Hayworth in 1973. The text is a combination of factual reconstruction combined with fan admiration. Hayworth is made to seem a timid helpless victim, in constant need of protection. Vulnerable and manipulated, she rose from bit player to screen goddess only to sink again in a swamp of scandal and notoriety. This latter period is largely overlooked by the author, who concentrates on the period when she was an actual princess and a screen queen. The book is illustrated and an index is provided.

When the recorded events of Hayworth's life are recalled, their range and uniqueness would indicate a biography rich in dramatic irony and incident. The cost of her fame, her ultimate destiny, her failures as a woman/mother/wife—all these potentially powerful prospects are bypassed in favor of a fan's appreciation. Will the real Rita Hayworth please stand up? In this volume she apparently cannot. Nevertheless, the star and her story are so fascinating that even so selected a factual recall as this is of some interest. Acceptable.

5253 *The Rivals of D. W. Griffith: Alternate Auteurs 1913-1918.* edited by Koszarski, Richard. 60 p. paper illus. Minneapolis: Walker Art Center, 1976.

This catalogue was published in conjunction with a film program offered at the Walker Art Center in Minneapolis in 1976. The purpose of the program was to point out that D. W. Griffith was not alone in synthesizing and using pioneering filmmaking techniques. By selecting examples from the work of other artists, Koszarski tries to show the total creativity that characterized the film industry from 1913 to 1918.

An introduction and a final section on lost films of the period frame what is essentially a collection of notes on 20 films. The catalogue is nicely illustrated and contains a three—part bibliography (history, art-technique, and biography).

This short volume offers some rich historical information that will appeal to scholars, historians, and film buffs. The selection, organization and arrangement of the material is quite impressive. Recommended.

5254 *Rivette: Texts and Interviews.* edited by Rosenbaum, Jonathan. 101 p. paper London: British Film Institute; (Zoetrope in the USA), 1977.

Two interviews with Jacques Rivette followed by four texts/articles by the director comprise the text of this short, original volume. The articles include: "Letter on Rossellini," "The Hand," "Montage," and "For the Shooting of Les Filles du Feu." A bio-filmography and a bibliography, both quite detailed, are added.

Rivette is one of the least appreciated New Wave directors, probably because of the unavailability of his films. The intent of this volume is to focus critical attention on the filmmaker and his work. In that context, it is quite successful.

5255 *The RKO Gals.* by Parish, James Robert. 896 p. illus. New Rochelle, N.Y.: Arlington House, 1974.

Author Parish continues his production of film actress biographies in this pleasing volume. Using the same format of biography, filmography and stills that he used in *The Paramount Pretties, The Fox Girls, The Slapstick Queens, Good Dames* and *The MGM Stock Company,* he offers as subjects here 14 actresses who began their careers at the RKO Studios. Included are Ann Harding, Constance Bennett, Irene Dunne, Ginger Rogers, Katharine Hepburn, Anne Shirley, Lucille Ball, Joan Fontaine, Wendy Barry, Lupe Valez, Maureen O'Hara, Jane Russell, Barbara Hale and Jane Greer.

The biographies are factual, stressing career rather than private life. Illustrations are well reproduced and the filmographies contain very complete listings of cast and production credits. Other than Katharine Hepburn and Lucille Ball, the RKO actresses are a group new to published biography. The amount of information offered, the unfamiliarity of most of the material, and the efficient manner of presentation are the major qualities of this volume. The excellent production of the book by the publisher is also noteworthy. Compared to other similar collective biographies which treat only five or six subjects, this one with 14 is a bargain. In addition, there are appendixes on the history of the RKO Studios and selected executives and producers who functioned there. Acceptable.

5256 *RKO Radio Pictures of 1931-1935.* edited by Gordon, R. F. New York: Gordon Press, 1976.

5257 *The Road to Hollywood.* by Hope, Bob; and Thomas, Bob. 271 p. illus. Garden City, N.Y.: Doubleday, 1977.

This three-part volume is subtitled "My Forty-Year Love Affair With the Movies," and consists of an autobiographical section, a critical evaluation of Hope's films by Bob Thomas, and a final filmography offering casts, credits and synopses.

The section by Hope consists of many jokes, wisecracks, and one-liners strung onto a biographical framework. Hope claims authorship, but it all sounds suspiciously like his army-of-gag writers' typical output. Thomas' critique is superficial, at best.

This is another instance of the manufactured humor and comment that has typified Hope's public persona for 40 years. Its contents may be appreciated by those who think of Hope as a funny man.

5258 THE ROBE. 18 p. paper illus. New York: ABC Vending Corp., 1953.

The story of the 1953 film is told in several introductory pages of this souvenir book which features pictures spread over a double page, thus simulating a wide-screen image. Since this was the first film in Cinemascope, there is also an article explaining the process. In addition to the cast and production credits, there is an article by Lloyd C. Douglas entitled "Why I Wrote *The Robe.*" One final section takes the reader "Behind the Scenes With the People Who Bring You THE ROBE."

5259 *Robert Aldrich.* edited by Henstell, Bruce. 27 p. paper Washington, D.C.: American Film Institute, 1972.

In November, 1972, Robert Aldrich visited the AFI Center in Beverly Hills to discuss his film, THE DIRTY DOZEN (1967). The first section concentrates on the film, another discusses general topics in filmmaking. A bibliography and a filmography are included.

5260 *Robert Aldrich: A Guide to References and Resources.* by Silver, Alain; and Ward, Elizabeth. 172 p. Boston: G.K. Hall, 1979.

While the name, Robert Aldrich, is a familiar one to anyone concerned with film, much of his work is either unknown or credited to someone else—often Robert Wise. Aldrich is a director-writer-producer whose career spans almost four decades. This reference guide, which had its genesis in a masters thesis, covers all aspects of Aldrich's career most adequately. It begins with a biography and a critical survey. Next the films directed and produced by Aldrich are described in detail with casts, credits, and notes given. A bibliography which separates general writing from that on specific individual films follows. Aldrich's film-related activities are noted along with a distributor list. An interview of Aldrich by Silver along with an author index and a film index completes the book.

Since Aldrich is a colorful filmmaker who has enjoyed the successes and failures that inevitably accompany a long career in a difficult business, any volume devoted to him is certain to be of interest. The elements presented here have been carefully selected and arranged, resulting in a solid reference book that can also be enjoyed as a browsing/reading experience.

5261 *Robert Aldrich.* edited by Combs, Richard. 76 p. paper illus. London: British Film Institute, 1978.

Includes a filmography and biographical references.

5262 *Robert Aldrich.* edited by Combs, Richard. New York: Zoetrope, 1979.

5263 *Robert Altman: American Innovator.* by Kass, Judith M. 282 p. paper illus. New York: Popular Library, 1978.

In this hurriedly prepared paperback, an introductory essay precedes chapter examinations of each of Robert Altman's film from THE DELINQUENTS (1957) to THREE WOMEN (1977).

In each instance there is a plot summary, background information, author comment, critical reaction, and some illustrations. The latter are murky and hard to interpret at times. A filmography giving full cast and production credits completes the book.

Since this is the only book on Altman currently available, it will have to do until a carefully researched and written one appears.

5264   *Robert Altman.* edited by Reed, Rochelle. 24 p. paper illus. Washington, D.C.: American Film Institute, 1975.

While he was making NASHVILLE (1975), director Robert Altman appeared for an interview at the AFI Center for Advanced Film Studies on December 4, 1974. Two days before the meeting, students at the Center viewed three Altman films: BREWSTER MCCLOUD (1970), MCCABE AND MRS. MILLER (1970), and THIEVES LIKE US (1973) . Just prior to the interview Altman showed them three reels of NASHVILLE. The conversation which followed this preparation is reprinted here. A filmography is added.

5265   *Robert Benchley: His Life and Good Times.* by Rosmond, Babette. 239 p. illus. New York: Doubleday, 1969.

Robert Benchley the humorous writer for *Vanity Fair* and *The New Yorker* later went to Hollywood to appear in films. His major ability was to give importance to many supporting or bit comedy roles. In addition he made a series of short subjects in the thirties which are cherished in the memory of those who saw them originally. Viewed today, they may not seem so humorous. Contains film stills, cartoons, and a list of his short films.

5266   *Robert Benchley.* by Yates, Norris W. 175 p. New York: Twayne Publishers, 1968.

This volume concentrates on Benchley as a writer, with scant mention of his career in films and on radio. The author points out that the "Genial Boob" characterization used in films was derived from his humorous writings done in the earlier decade. Personal biographical elements are also minimized with major attention focused on his career as author, columnist, critic, and humorist. Acceptable.

5267   *Robert Benchley: A Biography.* by Benchley, Nathaniel. 258 p. illus. New York: McGraw-Hill, 1955.

The author is the eldest son of Robert Benchley.

5268   *Robert Bresson: The Complete Screenplays—Volume 1.* edited by Michelson, Annette. New York: Urizen, 1980.

5269   *Robert Donat: A Biography.* by Trewin, J. C. 252 p. illus. London: Heinemann, 1968.

This book provides support for the argument that one can write an unexciting biography about an exciting actor. The text and the list of Donat's stage and screen roles will remind the reader of this fine actor's many character creations. The films from his early role in THE PRIVATE LIFE OF HENRY VIII (1933) to his final appearance in THE INN OF THE SIXTH HAPPINESS (1958) are mentioned. Four of his films—THE 39 STEPS (1935), THE CITADEL (1938), THE GHOST GOES WEST (1936), and GOODBYE, MR. CHIPS (1939)—are considered by many to be classics and his contribution to them is not to be minimized.

5270   *Robert E. Sherwood: Film Critic.* by Sherwood, Robert E. 359 p. Brooklyn, N.Y.: Revisionist Press, 1973.

5271   *Robert Flaherty: A Guide to References and Resources.* by Murphy, William T. 171 p. Boston: G.K. Hall, 1978.

This volume on the life and films of Robert Flaherty follows the established pattern of *The Guide to References and Resources* series. It offers all the elements necessary for an understanding and study of the documentary filmmaker—a biographical essay, a critical survey, a detailed filmography, a bibliography, work and writings by Flaherty, archival sources, film distributors, an author index, and a film title index.

The author's success in providing a concentrated biography, many helpful annotations, and a fine critical evaluation of Flaherty's films makes this volume worthy of attention by historians, authors, and scholars.

5272   *Robert Helpmann.* by Walker, Kathrine S. 126 p. illus. London: Rockcliff, 1957.

Robert Helpmann, a ballet dancer from Australia, is probably best known for his performance in the film, THE RED SHOES (1948). In addition to acting on stage and choreographing, he has appeared occasionally in films since his debut in ONE OF OUR AIRCRAFT IS MISSING (1942).

5273 *Robert Mitchum.* by Belton, John. 159 p. paper illus. New York: Pyramid, 1976.

In this excellent survey, the films of Robert Mitchum, from HOPPY SERVES A WRIT (1943) to FAREWELL, MY LOVELY (1975), are examined using factual information, description, critical evaluation and photographic support. Supplementing the text and the clearly reproduced visuals are a bibliography, a filmography, and an index.

This is another fine book in the impressive *Pyramid* series. Applying Belton's sharp critical sense to the work of a colorful and underrated actor such as Mitchum has resulted in an entertaining, informative evaluation. Recommended.

5274 *Robert Mitchum on the Screen.* by Marill, Alvin H. 246 p. illus. New York: A. S. Barnes, 1978.

In recent years the quality of Robert Mitchum's screen performances has been recognized—if somewhat belatedly. This volume reminds the reader of the range of his roles and the unique quality he brought to many of them.

After an introductory biographical chapter, the text reviews his 95 films from BORDER PATROL (1943) to THE BIG SLEEP (1978). For each there are cast names, production credits, stills, plot synopsis, critical quotes and occasional comments by the author. An index is provided.

As a review of a long career and as a reminder of Mitchum's underrated acting ability, the book is quite successful. It will please most readers. Acceptable.

5275 *The Robert Mitchum Story.* by Tomkies, Mike. 271 p. illus. Chicago: Regnery, 1972.

The subtitle for this one originally was "It Sure Beats Working," and it gives a clue to the tone of the book. Mitchum always had a colorful and smart way with words and Tomkies uses that talent to give an enlightening portrait of a unique man.

5276 *Robert Morley: A Reluctant Autobiography.* by Morley, Robert; and Stokes, Sewell. 285 p. illus. New York: Simon & Schuster, 1966.

The subtitle of this book has been aptly chosen by Mr. Morley or his publisher. At the time of publication, Morley had appeared in at least 40 films—from MAIRE ANTOINETTE (1937) to HOTEL PARADISO (1966). In this wordy autobiography Morley writes

a few meager sentences about five of these films. For shame, Mr. Morley.

5277 *The Robert Morley Bedside Reader.* by Morley, Robert. 207 p. illus. Chicago: Henry Regnery, 1976.

This witty and entertaining collection of short articles taken from various periodicals provides a portrait of Robert Morley offstage. Attention is given to his travels, opinions, reactions, relatives, etc., but little is offered about his major occupation—acting. Films are barely mentioned and plays get only a bit more attention.

What is offered, however, is indirect biography—scattered fragments which the reader must assemble. Morley is a civilized English gentleman who has the talent, maturity, and intelligence to translate ordinary events into rewarding reading experiences. Acceptable.

5278 *Robert Redford.* by Reed, Donald A. 185 p. paper illus. New York: Popular Library, 1975.

This over-sized paperback calls itself "A Photographic Portrayal of the Man and His Films." It is really a "Films of..." volume in which each of Redford's films is described by stills, cast, and synopsis. Added are a biographical section and coverage of Redford's work in television and the theatre. The more than 200 visuals provide the substance here.

5279 *Robert Redford.* by Hanna, David. 185 p. paper illus. New York: Nordon Publications (A Leisure Book), 1975.

Subtitled "The Super Star Nobody Knows," this volume combines biographical data with character analysis to provide an interesting study. Since it was written without Redford's cooperation, its total validity may be somewhat questionable.

The author has made good use of his many sources, using numerous quotes throughout and giving the impression of a personal acquaintance with Redford. Although Hanna establishes the external persona of Redford very well, the private man remains hidden.

Two sections of photographs are limited to shots of Redford as actor-celebrity. Nothing is shown of his early life. This volume resembles an uncompleted jigsaw puzzle with only a partial image exposed. Since Redford himself controls the remaining pieces, we will have to wait for his participation for a totally satisfying portrait. In the interim this book is acceptable.

5280 *Robert Redford.* by Paige, David. 31 p. paper illus. Mankato, Minn.: Creative Education, 1977.

A superficial biography written for the very young reader.

5281 *Roberto Rossellini.* by Guarner, Jose Luis. 144 p. illus. New York: Praeger, 1970.

This is an unusual book in that it is a scholarly examination of the films of Rossellini rather than the biography the title may suggest. Written in a formal style lacking any lightness, the value of the book lies in the presentation of the Rossellini films that we have not seen in America. Although the author makes no division, the films seem to fall into periods—the early classics, the Bergman films, the Indian period, the transitional films, and the recent historical films. Each film is prefaced by a plot summary, followed by a serious discussion and analysis. No background to the making of the film is given.

Very few outside sources are quoted. The critical reception or popular success of the films is nowhere noted. The pictures used are excellent but many times players are not identified. Omissions such as Fellini's screenwriting contribution to the classics, ROME, THE OPEN CITY (1945), and PAISAN (1946), are numerous. A filmography and a bibliography are given. An important book because of the scarcity of material available on this director, but a disappointing, cold analytical experience because of the author's intensely pedantic approach.

5282 ROBIN AND MARIAN. by Goldman, James. 186 p. paper illus. New York: Bantam, 1976.

Script of the 1976 film directed by Richard Lester. A long introduction by the author precedes the script. Partial cast and production credits are noted.

5283 *Robot: The Mechanical Monster.* by Annan, David. III p. paper illus. New York: Bounty (Crown), 1976.

This volume is concerned with mechanical men and women as they have appeared in myth, legend and, most prominently, in films. A broad interpretation is given to the term "mechanical monster," and included in the category are the robot girl from METROPOLIS (1926), the computerized people from WESTWORLD (1974), and the monster from the many FRANKENSTEIN films along with similar man-made creations from other films.

The many illustrations, which include several small full-color posters, are well selected and reproduced. No indexis provided. The volume should be popular with its intended audience—the young reader who never tires of science fiction films. Acceptable.

5284 *Rock On Film.* by Ehrenstein, David; and Reed, Bill. 276 p. illus. paper New York: Delilah, 1982.

5285 *Rocks on the Roof.* by Backus, Jim. 190 p. illus. New York: G. P. Putnam's, 1958.

Best known as the voice of Mr. Magoo in the UPA cartoons, Jim Backus has appeared in films since the early forties, usually in a supporting comedy role.

5286 ROCKY and ROCKY II. by Stallone, Sylvester. unpaginated paper illus. Los Angeles: Fotonovel, 1979.

This *Fotonovel* (see series entry) contains 375 stills, some original film dialogue, connecting narrative, and cast credits for the 1979 film, ROCKY II which was directed by Sylvester Stallone. Included also is an abbreviated version of the original 1977 ROCKY in the same format. This film was directed by John Avilosen.

5287 *The Rocky Horror Picture Show Book.* by Henkin, Bill. 239 p. paper illus. New York: Hawthorn, 1979.

This volume tries to explain and also pay homage to the cult film, THE ROCKY HORROR SHOW (1975), using an oversize format, many illustrations, cast profiles, critical reaction, and some music and lyrics.

5288 *Rodgers and Hart: Bewitched, Bothered and Bewildered.* by Marx, Samuel; and Clayton, Jan. 287 p. illus. New York: G. P. Putnams, 1976.

Thisdual biography is called "an anecdotal account" by its authors, both of whom knew Richard Rodgers. This acquaintanceship has apparently hindered or limited the authors in their portrait of him. Not so with Larry Hart, however; he emerges as the fascinating, loveable but ultimately tragic hero of this volume. According to the authors, the major cause of his long unhappiness was his homosexuality.

Although the emphasis is on theatrical musicals, some attention is given to the original music written by Rodgers and Hart specifically for films. Included are AND THEN WE WROTE (a short film made in the late twenties), THE HOT HEIRESS (1931), THE PHANTOM PRESIDENT (1932), LOVE ME TONIGHT (1932), HOLLYWOOD PARTY (1934), HALLELUJAH, I'M A BUM (1933), THE DANCING PIRATE (1935, another short film), THEY MET IN ARGENTINA (1941), MISSISSIPPI (1935). Several of their theatrical successes were also brought to the screen: TOO MANY GIRLS (1940), EVERGREEN (1935), I MARRIED AN ANGEL (1942), HIGHER AND HIGHER (1943), ON YOUR TOES (1939), and PAL JOEY (1957).

Included in the volume are some illustrations and an index. Missing are such essentials as a theatre chronology and a filmography. Acceptable.

5289 *Roger Corman—The Millenic Vision.* by Will, David; and Willemen, Paul. 102 p. paper illus. Edinburgh: Edinburgh Film Festival, 1970.

This collection of essays by the authors along with David Pirie and Lynda Myles was published by the Edinburgh Film Festival in association with *Cinema* magazine. It is the first volume to examine Corman's films in a serious manner. Dividing them into four general categories makes the authors' attempts to examine Corman's world view, his major themes, and his film style most successful. The photographs used are excellent, there is good filmography, and a biographical sketch is given.

5290 *Roger Moore's James Bond Diary.* by Moore, Roger. 184 p. paper illus. Greenwich, Conn.: Fawcett, 1973.

Written during the filming of LIVE AND LET DIE (1973), this diary is a day-to-day (84 in all) account of Moore's experiences in portraying James Bond for the first time. The style of the book is a combination of subtle English humor and mocking self-deprecation. Easy and enjoyable to read, the text does contain some general observations on filmmaking, acting, and celebrity. Of special interest are two sections of illustrations, which help to identify personalities, locations, etc. The book is a pleasant surprise that will please those adults who enjoy the humor implicit in the fictional and film character of James Bond. Moore captures much of the same spirit in his diary.

5291 *The Role of Film in Development.* by Hopkinson, Peter. and 52 p. paper Paris: UNESCO, 1971.

This book, number 64 in the UNESCO *Reports and Papers on Mass Communications* series, is concerned with the ways that films can be used in the development of the newer emerging countries. Development is defined here as "making more fully productive the huge but hitherto underutilized potential wealth of a country's human and natural resources." A minicourse in film genre and its use is offered along with some appendixes on production, costs, training, film terminology and script samples. Acceptable.

5292 *The Role of Sponsored Motion Pictures in the High School.* by Williams, DeLoss; and Finn, James D. 26 p. paper Los Angeles: University of Southern California, Dept. of AV Education, 1961.

The final report of an investigation, this paper includes tables, diagrams and text.

5293 *Roll 'Em: Behind the Scenes in Early Motion Picture Days.* by Roberts, Thomas Benton. 118 p. illus. New York: Vantage Press, 1976.

Thomas Benton Roberts' association with Hollywood and filmmaking was that of a nautical advisor. From 1932 to 1958 he participated in the making of several thousand films by renting or driving boats, building nautical props, helping with special effects, and acting as general advisor on boat sequences. In this volume he recalls incidents from a very unusual career. Unfortunately the memoir provided by the author is a personalized one, punctuated with asides about himself and his family that are of minimal interest. The stories that he tells of Hollywood are mild and depend upon celebrity name-dropping rather than narrative style for their appeal. Since the visuals provided are quite small and many are poorly reproduced, they offer little support to the weak text. No index is provided.

This volume is quite harmless and may even please some readers. Acceptable.

5294 *Roman Polanski: A Guide to References and Resources.* by Bisplinghoff, Gretchen; and Wexman, Virginia Wright. 116 p. Boston: G. K. Hall, 1979.

This reference book on Roman Polanski follows the general structure of the series. A short biography, which successfully avoids emphasizing the sensational, introduces the information sources, the major section of which is an annotated bibliography arranged yearly from 1958 to 1978. Also included are a critical survey of Polanski; a filmography with synopses, credits, notes and awards; a list of Polanski's performances and writings; distributor names; and archival sources for additional research. A film index and an author index complete the volume.

CHINATOWN (1974) is the Polanski film that apparently has fascinated most writers although his other features, KNIFE IN THE WATER (1962), MACBETH (1971), REPULSION (1965), CUL-DE-SAC (1966), and ROSEMARY'S BABY (1968), are also well covered by the literature.

Polanski has made relatively few films to date but they are all memorable. Any reader seriously interested in his work should begin with this comprehensive reference.

5295 *Roman Polanski.* edited by Reed, Rochelle. 24 p. paper illus. Washington, D.C.: American Film Institute, 1974.

Roman Polanski was finishing his work on CHINATOWN (1974) when this interview was made on March 20, 1974. A filmography is appended.

5296 *The Roman Polanski Story.* by Kiernan, Thomas. 262 p. illus. New York: Delilah/Grove Press, 1980.

Roman Polanski has publically refuted much of what author Thomas Kiernan has included in this obviously unauthorized biography. Nevertheless, the story related here holds enormous interest. Kiernan claims his sources to be the various members of the Polanski circle—a Polish expatriate group of filmmakers. Using their input and the usual research sources, he traces Polanski's life from his birth in Paris in 1933 to the completion of his film, TESS (1979). Some of the text deals with bizarre sexual matters that have provided gossip and innuendo about Polanski for years. The author is not hesitant in supplying conjecture and color to some of his factual material. Illustrations are provided, but there is no index or filmography.

This is strong biographical material that will fascinate any one familiar with Polanski's films. How much of the private life revealed here appears in the films is a puzzle for future biographers to solve.

5297 *The Romance of Motion Picture Production.* by Royal, Lee. 72 p. illus. Los Angeles: Royal, 1920.

5298 *The Romance of the Movies.* by Wood, Leslie. London: Heinemann, 1937.

Long out of print, this book was an early version of the 1947 *The Miracle of the Movies.*

5299 *The Romance of the Talkies.* by Allighan, Garry. 104 p. illus. London: Claude Stacey, 1929.

Examines the early talking picture era, pointing out its inevitability, popularity, rapid acceptance and its implications for the industry and for society. Includes statistics, technical details, theatre architecture, performers, etc.

5300 *Romanian Animation Films Catalogue 1972.* paper illus. Bucharest: Romania Film, 1973.

A catalog in three languages (English, French, German) that gives data and description about cartoons, cut-outs, puppets, and other forms of animated films created in Romania.

5301 ROMEO AND JULIET. 34 p. paper illus. New York: National Publishers, 1968.

There are only a few colored stills in the center section of this souvenir book based on the 1968 film which utilized color photography so well. The black and white photographs are devoted to the usual topics: stills, cast members, sets, etc. The production under Franco Zefferelli's direction is discussed. Other supporting cast and production credits are noted.

5302 ROMEO AND JULIET. by Shakespeare, William. 290 p. illus. New York: Random House, 1936.

This volume was published simultaneously with the appearance of the 1936 film version of ROMEO AND JULIET. It contains chapters written by Norma Shearer (Juliet), Leslie Howard (Romeo), John Barrymore (Mercutio), Cedric Gibbons (settings), Adrian (costumes), etc. Shakespeare's play and the film script are included.

5303 *Ronald Colman.: A Very Private Person.* by Colman, Juliet Benita. 294 p. illus. New York: Morrow, 1975.

This biography, written by the subject's daughter, covers Ronald Colman's career from his early days as a shipping clerk to his final film in 1957. Colman is characterized as an extremely shy man whose acting ability and distinctive voice gave him lengthy careers in films, on radio and on television. The author knew her father only as a child and relies on the anecdotes, reminiscences and memories of Colman's contemporaries. Apparently his screen image of a principled gentleman extended to his personal life. Included are a filmography, a bibliography, a list of theatre appearances, some illustrations and an index. Acceptable.

5304 *Ronald Colman.* Wild, Roland.

This biography of Ronald Colman covers his early career and gives minimal attention to his success in talking pictures.

5305 *Rosalind Russell.* by Yanni, Nicholas. 160 p. paper illus. New York: Pyramid, 1975.

A critical survey of Rosalind Russell's career as a film actress is offered in this fine original paperback. Beginning with EVELYN PRENTICE (1934), the author discusses Russell's 51 films ending with MRS. POLLIFAX—SPY (1971). The only attention paid to her personal life comes in a short epilogue entitled "The Private Lady." The evaluations of Russell's work are often quite subjective, but Yanni does succeed in avoiding the adoring-fan approach; at time he states she was miscast or her interpretation was wrong, and he even accuses her of overacting several times. As usual with the *Pyramid* series, the visual selection and reproduction are top-notch. A bibliography, a filmography and an index are added. Recommended.

5306 THE ROSE: An Illustrated Book. by Watson, Diane Masters. 98 p. paper illus. New York: Twenty First Century Communications, 1979.

Although this original paperback is called a novel, it is composed mostly of visuals taken from the 1979 film, THE ROSE. The terse narrative serves primarily as an explanation and continuity for the intriguing photographs, many of which are reproduced in full color. A different form of film book, this one falls somewhere between the souvenir book and the photonovel. It is carefully produced and summarizes the film in an attractive fashion.

5307 *Rossellini: The War Trilogy.* by Rossellini, Roberto. paper illus. New York: Grossman, 1973.

Contains the following scripts: OPEN CITY (1945), (also known as ROME, OPEN CITY); PAISAN (1946); GERMANY, YEAR ZERO (1947).

5308 *Rotha on the Film: A Selection of Writings on the Cinema.* by Rotha, Paul. 338 p. Fair Lawn, N.J.: Essential Books, 1958.

This book is a series of articles written between 1928 and 1957, which the author has divided into four general groupings: general film topics, specific motion pictures, problems of the documentary, and problems of the British film industry. The sources of the material are magazines and journals, for the most part British. Most of the articles are still of great interest but those on the documentary and the British film industry will have a limited appeal. Some illustrations are included and there are both name and general indices. The intelligence, background, and writing ability that Rotha brings to the field of film literature makes everything he has written important. This book is no exception. Some of the material will not excite the general reader of today. There is no index.

5309 *Rouben Mamoulian: Style is the Man.* edited by Silke, James R. 35 p. paper illus. Washington, D.C.: The American Film Institute, 1971.

A transcription of an interview with Mamoulian held in April 1970 at the AFI Center in Beverly Hills. Includes a bibliography, a filmography, and a listing of the stage productions that Mamoulian was involved with. The book has an index-guide to the topics discussed during the interview and a few illustrations. Acceptable.

5310 *Roy Rogers, King of the Cowboys.* by Roper, William L. 182 p. illus. Minneapolis: Denison, 1971.

A title in the *Men of Achievement* series, this biography of "The King of the Cowboys," Roy Rogers, was written for the young reader. Illustrations and a bibliography accompany the text.

5311 *The Royal Ballet on Stage and Screen: The Book of the Royal Ballet Film.* edited by Moiseiwitsch, Maurice; and Warman, Eric. 56 p. illus. London: William Heinemann, 1960.

Analysis and coverage of the ballets "Swan Lake," "Firebird," and "Ondine" as filmed by the Rank Organization.

5312 *Rudolph Valentino: The Man Behind the Myth.* by Oberfirst, Robert. 320 p. illus. New York: Citadel Press, 1962.

"He was a man of physical beauty, but a boy at heart. Without the strong, wise guidance of his mother he was lost, as would be any boy in playland." The paragraph above is typical of the gushy, schoolgirl style used in this biography. There is no author hesitancy in reconstructing fictional conversations and happenings. The recreations of bedroom scenes are ludicrous and laughable. Another bonus from the author is the 12-page section reprinting Valentino's favorite poems.

The documentation and interpretation of well-known facts about his early career are omitted or distorted into romantic, saccharine adventures. Was it not the shame of his arrest and several days in jail that sent him in flight to the West Coast? Did Mae Murray advance the money for his jail bond? This book gives as his only reason a determination to become a farmer in the west. The pictures are average and there is no index. This is biographical writing of such poor quality that it makes one want to reconsider the slanderous Steiger-Mank paperback or the padded Shulman tome on Valentino. At least the fictions and sexual insinuations found in those volumes were titillating.

5313   *Rudolph Valentino.* by Walker, Alexander. 127 p. illus. New York: Stein and Day, 1976.

One may approach another biography of Valentino with apprehension—what more can be said? Since film critic Alexander Walker has two successful film books, *Stardom: The Hollywood Phenomenon* and *Hollywood U.K.*, to his credit, curiosity may also exist as to his handling of the Valentino story. Ultimately it is the author's ability at synthesizing the available biographical data surrounding the legend that will determine the book's quality. In this effort Walker has some mixed success; he has taken all the known events of Valentino's life and woven them into a relatively clear portrait of the romantic actor. In describing and evaluating Valentino's film style and effect, he is perceptive, objective and critically on-target. Only his treatment of the rumor and gossip surrounding his subject is weak. For example, much conjecture still exists about Valentino's sexual nature off-screen; Walker's conclusion is that it was extremely low key, with Valentino making no demands on his wives—a flat, unsatisfactory explanation at best.

Many illustrations accompany the text and the book is indexed. Acceptable.

5314   *Rudolph Valentino Paper Dolls.* by Tierney, Tom. 32 p. paper illus. New York: Dove, 1979.

Tierney repeats his Hollywood paperdoll format here using Rudolph Valentino and 22 authentic costumes from his films, and elsewhere. Ten films are represented along with Nijinsky as Valentino, an Indian chief and a vaudeville dancer. A short biography appears on the inside cover.

5315   *Rudy: An Intimate Portrait of Rudolph Valentino by His Wife.* by Rambova, Natacha. 224 p. illus. London: Hutchinson, 1927.

A reminiscence of Valentino's life and career constitutes the first part of this book. Included here are short sketches of the famous Hollywood personalities prominent during the early twenties. The second part deals with supposed messages received from Valentino after his death.

5316   *Rules for Use in the Cataloguing Department of the National Film Archive.* by Grenfell, David; and Kula, Sam; and Carroll, Jeanne. 46 p. paper illus. London: British Film Institute, 1960.

This is the fifth edition of a work that appeared originally around 1950. It formulates rules for placing entries in the title catalog, the news film catalog, and in indexes. Proper alphabetizing and capitalization are described. Appendixes consider procedures, definitions, abbreviations, credits, classifications, headings, types of cards used. Some sample cards and an index complete the volume. A most useful reference for all libraries having film collections.

5317   RULES OF THE GAME. by Renoir, Jean; and Koch, Karl; and Francois, Camille. 172 p. illus. New York: Simon & Schuster, 1970.

Script of the 1939 film directed by Renoir. Contains cast credits and seven articles: 1) "The Birth of RULES OF THE GAME," an interview with Renoir; 2) "The Era of the Auteur," an interview with Renoir; 3) Interview in Sologne; 4) "A Certain Grace: Jean Renoir"; 5) "Alain Resnais and Richard Roud"; 6) "An Intimate Chamber Piece: Joel W. Finler"; and 7) "Historical Note."

5318   *Run Through: A Memoir.* by Houseman, John. 507 p. illus. New York: Simon and Schuster, 1972.

The memoir runs from 1902 to 1942, with the greatest attention given to the decade of the thirties. The attraction for many readers will be the portrait of Orson Welles as a teen-aged actor, director, producer and radio performer. The final portion of the book will be of most interest to film enthusiasts. Houseman went to Hollywood with Welles and his account of the evolution of CITIZEN KANE (1941) is fascinating. He worked in the film industry with others but those experiences are not covered in this volume. His productions include: THE BLUE DAHLIA (1946), LETTER FROM AN UNKNOWN WOMAN (1948), JULIUS CASESAR (1953), LUST FOR LIFE (1956), THE BAD AND THE BEAUTIFUL (1952), among others.

Houseman's partial biography needs no further endorsement here. A brilliant book, it was given wide critical praise and was the recipient of several honors. Its contribution to film literature is the reason for its inclusion in this book. By furnishing the Welles portrait, the information on such pre-CITIZEN KANE films as TOO MUCH JOHNSON (1938), and confirming much of Kael's argument, he helps to add to the legend and importance of Welles and CITIZEN KANE. The book has fine illustrations and is indexed.

5319 *Running a School Film Society.* by Smith, Jack. 5 p. London: Society of Film Teachers, 1958.

A short pamphlet that deals with such topics as finance, choice of films, presentation, and teaching appreciation. A sample program note for Jacques Tati's JOUR DE FETE (1947) is included.

5320 *Running Away from Myself.* by Deming, Barbara. 210 p. illus. New York: Grossman Pub., 1969.

The underlying premise of this book is that film reflects society, not as a mirror but as a visualizer of our dreams both pleasant (wishes) and unpleasant (fears). Films used to illustrate this thesis are taken largely from the forties (with a few from the thirties). With such character genres as the war hero, the possessive heroine, the success boy, the restless, the lost, the tough, the nihilist, and the comic heroes, the author presents a rather hopeless dream portrait. Whether or not the reader will agree with the author's theory, he will be stimulated and absorbed by the analysis and suggestion offered. There are illustrations and a filmography. A good example of the possible use of the entertainment film in psychological study, this book is recommended for the more mature reader.

5321 *Russel Harty Plus.* by Harty, Russel. 177 p. illus. London: Elm Tree Books, 1974.

Harty is a television talk show host and his book includes material on David Niven, Michael Caine, Tony Curtis, June Havoc and Oliver Reed.

5322 THE RUSSIAN ADVENTURE. by Okon, May. 32 p. paper illus. New York: Perry Sales, Ltd., 1966.

This is the souvenir book of a travelogue of Russia that was produced in the Cinerama format and was narrated by Bing Crosby. Consisting mostly of stills from the 1966 film, the book illustrates a circus, a ballet, a whale hunt, the Moiseyev dancers, a boar hunt, reindeer races, etc. One page is devoted to Crosby, another to the producers, and the center section contains a map of Russia.

5323 *Russian-English Dictionary of Science, Technology and the Art of Cinematography.* compiled by Telberg, Val G. 103 p. New York: Telbeg Book Corp., 1964.

5324 *Russian Film Catalogues (No. 5 and No. 8).* 104 & 99 p. paper illus. Moscow: Sovexport Film, n.d.

No dates appear on these catalogs, but they seem to have been published during the sixties. Designed to promote the sale of films in Russia and other lands, the books contain annotations in Russian, English, and French. Films are arranged according to topic/subject: peace, friendship, cooperation among people; people, events, and the times; science and engineering; culture and art; natural history and people; sports; cartoons, puppet films; and television films.

5325 *Sabu of the Elephants.* by Whittingham, Jack. 124 p. illus. London:, 1938.

This biography of Sabu Dastagir contains a preface by Alexander Korda.

5326 *Sabu, the Elephant Boy.* by Flaherty, Frances; and Leacock, Ursula. 94 p. illus. London: J. H. Dent, 1938.

This account of the 1937 period during which ELEPHANT BOY was being made by Robert Flaherty includes material about the discovery of Sabu Dastagir, who rose from stable boy to international film actor. Legends and stories about elephants are also included.

5327 *Sacha Guitry: The Last Boulevardier.* by Harding, James. 277 p. illus. New York: Scribners, 1968.

A biography of the French actor-producer-director which includes a filmography.

5328 *Sacha Guitry.* by Knapp, Bettina. 245 p. illus. Boston: Twayne, 1981.

5329 *Saddle Aces of the Cinema.* by Rainey, Buck. 307 p. San Diego: A. S. Barnes, 1980.

This collective biography of 15 movie cowboys treats some familiar subjects along with others who are relatively unknown or forgotten. Thus, Tom Mix and Gene Autry appear along with Wally Wales, Reb Russell, Al Hoxie, and Fred Thompson. For each there is an essay, some illustrations, and a filmography. Since cowboy films were ground out with almost weekly regularity at times, the filmographies tend to be quite lengthy. A film index and a name index complete this specialized book, which may appeal to western film devotees.

5330 *Sadism in the Movies.* by De Coulteray, George. 400 p. illus. New York: Medical Press of N.Y., 1965.

A candidate for the pornographic fast buck, this book furnishes nearly 200 pages of text devoted to a cataloging of sadistic themes. A not-always-successful attempt is made to link these themes with scenes or actions in films. On many occasions the author seems to be stretching credulity to find examples. THE VIKINGS (1958), incidentally, provides much of his material. The latter portion of the book contains several hundred pornographic illustrations of the themes, most of which are poorly reproduced, and even in some cases, quite indistinct. There is no index and none of the illustrations are identified. Some of the text is interesting (e.g., "Hitchcock confuses, for his repulsive ethical purposes, sadism and misogyny") but the book is such a poor overall treatment of the subject that it cannot be recommended to anyone except the overly prurient.

5331 *The Saga of Buck Jones.* by Rainey, Buck. 126 p. illus. Los Angeles: Western Film Collector Press, 1975.

5332 *The Saga of Special Effects.* by Fry, Ron; and Fourzon, Pamela. 212 p. illus. Englewood Cliffs, N.J.: Prentice Hall, 1977.

Called in its subtitle "The Complete History of Cinematic Illusion, from Edison's Kinetoscope to Dynamation, Sensaround... and Beyond," this volume offers one of the best overviews of motion picture special effects published to date. Using a historical framework, the authors explain by word and picture how special effects have been created by studio technicians to give the impression of reality to the improbable or the impossible. Chapters are devoted to the infant industry, the silent era, the thirties, World War II, the "creature-ridden" fifties, the "spectacular" sixties and the "disaster" seventies.

An appendix lists those films nominated for Academy Awards for special effects, with the winners indicated. A short bibliography and an index complete the book. The illustrations, an essential element of the book, are most helpful in explaining the various processes employed.

Special effects are one of the most intriguing elements of filmmaking; their use creates a kind of magic that can be found in no other medium. This volume, which is comprehensive, readable, and informative, presents a superb explanation and history of these unique illusions. Highly recommended.

5333 *Saint Cinema.* by Weinberg, Herman G. 366 p. paper illus. New York: Drama Book Specialists, 1973.

A collection of articles on film written during the preceding 40 years. The approach is artistic, theoretical, and intellectual and deals almost exclusively with the art film and the serious artist. Most entertaining are the pieces entitled "Coffee, Brandy, and Cigars" taken from *Film Culture.* They are a potpourri of unrelated thoughts and ramblings on cinematic topics. The book is quite special, but could be very rewarding to the right reader.

5334 SAINT JOAN. by Shaw, George Bernard. 162 p. illus. Seattle, Wash.: University of Washington Press, 1968.

The unfilmed script of Shaw's play, edited by Bernard F. Dukore.

5335 SALESMAN. by Maysles, Albert; and Maysles, David; and Zwerin, Charlotte. 128 p. paper illus. New York: Signet Books, 1969.

Script of the 1961 film directed by Albert and David Maysles. Contains cast credits, a filmography, and an introduction by Harold Clurman.

5336 SALT OF THE EARTH: The Story and Script of the Film. by Biberman, Herbert. 373 p. illus. Boston: Beacon Press, 1965.

The story of the great difficulty surrounding the making, distribution, and showing of a motion picture, this volume addresses itself to freedom of speech. Can a film which takes a strong minority stand on a controversial issue survive? Can the men responsible for the film statement also be allowed to exist professionally? The author, one of the Hollywood Ten (and the husband of Gale Sondergaard), tells the story of this struggle, which culminates in the trial of some 60 defendants accused of conspiracy and violation of anti-trust laws. Some stills and a script of the film complete the book. Specialized as to its film topic, the book is generalized in its theme, which is freedom of the screen. An important book for all advanced readers.

5337 SALT OF THE EARTH. by Wilson, Michael. 191 p. Old Westbury, N.Y.: Feminist Press, 1978.

Includes a long commentary by Deborah S. Rosenfelt and several articles about the making of the film.

5338 SALTWATER FLATS, A Silent Film. by Blotnick, Elihu. 64 p. illus. paper Berkeley, Calif.: California Street, 1975.

5339 *Sam Peckinpah: Master of Violence.* by Evans, Max. 92 p. illus. Vermillion, S.D.: Dakota Press, 1972.

This is not a biography, nor is it a study of Peckinpah's films. It is a series of disconnected anecdotes, comments, and descriptions about the making of THE BALLAD OF CABLE HOGUE (1970). The author has known Peckinpah for almost a decade and was invited to work with him on HOGUE. This volume tells something of Peckinpah's methods, the reactions of people to him, and his lifestyle. Some spare background information about his other films appears in opening and closing chapters.

The illustrations are unimpressive, except as a reminder to the reader that the director was responsible for RIDE THE HIGH COUNTRY (1962), THE WILD BUNCH (1969), MAJOR DUNDEE (1965), STRAW DOGS (1971), and THE GETAWAY (1972). JUNIOR BONNER (1973) is mentioned, but no illustration is given. At best this is pleasant reading—chatty, fragmented and subjective—and it gives some insight into Peckinpah and his directorial skills; at worst it is an inflated magazine piece. Acceptable.

5340 *see 5339*

5341 *Samuel Fuller.* by Hardy, Phil. 144 p. paper illus. New York: Praeger, 1970.

From 1949 to 1967, Samuel Fuller made quality action films on very low budgets—SHOCK CORRIDOR (1963), RUN OF THE ARROW (1956), etc. As a detailed examination of the relatively unknown writer-producer-director and his work, this book divides the films into five subject or theme categories: an American dream, journalism and style, an American reality, Asia, and the violence of love. In each section the individual films are summarized and analyzed. As a result the reader receives not only accounts of the films, but also a composite portrait of Fuller. His influence on Godard is mentioned. Excellent stills are scattered throughout the book, not always alongside the film being examined . A filmography including television work is appended. There is no index. This book should hasten a belated recognition of Fuller.

5342 *Samuel Fuller.* edited by Will, David; and Wollen, Peter. 128 p. paper illus. Edinburgh: Scottish International Review, 1969.

An anthology about Fuller with essays, articles, an interview, a biography and a filmography.

5343 *Samuel Fuller.* by Garnham, Nicholas. 176 p. paper illus. New York: Viking, 1972.

The premise that Welles, Mankiewicz and Fuller are the clearest American examples of auteur theory begins this examination of Samuel Fuller's work. The approach to the films is as a total body of work rather than as individual statements. A broad overview describes the influences, settings, camera techniques, editing, and themes found in the films and provides the base for what follows. In succeeding chapters, the continual appearance of large themes such as the individual, love, society, national identity, energy and, finally, madness is noted.

A concluding section suggests the influence that Fuller has had on Godard. The filmography which closes the book is detailed and helpful in recalling the films, most of which were low-budget B films. The cult which has grown about Fuller and his work should find strong support in this well-written and different examination. The arguments are logical and objective in spite of the author's obvious admiration for his subject. Picture quality is only fair and no index is provided. Recommended.

5344 *Samuel Goldwyn.* by Epstein, Lawrence J. Boston: Twayne, 1981.

5345 *Samuel Goldwyn Presents.* by Marill, Alvin H. 320 p. illus. New York:

A. S. Barnes, 1976.

This detailed filmography of 80 Samuel Goldwyn productions begins with THE ETERNAL CITY (1923) and ends with PORGY AND BESS (1959). In between are classic films such as WUTHERING HEIGHTS (1941), THE LITTLE FOXES (1941) and THE BEST YEARS OF OUR LIVES (1946), along with some forgotten clinkers like ONE HEAVENLY NIGHT (1930), WE LIVE AGAIN (1934) and I WANT YOU (1951). Marill has provided a fine coverage of the films by giving a plot synopsis, several stills, cast and production credits, critical quotes, and background information. However, a reading of the text suggests that he has obtained most of his material from previous writings rather than a re-viewing of the films. It is undeniable that Goldwyn's product was characterized by careful casting, good direction, and expensive production values. The films reflect a uniform quality and care but they are largely products of their time and the majority of them seem quite dated when viewed today.

Supporting elements include a short introductory biography, a portrait gallery of Goldwyn stars and filmmakers, a list of radio and television versions of the films, and an index.

Unfortunately the text does not examine the films in today's terms; however, it does contain an abundance of information and nostalgia that makes for a rewarding reading experience and for a useful reference work. Acceptable.

5346   *Samuel Goldwyn, The Producer and His Films.* by Griffith, Richard. 48 p. paper illus. New York: Museum of Modern Art, 1956.

A brief biographical sketch followed by film notes on approximately two dozen Goldwyn productions make up this booklet. Originally issued in 1956 to accompany a showing of Goldwyn films at the Museum of Modern Art, it is still pertinent because of the revivals of the films and their frequent appearance on TV. As with all of Richard Griffith's work, the material is authoritative, interesting, and structured. The illustrations are few in number and fair in quality. The list of the independent productions of Samuel Goldwyn which concludes the booklet is an excellent reminder of Goldwyn's contribution to motion pictures. Recommended as general reading and as background to the Goldwyn films.

5347   *The Samurai Film.* by Silver, Alain. 242 p. illus. New York: A. S. Barnes, 1977.

A genre unfamiliar to most western film viewers is given detailed treatment in this volume. Combining history and criticism, the author presents a study of a film genre indigenous to the Japanese cinema. A few of Kurosawa's samurai films—RASHOMON (1950), SEVEN SAMURAI (1954), THRONE OF BLOOD (1951), YOJIMBO (1961), and SANJURO (1962)—are known in America but the work of other directors in this genre is not. Covered here are films of Hideo Gosha, Hiroshi Inagaki, Kihachi Okamoto, and Masahiro Shinoda.

Opening sections deal with the samurai in history, in fiction, in legend and in art. Genre types, the alien hero and the slayers, are considered in individual chapters, as are Kurosawa and Gosha.

Supporting elements are excellent. They include a fascinating glossary of Japanese terms, a bibliography, an index and several filmographies (one for directors, another for series films), and a final chronological listing of samurai films from 1950 to 1972. The illustrations which complement the text are well-selected but their reproduction quality is variable.

An impressive treatment of an unusual film topic is offered here. The book should please anyone interested in the serious study of cinema. In addition, its value as a reference work is considerable. Recommended.

5348   SAN FRANCISCO. by Loos, Anita. 205 p. illus. Carbondale, Ill.:Southern Illinois Press, 1979.

A reading version of Loos's original script including added scenes and retakes. The volume also offers a short preface along with cast and credits. The 1936 film was directed by W.S. Van Dyke.

5349   *Sand in My Mink.* by Donlan, Yolande. 144 p. illus. London: MacGibbon and Kee, 1955.

Yolande Donlan is an American actress who achieved fame on the London stage and in British films. Active during the fifties and sixties, she offers an account of her travels in Europe and North Africa in this volume. She is married to Val Guest, the writer-director-producer.

5350   THE SAND PEBBLES. by Graham, Bruce. 32 p. paper illus. New York: Alsid Distributors, 1966.

The problems of reproducing "China in the 20's" are detailed in this souvenir book. How the production was begun under the guidance of producer-director Robert Wise is noted. There are some attractive full-page color portraits of the stars and other cast credits and production names are given. One of the more interesting sections pertains to the building of the gunboat, "The San Pablo."

5351 *Santiago Alvarez.* edited by Chanan, Michael. 70 p. paper New York: Zoetrope, 1981.

Alvarez is a Cuban documentary filmmaker whose work includes agit-prop cinema. He produced some Cuban newsreels for Noticiero.

5352 SARABAND FOR DEAD LOVERS: The Film and its Production. 107 p.illus. London: Convoy Pub., 1948.

This is a superior account of the production of a film called SARABAND (1948) in the United States. A visual sample of the components is offered the reader—the publicity stills, the story boards, a page of the original script, the art sketches for a scene, a section of the musical score, costume designs, and finally a section of a scenario. Illustrations, photos, credit lists are all excellent. Recommended as both interesting, informative material and as a model for producers who prepare similar publications.

5353 *Sarah Bernhardt.* by Emboden, William. 176 p. illus. New York: Macmillan, 1975.

This volume is noted since it contains two chapters which deal with Sarah Bernhardt's films. How an aging legendary actress used a new medium to insure immortality makes fascinating reading and viewing. The book is a pictorial history of Bernhardt with emphasis, naturally, on her stage roles.

5354 *Sarah Bernhardt; The Art within the Legend.* by Taranow, Gerda. 287 p. illus. Princeton, N.J.: Princeton University Press, 1972.

It is the art of Sarah Bernhardt that the author is concerned with here rather than the biography. Divided into sections which treat voice, pantomime, gesture, spectacle, roles and repertoire, the book offers as appendices a filmography, an audiography, and a bibliography. It is because of the filmography that the book is noted here.

5355 *Saturday Afternoon at the Bijou.* by Zinman, David. 511 p. illus. New Rochelle, N.Y.: Arlington House, 1973.

One of three books that treat similar material, the series films which usually occupied half of the double bills during the 1930's and 1940's. *The Great Movie Series* and *A Thousand and One Delights* are the others. This entrant in the competition has some omissions and inconsistencies that lessen its effectiveness.

The title is somewhat misleading, since Zinman's concern is more with a survey of series films rather than with Saturday matinee film material. There is an appreciable difference. Starting with the Tarzan films, he discusses, in turn, The Wolf Man, Frankenstein's monster, The Invisible Man, The Mummy, Planet of the Apes, Gene Autry, The Cisco Kid, Hopalong Cassidy, The Three Musketeers, Sherlock Holmes, The Saint, The Falcon, The Thin Man, Crime Doctor, Charlie Chan, Mr. Moto, Fu Manchu, James Bond, Dr. Kildare, Dr. Christian, Doctor in the House, Andy Hardy, Henry Aldrich, Blondie, Nancy Drew, Mexican Spitfire, Torchy Blane, The Dead End Kids, Lassie and Our Gang. Selective, to be sure, but why some of these over Ma and Pa Kettle, Abbott and Costello, Maisie, Philo Vance, The East Side Kids, The Bowery Boys, the Carry-On Films, or The Three Stooges? Why the inclusion of the British doctor series, the James Bond series, or the Planet of the Apes films, all of which appeared from the mid-50's to late 60's, but none of which was a Saturday matinee series?

For each series, a single film is described in some detail to convey the flavor of the series. A complete filmography follows each chapter and more than 250 photographs aid greatly in the descriptions. The text is chatty, informative, and full of factual trivia. It makes for enjoyable reading, and that Zinman is a dedicated film buff is obvious on every page. His affection for these old mediocre films is apparently limitless. The book is indexed and there is a short selected bibliograhy.

While one can appreciate and approve Zinman's ardor for the series films, this tribute is a little late and a little less than some earlier volumes. However, it does have both reference and entertainment values.

5356 *The Saturday Evening Post* Movie Book. edited by Flythe, Starkey, Jr. 152 p. illus. Indianapolis: Curtis, 1979.

This anthology of articles and illustrations comes from the pages of *The Saturday Evening Post*. High spots of Hollywood history are covered from 1902 to 1974 and include most of the legendary names. The policy of the magazine was to use short, one-page articles along with short stories. A dozen *Post* stories used as the basis for films are here along with numerous short pieces, some purportedly written by Hollywood personalities.

Paintings by Norman Rockwell appear throughout.

5357   SATURDAY MORNING. by MacKenzie, Kent; and Goldsmith, Gary. 143 p. paper illus. New York: Avon Books, 1971.

Script of the 1971 film directed by Kent Mackenzie. Contains cast credits, production credits, and an introduction by the producer-director, Kent Mackenzie.

5358   *Saturday Morning Cinema.* by Members of the Children's Film Foundation. 52 p. paper illus. London: Children's Film Foundation, 1969.

This volume, which is subtitled "25 Years of Films for Children—The Children's Film Foundation Moves into the Seventies," is a combination of text and filmography. Opening sections describe the history, activities, and services of the CFF. The mid-section contains a catalog-filmography of CFF films —title, number of reels, color, format, synopsis, credits, cast, awards, and a still are given for each. A financial report, sections on the audience, and the international distribution of CFF films complete the volume. In 1972 the catalog was separated from the text material and issued separately.

5359   SATURDAY NIGHT FEVER - Official Authorized Scrapbook. 64 p. illus. New York: Paradise Press (Castle), 1978.

This heavily illustrated book has four articles on John Travolta, the females in the film, the Bee Gees and producer Robert Stigwood.

5360   *Satyajit Ray: Our Films, Their Films.* by Ray, Satyajit. 219 p. New Delhi: Orient Longman, 1976.

The title given to this collection of 25 essays aptly describes its content—filmmaker Satyajit Ray's comments on the cinema of India and other nations. Included in the latter category are Italy, United States, England, Russia, and Japan.

Since the author is so closely associated with the Indian film, much of the volume approaches a kind of indirect autobiography. Ray's personal approach is noted along with his reaction to and appreciation of other filmmakers. The volume is indexed.

Among other things, the book offers a taste of autobiography, philosophy, national cinema, film criticism, director appreciation, and eastern culture. It

can appeal to the reader on several levels. Recommended.

5361   *Savage Cinema.* by Witcombe, Rick Trader. 95 p. paper illus. New York: Bounty, 1975.

This survey of screen violence consists of a serious, interpretive text and a collection of sensationalized visuals. The latter are mostly stills with a few examples of movie poster art added. Sex, nudity, perversion, sadism and aggression are featured predominately in the photographs, which vary considerably in their clarity and sharpness. The reader may sense a contradiction between the sensible analytical text and the shocking illustrations. Are they really necessary or were they added to sell the volume? Argument can be offered either way. The limits of aggression and violence have yet to be established. The volume is without an index or a table of contents. Acceptable for mature adults.

5362   SAVAGES. by Trow, George S.; and O'Donoghue, Michael. 152 p. paper illus. New York: Evergreen, 1973.

Script of the 1973 film directed by James Ivory. Includes an introduction by James Ivory, and "A Motion Picture Treatment," by James Ivory, George S. Trow, and Michael O'Donoghue.

5363   SAVAGES, SHAKESPEARE WALLAH. by Ivory, James. 152 p. paper illus. London: Plexus, 1973.

Contains scripts and articles for: SAVAGES, (1973); and SHAKESPEARE WALLAH (1965).

5364   *Sawed-Off Justice.* by Franklin, Lynn; and Green, Maury. illus. New York: G. P. Putnam's, 1976.

Crimes committed in Beverly Hills are described by a retired member of the police force. Punishment is rare because of overly lenient judges who succumb easily to pressure.

5365   "Say... Didn't You Used To Be George Murphy?". by Murphy, George; and Lasky, Victor. 438 p. illus. New York: Bartholomew House, 1970.

This autobiography could have been so much better. The author displays a talent for rationalizing, underplaying, or for overlooking all the questionable happenings in his career and emphasizing only the good or saleable points. This approach may serve as pre-election fodder but it does not make a good biography. Do all political candidates in California publish biographies in election years?

The emphasis throughout reflects the Right Republican Establishment and pays constant tribute to its most publicized representatives. The comments about Murphy's films are quite good; it is a shame they are surrounded by the one-sided prejudiced verbiage about a public political fiction rather than an honest look at a human being. This book is indexed and has a few uninteresting photographs. Acceptable only for the film comment.

5366 *Scandal and Parade: The Theater of Jean Cocteau.* by Oxenhandler, Neal. 284 p. illus. New Brunswick, N.J.: Rutgers University Press, 1957.

5367 *Scandinavian Film.* by Hardy, Forsyth. 94 p. illus. London: Falcon Press, 1952.

An area of filmmaking largely overlooked until recently has been Danish, Swedish, and Norwegian films, which are discussed from the historical and critical viewpoint in this slim volume. Somewhat dated, it has value for the advanced, dedicated student or researcher. Appreciation of European films demands background and thus this book is not for the casual or general reader.

5368 *Scarlett Fever.* by Pratt, William; and Bridges, Herb. 323 p. illus. New York: Macmillan, 1977.

Called "The Ultimate Pictorial Treasure of Gone With the Wind," this attractive volume deals first with the book, then the film, and finally, the years following its first showing in 1939. Conjecture about a sequel, and GONE WITH THE WIND on television are the book's final topics.

Using the collection of GONE WITH THE WIND memorabilia owned by Herb Bridges, the book covers all aspects of the film—its time in American history, the players, behind the scenes stories, stills, designs, studio shots, etc. A bibliography and an index are included.

Everything anyone would want to know about GONE WITH THE WIND probably can be found here. The result is an overabundance of work and picture information that may have the same effect as an overindulgence in any pleasure—weariness, discomfort and ennui.

5369 *Scarlett O'Hara's Younger Sister.* by Keyes, Evelyn. 318 p. paper illus. Secaucus, N.J.: Lyle Stuart, 1977.

Evelyn Keyes has written a book designed to titillate and tantalize readers in search of celebrity expose. In telling of her adventures with the high and mighty of Hollywood (DeMille, Harry Cohn, John Huston, Kirk Douglas, Charles Vidor, Mike Todd, etc.,) she leaves no sexual stone (or bedspread) unturned. The great difference here is that she names the participants in most of her love scenes both on and off the screen.

In between the romantic liaisons, there is a rather pathetic story of a performer with average acting skills trying to make it in Hollywood. The compromises and insults—verbal and physical—that she endured to establish her slight celebrity are depressing. Almost as sad are her four adventures in matrimony; life with a quartet of difficult, erratic, tempermental male prima donnas was apparently not much fun either. Author Keyes sums it all up nicely in her opening G.B. Shaw quote about the two tragedies in life being not getting your heart's desire or actually getting it.

The volume contains an index and two picture sections. This is a frank, fascinating memoir. Readers won't be disappointed.

5370 *Scarlett, Rhett, and a Cast of Thousands.* by Flamini, Roland. 355 p. illus. New York: Macmillan, 1975.

The research for this book which is subtitled "The Filming of GONE WITH THE WIND" included more than one hundred interviews, a review of four years of newspaper and periodical articles, and a reading of the unpublished letters of the original novel's author, Margaret Mitchell.

With great attention to detail and by use of a breezy journalistic style, Flamini has recalled much of the true-life fantasy that characterized the making of the film. From the novel's status as "an unwanted property" to the film's Atlanta premiere, the story is related as a series of crises that will cause the reader to wonder how the film was ever completed.

Surrounding this fast-moving account of spectacular Hollywood filmmaking in the thirties is a group of illustrations that have been intelligently selected and beautifully reproduced. They serve to identify clearly the many characters who populate the incidents and intrigues related in the text. An index is also provided.

Given the intelligent treatment of a legendary story, along with a superb collection of visuals, most readers will find this book an immediate attraction and an ultimately satisfying experience. Recommended.

5371 *Scavullo on Men.* by Scavullo, Fran-
scesco. 186 p. illus. New York: Random House, 1977.

Forty notable men are photographed and interviewed in this attractive volume. Strangely, only a
few are from the world of motion pictures—Robert
Altman, Alan Bates, Robert Evans, Milos Forman,
Christopher Reeve, and Henry Winkler.

Scavullo's questions are sharply to-the-point and his
photographs are revealing.

5372 *Scenario Writing and Producing for
the Amateur.* by Gleason, Marion
Norris. 308 p. Boston: 1929.

Contains material on the dramatic construction of a
scenario, how to write the scenario continuity, the
home movie, the children's scenario, a holiday scenario, scenarios for organized groups, the experimental field, and directing the amateur motion
picture production.

5373 *Scenarios! Scenarios! Scenarios!* by
Horn, Donald R. 94 p. paper illus.
Philadelphia: Chilton, 1963.

This title in the *Modern Camera Guide* series offers
stories, incidents, gimmicks, tricks, and other
suggestions for writing scripts that will result in interesting and unusual amateur films.

5374 *Scene Design for Stage and Screen.*
by Larson, Orville K. 334 p. illus.
East Lansing, Mich.: Michigan
State University Press, 1961.

An anthology of readings on the aesthetics and methodology of scene design for the performing arts.

5375 *Scenery for Cinema.* by Koenig,
John. 94 p. illus. Baltimore: Baltimore Museum of Art, 1942.

Based on the exhibition, "Scenery for Cinema," held
at the museum from January to March in 1942. The
volume offers a survey of film history, the development of movie settings, plans and sketches for THE
KING STEPS OUT (1936), models of sets, techniques
of construction, painting, lighting, set dressing,
tricks in the movies, interior and exterior settings,
musical numbers, costume design, etc. Many illustrations are included.

5376 SCENES FROM A MARRIAGE. by
Bergman, Ingmar. 199 p. illus. New
York: Pantheon, 1974.

Script of the 1974 film directed by Bergman. Originally prepared as a six-part series for Swedish television, SCENES FROM A MARRIAGE (1974) has been
edited into a shorter film for showings in commercial theatres throughout the world. Told in six
scenes, it is the story of a seemingly perfect marriage
gone sour. Bergman provides a short introduction to
the film script, and there are some photographs from
the original television production.

5377 SCENT OF MYSTERY. by Williams,
Dick. 32 p. paper illus. 1959.

This souvenir book was published to accompany
showings of a 1959 filmwhich used a process called
"Scentavision" or "Smell-O-Vision." Presented by
Mike Todd, Jr., this was the process which flooded
the theatre with synthetic smells correlated to some
action or person on the screen. In this film it is the
smell of the perfume that the killer wears which
proves her undoing. The plot, the process, the cast,
and the actual filming are shown and described. A
cardboard recording of two musical selections from
the film is included with the book. Cast and production credits are noted. If for no other reason, the
book is noted here as proof that the process and the
film were actually tried out for one brief period. The
public rejected the concept of smelling its movies
and the film was re-released without the smells and
with a new title, HOLIDAY IN SPAIN (1959). The
public was consistent—it still ignored the film.

5378 *Schnozzola.* by Fowler, Gene. 287 p.
paper illus. New York: Perma
Books, 1953.

This beautifully written biography covers only a
portion of the Durante legend; the last 20 years are
missing. Attention to films is minimal and the book
can only be recommended here as supplementary
material to the book about the Durante film career
that is still to be written. It is ironic that reference
works and biographers ignore Durante's film work
for the most part. Admittedly his impact in films has
never been as great as his appearances in clubs, on
Broadway, and TV. However, the number of his
films is quite large (almost 50) and his performances
in some of them are quite impressive.

5379 *Scholastic's Literature of the Screen
(A series).* edited by Maynard, Rich-
ard A. illus. New York: Scholastic
Book Services, 1974- .

The initial publications of this series are: (1) *Identity,* which contains print versions (scripts) of the following films: THAT'S ME (1961), Walter Stuart; THE LONELINESS OF THE LONG-DISTANCE RUNNER (1962), Tony Richardson; COOL HAND LUKE (1967), Stuart Rosenberg; and UP THE DOWN STAIRCASE (1967), Robert Mulligan; (2) *Power,* which contains print versions (scripts) of the following films: MR. SMITH GOES TO WASHINGTON (1939), Frank Capra; A FACE IN THE CROWD (1957), Elia Kazan; and THE CANDIDATE (1972), Michael Ritchie; (3) *Men and Women,* which contains print versions (scripts) of the following films: SPLENDOR IN THE GRASS (1961), Elia Kazan; THE FAMILY WAY (1967), Roy Boulting; and NOTHING BUT A MAN (1964), Michael Roemer; (4) *Values in Conflict,* which contains print versions (scripts) of the following films: HIGH NOON (1952), Fred Zinnemann; THE HUSTLER (1961), Robert Rossen; and THE SAVAGE INNOCENTS (1961), Nicholas Ray. A teacher's guide for each of the above volumes contains study guides for all the films along with distributor information and a short bibliography.

5380   *The School and the Art of Motion Pictures.* by Mallery, David. 101 p. paper Boston: National Association of Independent Schools, 1964.

After a discussion of the relatively recent acceptance of the feature film as a teaching material in the schools, this small volume discusses some quality films which are suitable for academic use. The films are arranged by category or genre—the art of the film, novel into film, stage to screen, biography on film, the western, the musical, etc. Each film is given a paragraph of descriptive evaluation. For each category there is an extended discussion. An index and a short listing of rental libraries conclude the book.

This is one of the best volumes on this particular subject. It is unthinkable that any secondary school should not include film in its curriculum today. This book will assist greatly in that endeavor. It is well written, concise and its selection of basic films cannot be seriously challenged. This is an essential book.

5381   *Sci-Fi Now.* by Frank, Alan. 80 p. paper illus. London: Octopus, 1975.

Another entry in the *Octopus Film* series, this volume carries thesubtitle, "Ten Exciting Years of Science Fiction from 2001 to Star Wars."

Many illustrations, mostly in color, and an index accompany the text.

5382   *Science Fiction: Studies in Film.* by Pohl, Frederick; and Pohl, Frederik, IV. 364 p. illus. paper New York: Ace, 1981.

A chronological history of the science fiction film, from A TRIP TO THE MOON (1902) to STAR TREK (1980). About 70 films are treated in detail and others are mentioned. Supporting material is good and there are illustrations. No index is provided.

5383   *Science-Fiction and Horror Movie Posters in Full Color.* edited by Adler, Alan. 48 p. paper illus. New York: Dover, 1977.

This collection of 48 full-color posters emphasizes the hard sell usually given exploitation features. Excepting KING KONG (1933), THE WAR OF THE WORLDS (1952), and a few others, most of the films are low-cost shockers like THE GIANT CLAW (1957), THE MOLE PEOPLE (1956), ATTACK OF THE PUPPET PEOPLE (1958), etc.

Each poster is attractively reproduced, but unfortunately the pages are printed on both sides so that two books would be necessary to display all the posters. The editor has supplied notes about all the films in an introductory section. Acceptable.

5384   *The Science Fiction Book.* by Rottensteiner, Franz. 160 p. paper illus. New York: New American Library, 1977.

Contains a chapter on science fiction films.

5385   *Science Fiction Film.* by Gifford, Denis. 160 p. paper illus. New York: Dutton, 1970.

Another superior volume from the author of *Movie Monsters,* this one has more than 120 illustrations of robots, rockets, and Flash Gordon. The classic science fiction films are noted.

5386   *Science Fiction Film Awards.* by Reed, Donald A.; and Pattison, Patrick. La Habra, Calif.: ESE, California, 1980.

5387   *Science Fiction Films.* edited by Atkins, Thomas R. 101 p. paper illus. New York: Monarch, 1976.

If the goal of this volume is "to offer a reevaluation of science fiction on the screen," then perhaps a subtitle should have been used. Seven essays consider specific examples of the science fiction film as well as certain motifs, trends, characteristics and sub-genres. Films such as THE INVASION OF THE BODY SNATCHERS (1956), METROPOLIS (1926), and SOLA-RIS (1972) receive individual analysis, while other sections employ a somewhat broader approach to the central topic and include such elements as interviews with Fritz Lang and Don Siegel. Accompanying the diversified text is an impressive collection of stills and a selected bibliography.

Because of the complexity of this particular film topic, the reader may be disappointed to find the small sampling offered here. The high quality of the few offerings may not satisfy those in search of the overview/survey suggested by the title. Acceptable.

5388   *Science Fiction Gold.* by Saleh, Dennis. 192 p. paper illus. New York: McGraw-Hill, 1979.

The subtitle, "Film Classics of the 50's," accurately describes the content of this original paperback. After a short foreword by Ray Harryhausen, fourteen films are recalled via illustration, plot, comment and background information. Cast and credits are noted in a concluding filmography.

Most of the text deals with a retelling of the plot or background information, with only a modest attempt at critical evaluation made. Although the word "gold" in the title may suffice for the author, some of the films noted here did not gather a majority of favorable reviews when they first appeared. Time has not helped, either, for THE BEAST FROM 20,000 FATHOMS (1953), WHEN WORLDS COLLIDE (1951) and IT CAME FROM OUTER SPACE (1953) are still difficult to sit through. Another disappointment is the variation in clarity of the full-page illustrations. The result is a mediocre volume that is acceptable mostly for nondiscriminating science fiction film fans.

5389   *Science Fiction in the Cinema.* by Baxter, John. 240 p. illus. New York: A. S. Barnes, 1970.

Starts with Melies and explores this film genre with illustrations and absorbing text. Looks at many classic films, both silent and sound. There is some similarity with the horror category but science fiction has sufficient uniqueness to warrant individual attention. Has an extended filmography and a short bibliography. (One minor reservation is the cramped look of the stills; perhaps in future editions, the book will get the larger production format it deserves.) Highly recommended.

5390   *Science Fiction in the Movies.* by Pickard, Roy. 160 p. illus. London: Muller, 1978.

Pickard provides his usual encyclopedic treatment for science fiction films here.

5391   *Science Fiction Movies.* by Strick, Philip. 160 p. illus. London: Octopus, 1976.

A well-produced and well-written overview of the science fiction film genre is provided in this volume from the *Movie Treasury* series. In treating his selection of examples, Strick emphasizes what the film says, how it says it, and how convincing it is to him.

Using many fine illustrations, some in color, he deals with some familiar topics—outer space, beasts, time manipulation, other worlds, future worlds, etc. An index of film titles is added.

5392   *The Science Fictionary: An A-Z Guide to SF Authors, Films, TV Shows.* by Naha, Ed. paper illus. New York: Seaview (Harper and Row), 1980.

5393   *The Scientific Film in Germany.* by Wolf, Gotthard. 80 p. illus. Wuppertal: Lucas, 1958.

Translated from the German language, this volume deals with the scientific applications of cinematography.

5394   *Scooper.* by McCallum, John D. 274 p. illus. Seattle: Wood and Reber, 1960.

An authorized biography of Scoop Conlon, a reporter, publicist, and friend of many Hollywood personalities during the silent screen era.

5395   *Scoring for Films.* by Hagen, Earle. 253 p. illus. New York: Criterion Music Corp., 1971.

An advanced technical book that still has certain values for the lay person interested in knowing more about the writing of music for films or television. Its stated purpose is "to orient the reader with the problems, possibilities and language of film or music composition." A very short history of movie music introduces the text which is divided into three major sections: 1) The Mechanics and Vocabulary of Film Composition; 2) The Psychology of Creating Music for Films; and 3) The Responsibilities of the Composer. A few summary statements and a valuable glossary conclude the book. Throughout there are many illustrations, charts, music pages, script pages, and tables.

The second (Psychology) section features a symposium which proposes four provocative questions to film composers Alfred Newman, Jerrald Goldsmith, Hugo Friedhofer, Quincy Jones, and Lalo Schifrin. Their replies differ as widely as their musical styles. One further bonus is the inclusion of two 7-inch recordings which contain musical segments from actual film sound tracks conducted and narrated by Hagen. These are coordinated with the text. The author has provided a service to the musician and the lay person that is soundly based on his teaching and professional experience of scoring more than 2000 television episodes.

The stated purpose of the book is more than accomplished by the logical presentation of his text and the support of the visuals and the recordings. It is a fine teaching-learning package presented with efficiency and enthusiasm. Highly recommended.

5396 *Scott Fitzgerald.* by Turnbull, Andrew. 372 p. paper illus. New York: Ballantine, 1962.

This biography briefly covers Fitzgerald's first trip to Hollywood in 1927 and the latter years (1937-1940) that he spent there.

5397 SCOTT OF THE ANTARCTIC: The Film and Its Production. by James, David. 151 p. illus. London: Convoy Pub., 1948.

This is an account of the planning and production of SCOTT OF THE ANTARCTIC (1948)—the story, the schedule, studio work, including research, the location shooting in Antarctica and Switzerland, and the final studio work. Biographies of the artists concerned are given along with a section on how the music for the film was written. This is one of the better accounts of the making of a particular film. It is unfortunate that the film is not more widely known in America.

5398 *Scoundrel Times.* by Hellman, Lillian. Boston: Little, Brown, 1976.

The "scoundrels" in the book's title refer to those persons who remained silent, embarrassed, or became informers to the House Un-American Activities Committee in the early 50's. Hellman was a model, of course, in her refusal to answer questions about anyone but herself. In this short memoir she describes events before, during, and after the investi-

gations.

Many Hollywood personalities were involved in the congressional witchhunts of the McCarthy period.

5399 *Scream Queens: Heroines of the Horrors.* by Beck, Calvin Thomas. 343 paper illus. New York: Collier-Macmillan, 1978.

The purpose of this collective biography is to acknowledge the contribution of actresses to the horror film genre. An overview precedes the 29 biographies which are written in the "... and next she appeared in ..." style with many review and interview quotes added to break up the monotony of the narrative line. Very little author interpretation is offered, with most critical comment depending upon the selected review excerpt. Illustrations are plentiful and both a bibliography and an index are provided.

The book comes nowhere near the achievement of its goal. Only the selection of some neglected performers (May McAvoy, Laura La Plante, Mae Clarke, Faith Domergue, Hazel Court, Barbara Steele etc.) gives any distinction to a pedestrian collective biography.

5400 *Screen Achievement Records Bulletin.* compiled by Academy of Motion Picture Arts & Sciences. 2 volumes paper Beverly Hills: The Academy of Motion Picture Arts & Sciences, 1977.

According to the Academy, this computer generated publication will appear three times each year and as a comprehensive cumulative annual volume.

Section I (volume 1) contains an alphabetical list of film titles with full credits supplied for each. Section II (volume 1) lists individual credits by craft; Section III (volume 2) lists releases by company; and the final Section IV (volume 2), is a master list of individuals with references to their films and credits.

The pages, reproduced in typewritten capital letters, are filled with specialized, specific information that might be difficult to locate elsewhere. Note that this publication appeared in 1979 as *The Annual Index to Motion Picture Credits.*

5401 *Screen Acting.* by Marsh, Mae. 129 p. illus. Los Angeles: Photostar, 1921.

A chatty account of silent screen acting which treats such topics as beauty, expression, make-up, costuming, chin, eyes, seven qualities, emphasis, prepression, film shots, etc. The author also discusses her discoverer, D. W. Griffith, and describes the home life of a star.

5402   *Screen Acting, Its Requirements and Rewards.* by Klumph, Inez; and Klumph, Helen. 243 p. illus. New York: Falk, 1922.

Contains portraits, assistance, and advice from silent film stars such as Lillian Gish, Colleen Moore, Lon Chaney, Valentino, Milton Sills, Ruth Roland, etc.

5403   *Screen Ads (A Series).* by Barbour, Alan. paper illus. Kew Gardens N.Y.: Screen Facts, 1965- .

Alan Barbour, a film buff, collector and author, created a series of profusely illustrated paperback volumes dealing with serials, screen ads, westerns, older films, etc.

The following titles were among those published: *Great Serial Ads*, 1965; *Screen Ads Monthly*, 4 issues, 1967-68; *Movie Ads of the Past*, 1966; *The Wonderful World of 'B' Films*, 64 pages, 1968; *Thrill After Thrill*, 1971.

5404   *The Screen Arts.* by Fischer, Edward. 184 p. New York: Sheed & Ward, 1960.

This volume is designed as a guide to film and television appreciation. Using broad topics such as artistic truth, film grammar, the art of the writer, director, and actor, the author suggests some standards for judging film and television quality. The major focus is on film, with television relegated to two short chapters. Many of the comments and examples indicate the religious orientation of the author. For the neophyte in film study the book has value. Other more experienced readers will find much of the text a bit naive.

5405   *Screen Education.* by Hodgkinson, Anthony. paper New York: UNESCO, 1963.

How to teach a critical approach to film and television is the theme of this paperback. Somewhat pedantic in style, the book is still of great value to educators.

5406   *Screen Education for Schools: An Introduction for Cinema and Television Studies.* by Richardson, Alex. 60 p. paper London: Schoolmaster, 1967.

5407   *Screen Education in Canadian Schools.* edited by Canadian Education Association, Information Division. 48 p. paper illus. Toronto: Canadian Education Association, 1969.

5408   *Screen Education Year Book 1966.* edited by Mainds, Roger. 217 p. illus. London: Society for Education in Film and TV, 1966- .

Contains essays on filmmaking and film study. THE SEARCHERS (1956) is examined in great detail—distributor, production company, producer, leading players, running time, synopsis, biographies of leading actors, filming and location notes, and discussion of main characters. Finally, the humor-technique and the message of the film are explored. In addition to THE SEARCHERS, eight other films suitable for young people are outlined. Many references for supportive materials are given: film distributors, book reviews, bibliography, list of directors, etc. The 1965 edition contains one section of short films and another section on children as filmmakers.

5409   *Screen Education Yearbook—1969.* edited by Mainds, Roger. 181 p. paper illus. London: Society for Education in Film and TV, 1969.

This annual journal contains articles, director filmographies, biographies, book reviews, addresses, periodical guides, distributor lists, film criticisms, and other information of concern to film users. Although much of the information is pertinent only in Britain, there is still enough to warrant inclusion in other film collections. Acceptable.

5410   *Screen Experience: An Approach to Film.* edited by Feyen, Sharon. 273 p. paper illus. Dayton, Ohio: Pflaum, 1969.

Although this volume was probably designed as an aid to educators and media specialists, it should have appeal to a much wider audience. The beginning is a short history of film styles followed by a consideration of the film today and tomorrow. Literary and stage adaptations are explored as are short films, the western, the comedy, and the documentary. Film direction, editing, grammar, and properties all receive chapter attention, along with "How to Organize a Film Series" and "How to Program

Films." Chapters have bibliographies, questions for discussion, and suggested projects.

Illustrations and the recommended books/films used throughout are excellent. The appendix which has a general heading of "Practical Information" includes an annotated list of films mentioned in the text, an excellent bibliography, and an index of film titles. A vital, necessary book. Highly recommended.

5411 *Scream Gems.* by Baraket, Mark. 143 p. paper illus. New York: Drake, 1977.

A personal selection of assorted international science fiction, horror and fantasy films, accompanied by drawings and stills.

5412 *Screen Greats* (A Series). edited by Smith, Millburn. paper illus. New York: Barven Publications, 1972.

This promising publishing venture made its appearance with ten issues of a periodical which resembled the *Citadel* series in many ways. Each issue was devoted to a personality or a team and consisted mostly of stills, portraits, and candids. A filmography was given at the end of each volume. The number of pages averaged about 60.

These volumes were better in many ways than the Primestyle Michael Burrows books or the Cinefax series of the late sixties.

5413 *The Screen Image of Youth: Movies about Children and Adolescents.* by Goldstein, Ruth M.; and Zornow, Edith. 361 p. illus. Metuchen, N.J.: Scarecrow, 1980.

Basically this is a reference-filmography; it also considers the changing image of the child and adolescent (anyone under 20) over several decades. More than 350 films (features, TV movies, documentaries) in which there is a significant child/adolescent character are considered. The films are arranged alphabetically by title under 15 subject categories—growing pains, teachers and school, religion, death, delinquency and crime, etc. The annotation provided for each consists largely of a plot synopsis, but informative critical comments and evaluations are added. Often the films are cross-referenced under several headings. A distributor list, a bibliography, a category index, and a title index complete the book.

The authors, who wrote *Movies For Kids*, are specialists in this area and their expertise is evident throughout this exceptional filmography. Recommended.

5414 *Screen Monographs I.* New York: Arno Press, 1970.

Contains "The Art of Cineplastics" (by Elie Faure, 63 p.); "The Technique of the Film" (Bernard Gordon and Julian Zimet, 24 p.); and "Parnassus to Let" (Eric Walter White, 48 p.).

5415 *Screen Monographs II.* illus. New York: Arno Press, 1970.

Includes: "The Crisis of the Film" (by John Gould Fletcher, 35 p.); "The Photo Drama" (William Morgan Hannon, 64 p.); "See and Hear" (Will H. Hays, 63 p.); and "The American Influence in France" (Philippe Soupault, 23 p.).

5416 *A Screen of Time: A Study of Luchino Visconti.* by Stirling, Monica. 296 p. illus. New York: Harcourt, Brace, Jovanovich, 1979.

Monica Stirling supplies both a detailed political and social setting for her impressive biography of Italian film director, Luchino Visconti. His work in opera and the theatre is noted along with his films from OSSESSIONE (1942) to THE INTRUDER (1976). Consideration of the latter is very general and takes up less than half the book. The text concentrates on the life of a general theatrical artist as it relates to music, art, history, literature, politics, etc.

Stirling is also discreetly reluctant concerning Visconti's private life. Although she was close to him as observer and interviewer during his last months, she dwells on the artistic rather than the personal. Illustrations, a bibliography, and an index are included.

5417 *Screen Personalities Of 1933.* by Trotta, Vincent; and Lewis, Cliff. 109 p. illus. Gordon Press, 1976 (1933).

These "intimate glimpses into the lives of movie stars" were first published in 1933 by Grosset and Dunlap, N.Y.

5418 *Screen Personalities.* by Trotta, Vincent; and Lewis, Cliff. 109 p. illus. New York: Grosset and Dunlap, 1933.

Pictures and stories about the lives of such early talking-picture stars as Garbo, Jolson, Harlow, Dietrich, West, the Bennetts, Arliss, the Barrymores, etc.

5419 *Screenplay—The Foundations of Screenwriting.* by Field, Syd. 212 p. paper New York: Delta, 1979.

Subtitled "A Step-by-Step Guide from Concept to Finished Script," this original paperback discusses subject, character, sequence, plot, scene, form, etc. Field defines the screenplay, tells how to build it, write it and then market the final product. The text includes many examples along with a clear sequential development that encourages the aspiring writer to begin. Syd Field is a writer-producer who also teaches screenwriting; his experience in both fields serves the reader well.

5420 *The Screen Plays of Lina Wertmuller.* by Wertmuller, Lina. 334 p. illus. New York: Quadrangle, 1977.

Critic John Simon provides an introduction to this collection of scripts written by Lina Wertmuller. Included are THE SEDUCTION OF MIMI (1974), LOVE AND ANARCHY (1974), SWEPT AWAY (1975), and SEVEN BEAUTIES (1976).

5421 *Screen Reader Number 1.* paper illus. New York: Zoetrope, 1978.

Carrying a subtitle of "Cinema/Ideology/Politics," this anthology contains material originally published in *Screen* in 1971-1973. The three major topics include a debate between *Cahiers du Cinema* and *Cinethique*, a debate on realism, and questions of progressive aesthetics in the Soviet Union in the 1920s.

5422 *Screen Test.* by Bowen, Peter; and Hayden, Martin; and Reiss, Frank. 303 p. paper illus. Baltimore: Penguin Books, 1975.

Here is another example of a superior quiz book about the movies. Previously the outstanding ones featured large half-page stills. This one relies a bit more on the careful phrasing and construction of provocative, memory-jogging questions, but it too employs the photograph question/identification. The quizzes appear in 16 category chapters, which have mostly genre titles, e.g., Westerns, Spies, Horrors, etc. Answers appear at each chapter's end. In addition to straight questions, there are multiple choices, identifications, fill-in-the-blanks, completion, true or false and other forms of testing. What gives this volume distinction is the care and research that must have gone into the preparation of the questions. This is evidenced by the wording, content and arrangement of each puzzler.

Production qualities are outstanding. Printed on high quality paper, the book also is distinguished by very fine reproduction of its visuals. A bibliography is appended. While it cannot be called essential, its excellence will add the right touch of amusement and will help balance all the serious scholarly texts being written today. Readers will enjoy it enormously. Recommended.

5423 *Screen Tests: A Diary.* by Malanga, Gerard; and Warhol, Andy. 216 p. paper illus. New York: Kulchur (Citadel), 1967.

This volume deals with the screen tests of 54 personalities who appeared in Warhol's films.

5424 *Screen Violence and Film Censorship: A Review of Research.* by Brody, Stephen. 179 p. paper London: Her Majesty's Stationery Office, 1977.

This review is Home Office Research Study No. 40.

5425 *Screen World: Volume 19.* by Willis, John. 256 p. illus. New York: Crown Pub., 1968.

This reference annual is a pictorial and statistical record of films released during the year 1967. For each film the cast, credits, and other facts are given in addition to one or more stills from the film. A biographical data section on several hundred actors is included as is an obituary section. The index is very detailed with over 5000 entries. Picture quality is excellent and the book is ideal for browsing. Recent editions are available from Crown while Biblo & Tannen have reprinted early volumes. A vital reference book.

5426 *The Screen Writer Looks at the Screen Writer.* by Froug, William. 352 p. New York: Macmillan, 1972.

The purpose of this volume is to further the recognition of the screen writer who has a past history of neglect, abuse and professional oblivion. Putting down the auteur theory as being almost impossible within the Hollywood structure of filmmaking, Froug makes a strong argument for the emergence of the writer into the economic mainstream. One bit of evidence he offers is the current publication of many modern and classic scripts. The quality of the film is often found in the script before directorial style is superimposed upon it: "Style follows content and is meaningless without it."

The format of the book is a collection of interviews

by Froug with the following screen writers: Lewis John Carlino, William Bowers, Walter Brown Newman, Jonathan Axelrod, Ring Lardner, Jr., I. A. L. Diamond, Buck Henry, David Giler, Nunnally Johnson, Edward Anhalt, Stirling Silliphant, and Fay Kanin. The mixture of names, semi-names, and unknowns seems intended to support Froug's argument. Each interview is preceded with the writer's credits, a lengthy background article, and a sample script page. Anyone interested in filmmaking is referred to this collection of views on screen writing. Its importance is argued with intelligence and balance, and the result is a clarification of questions dealing with theory, aesthetics and process. Highly recommended.

5427 *The Screen-Writer's Handbook.* by Nash, Constance; and Oakey, Virginia. 149 p. paper New York: Barnes and Noble, 1978.

This volume follows the outline of its subtitle, "What to Write, How to Write It, Where to Sell It." After discussing the elements of characterization, dialogue and style, the authors treat the actual writing (organization, style, terminology, draft, rewrite) and script format (title page, typewriter settings, variations, number of copies, etc.). Concluding sections are devoted to interviews, excerpts, and practical business advice. The book is indexed.

An abundance of valuable direction-advice-information is provided in this small and modest volume. Along with the step-by-step guidance, there are sample pages, agent directories, contracts, and writer's guild information. A treasury of useful reference, suggestion and example can be found here by the beginning writer. Recommended.

5428 *Screen Writing and Production Techniques.* by Curran, Charles W. 240 p. illus. New York: Hastings House, 1958.

Subtitled "The Non-Technical Handbook for TV, Film and Tape," this volume appeared in 1952 as *The Handbook of Motion Picture Technique for Business Men* and in 1953 as *The Handbook of TV and Film Technique.*

5429 *Screen Writing for Narrative Film and Television.* by Miller, William. 256 p. New York: Hastings House, 1980.

A title in the *Communication Arts* series, this text provides a guide to creative writing for films and television. There are sequential chapters on creativity, narrative structure, narrative techniques, characterization, sequences, scenes, themes, settings, sound, comedy, adaptation. A final chapter deals with nonnarrative films. Appendixes, reference, a filmography and an index complete the book.

The author, a professor from Ohio, provides an informative, readable explanation of the elements and the processes involved in the writing of worthy scripts.

5430 *Screening Out the Past.* by May, Larry. 304 p. illus. New York: Oxford University Press, 1980.

The theme of this volume, which is subtitled "The Birth of Mass Culture and the Motion Picture Industry", is that the industry both reflected and contributed to the change in America from Victorian life.

As part of his primary evidence, the author uses the "Victorian" films of D. W. Griffith, as contrasted to the "modern" ones of Mary Pickford, Douglas Fairbanks and, ultimately, Cecil B. DeMille. Sociological changes that took place concurrently with the rise of the motion picture industry are documented.

May's study is accompanied by many pages of notes, some tables, and an index. Using a particular industry and its product as a source for the writing of history is a relatively new method of research. Although his subject-thesis is not a new one, he has researched it with scholarly thoroughness.

5431 *Screening the Novel.* by Miller, Gabriel. 208 p. illus. New York: Ungar, 1980.

The Ungar *Film Library* series continues its investigationsinto the relationships between literature and film with this volume, which is subtitled "Rediscovered American Fiction in Film."

Eight popular films and the neglected novels from which they were adapted form its content. SUSAN LENOX; HER FALL AND RISE (1931), THE POSTMAN ALWAYS RINGS TWICE (1946), THEY SHOOT HORSES DON'T THEY? (1969), THE TREASURE OF THE SIERRA MADRE (1948), PATHS OF GLORY (1957), and THE PAWNBROKER (1965) are films made from novels having the same titles. HESTER STREET (1975) is based on *Yekl: A Tale of the New York Ghetto*, while THE GANGSTER (1957) was taken from *Low Company.* Each essay gives emphasis to the intent of the original author and to the challenges faced by the film's director. Supplementing the text are chapter notes, illustrations, a bibliography, a distributor list and an index.

This volume advances the study of film and literature. The comparative analysis employed is perhaps the ideal method to investigate the relative strengths and weaknesses of each book or film and, ultimately, each medium.

5432 *Screening the Sexes: Homosexuality in the Movies.* by Tyler, Parker. 384 p. paper illus. New York: Holt, Rinehart, Winston, 1972.

The trend of many of our well-known writers to come "out-of-the-closet" gets another push forward with this newest Parker Tyler volume. His position is quite similar to that of the gay militants. Combining super-intellectuality with gutter language, analysis with gossip, and criticism with camp, he creates a fascinating book. It is not always easy to comprehend Tyler but here he is clearer than usual. Believing that films reflect behavior, myth, hidden desires, and so on, he analyzes many films to support his sexual freedom thesis and to enlighten filmgoers who may never have realized what they were seeing.

Most of the films are of recent, post-60's vintage and this gives him richer subjects with which to work. Joe Cairo in THE MALTESE FALCON (1940) or Franklin Pangborn in any film get some mention, but the strongest guns are saved for the STAIRCASE (1969), THE KILLING OF SISTER GEORGE (1969), BOYS IN THE BAND (1970), PERFORMANCE (1970) (1969), FELLINI SATYRICON (1969), MIDNIGHT COWBOY (1969) and others. Some unexpected titles also get the critical scalpel from the author—THE WIZARD OF OZ (1939), PERILS OF PAULINE (1967), HUSBANDS (1970), etc. This is a writing performance that merits attention and applause. Highly recommended.

5433 *The Screenplay as Literature.* by Winston, Douglas Garrett. 240 p. illus. Cranbury, N.J.: Fairleigh Dickinson University Press, 1973.

Because of this book's title, the reader might expect a discussion of published screenplays considered as a genre of literature; if so he will be severely disappointed. Instead the author has revived some rather familiar material and attempted to tie it in with a consideration of film as a literary form. A more appropriate title might have been *Literature and Film* or *Film and Literature*, but unfortunately both have already been used.

Starting with a review of film language and grammar, the author considers such topics as neo-realism, stream of consciousness, existentialism, psychoanalytic technique, and the plotless screenplay. The work of Bresson, Bergman, Antonioni, and Fellini in original writing, collaboration, and adaptation is considered. After a closing section on underground films, a summary and some conclusions are offered. Text references, a bibliography and an index complete the book. Seven small illustrations add little to the text.

While the author's intent seems clear (he wants certain films to be considered as seriously as certain pieces of literature), his arguments and his methodology are often confusing. Screenplay and film are synonymous in much of the writing; attention to the complex process of changing script to film is minimal and, finally, the vacillation between film and literature weakens the author's case. The familiarity of much of this presentation along with its misleading title and a relatively high price will make this book a disappointment to many readers. It is acceptable only if the purchaser is fully aware that it is discussion of film literature and it is not a critical survey of published screenplays as listed in the *Cinema Booklist* series or in McCarty's *Checklist*.

5434 *Screenplays by Michelangelo Antonioni.* by Antonioni, Michelangelo. 361 p. illus. New York: Orion Press, 1963.

Contains: IL GRIDO (1957), L'AVVENTURA (1960), LA NOTTE (1961), and L'ECLISSE (1962).

5435 *Screenwriter: The Life and Times of Nunnally Johnson.* by Stempel, Tom. 269 p. illus. San Diego: A. S. Barnes, 1980.

Nunnally Johnson was a well known and respected screenwriter who spent most of his career at the 20th Century Fox Studio. This study concentrates mostly on his professional work, ranging from ROUGH HOUSE ROSIE (1927) to THE DIRTY DOZEN (1967). The material put forth by Stempel has been adequately researched and is presented in a logical, easy-to-use arrangement: overview, notes, filmography, stage plays, bibliography and index. The actual text is rather short and eliminates any detailed personal portrait of the man. The volume by Nora Johnson on her father, *Flashback*, deals more deeply with Johnson the person.

5436 *The Screenwriter as Collaborator: The Career of Stewart Stern.* by Brown, Kent R. New York: Arno, 1980.

This title in the *Dissertations on Film* series examines the career of screenwriter Stewart Stern from 1948 to 1971. Stern's personal comments via interviews are included and a few of his films are treated in detail.

5437 *The Screenwriters Guide.* by Burr, Keith. 96 p. paper New York: Zoetrope, 1981.

A guide to help the sale of film and TV scripts. Contains a list of 500 film/TV producers with their address and phone number.

5438 *Screwball: The Life of Carole Lombard.* by Swindell, Larry. 324 p. illus. New York: William Morrow, 1975.

It is probably impossible to capture the style and charisma of Carole Lombard in print. She had a flair for life, and with her offbeat, original outlook, was a fine example of women's liberation long before the movement became prominent.

Her life and her career, including marriages to William Powell and Clark Gable, are described with affection and warmth in this detailed biography by Larry Swindell.

Illustrations and a filmography accompany this portrait of the queen of screwball comedy.

5439 *Script Continuity and the Production Secretary in Film and TV.* by Rowlands, Avril. 160 p. paper illus. New York: Hastings House, 1977.

The person who keeps a written account of the shooting done by a film or TV unit is known by many titles—script girl, continuity clerk, etc. Often this person also acts as a production secretary whose assignments may be quite varied. One of the *Media Manuals* series, this volume considers the two responsibilities separately while recognizing they are often performed simultaneously.

The continuity section considers such topics as sequence shooting, the script, shot definition, vocabulary, continuity of action and dialogue, continuity report sheets, etc. In the section devoted to the production secretary, there is information, advice and guidance on script, actors, extras, children, animals, location filming, housing, travel, food, costumes, makeup, etc. Other sections are devoted to the filming schedule, shooting, post-synchronizing, graphics, dubbing, and copyright. A glossary and some suggestions for further reading complete the book. The many illustrations, most of which are either cartoon drawings, diagrams, or charts, are quite helpful.

In a clear, logical exposition, the role of an important member of a film unit is defined and described

here. The book will be helpful in a wide variety of circumstances. Recommended.

5440 *Script Models: A Handbook for the Media Writer.* by Lee, Robert E.; and Misiorowski, Robert. 96 p. New York: Hastings House, 1978.

The first section of this handbook/stylebook contains specimen pages of scripts for filmstrips, multimedia presentations, nontheatrical and theatrical films, television and radio. Closing pages offer information, advice, a glossary and a bibliography for the writer. The text is presented in typewriter script so that each specimen resembles an original excerpt. For the writer wishing to prepare a script for any of the nonprint media, the volume will be very useful. As a text for courses in scriptwriting, it will be hard to better this excellent overview. Recommended.

5441 *Script Writing for Short Films.* by Beveridge, James A. 45 p. paper illus. New York: UNESCO, 1969.

A brief discussion of script writing which treats topics such as audience, objectives, sponsors, research, budget, production crew, dialogue, showmanship, etc. Certain unique problems of the short film are examined and some solutions are offered. There are script excerpts from JAI JAWAN, THE DREAMS OF MAUJIRAM, PHOEBE (1964), and POISONS, PESTS, AND PEOPLE (1960). Two storyboard outlines are shown and recent films which illustrate the concepts developed in the text are listed. As usual with most UNESCO publications, this one may be difficult to obtain but the effort is worthwhile. It is a most effective, concise summary of scripting for the short film. Highly recommended.

5442 *Scriptwriting for Animation.* by Hayward, Stan. 160 p. paper illus. New York: Focal, 1977.

Another addition to the excellent *Media Manuals* series, this volume deals exclusively with the writing of scripts for animated films. Employing the usual structure of the series, the text is broken down into many elements, each of which is treated as an entity, i.e., the storyboard, animating by machine, transitions, the voice track, copying machine, advertising commercials, etc. When they are ordered, they present a comprehensible guide to scripting animated films.

As always the illustrations are superb and there is a helpful glossary. Contains a bibliography and a complete storyboard sequence.

5443 *Scriptwriting for the Audio-Visual Media.* by Edmonds, Robert. 185 p. paper illus. New York: Teachers College Press, 1978.

The audiovisual media referred to in the title consists of radio, television, filmstrips, slidefilms and, of course, films. It is the latter which receives the greatest attention, with sections devoted to writing both the fiction and nonfiction film. In addition to providing basic data and helpful advice, the author includes sample scripts for several different types of films.

Since Edmonds is a filmmaker with impressive credits, much of what he offers is based on personal experience. A final chapter describes the writer's market and offers suggestions on how to get a job. A glossary is appended.

5444 *see 5445*

5445 SCROOGE. by Donaldson, Elaine. 128 p. illus. Nashville: AuroraPublishers, 1970.

This attractive book designed for children will also appeal to a more mature audience. It is a retelling of Dickens' *A Christmas Carol* but is based on the script for the film SCROOGE (1970), written by Leslie Bricusse. The script adaptation by Donaldson is beautifully complemented by two sets of visuals— the first is a series of fascinating line drawings by Ronald Searle, while the other consists of carefully reproduced stills from the film. The book comes in a cardboard box jacket which has a full-color Searle drawing that catches the eye. The production given to all elements of this collaboration is outstanding. Highly recommended.

5446 *Scruffy.* by Burbidge, Claude. 160 p. illus. London: Hurst and Blackett, 1937.

Scruffy was a dog who appeared in several films during the thirties. The subtitle tells it all: "Adventures of a Mongrel in Movieland."

5447 *Scrutiny of the Cinema.* by Hunter, William. 87 p. illus. London: Wishart & Co., 1932.

An introductory article on film criticism is followed by discussions of particular films of the twenties and early thirties. Attention is paid to avant-garde films and documentaries and to such directors as Eisenstein, Lang, Clair, Pabst, Feydor, Chaplin, and Pudovkin. The book ends with an essay on sound.

Interesting material.

5448 *The Seal of Dracula.* by Pattison, Barrie. 136 p. paper illus. New York: Bounty, 1975.

A study of a subset of the horror film genre, this book classifies vampires under several headings— national origins, occupations, political beliefs, silent films, talkies, etc. A solid text explores the many interpretations of vampires that have appeared in films for more than 70 years. It is the visuals— consisting of stills and posters—that will attract and excite readers. Reproduction of them is quite good and several in full color are most effective. Selection, however, is another matter, with an obvious emphasis on nudity and sex predominating. The argument in the text that vampirism is a form of sexual activity may justify the selection. A filmography concludes the volume. With a well-researched text, a topic of apparently inexhaustible fascination, and all those provocative visuals, this book is sure to please and entertain many readers. Recommended for mature adults.

5449 *Sean Connery: Gilt-Edged Bond.* by Gant, Richard. 109 p. paper illus. London: Mayflower, 1967.

An early biography of the actor who is both blessed and cursed by the character James Bond that he created.

5450 SEARCH FOR PARADISE. 20 p. paper illus. New York: Cinerama Publishers, 1957.

This is a souvenir book of the 1957 Cinerama adventure that featured Lowell Thomas as he explored Ceylon, the Hunza River and Valley, the Indus River, Kashmir, and Nepal. Dimitri Tiomkin's music is acknowledged and the diagram of the three-projector system of Cinerama is included. Photography throughout is disappointing.

5451 *The Search for Sam Goldwyn: A Biography.* by Easton, Carol. 304 p. illus. New York: William Morrow, 1975.

The fact that Carol Easton had difficulty finding people who would cooperate with her in the writing of this unauthorized biography is evident in both her content and attitude. Her irritation with the Goldwyn family is noted frequently and probably contributed to the negative portrait of Goldwyn she presents. Her research is spotty and omits large segments of Goldwyn history. She retells many standard Goldwyn anecdotes which may be truth—or perhaps part of the legendary myth that was built about the movie mogul.

Illustrations and a bibliography accompany this limited biography.

5452 *Seastrom and Stiller in Hollywood.* by Pensel, Hans. 106 p. illus. New York: Vantage Press, 1969.

Originally written as a master's thesis at the University of California, this volume is based largely on Swedish and Danish source material. The aim of the work is to acquaint the reader with the contributions of both men and the text is written in a scholarly but effectively simple style. Illustrations are fine and filmographies of both directors and a bibliography are given.

5453 *A Seat at the Cinema.* by Manvell, Roger. 192 p. illus. London: Evans Brothers, 1951.

An explanation of how films are made is given in this book. Manvell talks of the technicians and specialists, gives examples from shooting scripts, and pays tribute to Griffith, Flaherty, Eisenstein and Melies. The commercial aspect of filmmaking is also treated. Although this volume is dated, Manvell's observations remain valid.

5454 *Second Sight: Notes on Some Movies, 1965-1970.* by Schickel, Richard. 351 p. New York: Simon and Schuster, 1972.

Richard Schickel was the film critic for *Life* magazine during the years 1965-1970. The collection of reviews in this volume represents about half of all he wrote for the magazine. The unusual technique of adding a second and later evaluation to the original adds a provocative dimension to the reviews: a film critic rereading his first opinions and judging how well they have stood the test of time. A lengthy introduction combines some Schickel career history with the development of his aesthetic for reviewing films.

The reader may take exception to Schickel's comments. Why, for example, does he dislike Fellini so?— "His is a mind of truly stupefying banality." But one can only admire his candid evaluations of his own writing— "Not, I'm afraid, a very good performance on my part," or "I overpraised this movie," or "Sometimes I feel like cutting my tongue out." A critic capable of such introspection can't be all bad.

The book reviews many of the important films which appeared in the latter half of the sixties, and there is an index to make the volume more serviceable. Schickel writes in a style which avoids obfuscation, intellectual boasting, and bandwagon-joining. He is clear, economical, and always his own man. This is an entertaining collection of the writings of a critic who has yet to experience the fame and celebrity that lesser critics now enjoy. Because of its uniqueness and the balance it provides to other existing criticism, the book is recommended.

5455 *Second Wave.* edited by Wood, Robin. 144 p. paper illus. New York: Praeger, 1970.

This book contains critical pieces on directors whose work follows the French "New Wave" group in both time and inspiration. Included are: Dusan Makavejev (by Robin Wood); Jerzy Skolimowski (Michael Walker); Nagisa Oshima (Ian Cameron); Ruy Guerra (Michel Ciment); Glauber Rocha (Michel Ciment); Gilles Groulx (Robert Daudelin); Jean-Pierre Lefebvre (Jean Chabot); and Jean-Marie Straub (Andi Engel). Filmographies of all the directors listed above have been compiled by Elizabeth Cameron and are given at the back of the book.

5456 *The Second Whole Library Catalog.* by Films, Inc. Staff. 144 p. paper illus. Wilmette, Ind.: Films, Inc., 1974.

An oversized film catalog patterned after the *Whole Earth Catalog* series, this volume contains material on films, booking, programming, equipment, books, periodicals and other assorted topics pertinent to film use and study. All of the content is selected: for example, the films are limited to those distributed by Films, Inc. and often the books cited are the well-publicized titles rather than more appropriate but lesser known volumes. In spite of the limitations, the catalog is a pleasure to read and does offer useful ideas, suggestions, and information.

Many classic feature films are noted as being available on a five-year lease in the book. To aid the user there are separate indexes for programming, subjects and film titles. The volume is profusely illustrated with stills, drawings, sketches, etc. Highly recommended.

5457 *The Secret Happiness of Marilyn Monroe.* by Dougherty, James E. 150 p. paper illus. Chicago: Playboy Press, 1976.

In writing this memoir of his marriage to Marilyn

789

Monroe, James Dougherty makes himself very clear when he says, "She had an identity she was never ashamed of as my wife."

From their first dates in 1941 until their divorce in 1946, the author recalls details, conversations and incidents that describe their times together. The latter portions of the book are devoted to his observations of her climb to stardom after their divorce. He explains his years of silence as a protection of his children by a second marriage.

Several illustrations are included but the book is not indexed.

Although this volume appears after so many others about Monroe, it does offer something unique. It is a firsthand, affectionate memoir, written with good taste, that tells of a young marriage, its partners, and their capitulation to ambition. Acceptable.

5458   *The Secret Life of Tyrone Power.* by Arce, Hector. 291 p. paper illus. New York: Bantam, 1979.

What has made this biography of Tyrone Power a bestseller is the revelation that he was a bisexual who couldn't say "no" to anyone. The portrait provided by Arce, who has apparently researched his subject carefully, is that of a passive actor who was dominated by strong-willed directors and lovers for most of his life. His personality was kind, gentle, courteous and considerate. What he lacked was a driving ambition for better parts, and, as a result, he played the same kind of innocuous role constantly until his career began to fade. An exception may have been Billy Wilder's WITNESS FOR THE PROSECUTION (1957) which indicated some of Power's acting potential.

It is unfortunate that Arce has over-emphasized the sexual side of the actor—the matter of bisexuality seems much more important to the author than it, apparently, ever was to the actor.

A bibliography and some illustrations are added.

5459   *The Secret Life of Walter Winchell.* by Stuart, Lyle. 253 p. New York: Boars Head Books, 1953.

In creating the negative portrait of Walter Winchell, the author becomes that which he condemns—an irresponsible writer using words as weapons of vengeance. His style is emotional, lightweight and gives the audience a character to loathe. How much of the content is valid remains a task for the researcher. Interesting for the strong, cruel portrait provided, but only of peripheral interest to film readers.

5460   *Secrets of Film and Television.* by Hill, Gordon. 128 p. illus. Sevenoaks, England: Hodder and Stoughton, 1981.

Written for children, this book is a bit more detailed than most such volumes.

5461   SECRETS OF LIFE. by Platt, Rutherford; and Walt Disney Studios. 124 p. illus. New York: Simon and Schuster, 1957.

Based on the Disney True-Life Adventure, SECRETS OF LIFE (1956), this volume was another translation of screen material into a children's volume.

5462   *Secrets of the Stars.* by Myers, Denis. 143 p. illus. London: Odhams, 1952.

Heavily illustrated fan magazine material on the lives, careers and loves of the stars.

5463   *Secular Films and the Church's Ministry.* by Summers, Stanford. 64 p. paper illus. New York: Seabury Press, 1969.

5464   *See and Hear.* by Hays, Will. 63 p. illus. New York: Motion Picture Producers and Distributors of America, 1929.

A brief history of motion pictures and the development of sound written in 1929. Reprinted in *Screen Monographs II.*

5465   *See No Evil.* by Vizzard, Jack. 381 p. New York: Simon & Schuster, 1970.

After a Jesuit school training, the author spent 25 years with the Hollywood Code office. This volume is a raucous and racy account of censorship during those years and decidedly not a pedantic recitation of court statistics. The reader may be persuaded of Hollywood's ability to corrupt. The stories concerning various films are told in an entertaining manner, sacrificing detail and analysis for entertainment value. Yet the cumulative effect the book has should not be minimized—the reader is given a fascinating in-depth look at the behind-the-scenes operation of the Production Code Office.

The author's intelligence and style are evident in such statements as "The Code was an instrument designed to present reality on the screen not as it was, but as it should be"; or "In an act of mercy,

Valenti put a gun to the poor thing's (the Code's) head, and gave it the coup de grace. It went out without a whimper." No illustrations or index, but the Production Code and a few notes are appended. Entertaining, informative, and a different view of a subject that has only had scholarly treatment up to now.

5466 *The Seed Catalog: A Guide to Teaching/Learning Materials.* by Schrank, Jeffrey. 374 p. paper illus. Boston: Beacon, 1974.

The imaginative, unpredictable author of *Teaching Human Beings* enlarges the scope and treatment of his original theme, suggesting ideas, activities and materials for classroom use in this new volume. In a stimulating text, he includes separate sections on publications, organizations, periodicals, audio, film, video, games, multi-media and devices. The section on film offers rental cost comparisons, many excellent film evaluations, distributor evaluations, feature film sources, specialized film distributors (annotated), and selected film reference works. All of the sections are impressive except the last—which treats only a few titles/sources, which are poorly chosen. For example, the cited *Cinemabilia* film book catalog cannot compare with the omitted Larry Edmund's *Cinema.*

The intent of the book is praiseworthy; for the most part, its achievement is both rewarding and satisfying. It is a thoughtful, modern volume highly recommended for all educational institutions. The imaginative teacher will love it. It is also valuable for use with community discussion groups, in-service courses—in fact almost anywhere the teaching/learning process is occurring.

5467 *Seeing Stars.* by Wagner, Charles L. 403 p. illus. New York: G. P. Putnam's, 1940.

Wagner recalls the film stars he has known.

5468 *Seeing the Light.* by Broughton, James. 80 p. paper illus. San Francisco: City Lights Books, 1977.

James Broughton is an independent, avant-garde filmmaker-poet who offers philosophy, advice, proverbs, definitions, and other thoughts on filmmaking in this unusual book.

His statements are short, isolated bits that ultimately summarize his view of the creative process in filmmaking.

A filmography and a bibliography of his work complete his stimulating, sometimes inspirational message.

5469 *Seeing With Feeling.* by Lacey, Richard. 118 p. paper illus. Philadelphia: W. B. Saunders, 1972.

Lacey's major topic, "Film in the Classroom," is the subtitle of this useful book. He begins with the premise that films by themselves do not "work" —it is the experience provided with the film that either works or does not. While there are no certainties in film study methodologies, the author suggests some as starting points and encourages the development of other unique individual methods by teachers who use films.

A general overview on film use is followed by a provocative section called "What To Do When the Lights Go On." The major portion of the text is devoted to "The Image-Sound Skin" and some related classroom procedures. The "Skin" concept is defined as the basis of a collaborative approach to integrate feeling and intuition with the intellectual concerns of a film. Closing sections of the text anticipate certain problems in gaining acceptance of film study procedures in schools and suggest measures to gain understanding and support. Some appendixes on literature, periodicals, and film sources complete the book. Illustrations consist of stills taken mostly from the films mentioned in the text.

Different approaches to film study derived in part from educational research concepts and philosophy are the concern of this book. The pioneer works of Culkin, Mallery, Sullivan, Sohn, Lowndes and others have suggested much of what is offered here. The service provided by Lacey is one of synthesis and justification. The book is certainly essential for all schools and colleges that offer film courses. Anyone using films will find the suggestions quite valuable for developing programs. Highly recommended.

5470 *Seeking the Bubble.* by Knight, Esmond. illus. London: Hutchinson, 1944.

Esmond Knight is a British actor who graduated to character parts after some starring roles in films of the thirties.

5471 *Seen Any Good Dirty Movies Lately?* by Arnold, James. 118 p. paper illus. Cincinnati, Ohio: St. Anthony Messenger Press, 1972.

The constant search for fresh critical insight in evaluating films may be satisfied for the moment by this modest but rather significant book. Arnold is the movie critic for the *Milwaukee Journal*, several Catholic newspapers, and *St.Anthony Messenger* magazine. His approach is based on the issue of morality in films, in addition to the usual aesthetics. As his guide he quotes sociologist Andrew Greeley: "I believe that love is at the core of the universe; that man is estranged essentially because of his inability to respond to love since he is estranged from love; this estrangement is ended by the intervention of Love in the Person of the Son of Man. ...Love and life are proclaimed by celebrating. The most appropriate human relationship is friendship, ...because it mirrors love... Man's role is to strive so that the world may be pervaded by friendship. Whenever men come together in friendship, the spirit of loving life is present in their midst, inspiring them to break out of the bonds of hesitation, doubt, and distrust in order that they might be for one another."

Films such as Fellini's CABIRIA (1957) and 8-1/2 (1963) or MIDNIGHT COWBOY (1969) are considered moral when applied against the life-friendship-love aesthetic above. Sex and love in films, what films tell our youth, and whether parents should forbid films for their children are other topics discussed with intelligence, wit and sensitivity. The closing section reprints Arnold's reviews of films that caused some moral flurry when the first appeared. His response to them is offered as a guide for laymen to use in coping with films yet to appear.

The book has many fine illustrations and is indexed. How such quality can be placed in an original paperback film book and sold at a very low cost is a lesson for other publishers to study. Highly recommended.

5472 *Seen any Good Movies Lately?* by Zinsser, William K. 239 p. Garden City, N.Y.: Doubleday, 1958.

The author served from 1954 to 1958 as a motion picture critic for the *New York Herald Tribune*. These humorous pieces are a result of his experiences in preparing and writing over 600 reviews and columns. The author's style is reminiscent of Benchley, Perelman, and Ace. He uses an irreverent, exposing and critical approach to Hollywood press-agentry, motion picture promotion tours, film script cliches, the western film genre, and other similar topics. His closing discussion turns quite serious when he talks of the precariousness of being a serious film reviewer. The book is amusing but hardly distinguished reading material.

5473 *Seesaw: A Dual Biography of Anne Bancroft and Mel Brooks.* by Holtzman, William. illus. New York: Doubleday, 1979.

'Seesaw" is a title word from Anne Bancroft's stage play and it also applies to the author's method. In this unauthorized dual biography, he seesaws between the two. The material is familiar, but Holtzman has the ability to make some of it seem fresh.

Films, roles, critical quotes, anecdotes, factual narrative and illustrations are combined to provide portraits of the pair. Biographies such as this one are usually limited because of the nonparticipation of the subjects.

5474 *Selected Articles on Censorship of the Theater and Moving Pictures.* compiled by Beman, Lamar T. 385 p. New York: Ozer, 1971 (1931).

This reprint of a 1931 volume, originally published by H. W. Wilson Company and now published as part of the series, *Moving Pictures—Their Impact on Society*, deals with both film and theater. The film portion resembles a printed debate; a brief with affirmative and negative arguments is presented first. It is followed by a general bibliography and then separate references for the affirmative and negative sides.

A general discussion consisting of articles from *Scientific Monthly*, *New York Times*, and *Educational Screen* is followed by an affirmative discussion section (*World's Work*, *Bookman*, etc.) and the negative section (*Review of Reviews*, *Cleveland Plain Dealer*, etc.). Of interest to scholars, researchers, and historians only.

5475 *Selected Attempts at Stereoscopic Moving Pictures and Their Relationship To The Development of Motion Picture Technology, 1852-1903.* by Gosser, H. Mark. illus. New York: Arno Press, 1977.

Written in 1975 at Temple University in partial fulfillment of the masters program, this study traces the historical development of stereoscopic (3-D) film projection. The author has provided the reader not only with comprehensive examination of stereoscopy as a form of cinema technology, but also has analyzed its relationship to the growth of film apparatus. This title appears in the *Dissertations on Film* series

5476 *Selected Bibliography of Volumes Relating to the Creative Aspects of Motion Picture Production.* compiled by U.S. Naval Photographic Science Laboratory. 28 p. paper Washington, D.C.: Bureau of Aeronautics, United States Navy,

1945.

5477 *Selected Letters of Raymond Chandler.* edited by MacShane, Frank. 501 p. New York: Columbia University Press, 1981.

Fascinating insight into the person of Raymond Chandler and his career as author and screen writer is provided by this collection of letters. Anyone who likes Chandler's work will find this book a rich, satisfying literary feast.

5478 *Selected List of Catalogues for Short Films and Filmstrips.* compiled by Department of Mass Communications, UNESCO. 36 p. paper Paris: UNESCO, 1964.

A revised edition of the 1955 publication, *Catalogues of Short Films and Filmstrips: Selected List.*

5479 *Selected Mental Health Audiovisuals.* compiled by National Clearinghouse for Mental Health Information. paper Rockville, Md.: National Institute of Mental Health, 1979.

A catalog of more than 2000 nonprint materials on mental health, including many films. Short annotations are supplied along with much other information.

5480 *Selecting Instructional Media.* by Sive, Mary Robinson. 268 p. Littleton, Colo.: Libraries Unlimited, 1978.

Subtitled "A Guide to Audiovisual and Other Instructional Media Lists," this reference offers comprehensive lists by subject area and by type of medium. Of course, many references for films can be found. Essential for educators, this volume is also very useful to anyone concerned with film in an instructional setting.

5481 *Selection and Use of Kodak and Eastman Motion Picture Film.* 47 p. paper illus. Rochester, N.Y.: Eastman Kodak, 1972.

This booklet provides information about the essential characteristics of both black and white and color motion picture films along with some suggestions for the care and handling of films. Topics covered include choosing a film, emulsion characteristics, filters, printing systems, processing, sound systems, physical characteristics, cores, spools, winding, packaging, storage, care, and American National Standards Institute (ANSI) standards. A list of recommended practices and standards published in *The Society of Motion Picture and Television Engineers Journal* is added. Although some of the text may be too specialized or technical for the general reader, much of the information given is clear, practical and useful. As always with Kodak publications, the illustrative materials are superb. For filmmakers this volume would be most helpful in the selection of the proper film stock for a particular purpose. Recommended.

5482 *Selection and Use of Kodak and Eastman Motion Picture Films.* edited by Kodak Staff. 44 paper illus. Rochester, N.Y.: Kodak, 1980.

A guide to motion picture films which notes their characteristics and offers information on emulsions, filters, printing, processing, sound, cores, spools, and packaging.

5483 *A Selection of Films for Family Planning Programmes.* compiled by International Planned Parenthood Federation. 66 p. paper London: International Planned Parenthood Federation, 1973.

Contains an introduction, a subject index, an alphabetical index, a geographical index, along with data and production information about the films. The annotations contain warnings about use of the films since they deal with birth control, contraception, etc.

5484 *A Selection of Films on Mental Health.* edited by Pilkington, T. L. 164 p. paper London: World Federation for Mental Heatlh, 1968.

Written in three languages (English, German, French) this catalog devotes a single pageto each film, giving its title, date, distributor, an annotation, and the suggested audience.

5485 *The Selective Guide to Audiovisuals for Mental Health and Family Life Education.* edited by Neher, Jack. 511 p. paper Indianapolis, Ind.: Academic Media, 1979.

This volume lists 350 recent filmstrips, videotapes and audiotapes with bibliographic information, a description, an evaluation, and suggestions for audience use.

Indexes are by subject and by title, while the entries themselves appear under 21 different headings.

5486 *Self and Cinema: A Transformalist Perspective.* by Houston, Beverle; and Kinder, Marsha. 480 p. paper illus. Pleasantville, N.Y.: Redgrave, 1980.

In this volume the authors adapt selected theories and apply them to recent films: the theories of— Freud and Jung to PERSONA (1967) and THE RITUAL (1969), Marxism and feminism to WEEKEND (1967) and SEVEN BEAUTIES (1975), etc. Other theories considered are behaviorism, phenomenological criticism, archetypical criticism, structuralism, and cinesemiology.

5487 *Self Creations: 13 Impersonalities.* by Morgan, Thomas B. 247 p. New York: Holt, Rinehart & Winston, 1965.

The "self creations" are more interviews with 13 celebrities from all fields taken from the file of a journalist. The motion picture personalities include Gary Cooper, Elia Kazan, and John Wayne. An unusual feature is the followup reaction of the subject to the published interview. Of limited interest.

5488 *The Self-Enchanted. Mae Murray: Image of an Era.* by Ardmore, Jane. 262 p. illus. New York: McGraw, Hill, 1959.

The title of this biography has been wisely chosen. Certainly the portrait of this silent screen star reflects the age and setting in which she achieved her celebrity. Written with compassion and understanding for the subject's faults and virtues, the story contains much interesting peripheral material about other personalities such as Valentino, von Stroheim, Robert Leonard, and John Gilbert. If Miss Murray's memory is correct, other accounts of Valentino's arrival in Hollywood are untrue. Pictures used throughout are excellent and illustrate the flamboyant lifestyle of a famous actress in the twenties. The book combines nostalgia with intelligent biography. As a result it will appeal to many readers and is recommended.

5489 *Self-Policing of the Movie and Publishing Industry.* edited by House Committee on Post Office and Civil Service. 178 p. paper Washington, D.C.: U.S. Government Printing Office, 1960.

Report of a hearing held before the Subcommittee on Postal Operations of the Committee on Post Office and Civil Service, House of Representatives, 86th Congress, second session.

5490 *Self-Portrait.* by Tierney, Gene; and Herskowitz, Mickey. 244 p. paper illus. New York: Berkley, 1980.

Using a flashback format, Gene Tierney begins her autobiography in 1958, the year that she attempted suicide and ended up in the Menninger Clinic. Then it's back to 1938 when she was offered her first film contract. The rest is a kind of tragic fairy tale that includes celebrity, royalty, millionaires and finally, mental illness. The latter apparently was caused by marital failure, paternal disillusionment, and the birth of a retarded child.

Tierney tells all of this in a simple unsparing way: it seems to suggest that after seven years in and out of mental institutions, she has found enough inner peace to accept herself and her life without submitting to depression or self-pity.

The 36 films she appeared in are noted in a filmography, and some are mentioned in the text. Illustrations appear in a center section.

Tierney's story has all the elements of exaggerated soap opera. It is redeemed and made sympathetic by the simple, unaffected approach of the author.

5491 *Self Portrait.* by Ray, Man. 398 p. illus. London: Andre Deutsch, 1963.

5492 *Self-Portrait with Friends: The Selected Diaries of Cecil Beaton, 1926-1974.* edited by Buckle, Richard. 435 p. illus. New York: New York Times Books, 1979.

A selection from six previously published Beaton diaries, this volume also offers 24 Beaton portraits of the rich and famous—Garbo, Olivier, Jackie, Coco, et al.

5493 *Selling Dreams.* by Welsh Art Council. 84 p. illus. paper Forest Groves, Ore.: International Scholarly Book Service, 1980.

5494 *Selznick.* by Thomas, Bob. 361 p. illus. Garden City, N.Y.: Doubleday, 1970.

The Selznick referred to is, of course, David, the producer of the numerous lengthy memos, the quality pictures in the early thirties and the milestone film, GONE WITH THE WIND (1939). In addition to a fully realized portrait of David, the book tells much about his brother, Myron, and his father, Lewis. Crammed with story, legend, incident, and anecdote (sometimes adapted freely and almost totally from other sources, e.g., Ben Hecht's *A Child of the Century*), the book covers not only a life story but a quick history of Hollywood picture production.

Most of the illustrations are very good except for a few which resemble enlarged newspaper plate reprints. The appendix includes a filmography along with stills from the various pictures which Selznick produced. A commendable achievement consistent in quality and production with the author's earlier volumes on Cohn and Thalberg; highly recommended.

5495 *The Selznick Players.* by Bowers, Ronald. 255 p. illus. New York: A. S. Barnes, 1976.

This volume is a collective actor biography supplemented by diverse material about David O. Selznick and his production company. The performers selected for chapter biographies are Ingrid Bergman, Vivien Leigh, Joan Fontaine, Jennifer Jones, Dorothy McGuire, Joseph Cotten, Gregory Peck, and Shirley Temple. Eight other Selznick actors are mentioned in an appendix.

A long introductory chapter is devoted to Selznick as the prototype of the independent producer in Hollywood during the thirties. The story of making GONE WITH THE WIND (1939) is retold in a second chapter and the appendix lists Academy Award nominations of the Selznick pictures and players along with top grossing Selznick films. For each of the main subjects filmographies are provided and the book is nicely illustrated. A bibliography and an index complete the volume.

The biographies, which tend to be factual rather than critical, use quotations, press releases and other public records to a great extent. They are brisk, readable accounts and will satisfy seekers of film star data/information. Anyone searching for character analysis or performance evaluations will have to look elsewhere. Acceptable.

5496 *Semiotics of Cinema.* by Lotman, Juri. 106 p. paper Ann Arbor, Mich.: University of Michigan, 1976.

This volume was translated from the Russian and is number 5 in the *Michigan Slavic Contributions* series. A bibliography is included.

5497 *Semiotics of Films.* edited by Eschlack, Achim; and Rader, Wendelin. 203 p. New York: K. G. Saur, 1978.

5498 *Sergei Eisenstein: An Investigation into His Films and His Philosophy.* by Moussinac, Leon. 226 p. paper illus. New York: Crown, 1970.

Beginning with a long essay by the author, the volume also contains articles and comment by Eisenstein, some excerpts from his film treatments, letters, a few short critical essays, a bio-filmography, a bibliography and an index. The title sums up quite well a book that will please the growing Eisenstein cult. Translated from the French, it is a total and penetrating study of the famous director. Recommended.

5499 *Sergei Eisenstein and Upton Sinclair: The Making and Unmaking of* QUE VIVA MEXICO. edited by Geduld, Harry M.; and Gottesman, Ronald. 512 p. illus. Bloomington, Ind.: Indiana University Press, 1970.

This large volume is a collection of original source material from which the authors have attempted to derive the story of the abortive attempt to film QUE VIVA MEXICO (1933) (usually called THUNDER OVER MEXICO). Principals involved were Eisenstein, the Soviet and the Mexican Governments, and Upton Sinclair. The book is complex, difficult to follow at times, and not totally successful in its attempt to ascertain why the film was never finished.

5500 *Sergei M. Eisenstein: A Biography.* by Seton, Marie. 533 p. illus. New York: A. A. Wyn, 1952.

Written by a personal friend, this lengthy biography of Eisenstein is a definitive one. It offers an explanation of his work and an examination of his influence, along with a disclosure of the political tensions which affected him. It is detailed and, along with many photographs, offers a collection of Eisenstein's sketches. Essential for any serious study of Eisenstein.

5501 *The Serials.* by Stedman, Raymond W. 514 p. illus. Norman, Okla.: University of Oklahoma Press, 1971.

Only a third of this volume pertains to film. It touches on the silent serials of Pearl White, Ruth Roland and others and concentrates on the sound serials of the thirties. Other sections are devoted to radio and TV serials. The reference material in the appendices is excellent.

5502 *Serials (A Series).* by Barbour, Alan. varies paper illus. Kew Gardens, N.Y.: Screen Facts, 1965- .

Alan Barbour, a film buff, collector and author, created a series of profusely illustrated paperback volumes dealing with serials, screen ads, westerns, older films, etc. The following titles were among those published: *The Serial: Volume I*, 297 pages, 1967; *Great Serial Ads*, 1965; *The Serial: Volume 2*, 299 pages, 1968; *Serial Pictorial*, 8 different titles, 16 pages each—THE ADVENTURES OF CAPTAIN MARVEL (1941), THE MASKED MARVEL (1943), DARKEST AFRICA (1936), SPY SMASHER (1942), DRUMS OF FU MANCHU (1940), ZORRO'S FIGHTING LEGION (1939), SECRET AGENT X-9 (1945); *Roy Barcroft: Scenes from His Films*; *Serial Quarterly*, 7 issues, 1966-1967; *Serial Showcase*, 1968; *The Serials of Columbia*, 1967; *The Serials of Republic*, 1965; *Old Movies: The Serial*, 2 volumes, 64 pages, 1969, 1970; *Screen Ads Monthly*, 4 volumes, 1967, 1968; *Thrill After Thrill*, 1971.

5503 *Series, Serials, and Packages. Vol. 12, Issue #2.* edited by Fliegelman, Avra. 414 p. New York: Broadcast Info. Bureau, 1971.

Another excellent reference book about television programming of filmed material; in this case, the films are series, serials, and packages. The first section is a title index listing series films running from 20 seconds to 120 minutes. They are arranged in time division (1 hour, one-half hour, 15 minutes), with appropriate subject headings under each division. Adventure, documentary, drama, mystery, and interview are some of the subject headings to be found. For each series the following information is offered: title, stars, story line, number of films available or planned, running time, black and white or color, gauge, year produced, leasing fee range, markets open, sponsors, producer, distributor.

A second section lists foreign language series arranged alphabetically by language from Arabic to Yugoslav. Other sections include series available for cable television, a total title index and a listing of film sources. As a reference source on TV serials and series, the book is invaluable.

5504 THE SERPENT'S EGG. by Bergman, Ingmar. 123 p. illus. New York:Pantheon, 1977.

Script of the 1977 film written and directed by Ingmar Bergman.

5505 *The Serpent's Eye: Shaw and the Cinema.* by Costello, Donald P. 209 p. illus. Notre Dame, Ind.: University of Notre Dame Press, 1965.

An examination of George Bernard Shaw's views on cinema and their effect on the subsequent transferrence of certain of his plays to motion pictures are the major topics of this book. Throughout the book, the figure of producer Gabriel Pascal looms large since he was responsible for four films of Shaw's plays: PYGMALION (1938), MAJOR BARBARA (1940), CAESAR AND CLEOPATRA (1945), and ANDROCLES AND THE LION (1953). The first three films each receive a chapter of detailed analysis. The author, a Notre Dame professor, writes in an enlightened, scholastic style. Obviously researched with care, the book contrasts Shaw's cinema theories with the success or failure of the films to which they were applied. Pictures used throughout are related to the textual material.

Especially commendable is the appendix which includes a Shaw filmography, sample scenes and scenarios, and a comparison of the play, the printed screen version, and the transcribed sound track of a portion of PYGMALION. An extended bibliography and an index are included. Very specialized material that has some implication for broader areas of film preparation. Admirable work done by an able scholar.

5506 *Seven Daughters of the Theatre.* by Wagenknecht, Edward. 234 p. illus. Norman, Okla.: University of Oklahoma Press, 1964.

Included as a cinema book because the author offers a study of Marilyn Monroe along with those of Sarah Bernhardt, Ellen Terry, Julia Marlowe, Isadora Duncan, Mary Garden, and Jenny Lind. His estimation of Monroe's potential as a serious actress is a thoughtful tribute.

5507 *The Seven Deadly Sins of Hollywood.* by Wiseman, Thomas. 222 p. illus. London: Oldburne Press, 1957.

Here is a collection of trivial celebrity interviews peppered with comments such as—Liberace: "His personality is outshone by his tailor's" ; Rossano Brazzi: "A male Diana Dors" ; Susan Hayward: "A girl with a will of stainless steel and the appetite of a truck driver"; Orson Welles: "An artistic nymphomaniac"; Darryl Zanuck: "Looked like a humanised ferret in a Disney film"; and Victor Mature: "A man saved by the Bible."

The author is a columnist for the *London Evening Standard* and although the title refers to "a new appraisal of Hollywood," the reportage covers the world scene. Written nearly 15 years ago, many of the quotations are either amusing or sad, and sometimes both, as in the cases of Monroe and Mansfield. The supposed climax of the book, the listing of the seven deadly sins of Hollywood, is contrived and rather unnecessary. The excellence of the accompanying photographs underlines the shallowness of the text. This is amusing surface trivia. Where else is there a book containing an interview with Vera Hruba Ralston?

5508 *The Seven Lively Arts.* by Seldes, Gilbert. 306 p. New York: Sagamore Press, 1957 (1924).

A slightly revised version of early Seldes (1924), this volume has a few essays on motion pictures. The subjects include Mack Sennett, Keystone, Chaplin, Griffith, and movie moguls. Other portions of the book concern vaudeville, comic strips, popular music, etc. For supplementary use only.

5509 SEVEN SAMURAI. by Hashimoto, Shinolou; and Oguni, Hideo; and Kurosawa, Akira. 224 p. paper illus. New York: Simon & Schuster, 1970.

Script of the 1954 film directed by Kurosawa. Contains cast credits and an introduction by Donald Richie.

5510 *Seventeen Interviews: Film Stars and Superstars.* by Miller, Edwin. 384 p. illus. New York: Macmillan, 1970.

This collection of short interviews taken from the pages of *Seventeen* features stars, superstars, and almost-stars—over 50 of them, mostly film personalities, with a few in the world of music and dance. The articles are written more seriously than those created for fan magazines but still remain surface portraits with all controversial topics carefully avoided. Since they were designed for readers of *Seventeen*, one can only assume that the readership of that magazine is much younger than its name indicates. Perhaps the rationale for these articles is to provide models for young people to emulate. The more mature reader who is familiar with the Rex Reed type of interview will be very disappointed. All

others beware of the nonsatisfying mixture of blandness and sugar.

5511 1776. 24 p. paper illus. New York: Souvenir Publications, 1972.

An article entitled "1776—The Way It Was and Is!!!" attempts to provide background to the film by contrasting historical fact with legend and myth. Jack L. Warner, who never misses an opportunity to occupy center stage, receives two pages of profile and tribute. Illustrations are in both black and white and color, with the latter group fuzzy and out of focus. In the centerfold there is a reproduction of The Declaration of Independence with the signers designated. A second article, "The Spirit of 1776," relates the filming of the original play. Capsule biographies of the cast are presented in a unique way with leading players first, followed by groupings of the delegates arranged according to the state they represented. Production credits are also listed.

5512 THE SEVENTH SEAL. by Bergman, Ingmar. 82 p. paper illus. London: Lorrimer Pub. Co., 1968.

Script of the 1956 film directed by Bergman. Contains cast credits and an introduction by Bergman.

5513 THE SEVENTH VOYAGE OF SINBAD. 12 P. illus. 1958.

The emphasis in this short souvenir book is on the special effects used in the 1958 film. They are explained in a section entitled "This is Dynamation" which describes the duel between Sinbad and a skeleton, and other unusual sequences from the film. The story is outlined and cast and production credits are noted. Most of the illustrations are fuzzy and out of focus. It is somewhat ironic that Bernard Herrmann's score, a soundtrack recording rarity at this writing, is merely acknowledged.

5514 *75 Years of Indian Cinema.* by Rangoonwalla, Firoze. 168 p. illus. New Delhi: Indian Book Co., 1975.

This history attempts to document the growth of cinema in India for the past 75 years. Attention is given to films, personalities, technological developments and the Indian film industry. The text is arranged chronologically by decades with chapters devoted to: Beginnings (1896-1899); A Decade of Shorts (1900-1909); Feature Film, in Embryo (1910-1919); Silent Era, in Bloom (1920-1929); Talkie Comes and Conquers (1930-1939); War, Freedom and After (1940-1949); New Tastes (1950-1959); and Back to Adolescence? (1960-present). A center section of illustrations and an index complete the book.

The author has researched the material carefully and arranged it into a pedantic informational flow. Since most American readers will lack familiarity with the titles and the persons discussed, their reading pleasure will be minimal. Those interested in the national cinema of India will find this book to be a rich source of information. Acceptable.

5515   *Seventy Years of Cinema.* by Cowie, Peter. 287 p. illus. New York: A. S. Barnes, 1969.

This book is a year-by-year look at the motion picture, with emphasis on those films which have been influential trend-makers. For example, the year 1948 offers detailed plot description, analysis, cast and production credits for THE BICYCLE THIEF, THE TREASURE OF SIERRA MADRE, and THE LADY FROM SHANGHAI. Capsule attention is given to THE FALL-EN IDOL, KEY LARGO, LOUISIANA STORY, THE NAKED CITY, THE PIRATE, RED RIVER, LA TERRA TREMA, UNFAITHFULLY YOURS, and THE WINS-LOW BOY. Short films noted are VAN GOGH and A DIVIDED WORLD. The final portion of each yearly account contains a few facts of interest—births, deaths, technological developments, etc. The book appears to be equally divided into text and pictorial portions.

The picture selection and reproduction are very good. The author is very subjective in his selection and some of his analyses (e.g., STRANGERS ON A TRAIN, (1951) are rather unusual. His opinions are strong. Readers may quarrel with his evaluation of PSYCHO (1960) ("Hitchcock's greatest film" and "The most intelligent and disturbing horror film ever made"). Although there are some minor errors, this is, overall, a provocative, entertaining book with excellent reference value. Recommended.

5516   *Several Aspects of Belgian Cinema.* by bolen, Francis. 22 p. paper Brussels: Ministry of Culture, 1971.

This short paper translated from the French deals with the history of the Belgian cinema.

5517   *Sex Education on Film.* by Singer, Laura J.; and Buskin, Judith. 170 p. paper New York: Teachers College Press, 1971.

Subtitled "A Guide to Visual Aids and Programs," this volume considers over 110 titles dealing with some aspect of sex education. Included in the group are 85 films, along with some filmstrips and slide sets. The titles are classified under subject headings

such as family relationships, physical and emotional development, creation of life, masculinity and femininity, attitudes and values, marriage, and philosophy of sex education. A sample program is offered, and there is an age and socioeconomic group index to the films. An alphabetical listing by title concludes this helpful reference.

The annotations are both descriptive and evaluative with suggestions made as to possible use, methodology, etc. A set of questions accompanies the introduction to each unit. Distributors of the various media are noted along with other resource agencies which supply printed materials. This is a valuable reference book that belongs in all school libraries. The arrangement facilitates finding pertinent material in this sensitive subject area, and the evaluations give needed direction for its possible use. Recommended.

5518   *Sex Goddesses of the Silent Screen.* by Zierold, Norman. 207 p. illus. Chicago, Ill.: Henry Regnery, 1973.

The sex goddesses are Theda Bara, Barbara Lamarr, Pola Negri, Mae Murray, and Clara Bow. An essay which combines biographical and critical elements is given for each, as are separate filmographies. Acceptable.

5519   *Sex in the Movies.* by Walker, Alexander. 284 p. paper illus. Baltimore: Penguin Books, 1968.

This is the title given for the paperback edition of *The Celluloid Sacrifice.*

5520   *Sex on Celluloid.* by Milner, Michael. 224 p. paper illus. New York: Macfadden Books, 1964.

With the arrival of almost complete screen freedom, much of this book seems dated now. But if viewed as a past history and as a discussion of why some films were made in a certain way, it has value. The book itself is a blend of data, analysis, and sensationalism—as though someone had decided to spice up a scholarly dissertation. The pictures are badly reproduced. Much of the comment on various films is quite interesting and anyone who is concerned with censorship will be rewarded.

5521   *The Sex People.* by Kronhausen, Phyllis; and Kronhausen, Eberhard. 265 p. paper Chicago: Playboy Press, 1975.

The authors continue their exploration of the sexual revolution, a subject they reported upon in six previously published books. Here they turn their attention to sexual entertainments such as shows and movies. Included are conversations with producers (Jim Mitchell, Art Mitchell, Terry Sullivan, etc.) and performers (Linda Lovelace, Georgina Spelvin, Marilyn Chambers, Tina Russell, Maria Schneider, Harry Reems, Marc Stevens).

All of this is presented as sociological reportage— "a professional view...." The text resembles the better hardcore novel for the most part and seems designed for the erotic titillation of the reader rather than for education or enlightenment.

5522 *Sex, Psyche, Etcetera in the Film.* by Tyler, Parker. 239 p. New York: Horizon Press, 1969.

This most recent collection of Tyler's writings continues his consistent peformance as one of the most rewarding writers on film. The articles, written originally for several small magazines, are collected in four categories: sex ritual, the modern psyche, the artist in crisis, and film aesthetics. Because of Tyler's style, interests, and standards, the articles read as a total statement instead of disparate comments.

As usual the topics are surprising, unexpected and, at times, quite far out. For example, the analysis for GALLANT BESS (1946) may even stun the creators of this film. Orson Welles, Chaplin, Fellini, Bergman, Antonioni, and Warhol are among those given attention by Tyler. The major focus is on current films, mostly the experimental and the unusual ones. Perhaps the most disappointing piece is the defense of I AM CURIOUS (YELLOW) (1967). There are no illustrations in this book but it is indexed. This is a major critical collection that will appeal to some readers but will be much too difficult for many others.

5523 *Sexual Alienation in the Cinema: The Dynamics of Sexual Freedom.* by Durgnat, Raymond. 320 p. illus. London: Studio Vista, 1972.

5524 *Sexual Stratagems: The World of Women in Film.* edited by Erens, Patricia. 336 p. illus. New York: Horizon, 1979.

Patricia Erens has divided this anthology into two major sections: The Male-directed Cinema, and The Women's Cinema. In the first she considers images, distortions, and specific films directed by men— DAMES (1934), MADAME DE (1954), TWO OR THREE THINGS I KNOW ABOUT HER (1967), LUCIA (1968), etc. In the second, longer section she treats certain female directors (Alice Guy Blache, Esther Shub, Maya Deren, Germaine Dulac, Leni Riefenstahl and Mai Zetterling) and selected films directed by women—MAEDCHEN IN UNIFORM (1931), A VERY CURIOUS GIRL (1969), JEANNE DIELMAN (1975), etc. Many pages of female director filmographies and a lengthy bibliography complete the book.

This anthology accomplishes several things; it presents an overview of the feminist aesthetic in films, a familiarization with unknown female directors, and an evaluation of films dealing positively and negatively with women. A good collection of photographs supports the well-selected and arranged articles. Recommended.

5525 *Sexuality in the Movies.* edited by Atkins, Thomas R. 244 p. illus. Bloomington, Ind.: Indiana University Press, 1975.

This anthology is divided into three parts: social and cultural perspectives (e.g., censorship, ratings, morality, sexual fantasies), categories and genres (e.g., popular films, flesh films, monster films, films with homoesexual themes, european films) and contemporary landmarks, e.g., I AM CURIOUS YELLOW (1967); MIDNIGHT COWBOY (1969); CARNAL KNOWLEDGE (1971); DEEP THROAT (1972); LAST TANGO IN PARIS (1974); CRIES AND WHISPERS (1974). The strengths and weaknesses usually inherent in the anthology format are present here. A good overall structure has been filled out by contributions which vary somewhat in their effectiveness, e.g., Lenning's "History of Censorship" is excellent while Gene D. Phillips' article seems familiar, covering much the same homosexual-theme material that Parker Tyler did in *Screening the Sexes.* Missing also is any connective narrative that would make this a more unified whole rather than several disparate articles on a general large theme.

These are minor reservations to a mostly successful survey. An outstanding feature of the book is the collection of photographs used to complement the text. Carefully reproduced, they have obviously been selected with care and good taste. In both text and illustration, sensationalism is absent. In summary this is an attractive book that treats a controversial subject with intelligence and sensitivity. Its visuals are superb and most of the text is quite rewarding. Recommended for mature adults.

5526 *The Sexy Cinema.* by Strick, Marv; and Lethe, Robert. 192 p. illus. Los Angeles: Sherbourne, 1974.

A historical survey of eroticism in the cinema, this volume discusses how sex was shown/implied on screen by directors, actors, scripts, etc. More than 100 illustrations accompany this popularized overview of sex in cinema.

5527 *Seymour Stern: American Film Historian.* by Fosterer, Selig. Brooklyn, N.Y.: Revisionist Press, 1980.

5528 *The Shadow and Its Shadow.* edited by Hammond, Paul. 133 p. paper London: British Film Institute; New York: Zoetrope, 1978.

This anthology, subtitled "Surrealist Writings on Cinema," consists of statements by Aragon, Artaud, Breton, Brunius, Bunuel, Ado Kyrou and Man Ray. The Manifesto for L'AGE D'OR (1930) is included. Several of the articles have never been published in English before.

5529 *The Shadow of an Airplane Climbs the Empire State Building.* by Tyler, Parker. 248 p. Garden City, N.Y.: Doubleday, 1972.

Parker Tyler resembles Marshall McLuhan (whom he deprecates whenever possible) in that he explores but does not explain. In this frustrating collection of intellectual obfuscation, Tyler is supposedly seeking a theory of world film. Congratulations are extended to those who can find it here. The last few paragraphs contain such world-shaking statements as "So, film makers, I make an envoi: Hold to the sprocket holes of the images dictated to you by your own voices, your personal and peculiar voices, and no other voices. This is your hope and, of course, my theory."

Many of the films analyzed or used as arguments by Tyler are quite obscure. This becomes a tactic to intimidate the reader; select the unknown, pontificate about it, and leave the reader with self-doubt. There may be those who have the time, energy, or curiosity to wade through this volume. May their effort and patience be rewarded—although it is unlikely. Not recommended unless it is used as an example of film criticism which, if it appears with any frequency, will kill off the art.

5530 *The Shadow of Sound.* by Gregg, Eugene S. 174 p. New York: Vantage, 1968.

A discussion of what happened with the invention and acceptance of talking pictures.

5531 *Shadow Theatre and Shadow Films.* by Reiniger, Lotte. 128 p. illus . New York: Watson-Guptill, 1970.

Two art forms and their use in the classroom explained by a master practitioner.

5532 *Shadowland.* by Arnold, William. 260 p. illus. New York: McGraw-Hill, 1978.

Many of the strong dramatic events that made *Will There Ever Be a Morning?* so unforgettable are recovered in this volume by investigative reporter Arnold. The difference between the two volumes, he infers, is that which exists between fact and fictionalized biography. Labeling the earlier book "a number of sensational scenes" invented by Jean Ratcliffe, he minimizes the half dozen years that Ratcliffe lived with Frances Farmer. He opts instead for documentation, conjecture, and hearsay, telling his story in a cool reportorial fashion. The result is still an engrossing biography that will enrage and sadden the reader. It is modern tragedy, with the practitioners of psychiatry/mental health as chief villains. A few illustrations illuminate the text.

Arnold has given the Frances Farmer story greater dimension by his exploration of possible political motives for her placement in mental institutions, and by his belief that she was lobotomized. His carefully wrought analyses and conclusions are major strengths in a disturbing book that deserves the attention of the serious reader.

5533 *Shakespeare and the Film.* by Manvell, Roger. 172 p. illus. New York: Praeger, 1971.

Shakespeare on silent film was covered by Robert Hamilton Ball, and Manvell concentrates on sound films in this book. A short chapter acknowledges the silents and is quickly followed by analyses of the Pickford-Fairbanks' THE TAMING OF THE SHREW (1929), Reinhardt's A MIDSUMMER NIGHT'S DREAM (1935), Cukor's ROMEO AND JUILET (1936) and Czinner's AS YOU LIKE IT (1936). Laurence Olivier, Orson Welles, and Akira Kurosawa are accorded individual chapters as are the Russian and Italian Shakespeare films. Attention is given to two adaptations of "Julius Caesar" and to recent translations of specific stage productions to film. Peter Brook's 1970 film of KING LEAR is discussed in detail as the most recent Shakespearian film. A filmography with extensive cast credits, a selected bibliography and an index conclude the book.

Each of the films is represented by some stills which are brilliantly reproduced in most cases. The visuals here help to interpret much of the text and are an essential ingredient of the book. As with all of Manvell's work, the text is scholarly, readable, thorough, and linear. Production work, especially with the visuals, is outstanding. This is a beautiful book that is recommended to all.

5534 *Shakespeare on Film.* by Jorgens, Jack J. 337 p. illus. Bloomington, Ind.: Indiana University Press, 1977.

To an enthusiasm for Shakespeare and for film, the author has added an enormous research effort and considerable interpretive skills. The result is this impressive volume, which explores and contemplates the use of Shakespeare's plays as material for the cinema.

Following an introduction which clearly states the author's purposes, methods, and goals, the text offers individual chapters on each of 16 different films. Some duplication of the original plays occurs as two film versions of *Othello, Hamlet,* and *A Midsummer Night's Dream* are considered along with several interpretations of *Macbeth.*

The appendix offers credits and outlines of the films in which a correlation is made between the sequences of the films and the acts of the plays. Notes for each of the chapters follow and the book concludes with a general index. Frame enlargements are used to provide visual illustration for the text.

It is unusual to find a scholarly volume that has the potential to attract a wide readership. This is such a book, for not only can it be used in secondary schools and colleges, but it also will appeal immensely to anyone interested in the relationship between film and literature. Highly recommended.

5535 *Shakespeare on Film: An Index to William Shakespeare's Plays on Film.* by Morris, Peter. 30 p. paper illus. Ottawa, Ontario: Canadian Film Institute.

A survey of about 50 films from THE TAMING OF THE SHREW (1928) to KING LEAR (1971), this volume also contains an essay on silent-film versions of Shakespeare, a filmography, and a discussion of the various approaches used in filming the plays.

5536 *Shakespeare on Silent Film: A Strange Eventful History.* by Ball, Robert Hamilton. 403 p. illus. New York: Theatre Arts Books, 1968.

An impressive, scholarly work, this volume traces the use of Shakespeare's plays as material for the

silent film. During the early film era, Shakespeare's plays were brought to the masses and, in return, a certain respectability was brought to film. Included in the volume are rare illustrations, portions of scenarios, and screen titles from the Shakespeare films. Extended notes, a title index, and a general index are included.

Should the McLuhanites worry, the author recognizes the differences between a silent film and a live production of the plays. "Inadequate, even ridiculous as was Shakespeare on silent film, not art, not good entertainment, it was the necessary preparation for something better." This is an excellent example of research in films done by a qualified scholar, with impressive reportage of his findings. This volume is highly recommended for scholars.

5537 SHAKESPEARE WALLAH. by Jhabvala, R. Prawer; and Ivory, James. 152 p. paper illus. New York: Evergreen, 1973.

Script of the 1965 film directed by Ivory. Includes an introduction by James Ivory.

5538 *The Shame and Disgrace of* COLONEL BLIMP. by Robson, E.W.; and Robson, M.M. 31 p. illus. London: Sidneyan Society, 1944.

The authors of *The Film Answers Back* take on COLONEL BLIMP (1943) for the portrait of a sympathetic German (Anton Walbrook), among other things.

5539 *The Shattered Silents: How the Talkies Came to Stay.* by Walker, Alexander. 218 p. illus. New York: William Morrow, 1979.

Similar in content to Harry Geduld's *The Birth of the Talkies,* this study by Alexander Walker examines the effects that sound motion pictures had on actors, studios, moguls, sound engineers, writers, etc. The period of transition was from 1926 to 1929, and Walker conveys the drama, shock, excitement and confusion of those years. Typical of Walker's scholarship is his use of the many film trade journals in relating his story.

A selected filmography (1925-1929), a bibliography, an index, and over 30 pages of illustrations add to the high quality of this book. A definitive study of a crucial period in Hollywood history.

5540 *Shelley Also Known As Shirley.* by Winters, Shelley. 511 p. illus. New

York: William Morrow, 1980.

If there is such a thing as autobiographical overkill, this volume may be a prime example. Shelley Winters spends over 500 pages talking about herself and only gets her story as far as MAMBO (1954) and her divorce from Vittorio Gassman. In a manner that befits her public image, she tells about her early struggles, affairs, marriages, stage roles, screen appearances, etc., in a brash, flashy manner designed to draw and keep attention. Though she is shy about specific dates, there is no hesitation in naming people. This results in perhaps the most interesting part of her tale—her impressions of fellow actors and filmmakers. Whether one is entertained by her candid, outspoken recital will depend on one's appetite for a Cinderella story spiced with gossip and celebrity characters. No one can fault her for not trying to turn in a good performance, whether on screen or on paper. It's only that, every so often, it seems she's trying too hard.

Unfortunately, no index or filmography is provided. There are more than 100 good illustrations which complement the text nicely.

5541 *The Sherlock Holmes File.* by Pointer, Michael. 168 p. illus. New York: Clarkson N. Potter (Crown), 1977.

A nourishing feast of text and visuals is provided for Sherlock Holmes aficionados in this unusual volume. Although the jacket subtitle reads "The Many Personae of Sherlock Holmes on Stage, in Film and in Advertising," this is only a partial account of the content. Literature, television, recordings, and other media are also considered.

Since the author is dealing with various actors who have portrayed either Holmes or Dr. Watson, his text must depend upon the visuals. About 175 are provided and they show Holmes pictured in stage photographs, film stills, posters, record jackets, etc. Special chapters are devoted to Holmes' disguises, the settings of his activities, *The Hound of the Baskervilles* (seven films and two television versions), and the 1968 recreation of the Holmes-Moriarty death struggle at the Reichenback Falls. The appendix lists 54 stage productions, 115 silent films, 200 sound films, 34 radio programs/series, and 10 television programs/series. The volume is indexed.

To the Sherlock Holmes devotee, this volume is absolutely essential. The general reader will be quickly caught by the Holmes fever because of the intelligent and entertaining treatment provided here. Highly recommended.

5542 *Sherlock Holmes on the Screen.* by Pohle, Robert W., Jr.; and Hart, Douglas C. 260 p. illus. New York: A.S. Barnes, 1977.

Since 1903 there have been over 150 Sherlock Holmes films, as well as a considerable number of Holmes parody films. In this volume the authors survey the film careers of Holmes and his companion, Dr. Watson, from SHERLOCK HOLMES BAFFLED (1903) to THEY MIGHT BE GIANTS (1971). The arrangement of the films is a chronological one with occasional interruptions about the actors identified with playing Sherlock Holmes. Given for most films are the title, credits, cast, synopsis, comment, and a few review excerpts. In the case of the actors, such things as their physical appearance, acting technique, and public image are considered along with some biographical data. Basil Rathbone, John Barrymore, Raymond Massey, Peter Cushing, and Christopher Lee are analyzed in some detail. In addition to the English language films, coverage is extended to a few German and Czech films. A final chapter treats Sherlock Holmes on television. A bibliography and an index are included along with a good collection of appropriate visuals that convey the many physical interpretations of Conan Doyle's detective.

By combining a topic of lasting interest with careful research, logical arrangement and intelligent interpretation, the authors have come up with a volume that will please a wide audience. It is also a natural for the study of the relationship between literature and film. Finally, its value as a reference book is obvious. Recommended.

5543 *Shinde's Dictionary of Cine Art and Film Craft.* edited by Shinde, M.K. 176 p. illus. Bombay: Shatkal, 1963.

An Indian dictionary of terms and topics encountered in films and filmmaking.

5544 *Shirley Temple.* by Eby, Lois. 143 p. paper Derby, Conn.: Monarch Books, 1962.

The subtitle tells it all: "The Amazing Story of the Child Actress Who Grew Up to Be America's Fairy Princess." This paperback ends with her marriage in 1950 to Charles Black; her short political career is not covered. There is a biography of Elizabeth Taylor by John B. Allan in this same series.

5545 *Shirley Temple.* by Windeler, Robert. 160 p. illus. London: W. H. Allen, 1975.

A biography of Shirley Temple that includes illustrations, an index, and a filmography.

5546 *Shirley Temple.* by Basinger, Jeanine. 158 p. paper illus. New York: Pyramid, 1975.

Books about Shirley Temple have been few. Most of them were published during the height of her popularity in the thirties. Here is the first volume to examine her film roles while also describing the private life of the most popular child star in motion picture history. Since Temple's life was carefully programmed both off screen and on, there is an antiseptic, too-good-to-be-true quality in the recollection of her Hollywood days. Apparently she did everything right and was without blemish.

Her films, however, are another matter, ranging as they do from charming to horrible. Author Basinger evaluates them quite objectively, e.g., "Shirley's performance is competent but lackluster" (DIMPLES, 1936); "One of Shirley Temple's best films" (WEE WILLIE WINKIE, 1937); "She was as out-of-place as Lassie would have been in 'Private Lives'" (KATHLEEN, 1941). The illustrations provide full coverage of films and events providing a visual record of the maturing of a talented, captivating little girl into an active, outspoken champion of Republican Party dogma. A biography, a filmography and an index are included. Recommended for all collections.

5547 *Shirley Temple Dolls and Collectibles.* by Smith, Patricia. 2 Volumes illus. Paducah, Ky.: Collector Books, 1977.

Shirley Temple was an early example of a performer whose likeness was merchandized in a great many ways. These two volumes by Patricia Smith list hundreds of Shirley Temple dolls and toys. Values for the items are suggested. Lorraine Burdick, author of *The Shirley Temple Scrapbook*, has also written a book on the collectibles entitled *Shirley Temple's Dolls and Related Delights* (Hobby House, 1977).

5548 *The Shirley Temple Scrapbook.* by Burdick, Loraine. 160 p. illus. Middle Village, N.Y.: Jonathan David, 1975.

The title of this volume is most appropriate since its contents are samplings of the elements which comprise a critical biography or appreciation. Bits of biography, filmography, career survey and celebrity-personality investigation appear in abbreviated form.

Written by a former president of the Shirley Temple Fan Club, the book is a tribute made up of material indigenous to such admiring organizations. The biography is skeletal, illustrations are uniformly flattering, critical evaluation of the films and Temple's performances in them is absent. Film plot outlines are condensed to a sentence or so, and any sociological considerations of the public adoration for Shirley Temple in the 1930s remains unexplored.

What we have then is a series of charming photographs linked together by a bland subjective text which tells little about an American legend and phenomenon. Nondiscriminating nostalgia buffs will find pleasure in this visual tribute, but the serious reader will have to refer to the book by Jeanine Basinger or await the serious study that Shirley Temple and her era deserve. Acceptable.

5549 THE SHOES OF THE FISHERMAN. 34 p. paper illus. New York: National Publishers, 1968.

Many photographs, both stills and candids, tell the story of the 1968 film and its production in this souvenir book. Some attention is given to director Michael Anderson, producer George Englund, and star Anthony Quinn. The author of the novel upon which the film is based, Morris West, is also profiled. Supporting cast and production credits are noted.

5550 *The Shoestring Animator: Making Animated Films with Super Eight.* by Grush, Byron. 160 p. illus. Chicago: Contemporary Books, 1981.

5551 *Shoot-Em-Ups.* by Adams, Les; and Rainey, Buck. 633 p. illus. New Rochelle, N.Y.: Arlington House, 1978.

The subtitle to this large volume reads, "The Complete Reference Guide to Westerns of the Sound Era." Although "complete" may give pause to some users, the book certainly attempts to cover its subject in comprehensive fashion. After a chapter on the silent western, the period from 1928 to 1977 is broken into four- or five-year intervals which are described with a title and short explanation—e.g. 1933-1937, The Golden Years (Familiar Faces and Fast Guns).For each interval, a critical essay covering the period precedes a filmography arranged on a year-by-year basis. For instance, in the above section, the films which appeared in 1933 are arranged according to their release date and each is given a numerical sequence number. This procedure is then repeated for 1934, 1935, 1936, and 1937. For each of the films listed, the following information is given: studio, release date, running time, cast, director, original story author, screenplay writer, and producer. Stills from many of the films appear throughout the book.

Access to the films is provided by an alphabetical title listing which is followed by the year of release and numerical sequence number.

Anyone searching for information about specific films in the western genre would do well to consult this reference first. It provides information that is difficult to obtain elsewhere; in addition, the twelve narratives which introduce each chapter-period provide a refreshing critical history. Recommended.

5552 *Shoot First! Assignments of a Newsreel Cameraman.* by Noble, Ronald. 271 p. illus. London: Harrap, 1955.

5553 *Shooting Scripts.* by Cornford, Adam. illus. paper San Francisco: Black Stone, 1979.

5554 *Shooting Star: A Biography of John Wayne.* by Zolotow, Maurice. 416 p. illus. New York: Simon & Schuster, 1974.

Although it was a late entry in the John Wayne biography sweepstakes, this volume is the best of the group. Wayne's cooperation has enabled Zolotow to explore in much more detail the actor's rise from stuntman to superstar. Personal qualities and characteristics are examined and an intimate portrait is presented. The marriages, male camaraderie, relationship with John Ford, politics, and the battle with cancer are covered along with an abundance of unfamiliar anecdotes and incidents. A center section of photographs and an index support the text. The biography is a sympathetic yet objective study of a film performer whose personal life seems a blurred reflection of his screen image. Recommended.

5555 *Shooting Without Stars.* by Hornby, Clifford. 252 p. illus. London: Hutchinson, 1940.

An account of making RHODES OF AFRICA (1936).

5556 *The Short Film: An Evaluative Selection of 500 Films.* by Rehrauer, George. 199 p. illus. New York: Macmillan, 1975.

This is a source book of 500 short (under 60 minutes) films that have been recommended by experts, evaluation groups and other authorities in more than 36 books. The films considered are those that have wide appeal and can be used with a variety of audiences. Arranged alphabetically by title, the 500 entries offer the following information for each film: release date, producer-distributor, running time, the absence of narration/dialogue, type of film, color or black and white, content description, suggested audiences, areas of use and recommending sources. This latter information is keyed to an annotated bibliography of the 36 books used in determining the films. By reference to the bibliography, evaluations and suggestions for use may be located with ease. A detailed subject index, extensively cross-referenced, is also provided. Stills from more than 50 of the films are used to convey the pictorial style of each. The goal of the volume is to provide information about those short films which have been accepted as representative of the best in the genre. The selection process necessitated the use of a large number of responsible reviewers, and in most cases, the test of time—the continuing approval of audiences.

5557 *Short Films.* edited by Information Film Service. 290 p. paper illus. Prague: Ceskoslovensky Film Export Praha, 1972.

The films in this Czechoslovakian film catalog are arranged by subject area—education, mining, power, pediatrics, legumes, etc. For each film there is a description which appears in three languages (English, French and German).

5558 *A Short History of the Hungarian Cinema.* by Nemeskurty, Istvan. 41p. illus. New York: Zoetrope, 1981.

Fifty five years of Hungarian film history presented in succinct, terse fashion using text and illustration.

5559 *A Short History of the Movies.* by Mast, Gerald. 432 p. illus. New York: Bobbs-Merrill, 1971.

The evolution of film from its beginnings to today's art form is related in this book. It emphasizes important directors and their key films. The business, technology and sociology of the motion picture are treated.

5560 *Short Lives: Portraits in Creativity and Self-Destruction.* by Matson, Katinka. 436 p. paper illus. New York: William Morrow, 1980.

Although the purported intention of this collective biography is to investigate why certain creative people engage in self-destruction, that goal is hardly realized. Instead, some 31 capsule biographies are offered in a superficial, sentimental text.

Subjects include Montgomery Clift, James Dean, Marilyn Monroe, Judy Garland, etc.

5561 *Short Stories on Film.* by Emmens, Carol A. 345 p. Littleton, Colo.: Libraries Unlimited, 1978.

It is always rewarding to discover the publication of a useful, carefully written reference book about films. *Short Stories on Film* is such a volume. It is a bibliography arranged alphabetically by author surname of short stories that have been made into films. Each entry contains the author's name, the short story title, the film title, the original source if any, running time, color format, date of release, director, producer, distributor, cast, and a short plot outline—often only one sentence. The only reservation one may have about this material is the quality of these plot summaries. They can occasionally be a bit misleading to those unfamiliar with the films.

Further access to the information is provided by a story title index and a film index which appear in the book's final pages.

The treatment and arrangement that has been accorded this reference material is excellent. Certainly the book will become a standard work to be placed alongside Enser's *Filmed Books and Plays.* It should be a cause for gladness for anyone concerned with the relationship between film and literature. Highly recommended.

5562 *Short Story/Short Film.* by Marcus, Fred H. 447 p. illus. Englewood Cliffs, N.J.: Prentice-Hall, 1977.

The practice of using short stories as a source for film material is a relatively new one. In this volume some 15 examples of film adaptations are explored in detail. Included are: YOUNG GOODMAN BROWN (1973), THE LOTTERY (1969), BARTLEBY (1969), THE UPTURNED FACE (1973), DR. HEIDEGGER'S EXPERIMENT (1969), THE BET (1967), THE LADY OR THE TIGER (1969), THE MASQUE OF THE RED DEATH (1970), A TIME OUT OF WAR (1954), AN OCCURRENCE AT OWL CREEK BRIDGE (1962), THE UNICORN IN THE GARDEN (1953), THE GARDEN PARTY (1974), and STICKY MY FINGERS, FLEET MY FEET (1970).

The original short story and either a screenplay, a continuity, a shot analysis or a storyboard are offered for comparison. In several instances more than one adaptation is offered, as are critiques of the film. Final pages include appendices of awards, film data, distributors, additional films, a glossary of film terms, and a selected bibliography. In addition to the storyboards, a selection of stills from the films is included.

This work will remind some readers of the *From Fiction to Film* series, whose format is similiar to that employed by Marcus here. However, his treatment of the relationship between film and literature as exemplified by these 15 short stories and films is most welcome. The volume should be embraced by teachers on the secondary and college level. Recommended.

5563 *A Short Time for Insanity: An Autobiography.* by Wellman, William. 276 p. illus. New York: Hawthorn Books, 1974.

Using a stream-of-consciousness technique, director William Wellman recalls some selected incidents in what he calls his autobiography. It is a very fragmented, partial account of an eventful life. Lying on a hospital bed, he remembers in a drug-induced haze his start in films, the making of WINGS (1927), THE CALL OF THE WILD (1935), and THE STORY OF G.I. JOE (1945). Mostly his narrative rambles and concerns itself with personal incidents rather than professional career.

The man is witty, cynical, warm and honest in his writing. The lengthy filmography will cause the reader to regret the lack of attention given to Wellman's career. The index may be of some assistance in locating specific information in this verbose, rambling text. Wellman is a director to be appreciated. Apparently the tribute must come from another writer who can discern the important amid the trivial; until such a critical study appears, this volume, althougha disappointment, is acceptable.

5564 *Shorthand with Champagne.* by Ruby, Edna. 246 p. Cleveland: World, 1966.

A public stenographer tells of her experiences with film stars.

5565 *Shots in the Dark.* edited by Manvell, Roger. 268 p. illus. London: Allen Wingate, 1951.

A collection of reviews on films released in Great Britain over a three -year period (1949-1951). Nearly all of the films are well-known and the comments of 27 British critics are refreshing to read.

5566 *Should Christians Attend Movies?* by Lindsay, Gordon. Dallas, Texas: Christ Nations.

5567   *Show Biz: From Vaude to Video.* by Green, Abel; and Laurie, Joe, Jr. 612 p. New York: Holt, 1951.

Show business in the first 50 years of this century is the theme of this volume. Its pertinence for film collections is that it also parallels the first 50 years of motion-picture history. The two authors were closely identified with *Variety*, the weekly show business newspaper—Green as Editor and Laurie as writer. While the literary style is refreshing, breezy, and alive, it is more formal here than one might expect from *Variety* writers. Some of the famous "Varietyese" is used, but in moderation. To make certain no one is confused, a glossary is included.

This book is proof that history can be both informative and entertaining. Much attention is given to the growth of the motion picture, with the emphasis on the commercial side rather than the aesthetic or artistic. Since there is an extended index, the book is a fine reference source. No illustrations are included, but, considering the range of the subject, selection would be almost impossible. This is an excellent and important book that can fit many needs—reference, history, sociology, entertainment, to name a few—and is highly recommended. It should be updated as soon as possible to cover the last 30 years of show biz.

5568   *The Show Biz Trivia Quiz Book.* edited by Moore, Thomas W. 192 p. paper New York: Pocket Books, 1976.

The nearly 1000 questions offered in this quiz book are grouped under four headings: Films, Radio, Television, and Music. Each group is further subdivided into Elementary, Intermediate, Graduate and Bonus questions. A rather elaborate structure for playing a championship game of trivia is also suggested. The 268 questions on films are all straightforward answer questions—no variations are used, although some questions have several parts. Answers appear in the book's final pages.

An acceptable recreation that will please trivia addicts.

5569   *Show Business: Stars of the World of Show Business.* by Towers, Harry A. 110 p. illus. London: Low, Marston, 1949.

Deals with film, theatre and radio, with the emphasis on British performers such as Olivier, Jean Simmons, Trevor Howard, Googie Withers, etc.

5570   *Show Business Laid Bare.* by Wilson, Earl. 336 p. illus. New York: G. P. Putnam's, 1974.

This is a hypocritical book that purports to examine various aspects of show business but whose obvious intent is to provide sexual titillation, innuendo, and satisfaction for the sensation-seeker. Using today's social standards as the explanation for changes in films, the stage, nightclub acts and personal lifestyles, Wilson gives many examples of permissive behavior. Hypocrisy constantly surfaces in his pretense of shock, disapproval, surprise, etc., at certain of these revelations, when it is patently obvious there is a primary financial motive in his disclosure of them.

Some of the subjective matter indicates the level on which he writes: The Shack-Up Society, The Coke Scene, The Genitalia Generation, etc. Individuals given special attention include Sarah Miles, Burt Reynolds, Marlon Brando, Woody Allen, Elliott Gould, Carol Lynley, Cheri Caffaro, Marilyn Monroe, John F. Kennedy, Edith Piaf, and Marlene Dietrich. A center section contains some suggestive/unattractive photographs which offer further evidence of the author's ability and interest. This is a volume that is acceptable as a sociological example of reader-publisher taste in the seventies. It adds little to any film history, but it will be popular with many readers. The carefully worded title alone will insure that.

5571   *The Show Business Nobody Knows.* by Wilson, Earl. 415 p. illus. Chicago: Cowles Book Co., 1971.

Wilson begins his book with: "Today almost everybody knows almost everything about show business," Then he launches into an uninspired retelling of familiar gossip column material, treating all aspects of show business—night clubs, recordings, films, the big bands, the new black stars, television, etc. Because of the predominance of so many film names in the text, the book is considered here.

Extended attention is given to the Burton-Taylor affair, Bergman-Rossellini, Marie MacDonald, Jayne Mansfield, the Barrymores, Bogart-Bacall, Robert Mitchum, Marilyn Monroe, Dean Martin, Lena Horne, and Sammy Davis, Jr. Many other film personalities are mentioned in short humorous anecdotes or narrative examples. The text tends to be hypocrisy, the author pretending shock and surprise at the behavior of his subjects, then betraying his cynicism a few paragraphs later. A picture section provides momentary relief and there is an index that might help scholars or researchers.

Perhaps the most disheartening things about the book are the respectful production and prolonged exploitation given to this tired material. When quickie paperback material is given such full publisher treatment, it is ultimately the purchaser-reader who feels cheated. Not recommended.

5572 *Show People.* by Tynan, Kenneth. 317 p. New York: Simon & Schuster, 1980.

In this collective biography, British critic Kenneth Tynan writes about people he personally admires—people he would invite to an ideal dinner party.

The mixture of show business entertainers may be chemically risky since his company includes Ralph Richardson, Mel Brooks, Louise Brooks, Johnny Carson, and playwright Tom Stoppard. In print, however, the group is fine when hosted by Tynan.

An experienced interviewer, Tynan uses wit, intelligence and taste in the revealing of his subjects. His talent as a writer has not been seen to such advantage in a long time.

This beautifully written, entertaining book is highly recommended.

5573 *Showboat.* by Kreuger, Miles. 246 p. illus. New York: Oxford University Press, 1977.

In this history-appreciation of an American classic musical, the author treats both the stage presentations and the films inspired by Edna Ferber's novel. The first film (1929) was made by Universal at the beginning of the sound era and was followed by a "definitive" Universal version in 1936 and a MGM color remake in 1951. Each film receives detailed coverage and analysis via text and illustrations. Complete film casts and songs appear in an appendix. The book is indexed.

Some indication of Kreuger's careful research can be seen by his inclusion of a short one-reel film, CAPTAIN HENRY'S RADIO SHOW (1933), derived from the radio program "The Maxwell House Showboat," which in turn was another spinoff of Ferber's *Showboat.*

Specialized research made pleasant and popular by the obvious intelligence, affection and hard work of the author. Recommended.

5574 *Showcase.* by Newquist, Roy. 412 p. illus. New York: William Morrow, 1966.

Twenty-five show business professionals are interviewed in this volume. Included are actors, directors, writers, producers and designers. The questions include such topics as starting in show business, preparing for a role, differences in audiences, effect

of critics, etc.

Subjects who have worked in films include Julie Andrews, Hume Cronyn, Sammy Davis, Agnes de Mille, Edith Evans, Janet Gaynor, John Gielgud, George Grizzard, Julie Harris, Helen Hayes, Danny Kaye, Ernest Lehman, Jack Lemmon, Mike Nichols, Peter O'Toole, Robert Preston, Rosalind Russell, and Jessica Tandy.

A line drawing of the subject by Irma Selz precedes each interview, and Brooks Atkinson has supplied an introduction. Acceptable.

5575 *Showdown: Confronting Modern America in the Western Film.* by Lenihan, John H. 202 p. illus. Urbana, Ill.: University of Illinois Press, 1980.

In this unusual study, based upon his Ph.d. dissertation, Lenihan's thesis is that the post-World War II western films mirror such major American issues as the cold war, racism, individuality, social progress, alienation, committment, and social conformity. Using a sampling that is large rather than selected, he argues that films made for a mass audience are more representative of American society's thinking than ideas found in a few intellectual examples. He does use specific films, however, to make his points. For example, is HIGH NOON (1952) an allegory for the small town of Hollywood versus the HUAC?

Supporting the thought-filled text are a long bibliography, a chronological list of western films, and two indexes.

5576 *Sidney.* by Hoffman, William. 175 p. illus. New York: Lyle Stuart, 1971 .

This is another unauthorized Poitier biography. The well-documented struggle from an early life in the Bahamas and Florida to New York and Hollywood is again noted. His numerous films are discussed but there is no index, filmography, etc. to facilitate reference. Affectionate, limited and premature. This one is for die-hard Poitier fans only.

5577 *Sidney Lumet: A Guide to References and Resources.* by Bowles, Stephen E. 151 p. Boston: G.K. Hall, 1979.

In this volume on director Sidney Lumet, there are some discernible departures from the usual structure of the books in the *Guide to References and Resources* series. The longest section is devoted to the synopses, credits, and notes of his 25 films from TWELVE ANGRY MEN (1957) to EQUUS (1977). The biographical and critical survey sections are also comparatively long. Much shorter this time is the bibliography which consists of 57 entries, most of which are accompanied by lengthy annotations. In the section that follows, review and reference citations for each film are simply placed under the film title. Distributor information, a list of Lumet's performances and writings, a title index, and a name index complete the volume.

Because of the extended attention given to certain elements of this guide, it becomes as much an appreciation as a reference book. On either level it is quite successful.

5578 *Sidney Poitier: The Long Journey.* by Ewers, Carolyn H. 126 p. paper illus. New York: Signet Books, 1969.

This short paperback biography is frankly affectionate but occasionally blinded toward its subject. Poitier emerges as a hero of enormous proportion with the few human frailties mentioned either excused or rationalized by the infatuated authoress. The story is surface and sketchy but interesting, nevertheless. The illustrations are adequate. No index or filmography is offered. The Poitier films are given quick coverage with a few exceptions. In summary, this is an extended biographical sketch, supplemented by a few pictures. It is not an in-depth analysis of a public figure or even good biographical writing, but it is entertaining reading.

5579 *Sidney Poitier.* by Paige, David. 31 p. paper illus. Mankato, Minn.: Creative Education, 1976.

A superficial biography written for very young readers.

5580 *Sight and Sound* (A Periodical).

Sight and Sound, one of the world's foremost film periodicals, is available on microfilm from World Microfilms Publications, London. The period covered is 1932 to date.

5581 *Sight, Sound and Society: Motion Pictures and Television in America.* edited by White, David Manning; and Averson, Richard. 466 p. Boston, Mass.: Beacon Press, 1968.

Although this is primarily an anthology in the field of mass communication, there is sufficient emphasis on motion pictures to warrant its inclusion here. The theme is an examination of the ongoing relationships between motion pictures, television and American social institutions. Aspects considered include the audience, the message, the communicators, controversial issues, and a look at the future of the sight and sound situation. The theme of the book is carried out by the excellent choice of articles. A valuable bibliography is appended. Recommended for all readers.

5582 *Sight-Sound-Motion.* by Zettl, Herbert. 400 p. illus. Belmont, Calif.: Wadsworth, 1973.

A five-dimensional approach to image communication: light, space, time, motion and sound. Employing information from the fields of art theory, psychology of perception, film theory, film direction and editing and so on, the book attempts to give an understanding of film and television aesthetics and their use. Almost 1000 illustrations are used, with some in color. A glossary, bibliography and index are also included.

5583 *Sights and Sounds of Cinema.* by Edmonds, Robert. New York: Teachers College, 1981.

5584 *The Signet Book of Movie Lists.* edited by Rovin, Jeff. 184 p. paper illus. New York: Signet (New American Library), 1979.

Another collection of lists about movie topics—stars, films, economics, awards, soundtrack recordings, directors, genres, gossip, etc.

5585 *Signs and Meaning in the Cinema.* by Wollen, Peter. 168 p. paper illus. Bloomington, Ind.: Indiana University Press, 1969.

This is a book that deals with semiology and the cinema. One possible definition of semiology is "the art of using signs in signaling or in expressing thought." It considers also what constitutes a sign and which laws govern them. After examining two major influences, Eisenstein and auteur theory, which determine much of today's film aesthetics and film criticism, the author makes an argument for the re-investigation of film aesthetics, using semiology as an analytical tool.

This is a stimulating volume for the advanced student, the cinema-philosopher or the doctoral candidate searching for thesis material. It is theoretical, somewhat pedantic, and demands both a philosophical and cinema background for complete comprehension. Its argument is well-organized, adequately defended, and intelligently documented. A major contribution to film literature but with a limited appeal.

5586 *The Silence of God: Creative Response to the Films of Ingmar Bergman.* by Gibson, Arthur. 171 p. New York: Harper & Row, 1969.

An analysis of seven Bergman films along with a brief synopsis of each plot forms the structure of this book. A recurrent theme in the films, the silence of God, is examined by the author, who is a professor of theology. The films discussed are: THE SEVENTH SEAL (1956), WILD STRAWBERRIES (1957), THE MAGICIAN (1958), THROUGH A GLASS DARKLY (1961), WINTER LIGHT (1962), THE SILENCE (1963), and PERSONA (1966). For the person who is currently experiencing the films, the book should be an invaluable aid to their appreciation. Because the Bergman films demand it, the approach is intellectual, theoretical, religious and philosophical. The book is recommended for those making a serious study of either Bergman or any of the seven films. Casual readers may find the book rather heavy going.

5587 *The Silent Cinema.* by O'Leary, Liam. 160 p. paper illus. New York: Dutton, 1965.

Another excellent volume in the *Dutton Pictureback* series, this one is characterized by the many rarely seen stills of the silent motion picture era (1895-1927). The accompanying text is spare but most informative; it describes the growth of the motion picture from the one-reel film to the mature film art of the late silent era. Since silent films spoke a universal language, the viewpoint is worldwide—not exclusively American. When pictures, text, subject matter, art arrangement and production are all of such high quality as found in this small volume, it is not surprising that this book might be considered a basic one. Highly recommended.

5588 *Silent Cinema: An Annotated Critical Bibliography.* by Phillips, Leona R. New York: Gordon Press, 1977.

5589 *The Silent Clowns.* by Kerr, Walter. 373 illus. New York: Knopf, 1975.

This oversized, beautifully produced book provides a detailed study of American silent film comedy. With over 400 carefully reproduced stills, Walter Kerr composes his subject in a logical, developmental fashion; he chooses as his beacons Chaplin, Keaton, Lloyd, Langdon, and Laurel and Hardy, and interweaves their accomplishments with historical context from turn-of-the-century Melies films to Chaplin's MODERN TIMES (1935). Of course, the

work of many other comedians is also considered.

Kerr brings all his talents, resources and enthusiasm to his study, offering comment, theory, analysis, information and even conjecture. He identifies the sources of the excellent illustrations and provides an index.

Although some of the material has appeared in earlier books by other writers, Kerr has synthesized it into an impressive, loving statement on silent film comedy and its practitioners.

5590 *Silent Heroes Speak Today: What Yesterday's Stars of the Silver Screen Might Say if They Were Here Today.* 26 p. paper illus. Kansas City, Mo.: Hallmark, 1972.

Satire and humor about the silent screen in the form of a greeting card/book to be given or sent to the unsuspecting.

5591 SILENT MOVIE. by Brooks, Mel; and Clark, Ron; and DeLuca, Rudy; and Levinson, Barry. 198 p. paper illus. New York: Ballantine, 1976.

Script of the 1976 film directed by Mel Brooks. Four flip books are provided by placement of photographs at the upper and lower corners of the book. Illustrations are identified and partial cast and production credits are given. Since there is no dialogue in the film, the script describes the various shots and titles used.

5592 *Silent Movies: A Picture Quiz Book.* by Appelbaum, Stanley. 216 p. paper illus. New York: Dover Publications, 1974.

In what is apparently a series, the author and publisher have succeeded one more time in publishing a quality picture volume at a modest cost. Some 212 stills are well reproduced in this collection from the silent screen era. They are arranged by personality (e.g., Harold Lloyd) or by topic (e.g., Serials), with about eight half-page stills provided for each. Some quiz questions which may attract readers or buyers are provided, but the collection of visuals is strong enough to warrant acquisition of the book. Answers to the questions and indexes to the personalities and the films are provided. Here is a superior collection of stills which define an era quickly and entertainingly. Enthusiastically recommended.

5593 *The Silent Partner.* by Lyons, Timothy James. 256 p. New York:

Arno, 1974.

Subtitled "The History of the American Film Manufacturing Company 1910-1921," this volume is a title in the *Dissertations on Film* series and was written to fulfill one of the requirements for an advanced degree at the University of Iowa in 1972. It begins with the historical thesis that small motion picture companies have always joined together to form large companies, and eventually these giants have always faced the challenge of other small companies. The American Film Manufacturing Company is used as an illustration of this thesis.

In relating the company's history, the author examines human elements, technical aspects, economic factors and the ultimate product—the films. An opening chapter describes the industry in which the company was founded and operated. Successive chapters deal with business, personnel, and film product. Some conclusions, a bibliography and appendices are added. A few tables of data supplement the text. Of primary interest to historians and scholars, this volume is an example of satisfying historical research. Acceptable.

5594 *The Silent Picture: A Periodical.* illus. New York: Arno, 1977.

The Silent Picture was a quarterly that used interviews, filmographies and bibliographies to supplement its articles devoted to the art and history of the silent films.

All 49 issues (volumes 1 to 19) have been gathered in this single volume which has a comprehensive index.

5595 *Silent Snow, Secret Snow.* by Barrett, Gerald R.; and Erskine, Thomas L. 193 p. paper illus. Encino, Cal.: Dickenson Publish. Co., 1972.

The first of a new series titled *From Fiction to Film* (see also AN OCCURRENCE AT OWL CREEK BRIDGE). An introduction by Barrett is followed by Conrad Aiken's short story, "Silent Snow, Secret Snow." The gradual withdrawal of a young boy into his own private world of fantasy is the story's theme. A dozen critical articles about the author and his short story are offered next.

The second section deals with a 17-minute film made from the story in 1966 by director Gene Kearney. A preface entitled "Shot Analysis" explains shots, transitions, camera movement, camera angles and sound. This information is used throughout the Movscript, which follows. Final sections include five articles about the film and some suggestions for written assignments.

Everything about the series looks promising. This book is evidence of thoughtful planning combined with intelligent selection and good production. Schools and colleges can use this approach to film and literature study with a predictable success. Highly recommended.

5596 *Silent Star.* by Moore, Colleen. 262 p. illus. Garden City, N.Y.: Doubleday, 1968.

The autobiography of Colleen Moore, with emphasis on the 1915-1930 period in Hollywood. Miss Moore is factual and rather unemotional in her comments about herself and other celebrities of that period. The gossip, opinion, and legend that she relates is told in a cool, positive, nonmalicious way. She does offer an informative surface look at Hollywood during the golden age of the silent screen. Some very effective illustrations add immeasureably to her story. The book has value for screen historians and will charm those interested in memorabilia of the silent screen. There is no index.

5597 *Silent Stars, Sound Stars, Film Stars.* by Town, Harold B. 128 p. illus. Toronto: McClelland and Stewart, 1971.

Mostly portraits, caricatures, etc., of moving pictures performers.

5598 *The Silent Voice—A Sequel: The Golden Age of the Cinema.* by Lennig, Arthur. 158 p. paper Troy, N.Y.: Arthur Lenning, 1967.

The author plans to revised and combined this volume with an earlier book, *The Silent Voice.* Lennig is responsible for the following books on film: *Film Notes* (1960); *Classic of the Film* (1965); *The Silent Voice* (1966); *The Silent Voice—A Sequel* (1967); *The Silent Voice—A Text* (1969); and *The Sound Film—An Introduction* (1969). The industrious reader may locate copies of these books in film bookshops, but they are rare indeed. Mr. Lennig's contributions to film literature are all of high quality and one hopes that his work becomes more readily available.

5599 *Silents to Sound.* by Schoen, Juliet P. 185 p. illus. New York: Four Winds Press, 1976.

The challenge of covering "A History of the Movies" in less than 100 pages is satisfied in this volume designed for young people. The topics treated have been selected with intelligence and are presented with taste and appeal. Although the scholar might argue over certain emphases and carp over other omissions, the total story presented is a most adequate one. It is a reasonable history of the movies.

The illustrations are very good with many classic/familiar visuals included. An index completes the volume.

For the beginner this is an ideal introduction to the history of the motion picture. Well written and produced, it should motivate the reader to seek further literature about the cinema. Recommended.

5600 *The Silver Screen.* by Allen, Kenneth S. 67 p. illus. London: The Children's Book Club, 1948.

5601 *Silver Spoon: Being Extracts from Random Reminiscences of Lord Grantley.* by Grantley, Richard; and Wood, Mary; and Wood, Alan. 239 p. illus. London: Hutchinson, 1954.

Includes chapters on going into films, Swanson and Korda, working with Wilcox, and the Pinewood studios.

5602 THE SILVER STREAK. by Whately, Roger; and O'Donnell, Jack and and Hanemann, H. W. and Script of the 1934 film directed by Tommy Atkins. The RKO film featured Charles Starrett and was based on an unpublished story of Whately. 268 p. illus. Los Angeles: Haskell-Travers, 1935.

5603 *The Simple Art of Making Films.* by Rose, Tony. 294 p. illus. London: Focal Press, 1957.

5604 *Simple Film Animation With and Without a Camera.* by Bourgeois, Jacques; and Hobson, Andrew; and Hobson, Mark. 110 p. illus. paper New York: Sterling/Drake, 1979.

A combined edition of *Film Animation as a Hobby* and *Animating Films Without a Camera.*

5605 *The Simplification of American Life: Hollywood Films of the 1930's.* by Paine, Jeffery Morton. 305 p. New York: Arno Press, 1977.

Written in 1971 at Princeton University in partial fulfillment of the doctoral program, this analysis of Depression-era films examines the cultural role of American movie themes during that historical period. The evolution of new American values and perceptions of the thirties are traced in the historical record of film topics which the author identifies as forming a streamlining of the American view of life. By using a substantial number of materials to support his historical survey, the author has provided a scholarly analysis of Depression-era films. This title appears in the *Dissertations on Film* series.

5606 *Simply Super 8: A Basic Guide to Moviemaking.* by Sherman, Roger M.; and Schonhaut, Barry. 208 p. paper illus. Boston: Little, Brown, 1977.

A basic guide to super 8 filmmaking has been provided by two professionals in this volume. All of the basics—equipment, techniques, lighting, lenses, sound, editing, animation, filming nature, splicing, sound filming, time lapse—are explained with clarity and judgment.

Line drawings add to the exposition, as does a bibliography, an index, and a list of manufacturers/suppliers.

5607 *Sinatra.* by Douglas-Home, Robin. 64 p. illus. New York: Grosset & Dunlap, 1962.

This short volume is more a profile that a fullblown biography. Although some life-story line exists, much of the volume attempts to paint a picture of Sinatra the multi-artist as he existed in 1961. In that effort, the author is mostly successful. He does describe the person instead of the image. A brief section on films, some candid photos of Sinatra at work and play, and the well-written text are the book's assets. This is not a cinema biography, but it will supplement other sources till a good one comes along.

5608 *Sinatra: Twentieth-Century Romantic.* by Shaw, Arnold. 371 p. illus. New York: Holt, Rinehart, & Winston, 1968.

The life of Frank Sinatra as it has been reported by the press, magazines, and books is presented here. No attempt is made by the author to "explain" the Sinatra personality or charisma. The volume reads as Sinatra's social and professional diaries might. Much attention is given to the "recording" or "musical" side of the career. The films are mentioned briefly but little is related about the making of them, their reception, or Sinatra's preparation for them.

The author's style is monotonous and cannot communicate the excitement of his subject. No film stills are used although there are a few newspaper type photos. In the appendix, a bare listing of his film titles takes a page and a half, while "Sinatra As a Recording Artist" receives six and one-half pages. That ratio is indicative of the book. Film buffs should beware of this one. Recommended only as a third-hand source of information.

5609 *Sinatra.* by Sciacca, Tony. 248 p. paper illus. New York: Pinnacle, 1976.

This original paperback is an unauthorized biography that will probably displease its subject, Frank Sinatra. Written in a terse journalistic style, the book presents the many faces, moods and talents of Sinatra in a dispassionate recital. Admitting to a positive bias at the beginning of his research, the author quickly became objective toward his hero. His final conclusion was that Sinatra typifies the artist who feels he owes the public only one thing—a performance with a voice. His personal life is strictly his own. This approach to telling the story of a complex man has served Sciacca well. Predictably, the well-publicized years in Sinatra's life—with Ava Gardner, Mia Farrow, etc.—receive the most attention. Relationships with his parents, his first wife and his children remain secret—further evidence of Sinatra's insistence on a private personal life.

A few illustrations appear in a center section. Unfortunately there is no index or other supporting reference material.

An absorbing portrait of a legendary performer is given in this well-written volume which will please most readers. Although information sources were limited, the author has synthesized a character that may be a fairly accurate reflection of the real Frank Sinatra. Acceptable.

5610 *Sinatra: An Unauthorized Biography.* by Wilson, Earl. 361 p. paper illus. New York: Signet, 1976.

This is the unauthorized biography that caused Frank Sinatra to sue Earl Wilson for 3 million dollars. Why Sinatra was upset is curious since there were several earlier unauthorized biographies (not nearly as good as this one) which went unnoticed by Sinatra.

If there is a fault with this volume, it is that Wilson tells too much. In very detailed fashion he relates the rise, fall, and the regaining of Sinatra's mass popularity.

The Jekyll-Hyde personality and behavior of the singer is noted over and over again in narrative and anecdote.

Wilson was around when it was happening and he knows the story firsthand. He shares it—in part—with the reader in an entertaining, if somewhat long-winded, portrait.

5611 *Sinatra's Women.* by Romero, Gerry. 224 p. paper illus. New York: Manor Books, 1976.

Another unauthorized biography of Frank Sinatra, this one is different in that it is structured around the females in his life.

There are individual chapters devoted to his mother, his wives (Nancy, Ava, Mia, and Barbara), his romances (Turner, Bacall, Novak, Prowse, Monroe), his daughters (Nancy, Jr. and Tina), and his singing style mentors (Billie Holiday and Mabel Mercer).

The approach works, in that the familiar story remains fresh and interesting. A few pictures and a bibliography complete this above average original paperback.

5612 *Sinema: American Pornographic Films and the People Who Make Them.* by Turan, Kenneth; and Zito, Stephen F. 244 p. illus. New York: Praeger, 1974.

This is the first volume by a prestige publisher on the motion picture genre that surfaced from the underground during the seventies. Although it employs the same material and approach found in earlier original paperbacks such as *The Celluloid Love Feast* and *Contemporary Erotic Cinema*, the approach here is somewhat more factual, analytical and scholarly. In addition to the familiar, inevitable interviews with directors (Russ Meyer, David F. Friedman, Radley Metzger, Bill Osco, Gerard Damiano, the Mitchell Brothers, Wakefield Poole, Cal Culver) and performers (Marsha Jordan, Mary Rexroth, Pat Rocco, John Holms aka Long Johnny Wadd, Marilyn Chambers, Harry Reems), an attempt is made to trace the evolution of the erotic film.

Starting with FATIMA'S DANCE in the 1890s, films throughout the years contained erotic content and aroused censorship groups. Social significance themes were quickly employed to protect the "sensational" content of films. White slavery, drug addiction, venereal disease, sex education, etc., were topics used to disguise the sexual content of certain films. Sociological films about life in nudist camps were plentiful. Probably the most infamous films were the stag reels made for showing to selected private audiences. Russ Meyer's THE IMMORAL MR. TEAS (1959) was the first erotic feature film to play in an appreciable number of commercial movie houses with great financial success. With the loss of regular audiences to TV, producers and distributors used more daring in their films with the eventual surfacing of the hard and soft-corepornographic films we have today. It is this latter-day phenomenon that the authors treat in detail.

Their survey is limited to American films and their final conclusions are downbeat as to the future of porno films. Naturally the text contains material which will be offensive to some readers and unsuitable for younger ones. Pictures include some nudity and soft-core illustrations. The topic of pornographic films has some pertinence for anyone interested in the art of the motion picture. In this volume, as in previous ones, the important aspects such as the psychology, effect on other films, the audience, content, etc., are frequently neglected in favor of the more sensational elements. Just as in those early films, the social significance is present but given a supporting role to the sexual content. It is acceptable for mature adults.

5613 *Sing As We Go.* by Fields, Gracie. 216 p. illus. London: World Distributors, 1960.

The autobiography of the British music hall singer and comedienne who appeared in films during the thirties and forties. After many successful British films, which included SALLY IN OUR ALLEY (1931), THE SHOW GOES ON (1937), and KEEP SMILING (1938), she went to Hollywood and made films such as HOLY MATRIMONY (1943), MOLLY AND ME (1945) and PARIS UNDERGROUND (1945). Her contributions to public morale during the Depression and during World War II endeared her to audiences all over the world.

5614 *The Singing Cowboys.* by Rothel, David. 272 p. illus. New York: A. S. Barnes, 1978.

This collective biography-appreciation treats such western musical stars as Gene Autry, Tex Ritter, Roy Rogers, Eddie Dean, Jimmy Wakely, Monte Hale, and Rex Allen. In individual chapters, each is represented by a biographical sketch, a general and often personal appreciation, a nicely annotated filmography, and a discography where possible. Several of the subjects cooperated with the author via interviews. One shorter chapter is devoted to the less successful singing cowboys: Dick Foran, Fred Scott, George Houston, Smith Ballew, Jack Randall, Tex

Fletcher, Dusty King, James Newell and Bob Baker. Illustrations are varied and indicate a careful search of diverse sources by the author. A bibliography and an index complete the book.

The singing cowboy films are a fascinating subgenre —certainly worth the attention and affection that Rothel has given them here. Since each biography has been written with a personal approach, there is an author tendency to be worshipful or overly cautious in telling the stories of these men. To him they remain the heroes they once were on the screen. Acceptable.

5615 SINGIN' IN THE RAIN. by Comden, Betty; and Green, Adolph. 75 p. paper illus. New York: Viking, 1972.

Script of the 1951 film directed by Stanley Donen and Gene Kelly. Contains an introductory article by Betty Comden and Adolph Green, cast and credits.

5616 *Single Bed for Three: A* LAWRENCE OF ARABIA Notebook. by Kent, Howard. 208 p. illus. London: Hutchinson, 1963.

5617 *Sinners and Supermen.* by Nolan, William F. 192 p. paper North Hollywood, Calif.: All Star Books, 1965.

A series of profiles written originally for magazines, this small paperback contains a few subjects who are associated with films. Included are pieces on Brando, Preminger, Welles, Sellers, Dean Martin, and Howard Hughes. Profiled authors who have had their works adapted for films include Ray Bradbury, Ian Fleming, Rod Serling, Raymond Chandler, Ben Hecht and James Thurber. The author's work is designed for mass magazines and the few editorial comments and opinions presented are harmless. Each profile is short, matter of fact, and largely part of the record. The book's service is in bringing it together in a condensed, efficient form for the person who has need of a quick biography . This paperback suggests a format for film biographies that is seldom used. Until others come along, readers may find some value or interest in this modest paperback.

5618 *Sir Charlie.* by Hoyt, Edwin P. 206 p. illus. London: Robert Hale, 1977.

An unauthorized biography of Charlie Chaplin, this volume offers text, illustrations, a bibliography, and an index.

5619 *Sir Donald Wolfit CBE.* by Harwood, Ronald. illus. London: Secker and Warburg, 1971.

Wolfit is an extrovert stage and film actor who specializes in bravura roles. An early autobiography called *First Interval* appeared in 1954.

5620 *Sir Larry, The Life of Laurence Olivier.* by Kiernan, Thomas. New York: Times, 1981.

5621 *Sirk On Sirk.* by Sirk, Douglas; and Halliday, Jon. 176 p. paper illus. New York: Viking, 1972.

Douglas Sirk is a little-known director whose films have been enjoyed by large audiences for many years. They are now appearing with annoying regularity on television and certain titles need a rest. This is, of course, a sort of belated tribute to Sirk. A sampling of his film titles will give the reader some idea of his metier: WRITTEN ON THE WIND (1956), IMITATION OF LIFE (1959), MAGNIFICENT OBSESSION (1954), THE TARNISHED ANGELS (1957), LURED (1947), TAKE ME TO TOWN (1953). Apparent from this sampling is a Universal-Ross Hunter audience type of film and this was Sirk's kind of operation. After starting with German theatre and films, he came to America in 1937 and worked for Columbia (1942-48) and Universal (1950-58). He now lives in Switzerland and this collection of interviews conducted by Halliday took place there in 1970.

The interviews cover, in chronological fashion, the German theatre, German films, France and Holland, the Columbia period, the Universal period, and his retirement. The bio-filmography at the book's end is an interesting article by itself. In outline form, it describes Sirk's films and tells enough of his life to give a satisfying portrait of a professional. The structure of the book works very well.

Illustrations are a bit small at times but mostly acceptable. A non-bibliography is included ("non" because it includes so little written on Sirk and so much more on some of the personalities with whom he worked). Very nicely done; recommended.

5622 *Six European Directors: Essays on the Meaning of Film Style.* by Harcourt, Peter. 287 p. paper Baltimore: Penguin, 1974.

In this volume of original film criticism, the author examines the work of Eisenstein, Renoir, Bunuel, Bergman, Fellini and Godard. Surrounding the individual essays on each of the above directors are two articles—the first on film criticism and the second on film style. Notes and references to the chapters and an index are provided. Harcourt's analysis

of selected themes, moments, and characters from the director's work demands some prior knowledge and film experience. It is difficult to comprehend his analysis of Bergman without having seen or studied the films.

For serious readers and students, this volume is a rare intellectual experience. Those looking for an entertainment will find the sober, no-nonsense approach to film style and criticism a bit heavy. Recommended for mature adults.

5623 *Six Gun Heroes: A Price Guide to Movie Cowboy Collectibles.* by Hake, Theodore L.; and Cauler, Robert D. 139 p. paper illus. Des Moines, Ia.: Wallace-Homestead Book Company, 1976.

The collectibles mentioned in the title refer to posters, books, cards, programs, toys, jewelry, buttons, and other items. Stars treated in the volume include Hopalong Cassidy (William Boyd), Gene Autry, Roy Rogers, The Lone Ranger and Tom Mix. The number of collectibles listed for each varies and the book is enlarged by the inclusion of a tribute to John Wayne, a photo gallery of western heroes and a quiz. There are biographical portraits of each of the above-mentioned stars along with complete filmographies. It is the pictures and prices of the collectibles, however, which provide this book's uniqueness.

5624 *The Six-Gun Mystique.* by Cawelti, John G. 138 p. paper Bowling Green, Ohio: Bowling Green University Popular Press, 1970.

In this long essay, Cawelti has used the western story, novel, and film to formulate some basic principles about the interpretation of popular formula narrative and drama. Other genres such as gangster, spy, or science fiction, could have been used for this purpose. The emphasis is on the form of the genre and diverse analyses or explanations of it. Typical of the ideas discussed are these two: a major focus of the western is the justification of acts of violent aggression; and the distinctive characteristic of the cowboy hero isnot his possession of a symbolic weapon but the way in which he uses it. According to the author, the components of a western are (1) setting, (2) complex of characters (the civilized group, the threatening group and the heroes), and (3) types of situations and patterns of action. Each of these elements is discussed in some detail. Although it seems that the author occasionally devotes too much attention to the obvious, most of the essay offers provocative reading and stimulating analysis. Some exception can be made to the several appendices which offer supportive material that has been arranged poorly. For example, the director list lacks any organizational structure and the dates for many films are missing. Other sections are also poorly presented. The materials for a fine book are evident here. Greater attention to their arrangement and presentation would have helped the text enormously. Acceptable.

5625 *Six Guns and Society.* by Wright, Will. 217 p. Berkeley: University of California Press, 1975.

The general purpose of this volume, which is subtitled "A Structural Study of the Western," is to show that the genre has some redeeming social value. The author argues that if a myth such as the western remains popular, it must offer a symbolic meaning to viewers; it must address itself to describing the viewer and his society.

After a deceptively easy introduction, Wright begins a systematic, serious study that involves abstract structural theory, economical and political history, and many detailed analyses of western films. Topics include the structure of myth, myth as a narrative of social action, and myth and meaning. In a discussion of the structure of the western film, four types are noted: the classical plot, the vengeance variation, the transition theme, and the professional plot. A short bibliography, an appendix, and an index complete the book.

As indicated above, this volume is not for the casual reader or browser. It is an in-depth study of a film genre that will appeal to the serious student and the western film devotee. Acceptable.

5626 *Six Men.* by Cooke, Alistair. 205 p. illus. New York: Knopf, 1977.

Alistair Cooke has chosen six men he knew and admired for this collective biography: Charles Chaplin, Humphrey Bogart, H. L. Mencken, Adlai Stevenson, Bertrand Russell and Edward VIII.

A journalist in several media, Cooke has admirable talents in selecting what is important about his subjects and retelling it in a theatrical style. He writes with erudition, wit and grace; those familiar with his introductions to "Masterpiece Theatre" will know what to expect. A portrait of each subject accompanies the text.

5627 *Six Talks on G. W. Pabst: The Man, the Director, the Artist.* by Bachman, Gideon. 94 p. paper New York: Group For Film Study, 1955.

The author is also responsible for *The Work of Luis*

Bunuel, an eleven page booklet, No. 27, in the same series.

5628 *16mm Films.* compiled by Cape Provincial Library. 485 p. paper Capetown: Cape Provincial Library Service, 1969.

A film catalog which contains an introduction, a subject guide, a subject catalog (Dewey), a list of story films and a general title index. The annotations provided for the hundreds of films are descriptive rather than evaluative. A 39-page supplement to this large catalog appeared in 1971.

5629 *16mm Sound Motion Pictures.* by Offenhauser, William H. 580 p. illus. New York: Wiley, 1949.

Everything anyone ever wanted to know about 16mm film.

5630 *16mm Distribution.* compiled by Trojan, Judith; and Covert, Nadine. 181 p. paper New York: Educational Film Library Association, 1977.

When you have finished making your own film, how do you arrange to get it shown and distributed?

This volume addresses that question in the form of articles and speeches adapted from an 1976 conference on film distribution. Topics include the market, the audience, contracts, legal considerations, commercial distribution, university distribution, tele-markets, etc. Valuable appendixes offer a bibliography, a list of film festivals, showcases, periodicals, conferences, and sources of mailing lists.

The volume provides practical guidance and assistance to the low-budget filmmaker in search of recognition and success.

5631 *Sixteen MM Film Cutting.* by Burder, John. 158 p. paper illus. New York: Hastings House, 1975.

John Burder supplies additional information to that offered in his 1968 book, *The Technique of Editing 16mm Films*, in this manual. He has organized his presentation of techniques and procedures into about 70 separate sections, each of which is presented with clarity and illustration. Topics include hardware, rushes, simple joins, special effects, first assembly, lab instructions, etc.

As usual with this series, the presentation is a direct, no-nonsense one that stresses economy and practicality. A short bibliography and a glossary complete the book.

5632   *Sixty Years of Hollywood.* by Baxter, John. 254 p. illus. New York: A. S. Barnes, 1973.

The reader may not always agree with Baxter's critical appraisals but it is hard not to be impressed by the quality and freshness of his writing. In this volume he has used those films he thinks have been important to Hollywood and its image. Thus he selects CAPTAIN FROM CASTILE, CROSSFIRE, and CRY WOLF for the year 1947. The 60 years in the title are selected from the period 1894 to 1971.

Some films not only receive critical attention, but the cast, the director, some production crew, and the studio are mentioned. Others merely indicate the director. Many nicely reproduced illustrations complement the text and an index is provided. This volume is satisfying in several respects—it is a history of sorts, an anthology of film reviews, a photo book, and most of all, an entertainment. A different kind of film book, this one succeeds on all counts. Recommended.

5633   *Sixty Years of 16mm Film (1923-1983): A Symposium.* 220 p. paper Evanston, Ill.: Film Council of America, 1954.

The title notwithstanding, this book was published by the now defunct Film Council of America in 1954. An early attempt to survey the field of the 16mm film, the volume was most comprehensive and rather successful in its endeavor. Articles on the use of 16mm film in schools, colleges, adult education, government industry, agriculture, labor, churches, libraries and museums are presented. Sections on production, distribution, exhibition, evaluation, and cataloging are also included. While some of the material is either dated or no longer applicable, a much larger portion is still pertinent. Since the appearance of Waldron's volume in 1949 and this one, there has been a void in this film area. Until an up-to-date survey appears, interested libraries and users may consider this volume. Acceptable.

5634   *Sixty Years of Vamps and Camps.* by Hudson, Richard M. illus. New York: Drake, 1974.

This scrapbook of "Visual Nostalgia of the Silver Screen" is dedicated to the man who streaked through the Academy Awards in 1974, an indication of the approach used.

Hudson's text is negligible but many of the 700 black and white visuals he supplies are happily unfamiliar and cover about 70 years of Hollywood in stills, publicity shots, posters, magazine covers, etc. Arranged under rather large general headings, the illustrations show sex gods and goddesses, incredible costumes, film sirens, Bette Davis in BEYOND THE FOREST (1949), etc. Martha Raye supplies the introduction to this light "campy" diversion.

5635   *Skouras: King of the Fox Studios.* by Curti, Carlo. 311 p. paper Los Angeles: Holloway House Pub. Co., 1967.

Purportedly an unauthorized biography of Skouras, this book devotes only the first of three sections to its title subject. The remaining two are given to Marilyn Monroe and to Elizabeth Taylor as CLEOPATRA (1963). The Skouras section is straight factual reporting, as is the re-telling of Taylor-Burton-CLEOPATRA saga. The portion on Monroe is scandal-mongering in the old *Confidential* magazine style. It is a distasteful, ill-advised, nondocumented collection of stories about Monroe's life and career. This account makes Irving Shulman read like Louisa May Alcott. An objective biography of Skouras would be welcome; unfortunately, this is not it. In addition it tries to make a fast dollar on a lady who can no longer defend herself. A sad book in so many ways.

5636   *The Sky and the Stars: The Memoirs of Albert Prejean.* by Prejean, Albert. 216 p. illus. London: Harvill, 1956.

Albert Prejean was a French actor and stuntman whose acrobatic skill was used in many films from 1921 to 1957. Director Rene Clair used him frequently to good advantage. Photographs and stills are included in this autobiography.

5637   *The Slapstick Queens.* by Parish, James Robert. 298 p. illus. New York: Barnes, 1973.

This volume is really a 5-in-1 version of the *Citadel* series. In abbreviated form it offers *The Films of* ... Marjorie Main, Martha Raye, Joan Davis, Judy Canova, and Phyllis Diller. The format is consistent: an introductory essay which is part biography and part critical review is followed by a picture gallery arranged in chronological fashion. A filmography with full cast and production credits for each film follows.

The text is well researched and blends reviews, quotations, comment and straight information to give both a personal and professional portrait. For the most part, these portions of the book are successful. The picture sections are surprisingly good. While there are still a few dark pictures, the majority are clearly reproduced with the contrast values apparently under control. Occasionally there is an indication of poor layout policy with a single small illustration taking up an entire page that might accommodate at least two or three other visuals.

When one considers the very few slapstick queens of the screen, it is readily apparent why Parish had to include such as Phyllis Diller. Lucille Ball and Carol Burnett are television slapstick artists whose films do not reflect that facet of their talent.

In any event, it is a pleasure to see this tribute paid to at least four great comediennes. In his coverage of these few neglected ladies, Parish has provided pleasure, information, and nostalgia that cannot fail to win a large and appreciative audience. Recommended.

5638   *Slow Fade to Black.* by Cripps, Thomas. 447 p. paper illus. New York: Oxford University Press, 1977.

Subtitled "The Negro In American Film, 1900-1942," this thoroughly researched study traces the nation's and Hollywood's changing attitudes towards the black during the first four decades of this century. The story of the black image is related from a new positive recognition in the very early films to the menial servant-slave of the twenties and thirties and then finally to the quiet revolution of the forties. Many pages of notes, some illustrations, and indexes support the text.

Thomas Cripps is able to assess, interpret, clarify and argue his subject with logic, intelligence and, of course, some solid background research. This is a definitive study.

5639   *Sluts, Saints and Superwomen Sinners.* by Harvey, James. 160 p. paper Los Angeles, Calif.: Edka Books, 1967.

Among the women who are discussed and demeaned by this trashy book are Zsa Zsa Gabor, Ingrid Bergman, and Elizabeth Taylor. Nothing new is divulged about the facts of their lives, which are already well recorded. What the author does contribute is the leer and the innuendo, along with a lot of suggestive wording. A cheap, untalented retelling that makes a scandal in high places a bore. Noted for the record.

5640   SMALL CHANGE. by Truffaut, Francois. New York: Grove, 1977.

The short script of the 1976 film directed by Francois Truffaut.

5641   *Small-Town Motion Pictures and Other Sketches of Franklin County, Maine.* by Hoar, Jay S. 92 p. illus. Farmington, Maine: Knowlton and McLeary, 1969.

5642   *Snakes and Ladders: A Memoir.* by Bogarde, Dirk. 339 p. illus. New York: Holt, Rinehart, Winston, 1979.

Following the critical success of his first volume, *A Postillion Struck By Lightning*, Dirk Bogarde continues his autobiography in this equally satisfying volume. Starting with military service in World War II, his story continues up to 1970, the year of his appearance in Visconti's DEATH IN VENICE. During that period he appeared in VICTIM (1961), THE SERVANT (1963), KING AND COUNTRY (1964), DARLING (1965), and THE DAMMED (1969). He writes of his acquaintance with Luchino Visconti, Joseph Losey, George Cukor, Judy Garland, Kay Kendall, Noel Coward, Julie Christie and others. There are illustrations, a filmography, and an index to accompany this witty, elegant memoir.

5643   SNOW WHITE AND THE SEVEN DWARFS. edited by Solomon, Jack, Jr. 228 p. illus. New York: Viking, 1979.

The story of the classic animated film, SNOW WHITE AND THE SEVEN DWARFS (1937), and how it was made are told in this oversized volume. Using more than 400 attractively reproduced visuals, the book treats technical details, animation artists, and the creative process of animated filmmaking. Visuals include some full-color reproductions, along with sketches, schematic drawings, storyboards, and paintings. Appealing on several levels, the book, like the film, will delight a wide audience.

5644   SO DEAR TO MY HEART. edited by Walt Disney Productions. 125 p. illus. New York: Simon and Schuster, 1950.

A *Golden Story Book* based on the Disney film, SO DEAR TO MY HEART (1948), which, in turn, was based on the novel by Sterling North.

5645   *So Long Until Tomorrow.* by Thomas, Lowell. 317 p. illus. New York: William Morrow, 1977.

Known mostly as a broadcaster, author and world traveler, Lowell Thomas was an officer in Cinerama, Inc. and narrated parts of their films. His memoirs describe his active, event-filled career.

5646   *So You Think You Know Movies?* by Kennedy, Donald. 160 p. paper illus. New York: Ace, 1970.

There are three groups of trivia tests in this paperback. Questions are general in the first group, based on photographs in the second, and about personalities in the third. The questions are adequate, the pictures are poor, and the production is below pulp magazine standards. Some amusement for a single usage.

5647   *The Social Aspects of the Cinema— Monograph Number Five.* 237 p. Rome: International Educational Cinematographic Institute, 1934.

The text is divided into six parts: A World Enquiry; The Cinematograph and Crime; Vital Aspects of the Cinema; Cinema and Adolescence: The Child and the Cinema; Social Propaganda Films; Study and Research.

5648   *The Social Conduct and Attitudes of Movie Fans.* by Shuttleworth, Frank K.; and May, Mark A. New York: Arno Press, 1970 (1933).

In this Payne Fund Study, attitude tests were administered to 200 children divided equally into two groups—the first, moviegoers, and the second, non-moviegoers. Teacher ratings, conduct records, and a sociogram-type game were also used. The results were relatively inconclusive. Another Payne Fund Study, *Motion Pictures and the Social Attitudes of Children*, is bound with this volume.

5649   *The Social History of Art: Volume 4: Naturalism, Impressionism, The Film Age.* by Hauser, Arnold. 2 vol. 1022 p. illus. New York: Knopf, 1952.

The section on "The Film Age" considers that period in its larger historical context.

5650   *see 5651*

5651   *Social Sciences and Humanities Index.* New York: H. W. Wilson, Co., 1920- .

This quarterly index considers over 200 scholarly periodicals in the social sciences and humanities fields. An annual bound volume is published as are cumulated indexes from time to time. From 1920 to 1956 this reference was called *The International Index.* From 1907 to 1919 it was titled *The Readers' Guide to Periodical Literature Supplement.* Look under "Moving Picture" and "Film."

5652   *Society for Education in Film and Television Publications.* paper illus. London: SEFT, 1950- .

An organization formed in 1950 to develop film and television appreciation with children and young people, the Society for Education in Film and Television publishes two journals. *Screen*, a quarterly which has had other titles since its origin in 1960, often resembles a paperback book since it treats one topic per issue, e.g., "Brecht and a Revolutionary Cinema," and "Cinema Semiotics and the Work of Christian Metz." *Screen Education* deals with film study at a variety of levels and in differing educational contexts. The topic of an entire recent issue was "CSE Film Study: Problems and Approaches."

5653   *Society of Film and Television Arts Publications.* paper illus. London: SFTA, 1960- .

This organization publishes the *SFTA Journal* currently appearing three times per year. Selected issues noted here treated such film topics as: The Individual Approach in Film and Television (1962), Regional Theatre and Film and Television (1962), Sex and Violence in Film and Television (1964), Spies on the Screen (1966), Editing: Film and Television (1966), The Short and Factual Film in Britain (1967), Wild Life: Film and Television (1968), Economics of British Film Production (1968), Shakespeare on the Screen (1969), The National Film Archive (1970), The Film Festival Explosion (1970), Censorship: The Changing Mood (1971), SFTA Awards (1972), The British Film Industry (1972), and John Grierson (1972).

5654   *Sociology of Film.* by Mayer, J. P. 328 p. illus. London: Faber & Faber, 1946.

Following a general chapter on the problems of sociology of film, there is a consideration of the universal, popular audience. A few chapters are devoted to children's and adolescents' reactions to films. The content of films and adult reaction to films concludes the volume. The final recommendations on censorship and control are provocative, and, by today's standards, unpopular. The arguments offered are well supported by the author's research.

There are many detailed interview reactions given in the body of the book and their value today is questionable. Perhaps a statistical summary might have been preferable. A sample survey form may be found in the appendix. All the methodology has roots in the earlier Payne Fund Studies. (The author published a follow-up study to this one called *British Cinemas and their Audiences* in 1949.) For those interested in audience research, this volume will have some value.

5655 *The Sociology of Film Art.* by Huaco, George A. 229 p. New York: Basic Books, 1965.

Three distinct film waves of the past are subject material for this text: German expressionist films (1920-1931), Soviet expressive realism films (1925-1930), and Italian neo-realism (1945-1955). Certain sociological hypotheses are presented and then applied to each of the three film groups to see if they are valid for that group. Final conclusions are given. Although it may sound a bit foreboding in description, the study is totally absorbing. A stimulating use of film in research, the text is well documented with chapter notes, a bibliography, and an index.

5656 *Sodom and Gomorrah: The Story of Hollywood, Los Angeles.* by Knepper, Max. 236 p. Los Angeles: End Poverty League, 1935.

With a preface by Upton Sinclair, this personal publication deals with moral and religious matters in the film capital during the early thirties.

5657 *The Solid Gold Sandbox.* by Bonderoff, Jason. 178 p. paper illus. New York: Pinnacle, 1975.

The front cover of this book adds the following to the main title: "Or How To Make It as a Child Star in the Super Competitive World of Dazzling Darlings of Stage, Screen, and Television." Mentioned briefly are Margaret O'Brien, Tatum O'Neal, Linda Blair, Jackie Coogan, Richard Thomas, and Patty Duke. Much of the text is about child actors in daytime television serials.

5658 *Solid Goldie.* by Berman, Connie. 128 p. illus. paper New York: Simon and Schuster (Fireside), 1981.

A nicely produced and illustrated biography of Goldie Hawn.

5659 SOLOMON AND SHEBA. 18 p. paper illus. 1952.

One of the opening sections in this souvenir book, entitled "Unforgettable Moments," gives the readers some idea of the 1952 film being described. The large 70mm super Technirama process, a cast of thousands, Yul Brynner, Gina Lollobrigida, and King Vidor are some of the subjects considered by the book. Some fuzzy illustrations attempt to link sequences from the film to biblical sources.

5660 *Some Are Born Great.* by St. Johns, Adela Rogers. 297 p. Garden City, N.Y.: Doubleday, 1974.

Subtitled "Lively and Controversial Tales of Some of the Extraordinary Women of Our Time," this is a collection of nine tributes. Among those singled out are Judy Garland and Marion Davies. Other Hollywood names are mentioned—Billie Dove, Lilyan Tashman, Edmund Lowe, et al. A reporter with a firsthand knowledge of her subjects should do better than this. No illustrations or index either.

5661 *Some Enchanted Egos.* by Zec, Donald. 279 p. illus. New York: St. Martin's Press, 1973.

Donald Zec is a reporter, feature writer and columnist for London's *Daily Mirror*. In this collection of interviews, his constant intention is to puncture the myth and ego of his subjects, and in some cases, he succeeds easily. Names on his list are numerous and include Omar Sharif, Raquel Welch, Shelley Winters, Elizabeth Taylor, Tony Curtis, Paul Newman and Frank Sinatra ("a pair of eyes that might look good on a asp...").

Better than most books of this type, this operation moves so quickly and amusingly that you may not notice the knife.

5662 *Some Interesting People and Times.* by Wallace, Irving. paper illus. New York: Dale, 1978.

The author supplies a nostalgic look at the 1940s in this original paperback.

5663 SOME LIKE IT HOT. by Wilder, Billy; and Diamond, I. A. L. 144 p. paper illus. New York: Signet Books, 1959.

Script of the 1959 film directed by Wilder. Contains cast credits.

5664 *Some of My Best Friends Are People.* by Moger, Art. 156 p. illus. Boston: Challenge, 1964.

Memoirs of a press agent who worked at Warner

Brothers for more than 20 years. Contains many anecdotes about stars at Warners.

5665 *Some Properties of Estar Base Motion Picture Films.* edited by Kodak Staff. paper illus. Rochester, N.Y.: Kodak, 1975.

This booklet describes the difference between triacetate and Estar base films.

5666 *Some Time in the Sun.* by Dardis, Tom. 274 p. illus. New York: Scribners, 1976.

A view of the relationship that existed between Hollywood and five famous authors constitutes the general theme of this volume. The adventures of distinguished literary figures in Hollywood have been treated in earlier books; in this volume, however, research, letters, script excerpts, investigation and interviews have been combined with a writer's style and viewpoint to create a new interpretation of the literary giant at work in Hollywood.

Five authors are considered: F. Scott Fitzgerald, Nathanael West, William Faulkner, Aldous Huxley, and James Agee. Put to rest is the old cliche about artists selling themselves for Hollywood gold. For the most part the writers were fascinated by the exploration of a new medium and took the reponsibilities assigned to them seriously. True, it was the money that originally brought them to Hollywood, but screenwriting became the focus of each of their lives for long periods of time, and they gave value for the monies received.

Supporting this original study are a few pictures of the five men, a lengthy bibliography, chapter notes and an index. This volume will appeal to the reader interested in film/literature. It is an investigation crammed with information, detail, anecdote and comment that offers some new insights about screenwriting during Hollywood's Golden Age. Recommended.

5667 *Sometimes I Wonder.* by Carmichael, Hoagy; and Longstreet, Stephen. 312 p. illus. Folkestone, Kent, England: Redman, 1966.

Carmichael, who is best known as the composer of "Stardust," has had careers as a lawyer, pianist, singer, composer, and actor. In the latter capacity, he has appeared frequently on radio, television and in films. His more important films include TO HAVE AND HAVE NOT (1944), THE BEST YEARS OF OUR LIVES (1946), and YOUNG MAN WITH A HORN (1950). He wrote music for such films as EVERY DAY'S A HOLIDAY (1938), MR. BUG GOES TO TOWN (1942), and THREE FOR THE SHOW (1955).

5668 *Son of Famous Monsters of Filmland.* by Ackerman, Forrest J. 162 p. paper illus. New York: Paperback Library, 1965.

Here is a second collection of horror stills thinly connected by a contrived text. There are occasional exceptions, for example a survey by author Robert Bloch—PSYCHO (1960)— of important fright films. The pictures are all a safe bet to amuse and entertain. A pleasant luxury; not an essential.

5669 *Son of Groucho.* Marx, Arthur.

Arthur Marx is a man burdened through his lifetime with an enormous problem—Groucho. The relationship between famous fathers and sons has been documented many times: Keenan-Ed Wynn, Edward G. Robinson, Jr.-Sr., Michael-Charles Chaplin, Jr.-Sr., etc. Some offspring come to terms with the problem, others go down to defeat via drugs, alcohol, and public scandal. Arthur Marx has accepted his fate as the son of Groucho with a minimum of self-pity, but uses this volume to make his own claim for personal recognition. It is not a persuasive case because the book's major appeal is still Groucho, not Arthur.

The author provides a revealing and quite objective portrait of Groucho. At times, the technique is interesting. Some negative quality about Groucho is mentioned—almost externally—and then Arthur comes to Groucho's defense as a forgiving understanding son. In this manner Groucho is depicted as being stingy, foolish, insecure, cynical, and unloving. His inability to give himself via affection or understanding to those in his immediate family is emphasized, as is his constant need for "a victim" for his insult-wit. A few pictures of father and son appear in the book's center section.

The final effect of the book is probably not what the author intended. Most readers will ignore Arthur Marx, his story and his achievements, in favor of the larger-than-life legend that he was blessed/cursed with as a parent. The exorcism of Groucho is an act of which the author seems incapable. Most readers will enjoy this most recent attempt. Recommended with a small warning. Like most of his remarks, Groucho's comments about women and sex are calculated to surprise, insult and shock. At times he is quite a dirty old man.

5670 *Son of The Compleat Motion Picture Quiz Book.* by Trigg, Harry L.; and Trigg, Yolanda L. 281 p. paper New

York: Doubleday, 1977.

Here we have a motion picture quiz book that is a sequel to the authors' earlier (1975) volume. The mixture is as usual—about 200 quizzes in a variety of formats. Answers appear in the back of the book. The generalization about sequels applies here.

5671 *SONG OF NORWAY.* 28 p. paper illus. New York: A B C Pictures Corp., 1970.

Most of the attention in this souvenir book is focused on composor Edvard Grieg, whose life and music were the inspiration of the play upon which the 1970 film is based. Cast and production credits are given.

5672 *Song of Wild Laughter.* by Couffer, Jack. 190 p. illus. New York: Simon & Schuster, 1963.

An expose of techniques, practices, and abuses employed to make the Disney *True-Life* series, as told by a cameraman-director. Somewhat disillusioning.

5673 *Songs from Hollywood Musical Comedies, 1927 to Present: A Dictionary.* by Woll, Allen I. 251 p. New York: Garland, 1976.

This is volume 44 in the Garland *Reference Library in the Humanities* series. Using typewritten manuscript which has been reduced to book page size, the volume consists of four parts, the first of which is an alphabetical listing of over 7000 song titles. Following each title is a number which refers to one of the 1186 films listed in part two. Entries here note year of release, stars, director, writer-composer, and, in specific cases, song titles. If a soundtrack recording is available, company name and record number are indicated. A chronology of the Hollywood musical from THE JAZZ SINGER (1927) to FUNNY LADY (1975) comprises the third section, while the final part lists the composers and lyricists with numerical references to the second, or film title, section. A bibliography, directions on use, and an introductory essay appear in the book's front pages.

The material presented here and its easy, convenient arrangement are to be admired. A useable reference to a group of popular songs, the book will satisfy many questions or inquiries posed to librarians. One small reservation is the lack of a recording company name list. It is difficult to decode such acronyms as EOH, JJA, PRW, etc. This volume is highly recommended.

5674 *Sons Come and Go, Mothers Hang In Forever.* by Saroyan, William. New York: McGraw-Hill, 1976.

These memoirs of William Saroyan include his first taste of celebrity in Hollywood.

5675 *Soon To Be a Major Motion Picture.* by Gershuny, Theodore. 362 p. illus. New York: Holt Rinehart & Winston, 1980.

This volume about the filming of ROSEBUD (1975) is subtitled, "The Anatomy of an All-Star Big-Budget Multimillion-Dollar Disaster." The stars include Robert Mitchum, Peter O'Toole, Richard Attenborough, Peter Lawford, John Lindsay and, most importantly, director Otto Preminger.

The author, who ingratiated himself with Preminger and wished he had not, was present from the 1974 start to note the locations, logistics problems, personality clashes, and assorted other mayhems. Gershuny's view of the process and the people becomes more cynical with each page. The general theme is the wonder that films ever get made at all.

An appendix, an index and a section of illustrations accompany this sour look at the world of commercial filmmaking.

5676 *Sophia.* by Zec, Donald. 263 p. illus. New York: David McKay, 1975.

This volume is appropriately called an intimate biography. Written with the cooperation of the subject, it is franker than most such accounts. The book tells of Sophia Loren's rise from an illegitimate child in a Naples slum to a world famous film star. No hesitancy is evident in noting that her early successes were based on the unrestrained use of her physical endowments. After her career was launched under Carlo Ponti's guidance, the major problem was avoiding romantic liaisons with some of her love-smitten costars—especially Cary Grant and Peter Sellers. The drawn-out Ponti bigamy accusation and the difficulties in having children receive extended attention. Fortunately there is information on many of her films which helps to balance the domestic problems. Two pictorial sections, an abbreviated filmography, and an index are also included.

The portrait of Sophia Loren provided by Donald Zec is that of a woman who understands herself and her life. A final quote sums up nicely: "The World makes stars, I make... the best spaghetti vongole in Italy." Recommended for mature adults. Some of the text may be unacceptable for younger readers.

5677   *Sophia, Living and Loving: Her Own Story.* by Hotchner, A. E. 244 p. paper illus. New York: Bantam, 1979.

With a collection of problems that could be right out of a Dickens or Alger novel, Sophia Loren's story tends toward Italian melodrama. Poverty, illegitimacy, bigamy, miscarriage, theft, kidnapping, banishment, and other assorted misfortunes are overcome with love, courage, ambition, pride, achievement and basic wisdom.

The author, known for his biographies of Doris Day and Ernest Hemingway, does not seem to capture this subject as totally as he did the earlier two. For his material, he has used four months of interviews with the actress. Loren was smart enough to demand control of any authorized biography in her continuing effort to perpetuate her own legend. As a result, this account seems like an attempt of a fortyish film star to establish a positive reputation upon which she can base her remaining years as a public performer. As a memoir and also a reminder, the book is a pleasant enough inspirational account of an earth goddess. Comments from family members and some illustrations accompany the story. No index or filmography is provided.

5678   *Sophia Loren.* by de Laborderie, Renaud. 48 p. paper illus. Manchester: World Distributors, 1964.

This volume carries the subtitle "Renaud de Laborderie Spotlights in Words and Pictures the Career of the Remarkable Sophia Loren."

5679   *Sophia Loren: In the Camera's Eye.* by Shaw, Stan. 160 p. illus. New York: Exeter, 1979.

5680   *The Sophia Loren Story.* by Reid, Gordon. 64 p. paper illus. London: EURAP, 1958.

This title in the *Film Star Biographies* series includes a filmography.

5681   *see   5680*

5682   *see   5683*

5683   THE SORROW AND THE PITY. by Ophuls, Marcel; and Harris, Andre. 184 p. illus. New York: Outerbridge & Lazard, 1972.

Script of the 1970 film directed by Ophuls. Contains an introduction by Stanley Hoffman, along with bio-graphical and appendix material by Mireille Johnston.

5684   *The Soul of the Moving Picture.* by Bloom, Walter. 168 p. illus. New York: Dutton, 1924.

Translated from the German, this volume is an introduction to moving pictures as an art form, with attention given to its potentials. Topics include tools, texts, tricks, scene, setting, poetry, adaptation, paths to art, etc. Many stills accompany the text, which emphasizes the contributions made to film art by the German cinema.

5685   *Souls Made Great Through Love and Adversity: The Film Work of Frank Borzage.* by Lamster, Frederick. 242 p. illus. Metuchen, N.J.: Scarecrow, 1981.

An in-depth study of the films of Frank Borzage, once called D. W. Griffith's successor. His melodramatic films lost popularity with the arrival of realism in the forties. Here the films are discussed chronologically with a filmography, a bibliography and an index following.

5686   *Sound: Magnetic Sound Recording for Motion Pictures.* by da Silva, Paul. 58 p. paper illus. Rochester: Eastman Kodak, 1977.

This typically excellent *Kodak* guide, written for both student and professional deals with the preparation and production of effective magnetic sound tracks. An older (1969) similar title also published by Kodak was *Basic Magnetic Sound Recording for Motion Pictures.*

5687   *Sound and the Cinema: The Coming of Sound to the American Film.* edited by Cameron, Evan William. 223 p. paper Pleasantville, N.Y.: Redgrave, 1979.

This anthology is an account of the effect the coming of sound had on the art and industry of motion pictures. A first section discusses the revolution brought about by the new technology, while the second consists of recollections by Hal Mohr, Frank Capra, Rouben Mamoulian, Julius J. Epstein, Walter Reisch, and Bernard Herrmann. Closing chapters are concerned with the European influence from 1925 to 1940 and an analysis of the sound in two films, APPLAUSE (1929) and CITIZEN KANE (1941).

5688 *Sound and the Documentary Film.* by Cameron, Ken. 150 p. illus. London: Pitman, 1947.

The first portion of this volume is devoted to views and comments on documentary film, accompanied by much cynicism about the "name celebrities" of the field. The latter sections deal with sound recording techniques and provide a good technical reference.

5689 *Sound for Your Color Movies.* by Cushman, George W. 95 p. paper illus. New York: Amphoto, 1958.

How to choose and use the right equipment for amateur sound motion pictures.

5690 *The Sound Motion Picture in Science Teaching.* by Rulon, P. J. New York: Johnson Reprints, 1980 (1933).

A reprint of volume 20 in the *Harvard Studies in Education* series.

5691 *Sound Motion Pictures, from the Laboratory to Their Presentation.* by Brooks, Harold. 401 p. illus. Garden City, N.Y.: Doubleday, Doran, 1929.

5692 *Sound Motion Pictures, Recording and Reproducing.* by Cameron, James R. 617 p. illus. Coral Gables, Florida: Cameron, 1947.

Another Cameron text, with attention given to cinematography, sound apparatus, motion picture studio activities, film laboratory practice, etc. This was the 6th edition of this particular title, which contained almost 1000 pages when the 8th edition appeared in 1959.

5693 THE SOUND OF MUSIC. by Lubalin, Herb; and Liebling, Howard. 48 p. paper illus. New York: National Publishers, 1965.

The first and longer section of this souvenir book is a retelling of the story with accompanying color stills from the 1965 film. The second part spotlights the cast, the composers, and the production personnel of the film. The black and white photographs used in this section provide a marked contrast to the earlier color stills. The book, like the film, seems aimed at the emotion rather than the intellect.

5694 *The Sound of Their Music: The Story of Rodgers and Hammerstein.* by Nolan, Frederick. illus. New York: Walker & Co., 1978.

Although this dual biography deals mostly with the theatrical writing and productions of Richard Rodgers and Oscar Hammerstein II, some film names and references do appear in the text. Nearly all of the team's musicals were transferred to film and they wrote the original score for STATE FAIR (1945).

5695 *Sound Pictures and Trouble Shooter's Manual.* by Cameron, James; and Rider, John. 1120 p. illus. Manhattan Beach, N.Y.: Cameron, 1930.

Another large handbook-manual designed for the professional technician of the thirties.

5696 *Sound Projection.* by Miehling, Rudolph. 528 p. illus. New York: Mancall, 1929.

A technical book which deals with the nature, use and manipulation of sound in motion picture projection. Generators, amplifiers, electricity, sound heads, etc., are treated in the text.

5697 *Sound-Recording for Films: A Review of Modern Methods.* by Elliott, W. F. 134 p. illus. London: Pitman, 1937.

A state-of-the-art report covering the first decade of sound films.

5698 *Sound Recording for Motion Pictures.* by Frater, Charles B. 210 p. paper illus. San Diego: A. S. Barnes, 1979.

This is a title in a series of original paperbacks on professional motion picture techniques called *Screen Textbooks* Using text, illustrations, diagrams charts, graphs and tables, the book covers the sound equipment available today and how it is used. Topics include sound waves, electricity, synchronous sound recording, transfer from tape to film, editing sound, dubbing, optical sound transfer and the magra tape recorders.

The volume, which is indexed, is most appropriate for the professional. Advanced students will also find it helpful in understanding and using sound in films.

5699 *Sound Sense For Movie Makers.* by Watson, Ivan. illus. Dobbs Ferry, N.Y.: Morgan & Morgan, 1975.

This book is an example of selected information made inappropriate because of technology. Written before sound cameras were so accessible, the text deals only with the older silent cameras. Nevertheless, it does offer an abundance of other information that remains pertinent.

5700 *Sounds and Images: Radio, Television, Film.* by Heath, Ray Brian. 96 p. illus.

This textbook, designed for British secondary schools, deals in part with film.

5701 *Sounds for Silents.* by Hofmann, Charles. illus. New York: Drama Book Shop, 1970.

Written by the piano accompanist to the silent films shown at the Museum of Modern Art, this short book covers a neglected topic in cinema literature. Some sample scores, a plastic disc and a foreword by Lillian Gish are among the positive features. The few pages and the high price are negatives. The small plastic disc has music from THE LONEDALE OPERATOR (1911), BIRTH OF A NATION (1915), BROKEN BLOSSOMS (1918), PETER PAN (1924), and PASSION OF JOAN OF ARC (1928).

5702 *Soundtrack: The Music of the Movies.* by Evans, Mark. 302 p. illus. New York: Hopkinson and Blake, 1975.

A thorough exploration of film music is offered in this affectionate tribute to a heretofore neglected film aesthetic. Beginning with short sections on the music of the silent film and the early talkies, the text progresses quickly to the Golden Age of Film Music (1935-1950). This period is covered by separate consideration of many outstanding composers active during this time. Discussions of the fifties, pop music in films, the functions of a film score, and ethics, aesthetics, fables and folklore complete the text. A glossary and an index are added along with some small illustrations, composer portrait sketches, and score excerpts.

Not only does this volume offer information, evaluation, and appreciation of its subject, but it also provides a historical perspective that will answer many reference questions. Although it is not as comprehensive as Limbacher's *Film Music*, this volume is a more readable, unified statement. Recommended.

5703 *Sources of Meaning in Motion Pictures and Television.* by Pryluck, Calvin. 241 p. illus. New York: Arno Press, 1976.

Written in 1973 at the University of Iowa in partial fulfillment of the doctoral program, this work provides a "theory of the film" which emphasizes the semiotic and film language areas of film theory. The author proposes a new, broad-based approach to film theory which is applicable to a variety of film uses including educational and entertainment films. This title appears in the *Dissertations on Film* series.

5704 *Sources of Motion Pictures and Filmstrips.* by 22 p. paper Rochester, N.Y.: Eastman Kodak, 1972.

Selected sources of motion pictures and filmstrips are noted in this booklet. Local, regional and national distributors are discussed along with university film libraries. After some general catalogs are described, more specialized listings are suggested under ten specific subject areas: agriculture, business, ecology, religion, etc. A useful reference for all collections.

5705 *The South and Film.* by French, Warren. 200 p. Jackson, Miss.: University Press of Mississippi, 1981.

5706 SOUTH PACIFIC. by Skouras, Thana. 48 p. illus. New York: Lehmann Publishers, 1958.

An unusual feature of this souvenir book is the information contained on the front and back endpapers. It is a listing of all the awards and nominations that the entire personnel, both on screen and behind the cameras, have received. The stage and theatre awards accorded the original New York production are also noted. James Michener discusses his original short story and Brooks Atkinson offers a biographical sketch of Rodgers and Hammerstein, who follow with statements of their own. Buddy Adler, the producer, introduces the center section which is a visualized or story-board version of the 1958 film. Shots are described, notations about lighting, costume design and set decorations are noted, and the pages are supposed to resemble a romantic idea of a film script. The remainder of the volume is devoted to the director, the cast, the score, the color work, set decoration, costume, and dance. A section describing the Todd-AO film process gives a chronology of important dates in the history of motion picture technology.

This volume is so far superior to most of the others

in this genre that it merits the detailed discussion above. If a souvenir book is to be published, this is one very fine way of doing it.

5707 SOUTH SEAS ADVENTURE. 20 p. paper illus. New York: Cinerama Publishers, 1958.

In this souvenir book a few miscellaneous articles about the South Seas are accompanied by some rather poor photographs of the locales. Historical background is given, but the reader interest will probably center on the diagram of the three-projector system of Cinerama. Producer Carl Dudley and composer Alex North are mentioned.

5708 *Souvenir Programs of 12 Classic Movies 1927-1944.* edited by Kreuger, Miles. 236 p. paper illus. New York: Dover, 1977.

Supplement One of *Cinema Booklist* contained reviews of more than 100 souvenir books, mostly for films made after World War II. The production of these volumes was rather elaborate, employing full-color pictures, hardbound covers, etc. Earlier programs were much simpler, and this interesting volume reproduces 12 of them from the first decade or so of talking pictures. The following films are represented: THE JAZZ SINGER (1927), THE BROADWAY MELODY (1929), THE LOVE PARADE (1929), ALL QUIET ON THE WESTERN FRONT (1930), GRAND HOTEL (1932), DINNER AT EIGHT (1933), CAPTAINS COURAGEOUS (1937), THE GOOD EARTH (1937), LOST HORIZON (1937), GONE WITH THE WIND (1939), THE GREAT DICTATOR (1940), and CITIZEN KANE (1941).

The programs are unique historical documents which offer information heretofore not widely published. Selection, which includes musicals, comedies and dramas, has been made with taste and intelligence. Reproduction quality is good.

The programs will enrich any current viewing of these classic films. A wide audience which includes students, writers, scholars and buffs will find the collection to be an informational and nostalgic treasure. Highly recommended.

5709 *The Soviet Censorship.* edited by Dewhirst, Martin; and Farrell, Robert. 170 p. Metuchen, N.J.: Scarecrow, 1973.

This book is the record of a symposium organized by the Institute for the Study of the USSR in cooperation with Radio Liberty. The participants were recent emigres and defectors who spoke about the network of Soviet censorship. There is one chapter devoted to specific examples of censorship in the Soviet cinema, but much of the remaining text is also pertinent. The participants, a bibliography, a list of USSR newspapers and periodicals and a name index complete the volume.

5710 *Soviet Cinema.* by Dickinson, Thorold; and De La Roche, Catherine. 136 p. illus. London: Falcon Press, 1948.

In this general survey of Soviet cinema (up to 1947), each author covers a different period: the sound era, De La Roche; the silent era, Dickinson. Many fine illustrations.

5711 *Soviet Cinema.* by Arossev, A. 326 p. illus. Moscow: Voks Publishing, 1935.

This scarce volume is noted here because of its historical importance. It emphasizes a 15-year period of the Soviet film, 1920-1935, combining pictures and text of the films, directors, actors, and other artisans. The many unusual pictures throughout are fascinating from both an historical and a technical viewpoint. The text alternates between being quaint, predictable, and amusing. Cecil B. DeMille's tribute to the Soviet film, for example, appears alongside John Howard Lawson's. Anyone studying Soviet film should be familiar with this volume. Recommended highly.

5712 *Soviet Cinema: Directors and Films.* by Birkos, Alexander S. 344 p. illus Hamden, Conn.: Archon Books, 1976.

In this reference volume the author provides access to the directors and films of the Soviet Cinema with a concentration on the period from 1918 to 1975. A short introduction provides the historical framework for the content. Immediately following there are over a hundred biographical entries of varying length arranged alphabetically by director surname. Each offers birthdate, date of death if pertinent, geographical area of operation in the Soviet Union, a descriptive essay, and a filmography. Apparently many of the Soviet directors also had careers as actors. The second section is an alphabetical listing of selected film titles. In most instances the title, year of release, director, studio and a short description are offered. An annotated bibliography concludes the volume, which also contains a few illustrations.

The author has assembled information that is difficult to obtain. The volume will be of inestimable aid to anyone concerned with the Soviet cinema.

5713 *Soviet Cinema.* by Marshall, Herbert. 40 p. paper illus. London: Russia Today Society, 1945.

5714 *The Soviet Film Industry.* by Babitsky, Paul; and Rimberg, John. 377 p. New York: Praeger, 1955.

An account of how the Soviet studios operate via fear, coercion, trial-and-error, political pressures, and interference. In the films from 1922 to 1954, the happy ending always occurs. The same is not true for the Soviet film artisans. The book includes an analysis of heroes and villains in Soviet films from 1923 to 1950. Several indices of Russian films, persons, subjects, and directors are given.

5715 *Soviet Films: Principal Stages of Development.* by Pudovkin, V.; and Alexandrov, G.; and Piryev, I. 56 p. illus. Bombay: People's Publishing House, 1951.

5716 *Soviet Films, 1938-1939.* by Fink, V. 124 p. illus. Moscow: State Publishing House for Cinema Literature, 1939.

5717 *The Soviet Screen.* by Eisenstein, Sergei. 35 p. paper illus. Moscow: Foreign Languages Publishing House, 1939.

5718 *Space Monsters: From Movies, TV, and Books.* by Simon, Seymour. 80 p. illus. New York: Lippincott, 1977.

Designed for children, this is the usual overview of media monsters.

5719 *Spaghetti Westerns: Cowboys and Europeans from Karl May to Sergio Leone.* by Frayling, Christopher. 304 p. illus. Boston: Routledge and Kegan Paul, 1981.

An extended critical analysis of the Italian western, 1965 to 1974. Attention is given to Sergio Leone's films which starred Clint Eastwood and there is an attempt to place this subgenre into a historical-political context. Unusual and quite thorough.

5720 *Spain Again.* by Bessie, Alvah. 228 p. paper illus. Corte Madera, Calif.: Chandler & Sharp, 1975.

Screenwriter Alvah Bessie was one of the Hollywood Ten jailed for contempt during the late forties. Earlier he had participated in the Spanish Civil War, and in 1967, was able to go back to Spain again to make a film. Ironically, the subject was the return of a veteran of the Abraham Lincoln Brigade to Spain. Although the film is almost unknown, it won Spain's Master Award in 1968. The question raised by Bessie here is whether it was honorable to go to Spain again.

5721 *The Spanish Cinema, 1970.* compiled by Uniespana. 253 p. paper illus. Madrid: Uniespana, 1970.

A catalog of Spanish films with a text translated from Spanish to English by the Berlitz School.

5722 SPARTACUS. by Marguiles, Stan. 30 p. illus. 1960.

In this souvenir book an opening article entitled "Portrait of a Production" is followed by "Spartacus, Rebel Against Rome" by C. A. Robinson, Jr. Several pages discuss gladiators and the role they played in ancient Rome. One complete section is devoted to those artisans "On the Other Side of the Camera" and there is a fold-out art section on the individual stars of the 1960 film. Supporting cast and production credits are noted.

5723 *Speaking Candidly: Films and People in New Zealand.* by Mirams, Gordon. 242 p. illus. Hamilton, New Zealand: Paul's Book Arcade, 1945.

This volume, written as a defense of and prophecy about films in New Zealand, deals with the industry and film's effect on the movie audience. It includes such topics as going to pictures, what movies do to us, Hollywood makes history, movies go to war, British and foreign movies, adjectival industry, a case for critics, newsreels, documentaries, from studio to screen, etc.

5724 *Special Effects in Cinematography.* by Bulleid, H. A. V. 264 p. illus. London: Fountain Press, 1954.

This is an earlier, simpler and less comprehensive exploration of special effects in filming than the one given by Fielding. The topics treated here are such basics as camera speeds, animation, superimposition, split screen, optical effects, mirrors, sound, etc. Only in one short chapter does the author consider optical printing, mattes, back projection and more sophisticated processes. The volume is good as an introduction or supplement to the Fielding book. It has a somewhat limited value by itself because of its restricted coverage of its subject matter. Today most filmmakers assume that what is labelled special effects here is really basic cinematography.

5725 *Special Effects in Motion Pictures.* by Clark, Frank P. 283 p. illus. New York: Society of Motion Picture and Television Engineers, 1966.

Some methods for producing mechanical special effects are given along with an account of their development and application.

5726 *Special Effects in the Movies: How Do They Do It.* by Culhane, John. 192 p. illus. New York: Ballanatine, 1981.

With over 400 illustrations this volume explores the film labs, techniques, and tricks used to fascinate audiences. It also pays tribute to the artists who create the special effects.

5727 *Special Effects, Volume II.* by Hutchinson, David. illus. paper NewYork: Starlog, 1980.

An original paperback series devoted to explaining and exploring special effects. Volume III appeared in 1981.

5728 *A Special Kind of Magic.* by Newquist, Roy. 156 p. illus. Chicago: Rand McNally & Co., 1967.

Extended interviews with Spencer Tracy, Katharine Hepburn, Stanley Kramer, Sidney Poitier, and Katherine Houghton are the substance of this volume. The framework for the interviews was the making of the film, GUESS WHO'S COMING TO DINNER? (1967) It is the Hepburn interview, and the ones with Kramer and Tracy, that give the volume its importance. The questioning is unobtrusive, spare and intelligent, while the replies give the reader confirmation of the subjects' wisdom and experience.

Although there is a trace of drum-beating for the film about this book, it never diminishes the fascination of the three major subjects. Although it is not an essential, this volume is recommended for most readers.

5729 *Spectacular: The Story of Epic Films.* by Cary, John. 160 p. paper illus. Secaucus, N.J.: Castle Books (DerbiBooks), 1974.

A survey of the epic film genre is provided in this oversized, spiral-bound volume. Beginning with such early silent spectaculars as QUO VADIS (1901) and CABIRIA (1913), the text progresses to Griffith, DeMille, and some of the major film epics of the sound era—GONE WITH THE WIND (1939), QUO VADIS (1951), LAWRENCE OF ARABIA (1962), DOCTOR ZHIVAGO (1965) and others. One chapter is devoted to an extended interview with Robert Wise about the making of HELEN OF TROY (1954). A selected filmography which gives casts, credits, and other data concludes the volume. The well-selected visuals include full-color pages, stills, portraits, double pages, advertisements, etc. The spiral binding does not facilitate the use of the book. Turning the pages becomes awkward and they often tear, because of the punched holes. Acceptable.

5730 *Speed: Cinema of Motion.* by Adrian, Werner. III p. paper illus. New York: Bounty (Crown), 1975.

An examination of speed and motion in films, this volume considers five large categories: steam, rail and iron; sea, undersea and air; bike; saddle, coach and car; and human grace, outer space.

Emphasis is on the visuals, which have been well selected and nicelyreproduced. The accompanying text and picture captions are rather basic, suggesting ideas and themes but never exploring them in any depth. The book is not indexed.

With its sampling of selected ways in which speedmotion has been utilized in films, this volume provides an adequate introduction to an important theme. However, the topic deserves a much more structured and carefully considered exposition than that provided here. Acceptable.

5731 *Spellbound in Darkness.* by Pratt, George C. 576 p. paper illus. Greenwich, Conn.: New York Graphic Society, 1973.

Originally published in 1966 as a unique two-volume college text, the present version has had 66 photographs added, and the material has been redesigned into a single large volume. Subtitled "A History of the Silent Film," the book is a collection of readings which cover a variety of actors, directors, and films from 1896 to 1929. Melies, Porter, Griffith, Chaplin, Sennett, DeMille, von Stroheim, Flaherty, Dreyer, and Lubitsch are discussed along with the films and topics that were the major elements of the silent era. The author provides a commentary to many of the articles which explains and enhances their contribution to the historical account being presented. Picture reproduction is excellent and there is a helpful index provided.

While this volume is not a history in the usual sense, it provides much more than the usual straightforward narrative approach. All of the elements combine to create a memorable tribute to the silent screen. Its appearance as a trade book can only be applauded. Highly recommended.

5732 *Spencer Tracy.* by Swindell, Larry. 319 p. illus. New York: World Pub. Co., 1969.

This excellent film biography has several commendable qualities—the telling of a complex life story with taste and dignity, the observance of an objective view, an ability to separate the important from the trivial, and, finally, an admission that no one could ever "know" Spencer Tracy. The early years from 1900 to 1920 are covered quickly, as are the theater years of 1921 to 1930. Emphasis is on the screen years from 1930 to 1967. His marriage, the relationships with Loretta Young and Katharine Hepburn, his films, and his behavior are all discussed. The author is never hesitant to evaluate a film or a performance. Good illustrations and a filmography are included. This is superior biography on all counts and is highly recommended.

5733 *Spencer Tracy.* by Tozzi, Romano. 159 p. paper illus. New York: Pyramid Books, 1973.

After several recent books on Spencer Tracy and Katharine Hepburn, what can there be left to add? Romano Tozzi has responded to this problem by summarizing the Tracy career with mostly factual descriptive accounts of his films. He has avoided any in-depth critical analysis and much of Tracy's personal life. For example, his alcoholism, his harassment of Irene Dunne, and his difficult behavior are all ignored. To suggest once again that Elia Kazan's inexperience as a film director was responsible for the failure of THE SEA OF GRASS (1947) is to perpetuate an inaccuracy. A reliance on incorrect information previously published in another Tracy biography plus inadequate research probably explains its appearance here.

The quality of picture selection and reproduction is up to the high standard characteristic of the *Pyramid* series. A filmography, a bibliography and an index complete the volume. The difficulties of being a late arrival in the film book sweepstakes are appar-

ent in this volume. Although these visuals are fine, and the other elements are nicely supportive, the text is often vulnerable and lacks critical insight. Acceptable.

5734 *The Spine Chillers.* by Welsh, Paul. 68 p. paper illus. Ilfracombe, England: Stockwell, 1975.

This original paperback is a collective biography of Lon Chaney, Jr., Peter Cushing, Christopher Lee, and Vincent Price.

5735 SPLENDOR IN THE GRASS. by Inge, William. 121p. paper illus. New York: Bantam Books, 1961.

Script of the 1961 film directed by Elia Kazan.

5736 *Splinters from Hollywood Tripods.* by Miller, Virgil E. 139 p. illus. New York: Exposition Press, 1964.

Some rambling memoirs of a Hollywood cameraman who worked with Chaney on HUNCHBACK OF NOTRE DAME (1922) and PHANTOM OF THE OPERA (1925). From then on his work seems to have gone downhill, ending with a five-year stint as TV cameraman with Groucho Marx, Art Baker and Edgar Bergen. The book rambles (or splinters) and much space is devoted to the author's poems. Most readers will wish that he had concentrated on the important films and personalities that he knew during his career. He writes in fan magazine style and does nothing to avoid cliches. What could have been an important memoir and contribution to film literature becomes a less-than-mediocre personal recollection. Except for those historians who are willing to wade through much dross to find a few nuggets of film history, this book is not recommmended.

5737 *Split Focus.* by Hopkinson, Peter. 119 p. illus. London: Rupert Hart-Davis, 1969.

Peter Hopkinson is an English filmmaker who began his career with home movies at a very early age. When he was 16, he began working at the film studios, and later worked with Gracie Fields, George Formby, King Vidor, and Alexander Korda. In World War II he served with distinction as a cameraman through many different campaigns. After the war he worked for The March of Time and has since produced documentaries for television. The self-image that Hopkinson presents is a most admirable one. He is a dedicated professional who believes in such rare virtues as integrity of purpose, honesty, modesty, and justice. In addition to presenting himself, he is able to describe the world he is photographing. A specialized book about a little known filmmaker, but a very rewarding reading experience. Recommended.

5738 *The Spoken Seen: Film and the Romantic Imagination.* by McConnell, Frank D. 195 p. illus. Baltimore: Johns Hopkins University Press, 1975.

In this provocative discussion of film aesthetics, the author relates the narrative motion picture to poetry and modern fiction. In doing so, he considers reality, automatons, politics, genres and film actor stardom, making persuasive arguments for a personal theory of film.

His structure is a logical one and the text is written to challenge and stimulate thought rather than to impress or confuse the reader. He uses many films, most of which are familiar, to illustrate his concepts and ideas. A few visuals are added and there is a helpful index.

This is an excellent, thoughtful discussion that will engender very positive reactions from mature readers. Highly recommended.

5739 *The Sponsor's Guide to Filmmaking.* by Trachtenberg, Leo. 145 p. illus. New York: Hopkinson & Blake, 1978.

This is a guide for business/industry executives faced with the prospect of film sponsorship. In twelve terse chapters the author tells how sponsored films are made, promoted, and distributed. His text is characterized by common sense suggestions based on goals or economy and efficiency in filmmaking. Topics discussed include choosing a producer, defining your audience, setting costs, contracts, scripts, shooting, post-shooting, promotion, distribution, etc. Appendixes include a glossary, along with lists of film distributors, organizations, directories, and competitions.

5740 *The Sponsored Film.* by Klein, Walter J. 210 p. New York: Hastings House, 1976.

In his introduction the author states "a sponsored film is a moving picture, in any form, paid for by anyone controlling its content and shown for public entertainment or information." He provides a survey of such films, considering their origin, purchase, sales, production, management, restrictions, etc. Practical information such as a sample contract, specifications, distribution centers, and several organization rosters are included in an appendix. The book is indexed.

This is a much needed survey on a film genre badly neglected in cinema literature. The text includes experiences and anecdotes along with exposition, description and data; as a result the coverage is quite comprehensive. Writing in a clear conversational style, the author emphasizes key concepts and statements by italicizing them. Throughout the reader will sense that this is the presentation of an experienced teacher who loves his subject. He also knows how best to explain it to the interested reader. Recommended.

5741 *Spotlight on Film: A Primer for Film-Lovers.* by Larsen, Egon. 301 p. illus. New York: Gordon Press, 1976 (1950).

This volume presents a general overview of the techniques used to make motion pictures. It was published in London in 1950 by Parrish.

5742 *Spotlight on Films: A Primer for Film-Lovers.* by Larsen, Egon. 301 p. illus. London: Max Parrish, 1950.

Cinematic language and technical developments are emphasized in this study of films and filmmaking, 1903-1949.

5743 *Springtime in Italy: A Reader on Neo-realism.* edited by Overby, David. 242 p. Hamden, Conn.: Archon, 1979.

David Overby provides a lengthy introduction to this anthology on neo-realism in the Italian film. The text itself consists of 17 articles, essays, discourses, etc., by filmmakers and writers associated with the neo-realism era in Italian film history: Visconti, de Sica, and Rossellini among them.

The author has selected and translated the articles from the original Italian, in addition to setting an appropriate framework for their presentation. A filmography, a bibliography and notes accompany the text.

5744 *Squadron of Death: A Description of Aeroplane Work For Film Purposes.* by Grace, Dick. 304 p. illus. New York: Doubleday, Doran, 1929.

Memoirs of a World War I aviator and stunt flier who worked in several films including WINGS (1927).

5745 *Stage and Film Decor.* by Myerscough-Walker, Raymond. 192 p. illus. London: Pitman, 1940.

The second section of this volume deals with film design and treats such topics as form, tone, lighting, materials, models, architecture, etc. The work of British designers such as Vincent Korda, Edward Carrick and Laurence Irving is discussed.

5746 *Stage and Screen.* by Shelley, Frank. 55 p. illus. London: Pendulum, 1947.

Evaluations of the stage and screen art of various performers.

5747 *Stage and Screen.* by Brazier, Marion H. 130 p. illus. Boston: M. H. Brazier, 1920.

Contains comments on the various aspects of the silent motion picture—artistic quality, morality, film music, censorship, use of the camera, etc. Writers, stage actors, film directors and others are quoted. The author also offers recollections of many films and actors from the early silent screen era.

5748 *The Stage and the School.* by Ommanney, Katherine A.; and Ommanney, Pierce C. 571 p. illus. New York: McGraw-Hill, 1950.

This pioneer textbook contains four chapters on motion pictures and indicates that much of what we consider new in film education may not be so. Chapter titles are 1) "Motion Picture History," 2) "Motion Picture Production, (Including Classroom Production!)," 3) Motion Picture Acting," and 4) "Shopping for Films." In the appendix there is a bibliography and a list of 100 "fine" films. Listed here as an historical source for researchers or historians.

5749 *The Stage/Screen Debate: A Study in Popular Aesthetics.* by Waller, Gregory A. 426 p. New York: Garland, 1982.

A title in the *Dissertations on Film* series.

5750 *Stage to Screen, Theatrical Method from Garrick to Griffith.* by Vardac, A. Nicholas. 283 p. illus. New York: Benjamin Blom, 1968 (1949).

An attempt to trace the influence that the 19th-century stage had upon early motion pictures is made in this volume. By describing theatres, staging methods, the melodrama and the spectacle, the author points out the contribution of each to early films. For example, melodrama led toward cinematic construction while spectacle led toward the photographic composition.

The first and longer section of the book deals with the 19th-century theatre, while the concluding section attempts to trace various elements found in the early films back to theatrical origins or sources mentioned previously. A few average illustrations are used. This is a scholarly—doctoral research-type presentation that will have limited interest for the general audience. It has interest and value for advanced students.

5751 STAGECOACH. by Nichols, Dudley. 152 p. paper illus. New York: Simon & Schuster, 1971.

Script of the 1938 film directed by John Ford. Includes: cast, production credits, and "Stage to Lordsburg" by Ernest Haycox (original short story).

5752 A STAIN ON HIS CONSCIENCE. by Schreivogel, Paul A. 20 p. paper illus. Dayton, Ohio: Pflaum, 1970.

A study guide for the 1968 film directed by Dusan Vukotic. Found in *Films in Depth* and also available separately.

5753 *Stan: The Life of Stan Laurel.* by Guiles, Fred Lawrence. 240 illus. New York: Stein and Day, 1980.

Not much new is divulged here in this latest biography of Stan Laurel. Since John McCabe has covered the territory so thoroughly, it remains for Guiles to use style to minimize familiarity. This he does rather well, as he describes the dark side of the comedian—the self-destructive alcoholic addicted to the pursuit and seduction of females. The illustrations, a filmography, a bibliography and an index support the text nicely.

5754 *Stan Brakhage, Ed Emshwiller.* edited by Reed, Rochelle. 24 p. paper illus. Washington, D.C.: American Film Institute, 1973.

Stan Brakhage took part in a 1972 summer seminar at the AFI Center in Beverly Hills; Ed Emshwiller preceded him by a year in a similar session. Edited transcripts of both discussions are given here. Acceptable.

5755 *A Standard Glossary for Film Criticism.* by Monaco, James. 32 p. paper New York: Zoetrope, 1975.

This short selected list of 260 words and phrases commonly encountered in film criticism has been carefully prepared. The terms are well chosen and their definitions are clear, succinct, and largely devoid of technical jargon. Another positive feature is the extensive cross-referencing which facilitates user understanding.

The booklet is a most helpful aid that can be used to advantage in a variety of situations. It should also help in the standardization of film terminology. Acceptable.

5756 *The Standards and Policy of the National Board of Review.* edited by National Board of Review of Motion Pictures. 20 p. paper New York: National Board of Review of Motion Pictures, 1916.

The National Board of Review (originally called the National Board of Censorship) had as its goal the search for ways to improve the artistic, moral and social aspects of motion pictures. This publication is a statement of their policy and standards during the formative years of the Board.

5757 *Standards for Cataloging Non-Print Materials.* compiled by Association for Educational Communications and Technology. 56 p. paper Washington, D.C.: National Education Association, 1971.

This booklet, which is revised at irregular intervals, contains material on cataloging films.

5758 *Standards for School Media Programs.* compiled by American Association of School Librarians. 80 p. paper Washington, D.C.: National Education Association, 1969.

This volume, which is revised at irregular intervals, suggests standards in terms of numbers and space based on school size, student body, and faculty. Attention is given to films in the school media program.

5759 *Standards of Photoplay Appreciation.* by Lewin, William; and Frazier, Alexander. 100 p. illus. Summit, N.J.: Educational and Recreational Guides, 1957.

Designed for high school use, this volume includes a photoplay approach to Shakespeare's play, *Julius Caesar*, along with bibliographies and illustrations.

5760 *Stanley Baker: Portrait of an Actor.* by Storey, Anthony. 160 p. illus. London: W.H. Allen, 1977.

A biography of the Welsh actor who appeared in many British films from 1941 to 1972. His films include THE GUNS OF NAVARONE (1961), ZULU (1963), ACCIDENT (1967), and WHERE'S JACK (1968). Baker died in 1976.

5761 *Stanley Donen: Director.* compiled by Davies, Brenda. 8 p. paper London: British Film Institute, 1969.

5762 *Stanley Donen and His Films.* by Casper, Joseph A. 288 p. illus. San Diego, Calif.: A. S. Barnes, 1981.

5763 *Stanley Kramer, Film Maker.* by Spoto, Donald. 367 p. paper illus. New York: G. P. Putnam's, 1978.

This is not a biography but a review of Stanley Kramer's 34 films from SO THIS IS NEW YORK (1948) to THE DOMINO PRINCIPLE (1976). Each is presented in a separate chapter that contains illustrations, plot description, critical analysis and background information. Perhaps the key to Kramer's work and career is found in his statement, "I'll accept the blame for the box office failures but I'd also like the credit for aiming at quality." Kramer has been called a red, a red baiter, a liberal, a boy wonder, the anti-Christ, a cinema auteur, a questioner, a gambler, an anti-American, and many other names. This is testimony to the vigor, daring, enthusiasm and talent that he brought to his films, 14 of which he directed. A filmography and an index are added.

Donald Spoto does not indicate the enthusiasm for this study that was so evident in his earlier book, *The Art of Alfred Hitchcock.* He has provided a competent but unexciting review of a major American filmmaker.

5764 *Stanley Kubrick: A Guide to References and Sources.* by Coyle, Wallace. 160 p. Boston: G. K. Hall, 1980.

Although he has made only 11 feature films, Stanley Kubrick is considered a leading director. This book, a title in the *Guide to References and Resources* series, provides access to the world of Kubrick. It consists of biographical background, a critical essay, a long annotated filmography, a bibliography, Kubrick's writing, archival sources, film distributors, and two indexes.

While some reservation may exist about the critical essay, the remaining elements are almost pure information and are presented objectively. References given here for Kubrick are abundant, with 614 noted. For anyone interested in the director, this is an ideal place to begin.

5765 *Stanley Kubrick: A Film Odyssey.* by Phillips, Gene D. 189 p. paper illus. New York: Popular Library, 1975.

The *Big Apple* series reinforces its initial impression with this fine review of Stanley Kubrick's films. Beginning with a short film created and produced entirely by himself, DAY OF THE FIGHT (1951), the volume details each of Kubrick's succeeding eleven films, ending with some notes on BARRY LYNDON (1975) which was in production as the book was written.

Although major attention is given to a detailed retelling of the plots, there is also background information and critical comment offered. Thus, the reader familiar with the films will still find sufficient substance here to warrant his attention.

The many illustrations are well reproduced. A bibliography and a filmography complete the book. A thorough review of Kubrick's films is provided by both text and visuals. The volume is an objective evaluation, made so by some excellent critical analyses. Recommended.

5766 *Stanley Kubrick Directs.* by Walker, Alexander. 272 p. paper New York: Harcourt, Brace, Jovanovich, 1971.

This excellent account of the work and persona of Kubrick appears at a time when the director's reputation is quite high. From his first films, FEAR AND DESIRE (1953) and KILLER'S KISS (1955), to his later works, 2001: A SPACE ODYSSEY (1969) and A CLOCKWORK ORANGE (1971), he has never failed to bring artistry, excitement, and controversy to the film medium. His filmography (when this book was published) was rather short; it included, in addition to the above, PATHS OF GLORY (1958), SPARTACUS (1960), LOLITA (1962), DR. STRANGELOVE (1958), and two early documentary short films.

The first portion of this book gives a narrative account of his career and films. Style and content are discussed next and the major portion of the book is devoted to detailed analyses of three films: PATHS OF GLORY, DR. STRANGELOVE and 2001: A SPACE ODYSSEY. It should be noted that only a few descriptive pages are devoted to A CLOCKWORK ORANGE since it was in production when this book was being prepared. The text is impressive and treats Kubrick and his films with affection and respect. The photographs range from average to excellent, although many of them are too small to be effective. The book should be very popular with young people.

5767 STAR!. by Newman, Howard. 48 p. paper illus. New York: National Publishers, 1968.

This souvenir book is presented as a scrapbook devoted to a female star, Gertrude Lawrence. Using candids, stills and studio photographs, there is a mixture of the originals with Gertrude Lawrence and the 1968 film shots with Julie Andrews. Old program covers and caricatures are also used, along with reprints of news articles about the filming and about Miss Lawrence. This intermingling of the old and the new is an imaginative and clever approach to a screen biography. Major cast members are given special attention and full supporting cast and production personnel are listed.

5768 *Star Acting: Gish, Garbo, Davis.* by Affron, Charles. 354 p. illus. New York: Dutton, 1977.

This study of screen acting uses more than 750 frame enlargements from the films of Lillian Gish, Greta Garbo, and Bette Davis. It begins with a rather vulnerable general discussion and then uses selected films of the trio named above. The actresses were chosen in order to provide a continuum from the first major features of the silent era to the decline of Hollywood in the early 50s. The three subjects are, of course, ideal examples of different film personalities, and the author indicates how each tried to expand the art of screen acting. Some attention is given to directors D. W. Griffith, King Vidor, Victor Seastrom and William Wyler, but the emphasis is on the star. A few films are analyzed in depth while many others are discussed more briefly. The frame enlargements are of excellent quality and are extremely helpful in supporting the author's argument. Detailed filmographies, a bibliography and an index are also provided.

This unusual and provocative analysis employs two dependable elements: a trio of legendary film stars and a recreation of some classic films. Its major weakness is the minimizing of the director's role; surely Cukor, Mamoulian, Mankiewicz, etc., contributed more than one might sense from the text. There is still enough thoughtful selection, intelligent arrangement and original analysis to provide a rewarding reading experience. Recommended.

5769 *Star Babies.* by Strait, Raymond. 231 p. illus. New York: St. Martin's Press, 1980.

What it's like to have a celebrity as a parent is told in *National Enquirer* style, with each offspring telling a story that resembles a confidence rather than a reminiscence. The author offers minimal assistance in providing form for the stories. Included as subjects are the children of Mario Lanza, Judy Garland, Vic Damone, Pat Boone, Tom Mix, Dorothy Lamour, David O. Selznick, Lou Costello, Jack Albertson, Lloyd Bridges, Gordon MacRae, Rosemary Clooney, Will Geer, and Andre Previn.

5770 *A Star Danced.* by Lawrence, Gertrude. and 231 p. illus. London: W. H. Allen, 1945.

An autobiography of the British stage star who appeared occasionally in films. Her motion pictures include: THE BATTLE OF PARIS (1912), REMBRANDT (1936), MEN ARE NOT GODS (1937), and THE GLASS MENAGERIE (1950). She mentions none of these but does indicate that she played a role in NO FUNNY BUSINESS (1933). The book is not indexed and there are no illustrations. See also *Gertrude Lawrence As Mrs. A.*

5771 *Star Gazer: Andy Warhol's World and His Films.* by Koch, Stephen. 155 p. illus. New York: Praeger, 1973.

The Warhol phenomenon is explored in this book, which happily gives major attention to his films. The decade from 1963 to 1973 saw the production of many experimental films either by Warhol or by Paul Morrissey, a member of his entourage. After a short introductory chapter, the silent films are discussed. Major ones which receive analysis include BLOW-JOB (1964), HAIRCUT (1964), EMPIRE (1964), SLEEP (1963), KISS (1963), EAT (1963), and others. The sound films discussed include HARLOT (1965), BEAUTY 2 (1965), KITCHEN (1965), VINYL (1965), HEDY (1965), MY HUSTLER (1965), THE CHELSEA GIRLS (1966), THE LOVES OF ONDINE (1968), NUDE RESTAURANT (1968) and LONESOME COWBOYS (1968). In 1968 Warhol was nearly killed in a shooting and since that time apparently has produced little if any film. His partner of sorts, Paul Morrissey, is probably responsible for FLESH (1968), TRASH (1970), WOMEN IN REVOLT (1972), HEAT (1972), and AMOUR (1973). A long but still incomplete filmography and an index conclude the book. One small section of illustrations only increases one's desire to see more of this experimental filmmaker's work.

Warhol's films of the sixties presaged the freedom that commercial films have had in the seventies. His influence on both content and technique can be documented by studying and re-viewing his films. This volume notes much of his total contribution and serves nicely as a record of his early provocative work. Highly recommended for mature adults. The emphasis on sexual behavior in the films makes the volumes unsuitable for young readers.

5772 *A Star Is a Star Is a Star: The Lives and Loves of Susan Hayward.* by Anderson, Christopher P. 269 p. illus. New York: Doubleday, 1980.

This biography suffers by appearing concurrently with Beverly Linet's *Susan Hayward: Portrait of a Survivor.* Anderson employs an annoying format: he invents endless dialogue, making this almost a work of fiction. His research of Hayward seems partial and limited, based primarily on newspaper sources, e.g., the Hayward-Barker divorce case and testimony. The lady deserves better treatment than that provided by Andersonin this book.

5773 *Star Maker: The Story of D. W. Griffith.* by Croy, Homer. 210 p. illus. New York: Duell, Sloan & Pearce, 1959.

This is one of the few total biographies of Griffith ever published. Many other books devote anecdotes, segments, and chapters to him, but this one attempts the total story. For the most part, it misses. The story of his life is told with reconstructed dialogue, stock situations made of what certainly were complex relationships, and a total simplification of a life that certainly was not simple. The volume seems to have been designed for a juvenile audience. A small number of photos does little to help the narrative. Even the two-page index seems short and simplified. Acceptable for young people.

5774 *Star Portrait: Intimate Life Stories of Famous Film Stars.* by Booch, Harrish S.; and Doyle, Karing. 152 p. illus. Bombay: Lakhani Book Depot, 1962.

India's top film stars are pictured and profiled in this volume.

5775 *see 5774*

5776 *Star Quality.* by McClure, Arthur F.; and Jones, Ken D. 285 p. illus. New York: A. S. Barnes, 1974.

Some confusion seems to exist concerning the subtitle for this volume. The dust jacket offers "The Great Actors and Actresses of Hollywood," while the title page gives "Screen Actors from the Golden Age of Films." The latter is more appropriate since the book deals with those film performers who were more than featured players but were never considered superstars. Patricia Ellis, Patrick Knowles, and Inger Stevens are examples used in the introduction. In the first section 79 performers are presented with a one-page biography and a still. The second section contains almost 400 portraits, each having a caption with subject name, birthdate, birth place, and, if applicable, date of death.

Of course, choice and placement are the author's prerogative, but to place Kane Richmond, Milburn Stone, Lyle Talbot, and Grant Withers in the more important Section I, while Lew Ayres, George Brent, Jeff Chandler, Montgomery Clift, Broderick Crawford, Dan Dailey, and others are represented only by an individual portrait in Section II may seem a distortion of importance or ability. The women fare no better; in the portrait-only section we find, for example, Madeleine Caroll, Jean Arthur, Lauren Bacall, and Cyd Charrise, while biographies and portraits are provided for Judy Canova, Frances Dee, Irene Hervey, Rita Johnson, Rochelle Hudson, etc. Errors and omissions can be found: page 254 shows a still of Dale Robertson captioned as Cliff Robertson; the Francis Farmer biography omits mention of her marriage to Leif Erickson; and Charles Bickford's second picture was not ANNA CHRISTIE (1930), as stated, but HELL'S HEROES (1929), as recorded in Bickford's autobiography.

While these may be minor matters, the photographs are not. For the most part, they are well selected, although the use of two-shots and three-shots instead of portraitsis occasionally disconcerting. Reproduction quality is above average. This book's intended audience of film buffs and fans will probably be pleased with the material and its presentation. For the reasons suggested above, others may not react as positively. Acceptable.

5777 *Star Shots.* by Engstead, John. 250 p. illus. New York: Dutton, 1978.

A lot of studio portrait photography combined with a small amount of modest biographical memoir is the substance of this pleasing volume. John Engstead has been associated with film celebrities since the mid-twenties and he's photographed most of them. Currently he is primarily concerned with television shows.

The format of the book is a simple one: as he recalls meeting and working with Hollywood actors, Engstead presents selected portraits that correlate with his stories. The text includes bits of history, gossip, opinion, professional advice, and some unobtrusive personal biography. The latter is so underplayed as to be almost hidden within the text and pictures. Engstead, one of Hollywood's most famous photographers, is apparently a very modest man.

Anyone who has a fondness for Hollywood's Golden Era will be captivated by this volume. The many attractive visuals are reproduced with careful clarity, and the accompanying story is told with a professional's taste and discrimination. Recommended.

5778 *Star-Spangled Kitsch.* by Brown, Curtis F. 202 p. paper illus. New York: Universe, 1976.

The ultimate in bad taste in the movies and elsewhere is the subject of this expose.

5779 *Star Stats: Who's Whose in Hollywood.* by Marx, Kenneth S. 436 p. paper Los Angeles: Price/Stern/Sloan, 1979.

This volume is a computer printout of several hundred biographical summaries of film performers (birthdate, place, father, mother, sister, brother, married, son, daughter, romance, friend, residence, possession, biography, Academy Award nomination/winner, comment, credit, etc.). A cross reference index, a three page history of the film business, studio hierarchies, and a comprehensive listing of birthdates complete the volume.

The value of this reference is quite limited. Most of the information given here is available elsewhere (i.e., *International Motion Picture Almanac*), and the provision of a fewselected credits is a misjudgment. Why bother indicating that Sandra Dee has four credits—UNTIL THEY SAIL (1957), A SUMMER PLACE (1959), TAMMY AND THE DOCTOR (1963), and TAKE HER SHE'S MINE (1964)— when the actress appeared in more than 25 films? And the need to find out the name of a star's stepfather seems a bit remote.

5780 *The Star Treatment.* by Stelzer, Dick. 213 p. Indianapolis, Ind.: Bobbs Merrill, 1977.

The subject of this unusual volume is psychotherapy, and within its pages 23 celebrities talk about their experiences with it. After the setting of each interview has been briefly described, Stelzer presents the conversation as a statement rather than a question-and-answer session. Subjects who have been associated with filmmaking include Mel Brooks, Rod Steiger, Lee Grant, Bruce Dern, Shelley Winters, Blake Edwards, and others.

The essays vary in length and style, depending in part upon the persona of the interviewee. All possess some elements of interest and the book's total endorsement of psychotherapy's value is commendable. Acceptable.

5781 *The Star Trek Compendium.* by Asherman, Allan. 256 p. illus. New York: Wallaby, 1981.

All about the TV "Star Trek" phenomenon—includes some information on STAR TREK—THE MOTION PICTURE (1980).

5782 STAR TREK—THE MOTION PICTURE Books.

In addition to the usual titles concerned with the production of STAR TREK—THE MOTION PICTURE (1979), some 16 separate publishing projects were tied in with the film. Titles included: *The 1980 Star Trek Calendar, The Official U.S.S. Enterprise Officer's Date Book for 1980, The Star Trek, Make-Your-Own Costume Book, Star Trek Speaks, Star Trek Spaceflight Chronology, The Star Trek Peel-Off Graphics Book, The Star Trek Iron-On Transfer Book, The Official Blueprints from Star Trek—the Motion Picture, The Great Star Trek Trivia Book, Star Trek—the Making of Star Trek the Motion Picture, The Star Trek Pop-up Book; and The U.S.S. Enterprise Punch-out Book.* The above represents only one aspect of the merchandising that accompanies certain films.

5783 STAR WARS: The Making of the Movie. by Weinberg, Larry. 70 p. illus. New York: Random House, 1980.

A book designed for very young readers.

5784 *The* STAR WARS Album. 78 p. paper illus. New York: Ballantine, 1977.

A behind-the-scenes look at the production of STAR WARS (1977), this original paperback contains interviews, stills, a genre history, a glossary, production shots, drawings, and a linking text. Attention is given to the special effects used in the film.

5785 *The* STAR WARS Book. compiled by Titelman, Carol W. 128 p. paper illus. New York: Ballantine, 1977.

This large format paperback contains the complete screenplay of STAR WARS (1977), along with production paintings, costume sketches, stills of the characters on sets, storyboards for the animated sequences, a discussion of the special effects, color reproduction of posters, information on the advertising and merchandizing of the film, cartoons, drawings, etc.

5786 *Stardom: The Hollywood Phenomenon.* by Walker, Alexander. 392 p. illus. New York: Stein & Day, 1970.

This book by the film critic of the *London Evening Standard* is about stardom and ranges in its explorations from Florence Lawrence to today's instant stars or anti- stars. While today's films are said to be a director's statement, the films of yesterday were, for the most part, star-based. Attention is given to Gish, Chaplin, Fairbanks Sr., Garbo, Negri, Valentino, Gilbert, Davis, Crawford, Gable, and Wayne. Bibliographic references are excellent. Interesting, but hardly essential.

5787 *Stardust in Hollywood.* by Gordon, Jan; and Gordon, Cora. 300 p. illus. London: Harrad, 1930.

An account of a visit to Hollywood, along with observations of the various filmmakers of the period at their work.

5788 *Stargazer: Andy Warhol and His Films.* by Koch, Stephen. 216 p. illus. New York: Praeger, 1973.

An attempt to analyze the Warhol films by relating them to the development of the underground film movement. Much meaning is read into the films, and for those enthusiasts who enjoy film without rationale, message, merit or technique, the book may be rewarding. Others may not have the patience, as many viewers did not for the films.

5789 *Starmaker: The Autobiography of Hal Wallis.* by Wallis, Hal; and Higham, Charles. 240 p. illus. New York: Macmillan, 1980.

In his long career as a Hollywood filmmaker, Hal Wallis has been responsible for producing many excellent films and discovering/introducing/developing numerous movie personalities. Among the latter are Elvis Presley, Dean Martin, Jerry Lewis, Shirley MacLaine, Humphrey Bogart, Errol Flynn, Charlton Heston, Kirk Douglas, and others. He has produced more than 100 films for Warner Brothers, Paramount and as an independent. Many of these are regarded as classics.

His story is related rapidly in less than 200 pages. Added is a selection of interoffice memos, a chronological listing of his films, an index and some illustrations. With such a rich record of accomplishment, it is no surprise that this volume is like an hor d'oeuvre rather than the main course. Most things are covered briefly and although the reader may gain some sense of Hal Wallis and his career, a feeling of much-more-to-tell remains. The book is almost a "Coming Attraction" of the detailed study of Wallis that should be written.

5790   *Starring Elvis.* edited by Bowser, James W. 256 p. paper illus. New York: Dell, 1977.

Abbreviated novelizations of 13 of Elvis Presley's 33 films are offered in this illustrated paperback. Noted here as an example of the diversity of books published about Elvis.

5791   *Starring Fred Astaire.* by Green, Stanley; and Goldblatt, Burt. 436 p. illus. New York: Dodd, Mead, 1973.

This coffee-table volume offers a comprehensive assessment of Fred Astaire's career on stage, in films, on radio and television, and on recordings. Using almost 1000 photographs, the book is a descriptive history of Astaire's half-century as a star performer. The text blends information, comment, review excerpts, plot synopses, credits, segments of dialogue, background information, etc. It is the visual collection, however, which provides the greatest appeal. The illustrations are well selected and include some rare photographs from Astaire's personal collection. Recommended.

5792   *Starring John Wayne.* by Fernett, Gene. 192 p. illus. Coca, Fla.: Cinememories, 1969.

A pictorial filmography.

5793   *Starring Miss Barbara Stanwyck.* by Smith, Ella. 340 p. illus. New York: Crown, 1973.

Ms. Smith and her publishers are to be congratulated in finally producing a quality product that more than equals the best of the *Citadel* series. Emphasis here is on the films and recenttelevision work and not on personal biography. Following a short introductory chapter about Stanwyck's early life and

Broadway career, the text gets quickly to her first film, BROADWAY NIGHTS (1927). Each of her succeeding films is described by the author, other professionals or by excerpts from reviews. Ms. Smith paints a positive picture throughout and many of the quotations also pay tribute to the strength, the no-nonsense approach and the good-gal quality of Stanwyck at work. The illustrations are all outstanding; many full-page portraits are especially beautiful. They confirm that for more than four decades, Stanwyck has been a handsome woman. Reproduction quality is in keeping with the visual content. There is a long filmography, a list of the star's awards and honors, and an index.

The reader who is searching for biography will have to find it elsewhere—e.g., *The Life of Robert Taylor* —but those interested in the artistry of this durable performer will be rewarded by this volume. While the text lacks critical analyses, it does offer detailed descriptions, some firsthand recollections, and the opportunity to observe the evolution of a starlet into a serious, mature artist of impressive stature. The visuals alone qualify this volume for recommendation.

5794   *Starring Robby Benson: The Official Robby Benson Scrapbook.* by White, Dana. New York: School Book Service, 1979.

5795   *Starring Robert Benchley: Those Magnificent Movie Shorts.* by Redding, Robert. 209 p. illus. Albuquerque: University of New Mexico Press, 1973.

During his 17 years in Hollywood, Robert Benchley appeared in 38 feature films and 48 short films and contributed to the scripts of 14 films. This volume is a well-researched, scholarly study of Benchley's life and work as exemplified by his 48 short films. Using the argument that the short films were based primarily on his written work, Redding evaluates the films and Benchley's effect on the film industry. After opening sections which recall his career as a drama critic and writer of humorous pieces, major attention is given to the methods he used to translate his humor into cinematic terms. Benchley's short films were an auteur operation to a large degree, since he wrote, acted and directed most of them. His style and content resisted direction or control by others.

The text is supported by meticulously detailed notes, a filmography, a bibliography, and a good index. The few stills serve to show the character Benchley portrayed in the shorts. Benchley probably would have been shocked at this pedantic, scholarly analysis of his work. Its reception by readers will varyfor the same reason—in-depth analysis of comedy is never as satisfying as the original art. Acceptable.

5796 *The Stars.* by Morin, Edgar. 192 p. paper illus. New York: Grove Press, 1960.

An investigation and analysis of the star system, whichhas been a component of films since Florence Lawrence, is the subject of this volume. The system is viewed historically, psychologically, economically, sociologically, and cinematically. It is the sociological (fans, clubs, etc.) that will probably cause the most disbelief by the sophisticated reader of today; however, consider the recent MGM auction of properties. James Dean is singled out as a case study in the star system. The selection of stills used is outstanding but their reproduction is poor in many cases.

This volume, published in 1960, seemingly was the prototype for the many others that followed from other publishers in the late sixties. Interesting in execution and absorbing in content.

5797 *The Stars.* by Schickel, Richard. 287 p. illus. New York: Dial Press, 1962.

This is a pictorial survey of American film stardom viewed over four decades (1920-1960). Almost all of the personalities entitled to the designation of film stars are represented as are a few of lesser magnitude. Missing are Kirk Douglas (if Heston and Lancaster, why not Douglas?), Debbie Reynolds (why June Allyson?), Olivia De Havilland (with two Academy Awards?), Loretta Young, and Irene Dunne. Since the book stops at 1960, Newman, Burton, Streisand and Poitier are not listed.

The pictures are quite pleasing and reproduced with adequate fidelity. The text is opinionated and vulnerable on occasion and errors abound. (Reference is made to DeMille's KING OF KINGS in 1936, and to the Marx Brothers' film, THREE WISE FOOLS.) The book has been reproduced in several lower-priced editions. Recommended.

5798 *Stars.* by Dyer, Richard. paper illus. London: British Film Institute; New York: Zoetrope, 1979.

Dyer's topic this time is film celebrity, identified by both the sociological and semiotic approach. The first says stars give films significance while the second says the stars are only important because of the films in which they appear. The argument is expanded by the use of many specific examples.

5799 *see* *5798*

5800 *Stars and Featured Players of Paramount of 1930-1931.* edited by Gordon, R. F. New York: Gordon Press, 1976.

5801 *Stars and Films of 1937 and 1938.* edited by Watts, Stephen. 2 volumes 208 p.; 208 p. illus New York: Gordon Press, 1976 (1937-38).

Published originally in London, these yearbooks contain illustrations, articles, reviews, etc.

5802 *Stars and Stars: Famous Faces and the Zodiac.* by Lynen, S. paper illus.

Some famous people and their "real" personality as foretold by the stars.

5803 *Stars and Strikes.* by Ross, Murray. 233 p. New York: Columbia University Press, 1941.

The unionization of Hollywood is related by tracing the development of both the craft and the artist unions. The factual is emphasized (tables, statistics, etc.) while the human factors (competition, scandals, graft) are overlooked. Interesting, impartial, but pedantic.

5804 *Stars and Their Cars.* by Barris, George. 143 p. paper illus. Hollywood, Calif.: Laufer Co., 1973.

The author of this unusual paperback is a specialist who "customizes" cars to fit specific personalities. He describes the work he has done for such stars as Steve McQueen, Elvis Presley, David Carradine, Clint Eastwood, Paul Newman, James Garner, Ann-Margret, and others. Rock music artists are abundantly represented along with assorted TV performers. A sampling of his customizing is shown in a center section of photographs. A harmless and unessential volume.

5805 *Stars Beyond: A Biographical Graveside to Hollywood's Greats.* by Perry, Jim. Yuma, Ariz.: Perry, 1980.

5806 *Stars in My Eyes... Stars in My Bed.* by Bacon, Nancy. 216 p. paper illus. New York: Pinnacle, 1975.

This sleazy volume lives up to its cover blurbs of being scandalous, outrageous and unbelievable; added to these descriptions should be unethical, unkind, self-serving and vindictive . What Nancy Bacon offers here are kiss-and-tell accounts of a few selected love affairs and one-night-stands with some male celebrities. Sexual aspects are emphasized to such a degree that a reader may question the author's ability to sustain another kind of relationship.

Variation in the book is provided by sordid recollections of personalities such as Marilyn Monroe, Laurence Harvey, Jayne Mansfield, Judy Garland, and Sharon Tate—all of whom are unable to defend their reputations at this point. Bacon is aware that authors cannot be sued for libel by dead people and thus she divulges privileged private information indiscriminately. Shades of *Confidential* magazine and *Hollywood Babylon* are combined with the author's consistent lack of taste to provide another bestseller about the scandalous life of Hollywood celebrities. Interested persons should make their own decision on this book.

5807   *Stars in My Hair.* by Denham, Reginald. 256 p. illus. London: Werner Laurie, 1958.

This is the autobiography of a British actor-writer-director who worked both on stage and screen. His films appeared mostly in the thirties, but some of his later plays were also made into films.

5808   *Stars of Australian Stage and Screen.* by Porter, Hal. 304 p. illus. San Francisco: Tri-Ocean Books, 1965.

The Australian cinema is represented in this volume by both its filmmakers and its films.

5809   *Stars of the Movies and Featured Players.* 252 p. illus. Hollywood: Hollywood Publicity Company, 1927.

This volume contains 250 portraits of film actors of the silent screen era.

5810   *Stars of the Photoplay.* 254 p. illus. Chicago: Photoplay Magazine, 1924.

The cover of this collective biography reads, "Art Portraits of Famous Film Favorites with Short Biographical Sketches."

5811   *Stars of the Screen.* by Bermingham, Cedric. 201 p. illus. London: H. Joseph, 1931.

This is one of four volumes which appeared as year-books from 1930 to 1934. Coverage, usually from 150 to 100 subjects, includes players from American, British, and German screens along with the usual lists of awards, films, new actors, etc.

5812   *Stars of the Screen 1931.* edited by Bermingham, Cedric O. 201 p. illus. New York: Gordon Press, 1976 (1931).

Originally published in London, this volume contains short biographies of more than 100 actors along with photos and other biographical material.

5813   *Stars of the Twenties.* by Abbe, James; and Early, Mary Dawn. illus. New York: Viking, 1975.

More than 105 portraits by famed photographer James Abbe make up the substance of this attractive volume. Lillian Gish provides an introduction to the superb collection and there is an accompanying text by Mary Dawn Early. Many of the subjects are film personalities; they become objects of great beauty when observed by James Abbe.

5814   *see   5813*

5815   *see   5813*

5816   *Stars Off Gard.* by Gard, Alex. 63 p. illus. New York: Scribners, 1947.

A collection of 50 caricatures, mostly of stars from Hollywood's golden era.

5817   *Stars on the Crosswalks.* by Halliday, Ruth S. 100 p. paper illus. Sherman Oaks, Calif.: Mitock, 1958.

A 1958 guide to Hollywood, including restaurants, housing, tourist information, points of interest, etc.

5818   STATE OF SIEGE. by Solinas, Franco. 214 p. paper illus. New York: Ballantine, 1973.

Script of the 1972 film directed by Constantine Costa-Gavras. This book is divided into two parts: "Reflections" (containing various articles about the making of the film including an interview with the director and the scriptwriter) and "Documents" (containing various articles on internal politics in Chile). Also includes cast and production credits and bibliography.

5819 *The State of the Art of Instructional Films.* by Hoban, Charles F. 34 p. paper Stanford, Calif.: ERIC, Stanford University, 1971.

Hoban, the author of *Instructional Film Research: 1918-1950*, provides an update on teaching films.

5820 STAVISKY. by Semprun, Jorge. 163 p. paper illus. New York: Viking, 1975.

Script of the 1974 film directed by Alain Resnais. Contains cast and production credits, an introduction by Richard Seaver and an interview with Resnais.

5821 *Steady Barker.* by Barker, Eric. illus. London: Secker and Warburg, 1956.

Eric Barker is a radio comedian who appeared in many British films from the late thirties to the early seventies.

5822 *Step Right Up! I'm Gonna Scare the Pants off America.* by Castle, William. 275 p. illus. New York: G. P. Putnam's, 1976.

William Castle, like Roger Corman, had the talent to make very successful films with small budgets. Most of his output was in the horror genre—MACABRE (1958), THE TINGLER (1960), HOMICIDAL (1961), STRAIGHT-JACKET (1964), THE NIGHT WALKER (1965), I SAW WHAT YOU DID (1965), ROSEMARY'S BABY, etc. His autobiography resembles his films in its terse, economical, modest, yet completely entertaining approach to his story. Using much wit and humor, he recalls many anecdotes from his three decades in Hollywood. As indicated in his title, he is a pitchman who knows how to sell his product to an audience.

His memoirs are fun to read and many inadvertently draw attention to some of his overlooked films.

5823 *Stephen King's Danse Macabre.* by King, Stephen. illus. New York: Everest House, 1980.

Author Stephen King discusses books, movies and television programs of the horror genre.

5824 *Steps in Producing and Costing a Business Film.* compiled by Audiovisual Committee. 21 p. paper New York: Association of National Advertisers, 1962.

5825 *Steps in Time.* by Astaire, Fred. 338 p. illus. New York: Harper & Brothers, 1959.

If the reader is looking for a frank, soul-searching, confessional-type autobiography, he will be disappointed in this book. In print Astaire is a shy, introverted, polite gentleman who believes in personal privacy. He relates a chronological factual story which is punctuated only by positive comments or judgments.

The book's strength lies in his descriptions of the 30 musical films he made. (FINIAN'S RAINBOW was done in 1968. His nondancing roles in ON THE BEACH (1959) and THE NOTORIOUS LANDLADY (1962) were done after the musicals.) It is unfortunate that there is a repetitive sameness to these accounts of making film musicals, e.g., initial idea, rehearsal, nice people, more work, and finally gratifying results. More detail and technical description would have been welcome. Illustrations are modest as is the index and a bare listing of his films. This is not a book about the greatest film dancer in the world—it is the modest, careful, almost reluctant life story of a man who says in closing, "I just dance...."

5826 *Stereo Views.* by Chandler, Arthur. 32 p. paper San Francisco: Troubador, 1978.

Although not a film book per se, this oversized paperback approximates the effect of three dimensional films. Using a collection of 3-D drawings/views, along with a set of glasses, the viewer can experience an illusion of depth. A short essay introduces the collection.

5827 *Sternberg.* edited by Baxter, Peter. 144 p. paper illus. London: British Film Institute (New York: Zoetrope), 1980.

This appreciation of director Josef von Sternberg is in the form of an anthology. Sixteen articles, along with an introduction, a filmography, and a selected bibliography, are offered.

The essays are varied and treat different aspects of Von Sternberg's career—method, style, Dietrich, legend, reality, etc.

5828 *Steve Martin: The Unauthorized Biography.* by Lenburg, Greg; and Skretvedt, Randy; and Lenburg,

Jeff. 139 p. paper illus. New York: St. Martin's Press, 1980.

Steve Martin's first major film, THE JERK (1979),was a large commercial success. More films from this unusual comedian will help to define his potential in the medium. At this point his audience is specialized and fickle.

5829   *Steve Martin—An Unauthorized Biography.* by Daly, Marsha. 212 p. paper illus. New York: Signet/NAL, 1980.

A section of photographs accompanies this unauthorized biography.

5830   *Steve McQueen: Star on Wheels.* by Nolan, William. 143 p. paper New York: Berkley (Medallion Books), 1972.

Equal time is given to McQueen's racing and professional experiences. The biographical portion is largely factual, with a sprinkling of statements from McQueen obtained during several interviews done originally for a racing magazine. This appears to be a spinoff of that material supplemented with additional information obtained from McQueen's friends and professional associates.

The films are mentioned ever so quickly, with only BULLITT (1968) and LE MANS (1971) getting extended coverage. No critical judgments are made about the films and the book closes with what already seems an ironic tribute to the lasting McQueen marriage to Neile Adams. There are no illustrations, filmography or index.

If the reader skips over the racing portions, he will have the equivalent of a magazine article on McQueen's life and career. While this biographical content is similar in style to that found in some higher priced volumes, it is too abbreviated to serve as anything but a temporary source. Until a fuller treatment of McQueen is written, this book is acceptable.

5831   *Steve McQueen: The Unauthorized Biography.* by McCoy, Malachy. 233 p. illus. Chicago: Henry Regnery, Co., 1974.

The latest entry in the series of unauthorized biographies published by Regnery—previous subjects include Cary Grant, Marlon Brando, James Cagney and John Wayne—is an improvement on the others. In addition to using public records for his information, the author has added possible interpretation,

criticism and evaluation of his material.

He is positive in his approach and often sees qualities in McQueen's performances that only a doting fan could discern. Using many details and quotations, he traces the star's life from an Indianapolis birth in 1930 to the making of THE GETAWAY in El Paso during the spring of 1972. The filmography of less than two dozen films confirms McQueen's fast rise to star status. A short index is added and there are a few well-reproduced stills in the center section. The combination of detailed research and professional knowledge has enabled McCoy to offer biography of substance. It is weakened only by the nonparticipation of the subject and the fondness of the author for same. Acceptable.

5832   *Stewart Granger: Sparks Fly Upward.* by Granger, Stewart. 416 p. illus. New York: G. P. Putnam's, 1981.

Granger could not tolerate or understand the Hollywood system. This autobiography devotes much space to a dissection of the studios and the Hollywood society of the late forties. He is frank about himself and tells numerous anecdotes about his co-workers. A lively story.

5833   STILL LIGHT Film Notes and Plates. by Beavers, Robert. 27 p. paper illus. Florence, Italy: Il Torchio, 1971.

Jonas Mekas supplies the introduction to this volume, which was written by a fellow experimental filmmaker.

5834   *Still Seeing Things.* by Brown, John Mason. 335 New York: McGraw-Hill, 1950.

John Mason Brown was a film critic for *The Saturday Review of Literature* from 1948 to 1950. His reviews are reprinted here. Other collections of his criticism can be found in *Seeing Things* (1946), *Seeing More Things* (1948), and *As They Appear* (1952).

5835   *Stills.* paper New York: Museum of Modern Art.

See Motion Picture Stills.

5836   *Stills From a Moving Picture.* by Glazier, Lyle. illus. paper Buffalo, N.Y.: Paunch, 1974.

5837   *The Stooge Chronicles.* by Forrester, Jeffrey. III p. illus. Chicago: Triumvirate, 1981.

More information about the Three Stooges.

5838 *Stop, Look, and Write! Effective Writing Through Pictures.* by Leavitt, Hart Day; and Sohn, David A. 223 p. paper illus. New York: Bantam Books, 1964.

This paperback provides exercises in visual literacy designed to teach the reader how to see life as a good photographer does. Using the work of noted photographers, the reader is urged to translate what he sees into words. The relationship between visuals and words is the base upon which all good screenplays rest.

5839 *Stop the Presses.* by Barris, Alex. 211 p. illus. New York: A. S. Barnes, 1976.

In this volume, which is subtitled "The Newspaperman in American Film," a survey of hundreds of selected sound films is offered. What they have in common is the presence of a character who is a reporter, journalist, columnist, editor or publisher. To trace the evolution of the newspaperman in film, the author chooses a few general headings—The Reporter as Crimebuster, as Scandal-Monger, as Crusader, as Human Being, as Villain, Overseas, etc. Under each heading he reviews the plots of appropriate films, adding some brief critical comment. Much of the book's space is devoted to stills from the films and rightly so. Since they have been well selected and clearly reproduced, they constitute the book's major attraction.

The text is another matter. Although the author is certainly well informed on sound films, he is a bit shaky in other areas of film history. In the introduction he says, "If there was any great (or even reasonably entertaining) silent newspaper movie, it fails to come to mind." Had he looked at the subject index of *The American Film Institute Catalog 1921-1930*, he would have found hundreds of titles listed under "Newspapers" or "Reporter" or "Columnist," etc. Serious readers may feel he missed a fine opportunity by not using his basic material to describe a film genre rather than examining a film character with limited dimensions. Finally, a major omission is a film title index. The performer index provided is of limited value to most researchers; a title index is preferable in many cases.

In summary the author has provided an entertainment rather than a serious study. His subject has wide appeal and his treatment of it is adequate.

5840 *Stories into Film.* edited by Kittredge, William; and Krautzer, Steven M. 286 p. paper New York: Harper and Row, 1979.

This anthology is an example of a different approach to film literature. It offers nine stories which were used as the basis for successful films: FREAKS (1932), IT HAPPENED ONE NIGHT (1934), STAGECOACH (1939), THE WILD ONE (1954), REAR WINDOW (1954), THE HUSTLER (1961), THE MAN WHO SHOT LIBERTY VALANCE (1962), BLOW-UP (1966), and 2001: A SPACE ODYSSEY (1968). A general introduction is provided along with head notes for each story, with the concern of both being the transformation of fiction into film. Further support of this theme is provided by two lengthy bibliographies and detailed cast-credit lists for the films. Film rental sources are also noted.

This volume can be used and enjoyed in a variety of ways. Most preferable, of course, would be a combination of viewing, reading, and discussing. Since the films are familiar to many, reading alone might also be pleasurable for some.

5841 STORM IN THE WEST. by Lewis, Sinclair; and Schary, Dore. 192 p. New York: Stein & Day, 1963.

A fictional screenplay-allegory with western stereotypes of good guys and bad guys used to represent personalities of World War II—Stalin, Hitler, etc. It was never filmed as it was considered too controversial.

5842 *Story and Discourse: Narrative Structure in Fiction and Film.* by Chatman, Seymour. 277 p. illus. Ithaca, N.Y.: Cornell University Press, 1978.

Narrative, according to Seymour Chatman, may be divided into story (the what) and discourse (the way). In this book he treats both film narrative and literary narrative as he develops an argument/theory which he presents diagramatically on the final page of his text. Among the topics discussed under "story" are events and existence; under "discourse", nonnarrated stories and covert versus overt narrators. An introduction and a conclusion frame the development of this theory-model-structure nicely.

The author acknowledges that "theory makes heavy reading and the theorist owes his audience a special obligation to summarize and take stock." Chatman apparently appreciates the difficulty a lay reader may have with this subject; he strives for a clarity of thought and expression in his text and avoids the temptation to speak only to the scholar. The result is a theory-book that, with some effort and patience on the part of the reader, is ultimately comprehensible, enlightening, and satisfying. Recommended.

5843   *The Story Behind* THE EXORCIST. by Travers, Peter; and Reiff, Stephanie. 246 p. illus. New York: Crown, 1974.

A behind-the-scenes account of the making of one of the most controversial films in recent years is given in this book. With the help of over 100 well-selected photographs, the authors trace the film's creation from the actual 1949 case upon which author William Peter Blatty based his novel to the 1974 Academy Award ceremonies which largely ignored the film in its prize-giving. Under the title, "Cast of Characters," short biographies of Blatty, director William Friedkin, and cast members introduce the text. The Roman Catholic ritual for exorcism is reprinted in the appendix along with the official credits for the film and an index.

Interviews, research, reviews of the film, quotations, the McCambridge-Dietz controversies—all these were used as material for this account, and, in general, are integrated well in describing the film's creation. Unfortunately the edge has been taken off much of this material by the wide publicity and coverage the film received and by the paperback account offered by author-producer Blatty, which has circulated quickly and widely. This account will satisfy anyone who is interested in THE EXORCIST (1973). It will probably be much appreciated in the years to come when the quality of the film can be assessed without the emotional bias that attended its first appearance. Acceptable.

5844   *Story Into Film.* by Ruchti, Ulrich; and Taylor, Sybil. New York: Dell, 1978.

5845   *Story Line: Recollections of a Hollywood Screenwriter.* by Coffee, Lenore. 212 p. illus. London: Cassell, 1973.

5846   THE STORY OF ADELE H. by Truffaut, Francois. 191 p. paper illus. New York: Grove. 1976

The script of the film is accompanied by 128 stills, a foreword by the director, and some notes.

5847   *The Story of Bing Crosby.* by Crosby, Edward (Ted). 239 p. illus. New York: World (Forum Books), 1946.

This is a revised, post-war edition of *Bing*, by Ted and Larry Crosby, which was first published in 1937. It contains an affectionate biography, a filmography, and a discography.

5848   *The Story of Bishop's Stortford's Cinemas.* by Smith, Joe G. 25 p. paper Bishop's Stortford, Hertfordshire, England: Joe G. Smith, 1978.

An example of historical film literature published at the local level.

5849   *The Story of Cuddles: My Life Under the Emperor Francis Joseph, Adolf Hitler, and the Warner Brothers.* by Sakall, S. Z. 231 p. illus. London: Cassell, 1954.

5850   *The Story of Films.* by Vereker, Barbara. 128 p. illus. London: Hutchinson, 1961.

The author is a film critic who discusses filmmaking, studio production, filmmakers, criticism, economics, etc., in a volume designed for the young reader.

5851   *The Story of Lassie.* by Weatherway, Rudd B.; and Rothwell, John H. 126 p. illus. New York: Duell, Sloan and Pearce, 1950.

Lots of illustrations accompany this story of how Lassie was found and trained to become a famous animal performer in films. The television series came much later.

5852   *The Story of the Cinema.* by Du Feu, Helen. 96 p. illus. London: Wayland, 1974.

This survey, a title in the *Eyewitness* series, was designed for younger readers. It contains text, illustrations, a bibliography, and anindex.

5853   *The Story of the Cinema.* by Shipman, David. 800 p. Sevenoaks, England: Hodder and Stoughton, 1980.

5854   *The Story of the Danish Film.* by Neergaard, Ebbe. 119 p. paper illus. Copenhagen: Danish Institute, 1963.

A history of the Danish film, this volume covers the period from 1896 to 1962. Personality description, industry statistics, and critical analyses of films are given. A short index along with a listing of authors whose literary works were adapted for Danish films appear. An interesting book that will have limited appeal because of its unfamiliar subject material.

5855 *The Story of the Films.* by Kennedy, Joseph P. 377 p. illus. New York: A. W. Shaw Co., 1928.

In the late twenties some 14 leaders of the film industry spoke to students at the Harvard Business School. Appearing were William Fox, Jack Warner, Will Hays, Adolph Zukor, Marcus Loew, etc. Each presented one aspect of the industry at that time. This is the edited version of those presentations, introduced by Joseph Kennedy, Sr.

5856 *The Story of the Hollywood Film Strike in Cartoons.* by Price, Gene; and Kistner, Jack. paper illus. Hollywood: Local 644, 1945.

A rare, mimeographed collection of cartoons and caricatures pertinent to the film strike of 1945. Price has supplied the visuals, which make up most of the content of this oversized volume.

5857 *The Story of the Making of* BEN HUR. 36 p. illus. New York: Random House, 1959.

Issued as a program to accompany showing of BEN HUR (1959), this volume has several interesting sections. They include the history of the book, actor biographies, a profile on William Wyler, the actual production sets, wardrobe, music, photography and credits. In addition, the book is filled with pictures from the film and candids of the filming. The information here is factual and not critical since it came from the MGM publicity mills. Discounting prejudiced selectivity, the book is an acceptable sample of a genre of film literature.

5858 *The Story of the Men in* ALL THE PRESIDENT'S MEN. by Dexter, Paul L. 170 p. paper New York: Award Books, 1976.

A collective biography, this original paperback offers Robert Redford, Dustin Hoffman, Jason Robards, and Martin Balsam as subjects. To date, book material on these four actors is relatively scarce; even though this coverage is superficial, it is wel-

come at this point.

5859 *The Story of* THE MISFITS. by Goode, James. 331 p. illus. Indianapolis, Ind.: Bobbs-Merrill Co., 1963.

This is an account of the making of THE MISFITS (1963), a film that is famous for a variety of reasons, most of them depressing. Author Goode recounts in a diary fashion certain external descriptions of the events concerned with the production. It is all rather surface coverage and adds little to what is already film lore.

The author seems fascinated with names and the book resembles a testimonial to all the persons involved in the film, from grip to script girl. There is little analysis given as the author concentrates on the factual and the quotable. Is it possible the author had to have someone's stamp of approval in order to gain access to the filming? The material suggests such a condition. The book is not indexed and the picture section consists of candid shots taken during the shooting.

5860 *The Story of* TOMMY. by Barnes, Richard; and Townsend, Peter. 129p. illus. Tuickenham, England: Eel Pie, 1977.

The story of TOMMY (1977) retold with many full-color illustrations.

5861 *The Story of Walt Disney.* by Miller, Diane Disney; and Martin, Pete. 247 p. illus. New York: Henry Holt & Co., 1956.

Told by his daughter, this biography of Disney is earlier and official as compared with Schickel's recent unflattering and unapproved portrait, *The Disney Version.* It is continually disconcerting to read "father" instead of "Disney" or "Walt" for more than 200 pages. Another disadvantage is the author's inability to be anything but positive. Other offspring-biographers have achieved objectivity in writing about their parents (John Lahr, Marguerite Taylor, etc.) but no such quality is evident here. The factual data given has value as historical documentation of the Disney Empire and how it was formed. There are a few poorly chosen and poorly reproduced photographs but there is no index. This is a rather ordinary biography that needs the charm or creativity found in some of Disney's films. Its greatest value is as a contrast to be read along with the Schickel book.

5862 *Story Telling and Mythmaking: Images from Film and Literature.* by McConnell, Frank. 303 p. illus. New York: Oxford University Press, 1979.

The author sees narrative literature and films as expressions of humanity's self-definition. He examines both forms as they exist in four categories: epic, romance, melodrama and satire. Similar heroes in both forms are identified and discussed: *Don Quixote,*—The GODFATHER, *The Metamorphosis,* — TAXI DRIVER (1976), *Gulliver's Travels,*—KING KONG (1933), etc.

The discussion is pedantic and, as might be expected, the many references to literature demand considerable reader background. Some of McConnell's thoughts and conclusions seem farfetched, but his serious treatment of a unique topic deserves admiration.

5863 *Straight Shooting.* by Stack, Robert. 292 p. illus. New York: Macmillan, 1980.

Robert Stack is always the gentleman and retains his public image throughout this autobiography. Although his life has been crammed with both incidents and colorful personalities, he presents his memoirs in a matter-of-fact, low-key fashion—no scandal, no excitement—just positive, admiring portraits and anecdotes of the Hollywood people he grew up with. It's hard to quarrel with such a friendly book, but it's also interesting to think about the book Stack might have written if he were like Shelley Winters.

5864 *The Strange Case of Alfred Hitchcock, or, The Plain Man's Hitchcock.* by Durgnat, Raymond. 419 p. illus. Cambridge, Mass.: MIT Press, 1975.

Is Hitchcock the master of the aesthetic touch? Is he a dark Roman Catholic moralist? Or is he an entertainer whose work occasionally approaches significant art? Durgnat treats all of these possibilities with an emphasis on the "entertainer" approach to Hitchcock's films. A short biographical chapter which identifies 13 career phases introduces this study of Hitchcock's films. After discussing the moral codes and patterns which pervade Hitchcock's work, the films are discussed individually. This portion of the text is put forth as the "evidence" for Durgnat's critical observations. Although the films are presented in a vertical-chronological arrangement, much cross-referencing with regard to theme, genre, action, character, etc., is employed. Thus the relationship of a specific film to certain films of other directors and to the Hitchcock corpus is effectively established. A selection of stills appears in the center section; a bibliography, a filmography arranged alphabetically by title, and a solid index complete the book.

The alternate title is puzzling since Durgnat does not write for the plain man—his work has always demanded background, concentration and sophistication in film matters. Many of the ideas presented here seem original products of an intellectual critic who is exploring familiar territory with an open mind. What Durgnat deduces from his unique examination of the evidence cannot help but fascinate and reward many readers. Recommended.

5865 *Stranger and Friend: The Way of an Anthropologist.* by Powdermaker, Hortense. 315 p. New York: W. W. Norton, 1967.

The anthropologist/author is best known for her 1950 study of the Hollywood power structure, *Hollywood, the Dream Factory.* In this volume she elaborates on some of her Hollywood experiences.

5866 *Straub.* by Roud, Richard. 176 p. paper illus. New York: Viking, 1972.

At 38, Jean-Marie Straub had made five films: MACHORKA-MUFF (1963), NOT RECONCILED (1965), CHRONICLE OF ANNA MAGDELANA BACH (1968), THE BRIDEGROOM, THE ACTRESS, AND THE PIMP (1968), and OTHON (1969). Although he is French, he has chosen to work in Germany and Italy for political reasons. Known as an underground revolutionary, he uses an almost stationary camera and non-narrative structures in his films.

This volume analyzes each of his films critically, contains quotes from interviews, and includes the entire script of NOT RECONCILED. A filmography appears at the book's end and there are sufficient illustrations to suggest the filmmaker's style.

This volume, as Roud states, is a bit premature. It is a fine gesture to introduce new artists to the public but those selected for this honor should perhaps not be as obscure as Straub. Far more deserving are other filmmakers whose work is already proven: Saul Bass, Frederick Wiseman, the Maysles Brothers, etc. The quarrel here is with the subject selection and not with treatment. In all fairness, the book is well done and will interest young filmmakers.

5867 *A Streak of Luck: The Life and Legend of Thomas Alva Edison.* by Conot, Robert. 500 p. illus. New York: Seaview, 1979.

A well-written biography of Thomas Alva Edison, this book is based in part on material in the Edison Archives previously unavailable. The exhausting research of this information enabled Conot to put forth a very warts-and-all portrait of the eccentric inventor——a visionary, a wheeler-dealer, an inept engineer, and a showoff——among other things.

Edison was ambitious; he held over 1000 patents for inventions, but he was greedy, egotistical, and often difficult. This is probably the best biography of Edison written to date. Recommended.

5868 *The Street Where I Live.* by Lerner, Alan Jay. 333 p. illus. New York: W. W. Norton, 1978.

For many people this will be a very special book—one to be treasured and shared with others who appreciate the American musical theatre. In a way it is a collective biography of three Lerner and Loewe musicals, "My Fair Lady" (play), GIGI (film) and "Camelot" (play). How the creative talents of dedicated professionals are merged into a successful production is conveyed by anecdotes, description, opinion, and actual fact. All three musicals were eventually seen on the screen, but GIGI (1958) is the only motion picture discussed here. Three familiar screen actors—Rex Harrison, Julie Andrews and Richard Burton—did appear on the Broadway stage in the other two plays.

These famous musicals will also be recalled by reading the entire Lerner lyrics which appear in the final pages. The book is illustrated and an index is provided.

In this volume Alan Jay Lerner has shared his experiences in creating three classic American musicals. The affection with which they are held by millions of people will be reinforced by his warm personal memoir. Recommended.

5869 *Streisand.* by Black, Jonathan. 187 p. paper illus. New York: Leisure Books, 1975.

This entertaining biography was unauthorized and thus had to depend mostly on factual matters of record. The blending of this public material with a connecting narrative is done with an intelligence and taste rarely found in original paperback volumes.

Streisand's life is recalled from her birth in 1942 to her preparation for the film, A STAR IS BORN, in 1975. In addition to her films, attention is given to her recordings and her television appearances. A few illustrations appear in a center section. No index is provided.

Despite certain fan magazine elements such as recreated conversations, testimonials from Streisand Club Members, etc., the book presents a clear portrait of a determined, ambitious, talented female who achieved superstardom "her way." Acceptable.

5870 *see* 5869

5871 *Streisand: The Woman and the Legend.* by Spada, James; and Nickens, Christopher. 250 p. illus. New York: Doubleday, 1981.

An admiring but unauthorized biography that relates Streisand's success on stage, in films and on records. Based on interviews, the volume is heavily illustrated. Nickens is editor of *Barbra*, a quarterly fan magazine devoted to the superstar.

5872 *Stroheim.* by Finler, Joel W. 144 p. illus. Berkeley, Calif.: University of California Press, 1968.

Stroheim's association with films such as INTOLERANCE (1916), GREED (1923), LA GRANDE ILLUSION (1937) and SUNSET BOULEVARD (1950) assure his position in cinema history. This book explores his directorial style, his legendary extravagances, the decadence of his films, and the similarities between them. The major portion is devoted to a detailed analysis of his masterpiece, GREED. Based on existing stills of the excised material, on Stroheim's script, and on the novel, *McTeague*, a comparison between the original 24-reel version and the final 10-reel version is attempted.

The other films are given some attention, but his career as an actor is largely overlooked. A filmography and a short bibliography are included. An essential book for the serious cinema student and fascinating reading for the general audience. Certainly, the volume will generate a reader interest in viewing or re-viewing GREED.

5873 *Stroheim: A Pictorial Record of His Nine Films.* by Weinberg, Herman G. 259 p. paper illus. New York: Dover, 1975.

In addition to books on Ernst Lubitsch and Josef von Sternberg, Herman Weinberg is also known for his complete reconstruction via stills of two mutilated von Stroheim films, GREED (1923) and WEDDING MARCH. In this volume he has provided a pictorial summary of the nine films that von Stroheim directed, including these two. Each film is introduced by a short essay which includes a synopsis, cast, production credits, background notes and other information. Full-page reproductions of stills from the films are arranged in narrative order and accompanied by brief captions; at times the original subtitles are used.

Except in very few instances, the reproduction of the more than 200 visuals is remarkably clear and sharp. Some original publicity material—posters, programs, etc.—is also shown. A final section indicates some of von Stroheim's unrealized projects. All elements blend here: the careful production and, most of all, the marvelous stills. This is a handsome volume. Highly recommended.

5874   *The Strongman.* by Bonomo, Joe. 352 p. paper illus. New York: Bonomo Studios, 1968.

The career of a Hollywood stuntman who was also a physical culture devotee is the subject of this unusual pictorial autobiography. Along with a naive, simple narrative, the book has a large number of illustrations—750 of them according to the author—that provide the major attraction.

Bonomo's film career was at its height in the twenties and the illustrations are primarily from this era. The emphasis naturally is on action and stunt work. The title cards which introduce each chapter will delight mature readers. This is a book to be read for entertainment—as autobiography it suffers from a text which is Horatio Alger and Narcissus in equal parts. Recommended as recreational reading.

5875   *Structural Film Anthology.* by Gidal, Peter. 140 p. paper London: British Film Institute; (Zoetrope in U. S.), 1976.

In the introductory chapter, Peter Gidal states, "Structural/materialist films are at once object and procedure. Some are clearly, blatantly of a whole, others work as obvious fragments, non-beginning-non-end films. Both rely on an aesthetic that tries to create didactic works." The rest of that chapter puts forth, in rather complex technical language, the theory and definition of structural/materialist film. Following this there is a section on abstract film and then some twenty films/filmmakers receive individual attention from a diversity of authors in the form of notes, interviews, letters, essays, etc.

This is a difficult volume for the average person to

handle or appreciate since its requirements for comprehension are so great. The film theorist or the academician looking for fresh material will probably respond to some of it. Acceptable.

5876   *The Structure of American Industry.* by Adams, Walter. 608 p. illus. New York: Macmillan, 1961.

This is the third edition of a volume that contains case studies and a bibliography pertinent, at times, to the motion picture industry.

5877   *The Structure of John Ford's* STAGECOACH. by Warfield, Nancy. 30 p. paper illus. New York: Little Film Gazette, 1974.

A collection of materials about John Ford and his film, STAGECOACH (1939), appears in this volume. They include a short essay by the author, several glossy stills from the film mounted by hand, an article by Dudley Nichols, a comparison of the short story source, "Stage to Lordsburg," with the film, and some explanatory notes. A lengthy bibliography for John Ford, mostly taken by permission from work done by Gillian Hartnoll and Mel Schuster, completes the book. All of this presents rather specialized material.

5878   *Student Film Festivals/Awards.* by Elsas, Diana; and Kelso, Lulu. 11 p. paper Washington, D.C.: American Film Institute, 1977.

This title in the *Factfile* series lists 34 festival and awards programs that are either intended for students or have a student category. Full bibliographic information is given for each, and a list of publications/sources that might be helpful is added.

5879   *Students Make Motion Pictures.* by Booker, Floyde E.; and Herrington, Eugene H. Washington, D.C.: American Council on Education, 1941.

A report on student filmmaking in the Denver schools.

5880   *Studies in Documentary.* by Lovell, Alan; and Hiller, Jim. 176 p. paper illus. New York: Viking, 1972.

The title of this book may be adequate but it is also misleading. The names of John Grierson and Humphrey Jennings should be in the title, or at least in the subtitle, since the two major essays are devoted to these two personalities, and they dominate the book. Such associates of Grierson as Edgar Anstey, Alberto Cavalcanti, Sir Arthur Elton, Stuart Legg, Paul Rotha, Henry Watt and Basil Wright are given short biographical sketches.

Completing the book is a third essay called "Free Cinema" —a name given to six programs of documentary film given between 1956-59 at the National Film Theatre. It included classic films by directors such as Lindsay Anderson, Tony Richardson, Karel Reisz, Norman McClaren, Georges Franju, Roman Polanski, and others.

This is a critical history of the British documentary film with emphasis on two of its greatest artists. Partial filmographies for Jennings and Grierson are included, as are credits for the films in the Free Cinema program. The accompanying visuals are too dark and lack proper contrast values. This is specialized material that will please a small American audience. Recommended.

5881 *Studies in the Arab Theater and Cinema.* by Landau, Jacob M. 290 p. illus. Philadelphia: University of Pennsylvania Press, 1958.

The major portion of this book is devoted to Arab theatre. The 50 pages dealing with the Arab cinema cover such areas as history, development, production, acting, and themes. A very specialized book noted here for scholars and historians.

5882 *The Studio.* by Dunne, John Gregory. 255 p. New York: Farrar, Straus & Giroux, 1968.

A penetrating, fish-eye look at a major studio in a period of transition is the topic of this book. The author was given entry into a rather closed organization, the 20th-Century-Fox Studios, for one year. His goal was to find "something of the state of the mind called Hollywood." The last of the big budget movies—(HELLO, DOLLY (1969); DR. DOLITTLE (1967), and STAR (1968), for example)—were the concerns of the studio during this period. The volume reads in cinema-verite style and is populated with real people—no pseudonyms are used.

Most editorial comment is made within the context of the reporting. The author's objectivity is suspect throughout. Most revealing at times, the book is without sentiment and approaches its title subject as it would a dinosaur living in 1967. The volume is good reporting and fascinating reading. While not a basic book, it has much to recommend it.

5883 *Study Extract Catalogue.* compiled by British Film Institute. paper London: British Film Institute, 1969.

A catalog that lists all extracts available from the BFI Distribution Library. Credits, running times, plot summaries, etc., are given. A supplement to the above catalog was published in 1971. This is a service that is hard to find in the United States (with the possible exception of Teaching Film Custodians, located now at Indiana University Audiovisual Center). It makes short excerpts from films available for study, e.g., BRIEF ENCOUNTER, 8 min., David Lean; THE MAGNIFICENT AMBERSONS, 12 min., Orson Welles; VIRIDIANA, 20 min., Luis Bunuel; WILD STRAWBERRIES, 18 min., Ingmar Bergman.

5884 *Study Guide for* AMERICA AT THE MOVIES. edited by Cinema Five. 8 p. paper New York: Cinema five, 1976.

This study guide for the film AMERICA AT THE MOVIES (1976) contains introductory notes for the user, suggested activities for before and after the showing of the film, a glossary, bibliographies for each of the five sections of the film, and some background information.

5885 *The Study of Film as an Art Form in the American Secondary Schools.* by Selby, Stuart Alan. 262 p. New York: Arno Press, 1978.

Written in 1963 at Columbia University's Teachers College in partial fulfillment of the doctoral program, this study is a forerunner in film education research, concentrating on instruction techniques as well as curriculum content in the secondary school. Through an historical survey, the author examines the role of film education from its early conception in the 1930s to present day by investigating its subservient relationship to English/Literature curricular units. He also traces the development and transition of objectives within the secondary film instruction curriculum. This title is included in the *Dissertations on Film* series.

5886 *A Study of the German Film 1915-1919.* by Prels, Max Kino. 80 p. illus. New York: Gordon Press, 1976 (1919).

Orignally published in 1919 by Biclefeld, V. Hagen and Klasing, Germany.

5887   *A Study of the Non-Linearity Variable in Filmic Presentation.* by Allen, William H.; and Cooney, Stuart M. 157 p. paper illus. Los Angeles: UCLA Research Division Department of Cinema, 1963.

William Allen was one of the most active researchers in the audiovisual field during the period that followed World War II. This study is typical of the many investigations he made in the film medium.

5888   *A Study of Verbal Accompaniments to Educational Motion Pictures.* by Westfall, Leon H. 68 p. paper New York: AMS Press, 1972 (1934).

This is a reprint of the author's thesis, which appeared originally as number 617 in the series *Contributions to Education,* published in 1934 by Teachers College of Columbia University. A bibliography is included.

5889   *A Study to Determine the Relative Effectiveness of Filmed Demonstrations: in Teacher Education For a New High School Mathematics Curriculum.* by Van Horn, Charles. 55 p. paper Urbana, Ill.: University of Illinois, 1961.

A report on a study of the use of film in education which is typical of many investigations conducted at American universities during the sixties.

5890   *Studying Visual Communication.* by Worth, Sol. 188 p. Philadelphia: University of Pennsylvania Press, 1981.

Eight essays which are concerned with the acceptance of film as a communication. Worth was a professor of communications and his writing deals with theories, semiotics, aesthetics and other concerns of academe.

5891   *Stunt: The Story of the Great Movie Stunt Men.* by Baxter, John. 320 p. illus. New York: Doubleday, 1974.

Using a combination of history, research and interviews, John Baxter has provided a solid overview of professional stunting in films. He begins with the early amateurs, who were either drunks or reckless opportunists in need of money. Stunting became a profession (or, an art) in the twenties and has continually been refined to the present day. Some of the famous names associated with this dangerous occupation are Tom Mix, Douglas Fairbanks, the Keystone Cops, Pearl White, Harold Lloyd, and Harry Houdini. Interviews and quotations from William Duncan, Edgie Polo, Richard Talmadge, Richard Grace, Yakima Canutt and others are integrated into the text. Types of stunts are described, as are genres of films requiring this work—African, aircraft, magic, nightmare, epic, swashbucklers, auto driving, etc. Final chapters look at the professional stuntman in films today.

Illustrations are selected primarily to explain and expand the text. Reproduction of them is adequate. Some source notes, a few bibliographic comments, and an index complete the book. This specialized study is acceptable for all readers. See also *Stunting in the Cinema* and *Locklear: The Man Who Walked on Wings.*

5892   *Stunting in the Cinema.* by Wise, Arthur; and Ware, Derek. 248 p. illus. New York: St. Martin's Press, 1973.

Stunting is defined here as a spectacular visual act that "involves a certain danger to the performer which he can only overcome by skill." In this survey some history is interwoven with accounts of various stunts and the personalities, animals, and vehicles involved. The stuntman is a professional whose approach to his work is meticulously planned and studied. His work, rewards, image, and satisfactions are noted. Although 38 photographs and ten line illustrations are provided, the book would be enhanced by more. There is a lengthy bibliography and many chapter notes are provided. The index is also very detailed.

In summary this is a well-written and researched presentation of a specialized element of filmmaking. Not only have the authors drawn on their own wide experience, but also they have given support to the text by many examples found in the literature. Their affection and respect for stunting and the care they have exercised in making their presentation results in a most unusual book. Recommended.

5893   *Stuntman: The Autobiography of Yakima Canutt.* by Canutt, Yakima; and Drake, Oliver. 252 p. illus. New York: Walker and Company, 1979.

The author, now in his eighties, has had a long career in Hollywood as an actor, director, and stuntman. Beginning with silent films in the early twenties, Canutt was working as recently as 1976, in EQUUS. He introduces his story with one of his most impressive achievements—the chariot race in BEN

HUR (1959). Then, following a chronological structure, he recalls many of the films, actors, and stunts that were part of his professional life. Illustrations, a filmography, and an index accompany the text.

Canutt is a gracious man throughout his memoirs, being much more lavish with his compliments than with his complaints. He recalls most of the celebrities with whom he worked as brave, cooperative, macho men. If he gives the reader too much detail about the various stunts, it can be blamed on his pride in a unique profession. Unfortunately, unless the reader can recall with accuracy the individual stunts in each film, the many descriptions become rather academic and somewhat repetitious.

This is a pleasant book that lacks the excitement one might expect from a lifetime of stunting. Perhaps the ideal format for Canutt's life is a compilation film with his voice-over narration. Until such a film appears, this volume will please most readers.

5894 *Style In Motion.* by White, Nancy; and Esten, John. illus. New York: Crown, 1979.

A collection of 160 photographs by Munkacsi, the noted photographer for *Harper's Bazaar*, is presented in this oversized volume. The period covered is 1920-1950 and some film personalities appear as subjects.

5895 *Styles of Radical Will.* by Sontag, Susan. 274 p. New York: Farrar, Straus & Giroux, 1969.

This volume of critical writings covers the broad field of arts. In it are Sontag's observations on Godard, on Bergman's PERSONA (1966) and the theatre's nature as opposed to that of the film.

5896 *Subject Collections (a Partial Film Reference).* edited by Ash, Lee; and Lorenz, Denis. New York: Bowker, 1967.

This is a guide to special book collections found in university, college, public and special libraries in the United States and Canada. Those libraries which have special film literature collections are listed under the subject heading "Moving Pictures."

5897 *Subject Directory of Special Libraries and Information Centers, Vol. 2.* edited by Young, Margaret; and Young, C. Harold; and Kruzas, Anthony T. 194 p. Detroit: Gale Research Co., 1977.

The fourth edition of the *Subject Directory of Special Libraries* consists of five volumes which cover special libraries, research libraries, information centers, archives and data centers maintained by government agencies, business, industry, newspapers, educational institutions, nonprofit organizations and societies. This particular volume is the second of the group and is titled *Education and Information Science Libraries*; it includes audiovisual, picture, publishing, rare book and recreational libraries.

Each type of library is treated separately in two chapters—the first for those institutions found in the United States, the second for Canadian libraries. A typical entry offers name, classification of library, address, phone number, director's name, staff size, subject coverage, number and type of holdings, services, and remarks. Other pertinent information appears in certain selected entries.

Opening sections display the questionnaire from which the entry information was obtained along with an explanation of the many abbreviations used throughout. Separate alternate name indexes for the United States and Canada conclude the volume.

A selection of the total number of film libraries to be found in North America appears under the audiovisual heading. Although the listing is a partial one, the user will discover both general and specific information that cannot be found elsewhere. Acceptable.

5898 *Subsidiary Rights and Residuals.* edited by Taubman, Joseph. 199 p. paper New York: Federal Legal Publications, 1968.

The economic return on the continued use of a creative work is the topic considered here. It is a collection of articles based on a forum held in 1965 on the problem of residuals. Both current and past practices of payment in most mass media are detailed here. Very specialized but should be noted by anyone concerned with the economics of films and filmmaking.

5899 *Success Tips from Young Celebrities.* by Reed, Dena. 159 p. illus. New York: Grosset & Dunlap, 1967.

The newer stars of the sixties—Patty Duke, George Maharis, Bobby Darin, etc.—tell how to succeed in show business. Some biographical information is included.

5900 *Successful Film Writing.* by Margrave, Seton. 216 p. illus. London: Methuen, 1936.

Film writing as illustrated by THE GHOST GOES WEST (1936). Contains: "Sir Tristram Goes West," a short story by Eric Keown; a first treatment of the story; and the final scenario for THE GHOST GOES WEST.

5901   *Sudan Sand.* by Treatt, S. C. 251 p. illus. London: Harrad, 1930.

An early account of filming the Baggara Arabs.

5902   THE SUGARLAND EXPRESS—*Spielberg; Barwood and Robbins; Zsigmond.* by Reed, Rochelle. 44 p. paper illus. Washington, D.C.: American Film Institute, 1974.

This issue of the *Dialogue on Film* series is concernedwith the making of THE SUGARLAND EXPRESS (1974). On November 14, 1973, director Steven Spielberg was interviewed. Writers Hal Barwood and Matthew Robbins appeared on February 13, 1974. The interview with Vilmos Zsigmond was held on March 2, 1974. This final interview is excerpted to include only those comments pertinent to THE SUGARLAND EXPRESS.

5903   *Sun and Shadow.* by Aumont, Jean Pierre. 315 p. illus. New York: W. W. Norton, 1977.

To American audiences Jean Pierre Aumont has always been the French actor who not only possessed continental poise and charm but who could play a variety of roles with competence. Never an exciting performer, he was heroically/romantically believable in the many screen roles he portrayed. This autobiography indicates a far greater range and depth to the man than his screen image might suggest. He is a prolific writer, a stage actor of considerable skill and, apparently, a workaholic who is dedicated to practicing, sharpening and perfecting his skills and talents.

He traces his life from early Paris stage appearances in the thirties to Broadway, Hollywood, World War II, and a final international career. His marriages to Maria Montez and Marisa Pavan are included, as are many personal and professional encounters with famous names. A center section of illustrations, a list of his plays and films and an index complete the volume.

If the reader accepts the adage that "less is more," he will appreciate Aumont's low-key recital of a remarkable life filled with incident and personalities. The longevity of his acting career is probably due to his ability to make difficult roles seem so easy to perform. That same skill can be found in his writing,

which is relaxed, effortless and quite charming. In reality it is Aumont diligently perfecting one of his considerable talents once again. Recommended.

5904   SUNDAY BLOODY SUNDAY. by Gilliatt, Penelope. 135 p. New York: Viking, 1972.

Script of the 1971 film directed by John Schlesinger. Contains cast and production credits.

5905   SUNDAY LARK. by Schreivogel, Paul. 20 p. paper illus. Dayton, Ohio: Pflaum, 1970.

A study guide for the 1964 film directed by Sanford Semel.

5906   *Sunday Night at the Movies.* by Jones, G. William. 126 p. paper illus. Richmond, Va.: John Knox Press, 1967.

One of the purposes of this paperback is to help advance film literacy in church audiences. Although its religious origin is obvious throughout, the book has much general material that can be transferred to nonreligious situations. In addition to film aesthetics, other topics discussed are film selection, physical conditions for film showings, discussion techniques, etc. A bibliography, a film list, and some rental sources complete the book, which will probably be most helpful in setting up discussion programs. Other users may also findmuch of value here if they are willing to engage in a process of selection and transfer.

5907   *The Sunday Times Guide to Movies on Television.* by Allan, Angela; and Allan, Elkan. 398 p. London: Times Newspapers Ltd., 1973.

The British equivalent to the Scheuer and Maltin books, this volume employs more wit in its reviews than either of its American counterparts. For example, the ratings are listed as follows: Cancel all other engagements; Catch it if you can; If you've nothing better to do; Find something better to do; Don't waste your time; Ring up and complain.

The annotations are also quite entertaining. For example, the one on MEET ME IN ST. LOUIS reads: "Judy Garland was delightful under the spell of Vincente Minnelli in 1946 (two years before they had Liza) as one of a well-to-do St. Louis family at the time of the World's Fair there. Pa was Leon Ames, Ma was Mary Astor, and Tom Drake was 'The Boy Next Door,' Other songs include: 'The Trolley

Song,' and 'Have Yourself a Merry Little Christmas.'" Color.

An alternate title index is also provided. It should be noted that this volume was not easily available in England, and probably has to be ordered from the publisher.

5908 SUNRISE AT CAMPOBELLO. 24 p. paper illus. New York: David March, 1960.

Other than a few articles about the backgrounds and the writing of the play by Dore Schary, the content of this souvenir book consists of the usual items: major cast acknowledgement to Ralph Bellamy and Greer Garson, major production credits to producer-writer Dore Schary and director Vincent Donehue, and shorter recognition to the supporting players. The production, story, and some highlights of the 1960 film are also presented.

5909 *Sunshine and Shadow.* by Pickford, Mary. 382 p. illus. Garden City, N.Y.: Doubleday, 1955.

In some ways this autobiography is exactly what a reader would expect from America's Sweetheart, but with a few pleasant surprises. There is some attempt at both personal and professional evaluation and sufficient attention is given to her films. The book has many, many fine illustrations which are correlated nicely with the book, being placed at strategic places rather than lumped together in one grouping. An introduction by Cecil B. DeMille is another asset.

While Miss Pickford emerges as a super-heroine, her account here is realistic, fast-moving, and told with an emotion that is never excessive. The cynical reader may pick this book up expecting to scoff or to choke on sweetness but will remain to admire the businesslike approach to an autobiography. This is one of the better life stories of Hollywood.

5910 *Super 8: The Modest Medium.* by Gunter, Jonathan F. 93 p. paper illus. New York: Unipub, 1976.

Commissioned by UNESCO, this short volume has as its goal a review of the 8mm film medium. It includes recent developments as it notes the transformation of the medium from an amateur's device into a professional tool that seems admirably suited for television use.

Three chapters make up the body of the monograph: 8mm Film and Its Context; The Range of 8mm Hardware; and 8mm in Relation to Other Media. A bibliography and an index of technical terms are added. The volume contains some illustrations.

In his clearly stated observations and carefully selected information, the author makes a strong case for the intelligent use of this medium. Its potential is far greater than currently recognized, and this volume suggests ways to increase its acceptance as a major communication tool. This excellent discussion has pertinence for a large, diverse audience. Recommended.

5911 *The Super 8 Book.* by Lipton, Lenny. 308 p. paper illus. San Francisco: Straight Arrow, 1975.

In his earlier book, *Independent Filmmaking*, Lenny Lipton treated several film gauges; here his attention is given exclusively to super 8. He divides his text into seven major headings; Format, Cameras, Sound, Processing and Striping, Editing, Prints, and Projection. Under each there are subheadings which structure the volume as both a text and a reference work. Retrieval of specific information is made easier by the addition of a detailed index, a directory of products andservices, and a list of periodicals. It is also facilitated by marking each page edge with the appropriate heading; thus the section on sound, for example, can be found quickly by simply flipping the book's edge with the thumb.

Correlated with the main text are 200 drawings, illustrations, tables and charts. They are most helpful in explaining or expanding certain complex operations which occur in super 8 filmmaking.

Lipton's knowledge of his subject has been combined with his skill at communication to create a definitive book for the amateur or independent filmmaker. It has depth, clarity, and detail; best of all, it is both practical and easy to use. Highly recommended.

5912 *Super 8 Filmmaking from Scratch.* by McClain, Bebe Ferrell. 226 p. paper illus. Englewood Cliffs, N.J.: Prentice-Hall, 1978.

An organized approach to super 8mm filmmaking is offered in this well-designed volume. Using a step-by-step approach, each of the essential production procedures——planning, shooting, editing——are covered in depth. In addition there is information about film types, equipment, sound, spontaneous filmmaking, effects, labs, etc. An equipment list and an index complete the volume, which is generously illustrated.

The essential information that theaspiring filmmaker needs to know in order to begin super 8 filmmaking is given in an attractive, carefully structured presentation. An enormous amount of detailed instruction and practical advice is contained within its pages. Recommended.

5913   *The Super 8 Filmmmaker's Handbook.* by Matzkin, Myron A. 320 p. illus. New York: Amphoto, 1976.

In this handbook, which has over 200 illustrations and diagrams, Matzkin offers a comprehensive survey of super 8 filmmaking. All the basics are covered in addition to those variations that only the experienced professional can offer. As usual, the author is clear, practical, and thorough in the material he has chosen to present. Much of what appears here can be applied to other film gauges.

5914   *Super 8mm Movie Making Simplified.* by Matzkin, Myron A. 100 p. illus. Englewood Cliffs, N.J.: Prentice-Hall, 1975.

An oversized volume in the *Modern Photo Guide* series, this book deals with equipment, fundamentals, lighting, special effects, editing, titling, projection, sound, etc. Matzkin is a professional filmmaker—teacher and this guide is up to his usual high standard. Four pages of full-color illustrations are added.

5915   *Super Films.* by Parlato, Salvator J., Jr. 354 p. illus. Metuchen, N.J.: Scarecrow, 1976.

The attempt here was to produce a filmography of live and animated short educational films that had been awarded one or more festival prizes. Covering the period from 1935 to 1975 films are arranged alphabetically by title. In addition to the visual bibliographic data, each entry offers a descriptive annotation derived from producer-supplied information. Access to the films is by a topical index and a general subject index. Festivals are listed along with a company-title index and a list of film company addresses.

The structure employed here is similar to Rehrauer's earlier volume, *The Short Film*, except that the methodology used for selection in that volume may be more justifiable than a simple listing of easily obtained film titles. Parlato's festival roster is partial, the film data given is often contradictory with that found elsewhere, and the annotations reflect producer vagaries. A good idea that may have been rushed into print without proper thought and preparation seems to describe this volume.

5916   *The Super Secs.* by Marchak, Alice; and Hunter, Linda. 253 p. Los Angeles: Charles, 1975.

What its like to be a secretary to a super star is described in this lightweight book written by two such employees. Marchak has been Marlon Brando's secretary for about two decades, while Hunter works for Blake Edwards and Julie Andrews. For this book they recount their experiences with almost total recall—Brando's Oscar refusal, the Andrews-Edwards wedding, world travel, etc. The result is not as dull as one might predict—in fact, the employer-employee relationships present a different side of show business to the public.

5917   *Super Stars.* by Walker, Alexander. 64 p. paper illus. Oxford, England: Phaidon; New York: Dutton, 1978.

A giant poster book featuring film stars from 1910 to 1977, selected and introduced by Alexander Walker.

5918   *Super Stars of the '70s.* by Castell, David. 95 p. paper illus. London: Barnden Castell Williams, 1975.

After an opening discussion of the term "superstar," the author reviews film actors prominent during the first half of this decade by assigning them into categories. First Choice: Eastman, McQueen, Redford, Newman, Hackman, Caan, et al. Home Produce: British Actors—Connery, R. Moore, Michael York, Donald Sutherland, Oliver Reed, Glenda Jackson, et al. Place Your Bets: Future Stars—Karen Black, Elton John, et al. Household Names: Taylor, Burton, Burt Reynolds, Brando, et al. The Trojans: Wayne, Lancaster, Douglas, Heston, Peck, et al. A list of fan clubs and a suspicious bibliography which promotes the publisher's products complete the book. Illustration quality is above average. Acceptable.

5919   *Superman: Serial to Cereal.* by Grossman, Gary. 320 p. paper illus. New York: Popular Library, 1977.

This volume traces the journey of the character, Superman, from the pages of *Action Comics* to radio, films and television. Emphasis is on the latter media with varying attention given to a sampling of the many episodes. George Reeves, the actor who played Superman for more than six years, receives extended biographical treatment, as does another Superman interpreter, Kirk Alyn.

The volume suffers from a lack of material organization and an index. Other than the filmographies in the appendix, reference value is negligible and the reader may have to wade through a sea of trivia in order to find specific information. Illustrations tend to be murky and not always pertinent to the text. It should be noted that the book does not treat the 1979 film, SUPERMAN.

5920 SUPERMAN Blueprints. 2 books illus. paper New York: Warner, 1979.

5921 *Superman Books*. New York: Warner, 1978.

A discernible trend in film literature is the publication of many tie-in books timed with the release of a high-budget, specialized film. SUPERMAN (1978) was accompanied by *The Superman Cutouts, The Superman Blueprints, The Superman Portfolio*, and *Your Superman Telephone and Address Book*.

5922 *The Supernatural Movie Quiz Book*. by Rovin, Jeff. 94 p. paper illus. New York: Drake, 1977.

Would you believe a subgenre quiz book? Here are 41 quizzes featuring ghosts, vampires, witches, and other assorted creatures. Stills and answers accompany the quizzes.

5923 *Surrealism and Film*. by Matthews, J. H. 198 p. illus. Ann Arbor, Mich.: University of Michigan Press, 1971.

A lengthy introductory discussion of the surrealist viewpoint in general is followed by an enumeration of those qualities the surrealist looks for and expects in films. The body of the book examines, describes, and evaluates films, scripts, and filmmakers that have pertinence for the surrealist. A final chapter is devoted to Luis Bunuel. Included are many explanatory footnotes and a detailed index. The illustrations are a distinct disappointment, both because of the small obvious selection and their reproduction. The idea of using mono-blue color on the visuals may suggest surrealism but it diminishes the value of the photographs.

The pedantic text is another matter. It is scholarly, well researched, and impressive in its choice and treatment of topic. While it may please the artist/scholar, much of it may be a challenge to the average reader. It almost demands some prior knowledge of surrealism, many remote films, and the French school of avant-garde filmmakers from the twenties.

5924 *Surrealism and Spain, 1920-1936*. by Morris, Cyril Brian. 291 p. illus. Cambridge, London: Cambridge University Press, 1972.

Contains material on surrealism in films.

5925 *Surrealism and the Cinema*. by Gould, Michael. 171 p. illus. New York: A. S. Barnes, 1976.

The surrealism movement which flowered during the twenties had its effect on other art forms. In this volume Michael Gould examines selected films and certain directors in an effort to show the effect of surrealism on the motion picture.

An introductory chapter discusses the artists and paintings that are identified with the movement. An explanation of the movement's characteristics is followed by their identification in films. Film directors Luis Bunuel, Josef von Sternberg, Alfred Hitchcock, and Samuel Fuller receive individual attention. Final chapters are devoted to the animated film and the experimental film. A bibliography and an index are added. The illustrations are well selected but the quality of their reproduction varies a great deal.

In this unique volume, the author has used his research and analytical ability to formulate a convincing statement concerning surrealism in films. It will appeal to readers who desire a deeper background in the understanding and appreciation of the film form. Recommended.

5926 *Surrealists and Surrealism*. by Picon, Gaetan. 231 p. illus. New York: Rizzoli, 1977.

This rich, ornate art book explores the effect that surrealists have had on the arts. A chapter on surrealist films appears in the text which treats the movement and its major artists. Illustrations are beautifully reproduced.

5927 *A Survey of British Research in Audiovisual Aids 1945-1971*. by Coppen, Helen. 271 p. paper London: National Committee for Audio-Visual Aids in Education and Educational Foundation for Visual Aids, 1972.

Section 5 of this survey deals with motion picture films—both instructional and other types. About 24 research projects are described by purpose, procedure, and conclusion. Section 9, which treats multimedia or combined media systems, also mentions film. A supplement covering 1972-1973 is similarly structured and, in addition, contains a cumulative index, 1945-1973.

5928   *A Survey of Motion Picture, Still Photography and Graphic Arts Instruction.* by Horrell, William C. 55 p. paper illus. Rochester, N.Y.: Eastman Kodak, 1971.

The fourth edition of this guide to visual instruction in American and Canadian colleges, universities, technical institutes and schools of photography is based upon responses from 2500 U.S. and 60 Canadian schools. Information is given regarding courses, faculty, degrees, philosophies, graduates and many other topics. The purpose of the volume is to provide guidance for those wishing to study filmmaking, photography or graphic arts beyond the high school level. This is an essential reference for school libraries and it is appropriate for other collections as well. The annual AFI guide to college courses in film is another valuable information source on this subject.

5929   *Susan Hayward—The Divine Bitch.* by McClelland, Doug. 221 p. paper illus. New York: Pinnacle Books, 1973.

A strong case for the acceptance of Susan Hayward as one of Hollywood's greatest actresses is made by the author in this career exploration. The volume cannot, in all fairness, be called a biography, since the major portion of the text is devoted to Hayward's films and professional activities. There is a smattering of biographical information but it is incidental to the evaluation of Hayward's work. From an appearance in HOLLYWOOD HOTEL in 1936 to her last few television appearances in 1972, Hayward always made her opportunities count. Ever the professional, she was ambitious, determined, and most important, talented.

If the reader shares McClelland's admiration and affection for Hayward's work, he will find this volume most pleasing. Those searching for an objective evaluation may be disappointed, since Hayward is the perennial heroine here and can do no wrong. Any blame is continually placed elsewhere and the resultant portrait is a rather predjudiced one. However, the detailed description of her film work represents impressive research and is most entertaining to read. An index, a filmography, and a small center section of visuals add to the book's appeal. Recommended for all mature readers.

5930   *Susan Hayward: Portrait of a Survivor.* by Linet, Beverly. and 337 p. illus. New York: Atheneum, 1980.

Beverly Linet, the author of an Alan Ladd biography, gives her attention to a stronger, more colorful subject here. By interviews and research, she follows the struggles of Susan Hayward from a penniless childhood in Brooklyn to her final triumphant appearance at the 1974 Academy Awards. Along the way are romances, marriages, attempted suicide, studio battles, personal feuds—all the elements that make a realistic, down-to-earth, gusty heroine, which Hayward apparently was. A fine set of illustrations accompanies the story.

This biography is a fast, terse reading experience whose organization and clarity may obscure the difficult work that Linet has done. She writes with a style that indicates her experience and expertise in interpreting Hollywood to a mass audience.

5931   *Suspense in the Cinema.* by Gow, Gordon. 167 p. paper illus. New York: A. S. Barnes, 1968.

Many examples of suspense in foreign and American films are explored in this book. Although no specific definition of suspense is offered, the term in a cinematic sense is described, categorized, and illustrated. Some of the examples used are fascinating while other classic examples are conspicuously missing from the discussion. The category headings lack consistency, ranging from a condition ("Isolation") to a genre ("Among Thieves"). Illustration titles were not well-printed in the copy examined, a portion of the words being cut off the page. In short, a topic of great interest handled with indifference.

5932   *Swanson on Swanson.* by Swanson, Gloria. 535 p. illus. New York: Random House, 1980.

Those who appreciate the persona of Gloria Swanson—sharp, clear, egocentric, proud, opinionated, determined, shrewd and witty—will enjoy her autobiography. Using a no-nonsense style, she recalls her rise from a teen-aged movie player to cinema royalty, and her enduring career. Her memoir is filled with accounts of her films, six marriages, co-workers, personal views, and Hollywood as it was. The uninitiated may become impatient with Swanson's demands for admiration—she reminds the reader constantly of her beauty, charm, allure, longevity, business acumen, and innate wisdom on various topics. The only thing she still doesn't seem to understand fully is herself.

5933   *The Swashbucklers.* by Parish, James Robert; and Stanke, Don E. 672 p. illus. New Rochelle, N.Y.: Arlington House, 1976.

This collective biography is devoted to eight male film stars who could portray "a swaggering swordsman" with style and popular appeal. Although many other actors have appeared as swashbucklers, those singled out for detailed examination here are Ronald Colman, Tony Curtis, Douglas Fairbanks, Sr., Errol Flynn, Stewart Granger, Victor Mature, Tyrone Power, and Cornel Wilde. The selection is a sound one, for though there have been multiple books on Fairbanks and Flynn, the biographical coverage on the other six has been slight.

In each instance there is carefully selected material about the subject's personal life and a rather full coverage of his films. Plots are summarized and critical evaluations of performances are offered. Illustrations, a detailed filmography, and some footnotes complete each biography.

Although the unifying theme of swashbuckling serves as little more than an excuse to gather these selected subjects for biographical examination, the individual portraits are quite satisfying. Obviously the authors are able to offer more personal detail about the deceased heroes—Fairbanks, Flynn, and Colman—than the others. However, the coverage on the others is more than adequate, with matters of public record effectively integrated into each story.

The volume can be used effectively to satisfy both reference and reader needs. Selection, content, and presentation are consistently impressive throughout the many pages. Just as the swashbucklers who are profiled within did earlier, this book is sure to please a large audience. Recommended.

5934 *Swastika: Cinema of Oppression.* by Phillips, Baxter. III p. paper illus. New York: Warner Books, 1976.

An examination of the ways that several nations used film to influence the minds of their people is offered in this volume. Beginning with Russia and Eisenstein, the author also considers film production under such leaders as Lenin, Stalin, Mussolini, Hitler, Franco, and Hirohito. Coverage is fragmented and brief, but some insight into the political use of film is offered. The selection of the illustrations seems limited to a relatively few films; there are far too many from POTEMKIN (1925). The quality of reproduction for the visuals is good. Unfortunately, no index is provided. Acceptable.

5935 *Sweden I.* by Cowie, Peter. 224 p. paper illus. New York: A. S. Barnes, 1970.

This guide to Swedish films and filmmakers is an idealreference work. There are 250 entries alphabeti-

cally arranged according to Swedish title or name; included are directors, players, technicians and 70 important films. The filmographies for the players are limited to Swedish films but the entire body of work of the directors is listed. Almost half of the book is taken up with a detailed index which lists both Swedish and English titles. The book is profusely illustrated with many fine stills and portraits.

5936 *Sweden II.* by Cowie, Peter. 256 p. paper illus. New York: A. S. Barnes, 1970.

The subtitle of this book is "A Comprehensive Assessment of the Themes, Trends, and Directors in Swedish Cinema." It is an expansion and revision of Cowie's earlier work, *Swedish Cinema.* More directors are treated in this volume but the filmographies and film plot outlines have been transferred to *Sweden I.* The production, including a lengthy bibliography and many illustrations, is excellent. This volume is an admirable companion to *Sweden I.*

5937 *Swedish Cinema.* by Cowie, Peter. 224 p. paper illus. New York: A. S. Barnes, 1966.

The two golden periods of Swedish cinema are explored in this volume. During the first period of 1914-1921, it is the films of Victor Sjostrom and Mauritz Stiller which dominate. Ingmar Bergman is largely responsible for the second period, the mid-fifties to the present. Some attention is given to a few other directors, but the three mentioned above receive the most coverage, with Bergman's section occupying almost half of the book. The text is both descriptive and evaluative. Although many of the non-Bergman films are not familiar, the accounts given of them arouse reader interest. Stills are excellent and a filmography of the major directors is included. Recommended.

5938 *The Swedish Film Institute.* by Swedish Film Institute. 20 p. paper Stockholm: Svenska Film Institute, 1965.

The Swedish Film Institute is a foundation formed by an 1963 agreement between the government and the film industry. Television, taxes, a limited audience and other factors were killing the film industry when the 1963 Reform was adopted. The details of the agreement as well as its subsequent effects are spelled out in this short booklet. Noted here as an example of governmental cooperation with a threatened film industry.

5939   *Swedish Films.* by Lauritzen, Einar. 32 p. paper illus. New York:Museum of Modern Art, 1962.

A short survey of Swedish films from 1909 to 1957, this booklet was prepared in connection with a special showing of the films at the Museum. Although it is partial in its coverage, the information, both picture and text, is excellent. Both description and evaluation of the films are offered. Because of the limited survey and the date of publication, the book has its greatest value as a secondary reference.

5940   *Swedish Films 1978.* edited by Hylten-Cavallius, Gun. 120 p. paper illus. Stockholm: Swedish Film Institute, 1978.

An annual survey of films made in Sweden, this volume contains illustrations and tables.

5941   *Sweet and Lowdown: America's Popular Song Writers.* by Craig, Warren. 645 p. Metuchen, N.J.: Scarecrow, 1978.

For anyone interested in popular music, this volume is pure pleasure. It offers abbreviated biographies of 145 American songwriters arranged alphabetically. Each entry contains a chronological listing of the composer's songs and the show/film/TV program for which they were originally written. Additional access to the songs is provided by a title index and a production index. Appendixes offer comparative ratings, a bibliography of sources, and a general bibliography.

Music written specifically for films is given superb coverage in this most welcome reference book.

5942   SWEET CHARITY. by Rothman, Jay. 48 p. paper illus. 1969.

Someoutstanding color photography is to be found in this souvenir book. After a brief history of the story, from Fellini to Broadway to film, the leading cast members are profiled. In addition there are sections devoted to the songs, dances, set decorations, costume design, and finally to the director, Bob Fosse, and the producer, Robert Arthur. Other cast and production credits are also noted.

5943   SWEET SWEETBACK'S BAADASSSSS SONG. by Van Peebles, Melvin. 192 p. paper illus. New York: Lancer Books, 1971.

Script of the 1971 film directed by Van Peebles.

5944   *Sweetheart: The Story of Mary Pickford.* by Windeler, Robert. 226 p. illus. New York: Praeger, 1974.

In this detailed biography of Mary Pickford, the author offers nothing new or startling. The service he provides is the organization of public materials on his subject augmented by material gained via numerous interviews with Pickford acquaintances. Apparently no communication between author and subject took place. Most of the Pickford quotations are from her autobiography, *Sunshine and Shadow.*

The portrait of Pickford as an ambitious, intelligent actress blessed with timing, a sharp mother and agent, and a sound business sense is well known. What the author has provided is embellishment and polishing of the facts and legends which surround this lady. The book is written in a totally positive style—nothing Pickford says or does in the story seems negative or unpleasant. Thus, the reader receives a biased portrait that becomes a bit too bland to maintain reader interest. The background material about early filmmaking in New York and Hollywood is far more exciting. The selection and reproduction of the illustrations is excellent; a filmography and an index are other assets. As a competent but rather unexciting biography, this volume is acceptable. However, it is stronger as a portrait of the early motion picture industry and, on that basis, can be recommended.

5945   THE SWIMMER. by Perry, Eleanor. 127 p. New York: Stein & Day, 1967.

Novelized script of the 1967 film directed by Frank Perry.

5946   *The Swing Era 1936-1937.* edited by Payne, Philip W.; and Hall, Ben H. 72 p. illus. New York: Time-Life Records, 1970.

This book was designed as part of a records-book package that was one of a series which surveyed popular music. Subtitled "The Movies: Between Vitaphone and Video," Ben H. Hall's text recalls the period in which the recordings first appeared. Using many well-reproduced stills of thirties filmmaking, the narrative begins with the end of the silent era— THE JAZZ SINGER (1927)—and ends with JOLSON SINGS AGAIN (1949). Some attempt is made to link the book and records by noting the use of swing bands in the films of the thirties and forties. Detailed biographies of two bandleaders, Benny Goodman and Fletcher Henderson, are included along with some discographies.

Excellent production has been given to the mediocre

essay-recollection presented here. Lacking any organization, the author rambles on about the golden era of Hollywood, omitting essentials, emphasizing personal enthusiasms (e.g., Margaret Dumont), and superimposing the swing band coverage on what is basically a historical overview of two decades. Errors such as attributing JOLSON SINGS AGAIN to Warner Bros. rather than Columbia, using "Swing Concerto" for Artie Shaw's "Concerto for Clarinet," and placing events out of chronological sequence weaken Hall's personalized memoir-history. The pictures, however, make the book acceptable.

5947 *Swingin' Dors.* by Dors, Diana. 186 p. paper illus. London: World Distributors, 1960.

The story of a British sex symbol who appeared in many films since her debut in THE SHOP AT SLY CORNER (1946). Working both in Europe and Hollywood, she graduated from lead parts to character roles in her more recent films. Written immediately after she had reached her greatest celebrity, the book covers only the first portion of her career. Today she is still active as a performer in bit roles—HANNIE CAULDER (1971), for example—and as a leading character actress in films for television, e.g., NURSE WILL MAKE IT BETTER (1975).

5948 *Swordsmen of the Screen: From Douglas Fairbanks to Michael York.* by Richards, Jeffrey. 296 p. illus. Boston: Routledge and Kegan Paul, 1977.

This volume is a survey-analysis of a film genre, the swashbuckler, and those male performers who created memorable roles within it. The treatment is a historical one that begins with a description of the genre and its heroes. Next it offers hundreds of examples involving such character classifications as knights, musketeers, adventurers, cavaliers, conquistadores, masked avengers, folk heroes, highwaymen, sheikhs, and pirates.

A bibliography, a title index and a general index conclude the book. A generous number of illustrations accompanies the text.

As a title in the *Cinema and Society* series, this volume is most welcome. It offers an intelligent, balanced treatment of an easily identifiable film genre. Supporting elements—particularly the fine visuals—add to the overall quality of the book. It should appeal to a broad general audience. Recommended.

5949 *Sybil Thorndike.* by Trewin, John Courtenay. 123 p. illus. London: Rockliff, 1955.

Sybil Thorndike made only a very few films from the twenties through the sixties. This volume is an illustrated study of her work, with a list of both stage and screen appearances up to the mid-fifties.

5950 *see 5949*

5951 *Sybil Thorndike (Casson).* by Sprigge, Elizabeth. 348 p. illus. London: Gollancz, 1971.

Sybil Thorndike has provided the foreword to this biography which covers her many stage appearances and the few films she has made.

5952 *Sydney Pollack.* by Taylor, William R. 170 p. illus. Boston: Twayne, 1981.

5953 *Symbolic Leaders: Public Dramas and Public Men.* by Klapp, Orrin E. 272 p. Chicago: Aldine Publishing Co., 1964.

According to the publisher, this book "is a probing and provocative analysis of the process of public drama and of the actors who play the leading roles...." A symbolic leader is one who functions primarily through his image or meaning. Film personalities mentioned are Monroe, Bankhead, Mae West, Will Rogers, John Barrymore, Chaplin, Elvis, Sinatra, Valentino and many others. While not a pure film book, the concept of leadership via public image is a challenging question.

5954 *Systems Film Catalog.* paper Cleveland, Ohio: Association for Systems Management, 1977.

5955 *TAB Books (a Series).* Illus. Blue Ridge Summit, Pa.

TAB publishes an impressive series of volumes addressed to the practical, how-to-do-it side of filmmaking.

Some titles are: *Music Scoring for TV and Motion Pictures*, *Professional Filmmaking*, *The Amateur Filmmakers Handbook of Sound Synchronization and Scoring*, *How to Prepare a Production Budget for Film and Video Tape*, *How to Repair Movie and Slide Projectors*, and *Don't Look at the Camera.*

Although TAB specializes in areas other than filmmaking (radio, electronics, hobbies, solar energy, etc.), occasionally they offer the only information in print on a film topic. Their books are easy to read.

5956 *Tackle Movie-Making This Way.* by Rose, Tony. 119 p. paper illus. London: S. Paul, 1960.

5957 *Take It from Me.* by Edwards, Jimmy. illus. London: Werner Laurie, 1953.

Jimmy Edwards is a British comedian who appears on stage, radio, and in films.

5958 *Take My Life.* by Cantor, Eddie; and Ardmore, Jane Kesner. 288 p. illus. Garden City, N.Y: Doubleday, 1957.

Although this volume is mostly about the stage and is only peripheral to film matters, some insights into the lives of personalities who have worked in both mediums are given. Fanny Brice, Al Jolson, Irving Berlin, Will Rogers, W. C. Fields, Ben Schulberg and Samuel Goldwyn all receive special attention. Surprisingly well-written in parts, the book has little pertinence for film historians except as background material.

5959 *Take Them Up Tenderly.* by Harriman, Margaret. 266 p. New York: Knopf, 1944.

A collective biography made up of "Profiles" from *The New Yorker* magazine. Most directly related to films are Hollywood agent Leland Hayward, attorney Fanny Holtzmann, Helen Hayes and Mary Pickford. Other subjects include Moss Hart, Rodgers and Hart, Oscar Hammerstein II, Cole Porter, Lillian Hellman, and others.

5960 *Take Two: A Life in Movies and Politics.* by Dunne, Philip. 355 p. illus. New York: McGraw-Hill, 1980.

Philip Dunne has had a long career in Hollywood as both screenwriter and director. Since most of his work was done at the Twentieth Century Fox studios, it is not surprising to find such personalities as Darryl Zanuck, Spyros Skouras, Tyrone Power, Joe Mankiewicz, John Ford, Buddy Adler, etc., having prominent roles in his story. Dunne recalls the golden years of Hollywood, 1930-1955, with special attention to the witch hunts that characterized the last decade of that period.

His opinions and recollections are of some interest but lack the cohesiveness and dramatic excitement

necessary to grip the reader. In this sense the book is flawed in the same way that the films Dunne directed are, e.g., HILDA CRANE (1956), TEN NORTH FREDERICK (1958), BLUE DENIM (1959), WILD IN THE COUNTRY (1962), etc. He was apparently more successful when he allowed someone else to interpret his words and thoughts.

An index and some illustrations are supplied, but a much-needed filmography is missing. Dunne's memoir is filled with personalities and anecdotes but it is only sporadically interesting.

5961 *The Taking and Showing of Motion Pictures for the Amateur.* by Cameron, James. 238 p. illus. New York: Cameron Publishing, 1927.

5962 TAKING OFF. by Forman, Milos; and Klein, John; and Guare, John and and Carriere, Jean-Claude. 220 p. paper illus. New York: Signet, 1971.

Script of the 1971 film directed by Forman. Contains cast credits and production credits together with two articles: "How I Came to America to Make a Film and Wound Up Owing Paramount $140,000" (Foreman) and "Getting the Great Ten Percent: An Interview with Milos Foreman" (Harriet R. Polt).

5963 *Tall, Dark and Gruesome: An Autobiography.* by Lee, Christopher. 286 p. illus. London: W. H. Allen, 1977.

This autobiography of horror film star Christopher Lee contains illustrations and an index.

5964 *The Tale of the Tales: The Beatrix Potter Ballet.* by Godden, Rumer. 208 p. illus. New York: Frederick Warne, 1971.

Rumer Godden was asked to record the making of the movie-ballet that combined five of the Beatrix Potter stories. The result is a report that includes interviews, observations, impressions and many color illustrations. The film, shown, here under the title PETER RABBIT AND TALES OF BEATRIX POTTER (1971), featured the Royal Ballet. Everything about this book is first-rate: text (Ms. Godden is an expert on Beatrix Potter), sketches, designs, stills, and production. Highly recommended.

5965 *A Talent For Luck: An Autobiography.* by Strauss, Helen. 302 p. illus. New York: Random House, 1979.

After working in the film business, Helen Strauss became the head of the literary department of the William Morris Agency and in that capacity met many celebrities. Later she was involved in creating the "package" —a combination of vehicle and personnel sold as a unit. Her clients included many famous names (Dietrich, Bankhead, Astaire, etc.) and in this autobiography she speaks openly and honestly about them.

5966 *A Talent to Amuse.* by Sheridan, Morley. 453 p. illus. New York: Doubleday, 1969.

A biography of Noel Coward that includes a chronology, a bibliography, and an index.

5967 THE TALES OF HOFFMAN. by Gibbon, Monk. 99 p. illus. London: Saturn Press, 1951.

A study of the 1951 film.

5968 *The Talkies.* by Krows, Arthur E. 245 p. illus. New York: Henry Holt, 1930.

An early popularized explanation of how talking films developed. There is some discussion of stage-screen relationships, along with nontechnical explanations of early sound techniques.

5969 *The Talkies.* by Scotland, John. 194 p. illus. London: Crosby Lockwood, 1930.

One of the early books written to explain the development and the technique of sound motion pictures. Of historical interest, this volume has some rare photographs.

5970 *The Talkies.* by Griffith, Richard. 360 p. paper illus. New York: Dover, 1971.

This collection of 150 articles and hundreds of illustrations from *Photoplay* magazine (1928-1940) is a most rewarding film book. Selected, arranged and written by Richard Griffith, the book should surprise no one with its intelligence, its total effect, and its coverage. Griffith places the articles in categories entitled: 1) Stars, Comedians, Child Stars, Support; 2) Living and Working in Movieland; 3) The Fans and Their Magazine; 4) Pictures and Trends.

The text is fan magazine writing of the thirties—quaint, exaggerated, emotional, and mythical for the most part. Picture quality varies considerably, with many dark reproductions in evidence, yet other il-

lustrations are very clear copies of the original materials. One especially effective feature is the inclusion of feature film advertisements. Adding product advertising is questionable but probably could not be avoided because of production problems. The thoroughness of Griffith is indicated once again in the impressive index.

The book has many values—as history, reference, nostalgia, and as pure entertainment. It is enthusiastically recommended. A joy for all patrons to discover and far superior to the earlier *Hollywood and The Great Fan Magazines.*

5971 *The Talkies Era: A Pictorial History of Australian Sound Film Making, 1930-1960.* by Reade, Eric. 127 p. illus. Melbourne: Lansdowne, 1972.

5972 *Talking About Films.* by Das Gupta, Chidananda. Columbia, Mo.: South Asia Books, 1981.

5973 *Talking about the Cinema.* by Kitses, Jim; and Mercer, Ann. 98 p. paper illus. London: British Film Institute, 1966.

The subtitle, "Film Studies for Young People," shows the concern of this volume. Using the experiences of many teachers and students, the authors have utilized their comments, reactions, feelings, etc., to frame an introductory 12-week course in film study. After the second and third terms are briefly described, some conclusions are offered. Appendixes note other film courses, information sources, and an index to selected films. This pioneer work may remind the reader of some more recent works. Much of what is said is still pertinent, and the book remains a valuable source volume for educators.

5974 *The Talking Clowns.* by Manchel, Frank. 129 p. illus. New York: Franklin Watts, 1976.

Subtitled "From Laurel and Hardy to the Marx Brothers," this volume is intended to introduce several legendary screen performers to young readers. In addition to the above teams, the text also treats Mae West and W. C. Fields. Each is given a general treatment that combines elements of biography, motion picture history, and criticism. Accompanying the text are some clearly reproduced illustrations, a bibliography, and an index.

Author Manchel, an experienced hand at writing film books for juveniles, provides another carefully prepared and written text. As usual, he is able to capture the essence and appeal of his subjects in a minimum number of pages.

The inclusion of Mae West as a "Talking Clown" may be controversial; strong arguments against such a classification come immediately to mind. Acceptable.

5975   *Talking Movies.* by Cameron, James. 115 p. illus. New York: Cameron Publishing, 1927.

5976   *Talking of Films.* by Minney, Rubeigh J. 80 p. paper London: Home and Van Thal, 1947.

A short discussion of the British film industry—its stars, writers, producers, problems, markets, costs, potentials, etc.

5977   *Talking Pictures: Screenwriters in the American Cinema.* by Corliss, Richard. 398 p. Woodstock, N.Y.: Overlook Press, 1974.

The structure of this ambitious volume is somewhat similar to that of *The American Cinema* by Andrew Sarris, who has provided the preface here. Corliss has divided selected American screenwriters from the period of 1927 to 1973 into five groups: "The Author-Auteurs", "The Stylists", "Themes in Search of a Style", "The Chameleons", and "A New Wind from the East". Each group is introduced by a short statement, after which the writers are considered individually. A basic total filmography listing film title, year, and coauthor, if any, introduces each writer section. One or more films representative of the writer's work are described and evaluated. For example, Joseph L. Mankiewicz is represented by A LETTER TO THREE WIVES (1949), ALL ABOUT EVE (1950), and THE BAREFOOT CONTESSA (1954). The films used for the text have extended cast and professional credits in a separate filmography at the book's end.

The treatment resembles a series of critical reviews which emphasize the writing of the script rather than a film's other aesthetic qualities. The analysis and critical opinion offered is copious, varied subjective, and controversial. The reader who comes to this book with knowledge and experience in film matters will be fascinated. There are enough modern films considered to attract the younger reader. Recommended.

5978   *Talking Pictures.* by Brown, Bernard. 309 p. illus. London: Pitman, 1933.

A practical and popular account of the principles of construction and operation of the apparatus used in making and showing sound films.

5979   *Talking Pictures, How They Are Made and How to Appreciate Them.* by Kiesling, Barrett C. 332 p. illus. Richmond, Va.: Johnson Pub. Co., 1937.

Details the steps in making and distributing a motion picture from story selection to final cut. A glossary of technical/trade terms is given along with illustrations. The "appreciation" portion is weak.

5980   *Talking Shadows.* by Jester, Ralph. 64 p. illus. Evanston, Ill.: Row, Peterson, 1942.

An early discussion of the way the Hollywood motion picture worked.

5981   *The Tall American: The Story of Gary Cooper.* by Gehman, Richard. 187 p. illus. New York: Hawthorn, 1963.

Written for juveniles, this biography contains some original illustrations by Albert Micale and a title page illustration by Cooper's daughter, Maria.

5982   *Tall Tales From Hollywood.* by Garnett, Tay. 96 p. New York: Liveright, 1932.

5983   *Tallulah.* by Gill, Brendan. 287 p. illus. New York: Holt, Rinehart & Winston, 1972.

This oversized book contains much information in both text and pictures about Tallulah Bankhead's films. There are stills from a few early silents and large full pictures from her later sound films. The book begins with a long biographical essay that is peppered with Bankhead's "one liners" and bits of scandal and gossip. In a second section, an album of personal, professional and news pictures reiterates the life story. Small illustrations accompany the essay and short explanations identify the visuals in the second part. A chronology of her professional activities (including her films) and an index complete the book. The subject is ever-fascinating, the stories are still amusing and the picture collection is superb. Recommended.

5984   *Tallulah, Darling.* by Brian, Denis. 285 p. paper illus. New York: Pyramid, 1972.

A paperback biography, reissued in 1980 as hardcover, that captures many of the anecdotes, stories, and pronouncements of Tallulah. Based on 150 interviews of persons acquainted with Bankhead in one way or another, the text also includes a 1966 interview with the subject herself. It is packed with quotations, many of them taken from Bankhead's 1952 autobiography, *Tallulah*. The films are mentioned in some depth and there are two sections on LIFEBOAT (1944) and A ROYAL SCANDAL (1945) that will add to anyone's appreciation of those films.

While the portrait is not always flattering, it is consistently affectionate. A few pictures and an index are included. This volume is as enjoyable as some of the other narrative biographies and is only surpassed by Brendan Gill's picture-volume. Recommended.

5985 *Tallulah, Darling of the Gods.* by Tunney, Kiernan. 228 p. illus. New York: Dutton, 1973.

Another Bankhead book, this one by an Irish playwright and critic. In 1947 he came to visit Bankhead to persuade her to perform in one of his comedies. He writes of that first instance and others that followed over the next 20 years. How much of the memoir is valid has been questioned by those who were part of Bankhead's menage. They either deny having seen him or only acknowledge his presence at one or two dinners.

The account is a personal, intimate one and tries to describe the personality rather than recall the professional triumphs and failures. Acceptable—with a question about its authenticity.

5986 *The Talmadge Girls.* by Loos, Anita. 204 p. illus. New York: Viking, 1978.

In this short volume there are five leading ladies—Peg Talmadge, her three daughters (Norma, Constance, Natalie) and Anita Loos. Their stories are told against the background of the twenties Hollywood in an entertaining 135 pages. The rest of the book consists of some good photos and an unnecessary Loos script (68 pages) for Constance, A VIRTUOUS VAMP (1919). An index would have been helpful.

More than a collective biography, this is another Loos memoir of a fantasy town with strong characters, odd lifestyles, and assorted crazies.

5987 *The Talmadge Sisters, Norma, Constance, Natalie.* by Talmadge, Margaret. 245 p. illus. Philadelphia:

Lippincott, 1924.

An early collective biography of the screen sisters, written with protective care, by their mother. Includes filmographies and some attention to Buster Keaton, who was married to Natalie.

5988 THE TAMING OF THE SHREW. 32 p. paper illus. 1967.

After a short introductory section on the background of the 1967 film, this souvenir book tells the story with a minimum of narrative and a maximum of photographs, some of them full-page illustrations. There are also full-page portraits of Elizabeth Taylor, Richard Burton, and director Franco Zeffirelli. The supporting cast and production personnel are noted, with special attention given to the designers and scriptwriters.

5989 *Tara Revisited.* by Vance, Malcolm. 224 p. paper illus. New York: Charter, 1976.

An unusual format is employed in this original paperback, which delivers something somewhat different than "the inside story of what happened to the stars of GONE WITH THE WIND." As promised on the jacket, it offers a collective biography of the stars, principals, supporting actors, minor cast players and filmmakers who were involved in the 1939 classic film. Coverage varies with Gable, Leigh, de Havilland and Howard receiving full attention while Cliff Edwards, Eric Linden and Jackie Moran are each given a page or two. The term "inside story" is an exaggeration since the information offered here is largely public record and rather familiar. What Vance has done is provide some background of the film along with the biographical sketches and filmographies of those filmmakers who had the good fortune to be associated with the most popular motion picture ever made in Hollywood.

5990 *The Tara Treasury: A Pictorial History of* GONE WITH THE WIND. by Gardner, Gerald; and Gardner, Harriet Modell. 192 p. illus. Westport, Conn.: Arlington House, 1980.

Another GONE WITH THE WIND (1939) album of history, facts, memories, and trivia is presented here. With some fine illustrations accompanying a rather biased/dated-selected text, the authors cover familiar ground in the problems, personalities, and publicity that accompanied the production of the film. For fans of GONE WITH THE WIND, this book may be a treasury; others will find it only partly satisfying.

5991 *Tarzan of the Movies.* by Essoe, Gabe. 208 p. illus. New York: Citadel Press, 1968.

This picture book traces the line of Tarzans from the silents to the talkies and finally to television. An introduction which highlights the life of Edgar Rice Burroughs and gives some background about the Tarzan character is offered by Burroughs' daughter. There were 40 Tarzan films produced and the role was played by 14 different actors. The book not only covers these performances but also includes some Tarzan spin-offs, e.g., KING OF THE JUNGLE (1933) etc. The text is both critical and descriptive; the quality of the stills varies greatly. A fascinating book that will attract most readers.

5992 *Tax Shelters After Tax Reform.* edited by Shapiro, Ruth G. 315 p. New York: Practising Law Institute, 1977.

A legal volume that includes material on motion picture tax shelters.

5993 *Taxation of the Motion Picture Industry.* by Kopple, Robert C.; and Stiglitz, Bruce M. Washington, D.C.: Bureau of National Affairs, 1978.

5994 *Teach Yourself Film-Making.* by Hill, Roger. 149 p. London: English Universities Press, 1970.

Both the technical and the creative side of filmmaking are considered in this book. Topics include camera, film, projector, editing, etc.

5995 *Teach Yourself The Cinema.* by Reader, Keith. New York: McKay, 1979.

5996 *Teaching a Critical Approach to Cinema and TV.* by UNESCO. paper New York: UNESCO Public Center, 1967.

5997 *Teaching about the Film.* by Peters, J. M. L. 120 p. illus. New York: UNESCO, 1961.

Teachers will find two valuable divisions in this small treasure. The first deals with the content of the film education and the second is concerned with techniques, methodology, and goals of film-teaching. The book uses all the shots which make up a total scene from THE FALLEN IDOL (1949) to illustrate editing, camera placement, etc. This clear, excellent presentation of material is characteristic of the approach used throughout. Although many references are European, this is still an essential volume for anyone concerned with film education.

5998 *Teaching by Projection.* by Judd, Stephen R. 170 p. London: Focal, 1963.

5999 *Teaching Film Animation to Children.* by Andersen, Yvonne. 112 p. illus. New York: Van Nostrand, Reinhold, 1970.

Miss Andersen, the director of the Yellow Ball Workshop in Lexington, Massachusetts, explains some of the techniques she has developed for helping children express themselves through film. The emphasis is upon simplicity, ease, economy and creativity. Different types of animation are described: cutouts, flip cards, clay, drawing on film, etc. Photography and sound techniques are covered as is the organization and administration of a workshop along with the necessary equipment and materials. The step-by-step illustrations are uniformly good. Highly recommended.

6000 *The Teaching Film in Primary Education.* by Mass Communication Techniques Division, UNESCO. 51 p. paper Paris: UNESCO, 1963.

Published as number 39 in the *Reports and Papers on Mass Communication* series.

6001 *Teaching History With Film.* by O'-Connor, John E.; and Jackson, Martin A. 74 p. paper illus. Washington, D.C.: American Historical Association, 1974.

This booklet, number two in a series entitled *Discussions on Teaching*, deals with many aspects of teaching history with film. After a rationale is offered, specific applications using films as either 1) a source of information, 2) motivation for study and discussion, or 3) historical documentation and interpretation, are discussed. Practical suggestions for classroom procedures are also noted. The book's final pages offer a glossary, a bibliography, a filmography, and a distribution list. This is a basic book that should be helpful to the beginning teacher. Some of the information is either dated or too elementary, but the general intent of the book is laudable.

6002 *Teaching Human Beings.* by Schrank, Jeffrey. 192 p. paper Boston: Beacon Press, 1972.

The subtitle of this book is "101 Subversive Activities for the Classroom." Since many of these activities deal with film, the book is considered here. Six major topics make up the book's contents: sense education, hidden assumptions, violence and the violated, chemicals and the body (drugs), learning about death, and subversive activities. An annotated evaluative filmography follows each of the sections. In addition, there are discussion suggestions, a bibliography, and a sampling of the activities mentioned in the subtitle.

"Subversive" in the context of this book means the use of those simulation games, group encounters, books, and films that seldom appear in a traditional classroom. Teachers wishing to improve the daily school experience for their students will find stimulating and rewarding material here. Excellent for the professional shelf in all school situations and the college-university crowd could profit from this volume even more.

6003 *Teaching in the Dark.* by Kuhns, William; and Carr, John. paper illus. Dayton, Ohio: Pflaum.

6004 *The Teaching of Film: A Report and Some Recommendations.* by Cinema Consultative Committee. 16 p. paper London: British Board of Film Censors, 1959.

An early British report urged a planned, financially supported approach to film study in England and Scotland. The Committee argued for film study courses in the training colleges and requested that a degree program be established. It was their hope that the film industry would offer support. Noted here for the record, but it may help those teachers and schools who are considering film study for their curriculum.

A similar title, *Teaching Film: A Guide to Classroom Method,* is worth noting. Written by Grace Greiner, and published by the British Film Institute in 1955, this 32-page book outlines the task of teaching film and considers its implementation in the infants school, the junior school, and the secondary school. The role of the film teacher is outlined in a final chapter. A bit dated but still acceptable.

6005 *Teaching Program: Exploring the Film.* by Kuhns, William; and Stanley, Robert. 94 p. paper illus. Day-

ton, Ohio: Pflaum, 1968.

6006 *Teaching the Screen Language.* by Hodgkinson, Anthony W. 33 p. paper Concord, Mass.: The New England Screen Education Association, 1976.

Although it was written in 1965, this short statement on a "basic method" of teaching screen language has been revised and serves as author Hodgkinson's current response to the "murky mixtures of Metz and Barthes" so prevalent in film appreciation courses today. Stated simply, he thinks of film as a means of expression and communication having an identifiable vocabulary and syntax. Vocabulary consists of shots which have sound, motion, and visual qualities; syntax is the arrangement and punctuation of the shots via editing and transitions. Many films are suggested as examples of the concepts discussed.

Refreshing in its clarity yet impressive by its embodiment of so much thoughtful content, this small volume should be required reading for all film teachers and students. Highly recommended.

6007 *Teaching with Films.* by Fern, George H.; and Robbins, Eldon. 146 p. Milwaukee: Bruce, 1946.

6008 *Technical Handbook of Mathematics for Motion Picture Music Synchronization.* by Raksin, Rudy. 87 p. paper illus. Sherman Oaks, Calif.: R-Y Publishing Co., 1972.

6009 *The Technique of Documentary Film Production.* by Baddeley, W. Hugh. 268 p. illus. New York: Hastings House, 1969.

In this volume, planning, scripting, casting, music, makeup and other production matters are applied to the factual film. A glossary and index are given. Practical, clear, well organized and comprehensive.

6010 *The Technique of Editing 16mm Films.* by Burder, John. 152 p. illus. New York: Hastings House, 1968.

A thorough discussion of the essential editing process, this book covers film, equipment and facilities. It is a how-to-do-it book that avoids theory. Diagrams, a glossary and an index are given.

6011 *Technique of Eroticism.* by Lo Duca, Giuseppe. 230 p. London:

Eros Library, 1963.

Translated by Alan Hull Walton, this volume deals with moral and religious aspects of sexual films and themes.

6012   *The Technique of Film and Television Make-up.* by Kehoe, Vincent J.R. 260 p. illus. New York: Hastings House, 1969.

Make-up that must be photographed in both color and black-and-white has led to many changes in make-up techniques which are noted in this revised volume. Here is a compact handbook containing much information, diagrams, pictures, charts, formulas, sources, etc. The book is indexed.

6013   *The Technique of Film Animation.* by Halas, John; and Manvell, Roger. 360 p. illus. New York: Hastings House, 1968.

This is a standard classic volume in its field, originally published in 1959, covering all aspects of the animated film in a readable, informative and entertaining manner. Many illustrations and drawings combined with an intelligent text (Manvell's contribution?) make the volume an outstanding example of the technical book that can also be read for pleasure. The book has been revised in 1968 to include such new developments as computer animation. There are tables of data, a list of animated films, a glossary, a book list, and an index. Most impressive.

6014   *The Technique of Film Editing.* by Reisz, Karel; and Millar, Gavin. 411 p. illus. New York: Hastings House, 1968.

If a book's eligibility for classic status is based on its continual sales, its many editions, its translations into other languages, and its general excellence, this volume is a classic of its type. Written in 1953, it is still most pertinent and valuable. This enlarged and updated edition is the 15th. The author's style is both literate and nontechnical. Included is an early history of the development of editing citing mostly the work of Griffith, Pudovkin, and Eisenstein. Scenes from BIRTH OF A NATION (1915), CITIZEN KANE (1941), BREATHLESS (1959), SHOOT THE PIANO PLAYER (1960), BRIGHTON ROCK (1947), and many other films are used as examples of the editing principle. Photographs and script pages are given throughout. There is a glossary and an index. Consistently excellent and highly recommended.

6015   *The Technique of Film Music.* by Huntley, John; and Manvell, Roger. 299 p. illus. New York: Focal Press, 1967.

A rather specialized book that covers music in both the silent and the sound eras, this volume also discusses the function of music in films. In addition, the work of the music director, the sound technician, and the composer is described. Appendices include an outline history of music in films from 1895 to 1955, an extended bibliography on film music and an index. The appendix devoted to recordings of film music is of limited value because of record deletion from catalog and British trademarks and serial numbers. A most worthwhile book for those readers with a concentrated interest in the topic. Nonmusicians may find it a bit too technical.

6016   *The Technique of Lighting for Television and Motion Pictures.* by Millerson, Gerald. 366 p. illus. New York: Hastings House, 1972.

This book is part of a series which the publishers call *The Library of Communication Techniques.* A study of the art of creative lighting, it covers introductory topics such as the nature of light, the eye, the camera and the visual world. Basic principles and tools of lighting lead to more advanced chapters on portraiture, still life, persuasive lighting, and lighting of scences. Motion picture and television techniques, lighting effects and picture control are discussed in the final sections. Some suggestions for further reading are made and there is an adequate index to the material in the book.

Any book on lighting must contain visuals which illustrate techniques and concepts. Not only is this volume rich in such pictures, but the high standard of photo reproduction which characterizes this series is once again evident. Tables, charts, diagrams, and graphs help support and interpret the text also.

This is a specialized technical book that will be of great assistance to the advanced amateur and the professional.

6017   *The Technique of Screenplay Writing.* by Vale, Eugene. 306 p. New York: Grosset & Dunlap, 1972 (1944).

An updating of a well-known work that appeared originally in 1944. Considered by many to be one of the standard works on writing screenplays, the new volume uses films such as EASY RIDER (1969), MIDNIGHT COWBOY (1969), DOCTOR ZHIVAGO (1965), AIRPORT (1970) and BONNIE AND CLYDE (1967) to explain various points and techniques.

The author's philosophy is evident in his use of the Delacroix quotation: "First learn to be a craftsman. It won't keep you from being a genius." That advice is applicable for the would-be-filmmakers of today. Vale divides his text into three major divisions: the form, the dramatic constitution, and the story. Within each category, he discusses the pertinent elements. For example, under form, such elements as film language, space, picture, time, sound, and information sources are explained. A fascinating diagram comparing the forms of books, plays and films is typical of the provocative and valuable material offered. The other two sections are similar in structure. At all times the text is clear, sequential, and non-pedantic. Frequent references are made to well-known films to support statements. The book is not illustrated, but a good index is offered. The logical development, clarity, and practical advice make this volume valuable to anyone interested in writing for the screen.

6018 *The Technique of Special Effects Cinematography.* by Fielding, Raymond. 398 p. illus. New York: Hastings House, 1968.

This is a definitive work on the tricks of the cinematographic trade. Using many illustrations and diagrams, the author describes various types of special effects such as miniatures, glass shots, optical printing, mirror shots, rear projection, front projection, matte shots, aerial image printing, etc.

The book assumes that the reader has some basic knowledge of cinematography, but much of the content will be comprehensible and of value to the novice. The illustrations are fine and there is an impressive bibliography. Although the entire special effects field is not completely covered, there is enough here to recommend this book enthusiastically.

6019 *The Technique of the Film Cutting Room.* by Walter, Ernest. 282 p. illus. New York: Hastings House, 1969.

Text, charts, drawings, and a glossary all combine to describe the activities and responsibilities of the film cutting room.

6020 *The Technique of the Motion Picture Camera.* by Souto, H. Mario Raimondo. 263 p. illus. New York: Hastings House, 1967.

The various components such as the intermittent

mechanism, the viewing system, the shutter, the motor, the controls, etc. are described in this book about motion picture cameras (16mm and 35mm). Some slight attention is given to actual shooting techniques. This volume may be of interest to the professional, but it is too specialized for others.

6021 *Technique of the Photoplay.* by Sargent, Epes Winthrop. 398 p. illus. New York: Moving Picture World, 1916.

This is the 3rd edition of an early volume on writing silent film scripts. The text consists of a collection of the author's weekly columns from *Moving Picture World* and considers many aspects of photoplay construction.

6022 *Technique of the Photoplay.* by Palmer, Frederick. 330 p. Hollywood: Palmer Institute of Authorship, 1924.

An early manual on writing screenplays for the silent film.

6023 *The Technique of the Photoplay.* by Pepper, Dick L. 254 p. Clacton-on-Sea, Great Britain: East Essex Printing Works, 1925.

Advice and direction on writing scripts for silent films.

6024 *The Technique of the Sound Studio.* by Nisbett, Alec. 528 p. illus. New York: Hastings House, 1971.

General principles of sound reproduction for stereo, film, TV, and radio are the concern of this book. Studios, microphones, sound quality, volume, editing, fades and mixes, sound effects, echo and distortion are a few of the topics discussed. Comprehensive and readable, the volume includes diagrams, a glossary and an index.

6025 *The Technique of Wildlife Cinematography.* by Warham, John. 222 p. illus. London: Focal Press, 1966.

This volume on the specific application of cinematography to photographing animals contains plates, tables, diagrams, and a bibliography.

6026 *A Technological History of Motion Pictures and Television.* edited by Fielding, Raymond. 255 p. illus. Berkeley, Calif.: University of California Press, 1967.

This anthology, taken from the pages of the *Journal of the Society of Motion Picture and Television Engineers*, is an excellent book that will probably be used more for reference and browsing than for actual reading. The development of the technology of both motion pictures and television is traced from early articles published by inventors, engineers, and historians. The book is a treasure of rare photographs and drawings of models, devices, films and documents. The entire collection is superb and needed. However, most users will find reading the accounts of technological discoveries and advances pretty heavy going.

6027   *Teleplay.* by Trapnell, Coles. 245 p. San Francisco: Chandler Pub. Co., 1967.

A good introduction to script writing with attention given to theory and mechanics.

6028   *TV and Film Production Data Book.* by Pittaro, Ernest. 448 p. illus. New York: Morgan & Morgan, 1959.

Describes cameras, projectors, lighting, and other equipment. Some operation procedures are given along with many tables of data, statistics, etc., all vintage 1959.

6029   *TV and Screen Writing.* edited by Yoakem, Lola Goelet. 124 p. Berkeley, Calif.: University of California Press, 1958.

Seventeen writers, most of whom have screen credits, offer advice to the aspiring writer. In addition to the basic principles of screen writing, the various story genres are discussed, as are potential markets and contracts.

6030   *TV Feature Film Source Book.* 715 p. paper New York: Broadcast Information Bureau, 1972.

This excellent reference annual lists all the feature films which are available for showing on television. Arranged alphabetically by title, each film entry offers the following information: film title; stars; type of film; year of release; annotation, story line; running time; black-and-white or color; width in millimeters.; original producer; original distributor; TV distributor.

For anyone dealing with film study, film bookings, or simply general reference, this book is a bountiful treasure of information.

6031   *TV "Free" Film Source Book, Vol. 12, Issue 3.* edited by Fliegelman, Aura. 340 p. paper New York: Broadcast Information Bureau, Inc., 1971.

This is indeed a source book. In the first of three major sections, the reservoir of free television films is subdivided into three categories according to running time—one-hour films, half-hour films and 15-minute films. The one-hour division, for example, lists films having a running time between 31 minutes and 60 minutes. Major subject headings are provided under each time category—arts, space, sports, religious, travel, etc.—and the individual films are listed under these headings.

The following information is offered for each film: title; a short annotation; running time; black-and-white or color; charges; markets open; restrictions; underwriter; distributor.

Titles of all the films are arranged in an alphabetical listing in Section II, while the final section lists sources of the films. The book is a most complete and valuable index to free films.

6032   *TV Key Movie Guide.* edited by Scheuer, Steven H. 403 p. New York: Bantam Books, 1966.

This paperback describes and rates over 6900 films. See *Movies on TV.*

6033   *TV Key Movie Reviews and Ratings.* edited by Scheuer, Steven H. New York: Bantam Books, 1961.

See *Movies on TV.*

6034   *TV Movie Almanac and Ratings (1958-1959).* edited by Scheuer, Steven H. 244 p. paper illus. New York: Bantam Books, 1959.

This paperback describes and rates over 5000 films. See *Movies on TV.*

6035   *TV Movies.* by Maltin, Leonard. 536 p. paper illus. New York: Signet Books, 1970.

In this valuable reference, there are some 8000 films listed. Given with each is the title, running time, some cast names, and a short synopsis. A rating by Mr. Maltin is also offered. An essential book whose price is right.

6036 *Television, Radio, Film for Churchmen.* edited by Jackson, B. F. Nashville, Tenn.: Abingdon Press, 1969.

This is volume No. 2 in the *Communication for Churchmen* Series.

6037 *Television Seminar—NBC.* edited by Reed, Rochelle. 24 p. paper illus. Washington, D.C.: American Film Institute, 1973.

Thomas Sarnoff, accompanied by a panel of NBC executives, discusses the making and use of films for television. A transcript of a meeting held in January 1973. Acceptable.

6038 *Television's Classic Commercials.* by Diamant, Lincoln. 305 p. illus. New York: Hastings House, 1971.

Written by a man who had careers in publishing, broadcasting, and advertising, this book looks at 69 classic television commercials which appeared from 1948-1958, the so-called "Golden Years" of television. The awarding of classic status by the American Television Commericals Festival judges basically rests upon three criteria: longevity, memorability, and influence on later techniques. A short historical account of the development of the American commercial is given first. Then the 69 commericals are arranged under subject headings such as food, tobacco, apparel, cars and trucks, etc. The description of each film includes a television screen still, the technique used, length, number of words, the air date, advertiser, agency, producer, and other creative personnel involved. Of major importance is the reproduction of the full script with each shot and accompanying audio noted. A final paragraph of background information completes each entry. Three appendices indicate dollar expenditures in advertising and a fourth reproduces the world's first commercial, an audio message broadcast on August 28, 1927 over Radio Station WEAF in New York City. A glossary of more than 500 terms used in broadcasting completes the book.

The importance of this book is obvious if one considers the social impact the TV commercial has had on our society. Furthermore, since most commercials are shot as film initially and contain the newest filmmaking techniques, the provision of 69 full scripts for filmmakers to study is an offering to be appreciated. Content, arrangement, production and supporting text are all first rate. Many of the *Hastings House* books are prepared with a publishing longevity in mind and this one is no exception. It should be popular, useful, and in-print for many years to come. Recommended enthusiastically for all.

6039 *Tell It On The Mountain.* by Lasky, William R.; and Scheer, James F. 271 p. paper illus. Old Tappan, N.J.: Revell, 1977.

The author is the younger son of film pioneer, Jesse L. Lasky. Unlike his brother, Jesse, Jr., William was a failure until he discovered religion. In this book he combines his life story with that of his parents. It is a painful, honest autobiography that gives detailed portraits of Lasky, Sr. and his Hollywood activities. A misfit in the motion picture industry, the author tells of the religious experiences and philosophies that have brought him satisfaction.

6040 *Tell It to Louella.* by Parsons, Louella. 316 p. illus. New York: G. P. Putnam's, 1961.

The further adventures of "the gay illiterate." Louella Parsons was most powerful during Hollyood's golden years. Her rapid loss of prestige, influence, and status is not part of this story.

6041 *Telling It Again and Again Repetition in Literature and Film.* by Kawin, Bruce F. 197 p. Ithaca, N.Y.: Cornell University Press, 1972.

As indicated in the subtitle, this volume concerns itself with the use of repetition for effect. The literature of Gertrude Stein and Samuel Beckett are obvious examples. Many other examples in literature are cited and if this volume had appeared in the fifties or earlier, it would have concerned itself with literature exclusively. However, now the works of Eisenstein, Bunuel, Bergman, Resnais and other filmmakers are considered. Acceptable.

6042 *Telly Savalas: TV's Golden Greek.* by Daly, Marsh. 156 p. paper illus. New York: Berkley, 1975.

Although Telly Savalas has been appearing regularly in films since MAD DOG COLL (1960), it was the 1973 television program, "KOJAK," which made him an international star. In this surface overview of his life, some attention is given to his film work. A few illustrations are added but the other supporting essentials (filmography, index, etc.) are missing.

6043 *10-1/2.* by Stevens, Marc. 288 p. paper New York: Zebra, 1975.

Marc Stevens is one of the more recognizable male

stars of pornographic films. In this rambling memoir, he tells about his life, his proportions, coworkers, the porn film industry and other assorted items, most of them sexual. Al Goldstein, the editor of *Screw Magazine*, sets the mood in his introduction. Arousing or filthy—depending on where the reader sits.

6044   THE TEN COMMANDMENTS. 28 p. paper illus. New York: GreenstoneCo., 1956.

The emphasis is on director Cecil B. DeMille in this souvenir book which opens with some excerpts from a DeMille address made in 1956. Full-page printings by Arnold Friberg in color are used to tell the story of the 1956 film. Although the cast members are grouped three to a page, greater attention is given to biographies of director-producer DeMille, coproducer Henry Wilcoxon, and composer Elmer Bernstein. Some mention is made of the enormous amount of research that was done for the film. See also *Moses and Egypt* for more information on the research.

6045   *Ten Film Classics: A Re-viewing.* by Murray, Edward. 183 p. paper illus. New York: Ungar, 1978.

In an attempt to answer the question, "what makes a movie a classic?" Edward Murray selects ten films and examines them in a theoretical, historical, and biographical context. By combining critical approaches he provides in-depth analyses of POTEMKIN (1925), CITIZEN KANE (1941), THE BICYCLE THIEF (1948), IKURU (1952), LA STRADA (1954), ON THE WATERFRONT (1954), WILD STRAWBERRIES (1957), L'AVVENTURA (1959), THE 400 BLOWS (1959) and BONNIE AND CLYDE (1967).

Notes, a bibliography, a directors' filmography, distributors, and an index support Murray's criticism.

6046   *Ten Lessons in Film Appreciation.* by Murray, John. Melbourne: Georgian House, 1966.

6047   *Ten Million Photoplay Plots.* by Hill, Wycliffe A. 100 p. Los Angeles: Photodrama Company, 1919.

This early volume claims to be the "Master Key to All Dramatic Plots."

6048   *Ten Years in Paradise.* edited by Scaramazza, Paul A. 289 p. paper illus. New York: Cinemabilia (Pleasant Press), 1974.

In this volume more than 4200 feature film reviews that originally appeared from 1920 to 1930 in *Photoplay* magazine have been gathered. Early reviews from 1920 to 1923 have been edited into a few succinct sentences to match the capsule review format that the magazine used during the period 1923 to 1930. Thus, the reviews represent the complete *Photoplay* coverage of the golden age of silent films and the early sound years. The evidence presented here indicates that review opinion was often prejudiced, uninformed and commercially biased, e.g., "THE WEDDING MARCH (Paramount): Von Stroheim's romance of old Vienna, dressed up with some repellent scenes and characters. Some good moments, but, as a whole, a waste of time, money and talent." Some of the humor seems to predict the one-liners typical of the current *New York Times* TV movie reviews, e.g., "WEST OF ZANZIBAR (MGM): Lon Chaney goes cripple again. So does the plot."

The films are arranged alphabetically by title under the year in which they were reviewed. After each capsule comment, the month of release is noted. A total index of all film titles indicates the director and the page on which the review appears. A selection of *Photoplay* covers provides the illustrative material and a short addenda offers a few comments and omissions. Although its greatest appeal will be to the informed, dedicated silent film buff, the volume will please a variety of audiences—researchers, nostalgia lovers, students, etc. The coverage is impressive and the arrangement makes for easy reference use. Recommended.

6049   *Ten Years of British Short Films Abroad.* edited by Dunbar, Robert. 88 p. paper London: National Panel For Film Festivals, 1976.

The subtitle tells it all: "A Survey of Past Successes, Present Problems, and Future Action, and a Guide to 100 Film Festivals with Lists of Prize Winners."

6050   *Ten Years of Films on Ballet and Classical Dance, 1956-1965.* by UNESCO. 105 p. paper illus. Paris: UNESCO, 1968.

This catalogue is a sampling of films on ballet, classical and modern dance from many countries. It limits itself to films which are "pure dance" rather than biographies, how-to-dance films, or folk dance films. After a short introduction by Agnes Bleier-Brody, an alphabetical listing by country follows. Under each, one or more dance films originated in that country are described. Included in the description are the names of those responsible for the production, choreography, music, libretto, decor, direction, and principal roles. Film characteristics of length, gauge, color, black and white are given along with distributor information. A last section offers some information about the subject of the film. Several indexes complete the book: the first lists the films by country (really a table of contents), the second is an index of choreographers and the third, an index of composers.

Although the book refers to films which are eighteen more years old, they are still pertinent to many persons concerned with the study of dance, music, and allied arts.

6051 *Ten Years of People's Poland.* by Grodzicki, August; and Merz, Irena. 62 p. paper illus. Warsaw: Polonia Publishing House, 1955.

A survey of theatre and film in Poland that covers the years from 1945 to 1955.

6052 *Tendencies for Monopoly in the Cinematograph Film Industry.* by Cinematograph Film Council Committee. 41 p. paper London: H.M. Stationery Office, 1944.

6053 *Tenets for Movie Viewers.* by Gardiner, Harold Charles; and Walsh, Moira. 56 p. paper New York: America Press, 1962.

6054 *Tennessee Williams: Memoirs.* by Williams, Tennessee. 264 p. illus. New York: Doubleday, 1975.

Tennessee Williams' novel, *The Roman Spring of Mrs. Stone*, and many of his plays and short stories have been made into films. For THE GLASS MENAGERIE (1950), A STREETCAR NAMED DESIRE (1951), THE ROSE TATTOO (1955), BABY DOLL (1956), SUDDENLY LAST SUMMER (1959), THE FUGITIVE KIND (1960), and BOOM! (1968), he also participated in the writing of the screenplays.

Since he is known primarily as a stage dramatist, it is that aspect of his professional career that he emphasizes; but even those sections are overshadowed by his brave attempt to explain his private life and personality to the reader. For the most part he is unsparing with himself and others. His talent as a dramatic writer is employed in this book with skill and a sense of showmanship as he recalls, in a nonlinear fashion, those events and persons who affected his life and career.

The illustrations which appear throughout the book complement the narrative most effectively. The visualization of the young writer, his family and his friends helps to create an intimacy between the author and reader. A detailed index adds considerably to the book's overall quality.

Since Williams devotes a considerable portion of the text to his homosexual activities, the volume may not please certain readers. Others may find these sections to be a key toward a further understanding of the man and his writing.

Like all his work, this volume is written with much beauty and an absence of fear. It will be a rewarding reading experience for those who have appreciated his plays and stories. For others who have yet to discover his artistry, the book can provide an excellent introduction to the most complex and fascinating dramatist that has appeared in this century thus far. Highly recommended.

6055 *Tennessee Williams and Film.* by Yacowar, Maurice. 168 p. illus. New York: Frederick Ungar, 1977.

In this study of films derived from the plays and stories of Tennessee Williams, the author uses a chronological arrangement beginning with THE GLASS MENAGERIE (1950) and ending with THE LAST OF THE MOBILE HOT-SHOTS (1969). A total of 15 works is examined, with special attention given to the changes made in transferring the original material to the screen. In addition to analyzing the actions and motivations of the characters, the text offers many valid evaluations of the performers who interpreted the unforgettable Williams characters on the screen.

Supporting the text are a filmography, chapter notes, a bibliography, and an index. A center pictorial section offers nine stills from the films.

Given the basic richness of Tennessee Williams' work, the author has embellished it further by his perceptive analyses of both the original and the screen version. Although Yacowar's approach is that of a respectful scholar, his text provides a provocative exploration that will hold the reader's attention completely. Highly recommended.

6056 *Tenth Year of State Awards for Film, 1962.* edited by India Ministry of Information and Broadcasting. 31 p. paper New Delhi: Ministry of Information and Broadcasting, 1963.

6057 *Terence Macartney-Filgate: The Candid Eye.* edited by Gobeil, Charlotte. 34 p. illus. Ottawa: Canadian

Film Institute, 1966.

This appreciation contains an interview, a filmography, and critical comments about this Canadian documentary filmmaker. The Candid Eye was a unit of the National Film Board of Canada in which Macartney-Filgate was a leading member from 1957 to 1960.

6058   *Terrors of the Screen*. by Manchel, Frank. 122 p. illus. Englewood Cliffs, N.J.: Prentice-Hall, 1970.

Aimed primarily at a juvenile audience, this book covers the horror genre of films in a broad sense. Complemented by a fine selection of stills, most of which are reproduced with excellent fidelity, the text is a bit uneven in its emphases (Chaney) and omissions—THE DEVIL DOLL (1936), DR. X (1932), THE HAUNTING (1963)—but no volume on horror can ever satisfy completely.

Note: Two other fine volumes designed for younger readers by Dr. Manchel are: *When Pictures Began to Move* and *When Movies Began to Speak.*

6059   *Tex Avery: King of Cartoons*. by Adamson, Joe. 237 p. paper illus. New York: Popular Library (Big Apple Books), 1975.

A brief history of the animated cartoon introduces this appreciation of Tex Avery. From his first cartoons made for Warner Brothers in 1935 to his later MGM films of the fifties, his career as an animation artist is covered. Detailed attention is given to a description-analysis of the many cartoons he worked on, supervised, or directed. An interview with Michael Maltese describes the working habits at the Warner cartoon studio. In a second interview, Heck Allen, the story man for many of Avery's cartoons, reminisces about the animation industry while a final interview is a composite of three sessions held with Avery himself between 1969 and 1971.

A long Avery filmography with evaluations in the form of star ratings is added along with some final comments. Since most of the visuals are apparently frame blowups, the quality of the illustrations is often fuzzy.

Although the reader may have some initial difficulty in coordinating the disparate elements in this volume, the final result should be a greater understanding and appreciation of the animator and his art. Highly recommended.

6060   *Thalberg—Life and Legend*. by Thomas, Bob. 415 p. illus. Garden City, N.Y.: Doubleday, 1969.

The biography of a highly regarded Hollywood legend. At 20, Thalberg was head of production at Universal. By the mid-twenties, he and Louis B. Mayer were operating the Metro-Goldwyn-Mayer studios. During his reign he was responsible for producing many of the classic MGM films—THE BIG PARADE (1925), THE MERRY WIDOW (1925) ANNA CHRISTIE (1930), MUTINY ON THE BOUNTY (1935), GRAND HOTEL (1932), A NIGHT AT THE OPERA (1935), THE GOOD EARTH (1937), CAMILLE (1936), etc. Bob Thomas, a Hollywood columnist for Associated Press and author of biographies on Harry Cohn and David Selznick, does not have as controversial or colorful a subject in this volume. Thalberg was ambitious, hardworking and, apparently, clean-living. Mr. Thomas has no scandal to relate and is content to describe a happy marriage to Norma Shearer and, of course, to the motion picture industry. Thalberg's infrequent emotional moments are saved for von Stroheim and Mayer.

The volume has been handsomely produced, with many photographs, an annotated filmography of many Thalberg films, a bibliography, an index, and a list of nominations and awards won by the films. Like its subject, the book lacks a certain outer excitement, but the wealth of quiet, rich material underneath will still fascinate most readers. How much has not been told is interesting to contemplate. Highly recommended.

6061   *Thank You for Having Me*. by Lejeune, Caroline A. 255 p. London: Hutchinson, 1964.

The reminiscences of a pioneer English film critic for whom emotion was more important than film theory or aesthetics. She helped to popularize films and film criticism in England. Although she speaks of Korda, Hitchcock, Howard, Clair and Renoir, she spends much time talking about her personal and home life.

6062   *That Kelly Family*. by McCallum, John. 229 p. illus. New York: Barnes, 1957.

Princess Grace and her family.

6063   *That Kid—The Story of Jerry Lewis*. by Gehman, Richard. 192 p. paper illus. New York: Avon Books, 1964.

A paperback biography of Jerry Lewis, a rather neglected subject in American cinema literature. Much more has been written in French.

6064 *That Marvel—The Movie.* by Van Zile, Edward Sims. 229 p. New York: G. P. Putnam's, 1923.

The subtitle in 1923 reads "A Glance at Its Reckless Past, Its Promising Present, and Its Significant Future." After an early factual history is presented, some arguments are given concerning the good and evil potentials of film. An appendix is made up of statistics of the period.

6065 *That's Hollywood.* by Carpozi, George, Jr. 5 vols. paper New York: Manor Books, 1978.

In what may become a series, George Carpozi has written five collective biographies about personalities from Hollywood's golden era.

Each volume is entitled, *That's Hollywood*, with a numeral following the title: 1. *The Matinee Idols*, 2. *The Love Goddesses*, 3. *The Magnificent Entertainers*, 4. *The Great Ladies of Hollywood*, 5. *The Distinguished Performers*.

6066 *Theater and Film.* by Manvell, Roger. 303 p. illus. Rutherford, N.J.: Fairleigh Dickinson University Press, 1979.

Roger Manvell has been writing film books since the forties. In both his choice of subject and his treatment of it, he is usually ahead of the field. Occasionally, he'll lend his name to something like *Love Goddess of the Movies*, but usually he deals with the relationship between films and such topics as war, Shakespeare, television, the public, animation, etc. Here he considers film and theatre.

The investigation consists of two parts: a comparative study of the two forms, and then some selected examples of adaptations from stage to screen, e.g., Shaw's *Pygmalion*, Euripides' *Electra*, Chekov's *Three Sisters*, O'Neill's *Long Day's Journey Into Night*, William's *A Streetcar Named Desire*, and several others.

Acknowledgement of earlier studies by Allardyce Nicoll and Andre Bazin is made in an appendix. A discography, a bibliography, an index, and a selected list of dramatists whose plays have been filmed complete the book.

Reading Roger Manvell's work has always been a rewarding pleasure. This one is no exception.

6067 *Theatre: Stage to Screen to Television.* by Leonard, William Torbert. 2 volumes 1,812 p. Metuchen, N.J.: Scarecrow, 1981.

Three hundred and twenty seven plays are considered in their path from stage to screen to television, synopsis, comment, casts, credits, songs, authors, prizes etc. are noted.

6068 *Theatre and Cinema Architecture.* edited by Stoddard, Richard. 368 p. Detroit: Gale Research, 1978.

This is a unique bibliography which notes information sources for theatre and cinema architecture. There are three divisions: General References (25 entries), Theatre Architecture (1561 entries), and Cinema Architecture (238 entries). The latter section divides its entries under the categories of general references, France, Germany, Great Britain, United States, and Other Countries. Many of the entries are annotated, offering both descriptive and evaluative comments. Indexes for authors, architects and designers, theatres and cinemas, and subjects are added.

As indicated, this is very specialized information that will have a limited use. It is presented in an efficient, easy format and should be of great assistance to the interested scholar/user. Acceptable.

6069 *Theatre and Motion Picture Houses.* by Meloy, Arthur S. 120 p. illus. New York: The Architect's Supply and Publishing Company, 1916.

A practical treatise on the proper planning and construction of theatre and motion picture houses, containing useful suggestions, rules and data for the benefit of architects, prospective owners, etc. Illustrated by the author.

6070 *Theatre, Film and Television Biographies Master Index.* edited by La Beau, Dennis. 477 p. Detroit: Gale Research, 1979.

An index to 44 biographical sources is provided by this book. The 18 sources that deal specifically with filmmakers are *A Biographical Dictionary of Film*, *A Companion to the Movies*, *Dictionary of Film Makers*, *Filmarama*, *The Filmgoer's Companion*, *Hollywood Players*, *International Motion Picture Almanac*, *The MGM Stock Company*, *Motion Picture Performers*, *The Movie Makers*, *The Oxford Companion to Film*, *They Had Faces Then*, *Twenty Years of Silents*, *The Versatiles*, *Who Was Who on Screen*, *Who's Who in Hollywood*, *Women Who Make Movies*, and *The World Encyclopedia of Film*. This is a selected group of references which omits *Classics of the Silent Screen*, *Motion Picture Directors*, *The Hollywood Album*, *50 Major Film Makers*,

Star Quality and other collective biographies, all of which offer at least 50 entries. Often the quality and content found in the omitted volumes is better than in certain selected titles such as *The World Encyclopedia of Film, A Companion to the Movies*, etc.

The presence of books dealing with theatre (18 titles) and television (one title) may help the researcher since many filmmakers are active in those media. The same is true of the remaining two cross-media volumes, *The ASCAP Biographical Dictionary of Composers, Authors, and Publishers* and *Celebrity Register*. For example, information about Frank Loesser can found in the ASCAP title and also in certain film and theatre volumes. Hundreds of obscure players are listed in the index and the researcher will be helped greatly. Quick access to many popular sources of biographical information is provided by this concise, easy-to-use volume. Recommended.

6071   *The Theatre of Science.* by Grau, Robert. 465 p. illus. New York: Benjamin Blom, 1969 (1914).

Subtitled, "A Volume of Progress and Achievement in the Motion Picture Industry," this historical account covers the period from 1876 to 1914. It considers many aspects such as music, the press, the stage, producers, directors, actors, etc. More than 87 pages of unusual photographs are a part of this informal, chatty and quite entertaining history. It is unforgivable that the current publishers did not provide an index. This book is an excellent, overlooked early history of motion pictures.

6072   *The Theatre, the Cinema and Ourselves.* by Andrews, Cyril Bruyn. 52 p. illus. London: Clarence House, 1947.

A short volume of British criticism, comment and a comparison of acting techniques.

6073   *The Theatrical Distribution of Cultural Films.* by Leglise, Paul. 137 p. paper Strasbourg, France: Council of Europe, 1967.

A cultural film is defined as "one which imparts fresh knowledge or makes a valuable contribution to the intellectual heritage of mankind." This book considers only short films, full length documentaries, or children's films which have been shown in public cinemas to a paying audience. Feature films are not treated. The experiments and projects dealing with such cultural films are noted along with national legislation and international agreements. A general chapter on the cultural film concludes the work. This is an excellent survey with much meaning, implication and information for those dealing with film education.

6074   *Their Hearts Were Young and Gay.* by Best, Marc. 256 p. illus. New York: A. S. Barnes, 1975.

In *Those Endearing Young Hearts* Marc Best offered 50 child film actors as subjects for a collective biography. In this sequel he has added 40 more, arranging them in alphabetical order, and noting such biographical material as date and place of birth, education, entrance into show business, hobbies, personal characteristics, and a list of credits. Several hundred illustrations consisting of portraits and stills supplement the data.

6075   *Themes: Short Films for Discussion.* by Kuhns, William. illus. Dayton, Ohio: Pflaum, 1968.

The contents of this book may vary since it has recently become a loose-leaf book with periodic supplements. A total of 134 short films will be included in the latest edition—the original book (82 films) plus Supplement One (30 films) and Supplement Two (22 films). For each short film, a synopsis, technical data, distributor information, and discussion questions are provided. Some introductory material and suggestions are also given. An excellent aid for schools.

6076   *Themes Two.* by Kuhns, William. 192 p. paper illus. Dayton, Ohio: Pflaum, 1974.

After a period of several years, William Kuhns has provided a sequel to his earlier work, *Themes: Short Films for Discussion.* Although the production format has been changed from looseleaf to paperback, the content is still very impressive. The author has selected 100 films and provided a narrative outline of each. Gone are the sections on possible use and suggested questions. Credits and descriptive information are still given at the beginning of each review. The appendices offer information about distributors, books on film, and themes of the films. Some small illustrations are sprinkled throughout the book.

Information about recommended short films is always welcome and in Kuhn's case, doubly so. He writes with an intelligence that only comes with experience, background and dedication. An essential book.

6077 *Then and Now: The Story of the Motion Picture.* by Strong, Harry H. 45 p. illus. Toledo, Ohio: Strong Electric Co., 1943.

A short history of cinematography and world cinema.

6078 *Theodore Huff, American Film Historian.* by Wishniac, Vance L. Brooklyn, N.Y.: Revisionist, 1980.

Theodore Huff, a writer-teacher-historian, is perhaps best known for his biography of Charlie Chaplin.

6079 *Theology Through Film.* by Hurley, Neil P. 212 p. illus. New York: Harper & Row, 1970.

"The motion picture enjoys a psychological and pedagogical experience that has as yet not been matched by a corresponding effectiveness in the modes of religious communication. Today, access to films allows the religious leader/educator to compare his 'message' with that expounded by others." These statements are taken from the provocative introduction to this remarkable book.

In the body of the work, chapters are devoted to such ideas as man in secular society, inner man, freedom, conscience, sex, evil, death, grace, sacrificial love, and the future. In each chapter, films are correlated with the theme being explored. For example, the chapter on society uses LILIES OF THE FIELD (1963), A TASTE OF HONEY (1962), MIDNIGHT COWBOY (1969), CATCH 22 (1970), IL SORPASSO (1962), THE ISLAND (1961), THE APU TRILOGY (1954), RULES OF THE GAME (1939) and other films. A final section deals with the teaching of theology. Chapters are footnoted and there is an index. Pictorial illustrations are well chosen and well reproduced.

For those critics who decry the lack of "serious" writing on cinema, this book is a fine response. If offers intelligence without conceit, readability without compromise, and now-ness without faddishness. It is stimulating reading that will be of value and interest to a wide audience. Highly recommended.

6080 *Theories of Authorship.* edited by Caughie, John. 316 p. illus. London: Routledge and Kegan Paul, 1981.

This BFI reader is concerned with film authorship. The first section entitled "Auteurism" contains 6 articles on theory and seven on director John Ford. The second, "Auteurstructuralism," consists of seven articles, while the last part, "Fiction of the Author/Author of the Fiction" contains ten articles.

6081 *Theories of Film.* by Tudor, Andrew. 168 p. paper illus. New York: Viking Press, 1973.

An exploration of a wide field of film theory is presented in this volume. Beginning with the work of Sergei Eisenstein, the text also discusses the theories of John Grierson, Andre Bazin, Siegfried Kracauer, Rudolf Arnheim and others. Attention is also given to the auteur and the genre theories. In addition to analyzing these selected theories, Tudor also tries or tests them but comes to no startling or radical conclusions. He finds the theories to be contradictory, partial, inadequate, and even incorrect; but they do contain mutual elements which suggest that a satisfactory theory might be evolved.

He believes theorizing is essential, that the focus should be on "What is" rather than "What should be" and that models of film theory are the first priority in formulating a satisfactory film theory. The illustrations are adequate and a bibliography is included. Recommended.

6082 *Theories of Mass Communication.* by De Fleur, Melvin L. New York: McKay, 1966.

One chapter is devoted to film.

6083 *The Theory and Practice of the Cine-Roman.* by Van Wert, William F. 382 p. New York: Arno Press, 1978.

Written in 1975 at Indiana University in partial fulfillment of the doctoral program, this study of the New Wave French cinema examines the work of several directors who have created a literary cinema employing the film-novel technique. The films of Alain Resnais, Agnes Varda, and Alain Robbe-Grillet are among the numerous ones analyzed by the author. Details on film production and distribution are presented in an economic analysis of the works of these artists. This title is included in the *Dissertations on Film* series.

6084 *Theory of Film: The Redemption of Physical Reality.* by Kracauer, Siegfried. 364 p. paper illus. New York: Oxford University Press, 1960, 1965.

According to the author, the concern of this volume is "black and white film as it grows out of photography." Its purpose is to give an understanding of the "intrinsic nature of photographic film." If motion pictures are an extension of photography, they share the same relationship with the available physical world and justify themselves when they depict this physical reality. Films are most valid when they indicate the world that is available to our eyes. These are some of the basic beliefs and concerns of the author, who devotes the remainder of his book to an exploration and defense of these theories.

This is not an easy book to read and will demand a wide intellectual background, a strong determination and much endurance. It is a pedantic, serious, in-depth, verbose systematic analysis of film aesthetics. The book is illustrated and contains notes, a bibliography and an index.

6085   *A Theory of Film Language.* by Salvaggio, Jerry Lee. New York: Arno, 1980.

This title in the Dissertations on Film series deals with the nature of spatial-temporal signification in the film narrative. This is the communication process in which a filmmaker uses spatial-temporal codes and the audience decodes them according to the filmmaker's intention.

6086   *Theory of Film Practice.* by Burch, Noel. 172 p. illus. New York: Praeger, 1973.

This complex series of arguments, opinions, and derivations on film theory and aesthetics had their first appearance in *Cahiers du Cinema.* Burch has arranged them under headings such as Basic Elements, Dialectics, Perturbing Factors, and Reflections on Film Subjects.

The author attempts to close the gap between the theory and the practice of filmmaking but the endeavor does not quite succeed. The difficult writing sytle is an intellectual hurdle that few will attempt to master. For example: "Taken in its most elementary sense (which was how Eisenstein certainly took it), 'dialectics' may convey a meaningful image of the conflictual organization to which these elementary parameters have been subjected by nearly every consequential filmmaker in his or her search for 'unity through diversity'..." While this verbiage may be fine for the dedicated theoretician, it is probably a bit too concentrated for the young impatient filmmaker.

The book is indexed and there are a few illustrations. Many of the examples of films in the text are French, and familiarity with them will help in appreciating the text.

6087   *A Theory of Semiotics.* by Eco, Umberto. 368 p. illus. Bloomington, Ind.: Indiana University Press, 1976.

6088   *The Theory of Stereoscopic Transmission and Its Application to the Motion Picture.* by Spottiswoode, Raymond; and Spottiswoode, Nigel. 177 p. illus. Berkeley, Calif.: University of California Press, 1953.

Issued when 3-D films were being made by Hollywood studios, this explanation includes some stereoscopic images and a viewer. Bibliographical footnotes accompany the text.

6089   *Theory of the Film: Character and Growth of a New Art.* by Balazs, Bela. 291 p. illus. London: Dennis Dobson, 1952.

Translated from the Hungarian, this volume is an early attempt to approach an aesthetic of film art. Although it was updated by the author prior to translation, many of the ideas seem overly familiar to us today. References to certain forgotten films also distract from its effectiveness. Reading a short chapter on the potential of film opera is interesting to us today since we have had several decades of film experience with which we can test the author's prognostications and theories. All elements of film are considered and it is surprising how many terms (kitsch?), ideas, and opinions seem to have originated with this author. Some photographs are included.

The volume can be read with ease and pleasure. If one can overlook its age and regard it as a pioneer work still valid, the reading experience will be rewarding.

6090   *There Must Be a Lone Ranger.* by Calder, Jenni. 241 p. illus. New York: Taplinger, 1975.

The general theme of this book is well expressed in its subtitle, "The American West in Film and Reality." Using examples from many films produced from 1903 to 1972, the author has compared film incidents, locales, and characters to their actual real-life counterparts. Chapters are devoted to specific topics—the frontier, indians, the law, women, the range, violence, etc. Chapter notes, a chronological film list, a bibliography and an index complete the work. A center section contains a few photographs.

The author's interest in and affection for this film genre is shown by the careful attention she gives to detail. All aspects of the western are considered with a critical objectivity and respect rarely found in such analyses. A minor criticism may be made of the visuals. The wisdom of including such a small sampling of illustrations is questionable. Certainly the comparative nature of this study warrants many more than those provided. Perhaps the few offered should have been eliminated because of the unsatisfied feeling they produce. The text, however, is so strong in its detailed double portrait of the American West that most readers will be both stimulated and satisfied. Recommended.

6091 THERE'S NO BUSINESS LIKE SHOW BUSINESS. 16 p. paper illus. 1954.

After a short plot synopsis, the starring members of the cast and songwriter Irving Berlin are each given one page of attention in this souvenir book. Ethel Merman, Donald O'Connor, Marilyn Monroe, Dan Dailey, Johnny Ray and Mitzi Gaynor are spotlighted. The supporting cast is listed but there are no technical or production credits. Photographs are in black and white and the book's inexpensive appearance suggests that it was a rapidly produced afterthought.

6092 *They Call Me the Show Biz Priest.* by Perrella, Robert. 274 p. paper illus. New York: Pocket Books, 1973.

Father Robert Perrella is a Catholic priest whose parish is made up of show business personalities from all religious backgrounds. In this paperback reprinting of the original Trident book, he recalls via anecdote, narrative and comment almost 30 years as a confidant of the stars. There are vignettes of Sinatra, Durante, Martha Raye, Jane Wyman, Lucille Ball, Perry Como and many, many others.

The book presents positive, flattering portraits of its many characters along with autobiographical data that is copious but subtly presented and nonintrusive. The author has probably had much experience in telling selected stories about his famous acquaintances, and this volume is a lengthy testimony to his skill as an entertaining name-dropper. Acceptable.

6093 *They Came to My Studio: Famous People of Our Time.* by Vivienne. 172 p. illus. London: Hall, 1956.

6094 *They Didn't Win the Oscars.* by Libby, Bill. 236 p. illus. Westport, Conn: Arlington House, 1980.

A book devoted to Oscar losers, this volume promises the answer to the same nagging question that rises each year after the awards—why did they lose?

After an introduction, the text offers lists of Oscar nominees and winners (1927-1979), fan lists, critic lists, nomination breakdowns, etc. The rest of the text consists of familiar factual material or subjective emotional reaction to moments in films.

What is outstanding here is the collection of visuals. Reproduced with remarkable clarity, the stills will recall the losers far better than the words provided.

6095 *They Had Faces Then.* by Springer, John; and Hamilton, Jack D. 342 p. illus. Secaucus, N.J.: Citadel, 1974.

John Springer has chosen to concentrate on female superstars, stars and starlets of the 1930s in this attractive collection of 940 photographs. Supporting the visuals is an affectionate, nostalgic text that entertains more than informs. Emphasis throughout the book is on a Hollywood specialty absent in most female performers of today—glamour via style, beauty, charisma and radiance. In the closing section of the book, Jack D. Hamilton has provided short biographic sketches of the actresses containing data on marriages, divorces, wealth, career rises and declines, suicides, etc. Acceptable.

6096 THEY MIGHT BE GIANTS. by Goldman, James. 152 p. illus. New York: Lancer, 1970.

Script of the 1970 film, which was directed by Anthony Harvey.

6097 THEY SHOOT HORSES DON'T THEY? by Thompson, Robert E. 319 p. paper New York: Avon Books, 1969.

Script of the 1969 film directed by Sydney Pollack. Contains the short novel by Horace McCoy.

6098 *They Went Thataway.* by Horwitz, James. 281 p. illus. New York: Dutton, 1976.

The author, who thinks of himself as a front-row kid at the movies, describes his adventures as he searches for his boyhood heroes today. After two introductory chapters which tell about his infatuation with western films, he sets out to find the actor-characters who were heroes in those films. Although he is too late for many of them, he was successful in talking to such western film stars as Gene Autry, Sunset Carson, Charles Starrett, Russell Hayden, Joel McCrea, Rex Allen, Jimmy Wakely, Duncan Renaldo, and Tim McCoy.

The encounters are not reported in the usual interview fashion but appear as the casual conversations one might find in a novel. In fact, the entire book may be read as a western trip scenario starring an unknown lead but featuring an all-star supporting cast. Interwoven into the plot are short biography-appreciations of many western actors, all of whom have had a past influence on the author-hero.

The book uses posters and advertising cards from the western films as illustrations. There is no index.

In this unusual and entertaining book, Horwitz has said a great deal about westerns, America, actors, media, and many other topics in a most ingenious way. He has employed a deceptively simple story to explore some rather large ideas. Recommended.

6099   *They're Playing Our Song.* by Wilk, Max. 295 p. New York: Atheneum, 1973.

The 21 songwriters profiled in this collective biography have all had some connection with motion pictures. Using interviews, research data, public information and personal experience, Wilk has created some lively character sketches. Included are separate chapters on Jerome Kern, Bert Kalmar and Harry Ruby, Vincent Youmans, Dorothy Fields, Lorenz Hart, Richard Rogers, Oscar Hammerstein, Ira Gershwin, Richart Whiting, Leo Robin, Betty Comden, Harry Warren, Johnny Mercer, Harold Arlen, Jule Styne, Sammy Cahn, Saul Chaplin, E. Y. Harburg, Stephen Sondheim, Frank Loesser, and Irving Berlin. A potentially fine and useful book has been diminished by the omission of an index to its large amount of data and information. The reader must search at random for any specific information on song titles, films, shows, etc. Acceptable.

6100   *Things I Don't Remember.* by De Casalis, Jeanne. illus. London: Heinemann, 1953.

Jeanne De Casalis is a British actress who appeared in films during the thirties and forties.

6101   *The Things I Had to Learn.* by Young, Loretta; and Ferguson, Helen. 256 p. illus. Indianapolis: Bobbs-Merrill, 1961.

Certain film stars who participate in so-called autobiographical attempts have an uncanny ability to envision themselves as psychological and spiritual leaders for the unwary reader. Loretta Young is a case in point. Instead of concentrating on the important element, her career in the motion picture industry, she offers advice, gratitude, thanks, acknowledgment, counseling service, etc. She is intent on reinforcing the fiction of her public image. An incomplete and carelessly prepared filmography completes this disappointing book. There is no index. Not recommended.

6102   THINGS TO COME. by Wells, H. G. 155 p. New York: Macmillan, 1935.

Script of the 1935 film directed by William Cameron Menzies. Contains an introduction by H. G. Wells.

6103   *Things to Come.* by Menville, Douglas; and Reginald, R. 212 p. illus. New York: Times Books, 1977.

This volume, which is subtitled "An Illustrated History of the Science Fiction Film," provides a survey that is factual, descriptive and critical. Beginning with a section on silent films (1895-1929), the authors devote one chapter to the Golden Era (1930-1949), and then separate chapters to each decade that followed, up to 1977. They have obviously seen most of the films they discuss. The usual detailed plot descriptions are present but it is the critical evaluations which distinguish this survey from earlier ones. There is an attempt to identify those qualities in each film which make it eligible for consideration in this genre study.

Equally important is the selection and reproduction of the hundreds of illustrations found throughout the book. They often give the reader the visual information necessary for a fuller comprehension of the text and the films. A bibliography and an index complete the volume.

The author's affection, knowledge and concern with the science fiction film is constantly evident in this entertaining, well- organized, and informative survey. Recommended.

6104   THE THIRD MAN. by Greene, Graham. 134 p. paper illus. New York: Simon & Schuster, 1968.

Script of the 1949 film directed by Carol Reed. Contains cast credits, an introduction by Andrew Sinclair, and a paragraph about each of the major characters.

6105   *The Third Time Around.* by Burns, George. 219 p. illus. New York: Putnams, 1980.

George Burns is making up for all those silent years as Gracie's partner. Currently he is chattering his head off on television, in films and in books like this one, his second autobiographical memoir. It's mostly the same mixture as that in *Living It Up*—anecdotes, tall stories, and one-liners about the early days, recent films, life with Gracie, etc. A few of Burns and Allen's classic routines are also recalled.

Burns is always "on" and, if the reader loves him as much as millions of others apparently do, this book will please and entertain.

6106 *Third Time Lucky.* by Donlan, Yolande. 245 p. illus. New York: Dial, 1976.

Yolande Donlan is an American girl whose greatest fame was achieved in British films and theatre. In this autobiographical memoir, she concentrates on her early years in Hollywood. A character-actor father, a French opera singer mother, other eccentric relatives, and an all-star cast—Gable, Barrymore, Hayworth, etc.—figure largely in her story. Her own professional achievements are considerable. In a long, colorful career, she has worked with and met many celebrated performers. Her affection for show business and its denizens is evident throughout this volume. Written in a positive, often comic style, the book is a satisfying recollection of biographical incidents, colorfully interpreted.

Some good illustrations are provided, but there is no index or filmography. See also *Sand in My Mink.* Acceptable.

6107 *Third World Cinema.* by Elsas, Diana; and Fabien, Rosemarie. 27 p. paper Washington, D.C.: American Film Institute, 1977.

As defined here the Third World includes Africa (non-Arab), Latin America, India, and Southeast Asia. The topics covered include organizations concerned with Third World film, film study, archives, festivals, distributors, bibliography and periodicals. This useful reference is a title in the *Fact File* series.

6108 *Thirty From The Thirties.* compiled by Tierney, Tom. 128 p. paper illus. Englewood Cliffs, N.J.: Prentice-Hall, 1976.

A coloring book of paperdoll cut-outs, this oversized paperback features 30 film stars from the 1930s, with six movie costumes for each. Ginger Rogers, Joan Crawford, Bette Davis, Garbo, Errol Flynn, Fred Astaire, Fay Wray and the Marx Brothers are among those present. The costumes are carefully reproduced from the stars' most famous roles. A history of costume design, brief star biographies and some trivia quizzes complete the book.

6109 *Thirty Thousand Miles for the Films.* by Barkas, Natalie. 197 p. illus. London: Blackie, 1937.

An account of the making of RHODES OF AFRICA (1936).

6110 *Thirty Years of the Ten Best.* compiled by National Board of Review of Motion Pictures. paper illus. New York: National Board of Review, 1959.

6111 *Thirty Years of Treason.* edited by Bentley, Eric. 991 p. paper New York: Viking, 1973.

This collection of excerpts from hearings held by the House Committee on Un-American Activities covers the period 1938 to 1968. The intention is to show the evolution of HUAC from an investigating panel which operated in a dignified sensitive way into a menacing governmental agency which was a potential threat to every creative person. It is, the publishers say, a warning for the future. The inquiry into Communistic infiltration of the motion picture industry involved Adolph Menjou, Robert Taylor, Ronald Reagan, Gary Cooper, John Howard Lawson, Edward Dmytryk, Emmet Lavery, Ring Lardner, Jr., Larry Parks, Sterling Hayden, Jose Ferrer, Budd Schulberg, Elia Kazan, Edward G. Robinson, Lionel Stander and Lee J. Cobb. An index facilitates access. It is difficult to imagine users reading this large volume as a totality; its greatest use will probably be for reference and as such it can be recommended.

6112 *This Book Is a Movie.* edited by Bowles, Jerry G.; and Russel, Tony. 320 p. paper illus. New York: Delta, 1971.

Contrary to the title, this book is not a movie: it is a collection of examples of the way some people are using words, numbers and other symbols as a visual element in their poetry.

6113 *This Film Business.* by Messel, Rudolph. 295 p. illus. London: Ernest Benn, 1928.

This volume explores diverse elements of the film business just prior to the emergence of the sound film. Included are sections on history, Griffith, von Stroheim, GREED (1923), METROPOLIS (1928), the domination of the Hollywood film, abstract film, the future/function of film as an art form, film as a social force, etc.

6114 *This For Remembrance.* by Clooney, Rosemary; and Strait, Raymond. 250 p. illus. Chicago: Playboy Press, 1977.

Its all here—success, celebrity, tragedy, inspiration, love, suffering, despair, recovery, a happyending—in this volume subtitled "The Autobiography of Rosemary Clooney, an Irish-American Singer." In what seems to be an edited tape transcript, Clooney recalls her climb to success, marriage to Jose Ferrer, and a sixties breakdown leading to the isolation cell of a psychiatric ward. At this writing she is professionally active again, apparently recovered and at peace with herself.

Clooney is noted mostly as a singer, but has appeared in a number of films. THE STARS ARE SINGING (1953), HERE COME THE GIRLS (1953), RED GARTERS (1954), WHITE CHRISTMAS (1954), and DEEP IN MY HEART (1954). Her appreciable talents were never utilized by Hollywood.

6115   THIS IS CINERAMA. 20 p. paper illus. New York: Cinerama Publishers, 1954.

Lowell Thomas narrated much of this first film in the Cinerama process. It began with the well-remembered roller coaster ride which was followed by sequences designed to show the potential of this new process. Four pages of description of the process introduce the program of this pioneer film. The second section (or act) of the 1954 film was a flightacross the United States.

6116   *This is Where I Came In.* by Clarke, T. E. B. 206 p. illus. London: Michael Joseph, 1974.

An autobiography and reminiscence by a British screenwriter whose credits include JOHNNY FRENCHMAN (1945), HUE AND CRY (1946), PASSPORT TO PIMLICO (1949), THE MAGNET (1950), THE LAVENDER HILL MOB (1951), THE TITFIELD THUNDERBOLT (1952), THE RAINBOW JACKET (1954), ALL AT SEA (1957) and other films.

6117   *This Is Where We Came In.* by Knelman, Martin. 176 p. paper Toronto: McClelland & Stewart, 1977.

This look at Canadian films, written by a film critic, treats a range of topics—history, industry, films, directors etc. The comments indicate a considerable background in the growthand development of the Canadian film industry, while the criticism seems sharp, personal and informed. Unfortunately most of the Canadian films are unfamiliar and the author's skill as a critic may be difficult for an American reader to appreciate.

6118   *This Laugh Is on Me: The Phil Silvers Story.* by Silvers, Phil; and Saffron, Robert. 276 p. illus. Englewood Cliffs, N.J.: Prentice-Hall, 1973.

Phil Silvers is one of the last examples of a performer who paid his dues in all forms of show business. Starting as a Gus Edwards vaudeville act, he later appeared in burlesque, radio, films, television and the theatre. He recalls his many careers with short anecdotes that are affectionate more often than not. That he is essentially a sad man off stage is continually apparent, although Silvers never labors this point or asks for reader sympathy. Thankfully, his film career is treated to full coverage, from TOM, DICK, AND HARRY (1942) to THE BOATNICKS (1970). Most of his films receive individual mention, and his evolution from the best-friend Binky character to the fast-talking, larcenous Bilko character is nicely developed. There are two sections of pictures which are adequately chosen and reproduced. No index or chronology of appearances is provided, and therefore the book has little reference value.

As a portrait of a comic who was more successful on stage than off, the book is interesting and entertaining. The underlying theme of sadness that permeates the book may dampen some reader appreciation, but the mature audience that grew up with Binky, Bilko, and Silvers will enjoy it anyway. Acceptable for adults.

6119   *This Life.* by Poitier, Sidney. 374 p. illus. New York: Alfred A. Knopf, 1980.

In writing about his life, from his childhood in the Bahamas to his position as a director/actor who can choose his work in the eighties, Sidney Poitier tells a story rich in incident but lacking in drama. Told in a cool, tranquilized style that combines his Caribbean language patterns with occasional actor-writer jargon, his story contains elements of luck, ambition, integrity, dedication, aggressiveness, modesty, and candor. He sees his career and success primarily as a pioneering wedge into the film profession for young black people. Some illustrations are included, but unfortunately there is no index or filmography for reader reference.

The man presented in this volume is admirable for many reasons. He addresses the reader in an informal personal style that is disarming in itself. Coupled with a success based on hardwork, grit and determination, the result, like the actor's work, is easy to admire.

6120 *This Loving Darkness: The Cinema and Spanish Writers, 1920-1936.* 194 p. illus. New York: Oxford University Press, 1980.

6121 *This Was Hollywood.* by Day, Beth. 287 p. illus. New York: Doubleday, 1960.

A memoir of the legendary capital of the film world, this book is affectionate, nostalgic, and quite romantic. Admitting that by 1960 Hollywood had vanished, the author returns primarily to the period of the thirties and forties for her documentary account. Although she is not always correct, the author does provide an antiseptic, positive look at people and studio operations during the golden years. The narrative is chatty, noncontroversial and bland. A group of fine pictures is included but there is no index. Some readers may find this book entertaining but it adds little to the body of film literature.

6122 *This Was Show Business.* by Peck, Ira; and Springer, John. 74 p. paper illus. New York: Literary Enterprises, 1956.

Noted here primarily as one of the first picture books combining a literate text by the always dependable John Springer and some excellent visuals. Subjects are divided between films, radio, the stage, etc., but most appeared at some time in films. This volume has been out of print for years but it would be even more fascinating today if it were reprinted.

6123 *This Year of Films.* compiled by Hammond, Ion. 127 p. paper illus. London: Dewynters, 1946.

Reviews, critical quotes, and stills from films of the mid-forties.

6124 *This You Won't Believe.* by Griffith, Corinne. 115 p. paper New York: Frederick Fell, 1972.

The outside cover of this, Corinne Griffith's tenth publication, suggests that the book is a collection of tales about herself and her circle of celebrity friends. Well, she does mention Randolph Scott, Dorothy McGuire, Gene Autry, Roy Rogers, John Wayne, Cary Grant, Eva Marie Saint, in sentences such as: "Among my first customers were..." "He directed pictures which starred...." "I ran into..."

The book rambles along chattily, saying very little in a folksy and down-to- earth way. Most readers will lose interest quickly.

6125 THOROUGHLY MODERN MILLIE. 26 p. paper illus. New York: Universal Pictures, 1967.

The twenties are discussed by producer Ross Hunter on the inside covers of this short but visually attractive souvenir book. In an overly cute, and ultimately sickening fashion, using a phone call type of dialogue between two flappers, the plot is related. Songs from the 1967 film provide the opportunity to use full-page photographs in color as each advances the plot. The latter section of the book is devoted to cast biographies and some selected production people: director George Roy Hill, arranger Andre Previn and composer Elmer Bernstein, among others.

6126 *Those Endearing Young Charms.* by Best, Marc. 279 p. illus. New York: A. S. Barnes, 1971.

In the preface, author Best says, "It seems absurd that out of the countless volumes of film literature that have been published, none whatsoever has given due regard to the youngsters of celluloid." This statement is indicative of the carelessness that characterizes this volume. Norman Zierold's *The Child Stars*, published in 1965, covers some of the same ground and does it much better than Best. There is no definition for the phrase "child performer." Many of the subjects continued making films during their teens and into adulthood, e.g., Natalie Wood, Jackie Cooper, Roddy McDowall, Dean Stockwell.

Although it is not stated, the cutoff age for the filmographies appears to be age fourteen. Fifty of the "most notable child performers" are treated with a short text, a studio portrait, and some film stills. The subjects are selected in a mysterious manner, with omissions such as Durbin, Garland, the Mauch Twins, Gloria Jean, Elizabeth Taylor, Sabu, Leon Janney, and Bobby Breen. Included are such dubious "notables" as Peter Miles, Philippe De Lacy and Joan Carroll.

The filmographies are very selective lists of only the more widely known films or those for which the author was able to furnish stills. Some inane material about hobbies, schools and civic activities reads like studio publicity. The remainder of the uninspired text is descriptive and never critical. Picture reproduction is adequate.

A comprehensive, carefully researched study on child performers would be a welcome addition to film literature. Zierold is limited in his coverage and lacks illustrations. Best offers an unexplained, haphazard, dull approach and some interesting illustrations. A disappointing volume that is acceptable only as a temporary stop-gap.

6127   *Those Fabulous Film Factories: The History of Motion Picture Studios in California.* by Torrence, Bruce. 240 p. illus. Layton, Utah: Peregrine Smith, 1981.

6128   *Those Fabulous Movie Years: The 30s.* by Trent, Paul. 192 p. illus. Barre, Mass: Barre Publishing, 1975.

With the use of more than 300 stills and photographic portraits, the author has created a tribute to the stars, directors and films of the thirties. Beginning with TOL'ABLE DAVID (1930), his survey is personal and selective but manages to include nearly all of the classic and popular favorites. The arrangement of the films is chronological by year of appearance. Biographical and illustrative material on the directors and actors is placed next to the write-up of one of their well-known films.

Retrieval of information about personalities is difficult. The table of contents provides only minimum help. On what pages are Busby Berkely, MR. DEEDS GOES TO TOWN, or Noel Coward mentioned? Indexes for names and titles are essential elements missing from this volume. A listing of the films given full-page prominence in the text completes the book. The selection of stills is outstanding, recreating many memorable scenes from Hollywood's golden era. The full-color pictures are beautiful examples of early color photography. Reproduction of the black and white stills is above average.

Here is a fascinating pictorial volume that will interest and please a wide range of readers. Text, visuals and production are of high quality. However, the absence of an index greatly weakens the potential of the book for reference. Recommended with the above-noted reservation.

6129   *Those Great Movie Ads.* by Morella, Joe; and Epstein, Edward Z. and and Clark, Eleanor. 320 p. illus. New Rochelle, N.Y.: Arlington House, 1972.

The popular success of a motion picture depends, according to Judith Crist in her introduction to this book, on "producer's sell" and "word of mouth." Promotion ads figure largely in both factors, and it is the concern of this book to explore the many aspects of film advertising.

Using reprinted ads from a variety of sources—newspapers, magazines, billboards, posters, testimonials, endorsements, press books—the authors have put together a fascinating collection of memorabilia. What is lacking is a general structure

that will indicate to the reader some discernible pattern or approach to the collection. The major narrative section, "A Brief Look at Movie Advertising," pops up towards the middle, while "Logos," "Schmeer," and "Critic's Quotes" begin the book and "Walt Disney," "Fan Quiz," and "Turnaround Campaigns" end it. Reproduction of the illustrations and ads varies considerably from excellent to awful (see montages on p. 158, 228, 279). No index is provided.

How important these reservations are to the reader is debatable. The main attraction here is the ads and anything else is icing. Nevertheless, for the serious reader, a bit more quality could have resulted from editor attention to possible reference use, historical arrangement or acknowledgment, and possible improvement of ad reproduction. The potential popularity of this book is not in question; it is likely to be a reader favorite. Recommended.

6130   THOSE MAGNIFICENT MEN IN THEIR FLYING MACHINES. 34 p. paper illus. New York: 20th Century Fox, 1965.

Produced with much the same spirit and approach as the film, this souvenir book tells the story in a 1910 gazette form. Many shots from the 1965 film are used as illustrations and the fashions of the period are given special attention. An outstanding feature is an art portfolio by artist Ronald Searle. Cast and production credits are given and there is a players gallery showing the leading actors in the large cast.

6131   *Those Philadelphia Kellys.* by Lewis, Arthur H. 288 p. illus. New York: William Morrow, 1977.

This volume is called a family biography and carries the subtitle, "With a Touch of Grace." In addition to the former film star, the family included a vaudeville headliner (Walter Kelly, "The Virginia Judge"), a Pulitzer Prize winning playwright (George Kelly— "Craig's Wife," "The Show-Off," "The Torch Bearers," etc.), and an Olympic gold medalist (John Kelly). Attention is given to them and many other colorful Kellys in this racy, entertaining book.

The author's approach is that of investigative reporter and he spares few images or feelings. The portrait of Grace placed against that of her unusual family makes more sense than all the previous fan biographies written about her. Illustrations are provided and the book is indexed.

Most of the individuals who comprise the Kelly family are fascinating subjects for biography; certainly the material about Grace is superior to anything published thus far. Recommended.

6132 *Those Scandalous Sheets of Hollywood.* by Lee, Ray. 185 p. paper Van Nuys, Calif.: Venice Publishing, 1972.

The Hollywood scandals appear again for their annual resurrection in this exploitation paperback. The assortment this round is Flynn, Chaplin, Arbuckle, Lana Turner, Valentino, William Desmond Taylor, and a pair of less-abused subjects—Clara Bow and Ramon Novarro. That readers can still find this material of interest is puzzling. They obviously do, based on the number of printed rehashes that have appeared.

6133 *Those Who Died Young.* by Sinclair, Marianne. 192 p. paper illus. New York: Penguin, 1979.

A collective biography of "Cult Heroes of the 20thCentury," this oversized volume contains profiles of Valentino, Harlow, Monroe, Garfield, Clift, Dean, Presley and Lombard.

6134 *Thou Swell, Thou Witty: The Life and Lyrics of Larry Hart.* edited by Hart, Dorothy. 191 p. illus. New York: Harper & Row, 1976.

The lyrics of more than 50 songs that Larry Hart wrote are accompanied by a whitewashed biography and some remembrances by friends in this attractive volume.

Dorothy Hart, the sister-in-law of the lyricist, is very protective in the material she has provided.

6135 *Thought Control in the U.S.A.* 432 p. New York: Garland, 1947.

This Garland reprint gathers together six pamphlets which offer a summary-transcript of the conference sponsored by the Hollywood Arts, Sciences and Professions from July 9 to July 13, 1947. It consists of speeches, remarks, statements, etc., against the "unwarranted intrusion" of the House Un-American Activities Committee into Hollywood affairs. The HUAC hearings began later that year.

6136 *A Thousand and One Delights.* by Barbour, Alan G. 177 p. illus. New York: Macmillan, 1971.

This picture book is in the form of a memoir of the author's favorite films of the forties. Meant as an entertainment, the book begins with a tribute to Jon Hall and Maria Montez, then follows with chapters on Abbott and Costello, reissues of thirties films, horror films, comedies, films from the Monogram Studio, serials, the B mystery, the B western, the swashbuckler films, John Wayne, and finally big budget films. The criterion for inclusion in Barbour's list is simple—a film that he saw in the forties which he remembers with great pleasure.

The brief text is relaxed, chatty and informative. Picture selection and reproduction are above average. The book is not indexed. Although not essential, this volume will provide much reading and browsing pleasure for readers.

6137 *Three British Screenplays.* edited by Manvell, Roger. 299 p. illus. London: Methuen, 1950.

Contains cast credits, an introduction by Frank Launder and Roger Manvell, a list of technical terms, and the screenplays of BRIEF ENCOUNTER (1945), ODD MAN OUT (1947), and SCOTT OF THE ANTARCTIC (1948).

6138 *Three Classic Silent Screen Comedies Starring Harold Lloyd.* by McCaffrey, Donald W. 264 p. illus. Rutherford, N.J.: Fairleigh Dickinson University Press, 1976.

Based upon the author's doctoral dissertation written in 1962, this volume deals with GRANDMA'S BOY (1922), SAFETY LAST (1923), and THE FRESHMAN (1925). The films are handled as a group rather than individually, as the author examines story, exposition, development, climax, and resolution. Detailed analysis of shots, techniques, gestures, props, etc., are given. An overall observation summarizes the close scrutiny given the three films.

Supporting the investigation are an introductory biographical-background chapter, an account of a 1965 interview with Lloyd, a listing of sequences found in the three films, a Lloyd filmography, a bibliography, and an index. The illustrations provided vary somewhat in quality, with overexposure and a lack of clarity as major flaws.

Up to now the films studied by McCaffrey have not been generally available for showing or study. Without actually viewing them, a reading of this book would have limited value for most people. Too often the book gives evidence of its origin—a research study designed for a committee of specialized scholars/readers. Acceptable.

6139 THREE COMRADES. by Fitzgerald, F. Scott; and Paramore, Edward A.;

and Mankiewicz, Joseph. 289 p. illus. Carbondale, Ill.: Southern Illinois University Press, 1978.

This is the script of the 1938 film that Fitzgerald wrote based on the novel by Erich Maria Remarque. Later director Mankiewicz and Edward Paramore rewrote about two-thirds of Fitzgerald's screenplay, so the finished film really represents a collaboration.

6140   *3-D Kinematography and New Screen Techniques.* by Cornwell-Clyne, Adrian. 266 p. illus. London: Hutchinson's Scientific and Technical Publications, 1954.

6141   *Three European Directors.* edited by Wall, James M. 224 p. Grand Rapids, Mich.: Wm. B. Eerdmans, 1973.

A three-part anthology that contains: "Francois Truffaut—Auteur of Ambiguity," by James M. Wall; "Fellini's Film Journal," by Roger Ortmayer; and "Luis Bunuel and the Death of God," by Peter P. Schillaci. Separate bibliographies are provided for each section, and there are filmographies given for Truffaut and Bunuel. The popularity of the three directors is both an advantage and a disadvantage; any articles are bound to be of some interest, but the material also seems very familiar. Acceptable.

6142   *The Three Faces of Film.* by Tyler, Parker. 150 p. illus. New York: Thomas Yoseloff, 1960.

With four exceptions, this is a collection of individual magazine pieces assembled together under three general headings: the art, the dream, and the cult. As usual with Tyler's criticism, the style is alternately stimulating and verbose, alienating and supportive, clear and murky. Much of his attention is directed to the avant-garde or experimental film, to the relationship between film and modern art, and to the myth and meanings found in motion pictures.

There are three sections of illustrations, all of which aid the reader's comprehension of Tyler's message. The book is indexed. This is not easy criticism, but for the advanced or mature reader of film literature, it is rewarding. A full appreciation of Tyler demands background and certain reading and viewing experiences that many readers do not possess. For some, therefore, the book will be a frustrating put-on while others will find it serious, exhilarating, and different.

6143   *Three Films.* by Bergman, Ingmar. 143 p. paper illus. New York: Grove Press, 1970.

Contains: THROUGH A GLASS DARKLY (1961), WINTER LIGHT (1962), and THE SILENCE (1963). Note: This book is called *A Film Trilogy* in its hardbound edition.

6144   *365 Nights in Hollywood.* by Starr, Jimmy. 365 p. Hollywood: David Graham Fischer Corp., 1926.

6145   THREE LITTLE PIGS. edited by Walt Disney Studio Staff. 62 p. illus. New York: Blue Ribbon Books, 1933.

In this early example of the translation of film to book, the folklore story of the three little pigs is told by a text and illustrations supplied by the staff of the Disney Studios. Some of the visuals are in color and the cover is taken from the Walt Disney Silly Symphony series. See also Walt Disney Books.

6146   *Three Major Screenplays.* by Wald, Malvin; and Werner, Michael. 394 p. paper illus. New York: Globe Book Co., 1973.

This textbook contains the following: 1)Introduction, 2) "Screenplay Terms" —A Glossary of Moviemaking Terminology, 3) "The Student as Filmmaker" —A Practical Discussion of Some of the Basic Problems in Making Films, 4)Screenplay of THE OX BOW INCIDENT (1943), 5) Screenplay of HIGH NOON (1952), 6)Screenplay of LILIES OF THE FIELD (1963), and 7) A Film Lover's Bibliography. Each of the three screenplays is preceded by "About the Author," and "About the Screenplay," and is followed by "What the Critics Said," and "To Enrich Your Reading." A teacher's guide for using the book as a classroom text is also available.

6147   *Three Men and a Gimmick.* by Hirst, Robert. 125 p. Kingswood, England: The World's Work, 1957.

A collective biography with Peter Cushing, Terry Thomas, and Arthur Askey as subjects.

6148   *Three-Quarter Face: Reports & Reflections.* by Gilliatt, Penelope. 282 p. New York: Coward, McCann & Geoghegan, 1980.

This collection of reviews and profiles is taken largely from *The New Yorker*. The book is flawed by Gilliatt's style and approach to her subjects. Her job as critic apparently has led her to have a distorted idea of her talent, critical position, and influence. At times she is either pretentious, self-serving, boring, or narcissistic. The result is a minor, disappointing book, even with a cast that includes Hitchcock, Ford, Woody Allen, Fellini, and Bunuel.

6149 *Three Screenplays.* by Bunuel, Luis. 245 p. illus. New York: Orion Press, 1969.

Contains cast credits and scripts of VIRIDIANA (1961), THE EXTERMINATING ANGEL (1962), and SIMON OF THE DESERT (1965).

6150 *Three Screenplays.* by Fellini, Federico. 288 p. paper illus. New York: Orion Press, 1970.

Includes: I VITELLONI (1953), IL BIDONE (1955), and THE TEMPTATIONS OF DOCTOR ANTONIO (1961), and cast credits.

6151 *Three Screenplays.* by Rossen, Robert. 274 p. paper illus. New York: Doubleday, 1972.

Contains: ALL THE KINGS MEN (1949), THE HUSTLER (1961), LILITH (1963); a list of the screenplays written by Rossen; a list of the films directed by Rossen.

6152 *Threshold: The Blue Angel's Experience.* by Herbert, Frank. 153 p. paper illus. New York: Ballantine, 1973.

This volume includes the narration and more than 100 stills from the documentary film about the flying team of six U.S. Navy men. Credits for the film are provided.

6153 *The Thrill of It All.* by Barbour, Alan G. 204 p. illus. New York: Macmillan, 1971.

This pictorial history of the B western disposes of the first two decades of films in one brief opening chapter. The cowboy stars of the early thirties— Buck Jones, Tim McCoy, Hoot Gibson, Tom Tyler, Ken Maynard and Bob Steele—are introduced next. John Wayne receives one chapter to himself while Gene Autry, Roy Rogers, William Boyd, and others share sections. The villains, serials, cowboy trios, singing cowboys, and the eventual demise of the B western are some of the other topics discussed.

As with the other Barbour books, the purpose is primarily entertainment. However, a little more effort could have increased the overall value of this book. The addition of some indexes, some expansion of the chapter introductions and a tighter organization of the material would have helped a great deal

without altering the initial concept of the book. Picture quality is quite good and the brief text, emotional at times, is always readable and informative. The book is not essential but will please many readers. Young people will enjoy it especially.

6154 *The Thriller.* by Davis, Brian. 160 p. paper illus. New York: Dutton, 1973.

This is the most recent of the excellent Studio Vista *Pictureback* series and is a most welcome addition. Using 1946 as a starting point, the author traces the evolution of the thriller from the documentary-realism of the late forties to the stark crime, detective, and spy films of the seventies. The use of this film genre to expose and explore social and political problems is considered, as are two of its major elements—the robbery and the chase. Davis' conclusion provides a chill of its own. If films reflect reality, he states, there is not much that can be said for the post-World War II world.

The emphasis here is on the visuals and they are well reproduced, as in all the volumes of this series. In addition, it is Davis' text, which is literate, critical and inclusive, that surprises and pleases. Not only is the volume an entertainment, but in its examination of a popular film genre, it makes several provocative and important statements. The index provides some reference value, too. Here is another exemplary combination of visuals, text and production. Highly recommended.

6155 *Thriller Movies.* by Hammond, Lawrence. 160 p. illus. London: Octopus Books, 1974.

Here is another book in the *Movie Treasury* series that examines a major movie genre, the thriller. Defined broadly as films of suspense and mystery, the genre in this book includes detective films— FAREWELL MY LOVELY (1975), THE BIG SLEEP (1946), THE MALTESE FALCON (1941), SHAMUS (1973), GUMSHOE (1972), etc.; gangster films—THE GODFATHER (1972), THE BIG HEAT (1953), KEY LARGO (1948), THE DESPERATE HOURS (1955), etc.; science fiction films—2001: A SPACE ODYSSEY (1968), A CLOCKWORK ORANGE (1971), METROPOLIS (1928), etc.; and certain films which challenge any single classification— CITIZEN KANE (1941), DR. STRANGELOVE (1964), LIFEBOAT (1944), THE MAGNIFICENT AMBERSONS (1942), etc.

The book is characterized by imbalance. A large percentage of the visuals is taken from only a few films. Entire chapters are given to the films of Orson Welles, Alfred Hitchcock and Stanley Kubrick, while other directors who specialize in thrillers—

Samuel Fuller, Michael Curtiz, Howard Hawks, etc. —are not mentioned. The text relies mostly on retelling the plots of selected films, avoiding any indepth analysis of the genre.

Although the visuals are clearly reproduced, with many in color, their captions are notoriously weak. Many well-known performers are not identified even when they are the only figure in or a major part of the visual. For example, Alan Arkin is not named but called "a mysterious intruder" in a full-page illustration. Others predominantly shown but not identified included Raymond Burr, Farley Granger, John Dahl, Kent Smith, Anne Francis, Robert Ryan, John Gavin. One caption notes William Wyler "visiting" actors on the set. The film being made was THE DESPERATE HOURS (1955), which Wyler produced and directed. Stanley Donen is spelled Stanley Doners in another. Aimed for a nondiscriminating audience, this volume has little to offer but its visuals. Acceptable.

6156 *Through Navajo Eyes.* by Worth, Sol; and Adair, John. 286 p. illus. Bloomington, Ind.: Indiana University Press, 1972.

This book is a rarity, and a find. An account of a study of Navajo Indians using the major fields of anthropology and film communication may suggest a doctoral thesis made palatable for publication, but this book is much more than that. Under grants from the National Science Foundation and the Annenberg School of Communications, the author's goal was to teach filmmaking and editing to a group of Navajos. It was hoped that these abilities would enable them to depict themselves and their culture via film. Two aspects of the project emerge: first, the training stage and then the analysis stage. Since both authors have had many similar experiences with other ethnic groups, comparison is frequent and sometimes surprising.

The films made are described in detail at the close of the book and there are frame enlargements to supplement the written account. A valuable bibliography lists works that have pertinence to either one or both of the two major disciplines used. To round out the study completely, a full index is given.

The book should serve as a model for many future studies which can use film communication with another discipline. Many findings are stated, and yet some new questions or problems are developed. For example, one initial question raised by an older leader comes to mind: how would making films help the Navajo? A typical problem for the authors was the impossibility of translating the film images into the printed word.

For anyone concerned with teaching or using filmmaking with small groups, the book has much to offer and suggest. It shows a use of film not often treated in other volumes.

6157 THUNDERBALL. 34 p. paper illus. New York: Program Publishing Co., 1965.

A few color photographs are sprinkled in with the black and white stills which predominate in this souvenir book. Some background is given but the major emphasis is on detailing James Bond's exploits in this 1965 film. As with the films, there is much female body exposure. Cast and production credits are barely mentioned.

6158 *Tim McCoy Remembers the West.* by McCoy, Tim; and McCoy, Ronald. 274 p. illus. New York: Doubleday, 1977.

Although he speaks of his career as a Hollywood cowboy star, Tim McCoy devotes most of this autobiography to describing the West as he knew it. He tells stories about his friendly association with Indians at the turn of the century; his appearances in road shows, the circus, and his wild west show; making films in Hollywood; and travelling throughout the world. Illustrations and index accompany this account of a full, rich life.

6159 TIME BANDITS. by Palin, Michael; and Gilliam, Terry. 160 p. illus. London: Hutchinson, 1981.

A script of the 1981 film directed by Terry Gilliam.

6160 *Time Exposure.* by Beaton, Cecil. 134 p. paper illus. New York: Scribners, 1946.

Another Beaton collection of portraits and photographs of celebrities.

6161 *The Time of the Toad: A Study of Inquisition in America and Two Related Pamphlets.* by Trumbo, Dalton. 161 p. paper illus. New York: Harper and Row, 1972.

Written by one of the Hollywood Ten, this volume contains: *The Time of the Toad*, a short essay originally published in the early fifties; *The Devil in the Book*, another short essay originally published in 1956; and *Honor Bright and All That Jazz*.

All three deal with Communism in the United States, blacklisting, the HUAC investigations, and the motion picture industry.

6162 TIME PIECE. by Schreivogel, Paul. 20 p. paper illus. Dayton, Ohio: Pflaum, 1970.

A study guide for the 1966 film directed by Jim Hensen.

6163 *The Times We Had.* by Davies, Marion. 276 p. illus. Indianapolis: Bobbs-Merrill, 1975.

Many people think that Marion Davies was the inspiration for the Susan Alexander character in CITIZEN KANE (1941). This warm, revealing autobiography should dispel this untruth. Davies not only was a talented comedienne, but she also was William Randolph Hearst's lover- partner for several decades.

Beginning with an apologetic disclaimer by Orson Welles, the volume skims over Davies' early life to concentrate on the period suggested by the subtitle, "The Years with William Randolph Hearst."

The text was taken from tapes recorded by the actress from 1951 to 1961. Supplementing the intelligently edited transcription of these oral memoirs are comments, identifications and corrections by the editors. An abundance of well-selected visuals captures and reflects the flavor of the period. Reproduction of them, however, varies from excellent to poor.

In this volume, the author has written about her greatest role—that of a combination actress-lover-mistress-celebrity. Parts such as this demand unusual talents and human qualities. Apparently Davies had both in abundance. The volume is delightful in both text and visuals, and the author's recollections of her filmmaking experiences will bring pleasure to film buffs.

The disproving of the CITIZEN KANE myth also brings the book importance and distinction. It is a modest biographical treasure that reflects its author's approach to life. Highly recommended.

6164 *A Title Guide to the Talkies.* by Dimmitt, Richard. 2133 p. Metuchen, N.J.: Scarecrow Press, 1965.

These two volumes list in alphabetical order 16,000 feature-length films made from October 1927 until December 1963. Following each entry there is a copyright or release date, the name of the copyright applicant and the source material of the film—book, play, original, etc. The reference is designed primarily to direct interested readers to this original source material. To facilitate this service, the author name, publisher, date, and pagination are given. The sources of Dimmitt's information are noted after each entry. Finally, an index of author names is given. This massive reference work is impressive in its scope and coverage.

6165 *A Title Guide to the Talkies: 1964 to 1974.* by Aros, Andrew A. 344 p. Metuchen, N.J.: Scarecrow, 1977.

This is a continuation of Richard B. Dimmitt's original two-volume work which covered the period.1927 to 1963. Its purpose is to indicate the original work upon which a film is based. The entries indicate film title, year of copyright, company, producer, screenwriter(s), director, and the original literary work including its author and often the publisher and date. The sources of Aros' information are indicated and an index of writers is furnished.

Aros has expanded and improved Dimmitt's pioneer work, which remains a basic reference.

6166 *Titling Your Color Movies.* by Moore, James W. 96 p. paper illus. New York: A. S. Barnes, 1958.

6167 TO BE ALIVE. by Reid, Alastair. 90 illus. New York: Macmillan, 1966.

The theme and pictures in this volume are taken directly from the film, TO BE ALIVE, which was exhibited at the New York World's Fair in 1964-65. For this book some free verse by poet Alastair Reid has been added. The visuals are all of exceptionally high quality and the added text is acceptable but a bit pretentious. The book will not have much meaning for those who did not see the original which was projected on three screens.A reminder of the power, effectiveness, and popularity of the film, this volume has a limited value.

6168 *To Be Continued.* by Weiss, Ken; and Goodgold, Ed. 341 p. illus. New York: Crown, 1972.

Some 220 sound serials of the period 1929 to 1956 are the subject of this attractive volume. Arranged chronologically by individual years, each serial is described by name, number of episodes, studio, director, cast members, a short synopsis and several stills. The famous serials receive extended annotation and a greater number of illustrations.

The text reflects the enthusiasm and fondness that the authors have for their subject. Pictures are plentiful, nicely chosen, and well reproduced. The indexes are arranged in two ways: a chronological listing of the titles by year of release, and then a general alphabetical index which includes all the titles.

An example of fascinating subject material treated with knowledge and admiration, and arranged in an attractive usable manner, this volume is pleasant reading and an easy reference tool. Recommended.

6169 *To Elvis with Love.* by Canada, Lena. illus. New York: Everest House, 1978.

6170 *To Encourage the Art of the Film: The Story of the British Film Insitute.* by Butler, Ivan. 208 p. illus. London: Robert Hale, 1971.

The history of the British Film Institute is divided into convenient sections, each dealing with a specific aspect or function. Topics such as the organization and administration from 1933 to 1970, preservation of films, education, film presentations, production of film, distribution of films, publications, and film societies are treated individually rather than in a continuing narrative. The appendixes include an organization chart, lists of BFI officials, a chronological listing of the film programs given by the Institute, the speakers who have participated in the John Player Lecture Series, and the features shown at the London Film Festival from 1957 to 1970. The book is indexed in detail and many illustrations correlatenicely with the text.

This is a specialized book that will have a limited appeal, but it has implications for even the smallest film library since many of the functions delineated here are repeated in those libraries. Recommended.

6171 *To Find an Image.* by Murray, James. 205 p. illus. Indianapolis: Bobbs-Merrill, 1973.

Subtitled "Black Films from Uncle Tom to Super Fly," this volume is a collection of history, survey, interviews, and filmography. Thus the subject of black cinema is covered from several approaches. Emphasis is on the recent changes which have occurred in content, character, and performer in films featuring blacks. Performers such as Sidney Poitier, Diahann Carroll, Jim Brown and Godfrey Cambridge are discussed. Interviews with black filmmakers Gordon Parks, Melvin Van Peebles, Ossie Davis, William Greales and St. Clair Bourke are also included. A few summary chapters are devoted to an evaluation of current black cinema and to offering some predictions about its future.

An unusual appendix offers separate sections of data noting people and films affecting black cinema. Re-

presentative black directors, producers, screenwriters, scores, and film production companies are also noted. Blacks who have received Academy Award nominations are listed, and there is an index. Sixteen pages of pictures are only average in selection and quality and contain several fuzzy or murky shots of older material or performers, e.g., Bill Robinson, LIFEBOAT (1944), CASABLANCA (1943), John Killens, etc.

This is a welcome addition to the recent volumes which have appeared on blacks in film. It addresses itself primarily to the present and provides much information and data that the others do not. Recommended.

6172 TO HAVE AND HAVE NOT. by Faulkner, William; and Furthman, Jules. paper illus. Madison, Wisc.: University of Wisconsin Press.

Script of the 1944 film which was directed by Howard Hawks. This volume was edited by Bruce Kawin.

6173 TO KILL A MOCKINGBIRD. Foote, Horton.

Screenplay of the 1962 film directed by Robert Mulligan, with a word from Harper Lee, author of the novel.

6174 *To See the Dream.* by West, Jessamyn. 314 p. New York: Harcourt, 1957.

A journal written during the year that author West acted as script writer and advisor to William Wyler during the filming of her book *The Friendly Persuasion.* Charming, well-written and as pleasing as the film which resulted.

6175 *To the Distant Observer.* by Burch, Noel. 387 p. illus. Berkeley, Calif.: University of California Press, 1979.

Using a historical approach, Noel Burch treats many aspects of the Japanese cinema that are individual and unique. Using culture, society, politics, militarism, post-war democratization and other topics, the author tries to show their influence and effect on the development of a national cinema. Burch's main concern is the difference between the dominant modes of Western and Japanese cinema. To this end the works of prominent film directors are analyzed in detail. The average reader will find this volume a challenge; it requires background, understanding and hard work for comprehension. For example, familiarity with film theory, aesthetics, and terms such as "diegetic process," "profilmic space," "alterity cut," and "decoupage" are necessary.

Illustrations, a bibliography, director filmographies, archive holdings, a title index and a name index complete the study. The book is most impressive but rather exhausting to study, read and/or use.

6176 *Together Again: The Great Movie Teams.* by Kanin, Garson. illus. New York: Grosset & Dunlap, 1980.

Twenty Hollywood teams are selected for this collective biography. An attempt is made to analyzed the reason for teams' success. The many variables lean to a general conclusion of chemistry, testing, and the relationship balance that brings out the best in each partner. Short biographies are given along with 750 illustrations.

Among the teams discussed are Pickford-Fairbanks, Woody Allen-Diane Keaton, Tracy-Hepburn, Garbo-Gilbert, Bogart-Bacall, Laurel & Hardy, Astaire-Rogers, Rooney-Garland, Macdonald-Eddy, Olivier-Leigh, Burton-Taylor, Loy-Powell, and the Marx Brothers.

6177 TOM JONES. by Osborne, John. 192 p. paper illus. New York: Grove Press, 1964.

Script of the 1963 film directed by Tony Richardson. Contains cast credits.

6178 TOM JONES. by Osborne, John. 142 p. illus. Salem, N.H.: Faber and Faber, 1980.

A script of the 1963 film directed by Tony Richardson.

6179 *Tom Swift and His Electric English Teacher.* by Poteet, G. Howard. 96 p. paper illus. Dayton, Ohio: Pflaum, 1973.

A media catalog reminiscent of the *Whole Earth* series, this volume is divided into sections devoted to a specific medium—radio, film, television, print, slides, etc. The subdivisions in each section indicate the book's design for use by classes in English, e.g., general, language, literature, and composition. The film section contains advertisements for books, prints, stills, filmstrips, etc., along with informational abstracts, articles and bits.

Selection seems personal, with a noticeable emphasis on Pflaum products; although they are undeniably excellent, the volume becomes somewhat suspect when it resembles an advertising piece rather than

an objective collection. Other than this specific reservation, the book is fun to read and valuable to own; its suggestions, hints and bibliographic references alone make it an essential for all alert English teachers if not also for their classes. Highly recommended for school use.

6180 *Tommy Steele.* by Kennedy, John. 189 p. illus. London: Transworld Publications, 1959.

An early biography of the pop singer prepared by his publicity agent. Steele first appeared in films during the late fifties—KILL ME TOMORROW (1957), THE TOMMY STEELE STORY (1957), THE DUKE WORE JEANS (1958) and TOMMY THE TOREADOR (1959). His later films made in Hollywood and Britain are not treated here.

6181 *see 6180*

6182 *Toms, Coons, Mulattos, Mammies and Bucks.* by Bogle, Donald. 260 p. illus. New York: Viking, 1973.

Subtitled "An Interpretive History of Blacks in American Films," this volume documents the changes in the portrait of the black in film over its 70-year history. Beginning with UNCLE TOM'S CABIN (1903), it covers the silent era to THE BIRTH OF A NATION (1915) and the remainder of the twenties when blacks portrayed comic jesters. The black as a servant was the theme of the thirties, while the forties saw him first as a musical entertainer and then as a problem personality. The fifties brought forth the first black film stars, and the sixties repeated in depth some of the problems which were merely approached in the forties. Black militants and the black films are themes for the seventies.

This volume is one of the best treatments of the topic thus far. It repeats some of Noble and Mapp but has much to say in addition. Recommended.

6183 *Tony Hancock.* by Oakes, Philip. 96 p. illus. London: Woburn Press, 1975.

A title in *The Entertainers* series, this is the biography of the British comedian, Tony Hancock, who appeared unsuccessfully in a few films. The text offers a brief overview of his life and career, but *Hancock* by Freddie Hancock and David Nathan, written in 1969, offers a more fully dimensioned portrait.

6184 *Too Much Too Soon.* by Barrymore, Diana; and Frank, Gerold. 380 p.

illus. New York: Henry Holt, 1957.

Although her film career was a brief one, the author sprinkles this autobiography with enough motion picture names and anecdotes to warrant its inclusion here. As a young, inexperienced actress, she made several mediocre films in the early forties. The remaining years of her short life were spent in attempts to make a comeback on the stage. Her battle with alcoholism and her romantic encounters are described in some detail. This volume was published before her death in 1960. There are a few interesting pictures but no index.

6185   *Too Young to Die.* by Fox-Sheinword, Patricia. 356 p. illus. New York: Weather Vane, 1979.

Among the author's credits are a book, *Husbands and Other Men I've Played With,* and two essays: "Where You Never Thought You'd Be—In A Gay Marriage," and "My Last Date with a Teen-ager." Here she offers a chronological collective biography of 31 celebrities who died young—from Valentino (1926) to Presley (1977). The predictable film names are present: Harlow, Lombard, Garfield, Dean, Monroe, Cliff, Garland, and Mineo.

Most of the text seems derivative and familiar. Illustrations, filmographies and other credits are added.

6186   *Top Hat and Tails: The Story of Jack Buchanan.* by Marshall, Michael. 271 p. illus. North Pomfret, Vt.: Hamish Hamilton, 1978.

If Jack Buchanan had done no film other than THE BAND WAGON (1953), he would still be appreciated by filmgoers the world over for his performance in that musical. Fortunately he made many other motion pictures including AULD LANG SYNE (1917), MONTE CARLO (1930), BREWSTER'S MILLIONS (1935), AS LONG AS THEY'RE HAPPY (1955) and THE FRENCH THEY ARE A FUNNY RACE (1957). Most of his films were of British origin. This volume traces his life and career from an appearance on the variety stage in 1911 to his death in 1957. A sophisticated urban personality and a multi-talented performer, Buchanan was admired by public and critics alike. Active in theatre, films, television, recordings, and radio, he was an actor who never stopped working at his craft. The author captures Buchanan's personal charm as well as the flavor of the entertainment world in which he performed.

Supporting the affectionate text are a career chronology, a discography, a bibliography, some fine illustrations, an index, and an introduction by Fred Astaire. Everything in this biography blends to

give the reader the uniquely rich and rewarding experience of meeting Jack Buchanan, a legendary performer. Recommended.

6187   TORA! TORA! TORA!. 36 p. paper illus. New York: 20th Century Fox, 1970.

This souvenir book considers the 1970 film as two separate stories and two separate films—the American and the Japanese. The historical background is shown by artwork and by newspaper headlines. Cast and credits are listed separately.

6188   *The Total Film-Maker.* by Lewis, Jerry. 208 p. illus. New York: Random House, 1971.

The term, "total film-maker" may apply to Griffith, Welles, or Chaplin, but to apply that same title to the rather short presentation of ideas, comments, and ramblings presented here is both immodest and a bit fraudulent. Based upon lectures given to a group of graduate students at the University of Southern California, the book is composed of anecdotes, personal recollections and observations, practical advice, and philosophy. In broad terms Lewis considers the producer, the writer, the actor and the stage crew. Activities such as pre-planning, actual filming, cutting the film, creating and recording the musical score, and distributing the film are also treated. The closing portion of the volume analyzes the art of comedy, with Lewis selecting Chaplin, Stan Laurel, and Jackie Gleason as his personal "greats."

Since it was based on edited audio tapes of the lectures, the book gives evidence of its origin. It lacks strong continuity and conciseness, and seems extemporaneous rather than tightly structured.

As a statement on filmmaking by Jerry Lewis, the volume is not disagreeable. Lewis writes in the same manner as he speaks on the informal talk shows of television. He is opinionated, charming, aggressive, and knowledgeable. As in all his other media appearances, readers will either love him or loathe him. You can toss a coin on this one.

6189   *The Tough Guys.* by Parish, James Robert. 635 p. illus. New Rochelle, N.Y.: Arlington House, 1976.

The tough guys of this collective biography are James Cagney, Kirk Douglas, Burt Lancaster, Robert Mitchum, Paul Muni, Edward G. Robinson, and Robert Ryan. Each is given biographical coverage in a separate section which includes narrative, illustrations, and a detailed filmography. An overall index completes the volume.

Within the limits of unauthorized biography, it is hard to imagine anyone who can equal or even compete with Parish's expertise. Selection, style, knowledge and probably even instinct seem to guide him in structuring these life stories. His judgment in either eliminating scandal-gossip-innuendo or handling it with taste and discretion is constantly evident. Perhaps his greatest service is the provision of standard, relatively objective coverage in his many volumes of collective biography. For example, in this particular volume, comparison is possible between the seven subjects since they are presented by one author-editor rather than seven of varying abilities.

Illustrations are above average throughout and they have been carefully reproduced. Chalk up still another success for Parish. This one should please a wide audience and is recommended.

6190 *Tough Guys and Gals of the Movies.* by Edelson, Edward. 133 p. illus. New York: Doubleday, 1978.

Written for young readers, this volume examines the different types of tough guys and gals found in films. Emphasis is placed on the careers of Humphrey Bogart, James Cagney and Edward G. Robinson. Although many other macho stars such as Wayne, Cooper, Gable, Flynn, Widmark, von Stroheim, Duryea, etc., receive attention, the gals of the title get only scant attention; a final short chapter mentions Harlow, Bette Davis, Crawford, Mary Astor, Bacall, Bankhead, Dietrich, Lupino, Rosiland Russell and Stanwyck. An index and some illustrations help somewhat.

Since this is a surface overview of very personal selections (where are Claire Trevor, Susan Hayward, Mercedes McCambridge, Shelley Winters, Aldo Ray, Rod Steiger, William Bendix, Lee Van Cleef, Broderick Crawford, etc?), it is limited in both information and coverage of its stated topic.

6191 *Toward a Concept of Cinematic Literature: An Analysis of* HIROSHIMA MON AMOUR. by Etzkowitz, Janice. New York: Garland, 1982.

A title in the *Dissertations on Film* series.

6192 *Toward a Definition of the American Film Noir (1941-1949).* by Karimi, A. M. New York: Arno Press, 1976.

Written in 1970 at the University of Southern California in partial fulfillment of the doctoral program,

this study explores the "film noir," tracing its historical influence on the American films of the forties. The author, in analyzing this film format as an accurate sociological reflection of the period portrayed, extends his research by including a filmography for the film noir scholar. This title appears in the *Dissertations on Film* series.

6193 *Toward a Film Humanism.* by Hurley, Neil P. 212 p. paper illus. New York: Delta Books, 1975.

A new title has been given to this paperback reprint of Hurley's *Theology Through Film.*

6194 *Toward a Semiotic Theory of Visual Communication in the Cinema.: A Reappraisal of Semiotic Theories from a Cinematic Perspective and a Semiotic Analysis of Color Signs and Communications in the Color Films of Alfred Hitchcock.* by Kindem, Corham Anders. New York, Arno, 1980.

The semiotic theories of deSaussure, Peirce, and Eco are tested by examining color signs and communications in the color films of Alfred Hitchcock.

6195 *Toward a Sociology of the Cinema.* by Jarvie, I. C. 394 p. London: Routledge and Kegan Paul, 1970.

British edition title; see *Movies and Society.*

6196 *Toward a Structural Psychology of Cinema.* by Carroll, John M. 224 p. Hawthorne, N.Y.: Mouton, 1980.

A title in the *Approaches to Semiotics* series.

6197 *Tower of Babel: Speculations on the Cinema.* by Rhode, Eric. 214 p. New York: Chilton Books, 1966.

This is an interesting theoretical discussion that will take on increased meaning and pleasure if one is familiar with the films of its director-subjects. To acquire this film experience is a challenge, since the directors considered are Vigo, Bresson, Eisenstein, Jennings, Lang, Rivette, Fellini, Resnais, Ophuls, Wajda, and Satyajit Ray. Using this international sampling, an attempt is made to contrast the temperament and ideology of each of the directors by obtaining from their films an idea of how the director actually sees society and politics and how he would prefer to see them. Not an easy task, the work of the author becomes quite subjective, and most vulnerable on occasion. A provocative book for the advanced film scholar reader.

6198   TOYS. by Schreivogel, Paul A. 20 p. paper illus. Dayton, Ohio: Pflaum, 1970.

A study guide for the 1967 film directed by Grant Munro.

6199   *Tracy and Hepburn.* by Kanin, Garson. 307 p. New York: Viking, 1971.

Is there anyone who hasn't seen, heard about or read this book? It was given a mammoth publicity campaign, was reviewed in periodicals, newspapers and magazines, went through several printings in the hardcover version, and then appeared in paperback. In this case, it was much ado about something; the book is a very good one.

Based largely on reminiscences of his social and professional interactions with the pair, Kanin alternates the spotlight between the two, sometimes allowing them to share an anecdote. The author makes no attempt to be objective and both stars have positive sympathetic roles in his story. His memory and critical judgment are not always convincing: for example, "The film (SEA OF GRASS (1947) was a success in every way" ; "The result (STATE OF THE UNION(1948)) was a disappointment." In telling a long story about Hepburn and Cary Grant, the author makes numerous mentions of a film he calls MEMORY OF LOVE in which Grant appeared with Carole Lombard. The film referred to was IN NAME ONLY (1939), had a different story than that attributed to it here, and was made the year before PHILADELPHIA STORY (1940); these are some facts that Kanin has confused in his account. but this is a minor matter. Weakness in their scripts was never a problem—it was the star quality of the subjects that attracted audiences to their films. The same condition prevails here.

No index or illustrations are provided. Recommended.

6200   *Traditions of Independence: British Cinema in the Thirties.* by Willemen, Paul. edited by Macpherson, Don; 226 p. New York: Zoetrope, 1980.

There are five sections in this anthology: (1) The Thirties and the Seventies; (2) Censorship and the Law; (3) The Labour Movement and Oppositional Cinema; (4) Avant-Garde/Art/Criticism; and (5) Amateur Films. Each section offers many short pieces.

6201   *The Tragic Secret Life of Jayne Mansfield.* by Strait, Raymond. 207 p. illus. Chicago: Regnery, 1974.

In death as in real life, Jayne Mansfield is following in the shadow of Marilyn Monroe. Several volumes which deal with Mansfield and her rapid rise and fall have recently appeared. This is one of the most sensationalized as well as one of the most fascinating. Written by the man who was her press secretary for 10 years, the book contains special material not available to other biographers. Although the author shows compassion and affection for his subject, he is able to maintain an admirable objectivity; as a result, a fully dimensioned, complex portrait emerges—one which differentiates the private and public life of a celebrity until that unhappy time when they become inseparable. Not only does the author suggest a motivation for Mansfield's bizarre behavior, but he also is more than competent in describing the show business world that first welcomed and ultimately destroyed this unusual woman.

The pictures are well reproduced, but the selection is too small and certainly could have been more comprehensive. The lack of an index is regrettable, suggesting as it does a weakness in belief in the importance of the author's subject. As a readable, sensationalized account of a modern day tragedy, the book will appeal to many curious readers. For those willing to probe beyond the author's external narrative, the book offers some damning views of fame in today's society. Acceptable for mature adults.

6202   *Training Film Profiles.* 8 volumes illus. New York: Olympic Media Information, 1968-1975.

These eight volumes evaluate more than 2000 films, filmstrips, kits, etc., produced from 1967 to 1975. Emphasis is placed on the effectiveness of the medium as an instructional aid. All levels of education are represented in the examined materials, which teach attitudes and concepts rather than technical skills. Many films are included in this valuable selection-evaluation aid. The high cost of the volumes may make them prohibitive for many institutions.

Olympic Media Information also publishes two other aids. *Hospital/Health Care Training Media Profiles* deals with evaluations of audiovisual materials designed specifically for hospital educators, community colleges with allied health courses, and vocational-technical schools. Each volume is made up of six bimonthly editions. Currently available are three volumes covering 1974 to 1976. *Educational Media Catalogs on Microfiche* is a collection of 300 current catalogs reproduced page by page on approximately 150 NMA-format fiche. They are indexed by distributor name.

6203 *Transcendental Style in Film—Ozu, Bresson, Dreyer.* by Schrader, Paul. 194 p. illus. Los Angeles: University of California Press, 1972.

By analyzing examples from the films of three directors—Yasujiro Ozu, Robert Bresson, and Carl Dreyer—the author attempts to develop a theory about film style which can express the sacred and the holy. This attempt to create a religious aesthetic for film is admirable but demanding and ultimately exhausting. By using many philosophical, religious, and aesthetic concepts and references, the author attempts to define or describe transcendental style.

Each of the three director sections is quite detailed and the reader may wonder how much of what is being discussed was truly the director's intent. Extended footnotes and impressive bibliographies are provided in the appendix. The book is also illustrated and indexed. This is a scholarly attempt to link religion, art, and film by philosophical discussion and conjecture. The text will prove difficult for most readers and the ultimate reaction will probably be frustration or confusion rather than satisfaction.

Others may prefer Butler's *Religion in the Cinema*, Hurley's *Theology Through Film*, or *Celluloid and Symbols* by Cooper and Skrade.

6204 *Transylvanian Catalog.* by Lamberti, Mark. 72 p. paper illus. Mount Vernon, N.Y.: Audio Brandon Films, 1974.

This fascinating catalog of horror, science fiction and occult films has much to recommend it. The films are arranged in chapters devoted to categories such as bats and bloodsuckers, atomic era monsters, beasts, creatures of science, etc. An alphabetical title index helps to provide access to the individual films. The text, consisting of chapter introductions and film annotations, is informative, practical, and often amusing. Visuals, as usual with this genre, are often better than the films they represent. The total approach to the subject provided by this catalog could not be more appropriate. Here is another Audio Brandon catalog that will amuse and inform a wide audience. Highly recommended.

6205 TRAPEZE. 16 p. paper illus. 1956.

Attention is focused on personalities in this souvenir book. Burt Lancaster, Tony Curtis, and Gina Lollobrigida each receive several pages for biographical data, and supporting players Katy Jurado and Thomas Gomez are alloted single pages. Director Carol Reed, producer Harold Hecht, and writer James Hill get a page each. Very little of the book is devoted to either background or filmmaking but several scenes from the 1956 film are used as illustrations and there is a very short plot outline.

6206 *Travolta Super Star Special.* 48 p. paper illus. London: IPC Magazines, 1978.

A paperback biography of John Travolta that includes some full-color illustrations.

6207 *Travolta to Keaton.* by Reed, Rex. 222 p. illus. New York: William Morrow, 1979.

What more can be said about Rex Reed's books? No sizeable middle ground exists—readers either love him or loathe him. As a self-appointed critic and social historian, his articles reflect an excessive adoration of the past (performers and films) and a deep suspicion of the present. In this book we receive one article on Las Vegas and 33 interviews, many of which have appeared earlier in other publications. Some of the material discussed is dated but the bulk of Reed's observation and comment is cynical, witty, bitchy and most important, amusing.

He apparently has such southern charm and openness that his subjects drop their defenses and willingly divulge information-opinion that is usually not grist for the interview mills.

A large audience finds that reading and listening to Rex Reed is a great deal of fun. This volume should reinforce that opinion.

6208 *Travolta! A Photo Bio.* by Reeves, Michael. 272 p. paper illus. New York: Jove, 1978.

In providing 23 chapters generously filled with text and over 100 illustrations, Reeves covers Travolta's life and career up to GREASE (1978). Designed to compete with other mass market books on the actor, this one is nicely produced, adequately written and much less expensive. Most readers will respond primarily to the illustrations, which are well selected and reproduced.

6209 THE TREASURE OF THE SIERRA MADRE. by Huston, John. 208 p. paper illus. Madison, Wisc.: University of Wisconsin Press, 1979.

James Naremore provides an introduction-analysis

of the script and the final film.

6210   *A Tree is a Tree.* by Vidor, King. 315 p. illus. New York: Harcourt, Brace, 1953.

A rather external biography, this story traces the life of King Vidor from adolescent ticket-taker to Hollywood director. As a young helper in a nickelodeon who had to watch BEN-HUR (the early Italian 2 reeler) 147 times, he later was responsible for THE BIG PARADE (1925), THE CROWD (1928), HALLELUJAH (1929), and OUR DAILY BREAD (1934). In addition to many other films, each of the above films is treated in some detail. RUBY GENTRY (1952) is the most recent film considered.

The book is not so much a biography as a series of anecdotes, comments, and opinions arranged chronologically. Vidor the professional emerges but Vidor the person is still quite unknown at the book's conclusion. This is one of the better books about Hollywood as seen from the director's chair. The approach and the evaluations are seemingly honest. Nothing sensational or malicious is included. What is related, however, is quite informative and diverting. Recommended for the background given and for its portrait of Hollywood from 1925 to 1950. Historians and film buffs will enjoy this one.

6211   THE TRIAL. by Welles, Orson. 176 p. paper illus. New York: Simon & Schuster, 1970.

Script of the 1962 film directed by Welles. Contains introductory comments by Welles and cast credits.

6212   *Tribute to Mary Pickford.* by Cushman, Robert B. 16 p. paper illus. Washington, D.C.: The American Film Institute, 1970.

This paperback on Pickford consists of an introductory essay about her career which is both factual and critical, an account of her short films made at Biograph, and film notes on nine of her feature films. A complete filmography of 141 short films and 52 features concludes the tribute. This book presents a portrait of Pickford that is not available elsewhere. Illustrations are fine and the content is excellent. Recommended.

6213   *Tribute to the King of Rock and Roll: Remembering You.* illus. London: IPC Magazines, 1977.

6214   *Trick Effects with the Cine Camera.* by Bulleid, Henry A. 79 p. paper

illus. London: Link House, 1937.

A title in the *Amateur Cine World* series by the author who later wrote a fuller treatment for the professional on the same subject, *Special Effects in Cinematography* (1954).

6215   TRILOGY: An Experiment in Multi-Media. by Capote, Truman; and Perry Eleanor ; and Perry, Frank. 276 p. illus. New York: Macmillan, 1969.

This unusual volume contains: 1) an introduction by John Culkin; 2) separate articles by each of the authors; 3) the original short stories by Capote upon which the film was based ("Miriam," "Among the Paths to Glory," and "A Christmas Memory"); and 4) the script for the above stories written by Eleanor Perry. Together these items make an interesting collection that can be used most effectively with a viewing of the film.

6216   TRIO. by Maugham, S. and Sherriff, R.; and Langley, Noel. 156 p. illus. Garden City, N.Y.: Doubleday, 1950.

Script of the 1950 film directed by Ken Annakin and Harold French. Contains the following short stories by Somerset Maugham and the screenplays made from them: "The Verger" (Annakin), "Mr. Know-All" (Annakin), and "Sanitorium" (French).

6217   TRISTANA. by Bunuel, Luis. 144 p. paper illus. New York: Simonand Schuster, 1971.

Script of the 1970 film directed by Bunuel. Contains an introductory article by J. Francisco Aranda, cast and credits.

6218   *Trivia and More Trivia.* by Goodgold, Edwin; and Carlinsky, Dan. 268 p. illus. Secaucus, N.J.: Castle Books, 1966.

This volume contains 1001 questions and answers about "those thrilling days of yesteryear." A variety of formats is employed: a dictionary of questions, quotations, connoisseur questions, a photo-quiz, matching, and a crossword puzzle. A large percentage of the material deals with films and film personalities.

6219   THE TROJAN WOMEN 22 p. paper illus. New York: Raydell Publishing, 1971.

Reference to the play by Euripides and "A Director's Note" by Michael Cacoyannis are the two leading articles in this souvenir book. The remaining pages are devoted to shots from the 1971 film, pages on each of the leading stars—Katharine Hepburn, Vanessa Redgrave, Irene Papas, Genevieve Bujold, and a biographical sketch of Cacoyannis. Some candid photos made during the filming are also shown and supporting cast and other production credits are noted.

6220 *THE TROJAN WOMEN.* by Cacoyannis, Michael. 116 p. paper illus. New York: Bantam Books, 1971.

Script of the 1971 film directed by Cacoyannis. Contains cast credits and is divided into four sections: 1) A Pacifist in Periclean Athens (Edith Hamilton); 2) *The Trojan Women* of Euripides (translated by Edith Hamilton); 3) Director's Note (Michael Cacoyannis); 4) Screenplay for THE TROJAN WOMEN (Michael Cacoyannis).

6221 *The True Book about Films.* by Harrison, Richard M. 142 p. illus. London: Muller, 1956.

A textbook designed for young readers.

6222 *True Britt.* by Ekland, Britt. 245 p. illus. Englewood Cliffs, N.J.: Prentice-Hall, 1981.

A romantic autobiography of a minor film actress who lives for love. In her search she recalls ex-husband Peter Sellers and ex-lover Warren Beatty.

6223 *The True Story of Jean Harlow, Hollywood's All-time Sex Goddess.* edited by Nystedt, Bob. 66 p. paper illus. Skokie, Ill.: Publishers' Development Corp., 1964.

Published to counter-balance the portrait given in Irving Shulman's *Harlow*, this volume consists of memoirs "as told by those who knew her best." It includes contributions by Ben Lyon, Maureen O'Sullivan, Adela Rogers St. Johns, Kay Mulvey and others.

6224 *Truffaut.* by Allen, Don. 176 p. paper illus. New York: Viking Press, 1974.

Don Allen presents a detailed study of 13 Truffaut films—the last being LA NUIT AMERICAINE (1973), released in the United States and Great Britain as DAY FOR NIGHT. The films are characterized as autobiographical, pessimistic, and preoccupied with recurring themes. Although the author is open in his admiration of Truffaut, he tries to be critically honest. In addition to treating the films together in pointing out their similarities in plot, action and themes, Allen also examines them individually. The films are arranged chronologically (except for the Antoine Doinel quartet), with a chapter devoted to each. A filmography and some illustrations complete the book.

The investigation and evaluations contained here are commendable in content, style and format. The book is a late entry, however, since Graham Petrie's *The Cinema of Francois Truffaut* and C. G. Crisp's *Francois Truffaut* cover very similar material and include some of the same film stills offered here. As an intelligent, satisfying guide to Truffaut's work, this volume can be recommended.

6225 *The Truth About Elvis.* by Stearn, Jess. illus. New York: G.P. Putnam, 1980.

6226 *The Truth About the Movies—By The Stars.* edited by Hughes; Laurence. 543 p. illus. New York: Gordon Press, 1976 (1924).

Photos and articles by stars, directors and producers of the twenties. Originally published by Hollywood Publishing in 1924.

6227 *The Truth Game.* by Hallowell, John. 253 p. New York: Simon & Schuster, 1969.

The truth game of the title, supposedly originated by Melina Mercouri, is the old parlor game of likening people to other animals, vegetables, or minerals. It is played by the author during several of the interviews contained in this collection. The subjects are the Newmans, Doris Day, Raquel Welch, Kim Novak, Rita Hayworth, Barbra Streisand, Rona Barrett, Andy Warhol, and others. Several articles on show business topics complete the book.

The interviews are dull and perform a disservice to the stars. Rather than describing his subjects in illuminating or revealing prose, Hallowell allows his personal reaction to the subjects to govern the content. Thus, at times, the writing style is amateur-awestruck and, at other times, it is unmotivated-bitchy. The nondiscriminating reader may be amused; others will be merely annoyed.

6228 *Tryin' to Get to You: The Story of Elvis Presley.* by Harms, Valerie. illus. New York: Atheneum, 1979.

6229 *Turn On to Stardom.* by Nicholson, Dianne. 192 p. paper New York: Cornerstone Library, 1968.

Directed at those who have an urge to perform professionally, this book includes many interviews with experts and sets forth some guidelines for action. The qualities necessary to become a performer are delineated: knowing yourself, both physically and emotionally, is the most essential requisite. The possibilities for a performer are listed: theatre, variety, burlesque, opera, concert, television, films, or recordings. How one prepares by training voice, body, and mind is covered, and other sections are devoted to a how-to-do-it approach to getting a job: the places, the trade publications, the photos, resumes, auditions, unions, agents, schools, etc. The final chapter concerns perseverance, timing, existing, and morals.

If the book is rather light on dissuading young people from a career in show business, it is quite thorough in covering the basic elements in preparing for such a career.

6230 *The Turned-on Hollywood Seven: Jackie Remembers Our Gang.* by Taylor, Jackie Lynn; and Fries, Jack. 76 p. paper illus. Toluca Lake, Calif.: Pacifica, 1970.

The author appeared in five LITTLE RASCALS films during 1934 and today works in local television that covers Southern California. She also hosted a television revival of the shorts.

6231 *Turning Kids on to Print Using Nonprint.* by Thomas, James L. 168 p. illus. Littleton, Colo.: Libraries Unlimited, 1978.

How to use the local production of audiovisual materials as a motivation for reading is the theme of this book. After explaining the construction of storyboards, the key element in media production, the author devotes individual chapters to filmstrips, 8mm films, television programs, transparencies, and dioramas. For each there are objectives, strategies, definitions, materials, costs, procedures, a bibliography, follow-up activities, and a list of equipment/materials suppliers. A general bibliography and an index complete the volume, which is illustrated.

A need for this kind of book has existed for a long time. Professor Thomas has presented his arguments in a most efficient and persuasive manner. This volume, highly recommended for all K-12 schools, should also be required reading for all teacher candidates.

6232 *TV and Movie Puzzles.* 544 p. illus. paper New York: Playmore and Prestige, 1981.

6233 *TV Broadcasts on Films and Filmmakers.* edited by Monty, Ib. 90 p. paper Copenhagen: Det Danske Filmmuseum, 1972.

A catalog published for the International Federation of Film Archives by the Danish Film Museum.

6234 *Twayne's Theatrical Arts Series.* edited by French, Warren. illus. Boston: Twayne, 1977- .

This series, which carries a subdivision title of "The Giants of the Modern Cinema," provides in-depth critical studies and surveys of the work of selected directors.

Chosen as subjects thus far are: Abel Gance, Jean-Luc Godard, Luis Bunuel, Frank Capra, Rene Clair, Grigori Kosintsev, Fritz Lang, Joseph Losey, Mike Nichols, Laurence Olivier, G. W. Pabst, Pier Paolo Pasolini, Alain Resnais, Leni Riefenstahl, Nicholas Roeg, Ken Russell, Douglas Sirk, Francois Truffaut, Peter Watkins, and Billy Wilder.

The books, written by qualified authors, scholars, and historians, are well researched and documented with an abundance of intelligent critical comment. Notes, illustrations, a bibliography, a filmography and an index accompany the text.

These studies form a notable contribution to the literature of the motion picture.

6235 *Twelve Directions: Some Films and Filmmakers from the Royal College of Art.* by Freeth, Martin. 40 p. paper illus. Hampshire, Christchurch: Hurad, 1969.

Interviews with twelve students from the Film and TV School of the Royal College of Art on the films they have made or are making.

6236 *20th Century Fox Memorbilia Catalog.* by Sotheby, Parke-Bernet Galleries. 275 p. paper illus. Los Angeles: Sotheby, Parke-Bernet,

1971.

The title page reads "Movie Memorabilia—inactive properties including furniture, decorative objects, paintings, posters, set sketches and other decorations, full-size and model boats and ships, airplanes, model trains." This was the catalog required for admission to the auction of the 20th Century Fox props held in February, 1971. Not only does it contain illustrations of the properties butmany stills from the Fox films are included.

6237 *Twenty Best Film Plays.* edited by Gassner, John; and Nichols, Dudley. 1112 p. New York: Crown Pub., 1943.

Contains scripts of: MRS. MINIVER (1942), REBECCA (1940), THE GRAPES OF WRATH (1940), HERE COMES MR. JORDAN (1941), HOW GREEN WAS MY VALLEY (1941), IT HAPPENED ONE NIGHT (1934), THE GOOD EARTH (1937), MR. SMITH GOES TO WASHINGTON (1939), THIS LAND IS MINE (1943), ALL THAT MONEY CAN BUY (1941), MY MAN GODFREY (1936), LITTLE CAESAR (1930), WUTHERING HEIGHTS (1939), THE WOMEN (1939), THE FIGHT FOR LIFE (1940), THE LIFE OF EMILE ZOLA (1937), YELLOW JACK (1938), MAKE WAY FOR TOMORROW (1937), STAGECOACH (1939), JUAREZ (1939), and FURY (1936).

6238 *Twenty Films to Use in Junior Film Societies.* by Hodgkinson, A. W. 55 p. paper illus. London: British Film Institute, 1953.

Another pioneering work by a creative professor of film study.

6239 *Twenty Five Thousand Sunsets: The Autobiography of Herbert Wilcox.* by Wilcox, Herbert. 233 p. illus. London: Bodley Head, 1967.

Wilcox is the veteran film producer-showman-director who has been an influence in the British film industry for several decades. In this rather emotional but selective autobiography, he accents those matters which represent the high points of his career while minimizing, forgetting, or omitting certain low points. Much attention is given to his wife, Anna Neagle, and to the films they made together. This is an average biography that will have a minimal interest for American readers. Historians and scholars will appreciate it much more.

6240 *25 Years of Film: Reminiscences and Reflections of a Critic.* by Doyle, George Ralph. 270 p. illus. London:

Mitre Press, 1936.

An amusing account of the experiences and memories of a film critic, this volume also provides a survey of the first three decades of film in London. In a flippant, entertaining style, Doyle uses facts, arguments, and abuses to make his points. The style is rambling and digression abounds, but the book is never dull. Especially fine is the naming of 100 notable films and the accompanying comments.

6241 *Twenty-Five Years of Films: Reminiscences and Reflections of a Critic.* by Doyle, G. R. 288 p. illus. London: Mitre, 1936.

Alexander Korda supplies the foreword to this consideration of many aspects of the film art. In the first section Doyle covers the story and script, the filming, the players, the directors, the films, their presentation and publicity. More philosophical in the second part, he talks about what is wrong with films, developing a reasonable attitude toward them, and finally, treats the mechanism of film and the principles of cinematography.

6242 *Twenty-Four Times a Second: Films and Film-Makers.* by Pechter, William S. 324 p. New York: Harper & Row, 1971.

The essays in this collection are derived from articles dating from 1960-1970 and appeared in magazines such as *Commentary, Commonweal, Kenyon Review, Film Quarterly, Film Comment,* etc. Thus they represent a more leisurely, thoughtful effort than does, for example, the review prepared for a newspaper or magazine with publication deadlines. The time advantage does not always work in the author's favor. The films evaluated are predictable—BREATHLESS (1959), LA DOLCE VITA (1961), L'AVVENTURA (1960), FIVE DAY LOVER (1961), LAST YEAR AT MARIENBAD (1961), 8-1/2 (1963), etc. The directors assessed are no surprise either—Bergman, Hitchcock, Godard, Renoir, etc. Capra is the unusual exception. Two other writers of film criticism, James Agee and Robert Warshow, are paid tribute. There is an index.

The author tries to tackle the significant issues of film criticism. As an example, he seems to reject the technical, fragmented approach in favor of an appreciation of film totality. His arguments are not always persuasive or successful. At times he is vague and unfocused, while at other times he concentrates on puns and humor rather than content. Also, one wishes he had addressed himself to less familiar materials. This is a book that promises more than it eventually delivers.

6243 *27 Major Film Classics.* edited by Museum of Modern Art. 19 p. paper illus. New York. Museum of Modern Art, 1967.

An announcement which details the collection of 27 films donated to the museum by Janus Films.

6244 *Twenty Years A-Growing.* by Thomas, Dylan. 91 p. London: J. M. Dent, 1964.

An unfilmed script by Dylan Thomas based on a story by Maurice O'Sullivan. The locale is the Blasket Islands of Ireland.

6245 *Twenty Years of British Film 1925-1945.* by Balcon, Michael; and Hardy, H. Forsyth; and Lindgren, Ernest; and Manvell, Roger. 116 p. illus. London: Falcon Press, 1947.

An illustrated survey of British films made over two decades; both entertainment features and documentaries are included.

6246 *Twenty Years of Cinema in Venice.* 698 p. illus. Rome: Edizioni dell'Ateneo, 1952.

This is a history of the Venice Film Festival, the International Exhibition of Cinematographic Art, which began in 1932. The films presented over the two decades and the evolution of film art over the same period are the themes of this book. There are many interesting articles, 336 stills, and a lot of administrative back-slapping.

6247 *Twenty Years of Polish Cinema Film 1947-1967.* 152 p. illus. Warsaw: Art and Film Pub., 1969.

A beautiful, oversized picture book with English text. A visual delight.

6248 *Twenty Years of Silents.* by Weaver, John T. 514 p. Metuchen, N.J.: Scarecrow Press, 1971.

Serves as a handy guide to the screen credits of the actors, actresses, directors and producers of silent films. Designed for quick reference, it lists players alphabetically, with their film credits presented chronologically by year of release. Directors' and producers' credits are presented in the same manner. Also included are listings of vital statistics and silent film studio corporations and distributors. Recommended.

6249 *Twiggy and Justin.* by Whiteside, Thomas. 136 p. paper illus. New York: Manor Books, 1972.

This paperback is subtitled, "The Inside Story of the Rise to Stardom of the 90-Pound Beauty," and is based on material which appeared originally in *The New Yorker*. Its portrait of the two title characters may be of moderate interest to some, but since it was written before THE BOY FRIEND (1971), it has little pertinence for film collections. Production quality is poor and the book is noted here as a matter of record.

6250 *Twinkle, Twinkle Movie Star!* by Brundidge, Harry T. 284 p. illus. New York: Dutton, 1930.

A collection of 31 interviews along with a portrait of each subject. Included are such performers as Renee Adoree, George Bancroft, Richard Dix, William Powell, Lupe Velez, and others.

6251 TWO FOR THE ROAD. by Raphael, Frederic. 142 p. New York: Holt, Rinehart, & Winston, 1967.

Script of the 1966 film directed by Stanley Donen.

6252 *Two for the Show: Great Comedy Teams.* by Burr, Lonnie. 256 p. illus. New York: Julian Messner, 1979.

In this collective biography, comedyteams such as Laurel and Hardy, Burns and Allen, Abbott and Costello, Martin and Lewis, and the Marx Brothers are discussed. In addition to the text, there is a glossary, a chronology, a bibliography, an index, and some illustrations.

6253 *200 Cine Tips.* by Voogel, Emile; and Keyser, Peter. paper illus. London: Fountain Press, 1977.

With its pages made to resemble a strip of film, this book offers some 200 "frames" of filmmaking advice. The suggestions are arranged sequentially and in groups under the following headings: Ten Commandments, Avoiding Mistakes, Getting Good Pictures, Artificial Light, Titling, Editing, Sound and Projection. The volume, which is well illustrated, should please most amateur filmmakers.

6254 *The Two Hundred Days of 8-1/2.* by Boyer, Deena. 218 p. illus. New York: Macmillan, 1964.

A day-by-day account of the making of Fellini's 8-1/2 (1963) by the woman who acted as the "on-set press officer" for the production. Photographs include stills from the film and candids of the actual shooting. An afterword is provided by Dwight MacDonald. All are fascinating. As a well-produced diary of the making of a classic film, this book has a certain importance.

6255 *Two-Hundred Thousand Feet: The Edge of the World.* by Powell, Michael. 334 p. illus. New York: Dutton, 1938.

An account of making the film THE EDGE OF THE WORLD (1937) and of life on the island of Foula. A well-written, sometimes racy account.

6256 TWO-LANE BLACKTOP. by Wurlitzer, Rudolph; and Corry, Will. 160 p. paper illus. New York: Award Books, 1971.

Script of the 1971 film directed by Monte Hellman. Contains cast of characters; production staff credits; introduction: An Interview with Blacktop Director Monte Hellman; and production notes.

6257 *The Two Lives of Errol Flynn.* by Freedland, Michael. 257 p. paper illus. New York: Bantam, 1978.

Although this biography of Errol Flynn is purportedly based on interviews with a selected group of people who knew him, not much new material is disclosed. The actor had a softer, nonmachismo side, hated his mother, and may have been a racist. These private life items are the contrast to the public image.

Much of the text is familiar and Freedland's style does not bring any needed freshness. Retelling the facts of Flynn's charisma, lechery, and ultimate debauchery at this time is almost approaching cliche. A few illustrations do not help.

6258 *The Two of Us.* by McCambridge, Mercedes. 182 p. illus. London: P. Davies, 1960.

A relatively unknown autobiography of the actress.

6259 *The Two of Us.* by Martin, Tony; and Charisse, Cyd. 286 p. illus. New York: Mason/Charter, 1976.

Using the format of alternating subject chapters, as employed by Garson Kanin in *Tracy and Hepburn*, this dual autobiography follows the careers of Tony Martin and Cyd Charisse through show business adventures in Hollywood, Las Vegas, Europe and other world locations. Since the peaks in their careers were not simultaneous, common events appear in different places. For example, Cyd tells of first meeting Tony on page 125 while his story of their initial meeting takes place on page 232. The structure really provides for two independent stories that converge only in the final pages.

Both authors recall incident, anecdote, impression and coversation with apparent ease. Famous names appear with consistent regularity as Martin recalls Hollywood during the thirties and early forties, while Charisse takes care of the late forties and the fifties.

The reading is pleasant and reaction to the book may be proportional to one's feelings about the subjects; certainly the more sympathetic portrait is of Cyd Charisse. There is no index or filmography but some helpful illustrations are included. Acceptable.

6260 TWO OR THREE THINGS I KNOW ABOUT HER: Analysis of a Film by Jean-Luc Godard. by Guzzetti, Alfred. illus. Boston: Harvard University Press, 1980.

A frame-by-frame analysis of Godard's film.

6261 *Two Reels and a Crank: From Nickelodeon to Picture Palaces.* by Smith, Albert E.; and Koury, Phil A. 285 p. illus. Garden City, N.Y.: Doubleday, 1952.

The rough-and-tumble early days of motion picture invention, production, and distribution are recalled in this book. During the late 1890's Albert Smith was inventing projectors, pirating films, faking scenes and otherwise engaging in the cut-throat rivalries of those days. He helped to establish Vitagraph Pictures at the same time. In 1925 Smith sold Vitagraph to Warners and retired. He was given an honorary Oscar in 1948 as a film pioneer.

In this memoir, fascinating portraits of Thomas Edison, Mary Pickford, and John Bunny are presented. A lengthy list of personalities developed or employed by Smith's Vitagraph Studio is included. His indictment of the early Samuel Goldwyn's business practices is particularly stinging. This is a pleasing, well-written reminiscence that recreates a period from firsthand knowledge. While general interest in this history may be mild, any reader will be rewarded by the lively, virile accounts supplied by the author.

6262 *Two Russian Screen Classics.* 102 p. paper illus. New York: Simon &

Schuster, 1973.

Contains cast, production credits, and introductions to MOTHER (1925); EARTH (1930).

6263 *Two Screenplays.* by Cocteau, Jean. 147 p. illus. New York: Orion Press, 1968.

Two filmscripts directed by Cocteau. Contains cast credits; an introduction by Cocteau; and THE BLOOD OF A POET (1930) and THE TESTAMENT OF ORPHEUS (1959).

6264 *Two Screenplays.* by Visconti, Luchino; and d'Amico, Suso Cocchi. 186 p. illus. New York: Orion Press, 1970.

Scripts of two films directed by Visconti. Contains LA TERRA TREMA (1947), and SENSO (1954), and cast credits.

6265 *Two Stars for God.* by Petersen, William J. 191 p. paper illus. New York: Warner, 1974.

The two stars in this instance are Dale Evans Rogers and Anita Bryant. Although the theme is how these two women found abiding faith in God, there is an abundance of autobiographical material included.

It should be noted that each has written one or more books which have sold over a million copies. Most famous is Bryant's *Mine Eyes Have Seen the Glory* and Evans' *Angel Unaware.*

Noted for the biographical material on Dale Evans Rogers.

6266 2001— A SPACE ODYSSEY. 22 p. paper illus. New York: National Publishers, 1968.

This souvenir book is unusual in several ways: it has been produced in an elongated shape, it has tissues alternating with its pages, and it is quite difficult to handle. Much of the material in the volume is fine; excellent illustrations, and pages devoted to director Stanley Kubrick, original author Arthur C. Clarke, stars Keir Dullea, Gary Lockwood and Hal, the computer. Other cast and production credits are given.

6267 2001 — A SPACE ODDYSSEY. by Geduld, Carolyn 87 p. paper Bloomington, Ind.: Indiana University Press, 1973.

One of the first group of *Filmguides,* this short

volume contains the following elements: film credits, a plot outline, a summary of director Kubrick's career, a chronological account of the production, a lengthy analysis and a summary critique. A brief filmography, an excellent bibliography, and a single rental source form the book's final pages. The information offered is most impressive. All aspects of this classic but controversial film are covered, including critical reception. Any viewing of 2001: A SPACE ODYSSEY (1968) will be greatly enriched by use of this volume before and after the film experience.

The Kubrick filmography should have been enlarged to include the cast and production credits. The book is a most welcome addition to those already published on the film and will be an invaluable aid to those studying it in future years. Highly recommended.

6268 *Tycoons and Locusts: A Regional Look at Hollywood Fiction of the Thirties.* by Wells, Walter. 139 p. illus. Carbondale: Southern Illinois University Press, 1973.

6269 *Tynan Right and Left.* by Tynan, Kenneth. 479 p. New York: Atheneum, 1968.

The cinema reviews by Tynan occupy approximately one-eighth of the total book. But since this is a sampling of film writing by this erudite, brilliant critic, it is noted here. Superior film criticism.

6270 *Tyrone Power: The Last Idol.* by Lawrence, Fred. 471 p. illus. New York: Doubleday, 1979.

Since this biography is "official" in the sense that it was written with the cooperation of Tyrone Power's sister, wives, and daughters, it is not surprising that it is a mostly positive, admiring portrait. Power's weaknesses, excesses and his bisexuality are minimized, while his potential and position as a major film star are somewhat exaggerated. Lawrence blames his slide from fame and his early death on the "idol" syndrome acquired early in his career.

The book includes many illustrations, a filmography, a bibliography, and an index.

6271 *The UFO Movie Quiz Book.* by Rovin, Jeff. 165 p. paper illus. New York: Signet, 1978.

There must be a large audience for quiz books such as this one. Signet also publishes such titles as *From the Blob to Star Wars, The Trekkie Quiz Book, The*

Official TV Trivia Quiz Book (2 volumes), *The Official Movie Trivia Quiz Book*, *The Nostalgia Quiz Book* (3 volumes), *The Elvis Presley Quiz Book*, *The Beatles Quiz Book*, *The Sports Nostalgia Quiz Book* (2 volumes), etc. 101 quizzes areprovided along with answers, photos and an introduction by director Robert Wise. Formats include matching, multiple choice, fill-in-the-blanks, and questions, while topics cover specific films, directors, and TV series.

6272 *Ulrich's International Periodicals Directory.* New York: Bowker, 1932-

This directory considers international periodicals arranged according to subject. It gives all the data necessary for subscription or information requests. Under "Motion Pictures" (pages 986-992), the 1970 directory cited periodicals which ranged alphabetically from *ABC Film Review* to *Zhurnal Nauchnoi I. Prikladnoi.* The directory is now published annually with quarterly supplements available. Most interesting to readers of film literature is the list of periodicals which have ceased publication since the last edition.

6273 ULYSSES. 32 p. paper illus. New York: National Publishers, 1967.

This oversized souvenir book features many full-page illustrations in addition to a rather long synopsis of the 1967 film. Author James Joyce receives some attention, as do the actors in the film, Milo O'Shea, Barbara Jefford, Maurice Roeves, T.P. McKenna, and Anna Manahan. Both the executive producer, Walter Reade, Jr., and the director, Joseph Strick, are spotlighted. The book closes with an excerpt from Molly's soliloquy.

6274 UN CHIEN ANDALOU. by Bunuel, Luis; and Dali, Salvador. 43 p. paper illus. New York: Simon & Schuster, 1968.

Script of the 1928 film directed by Bunuel. Also contains cast credits and four articles: Jean Vigo on UN CHIEN ANDALOU; Cyril Connolly on UN CHIEN ANDALOU; original shooting script; and final screen version. Appears in the same volume as L'AGE D'OR (1930).

6275 UNDER MILK WOOD. by Sinclair, Andrew; and Thomas, Dylan. 95 p. paper illus. New York: Simon and Schuster, 1972.

Script of the 1972 film directed by Sinclair. Contains "Milk Wood and Magic" by Andrew Sinclair, cast and credits.

6276 *Underground Film: A Critical History.* by Tyler, Parker. 249 p. illus. New York: Grove Press, 1969.

The author states early in this volume that his purpose is "to show what the exact personality of the underground films is," and "how its traits exist in a historical perspective...." By a series of examples of films from the preceding five decades, Tyler does indicate in many ways the debt of today's underground films to the many avant-garde films which were made long before the sixties. As is usual in Tyler's books, the text is witty, intellectual, and most provocative. Not for the casual or general reader, it is for the cinematist who is searching for new ideas and interpretations. Photographs are reproduced with fidelity, and a film list of key works from 1915 to 1969 is included.

6277 *Underscore.* by Skinner, Frank. 239 p. illus. Hackensack, N.J.: Wehman Bros., 1961.

The author, a composer of music for many films, indicates his personal method of writing film scores.

6278 *Understanding Media: The Extensions of Man.* by McLuhan, Marshall. 365 p. paper New York: McGraw-Hill, 1964.

McLuhan's most important work, which summarizes his theories and observations about media. A major point made is that all media are extensions of the human body: the telephone is an extension of the ear, the automobile an extension of the legs, etc.

6279 *Understanding Movies.* by Gianetti, Louis D. 217 p. paper illus. Englewood Cliffs, N.J.: Prentice-Hall, 1972.

The author's intent is "to help the moviegoer understand some of the complex elements" of film. Individual chapters are devoted to the basic techniques that directors have used to convey meaning—picture, movement, editing, sound, drama, literature and theory. A solid glossary and a detailed index complete the book. Good illustrations and helpful diagrams appear throughout. Under each heading, the author discusses many concepts or ideas. For each he tries to describe or show one film example to illuminate his point.

Books on aesthetics can get overly pedantic or so convoluted that they strain reader patience. Not so here; this readable book is straightforward, intelligent and informative. An example of the book's excellence is the chapter on theories which provides one of the best summaries currently available. Highly recommended.

6280 *Understanding Sound, Video and Film Recording.* by Overman, Michael. 142 p. illus. Blue Ridge Summit, Pa: Tab Books, 1978.

A history of sound recording is presented here with individual chapters on film and television sound appearing in the closing sections of the volume. The author's intent throughout is to tell how the major developments in sound recording occurred and how these developments work. From the barrel organ to the video disc, he offers historical background and technical explanation.

Illustrations consist of line drawings which describe in visual fashion the events and discoveries treated in the text. An index is provided.

The reader who is searching for basic information on general sound recording topics will probably find a satisfactory explanation in this book. It is well written and succeeds nicely in achieving its modest goals. Acceptable.

6281 *Understanding the Film.* by Johnson, Ron; and Bone, Jan. 248 p. paper illus. Skokie, Ill.: National Textbook Company, 1976.

This title, taken from the *Language Arts* series published by the National Textbook Company, has as its goal the transformation of the moviegoer into the film viewer. To do this it concentrates on film definition, personnel, filmmaking, viewing, perception, film language, script construction, film evaluation, and specific directors. An appendix offers about 200 brief annotations for American, foreign and short films that are recommended for viewing. Illustrations are plentiful, well selected and carefully reproduced. The lack of an index seriously limits the general use of the book.

The elements needed for an introduction to the serious study of film are all present in the text. Written with a discernible, intelligent structure, the volume offers an entertaining, nonpedantic approach. Unfortunately, because of the missing index, the book becomes acceptable rather than recommended.

6282 *Understanding the Mass Media: A Practical Approach for Teaching.* by Tucker, Nicholas. 198 p. Cambridge: Cambridge University Press, 1980.

6283 *Underwater Photography.* by Rebikoff, Dimitri, and Cherney, Paul. 144 p. paper illus. New York: Amphoto, 1972.

Addressed to both the professional and the semiprofessional, this book explains techniques, equipment, tricks, problems, and materials of underwater photography.

6284 *Underworld U.S.A.* by McArthur, Colin. 176 p. illus. London: Secker & Warburg, 1972.

The re-evaluation of the American cinema begun by the *Cahiers* critics and then taken up by *Movie* and Andrew Sarris suggests the presence of auteurs in that cinema. McArthur argues that recent critical attention overlooks far more important elements; for example, the force and function of the genres—western, gangster, musical. This volume addresses itself to the American gangster films, a genre to which he adds a sub-set called Thrillers. His rationale is that the two forms are interrelated by their iconography, personnel, mood, and theme.

A few introductory chapters discuss the elements, the development, and the historical background for the gangster film. To support his thesis, the author analyzes certain films of nine directors, allowing one chapter for each: Fritz Lang, John Huston, Jules Dassin, Robert Siodmak, Elia Kazan, Nicholas Ray, Samuel Fuller, Don Seigel and Jean-Pierre Melville. The inclusion of this latter director is justified as an example of an American genre transferred to Europe. Supporting the text rather well is a fine selection of stills. One may cause some puzzlement —why a full-page still from SINGIN' IN THE RAIN (1952) to preface the introduction? An index to film titles and a general index complete the book.

When the author states that there is only the scantiest of material on John Huston, one questions his research. Two full-length books come to mind— *John Huston, King Rebel* and *John Huston: A Pictorial Treasury of His Films*—in addition to interviews (*Interviews with Film Directors*) and observations (*Picture*, by Lillian Ross).However, his total theme is provocative and the structure of the book is well designed to support his argument. For the most part it is informative and enjoyable. The book is not essential, but it will please many readers.

6285 *Unemployment Problems in American Film Industry.* by Subcommittee on Labor. 105 p. paper illus. Washington, D.C.: U.S. Government Printing Office, 1972.

A record of the hearings, held in Los Angeles on October 29 and 30, 1971, during the first session of the 92nd Congress.

6286 *Unholy Fools, Wits, Comics, Disturbers of the Peace.* by Gilliatt, Penelope. 384 p. illus. New York: Viking, 1973.

A selection of Gilliatt's theatre and film criticism written both here and in England during the last dozen or so years. The range of films is wide, including the work of master directors like Bergman, Kubrick and Renoir, but it is the comedy films that seem to inspire the author. Her method is simple, logical, and effective. Opening portions of the reviews recall the film, the plot and the acting in an effort to duplicate the viewing experience; she follows with witty, honest, and often profound analysis.

Gilliatt may be an acquired taste but she is a most rewarding writer for those who appreciate her critical abilities. The theater reviews include works by Shaw, Pirandello, Brecht, Beckett, and Pinter. Recommended.

6287 *The Unimportance of Being Oscar.* by Levant, Oscar. 255 p. illus. New York: G. P. Putnam's, 1968.

There is a sprinkling of Hollywood film anecdotes in this Levant collection of memories and observations. Funny, irreverent, and often brilliant.

6288 *United Artists: The Company Built by the Stars.* by Balio, Tino. 323 p. illus. Madison, Wisc.: University of Wisconsin Press, 1976.

In 1919 the United Artists Corporation was founded by Mary Pickford, Charlie Chaplin, Douglas Fairbanks, and D. W. Griffith. The rationale for the company was to make and distribute films of high quality made by the founders and others. During the twenties, under the leadership of Joe Schenk, filmmakers such as Goldwyn, Swanson, Valentino, and Keaton were brought in. During the thirties and forties a battle for survival ensued; today the company is thriving.

In this volume, which is based in part on a collection of United Artists papers housed at the State Historic Society of Madison, the author traces the history of the company from its beginning to its resurgence in 1949.

Of equal importance with the text are the appendixes which include: (1) a listing of United Artists films from 1919 to 1950; (2) the producers affiliated with the company along with their films; (3) Walt Disney cartoons; (4) income history; (5) dividend payments; and (6) capital stock purchased by the company. A description of the United Artists collection of papers, some notes, and an index complete the volume.

This is a detailed informational study that will serve a limited audience. While it has some reference value, much of it is too specialized and only of interest to the student or the researcher. Acceptable.

6289 *United Nations Film Footage Library Index.* compiled by Radio and Visual Services, United Nations 80 p. paper New York: Office of Public Information United Nations, 1958.

6290 *U.S. Government Films.* by National Audiovisual Center. 165 p. Washington, D.C.: General Services Administration, 1969.

This is a catalog of motion pictures and filmstrips for sale by the National Audiovisual Center in Washington, D.C. The films are annotated and listed under subject headings. A consolidated title listing is given at the book's conclusion. A useful reference.

6291 *U.S. Government Films for Public Educational Use: Circular Number 742.* by Reid, Seerley; and Grubbs, Eloyse. 532 p. Washington, D.C.: Government Printing Office, 1968.

This is a selective list of about 6000 films and filmstrips which are the property of the Federal government (who controls distribution and reproduction rights). Also given are some of those which are merely presented by the government and to which the government has only limited distribution rights.

Included with each film is its source, its loan-rental-purchase data, and its TV clearance, if any. Each entry also has a nonevaluative summary, and a physical description which includes factors such as running time, audio format, color format, gauge, and order number. A list of sources for obtaining the films is included. The lengthy subject index is easy to use.

6292 *Universal Film Lexicon 1932.* edited by Arnau, Frank. 776 p. illus. New York: Gordon Press, 1976 (1932).

A reference yearbook in French, English and German that offers an alphabetical index to film topics. Originally published in London and Berlin.

6293   *Universal Pictures.* by Fitzgerald, Michael G. 766 p. illus. New Rochelle, N.Y.: Arlington House, 1977.

The subtitle of this large reference book about the Universal Studios describes its contents: "A Panoramic History in Words, Pictures and Filmographies." It begins with a selected historical overview arranged by film genre. A short section which follows lists the Academy Award nominations (and winners) received by Universal films and personnel. The short biographies of 72 Universal performers which appear next serve to introduce the largest section of the book—The Universal Studios Sound Filmography. Arranged chronologically, each year's film production from 1930 to 1976 is noted. Credits, cast names, technical data and a plot summary are given. The short subjects and featurettes made by the studio are also identified. An index completes the volume.

Accompanying all this information is a collection of nearly 600 illustrations, most of which are film stills. Their reproduction is clear but the black and white contrast values used have provided some darkish/dull-toned visuals.

A few questions can be raised about the author's judgments in the opening historical section. For example, did Universal make the most enjoyable and realistic musical of all the Hollywood studios; should stills from GUNG HO (1943) and GANG (1945) appear in the musical film section; why list CAN'T HELP SINGING (1944) as a "western of interest" when it has been described earlier as "strictly musical all the way;" why is there minimal text on certain major films—SHENANDOAH (1965), THE GLENN MILLER STORY (1955), MY LITTLE CHICKADEE (1940), BACK STREET (1932, 1941, 1961), THE OLD DARK HOUSE (1932), PILLOW TALK (1959), etc.—while others of lesser historical importance receive much more notice—THE THRILL OF IT ALL (1963), APPOINTMENT FOR LOVE (1941), THE PRIVATE WAR OF MAJOR BENSON (1955), IN SOCIETY (1944), THE HOUSE OF FRANKENSTEIN (1944), etc.?

Enough other examples can be found to suggest that the historical portions of the volume are the weakest. Since the author created this massive reference in less than two years, it is not surprising that the factual sections rather than the interpretive ones supply the book's strength. The biographies and the long filmography will be appreciated as major reference and research aids.

6294   *Universal Pictures in the Twenties and Thirties.* edited by Gordon, R. F. 2 volumes New York: Gordon Press, 1976.

6295   *University Advisory Committee Seminar.* edited by Reed, Rochelle. 24 p. paper illus. Washington, D.C.: The American Film Institute, 1972.

A meeting was held at the AFI Center in Beverly Hills in August, 1972, to explore the relationship between the AFI and the academic film community. The transcript published here is of the morning session which was enriched by the participation of Charlton Heston, Alfred Hitchcock, George Seaton, George Stevens, and Robert Wise. A list of suggested films is appended. Acceptable.

6296   *University and College Film Collections.* compiled by Indiana University Audio-Visual Center. 75 p. paper New York: Educational Film Library Association, 1974.

This is the third edition of a directory originally compiled by Allan Mirwis of Indiana University. From questionnaires the following information was gathered for more than 400 film libraries: the name of the institution housing the collection, address, person in charge of collection, telephone number, free-loan policy, rental policy, number of titles and prints, catalog frequency and availability, and additional information. An opening section lists those film collections with out-of-state rental policies, with any restriction noted. The main body of the book uses an alphabetical state-by-state listing of the collections with the above information provided for each. This specialized information can be used in a variety of ways. The book is another example of the unique service offered to the professions of education and librarianship by EFLA. It would also seem to be an essential for the marketing departments of book and film producers.

6297   *The Unkindest Cuts: The Scissors and the Cinema.* by McClelland, Doug. 220 p. illus. New York: A. S. Barnes, 1972.

The idea of writing a book about the arbitrary cutting of scenes and even entire performances from completed films is intriguing. The author states that he will not consider the usual cutting done by film editors or censors but only that done by directors, producers, leading actors or even exhibitors. This is a dangerous assertion since only the person making the cut knows the true rationale. As a result guidelines are not always followed. He does use the well-known examples—GREED (1923), THE MAGNIFICENT AMBERSONS (1942), A STAR IS BORN (1954), and THE RED BADGE OF COURAGE (1951). Other lesser known excisions are also described, but there is always a large difference between the total footage shot and the release print. The author includes here many instances of what appeared to be normal rearrangement or assessment of primary material. Surely it is not always arbitrary or capricious to try to improve a creative effort by editing, trimming, or shortening. Stories of films which were rescued by post-preview cutting are legion and include such items as LOST HORIZON (1937), THE SIN OF MADELON CLAUDET (1931), and A NIGHT AT THE OPERA (1935). The great unfairness comes about in tampering with a film that has been released and reviewed—i.e., CLEOPATRA (1963), EXODUS (1960), LAWRENCE OF ARABIA (1962), etc.

Another reservation about the volume concerns the constant intrusion of the author's personal opinion of performances— Phyllis Newman is a giddy guts who was mighty lucky to marry Adolph Green, or Eva Marie Saint and Warren Beatty were at the kitchen sink when charm was passed out. The putdown may be amusing to read but is it appropriate to the subject matter here?

If the author's substitution of hearsay, gossip, and opinion for research and his digressions from the major theme or purpose of the book can be overlooked, the reader will find many fascinating examples of film cuts told with supporting background information. The book is illustrated with scenes that never appeared on the screen. Reproduction quality of these stills varies widely and the size of some diminishes their effect considerably. A lengthy index is provided.

Since most of the previously published material on this topic dealt primarily with official censorship, the broader approach of this book is appreciated. Although it is flawed, non-discriminating readers will appreciate its contents and film buffs will enjoy re-viewing the many legends concerning discarded film treasure. Generally recommended.

6298   THE UNQUIET DEATH OF JULIUS AND ETHEL ROSENBERG. by Goldstein, Alvin H. illus. Westport, Conn.: Lawrence Hill and Company, 1975.

Contains the text and photographs from the 1975 television documentary written and directed by Alvin H. Goldstein. A preface to the book is provided by Nat Hentoff.

6299   *Unreal Reality: The Cinema of Harry Kumel.* by Soren, David. Columbia, Mo.: Lucas, 1979.

Kumel is a Belgian filmmaker who works for TV and teaches in a Dutch film School. His films include: MONSIEUR HAWARDEN (1968), DAUGHTERS OF DARKNESS (1971), and MALPERTUIS (1972).

6300   UP AGAINST IT: A Screenplay for the Beatles. by Orton, Joe. 88 p. paper New York: Grove, 1979.

In 1967 the Beatles hired playwright Joe Orton ("Entertaining Mr. Sloane," "Loot," "What the Butler Saw") to write a filmscript to follow HELP (1965).

The unfilmed scenario is reproduced here along with background information by John Lahr. Typical of Orton's approach is his original ending—the Beatles wed the same woman and all head off for the same marriage bed.

6301   *Up and Down the Line.* by Train, Jack. 256 p. illus. London: Odhams Press, 1956.

Autobiography of the British stage and radio star, who appeared in SHOWTIME (1948).

6302   UP IN SMOKE. by Cheech and Chong. paper illus.

An oversized paperback with many stills. Based on the successful film, UP IN SMOKE (1979). Total appreciation will depend upon an acquaintance with the drug culture.

6303   *Up in the Clouds, Gentlemen Please.* by Mills, John. 320 p. illus. New Haven, Conn.: Ticknor and Fields, 1981.

A mild, polite autobiography of an actor who typifies the Englishman in all his film roles. Some anecdotes about his professional friends lend a bit of excitement.

6304   *Upton Sinclair Presents William Fox.* by Sinclair, Upton. 371 p. New York: Arno Press, 1970 (1933).

This is an emotional book written at William Fox's request and originally published by the author. It is an obvious, prejudiced semibiography that reads like the confessions of an overconfident financial wheeler-dealer. Surely this book holds the record for numerical symbols and statistics ever to appear in any biography. After a career which began with

$1600 investment in a nickelodeon and ended with a prison term, today William Fox is a relatively forgotten mogul. Yet he established the Fox Studios and at one time had a personal fortune exceeding 40 million dollars.

Told practically in the first person, this volume will do little to preserve his memory since some of it reads like bankruptcy testimony. The rest is a diatribe against Wall Street bankers and lawyers. There are no illustrations and there is no index. Although Sinclair's writing is passionate, the complexity and intricacies of Fox's financial maneuvering will strain the patience of most readers. For historians and researchers only.

6305   *The Use of Audio-visual Aids In Education For International Understanding.* edited by Bucknell, Jack. 106 p. paper Paris: UNESCO, 1965.

This is the report and recommendations of an international seminar held in Hungary during August, 1965. It was organized by the UNESCO Institute For Education.

6306   *The Use of Film in the Teaching of English.* by Ontario Institute for Studies in Education 184 p. paper illus. Toronto: Ontario Institute for Studies in Education, 1971.

This report is number 8 in the *Curriculum* series published by the institute.

6307   *The Use of Mobile Cinema and Radio Vans in Fundamental Education.* 192 p. paper illus. London: Film Centre; New York: UNESCO, 1949.

6308   *The Use of Short 8mm Films in European Schools.* by Lefranc, Robert. 134 p. paper illus. Strasbourg: Council for Cultural Cooperation, 1967.

6309   *The Use of the Film.* by Wright, Basil. 72 p. London: The Bodley Head, 1948.

A look at motion picture production in Britain and a short argument about what films should be and do. The social importance theory of film is stressed.

6310   *The Uses of Film in the Teaching of English.* by English Study Commit-

tee, Office of Field Development. Ontario, Canada: Institute for Studies in Education, 1971.

6311   *Using Films: A Handbook for the Program Planner.* edited by Limbacher, James L. 130 p. paper New York: Educational Film Library Association, 1967.

This elementary collection of obvious articles for the novice in film use is a disappointment. Some of the material and the suggested approaches are not pertinent for today's sophisticated readers. To the experienced professional, the selection of articles may seem biased. Are the author biographies really necessary? A book of very limited value.

6312   *Using Mass Media in the Schools.* by Boutwell, William D. 292 p. New York: Appleton Century, 1962.

Prepared by the Committee on the Use of Mass Media of the National Council of English Teachers, this anthology was produced by consultants, experts, authorities, etc.,—a typical sixties committee operation. It contains "The Anatomy of Motion Pictures" by Arthur Knight, "Development of Taste in Movies" by Howard A. Burton and "We Evaluate Hollywood Films" by Mary Alice Uphoff. Other articles on mass media make reference to film, as do a few appendixes.

6313   *Using Projectors.* by Film Section, NCB. 35 p. paper illus. London: National Coal Board, 1965.

Contains tables, diagrams, and a bibliography.

6314   *Using Your Nation's Capital.* edited by Caffrey, Ann Gourley. 214 p. paper illus. Washington D.C.: United States Office Of Education, 1978.

This volume, which is subtitled "An Indexed Guide To Multimedia Resources In Washington, D.C.," provides information about 109 agencies/organizations. Each entry includes the organization name, address, telephone number, its purpose-function, and a sampling of its media offerings. For example, the National Gallery Of Art entry notes the following media; color reproductions, slides, filmstrips, films, exhibits, multimedia programs, reproductions, catalogs, books, and booklets. As indicated, only a few titles—a sampling—are mentioned. The author suggests contacting each agency for their available media. A final subject index provides access to individual areas or topics which may not be apparent from the agency's name.

Because of the efficient way it provides information about the enormous collection of multimedia that is available to everyone through those 109 agencies/organizations, this small reference book is recommended.

6315 *Ustinov in Focus.* by Thomas, Tony. 192 p. paper illus. New York: A. S. Barnes, 1971.

The emphasis in this tribute to Ustinov is on his film work as director, actor and writer. A large introductory section deals with Ustinov as a person—a biographical sketch touching on his early career, his family life, and his attitude towards himself and his work. The second section deals in chronological fashion with those films to which he has made some contribution. The appendices include a listing of his plays, his books, and his recordings.

Some of the book is based on interviews and visits with Ustinov; these are the strongest portions. When the author gives his personal reaction to the films, the text loses critical perspective in favor of some gushy tribute. Illustrations are excellent and the book should please all admirers of the multi-talented Ustinov. Recommended.

6316 *Vachel Lindsay: The Poet as Film Theorist.* by Wolfe, Glenn Joseph. 191 p. New York: Arno, 1973.

One of the doctoral dissertations on film topics which are reproduced by Arno exactly as submitted to the degree-granting institutions. Probably the first American to advance a theory of film was the poet-writer, Vachel Lindsay, in *The Art of the Moving Picture.* This study concentrates on Lindsay's film writings and looks at the factors which influenced him; his interest in many arts—sculpture, painting, architecture, etc.—and his concern with religion, politics, society, and his fellow man, all of which had an effect on his interpretation of film as art.

The first section deals with his social views, ideas on art, and his religious beliefs. Social problems and how film could help in solving them is considered next. Other sections indicate the relationships between Lindsay's social beliefs and his theories on the arts, including film. A final section compares Lindsay's theories and those of his contemporaries. A bibliography is included.

6317 *Val Lewton: The Reality of Terror.* by Siegel, Joel E. 176 p. paper illus. New York: Viking, 1973.

This long awaited book on the films that Val Lewton produced during the forties is completely satisfying; in most ways it is equal to the quality of the previous volumes in the fine *Cinema One* series. An account of Lewton's life and work opens the book. Included here are references to older interviews, letters, reminiscences of people who worked with Lewton, and background information about making the films. The films themselves occupy the second portion of the book. Cast and production credits are given, with a short plot synopsis and some production data. A critical essay follows in which the author evaluates in depth the strengths and weaknesses of each film.

Lewton's films number only 14 and some of the later ones were quite undistinguished, but the popularity, the frequency on TV, and the critical rediscovery of I WALKED WITH A ZOMBIE (1943), THE SEVENTH VICTIM (1943), ISLE OF THE DEAD (1945), THE BODY SNATCHERS (1945) and others more than justify this book's attention. Siegel has written with enthusiasm, respect, and a scholar's eye. Along with the comprehensive coverage of a relatively short career, he has included bits of information which fascinate and surprise, e.g., was Hitchcock's shower scene in PSYCHO (1960) really lifted or suggested by Lewton's THE SEVENTH VICTIM?

The illustrations are disappointing, not so much in their selection as in their reproduction. Many are given only a third of a page and in some there is too much contrast, the black being far too dark. The book is not indexed but there is a list of Lewton's credits to 1937, compiled by himself. By his sympathetic understanding of his subject, Siegel has provided a tribute to Lewton unlike any received in his lifetime. A fine book.

6318 *Vale of Laughter.* by Travers, Ben. 251 p. illus. London: Geoffrey Bles, 1957.

The autobiography of a playwright whose farces were adapted for filming in the thirties.

6319 *Valentine and Vitriol.* by Reed, Rex. 280 p. illus. New York: Delacorte, 1977.

Rex Reed returns to what he does best—interviewing people—in this collection of pieces originally written either for his syndicated column or *The Ladies Home Journal.* By dividing his subjects into four categories, he gives some hint of his feeling for them. Under "The Goddesses" we find Elizabeth Taylor, Sophia Loren, and Audrey Hepburn—a trio he adores. "The Heroes" and "The Survivors" contain mostly admiring interviews, while the final section,

"The New Breed," provides him with a few opportunities for the vitriol promised in the title. Rex Reed has apparently discontinued the original "bitchy" style evident in his first few books in favor of a mellower, more mature and accepting type of observation.

An introduction by Liz Smith and an article about the author's daily rounds precede the interview sections. A few of the illustrations show the photogenic author with certain of his subjects.

Reed's working style remains quite personal; his reaction to his subject is as important as what the subject says and does. This collection is readable, enjoyable, and ultimately, forgettable. As light entertainment that will please a large audience, the book can be recommended.

6320   *Valentino.* by Shulman, Irving. 499 p. illus. New York: Trident Press, 1967.

Approximately one half of this book, the central section, is biographical. Surrounding this portion is a long, detailed account of Valentino's funeral, some post-death reporting about his estate and finances, and finally a retelling of the spiritual and ritualistic activities of his devoted fans.

The middle section constitutes the book's strength. Shulman has practiced a bit more restraint here than in *Harlow*, for although the message is clear, it is related with discretion and sensitivity. The biographical coverage is based on documented facts and seems valid. Occasionally there is an allowance for reader interpretation as opposed to dogmatic statement by the author. The few pictures and the padding are disappointing as is the lack of an index. Since the central section is acceptable, this volume is certainly preferable to several of the other published biographies of this legendary figure.

6321   *Valentino.* by Steiger, Brad; and Mank, Chaw. 192 p. paper illus. New York: Macfadden Bartell, 1966.

Although the cover of this sensationalized biography advises that the book includes photographs from Valentino's own private scrapbook, the total of 18 small shots contains only two possibly rare photos. The entire volume promises more than it ever delivers. Using conjecture, innuendo, and rampant imagination, the authors recreate incidents and private conversations which they then present as if privy to tape recordings or transcripts which do not exist. This volume is a sample of unfair and offensive biography using a legendary subject who cannot

retaliate.

6322   *Valentino: A Biography.* by Arnold, Alan. 165 p. illus. New York: Library Publications, 1954.

An out-of-print and hard-to-find biography.

6323   *Valentino.* by Tajiri, Vincent. 150 p. paper illus. New York: Bantam, 1977.

A pedestrian retelling of the Valentino life and career, this original paperback covers all the familiar facts and fancies about the screen's legendary lover. What it lacks is any attempt to give motivation for Valentino's rapid climb to fame and his mishandling of his celebrity status. The item of conjecture which is a major interest today—Valentino's personal sex life—is almost unmentioned in this account. A filmography, illustrations, and an index accompany the text.

6324   *Valentino As I Knew Him.* by Ullman, S. George. 218 p. illus. New York: A. L. Burt Co., 1926.

Perhaps a better title to this biography might be "Valentino as I Would Like Him to Be Remembered." Written by Valentino's friend, mentor, and business manager, the book is an affectionate, positive, rhapsodic tribute more than a biography. Anything which might tarnish the legend is omitted—the early life, the marriage difficulties, etc. The resulting partial story is redundant in its praise and becomes monotonous as the reader waits for Valentino to behave like a human being instead of a potential legend. Ullman was still doing his job after Valentino's death. The pictures used are fine. There is no index. Although interest in Valentino still exists, this book no longer serves any great value except to historians and scholars.

6325   *Valentino! The Love God.* by Botham, Noel; and Donnelly, Peter. 250 p. paper illus. New York: Ace, 1976.

Purportedly based on interviews of those who knew Valentino, this biography by two British writers was published here to coincide with the release of Ken Russell's film. The story is the same—gigolo to superstar—but the subject—a man loved by unseen millions but not loved by any one particular person—remains absorbing. The scandal-tabloid approach suits the material.

6326 *Valentino, the Unforgotten.* by Peterson, Roger C. 256 p. illus. Los Angeles: Wetzel, 1937.

6327 *Valley of the Cliffhangers.* by Mathis, Jack. 448 p. illus. Northbrook, Ill.: Jack Mathis Advertising, 1975.

This elaborate oversized volume celebrates the 66 serials produced by Republic Studios from 1935 to 1955. Each serial is described by a detailed text, many stills, portraits of the featured actors, frame enlargements of the titles, and a full cast listing. Not only does the text relate the chapter plots, but it also offers background information about each production along with some critical observation and comment. Supporting this abundance of information is a table of the technical credits for the serials and a complete index to the text.

The reader will make some fascinating discoveries—the presence of certain aspiring performers in the films (Jennifer Jones, Carole Landis, Marguerite Chapman, Rod Cameron, Tom Neal, Bruce Bennett, John Carroll, etc.) and some older actors who were nearing the end of their careers (Bela Lugosi, Lionel Atwill, Noah Beery, Sr., William Farnum, etc.). The continual presence of the same supporting actors (Eddie Parker, David Sharpe, Tom Steele, Dale Van Sickel, etc.) in the serials and the concentration on a relatively few geographical areas (the jungle, the West, the Canadian Rockies, and outer space) may also be observed.

This attractive volume is an ideal gift for a film buff. It offers an abundance of information in addition to being a rewarding reading adventure. Recommended.

6328 *Values in Conflict.* edited by Maynard, Richard A. 160 p. paper illus. New York: Scholastic Book Services, 1974.

This volume contains scripts of the following films: HIGH NOON (1952), Fred Zinnemann; THE HUSTLER (1961), Robert Rossen; and THE SAVAGE INNOCENTS (1961), Nicholas Ray.

6329 *The Vampire Cinema.* by Pirie, David. 176 p. illus. New York: Crescent, 1977.

An excellent study and survey of a film subgenre is provided by David Pirie, a British film critic, in this attractive volume. He begins with a review of the vampire in legend and literature, followed by an account of certain silent films dealing with vampirism. The remaining portion of the text categorizes the vampire film according to country of origin: the American, the British, and the Latin. One chapter, which apparently transcends any national boundary, is that of the sex vampire.

In his exploration of this subgenre, Pirie discusses a number of films which are either unfamiliar or which have undergone so many content/title changes as to make them unrecognizable. His treatment emnphasizes critical analysis rather than plot retelling which results in an absorbing study. The illustrations (nearly 200 of them) are superb, arousing both the morbid curiosity and the general visual interest of the reader. An index and a bibliography complete this fascinating book. Recommended.

6330 *The Vampire Film.* by Silver, Alain; and Ursini, James. 238 p. illus. Cranbury, N.J.: A. S. Barnes, 1975.

This book consists of two major parts: a survey of the vampire in film and literature and a filmography and bibliography. The opening survey considers the sources of the legends, myths, and superstitions which surround vampirism. The male vampire and the female vampire are each discussed separately. Concluding the survey is a recognition and description of certain emerging traditions in the genre.

The filmography is a selected one emphasizing mostly Eastern European vampires, while the bibliography notes many books and periodical articles. An index to the film titles is added.

An abundance of stills supports the text. Although their reproduction is adequate, their selection seems a bit unbalanced, with as many as five stills from one film (SANTO Y BLUE DEMON CONTRA DRACULA Y EL HOMBRE LOBO, 1973) not mentioned in the text to none for films treated in some detail (TERROR IN THE CRYPT, 1963). The placement of the stills throughout the filmography makes its use quite difficult. Many of the foreign titles are cross-listed under alternates or translations, and splitting annotations to provide space for the visuals seems poor production planning.

The text with its supporting material is sufficiently strong and original to attract devotees of this genre. Acceptable.

6331 *Van Dyke and the Mythical City of Hollywood.* by Cannom, Robert. 424 p. illus. Culver City, Calif.: Murray and Gee, 1948.

This book is more a tribute to director W. S. Van Dyke than a biography. In addition to the Van Dyke story, it includes a filmography and anecdotes about MGM personalities such as Norma Shearer, Myrna

Loy, Jeanette MacDonald, Nelson Eddy, etc. A bit too much worship but still most interesting.

6332 *Van Johnson: The Luckiest Guy in the World.* by Beecher, Elizabeth. 248 p. illus. Racine, Wisc.: Whitman, 1947.

Contains drawings of Johnson by Henry Vallely.

6333 *Van Nostrand Reinhold Manual of Film-Making.* by Callaghan, Barry. 164 p. illus. New York: Van Nostrand Reinhold, 1973.

This well-organized textbook covers the elements of filmmaking in a ordered sequence of 14 chapters. Designed for the advanced amateur who can operate in a professional or semiprofessional surrounding, the text considers such topics as script, camera, film stocks, lighting, exposure, cameras, sound, labs, editing, and presentation. A glossary, an index and a list of suggested books are provided.

Many visuals, charts, and diagrams support the rather formal, informational text. The photographs lose effectiveness because of their small size. For example, the high and low angle shots shown on page 71 deserve either enlargement or replacement by more suitable visuals. The enlarged frames given on pages 51-52 seem to lack sharpness and focus, and although they are presented to show control in color printing, some care should be taken to insure clarity of image too.

The detail, thoroughness, and presentation of the text is impressive. Technical discussions are avoided for the most part, and the expertise of the author in providing succinct practical explanations is constantly evident. Recommended. Colleges offering filmmaking courses may wish to consider this book as a basic text.

6334 *Variety Film Reviews 1907-1980.* 15 volumes New York: Garland, 1982.

Announced for 1982, this publishing project will consist of 15 oversized volumes (650 pages each) of reviews, 1 title index volume, and 4 volumes devoted to credit indexing.

6335 *Variety International Show Business Reference.* edited by Kaplan, Mike. 1135 p. New York: Garland, 1981.

This show business reference book contains almost 6000 minibiographies; winners and nominees for Oscar, Emmy, Tony and Grammy awards; cast and credits for films reviewed in *Variety* from January 1,

1976 to December 31, 1980; a necrology of show business and many other categories of information.

6336 *Variety Music Cavalcade: Musical-Historical Review 1620-1969.* by Mattfeld, Julius. 713 p. Englewood Cliffs, N.J.: Prentice-Hall, 1971.

As well as a yearly summary of the most popular songs, the book also gives a capsule entertainment history of each year. Obviously films receive much attention. Early years are telescoped. Each song entry includes the title, composer, librettist, publisher, copyright date, and, if pertinent, the medium in which it first appeared. For example: "True Love" (film: HIGH SOCIETY), w., m., (words, music) Cole Porter, Buxton Hill Music Corp., cop. 1955 and 1956." It should be noted that this is a partial listing and does not contain all published popular songs. An index of the titles considered is most helpful. This is a unique reference that can be most valuable. It will probably answer most questions on the topic of popular music from films.

6337 *Variety Obits: An Index to Obituaries in Variety, 1905-1978.* compiled by Perry, Jeb H. 311 p. Metuchen, N.J.: Scarecrow, 1980.

This is an index of approximately 15,000 entries, each representing an obituary that appeared in *Variety*, a weekly theatrical journal, from 1905 to 1978. The persons listed worked in production-related areas of motion pictures, television, theatre, radio, minstrel shows, and vaudeville. Business people are omitted.

Each entry consists of the professional name, occasionally the real name, age at death, date of death, the principal profession, the *Variety* date and page of the obituary.

6338 *Variety's Complete Reference Book of Major U.S. Showbusiness Awards.* edited by Kaplan, Mike. 500 p. New York: Garland, 1982.

Deals with the Oscars, the Emmys, the Tonys, the Grammys, the Pulitzer Prize plays, etc. Winners and nominees are given up through 1981.

6339 *Vaudeville and Film 1895-1915: A Study in Media Interaction.* by Allen, Robert C. New York: Arno, 1980.

The author refutes some of the legends about the relationship between vaudeville and early films. A title in the *Dissertations on Film* series.

6340 *Vaudeville Pattern.* by Ripley, A. Crooks. 123 p. illus. London: Brownlee, 1947.

Contains material on the British film.

6341 *The Vaudevillians.* by Smith, Bill. 278 p. illus. New York: Macmillan, 1976.

A collective biography of entertainers who first gained fame in vaudville, this book also offers a short history, a glossary and an index. Each of the 30 subjects receives a short chapter that covers life and career. Those that are also known for film work include George Jessel, Edgar Bergen, Milton Berle, George Burns, Jack Haley, Harry Ritz, Ken Murray and Rudy Vallee.

6342 *Venus in Hollywood: The Continental Enchantress from Garbo to Loren.* by Bruno, Michael. 275 p. illus. New York: Lyle Stuart, 1970.

An example of an unfocused, padded book that has a meaningless title and similar content. It abounds in trivia, unnecessary information (e.g., the old production code), and many questionable critical statements, and has an uninspired photograph collection. The index and a bibliography help a bit but the book is beyond saving. Forget this one.

6343 *The Verdict.* by Knef, Hildegarde. 377 New York: Farrar, Straus & Giroux, 1976.

Knef's first venture into autobiography, *The Gift Horse*, was a critical and popular success. This new supplement is made of much stronger content—the observations of a woman dying of cancer. In 1973 her 56th operation was performed. The book is about all these operations along with her pitiless appraisal of life. As a survivor filled with fury, anger, courage, self-discipline and a passion to live, Knef remains an unforgetable actress, singer and author.

6344 *Veronica: The Autobiography of Veronica Lake.* by Lake, Veronica; and Bain, Donald. 248 p. illus. London: W. H. Allen, 1969.

The story of a studio-manufactured screen personality, this book is more candid and revealing than most autobiographies. From her appearance in some short comedies to her recent efforts on the stage, Veronica Lake reviews her life in a frank, unsenti-

mental, and rather cynical style.

The book is flawed by some poor taste in relating certain sexual incidents. It is most effective when Miss Lake is describing her likes and dislikes—in the latter case, Frederic March, Mitchell Leisen, and Constance Moore are the major targets. There are a few illustrations and an index of personalities. The material of Miss Lake's life is rich enough to support a fine book. This is not it, since it settles for shock and sensationalism rather than the mature backward look needed.

6345 *The Versatiles.* by Twomey, Alfred E.; and McClure, Arthur F. 304 p. illus. New York: A. S. Barnes, 1969.

The subtitle for this volume is "A Study of Supporting Character Actors and Actresses in the American Motion Picture, 1930-1955." The word "study" is misleading since the narrative is minimal. In the first section approximately 400 players receive attention via a picture and a biography. Some 200 more are covered briefly by a photograph and a few picture credits in the latter section. The arrangement is alphabetical in both cases and unless the name of the performer is known, the reference value of this book is negligible. A better reference arrangement of the same material is offered in the poorly produced *Who is That*. No total index is provided, and the balance is poor with many major supporting players appearing in the second section while relative unknowns are given space in the extended first section. A distinct disappointment.

6346 *The Very Merry Moira.* by Lister, Moira. 189 p. illus. London: Hodder and Stoughton, 1969.

In this autobiography the author tells of her appearances on the stage in Africa and London. Her later success as a leading lady in many British films and on television is also noted.

6347 *Victor Saville.* by Rollins, Cyril B.; and Wareing, Robert J. 24 p. paper illus. London: British Film Institute, 1972.

Saville was a producer-director responsible for many glossy, stylish British films during the thirties. In the early forties he emigrated to Hollywood, where he was active for a decade or so. The last film he produced was THE GREENGAGE SUMMER (1965). In this booklet, published for a 1972 retrospective, there is a biography, an interview, and a filmography. Acceptable.

6348 *A Victorian in Orbit.* by Hardwicke, Sir Cedric; and Brough, James. 311 p. illus. Garden City, N.Y.: Doubleday, 1961.

Sir Cedric looks dispassionately at himself, as apprentice and player, in this wry, irreverent memoir. As expected, he is pro-stage and anti-Hollywood. At least he is not bitter.

6349 THE VICTORS. 32 p. paper illus. New York: Columbia Pictures, 1963.

An introduction by director Carl Foreman, in which he describes the making and the meaning of the 1963 film, is among several interesting articles in this very fine souvenir book. "The Blitz—22 Years Later" by Quentin Reynolds, and "From Book to Box Office" by Alex Baron, author of the original novel, are two other good features. The illustrations are in black and white and some are reproduced on a very thin paper. Cast biographies are grouped three to a page and supporting cast and production credits are given.

6350 *Victory in My Hands.* by Russell, Harold; and Rosen, Victor. 280 p. New York: Creative Age, 1949.

Russell is known for his role in THE BEST YEARS OF OUR LIVES (1946).

6351 *Video Source Book.* edited by Reed, Maxine K. 1260 p. Detroit: Gale Research Co., 1980.

A listing of pre-recorded video programs that includes many films originally made for theatrical showing. Formats, casts, times, plots, etc. are offered along with other information on use, subjects, distribution and suggested audiences.

6352 *Vietnam on Film: From* THE GREEN BERETS to APOCALYPSE NOW. by Adair, Gilbert. 208 p. illus. New York: Proteus, 1981.

Intelligent, witty criticism applied to Vietnam War films. The author does not take full advantage of the potential of his topic. But what he offers is quite good.

6353 *The View from the Sixties.* by Oppenheimer, George. 273 p. New York: David McKay, 1966.

A well-written reminiscence by a former Hollywood script writer who has become a newspaper critic in recent years. The period recalled is roughly the decade from 1935 to 1945 and deals with Goldwyn, MGM, and Columbia. Certain of his war experiences are also related. While this is not an essential volume, it has an intelligence and style that will please most readers.

6354 *A Viewer's Guide to Film Theory and Criticism.* by Eberwein, Robert T. 235 p. Metuchen, N.J.: Scarecrow, 1979.

An overview of the work of 20 major film theorists is offered in a readable text here. Beginning with "pioneers" such as Lindsay, Munsterberg, Kracauer, etc., the subjects include such moderns as Joan Mellen, Christian Metz, and Peter Wollen. Accompanying this excellent introduction to film theory is a lengthy bibliography, a general index, and a film index. For readers who wish to be well-informed on film theory, this volume is a very good place to start.

6355 *The Viewing of Oneself Performing Selected Motor Skills in Motion Pictures...* by Smith, Hope M.; and Clifton, Marguerite A. 20 p. paper Los Angeles: University of California, 1961.

The remaining portion of the title of this unusual study is "And Its Effect upon the Expressed Concept of Self in Movement."

6356 *Viewing Tastes of Adolescents in Cinema and Television.* by Barclay, John B. 73 p. paper illus. Glasgow: Scottish Educational Film Association, 1961.

6357 *Viking Eggeling 1880-1928, Artist and Filmmaker: Life and Work.* by O'Konor, Louise. 300 p. illus. Stockholm: Almqvist and Wiksell, 1971.

Eggeling is usually cited as the maker of DIAGONAL SYMPHONY, a 7-minute abstract experimental film made in 1921. O'Konor gives a biographical essay, a collection of Eggeling's writings, some descriptions of his artistic works, and a lengthy outline of DIAGONAL SYMPHONY. Some of the text is concerned with the relationship between Hans Richter and Eggeling and involves feuds, forgeries, and friendships. A specialized work.

6358 THE VIKINGS. 18 p. (paper) illus. New York: Progress Lithographers, 1958.

Opening sections of this souvenir book include the synopsis of the 1958 film and several pages devoted to "Experts Behind The Vikings." Kirk Douglas contributes an article entitled "On Making a Movie" and there are the usual full-page biographies of Douglas, Tony Curtis, Ernest Borgnine, and Janet Leigh. Stills from the film are included and supporting cast and other production credits are given.

6359 *Vincent Price.* by Price, Vincent. 118 p. illus. Garden City, N.Y.: Doubleday, 1978.

A title in the *All I Want to Know About* series, this autobiography by Vincent Price should have enormous appeal to the juveniles for whom it was written. Price has written four previous volumes, mostly about his nontheatrical interests—collecting art and cooking. Here he tells a romanticized, selected, factual account of his professional life. Fortunately Price apparently has the ability to laugh at both himself and some of his roles. This makes what is essentially an ego trip somewhat palatable.

The book is indexed and heavily illustrated—mostly with portraits of Price. There is no filmography or play list even though the subtitle reads, "His Movies, His Plays, His Life."

Price should be professional enough to recognize that there exists an enormous juvenile audience that knows and admires him because of the never-ending reruns of his theatrical features. They deserve more than this sugary recall of a rich theatrical life.

6360 *Vincent Price Unmasked.* by Parish, James Robert; and Whitney, Steven. 266 p. illus. New York: Drake, 1974.

Since this volume is a combination of the life and careers of Vincent Price, its structure is a logical one: biography, theatre, films, radio, TV and authorship. For the most part the biography is a factual narrative which describes Price's many activities and interests. The style consists of "Price's next film was.... He traveled to Maine for.... Before he left for New York...," etc. "Alma Reed cared for Vincent very much...." "Price and Edith Barrett were inseparable...." "Things were functioning less well on the home scene. On May 10, 1948 Edith Barrett was granted a divorce...." "Vincent and Mary share a love of art, a love of fine cooking, and a love for their work...." "On August 8, 1949 Vincent and Mary were wed...."

Cast and credits are given in the theatre section; the filmography adds some critical evaluation and background to the cast and credit notations. A simple listing of network, date, show name and type of show is given in the radio-TV section. Price's cookbooks, art books and the autobiography are annotated in the final section. No index is provided, but three sections of visuals appear in the book. The front and back endpapers show Price in 16 screen roles; the photographs have been well selected and clearly reproduced.

The reference sections on Price's several careers along with the visuals are the strong elements in this book. The biographical portion is so mild, cautious and bland that it is puzzling why major attention was given to it in terms of page space. It might have been wiser to emphasize Price's on-screen excitement by a more critical examination of that work and relegate the biography to an introductory chapter or chronology. Acceptable.

6361 *Vincente Minnelli.* by De La Roche, Catherine. 40 p. paper New Zealand Film Institute (Film Culture, USA).

A brief biography followed by critical reviews of 25 Minnelli films dating from 1942 to 1959. Production credits and casts are given. The evaluations are questionable and the attention given the films is quite uneven (e.g., almost five pages are devoted to ZIEGFELD FOLLIES (1945) while THE BAND WAGON (1953) gets a short page and a half). If there is nothing else available, this booklet might be of some small interest as a partial reference.

6362 *Vincente Minnelli and the Film Musical.* by Casper, Joseph Andrew. 192 p. illus. New York: A. S. Barnes, 1977.

Two separate topics are interwoven in a critical study that has been carefully researched and logically structured. First, an important genre of American film, the musical, is analyzed using Vincente Minnelli's musicals as the major data. Paralleled with this investigation is a critical appreciation of Minnelli which discusses his background, themes, planning, direction, visual design, and music and dance integration. A final chapter summarizes Minnelli's achievements and his contribution to the musical film genre. The status of the genre itself is undetermined at this time according to the author.

The films which serve as examples/models include CABIN IN THE SKY (1942), I DOOD IT (1943), MEET ME IN ST. LOUIS (1944), YOLANDA AND THE THIEF (1945), THE ZIEGFELD FOLLIES (1945), THE PIRATE (1948), AN AMERICAN IN PARIS (1951), THE BAND WAGON (1953), BRIGADOON (1954), KISMET (1955),

GIGI (1958), BELLS ARE RINGING (1960) and ON A CLEAR DAY YOU CAN SEE FOREVER (1970).

Visuals are clearly reproduced and the text is supported by notes, a bibliography, a filmography, and an index.

The treatment afforded a film genre in this volume represents intelligent, helpful analysis. Combining it with a superb evaluation and appreciation of a major American filmmaker results in a creative approach to film criticism that is rare in the literature. Recommended.

6363 *Vintage Films.* by Crowther, Bosley. 237 p. illus. New York: Putnam, 1977.

In 1967 Bosley Crowther wrote *The Great Films: 50 Golden Years of Motion Pictures.* This volume is subtitled "50 Enduring Motion Pictures" and is structured in the same manner. Using as his criteria "...outstanding achievements...that have stood the test of time...and merit continuing presentation for the pleasures and enlightenment they can afford..." he offers a selection which ranges from THE BROADWAY MELODY (1929) to THE GODFATHER II (1974). Placed in chronological order, each film is represented by an essay which is both descriptive and critical, plus a few stills. An index completes the volume.

When examined with respect to his stated criteria, Crowther's choices are unassailable. What argument—other than familiarity—can be raised against THE WIZARD OF OZ (1939), STAGECOACH (1939), CASABLANCA (1942), ALL ABOUT EVE (1950), SINGIN IN THE RAIN (1952), A STAR IS BORN (1954) and DR. STRANGELOVE (1964)?

Although they contain information and interpretation, the essays offer few controversial ideas and, as a result, are pleasant but bland reading. Photograph reproduction is excellent. The affectionate and courteous treatment of 50 famous films that Crowther offers should please most readers. Acceptable.

6364 *Violations of the Child Marilyn Monroe.* by H. P. S. (Anonymous) 159 p. illus. New York: Bridgehead Books, 1962.

If you are willing to believe that this book was written by a psychiatrist, and that it was he who called her just before her death, you may believe the rest of this familiar narrative. It concentrates on the years from six to eleven in Monroe's childhood and the emphasis is on the oft-reported sexual incidents. Mention is made of other times in her career, of her marriages, affairs, and professional insecurities. The book is illustrated by some vulgar line drawings. A quick-buck, bad-taste book noted here for the record.

6365 *Violence and the Mass Media.* edited by Larsen, Otto N. 310 p. paper New York: Harper and Row, 1968.

This volume is a part of the *Readers in Social Problems,* series and it deals with violence as it exists in all the media. There are several articles pertinent to film. They include: "Violence in the Cinema" by Philip French; "The Morality Seekers: A Study of Organized Film Criticism in the United States" by Jack Schwartz; "New Movie Standards: General Film Code, Not Specific Bans" by Louis Chapin. The general articles are all excellent, and although the major emphasis is on television and comic books, the above articles can serve as an introduction to violence in film. Recommended.

6366 *Violence in the Arts.* by Fraser, John. 192 p. New York: Cambridge University Press, 1974.

This essay deals not only with films but also with novels, short stories, nonfiction books, theatre and other creative art forms. The author notes our contradictory attitudes toward violence and suggests some of the events in our recent history which may have caused them. Examples of violence in the arts and reactions to them are cited—such as our inconsistent feelings toward victims of violence.

As indicated, films occupy only a part of the author's attention; however, there is much in his general statement on violence that is applicable to films. Readers may experience occasional difficulty in determining whether an italicized title refers to a film or its literary source, since the director or writer is not always indicated. There are many helpful notes provided for the text and an index is added. In today's society violence affects us all. Fraser has provided a provocative survey and analysis in this clearly written volume. It is highly recommended for mature audiences.

6367 *Violence on the Screen.* by Glucksmann, Andre. 78 p. paper London: British Film Institute, 1971.

A translation from the original French version, this volume has as its subtitle "A Report on Research into the Effects on Young People of Scenes of Violence in Films and Television." It includes a foreword by Paddy Whannel and an afterword by Dennis Howitt that sums up the research done in this area from 1966-1970. Bibliographic notes follow these sections. Glucksmann begins by surveying opinion on violence. Impact, effect, sociological variables, determination of effect, experimental study of violence, and a cultural approach to the effect of screen violence are other topics he considers. A final summary is followed by 153 bibliographic footnotes. This is a carefully researched and written summary that has value for teachers, students, librarians, parents, etc. Highly recommended.

6368 *Violent America: The Movies, 1946-1964.* by Alloway, Lawrence. 95 p. illus. New York: The Museum of Modern Art, 1971.

In the spring of 1969, the Museum of Modern Art presented a series of 35 films, entitling the group, "The American Action Film 1946-1964." This volume discusses these films, examining their heroes, villains, females, and actors. Such topics as "The Pleasure of Tragedy/The Appeal of Violence" , "Cartharsis Via Film," Film As a Formulaic Art" and others are treated.

As is usual with MOMA publications, the text and production values are excellent. Many full-page stills are used in this slightly oversized volume. A final filmography with accompanying comment is also impressive. Copious footnotes add to the quality of the text.

6369 THE VIRGIN SPRING. by Isaksson, Ulla. 114 p. paper illus. New York: Ballantine Books, 1960.

Script of the 1959 film directed by Ingmar Bergman. Contains biographical sketches of Bergman and Isaksson.

6370 *Virgins, Vamps, and Flappers.* by Higashi, Sumiko. 226 p. illus. Montreal: Eden Press, 1978.

This unpublicized volume tackles an unusual subject, "The American Silent Movie Heroine," but offers some pedestrian, almost familiar findings. The author uses the stereotypes of her title in an examination of films and actresses (Gish, Pickford) of the silent era approached from the feminist point of view. The transition from Victorian female to liberated jazz-age woman on screen is described. An assessment of the screen's reflection of reality is attempted.

A well-researched text (the author looked at more than 165 films), a few fuzzy illustrations, detailed chapter notes, a long bibliography, a filmography and an index all testify to Higashi's thoroughness.

Her review is impressive but the findings are a bit anticlimactic.

6371 *Visconti.* by Nowell-Smith, Geoffrey. 189 p. illus. Garden City, N.Y.: Doubleday, 1968.

The focus is on the films of Visconti. Considered singly, they are arranged in a related order rather than a strict chronological one; thus, THE LEOPARD (1963) appears with SENSO (1953) as examples of Visconti's treatments of historical themes and the baroque. The most recent film examined here is VAGHE STELLE DELL 'ORSA (1965) which was also known both as OF A THOUSAND DELIGHTS and SANDRA.

The analyses are stimulating, well-documented, and consistent with auteur theory. They define both the artist and his films with a high degree of success. Illustrations are above average in reproduction quality. A filmography which includes some of the short films (e.g., an episode of the 1962 film BOCCACCIO '70) is also given. As a partial study of Visconti, the book is a definite contribution. His masterpieces THE DAMNED (1969) and DEATH IN VENICE (1970) provide much additional material for a full consideration of this major director. Recommended.

6372 *Vision in Motion.* by Moholy-Nagy, Laszlo. 371 p. illus. Chicago: Theobald, 1956.

A theoretical discussion of film aesthetics. Many illustrations.

6373 *Visionary Film.* by Sitney, P. Adams. 452 p. illus. New York: Oxford University Press, 1974.

The topic of the American avant-garde film is covered in several ways in this impressive book. Both a historical and an analytical approach are employed. In addition, the work of 24 famous American filmmakers is discussed in detail. Chapter notes and references aregiven and a useful index is provided. The avant-garde film has been by such terms as film poem, experimental, underground, independent and new American cinema. Sitney considers the development of this film genre from the twenties to the seventies, emphasizing the post-40's work of Kenneth Anger, Stan Brakhage, Maya Deren, Gregory Markopolous, Jonas Mekas, Jack Smith, Andy Warhol and others. The influence that the filmmakers exercised over each other and on the commercially produced film is noted. Unifying this material is the author's major theme, the identification of a visionary strain in the complex world of the American avant-garde film.

Surpassing earlier volumes, such as Battock's *The New American Cinema*, Renan's *An Introduction to the American Underground Film*, and Tyler's *Underground Film*, in scope and execution, this book stands with Youngblood's *Expanded Cinema* as essential reading for anyone interested in film as an art form. The challenge of creating order and meaning out of a disorganized, often chaotic art field has been handled most successfully by Sitney. His explanations, arguments and descriptions are clear and his knowledge of his subject is wide and has depth. The 66 illustrations provided are good, but a volume such as this seems to warrant many more. In summary, this is an important, serious work that is a fine contribution to film literature. Highly recommended for mature readers.

6374   *Visions of Tomorrow: Great Science Fiction from the Movies.* by Edelson, Edward. 117 p. illus. New York: Doubleday, 1975.

This hardbound book appeared in paperback as *Great Science Fiction from the Movies.*

6375   *Visions of Yesterday.* by Richards, Jeffrey. 391 p. illus. London: Routledge and Kegan Paul, 1973.

This volume is an examination of the cinema from the viewpoints of mythology and ideology. The author argues that in giving identity, purpose, and meaning to a movement, myths "shape the attitudes and determine the outlook of the adherents." It is the popular arts—especially film—that can tell us about people and their beliefs. Here the author uses films as a source of social history.

Under a general heading of Cinema of the Right, Richards explores American Populism (Ford, Capra, McCarey), British Imperialism, and German National Socialism. After some conclusions about these three conservative movements as reflected in films, the book offers separate filmographies and several indexes. Illustrations are plentiful and are carefully reproduced.

This is an excellent volume that is relatively unknown in America. It provides a promising model for future film research. Highly recommended.

6376   *The Visual Artist and the Law.* by Associated Councils of the Arts. 100 p. paper New York: Associated Councils of the Arts, 1972.

A monograph covering copyright, galleries, museums, publishers, taxes, sales, etc. Contains a list of organizations.

6377   *The Visual Arts Today.* edited by Krepes, Gyorgy. 195 p. New York: Braziller, 1965.

6378   *Visual Education? The Serious Student's Guide to Social Misinformation.* by Johnston, Winifred. 55 p. illus. Norman: Cooperative Books, 1941.

The author is again concerned with film and propaganda. This is a proper sequel to her earlier *Memo on the Movies* (1939).

6379   *Visual Scripting.* by Halas, John. 144 p. illus. New York: Hastings House, 1976.

This volume is a collection of 14 articles by different writers on the preparation of films from a visual point of view. Emphasizing the animated film, the text also notes techniques and recent technology that affect all kinds of filmmaking. The storyboard is used throughout to present examples and to explain the methods used by the contributors. Since these authors represent nine countries, the book's approach is broadly international rather than provincial.

The text, which was arranged by John Halas, offers much valuable practical information. Most impressive is a fine collection of illustrations which complements the verbal material. There is also a final index.

A rich source of film information intelligently arranged and attractively presented. Recommended.

6380   *Visual Thinking.* by Arnheim, Rudolph. 345 p. illus. Berkeley, Calif.: University of California Press, 1969.

Arnheim's concern here is with visual perception as a cognitive activity. In earlier works, one of his theses was that all artistic activity is a form of reasoning—a combination of perception and thought. This volume is a continuation of that idea with visual perception as the major area of analysis. He draws on philosophy, research, science and art for his arguments. The book is illustrated and indexed. While it is not a film book in the strict sense, it is noted here for its value to educators, filmmakers and researchers.

6381   *Visualize.* by Anderson, David R.; and Wilburn, Gary; and Kuhns,

William; and Stanley, Robert; and Jewell, Wayne. paper illus. Dayton, Ohio: Pflaum, 1971.

This kit consists of five components: 1) "Exploring the Film" by William Kuhns and Robert Stanley; 2) "Visualize" —Student Manual; 3) "Visualize" —Instructor Manual by David Anderson and Gary Wilburn; 4)Photo Language—A Collection of 16 Still Pictures—approximately 6 inches x 9 inches in size; 5) A 3-minute super-8 film called ONE IS THE LONELIEST NUMBER.

The purpose, or use, of the kit is to assist in a course on visual language, the goal of which is improved communication and self- expression. It is suggested that culminating activities for the course be a slide presentation and an 8mm film.

The attempt to provide a more effective way of teaching visual skills is most commendable. The proposed course seems both workable and enjoyable for all participants including the teacher.

6382 *Viva Vamp.* by Flora, Paul. illus. New York: David McKay, 1959.

This is an amusing collection of photographs put together "in praise of vamps from Theda Bara to Marilyn Monroe." Flora has added some line drawings to surround the stills, and Ogden Nash has contributed a foreword. Picture selection is good but the reproduction is most variable. Certain shots are much too small to be effective. There is no index.

6383 VIVA ZAPATA. by Steinbeck, John. 150 p. paper illus. New York:Viking, 1975.

Script of the 1952 film directed by Elia Kazan. Contains two essays entitled "Steinbeck's Zapata: Rebel Versus Revolutionary" and "A Note on the Script." Sections called "Steinbeck's Screenplays and Productions" and "Steinbeck's Films," along with complete script, cast and credits, are included. There is a bibliography at the end.

6384 *Viveka... Viveca.* by Lindfors, Viveca. New York: Everest House, 1981.

Four marriages, three children, a long successful career in theatre and film—all this provides actress Viveca Lindfors with strong material for a dramatic, candid autobiography.

6385 *Vivien Leigh: A Bouquet.* by Dent, Alan. 219 p. illus. London: Hamilton, 1969.

6386 *Vivien Leigh: A Biography.* by Edwards, Anne. 319 p. illus. New York: Simon and Schuster, 1977.

The brilliance of this biogrpahy is almost immediately apparent. Anne Edwards selected a subject which intrigued her and then began her search for material using persons and material that were formerly unavailable. She has written a biography that is compassionate yet objective.

From the middle-class British society in India to world celebrity and a tragic death, the story of Vivien Leigh is an absorbing one. The author has reconstructed the life of a complex personality with full attention to her ambition, weaknesses, pride, temper, and capacity to live and love. Often frank and revealing, the text successfully avoids sensationalism. In the broad total portrait provided, the scandalous elements are few and relatively minor. A few illustrations, a theatre chronology, a filmography, a list of radio appearances and an index are included.

As with her biography of Judy Garland, Anne Edwards has an understanding of the triumphs and tragedies that are indigenous to female performers. She has provided an excellent biographical study that will attract readers for years to come. Highly recommended.

6387 *The Voice: The Story of an American Phenomenon.* by Kahn, E. J., Jr. 125 p. illus. New York: Harper, 1947.

An early biography of Frank Sinatra.

6388 *The Voice of the Film.* by McKay, Herbert C. 80 p. illus. New York: Falk, 1930.

Used as a text by the New York Institute of Photography, this older volume offers "a simple description of the processes used in making films with synchronized sound."

6389 *Voices from the Japanese Cinema.* by Mellen, Joan. 295 p. paper illus. N.Y.: Liveright, 1975.

Joan Mellen's three previous volumes indicate the appearance of a stimulating writer-scholar. This new volume provides further evidence of her continuing growth as an author. Using still another form—the interview—she has provided a view of an important national cinema by talking to 15 Japanese filmmakers. The translated interviews follow an excellent overview of the Japanese cinema which combines film history, backgrounds for the interviews, and her personal reactions to the artists she met.

Filmmakers interviewed include Daisuke Ito, Akira Kurosawa, Mme. Kashiko Kawakita, Kaneto Shindo, Tadashi Imai, Kon Ichikawa, Masaki Kobayashi, Setsu Asakura, Kiroshi Teshigahara, Susumu Hani, Sachiko Hidari, Toichiro Narushima, Masahiro Shinoda, Nagisa Oshima, and Shuji Terayama. Illustrations include pictures of the artists at work and stills from their films. The book also contains a detailed index.

All the qualities that make a worthwhile film book are present here—intelligence, preparation, background, style, arrangement, etc. Although the topic may be of limited interest to general readers, it will fascinate and reward those researchers, students, historians and teachers concerned with the Japanese cinema.

6390   *Voices of Film Experience: 1894 to the Present.* edited by Leyda, Jay. 544 p. New York: Macmillan, 1977.

This anthology presents more than 600 actors, writers, designers, composers, producers, and directors expressing selected views on films and filmmaking. Participants are arranged alphabetically by surname with James Agee first and Adolph Zukor last. The length of each contribution varies, with some subjects being quoted from more than one essay, interview, or autobiographical source. The result is fascinating if somewhat disjointed reading. Selection by Leyda seems to have been made with an emphasis on reader enjoyment rather than on the formulation of any themes or philosophies. This makes for a very entertaining text that offers not only information, but also a chance to browse indiscriminately among the many filmmakers present here. A most helpful index has been provided and there are short identifications given for each of the speakers. An impressive list of sources from which Leyda selected his statements runs over 26 pages in length.

Because it requires so little reader effort to obtain maximum enjoyment from this book, the ability of the editor in locating and selecting the appropriate material may be overlooked. Jay Leyda has made the greatest contribution to this fine collection. Recommended.

6391   *see*   *6392*

6392   *von Stroheim.* by Curtiss, Thomas Quinn. 357 p. illus. New York: Farrar, Straus & Giroux, 1971.

In the introduction to this biography, the author states that he was a close friend and frequent companion of von Stroheim for many years—from about 1940 to 1957. The relationship has not been realized by the author in his book. His straightforward narrative includes some awkward reconstructed conversations but not much personal insight or comment about a friend. Other than a few anecdotes, not much of the book is new information. Peter Noble's 1951 biography, *Hollywood Scapegoat* and Joel Finler's 1968 *Stroheim* covered the same ground.

The production of the book is another matter. The dust jacket is striking, with two eye-catching illustrations of von Stroheim, and there are an attractive inner-cover picture, a most impressive typesetting and arrangement, and, finally, many beautifully reproduced stills. The production more than makes up for the disappointing text.

An account of the first screening of the uncut 42-reel version of GREED (1923) and a filmography of von Stroheim as director and actor make up the appendix. There is no index. What should have been a definitive work emerges as a retelling of the familiar, enhanced and saved by superior production values. Recommended.

6393   *W. C. Fields: His Follies and His Fortunes.* by Taylor, Robert Lewis 340 p. illus. Garden City, N. Y.: Doubleday, 1949.

This is an affectionate, emotional tribute to Fields written with a comprehension of the social framework that surrounded him. Many anecdotes, stories, and legends are told as well as descriptions of some of his films, his comedy techniques, and his antisocial behavior. The few photographs are only average and there is no index. But never mind, the biography is so richly woven by an author of considerable talent that little else matters here. If this book is read concurrently with *The Films of W. C. Fields* the reader will have a extraordinary experience in film biography. Highly recommended.

6394   *W. C. Fields—By Himself.* by Fields, W. C.; and Fields, Ronald J. 510 p. illus. Englewood Cliffs, N.J.: Prentice-Hall, 1973.

There is a wealth of original material in this collection of letters, notes, scripts, and articles by W. C. Fields. A subtitle calls it "His Intended Autobiography" but this is wishful thinking on the part of Fields' grandson, Ronald, who cataloged, annotated, and provided linking commentary for the papers. Some sections are detailed and rather complete—such as the early pre-Ziegfeld years when Fields was developing his artistry as a vaudeville juggler. But the twenties and the thirties are only covered superficially. Some detail returns with the forties, and this suggests that the material available was in direct proportion to Fields' contact with his family.

The letters indicate that Fields' generosity was greater than legend has it, and that his wife, Hattie, was a rather unloving and demanding woman. The relationship between Fields and his only son is distant, with some anemic effort at reconciliation during the forties. This late tenuous reunion between father and son appears to have been effected by Claude, Jr.'s acceptance of his father's celebrity and by his wife, Ruth, who ingratiated herself with the comedian. Carlotta Monti, Fields' mistress, who wrote *W. C. Fields and Me*, is given a nasty brushoff in two letters from Fields. The last was written from the sanitarium in which he died on December 7, 1946.

In spite of what seems like biased selection designed to suggest a family relationship that never was, the volume offers many evidences of Fields' personality, intelligence, wit, and hangups.

The illustrations vary in their effectiveness, the early vaudeville poses having an excellence that far surpasses the uninspired group from the sound film era. Many of Fields' drawings of himself are reproduced.

This collection of Fields materials is certain to interest and please many readers and fans. But the book promises more than it ultimately delivers andis weakened both by the absence of a strong linking commentary and by a suggested family image that reads as fabrication. Recommended.

6395 *W. C. Fields.* by Yanni, Nicholas. 157 p. paper illus. New York: Pyramid, 1974.

The life and career of W. C. Fields is related in this well-illustrated book, a title in the *Illustrated History of the Movies* series. A bibliography, a filmography, and an index supplement the author's coverage of Fields' films and folklore. This is another excellent addition to the series.

6396 *W. C. Fields and Me.* by Monti, Carlotta. 221 p. illus. Englewood Cliffs, N. J.: Prentice-Hall, 1971.

This memoir was written by a lady who was Field's mistress for 14 years. During that time she was content to be both the target of much of his sarcasm as well as the recipient of some rare Fieldsian tenderness. "Woody," as she called him, was the same person off screen as he was on—mean, vindictive, crochety, larcenous and shifty. Add to these qualities those of frugality and suspicion, and Miss Monti becomes eligible for a martyr's award. She says at times he was also lovable, kind, sweet, thoughtful

and generous.

The book is crowded with anecdotes that read like episodes from a Field's film, and "Woody's" pet hates are noted as are his famous aliases— "Claude Nesselrode" and "A Pismo Clam," being two of them. The book is funny, clever, frank, revealing, intimate and, yet, quite sad; Miss Monti is still a loser. All in all, it is a most welcome addition to the literature we have on Fields.

6397 *The Wajda Trilogy.* by Wajda, Andrzej. 239 p. paper illus. New York: Simon and Schuster, 1972.

Contains script, cast and production credits for: ASHES AND DIAMONDS (1958), KANAL (1955), A GENERATION (1954), with an introduction by Boleslaw Sulik.

6398 *Walking the Tightrope: The Private Confessions of a Public Relations Man.* by Rogers, Henry C. 256 p. New York: Morrow, 1980.

Henry Rogers began as an assistant press agent in the Hollywood of the thirties. He soon represented such stars as Rita Hayworth, Joan Crawford, Claudette Colbert, etc. In this memoir, he includes many positive stories about his celebrity clients—as any self-respecting public relations man should do.

6399 *Wallace Reid.* by Reid, Bertha Westbrook. 104 p. illus. New York: Sorg, 1923.

Published shortly after his death, this is a biography of Wallace Reid related by his mother. Emphasis is on his childhood, with minimum attention given to matters of interest such as his career in films. The text is defensive and omissive.

6400 *Wallflower at the Orgy.* by Ephron, Nora. 173 p. paper New York: Bantam, 1980 (1970).

Among this collection of articles are interviews, essays and an account of the location shooting of CATCH 22 (1970).

6401 *Walt Disney: Young Movie Maker.* by Hammontree, Marie. 200 p. illus. Indianapolis: Bobbs Merrill, 1969.

A title in the *Childhood of Famous Americans* series, this biography of Walt Disney concentrates on his boyhood. The book, designed for young readers, is illustrated by Fred Irvin.

6402 *Walt Disney's Treasury of Children's Classics.* edited by Geis, Darlene. 307 p. illus. New York: Harry Abrams, 1978.

Dedicated to Walt Disney, this book is a collection of 17 children's stories that have all been made into films by the Disney Studios. Using hundreds of full-color illustrations from the films, the pages recreate the Disney versions of *Cinderella, Snow White, Peter Pan, Bambi,* etc. For each there is a page or so which tells about the making of the film.

The outstanding production given to this volume along with the intelligent selection and editing done by Darlene Geis, plus, of course, the Disney visuals, make this a book that adults will admire and children will cherish.

6403 *Walt Disney: The Art of Animation.* by Thomas, Bob. 185 p. illus. New York: Simon & Schuster, 1958.

Designed as a children's book, this beautifully produced volume should appeal to any reader interested in animation in films. The illustrative examples are taken from the Disney library of animated motion pictures, the narrative is simple but never condescending, and the contents are quite inclusive. Each of the elements of animated films is discussed in a separate chapter—layout, animation, background and color, music, sound, etc.

In the final sections there is a glossary of animation terms, a compilation of credits for the Disney animated features, and a list of Academy Awards given to the Disney Studios. All of this sounds like an overdose of Disney and his artists, but when the longevity, quality, and popularity of the Disney output is considered, the reader may forgive the exclusiveness of the book. The excellence of illustration, text and production qualify this volume for children and young adults. Recommended.

6404 *Walt Disney: Magician of the Movies.* by Thomas, Bob. 176 p. illus. New York: Grosset and Dunlap, 1966.

This is a short biography written for children and published without illustrations. A few badly-drawn sketches are used to introduce chapters. The narrative is rather fictional in that it improvises dialogue, omits all human dimension, and does not present a balanced view of the man. A disservice to Disney and, above all, to the children who might read this.

6405 *Walt Disney.* by Larson, Norita. illus. Mankato, Minn.: Creative Education, 1975.

A brief biography of Walt Disney written for young readers. Illustrations are by Harold Henriksen, not Disney.

6406 *Walt Disney: An American Original.* by Thomas, Bob. 379 p. illus. New York: Simon and Schuster, 1976.

This biography divides the lifetime of Walt Disney into five eras: The Midwest Years (1901-1923), The Cartoon Maker (1923-1934), Toward a New Art (1934-1945), Stretching the Horizon (1945-1961), and The Distant Reach (1961-1966). The typical Bob Thomas biographical method is employed: material and data of record, combined with many subject quotations to form a chronological narrative. In this case Thomas had the cooperation of Disney's production company, family, and friends.

Critical comment is minimized in favor of a descriptive recreation of actions and events. The result is a workman-like, pleasing biography that informs but never involves the reader. The detail provided, however, should be acknowledged and appreciated. A center section of illustrations and an index are included.

Compared to Schickel's *The Disney Version,* Bob Thomas' portrait of Disney seems carefully laundered. As promised in the title, the book does cover a lifetime of ambition and achievement by an American original. Recommended.

6407 *Walt Disney.* by Walker, Greta. illus. New York: G. P. Putnam's, 1977.

A title in the *See and Read* series, this biography of Walt Disney was designed for children in grades kindergarten to three. Illustrations are by Ruth Sanderson, not Disney.

6408 *Walt Disney: Master of Make Believe.* by Montgomery, Elizabeth R. 96 p. illus. Champaign, Ill.: Garrard 1971.

A biography of Walt Disney which stresses his contribution to the film art and industry. Written for a juvenile audience as a title in the *Americans All* series, the book is illustrated by Vic Mays, not Disney.

6409 *Walt Disney.* edited by Wisdom Staff. 34 illus. Beverly Hills: Wisdom, 1959.

Although *Wisdom* was a periodical, its format was that of a hardbound book. The issue of December, 1959 (Volume 32) concentrated on Walt Disney.

Along with some fine illustrations it contains the following articles: Walt Disney: A Biography; Animated Cartoon World of Walt Disney; Animated Feature Length World of Walt Disney; The Art of Animation; Live-Action Movie World of Walt Disney; Disneyland; Wisdom of Walt Disney.

6410 *Walt Disney: A Guide to Reference and Resources.* by Bron, Elizabeth Lee; and Gartley, Lynn. 226 p. Boston: G. K. Hall, 1979.

Walt Disney functioned as a producer rather than a director, yet his personal imprint ison each of the Disney films made under his tenure. This reference book consists of two major sections and several short supporting chapters. A brief biography and a critical essay precede a lengthy filmography of 85 Disney feature films. For each there is a detailed synopsis, complete credits, running time, release dates, distribution company, etc. The bibliography which follows consists of 640 items arranged chronologically by year. Annotations provided for most of the entries are descriptive rather than critical. Concluding sections of the book include a list of Walt Disney's TV performances, some selected articles he wrote, two archival sources, a distributor list, an author index, and a film title index.

A bit more explanation of their work by the authors would have been helpful. Sources, limits of selection, difficulties, etc., would be of interest. For example, the bibliography is apparently a selected one, or else why would an important source such as volume 56 of the magazine, *Wisdom*, which dealt mostly with Walt Disney, be missing? Nevertheless, there is an abundance of information here for the reader in search of material on Disney or his films. This reference is easy to use and often enjoyable to read.

6411 *Walt Disney: Young Movie Maker.* by Tree, Marie Hammon. 200 p. illus. New York: Bobbs-Merrill, 1969.

A biography of Walt Disney written for young people, this book contains illustrations by Fred Irvin. It covers Disney's life up to the opening of the 1955 Disneyland and includes a glossary and a chronology.

6412 *see* 6405

6413 *Walt Disney: The Master of Animation.* by Kurland, Gerald. paper illus. Charlotteville, N.Y.: SamHar, 1972.

A title in the *Outstanding Personalities* series, this biography was designed for young readers.

6414 *Walt Disney Animated Features and Silly Symphonies.* by Foster, Alan D. 192 p. illus. New York: Abbeville, 1980.

6415 *Walt Disney Books.* illus. New York: Golden Press.

As indicated in Munsey's *Disneyana: Walt Disney Collectibles*, the use of the Disney characters for merchandising various articles goes back to the twenties. Books have always been an attractive part of this market and range from the well-produced *Big Golden Books* to cheap comic magazines. A few examples of the *Big Golden Books* are annotated in this volume. *Cinderella*, *Mary Poppins*, *Peter Pan*, *Alice in Wonderland*, *Snow White and the Seven Dwarfs*, *Winnie the Pooh*, *Bambi*, and *Pinocchio*.

Other series published by Golden Press feature similar books. A sampling of the constantly changing inventory of Disney-inspired books might include: *Bambi's Fragrant Forest*, *Disney's Favorite Stories*, *Walt Disney's Nursery Tales*, *The Plot to Capture Robin Hood*, *Mickey Mouse in the Wild West*, *The Walt Disney Songbook*, *Robin Hood*, *Uncle Remus Stories*, *The New Walt Disney Treasury*, *Mickey Mouse Cookbook*, *Walt Disney's Storyland*, *The Giant Walt Disney Word Book*, *Lady and the Tramp*, *Pluto's Farm Fun*, *Goofy's Forest Fun*, *Donald Duck's World Tour*, *Walt Disney's Fairy Tale Friends*. It has been estimated that over 1000 different titles have appeared to date.

The Disney characters appear also under other publishers' imprints, e.g., Random House, Blue Ribbon Books, Scholastic Book Services, etc. In *Cinema Booklist*, three such titles were annotated: *Three Little Pigs*, *Snow White and the Seven Dwarfs*, and *The Happiest Millionaire*. Novelized versions of such Disney films as HERBIE RIDES AGAIN (1974) are also published by Scholastic Book Services.

6416 *Walt Disney Magic Moments.* by Arseni, Ercole; and Bosi, Leone; and Marconi, Massimo. 191 p. illus. Walt Disney Productions & Arnoldo Mondadori Editions, Milan, 1973.

Over 500 illustrations, many of which are reproduced in full color, are the substance of this entertaining volume. Tracing in word and picture the history of the Disney empire, the book features the predictable Disney characters—Mickey Mouse, Minnie Mouse, Pluto, Donald Duck, etc. Acceptable.

6417 *The Walt Disney Parade.* compiled by Walt Disney Studios. 176 p. illus. Garden City, N. Y.: Doubleday, 1940.

A collection of characters and stories taken from the Walt Disney animated shorts and features designed for children. Noted here for the many illustrations/stills that are included, some of which are in color. Contents include Brave Little Tailor, Little Hiawatha, The Practical Pig, Donald's Ostrich, Donald's Penguin, Goofy and Wilbur, Snow White and the Seven Dwarfs, Society Dog Show, The Ugly Duckling, Timid Elmer, The Hockey Champ, Farmyard Symphony, Sea Scouts, and Pinocchio.

6418 *The Walt Disney Story of* OUR FRIEND THE ATOM. by Walt Disney Productions. 128 p. illus. New York: Dell, 1956.

A book based on the Disney film, OUR FRIEND THE ATOM (1956).

6419 *Walt Disney's* AFRICAN LION. by Algar, James. 74 p. illus. New York: Simon and Schuster, 1956.

A title in the TRUE LIFE ADVENTURE series, published as a *Documentary Art* book for children. The book is based on Disney's film, THE AFRICAN LION (1955), from which the illustrations aretaken.

6420 *Walt Disney's* BAMBI. by Walt Disney Productions. 28 p. illus. New York: Simon & Schuster, 1949.

Designed for children, this volume is based on the original story by Felix Salten as interpreted by Disney. The illustrations are derived from the 1949 film and are in color.

6421 *Walt Disney's* CINDERELLA. by Walt Disney Productions. 28 p. illus. New York: Simon & Schuster, 1950.

Both the story and the illustrations in this children's book were adapted from the Walt Disney film, CINDERELLA (1950). As is usual with the *Big Golden Book* series, the illustrations are in color. See also

Walt Disney books.

6422 *Walt Disney's* FANTASIA. by Taylor, Deems. 157 p. illus. New York: Simon and Schuster, 1940.

Published simultaneously with the film's first release, this volume combines illustration and text. Deems Taylor, who narrated the film, does a similar job here in print and is assisted by a foreword by Leopold Stokowski.

6423 *Walt Disney's* LIVING DESERT. edited by Disney Productions. 73 p. illus. New York: Simon and Schuster, 1956.

A *Documentary Art* book based on the Disney *True-Life Adventure* film, THE LIVING DESERT (1953).

6424 *Walt Disney's* MARY POPPINS. edited by McHargue, Georgess. 46 p. illus. New York: Golden Press, 1964.

The text of this title in the *Big Golden Book* series has been adapted by Georges McHargue from the film and the original story by P. L. Travers. Full-color stills from the Walt Disney film, MARY POPPINS (1964), and some original line drawings by Betty Fraser and Craig Pineo are well reproduced throughout the book. See also Walt Disney Books.

6425 *Walt Disney's* MARY POPPINS. edited by Walt Disney Productions unpaginated illus. New York: Golden Books, 1966.

A storybook for children based on the Walt Disney film, MARY POPPINS (1964).

6426 *Walt Disney's* PETER PAN. by Barrie, James M. 27 p. illus. New York: Golden Press, 1952.

Adapted from the Walt Disney film, PETER PAN (1953), this title in the *Big Golden Book* series uses illustrations by the Walt Disney Studio, with pictures adapted by John Hench and Al Demster. The classic story is presented in a simplified style, apparently with permission from the James M. Barrie Estate. The many illustrations are in full color and are quite attractive. See also Walt Disney Books.

6427 *Walt Disney's* SNOW WHITE AND THE SEVEN DWARFS. 40 p. illus. New York: Random House, 1973.

This title in the Disney *Wonderful World* series does

not list an author. It is a simplified retelling of the fairy tale, using a minimum text and maximum illustrations, adapted, of course, from Disney's first feature-length cartoon, SNOW WHITE AND THE SEVEN DWARFS (1937). The visuals are attractively presented in full color. See also Walt Disney Books.

6428 *Walt Disney's* SNOW WHITE AND THE SEVEN DWARFS. edited by Walt Disney Studios. unpaginated paper illus. New York: Harmony, 1980.

More than 100 full-color illustrations taken from SNOW WHITE AND THE SEVEN DWARFS (1938) appear in this title from the *Disney Read-Aloud Film Classics* series. A few words of dialogue or narrative appear under the illustrations,and there is a short introduction.

6429 *Walt Disney's* THE JUNGLE BOOK. edited by Walt Disney Studios. unpaginatd paper illus. New York: Harmony, 1980.

More than 100 full-color illustrations taken from THE JUNGLE BOOK (1967) appear in this title from the *Disney Read-Aloud Film Classics* series. A few words of dialogue or narrative appear under the illustrations. According to the publishers, the series, designed for children of all ages, will eventually include all of the Disney classics.

6430 *Walt Disney's* THREE LITTLE PIGS. edited by Brenner, Barbara. 40 p. illus. New York: Random House, 1972.

A more recent example of the use of the Disney-created folklore characters is shown in this children's book, a title in the *Disney Wonderful World of Reading* series. Using large colored visuals adapted from Disney's cartoon short, THE THREE LITTLE PIGS (1933), the story is retold with a minimum amount of words and a maximum number of illustrations.

6431 *Walt Disney's Uncle Remus Stories.* by Palmer, Marion. 92 p. illus. New York: Simon and Schuster, 1947.

Another *Giant Golden Book* which utilizes the characters and backgrounds from the Disney films which were based on the original Uncle Remus stories by Joel Chandler Harris. Best known is SONG OF THE SOUTH (1947).

6432 *Walt Disney's* VANISHING PRAIRIE. by Bromfield, Louis. 73 p. illus. New York: Simon and Schuster, 1956.

A *True-Life Adventure* book based on the Disney film, THE VANISHING PRAIRIE (1954).

6433 *Walt Disney's America.* by Finch, Christopher. 302 p. illus. New York: Abbeville, 1978.

This volume explores the ways in which Walt Disney was "formed" by America and how, in his films, he gave defintive American form to subjects from European folklore. Many illustrations and a Disney career chronology are included.

6434 *see 6422*

6435 *Walter Forde.* edited by Brown, Geoff. 51 p. paper London: British Film Institute, 1977.

A collection of articles in tribute to Walter Forde, a silent film comedian who later became a director of many British feature films.

6436 *Wanderer.* by Hayden, Sterling. 407 p. paper New York: Bantam Books, 1965.

Although the author has made over 45 motion pictures, the attention given to this aspect of his life in this autobiography is minimal and offered apologetically. It is true that most of his films are minor ones but he did make THE ASPHALT JUNGLE (1950) and DR. STRANGELOVE (1963). The book tells of his love of the sea and sailing, his confession of Communist party activity to the House Committee on Un-American Activities, and his wartime career. It is not the story so much as the author's honest, masculine style that makes the book noteworthy. While it offers very little about film, it does give the reader a fully realized picture of a film actor who was not in the usual mold. Excellent reading.

6437 WAR AND PEACE. by Stern, Harold. 34 p. paper illus. New York: National Publishers, 1968.

This is a souvenir book of the 1968 Russian-made film which was shown in two parts and had a total running time of more than six hours. It should not be confused with the 1956 film directed by King Vidor which starred Henry Fonda and Audrey Hepburn. The plot is described with the help of stills, and a later section tells about the making of the film.

Author Leo Tolstoy receives an extended biographical treatment and there is even one page devoted to the Walter Reade Organization, the distributor responsible for bringing the film to America. Cast principals and production personnel are noted.

6438   *War and Society: A Teacher's Handbook.* by The Schools Council, the Nuffield Foundation Humanities Project. 100 p. paper London: Heinemann, 1970.

Suggests a variety of media that can be used in discussing particularwars in an educational setting. Films, tapes, fiction and other forms are noted.

6439   *The War Film.* by Butler, Ivan. 191 p. illus. New York: A. S. Barnes, 1974.

In this study of a film genre, Ivan Butler has provided a survey which considers the films in the order of their release date. Using American and British films for the most part, the text follows a chronological film history structure in its examination. Starting with silent films, the narrative progresses quickly to BIRTH OF A NATION (1914), and the World War I period. The twenties and thirties are viewed as periods of war nostalgia (WHAT PRICE GLORY?—1926) and disillusionment (ALL QUIET ON THE WESTERN FRONT—1930). The World War II period saw a great number of films produced for purposes of morale, interpretation, and propaganda. The postwar films and those that dealt with the Korean War are treated next. Final pages of the text are devoted to MASH (1970), PATTON (1970) and JOHNNY GOT HIS GUN (1971).

A most helpful arrangement of the war films is provided in a listing by specific war. Napoleonic Wars (1803-15), the American Civil War (1861-65), the First World War (1914-1918), the Spanish Civil War (1936-39), the Second World War (1939-45), the Korean War (1950-53), Vietnam and the Atomic Threat (1945- ?) are the headings used. An index completes the volume. Picture selection and reproduction are adequate.

Butler writes with a thorough background and knowledge of this genre, which in some cases is a difficult one to define, since war may be incidental to the plot of a film. For example, THE LADY VANISHES (1938) is treated, but WATERLOO BRIDGE (1940) is not. However, the selection of war films presented is a large, valid group and Butler's discussion of them is provocative and often disturbing. Acceptable.

6440   *The War Film.* by Kagan, Norman. 160 p. paper illus. New York: Pyramid, 1974.

The *Pyramid Illustrated History of the Movies* series is consistent not only in the topics it covers but also in the quality of writing among its titles. With so many volumes about the war film appearing in 1974, it is gratifying to see the topic handled with such intelligence and style as in this volume. The genre is examined in a partially chronological arrangement, i.e., World War I, the period between, World War II, the Korean War, and the Vietnam War. The Comedy of War and Anti-War Films are considered in separate chapters, as are two classics: THE BIRTH OF A NATION (1915) and SHOULDER ARMS (1918). A rather selected filmography, a bibliography and an index complete the volume.

Using only the fiction film, the author's criteria in evaluating a film are the questions: Are war films ever true to war? to history? to film? to their time? to art? to themselves? The answering of these questions sets up a rather demanding task but they do offer a valid method for approaching this genre. The many illustrations which appear throughout the book are adequately reproduced. Recommended.

6441   THE WAR GAME. by Watkins, Peter. paper illus. New York: AvonBooks, 1967.

Script of the 1967 film directed by Watkins.

6442   *War Movies.* by Perlmutter, Tom. 160 p. paper illus. Secaucus, N.J.: Castle Books (DerbiBooks), 1974.

An oversized spiral-bound study of war films, this volume combines a well-written text with a fine collection of visuals. Employing history, description and criticism, the author covers all aspects of the genre most effectively. A chapter written by Derek Ware on special effects in war films is added. The visuals are made up of stills, frame enlargements, posters, one-sheets and other forms of film publicity. Most are clearly reproduced, and they cover a large number of selected war films. A few are in color, and there are ten double-page fold-outs. The spiral binding may cause some difficulty in use, but the content is so absorbing that most readers will not mind the difficulty in turning pages. Highly recommended.

6443   *War on Film: The American Cinema and World War I, 1914-1941.* by Isenberg, Michael T. Madison, N.J.: Fairleigh Dickinson University Press, 1981.

An argument for the use of films as historical documentation is made as the author shows how films from 1914 to 1941 reflected American opinion and attitude toward World War I.

6444 *The War/Peace Film Guide.* by Dougall, Lucy. 51 p. paper Berkeley, Calif.: World Without War Council, 1970.

This guide is an annotated list of some 100 films which deal with war. The short films are divided into nine categories: 1) The Human Cost of War, 2) Psychological and Social Roots of War, 3) Non-Violence and Personal Witness, 4) Conscientious Objection and the Draft, 5) The Arms Race and the Effects of Nuclear War, 6) International Organization and World Law, 7) World Development and World Community, 8) U.S. Foreign Policy, and 9) Area Studies—China, Vietnam. In adition, 24 feature-length films are described, some programming suggestions are given and a bibliography is added. Sources for renting or buying the films are also listed. A very fine reference book for both general and special usage.

6445 *War/Peace Film Guide.* by Dougall, Lucy. 124 p. paper Chicago: World Without War Publications, 1973.

This is a revised and enlarged edition of Lucy Dougall's original guide. Beginning with a subject index to films, the author offers suggestions for programs including discussion guides, background literature, room arrangements, program formats, study units, activities, training series, etc.

Film annotations are divided into four groups: features, short films and documentaries, films on China and films for children. There are separate bibliographies for children and adults. Other chapters indicate sources for study guides, study units, curricula, film catalogs, etc. Film sources and a title index to all the films complete the book. The generous quantity and high quality of the material in this volume make it an excellent resource. Highly recommended.

6446 *The War That Hitler Won.* by Herzstein, Robert Edwin. 491 p. illus. New York: G. P. Putnam's, 1978.

Subtitled "The Most Infamous Propaganda Campaign in History," this volume contains several chapters on the use of newsreels, features, and shorts by the Third Reich. Films such as JUD SUSS (1940), CAMPAIGN IN POLAND (1940), VICTORY IN THE WEST (1941), RETURN (1941), REQUEST CONCERT (1940) and KOLBERG (1945) are described in detail.

6447 *The War, the West and the Wilderness.* by Brownlow, Kevin. 602 p. illus. New York: Knopf, 1978.

Film historian Kevin Brownlow continues to devote himself to the silent film era, a period he examined so successfully in *The Parade's Gone By.* Using the three general headings of the title, he discusses a number of films, persons, and events connected to each. For example, under war, there are short essays on propaganda, Chaplin, pacifism, Griffith, von Stroheim, WHAT PRICE GLORY? (1926), WINGS (1927), etc. His usual meticulous preparation (film viewing, literature examination, interviews, and other types of research) has gone into the writing of these pieces. The result is a collection which puts forth new insights into an important period of film history. Since the essays are so well documented and told with such admiring enthusiasm, their credibility is strong. The text is greatly enhanced by rare illustrations which have been reproduced with care. They give a visual evidence about the period which corresponds closely with Brownlow's words. Sources, notes, and an index complete the volume.

There are few books in the flood of cinema literature that have any potential to last for more than their original edition. This is an important book which should waste little time in becoming a classic title that will be read, reread, quoted, and listed in film bibliographies. It is an essential for those seriously interested in film study.

6448 *Warner Brothers.* by Higham, Charles. 232 p. illus. New York: Charles Scribner's Sons, 1975.

The subtitle of this volume reads: "A History of the Studio: Its Pictures, Stars, and Personalities." Missing are two essential words— "selected" and "critical." Higham covers the early life of the founding Warner brothers and then concentrates on the movie-making years from 1918 to 1954. The structure is a chronological one with data, opinion, anecdote or interpretation used to flesh out the factual recital. The book is indexed and a pictorial section is included.

While some of the anecdotal material is fascinating and absorbing, the omission, misplacement, or incorrectness of important elements of the Warner Bros. story is most disturbing. Ida Lupino gets mentioned only once—as a cast member of THEY DRIVE BY NIGHT (1940). John Huston's work on the script, George Raft's refusal of the lead and the final use of Humphrey Bogart in HIGH SIERRA (1939) are not mentioned. (The pairing of Huston and Bogart in this film led to THE MALTESE FALCON (1941) and the Bogart legend.) No mention is made of the films that

Errol Flynn made prior to CAPTAIN BLOOD (1935). By this omission, the reader is led to believe that CAPTAIN BLOOD was his second film. The sequence of his films is in actual error again on page 123 when Higham states his next film after CHARGE OF THE LIGHT BRIGADE (1936) was THE ADVENTURES OF ROBIN HOOD (1938). In between these two were THE PRINCE AND THE PAUPER (1937), GREEN LIGHT (1937), ANOTHER DAWN (1937), and THE PERFECT SPECIMEN (1937). The chronology is shaky and misleading throughout. For example, page 103 suggests that GOLD DIGGERS OF 1933 (1933) preceded 42ND STREET (1933). It was in fact the immediate success of 42ND STREET that led to making GOLD DIGGERS OF 1933. A collection of stills arranged in a roughly chronological order places THE MALTESE FALCON (1941) in with some early thirties' films. In the still from PUBLIC ENEMY (1931) Edward Woods is incorrectly identified as Donald Cook.

While the book gives the reader a valid impression of the philosophy, tempo, methods and attitude of the studio, it disappoints in its casual, careless treatment of important factual material and in its critical selection and evaluation of both people and films. Ted Sennett's *Warner Brothers Presents* covers much of this same material with more care and style, while volumes such as Zierold's *The Moguls* and French's *The Movie Moguls* cover the biographical aspects of the brothers Warner. Jack Warner's autobiography, *My First 100 Years in Hollywood*, is also valuable in this respect. In summary, this volume is a late entry that offers some anecdotal material that is new, a lot that is old, and too much that is carelessly chosen or presented. Acceptable with the above reservations.

6449 *Warner Brothers Anniversary Book.* edited by Wilson, Arthur. 192 p. paper illus. New York: Dell, 1973.

A filmography of the feature films made by the Warner Bros. Studio arranged chronologically from 1917 to 1972, this volume also includes more than 150 stills. There is an introduction by Willard Van Dyke and a critical essay by Arthur Knight. Cast and credits are given for each film, and an alphabetical index of film titles concludes the volume.

6450 *The Warner Brothers Cartoons.* by Friedwald, Will; and Beck, Jerry. 287 p. illus. Metuchen, N.J.: Scarecrow 1981.

A filmography of over 850 cartoons from the LOONEY TUNES and MERRIE MELODIES series. Arranged according to release data from 1929 to 1969, the entries contain credits and a plot synopsis. Arranged according to release dates from 1929 to 1969, the entries contain credits and a plot synopsis.

6451 *Warner Brothers Directors.* by Meyer, William R. 381 p. illus. New Rochelle, N.Y.: Arlington House, 1978.

Subtitled "The Hard-Boiled, the Comic, and the Weeper," this is a collective biography of 19 directors, all of whom helped to make Warner Brothers a leading studio during Hollywood's golden age. Although they worked for other studios, it was at Warners that most created their finest films. The subjects include Lloyd Bacon, Busby Berkeley, Curtis Bernhardt, Alan Crosland, Michael Curtiz, Delmer Daves, William Dieterle, Peter Godfrey, Edmund Goulding, Howard Hawks, John Huston, William Kieghley, Mervyn LeRoy, Anatole Litvak, Jean Negulesco, Irving Rapper, Vincent Sherman, Raoul Walsh, and William Wellman. For each there is an individual chapter which includes an essay recalling in chronological order the subject's films, some selected biographical information, a set of clearly reproduced stills and a filmography. The text of the essay dwells on careers rather than personal lives and is strengthened by the inclusion of Meyer's comments and quotations from other authors. An index is provided.

The volume pays tribute to a group of men responsible for creating a large number of commercially successful films within the Hollywood studio structure. Many of these films still bring pleasure to a large audience. Belated recognition of some major Hollywood talents is offered in this volume, whichshould appeal to both the general reader and the film buff. The book is also a helpful reference source. Recommended.

6452 *Warner Brothers Presents.* by Sennett, Ted. 428 p. illus. New Rochelle, N.Y.: Arlington House, 1971.

The two decades from 1930 to 1950 saw the Warner Brothers Studios produce an enormous number of films, many of which have become classic legacies from Hollywood's Golden Years. Sennett's book is a tribute to Warner Brothers, to stars created there and, ultimately, to the Warner's stock company— Frank McHugh, Glenda Farrell, Alan Hale, etc.

Warner's triumphant gamble with THE JAZZ SINGER (1927) set the stage for the recruitment of the Warners Company of actors, most of whom are identified by capsule career sketches. The films, the obvious focus of the text, are efficiently categorized in individual chapters dealing with the following genres: crime and social problems, musical comedy, mystery-melodrama, man's work, war, and classic-biography. Remaining sections list brief paragraphs for many of the behind-the-scenes personnel at Warners during these years—directors, cameramen, composers, etc. There is a bibliography, a listing of awards received, and a briefly annotated filmography of all the Warners and First National films which appeared during the twenty-year period. An index to this massive work is also provided. The sections dealing with the films are illustrated with many representative and well- chosen stills. Reproduction quality is uniformly high.

Aside from the author's great affection for his subject, other positive qualities of this book include the meticulous coverage, the convenient and thoughtful arrangement, and the production quality. The appeal of the book is exceptionally wide. The likely tendency to assign it to reference would deprive a large potential audience of much reading pleasure, nostalgia, and background information of today's television viewing. With the Warners Film Library a primary candidate for transfer into video-cassettes, the book can only appreciate in value and importance. This is an outstanding volume.

6453 *The Warner Brothers Story.* by Hirschhorn, Clive. 480 p. illus. New York: Crown 1979.

Anyone who grew up with Warner Brothers films will admire this oversized recall of that studio, its product, and its stars. In chronological order from 1918 to 1978, some 1800 films are listed with cast, background information, at least one illustration, and a few major credits. The format is similar to *MGM Story* and *Universal Pictures* and provides a valuable annotated filmography for a major Hollywood studio. Picture reproduction is consistently excellent although some images are too small for total comprehension. A detailed index helps to locate specific names. This is a volume that is really "difficult to put down." Its recall of so many great films and fine actors is immensely pleasing.

6454 *Warren Beatty.* by Burke, Jim. 182 p. paper illus. New York: Tower, 1976.

Although this unauthorized biography is based largely on previously published sources, it has been assembled with a wicked humor that seems suitable to its subject. Warren Beatty is portrayed as a self-serving, egotistical, often neurotic actor-producer who just happened to produce two box office bonanzas, BONNIE AND CLYDE (1967) and SHAMPOO (1975). HEAVEN CAN WAIT, Beatty's gigantic moneymaker, came out in 1978 after Burke's book was published.

Using the theme of sex and politics throughout, the author offers large doses of suggestion, innuendo, and conjecture along with his factual material. The result is fun to read, even if it often seems like a bad novel rather than a biography. This is a lively reconstruction which might be considered as a trailer for a most colorful biography.

6455 *Warren Beatty: Lovemaker Extraordinary.* by Munshower, Suzanne L. 138 p. paper illus. London: Everest, 1976.

6456 *The WAFL Book.* edited by Epler, Greg. 191 p. paper illus. Washington, D.C.: Washington Area Filmmakers League, 1978.

Subtitled "A Guide to Film and Video in the Washington, D.C. Area," this volume is published by WAFL (the Washington Area Filmmakers League). It contains five sections: a directory of individuals possessing filmmaking/video skills; a listing of local film/video services; suggestions on using the capital city for film/video-related activities; a listing of film/video schools and organizations; and a bibliography. A group of advertisements appears in the book's final pages.

This volume will serve with efficiency those persons who have proximity to our nation's capital. Some of the information has general usage and appeal.

6457 *Watching Films.* by Sproxton, Vernon. and A reprint of the 1948 volume originally published by SCM Press, London. Philadelphia: R. West, 1979 (1948).

6458 *Water, World, and Weissmuller: A Biography.* by Onyx, Narda. 330 p. illus. Los Angeles: VION, 1964.

A biography of the actor who is most closely associated with the screen image of Tarzan.

6459 WATERLOO. 32 p. paper illus. London: Sackville Publishers, 1970.

This souvenir book is listed even though it was not published in United States and may be most difficult to obtain. Certain films which are financial and critical disasters in this country are more successful in Europe where they are given reserved seat showings. (PAINT YOUR WAGON is good example.)

Most of this volume is given to illustrations of the battle scenes. There is some attention to backgrounds, story, and production including a map of

Waterloo as of June 18, 1815. There are some short biographies of the producer and director; cast and other production credits are noted.

6460 *The Waves at Genji's Door: Japan Through Its Cinema.* by Mellen, Joan. 463 p. illus. New York: Pantheon Books, 1976.

Joan Mellen's goal in this volume is to reintroduce the Japanese film, which she considers to be "...the finest national cinema in existence." Using a historical, social, and political base, the text traces the growth and evolution of the Japanese film from the twenties to the present. In considering a film, the author usually examines not only the film's time-setting, but also the time of its production, and the film's importance to the history of the Japanese cinema. Such topics as feudalism, militarism, women, samurai, World War II, the family, and political cinema are examined. Singled out for extended attention are the films of directors such as Mikio Naruse, Kenji Mizoguchi, Yasujiro Ozu, Akira Kurosawa, Keisuke Kinoshita, Tadashi Imai, Misaki Kobayashi, Kon Ichikawa, Masahiro Shinoda, Shohei Imamura, Nagisa Oshima and Susuma Hani.

A fine selection of illustrations and a detailed index accompany the unique investigation and commentary that Mellen has provided. Acknowledging the earlier work of Donald Richie, she also expands her own exploration of the Japanese film (see *Voices From the Japanese Cinema*) to that of the Japanese nation. With a missionary's effort and enthusiasm, Mellen has created another valuable contribution to cinema literature. Recommended.

6461 *The Way I See It.* by Cantor, Eddie. 204 p. Englewood Cliffs, N.J.: Prentice-Hall, 1959.

Not a biography but a collection of advice, philosophy, reminiscence, and opinion. The best chapter is the one in which he names those performers he considers the greatest.

6462 *The Way of All Flesh Tones: A History of Color Motion Picture Processes, 1895-1929.* by Nowotny, Robert A. 359 p. New York: Gordon, 1982.

A title in the *Dissertations on Film* series.

6463 *A Way of Seeing.* by Barson, Alfred T. 218 p. Amherst, Mass.: University of Massachusetts Press, 1972.

In this study, begun as a doctoral dissertation, Bar-

son attempts to define the sources that influenced Agee's work, and to chart the rise and fall of his work. Since it is a bit easier to deal with the novel, the essay, or similar forms than with the film reviews or scripts, the analysis tends toward the former. *Let Us Now Praise Famous Men, A Death in the Family,* and *The Morning Watch* receive a good share of the attention. In a final chapter, Barson argues that the film adaptations on which Agee was working at the time of his death represented a decline in his artistry. Be that as it may, Agee is known widely for his writing on film, and it is for that reason the book is considered here. There is enough about Agee's film writing, his beliefs, philosophies, and his life to warrant consideration by film scholars.

6464 *WDR and the Arbeiter Film: Fassbinder, Ziewer, and Others.* by Collins, Richard; and Porter, Vincent. 174 p. illus. New York: Zoetrope, 1981.

WDR is a TV station in Cologne that developed the "worker film". Filmmakers and their films are discussed.

6465 *We All Go to the Pictures.* by Lowe, Thomas A. 214 p. illus. London: William Hodge, 1937.

A collection of comment, criticism and caricatures (by Coca).

6466 *We Barrymores.* by Barrymore, Lionel; and Shipp, Cameron. 311 p. illus. New York: Appleton-Century-Crofts, 1951.

The Barrymores descend from a theatrical family and it is not surprising that Lionel evidences the loyalty they had to the stage. He does give recognition and homage to films—one chapter is called "Don't Sell Movies Short" —but the appendix is reserved for his stage vehicles and not his films. Emphasis is on Lionel, with John and Ethel finishing in that order. One wishes Lionel had told more about his directing experiences, the many actors with whom he worked, and his 25 years in Hollywood. An early chapter relates his experiences with D. W. Griffith at Biograph. The book is indexed and there are a few photographs. Acceptable.

6467 *We Followed Our Hearts to Hollywood.* by Kimbrough, Emily. 210 p. illus. New York: Dodd, Mead, 1943.

In 1943 the author and Cornelia Otis Skinner were asked by Paramount Pictures to write the dialogue for a film based on their book, *Our Hearts Were Young and Gay*. This volume tells of their adventures in Hollywood. It is written in a light comic style that is also reflected in the line drawings supplied by Helen E. Hokinson. Although the account is studded with film names, not much specific information is offered. The book is noted here because of its selected impressions of Hollywood during the World War II era.

6468   *We Have Come for Your Daughters; What Went Down on the Great Medicine Ball Caravan.* by Grissom, John, Jr. 254 p. illus. New York: William Morrow, 1972.

A caravan of hippies, supported by Warner Brothers, traveled across the United States and then flew to England. The idea was to film the tour and come up with a SON OF WOODSTOCK. Unfortunately, talent was minimal and drugs were abundant. This volume covers pretty much the same ground as Forcade's book, *Caravan of Love and Money.* Grissom traveled with the group and reports firsthand the debacle, with the Warner executives getting a very negative notice. It happened only once and probably never will again. For that reason, it may interest some readers. Acceptable.

6469   *We Made a Film in Cyprus.* by Lee, Laurie; and Keene, Ralph. 92 p. illus. London: Longmans Green, 1947.

An account of the making of the documentary film, CYPRUS IS AN ISLAND (1946).

6470   *We Make the Movies.* edited by Naumburg, Nancy. 284 p. illus. New York: W. W. Norton & Co., Inc., 1937.

This is a collection of articles written by the creative artists who combine their talents to make motion pictures. Represented are the producer (Jesse Lasky), the screen writer (Sidney Howard), the director (John Cromwell), the actress (Bette Davis), the actor (Paul Muni), the composer (Max Steiner), and others. All of the contributors receive a biographical sketch and there is a rather good glossary of terms given. Somewhat dated material today but still of interest to students, historians, and nostalgia seekers.

6471   *We Remember Elvis.* by Hill, Wanda June. 140 p. illus. Palos Verdes, Calif.: Morgan Press, 1978.

This attractive memoir was written by a friend, employee, fan, and admirer of Elvis Presley. She met her idol on the set of KISSIN' COUSINS (1964) and remained in contact with him over the next 15 years. She attributes his death to cancer.

Included here are her recollections, along with those of other friends. The book is amemorial, as the title suggests, since the reminiscences are all affectionate and positive. The center section consists of 68 photographs, most of which are from private collections, including the author's. Of special interest is the transcript of interview tapes that were made with Elvis and the author between November 1976 and 1977.

For Elvis fans this attractive, well-intentioned memoir is a must. The serious historian may have some reservation, mostly about the objectivity, memory, conjecture and romanticism of the author.

6472   *We Thought We Could Do Anything.* by Ephron, Henry. 211 p. illus. New York: W. W. Norton, 1977.

Subtitled "The Life of Screenwriters Phoebe and Henry Ephron," this memoir concentrates on the Hollywood experiences of the couple. After writing a Broadway hit, "Three's a Family," they were employed in 1944 by various studios where they wrote such screenplays as THE JACKPOT (1950), ON THE RIVIERA (1951), THERE'S NO BUSINESS LIKE SHOW BUSINESS (1954), DADDY LONG LEGS (1955), CAROUSEL (1956), and THE DESK SET (1957). Later Henry functioned as a producer. Their hectic life as playwrights, producers, scriptwriters, was intensified by the difficulties of raising a family. The story of what was an ideal collaboration is told with good humor and a continual appreciation of their good fortunes. An epilogue by daughter Nora Ephron closes the book. Illustrations are provided but there is no index. Acceptable.

6473   *We're In the Money: Depression America and Its Films.* by Bergman, Andrew. 200 p. illus. New York: New York University Press, 1971.

This adaptation of a doctoral study treats the films of the depression decade in two parts. The years 1930-1933 spotlight gangsters, shyster lawyers and politicians, the Marx Brothers, W. C. Fields, "anarchy' films, the worldly women, the street women, and the musicals. The second and longer part dealing with 1933 to 1939 treats King Kong, the G-man, the cowboy, the social themes of Warner films, Frank Capra, screwball comedy, the mob, and the juvenile delinquent. References and notes are given for each of these subsections in the book's appendix in addition to a listing of the films discussed and a general bibliography.

As a different approach to the study of film, the book is most welcome. The author makes a strong case for using films to explain or identify an era in American history and indicates the service they performed for a distressed nation. Because of its origins certain portions of the book may be a bit intellectual for the reader in search of a nostalgic look at some films of the 30's, but there is more than enough entertainment value here to make the book valuable. Recommended.

6474 WEEKEND. by Godard, Jean-Luc. 188 p. paper illus. New York: Simon and Schuster, 1972.

Contains: WEEKEND (1968); WIND FROM THE EAST (1969); "Godard and WEEKEND" by Robin Wood; "WIND FROM THE EAST, or Godard and Rocha at the Crossroads" by James Roy MacBean; casts and credits.

6475 *Weep No More My Lady.* by Deans, Mickey; and Pinchot, Ann. 247 p. illus. New York: Hawthorn Books, 1972.

The only contribution that Mickey Deans apparently can make to the Garland legend is to tell of those last months of her life. This he attempts to do but with a decided lack of sensitivity, talent, and objectivity. The non-Deans portions of Garland's life are retold in a researcher fashion and perhaps this is Ms. Pinchot's portion of the book. It is not much better. The book covers in flashback format the many well-known incidents in Garland's career and attempts a reply to Mel Torme's book, *The Other Side of the Rainbow.* Most of the narrative is about the last months with Deans. The illustrations tell a stronger story than the author's.

This book resembles many of the later personal appearances of Garland. Late again, finally she's there, but surrounded by "takers" pushing her on stage against her will; and this is not the Garland the audience paid to see. Not recommended.

6476 *Weimar: A Cultural History 1918-1933.* by Laqueur, Walter. 308 p. illus. New York: G. P. Putnam's, 1974.

The evocation of a specific period in German history with special attention to its culture is the theme of this volume. The worlds of art, theatre, music and literature are considered along with the burgeoning German film industry. The latter inspired the world with different approaches, adult themes, and ad-

vanced techniques culminating in such classics as THE CABINET OF DR. CALIGARI (1919), THE LAST LAUGH (1914), and THE BLUE ANGEL (1929). Filmmakers such as Fritz Lang, F. W. Murnau, Ernst Lubitsch, Dietrich, Pola Negri, and G. W. Pabst are mentioned throughout this survey. The book concludes in the early thirties when most of the motion picture talent had been lured to Hollywood. Nazi Germany was emerging as the Weimar Era faded.

While this is not a film book per se, the author's recognition of film's role and importance in Weimar Germany makes it a resource that film scholars and historians will want to consider. Anyone picking it up will find it hard not to become involved with the Germany of CABARET (1972) and THE BLUE ANGEL (1929).

6477 *Werner Herzog: Screenplays, Number I.* edited by Greenberg, Alan. 192 p. New York: Tanam, 1980.

Includes AGUIRRE THE WRATH OF GOD (1973), EVERY MAN FOR HIMSELF AND GOD AGAINST ALL (1975), and LAND OF SILENCE AND DARKNESS (1971).

6478 *Werner Krauss.* by Goetz, W. New York: Gordon Press, 1976.

6479 *West Coast Theatrical Directory.* 324 p. paper illus. San Jose, Calif.: Gousha/Times Mirror, 1972.

This directory covers not only LosAngeles and San Francisco, but also Nevada, Hawaii and has some large company representation for Chicago, Nashville, and New York City. It contains listings of firms and individuals from all entertainment areas—agents, production companies, distributors, public relations firms, schools, etc. An acceptable film reference.

6480 WEST SIDE STORY. 40 p. paper illus. New York: Program Publishing Co., 1961.

Because of the many creative talents involved in the 1961 film, much information about personalities is offered in this souvenir book. In addition to the usual sections on the story, its origin and the film-making, there is a short article by Hollis Alpert. Individual pages are presented for Natalie Wood, Richard Beymer, Russ Tamblyn, Rita Moreno, and George Chakiris, as well as for directors Robert Wise and Jerome Robbins, writer Ernest Lehman, and composer Leonard Bernstein. The stills are mostly in black and white although there is an attractive centerfold in full color. The Sharks and the

Jets get individual pages and other cast and production credits are noted.

6481 *The Western: An Illustrated Guide.* by Eyles, Allen. 183 p. paper illus. New York: A. S. Barnes, 1967.

This is an unusual reference book that concerns itself exclusively with the western film. The volume consists of an alphabetical arrangement of 358 actors, fictional characters, real persons, directors—in short, people of the westerns. With each, some background and evaluation is usually offered.

The second portion of the book is a title index of western films. Following each title are numbers which indicate in order the players, behind-the-camera personnel, and other references from the first 358 sections. The illustrations are small in size since several are used for each page in a montage arrangement. While the author's opinions and his selections are sometimes questionable, the book can offer pleasurable moments to the film enthusiast by its thoughtful comment on the "western" people.

6482 *The Western: From Silents to Cinerama.* by Fenin, George N.; and Everson, William K. 362 p. illus. New York: Bonanza Books, Crown Pub., 1962.

A rather complete coverage of a motion picture genre, that is to some, Hollywood's most important, this volume is commendable on several counts. The content is excellent, and it is in a beautifully produced book. The pictures blend nicely with the text and are used with some attention to art and production design. The photographs are well chosen and include some rarely seen shots. Chronological in its approach, the book offers an opening analysis of the western's ingredients and influence, then covers the period from THE GREAT TRAIN ROBBERY (1903) to HOW THE WEST WAS WON (1962). An attractive book. Recommended.

6483 *The Western.* by Eyles, Allen. 207 p. illus. New York: A. S. Barnes, 1975.

This is a revised and expanded edition of the dictionary-type volume that first appeared in 1967 and contained 358 entries. The number has been enlarged to 404 here and still includes stars, directors, supporting players, composers, stuntmen, etc.—anyone whose work in westerns has been notable or noticeable. The second section offers an index of more than 2500 film titles, which are cross-referenced to the first section. Thus HIGH PLAINS DRIFTER (1973) offers references to the Clint Eastwood entry and to a picture of Eastwood. Each of the major entries offers a few crisp, succinct sentences and a filmography limited to western films. Illustrations are plentiful and are well reproduced. Here is an excellent reference book that has been appreciably improved in this revised edition. Recommended.

6484 *The Western: From Silents to the Seventies.* by Fenin, George N.; and Everson, William K. 396 p. illus. New York: Grossman, 1973.

This is an expanded and revised edition of the original volume, which was subtitled "From Silents to Cinerama." New sections on the "spaghetti" western and the western made in Japan have been added, along with a survey of the western films from 1962 to 1972. Changes in plot and character image are noted in detail in this latter section, such items as Warhol's LONESOME COWBOYS (1968), George Englund's ZACHARIAH (1971) and Dennis Hopper's THE LAST MOVIE (1971) included. The original comment still applies, this is an attractive book. Recommended.

6485 *The Western (A Series).* by Barbour, Alan. paper illus. Kew Gardens, N.Y.: Screen Facts, 1965- .

Alan Barbour, a film buff, collector, and author, created a series of profusely illustrated paperback volumes dealing with serials, screen ads, westerns, older films, etc. Some were unpaginated.

The following titles were among those published: *Hit the Saddle*, 1969; *The 'B' Western*, 64 pages, 1966; *Old Movies: The Western*, 3 volumes, 64 pages each.

6486 *The Western Film.* by Silver, Charles. 160 p. paper illus. New York: Pyramid, 1976.

A title in the Pyramid *Illustrated History of the Movies* series, this volume deals with the films, actors, and directors associated with the genre. It is heavily illustrated and contains a filmography, a bibliography and an index.

6487 *Western Films: An Annotated Critical Bibliography.* by Nachbar, John G. 98 p. New York: Garland Publishing, 1975.

Articles and books are placed under ten categories in this bibliography: Selected Reference Sources; Western Film Criticism, Pre-1950; Specific Western Films; Western Film Performers; Makers of Western Films; Western Film History; Theories of Western Film; The Western Audience; Comparative Studies; and Westerns in the Classroom.

The choice of entries is a selected one. Each has an adequate descriptive annotation, but critical comment appears only occasionally. A subject index and an author index complete the work.

This is a selected, specialized reference. It should be invaluable to anyone engaged in the study-research of the western film genre.

6488 *The Western Films of John Ford.* by Place, J. A. 246 p. illus. Secaucus, N.J.: Citadel, 1974.

In a departure from the usual format, this *Citadel* volume examines selected John Ford films in a critical fashion. In chronological order, the following films are treated by text, stills, casts, and credits: STRAIGHT SHOOTING (1917), THE IRON HORSE (1924), THREE BADMEN (1926), STAGECOACH (1939), DRUMS ALONG THE MOHAWK (1939), MY DARLING CLEMENTINE (1946), FORT APACHE (1948), THREE GODFATHERS (1948), SHE WORE A YELLOW RIBBON (1949), WAGONMASTER (1950), RIO GRANDE (1950), THE SEARCHERS (1956), THE HORSE SOLDIERS (1959), SERGEANT RUTLEDGE (1966), TWO RODE TOGETHER (1961), and THE MAN WHO SHOT LIBERTY VALANCE (1962).

Although the Ford westerns have been treated extensively in previous volumes, the many visuals used here, along with a valid critical appraisal, make this one of Citadel's better efforts.

6489 *Western Movies.* edited by Pilkington, William T.; and Graham, Don. 157 p. illus. Albuquerque, N. M.: University of New Mexico Press, 1979.

This anthology offers a survey of fourteen selected western films ranging from THE VIRGINIAN (1929) to THE MISSOURI BREAKS (1976). The films which are identified as "landmarks" of the genre also include STAGECOACH (1939), FORT APACHE (1948), HIGH NOON (1952), SHANE (1953), HUD (1963), RIO BRAVO (1959), THE WILD BUNCH (1969), LITTLE BIG MAN (1970), A MAN CALLED HORSE (1970), THE GREAT NORTHFIELD MINNESOTA RAID (1972), and ULZANA'S RAID (1972). The twelve essays are previously published pieces from various contributors including each of the editors, who also provide an introduction. There is a selected bibliography and some line drawing illustrations by Laura Butler. Chapter notes follow some of the essays.

Many of the volumes previously published on the

western film devote themselves to a general overview of the genre. The strength of this volume is the provision of some lengthy and sustained examinations of individual films. The editors' identification of critical approaches to the western film embellishes the diverse, informative reviews that follow. Acceptable.

6490 *Western Movies.* by Clapham, Walter C. 160 p. illus. Secaucus, N.J.: Octopus Books, 1974.

This survey of a film genre is a volume in the *British Movie Treasury* series and covers westerns from THE GREAT TRAIN ROBBERY (1903) to BUTCH CASSIDY AND THE SUNDANCE KID (1969). The text discusses historical backgrounds, film production, and the actors and directors who specialize in western films. Illustrations are well chosen, with many appearing in full color. An index of film titles and a general index complete the book.

6491 *Western Stars of Television and Film.* by Ferguson, Ken; and Ferguson, Sylvia. illus. London: Purnell, 1967.

6492 *Westerns.* by Warman, Eric; and Vallance, Tom. 151 p. illus. London: Golden Pleasure Books, 1964.

6493 *The Westerns: A Picture Quiz Book.* by Cocci, John. 128 p. paper illus. New York: Dover, 1976.

Although this is a quiz book, it is the 238 well-reproduced stills that are the main attraction. The visuals are taken from films made from 1903 to 1975 and include many Hollywood stars. A title index and a performer index make identification easy, as do the answers to the questions which are given in the closing pages. This is an attractive volume that has a dual appeal; as a game-recreation or as a review of a major Hollywood genre, it should please most readers. Recommended.

6494 *Westerns: Aspects of a Movie Genre.* by French, Philip. 176 p. paper illus. New York: Viking Press, 1973.

In this examination of a film genre, the author enumerates the changes that have appeared in the plots, the characters, the attitudes, etc., in the post-World War II western. He argues that innocence has been replaced by psychological motivation, nostalgic conservatism by radical chic, and the prairie by urban skyscrapers. Specific chapters deal with the reflection of political attitudes in the western, the evolution of the hero, villain, woman and child characters, the attitudes expressed towards blacks and Indians, and the changing background for the western. Not only does the author summarize the postwar western, but he also offers a list of 20 of his personal post-1947 favorites. The illustrations are barely adequate; many are dark and lack clarity and sharpness. A director's filmography and a bibliography complete the volume.

This volume of film criticism based on a genre approach is bright, original, and well written. French's clarity in explaining his purpose and in his fulfillment of it should be appreciated, and his contribution to the literature of the western film genre is most welcome. Recommended.

6495 *Westerns.* by Vallance, Tom. edited by Warman, Eric; 151 p. illus. London: Golden Pleasure Books, 1964.

Special attention is given to such classic westerns as STAGECOACH (1939), UNION PACIFIC (1939), HIGH NOON (1952), THE MAGNIFICENT SEVEN (1960), THE OX BOW INCIDENT (1943), 3:10 TO YUMA (1957), THE GUNFIGHTER (1950), RED RIVER (1948), and HOW THE WEST WAS WON (1963). The remainder of the text is devoted to the directors, actors, writers, villains, and other denizens of the western film genre.

6496 *Westerns: Film Album Number 1.* by Eyles, Allen. 52 p. paper illus. London: Ian Allen, 1971.

A chronological picture gallery with brief text under each visual.

6497 *The Westmores of Hollywood.* by Westmore, Frank; and Davidson, Muriel. 256 p. illus. Philadelphia: J. B. Lippincott, 1977.

The three major elements of this volume—the Westmore clan's biography, Hollywood behind the scenes, and the art of screen makeup—have been blended into a most pleasurable reading experience. The male contingent of the Westmore family consisted of father George, and brothers Mont, Perc, Ern, Wally, Bud, and Frank. Their individual lives and careers receive attention but the major story and viewpoint is that of the youngest son, Frank, who was constantly in awe of his brothers.

Since each brother was associated with a different studio during the Golden Age of Hollywood, the task of providing makeup to the outstanding stars fell almost exclusively to the Westmores. They were

aides, associates, confidants, friends and lovers to Hollywood's famous. Many anecdotes are related which illuminate the informal off-screen personalities of the stars. Within these stories there is also much detailed explanation of the art of screen makeup.

The volume is nicely illustrated and includes the Westmore family tree, which will help the reader to keep the large cast of characters straight. A substantial index is provided.

The male members of the Westmore family have the major roles in this drama about the profession of screen makeup. With many prominent Hollywood stars appearing in supporting parts, the result is one of the best books about Hollywood. Recommended.

6498 WESTWORLD. by Crichton, Michael. 107 p. paper illus. New York:Bantam, 1973.

Script of the 1973 film directed by Crichton. Contains a foreword by Saul David, former story editor at MGM, an article written by author/director Crichton entitled "Shooting Westworld" ; and cast and credits.

6499 *What Becomes A Legend Most? The Black Glama Story.* by Rogers, Peter. 80 p. illus. New York: Simon & Schuster, 1979.

In 1968 breeders of black minks hired Peter Rogers to develop an advertising program to promote their product. Using pictures by Richard Avedon and Bill King, he devised the "What Becomes a Legend Most?" campaign, which consisted of full-page layouts with famous females posing in black mink furs. They were unidentified, with only the logo accompanying the photo. A decade of the photos appear here along with some background information by adman Rogers.

6500 *What Can She Be? A Film Producer.* by Goldreich, Gloria; and Goldreich, Esther. illus. New York: Lothrop, 1977.

The authors have written a series of career guidance books for young female readers. Each book treats a different vocation—farmer, geologist, lawyer, legislator, physician, newscaster, veterinarian, architect, etc. This volume is about the varied and exciting work of a female producer of special films for television.

6501 *What is a City?.* paper Boston: Boston Public Library, 1972.

A bibliography and filmography about urban life. It uses headings such as victims of the city, a place to earn a living, cities of the future, etc.

6502 *What Is a Film?* by Manvell, Roger. 184 p. illus. London: MacDonald, 1965.

Roger Manvell is one of the few writers on cinema who could go over such familiar territory and emerge with a successful book. In considering all aspects of film (history, direction, economics, etc.) he has used modern examples in order to appeal to the new cinema public. In a brief, efficient way he has touched all bases in this small book. As usual, Manvell's illustrations are excellent and, it would appear, every name and title mentioned is indexed. As an introduction to or an overview of film, this is an excellent book. The sophisticated reader may find it too familiar but the beginner will be rewarded.

6503 *What is Cinema Verite?* by Assari, M. Ali; and Paul, Doris A. 208 p. illus. Metuchen, N.J.: Scarecrow, 1979.

Originally Cinema Verite was a documentary filmmaker's attempt to capture life or truth with a camera rather then staging it. Arguments about the participation of the filmmaker were immediate. This volume considers the diverse viewpoints of selected practitioners—Dziga Vertov, Robert Flaherty, Jean Rouch, Richard Leacock, Mario Ruspoli, Jacques Rozier, Chris Marker, Albert Maysles, William C. Jersey and others—in its attempt to discover what Cinema Verite is.

The text consists of an introductory essay, some history, a discussion of two schools of Cinema Verite (American and French), some variations, and a concluding chapter. A filmography, a bibliography, and an index complete the book. There are very few illustrations.

6504 *What is Cinema? Volume I.* by Bazin, Andre 183 p. illus. Berkeley, Calif.: University of California Press, 1967.

This volume is one of the most important books on cinema aesthetics. Andre Bazin was editor of *Cahiers du Cinema*, a mentor of many New Wave directors, and one of the most respected and influential film critics in the decade following World War II. This selection of his writings was made and translated by Hugh Gray. In a style which may be difficult to read and comprehend, Bazin addresses himself to his ultimate wish, the elimination of anything which might interfere with or hamper the relationship of viewer and film.

The theories of montage put forth by the Russian school of directors in the twenties are re-evaluated with a deadly logic and simple clarity: "Montage is the creation of a sense or meaning not proper to the images themselves but derived exclusively from their juxtaposition." For advanced students, and intellectual film buffs, this small volume will be a treat. The general reader will find Bazin's theories and comments a bit heavy.

6505 *What is Cinema? Volume II.* by Bazin, Andre. 200 p. Berkeley: University of California Press, 1971.

Another collection of the writings of the highly regarded French critic Andre Bazin, this volume deals with specifics rather than the aesthetics theory of the first book. Italian neo-realism, certain films of Italy, LA TERRA TREMA (1948), BICYCLE THIEF (1949), UMBERTO D (1955), CABIRIA (1957), and some Italian directors—Visconti, De Sica, Fellini, and Rossellini—are discussed. Another section analyzes the work of Chaplin, emphasizing two films, LIMELIGHT (1947) and MONSIEUR VERDOUX (1952). Final sections treat the American western and the pin-up girl, the book *Eroticism in the Cinema*, and Jean Gabin. The book is indexed.

As with Volume One, the text is informative, provocative, readable and ultimately rewarding. It is an excellent collection of cinema criticism that is highly recommended.

6506 *What is Wrong with the Movies?* by Rice, John R. 117 p. paper Grand Rapids, Mich.: Zondervan, 1938.

An early personally published attack on films and the film industry of the thirties. The author is generous with adjectives such as wicked, notorious, greedy, sinful, etc.

6507 *What Shall We Do Tomorrow?* by Bell, Mary Hayley. 235 p. illus. Philadelphia: Lippincott, 1969.

Reminiscences of the Mills family—John, Hayley, and Juliette—written by Mother Mary. Traces their lives from India to wartime London to Disney and Hollywood.

6508 *What Shocked the Censors.* by National Council on Freedom from Censorship. 98 p. paper New York:

The National Council on Freedom from Censorship, 1933.

A complete record of cuts in motion picture films ordered by the New York State censors from January, 1932 to March, 1933.

6509 *What the Censor Saw.* by Trevelyan, John. 276 p. illus. London: Michael Joseph, 1973.

John Trevelyan spent more than two decades as part of the British Board of Censors. In this volume he provides a history of the Board and describes the work of a censor, using many specific examples. He also offers some personal thoughts on the subject of censorship. In a sense much of text is a biographical memoir, since it offers an indirect portrait of Trevelyan. Censorship in the United States is also considered. Source notes, a few illustrations, appendixes (codes), and an index complete the book.

6510 *What the Stars Told Me: Hollywood In Its Heyday.* by Zeltner, Irwin. 182 p. Jericho, N.Y.: Exposition Press, 1971.

The memoirs, correspondence and reminiscences of press agent Irwin Zeltner make up the content of this book.

6511 *What's Wrong With the Movies?* by Lane, Tamar. 254 p. New York: Jerome S. Ozer, 1971 (1923).

Tamar Lane is the author of *The New Technique of Screen Writing* which appeared some 13 years after this volume was published by the Waverly Company in Los Angeles. It is a book of criticism and comment about all aspects of motion pictures, encompassing producers, authors, critics, morals, players, the church, etc. Most of it is quite enjoyable to read, although Lane was not the most perceptive of critics. Acceptable.

6512 *Whatever Became Of?* by Lamparski, Richard. 207 p. paper illus. New York: Ace Pub. Co., 1967.

This collection of pairs of then-and-now photographs along with a capsule reprise of the career of each subject is included here because of the presence of many former film personalities in it. The book belongs in the nostalgia-trivia category and will have strong appeal for certain readers. Further volumes of *Whatever Became Of* are available.

6513 *Whatever Became of ...? Volume 2.* by Lamparski, Richard. 207 p. paper illus. New York: Ace, 1968.

6514 *Whatever Became of...? Volume 3.* by Lamparski, Richard. 206 p. illus. New York: Crown, 1971.

6515 *Whatever Became of...? (vol. 4).* by Lamparski, Richard. 207 p. illus. New York: Crown, 1973.

This is the fourth book in the series that Lamparski began in 1967 and is consistent with the format established in that volume. One hundred celebrities who are no longer in the limelight are profiled and quoted in short two-page mini-biographies. Most of them are film personalities. A pair of pictures shows them first at the peak of their fame and then as they look today.

The books do have a fascination for the curious, and although the second photograph in nearly every instance is both disillusioning and disturbing, the reader continues to look at page after page. Each experience is similar to five minutes of the Good-Will Hour when the subject is misfortune and/or old age. The reader can expose himself vicariously to shock after shock as he sees how the mighty have changed or fallen. The popularity of the format is unquestionable. Many printings and subsequent paperback editions attest to this fact. An overlooked quality of the books is their reference value. In addition to offering a kind of macabre entertainment, Lamparski has provided information not available elsewhere. Recommended.

6516 *Whatever Became of...? (vol. 5).* by Lamparski, Richard. 207 p. illus. New York: Crown, 1975.

Lamparski continues his highly successful combination of mini-biography and nostalgia in this fifth volume of the series. The format is consistent: a picture of the subject at the height of his or her celebrity contrasted with a current photograph. Accompanying this visual shock-disillusionment is a text which recalls in brief some biographical data and career highlights. Closing sentences describe the current activities of the subject and occasionally offer a philosophical quote about life, career or fleeting fame.

Once again the majority of subjects have been concerned in some way with films. Photographic work is above average and a table of contents lists the subjects alphabetically by last name, although they appear in a random arrangement throughout the book. The choices and their treatment will continue to fascinate readers. In addition the book can serve as a limited reference source. Recommended.

6517 *Whatever Happened to Hollywood?* by Lasky, Jesse L., Jr. 349 p. illus. New York: Funk & Wagnalls, 1974.

As the son of a pioneer Hollywood mogul, Jesse Lasky should have a richly stocked storehouse of memories, anecdotes, stories and impressions. Based on the material he presents here, he either wore blinders during much of his early life or he is a soul of utter discretion. In this memoir he recalls many incidents with a sugar-coated text, e.g., "Having Hedy in that part was everybody's good luck...," "The selection of Angela Lansbury to play the older sister was perfect....," "Miss Harlow had amused herself with an altar boy in the temple of her fame...."

Much attention is given to his work with Cecil B. DeMille, and although he has writing credits for many films, most of them are only briefly discussed and some not at all. For example no mention is made of WHITE PARADE (1934), ATTACK (1944), PEARL OF THE SOUTH PACIFIC (1955), THE WIZARD OF BAGDAD (1961), THE SINGING HILL (1941), PIRATES OF TORTUGA (1961), etc. A kind of fuzzy innocence pervades most of the narrative, which needs the stimulation of either some interesting material or a cynical, acid interpretation of the bland tales told here. Perhaps the author was intimidated by the brassiness of his father's autobiography, *I Blow My Own Horn.* The illustrations once again emphasize a bias in selection. Although there are many photographs, they do not always advance the story of Jesse Lasky, Jr. Much attention is again offered to DeMille. The volume is indexed.

The title is a disappointing misnomer, for the volume is not an explanation of what happened to Hollywood but a recitation of selected incidents in the life of Jesse Lasky, Jr. A further disappointment comes from expecting an author with a rich background and long writing experience to generate a more exciting narrative than this. Parts of it are mildly entertaining but the author seems far too modest about himself, his life and his accomplishments. He succeeds in convincing the reader that the story he tells is really not important. Acceptable.

6518 *When Elvis Died.* by Gregory, Neal; and Gregory, Janice. 229 p. illus. Washington, D.C.: Constitutional Press, 1980.

This report on how the media treated the death of Elvis Presley is subtitled "A Chronicle of National and International Reaction to the Passing of an American King." It includes obits, editorials, measures of print space and air time given to the death, etc. A bibliography, an index and a few illustrations conclude the study.

6519 *When I Was Young.* by Massey, Raymond. 271 p. illus. Boston: Little, Brown, 1976.

This first volume of autobiography traces Raymond Massey's life up to age 25. At that point he decided to become an actor. Although the memoir is written with almost total recall, it offers only a mildly pleasant collection of impressions, stories, and portraits of people. Massey's impressive theatrical career is detailed in another volume, *A Hundred Different Lives.*

6520 *When Movies Began to Speak.* by Manchel, Frank. 76 p. illus. Englewood Cliffs, N.J.: Prentice-Hall, 1969.

Dr. Manchel continues to write noncomprehensive but informative and entertaining surveys of film topics. In this instance, he continues his history from the introduction of sound to the late sixties. Included are such topics as the development of sound, some pioneers (Lee De Forest and his audio amplifier, for example), directors, and films. Unionization, war films, the end of the Star system, the McCarthy era, the invasion of foreign films, and the effect of television on the film industry are also treated. The book is illustrated by James Caraway. This is another in the series that Dr. Manchel has created for a young audience. Recommended.

6521 *When Pictures Began to Move.* by Manchel, Frank. 76 p. illus. Englewood Cliffs, N.J.: Prentice-Hall, 1969.

The title may be somewhat misleading, since the book covers film history from prescreen days up to the middle twenties. Perhaps because the subject is technical, the text here lacks the sparkle of other Manchel books. The author does not receive much assistance from the production either, several of the illustrations being far too dark and murky. Line drawings by James Caraway are few and rather uninspired.

The first half includes the prescreen gadgets, the early projectors and cameras, pioneers, the Trust, early companies and films. In the second half, the emphasis is on people, with Fairbanks, Pickford, Sennett, Chaplin and Griffith predominating. The post-World War I film schools of German impressionism and Russian realism are described and the book ends with the French avant-gardists, Garbo, von Stroheim, von Sternberg and Flaherty. A bibliography and an index are added.

Because of the scope of the book, it may be unfair to carp about emphases, omissions, treatment. Certainly, if the intention is to create an appetite for further inquiry into film history, the book is most adequate.

6522 *When the Lights Go Down.* by Kael, Pauline. 592 p. New York: Holt, Rinehart & Winston, 1980.

Two-hundred movie reviews by Pauline Kael that appeared in *The New Yorker* from 1975 to 1979 are collected here. Many people think her the most influential film critic of recent years, and the reviews reprinted here support their opinion. She is the total professional, in that she is dedicated, enthusiastic, informed, and unique in regard to film criticism. She continues to set higher standards for everyone concerned with film appreciation.

6523 *When the Moon Shone Bright on Charlie Chaplin.* by Isaac, Frederick. 108 p. illus. Melksham, England: Venton, 1978.

This biography of Charlie Chaplin contains text, illustrations, a filmography, and a bibliography.

6524 *When the Movies Began: First Film Stars.* by Marvin, Edgar. Morristown, N.J.: Silver Burdett, 1978.

A history designed for young readers.

6525 *When the Movies Were Young.* by Griffith, Mrs. D. W. 256 p. illus. New York: Benjamin Blom, 1968 (1925).

Readers of this book may be surprised to find that it covers the period from author Linda Arvidson's first encounter with her future husband to his start of the production of BIRTH OF A NATION (1915). A romantic, emotional, somewhat gushy account of early moviemaking first published in 1925, the book is crowded with silent screen names. Given special attention is Mary Pickford.

6526 *When the Shooting Stops...the Cutting Begins: A Film Editor's Story.* by Rosenblum, Ralph; and Karen, Robert. 260 p. illus. New York: Vik-

ing, 1979.

Although this volume deals with the profession of film editing, it is also a biography of sorts. Rosenblum began his career with the Office of War Information. Since then, he has worked on documentaries with Robert Flaherty, in television, and finally with directors such as Ivan Passer, Sidney Lumet, William Friedkin, Larry Pierce, Mel Brooks, and Woody Allen. Using anecdotes, stories and examples from more than 30 years of experience, Rosenblum defines the film editor (himself) and his craft, with sensitivity, wit, and compassion. Illustrations and an index accompany this revealing book.

6527 *When the Smoke Hit the Fan.* by Bellamy, Ralph. 318 p. illus. New York: Doubleday, 1979.

Ralph Bellamy has been in show business for almost 60 years. In this earnest, no-nonsense autobiography, he recalls a career packed with incidents, personalities, and different roles. Bellamy has paid his dues in tents, vaudeville, theatre, radio, films, and television. He is proud to be an actor, a feeling that pervades most of this book.

6528 *Where There's Life, There's Bob Hope.* by Guild, Leo. 96 p. paper illus. Los Angeles: Petersen, 1957.

6529 *Where We Came In: Seventy Years of the British Film Industry.* by Oakley, C. A. 245 p. illus. London: Allen & Unwin, 1964.

An interesting history of British films from 1895 to 1960, this book provides an admirable framework for a subsequent reading of the Rank, Korda, Balcon and Hitchcock volumes. Many of the names mentioned in the earlier sections will be unfamiliar. The stills used throughout reflect largely the post-World War II golden period of English films. An unusual feature is the 13-page outline history—a year-by-year sequence of events—which is placed as a foreword to the main text. A short introduction and an index make up the remainder of the volume. The book is an essential for historians. Other reader reaction will vary with specific interests and background.

6530 *Where's the Rest of Me? The Ronald Reagan Story.* by Reagan, Ronald; and Hubler, Richard G. 316 p. New York: Duell, Sloan & Pearce, 1965.

Here is a controversial autobiography of a film actor whose activities in the industry's unions and organizations led to his political career. Much attention is given to his film career, which spanned several decades. The accounts of his work with the Screen Actors Guild, the fight against the Communist take-over, and the struggle between the various unions for power are discussed; an opposing view of the much documented House Un-American Activities Committee hearings in 1947 is also presented.

Author Reagan makes a persuasive and attractive case for himself and his ideas. He is generous to his co-workers and apparently tries to look at himself objectively. However, a rather flat picture emerges —all virtues and no faults. The appendix is a short summary of Reagan's political philosophy. An index is included but there are no illustrations. As a contribution to film history, the book is very good: it concentrates on filmmaking both on-camera and behind the scenes. As biography, it is only average.

6531   *Which One's Cliff? (Richard): An Autobiography.* by Richard, Cliff. 189 p. illus. London: Hodder and Stoughton, 1977.

6532   *The White Album.* by Didion, Joan. New York: Simon & Schuster, 1979.

A collection of 20 essays originally published from 1968-78 in periodicals (*Esquire, Life, The Saturday Evening Post*), this volume includes some material on working and living in Hollywood and a take-off on film criticism, "In Hollywood."

6533   *White Mane.* by Lamorisse, Albert. unpaginated paper illus. New York: Dutton, 1954.

A picture book derived from Lamorisse's 1953 film, CRIN BLANC.

6534   *White Russian, Red Face.* by Danischewsky, Monja. 192 p. illus. London: Victor Gollancz, Ltd., 1966.

This is the biography of a Russian writer-producer who began his British film career in the early thirties. His early responsibility was publicity work for various British studios; later he was a producer of such films as WHISKY GALORE (1948), THE GALLOPING MAJOR (1950), THE BATTLE OF THE SEXES (1961), TWO AND TWO MAKE SIX (1961). In 1964 he wrote the screenplay of TOPKAPI. Although many famous British film names appear in the latter portion of the volume, the period of the author's major film activity, 1948 to 1964, is covered in only a few pages. The photographs are of the author's family and there is an index.

Since the film-related content is minimal, the style is self-congratulatory and there are no pertinent illustrations or indexes, the book has very little importance for film study. Not recommended.

6535   *Whither Indian Film.* edited by Round Table on Whither Indian Film, Delhi, 1967. 34 p. paper Delhi: Indian Institute of Mass Communications, 1968.

A report of a conference held on October 11, 1967, dealing with the motion picture industry of India, and sponsored by the Indian Institute of Mass Communications in New Delhi.

6536   *Who Could Ask for Anything More?* by Merman, Ethel; and Martin, Pete. 252 p. Garden City, N.Y.: Doubleday, 1955.

Merman has never had the success in films that she enjoyed on the musical comedy stage. In this brisk, flippant autobiography she does give sufficient attention to her films to warrant some notice here. The first film she made was a short for Warners in 1929. The films she talks about are WE'RE NOT DRESSING (1934), ALEXANDER'S RAGTIME BAND (1934), ANYTHING GOES (1936), CALL ME MADAM (1953) and THERE'S NO BUSINESS LIKE SHOW BUSINESS (1954). Since she was a supporting player in the early films, much of her material landed on the cutting room floor. Her big number, "The Animal in Me," in WE'RE NOT DRESSING took weeks to film, included 40 elephants, kangaroos and sundry other animals. It did not appear in the final print.

This is flashy, surface autobiography typical of the early fifties Pete Martin school of writing. No index, no illustration, no filmography—just Merman and Martin. It is harmless, occasionally informative (as above), and acceptable.

6537   WHO IS HARRY KELLERMAN AND WHY IS HE SAYING THOSE TERRIBLE THINGSABOUT ME? by Gardner, Herb. 156 p. paper illus. New York: Signet Books,1971.

Script of the 1971 film directed by Ulu Grosbard. Contains cast credits.

6538   *Who Is That?* by Meyers, Warren B. 63 p. illus. New York: Personality Posters, 1967.

Although it deserves better production standards than were applied to it in this edition, this book will delight many readers. Subtitled "The Late Late Viewer's Guide to the Old Old Movie Players," this collection of photos will poke the memories of any serious filmgoer. These are the supporting actors whose faces are so recognizable and whose names are so unknown to most audiences. The faces are placed in categories based on the roles usually portrayed, such as "tough tomatoes," "society ladies," "bad guys," "clean old men," etc. An index of names is included.

The topic/idea of this book is most commendable but the production is slipshod. Omissions (Bert Freed, Robert Barrat), misspellings (Hines for Hinds), and questionable categorizing (Irene Ryan as a tough tomato?) all diminish the quality. However, it is still invaluable as both a personal and professional reference. Recommended because of the scarcity of this type of information.

6539 *Who Killed Marilyn?* by Sciacca, Tony. 222 p. paper illus. New York: Manor Books, 1976.

In this book the author's thesis is that Marilyn Monroe was murdered because of her friendships with men at the top of this country's power structure. On the cover, the subtitle reads, "And Did the Kennedys Know?"

Using speculation and theory superimposed on gossip, rumor, and fact, the author favors the likelihood that either (1) the murder was committed by someone around the Kennedys without their knowledge, or (2) that it was done by right-wingers hoping to disgrace the Kennedys. The case that Sciacca presents is most persuasive, and offers such realistic evidence as the autopsy report. This is followed, incongruously, by a Monroe filmography. A few visuals appear in a center section.

Aimed at the nonsophisticated reader, this volume is acceptable.

6540 *Who Played Who in the Movies: An A-Z.* by Pickard, Roy. 248 p. illus. New York: Shocken, 1981.

An alphabetical arrangement of real and fictional characters who have been the subject of a motion picture. Each entry lists actors and films relating to the characters.

6541 *Who Threw That Pie? The Birth of Movie Comedy.* by Quackenbush, Robert. 48 p. illus. Chicago: Albert Whitman, 1979.

A survey of silent film comedy designed for the young reader.

6542 *Who Was That Masked Man? The Story of The Lone Ranger.* by Rothel, David. 256 p. illus. New York: A. S. Barnes, 1976.

The history of The Lone Ranger as he appeared in the mass media is detailed in this volume. Print, radio, and television predominate with only a few films mentioned. They include two 15-chapter serials made by Republic Studios—THE LONE RANGER (1938) and THE LONE RANGER RIDES AGAIN (1939) —and a pair of feature films, THE LONE RANGER (1956), released by Warner Brothers, and THE LONE RANGER AND THE LOST CITY OF GOLD (1958), released through United Artists.

The sections devoted to the films are quite short and are accompanied by stills, posters, etc. In general the volume is nicely illustrated and a helpful index is provided.

The book will have an appeal for a specialized audience interested in the development of a major western hero-myth.

6543 *Who Was When?* by De Ford, Miriam A.; and Jackson, Joan S. 184 p. New York: Wilson, 1976.

This is the third edition of a reference which is concerned with "when?" Entries for some 10,000 individuals who lived from 500 B.C. to 1974 are arranged chronologically by date and field of activity. Since moving pictures have been with us for less than a century, the book has minimal value for film reference.

6544 *Who Was Who in the Theatre (1912-1976).* edited by Parker, John. 2664 p. (4 vols). Detroit: Gale Research, 1978.

This collective biography offers 4100 biographical sketches of individuals who were formerly active in the English-speaking theatre during the period from 1912 to 1972. Included are deceased persons, along with those who have retired or sought total careers in other media. Although performers constitute the majority of the entries, writers, directors, critics, producers, etc., are also listed.

These four volumes are a compilation from 15 previous editions of *Who's Who in the Theatre*, issued in England by Pitman Publishing Ltd. between 1912 and 1972. Where appropriate, death dates up to 1976 have been added. The importance of this reference to film literature is that so many of the individuals treated here were also active in making films.

A typical entry gives the subject's name, occupation, birthplace and date, education, marital history, professional credits, and supplementary information such as awards, hobbies, mailing address, clubs, favorite roles, etc. Sampling the entries indicates a need for much more extensive editing to provide a consistency, fullness, currency and accuracy that is frequently missing. For example: why continue to note a mailing address for Charles Bickford when he died in 1967; the address given for Fred Astaire is that of the RKO Studios, which have not existed since the early fifties; why not update the films mentioned to include the noteworthy ones rather that the earliest? It is recognized that the reference is basically a theatrical one but if any film information is offered—as it is—shouldn't it be of high quality? Selected films are listed for some persons and not for others, i.e., Reginald Gardiner, Steven Geray, etc. The thin line between who is still active on stage and who is not is often puzzling. For example, why "retire" Elia Kazan and Margot Fonteyn (included here) and still regard an octogenarian like Walter Pidgeon (excluded here) as active? Why not note that Barbara Stanwyck's marriage to Robert Taylor ended in divorce? Here she remains married to him.

In summary, this set of reference books is most valuable for theatre/performing arts collections. The stage work of its many subjects is treated in adequate detail and it will save the researcher much time. However, as a source for any other type of biographical information, it is often dated, partial or misleading.

6545 *Who Was Who on Screen.* by Truitt, Evelyn Mack. 363 p. New York: Bowker, 1974.

This most useful reference book is a unique, detailed necrology of over 6000 film performers. The period covered is 1920 to 1971, and most entries offer the birthdate; birthplace; date, place, and cause of death; the different media in which the subject performed; marriages; divorces; and an occasional bit of biographical information. The major portion of each entry is a filmography, arranged chronologically with title and date indicated. Two small reservations occur upon perusal. The information offered is not always consistent. Marriages and divorces are not noted in all cases (e.g., no mention is made of Marilyn Monroe's first marriage to Jim Dougherty). The added informational bits are puzzling as to the basis for their inclusion (e.g., Paul Lukas "appeared in both stage and screen versions of WATCH ON THE RHINE, receiving New York Drama League Award for the stage role and the Academy Award in 1943 for best actor in the film version." Others of equal

or greater fame Tyrone Power, Rudolph Valentino, Mario Lanza, Stan Laurel, etc., receive far less annotation.) These inconsistencies and errors are very minor reservations to a major reference work. The author has aimed for accuracy, wide coverage and ease of use. In all of these, she has succeeded most admirably. Highly recommended.

6546 *Who Wrote the Movie and What Else Did He Write?* edited by Spigelgass, Leonard. 491 p. Los Angeles: Academy of Motion Picture Arts & Sciences, 1970.

After short introductions by Gregory Peck and the editor, this fine reference work lists in its first section some 2000 authors alphabetically. Under each is listed any film in which he participated as a writer. Other writings, publications, and award information for the individual are noted. For example, the section on Arthur Miller lists screen credits, produced plays, published works and miscellaneous data. The second section is a film title index with about 13,000 entries. Beneath each are given the writers of the film, the producing or distribution company, the year of release, and other titles by which the picture may be known.

The final section is a listing of writing awards and nominations including the Academy Awards, the Screen Writers Guild Awards, and the Writers Guild of America, West Screen Branch Awards. An index is provided for the awards section. Note: the time period covered by this index is 1936-1969.

6547 *Who's Afraid of Elizabeth Taylor?* by Maddox, Brenda. 252 p. illus. New York: M. Evans, 1977.

The author states that her intent is not a biography but an exploration of private life versus public myth. As an added bonus she also promises to discuss "how women and sex have changed from the forties to the seventies." Her method is to compare Taylor's film roles and experiences with those in her private life. The treatment is somewhat biased (Elizabeth Taylor would not grant any interviews) but Maddox has researched her subject carefully; as a result the volume is a lively recap of the Taylor life and legend.

A center section offers a few pictures and there is a listing of Taylor's films. No index is provided.

The text offers little new material. It is the author's critical-analytical approach that makes the volume worth reading. Acceptable.

6548 *Who's on First.* by Anobile, Richard. 256 p. illus. New York: Darien

House, 1972.

This is one of what is apparently a series—*Verbal and Visual Gems From the Films of* ...., first the Marxes, then W. C. Fields, and now Abbott and Costello.

After a preface by Howard Thompson and an introduction by Carol Burnett (who believes that the boys will be rediscovered), Anobile presents his compilation of frame blow-ups and accompanying dialogue. Probably the most famous bit is the "Who's on First" routine that the team used in burlesque, on Broadway, radio, and finally in films. The films are selected from the Universal group, and the excerpts indicate the kind of slapstick and verbal humor that amused audiences in the forties. It will please most readers.

6549 *Who's Who in America.* edited by Marquis Staff. 3614 p. New York: Marquis Who's Who, 1980.

The most interesting aspect of this collective biography is the selection of the subjects, which is apparently done in several ways. Persons in certain positions (e.g., state governors) are automatic inclusions, some are elected by a board who engage "in a judicious process of evaluation," and others must be of reference interest (one in 3000 Americans). Once selected, the information offered may come from the subject via questionnaire, from public records and other diverse sources. "America" is interpreted in a very wide sense and some of the deceased subjects belong more appropriately in *Who Was Who*. Many film personalities are represented in biographies supplied, one suspects, by their press agents.

6550 *Who's Who in Filmland.* compiled by Reed, Landford; and Spiers, Hetty. 344 p. illus. London: Chapman and Hall, 1931.

A yearbook which was begun in 1928 and appeared only three times. It includes biographies and portraits of individuals who were active in the international film industries of the late twenties and early thirties. More than a thousand are treated in each volume, which also contains articles on film topics.

6551 *Who's Who in Hollywood 1900-1976.* by Ragan, David. 864 p. New Rochelle, N.Y.: Arlington House, 1977.

The 20,000 entries found in this biographical reference work are divided into five general sections— Living Players, Players Who Died (1900-1974), Players Who Died in 1975 and 1976, Lost Players, and

Lost Child Players. With this arrangement it may be necessary for the searcher to look in several or all of the sections in order to locate a specific name.

In the first and longest section, bits of information are offered in nonconsistent, random fashion. Some entries contain ages, birthdates, marriages and other personal data while others offer only a sampling of film credits. Each does note the state, region, section or country in which the player currently resides. The imbalance of attention given to each entry may cause confusion for the uninformed user. For example, Louis Jordan, Anthony Perkins, and Joseph Cotten each receive about ten lines while Kurt Kreuger is given 75 lines, Vera Zorina 68 lines, and Jean Peters 91 lines. The writeups on the latter three make for entertaining nostalgia but the question of film career-contribution arises. Does Vera Zorina's few years of forgettable film acting compare with Perkins' major performances given over the last 25 years? Does it deserve seven times as much attention?

A more equitable apportionment is used with the deceased players in the second section. Entries are consistent here in providing the age and the date of death. Publication logistics probably account for the 1975-76 necrology which follows. Concluding sections list players the author identifies as "lost," since he was unable to obtain information about their current location or activities.

The book is a mixture of pleasure and disappointments; certainly the longer write-ups, which resemble Lamparski's *Whatever Became Of* series, are readable nostalgia, but the selectivity, inconsistency, and imbalance of the entries do not make a very valuable film reference. Acceptable.

6552 *Who's Who in Show Business.* 542 p. illus. Rye, N.Y.: B. Klein Publications, 1971.

A directory of the entertainment world, this volume contains a listing of performers along with the names and addresses of their agents or representatives. All fields of entertainment are covered and the range of personalities is world wide. An acceptable film reference.

6553 *Who's Who in the Film World.* compiled by Justice, Fred C.; and Smith, Tom R. 229 p. illus. Los Angeles: Film World, 1914.

Biographical sketches "with photographic reproductions of prominent men and women who through their genius and untiring energy have contributed so greatly toward the building of the moving picture industry."

6554 *Who's Who in the Soviet Cinema.* compiled by Dolmatovskaya, Galina; and Shilova, Irina. 685 p. illus. Moscow: Progress; Chicago: Imported Publications, 1979.

Seventy biographical sketches of Russian film directors and actors are provided in this imported volume. In the first part, 35 directors, listed alphabetically by surname, are described by Galina Dolmatovskaya, with biographical data, critical comment, a filmography and illustrations. The initial portrait which introduces each essay reappears on each page in reduced size, making it easy for the reader to learn/memorize the unfamiliar subject's face. There are also stills from the films which provide slight evidence of their content, theme or structure.

The second section on the actors is similarly presented by Irina Shilova. Translation from original Russian has been accomplished with most of the essays reading like a carefully composed high school English composition. However, content rather than style is important here, and this volume satisfies that criterion easily. It is a unique reference book that helps to fill an open, unknown area in world cinema literature. Recommended.

6555 *Who's Who in the Theatre.* edited by Herbert, Ian. 1389 p. Detroit: Gale Research, 1976.

The 16th edition of this standard reference work includes such theatrical information as playbills for 1971-1975 for New York, London, Stratford-On-Avon, Chichester, and Stratford, Ontario, along with lists of New York and London theatres, long-run plays, working dimensions of theatres, etc. The sections pertinent to film research include the lengthy, up-to-date biographies which make up the major portion of the book, an obituary, and the names of performers treated in previous editions who may still be active.

Since most of today's performers do appear in several media, the biographical portion offers a rich source of information about actors, directors, writers, composers, etc. The usual data given in each of the more than 2500 entries includes birthdate, birthplace, parents, education, marriages, other occupations, chronological theatrical appearances, a sampling of film and television work, recreations, and address. The above information is presented as factual data without comment; no attempt is made at evaluation, interpretation or criticism. The obituary notes those performers who died between 1971

and 1976.

This is a valuable reference work that will serve a wide variety of library patrons. It provides background information on filmmakers that cannot be found elsewhere. Recommended.

6556 *Who's Who of the Horrors and Other Fantasy Films.* by Hogan, David J. 279 p. illus. San Diego: A. S. Barnes, 1980.

Subtitled "The International Personality Encyclopedia of the Fantastic Film," this volume is a selected list of personalities associated with one or more horror-fantasy-sci-fi films. With such a broad base, we find entries for nonhorror people like James Stewart, Victor Mature, Ida Lupino, Fred MacMurray, Olivia de Havilland, Cary Grant, etc. The connection, however, brief and infrequent, with the title is noted in each case. With such a wide umbrella topic, almost any actor lasting a decade or so in Hollywood would probably be eligible.

The annotations are short, occasionally critical, and there is a chronological filmography appended. Calling the latter "an index" is misleading since the reader would have to know the year to find the title to find the text reference. A puzzling book as to purpose, selection and format, this one was, apparently, assembled for nondiscriminating film buffs.

6557 *Who's Who on the Screen.* compiled by Fox, Charles D.; and Silver, Milton L. 415 p. illus. New York: Ross, 1920.

A mixture of items, mostly biographical, that treat actors, directors, producers, and studios/production companies. In addition there are articles, stills, cartoons, an album of Marion Davies paintings, and an index.

6558 *Whodunit? Hollywood Style.* by Nuetzel, Charles. 169 p. paper Beverly Hills, Calif.: Book Co. of America, 1965.

Once again the major Hollywood scandals are retold, this time with more detail and disclosure. Chronologically arranged, the misfortunes of Fatty Arbukle, William Desmond Taylor, Jean Harlow, Thelma Todd, Lana Turner and Marilyn Monroe are related along with all possible interpretations and suspicions as to what really happened.

Since the scandals have a relationship to economics, sociology and censorship, the book is noted. If information about the major Hollywood scandals is desired, this volume offers a quick efficient way to find it. Be aware that the book is not an example of good taste. It was designed for other than serious readers.

6559 *The Whole Sex Catalogue.* edited by Hurwood, Bernhardt J. 319 p. paper illus. New York: Pinnacle, 1975.

A collection of visualized information on all aspects of sex and sexual behavior, this "X"-rated volume contains a short chapter on sex in films. It deals mostly with porno films.

6560 *The Whole Truth and Nothing But.* by Hopper, Hedda; and Brough, James. 331 p. illus. Garden City, N.Y.: Doubleday, 1963.

This is the second and lesser of the Hopper books. Largely an expansion of some of the more celebrated Hollywood headlines and legends, this book is more scandalous and less restrained than most of its type. It is believed that a libel suit stemming from this book won Michael Wilding an out-of-court settlement. The usual fan magazine gossip elements are here—hints, innuendo, suggestion, guesses. There is a small group of illustrations that are quite unusual.

The informed and sophisticated who can read between the carefully phrased lines will enjoy the game presented here. Others may wonder what certain stories are really about. The book may stand with one or two others as a good example of the typical output of that Hollywood dinosaur, the powerful gossip columnist. It is fascinating trash that did appeal to and will continue to interest a large readership.

6561 *The Whole World in His Hands: A Pictorial Biography of Paul Robeson.* by Robeson, Susan. Secaucus, N.J.: Citadel, 1981.

Robeson's granddaughter has compiled this pictorial tribute. More than 200 photographs are included.

6562 WHOLLY COMMUNION. paper illus. London: Lorrimer, 1965.

Script of the 1966 film directed by Peter Whitehead. A film of a poetry reading held at Albert Hall in 1965. Featured in the film are Allen Ginsberg, Laurence Ferlinghetti, Gregory Corso and others. Introduction by Alexis Lykiard. Notes by Peter Whitehead.

6563 *Who's Who in American Film Now.* by Monaco, James; and Boonshoft, Sharon. 200 p. illus. New York: Zoetrope, 1980.

A dictionary of 4700 names arranged under the various film crafts-costume designers, editors, stunts, directors, etc. Selected film credits follow each entry.

6564 *Who's Who in American Films and Television.* by Arthur Knight. Los Angeles: Standard Who's Who, 1982.

Announced as having 10,000 entries.

6565 *Who's Who in the Film World of 1914.* edited by Justice, Fred C.; and Smith, T. R. 229 p. illus. New York: Gordon Press, 1976 (1914).

Published originally by Film World, Los Angeles in 1914, this volume carried this subtitle "Being Biographies with Photographic Reproductions of Prominent Men and Women Who Through Their Genius and Untiring Energy Have Contributed so Greatly Toward the Up Building of the Motion Picture Industry."

6566 *A Who's Who of British Film Actors.* by Palmer, Scott. 568 p. Metuchen, N.J.: Scarecrow, 1981.

An alphabetical listing of 1420 British film actors with brief biographical information and a chronological filmography given for each.

6567 *Why A Duck? Visual and Verbal Gems from the Marx Brothers' Movies.* edited by Anobile, Richard J. 288 p. paper illus. New York: Darien House, 1971.

The subtitle tells it all. This book uses photographs and dialogue excerpts from the nine early Marx Brothers films—COCONUTS (1929), to THE BIG STORE (1941). Stills and frame enlargements make up the more than 600 visuals which attempt to stimulate the classic moments in these films. A pleasant entertainment.

6568 *Why Me? An Autobiography.* by Gargan, William. 311 p. illus. Garden City, N.Y.: Doubleday, 1969.

" Inspirational, moving, heart-warming" —these are publishers' words reserved for autobiographies

941

like this one. Gargan was "King of the B Pictures" in Hollywood during the thirties and forties and, as Martin Kane, was one of television's first series personalities. He was also a worker for the American Cancer Society. Some attention is given to films. He has kind words for Leslie Howard, the Irish clan (Pat O'Brien, Spencer Tracy, Frank McHugh, and others) and Carole Lombard, but really bad-mouths Charles Laughton.

Gargan comes out as a man of admittedly minor talent who was both aggressive and lucky. His two major roles—ANIMAL KINGDOM (1932) and "Martin Kane"—both occurred at the infancies of new media. The illustrations are mediocre. The book is not indexed and the emphasis is on Gargan's laryngectomy and rehabilitation. Minimum interest for film collections.

6569 *Wide Eyed in Babylon.* by Milland, Ray. 264 p. illus. New York: William Morrow, 1974.

In this road company version of *The Moon's a Balloon*, Ray Milland travels a path similar to David Niven's. From Welsh boyhood to His Majesty's Horseguards and on to a film career is the plot in which he appears. Like almost all of his 200 films, his performance here is bland, passive and frail. He attempts to liven up the anemic text by being bawdy, using naughty words, describing his bladder functions in detail, hating gay people and adapting well-known stories and characters to fit his purpose. On page two, Milland states "it was simply a matter of opportunity...," a statement which explains a 44-year stay in Hollywood.

The greater part of this volume is concerned with Milland's youth and early adulthood. London, Hollywood and a few of the 200 films get a fast shuffle. He admires Dorothy Lamour (she's alive), hates Hedda Hopper (she's dead), and is proud of his work in THE LOST WEEKEND (1945). Other than a few short anecdotes about his recent activities, the narrative ends with the Academy Award in 1946.

There are some illustrations, but no index is provided. Two questions might occur to the reader who wades through this disappointing memoir: Would I like to meet Ray Milland? Given his "opportunity," would another actor have made something more of it? The answers will be uncomplimentary to Ray Milland. Acceptable only because this autobiography is the only material currently available on Milland.

6570 *Wide Screen Cinema and Stereophonic Sound.* by Wysotsky, Michael Z. 284 p. illus. New York:

Hastings House, 1970.

An account of wide screen, panoramic, circular, and other systems of cinema production developed by Russian technologists is the subject of this translated book. The stereophonic sound for each is described also.

6571 *Wild Animal Actors.* by Christeson, Frances M.; and Christeson, Helen M. 157 p. illus. Chicago: Albert Whitman, 1936.

A collection of stories about animals who take part in motion pictures. Frank Buck provides an introduction to this volume, which is designed for young readers.

6572 THE WILD CHILD. by Truffaut, Francois; and Gruault, Jean. 189 p. paper illus. New York: Pocket Books, 1973.

Script of the 1970 film directed by Truffaut. Contains an article entitled "About Truffaut" by Linda Lewin and "How I Made THE WILD CHILD", by Truffaut; also cast and production credits.

6573 WILD STRAWBERRIES. by Bergman, Ingmar. 120 p. paper illus. New York: Simon & Schuster, 1970.

Script of the 1958 film directed by Bergman.

6574 *Wilfred Pickles Invites You to Have Another Go.* by Pickles, Wilfred. 135 p. illus. London: David and Charles, 1978.

Known for his lengthy career in British radio and television, Wilfred Pickles has appeared in a few films, i.e., BILLY LIAR (1963), THE FAMILY WAY (1966) etc. His first autobiography, *Between You and Me*, was published in 1949.

6575 *Will Acting Spoil Marilyn Monroe?* by Martin, Pete. 128 p. illus. Garden City, N.Y.: Doubleday, 1956.

A long, extended article with many supporting pictures, this writing is partly biographical. It includes quotes from Monroe herself, her directors, co-workers, and others. An attempt is made at analyzing the Monroe charisma, but, as with most other such attempts, there is an overemphasis on a rather singular theory, that of sexual attraction. As seen today, Monroe's performances indicate much more. As supporting material to the later biographies, this volume has much merit. The writing is breezy, entertaining, and not enraptured with its subject. Most readers will enjoy this, although the later and major portion of the Monroe saga is not covered.

6576 *Will Rogers.* by Day, Donald. 370 p. illus. New York: David McKay, 1962.

Since Donald Day acted as editor of Will Rogers' autobiography, it is not surprising to find him mining the same material for this biography. This volume differs in that the narrative line here is more distinct. Much use is made, however, of Rogers' book. The account of the silent films is almost negligible and the short chapter on the sound films, "Playing Himself in the Talkies," takes up only nine pages and does not deal directly with the filmmaking, but more with personalities like Shirley Temple, Bill Robinson, Irvin Cobb, and John Ford. The book is indexed and contains a few illustrations. From a film viewpoint, this is a disappointing biography.

6577 *Will Rogers: Ambassador of Good Will, Prince of Wit and Wisdom.* by O'Brien, P. J. 288 p. illus. Chicago: John C. Winston, 1936.

This biography arranges its materials in a convenient fashion. Chapter headings such as "Rogers on the Stage," "Rogers and Politics," "Rogers As Writer," make specific information easier to obtain. In the chapter on "Rogers in the Moving Pictures," his film career is traced from the 1919 film, LAUGHING BILL HYDE, to STEAMBOAT ROUND THE BEND in 1935. He made 24 silent films and 19 sound films, with all of the latter becoming financial successes. Probably his most famous screen roles were in DAVID HARUM (1934) and STATE FAIR (1933).

Other than the chapter indicated, the rest of the biography is a dated tribute that is fan-magazine-factual rather than a thoroughly researched portrait. There is no index. The pictures are effective in recreating the era of Will Rogers.

6578 *Will Rogers: His Wife's Story.* by Rogers, Betty. 318 p. paper illus. Norman, Okla.: University of Oklahoma Press, 1979 (1941).

First published in 1941, this biography offers a personal view of Will Rogers by his wife, Betty. An admiring, positive memoir rather than an objective review of a life and career, the book traces Rogers' life from his birth in 1897 in the Cherokee Nation Territory up to the fatal plane crash of 1935 in Alaska. Some mention is made of his filmmaking activities.

An index, additional illustrations and a foreword by Reba Collins have been provided for this new edition.

6579 *Will Rogers: The Man and His Times.* by Ketchum, Richard M. 448 p. illus. New York: American Heritage, 1973.

This biography of Rogers is interesting on several counts. First, more than 400 illustrations are used in the volume, and secondly, a recording entitled "The Voice of Will Rogers" is available with the book. Coverage of the films is found in both text and stills.

6580 *Will Rogers.* by Alworth, E. Paul. 140 p. Boston: Twayne, 1974.

This appreciation is part of the Twayne's *United States Authors* series. Its emphasis is on the qualities and factors that made Will Rogers into America's most celebrated humorist. He was one of the first entertainers to use all of the mass media with success; stage, screen, radio, newspapers, and books seemed to be natural vehicles for his personal observations.

Only the briefest mention is made of his films in a text that deals mostly with Roger's life and character, along with an analysis of his style of humor. Notes and references accompany the text. A selected bibliography and an index are included.

The material presented helps to explain Roger's appeal to all types of audiences. His success as a film performer can be traced to the elements discussed by the author in this well-documented study. Acceptable.

6581 *Will Rogers, Cowboy Philosopher.* by Montgomery, Elizabeth Rider. 96 p. illus. Champaign, Ill.: Garrard, 1970.

Designed for the young reader, this title in the *Americans All* series deals in very general terms with the life of Will Rogers. For example, only a few short paragraphs are devoted to his film activities. Illustrations are a mixture of pictures and drawings.

6582 *Will Rogers Rode the Range.* by Axtell, Margaret S. 168 p. illus. Phoenix, Ariz.: Allied Printing, 1972.

Biographical references and illustrations accompany this story of the cowboy philosopher.

6583 *The Will Rogers Scrapbook.* edited by Sterling, Bryan B. 190 p. illus. New York: Grosset & Dunlap, 1976.

This period-styled scrapbook includes a short Rogers' autobiography, some antique illustrations, interviews with friends and coworkers, and other material about the cowboy humorist.

6584 *Will Rogers: The Cowboy Who Walked with Kings.* by Bennett, Cathereen L. 71 p. illus. Minneapolis, Minn.: Lerner, 1971.

A biography of the cowboy who became a humorist-actor-philosopher, this illustrated volume was designed for younger readers.

6585 *Will the Old Bob Turnbull Please Drop Dead?* by Turnbull, Bob. 93 p. paper Elgin, Ill.: David C. Cook, 1970.

The cover of this original paperback asks the question, "Why does a movie actor turn minister?" Listed as an actor who earned top credits in film features, television and theatre, Bob Turnbull gave it all up to become "the Chaplain of Waikiki Beach." He is also a member of the Honolulu Vice Squad. Other than DRAGSTRIP RIOT (1958), no other film is named. The reader is forced to wonder what those other top credits were, since most actor reference books do not list a Bob Turnbull.

The phenomenon of show business people finding religious salvation and then publicizing their discoveries is increasing in frequency. Minimized or eliminated is the fact that these conversions usually occur when careers are waning, finished or hopeless, e.g., Pat Boone, Betty Hutton, Mickey Rooney, Dale Evans Rogers, Ethel Waters, Cliff Richards, and Colleen Townsend. This volume is apparently designed for an audience that enjoys stories about renouncing the fast, worldly celebrity existence in favor of a life more closely approaching their own. It is not pertinent for film readers.

6586 *Will There Really Be A Morning?* by Farmer, Frances. 318 p. illus. New York: G. P. Putnam's, 1972.

This autobiography lingers in the mind long after it has been set aside. Much of what it relates is not pleasant or attractive. Farmer's family life, her early professional career, her stay in mental institutions and her final rehabilitation are the substance of the book. These major threads of Miss Farmer's life are interwoven with honesty and artistry. Much of the book is shocking: the author's description of the behavior of her fellow steerage passengers, of the inhabitants and life within a mental institution, and of a lesbian rape make strong reading.

The author describes her career in Hollywood in some detail. Only four photographs are included but they are carefully selected to supplement the story. This is very powerful writing that will appeal to mature readers. Highly recommended.

6587 *William Friedkin.* edited by Reed, Rochelle. 36 p. paper illus. Washington, D.C.: American Film Institute, 1974.

A long interview with director William Friedkin was held in 1974 at AFI headquarters in California. The record of the four-hour session is printed here along with Friedkin's short but impressive filmography.

6588 *William Goldman's Story of* A BRIDGE TOO FAR. by Goldman, William. paper illus. New York: Dell, 1977.

This original paperback is a mixture of elements all linked to the film, A BRIDGE TOO FAR (1977). An introduction entitled "Reflections on Filmmaking in General and A BRIDGE TOO FAR Very Particularly" discusses screenwriting, director Richard Attenborough, and producer Joseph Levine. Following this is a section which tells the plot of the film using many captioned photos. Concluding the book are statements by and candid photographs of each of the leading performers in the film. Several real life heroes are also quoted. They talk about their roles, attitudes, and feelings about the film. A list of the players and the filmmakers appears as a frontispiece to the book.

6589 *William Henry Fox Talbot.* by Arnold, H. J. P. "Douglas" . 383 p. illus. Salem, N.H.: Hutchinson, 1977.

This carefully written and attractively produced biography of William Henry Fox Talbot has several outstanding features. Its subject has been thoroughly researched from original sources, and it is comprehensive in its scope; life, career, times, historical significance, etc., are all here. In addition there are excellent illustrations, footnotes, references, chapter notes, appendixes, and a detailed index.

The contribution that Talbot made to photography is well documented in this scholarly volume. A dominant figure in film history has been well served by H. J. P. Douglas Arnold.

6590 *William Henry Fox Talbot: Father of Photography.* by Booth, Arthur H. 119 p. illus. London: Barker, 1965.

6591 *William Holden.* by Holtzman, Will. 160 p. paper illus. New York: Pyramid, 1976.

From his first appearance in GOLDEN BOY (1939) to 21 HOURS AT MUNICH (1977), William Holden was a leading film actor. His career is covered in detail in this volume.

Using many well-selected visuals and a critical text, the author shows Holden as an independent, complex man whose film acting escapes easy categorization. Holden played in films ranging from musicals and drawing room comedies to violent action adventures. All are critically examined here. A bibliography, a filmography, and an index are included.

In his initial sentence, the author states, "There is no William Holden, only William Holden films." For this volume that is true, for no personal portrait is attempted. Other than a few Holden quotations introducing each section, the off-screen view of Holden is minimal.

The production standards of the *Pyramid* series are maintained in this volume. Acceptable.

6592 *William Peter Blatty on* THE EXORCIST—From Novel to Film. by Blatty, William Peter. 376 p. paper illus. New York: Bantam, 1974.

As writer and producer of the film, and as the author of the original novel upon which the film was based, William Peter Blatty is totally justified in featuring his name in this book's title. His contribution to the success of the film was not a small one. In this volume he tells of how he wrote the book, the initial efforts to get it filmed and the final arguments and compromises that were necessary to get it into production.

The first draft of the screenplay is given along with the rationale for the changes that were made in the final version. A transcript of the final film with scene settings is included along with the cast and production credits. A center section of photographs is helpful, especially to those who have not seen the film.

Now that the initial excitement over the film has subsided, it will be interesting to see whether the film becomes a classic of its genre. Since it seems certain to attain that status, this book about its making becomes a most important document. Not only is it an absorbing account of filmmaking, but also its specific subject matter has a great fascination. Add

the element of the film's continuing popularity and the importance of this book is established. Highly recommended.

6593 *William Wyler.* by Madsen, Axel. 456 p. illus. New York: Thomas Y. Crowell, 1973.

The cooperation of William Wyler is evident throughout this authorized biography and adds an authenticity and detail seldom found in such volumes. Beginning with his early years in Europe, the narrative progresses quickly to the all-important offer from his relative, Carl Laemmle, to come to America and take a job with Universal Films in New York City. A career on the West Coast making westerns followed soon after, and by the early thirties Wyler was experienced enough to direct successful sound films. From the mid-thirties to the seventies he remained one of the most honored and sought-after directors.

The volume describes his films, their making, and Wyler's relationships with the performers appearing in them. Detail, anecdote, and frank appraisals characterize this recall of Wyler's many films; although Wyler's personal life is given slight attention, the section on his marriage to Margaret Sullavan is enough to indicate what life with a female film star was like in the thirties. Chapternotes, a list of awards, a filmography and an index complete the book. Like Wyler's films, this volume is a beautifully crafted work—complete with sensitive attention to detail, entertaining and ultimately rewarding. Highly recommended.

6594 *Willowbrook Cinema Study Project.* by Amelio, Ralph J. 84 p. paper Dayton, Ohio: Pflaum, 1969.

A course on film designed for high school juniors and seniors, this booklet emphasizes viewing and discussion of features and short films. It was developed from materials used at Willowbrook High School, Villa Park, Illinois. A very fine annotated bibliography is given.

6595 *Wim Wenders.* by Dawson, Jan. 32 p. paper illus. Toronto: Festivals of Festivals; U.S.A.: Zoetrope, 1976.

An interview of Wim Wenders conducted by Jan Dawson begins the oversized booklet. A selection of Wender's critical writing follows and discusses L'ENFANT SAUVAGE (1969), Eddie Constantine, and some Van Morrison recordings. Wender's filmography (1967 to 1976) is appended.

6596   *Winchell: His Life and Times.* by Klurfeld, Herman. 211 p. illus. New York: Praeger, 1976.

A dispassionate account of Walter Winchell and his career is offered in this biography. Written by a man who served as Winchell's ghostwriter for 27 years, the book is crammed with firsthand fact, knowledge, observation and anecdote. True to his experience as a columnist, the author avoids verbosity and makes each word in his text count. His is an exceedingly spare style of writing.

Klurfeld tries to be objective about his subject and, after almost three decades of association, this is not an easy task. In most instances he succeeds in presenting an unbiased portrait of the colorful columnist. The closing summary evaluation of Winchell that he presents is quite effective and believable. A few pictures and an index support the terse text; unfortunately there is no bibliography.

There have been several earlier biographies and one autobiography of Winchell, none of which were completely successful. This one supplies certain qualities that the others lacked—access to the subject, objectivity, and a style appropriate to the material. However, almost no attention is given here to Winchell's Hollywood and TV activities—even Ben Bernie and the famous feud are ignored. Acceptable.

6597   *Winchell.* by Thomas, Bob. 288 p. illus. Garden City, N.Y.: Doubleday, 1971.

The author of *King Cohn, Thalberg* and *Selznick* tackles another colorful subject in this biography. Walter Winchell was one of the most powerful and controversial columnists in America during the thirties. Over 800 newspapers carried his column and his Sunday night radio broadcasts captured millions of listeners.

He covered the Broadway-Hollywood scene for more than two decades. Emphasis here is on the international celebrities rather than the many movie names that used to populate his column. A short photography section is provided and the book is indexed. Along with Louella Parsons, Winchell's history consists of early ambition, gossip, power, vendetta, and a precipitous fall from public view. Peripheral material for film history. See also *The Secret Life of Walter Winchell.*

6598   *Winchell Exclusive.* by Winchell, Walter. 332 p. illus. Englewood Cliffs, N.J.: Prentice-Hall, 1975.

Shortly before his death, Walter Winchell be-

queathed his autobiographical writings to his attorney, Ernest Cuneo, who introduces them here. Starting with his birth in 1897, the account of Winchell's life and career is told in short fragments, each with a different title. Thus the writer can digress with regularity and still not neglect the main subject since all of the digressions were Winchell's subject matter at some time.

The illustrations are mostly well-selected candids that show several aspects of Winchell's personality. The volume is indexed. Since Winchell often wrote about the Hollywood scene and appeared in several films, his autobiography is noted here. It is acceptable.

6599   *Winchester's Screen Encyclopedia.* edited by Miller, Maud M. 404 p. illus. London: Winchester Publications, 1948.

In addition to a who's who of 1000 biographical entries, this volume treats Korda, Rank, films in Great Britain, stars and their public, the making of films, film music, documentary films, the "specialized" cinema, children at the cinema, etc. A glossary, an index, and other statistical information are also offered.

6600   *The Wind at My Back.* by O'Brien, Pat. 286 p. paper illus. New York: Avon Books, 1967.

If the reader can overlook the professional Irishman and focus on the professional actor, he will enjoy this biography. Filled with anecdotes, opinions, and observations, the book is surprisingly consistent in its retelling of a long career in films. There are a few social and geographical digressions but most of the story is concerned with professional matters. Some of it is surprising; for example, between 1950 and 1964, O'Brien made only four films for major Hollywood studios. The many pictures made during the prior two decades which haunt us on television have surrounded us with a mistaken impression that O'Brien is ever active. His theory is that he was being punished after 1950 for some unknown offense.

The small picture section disappoints as much as the text pleases. A filmography and an index would have helped greatly. There is so much that is interesting and informative about the book, it is sad that some editor did not have the foresight to make it more pertinent to film literature and study. It is still one of the better film actor biographies available.

6601   WINDJAMMER. by Hardiman, James W. 62 p. illus. New York:

Random House, 1958.

This souvenir book describes a 1958 film-travelogue that was done in the Cinemiracle process and was directed by documentary filmmaker, Louis de Rochemont. The story of the cruise is related by the participants, the cadets and the captain, and is supplemented by maps and illustrations. An interesting section deals with the superstitions which surround any sailing of the seas. Director de Rochemont is profiled and other cast and production credits are noted. The book creates the same feeling in the reader that the film did—a pleasant, visually rewarding trip that lacked any great excitement.

6602 *Window on Hong Kong: A Sociological Study of the Hong Kong Film Industry and Its Audience.* by Jarvie, I. C. 223 p. illus. Hong Kong: Centre of Asian Studies, University of Hong Kong, 1977.

Film sociologist Jarvie turns up in unexpected places and his studies are always welcome. Here, the title tells what he's about, and to his text he's added illustrations, tables, a bibliography, and an index.

6603 *Wings on My Feet.* by Henie, Sonja. 177 p. illus. New York: Prentice-Hall, 1940.

The first portion of this book is early biography while the second offers instruction on ice skating.

6604 *Wings on the Screen: A Pictorial History of Air Movies' 1928-1978.* by Skogsberg, Bertil. 192 p. illus. San Diego, Calif.: A. S. Barnes, 1981.

6605 *Winners of the West: The Sagebrush Heroes of the Silent Screen.* by Lahue, Kalton C. 353 p. illus. New York: A. S. Barnes, 1970.

Some 38 film personalities who were known for their performances in silent westerns are professionally profiled in this volume. The group includes both men and women. Each profile is composed of a few stills, and an account of the film career of the subject. No attempt is made to personalize the actor. A few lesser known actors are accorded a picture and a paragraph in a concluding group section.

Picture quality is quite variable and sizes tend to half or three-quarter page. There are very few full-page illustrations. The book's physical dimensions are smaller than the usual picture book and thus the picture size and subjects are reduced considerably.

An objectionable trend may be starting with this book in which two full-page portraits are devoted to its dedication—the author's wife and a script writer who assisted. Poor production and pedestrian subject treatment make this book barely suitable.

6606 *Wisconsin/Warner Brothers Screenplay Series.* edited by Balio, Tino. paper illus. Madison, Wisc.: University of Wisconsin Press, 1979- .

In 1979 an attractive script series, derived from the classic Warner Brothers films, was introduced. Tino Balio is the general editor, assisted by another editor in charge of each volume, and an editorial committee consisting of Dudley Andrew, John G. Cawelti, and Dore Schary.

The series has announced plans for the forthcoming scripts: THE JAZZ SINGER (1928), MYSTERY OF THE WAX MUSEUM (1933), THE TREASURE OF THE SIERRA MADRE (1948), THE ADVENTURES OF ROBIN HOOD (1938), AIR FORCE (1943), FORTY-SECOND STREET (1933), GOLD DIGGERS OF 1933 (1933), THE GREEN PASTURES (1936), HEROES FOR SALE (1933), HIGH SIERRA (1941), I AM A FUGITIVE FROM A CHAIN GANG (1932), LITTLE CAESAR (1930), MILDRED PIERCE (1945), MISSION TO MOSCOW (1943), THE PUBLIC ENEMY (1931), THE ROARING TWENTIES (1939), TO HAVE AND HAVE NOT (1944), WHITE HEAT (1949), YANKEE DOODLE DANDY (1942), ARSENIC AND OLD LACE (1944), THE BIG SLEEP (1946), BLACK FURY (1935), BLACK LEGION (1936), THE CABIN IN THE COTTON (1932), CAPTAIN BLOOD (1935), THE CORN IS GREEN (1945), DARK VICTORY (1939), FIVE STAR FINAL (1931), FOOTLIGHT PARADE (1933), THE FOUNTAINHEAD (1949), KEY LARGO (1948), MARKED WOMAN (1937), A MIDSUMMER NIGHT'S DREAM (1935), THE PETRIFIED FOREST (1936), SERGEANT YORK (1941), TAXI (1932), WATCH ON THE RHINE (1943), WILD BOYS OF THE ROAD (1933).

6607 *The Wisdom of Bruce Lee.* by Dennis, Felix; and Hutchinson, Roger. 168 p. paper illus. New York: Pinnacle, 1976.

Written for the admirers and imitators of the late martial arts exponent, Bruce Lee, this appreciation adds little to previous books. Lee lived a short violent life, appeared in Kung Fu films, on television and was a teacher-pal to a few Hollywood macho types. Illustrations and a bibliography are added.

6608 *The Wit and Wisdom of Hollywood.* by Wilk, Max. 330 p. New York: Atheneum, 1971.

A collection of gags, jokes, anecdotes, toasts, stories, insults, quotes, etc., taken mostly from the Golden Age of Hollywood. Predictably, Goldwyn gets a good share but many other familiar names also get their opportunity to be witty. The wisdom the title mentions is hard to discover. Entertaining, funny, and sad to think that the era which generated this humor has vanished forever.

6609 *The Wit and Wisdom of Mae West.* edited by Weintraub, Joseph. 94 p. illus. New York: G. P. Putnam's, 1967.

This short book contains both pictures and quotations of Mae West. It resembles a mini-version of *The Films of Mae West.* In the brief time required to go through it, the reader can quickly grasp the West charisma. Many other elaborate books do not illuminate their subjects half so well. The quotes and the pictures are amusing and will please most readers.

6610 *Wit and Wisdom of the Moviemakers.* edited by Colombo, John Robert. 192 p. illus. London: Hamlyn, 1979.

An anthology of humorous quotations.

6611 *With a Cast of Thousands.* by Zimmer, Jill Schary. 525 p. New York: Stein & Day, 1963.

Subtitled, "A Hollywood Childhood," this book details the life of the daughter of producer-writer Dore Schary during the forties and fifties. For some of these years, Schary was the head of MGM. Across its pages are sprinkled many famous Hollywood and Washington names, all viewed through the eyes of an atypical adolescent girl. No index or pictures are included. As a sociological study of childhood in the upper echelons of the Hollywood caste system, the volume has some slight merit. Otherwise it is entertaining trivia.

6612 *With A Hays Nonny Nonny.* by Paul, Elliot; and Quintanilla, Luis. 188 p. illus. New York: Random House, 1942.

An early diatribe about the Hays Code and Hollywood censorship, this book considers the stories of the Old Testament as potential screen material. One by one they are eliminated because of their unacceptability according to the Code, or their unsuitability for a mass entertainment audience. There is a wealth of comment about motion picture writing/

making circa 1940. Since many of the author's suggestions are now standard procedures, the book has a certain historical value but it is not very pertinent to filmmaking today. The argument is made with humor and some fine line sketches accompany the text. The book will have appeal for anyone interested in censorship. Acceptable.

6613 *With Eisenstein in Hollywood: A Chapter of Autobiography.* by Montagu, Ivor. 356 p. paper illus. Berlin: Seven Seas Publishers, 1968.

During the thirties famous people from all over the world came to Hollywood to observe, write, act or direct. Among these was the Russian director, Eisenstein. The account told here is of the writing of two scenarios, SUTTER'S GOLD and AN AMERICAN TRAGEDY, which were never filmed. Three persons were involved in the collaboration: Montagu, Eisenstein and Grigory Alexandrov. The record of their adventures during the heyday of Hollywood makes up about half of the volume with the scenarios filling the remainder. A few photographs of limited interest to most readers are added.

6614 *With Prejudice: Almost an Autobiography.* by Fairlie, Gerard. 255 p. illus. London: Hodder and Stoughton, 1952.

Gerard Fairlie is a writer whose screen credits include ALIAS BULLDOG DRUMMOND (1935), CHARLIE CHAN IN SHANGHAI (1935), and CONSPIRATOR (1950).

6615 *With the Movie Makers.* by Stearns, Myron M. 192 p. illus. Boston: Lothrop, Lee & Shepard, 1923.

Written for an unsophisticated audience, this volume describes studio filmmaking in the twenties. In addition, the author treats such broad topics as how do you watch the movies?, tricks, pioneer day, American films abroad, the world through a camera, developing an appreciation for films, etc. The production of two films at the Cosmopolitan Studios in New York is described: HUMORESQUE (1920) and INSIDE THE CUP (1921). Some of the illustrations are taken from the author's own productions.

6616 *With Those Eyes.* by Morgan, Michele; and Routier, Marcelle. 305 p. illus. London: W. H. Allen, 1978.

Remember Michele Morgan? She's the leading lady of THE FALLEN IDOL (1948) and also Frank Sinatra's costar in HIGHER AND HIGHER (1943). Of course,

948

she's a beautiful French film star who has appeared in films since ORAGE (1936). In this autobiography, translated from the French language, she recalls her life and long career with text and a few pages of pictures.

6617 *With Two Wheels and a Camera.* by Kopperl, Bert. 242 p. illus. Hicksville, N.Y.: Exposition, 1979.

A victim of polio in 1945, the author established a photography business in Palm Springs soon after. Eventually his clients included some of Hollywood's biggest names: Gable, Tracy, Bogart, Bacall, Peck, Hope, Hayworth, etc. Before his paralysis he had taken some shots of Alan Ladd, who remained a personal friend. His pictures were taken from a wheelchair and have included subjects other than film stars; 64 of them are included in this inspirational story of courage and talent.

6618 *Without Makeup: Liv Ullman.* by Outerbridge, David E. 160 p. illus. New York: Morrow, 1979.

This oversized photo-biography of actress Liv Ullman contains the distillation of a five-month interview along with over 250 clearly reproduced visuals. The latter consist mostly of candids, portraits, and stills from films and plays. Predictably, Ullman's association with Ingmar Bergman is a major element. In one sense, this is a variation on *The Films of...* books; in another, it is a long, illustrated interview. It is well produced and should appeal to anyone interested in Liv Ullman or Ingmar Bergman.

6619 *Without Veils: The Intimate Biography of Gladys Cooper.* by Stokes, Sewell. 243 p. illus. London: P. Davies, 1953.

A biography of the actress, with an introduction by W. Somerset Maugham.

6620 *Wiv a Little Bit O'Luck.* by Holloway, Stanley; and Richards, Dick. 223 p. illus. New York: Stein & Day, 1967.

Mostly "Alfred Doolittle" on and off the legitimate stage, this book has one chapter in which Holloway discusses the films he has made. Throughout are anecdotes concerning film celebrities. Limited interest to most readers.

6621 THE WIZ Scrapbook. by Anobile, Richard. 144 p. paper illus. New York: Berkley, 1978.

Richard Anobile, who is known for his print recreations of classic films, here documents in words and pictures the production of a new film. As an introduction, he recalls a few historical bits about the Oz stories as books, plays and films. The major portion of the book is devoted to the preparation, rehearsal, and shooting of the 1978 film, which was based on a successful all-black stage show. Anobile's text and his selection of over 200 visuals—many in full color—provide an interesting account of seventies filmmaking. It should be noted that THE WIZ (1978) cost about 25 million dollars to make but proved to be an enormous box office failure.

6622 THE WIZARD OF OZ. edited by Elias, Horace J. 127 p. paper illus. New York: Grosset & Dunlap, 1976.

This paperback is noted here because it includes almost 250 stills from the motion picture THE WIZARD OF OZ (1939).

6623 *The Wolf Man.* by Thorne, Ian. 47 p. illus. Mankato, Minn.: Crestwood House, 1977.

A survey of the werewolf in films, designed for young readers.

6624 *The Woman at the Well.* by Rogers, Dale Evans. 191 p. illus. Old Tappan, N.J.: Fleming Revell Co., 1970.

According to the publisher, there are over 150,000 copies of this book in print. In addition, this is the tenth book written by Dale Evans Rogers, known as an entertainer via films, radio, television and personal appearances. It is an autobiography told with many references to her religious beliefs.

After a short career as a singer, she arrived in Hollywood at the age of 28. In a short section she discusses her early career, the westerns made at Republic with Roy Rogers, Gabby Hayes, and the Sons of the Pioneers. Her divorce and subsequent marriage to Rogers finishes the film section. The remaining portion of the book is concerned with family, church, religion and patriotism. It is hard to go too far wrong with that quartet and author Evans evidently knows it.

There is apparently an audience for this kind of book and it is easy to understand its appeal to a segment of the reading public. A picture book autobiography, *Dale*, covers almost the same material. The author's style is folksy and she stresses honesty and objectivity in viewing her life. However, the continual sermonizing negates the warm effect of her narrative skill. A few illustrations are provided.

6625 WOMAN IN THE DUNES. by Abe, Kobe. 96 p. paper illus. New York: Trident Press, 1966.

Script of the 1964 film directed by Hiroshi Teshigahara. Contains cast credits and a preface.

6626 *Womanhood Media.* by Wheeler, Helen. 335 p. Metuchen, N.J.: Scarecrow Press, 1972.

This volume is noted here as a reference for films on or about topics of concern for the Woman's Liberation Movement. In a section entitled "Non-Books: Audio-Visual," the reader will find both short films and feature films listed along with other materials such as posters, filmstrips, and recordings. The list is very selective and anyone familiar with films may find argument with both selections and omissions. However, all the titles are of interest, in that they explore a wide range of topics, problems, and history.

There is much other material in the volume, with attention to the films being rather minor. For instance, the basic book collection is an annotated list of 318 volumes. Certainly there are enough films to warrant individual attention. This is a minor reservation to a volume that will assist many persons in locating materials on womanhood.

6627 *Women and Film: A Bibliography.* by Kowalski, Rosemary Ribich. 278 p. Metuchen, N.J.: Scarecrow Press, 1976.

This bibliography consists of 2302 consecutively numbered entries which appear under four major headings: Women as Performers; Women as Filmmakers; Images of Women; and Women Columnists and Critics. The first three headings are further subdivided using such divisions as reference works, specific works, and catalogues; each of these sections arranges its entries alphabetically by author surname or by the title of the work. A final subject index uses the entry number rather than the page number.

A scattering of annotations ranging from a few words to a full paragraph appear throughout. The quality varies greatly and entries are sometimes incorrect (see no. 899 on Mary Pickford).

Much of this material is available in other sources which offer greater detail, a higher quality of writing, and a better arrangement.

6628 *Women And Film/Television.* by Elsas, Diana; and Kelso, Lulu. 9 p.

paper Washington, D.C.: American Film Institute, 1977.

A title in the *Factfile* series, this booklet lists basic sources relevant to the subject of women and film/ television. Included are organizations, books, pamphlets, bibliographies, filmographies, distributors of women's films, and special programs.

6629 *Women and Their Sexuality in the New Film.* by Mellen, Joan. 255 p. illus. New York: Horizon Press, 1973.

An examination of the treatment of women and their sexuality in modern films is offered in this provocative volume. Using a variety of approaches to her subject, the author offers some controversial conclusions and opinions on films, directors and producers. Certain directors receive extended treatment—Bergman, Bertolucci, Rohmer, Reich, Bunuel, Visconti, Rydell, and Kershner. The major topics explored are sexuality, lesbianism, and sexual politics. One chapter on Mae West discusses her screen image over four decades. In addition to the personalities, many films are analyzed in some detail to illustrate the distorted reflection of women the author finds in them. Stills from about 40 of the films are adequately reproduced and complement the text. Recommended.

6630 *Women and the Cinema.* edited by Kay, Karyn; and Peary, Gerald. 464 p. paper illus. New York: Dutton, 1977.

This is "A Critical Anthology" of 45 essays about women and film. Written by an impressive group of authors, the pieces are presented under seven major headings: Feminist Perspectives, Actresses, Women in American Production, Experimentalists and Independents, Women and Political Films, Polemics, and Feminist Film Theory. A bibliography follows each section. Filmographies, illustrations, a general bibliography, an index, and contributor identifications complete the book.

Anyone interested in the topic could not find a better beginning than this volume. The casual reader will also find much of the content to be both enlightening and entertaining.

6631 *Women Have Been Kind: The Memoirs of Lou Tellegen.* by Tellegen, Lou. 305 p. illus. New York: Vanguard, 1931.

The autobiography of a Dutch stage actor who made many silent films for Paramount, Vitagraph and Fox. At one time he was married to Geraldine Farrar, an opera singer who also appeared in silent films.

6632 *Women in Film Noir.* by Kaplan, E. Ann. 132 p. paper illus. London: British Film Institute (New York: Zoetrope), 1980.

Here is an anthology which considers the place of women in film noir. Films examined include KLUTE (1971), MILDRED PIERCE (1945), THE BLUE GARDENIA (1953), GILDA (1946), and DOUBLE INDEMNITY (1944). Illustrations and a filmography conclude the book.

Much of the analysis is heavy going and ultimately suggests the dangers of over-interpretation of the filmmaker's purpose and intent.

6633 *Women in Focus.* by Betancourt, Jeanne. 186 p. paper illus. Dayton, Ohio: Pflaum, 1974.

This welcome addition to the film reference shelf notes films which present real women rather than stereotypes. An alphabetical title index of the films is followed by an index of the filmmakers represented along with their specific films. Making up the major portion of the book are the informative, well-written annotations of the films. Each gives film data, a pertinent recent quotation, an analytical, critical annotation, and some suggested feminist reading. A theme index, some programming suggestions, a bibliography and a distributor list complete the book. The book is illustrated with stills and pictures of the filmmakers.

The intelligence, selection, arrangement and production evidenced in this volume are most impressive. Not only does the content meet an existing need, but also the ease and efficiency of use of its many sections make it an outstanding new volume in the film reference category. Highly recommended.

6634 *Women on the Hollywood Screen.* by Manchel, Frank. 122 p. illus. New York: Franklin Watts, 1977.

In this volume designed for young people, Frank Manchel traces the screen image of the American woman as it changes from sweetheart-wife-mother to the independent female of today. Using a cast of familiar stars, the text mirrors not only the evolution of the female screen image, but also the changing economics of the American motion pictureindustry.

The approach employed is chronological. After a fine introductory chapter, individual sections are de-voted to images from the silent screen, the early sound era, the golden age, the period of decline and the ongoing reorganization of the industry. Illustrations are plentiful, well selected and nicely reproduced. A bibliography and an index complete the volume.

A film topic of current interest has been treated with care, sensitivity and intelligence by the author. The reader of this volume will not only be richly entertained, but will also be rewarded by a superb exposition of modern social dilemma. Highly recommended.

6635 *The Women We Wanted To Look Like.* by Keenan, Brigid. 224 p. illus. New York: St. Martin's Press, 1978.

A panorama of styles and fashion, this volume covers the period from the twenties to the seventies. Many of the women and designers shown or mentioned are associated with motion pictures.

6636 *Women Who Make Movies.* by Smith, Sharon. 307 p. paper illus. New York: Hopkinson and Blake, 1975.

The author of this book has two major goals in mind: first, a historical overview of women in film-making and then, identification of the women currently active as filmmakers. Beginning with some of the earliest films made around 1896, Smith singles out a French woman, Alice Guy Blache, for individual attention. The following section on the United States includes directors, writer, editors, and avant-gardists. Lois Webber, Nell Shipman, Ruth Ann Baldwin, and the more familiar Anita Loos, Mabel Normand, Lillian Gish, Nazimova, Mary Pickford and Gloria Swanson are some of the women considered in the silent era. Dorothy Arzner, Ida Lupino and a very few others represent the sound era. There are interviews with Barbara Loden, Faith Hubley, and Shirley Clarke, along with material on Elaine May, Susan Sontag, Stephanie Rothman, Shirley MacLaine, Francine Parker, Jane Fonda, Hannah Weinstein, Eleanor Perry, and many others.

Remaining chapters in the historical section are devoted to a worldwide survey ranging from Africa to West Germany. The second portion is a collection of mini-biographies of critically recognized women filmmakers who operate outside of the commercial Hollywood structure. Arranged alphabetically they offer selected brief information about the subject with major accomplishments noted. A listing of women filmmakers throughout the United States constitutes the third section. It is similar to the middle portion, but the annotations here are much shorter—usually only a sentence. Concluding portions of the book are a list of concerned organizations, distributors, a bibliography, and an index. A selection of photographic portraits of women filmmakers adds to the quality of the book.

A neglected but currently pertinent subject is handled with competence and intelligence. The author's approach is a bit overly intense and serious,but perhaps at this time the subject demands such treatment. Research, interest, and thought are evident in both text, supporting material, arrangement and production. This is a welcome reference-reader. Recommended.

6637   *Women's Films: A Critical Guide.* compiled by Audiovisual Center Personnel. 121 p. paper illus. Bloomington, Ind.: Indiana University, 1975.

After an introduction and a definition, this volume offers critical annotations and information about 170 or so "women's films," arranged under topic headings such as abortion, rape, day care, working mothers, etc. Each entry notes the title, running time, color format, purchase/rental information, date of release, director and distributor. The annotations, which are both descriptive and critical, are preceded by explanations of each topic heading. A title index, a distributor's index, and a bibliography are included.

The book is a result of the work of a volunteer screening committee who use a modified EFLA (Educational Film Library Association) sheet for their evaluations. Committee reports were synthesized into the final form presented here by Carolyn Geduld.

Everyone connected with this volume can feel pride in their accomplishment. It is an outstanding example of what professionals can create when they work for a common cause. The volume provides a most valuable information source on topics of immediate concern to all people, especially women. Highly recommended.

6638   *Women's Films in Print.* by Dawson, Bonnie. 165 p. paper San Francisco: Bootlegger Press, 1975.

This directory describes 800 films which represent the work of 370 women filmmakers. Only 16mm films currently available for sale or rental are listed. The filmography is arranged alphabetically by filmmaker name—thus, under Bauman, Suzanne, we

find BUTTON, BUTTON (1968), THE CABINET (1972), JOANJO: A PORTUGUESE TALE (1970), MANHATTAN STREET BAND and WHY THE SUN AND MOON LIVE IN THE SKY (1971). For each a short annotation is provided. At times an excerpt from a review is used. In addition to the release date, running time, distributor, color format, sound format, rental cost and purchase price are noted. Final sections include distributor addresses, a bibliography, a title index, and a subject index.

This is a helpful resource that is carefully arranged to provide easy access and retrieval. The annotations are very short, but they usually provide enough information to determine whether any further consideration of the film is desirable. An attractive, useful book. Recommended.

6639   *The Women's Movement Media: A Source Guide.* by Harrison, Cynthia Ellen. 250 p. New York: R.R. Bowker, 1975.

Includes films related to the women's movement.

6640   *The Wonder Album of Filmland.* Winchester, Clarence.

This pictorial survey of the screen was originally printed in London in 1933.

6641   *The Wonderful World of B Films.* compiled by Barbour, Alan G. paper illus. Kew Gardens, N.Y.: Screen Facts, 1968.

Mostly a collection of stills from B films.

6642   *The Wonderful World of Cliff Richard.* by Ferrier, Bob. 246 p. illus. London: Peter Davies, 1964.

The story of the youthful pop singer who, after a rapid rise to success as a recording, film and television performer, was to become a fervent advocate of religious salvation in the late sixties. This volume deals with his early successes. Among his films are SERIOUS CHARGE (1959), EXPRESSO BONGO (1960), THE YOUNG ONES (1961), SUMMER HOLIDAY (1963) and WONDERFUL LIFE (1964). See also *New Singer New Song.*

6643   THE WONDERFUL WORLD OF THE BROTHERS GRIMM. 32 p. illus. New York: Metro Goldwyn Mayer Co., 1962.

This souvenir book is devoted to the first film produced in the 3-camera Cinerama process by a major studio, Metro-Goldwyn-Mayer. The Cinerama process is discussed in an introductory article which is followed by some watercolor portraits of the many stars who appear in the 1962 film. The story is related with a short narrative and many colored stills from the film, some taking a double page. The background of the Grimm stories and their adaptation to film form is related. Producer George Pal and director Henry Levin are given special attention and the remaining cast and production credits are noted.

6644 WOODSTOCK. 48 p. paper illus. New York: Concert Hall Publications, 1971.

The influence of McLuhan can be detected in this souvenir book which consists almost exclusively of pictures of the artists and audience at the Woodstock Concert. The illustrations are fascinating, well chosen, and nicely reproduced. A short list of performer and production credits is included.

6645 *Woody Allen: A Biography.* by Guthrie, Lee. 160 p. illus. New York: Drake, 1978.

Since the subject of this biography has successfully resisted invasion of his private life, the author had to be content with factual material of record. Woody Allen's achievements, quotations, comedy routines, etc., are used to explain the artist. Obviously, only a surface sketch results. There is little analytical depth given to either the biographical data or to the selected comedy content.

The short volume is illustrated, indexed and contains both a bibliography and an annotated list of Allen's work. Allen deserves a better biography-appreciation than the one provided here. A stronger attempt was made by Eric Lax in *On Being Funny: Woody Allen and Comedy.*

6646 *Woody Allen: An Illustrated Appreciation of the Man and His Talent.* by Palmer, Myles. 128 p. paper illus. New York: Proteus, 1980.

A review of Woody Allen's films accompanied by more than 50 candid photos and stills. The text is somewhat superficial and suggests that this is more of a scrapbook than a serious study.

6647 *Woody Allen: Clown Prince of American Humor.* by Adler, Bill; and Feinman, Jerry. 178 p. paper illus. New York: Pinnacle Books, 1975.

This is an unauthorized biography of "Woody Allen Alias Allen Konigsberg a/k/a The Funniest Man Alive Today." Rather than emphasize biographical data, the authors have chosen analysis and criticism of Allen's writing, routines, characters and other creative efforts. Written with an undisguised admiration for the subject, the book discusses in fine detail the commercial comic character that Allen plays for the public. Woody Allen offstage intrigues the authors, but for the most part, they are not as successful in defining this facet of their subject.

A center section of illustrations consists of three dozen tiny photographs which seem carelessly selected and reproduced.

This tribute to Woody Allen will be greeted with enthusiasm by aficionados, while other readers will be introduced to the most original comedian currently active in films. Although one wishes the book had been prepared with more detail and care, its appearance is welcomed. Recommended.

6648 *Woody Allen.* by Palmer, Myles. 128 p. paper illus. New York: Proteus, 1980.

6649 *Woody Allen: Clown Prince of American Humor.* by Adler, Bill; and Feinman, Jeffrey. 178 p. paper illus. New York: Pinnacle, 1975.

In six chapters this unauthorized biography of Woody Allen gives an overview of his life and career. From his start as a writer, through the night club years, up to his position as a major filmmaker, the sensitive hard-working intellectual person is described. Since this appreciation ends at 1975, his later successes are not included. Some murky illustrations appear in a center section and a final chapter is devoted to "The Written Wisdom of Witty Woody."

As an introduction to Woody Allen, this volume is temporarily acceptable. However, the man is such a complex blending of talent, creativity, personality, ability and energy that a satisfactory biography probably could only be written with Allen's cooperation.

6650 *Woody Allen and His Comedy.* by Lax, Eric. 242 p. illus. London: Elm Tree/Hamish Hamilton, 1976.

This appreciation of Woody Allen combines biography, description, criticism, script excerpts, quotations and illustrations in an attempt to define the artist and his comedy. Since Allen cooperated with the author, the material has newness and appeal.

Much attention is given to the early films and to his night club appearances. An index is provided.

With Woody Allen's continuing success as a film-maker with audiences and critics, this volume can only increase in popularity. The enormous interest of Allen's fans will be satisfied nicely, if momentarily, by Lax's carefully prepared tribute. Recommended.

6651 *Woody Allen's* PLAY IT AGAIN SAM. edited by Anobile, Richard J. 192 p.paper illus. New York: Grosset & Dunlap, 1977.

Using more than 1000 frame enlargements, Richard Anobile has recreated PLAY IT AGAIN SAM (1972). The original dialogue appears beneath the appropriate frame. An introduction and an interview with director Herbert Ross accompany this version of the Woody Allen comedy film.

6652 *Word and Image: History of the Hungarian Cinema.* by Nemeskurty, Istvan. 245 p. illus. Budapest: Corvina Press, 1968.

From 1899 to the mid-sixties is the range of this history of Hungarian cinema—a quite unfamiliar topic. The text is well-written and the reproduction of stills from the films is outstanding in sharpness and clarity. The evidence presented by the stills suggest that a Western showing of the best of these films is in order. It is difficult to evaluate the text when the films discussed are so unknown. Title, director, and actor lists taken from Hungarian features made between 1945 and 1966 are appended as is an index of all the films mentioned throughout. This volume will probably appeal only to a very small group because of its largely unknown subject material.

6653 *Word Is Out: Stories of Some of Our Lives.* by Adair, Nancy; and Adair, Casey. 337 p. paper illus. New York: Delta, 1978.

In preparing the film WORD IS OUT (1978), about 150 homosexual men and women were interviewed on videotape. From that group 26 were selected and reinterviewed for the final film. This volume includes an introduction, the complete uncut text of those 26 interviews, an essay on making the film, and a lengthy bibliography of gay literature.

6654 *The Work of Dorothy Arzner.* edited by Johnston, Claire. 34 p. paper London: British Film Institute (Zoetrope in U.S.), 1975.

The subtitle of this short booklet, "Towards a Feminist Cinema," indicates the approach employed by the authors and editors. Divided into two sections, the text consists of a pair of short essays (why Arzner is important in film history) and one interview (who Arzner is). A filmography completes the work.

Most readers will find this booklet pertinent to a reevaluation of Arzner's films in the light of today's feminist movement. The essays are intelligent and responsible criticism, while the interview presents a strong, forceful woman. Recommended.

6655 *The Work of the Film Director.* by Reynertson, A. J. 256 p. illus. New York: Hastings House, 1970.

This is one of the few volumes on film aesthetics considered from a director's viewpoint. Its major theme, obviously, is the work or technique required of a film director. Both the technical and creative demands are noted. Topics such as as sound, composition, time, design, and characters are given attention and a good glossary of terms is included. Aimed primarily at the advanced amateur and the professional, the book is recommended for schools offering courses in film production.

6656 *The Work of the Industrial Film Maker.* by Burder, John. 255 p. illus. New York: Hastings House, 1973.

The industrial film is usually a sponsored one designed to sell, train, convince, explain or instruct; entertainment is not its primary function. This practical volume begins by discussing the rationale for the industrial film and follows this with a sequential explanation of how the films are made and eventually used. Sections on planning, pre-production activities, film stock, equipment, actual production and post-production are included. A glossary and an index complete the book.

A few illustrations accompany the text which is designed for understanding. The discussion of A and B rolls, for example, is presented with a clarity one seldom finds in print. Within the glossary, there is further evidence of the author's aim of providing comprehensible explanations of filmmaking terms. Although its topic is of concern to persons in a position to make industrial films, the book will also appeal to the individual interested in filmmaking. Its presentation is logical, encouraging and informative. Recommended, although the title may scare off some readers.

6657 *The Work of the Motion Picture Cameraman.* by Young, Freddie;

and Petzold, Paul. 245 p. illus. New York: Hastings House, 1972.

Here is a technical book that is also a pleasure to read as a leisure activity. Written via audio tapes by Freddie Young, it is unusual in several ways. Some biographical information and a filmography for Young appear at the book's opening, introducing the author and establishing his credentials. His expertise is given further reinforcement by the selection of visuals, which include both film stills and production shots.

The rest is also praiseworthy, a blend of technical information, observation, and advice based upon experience. Diagrams are used constantly to help explain postitions, movements, or concepts. The topics covered are filmmakers, cameras, lenses, lighting, preliminaries to filming, camera techniques, studio and location filming, artificial backgrounds, marine sequences, etc. A glossary and an index complete the book.

This is another volume of high quality in the *Hastings House* series. All the elements combine to createwhat will inevitably become a standard work going through many printings and subsequent editions. Highly recommended.

6658 *The Work of the Science Film Maker.* by Strasser, Alex. 306 p. illus. New York: Hastings House, 1973.

Strasser is an experienced professional whose concern here is to indicate how specific equipment and certain techniques may be used in the making of specialized films. The range of possibilities he discusses is wide and includes both the scientific film and the industrial-technological film. As in all of the *Hastings House* series, the illustrations are outstanding and supplement the excellent text in fine fashion. An appendix, glossary, bibliography and an index are included. Highly recommended.

6659 *Working for the Films.* edited by Blakeston, Oswell. 207 p. London: Focal Press, 1947.

In this book some 19 people talk about their jobs in British filmmaking. Such names as David Lean, Eric Portman and Alberto Cavalcanti are represented. Most of the others are unfamiliar, performing tasks such as continuity girl, sound man, film publicist, etc. The purpose seems to be vocational guidance, since most speak of difficulties, ambitions, responsibilities, rewards and opportunities.

The information is rather general and has little pertinence today since it describes the British film industry of the late forties. Little is said of the restrictive practices and regulations which obviously affect employment in films. With the widespread unemployment in the film industry at this point, the book can be interpreted only as theoretical advice. Because of its age, its British origin, and its outdated industry view, the book is recommended only for background reading and information, not for up-to-date guidance.

6660 *Working Papers on the Cinema: Sociology and Semiology.* edited by Wollen, Peter. 36 p. paper London: British Film Institute, 1969.

This collection includes the following papers: "An Approach to the Sociology of Film," by Terry Lovell; "Sociological Perspectives on Film Aesthetics," by Andrew Tudor; "Cinema and Semiology: Some Points of Contact," by Peter Wollen; "Semiology and the Cinema," by Frank West; and "Literary Criticism and the Mass Media with Special Reference to the Cinema," by Paul Filmer. First presented at BFI seminars, they were intended as catalysts to discussion rather than as complete finalized statements. Some bibliographical notes are appended. Acceptable.

6661 *Working with Kazan.* by Frazer, John; and Reed, Joseph W., Jr. edited by Basinger, Jeanine; Unpaginated. paper illus. Middletown, Conn.: Wesleyan University Press, 1973.

Published as part of a retrospective showing of Kazan's films at Wesleyan University, this booklet has a short introduction, followed by a chronology of Kazan's theatre work. His career as a director in films is noted next with complete cast and production credits given for each film. The major part of the text follows and is made up of recollections of some professionals who have worked with Kazan. They include writers, actors, and other directors. Since most of the comments were solicited for this specific honorary occasion, the tone of the articles is mostly positive, complimentary and even, at times, worshipping. A one-sided portrait emerges, but some interesting material about Kazan's directorial methods is offered. The photographs are excellent, and until a more complete and objective volume is available this one can be recommended. See also *Kazan on Kazan* and *Elia Kazan On What Makes A Director*.

6662 *World Communications.* edited by UNESCO. 533 p. New York: Unipub, 1975.

The press, radio, television and film situations of

some 200 countries are described in this UNESCO survey. An introductory section discusses the media in general terms. The seven sections which follow and treat the material geographically by continent/area include Africa, North America, South America, Asia, Europe, Oceania, and the USSR. The individual country entries are structured similarly—statistical information precedes the general comments about each medium within the country. For example, French Guiana, with a population of 51,000 and an area of 91,000 square kilometers, has nine cinemas with a total seating capacity of 3400 persons. The total annual attendance at films is 700,000 and the annual visits per person are 14. Mostly French films are shown. Statistics are provided for those countries which produce films.

The information in this volume is supplied to UNESCO by the governments of the various countries. This is the fifth edition of this volume and it includes changes reported since 1965. Two new categories are introduced—space communication, and professional training/organizations. The book remains an essential reference.

6663 *World Directory of Stockshot and Film Production Libraries.* by Chittock, J. 72 p. Elmsford, N.Y.: Pergamon Publications, 1969

6664 *World Directory Of Stockshot and Film Production Libraries.* edited by Royal Film Archive of Belgium. 63 p. paper illus. Elmsford, N.Y.: Pergamon, 1969.

This directory of moving picture collections was compiled under the direction of M. Jacques Ledoux and was published for the International Film and Television Council.

6665 *World Encyclopedia of the Film.* edited by Cawkwell, Tim; and Smith, John M.

There are two main elements in this encyclopedia: the cast and credits for about 20,000 films, and an international biographical dictionary with about 2000 entries. The book goes up to 1971 and offers rather complete filmographies for selected directors. Silent film is somewhat neglected and the directors may be a bit overemphasized, but these are minor faults. The volume is an excellent reference work, easy and pleasant to use. Highly recommended.

6666 *World Film and TV Study Resources.* by Rose, Ernest D. 421 p.

Germany: Friedrich-Ebert-Stiftung (Journal of University Film Association in U.S.), 1974.

This unusual book has as its subtitle "A Reference Guide to Major Training Centers and Archives." Its contents are arranged geographically by continents, then alphabetically by country. For example, under Asia and Oceania, an entry for New Zealand shows four institutions: National Film Library, Victoria University of Wellington, University of Canterbury, and University of Auckland. Data supplied varies and may include such items as personnel, address, phone, holdings, courses, programs, costs, subsidies, descriptive narrative, etc.

When used with the *AFI Guide to College Courses in Film and Television*, this volume should help anyone interested in locating schools and archives that deal specifically with television and film studies. Recommended.

6667 *World Film Directory: Agencies Concerned with Educational, Scientific, and Cultural Films.* compiled by Department of Mass Communications, UNESCO. 68 p. paper Paris: UNESCO, 1962.

This volume is number 35 in the series, *Reports and Papers on Mass Communication.*

6668 *The World Film Encyclopedia, a Universal Screen Guide.* edited by Winchester, Clarence. 512 p. illus. London: The Amalgamated Press, 1933.

This anthology tries to cover many subjects, among them history, fashion, censorship, make-up, collective biography, awards, casts, amateur cinema, film clubs, film production, newsreels, film terms, etc.

6669 *World Film Encyclopedia 1933.* edited by Winchester, Clarence. 512 p. illu. Gordon Press, 1976 (1933).

An early encyclopedia with many contributing authors, this volume was originally published by Amalgamated Press in London in 1933.

6670 *World Filmography 1967.* edited by Cowie, Peter. 688 p. illus. New York: A. S. Barnes, 1977.

In this volume, the editors have provided a comprehensive guide to several thousand feature films which were released internationally during 1967.

Some 45 countries are listed in alphabetical order, beginning with Algeria and ending with Yugoslavia. For each there is a national filmography for 1967 arranged alphabetically by original title. Coproductions and information about other filmmaking activities appears at the end of each filmography.

A typical entry in the filmography gives the film title, an English translation where necessary, director, screenwriter, literary source, film editor, color format, cameraman, music composer, producer, distributor, the leading players and a single-sentence plot summary. Occasionally such items as makeup, special songs, assistant directors, etc., are noted. Selected stills from the films appear throughoutthe book and are carefully reproduced. An index to alternative and translated titles along with an index to directors completes the book.

A gap of eight years (1969 to 1977) from initial research to publication gives some indication of the enormity of this series, which could ultimatelynumber more then 70 volumes.

This first volume is most impressive in its scope, arrangement, and treatment. Because of the impressive production values present, there is an attractiveness that is rare in reference books. Most importantly, an enormous amount of film information has been provided in a form that is both easy and pleasant to use. This is a project that deserves encouragement and support. Highly recommended.

6671 *World Filmography 1968.* edited by Cowie, Peter. 723 p. illus. New York: A. S. Barnes, 1977.

This volume continues the ambitious project described under *World Filmography 1967.* Once again the thousands of feature films made during the year 1968 by some 49 countries are presented in an international filmography. The arrangement and the information offered is similar to the 1967 volume.

For this book, however, the scope has been enlarged to include the Ivory Coast, Mexico, Morocco, Niger, and Senegal. Algeria, which appeared in the 1967 volume, is no longer listed. It might help the user and ultimately the series if some explanation were given for additions and deletions in future editions.

The book remains an admirable reference and is recommended.

6672 *The World I Lived In.* by Jessel, George; and Austin, John. 213 p. illus. Chicago: Henry Regnery, 1975.

George Jessel had careers in all facets of show business, including acting in and producing motion pic-

tures. In this autobiography he discusses both these latter activities. His explanation of why he did not make THE JAZZ SINGER (1927) offers an interesting sidelight on that historic film. In another section he discusses his career as a producer at 20th Century Fox from 1943 to 1953.

Jessel has never been shy or retiring and the chutzpah that enabled him to succeed in so many areas is evident here. He is the literary con man: dropping names, divulging personal intimacies, offering confidences, and making the reader feel he is getting a treat instead of a treatment. All this is done with enough wit, wisdom and determination so that most readers will probably enjoy the selected memoirs provided here. Predictably the illustrations show Jessel in close association with some of the world's best-known personalities. An index is provided.

If Jessel could have turned off his perennial routine long enough to write in depth about his film career, the result could have been an impressive film book. As it is, thanks are in order for the short glimpses contained here. Acceptable.

6673 *The World in a Frame: What We See in Films.* by Braudy, Leo. 274 p. New York: Anchor Press/Doubleday, 1976.

Here is a serious, scholarly statement on film theory that has as its goal the improvement of the reader's critical judgment and appreciation of films. It deals with three large general ideas—the place of objects in films and how they gain significance (open and closed visual form), the influence of tradition and convention on films (narrative thematic form), and the varieties of connection possible with the faces and bodies on the screens (personalities who disrupt form arrangements).

In his argument, the author makes references to art films, other art forms, popular films, performers, directors, film criticism, etc. A strong background of experience and education in film matters is almost essential for the appreciation of Braudy's message. The qualified reader will find a text with thought, idea, concept and suggestion. Others may be somewhat discouraged by the mental effort required. Recommended.

6674 *The World Is My Cinema.* by Robson, E. W.; and Robson, M. M. 205 p. illus. London: The Sidneyan Society, 1947 (1940).

This warning about the possible negative effects of film content upon society was first published in 1940.

6675 *World List of Film Periodicals and Serials.* 127 p. Brussels: La Cinematheque de Belgique, 1955.

Out of date now but listed here to show the possibility and need for such a publication. Periodicals are listed alphabetically by country of origin. A general alphabetical index of titles and a subject index are also given. This is a model to emulate (and as soon as possible). A short supplement to the above was published in 1957.

6676 *World List of Films on Bees and Beekeeping.* compiled by Bee Research Association. 67 p. paper Gerrard Cross Bucks, England: Bee Research Association, 1973.

Almost 300 films are noted in this catalog, which offers entries under three large categories: biology of bees, beekeeping, and economic uses-products of bees. The titles are also listed alphabetically, by country, and by distributor. Noted here as an example of a specialized filmography that is efficiently arranged and apparently comprehensive in its coverage.

6677 *The World of Animation.* edited by Kodak Staff. 152 p. illus. Rochester, N.Y.: Kodak, 1979.

All aspects of animation are covered in this attractive book—history, filmmaking, budgets, studio animation, personal production, your own animation stand, equipment, materials, etc. Like most of Kodak's major efforts, the book is copiously illustrated with full-color, black and white, and line-drawing visuals.

6678 *World of Children Films.* compiled by White House Conference on Children. 18 p. paper Washington, D.C.: U.S. Government Printing Office, 1970.

6679 *The World of Communications: Audiovisual Media.* by Hauenstein, A. Dean; and Bachmeyer, Steven A. 346 p. illus. Bloomington, Ill.: McKnight, 1975.

This communications text was designed for secondary schools and deals primarily with radio, recordings, motion pictures, theatre, and television. Although the section on motion pictures is short, many other portions of the book have pertinence—writing, casting, production, marketing, equipment,

careers, etc. The book can serve nicely as a basic introduction to advanced courses on the individual media. See also *Making Motion Pictures.*

6680 *The World of Entertainment.* by Fordin, Hugh. 566 p. paper illus. New York: Equinox (Avon), 1975.

It will be impossible for any film buff to resist this attractive book, which carries the subtitle "Hollywood's Greatest Musicals" and deals with the Freed Unit at MGM.

In Hollywood since 1929, Arthur Freed was a songwriter who graduated to producing most of the major musicals to emerge from Hollywood. This volume contains detailed information on some forty of them, ranging from THE WIZARD OF OZ (1939) to THE BELLS ARE RINGING (1960).

The text is based on the author's diligent research, which included many interviews and complete access to Freed's archives. The result is a minutely detailed, nonsensationalized recall of the famous musicals and the artists who made them.

Illustrations have been reduced in size for this paperback edition but remain effective. A Freed filmography and a song catalogue complete the work.

Not only is this volume a fitting memorial to Arthur Freed, but it is also a distinct service to all those who love Hollywood musicals, i.e., the large audiences who recently embraced THAT'S ENTERTAINMENT (1974) and THAT'S ENTERTAINMENT, PART TWO (1976), both of which consisted mostly of extracts from Freed's productions. This is a volume that will bring unending pleasure to many readers. Highly recommended.

6681 *The World of Fanzines.* by Wertham, Fredric. 144 p. illus. Carbondale, Ill.: Southern Illinois University Press, 1973.

6682 *The World of Film.* by Stewart, Bruce. 75 p. illus. Richmond, Virginia: John Knox Press, 1972.

Intended as an introduction to film, this short volume contains abbreviated and superficial accounts of film history, filmmaking, film sociology, aesthetics, and film content. The few chapters are written in a concise, literate style that almost conceals some of the questionable content: e.g., 1) "3-D soon enough will become as normal to films as sound and color"; 2) "Film will have flopped over into propaganda which is always fatal"; and 3) "The barbed wit of PASSPORT TO PIMLICO (1949),

THE LAVENDER HILL MOB (1951), THE LADY KILL-ERS (1955)... puzzled the Americans."

Much of the presentation is supported by citing film examples and, when Stewart writes about them subjectively, the text improves considerably. The illustrations appear in four groupings and are interesting and well reproduced. Nothing about this volume is sufficiently outstanding to warrant immediate acquisition. The topics are covered in greater depth in many other earlier works and the author's style is not individualistic enough to make the book unique. Acceptable.

6683 *The World of Film and Filmmakers: A Visual History.* edited by Allen, Don. 240 p. illus. New York: Crown, 1979.

This oversized coffee table book offers a visualized introduction to the world of motion pictures from their earliest days to the present. The text, a joint effort by a group of well-known filmmakers, treats history, industry, production, technique, technology, directors, critical appreciation, aesthetics, etc. A biographical who's who, a glossary of film terms, and an index are added.

All of the above seems to support the important feature of the book, the 350 or so visuals. In color and black-and-white, they include stills, posters, diagrams, charts, photographs, etc. Reproduction quality is somewhat variable causing a well-chosen set of illustrations to be diminished in effectiveness.

6684 *The World of Film and Filmmakers: A Visual History.* edited by Allen, Don. New York: Crown, 1979.

6685 *The World of Jacqueline Susann.* by Hanna, David. 217 p. paper illus. New York: Manor, 1975.

David Hanna is a pro at writing "instant" biographies, as this one on the late Jacqueline Susann shows.

6686 *World of Laughter: The Motion Picture Comedy Short 1910-1930.* by Lahue, Kalton C. 240 p. Norman, Okla.: University of Oklahoma Press, 1966.

A discussion of the many topics surrounding the production, distribution and exhibition of the comedy short during the period 1910-1930. The author's estimate of 40,000 comedy films produced would indicate that any coverage of this enormous output must be subjective and selective. In a most valuable appendix, all the silent comedies of these teams or individuals are given: Billy Bevan, Chaplin, Keaton, Langdon, Laurel and Hardy, Harold Lloyd, Our Gang, Snub Pollard, Larry Semon and Ben Turpin. The book obviously was a labor of love and the author's respect for the art of the silent film comedy is evident throughout. Especially effective is an analysis of this art form which avoids the intellectual-aesthetic approach, using instead descriptions of what happened on the screen and subsequently to the audience. A short bibliography is appended. Recommended as a basic book in film study. Interesting to the general reader, the film buff and the scholar.

6687 *The World of Luis Bunuel.* by Mellen, Joan. 428 p. paper illus. New York: Oxford University Press, 1978.

In paying tribute to Luis Bunuel, the always impressive Joan Mellen has put together a fine anthology subtitled "Essays in Criticism." Beginning with her overview of Bunuel's career, she follows with major sections entitled biographical glimpses, Bunuel the filmmaker, and the Bunuel films. A final section is produced by a "Debate" on THE DISCREET CHARM OF THE BOURGEOISIE (1972), with John Simon, Charles Thomas Samuels, Raymond Durgnat, and Irving Louis Horowitz participating. A filmography, illustrations and an index complete the anthology. As a description of what is offered, the title is well chosen. Anyone interested in Bunuel couldn't find anything much better than this collection.

6688 *A World of Movies.* by Lawton, Richard. 383 p. paper illus. New York: Delacorte Press, 1974.

Continuing the work that he began in two previous volumes—*The Image Makers* and *Grand Illusions*—Lawton has once again gathered a collection of beautiful portraits, production shots, and stills. As he states in his subtitle, they illustrate "70 Years of Film History." The arrangement is simple and logical. An introduction by Ella Smith offers a short review of motion picture history. Two major sections—The Silents and The Talkies—make up the main body of the book. A listing of the winners in the major categories of the Academy Awards and an index complete the work.

The major ingredient here is the photographs, and they are most satisfying. Over 30 pages in full color add a richness to the hundreds of carefully selected black and white visuals. Most are unfamiliar and the arrangement-layout accorded them is impressive.

Obviously clarity was an absolute requisite; it is hard to find any illustration which has not been carefully reproduced. Some brief captions and a text provide a continuity to the pictures and the book.

The selection, treatment, and final production of this volume is outstanding. It cannot fail to captivate any reader who has the slightest interest or background in film. Highly recommended.

6689   WORLD OF PLENTY. by Knight, Eric. 62 p. paper illus. London: Nicholson & Watson, 1945.

Script of the 1942 film, which was directed by Paul Rotha.

6690   *The World of Raymond Chandler.* edited by Gross, Miriam. 190 p. illus. New York: A and W Publishers, 1977.

Aside from being the creator of the private detective, Philip Marlowe, Raymond Chandler also wrote screenplays based on other writer's works—DOUBLE INDEMNITY (1944), STRANGERS ON A TRAIN (1951), etc. This anthology explores via 15 articles and essays the work and career of the writer.

Several deal directly with his screen work and Hollywood assignments. The remainder tell much about his writing achievements and their increasing influence on American literature. Many of the illustrations are film stills and a Chandler bibliography is included.

Anyone who has enjoyed the numerous Marlowe movies and books will relish these memoirs of Raymond Chandler. They provide a behind-the-scenes look at a most unusual man and also help to recall many classic scenes and characters that are part of Chandler's literary legacy to us. Recommended.

6691   *The World of Robert Flaherty.* by Griffith, Richard. 165 p. illus. Boston: Little, Brown, 1953.

The world of Flaherty consists of the Pacific: MOANA (1926), TABU (1931), WHITE SHADOWS (1928); Hudson Bay: NANOOK OF THE NORTH (1922); Ireland: MAN OF ARAN (1934); India: ELEPHANT BOY (1937); and the United States: THE LAND (1940), LOUISIANA STORY (1948). One chapter is devoted to each of the above locations as Griffith gives background to the making of each of Flaherty's films. Using letters, quotations, and portions of other books in addition to his own comments, the author documents Flaherty's continuing search for the "spirit of man."

The illustrations, taken from the collection of the Museum of Modern Art, are classic and add considerably to the book. There is no index. For those interested in Flaherty and/or the documentary film, the book is a fine compilation of textual and illustration material. The general reader may find the book somewhat dated and not pertinent to today's documentary filming.

6692   *The World of Tennessee Williams.* edited by Leavitt, Richard F. 169 p. illus. New York: G. P. Putnam's, 1978.

Basically this is a biographical picture book with some connecting narrative. The illustrations, most of which are unfamiliar and uniformly interesting, consist of photographs, newspaper and letter reproductions, stage and film stills, production shots, set designs, posters, etc. They are linked by an admiring review of the life and career of the author-playwright. Since Williams is also represented by motion picture versions of his work, the book will be of interest to film scholars. A bibliography and an index complete the visual biography.

6693   *A World On Film: Criticism and Comment.* by Kauffmann, Stanley. 437 p. New York: Harper & Row, 1966.

The reviews and articles in this book are from the period of 1958-1965. Most of them appeared in *The New Republic* and, one assumes, were responsible for Mr. Kaufmann's later appointment as a *New York Times'* drama critic. The reviews, which cover a surprising number of important films, are arranged according to topic or country and not chronologically. Thus, reviews of the films made from Tennessee Williams' plays are together, as are those directed by Ingmar Bergman.

Mr. Kaufmann's style is scholarly, opinionated, prejudiced and rather humorless. He has certain dislikes that he attacks with style and regularity—Dean Martin, Burl Ives, Burt Lancaster, dubbing, etc. He is also prone to repeat his enthusiasms—Brando, Lemmon, Antonioni, et al. The book can be fascinating reading for a variety of reasons. Regardless of the strong and sometimes questionable opinions, the writing is intelligent, thoughtful, and indicates an author of considerable background and education. Film buffs, TV viewers, students, teachers can all find much of value here.

6694   *World Survey of Motion Picture Theater Facilities.* compiled by U.S. Business and Defense Services Administration. 5 p. Washington, D.C.: U.S. Government Printing Office, 1960.

6695 *The World Viewed: Reflections on the Ontology of Film.* by Cavell, Stanley. 174 p. paper New York: Viking, 1971.

For 25 years, going to the movies was a weekly experience for Stanley Cavell. Around 1960 his attendance habit and his relation to films changed. His desire "to come to terms with movies" has resulted in the philosophical-aesthetic explorations of this unusual book. It poses questions such as "Why are films important?"; "What happens to reality when it is projected and screened?"; "What does the silver screen screen?"; "What is the cinema's way of satisfying the myth?".

The author is a professor of aesthetics and philosophy at Harvard, and his frequent references to Bazin, Wittgenstein, Baudelaire, Nietzsche, Heidegger, Rousseau and others presuppose a background on the part of the reader. An extended section of footnotes follows the text and will assist or rescue some readers. For the intellectuals who can partake of this philosophical smorgasbord with ease and pleasure, the book is a publishing rarity today. Others will find the going quite heavy but may be rewarded with sufficient prodding and provocation toward a possible reexamination of their own views about film.

6696 *World Wide Encyclopedia of Film Awards.* edited by Darino, E. paper New York: E. Darino.

Apparently the enterprising E. Darino published his own book which contains "6000 titles and 5000 names of 396 awards granted to all kinds of films all over the world." Predictably, some of the larger publishers (i.e., Gale) offer much the same information.

6697 *World-Wide Influence of the Cinema: A Study of Official Censorship and the International Cultural Aspects of Motion Pictures.* by Harley, John Eugene. 320 p. Los Angeles: University of Southern California Press, 1940.

In this early study which explores the relationship between films and governments, an attempt is made to show what various countries have done to control or censor films. Recognizing the power of films to affect audiences, the book describes film as a vital force in both national and world affairs. Using the United States as a major example, both official and unofficial censorship are cited. Attention is given to certain agencies which have a vested interest in films, sometimes only in a peripheral way. The book concludes with chapters on cultural, documentary, and educational films, and a discussion of international commerce in films.

6698 *The World's Greatest Monster Quiz.* by Carlinsky, Don; and Goodgold, Edwin. 122 p. paper illus. New York: Berkley, 1975.

A collection of quizzes on horror films.

6699 *Worshippers of the Silver Screen.* by Sumrall, Lester F. 64 p. illus. Grand Rapids, Mich.: Zondervan, 1940.

Another anti-motion-picture volume from Zondervan, this one discusses the havoc caused to American life by the money-mad denizens of Hollywood.

6700 WR MYSTERIES OF THE ORGANISM. by Makavejev, Dusan 144 p. paper illus. New York: Avon Books, 1972.

Script of the 1971 film directed by Makavejev. Contains cast and production credits; film festivals entered and awards won; an interview with Makavejev by Phillip Lopate and Bill Zavatsky.

6701 *The Writer and the Screen.* by Rilla, Wolf. 190 p. paper New York: William Morrow, 1974.

Subtitled "On Writing for Film and Television," this volume was written by Wolf Rilla, the director of VILLAGE OF THE DAMNED (1960) and many other films. He also teaches at the London Film School. Here he explains and examines requirements for screenwriting by considering such elements as the image, the word, the writer, the screenplay, films of fact, television and the marketplace. Examples of a story outline, a screenplay, and a television play are included in the appendix. The book is indexed.

The author's wide experience, along with his impressive literary skill, make this comprehensive introduction to screenwriting both readable and rewarding. Recommended.

6702 *Writers' Congress, Proceedings, October, 1943.* edited by Writers' Congress Continuation Committee. 663 p. paper Berkeley, Calif.: University of California Press, 1944.

An account of the conference held in October, 1943,

under the sponsorship of the Hollywood writers' mobilization and the University of California Press. Much of the attention is directed toward the role of the writer in World War II.

6703   *Writer's and Artist's Yearbook— 1980.* edited by Adam and Charles Black Co. 496 p. paper London: Adam and Charles Black, 1980.

A yearbook in its 73rd year, this volume is a reference for writers. It offers articles and advice along with information on suggested markets, societies, bibliographies, taxes, rights, copyright, etc.

6704   *Writers Guild 1979 Directory.* edited by Rivkin, Allen. paper Los Angeles: Writers Guild of America, 1979.

This announced directory will list the credits of more than 1000 writers. Issued at irregular intervals, it is an alphabetical arrangement of subject names, with their agency, address, telephone, and recent writing credits. Those not represented by agencies offer their home address and phone number. Credits noted include television shows, pilots, prizes, features, shorts, etc.

6705   *Writing about Literature and Film.* by Bryan, Margaret B.; and Davis, Boyd H. 192 p. paper illus. New York: Harcourt, Brace, Jovanovich, 1975.

6706   *Writing For and About Film.* by Hurley, Gerard T. 43 p. paper illus. New York: Harper & Row, 1975.

A short introduction on how to write scripts, adapt literature, or write about film, this paperback was designed for use with students. Exercises, discussion topics, illustrations, and a bibliography accompany the terse text.

6707   *Writing for Film and Television.* by Bronfeld, Stewart. 144 p. Englewood Cliffs, N.J.: (Spectrum) Prentice-Hall, 1981.

A solid practical guide to the mechanics of screenwriting.

6708   *Writing for the Films.* by Fawcett, L'Estrange. 107 p. London: Pitman, 1937.

6709   *Writing for the Screen.* by Jackson, Arrar. 144 p. London: Black, 1929.

Jackson's text is divided into three sections: the story, the scenario, and miscellaneous Matters. Topics such as technique, prospects, mechanics, continuity, construction, synopsis, commercial prospects, etc., are discussed. She also includes excerpts from her script for THE MISTAKE MASTER.

6710   *Writing for the Screen (With Story, Picture Treatment, and Shooting Script).* by Beranger, Clara. 199 p. Dubuque, Iowa: W. C. Brown, 1950.

6711   *Writing on Life.* by Barnett, Lincoln. 383 p. New York: Sloane, 1951.

Before he presents these 16 autobiographical interviews, the author describes the background surrounding each meeting. The subjects include Astaire, Crosby, Tennessee Williams, Jerry Geisler, Charles Brackett, Billy Wilder and Ingrid Bergman. Barnett liked them all.

6712   *Writing the Photoplay.* by Essenwein, Joseph B.; and Leeds, Arthur. 374 p. Springfield, Mass.: Home Correspondence School, 1913.

6713   *Writing the Script: A Practical Guide for Films and Television.* by Root, Wells. 195 p. paper New York: Holt, Rinehart & Winston, 1980.

If it is possible to have a "hot" volume on screenwriting, this is it. Inspired by a course he gave at UCLA, the author, who is an experienced professional, employs a variety of approaches: criticism, legend, standard rules, exceptions, practical considerations, etc. Root tries to show how the various elements of screenwriting are blended into an acceptable final product. He is practical, down-to-earth, and even mercenary in describing the business of writing scripts.

6714   *The Writings of Robert Smithson: Essays with Illustrations.* edited by Holt, Nancy. 331 p. paper illus. New York: New York University Press, 1979.

Robert Smithson was a modern artist who influenced many creative people in diverse fields by his work and his writing. In this collection over 200 photographs accompany his essays, which occasionally deal with film and cinema.

6715 *Xaviera Meets Marilyn Chambers.* by Hollander, Xaviera; and Chambers, Marilyn. 201 p. paper New York: Warner Books, 1976.

This is fantasy pornography as purportedly expressed by the author of *The Happy Hooker* and the Ivory Snow star of BEHIND THE GREEN DOOR when they met for a week in Toronto. The sexual talk is nonstop and no erotic subject is overlooked; as a result, the two females seem rather limited—at least intellectually.

6716 YANKEE DOODLE DANDY by Buckner, Robert; and Joseph, Edmund. 192 p. illus. Madison, Wisc.: University of Wisconsin Press, 1981.

The script of the 1942 film directed by Michael Curtiz.

6717 *A Year in Review.* by Motion Picture Association of America. 35 p. paper illus. New York: Motion Picture Association of America, 1968.

6718 *A Year in the Dark: Journal of a Film Critic 1968-69.* by Adler, Renata. 355 p. New York: Random House, 1969.

This book contains approximately 130 film reviews and 50 essays about motion pictures all of which appeared in the *New York Times* during 1968-69. In a thoughtful introduction, Miss Adler gives background and experiences that were part of her 14 months as a movie critic. The reviews are unique, incisive and written with style. An outstanding sampling of film criticism, the collection will bring pleasure and joy to most readers. Highly recommended.

6719 *The Year's Work in the Film—1949.* edited by Manvell, Roger. 104 p. paper illus. London: Longmans, Green, 1950.

This was the first issue of what was planned as an annual publication of the British Council. After two years the annual was apparently discontinued. The first volume contained material on Carol Reed, the feature film, the documentary, the specialized film, the British film abroad, film decor, the British Film Institute, film books, film music, and festival awards won by British films. The 1950 yearbook published in 1951 paid tribute to Sir Michael Balcon, in addition to covering the topics listed above.

6720 *Yearbook of the Canadian Motion Picture Industry.* illus. Toronto: Film Publications of Canada, 1951- .

With the addition of a television section in the early sixties, the name of the yearbook became *The Yearbook of the Canadian Entertainment Industry.*

6721 *Yes, Mr. DeMille.* by Koury, Phil. 319 p. New York: G. P. Putnam's, 1959.

A series of anecdotes and legendary stories about DeMille arranged in a somewhat chronological fashion, this book gives a different perspective on the famous director than the others which are available. It stresses his ego, tyranny, power, and quick but caustic wit; his association with the Bible and yes-men; and petty economies, the costuming of his female stars, and his long-suffering staff. Although the content is critical, the final portrait is respectful and even affectionate. The book is not indexed and there are no illustrations. Enjoyable light reading.

6722 *Yesterday's Clowns.* by Manchel, Frank. 154 p. illus. New York: Franklin Watts, 1973.

Several short biographical sketches of master comedians of the silent screen are offered in this volume designed for young people. The book contains separate chapters devoted to Max Linder, Charlie Chaplin, Buster Keaton, Harold Lloyd, and Harry Langdon. The school of Keystone comedy is represented by Mack Sennett.

The essays are brief, dwelling mostly on career and style rather than offering detailed analyses of films. Many other personalities appear in these short biographies, which collectively describe the rise of silent film comedy during the decade from 1915 to 1925. As usual with the Manchel books, the visuals have been selected with care. Reproduction of them is above average in most instances. A good bibliography is added. Recommended for children and young adults.

6723 *The Yiddish Film.* edited by Gordon, R. F. New York: Gordon Press, 1977.

6724 *You Call Me Chief: Impressions of the Life of Chief Dan George.* by Mortimer, Hilda; and George, Chief Dan. New York: Doubleday, 1981.

A biography of the American Indian who became a film actor at age 71.

6725 *You Can Get There From Here.* by MacLaine, Shirley. 249 p. New York: W. W. Norton, 1975.

In this autobiographical report, the reader is taken behind the scenes of an ill-fated television series, a doomed political campaign and a sobering trip into China. Placed within the reportage of these three events are the elements of biography that present a partial picture of a complex personality.

MacLaine's writing style and her ability at observation and selection are as acute here as in her first book. She is quite subjective with the persons and events that affect her life. Her comments on television, Sheldon Leonard, George McGovern, political conventions, the dozen female companions she took to China—even her parents—are consistently sharp, informative and prejudiced. What she says is so carefully stated and placed within the context of her accounts that the involved reader may find it difficult to separate opinion from reportage, all of which makes for a provocative experience. The lady knows her business—which is pleasing an audience. Whether on stage, on films, or in print Shirley MacLaine is a consistently dependable performer. This volume is one more example of her knowledge, intelligence and ability. Recommended.

6726 *You Can Make It: An Insider's Guide to a Hollywood Career.* by Callow, Ridgeway. 88 p. illus. Nevada City, Calif.: You Can Make It Enterprises, 1981.

6727 *You Must Remember This.* by Wagner, Walter. 320 p. New York: G. P. Putnam's, 1975.

This collection of 24 interviews is subtitled "Oral Reminiscences of the Real Hollywood" and it features some unique and unusual subjects. Included are sessions with Mary Pickford, Minta Durfee Arbuckle, John Ford, Claire Windsor, George Jessel, Douglas Fairbanks, Jr., Frances Goldwyn, Jimmie Fidler, Richard Arlen, Darla Hood, Jesse Lasky, Jr., Lew Ayres, Ken Murray, Anne Rutherford, Sue Carol, Edith Head, Martin Rackin, Stanley Kramer and Jack Lemmon. Less familiar subjects include Walter 'Cap' Field (the world's oldest extra), Eddie LeVeque (the last of the Keystone Kops), Gaylord Carter (an artist at the great Wurlitzer organ), Ward Kimball (producer-director at the Disney Studios) and Mike Medavoy (United Artists vice president).

Each reminiscence is preceded by a short introductory section which describes the subject and the setting. Wagner's questions have been eliminated and each section reads like a personal statement rather than a question-and-answer session. With at least two exceptions (Rackin and Ford), most of the content consists of rather mild recollections of the Hollywood that was. The reader may surmise that time and distance from that period has lent obvious enchantment; the real Hollywood was a lot tougher and rougher than the fairyland described here. Nevertheless, the illusions and self-serving memories make pleasant nostalgic reading. Acceptable.

6728 *You Must Remember This—The Filming of* CASABLANCA. by Francisco, Charles. 216 p. illus. Englewood Cliffs, N.J.: Prentice-Hall, 1980.

Quite a bit is told about CASABLANCA (1943), from its origin as an unproduced stage play, "Everybody Comes to Rick's," to its current position as one of the three most popular films ever made. Some of Francisco's information seems like padding (actor biographies, for example), but much of what he tells here will be enormously pleasing to admirers of the film.

A few illustrations and an index are added to this entertaining account.

6729 *You Won't Be So Pretty (But You'll Know More).* by Landis, Jessie Royce. 256 p. illus. London: W. H. Allen, 1954.

An autobiography of the character actress, most of whose important films—TO CATCH A THIEF (1955), NORTH BY NORTHWEST (1959), etc., were made after this book appeared.

6730 *You're Only Human Once.* by Moore, Grace. 275 p. Garden City, N.Y.: Doubleday, 1944.

This autobiography of an opera star who became a glamorous motion picture personality is noted here since it contains two chapters on Hollywood. Miss Moore is candid, honest, and without malice as she recalls her short but meteoric career in the films.

6731 *The Young Actor's Guide to Hollywood.* by Benner, Ralph; and Clements, Mary Jo. 185 p. illus. New York: Coward-McCann, 1964.

According to the publisher's blurb on the jacket, this is "a complete key to getting into movies and TV, with authoritative advice on training, agents, studios, resumes, photographs, grooming, and Hollywood jobs, residences and social life." When the book is opened, there is a list of cab fares from Hollywood and Vine to the various studios, along with a street map. All of this greets the reader before the text.

Books such as this are suspect for many reasons. They are designed to capture a "quick buck" from unknowing youth. They are false not so much by what they say as by what they omit. Financial information is now historical and nostalgic. Chapter titles such as "Your Big Break" or "Can You Succeed in Hollywood?" are indicative of the content. Some of the advice is valid but much of it is filler designed to pad out a book. There is no index. In addition the emphasis is somewhat unbalanced. Considering the current dissolution of what was once Hollywood, the volume does not seen very pertinent. Forget this one.

6732 *Young Animators and Their Discoveries.* by Larson, Rodger; and Hofer, Lynne; and Barrios, Jaime. 159 p. illus. New York: Praeger, 1973.

Subtitled "A Report from Young Filmmakers Foundation," this collection of interviews with a dozen young filmmakers will have great appeal for adolescents and young adults. In the nine interviews of either individuals or teams, many styles and forms of animation are discussed—three-dimensional, cutouts, cels, scratch film, painted film, etc. Each animator speaks of his philosophy and experiences with one or more of these animation types.

Some introductory material on animation is provided, as well as a concluding glossary, bibliography and index. Illustrations are plentiful, although not all are titled, which may cause some confusion for the reader. This is not a how-to-do-it book although certain of its sections do provide a kind of instruction. It is more an account of the creative filmmaking adventures that a group of young people have enjoyed. As motivation for experimentation in filmmaking, the book is excellent. Recommended.

6733 *Young Cinema.* by Children's Film Foundation. 20 p. paper illus. London: Children's Film Foundation, 1972.

An explanation of the Children's Film Foundation (CFF) is offered by its chairman and chief executive, Sir John Davis, at the beginning of this collection of articles. Critic Margaret Hinxman offers further information on the CFF, its films, children's filmgoing habits, film content, and opportunities for new talent. Peter King, finance chairman, tells how the CFF works, while Percy Livingstone describes the distribution system for CFF films. The international scene is explained by Henry Geddes and a summary of some audience research concludes the book.

The importance of CFF and its possible use as a model by other nations should be emphasized. For the past 25 years it has brought suitable filmgoing experiences of high quality to children, not only in Great Britain but also in other lands. The absence of CFF films on American screens and in American schools is an enigma. Recommended. See also *Saturday Morning Cinema* and *Children's Film Foundation Catalogue and Index of Films.*

6734 *Young Film Makers.* by Rees, Sidney; and Waters, Don. 20 p. paper illus. London: Society for Education in Film and TV, 1963.

This publication was called *Film Making in School* in 1960.

6735 *Young Filmmakers.* by Larson, Rodger; and Meade, Ellen. 190 p. illus. New York: Dutton, 1969.

The author expresses his philosophy toward filmmaking when he announces the two film directors he admires most, D. W. Griffith and Andy Warhol. His reason is that they both approached film as though no one had ever made a movie before. It is this attitude he advocates for the neophyte filmmaker. Discussed are films made both with and without a camera, film stocks, cameras, scripts, editing, etc.

The approach is not a step-by-step "how-to-do-it" but is instead an offering of many possibilities. Numerous pictures illustrate the text beautifully and there is an index and glossary. Encouraging creativity and experimentation, the book is so competent and enthusiastic that it cannot fail to appeal to all would-be filmmakers. Highly recommended.

6736 *Young Gemini.* by McCowen, Alec. III p. illus. New York: Atheneum, 1979.

The early life of British stage and film actor Alec McCowen.

6737 *Young Judy.* by Dahl, David; and Kehoe, Barry. 250 p. illus. New York: Mason/Charter, 1975.

" To Frank and Ethel Gumm must go the eternal credit for the qualities Frances (Judy Garland) possessed as a person and as a performer. Frank gave her the depth of feeling; Ethel single-handedly brought about her success. She had it all by 1935."

This quotation summarizes the authors' research into Judy Garland's formative years (1922 to 1935). This book is a reconstruction of those years and deals with the Gumm family as they moved from Grand Rapids to Lancaster, Calif., and finally to Los Angeles and Hollywood.

The family consisted of the parents, Frank and Ethel, and the three daughters, Mary Jane, Virginia and Frances. Affecting the lives of all five was the problem of Frank Gumm's homosexuality. The authors' thesis is that the father's problem determined the behavior of his wife to a large extent. She sought escape from her unhappy liaison by seeking opportunities for the Gumm sisters at first, and eventually for Frances Gumm-Judy Garland alone. Many of Garland's later problems, attitudes, and actions, according to the authors, can be traced to her father's apparent sexual preferences. Much detail appears in the book, and the time continuum is often interrupted with article-newspaper quotes about Garland's life after she attained stardom. The illustrations are taken from private sources are well selected; understandably their reproduction quality varies considerably.

The book is not indexed, but a chronology of Garland's early appearances as a performer is included. Chapter notes and a lengthy bibliography complete the book. This is a specialized, unusual book that evidences some diligent researching. Considered as both a reconstruction of a period and as a contemplation of the influence of parents upon their children, the volume is a success. Its appeal to Garland fans is undeniable, and the issue of homosexuality will not lose many general readers either. This is a unique book that offers a newer and perhaps more valid explanation of a show business legend. Recommended for mature adults.

6738 *Young Soviet Film Makers.* by Vronskaya, Jeanne. 127 p. illus. London: George Allen & Unwin, 1972.

This survey covers the period from about 1955 to 1970, and chronicles the rise of Soviet film artists in the post-Stalin era. The films discussed are unfamiliar to Western audiences. Beginning with a short history, the book quickly enters on a discussion of the new filmmakers. Vronskaya considers them as controversial young intellectuals and describes the departure from social realism and the appearance of comedies. The popular actors and films are indicated. Filmmaking by national minority groups, such as those in Georgia, Armenia, Azerbaidzhan, Lithuania, Moldavia and the Steppes, is described.

The appendices which support this broad survey are well chosen: a list of Soviet studios, a chronological list of the important films (1956-1972), filmographies, a short bioliography, and an index. There are many stills and most are adequately reproduced. This small volume apparently offers both quality and quantity. This is stated with reservation since judgement of the validity of the author's work would require an unusual expertise in modern Soviet film. It does bring to the attention of the Western world, however, artists whose works deserve a greater audience. Recommended.

6739 *The Young Turks.* by Seemayer, Stephen. 160 p. illus. Los Angeles: Astro Artz, 1981.

6740 YOUNG WINSTON. 22 p. paper illus. New York: Columbia Pictures, 1972.

An article by Barry Norman introduces the 1972 film in this souvenir book which features some very attractive color photography. The remaining pages are devoted to actors Robert Shaw, Anne Bancroft, and Simon Ward and to the characters they portray. Producer Carl Forman and director Richard Attenborough are profiled and supporting cast and production credits are listed.

6741 YOUNG WINSTON. by Foreman, Carl. 157 p. paper illus. New York: Ballantine Books, 1972.

Script of the 1972 film. Contains cast credits and an introduction by the director, Richard Attenborough.

6742 *The Youngest Son.* by Montagu, Ivor. 384 p. illus. London: Lawrence P. Wishart, 1970.

This is the biography of a man concerned with both the art and business of making films. Known also as a film theorist, he became fascinated with the Russian filmmakers in the late twenties. Although his most important work took place later, this volume covers the formative period of his life—1904 to 1927.

Montagu has had a long career in films as an editor, importer, distributor, exhibitor, producer, director, writer, critic, and translator. During the thirties he worked with Hitchcock and Eisenstein and was active in the Spanish Civil War and World War II. He is the author of *Film World.*

6743 *Your Book of Film Making.* by Priest, Christopher. 80 p. illus. London: Faber and Faber, 1974.

6744 *Your Book of Film Making.* by Priest, Christopher. Levittown, N.Y.: Transatlantic, 1974.

Film making for the Junior High School student.

6745 *Your Career in Film Making.* by Gordon, George N.; and Falk, Irving A. 224 p. illus. New York: Julian Messner, 1969.

A short history of motion pictures followed by a survey of filmmaking today. Sprinkled with quotes from professionals, some reasonable career advice, and much factual information.

6746 *Your Career in Motion Pictures, Radio, Television.* by Jones, Charles R. 255 p. New York: Sheridan House, 1949.

6747 *Your Career in Theater, Radio, Television, or Filming.* by Allosso, Michael. 191 p. paper illus. New York: Arco, 1978.

This book, designed for young adults, first appeared in 1976 as *Exploring Theater and Media Careers.* The section on filmmaking deals with the production and distribution of films, with information provided on job descriptions, qualifications, opportunities, salaries, etc. Obviously, some of this data becomes invalid quickly. A glossary, a bibliography and a list of professional associations completes this very general overview of employment in the media fields.

6748 *Your Film and the Lab.* by Happe, L. Bernard. 208 p. illus. New York: Hastings House, 1974.

Everything you've ever wanted to know about film laboratories is explained in this volume by the dependable and often encyclopedic L. Bernard Happe. Using 97 separate sections, he discusses such topics as answer prints, optical printers, negative storage, title areas, printing opticals, cue marks, A and B cutting, enlargement printing, reduction printing, film on television, laboratory charges, and budgeting, among many others.

As usual his text is detailed, comprehensive and succinct—when one considers what is being described. Many easy-to-follow illustrations help the reader to understand some of the more complex operations performed by the labs. A glossary and some suggested reading complete the volume. The 97 topics listed in the table of contents serve nicely as an index.

This is another excellent volume in the *Media Manual* series. It is highly recommended for the professional filmmaker and can be used profitably by anyone who plans to deal with a film lab.

6749 *Your Instant Guide To Movie Making.* by Cleave, Alan. 63 p. paper illus. London: Fountain, 1977.

6750 *Your Introduction to Film: T.V. Copyright, Contracts, and Other Law.* by Minus, Johnny; and Hale, William S. 232 p. paper illus. Hollywood: Seven Arts Press, 1973.

6751 *Your Introduction to Film and TV Law.* by Minus, Johnny; and Hale, William Storm. illus. Hollywood, Calif.: Seven Arts Press, 1972.

An introductory volume on film and television law, the book deals with such topics as contracts, copyright, right of privacy, taxation, FCC, libel, guilds, unions, forms, obscenity, etc. The authors were responsible for *The Movie Industry Book.*

6752 *Yours Faithfully.* by Henson, Leslie L. 180 p. illus. London: John Long, 1948.

Henson was a British stage actor known for his gravel speech and his bulging fish-eyes. Noted for appearing mostly in farces on the London stage, he also appeared occasionally in films from 1916 to 1956. See also his earlier autobiography, *My Laugh Story.*

6753 *Yours Indubitably, Etc.* by Hare, Robertson. 192 p. illus. London: Robert Hale, 1956.

An autobiography of the actor-comic who appeared in many films during his long career. During the thirties his films were mostly adaptations of stage farces; later he was stereotyped as a balding, put-upon little man. Still active during the sixties, he had roles in CROOKS ANONYMOUS (1962) and HOTEL PARADISO (1966).

6754 *The Yugoslav Short Film.* 64 p. paper illus. Beograd: Savet Filmske Industrie, 1962.

An annual catalog of short films made in Yugoslavia described in English, French, and Yugoslavian. The subjects include political life, social life, history, economics, nature, cartoons, etc.

6755   Z. 14 p. paper illus. 1970.

This short souvenir book furnishes some background for the film by discussing the Lambrakis Affair which served as original source material. Characters from the 1970 film are shown, some press comments are quoted, and some stills from the film presented. Cast and production credits complete the book.

6756   *Z is for Zagreb.* by Holloway, Ronald. 128 p. illus. New York: A. S. Barnes, 1972.

The artists who are the foundation of the Zagreb Studios—such as Dusan Vukotic, Boris Kolar, or Ante Zaninovic—are a relatively unfamiliar group in America. Their films which emanate from the Zagreb Cartoon Studio in Yugoslavia are more widely known. This book is about both. It starts with a short history of the studio which had its beginning in the late forties. Short biographies consist of factual/statistical data rather than narrative, but it is the final section which will have the most value and appeal. Entitled "A Guide to Zagreb Cartoons (1956-70)," it is a chronological listing of the Zagreb output, with individual films arranged each year in a preferential ranking. Credits and a brief story annotation are given for each. The ranking via position in each year's listing serves as the only evaluation. The distributors of the Zagreb films in countries all over the world are listed on a closing page. The drawings used in the book are all reproduced in black and white and probably lose a great deal in the absence of color. The book jacket has some color illustrations which are most effective. An index is provided.

This is special material that will appeal to those familiar with the excellence of the cartoons. It is difficult to generate a great deal of enthusiasm for the films with the sparse evaluations and the visual representation given here. Acceptable.

6757   *Zanuck: Hollywood's Last Tycoon.* by Guild, Leo. 255 p. illus. paper Los Angeles,: Holloway House, 1970.

Disproportionate attention is given to topics such as Marilyn Monroe's career and the Taylor-Burton relationship in this sketchy biography. As a result, the portrait of Zanuck is interrupted with what appear to be sensationalized digressions. As in most of the Holloway House series, the photographs are superb, although their selection again appears influenced by attempts at innuendo or sexual suggestion, e.g., the stills for TOBACCO ROAD (1941) and THE RAZOR'S EDGE (1946). This is an acceptable work flawed by

attempts to capture a nondiscriminating mass audience.

6758   *Zavattini: Sequences from a Cinematic Life.* by Zavattini, Cesare. 297 p. illus. Englewood Cliffs, N.J.: Prentice-Hall, 1970.

Zavattini is the writer of many film scripts including UMBERTO D (1952), MIRACLE IN MILAN (1950), BICYCLE THIEF (1948), SHOESHINE (1946), and SUNFLOWER (1970). Much of his screen work has been with Vittorio DeSica, to whom this book is dedicated. The volume is a series of comments written in diary form. A novel compressed into 30 pages is included, too. Film matters are mentioned only briefly and, therefore, the book is of limited interest for most cinema students. There are only a few photos and no index or filmography is included.

6759   *Zen Showed Me the Way.* by Hayakawa, Sessue. 256 p. illus. Indianapolis: Bobbs-Merrill, 1961.

Here is the autobiography of the famous Japanese actor. His career in silent films and his return to the United States after success in Europe are noted. As indicated, the role of Zen in his life is stressed.

6760   *Zombie: The Living Dead.* by London, Rose. 111 p. paper illus. New York: Bounty Books (Crown), 1976.

This volume is concerned with films about the undead. Included are mummies, vampires, living skeletons, ghosts, ventriloquist's dummies, revived corpses, zombies, etc. The approach is a popularized one rather than a serious study; thus, there is no index, filmography, bibliography etc. This is a book designed for the nondiscriminating reader who is not yet tired of horror film surveys in print. Acceptable.

6761   *Zsa Zsa Gabor.* by Frank, Gerold. 286 p. paper illus. New York: Crest, 1960.

This is a paperback reprinting of the original World publication, a biography of a complex woman who collects men, jewels and husbands in approximately that order. Her candor combined with a European wisdom and experience made her a welcome relief from the typical girl-next-door personality prominent in the forties and fifties—e.g., Doris Day, June Allyson, Jane Wyatt, and Harriet Nelson. Her public image was that of a beautiful, wordly woman whose attitudes, standards and morals were quite unconventional.

She has appeared in quite a few films—most of them forgotten, except as early morning TV revivals, the exception being John Huston's MOULIN ROUGE (1952), in which she played Jane Avril. She discusses her film roles briefly in this book, which also contains her detailed portrait of George Sanders—a character as unique as Zsa Zsa. Some illustrations appear in a center section. Since this was a very early entry in the celebrity biography rush of the sixties, it lacks an index and a filmography and concentrates instead on romantic sensationalism. Acceptable.

6762 ZUCKERKANDL. by Hutchins, Robert M. 57 p. paper illus. New York: Grove Press, 1968.

A book version of the animated film with drawings.